CASES AND MATERIALS

ON

THE
LAW OF EMPLOYMENT
DISCRIMINATION

THIRD EDITION

By

JOEL WM. FRIEDMAN
Professor of Law
Tulane Law School

GEORGE M. STRICKLER, JR.
Professor of Law
Tulane Law School

Westbury, New York
THE FOUNDATION PRESS, INC.
1993

Library of Congress Cataloging-in-Publication Data

Friedman, Joel William, 1951–
    Cases and materials on the law of employment discrimination / by
Joel Wm. Friedman, George M. Strickler, Jr. — 3rd ed.
        p.   cm. — (University casebook series)
    Includes index.
    ISBN 0–88277–974–5
    1. Discrimination in employment—Law and legislation—United
States—Cases. I. Strickler, George M. II. Title. III. Series.
KF3464.A7F74   1992
344.73'01133—dc20
[347.3041133]   92–20401

 TEXT IS PRINTED ON 10% POST
CONSUMER RECYCLED PAPER

 PRINTED WITH
SOY INK™

F. & S. Cs.Employ.Discrim. 3rd Ed. UCS
2nd Reprint—1994

TO
VIVIANE SHELI
JWF

JAMES A. LIGHTFOOT
GMS, Jr.

*

PREFACE

The nineteen years since the enactment of the omnibus 1964 Civil Rights Act has witnessed an explosion of administrative, legislative and judicial responses to the challenge of eradicating job discrimination and achieving equal employment opportunity for all workers in the United States. The materials herein seek to explore how the three branches of the federal and, to a lesser degree, state governments have attempted to make and enforce decisions that frequently involve controversial social policy as well as technical juridical judgments. In our experience, many students are attracted to a course in Employment Discrimination Law precisely because it offers them the opportunity to evaluate how different governmental institutions have addressed many inherently interesting and intellectually challenging issues steeped in social policy considerations. There are also, of course, a group of students who take an Employment Discrimination course with the intent of pursuing a career interest in this specialized field. Other students choose to study Employment Discrimination Law because the rich body of U.S. Supreme Court opinions in this area offers them more of a chance to analyze that Court's work than is available in many other courses. With this in mind, we have concluded that an effort to concentrate solely on providing a digest of the applicable legal rules serves the interests of neither the majority of our students nor their instructors. Accordingly, the book was developed with three goals in mind: First, to expose the students to the substantive law and, in so doing, improve their skills in statutory construction and case analysis. Second, to go beyond the decisions on the merits and examine the policy conflicts underlying the legal issues and evaluate the choices that were made. Third, because of the significant contribution to this body of caselaw by the U.S. Supreme Court, many of its opinions are used as a means of examining how the Court is functioning, on a substantive and methodological level, in one specialized field.

To accomplish these three goals, we have provided both hypothetical problems and specific interrogatories to raise issues discussed in and suggested by the statutes and cases and to generate discussion of other policy oriented and jurisprudential questions. Both were made available so that the instructor can choose the approach with which she or he is most comfortable. In addition, where certain portions of the course material demand it, background information is provided in narrative form.

Choosing the principal cases is always a difficult task. We have included, of course, all of the landmark opinions in this area. In addition, however, we have sought to include many very recent federal appellate court opinions that both raise important, novel and interesting issues and address them in a scholarly and pedagogically effective manner. To keep the size of this book within manageable limits, however, an effort has been made to avoid an encyclopedic approach. Accordingly, extensive string citations to cases and other authorities have been omitted in favor of providing a wider range of problems and questions. Finally, while this book is designed for a three hour course, there are several chapters which can be deleted to provide an integrated set of materials for a two hour course or seminar.

Cases and statute citations, as well as footnotes, of the court and commentators have been omitted without so specifying; numbered footnotes are from the original materials and retain the original numbering; lettered footnotes are those of the authors.

J.W.F.
G.M.S. JR.

New Orleans, La.
January, 1983

PREFACE TO THE SECOND EDITION

The continuing accumulation of employment discrimination decisions and particularly the Supreme Court's willingness to return again and again to the area have led us to offer a second edition of this casebook which is now three years old.

Our experience with the first edition has convinced us that the basic organization of the book was sound and we have retained that organization in this edition. Our goals for the book have also remained essentially those we had in 1983. We designed the book to support a comprehensive survey course in an important species of labor law. We also wanted to provide materials that would allow the examination of the policy conflicts underlying both the passage of the modern civil rights statutes and their construction by the courts.

Because we were essentially satisfied with the structure of the original edition, updating the materials has created some difficulty. We realize that most teachers who will be using this book will do so in the context of a single two or three hour course. Simply adding the new decisions and developments to the existing material would have produced an overlong, unwieldy book. But because of developments in the law, we could not avoid expansion of some chapters, that on affirmative action being one example. Our response to the problem of keeping the book in manageable limits has been to compress more material into notes and textual discussion rather than to severely edit the principal cases. We have also shortened the chapter on class actions, which, as interesting as it was to one of us, is probably not covered in many courses.

Most of the principal cases from the first edition and the 1985 Supplement have been retained in this edition. Cases that have been overruled have, of course, been replaced. In several instances we have added cases that addressed previously unresolved issues and have substituted new decisions for those which we found did not "teach well." We also decided that, rather than rely on note material to cover some subjects, a principal case should be inserted.

We hope the new edition will prove to be an effective instructional tool.

G.M.S. Jr.
J.W.F.

New Orleans, Louisiana
November, 1986

*

PREFACE TO THE THIRD EDITION

Five years have passed since publication of the second edition of this casebook and this period has been marked by a significant level of legislative and judicial activity in the area of employment discrimination law. Not only did Congress pass the Americans With Disabilities Act (a comprehensive enactment addressing the employment rights of disabled individuals), but as evidence of its increasingly confrontational relationship with the Supreme Court, enacted several significant amendments to the Age Discrimination In Employment Act, the Rehabilitation Act and Title VI of the 1964 Civil Rights Act designed to overturn recent Supreme Court interpretations of these statutes. The most dramatic instance of this confrontation can be found in the passage of the 1991 Civil Rights Act in direct response to several Supreme Court rulings concerning the allocation of burdens of proof in Title VII cases, collateral review of affirmative action plans and the scope of the 1866 Civil Rights Act.

As a result of these important jurisprudential developments, and in response to our own experience teaching with these materials, this new edition contains several organizational changes in addition to the obvious substantive modifications. The most important organizational change is found in the new Chapter 3. We have attempted in this one chapter to combine the elements of Chapters 2 and 3 of the second edition so that the cases addressing the methods of proving disparate treatment and disproportionate impact claims are linked with those cases in which the theoretical bases for these evidentiary frameworks are articulated and explained. We also have eliminated the independent chapter on remedies and shifted the discussion of remedial issues associated with the different statutes into the chapters dealing with each of the statutes. With respect to substantive developments, we have added a significant amount of new Note materials, deleted several principal cases and inserted many new and important principal cases. We hope that these substantive changes, as well as the organizational realignment of materials will add to the teachability of these materials.

J.W.F.
G.M.S. Jr.

New Orleans, La.
August, 1992

*

ACKNOWLEDGMENTS

We wish to thank the following authors and copyright holders for permitting the inclusion of portions of their publications in this book.

Fisher, Franklin M., "Multiple Regression in Legal Proceedings," Columbia Law Review, Vol. 80, pp. 702, 705–06 (1980). Reprinted with permission of the Columbia Law Review.

Kanowitz, Leo, "Sex Based Discrimination in American Law III," Hastings Law Review, Vol. 20, pp. 305, 310–313 (1968); reprinted at L. KANOWITZ, WOMEN AND THE LAW: THE UNFINISHED REVOLUTION 103–105 (1969). Reprinted by permission of the publisher.

Reiss, Michael, "Requiem for an 'Independent Remedy': The Civil Rights Acts of 1866 and 1871 As Remedies for Employment Discrimination," Southern California Law Review, Vol. 50, pp. 961, 971–974 (1977). Reprinted with permission of the Southern California Law Review.

Preparation of this casebook was aided by the invaluable research assistance and proofreading of Sigrid K.J. Bonner, Tulane '92 and Terrence C. Gorman, Tulane '94. Special thanks to Camella Dimitri and Viviane Stoleru for their invaluable assistance and support.

*

SUMMARY OF CONTENTS

PART I. INTRODUCTION: THE RESPONSE TO EMPLOYMENT DISCRIMINATION PRECEDING THE ENACTMENT OF TITLE VII OF THE 1964 CIVIL RIGHTS ACT [1]

PART II. TITLE VII OF THE CIVIL RIGHTS ACT OF 1964

PART III. OTHER FEDERAL ANTI–DISCRIMINATION LEGISLATION

PART IV. AFFIRMATIVE ACTION [1021]

PART V. THE PRESIDENTIAL RESPONSE TO DISCRIMINATION: EXECUTIVE ORDERS [1219]

APPENDIX

SUMMARY OF CONTENTS

ANALYTICAL TABLE OF CONTENTS

PART I. INTRODUCTION: THE RESPONSE TO EMPLOYMENT DISCRIMINATION PRECEDING THE ENACTMENT OF TITLE VII OF THE 1964 CIVIL RIGHTS ACT

PART II. TITLE VII OF THE CIVIL RIGHTS ACT OF 1964

TABLE OF CONTENTS

PART III.   OTHER FEDERAL ANTI–DISCRIMINATION LEGISLATION

TABLE OF CONTENTS

TABLE OF CASES

Principal cases are in italic type. Non-principal cases are in roman type. References are to Pages.

*

CASES AND MATERIALS

ON

THE
LAW OF EMPLOYMENT
DISCRIMINATION

*

Part I

INTRODUCTION: THE RESPONSE TO EM-PLOYMENT DISCRIMINATION PRECED-ING THE ENACTMENT OF TITLE VII OF THE 1964 CIVIL RIGHTS ACT

Our legal system places numerous restraints on the terms and conditions employers and employee organizations may impose on employees and applicants for employment. The First Amendment to the United States Constitution and similar provisions in most state constitutions have been construed generally to prohibit the denial of public employment to persons because of their speech or beliefs. The federal government and some states have enacted legislation, such as the Occupational Safety and Health Act, directly affecting the conditions of the work place. In the Fair Labor Standards Act, Congress has created a statutory floor to the compensation that may be paid certain classes of wage earners and has prohibited altogether the employment of children in industry. The National Labor Relations Act and the Railway Labor Act were passed to prohibit employer interference with employee organization and to promote collective bargaining. Unions in turn are prohibited by the Landrum–Griffin Act from interfering with their members' right to speak out and seek internal political redress within the unions.

In addition to such statutory restraints, the employment relationship is often hedged by limitations of a contractual nature, ranging from collective bargaining agreements applying to thousands of employees and multiple employers, to the individual one-of-a-kind deals struck by first round picks in the National Football League draft and the teams which have obtained the rights to negotiate with them. Courts have at times imposed limits on the employer's freedom of action, even where no explicit contract exists, by finding implied contracts based on public policy or the course and history of the particular employment relationship.

The subject of this casebook is another type of legal restraint placed on employers and unions by legislatures and courts—the prohibition of certain employment actions based on characteristics of employees other than job performance or ability. The law of employment discrimination as so defined is in large part of very recent origin. Indeed, the bulk of the material contained in this book relates to legislative and judicial developments occurring after July, 1965, the effective date of Title VII of the 1964 Civil Rights Act. But in some circumstances, employment discrimination against racial minorities

1

and women was prohibited even before 1964. The legal basis for such prohibitions is the subject of the following materials.

SECTION A. THE CONSTITUTION

Section 1 of the Fourteenth Amendment to the United States Constitution provides in part that:

> No State shall make or enforce any law which shall abridge the privileges or immunities of citizens of the United States; nor shall any State deprive any person of life, liberty, or property, without due process of law; nor deny to any person within its jurisdiction the equal protection of the laws.

KERR v. ENOCH PRATT FREE LIBRARY OF BALTIMORE CITY

United States Court of Appeals, Fourth Circuit, 1945.
149 F.2d 212, cert. denied, 326 U.S. 721, 66 S.Ct. 26, 90 L.Ed. 427 (1945).

SOPER, CIRCUIT JUDGE.

This suit is brought by Louise Kerr, a young Negress, who complains that she has been refused admission to a library training class conducted by The Enoch Pratt Free Library of Baltimore City to prepare persons for staff positions in the Central Library and its branches. It is charged that the Library is performing a governmental function and that she was rejected in conformity with the uniform policy of the library corporation to exclude all persons of the colored race from the training school, and that by this action the State of Maryland deprives her of the equal protection of the laws in violation of § 1 of the Fourteenth Amendment of the Constitution of the United States and of the Civil Rights Act codified in 8 U.S.C.A. § 41. She asks for damages, as provided in that act, 8 U.S.C.A. § 43, for a permanent injunction prohibiting the refusal of her application, and for a declaratory judgment to establish her right to have her application considered without discrimination because of her race and color. Her father joins in the suit as a taxpayer, and asks that, if it be held that the library corporation is a private body not bound by the constitutional restraint upon state action, the Mayor and City Council of Baltimore be enjoined from making contributions to the support of the Library from the municipal funds on the ground that such contributions are ultra vires and in violation of the Fourteenth Amendment since they constitute a taking of his property without due process of law.

The defendants in the suit are the library corporation, nine citizens of Baltimore who constitute its board of trustees, the librarian and the Mayor and City Council of Baltimore. The defendants first named defend on two grounds: (1) That the plaintiff was not excluded from the Training School solely because of her race and color; and (2) that the Library is a private corporation, controlled and managed by the board of trustees, and does not perform any public function as a representative of the state. The municipality joins in the second defense and also denies that its appropriations to the Library are ultra vires or constitute a taking of property without due process of law. The District Judge sustained all of the defenses and dismissed the suit.

In our view it is necessary to consider only the first two defenses which raise the vital issues in the case. It is not denied that the applicant is well qualified to enter the training school. She is a native and resident of Baltimore City, twenty-seven years of age, of good character and reputation, and in good health. She is a graduate with high averages from the public high schools of Baltimore, from a public teachers' training school in Baltimore, has taken courses for three summers at the University of Pennsylvania, and has taught in the elementary public schools of the City. We must therefore consider whether in fact she was excluded from the training school because of her race, and if so, whether this action was contrary to the provisions of the federal constitution and laws.

There can be no doubt that the applicant was excluded from the school because of her race. The training course was established by the Library in 1928, primarily to prepare persons for the position of library assistant on the Library staff. There is no other training school for librarians in the state supported by public funds. Applicants are required to take a competitive entrance examination which, in view of the large number of applications for each class, is limited to fifteen or twenty persons who are selected by the director of the Library and his assistants as best qualified to function well in the work in view of their initiative, personality, enthusiasm and serious purpose. Members of the class are paid $50 monthly during training, since the practical work which they perform is equivalent to part time employment. In return for the training given, the applicant is expected to work on the staff one year after graduation, provided a position is offered. All competent graduates have been in fact appointed to the staff as library assistants, and during the past two or three years there have been more vacancies than graduates.

During the existence of the school, more than two hundred applications have been received from Negroes. All of them have been rejected. On June 14, 1933, the trustees of the Library formally resolved to make no change in the policy, then existing, not to employ Negro assistants on the Library service staff "in view of the public criticism which would arise and the effect upon the morale of the staff and the public." This practice was followed until 1942 when the trustees engaged two Negroes, who had not attended the Training School, as technical assistants for service in a branch of the Library which is patronized chiefly by Negroes. There are in all seventy senior and eighty junior library assistants employed at the Central Building and the twenty-six branches. There is no segregation of the races in any of them and white and colored patrons are served alike without discrimination. The population of Baltimore City is approximately eighty per cent white and twenty per cent colored.

Notwithstanding the appointment of two colored assistants in one branch of the Library, the board of trustees continued to exclude Negroes from the Training School for the reasons set forth in the following resolution passed by it on September 17, 1942:

"Resolved that it is unnecessary and unpracticable to admit colored persons to the Training Class of The Enoch Pratt Free Library. The trustees being advised that there are colored persons now available with adequate training for library employment have given the librarian authority to employ such personnel where vacancies occur in a branch or branches with an established record of preponderant colored use."

It was in accordance with this policy that the application made by the plaintiff on April 23, 1943, was denied.

The view that the action of the Board in excluding her was not based solely on her race or color rests on the contention that as the only positions as librarian assistants, which are open to Negroes, were filled at the time of her application, and as a number of adequately trained colored persons in the community were then available for appointment, should a vacancy occur, it would have been a waste of her time and a useless expense to the Library to admit her. The resolution of September 17, 1942, and the testimony given on the part of the defendants indicate that these were in fact the reasons which led to the plaintiff's rejection, and that the trustees were not moved by personal hostility or prejudice against the Negro race but by the belief that white library assistants can render more acceptable and more efficient service to the public where the majority of the patrons are white. The District Judge so found and we accept his finding. But it is nevertheless true that the applicant's race was the only ground for the action upon her application. She was refused consideration because the Training School is closed to Negroes, and it is closed to Negroes because, in the judgment of the Board, their race unfits them to serve in predominantly white neighborhoods. We must therefore determine whether, in view of the prohibition of the Fourteenth Amendment, the Board is occupying tenable ground in excluding Negroes from the Training School and from positions on the Library's staff.

The District Judge found that the Board of Trustees controls and manages the affairs of the Library as a private corporation and does not act in a public capacity as a representative of the state. Hence he held that the Board is not subject to the restraints of the Fourteenth Amendment which are imposed only upon state action that abridges the privileges or immunities of citizens of the United States or denies to any person the equal protection of the laws. His opinion reviews at length the corporate history of the institution and applies the rule, enunciated in state and federal courts, that to make a corporation a public one its managers must not only be appointed by public authority, but subject to its control.

The Court of Appeals of Maryland has used this test in somewhat similar cases and has held corporations to be private in character although public funds have been placed at their disposal to aid them in serving the public in the exercise of functions which could appropriately be performed by the state itself. For example, the rule was applied in Clark v. Maryland Institute, 87 Md.643, 41 A. 126, where a colored youth was refused admission to an educational institution to which he had been appointed by a member of the City Council of Baltimore under a contract between the City and the Institute which authorized each member of the Council to make one appointment in consideration of an annual appropriation by the City of $9,000 per year for the education of the pupils. It was held that the Institute was within its rights in excluding colored persons because it was a private corporation and not an agency of the state, subject to the provisions of the Fourteenth Amendment.

These decisions are persuasive but in none of them was the corporation under examination completely owned and supported from its inception by the state as was the library corporation in the pending case. Moreover, a federal question is involved which the federal courts must decide for themselves so that a final and uniform interpretation may be given to the Constitution, the supreme law of the land; and in the performance of this duty in the pending case, we should not be governed merely by technical rules of law, but should appraise the facts in order to determine whether the board of trustees of the library corporation may be classified as "representatives of the state to such an extent and in such a sense that the great restraints of the Constitution set limits to their action." Nixon v. Condon, 286 U.S. 73, 88, 89, 52 S.Ct. 484, 487, 76 L.Ed. 984, 88 A.L.R. 458.

With this test in view, we must examine the legal background and the activities of the Library. It was established in 1882 through the philanthropy of Enoch Pratt, a citizen of Baltimore. His purpose was to create an institution which would belong to the City of Baltimore and serve all of its people; but he was fearful lest its management might fall into the hands of local politicians who would impair its efficiency by using it for selfish purposes. Accordingly, he erected and furnished a central library building at a cost of $225,000 and provided a fund of $833,000 and gave them to the city on condition that the city would create a perpetual annuity of $50,000 to be paid to the Board of Trustees for the maintenance of the Library and the erection and maintenance of four branches. But he also made it a condition of the gift that a Board of Trustees, to be selected by him from the citizens of Baltimore, be incorporated, with the power to manage the Library and fill all vacancies on the Board irrespective of religious or political grounds, and with the duty to make an annual report to the city showing the proceedings, the condition of the Library, and its receipts and disbursements for the year. These conditions were met; the corporation was formed, and the conveyances by gift were made to and accepted by the city which assumed the required obligations.

* * *

The Library was managed and conducted in accordance with these provisions until the year 1907 when Andrew Carnegie gave the city $500,000 for the erection of twenty additional branch buildings on the sole condition that the city should provide the sites and an annual sum of not less than ten per cent of the cost of the buildings for mainte-nance. The city accepted the gift upon these conditions by Ordinance No. 275 of May 11, 1907, and directed that the annual appropriation be expended by the trustees for the branch libraries in such manner as might be specified by the city from year to year in its ordinance of estimates. The legislature impliedly ratified the gift by the Act of 1908, Ch. 144, by enacting an amendment to the city charter empower-ing the city to appropriate and pay over such sums as it might deem proper for the equipment, maintenance or support of the library, provided that the title of ownership to the property should be vested in the Mayor and City Council of Baltimore.

By the year 1927 the central library had outgrown its quarters and the Legislature of the state, by the Act of 1927, Ch. 328, authorized the city, if the voters should approve, to issue bonds in the sum of $3,000,-000 for the acquisition of additional real estate and the erection of a new building for a free public library in Baltimore City. The bond issue was authorized by Ordinance No. 1053 of April 13, 1927, which was submitted to and approved by the voters. Thereafter the city acquired the necessary land and erected thereon a modern library which constitutes the central building of the institution. Ordinance No. 1195, approved December 16, 1930, authorized the incorporation into the new site of the land previously occupied by the central building. The building has been completed and has been in use for some years past. The Library now includes this central building and twenty-six branches.

The existing fiscal arrangement between the city and the Library throws strong light on the question now under consideration. The work of the Library has been so expanded and its usefulness to the people of Baltimore has been so clearly demonstrated under the management of the Board of Trustees that the city has gradually increased its annual appropriations until they far exceed the obli-gations assumed by it under the gifts from Enoch Pratt and Andrew Carnegie.

* * *

Until ten years ago the appropriations made by the city were turned over to the trustees to be expended for library purposes; but for the past ten years all disbursements from city appropriations are made through the City Bureau of Control and Accounts on vouchers submitted by the trustees to the Bureau for payment. Salary checks are issued by the city's payroll officer and charged against the Library's appropriation. Library employees are not under the city's merit system, but their salaries conform to the city's salary scale and if an increase in salary or the creation of a new position is desired, the trustees are obliged to take up the matter with the Board of Estimates. The trustees submit an itemized budget to the city which is reviewed by the city's budget committee and the library budget is included in the regular city budget. All of the income of the Library is thus received from and disbursed by the city with the exception of an annual income of special gifts which has recently averaged from $6,000 to $8,000 annually, or about one per cent of the city's outlay.

* * *

From this recital certain conclusions may be safely drawn. First. The purpose which inspired the founder to make the gift and led the state to accept it, was to establish an institution to promote and diffuse knowledge and education amongst all the people.

Second. The donor could have formed a private corporation under the general permissive statutes of Maryland with power both to own the property and to manage the business of the Library independent of the state. He chose instead to seek the aid of the state to found a public institution to be owned and supported by the city but to be operated by a self perpetuating board of trustees to safeguard it from political manipulation; and this was accomplished by special act of the legislature with the result that the powers and obligations of the city and the trustees were not conferred by Mr. Pratt but by the state at the very inception of the enterprise. They were in truth created by the state in accordance with a plan which was in quite general operation in the Southern and Eastern parts of the United States at the time.*

Third, during the sixty years that have passed since the Library was established, the city's interests have been greatly extended and increased, as the donor doubtless foresaw would be the case, until the existence and maintenance of the central library and its twenty-six branches as now conducted are completely dependent upon the city's voluntary appropriations. So great have become the demands upon the

---

* We learn from Joeckel, The Government of the American Public Library, University of Chicago Press, 1935, that the oldest form of free public library existent today is that having a corporate existence. Accurate description of the libraries comprising this group is impossible because of the many variations of legal detail but the essential distinction between these and other public libraries lies in the fact that control and sometimes ownership is vested wholly or in part in a corporation, association or similar organization which is not part of the municipal or other government. Frequently there is some form of contractual relationship between the corporation and the city. But regardless of legal organization, these libraries all render service freely to all citizens on precisely the same terms as public libraries under direct municipal control. No less than 56 or 17% of all the public libraries in American cities having a population in excess of 30,000 fall into this category. Geographically these libraries are confined to the East and especially to the South where more than one-third of the cities in the 30,000 or over population group are served by libraries of this type. The Enoch Pratt Free Library belongs to this group.

city that it now requires the budget of the Library to be submitted to the municipal budget authorities for approval and in this way the city exercises a control over the activities of the institution.

We are told that all of these weighty facts go for naught and that the Library is entirely bereft of governmental status because the executive control is vested in a self perpetuating board first named by Enoch Pratt. The District Court held that Pratt created in effect two separate trusts, one in the physical property, of which the city is the trustee, and the other a trust for management, committed to the board of trustees, and that the purpose and effect of the act of the legislature "was merely to ratify and approve the agreement between Mr. Pratt and the city, and to give the necessary authority of the state to the city to carry out the agreement"; and that the practical economic control of the Library by the city, by virtue of its large voluntary contributions, is immaterial, because "the problem must be resolved on the basis of the legal right to control and not possible practical control through withholding appropriations."

We do not agree with this analysis of the situation ... It is our view that although Pratt furnished the inspiration and the funds initially, the authority of the state was invoked to create the institution and to vest the power of ownership in one instrumentality and the power of management in another, with the injunction upon the former to see to it that the latter faithfully performed its trust. We know of no reason why the state cannot create separate agencies to carry on its work in this manner, and when it does so, they become subject to the constitutional restraints imposed upon the state itself.

We think that the special charter of the Library should not be interpreted as endowing it with the power to discriminate between the people of the state on account of race and that if the charter is susceptible of this construction, it violates the Fourteenth Amendment since the Board of Trustees must be deemed the representative of the state. The question of interpretation is not unlike that which was before the Supreme Court in Steele v. Louisville & N. R. Co., 323 U.S. 192, 65 S.Ct. 226, where it was held that a labor union which was empowered by the Federal Railway Labor Act to represent a whole craft of employees could not discriminate against Negro members thereof.

* * *

For like reasons we think that the charter of the Library which empowers the Board of Trustees to manage the institution for a benevolent public purpose should not be construed to authorize them to pass a regulation in respect to the appointment of its agents which violates the spirit of the constitutional prohibition against race discrimination. Nor do we assume that the act would be so interpreted by the Court of Appeals of Maryland which in Mayor & c. v. Radecke, 49 Md.217, 33 Am.Rep. 239, pointed out the duty of the courts to look beneath the language of an act to find the true purpose of a grant of legislative power. In that case the court said: "While we hold that this power of control by the Courts is one to be most cautiously exercised, we are yet of opinion there may be a case in which an Ordinance passed under grants of power like those we have cited, is so clearly unreasonable, so arbitrary, oppressive or partial, as to raise the presumption that the Legislature never intended to confer the power to pass it, and to justify the Courts in interfering and setting it aside as a plain abuse of authority."

In any event, it is our duty in this case in passing upon the nature of the library corporation and its relationship to the state not to be guided by the technical rules of the law of principal and agent, but to apply the test laid down in Nixon v. Condon, 286 U.S. 73, 52 S.Ct. 484, 76 L.Ed.2d 984, 88 A.L.R. 458, to which we have already referred. There the Supreme Court held that an executive committee of a political party, which had been authorized by a Texas statute to determine the qualification of the members of the party, was not acting merely for the political organization for which it spoke but was acting as a representative of the state when it excluded Negroes from participation in a primary election. In declaring that this action was subject to the condemnation of the Fourteenth Amendment the court said (286 U.S. at pages 88, 89, 52 S.Ct. at page 487, 76 L.Ed. 984, 88 A.L.R. 458):

"* * * The pith of the matter is simply this, that, when those agencies are invested with an authority independent of the will of the association in whose name they undertake to speak, they become to that extent the organs of the state itself, the repositories of official power. They are then the governmental instruments whereby parties are organized and regulated to the end that government itself may be established or continued. What they do in that relation, they must do in submission to the mandates of equality and liberty that bind officials everywhere. They are not acting in matters of merely private concern like the directors or agents of business corporations. They are acting in matters of high public interest, matters intimately connected with the capacity of government to exercise its functions unbrokenly and smoothly. Whether in given circumstances parties or their committees are agencies of government within the Fourteenth or the Fifteenth Amendment is a question which this court will determine for itself. It is not concluded upon such an inquiry by decisions rendered elsewhere. The test is not whether the members of the executive committee are the representatives of the state in the strict sense in which an agent is the representative of his principal. The test is whether they are to be classified as representatives of the state to such an extent and in such a sense that the great restraints of the Constitution set limits to their action."

For further application of this principle, see Smith v. Allwright, 321 U.S. 649, 64 S.Ct. 757, 88 L.Ed. 987.

We have no difficulty in concluding that in the same sense the Library is an instrumentality of the State of Maryland. Even if we should lay aside the approval and authority given by the state to the library at its very beginning we should find in the present relationship between them so great a degree of control over the activities and existence of the Library on the part of the state that it would be unrealistic to speak of it as a corporation entirely devoid of governmental character. It would be conceded that if the state legislature should now set up and maintain a public library and should entrust its operation to a self perpetuating board of trustees and authorize it to exclude Negroes from its benefits, the act would be unconstitutional. How then can the well known policy of the Library, so long continued and now formally expressed in the resolution of the Board, be justified as solely the act of a private organization when the state, through the municipality, continues to supply it with the means of existence.

The plaintiff has been denied a right to which she was entitled and the judgment must be reversed and the case remanded for further proceedings.

Reversed and remanded.

NOTES FOR DISCUSSION

1. The Civil Rights Act, 8 U.S.C. § 41, referred to by the Fourth Circuit in *Kerr*, was the predecessor to the current 42 U.S.C. § 1983. That Act, passed in 1871, provides a federal cause of action for any person whose constitutional or federal statutory rights have been violated by any person acting "under color of any statute, ordinance, regulation, custom or usage, of any State or Territory * * *." Section 1983 thus creates no substantive rights but does furnish a federal cause of action against public officials and state and local governments for the violation by such officials or entities of rights insured by the constitution or by federal statutes. Section 1983 is by far the frequently utilized of the Reconstruction Era civil rights statutes. Its application in the employment discrimination context is discussed in Chapter 8, Section B, *infra*.

2. What is "the spirit of the constitutional prohibition against race discrimination" referred to by the Fourth Circuit? See Strauder v. West Virginia, 100 U.S. (10 Otto) 303, 25 L.Ed. 664 (1880). If the library had a policy of admitting only men to the training program, would Kerr have had a claim under the Fourteenth Amendment? In Reed v. Reed, 404 U.S. 71, 92 S.Ct. 251, 30 L.Ed.2d 225 (1971) the Supreme Court held a state probate law that gave an absolute preference for men over women for appointment as estate administrators violated the equal protection clause of the Fourteenth Amendment. The Supreme Court has not, however, applied the same constitutional test to distinctions drawn on the basis of gender as it has to state action on the basis of race. For a discussion of the level of judicial scrutiny applied to state action based on gender as contrasted with state action based on race see Personnel Administrator of Massachusetts v. Feeney, *supra*, Chapter 8B.

3. The Fifth Amendment provides in part that "[n]o person shall be * * * deprived of life, liberty, or property, without due process of law * * *." The due process clause has consistently been interpreted as forbidding the federal government from denying equal protection of the laws. In Davis v. Passman,

442 U.S. 228, 99 S.Ct. 2264, 60 L.Ed.2d 846 (1979), the Court held that a female employee of a U.S. Congressman who was discharged when the Congressman determined that "it was essential" her position be filled by a man, stated a cause of action for back pay and damages under the Fifth Amendment.

> "To withstand scrutiny under the equal protection component of the Fifth Amendment's Due Process Clause, 'classifications by gender must serve important governmental objectives and must be substantially related to achievement of those objectives.'" * * * The equal protection component of the Due Process Clause thus confers on petitioner a federal constitutional right to be free from gender discrimination which cannot meet these requirements.

442 U.S. at 234–235, 99 S.Ct. at 2271–2272 (quoting Califano v. Webster, 430 U.S. 313, 97 S.Ct. 1192, 51 L.Ed.2d 360 (1977)) (footnotes omitted). Under what circumstances might discrimination against employees based on race or sex "serve important governmental objectives?" What about age? See, Vance v. Bradley, 440 U.S. 93, 99 S.Ct. 939, 59 L.Ed.2d 171 (1979) (age 60 retirement requirement for Foreign Service personnel held not violative of Fifth Amendment equal protection because it removes from the service those who are sufficiently old that they may be less equipped or less ready than younger employees to face the rigors of overseas duty).

4. The Fourteenth Amendment applies on its face only to states, but has been consistently interpreted as applying to any non-federal public body. Thus, the employment practices of cities, and other political subdivisions, as well as of agencies of the state itself, constitute state action for purposes of Fourteenth Amendment coverage. The "state action" requirement of the Fourteenth Amendment and the "under color of law" requirement of § 1983 are frequently treated as being one-and-the-same. See, United States v. Classic, 313 U.S. 299, 326, 61 S.Ct. 1031, 1043, 85 L.Ed.2d 1368 (1941) ("Misuse of power, possessed by virtue of state law and made possible only because the wrongdoer is clothed with the authority of state law is action taken 'under color of state law.'"); United States v. Price, 383 U.S. 787, 794 n.7, 86 S.Ct. 1152, 1156 n.7, 16 L.Ed.2d 267, 272 n.7 (1966) ('under color' of law consistently treated as same thing as 'state action' required under 14th Amendment). The Supreme Court has stated, however, that the concepts "denote two separate areas of inquiry." Flagg Brothers, Inc. v. Brooks, 436 U.S. 149, 155–56, 98 S.Ct. 1729, 1732–33, 56 L.Ed.2d 185 (1978). In Lugar v. Edmondson Oil Co., Inc., 457 U.S. 922, 102 S.Ct. 2744, 73 L.Ed.2d 482 (1982), the Court explained that "under color of state law" means that the individual has acted with knowledge of and pursuant to law, but that such conduct by itself would not be state action. 457 U.S. at 935 n.18, 102 S.Ct. at 2752. Conduct which constitutes state action will, however, always satisfy the "color of law" requirement. Ibid. Because of the myriad ways in which the public and private sectors of society interact, a persistent problem has been in determining what constitutes sufficient state involvement to render an activity "state action." See, Graseck v. Mauceri, 582 F.2d 203, (2d Cir.1978), cert. denied, 439 U.S. 1129, 99 S.Ct. 1048, 59 L.Ed.2d 91 (1979) ("one of the more slippery and troublesome areas of civil rights litigation").

In Burton v. Wilmington Parking Authority, 365 U.S. 715, 81 S.Ct. 856, 6 L.Ed.2d 45 (1961), the Court found state action in the racially discriminatory operation of a privately-owned restaurant that leased space from a publicly-owned parking garage, because the state had "so far insinuated itself into a position of interdependence with the restaurant that it must be recognized as a joint participant in the challenged activity." 365 U.S. at 725, 81 S.Ct. at 861. But in Moose Lodge No. 107 v. Irvis, 407 U.S. 163, 92 S.Ct. 1965, 32 L.Ed.2d 627 (1972), the Court held that state licensing of a private club did not constitute sufficient state action to make racial discrimination by the club violative of the Fourteenth Amendment. The Court noted that the state licensing did not "foster or encourage" discrimination and distinguished *Burton* on the ground that the Moose Lodge was not located on public property and did not have the sort of "symbiotic relationship" with the state enjoyed by the restaurant. 407 U.S. at 175, 92 S.Ct. at 1972.

In Blum v. Yaretsky, 457 U.S. 991, 102 S.Ct. 2777, 73 L.Ed.2d 534 (1982), a case challenging the discharge and transfer of patients from state regulated private nursing homes, the Court held that in order to establish state action the plaintiff must prove that the state "has exercised coercive power or has provided such significant encouragement, either overt or covert, that the choice must be in law deemed that of the State." 457 U.S. at 1004, 102 S.Ct. at 2785. Extensive state regulation of a private entity does not make it a state actor. Blum v. Yaretsky, *supra*; Jackson v. Metropolitan Edison Co., 419 U.S. 345, 95 S.Ct. 449, 42 L.Ed.2d 477 (1974). But see, Roberts v. Louisiana Downs, Inc., 742 F.2d 221 (5th Cir.1984) (state action where state regulation is directly linked to challenged conduct). Nor will dependency on state funding make the state responsible for the actions of an otherwise private entity. See also, Rendell–Baker v. Kohn, 457 U.S. 830, 102 S.Ct. 2764, 73 L.Ed.2d 418 (1982) (school's discharge of teacher was not state action although 90–99% of school's funding came from public sources); Blum v. Yaretsky, *supra* (nursing home's discharge of patients not state action even though state subsidized operating costs and paid medicaid for more than 90% of its patients).

In N.C.A.A. v. Tarkanian, 488 U.S. 179, 109 S.Ct. 454, 102 L.Ed.2d 469 (1988) the Supreme Court held that a private association's investigation and findings regarding the activities of a basketball coach on the basis of which the state university suspended the coach, did not constitute state action under the Fourteenth Amendment nor action under color of state law for purposes of Section 1983. The Court reasoned that NCAA could not be deemed a state actor because it possessed no power by virtue of state law and that the university's actions, though influenced by the NCAA, did not turn the association's conduct into action under color of state law since the university was not bound to adopt the NCAA's rulings or standards.

In *Rendell–Baker, Blum* and *Tarkanian* the Court emphasized that the challenged conduct was not that of public officials or encouraged by state laws or policies. In light of the recent Supreme Court decisions, would *Kerr* be decided the same way today? With *Kerr* compare Gilliard v. New York Public Library System, 597 F.Supp. 1069, 1074–75 (S.D.N.Y.1984) (discharged employee's § 1983 suit against publicly funded library dismissed for lack of state action because of lack of control of city over personnel matters).

5. In *Kerr*, the defendant conceded a racially discriminatory employment policy while apparently denying that plaintiff was refused admission to the training program because of that policy. But if the library had no formalized rule excluding blacks from the program, what kind of evidence would Kerr have had to present to prove that she was denied admission because of her race? Would the fact that, during the training school's existence, all 200 applications by blacks had been rejected be sufficient for a finder of fact to conclude that Kerr had been denied admission because of her race? Should

such evidence even be admissible to prove discrimination against Kerr? See Chapter 2C, *infra*.

6. Does the Fourth Circuit's reversal and remand for further proceedings mean that Kerr should be placed in the training program? What if all the positions in the program have been filled? If Kerr has an absolute constitutional right not to be discriminated against because of her race, what is the appropriate measure of relief? See, Chapter 8D, *infra*.

SECTION B.   FEDERAL CIVIL RIGHTS LEGISLATION AND EXECUTIVE ACTION

Following the Civil War, Congress passed a series of statutes intended to implement the commands of the Thirteenth, Fourteenth and Fifteenth Amendments by providing protection for black citizens from their former masters. The Reconstruction civil rights statutes were not, however, sympathetically received by the Supreme Court. In 1873 in The Slaughter-house Cases, 83 U.S. (16 Wall.) 36, 21 L.Ed. 394 (1873), the Court upheld the validity of a Louisiana law which created a monopoly for a private slaughterhouse. A majority of the Court held that the law did not abridge the privileges and immunities of Louisiana citizens under the Fourteenth Amendment because such privileges and immunities encompassed only those rights which grew directly out of the relationship between the citizen and the national government, such as the right to sue in federal court, and did not include fundamental individual rights which arose only from state citizenship. The decision, though not directly involving the civil rights statutes, nonetheless affected them, because the Court construed the constitutional basis for much of the civil rights legislation in the narrowest possible way. *The Slaughter-house Cases* was followed shortly by United States v. Cruikshank, 92 U.S. (2 Otto) 542, 23 L.Ed. 588 (1876), where the Court held that an indictment under a section of the post-war statutes, which charged that defendants conspired to prevent black citizens from assembling, was defective because of the failure to allege that the right to assemble grew out of the black citizens' relation to the federal government. Applying the *Slaughter-house* doctrine to a statute, the Court held that the right to assemble peacefully was not an attribute of national citizenship unless the assemblage was for the purpose of petitioning the federal government. But even more significantly, the Court also announced that the first section of the Fourteenth Amendment consisted only of restrictions on the states and did not "add anything to the rights which one citizen has under the constitution against another." It followed that legislation founded on the Fourteenth Amendment could not reach private action. The combination of the narrow construction of the privileges and immunities clause in *The Slaughter-house Cases* and the elimination of private action from the reach of the Fourteenth Amendment in *Cruikshank* foreshadowed the effective negation of all the Reconstruction civil rights statutes.[a]

[a] A good account of the post war civil rights legislation and of its judicial destruction is contained in Gressman, The Unhappy History of Civil Rights Legislation, 50 Mich.L.Rev. 1323 (1952).

One of the series of legislative efforts which could have become a vehicle for protecting the employment rights of blacks was the Civil Rights Act of 1866, which provided that all citizens, without regard to color, were entitled in every state to the same right to contract, sue, give evidence, and to take, hold and convey property, and to the equal benefits of all laws for the security of persons and property as was enjoyed by white citizens. In 1903, a federal grand jury in Arkansas indicted a number of individuals for conspiring to violate the rights of black citizens protected by the 1866 Act. The indictment stated that a lumber mill in White Hall, Arkansas had employed eight black citizens as "laborers and workmen" such employment "being a right similar to that enjoyed in said state by the white citizens thereof." The indictment further alleged that:

> defendants being then and there armed with deadly weapons, threatening and intimidating the said workmen there employed, with the purpose of compelling them, by violence and threats and otherwise, to remove from said place of business, to stop said work, and to cease the enjoyment of said right and privilege, and by then and there wilfully, deliberately, and unlawfully compelling [the employees] to quit said work and abandon said place and cease the free enjoyment of all advantages under said contracts, the same being so done by said defendants and each of them for the purpose of driving [the employees] from said place of business and from their labor because they were colored men and citizens of African descent * * *.

A demurrer to the indictment on the ground that the offense created by the Civil Rights Act was not within the jurisdiction of the federal courts was overruled and the respondents were convicted. On appeal, the Supreme Court reversed. Hodges v. United States, 203 U.S. 1, 27 S.Ct. 6, 51 L.Ed. 65 (1906). The Court held that since the attempt to protect the employment rights of the black workers was directed against *private action*, the Fourteenth Amendment provided no basis for the prosecution. The Thirteenth Amendment, which outlawed slavery, was equally inapplicable because interference with an employee's right to contract was not the equivalent of forcing him into slavery or involuntary servitude. Concluding that neither the federal constitution, nor the laws passed pursuant thereto secured " 'to a citizen of the United States the right to work at a given occupation or particular calling free from injury, oppression, or interference by individual citizens,' " the court held that "the United States court had no jurisdiction of the wrongs charged in the indictment." The section of the 1866 Act at issue in *Hodges* has survived as 42 U.S.C. § 1981.[b] Small wonder,

b It is unclear why the Court in *Hodges* did not declare the 1866 Act unconstitutional as an unlawful assumption of state powers in violation of the 10th Amendment, as it did with other civil rights legislation in The Civil Rights Cases, 109 U.S. 3, 3 S.Ct. 18, 27 L.Ed. 835 (1883). Justice Harlan in his dissent in *Hodges* commented that "if [the majority opinion's]

however, that it and other of the post-war statutes remained deadletters during the first two thirds of this century. A modern resurrection of the 1866 Act, beginning with the decision in Jones v. Alfred H. Mayer Co., 392 U.S. 409, 88 S.Ct. 2186, 20 L.Ed.2d 1189 (1968), is described in Chapter 8A, *infra.*

After the practical nullification of the civil rights statutes by the Court, federal efforts to eliminate employment discrimination in the first half of this century were half-hearted at best. Religious discrimination in federal employment was prohibited by a civil service rule as early as 1883 (U.S. Civil Service Commission, Rule VIII, 1883), but not until 1940 was discrimination on the basis of race against federal employees and applicants for employment specifically barred. Ramspeck Act, 54 Stat. 1211, 1940, 5 U.S.C. § 631a, 1958.

In 1941 President Roosevelt issued Executive Order 8802, 6 Fed. Reg. 3,109 (1941) which "reaffirmed" the policy of the United States against "discrimination in the employment of workers in defense industries or government because of race, creed, color, or national origin." [c] The order established the Committee on Fair Employment Practice which could "receive and investigate complaints of discrimination" and "take appropriate steps to redress grievances which it finds to be valid." Those "appropriate steps" were not spelled out in subsequent Executive Orders, however, and the Committee was never given direct means of enforcing any directives it might issue. Twenty years later, President Kennedy issued Executive Order No. 10,925, 26 Fed. Reg. 1,977 (1961) which created the President's Committee on Equal Employment Opportunity, an agency charged with the responsibility of effectuating equal employment opportunity in government employment and in private employment on government contracts. Executive Order 10,925 was a dramatic break with the past. For while certain orders had imposed on government contractors an obligation not to discriminate on the basis of race, creed, color, or national origin, the Kennedy order required contractors to take affirmative action to make the policy effective and gave the Committee real enforcement powers. The Committee was authorized to: (a) publish the names of noncomplying contractors and unions; (b) recommend suits by the Department of Justice to compel compliance with contractual obligations not to discriminate; (c) recom-

scope and effect are not wholly misapprehended by me, the court does adjudge that Congress cannot make it an offense against the United States for individuals to combine or conspire to prevent, even by force, citizens of African descent, solely because of their race, from earning a living." 203 U.S. at 8, 27 S.Ct. at 16.

[c] President Roosevelt was embarrassed into acting by the threat of a mass demonstration in Washington organized by A. Philip Randolph, President of the Brotherhood of Sleeping Car Porters, to protest racial discrimination by defense contractors. The march was scheduled for July 1, 1941. The administration, fearing international repercussions from such a demonstration, sought to dissuade Randolph, but he and other black leaders refused to cancel the march without a public commitment from the President to use his powers to obtain equal employment opportunity. Finally, on June 25th, the President promulgated Executive Order 8802. See Rochames, Race, Jobs & Politics 17–21 (1953); Comment, The Development of Modern Equal Employment Opportunity and Affirmative Action Law: A Brief Chronological Overview, 20 Howard L.J. 74, 75 (1977).

mend criminal actions against employers supplying false compliance reports; (d) terminate the contract of a noncomplying employer; and (e) forbid contracting agencies to enter into contracts with contractors guilty of discrimination. The work of the Committee and its successor agency, the Office of Federal Contract Compliance Programs, will be examined in Part V, *infra*.

SECTION C. FEDERAL LABOR STATUTES
STEELE v. LOUISVILLE & NASHVILLE RAILROAD CO.

Supreme Court of the United States, 1944.
323 U.S. 192, 65 S.Ct. 226, 89 L.Ed. 173.

MR. CHIEF JUSTICE STONE delivered the opinion of the Court.

The question is whether the Railway Labor Act, 45 U.S.C.A. § 151 et seq., imposes on a labor organization, acting by authority of the statute as the exclusive bargaining representative of a craft or class of railway employees, the duty to represent all the employees in the craft without discrimination because of their race, and, if so, whether the courts have jurisdiction to protect the minority of the craft or class from the violation of such obligation.

The issue is raised by demurrer to the substituted amended bill of complaint filed by petitioner, a locomotive fireman, in a suit brought in the Alabama Circuit Court against his employer, the Louisville & Nashville Railroad Company, the Brotherhood of Locomotive Firemen and Enginemen, an unincorporated labor organization, and certain individuals representing the Brotherhood. The Circuit Court sustained the demurrer, and the Supreme Court of Alabama affirmed. We granted certiorari, the question presented being one of importance in the administration of the Railway Labor Act.

The allegations of the bill of complaint, so far as now material, are as follows: Petitioner, a Negro, is a locomotive fireman in the employ of respondent railroad, suing on his own behalf and that of his fellow employees who, like petitioner, are Negro firemen employed by the Railroad. Respondent Brotherhood, a labor organization, is, as provided under § 2, Fourth of the Railway Labor Act, the exclusive bargaining representative of the craft of firemen employed by the Railroad and is recognized as such by it and the members of the craft. The majority of the firemen employed by the Railroad are white and are members of the Brotherhood, but a substantial minority are Negroes who, by the constitution and ritual of the Brotherhood, are excluded from its membership. As the membership of the Brotherhood constitutes a majority of all firemen employed on respondent Railroad, and as under § 2, Fourth, the members because they are the majority have the right to choose and have chosen the Brotherhood to represent the craft, petitioner and other Negro firemen on the road have been required to accept the Brotherhood as their representative for the purposes of the Act.

On March 28, 1940, the Brotherhood, purporting to act as representative of the entire craft of firemen, without informing the Negro firemen or giving them opportunity to be heard, served a notice on respondent Railroad and on twenty other railroads operating principally in the southeastern part of the United States. The notice announced the Brotherhood's desire to amend the existing collective bargaining agreement in such manner as ultimately to exclude all Negro firemen from the service. By established practice on the several railroads so notified only white firemen can be promoted to serve as engineers, and the notice proposed that only "promotable", i.e., white, men should be employed as firemen or assigned to new runs or jobs or permanent vacancies in established runs or jobs.

On February 18, 1941, the railroads and the Brotherhood, as representative of the craft, entered into a new agreement which provided that not more than 50% of the firemen in each class of service in each seniority district of a carrier should be Negroes; that until such percentage should be reached all new runs and all vacancies should be filled by white men; and that the agreement did not sanction the employment of Negroes in any seniority district in which they were not working. The agreement reserved the right of the Brotherhood to negotiate for further restrictions on the employment of Negro firemen on the individual railroads. On May 12, 1941, the Brotherhood entered into a supplemental agreement with respondent Railroad further controlling the seniority rights of Negro firemen and restricting their employment. The Negro firemen were not given notice or opportunity to be heard with respect to either of these agreements, which were put into effect before their existence was disclosed to the Negro firemen.

Until April 8, 1941, petitioner was in a "passenger pool", to which one white and five Negro firemen were assigned. These jobs were highly desirable in point of wages, hours and other considerations. Petitioner had performed and was performing his work satisfactorily. Following a reduction in the mileage covered by the pool, all jobs in the pool were, about April 1, 1941, declared vacant. The Brotherhood and the Railroad, acting under the agreement, disqualified all the Negro firemen and replaced them with four white men, members of the Brotherhood, all junior in seniority to petitioner and no more competent or worthy. As a consequence petitioner was deprived of employment for sixteen days and then was assigned to more arduous, longer, and less remunerative work in local freight service. In conformity to the agreement, he was later replaced by a Brotherhood member junior to him, and assigned work on a switch engine, which was still harder and less remunerative, until January 3, 1942. On that date, after the bill of complaint in the present suit had been filed, he was reassigned to passenger service.

Protests and appeals of petitioner and his fellow Negro firemen, addressed to the Railroad and the Brotherhood, in an effort to secure relief and redress, have been ignored. Respondents have expressed their intention to enforce the agreement of February 18, 1941, and its subsequent modifications. The Brotherhood has acted and asserts the right to act as exclusive bargaining representative of the firemen's craft. It is alleged that in that capacity it is under an obligation and duty imposed by the Act to represent the Negro firemen impartially and in good faith; but instead, in its notice to and contracts with the railroads, it has been hostile and disloyal to the Negro firemen, has deliberately discriminated against them, and has sought to deprive them of their seniority rights and to drive them out of employment in their craft, all in order to create a monopoly of employment for Brotherhood members.

The bill of complaint asks for discovery of the manner in which the agreements have been applied and in other respects; for an injunction against enforcement of the agreements made between the Railroad and the Brotherhood; for an injunction against the Brotherhood and its agents from purporting to act as representative of petitioner and others similarly situated under the Railway Labor Act, so long as the discrimination continues, and so long as it refuses to give them notice and hearing with respect to proposals affecting their interests; for a declaratory judgment as to their rights; and for an award of damages against the Brotherhood for its wrongful conduct.

The Supreme Court of Alabama took jurisdiction of the cause but held on the merits that petitioner's complaint stated no cause of action.[1] It pointed out that the Act places a mandatory duty on the Railroad to treat with the Brotherhood as the exclusive representative of the employees in a craft, imposes heavy criminal penalties for willful failure to comply with its command, and provides that the majority of any craft shall have the right to determine who shall be the representative of the class for collective bargaining with the employer. It thought that the Brotherhood was empowered by the statute to enter into the agreement of February 18, 1941, and that by virtue of the statute the Brotherhood has power by agreement with the Railroad both to create the seniority rights of petitioner and his fellow Negro employees and to destroy them. It construed the statute, not as creating the relationship of principal and agent between the members of the craft and the Brotherhood, but as conferring on the Brotherhood plenary authority to treat with the Railroad and enter into contracts fixing rates of pay and working conditions for the craft as a whole without any legal obligation or duty to protect the rights of minorities from discrimination or unfair

---

1. The respondents urge that the Circuit Court sustained their demurrers on the ground that the suit could not be maintained against the Brotherhood, an unincorporated association, since by Alabama statute such an association cannot be sued unless the action lies against all its members individually, and on several other state-law grounds. They argue accordingly that the judgment of affirmance of the state Supreme Court may be rested on an adequate non-federal ground. As that court specifically rested its decision on the sole ground that the Railway Labor Act places no duty upon the Brotherhood to protect petitioner and other Negro firemen from the alleged discriminatory treatment, the judgment rests wholly on a federal ground, to which we confine our review.

treatment, however gross. Consequently it held that neither the Brotherhood nor the Railroad violated any rights of petitioner or his fellow Negro employees by negotiating the contracts discriminating against them.

If, as the state court has held, the Act confers this power on the bargaining representative of a craft or class of employees without any commensurate statutory duty toward its members, constitutional questions arise. For the representative is clothed with power not unlike that of a legislature which is subject to constitutional limitations on its power to deny, restrict, destroy or discriminate against the rights of those for whom it legislates and which is also under an affirmative constitutional duty equally to protect those rights. If the Railway Labor Act purports to impose on petitioner and the other Negro members of the craft the legal duty to comply with the terms of a contract whereby the representative has discriminatorily restricted their employment for the benefit and advantage of the Brotherhood's own members, we must decide the constitutional questions which petitioner raises in his pleading.

But we think that Congress, in enacting the Railway Labor Act and authorizing a labor union, chosen by a majority of a craft, to represent the craft, did not intend to confer plenary power upon the union to sacrifice, for the benefit of its members, rights of the minority of the craft, without imposing on it any duty to protect the minority. Since petitioner and the other Negro members of the craft are not members of the Brotherhood or eligible for membership, the authority to act for them is derived not from their action or consent but wholly from the command of the Act. Section 2, Fourth, provides: "Employees shall have the right to organize and bargain collectively through representatives of their own choosing. The majority of any craft or class of employees shall have the right to determine who shall be the representative of the craft or class for the purposes of this Act * * *." Under § 2, Sixth and Seventh, when the representative bargains for a change of working conditions, the latter section specifies that they are the working conditions of employees "as a class." Section 1, Sixth, of the Act defines "representative" as meaning "Any person or * * * labor union * * * designated either by a carrier or a group of carriers or by its or their employees, to act for it or them." The use of the word "representative," as thus defined and in all the contexts in which it is found, plainly implies that the representative is to act on behalf of all the employees which, by virtue of the statute, it undertakes to represent.

By the terms of the Act, § 2, Fourth, the employees are permitted to act "through" their representative, and it represents them "for the purposes of" the Act. Sections 2, Third, Fourth, Ninth. The purposes of the Act declared by § 2 are the avoidance of "any interruption to commerce or to the operation of any carrier engaged therein," and this aim is sought to be achieved by encouraging "the prompt and orderly settlement of all disputes concerning rates of pay, rules, or working conditions." These purposes would hardly be attained if a substantial minority of the craft were denied the right to have their interests considered at the conference table and if the final result of the bargaining process were to be the sacrifice of the interests of the minority by the action of a representative chosen by the majority. The only recourse of the minority would be to strike, with the attendant interruption of commerce, which the Act seeks to avoid.

Section 2, Second, requiring carriers to bargain with the representative so chosen, operates to exclude any other from representing a craft. The minority members of a craft are thus deprived by the statute of the right, which they would otherwise possess, to choose a representative of their own, and its members cannot bargain individually on behalf of themselves as to matters which are properly the subject of collective bargaining.

* * *

Unless the labor union representing a craft owes some duty to represent non-union members of the craft, at least to the extent of not discriminating against them as such in the contracts which it makes as their representative, the minority would be left with no means of protecting their interests, or indeed, their right to earn a livelihood by pursuing the occupation in which they are employed. While the majority of the craft chooses the bargaining representative, when chosen it represents, as the Act by its terms makes plain, the craft or class, and not the majority. The fair interpretation of the statutory language is that the organization chosen to represent a craft is to represent all its members, the majority as well as the minority, and it is to act for and not against those whom it represents.[3] It is a principle of general application that the exercise of a granted power to act in behalf of others involves the assumption toward them of a duty to exercise the power in their interest and behalf, and that such a grant of power will not be deemed to dispense with all duty toward those for whom it is exercised unless so expressed.

We think that the Railway Labor Act imposes upon the statutory representative of a craft at least as exacting a duty to protect equally the interests of the members of the craft as the Constitution imposes upon a legislature to give equal protection to the interests of those for whom it legislates. Congress has seen fit to clothe the bargaining representative with powers comparable to those possessed by a legislative body both to create and restrict the rights of those whom it represents, but it has also imposed on the representative a corresponding duty. We hold that the language of the Act to which we have

---

3. Compare the House Committee Report on the N.L.R.A. (H. Rep. No. 1147, 74th Cong., 1st Sess., pp. 20–22) indicating that although the principle of majority rule "written into the statute books by Congress in the Railway Labor Act of 1934" was to be applicable to the bargaining unit under the N.L.R.A., the employer was required to give "equally advantageous terms to nonmembers of the labor organization negotiating the agreement."

referred, read in the light of the purposes of the Act, expresses the aim of Congress to impose on the bargaining representative of a craft or class of employees the duty to exercise fairly the power conferred upon it in behalf of all those for whom it acts, without hostile discrimination against them.

This does not mean that the statutory representative of a craft is barred from making contracts which may have unfavorable effects on some of the members of the craft represented. Variations in the terms of the contract based on differences relevant to the authorized purposes of the contract in conditions to which they are to be applied, such as differences in seniority, the type of work performed, the competence and skill with which it is performed, are within the scope of the bargaining representation of a craft, all of whose members are not identical in their interest or merit. Without attempting to mark the allowable limits of differences in the terms of contracts based on differences of conditions to which they apply, it is enough for present purposes to say that the statutory power to represent a craft and to make contracts as to wages, hours and working conditions does not include the authority to make among members of the craft discriminations not based on such relevant differences. Here the discriminations based on race alone are obviously irrelevant and invidious. Congress plainly did not undertake to authorize the bargaining representative to make such discriminations.

The representative which thus discriminates may be enjoined from so doing, and its members may be enjoined from taking the benefit of such discriminatory action. No more is the Railroad bound by or entitled to take the benefit of a contract which the bargaining representative is prohibited by the statute from making. In both cases the right asserted, which is derived from the duty imposed by the statute on the bargaining representative, is a federal right implied from the statute and the policy which it has adopted. It is the federal statute which condemns as unlawful the Brotherhood's conduct. "The extent and nature of the legal consequences of this condemnation, though left by the statute to judicial determination, are nevertheless to be derived from it and the federal policy which it has adopted." Deitrick v. Greaney, 309 U.S. 190, 200, 201, 60 S.Ct. 480, 485, 84 L.Ed. 694.

So long as a labor union assumes to act as the statutory representative of a craft, it cannot rightly refuse to perform the duty, which is inseparable from the power of representation conferred upon it, to represent the entire membership of the craft. While the statute does not deny to such a bargaining labor organization the right to determine eligibility to its membership, it does require the union, in collective bargaining and in making contracts with the carrier, to represent non-union or minority union members of the craft without hostile discrimination, fairly, impartially, and in good faith. Wherever necessary to that end, the union is required to consider requests of non-union members of the craft and expressions of their views with respect to collective bargaining with the employer and to give to them notice of and opportunity for hearing upon its proposed action.

* * *

In the absence of any available administrative remedy, the right here asserted, to a remedy for breach of the statutory duty of the bargaining representative to represent and act for the members of a craft, is of judicial cognizance. That right would be sacrificed or obliterated if it were without the remedy which courts can give for breach of such a duty or obligation and which it is their duty to give in cases in which they have jurisdiction. * * * there can be no doubt of the justiciability of these claims. As we noted in General Committee v. Missouri–Kansas–Texas R. Co., supra, 320 U.S. 331, 64 S.Ct. 150, the statutory provisions which are in issue are stated in the form of commands. For the present command there is no mode of enforcement other than resort to the courts, whose jurisdiction and duty to afford a remedy for a breach of statutory duty are left unaffected. The right is analogous to the statutory right of employees to require the employer to bargain with the statutory representative of a craft, a right which this Court has enforced and protected by its injunction in Texas & N. O. R. Co. v. Brotherhood of Railway & S. S. Clerks, 281 U.S. 556, 557, 560, 50 S.Ct. 429, 430, 74 L.Ed. 1034, and in Virginian R. Co. v. System Federation, 300 U.S. 548, 57 S.Ct. 599, 81 L.Ed. 789, and like it is one for which there is no available administrative remedy.

We conclude that the duty which the statute imposes on a union representative of a craft to represent the interests of all its members stands on no different footing and that the statute contemplates resort to the usual judicial remedies of injunction and award of damages when appropriate for breach of that duty.

The judgment is accordingly reversed and remanded for further proceedings not inconsistent with this opinion.

Reversed.

MR. JUSTICE BLACK concurs in the result.

MR. JUSTICE MURPHY, concurring.

The economic discrimination against Negroes practiced by the Brotherhood and the railroad under color of Congressional authority raises a grave constitutional issue that should be squarely faced.

The utter disregard for the dignity and the well-being of colored citizens shown by this record is so pronounced as to demand the invocation of constitutional condemnation. To decide the case and to analyze the statute solely upon the basis of legal niceties, while remaining mute and placid as to the obvious and oppressive deprivation of constitutional guarantees, is to make the judicial function something less than it should be.

The constitutional problem inherent in this instance is clear. Congress, through the Railway Labor Act, has conferred upon the union selected by a majority of a craft or class of railway workers the power to represent the entire craft or class in all collective bargaining matters. While such a union is essentially a private organization, its power to represent and bind all members of a class or craft is derived solely from Congress. The Act contains no language which directs the manner in which the bargaining representative shall perform its duties. But it cannot be assumed that Congress meant to authorize the representative to act so as to ignore rights guaranteed by the Constitution. Otherwise the Act would bear the stigma of unconstitutionality under the Fifth Amendment in this respect. For that reason I am willing to read the statute as not permitting or allowing any action by the bargaining representative in the exercise of its delegated powers which would in effect violate the constitutional rights of individuals.

If the Court's construction of the statute rests upon this basis, I agree. But I am not sure that such is the basis. Suffice it to say, however, that this constitutional issue cannot be lightly dismissed. The cloak of racism surrounding the actions of the Brotherhood in refusing membership to Negroes and in entering into and enforcing agreements discriminating against them, all under the guise of Congressional authority, still remains. No statutory interpretation can erase this ugly example of economic cruelty against colored citizens of the United States. Nothing can destroy the fact that the accident of birth has been used as the basis to abuse individual rights by an organization purporting to act in conformity with its Congressional mandate. Any attempt to interpret the Act must take that fact into account and must realize that the constitutionality of the statute in this respect depends upon the answer given.

The Constitution voices its disapproval whenever economic discrimination is applied under authority of law against any race, creed or color. A sound democracy cannot allow such discrimination to go unchallenged. Racism is far too virulent today to permit the slightest refusal, in the light of a Constitution that abhors it, to expose and condemn it wherever it appears in the course of a statutory interpretation.

NOTES AND PROBLEMS FOR DISCUSSION

1. What was the "grave constitutional issue" which Justice Murphy in his concurring opinion wished to see "squarely faced?" Would the adoption by the Court of a constitutional basis for its decision have been of any practical benefit to the plaintiff class? The complaint in *Steele* prayed for an injunction prohibiting enforcement of the agreement between the Brotherhood and the Railroad and prohibiting the Brotherhood from acting as the plaintiffs' representative so long as it refused to give them notice and a hearing with respect to actions affecting their interests. Why didn't the plaintiffs request an injunction requiring the Brotherhood to accept blacks as members? What relief does the Court actually afford the plaintiffs?

2. In BROTHERHOOD OF RAILROAD TRAINMEN v. HOWARD, 343 U.S. 768, 72 S.Ct. 1022, 96 L.Ed. 1283 (1952), black train porters complained

that the segregated, all-white Brotherhood of Railroad Trainmen representing the craft of brakemen had entered into an agreement with the employer, the effect of which was to abolish the job of train porter and assign all porter functions to brakemen. The case differed from *Steele* in that the plaintiffs were not members of the bargaining unit represented by the defendant union, but were members of a different craft and were represented by a union of their own choosing. The question thus posed was whether the defendant union owed any duty under the Railway Labor Act not to discriminate against black employees which it did not represent as bargaining agent. In a brief opinion the majority, relying on *Steele*, concluded that "[t]he Federal Act thus prohibits bargaining agents it authorizes from using their position and power to destroy colored workers' jobs in order to bestow them on white workers." 343 U.S. at 774, 72 S.Ct. at 1025. In dissent, Justice Minton, joined by Chief Justice Reed, argued that:

> The majority reaches out to invalidate the contract, not because the train porters are brakemen entitled to fair representation by the Brotherhood, but because they are Negroes who were discriminated against by the carrier at the behest of the Brotherhood. I do not understand that private parties such as the carrier and the Brotherhood may not discriminate on the ground of race. Neither a state government nor the Federal Government may do so, but I know of no applicable federal law which says that private parties may not. That is the whole problem underlying the proposed Federal Fair Employment Practices Code. Of course, this Court by sheer power can say this case is *Steele*, or even lay down a code of fair employment practices. But sheer power is not a substitute for legality.

343 U.S. at 777–778, 72 S.Ct. at 1027.

In light of *Steele*, what was the source of the union's duty not to discriminate against employees it did not represent? In CONLEY v. GIBSON, 355 U.S. 41, 78 S.Ct. 99, 2 L.Ed.2d 80 (1957), the *Steele* doctrine of fair representation was extended to apply to a union's failure to protect black employees in the bargaining unit from unilateral action by the employer. In that case the railroad eliminated forty-five jobs held by blacks in violation of a contract with the Brotherhood of Railway Clerks whose all-white local accepted the employer's excuses and refused to process grievances filed by the displaced employees. Because the district court dismissed the case on jurisdictional grounds, the Supreme Court could hold no more than that the complaint stated a cause of action under the Railway Labor Act. 355 U.S. at 45, 78 S.Ct. at 101. Thus the question of exactly what relief black employees were entitled to against union or employer under the Act remained unanswered.[a] Could, for example, the employer be required to reinstate black employees discharged on racial grounds because of the union's failure to fairly represent? Also left open by *Steele* and its progeny was the question of whether a union had an obligation to protest racially discriminatory employment practices preexisting the union's status as bargaining agent under the RLA. See Clark v. Norfolk & Western Railway, 37 L.R.R.M. 2685 (W.D.Va.1956); Richardson v. Texas & New Orleans Railroad Co., 242 F.2d 230 (5th Cir.1957).

[a] On remand from the Supreme Court, seven years after the elimination of the black jobs, the district court is reported to have granted the defendants' motion to dismiss as to deceased plaintiffs and a motion for summary judgment as to the remaining plaintiffs' class action. See Herring, The "Fair Representation" Doctrine: An Effective Weapon Against Union Racial Discrimination?, 24 Md.L.Rev.113, 127 (1964).

3. The development of the fair representation doctrine occurred chiefly in litigation under the Railway Labor Act arising in the southern railroad industry. That development began with the filing of the *Steele* case and its federal court companion, Tunstall v. Brotherhood of Locomotive Firemen and Enginemen, Ocean Lodge No. 76, 323 U.S. 210, 65 S.Ct. 235, 89 L.Ed. 187 (1944) in the early 1940s. It was not until 1955, however, that unions acting as bargaining agents under the National Labor Relations Act were held to have the same obligations toward minority employees that the railroad unions bore under the RLA. In Syres v. Oil Workers Intern. Union, Local No. 23, 223 F.2d 739 (5th Cir.1955), reversed, 350 U.S. 892, 76 S.Ct. 152, 100 L.Ed. 785 (1955), an all-black local filed suit against its white counterpart for injunctive relief and damages, alleging that the white union caused the employer to maintain segregated job classifications which relegated black workers to the lowest paying, least desirable positions. The Fifth Circuit affirmed the dismissal of the suit as one merely arising from a dispute between the locals, and involving no federal question. The Supreme Court reversed in a one sentence per curiam opinion citing *Steele* and Brotherhood of Railroad Trainmen v. Howard. In Humphrey v. Moore, 375 U.S. 335, 84 S.Ct. 363, 11 L.Ed.2d 370 (1964), the Court stated explicitly that a union operating under the NLRA has the same "responsibility and duty of fair representation" as that imposed on unions by the RLA. The National Labor Relations Board in Metal Worker's Union (Hughes Tool Co.), 147 N.L.R.B. 1573 (1964) held that a union's breach of its duty to fairly represent black workers constituted a violation of the NLRA, and warranted rescission of the union's certification as exclusive bargaining agent. See also Local Union 12, United Rubber, Cork, Linoleum and Plastic Workers v. National Labor Relations Board, 150 N.L.R.B. 312 (1964), enforced, 368 F.2d 12 (5th Cir.1966) (union's refusal to process grievances based on belief that employee's discriminatory job conditions should continue found to be violation of duty of fair representation), and Houston Maritime Association, 168 N.L.R.B. 615 (1967) (duty of fair representation breached by union's policies which perpetuated effects of past discrimination). But in Handy Andy, Inc., 228 N.L.R.B. 447 (1977), the Board ruled that certification would not be withheld because of a union's history of discriminatory activities in *other* bargaining units.

4. *Steele* and the cases discussed above addressed the problem of racial discrimination by the employer initiated or tolerated by unions endowed with powers by the national labor laws. As a natural corollary to the fair representation cases, the practice of racial segregation of union membership itself came under attack. In James v. Marinship Corp., 25 Cal.2d 721, 155 P.2d 329 (1944) and Williams v. International Brotherhood of Boilermakers, Iron Shipbuilders & Helpers of America, 27 Cal.2d 586, 165 P.2d 903 (1946), all-white locals of the Boilermakers created segregated auxiliary locals for black employees and then sought to enforce closed shop agreements with employers by demanding discharge of black workers who refused to join such auxiliaries. The district court in *James* enjoined enforcement of the closed shop contracts against the black employees and also enjoined the white local from "refusing to admit into membership in said Local 6 on the same terms and conditions as white persons * * * plaintiffs and other Negro workers similarly situated." The California Supreme Court, basing its decision in part on the public policy of the state and in part on the special status of the unions as exclusive bargaining agents under the NLRA, affirmed and held that a union could not enforce a closed shop agreement while at the same time closing its membership. The court interpreted the district court's order, however, not as requiring the white local to admit

black members, but only as prohibiting the union from maintaining *both* a closed shop and an arbitrarily closed or partially closed union. 155 P.2d at 342. The court's opinions in both *James* and *Williams* were expressly contingent on the findings that the black auxiliaries were inferior in status and authority to the white locals, thus leaving open the question whether a union with "separate but equal" segregated locals could enforce a closed shop contract against workers refusing to join a segregated local. In Betts v. Easley, 161 Kan. 459, 169 P.2d 831 (1946), the Kansas Supreme Court enjoined the Brotherhood of Railway Carmen, which had established racially segregated locals after becoming the certified bargaining agent for employees of the Santa Fe Railway, from acting as a bargaining agent for black employees as long as the latter "were not given equality in privileges and participation in union affairs." But in Oliphant v. Brotherhood of Locomotive Firemen and Enginemen, 262 F.2d 359 (6th Cir.1958), cert. denied, 359 U.S. 935, 79 S.Ct. 648, 3 L.Ed.2d 636 (1959), where black employees sought an order requiring their admission to an all-white union on the ground that, as their recognized bargaining agent, it had negotiated a contract detrimental to their interests, the district court and court of appeals dismissed the complaint, finding the Brotherhood's certification under the RLA insufficient to make its discriminatory conduct the equivalent of government action. The Supreme Court denied review "in view of the abstract context in which the questions sought to be raised are presented in this record."

SECTION D. STATE LAW

Commencing in the 1940's, a number of states enacted fair employment practice statutes to combat discrimination in employment. These statutes took one of two forms: (1) those which expressed a public policy against discrimination in employment, but contained no remedial provisions, and (2) those which defined prohibited employment practices and provided an enforcement mechanism.[a] A series of statutes [b] enacted by the State of New York typified the second type of act: the New York laws, variously applicable to employers, employment agencies, and labor organizations, defined unlawful discrimination to include the refusal of an employer to hire or to discharge from employment because of an individual's race, color or creed. Discrimination with regard to "compensation or terms of employment" was also prohibited and labor unions were forbidden to discriminate against either their members or employers because of race, creed or color. Most importantly, the New York laws provided for enforcement by the State Commission for Human Rights. Upon the filing of a complaint of discrimination, the Commission was authorized to investigate, conduct hearings, issue judicially enforceable cease and desist orders and take other affirmative action.[c] Violators of the acts were subject to criminal

---

[a] For a comprehensive survey of state legislation as of 1949, see Note, Fair Employment Practices—A Comparison of State Legislation and Proposed Bills, 24 N.Y.U.L.Q. 398 (1949).

[b] See, e.g., N.Y. Civil Rights Law, ch. 6, §§ 40–43; N.Y. Executive Law, ch. 18, §§ 290–301; N.Y. Labor Laws, ch. 31,

§ 220–e; N.Y. Penal Law, ch. 40, §§ 700–701, 514.

[c] Under N.Y. Executive Law, ch. 18, §§ 295–297, the Commission was authorized to issue cease and desist orders upon a finding that a violation was occurring; to order reinstatement, back pay, restoration

prosecution as well as civil liability.   An individual discriminated against by a labor union enjoyed a private right of action for damages, but when a labor organization was not implicated, the individual's exclusive remedy was before the Commission.

In RAILWAY MAIL ASSOCIATION v. CORSI, 326 U.S. 88, 65 S.Ct. 1483, 89 L.Ed. 2072 (1945), an association of postal workers which limited its membership to "Caucasians and native American Indians" charged that the New York statute prohibiting discriminatory exclusion from membership violated due process by denying to the group the right to select its own membership.   Citing State v. Louisville & Nashville Railroad Co. and Tunstall v. Brotherhood of Locomotive Firemen and Engineers, a unanimous Supreme Court declared there was "no constitutional basis for the contention that a state cannot protect workers from exclusion solely on the basis of race, color or creed by an organization * * *."   Significantly, the Court did not refer to Hodges v. United States, In *The Slaughter-house Cases* or any other judicial nullifications of federal civil rights legislation.   But if a state was not constitutionally barred from prohibiting discrimination by private associations, could there be any constitutional barrier to such action by the federal government?

Following passage of the Civil Rights Act of 1964 a number of states enacted employment discrimination laws that replicated or were very similar to Title VII of the federal act.   The relation of such state statutes to federal employment discrimination litigation is discussed in Chapter 4, *infra*.

of or admission to union membership; and
to order payment of compensatory damages.

Part II

TITLE VII OF THE CIVIL RIGHTS ACT OF 1964

Chapter 1

AN OVERVIEW OF THE SUBSTANTIVE PROVISIONS

Of the several pieces of legislation enacted by Congress to promote the goal of equal employment opportunity, none has been the basis for more litigation, nor the subject of more intense and wideranging judicial and academic scrutiny, than Title VII of the Civil Rights Act of 1964,[a] as amended by the Equal Employment Opportunity Act of 1972[b], the Pregnancy Discrimination Act of 1978[c], and the Civil Rights Act of 1991.[d] The explosion of litigation that followed the enactment of Title VII can be traced, at least in part, to the expansive language Congress used to define the classes of persons and employment-related decisions subject to the Act's substantive proscriptions. Title VII prohibits employers, unions and employment agencies from discriminating with respect to a broadly defined class of employment-related decisions on the basis of five specifically enumerated classifications—race, color, religion, national origin and sex. It also created the Equal Employment Opportunity Commission (EEOC), a five member, presidentially-appointed agency, to administer and interpret its provisions. The following selection of cases and note materials addresses several issues relating to the coverage of this statute.

SECTION A. COVERED ENTITIES

Read Sections 701(a)–(i), 703(a)–(c), and 717(a) of Title VII.[e]

[a] The 1964 Civil Rights Act, Pub.L. 88–352; 78 Stat. 241; 42 U.S.C. §§ 1971, 1975a–d, 2000a et seq., is an omnibus civil rights statute designed to prohibit discrimination in, inter alia, public accommodations and facilities, participation in federally assisted programs, and education, as well as in employment.

[b] Pub.L. 92–261, 86 Stat. 103, 42 U.S.C. § 2000e et seq.

[c] Pub.L. 95–555, 92 Stat. 2076, 42 U.S.C. § 2000e(k).

[d] Pub.L. 102–166, 105 Stat. 1071, 42 U.S.C. § ——.

[e] All references to Title VII will be made to the Act's original section numbers rather than to the parallel U.S. Code citations.

1. Employers

Title VII prohibits three types of employment-related institutions—employers, employment agencies, and unions—from engaging in discriminatory employment practices. Section 701(b) defines "employer" as [1] a "person," [2] "engaged in an industry affecting commerce," [3] who has at least fifteen employees for twenty weeks during the current or preceding calendar year. The broadly worded definitions in § 701 of "person" and "industry affecting commerce" clearly reflect Congress' desire to maximize the scope of Title VII's jurisdiction since they result in the inclusion of virtually all organizational structures used to further business purposes within the statutory definition of "employer." Consequently, the only significant limitation on the definition of this term is the requirement that an "employer" have fifteen "employees" within the prescribed time period. Moreover, while the Act originally required a covered employer to have twenty-five employees, the reduction of this requirement to fifteen employees effected by the 1972 Amendments is further evidence of the legislature's desire to expand the reach of Title VII. Several interpretative questions, nevertheless, have arisen in connection with this minimum employee requirement.

**EQUAL EMPLOYMENT OPPORTUNITY COMMISSION
v. RINELLA & RINELLA**

United States District Court, Northern District of Illinois, 1975.
401 F.Supp. 175.

WILL, DISTRICT JUDGE.

* * * Arlene Nagy was employed by the defendants as a legal secretary from January 1971 to March 1973, when she resigned and from October 1973, when she was rehired, to July 10, 1974 when she was discharged. From March of 1974, she was also a member of Women Employed, an Illinois not-for-profit corporation whose purpose is to oppose discrimination based on sex and otherwise to work to improve the employment status and working conditions of women in Chicago, Illinois.

Between March 1973 and July 30, 1974, Ms. Nagy engaged in various activities in opposition to what she alleges to be unlawful employment practices by Rinella & Rinella, which discriminated against women. These activities included joining Women Employed, soliciting other women employees of Rinella & Rinella to join Women Employed, attending meetings and participating in the activities of Women Employed, and publicly alleging that Rinella & Rinella discriminated on the basis of sex in its health insurance benefits. On July 30, 1974, Samuel A. Rinella, the owner of the law firm, discharged Ms. Nagy because of her participation in these activities.

Women Employed, on August 26, 1974, filed a charge with the Commission stating that Rinella & Rinella, in violation of Section 704(a) of Title VII, 42 U.S.C. § 2000e–3(a), intentionally discriminated against Arlene Nagy by unlawfully discharging her, and that the firm, by and through its partner, Samuel Rinella, intentionally discriminated against other female employees by interrogating them concerning their membership in Women Employed and threatening to discharge them if they joined or participated in the activities of Women Employed. The Commission conducted a preliminary investigation and the District Director of the Commission's Chicago District Office concluded, in accordance with Section 706(f)(2), that prompt judicial action in the form of preliminary relief was necessary to carry out the purposes of Title VII. Consequently, on October 7, 1974, the Commission filed a petition for preliminary relief against Rinella & Rinella pursuant to Section 706(f)(2) * * *.

During the pendency of this action, on February 24, 1975, the Commission under the signature of a deputy director of the Chicago District Office, issued a right-to-sue letter to Women Employed. Thereafter, on March 4, 1975, Women Employed, as agent for and on behalf of Arlene Nagy, and Arlene Nagy, filed the second lawsuit under Section 706(f)(1) of Title VII * * *.

The defendants have filed motions to dismiss both lawsuits raising numerous alleged jurisdictional and procedural deficiencies. Specifically, their totally non-frivolous claims include:

> 1. The court is without subject matter jurisdiction in that:
>
> a. The defendant does not qualify as an employer engaged in an industry affecting interstate commerce.
>
> b. The defendant has not continuously employed fifteen (15) or more persons.

* * *

For the reasons set forth hereinafter, we find none of defendants' arguments offered in support of their motions to be meritorious and, accordingly, their motions to dismiss will be denied.

The plaintiffs allege that the defendant law firm is an employer within the meaning of Section 701(b) of Title VII, and is, therefore, subject to the proscriptions of the Civil Rights Act of 1964. The term "employer" is defined by the Act as:

> * * * a person engaged in an industry affecting commerce who has fifteen or more employees for each working day in each of twenty or more calendar weeks in the current or preceding calendar year, and any agent of such person * * *.

Title VII goes on to define an "employee" in almost unrestricted terms:

> The term "employee" means an individual employed by an employer * * *.

The defendants admit that they employed at least eleven employees during the relevant period consisting of secretaries and other clerical personnel and law clerks. Ms. Nagy's status as an employee is contested by the defendants; however, it would appear that she constituted a twelfth employee. The firm also included a group of lawyers which ranged from six to eight during the period under investigation. It is the defendants' contention that, due to the nature of these attorneys' status, they were independent contractors and not employees of the firm. As such, defendants contend, their numbers may not be applied toward reaching the required fifteen employees, and, accordingly, the firm is beyond the purview of Title VII.

The defendants argue that a primary consideration in determining whether an individual is an employee is whether the employer had the power to direct, control and supervise the employee in the performance of his work. The defendants contend that the element of control is not present here. They stress that the lawyers associated with the firm divide fees on the basis of productivity pursuant to a pre-arranged agreement providing for periodic salary draws, that the attorneys have no fixed office hours, set their own vacation schedules, and fix the fees in those cases for which they have responsibility. They further claim that the lawyer to whom a case is assigned is solely responsible for working on that case and does not receive instructions or guidance.

While the defendants' representations would indicate that, as professionals, the attorneys associated with Rinella & Rinella are subject to minimal direct supervision, the conclusion that the defendants would have us accept—that professional employment situations are not covered by Title VII—clearly is not the case. That sections 701, 703 and 704(a) of Title VII were intended to reach "professionals" is borne out by the legislative history of the 1972 amendments to Title VII.

* * *

The courts also have found little distinction between professional and nonprofessional job situations, concluding that, since the primary objective of Title VII is the elimination of the major social ills of job discrimination, discriminatory practices in professional fields are not immune from attack.

Accordingly, we do not find that the greater independence and authority generally afforded attorneys associated with smaller law firms precludes their being employees of the firm. Rather, the court must examine the totality of the firm's arrangements to determine whether an employer-employee relationship in fact exists. In the instant case, the evidence overwhelmingly supports a finding that the attorneys associated with Samuel Rinella in Rinella & Rinella are employees.

Samuel Rinella admits to being the sole owner of the firm of Rinella & Rinella. All of the other attorneys are associated with him in the practice of law. Samuel Rinella hires each of his associates and he has the authority to fire them. Samuel Rinella maintains that the reason that he has associates is to accommodate the amount of business he attracts and so he can have control over the cases.

Samuel Rinella refers significant numbers of his cases to his associates. * * * Associates' cases which are not referred directly from Samuel Rinella are also apparently considered firm work as most of the associates deposit the fees from their own cases in the firm bank account * * *.

Samuel Rinella also exerts considerable control over the compensation paid to those associated with his firm. While the attorneys' compensation, regular or bi-weekly salary draws out of the firm account with quarterly adjustments, is the result of negotiation and mutual agreement between Samuel Rinella and the individual attorney, no one disputes that Samuel Rinella has the final say with respect to the sums involved. The lawyers' compensation strongly resembles a salary in that it is regular and in round numbers, and there is no indication that an attorney has ever returned money to the firm following a quarterly adjustment or paid any interest. These factors controvert the defendants' suggestion that the draws are merely loans to independent contractors based upon expected earnings. Samuel Rinella also determines and pays the salaries of all secretarial and clerical employees.

* * *

Finally, all outward appearances to the public indicate that the attorneys are employed by the firm. The list of names on the law office's outer door, as well as the letterhead on the firm's stationery and billhead, suggest that the attorneys are working for the firm. The firm's stationery and billhead are apparently used by the associates on their own cases as well as those referred to them by Samuel Rinella. The firm's listings in various legal directories also suggest that the associates are employees. Since the firm is not a partnership, and the associates are not listed as "of counsel," it is only reasonable to conclude that they are employed by the firm.

Based upon all of these considerations, it is inconceivable that the associates of Rinella & Rinella could be considered anything but employees of the firm. Added to the secretarial and other clerical employees whom defendants concede to be employees within the meaning of Title VII, the law firm does employ more than the requisite fifteen employees, and therefore comes within its coverage.

The defendants contend that they are not engaged in an industry affecting interstate commerce due to the local nature of their business which involves predominately divorce litigation. Few cases have dealt with whether the practice of law affects commerce. Of particular note is the National Labor Relations Board's decision in Evans and Kunz, Ltd., 194 NLRB 1216 (1972), involving unfair labor charges levied against a small Phoenix law firm which confines most, if not all, of its activities to the practice of law solely within the state of Arizona. In that case, the Board upheld the Trial Examiner's decision that the firm was engaged in operations affecting commerce within the meaning of the National Labor Relations Act, wherein "affecting commerce" is similarly defined. The Board, however, exercised its discretion and declined to assert its jurisdiction concluding that "the effect of a labor dispute on commerce is not sufficiently substantial to warrant the exercise of jurisdiction." While we do not find the Board's decision defining jurisdiction in the context of a different statute with different policies and purposes to be controlling here, we do find its determination that a predominantly local law firm affects commerce to be germane and instructive.

* * * [I]n keeping with the general principle that remedial legislation such as Title VII should be liberally construed for jurisdictional purposes, we find that the dynamics inherent in a general law practice necessarily affects interstate commerce. This is especially so in light of the cases interpreting the interstate commerce requirements of the Civil Rights Act of 1964, most notably, Katzenbach v. McClung, 379 U.S. 294, 85 S.Ct. 377, 13 L.Ed.2d 290 (1964), which held that Ollie's Barbeque, a family owned restaurant catering only to local trade, was within the definition of commerce contained in Title II of the Civil Rights Act of 1964.

The incidents of interstate commerce are far more apparent in the instant case than they were in Katzenbach v. McClung and many of its progeny. Notwithstanding the defendants' divorce orientation, they admit that their practice encompasses other types of business, i.e., corporate, probate and real estate. They further admit that various attorneys travel out of state on firm business. Samuel Rinella, for instance, travelled to London, England and to Arizona, and Richard Rinella travelled to Washington, D.C. The firm's long distance phone bill in calendar year 1974 was $1,277.01; its out-of-state travel expenses amounted to approximately $2,000 for the same year. The firm also purchased both office intercommunication equipment from an out-of-state company for $8,400, and law and reference books from out-of-state publishers billed at approximately $2,500. These various factors establish that Rinella & Rinella indeed affects interstate commerce and, accordingly, is subject to the proscriptions of Title VII.

* * *

In summary, defendants' motion to dismiss for lack of jurisdiction * * * [is] denied. Cause No. 74 C 2861 and Cause No. 75 C 702 will be consolidated for the purpose of further discovery and trial if necessary. An order consistent with the foregoing will enter.

NOTES AND PROBLEMS FOR DISCUSSION

1. Would the result in the principal case have been different if all the attorneys in the defendant law firm had been partners? See Burke v. Friedman, 556 F.2d 867 (7th Cir.1977). Is a general rule the best approach or should decisions be made on an ad hoc basis? The EEOC has embraced the "economic realities" test, under which it looks to the economic realities of the plaintiff's employment situation, especially his or her ownership and management interest in the business. See EEOC Dec. No. 85–4, 53 L.W. 2492 (Apr. 9, 1985). The Tenth Circuit, however, in Wheeler v. Main Hurdman, 825 F.2d 257 (10th

Cir.1987), rejected both the "economic realities" and "control" tests in favor of a general rule that bona fide general partners are not employees within the meaning of the statute. The court indicated that "bona fide general partners" were distinguishable from "employees" by their (1) participation in profits and losses; (2) exposure to liability; (3) investment in the firm; (4) partial owner-ship of firm assets; and (5) voting rights. Yet another court, applying Title VII jurisprudence to an age discrimination claim brought under the ADEA, con-cluded that an employer's classification of an individual as a partner should not be dispositive of the determination of that individual's status. Rather, it reasoned, the classification of an individual as an employee or employer should reflect a consideration of (a) the individual's ability to control and operate the business, (b) whether the individual's compensation was based on profit sharing; and (c) whether the individual enjoyed some measure of job security. Caruso v. Peat, Marwick, Mitchell & Co., 664 F.Supp. 144, 149–50 (S.D.N.Y.1987). For a suggestion that treating partners as "employees" is consistent with the pur-poses of Title VII, see Note, Applicability of Federal Antidiscrimination Legisla-tion to the Selection of a Law Partner, 76 Mich.L.Rev. 282 (1977).

2. Jane Baker claims that she was refused a position as night manager by Pine Valley Motor Lodge on the basis of her sex. Pine Valley is a small, local business with only 10 employees. It is a wholly owned subsidiary, however, of Great American Hotel & Motel, Inc., a corporation with over one thousand employees. After Baker filed a Title VII action against Pine Valley, the defendant moved to dismiss the case on the ground that it was not an employer within the meaning of the statute. How should the court rule on this motion? See Armbruster v. Quinn, 711 F.2d 1332 (6th Cir.1983); Watson v. Gulf & Western Industries, 650 F.2d 990 (9th Cir.1981); Baker v. Stuart Broadcasting Co., 560 F.2d 389 (8th Cir.1977). Any different result if Pine Valley's payroll also included six part-time employees? See Pascutoi v. Washburn–McReavy Mortuary, Inc., 11 FEP Cases 1325 (D.Minn.1975). What if each of these six also had another job? See Thurber v. Jack Reilly's, Inc., 717 F.2d 633 (1st Cir.1983), cert. denied, 466 U.S. 904, 104 S.Ct. 1678, 80 L.Ed.2d 153 (1984). What if they were unpaid volunteers? See Tadros v. Coleman, 717 F.Supp. 996 (S.D.N.Y.1989), affirmed without discussion, 898 F.2d 10 (2d Cir.1990); Smith v. Berks Community Television, 657 F.Supp. 794 (E.D.Pa.1987). If unpaid vol-unteers are held not to fall within the meaning of "employee", does this mean that they are not entitled to protection under Title VII or does it mean only that an employer who does not have fifteen statutory employees without them is not covered by the statute?

3. Bill Montes claims that on July 5, 1978, he was denied a promotion by his employer, Kondet Industries, Inc. because he is an Hispanic. He filed a timely charge of national origin and race discrimination with the EEOC on October 15, 1978. On December 1, 1978, Kondet was taken over by Amalga-mated Production Company. Montes timely filed an amended charge against Amalgamated on January 1, 1979. Amalgamated subsequently moved to dismiss the complaint for failure to state a claim and for lack of subject matter jurisdiction. What result? Should this issue be left to private negotiation? Would the affected employees be a party to such negotiations? What effect would a rule imposing liability have or transferability of businesses? Could Montes have obtained an effective remedy from the prior owner? See In Re National Airlines, Inc., 700 F.2d 695 (11th Cir.1983); Trujillo v. Longhorn Mfg. Co., 694 F.2d 221 (10th Cir.1982); Dominguez v. Hotel Union, Local 64, 674 F.2d 732 (8th Cir.1982); EEOC v. MacMillan Bloedel Containers, Inc., 503 F.2d 1086

(6th Cir.1974); Brown v. Evening News Association, 473 F.Supp. 1242 (E.D.Mich.1979). What if the EEOC charge had been filed on December 15, 1978? See Rabidue v. Osceola Refining Co., 805 F.2d 611 (6th Cir.1986), cert. denied, 481 U.S. 1041, 107 S.Ct. 1983, 95 L.Ed.2d 823 (1987). See generally, Barksdale, Successor Liability Under the National Labor Relations Act and Title VII, 54 Tex.L.Rev. 707 (1976).

4. Can the discharged employee of a McDonald's franchise bring a Title VII claim against McDonald's as well as against the owner/operator of the franchise? Assume that the franchisor conducts intermittent inspections of all franchises to ensure that the franchises adhere to standardized operating standards and details and that the franchisor has the authority to terminate an individual's franchise. See Evans v. McDonald's Corp., 936 F.2d 1087 (10th Cir.1991); Kennedy v. McDonald's Corp., 610 F.Supp. 203 (S.D.W.Va.1985). Suppose that after her discharge, this employee moved to Moscow and obtained a job with the McDonald's on Pushkin Square. Could she bring a claim under Title VII against either McDonald's or the owner/operator of the franchise if she was subsequently discharged on the basis of her sex? See § 702(b) and the discussion at Note 5 after *Mississippi College* in § D of this Chapter, *infra* at 79–81.

5. Section 701(b) includes "agents" of § 701(a) "persons" within the class of covered employers. Accordingly, an employer with less than fifteen employees can be covered by the Act if it is viewed as the agent of an organization with more than 15 employees. See e.g., Owens v. Rush, 636 F.2d 283 (10th Cir.1980) (claim against County Sheriff, whose office employed fewer than 15 persons, is cognizable under Title VII as Sheriff is under contract of, and is therefore an agent of County, and County satisfied minimum employee requirement). Does this provision also mean that a company can be liable under Title VII for the discriminatory acts of its employees? Would it matter whether the discriminator was a supervisory or non-supervisory employee? What about the employer's prior knowledge of, or response to the discriminatory conduct? See Meritor Savings Bank, FSB v. Vinson, *infra,* at 408. Note, however, the absence in § 717 (the provision extending Title VII to federal government employees) of analogous "agent" language. Did Congress intend to apply a different rule to federal employers?

6. As originally enacted, Title VII did not apply to the employment practices of federal, state or local government employers. The 1972 amendments, however, broadened the definition of "person" in § 701(a) to include state and local governments, governmental agencies, and political subdivisions. In addition, the 1972 enactment added a new provision, § 717, bringing many federal government employees within the purview of Title VII. Coverage for federal employees, however, was limited by the express terms of § 717(a) to employees or applicants for employment in (1) executive agencies, and (2) those units of the legislative and judicial branches having positions in the competitive service. But as part of the amendments to Title VII contained in the 1991 Civil Rights Act, Congress expanded the applicability of the substantive (though not remedial or procedural) terms of Title VII to encompass employees of the U.S. House of Representatives and the agencies of the legislative branch. Section 117 of the 1991 Act extends the coverage of Title VII to all employees of the House, any employing authority of the House and any instrumentality of the Congress. This provision also lists the Capitol Architect, the Congressional Budget Office, the Government Printing Office, the Office of Technology Assessment and the U.S. Botanic Garden as among the instrumentalities of the

Congress. The remedies and procedures for enforcing the substantive rights of House employees are governed exclusively by the terms of the House Fair Employment Practices Resolution adopted in 1988, or any other subsequently adopted provision that continues the effect of this resolution and which is enacted by the House in the exercise of its rulemaking authority. The remedies and procedures applicable to complaints by employees of Congressional instrumentalities are to be established by the chief official of each instrumentality and are the exclusive means of enforcing the rights enjoyed by such employees under Title VII and the GERA. The Act contains no provision for judicial review of Title VII claims by employees of either the House or legislative agencies.

The rights of Senate employees and presidential appointees are addressed by another portion of the 1991 legislation—an associated statute entitled the Government Employee Rights Act of 1991 (GERA). This Act provides that the substantive terms of Title VII, as amended, apply to all employment-related decisions affecting Senate employees (defined as incumbent and former employees as well as applicants for employment) and presidential appointees (a term defined to include employees of all units of the executive branch, including the Executive Office, but excluding appointees whose appointments are made with the advice and consent of the Senate and members of the uniformed services). It also incorporates the Senate's commitment to Rule XLII of the Standing Rules of the Senate, which prohibits members and employee from discriminating against individuals with respect to all terms and conditions of employment on the basis of, *inter alia*, the five classifications mentioned in Title VII. While Senate employees and presidential appointees enjoy the substantive protections of Title VII, they are not entitled to a judicial trial of their claims. Rather, exclusive jurisdiction over complaints by Senate employees is assigned to the newly created Office of Senate Fair Employment Practices, with review of its decisions going to the Senate Ethics Committee and, thereafter, to the Federal Circuit Court of Appeals. Similarly, presidential appointees alleging a violation of the GERA can either file a charge with the EEOC or with a body designated by a presidential Executive Order, with review from either of these sources to the Federal Circuit Court of Appeals. And since § 102 of the 1991 Act limits recovery of punitive damages to private sector employees, this form of relief is unavailable to Senate employees and presidential appointees.

The Supreme Court upheld the constitutionality of the extension of Title VII to state and local government entities in Fitzpatrick v. Bitzer, 427 U.S. 445, 96 S.Ct. 2666, 49 L.Ed.2d 614 (1976). Rejecting the claim that awards of money judgments for back pay or attorneys' fees infringed upon state sovereignty guaranteed by the Eleventh Amendment, the Court held that enactment of the statutory amendment was a proper exercise of Congress' enforcement power under § 5 of the Fourteenth Amendment. For a thorough discussion of the constitutional challenges to Title VII's extension to public employment, see Note, Title VII and Public Employers: Did Congress Exceed Its Powers?, 78 Col.L.Rev. 372 (1978).

7. While § 701(a) includes state and local governments within the meaning of "employer", § 701(f) expressly excluded elected officials, members of their personal staff, their immediate legal advisors and policy-making level appointees (unless they were subject to state or local civil service laws) from the operation of Title VII. Section 321 of the GERA, as part of the 1991 Civil Rights Act, eliminated this exclusion as to all but elected officials. Thus, individuals appointed by elected officials to their personal staff, as their legal

advisors or as policy-making officials are now protected under Title VII and can enforce these rights by filing a complaint with the EEOC, with review to a U.S. Court of Appeals.

8.   William Sheraton, a black attorney, is engaged in the private practice of criminal defense law. He claims that the trial judges in his jurisdiction do not appoint black attorneys to represent indigents in criminal cases. Attorneys receiving such appointments are paid under a local Criminal Justice Act. Mr. Sheraton files an action against the State under Title VII alleging that he is being discriminated against on the basis of his race. The State responds with a motion to dismiss. What result? See Thompson v. District of Columbia, 25 FEP Cases 943 (D.D.C.1980), affirmed, 672 F.2d 897 (D.C.Cir. 1981).

9.   Camella Dimitri is a secretary for Lois Ann, Inc., a producer of computer software products. Lois Ann has thirteen employees in its Los Angeles office and three sales representatives. The sales representatives do not work out of the corporate office. They sell other product lines besides those of Lois Ann and are paid no salary apart from commissions received for products sold. Ms. Judge brought a Title VII action against Lois Ann alleging that she was subjected to sexual harassment by Lois Ann's President, Alan Kopolow. Lois Ann files a motion to dismiss. What result? See Armbruster v. Quinn, 711 F.2d 1332 (6th Cir.1983).   *Dismissed*

2.   Employment Agencies

What are 5

GREENFIELD v. FIELD ENTERPRISES, INC.

United States District Court, Northern District of Illinois, 1972.
4 FEP Cases 548.

McGARR, DISTRICT JUDGE.

The plaintiffs describe themselves as six " * * * female members of the employment market in the Chicago area * * * over twenty-one years of age."   The defendants are corporations in the business of publishing newspapers and particularly newspapers containing classified advertisement sections in the Chicago area. The complaint alleges that these classified advertisement sections contain help-wanted listings under separate male and female headings without reference to whether sex is a bona fide occupational qualification reasonably necessary to the normal operation of the advertiser's business or enterprise.   It is contended that this practice is a violation of Title VII of the Civil Rights Act of 1964 and particularly Section 703(b):

> It shall be an unlawful employment practice for an employment agency to fail or refuse to refer for employment, or otherwise to discriminate against, any individual because of his race, color, religion, sex, or national origin, or to classify or refer for employment any individual on the basis of his race, color, religion, sex, or national origin.

The definition of the phrase "employment agency" used in this section is found elsewhere in the same statute. Paragraph (c) reads in pertinent part as follows:

The term "employment agency" means any person regularly undertaking with or without compensation to procure employees for an employer or to procure for employees opportunities to work for an employer and includes an agent of such person.   * * *

Plaintiffs allege that the publication of said listings causes them irreparable injury by depriving them of equal access to employment where sex is not a bona fide occupational qualification.   * * * The complaint seeks a preliminary and permanent injunction against the defendants, prohibiting the listing of jobs under male and female headings where sex is not a bona fide occupational qualification.

Defendants have filed motions variously denominated motion to strike or dismiss, or motions for judgment on the pleadings, all seeking a final disposition of the case based on the contention that the complaint fails to state a cause of action cognizable before this court. * * *

* * *

The paramount issue in the adjudication of the motions now under consideration by this court involves the question whether the language of the statute controlling here, in its reference to employment agencies, was intended to apply, and does apply, to newspapers publishing classified ads.   * * *

At the outset, we must examine Section 703(b), and consider it together with the definition of the term employment agency in Section 701(c).   Those sections, together with such light as the legislative history may throw upon them, control this court's decision on these motions.   To the extent that it is helpful, we must also consider the single case which seems closely in point, Brush v. San Francisco Newspaper Printing Co., 315 F.Supp. 577, and the equally relevant consideration that the Equal Employment Opportunity Commission, the agency charged with the administration of Title VII, has concluded that utilization by the employer of classified advertising such as is complained of here, is covered by Title VII, and has so stated as follows:

"Job Opportunity Advertising. It is a violation of Title VII for a help-wanted advertisement to indicate a preference, limitation, specification, or discrimination based on sex unless sex is a bona fide occupational qualification for the particular job involved. The placement of an advertisement in columns classified by publishers on the basis of sex, such as columns headed 'Male' or 'Female', will be considered as expression of a preference, limitation, specification or discrimination based on sex."

The administrative interpretation of the Act by the enforcing agency is entitled to great deference. It is not, however, precisely in point in this case, nor is it, in the last analysis, binding upon the court.

The brief of the Equal Employment Opportunity Commission refers to an ancillary provision of the statute for the light it presumably throws on the issues here. It sets out the relevant portion of Section

704(b) of Title VII. The pleadings do not rely upon this section, and it has not otherwise been injected into the case except by this reference in the brief of the Equal Employment Opportunity Commission. Because it refers to printing and advertising, it seems apt at first glance. However, it throws no light on the principal issue, since it, too, is a section limited in its application to "an employment agency." We thus revert to the necessity of determining whether in the conduct of the activities complained of in the complaint, the newspaper defendants are employment agencies as contemplated by the statute.

In examining Section 701(c) of the Act, which defines employment agency, we note that it begins with the phrase "any person." Corporations are included in the meaning of the word person. The section goes on, " * * * regularly undertaking with or without compensation to procure employees for an employer or to procure for employees opportunities to work for an employer. * * * " This definition clearly describes the activities of an employment agency in the traditional and generally accepted sense of that term, that is, any agency in the business of finding jobs for its worker clientele and finding workers for its employer clientele. Nothing in the statute or legislative history suggests a broader or different meaning. Only the most forced and tortured construction of those words could bring within that definition a newspaper publishing corporation which, as part of its publishing activities, accepts and lists classified ads for compensation.

The final relevant phrase of the definition of the term employment agency, after defining this phrase in the words set forth above, concludes by saying, " * * * and includes an agent of such person. * * * " Plaintiffs' brief makes the point that if the newspapers in their classified ad activities are not employment agencies, that they certainly are the agents of employment agencies, and thus come within the statutory definition. The matter again is one of statutory construction. The definition of employment agency refers to a person regularly undertaking to procure employees for an employer or to procure opportunities to work for employees. Persons are defined by the statute as individuals, unions, partnerships, associations, corporations, legal representatives, mutual companies, joint stock companies, trusts, unincorporated associations, trustees, etc. This variety of legal entities having been included in the definition of persons, it made clear and obvious sense for the statutory draftsmen to inject into the description of activities by such persons constituting them as employment agencies in the traditional and recognized sense, the notion that entities in the business world act through and are responsible for the actions of their agents. Therefore, the meaning of the phrase, " * * * includes an agent of such person * * * " must necessarily mean an agent of such person engaged in the same activity as brings the person within the definition of the term employment agency. This, again, is the regular undertaking of procuring employees for an employer client or employers for employee clients. While the publishing of classified advertising may further the business of employment agencies, it does not constitute the business of employment agencies. The assistance that the newspapers may or may not furnish to their customers in the course of servicing their advertising requirements as set forth on page four of plaintiffs' memorandum may indeed constitute the newspaper defendants a link in the job procurement chain, may indeed make them indispensible to the successful operation of employment agencies. But these activities do not make them employment agencies themselves. Therefore, and for these reasons, this court agrees with the conclusions of District Judge Swygert in Brush v. San Francisco Newspaper Printing Co. In addition, as set forth in that opinion, the legislative history of the section under consideration is consistent with this interpretation, and while not controlling as a matter of statutory construction, lends support to the conclusions here reached. * * *

On the other side of this issue, and quite to the contrary, is the position of the Equal Employment Opportunity Commission. * * *

In view of the clear limitation of the applicable statute to employers and employment agencies, the Equal Employment Opportunity Commission Guideline must be similarly limited in its application. Thus read, it is appropriately promulgated, but not of probative value in this case.

If read in the broader sense that it was intended to extend Title VII to newspapers, it is obvious that this guideline promulgated by the Equal Employment Opportunity Commission is contrary to the interpretation of that section indicated in the earlier portions of this opinion. * * *

* * *

The plaintiffs' brief and the *amicus* brief contain much material suggesting the impropriety and undesirability of the separate classification by sex of help-wanted and employment opportunity ads. Much of this material is persuasive. It is the business and jurisdiction of this court to decide only the applicability of the statute upon which the cause of action here under consideration is predicated. That statute has been determined to be non-applicable and for this reason this court has no jurisdiction. It seems appropriate to suggest, however, to the defendant, however gratuitously, that the position of the plaintiffs is an idea whose time has come and that serious consideration be given to a revision of the classification practices in employment advertising without reference to and free from the compulsion of the jurisdiction of the court.

The several motions of the defendants to strike and dismiss and for judgment on the pleadings are hereby granted.

NOTES AND PROBLEMS FOR DISCUSSION

1. Would a contrary result in *Greenfield* have created a constitutional problem? In Pittsburgh Press Co. v. Pittsburgh Commission on Human Relations, 413 U.S. 376, 93 S.Ct. 2553, 37 L.Ed.2d 669 (1973), the Supreme Court

upheld a state court order forbidding newspapers from publishing "help-wanted" advertisements in sex-designated columns except for jobs exempt from the provisions of a city antidiscrimination ordinance. The Court rejected the newspaper's claim that the court order infringed upon its constitutional right to free speech, on the ground that the First Amendment does not protect commercial advertising. Three years later, however, in Virginia State Pharmacy Board v. Virginia Citizens Consumer Council, Inc., 425 U.S. 748, 96 S.Ct. 1817, 48 L.Ed.2d 346 (1976), the Court indicated that its prior ruling in *Pittsburgh Press* was limited by the fact that the restriction on publication in that case applied only to otherwise illegal (sex discriminatory) commercial speech. The Court then struck down a Virginia statute which declared it unprofessional conduct for a licensed pharmacist to advertise prescription drug prices and specifically stated that commercial speech is entitled to some measure of First Amendment protection.

2. The court in *Greenfield* dealt with only one of the interpretative questions arising out of the statutory definition of employment agency. In addition to the "regularly undertaking" requirement discussed in *Greenfield*, 701(c) demands that an employment agency procure "employees" for an "employer". Accordingly, issues concerning the interpretation of these two words previously discussed in connection with suits against employers also must be examined in the employment agency context.

(a) Does Title VII apply, for example, to transactions between a statutory employment agency and a client with fewer than fifteen employees? See Shrock v. Altru Nurses Registry, 810 F.2d 658 (7th Cir.1987) (agency referring nurses to private patients or to doctors acting on behalf of their patients does not procure employees for an "employer"). In a 1988 policy statement, however, the EEOC declared that an employment agency will be covered with respect to all of its activities, including those involving employers with less than 15 employees, as long as it regularly procures employees for at least one covered employer. EEOC Policy Statement No. 915.030 (July 11, 1988).

(b) Section 701(c) imposes no size limitation on covered employment agencies. Note, however, that an employment agency also may qualify as an employer under § 701(b) vis-a-vis its own staff and thus be subject to the provisions of § 703(a) as well as § 703(b).

3. Is a law school placement office a statutory employment agency? If so, must it ensure that all prospective employers using its facilities or services employ non-discriminatory recruitment and hiring practices? See Kaplowitz v. University of Chicago, 387 F.Supp. 42 (N.D.Ill.1974). Cf. Dumas v. Town of Mt. Vernon, 436 F.Supp. 866 (S.D.Ala.1977), affirmed in relevant part, reversed in part, 612 F.2d 974 (5th Cir.1980)) (County Personnel Board that tested, interviewed and certified job applicants for jobs with the defendant Town is an employment agency.) What about a State Board of Bar Examiners? See George v. New Jersey Bd. of Veterinary Medical Examiners, 794 F.2d 113 (3d Cir.1986) (state board of veterinary medical examiners is neither an employer nor employment agency within meaning of Title VII).; Tyler v. Vickery, 517 F.2d 1089 (5th Cir.1975), cert. denied, 426 U.S. 940, 96 S.Ct. 2660, 49 L.Ed.2d 393 (1976).

4. Note that while the court in *Greenfield* indicated that the EEOC's interpretation of the statute was entitled to "great deference," it ultimately rejected the EEOC position. On what basis should a court refuse to give

deference to an expert administrative agency determination? What was the basis for refusing to defer to the EEOC in *Greenfield?*

3. Labor Organizations

Sections 701(d) and (e) define "labor organization" in such general terms that there are few reported cases dealing with the application of Title VII to unions. A statutory union must either (a) operate a hiring hall that procures employees for a statutory employer; or (b) have fifteen members *and* either (1) be a certified or otherwise recognized bargaining representative of employees of a statutory employer, or (2) be affiliated with a body that represents or is actively seeking to represent employees of a statutory employer. The statute, therefore, covers international, national, and state as well as local bodies. In addition, the statute applies to agents of covered unions.

LOCAL NO. 293 OF IATSE v. LOCAL NO. 293–A OF IATSE

United States Court of Appeals, Fifth Circuit, 1976.
526 F.2d 316.

BELL, CIRCUIT JUDGE.

This is an appeal from the grant of a partial summary judgment ordering the merger of two segregated local unions. The district court held the maintenance of segregated locals to be violative of Title VII of the Civil Rights Act of 1964. The court also denied a motion to dismiss for lack of jurisdiction. Finding the latter ruling erroneous, we reverse.

Appellee Local 293 is a predominantly white union with over 90 members. Local 293–A is a predominantly black union having fewer than 10 members, two of whom are white. Both unions operate in the same geographical area of New Orleans and have existed as separate locals for many years. Each local is affiliated with the International Alliance of Theatrical Employees and Moving Picture Operators of the United States and Canada (IATSE).

Local 293 and its members brought this action claiming that the failure and refusal of Local 293–A to merge has denied Local 293 the opportunity to enter into collective-bargaining agreements with many employers and has denied many employees the right to be represented by any labor organization. This was caused by both unions seeking contracts with the same employer. Plaintiffs also alleged in conclusionary terms, that Local 293–A discriminated against them on the grounds of race and color. Both injunctive relief and damages were sought. Without an evidentiary hearing and on a bare record, the district court ordered the merger of the two unions but reserved ruling on the damage claim until a trial on the merits.

* * *

At the outset it is observed that Local 293 makes no claim that Local 293–A "maintains or operates a hiring hall or hiring office."

Absent such an allegation, Local 293 must show that the membership of Local 293–A satisfies the minimum membership requirement of the Act.

Appellant contended in its motion to dismiss for lack of jurisdiction that it had fewer than 15 members and thus was not subject to the Act. Indeed, plaintiffs alleged that appellant-defendant had fewer than ten members. The district court denied the motion without explanation.

A review of the legislative history of 42 U.S.C.A. § 2000e(e) leads this court to the conclusion that Congress intended to exempt small local labor organizations of the type here at issue. The jurisdictional requirements of 42 U.S.C.A. § 2000e(e) were copied nearly verbatim from the Labor–Management Reporting and Disclosure Act of 1959. There was, however, one notable change. The 1959 Act contained no requirement that a labor organization be of a certain size in order to be regulated. In originally limiting Title VII's coverage to 100–member labor organizations (since reduced to 15 members) we must assume that Congress intended to restrict its regulation short of the power invested in it by the Commerce Clause.

Local 293 asserts, however, that the Act applies to Local 293–A because of the affiliation with the International, IATSE. It is claimed that IATSE exercises "sufficient control" over the membership and transfer policies of the local to allow the aggregation of membership numbers in reaching the jurisdictional minimum. * * *

This approach of aggregating International and Local memberships may be likened to the "substantial identity" theory advanced in United States v. Jacksonville Terminal Co., M.D.Fla., 1972, 351 F.Supp. 452. In that case private plaintiffs brought an action against several international unions and their locals, some of whom had fewer than 25 members. The district court found jurisdiction over the locals because there existed,

> " * * * such a substantial identity between the members of defendant unions in the employ of the Terminal and the various and respective national and international labor organizations of which they are members [as to be] indistinguishable for the purposes of 42 U.S.C. § 2000e(d), (e) and (h)."

We note that the instant case involves only one defendant local. The International, IATSE, was not joined as a party defendant as was the case in *Jacksonville Terminal.* Without deciding the propriety of the "substantial identity" or "substantial control" test, we hold that no such theory of jurisdiction may be advanced absent joinder of the International as a party defendant. Once this is done, there must be some showing to support the claim of substantial identity.

We conclude that the district court erred in denying the motion to dismiss for lack of jurisdiction.

Reversed and remanded for further proceedings not inconsistent herewith.

NOTES AND PROBLEMS FOR DISCUSSION

1. Why was the plaintiff's failure to join the International Union fatal to the court's exercise of jurisdiction? The court states that Congress intended to exclude small local unions from the compass of Title VII, but suggests nevertheless that where there is a substantial identity of members between two locals (as in the cited case of *Jacksonville Terminal*), or where the International exercises substantial control over the activities of the local, jurisdiction may attach. What does the court mean by this? Is it saying that in the presence of such a connection, the otherwise exempt local will be viewed as satisfying the jurisdictional minimum member requirement and thus be subject to liability under the Act? Or is it suggesting that where such a close connection exists, the International (or other related local union) should be liable for the acts of the local? Isn't there a significant difference between these two interpretations? For example, wouldn't the plaintiff prefer to have the presumably deeper pocket of the International available to satisfy any judgment? And in deciding which of these alternatives was intended by the court, consider that if the court was not considering imposing liability on the International, why did it insist that the International be joined as a party defendant? There would seem to be little if any reason to require the joinder of the International if the court intended to limit liability to the originally named local. (The parallel issue for subsidiary and parent employers is presented, *supra,* at page 34, Note 2.) Accordingly, then, it is important to determine the circumstances or standard under which an International should be held liable for the discriminatory practices of an affiliated local union.

   This question was addressed in BERGER v. IRON WORKERS REINFORCED RODMEN LOCAL 201, 843 F.2d 1395 (D.C. Cir. 1988), cert. denied, 490 U.S. 1105, 109 S.Ct. 3155, 104 L.Ed.2d 1018 (1989). The court began by noting that Section 301 of the LMRA sets forth a common law agency test to govern the liability of Internationals for their affiliated locals' collective bargaining agreement violations. It then extended this standard to cover liability for conduct in violation of Title VII, thereby rejecting the plaintiff's claim that liability under civil rights statutes should be more expansive because these statutes created an affirmative duty on the part of international unions to eliminate discrimination. In the absence of any statutory language on this matter, the court could not discern any Congressional intent to hold international unions under any special standard of liability for the failings of their locals with regard to civil rights. It reasoned, therefore, that a union's liability for the acts of another was to be determined under common law agency principles. Accordingly, it held that an International could be held vicariously liable only for the discriminatory practices of a local union with which it enjoyed an agency relationship. It did add, however, that there might be circumstances in which a union's failure to act in opposition to the discriminatory practices of an entity with which it did not have an agency relationship might be an independent basis for liability under Title VII.

2. Charles Embry claims that he was denied membership by the Independent Drugstore Workers Union # 2 solely on the basis of his race. The Union has 50 members, consisting of all ten of the employees of each of the five independent drugstores with whom it engages in collective bargaining. How should the trial court rule on the defendant Union's motion to dismiss Embry's Title VII suit for lack of jurisdiction or failure to state a cause of action? See Renfro v. Office and Professional Employee's International Union, Local 277, 545 F.2d 509 (5th Cir.1977). In a 1988 policy statement, the EEOC declared

that as long as a labor organization deals with at least one statutory employer, it is covered by Title VII with respect to all of its activities, including those involving employers with less than the statutory minimum number of employees. EEOC Policy Statement No. 915.030 (July 11, 1988).

3. Sally Jones is employed as an administrative assistant by a local union. The union is the exclusive bargaining representative for hundreds of hotel and motel employees and has a staff of ten full time employees. Sally claims that the union has refused to promote her because of her sex. Can she state a cause of action under any section of Title VII? What if the union's activities are governed by a board of directors made up of fifty members, all of whom are full time employees of the hotels and restaurants organized by this union and all of whom are paid on a per diem basis by the union for the days they conduct union business, such as the investigation of all grievances? See Chavero v. Local 241, 787 F.2d 1154 (7th Cir.1986). See also §§ 703(a)(1), (c)(1).

4. Are public sector unions within the reach of Title VII? In EEOC v. CALIFORNIA TEACHERS' ASSOCIATION, 534 F.Supp. 209 (N.D.Cal.1982), the defendant, a union representing public school teachers in California, claimed that it was not engaged in an industry affecting commerce (as required by § 701(d)) and thus was not a statutory labor organization. Section 703(e) provides that a union can satisfy the § 701(d) standard if it represents employees of an employer that is engaged in an industry affecting commerce. In addition, § 701(h) includes "any governmental industry, business or activity" within its definition of industry affecting commerce. The combination of §§ 701(e) and (h), the plaintiff contended, demonstrated Congress' determination that public sector unions affect interstate commerce. The court rejected this argument. Governmental employers were added to § 701(h) as part of the 1972 amendments to Title VII, an enactment initiated pursuant to Congress' authority under § 5 of the fourteenth amendment, not the commerce clause. Since Congress did not consider the commerce clause in amending § 701(h), the court reasoned, the legislature cannot be deemed to have found that every governmental entity is an industry affecting commerce. Accordingly, the court concluded, the statute also cannot be read to include a presumption that all public sector unions satisfy the "industry affecting commerce" requirement. The court then allocated to the plaintiff the duty of proving the requisite nexus with interstate commerce by proving either that the union was itself an industry affecting commerce or that it represented employees of an employer engaged in an industry affecting commerce. Will it be difficult for the EEOC to carry that burden? But see Graves v. Methodist Youth Services, Inc., 624 F.Supp. 429 (N.D.Ill.1985) (local social service agency providing free services is *not* engaged in an industry or activity affecting interstate commerce; $175 in annual long distance telephone charges and purchase of office supplies from out-of-state supplier are *de minimis* and do *not* affect interstate commerce).

5. Should the successorship issue discussed in connection with employers be applied to unions? In EEOC v. LOCAL 638, 700 F.Supp. 739 (S.D.N.Y.1988), the court held that the defendant local union was subject to the terms of a federal district court's order requiring another local to stop discriminating where the two locals had been merged by order of the International union. The court reasoned that the successorship doctrine previously applied to employers in the NLRA and Title VII contexts was equally applicable to unions in the Title VII context. It stated that the defendant local's duty to comply with the judicial order survived the merger because the local named in that judicial order ceased to have any independent existence after the merger and because

the defendant local inherited all the assets, operations, records and collective bargaining responsibilities of the merged local. The trial court also relied on the fact that the defendant local had notice of the judicial order and the other local's obligations under it. To not hold the defendant to the terms of the order, the trial judge indicated, would nullify the federal court's order and encourage future "mergers" in an attempt to evade judicial orders and judgments.

4. "Individuals" vs. "Employees"

MITCHELL v. TENNEY

United States District Court, Northern District of Illinois, 1986.
650 F.Supp. 703.

MEMORANDUM AND ORDER

Moran, District Judge.

Plaintiff Harold L. Mitchell, Jr. ("Mitchell") filed this action against defendants Richard E. Tenney ("Tenney"), Pioneer Commodities, Inc. ("Pioneer") and Agri–Econ, Inc. ("Agri") alleging a federal claim and various pendent state claims. Specifically, Mitchell contends that Pioneer and Tenney discriminated against him on the basis of his race in violation of Title VII of the Civil Rights Act of 1964. * * *

All defendants joined in filing a motion for summary judgment on the Title VII claim * * *. The defendants argue that Mitchell was not an employee of Pioneer but an independent contractor. As such, any claim of race discrimination under Title VII must fail, defendants argue, because an employer/employee relationship is a threshold requirement in all Title VII actions. Therefore, defendants state that they are entitled to judgment as to the Title VII claim. * * * Because Mitchell's status with Pioneer could be that of an employee, and in any case common law employee status is not a prerequisite for a Title VII plaintiff such as Mitchell, defendants' motion for summary judgment on the Title VII claim is denied. * * *

Mitchell's Title VII claim involves discriminatory acts in which Pioneer and Tenney allegedly engaged. Only facts pertaining to the issue of Mitchell's employment relationship with Pioneer are relevant to this summary judgment motion. The parties have engaged in discovery solely on that question. Mitchell's amended complaint sets forth a detailed history of his relationship and association with Pioneer, Agri and Tenney. The depositions of Mitchell and Tenney provide additional facts.

Pioneer is a futures commission merchant ("FCM") registered with the Commodity Futures Trading Commission ("CFTC"). Its principal business activities include (1) buying and selling commodity futures for its customers; (2) investing customer funds, and (3) conducting seminars for customers regarding commodities trading. * * *

Mitchell began working for Pioneer on April 15, 1977 as an associated person ("AP"). Mitchell described an AP as "one who would take orders from the public and transmit those orders to the floors of the appropriate exchanges". Mitchell was licensed with the CFTC as an AP affiliated with Pioneer. As an AP, Mitchell placed orders for Pioneer. He could not place orders in his own name or in the name of another FCM.

Mitchell performed his duties as AP for Pioneer at its office in Chicago. Equipment, furniture, and supplies such as stationery were furnished by Pioneer at its expense. Mitchell solicited customers to trade in commodities on the telephone (all but one phone line furnished by Pioneer) and by direct mail to potential or former customers of Pioneer.

Mitchell was paid on a commission basis. Pioneer unilaterally set the rate (55–60%) at which Mitchell would be paid, based upon the volume of sales he generated. From a gross commissions amount, Pioneer deducted any advancements it paid to Mitchell and certain recurring expenses such as health insurance premiums for the group health plan which Pioneer made available. Mitchell was also charged for other business expenses: postage, photocopy charges and phone charges. Pioneer did not deduct any employment taxes from Mitchell's commission checks.

Mitchell set his own working hours and while working did not have an immediate supervisor "stand[ing] over [his] shoulder". However, Tenney testified about the period (April 1983–September 1983) when he took over supervision of the Chicago office due to problems with Melvin Brown, vice-president of Pioneer and the supposed supervisor of this office. During this time, Mitchell called Tenney to report if he would be late, and Tenney threatened sanctions for tardiness, such as charging Mitchell 25% for every order Tenney had to write for Mitchell while covering Mitchell's phone line and accounts. Tenney also testified that any market letters sent out by Mitchell on Pioneer's stationery had to be shown to him first. Further, after Tenney began supervising the Chicago office "nothing went out of there without [Tenney] knowing about it". Tenney stated he had a right to see all the materials mailed by Pioneer's APs because an FCM may ultimately be liable for acts of an AP.

On December 8, 1983, Mitchell received a letter from Pioneer's attorney notifying him that Pioneer's Chicago office was closed and that Mitchell's employment was terminated. Mitchell contends that his termination was racially motivated, a violation of Title VII.

DISCUSSION

1. Who May Be a Title VII Plaintiff?

Defendants have focused their attention on the common law distinction between "employees" and "independent contractors." They urge that the record clearly shows that Mitchell was an independent contractor, and maintain that the independent contractors are not protected by Title VII. Mitchell contends that the specific label given an individual by an employer is not dispositive of his status. He argues that given the degree of control defendants exercised over him, he was an employee. Alternatively, he contends that even if he was not an employee in the traditional sense, nevertheless he still may bring this action under Title VII. Title VII was intended to protect any individual against the specific acts of which Mitchell complains, not only traditional common law employees but also others aggrieved by discrimination affecting employment opportunities.

Some courts, in attempting to determine whether an individual may sue under Title VII, have used as a framework of analysis the so-called "economic realities test" formulated by the District of Columbia Circuit in Spirides v. Reinhardt, 613 F.2d 826 (D.C.Cir.1979). That test is essentially an application of the common law rules for distinguishing between a "servant" and an "independent contractor" to the Title VII context. *Spirides* held that Title VII did not protect an independent contractor from discrimination in employment. 613 F.2d at 829. The Seventh Circuit mentioned, and appeared to endorse, the *Spirides* approach in Unger v. Consolidated Foods Corp., 657 F.2d 909, 915 n. 8 (7th Cir.1981), vacated on other grounds, 456 U.S. 1002, 102 S.Ct. 2288, 73 L.Ed.2d 1297 (1982), on remand, 693 F.2d 703 (7th Cir.1982), cert. denied, 460 U.S. 1102, 103 S.Ct. 1801, 76 L.Ed.2d 366 (1982), and referred to "economic realities" again in EEOC v. Dowd & Dowd, Ltd., 736 F.2d 1177, 1178 n. 2 (7th Cir.1984).

Nevertheless, in this circuit the common law distinction between servants and independent contractors does not control the question of who may bring a Title VII action. *Unger* actually held that some persons ostensibly classified as independent contractors were employees for purposes of employment discrimination. A sales representative with a six-state territory, whose contract called her an independent contractor and who was paid entirely by commission, came within the class of persons Title VII was intended to protect and therefore was a proper plaintiff under the statute. *Dowd* dealt with the question of who is a proper Title VII defendant, i.e., who is an "employer" under 42 U.S.C. § 2000e(b), and did not cite *Spirides*. More recently, in Doe v. St. Joseph's Hospital of Fort Wayne, 788 F.2d 411 (7th Cir.1986), the court expressly held that a plaintiff who admitted that she was not an employee of the defendant was not barred from bringing a Title VII action.

In *Doe,* a physician sought to sue a hospital which had denied her staff privileges under Title VII. She did not dispute that she was not an employee of the hospital under the test which separates employees from independent contractors. Instead, she argued that denial of hospital staff privileges on the basis of sex was a practice Congress intended to prohibit when it enacted Title VII. Such conduct by the hospital interfered with the physician's employment opportunities, namely her ability to be employed by patients who needed the care and facilities which that hospital provided. The court agreed, holding that analysis should focus on whether the defendant had the power to affect the plaintiff's access to employment opportunities in a discriminatory manner, not whether the plaintiff was technically the defendant's employee.

Defendants here are not entitled to judgment as a matter of law under either the "economic realities test" of *Spirides* nor the "affecting employment opportunities" analysis of *Doe*. The amount of control defendants exercised over Mitchell is disputed. Defendants have not demonstrated that a trier of fact could not find sufficient control to characterize Mitchell as an employee of Pioneer. Alternatively, if we approach the facts from the perspective outlined in *Doe,* assuming that Mitchell's customers employed him rather than Pioneer, there is no question that Pioneer had the power to affect Mitchell's ability to attract customers, and so his employment opportunities. Either way, his termination, if it was discriminatory, was the kind of discriminatory conduct Congress intended to protect him from by passing Title VII.

2. Was Mitchell an Employee?

The "economic realities test" calls for application of general principles of the law of agency to undisputed or established facts. All circumstances surrounding the work relationship must be considered, no one factor being determinative. Ultimately, the most important factor is the extent of control which an employer may exercise over a worker's performance of the job. Id.[1] See also Restatement (Second) of Agency §§ 2; 220(2)(a) (1958). "Where an employer has the right to control and direct the work of an individual not only as to the result to be achieved, but also as to the details by which that result is achieved, an employer/employee relationship is likely to exist." *Spirides,* 613 F.2d at 831–832.

Defendants argue that summary judgment is appropriate because there is no genuine issue of material fact regarding the employment relationship between the parties. Tenney stated in his deposition that he considered Mitchell an independent contractor. In fact, he was advised by legal counsel not to treat APs like Mitchell as employees in the traditional sense. Further, Tenney points to the fact that Mitchell

---

1. Additional matters of fact that an administrative agency or reviewing court may consider include, among others: (1) the kind of occupation, with reference to whether the work usually is done under the direction of a supervisor or is done by a specialist without supervision; (2) the skill required in the particular occupation; (3) whether the "employer" or the individual in question furnishes the equipment used and the place of work; (4) the length of time during which the individual has worked; (5) the method of payment, whether by time or by the job; (6) the manner in which the work relationship is terminated, i.e., by one or both parties, with or without notice and explanation; (7) whether annual leave is afforded; (8) whether the work is an integral part of the business of the "employer"; (9) whether the worker accumulates retirement benefits; (10) whether the "employer" pays social security taxes; and (11) the intention of the parties. *Spirides,* 613 F.2d at 832.

worked independently and without supervisory control. Defendants also point to the method of compensating Mitchell to support their conclusion that Mitchell is clearly an independent contractor.

The lengthy depositions taken in this case show that APs work like most salespersons. Their ability to cultivate customers and interest them in commodities trading is largely a product of their personal style and expertise developed after working in the commodities business. The federal regulatory scheme which governs the activities of APs and FCMs imposes a considerable amount of mutual dependence. APs cannot make trades for customers without an affiliation with an FCM. APs may work only with one FCM at a time. Any accounts and customers APs obtain are customers of the FCM, not of the AP. Any market information APs provide to their customers is transmitted under the FCM's name. Confirmation statements for each customer's trading activity must be maintained by the FCM's, not the AP's. The FCMs are ultimately liable for much of the work done by the APs while in their employ. In short, APs work for an FCM and are the essence of its business. Through APs the FCMs contact and serve their customers.

Pioneer labeled Mitchell an independent contractor and preferred to consider him as such. But labels given an individual are not dispositive of the individual's employment status. They are only one factor in the analysis. Looking at the control factor, as the *Spirides* court emphasized, Mitchell's performance of his job more closely resembles the work of an employee. Pioneer and Tenney may not have exerted control or some type of supervision over Mitchell on a daily basis. However, according to the deposition testimony Tenney believed he had the right to, and in fact did, exercise control over Mitchell on a number of occasions. Mitchell's status resembles that of the saleswoman in *Unger* in several respects, including economic and managerial control and payment of some business expenses, and that court found her to be an employee for purposes of bringing a Title VII action. Defendants have not established beyond dispute that Mitchell was not an employee of Pioneer.

3.   Was Mitchell Within the Class of Persons Title VII Protects?

More importantly, employee status is not necessarily the primary focus of, nor a threshold requirement to maintaining, a Title VII action. While an individual's status with an employer is not unimportant, the focus must be on whether the defendant can subject him to the type of acts Title VII was intended to prohibit. The purpose of Title VII is to eliminate hiring, firing and other practices relating to employment opportunities which are discriminatorily motivated. The language of Title VII is broad.   * * *

There are no indications that "any individual" should be read to mean only an employee of an employer, as those terms are used in the law of agency. Title VII should be construed "liberally so as to further

the goals and purposes of eliminating discrimination in employment."
Unger, 657 F.2d at 915 n. 8.   Moreover, the language of Title VII
indicates that Congress intended to prohibit employers, labor organizations and employment agencies from exerting any power they may have
to foreclose, on discriminatory grounds, any individual's access to
employment opportunities which would otherwise be available.

Defendants rely on the language in 42 U.S.C. § 2000e(f) for their
conclusion that Mitchell must be an employee to maintain a Title VII
action.   However, this section does not provide any definition for
"employee" other than to state that "[an] employee [is] an individual
employed by an employer."   42 U.S.C. § 2000e(f).[2]   Moreover, in the
provisions which define the private right of action at stake here, the
statute does not speak of "employee," but rather uses the phrases "any
individual" and "person aggrieved."   § 2000e–2(a); § 2000e–5(e), (f)(1),
and (f)(3).   In *Doe,* the Seventh Circuit noted that the "common law
independent contractor/employee test," which is at the heart of the
defendants' argument, "is often not applied to antidiscrimination legislation because 'it is considered inconsistent with the remedial purpose
behind such legislation.' " 788 F.2d at 425 n. 28.   The court in *Doe*
emphasized giving a plaintiff the opportunity to show that Title VII
was intended to protect persons from the acts of discrimination by an
employer or discriminatory interference with employment opportunities which he or she suffered.   788 F.2d at 426.

The Seventh Circuit in *Doe* held that it would be contrary to the
legislative intent behind Title VII to summarily conclude that certain
individuals not meeting a technical definition of "employee" from
common law agency are foreclosed from seeking relief for alleged acts
of discrimination in employment.   In Armbruster v. Quinn, 711 F.2d
1332 (6th Cir.1983), the Sixth Circuit Court of Appeals formulated a
variation on the economic realities test which focuses on

> the economic realities underlying the relationship between the
> individual and the principal in an effort to determine whether that
> individual is likely to be susceptible to the discriminatory practices
> which * * * [Title VII] was designed to eliminate.

711 F.2d at 1340.   The court's reasoning in *Doe* tracks the *Armbruster*
court's emphasis on a plaintiff's exposure to harm in his compensation,
or in the terms, conditions or privileges of his employment, from an
employer's discriminatory practices.   The employer need not have been
the plaintiff's employer in terms of agency law, as long as it is an
"employer" within the definition of the statute, and its acts had a

---

2. While the term "employer" is defined in Title VII, 42 U.S.C. § 2000e(b),
that statute sheds no light on the issue
here. An employer is defined as "a person
engaged in an industry affecting commerce
who has fifteen or more employees during
a specified period."   The Seventh Circuit
has already indicated that the definition of
"employee" for purposes of determining
the number of "employees" a business has
does not necessarily control the question of
who is eligible to sue under Title VII.   See
Dowd, 736 F.2d at 1178 n. 2.

discriminatory effect on the plaintiff's employment.   Cf. 42 U.S.C. § 2000e–2(a)(1).

In *Doe* the physician admitted that her patients, not the hospital, employed her.   She nevertheless contended that Title VII protected her against a hospital's denial of staff privileges on the basis of her sex, since such a denial restricted the opportunities she would otherwise have for patients to employ her.   The Seventh Circuit held that she stated a claim, despite the hospital's protests that she could still function quite adequately as a physician without those privileges.   The hospital pointed out that nothing prevents a physician from having privileges at more than one hospital at a time, so that she presumably retained her other privileges elsewhere, plus the ability to treat patients in her office.   The court found that loss of one set of staff privileges was enough to significantly affect her employment opportunities.

Pioneer's power to cut off Mitchell's chances at customers was far greater than the power the hospital had over the physician in *Doe*.   An AP in commodities, unlike a physician, cannot have "privileges" at more than one FCM at a time.   Neither can he carry out his profession, making trades for customers, at an office of his own.   To trade for others, he must have an affiliation with an FCM.   If the plaintiff in *Doe* had a claim under Title VII, then so does Mitchell.

We do not, of course, presume that defendants in fact closed their Chicago office in order to discriminate against Mitchell.   Defendants chose to rest their motion on the ground that even if Mitchell's termination was discriminatory, he is not a proper Title VII plaintiff.   But defendants have not eliminated all dispute about facts which could make Mitchell their employee.   And if he was not, then his customers employed him, in which case defendants had the power to significantly restrict Mitchell's employment opportunities by foreclosing his access to customers.   If defendants discharged him on account of his race, Title VII protects him against such a discharge.   Therefore, defendant's summary judgment motion is denied * * *.

NOTES AND PROBLEMS FOR DISCUSSION

1.   The trial court in the principal case, relying on its circuit court's ruling in *Doe,* suggests that a plaintiff can assert a claim against a defendant who is not his employer when that defendant interferes with the plaintiff's opportunity for employment relationships with third parties who also are not the plaintiff's employer.   Are these courts correct in concluding that a common law employment relationship is not essential to a Title VII claim?   Is their analysis supported by the presence of the term "individual" in § 703(a)?   Is prohibiting "interference with employment opportunities" by an entity with which the plaintiff does not share a traditional employment relationship consistent with the antidiscrimination policies of the statute?   Could it be argued that the use of "individual", rather than "employee", was intended to include former employees or applicants for employment within the protection of the statute but, at the same time, to limit the scope of the statute to disputes between

prospective, incumbent or former partners to a traditional employment relationship? The Fifth Circuit, while not ruling on whether Title VII prohibits discriminatory interference with employment relationships with a third party, nevertheless suggested that if it were to recognize such a claim, it would be limited to situations where the opportunities interfered with by the defendant were in the nature of employment relationships as determined by application of the economic realities test. Thus, in DIGGS v. HARRIS HOSPITAL–METHODIST, INC., 847 F.2d 270 (5th Cir.1988), where the defendant hospital's termination of the plaintiff physician's staff privileges interfered with her opportunity to provide services to her private patients, the court suggested that a third party interference claim would not lie since the plaintiff's relationship with her patients was not one of employment and, therefore, that the hospital did not interfere with an employment relationship opportunity. Accord, Mitchell v. Frank R. Howard Memorial Hospital, 853 F.2d 762 (9th Cir.1988), cert. denied, 489 U.S. 1013, 109 S.Ct. 1123, 103 L.Ed.2d 186 (1989). But see Vakharia v. Swedish Covenant Hospital, 765 F.Supp. 461 (N.D.Ill.1991) (agreeing that a plaintiff nurse alleging interference by defendant hospital with employment opportunities with her patients must establish existence of employment relationship between herself and the patients, but rejecting *Frank R. Howard* court's ruling that doctor-patient relationship is not an employment relationship). Assuming an employment relationship is required, is it necessary that the third party be a statutory employer, i.e., have fifteen employees, etc?

While the courts in the above mentioned cases clearly indicated that the defendant need not be the *plaintiff's* employer, they presumably did not intend to relieve the plaintiff of the burden of establishing that the defendant is *someone's* employer, i.e., that the defendant satisfies the statutory definition of employer. This issue came up in an interesting context in GRAVES v. WOMEN'S PROFESSIONAL RODEO ASSOCIATION, INC., 708 F.Supp. 233 (W.D.Ark.1989), affirmed, 907 F.2d 71 (8th Cir.1990). There, the plaintiff, a 19 year old male, alleged that he was denied membership in the defendant association on the basis of his sex. The defendant, whose bylaws explicitly limited eligibility for membership to women, was a nonprofit association that organized female rodeo contestants and sanctioned rodeo events. The WPRA did not impose any requirements with respect to the number of rodeos its members were required to compete in, nor did it require participation in any particular rodeo. The plaintiff alleged that by denying him membership, the defendant deprived him of the opportunity "to earn a living in his chosen field, i.e., professional rodeo barrel racing." Id., at 235. On a motion for summary judgment, the defendant sought dismissal of the complaint on the ground that it was not an employer within the meaning of Title VII. The trial and appellate courts correctly reasoned that this motion required a two step analysis. First, the courts had to resolve whether the defendant was a statutory employer. Then, if so, whether the plaintiff established that the defendant had interfered with an employment opportunity. As it turned out, the plaintiff did not dispute the fact that the defendant had only two traditional employees. He maintained, however, that the association's members should be deemed employees for jurisdictional purposes because of the pervasive degree of control exerted by the defendant over the means and manner of work of its members. In a sense, then, the plaintiff sought to rely on the existence of a non-traditional employment relationship to satisfy both prongs of the analysis, i.e., that the defendant was an employer and that the defendant had interfered with employment opportunities. Both courts rejected this argument, noting that the jurisdictional requirement of § 701(b) refers explicitly to the existence of fifteen "employees", whereas the substantive antidiscrimination provisions of § 703(a) refer to "any individual". Accordingly, they held, the plaintiff was required to establish that the defendant employed fifteen employees before the court would reach the issue of whether the defendant had interfered with the plaintiff's employment opportunities with a third party. With respect to the jurisdictional issue, the courts concluded that while the defendant association did exert a significant degree of control over where its members could work, as other courts had held in other cases involving licensing boards that exert control over access to the job market, this degree of control was not enough, *per se,* to establish the employment relationship required by § 701(b). Finally, while the appellate court terminated its analysis by concluding that the defendant was not a statutory employer, the trial court added that even if the defendant had been deemed to be a statutory employer, the plaintiff had established only that the defendant interfered with his ability to participate in a competition for prize money and not that the defendant had interfered with a potential employment relationship. On this latter question, then, the trial court echoed the views of the Fifth and Ninth Circuits in *Diggs* and *Mitchell.*

2. Can a prisoner in a state institution who alleges that he was denied a position in the prison's library because of his race assert a cognizable Title VII claim against the prison? Would it matter if obtaining that position also would entitle him to status as an employee of the state library? In BAKER v. McNEIL ISLAND CORRECTIONS CENTER, 859 F.2d 124 (9th Cir.1988), the Ninth Circuit, in a case of first impression concerning the applicability of Title VII to prison inmates, reversed a trial court order that had granted the defendant's motion to dismiss for failure to state a claim. The Ninth Circuit reasoned that since the prison controlled the means and manner of the performance of the inmate position—the most important factor in determining whether an employment relationship existed—this strongly suggested to them that the plaintiff was an employee of the defendant. Thus, they reasoned, they could not be convinced at this time that the plaintiff could offer no set of facts to prove that he was entitled to relief. Moreover, as there was a suggestion of some employment relationship between state librarians and the inmate, the court was not willing to conclude that the plaintiff could offer no set of facts to support a finding of liability. Finally, the court noted that the plaintiff might also be able to prove that he was denied a "training" opportunity which is also covered by the antidiscrimination provisions of Title VII. Accordingly, it reversed the dismissal of the complaint and remanded the case for further proceedings.

SECTION B. COVERED EMPLOYMENT DECISIONS

Sections 703(a)–(c) set forth the substantive limitations placed by Title VII on employers, employment agencies, and labor organizations. Once again, Congress' use of broad language in these provisions reflected its desire to bring almost all employment-related decisions made by these three entities within the scope of the statute's proscriptions. The following case illustrates the breadth of the antidiscrimination mandate.

HISHON v. KING & SPALDING

Supreme Court of the United States, 1984.
467 U.S. 69, 104 S.Ct. 2229, 81 L.Ed.2d 59.

CHIEF JUSTICE BURGER delivered the opinion of the Court.

We granted certiorari to determine whether the District Court properly dismissed a Title VII complaint alleging that a law partnership discriminated against petitioner, a woman lawyer employed as an associate, when it failed to invite her to become a partner.

I

A

In 1972 petitioner Elizabeth Anderson Hishon accepted a position as an associate with respondent, a large Atlanta law firm established as a general partnership. When this suit was filed in 1980, the firm had more than 50 partners and employed approximately 50 attorneys as associates. Up to that time, no woman had ever served as a partner at the firm.

Petitioner alleges that the prospect of partnership was an important factor in her initial decision to accept employment with respondent. She alleges that respondent used the possibility of ultimate partnership as a recruiting device to induce petitioner and other young lawyers to become associates at the firm. According to the complaint, respondent represented that advancement to partnership after five or six years was "a matter of course" for associates "who receive[d] satisfactory evaluations" and that associates were promoted to partnership "on a fair and equal basis." Petitioner alleges that she relied on these representations when she accepted employment with respondent. The complaint further alleges that respondent's promise to consider her on a "fair and equal basis" created a binding employment contract.

In May 1978 the partnership considered and rejected Hishon for admission to the partnership; one year later, the partners again declined to invite her to become a partner.[1] Once an associate is passed over for partnership at respondent's firm, the associate is notified to begin seeking employment elsewhere. Petitioner's employment as an associate terminated on December 31, 1979.

B

Hishon filed a charge with the Equal Employment Opportunity Commission on November 19, 1979, claiming that respondent had

---

1. The parties dispute whether the partnership actually reconsidered the 1978 decision at the 1979 meeting. Respondent claims it voted not to reconsider the question and that Hishon therefore was required to file her claim with the Equal Employment Opportunity Commission within 180 days of the May 1978 meeting, not the meeting one year later, see 42 U.S.C. § 2000e–5(e). The District Court's disposition of the case made it unnecessary to decide that question, and we do not reach it.

discriminated against her on the basis of her sex in violation of Title VII of the Civil Rights Act of 1964. Ten days later the Commission issued a notice of right to sue, and on February 27, 1980, Hishon brought this action in the United States District Court for the Northern District of Georgia. She sought declaratory and injunctive relief, back pay, and compensatory damages "in lieu of reinstatement and promotion to partnership." This, of course, negates any claim for specific performance of the contract alleged.

The District Court dismissed the complaint on the ground that Title VII was inapplicable to the selection of partners by a partnership.[2] A divided panel of the United States Court of Appeals for the Eleventh Circuit affirmed. We granted certiorari and we reverse.

II

At this stage of the litigation, we must accept petitioner's allegations as true. A court may dismiss a complaint only if it is clear that no relief could be granted under any set of facts that could be proved consistent with the allegations. The issue before us is whether petitioner's allegations state a claim under Title VII * * *.

A

Petitioner alleges that respondent is an "employer" to whom Title VII is addressed. She then asserts that consideration for partnership was one of the "terms, conditions, or privileges of employment" as an associate with respondent.[4] If this is correct, respondent could not base an adverse partnership decision on "race, color, religion, sex, or national origin."

Once a contractual relationship of employment is established, the provisions of Title VII attach and govern certain aspects of that relationship.[5] In the context of Title VII, the contract of employment may be written or oral, formal or informal; an informal contract of employment may arise by the simple act of handing a job applicant a shovel and providing a workplace. The contractual relationship of employment triggers the provision of Title VII governing "terms, condi-

---

2. The District Court dismissed under Fed.Rule Civ.Proc. 12(b)(1) on the ground that it lacked subject-matter jurisdiction over petitioner's claim. Although limited discovery previously had taken place concerning the manner in which respondent was organized, the court did not find any "jurisdictional facts" in dispute. See Thomson v. Gaskill, 315 U.S. 442, 446, 62 S.Ct. 673, 675, 86 L.Ed. 951 (1942). Its reasoning makes clear that it dismissed petitioner's complaint on the ground that her allegations did not state a claim cognizable under Title VII. Our disposition makes it unnecessary to consider the wisdom of the District Court's invocation of Rule 12(b)(1), as opposed to Rule 12(b)(6).

4. Petitioner has raised other theories of Title VII liability which, in light of our disposition, need not be addressed.

5. Title VII also may be relevant in the absence of an existing employment relationship, as when an employer *refuses* to hire someone. See § 2000e–2(a)(1). However, discrimination in that circumstance does not concern the "terms, conditions, or privileges of employment," which is the focus of the present case.

tions, or privileges of employment." Title VII in turn forbids discrimination on the basis of "race, color, religion, sex, or national origin."

Because the underlying employment relationship is contractual, it follows that the "terms, conditions, or privileges of employment" clearly include benefits that are part of an employment contract. Here, petitioner in essence alleges that respondent made a contract to consider her for partnership.[6] Indeed, this promise was allegedly a key contractual provision which induced her to accept employment. If the evidence at trial establishes that the parties contracted to have petitioner considered for partnership, that promise clearly was a term, condition, or privilege of her employment. Title VII would then bind respondents to consider petitioner for partnership as the statute provides, i.e., without regard to petitioner's sex. The contract she alleges would lead to the same result.

Petitioner's claim that a contract was made, however, is not the only allegation that would qualify respondent's consideration of petitioner for partnership as a term, condition, or privilege of employment. An employer may provide its employees with many benefits that it is under no obligation to furnish by any express or implied contract. Such a benefit, though not a contractual *right* of employment, may qualify as a "privileg[e]" of employment under Title VII. A benefit that is part and parcel of the employment relationship may not be doled out in a discriminatory fashion, even if the employer would be free under the employment contract simply not to provide the benefit at all. Those benefits that comprise the "incidents of employment," S.Rep. No. 867, 88th Cong., 2d Sess. 11 (1964),[7] or that form "an aspect of the relationship between the employer and employees," Allied Chemical & Alkali Workers v. Pittsburgh Plate Glass Co., 404 U.S. 157, 178, 92 S.Ct. 383, 397, 30 L.Ed.2d 341 (1971),[8] may not be afforded in a manner contrary to Title VII.

6. Petitioner not only alleges that respondent promised to consider her for partnership, but also that it promised to consider her on a "fair and equal basis." This latter promise is not necessary to petitioner's Title VII claim. Even if the employment contract did not afford a basis for an implied condition that the ultimate decision would be fairly made on the merits, Title VII itself would impose such a requirement. If the promised consideration for partnership is a term, condition, or privilege of employment, then the partnership decision must be without regard to "race, color, religion, sex, or national origin."

7. Senate Report 867 concerned S. 1937, which the Senate postponed indefinitely after it amended a House version of what ultimately became the Civil Rights Act of 1964. See 110 Cong.Rec. 14,602 (1964). The report is relevant here because S. 1937

contained language similar to that ultimately found in the Civil Rights Act. It guaranteed "equal employment opportunity," which was defined to "include all the compensation, terms, conditions, and privileges of employment." S.Rep. No. 867, 88th Cong., 2d Sess. 24 (1964).

8. *Allied Chemical* pertains to Section 8(d) of the National Labor Relations Act (NLRA), which describes the obligation of employers and unions to meet and confer regarding "wages, hours, and other terms and conditions of employment." 49 Stat. 452, as added, 29 U.S.C. § 158(d). The meaning of this analogous language sheds light on the Title VII provision at issue here. We have drawn analogies to the NLRA in other Title VII contexts, see Franks v. Bowman Transportation Co., 424 U.S. 747, 768–770, 96 S.Ct. 1251, 1266–1267, 47 L.Ed.2d 444 (1976), and have noted that certain sections of Title VII were

Several allegations in petitioner's complaint would support the conclusion that the opportunity to become a partner was part and parcel of an associate's status as an employee at respondent's firm, independent of any allegation that such an opportunity was included in associates' employment contracts. Petitioner alleges that respondent's associates could regularly expect to be considered for partnership at the end of their "apprenticeships," and it appears that lawyers outside the firm were not routinely so considered.[9] Thus, the benefit of partnership consideration was allegedly linked directly with an associate's status as an employee, and this linkage was far more than coincidental: petitioner alleges that respondent explicitly used the prospect of ultimate partnership to induce young lawyers to join the firm. Indeed, the importance of the partnership decision to a lawyer's status as an associate is underscored by the allegation that associates' employment is terminated if they are not elected to become partners. These allegations, if proved at trial, would suffice to show that partnership consideration was a term, condition, or privilege of an associate's employment at respondent's firm, and accordingly that partnership consideration must be without regard to sex.

B

Respondent contends that advancement to partnership may never qualify as a term, condition, or privilege of employment for purposes of Title VII. First, respondent asserts that elevation to partnership entails a change in status from an "employee" to an "employer." However, even if respondent is correct that a partnership invitation is not itself an offer of employment, Title VII would nonetheless apply and preclude discrimination on the basis of sex. The benefit a plaintiff is denied need not *be* employment to fall within Title VII's protection; it need only be a term, condition, or privilege *of* employment. It is also of no consequence that employment as an associate necessarily ends when an associate becomes a partner. A benefit need not accrue before a person's employment is completed to be a term, condition, or privilege of that employment relationship. Pension benefits, for example, qualify as terms, conditions, or privileges of employment even though they are received only after employment terminates. Arizona Governing Committee for Tax Deferred Annuity & Deferred Compensation Plans v. Norris, 463 U.S. 1073, ___, 103 S.Ct. 3492, ___, 77 L.Ed.2d 1236 (1983). Accordingly, nothing in the change in status that advancement to partnership might entail means that partnership consideration falls outside the terms of the statute. See Lucido v. Cravath, Swaine & Moore, 425 F.Supp. 123, 128–129 (SDNY 1977).

expressly patterned after the NLRA, *see* Albemarle Paper Co. v. Moody, 422 U.S. 405, 419, 95 S.Ct. 2362, 2372, 45 L.Ed.2d 280 (1975).

9. Respondent's own submissions indicate that most of respondent's partners in fact were selected from the ranks of associates who had spent their entire prepartnership legal careers (excluding judicial clerkships) with the firm.

Second, respondent argues that Title VII categorically exempts partnership decisions from scrutiny. However, respondent points to nothing in the statute or the legislative history that would support such a *per se* exemption.[10] When Congress wanted to grant an employer complete immunity, it expressly did so.[11]

Third, respondent argues that application of Title VII in this case would infringe constitutional rights of expression or association. Although we have recognized that the activities of lawyers may make a "distinctive contribution * * * to the ideas and beliefs of our society," NAACP v. Button, 371 U.S. 415, 431, 83 S.Ct. 328, 337, 9 L.Ed.2d 405 (1963), respondent has not shown how its ability to fulfill such a function would be inhibited by a requirement that it consider petitioner for partnership on her merits. Moreover, as we have held in another context, "[i]nvidious private discrimination may be characterized as a form of exercising freedom of association protected by the First Amendment, but it has never been accorded affirmative constitutional protections." Norwood v. Harrison, 413 U.S. 455, 470, 93 S.Ct. 2804, 2813, 37 L.Ed.2d 723 (1973). There is no constitutional right, for example, to discriminate in the selection of who may attend a private school or join a labor union. Runyon v. McCrary, 427 U.S. 160, 96 S.Ct. 2586, 49 L.Ed.2d 415 (1976); Railway Mail Association v. Corsi, 326 U.S. 88, 93–94, 65 S.Ct. 1483, 1487–1488, 89 L.Ed. 2072 (1945).

III

We conclude that petitioner's complaint states a claim cognizable under Title VII. Petitioner therefore is entitled to her day in court to prove her allegations. The judgment of the Court of Appeals is reversed, and the case is remanded for further proceedings consistent with this opinion.

It is so ordered.

JUSTICE POWELL, concurring.

10. The only legislative history respondent offers to support its position is Senator Cotton's defense of an unsuccessful amendment to limit Title VII to businesses with 100 or more employees. In this connection the Senator stated: "[W]hen a small businessman who employs 30 or 25 or 26 persons selects an employee, he comes very close to selecting a partner; and when a businessman selects a partner, he comes dangerously close to the situation he faces when he selects a wife." 110 Cong.Rec. 13,085 (1964); accord 118 Cong. Rec. 1524, 2391 (1972).

Because Senator Cotton's amendment failed, it is unclear to what extent Congress shared his concerns about selecting partners. In any event, his views hardly conflict with our narrow holding today: that in appropriate circumstances partnership consideration may qualify as a term, condition, or privilege of a person's employment with an employer large enough to be covered by Title VII.

11. For example, Congress expressly exempted Indian tribes and certain agencies of the District of Columbia, 42 U.S.C. § 2000e(b)(1), small businesses and bona fide private membership clubs, § 2000e(b)(2), and certain employees of religious organizations, § 2000e–1. Congress initially exempted certain employees of educational institutions, § 702, 78 Stat. 255 (1964), but later revoked that exemption, Equal Employment Opportunity Act of 1972, § 3, 86 Stat. 103.

I join the Court's opinion holding that petitioner's complaint alleges a violation of Title VII and that the motion to dismiss should not have been granted. Petitioner's complaint avers that the law firm violated its promise that she would be considered for partnership on a "fair and equal basis" within the time span that associates generally are so considered.[1] Petitioner is entitled to the opportunity to prove these averments.

I write to make clear my understanding that the Court's opinion should not be read as extending Title VII to the management of a law firm by its partners. The reasoning of the Court's opinion does not require that the relationship among partners be characterized as an "employment" relationship to which Title VII would apply. The relationship among law partners differs markedly from that between employer and employee—including that between the partnership and its associates.[2] The judgmental and sensitive decisions that must be made among the partners embrace a wide range of subjects.[3] The essence of the law partnership is the common conduct of a shared enterprise. The relationship among law partners contemplates that decisions important to the partnership normally will be made by common agreement, see, e.g., Memorandum of Agreement, King & Spalding, App. 153–164 (Respondent's partnership agreement), or consent among the partners.

Respondent contends that for these reasons application of Title VII to the decision whether to admit petitioner to the firm implicates the constitutional right to association. But here it is alleged that respondent as an employer is obligated by contract to consider petitioner for partnership on equal terms without regard to sex. I agree that enforcement of this obligation, voluntarily assumed, would impair no right of association.[4]

1. Law firms normally require a period of associateship as a prerequisite to being eligible to "make" partner. This need not be an inflexible period, as firms may vary from the norm and admit to partnership earlier than, or subsequent to, the customary period of service. Also, as the complaint recognizes, many firms make annual evaluations of the performances of associates, and usually are free to terminate employment on the basis of these evaluations.

2. Of course, an employer may not evade the strictures of Title VII simply by labeling its employees as "partners." Law partnerships usually have many of the characteristics that I describe generally here.

3. These decisions concern such matters as participation in profits and other types of compensation; work assignments; approval of commitments in bar association, civic or political activities; questions of billing; acceptance of new clients; questions of conflicts of interest; retirement programs; and expansion policies. Such decisions may affect each partner of the firm. Divisions of partnership profits, unlike shareholders' rights to dividends, involve judgments as to each partner's contribution to the reputation and success of the firm. This is true whether the partner's participation in profits is measured in terms of points or percentages, combinations of salaries and points, salaries and bonuses, and possibly in other ways.

4. The Court's opinion properly reminds us that "invidious private discrimination * * * has never been afforded affirmative constitutional protections." Op., at 2235. This is not to say, however, that enforcement of laws that ban discrimination will always be without cost to other values, including constitutional rights. Such laws may impede the exercise of personal judgment in choosing one's associates or colleagues. See generally, Fallon, To Each According to His Ability, From None According to His Race: The Concept of

In admission decisions made by law firms, it is now widely recognized—as it should be—that in fact neither race nor sex is relevant. The qualities of mind, capacity to reason logically, ability to work under pressure, leadership and the like are unrelated to race or sex. This is demonstrated by the success of women and minorities in law schools, in the practice of law, on the bench, and in positions of community, state and national leadership. Law firms—and, of course, society—are the better for these changes.

NOTES AND PROBLEMS FOR DISCUSSION

1. In Lucido v. Cravath, Swaine & Moore, 425 F.Supp. 123 (S.D.N.Y.1977), discussed in the principal case, the trial judge refused to recognize "any First Amendment privacy or associational rights for a commercial, profit-making business organization" such as a law firm. Moreover, the court added, even if such a constitutional guarantee existed, the application of Title VII to the partnership selection process did not violate that right since it did not prevent the partners from associating for political, social, and economic goals. Does the right to freedom of association extend beyond a group's exercise of protected First Amendment rights of speech and petition? In Heart of Atlanta Motel, Inc. v. United States, 379 U.S. 241, 85 S.Ct. 348, 13 L.Ed.2d 258 (1964), the Supreme Court declared that Title II of the 1964 Civil Rights Act, which prohibits discrimination or segregation on the basis of race, color, religion or national origin by certain places of public accommodation, did not infringe upon constitutional guarantees of personal liberty or due process. A town zoning ordinance restricting land use to one-family dwellings was challenged in Village of Belle Terre v. Boraas, 416 U.S. 1, 94 S.Ct. 1536, 39 L.Ed.2d 797 (1974). The ordinance's definition of "family" precluded occupancy of a single dwelling by more than two unrelated persons but permitted occupancy by an unlimited number of persons related by blood, marriage and adoption. Plaintiffs, six unrelated college students seeking to reside in a single home, claimed that the ordinance infringed upon their constitutional rights of privacy and association. The Supreme Court summarily rejected this contention. Subsequently, however, in Moore v. City of East Cleveland, 431 U.S. 494, 97 S.Ct. 1932, 52 L.Ed.2d 531 (1977) the Court ruled that a housing ordinance permitting only certain categories of related persons to live together constituted an intrusive regulation of family life and therefore infringed upon the freedom of personal choice in marriage and family matters protected by the Constitution. Nevertheless, the Court added, the statute could survive constitutional attack if it served an

Merit in the Law of Antidiscrimination, 60 Boston Univ.L.Rev. 815, 844–860 (1980). Impediments to the exercise of one's right to choose one's associates can violate the right of association protected by the First and Fourteenth Amendments. Cf. NAACP v. Button, 371 U.S. 415, 83 S.Ct. 328, 9 L.Ed.2d 405 (1963); NAACP v. Alabama, 357 U.S. 449, 78 S.Ct. 1163, 2 L.Ed.2d 1488 (1958).

With respect to laws that prevent discrimination, much depends upon the standards by which the courts examine private decisions that are an exercise of the right of association. For example, the courts of appeals generally have acknowledged that respect for academic freedom requires some deference to the judgment of schools and universities as to the qualifications of professors, particularly those considered for tenured positions. Lieberman v. Gant, 630 F.2d 60, 67–68 (CA2 1980); Kunda v. Muhlenberg College, 621 F.2d 532, 547–548 (CA3 1980). Cf. Regents of the University of California v. Bakke, 438 U.S. 265, 311–315, 98 S.Ct. 2733, 2759–2761, 57 L.Ed.2d 750 (1978) (opinion of Justice Powell). The present case, before us on a motion to dismiss for lack of subject matter jurisdiction, does not present such an issue.

important governmental interest. Should the rights of associational privacy extend beyond marriage and family life matters to commercial relationships? If so, should this right overwhelm the government interest in eradicating employment discrimination embodied in Title VII? Are you persuaded by the Court's treatment of these issues in *Hishon*? For an interesting discussion of these questions, see Raggi, An Independent Right to Freedom of Association, 12 Harv.Civ.R.–Civ.L.L.Rev. 1 (1977).

2. In his concurring opinion, Justice Powell appears to wish to limit the Court's opinion by suggesting that Title VII would not apply to the business relationship among partners. His opinion implies that although the plaintiff Hishon was protected as a statutory "employee" while she was an associate (and therefore was entitled to nondiscriminatory treatment of the partnership decision—a privilege of employment), if she were to become a partner, Title VII would not apply to the manner in which the partnership treated her, since her status would change from "employee" to "employer". Does this mean, for example, that the level of her participation in profits could be set lower than that awarded to a similarly situated male partner? If so, does she really enjoy an equal right to partnership consideration? Would it make a difference if the profit participation differential was instituted one minute or one month or one decade after the partnership decision? But consider the reasoning in cases such as *Mitchell* and *Doe, supra*, that the plaintiff does not have to be an "employee" of the defendant "employer." Could a partner claim that his or her employment opportunities have been interfered with by the defendant and therefore state a claim under Title VII? Should the line be drawn to prevent an "owner" from bringing a Title VII claim against his or her business? Considering the realities of the modern, large law firm, is it appropriate to classify partners as owners rather than as employees? Should there be some limit to governmental intrusion into the partnership relationship? Finally, would the result in *Hishon* have changed if the plaintiff had been an associate in a different law firm, seeking a lateral move to the partnership level?

There was no question in *Hishon* as to whether the defendant was a statutory employer. But what would the Court have done if the defendant law firm had been organized as a professional corporation rather than as a partnership and if all the workers had been shareholders in that corporation? In EEOC v. Dowd & Dowd, Ltd., 736 F.2d 1177 (7th Cir.1984), the court held that shareholders of a professional corporation engaged in the practice of law were not employees within the meaning of Title VII. The court interpreted Justice Powell's opinion in *Hishon* as implying that partners were owners and not employees and added that shareholders of a professional corporation should be similarly viewed.

3. Peroni Macaroni Co. restricts the sale of its corporate stock to persons of Italian ancestry. Does this violate Title VII? Would your answer change if Peroni required all of its stockholders to be full-time employees but did not make stock ownership a condition of employment? What if it gave stockholder employees certain benefits that were not provided to nonshareholder employees, such as the exclusive right to managerial positions, guaranteed overtime and hourly wage premiums? Could the company restrict eligibility for corporate officership and membership on the board of directors to shareholder employees? See Bonilla v. Oakland Scavenger Co., 697 F.2d 1297 (9th Cir.1982), cert. denied, 467 U.S. 1251, 104 S.Ct. 3533, 82 L.Ed.2d 838 (1984), on remand sub nom., Martinez v. Oakland Scavenger Co., 680 F.Supp. 1377 (N.D.Ca.1987).

SECTION C. PROSCRIBED BASES OF CLASSIFICATION

The protections of Title VII extend to all persons.[a] The statute prohibits discrimination by employers, unions and employment agencies against "any individual". This does not mean, however, that all forms of discrimination are prohibited by this enactment. Title VII prohibits covered employment institutions from discriminating with respect to covered employment decisions on the basis of only five classifications—race, color, religion, sex and national origin. Thus, for example, while an alien, blind person or minor can assert a claim under Title VII alleging discrimination on the basis of national origin, race, or sex, the statute does not support a claim of discrimination on the basis of alienage, handicap, or age. Specific problems associated with each of the protected classifications are examined *infra* at 333–458.

SECTION D. EXEMPTIONS

Read Sections 701(b)(1), (2); 702; 703(e)(2), (f), (i).

The broad coverage of Title VII is subject to a few statutorily created exemptions. Indian tribes and bona fide private membership clubs are immune from Title VII liability. Businesses located on or near Indian reservations are permitted to give preferential treatment to Indians living on or near a reservation. Discrimination also is permitted against members of the Communist Party or Communist-front organizations and against alien employees of American businesses located abroad. State and federal statutes creating preferences for veterans enjoy a similar exemption from the provisions of Title VII. The most controversial of these exemptions is the immunity accorded religious institutions under § 702.

EQUAL EMPLOYMENT OPPORTUNITY COMMISSION v. MISSISSIPPI COLLEGE

United States Court of Appeals, Fifth Circuit, 1980.
626 F.2d 477, cert. denied, 453 U.S. 912, 101 S.Ct. 3143, 69 L.Ed.2d 994 (1981).

CHARLES CLARK, CIRCUIT JUDGE.

The Equal Employment Opportunity Commission [EEOC] appeals the district court's denial of its petition seeking enforcement of a subpoena issued in connection with its investigation of a charge of discrimination filed against Mississippi College [College]. At issue is a significant interplay between the effective enforcement of Title VII and the religious protections of the first amendment. We vacate the judgment appealed from and remand the action to the district court.

---

[a] Two relatively minor exceptions to this rule are found at §§ 702 and 703(f). See *infra*, at Section D of this Chapter.

I. FACTS

A. *The College*

Mississippi College is a four-year coeducational liberal arts institution located in Clinton, Mississippi. The College is owned and operated by the Mississippi Baptist Convention [Convention], an organization composed of Southern Baptist churches in Mississippi.

The Convention conceives of education as an integral part of its Christian mission. It acquired the College in 1850 and has operated it to the present day to fulfill that mission by providing educational enrichment in a Christian atmosphere. As part of its policy, Mississippi College seeks to assure that faculty and administrative officers are committed to the principle that "the best preparation for life is a program of cultural and human studies permeated by the Christian ideal, as evidenced by the tenets, practices and customs of the Mississippi Baptist Convention and in keeping with the principles and scriptures of the Bible." In accordance with this purpose, the College has a written policy of preferring active members of Baptist churches in hiring. The evidence the College presented to the district court indicates that approximately ninety-five percent of the college's full-time faculty members are Baptists. The evidence also shows that eighty-eight percent of the College's students are Baptists. The undergraduate curriculum for all students, regardless of major, includes two courses in which the Bible is studied, and all students are required to attend chapel meetings held twice weekly. The College's facilities include prayer rooms available for use by the students and the College employs a full-time director of Christian activities. Because no woman has been ordained as a minister in a Southern Baptist church in Mississippi, the College hires only males to teach courses concerning the Bible.

B. *The Charging Party*

Dr. Patricia Summers, the charging party, obtained part-time employment with the College as an assistant professor in the psychology department for the 1975–76 school year. While employed by the College, Summers learned of a vacancy in the full-time faculty of the department of educational psychology created by the departure of Raymond Case, an experimental psychologist. She expressed her desire both orally and in writing to be considered for the position, but she was not interviewed by College officials. Instead, the College hired William Bailey to fill the vacant position. When Summers inquired why she had not been considered for the vacancy, the Vice President of Academic Affairs informed her that the College sought someone with a background in experimental psychology.

In May 1976, Summers filed a charge of discrimination with the EEOC, alleging that Mississippi College had discriminated against her on the basis of sex in hiring someone to fill the vacant full-time position in the psychology department. She later amended her charge to include the additional allegations that the College discriminated against women as a class with respect to job classifications, promotions, recruitment, and pay and that it discriminated on the basis of race in recruiting and hiring.

The evidence before the district court demonstrates that Summers had received a doctoral degree in education from the University of Virginia with a major in counseling and had engaged in post-doctoral studies at Harvard University and other nationally recognized schools. In an affidavit filed with the court, Summers averred that she previously had taught experimental psychology. The President of Mississippi College, Dr. Lewis Nobles, stated both in an affidavit filed with the EEOC and in his testimony before the district court that the College sought to fill the vacancy with an experimental psychologist, that Bailey had been trained in this field, and that Summers' experience was in clinical psychology. Nobles also stated that an additional factor in the College's selection of Bailey was that he was a Baptist, while Summers was not. Although Summers had been baptized in the Baptist faith while a child, she joined the Presbyterian church, the faith of her husband, when she married in 1970.

Although the College did not hire Summers to fill the vacant full-time position, it did offer to renew her part-time contract for the 1976–77 school year at an increased salary. In offering to renew her contract the College did not indicate that it had any objections to her religious views.

C.   *The Subpoena Enforcement Proceedings*

The College refused to comply voluntarily with the EEOC's request for information that the Commission considered necessary to investigate Summers' charge. * * * The College responded to the subpoena by filing a petition with the EEOC seeking revocation of the subpoena. The EEOC denied the College's petition. The College still declined to comply with the subpoena and the EEOC brought this action in the district court seeking enforcement of the subpoena under § 710 of Title VII.[4] After a hearing on the merits, the district court denied enforcement of the petition.

* * *

On this appeal the EEOC contends that the district court erred in denying its petition for enforcement. First, it asserts that Summers,

---

4. Section 710 of Title VII grants to the EEOC, for the purposes of any hearing or investigation it conducts, the same investigatory powers exercised by the National Labor Relations Board under 29 U.S.C. § 161. Thus § 710 empowers the district court within whose jurisdiction either the EEOC is conducting its inquiry or the person resides against whom enforcement of the subpoena is sought to order any person who refuses to obey a subpoena issued by the EEOC to appear before the EEOC, to produce evidence if so ordered, or to give testimony concerning the matter under investigation. Any failure to obey is punishable as a contempt of court. *See* 29 U.S.C. § 161.

although white, can assert a charge of race discrimination against the College because she has standing to assert discrimination that affects her "working environment." Second, it argues that § 702 does not exempt race or sex discrimination by a religious education institution from the scope of Title VII. Third, it maintains that its investigation of the College's hiring practices violates neither the establishment clause nor the free exercise clause of the first amendment.

II. SUMMERS' STANDING TO ASSERT A CHARGE OF RACIAL DISCRIMINATION

* * *

We conclude that § 706 of Title VII permits Summers to file a charge asserting that Mississippi College discriminates against blacks on the basis of race in recruitment and hiring.[8] Our decision today does not allow Summers to assert the rights of others. We hold no more than that, provided she meets the standing requirements imposed by Article III, Summers may charge a violation of her own personal right to work in an environment unaffected by racial discrimination.

* * *

III. SECTION 702 OF TITLE VII

Section 702 of Title VII exempts from the application of Title VII religious educational institutions "with respect to the employment of individuals of a particular religion to perform work connected with the carrying on by such * * * educational institution * * * of its activities." 42 U.S.C. § 2000e–1.

The EEOC contends that § 702 only exempts from the coverage of Title VII discrimination based upon religion, not discrimination predicated upon race, color, sex, or national origin. It argues that the College's mere assertion that it declined to hire Summers because of her religion should not prevent it from investigating to determine if the College used Summers' religion as a pretext for some other form of discrimination. The College asserts that its hiring decision falls squarely within the statutory exemption created by § 702.

This court previously rejected the argument that the exemption provided by § 702 applies to all of the actions of a religious organization taken with respect to an employee whose work was connected with its "religious activities." See McClure v. Salvation Army, 460 F.2d 553 (5th Cir.), cert. denied, 409 U.S. 896, 93 S.Ct. 132, 34 L.Ed.2d 153 (1972). In *McClure* we restricted the application of that exemption to a reli-

---

8. We decide only the issue before us of whether a white employee can charge her employer with discriminating against blacks in violation of Title VII. We expressly pretermit the question of whether any form of discrimination other than racial discrimination can be charged by a person who is not a member of the group against whom the discrimination is directed. We likewise pretermit and intimate no opinion concerning Summers' adequacy as a class representative for any blacks against whom the College may have discriminated.

gious organization's discrimination in employment against an individual on the basis of religion, stating:

> The language and the legislative history of § 702 compel the conclusion that Congress did not intend that a religious organization be exempted from liability for discriminating against its employees on the basis of race, color, sex or national origin with respect to their compensation, terms, conditions or privileges of employment.

The College argues first that once it showed (1) an established policy of preferring Baptists in its hiring decisions, (2) that the individual hired for the position was Baptist, and (3) that the charging party was not a Baptist, § 702 prevented the EEOC from investigating further the charge of discrimination. *McClure* did not address the EEOC's authority to investigate an individual charge of race or sex discrimination asserted against a religious institution that presents evidence showing that it made the challenged employment decision on the basis of an individual's religion. We conclude that if a religious institution of the kind described in § 702 presents convincing evidence that the challenged employment practice resulted from discrimination on the basis of religion, § 702 deprives the EEOC of jurisdiction to investigate further to determine whether the religious discrimination was a pretext for some other form of discrimination. This interpretation of § 702 is required to avoid the conflicts that would result between the rights guaranteed by the religion clauses of the first amendment and the EEOC's exercise of jurisdiction over religious educational institutions.

The College argues second, and more broadly, that the employment relationship between a religious educational institution and its faculty is exempt from Title VII. It relies on *McClure's* holding that the relationship between a church and its ministers was not intended by Congress to be covered by Title VII. The College's reliance on *McClure* as support for this argument is misplaced.

In *McClure* this court expressly restricted its decision to the context of the church-minister relationship. We concluded that matters touching the relationship between a church and its ministers, including the selection of a minister, determination of salary, and assignment of duties and location, are "matters of church administration and government and thus, purely of ecclesiastical cognizance." The facts distinguish this case from *McClure*. The College is not a church. The College's faculty and staff do not function as ministers. The faculty members are not intermediaries between a church and its congregation. They neither attend to the religious needs of the faithful nor instruct students in the whole of religious doctrine. That faculty members are expected to serve as exemplars of practicing Christians does not serve to make the terms and conditions of their employment matters of church administration and thus purely of ecclesiastical concern. The employment relationship between Mississippi College and its faculty and staff is one intended by Congress to be regulated by Title VII.

Because the College is not a church and its faculty members are not ministers, *McClure's* construction of Title VII does not bar the EEOC in the instant case from investigating Summers' allegations that the college engages in class discrimination against women and blacks.[10] However, as pointed out above, § 702 may bar investigation of her individual claim. The district court did not make clear whether the individual employment decision complained of by Summers was based on the applicant's religion. Thus, we cannot determine whether the exemption of § 702 applies. If the district court determines on remand that the College applied its policy of preferring Baptists over non-Baptists in granting the faculty position to Bailey rather than Summers, then § 702 exempts that decision from the application of Title VII and would preclude any investigation by the EEOC to determine whether the College used the preference policy as a guise to hide some other form of discrimination. On the other hand, should the evidence disclose only that the College's preference policy could have been applied, but in fact it was not considered by the College in determining which applicant to hire, § 702 does not bar the EEOC's investigation of Summers' individual sex discrimination claim.

IV. FIRST AMENDMENT QUESTIONS

The EEOC contends that the district court erred in concluding that application of Title VII to a religious educational institution would foster the excessive government entanglement with religion prohibited by the establishment clause and would impermissibly burden the institution's practice of its religious beliefs in violation of the free exercise clause.

A. Establishment Clause

The establishment clause of the first amendment prohibits Congress from enacting any law "respecting an establishment of religion."

---

10. The College has asserted both before this court and before the district court that its desire to employ Southern Baptists whenever possible to facilitate the carrying out of its religious mission has resulted in its adoption of several recruiting and employment practices that tend to have a disparate impact upon women and blacks. The College contends, for example, that it recruits faculty members through the Association of Baptist Colleges, the member colleges of which have predominantly white student bodies. To the extent that this employment practice is based upon religious discrimination, § 702 exempts it from the application of Title VII. However, any choice by the College to recruit only among Baptist colleges that are predominantly white as opposed to all Baptist colleges is not protected by § 702 and could be investigated by the EEOC. Also, § 702 does not prevent the EEOC from investigating whether the College discriminates against any blacks who may apply from the schools at which it does recruit. The determination of which of the College's employment practices are based upon religious discrimination and therefore exempt under § 702 can best be made by the district court on remand. On remand the College should be granted a further opportunity to present evidence demonstrating which parts of the information sought concern practices based upon religious discrimination.

In determining whether a congressional enactment violates the establishment clause, the Supreme Court has examined three principal criteria: (1) whether the statute has a secular legislative purpose, (2) whether the principal or primary effect of the statute is neither to advance nor to inhibit religion, and (3) whether the statute fosters "an excessive government entanglement with religion." Lemon v. Kurtzman, 403 U.S. 602, 612–13, 91 S.Ct. 2105, 2111, 29 L.Ed.2d 745, 752 (1971). The College does not contend that Title VII has no secular legislative purpose or that it inhibits or advances religion as its primary effect. We therefore focus our inquiry upon the third criteria: whether the statute fosters an excessive entanglement with religion.

In *Lemon* the Court evaluated three factors in determining whether government entanglement with religion is excessive:

> the character and purposes of the institutions that are benefited, the nature of the aid that the State provides, and the resulting relationship between the government and the religious authority.

Although the Supreme Court generally has construed the establishment clause in the context of governmental action that benefited a religious activity, it is now clear that the establishment clause is implicated by a statute that potentially burdens religious activities. See N.L.R.B. v. Catholic Bishop of Chicago, 440 U.S. 490, 500–502, 99 S.Ct. 1313, 1319–20, 59 L.Ed.2d 533, 541–542 (1979). The three-prong test employed in *Lemon* to determine whether government entanglement is excessive applies with equal force to such cases.

The evidence presented to the district court makes it readily apparent that the character and purposes of the College are pervasively sectarian. The purpose of the College is to provide a college education in an atmosphere saturated with Christian ideals. The College is formally affiliated with the Mississippi Baptist Convention. Indeed, the College exists primarily to serve the evangelical mission of the Convention. The Convention selects the Board of Trustees that exercises effective control over the College.

The nature of the burden that might be imposed upon the College by the application of Title VII to it is largely hypothetical at this stage of the proceedings. The information requested by the EEOC's subpoena does not clearly implicate any religious practices of the College. The College's primary concern is that the EEOC's investigation will not cease should it comply with the subpoena, but instead will intrude further into its operations. The College worries that the EEOC will seek to require it to alter the employment practices by which it seeks to ensure that its faculty members are suitable examples of the Christian ideal advocated by the Southern Baptist faith. These hypothetical concerns are of limited validity. As noted previously, the exemption granted to religious institutions by § 702 of Title VII must be construed broadly to exclude from the scope of the act any employment decision made by a religious institution on the basis of religious discrimination. This construction of § 702 largely allays the College's primary concern that it will be unable to continue its policy of preferring Baptists in hiring. The only practice brought to the attention of the district court that is clearly predicated upon religious beliefs that might not be protected by the exemption of § 702 is the College's policy of hiring only men to teach courses in religion.[12] The bare potential that Title VII would affect this practice does not warrant precluding the application of Title VII to the College. Before the EEOC could require the College to alter that practice, the College would have an opportunity to litigate in a federal forum whether § 702 exempts or the first amendment protects that particular practice. We thus determine that, in the factual context before us, the application of Title VII to the College could have only a minimal impact upon the College's religion based practices.

The relationship between the federal government and the College that results from the application of Title VII does have limits both in scope and effect. It is true that the subpoena issued to the College by the EEOC presages a wide ranging investigation into many aspects of the College's hiring practices. Furthermore, should the EEOC conclude that cause exists to believe that the College discriminates on the basis of sex or race, the College in all likelihood would be subjected to a court action if it did not voluntarily agree to alter its actions. The College would, however, be entitled to a de novo determination of whether its practices violate Title VII. In that action the College could reassert the protection of the first amendment prior to being ordered to amend its practices. If the challenged employment practices survived the scrutiny of the district court, the EEOC could not attack again those particular practices absent some change in circumstances.

Although the College is a pervasively sectarian institution, the minimal burden imposed upon its religious practices by the application of Title VII and the limited nature of the resulting relationship between the federal government and the College cause us to find that application of the statute would not foster excessive government entanglement with religion. Employment practices based upon religious discrimination are exempt under § 702 from the coverage of Title VII and the College could not be required to alter any of its other employment practices until it exercised its opportunity to justify those practices on first amendment grounds before a federal district court. Because no religious tenets advocated by the College or the Mississippi Baptist Convention involve discrimination on the basis of race or sex, an investigation by the EEOC will only minimally intrude upon any of the College's or Convention's religious beliefs. No ongoing interference with the College's religious practices will result from an EEOC investigation of the charge filed by Summers. Therefore, we conclude that

---

12. In his testimony before the district court Dr. Nobles explained that the practice of not hiring women to teach religion courses was based upon Bible scriptures indicating that pastors and deacons should be men. He testified that to his knowledge no member church of the Mississippi Baptist Convention had an ordained woman preacher.

imposing the requirements of Title VII upon the College does not violate the establishment clause of the first amendment.

B.   *The Free Exercise Clause*

The free exercise clause of the first amendment proscribes any congressional legislation "prohibiting the free exercise" of religion.

In determining whether a statutory enactment violates the free exercise of a sincerely held religious belief, the Supreme Court has examined (1) the magnitude of the statute's impact upon the exercise of the religious belief, (2) the existence of a compelling state interest justifying the burden imposed upon the exercise of the religious belief, and (3) the extent to which recognition of an exemption from the statute would impede the objectives sought to be advanced by the state.

As discussed previously, the impact of Title VII upon the exercise of the religious belief is limited in scope and degree. Section 702 excludes from the scope of Title VII those employment practices of the College that discriminate on the basis of religion. We acknowledge that, except for those practices that fall outside of Title VII, the impact of Title VII on the College could be profound. To the extent that the College's practices foster sexual or racial discrimination, the EEOC, if unable to persuade the College to alter them voluntarily, could seek a court order compelling their modification, imposing injunctive restraints upon the College's freedom to make employment decisions, and awarding monetary relief to those persons aggrieved by the prohibited acts. However, the relevant inquiry is not the impact of the statute upon the institution, but the impact of the statute upon the institution's exercise of its sincerely held religious beliefs. The fact that those of the College's employment practices subject to Title VII do not embody religious beliefs or practices protects the College from any real threat of undermining its religious purpose of fulfilling the evangelical role of the Mississippi Baptist Convention, and allows us to conclude that the impact of Title VII on the free exercise of religious beliefs is minimal.

Second, the government has a compelling interest in eradicating discrimination in all forms. Congress manifested that interest in the enactment of Title VII and the other sections of the Civil Rights Act of 1964. The proscription upon racial discrimination in particular is mandated not only by congressional enactments but also by the thirteenth amendment. We conclude that the government's compelling interest in eradicating discrimination is sufficient to justify the minimal burden imposed upon the College's free exercise of religious beliefs that results from the application of Title VII.

Moreover, we conclude that creating an exemption from the statutory enactment greater than that provided by § 702 would seriously undermine the means chosen by Congress to combat discrimination and is not constitutionally required. Although the number of religious educational institutions is minute in comparison to the number of employers subject to Title VII, their effect upon society at large is great because of the role they play in educating society's young. If the environment in which such institutions seek to achieve their religious and educational goals reflects unlawful discrimination, those discriminatory attitudes will be perpetuated with an influential segment of society, the detrimental effect of which cannot be estimated. Because the burden placed upon the free exercise of religion by the application of Title VII to religious educational institutions is slight, because society's interest in eradicating discrimination is compelling, and because the creation of an exemption greater than that provided by § 702 would seriously undermine Congress' attempts to eliminate discrimination, we conclude the application of Title VII to educational institutions such as Mississippi College does not violate the free exercise clause of the first amendment.

* * * We vacate the district court's findings of fact, its conclusions of law, and its initial opinion and remand for further proceedings consistent with this opinion. We specifically note that on remand the district court * * * should allow the parties to present further evidence demonstrating which employment practices of Mississippi College are exempt from the coverage of Title VII under § 702 as construed by this opinion. We leave for resolution by the district court on remand the question of what portions of the EEOC's subpoena should be enforced.

Vacated and Remanded.

NOTES AND PROBLEMS FOR DISCUSSION

1. As originally enacted in 1964, § 702 permitted discrimination by religious institutions only with respect to the employment of individuals connected with the institution's religious activities. The 1972 amendments broadened this exemption to cover all secular as well as religious activities of religious organizations. Both enactments, however, permit discrimination only on religious grounds. Is the scope of the exemption as amended consistent with the interests § 702 was designed to serve? Does it reach a proper balance between the inevitably competing constitutional interests in permitting free exercise but prohibiting the establishment of religion?

(a) Should a religious organization be immune from Title VII liability with respect to its secular activities or does such a broad exclusion conflict with the establishment clause of the First Amendment? Why should a religious sect that owns and operates a restaurant or radio station be permitted to limit employment in those establishments to members of its sect? See King's Garden, Inc. v. Federal Communications Commission, 498 F.2d 51 (D.C.Cir. 1974), cert. denied, 419 U.S. 996, 95 S.Ct. 309, 42 L.Ed.2d 269 (1974). Would it make a difference if the church's secular undertaking was a nonprofit activity? In CORPORATION OF PRESIDING BISHOP OF THE CHURCH OF JESUS CHRIST OF LATTER–DAY SAINTS v. AMOS, 483 U.S. 327, 107 S.Ct. 2862, 97 L.Ed.2d 273 (1987), the members of the Supreme Court unanimously agreed that the application of § 702 to a religious institution's nonprofit activities did not violate the establishment clause of the First Amendment. The respondent had been discharged from his position as building engineer of a nonprofit gymnasium facility run by the petitioner, a religious entity associated with the

Mormon Church. The discharge was predicated on the respondent's failure to qualify for a certificate attesting to his membership in the Church. In response to the employee's Title VII claim that his discharge constituted unlawful religious discrimination, the defendant asserted a § 702 exemption from religious discrimination liability. (The trial court had found that the plaintiff's duties involved solely nonreligious activity.) In his majority opinion, Justice White stated that § 702 served the secular purpose of minimizing governmental interference with the decision-making processes of religious institutions. He added that its application to nonprofit activities of such religious institutions did not have the primary effect of advancing religion since it merely permitted, but did not require, the church to engage in this type of secular endeavor. Thus, White reasoned, any advancement of religion that would be occasioned by the use of the gymnasium would be attributed to (i.e., accomplished by) the activities of the church and not the government.

Justice Brennan, in a concurring opinion joined in by Justice Marshall, emphasized his understanding of the limited scope of the Court's ruling. He stated that a reasonable accommodation to a religion's need to exercise its religious beliefs, as well as its need to define and maintain its religious character, was satisfied by permitting religious institutions to discriminate on the basis of religion only with respect to religious activities. The application of this principle, in turn, required ad hoc determinations of the religious or secular character of each challenged activity. Yet such determinations result in government entanglement in religious affairs and, he added, might chill religious activity, at least with respect to those activities whose religious or secular classification by a court cannot be predicted by the church. Thus, he concluded, the requirement of a case-by-case analysis for all activities was constitutionally unacceptable. Nevertheless, Brennan added, as the risk of chilling religious organizations was most likely to arise with respect to such institutions' nonprofit activities (since nonprofit activities are more likely than commercial activities to be seen as infused with some religious purpose), it was reasonable to avoid this chilling effect by automatically categorizing all nonprofit activities as religious in nature and thus constitutionally subject to the § 702 exemption. Therefore, since the instant activity was indisputably a not-for-profit endeavor, he concluded that an individual determination of its religious character was not required and thus agreed with the majority's conclusion that § 702 could be constitutionally applied in this case. On the other hand, Justice Brennan left little doubt that he would have required an *ad hoc* determination of the religious character of the enterprise had it not been a nonprofit affair. Is it really very helpful to characterize activities as religious depending on whether or not they are viewed as nonprofit? Consider that, at least for tax purposes, an activity or organization is determined to be nonprofit on the basis of the nature and purpose of its activities and not according to the financial bottom line.

Justices Blackmun and O'Connor also filed separate concurring opinions, underscoring their understanding that the constitutionality of the application of § 702 to for-profit activities remained unanswered by the majority's opinion. Justice O'Connor added that the majority had applied the wrong analysis in determining whether the application of § 702 to nonprofit activities violated the establishment clause. Specifically, she stated, the majority's distinction between state action that permits religious groups to advance their religious beliefs and state action that directly promotes religion served "to obscure far more than to enlighten" since almost any government benefit to religion could be characterized simply as conduct that allows the religion to advance its own belief and thereby escape establishment clause scrutiny. She preferred to recognize that any government action immunizing religious organizations from a generally applicable statutory obligation has the effect of advancing religion and that the real question was whether the government's action is intended to and has the effect of conveying an endorsement of religion. With respect, then, to non-profit activities, Justice O'Connor concluded, the fact that such activities are likely to be involved with the institution's religious mission should persuade an objective observer that § 702 was intended to serve as an accommodation of the exercise of religious beliefs (by lifting from religious organizations the burden of demonstrating that each nonprofit activity is religious in nature) and not as an endorsement of religion.

Would the result in *Amos* have changed if the church's undertaking had been directly subsidized by governmental funds? In DODGE v. THE SALVATION ARMY, 48 EPD ¶ 38,619 (S.D.Miss.1989), the plaintiff was terminated from her job as Victims Assistance Coordinator because she was a member of a Satanic sect and had used the copy machine at the Salvation Army office to reproduce and disseminate Satanic materials. The defendant Army contended that her action was contrary to its religious purposes and, therefore, that its conduct was immunized by the religious exemption of § 702. The trial court noted that § 702 applied to this case since the Army was a religion and so, per *Amos*, it was permitted to terminate any of its employees on the basis of religion, regardless of whether their duties were secular or not. But, the court added, there was a difference in this case. The plaintiff's position was funded predominantly, if not exclusively, by a combination of grants from the federal and state governments. This led the court to distinguish the instant case from *Amos* and to conclude that the application of § 702 to the facts of this case violated the establishment clause. The court reasoned that the effect of the government substantially, if not exclusively, funding a position and then letting the beneficiary choose the holder of that position on the basis of religion had the effect of advancing religion and creating excessive government entanglement with religion in violation of the establishment clause. For more on the constitutionality of § 702, see Lupu, Free Exercise Exemption and Religious Institutions: The Case Of Employment Discrimination, 67 B.U.L.Rev. 391 (1987); Note, The Constitutionality of the 1972 Amendment to Title VII's Exemption for Religious Organizations, 73 Mich.L.Rev. 538 (1975).

In light of the Court's ruling in *Amos*, should § 702 apply to the employment practices of the Christian Science Monitor? See Feldstein v. Christian Science Monitor, 555 F.Supp. 974 (D.Mass.1983).

In ALLEGHENY COUNTY v. ACLU, GREATER PITTSBURGH CHAPTER, 492 U.S. 573, 109 S.Ct. 3086, 106 L.Ed.2d 472 (1989), a case involving the display of a creche and menorah on public property, a majority of the Court, in a series of opinions, agreed on a refinement of the definition of governmental action that unconstitutionally advances religion in violation of the establishment clause. The majority concluded that it should determine whether the challenged governmental practice has the purpose or effect of "endorsing" religion. It stated that the establishment clause precludes the government from "conveying or attempting to convey a message that religion or a particular religious belief is favored or preferred." The majority added that *any* endorsement is invalid because "it sends a message to nonadherents that they are outsiders, not full members of the political community, and an accompanying message to adherents that they are insiders, favored members of the political community." Does this statement of the establishment clause standard change the result in the cases discussed in this Note?

(b) On the other hand, does the exercise of government control over the relationship between a religious institution and employees associated exclusively with its religious functions infringe upon the institution's right of free exercise? The principal case examined two related aspects of this problem: (1) Whether there are circumstances under which Title VII was not intended to restrict the employment relationship between the parties; and (2) In those circumstances where Title VII does apply to religious institutions, the extent to which such regulation is consistent with the limitations on government conduct imposed by the free exercise clause of the First Amendment.

The former statutory issue was the focus of the court's attention in McClure v. Salvation Army, 460 F.2d 553 (5th Cir.1972), cited in the principal case. There, the plaintiff, a commissioned officer with the status of ordained minister in the Salvation Army, alleged that she had suffered salary and assignment discrimination because of her sex. The court, after noting that the Salvation Army was a church, ruled that Congress did not intend for Title VII to regulate the employment relationship between a church and its ministers. The court acknowledged, however, that its interpretation of Congressional intent was prompted by its conclusion that a contrary interpretation of the statute would conflict with the principles embodied in the free exercise clause of the First Amendment. *McClure* was distinguished in *Mississippi College*, however, on the ground that in the latter case the defendant College was not a church and the plaintiff was not a minister. On the other hand, in Rayburn v. Seventh–Day Adventists, 772 F.2d 1164 (4th Cir.1985), the court extended the *McClure* rationale to the claim of a female member of the church who had been denied a pastoral staff position of associate pastor by one of the Adventist churches on the basis of her sex. The position of associate pastor could be held by an ordained minister or a person (male or female) who had received seminary training but had not been ordained. The Adventist Church, however, did not permit women to stand for ordination. The court concluded that the *McClure* "ministerial exception" turned not on the presence of ordination but on the function of the position. It held that the exception should apply whenever the employee's "primary duties consist of teaching, spreading the faith, church governance, supervision of religious order, or supervision or participation in religious ritual and worship;" i.e., whenever "the position is important to the spiritual and pastoral mission of the church." Id., at 1169.

Would *McClure* or *Rayburn* support a defense motion to dismiss a claim of sex discrimination brought by an editorial employee against a church-affiliated publishing house that publishes and sells religious materials for the sole purpose of carrying out the church's ministry? See EEOC v. Pacific Press Publishing Association, 676 F.2d 1272 (9th Cir.1982). What about a theology teacher's claim against a religious seminary? Would it make a difference if the teacher also was a minister of that faith? In MAGUIRE v. MARQUETTE UNIVERSITY, 627 F.Supp. 1499 (E.D.Wis.1986), affirmed, 814 F.2d 1213 (7th Cir.1987), the defendant refused to hire a Catholic woman as an associate professor of theology because she was not a Jesuit (an order of the Catholic Church composed solely of men) and because of its perceptions of her views concerning the moral theology of abortion. The plaintiff filed a sex discrimination charge under Title VII and the defendant claimed that its policy was exempted from statutory scrutiny by the operation of § 703(e)(2). The trial court acknowledged that Marquette clearly constituted a religiously-supported and controlled educational institution within the meaning of § 703(e)(2). It then suggested that the position of theology professor at such an institution approached the relationship between a religion and its minister and held that judicial interference with the decision to hire a theology professor would deprive the defendant of its free exercise rights and constitute an establishment of religion by fostering excessive government entanglement with religion. The court also addressed the defendant's claim that the plaintiff's theological position on abortion indicated that she was not a Catholic and that, therefore, pursuant to § 703(e)(2) the University could refuse to hire a non-Catholic. The trial judge concluded that resolving this question would require him to determine whether the plaintiff was a Catholic and that such a determination was itself prohibited by the free exercise and establishment clauses. The court, however, did not examine the interesting question of whether a religious institution's religiously-premised policy of not hiring women (i.e., the policy of reserving positions for Jesuits, an all male order) was subject to Title VII attack. On appeal, the Seventh Circuit affirmed the trial court's order in *Maguire* on a very narrow ground and thereby avoided determining whether Marquette and the subject employment decision were covered by the § 702 exemption. It held that even if sex had played some role in the decision not to hire the plaintiff, it was not "the motivating or substantial factor" behind her rejection. Since both sides admitted that the plaintiff was rejected largely because of her views on abortion, the appeals court concluded that this same decision would have been reached had the plaintiff been a man. Thus, it concluded, she had failed to establish a claim of sex discrimination. What if a minister taught history rather than theology? See EEOC v. Southwestern Baptist Theological Seminary, 651 F.2d 277 (5th Cir.1981), cert. denied, 456 U.S. 905, 102 S.Ct. 1749, 72 L.Ed.2d 161 (1982). See generally, Note, Equal Employment or Excessive Entanglement? The Application of Employment Discrimination Statutes to Religiously Affiliated Organizations, 18 Conn.L.Rev. 581 (1986).

As to the second statutory issue, the court in *Mississippi College* concluded that where the defendant presents convincing evidence that its challenged employment decision was based on religious considerations, the free exercise clause precludes further investigation by the EEOC even if the plaintiff claims that religion is merely a pretext for a proscribed form of discrimination. Does this represent an appropriate accommodation of the competing statutory and constitutional principles where the employee is not connected directly with the organization's religious activities? Is the Court's ruling in *Amos* relevant here? For an interesting discussion of the constitutional implications of § 702's application to "nonreligious" activities see Note, Religious Discrimination and The Title VII Exemption For Religious Organizations: A Basic Values Analysis For the Proper Allocation of Conflicting Rights, 60 So.Cal.L.Rev. 1375 (1987).

2. Suppose a religious institution provided a fringe benefit to "head of household" employees and that this benefit was given only to single employees and married male employees because, according to its religious beliefs, the husband is the head of the household. Can a married female employee who is denied that benefit bring a Title VII sex discrimination claim? Is this a form of religious discrimination that, through the operation of § 702, exempts the institution from Title VII scrutiny? If not, would applying the statute in this situation nevertheless violate the First Amendment? The issue of whether sex discriminatory policies mandated by religious belief are immunized by § 702 was mentioned (in footnote 12), but not seriously considered by the court in *Mississippi College*. But in EEOC v. FREMONT CHRISTIAN SCHOOL, 781

F.2d 1362 (9th Cir.1986), where the defendant school implemented the afore-mentioned type of sex-based head of household fringe benefit policy, the court rejected the church owned and operated school's § 702 and constitutional law defenses. On the statutory question, the court said simply that the statute only exempted religious classifications and that this was a policy that discriminated on the basis of sex. Then, noting that the Church had voluntarily dropped a similarly sex-based policy concerning wages, the court concluded that forcing the Church to abandon this discriminatory fringe benefit policy would only "minimally, if at all" interfere with the practice of its religious beliefs. Thus, in light of the government's substantial interest in ensuring equal employment opportunity, the application of the statute to the Church in this situation was held not to violate the First Amendment free exercise guarantee. Contrarily, in Dayton Christian Schools, Inc. v. Ohio Civil Rights Commission, 766 F.2d 932 (6th Cir.1985), reversed on other grounds, 477 U.S. 619, 106 S.Ct. 2718, 91 L.Ed.2d 512 (1986), the Sixth Circuit ruled that application of an Ohio antidis-crimination statute (which did not contain a provision analogous to § 702) to a religious school's decision not to rehire a pregnant teacher would violate the First Amendment free exercise and establishment of religion clauses as made applicable to the States by the Fourteenth Amendment. Initially, the teacher had been informed that the decision not to rehire her was founded on the school's religiously-based desire to have a mother with pre-school age children at home. After learning of this decision, the teacher consulted an attorney, who communicated with the school and threatened legal action for violation of state and federal antidiscrimination statutes. Shortly thereafter, the teacher was discharged for consulting the attorney. A letter explaining the discharge stated that the teacher was terminated for failing to follow the Biblical Chain-of-Command, a biblical concept that was interpreted by the school as requiring the internal peaceful resolution of differences in order to maintain a united front. After the teacher had a filed a complaint under state law with the state Civil Rights Commission, the school brought a § 1983 action to enjoin that state agency from exercising jurisdiction over the school and for a declaratory judgment that enforcement of the statute by the Commission in this circum-stance violated the First and Fourteenth Amendments. The Sixth Circuit first noted the trial court findings that the school was a religious institution and that nonrenewal of the teaching contract for violating the Chain-of-Command was consistent with and compelled by the school board's sincerely held religious beliefs. On the basis of these facts and its evaluation of the importance of religion in the school's educational process and the unique role of the teacher in promoting the school's religious mission, the appellate court concluded that the exercise of jurisdiction by the state agency was unacceptably burdensome on the school board's exercise of religion. Moreover, it added, this burden was not overcome by the state's substantial interest in eradicating discrimination as accommodating the board's religious beliefs in this case resulted in only a limited interference with the state's ability to prohibit discrimination because the state still would be able to prohibit religious institutions from engaging in non-religious discrimination. The Supreme Court reversed, ruling that the trial court should have abstained from adjudicating the case under the federal-ism-premised abstention principles enunciated in Younger v. Harris. The Court stated that "however Dayton's constitutional claim should be decided on the merits, the Commission violates no constitutional rights by merely investi-gating the circumstances of Hoskinson's discharge in this case, if only to ascertain whether the ascribed religious-based reason was in fact the reason for the discharge." It was sufficient, the Court ruled, that the constitutional claims could be raised in state court judicial review of the anticipated administrative proceedings.

3. Section 702 states that Title VII shall not apply to religious institutions with respect to the employment of "individuals of a particular religion." Suppose a Catholic school hires a Protestant lay teacher, but subsequently refuses to renew her contract when it discovers that she has remarried. Can she file a claim of religious discrimination? Assume the school admits that its decision was not based on the fact of her formal affiliation with the Protestant Church, but, rather, maintains that she was denied reappointment solely because she engaged in conduct (remarriage) that is inconsistent with the Catholic Church's religious precepts. In LITTLE v. WUERL, 929 F.2d 944 (3d Cir.1991), the court agreed with the defendant school that the statutory grant of permission to employ persons "of a particular religion" includes permission to employ only those individuals whose beliefs and conduct are consistent with the employer's religious precepts. The court added that its conclusion was influenced by the fact that a contrary decision would raise sensitive First amendment free exercise and establishment clause concerns. The Americans With Disabilities Act, a comprehensive federal law prohibiting discrimination against individuals with disabilities, expressly provides that religious entities can require all applicants and employees to conform to its religious tenets. See Part III, Chapter 11, Section B. *infra.*

4. The Friendship, Commerce and Navigation Treaty between the U.S. and Japan provides that companies of either nation are permitted to hire certain classes of employees "of their choice". Two separate actions were brought against American-incorporated wholly-owned subsidiaries of Japanese companies claiming that the subsidiaries' policies of filling these positions solely with male Japanese citizens violated Title VII. The defendant subsidiaries contended that the Treaty immunized them from the application of local antidiscrimination law. In Spiess v. C. Itoh & Co., 643 F.2d 353 (5th Cir.1981), vacated and remanded in light of Sumitomo Shoji America, Inc. v. Avagliano, 457 U.S. 1128, 102 S.Ct. 2951, 73 L.Ed.2d 1344 (1982), the Fifth Circuit found the Treaty applicable to an American subsidiary of a foreign corporation and held that the Treaty provision permitting Japanese companies to hire executives "of their choice" did exempt the company from American domestic employment discrimination laws. It reasoned that subsequently enacted federal legislation invalidates extant treaty obligations only when congressional intent to do so is clearly expressed and that no evidence of such an intent was manifested in Title VII. In Avagliano v. Sumitomo Shoji America, Inc., 638 F.2d 552 (2d Cir.1981), the Second Circuit also ruled that the Treaty applied to American-incorporated subsidiaries of Japanese companies, but concluded that the Treaty did not exempt such subsidiaries from the provisions of Title VII. The Supreme Court reversed the appellate court, 457 U.S. 176, 102 S.Ct. 2374, 72 L.Ed.2d 765 (1982), holding that the Treaty was not intended to cover locally-incorporated subsidiaries of foreign companies. Accordingly, it did not reach the question of whether the treaty superseded domestic law. Nevertheless, there was no contention in *Sumitomo* that the Japanese parent controlled the subsidiary's personnel policies nor that it had dictated the citizenship preference. Would this make a difference? See Fortino v. Quasar Co., 950 F.2d 389 (7th Cir.1991) (subsidiary in such instance should be permitted to invoke parent's treaty rights since forbidding the subsidiary from following the parent's orders concerning citizenship preferences would have the same effect on the parent as forbidding the parent from imposing such a preference).

The Treaty of Friendship, Commerce and Navigation of 1956 between the United States and Korea, like the treaty with Japan, grants to Korean corporations the unfettered right to engage and terminate certain executive employees "of their choice". In MACNAMARA v. KOREAN AIR LINES, 863 F.2d 1135 (3d Cir.1988), cert. denied, 493 U.S. 944, 110 S.Ct. 349, 107 L.Ed.2d 337 (1989), an American citizen employed by the defendant in a managerial position was replaced with a Korean national. The American citizen filed a claim of race discrimination under Title VII. The Third Circuit construed the language of the treaty to guarantee to Korean corporations the right to manage their business in the host country with their own nationals. The court, therefore, concluded that the treaty was intended to provide Korean corporations with the right to discriminate on the basis of citizenship. It also stated, however, that the treaty was not designed to insulate Korean businesses from domestic legislation prohibiting discrimination on such other bases as race or national origin. Noting that Title VII does not prohibit citizenship discrimination, the court found no conflict between the treaty and the application of Title VII to intentional cases of racial or national origin discrimination. The Third Circuit did add, however, that the application of a citizenship requirement by a business from a country, perhaps like Korea, with a largely racially homogeneous population, could result in disproportionate impact discrimination against members of a particular racial group. In such a context, the citizenship requirement would mean that almost all of the foreign corporation's managerial employees would be of the same national origin or race. Thus, since the Treaty guaranteed the right to hire one's own nationals for managerial positions while Title VII proscribed citizenship requirements that disproportionately exclude members of a particular racial or national origin group, the court concluded that a conflict did exist between the statute and treaty. To resolve this conflict, the court ruled that the statute had to yield to the treaty and held, therefore, that the treaty immunized the defendant from any disproportionate impact-based challenge to its citizenship preference. See also Fortino v. Quasar Co., 950 F.2d 389 (7th Cir.1991) (treating permitting Japanese corporations to invoke citizenship preference would be nullified by permitting American plaintiff to bring intent or impact-based claim of national origin discrimination; court also notes absence of evidence of preferential treatment in favor of Japanese–Americans); Lemnitzer v. Philippine Airlines, 783 F.Supp. 1238 (N.D.Cal.1991) (Air Transport Agreement between U.S. and Republic of the Philippines achieved treaty status and language permitting defendant, a subsidiary of the Philippine government, to "bring in" managerial employees for its U.S. operations exempts airline from operation of Title VII and so airline is free to implement preference for individuals of Philippine citizenship or national origin).

In the absence of a treaty, is a foreign corporation doing business in the U.S. a statutory "employer" so that its American employees are covered by the provisions of Title VII? See Ward v. W & H Voortman, Ltd., 685 F.Supp. 231 (M.D.Ala.1988); Note, Commercial Treaties and the American Civil Rights Laws: The Case of Japanese Employers, 31 Stan.L.Rev. 947 (1979).

5. Prior to the enactment of the 1991 Civil Rights Act, § 702 provided, *inter alia*, that Title VII did not apply to "the employment of aliens outside any State." It was unclear from this language, however, whether Congress meant to exclude both aliens and U.S. citizens employed abroad by an American corporation from the protections of the statute. Lurking in the background of this interpretive question was the traditional rule of statutory construction that

federal legislation, unless a contrary intent appears, is intended to apply solely within the territorial limits of the U.S. In EEOC v. ARABIAN AMERICAN OIL CO., 499 U.S. ___, 111 S.Ct. 1227, 113 L.Ed.2d 274 (1991), the Supreme Court construed § 702 in light of this general presumption against extraterritorial application of American statutory law, concluded that the presumption had not been rebutted by a "clearly expressed" affirmative intention to extend coverage beyond U.S. territorial limits and, therefore, ruled that Title VII did not apply outside of the U.S. Among the reasons offered by the six member majority, speaking through the Chief Justice, was the notion that since the statutory definition of "employer" did not suggest that Congress meant to distinguish between American and foreign employers, applying Title VII extraterritorially would mean that the law also would apply to foreign corporations employing Americans overseas. Imposing American domestic law upon foreign corporations operating in foreign commerce, the Court declared, would raise difficult issues of international law and it was not prepared to ascribe a policy with such an impact to Congress solely on the basis of the terminology of § 702. Moreover, the Court continued, if Congress had intended to rebut the presumption against extraterritoriality, it would have directly addressed the issue, as it did, for example, when it amended the ADEA to apply abroad. The explicit provision of extraterritorial application in that (and other) statutes, the Court reasoned, demonstrated that Congress was aware of the need to make a "clear statement" of extraterritoriality and that it knew how to make such a statement.

In 1991, Congress reversed, in large part, the ruling in *Arabian American* as part of a major legislative overhaul of several Supreme Court interpretations of Title VII. With respect to the employment of American citizens in foreign countries, it did so by expressly addressing the concerns articulated by the Court in *Arabian American*. Section 109(a) of the 1991 Act amends the statutory definition of "employee" contained in § 701(f) of Title VII to include U.S. citizens employed in a foreign country. At the same time, however, § 109(b) of the 1991 statute limits the breadth of this change by adding new subsection "(b)" to § 702 of Title VII and providing therein that Title VII will not apply to an employee in a foreign workplace if compliance with the requirements of Title VII would result in a violation of domestic law. The newly enacted § 702(b) also extends the application of Title VII to foreign incorporated businesses that are controlled by U.S. companies. It provides that the employment practices of foreign corporations controlled by American employers will be "presumed to be engaged in by" the American parent. It also sets forth four factors that shall be used to determine the existence of the requisite control. Not surprisingly, these factors relate to centrality of control over operations, management, labor relations and ownership. Presumably, then, § 702(b) was intended to make the American parent company liable for the acts of its foreign subsidiary. But it is not clear from the statutory language whether the American employee can also state a claim against the American-controlled foreign company. Is it significant, in resolving this ambiguity, that the definition of "employer" in § 701(b) of Title VII is not expressly limited to American companies? On the other hand, beyond the obvious difficulty of obtaining personal jurisdiction over a foreign company in a U.S. court, any attempt at extraterritorial enforcement of the statute over a foreign company is complicated by the absence in the Act of either any venue provision for foreign employers or any provision for extraterritorial EEOC subpoena power. Finally, by referring only to foreign "corporations" in § 702(b), did

Congress intend to exclude other forms of foreign business enterprises such as joint ventures?

6. Private membership clubs are exempted from the definition of employer in § 701(b)(2). Does this provision prevent an employee of a credit union from filing a claim under Title VII against his employer? See Quijano v. University Federal Credit Union, 617 F.2d 129 (5th Cir.1980). What about the employee of a private retirement and nursing home sponsored by, and whose admittees must be members or the spouses of members of, a private membership club? See Fesel v. Masonic Home of Delaware, Inc., 428 F.Supp. 573 (D.Del.1977).

7. Does the existence of the § 702 exemption *ipso facto* demonstrate that nonprofit or charitable institutions are covered by § 703(a) if the plaintiff can prove that they affect interstate commerce? See Martin v. United Way of Erie County, 829 F.2d 445 (3d Cir.1987) (local United Way is engaged in an industry that affects commerce and "Congress intended to cover all activities affecting commerce, to the extent permitted by the Constitution, regardless of whether they are operated for non-profit or charitable purposes.").

Chapter 2

DEFINING AND PROVING DISCRIMINATION

SECTION A. INTRODUCTION

1. A General Overview

As the materials in the preceding chapter indicate, the intricate nature of Title VII's definitional and substantive provisions reflects Congress' desire to place a wide range of institutions and employment practices within the reach of the statute's antidiscrimination principle. While the statute sets forth an extensive list of unlawful employment practices, the word "discriminate" is contained within the definition of each group of proscribed policies. A reexamination of the definitional provisions, however, reveals that Congress did not provide a definition of this critical term. Is the meaning of discrimination so obvious that the concept does not need to be defined? Surely, no one would doubt that an employer's refusal to hire a qualified woman simply because of its determination that women belong at home, and not in the work force, would be prohibited by Title VII. But one can imagine that after the passage of more than a quarter century since the enactment of this statute, most employers have progressed to a point where it is relatively rare to find such blatantly discriminatory policies in existence. Yet, other perhaps more indirect, less obvious or less intentionally invidious policies might also produce injuries of the type Title VII was intended to guard against and remedy. For example, what if the employer rejected a woman because she failed to meet the company's policy that all employees be at least 5'9" tall and weigh 150 pounds? Would your opinion change if the employer could prove that it would be happy to hire any woman who satisfied this height and weight requirement? Is a company, 95% of whose employees are women, discriminating on the basis of sex when it refuses to hire pregnant women or married women with pre-school aged children? Suppose a female employee could prove that the company president had told her that she had been discharged because she "took too long to make important decisions; you acted like a typically indecisive woman"? What about an employer who refuses to hire any job applicant with an arrest record? with facial hair? Finally, assume the employer admittedly refused to hire Blacks before the effective date of Title VII but abolished that policy after Title VII was enacted. Is this company violating Title VII by granting promotions on the basis of total years of service with the firm?

The absence of any statutory definition of discrimination left the task of formulating a workable concept of discrimination to the courts.

This proved to be a more involved undertaking than might reasonably have been anticipated. While discrimination may appear, at first blush, to be a relatively straightforward concept, as the preceding paragraph suggests, it can manifest itself in subtle and indiscernible, as well as conspicuous ways. For a quarter of a century, the Supreme Court struggled with the task of formulating and refining a framework for analyzing discrimination claims. By 1981, its analysis had evolved to the point where it was comprehensive in scope, clearly articulated and reasonably well accepted and understood. During its 1989 term, however, the Court, in a series of cases, significantly (some might say, radically) altered its approach to many aspects of this general issue. These opinions so dramatically changed the legal landscape that Congress passed the 1991 Civil Rights Act, in principal part, for the expressly stated purpose of returning to the pre–1989 jurisprudence. The succeeding sections of this Chapter will document and examine the results of this confrontation between the legislative and judicial branches. Before moving to that discussion, however, it is important to consider the prefatory question of whether the provisions of the 1991 Act should apply to pre-existing claims, i.e., whether it should apply to pending cases filed before the date of enactment and/or to post-Act filings that challenge pre-Act conduct.

2. Retroactive Application of the 1991 Civil Rights Act

President Bush signed the 1991 Civil Rights Act into law on November 21, 1991. Immediately thereafter, plaintiffs in pending cases sought to amend their complaints to add jury demands and requests for compensatory and punitive damages, as well as to invoke the evidentiary and other changes wrought by the 1991 Act. This, of course, raised the important threshold question of whether some or all of the provisions of the 1991 statute should apply to challenges to pre-Act conduct asserted in suits filed either before or after the date of enactment.

There are several provisions in the 1991 statute that address, albeit in either oblique or limited fashion, the question of retroactivity. Section 402(a) provides that "[e]xcept as otherwise specifically provided, this Act and the amendments made by this Act shall take effect upon enactment." This proviso clearly was designed to refer to language in § 402(b), which declares, in effect, that the statute shall not apply to the remanded portion of the *Wards Cove* litigation, and in § 109(c), which expressly provides that the amendments concerning extraterritorial application of Title VII shall not apply to conduct occurring before the date of enactment. Additionally relevant, perhaps, is the combination of § 102(a), which permits only a "complaining party" to seek monetary damages and a jury trial, and § 102(d)(1), which defines "complaining party" as, *inter alia*, a person who "may bring" (as opposed to "may bring or has brought") an action under Title VII. Thus, while the statute expressly precludes retroactive application in specified instances, the general issue is not clearly resolved. As the caselaw demonstrates, one can draw conflicting inferences from this textual pattern.

The legislative history is similarly unhelpful. A group of Republican legislators drew up one set of interpretive memoranda, while Democratic Senators and Representatives proffered their own interpretive memoranda, all of which appear to have been prepared merely to reflect the kind of legislation their proponents would have preferred to enact. Notwithstanding, or perhaps because of, the existence of this partisan rhetoric, the compromise legislation that ultimately was enacted contains a unique provision through which Congress attempted to codify an exclusive legislative history. Yet while § 105(b) states that only one specified interpretive memorandum shall be considered or relied upon as legislative history in construing the terms of the statute, it is unlikely that courts will refrain from considering the legislative debates on and explicit terms of antecedent legislative efforts, such as the 1990 Civil Rights Act, which was passed by Congress but vetoed by President Bush, or H.R.1, the predecessor to the bill that ultimately became the 1991 Act. While both of these predecessor bills expressly stated that their provisions were to have retroactive effect, this language was eliminated as part of the compromise necessary to ensure the enactment of the statute in 1991. Moreover, to further complicate matters, in his signing statement, President Bush directed federal agencies to adopt the position that § 402(a) should be construed to mean that the Act does not apply to cases that were filed prior to the date of enactment.

The EEOC has adopted, at least in part, the President's view. In a policy directive issued to agency personnel, the EEOC Chair declared that the Act applies only to cases involving conduct that occurred on or after the statute's date of enactment and, therefore, that it will seek compensatory and punitive damages under the 1991 Act only as to cases challenging conduct that occurred after the date of enactment.[a] The express limitation to damage claims suggests that the EEOC intends to offer a series of directives concerning the retroactive effect of various provisions of the statute. The issuance of these sorts of directives also raises the interesting question of the degree of deference courts will and should accord opinions that rest not on the EEOC's expertise in Title VII matters, but, rather, on the agency's interpretation of Supreme Court jurisprudence generally concerning the retroactivity of legislation. See United States v. Department of Mental Health, County of Fresno, 785 F.Supp. 846 (E.D.Cal.1992) (EEOC directive is not entitled to deference normally accorded statements of administrative agencies in their area of expertise as EEOC's expertise is not in the area of statutory interpretation); Lute v. Consolidated Freightways, Inc., 789 F.Supp. 964 (N.D.Ind.1992) (Id.); Carpenter v.

---

[a] Daily Labor Report (January 2, 1992).

Ford Motor Co., 58 EPD ¶ 41,406 ___ F.Supp. ___, (N.D.Ill.1992) (Id.);
Lee v. Sullivan, 787 F.Supp. 921 (N.D.Cal.1992) (Id.).

The courts are split on whether the Act should apply to pre-existing claims, largely because of the ambiguous posture of the statutory text, legislative history and Supreme Court jurisprudence on the general question of retroactivity. One trial judge poignantly captured the frustration felt by many of his colleagues in attempting to resolve this issue. In King v. Shelby Medical Center, 779 F.Supp. 157 (N.D.Ala. 1991), Judge Acker observed that:

> [E]very federal court in the United States is now faced with the problem which this * * * amendment presents. Why? Because Congress in this new civil rights legislation punted on the question of whether or not the Act applies retroactively. Many senators and congressmen have deliberately tried to create a "legislative history" to support their personal views on this question, but the fact is that Congress, for no good reason, deliberately chose not to include in the statute itself a provision either for retroactive or for prospective-only application.

The Supreme Court has issued opinions that take apparently contrary positions on the retroactivity issue. One of these two lines of cases is exemplified by the ruling in Bradley v. School Board of City of Richmond, 416 U.S. 696, 94 S.Ct. 2006, 40 L.Ed.2d 476 (1974), where the Court held that a statute enacted during the pendency of a case is presumed to apply unless a contrary intention appears in the statute or where application of the statute would result in manifest injustice. At the same time, in cases such as Bowen v. Georgetown University Hospital, 488 U.S. 204, 109 S.Ct. 468, 102 L.Ed.2d 493 (1988), the Court has held that there is a strong presumption *against* retroactivity. This presumption, the Court has noted, can only be rebutted by "clear terms to the contrary ... [where the] words used are so clear, strong, and imperative that no other meaning can be annexed to them, or unless the intention of the legislature cannot be otherwise satisfied." United States v. Heth, 7 U.S. (3 Cranch) 399, 413, 2 L.Ed. 479 (1806). As recently as 1990, the Supreme Court recognized the "apparent tension" between these two lines of cases. In Kaiser Aluminum & Chemical Corp. v. Bonjorno, 494 U.S. 827, ___, 110 S.Ct. 1570, 1577, 108 L.Ed.2d 842, 854 (1990), the Court referred to the "generally accepted axiom that retroactivity is not favored in the law" and added that "Congressional enactments and administrative rules will not be construed to have retroactive effect unless their language requires this result." Nevertheless, it also refused to relieve this "tension" since it found that Congress had clearly manifested its intention to preclude retroactive application of the amendments at issue, and, therefore, that retroactivity would be denied under either presumption.

The *Bowen-Bradley* conflict, however, may be reconcilable. As mentioned in the preceding paragraph, the *Bradley* Court stated that the presumption in favor of retroactivity can be rebutted by a showing that retroactive application would produce a manifest injustice. The Court also listed three factors to consider in determining whether application of the new enactment would result in such an injustice: (1) the nature and identity of the parties, (2) the nature of their rights, and (3) the nature of the impact the change in law would have upon those rights. The Court's choice of these factors suggests that where the new statute affects the vested substantive rights and obligations of the parties and/or changes the legal effect of prior conduct, as opposed to making procedural or remedial changes, retroactive application will effect a manifest injustice and, therefore, the statute should apply only prospectively. Substantive changes should be less amenable to retroactive application than procedural or remedial alterations since they more directly impinge upon a party's reliance interests. A party is more likely to change its pre-litigation conduct in the face of a change in the relevant substantive legal rules than in response to a modification of the procedural or remedial regime. It is also arguable, however, that a party might adapt its pre-litigation and litigation strategy to such "procedural" changes as the right to a jury trial, the availability of compensatory or punitive damages, or a variation in the governing evidentiary burden. Nevertheless, if the substantive/procedural dichotomy is, in fact, determinative of a finding of manifest injustice, then statutory changes affecting substantive matters will not apply retroactively under either presumption. Of course, if the courts adopt this approach, they will have to undertake a separate evaluation of each of the changes effected by the new statute. This, in turn, could result in retroactive application of some provisions and purely prospective application of others.

At least three circuit court panels have adopted this approach in connection with the 1991 Act. In MOZEE v. AMERICAN COMMERCIAL MARINE SERVICE COMPANY, 963 F.2d 929 (7th Cir.1992), a Seventh Circuit panel ruled that *Bradley* and *Bowen* could be reconciled by applying the *Bowen* presumption to statutory changes affecting substantive rights and obligations regardless of whether retroactivity is sought on appeal or on remand. It also stated that the *Bradley* presumption should apply to procedural issues (such as the right to a jury trial and the recovery of damages) where appellate resolution of the substantive issues resulted in a retrial of the entire case, although not where reconsideration is ordered only for a portion of the case. In VOGEL v. CITY OF CINCINNATI, 959 F.2d 594 (6th Cir.1992), the Sixth Circuit stated that while it had found the *Bradley* presumption to be controlling on several occasions, the cases also indicated that "*Bradley* should be read narrowly and should not be applied in contexts where 'substantive rights and liabilities', broadly construed, would be affected." It then summarily concluded that retroactive application of the statute (without referring to any particular provision thereof) would affect substantive rights and liabilities of the parties and, therefore, ruled that the statute would not apply retroactively. The Fifth Circuit, in JOHNSON v. UNCLE BEN'S, INC., 965 F.2d 1363 (5th Cir.1992), stated that it would "follow the canon that statutes affecting substantive rights are ordinarily addressed to the future and are to be given prospective effect only." Id., at 1374. See also Fray v. Omaha World Herald Co., 960 F.2d 1370 (8th Cir.1992) (Heaney, J., dissenting) (refusing to choose between alternative presumptions and preferring to rule on the basis of the common thread between the two lines of cases— an "overriding concern for fairness", i.e, whether retroactive application would interfere with vested rights); Brown v. Amoco Oil Co., 793 F.Supp. 846 (N.D.Ind.1992) (interpreting *Mozee* as permitting provision-by-provision analysis of statutory changes and, noting the dictum in *Mozee* suggesting that procedural changes should be subjected to *Bradley* presumption, ruling that the mixed motive and punitive damage provisions relating to Title VII claims and the provision relating to § 1981 claims are substantive and cannot be applied retroactively and that the compensatory damage and jury trial provisions are procedural in nature and can apply retroactively); Manning v. Moore Business Forms, Inc., 58 FEP Cases 1228 (W.D.Wis.1992) (applying damage and jury trial provisions retroactively to Title VII count per *Bradley* presumption but denying retroactivity to substantive change to § 1981 per *Bowen* presumption).   But in LUDDINGTON v. INDIANA BELL TELEPHONE, 966 F.2d 225 (7th Cir.1992) another Seventh Circuit panel, citing the decision in *Mozee* for the proposition that the 1991 Act is not to be given retroactive effect, nevertheless stated that it would address the issue of retroactivity "as if it were an open question in this circuit."   It then concluded that a rebuttable presumption against retroactivity should be applied to both substantive and nonsubstantive changes. The panel reasoned that changes in remedies, procedures and evidence "can have as profound an impact on behavior outside the courtroom as avowedly substantive changes" since "[t]he amount of care that individuals and firms take to avoid subjecting themselves to liability whether civil or criminal is a function of the severity of the sanction, and when the severity is increased they are entitled to an opportunity to readjust their level of care in light of the new environment created by the change." Id., at 229.

Other courts of appeals have employed this analysis in cases arising under other statutes. See Lussier v. Dugger, 904 F.2d 661 (11th Cir.1990); Federal Deposit Insurance Corp. v. New Hampshire Insurance Co., 953 F.2d 478 (9th Cir.1991) (concept of limited retroaction for non-substantive statutory changes termed "persuasive"); Federal Deposit Insurance Corp. v. Wright, 942 F.2d 1089, 1095 n.6 (7th Cir.1991) ("tension between the two lines of precedent is negated because, under *Bradley*, a statute will not be deemed to apply retroactively if it would threaten manifest injustice by disrupting vested rights."); Arnold v. Maynard, 942 F.2d 761, 762 n.2 (10th Cir.1991) (*Bowen* presumption applies to statute affecting substantive rights and liabilities but "presumption has always been to the contrary with respect to statutes that address matters of procedure and jurisdiction."). Nevertheless, it was just this possibility of "partial retroactivity" that caused one trial court

to deny retroactive application to the entirety of the 1991 statute. See
Doe v. Board of County Commissioners, 783 F.Supp. 1379 (S.D.Fla.1992).
See also Kemp v. Flygt Corporation, 791 F.Supp. 48 (D.Conn.1992)
(while noting that portions of the 1991 Act could be applied retroactively, court states it is "unwilling to hold that some of the Act is
retroactive and some is not. To embark on such a course armed with
the Act's [ambiguous] legislative history would be folly."). But see
Joyner v. Monier Roof Tile, 784 F.Supp. 872 (S.D.Fla.1992) (criticizing
Doe court for rejecting partial retroactivity as a "piece-meal approach"
and stating, in dictum, that it was prepared to give retroactive effect
only to procedural or remedial changes effected by statute).

In light of the ambiguous statutory text and unique legislative
history of the 1991 Act, it is not surprising to find that the ruling on
retroactivity by the overwhelming majority of lower courts is a function
of that court's choice of Supreme Court precedent. Thus, for example,
where the courts have chosen to adhere to the *Bradley* presumption in
favor of retroactivity, most have ruled in favor of retroactive application. See e.g., Mojica v. Gannett Co., 779 F.Supp. 94 (N.D.Ill.1991) (in
absence of legislative indication to rebut presumption, the fact that
overturning Supreme Court interpretations of an existing statute was
the *raison d'etre* of the statute supports retroactivity; furthermore, in
view of the public, as well as private, interests affected by this new
statute, and the fact that the parties should not be viewed as having a
"substantial" right to a court trial, retroactive application would not
work a manifest injustice. Accordingly, the plaintiff was permitted to
amend the complaint to include a jury demand, as well as a request for
compensatory and punitive damages.); Stender v. Lucky Stores, Inc.,
780 F.Supp. 1302 (N.D.Cal.1992) (statute applies retroactively because
the specific exceptions to retroactivity contained in §§ 402(b) and 109(c)
would be meaningless if Congress had not intended the remainder of
the statutory provisions to apply to pending cases; moreover, restora-
tive legislation should be presumed to have retroactive effect and all
but one of the courts that have addressed the issue have concluded that
the Civil Rights Restoration Act of 1987—which was designed to overrule the Court's ruling in *Grove City College* and whose text is silent on
the question of retroactivity—should apply to cases pending at the time
of its enactment. Additionally, all of the *Bradley* factors weigh against
a finding of manifest injustice, i.e., the statute (1) involves matters of
great public concern (remedying discrimination and promoting equality), (2) does not infringe upon the defendant's unconditional rights since
the defendant has no unconditional right to limit plaintiffs to a particular type of remedy, and (3) does not change the substantive law by
merely changing the nature of plaintiff's proof and the available
remedies.); King v. Shelby Medical Center, 779 F.Supp. 157 (N.D.Ala.
1991) (as statutory provision of right to jury trial is purely procedural
and amendment to § 1981 simply restores law to pre-*Patterson* state,
retroactive application of these changes does not result in manifest
injustice); Thakkar v. Provident National Bank, 1991 WL 274827

(E.D.Pa.1991) (applying *Bradley* presumption and "assuming", without discussion, that statute applies retroactively) and Davis v. Tri–State Mack Distributors, Inc., 57 FEP Cases 1025 (E.D.Ark.1991) (1991 Act should apply retroactively to the request by plaintiff for expert witness fees because of statute's remedial purposes and the absence of any statutory language against retroactive application). But see McCullough v. Consolidated Rail Corp., 785 F.Supp. 1309 (N.D.Ill.1992) (retroactivity should be denied under either presumption; creation of new right to recover damages indicates that retroactivity would result in manifest injustice under *Bradley*); Doe v. Board of County Commissioners, 783 F.Supp. 1379 (S.D.Fla.1992) (plaintiff sought leave to amend Title VII claim alleging a racially discriminatory discharge to add jury demand, request for monetary damages and § 1981 claim; applying *Bradley* presumption would require partial retroactivity as request for jury and monetary damages in Title VII claim is purely procedural or remedial and consequently would not result in manifest injustice, whereas request to add § 1981 claim would affect substantive rights and therefore would create manifest injustice and this court "declines to take such a piece-meal approach".); Maddox v. Norwood Clinic, Inc., 783 F.Supp. 582 (N.D.Ala.1992) (applying *Bradley* analysis and ruling that retroactive application of substantive change permitting damage recovery would result in manifest injustice); and Sorlucco v. New York City Police Department, 780 F.Supp. 202 (S.D.N.Y.1992) (retroactivity denied under *Bradley* rule because invocation of jury trial provision after trial was completed would result in manifest injustice).

On the other hand, where the courts have chosen to follow the presumption against retroactivity articulated in *Bowen,* they have declined to accord the statute retroactive application. See Johnson v. Uncle Ben's, Inc., 965 F.2d 1363 (5th Cir.1992) (1991 Act makes substantive changes and so should be denied retroactive effect, especially since this case is pending on appeal and was filed and decided by the trial court before 1991 statute was enacted); Luddington v. Indiana Bell Telephone Co., 966 F.2d 225 (7th Cir.1992) (provision of 1991 Act expanding coverage of § 1981 denied retroactive effect, at least as to cases filed prior to the Act's effective date); Vogel v. City of Cincinnati, 959 F.2d 594 (6th Cir.1992) (retroactive application would affect parties' substantive rights); Van Meter v. Barr, 778 F.Supp. 83 (D.D.C.1991) (FBI agent denied leave to amend complaint to include a claim for compensatory damages and a request for a jury trial in a case that had been filed more than nine months before the enactment of the new statute. At least as to claims by federal employees, neither statutory text nor legislative history is sufficiently demonstrative of intent to apply statute to pending cases to rebut presumption against retroactivity. Federal, unlike private sector, employees are required to raise discrimination claims with the employing agency prior to initiating suit. This difference was not affected by the 1991 legislation and to permit federal employees to insert claims for monetary relief at the judicial stage without providing the employing agency the opportunity to resolve such claims at the administrative level would be inconsistent with the legislative enforcement scheme for federal employees, a condition upon which the federal waiver of sovereign immunity was based. Nothing in the 1991 Act reflected Congress' desire to broaden its waiver of sovereign immunity or to expand the jurisdiction of federal courts to hear compensatory damage claims in cases where that issue had not been considered administratively. Court reserves decision, however, on whether the statute could apply to cases where the aggrieved had filed the administrative complaint, but not the lawsuit, prior to the enactment of the statute. Finally, language in § 102(d) defining "complaining party" as an individual who "may" bring suit indicates that Congress intended to preclude application of the statute to individuals who already have brought such actions.); Khandelwal v. Compuadd Corporation, 780 F.Supp. 1077 (E.D.Va.1992) (denying retroactivity; *Bowen* presumption should apply because it is a more recent case and Fourth Circuit appears to favor it); West v. Pelican Management Services Corp., 782 F.Supp. 1132 (M.D.La.1992) (denying retroactivity per *Bowen* and stating that language in §§ 402(b) and 109(c) specifically denying retroactivity does not lead to inference that remainder of statute should be granted retroactive effect but, rather, merely indicates that Congress was "seeking additional assurances" that retroactivity would be denied in these two situations. Court also notes that both vetoed 1990 legislation and predecessor bill to 1991 statute contained provisions clearly providing for retroactivity and that these provisions were not part of final statutory language.); Johnson v. Rice, 58 FEP Cases 31 (S.D.Ohio 1992) (denying retroactive application on ground that *Bowen* precludes retroactivity for substantive changes and amendment permitting monetary damage awards creates a new liability and, thus, is a substantive amendment); High v. Broadway Industries, Inc., 57 FEP Cases 1159 (W.D.Mo.1992) (denying retroactivity per *Bowen* presumption and in light of EEOC Guideline) and Hansel v. Public Service Co. of Colorado, 778 F.Supp. 1126 (D.Colo.1991) (denying retroactive effect on basis of *Bowen* presumption, noting that Act was signed on last day of trial, no textual language supports retroactivity and legislative history is ambiguous.).

In FRAY v. THE OMAHA WORLD HERALD CO., 960 F.2d 1370 (8th Cir.1992), the Eighth Circuit noted that the *Bowen* presumption was the better rule, but added that retroactivity should be rejected under either presumption. In refusing to apply the 1991 Act to an appeal from a jury verdict rendered in favor of the plaintiff in a case brought under § 1981, the court concluded that neither the text nor legislative history provided clear evidence of Congressional intent to rebut the *Bowen* presumption against retroactivity. Additionally, however, while admitting that the legislative history and text reflected a determination by Congress to leave this issue to the judiciary, a majority of the panel reasoned that the fact that a predecessor bill mandating retroactivity had been vetoed and that a subsequent bill omitting a mandate for retroactivity was enacted constituted sufficient evidence of statutory direction to rebut the *Bradley* presumption in favor of retroactivity. In dissent, Jude Heaney replied that it was clear from the legislative history that Congress was split on the question of retroactivity and that Congress' sole intention was to leave the retroactivity decision to the courts. Rather than attempting to choose between *Bowen* and *Bradley,* he preferred to adopt a test that he said fit within the common strain of the two cases; i.e., whether or not retroactivity would interfere with vested rights. In his view, retroactive application of the 1991 statute would only restore the rights enjoyed by the parties at the time the suit was filed. Accordingly, he concluded that the statute should be given retroactive effect.

The foregoing cases all have examined whether the Act should apply to cases pending at the trial level. Should a different analysis concerning retroactivity be employed when the question of retroactivity is raised on appeal after the case has been tried on the merits? This issue was addressed by the Seventh Circuit in MOZEE v. AMERICAN COMMERCIAL MARINE SERVICE COMPANY, 963 F.2d 929 (7th Cir.1992). In this case, the trial court's findings in favor of the plaintiffs' individual and class-based claims under Title VII and § 1981 were subjected to an interlocutory appeal. The appellate court affirmed the trial judge's rulings with respect to the plaintiffs' individual and class claims challenging the employer's discharge and promotion practices under Title VII, reversed the ruling in favor of the plaintiffs' discharge-based claims under § 1981 and vacated and remanded the class claims regarding the employer's discipline procedures. All of these rulings were issued prior to the enactment of the 1991 Act. After the passage of the new statute, and while a petition for rehearing was pending before it, the circuit panel requested additional briefing on the possible applicability of the 1991 Act. In light of the procedural posture of the case, the court reasoned, it was necessary to determine whether the Act apply retroactively on appeal and/or on remand. After concluding that the text and legislative history of the statute were unhelpful in determining whether Congress intended for the statute to have retroactive effect, the court turned to the Supreme Court jurisprudence on retroactivity. It concluded that the *Bradley* and *Bowen* lines of cases could best be reconciled by applying the *Bowen* presumption against retroactivity to statutory changes affecting substantive rights and liabilities at any stage of the proceedings. With respect to procedural changes, the court reasoned that while the *Bradley* presumption in favor of retroactivity was generally the appropriate standard, applying changes such as the right to a jury trial **on appeal** could result in a new trial of previously litigated issues, a result which, in the court's view, rose to the level of manifest injustice. Consequently, the court ruled, the *Bowen* presumption would apply to statutory changes affecting most procedural rules once the matter is on appeal. The court left the door slightly ajar by noting that *Bradley* might apply to damage provisions. It quickly added, however, that since the provisions in the 1991 Act concerning compensatory and punitive damages were not part of the interlocutory appeal, it did not have to rule on that question. Accordingly, in the absence of a clear legislative statement concerning retroactivity, the court held that none of the provisions of the 1991 Act would be applied to change its disposition of the issues on appeal from the trial court. It added, however, that where an appellate court's rulings resulted in a remand of the entire proceedings, statutory changes that only regulate trial proceedings and do not define the scope of a party's substantive rights or liabilities, such as the right to collect damages and the right to a jury trial, should apply to the new trial. Nevertheless, the court continued, where the remand did not require reconsideration of the entirety of the plaintiff's complaint, but, as in the instant case, resulted in a retrial of only a portion of the original proceeding, retroactivity would be inequitable and confusing and, therefore, would be denied. To do otherwise, the court stated, would mean that the remanded claims would be governed by different law than those claims which were not part of the remand order. See also Johnson v. Uncle Ben's, Inc., 965 F.2d 1363 (5th Cir.1992) (1991 Act should not be applied to a case pending on appeal that was filed and decided by the trial court before the enactment of the statute).

Another panel of the Seventh Circuit, however, citing *Mozee* as authority for the proposition that the 1991 Act was not to be accorded retroactive impact, stated that the presumption against retroactivity was a component of the traditional conception of the rule of law irrespective of whether the statute affected substantive or nonsubstantive rights. Nonsubstantive changes in remedies, procedures and evidence, the panel reasoned, "can have as profound an impact on behavior outside the courtroom as avowedly substantive changes" because "[t]he amount of care that individuals and firms take to avoid subjecting themselves to liability whether civil or criminal is a function of the severity of the sanction, and when the severity is increased they are entitled to an opportunity to readjust their level of care in light of the new environment created by the change." It then held that the provision of the 1991 Act reversing the Court's interpretation of § 1981 in *Patterson* should not be given retroactive effect, at least at to cases filed before the effective date of the 1991 statute. Luddington v. Indiana Bell Telephone, 966 F.2d 225, 229 (7th Cir.1992).

Finally, while most courts agree that the retroactivity question also must be addressed in post-Act-filed cases challenging pre-Act conduct, they disagree with respect to their answer to this question. Compare Jaekel v. Equifax Marketing, ____ F.Supp. ____, 1992 WL 143725 (E.D.Va.1992) (applying damages and jury trial provisions retroactively) with Crumley v. Delaware State College, ____ F.Supp. ____, 1992 WL 142243 (D.Del.1992) (denying retroactivity and noting that date of challenged conduct, rather than date of filing, is crucial factor in determining whether retroactivity issue must be resolved) and Neibauer v. Philadelphia, College of Pharmacy, ____ F.Supp. ____, 1992 WL 151321

(E.D.Pa.1992) (Id.).   But see Great American Tool & Manufacturing Co. v. Adolph Coors Company, Inc., 780 F.Supp. 1354 (D.Colo.1992) (no issue of retroactive application since case filed post-enactment).

SECTION B. INTENTIONAL DISCRIMINATION AGAINST THE INDIVIDUAL: DISPARATE TREATMENT

1. The Conceptual Framework

The most easily recognized form of discrimination occurs when an employer, union or employment agency intentionally treats people differently because of their race, color, religion, sex or national origin. In a series of cases spanning a decade, the Supreme Court struggled with the problem of setting forth a clearly stated evidentiary scheme to guide the parties in prosecuting and defending, and the lower courts in analyzing, what the Court denominated "disparate treatment" claims, i.e., those containing allegations of intentional discrimination.   The clearest articulation of the fruits of that struggle is contained within the following opinion.

TEXAS DEPARTMENT OF COMMUNITY AFFAIRS v. BURDINE
Supreme Court of the United States, 1981.
450 U.S. 248, 101 S.Ct. 1089, 67 L.Ed.2d 207.

JUSTICE POWELL delivered the opinion of the Court.

This case requires us to address again the nature of the evidentiary burden placed upon the defendant in an employment discrimination suit brought under Title VII of the Civil Rights Act of 1964.   The narrow question presented is whether, after the plaintiff has proved a prima facie case of discriminatory treatment, the burden shifts to the defendant to persuade the court by a preponderance of the evidence that legitimate, nondiscriminatory reasons for the challenged employment action existed.

I

[Respondent was employed as an accounting clerk in a division of the Petitioner Department that was funded completely by the federal government.   To retain this funding, the Petitioner was forced to reduce its staff, which it accomplished by firing Respondent and two other employees, while retaining one male employee.   Before her termination, Respondent had been denied a promotion to a supervisory position.   She brought the instant action alleging that the failure to promote and subsequent decision to terminate her were the result of sex discrimination in violation of Title VII.   The District Court, after a bench trial, ruled in favor of the defendant, finding no evidence to support plaintiff's claim that either decision had been based on gender discrimination.]

The Court of Appeals for the Fifth Circuit reversed in part.   The court * * * affirmed the District Court's finding that respondent was not discriminated against when she was not promoted. The Court of Appeals, however, reversed the District Court's finding that Fuller's testimony sufficiently had rebutted respondent's prima facie case of gender discrimination in the decision to terminate her employment at PSC. The court reaffirmed its previously announced views that the defendant in a Title VII case bears the burden of proving by a preponderance of the evidence the existence of legitimate nondiscriminatory reasons for the employment action and that the defendant also must prove by objective evidence that those hired or promoted were better qualified than the plaintiff. The court found that Fuller's testimony did not carry either of these evidentiary burdens. It, therefore, reversed the judgment of the District Court and remanded the case for computation of backpay. Because the decision of the Court of Appeals as to the burden of proof borne by the defendant conflicts with interpretations of our precedents adopted by other courts of appeals, we granted certiorari. We now vacate the Fifth Circuit's decision and remand for application of the correct standard.

II

In McDonnell Douglas Corp. v. Green, we set forth the basic allocation of burdens and order of presentation of proof in a Title VII case alleging discriminatory treatment. First, the plaintiff has the burden of proving by the preponderance of the evidence a prima facie case of discrimination. Second, if the plaintiff succeeds in proving the prima facie case, the burden shifts to the defendant "to articulate some legitimate, nondiscriminatory reason for the employee's rejection." Third, should the defendant carry this burden, the plaintiff must then have an opportunity to prove by a preponderance of the evidence that the legitimate reasons offered by the defendant were not its true reasons, but were a pretext for discrimination.

The nature of the burden that shifts to the defendant should be understood in light of the plaintiff's ultimate and intermediate burdens. The ultimate burden of persuading the trier of fact that the defendant intentionally discriminated against the plaintiff remains at all time with the plaintiff. See Board of Trustees of Keene State College v. Sweeney. See generally 9 Wigmore, Evidence § 2489 (3d ed. 1940) (the burden of persuasion "never shifts"). The *McDonnell Douglas* division of intermediate evidentiary burdens serves to bring the litigants and the court expeditiously and fairly to this ultimate question.

The burden of establishing a prima facie case of disparate treatment is not onerous. The plaintiff must prove by a preponderance of the evidence that she applied for an available position, for which she was qualified, but was rejected under circumstances which give rise to an inference of unlawful discrimination.[6] The prima facie case serves an important function in the litigation: it eliminates the most common

---

6. In the instant case, it is not seriously contested that respondent has proved a prima facie case. She showed that she was a qualified woman who sought an available position, but the position was left open for several months before she finally was rejected in favor of a male who had been under her supervision.

nondiscriminatory reasons for the plaintiff's rejection. * * * Establishment of the prima facie case in effect creates a presumption that the employer unlawfully discriminated against the employee. If the trier of fact believes the plaintiff's evidence, and if the employer is silent in the face of the presumption, the court must enter judgment for the plaintiff because no issue of fact remains in the case.[7]

The burden that shifts to the defendant, therefore, is to rebut the presumption of discrimination by producing evidence that the plaintiff was rejected, or someone else was preferred, for a legitimate, nondiscriminatory reason. The defendant need not persuade the court that it was actually motivated by the proffered reasons. It is sufficient if the defendant's evidence raises a genuine issue of fact as to whether it discriminated against the plaintiff.[8] To accomplish this, the defendant must clearly set forth, through the introduction of admissible evidence, the reasons for the plaintiff's rejection.[9] The explanation provided must be legally sufficient to justify a judgment for the defendant. If the defendant carries this burden of production, the presumption raised by the prima facie case is rebutted,[10] and the factual inquiry proceeds to a new level of specificity. Placing this burden of production on the defendant thus serves simultaneously to meet the plaintiff's prima facie case by presenting a legitimate reason for the action and to frame the factual issue with sufficient clarity so that the plaintiff will have a full and fair opportunity to demonstrate pretext. The sufficiency of the defendant's evidence should be evaluated by the extent to which it fulfills these functions.

7. The phrase "prima facie case" may denote not only the establishment of a legally mandatory, rebuttable presumption, but also may be used by courts to describe the plaintiff's burden of producing enough evidence to permit the trier of fact to infer the fact at issue. 9 Wigmore, Evidence § 2494 (3d ed. 1940). *McDonnell Douglas* should have made it apparent that in the Title VII context we use "prima facie case" in the former sense.

8. This evidentiary relationship between the presumption created by a prima facie case and the consequential burden of production placed on the defendant is a traditional feature of the common law. "The word 'presumption' properly used refers only to a device for allocating the production burden." F. James & G. Hazard, Civil Procedure § 7.9, at 255 (2d ed. 1977) (footnote omitted). See Fed.Rule Evid. 301. Usually, assessing the burden of production helps the judge determine whether the litigants have created an issue of fact to be decided by the jury. In a Title VII case, the allocation of burdens and the creation of a presumption by the establishment of a prima facie case is intended progressively to sharpen the inquiry into the elusive factual question of intentional discrimination.

9. An articulation not admitted into evidence will not suffice. Thus, the defendant cannot meet its burden merely through an answer to the complaint or by argument of counsel.

10. In saying that the presumption drops from the case, we do not imply that the trier of fact no longer may consider evidence previously introduced by the plaintiff to establish a prima facie case. A satisfactory explanation by the defendant destroys the legally mandatory inference of discrimination arising from the plaintiff's initial evidence. Nonetheless, this evidence and inferences properly drawn therefrom may be considered by the trier of fact on the issue of whether the defendant's explanation is pretextual. Indeed, there may be some cases where the plaintiff's initial evidence, combined with effective cross-examination of the defendant, will suffice to discredit the defendant's explanation.

The plaintiff retains the burden of persuasion. She now must have the opportunity to demonstrate that the proffered reason was not the true reason for the employment decision. This burden now merges with the ultimate burden of persuading the court that she has been the victim of intentional discrimination. She may succeed in this either directly by persuading the court that a discriminatory reason more likely motivated the employer or indirectly by showing that the employer's proffered explanation is unworthy of credence.

III

In reversing the judgment of the District Court that the discharge of respondent from PSC was unrelated to her sex, the Court of Appeals adhered to two rules it had developed to elaborate the defendant's burden of proof. First, the defendant must prove by a preponderance of the evidence that legitimate, nondiscriminatory reasons for the discharge existed. Second, to satisfy this burden, the defendant "must prove that those he hired * * * were somehow *better* qualified than was plaintiff; in other words, comparative evidence is needed."

A

The Court of Appeals has misconstrued the nature of the burden that *McDonnell Douglas* and its progeny place on the defendant. We stated in *Sweeney* that "the employer's burden is satisfied if he simply 'explains what he has done' or 'produc[es] evidence of legitimate nondiscriminatory reasons.'" It is plain that the Court of Appeals required much more: it placed on the defendant the burden of persuading the court that it had convincing, objective reasons for preferring the chosen applicant above the plaintiff.

The Court of Appeals distinguished *Sweeney* on the ground that the case held only that the defendant did not have the burden of proving the absence of discriminatory intent. But this distinction slights the rationale of *Sweeney* and of our other cases. We have stated consistently that the employee's prima facie case of discrimination will be rebutted if the employer articulates lawful reasons for the action; that is, to satisfy this intermediate burden, the employer need only produce admissible evidence which would allow the trier of fact rationally to conclude that the employment decision had not been motivated by discriminatory animus. The Court of Appeals would require the defendant to introduce evidence which, in the absence of any evidence of pretext, would *persuade* the trier of fact that the employment action was lawful. This exceeds what properly can be demanded to satisfy a burden of production.

The court placed the burden of persuasion on the defendant apparently because it feared that "[i]f an employer need only *articulate*—not prove—a legitimate, nondiscriminatory reason for his action, he may compose fictitious, but legitimate, reasons for his actions." We do not believe, however, that limiting the defendant's evidentiary obligation to a burden of production will unduly hinder the plaintiff. First, as noted above, the defendant's explanation of its legitimate reasons must be clear and reasonably specific. This obligation arises both from the necessity of rebutting the inference of discrimination arising from the prima facie case and from the requirement that the plaintiff be afforded "a full and fair opportunity" to demonstrate pretext. Second, although the defendant does not bear a formal burden of persuasion, the defendant nevertheless retains an incentive to persuade the trier of fact that the employment decision was lawful. Thus, the defendant normally will attempt to prove the factual basis for its explanation. Third, the liberal discovery rules applicable to any civil suit in federal court are supplemented in a Title VII suit by the plaintiff's access to the Equal Employment Opportunity Commission's investigatory files concerning her complaint. Given these factors, we are unpersuaded that the plaintiff will find it particularly difficult to prove that a proffered explanation lacking a factual basis is a pretext. We remain confident that the *McDonnell Douglas* framework permits the plaintiff meriting relief to demonstrate intentional discrimination.

B

The Court of Appeals also erred in requiring the defendant to prove by objective evidence that the person hired or promoted was more qualified than the plaintiff. *McDonnell Douglas* teaches that it is the plaintiff's task to demonstrate that similarly situated employees were not treated equally. The Court of Appeals' rule would require the employer to show that the plaintiff's objective qualifications were inferior to those of the person selected. If it cannot, a court would, in effect, conclude that it has discriminated.

* * *

The views of the Court of Appeals can be read, we think, as requiring the employer to hire the minority or female applicant whenever that person's objective qualifications were equal to those of a white male applicant. But Title VII does not obligate an employer to accord this preference. Rather, the employer has discretion to choose among equally qualified candidates, provided the decision is not based upon unlawful criteria. The fact that a court may think that the employer misjudged the qualifications of the applicants does not in itself expose him to Title VII liability, although this may be probative of whether the employer's reasons are pretexts for discrimination.

IV

In summary, the Court of Appeals erred by requiring the defendant to prove by a preponderance of the evidence the existence of nondiscriminatory reasons for terminating the respondent and that the person retained in her stead had superior objective qualifications for the position. When the plaintiff has proved a prima facie case of discrimination, the defendant bears only the burden of explaining clearly the nondiscriminatory reasons for its actions. The judgment of the Court of Appeals is vacated and the case is remanded for further proceedings consistent with this opinion.

It is so ordered.

NOTES AND PROBLEMS FOR DISCUSSION

1. The principal case is the fourth in a line of opinions, each of which dealt with the allocation of evidentiary burdens in disparate treatment claims. In McDonnell Douglas v. Green (cited, appropriately, in the first sentence of the substantive portion of *Burdine*), 411 U.S. 792, 93 S.Ct. 1817, 36 L.Ed.2d 668 (1973), the Court took its first step in this extended journey. This case involved a black mechanic who had been laid off during a general reduction in the employer's work force. He protested that this action, as well as the company's general hiring practices, was racially biased. As a further display of his protest, he and others illegally stalled their cars on the main roads leading to the company's plant in order to block access to it at the time of the morning shift change. A few weeks after the "stall-in", the company publicly advertised for qualified mechanics, but turned downed Green's application because of his participation in the "stall-in". He then filed the instant suit alleging that the company had refused to rehire him because of his race and involvement in the civil rights movement. The Court began its analysis of the case by stating that "the critical issue before us concerns the order and allocation of proof in a private, non-class action challenging employment discrimination." It then outlined the elements of a plaintiff's prima facie case. In now classic language, the Court stated that a plaintiff "may" establish a prima facie claim of discrimination by showing that (1) he is a member of a protected classification; (2) he applied and was qualified for the employment opportunity in question; (3) he was rejected; and (4) the position remained open after his rejection and the employer continued to seek applicants from individuals of his qualifications. The Court quickly added that while this was a generally applicable formula, it was not intended as an inflexible standard, each of whose criteria necessarily had to govern the disposition of the myriad of varying factual situations that could arise in Title VII cases. It then stated that once the prima facie case is established, "the burden then must shift to the employer to articulate some legitimate, nondiscriminatory reason for the employee's rejection....[T]his suffices to discharge [defendant's] burden of proof at this stage and to meet [plaintiff's] prima facie case of discrimination." It noted, however, that if the defendant sustains this burden, the plaintiff must be afforded the opportunity to "show" that the defendant's stated reason was pretextual. Finally, the Court remanded the case for retrial consistent with this tripartite evidentiary formula, suggesting that the plaintiff might be able to establish pretext by proving, *inter alia*, that white employees who had been involved in acts against the company of comparable seriousness were nevertheless rehired or retained.

Unfortunately, this opinion caused confusion among the lower courts as they attempted to discern the precise contours of this blueprint. For example, with respect to a plaintiff's prima facie showing that she was "qualified" for the position, did the Court intend to require a plaintiff to prove that she was better qualified than the successful applicant? Equally qualified? Or, would it be sufficient to establish that she possessed the minimum qualifications prescribed for the job? Should the employer's use of subjective criteria affect the nature of the plaintiff's showing? (For a detailed discussion of these issues see Note 2, *infra*, at 99–100.) Three interrelated questions also were raised with respect to the evidentiary impact of establishing a prima facie case. First, what was the precise nature of the defendant's "burden of proof"? Much of the confusion surrounding this issue was caused by the *McDonnell Douglas* Court's use of the word "articulate," rather than "prove" or "produce evidence of" to describe the burden placed on the defendant to "meet" the prima facie showing. Did the Court intend to require the defendant to prove the existence of a nondiscriminatory explanation? Did it impose the lesser burden of producing credible evidence of such an explanation? Or could this requirement be met merely through an allegation in the pleading or by argument of counsel? Second, what factual issue is to be addressed by the defendant's offer of proof? In stating that the defendant must articulate "some" legitimate, nondiscriminatory justification, did the Court mean to require the defendant to offer evidence of a single nondiscriminatory justification or to negate the presence of any discriminatory motive? Finally, what is the effect of establishing a prima facie case when the defendant does not discharge whatever burden has been imposed upon it? Is the court compelled to issue a judgment in favor of the plaintiff? In other words, does the prima facie case produce a presumption or an inference of discrimination?

In the two cases following *McDonnell Douglas*, Furnco Construction Corp. v. Waters, 438 U.S. 567, 98 S.Ct. 2943, 57 L.Ed.2d 957 (1978), and Board of Trustees of Keene State College v. Sweeney, 439 U.S. 24, 99 S.Ct. 295, 58 L.Ed.2d 216 (1978), the Court attempted, unsuccessfully, to clear up the confusion on each of these questions. Consequently, the Court, as noted in the first sentence of its opinion in *Burdine*, once again had to step into this evidentiary breach. In this, its fourth, though not final, sojourn, (see *Aikens*, *infra* at 113), the Court did manage to more clearly articulate its thinking with respect to both the prima facie and defense cases. How were these matters resolved? For further discussion and analysis of the Court's treatment of the evidentiary matters discussed in this Note, see Belton, Burdens of Pleading and Proof In Discrimination Cases: Toward a Theory of Procedural Justice, 34 Vand.L.Rev. 1205 (1981); Friedman, The Burger Court and the Prima Facie Case in Employment Discrimination Litigation: A Critique, 65 Corn.L.Rev. 1 (1979); Mendez, Presumptions of Discriminatory Motive in Title VII Disparate Treatment Cases, 32 Stanf.L.Rev. 1129 (1980).

2. In *McDonnell Douglas*, *Furnco* and *Sweeney*, the Court required the defendant to articulate some "legitimate, nondiscriminatory reason" for its action. The *Burdine* Court added that this explanation must be "legally sufficient." Does this mean something other than "nondiscriminatory"? If so, under what standard must the reason be legitimate? Would it be sufficient for a court to conclude that the justification is silly? unethical? violative of some other statute or common law principle? See Curler v. City of Fort Wayne, 591 F.Supp. 327 (N.D.Ind.1984). What if the employer's articulated defense consists of evidence of its subjective evaluation of the worker's performance in a case involving a refusal to reinstate after layoff or a promotion? Compare IMPACT v. Firestone, 893 F.2d 1189 (11th Cir.), cert. denied, ___ U.S. ___, 111 S.Ct. 133, 112 L.Ed.2d 100 (1990) (employer's statement that plaintiff was not the "best qualified," without an explanation of the qualifications actually used by the employer to reach this determination, is not sufficiently specific, under *Burdine*, to afford plaintiff a full and fair opportunity to show that this reason is a pretext) and Miles v. M.N.C. Corp., 750 F.2d 867 (11th Cir.1985) (where subjective evaluation was made by a white supervisor in absence of guidelines

for evaluating performance and without either written work evaluations or regular checks on employee work habits, court finds situation a "ready mechanism for racial discrimination" and that this justification, without more, did not rebut the prima facie case) with Verniero v. Air Force Academy School Dist. No. 20, 705 F.2d 388 (10th Cir.1983) (subjective evaluation of applicant's ability to get along with co-workers did rebut the prima facie case).

Can bureaucratic inefficiency, employee ineptitude and an inadequate budget constitute "legitimate" explanations for actions which would otherwise constitute disparate treatment? In HILL V. MISSISSIPPI STATE EMPLOYMENT SERVICE, 918 F.2d 1233 (5th Cir.1990), the Court of Appeals held that a state employment service's explanation that its failure to refer a black applicant to various open positions for which she was qualified (while referring whites who had not even listed such positions on their applications) resulted from red tape and employee error must be accepted. The plaintiff through statistical evidence showed that black applicants were referred to fewer jobs than comparable white applicants. The district court found that the agency's excuse of employee error and bureaucratic bumbling was not a pretext for intentional discrimination. Expressing discomfort with the idea that general inefficiency could be raised as a defense by employers for any action that might otherwise be discriminatory, the Court of Appeals nevertheless concluded that discriminatory animus could not be inferred from inefficiency and that inefficiency could not be punished under Title VII.

In dissent, Judge Rubin challenged the majority's conclusion that agency's inefficiency was in fact racially neutral.

> "The MSES has not shown a single instance in which its inefficient system favored black employees ... Presumably so inefficient a system would sometimes result in a neglect or oversight of white applicants. The evidence shows that the MSES system is inefficient only when it fails to refer black employees."

918 F.2d at 1243.

3. The Court stated in *McDonnell Douglas*, and reaffirmed in the three subsequent cases, that if the defendant rebuts the plaintiff's prima facie case, the plaintiff still can prevail if it can prove that the defendant's "stated reason for [plaintiff's] rejection was in fact pretext." As mentioned in Note 1, the Court suggested in *McDonnell Douglas* that the plaintiff might be able to establish pretext by proving that otherwise similarly situated nonblack employees had not been refused reemployment. The Court also noted, however, that "statistics as to [defendant's] employment policy and practice may be helpful" in making this determination and that "the racial composition of defendant's labor force is itself reflective of restrictive or exclusionary practices." The Court cautioned, however, that "such general determinations, while helpful, may not be in and of themselves controlling as to an individualized hiring decision." 411 U.S. at 805, 933 S.Ct. at 1826, 36 L.Ed.2d at 679 n.19. Similarly, in *Furnco*, the Court declared that evidence proffered by the defendant relating to the racial mix of the its workforce "is not wholly irrelevant on the issue of intent" and that a trial court is "entitled to consider the racial mix of the work force when trying to make the determination as to [the defendant's] motivation." 438 U.S. at 579–80; 98 S.Ct. at 2951, 57 L.Ed.2d at 969. Moreover, the lower appellate courts have ruled that statistical evidence can help establish a prima facie case, even though it may not be directly probative of any of the four specific elements set forth in McDonnell Douglas. See e.g., Gilty v. Village of

Oak Park, 919 F.2d 1247, 1253 n.8 (7th Cir.1990); Smith v. Horner, 839 F.2d 1530, 1536 n.8 (11th Cir.1988); Diaz v. American Telephone & Telegraph, 752 F.2d 1356 (9th Cir.1985).

In International Brotherhood of Teamsters v. United States, 431 U.S. 324, 339 n.20, 97 S.Ct. 1843, 1857 n.20, 52 L.Ed.2d 396, 418 n.20 (1977), a case involving a claim of class-based disparate treatment, the Court offered a probability-based explanation of the probative value of statistics generally in disparate treatment cases. The Court stated that "[s]tatistics showing racial or ethnic imbalance are probative * * * only because such imbalance is often a telltale sign of purposeful discrimination; absent explanation, it is ordinarily to be expected that nondiscriminatory hiring practices will in time result in a workforce more or less representative of the racial and ethnic composition of the population in the community from which employees are hired." Simply put, the Court's theory can be reduced to two propositions. First, that where there is an otherwise unexplained departure from the expected results of the rules of probability, it is reasonable for a factfinder to conclude that this general pattern was the product of discrimination. Second, proof of this general pattern tends also to establish that the defendant's decision in the individual case was the consequence of discrimination. But precisely because the probative force of the nexus between a general pattern and an individual decision is not likely to be very strong, few, if any, individual disparate treatment cases are proved by such evidence alone. Thus, even when it is available, statistical evidence usually is tendered as a supplement, rather than a substitute, for direct evidence. See e.g., Smith v. Horner, 839 F.2d 1530, 1536 n.8 (11th Cir.1988) (statistics in an individual disparate treatment case can be relevant, but cannot alone establish a prima facie case). Moreover, in many disparate treatment cases, no statistical pattern may exist or, because the work force is so small or the job qualifications so unique, statistically significant data may be unavailable. By way of comparison, statistical evidence plays a crucial, albeit different, role in both class-based claims of intentional discrimination and allegations of nonintentional discrimination. Consequently, a detailed analysis of statistical methodology in employment discrimination litigation will be found in Sections B and C, *infra*.

4.   Henry Wilson, a male African–American, was refused employment as a bricklayer by Supreme Contracting, Inc. After successfully completing the job interview and reference check portions of the application process, Wilson was sent to the company physician for a routine physical examination. The doctor reported to the personnel supervisor that Mr. Wilson was not physically qualified because of a previously undetected heart defect. Mr. Wilson's concern over such a finding led him to consult his own doctor, whose examination showed that Mr. Wilson was in perfect health. Mr. Wilson brought a letter to that effect from his physician to the plant personnel supervisor. The supervisor, however, refused to reconsider Wilson, stating that company policy precluded re-examination of applicants found unfit by the plant doctor. Two days later, the plant hired a white man for the bricklaying position sought by Wilson. Can Wilson establish a prima facie violation of Title VII? What arguments could the employer assert in response? Could plaintiff ultimately succeed on the merits? Would it make any difference if the plaintiff could persuade the factfinder that the company physician made a mistake? What if the plaintiff could show that only 5% of the bricklayers employed by Supreme Contracting are black, even though Blacks constitute 35% of the population of

the surrounding community? See Weaden v. American Cyanamid Co., 14 FEP Cases 533 (N.D.Fla.1976).

5. Must the plaintiff in a disparate treatment case allege and prove that the defendant was motivated by a hostile racial, or other class-based, prejudice? Suppose, for example, an employer refrained from evaluating the performance of an African–American employee and counseling her about deficiencies in her work to avoid the possibility of a confrontation and charges of racial discrimination. Other employees were annually evaluated, their performance rated and then counseled about deficiencies. After several years the employer, under a cost-reduction program, laid off the two lowest performers in each department. The two that were chosen were this African–American employee and a white employee. Can she successfully bring a claim of disparate treatment against the employer? See Vaughn v. Edel, 918 F.2d 517 (5th Cir.1990) (while plaintiff's race did not directly motivate the discharge, she was treated differently because of her race during the years of her employment in that she was not afforded "the same opportunity to improve her performance, and perhaps her relative ranking" that was provided to white employees; the fact that the employer's reluctance to criticize or counsel her about her deficiencies was motivated by benign self-interest rather than racial hostility or prejudice was irrelevant.)

Disparate treatment claims, of course, may also be raised against unions. Section 703(c) sets forth three classes of prohibited union employment practices. The first two categories deal predominantly with actions taken by the union directly against either its members or membership applicants. Subsection (1), for example, makes it an lawful employment practice for a union "otherwise to discriminate against any individual" on the basis of the five proscribed classifications. Subsection (3), however, prohibits a union from doing anything to "cause or attempt to cause an employer" to violate the statute. These two provisions raise the interesting question of the extent of a union's duty to oppose employer discriminatory conduct. For example, does a union's acquiescence to, as opposed to participation in or instigation of, employer misconduct subject the union to liability? The Supreme Court had an opportunity to examine this problem in the following case.

GOODMAN v. LUKENS STEEL COMPANY

Supreme Court of the United States, 1987.
482 U.S. 656, 107 S.Ct. 2617, 96 L.Ed.2d 572.

Justice White delivered the opinion of the Court.

In 1973, individual employees of Lukens Steel Company (Lukens) brought this suit on behalf of themselves and others, asserting racial discrimination claims under Title VII of the Civil Rights Act of 1964 * * * against their employer and their collective-bargaining agents, the United Steelworkers of America and two of its local unions (Unions).

After a bench trial, the District Court * * * concluded that the Unions were * * * guilty of discriminatory practices, specifically in failing to challenge discriminatory discharges of probationary employees, failing and refusing to assert instances of racial discrimination as grievances, and in tolerating and tacitly encouraging racial harassment. The District Court entered * * * injunctive orders against * * * the Unions, reserving damages issues for further proceedings. * * * [T]he Unions appealed, challenging the District Court's liability conclusions * * *.

The Court of Appeals * * * affirmed the liability judgment against the Unions. * * * The Unions' petition * * * claimed error in finding them liable under Title VII * * *. * * *

* * *

II

This case was tried for 32 days in 1980. One-hundred fifty-seven witnesses testified and over 2,000 exhibits were introduced. On February 13, 1984, the District Court filed its findings and conclusions. In an introductory section discussing the relevant legal principles, the trial judge discussed, among other things, the nature of "disparate treatment" and "disparate impact" cases under Title VII, recognizing that in the former the plaintiff must prove not only disparate treatment, but trace its cause to intentional racial discrimination, an unnecessary element in disparate impact cases. * * *

The District Court proceeded to find that the company had violated Title VII in several significant respects, including the discharge of employees during their probationary period, the toleration of racial harassment by employees, initial job assignments, promotions, and decisions on incentive pay. * * *

Similarly, the Unions were found to have discriminated on racial grounds in violation of * * * Title VII * * * in certain ways: failing to challenge discriminatory discharges of probationary employees; failure and refusal to assert racial discrimination as a ground for grievances; and toleration and tacit encouragement of racial harassment.

What the conduct of the Unions had been and whether they had treated blacks and whites differently were questions of historical fact that Federal Rule of Civil Procedure 52(a) enjoins appellate courts to accept unless clearly erroneous. So is the issue of whether the Unions intended to discriminate based on race. The Court of Appeals did not set aside any of the District Court's findings of fact that are relevant to this case. That is the way the case comes to us, and both courts below having agreed on the facts, we are not inclined to examine the record for ourselves absent some extraordinary reason for undertaking this task. Nothing the Unions have submitted indicates that we should do so. * * * Unless there are one or more errors of law inhering in the judgment below, as the Unions claim there are, we should affirm it.

The Unions contend that the judgment against them rests on the erroneous legal premise that Title VII * * * [is] violated if a Union passively sits by and does not affirmatively oppose the employer's racially discriminatory employment practices. It is true that the District Court declared that mere Union passivity in the face of employer discrimination renders the Union liable under Title VII * * *.[10] We need not discuss this rather abstract observation, for the court went on to say that the evidence proves "far more" than mere passivity.[11] As found by the court, the facts were that since 1965, the collective-bargaining contract contained an express clause binding both the employer and the Unions not to discriminate on racial grounds; that the employer was discriminating against blacks in discharging probationary employees, which the Unions were aware of but refused to do anything about by way of filing proffered grievances or otherwise; that the Unions had ignored grievances based on instances of harassment which were indisputably racial in nature; and that the Unions had regularly refused to include assertions of racial discrimination in grievances that also asserted other contract violations.[12]

In affirming the District Court's findings against the Unions, the Court of Appeals also appeared to hold that the Unions had an affirmative duty to combat employer discrimination in the workplace. But it, too, held that the case against the Unions was much stronger than one of mere acquiescence in that the Unions deliberately chose not to assert claims of racial discrimination by the employer. It was the Court of Appeals' view that these intentional and knowing refusals discriminated against the victims who were entitled to have their grievances heard.

The Unions submit that the only basis for any liability in this case under Title VII is § 703(c)(3), which provides that a Union may not "cause or attempt to cause an employer to discriminate against an individual in violation of this section," and that nothing the District Court found and the Court of Appeals accepted justifies liability under this prohibition. We need not differ with the Unions on the reach of § 703(c)(3), for § 703(c)(1) makes it an unlawful practice for a Union to

---

10. * * * [T]his statement must have been addressed to disparate impact, for discriminatory motive is required in disparate treatment Title VII cases * * *. See Teamsters v. United States.

11. The District Court commented that there was substantial evidence, related to events occurring prior to the statute of limitations period, which "casts serious doubt on the unions' total commitment to racial equality." The District Court noted that it was the company, not the Unions, which pressed for a nondiscrimination clause in the collective-bargaining agreement. The District Court found that the Unions never took any action over the segregated locker facilities at Lukens and did not complain over other discriminatory practices by the company. The District

Court found that when one employee approached the president of one of the local unions to complain about the segregated locker facilities in 1962, the president dissuaded him from complaining to the appropriate state agency. The District Court, however, found "inconclusive" the evidence offered in support of the employees' claim that the Unions discriminated against blacks in their overall handling of grievances under the collective-bargaining agreement.

12. The District Court also found that although the Unions had objected to the company's use of certain tests, they had never done so on racial grounds, even though they "were certainly chargeable with knowledge that many of the tests" had a racially disparate impact.

"exclude or to expel from its membership, *or otherwise to discriminate against,* any individual because of his race, color, religion, sex, or national origin." Both courts below found that the Unions had indeed discriminated on the basis of race by the way in which they represented the workers, and the Court of Appeals expressly held that "[t]he deliberate choice not to process grievances also violated § 703(c)(1) of Title VII." The plain language of the statute supports this conclusion.

* * *

The Unions insist that it was error to hold them liable for not including racial discrimination claims in grievances claiming other violations of the contract. The Unions followed this practice, it was urged, because these grievances could be resolved without making racial allegations and because the employer would "get its back up" if racial bias was charged, thereby making it much more difficult to prevail. The trial judge, although initially impressed by this seemingly neutral reason for failing to press race discrimination claims, ultimately found the explanation "unacceptable" because the Unions also ignored grievances which involved racial harassment violating the contract covenant against racial discrimination but which did not also violate another provision. The judge also noted that the Unions had refused to complain about racially based terminations of probationary employees, even though the express undertaking not to discriminate protected this group of employees, as well as others, and even though, as the District Court found, the Unions knew that blacks were being discharged at a disproportionately higher rate than whites. In the judgment of the District Court, the virtual failure by the Unions to file any race-bias grievances until after this lawsuit started, knowing that the employer was practicing what the contract prevented, rendered the Unions' explanation for their conduct unconvincing.[13]

As we understand it, there was no suggestion below that the Unions held any racial animus against or denigrated blacks generally. Rather, it was held that a collective bargaining agent could not, without violating Title VII, * * * follow a policy of refusing to file grievable racial discrimination claims however strong they might be and however sure the agent was that the employer was discriminating against blacks. The Unions, in effect, categorized racial grievances as unworthy of pursuit and, while pursuing thousands of other legitimate grievances, ignored racial discrimination claims on behalf of blacks,

13. The District Court also rejected the Unions' argument that much of the workers' case involved discrimination by the company in making initial job assignments, and that it had no control over those assignments. The court found that once hired, new employees were entitled to the protection of the collective-bargaining agreement, including the protection afforded by the non-discrimination clause:

"To require blacks to continue to work in lower paying and less desirable jobs, in units disparately black, is to discriminate against them in violation of the collective bargaining agreement (and, of course, also in violation of Title VII). It is very clear, on the record in this case, that the defendant unions never sought to avail themselves of this rather obvious mechanism for protecting the interests of their members."

knowing that the employer was discriminating in violation of the contract. Such conduct, the courts below concluded, intentionally discriminated against blacks seeking a remedy for disparate treatment based on their race and violated * * * Title VII * * *. As the District Court said, "A union which intentionally avoids asserting discrimination claims, either so as not to antagonize the employer and thus improve its chances of success on other issues, or in deference to the perceived desires of its white membership, is liable under * * * Title [VII] * * *, regardless of whether, as a subjective matter, its leaders were favorably disposed toward minorities."

The courts below, in our view, properly construed and applied Title VII * * *. Those provisions do not permit a union to refuse to file any and all grievances presented by a black person on the ground that the employer looks with disfavor on and resents such grievances. It is no less violative of * * * [this law] for a union to pursue a policy of rejecting disparate treatment grievances presented by blacks solely because the claims assert racial bias and would be very troublesome to process.

* * * [T]he judgment of the Court of Appeals is affirmed.

It is so ordered.

JUSTICE BRENNAN, with whom JUSTICE MARSHALL and JUSTICE BLACKMUN join, concurring in part and dissenting in part.

I join Part II of the Court's opinion, affirming the Court of Appeals' decision that the Unions engaged in race discrimination in violation of * * * Title VII of the Civil Rights Act of 1964. * * *

* * *

JUSTICE POWELL, with whom JUSTICE SCALIA joins, and with whom JUSTICE O'CONNOR joins as to Parts I through IV, concurring in part and dissenting in part.

* * * I dissent, however, from Part II of the Court's opinion, that affirms the judgment against the Unions for violating * * * Title VII of the Civil Rights Act of 1964. The ambiguous findings of the District Court, accepted by the Court of Appeals for the Third Circuit, do not provide adequate support for the Court's conclusion that the Unions engaged in intentional discrimination against black members. Neither of the courts below specifically found that the Unions were motivated by racial animus, or that they are liable to black members under the alternate Title VII theory of disparate impact. Accordingly, I would remand to permit the District Court to clarify its findings of fact and to make additional findings if necessary.

I

Close examination of the findings of the District Court is essential to a proper understanding of this case. The plaintiffs, blacks employed by the Lukens Steel Company, sued the United Steelworkers of America and two of its local unions (Unions) for alleged violations of * * * Title VII. The plaintiffs' allegations were directed primarily at the Unions' handling of grievances on behalf of black members. The District Court found that "[t]he steady increase in grievance filings each year has not produced a corresponding increase in the capacity of the grievance-processing system to handle complaints." Consequently, the court found, the Unions gave priority to "[s]erious grievances"— that is, "those involving more than a four-day suspension, and those involving discharges." In an effort to reduce the backlog of grievances, the Unions disposed of many less serious grievances by simply withdrawing them and reserving the right to seek relief in a later grievance proceeding. The District Court found "no hard evidence to support an inference that these inadequacies disadvantage blacks to a greater extent than whites." The incomplete evidence in the record suggests that the percentage of grievances filed on behalf of black employees was proportional to the number of blacks in the work force. Of the relatively few grievances that proceeded all the way to arbitration, the District Court found that the number asserted on behalf of black members was proportional to the number of blacks in the work force. Moreover, black members had a slightly higher rate of success in arbitration than white members. In sum, the District Court found that "plaintiffs' generalized evidence concerning perceptions about racial inequities in the handling of grievances does not, without more, establish a prima facie case * * *." [1]

The District Court concluded, however, that the plaintiffs were "on firmer ground" in challenging the Unions' "repeated failures, during the limitations period, to include racial discrimination as a basis for grievances or other complaints against the company." Beginning in 1965, the Unions' collective-bargaining agreements with the employer prohibited discrimination on the basis of race against any employee, permanent or probationary. It is undisputed that the Unions "were reluctant to assert racial discrimination as a basis for a grievance." The court found the Unions' explanation for this reluctance facially reasonable. The Unions observed that employees were more likely to obtain relief if a grievance based on racial discrimination was framed as a violation of another provision of the collective-bargaining agreement that did not require proof of racial animus. Moreover, when faced with an allegation of racial discrimination, "the company tended 'to get its back up' and resist [the] charge." The court nevertheless rejected the Unions' explanation, for two reasons. First, the court found that the Unions "virtually ignored" the "numerous instances of harassment, which were indisputably racial in nature, but which did not otherwise plainly violate a provision of the collective bargaining

---

1. The District Court found that black union members "actively participated" in union meetings and affairs. A black member served as chairman of the grievance committee, and other black members served on the committee. The percentage of black shop stewards, the Union's primary representatives in the grievance process, frequently exceeded the percentage of black members in the bargaining unit.

agreement." Second, the court concluded that "vigorous pursuit of claims of racial discrimination would have focused attention upon racial issues and compelled some change in racial attitudes," and that the Unions' "unwillingness to assert racial discrimination claims as such rendered the non-discrimination clause in the collective bargaining agreement a dead letter."

The District Court also found that the Unions had adopted a policy of refusing to process any grievances on behalf of probationary employees, despite the fact that the collective-bargaining agreement prohibited employers from discriminating against any employee, permanent or probationary, on the basis of race. The Unions adhered to this policy, the court found, even though they "knew that blacks were being discharged * * * at a disproportionately higher rate than whites." Finally, the court found that the Unions failed to object to written tests administered by the employer on the ground that it had a disparate impact on black members, even though they "were certainly chargeable with knowledge that many of the tests * * * were notorious in that regard." The court found, however, that the Unions objected to "tests of all kinds," on the ground that they gave an unfair advantage to younger employees who had recently completed their formal education.

The Court of Appeals accepted each of the District Court's findings of fact and affirmed the judgment against the Unions. The appellate court concluded that the Unions' "deliberate choice not to process grievances" violated Title VII "because it discriminated against the victims who were entitled to representation." * * *

II

A

As the Court recognizes, * * * a valid claim under Title VII must be grounded on proof of disparate treatment or disparate impact. A disparate treatment claim * * * requires proof of a discriminatory purpose. Teamsters v. United States, 431 U.S. 324, 335–336, n. 15, 97 S.Ct. 1843, 1854–1855, n. 15, 52 L.Ed.2d 396 (1977). Of course, " '[d]iscriminatory purpose' * * * implies more than intent as volition or intent as awareness of consequences." Personnel Administrator of Mass. v. Feeney, 442 U.S. 256, 279, 99 S.Ct. 2282, 2296, 60 L.Ed.2d 870 (1979) (citation omitted). It implies that the challenged action was taken "at least in part 'because of,' not merely 'in spite of,' its adverse effects upon an identifiable group." Ibid. The Court concedes that "there was no suggestion below that the Unions held any racial animus against or denigrated blacks generally." It nevertheless concludes that the Unions violated Title VII * * * because they "refuse[d] to file any and all grievances presented by a black person on the ground that the employer looks with disfavor on and resents such grievances," and "pursue[d] a policy of rejecting disparate treatment grievances presented by blacks solely because the claims assert racial bias and would be very troublesome to process," ibid. In my view, this description of the

Union's conduct, and thus the Court's legal conclusion, simply does not fit the facts found by the District Court.

The Unions offered a nondiscriminatory reason for their practice of withdrawing grievances that did not involve a discharge or lengthy suspension. According to the Unions, this policy, that is racially neutral on its face, was motivated by the Unions' nondiscriminatory interest in using the inadequate grievance system to assist members who faced the most serious economic harm. The District Court made no finding that the Unions' explanation was a pretext for racial discrimination. The Unions' policy against pursuing grievances on behalf of probationary employees also permitted the Unions to focus their attention on members with the most to lose. Similarly, the Unions' stated purpose for processing racial grievances on nonracial grounds—to obtain the swiftest and most complete relief possible for the claimant, was not racially invidious. The Unions opposed the use of tests that had a disparate impact on black members, although not on that ground. Their explanation was that more complete relief could be obtained by challenging the tests on nonracial grounds. The District Court made no finding that the Unions' decision to base their opposition on nonracial grounds was motivated by racial animus.[2] Absent a finding that the Unions intended to discriminate against black members, the conclusion that the Unions are liable under * * * the disparate treatment theory of Title VII is unjustified.

B

Although the District Court stated that the plaintiffs raised both disparate treatment and disparate impact claims, it did not make specific findings nor did it conclude that the plaintiffs are entitled to

---

2. Of course, an inference of discriminatory intent may arise from evidence of objective factors, including the inevitable or foreseeable consequences of the challenged policy or practice. Personnel Administrator of Mass. v. Feeney, 442 U.S. 256, 279, n. 25, 99 S.Ct. 2282, 2296, n. 25, 60 L.Ed.2d 870 (1979); Arlington Heights v. Metropolitan Housing Dev. Corp., 429 U.S. 252, 266, 97 S.Ct. 555, 564, 50 L.Ed.2d 450 (1977). But when "the impact is essentially an unavoidable consequence of a * * * policy that has in itself always been deemed to be legitimate, * * * the inference simply fails to ripen into proof." Personnel Administrator of Mass. v. Feeney, supra, 442 U.S., at 279, n. 25, 99 S.Ct., at 2296, n. 25.

The District Court did not expressly rely on any inference of racial animus drawn from the consequences of the Unions' grievance policies. Indeed, it appears that the District Court imposed liability for intentional discrimination without finding that the Unions acted, or failed to act, with the purpose of harming black members.

The District Court's primary justification for imposing liability was that "mere union passivity in the face of employer-discrimination renders the unions liable under Title VII * * *." It then stated:

"Moreover, the evidence in this case proves far more than mere passivity on the part of the unions. The distinction to be observed is between a union which, through lethargy or inefficiency simply fails to perceive problems or is inattentive to their possible solution (in which case, at least arguably, the union's inaction has no connection with race) and a union which, aware of racial discrimination against some of its members, fails to protect their interests."

Far from inferring racial animus from the foreseeable consequences of the Unions' inaction, the District Court merely stated its view that union passivity—whether deliberate or inadvertent—is a basis for liability without regard to the Unions' purpose or intent.

recover under a disparate impact theory. Indeed, the limited amount of statistical evidence discussed by the District Court indicates that the Unions' grievance procedures did not have a disparate impact on black members. Moreover, neither the District Court nor the Court of Appeals considered the validity of potential defenses to disparate impact claims. For example, before the court properly could have held the Unions liable on a disparate impact theory, the court should have considered whether the Unions' practices were justified by the doctrine of business—or union—necessity. See Griggs v. Duke Power Co. The court also should have considered arguments that some of the challenged practices, such as the Unions' refusal to pursue grievances of probationary employees, were justifiable as part of a bona fide seniority system.[3] Because this Court is reluctant to consider alternative theories of liability not expressly passed upon by the lower courts, I would remand to the District Court to permit it to consider whether the Unions are liable under a disparate impact theory.

III

The Court does not reach the question whether a union may be held liable under Title VII for "mere passivity" in the face of discrimination by the employer, because it agrees with the courts below that the record shows more than mere passivity on the part of the Unions. I disagree with that conclusion, and so must consider whether the judgment can be affirmed on the ground that Title VII imposes an affirmative duty on unions to combat discrimination by the employer.

The starting point for analysis of this statutory question is, as always, the language of the statute itself. Section 703(c), the provision of Title VII governing suits against unions, does not suggest that the union has a duty to take affirmative steps to remedy employer discrimination. Section 703(c)(1) makes it unlawful for a union "to exclude or to expel from its membership, or otherwise to discriminate against, any individual because of his race, color, religion, sex, or national origin." This subsection parallels § 703(a)(1), that applies to employers. This parallelism, and the reference to union membership, indicate that § 703(c)(1) prohibits direct discrimination by a union against its members; it does not impose upon a union an obligation to remedy discrimination by the *employer*. Moreover, § 703(c)(3) specifically addresses the union's interaction with the employer, by outlawing efforts by the union "to cause or attempt to cause an employer to discriminate against an individual in violation of this section." If Congress had intended to impose on unions a duty to challenge discrimination by the employer, it hardly could have chosen language more ill-suited to its purpose. First, "[t]o say that the union 'causes' employer discrimination simply by allowing it is to stretch the meaning of the word beyond its limits." 1 A. Larson & L. Larson, Employment Discrimination,

---

3. Although these defenses do not appear to have been raised by the Unions in courts below, this is not surprising in view of the fact that the plaintiffs did not present evidence or legal arguments to support a disparate impact theory.

§ 44.55, p. 9–40 (1985). Moreover, the language of § 703(c)(3) is taken *in haec verba* from § 8(b)(2) of the National Labor Relations Act (NLRA). That provision of the NLRA has been held not to impose liability for passive acquiescence in wrongdoing by the employer. Indeed, well before the enactment of Title VII, the Court held that even encouraging or inducing employer discrimination is not sufficient to incur liability under § 8(b)(2).

In the absence of a clear statement of legislative intent, the Court has been reluctant to read Title VII to disrupt the basic policies of the labor laws. See Trans World Airlines, Inc. v. Hardison, 432 U.S. 63, 79, 97 S.Ct. 2264, 2274, 53 L.Ed.2d 113 (1977). Unquestionably an affirmative duty to oppose employer discrimination could work such a disruption. A union, unlike an employer, is a democratically controlled institution directed by the will of its constituents, subject to the duty of fair representation. Like other representative entities, unions must balance the competing claims of its constituents. A union must make difficult choices among goals such as eliminating racial discrimination in the workplace, removing health and safety hazards, providing better insurance and pension benefits, and increasing wages. The Court has recognized that "[t]he complete satisfaction of all who are represented is hardly to be expected." Ford Motor Co. v. Huffman, 345 U.S. 330, 338, 73 S.Ct. 681, 686, 97 L.Ed. 1048 (1953). For these reasons unions are afforded broad discretion in the handling of grievances. Union members' suits against their unions may deplete union treasuries, and may induce unions to process frivolous claims and resist fair settlement offers. The employee is not without a remedy, because union members may file Title VII actions directly against their employers. I therefore would hold that Title VII imposes on unions no affirmative duty to remedy discrimination by the employer.

* * *

JUSTICE O'CONNOR, concurring in the judgment in No. 85–1626 and dissenting in No. 85–2010.

* * * I join Parts I through IV of Justice Powell's opinion concurring in part and dissenting in part, as to No. 85–2010.

NOTES AND PROBLEMS FOR DISCUSSION

1. Do the members of the majority and the three dissenters differ on more than the evidentiary level necessary to support a finding of intentional discrimination? Do they disagree, for example, on the legal issue of whether union officials have an affirmative duty to challenge allegedly discriminatory conduct on the part of the employer? See Johnson v. Palma, 931 F.2d 203 (2d Cir.1991)(union's refusal to process a grievance because it did not want to violate company policy of not proceeding with discrimination-related grievance while grievant was pursuing a complaint before the state fair employment agency constituted unlawful retaliation in violation of § 704(a); refusal to file grievance because employer looks with disfavor on it is, per *Lukens*, unlawful

and while *Lukens* did not resolve whether union passivity in face of company policy is a permissible justification for union's conduct, union's actions in this case constituted more than mere passivity).

2. The collective bargaining agreement in *Goodman* contained an anti-discrimination clause. In the absence of such a clause, how should the courts deal with a Title VII claim against a union based on the existence of a discriminatory provision in a collective bargaining agreement? Several circuit courts have held, in general terms, that in negotiating a collective agreement, a union has an affirmative duty to bargain to *try to* eliminate discriminatory contractual provisions. See Jackson v. Seaboard Coast Line Railroad Co., 678 F.2d 992 (11th Cir.1982); Terrell v. United States Pipe & Foundry Co., 644 F.2d 1112 (5th Cir.1981), vacated and remanded for reconsideration on other grounds, 456 U.S. 968, 102 S.Ct. 2229, 72 L.Ed.2d 841 (1982); Burwell v. Eastern Air Lines, Inc., 633 F.2d 361 (4th Cir.1980); Macklin v. Spector Freight Systems, Inc., 478 F.2d 979 (D.C.Cir.1973). In *Macklin* and *Jackson,* the courts imposed liability on the union where the collective agreements were found to be discriminatory, primarily on the ground that the union was a party to the contract. In *Terrell,* where evidence of the bargaining history was available, the Fifth Circuit analyzed that history to determine whether the union had "taken every reasonable step to bring employment practices into compliance with the law." Nevertheless, the court in *Burwell* reasoned, where the union had not taken every such reasonable step, it could avoid liability if it established that it had merely acquiesced in a practice or provision that was imposed by the company and which it had no realistic power to stop. Applying this dual standard, the court in Martinez v. Oakland Scavenger Co., 680 F.Supp. 1377, 1398–99 (N.D.Cal.1987) held that where the union succeeded in narrowing the scope of a discriminatory provision (but not in removing it entirely from the contract), the union was not liable for this discriminatory practice. Additionally, where the bargaining history revealed that the union had sought to eliminate another discriminatory provision in the contract, but that the employer consistently rejected its proposals, the union had found to have made a bona fide attempt to eliminate the discriminatory practice and therefore was relieved of liability under Title VII.

3. Several courts have noted that the labor law concept of a union's duty of fair representation has some application in the Title VII context. The duty of fair representation was read into § 9 of the National Labor Relations Act as a corollary to the status accorded unions by that provision as exclusive bargaining representative of all members of the bargaining unit. See e.g., Vaca v. Sipes, 386 U.S. 171, 87 S.Ct. 903, 17 L.Ed.2d 842 (1967). The duty requires the union to fairly and impartially represent all members of the bargaining unit and prohibits conduct found to be arbitrary, discriminatory or in bad faith. Where the union's conduct is shown to be based on the individual member's race, religion, color, sex or national origin, such a breach of the duty of fair representation has been held to subject the union to liability under Title VII. See Martin v. Local 1513 and Dist. 118 of the IAMAW, 859 F.2d 581, 584 (8th Cir.1988); Farmer v. ARA Services, Inc., 660 F.2d 1096, 1103–1104 (6th Cir. 1981).

2. The Plaintiff's Burden: Proof of the Prima Facie Case and Pretext

UNITED STATES POSTAL SERVICE BOARD OF GOVERNORS v. AIKENS

Supreme Court of the United States, 1983.
460 U.S. 711, 103 S.Ct. 1478, 75 L.Ed.2d 403.

JUSTICE REHNQUIST delivered the opinion of the Court.

Respondent Louis Aikens filed suit under Title VII of the Civil Rights Act of 1964, claiming that petitioner, the United States Postal Service, discriminated against him on account of his race. Aikens, who is black, claimed that the Postal Service had discriminatorily refused to promote him to higher positions in the Washington, D.C. Post Office where he had been employed since 1937. After a bench trial, the District Court entered judgment in favor of the Postal Service, but the Court of Appeals reversed. We vacated the Court of Appeals' judgment and remanded for reconsideration in light of Texas Department of Community Affairs v. Burdine.

On remand, the Court of Appeals reaffirmed its earlier holding that the District Court had erred in requiring Aikens to offer direct proof of discriminatory intent. It also held that the District Court erred in requiring Aikens to show, as part of his *prima facie* case, that he was "as qualified or more qualified" than the people who were promoted. 665 F.2d 1057, 1058, 1059 (CADC 1981) (Per Curiam). We granted certiorari.[1]

The Postal Service argues that an employee who has shown only that he was black, that he applied for a promotion for which he possessed the minimum qualifications, and that the employer selected a nonminority applicant has not established a *"prima facie"* case of employment discrimination under Title VII. Aikens argues that he submitted sufficient evidence that the Postal Service discriminated against him to warrant a finding of a *prima facie* case.[2] Because this

1. We have consistently distinguished disparate treatment cases from cases involving facially neutral employment standards that have disparate impact on minority applicants. See, e.g., Texas Department of Community Affairs v. Burdine, 450 U.S. 248, 252 n. 5, 101 S.Ct. 1089, 1093 n. 5, 67 L.Ed.2d 207 (1981); McDonnell Douglas Corp. v. Green, 411 U.S. 792, 802 n. 14, 93 S.Ct. 1817, 1824 n. 14, 36 L.Ed.2d 668 (1973).

2. Aikens showed that white persons were consistently promoted and detailed over him and all other black persons between 1966 and 1974. Aikens has been rated as "an outstanding supervisor whose management abilities are far above aver-

age." App. 8. There was no derogatory or negative information in his Personnel Folder. He had more supervisory seniority and training and development courses than all but one of the white persons who were promoted above him. He has a Masters Degree and has completed three years of residence towards a Ph.D. Aikens had substantially more education than the white employees who were advanced ahead of him; of the 12, only two had any education beyond high school and none had a college degree. He introduced testimony that the person responsible for the promotion decisions at issue had made numerous derogatory comments about blacks in general and Aikens in particular. If the case was fully tried on the merits, it is surprising to find the parties and the Court of Appeals still addressing the question whether Aikens made out a *prima facie* case. We think that by framing the issue in these terms, they have unnecessarily evaded the ultimate question of discrimination *vel non.*[3]

By establishing a *prima facie* case, the plaintiff in a Title VII action creates a rebuttable "presumption that the employer unlawfully discriminated against" him. Texas Department of Community Affairs v. Burdine, 450 U.S. 248, 254, 101 S.Ct. 1089, 1094, 67 L.Ed.2d 207 (1981). See McDonnell Douglas Corp. v. Green, 411 U.S. 792, 93 S.Ct. 1817, 36 L.Ed.2d 668 (1973). To rebut this presumption, "the defendant must clearly set forth, through the introduction of admissible evidence, the reasons for the plaintiff's rejection." *Burdine,* supra, 450 U.S., at 255, 101 S.Ct., at 1094. In other words, the defendant must "produc[e] evidence that the plaintiff was rejected, or someone else was preferred, for a legitimate, nondiscriminatory reason." Id., at 254, 101 S.Ct., at 1094.

But when the defendant fails to persuade the district court to dismiss the action for lack of a *prima facie* case,[4] and responds to the plaintiff's proof by offering evidence of the reason for the plaintiff's rejection, the fact finder must then decide whether the rejection was discriminatory within the meaning of Title VII. At this stage, the *McDonnell–Burdine* presumption "drops from the case," id., at 255, n. 10, 101 S.Ct., at 1095, n. 10, and "the factual inquiry proceeds to a new level of specificity." Id., at 255, 101 S.Ct., at 1095. After Aikens presented his evidence to the District Court in this case, the Postal Service's witnesses testified that he was not promoted because he had turned down several lateral transfers that would have broadened his Postal Service experience. The District Court was then in a position to decide the ultimate factual issue in the case.

The "factual inquiry" in a Title VII case is "whether the defendant intentionally discriminated against the plaintiff." *Burdine,* supra, at 253, 101 S.Ct., at 1093. In other words, is "the employer * * * treating 'some people less favorably than others because of their race, color, religion, sex, or national origin.' " Furnco Construction Corp. v. Waters, 438 U.S. 567, 577, 98 S.Ct. 2943, 2949, 57 L.Ed.2d 957 (1978), quoting Int'l Brotherhood of Teamsters v. United States, 431 U.S. 324, 335, n.

District Court were to find, on the basis of this evidence, that the Postal Service did discriminate against Aikens, we do not believe that this would be reversible error.

3. As in any lawsuit, the plaintiff may prove his case by direct or circumstantial evidence. The trier of fact should consider all the evidence, giving it whatever weight and credence it deserves. Thus, we agree with the Court of Appeals that the District Court should not have required Aikens to submit direct evidence of discriminatory intent. See International Brotherhood of

Teamsters v. United States, 431 U.S. 324, 358 n. 44, 97 S.Ct. 1843, 1866 n. 44, 52 L.Ed.2d 396 (1977) ("[T]he *McDonnell Douglas* formula does not require direct proof of discrimination").

4. It appears that at one point in the trial the District Court decided that Aikens had made out a *prima facie* case. When Aikens concluded his case in chief, the Postal Service moved to dismiss on the ground that there was no *prima facie* case. The District Court denied this motion.

15, 97 S.Ct. 1843, 1854, n. 15, 52 L.Ed.2d 396 (1977). The *prima facie* case method established in *McDonnell Douglas* was "never intended to be rigid, mechanized, or ritualistic. Rather, it is merely a sensible, orderly way to evaluate the evidence in light of common experience as it bears on the critical question of discrimination." *Furnco,* supra, 438 U.S., at 577, 98 S.Ct., at 2949. Where the defendant has done everything that would be required of him if the plaintiff had properly made out a *prima facie* case, whether the plaintiff really did so is no longer relevant. The district court has before it all the evidence it needs to decide whether "the defendant intentionally discriminated against the plaintiff." *Burdine,* supra, 450 U.S., at 253, 101 S.Ct., at 1093.

On the state of the record at the close of the evidence, the District Court in this case should have proceeded to this specific question directly, just as district courts decide disputed questions of fact in other civil litigation.[5] As we stated in *Burdine:*

> "The plaintiff retains the burden of persuasion. [H]e may succeed in this either directly by persuading the court that a discriminatory reason more likely motivated the employer or indirectly by showing that the employer's proffered explanation is unworthy of credence." 450 U.S., at 256, 101 S.Ct., at 1095.

In short, the district court must decide which party's explanation of the employer's motivation it believes.

All courts have recognized that the question facing triers of fact in discrimination cases is both sensitive and difficult. The prohibitions against discrimination contained in the Civil Rights Act of 1964 reflect an important national policy. There will seldom be "eyewitness" testimony as to the employer's mental processes. But none of this means that trial courts or reviewing courts should treat discrimination differently from other ultimate questions of fact. Nor should they make their inquiry even more difficult by applying legal rules which were devised to govern "the allocation of burdens and order of presentation of proof," *Burdine,* supra, at 252, 101 S.Ct., at 1093, in deciding this ultimate question. The law often obliges finders of fact to inquire into a person's state of mind. As Lord Justice Bowen said in treating this problem in an action for misrepresentation nearly a century ago:

> "The state of a man's mind is as much a fact as the state of his digestion. It is true that it is very difficult to prove what the state of a man's mind at a particular time is, but if it can be ascertained it is as much a fact as anything else." Eddington v. Fitzmaurice, 29 Ch.Div. 459, 483 (1885).

The District Court erroneously thought that respondent was required to submit direct evidence of discriminatory intent, see n. 3, supra, and erroneously focused on the question of *prima facie* case

---

5. Of course, the plaintiff must have an adequate "opportunity to demonstrate that the proffered reason was not the true reason for the employment decision," but rather a pretext. *Burdine,* supra, at 256, 101 S.Ct., at 1095. There is no suggestion in this case that Aikens did not have such an opportunity.

rather than directly on the question of discrimination. Thus we cannot be certain that its findings of fact in favor of the Postal Service were not influenced by its mistaken view of the law. We accordingly vacate the judgment of the Court of Appeals, and remand the case to the District Court so that it may decide on the basis of the evidence before it whether the Postal Service discriminated against Aikens.

It is so ordered.

JUSTICE MARSHALL concurs in the judgment.

JUSTICE BLACKMUN, with whom JUSTICE BRENNAN joins, concurring.

I join the Court's opinion. I write to stress the fact, however, that, as I read its opinion, the Court today reaffirms the framework established by McDonnell Douglas Corp. v. Green, 411 U.S. 792, 93 S.Ct. 1817, 36 L.Ed.2d 668 (1973), for Title VII cases. Under that framework, once a Title VII plaintiff has made out a prima facie case and the defendant-employer has articulated a legitimate, nondiscriminatory reason for the employment decision, the plaintiff bears the burden of demonstrating that the reason is pretextual, that is, it is "not the true reason for the employment decision." Texas Dept. of Community Affairs v. Burdine, 450 U.S. 248, 256, 101 S.Ct. 1089, 1095, 67 L.Ed.2d 207 (1981). As the Court's opinion today implies, ante, at 1481, this burden "merges with the ultimate burden of persuading the court that [the plaintiff] has been the victim of intentional discrimination." 450 U.S., at 256, 101 S.Ct., at 1095.

This ultimate burden may be met in one of two ways. First, as the Court notes, a plaintiff may persuade the court that the employment decision more likely than not was motivated by a discriminatory reason. Ante, at 1481 and 1483. In addition, however, this burden is also carried if the plaintiff shows "that the employer's proffered explanation is unworthy of credence." *Burdine*, 450 U.S., at 256, 101 S.Ct., at 1095, citing *McDonnell Douglas*, 411 U.S., at 804–805, 93 S.Ct., at 1825–26. While the Court is correct that the ultimate determination of factual liability in discrimination cases should be no different from that in other types of civil suits, ante, at 1483, the *McDonnell Douglas* framework requires that a plaintiff prevail when at the third stage of a Title VII trial he demonstrates that the legitimate, nondiscriminatory reason given by the employer is in fact not the true reason for the employment decision.

NOTES AND PROBLEMS FOR DISCUSSION

1. On remand, the trial court found that the plaintiff had not established that the employer's explanation for its failure to promote him was a pretext for discrimination. Aikens v. Bolger, 33 FEP Cases 1697 (D.D.C.1984).

2. Although the majority in *Aikens* avoids saying so directly, is there any doubt that the plaintiff established a *prima facie* case under the *McDonnell Douglas–Burdine* formula? The *prima facie* case was described in *McDonnell Douglas* and *Burdine* in the context of refusal-to-hire and denial-of-promotion claims. According to those decisions the plaintiff must establish: (1) that he

belongs to a minority protected by Title VII; (2) that he applied for and was qualified for a job that the employer sought to fill; (3) that he was rejected for the position; and (4) that the employer, after rejecting the plaintiff, continued to seek applicants from persons of the plaintiff's qualifications. Those elements of a *prima facie* case are not adaptable to all proof patterns which can arise in disparate treatment cases. See, e.g., Lams v. General Waterworks Corp., 766 F.2d 386 (8th Cir.1985) (*McDonnell Douglas* formula of little use in deciding promotion claim by employees who were not considered for promotion because they did not know of vacancy until position was filled). Must a plaintiff show that she was within a racial minority in the employer's work force in order to establish a *prima facie* case of racial discrimination in promotion? See, Legrand v. Trustees of University of Arkansas at Pine Bluff, 821 F.2d 478 (8th Cir.1987), cert. denied, 485 U.S. 1034, 108 S.Ct. 1592, 99 L.Ed.2d 907 (1988) (not an essential element of prima facie case that plaintiff prove he is in minority group: overall circumstances may dictate that inference of discrimination based on race has been established). Must the plaintiff prove that the employer sought to fill the vacancy after discharging him in order to establish a *prima facie* case of disparate treatment in termination? What if the plaintiff's theory is that a white employee would not have been discharged under similar circumstances? See, Beaven v. Commonwealth of Kentucky, 783 F.2d 672 (6th Cir.1986). Should the fact that a female employee was discharged by a female supervisor and replaced by a female bar her from making out a prima facie case of sex discrimination? In such circumstances what is the function of the prima facie case? See, Veatch v. Northwestern Memorial Hospital, 730 F.Supp. 809 (N.D.Ill.1990). See also, EEOC v. Metal Service Co., 892 F.2d 341, 348 (3d Cir.1990) (courts should be sensitive to the myriad of ways that inference of discrimination can be created).

In order to establish a prima facie case under *McDonnell Douglas* and *Burdine*, the plaintiff must prove that she was "qualified" for the position that she was denied. But how should "qualified" be defined? Must the plaintiff prove that she was performing at a level that met her employer's reasonable expectations? Compare, Lovelace v. Sherwin—Williams Co., 681 F.2d 230, 244–45 (4th Cir.1982) with Bienkowski v. American Airlines, Inc., 851 F.2d 1503, 1505–1506 (5th Cir.1988). Courts have divided over the role that subjective qualifications for a job ("leadership," "likability," "loyalty,") can play in determining whether a prima facie case has been made out. Several circuits have held that, because subjective factors are more likely to mask discrimination and are harder to evaluate, where both objective and subjective criteria make up the job qualifications, the plaintiff need only show that he satisfies the *objective* criteria for the job to show that he is qualified; the employer must assert the alleged failure to satisfy the subjective standards as part of the rebuttal. See, Weldon v. Kraft, Inc., 896 F.2d 793, 798 (3d Cir.1990); Burrus v. United Telephone Co. of Kansas, Inc., 683 F.2d 339, 342 (10th Cir.), cert. denied, 459 U.S. 1071, 103 S.Ct. 491, 74 L.Ed.2d 633 (1982); Lynn v. Regents of University of California, 656 F.2d 1337, 1344–45 (9th Cir.1981), cert. denied, 459 U.S. 823, 103 S.Ct. 53, 74 L.Ed.2d 59 (1982). But see, Hill v. Seaboard Coast Line R. Co., 885 F.2d 804, 809 (11th Cir.1989) ("We have not held that plaintiff need meet only the employer's objective criteria in order to establish that prong of a prima facie case").

Should the plaintiff's lack of qualifications, not known by the employer at the time of discharge (because of plaintiff's falsification of his resume and employment application), prevent him from making out a prima facie case?

Compare, Smith v. General Scanning, Inc., 876 F.2d 1315, 1319 (7th Cir.1989) (plaintiff's resume fraud had nothing to do with his termination since it surfaced after suit filed; whether employer discriminated against him must be decided solely with respect to reason given for his discharge) with Livingston v. Sorg Printing Co., 49 FEP Cases 1417, 1418 (S.D.N.Y.1989) (employee's admission that he made misrepresentations on employment application bars him from making out prima facie case, even though employer was not aware of misrepresentations at time of discharge). Which is the better rule?

3. *McDonnell Douglas*, *Burdine* and *Aikens* emphasize that, once an employer has articulated a non-discriminatory reason for the challenged action, the plaintiff must be given a "fair opportunity" to show that the employer's justification was "pretextual." The Court's requirement in *Burdine* that "the defendant's explanation of its legitimate reasons * * * be clear and reasonably specific," 450 U.S. at 258, 101 S.Ct. at 1096, affords the plaintiff some protection against reasons so nebulous or vague as to make disproving them impossible. Generally, the more subjective the standard by which employees or applicants are to be judged and the more informal the manner in which they are evaluated, the more likely that the court will find the employer's justifications pretextual when faced with evidence from which discrimination could be inferred. See, Farber v. Massillon Board of Educ., 917 F.2d 1391, 1399 (6th Cir.1990), cert. denied, ___ U.S. ___, 111 S.Ct. 2851, 115 L.Ed.2d 1019 (1991) (use of subjective criteria was "merely a poor disguise for discriminatory action); Robbins v. White–Wilson Medical Clinic, Inc., 660 F.2d 1064, 1067 (5th Cir. 1981), vacated and remanded on other grounds, 456 U.S. 969, 102 S.Ct. 2229, 72 L.Ed.2d 842 (1982) (employer's rejection of applicant because of her "yucky" attitude legally insufficient when viewed in context of evidence in plaintiff's prima facie case). Should use of a subjective evaluation system that allows judgments which may be tainted by unlawful prejudice to control employment decisions constitute a *per se* violation of Title VII? See Price Waterhouse v. Hopkins, *infra* at 129.

A plaintiff cannot prove that an employer's stated reasons are pretextual merely by showing that the employer was mistaken or relied on incorrect information. Only if the employer's articulated reason is shown to be a pretext for accomplishing a discriminatory purpose will the plaintiff prevail. Thus, a sincere, though mistaken, suspicion of dishonesty would satisfy the employer's *Burdine* burden. See, Williams v. Southwestern Bell Telephone Co., 718 F.2d 715, 717–718 (5th Cir.1983) ("The trier of fact is to determine the defendant's intent, not adjudicate the merits of the facts or suspicions upon which it is predicated."); Pollard v. Rea Magnet Wire Co., 824 F.2d 557 (7th Cir.), cert. denied, 484 U.S. 977, 108 S.Ct. 488, 98 L.Ed.2d 486 (1987) ("A reason honestly described but poorly founded is not a pretext, as that term is used in the law of discrimination."); Bechold v. IGW Systems, Inc., 817 F.2d 1282 (7th Cir.1987) (honestly held belief, even if not reasonable, does not *per se* prevent the employer from showing a legitimate reason for discharge).

One circumstance that will usually justify a finding of pretext is a change in the employer's explanation for the challenged action between the action and trial. See, Estes v. Dick Smith Ford, Inc., 856 F.2d 1097 (8th Cir.1988) (where employer told EEOC that plaintiff had been terminated because of reduction in force, but at trial contended that discharge was due to poor work performance, changed explanation might persuade trier of fact to infer that employer was not telling the truth in either explanation); Schmitz v. St. Regis Paper Co., 811 F.2d 131 (2d Cir.1987) (changed reason for discharge is circumstantial evidence that real reason is being concealed). A finding that one of several non-discriminatory reasons put forward by the employer is false, will not mandate that the other reasons are also false but such an inference by the trier of fact is permissible. Roebuck v. Drexel University, 852 F.2d 715 (3d Cir.1988); Sims v. Cleland, 813 F.2d 790 (6th Cir.1987) (rejection as false of one reason promotion denied plaintiff does not impugn alternative reason that another employee promoted because of his hard work and dedication).

4. In his concurring opinion in *Aikens*, Justice Blackmun characterized the majority's opinion as reaffirming the *Burdine* formula, under which the plaintiff must prevail if it proves that the defendant's proffered reason is in fact not "the true reason" for its challenged decision. But what if the plaintiff convinces the trier of fact that the defendant did not actually rely on its proffered reason yet does not offer evidence sufficient to convince the court that the defendant was motivated by discriminatory animus? On this issue consider the following cases.

TYE v. BOARD OF EDUCATION OF POLARIS JOINT VOCATIONAL SCHOOL DISTRICT

United States Court of Appeals, Sixth Circuit, 1987.
811 F.2d 315, cert. denied, 484 U.S. 924, 108 S.Ct. 285, 98 L.Ed.2d 246 (1987).

Before MERRITT, GUY and NORRIS, CIRCUIT JUDGES.

MERRITT, CIRCUIT JUDGE.

Ann Tye, plaintiff-appellant, appeals from a judgment in favor of defendant Polaris Board of Education and other individual defendants in her Title VII sex discrimination suit. In this appeal, Ms. Tye contends that the trial court erred in law and fact by finding the defendants' proof sufficient to rebut both her *prima facie* case and her proof of pretext. The Board cross-appeals the denial of attorney's fees and restrictions placed on pre-trial discovery. For the reasons stated below, we now reverse and remand.

Ann Tye was employed by the Board of Education of the Polaris Joint Vocational School District as a vocational guidance counselor for three years from September 1979 through June 1982. Ms. Tye's employment for this period was obtained under a series of one-year limited contracts. In March, 1982, fiscal constraints forced the Board to eliminate a number of staff positions throughout the district. As part of this cutback, two of the four vocational guidance counselor positions at Ms. Tye's school were slated for elimination. One of these positions was eliminated by attrition, and the other by non-renewal of appellant's contract. One of the two surviving positions was filled by Mr. Ernest Mason, a former coworker of the appellant. This action is based on the decision of Dr. Richard Mueller, the school superintendent, to recommend renewal of Mr. Mason's contract instead of Ms. Tye's. In this context, non-renewal of a contract is tantamount to a dismissal and constitutes an actionable employment decision under Title VII.

* * *

The basic issue here is whether an employer may prevail when he stipulates to untrue reasons given to rebut a *prima facie* case and then refuses to give any coherent and understandable reason—subjective or objective—for an employment decision covered by Title VII.

Since it was obvious that Ms. Tye established a *prima facie* case,[1] the trial court focused solely on the defendant's reasons for the employment action. In order to meet its burden at this point the Board had to produce admissible evidence that Mr. Mason was preferred for a legitimate, nondiscriminatory reason. The purpose of this stage of the proceeding is two-fold: it is necessary to rebut the inference of discrimination that attaches upon proof of a *prima facie* case, and it narrows the range of explanations that the plaintiff must disprove in order to show pretext. Thus, while this burden is only one of production and not persuasion, it is elementary that the evidence produced must be clear, reasonably specific, and legally sufficient to justify a judgment for the defendant if not disproved by the plaintiff. If the employer fails to carry this burden, the plaintiff is entitled to judgment as a matter of law.

If the defendant successfully articulates a legitimate reason, however, the presumption of discrimination imposed by *McDonnell Douglas* disappears. See U.S. Postal Service Board of Governors v. Aikens. At this stage, a Title VII trial is procedurally indistinguishable from any other civil trial. The shifting burdens have run their course, and the trial court must now turn its attention to the ultimate question of fact: Did the defendant intentionally discriminate against the plaintiff? At

---

1. Appellees' argue that because Ms. Tye was terminated as part of a reduction in force, this circuit's decision in LaGrant v. Gulf & Western Manufacturing Co., 748 F.2d 1087 (6th Cir.1984), requires her to present additional evidence in her *prima facie* case. *LaGrant* holds that an ADEA plaintiff who cannot prove that he was replaced by a younger person in a reorganization or reduction in force, must present in his *prima facie* case some "direct, circumstantial, or statistical evidence that age was a factor in his termination." However, because of the differing factual and statutory bases presented by the two cases, it is clear that the *LaGrant* holding is inapposite to Ms. Tye's case.

As this circuit has previously noted, important differences exist between the type of discrimination actionable under Title VII and age discrimination under the ADEA.

The progression of age is a universal human process. In the very nature of the problem, it is apparent in the usual case, absent any discriminatory intent, discharged employees will more often than not be replaced by those younger

than they, for older employees are constantly moving out of the labor market, while younger ones move in. This factor of progression and replacement is not necessarily involved in cases involving the immutable characteristics of race, sex, and national origin.

Laugesen v. Anaconda Co., 510 F.2d 307, 313 n. 4 (6th Cir.1975). Because of these differences, cases interpreting the procedural framework under one statute are not automatically applicable to the other. See LaGrant v. Gulf & Western Manufacturing Co., 748 F.2d 1087, 1090 (6th Cir.1984) (citing cases that reject strict application of *McDonnell Douglas* to ADEA claims).

Furthermore, when the *LaGrant* opinion is examined closely, it is apparent that it is factually inapposite as well. The plaintiff in *LaGrant* failed to prove an essential element of his *prima facie* case, namely, that he was replaced by a younger person. In this case, Ms. Tye has conclusively established that she was replaced by a male, Mr. Ernest Mason. Thus the circumstances that led the *LaGrant* court to add an additional element to the plaintiff's *prima facie* case are not present here.

this last stage, sufficiency of the parties' proof as to the intermediate *McDonnell Douglas* burdens is usually no longer an issue. Yet, the trial court's decisions regarding these intermediate burdens cannot be shielded from appellate review simply because the court ignored its error and proceeded with the proof. An unrebutted *prima facie* case entitles the plaintiff to judgment as a matter of law, and a trial court's failure to grant such relief may be redressed on appeal. With this procedural framework in mind, we now turn to the issues presented by this case.

Ms. Tye contends that the reasons proffered by the Board for her non-renewal were insufficient to meet the intermediate burden described above. Reviewing the record as a whole, we find that the District Court was correct in finding the defendants' proof sufficient. To meet their burden, the defendants submitted a list of ten reasons for the decision:

    1. A statutory right to non-renew limited contracts such as Ms. Tye's;

    2. The collective bargaining agreement covering Ms. Tye's employment allowed for non-renewal;

    3. Declining enrollment;

    4. Fiscal cutbacks;

    5. Multiple certification of staff;

    6. Staff diversity and complement;

    7. Employee demeanor and attitude;

    8. Employee interaction with other faculty;

    9. Program changes at the school;

    10. Superintendent Richard Mueller's subjective feelings and impressions.

Since the "employment decision" under review here is the choice to renew Mr. Mason instead of Ms. Tye, it is clear that reasons one through four in the list above are irrelevant. These reasons explain only why staff reductions were made, not why the plaintiff was singled out. Evidence offered to meet the intermediate burden of production must articulate a legitimate, non-discriminatory reason "why someone else was preferred." *Burdine.* Since these four reasons explain only why staff reductions were made and not why Ms. Tye was chosen to go, they are legally insufficient to rebut a *prima facie* case of discrimination in this context.

Before considering the other six reasons on the list, it is important to note that the list itself was introduced into evidence as part of a stipulation. Later in the trial, Dr. Richard Mueller completely contradicted all of these reasons.[2] Since Dr. Mueller had unilateral authority

---

2. Dr. Mueller testified that he did not actually have a reason for recommending Ms. Tye's non-renewal in April, 1982, and that the stipulated reasons were "reconstructed" specifically for this litigation:

over recommendations for non-renewal, it is obvious from his testimony that these stipulated reasons were in fact untrue. Furthermore, Dr. Mueller's statement that he did what he thought was best for Polaris [3] is a subjective reason which is legally insufficient to rebut Ms. Tye's *prima facie* case. Therefore, if the stipulations had not been introduced and Dr. Mueller's testimony alone had been used to meet the defendant's intermediate burden, Ms. Tye would have been entitled to judgment on an unrebutted *prima facie* case.

Since the stipulations *were* admitted into evidence, however, the *McDonnell Douglas* burdens vanished before the time Dr. Mueller testified. Chronologically, the contrary testimony could only support the plaintiff's case on pretext, and could not negate the burden of production which the defendant met previously. It is clear that *Burdine* allows the defendant to satisfy his intermediate burden by offering an untrue reason for the decision. If an untrue explanation is offered, so the reasoning goes, the plaintiff may prove pretext by attacking the employer's motive for offering an untrue reason. Accordingly, we find that defendants' intermediate burden was met when reasons four through nine were admitted into evidence.

A Title VII trial does not end, however, when the defendant meets his intermediate burden: the plaintiff next has an opportunity to show that the proffered reasons are a pretext for discrimination. Evidence introduced at the intermediate stage is taken on its face, while the ultimate question of intentional discrimination can only be answered by ascertaining the truth of the proffered reasons.

* * *

Thus, the plaintiff may indirectly prove intentional discrimination by showing that the defendants' justifications are untrue and therefore must be a pretext. Although the District Court's finding of no pretext in Ms. Tye's case must be accorded deference as a finding of fact, it may

Q You are telling the Court that you have no reasons for recommending Tye's non-renewal in April of 1982?

A In April, 1982, under the Ohio Revised Code, I did not have to give reasons or make up reasons, or write them down, so I cannot testify, since I am under oath, to any reasons that existed in April of 1982, because I did not have to, *nor did I have a reason in April of 1982.*

Q So you really did not have any specific reason in mind when you recommended Tye's non-renewal?

A *That is what I testified to,* although the way up to a point in time until I was required in Federal Court to give consid-

eration or try to reconstruct under the Ohio Revised Code, and I have given testimony of subjective reconstructed considerations that I believe that, as a human being, I gave to the best of my ability.

Appendix at 242 (cross-examination of Dr. Richard Mueller) (emphasis supplied). Dr. Mueller's subsequent testimony contradicted even these reconstructed reasons. Dr. Mueller denied any attempt to compare Ms. Tye to Mr. Mason on qualifications (Appendix at 419), personnel files (Appendix at 417), supervisor's assessments (Appendix at 407), or "subjective" factors (Appendix at 247–48).

3. Appendix at 434.

be overturned on appeal when it is based on contradictory and evasive testimony:

* * *

Under the formulation of the "clearly erroneous" rule announced in United States v. United States Gypsum Co., 333 U.S. 364, 395, 68 S.Ct. 525, 92 L.Ed. 746 (1948), the reviewing court must be left with a "definite and firm conviction that a mistake has been committed." We are so convinced in this case. The individual whose state of mind is at issue here, Dr. Richard Mueller, clearly stated that he had no specific reason for selecting Ms. Tye for non-renewal in April, 1982. He testified that he made no attempt to compare Ms. Tye to her co-workers on *any* basis prior to selecting her for non-renewal. Dr. Mueller specifically disavowed any comparison based on qualifications, personnel files, supervisor's assessments, or "subjective" factors.

Appellees cite the decision of this circuit in Grano v. Department of Development of City of Columbus, to support the action taken by Dr. Mueller. *Grano,* however, is distinguishable on its facts. In *Grano,* a male employee was selected for promotion over a female who had equal objective qualifications. The employer, who was familiar with the plaintiff's work, did not interview her and based his decision solely on his subjective assessment of her qualifications. In the instant case, Dr. Mueller was not Ms. Tye's immediate supervisor and did not have the personal knowledge possessed by the decisionmaker in *Grano.* Here, the defendant could have obtained this information by consulting the personnel files or Ms. Tye's supervisor, Mr. Kenneth Collier. He chose to do neither. Subjective reasons are sufficient if they result from investigation into the employee's character and performance, but preferences cannot be sufficient if they simply emanate from the subconscious of the decisionmaker without any specific basis.

The District Court found that Dr. Mueller non-renewed Ms. Tye "without a thought process" because he was relying on a state statute that allowed him to take such action without providing notice to the employee. Whatever the effect of the state statute, it is impossible for Dr. Mueller to have chosen Mason over Tye without any reason whatever. Dr. Mueller did not flip a coin or draw lots—he made a choice. The comparison may have been subconscious and based on intangible factors, but it must have occurred.

Where a decisionmaker does not possess any information on which to choose between two individuals, it is well advised for him to gather information from whatever sources are available. Where no such attempt is made, and the employer gives evasive and contradictory testimony regarding the choice, he runs the risk that a Title VII plaintiff will be able to prove pretext. Ms. Tye achieved precisely that by disproving all of the defendants' proffered reasons. Therefore, the District Court should have entered judgment for Ms. Tye in this case.

Since we hold that Ms. Tye was indeed the victim of impermissible discrimination, it is unnecessary to consider the defendants' cross-appeal for attorney's fees. We also dismiss defendants' evidentiary claim regarding restricted discovery on the issue of Ms. Tye's motivation. The fact that a union encourages one of its members to vindicate her rights is not material where it is clear that her rights were indeed violated.

In light of the foregoing, we reverse the judgment below and remand to the District Court for such relief as may be appropriate in this case.

Norris, Circuit Judge, dissenting.

In my view, this appeal should be resolved by reference to our opinion in LaGrant v. Gulf & Western. Analysis of and adherence to the rationale underlying that opinion leads to the inescapable conclusion that Ms. Tye did not make out a *prima facie* case.

In this case and in *LaGrant,* there was a reduction in force with the plaintiff in both having been laid off and complaining that the decision to retain another specific employee was the product of discrimination. In each case, the plaintiff attempted to establish a *prima facie* case by showing (1) membership in the protected class, (2) discharge, (3) qualification for the position, and (4) replacement by a person who was younger or a member of the opposite sex.

In *LaGrant,* we held that this *McDonnell Douglas* four-step progression to a *prima facie* case, while appropriate in the usual termination and replacement situation where no position is eliminated and the position left open by the plaintiff's discharge is filled by another, is not applicable in a reduction in force situation since the plaintiff is not replaced. Thus, in a reduction in force situation, other evidence must be substituted for the fourth element (replacement) in order for there to be sufficient circumstantial evidence from which an inference of discrimination can be drawn, and a *prima facie* case made out.

The rationale of *LaGrant* is applicable here since we are confronted with a similar evidentiary consideration. The ultimate fact to be proved in discrimination cases is intentional discrimination, and direct evidence of that ultimate fact is rarely available. The evidentiary litany of *McDonnell Douglas* and its progeny recognizes the reality that proof of intentional discrimination will almost always have to depend upon circumstantial evidence. The *prima facie* case stage of the litany is a way of measuring the quality of circumstantial evidence that is required to raise an inference of intentional discrimination that is strong enough to go to a jury (*i.e.,* that would survive a motion for summary judgment or for directed verdict). *LaGrant* speaks to the sufficiency of circumstantial evidence required to raise an inference of intentional discrimination, in the context of a reduction in force, as distinguished from termination and replacement.

In *LaGrant,* this court correctly perceived the evidentiary framework of reduction in forces cases. In the termination and replacement situation, when a woman is replaced by a man, that fact, in concert with a showing that (1) she was a member of the protected class, (2) was discharged, and (3) was qualified, is sufficient to ground an inference of discriminatory treatment. By contrast, when, due to conceded economic necessity, one of two positions (one held by a man, the other by a woman) is eliminated, and the male is retained and the woman is terminated, the *LaGrant* rationale says that these reduction in force circumstances do not raise an inference of intentional discrimination. The reason for the distinction is apparent; the two situations are vastly different, qualitatively. It is the replacement of a woman by a man that is the suspect circumstantial evidence; that exercise both disfavors the woman and prefers the man. By contrast, when there is a reduction in force, only the act of disfavor is present; the man simply retains the status he already had. While one might argue that retaining the man also amounts to preferential conduct, that argument was rejected in *LaGrant* to the extent that retention in concert with termination was deemed not to be circumstantial evidence of intentional discrimination, in comparison with the combination of replacement and termination, which will ground a reasonable inference of intentional discrimination, when the other *McDonnell Douglas* factors are also present.

I am unpersuaded by the distinction attempted to be drawn between this case and *LaGrant,* in footnote one of the majority opinion, since the statement that "Ms. Tye has conclusively established that she was replaced by a male," is not an accurate characterization of the evidence as set out in the majority opinion's recitation of facts.

Accordingly, because Ms. Tye did not satisfy her burden of establishing a *prima facie* case, our inquiry should conclude at that point, and result in affirmance of the district court.

BENZIES v. ILLINOIS DEPARTMENT OF MENTAL HEALTH AND DEVELOPMENTAL DISABILITIES

United States Court of Appeals, Seventh Circuit, 1987.
810 F.2d 146, cert. denied, 483 U.S. 1006, 107 S.Ct. 3231, 97 L.Ed.2d 737 (1987).

Before POSNER and EASTERBROOK, CIRCUIT JUDGES, and PARSONS, SENIOR DISTRICT JUDGE.[*]

EASTERBROOK, CIRCUIT JUDGE.

Bonnie Benzies, who holds a Ph.D. in psychology, was classified as a Psychologist III in the Illinois Department of Mental Health and Developmental Disabilities. She wanted a promotion to Supervising Psychologist I, a position with higher pay. Illinois civil service rules

[*] The Hon. James B. Parsons, of the Northern District of Illinois, sitting by designation.

allow promotions to occur in two ways: competition to fill vacancies, and "upgrading" of a job to reflect more accurately the incumbent's tasks. Before she acquired her Ph.D. Benzies failed twice to obtain a competitive promotion, each time being assured that a Ph.D. was necessary. When she had obtained her Ph.D. she asked for a "job audit" as a foundation for upgrading. Civil service personnel audited her work, found that she was not supervising other psychologists, and concluded that she was not eligible for non-competitive promotion. Meanwhile the Department had promoted four male psychologists—two without Ph.D.s—through the non-competitive audit and upgrade process. Benzies quit in disgust and complained to the EEOC. After that agency issued her right-to-sue letter, she filed this action under Title VII of the Civil Rights Act of 1964, 42 U.S.C. § 2000e et seq.

The district court held a bench trial and concluded that the Department had not engaged in intentional discrimination. The Department argued that the process of non-competitive upgrading is mechanical, that neutral rules govern who is promoted. Any psychologist with supervisory duties will be promoted; none without will be; the four men had supervisory duties, and Benzies did not, the Department insisted. The district court doubted this explanation but stated: "the court cannot say that it is more probably true than not true that the reasons advanced by the defendant for the promotion of [the four men] are pretext and were not sex-neutral."

Aware that such findings, even on the ultimate issue, are all but conclusive, see Pullman–Standard v. Swint, 456 U.S. 273, 102 S.Ct. 1781, 72 L.Ed.2d 66 (1982); Anderson v. City of Bessemer City, 470 U.S. 564, 573–76, 105 S.Ct. 1504, 1511–13, 84 L.Ed.2d 518 (1985), Benzies directs her fire against what she believes is a mistake of law in the district court's opinion. The court stated that the plaintiff "has the ultimate burden of persuading the court that the reasons advanced [for the decision under attack] are a pretext *and* that a substantial or motivating factor in the defendant's decision was discrimination and but for that discrimination, the plaintiff would have been appointed." (Emphasis added.) Benzies insists that *and* should have been *or*.

This does not make any difference. The district court concluded both that the reasons the Department gave were not pretexts and that the Department did not act with discriminatory intent. Conjunctive versus disjunctive became immaterial. Witnesses testified that the process of non-competitive promotion is mechanical. The district court expressed doubts, on which Benzies plays, but a doubt is not the same thing as a favorable finding. Neither finding is clearly erroneous.

Just in case, we add that Benzies is wrong on the law. The plaintiff must show that intentional discrimination caused the employer to take some unfavorable action. See United States Postal Service Board of Governors v. Aikens; Texas Department of Community Affairs v. Burdine. To have any hope of showing this, the plaintiff must puncture a neutral explanation the employer offers for its conduct.

Benzies argues that if the plaintiff does so—in the argot, shows that the explanation is a "pretext"—then the district court must infer that the employer acted with discriminatory intent. Not so. A demonstration that the employer has offered a spurious explanation is strong evidence of discriminatory intent, but it does not compel such an inference as a matter of law. The judge may conclude after hearing all the evidence that neither discriminatory intent nor the employer's explanation accounts for the decision.

A public employer may feel bound to offer explanations that are acceptable under a civil service system, such as that one employee is more skilled than another, or that "we were just following the rules." The trier of fact may find, however, that some less seemly reason—personal or political favoritism, a grudge, random conduct, an error in the administration of neutral rules—actually accounts for the decision. Title VII does not compel every employer to have a good reason for its deeds; it is not a civil service statute. Unless the employer acted for a reason prohibited by the statute, the plaintiff loses. The failure of an explanation to persuade the judge supports an inference that a bad reason accounts for the decision, but it is not invariably conclusive; the presence of a sufficient explanation, however, is dispositive against the plaintiff. (A "sufficient" explanation is one that would produce the same decision whether or not the prohibited characteristic played some role.)

Benzies wants us to treat any failure of the employer's chosen explanation as leaving the prima facie showing of discrimination unrebutted, compelling judgment in the employee's favor. *Aikens* establishes, however, that after the case has been tried the apparatus of prima facie case and response is no longer determinative. Once a disparate treatment case has been tried, the question that matters is whether the plaintiff established that the employer's use of a criterion forbidden by statute caused an adverse decision. So Benzies does not have a legal ground that compels the district court to reexamine its conclusions.

Although we conclude that the district court's findings are not clearly erroneous, we share that court's doubt about the Department's conduct. The Department has never had a female supervising psychologist, and the record would have supported a finding that Benzies got the runaround for reasons related to her sex rather than to her talents and accomplishments. The Department's defense at trial was that, when Benzies demanded a job audit, she was not supervising anyone. That may be true, but it does not explain why men were given supervisory tasks and women were not. A "neutral" rule paying supervisors more than other employees is not neutral in application if only men are given supervisory tasks. The conclusion that the decisions to upgrade the four men, and not Benzies, were correct under the rules given each employee's duties does not respond to a claim that the Department discriminated in the assignment of the supervisory duties that were indispensable to being promoted.

The district judge did not explicitly discuss the reasons the men were assigned the duties that made promotions possible, while Benzies was not. Much of Benzies's brief tries to show that she should have been given supervisory duties, making a promotion possible. Fed. R.Civ.P. 52(a) requires the district court to make findings on all contested issues that are important to the outcome. A review of the record in this case shows why the district court did not address this potentially dispositive question: it was not raised at trial. The pretrial orders do not mention, as issues for trial, disputes about the assignment of duties to the psychologists. The principal pretrial order, drafted by the Department, poses a series of questions about the nature of the audit and upgrade process. Benzies filed a supplemental pretrial order presenting one more question about the audit process. She did not ask the court to consider the assignment of duties. The pretrial order establishes the issues for decision, and it is too late for appellate counsel to reshape the case. See Erff v. Markhon Industries, Inc., 781 F.2d 613 (7th Cir.1986). If issues about the failure to assign supervisory duties to Benzies were before the district judge at all, they were presented too obliquely to require a response. Each party must sharpen his own claims; those left in amorphous form by counsel need not be honed and decided by the judge. Benzies is bound by the litigation strategy in the district court. The judge addressed and resolved the matters presented to him. We are not sure that Benzies received her due from the State of Illinois, but we have no doubt that she received her due from the district court.

AFFIRMED.

NOTES AND PROBLEMS FOR DISCUSSION

1. In both Tye v. Board of Education and Benzies v. Illinois Dept. of Mental Health the employer's articulated reason for its decision regarding the plaintiff's employment was found to be false. The Sixth and Seventh Circuits differ widely on the legal significance of that finding. Which view is more consistent with the purpose of the *McDonnell–Douglas–Burdine* proof model? Does *Aikens* compel the result in *Benzies* as suggested by Judge Easterbrook? With the principal cases compare, MacDissi v. Valmont Industries, Inc., 856 F.2d 1054 (8th Cir.1988) (as a matter of both common sense and federal law, an employer's submission of a discredited explanation for firing plaintiff is itself evidence which may persuade the trier of fact that unlawful discrimination occurred) and Connell v. Bank of Boston, 924 F.2d 1169 (1st Cir.1991) (in age discrimination case, plaintiff must prove age bias, not simply refute or cast doubt on employer's explanation for discharge: question is whether the employee was discharged because of age, not whether the discharge decision could be second-guessed).

2. In light of Judge Easterbrook's expressed doubt about the reason Benzies was not assigned supervisory duties and his conclusion that the record, even as it stood, would support a finding of discrimination, does any rule or policy prevent a remand to the district court with instructions that the trial judge make additional findings on the supervisory assignments issue? Other

than a "sporting" theory of litigation, is there any reason that a party should always "be bound" by her litigation strategy?

3. Proof of Causation

PRICE WATERHOUSE v. HOPKINS

Supreme Court of the United States, 1989.
490 U.S. 228, 109 S.Ct. 1775, 104 L.Ed.2d 268.

JUSTICE BRENNAN announced the judgment of the Court and delivered an opinion, in which JUSTICE MARSHALL, JUSTICE BLACKMUN, and JUSTICE STEVENS join.

Ann Hopkins was a senior manager in an office of Price Waterhouse when she was proposed for partnership in 1982. She was neither offered nor denied admission to the partnership; instead, her candidacy was held for reconsideration the following year. When the partners in her office later refused to repropose her for partnership, she sued Price Waterhouse under Title VII of the Civil Rights Act of 1964, 78 Stat. 253, as amended, 42 U.S.C. § 2000e *et seq.,* charging that the firm had discriminated against her on the basis of sex in its decisions regarding partnership. Judge Gesell in the District Court for the District of Columbia ruled in her favor on the question of liability, and the Court of Appeals for the District of Columbia Circuit affirmed. 825 F.2d 458 (1987). We granted certiorari to resolve a conflict among the Courts of Appeals concerning the respective burdens of proof of a defendant and plaintiff in a suit under Title VII when it has been shown that an employment decision resulted from a mixture of legitimate and illegitimate motives.

I

At Price Waterhouse, a nationwide professional accounting partnership, a senior manager becomes a candidate for partnership when the partners in her local office submit her name as a candidate. All of the other partners in the firm are then invited to submit written comments on each candidate—either on a "long" or a "short" form, depending on the partner's degree of exposure to the candidate. Not every partner in the firm submits comments on every candidate. After reviewing the comments and interviewing the partners who submitted them, the firm's Admissions Committee makes a recommendation to the Policy Board. This recommendation will be either that the firm accept the candidate for partnership, put her application on "hold," or deny her the promotion outright. The Policy Board then decides whether to submit the candidate's name to the entire partnership for a vote, to "hold" her candidacy, or to reject her. The recommendation of the Admissions Committee, and the decision of the Policy Board, are not controlled by fixed guidelines: a certain number of positive comments from partners will not guarantee a candidate's admission to the partnership, nor will a specific quantity of negative comments necessarily defeat her application. Price Waterhouse places no limit on the number of persons whom it will admit to the partnership in any given year.

Ann Hopkins had worked at Price Waterhouse's Office of Government Services in Washington, D.C., for five years when the partners in that office proposed her as a candidate for partnership. Of the 662 partners at the firm at that time, 7 were women. Of the 88 persons proposed for partnership that year, only 1—Hopkins—was a woman. Forty-seven of these candidates were admitted to the partnership, 21 were rejected, and 20—including Hopkins—were "held" for reconsideration the following year.[1] Thirteen of the 32 partners who had submitted comments on Hopkins supported her bid for partnership. Three partners recommended that her candidacy be placed on hold, eight stated that they did not have an informed opinion about her, and eight recommended that she be denied partnership.

In a jointly prepared statement supporting her candidacy, the partners in Hopkins' office showcased her successful 2–year effort to secure a $25 million contract with the Department of State, labeling it "an outstanding performance" and one that Hopkins carried out "virtually at the partner level." Despite Price Waterhouse's attempt at trial to minimize her contribution to this project, Judge Gesell specifically found that Hopkins had "played a key role in Price Waterhouse's successful effort to win a multi-million dollar contract with the Department of State." Indeed, he went on, "[n]one of the other partnership candidates at Price Waterhouse that year had a comparable record in terms of successfully securing major contracts for the partnership."

The partners in Hopkins' office praised her character as well as her accomplishments, describing her in their joint statement as "an outstanding professional" who had a "deft touch," a "strong character, independence and integrity." Clients appear to have agreed with these assessments. At trial, one official from the State Department described her as "extremely competent, intelligent," "strong and forthright, very productive, energetic and creative." Another high-ranking official praised Hopkins' decisiveness, broadmindedness, and "intellectual clarity"; she was, in his words, "a stimulating conversationalist." Evaluations such as these led Judge Gesell to conclude that Hopkins "had no difficulty dealing with clients and her clients appear to have been very pleased with her work" and that she "was generally viewed as a highly competent project leader who worked long hours, pushed vigorously to

1. Before the time for reconsideration came, two of the partners in Hopkins' office withdrew their support for her, and the office informed her that she would not be reconsidered for partnership. Hopkins then resigned. Price Waterhouse does not challenge the Court of Appeals' conclusion that the refusal to repropose her for partnership amounted to a constructive discharge. That court remanded the case to the District Court for further proceedings to determine appropriate relief, and those proceedings have been stayed pending our decision. We are concerned today only with Price Waterhouse's decision to place Hopkins' candidacy on hold. Decisions pertaining to advancement to partnership are, of course, subject to challenge under Title VII. Hishon v. King & Spalding.

meet deadlines and demanded much from the multidisciplinary staffs with which she worked."

On too many occasions, however, Hopkins' aggressiveness apparently spilled over into abrasiveness. Staff members seem to have borne the brunt of Hopkins' brusqueness. Long before her bid for partnership, partners evaluating her work had counseled her to improve her relations with staff members. Although later evaluations indicate an improvement, Hopkins' perceived shortcomings in this important area eventually doomed her bid for partnership. Virtually all of the partners' negative remarks about Hopkins—even those of partners supporting her—had to do with her "interpersonal skills." Both "[s]upporters and opponents of her candidacy," stressed Judge Gesell, "indicated that she was sometimes overly aggressive, unduly harsh, difficult to work with and impatient with staff."

There were clear signs, though, that some of the partners reacted negatively to Hopkins' personality because she was a woman. One partner described her as "macho"; another suggested that she "overcompensated for being a woman"; a third advised her to take "a course at charm school". Several partners criticized her use of profanity; in response, one partner suggested that those partners objected to her swearing only "because it[']s a lady using foul language." Another supporter explained that Hopkins "ha[d] matured from a tough-talking somewhat masculine hard-nosed mgr to an authoritative, formidable, but much more appealing lady ptr candidate." But it was the man who, as Judge Gesell found, bore responsibility for explaining to Hopkins the reasons for the Policy Board's decision to place her candidacy on hold who delivered the *coup de grace:* in order to improve her chances for partnership, Thomas Beyer advised, Hopkins should "walk more femininely, talk more femininely, dress more femininely, wear make-up, have her hair styled, and wear jewelry."

Dr. Susan Fiske, a social psychologist and Associate Professor of Psychology at Carnegie–Mellon University, testified at trial that the partnership selection process at Price Waterhouse was likely influenced by sex stereotyping. Her testimony focused not only on the overtly sex-based comments of partners but also on gender-neutral remarks, made by partners who knew Hopkins only slightly, that were intensely critical of her. One partner, for example, baldly stated that Hopkins was "universally disliked" by staff, and another described her as "consistently annoying and irritating"; yet these were people who had had very little contact with Hopkins. According to Fiske, Hopkins' uniqueness (as the only woman in the pool of candidates) and the subjectivity of the evaluations made it likely that sharply critical remarks such as these were the product of sex stereotyping—although Fiske admitted that she could not say with certainty whether any particular comment was the result of stereotyping. Fiske based her opinion on a review of the submitted comments, explaining that it was commonly accepted practice for social psychologists to reach this kind of conclusion without having met any of the people involved in the decisionmaking process.

In previous years, other female candidates for partnership also had been evaluated in sex-based terms. As a general matter, Judge Gesell concluded, "[c]andidates were viewed favorably if partners believed they maintained their femin[in]ity while becoming effective profession-al managers"; in this environment, "[t]o be identified as a 'women's lib[b]er' was regarded as [a] negative comment." In fact, the judge found that in previous years "[o]ne partner repeatedly commented that he could not consider any woman seriously as a partnership candidate and believed that women were not even capable of functioning as senior managers—yet the firm took no action to discourage his comments and recorded his vote in the overall summary of the evaluations."

Judge Gesell found that Price Waterhouse legitimately emphasized interpersonal skills in its partnership decisions, and also found that the firm had not fabricated its complaints about Hopkins' interpersonal skills as a pretext for discrimination. Moreover, he concluded, the firm did not give decisive emphasis to such traits only because Hopkins was a woman; although there were male candidates who lacked these skills but who were admitted to partnership, the judge found that these candidates possessed other, positive traits that Hopkins lacked.

The judge went on to decide, however, that some of the partners' remarks about Hopkins stemmed from an impermissibly cabined view of the proper behavior of women, and that Price Waterhouse had done nothing to disavow reliance on such comments. He held that Price Waterhouse had unlawfully discriminated against Hopkins on the basis of sex by consciously giving credence and effect to partners' comments that resulted from sex stereotyping. Noting that Price Waterhouse could avoid equitable relief by proving by clear and convincing evidence that it would have placed Hopkins' candidacy on hold even absent this discrimination, the judge decided that the firm had not carried this heavy burden.

The Court of Appeals affirmed the District court's ultimate conclu-sion, but departed from its analysis in one particular: it held that even if a plaintiff proves that discrimination played a role in an employment decision, the defendant will not be found liable if it proves, by clear and convincing evidence, that it would have made the same decision in the absence of discrimination. 825 F.2d, at 470–471. Under this approach, an employer is not deemed to have violated Title VII if it proves that it would have made the same decision in the absence of an impermissible motive, whereas under the District Court's approach, the employer's proof in that respect only avoids equitable relief. We decide today that the Court of Appeals had the better approach, but that both courts erred in requiring the employer to make its proof by clear and convincing evidence.

II

The specification of the standard of causation under Title VII is a decision about the kind of conduct that violates that statute. According to Price Waterhouse, an employer violates Title VII only if it gives decisive consideration to an employee's gender, race, national origin, or religion in making a decision that affects that employee. On Price Waterhouse's theory, even if a plaintiff shows that her gender played a part in an employment decision, it is still her burden to show that the decision would have been different if the employer had not discriminated. In Hopkins' view, on the other hand, an employer violates the statute whenever it allows one of these attributes to play any part in an employment decision. Once a plaintiff shows that this occurred, according to Hopkins, the employer's proof that it would have made the same decision in the absence of discrimination can serve to limit equitable relief but not to avoid a finding of liability.[2] We conclude that, as often happens, the truth lies somewhere in-between.

2. This question has, to say the least, left the Circuits in disarray. The Third, Fourth, Fifth, and Seventh Circuits require a plaintiff challenging an adverse employment decision to show that, but for her gender (or race or religion or national origin), the decision would have been in her favor. See, e.g., Bellissimo v. Westinghouse Elec. Corp., 764 F.2d 175, 179 (CA3 1985), cert. denied, 475 U.S. 1035, 106 S.Ct. 1244, 89 L.Ed.2d 353 (1986); Ross v. Communications Satellite Corp., 759 F.2d 355, 365–366 (CA4 1985); Peters v. City of Shreveport, 818 F.2d 1148, 1161 (CA5 1987); McQuillen v. Wisconsin Education Assn. Council, 830 F.2d 659, 664–665 (CA7 1987). The First, Second, Sixth, and Eleventh Circuits, on the other hand, hold that once the plaintiff has shown that a discriminatory motive was a "substantial" or "motivating" factor in an employment decision, the employer may avoid a finding of liability only by proving that it would have made the same decision even in the absence of discrimination. These courts have either specified that the employer must prove its case by a preponderance of the evidence or have not mentioned the proper standard of proof. See, e.g., Fields v. Clark University, 817 F.2d 931, 936–937 (CA1 1987) ("motivating factor"); Berl v. Westchester County, 849 F.2d 712, 714–715 (CA2 1988) ("substantial part"); Terbovitz v. Fiscal Court of Adair County, Ky., 825 F.2d 111, 115 (CA6 1987) ("motivating factor"); Bell v. Birmingham Linen Service, 715 F.2d 1552, 1557 (CA11 1983). The Court of Appeals for the D.C. Circuit, as shown in this case, follows the same rule except that it requires that the employer's proof be clear and convincing rather than merely preponderant. 263 U.S.App.D.C. 321, 333–334, 825 F.2d 458, 470–471 (1987); see also Toney v. Block, 227 U.S.App.D.C. 273, 275, 705 F.2d 1364, 1366 (1983) (Scalia, J.) (it would be "destructive of the purposes of [Title VII] to require the plaintiff to establish * * * the difficult hypothetical proposition that, had there been no discrimination, the employment decision would have been made in his favor"). The Court of Appeals for the Ninth Circuit also requires clear and convincing proof, but it goes further by holding that a Title VII violation is made out as soon as the plaintiff shows that an impermissible motivation played a part in an employment decision—at which point the employer may avoid reinstatement and an award of backpay by proving that it would have made the same decision in the absence of the unlawful motive. See, e.g. Fadhl v. City and County of San Francisco, 741 F.2d 1163, 1165–1166 (CA9 1984) (Kennedy, J.) ("significant factor"). Last, the Court of Appeals for the Eighth Circuit draws the same distinction as the Ninth between the liability and remedial phases of Title VII litigation, but requires only a preponderance of the evidence from the employer. See, e.g., Bibbs v. Block, 778 F.2d 1318, 1320–1324 (CA8 1985) (en banc) ("discernible factor").

A

In passing Title VII, Congress made the simple but momentous announcement that sex, race, religion, and national origin are not relevant to the selection, evaluation, or compensation of employees.[3] Yet, the statute does not purport to limit the other qualities and characteristics that employers *may* take into account in making employment decisions. The converse, therefore, of "for cause" legislation,[4] Title VII eliminates certain bases for distinguishing among employees while otherwise preserving employers' freedom of choice. This balance between employee rights and employer prerogatives turns out to be decisive in the case before us.

Congress' intent to forbid employers to take gender into account in making employment decisions appears on the face of the statute. In now-familiar language, the statute forbids an employer to "fail or refuse to hire or to discharge any individual, or otherwise to discriminate with respect to his compensation, terms, conditions, or privileges of employment," or to "limit, segregate, or classify his employees or applicants for employment in any way which would deprive or tend to deprive any individual of employment opportunities or otherwise adversely affect his status as an employee, *because of* such individual's * * * sex." (emphasis added).[5] We take these words to mean that gender must be irrelevant to employment decisions. To construe the words "because of" as colloquial shorthand for "but-for causation," as does Price Waterhouse, is to misunderstand them.[6]

But-for causation is a hypothetical construct. In determining whether a particular factor was a but-for cause of a given event, we

---

3. We disregard, for purposes of this discussion, the special context of affirmative action.

4. Congress specifically declined to require that an employment decision have been "for cause" in order to escape an affirmative penalty (such as reinstatement or backpay) from a court. As introduced in the House, the bill that became Title VII forbade such affirmative relief if an "individual was * * * refused employment or advancement, or was suspended or discharged *for cause.*" H.R. 7152, 88th Cong., 1st Sess. 77 (1963) (emphasis added). The phrase "for cause" eventually was deleted in favor of the phrase "for any reason other than" one of the enumerated characteristics. See 110 Conger. 2567–2571 (1964). Representative Celler explained that this substitution "specif[ied] cause"; in his view, a court "cannot find any violation of the act which is based on facts other * * * than discrimination on the grounds of race, color, religion, or national origin." Id., at 2567.

5. In this Court, Hopkins for the first time argues that Price Waterhouse violat-ed § 703(a)(2) when it subjected her to a biased decisionmaking process that "tended to deprive" a woman of partnership on the basis of her sex. Since Hopkins did not make this argument below, we do not address it.

6. We made passing reference to a similar question in McDonald v. Santa Fe Trail Transportation Co., * * * where we stated that when a Title VII plaintiff seeks to show that an employer's explanation for a challenged employment decision is pretextual, "no more is required to be shown than that race was a 'but for' cause." This passage, however, does not suggest that the plaintiff *must* show but-for cause; it indicates only that if she does so, she prevails. More important, *McDonald* dealt with the question whether the employer's stated reason for its decision was *the* reason for its action; unlike the case before us today, therefore, *McDonald* did not involve mixed motives. This difference is decisive in distinguishing this case from those involving "pretext."

begin by assuming that that factor was present at the time of the event, and then ask whether, even if that factor had been absent, the event nevertheless would have transpired in the same way. The present, active tense of the operative verbs of § 703(a)(1) ("to fail or refuse"), in contrast, turns our attention to the actual moment of the event in question, the adverse employment decision. The critical inquiry, the one commanded by the words of § 703(a)(1), is whether gender was a factor in the employment decision *at the moment it was made.* Moreover, since we know that the words "because of" do not mean "*solely* because of," [7] we also know that Title VII meant to condemn even those decisions based on a mixture of legitimate and illegitimate considerations. When, therefore, an employer considers both gender and legitimate factors at the time of making a decision, that decision was "because of" sex and the other, legitimate considerations—even if we may say later, in the context of litigation, that the decision would have been the same if gender had not been taken into account.

To attribute this meaning to the words "because of" does not, as the dissent asserts, divest them of causal significance. A simple example illustrates the point. Suppose two physical forces act upon and move an object, and suppose that either force acting alone would have moved the object. As the dissent would have it, *neither* physical force was a "cause" of the motion unless we can show that but for one or both of them, the object would not have moved; to use the dissent's terminology, both forces were simply "in the air" unless we can identify at least one of them as a but-for cause of the object's movement. Events that are causally overdetermined, in other words, may not have any "cause" at all. This cannot be so.

We need not leave our commonsense at the doorstep when we interpret a statute. It is difficult for us to imagine that, in the simple words "because of," Congress meant to obligate a plaintiff to identify the precise causal role played by legitimate and illegitimate motivations in the employment decision she challenges. We conclude, instead, that Congress meant to obligate her to prove that the employer relied upon sex-based considerations in coming to its decision.

Our interpretation of the words "because of" also is supported by the fact that Title VII does identify one circumstance in which an employer may take gender into account in making an employment decision, namely, when gender is "bona fide occupational qualification [(BFOQ)] reasonably necessary to the normal operation of th[e] particular business or enterprise." The only plausible inference to draw from this provision is that, in all other circumstances, a person's gender may not be considered in making decisions that affect her. Indeed, Title VII even forbids employers to make gender an indirect stumbling block to employment opportunities. An employer may not, we have held, condition employment opportunities on the satisfaction of facially neutral

---

7. Congress specifically rejected an amendment that would have placed the word "solely" in front of the words "because of." 110 Conger. 2728, 13837 (1964).

tests or qualifications that have a disproportionate, adverse impact on members of protected groups when those tests or qualifications are not required for performance of the job.

To say that an employer may not take gender into account is not, however, the end of the matter, for that describes only one aspect of Title VII. The other important aspect of the statute is its preservation of an employer's remaining freedom of choice. We conclude that the preservation of this freedom means that an employer shall not be liable if it can prove that, even if it had not taken gender into account, it would have come to the same decision regarding a particular person. The statute's maintenance of employer prerogatives is evident from the statute itself and from its history, both in Congress and in this Court.

To begin with, the existence of the BFOQ exception shows Congress' unwillingness to require employers to change the very nature of their operations in response to the statute. And our emphasis on "business necessity" in disparate-impact cases, see *Watson* and *Griggs,* and on "legitimate, nondiscriminatory reason[s]" in disparate-treatment cases, results from our awareness of Title VII's balance between employee rights and employer prerogatives. In *McDonnell Douglas,* we described as follows Title VII's goal to eradicate discrimination while preserving workplace efficiency: "The broad, overriding interest, shared by employer, employee, and consumer, is efficient and trustworthy workmanship assured through fair and racially neutral employment and personnel decisions. In the implementation of such decisions, it is abundantly clear that Title VII tolerates no racial discrimination, subtle or otherwise."

When an employer ignored the attributes enumerated in the statute, Congress hoped, it naturally would focus on the qualifications of the applicant or employee. The intent to drive employers to focus on qualifications rather than on race, religion, sex, or national origin is the theme of a good deal of the statute's legislative history. An interpretive memorandum entered into the Congressional Record by Senators Case and Clark, comanagers of the bill in the Senate, is representative of this general theme.[8] According to their memorandum, Title VII "expressly protects the employer's right to insist that any prospective applicant, Negro or white, must meet the applicable job qualifications. Indeed, the very purpose of title VII is to promote hiring on the basis of job qualifications, rather than on the basis of race or color."[9]   110

---

8. We have in the past acknowledged the authoritativeness of this interpretive memorandum, written by the two bipartisan "captains" of Title VII. See, e.g., Firefighters v. Stotts, 467 U.S. 561, 581, n. 14, 104 S.Ct. 2576, 2589, n. 14, 81 L.Ed.2d 483 (1984).

9. Many of the legislators' statements, such as the memorandum quoted in text, focused specifically on race rather than on gender or religion or national origin. We do not, however, limit their statements to the context of race, but instead we take them as general statements on the meaning of Title VII. The somewhat bizarre path by which "sex" came to be included as a forbidden criterion for employment—it was included in an attempt to *defeat* the bill, see C. & B. Whalen, The Longest Debate: A Legislative History of the 1964 Civil Rights Act 115–117 (1985)—does not persuade us that the legislators' state-

Conger. 7247 (1964), quoted in Griggs v. Duke Power Co., supra, at 434. The memorandum went on: "To discriminate is to make a distinction, to make a difference in treatment or favor, and those distinctions or differences in treatment or favor which are prohibited by section 704 are those which are based on any five of the forbidden criteria: race, color, religion, sex, and national origin. Any other criterion or qualification for employment is not affected by this title." 110 Conger. 7213 (1964).

Many other legislators made statements to a similar effect; we see no need to set out each remark in full here. The central point is this: while an employer may not take gender into account in making an employment decision (except in those very narrow circumstances in which gender is a BFOQ), it is free to decide against a woman for other reasons. We think these principles require that, once a plaintiff in a Title VII case shows that gender played a motivating part in an employment decision, the defendant may avoid a finding of liability [10] only by proving that it would have made the same decision even if it

ments pertaining to race are irrelevant to cases alleging gender discrimination. The amendment that added "sex" as one of the forbidden criteria for employment was passed, of course, and the statute on its face treats each of the enumerated categories exactly the same.

By the same token, our specific references to gender throughout this opinion, and the principles we announce, apply with equal force to discrimination based on race, religion, or national origin.

10. Hopkins argues that once she made this showing, she was entitled to a finding that Price Waterhouse had discriminated against her on the basis of sex; as a consequence, she says, the partnership's proof could only limit the relief she received. She relies on Title VII's § 706(g), which permits a court to award affirmative relief when it finds that an employer "has intentionally engaged in or is intentionally engaging in an unlawful employment practice," and yet forbids a court to order reinstatement of, or backpay to, "an individual * * * if such individual was refused * * * employment or advancement or was suspended or discharged *for any reason other than* discrimination on account of race, color, religion, sex, or national origin." 42 U.S.C. § 2000–5(g) (emphasis added). We do not take this provision to mean that a court inevitably can find a violation of the statute without having considered whether the employment decision would have been the same absent the impermissible motive. That would be to interpret § 706(g)—a provision defining *remedies*—to influence the substantive commands of the statute. We

think that this provision merely limits courts' authority to award affirmative relief in those circumstances in which a violation of the statute is not dependent upon the effect of the employer's discriminatory practices on a particular employee, as in pattern-or-practice suits and class actions. "The crucial difference between an individual's claim of discrimination and a class action alleging a general pattern or practice of discrimination is manifest. The inquiry regarding an individual's claim is the reason for a particular employment decision, while 'at the liability stage of a pattern-or-practice trial the focus often will not be on individual hiring decisions, but on a pattern of discriminatory decision-making.' " Cooper v. Federal Reserve Bank of Richmond, * * * quoting Teamsters v. United States * * *.

Without explicitly mentioning this portion of § 706(g), we have in the past held that Title VII does not authorize affirmative relief for individuals as to whom, the employer shows, the existence of systemic discrimination had no effect. See Franks v. Bowman Transportation Co. * * *; Teamsters v. United States * * *; East Texas Motor Freight System, Inc. v. Rodriguez * * *. These decisions suggest that the proper focus of § 706(g) is on claims of systemic discrimination, not on charges of individual discrimination. Cf. NLRB v. Transportation Management Corp., * * * (upholding the National Labor Relations Board's identical interpretation of § 10(c) of the National Labor Relations Act, 29 U.S.C. § 160(c), which contains language almost identical to § 706(g)).

had not allowed gender to play such a role. This balance of burdens is the direct result of Title VII's balance of rights.

Our holding casts no shadow on *Burdine,* in which we decided that, even after a plaintiff has made out a prima facie case of discrimination under Title VII, the burden of persuasion does not shift to the employer to show that its stated legitimate reason for the employment decision was the true reason. We stress, first, that neither court below shifted the burden of persuasion to Price Waterhouse on this question, and in fact, the District Court found that Hopkins had not shown that the firm's stated reason for its decision was pretextual. Moreover, since we hold that the plaintiff retains the burden of persuasion on the issue whether gender played a part in the employment decision, the situation before us is not the one of "shifting burdens" that we addressed in *Burdine.* Instead, the employer's burden is most appropriately deemed an affirmative defense: the plaintiff must persuade the factfinder on one point, and then the employer, if it wishes to prevail, must persuade it on another. See NLRB v. Transportation Management Corp., 462 U.S. 393, 400, 103 S.Ct. 2469, 2473, 76 L.Ed.2d 667 (1983).[11]

Price Waterhouse's claim that the employer does not bear any burden of proof (if it bears one at all) until the plaintiff has shown "substantial evidence that Price Waterhouse's explanation for failing to promote Hopkins was not the 'true reason' for its action" merely restates its argument that the plaintiff in a mixed-motives case must squeeze her proof into *Burdine's* framework. Where a decision was the product of a mixture of legitimate and illegitimate motives, however, it simply makes no sense to ask whether the legitimate reason was "*the* 'true reason'" for the decision—which is the question asked by *Burdine.* See *Transportation Management,* supra, at 400, n. 5.[12] Oblivious

---

11. Given that both the plaintiff and defendant bear a burden of proof in cases such as this one, it is surprising that the dissent insists that our approach requires the employer to bear "the ultimate burden of proof." Post, at 10. It is, moreover, perfectly consistent to say *both* that gender was a factor in a particular decision when it was made *and* that, when the situation is viewed hypothetically and after the fact, the same decision would have been made even in the absence of discrimination. Thus, we do not see the "internal inconsistency" in our opinion that the dissent perceives. See post, at 6–7. Finally, where liability is imposed because an employer is unable to prove that it would have made the same decision even if it had not discriminated, this is not an imposition of liability "where sex made no difference to the outcome." Post, at 6. In our adversary system, where a party has the burden of proving a particular assertion and where that party is unable to meet its burden, we assume that that assertion is inaccurate.

Thus, where an employer is unable to prove its claim that it would have made the same decision in the absence of discrimination, we are entitled to conclude that gender *did* make a difference to the outcome.

12. Nothing in this opinion should be taken to suggest that a case must be correctly labeled as either a "pretext" case or a "mixed motives" case from the beginning in the District Court; indeed, we expect that plaintiffs often will allege, in the alternative, that their cases are both. Discovery often will be necessary before the plaintiff can know whether both legitimate and illegitimate considerations played a part in the decision against her. At some point in the proceedings, of course, the District Court must decide whether a particular case involves mixed motives. If the plaintiff fails to satisfy the factfinder that it is more likely than not that a forbidden characteristic played a part in the employment decision, then she may prevail only if

to this last point, the dissent would insist that *Burdine's* framework perform work that it was never intended to perform. It would require a plaintiff who challenges an adverse employment decision in which both legitimate and illegitimate considerations played a part to pretend that the decision, in fact, stemmed from a single source—for the premise of *Burdine* is that *either* a legitimate *or* an illegitimate set of considerations led to the challenged decision. To say that *Burdine's* evidentiary scheme will not help us decide a case admittedly involving *both* kinds of considerations is not to cast aspersions on the utility of that scheme in the circumstances for which it was designed.

* * *

C

In saying that gender played a motivating part in an employment decision, we mean that, if we asked the employer at the moment of the decision what its reasons were and if we received a truthful response, one of those reasons would be that the applicant or employee was a woman.[13] In the specific context of sex stereotyping, an employer who acts on the basis of a belief that a woman cannot be aggressive, or that she must not be, has acted on the basis of gender.

Although the parties do not overtly dispute this last proposition, the placement by Price Waterhouse of "sex stereotyping" in quotation marks throughout its brief seems to us an insinuation either that such stereotyping was not present in this case or that it lacks legal relevance. We reject both possibilities. As to the existence of sex stereotyping in this case, we are not inclined to quarrel with the District Court's conclusion that a number of the partners' comments showed sex stereotyping at work. As for the legal relevance of sex stereotyping, we are beyond the day when an employer could evaluate employees by assuming or insisting that they matched the stereotype associated with their group, for " '[i]n forbidding employers to discriminate against individuals because of their sex, Congress intended to strike at the entire spectrum of disparate treatment of men and women resulting from sex stereotypes.' " Los Angeles Dept. of Water & Power v. Manhart, 435 U.S. 702, 707, n. 13, 98 S.Ct. 1370, 1375, n. 13, 55 L.Ed.2d

---

she proves, following *Burdine*, that the employer's stated reason for its decision is pretextual. The dissent need not worry that this evidentiary scheme, if used during a jury trial, will be so impossibly confused and complex as it imagines. Juries long have decided cases in which defendants raise affirmative defenses. The dissent fails, moreover, to explain why the evidentiary scheme that we endorsed over ten years ago in *Mt. Healthy* has not proved unworkable in that context but would be hopelessly complicated in a case brought under federal antidiscrimination statutes.

13. After comparing this description of the plaintiff's proof to that offered by the concurring opinion, * * * we do not understand why the concurrence suggests that they are meaningfully different from each other * * *. Nor do we see how the inquiry that we have described is "hypothetical" * * *.

It seeks to determine the content of the entire set of reasons for a decision, rather than shaving off one reason in an attempt to determine what the decision would have been in the absence of that consideration. The inquiry that we describe thus strikes us as a distinctly non-hypothetical one.

657 (1978), quoting Sprogis v. United Air Lines, Inc., 444 F.2d 1194, 1198 (CA7 1971). An employer who objects to aggressiveness in women but whose positions require this trait places women in an intolerable and impermissible Catch-22: out of a job if they behave aggressively and out of a job if they don't. Title VII lifts women out of this bind.

Remarks at work that are based on sex stereotypes do not inevitably prove that gender played a part in a particular employment decision. The plaintiff must show that the employer actually relied on her gender in making its decision. In making this showing, stereotyped remarks can certainly be *evidence* that gender played a part. In any event, the stereotyping in this case did not simply consist of stray remarks. On the contrary, Hopkins proved that Price Waterhouse invited partners to submit comments; that some of the comments stemmed from sex stereotypes; that an important part of the Policy Board's decision on Hopkins was an assessment of the submitted comments; and that Price Waterhouse in no way disclaimed reliance on the sex-linked evaluations. This is not, as Price Waterhouse suggests, "discrimination in the air"; rather, it is, as Hopkins puts it, "discrimination brought to ground and visited upon" an employee. By focusing on Hopkins' specific proof, however, we do not suggest a limitation on the possible ways of proving that stereotyping played a motivating role in an employment decision, and we refrain from deciding here which specific facts, "standing alone," would or would not establish a plaintiff's case, since such a decision is unnecessary in this case. But see post, at 17 (Justice O'Connor, concurring in judgment).

As to the employer's proof, in most cases, the employer should be able to present some objective evidence as to its probable decision in the absence of an impermissible motive.[14] Moreover, proving "that the same decision would have been justified * * * is not the same as proving that the same decision would have been made." *Givhan*, 439 U.S., at 416, 99 S.Ct. at 697, quoting Ayers v. Western Line Consolidated School District, 555 F.2d 1309, 1315 (CA5 1977). An employer may not, in other words, prevail in a mixed-motives case by offering a legitimate and sufficient reason for its decision if that reason did not motivate it at the time of the decision. Finally, an employer may not meet its burden in such a case by merely showing that at the time of the decision it was motivated only in part by a legitimate reason. The very premise of a mixed-motives case is that a legitimate reason was present, and indeed, in this case, Price Waterhouse already has made this showing by convincing Judge Gesell that Hopkins' interpersonal problems were a legitimate concern. The employer instead must show that its legitimate reason, standing alone, would have induced it to make the same decision.

---

14. Justice White's suggestion, * * *, that the employer's own testimony as to the probable decision in the absence of discrimination is due special credence where the court has, contrary to the employer's testimony, found that an illegitimate factor played a part in the decision, is baffling.

III

The courts below held that an employer who has allowed a discriminatory impulse to play a motivating part in an employment decision must prove by clear and convincing evidence that it would have made the same decision in the absence of discrimination. We are persuaded that the better rule is that the employer must make this showing by a preponderance of the evidence.

* * *

Significantly, the cases from this Court that most resemble this one, *Mt. Healthy and Transportation Management,* did not require clear and convincing proof. *Mt. Healthy,* 429 U.S., at 287, 97 S.Ct., at 576; *Transportation Management,* 462 U.S., at 400, 403, 103 S.Ct. 2475. We are not inclined to say that the public policy against firing employees because they spoke out on issues of public concern or because they affiliated with a union is less important than the policy against discharging employees on the basis of their gender. Each of these policies is vitally important, and each is adequately served by requiring proof by a preponderance of the evidence.

Although Price Waterhouse does not concretely tell us how its proof was preponderant even if it was not clear and convincing, this general claim is implicit in its request for the less stringent standard. Since the lower courts required Price Waterhouse to make its proof by clear and convincing evidence, they did not determine whether Price Waterhouse had proved by a *preponderance of the evidence* that it would have placed Hopkins' candidacy on hold even if it had not permitted sex-linked evaluations to play a part in the decision-making process. Thus, we shall remand this case so that that determination can be made.

IV

The District Court found that sex stereotyping "was permitted to play a part" in the evaluation of Hopkins as a candidate for partnership. 618 F.Supp., at 1120. Price Waterhouse disputes both that stereotyping occurred and that it played any part in the decision to place Hopkins' candidacy on hold. In the firm's view, in other words, the District Court's factual conclusions are clearly erroneous. We do not agree.

In finding that some of the partners' comments reflected sex stereotyping, the District Court relied in part on Dr. Fiske's expert testimony. Without directly impugning Dr. Fiske's credentials or qualifications, Price Waterhouse insinuates that a social psychologist is unable to identify sex stereotyping in evaluations without investigating whether those evaluations have a basis in reality. This argument comes too late. At trial, counsel for Price Waterhouse twice assured the court that he did not question Dr. Fiske's expertise and failed to challenge the legitimacy of her discipline. Without contradiction from

Price Waterhouse, Fiske testified that she discerned sex stereotyping in the partners' evaluations of Hopkins and she further explained that it was part of her business to identify stereotyping in written documents. We are not inclined to accept petitioner's belated and unsubstantiated characterization of Dr. Fiske's testimony as "gossamer evidence" based only on "intuitive hunches" and of her detection of sex stereotyping as "intuitively divined." Nor are we disposed to adopt the dissent's dismissive attitude toward Dr. Fiske's field of study and toward her own professional integrity.

Indeed, we are tempted to say that Dr. Fiske's expert testimony was merely icing on Hopkins' cake. It takes no special training to discern sex stereotyping in a description of an aggressive female employee as requiring "a course at charm school." Nor, turning to Thomas Beyer's memorable advice to Hopkins, does it require expertise in psychology to know that, if an employee's flawed "interpersonal skills" can be corrected by a soft-hued suit or a new shade of lipstick, perhaps it is the employee's sex and not her interpersonal skills that has drawn the criticism.[15]

Price Waterhouse also charges that Hopkins produced no evidence that sex stereotyping played a role in the decision to place her candidacy on hold. As we have stressed, however, Hopkins showed that the partnership solicited evaluations from all of the firm's partners; that it generally relied very heavily on such evaluations in making its decision; that some of the partners' comments were the product of stereotyping; and that the firm in no way disclaimed reliance on those particular comments, either in Hopkins' case or in the past. Certainly a plausible—and, one might say, inevitable—conclusion to draw from this set of circumstances is that the Policy Board in making its decision did in fact take into account all of the partners' comments, including the comments that were motivated by stereotypical notions about women's proper deportment.[16]

Price Waterhouse concedes that the proof in *Transportation Management, supra,* adequately showed that the employer there had relied on an impermissible motivation in firing the plaintiff. But the only evidence in that case that a discriminatory motive contributed to the plaintiff's discharge was that the employer harbored a grudge

---

15. We reject the claim, advanced by Price Waterhouse here and by the dissenting judge below, that the District Court clearly erred in finding that Beyer was "responsible for telling [Hopkins] what problems the Policy Board had identified with her candidacy." This conclusion was reasonable in light of the testimony at trial of a member of both the Policy Board and the Admissions Committee, who stated that he had "no doubt" that Beyer would discuss with Hopkins the reasons for placing her candidacy on hold and that Beyer "knew exactly where the problems were" regarding Hopkins.

16. We do not understand the dissenters' dissatisfaction with the District Judge's statements regarding the failure of Price Waterhouse to "sensitize" partners to the dangers of sexism. Made in the context of determining that Price Waterhouse had not disclaimed reliance on sex-based evaluations, and following the judge's description of the firm's history of condoning such evaluations, the judge's remarks seem to us justified.

toward the plaintiff on account of his union activity; there was, contrary to Price Waterhouse's suggestion, no direct evidence that that grudge had played a role in the decision, and in fact, the employer had given other reasons in explaining the plaintiff's discharge.   If the partnership considers that proof sufficient, we do not know why it takes such vehement issue with Hopkins' proof.

Nor is the finding that sex stereotyping played a part in the Policy Board's decision undermined by the fact that many of the suspect comments were made by supporters rather than detractors of Hopkins. A negative comment, even when made in the context of a generally favorable review, nevertheless may influence the decisionmaker to think less highly of the candidate; the Policy Board, in fact, did not simply tally the "yes's" and "no's" regarding a candidate, but carefully reviewed the content of the submitted comments.   The additional suggestion that the comments were made by "persons outside the decisionmaking chain" * * * —and therefore could not have harmed Hopkins—simply ignores the critical role that partners' comments played in the Policy Board's partnership decisions.

Price Waterhouse appears to think that we cannot affirm the factual findings of the trial court without deciding that, instead of being overbearing and aggressive and curt, Hopkins is in fact kind and considerate and patient.   If this is indeed its impression, petitioner misunderstands the theory on which Hopkins prevailed.   The District Judge acknowledged that Hopkins' conduct justified complaints about her behavior as a senior manager.   But he also concluded that the reactions of at least some of the partners were reactions to her as a *woman* manager.   Where an evaluation is based on a subjective assessment of a person's strengths and weaknesses, it is simply not true that each evaluator will focus on, or even mention, the same weaknesses. Thus, even if we knew that Hopkins had "personality problems," this would not tell us that the partners who cast their evaluations of Hopkins in sex-based terms would have criticized her as sharply (or criticized her at all) if she had been a man.   It is not our job to review the evidence and decide that the negative reactions to Hopkins were based on reality; our perception of Hopkins' character is irrelevant. We sit not to determine whether Ms. Hopkins is nice, but to decide whether the partners reacted negatively to her personality because she is a woman.

V

We hold that when a plaintiff in a Title VII case proves that her gender played a motivating part in an employment decision, the defendant may avoid a finding of liability only by proving by a preponderance of the evidence that it would have made the same decision even if it had not taken the plaintiff's gender into account.   Because the courts below erred by deciding that the defendant must make this proof by clear and convincing evidence, we reverse the Court of Appeals' judgment against Price Waterhouse on liability and remand the case to that court for further proceedings.

It is so ordered.

JUSTICE WHITE, concurring in the judgment.

* * *

Because the Court of Appeals required Price Waterhouse to prove by clear and convincing evidence that it would have reached the same employment decision in the absence of the improper motive, rather than merely requiring proof by a preponderance of the evidence as in *Mt. Healthy,* I concur in the judgment reversing this case in part and remanding. With respect to the employer's burden, however, the plurality seems to require, at least in most cases, that the employer submit objective evidence that the same result would have occurred absent the unlawful motivation. In my view, however, there is no special requirement that the employer carry its burden by objective evidence. In a mixed motive case, where the legitimate motive found would have been ample grounds for the action taken, and the employer credibly testifies that the action would have been taken for the legitimate reasons alone, this should be ample proof. This would even more plainly be the case where the employer denies any illegitimate motive in the first place but the court finds that illegitimate, as well as legitimate, factors motivated the adverse action.*

JUSTICE O'CONNOR, concurring in the judgment.

I agree with the plurality that on the facts presented in this case, the burden of persuasion should shift to the employer to demonstrate by a preponderance of the evidence that it would have reached the same decision concerning Ann Hopkins' candidacy absent consideration of her gender. I further agree that this burden shift is properly part of the liability phase of the litigation. I thus concur in the judgment of the Court. My disagreement stems from the plurality's conclusions concerning the substantive requirement of causation under the statute and its broad statements regarding the applicability of the allocation of the burden of proof applied in this case. The evidentiary rule the Court adopts today should be viewed as a supplement to the careful framework established by our unanimous decisions in McDonnell Douglas Corp. v. Green, and Texas Dept. of Community Affairs v. Burdine, for use in cases such as this one where the employer has created uncertainty as to causation by knowingly giving substantial weight to an impermissible criterion. I write separately to explain why I believe such a departure from the *McDonnell Douglas* standard is justified in the circumstances presented by this and like cases, and to express my views as to when and how the strong medicine of requiring the

---

* I agree with the plurality that if the employer carries this burden, there has been no violation of Title VII.

employer to bear the burden of persuasion on the issue of causation should be administered.

I

* * *

Like the common law of torts, the statutory employment "tort" created by Title VII has two basic purposes. The first is to deter conduct which has been identified as contrary to public policy and harmful to society as a whole. As we have noted in the past, the award of backpay to a Title VII plaintiff provides "the spur or catalyst which causes employers and unions to self-examine and to self-evaluate their employment practices and to endeavor to eliminate, so far as possible, the last vestiges" of discrimination in employment. Albemarle Paper Co. v. Moody, 422 U.S. 405, 417–418, 95 S.Ct. 2362, 2371–2372, 45 L.Ed.2d 280 (1975) (citation omitted). The second goal of Title VII is "to make persons whole for injuries suffered on account of unlawful employment discrimination." Id., at 418, 95 S.Ct., at 2372.

Both these goals are reflected in the elements of a disparate treatment action. There is no doubt that Congress considered reliance on gender or race in making employment decisions an evil in itself. As Senator Clark put it, "[t]he bill simply eliminates consideration of color [or other forbidden criteria] from the decision to hire or promote." 110 Conger. 7218 (1964). See also id., at 13088 (1964) (remarks of Sen. Humphrey) ("What the bill does * * * is simply to make it an illegal practice to use race as a factor in denying employment"). Reliance on such factors is exactly what the threat of Title VII liability was meant to deter. While the main concern of the statute was with employment opportunity, Congress was certainly not blind to the stigmatic harm which comes from being evaluated by a process which treats one as an inferior by reason of one's race or sex. This Court's decisions under the Equal Protection Clause have long recognized that whatever the final outcome of a decisional process, the inclusion of race or sex as a consideration within it harms both society and the individual. At the same time, Congress clearly conditioned legal liability on a determination that the consideration of an illegitimate factor *caused* a tangible employment injury of some kind.

Where an individual disparate treatment plaintiff has shown by a preponderance of the evidence that an illegitimate criterion was a *substantial* factor in an adverse employment decision, the deterrent purpose of the statute has clearly been triggered. More importantly, as an evidentiary matter, a reasonable factfinder could conclude that absent further explanation, the employer's discriminatory motivation "caused" the employment decision. The employer has not yet been shown to be a violator, but neither is it entitled to the same presumption of good faith concerning its employment decisions which is accorded employers facing only circumstantial evidence of discrimination. Both the policies behind the statute, and the evidentiary principles developed in the analogous area of causation in the law of torts, suggest that at this point the employer may be required to convince the factfinder that, despite the smoke, there is no fire.

We have given recognition to these principles in our cases which have discussed the "remedial phase" of class action disparate treatment cases. Once the class has established that discrimination against a protected group was essentially the employer's "standard practice," there has been harm to the group and injunctive relief is appropriate. But as to the individual members of the class, the liability phase of the litigation is not complete. See Dillon v. Coles, 746 F.2d 998, 1004 (CA3 1984) ("It is misleading to speak of the additional proof required by an individual class member for relief as being a part of the damage phase, that evidence is actually an element of the liability portion of the case") (footnote omitted). Because the class has already demonstrated that, as a rule, illegitimate factors were considered in the employer's decisions, the burden shifts to the employer "to demonstrate that the individual applicant was denied an employment opportunity for legitimate reasons." Teamsters v. United States, 431 U.S. 324, 362, 97 S.Ct. 1843, 1868, 52 L.Ed.2d 396 (1977). See also Franks v. Bowman Transportation Co., 424 U.S. 747, 772, 96 S.Ct. 1251, 1268, 47 L.Ed.2d 444 (1976).

The individual members of a class action treatment case stand in much the same position as Ann Hopkins here. There has been a strong showing that the employer has done exactly what Title VII forbids, but the connection between the employer's illegitimate motivation and any injury to the individual plaintiff is unclear. At this point calling upon the employer to show that despite consideration of illegitimate factors the individual plaintiff would not have been hired or promoted in any event hardly seems "unfair" or contrary to the substantive command of the statute. In fact, an individual plaintiff who has shown that an illegitimate factor played a substantial role in the decision in her case has proved *more* than the class member in a *Teamsters* type action. The latter receives the benefit of a burden shift to the defendant based on the *likelihood* that an illegitimate criterion was a factor in the individual employment decision.

There is a tension between the *Franks* and *Teamsters* line of decisions and the individual treatment cases cited by the dissent. Logically, under the dissent's view, each member of a disparate treatment class action would have to show "but-for" causation as to his or her individual employment decision, since it is not an element of the pattern or practice proof of the entire class and it is statutorily mandated that the plaintiff bear the burden of proof on this issue throughout the litigation. While the Court has properly drawn a distinction between the elements of a class action claim and an individual treatment claim, and I do not suggest the wholesale transposition of rules from one setting to the other, our decisions in *Teamsters* and *Franks* do indicate a recognition that presumptions shifting the burden of persuasion based on evidentiary probabilities and the policies behind the statute are not alien to our Title VII jurisprudence.

* * *

II

The dissent's summary of our individual disparate treatment cases to date is fair and accurate, and amply demonstrates that the rule we adopt today is a at least a change in direction from some of our prior precedents. We have indeed emphasized in the past that in an individual disparate treatment action the plaintiff bears the burden of persuasion throughout the litigation. Nor have we confined the word "pretext" to the narrow definition which the plurality attempts to pin on it today. *McDonnell Douglas* and *Burdine* clearly contemplated that a disparate treatment plaintiff could show that the employer's proffered explanation for an event was not "the true reason" either because it *never* motivated the employer in its employment decisions or because it did not do so in a particular case. *McDonnell Douglas* and *Burdine* assumed that the plaintiff would bear the burden of persuasion as to both these attacks, and we clearly depart from that framework today. Such a departure requires justification, and its outlines should be carefully drawn.

First, *McDonnell Douglas* itself dealt with a situation where the plaintiff presented no direct evidence that the employer had relied on a forbidden factor under Title VII in making an employment decision. The prima facie case established there was not difficult to prove, and was based only on the statistical probability that when a number of potential causes for an employment decision are eliminated an inference arises that an illegitimate factor was in fact the motivation behind the decision. In the face of this inferential proof, the employer's burden was deemed to be only one of production; the employer must articulate a legitimate reason for the adverse employment action. The plaintiff must then be given an "opportunity to demonstrate by competent evidence that the presumptively valid reasons for his rejection were in fact a coverup for a racially discriminatory decision." *McDonnell Douglas,* 411 U.S., at 805, 93 S.Ct., at 1826. Our decision in Texas Department of Community Affairs v. Burdine, also involved the "narrow question" whether, after a plaintiff had carried the "not onerous" burden of establishing the prima facie case under *McDonnell Douglas,* the burden of persuasion should be shifted to the employer to prove that a legitimate reason for the adverse employment action existed. As the discussion of *Teamsters* and *Arlington Heights* indicates, I do not think that the employer is entitled to the same presumption of good faith where there is direct evidence that it has placed substantial reliance on factors whose consideration is forbidden by Title VII.

The only individual treatment case cited by the dissent which involved the kind of direct evidence of discriminatory animus with which we are confronted here is United States Postal Service Bd. of Governors v. Aikens. The question presented to the Court in that case involved only a challenge to the elements of the prima facie case under *McDonnell Douglas* and *Burdine*, and the question we confront today was neither briefed nor argued to the Court. As should be apparent, the entire purpose of the *McDonnell Douglas* prima facie case is to compensate for the fact that direct evidence of intentional discrimination is hard to come by. That the employer's burden in rebutting such an inferential case of discrimination is only one of production does not mean that the scales should be weighted in the same manner where there *is* direct evidence of intentional discrimination. Indeed, in one Age Discrimination in Employment Act case, the Court seemed to indicate that "the *McDonnell Douglas* test is inapplicable where the plaintiff presents direct evidence of discrimination." Trans World Airlines, Inc. v. Thurston, 469 U.S. 111, 121, 105 S.Ct. 613, 621–622, 83 L.Ed.2d 523 (1985).

Second, the facts of this case, and a growing number like it decided by the Courts of Appeals, convince me that the evidentiary standard I propose is necessary to make real the promise of *McDonnell Douglas* that "[i]n the implementation of [employment] decisions, it is abundantly clear that Title VII tolerates no * * * discrimination, subtle or otherwise." In this case, the District Court found that a number of the evaluations of Ann Hopkins submitted by partners in the firm overtly referred to her failure to conform to certain gender stereotypes as a factor militating against her election to the partnership. The District Court further found that these evaluations were given "great weight" by the decisionmakers at Price Waterhouse. In addition, the District Court found that the partner responsible for informing Hopkins of the factors which caused her candidacy to be placed on hold, indicated that her "professional" problems would be solved if she would "walk more femininely, talk more femininely, wear make-up, have her hair styled, and wear jewelry." As the Court of Appeals characterized it, Ann Hopkins proved that Price Waterhouse "permitt[ed] stereotypical attitudes towards women to play a significant, though unquantifiable, role in its decision not to invite her to become a partner."

At this point Ann Hopkins had taken her proof as far as it could go. She had proved discriminatory input into the decisional process, and had proved that participants in the process considered her failure to conform to the stereotypes credited by a number of the decisionmakers had been a substantial factor in the decision. It is as if Ann Hopkins were sitting in the hall outside the room where partnership decisions were being made. As the partners filed in to consider her candidacy, she heard several of them make sexist remarks in discussing her suitability for partnership. As the decisionmakers exited the room, she was *told* by one of those privy to the decisionmaking process that her gender was a major reason for the rejection of her partnership bid. If, as we noted in *Teamsters*, "[p]resumptions shifting the burden of proof are often created to reflect judicial evaluations of probabilities and to conform with a party's superior access to the proof," one would be hard pressed to think of a situation where it would be more appropriate to require the defendant to show that its decision would have been justified by wholly legitimate concerns.

Moreover, there is mounting evidence in the decisions of the lower courts that respondent here is not alone in her inability to pinpoint discrimination as the precise cause of her injury, despite having shown that it played a significant role in the decisional process. Many of these courts, which deal with the evidentiary issues in Title VII cases on a regular basis, have concluded that placing the risk of nonpersuasion on the defendant in a situation where uncertainty as to causation has been created by its consideration of an illegitimate criterion makes sense as a rule of evidence and furthers the substantive command of Title VII. See, e.g., Bell v. Birmingham Linen Service, 715 F.2d 1552, 1556 (CA11 1983) (Tjoflat, J.) ("It would be illogical, indeed ironic, to hold a Title VII plaintiff presenting direct evidence of a defendant's intent to discriminate to a more stringent burden of proof, or to allow a defendant to meet that direct proof by merely articulating, but not proving, legitimate, nondiscriminatory reasons for its action"). Particularly in the context of the professional world, where decisions are often made by collegial bodies on the basis of largely subjective criteria, requiring the plaintiff to prove that *any* one factor was the definitive cause of the decisionmakers' action may be tantamount to declaring Title VII inapplicable to such decisions. See, e.g., Fields v. Clark University, 817 F.2d 931, 935–937 (CA1 1987) (where plaintiff produced "strong evidence" that sexist attitudes infected faculty tenure decision burden properly shifted to defendant to show that it would have reached the same decision absent discrimination); Thompkins v. Morris Brown College, 752 F.2d 558, 563 (CA11 1985) (direct evidence of discriminatory animus in decision to discharge college professor shifted burden of persuasion to defendant).

Finally, I am convinced that a rule shifting the burden to the defendant where the plaintiff has shown that an illegitimate criterion was a "substantial factor" in the employment decision will not conflict with other congressional policies embodied in Title VII. Title VII expressly provides that an employer need not give preferential treatment to employees or applicants of any race, color, religion, sex, or national origin in order to maintain a work force in balance with the general population. The interpretive memorandum, whose authoritative force is noted by the plurality, specifically provides: "There is no requirement in title VII that an employer maintain a racial balance in his work force. On the contrary, any deliberate attempt to maintain a racial balance, whatever such a balance may be, would involve a violation of title VII because maintaining such a balance would require an employer to hire or refuse to hire on the basis of race." 110 Conger. 7213 (1964).

Last Term, in Watson v. Fort Worth Bank & Trust, the Court unanimously concluded that the disparate impact analysis first enunciated in Griggs v. Duke Power Co., should be extended to subjective or discretionary selection processes. At the same time a plurality of the Court indicated concern that the focus on bare statistics in the disparate impact setting could force employers to adopt "inappropriate prophylactic measures" in violation of § 2000e–2(j). The plurality went on to emphasize that in a disparate impact case, the plaintiff may not simply point to a statistical disparity in the employer's work force. Instead, the plaintiff must identify a particular employment practice and "must offer statistical evidence of a kind and degree sufficient to show that the practice in question has caused the exclusion of applicants for jobs or promotions because of their membership in a protected group." The plurality indicated that "the ultimate burden of proving that discrimination against a protected group has been caused by a specific employment practice remains with the plaintiff at all times."

I believe there are significant differences between shifting the burden of persuasion to the employer in a case resting purely on statistical proof as in the disparate impact setting and shifting the burden of persuasion in a case like this one, where an employee has demonstrated by direct evidence that an illegitimate factor played a substantial role in a particular employment decision. First, the explicit consideration of race, color, religion, sex, or national origin in making employment decisions "was the most obvious evil Congress had in mind when it enacted Title VII." While the prima facie case under *McDonnell Douglas* and the statistical showing of imbalance involved in an impact case may both be indicators of discrimination or its "functional equivalent," they are not, in and of themselves, the evils Congress sought to eradicate from the employment setting. Second, shifting the burden of persuasion to the employer in a situation like this one creates no incentive to preferential treatment in violation of § 2000e–(2)(j). To avoid bearing the burden of justifying its decision, the employer need not seek racial or sexual balance in its work force; rather, all it need do is avoid substantial reliance on forbidden criteria in making its employment decisions.

While the danger of forcing employers to engage in unwarranted preferential treatment is thus less dramatic in this setting than in the situation the Court faced in *Watson,* it is far from wholly illusory. Based on its misreading of the words "because of" in the statute, the plurality appears to conclude that if a decisional process is "tainted" by awareness of sex or race in any way, the employer has violated the statute, and Title VII thus *commands* that the burden shift to the employer to justify its decision. The plurality thus effectively reads the causation requirement out of the statute, and then replaces it with an "affirmative defense."

In my view, in order to justify shifting the burden on the issue of causation to the defendant, a disparate treatment plaintiff must show by direct evidence that an illegitimate criterion was a substantial factor in the decision. As the Court of Appeals noted below, "[w]hile most circuits have not confronted the question squarely, the consensus among those that have is that once a Title VII plaintiff has demonstrated by direct evidence that discriminatory animus played a significant or substantial role in the employment decision, the burden shifts to the employer to show that the decision would have been the same absent discrimination." Requiring that the plaintiff demonstrate that an illegitimate factor played a substantial role in the employment decision identifies those employment situations where the deterrent purpose of Title VII is most clearly implicated. As an evidentiary matter, where a plaintiff has made this type of strong showing of illicit motivation, the factfinder is entitled to presume that the employer's discriminatory animus made a difference to the outcome, absent proof to the contrary from the employer. Where a disparate treatment plaintiff has made such a showing, the burden then rests with the employer to convince the trier of fact that it is more likely than not that the decision would have been the same absent consideration of the illegitimate factor. The employer need not isolate the sole cause for the decision, rather it must demonstrate that with the illegitimate factor removed from the calculus, sufficient business reasons would have induced it to take the same employment action. This evidentiary scheme essentially requires the employer to place the employee in the same position he or she would have occupied absent discrimination. Cf. Mt. Healthy Board of Education v. Doyle. If the employer fails to carry this burden, the factfinder is justified in concluding that the decision was made "because of" consideration of the illegitimate factor and the substantive standard for liability under the statute is satisfied.

Thus, stray remarks in the workplace, while perhaps probative of sexual harassment, see Meritor Savings Bank v. Vinson, cannot justify requiring the employer to prove that its hiring or promotion decisions were based on legitimate criteria. Nor can statements by nondecisionmakers, or statements by decisionmakers unrelated to the decisional process itself suffice to satisfy the plaintiff's burden in this regard. In addition, in my view testimony such as Dr. Fiske's in this case, standing alone, would not justify shifting the burden of persuasion to the employer. Race and gender always "play a role" in an employment decision in the benign sense that these are human characteristics of which decisionmakers are aware and may comment on in a perfectly neutral and nondiscriminatory fashion. For example, in the context of this case, a mere reference to "a lady candidate" might show that gender "played a role" in the decision, but by no means could support a rational factfinder's inference that the decision was made "because of" sex. What is required is what Ann Hopkins showed here: direct evidence that decisionmakers placed substantial negative reliance on an illegitimate criterion in reaching their decision.

It should be obvious that the threshold standard I would adopt for shifting the burden of persuasion to the defendant differs substantially from that proposed by the plurality, the plurality's suggestion to the contrary notwithstanding. The plurality proceeds from the premise that the words "because of" in the statute do not embody any causal requirement at all. Under my approach, the plaintiff must produce evidence sufficient to show that an illegitimate criterion was a substantial factor in the particular employment decision such that a reasonable factfinder could draw an inference that the decision was made "because of" the plaintiff's protected status. Only then would the burden of proof shift to the defendant to prove that the decision would have been justified by other, wholly legitimate considerations.

In sum, because of the concerns outlined above, and because I believe that the deterrent purpose of Title VII is disserved by a rule which places the burden of proof on plaintiffs on the issue of causation in all circumstances, I would retain but supplement the framework we established in *McDonnell Douglas* and subsequent cases. The structure of the presentation of evidence in an individual treatment case should conform to the general outlines we established in *McDonnell Douglas* and *Burdine*. First, the plaintiff must establish the *McDonnell Douglas* prima facie case by showing membership in a protected group, qualification for the job, rejection for the position, and that after rejection the employer continued to seek applicants of complainant's general qualifications. The plaintiff should also present any direct evidence of discriminatory animus in the decisional process. The defendant should then present its case, including its evidence as to legitimate, nondiscriminatory reasons for the employment decision. As the dissent notes, under this framework, the employer "has every incentive to convince the trier of fact that the decision was lawful." Once all the evidence has been received, the court should determine whether the *McDonnell Douglas* or *Price Waterhouse* framework properly applies to the evidence before it. If the plaintiff has failed to satisfy the *Price Waterhouse* threshold, the case should be decided under the principles enunciated in *McDonnell Douglas* and *Burdine,* with the plaintiff bearing the burden of persuasion on the ultimate issue whether the employment action was taken because of discrimination. In my view, such a system is both fair and workable and it calibrates the evidentiary requirements demanded of the parties to the goals behind the statute itself.

I agree with the dissent, that the evidentiary framework I propose should be available to all disparate treatment plaintiffs where an illegitimate consideration played a substantial role in an adverse employment decision. The Court's allocation of the burden of proof in Johnson v. Transportation Agency, 480 U.S. 616, 626–627, 107 S.Ct. 1442, 1449, 94 L.Ed.2d 615 (1987), rested squarely on "the analytical framework set forth in *McDonnell Douglas,*" which we alter today. It would be odd to say the least if the evidentiary rules applicable to Title VII actions were themselves dependent on the gender or the skin color of the litigants.

In this case, I agree with the plurality that petitioner should be called upon to show that the outcome would have been the same if respondent's professional merit had been its only concern. On remand, the District Court should determine whether Price Waterhouse has shown by a preponderance of the evidence that if gender had not been part of the process, its employment decision concerning Ann Hopkins would nonetheless have been the same.

JUSTICE KENNEDY, with whom THE CHIEF JUSTICE and JUSTICE SCALIA join, dissenting.

Today the Court manipulates existing and complex rules for employment discrimination cases in a way certain to result in confusion. Continued adherence to the evidentiary scheme established in *McDonnell Douglas* and *Burdine* is a wiser course than creation of more disarray in an area of the law already difficult for the bench and bar, and so I must dissent.

Before turning to my reasons for disagreement with the Court's disposition of the case, it is important to review the actual holding of today's decision. I read the opinions as establishing that in a limited number of cases Title VII plaintiffs, by presenting direct and substantial evidence of discriminatory animus, may shift the burden of persuasion to the defendant to show that an adverse employment decision would have been supported by legitimate reasons. The shift in the burden of persuasion occurs only where a plaintiff proves by direct evidence that an unlawful motive was a substantial factor actually relied upon in making the decision. * * * As the opinions make plain, the evidentiary scheme created today is not for every case in which a plaintiff produces evidence of stray remarks in the workplace.

Where the plaintiff makes the requisite showing, the burden that shifts to the employer is to show that legitimate employment considerations would have justified the decision without reference to any impermissible motive. The employer's proof on the point is to be presented and reviewed just as with any other evidentiary question: the Court does not accept the plurality's suggestion that an employer's evidence need be "objective" or otherwise out of the ordinary.

In sum, the Court alters the evidentiary framework of *McDonnell Douglas* and *Burdine* for a closely defined set of cases. Although Justice O'Connor advances some thoughtful arguments for this change, I remain convinced that it is unnecessary and unwise. More troubling is the plurality's rationale for today's decision, which includes a number of unfortunate pronouncements on both causation and methods of proof in employment discrimination cases. To demonstrate the defects in the plurality's reasoning, it is necessary to discuss first, the standard of causation in Title VII cases, and second, the burden of proof.

I

The plurality describes this as a case about the standard of *causation* under Title VII, but I respectfully suggest that the description is misleading. Much of the plurality's rhetoric is spent denouncing a "but-for" standard of causation. The theory of Title VII liability the plurality adopts, however, essentially incorporates the but-for standard.

The importance of today's decision is not the standard of causation it employs, but its shift to the defendant of the burden of proof. The plurality's causation analysis is misdirected, for it is clear that, whoever bears the burden of proof on the issue, Title VII liability requires a finding of but-for causation.

The words of Title VII are not obscure. The part of the statute relevant to this case provides that:

> "It shall be an unlawful employment practice for an employer—

> "(1) to fail or refuse to hire or to discharge any individual, or otherwise to discriminate against any individual with respect to his compensation, terms, conditions, or privileges of employment, *because of* such individual's race, color, religion, sex, or national origin." 42 U.S.C. § 2000e–2(a)(1) (emphasis added).

By any normal understanding, the phrase "because of" conveys the idea that the motive in question made a difference to the outcome. We use the words this way in everyday speech. And assuming, as the plurality does, that we ought to consider the interpretive memorandum prepared by the statute's drafters, we find that this is what the words meant to them as well. "To discriminate is to make a distinction, to make a difference in treatment or favor." 110 Conger. 7213 (1964). Congress could not have chosen a clearer way to indicate that proof of liability under Title VII requires a showing that race, color, religion, sex, or national origin caused the decision at issue.

* * *

What we term "but-for" cause is the least rigorous standard that is consistent with the approach to causation our precedents describe. If a motive is not a but-for cause of an event, then by definition it did not make a difference to the outcome. The event would have occurred just the same without it. Common law approaches to causation often require proof of but-for cause as a starting point toward proof of legal cause. The law may require more than but-for cause, for instance proximate cause, before imposing liability. Any standard less than but-for, however, simply represents a decision to impose liability without causation. As Dean Prosser puts it, "[a]n act or omission is not regarded as a cause of an event if the particular event would have occurred without it." W. Keeton, D. Dobbs, R. Keeton, & D. Owen, Prosser and Keeton on Law of Torts 265 (5th ed. 1984).

One of the principal reasons the plurality decision may sow confusion is that it claims Title VII liability is unrelated to but-for causation, yet it adopts a but-for standard once it has placed the burden of proof as to causation upon the employer. This approach conflates the question whether causation must be shown with the question of how it is to be shown. Because the plurality's theory of Title VII causation is ultimately consistent with a but-for standard, it might be said that my disagreement with the plurality's comments on but-for cause is simply academic.

* * *

Labels aside, the import of today's decision is not that Title VII liability can arise without but-for causation, but that in certain cases it is not the plaintiff who must prove the presence of causation, but the defendant who must prove its absence.

II

We established the order of proof for individual Title VII disparate treatment cases in McDonnell Douglas Corp. v. Green, and reaffirmed this allocation in Texas Dept. of Community Affairs v. Burdine. Under *Burdine,* once the plaintiff presents a prima facie case, an inference of discrimination arises. The employer must rebut the inference by articulating a legitimate nondiscriminatory reason for its action. The final burden of persuasion, however, belongs to the plaintiff. *Burdine* makes clear that the "ultimate burden of persuading the trier of fact that the defendant intentionally discriminated against the plaintiff remains at all times with the plaintiff." [3] I would adhere to this established evidentiary framework, which provides the appropriate standard for this and other individual disparate treatment cases. Today's creation of a new set of rules for "mixed-motive" cases is not mandated by the statute itself. The Court's attempt at refinement provides limited practical benefits at the cost of confusion and complexity, with the attendant risk that the trier of fact will misapprehend the controlling legal principles and reach an incorrect decision.

In view of the plurality's treatment of *Burdine* and our other disparate treatment cases, it is important first to state why those cases are dispositive here. The plurality tries to reconcile its approach with *Burdine* by announcing that it applies only to a "pretext" case, which it defines as a case in which the plaintiff attempts to prove that the employer's proffered explanation is itself false. This ignores the language of *Burdine,* which states that a plaintiff may succeed in meeting her ultimate burden of persuasion "*either* directly by persuading the court that a discriminatory reason more likely motivated the employer or indirectly by showing that the employer's proffered explanation is unworthy of credence." Under the first of these two alternative methods, a plaintiff meets her burden if she can "persuade the court that the employment decision more likely than not was motivated by a discriminatory reason." USPS Board of Governors v. Aikens, 460 U.S. 711, 717–718, 103 S.Ct. 1478, 1483, 75 L.Ed.2d 403 (1983) (Blackmun, J.,

---

3. The interpretive memorandum on which the plurality relies makes plain that "the plaintiff, as in any civil case, would have the burden of proving that discrimination had occurred." 110 Conger. 7214 (1964). Coupled with its earlier definition of discrimination, the memorandum tells us that the plaintiff bears the burden of showing that an impermissible motive "made a difference" in the treatment of the plaintiff. This is none other than the traditional requirement that the plaintiff show but-for cause.

concurring). The plurality makes no attempt to address this aspect of our cases.

Our opinions make plain that *Burdine* applies to all individual disparate treatment cases, whether the plaintiff offers direct proof that discrimination motivated the employer's actions or chooses the indirect method of showing that the employer's proffered justification is false, that is to say, a pretext. See *Aikens*, ("As in any lawsuit, the plaintiff may prove his case by direct or circumstantial evidence"). The plurality is mistaken in suggesting that the plaintiff in a so-called "mixed motives" case will be disadvantaged by having to "squeeze her proof into *Burdine's* framework." As we acknowledged in *McDonnell Douglas,* "[t]he facts necessarily will vary in Title VII cases," and the specification of the prima facie case set forth there "is not necessarily applicable in every respect to differing factual situations." The framework was "never intended to be rigid, mechanized, or ritualistic." *Aikens*, 460 U.S., at 715, 103 S.Ct., at 1482. *Burdine* compels the employer to come forward with its explanation of the decision and permits the plaintiff to offer evidence under either of the logical methods for proof of discrimination. This is hardly a framework that confines the plaintiff; still less is it a justification for saying that the ultimate burden of proof must be on the employer in a mixed motives case. *Burdine* provides an orderly and adequate way to place both inferential and direct proof before the factfinder for a determination whether intentional discrimination has caused the employment decision. Regardless of the character of the evidence presented, we have consistently held that the ultimate burden "remains at all times with the plaintiff." *Burdine*, 450 U.S., at 253, 101 S.Ct., at 1093.

Aikens illustrates the point. There, the evidence showed that the plaintiff, a black man, was far more qualified than any of the white applicants promoted ahead of him. More important, the testimony showed that "the person responsible for the promotion decisions at issue had made numerous derogatory comments about blacks in general and Aikens in particular." Yet the Court in *Aikens* reiterated that the case was to be tried under the proof scheme of *Burdine*. Justice Brennan and Justice Blackmun concurred to stress that the plaintiff could prevail under the *Burdine* scheme in either of two ways, one of which was directly to persuade the court that the employment decision was motivated by discrimination. *Aikens* leaves no doubt that the so-called "pretext" framework of *Burdine* has been considered to provide a flexible means of addressing all individual disparate treatment claims.

* * *

In contrast to the plurality, Justice O'Connor acknowledges that the approach adopted today is a "departure from the *McDonnell Douglas* standard." Although her reasons for supporting this departure are not without force, they are not dispositive. As Justice O'Connor states, the most that can be said with respect to the Title VII itself is that "nothing in the language, history, or purpose of Title VII *prohibits* adoption" of the new approach. Justice O'Connor also relies on analogies from the common law of torts, other types of Title VII litigation, and our equal protection cases. These analogies demonstrate that shifts in the burden of proof are not unprecedented in the law of torts or employment discrimination. Nonetheless, I believe continued adherence to the *Burdine* framework is more consistent with the statutory mandate. Congress' manifest concern with preventing imposition of liability in cases where discriminatory animus did not actually cause an adverse action, (opinion of O'Connor, J.), suggests to me that an affirmative showing of causation should be required. And the most relevant portion of the legislative history supports just this view. The limited benefits that are likely to be produced by today's innovation come at the sacrifice of clarity and practical application.

The potential benefits of the new approach, in my view, are overstated. First, the Court makes clear that the *Price Waterhouse* scheme is applicable only in those cases where the plaintiff has produced direct and substantial proof that an impermissible motive was relied upon in making the decision at issue. The burden shift properly will be found to apply in only a limited number of employment discrimination cases. The application of the new scheme, furthermore, will make a difference only in a smaller subset of cases. The practical importance of the burden of proof is the "risk of nonpersuasion," and the new system will make a difference only where the evidence is so evenly balanced that the factfinder cannot say that either side's explanation of the case is "more likely" true. This category will not include cases in which the allocation of the burden of proof will be dispositive because of a complete lack of evidence on the causation issue, cf. Summers v. Tice, 33 Cal.2d 80, 199 P.2d 1 (1948) (allocation of burden dispositive because no evidence of which of two negligently fired shots hit plaintiff). Rather, *Price Waterhouse* will apply only to cases in which there is substantial evidence of reliance on an impermissible motive, as well as evidence from the employer that legitimate reasons supported its action.

Although the *Price Waterhouse* system is not for every case, almost every plaintiff is certain to ask for a *Price Waterhouse* instruction, perhaps on the basis of "stray remarks" or other evidence of discriminatory animus. Trial and appellate courts will therefore be saddled with the task of developing standards for determining when to apply the burden shift. One of their new tasks will be the generation of a jurisprudence of the meaning of "substantial factor." Courts will also be required to make the often subtle and difficult distinction between "direct" and "indirect" or "circumstantial" evidence. Lower courts long have had difficulty applying *McDonnell Douglas* and *Burdine.* Addition of a second burden-shifting mechanism, the application of which itself depends on assessment of credibility and a determination whether evidence is sufficiently direct and substantial, is not likely to lend clarity to the process. * * *

Confusion in the application of dual burden-shifting mechanisms will be most acute in cases brought under § 1981 or the Age Discrimination in Employment Act (ADEA), where courts borrow the Title VII order of proof for the conduct of jury trials. See, e.g., Note, The Age Discrimination in Employment Act of 1967 and Trial by Jury: Proposals for Change, 73 Va.L.Rev. 601 (1987) (noting high reversal rate caused by use of Title VII burden shifting in a jury setting). Perhaps such cases in the future will require a bifurcated trial, with the jury retiring first to make the credibility findings necessary to determine whether the plaintiff has proved that an impermissible factor played a substantial part in the decision, and later hearing evidence on the "same decision" or "pretext" issues. Alternatively, perhaps the trial judge will have the unenviable task of formulating a single instruction for the jury on all of the various burdens potentially involved in the case.

I do not believe the minor refinement in Title VII procedures accomplished by today's holding can justify the difficulties that will accompany it. Rather, I "remain confident that the *McDonnell Douglas* framework permits the plaintiff meriting relief to demonstrate intentional discrimination." Although the employer does not bear the burden of persuasion under *Burdine*, it must offer clear and reasonably specific reasons for the contested decision, and has every incentive to persuade the trier of fact that the decision was lawful. Further, the suggestion that the employer should bear the burden of persuasion due to superior access to evidence has little force in the Title VII context, where the liberal discovery rules available to all litigants are supplemented by EEOC investigatory files. In sum, the *Burdine* framework provides a "sensible, orderly way to evaluate the evidence in light of common experience as it bears on the critical question of discrimination," *Aikens,* and it should continue to govern the order of proof in Title VII disparate treatment cases.[4]

III

The ultimate question in every individual disparate treatment case is whether discrimination caused the particular decision at issue. Some of the plurality's comments with respect to the District Court's

---

4. The plurality states that it disregards the special context of affirmative action. It is not clear that this is possible. Some courts have held that in a suit challenging an affirmative action plan, the question of the plan's validity need not be reached unless the plaintiff shows that the plan was a but-for cause of the adverse decision. See McQuillen v. Wisconsin Education Association Council, 830 F.2d 659, 665 (CA7 1987), cert. denied, 485 U.S. 914, 108 S.Ct. 1068, 99 L.Ed.2d 248 (1988). Presumably it will be easier for a plaintiff to show that consideration of race or sex pursuant to an affirmative action plan was a substantial factor in a decision, and the court will need to move on to the question of a plan's validity. Moreover, if the structure of the burdens of proof in Title VII suits is to be consistent, as might be expected given the identical statutory language involved, today's decision suggests that plaintiffs should no longer bear the burden of showing that affirmative action plans are illegal. See Johnson v. Transportation Agency, 480 U.S. 616, 626–627, 107 S.Ct. 1442, 1449, 94 L.Ed.2d 615 (1987).

findings in this case, however, are potentially misleading. As the plurality notes, the District Court based its liability determination on expert evidence that some evaluations of respondent Hopkins were based on unconscious sex stereotypes,[5] and on the fact that Price Waterhouse failed to disclaim reliance on these comments when it conducted the partnership review. The District Court also based liability on Price Waterhouse's failure to "make partners sensitive to the dangers [of stereotyping], to discourage comments tainted by sexism, or to investigate comments to determine whether they were influenced by stereotypes."

Although the District Court's version of Title VII liability is improper under any of today's opinions, I think it important to stress that Title VII creates no independent cause of action for sex stereotyping. Evidence of use by decision-makers of sex stereotypes is, of course, quite relevant to the question of discriminatory intent. The ultimate question, however, is whether discrimination caused the plaintiff's harm. Our cases do not support the suggestion that failure to "disclaim reliance" on stereotypical comments itself violates Title VII. Neither do they support creation of a "duty to sensitize." As the dissenting judge in the Court of Appeals observed, acceptance of such theories would turn Title VII "from a prohibition of discriminatory conduct into an engine for rooting out sexist thoughts." 825 F.2d 458, 477 (1987) (Williams, J., dissenting).

Employment discrimination claims require factfinders to make difficult and sensitive decisions. Sometimes this may mean that no finding of discrimination is justified even though a qualified employee is passed over by a less than admirable employer. In other cases, Title VII's protections properly extend to plaintiffs who are by no means model employees. As Justice Brennan notes, courts do not sit to determine whether litigants are nice. In this case, Hopkins plainly presented a strong case both of her own professional qualifications and of the presence of discrimination in Price Waterhouse's partnership process. Had the District Court found on this record that sex discrimination caused the adverse decision, I doubt it would have been reversible error. That decision was for the finder of fact, however, and the District Court made plain that sex discrimination was not a but-for cause of the decision to place Hopkin's partnership candidacy on hold.

---

5. The plaintiff who engages the services of Dr. Susan Fiske should have no trouble showing that sex discrimination played a part in any decision. Price Waterhouse chose not to object to Fiske's testimony, and at this late stage we are constrained to accept it, but I think the plurality's enthusiasm for Fiske's conclusions unwarranted. Fiske purported to discern stereotyping in comments that were gender neutral—e.g., "overbearing and abrasive"—without any knowledge of the comments' basis in reality and without having met the speaker or subject. "To an expert of Dr. Fiske's qualifications, it seems plain that no woman could *be* overbearing, arrogant, or abrasive: any observations to that effect would necessarily be discounted as the product of stereotyping. If analysis like this is to prevail in federal courts, no employer can base any adverse action as to a woman on such attributes." 825 F.2d 458, 477 (1987) (Williams, J., dissenting). Today's opinions cannot be read as requiring factfinders to credit testimony based on this type of analysis (opinion of O'Connor, J.).

Attempts to evade tough decisions by erecting novel theories of liability or multitiered systems of shifting burdens are misguided.

IV

The language of Title VII and our well-considered precedents require this plaintiff to establish that the decision to place her candidacy on hold was made "because of" sex. Here the District Court found that the "comments of the individual partners and the expert evidence of Dr. Fiske do not prove an intentional discriminatory motive or purpose," and that "[b]ecause plaintiff has considerable problems dealing with staff and peers, the Court cannot say that she would have been elected to partnership if the Policy Board's decision had not been tainted by sexually based evaluations." Hopkins thus failed to meet the requisite standard of proof after a full trial. I would remand the case for entry of judgment in favor of Price Waterhouse.

NOTES AND PROBLEMS FOR DISCUSSION

1. What exactly are the points of difference between Justice Brennan's plurality opinion and the concurring opinions of Justices White and O'Connor? Although Justice Brennan foreswears deciding what kind of evidence of discriminatory motivation "standing alone" would or would not shift the burden on causation to the employer, he suggests that all of the evidence presented by Ms. Hopkins—direct, circumstantial and expert opinion—was properly considered by the district court in deciding that sex was a "motivating factor" in the denial of partnership. Does Justice O'Connor agree? Is there disagreement as to the kind of evidence that will satisfy the employer's burden once it has shifted? Compare Justice Brennan's statement that "in most cases" the employer should present "objective" evidence as to its probable decision in the absence of an impermissible motive with Justice White's view that the employer's credible testimony alone "should be ample proof." Is there any practical significance to the dispute between the plurality and Justice O'Connor over the meaning of the "because of" language in Section 703?

2. In a plurality decision where no single rationale explaining the decision is adopted by five Justices, "the holding of the Court may be viewed as that position taken by those Members who concurred in the judgments on the narrowest grounds * * * ." Marks v. United States, 430 U.S. 188, 193, 97 S.Ct. 990, 993, 51 L.Ed.2d 260, 266 (1977) (quoting Gregg v. Georgia, 428 U.S. 153, 169 n.15, 96 S.Ct. 2909, 2923 n.15, 49 L.Ed.2d 859 (1976)). The "narrowest ground" has been variously defined as the one that departs least from the status quo and as the one applicable to the fewest number of cases. See, Note, The Precedential Value of Supreme Court Plurality Decisions, 80 Colum.L.Rev. 756, 763–64 (1980). What is the "narrowest ground" of *Price Waterhouse?*

3. Justice O'Connor argues that "mixed motive analysis" (and thus a shift in the burden of persuasion) is justified only where the plaintiff proves by "direct evidence that an illegitimate criterion was a substantial factor in the [employer's] decision." Before the decision in *Price Waterhouse* a number of circuits had adopted a "direct evidence" modification of the *McDonnell Douglas–Burdine* framework. That rule was first articulated by the Eleventh Circuit in Lee v. Russell County Board of Education, 684 F.2d 769, 774 (11th Cir.1982) and in Bell v. Birmingham Linen Service, 715 F.2d 1552, 1557 (11th

Cir.1983), cert. denied, 467 U.S. 1204, 104 S.Ct. 2385, 81 L.Ed.2d 344 (1984) (*McDonnell Douglas–Burdine* was "not intended to be a Procrustean bed within which all disparate treatment cases must be forced to lie."). Under the "direct evidence" doctrine, however, burden shifting occurred as a result of the presentation of credible direct evidence of discrimination, not as in *Price Waterhouse* from a finding by the trial judge of mixed motivation based on such evidence. See, Hill v. Metropolitan Atlanta Rapid Transit Authority, 841 F.2d 1533, 1539 (11th Cir.), modified on other grounds, 848 F.2d 1522 (11th Cir.1988) (presentation of credible direct evidence shifts burden of persuasion to employer to prove by a preponderance of the evidence that it would have made the same decision in absence of the discriminatory factor); Terbovitz v. Fiscal Court of Adair County, 825 F.2d 111, 115 (6th Cir.1987) (direct evidence of discrimination, if credited by the fact finder, removes the case from *McDonnell Douglas* because the plaintiff no longer needs the inference of discrimination that arises from the prima facie case). It is not clear whether this version of the "direct evidence doctrine" survives *Price Waterhouse*. Several Circuits, relying in part on Justice O'Connor's concurrence and in part on prior "direct evidence" jurisprudence have concluded that *Price Waterhouse* burden shifting is applicable only where the plaintiff has presented direct evidence. See, Lynch v. Belden & Co., 882 F.2d 262, 269 n.6 (7th Cir.1989), cert. denied, 493 U.S. 1080, 110 S.Ct. 1134, 107 L.Ed.2d 1040 (1990) ("absence of direct evidence ... makes inapplicable the Supreme Court's recent holding in *Price Waterhouse* "); Rossy v. Roche Products, Inc., 880 F.2d 621 (1st Cir.1989) (lack of direct evidence makes appropriate framework of *McDonnell Douglas*). Other circuits, on the basis of the plurality opinion, have suggested that "mixed motive" analysis is not dependent on direct evidence. See, Waltman v. International Paper Co., 875 F.2d 468, 481 (5th Cir.1989); Fragante v. Honolulu, 888 F.2d 591, 598 (9th Cir.1989), cert. denied 494 U.S. 1081, 110 S.Ct. 1811, 108 L.Ed.2d 942 (1990). Does Justice O'Connor's bright-line distinction between the burden-shifting effect of "direct evidence" of discrimination and other evidence which may convince the trier-of-fact that unlawful motivation was at work make sense? Why should not the burden shift once the district judge is convinced by any evidence in the case that unlawful discrimination was a motivating factor? Is it important that *Mount Healthy City School District Board of Education v. Doyle*, 429 U.S. 274, 97 S.Ct. 568, 50 L.Ed.2d 471 (1977), the First Amendment decision relied on by both the plurality Justices and Justice White, did not require direct evidence of unlawful motivation for burden shifting to occur? See, *North Mississippi Communications, Inc. v. Jones*, 874 F.2d 1064, 1069 (5th Cir.1989).

4. *Price Waterhouse* makes it important to define "direct evidence." In Jackson v. Harvard University, 900 F.2d 464 (1st Cir.), cert. denied, ___ U.S. ___, 111 S.Ct. 137, 112 L.Ed.2d 104 (1990) the plaintiff, a female professor who was denied tenure by the Harvard Business School, contended that her case fit within the *Price Waterhouse* framework because of a disparaging comment by the dean of the school concerning affirmative action and evidence that she was treated differently than a male candidate regarding the selection of the tenure review committee. The Court of Appeals refused to accept that either element of the plaintiff's proof constituted "direct evidence." That label was reserved for "evidence which, in and of itself, shows discriminatory animus." 900 F.2d at 467. What kind of evidence is that? Once direct evidence of discriminatory motivation is introduced by the plaintiff, what more must be established in order to shift the causation burden to the defendant? In Bruno v. City of

Crown Point, 950 F.2d 355 (7th Cir.1991), cert. denied, ___ U.S. ___, 112 S.Ct. 2998, 120 L.Ed.2d 874 (1992) a female applicant for a paramedic position was rejected in favor of a less experienced male applicant. Part of the plaintiff's proof at trial was that, of the seven applicants who were interviewed, only she was asked questions concerning her husband's attitude toward her work, her child care arrangements and whether it was "time to have more children." A jury found for plaintiff and awarded damages and the trial judge granted injunctive relief pursuant to Title VII. The Court of Appeals concluded that the questions asked plaintiff were based on sex-stereotypes, but went on to reverse the jury verdict on the ground plaintiff had failed to prove that gender played a part in the decision not to hire her. The court reasoned that it was not enough for plaintiff to prove that sex-stereotyped questions were asked during the selection process: the plaintiff must offer substantial evidence that the employer "relied" on the questions in making the hiring decision. The employer testified that he was satisfied with the plaintiff's answers to the questions and explained that he hired the male applicant because he had *less* experience than the other candidate, and could be "molded in the Crown Point way of doing things." According to the Court of Appeals, the plaintiff had not proved that the employer had relied on sex stereotypes and thus reversed. Did the Seventh Circuit misread *Price Waterhouse*? Does *Bruno* blur the distinction between mixed-motive and ordinary disparate treatment cases?

5. The plurality argues that its decision does not alter the *McDonnell Douglas–Burdine* model of proof for disparate treatment cases. But in a typical case where the plaintiff offers credible evidence that an illegal motivation played some role in the challenged decision and the employer offers credible evidence (beyond merely an "articulation") that its decision was based solely on legitimate factors, does *McDonnell Douglas–Burdine* have any applicability? For example, if the plaintiff in *Benzies v. Illinois Dept. of Mental Health,* supra, at, had argued that the denial of supervisory assignments was discriminatory, should the traditional disparate treatment model play any role in the district judge's analysis?

6. On remand from the Supreme Court's decision in *Price Waterhouse*, the district court held that the firm had failed to show by a preponderance of the evidence that it would have denied Ms. Hopkins' partnership even in the absence of sexually biased evaluations. The court ordered that the firm make Ms. Hopkins a partner effective July 1, 1990 and awarded back pay. The Court of Appeals affirmed. Hopkins v. Price Waterhouse, 737 F.Supp. 1202 (D.D.C.), affirmed, 920 F.2d 967 (D.C.Cir.1990). The relief aspects of the decision are discussed *infra* in Chapter 13.

7. One issue in *Price Waterhouse* on which all the Justices agreed was the relationship between the causation determination and liability under Title VII: if the employer satisfies its burden of proving that it would have made the same decision absent discriminatory motivation, there is no Title VII liability. In the Fall of 1991 Congress enacted and the President signed the Civil Rights Act of 1991, Pub.L. 102–166, 105 Stat. 1071 (1991) which was intended in part to reverse *Price Waterhouse*. Section 107 of the that Act amends Section 703 of Title VII (Unlawful Employment Practices) by adding the following subsection:

(m) Except as otherwise provided in this title, an unlawful employment practice is established when the complaining party demonstrates that race, color, religion, sex, or national origin was a motivating factor for any employment practice, even though other factors also motivated the practice.

The 1991 Act thus defines an unlawful employment practice to include any employment practice which is influenced in any manner by an unlawful motivation. But as the Act expands the scope of Title VII liability, it also restricts the kind of relief available in mixed-motive cases. Section 706(g) of Title VII generally provides for a wide range of remedies against an employer guilty of unlawful employment practices including reinstatement, back pay, compensatory and punitive damages. See Chapter 7, *infra*. Section 107 of the 1991 Act adds to Section 706(g) the following new subparagraph:

(B) On a claim in which an individual proves a violation under section 703(m) and a respondent demonstrates that the respondent would have taken the same action in the absence of the impermissible motivating factor, the court—

(i) may grant declaratory relief, injunctive relief (except as provided in clause (ii), and attorney's fees and costs demonstrated to be directly attributable only to the pursuit of a claim under section 703(m); and

(ii) shall not award damages or issue an order requiring any admission, reinstatement, hiring, promotion, or payment, described in subparagraph [706(A)].

Under the 1991 Act if a plaintiff proves that her discharge was in part the result of an unlawful motivation but the employer establishes to the court's satisfaction that, even absent the unlawful motivation, it would have discharged her anyway, the plaintiff may still be awarded a declaratory judgment, an injunction and attorney fees. What kind of declaratory relief would be appropriate? Would such a declaration have any practical effect on the employer? What injunctive relief might be appropriate? Does the new statute mean that a plaintiff who is not entitled to reinstatement, back pay or damages, may nevertheless be awarded an injunction prohibiting the employer from allowing the unlawful motivation to affect *other* employees in the future? The relief available under Title VII is discussed in Chapter 7, *infra*.

FINDINGS OF FACT AND APPELLATE REVIEW

Rule 52(a) of the Federal Rules of Civil Procedure requires the district judge, in actions tried without a jury, to make separate findings of fact and conclusions of law in support of her judgment. The Rule further provides that "[f]indings of fact, whether based on oral or documentary evidence, shall not be set aside unless clearly erroneous, and due regard shall be given to the opportunity of the trial court to judge of the credibility of the witnesses." The Supreme Court has held that "a finding is 'clearly erroneous' when although there is evidence to support it, the reviewing court on the entire evidence is left with the definite and firm conviction that a mistake has been committed." United States v. United States Gypsum Co., 333 U.S. 364, 395, 68 S.Ct. 525, 542, 92 L.Ed. 746, 766 (1948). Inherent in the clearly erroneous standard is the rule that a court of appeal does not try issues of fact *de novo* and does not set aside district court findings merely because, on the record before it, the appellate court would have reached a different conclusion.

The application of Rule 52 to findings of fact in employment discrimination cases is illustrated by ANDERSON v. CITY OF BES-SEMER, 470 U.S. 564, 105 S.Ct. 1504, 84 L.Ed.2d 518 (1985). In *Anderson* the district court found that the plaintiff had been denied employment because of her sex and that the employer's explanation for preferring a male applicant was pretextual. Critical to the district court's determination were findings that the plaintiff was better qualified for the position than the male applicant who was given the job and that the plaintiff, but not the male applicants, was seriously questioned concerning her spouse's feelings about her working. The Fourth Circuit reversed on the ground that the district court's subsidiary factual findings were clearly erroneous. The Supreme Court in turn granted review and reversed.

With respect to the qualifications of the two candidates for the position, the Court noted that the district court's finding was based on essentially undisputed documentary evidence regarding the respective backgrounds of the applicants and the duties of the position in question. The Court of Appeals, reading the same record differed with the district court as to the most important duties of the job in question and concluded that the male applicant was better qualified. The Supreme Court held that the court of appeals had overstepped its authority under Rule 52.

> Based on our own reading of the record, we cannot say that either interpretation of the facts is illogical or implausible. Each has support in inferences that may be drawn from the facts in the record; and if either interpretation had been drawn by a district court on the record before us, we would not be inclined to find it clearly erroneous. The question we must answer, however, is not whether the Fourth Circuit's interpretation of the facts was clearly erroneous, but whether the District Court's finding was clearly erroneous. The District Court determined that petitioner was better qualified, and, as we have stated above, such a finding is entitled to deference notwithstanding that it is not based on credibility determinations. When the record is examined in light of the appropriately deferential standard, it is apparent that it contains nothing that mandates a finding that the District Court's conclusion was clearly erroneous.

470 U.S. at 577, 105 S.Ct. at 1513.

As to the district court's finding that male candidates were not seriously questioned about the feelings of their wives toward the job in question, an issue on which there was conflicting testimony, the Court held that the Court of Appeals had failed to give due regard to the ability of the district judge to resolve conflicts in the oral testimony of witnesses and to make credibility determinations. Since the testimony of the witnesses that the district chose to believe was not "implausible on its face" and was not "contradicted by any reliable extrinsic evidence" the trial court's decision to credit the witness was not clearly erroneous.   470 U.S. at 579, 105 S.Ct. at 1514.

The Court concluded:

> [W]e do not assert that our knowledge of what happened 10 years ago in Bessemer City is superior to that of the Court of Appeals; nor do we claim to have greater insight than the Court of Appeals into the state of mind of the men on the selection committee who rejected the petitioner for the position of Recreation Director. Even the trial judge who has heard the witnesses directly and who is more closely in touch than the appeals court with the milieu out of which the controversy before him arises, cannot always be confident that he "knows" what happened. Often, he can only determine whether the plaintiff has succeeded in presenting an account of the facts that is more likely to be true than not. Our task—and the task of appellate tribunals generally—is more limited still: we must determine whether the trial judge's conclusions are clearly erroneous. On the record before us, we cannot say that they are.

470 U.S. at 580–81, 105 S.Ct. at 1514–15.

Until the passage of the Civil Rights Act of 1991, Title VII provided only equitable remedies. Most Title VII cases were thus tried to a judge sitting without a jury. The 1991 Act added compensatory and punitive damages to the remedies available under Title VII and the Act specifies that either party in a Title VII action may demand a jury trial if damages are claimed by the plaintiff. If anything, appellate courts give even greater deference to findings of fact by juries than by judges. The Seventh Amendment provides in part that: "No fact tried to a jury, shall be otherwise reexamined in any Court of the United States, than according to the rules of the common law." The courts have developed a "reasonableness" test for review of jury verdicts. A verdict will not be set aside unless, on the record before the court, reasonable minds could not have reached the verdict rendered. The evidence must be considered in the light most favorable to party who obtained the verdict and the winning party is entitled to all reasonable inferences from the evidence. See, Anderson v. Liberty Lobby, Inc., 477 U.S. 242, 106 S.Ct. 2505, 91 L.Ed.2d 202 (1986). Childress & Davis, Federal Standards of Review, Sec. 3.02 (2d Ed. 1991).

The practical effect of these standards of appellate review is to place a heavy burden on a party who would challenge a district court's fact-finding whether the fact-finder is a judge or jury. Judge Easterbrook was not exaggerating when he referred to a district court's fact findings in Benzies v. Illinois Department of Mental Health, *supra*, at 125 as "all but conclusive." It is thus highly important whether determinations by a district court are classified as findings of fact, conclusions of law or mixed questions of fact and law. In PULLMAN–STANDARD v. SWINT, 456 U.S. 273, 102 S.Ct. 1781, 72 L.Ed.2d 66

(1982) the Court held the question of unlawful intent in a Title VII case to be a "pure question of fact, subject to rule 52's clearly erroneous standard [of review]." The Court declined to address the question of the applicability of Rule 52 to mixed questions of law and fact— "questions in which historical facts are admitted or established, the rule of law is undisputed, and the issue is whether the facts satisfy the statutory standard * * *," but noted that the circuits were divided on this question. 456 U.S. at 289 n. 19, 102 S.Ct. at 1790 n. 19. Is there any doubt that in a mixed motivation case the question of whether unlawful motivation played a role in the challenged employment decision and the question whether the employer would have taken the same action absent discriminatory motivation are "pure" questions of fact? If such questions are submitted to a jury, is it likely that a panel composed of lay persons will be able to treat the questions separately and find, for example, that the employer was unlawfully motivated but also find that it would have made the same decision absent the unlawful motivation? Rule 49(a) of the Federal Rules of Civil Procedure allows the court to "require a jury to return only a special verdict in the form of a special written finding upon each issue of fact." Why might such a special verdict be useful in an employment discrimination case?

In a case tried under the *McDonnell Douglas–Burdine* formula, the district judge will normally be called on at the end of the plaintiff's case to determine whether he has put on a prima facie case. Is that ruling a "pure question of fact," a question of law, or a mixture of the two? Compare, Stanfield v. Answering Service, Inc., 867 F.2d 1290, 1293 (11th Cir.1989) (whether prima facie case made out "is essentially a factual question") with Gay v. Waiters' and Dairy Lunchmen's Union, Local 30, 694 F.2d 531, 539 (9th Cir.1982) (finding of no prima facie case is to be freely reviewed). In light of the Supreme Court's ruling in UNITED STATES POSTAL SERVICE v. AIKENS, *supra* at 113, does it matter? See generally, Calleros, Title VII and Rule 52(c): Standards of Appellate Review in Disparate Treatment Cases—Limiting the Reach of Pullman–Standard v. Swint, 58 Tul.L.Rev. 403 (1983); Childress & Davis, Federal Standards of Review, Sec. 2.24 (2d Ed. 1991).

4. The Defendant's Case

(a) General Rebuttal

If the plaintiff fails to put on sufficient proof to establish a prima facie case, the appropriate defense response is a motion for involuntary dismissal under Rule 41(b) of the Federal Rules of Civil Procedure (in cases tried without a jury), for a judgement as a matter of law (formerly called a directed verdict) under Rule 50(a) (in a jury case), or their state court equivalents.[1]

---

1. Where the defendant can show through the use of affidavits or material obtained in discovery that the plaintiff will not be able to establish a prima facie case

If the plaintiff has made out a prima facie case under the *McDon-nell Douglas–Burdine* formula, the defendant must come forward with admissible evidence showing a legitimate, non-discriminatory reason for the employment decision complained of by the plaintiff. Although the employer does not have the burden of proving that it's motivation was legitimate, the employer typically will not rest on a mere "articulation" of a non-discriminatory reason, but will put on all available evidence tending to show that it did not intend to discriminate. The trial court (judge or jury) must then decide the ultimate issue—whether the employer's reason was a pretext for unlawful discrimination. See *Aikens, supra* at 113. In a case where the court decides that the employer had "mixed motives" for its action, the trial court must also decide whether the employer would have reached the same decision absent the discriminatory motivation. See, *Price Waterhouse, supra* at 129.

The above material describes the large run of individual disparate treatment cases: the employer's case is essentially a denial that Title VII has been violated because the employer had a legitimate (i.e. not prohibited by Title VII) reason for its action. In the mixed motive case, the employer has the alternative defense that any unlawful motivation did not cause the action complained of.

Title VII does contain one affirmative defense that allows an employer to intentionally discriminate without liability. That defense, the bona fide occupational qualification, is discussed below.

(b) The Bona Fide Occupational Qualification

INTERNATIONAL UNION, UNITED AUTOMOBILE, AEROSPACE AND AGRICULTURAL IMPLEMENT WORKERS OF AMERICA, UAW v. JOHNSON CONTROLS, INC.

Supreme Court of the United States, 1991.
___ U.S. ___, 111 S.Ct. 1196, 113 L.Ed.2d 158.

JUSTICE BLACKMUN delivered the opinion of the Court.

In this case we are concerned with an employer's gender-based fetal-protection policy. May an employer exclude a fertile female employee from certain jobs because of its concern for the health of the fetus the woman might conceive?

I

Respondent Johnson Controls, Inc., manufactures batteries. In the manufacturing process, the element lead is a primary ingredient. Occupational exposure to lead entails health risks, including the risk of harm to any fetus carried by a female employee.

at trial, the defendant will be entitled to   Proc. Rule 52(a) thus avoiding a trial.
summary judgement under Fed.Rule Civ.

Before the Civil Rights Act of 1964 became law, Johnson Controls did not employ any woman in a battery-manufacturing job. In June 1977, however, it announced its first official policy concerning its employment of women in lead-exposure work:

"Protection of the health of the unborn child is the immediate and direct responsibility of the prospective parents. While the medical profession and the company can support them in the exercise of this responsibility, it cannot assume it for them without simultaneously infringing their rights as persons.

. . . . .

". . . . Since not all women who can become mothers wish to become mothers (or will become mothers), it would appear to be illegal discrimination to treat all who are capable of pregnancy as though they will become pregnant."

Consistent with that view, Johnson Controls "stopped short of excluding women capable of bearing children from lead exposure," but emphasized that a woman who expected to have a child should not choose a job in which she would have such exposure. The company also required a woman who wished to be considered for employment to sign a statement that she had been advised of the risk of having a child while she was exposed to lead. The statement informed the woman that although there was evidence "that women exposed to lead have a higher rate of abortion," this evidence was "not as clear ... as the relationship between cigarette smoking and cancer," but that it was, "medically speaking, just good sense not to run that risk if you want children and do not want to expose the unborn child to risk, however small . . . ."

Five years later, in 1982, Johnson Controls shifted from a policy of warning to a policy of exclusion. Between 1979 and 1983, eight employees became pregnant while maintaining blood lead levels in excess of 30 micrograms per deciliter. This appeared to be the critical level noted by the Occupational Health and Safety Administration (OSHA) for a worker who was planning to have a family. See 29 CFR § 1910.1025 (1989). The company responded by announcing a broad exclusion of women from jobs that exposed them to lead:

" ... It is [Johnson Controls'] policy that women who are pregnant or who are capable of bearing children will not be placed into jobs involving lead exposure or which could expose them to lead through the exercise of job bidding, bumping, transfer or promotion rights."

The policy defined "women ... capable of bearing children" as "all women except those whose inability to bear children is medically documented." It further stated that an unacceptable work station was one where, "over the past year," an employee had recorded a blood lead level of more than 30 micrograms per deciliter or the work site had yielded an air sample containing a lead level in excess of 30 micrograms per cubic meter.

II

In April 1984, petitioners filed in the United States District Court for the Eastern District of Wisconsin a class action challenging Johnson Controls' fetal-protection policy as sex discrimination that violated Title VII of the Civil Rights Act of 1964.   Among the individual plaintiffs were petitioners Mary Craig, who had chosen to be sterilized in order to avoid losing her job, Elsie Nason, a 50–year–old divorcee, who had suffered a loss in compensation when she was transferred out of a job where she was exposed to lead, and Donald Penney, who had been denied a request for a leave of absence for the purpose of lowering his lead level because he intended to become a father.

The District Court granted summary judgment for defendant-respondent Johnson Controls.   680 F.Supp. 309 (1988).   Applying a three-part business necessity defense derived from fetal-protection cases in the Courts of Appeals for the Fourth and Eleventh Circuits, the District Court concluded that while "there is a disagreement among the experts regarding the effect of lead on the fetus," the hazard to the fetus through exposure to lead was established by "a considerable body of opinion"; that although "expert opinion has been provided which holds that lead also affects the reproductive abilities of men and women ... [and] that these effects are as great as the effects of exposure of the fetus ... a great body of experts are of the opinion that the fetus is more vulnerable to levels of lead that would not affect adults"; and that petitioners had "failed to establish that there is an acceptable alternative policy which would protect the fetus."   The court stated that, in view of this disposition of the business necessity defense, it did not "have to undertake a bona fide occupational qualification's (BFOQ) analysis."

The Court of Appeals for the Seventh Circuit, sitting en banc, affirmed the summary judgment by a 7–to–4 vote.   886 F. 2d 871 (1989). The majority held that the proper standard for evaluating the fetal-protection policy was the defense of business necessity; that Johnson Controls was entitled to summary judgment under that defense; and that even if the proper standard was a BFOQ, Johnson Controls still was entitled to summary judgment.

The Court of Appeals first reviewed fetal-protection opinions from the Eleventh and Fourth Circuits.   See Hayes v. Shelby Memorial Hospital, 726 F. 2d 1543 (CA11 1984), and Wright v. Olin Corp., 697 F. 2d 1172 (CA4 1982).   Those opinions established the three-step business necessity inquiry: whether there is a substantial health risk to the fetus; whether transmission of the hazard to the fetus occurs only through women; and whether there is a less discriminatory alternative equally capable of preventing the health hazard to the fetus.   The Court of Appeals agreed with the Eleventh and Fourth Circuits that "the components of the business necessity defense the courts of appeals and the EEOC have utilized in fetal protection cases balance the interests of the employer, the employee and the unborn child in a manner consistent with Title VII."

* * *

We granted certiorari to resolve the obvious conflict between the ... Circuits on this issue, and to address the important and difficult question whether an employer, seeking to protect potential fetuses, may discriminate against women just because of their ability to become pregnant.[1]

III

The bias in Johnson Controls' policy is obvious. Fertile men, but not fertile women, are given a choice as to whether they wish to risk their reproductive health for a particular job. Section 703(a) of the Civil Rights Act of 1964 prohibits sex-based classifications in terms and conditions of employment, in hiring and discharging decisions, and in other employment decisions that adversely affect an employee's status. Respondent's fetal-protection policy explicitly discriminates against women on the basis of their sex. The policy excludes women with childbearing capacity from lead-exposed jobs and so creates a facial classification based on gender. Respondent assumes as much in its brief before this Court.

Nevertheless, the Court of Appeals assumed, as did the two appellate courts who already had confronted the issue, that sex-specific fetal-protection policies do not involve facial discrimination. These courts analyzed the policies as though they were facially neutral, and had only a discriminatory effect upon the employment opportunities of women.... The court assumed that because the asserted reason for the sex-based exclusion (protecting women's unconceived offspring) was ostensibly benign, the policy was not sex-based discrimination. That assumption, however, was incorrect.

First, Johnson Controls' policy classifies on the basis of gender and childbearing capacity, rather than fertility alone. Respondent does not seek to protect the unconceived children of all its employees. Despite evidence in the record about the debilitating effect of lead exposure on

---

1. Since our grant of certiorari, the Sixth Circuit has reversed a District Court's summary judgment for an employer that had excluded fertile female employees from foundry jobs involving exposure to specified concentrations of air-borne lead. See Grant v. General Motors Corp., 908 F. 2d 1303 (1990). The court said: "We agree with the view of the dissenters in Johnson Controls that fetal protection policies perforce amount to overt sex discrimination, which cannot logically be recast as disparate impact and cannot be countenanced without proof that infertility is a BFOQ.... Plaintiff ... has alleged a claim of overt discrimination that her employer may justify only through the BFOQ defense."

In Johnson Controls, Inc. v. Fair Employment & Housing Com'n, 218 Cal.App. 3d 517, 267 Cal.Rptr. 158 (1990), the court held respondent's fetal-protection policy invalid under California's fair-employment law.

the male reproductive system, Johnson Controls is concerned only with the harms that may befall the unborn offspring of its female employees.... Johnson Controls' policy is facially discriminatory because it requires only a female employee to produce proof that she is not capable of reproducing.

Our conclusion is bolstered by the Pregnancy Discrimination Act of 1978 (PDA), 42 U.S.C. § 2000e(k), in which Congress explicitly provided that, for purposes of Title VII, discrimination "on the basis of sex" includes discrimination "because of or on the basis of pregnancy, childbirth, or related medical conditions."[3] "The Pregnancy Discrimination Act has now made clear that, for all Title VII purposes, discrimination based on a woman's pregnancy is, on its face, discrimination because of her sex." Newport News Shipbuilding & Dry Dock Co. v. EEOC, 462 U.S. 669, 684, 103 S.Ct. 2622, 2631, 77 L.Ed.2d 89 (1983). In its use of the words "capable of bearing children" in the 1982 policy statement as the criterion for exclusion, Johnson Controls explicitly classifies on the basis of potential for pregnancy. Under the PDA, such a classification must be regarded, for Title VII purposes, in the same light as explicit sex discrimination. Respondent has chosen to treat all its female employees as potentially pregnant; that choice evinces discrimination on the basis of sex.

We concluded above that Johnson Controls' policy is not neutral because it does not apply to the reproductive capacity of the company's male employees in the same way as it applies to that of the females. Moreover, the absence of a malevolent motive does not convert a facially discriminatory policy into a neutral policy with a discriminatory effect. Whether an employment practice involves disparate treatment through explicit facial discrimination does not depend on why the employer discriminates but rather on the explicit terms of the discrimination.... The beneficence of an employer's purpose does not undermine the conclusion that an explicit gender-based policy is sex discrimination under § 703(a) and thus may be defended only as a BFOQ.

* * *

IV

Under § 703(e)(1) of Title VII, an employer may discriminate on the basis of "religion, sex, or national origin in those certain instances where religion, sex, or national origin is a bona fide occupational qualification reasonably necessary to the normal operation of that particular business or enterprise." We therefore turn to the question

---

3. The Act added subsection (k) to § 701 of the Civil Rights Act of 1964 and reads in pertinent part:

"The terms 'because of sex' or 'on the basis of sex' [in Title VII] include, but are not limited to, because of or on the basis of pregnancy, childbirth, or related medical conditions; and women affected by pregnancy, childbirth, or related medical conditions shall be treated the same for all employment-related purposes ... as other persons not so affected but similar in their ability or inability to work...."

whether Johnson Controls' fetal-protection policy is one of those "certain instances" that come within the BFOQ exception.

The BFOQ defense is written narrowly, and this Court has read it narrowly. See, e.g., Dothard v. Rawlinson, 433 U.S. 321, 332–337, 97 S.Ct. 2720, 2728–2731, 53 L.Ed.2d 786 (1977); Trans World Airlines, Inc. v. Thurston, 469 U.S. 111, 122–125, 105 S.Ct. 613, 622–624, 83 L.Ed.2d 523 (1985). We have read the BFOQ language of § 4(f) of the Age Discrimination in Employment Act of 1967 (ADEA), 29 U.S.C. § 623(f)(1), which tracks the BFOQ provision in Title VII, just as narrowly. See Western Air Lines, Inc. v. Criswell, 472 U.S. 400, 105 S.Ct. 2743, 86 L.Ed.2d 321 (1985). Our emphasis on the restrictive scope of the BFOQ defense is grounded on both the language and the legislative history of § 703.

The wording of the BFOQ defense contains several terms of restriction that indicate that the exception reaches only special situations. The statute thus limits the situations in which discrimination is permissible to "certain instances" where sex discrimination is "reasonably necessary" to the "normal operation" of the "particular" business. Each one of these terms—certain, normal, particular—prevents the use of general subjective standards and favors an objective, verifiable requirement. But the most telling term is "occupational"; this indicates that these objective, verifiable requirements must concern job-related skills and aptitudes.

The concurrence defines "occupational" as meaning related to a job. According to the concurrence, any discriminatory requirement imposed by an employer is "job-related" simply because the employer has chosen to make the requirement a condition of employment. In effect, the concurrence argues that sterility may be an occupational qualification for women because Johnson Controls has chosen to require it. This reading of "occupational" renders the word mere surplusage. "Qualification" by itself would encompass an employer's idiosyncratic requirements. By modifying "qualification" with "occupational," Congress narrowed the term to qualifications that affect an employee's ability to do the job.

Johnson Controls argues that its fetal-protection policy falls within the so-called safety exception to the BFOQ. Our cases have stressed that discrimination on the basis of sex because of safety concerns is allowed only in narrow circumstances. In Dothard v. Rawlinson, this Court indicated that danger to a woman herself does not justify discrimination. We there allowed the employer to hire only male guards in contact areas of maximum-security male penitentiaries only because more was at stake than the "individual woman's decision to weigh and accept the risks of employment." We found sex to be a BFOQ inasmuch as the employment of a female guard would create real risks of safety to others if violence broke out because the guard was a woman. Sex discrimination was tolerated because sex was related to the guard's ability to do the job—maintaining prison security. We also required in

Dothard a high correlation between sex and ability to perform job functions and refused to allow employers to use sex as a proxy for strength although it might be a fairly accurate one.

Similarly, some courts have approved airlines' layoffs of pregnant flight attendants at different points during the first five months of pregnancy on the ground that the employer's policy was necessary to ensure the safety of passengers. See Harris v. Pan American World Airways, Inc., 649 F.2d 670 (CA9 1980); Burwell v. Eastern Air Lines, Inc., 633 F.2d 361 (CA4 1980), cert. denied, 450 U.S. 965, 101 S.Ct. 1480, 67 L.Ed.2d 613 (1981); Condit v. United Air Lines, Inc., 558 F. 2d 1176 (CA4 1977), cert. denied, 435 U.S. 934, 98 S.Ct. 1510, 55 L.Ed.2d 531 (1978); In re National Airlines, Inc., 434 F.Supp. 249 (S.D.Fla.1977). In two of these cases, the courts pointedly indicated that fetal, as opposed to passenger, safety was best left to the mother. Burwell, 633 F.2d, at 371; National Airlines, 434 F.Supp., at 259.

We considered safety to third parties in Western Airlines, Inc. v. Criswell, supra, in the context of the ADEA. We focused upon "the nature of the flight engineer's tasks," and the "actual capabilities of persons over age 60" in relation to those tasks. Our safety concerns were not independent of the individual's ability to perform the assigned tasks, but rather involved the possibility that, because of age-connected debility, a flight engineer might not properly assist the pilot, and might thereby cause a safety emergency. Furthermore, although we considered the safety of third parties in Dothard and Criswell, those third parties were indispensable to the particular business at issue. In Dothard, the third parties were the inmates; in Criswell, the third parties were the passengers on the plane. We stressed that in order to qualify as a BFOQ, a job qualification must relate to the "essence," Dothard or to the "central mission of the employer's business," Criswell.

The concurrence ignores the "essence of the business" test and so concludes that "the safety to fetuses in carrying out the duties of battery manufacturing is as much a legitimate concern as is safety to third parties in guarding prisons (Dothard) or flying airplanes (Criswell)." By limiting its discussion to cost and safety concerns and rejecting the "essence of the business" test that our case law has established, the concurrence seeks to expand what is now the narrow BFOQ defense. Third-party safety considerations properly entered into the BFOQ analysis in Dothard and Criswell because they went to the core of the employee's job performance. Moreover, that performance involved the central purpose of the enterprise. Dothard ("The essence of a correctional counselor's job is to maintain prison security"); Criswell (the central mission of the airline's business was the safe transportation of its passengers). The concurrence attempts to transform this case into one of customer safety. The unconceived fetuses of Johnson Controls' female employees, however, are neither customers nor third parties whose safety is essential to the business of battery manufacturing. No one can disregard the possibility of injury to future children; the BFOQ, however, is not so broad that it transforms this deep social concern into an essential aspect of batterymaking.

Our case law, therefore, makes clear that the safety exception is limited to instances in which sex or pregnancy actually interferes with the employee's ability to perform the job. This approach is consistent with the language of the BFOQ provision itself, for it suggests that permissible distinctions based on sex must relate to ability to perform the duties of the job. Johnson Controls suggests, however, that we expand the exception to allow fetal-protection policies that mandate particular standards for pregnant or fertile women. We decline to do so. Such an expansion contradicts not only the language of the BFOQ and the narrowness of its exception but the plain language and history of the Pregnancy Discrimination Act.

The PDA's amendment to Title VII contains a BFOQ standard of its own: unless pregnant employees differ from others "in their ability or inability to work," they must be "treated the same" as other employees "for all employment-related purposes." This language clearly sets forth Congress' remedy for discrimination on the basis of pregnancy and potential pregnancy. Women who are either pregnant or potentially pregnant must be treated like others "similar in their ability ... to work." In other words, women as capable of doing their jobs as their male counterparts may not be forced to choose between having a child and having a job.

The concurrence asserts that the PDA did not alter the BFOQ defense. The concurrence arrives at this conclusion by ignoring the second clause of the Act which states that "women affected by pregnancy, childbirth, or related medical conditions shall be treated the same for all employment-related purposes ... as other persons not so affected but similar in their ability or inability to work." Until this day, every Member of this Court had acknowledged that "the second clause [of the PDA] could not be clearer: it mandates that pregnant employees 'shall be treated the same for all employment-related purposes' as nonpregnant employees similarly situated with respect to their ability or inability to work." California Federal S. & L. Assn. v. Guerra, 479 U.S. 272, 297, 107 S.Ct. 683, 698, 93 L.Ed.2d 613 (1987) (White, J., dissenting). The concurrence now seeks to read the second clause out of the Act.

* * *

We conclude that the language of both the BFOQ provision and the PDA which amended it, as well as the legislative history and the case law, prohibit an employer from discriminating against a woman because of her capacity to become pregnant unless her reproductive potential prevents her from performing the duties of her job. We reiterate our holdings in Criswell and Dothard that an employer must direct its concerns about a woman's ability to perform her job safely and efficiently to those aspects of the woman's job-related activities that fall within the "essence" of the particular business.[4]

V

We have no difficulty concluding that Johnson Controls cannot establish a BFOQ. Fertile women, as far as appears in the record, participate in the manufacture of batteries as efficiently as anyone else. Johnson Controls' professed moral and ethical concerns about the welfare of the next generation do not suffice to establish a BFOQ of female sterility. Decisions about the welfare of future children must be left to the parents who conceive, bear, support, and raise them rather than to the employers who hire those parents. Congress has mandated this choice through Title VII, as amended by the Pregnancy Discrimination Act. Johnson Controls has attempted to exclude women because of their reproductive capacity. Title VII and the PDA simply do not allow a woman's dismissal because of her failure to submit to sterilization.

Nor can concerns about the welfare of the next generation be considered a part of the "essence" of Johnson Controls' business. Judge Easterbrook in this case pertinently observed: "It is word play to say that 'the job' at Johnson [Controls] is to make batteries without risk to fetuses in the same way 'the job' at Western Air Lines is to fly planes without crashing." 886 F.2d, at 913.

Johnson Controls argues that it must exclude all fertile women because it is impossible to tell which women will become pregnant while working with lead. This argument is somewhat academic in light of our conclusion that the company may not exclude fertile women at all; it perhaps is worth noting, however, that Johnson Controls has shown no "factual basis for believing that all or substantially all women would be unable to perform safely and efficiently the duties of the job involved." Weeks v. Southern Bell Tel. & Tel. Co., 408 F.2d 228, 235 (CA5 1969), quoted with approval in Dothard, 433 U.S., at 333. Even on this sparse record, it is apparent that Johnson Controls is concerned about only a small minority of women. Of the eight pregnancies reported among the female employees, it has not been shown that any of the babies have birth defects or other abnormalities. The record does not reveal the birth rate for Johnson Controls' female workers but national statistics show that approximately nine percent of all fertile women become pregnant each year. The birthrate drops to two percent for blue collar workers over age 30. See Becker, From

---

4. The concurrence predicts that our reaffirmation of the narrowness of the BFOQ defense will preclude considerations of privacy as a basis for sex-based discrimination. We have never addressed privacy-based sex discrimination and shall not do so here because the sex-based discrimination at issue today does not involve the privacy interests of Johnson Controls' customers. Nothing in our discussion of the "essence of the business test," however, suggests that sex could not constitute a BFOQ when privacy interests are implicated. See, e.g., Backus v. Baptist Medical Center, 510 F.Supp. 1191 (E.D.Ark.1981), vacated as moot, 671 F.2d 1100 (CA8 1982) (essence of obstetrics nurse's business is to provide sensitive care for patient's intimate and private concerns).

Muller v. Oregon to Fetal Vulnerability Policies, 53 U.Chi.L.Rev., 1219, 1233 (1986). Johnson Controls' fear of prenatal injury, no matter how sincere, does not begin to show that substantially all of its fertile women employees are incapable of doing their jobs.

VI

A word about tort liability and the increased cost of fertile women in the workplace is perhaps necessary. One of the dissenting judges in this case expressed concern about an employer's tort liability and concluded that liability for a potential injury to a fetus is a social cost that Title VII does not require a company to ignore. It is correct to say that Title VII does not prevent the employer from having a conscience. The statute, however, does prevent sex-specific fetal-protection policies. These two aspects of Title VII do not conflict.

More than 40 States currently recognize a right to recover for a prenatal injury based either on negligence or on wrongful death. See, e.g., Wolfe v. Isbell, 291 Ala. 327, 333–334, 280 So.2d 758, 763 (1977); Simon v. Mullin, 34 Conn.Sup. 139, 147, 380 A.2d 1353, 1357 (1977). See also Note, 22 Suffolk U.L.Rev. 747, 754–756, and nn. 54, 57, and 58 (1988) (listing cases). According to Johnson Controls, however, the company complies with the lead standard developed by OSHA and warns its female employees about the damaging effects of lead. It is worth noting that OSHA gave the problem of lead lengthy consideration and concluded that "there is no basis whatsoever for the claim that women of childbearing age should be excluded from the workplace in order to protect the fetus or the course of pregnancy." 43 Fed. Reg. 52952, 52966 (1978). Instead, OSHA established a series of mandatory protections which, taken together, "should effectively minimize any risk to the fetus and newborn child." Id., at 52966. Without negligence, it would be difficult for a court to find liability on the part of the employer. If, under general tort principles, Title VII bans sex-specific fetal-protection policies, the employer fully informs the woman of the risk, and the employer has not acted negligently, the basis for holding an employer liable seems remote at best.

Although the issue is not before us, the concurrence observes that "it is far from clear that compliance with Title VII will preempt state tort liability." The cases relied upon by the concurrence to support its prediction, however, are inapposite. For example, in California Federal S. & L. Assn. v. Guerra, 479 U.S. 272, 107 S.Ct. 683, 93 L.Ed.2d 613 (1987), we considered a California statute that expanded upon the requirements of the PDA and concluded that the statute was not preempted by Title VII because it was not inconsistent with the purposes of the federal statute and did not require an act that was unlawful under Title VII. Here, in contrast, the tort liability that the concurrence fears will punish employers for *complying* with Title VII's clear command. When it is impossible for an employer to comply with both state and federal requirements, this Court has ruled that federal law pre-empts that of the States.   See, e.g., Florida Lime & Avocado Growers, Inc. v. Paul, 373 U.S. 132, 142–143, 83 S.Ct. 1210, 1217–1218, 10 L.Ed.2d 248 (1963).

* * *

If state tort law furthers discrimination in the workplace and prevents employers from hiring women who are capable of manufacturing the product as efficiently as men, then it will impede the accomplishment of Congress' goals in enacting Title VII.   Because Johnson Controls has not argued that it faces any costs from tort liability, not to mention crippling ones, the pre-emption question is not before us.   We therefore say no more than that the concurrence's speculation appears unfounded as well as premature.

The tort-liability argument reduces to two equally unpersuasive propositions.   First, Johnson Controls attempts to solve the problem of reproductive health hazards by resorting to an exclusionary policy. Title VII plainly forbids illegal sex discrimination as a method of diverting attention from an employer's obligation to police the workplace.   Second, the spectre of an award of damages reflects a fear that hiring fertile women will cost more.   The extra cost of employing members of one sex, however, does not provide an affirmative Title VII defense for a discriminatory refusal to hire members of that gender. Indeed, in passing the PDA, Congress considered at length the considerable cost of providing equal treatment of pregnancy and related conditions, but made the "decision to forbid special treatment of pregnancy despite the social costs associated therewith."   Arizona Governing Committee v. Norris, 463 U.S. 1073, 1084, n. 14, 103 S.Ct. 3492, 3499, n.14, 77 L.Ed.2d 1236 (1983) (opinion of MARSHALL, J.).   See Price Waterhouse v. Hopkins, 490 U.S. 228, 109 S.Ct. 1775, 104 L.Ed.2d 268 (1988).

We, of course, are not presented with, nor do we decide, a case in which costs would be so prohibitive as to threaten the survival of the employer's business.   We merely reiterate our prior holdings that the incremental cost of hiring women cannot justify discriminating against them.

VII

Our holding today that Title VII, as so amended, forbids sex-specific fetal-protection policies is neither remarkable nor unprecedented.   Concern for a woman's existing or potential offspring historically has been the excuse for denying women equal employment opportunities.   See, e.g., Muller v. Oregon, 208 U.S. 412, 28 S.Ct. 324, 52 L.Ed. 551 (1908).   Congress in the PDA prohibited discrimination on the basis of a woman's ability to become pregnant.   We do [*41] no more than hold that the Pregnancy Discrimination Act means what it says.

It is no more appropriate for the courts than it is for individual employers to decide whether a woman's reproductive role is more important to herself and her family than her economic role. Congress has left this choice to the woman as hers to make.

The judgment of the Court of Appeals is reversed and the case is remanded for further proceedings consistent with this opinion.

It is so ordered.

JUSTICE WHITE, with whom THE CHIEF JUSTICE and JUSTICE KENNEDY join, concurring in part and concurring in the judgment.

The Court properly holds that Johnson Controls' fetal protection policy overtly discriminates against women, and thus is prohibited by Title VII unless it falls within the bona fide occupational qualification (BFOQ) exception. The Court erroneously holds, however, that the BFOQ defense is so narrow that it could never justify a sex-specific fetal protection policy. I nevertheless concur in the judgment of reversal because on the record before us summary judgment in favor of Johnson Controls was improperly entered by the District Court and affirmed by the Court of Appeals.

I

In evaluating the scope of the BFOQ defense, the proper starting point is the language of the statute. Title VII forbids discrimination on the basis of sex, except "in those certain instances where . . . sex . . . is a bona fide occupational qualification reasonably necessary to the normal operation of that particular business or enterprise." For the fetal protection policy involved in this case to be a BFOQ, therefore, the policy must be "reasonably necessary" to the "normal operation" of making batteries, which is Johnson Controls' "particular business." Although that is a difficult standard to satisfy, nothing in the statute's language indicates that it could never support a sex-specific fetal protection policy.[1]

On the contrary, a fetal protection policy would be justified under the terms of the statute if, for example, an employer could show that exclusion of women from certain jobs was reasonably necessary to avoid substantial tort liability. Common sense tells us that it is part of the normal operation of business concerns to avoid causing injury to third parties, as well as to employees, if for no other reason than to avoid tort liability and its substantial costs. This possibility of tort liability is not hypothetical; every State currently allows children born alive to recover in tort for prenatal injuries caused by third parties, see W. Keeton, D. Dobbs, R. Keeton, & D. Owen, Prosser and Keeton on Law of Torts

---

1. The Court's heavy reliance on the word "occupational" in the BFOQ statute, *ante*, at 12, is unpersuasive. Any requirement for employment can be said to be an occupational qualification, since "occupational" merely means related to a job. See Webster's Third New International Dictionary 1560 (1976). Thus, Johnson Controls' requirement that employees engaged in battery manufacturing be either male or non-fertile clearly is an "occupational qualification." The issue, of course, is whether that qualification is "reasonably necessary to the normal operation" of Johnson Controls' business. It is telling that the Court offers no case support, either from this Court or the lower Federal Courts, for its interpretation of the word "occupational."

§ 55 p. 368 (5th ed. 1984), and an increasing number of courts have recognized a right to recover even for prenatal injuries caused by torts committed prior to conception, see 3 F. Harper, F. James, & O. Gray, Law of Torts § 18.3, pp. 677–678, n. 15 (2d ed. 1986).

The Court dismisses the possibility of tort liability by no more than speculating that if "Title VII bans sex-specific fetal-protection policies, the employer fully informs the woman of the risk, and the employer has not acted negligently, the basis for holding an employer liable seems remote at best." Such speculation will be small comfort to employers. First, it is far from clear that compliance with Title VII will pre-empt state tort liability, and the Court offers no support for that proposition. Second, although warnings may preclude claims by injured employees, they will not preclude claims by injured children because the general rule is that parents cannot waive causes of action on behalf of their children, and the parents' negligence will not be imputed to the children. Finally, although state tort liability for prenatal injuries generally requires negligence, it will be difficult for employers to determine in advance what will constitute negligence. Compliance with OSHA standards, for example, has been held not to be a defense to state tort or criminal liability. See National Solid Wastes Management Assn. v. Killian, 918 F.2d 671, 680, n. 9 (CA7 1990) (collecting cases); see also 29 U.S.C. § 653(b)(4). Moreover, it is possible that employers will be held strictly liable, if, for example, their manufacturing process is considered "abnormally dangerous." See Restatement (Second) of Torts § 869, comment b (1979).

Relying on Los Angeles Dept. of Water and Power v. Manhart, the Court contends that tort liability cannot justify a fetal protection policy because the extra costs of hiring women is not a defense under Title VII. This contention misrepresents our decision in Manhart. There, we held that a requirement that female employees contribute more than male employees to a pension fund, in order to reflect the greater longevity of women, constituted discrimination against women under Title VII because it treated them as a class rather than as individuals. We did not in that case address in any detail the nature of the BFOQ defense, and we certainly did not hold that cost was irrelevant to the BFOQ analysis. Rather, we merely stated in a footnote that "there has been no showing that sex distinctions are reasonably necessary to the normal operation of the Department's retirement plan." We further noted that although Title VII does not contain a "cost-justification defense comparable to the affirmative defense available in a price discrimination suit," "no defense based on the total cost of employing men and women was attempted in this case."

Prior decisions construing the BFOQ defense confirm that the defense is broad enough to include considerations of cost and safety of the sort that could form the basis for an employer's adoption of a fetal protection policy. In Dothard v. Rawlinson the Court held that being male was a BFOQ for "contact" guard positions in Alabama's maximum-security male penitentiaries. The Court first took note of the actual conditions of the prison environment: "In a prison system where violence is the order of the day, where inmate access to guards is facilitated by dormitory living arrangements, where every institution is understaffed, and where a substantial portion of the inmate population is composed of sex offenders mixed at random with other prisoners, there are few visible deterrents to inmate assaults on women custodians." The Court also stressed that "more [was] at stake" than a risk to individual female employees: "The likelihood that inmates would assault a woman because she was a woman would pose a real threat not only to the victim of the assault but also to the basic control of the penitentiary and protection of its inmates and the other security personnel." Under those circumstances, the Court observed that "it would be an oversimplification to characterize [the exclusion of women] as an exercise in 'romantic paternalism.' Cf. Frontiero v. Richardson, 411 U.S. 677, 684 (93 S.Ct. 1764, 1769, 36 L.Ed.2d 583)." Id., 433 U.S., at 335, 97 S.Ct., at 2729.

We revisited the BFOQ defense in Western Air Lines, Inc. v. Criswell, this time in the context of the Age Discrimination in Employment Act of 1967 (ADEA). There, we endorsed the two-part inquiry for evaluating a BFOQ defense used by the Fifth Circuit Court of Appeals in Usery v. Tamiami Trail Tours, Inc., 531 F.2d 224 (1976). First, the job qualification must not be "so peripheral to the central mission of the employer's business" that no discrimination could be " 'reasonably necessary to the normal operation of the particular business.' " Although safety is not such a peripheral concern [4] the inquiry " 'adjusts to the safety factor' "—" 'the greater the safety factor, measured by the likelihood of harm and the probable severity of that harm in case of an accident, the more stringent may be the job qualifications,' " (quoting Tamiami, supra, at 236). Second, the employer must show either that all or substantially all persons excluded " ' "would be unable to perform safely and efficiently the duties of the job involved," ' " or that it is " ' "impossible or highly impractical" ' " to deal with them on an individual basis. (quoting Tamiami, supra, at 235 (quoting Weeks v. Southern Bell Telephone & Telegraph Co., 408 F.2d 228, 235 (CA5 1969))). We further observed that this inquiry properly takes into account an employer's interest in safety—"when an employer establishes that a job qualification has been carefully formulated to respond to documented concerns for public safety, it will not be overly burdensome

4. An example of a "peripheral" job qualification was in Diaz v. Pan American World Airways, Inc., 442 F.2d 385(CA5), cert. denied, 404 U.S. 950, 92 S.Ct. 275, 30 L.Ed.2d 267 (1971). There, the Fifth Circuit held that being female was not a BFOQ for the job of flight attendant, despite a determination by the trial court that women were better able than men to perform the "non-mechanical" functions of the job, such as attending to the passen-gers' psychological needs. The court concluded that such non-mechanical functions were merely "tangential" to the normal operation of the airline's business, noting that "no one has suggested that having male stewards will so seriously affect the operation of an airline as to jeopardize or even minimize its ability to provide safe transportation from one place to another." 442 F.2d, at 388.

to persuade a trier of fact that the qualification is 'reasonably necessary' to safe operation of the business."

Dothard and Criswell make clear that avoidance of substantial safety risks to third parties is inherently part of both an employee's ability to perform a job and an employer's "normal operation" of its business. Indeed, in both cases, the Court approved the statement in Weeks v. Southern Bell Telephone & Telegraph Co., 408 F.2d 228 (CA5 1969), that an employer could establish a BFOQ defense by showing that "all or substantially all women would be unable to perform safely and efficiently the duties of the job involved." The Court's statement in this case that "the safety exception is limited to instances in which sex or pregnancy actually interferes with the employee's ability to perform the job," therefore adds no support to its conclusion that a fetal protection policy could never be justified as a BFOQ. On the facts of this case, for example, protecting fetal safety while carrying out the duties of battery manufacturing is as much a legitimate concern as is safety to third parties in guarding prisons (Dothard) or flying airplanes (Criswell).[5]

Dothard and Criswell also confirm that costs are relevant in determining whether a discriminatory policy is reasonably necessary for the normal operation of a business. In Dothard, the safety problem that justified exclusion of women from the prison guard positions was largely a result of inadequate staff and facilities. If the cost of employing women could not be considered, the employer there should have been required to hire more staff and restructure the prison environment rather than exclude women. Similarly, in Criswell the airline could have been required to hire more pilots and install expensive monitoring devices rather than discriminate against older employees. The BFOQ statute, however, reflects "Congress' unwillingness to require employers to change the very nature of their operations." Price Waterhouse v. Hopkins, 490 U.S. 228, 242, 109 S.Ct. 1775, 1786, 104 L.Ed.2d 268 (1989) (plurality opinion).

The Pregnancy Discrimination Act (PDA), contrary to the Court's assertion, did not restrict the scope of the BFOQ defense. The PDA was only an amendment to the "Definitions" section of Title VII, and did not purport to eliminate or alter the BFOQ defense. Rather, it merely clarified Title VII to make it clear that pregnancy and related conditions are included within Title VII's antidiscrimination provisions. As we have already recognized, "the purpose of the PDA was simply to make the treatment of pregnancy consistent with general Title VII

---

5. I do not, as the Court asserts, ante, at 14, reject the "essence of the business" test. Rather, I merely reaffirm the obvious—that safety to third parties is part of the "essence" of most if not all businesses. Of course, the BFOQ inquiry " 'adjusts to the safety factor.' " Criswell, 472 U.S., at 413, 105 S.Ct., at 2751 (quoting Tamiami, 531 F.2d, at 236). As a result, more strin-gent occupational qualifications may be justified for jobs involving higher safety risks, such as flying airplanes. But a recognition that the importance of safety varies among businesses does not mean that safety is completely irrelevant to the essence of a job such as battery manufacturing.

principles."   Arizona Governing Committee for Tax Deferred Annuity and Deferred Compensation Plans v. Norris, 463 U.S. 1073, 1085, n. 14, 103 S.Ct. 3492, 3499–3500, n. 14, 77 L.Ed.2d 1236 (1983).

* * *

In enacting the BFOQ standard, "Congress did not ignore the public interest in safety." Criswell, supra, at 419. The Court's narrow interpretation of the BFOQ defense in this case, however, means that an employer cannot exclude even pregnant women from an environment highly toxic to their fetuses. It is foolish to think that Congress intended such a result, and neither the language of the BFOQ exception nor our cases requires it.[8]

[Despite his disagreement with the majority, Justice White concluded that, on the state of the record, summary judgment was not appropriate because of disputes over material issues of fact.]

JUSTICE SCALIA, concurring in the judgment.

I generally agree with the Court's analysis, but have some reservations, several of which bear mention.

First, I think it irrelevant that there was "evidence in the record about the debilitating effect of lead exposure on the male reproductive system." Even without such evidence, treating women differently "on the basis of pregnancy" constitutes discrimination "on the basis of sex," because Congress has unequivocally said so. Pregnancy Discrimination Act of 1978.

Second, the Court points out that " Johnson Controls has shown no factual basis for believing that all or substantially all women would be unable to perform safely ... the duties of the job involved." In my view, this is not only "somewhat academic in light of our conclusion that the company may not exclude fertile women at all"; it is entirely

---

8. The Court's cramped reading of the BFOQ defense is also belied by the legislative history of Title VII, in which three examples of permissible sex discrimination were mentioned—a female nurse hired to care for an elderly woman, an all-male professional baseball team, and a masseur. See 110 Cong. Rec. 2718 (1964) (Rep. Goodell); id., at 7212–7213 (interpretive memorandum introduced by Sens. Clark and Case); id., at 2720 (Rep. Multer). In none of those situations would gender "actually interfere with the employee's ability to perform the job," as required today by the Court, ante, at 14.

The Court's interpretation of the BFOQ standard also would seem to preclude considerations of privacy as a basis for sex-based discrimination, since those considerations do not relate directly to an employee's physical ability to perform the duties of the job. The lower federal courts, how-
ever, have consistently recognized that privacy interests may justify sex-based requirements for certain jobs. See, e.g., Fesel v. Masonic Home of Delaware, Inc., 447 F.Supp. 1346 (Del.1978), aff'd, 591 F.2d 1334 (CA3 1979) (nurse's aide in retirement home); Jones v. Hinds General Hospital, 666 F.Supp. 933 (S.D.Miss.1987) (nursing assistant); Local 567 American Federation of State, County, and Municipal Employees, AFL–CIO v. Michigan Council 25, American Federation of State, County, and Municipal Employees, AFL–CIO, 635 F.Supp. 1010 (E.D.Mich.1986) (mental health workers); Norwood v. Dale Maintenance System, Inc., 590 F.Supp. 1410 (N.D.Ill.1984) (washroom attendant); Backus v. Baptist Medical Center, 510 F.Supp. 1191 (E.D.Ark.1981), vacated as moot, 671 F.2d 1100 (CA8 1982) (nursing position in obstetrics and gynecology department of hospital).

irrelevant. By reason of the Pregnancy Discrimination Act, it would not matter if all pregnant women placed their children at risk in taking these jobs, just as it does not matter if no men do so. As Judge Easterbrook put it in his dissent below, "Title VII gives parents the power to make occupational decisions affecting their families. A legislative forum is available to those who believe that such decisions should be made elsewhere." International Union, UAW v. Johnson Controls, Inc., 886 F.2d 871, 915 (CA7 1989) (Easterbrook, J., dissenting).

Third, I am willing to assume, as the Court intimates, that any action required by Title VII cannot give rise to liability under state tort law. That assumption, however, does not answer the question whether an action is required by Title VII (including the BFOQ provision) even if it is subject to liability under state tort law. It is perfectly reasonable to believe that Title VII has *accommodated* state tort law through the BFOQ exception. However, all that need be said in the present case is that Johnson has not demonstrated a substantial risk of tort liability—which is alone enough to defeat a tort-based assertion of the BFOQ exception.

Last, the Court goes far afield, it seems to me, in suggesting that increased cost alone—short of "costs . . . so prohibitive as to threaten survival of the employer's business,"—cannot support a BFOQ defense. I agree with JUSTICE WHITE's concurrence that nothing in our prior cases suggests this, and in my view it is wrong. I think, for example, that a shipping company may refuse to hire pregnant women as crew members on long voyages because the on-board facilities for foreseeable emergencies, though quite feasible, would be inordinately expensive. In the present case, however, Johnson has not asserted a cost-based BFOQ.

I concur in the judgment of the Court.

NOTES AND PROBLEMS FOR DISCUSSION

1. How does the Court resolve the question of whether a BFOQ defense can be founded on the cost to the employer of hiring in a non-discriminatory manner? The majority suggests that it might allow such a defense if the costs to the employer "would be so prohibitive as to threaten the survival of the employer's business." The four concurring justices would not place that severe a restriction on a cost-based BFOQ. What if the employer could show that its economic success in its particular industry was the result of employing only attractive women in customer contact jobs? Consider the following case.

WILSON v. SOUTHWEST AIRLINES CO.

United States District Court, Northern District of Texas, 1981.
517 F.Supp. 292.

Patrick E. Higginbotham, District Judge.

This case presents the important question whether femininity, or more accurately female sex appeal, is a bona fide occupational qualification ("BFOQ") for the jobs of flight attendant and ticket agent with Southwest Airlines. Plaintiff Gregory Wilson and the class of over 100 male job applicants he represents have challenged Southwest's open refusal to hire males as a violation of Title VII of the Civil Rights Act of 1964....

At the phase one trial on liability, Southwest conceded that its refusal to hire males was intentional.... Southwest contends, however, that the BFOQ exception to Title VII's ban on sex discrimination justifies its hiring only females for the public contact positions of flight attendant and ticket agent. The BFOQ window through which Southwest attempts to fly permits sex discrimination in situations where the employer can prove that sex is a "bona fide occupational qualification reasonably necessary to the normal operation of that particular business or enterprise." Id. Southwest reasons it may discriminate against males because its attractive female flight attendants and ticket agents personify the airline's sexy image and fulfill its public promise to take passengers skyward with "love." Defendant claims maintenance of its females-only hiring policy is crucial to the airline's continued financial success.

Since it has been admitted that Southwest discriminates on the basis of sex, the only issue to decide is whether Southwest has proved that being female is a BFOQ reasonably necessary to the normal operation of its particular business. As the application of § 703(e) depends, in large part, upon an analysis of the employer's "particular" business, it is necessary to set forth the factual background of this controversy as a predicate to consideration of Southwest's BFOQ defense. The facts are undisputed.

Factual Background

Defendant Southwest Airlines is a scheduled air carrier engaged in the transportation of passengers. Southwest's inaugural flight was June 18, 1971. It presently serves major cities in Texas, Oklahoma, Louisiana and New Mexico.

Southwest was incorporated in March of 1967 and filed its initial application with the Texas Aeronautics Commission ("TAC") in November of 1967 to serve the intrastate markets of Dallas, Houston and San Antonio. Southwest's proposed entry as an intrastate commuter carrier sparked a hostile reaction from the incumbent air carriers serving the Texas market. The airline's application to the TAC was bitterly contested and the original TAC decision to permit Defendant to begin serving Dallas, Houston and San Antonio was litigated for over four years through a succession of state and federal courts. The legal controversy was not resolved until December of 1970, when the U.S. Supreme Court denied the incumbent air carriers' petition for a *writ of certiorari*. According to Southwest's Chairman Herbert Kelleher, the airline in the interim had lost a commitment from a major insurance company to purchase $3 million of preferred stock; had lost a commitment for the sale of aircraft necessary to commence operations; had lost $2 million in subscriptions for stock by individual investors; and had spent over $530,000 in legal fees litigating the issue of its right to commence operations, all as a result of the defensive tactics of Southwest's competitors. In December of 1970, Southwest had $143 in the bank and was over $100,000 in debt, though no aircraft had ever left the ground.

Barely intact, Southwest, in early 1971, called upon a Dallas advertising agency, the Bloom Agency, to develop a winning marketing strategy. Planning to initiate service quickly, Southwest needed instant recognition and a "catchy" image to distinguish it from its competitors.

The Bloom Agency evaluated both the images of the incumbent competitor airlines as well as the characteristics of passengers to be served by a commuter airline. Bloom determined that the other carriers serving the Texas market tended to project an image of conservatism. The agency also determined that the relatively short haul commuter market which Southwest hoped to serve was comprised of predominantly male businessmen. Based on these factors, Bloom suggested that Southwest break away from the conservative image of other airlines and project to the traveling public an airline personification of feminine youth and vitality. A specific female personality description was recommended and adopted by Southwest for its corporate image:

> This lady is young and vital * * * she is charming and goes through life with great flair and exuberance * * * you notice first her exciting smile, friendly air, her wit * * * yet she is quite efficient and approaches all her tasks with care and attention. * * *

From the personality description suggested by The Bloom Agency, Southwest developed its now famous "Love" personality. Southwest projects an image of feminine spirit, fun and sex appeal. Its ads promise to provide "tender loving care" to its predominantly male, business passengers.[3] The first advertisements run by the airline featured the slogan, "AT LAST THERE IS SOMEBODY ELSE UP THERE WHO LOVES YOU." Variations on this theme have continued through newspaper, billboard, magazine and television advertisements during the past ten years.[4] Bloom's "Love" campaign was given a boost in 1974–1975 when the last of Southwest's competitors moved

---

3. According to an October, 1979 onboard marketing survey commissioned before this lawsuit was filed, 69.01% of the respondents were male, while 58.41% of all respondents listed their occupation as either professional/technical, manager/administrator, or sales. Only 49.75% of the passengers surveyed, however, gave "business" as the reason for their trip.

4. Unabashed allusions to love and sex pervade all aspects of Southwest's public image. Its T.V. commercials feature attractive attendants in fitted outfits, catering to male passengers while an alluring feminine voice promises inflight love. On board, attendants in hot-pants (skirts are now optional) serve "love bites" (toasted almonds) and "love potions" (cocktails). Even Southwest's ticketing system features a "quickie machine" to provide "instant gratification."

its operations to the new Dallas/Fort Worth Regional Airport, leaving Southwest as the only heavy carrier flying out of Dallas' convenient and fortuitously named, Love Field.

Over the years, Southwest gained national and international attention as the "love airline." Southwest Airlines' stock is traded on the New York Stock Exchange under the ticker symbol "LUV". During 1977 when Southwest opened five additional markets in Texas, the love theme was expanded to "WE'RE SPREADING LOVE ALL OVER TEXAS."

As an integral part of its youthful, feminine image, Southwest has employed only females in the high customer contact positions of ticket agent and flight attendant. From the start, Southwest's attractive personnel, dressed in high boots and hot-pants, generated public interest and "free ink." Their sex appeal has been used to attract male customers to the airline. Southwest's flight attendants, and to a lesser degree its ticket agents, have been featured in newspaper, magazine, billboard and television advertisements during the past ten years. Some attendants assist in promotional events for other businesses and civic organizations. Southwest flight attendants and ticket agents are featured in the company's in-flight magazine and have received notice in numerous other national and international publications.[5] The airline also encourages its attendants to entertain the passengers and maintain an atmosphere of informality and "fun" during flights. According to Southwest, its female flight attendants have come to "personify" Southwest's public image.

Southwest has enjoyed enormous success in recent years.[6] This is in no small part due to its marketing image. Though Southwest now enjoys a distinct advantage by operating its commuter flights out of "convenient" Love and Hobby Fields, the airline achieved a commanding position in the regional commuter market while flying "wing tip to wing tip" with national carriers who utilized the same airport, fares, schedules, and aircraft. The evidence was undisputed that Southwest's unique, feminized image played and continues to play an important role in the airline's success.[7]

Less certain, however, is Southwest's assertion that its females-only hiring policy is necessary for the continued success of its image and its business. Based on two onboard surveys, one conducted in October, 1979, before this suit was filed, and another in August, 1980, when the

---

5. For example, in 1974 a Southwest Airlines' flight attendant was featured on the cover of *Esquire* magazine as being "the best in America."

6. From 1979 to 1980, the company's earnings rose from $17 million to 28 million when most other airlines suffered heavy losses. As a percentage of revenues, Southwest's return is considered to be one of the highest in the industry.

7. Even Plaintiff Wilson in his original charge filed with the Equal Employment Opportunity Commission stated:

The airline [Southwest] does not hire male flight attendants and has built its business by attracting businessmen and employing attractive female flight attendants.

suit was pending,[8] Southwest contends its attractive flight attendants are the "largest single component" of its success. In the 1979 survey, however, of the attributes considered most important by passengers, the category "courteous and attentive hostesses" ranked fifth in importance behind (1) on time departures, (2) frequently scheduled departures, (3) friendly and helpful reservations and ground personnel, and (4) convenient departure times,[9] Defendant's Exh. 1 at 2 (¶ 17) and 39 (Question 14). Apparently, one of the remaining eight alternative categories, "attractive hostesses," was not selected with sufficient frequency to warrant being included in the reported survey results.

* * *

In evaluating Southwest's BFOQ defense, therefore, the Court proceeds on the basis that "love," while important, is not everything in the relationship between Defendant and its passengers. Still, it is proper to infer from the airline's competitive successes that Southwest's overall "love image" has enhanced its ability to attract passengers. To the extent the airline has successfully feminized its image and made attractive females an integral part of its public face, it also follows that femininity and sex appeal are qualities related to successful job performance by Southwest's flight attendants and ticket agents. The strength of this relationship has not been proved. It is with this factual orientation that the Court turns to examine Southwest's BFOQ defense.

* * *

[Judge Higginbottham's discussion of the legislative history and case law development of the BFOQ exception is omitted. Relying on Weeks v. Southern Bell Telephone & Telegraph Co., 408 F.2d 228 (5th Cir.1969) and Diaz v. Pan American World Airways, Inc., 442 F.2d 385 (5th Cir.1971), cert. denied, 404 U.S. 950, 92 S.Ct. 275, 30 L.Ed.2d 267 (1971), Judge Higginbotham reasoned that application of the BFOQ exception

---

8. The results of a briefer third survey conducted on March 10–11, 1981 at the request of Southwest's trial counsel cannot be considered. Conducted expressly to "determine" passenger preference for females in anticipation of trial, the survey showed bias and lacked statistical reliability for many reasons. Among other problems, the survey suffered from non-random sampling [passengers were sampled only at Love (Dallas) and Hobby (Houston) Fields, during the prime hours for business transportation (6:15–11:00 A.M.) and a disproportionately high (80%) number of males were included], and from a loaded setting [Southwest employed Kelly Temporary Services (59 of 60 interviewers were female) to conduct face-to-face interviews (the interviewers asked questions and recorded the responses) who identified themselves as agents of Southwest]. The survey also asked "loaded" and "double" ques-

tions, Question 10, for example, stated; "Southwest feels its 'Love Image' as featured by its attractive female flight attendants and ticket agents is one of the reasons people prefer to use Southwest over other airlines. If you could fly on another airline for the same price, out of the same airport, would you be as likely to use the services of Southwest, if Southwest changed this image—that is, would you be as likely to fly Southwest if they substituted males for some of the female flight attendants and ticket agents?" Given these deficiencies, and the failure to perform any test for statistical reliability, the survey conclusion that hiring males would have a negative impact on Southwest's business cannot be given weight.

9. Of the attributes reported, "delivering checked baggage promptly" ranked sixth in importance while "lower fares" ranked seventh.

to Title VII's prohibitions requires a two-part test: (1) does the particular job under consideration require that the worker be of one sex only; and, if so, (2) is that requirement reasonably necessary to the "essence" of the employer's business.]

Application of the Bona Fide Occupational Qualification to Southwest Airlines

Applying the first level test for a BFOQ, with its legal gloss, to Southwest's particular operations results in the conclusion that being female is not a qualification required to perform successfully the jobs of flight attendant and ticket agent with Southwest. Like any other airline, Southwest's primary function is to transport passengers safely and quickly from one point to another.[25] To do this, Southwest employs ticket agents whose primary job duties are to ticket passengers and check baggage, and flight attendants, whose primary duties are to assist passengers during boarding and deboarding, to instruct passengers in the location and use of aircraft safety equipment, and to serve passengers cocktails and snacks during the airline's short commuter flights. Mechanical, non-sex-linked duties dominate both these occupations. Indeed, on Southwest's short-haul commuter flights there is time for little else. That Southwest's female personnel may perform their mechanical duties "with love" does not change the result. "Love" is the manner of job performance, not the job performed.

While possession of female allure and sex appeal have been made qualifications for Southwest's contact personnel by virtue of the "love" campaign, the functions served by employee sexuality in Southwest's operations are not dominant ones. According to Southwest, female sex appeal serves two purposes: (1) attracting and entertaining male passengers and (2) fulfilling customer expectations for female service engendered by Southwest's advertising which features female personnel. As in *Diaz*, these non-mechanical, sex-linked job functions are only "tangential" to the essence of the occupations and business involved. Southwest is not a business where vicarious sex entertainment is the primary service provided. Accordingly, the ability of the airline to perform its primary business function, the transportation of passengers, would not be jeopardized by hiring males.

Southwest does not face the situation anticipated in *Diaz*[26] and encountered in [Fernandez v. Wynn Oil Co., 20 FEP Cases 1162 (C.D.Cal.1979)] where an established customer preference for one sex is so strong that the business would be undermined if employees of the

---

25. Southwest's argument that its primary function is "to make a profit," not to transport passengers, must be rejected. Without doubt the goal of every business is to make a profit. For purposes of BFOQ analysis, however, the business "essence" inquiry focuses on the particular service provided and the job tasks and functions involved, not the business goal. If an employer could justify employment discrimination merely on the grounds that it is necessary to make a profit, Title VII would be nullified in short order.

26. To reiterate, the Fifth Circuit in *Diaz*, supra, 442 F.2d at 389, announced that " * * * customer preference may be taken into account only when it is based on the company's inability to perform the primary function or service it offers."

opposite sex were hired. Southwest's claim that its customers prefer females rests primarily upon inferences drawn from the airline's success after adopting its female personality. But according to Southwest's own surveys, that success is attributable to many factors. There is no competent proof that Southwest's popularity derives directly from its females-only policy to the exclusion of other factors like dissatisfaction with rival airlines and Southwest's use of convenient Love and Hobby Fields. Nor is there competent proof that the customer preference for females is so strong that Defendant's male passengers would cease doing business with Southwest as was the case in *Fernandez*. In short, Southwest has failed in its proof to satisfy *Diaz's* business necessity requirement, without which customer preference may not give rise to a BFOQ for sex.

Southwest contends, nevertheless, that its females-only policy is reasonably necessary to the continued success of its "love" marketing campaign. Airline management testified that Southwest's customers will be disappointed if they find male employees after seeing only female personnel advertised. As a matter of law, this argument fails to support a BFOQ for sex. The court in *Diaz* emphasized that its test was one of business *necessity*, not business *convenience*. *Diaz*, supra, 442 F.2d at 388; Fernandez v. Wynn Oil Co., supra, 20 FEP at 1164. In Weeks v. Southern Bell Telephone and Telegraph Co., supra, 408 F.2d at 234–35, the Fifth Circuit expressly disapproved of the broad construction of the BFOQ exception in Bowe v. Colgate Palmolive Co., 272 F.Supp. 332, 362 (S.D.Ind.1967), aff'd in part and rev'd in part 416 F.2d 711 (7th Cir.1969) which would have permitted sex discrimination where sex was "rationally related to an end which [the employer] has a right to achieve—production, profit, or business reputation."

It is also relevant that Southwest's female image was adopted at its discretion, to promote a business unrelated to sex. Contrary to the unyielding South American preference for males encountered by the Defendant company in *Fernandez*, Southwest exploited, indeed nurtured, the very customer preference for females it now cites to justify discriminating against males. Moreover, the fact that a vibrant marketing campaign was necessary to distinguish Southwest in its early years does not lead to the conclusion that sex discrimination was then, or is now, a business *necessity*. Southwest's claim that its female image will be tarnished by hiring males is, in any case, speculative at best.

The few cases on point support the conclusion that sex does not become a BFOQ merely because an employer chooses to exploit female sexuality as a marketing tool, or to better insure profitability. In Guardian Capital Corp. v. New York State Division of Human Rights, 46 App.Div.2d 832, 360 N.Y.S.2d 937 (1974), *app. dismissed* 48 A.D.2d 753, 368 N.Y.S.2d 594 (1975) for example, the court prohibited an employer from firing male waiters to hire sexually attractive waitresses in an attempt to change the appeal of the business and boost sales. Similarly, in University Parking, Inc. v. Hotel and Restaurant Employees & Bartenders' Int'l Un., 71–2 Lab.Arb.Awards 5360 (1971) (Peck, Arb.), the arbitrator denied an employer's right to replace three waitresses with waiters in order to "upgrade" his business and respond to customer desires for "classier" French service. Merely because Southwest's female image was established in "good faith" [28] and has become its trademark does not distinguish Defendant's conduct from the discriminatory business decisions disapproved of in these cases.

Neither, in the final analysis, does Southwest's "battle-for-inches" with its competitors rise to the level of business *necessity*. *Diaz's* necessity test focuses on the company's ability "to perform the primary function or service it offers," not its ability to compete. As one court has noted in the context of racial discrimination, "[t]he expense involved in changing from a discriminatory system * * * [fails to constitute] a business necessity that would justify the continuation of * * * discrimination." Bush v. Lone Star Steel Co., 373 F.Supp. 526, 533 (E.D.Tex.1974); see also Robinson v. Lorillard Corp., 444 F.2d 791, 799 n. 8 (4th Cir.), cert. dismissed 404 U.S. 1006, 92 S.Ct. 573, 30 L.Ed.2d 655 (1971) ("dollar cost alone is not determinative"). Similarly, a potential loss of profits or possible loss of competitive advantage following a shift to non-discriminatory hiring does not establish business necessity under *Diaz*. To hold otherwise would permit employers within the same industry to establish different hiring standards based on the financial condition of their respective businesses. A rule prohibiting only financially successful enterprises from discriminating under Title VII, while allowing their less successful competitors to ignore the law, has no merit.

Southwest, however, has failed to establish by competent proof that revenue loss would result directly from hiring males. Analogous to the holding in Guardian Capital Corp. v. New York State Division of Human Rights, supra, 360 N.Y.S.2d at 938–39, an employer's mere "beforehand belief" that sex discrimination is a financial imperative, alone, does not establish a BFOQ for sex.

Conclusion

In rejecting Southwest's BFOQ defense, this court follows Justice Marshall's admonition that the BFOQ exception should not be permitted to "swallow the rule." See Phillips v. Martin Marietta Corp., 400 U.S. 542, 545, 91 S.Ct. 496, 498, 27 L.Ed.2d 613 (1971) (Marshall, J. concurring). Southwest's position knows no principled limit. Recognition of a sex BFOQ for Southwest's public contact personnel based on the airline's "love" campaign opens the door for other employers freely to discriminate by tacking on sex or sex appeal as a qualification for

---

28. Under Title VII, it is immaterial that Southwest's feminized marketing strategy was conceived and implemented in "good faith," not in a desire to discriminate against males. Even in cases of unintentional discrimination, the absence of bad motive or intent does not redeem employment practices with forbidden discriminatory consequences. See Griggs v. Duke Power Co., 401 U.S. 424, 432, 91 S.Ct. 849, 854, 28 L.Ed.2d 158 (1971); Vuyanich v. Republic National Bank, 78 F.R.D. 352, 358 (N.D.Tex.1978).

any public contact position where customers preferred employees of a particular sex.[29] In order not to undermine Congress' purpose to prevent employers from "refusing to hire an individual based on stereotyped characterizations of the sexes," see Phillips v. Martin Marietta Corp., supra, 400 U.S. at 545, 91 S.Ct. at 498, a BFOQ for sex must be denied where sex is merely useful for attracting customers of the opposite sex, but where hiring both sexes will not alter or undermine the essential function of the employer's business. Rejecting a wider BFOQ for sex does not eliminate the commercial exploitation of sex appeal. It only requires, consistent with the purposes of Title VII, that employers exploit the attractiveness and allure of a sexually integrated workforce. Neither Southwest, nor the traveling public, will suffer from such a rule. More to the point, it is my judgment that this is what Congress intended.

One final observation is called for. This case has serious underpinnings, but it also has disquieting strains. These strains, and they were only that, warn that in our quest for non-racist, non-sexist goals, the demand for equal rights can be pushed to silly extremes. The rule of law in this country is so firmly embedded in our ethical regimen that little can stand up to its force—except literalistic insistence upon one's rights. And such inability to absorb the minor indignities suffered daily by us all without running to court may stop it dead in its tracks. We do not have such a case here—only warning signs rumbling from the facts.

NOTES AND PROBLEMS FOR DISCUSSION

1. As noted in *Johnson Controls* and *Southwest Airlines* the BFOQ exception is interpreted narrowly and has been successfully utilized in only three contexts:

(a) Authenticity

The EEOC Guidelines provide that "[w]here it is necessary for the purpose of authenticity or genuineness, the Commission will consider sex to be a bona fide occupational qualification, e.g. an actor or actress." 29 C.F.R. § 1604.2 Being female has been found in a few cases to be a BFOQ for jobs the dominant purpose of which is to provide sexual titillation to male customers. See, St. Cross v. Playboy Club, Case No. CFS 22618–70 (New York Human Rights Appeal Board, 1971). One court has suggested that the "authenticity" rule would justify a BFOQ for Chinese nationality where necessary to maintain the authentic atmosphere of an ethnic Chinese restaurant. Utility Workers v. Southern California Edison Co., 320 F.Supp. 1262, 1265 (C.D.Cal.1970).

As in Southwest Airlines, efforts to justify discriminatory hiring practices on the basis of sexually stereotyped customer preferences have met with little success. In Fernandez v. Wynn Oil Co., the case distinguished by Judge Higginbotham in Southwest Airlines, the district court found that being a male was a BFOQ for the job of international marketing director for a company that

---

29. See Note: "Developments in the Law—Employment Discrimination and Ti-   tle VII of the Civil Rights Act of 1964," 84 Harv.L.Rev. 1109, 1185 (1971).

did extensive foreign business because the position involved attracting and transacting business with Latin American and Southeast Asian customers who were not comfortable doing business with women. The court found that hiring a female "would have totally subverted any business [the defendant] hoped to accomplish in those areas of the world." 20 FEP Cases at 1165. The Ninth Circuit reversed on the ground that foreign prejudice against women in business cannot justify non-enforcement of Title VII in this country. Fernandez v. Wynn Oil Co., 653 F.2d 1273 (9th Cir.1981). Cf. Avigliano v. Sumitomo Shoji America, Inc., 638 F.2d 552 (2d Cir.1981), reversed on other grounds 457 U.S. 176, 102 S.Ct. 2374, 72 L.Ed.2d 765 (1982) ("acceptability to those persons with whom the company or branch does business" is one factor to be considered in determining whether executive position in American branch of Japanese company can be restricted to Japanese national).

A minor, but certainly note-worthy, exception to the general rule that a BFOQ cannot be based in the discriminatory preference of customers, was established in Kern v. Dynalectron Corp., 577 F.Supp. 1196 (N.D.Tex.1983), affirmed, 746 F.2d 810 (5th Cir.1984) which held that an employer's requirement that helicopter pilots hired to fly into Mecca be of the Moslem faith (adopted to comply with Arabian Law which prohibits entry of non-Moslems into Mecca) is a BFOQ, exempt from the religious discrimination provisions of Title VII. The district courts' opinion also deserves at least Honorable Mention in the category of judicial understatement.

> The Defendants' burden of producing a legitimate reason for the existing discrimination is properly sustained through the application of the B.F.O.Q. exception to Kern's case. * * * [T]his Court held that Dynalectron has proven a factual basis for believing that *all* non-Moslems would be unable to perform this job safely. Specifically, non-Moslems flying into Mecca are, if caught, beheaded.

> * * * [T]he essence of Dynalectron's business is to provide helicopter pilots * * * [t]hus, the essence of Dynalectron's business would be undermined by the beheading of all the non-Moslem pilots based in Jeddah.

577 F.Supp. at 1200. But in Abrams v. Baylor College of Medicine, 581 F.Supp. 1570 (S.D.Tex.1984), affirmed in part, 805 F.2d 528 (5th Cir.1986), the court concluded that the "patronizing, paternalistic 'concerns' " of a medical school for the safety of Jewish staff members, did not justify, either under the BFOQ or business necessity rationales, its policy of excluding such employees from a program in Saudi Arabia. See, EEOC Decision No. 85–10 (1985), 38 FEP Cases 1873 (employer who refuses to hire woman for work in foreign country because it believes that country prohibits commingling of men and women in workplace will have its proffered reason for rejecting applicant viewed as pretextual unless it has "current, authoritative, and factual basis for its belief").

(b) Privacy

Employers have met with more success in basing BFOQ on customer desires where those desires are related to personal privacy and modesty. In Fesel v. Masonic Home of Delaware, Inc., 447 F.Supp. 1346 (D.Del.1978), affirmed, 591 F.2d 1334 (3d Cir.1979), numerous residents of a nursing home stated that they would leave if it abandoned its policy of hiring only female nurses. The court held that the home had sustained its burden of proving that the essence of its business would be undermined by employing members of the male sex:

While these attitudes may be characterized as "customer preference," this is, nevertheless, not the kind of case governed by the regulatory provision that customer preference alone cannot justify a job qualification based upon sex. Here personal privacy interests are implicated which are protected by law and which have to be recognized by the employer in running its business.

447 F.Supp. at 1352. See also, Jennings v. New York State Office of Mental Health, 786 F.Supp. 376 (S.D.N.Y.1992) (assignment policy at state mental health hospital which required that one orderly of same sex as patients be on duty at all times justified as BFOQ because duties of orderlies include assisting patients in intimate personal care); Backus v. Baptist Medical Center, 510 F.Supp. 1191 (E.D.Ark.1981), vacated on other grounds, 671 F.2d 1100 (8th Cir.1982) (hospital's exclusion of male nurses from obstetrics and gynecology department upheld as BFOQ); Jones v. Hinds General Hospital, 666 F.Supp. 933 (S.D.Miss.1987) (to preserve male patients' interests in privacy defendant allowed to restrict catheterization of male patients to male nurses). As part of the employer's burden of proving BFOQ based on the privacy rights of others, however, it will be required to show that no selective system of job assignments could be made which would protect privacy and allow the employment of members of both sexes). See, Jennings v. New York State Office of Mental Health, supra, 786 F.Supp. at 387 (requiring the presence on the ward of at least one [orderly] of same gender as patients is the least restrictive method to safeguard the privacy rights of the patients while respecting the [orderlies'] right to bid for job assignments.") Backus v. Baptist Medical Center, supra, 510 F.Supp. at 1197; Fesel v. Masonic Homes of Delaware, supra, 447 F.Supp. at 1351.

In Torres v. Wisconsin Dept. of Health and Social Services, 859 F.2d 1523 (7th Cir.1988) (en banc), cert. denied, 489 U.S. 1017, 109 S.Ct. 1133, 103 L.Ed.2d 194 (1989), and cert. denied, 489 U.S. 1082, 109 S.Ct. 1537, 103 L.Ed.2d 841 (1989), male prison guards challenged a policy that restricted certain guard positions in a maximum security women's prison to females. Prison officials justified the change in policy (previously males had been employed in all positions in the facility) on grounds of insuring inmate privacy and encouraging rehabilitation. The officials believed that, since a high percentage of the inmates had histories of abuse by males, providing the inmates with an environment free from the presence of males in positions of authority was necessary to foster the goal of rehabilitation. The district judge ruled that the BFOQ defense was not available to the defendants because the privacy interests of the prisoners could be protected, as they had been in the past, with measures short of denying jobs to men. With respect to the rehabilitation ground, the court determined that the defendants had offered no more than a theory of rehabilitation as justification of the BFOQ and that, without objective evidence either from empirical studies or otherwise supporting the theory, it could not support a BFOQ. A panel of the Seventh Circuit affirmed (838 F.2d 944), but on en banc rehearing, reversed. Emphasizing the necessity of innovation by prison officials, the court held that defendants had been required to meet an "unrealistic, and therefore unfair, burden" when they were required to produce objective evidence supporting the validity of the theory. The case was remanded for reevaluation of the entire record including appropriate deference to the decisions of the prison administrators. The dissenters argued that the majority had ignored the fact that the employer has the burden of proving the necessity of a BFOQ. In his dissent Judge Easterbrook stated:

When the burden is on the defendants, and the trier of fact has found the defendants' explanations shallow, an appellate court must accept that decision. We ought not take it as indisputable that women are different from men and use that premise to justify sex differences in employment. Congress thought otherwise; the district court found otherwise. Under the court's treatment of "necessity" a district judge may (perhaps is compelled to) accept an employer's bare opinion that segregation by sex is helpful.... the majority today says that sex may be a BFOQ in every female prison (maybe every prison) in America.

859 F.2d at 1536. See also, Hardin v. Stynchcomb, 691 F.2d 1364 (11th Cir.1982) (inmate privacy no justification for refusal to hire female jail guards).

(c) Safety

In DOTHARD V. RAWLINSON, 433 U.S. 321, 97 S.Ct. 2720, 53 L.Ed.2d 786 (1977), the Supreme Court struck down Alabama's height and weight requirements for prison personnel (see discussion *infra* at 214), the court upheld a regulation explicitly barring employment of females in 'contact positions' in male penitentiaries as a BFOQ. Citing the "rampant violence" and "jungle atmosphere" in the state's prisons, the Court stated that:

> The essence of a correctional counselor's job is to maintain prison security. A woman's relative ability to maintain order in a male maximum-security unclassified penitentiary of the type Alabama now runs could be directly reduced by her womanhood.
>
> * * *
>
> The likelihood that inmates would assault a woman because she was a woman would pose a real threat not only to the victim of the assault but also to the basic control of the penitentiary and protection of its inmates and the other security personnel. The employee's very womanhood would then directly undermine her capacity to provide the security that is the essence of a correctional counselor's responsibility.

433 U.S. at 335, 336, 97 S.Ct. at 2729, 2730. Since *Dothard*, efforts to exclude females from institutional positions in prisons on "personal privacy" or safety grounds have met with little success. See e.g., Gunther v. Iowa State Men's Reformatory, 612 F.2d 1079, 1085–86 (8th Cir.1980), cert. denied, 446 U.S. 966, 100 S.Ct. 2942, 64 L.Ed.2d 825 (1980) (since Iowa prison was not the "stygian spectre" involved in *Dothard*, it was unlawful to exclude females from contact positions); Griffin v. Michigan Department of Corrections, 654 F.Supp. 690 (E.D.Mich.1982) (neither prison security nor inmate privacy justified refusal to promote female to guard in men's prison). Cf. Torres v. Wisconsin Dept. of Health and Social Services, *supra*.

2. Concerns for authenticity, privacy and safety do not exhaust the reasons that an employer may prefer employees of a particular gender, ethnic background or religion.

May a school district justify its policy of assigning only male drivers to school buses transporting male Hasidic Jews on the ground that the Hasidim are forbidden to ride buses driven by women? Is the school district required by the free exercise clause of the First Amendment to make such assignments or is it prohibited from doing so by the establishment clause? See, Bollenbach v. Board of Education of Monroe–Woodbury Central School Dist., 659 F.Supp. 1450 (S.D.N.Y.1987). May a prison establish a specific religion as a BFOQ for the position of prison chaplain? See, Rasul v. District of Columbia, 680 F.Supp. 436 (D.D.C.1988).

If an airline cannot justify hiring only female flight attendants as necessary to its image, can it at least demand that its female attendants remain sexually attractive—i.e. slender? In Gerdom v. Continental Airlines, Inc., 692 F.2d 602 (9th Cir.1982), cert. denied, 460 U.S. 1074, 103 S.Ct. 1534, 75 L.Ed.2d 954 (1983), the Ninth Circuit rejected the defendants' argument that its weight restrictions for flight attendants (all of whom were female) was merely a sex-neutral "grooming" requirement outside of the purview of Title VII and held that the rule did not qualify as a BFOQ because, "Continental does not argue that only thin females can do the job." The airline's reliance on customer preference for slender female attendants was rejected for the same reasons as those expressed in *Wilson*. If the airline had employed male flight attendants who were subject to the same weight rules as the females, would the employer have to produce a business justification of any kind for its policy? Could an employer's desire that its employees be "real," i.e. biological, men or women, qualify as a BFOQ? Would such a defense be necessary for the employer who discharged an otherwise qualified transsexual? See, Ulane v. Eastern Airlines, Inc., 581 F.Supp. 821 (N.D.Ill. 1983), reversed, 742 F.2d 1081 (7th Cir.1984), cert. denied, 471 U.S. 1017, 105 S.Ct. 2023, 85 L.Ed.2d 304 (1985).

Where an employer desires that its female employees fit a particular "role model" can such a restriction constitute a BFOQ? In Chambers v. Omaha Girls Club, Inc., 834 F.2d 697 (8th Cir.1987) the plaintiff, a single woman, was discharged when she became pregnant because she violated the employer's rule prohibiting unmarried staff members from becoming parents. The court upheld the rule as a BFOQ. Should an employer's rule that its employees speak fluent English be analyzed as a BFOQ? See Fragante v. City of Honolulu, 888 F.2d 591, 597 (9th Cir.1989), cert. denied, 494 U.S. 1081, 110 S.Ct. 1811, 108 L.Ed.2d 942 (1990) (applicant denied employment as court clerk because of "heavy Filipino accent"; no violation of Title VII because "oral ability to communicate effectively in English" is reasonably related to normal operation of clerk's office); Stephen v. PGA Sheraton Resort, Ltd., 873 F.2d 276, 279 (11th Cir.1989) (termination of employee of Haitian origin who had difficulty speaking and understanding English was justified by business necessity).

3. Section 703(e), which permits discrimination where sex, religion or national origin is a BFOQ, omits race from these exceptions to Title VII's requirements. It is permissible to take race into account in order to remedy past discrimination, Fullilove v. Klutznick, 448 U.S. 448, 100 S.Ct. 2758, 65 L.Ed.2d 902 (1980), United Steelworkers of America v. Weber, 443 U.S. 193, 99 S.Ct. 2721, 61 L.Ed.2d 480 (1979) (Chapter 7, *infra*), but job assignments based on the racial stereotype that blacks work better with blacks constitutes a violation of Title VII. See Knight v. Nassau County Civil Service Commission, 649 F.2d 157 (2d Cir.), cert. denied, 454 U.S. 818, 102 S.Ct. 97, 70 L.Ed.2d 87 (1981); Miller v. Texas State Board of Barber Examiners, 615 F.2d 650 (5th Cir.), cert. denied, 449 U.S. 891, 101 S.Ct. 249, 66 L.Ed.2d 117 (1980). But where racial "authenticity" is a legitimate job requirement (a black actor for the role of Thurgood Marshall in a movie about his life) should not the employer have available a BFOQ-type defense?

SECTION C. NONINTENTIONAL DISCRIMINATION

The courts have recognized that the principles of Title VII can be violated by employment practices that do not result in overt differential treatment. Employment policies neutral on their face may deprive individuals of their statutory right to equal employment opportunity. Objective criteria can disqualify minority persons at a disproportionate rate because a history of societal discrimination has prevented many of them from achieving a competitive position in the labor force. The "disproportionate exclusionary impact" theory of discrimination, designed by the courts to address this problem, focuses primarily on the discriminatory impact of facially neutral policies rather than, as in disparate treatment cases, the intent underlying the defendant's action. Consequently, the nature of the proof required to establish the existence of this type of discrimination differs from that associated with claims of disparate treatment.

1. The Conceptual Framework

Read Section 703(k) of Title VII.

GRIGGS v. DUKE POWER CO.

Supreme Court of the United States, 1971.
401 U.S. 424, 91 S.Ct. 849, 28 L.Ed.2d 158.

MR. CHIEF JUSTICE BURGER delivered the opinion of the Court.

We granted the writ in this case to resolve the question whether an employer is prohibited by the Civil Rights Act of 1964, Title VII, from requiring a high school education or passing of a standardized general intelligence test as a condition of employment in or transfer to jobs when (a) neither standard is shown to be significantly related to successful job performance, (b) both requirements operate to disqualify Negroes at a substantially higher rate than white applicants, and (c) the jobs in question formerly had been filled only by white employees as part of a longstanding practice of giving preference to whites.

* * * [T]his proceeding was brought by a group of incumbent Negro employees against Duke Power Company. All the petitioners are employed at the Company's Dan River Steam Station, a power generating facility located at Draper, North Carolina. At the time this action was instituted, the Company had 95 employees at the Dan River Station, 14 of whom were Negroes; 13 of these are petitioners here.

The District Court found that prior to July 2, 1965, the effective date of the Civil Rights Act of 1964, the Company openly discriminated on the basis of race in the hiring and assigning of employees at its Dan River plant. The plant was organized into five operating departments: (1) Labor, (2) Coal Handling, (3) Operations, (4) Maintenance, and (5)

Laboratory and Test. Negroes were employed only in the Labor Department where the highest paying jobs paid less than the lowest paying jobs in the other four "operating" departments in which only whites were employed. Promotions were normally made within each department on the basis of job seniority. Transferees into a department usually began in the lowest position.

In 1955 the Company instituted a policy of requiring a high school education for initial assignment to any department except Labor, and for transfer from the Coal Handling to any "inside" department (Operations, Maintenance, or Laboratory). When the Company abandoned its policy of restricting Negroes to the Labor Department in 1965, completion of high school also was made a prerequisite to transfer from Labor to any other department. From the time the high school requirement was instituted to the time of trial, however, white employees hired before the time of the high school education requirement continued to perform satisfactorily and achieve promotions in the "operating" departments. * * *

The Company added a further requirement for new employees on July 2, 1965, the date on which Title VII became effective. To qualify for placement in any but the Labor Department it became necessary to register satisfactory scores on two professionally prepared aptitude tests, as well as to have a high school education. Completion of high school alone continued to render employees eligible for transfer to the four desirable departments from which Negroes had been excluded if the incumbent had been employed prior to the time of the new requirement. In September 1965 the Company began to permit incumbent employees who lacked a high school education to qualify for transfer from Labor or Coal Handling to an "inside" job by passing two tests—the Wonderlic Personnel Test, which purports to measure general intelligence, and the Bennett Mechanical Comprehension Test. Neither was directed or intended to measure the ability to learn to perform a particular job or category of jobs. The requisite scores used for both initial hiring and transfer approximated the national median for high school graduates.[3]

The District Court had found that while the Company previously followed a policy of overt racial discrimination in a period prior to the Act, such conduct had ceased. The District Court also concluded that Title VII was intended to be prospective only and, consequently, the impact of prior inequities was beyond the reach of corrective action authorized by the Act.

The Court of Appeals was confronted with a question of first impression, as are we, concerning the meaning of Title VII. After careful analysis a majority of that court concluded that a subjective test of the employer's intent should govern, particularly in a close case, and that in this case there was no showing of a discriminatory purpose in

3. The test standards are thus more stringent than the high school require- ment, since they would screen out approximately half of all high school graduates.

the adoption of the diploma and test requirements. On this basis, the Court of Appeals concluded there was no violation of the Act.

* * * In so doing, the Court of Appeals rejected the claim that because these two requirements operated to render ineligible a markedly disproportionate number of Negroes, they were unlawful under Title VII unless shown to be job related. We granted the writ on these claims.

The objective of Congress in the enactment of Title VII * * * was to achieve equality of employment opportunities and remove barriers that have operated in the past to favor an identifiable group of white employees over other employees. Under the Act, practices, procedures, or tests neutral on their face, and even neutral in terms of intent, cannot be maintained if they operate to "freeze" the status quo of prior discriminatory employment practices.

The Court of Appeals' opinion, and the partial dissent, agreed that, on the record in the present case, "whites register far better on the Company's alternative requirements" than Negroes.[6] This consequence would appear to be directly traceable to race. Basic intelligence must have the means of articulation to manifest itself fairly in a testing process. Because they are Negroes, petitioners have long received inferior education in segregated schools * * *. Congress did not intend by Title VII, however, to guarantee a job to every person regardless of qualifications. In short, the Act does not command that any person be hired simply because he was formerly the subject of discrimination, or because he is a member of a minority group. Discriminatory preference for any group, minority or majority, is precisely and only what Congress has proscribed. What is required by Congress is the removal of artificial, arbitrary, and unnecessary barriers to employment when the barriers operate invidiously to discriminate on the basis of racial or other impermissible classification.

* * * The Act proscribes not only overt discrimination but also practices that are fair in form, but discriminatory in operation. The touchstone is business necessity. If an employment practice which operates to exclude Negroes cannot be shown to be related to job performance, the practice is prohibited.

On the record before us, neither the high school completion requirement nor the general intelligence test is shown to bear a demonstrable relationship to successful performance of the jobs for which it was used. Both were adopted, as the Court of Appeals noted, without meaningful study of their relationship to job-performance ability. Rather, a vice president of the Company testified, the requirements

---

6. In North Carolina, 1960 census statistics show that, while 34% of white males had completed high school, only 12% of Negro males had done so.

Similarly, with respect to standardized tests, the EEOC in one case found that use of a battery of tests, including the Wonderlic and Bennett tests used by the Company in the instant case, resulted in 58% of whites passing the tests, as compared with only 6% of the blacks.

were instituted on the Company's judgment that they generally would improve the overall quality of the work force.

The evidence, however, shows that employees who have not completed high school or taken the tests have continued to perform satisfactorily and make progress in departments for which the high school and test criteria are now used.[7] The promotion record of present employees who would not be able to meet the new criteria thus suggests the possibility that the requirements may not be needed even for the limited purpose of preserving the avowed policy of advancement within the Company. * * *

The Court of Appeals held that the Company had adopted the diploma and test requirements without any "intention to discriminate against Negro employees." We do not suggest that either the District Court or the Court of Appeals erred in examining the employer's intent; but good intent or absence of discriminatory intent does not redeem employment procedures or testing mechanisms that operate as "built-in headwinds" for minority groups and are unrelated to measuring job capability.

The Company's lack of discriminatory intent is suggested by special efforts to help the undereducated employees through Company financing of two-thirds the cost of tuition for high school training. But Congress directed the thrust of the Act to the *consequences* of employment practices, not simply the motivation. More than that, Congress has placed on the employer the burden of showing that any given requirement must have a manifest relationship to the employment in question.

* * *

The Company contends that its general intelligence tests are specifically permitted by § 703(h) of the Act.[8] That section authorizes the use of "any professionally developed ability test" that is not "designed, intended *or used* to discriminate because of race * * *." (Emphasis added.)

The Equal Employment Opportunity Commission, having enforcement responsibility, has issued guidelines interpreting § 703(h) to permit only the use of job-related tests.[9] The administrative interpreta-

---

7. For example, between July 2, 1965, and November 14, 1966, the percentage of white employees who were promoted but who were not high school graduates was nearly identical to the percentage of nongraduates in the entire white work force.

8. Section 703(h) applies only to tests. It has no applicability to the high school diploma requirement.

9. EEOC Guidelines on Employment Testing Procedures, issued August 24, 1966, provide:

"The Commission accordingly interprets 'professionally developed ability test' to mean a test which fairly measures the knowledge or skills required by the particular job or class of jobs which the applicant seeks, or which fairly affords the employer a chance to measure the applicant's ability to perform a particular job or class of jobs. The fact that a test was prepared by an individual or organization claiming expertise in test preparation does not, without more, justion of the Act by the enforcing agency is entitled to great deference. Since the Act and its legislative history support the Commission's construction, this affords good reason to treat the guidelines as expressing the will of Congress.

* * *

Nothing in the Act precludes the use of testing or measuring procedures; obviously they are useful. What Congress has forbidden is giving these devices and mechanisms controlling force unless they are demonstrably a reasonable measure of job performance. Congress has not commanded that the less qualified be preferred over the better qualified simply because of minority origins. Far from disparaging job qualifications as such, Congress has made such qualifications the controlling factor, so that race, religion, nationality, and sex become irrelevant. What Congress has commanded is that any tests used must measure the person for the job and not the person in the abstract.

The judgment of the Court of Appeals is, as to that portion of the judgment appealed from, reversed.

Mr. Justice Brennan took no part in the consideration or decision of this case.

NOTES AND PROBLEMS FOR DISCUSSION

1. How does the concept of discrimination recognized by the Court in *Griggs* differ from the one examined in *McDonnell Douglas*? To what extent are these theories premised on different interpretations of the concept of equality?

2. Until the passage of the 1991 Civil Rights Act, there was substantial debate over whether there was any statutory authority for the recognition of a disproportionate impact-based cause of action under Title VII. Compare Gold, Griggs' Folly: An Essay On The Theory, Problems, And Origins Of The Adverse Impact Definition Of Employment Discrimination And A Recommendation For Reform, 7 Ind.Rel.L.J. 429 (1985) with Rutherglen, Disparate Impact Under Title VII: An Objective Theory of Discrimination, 73 Va.L.Rev. 1297 (1987). See also Blumrosen, Strangers in Paradise: Griggs v. Duke Power Co. and the Concept of Employment Discrimination, 71 Mich.L.Rev. 59 (1972). This dispute disappeared, of course, when Congress codified the impact model of discrimination in the 1991 enactment by adding new § 703(k)(1) to Title VII.

3. How much of a disproportionate impact must plaintiff show to establish a prima facie violation? The federal courts have not adopted a uniform quantitative standard for determining what constitutes a substantially disproportionate exclusionary impact. For a thorough and thoughtful discussion, see

tify its use within the meaning of Title VII."

The EEOC position has been elaborated in the new Guidelines on Employees Selection Procedures, 29 CFR § 1607, 35 Fed.Reg. 12333 (Aug. 1, 1970). These guidelines demand that employers using tests have available "data demonstrating that the test is predictive of or significantly correlated with important elements of work behavior which comprise or are relevant to the job or jobs for which candidates are being evaluated."

Shoben, Differential Pass–Fail Rates in Employment Testing: Statistical Proof Under Title VII, 91 Harv.L.Rev. 793 (1978).

On August 25, 1978, however, several federal agencies adopted a set of uniform testing guidelines to provide standards for ruling on the legality of selection procedures used by private and public employers subject to these agencies' rules. Section 4D, or the "four-fifths rule," provides that a selection rate for members of a protected group of less than 80% of the rate for the highest scoring group generally will create a prima facie case of disproportionate impact. This is only a rule of thumb; the agencies retain discretion to make adjustments in individual cases. See 4D, Fed.Reg. 38291, 297–98. The rule has been adopted by several courts. See Brown v. New Haven Civil Service Board, 474 F.Supp. 1256 (D.Conn.1979); Guardians Association v. Civil Service Commission, 630 F.2d 79 (2d Cir.1980); United States v. City of Chicago, 21 FEP Cases 200 (N.D.Ill.1979). The issue was discussed, though not resolved, by the Supreme Court in Watson v. Fort Worth Bank & Trust, 487 U.S. 977, 108 S.Ct. 2777, 101 L.Ed.2d 827 (1988). See Note 2 following *Watson, infra,* at ___.

4. Shortly after graduating from law school, James Stanton, a black man, failed the bar examination in the state in which he wanted to open up a private practice. He can prove that while 85% of the white applicants pass this examination, only 49% of all black applicants pass it. Can he successfully maintain a race discrimination claim under Title VII against the State Board of Bar Examiners? See Woodard v. Virginia Board of Bar Examiners, 598 F.2d 1345 (4th Cir.1979).

2. The Plaintiff's Case

Prior to the codification of the disproportionate impact theory of discrimination in the 1991 Civil Rights Act, the Supreme Court's recognition, or, some would say, creation of an impact-based theory of discrimination dramatically expanded the universe of employment decisions that could be, and were subjected to Title VII challenge. It also raised problems and controversies unique to this theoretical model. For example, suppose an employer adopted a multi-component selection policy under which all applicants for promotion were required to pass a battery of tests, undergo a personal interview and submit letters of recommendation. Further assume that the 90% of the white applicants, but only 35% of the black candidates, received promotions. But also assume that an unsuccessful candidate could not determine how important success on any of the individual components of the process was to the ultimate decision. Could such an unsuccessful black applicant successfully bring a *Griggs*-based claim? Alternatively, suppose the applicant could establish that 25% of the black applicants and 75% of the white applicants passed the tests, but that the employer could prove that as a consequence of its consideration of other factors, its work force was racially balanced? Could an African-American plaintiff establish a prima facie case? Do these two scenarios raise different issues? These and other questions associated with litigation of the plaintiff's case in disproportionate impact claims are addressed by the following cases.

Question - what is disparate impact?
effect on opportunity or
effect on result?

202   TITLE VII OF 1964 CIVIL RIGHTS ACT   Pt. 2

CONNECTICUT v. TEAL

Supreme Court of the United States, 1982.
457 U.S. 440, 102 S.Ct. 2525, 73 L.Ed.2d 130.

JUSTICE BRENNAN delivered the opinion of the Court.

We consider here whether an employer sued for violation of Title VII of the Civil Rights Act of 1964 may assert a "bottom line" theory of defense. Under that theory, as asserted in this case, an employer's acts of racial discrimination in promotions—effected by an examination having disparate impact—would not render the employer liable for the racial discrimination suffered by employees barred from promotion if the "bottom line" result of the promotional process was an appropriate racial balance. We hold that the "bottom line" does not preclude respondent-employees from establishing a prima facie case, nor does it provide petitioner-employer with a defense to such a case.

what about affirmative action?

I

Four of the respondents, Winnie Teal, Rose Walker, Edith Latney, and Grace Clark, are black employees of the Department of Income Maintenance of the State of Connecticut. Each was promoted provisionally to the position of Welfare Eligibility Supervisor and served in that capacity for almost two years. To attain permanent status as supervisors, however, respondents had to participate in a selection process that required, as the first step, a passing score on a written examination. This written test was administered on December 2, 1978, to 329 candidates. Of these candidates, 48 identified themselves as black and 259 identified themselves as white. The results of the examination were announced in March 1979. With the passing score set at 65,[3] 54.17 of the identified black candidates passed. This was approximately 68 percent of the passing rate for the identified white candidates.[4] The four respondents were among the blacks who failed the examination, and they were thus excluded from further consideration for permanent supervisory positions. In April 1979, respondents instituted this action in the United States District Court for the District of Connecticut against petitioners, the State of Connecticut, two state agencies, and two state officials. Respondents alleged, *inter alia*, that

---

3. The mean score on the examination was 70.4 percent. However, because the black candidates had a mean score 6.7 percentage points lower than the white candidates, the passing score was set at 65, apparently in an attempt to lessen the disparate impact of the examination.

4.

* * *

Petitioners do not contest the District Court's implicit finding that the examination itself resulted in disparate impact under the "eighty percent rule" of the Uniform Guidelines on Employee Selection Procedures adopted by the Equal Employment Opportunity Commission. Those guidelines provide that a selection rate that "is less than [80 percent] of the rate for the group with the highest rate will generally be regarded * * * as evidence of adverse impact."

petitioners violated Title VII by imposing, as an absolute condition for consideration for promotion, that applicants pass a written test that excluded blacks in disproportionate numbers and that was not job related.

More than a year after this action was instituted, and approximately one month before trial, petitioners made promotions from the eligibility list generated by the written examination. In choosing persons from that list, petitioners considered past work performance, recommendations of the candidates' supervisors and, to a lesser extent, seniority. Petitioners then applied what the Court of Appeals characterized as an affirmative action program in order to ensure a significant number of minority supervisors. Forty-six persons were promoted to permanent supervisory positions, 11 of whom were black and 35 of whom were white. The overall result of the selection process was that, of the 48 identified black candidates who participated in the selection process, 22.9 percent were promoted and of the 259 identified white candidates, 13.5 percent were promoted.[6] It is this "bottom-line" result, more favorable to blacks than to whites, that petitioners urge should be adjudged to be a complete defense to respondents' suit.

After trial, the District Court entered judgment for petitioners. The court treated respondents' claim as one of disparate impact under Griggs v. Duke Power Co., Albemarle Paper Co. v. Moody, and Dothard v. Rawlinson. However, the court found that, although the comparative passing rates for the examination indicated a prima facie case of adverse impact upon minorities, the result of the entire hiring process reflected no such adverse impact. Holding that these "bottom line" percentages precluded the finding of a Title VII violation, the court held that the employer was not required to demonstrate that the promotional examination was job related. The United States Court of Appeals for the Second Circuit reversed, holding that the District Court erred in ruling that the results of the written examination alone were insufficient to support a prima facie case of disparate impact in violation of Title VII. The Court of Appeals stated that where "an identifiable pass-fail barrier denies an employment opportunity to a disproportionately large number of minorities and prevents them from proceeding to the next step in the selection process," that barrier must be shown to be job related. We granted certiorari, and now affirm.

II

A

We must first decide whether an examination that bars a disparate number of black employees from consideration for promotion, and that has not been shown to be job related, presents a claim cognizable under Title VII. Section 703(a)(2) of Title VII provides in pertinent part:

---

6. The actual promotion rate of blacks was thus close to 170 percent that of the actual promotion rate of whites.

It shall be an unlawful employment practice for an employer—

* * *

(2) to limit, segregate, or classify his employees or applicants for employment in any way which would deprive or tend to deprive any individual of employment opportunities or otherwise adversely affect his status as an employee, because of such individual's race, color, religion, sex, or national origin.

Respondents base their claim on our construction of this provision in Griggs v. Duke Power Co., supra. * * *

Griggs and its progeny have established a three-part analysis of disparate impact claims. To establish a prima facie case of discrimination, a plaintiff must show that the facially neutral employment practice had a significantly discriminatory impact. If that showing is made, the employer must then demonstrate that "any given requirement [has] a manifest relationship to the employment in question," in order to avoid a finding of discrimination. *Griggs,* supra. Even in such a case, however, the plaintiff may prevail if he shows that employer was using the practice as a mere pretext for discrimination. See Albemarle Paper Co.; Dothard, supra.[7]

* * *

Petitioners' examination, which barred promotion and had a discriminatory impact on black employees, clearly falls within the literal language of § 703(a)(2), as interpreted by *Griggs.*[8] The statute speaks, not in terms of jobs and promotions, but in terms of *limitations* and *classifications* that would deprive any individual of employment *opportunities.*[9] A disparate impact claim reflects the language of § 703(a)(2) and Congress' basic objectives in enacting that statute: "to achieve equality of employment *opportunities* and remove barriers that have

---

7. Petitioners apparently argue both that the nondiscriminatory "bottom line" precluded respondents from establishing a prima facie case and, in the alternative, that it provided a defense.

8. The legislative history of the 1972 amendments to Title VII is relevant to this case because those amendments extended the protection of the Act to respondents here by deleting exemptions for state and municipal employers. That history demonstrates that Congress recognized and endorsed the disparate impact analysis employed by the Court in *Griggs.* Both the House and Senate reports cited *Griggs* with approval, the Senate Report noting that:

"Employment discrimination as viewed today is a * * * complex and pervasive phenomenon. Experts familiar with the subject now generally describe the problem in terms of 'systems' and 'effects' rather than simply intentional wrongs." In addition, the Section–by–Section Analyses of the 1972 amendments submitted to both houses explicitly stated that in any area not addressed by the amendments, present case law—which as Congress had already recognized included our then recent decision in *Griggs*—was intended to continue to govern.

9. In contrast, the language of § 703(a)(1), if it were the only protection given to employees and applicants under Title VII, might support petitioners' exclusive focus on the overall result. That subsection makes it an unlawful employment practice "to fail or refuse to hire or to discharge any individual, or otherwise to discriminate against any individual with respect to his compensation, terms, conditions or privileges of employment, because of such individual's race, color, religion, sex, or national origin."

operated in the past to favor an identifiable group of white employees over other employees." When an employer uses a nonjob-related barrier in order to deny a minority or woman applicant employment or promotion, and that barrier has a significant adverse effect on minorities or women, then the applicant has been deprived of an employment *opportunity* "because of * * * race, color, religion, sex, or national origin." In other words, § 703(a)(2) prohibits discriminatory "artificial, arbitrary, and unnecessary barriers to employment," that "limit * * * or classify * * * applicants for employment * * * in any way which would deprive or tend to deprive any individual of employment *opportunities*."

Relying on § 703(a)(2), *Griggs* explicitly focused on employment "practices, procedures, or tests," that deny equal employment "opportunity." We concluded that Title VII prohibits "procedures or testing mechanisms that operate as 'built-in headwinds' for minority groups." We found that Congress' primary purpose was the prophylactic one of achieving equality of employment "opportunities" and removing "barriers" to such equality. The examination given to respondents in this case surely constituted such a practice and created such a barrier.

Our conclusion that § 703(a)(2) encompasses respondents' claim is reinforced by the terms of Congress' 1972 extension of the protections of Title VII to state and municipal employees. See n. 8, supra. Although Congress did not explicitly consider the viability of the defense offered by the state employer in this case, the 1972 amendments to Title VII do reflect Congress' intent to provide state and municipal employees with the protection that Title VII, as interpreted by *Griggs,* had provided to employees in the private sector: equality of *opportunity* and the elimination of discriminatory *barriers* to professional development. The committee reports and the floor debates stressed the need for equality of opportunity for minority applicants seeking to obtain governmental positions. Congress voiced its concern about the wide-spread use by state and local governmental agencies of "invalid selection techniques" that had a discriminatory impact. *on opportunities?*

The decisions of this Court following *Griggs* also support respondents' claim. In considering claims of disparate impact under § 703(a)(2) this Court has consistently focused on employment and promotion requirements that create a discriminatory bar to *opportunities.* This Court has never read § 703(a)(2) as requiring the focus to be placed instead on the overall number of minority or female applicants actually hired or promoted. Thus Dothard v. Rawlinson, found that minimum statutory height and weight requirements for correctional counselors were the sort of arbitrary barrier to equal employment opportunity for women forbidden by Title VII. Although we noted in passing that women constituted 36.89 percent of the labor force and only 12.9 percent of correctional counselor positions, our focus was not on this "bottom line." We focused instead on the disparate effect that the minimum height and weight standards had on applicants: classify-

[handwritten margin notes: of course — not this would be ridiculous and does not strengthen court's argument]

But, only have to show if empl. is related (result if to dis-proportionally exclude)

ing far more women than men as ineligible for employment. Similarly, in Albemarle Paper Co. v. Moody, the action was remanded to allow the employer to attempt to show that the tests that he had given to his employees for promotion were job related. We did not suggest that by promoting a sufficient number of the black employees who passed the examination, the employer could avoid this burden. See also New York Transit Authority v. Beazer, 440 U.S. 568, 584, 99 S.Ct. 1355, 1365, 59 L.Ed.2d 587 (1979) ("A prima facie violation of the Act may be established by statistical evidence showing that an employment *practice* has the effect of denying members of one race equal access to employment *opportunities*.") (emphasis added).

In short, the District Court's dismissal of respondents' claim cannot be supported on the basis that respondents failed to establish a prima facie case of employment discrimination under the terms of § 703(a)(2). The suggestion that disparate impact should be measured only at the bottom line ignores the fact that Title VII guarantees these individual respondents the *opportunity* to compete equally with white workers on the basis of job-related criteria. Title VII strives to achieve equality of opportunity by rooting out "artificial, arbitrary and unnecessary" employer-created barriers to professional development that have a discriminatory impact upon individuals. Therefore, respondents' rights under § 703(a)(2) have been violated, unless petitioners can demonstrate that the examination given was not an artificial, arbitrary, or unnecessary barrier, because it measured skills related to effective performance in the role of Welfare Eligibility Supervisor.

B

The United States, in its brief as *amicus curiae*, apparently recognizes that respondents' claim in this case falls within the affirmative commands of Title VII. But it seeks to support the District Court's judgment in this case by relying on the defenses provided to the employer in § 703(h).[11] Section 703(h) provides in pertinent part:

> "Notwithstanding any other provision of this title, it shall not be an unlawful employment practice for an employer * * * to give and to act upon the results of any professionally developed ability test provided that such test, its administration or action upon the results is not designed, intended or used to discriminate because of race, color, religion, sex or national origin."

The Government argues that the test administered by the petitioners was not "used to discriminate" because it did not actually deprive disproportionate numbers of blacks of promotions. But the Government's reliance on § 703(h) as offering the employer some special haven for discriminatory tests is misplaced. We considered the relevance of

---

11. The Government's brief is submitted by the Department of Justice, which shares responsibility for federal enforcement of Title VII with the Equal Employment Opportunity Commission (EEOC). The EEOC declined to join this brief.

this provision in *Griggs*. After examining the legislative history of § 703(h), we concluded that Congress, in adding § 703(h), intended only to make clear that tests that were *job related* would be permissible despite their disparate impact. As the Court recently confirmed, § 703(h), which was introduced as an amendment to Title VII on the Senate floor, "did not alter the meaning of Title VII, but 'merely clarifie[d] its present intent and effect.'" American Tobacco v. Patterson, 456 U.S. 63, 73, n. 11, 102 S.Ct. 1534, 1539, n. 11, 71 L.Ed.2d 748 (1982), quoting 110 Cong.Rec. 12723 (remarks of Sen. Humphrey). A nonjob-related test that has a disparate racial impact, and is used to "limit" or "classify" employees, is "used to discriminate" within the meaning of Title VII, whether or not it was "designed or intended" to have this effect and despite an employer's efforts to compensate for its discriminatory effect. See *Griggs*.

In sum, respondents' claim of disparate impact from the examination, a pass-fail barrier to employment opportunity, states a prima facie case of employment discrimination under § 703(a)(2), despite their employer's nondiscriminatory "bottom line," and that "bottom line" is no defense to this prima facie case under § 703(h).

III

Having determined that respondents' claim comes within the terms of Title VII, we must address the suggestion of petitioners and some *amici curiae* that we recognize an exception, either in the nature of an additional burden on plaintiffs seeking to establish a prima facie case or in the nature of an affirmative defense, for cases in which an employer has compensated for a discriminatory pass-fail barrier by hiring or promoting a sufficient number of black employees to reach a nondiscriminatory "bottom line." We reject this suggestion, which is in essence nothing more than a request that we redefine the protections guaranteed by Title VII.[12]

---

12. Petitioners suggest that we should defer to the EEOC Guidelines in this regard. But there is nothing in the Guidelines to which we might defer that would aid petitioners in this case. The most support petitioners could conceivably muster from the Uniform Guidelines on Employee Selection Procedures (now issued jointly by the EEOC, the Civil Service Commission, the Department of Labor, and the Department of Justice), is *neutrality* on the question whether a discriminatory barrier that does not result in a discriminatory overall result constitutes a violation of Title VII. Section 1607.4C of the Guidelines, relied upon by petitioners, states that as a matter of *"administrative and prosecutorial discretion, in the usual case,"* the agencies will not take enforcement action based upon the disparate impact of any component of a selection process if the total selection process results in no adverse impact. (Emphasis added.) The agencies made clear that the "guidelines do not address the underlying question of law," and that an individual "who is denied the job because of a particular component in a procedure which otherwise meets the 'bottom line' standard * * * retains the right to proceed through the appropriate agencies, and into Federal court." In addition, in a publication entitled, "Adoption of Questions and Answers to Clarify and Provide a Common Interpretation of the Uniform Guidelines on Employee Selection Procedures," the agencies stated:

"Since the [bottom line] concept is not a rule of law, it does not affect the discharge by the EEOC of its statutory responsibilities to investigate charges of discrimination, render an administrative

Section 703(a)(2) prohibits practices that would deprive or tend to deprive "*any individual* of employment opportunities." The principal focus of the statute is the protection of the individual employee, rather than the protection of the minority group as a whole. Indeed, the entire statute and its legislative history are replete with references to protection for the individual employee. See, e.g., §§ 703(a)(1), (b), (c), 704(a). * * *

In suggesting that the "bottom line" may be a defense to a claim of discrimination against an individual employee, petitioners and *amici* appear to confuse unlawful discrimination with discriminatory intent. The Court has stated that a nondiscriminatory "bottom line" and an employer's good faith efforts to achieve a nondiscriminatory work force, might in some cases assist an employer in rebutting the inference that particular action had been intentionally discriminatory: "Proof that [a] work force was racially balanced or that it contained a disproportionately high percentage of minority employees is not wholly irrelevant on the issue of intent when that issue is yet to be decided." Furnco Construction Corp. v. Waters, 438 U.S. 567, 580, 98 S.Ct. 2943, 2951, 57 L.Ed.2d 957 (1978). See also Teamsters v. United States, 431 U.S. 324, 340, n. 20, 97 S.Ct. 1843, 1856–1857, n. 20, 52 L.Ed.2d 396 (1977). But resolution of the factual question of intent is not what is at issue in this case. Rather, petitioners seek simply to justify discrimination against respondents, on the basis of their favorable treatment of other members of respondents' racial group. Under Title VII, "A racially balanced work force cannot immunize an employer from liability for specific acts of discrimination." Furnco Construction Corp.

"It is clear beyond cavil that the obligation imposed by Title VII is to provide an equal opportunity for *each* applicant regardless of race, without regard to whether members of the applicant's race are already proportionately represented in the work force." Ibid. (emphasis in original).

It is clear that Congress never intended to give an employer license to discriminate against some employees on the basis of race or sex merely because he favorably treats other members of the employees' group. We recognized in Los Angeles Dept. of Water & Power v. Manhart, 435 U.S. 702, 98 S.Ct. 1370, 55 L.Ed.2d 657 (1978), that fairness to the class of women employees as a whole could not justify unfairness to the individual female employee because the "statute's focus on the individual is unambiguous." Similarly, in Phillips v. Martin Marietta Corp., 400 U.S. 542, 91 S.Ct. 496, 27 L.Ed.2d 613 (1971) (*per curiam*), we recognized that a rule barring employment of all married *women* with preschool children, if not a bona fide occupational qualification under § 703(e), violated Title VII, even though female applicants without preschool children were hired in sufficient numbers

---

finding on its investigation, and engage in voluntary conciliation efforts. Similarly, with respect to the other issuing agencies, the bottom line concept applies not to the processing of individual charges, but to the initiation of enforcement action."

that they constituted 75 to 80 percent of the persons employed in the position plaintiff sought.

Petitioners point out that *Furnco, Manhart,* and *Phillips* involved facially discriminatory policies, while the claim in the instant case is one of discrimination from a facially neutral policy. The fact remains, however, that irrespective of the form taken by the discriminatory practice, an employer's treatment of other members of the plaintiffs' group can be "of little comfort to the victims of * * * discrimination." Teamsters v. United States, supra. Title VII does not permit the victim of a facially discriminatory policy to be told that he has not been wronged because other persons of his or her race or sex were hired. That answer is no more satisfactory when it is given to victims of a policy that is facially neutral but practically discriminatory. Every *individual* employee is protected against both discriminatory treatment and against "practices that are fair in form, but discriminatory in operation." Griggs v. Duke Power Co. Requirements and tests that have a discriminatory impact are merely some of the more subtle, but also the more pervasive, of the "practices and devices which have fostered racially stratified job environments to the disadvantage of minority citizens." McDonnell Douglas Corp. v. Green.

IV

In sum, petitioners' nondiscriminatory "bottom line" is no answer, under the terms of Title VII, to respondents' prima facie claim of employment discrimination. Accordingly, the judgment of the Court of Appeals for the Second Circuit is affirmed, and this case is remanded to the District Court for further proceedings consistent with this opinion.

It is so ordered.

JUSTICE POWELL, with whom THE CHIEF JUSTICE, JUSTICE REHNQUIST, and JUSTICE O'CONNOR join, dissenting.

In past decisions, this Court has been sensitive to the critical difference between cases proving discrimination under Title VII by a showing of disparate treatment or discriminatory intent and those proving such discrimination by a showing of disparate impact. Because today's decision blurs that distinction and results in a holding inconsistent with the very nature of disparate-impact claims, I dissent.

I

Section 703(a)(2), provides that it is an unlawful employment practice for an employer to

> "limit, segregate or classify his employees or applicants for employment in any way which would deprive or tend to deprive any individual of employment opportunities or otherwise adversely affect his status as an employee, because of such individual's race, color, religion, sex, or national origin."

Although this language suggests that discrimination occurs only on an individual basis, in *Griggs* the Court held that discriminatory intent on the part of the employer against an individual need not be shown when "employment procedures or testing mechanisms * * * operate as 'built-in headwinds' for minority groups and are unrelated to measuring job capability." Thus, the Court held that the "disparate impact" of an employer's practices on a racial group can violate § 703(a)(2) of Title VII. In *Griggs* and each subsequent disparate-impact case, however, the Court has considered, not whether the claimant as an individual had been classified in a manner impermissible under § 703(a)(2), but whether an employer's procedures have had an adverse impact on the protected *group* to which the individual belongs.

Thus, while disparate-*treatment* cases focus on the way in which an individual has been treated, disparate-*impact* cases are concerned with the protected group. This key distinction was explained in *Furnco Construction Corp.* (Marshall, J., concurring in part):

> "It is well established under Title VII that claims of employment discrimination because of race may arise in two different ways. Teamsters v. United States, 431 U.S. 324, 335–336, n. 15, 97 S.Ct. 1843, 1854–1855, n. 15, 52 L.Ed.2d 396 (1977). An individual may allege that he has been subjected to 'disparate treatment' because of his race, or that he has been the victim of a facially neutral practice having a 'disparate impact' on his racial group."

In keeping with this distinction, our disparate impact cases consistently have considered whether the result of an employer's *total selection process* had an adverse impact upon the protected group.[2] If this case were decided by reference to the total process—as our cases suggest that it should be—the result would be clear. Here 22.9% of the blacks who entered the selection process were ultimately promoted, compared with only 13.5% of the whites. To say that this selection process had an unfavorable "disparate impact" on blacks is to ignore reality.

The Court, disregarding the distinction drawn by our cases, repeatedly asserts that Title VII was designed to protect individual, not group, rights. It emphasizes that some individual blacks were eliminated by the disparate impact of the preliminary test. But this argument confuses the *aim* of Title VII with the legal theories through which its aims were intended to be vindicated. It is true that the aim of Title VII is to protect individuals, not groups. But in advancing this commendable objective, Title VII jurisprudence has recognized two distinct

---

2. See Dothard v. Rawlinson, 433 U.S. 321, 329, 97 S.Ct. 2720, 2726–2727, 53 L.Ed.2d 786 (1977) (statutory height and weight requirements operated as a bar to *employment* of disproportionate number of women); Albemarle Paper Co. v. Moody, 422 U.S. 405, 409–411, 95 S.Ct. 2362, 2367–2368, 45 L.Ed.2d 280 (1975) (seniority system allegedly locked blacks into lower pay-ing jobs; applicants to skilled lines of progression were required to pass two tests); Griggs v. Duke Power Co., 401 U.S. 424, 431, 91 S.Ct. 849, 853, 28 L.Ed.2d 158 (1971) (tests were an absolute bar to transfers or hiring; the Court observed that all Congress requires is "the removal of artificial, arbitrary, and unnecessary barriers to *employment* * * *.") (emphasis added).

methods of proof. In one set of cases—those involving direct proof of discriminatory intent—the plaintiff seeks to establish direct, intentional discrimination against him. In that type case, the individual is at the forefront throughout the entire presentation of evidence. In disparate impact cases, by contrast, the plaintiff seeks to carry his burden of proof by way of *inference*—by showing that an employer's selection process results in the rejection of a disproportionate number of members of a protected group to which he belongs. From such a showing a fair inference then may be drawn that the rejected applicant, as a member of that disproportionately excluded group, was himself a victim of that process's " 'built-in head winds.'' *Griggs*. But this method of proof—which actually *defines* disparate impact theory under Title VII—invites the plaintiff to prove discrimination by reference to the group rather than to the allegedly affected individual.[3] There can be no violation of Title VII on the basis of disparate impact in the absence of disparate impact on a *group*.

In this case the plaintiff seeks to benefit from a conflation of "discriminatory treatment" and "disparate impact" theories. But he cannot have it both ways. Having undertaken to prove discrimination by reference to one set of group figures (used at a preliminary point in the selection process), the plaintiff then claims that *non* discrimination cannot be proved by viewing the impact of the entire process on the group as a whole. The fallacy of this reasoning—accepted by the Court—is transparent. It is to confuse the individualistic *aim* of Title VII with the methods of proof by which Title VII rights may be vindicated. The respondent, as an individual, is entitled to the full personal protection of Title VII. But, having undertaken to prove a violation of his rights by reference to group figures, respondent cannot deny petitioner the opportunity to rebut his evidence by introducing figures of the same kind. Having pleaded a disparate impact case, the plaintiff cannot deny the defendant the opportunity to show that there was no disparate impact. As the Court of Appeals for the Third Circuit noted in EEOC v. Greyhound Lines, 635 F.2d 188, 192 (CA3 1980):

> "no violation of Title VII can be grounded on the disparate impact theory without proof that the questioned policy or practice has had a disproportionate impact on the employer's workforce. This conclusion should be as obvious as it is tautological: there can be no disparate impact unless there is [an ultimate] disparate impact."

3. Initially, the plaintiff bears the burden of establishing a prima facie case that Title VII has been infringed. See Texas Dept. of Community Affairs v. Burdine. In a disparate-impact case, this burden is met by showing that an employer's selection process results in the rejection of a disproportionate number of members of a protected group. See Teamsters v. United States. Regardless of whether the plaintiff's prima facie case must itself focus on the defendant's overall selection process or whether it is sufficient that the plaintiff establish that at least one pass-fail barrier has resulted in disparate impact, the employer's presentation of evidence showing that its overall selection procedure does not operate in a discriminatory fashion certainly dispels any inference of discrimination. In such instances, at the close of the evidence, the plaintiff has failed to show disparate impact by a preponderance of the evidence.

Where, under a facially neutral employment process, there has been no adverse effect on the group—and certainly there has been none here—Title VII has not been infringed.

II

The Court's position is no stronger in case authority than it is in logic. None of the cases relied upon by the Court controls the outcome of this case.[5] Indeed, the disparate-impact cases do not even support the propositions for which they are cited. For example, the Court cites Dothard v. Rawlinson * * * and observes that "[a]lthough we noted in passing that women constituted 36.89 percent of the labor force and only 12.9 percent of correctional counselors, our focus was not on this bottom line. We focused instead on the disparate effect that the minimum height and weight standards had on applicants; classifying far more women than men as ineligible for employment." In *Dothard*, however, the Court was not considering a case in which there was any difference between the discriminatory effect of the employment standard and the number of minority members actually hired. The *Dothard* Court itself stated that

> "to establish a prima facie case of discrimination, a plaintiff need only show that the facially neutral standards in question *select* applicants *for hire* in a discriminatory pattern. Once it is shown that *the employment standards* are discriminatory in effect, the employer must meet 'the burden of showing that any given requirement [has] * * * a manifest relationship to the employment in question.' " (emphasis added).

The *Dothard* Court did not decide today's case. It addressed only a case in which the challenged standards had a discriminatory impact at the bottom line—the hiring decision. And the *Dothard* Court's "focus," referred to by the Court, is of no help in deciding the instant case.[6]

---

5. The Court concentrates on cases of questionable relevance. Most of the lower courts that have squarely considered the question have concluded that there can be no violation of Title VII on a disparate-impact basis when there is no disparate impact at the *bottom line*. See, e.g., EEOC v. Greyhound Lines, 635 F.2d 188 (CA3 1980); EEOC v. Navajo Refining Co., 593 F.2d 988 (CA10 1979); Friend v. Leidinger, 588 F.2d 61, 66 (CA4 1978); Rule v. Ironworkers Local 396, 568 F.2d 558 (CA8 1977); Smith v. Troyan, 520 F.2d 492, 497–498 (CA6 1975), cert. denied, 426 U.S. 934, 96 S.Ct. 2646, 49 L.Ed.2d 385 (1976); Williams v. City & Cty. of San Francisco, 483 F.Supp. 335 (N.D.Cal.1979); Brown v. New Haven Civil Service Board, 474 F.Supp. 1256 (D.Conn.1979); Lee v. City of Richmond, 456 F.Supp. 756 (E.D.Va.1978).

6. The Court cites language from two other disparate-impact cases. The Court

notes that in Albemarle Paper Co. v. Moody, the Court "remanded to allow the employer to attempt to show that the tests * * * given * * * for promotion were job related." But the fact that the Court did so without suggesting "that by promoting a sufficient number of black employees who passed the examination, the employer could avoid this hurdle," can hardly be precedent for the negative of that proposition when the issue was neither presented in the facts of the case nor addressed by the Court.

Similarly, New York Transit Authority v. Beazer, provides little support despite the language quoted by the Court. * * * In *Beazer*, the Court ruled that the statistical evidence actually presented was insufficient to establish a prima facie case of discrimination, and in doing so it indicated that it would have found statistical evi-

The Court concedes that the other major cases on which it relies, *Furnco,* and Phillips v. Martin Marietta Corp., "involved facially discriminatory policies, while the claim in the instant case is one of discrimination from a facially neutral policy." The Court nevertheless applies the principles derived from those cases to the case at bar. It does so by reiterating the view that Title VII protects *individuals,* not *groups,* and therefore that the manner in which an employer has treated other members of a group cannot defeat the claim of an individual who has suffered as a result of even a facially neutral policy. As appealing as this sounds, it confuses the distinction—uniformly recognized until today—between disparate *impact* and disparate *treatment.* Our cases, cited above, have made clear that discriminatory-impact claims cannot be based on how an individual is treated in isolation from the treatment of other members of the group. Such claims necessarily are based on whether the group fares less well than other groups under a policy, practice, or test. Indeed, if only one minority member has taken a test, a disparate-impact claim cannot be made, regardless of whether the test is an initial step in the selection process or one of several factors considered by the employer in making an employment decision.

III

Today's decision takes a long and unhappy step in the direction of confusion. Title VII does not require that employers adopt merit hiring or the procedures most likely to permit the greatest number of minority members to be considered for or to qualify for jobs and promotions. See Texas Dept. of Community Affairs v. Burdine; Furnco. Employers need not develop tests that accurately reflect the skills of every individual candidate; there are few if any tests that do so. Yet the Court seems unaware of this practical reality, and perhaps oblivious to the likely consequences of its decision. By its holding today, the Court may force employers either to eliminate tests or rely on expensive, job-related, testing procedures, the validity of which may or may not be sustained if challenged. For state and local governmental employers with limited funds, the practical effect of today's decision may well be the adoption of simple quota hiring.[8] This arbitrary method of employment is itself unfair to individual applicants, whether

---

dence of the number of applicants *and* employees in a methadone program quite probative. *Beazer* therefore does not justify the Court's speculation that the number of blacks and Hispanics actually employed were irrelevant to whether a case of disparate impact had been established under Title VII.

8. Another possibility is that employers may integrate consideration of test results into one overall hiring decision based on that "factor" *and* additional factors. Such a process would not, even under the Court's reasoning, result in a finding of discrimination on the basis of disparate impact unless the actual hiring decisions had a disparate impact on the minority group. But if employers integrate test results into a single-step decision, they will be free to select *only* the number of minority candidates proportional to their representation in the workforce. If petitioner had used this approach, it would have been able to hire substantially fewer blacks without liability on the basis of disparate impact. The Court hardly could have intended to encourage this.

or not they are members of minority groups. And it is not likely to produce a competent workforce. Moreover, the Court's decision actually may result in employers employing *fewer* minority members. As Judge Newman noted in Brown v. New Haven Civil Service Comm'n, 474 F.Supp. 1256, 1263 (D.Conn.1979):

> "[A]s private parties are permitted under Title VII itself to adopt voluntary affirmative action plans, * * * Title VII should not be construed to prohibit a municipality's using a hiring process that results in a percentage of minority policemen approximating their percentage of the local population, instead of relying on the expectation that a validated job-related testing procedure will produce an equivalent result, yet with the risk that it might lead to substantially less hiring." (citations omitted).

Finding today's decision unfortunate in both its analytical approach and its likely consequences, I dissent.

NOTES AND PROBLEMS FOR DISCUSSION

1. Does the Court's emphasis of individual interest terminology reflect a move away from the group interest-based theory of discrimination that it previously articulated in *Griggs?* Is the ruling in this case inconsistent with *Griggs* or does it simply shift the analysis of disproportionate impact to a different point in the selection process? If so, does this shift in emphasis reflect a changing conception of the notion of equality or nondiscrimination? See Friedman, Redefining Equality, Discrimination, And Affirmative Action Under Title VII: The Access Principle, 65 Tex.L.Rev. 41 (1986).

2. Do you agree with the dissent that there was no adverse effect on the group in this case? Is Justice Powell correct in assuming that a balanced bottom line dispels the inference of discrimination created by the plaintiff's prima facie showing? For a thorough discussion of *Teal* and its impact on the group interest concept that originated in *Griggs* see Blumrosen, The Group Interest Concept, Employment Discrimination, and Legislative Intent: The Fallacy of Connecticut v. Teal, 20 Harv.J.Leg. 99 (1983).

3. The New Bedford Police Department requires all applicants for police officer positions to meet a 5'6" minimum height requirement. When one of its female police officers retired, the City decided that it needed to replace her with another woman because of some particular aspects of the job dealing with female prisoners. Plaintiff Mary Landry scored so high on the mandatory exam that she was ranked first on the eligibility list. After the interview, however, she was rejected for failure to satisfy the minimum height requirement, as were the women who ranked second and third on the eligibility list. The fourth ranked woman received the job. Mary can prove that 80% of the men and 20% of the women in the relevant population satisfied the minimum height requirement. Can Mary successfully bring suit under Title VII? See Costa v. Markey, 706 F.2d 1 (1st Cir.1982), cert. denied, 464 U.S. 1017, 104 S.Ct. 547, 78 L.Ed.2d 722 (1983).

4. While disproportionate impact theory most obviously relates to the use of aptitude and intelligence examinations, it has been utilized to invalidate other objective employment standards such as minimum height and weight requirements, Dothard v. Rawlinson, 433 U.S. 321, 97 S.Ct. 2720, 53 L.Ed.2d 786

(1977) (sex discrimination); prior experience requirement, Chrisner v. Complete Auto Transit, Inc., 645 F.2d 1251 (6th Cir.1981) (sex discrimination); arrest record history, Gregory v. Litton Systems, Inc., 316 F.Supp. 401 (C.D.Cal.1970), affirmed as modified, 472 F.2d 631 (9th Cir.1972) (racial discrimination); garnishment experience, Johnson v. Pike Corp. of America, 332 F.Supp. 490 (C.D.Cal.1971) (racial discrimination); parentage of illegitimate children, Davis v. America National Bank of Texas, 12 FEP Cases 1052 (N.D.Tex.1971) (sex and race discrimination); and record of criminal conviction other than minor traffic offenses, compare Green v. Missouri Pacific Railroad Co., 549 F.2d 1158 (8th Cir.1977) with Richardson v. Hotel Corp. of America, 468 F.2d 951 (5th Cir. 1972).

Would an employer violate Title VII by refusing to hire persons with a history of drug use? See New York City Transit Authority v. Beazer, 440 U.S. 568, 99 S.Ct. 1355, 59 L.Ed.2d 587 (1979). What about a rule precluding spouses from working for the same employer? See Yuhas v. Libbey–Owens–Ford Co., 562 F.2d 496 (7th Cir.1977), cert. denied, 435 U.S. 934, 98 S.Ct. 1510, 55 L.Ed.2d 531 (1978). Can a gay employee state a *Griggs*-based Title VII claim based on an allegation that he was denied a promotion exclusively because of his sexual preference? Compare DeSantis v. Pacific Telephone & Telegraph Co., 608 F.2d 327 (9th Cir.1979) and Gay Law Students Association v. Pacific Telephone & Telegraph Co., 24 Cal.3d 458, 156 Cal.Rptr. 14, 595 P.2d 592 (1979), with Friedman, Constitutional and Statutory Challenges to Discrimination in Employment Based On Sexual Orientation, 64 Iowa L.Rev. 527, 566–68 (1979). Should the analysis of disproportionate impact claims be influenced by whether satisfaction of the challenged requirement is within or beyond the applicant's control?

In CHANEY v. SOUTHERN RAILWAY CO., 847 F.2d 718 (11th Cir.1988), a black employee was discharged after a drug test of his urine indicated the presence of marijuana. His expert witness testified that the particular drug test employed by the defendant was racially biased in that black people disproportionately obtain false positive results for drug use when it is used because they have higher levels of melanin in their urine than white people and that melanin fragments are misread by the test chemical as THC fragments, the marijuana indicator. The witness also indicated that alternative tests did not produce this racial impact. The trial court granted the defendant's Rule 41(b) motion on the ground that the plaintiff had not squarely presented a disproportionate impact claim in his pretrial order. It also stated that in light of the plaintiff's admission that he had used marijuana within two or three weeks of the time the test was taken, it had been established that the positive test result was the result of his admitted drug use and therefore that there was no need to examine the disproportionate impact claim. The Eleventh Circuit reversed on both grounds, holding that the plaintiff had sufficiently asserted an impact claim and, moreover, that his admission of marijuana use did not extinguish this claim. The court reasoned that since the company admitted that it would not have fired Chaney but for the positive test result, if the test in fact had a disproportionate exclusionary effect on blacks, the plaintiff would have stated a prima facie case. Accordingly, it remanded the case to the trial court for further consideration of the impact claim.

5. In LIVINGSTON v. ROADWAY EXPRESS, INC., 802 F.2d 1250 (10th Cir.1986), a 6'7" white male was rejected for employment as a truck driver pursuant to the defendant company's 6'4" maximum height limitation. The Tenth Circuit affirmed the trial court's dismissal of the complaint, concluding

that evidence of impact alone did not suffice to create a presumption of discrimination when the plaintiff is a member of a historically favored group. Rather, it held, where a member of a favored group alleges impact discrimination, the plaintiff "must show background circumstances supporting the inference that a facially neutral policy with a disparate impact is in fact a vehicle for unlawful discrimination." Since the plaintiff did not establish that the disproportionate impact of the height limitation was reflected in the actual workforce nor offer any other "background facts supporting the inference that Roadway Express is one of those unusual employers that discriminate against the majority . . . the only reasonable inference to be drawn from our common experience is that a maximum height restriction does not limit a male job applicant because of his sex but because of his height, a form of discrimination not prohibited by Title VII." 802 F.2d at 1252, 1253. The court also stated that *Teal* did not apply to cases where the plaintiff is a member of a favored group. Do you agree with this characterization of *Teal?*

For more than twenty five years after the issuance of its opinion in *Griggs,* the Supreme Court did not speak to the question of whether impact analysis was applicable to other than standardized employment selection criteria. In neither *Griggs* nor *Teal,* for example, did the Court differentiate between objective and subjective practices and procedures. Nor did it examine whether impact theory was limited to single factor employment criteria as opposed to multicomponent selection devices that generate an adverse impact. As a result, there was a significant amount of litigation raising the questions of whether impact analysis is properly applied to subjective criteria and/or to a multicomponent selection process. The Supreme Court finally addressed the former issue in the following case.

WATSON v. FORT WORTH BANK AND TRUST

Supreme Court of the United States, 1988.
487 U.S. 977, 108 S.Ct. 2777, 101 L.Ed.2d 827.

JUSTICE O'CONNOR delivered the judgment of the Court [and] the opinion of the Court as to Parts I, II–A, II–B, and III * * *.

This case requires us to decide what evidentiary standards should be applied under Title VII of the Civil Rights Act of 1964 in determining whether an employer's practice of committing promotion decisions to the subjective discretion of supervisory employees has led to illegal discrimination.

I

Petitioner Clara Watson, who is black, was hired by respondent Forth Worth Bank and Trust (the Bank) as a proof operator in August 1973. In January 1976, Watson was promoted to a position as teller in the Bank's drive-in facility. In February 1980, she sought to become supervisor of the tellers in the main lobby; a white male, however, was selected for this job. Watson then sought a position as supervisor of the drive-in bank, but this position was given to a white female. In February 1981, after Watson had served for about a year as a commercial teller in the Bank's main lobby, and informally as assistant to the supervisor of tellers, the man holding that position was promoted. Watson applied for the vacancy, but the white female who was the supervisor of the drive-in bank was selected instead. Watson then applied for the vacancy created at the drive-in; a white male was selected for that job. The Bank, which has about 80 employees, had not developed precise and formal criteria for evaluating candidates for the positions for which Watson unsuccessfully applied. It relied instead on the subjective judgment of supervisors who were acquainted with the candidates and with the nature of the jobs to be filled. All the supervisors involved in denying Watson the four promotions at issue were white.

Watson filed a discrimination charge with the Equal Employment Opportunity Commission. After exhausting her administrative remedies, she filed this lawsuit in the United States District Court for the Northern District of Texas.   * * *

The District Court addressed Watson's individual claims under the evidentiary standards that apply in a discriminatory treatment case. See McDonnell Douglas Corp. v. Green and Texas Department of Community Affairs v. Burdine. It concluded, on the evidence presented at trial, that Watson had established a prima facie case of employment discrimination, but that the Bank had met its rebuttal burden by presenting legitimate and nondiscriminatory reasons for each of the challenged promotion decisions. The court also concluded that Watson had failed to show that these reasons were pretexts for racial discrimination. Accordingly, the action was dismissed.

A divided panel of the United States Court of Appeals for the Fifth Circuit affirmed * * * the District Court's conclusion that Watson had failed to prove her claim of racial discrimination under the standards set out in McDonnell Douglas and Burdine, supra.[1] 798 F.2d 791 (1986).

Watson argued that the District Court had erred in failing to apply "disparate impact" analysis to her claims of discrimination in promotion. Relying on Fifth Circuit precedent, the majority of the Court of Appeals panel held that "a Title VII challenge to an allegedly discretionary promotion system is properly analyzed under the disparate treatment model rather than the disparate impact model." Other Courts of Appeals have held that disparate impact analysis may be

---

1. The dissenting judge argued that the District Court had abused its discretion in decertifying the broad class of black employees and applicants. He also argued that Watson had succeeded in proving that the Bank had discriminated against this class, and that the case should be remanded so that appropriate relief could be ordered.

applied to hiring or promotion systems that involve the use of "discretionary" or "subjective" criteria. See, e.g., Atonio v. Wards Cove Packing Co., 810 F.2d 1477 (CA9 1987) (en banc), on return to panel, 827 F.2d 489 (1987), cert. denied, No. 87–1388, 485 U.S. 989, 108 S.Ct. 1293, 99 L.Ed.2d 503 (1988), cert. pending, No. 87–1387; Griffin v. Carlin, 755 F.2d 1516, 1522–1525 (CA11 1985). Cf. Segar v. Smith, 238 U.S.App. D.C. 103, 738 F.2d 1249 (1984), cert. denied, 471 U.S. 1115, 105 S.Ct. 2357, 86 L.Ed.2d 258 (1985). We granted certiorari to resolve the conflict. 483 U.S. 1004, 107 S.Ct. 3227, 97 L.Ed.2d 734 (1987).

II

A

* * *

Several of our decisions have dealt with the evidentiary standards that apply when an individual alleges that an employer has treated that particular person less favorably than others because of the plaintiff's race, color, religion, sex, or national origin. In such "disparate treatment" cases, which involve "the most easily understood type of discrimination," Teamsters v. United States, the plaintiff is required to prove that the defendant had a discriminatory intent or motive. In order to facilitate the orderly consideration of relevant evidence, we have devised a series of shifting evidentiary burdens that are "intended progressively to sharpen the inquiry into the elusive factual question of intentional discrimination." Texas Department of Community Affairs v. Burdine. Under that scheme, a prima facie case is ordinarily established by proof that the employer, after having rejected the plaintiff's application for a job or promotion, continued to seek applicants with qualifications similar to the plaintiff's. The burden of proving a prima facie case is "not onerous," and the employer in turn may rebut it simply by producing some evidence that it had legitimate, nondiscriminatory reasons for the decision. If the defendant carries this burden of production, the plaintiff must prove by a preponderance of all the evidence in the case that the legitimate reasons offered by the defendant were a pretext for discrimination. We have cautioned that these shifting burdens are meant only to aid courts and litigants in arranging the presentation of evidence: "The ultimate burden of persuading the trier of fact that the defendant intentionally discriminated against the plaintiff remains at all times with the plaintiff." Id. See also United States Postal Service Bd. of Governors v. Aikens.

In Griggs v. Duke Power Co., this Court held that a plaintiff need not necessarily prove intentional discrimination in order to establish that an employer has violated section 703. In certain cases, facially neutral employment practices that have significant adverse effects on protected GROUPS have been held to violate the Act without proof that the employer adopted those practices with a discriminatory intent. The factual issues and the character of the evidence are inevitably somewhat different when the plaintiff is exempted from the need to prove intentional discrimination. The evidence in these "disparate impact" cases usually focuses on statistical disparities, rather than specific incidents, and on competing explanations for those disparities.

The distinguishing features of the factual issues that typically dominate in disparate impact cases do not imply that the ultimate legal issue is different than in cases where disparate treatment analysis is used. See, e.g., Washington v. Davis, 426 U.S. 229, 253–254, 96 S.Ct. 2040, 2054, 48 L.Ed.2d 597 (1976) (Stevens, J., concurring). Nor do we think it is appropriate to hold a defendant liable for unintentional discrimination on the basis of less evidence than is required to prove intentional discrimination. Rather, the necessary premise of the disparate impact approach is that some employment practices, adopted without a deliberately discriminatory motive, may in operation be functionally equivalent to intentional discrimination.

Perhaps the most obvious examples of such functional equivalents have been found where racially neutral job requirements necessarily operated to perpetuate the effects of intentional discrimination that occurred before Title VII was enacted. In *Griggs* itself, for example, the employer had a history of overt racial discrimination that predated the enactment of the Civil Rights Act of 1964. Such conduct had apparently ceased thereafter, but the employer continued to follow employment policies that had "a markedly disproportionate" adverse effect on blacks. The *Griggs* Court found that these policies, which involved the use of general aptitude tests and a high school diploma requirement, were not demonstrably related to the jobs for which they were used. Believing that diplomas and tests could become "masters of reality," which would perpetuate the effects of pre-Act discrimination, the Court concluded that such practices could not be defended simply on the basis of their facial neutrality or on the basis of the employer's lack of discriminatory intent.

This Court has repeatedly reaffirmed the principle that some facially neutral employment practices may violate Title VII even in the absence of a demonstrated discriminatory intent. We have not limited this principle to cases in which the challenged practice served to perpetuate the effects of pre-Act intentional discrimination. Each of oursubsequent decisions, however, like *Griggs* itself, involved standardized employment tests or criteria. See, e.g., Albemarle Paper Co. v. Moody (written aptitude tests); Washington v. Davis (written test of verbal skills); Dothard v. Rawlinson (height and weight requirements); New York City Transit Authority v. Beazer (rule against employing drug addicts); Connecticut v. Teal (written examination). In contrast, we have consistently used conventional disparate-treatment theory, in which proof of intent to discriminate is required, to review hiring and promotion decisions that were based on the exercise of personal judgment or the application of inherently subjective criteria. See, e.g., McDonnell Douglas Corp. v. Green (discretionary decision not to rehire individual who engaged in criminal acts against employer while laid off); Furnco Construction Corp. v. Waters (hiring decisions based on personal knowledge of candidates and recommendations); Texas Dept. of Community Affairs v. Burdine (discretionary decision to fire individual who was said not to get along with co-workers); United States Postal Service Bd. of Governors v. Aikens (discretionary promotion decision).

Our decisions have not addressed the question whether disparate impact analysis may be applied to cases in which subjective criteria are used to make employment decisions. As noted above, the Courts of Appeals are in conflict on the issue. In order to resolve this conflict, we must determine whether the reasons that support the use of disparate impact analysis apply to subjective employment practices, and whether such analysis can be applied in this new context under workable evidentiary standards.

B

The parties present us with stark and uninviting alternatives. Petitioner contends that subjective selection methods are at least as likely to have discriminatory effects as are the kind of objective tests at issue in *Griggs* and our other disparate impact cases. Furthermore, she argues, if disparate impact analysis is confined to objective tests, employers will be able to substitute subjective criteria having substantially identical effects, and *Griggs* will become a dead letter. Respondent and the United States (appearing as amicus curiae) argue that conventional disparate treatment analysis is adequate to accomplish Congress' purpose in enacting Title VII. They also argue that subjective selection practices would be so impossibly difficult to defend under disparate impact analysis that employers would be forced to adopt numerical quotas in order to avoid liability.

We are persuaded that our decisions in *Griggs* and succeeding cases could largely be nullified if disparate impact analysis were applied only to standardized selection practices. However one might distinguish "subjective" from "objective" criteria, it is apparent that selection systems that combine both types would generally have to be considered subjective in nature. Thus, for example, if the employer in *Griggs* had consistently preferred applicants who had a high school diploma and who passed the company's general aptitude test, its selection system could nonetheless have been considered "subjective" if it also included brief interviews with the candidates. So long as an employer refrained from making standardized criteria absolutely determinative, it would remain free to give such tests almost as much weight as it chose without risking a disparate impact challenge. If we announced a rule that allowed employers so easily to insulate themselves from liability under *Griggs*, disparate impact analysis might effectively be abolished.

We are also persuaded that disparate impact analysis is in principle no less applicable to subjective employment criteria than to objective or standardized tests. In either case, a facially neutral practice, adopted without discriminatory intent, may have effects that are indistinguishable from intentionally discriminatory practices. It is true, to be sure, that an employer's policy of leaving promotion decisions to the unchecked discretion of lower level supervisors should itself raise no inference of discriminatory conduct. Especially in relatively small businesses like respondent's, it may be customary and quite reasonable simply to delegate employment decisions to those employees who are most familiar with the jobs to be filled and with the candidates for those jobs. It does not follow, however, that the particular supervisors to whom this discretion is delegated always act without discriminatory intent. Furthermore, even if one assumed that any such discrimination can be adequately policed through disparate treatment analysis, the problem of subconscious stereotypes and prejudices would remain. In this case, for example, petitioner was apparently told at one point that the teller position was a big responsibility with "a lot of money ... for blacks to have to count." Such remarks may not prove discriminatory intent, but they do suggest a lingering form of the problem that Title VII was enacted to combat. If an employer's undisciplined system of subjective decisionmaking has precisely the same effects as a system pervaded by impermissible intentional discrimination, it is difficult to see why Title VII's proscription against discriminatory actions should not apply. In both circumstances, the employer's practices may be said to "adversely affect [an individual's] status as an employee, because of such individual's race, color, religion, sex, or national origin." 42 U.S.C. section 2000e–2(a)(2). We conclude, accordingly, that subjective or discretionary employment practices may be analyzed under the disparate impact approach in appropriate cases.

* * *

III

We granted certiorari to determine whether the court below properly held disparate impact analysis inapplicable to a subjective or discretionary promotion system, and we now hold that such analysis may be applied. We express no opinion as to the other rulings of the Court of Appeals.

Neither the District Court nor the Court of Appeals has evaluated the statistical evidence to determine whether petitioner made out a prima facie case of discriminatory promotion practices under disparate impact theory. It may be that the relevant data base is too small to permit any meaningful statistical analysis, but we leave the Court of Appeals to decide in the first instance, on the basis of the record and the principles announced today, whether this case can be resolved without further proceedings in the District Court. The judgment of the Court of Appeals is vacated, and the case is remanded for further proceedings consistent with this opinion.

It is so ordered.

JUSTICE KENNEDY took no part in the consideration or decision of this case.

JUSTICE BLACKMUN with whom JUSTICE BRENNAN and JUSTICE MARSHALL join, concurring in part and concurring in the judgment.

I agree that disparate-impact analysis may be applied to claims of discrimination caused by subjective or discretionary selection processes, and I therefore join Sections I, IIA, IIB, and III of the Court's opinion. * * *

JUSTICE STEVENS, concurring in the judgment.

* * *

Essentially for the reasons set forth in Parts II–B and II–C of Justice O'Connor's opinion, I agree that this question must be answered in the affirmative. * * *

NOTES AND PROBLEMS FOR DISCUSSION

1. While the Court unanimously agreed that impact analysis was applicable to subjective criteria, a majority of the Court did not rule on a related issue that had been raised by the parties, i.e., how multicomponent employment selection policies should be treated. Prior to the Court's ruling in *Watson,* the circuit courts had split on this issue. Compare Pouncy v. Prudential Insurance Co., 668 F.2d 795 (5th Cir.1982)(impact model inapplicable to multicomponent promotion policy where plaintiff offers evidence only of non-balanced "bottom line"; to prevail, plaintiff must establish discriminatory impact caused by a "specific practice") with Green v. USX Corp., 843 F.2d 1511 (3d Cir.1988), vacated and remanded in light of Wards Cove v. Atonio, 490 U.S. 1103, 109 S.Ct. 3151, 104 L.Ed.2d 1015 (1989) (expressly rejecting *Pouncy* analysis and holding that plaintiff need only show the disproportionate impact of the entire selection process and the fact that the disparity would not have occurred but for the cumulative hiring practice). In *Watson,* however, a four member plurality of the eight member Court (Justice Kennedy did not participate), consisting of Justices O'Connor, White, Scalia and the Chief Justice, briefly discussed this matter. The plurality declared that the plaintiff in a disproportionate impact case must isolate and identify the particular employment practice that is allegedly responsible for the discriminatory impact. The four other participating Justices did not expressly discuss this issue. While the participation of Justice Kennedy in the decision of the next principal case transformed the *Watson* plurality into a majority, the subsequent enactment of the 1991 Civil Rights Act resulted in a partial modification of the treatment of multicomponent personnel policies. See Note 1 after *Wards Cove,* infra, at 236.

2. Statistical proof plays different roles in treatment and impact cases. In the disproportionate impact case, the purpose of statistical evidence is to demonstrate the effect of the challenged procedure on different classes of persons. Where that effect can be demonstrated through relevant general population data, as was the case in *Griggs,* no statistical analysis of the disparity is necessary, because the legally relevant impact is defined in terms of that population. But in some impact cases, particularly those arising from employment tests, no general population data is available. Thus, if an employer's aptitude test is failed by 40% of all white applicants and 50% of all black applicants, the pass rates are known only for those applicants who actually

took the test.   The applicants form only a sample of those persons in the relevant job market.   Disparate impact in a sample drawn from the relevant population may not justify the conclusion that the test has a disparate impact on the population as a whole.   In other words, there may be no difference in pass rates between blacks and whites in the population and the difference in the sample may be the result of chance—i.e. the peculiar abilities of the individuals in the sample.   Courts have frequently assumed disparate impact on the population from the size of the disparity in the sample.   See United States v. Chicago, 549 F.2d 415, 429 (7th Cir.1977), cert. denied, 434 U.S. 875, 98 S.Ct. 225, 54 L.Ed.2d 155 (1977); Bridgeport Guardians, Inc. v. Members of Bridgeport Civil Service Commission, 482 F.2d 1333, 1335 (2d Cir.1973), cert. denied, 421 U.S. 991, 95 S.Ct. 1997, 44 L.Ed.2d 481 (1975); Chance v. Board of Examiners, 458 F.2d 1167, 1171 (2d Cir.1972).   The Uniform Guidelines on Employment Selection Procedure, 29 C.F.R. § 1607.4D, 28 C.F.R. § 50.14(4)D (1981), adopted by the EEOC and other federal agencies, utilizes an arbitrary four-fifths rule of thumb to assess impact.   Under this rule, a difference in pass rates between two racial, ethnic or sex groups is considered substantial if the pass rate for one group falls below four-fifths (80%) of the pass rate for the higher group.   Depending on the size of the relevant population and that of the sample, the application of such a rule of thumb, or any intuitive guess work as to impact, may be statistically unwarranted.   When only sample data is available, an inference of disparate impact on the population can only be based on a statistical analysis of the data to determine the likelihood that the observed pattern would occur by chance, if in fact there were no differences in the pass rates of the groups in the relevant population.   See Shoben, Differential Pass–Fail Rates in Employment Testing: Statistical Proof Under Title VII, 91 Harv.L.Rev. 793, 798, 805–11 (1978).

In the principal case, Justice O'Connor acknowledged that this standard has been "criticized on technical grounds", and "has not provided more than a rule of thumb for the courts."   She suggested that the courts have judged the significance of numerical disparities on an ad hoc basis because, in part, no consensus has developed around any alternative mathematical standard.   Thus, she concluded, "[a]t least at this stage of the law's development, we believe that such a case-by-case approach properly reflects our recognition that statistics 'come in infinite variety and ... their usefulness depends on all of the surrounding facts and circumstances.'" Does Justice O'Connor's stated preference for an *ad hoc* determination of whether the plaintiff has established a sufficiently disproportionate exclusionary impact cast doubt on the future viability of this quantitative standard?

3. The plurality predicates its decision to provide a "fresh" look at the applicable evidentiary standards on the "risk that employers will be given incentives to adopt quotas or to engage in preferential treatment" that is created by its extension of impact theory to subjective business practices.   It goes on to say that in § 703(j) Congress "clearly and emphatically expressed its intent that Title VII not lead to this result."   Is this a fair reading of this statutory provision?   Can it be said that the extension of impact theory to subjective practices would "require" an employer to grant preferential treatment on account of an imbalance in its workforce?

4. The question of the defendant's burden of proof was addressed by the plurality even though it admitted that neither lower court had ruled on whether or not the plaintiff had established a prima facie case of disproportionate impact.   Justice Stevens, in his concurring opinion, suggests that it was

both unnecessary and inappropriate for the Court to fashion such a dramatic change in the law under these circumstances. With whom do you agree?

WARDS COVE PACKING COMPANY, INC. v. ATONIO

Supreme Court of the United States, 1989.
490 U.S. 642, 109 S.Ct. 2115, 104 L.Ed.2d 733.

JUSTICE WHITE delivered the opinion of the Court.

* * *

I

The claims before us are disparate-impact claims, involving the employment practices of petitioners, two companies that operate salmon canneries in remote and widely separated areas of Alaska. The canneries operate only during the salmon runs in the summer months. They are inoperative and vacant for the rest of the year. In May or June of each year, a few weeks before the salmon runs begin, workers arrive and prepare the equipment and facilities for the canning operation. Most of these workers possess a variety of skills. When salmon runs are about to begin, the workers who will operate the cannery lines arrive, remain as long as there are fish to can, and then depart. The canneries are then closed down, winterized, and left vacant until the next spring. During the off season, the companies employ only a small number of individuals at their headquarters in Seattle and Astoria, Oregon, plus some employees at the winter shipyard in Seattle.

The length and size of salmon runs vary from year to year and hence the number of employees needed at each cannery also varies. Estimates are made as early in the winter as possible; the necessary employees are hired, and when the time comes, they are transported to the canneries. Salmon must be processed soon after they are caught, and the work during the canning season is therefore intense. For this reason, and because the canneries are located in remote regions, all workers are housed at the canneries and have their meals in company-owned mess halls.

Jobs at the canneries are of two general types: "cannery jobs" on the cannery line, which are unskilled positions; and "noncannery jobs," which fall into a variety of classifications. Most noncannery jobs are classified as skilled positions.[3] Cannery jobs are filled predominantly by nonwhites, Filipinos and Alaska Natives. The Filipinos are hired through and dispatched by Local 37 of the International Longshoremen Workers Union pursuant to a hiring hall agreement with the Local.

---

3. The noncannery jobs were described as follows by the Court of Appeals: "Machinists and engineers are hired to maintain the smooth and continuous operation of the canning equipment. Quality control personnel conduct the FDA-required inspections and recordkeeping. Tenders are staffed with a crew necessary to operate the vessel. A variety of support personnel are employed to operate the entire cannery community, including, for example, cooks, carpenters, store-keepers, bookkeepers, beach gangs for dock yard labor and construction, etc." 768 F.2d, at 1123.

The Alaska Natives primarily reside in villages near the remote cannery locations. Noncannery jobs are filled with predominantly white workers, who are hired during the winter months from the companies' offices in Washington and Oregon. Virtually all of the noncannery jobs pay more than cannery positions. The predominantly white noncannery workers and the predominantly nonwhite cannery employees live in separate dormitories and eat in separate mess halls.

In 1974, respondents, a class of nonwhite cannery workers who were (or had been) employed at the canneries, brought this Title VII action against petitioners. Respondents alleged that a variety of petitioners' hiring/promotion practices—e.g., nepotism, a rehire preference, a lack of objective hiring criteria, separate hiring channels, a practice of not promoting from within—were responsible for the racial stratification of the work force, and had denied them and other nonwhites employment as noncannery workers on the basis of race. Respondents also complained of petitioners' racially segregated housing and dining facilities. All of respondents' claims were advanced under both the disparate-treatment and disparate-impact theories of Title VII liability.

The District Court held a bench trial, after which it entered 172 findings of fact. It then rejected all of respondents' disparate-treatment claims. It also rejected the disparate-impact challenges involving the subjective employment criteria used by petitioners to fill these noncannery positions, on the ground that those criteria were not subject to attack under a disparate-impact theory. Petitioner's "objective" employment practices (e.g., an English language requirement, alleged nepotism in hiring, failure to post noncannery openings, the rehire preference, etc.) were found to be subject to challenge under the disparate-impact theory, but these claims were rejected for failure of proof. Judgment was entered for petitioners.

On appeal, a panel of the Ninth Circuit affirmed, but that decision was vacated when the Court of Appeals agreed to hear the case en banc. The en banc hearing was ordered to settle an intra-circuit conflict over the question whether subjective hiring practices could be analyzed under a disparate-impact model; the Court of Appeals held—as this Court subsequently ruled in Watson v. Fort Worth Bank & Trust—that disparate-impact analysis could be applied to subjective hiring practices. The Ninth Circuit also concluded that in such a case, "[o]nce the plaintiff class has shown disparate-impact caused by specific, identifiable employment practices or criteria, the burden shifts to the employer" to "prov[e the] business necessity" of the challenged practice. Because the en banc holding on subjective employment practices reversed the District Court's contrary ruling, the en banc Court of Appeals remanded the case to a panel for further proceedings.

On remand, the panel applied the en banc ruling to the facts of this case. It held that respondents had made out a prima facie case of disparate-impact in hiring for both skilled and unskilled noncannery positions. The panel remanded the case for further proceedings, instructing the District Court that it was the employer's burden to prove that any disparate-impact caused by its hiring and employment practices was justified by business necessity. Neither the en banc court nor the panel disturbed the District Court's rejection of the disparate-treatment claims.[4]

Petitioners sought review of the Court of Appeals' decision in this Court, challenging it on several grounds. Because some of the issues raised by the decision below were matters on which this Court was evenly divided in Watson v. Fort Worth Bank & Trust Co., supra, we granted certiorari, for the purpose of addressing these disputed questions of the proper application of Title VII's disparate-impact theory of liability.

II

In holding that respondents had made out a prima facie case of disparate impact, the court of appeals relied solely on respondents' statistics showing a high percentage of non-white workers in the cannery jobs and a low percentage of such workers in the noncannery positions. Although statistical proof can alone make out a prima facie case, see Teamsters v. United States; Hazelwood School Dist. v. United States, the Court of Appeals' ruling here misapprehends our precedents and the purposes of Title VII, and we therefore reverse.

"There can be no doubt," as there was when a similar mistaken analysis had been undertaken by the courts below in Hazelwood, "that the * * * comparison * * * fundamentally misconceived the role of statistics in employment discrimination cases." The "proper comparison [is] between the racial composition of [the at-issue jobs] and the racial composition of the qualified * * * population in the relevant labor market." Ibid. It is such a comparison—between the racial composition of the qualified persons in the labor market and the persons holding at-issue jobs—that generally forms the proper basis for the initial inquiry in a disparate-impact case. Alternatively, in cases

---

4. The fact that neither the District Court, nor the Ninth Circuit *en banc,* nor the subsequent Court of Appeals panel ruled for respondents on their disparate-treatment claims—i.e., their allegations of intentional racial discrimination—warrants particular attention in light of the dissents' comment that the canneries "bear an unsettling resemblance to aspects of a plantation economy." (Stevens, J., dissenting); (Blackmun, J., dissenting).

Whatever the "resemblance," the unanimous view of the lower courts in this litigation has been that respondents did not prove that the canneries practice intentional racial discrimination. Consequently, Justice Blackmun's hyperbolic allegation that our decision in this case indicates that this Court no longer "believes that race discrimination * * * against non-whites * * * is a problem in our society," is inapt. Of course, it is unfortunately true that race discrimination exists in our country. That does not mean, however, that it exists at the canneries—or more precisely, that it has been proven to exist at the canneries.

Indeed, Justice Stevens concedes that respondents did not press before us the legal theories under which the aspects of cannery life that he finds to most resemble a "plantation economy" might be unlawful. Thus, the question here is not whether we "approve" of petitioners' employment practices or the society that exists at the canneries, but rather, whether respondents have properly established that these practices violate Title VII.

where such labor market statistics will be difficult if not impossible to ascertain, we have recognized that certain other statistics—such as measures indicating the racial composition of "otherwise-qualified applicants" for at-issue jobs—are equally probative for this purpose. See, e.g., New York City Transit Authority v. Beazer, 440 U.S. 568, 585 (1979).[6]

It is clear to us that the Court of Appeals' acceptance of the comparison between the racial composition of the cannery work force and that of the noncannery work force, as probative of a prima facie case of disparate impact in the selection of the latter group of workers, was flawed for several reasons. Most obviously, with respect to the skilled noncannery jobs at issue here, the cannery work force in no way reflected "the pool of *qualified* job applicants" or the "*qualified* population in the labor force." Measuring alleged discrimination in the selection of accountants, managers, boat captains, electricians, doctors, and engineers—and the long list of other "skilled" noncannery positions found to exist by the District Court—by comparing the number of nonwhites occupying these jobs to the number of nonwhites filling cannery worker positions is nonsensical. If the absence of minorities holding such skilled positions is due to a dearth of qualified nonwhite applicants (for reasons that are not petitioners' fault),[7] petitioners' selection methods or employment practices cannot be said to have had a "disparate impact" on nonwhites.

One example illustrates why this must be so. Respondents' own statistics concerning the noncannery work force at one of the canneries at issue here indicate that approximately 17% of the new hires for medical jobs, and 15% of the new hires for officer worker positions, were nonwhite. If it were the case that less than 15–17% of the applicants for these jobs were nonwhite and that nonwhites made up a lower percentage of the relevant qualified labor market, it is hard to see how respondents, without more, cf. Connecticut v. Teal, 457 U.S. 440, 102 S.Ct. 2525, 73 L.Ed.2d 130 (1982), would have made out a prima facie case of disparate impact. Yet, under the Court of Appeals' theory, simply because nonwhites comprise 52% of the cannery workers at the cannery in question, respondents would be successful in establishing a prima facie case of racial discrimination under Title VII.

Such a result cannot be squared with our cases or with the goals behind the statute. The Court of Appeals' theory, at the very least, would mean that any employer who had a segment of his work force that was—for some reason—racially imbalanced, could be haled into

---

6. In fact, where "figures for the general population might * * * accurately reflect the pool of qualified job applicants," cf. Teamsters v. United States, we have even permitted plaintiffs to rest their prima facie cases on such statistics as well. See, e.g., Dothard v. Rawlinson.

7. Obviously, the analysis would be different if it were found that the dearth of qualified nonwhite applicants was due to practices on petitioner's part which—expressly or implicitly—deterred minority group members from applying for noncannery positions. See, e.g., Teamsters v. United States.

court and forced to engage in the expensive and time-consuming task of defending the "business necessity" of the methods used to select the other members of his work force. The only practicable option for many employers will be to adopt racial quotas, insuring that no portion of his work force deviates in racial composition from the other portions thereof; this is a result that Congress expressly rejected in drafting Title VII. See 42 U.S.C. § 2000e–2(j); see also Watson v. Fort Worth Bank & Trust Co., n. 2 (opinion of O'Connor, J.). The Court of Appeals' theory would "leave the employer little choice * * * but to engage in a subjective quota system of employment selection. This, of course, is far from the intent of Title VII." Albemarle Paper Co. v. Moody (Blackmun, J., concurring in judgment).

The Court of Appeals also erred with respect to the unskilled noncannery positions. Racial imbalance in one segment of an employer's work force does not, without more, establish a prima facie case of disparate impact with respect to the selection of workers for the employer's other positions, even where workers for the different positions may have somewhat fungible skills (as is arguably the case for cannery and unskilled noncannery workers). As long as there are no barriers or practices deterring qualified nonwhites from applying for noncannery positions, see supra, n. 6, if the percentage of selected applicants who are nonwhite is not significantly less than the percentage of qualified applicants who are nonwhite, the employer's selection mechanism probably does not operate with a disparate impact on minorities.[8] Where this is the case, the percentage of nonwhite workers found in other positions in the employer's labor force is irrelevant to the question of a prima facie statistical case of disparate impact. As noted above, a contrary ruling on this point would almost inexorably lead to the use of numerical quotas in the workplace, a result that Congress and this Court have rejected repeatedly in the past.

Moreover, isolating the cannery workers as the potential "labor force" for unskilled noncannery positions is at once both too broad and too narrow in its focus. Too broad because the vast majority of these cannery workers did not seek jobs in unskilled noncannery positions; there is no showing that many of them would have done so even if none of the arguably "deterring" practices existed. Thus, the pool of cannery workers cannot be used as a surrogate for the class of qualified job applicants because it contains many persons who have not (and would not) be noncannery job applicants. Conversely, if respondents propose to use the cannery workers for comparison purposes because they

8. We qualify this conclusion—observing that it is only "probable" that there has been no disparate impact on minorities in such circumstances—because bottom-line racial balance is not a defense under Title VII. See Connecticut v. Teal. Thus, even if petitioners could show that the percentage of selected applicants who are nonwhite is not significantly less than the percentage of qualified applicants who are nonwhite, respondents would still have a case under Title VII, if they could prove that some particular hiring practice has a disparate impact on minorities, notwithstanding the bottom-line racial balance in petitioners' work force. See Teal; see also n. 8, infra.

represent the "qualified labor population" generally, the group is too narrow because there are obviously many qualified persons in the labor market for noncannery jobs who are not cannery workers.

The peculiar facts of this case further illustrate why a comparison between the percentage of nonwhite cannery workers and nonwhite noncannery workers is an improper basis for making out a claim of disparate impact. Here, the District Court found that nonwhites were "overrepresent[ed]" among cannery workers because petitioners had contracted with a predominantly nonwhite union (Local 37) to fill these positions. As a result, if petitioners (for some permissible reason) ceased using Local 37 as its hiring channel for cannery positions, it appears (according to the District Court's findings) that the racial stratification between the cannery and noncannery workers might diminish to statistical insignificance. Under the Court of Appeals' approach, therefore, it is possible that *with no change whatsoever* in their hiring practices for noncannery workers—the jobs at issue in this lawsuit—petitioners could make respondents' prima facie case of disparate impact "disappear." But *if* there would be no prima facie case of disparate impact in the selection of noncannery workers absent petitioners' use of Local 37 to hire cannery workers, surely the petitioners' reliance on the union to fill the cannery jobs not at issue here (and its resulting "overrepresentation" of nonwhites in those positions) does not—standing alone—make out a prima facie case of disparate impact. Yet it is precisely such an ironic result that the Court of Appeals reached below.

Consequently, we reverse the Court of Appeals' ruling that a comparison between the percentage of cannery workers who are non-white and the percentage of noncannery workers who are nonwhite makes out a prima facie case of disparate impact. Of course,this leaves unresolved whether the record made in the District Court will support a conclusion that a prima facie case of disparate impact has been established on some basis other than the racial disparity between cannery and noncannery workers. This is an issue that the Court of Appeals or the District Court should address in the first instance.

III

Since the statistical disparity relied on by the Court of Appeals did not suffice to make out a prima facie case, any inquiry by us into whether the specific challenged employment practices of petitioners caused that disparity is pretermitted, as is any inquiry into whether the disparate impact that any employment practice may have had was justified by business considerations.[9] Because we remand for further

9. As we understand the opinions below, the specific employment practices were challenged only insofar as they were claimed to have been responsible for the overall disparity between the number of minority cannery and noncannery work-ers. The Court of Appeals did not purport to hold that any specified employment practice produced its own disparate impact that was actionable under Title VII. This is not to say that a specific practice, such as nepotism, if it were proved to exist,

proceedings, however, on whether a prima facie case of disparate impact has been made in defensible fashion in this case, we address two other challenges petitioners have made to the decision of the Court of Appeals.

A

First is the question of causation in a disparate-impact case. The law in this respect was correctly stated by Justice O'Connor's opinion last Term in Watson v. Fort Worth Bank & Trust:

> "[W]e note that the plaintiff's burden in establishing a prima facie case goes beyond the need to show that there are statistical disparities in the employer's work force. The plaintiff must begin by identifying the specific employment practice that is challenged.... Especially in cases where an employer combines subjective criteria with the use of more rigid standardized rules or tests, the plaintiff is in our view responsible for isolating and identifying the specific employment practices that are allegedly responsible for any observed statistical disparities."

Indeed, even the Court of Appeals—whose decision petitioners assault on this score—noted that "it is * * * essential that the practices identified by the cannery workers be linked causally with the demonstrated adverse impact." Notwithstanding the Court of Appeals' apparent adherence to the proper inquiry, petitioners contend that that court erred by permitting respondents to make out their case by offering "only [one] set of cumulative comparative statistics as evidence of the disparate impact of each and all of [petitioners' hiring] practices."

Our disparate-impact cases have always focused on the impact of *particular* hiring practices on employment opportunities for minorities. Just as an employer cannot escape liability under Title VII by demonstrating that, "at the bottom line," his work force is racially balanced (where particular hiring practices may operate to deprive minorities of employment opportunities), see Connecticut v. Teal, a Title VII plaintiff does not make out a case of disparate impact simply by showing that, "at the bottom line," there is racial *imbalance* in the work force. As a general matter, a plaintiff must demonstrate that it is the application of a specific or particular employment practice that has created the disparate impact under attack. Such a showing is an integral part of the plaintiff's prima facie case in a disparate-impact suit under Title VII.

Here, respondents have alleged that several "objective" employment practices (e.g., nepotism, separate hiring channels, rehire preferences), as well as the use of "subjective decision making" to select noncannery workers, have had a disparate impact on nonwhites. Re-

could not itself be subject to challenge if it had a disparate impact on minorities. Nor is it to say that segregated dormitories and eating facilities in the workplace may not be challenged under 42 U.S.C. § 2000e-2(a)(2) without showing a disparate impact on hiring or promotion.

spondents base this claim on statistics that allegedly show a disproportionately low percentage of nonwhites in the at-issue positions.   However, even if on remand respondents can show that nonwhites are
underrepresented in the at-issue jobs in a manner that is acceptable
under the standards set forth in Part II, supra, this alone will *not*
suffice to make out a prima facie case of disparate impact.   Respondents will also have to demonstrate that the disparity they complain of
is the result of one or more of the employment practices that they are
attacking here, specifically showing that each challenged practice has a
significantly disparate impact on employment opportunities for whites
and nonwhites.   To hold otherwise would result in employers being
potentially liable for "the myriad of innocent causes that may lead to
statistical imbalances in the composition of their work forces."   Watson
v. Fort Worth Bank & Trust.

Some will complain that this specific causation requirement is
unduly burdensome on Title VII plaintiffs.   But liberal civil discovery
rules give plaintiffs broad access to employers' records in an effort to
document their claims.   Also, employers falling within the scope of the
Uniform   Guidelines   on   Employee   Selection   Procedures,   29   CFR
§ 1607.1 et seq. (1988), are required to "maintain * * * records or other
information which will disclose the impact which its tests and other
selection procedures have upon employment opportunities of persons by
identifiable race, sex, or ethnic group[s.]" This includes records concerning "the individual components of the selection process" where there is
a significant disparity in the selection rates of whites and nonwhites.
Plaintiffs as a general matter will have the benefit of these tools to
meet their burden of showing a causal link between challenged employment practices and racial imbalances in the work force; respondents
presumably took full advantage of these opportunities to build their
case before the trial in the District Court was held.[10]

Consequently, on remand, the courts below are instructed to require, as part of respondents' prima facie case, a demonstration that
specific elements of the petitioners' hiring process have a significantly
disparate impact on nonwhites.

* * *

[That portion of the majority opinion addressing the burden of proof for
defendants is reproduced in Chapter III C 3, *infra* at ___.]

IV

For the reasons given above, the judgment of the Court of Appeals
is reversed, and the case is remanded for further proceedings consistent
with this opinion.

It is so ordered.

---

10. Of course, petitioners' obligation to
collect or retain any of these data may be
limited by the Guidelines themselves.   See
29   CFR   § 1602.14(b)   (1988)   (exempting
"seasonal" jobs from certain record-keep-
ing requirements).

JUSTICE BLACKMUN, with whom JUSTICE BRENNAN and JUSTICE MARSHALL join, dissenting.

I fully concur in Justice Stevens' analysis of this case. Today a bare majority of the Court takes three major strides backwards in the battle against race discrimination. It reaches out to make last Term's plurality opinion in Watson v. Fort Worth Bank & Trust, the law, thereby upsetting the longstanding distribution of burdens of proof in Title VII disparate-impact cases. It bars the use of internal workforce comparisons in the making of a prima facie case of discrimination, even where the structure of the industry in question renders any other statistical comparison meaningless. And it requires practice-by-practice statistical proof of causation, even where, as here, such proof would be impossible.

The harshness of these results is well demonstrated by the facts of this case. The salmon industry as described by this record takes us back to a kind of overt and institutionalized discrimination we have not dealt with in years: a total residential and work environment organized on principles of racial stratification and segregation, which, as Justice Stevens points out, resembles a plantation economy. This industry long has been characterized by a taste for discrimination of the old-fashioned sort: a preference for hiring nonwhites to fill its lowest-level positions, on the condition that they stay there. The majority's legal rulings essentially immunize these practices from attack under a Title VII disparate-impact analysis.

Sadly, this comes as no surprise. One wonders whether the majority still believes that race discrimination—or, more accurately, race discrimination against nonwhites—is a problem in our society, or even remembers that it ever was. Cf. City of Richmond v. J. A. Croson Co.

JUSTICE STEVENS, with whom JUSTICE BRENNAN, JUSTICE MARSHALL, and JUSTICE BLACKMUN join, dissenting.

I

* * *

Also troubling is the Court's apparent redefinition of the employees' burden of proof in a disparate impact case. No prima facie case will be made, it declares, unless the employees " 'isolat[e] and identif[y] the specific employment practices that are allegedly responsible for any observed statistical disparities' ". This additional proof requirement is unwarranted.[19] It is elementary that a plaintiff cannot recover upon proof of injury alone; rather, the plaintiff must connect the injury to an act of the defendant in order to establish prima facie that the

---

19. The Solicitor General's brief *amicus curiae* on behalf of the employers agrees: "[A] decision rule for selection may be complex: it may, for example, involve consideration of multiple factors. And certainly if the factors combine to produce a single ultimate selection decision and it is not possible to challenge each one, that decision may be challenged (and defended) as a whole."

defendant is liable.   Although the causal link must have substance, the act need not constitute the sole or primary cause of the harm.   Cf. Price Waterhouse v. Hopkins.   Thus, in a disparate impact case, proof of numerous questionable employment practices ought to fortify an employee's assertion that the practices caused racial disparities.[20]   Ordinary principles of fairness require that Title VII actions be tried like "any lawsuit."   Cf. USPS Board of Governors v. Aikens.   The changes the majority makes today, tipping the scales in favor of employers, are not faithful to those principles.

II

* * *

Statistical evidence of discrimination should compare the racial composition of employees in disputed jobs to that " 'of the qualified * * * population in the relevant labor market.' " (quoting Hazelwood School District v. United States).   That statement leaves open the definition of the qualified population and the relevant labor market. Our previous opinions, e.g., New York City Transit Authority v. Beazer; Dothard v. Rawlinson; Albemarle Paper Co. v. Moody; Griggs, demonstrate that in reviewing statistical evidence, a court should not strive for numerical exactitude at the expense of the needs of the particular case.

The District Court's findings of fact depict a unique industry. Canneries often are located in remote, sparsely populated areas of Alaska.   Most jobs are seasonal, with the season's length and the canneries' personnel needs varying not just year-to-year but day-to-day. To fill their employment requirements, petitioners must recruit and transport many cannery workers and noncannery workers from States in the Pacific Northwest.   Most cannery workers come from a union local based outside Alaska or from Native villages near the canneries. Employees in the noncannery positions—the positions that are "at issue"—learn of openings by word of mouth; the jobs seldom are posted or advertised, and there is no promotion to noncannery jobs from within the cannery workers' ranks.

In general, the District Court found the at-issue jobs to require "skills," ranging from English literacy, typing, and "ability to use seam micrometers, gauges, and mechanic's hand tools" to "good health" and a driver's license.[21]   All cannery workers' jobs, like a handful of at-issue

---

20.   The Court discounts the difficulty its causality requirement presents for employees, reasoning that they may employ "liberal civil discovery rules" to obtain the employer's statistical personnel records. Even assuming that this generally is true, it has no bearing in this litigation, since it is undisputed that petitioners did not preserve such records.

21.   The District Court found that of more than 100 at-issue job titles, all were skilled except these 15: kitchen help, waiter/waitress, janitor, oildock crew, night watchman, tallyman, laundry, gasman, roustabout, store help, stockroom help, assistant caretaker (winter watchman and watchman's assistant), machinist helper/trainee, deckhand, and apprentice carpenter/carpenter's helper.

positions, are unskilled, and the court found that the intensity of the work during canning season precludes on-the-job training for skilled noncannery positions. It made no findings regarding the extent to which the cannery workers already are qualified for at-issue jobs: individual plaintiffs testified persuasively that they were fully qualified for such jobs,[22] but the court neither credited nor discredited this testimony. Although there are no findings concerning wage differentials, the parties seem to agree that wages for cannery workers are lower than those for noncannery workers, skilled or unskilled. The District Court found that "nearly all" cannery workers are nonwhite, while the percentage of nonwhites employed in the entire Alaska salmon canning industry "has stabilized at about 47% to 50%." The precise stratification of the work force is not described in the findings, but the parties seem to agree that the noncannery jobs are predominantly held by whites.

Petitioners contend that the relevant labor market in this case is the general population of the " 'external' labor market for the jobs at issue." While they would rely on the District Court's findings in this regard, those findings are ambiguous. At one point the District Court specifies "Alaska, the Pacific Northwest, and California" as "the geographical region from which [petitioners] draw their employees," but its next finding refers to "this relevant geographical area for cannery worker, laborer, and other nonskilled jobs". There is no express finding of the relevant labor market for noncannery jobs.

Even assuming that the District Court properly defined the relevant geographical area, its apparent assumption that the population in that area constituted the "available labor supply," is not adequately founded. An undisputed requirement for employment either as a cannery or noncannery worker is availability for seasonal employment in the far reaches of Alaska. Many noncannery workers, furthermore, must be available for preseason work. Yet the record does not identify the portion of the general population in Alaska, California, and the Pacific Northwest that would accept this type of employment.[23] This deficiency respecting a crucial job qualification diminishes the usefulness of petitioners' statistical evidence. In contrast, respondents' evi-

---

22. Some cannery workers later became architects, an Air Force officer, and a graduate student in public administration. Some had college training at the time they were employed in the canneries.

23. The District Court's justification for use of general population statistics occurs in these findings of fact:

"119. Most of the jobs at the canneries entail migrant, seasonal labor. While as a general proposition, most people prefer full-year, fixed location employment near their homes, seasonal employment in the unique salmon industry is not comparable to most other types of

migrant work, such as fruit and vegetable harvesting which, for example, may or may not involve a guaranteed wage.

"120. Thus, while census data is *[sic]* dominated by people who prefer full-year, fixed-location employment, such data is *[sic]* nevertheless appropriate in defining labor supplies for migrant, seasonal work."

The court's rather confusing distinction between work in the cannery industry and other "migrant, seasonal work" does not support its conclusion that the general population composes the relevant labor market.

dence, comparing racial compositions within the work force, identifies a pool of workers willing to work during the relevant times and familiar with the workings of the industry. Surely this is more probative than the untailored general population statistics on which petitioners focus. Cf. *Hazelwood* ; *Teamsters*.

Evidence that virtually all the employees in the major categories of at-issue jobs were white,[24] whereas about two-thirds of the cannery workers were nonwhite,[25] may not by itself suffice to establish a prima facie case of discrimination.[26] But such evidence of racial stratification puts the specific employment practices challenged by respondents into perspective. Petitioners recruit employees for at-issue jobs from outside the work force rather than from lower-paying, overwhelmingly nonwhite, cannery worker positions. Information about availability of at-issue positions is conducted by word of mouth;[27] therefore, the maintenance of housing and mess halls that separate the largely white noncannery work force from the cannery workers, coupled with the tendency toward nepotistic hiring,[28] are obvious barriers to employment opportunities for nonwhites. Putting to one side the issue of business justifications, it would be quite wrong to conclude that these practices

24. For example, from 1971 to 1980, there were 443 persons hired in the job departments labeled "machinists," "company fishing boat," and "tender" at petitioner Castle & Cooke, Inc.'s Bumble Bee cannery; only three of them were nonwhites. In the same categories at the Red Salmon cannery of petitioner Wards Cove Packing Co., Inc., 488 whites and 42 nonwhites were hired.

25. The Court points out that nonwhites are "overrepresented" among the cannery workers. Such an imbalance will be true in any racially stratified work force; its significance becomes apparent only upon examination of the pattern of segregation within the work force. In the cannery industry nonwhites are concentrated in positions offering low wages and little opportunity for promotion. Absent any showing that the "underrepresentation" of whites in this stratum is the result of a barrier to access, the "overrepresentation" of nonwhites does not offend Title VII.

26. The majority suggests that at-issue work demands the skills possessed by "accountants, managers, boat captains, electricians, doctors, and engineers." It is at least theoretically possible that a disproportionate number of white applicants possessed the specialized skills required by some at-issue jobs. In fact, of course, many at-issue jobs involved skills not at all comparable to these selective examples. Even

the District Court recognized that in a year-round employment setting, "some of the positions which this court finds to be skilled, e.g., truckdriving on the beach, [would] fit into the category of jobs which require skills that are readily acquirable by persons in the general public."

27. As the Court of Appeals explained in its remand opinion:

"Specifically, the companies sought cannery workers in Native villages and through dispatches from ILWU Local 37, thus securing a work force for the lowest paying jobs which was predominantly Alaska Native and Filipino. For other departments the companies relied on informal word-of-mouth recruitment by predominantly white superintendents and foremen, who recruited primarily white employees. That such practices can cause a discriminatory impact is obvious."

28. The District Court found but downplayed the fact that relatives of employees are given preferential consideration. But "of 349 nepotistic hires in four upper-level departments during 1970–75, 332 were of whites, 17 of nonwhites," the Court of Appeals noted. "If nepotism exists, it is by definition a practice of giving preference to relatives, and where those doing the hiring are predominantly white, the practice necessarily has an adverse impact on nonwhites."

have no discriminatory consequence.[29]   Thus I agree with the Court of Appeals that when the District Court makes the additional findings prescribed today, it should treat the evidence of racial stratification in the work force as a significant element of respondents' prima facie case.

III

The majority's opinion begins with recognition of the settled rule that "a facially neutral employment practice may be deemed violative of Title VII without evidence of the employer's subjective intent to discriminate that is required in a 'disparate treatment' case."   It then departs from the body of law engendered by this disparate impact theory, reformulating the order of proof and the weight of the parties' burdens.   Why the Court undertakes these unwise changes in elementary and eminently fair rules is a mystery to me.

I respectfully dissent.

NOTES AND PROBLEMS FOR DISCUSSION

1.   Section 105(a) of the 1991 Civil Rights Act partially reversed the *Wards Cove* Court's ruling with respect to multifactor selection procedures.   It provides, in new § 703(k) of Title VII, that a plaintiff in a discriminatory impact must still prove that the particular practice that is being challenged generated the discriminatory impact.   In addition, however, it states that if the plaintiff can establish that individual components of a selection process "are not capable of separation for analysis," the prima facie showing can be based on the impact produced by the total process.   The statute offers no guidance as to the meaning of this key phrase.

2.   In *Wards Cove* the Supreme Court held that in a hiring/promotion case a comparison between the racial composition of the pool of qualified persons in the labor market and the racial composition of the population holding the at-issue jobs "generally forms the proper basis for the initial inquiry in a disparate impact case."   490 U.S., at 650, 109 S.Ct. at 2121.   The Court did not rule out other types of statistical comparisons to prove disparate impact.   *Wards Cove* does not mean, for example, that in a testing case the standard comparison of the racial composition of those taking the test and those passing the test has become invalid.   Nash v. Consolidated City of Jacksonville, 905 F.2d 355 (11th Cir.1990), cert. denied, ___ U.S. ___, 111 S.Ct. 967, 112 L.Ed.2d 1054 (1991).   The Third Circuit has held that, at least in some cases, applicant flow data remains an appropriate means of demonstrating the disparate impact of hiring practices.   Green v. USX Corp., 896 F.2d 801 (3d Cir.), cert. denied, ___ U.S. ___, 111 S.Ct. 53, 112 L.Ed.2d 29 (1990).   The Court of Appeals in *Green* reasoned that in selecting applicants for unskilled positions any able-bodied person should be competent to perform such a job and that applicant flow would accurately reflect the pool of such persons.

---

29.   The Court suggests that the discrepancy in economic opportunities for white and nonwhite workers does not amount to disparate impact within the meaning of Title VII unless respondents show that it is "petitioners' fault."   This statement distorts the disparate impact theory, in which the critical inquiry is whether an employer's practices *operate* to discriminate.   E.g., Griggs.   Whether the employer intended such discrimination is irrelevant.

In *Wards Cove* itself, on remand from the Supreme Court, the district court concluded that plaintiffs had failed to make out a prima facie case of disparate impact. The plaintiffs contended that nepotism influenced hiring in the skilled cannery positions and they proved that a substantial number of skilled workers were in fact related. The court found, however, that skilled workers were not hired on the basis of their relationships with other workers but on the basis of qualifications and available jobs. Atonio v. Wards Cove Packing Co., 54 FEP Cases 1623 (W.D.Wash.1991).

3. The Defenses

Disproportionate impact cases can be defended by demonstrating the inaccuracy or irrelevancy of plaintiff's statistical data. See, Wards Cove Packing v. Atonio, *supra*. Where the plaintiff has established that an employment practice has a disproportionate impact on a protected class, the employer may defend on the ground that the practice has a legitimate business purpose. Title VII also immunizes certain kinds of employment practices from a disproportionate impact attack. Those defenses are discussed below.

(a) Job Relatedness and Business Necessity

WARDS COVE PACKING COMPANY, INC. v. ATONIO
Supreme Court of the United States, 1989.
490 U.S. 642, 109 S.Ct. 2115, 104 L.Ed.2d 733.

* * *

[The facts of the case and the sections of the majority and dissenting opinions dealing with the plaintiff's burden of proof in a disparate impact case are reproduced in Chapter II C(2), supra, at 224. The Supreme Court instructed the courts on remand to require plaintiffs to demonstrate that "specific elements" of the employer's hiring process have a disproportionate impact on nonwhites.]

B

If, on remand, respondents meet the proof burdens outlined above, and establish a prima facie case of disparate impact with respect to any of petitioners' employment practices, the case will shift to any business justification petitioners offer for their use of these practices. This phase of the disparate-impact case contains two components: first, a consideration of the justifications an employer offers for his use of these practices; and second, the availability of alternate practices to achieve the same business ends, with less racial impact. See, e.g., Albemarle Paper Co. v. Moody, * * *. We consider these two components in turn.

(1)

Though we have phrased the query differently in different cases, it is generally well-established that at the justification stage of such a disparate impact case, the dispositive issue is whether a challenged practice serves, in a significant way, the legitimate employment goals of the employer. See, e.g., Watson v. Fort Worth Bank & Trust Co. * * *; New York Transit Authority v. Beazer * * *; Griggs v. Duke Power Co. * * * The touchstone of this inquiry is a reasoned review of the employer's justification for his use of the challenged practice. A mere insubstantial justification in this regard will not suffice, because such a low standard of review would permit discrimination to be practiced through the use of spurious, seemingly neutral employment practices. At the same time, though, there is no requirement that the challenged practice be "essential" or "indispensable" to the employer's business for it to pass muster: this degree of scrutiny would be almost impossible for most employers to meet, and would result in a host of evils we have identified above. * * *

In this phase, the employer carries the burden of producing evidence of a business justification for his employment practice. The burden of persuasion, however, remains with the disparate-impact plaintiff. To the extent that the Ninth Circuit held otherwise in its en banc decision in this case, * * *, or in the panel's decision on remand, * * * suggesting that the persuasion burden should shift to the petitioners once the respondents established a prima facie case of disparate impact—its decisions were erroneous. "[T]he ultimate burden of proving that discrimination against a protected group has been caused by a specific employment practice remains with the plaintiff *at all times.*" Watson, supra, * * * (O'Connor, J.) (emphasis added). This rule conforms with the usual method for allocating persuasion and production burdens in the federal courts, see Fed. Rule Evid. 301, and more specifically, it conforms to the rule in disparate-treatment cases that the plaintiff bears the burden of disproving an employer's assertion that the adverse employment action or practice was based solely on a legitimate neutral consideration. * * * We acknowledge that some of our earlier decisions can be read as suggesting otherwise. See *Watson,* * * * (Blackmun, J., concurring). But to the extent that those cases speak of an employers' "burden of proof" with respect to a legitimate business justification defense, see, e.g., Dothard v. Rawlinson, * * *, they should have been understood to mean an employer's production— but not persuasion—burden. Cf., e.g., NLRB v. Transportation Management Corp., 462 U.S. 393, 404, n. 7, 103 S.Ct. 2469, 2475 n. 7, 76 L.Ed.2d 667 (1983). The persuasion burden here must remain with the plaintiff, for it is he who must prove that it was "because of such individual's race, color," etc., that he was denied a desired employment opportunity. See 42 U.S.C. § 2000e–2(a).

(2)

Finally, if on remand the case reaches this point, and respondents cannot persuade the trier of fact on the question of petitioners' business necessity defense, respondents may still be able to prevail. To do so, respondents will have to persuade the factfinder that "other tests or selection devices, without a similarly undesirable racial effect, would also serve the employer's legitimate [hiring] interest[s];" by so demonstrating, respondents would prove that "[petitioners were] using [their] tests merely as a 'pretext' for discrimination." *Albemarle Paper Co.,* * * *; see also, *Watson* * * * (O'Connor, J.); * * * (Blackmun, J.). If respondents, having established a prima facie case, come forward with alternatives to petitioners' hiring practices that reduce the racially-disparate impact of practices currently being used, and petitioners refuse to adopt these alternatives, such a refusal would belie a claim by petitioners that their incumbent practices are being employed for nondiscriminatory reasons.

Of course, any alternative practices which respondents offer up in this respect must be equally effective as petitioners' chosen hiring procedures in achieving petitioners' legitimate employment goals. Moreover, "[f]actors such as the cost or other burdens of proposed alternative selection devices are relevant in determining whether they would be equally as effective as the challenged practice in serving the employer's legitimate business goals." *Watson,* supra, (O'Connor, J.). "Courts are generally less competent than employers to restructure business practices," Furnco Construction Corp. v. Waters, * * *; consequently, the judiciary should proceed with care before mandating that an employer must adopt a plaintiff's alternate selection or hiring practice in response to a Title VII suit.

* * *

Justice Stevens, with whom Justice Brennan, Justice Marshall, and Justice Blackmun join, dissenting.

Fully 18 years ago, this Court unanimously held that Title VII of the Civil Rights Act of 1964 prohibits employment practices that have discriminatory effects as well as those that are intended to discriminate. Griggs v. Duke Power Co., * * *. Federal courts and agencies consistently have enforced that interpretation, thus promoting our national goal of eliminating barriers that define economic opportunity not by aptitude and ability but by race, color, national origin, and other traits that are easily identified but utterly irrelevant to one's qualification for a particular job. Regrettably, the Court retreats from these efforts in its review of an interlocutory judgment respecting the "peculiar facts" of this lawsuit. Turning a blind eye to the meaning and purpose of Title VII, the majority's opinion perfunctorily rejects a longstanding rule of law and underestimates the probative value of evidence of a racially stratified work force.[4] I cannot join this latest sojourn into judicial activism.

4. Respondents comprise a class of present and former employees of petitioners, two Alaskan salmon canning companies. The class members, described by the parties as "nonwhite," include persons of Samoan, Chinese, Filipino, Japanese, and Alaska Native descent, all but one of whom are United States citizens. * * *, Fifteen years ago they commenced this suit, alleging that petitioners engage in hiring, job assignment, housing, and messing practices that segregate nonwhites from whites, in violation of Title VII. Evidence included this response in 1971 by a foreman to a college student's inquiry about cannery employment:

I

I would have thought it superfluous to recount at this late date the development of our Title VII jurisprudence, but the majority's facile treatment of settled law necessitates such a primer. This Court initially considered the meaning of Title VII in Griggs v. Duke Power Co., * * * in which a class of utility company employees challenged the conditioning of entry into higher paying jobs upon a high school education or passage of two written tests. Despite evidence that "these two requirements operated to render ineligible a markedly disproportionate number of Negroes,"[5] the Court of Appeals had held that because there was no showing of an intent to discriminate on account of race, there was no Title VII violation. Id., at 429. Chief Justice Burger's landmark opinion established that an employer may violate the statute even when acting in complete good faith without any invidious intent. * * *

* * *

The opinion in *Griggs* made it clear that a neutral practice that operates to exclude minorities is nevertheless lawful if it serves a valid business purpose. "The touchstone is business necessity," the Court stressed. * * * Because "Congress directed the thrust of the Act to the *consequences* of employment practices, not simply the motivation[,] * * * Congress has placed on the employer the burden of showing that any given requirement must have a manifest relationship to the employment in question." * * * (emphasis in original). Congress has declined to act—as the Court now sees fit—to limit the reach of this "disparate impact" theory, see Teamsters v. United States, * * *; indeed it has extended its application.[9] This approval lends added force to the *Griggs* holding.

" 'We are not in a position to take many young fellows to our Bristol Bay canneries as they do not have the background for our type of employees. Our cannery labor is either Eskimo or Filipino and we do not have the facilities to mix others with these groups.' " * * *

Some characteristics of the Alaska salmon industry described in this litigation—in particular, the segregation of housing and dining facilities and the stratification of jobs along racial and ethnic lines—bear an unsettling resemblance to aspects of a plantation economy. See generally Plantation, Town, and County, Essays on the Local History of American Slave Society 163–334 (E. Miller & E. Genovese eds. 1974). Indeed the maintenance of inferior, segregated facilities for housing and feeding nonwhite employees, * * *, strikes me as a form of discrimination that, although it does not necessarily fit neatly into a disparate impact or disparate treatment mold, nonetheless violates Title VII. See generally Brief for National Association for the Advancement of Colored People as *Amicus Curiae*. Respondents, however, do not press this theory before us.

5. This Court noted that census statistics showed that in the employer's State, North Carolina, "while 34% of white males had completed high school, only 12% of Negro males had done so. * * * Similarly, with respect to standardized tests, the EEOC in one case found that use of a battery of tests, including the Wonderlic and Bennett tests used by the Company in the instant case, resulted in 58% of whites passing the tests, as compared with only 6% of the blacks." * * *

9. Voting Rights Act Amendments of 1982, Pub.L. 97–205, 96 Stat. 131, 134, as amended, codified at 42 U.S.C. §§ 1973, 1973b (1982 ed. and Supp. V). Legislative reports leading to 1972 amendments to Title VII also evince support for disparate impact analysis. H.R.Rep. No. 92–238, pp.

The *Griggs* framework, with its focus on ostensibly neutral qualification standards, proved inapposite for analyzing an individual employee's claim, brought under § 703(a)(1), that an employer intentionally discriminated on account of race. The means for determining intent absent direct evidence was outlined in McDonnell Douglas Corp. v. Green, * * *, and Texas Dept. of Community Affairs v. Burdine, * * *, two opinions written by Justice Powell for unanimous Courts. In such a "disparate treatment" case, * * *, the plaintiff's initial burden, which is "not onerous," * * *, is to establish "a prima facie case of racial discrimination," * * *; that is, to create a presumption of unlawful discrimination by "eliminat[ing] the most common nondiscriminatory reasons for the plaintiff's rejection." * * * "The burden then must shift to the employer to articulate some legitimate, nondiscriminatory reason for the employee's rejection." * * * Finally, because "Title VII does not * * * permit [the employer] to use [the employee's] conduct as a pretext for the sort of discrimination prohibited by § 703(a)(1)," the employee "must be given a full and fair opportunity to demonstrate by competent evidence that the presumptively valid reasons for his rejection were in fact a coverup for a racially discriminatory decision." * * * While the burdens of producing evidence thus shift, the "ultimate burden of persuading the trier of fact that the defendant intentionally discriminated against the plaintiff remains at all times with the plaintiff." [13] * * *

Decisions of this Court and other federal courts repeatedly have recognized that while the employer's burden in a disparate treatment case is simply one of coming forward with evidence of legitimate business purpose, its burden in a disparate impact case is proof of an affirmative defense of business necessity.[14] Although the majority's

8, 20–22 (1971); S.Rep.No. 92–415, p. 5, and n. 1 (1971); accord Connecticut v. Teal, 457 U.S. 440, 447, n. 8, 102 S.Ct. 2525, 2531, n.8, 73 L.Ed.2d 130 (1982). Moreover, the theory is employed to enforce fair housing and age discrimination statutes. See Note, Business Necessity in Title VIII: Importing an Employment Discrimination Doctrine into the Fair Housing Act, 54 Ford. L.Rev. 563 (1986); Note, Disparate Impact Analysis and the Age Discrimination in Employment Act, 68 Minn.L.Rev. 1038 (1984).

13. Although disparate impact and disparate treatment are the most prevalent modes of proving discrimination violative of Title VII, they are by no means exclusive. * * * Moreover, either or both of the primary theories may be applied to a particular set of facts. See Teamsters v. United States.

14. See *McDonnell Douglas,* 411 U.S., at 802, n. 14, 93 S.Ct., at 1824, n. 14. See also, e.g., *Teal,* 457 U.S., at 446, 102 S.Ct., at 2530 ("employer must ... demonstrate

that 'any given requirement [has] a manifest relationship to the employment in question' "); New York City Transit Authority v. Beazer, 440 U.S. 568, 587, 99 S.Ct. 1355, 1366, 59 L.Ed.2d 587 (1979) (employer "rebutted" prima facie case by "demonstration that its narcotics rule ... 'is job related' "); Dothard v. Rawlinson, 433 U.S. 321, 329, 97 S.Ct. 2720, 2726, 53 L.Ed.2d 786 (1977) (employer has to "prov[e] that the challenged requirements are job related"); Albemarle Paper Co. v. Moody, 422 U.S. 405, 425, 95 S.Ct. 2362, 2375, 45 L.Ed.2d 280 (1975) (employer has "burden of proving that its tests are 'job related' "); *Griggs,* 401 U.S., at 432, 91 S.Ct., at 854 (employer has "burden of showing that any given requirement must have a manifest relationship to the employment"). Court of Appeals opinions properly treating the employer's burden include Bunch v. Bullard, 795 F.2d 384, 393–394 (CA5 1986); Lewis v. Bloomsburg Mills, Inc., 773 F.2d 561, 572 (CA4 1985); Nash v. Consolidated City of Jacksonville,

opinion blurs that distinction, thoughtful reflection on common-law pleading principles clarifies the fundamental differences between the two types of "burdens of proof." In the ordinary civil trial, the plaintiff bears the burden of persuading the trier of fact that the defendant has harmed her. * * * The defendant may undercut plaintiff's efforts both by confronting plaintiff's evidence during her case in chief and by submitting countervailing evidence during its own case. But if the plaintiff proves the existence of the harmful act, the defendant can escape liability only by persuading the factfinder that the act was justified or excusable. * * * The plaintiff in turn may try to refute this affirmative defense. Although the burdens of producing evidence regarding the existence of harm or excuse thus shift between the plaintiff and the defendant, the burden of proving either proposition remains throughout on the party asserting it.

In a disparate treatment case there is no "discrimination" within the meaning of Title VII unless the employer intentionally treated the employee unfairly because of race. Therefore, the employee retains the burden of proving the existence of intent at all times. If there is direct evidence of intent, the employee may have little difficulty persuading the factfinder that discrimination has occurred. But in the likelier event that intent has to be established by inference, the employee may resort to the *McDonnell/Burdine* inquiry. In either instance, the employer may undermine the employee's evidence but has no independent burden of persuasion.

In contrast, intent plays no role in the disparate impact inquiry. The question, rather, is whether an employment practice has a significant, adverse effect on an identifiable class of workers—regardless of the cause or motive for the practice. The employer may attempt to contradict the factual basis for this effect; that is, to prevent the employee from establishing a prima facie case. But when an employer is faced with sufficient proof of disparate impact, its only recourse is to justify the practice by explaining why it is necessary to the operation of business. Such a justification is a classic example of an affirmative defense.

Failing to explore the interplay between these distinct orders of proof, the Court announces that our frequent statements that the employer shoulders the burden of proof respecting business necessity "should have been understood to mean an employer's production—but

Duval Cty., Fla., 763 F.2d 1393, 1397 (CA11 1985); Segar v. Smith, 238 U.S.App.D.C. 103, 121, 738 F.2d 1249, 1267 (1984), cert. denied sub nom. Meese v. Segar, 471 U.S. 1115, 105 S.Ct. 2357, 86 L.Ed.2d 258 (1985); Moore v. Hughes Helicopters, Inc., a Div. of Summa Corp., 708 F.2d 475, 481 (CA9 1983); Hawkins v. Anheuser–Busch, Inc., 697 F.2d 810, 815 (CA8 1983); Johnson v. Uncle Ben's, Inc., 657 F.2d 750 (CA5 1981), cert. denied, 459 U.S. 967, 103 S.Ct. 293, 74 L.Ed.2d 277 (1982); contra Croker v. Boeing Co., 662 F.2d 975, 991 (CA3 1981) (en banc). Cf. Equal Employment Opportunity Comm'n Uniform Guidelines on Employee

not persuasion—burden." [18] * * * Our opinions always have emphasized that in a disparate impact case the employer's burden is weighty. "The touchstone," the Court said in *Griggs,* "is business necessity." * * * Later, we held that prison administrators had failed to "rebu[t] the prima facie case of discrimination by showing that the height and weight requirements are * * * essential to effective job performance," Dothard v. Rawlinson, * * *. I am thus astonished to read that the "touchstone of this inquiry is a reasoned review of the employer's justification for his use of the challenged practice. * * * [T]here is no requirement that the challenged practice be * * * 'essential,' '" * * *. This casual—almost summary—rejection of the statutory construction that developed in the wake of *Griggs* is most disturbing. I have always believed that the *Griggs* opinion correctly reflected the intent of the Congress that enacted Title VII. Even if I were not so persuaded, I could not join a rejection of a consistent interpretation of a federal statute. Congress frequently revisits this statutory scheme and can readily correct our mistakes if we misread its meaning. * * *

* * *

I respectfully dissent.

[The separate dissenting opinion of Justice Blackmun is included in Chapter II(C) *supra* at 224.]

WARDS COVE PACKING AND THE CIVIL RIGHTS ACT OF 1991

Despite Justice White's assurances to the contrary, *Wards Cove Packing* was widely viewed as having altered *Griggs* and substantially undermined disparate impact analysis. See, Player, Is Griggs Dead? Reflecting (Fearfully) on Wards Cove Packing Co. v. Atonio, 17 Fla. St. L. Rev. 1, 17 (1989); Strauss, Discriminatory Intent and the Taming of *Brown*, 56 U. of Chicago L. Rev. 935, 950 (1989) (*Wards Cove* "substantially modified the way *Griggs* is to be applied"); Murphy, Supreme Court Review, 5 Labor Lawyer 679, 681 (1989) (*Wards Cove* "drastically changed the rules in disparate impact cases."); Blumrosen, Society in Transition II: *Price Waterhouse* and the Individual Employment Discrimination Case, 42 Rutgers L.Rev. 1023, 1025 (1990) (*Wards Cove* "severely restricted the 'disparate impact' principle of Griggs v. Duke Power Co.").

Wards Cove Packing was a focal point of the Civil Rights Act of 1990 (S. 2104, H.R. 4000) which was designed to reverse it and four

Selection Procedures, 29 CFR § 1607.1 et seq. (1988).

18. The majority's only basis for this proposition is the plurality opinion in Watson v. Fort Worth Bank & Trust, * * * (1988), which in turn cites no authority. As Justice Blackmun explained in *Watson*, * * * (concurring in part and concurring in judgment), and as I have shown here, the assertion profoundly misapprehends the difference between disparate impact and disparate treatment claims.

The Court also makes passing reference to Federal Rule of Evidence 301. * * *. That Rule pertains only to shifting of evidentiary burdens upon establishment of a presumption and has no bearing on the substantive burdens of proof. * * *.

other employment discrimination decisions rendered during the 1989 term. The Act passed both houses of Congress but was vetoed by the President. The Senate's efforts to override the veto fell one vote short. In the Fall of 1991 Congress tried again. Although the Civil Rights Act of 1991, Pub.L. 102–166, 105 Stat. 1071 (1991) was targeted at the same five Supreme Court decisions and contained language very similar to the 1990 Act, the President signed the 1991 version which was the product of a compromise between the Administration and Senate sponsors of the Act. Among the stated purposes of the Act was "to codify the concepts of 'business necessity' and 'job related' enunciated by the Supreme Court in Griggs v. Duke Power Co. . . . and in other Supreme Court decisions prior to Wards Cove Packing Co. v. Atonio . . ."

Section 105 of the 1991 Act amends Section 703 (Unlawful Employment Practices) of Title VII by adding the following new subsection:

(k)(1)(A) An unlawful employment practice based on disparate impact is established under this title only if—

(i) a complaining party demonstrates that a respondent uses a particular employment practice that causes a disparate impact on the basis of race, color, religion, sex, or national origin and the respondent fails to demonstrate that the challenged practice is job related for the position in question and consistent with business necessity; or

(ii) the complaining party makes the demonstration described in subparagraph (C) with respect to an alternative employment practice and the respondent refuses to adopt such alternative employment practice.

* * *

(ii) If the respondent demonstrates that a specific employment practice does not cause the disparate impact, the respondent shall not be required to demonstrate that such practice is required by business necessity.

(C) The demonstration referred to by subparagraph (A)(ii) shall be in accordance with the law as it existed on June 4, 1989[the day before *Wards Cove Packing* was decided], with respect to the concept of 'alternate employment practice'.

The term "demonstrates" is defined in Section 104 of the Act as "meets the burdens of production and persuasion."

The 1990 Civil Rights Act that was vetoed by the President was accompanied by a full legislative history consisting of committee reports and Senate and House debate, much of which was directed at Wards Cove Packing. The 1991 Act was not preceded by legislative hearings or much debate. The Administration feared that the legislative history of the 1990 Act might be used by courts in interpreting the 1991 Act. Thus, as part of the compromise that led to its enactment, the 1991 Act contains an unusual statutory designation of legislative history in Section 105(b):

No statements other than the interpretive memorandum appearing at Vol. 137 Congressional Record S 15276 (daily ed. Oct. 25, 1991) shall be considered legislative history of, or relied upon in any way as legislative history in construing or applying, any provision of this Act that relates to Wards Cove—Business necessity/cumulation/alternative business practice.

The interpretive memorandum referenced in Section 105(b) states as follows:

INTERPRETIVE MEMORANDUM

The final compromise on S. 1745 agreed to by several Senate sponsors, including Senators DANFORTH, KENNEDY, and DOLE, and the Administration states that with respect to Wards Cove–Business necessity/cumulation/alternative business practice—the exclusive legislative history is as follows:

The terms "business necessity" and "job related" are intended to reflect the concepts enunciated by the Supreme Court in Griggs v. Duke Power Co., 401 U.S. 424, 91 S.Ct. 849, 28 L.Ed.2d 158 (1971), and in other Supreme Court decisions prior to Wards Cove Packing Co. v. Atonio, 490 U.S. 642, 109 S.Ct. 2115, 104 L.Ed.2d 733 (1989).

When a decision-making process includes particular, functionally-integrated practices which are components of the same criterion, standard, method of administration or test, such as the height and weight requirements designed to measure strength in Dothard v. Rawlinson, 433 U.S. 321, 97 S.Ct. 2720, 53 L.Ed.2d 786 (1977), the particular functionally-integrated practices may by analyzed as one employment practice.

NOTES AND PROBLEMS FOR DISCUSSION

1. The 1991 Act requires an employer whose challenged employment practice has been shown to have a disparate impact, to demonstrate that the practice is both "job related and consistent with business necessity." Those terms overlap but are not necessarily equivalent. An employment practice could be "job related" without being "necessitated" by the business. Prior to *Wards Cove Packing* the circuits varied widely on the kind of showing the employer had to make to satisfy the business necessity defense. In Robinson v. Lorillard Corp., 444 F.2d 791 (4th Cir.), cert. dismissed, 404 U.S. 1006, 92 S.Ct. 573, 30 L.Ed.2d 655 (1971) the court of appeals stated:

[T]he applicable test is not merely whether there exists a business purpose for adhering to a challenged practice. The test is whether there exists an overriding legitimate business purpose such that the practice is necessary to the safe and efficient operation of the business. Thus, the business purpose must be sufficiently compelling to override any racial impact; the challenged practice must effectively carry out the business purpose it is alleged to serve; and there must be available no acceptable alternative policies or practices which would better accomplish the business purpose advanced, or accomplish it equally well with a lesser differential racial impact.

444 F.2d at 798. In United States v. Bethlehem Steel Corp., 446 F.2d 652, 662 (2d Cir.1971), the court emphasized that "[n]ecessity connotes an irresistible demand. * * * [A practice] must not only directly foster safety and efficiency of a plant, but also be essential to those goals." Other circuits adopted a less restrictive interpretation of business necessity. In Contreras v. City of Los Angeles, 656 F.2d 1267 (9th Cir.1981), cert. denied, 455 U.S. 1021, 102 S.Ct. 1719, 72 L.Ed.2d 140 (1982) the Ninth Circuit held that employment tests that cause disparate impact "are impermissible unless shown, by professionally accepted methods, to be predictive of or significantly correlated with important elements of work behavior that comprise or are relevant to the job or jobs for which the candidates are being evaluated." 656 F.2d at 1276. See, Nolting v. Yellow Freight System, Inc., 799 F.2d 1192 (8th Cir.1986) (showing that an employee evaluation system "significantly served" the interest in quantity of production satisfied business necessity requirement). What version of the business necessity test should be applied under the 1991 Act? Does the interpretive memorandum help?

2.   Many disproportionate impact cases concern employment tests used by employers to screen job applicants for hiring or current employees for promotion or retention. See, Connecticut v. Teal, *supra* at 202. In Griggs v. Duke Power Co. the Court stated that to pass muster under Title VII a test with disproportionate impact "must measure the person for the job and not the person in the abstract." *Griggs*, 401 U.S. at 436, 91 S.Ct. at 856. A test which accurately predicts job performance is "valid"—i.e. does not violate Title VII despite its disproportionate impact.

Validation asks two fundamental questions. The first asks whether a relationship exists at all. If so, the second question is whether the relationship is strong enough to be useful.

R. M. Guion, Personnel Testing 131 (1965).

Validity refers to the degree to which a test correlates with a relevant measure or criterion of job performance. Unless those people who score relatively high on a test are also likely to perform better on the job, a test lacks validity for that purpose and is useless for selecting personnel for the job in question.

J. Kirkpatrick, Testing and Fair Employment 6–7 (1968).

The Uniform Guidelines for Employee Selection Procedures, 29 C.F.R. § 1607 (1990), promulgated by the EEOC and other federal agencies, describe three methods of validating employment tests.

Criterion–Related Validation

Criterion validation was described by the Fifth Circuit in United States v. Georgia Power Co., 474 F.2d 906, 912 (5th Cir.1973) as follows:

The most accurate way to validate an employment test is to administer the test to be validated to all applicants but proceed to select new employees without regard for their test achievement, and then, after an appropriate period of work experience, compare job performance with test scores.

* * * An alternative is "concurrent validation", a process in which a representative sample of current employees is rated, then tested, and their scores are compared to their job ratings.

The Uniform Guidelines describe a criterion-related study as consisting of "empirical data demonstrating that the selection procedure is predictive of or significantly correlated with important elements of job performance." 29 C.F.R. § 1607.5B. Of the three methods of validation, criterion-related validation is the only one which correlates test results with actual work performance and is thus considered preferable to methods based on less direct evidence. See, Bridgeport Guardians, Inc. v. Members of Bridgeport Civil Service Commission, 482 F.2d 1333, 1337 (2d Cir.1973), cert. denied, 421 U.S. 991, 95 S.Ct. 1997, 44 L.Ed.2d 481 (1975).

Content Validation

A test that measures the actual skills or knowledge used in the job has content validity. Thus, if the job consists of typing, a test that measures the applicant's typing proficiency would have content validity for that job. Evidence of the validity of a test by this method "should consist of data showing that the content of the selection procedure is representative of important aspects of performance on the job for which the candidates are to be evaluated." 29 C.F.R. § 1607.5B. Unlike criterion-related validity, content validation does not require correlation between success on the test and success in the job: a person who does well on typing tests may not perform well on the job. Content validation must, however, be based on a job analysis "of the important work behavior(s) required for successful performance and their relative importance and, if the behavior results in work product(s), an analysis of the work product(s)." 29 C.F.R. § 1607.14C(2). Courts have held that for a test to have content validity, it must measure "with proper relevant emphasis all or * * * most of the essential areas of knowledge and the traits needed for proper job performance." Bridgeport Guardians, Inc. v. Members of Bridgeport Civil Service Commission, 354 F.Supp. 778, 792 (D.Conn.), affirmed in pertinent part, reversed in part, 482 F.2d 1333 (2d Cir.1973), cert. denied, 421 U.S. 991, 95 S.Ct. 1997, 44 L.Ed.2d 481 (1975); Kirkland v. New York State Department of Correctional Services, 374 F.Supp. 1361, 1378 (S.D.N.Y.1974), affirmed in pertinent part, reversed in part, 520 F.2d 420 (2d Cir.1975), cert. denied, 429 U.S. 823, 97 S.Ct 73, 50 L.Ed.2d 84 (1976). Content validation can be used for tests which seek to measure specific skills or items of knowledge but is:

> not appropriate for demonstrating the validity of selection procedures which purport to measure traits or constructs, such as intelligence, aptitude, personality, common sense, judgment, leadership, and spatial ability. Content validity is also not an appropriate strategy when the selection procedure involves knowledge, skills, or abilities which an employee will be expected to learn on the job.

29 C.F.R. § 1607.14C(1).

Construct Validation

A construct validity study tests for abstract qualities or traits that are difficult to objectively measure but are, nonetheless, important characteristics for good job performance. Creativity, assertiveness or the ability to "get along" with others are the kinds of qualities or "constructs" which an employer might wish to test for but which are probably not susceptible to criterion or content related validation. The Uniform Guidelines outline the following procedure for construct validation: (1) a job analysis which identifies work behavior(s) required for successful job performance; (2) an identification of the construct(s) believed to underlie success in the critical job behavior(s); (3) a selection procedure which measures the important construct(s). 29 C.F.R. § 1607.14D(2). Finally,

> The user should show by empirical evidence that the selection procedure is validly related to the construct and that the construct is validly related to the performance of critical or important work behavior(s). The relationship between the construct as measured by the selection procedure and the related work behavior(s) should be supported by empirical evidence from one or more criterion-related studies involving the job or jobs in question which satisfy [the Guideline requirements for criterion-related validation].

29 C.F.R. § 1607.14D(3). The application of the Uniform Guidelines is discussed in the following case.

3. The 1991 Civil Rights Act also provides an interesting new twist to the conventional rebuttal stage of a disproportionate impact claim. Traditionally, if the defendant was able to sustain its burden of establishing job relatedness/business necessity, the plaintiff could still prevail if it could prove the existence of a less discriminatory, effective selection device. Prior to the Court's ruling in *Wards Cove*, the plaintiff was required only to prove that this less discriminatory device "would also serve the employer's legitimate interest in efficient and trustworthy workmanship." In *Wards Cove*, however, the Court used language which indicated that it was raising the stakes for plaintiffs by requiring a plaintiff to establish that the less discriminatory device was "equally effective" in achieving the employer's legitimate employment goals as, and no more costly than, the subject policy. The language of § 105 of the 1991 Act raises two questions in this regard. First, it states that the concept of "alternative employment practice" shall be interpreted in accordance with the law as it existed the day before the ruling was issued in *Wards Cove*. This suggests that Congress intended to reverse the *Wards Cove* requirement that the plaintiff establish that the less discriminatory alternative was equally effective as and no more costly than the challenged policy and, presumably, to reinstate the *Albemarle*-era construction of that term. Additionally, § 105 provides that a plaintiff can prevail by showing the existence of such an alternative only when the employer "refuses" (not "refused") to adopt that alternative device. This implies that the employer can escape liability completely, even where the plaintiff has otherwise established a prima facie case, merely by agreeing to adopt the plaintiff's proffered alternative as late as during the trial of the case. If this is the case, will the plaintiff be deemed to be a "prevailing party" for attorney fee awards purposes? Wouldn't the plaintiff argue that its litigation resulted in a positive change desired by the plaintiff—adoption of a less discriminatory test? The language of § 105 also suggests that proof of a less discriminatory alternative plus proof of refusal to adopt is enough *per se* to establish liability, irrespective of the issues of disporportionate impact and job-relatedness.

ALBEMARLE PAPER CO. v. MOODY

Supreme Court of the United States, 1975.
422 U.S. 405, 95 S.Ct. 2362, 45 L.Ed.2d 280.

Mr. Justice Stewart delivered the opinion of the Court.

[A class of present and former black employees challenged the defendant's policy of requiring applicants for employment in skilled lines of progression to pass two general ability tests. Just before trial, the company hired an industrial psychologist to study the job relatedness of its two tests. His study compared the test scores of current employees working in some of the skilled job groupings with supervisorial judgments of these employees' competence. A statistically significant correlation between an individual's supervisorial rating and scores on both tests was found in two of the ten job groupings examined by the psychologist. Additionally, when studied separately, a statistically significant correlation with supervisorial ratings was found in three job groupings for one of the tests and in seven of the ten groupings for the other examination. On the basis of this study, the trial court concluded that the defendant had carried its burden of proving that its tests were job related. On appeal, the U.S. Fourth Circuit Court of Appeals reversed, finding that the validation study was not sufficiently comprehensive to warrant a determination of job-relatedness.]

* * *

The EEOC has issued "Guidelines" for employers seeking to determine, through professional validation studies, whether their employment tests are job related. 29 CFR Part 1607. These Guidelines draw upon and make reference to professional standards of test validation established by the American Psychological Association. The EEOC Guidelines are not administrative "regulations" promulgated pursuant to formal procedures established by the Congress. But, as this Court has heretofore noted, they do constitute "[t]he administrative interpretation of the Act by the enforcing agency," and consequently they are "entitled to great deference." Griggs v. Duke Power Co.

The message of these Guidelines is the same as that of the Griggs case—that discriminatory tests are impermissible unless shown, by professionally acceptable methods, to be "predictive of or significantly correlated with important elements of work behavior which comprise or are relevant to the job or jobs for which candidates are being evaluated." 29 CFR § 1607.4(c).

Measured against the Guidelines, Albemarle's validation study is materially defective in several respects:

(1) Even if it had been otherwise adequate, the study would not have "validated" the Beta and Wonderlic test battery for all of the skilled lines of progression for which the two tests are, apparently, now

required. The study showed significant correlations for the Beta Exam in only three of the eight lines. Though the Wonderlic Test's Form A and Form B are in theory identical and interchangeable measures of verbal facility, significant correlations for one form but not for the other were obtained in four job groupings. In two job groupings neither form showed a significant correlation. Within some of the lines of progression, one form was found acceptable for some job groupings but not for others. Even if the study were otherwise reliable, this odd patchwork of results would not entitle Albemarle to impose its testing program under the Guidelines. A test may be used in jobs other than those for which it has been professionally validated only if there are "no significant differences" between the studied and unstudied jobs. 29 CFR § 1607.4(c)(2). The study in this case involved no analysis of the attributes of, or the particular skills needed in, the studied job groups. There is accordingly no basis for concluding that "no significant differences" exist among the lines of progression, or among distinct job groupings within the studied lines of progression. Indeed, the study's checkered results appear to compel the opposite conclusion.

(2) The study compared test scores with subjective supervisorial rankings. While they allow the use of supervisorial rankings in test validation, the Guidelines quite plainly contemplate that the rankings will be elicited with far more care than was demonstrated here. Albemarle's supervisors were asked to rank employees by a "standard" that was extremely vague and fatally open to divergent interpretations. * * * There is no way of knowing precisely what criteria of job performance the supervisors were considering, whether each of the supervisors was considering the same criteria or whether, indeed, any of the supervisors actually applied a focused and stable body of criteria of any kind.[32] There is, in short, simply no way to determine whether the criteria *actually* considered were sufficiently related to the Company's legitimate interest in job-specific ability to justify a testing system with a racially discriminatory impact.

(3) The Company's study focused, in most cases, on job groups near the top of the various lines of progression. In Griggs v. Duke Power Co., the Court left open "the question whether testing requirements that take into account capability for the next succeeding position or related future promotion might be utilized upon a showing that such long-range requirements fulfill a genuine business need." The Guidelines take a sensible approach to this issue, and we now endorse it:

"If job progression structures and seniority provisions are so established that new employees will probably, within a reasonable period of time and in a great majority of cases, progress to a higher level, it may be considered that candidates are being evaluated for jobs at that higher level. However, where job progression is not so

---

32. It cannot escape notice that Albemarle's study was conducted by plant officials, without neutral, on-the-scene oversight, at a time when this litigation was about to come to trial. Studies so closely controlled by an interested party in litigation must be examined with great care.

> nearly automatic, or the time span is such that higher level jobs or employees' potential may be expected to change in significant ways, it shall be considered that candidates are being evaluated for a job at or near the entry level."

The fact that the best of those employees working near the top of a line of progression score well on a test does not necessarily mean that that test, or some particular cutoff score on the test, is a permissible measure of the minimal qualifications of new workers entering lower level jobs. In drawing any such conclusion, detailed consideration must be given to the normal speed of promotion, to the efficacy of on-the-job training in the scheme of promotion, and to the possible use of testing as a promotion device, rather than as a screen for entry into low-level jobs. The District Court made no findings on these issues. The issues take on special importance in a case, such as this one, where incumbent employees are permitted to work at even high-level jobs without passing the company's test battery.

(4) Albemarle's validation study dealt only with job-experienced, white workers; but the tests themselves are given to new job applicants, who are younger, largely inexperienced, and in many instances nonwhite. * * * The EEOC Guidelines * * * provide that "[d]ata must be generated and results separately reported for minority and nonminority groups wherever technically feasible." In the present case, such "differential validation" as to racial groups was very likely not "feasible," because years of discrimination at the plant have insured that nearly all of the upper level employees are white. But there has been no clear showing that differential validation was not feasible for lower level jobs. More importantly, the Guidelines provide:

> "If it is not technically feasible to include minority employees in validation studies conducted on the present work force, the conduct of a validation study without minority candidates does not relieve any person of his subsequent obligation for validation when inclusion of minority candidates becomes technically feasible." * * *

For all these reasons, we agree with the Court of Appeals that the District Court erred in concluding that Albemarle had proved the job relatedness of its testing program and that the respondents were consequently not entitled to equitable relief.

* * *

Accordingly, the judgment is vacated, and these cases are remanded to the District Court for proceedings consistent with this opinion.

It is so ordered.

NOTES AND PROBLEMS FOR DISCUSSION

1. What kind of validation was attempted by the employer's expert? Does *Albemarle* equate job relatedness and business necessity? Consider the following.

ZAMLEN v. CITY OF CLEVELAND

United States Court of Appeals, Sixth Circuit, 1990.
906 F.2d 209.

Norris, Circuit Judge.

Plaintiffs appeal from an order of the district court entering judgment for defendants in this class action lawsuit alleging intentional discrimination under 42 U.S.C. § 1983, and municipal conduct causing a prohibited disparate impact under Title VII of the Civil Rights Act of 1964. The suit, which was brought on behalf of entry-level female firefighters in the City of Cleveland, challenged the rank-order written and physical capabilities selection examination established by the city as perpetuating the exclusion of women from firefighting positions. The district court granted defendants' motion for a directed verdict on the charge of intentional discrimination and, at the close of all the evidence, found for defendants on the Title VII claim.

* * *

I. BACKGROUND

Much has been written about historical discrimination based upon race, sex, and national origin in public service occupations such as law enforcement and firefighting.[1] In order to address the problem, many municipalities have employed rank-order written and physical abilities tests which ostensibly allow employers to select candidates who possess the highest degree of skills required to perform the job.[2] Although these tests have been designed to eliminate discriminatory hiring practices, some have been shown to have a disparate impact on women and, for that reason, are challenged.

Two claims are usually advanced in support of the argument that rank-order physical tests unfairly discriminate against women. First, it is said that these tests measure attributes in which men traditionally excel, such as speed and strength (anaerobic traits), while ignoring those in which women traditionally are said to excel, such as stamina and endurance (aerobic traits). Second, it is claimed that the tested attributes are not necessarily related to the skills which the specific job

---

1. See, e.g., Epstein, Women in the Firehouse: The Second Circuit Upholds a Gender–Biased Firefighters' Examination, 54 Brooklyn L.Rev. 511 (1988); Rutherglen, Disparate Impact Under Title VII: An Objective Theory of Discrimination, 73 Va. L.Rev. 1297 (1987); Canton, Adverse Impact Analysis Of Public Sector Employment Tests: Can a City Devise a Valid Test?, 56 U.Cin.L.Rev. 683 (1987); Colker, Rank–Order Physical Abilities Selection Devices for Traditionally Male Occupations as Gender–Based Employment Discrimination, 19 U.C. Davis L.Rev. 761 (1986).

2. In jurisdictions employing rank-order testing, candidates are graded on their test performance and an eligibility list is compiled in which scores are ranked from high to low. In contrast, tests administered on a pass/fail basis allow employers to select candidates from a pool of qualified applicants. Applicants may be chosen from the pool randomly or in accordance with an affirmative action policy.

requires. The examination at issue was challenged for precisely these reasons.

As of 1977, the city had never hired any woman firefighters. In that year, it hired Dr. Norman Henderson, a tenured professor of psychology at Oberlin College who had significant experience developing tests for various municipalities throughout the country, to design, administer and score an entry-level firefighter examination. Dr. Henderson was again hired to develop and administer an entry-level exam in 1980.

No women were hired after the 1977 and 1980 examinations were scored and the applicants ranked. Out of 911 applicants who took both the written and physical portions of the examination in 1980, 18 were female. Only one female, or 5.6% of the women who took the exam, scored high enough to be placed on the eligibility list. With a ranking of 634, however, she was too far down the list to be hired. In contrast, 787 male applicants, or 88.2%, were placed on the eligibility list.

In 1983, Dr. Henderson was once again hired by the city to design and administer an exam for firefighters. In light of the female applicants' poor performance on the 1977 and 1980 examinations, and in order to minimize any disparate impact which his previous examinations may inadvertently have had on female applicants, Dr. Henderson prepared a new job analysis. The purpose of this new job analysis was to:

(1) establish a list of tasks required of entry-level firefighters;

(2) determine the frequency with which each task is performed and its importance to acceptable job performance;

(3) group tasks into broad job dimensions;

(4) assess the knowledge, skills and abilities required for learning and adequately performing critical and highly important job tasks;

(5) determine overall knowledge, skills and abilities required for entry-level fire-fighters with respect to the above tasks; and

(6) identify and define abilities and skills to be tested based upon the above data.

He then compiled an initial tasks list based upon a 1974 survey of 271 Cleveland firefighters. In the survey, fire-fighters rated 95 fire-fighting tasks in terms of frequency and importance. This initial list was then reviewed in conjunction with the Ohio Trade and Industrial Education Fire Service Training Manual and tasks lists from other cities. Dr. Henderson then produced a revised list consisting of 150 tasks and submitted this list to Chief William E. Lee, Director of the Cleveland Fire Training Academy. Chief Lee pared this list down to a final checklist of 135 tasks. Dr. Henderson also prepared a list of 12 intellectual and perceptual abilities relevant to effective firefighting.

Based upon this initial research, Dr. Henderson developed final written and physical components of the examination. The written component was designed to test reading comprehension, the ability to follow directions, mathematical skills, and other forms of cognitive reasoning. The physical component consisted of three events:

Event 1: Overhead Lift—using a 33 lb. barbell, candidates must lift the barbell overhead repeatedly for one minute or up to a maximum of 35 lifts.

Event 2: Fire Scene Set Up and Tower Climb—while wearing a custom-tailored self-contained breathing apparatus, candidates must drag two lengths of standard 2 1/2" hose 180 feet (90 feet one way, drop coupling, run to the other end of the hose, pick up and return 90 feet, drop coupling in designated area), run 75 feet to pumper, remove a one-person ladder (approximately 35 lbs.) from the side of the pumper, carry the ladder into the fire tower, place it against the back rail of the first landing and continue up the inside stairwell to the fifth floor where a monitor observes the candidates' arrival. Then, candidates return to the first landing, retrieve the ladder and place it on the pumper.

Event 3: Dummy Drag—still wearing their self-contained breathing apparatus, candidates must drag a 100 lb. bag 70 feet (40 of which includes low headroom), turn and, still dragging the bag, return to the starting point.

After the test was developed, but before it was administered, the city embarked on a program to recruit and train female firefighters. As part of its recruitment program, the city provided potential female recruits with a free twelve-week training program. This program, which included a two and one-half hour physical and cognitive portion, began on February 14, 1983. The written portion of the training program was based primarily upon the 1982 edition of the ARCO Civil Service Test training manual. The physical portion, which was based primarily on the content of previous examinations, included training in such activities as dummy lift and carry, dummy drag, hose drag, tower run, fence climb, ladder lift, balance beam walk, and hose coupling. The program did not include training in the use of barbells, nor did the director of the program recommend to any of the women that she work with barbells prior to the examination.

One week before the actual physical examination, the city notified all applicants of the content of the examination, including the barbell event. The training program obtained a set of barbells which was made available to the applicants.

On April 30, 1983, the city administered the written portion of the test and, on May 7 and 13, the physical portion of the test. There were 3,612 applicants initially, but only 2,212 took the written part and 1,233 the physical part. Each portion of the examination was worth a raw score of 50 points with a maxim achievable score of 100. The raw scores on the written portion were adjusted by capping the scores from different sections, by awarding five extra points to qualifying veterans, by awarding ten extra points to city residents, and by adding up to six points to the scores of minority candidates. The minority adjustment was undertaken as a means of complying with a consent decree entered against the city in a suit by minority candidates alleging bias in hiring. Only those applicants with an adjusted score of at least 35 were eligible to take the physical portion of the exam.

Of the 285 females who took the written portion, 122 passed; of the 1,927 males who took the written examination, 1,206 passed. After taking the physical portion of the examination, 29 females scored high enough on both portions of the exam to be placed on the eligibility list while 1,069 males were placed on the list. However, the woman with the highest score still only ranked 334 on the eligibility list—too low to be hired. The class of 35 firefighters, therefore, contained no women.

On June 14, 1983, plaintiffs filed this class action. The principal defense was that the selection procedure was job-related and properly validated. A second, similar suit was initiated by the United States Government, and the two cases were consolidated for trial.

* * *

[Those portions of the opinion discussing the intentional discrimination claim and the exclusion of some of the plaintiffs' evidence are omitted.]

IV. ALLOCATION OF BURDENS

The purpose of Title VII is to achieve equality of employment opportunities through the eradication of employment barriers which discriminate on the basis of race, gender, religion, and other protected classifications. *Griggs v. Duke Power Co.* The Supreme Court has recognized that Title VII forbids not only overt discrimination "but also practices that are fair in form, but discriminatory in operation." *Griggs*, 401 U.S. at 431, 91 S.Ct. at 853. Employment practices which, although facially neutral, are discriminatory in practice have given rise to the theory of liability commonly known as the disparate impact theory. Under this basis for liability, a specific employment practice may be deemed violative of Title VII without proving the employer's subjective intent to discriminate. *Wards Cove Packing v. Atonio.* Here, plaintiffs proceeded under the disparate impact theory.

In *Albemarle Paper Co. v. Moody*, 422 U.S. 405, 95 S.Ct. 2362, 45 L.Ed.2d 280 (1975), the Supreme Court outlined the burdens of the parties in disparate impact cases:

> Title VII forbids the use of employment tests that are discriminatory in effect unless the employer meets "the burden of showing that any given requirement [has] ... a manifest relationship to the employment in question." [*Griggs v. Duke Power Co.*, 401 U.S. at 432, 91 S.Ct. at 854.] This burden arises, of course, only after the complaining party or class has made out a prima facie case of discrimination, i.e., has shown in effect that the tests in question select applicants for hire or promotion in a racial pattern signifi-

cantly different from that of the pool of applicants. See *McDonnell Douglas Corp. v. Green.* If an employer does then meet the burden of proving that its tests are "job related," it remains open to the complaining party to show that other tests or selection devices, without a similarly undesirable racial effect, would also serve the employer's legitimate interest in "efficient and trustworthy workmanship."

Albemarle, 422 U.S. at 425, 95 S.Ct. at 2375.

In *Wards Cove,* the Supreme Court clarified prior case law by pointing out that once a plaintiff has made out a prima facie case,[5] it is not the burden of persuasion which shifts to the employer; instead, at that point, the employer shoulders the burden of production, of producing evidence of a business justification: "The ultimate burden of proving that discrimination against a protected group has been caused by a specific employment practice remains with the plaintiff *at all times.*" *Wards Cove,* 490 U.S. at 659, 109 S.Ct. at 2126, 104 L.Ed.2d at 753 (citing *Watson v. Ft. Worth Bank & Trust Co.,* 487 U.S. 977, 108 S.Ct. 2777, 101 L.Ed.2d 827 (1988)).

Prior to *Wards Cove,* this circuit adopted the doctrine announced in *Spurlock v. United States Airline, Inc.,* which allows an employer to meet a lighter standard of proof of job-relatedness where the job at issue clearly requires a high degree of skill and the economic and human risks involved in hiring an unqualified applicant are great.

The district court specifically held that firefighting poses sufficient risks to the public's safety to invoke the *Spurlock* doctrine: "The risks to the public in terms of life, limb and property as a consequence of hiring an unqualified firefighter are great, resulting in a less heavy burden for demonstrating the job relatedness of the employment criteria." On appeal, plaintiffs contend that, since the *Spurlock* doctrine was intended to apply to jobs which require special skills or abilities "which are extremely difficult to define with significant precision and even harder—to the extent so identified—to test for or measure," *Davis v. City of Dallas,* 777 F.2d 205, 215 (5th Cir.1985), cert. denied, 476 U.S. 1116, 106 S.Ct. 1972, 90 L.Ed.2d 656 (1986), and since the 1983 examination at issue was designed to measure tangible, objective cognitive abilities and concrete physical capabilities, the district court improperly invoked this doctrine.

Actually, we need not decide whether the *Spurlock* doctrine was properly invoked since, in view of the Supreme Court's intervening opinion in *Wards Cove,* whether the district court lowered the city's burden of persuasion is no longer at issue. The city had only the burden of *producing* evidence to justify the use of its selection device. Since the city was found to have satisfied the *Spurlock* burden of

---

5. A plaintiff may present a prima facie case of discrimination under Title VII either by showing that the disputed practice has a disparate impact or, pursuant to the Uniform Guidelines on Employee Selection Procedures, 29 C.F.R. § 1607.4D (1985), that she was less than four-fifths as likely to be hired as an equally qualified man.

persuasion, and that burden is still more onerous than the burden of production which the city actually is obligated to bear under *Wards Cove*, the city, having met the heavier burden, necessarily satisfied the lighter burden. While one may produce without persuading, one cannot persuade without first producing. Accordingly, plaintiffs were not harmed by the district court's allocation of burdens.

V. ADEQUACY OF VALIDATION PROCEDURES AND FAILURE TO MEASURE AEROBIC CAPACITY

The standard of review in Title VII cases is strict. As this court recently recognized,

> [when] reviewing the district court's factual findings in a Title VII discrimination case, we may not reverse unless we find that the district court committed clear error. If the district court's account of the evidence is plausible ... the court of appeals may not reverse it even though ... it would have weighed the evidence differently.

Wrenn v. Gould, 808 F.2d 493, 499 (6th Cir.1987) (citing *Anderson v. Bessemer City*, 470 U.S. 564, 573, 105 S.Ct. 1504, 1511, 84 L.Ed.2d 518 (1985)).

The Equal Employment Opportunity Commission ("EEOC") has developed guidelines "to assist employers ... to comply with requirements of Federal law prohibiting employment practices which discriminate on grounds of race, color, religion, sex and national origin ... [and] to provide a framework for determining the proper use of tests and other selection procedures." 29 C.F.R. § 1607.1(B). Under the guidelines, employers may use three types of studies to validate an employee selection procedure: content, construct, or criterion-related validity studies. The particular device that is chosen depends upon the nature of the job, the way in which the test will be interpreted, and the type of data that is available.

* * *

[The court's description of the three types of validation studies is omitted. See, supra Note 2 at 246.]

The district court found that the 1983 examination was properly validated according to content, construct, and criterion validation principles. Nonetheless, plaintiffs attack the district court's finding on the ground that the test that Dr. Henderson developed was not properly validated and, in addition, did not test for all of the attributes he identified in his job analysis as important to an effective firefighter. Although Dr. Henderson recognized that successful firefighters must possess a high level of aerobic capacity and aerobic fitness, as well as muscle strength, muscular endurance, flexibility, coordination, muscle balance, and speed, the physical portion of the 1983 examination measured anaerobic—maximal speed and strength—but not aerobic—stamina or paced performance—traits.

We first note that there was substantial evidence before the district court supporting the conclusion that the examination was properly validated. Each event in the physical examination was designed to test a representative firefighting task. The barbell lift was designed to simulate the use of a pike pole to tear out ceilings. The fire scene set-up and tower climb event was intended to duplicate critical firefighting tasks performed where speed is the most critical factor, such as setting up ladders and climbing stairs. The dummy drag simulated the rescue of a disabled person under circumstances where heat and smoke make it difficult to stand upright. Although plaintiffs attack the content validity of these events as only superficially replicating an actual sequence of job tasks, an expert testified that these events did, in fact, simulate actual firefighting tasks. Plaintiffs may find fault with the way in which the district court came to certain conclusions but there is an insufficient basis for us to conclude that these conclusions are clearly erroneous.

Similarly, plaintiffs argue that there was insufficient evidence supporting the district court's conclusion that the examination was construct and criterion valid. However, plaintiffs ignore the substantial evidence before the district court, including Dr. Henderson's technical report correlating higher test scores with higher supervisor ratings as well as Dr. Henderson's further analyses, supporting the conclusion that the examination was construct and criterion valid.

Plaintiffs' most forceful argument is that the 1983 examination failed to measure attributes which are concededly important to effective firefighting, attributes in which it is often argued that women traditionally excel, such as stamina and endurance. By failing to test for these aerobic qualities, plaintiffs argue, Dr. Henderson devised an examination hopelessly biased in favor of male applicants who will almost always score higher than female applicants on tests which solely measure anaerobic qualities such as strength and speed.

A similar case was decided recently in the Second Circuit. In *Berkman v. City of New York*, 812 F.2d 52 (2d Cir.1987) ("Berkman IV"), plaintiffs argued that a firefighter exam used by the City of New York to select entry-level firefighters should be invalidated because it failed to measure aerobic capacity and placed undue emphasis on anaerobic performance. Recognizing that aerobic attributes are an important component of effective firefighting, the court nonetheless held that the city's failure to include events that test for such qualities did not invalidate the examination. While the court implied that an examination that included events which tested an applicant's aerobic energy system would be preferable, "[it] does not follow, however, that a physical test of the ability to perform simulated job tasks of firefighters, without a specific measurement of stamina, lacks validity to a degree that renders it vulnerable to a Title VII challenge." *Berkman*, 812 F.2d at 59.

While aerobic ability enables firefighters to sustain a consistent level of energy over a long period of time, speed and strength are critical at the initial stages of a fire where matters of life and death are most acute.   A firefighter who tires may be replaced by a fresh recruit but, as the Berkman court recognized, "if the first firefighters on the scene are deficient in the speed and strength necessary to handle their tasks, those in need of immediate rescue will not be comforted by the fact that those first on the scene might be able to sustain their modest energy levels for a prolonged period of time." *Berkman*, 812 F.2d at 60. Here, the district court concluded that anaerobic qualities are more important.   Certainly, we are unable to say a fire department is not entitled to select firefighters whose abilities enable them to act more effectively in the first moments of a fire.   Accordingly, although a simulated firefighting examination that does not test for stamina in addition to anaerobic capacity may be a less effective barometer of firefighting abilities than one that does include an aerobic component, the deficiencies of this examination are not of the magnitude to render it defective, and vulnerable to a Title VII challenge. *Berkman*, 812 F.2d at 59.

VI.   LESS RESTRICTIVE ALTERNATIVE

Finally, plaintiffs contend that a different scoring system—one which would eliminate the addition of variable numbers of minority points, the use of the capping system and the addition of veterans' points—would have raised the rank-order of women on the eligibility list and, thus, constitutes a less restrictive alternative.   Under *Wards Cove*, once the plaintiffs have shown that other nondiscriminatory means exist which could effectively serve the employer's legitimate interests, the employer must adopt them or risk the inference that the preferred test is a pretext for discriminatory conduct. *Wards Cove*.

The district court concluded that plaintiffs failed to demonstrate a less restrictive alternative, a conclusion with which we agree.   Although the use of a different scoring system might raise the rank-order of women on the eligibility list, given the fact that the woman with the highest test score still only ranked 334 on the eligibility list, and that the city only hired approximately forty firefighters each year, it is doubtful that any alternative scoring system would have had less of a disparate impact on women.   The evidence suggests that, at best, an alternative scoring system would result in female applicants ranking higher on the eligibility list, but still too low to actually be hired.   Since rescoring the examination is unlikely to result in higher numbers of successful female applicants, it is an insufficient reason to invalidate an otherwise lawful examination.

VII.   CONCLUSION

Because the examination did parallel the actual tasks which firefighters perform on the job, and the city did demonstrate a direct correlation between higher test scores and better job performance, the examination withstands plaintiffs' challenge. Accordingly, the judgment of the district court is affirmed.

NOTES AND PROBLEMS FOR DISCUSSION

1. As noted by the Sixth Circuit in *Zamlen*, prior to *Wards Cove Packing*, a number of circuits, relying on Spurlock v. United Airlines, Inc., 475 F.2d 216 (10th Cir.1972), had significantly relaxed the evidentiary burden in disparate impact cases on employers of those entrusted with "the lives and well-being" of the public. The *Spurlock* doctrine has not been explicitly approved by the Supreme Court. Should *Spurlock* influence interpretation of the business necessity standard in the 1991 Civil Rights Act?

2. Do *Zamlen* and *Berkman* mean that an employer is free to emphasize certain factors which favor male applicants in the selection procedure and deemphasize those equally job-related factors which favor female applicants without regard to how *relatively* important the factors are in performing the job? Compare, Brunet v. City of Columbus, 642 F.Supp. 1214 (S.D.Ohio 1986), appeal dismissed, 826 F.2d 1062 (6th Cir.1987), cert. denied, 485 U.S. 1034, 108 S.Ct. 1593, 99 L.Ed.2d 908 (1988) (physical test for firefighter placed undue emphasis on speed of limb movement and dynamic flexibility and underemphasized endurance) with Cleghorn v. Herrington, 813 F.2d 992 (9th Cir.1987) (physical ability test used to screen applicants for job of guarding nuclear facilities was properly validated even though test emphasized emergency duties rather than daily routine work which was largest component of job). If a physical test simulates certain tasks that are shown to be involved in the work, must the test even be formally validated to withstand a Title VII challenge? In United States v. City of Wichita Falls, 704 F.Supp. 709 (N.D.Tex.1988) the court upheld a physical agility test for police candidates that had not been validated through a formal study.

> A police officer's inability to perform any of the tasks could result in the death of that officer, another officer, or a civilian. Courts have recognized that a formal study need not be done to establish that a test accurately reflects the demands of a job. Evidence can be presented at trial, as in this case, which demonstrates that the test accurately reflects the qualities needed to perform a certain job. Thus, the physical agility test is "content valid," meaning the tasks performed in the test accurately simulate tasks performed by police officers.

704 F.Supp. at 714. But see, Nash v. Consolidated City of Jacksonville, 837 F.2d 1534 (11th Cir.1988) (fact that test was designed by qualified personnel familiar with jobs does not make test valid). To what extent should the nature of the employer's business allow "common sense" validation of employment criteria?

3. The plaintiffs' class in *Zamlen* was affected by the firefighters' test in two ways: (1) the content of the test resulted in a much smaller percentage of female than of male applicants attaining a passing score and (2) the use of test scores to rank applicants meant that, of those women who passed the test, most were ranked at the bottom of the list of acceptable candidates. Does the court satisfactorily explain the validation of the use of test scores to rank order candidates? With the principle case compare, Bridgeport Guardians, Inc. v. City of Bridgeport, 933 F.2d 1140 (2d Cir.), cert. denied, ___ U.S. ___, 112 S.Ct. 337, 116 L.Ed.2d 277 (1991) (in light of evidence that city failed to include

minorities on personnel review panels and rejected the recommendations of its own expert, its refusal to make police sergeant promotions from designated bands of scores and adherence to rank-order selection belies claim that its incumbent practices are non-discriminatory). See also, Colker, Rank Order Physical Abilities Selection Devices for Traditionally Male Occupations as Gender–Based Employment Discrimination, 19 U.C.Davis L.Rev. 761 (1986).

If minorities or women are disproportionately impacted by an employment test, one way to increase their number in the work force without abandoning the test is to set lower pass rates or cut off points for minorities and/or women. Such practices, referred to as race or sex "norming" are explicitly prohibited by Section 106 of the Civil Rights Act of 1991 which adds the following subsection to Section 703 of Title VII.

> (1) It shall be an unlawful employment practice for a respondent, in connection with the selection or referral of applicants or candidates for employment or promotion, to adjust the scores of, use different cutoff scores for, or otherwise alter the results of, employment related tests on the basis of race, color, religion, sex, or national origin.

In light of the general prohibitions in Section 703 was this section of the 1991 Act necessary?

4. Should the employer's burden in a disproportionate impact case be affected by the fact that the challenged practice perpetuates prior discrimination? In Walker v. Jefferson County Home, 726 F.2d 1554 (11th Cir.1984), the Court of Appeals noted that a nursing home's requirement of prior supervisory experience as a prerequisite for promotion to a supervisory position, though neutral on its face, impacted on black employees because of past discrimination in job assignments to supervisory positions and thus served to "freeze the status quo of prior discriminatory employment practices." In such a case the Court held that the employer should have a "heavy burden" of proving business necessity. The defendant failed to satisfy the burden because it did not prove that the job of supervisor was "highly skilled or that the economic and human risks involved as being an unqualified applicant [were] great." 726 F.2d at 1559. In United States v. Town of Cicero, 786 F.2d 331 (7th Cir.1986), the government challenged municipal ordinances which restricted city employment to persons who had been residents in the town for at least one year. The town was less than .05% black but adjoined two predominantly black communities. In its entire history the town had never employed a black. The district court denied a preliminary injunction on the ground that the ordinances were facially neutral. The Seventh Circuit reversed and remanded for reconsideration noting that under *Griggs*, even neutral practices cannot be maintained if they operate to freeze in the results of prior employment discrimination. To what extent should the rule of these "perpetuation" cases be affected by the 1991 Civil Rights Act?

An employer's reliance on an employment criteria as a business necessity may backfire and result in a finding of intentional discrimination if the criteria has not in fact been uniformly applied by the employer. In Kilgo v. Bowman Transportation Co., 789 F.2d 859 (11th Cir.1986) a trucking company argued that use of a one-year prior over-the-road experience requirement for new drivers was necessary for safety. The court of appeals concluded that even if the requirement was a business necessity and there was no less discriminatory alternative, the trial court's determination that the requirement was a pretext for intentional discrimination was not erroneous. The company had hired over

60 men who did not satisfy the prior experience requirement. See also, Davis v. Richmond, Fredericksburg & Potomac R. Co., 803 F.2d 1322 (4th Cir.1986) (prior experience requirement of such minimal value to employer given available training that it could only be pretext for discrimination). Proof of class-wide intentional discrimination, sometimes referred to as "pattern and practice" discrimination is discussed in Chapter 2D, *infra*.

(b) Bona Fide Seniority Systems

INTERNATIONAL BROTHERHOOD OF TEAMSTERS v. UNITED STATES

Supreme Court of the United States, 1977.
431 U.S. 324, 97 S.Ct. 1843, 52 L.Ed.2d 396.

MR. JUSTICE STEWART delivered the opinion of the Court.

This litigation brings here several important questions under Title VII of the Civil Rights Act of 1964. The issues grow out of alleged unlawful employment practices engaged in by an employer and a union. The employer is a common carrier of motor freight with nationwide operations, and the union represents a large group of its employees. The District Court and the Court of Appeals held that the employer had violated Title VII by engaging in a pattern and practice of employment discrimination against Negroes and Spanish-surnamed Americans, and that the union had violated the Act by agreeing with the employer to create and maintain a seniority system that perpetuated the effects of past racial and ethnic discrimination. In addition to the basic questions presented by these two rulings, other subsidiary issues must be resolved if violations of Title VII occurred—issues concerning the nature of the relief to which aggrieved individuals may be entitled.

I

The United States brought an action in a Tennessee federal court against the petitioner T.I.M.E.–D.C., Inc. (the company), pursuant to § 707(a) of the Civil Rights Act of 1964.[1] The complaint charged that

---

1. At the time of suit the statute provided as follows:

"(a) Whenever the Attorney General has reasonable cause to believe that any person or group of persons is engaged in a pattern or practice of resistance to the full enjoyment of any of the rights secured by this subchapter, and that the pattern or practice is of such a nature and is intended to deny the full exercise of the rights herein described, the Attorney General may bring a civil action in the appropriate district court of the United States by filing with it a complaint (1) signed by him (or in his absence the Acting Attorney General), (2)

setting forth facts pertaining to such pattern or practice, and (3) requesting such relief, including an application for a permanent or temporary injunction, restraining order or other order against the person or persons responsible for such pattern or practice, as he deems necessary to insure the full enjoyment of the rights herein described."

Section 707 was amended by § 5 of the Equal Employment Opportunity Act of 1972, 86 Stat. 107, 42 U.S.C. § 2000e–6(c) (1970 ed., Supp. V), to give the equal Employment Opportunity Commission, rather than the Attorney General, the authority to bring "pattern or practice" suits under

the company had followed discriminatory hiring, assignment, and promotion policies against Negroes at its terminal in Nashville, Tenn.[2] The Government brought a second action against the company almost three years later in a Federal District Court in Texas, charging a pattern and practice of employment discrimination against Negroes and Spanish-surnamed persons throughout the company's transportation system. The petitioner International Brotherhood of Teamsters (union) was joined as a defendant in that suit. The two actions were consolidated for trial in the Northern District of Texas.

The central claim in both lawsuits was that the company had engaged in a pattern or practice of discriminating against minorities in hiring so-called line drivers. Those Negroes and Spanish-surnamed persons who had been hired, the Government alleged, were given lower paying, less desirable jobs as servicemen or local city drivers, and were thereafter discriminated against with respect to promotions and transfers.[3] In this connection the complaint also challenged the seniority system established by the collective-bargaining agreements between the employer and the union. The Government sought a general injunctive remedy and specific "make whole" relief for all individual discriminatees, which would allow them an opportunity to transfer to line-driver jobs with full company seniority for all purposes.

The cases went to trial[4] and the District Court found that the Government had shown "by a preponderance of the evidence that

that section against private-sector employers. In 1974, an order was entered in this action substituting the EEOC for the United States but retaining the United States as a party for purposes of jurisdiction, appealability, and related matters. See 42 U.S.C. § 2000e–6(d) (1970 ed., Supp. V).

2. The named defendant in this suit was T.I.M.E. Freight, Inc., a predecessor of T.I.M.E.–D.C., Inc. T.I.M.E.–D.C., Inc., is a nationwide system produced by 10 mergers over a 17–year period. See United States v. T.I.M.E.–D.C., Inc., 517 F.2d 299, 304, and n. 6(CA5). It currently has 51 terminals and operates in 26 States and three Canadian Provinces.

3. *Line drivers*, also known as over-the-road drivers, engage in long-distance hauling between company terminals. They compose a separate bargaining unit at the company. C. Other distinct bargaining units include *servicemen*, who service trucks, unhook tractors and trailers, and perform similar tasks; and *city operations*, composed of dockmen, hostlers, and city drivers who pick up and deliver freight within the immediate area of a particular terminal. All of these employees were represented by the petitioner union.

4. Following the receipt of evidence, but before decision, the Government and the company consented to the entry of a Decree in Partial Resolution of Suit. The consent decree did not constitute an adjudication on the merits. The company agreed, however, to undertake a minority recruiting program; to accept applications from all Negroes and Spanish-surnamed Americans who inquired about employment, whether or not vacancies existed, and to keep such applications on file and notify applicants of job openings; to keep specific employment and recruiting records open to inspection by the Government and to submit quarterly reports to the District Court; and to adhere to certain uniform employment qualifications respecting hiring and promotion to line driver and other jobs.

The decree further provided that future job vacancies at any company terminal would be filled first "[b]y those persons who may be found by the Court, if any, to be individual or class discriminatees suffering the present effects of past discrimination because of race or national origin prohibited by Title VII of the Civil Rights Act of 1964." Any remaining vacancies could be filled by "any other persons," but the company obligated itself to hire one Negro or Spanish-surnamed person for every white person hired at any terminal until

T.I.M.E.–D.C. and its predecessor companies were engaged in a plan and practice of discrimination in violation of Title VII * * *." [5] The court further found that the seniority system contained in the collective-bargaining contracts between the company and the union violated Title VII because it "operate[d] to impede the free transfer of minority groups into and within the company." Both the company and the union were enjoined from committing further violations of Title VII.

With respect to individual relief the court accepted the Government's basic contention that the "affected class" of discriminatees included all Negro and Spanish-surnamed incumbent employees who had been hired to fill city operations or serviceman jobs at every terminal that had a line-driver operation.[6] All of these employees, whether hired before or after the effective date of Title VII, thereby became entitled to preference over all other applicants with respect to consideration for future vacancies in line-driver jobs.[7] Finding that members of the affected class had been injured in different degrees, the court created three subclasses. Thirty persons who had produced "the most convincing evidence of discrimination and harm" were found to have suffered "severe injury." The court ordered that they be offered the opportunity to fill line-driver jobs with competitive seniority dating back to July 2, 1965, the effective date of Title VII.[8] A second subclass included four persons who were "very possibly the objects of discrimination" and who "were likely harmed," but as to whom there had been no specific evidence of discrimination and injury. The court decreed that these persons were entitled to fill vacancies in line-driving jobs with competitive seniority as of January 14, 1971, the date on which the Government had filed its systemwide lawsuit. Finally, there were over 300 remaining members of the affected class as to whom there was "no evidence to show that these individuals were either harmed or not harmed individually." The court ordered that they be considered for

the percentage of minority workers at that terminal equaled the percentage of minority group members in the population of the metropolitan area surrounding the terminal. Finally, the company agreed to pay $89,500 in full settlement of any backpay obligations. Of this sum, individual payments not exceeding $1,500 were to be paid to "alleged individual and class discriminatees" identified by the Government.

The Decree in Partial Resolution of Suit narrowed the scope of the litigation, but the District Court still had to determine whether unlawful discrimination had occurred. If so, the court had to identify the actual discriminatees entitled to fill future job vacancies under the decree. The validity of the collective-bargaining contract's seniority system also remained for decision, as did the question whether any dis-

criminatees should be awarded additional equitable relief such as retroactive seniority.

5. The District Court's memorandum decision is reported at 6 FEP Cases 690 (1974) and 6 EPD ¶ 8979 (1973–1974).

6. The Government did not seek relief for Negroes and Spanish-surnamed Americans hired at a particular terminal after the date on which that terminal first employed a minority group member as a line driver.

7. See n. 4, supra.

8. If an employee in this class had joined the company after July 2, 1965, then the date of his initial employment rather than the effective date of Title VII was to determine his competitive seniority.

line-driver jobs [9] ahead of any applicants from the general public but behind the two other subclasses. Those in the third subclass received no retroactive seniority; their competitive seniority as line drivers would begin with the date they were hired as line drivers. The court further decreed that the right of any class member to fill a line-driver vacancy was subject to the prior recall rights of laid-off line drivers, which under the collective-bargaining agreements then in effect extended for three years.[10]

The Court of Appeals for the Fifth Circuit agreed with the basic conclusions of the District Court: that the company had engaged in a pattern or practice of employment discrimination and that the seniority system in the collective-bargaining agreements violated Title VII as applied to victims of prior discrimination. 517 F.2d 299. The appellate court held, however, that the relief ordered by the District Court was inadequate. Rejecting the District Court's attempt to trisect the affected class, the Court of Appeals held that all Negro and Spanish-surnamed incumbent employees were entitled to bid for future line-driver jobs on the basis of their company seniority, and that once a class member had filled a job, he could use his full company seniority—even if it predated the effective date of Title VII—for all purposes, including bidding and layoff. This award of retroactive seniority was to be limited only by a "qualification date" formula, under which seniority could not be awarded for periods prior to the date when (1) a line-driving position was vacant,[11] *and* (2) the class member, met (or would have met, given the opportunity) the qualifications for employment as a line driver.[12] Finally, the Court of Appeals modified that part of the District Court's decree that had subjected the rights of class members to fill future vacancies to the recall rights of laid-off employees. Holding

---

9. As with the other subclasses, there were a few individuals in the third group who were found to have been discriminated against with respect to jobs other than line driver. There is no need to discuss them separately in this opinion.

10. This provision of the decree was qualified in one significant respect. Under the Southern Conference Area Over–the–Road Supplemental Agreement between the employer and the union, line drivers employed at terminals in certain Southern States work under a "modified" seniority system. Under the modified system an employee's seniority is not confined strictly to his home terminal. If he is laid off at his home terminal he can move to another terminal covered by the Agreement and retain his seniority, either by filling a vacancy at the other terminal or by "bumping" a junior line driver out of his job if there is no vacancy. The modified system also requires that any new vacancy at a covered terminal be offered to laid-off line drivers at all other covered terminals be-

fore it is filled by any other person. The District Court's final decree, as amended slightly by the Court of Appeals, 517 F.2d 299, 323, altered this system by requiring that any vacancy be offered to all members of all three subclasses before it may be filled by laid-off line drivers from other terminals.

11. Although the opinion of the Court of Appeals in this case did not specifically mention the requirement that a vacancy exist, it is clear from earlier and later opinions of that court that this requirement is a part of the Fifth Circuit's "qualification date" formula.

12. For example, if a class member began his tenure with the company on January 1, 1966, at which time he was qualified as a line driver and a line-driving vacancy existed, his competitive seniority upon becoming a line driver would date back to January 1, 1966. If he became qualified or if a vacancy opened up only at a later date, then that later date would be used.

that the three-year priority in favor of laid-off workers "would unduly impede the eradication of past discrimination," id., at 322, the Court of Appeals ordered that class members be allowed to compete for vacancies with laid-off employees on the basis of the class members' retroactive seniority. Laid-off line drivers would retain their prior recall rights with respect only to "purely temporary" vacancies. Ibid.[13]

The Court of Appeals remanded the case to the District Court to hold the evidentiary hearings necessary to apply these remedial principles. We granted both the company's and the union's petitions for certiorari to consider the significant questions presented under the Civil Rights Act of 1964, 425 U.S. 990, 96 S.Ct. 2200, 48 L.Ed.2d 814.

II

In this Court the company and the union contend that their conduct did not violate Title VII in any respect, asserting first that the evidence introduced at trial was insufficient to show that the company engaged in a "pattern or practice" of employment discrimination. The union further contends that the seniority system contained in the collective-bargaining agreements in no way violated Title VII.

* * *

[The Court's discussion of the government's proof of post-Act intentional discrimination is omitted. See Chapter IID *infra*.]

B

The District Court and the Court of Appeals also found that the seniority system contained in the collective-bargaining agreements between the company and the union operated to violate Title VII of the Act.

For purposes of calculating benefits, such as vacations, pensions, and other fringe benefits, an employee's seniority under this system runs from the date he joins the company, and takes into account his total service in all jobs and bargaining units. For competitive purposes, however, such as determining the order in which employees may bid for particular jobs, are laid off, or are recalled from layoff, it is bargaining-unit seniority that controls. Thus, a line driver's seniority, for purposes of bidding for particular runs [25] and protection against layoff, takes into account only the length of time he has been a line driver at a particular terminal.[26] The practical effect is that a city driver or

---

13. The Court of Appeals also approved (with slight modification) the part of the District Court's order that allowed class members to fill vacancies at a particular terminal ahead of line drivers laid off at other terminals. See n.10, supra.

25. Certain long-distance runs, for a variety of reasons, are more desirable than others. The best runs are chosen by the line drivers at the top of the "board"—a list of drivers arranged in order of their bargaining-unit seniority.

26. Both bargaining-unit seniority and company seniority rights are generally limited to service at one particular terminal, except as modified by the Southern Conference Area Over–the–Road Supplemental Agreement. See n. 10, supra.

serviceman who transfers to a line-driver job must forfeit all the competitive seniority he has accumulated in his previous bargaining unit and start at the bottom of the line drivers' "board."

The vice of this arrangement, as found by the District Court and the Court of Appeals, was that it "locked" minority workers into inferior jobs and perpetuated prior discrimination by discouraging transfers to jobs as line drivers. While the disincentive applied to all workers, including whites, it was Negroes and Spanish-surnamed persons who, those courts found, suffered the most because many of them had been denied the equal opportunity to become line drivers when they were initially hired, whereas whites either had not sought or were refused line-driver positions for reasons unrelated to their race or national origin.

The linchpin of the theory embraced by the District Court and the Court of Appeals was that a discriminatee who must forfeit his competitive seniority in order finally to obtain a line-driver job will never be able to "catch up" to the seniority level of his contemporary who was not subject to discrimination.[27] Accordingly, this continued, built-in disadvantage to the prior discriminatee who transfers to a line-driver job was held to constitute a continuing violation of Title VII, for which both the employer and the union who jointly created and maintain the seniority system were liable.

The union, while acknowledging that the seniority system may in some sense perpetuate the effects of prior discrimination, asserts that the system is immunized from a finding of illegality by reason of § 703(h) of Title VII, 42 U.S.C. § 2000e–2(h), which provides in part:

> "Notwithstanding any other provision of this subchapter, it shall not be an unlawful employment practice for an employer to apply different standards of compensation, or different terms, conditions, or privileges of employment pursuant to a bona fide seniority * * * system, * * * provided that such differences are not the result of an intention to discriminate because of race * * * or national origin * * *."

It argues that the seniority system in this case is "bona fide" within the meaning of § 703(h) when judged in light of its history, intent, application, and all of the circumstances under which it was created and is maintained. More specifically, the union claims that the central purpose of § 703(h) is to ensure that mere perpetuation of *pre-Act* discrimination is not unlawful under Title VII. And, whether or not § 703(h) immunizes the perpetuation of *post-Act* discrimination, the

---

27. An example would be a Negro who was qualified to be a line driver in 1958 but who, because of his race, was assigned instead a job as a city driver, and is allowed to become a line driver only in 1971. Because he loses his competitive seniority when he transfers jobs, he is forever junior to white line drivers hired between 1958 and 1970. The whites, rather than the Negro, will henceforth enjoy the preferable runs and the greater protection against layoff. Although the original discrimination occurred in 1958—before the effective date of Title VII—the seniority system operates to carry the effects of the earlier discrimination into the present.

union claims that the seniority system in this litigation has no such effect. Its position in this Court, as has been its position throughout this litigation, is that the seniority system presents no hurdle to *post-Act* discriminatees who seek retroactive seniority to the date they would have become line drivers but for the company's discrimination. Indeed, the union asserts that under its collective-bargaining agreements the union will itself take up the cause of the post-Act victim and attempt, through grievance procedures, to gain for him full "make whole" relief, including appropriate seniority.

The Government responds that a seniority system that perpetuates the effects of prior discrimination—pre-Act or post-Act—can never be "bona fide" under § 703(h); at a minimum Title VII prohibits those applications of a seniority system that perpetuate the effects on incumbent employees of prior discriminatory job assignments.

The issues thus joined are open ones in this Court.[28] We considered § 703(h) in Franks v. Bowman Transportation Co., 424 U.S. 747, 96 S.Ct. 1251, 47 L.Ed.2d 444, but there decided only that § 703(h) does not bar the award of retroactive seniority to job applicants who seek relief from an employer's post-Act hiring discrimination. We stated that "the thrust of [§ 703(h)] is directed toward defining what is and what is not an illegal discriminatory practice in instances in which the post-Act operation of a seniority system is challenged as perpetuating the effects of discrimination occurring prior to the effective date of the Act." 424 U.S. at 761, 96 S.Ct., at 1263. Beyond noting the general purpose of the statute, however, we did not undertake the task of statutory construction required in this litigation.

(1)

Because the company discriminated both before and after the enactment of Title VII, the seniority system is said to have operated to perpetuate the effects of both pre- and post-Act discrimination. Post–Act discriminatees, however, may obtain full "make whole" relief, including retroactive seniority under Franks v. Bowman, supra, without attacking the legality of the seniority system as applied to them. *Franks* made clear and the union acknowledges that retroactive seniority may be awarded as relief from an employer's discriminatory hiring and assignment policies even if the seniority system agreement itself

---

28. Concededly, the view that § 703(h) does not immunize seniority systems that perpetuate the effects of prior discrimination has much support. It was apparently first adopted in Quarles v. Philip Morris, Inc., 279 F.Supp. 505 (E.D.Va.). The court there held that "a departmental seniority system *that has it genesis in racial discrimination* is not a *bona fide* seniority system." Id., at 517 (first emphasis added). The Quarles view has since enjoyed wholesale adoption in the Courts of Appeals.

Insofar as the result in Quarles and in the cases that followed it depended upon findings that the seniority systems were themselves "racially discriminatory" or had their "genesis in racial discrimination," 279 F.Supp., at 517, the decisions can be viewed as resting upon the proposition that a seniority system that perpetuates the effects of pre-Act discrimination cannot be bona fide if an intent to discriminate entered into its very adoption.

makes no provision for such relief.[29]   424 U.S., at 778–779, 96 S.Ct., at 1271.   Here the Government has proved that the company engaged in a post-Act pattern of discriminatory hiring, assignment, transfer, and promotion policies.   Any Negro or Spanish-surnamed American injured by those policies may receive all appropriate relief as a direct remedy for this discrimination.[30]

(2)

What remains for review is the judgment that the seniority system unlawfully perpetuated the effects of pre-Act discrimination.   We must decide, in short, whether § 703(h) validates otherwise bona fide seniority systems that afford no constructive seniority to victims discriminated against prior to the effective date of Title VII, and it is to that issue that we now turn.

The primary purpose of Title VII was "to assure equality of employment opportunities and to eliminate those discriminatory practices and devices which have fostered racially stratified job environments to the disadvantage of minority citizens."   McDonnell Douglas Corp. v. Green, 411 U.S. at 800, 93 S.Ct., at 1823.[31]   To achieve this purpose, Congress "proscribe[d] not only overt discrimination but also practices that are fair in form, but discriminatory in operation."   Id., at 431, 91 S.Ct., at 853.   Thus, the Court has repeatedly held that a prima facie Title VII violation may be established by policies or practices that

---

29.   Article 38 of the National Master Freight Agreement between The Company and the union in effect as of the date of the systemwide lawsuit provided:

"The Employer and the Union agree not to discriminate against any individual with respect to his hiring, compensation, terms or conditions of employment because of such individual's race, color, religion, sex, or national origin, nor will they limit, segregate or classify employees in any way to deprive any individual employee of employment opportunities because of his race, color, religion, sex, or national origin."

Any discrimination by the company would apparently be a "grievable" breach of this provision of the contract.

30.   The legality of the seniority system insofar as it perpetuates post-Act discrimination nonetheless remains at issue in this case, in light of the injunction entered against the union.   Our decision today in United Air Lines, Inc. v. Evans, 431 U.S. 553, 97 S.Ct. 1885, 52 L.Ed.2d 571, is largely dispositive of this issue.   Evans holds that the operation of a seniority system is not unlawful under Title VII even though it perpetuates post-Act discrimination that has not been the subject of a timely charge

by the discriminatee.   Here, of course, the Government has sued to remedy the post-Act discrimination directly, and there is no claim that any relief would be time barred.   But this is simply an additional reason not to hold the seniority system unlawful, since such a holding would in no way enlarge the relief to be awarded.   See Franks v. Bowman Transportation Co., 424 U.S. 747, 778–779, 96 S.Ct. 1251, 1271, 47 L.Ed.2d 444.   Section 703(h) on its face immunizes all bona fide seniority systems, and does not distinguish between the perpetuation of pre- and post-Act discrimination.

31.   We also noted in McDonnell Douglas:

"There are societal as well as personal interests on both sides of this [employer-employee] equation.   The broad, overriding interest, shared by employer, employee, and consumer, is efficient and trustworthy workmanship assured through fair and racially neutral employment and personnel decisions.   In the implementation of such decisions, it is abundantly clear that Title VII tolerates no racial discrimination, subtle or otherwise."   411 U.S. at 801, 93 S.Ct., at 1823.

are neutral on their face and in intent but that nonetheless discriminate in effect against a particular group.

One kind of practice "fair in form, but discriminatory in operation" is that which perpetuates the effects of prior discrimination.[32] As the Court held in Griggs: "Under the Act, practices, procedures, or tests neutral on their face, and even neutral in terms of intent, cannot be maintained if they operate to 'freeze' the status quo of prior discriminatory employment practices." 401 U.S., at 430, 91 S.Ct., at 853.

Were it not for § 703(h), the seniority system in this case would seem to fall under the Griggs rationale. The heart of the system is its allocation of the choicest jobs, the greatest protection against layoffs, and other advantages to those employees who have been line drivers for the longest time. Where, because of the employer's prior intentional discrimination, the line drivers with the longest tenure are without exception white, the advantages of the seniority system flow disproportionately to them and away from Negro and Spanish-surnamed employees who might by now have enjoyed those advantages had not the employer discriminated before the passage of the Act. This disproportionate distribution of advantages does in a very real sense "operate to 'freeze' the status quo of prior discriminatory employment practices." But both the literal terms of § 703(h) and the legislative history of Title VII demonstrate that Congress considered this very effect of many seniority systems and extended a measure of immunity to them.

Throughout the initial consideration of HR 7152, later enacted as the Civil Rights Act of 1964, critics of the bill charged that it would destroy existing seniority rights.[33] The consistent response of Title VII's congressional proponents and of the Justice Department was that seniority rights would not be affected, even where the employer had discriminated prior to the Act.[34] An interpretative memorandum placed in the Congressional Record by Senators Clark and Case stated:

> "Title VII would have no effect on established seniority rights. Its effect is prospective and not retrospective. Thus, for example, *if a business has been discriminating in the past and as a result has an all-white working force, when the title comes into effect the*

---

32. Local 53 Asbestos Workers v. Vogler, 407 F.2d 1047(CA5), provides an apt illustration. There a union had a policy of excluding persons not related to present members by blood or marriage. When in 1966 suit was brought to challenge this policy, all of the union's members were white, largely as a result of pre-Act, intentional racial discrimination. The court observed: "While the nepotism requirement is applicable to black and white alike and is not on its face discriminatory, in a completely white union the present effect of its continued application is to forever deny to Negroes and Mexican–Americans any real opportunity for membership." Id., at 1054.

33. E.g., H.R.Rep.No.914, 88th Cong., 1st Sess. 65–66, 71 (1963) (minority report); 110 Cong.Rec. 486–488 (1964) (remarks of Sen. Hill); id., at 2726 (remarks of Rep. Dowdy); id., at 7091 (remarks of Sen. Stennis).

34. In addition to the material cited in Franks v. Bowman Transportation Co., 424 U.S., at 759–762, 96 S.Ct., at 1261–1263, see 110 Cong.Rec. 1518 (1964) (remarks of Rep. Celler); id., at 6549 (remarks of Sen. Humphrey); id., at 6564 (remarks of Sen. Kuchel).

employer's obligation would be simply to fill future vacancies on a non-discriminatory basis. He would not be obliged—or indeed, permitted—to fire whites in order to hire Negroes, or to prefer Negroes for future vacancies, or, once Negroes are hired, to give them special seniority rights at the expense of the white workers hired earlier." 110 Cong.Rec. 7213 (1964) (emphasis added).[35]

A Justice Department statement concerning Title VII, placed in the Congressional Record by Senator Clark, voiced the same conclusion:

"Title VII would have no effect on seniority rights existing at the time it takes effect. If, for example, a collective bargaining contract provides that in the event of layoffs, those who were hired last must be laid off first, such a provision would not be affected in the least by Title VII. *This would be true even in the case where owing to discrimination prior to the effective date of the title, white workers had more seniority than Negroes.*" Id., at 7207 (emphasis added).[36]

While these statements were made before § 703(h) was added to Title VII, they are authoritative indicators of that section's purpose. Section 703(h) was enacted as part of the Mansfield–Dirksen compromise substitute bill that cleared the way for the passage of Title VII.[37] The drafters of the compromise bill stated that one of its principal goals was to resolve the ambiguities in the House-passed version of HR 7152. See, e.g., 110 Cong.Rec. 11935–11937 (1964) (remarks of Sen. Dirksen); id., at 12707 (remarks of Sen. Humphrey). As the debates indicate, one of those ambiguities concerned Title VII's impact on existing collectively bargained seniority rights. It is apparent that § 703(h) was drafted with an eye toward meeting the earlier criticism on this issue with an explicit provision embodying the understanding and assurances of the Act's proponents: namely, that Title VII would not outlaw such differences in treatment among employees as flowed from a bona fide

---

35. Senators Clark and Case were the "bipartisan captains" responsible for Title VII during the Senate debate. Bipartisan captains were selected for each title of the Civil Rights Act by the leading proponents of the Act in both parties. They were responsible for explaining their title in detail, defending it, and leading discussion on it. See id., at 6528 (remarks of Sen. Humphrey); Vaas, Title VII: Legislative History, 7 B.C.Ind. & Com.L.Rev. 431, 444–445 (1966).

36. The full text of the statement is set out in Franks v. Bowman Transportation Co., supra, at 760 n.16, 96 S.Ct., at 1262. Senator Clark also introduced a set of answers to questions propounded by Senator Dirksen, which included the following exchange:

"Question. Would the same situation prevail in respect to promotions, when

that management function is governed by a labor contract calling for promotions on the basis of seniority? What of dismissals? Normally, labor contracts call for 'last hired, first fired.' If the last hired are Negroes, is the employer discriminating if his contract requires they be first fired and the remaining employees are white?

"Answer. Seniority rights are in no way affected by the bill. If under a 'last hired, first fired' agreement a Negro happens to be the 'last hired,' he can still be 'first fired' as long as it is done because of his status as 'last hired' and not because of his race." 110 Cong.Rec. 7217 (1964). See *Franks*, supra, at 760 n.16, 96 S.Ct., at 1262.

37. See Franks v. Bowman, Transportation Co., supra, at 761, 96 S.Ct., at 1251; Vaas, supra, n. 35, at 435.

seniority system that allowed for full exercise of seniority accumulated before the effective date of the Act. It is inconceivable that § 703(h), as part of a compromise bill, was intended to vitiate the earlier representations of the Act's supporters by increasing Title VII's impact on seniority systems. The statement of Senator Humphrey, noted in *Franks*, 424 U.S. at 761, 96 S.Ct., at 1262, confirms that the addition of § 703(h) "merely clarifies [Title VII's] present intent and effect." 110 Cong.Rec. 12723 (1964).

In sum, the unmistakable purpose of § 703(h) was to make clear that the routine application of a bona fide seniority system would not be unlawful under Title VII. As the legislative history shows, this was the intended result even where the employer's pre-Act discrimination resulted in whites having greater existing seniority rights than Negroes. Although a seniority system inevitably tends to perpetuate the effects of pre-Act discrimination in such cases, the congressional judgment was that Title VII should not outlaw the use of existing seniority lists and thereby destroy or water down the vested seniority rights of employees simply because their employer had engaged in discrimination prior to the passage of the Act.

To be sure, § 703(h) does not immunize all seniority systems. It refers only to "bona fide" systems, and a proviso requires that any differences in treatment not be "the result of an intention to discriminate because of race * * * or national origin * * *." But our reading of the legislative history compels us to reject the Government's broad argument that no seniority system that tends to perpetuate pre-Act discrimination can be "bona fide." To accept the argument would require us to hold that a seniority system becomes illegal simply because it allows the full exercise of the pre-Act seniority rights of employees of a company that discriminated before Title VII was enacted. It would place an affirmative obligation on the parties to the seniority agreement to subordinate those rights in favor of the claims of pre-Act discriminatees without seniority. The consequence would be a perversion of the congressional purpose. We cannot accept the invitation to disembowel § 703(h) by reading the words "bona fide" as the Government would have us do.[38] Accordingly, we hold that an otherwise neutral, legitimate seniority system does not become unlawful under Title VII simply because it may perpetuate pre-Act discrimination. Congress did not intend to make it illegal for employees with

---

38. For the same reason, we reject the contention that the proviso in § 703(h), which bars differences in treatment resulting from "an intention to discriminate," applies to any application of a seniority system that may perpetuate past discrimination. In this regard the language of the Justice Department memorandum introduced at the legislative hearings, is especially pertinent: "It is perfectly clear that when a worker is laid off or denied a chance for promotion because under established seniority rules he is 'low man on the totem pole' he is not being discriminated against because of his race. * * * Any differences in treatment based on established seniority rights would not be based on race and would not be forbidden by the title." 110 Cong.Rec. 7207 (1964).

vested seniority rights to continue to exercise those rights, even at the expenses of pre-Act discriminatees.[39]

That conclusion is inescapable even in a case, such as this one, where the pre-Act discriminatees are incumbent employees who accumulated seniority in other bargaining units. Although there seems to be no explicit reference in the legislative history to pre-Act discriminatees already employed in less desirable jobs, there can be no rational basis for distinguishing their claims from those of persons initially denied *any* job but hired later with less seniority than they might have had in the absence of pre-Act discrimination.[40] We rejected any such distinction in *Franks*, finding that it had "no support anywhere in Title VII or its legislative history," 424 U.S. at 768, 96 S.Ct., at 1266. As discussed above, Congress in 1964 made clear that a seniority system is not unlawful because it honors employees' existing rights, even where the employer has engaged in pre-Act discriminatory hiring or promotion practices. It would be as contrary to that mandate to forbid the exercise of seniority rights with respect to discriminatees who held inferior jobs as with respect to later hired minority employees who previously were denied any job. If anything, the latter group is the more disadvantaged. As in *Franks*, " 'it would indeed be surprising if Congress gave a remedy for the one [group] which it denied for the other.' " Ibid., quoting Phelps Dodge Corp. v. NLRB, 313 U.S. 177, 187, 61 S.Ct. 845, 849, 85 L.Ed. 1271.[41]

---

39. The legislative history of the 1972 amendments to Title VII, summarized and discussed in Franks, 424 U.S. at 764–765, n.21, 96 S.Ct. at 1264; id., at 796–797, n.18, 96 S.Ct., at 1263 (Powell, J., concurring in part and dissenting in part), in no way points to a different result. As the discussion in Franks indicates, that history is itself susceptible of different readings. The few broad references to perpetuation of pre-Act discrimination or "de facto segregated job ladders," see, e.g., S.Rep.No.92–415, pp. 5, 9 (1971); H.R.Rep.No.92–238, pp. 8, 17 (1971), did not address the specific issue presented by this case. And the assumption of the authors of the Conference Report that "the present case law as developed by the courts would continue to govern the applicability and construction of Title VII," see *Franks*, supra, at 765 n.21, 96 S.Ct., at 1264, of course does not foreclose our consideration of that issue. More importantly, the section of Title VII that we construe here, § 703(h), was enacted in 1964, not 1972. The views of members of a later Congress, concerning different sections of Title VII, enacted after this litigation was commenced, are entitled to little if any weight. It is the intent of the Congress that enacted § 703(h) in 1964, unmistakable in this case, that controls.

40. That Title VII did not proscribe the denial of fictional seniority to *pre-Act* discriminatees who got no job was recognized even in Quarles v. Philip Morris, Inc., 279 F.Supp. 505 (E.D.Va.), and its progeny. Quarles stressed the fact that the references in the legislative history were to employment seniority rather than departmental seniority. Id., at 516. In Local 189, United Papermakers & Paperworkers v. United States, 416 F.2d 980(CA5), another leading case in this area, the court observed: "No doubt, Congress, to prevent 'reverse discrimination' meant to protect certain seniority rights that could not have existed but for previous racial discrimination. For example a Negro who had been rejected by an employer on racial grounds before passage of the Act could not, after being hired, claim to outrank whites who had been hired before him but after his original rejection, even though the Negro might have had senior status but for the past discrimination." Id., at 994.

41. In addition, there is no reason to suppose that Congress intended in 1964 to extend less protection to legitimate departmental seniority systems than to plant-wide seniority systems. Then, as now, seniority was measured in a number of ways, including length of time with the employ-

(3)

The seniority system in this litigation is entirely bona fide. It applies equally to all races and ethnic groups. To the extent that it "locks" employees into non-linedriver jobs, it does so for all. The city drivers and servicemen who are discouraged from transferring to line-driver jobs are not all Negroes or Spanish-surnamed Americans; to the contrary, the overwhelming majority are white. The placing of line drivers in a separate bargaining unit from other employees is rational, in accord with the industry practice, and consistent with National Labor Relations Board precedents.[42] It is conceded that the seniority system did not have its genesis in racial discrimination, and that it was negotiated and has been maintained free from any illegal purpose. In these circumstances, the single fact that the system extends no retroactive seniority to pre-Act discriminatees does not make it unlawful.

Because the seniority system was protected by § 703(h), the union's conduct in agreeing to and maintaining the system did not violate Title VII. On remand, the District Court's injunction against the union must be vacated.[43]

[The Court's discussion of the relief to be afforded victims of post-Act discrimination and the concurring and dissenting opinions of Justices Marshall and Brennan are omitted.]

NOTES AND PROBLEMS FOR DISCUSSION

1. Should *Teamsters* apply to seniority systems adopted *after* the passage of Title VII? After the decision in *Teamsters*, the EEOC took the position that a seniority system was protected under § 703(h) only if it was instituted *prior to* the effective date of the Act and only if evidence shows there was no discriminatory intent in the origin or maintenance of the system. The memorandum also stated that when the employer or a union was made aware—by means of a grievance, EEOC charge or the like—that the seniority system was "locking in" minorities or females, discriminatory intent would be inferred if the system was renegotiated when an alternative was available. EEOC Interpretive Memorandum quoted in Note, The Seniority System Exemption in Title VII: International Brotherhood of Teamsters v. United States, 6 Hofstra L.Rev. 585, 607–08

er, in a particular plant, in a department, in a job, or in a line of progression. See Aaron, Reflections on the Legal Nature and Enforceability of Seniority Rights, 75 Harv.L.Rev. 1532, 1534 (1962); Cooper & Sobol, Seniority and Testing under Fair Employment Laws: A General Approach to Objective Criteria of Hiring and Promotion, 82 Harv.L.Rev. 1598, 1602 (1969). The legislative history contains no suggestion that any one system was preferred.

42. See Georgia Highway Express, 150 N.L.R.B. 1649, 1651:"The Board has long held that local drivers and over-the-road drivers constitute separate appropriate units where they are shown to be clearly defined, homogeneous, and functionally

distinct groups with separate interests which can effectively be represented separately for bargaining purposes. * * * In view of the different duties and functions, separate supervision, and different bases of payment, it is clear that the over-the-road drivers have divergent interests from those of the employees in the [city operations] unit * * * and should not be included in that unit."

43. The union will properly remain in this litigation as a defendant so that full relief may be awarded the victims of the employer's post-Act discrimination. Fed. Rule Civ. Proc. 19(a). See EEOC v. MacMillan Bloedel Containers, Inc., 503 F.2d 1086, 1095(CA6).

(1978). But in AMERICAN TOBACCO CO. v. PATTERSON, 456 U.S. 63, 102 S.Ct. 1534, 71 L.Ed.2d 748 (1982), the Court held that § 703(h) is not limited to seniority systems predating passage of Title VII.

2. The Supreme Court has not directly addressed the question of what factors render a seniority system illegal under *Teamsters*. In James v. Stockham Valves & Fittings Co., 559 F.2d 310 (5th Cir.1977), cert. denied, 434 U.S. 1034, 98 S.Ct. 767, 54 L.Ed.2d 781 (1978), the Court of Appeals interpreted the decision as follows:

> As we read the *Teamsters* opinion, the issue whether there has been purposeful discrimination in connection with the establishment or continuation of a seniority system is integral to a determination that the system is or is not bona-fide * * * The Court's analysis suggests that totality of the circumstances in the development and maintenance of the system is relevant to examining that issue * * * In *Teamsters* the Court focused on four factors:
>
> > (1) whether the seniority system operates to discourage all employees equally from transferring between seniority units;
> >
> > (2) whether the seniority units are in the same or separate bargaining units (if the latter, whether that structure is rational and in conformance with industry practice);
> >
> > (3) whether the seniority system had its genesis in racial discrimination; and
> >
> > (4) whether the system was negotiated and has been maintained free from any illegal purpose.

559 F.2d at 351–352. Most post-*Teamsters* decisions have adopted the four-factor inquiry of *Stockham Valve*. See Sears v. Atchison, Topeka & Santa Fe Ry., Co., 749 F.2d 1451 (10th Cir.1984), cert. denied, 471 U.S. 1099, 105 S.Ct. 2322, 85 L.Ed.2d 840 (1985); Taylor v. Mueller Co., 660 F.2d 1116, (6th Cir.1981). Courts which have declared seniority systems illegal have generally found overt *post-Act* racial discrimination by the employer, union, or both. See, Wattleton v. International Broth. of Boilermakers, 686 F.2d 586 (7th Cir.1982), cert. denied, 459 U.S. 1208, 103 S.Ct. 1199, 75 L.Ed.2d 442 (1983); Veazie v. Greyhound Lines, Inc., et al., 35 EPD 34,832 (E.D.La.1983); Terrell v. United States Pipe and Foundry Co., 39 FEP Cases 571 (N.D.Ala.1985).

Should a court be able to infer discriminatory intent underlying a seniority system from evidence of the system's disproportionate impact on a protected class and its toleration by the employer and/or union? In PULLMAN–STANDARD v. SWINT, 456 U.S. 273, 102 S.Ct. 1781, 72 L.Ed.2d 66 (1982), the Court held that:

> Differentials among employees that result from a seniority system are not unlawful employment practices unless the product of an intent to discriminate. It would make no sense, therefore to say that the intent to discriminate required by § 703(h) may be presumed from such an impact. As § 703(h) was construed in *Teamsters*, there must be a finding of actual intent to discriminate on racial grounds on the part of those who negotiated or maintained the system.

Id. at 289, 102 S.Ct. at 1790. The Court also held that a finding of intent is a "pure question of fact subject to Rule 52's clearly erroneous standard" of review.

3. Should proof that a union favored departmental seniority and non-transferable seniority as a means of maintaining its all-white status preclude a finding that the system was bona fide? In Larkin v. Pullman–Standard Division, 854 F.2d 1549 (11th Cir.1988), vacated on other grounds, 493 U.S. 929, 110 S.Ct. 316, 107 L.Ed.2d 307 (1989) the court held that the union's racist motivation could not be imputed to the employer without independent evidence of the employer's intent. Not only was there no evidence that the employer acted with discriminatory intent in negotiating and maintaining non-transferable seniority, but there was evidence that the employer would have preferred no seniority rules at all. The company had accepted the seniority system as "a compromise negotiated and maintained without discriminatory intent." 854 F.2d at 1578. But if the union wanted the seniority system to maintain segregation and the company had no business purpose in maintaining the system, how can it be said that the "genesis" of the system was not racial discrimination? See Harvey v. United Transportation Union, 878 F.2d 1235, 1238 (10th Cir.1989), cert. denied, 493 U.S. 1074, 110 S.Ct. 1121, 107 L.Ed.2d 1028 (1990) (district court clearly erred in finding that seniority system did not have its genesis in racial discrimination where it ignored its own prior finding that seniority system was created when segregation was standard operating procedure).

CALIFORNIA BREWERS ASSOCIATION v. BRYANT

Supreme Court of the United States, 1980.
444 U.S. 598, 100 S.Ct. 814, 63 L.Ed.2d 55.

Mr. Justice Stewart delivered the opinion of the Court.

Title VII of the Civil Rights Act of 1964 makes unlawful, practices, procedures, or tests that "operate to 'freeze' the status quo of prior discriminatory employment practices." Griggs v. Duke Power Co., 401 U.S. 424, 430, 91 S.Ct. 849, 853, 28 L.Ed.2d 158. To this rule, § 703(h) of the Act, provides an exception:

> "[I]t shall not be an unlawful employment practice for an employer to apply different standards of compensation, or different terms, conditions, or privileges of employment pursuant to a bona fide seniority * * * system, * * * provided that such differences are not the result of an intention to discriminate because of race. * * * "

In Teamsters v. United States, 431 U.S. 324, 352, 97 S.Ct. 1843, 1863, 52 L.Ed.2d 396, the Court held that "the unmistakable purpose of § 703(h) was to make clear that the routine application of a bona fide seniority system would not be unlawful under Title VII * * * even where the employer's pre-Act discrimination resulted in whites having greater existing seniority rights than Negroes." [2]

The present case concerns the application of § 703(h) to a particular clause in a California brewery industry collective-bargaining agree-

---

2. United Air Lines, Inc. v. Evans, 431 U.S. 553, 97 S.Ct. 1885, 52 L.Ed.2d 571, extended this holding to preclude Title VII challenges to seniority systems that perpetuated the effects of discriminatory post-Act practices that had not been the subject of a timely complaint. See also International Brotherhood of Teamsters v. United States, 431 U.S. at 348, n.30, 97 S.Ct. at 1861.

ment. That agreement accords greater benefits to "permanent" than to "temporary" employees, and the clause in question provides that a temporary employee must work at least 45 weeks in a single calendar year before he can become a permanent employee. The Court of Appeals for the Ninth Circuit held that the 45–week requirement was not a "seniority system" or part of a "seniority system" within the meaning of § 703(h). 585 F.2d 421. We granted certiorari to consider the important question presented under Title VII of the Civil Rights Act of 1964. 442 U.S. 916, 99 S.Ct. 2835, 61 L.Ed.2d 282.

I

In 1973, the respondent, a Negro, filed a complaint in the United States District Court for the Northern District of California, on behalf of himself and other similarly situated Negroes, against the California Brewers Association and seven brewing companies (petitioners here), as well as against several unions. The complaint alleged that the defendants had discriminated against the respondent and other Negroes in violation of Title VII of the Civil Rights Act of 1964, 42 U.S.C. §§ 2000e et seq., and in violation of 42 U.S.C. § 1981.[3]

The complaint, as amended, alleged that the respondent had been intermittently employed since May 1968, as a temporary employee of one of the defendants, the Falstaff Brewing Corp. It charged that all the defendant employers had discriminated in the past against Negroes, that the unions had acted in concert with the employers in such discrimination, and that the unions had discriminated in referring applicants from hiring halls to the employers. The complaint further asserted that this historical discrimination was being perpetuated by the seniority and referral provisions of the collective-bargaining agreement (Agreement) that governed industrial relations at the plants of the seven defendant employers. In particular, the complaint alleged, the Agreement's requirement that a temporary employee work 45 weeks in the industry in a single calendar year to reach permanent status had, as a practical matter, operated to preclude the respondent and the members of his putative class from achieving, or from a reasonable opportunity of achieving, permanent employee status.[4] Finally, the complaint alleged that on at least one occasion one of the defendant unions had passed over the respondent in favor of more junior white workers in making referrals to job vacancies at a plant of one of the defendant employers.

3. The complaint also alleged, under 29 U.S.C. §§ 159 and 185, that the union defendants had breached their duty of fair representation by, among other things, negotiating "unreasonable privileges for some employees over others. * * * "

4. In this Court, the respondent emphasizes that he has not contended that there is anything illegal in classifying employees as permanent and temporary or in according greater rights to permanent than to temporary employees. His sole Title VII challenge in this respect has been to the 45–week rule on its face and as it has been applied by the defendant unions and employers.

The Agreement is a multiemployer collective-bargaining agreement negotiated more than 20 years ago, and thereafter updated, by the California Brewers Association (on behalf of the petitioner brewing companies) and the Teamsters Brewery and Soft Drink Workers Joint Board of California (on behalf of the defendant unions). The Agreement establishes several classes of employees and the respective rights of each with respect to hiring and layoffs. Three of these classes are pertinent here: "permanent," "temporary," and "new" employees.

A permanent employee is "any employee * * * who * * * has completed forty-five weeks of employment under this Agreement in one classification [5] in one calendar year as an employee of the brewing industry in [the State of California]." An employee who acquires permanent status retains that status unless he "is not employed under this Agreement for any consecutive period of two (2) years. * * * * "[6] A temporary employee under the Agreement is "any person other than a permanent employee * * * who worked under this agreement * * * in the preceding calendar year for at least sixty (60) working days. * * * " A new employee is any employee who is not a permanent or temporary employee.

The rights of employees with respect to hiring and layoffs depend in substantial part on their status as permanent, temporary, or new employees.[7] The Agreement requires that employees at a particular plant be laid off in the following order: new employees in reverse order of their seniority at the plant, temporary employees in reverse order of their plant seniority, and then permanent employees in reverse order of their plant seniority. Once laid off, employees are to be rehired in the reverse order from which they were laid off.

The Agreement also gives permanent employees special "bumping" rights. If a permanent employee is laid off at any plant subject to the Agreement, he may be dispatched by the union hiring hall to any other plant in the same local area with the right to replace the temporary or new employee with the lowest plant seniority at that plant.

Finally, the Agreement provides that each employer shall obtain employees through the local union hiring hall to fill needed vacancies. The hiring hall must dispatch laid-off workers to such an employer in the following order: first, employees of that employer in the order of their seniority with that employer; second, permanent employees registered in the area in order of their industry seniority; third, temporary

---

5. The Agreement classifies employees into brewers, bottlers, drivers, shipping and receiving clerks, and checkers. Under the Agreement, separate seniority lists have to be maintained for each of these classifications of employees. The respondent is a brewer.

6. An employee may also lose permanent status if he "quits the industry" or is discharged for certain specified reasons.

7. In addition, permanent employees are given preference over temporary employees with respect to various other employment matters, such as the right to collect supplemental unemployment benefits upon layoff, wages and vacation pay, and choice of vacation times.

employees in the order of their seniority in the industry; and fourth, new employees in the order of their industry seniority. The employer then "shall have full right of selection among" such employees.

The District Court granted the defendants' motions to dismiss the complaint for failure to state a claim on which relief could be granted. No opinion accompanied this order. A divided panel of the Court of Appeals reversed, 585 F.2d 421, concluding that the 45–week rule is not a "seniority system" or part of a "seniority system" within the meaning of § 703(h) of Title VII. In the appellate court's view the provision "lacks the fundamental component of such a system" which is "the concept that employment rights should increase as the length of an employee's service increases." 585 F.2d, at 426. The court pointed out that under the Agreement some employees in the industry could acquire permanent status after a total of only 45 weeks of work if those weeks were served in one calendar year, while others "could work for many years and never attain permanent status because they were always terminated a few days before completing 45 weeks of work in any one year." Id., at 426–427.

The Court of Appeals concluded that "while the collective bargaining agreement does contain a seniority system, the 45–week provision is not a part of it." Id., at 427:

> "The 45–week rule is simply a classification device to determine who enters the permanent employee seniority line and this function does not make the rule part of a seniority system. Otherwise any hiring policy (e.g., an academic degree requirement) or classification device (e.g., merit promotion) would become part of a seniority system merely because it affects who enters the seniority line."

Id., at 427, n.11.[8] Accordingly, the Court of Appeals remanded the case to the District Court to enable the respondent to prove that the 45–week provision has had a discriminatory impact on Negroes under the standards enunciated in Griggs v. Duke Power Co., 401 U.S. 424, 91 S.Ct. 849, 28 L.Ed.2d 158. 585 F.2d at 427–428.[9]

II

Title VII does not define the term "seniority system," and no comprehensive definition of the phrase emerges from the legislative history of § 703(h).[10] Moreover, our cases have not purported to delin-

---

8. The Court of Appeals also observed that "the 45–week requirement makes the system particularly susceptible to discriminatory application since employers and unions can manipulate their manpower requirements and employment patterns to prevent individuals who are disfavored from ever achieving permanent status." 585 F.2d, at 427. This danger, according to the court, is almost never present in any "true" seniority system, in which rights "usually accumulate automatically over time. * * *" Ibid.

9. The Court of Appeals directed the trial court on remand to consider as well the respondent's claims under 42 U.S.C. § 1981 and 29 U.S.C. §§ 159 and 185.

10. See 100 Cong.Rec. 1518, 5423, 7207, 7213, 7217, 12723, 15893 (1964). The example of a "seniority system" most fre-

eate the contours of its meaning.[11] It is appropriate, therefore, to begin with commonly accepted notions about "seniority" in industrial relations, and to consider those concepts in the context of Title VII and this country's labor policy.

In the area of labor relations, "seniority" is a term that connotes length of employment.[12] A "seniority system" is a scheme that, alone or in tandem with non-"seniority" criteria,[13] allots to employees ever improving employment rights and benefits as their relative lengths of pertinent employment increase.[14] Unlike other methods of allocating employment benefits and opportunities, such as subjective evaluations or educational requirements, the principal feature of any and every "seniority system" is that preferential treatment is dispensed on the basis of some measure of time served in employment.

Viewed as a whole, most of the relevant provisions of the Agreement before us in this case conform to these core concepts of "seniority." Rights of temporary employees and rights of permanent employees are determined according to length of plant employment in some respects, and according to length of industry employment in other respects. Notwithstanding this fact, the Court of Appeals concluded that the 45-week rule should not be viewed, for purposes of § 703(h), as part of what might otherwise be considered a "seniority system." For the reasons that follow, we hold that this conclusion was incorrect.

First, by legislating with respect to "systems"[15] of seniority in § 703(h), Congress in 1964 quite evidently intended to exempt from the normal operation of Title VII more than simply those components of any particular seniority scheme that, viewed in isolation, embody or effectuate the principle that length of employment will be rewarded. In order for any seniority system to operate at all, it has to contain

quently cited in the congressional debates was one that provided that the "last hired" employee would be the "first fired." Nowhere in the debates, however, is there any suggestion that this model was intended to be anything other than an illustration.

11. See Trans World Airlines, Inc. v. Hardison, 432 U.S. 63, 97 S.Ct. 2264, 53 L.Ed.2d 113; United Air Lines, Inc. v. Evans, 431 U.S. 553, 97 S.Ct. 1885, 52 L.Ed.2d 571; Teamsters v. United States, 431 U.S. 324, 97 S.Ct. 1843, 52 L.Ed.2d 396; Franks v. Bowman Transportation Co., 424 U.S. 747, 96 S.Ct. 1251, 47 L.Ed.2d 444.

12. Webster's Third New International Dictionary 2066 (unabridged ed. 1961) defines "seniority," in pertinent part, as the "status attained by length of continuous service * * * to which are attached by custom or prior collective agreement various rights or privileges * * * on the basis of ranking relative to others. * * *"

13. A collective-bargaining agreement could, for instance, provide that transfers and promotions are to be determined by a mix of seniority and other factors, such as aptitude tests and height requirements. That the "seniority" aspects of such a scheme of transfer and promotion might be covered by § 703(h) does not mean that the aptitude tests or the height requirements would also be so covered.

14. See E. Beal, E. Wickersham, & P. Kienast, The Practice of Collective Bargaining 430–431 (1972); Cooper & Sobol, Seniority and Testing Under Fair Employment Laws: A General Approach to Objective Criteria of Hiring and Promotion, 82 Harv.L.Rev.. 1598, 1602 (1969); Aaron, Reflections on the Legal Nature and Enforceability of Seniority Rights, 75 Harv.L.Rev.. 1532, 1534 (1962).

15. Webster's Third New International Dictionary 2322 (unabridged ed. 1961) defines "system," in pertinent part, as a "complex unity formed of many often diverse parts subject to a common plan or serving a common purpose."

ancillary rules that accomplish certain necessary functions, but which may not themselves be directly related to length of employment.[16] For instance, every seniority system must include rules that delineate how and when the seniority timeclock begins ticking,[17] as well as rules that specify how and when a particular person's seniority may be forfeited.[18] Every seniority system must also have rules that define which passages of time will "count" towards the accrual of seniority and which will not.[19] Every seniority system must, moreover, contain rules that particularize the types of employment conditions that will be governed or influenced by seniority, and those that will not.[20] Rules that serve these necessary purposes do not fall outside § 703(h) simply because they do not, in and of themselves, operate on the basis of some factor involving the passage of time.[21]

Second, Congress passed the Civil Rights Act of 1964 against the backdrop of this Nation's longstanding labor policy of leaving to the chosen representatives of employers and employees the freedom through collective bargaining to establish conditions of employment applicable to a particular business or industrial environment. It does not behoove a court to second-guess either that process or its products. Seniority systems, reflecting as they do, not only the give and take of free collective bargaining, but also the specific characteristics of a particular business or industry, inevitably come in all sizes and shapes. As we made clear in the Teamsters case, seniority may be "measured in a number of ways" and the legislative history of § 703(h) does not suggest that it was enacted to prefer any particular variety of seniority system over any other. 431 U.S., at 355, n. 41, 97 S.Ct., at 1865.

What has been said does not mean that § 703(h) is to be given a scope that risks swallowing up Title VII's otherwise broad prohibition of "practices, procedures, or tests" that disproportionately affect members of those groups that the Act protects. Significant freedom must be afforded employers and unions to create differing seniority systems.

---

16. See generally S. Slichter, J. Healy, & E. Livernash, The Impact of Collective Bargaining on Management 115–135 (1960).

17. By way of example, a collective-bargaining agreement could specify that an employee begins to accumulate seniority rights at the time he commences employment with the company, at the time he commences employment within the industry, at the time he begins performing a particular job function, or only after a probationary period of employment.

18. For example, a collective-bargaining agreement could provide that accumulated seniority rights are permanently forfeited by voluntary resignation, by severance for cause, or by nonemployment at a particular plant or in the industry for a certain period.

19. For instance, the time an employee works in the industry or with his current employer might not be counted for the purpose of accumulating seniority rights, whereas the time the employee works in a particular job classification might determine his seniority.

20. By way of example, a collective-bargaining agreement could provide that an employee's seniority will govern his entitlement to vacation time and his job security in the event of layoffs, but will have no influence on promotions or job assignments.

21. The examples in the text of the types of rules necessary to the operation of a seniority system are not intended to and do not comprise an exhaustive list.

But that freedom must not be allowed to sweep within the ambit of § 703(h) employment rules that depart fundamentally from commonly accepted notions concerning the acceptable contours of a seniority system, simply because those rules are dubbed "seniority" provisions or have some nexus to an arrangement that concededly operates on the basis of seniority. There can be no doubt, for instance, that a threshold requirement for entering a seniority track that took the form of an educational prerequisite would not be part of a "seniority system" within the intendment of § 703(h).

The application of these principles to the case at hand is straight-forward. The Agreement sets out, in relevant part, two parallel seniority ladders. One allocates the benefits due temporary employees; the other identifies the benefits owed permanent employees. The propriety under § 703(h) of such parallel seniority tracks cannot be doubted after the Court's decision in the *Teamsters* case. The collective-bargaining agreement at issue there allotted one set of benefits according to each employee's total service with the company, and another set according to each employee's service in a particular job category. Just as in that case the separation of seniority tracks did not derogate from the identification of the provisions as a "seniority system" under § 703(h), so in the present case the fact that the system created by the Agreement establishes two or more seniority ladders does not prevent it from being a "seniority system" within the meaning of that section.

The 45–week rule, correspondingly, serves the needed function of establishing the threshold requirement for entry into the permanent-employee seniority track. As such, it performs the same function as did the employment rule in *Teamsters* that provided that a line driver began to accrue seniority for certain purposes only when he started to work as a line driver, even though he had previously spent years as a city driver for the same employer. In *Teamsters*, the Court expressed no reservation about the propriety of such a threshold rule for § 703(h) purposes. There is no reason why the 45–week threshold requirement at issue here should be considered any differently.

The 45–week rule does not depart significantly from commonly accepted concepts of "seniority." The rule is not an educational standard, an aptitude or physical test, or a standard that gives effect to subjectivity. Unlike such criteria, but like any "seniority" rule, the 45–week requirement focuses on length of employment.

Moreover, the rule does not distort the operation of the basic system established by the Agreement, which rewards employment longevity with heightened benefits. A temporary employee's chances of achieving permanent status increase inevitably as his industry employment and seniority accumulate. The temporary employees with the most industry seniority have the first choice of new jobs within the industry available for temporary employees. Similarly, the temporary employees with the most plant seniority have the first choice of temporary employee jobs within their plant and enjoy the greatest security against "bumping" by permanent employees from nearby plants. As a general rule, therefore, the more seniority a temporary employee accumulates, the more likely it is that he will be able to satisfy the 45–week requirement. That the correlation between accumulated industry employment and acquisition of permanent employee status is imperfect does not mean that the 45–week requirement is not a component of the Agreement's seniority system. Under any seniority system, contingencies such as illnesses and layoffs may interrupt the accrual of seniority and delay realization of the advantages dependent upon it.[22]

For these reasons, we conclude that the Court of Appeals was in error in holding that the 45–week rule is not a component of a "seniority system" within the meaning of § 703(h) of Title VII of the Civil Rights Act of 1964. In the District Court the respondent will remain free to show that, in respect to the 45–week rule or in other respects, the seniority system established by the Agreement is not "bona fide," or that the differences in employment conditions that it has produced are "the result of an intention to discriminate because of race."

For the reasons stated, the judgment before us is vacated, and the case is remanded to the Court of Appeals for the Ninth Circuit for further proceedings consistent with this opinion.

It is so ordered.

MR. JUSTICE POWELL and MR. JUSTICE STEVENS took no part in the consideration or decision of this case.

MR. JUSTICE MARSHALL with whom MR. JUSTICE BRENNAN and MR. JUSTICE BLACKMUN join, dissenting.

In the California brewing industry, an employee's rights and benefits are largely dependent on whether he is a "permanent" employee within the meaning of the collective-bargaining agreement. Permanent employees are laid off after all other employees. If laid off at one facility, a permanent employee is permitted to replace the least senior nonpermanent employee at any other covered facility within the local area. Permanent employees are selected before temporary employees to fill vacancies. They have exclusive rights to supplemental unemployment benefits upon layoff and receive higher wages and vacation pay for the same work performed by other employees. Permanent employees have first choice of vacation times, less rigorous requirements for qualifying for holiday pay, exclusive access to veterans' reinstatement and seniority rights, and priority in assignment of overtime work among bottlers.

---

22. There are indications in the record of this case that a long-term decline in the California brewing industry's demand for labor is a reason why the accrual of seniority as a temporary employee has not led more automatically to the acquisition of permanent status. But surely, what would be part of a "seniority system" in an expanding labor market does not become something else in a declining labor market.

According to respondent's complaint, no Negro has ever attained permanent employee status in the California brewing industry.[1]

The provision of the collective-bargaining agreement at issue here defines a permanent employee as one "who * * * has completed forty-five weeks of employment * * * in one classification in one calendar year as an employee of the brewing industry in this State." An employee who works 44 weeks per year for his entire working life remains a temporary employee. By contrast, an employee who works 45 weeks in his first year in the industry attains permanent employee status. This simple fact belies the Court's conclusion that the 45–week requirement "does not depart significantly from commonly accepted concepts of 'seniority.' " Since I am unable to agree that the provision at issue is part of a "seniority system" under § 703(h) of Title VII, I dissent.

I

Neither Title VII nor its legislative history provides a comprehensive definition of the term "seniority system."[2] The Court is therefore correct in concluding that the term must be defined by reference to "commonly accepted notions about 'seniority' in industrial relations" and "in the context of Title VII and this country's labor policy." Those "commonly accepted notions," however, do not lead to the Court's holding today. And I believe that the relevant policies do not support that holding, but instead require that it be rejected.

The concept of "seniority" is not a complicated one. The fundamental principle, as the Court recognizes, is that employee rights and benefits increase with length of service. This principle is reflected in the very definition of the term, as found in dictionaries[3] and treatises and articles in the field of industrial relations.[4] To quote from a few of

---

1. In the present procedural posture of the case, of course, the allegations of the complaint must be accepted as true.

2. The legislative history does, however, provide a bit more guidance than the Court admits. The fact that the sole example of a seniority system given in the congressional debates is one in which rights increase with cumulative length of service is at least suggestive.

3. See, e.g., Webster's Third New International Dictionary 2066 (unabridged ed. 1961) ("a status attained by length of continuous service (as in a company * * *) to which are attached by custom or prior collective agreement various rights or privileges"); Random House Dictionary of the English Language 1299 (1966) ("priority, precedence, or status obtained as the result of a person's length of service"); Black's Law Dictionary 1222 (5th ed. 1979) ("As used with reference to job seniority, worker with most years of service is first pro-

moted within range of jobs subject to seniority, and is the last laid off, proceeding so on down the line to the youngest in point of service"); Ballentine's Law Dictionary 1160 (1969) ("the principle in labor relations that length of employment determines the order of layoffs, rehirings, and advancements").

4. See, e.g. Roberts' Dictionary of Industrial Relations 390 (1966) ("The length of service an individual employee has in the plant. * * * The seniority principle rests on the assumption that the individuals with the greatest length of service within the company should be given preference in employment"); United States Department of Labor, Bureau of Labor Statistics, Bulletin No. 908–11, p. 1 (1949) ("A seniority program aims to provide maximum security in employment to those with the longest service"); E. Dangel & I. Shriber, The Law of Labor Unions § 15 (1941) ("Seniority

the sources on which the Court purports to rely today: "Seniority is a system of employment preference based on length of service; employees with the longest service are given the greatest job security and the best opportunities for advancement." Aaron, Reflections on the Legal Nature and Enforceability of Seniority Rights, 75 Harv.L.Rev.. 1532, 1534 (1962). "The variations and combinations of seniority principles are very great, but in all cases the basic measure is length of service, with preference accorded to the senior worker." Cooper & Sobol, Seniority and Testing under Fair Employment Laws: A General Approach to Objective Criteria of Hiring and Promotion, 82 Harv.L.Rev. 1598, 1602 (1969). "Seniority grants certain preferential treatment to long-service employees almost at the expense of short-service employees. * * * [S]eniority is defined as length of service." E. Beal, E. Wickersham, & P. Kienast, The Practice of Collective Bargaining 430 (1972).

It is hardly surprising that seniority has uniformly been defined in terms of cumulative length of service. No other definition could accord with the policies underlying the recognition of seniority rights. A seniority system provides an objective standard by which to ascertain employee rights and protections, thus reducing the likelihood of arbitrariness or caprice in employer decisions. At the same time, it promotes stability and certainty among employees, furnishing a predictable method by which to measure future employment position. See, e.g., Sayles, Seniority: An Internal Union Problem, 30 Harv. Bus. Rev.. 55 (1952); C. Golden & H. Ruttenberg, The Dynamics of Industrial Democracy 128–131 (1973); Cooper & Sobol, supra, at 1604–1605.

The Court concedes this general point, recognizing that a " 'seniority system' is a scheme that, alone or in tandem with non-'seniority' criteria, allots to employees ever improving employment rights and benefits as their relative lengths of pertinent employment increase." In my view, that concession is dispositive of this case. The principal effect of the 45–week requirement is to ensure that employee rights and benefits in the California brewing industry are not "ever improving" as length of service increases. Indeed, cumulative length of service is only incidentally relevant to the 45–week rule. The likelihood that a

---

* * * is an employment advantage in the matter of the choice of and the right to work in one's occupation on the basis of an employee's length of service"); BNA, Collective Bargaining Contracts, Techniques of Negotiation and Administration with Topical Classification of Clauses 488 (1941) ("The term [seniority] refers to length of service with the employer or in some division of an enterprise"); Meyers, The Analytic Meaning of Seniority, Industrial Relations Research Association, Proceedings of Eighteenth Annual Meeting 194 (1966) ("Seniority is the application of the criterion of length of service for the calculation of relative equities among employees"); McCaffrey, Development and Administra-

tion of Seniority Provisions, Proceedings of New York University Second Annual Conference on Labor 132 (1949) ("seniority may be defined as the length of company-recognized service as applied to certain employer-employee relationships"); Christenson, Seniority Rights Under Labor Union Working Agreements, 11 Temple L. Q. 355 (1937) ("seniority is a rule providing that employers promote, lay-off and re-employ labor, according to length of previous service"). Cf. P. Selznick, Law, Society, and Industrial Justice 203 (1969) (referring to the " 'rather general feeling that a worker who has spent many years on his job has some stake in that job and in the business of which it is a part' ").

temporary employee will attain permanent employee status is largely unpredictable. The 45–week period, which is exclusive of vacation, leaves of absence, and time lost because of injury or sickness, represents almost 90% of the calendar year. Even if an employee is relatively senior among temporaries, his ability to work 45 weeks in a year will rest in large part on fortuities over which he has no control. The most obvious reason that employees have been prevented from attaining permanent employee status—a reason barely referred to by the Court— is that the brewing industry is a seasonal one. An employee may also be prevented from becoming permanent because of replacement by permanent employees or an employer's unexpected decision to lay off a particular number of employees during the course of a year.[5] It is no wonder that the accrual of seniority by temporary employees has not led with any regularity to the acquisition of permanent employee status.[6] In sum, the 45–week rule does not have the feature of providing employees with a reasonably certain route by which to measure future employment position. So understood, the 45–week rule has very little to do with seniority, for it makes permanent status turn on fortuities over which the employee has no control, not on length of service with the employer or in the relevant unit.

The Court avoids this conclusion by little more than assertion. It observes that the 45–week rule acts as a threshold requirement for entry onto the seniority track composed of permanent employees, but eliminates the force of that observation with the inevitable concession that such threshold requirements are not necessarily entitled to § 703(h) exemption.[7] It notes that the 45–week requirement "focuses on length of employment," and proceeds to the unexplained conclusion that it therefore "does not depart significantly from commonly accepted

5. Indeed, the agreement expressly provides that a permanent employee laid off at one facility will replace (or "bump") the temporary employee with the lowest *plant* seniority, even if that employee has more industry seniority than others. As a result, temporaries who are relatively senior in terms of industry seniority may have less opportunity to work 45 weeks in a calendar year than temporaries with less industry seniority but more plant seniority. Thus, it is simply not true that temporary employees obtain permanent employee status in order of cumulative length of employment, for the requisite 45 weeks is computed on the basis of service in the industry rather than in particular plants.

6. The Court acknowledges this point, but responds that a system which would fall within § 703(h) in an expanding labor market does not lose that status by virtue of the fact that the labor market is contracting. In the Court's words, however, the question is whether the 45–week rule is a part of a seniority system because it

"allots to employees ever improving employment rights and benefits as their relative lengths of pertinent employment increase." In that context it is surely relevant whether the 45–week provision does in fact operate to reward cumulative length of service, or serves instead as a virtually impassable barrier to advancement.

7. As the Court's own analysis suggests, the 45–week provision is entirely different from the seniority provisions involved in Teamsters v. United States, 431 U.S. 324, 97 S.Ct. 1843, 52 L.Ed.2d 396 (1977). At issue in that case was a seniority system granting some benefits on the basis of an employee's cumulative length of service with the company, and others on the basis of cumulative length of service in a particular job category. In both cases employee rights and benefits depended on total length of service in the relevant unit, not on the length of service within a calendar year.

concepts of 'seniority.'" And it adds that more senior temporary employees tend to have a greater opportunity to obtain work and thus to attain permanent status through 45 weeks of employment in a calendar year.

The Court's analysis, of course, is largely dependent on its conclusion that since the 45-week requirement is one measured by time of service, it does not depart from common concepts of seniority. That conclusion, however, is foreclosed by the Court's own definition of a seniority system as one in which employee rights increase with cumulative length of service—not length of service within a calendar year. The mere fact that the 45-week rule is in some sense a measure of "time" does not demonstrate a valid relation to concepts of seniority. Such a conclusion would make the § 703(h) exemption applicable to a rule under which permanent employee status is dependent on number of days served within a week, or hours served within a day.[8]

Nor is there much force to the suggestion that the 45-week requirement somehow becomes part of a seniority system because permanent employee status is more easily achieved by the more senior temporary employees. I could agree with the Court's decision if petitioners demonstrated that the collective-bargaining agreement actually operates to reward employees in order of cumulative length of service. But at this stage of the litigation there is no evidence that temporary employees attain permanent status in a way correlating even roughly with total length of employment. The mere possibility that senior temporary employees are more likely to work for 45 weeks is, in my view, insufficient.[9] It might as well be said that a law conditioning permanent employee status on the attainment of a certain level of skill is a "seniority" provision since skills tend to increase with length of service. A temporary employee is always subject to a risk that for some reason beyond his control, he will be unable to work the full 45 weeks and be forced to start over again.

II

Since the 45-week rule operates as a threshold requirement with no relation to principles of seniority, I believe that the rule is for analytical purposes no different from an educational standard or physical test which, as the Court indicates, is plainly not entitled to § 703(h) exemption. Accordingly, I think it clear that the 45-week requirement is not part of a "seniority system" within the meaning of § 703(h). But

8. For example, there can be no serious question that a provision making permanent status dependent on 7 days of work per week, or 12 hours per day, would not be part of a "seniority system" within the meaning of § 703(h).

9. I could understand, although I do not favor, a decision remanding this case for factual findings on the question whether temporary employees in fact acquire permanent status and, if so, whether they do so in order of cumulative length of service. In my view, it is extraordinary for the Court to conclude, in a factual vacuum and on the authority of nothing other than petitioners' word, that "the rule does not distort the operation of the basic system established by the Agreement, which rewards employment longevity with heightened benefits." See also n.5, supra.

if the question were perceived to be close, I would be guided by the familiar principle that exemptions to remedial statutes should be construed narrowly. "To extend an exemption to other than those plainly and unmistakably within its terms and spirit is to abuse the interpretative process and to frustrate the announced will of the people." Phillips Co. v. Walling, 324 U.S. 490, 493, 65 S.Ct. 807, 808, 89 L.Ed. 1095 (1945). The effect of § 703(h) is to exempt seniority systems from the general prohibition on practices which perpetuate the effects of racial discrimination. This exception is a limited one in derogation of the overarching purpose of Title VII, "the integration of blacks into the mainstream of American society," Steelworkers v. Weber, 443 U.S. 193, 202, 99 S.Ct. 2721, 2727, 61 L.Ed.2d 480 (1979). A statute designed to remedy the national disgrace of discrimination in employment should be interpreted generously to comport with its primary purpose; exemptions should be construed narrowly so as not to undermine the effect of the general prohibition. Today the Court not only refuses to apply this familiar principle of statutory construction, it does not even acknowledge it.

In my view, the Court's holding is fundamentally at odds with the purposes of Title VII and the basic function of the § 703(h) exemption. I dissent.[10]

NOTES AND PROBLEMS FOR DISCUSSION

1. Could a probationary period constitute a "seniority system" entitled to protection under § 703(h)? Assume the employer and the union negotiated as part of a collective bargaining agreement, a 60 day probation period for each "skilled" position in the plant. During the probation period the new employee may be removed from the position on the subjective determination of the supervisor that the employee will have difficulty becoming proficient at the work. After becoming permanent in the position, an employee may only be removed for malfeasance. Assume also that alleged failure during the probation period is the chief reason that only a relative handful of black employees have advanced to the skilled positions. Will the black employees be entitled to elimination of the probation system if they can prove a pattern of disparate treatment? Is a rule under which employees hired on the same day are ranked in seniority according to their scores on preemployment tests a "seniority system" within the meaning of § 703(h)? See, United States v. City of Cincinnati, 771 F.2d 161 (6th Cir.1985). Does a pay schedule that automatically increases each employee's pay annually without reference to the employee's actual length of service constitute a "seniority system"? See, Mitchell v. Jefferson County Board of Education, 56 FEP Cases 644, 936 F.2d 539 (11th Cir.1991). Is a contract provision requiring the employer to prefer active "surplus" employees for new positions over laid-off employees a "seniority

10. To decide this case we are not required to offer a complete definition of the term "seniority system" within the meaning of § 703(h). Nor are we called upon to canvass and evaluate rules "ancillary" to seniority systems. The question whether all of the rules listed by the Court, are part of a seniority system is not at all easy, and the Court's own reasoning demonstrates that its discussion of those rules is gratuitous and does little to advance analysis of the 45–week requirement. That requirement serves none of the functions of an "ancillary" rule.

system" covered by § 703(h)? See, Altman v. AT & T Technologies, Inc., 870 F.2d 386 (7th Cir.1989).

2. The Court in *California Brewers Ass'n* noted that on remand the plaintiff could still show that the 45–week rule was not a "bona fide" seniority system under § 703(h). Assume that the plaintiff is unable to prove that the rule was created or maintained for a discriminatory purpose, but does prove that it was used in a discriminatory fashion against him—i.e., that he was intentionally laid off because of his race to prevent him from obtaining permanent status. To what relief would he be entitled?

In FRANKS v. BOWMAN TRANSPORTATION CO., 424 U.S. 747, 96 S.Ct. 1251, 47 L.Ed.2d 444 (1976), the court held that § 703(h) does not preclude a court from awarding all appropriate relief, including retroactive seniority, to the victim of post-Act discrimination, notwithstanding the fact that the seniority system perpetuating that discrimination is not itself illegal. That decision was not affected by *Teamsters*. See Chapter 7B, *infra.*

3. A victim of post-Title VII discrimination in hiring or assignment must challenge the discrimination directly and cannot let the statute of limitations expire and then file a suit based upon the theory that an otherwise bona fide seniority system perpetuates the discrimination thus constituting a "continuing violation." United Air Lines, Inc. v. Evans, 431 U.S. 553, 97 S.Ct. 1885, 52 L.Ed.2d 571 (1977). But when should the limitation period for challenging a seniority system begin to run? When the seniority system is adopted or when it has its first impact on the plaintiff? See discussion in Chapter 4, *infra.*

SECTION D. INTENTIONAL DISCRIMINATION AGAINST A CLASS: PATTERN OR PRACTICE LITIGATION

HAZELWOOD SCHOOL DISTRICT v. UNITED STATES

Supreme Court of the United States, 1977.
433 U.S. 299, 97 S.Ct. 2736, 53 L.Ed.2d 768.

MR. JUSTICE STEWART delivered the opinion of the Court.

The petitioner Hazelwood School District covers 78 square miles in the northern part of St. Louis County, Mo. In 1973 the Attorney General brought this lawsuit against Hazelwood and various of its officials, alleging that they were engaged in a "pattern or practice" of employment discrimination in violation of Title VII of the Civil Rights Act of 1964, as amended.[1] The complaint asked for an injunction requiring Hazelwood to cease its discriminatory practices, to take affirmative steps to obtain qualified Negro faculty members, and to offer employment and give backpay to victims of past illegal discrimination.

1. Under 42 U.S.C. § 2000e–6(a), the Attorney General was authorized to bring a civil action "[w]henever [he] has reasonable cause to believe that any person or group of persons is engaged in a pattern or practice of resistance to the full enjoyment of any of the rights secured by [Title VII], and that the pattern or practice is of such a nature and is intended to deny the full exercise of [those rights.]" The 1972 amendments to Title VII directed that this function be transferred as of March 24, 1974, to the EEOC, at least with respect to private employers. § 2000e–6(c) (1970 ed. Supp. V); see also, § 2000e–5(f)(1) (1970 ed. Supp. V). The present lawsuit was instituted more than seven months before that transfer.

Hazelwood was formed from 13 rural school districts between 1949 and 1951 by a process of annexation. By the 1967–1968 school year, 17,550 students were enrolled in the district, of whom only 59 were Negro; the number of Negro pupils increased to 576 of 25,166 in 1972–1973, a total of just over 2%.

From the beginning, Hazelwood followed relatively unstructured procedures in hiring its teachers. Every person requesting an application for a teaching position was sent one, and completed applications were submitted to a central personnel office, where they were kept on file.[2] During the early 1960's the personnel office notified all applicants whenever a teaching position became available, but as the number of applications on file increased in the late 1960's and early 1970's, this practice was no longer considered feasible. The personnel office thus began the practice of selecting anywhere from 3 to 10 applicants for interviews at the school where the vacancy existed. The personnel office did not substantively screen the applicants in determining which of them to send for interviews, other than to ascertain that each applicant, if selected, would be eligible for state certification by the time he began the job. Generally, those who had most recently submitted applications were most likely to be chosen for interviews.[3]

Interviews were conducted by a department chairman, program coordinator, or the principal at the school where the teaching vacancy existed. Although those conducting the interviews did fill out forms rating the applicants in a number of respects, it is undisputed that each school principal possessed virtually unlimited discretion in hiring teachers for his school. The only general guidance given to the principals was to hire the "most competent" person available, and such intangibles as "personality, disposition, appearance, poise, voice, articulation, and ability to deal with people" counted heavily. The principal's choice was routinely honored by Hazelwood's Superintendent and the Board of Education.

In the early 1960's Hazelwood found it necessary to recruit new teachers, and for that purpose members of its staff visited a number of colleges and universities in Missouri and bordering States. All the institutions visited were predominantly white, and Hazelwood did not seriously recruit at either of the two predominantly Negro four-year colleges in Missouri.[4] As a buyer's market began to develop for public school teachers, Hazelwood curtailed its recruiting efforts. For the 1971–1972 school year, 3,127 persons applied for only 234 teaching vacancies; for the 1972–1973 school year, there were 2,373 applications

2. Before 1954 Hazelwood's application forms required designation of race, and those forms were in use as late as the 1962–1963 school year.

3. Applicants with student or substitute teaching experience at Hazelwood were given preference if their performance had been satisfactory.

4. One of those two schools was never visited even though it was located in nearby St. Louis. The second was briefly visited on one occasion, but no potential applicant was interviewed.

for 282 vacancies. A number of the applicants who were not hired were Negroes.[5]

Hazelwood hired its first Negro teacher in 1969. The number of Negro faculty members gradually increased in successive years: six of 957 in the 1970 school year; 16 of 1,107 by the end of the 1972 school year; 22 of 1,231 in the 1973 school year. By comparison, according to 1970 census figures, of more than 19,000 teachers employed in that year in the St. Louis area, 15.4% were Negro. That percentage figure included the St. Louis City School District, which in recent years has followed a policy of attempting to maintain a 50% Negro teaching staff. Apart from that school district, 5.7% of the teachers in the county were Negro in 1970.

Drawing upon these historic facts, the Government mounted its "pattern or practice" attack in the District Court upon four different fronts. It adduced evidence of (1) a history of alleged racially discriminatory practices, (2) statistical disparities in hiring, (3) the standardless and largely subjective hiring procedures, and (4) specific instances of alleged discrimination against 55 unsuccessful Negro applicants for teaching jobs. Hazelwood offered virtually no additional evidence in response, relying instead on evidence introduced by the Government, perceived deficiencies in the Government's case, and its own officially promulgated policy "to hire all teachers on the basis of training, preparation and recommendations, regardless of race, color or creed." [6]

The District Court ruled that the Government had failed to establish a pattern or practice of discrimination. The court was unpersuaded by the alleged history of discrimination, noting that no dual school system had ever existed in Hazelwood. The statistics showing that relatively small numbers of Negroes were employed as teachers were found nonprobative, on the ground that the percentage of Negro pupils in Hazelwood was similarly small. The court found nothing illegal or suspect in the teacher-hiring procedures that Hazelwood had followed. Finally, the court reviewed the evidence in the 55 cases of alleged individual discrimination, and after stating that the burden of proving intentional discrimination was on the Government, it found that this burden had not been sustained in a single instance. Hence, the court entered judgment for the defendants. 392 F.Supp. 1276 (E.D.Mo.).

The Court of Appeals for the Eighth Circuit reversed. 534 F.2d 805. After suggesting that the District Court had assigned inadequate weight to evidence of discriminatory conduct on the part of Hazelwood

---

5. The parties disagree whether it is possible to determine from the present record exactly how many of the job applicants in each of the school years were Negroes.

6. The defendants offered only one witness, who testified to the total number of teachers who had applied and were hired for jobs in the 1971–1972 and 1972–1973 school years. They introduced several exhibits consisting of a policy manual, policy book, staff handbook, and historical summary of Hazelwood's formation and relatively brief existence.

before the effective date of Title VII,[7] the Court of Appeals rejected the trial court's analysis of the statistical data as resting on an irrelevant comparison of Negro teachers to Negro pupils in Hazelwood. The proper comparison, in the appellate court's view, was one between Negro teachers in Hazelwood and Negro teachers in the relevant labor market area. Selecting St. Louis County and St. Louis City as the relevant area,[8] the Court of Appeals compared the 1970 census figures, showing that 15.4% of teachers in that area were Negro, to the racial composition of Hazelwood's teaching staff. In the 1972–1973 and 1973–1974 school years, only 1.4% and 1.8%, respectively, of Hazelwood's teachers were Negroes. This statistical disparity, particularly when viewed against the background of the teacher hiring procedures that Hazelwood had followed, was held to constitute a prima facie case of a pattern or practice of racial discrimination.

In addition, the Court of Appeals reasoned that the trial court had erred in failing to measure the 55 instances in which Negro applicants were denied jobs against the four-part standard for establishing a prima facie case of individual discrimination set out in this Court's opinion in McDonnell Douglas Corp. v. Green. Applying that standard, the appellate court found 16 cases of individual discrimination,[10] which "buttressed" the statistical proof. Because Hazelwood had not rebutted the Government's prima facie case of a pattern or practice of racial discrimination, the Court of Appeals directed judgment for the Government and prescribed the remedial order to be entered.[11]

We granted certiorari * * * to consider a substantial question affecting the enforcement of a pervasive federal law.

The petitioners primarily attack the judgment of the Court of Appeals for its reliance on "undifferentiated work force statistics to find an unrebutted prima facie case of employment discrimination." [12]

---

7. As originally enacted, Title VII of the Civil Rights Act of 1964 applied only to private employers. The Act was expanded to include state and local governmental employers by the Equal Employment Opportunity Act of 1972, 86 Stat. 103, whose effective date was March 24, 1972. See 42 U.S.C. §§ 2000e(a), (b), (f), (h) (1970 ed. Supp. V).

The evidence of pre-Act discrimination relied upon by the Court of Appeals included the failure to hire any Negro teachers until 1969, the failure to recruit at predominantly Negro colleges in Missouri, and somewhat inconclusive evidence that Hazelwood was responsible for a 1962 Mississippi newspaper advertisement for teacher applicants that specified "white only."

8. The city of St. Louis is surrounded by, but not included in, St. Louis County. Mo.Ann.Stat. § 46.145 (1966).

10. The Court of Appeals held that none of the 16 prima facie cases of individ-

ual discrimination had been rebutted by the petitioners. See 534 F.2d, at 814.

11. The District Court was directed to order that the petitioners cease from discriminating on the basis of race or color in the hiring of teachers, promulgate accurate job descriptions and hiring criteria, recruit Negro and white applicants on an equal basis, give preference in filling vacancies to the 16 discriminatorily rejected applicants, make appropriate backpay awards, and submit periodic reports to the Government on its progress in hiring qualified Negro teachers. Id., at 819–820.

12. In their petition for certiorari and brief on the merits, the petitioners have phrased the question as follows:

"Whether a court may disregard evidence that an employer has treated actual job applicants in a nondiscriminatory manner and rely on undifferentiated

The question they raise, in short, is whether a basic component in the Court of Appeals' finding of a pattern or practice of discrimination—the comparatively small percentage of Negro employees on Hazelwood's teaching staff—was lacking in probative force.

This Court's recent consideration in International Brotherhood of Teamsters v. United States, of the role of statistics in pattern-or-practice suits under Title VII provides substantial guidance in evaluating the arguments advanced by the petitioners. In that case we stated that it is the Government's burden to "establish by a preponderance of the evidence that racial discrimination was the [employer's] standard operating procedure—the regular rather than the unusual practice." We also noted that statistics can be an important source of proof in employment discrimination cases, since

> "absent explanation, it is ordinarily to be expected that nondiscriminatory hiring practices will in time result in a work force more or less representative of the racial and ethnic composition of the population in the community from which employees are hired. Evidence of long-lasting and gross disparity between the composition of a work force and that of the general population thus may be significant even though § 703(j) makes clear that Title VII imposes no requirement that a work force mirror the general population." Where gross statistical disparities can be shown, they alone may in a proper case constitute prima facie proof of a pattern of practice of discrimination. Teamsters, supra.

There can be no doubt, in light of the Teamsters case, that the District Court's comparison of Hazelwood's teacher work force to its student population fundamentally misconceived the role of statistics in employment discrimination cases. The Court of Appeals was correct in the view that a proper comparison was between the racial composition of Hazelwood's teaching staff and the racial composition of the qualified public school teacher population in the relevant labor market.[13] The

workforce statistics to find an unrebutted prima facie case of employment discrimination in violation of Title VII of the Civil Rights Act of 1964."

Their petition for certiorari and brief on the merits did raise a second question:

"Whether Congress has authority under Section 5 of the Fourteenth Amendment to prohibit by Title VII of the Civil Rights Act of 1964 employment practices of an agency of a state government in the absence of proof that the agency purposefully discriminated against applicants on the basis of race." That issue, however, is not presented by the facts in this case. The Government's opening statement in the trial court explained that its evidence was designed to show that the scarcity of Negro teachers at Hazelwood "is the result of purpose" and

is attributable to "deliberately continued employment policies." Thus here, as in International Brotherhood of Teamsters v. United States, 431 U.S. 324, 97 S.Ct. 1843, 52 L.Ed.2d 396, "[t]he Government's theory of discrimination was simply that the [employer], in violation of § 703(a) of Title VII, regularly and purposefully treated Negroes * * * less favorably than white persons." Id., at 335, 97 S.Ct., at 1854 (footnote omitted).

13. In Teamsters, the comparison between the percentage of Negroes on the employer's work force and the percentage in the general areawide population was highly probative, because the job skill there involved—the ability to drive a truck—is one that many persons possess or can fairly readily acquire. When special qualifications are required to fill particular

percentage of Negroes on Hazelwood's teaching staff in 1972–1973 was 1.4%, and in 1973–1974 it was 1.8%. By contrast, the percentage of qualified Negro teachers in the area was, according to the 1970 census, at least 5.7%.[14] Although these differences were on their face substantial, the Court of Appeals erred in substituting its judgment for that of the District Court and holding that the Government had conclusively proved its "pattern or practice" lawsuit.

The Court of Appeals totally disregarded the possibility that this prima facie statistical proof in the record might at the trial court level be rebutted by statistics dealing with Hazelwood's hiring after it became subject to Title VII. Racial discrimination by public employers was not made illegal under Title VII until March 24, 1972. A public employer who from that date forward made all its employment decisions in a wholly nondiscriminatory way would not violate Title VII even if it had formerly maintained an all-white work force by purposefully excluding Negroes.[15] For this reason, the Court cautioned in the

jobs, comparisons to the general population (rather than to the smaller group of individuals who possess the necessary qualifications) may have little probative value. The comparative statistics introduced by the Government in the District Court, however, were properly limited to public school teachers, and therefore this is not a case like Mayor v. Educational Equality League, 415 U.S. 605, 94 S.Ct. 1323, 39 L.Ed.2d 630, in which the racial-composition comparisons failed to take into account special qualifications for the position in question. Id., at 620–621, 94 S.Ct., at 1333–1334.

Although the petitioners concede as a general matter the probative force of the comparative work-force statistics, they object to the Court of Appeals' heavy reliance on these data on the ground that applicant-flow data, showing the actual percentage of white and Negro applicants for teaching positions at Hazelwood, would be firmer proof. As we have noted, see n.5, supra, there was not clear evidence of such statistics. We leave it to the District Court on remand to determine whether competent proof of those data can be adduced. If so, it would, of course, be very relevant. Cf. Dothard v. Rawlinson, 433 U.S. 321, 330, 97 S.Ct. 2720, 2721, 53 L.Ed.2d 786.

14. As is discussed below, the Government contends that a comparative figure of 15.4%, rather than 5.7%, is the appropriate one. But even assuming arguendo that the 5.7% figure urged by the petitioners is correct, the disparity between that figure and the percentage of Negroes on Hazelwood's teaching staff would be more than fourfold for the 1972–1973 school year, and

threefold for the 1973–1974 school year. A precise method of measuring the significance of such statistical disparities was explained in Castaneda v. Partida, 430 U.S. 482, 496–497, n.17, 97 S.Ct. 1272, 1281, n.17, 51 L.Ed.2d 498, n.17. It involves calculation of the "standard deviation" as a measure of predicted fluctuations from the expected value of a sample. Using the 5.7% figure as the basis for calculating the expected value, the expected number of Negroes on the Hazelwood teaching staff would be roughly 63 in 1972–1973 and 70 in 1973–1974. The observed number in those years was 16 and 22, respectively. The difference between the observed and expected values was more than six standard deviations in 1972–1973 and more than five standard deviations in 1973–1974. The Court in Castaneda noted that "[a]s a general rule for such large samples, if the difference between the expected value and the observed number is greater than two or three standard deviations," then the hypothesis that teachers were hired without regard to race would be suspect. 430 U.S. at 497 n.17, 97 S.Ct., at 1281 n.17.

15. This is not to say that evidence of pre-Act discrimination can never have any probative force. Proof that an employer engaged in racial discrimination prior to the effective date of Title VII might in some circumstances support the inference that such discrimination continued, particularly where relevant aspects of the decisionmaking process had undergone little change. Cf. Fed.Rule Evid. 406; Arlington Heights v. Metropolitan Housing Development Corp., 429 U.S. 252, 267, 97 S.Ct. 555,

Teamsters opinion that once a prima facie case has been established by statistical work-force disparities, the employer must be given an opportunity to show that "the claimed discriminatory pattern is a product of pre-Act hiring rather than unlawful post-Act discrimination."

The record in this case showed that for the 1972–1973 school year, Hazelwood hired 282 new teachers, 10 of whom (3.5%) were Negroes; for the following school year it hired 123 new teachers, 5 of whom (4.1%) were Negroes. Over the two-year period, Negroes constituted a total of 15 of the 405 new teachers hired (3.7%). Although the Court of Appeals briefly mentioned these data in reciting the facts, it wholly ignored them in discussing whether the Government had shown a pattern or practice of discrimination. And it gave no consideration at all to the possibility that post-Act data as to the number of Negroes hired compared to the total number of Negro applicants might tell a totally different story.[16]

What the hiring figures prove obviously depends upon the figures to which they are compared. The Court of Appeals accepted the Government's argument that the relevant comparison was to the labor market area of St. Louis County and the city of St. Louis, in which, according to the 1970 census, 15.4% of all teachers were Negro. The propriety of that comparison was vigorously disputed by the petitioners, who urged that because the city of St. Louis has made special attempts to maintain a 50% Negro teaching staff, inclusion of that school district in the relevant market area distorts the comparison. Were that argument accepted, the percentage of Negro teachers in the relevant labor market area (St. Louis County alone) as shown in the 1970 census would be 5.7% rather than 15.4%.

The difference between these figures may well be important; the disparity between 3.7% (the percentage of Negro teachers hired by Hazelwood in 1972–1973 and 1973–1974) and 5.7% may be sufficiently small to weaken the Government's other proof, while the disparity between 3.7% and 15.4% may be sufficiently large to reinforce it.[17]   In

564, 50 L.Ed.2d 450; 1 J. Wigmore, Evidence § 92, 2 id., §§ 302–305, 371, 375 (3d ed. 1940). And, of course, a public employer even before the extension of Title VII in 1972 was subject to the command of the Fourteenth Amendment not to engage in purposeful racial discrimination.

16. See n.13, supra, and n.21, infra. But cf. Teamsters, 431 U.S. at 364–367, 97 S.Ct., at 1868–1869.

17. Indeed, under the statistical methodology explained in Castaneda v. Partida, supra, 430 U.S., at 496–497, n.17, 97 S.Ct. 1272, at 1281, n.17, 51 L.Ed.2d 498, n.17, involving the calculation of the standard deviation as a measure of predicted fluctuations, the difference between using 15.4% and 5.7% as the areawide figure would be significant. If the 15.4% figure is taken as the basis for comparison, the expected number of Negro teachers hired by Hazelwood in 1972–1973 would be 43 (rather than the actual figure of 10) of a total of 282, a difference of more than five standard deviations; the expected number in 1973–1974 would be 19 (rather than the actual figure 5) of a total of 123, a difference of more than three standard deviations. For the two years combined, the difference between the observed number of 15 Negro teachers hired (of a total of 405) would vary from the expected number of 62 by more than six standard deviations. Because a fluctuation of more than two or three standard deviations would undercut the hypothesis that decisions were being made randomly with respect to race, 430

determining which of the two figures—or, very possibly, what interme-diate figure—provides the most accurate basis for comparison to the hiring figures at Hazelwood, it will be necessary to evaluate such considerations as (i) whether the racially based hiring policies of the St. Louis City School District were in effect as far back as 1970, the year in which the census figures were taken; [18] (ii) to what extent those policies have changed the racial composition of that district's teaching staff from what it would otherwise have been; (iii) to what extent St. Louis' recruitment policies have diverted to the city, teachers who might otherwise have applied to Hazelwood; [19] (iv) to what extent Negro teachers employed by the city would prefer employment in other districts such as Hazelwood; and (v) what the experience in other school districts in St. Louis County indicates about the validity of excluding the City School District from the relevant labor market.

It is thus clear that a determination of the appropriate comparative figures in this case will depend upon further evaluation by the trial court. As this Court admonished in Teamsters: "[S]tatistics * * * come in infinite variety * * *. [T]heir usefulness depends on all of the surrounding facts and circumstances." Only the trial court is in a position to make the appropriate determination after further findings. And only after such a determination is made can a foundation be established for deciding whether or not Hazelwood engaged in a pattern or practice of racial discrimination in its employment practices in violation of the law.[20]

We hold, therefore, that the Court of Appeals erred in disregarding the post-Act hiring statistics in the record, and that it should have remanded the case to the District Court for further findings as to the relevant labor market area and for an ultimate determination whether Hazelwood engaged in a pattern or practice of employment discrimina-

U.S. at 497 n.17, 97 S.Ct., at 1281 n.17, each of these statistical comparisons would reinforce rather than rebut the Government's other proof. If, however, the 5.7% areawide figure is used, the expected number of Negro teachers hired in 1972–1973 would be roughly 16, less than two standard deviations from the observed number of 10; for 1973–1974, the expected value would be roughly seven, less than one standard deviation from the observed value of 5; and for the two years combined, the expected value of 23 would be less than two standard deviations from the observed total of 15. A more precise method of analyzing these statistics confirms the results of the standard deviation analysis. See F. Mosteller, R. Rourke, & G. Thomas, Probability with Statistical Applications 494 (2d ed. 1970).

These observations are not intended to suggest that precise calculations of statistical significance are necessary in employing statistical proof, but merely to highlight the importance of the choice of the relevant labor market area.

18. In 1970 Negroes constituted only 42% of the faculty in St. Louis city schools, which could indicate either that the city's policy was not yet in effect or simply that its goal had not yet been achieved.

19. The petitioners observe, for example, that Harris Teachers College in St. Louis, whose 1973 graduating class was 60% Negro, is operated by the city. It is the petitioners' contention that the city's public elementary and secondary schools occupy an advantageous position in the recruitment of Harris graduates.

20. Because the District Court focused on a comparison between the percentage of Negro teachers and Negro pupils in Hazelwood, it did not undertake an evaluation of the relevant labor market, and its casual dictum that the inclusion of the city of St. Louis "distorted" the labor market statistics was not based upon valid criteria. 392 F.Supp. 1276, 1287 (E.D.Mo.).

tion after March 24, 1972.[21]   Accordingly, the judgment is vacated, and the case is remanded to the District Court for further proceedings consistent with this opinion.

It is so ordered.

[The concurring opinion of JUSTICE BRENNAN and dissenting opinion of JUSTICE STEVENS are omitted].

NOTES AND PROBLEMS FOR DISCUSSION

1.   The Supreme Court has established three models of proof for Title VII litigation.   Individual disparate treatment cases are governed by the *McDonnell Douglas–Burdine* formula.   Class disparate treatment cases, sometimes referred to as "pattern and practice" cases, follow the pattern established in *Teamsters* and *Hazelwood.*   Disproportionate impact cases are tried under the *Griggs* formula (as modified by *Wards Cove Packing*).   How does the employer's burden differ among the different theories?   The three theories are not, of course, mutually exclusive and it is quite common for more than one theory to be presented in the same case.   In *Wards Cove Packing,* for example, the plaintiffs presented evidence of both pattern and practice and disproportionate impact discrimination.   In *Watson v. Fort Worth Bank and Trust* the plaintiff relied on both disparate treatment and disproportionate impact theories.   In light of the Supreme Court's holding in *Watson* that disproportionate impact analysis can be applied to subjective employment decisions and the Court's dilution in *Wards Cove Packing* of the employer's burden in disproportionate impact cases, are the distinctions between the types of cases theoretical only?

2.   Contrasting an individual disparate treatment case with a pattern and practice case, the Supreme Court in COOPER v. FEDERAL RESERVE BANK, 467 U.S. 867, 104 S.Ct. 2794, 81 L.Ed.2d 718 (1984), noted:

> The crucial difference between an individual's claim of discrimination and a class action alleging a general pattern or practice of discrimination is manifest.   The inquiry regarding an individual's claim is the reason for a particular employment decision, while "at the liability stage of a pattern-or-practice trial the focus often will not be on individual hiring decisions, but on a pattern of discriminatory decisionmaking."

467 U.S. at 876, 104 S.Ct. at 2799 (quoting *Teamsters*).   Evidence of class wide discrimination is admissible in an individual case, but such evidence, even if very probative of class discrimination, does not establish that the individual plaintiff was a victim of such discrimination.   See, Gilty v. Village of Oak Park, 919 F.2d 1247, 1252 (7th Cir.1990) (evidence of pattern and practice discrimination no more than collateral to evidence of specific discrimination against plaintiff).   Cf. MacDissi v. Valmont Industries, Inc., 856 F.2d 1054 (8th Cir.1988) (even weak statistical proof has probative value in individual case).   In an individual disparate treatment case tried to a jury, should the trial judge have discretion to exclude statistical evidence purporting to show discrimination against the class of persons to which the plaintiff belongs on the ground that such evidence could confuse the jury?   See, Riordan v. Kempiners, 831 F.2d 690 (7th Cir.1987).

---

21. It will also be open to the District Court on remand to determine whether sufficiently reliable applicant-flow data are available to permit consideration of the petitioners' argument that those data may undercut a statistical analysis dependent upon hirings alone.

3.   The plaintiffs' statistical evidence in a pattern and practice case will be very similar to the plaintiffs' initial proof in a case tried under the disproportionate impact theory.   The function of the statistical proof in the two types of cases will, however, differ.   In a disproportionate impact case the statistical evidence is direct proof that the challenged practice or policy disproportionately affects the plaintiffs' class.   See, *Wards Cove Packing Co. v. Atonio, supra.*   In a pattern and practice case, by contrast, the statistical proof constitutes circumstantial evidence of intentional discrimination against a class of applicants or employees.   Does this difference in function of statistical evidence between the two types of cases mean that a different *kind* or *quality* of statistical evidence should be required to establish a prima facie case in cases tried under the different theories?   For example, in *Wards Cove Packing* the district court rejected the plaintiffs' disparate treatment claims and that ruling was not appealed.   Was there any necessary difference, however, between the *kind* of statistical evidence supporting the disparate impact claim and that presented on the "pattern and practice" claim?   How indeed could the same evidence establish a prima facie case of disparate impact and fail to establish a prima facie case of "pattern and practice" discrimination?   Several courts have suggested that, in pattern and practice cases, the trier of fact may demand proof by the plaintiff of a larger statistical deviation from what would have been expected absent discrimination than would satisfy the plaintiff's burden of proof in a disproportionate impact case.   See, Rivera v. City of Wichita Falls, 665 F.2d 531, 535 n.5 (5th Cir.1982) ("gross disparity" between minority percentage of employer's work force and minority percentage of relevant labor market required for prima facie case of intentional discrimination while only a "marked disproportion" required for disparate impact); Falcon v. General Telephone Co., 815 F.2d 317, 322 (5th Cir.1987) (disparities between Mexican–Americans in the available population and the percentage of Mexican–Americans in the employer's work force were not egregious enough to support an inference of discrimination); Nash v. Consolidated City of Jacksonville, 763 F.2d 1393, 1397 (11th Cir.1985), cert. denied, ___ U.S. ___, 111 S.Ct. 967, 112 L.Ed.2d 1054 (1991) (intent to discriminate against black firefighters could be inferred from city's testing procedures only if disparate impact was too obvious to be overlooked).   What could be the rationale of such decisions?

4.   In *Hazelwood* Justice Stewart, while not rejecting the government's general population statistics, concluded that the case should be remanded to allow the defendants to introduce applicant flow statistics which "might tell a totally different story."   In what way can applicant flow statistics tell a "different story"?   In Mister v. Illinois Central Gulf R. Co., 832 F.2d 1427, 1436 (7th Cir.1987), cert. denied, 485 U.S. 1035, 108 S.Ct. 1597, 99 L.Ed.2d 911 (1988) the Court of Appeals explained that, as a general matter, applicant flow statistics were to be preferred over general population comparisons because applicant statistics have a more direct relation to the actual hiring process.   He cautioned, however, that applicant flow could be affected by known discriminatory policies of the employer:

> [d]iscrimination affects the applicant pool in a way that makes the discrimination harder to detect.   The discriminating employer induces qualified blacks not to apply, and these non-applicants—victims of discrimination as much as the non-hired applicants—will make the employers hiring look "better" than it is.   An applicant pool analysis is biased against finding discrimination, if potential applicants know or suspect that the employer is

discriminating. If a study based on applicants nonetheless implies discrimination, this is potent evidence.

832 F.2d at 1436. See also, Washington v. Electrical Joint Apprenticeship & Training Committee, 845 F.2d 710 (7th Cir.), cert. denied, 488 U.S. 944, 109 S.Ct. 371, 102 L.Ed.2d 360 (1988) (where applicants may be discouraged by the selection process itself, disproportionate impact may be established from population statistics alone); Scoggins v. Board of Educ. of Nashville, 853 F.2d 1472 (8th Cir.1988) (relevant labor market may encompass more than applicants where employer recruited outside vicinity and where discriminatory practices may have driven black applicants away); Kilgo v. Bowman Transportation, Inc., 789 F.2d 859, 868–69 (11th Cir.1986) (rejection of applicant flow statistics in disproportionate impact case justified where employer's posted experience requirement was more likely to deter women than men from applying). Given the fact that the employers in *Wards Cove Packing* hired the noncannery employees from their home offices in Washington and Oregon, and not from villages in Alaska near the cannery locations, could applicant flow statistics for the noncannery positions establish any meaningful information about the actual pool of minorities available for these positions? How should the pool of persons available and qualified for noncannery positions be defined?

5. *Hazelwood* illustrates a common use of statistical comparisons in both pattern and practice and disproportionate impact cases. To prove that a practice or policy is discriminatory in design or effect the composition of the employer's work force (or in a hiring case, the pool of applicants) is compared to the composition of an outside "population." The difference between the work force composition and the composition of the population is used to prove the discriminatory effect in a disproportionate impact case and as circumstantial evidence of discriminatory intent in a disparate treatment case. The assumption underlying the evidentiary use of such comparisons is that, absent discrimination (effect or intent), the composition of the work force should reflect that of the outside population. Sometimes, as in *Hazelwood*, the composition of one of the relevant populations (the applicant pool) is unknown and the courts must assume that the composition of larger populations, such as the area work force, is sufficiently similar to the relevant pool for the proper inferences to be drawn. The relevance and probative value of this type of statistical evidence thus turns on the validity of the assumption about the outside population. The critical question is whether the proper outside population has been used for comparison with the work force statistics. What assumption was drawn in *Hazelwood* about the population of teachers in the St. Louis area?

Hazelwood also demonstrates the importance of "controlling" labor market statistics to provide a relevant population to compare with the employer's work force. Typically, gross labor market statistics must be controlled for both requisite skills and geographic scope.

Skill Prerequisites for the Job in Question

In JOHNSON v. TRANSPORTATION AGENCY, 480 U.S. 616, 107 S.Ct. 1442, 94 L.Ed.2d 615 (1987), (*infra* at 1181) the Court explained that an affirmative action plan that favored minorities could only be justified by proof of past discrimination and that such discrimination could not be inferred from a simple comparison of minorities already hired with those in the general population. The Court stated:

> [a] comparison of the percentage of minorities or women in the employer's work force with the percentage in the area labor market or general population is appropriate in analyzing jobs that require no special expertise, or training programs designed to provide expertise. When a job requires special training, however, the comparison should be with those in the labor force who possess the relevant qualifications.

480 U.S. at 632, 107 S.Ct. at 1452. See also, *Hazelwood* n.13; Boykin v. Georgia–Pacific Corp., 706 F.2d 1384, 1392 (5th Cir.1983), cert. denied, 465 U.S. 1006, 104 S.Ct. 999, 79 L.Ed.2d 231 (1984) (where unskilled persons are hired and then promoted on the basis of training received on the job, it is unnecessary to standardize data for qualifications); Green v. USX Corp., 896 F.2d 801 (3d Cir.), cert. denied, ___ U.S. ___, 111 S.Ct. 53, 112 L.Ed.2d 29 (1990) (since any able-bodied person should be able to competently perform such a job, applicant flow data will accurately reflect pool of such persons).

The difference between use of general population figures and adult work force figures will be small when the percentages of minority and majority persons working do not differ significantly. The choice of general population as opposed to adult work force statistics will be critical where the percentage of the minority in the population differs greatly from its percentage in the available work force. It is common for example for the percentage of women in the population to differ from the percentage of women in the adult work force. See, Dothard v. Rawlinson, 433 U.S. 321, 97 S.Ct. 2720, 53 L.Ed.2d 786 (1977) (women over 14 years of age comprised 52% of population of Alabama but only 37% of its total labor force).

Geographic Area

The geographic area used to define the statistical pool may also significantly affect its composition. In *Hazelwood* the Court of Appeals ruled that the relevant labor market included the entire Metropolitan Statistical Area of St. Louis as calculated by the Census Bureau. The Supreme Court remanded for a determination by the district court of whether the appropriate labor market for the school district included the city of St. Louis or, as contended by the school board, should be limited to the rural area surrounding the city. What should the district court consider in making this determination? In his dissent, Justice Stevens noted that the record of the case showed that one third of the teachers hired by the school district in 1972–73 lived in the city of St. Louis at the time of initial employment. 433 U.S. at 315 n.2, 97 S.Ct. at 2746 n.2. Should not that fact alone demonstrate that the city was properly included in the relevant labor market? In Clark v. Chrysler Corp., 673 F.2d 921, 928–929 (7th Cir.), cert. denied, 459 U.S. 873, 103 S.Ct. 161, 74 L.Ed.2d 134 (1982), the court determined the labor market for an employer which drew its labor force primarily from the county in which it was located, but also to some extent from peripheral areas, by weighing the minority availability statistics to reflect primarily the demographics of the employer's home county. See also, Markey v. Tenneco Oil Co., 707 F.2d 172 (5th Cir.1983) (racial composition of labor market for employer that drew work force from four-county area calculated by weighing black population of each county according to percentage of actual applicants from that county).

The relevant labor pool will vary for employers in the same locality and even from job to job within a plant depending primarily on the salary of the job in question and the relative scarcity of such jobs. The higher the salary and the greater the scarcity, the greater the commuting distance the job will justify. The fact that applicants are willing to relocate for some jobs may also significantly affect the limits of the labor pool. See Johnson v. Goodyear Tire & Rubber Co., 491 F.2d 1364 (5th Cir.1974).

In determining the appropriate comparison population, is there any danger in weighting an area according to the percentage of actual applicants from that area? See, United States v. Pasadena Independent School District, 43 FEP Cases 1319 (S.D.Tex.1987) (discussing difference between "Weighted Applicant Model" and "Gravity Model"). In *Wards Cove Packing,* the large majority of the minority cannery workers lived in Alaska near the cannery locations and, as noted by the dissent, were, by definition, available for seasonal work. In light of these circumstances, is it not a fair assumption that most of those employed in cannery positions who were qualified for noncannery jobs would be "available" for such positions? Could the relevant pool of those available for noncannery positions be determined by giving the percentage of qualified cannery workers substantially more "weight" than the percentage of qualified persons in the general labor market in the Pacific Northwest?

6. As used in *Hazelwood* the standard deviation is a "way to calculate the likelihood that chance is responsible for the difference between a predicted result and an actual result.... Statisticians tend to discard chance as an explanation for a result when deviations from the expected value approach two standard deviations." Payne v. Travenol Laboratories, Inc., 673 F.2d 798, 821 n.32 (5th Cir.), cert. denied, 459 U.S. 1038, 103 S.Ct. 451, 74 L.Ed.2d 605 (1982). Statistical significance also exists where it can be demonstrated that the probability of the discrepancy occurring by chance is no more than one in twenty. This is referred to as significant at the .05 level of significance. See White v. City of San Diego, 605 F.2d 455, 460 (9th Cir.1979). For large samples, the test of two or three standard deviations found by the Supreme Court to constitute sufficient proof of intentional discrimination in *Hazelwood* and in Castaneda v. Partida, 430 U.S. 482, 496–97 n.17, 97 S.Ct. 1272, 1281 n.17, 51 L.Ed.2d 498 (1977) "is essentially equivalent to a rule requiring significance at a level in the range below 0.05 or 0.01." Craik v. Minnesota State University Board, 731 F.2d 465, 476 n.13 (8th Cir.1984) (quoting Baldus & Cole, Statistical Proof of Discrimination, Sec. 9.03 at 297 (1980)). Despite *Hazelwood* and numerous lower court decisions holding that a discrepancy of two standard deviations or more is highly probative of discriminatory intent, courts have refrained from announcing a rule of law with respect to what level of statistical significance automatically gives rise to a rebuttable presumption of discrimination. In Watson v. Fort Worth Bank & Trust, *supra,* 487 U.S. at 994, 108 S.Ct. at 2789, the Supreme Court stated that "we have not suggested that any particular number of 'standard deviations' can determine whether a plaintiff has made out a prima facie case." See also, Palmer v. Schultz, 815 F.2d 84, 92 (D.C.Cir.1987) (noting that the Supreme Court has not established an "exact legal threshold at which statistical evidence, standing alone, establishes an inference of discrimination"); EEOC v. American National Bank, 652 F.2d 1176, 1192 (4th Cir.1981), cert. denied, 459 U.S. 923, 103 S.Ct. 235, 74 L.Ed.2d 186 (1982) ("courts should be extremely cautious in drawing any conclusions from standard deviations in the range of one to three"); Ottaviani v. State University of New York, *infra.* For a critical evaluation by statisticians of the

use of the binomial significance test, see Meier, Sacks and Zabell, What Happened in Hazelwood: Statistics, Employment Discrimination and the 80% Rule, 1984 Am. B. Found. Res. J., 139 (1984).

7. A precondition for use of the binomial distribution theory is the probability that the relevant comparison population has remained unchanged during the period in question. For example, in a hiring case it must be assumed that the applicant pool or the substitute population remains relatively the same over the period being studied. See, Lilly v. Harris–Teeter Supermarket, 720 F.2d 326, 336 n.18 (4th Cir.1983), cert. denied, 466 U.S. 951, 104 S.Ct. 2154, 80 L.Ed.2d 539 (1984). Where the population is constantly changing, however, the binomial theory based on averaged data is inappropriate. See, Arnold v. Postmaster General, 667 F.Supp. 6 (D.D.C.1987), reversed on other grounds, 863 F.2d 994 (D.C. Cir. 1988).

The use of the binomial distribution analysis is appropriate when evaluating whether an observed pattern of events, each with only two possible outcomes, such as the hiring of either a black or white person from the relevant population, is likely to have occurred at random. But many disparate treatment cases involve employment decisions, such as job assignment and wage setting, which have many possible outcomes. Such decisions may also be influenced by multiple factors. In such a case statistical evidence will be introduced to prove the fact and extent of the influence of a prohibited factor on the employment decision. Consider the following case.

OTTAVIANI v. UNIVERSITY OF NEW YORK AT NEW PALTZ

United States Court of Appeals, Second Circuit, 1989.
875 F.2d 365, cert. denied, 493 U.S. 1021, 110 S.Ct. 721, 107 L.Ed.2d 740 (1990).

PIERCE, CIRCUIT JUDGE.

This is an appeal from a judgment of the United States District Court for the Southern District of New York, Kram, J., in which the court found in favor of defendants on all of the Title VII claims asserted by individual faculty members and a class of similarly situated plaintiffs, following a lengthy bench trial. The decision of the district court is published in a thorough and lengthy opinion at 679 F.Supp. 288 (S.D.N.Y.1988).... Appellants contend the district court erred in its decision and principally attack the district court's treatment of the evidence presented in support of their Title VII claims. For the reasons that follow, we affirm.

BACKGROUND

This complicated Title VII suit was commenced by and on behalf of full-time, academic rank female faculty members at the State University of New York ("SUNY") at New Paltz ("the University") who were employed in the University's Division of Liberal Arts and Sciences at any time between academic years 1973 and 1984. The plaintiffs alleged that between 1973 and 1984, the University discriminated against female members of its faculty on the basis of gender in three separate categories: (1) placement in initial faculty rank at the University, (2) promotion into higher rank, and (3) salary. Judge Kram conducted a bench trial which extended over nine months on all of the plaintiffs' claims, and both parties presented extensive evidence to the court. For the sake of brevity, we will discuss only so much of the proceedings below as is relevant to our discussion of the key issues raised on appeal.

During the trial, the district court basically considered two types of evidence—objective statistical evidence and extensive "anecdotal" evidence. The statistical evidence presented by both sides consisted primarily of data produced by means of various "multiple regression analyses." Depending upon the party presenting the statistical evidence, the data was intended to either demonstrate or rebut the plaintiffs' claim of a pattern of ongoing discrimination against women within the University in all three of the contested categories.

A. The Statistical Evidence

Multiple regression analysis is a statistical tool commonly used by social scientists to determine the influence that various independent, predetermined factors (so-called "independent variables") have on an observed phenomenon (the so-called "dependent variable"). See Eastland v. Tennessee Valley Authority, 704 F.2d 613, 621 (11th Cir.1983), cert. denied, 465 U.S. 1066, 104 S.Ct. 1415, 79 L.Ed.2d 741 (1984); Fisher, Multiple Regression in Legal Proceedings, 80 Colum.L.Rev. 702, 705–06 (1980). In disparate treatment cases involving claims of gender discrimination, plaintiffs typically use multiple regression analysis to isolate the influence of gender on employment decisions relating to a particular job or job benefit, such as salary. See, e.g., Sobel v. Yeshiva Univ., 839 F.2d 18, 21–22 (2d Cir.1988); EEOC v. Sears, Roebuck & Co., 839 F.2d 302, 324–25 & n. 22 (7th Cir.1988); Palmer v. Schultz, 259 App. D.C. 246, 815 F.2d 84, 90–91 (D.C. Cir. 1987).

The first step in such a regression analysis is to specify all of the possible "legitimate" (i.e. nondiscriminatory) factors that are likely to significantly affect the dependent variable and which could account for disparities in the treatment of male and female employees. By identifying those legitimate criteria that affect the decision making process, individual plaintiffs can make predictions about what job or job benefits similarly situated employees should ideally receive, and then can measure the difference between the predicted treatment and the actual treatment of those employees. If there is a disparity between the predicted and actual outcomes for female employees, plaintiffs in a disparate treatment case can argue that the net "residual" difference represents the unlawful effect of discriminatory animus on the allocation of jobs or job benefits. D. Baldus & J. Cole, Statistical Proof of Discrimination § 3.2, at 94 (1980); id. § 8.02[1], at 245–46.[2]

---

2. Another way in which statisticians can measure the influence of gender on a particular employment decision is by using gender as one of the independent variables in a regression analysis. For each independent variable in a multiple regression analysis, the statistician calculates a coefficient, which is a measure of the effect that the variable has on the dependent variable being examined. If the regression coefficient for gender is sufficiently large, then it is probative of the impact that gender

In this case, the parties' statistical experts each determined what factors they thought were relevant to the setting of salaries and rank at the University, and used those factors as independent variables in their multiple regression analyses. By accounting for all of the "legitimate" factors that could affect salary and rank in general, the plaintiffs hoped to prove that there was a net "residual" difference or disparity between the predicted and actual salaries and rank of female faculty members that could only be attributed to ongoing gender discrimination within the University. Conversely, the defendants sought to attribute observed disparities in the pay and rank of male versus female faculty members to "legitimate" factors such as unequal job qualifications.

1. Plaintiffs' Proof of Salary Discrimination

a. Plaintiffs' Main Salary Study

The plaintiffs' main salary study was contained in Trial Exhibit 882 and purported to demonstrate the difference in salaries between male and female faculty members at New Paltz. According to the plaintiffs' statistical expert, Dr. Mary Gray, women actually earned from $1,036 to $2,277 less than their predicted salaries in each year of the class period. The defendants challenged these findings on several grounds, but principally attacked the plaintiffs' study for its failure to include certain independent variables which the defendants claimed were influential in the setting of faculty salaries at the University.

The plaintiffs' main salary study incorporated the following independent variables: (1) number of years of full-time teaching experience prior to hire at New Paltz; (2) number of years' teaching experience in academic rank at New Paltz; (3) possession of a doctorate degree; (4) number of years since obtaining the doctorate degree; (5) number of publications; (6) other experience prior to hire at New Paltz; and (7) years of full-time high school teaching experience. The plaintiffs' statistical expert, however, did not include academic rank variables in her main salary study such as prior rank, current rank, and years in current rank. Although Dr. Gray conceded that these three factors may influence salary decisions, she maintained that academic rank itself was subject to discrimination at New Paltz, and that the use of rank variables would therefore be inappropriate.

In connection with this assertion, the plaintiffs attempted to demonstrate that female faculty members were placed in lower academic ranks at New Paltz than their male counterparts, and promoted more slowly into higher academic ranks than their male counterparts, solely because of their gender.[3] The defendants' statistical expert, Dr. Judith Stoikov, responded by attempting to prove that rank at New Paltz was

has on the employment decision at issue. D. Baldus & J. Cole, supra, §§ 8.01 to 8.02[1], at 240–45.

3. There are four types of "academic rank" at New Paltz (1) professor, (2) associate professor, (3) assistant professor, and (4) instructor. Faculty members in one of these academic ranks either hold tenure or are on a "tenure track."

not discriminatory. After considering all the evidence as to rank, the district court rejected plaintiffs' proof as "unpersuasive," and concluded that plaintiffs had "failed to prove that rank at New Paltz was discriminatory." Ottaviani, 679 F.Supp. at 306.

The district court's rejection of plaintiffs' claims as to discrimination in rank at New Paltz had two important consequences for the plaintiffs' case. First, the court's ruling eliminated two of the contested categories of discrimination at New Paltz, and left the salary discrimination claim as plaintiffs' only remaining Title VII claim. Second, and equally important from the plaintiffs' perspective, the court's ruling "validated" academic rank as one of the legitimate factors to consider in accounting for salary disparities between male and female faculty members. Since the court considered the academic rank of faculty members to be a legitimate influencing factor on faculty salaries at New Paltz, and since the plaintiffs' main salary study failed to include academic rank variables, the court found the plaintiffs' principal study to be fundamentally flawed and less probative of discrimination than it otherwise might have been.

b. Plaintiffs' Other Salary Studies

Apart from their main salary study, the plaintiffs had also performed salary regressions which did include rank variables. Since these other studies did include what the court considered to be most of the relevant legitimate factors which could influence salary at New Paltz, the court accordingly looked primarily to these studies to determine whether the plaintiffs had made out a prima facie case of gender discrimination.

After considering and weighing all the evidence presented, the district court reached certain conclusions with respect to both the plaintiffs' and the defendants' statistical evidence. While the district judge found some of the plaintiffs' statistical evidence "persuasive," she thought that it was insufficient to establish a prima facie case of gender discrimination. On the other hand, the district judge did not believe that defendants' statistical evidence was sufficient to rebut the plaintiffs' discrimination claims altogether. Since the judge found the statistical evidence to be inconclusive one way or the other, she ruled that whether or not the plaintiffs could prevail on their discrimination claims would depend upon whether the totality of the evidence adduced at trial supported a finding of discrimination. Accordingly, the district judge next considered whether the extensive anecdotal evidence proffered by plaintiffs supported their claims of discrimination.

B. The Anecdotal Evidence

The anecdotal evidence at trial consisted of various narrative descriptions of events at the University which the plaintiffs contended illustrated or proved that the University had discriminated against its female faculty members. Specifically, the plaintiff class members sought to establish that: (1) the University did not have a viable affirmative action program; (2) New Paltz's methods for identifying and correcting existing salary inequities from 1973 to 1984 were either flawed or non-existent; (3) the University either retrenched or eliminated faculty positions to the detriment of its female faculty members; and (4) the University demonstrated a disdain for women's issues through its handling of the Women's Studies Program at New Paltz. Eleven witnesses also testified about individual instances of alleged salary discrimination at New Paltz, which the plaintiffs contended were illustrative of the administration's policies toward women as a whole.

On rebuttal, the defendants sought to negate the plaintiffs' claims through the specific testimony of University administrators and faculty members, and other types of anecdotal evidence. The defendants contended that such evidence demonstrated that there were nondiscriminatory reasons for all of the actions taken by the University during the period in question which negatively affected its female faculty members, and that none of the employment practices at issue were motivated by discriminatory animus.

After reviewing the anecdotal evidence, the district judge held that the plaintiffs had not proven their Title VII claims against the University. Although she found that the anecdotal evidence supported an inference of prima facie discrimination in a few of the individual class members' cases, in each of those cases she either accepted the defendants' explanations for the pay disparities, or found that the isolated incidents of discrimination were insufficient to support the class' claim of a pattern or practice of gender discrimination. Accordingly, the district court entered judgment in favor of defendants on all of the Title VII claims.

On appeal, the appellants contend that the district court erred in its treatment and analysis of the evidence in several key respects, and that as a result, the court's finding of no discrimination was erroneous. First, appellants challenge the district court's determination that the statistical evidence was inconclusive. Appellants contend that the statistical evidence adduced at trial was more than sufficient to establish a prima facie case of gender discrimination as a matter of law. Moreover, they also contend that the district judge's decision to allow allegedly "tainted" variables such as "rank" to be used in the multiple regression analyses minimized the overall impact of defendants' alleged discriminatory treatment of female faculty members, and resulted in weaker statistical proof. Appellants also take issue with the district court's rejection of the proffered anecdotal evidence of discrimination. Finally, appellants contend that the district court erroneously excluded or ignored evidence of pre-Title VII discrimination, in contravention of the Supreme Court's decision in Bazemore v. Friday, 478 U.S. 385, 92 L.Ed.2d 315, 106 S.Ct. 3000 (1986).

For the reasons that follow, we hold that Judge Kram did not clearly err in finding in favor of the defendants, and we affirm the decision of the district court.

DISCUSSION

We begin by noting that the district court correctly stated the familiar legal standards to be applied in Title VII cases. Since the plaintiff class herein had raised a "disparate treatment" claim under Title VII, the claimants bore the burden of not only establishing discriminatory intent on the part of SUNY administrators, but that "unlawful discrimination [was] a regular procedure or policy followed by [the University]." International Bhd. of Teamsters v. United States; see Coser v. Moore, 739 F.2d 746, 749 (2d Cir.1984) ("In order to prevail on their claim of a pattern and practice of discrimination, plaintiffs had to show by a preponderance of the evidence that [the defendant]'s 'standard operating procedure—the regular rather than the unusual practice' is to discriminate on the basis of sex.") (quoting Teamsters, 431 U.S. at 336).

* * *

A. Significance of Plaintiffs' Statistical Evidence

At trial, the plaintiffs herein contended that the statistical evidence alone was sufficient to establish a prima facie case of discrimination. According to plaintiffs, female faculty members were clearly treated less favorably than their male counterparts, and that unfavorable, disparate treatment was due solely to gender bias. The district court, however, found that the plaintiffs' statistical evidence was not "statistically significant" enough to establish a prima facie case of discrimination. For the reasons that follow, we conclude that the district court did not clearly err in ruling that the plaintiffs' proffered statistical evidence was not dispositive of their Title VII claims.

As discussed earlier, plaintiffs in a disparate treatment case frequently rely on statistical evidence to establish that there is a disparity between the predicted and actual treatment of employees who are members of a disadvantaged group, and to argue that such disparities exist because of an unlawful bias directed against those employees. Not all disparities, however, are probative of discrimination. Before a deviation from a predicted outcome can be considered probative, the deviation must be "statistically significant."

Statistical significance is a measure of the probability that a disparity is simply due to chance, rather than any other identifiable factor. Because random deviations from the norm can always occur, statisticians do not consider slight disparities between predicted and actual results to be statistically significant. As the disparity between predicted and actual results becomes greater, however, it becomes less likely that the deviation is a random fluctuation. When the probability that a disparity is due to chance sinks to a certain threshold level, statisticians can then infer from the statistical evidence, albeit indirectly, that the deviation is attributable to some other cause unrelated to mere chance. See D. Baldus & J. Cole, supra, § 9.42, at 191–93 (Supp.1987).

One unit of measurement used to express the probability that an observed result is merely a random deviation from a predicted result is the "standard deviation." The standard deviation "is a measure of spread, dispersion or variability of a group of numbers." D. Baldus & J. Cole, supra, at 359. Generally, the fewer the number of standard deviations that separate an observed from a predicted result, the more likely it is that any observed disparity between predicted and actual results is not really a "disparity" at all but rather a random fluctuation. Conversely, "[the] greater the number of standard deviations, the less likely it is that chance is the cause of any difference between the expected and observed results." Coates v. Johnson & Johnson, 756 F.2d 524, 536 n. 11 (7th Cir.1985). A finding of two standard deviations corresponds approximately to a one in twenty, or five percent, chance that a disparity is merely a random deviation from the norm, and most social scientists accept two standard deviations as a threshold level of "statistical significance." When the results of a statistical analysis yield levels of statistical significance at or below the 0.05 level, chance explanations for a disparity become suspect, and most statisticians will begin to question the assumptions underlying their predictions.

Cognizant of the important role that statistics play in disparate treatment cases, the Supreme Court has held that "[where] gross statistical disparities can be shown, they alone may in a proper case constitute prima facie proof of a pattern or practice of discrimination." Hazelwood School Dist. v. United States. The threshold question in disparate treatment cases, then, is: "[At] what point is the disparity in selection rates ... sufficiently large, or the probability that chance was the cause sufficiently low, for the numbers alone to establish a legitimate inference of discrimination"? Palmer, 815 F.2d at 92 (emphasis added). In answer to this question, "most courts follow the conventions of social science which set 0.05 as the level of significance below which chance explanations become suspect." D. Baldus & J. Cole, supra, § 9.02, at 291. The existence of a 0.05 level of statistical significance indicates that it is fairly unlikely that an observed disparity is due to chance, and it can provide indirect support for the proposition that disparate results are intentional rather than random.[6] By no means, however, is a five percent probability of chance (or approximately two standard deviations) considered an "exact legal threshold." Palmer, 815 F.2d at 92.

In the present case, the three salary studies which the district court considered most probative of a pattern or practice of discrimination produced a range of standard deviations between approximately

---

6. The commentators are careful to point out, however, that no matter how great the number of standard deviations is, statistical tests can never entirely rule out the possibility that chance caused the disparity. See Palmer, 815 F.2d at 91; D. Baldus & J. Cole, supra, § 9.42, at 191–93 (Supp. 1987).

one and five, and of the total thirty-three standard deviation measures cited, twenty-four exceeded two standard deviations.[7]   Significantly, however, nine of the measures cited fell below two standard deviations. Also, the negative residuals associated with being female were not significant in every year of the liability period.

Given the range of standard deviations associated with their salary regressions, the plaintiffs contended that the statistical evidence clearly gave rise to a presumption of discrimination.   As discussed earlier herein, however, although the district judge found the studies to be "persuasive," she nevertheless held that these levels of "statistical significance" alone were "not sufficiently high to support a prima facie claim of salary discrimination."   Ottaviani, 679 F.Supp. at 309.

On appeal, appellants argue inter alia that, as a matter of law, a finding of two standard deviations should be equated with a prima facie case of discrimination.   According to appellants, the district court therefore erred in finding that they had not met their burden of establishing a prima facie case.   In support of this argument, appellants point out that several courts have accepted two standard deviations as prima facie proof of discrimination.   See, e.g., Berger v. Iron Workers Reinforced Rodmen Local 201, 843 F.2d 1395, 1412 (D.C. Cir. 1988) ("if the likelihood that a fluctuation from expected results occurred by chance is five percent or less, a statistically significant difference is proved, and a prima facie case of discrimination is established"); Eldredge v. Carpenters 46 N. Cal. Counties JATC, 833 F.2d 1334, 1340 n. 8 (9th Cir.1987) (.045 level of statistical significance (approximately two standard deviations or 1 chance in 22) sufficient to give rise to an inference that discriminatory system rather than chance is responsible for women's lower admission rates to apprenticeship program), cert. denied, 108 S.Ct. 2857 (1988); Dalley v. Michigan Blue Cross/Blue Shield, Inc., 612 F.Supp. 1444, 1451 n. 18 (E.D.Mich.1985) ("Most courts and commentators have accepted the .05 level," or 1 in 20 probability, as indicative of statistical significance).   While appellants' argument that a finding of two standard deviations should be equated with a prima facie case of discrimination under Title VII is not without initial appeal, we are constrained to reject such a formal "litmus" test for assessing the legitimacy of Title VII claims.

It is certainly true that a finding of two to three standard deviations can be highly probative of discriminatory treatment.   As tempting as it might be to announce a black letter rule of law, however, recent Supreme Court pronouncements instruct that there simply is no minimum threshold level of statistical significance which mandates a

---

7. As discussed supra, two standard deviations corresponds roughly to a 1 in 20 chance that the outcome is a random fluctuation. Three standard deviations corresponds to approximately a 1 in 384 chance of randomness. Finally, a range of four to five standard deviations corresponds to a probability range of 1 chance in 15,786 to 1 chance in 1,742,160. M. Abramowia & I. Steigan, Handbook of Mathematical Functions, National Bureau of Standards, U.S. Government Printing Office, Applied Mathematics Series No. 55 (1966) (Tables 26.1, 26.2).

finding that Title VII plaintiffs have made out a prima facie case. See, e.g., Watson v. Fort Worth Bank & Trust, 487 U.S. 977, 108 S.Ct. 2777, 2789 n. 3, 101 L.Ed.2d 827 (1988) ("We have emphasized the useful role that statistical methods can have in Title VII cases, but we have not suggested that any particular number of 'standard deviations' can determine whether a plaintiff has made out a prima facie case in the complex area of employment discrimination."); see also Palmer, 815 F.2d at 92 (noting that Supreme Court has not established "an exact legal threshold at which statistical evidence, standing alone, establishes an inference of discrimination"); Coser v. Moore, 739 F.2d at 754 n. 3 (a significance level of 5% probability of chance "has no talismanic importance"); EEOC v. American Nat'l Bank, 652 F.2d 1176, 1192 (4th Cir.1981) ("courts of law should be extremely cautious in drawing any conclusions from standard deviations in the range of one to three"), cert. denied, 459 U.S. 923, 103 S.Ct. 235, 74 L.Ed.2d 186 (1982); D. Baldus & J. Cole, supra, § 9.4, at 188–89 (Supp. 1987) (courts should use tests of statistical significance only as "an aid to interpretation" and not as a "rule of law"). Accordingly, in accordance with Supreme Court pronouncements, we must reject appellants' suggestion that this court announce a rule of law with respect to what level of statistical significance automatically gives rise to a rebuttable presumption of discrimination.

* * *

The net import of Judge Kram's rulings regarding the significance of plaintiffs' statistical evidence is that she found the evidence to be "persuasive" but not dispositive. Contrary to appellants' assertions, it is clear from the district judge's rulings that she did not simply ignore the statistical evidence of discrimination presented by plaintiffs. The court found this evidence sufficient to cause her to deny the defendants' motion to dismiss at the end of plaintiffs' case, and to accept rebuttal evidence from the defendants. On rebuttal, however, the defendants were able to successfully undermine the plaintiffs' case by attacking the validity of the plaintiffs' statistical evidence, and by introducing statistical evidence of their own to negate the inference of discrimination that had been raised. Cf. Berger, 843 F.2d at 1416 ("Mere conjecture or general assertions of inadequacies in the opponent's statistical case, without demonstrating their effect on the results, will not suffice.").

Specifically, the defendants criticized the plaintiffs' most probative studies for excluding one factor which they claimed exerted a "highly significant positive influence[ ] on current salary," namely, whether a faculty member had held a prior, full-time administrative position at SUNY New Paltz before returning to full-time teaching. The defendants also criticized these studies because the salary regressions were "fitted" only to male faculty members, i.e., they used independent variables that were derived only from the male population. The district court noted in its opinion that a "males only regression" based exclusively on values existing only in the male population might have tended to overestimate the predicted salaries of certain female faculty members, because it might not have taken into account legitimate factors existing solely in the female population which could have affected the rate of pay for women teachers at the University.   See Ottaviani, 679 F.Supp. at 307.   If the predicted salary for a female faculty member was overestimated, this type of regression arguably would have overestimated the discrepancies between male and female salaries at the University.   Finally, the defendants criticized these studies because they inappropriately aggregated Instructors and Assistant Professors into a single "rank."   The defendants pointed out at trial that when the two ranks were combined into a single rank, the predicted salary of a female Instructor would essentially be based on the higher salary of an Assistant Professor, and hence the net residual difference between the predicted and actual salary of a female Instructor would be overstated.   Apart from these criticisms of plaintiffs' statistical evidence, the defendants also offered persuasive anecdotal evidence to negate the plaintiffs' claims of discriminatory animus. After considering all of the evidence presented, both statistical and anecdotal, the district court simply found that plaintiffs had failed to preponderate on their claims.

Recent Supreme Court precedent has made it clear that this court can reverse such a factual determination "only if it is clearly erroneous in light of all the evidence in the record or if it rests on legal error." Palmer, 815 F.2d at 101 (citing, inter alia, Bazemore, 478 U.S. 385, 106 S.Ct. 3000).   Especially in cases where statistical evidence is involved, " 'great deference is due the district court's determination of whether the resultant numbers are sufficiently probative of the ultimate fact in issue.' " EEOC v. Sears, Roebuck & Co., 839 F.2d at 310 (citation omitted).   As the Supreme Court cautioned in the Teamsters case, "statistics are not irrefutable; they come in infinite variety and, like any other kind of evidence, they may be rebutted.   In short, their usefulness depends on all of the surrounding facts and circumstances." 431 U.S. at 340, 97 S.Ct. at 1857.   The district judge herein gave due consideration to all of the evidence presented, and after reviewing the record, we do not perceive a convincing basis for finding her interpretation of that evidence to be clearly erroneous.   Accordingly, we affirm her rulings with respect to the statistical evidence presented.

B.   Use of Rank Variables

In conjunction with their attack on the district court's assessment of the sufficiency of plaintiffs' statistical evidence, appellants also challenge the district court's determination that "rank" was an appropriate factor to consider in assessing pay disparities between male and female faculty members.   According to appellants, if the court had rejected the rank variables and considered only those salary studies which excluded rank, then the number of standard deviations associated with their findings of discrimination would have been much greater, and their statistical proof would have been even more probative.

Although we recognize that the use of rank variables in testing for salary discrimination against women faculty members is not universally accepted, see Finkelstein, The Judicial Reception of Multiple Regression Studies in Race and Sex Discrimination Cases, 80 Colum.L.Rev. 737, 741–42 (1980); D. Baldus & J. Cole, supra, § 8.23, at 113–14 (Supp.1987), in Sobel v. Yeshiva University, this court specifically upheld the use of rank variables in a multiple regression analysis, stating that rank could be used as a legitimate factor in explaining pay disparities so long as rank itself was clearly not tainted by discrimination. As the plaintiffs' statistical expert, Dr. Mary Gray, explained in her own report: "In a bias-free system, one could use rank as a measure of productivity since the review process for promotion or hire should evaluate teaching, scholarship and service." (Emphasis added). See D. Baldus & J. Cole, supra, § 8.2, at 114. The question to be resolved, then, in cases involving the use of academic rank factors, is whether rank is tainted by discrimination at the particular institution charged with violating Title VII. Although appellants reiterate on appeal their claim that rank at New Paltz was tainted, it is clear that the district judge accepted and considered evidence from the parties on both sides of this issue, and that she rejected the plaintiffs' contentions on this point.

At trial, the plaintiffs failed to adduce any significant statistical evidence of discrimination as to rank. As the district court stated in its opinion, the plaintiffs' studies of rank, rank at hire, and waiting time for promotion "were mere compilations of data" which neither accounted for important factors relevant to assignment of rank and promotion, "nor demonstrated that observed differences were statistically significant." Ottaviani, 679 F.Supp. at 306. The defendants, on the other hand, offered persuasive objective evidence to demonstrate that there was no discrimination in either placement into initial rank or promotion at New Paltz between 1973 and 1984, and the district court chose to credit the defendants' evidence. Upon review of the record, we cannot state that the court's rulings in this regard were clearly erroneous. Accordingly, the district court's decision to focus primarily on those studies which included rank as an essential independent variable was not improper, and appellants' contentions to the contrary must be rejected. See Presseisen v. Swarthmore College, 442 F.Supp. 593, 614, 619 (E.D.Pa.1977) (inclusion of rank variable appropriate when evidence showed no discrimination with respect to hiring and promotion), aff'd mem., 582 F.2d 1275 (3d Cir.1978); see also EEOC v. Sears, Roebuck & Co., 839 F.2d at 327 (court's decision to focus generally on those regression analyses which did not omit "major factors" was proper); Rossini v. Ogilvy & Mather, Inc., 798 F.2d 590, 603–04 (2d Cir.1986) (trial court's reliance on studies which incorporated controversial variables not clearly erroneous, where court's decision came after "extensive testimony from experts on both sides of the issue").

C. Anecdotal Evidence

Appellants also contend on appeal that the district court did not give sufficient weight to the anecdotal evidence adduced at trial, and that the court should have rejected the explanations proffered by University administrators to explain pay and rank inequities as "pretextual." Our review of the anecdotal evidence, however, is limited to ascertaining whether the district judge committed clear error in making her findings. See Anderson v. City of Bessemer, 470 U.S. 564, 573, 105 S.Ct. 1504, 1511, 84 L.Ed.2d 518 (1985); Pullman–Standard v. Swint, 456 U.S. 273, 287, 102 S.Ct. 1781, 1789, 72 L.Ed.2d 66 (1982). It is not the function of this court to reweigh the evidence anew, particularly when findings by a district court are based on in-court credibility determinations. Rather, under the clearly erroneous standard, we may only reject findings by the trial court when we are left with the "definite and firm conviction that a mistake has been committed." United States v. United States Gypsum Co., 333 U.S. 364, 395, 68 S.Ct. 525, 542, 92 L.Ed.2d 746 (1948).

In this case, the district court found that the defendants had successfully rebutted the plaintiffs' anecdotal proof, and that, in any event, the anecdotal evidence on its face was too limited to prove class-wide discrimination. After reviewing the entire record, we do not think that the court's decision to credit the testimony of the defendants rather than that of the plaintiffs was clearly erroneous. Since the district court's "account of the evidence is plausible in light of the record viewed in its entirety," we may not overturn the findings of the court even if we might "have weighed the evidence differently," had we been sitting as the trier of fact. Accordingly, we affirm the findings of the district court with respect to the anecdotal evidence presented.

D. Bazemore Claim

In Bazemore v. Friday, 478 U.S. 385, 106 S.Ct. 3000, 92 L.Ed.2d 315 (1986), the Supreme Court held that employers have an obligation to eradicate employment discrimination that began prior to the effective date of Title VII (1972), if the discrimination continues into the post–1972 liability period. The Supreme Court also stated that statistical evidence of pre-Act discrimination can be probative of ongoing, post-Act discrimination.

On appeal, appellants contend that the district court erroneously excluded evidence of pre-Act discrimination in violation of the Supreme Court's dictates in Bazemore. In particular, appellants claim that the district judge improperly excluded Exhibit 990, which purported to document statistically significant evidence of discrimination as to initial faculty rank. This claim is without merit, however. At trial, the defendants objected to the admission of Exhibit 990 not because it was offered to prove pre-Act discrimination, but because it was unreliable and incomplete. While the weakness of statistical evidence should not ordinarily preclude its admission, see Bazemore, 478 U.S. at 400, the Supreme Court has recognized that some statistical evidence may be so unreliable as to be irrelevant, see id. at 400 n. 10; see also Penk v. Oregon State Bd. of Higher Educ., 816 F.2d 458, 465 (9th Cir.) ("Bazemore ... does not give blanket approval to the introduction of all evidence derived from multiple regression analyses."), cert. denied, 484 U.S. 853, 108 S.Ct. 158, 98 L.Ed.2d 113 (1987). Apparently the district judge herein thought that to be the case with respect to this particular exhibit, because she sustained the defendants' objection to its admission on the grounds that it was irrelevant and unduly confusing. Upon review of the record, we do not find the district court's decision to exclude the study to be clearly erroneous, and therefore we affirm the evidentiary ruling.

Moreover, we note that appellant's reliance on this court's decision in Sobel v. Yeshiva University as support for their more generalized, Bazemore-type claims is misplaced. In Sobel, the plaintiffs introduced evidence specifically designed to prove that women were discriminated against prior to the effective date of Title VII, and argued that "Yeshiva had a legal obligation to equalize women's salaries immediately upon application of Title VII to universities." 839 F.2d at 27. In the present case, even though the Supreme Court handed down its decision in Bazemore the same month that plaintiffs' trial was commenced, the plaintiffs did not introduce any statistical evidence of substance to prove that there was discrimination at New Paltz prior to the effective date of Title VII. Instead, nearly all of the plaintiffs' studies focused on the class liability period, which covered the years 1973 to 1984. This is in marked contrast to Sobel and Bazemore, wherein the plaintiffs offered direct, independent proof of pre-Act discrimination. Accordingly, we find appellants' arguments on this point generally to be without merit.

CONCLUSION

In sum, the burden of persuasion was on the plaintiffs to prove by a preponderance of the evidence that there was a pattern or practice of discrimination at SUNY New Paltz, and they failed to meet that burden. We have considered all of the arguments presented on appeal, and find them to be without merit. For the reasons stated above, the judgment of the district court is affirmed.

NOTES AND PROBLEMS FOR DISCUSSION

1. The function of multiple regression analysis of the kind used in *Ottaviani* has been described as follows:

> [O]ne might describe multiple regression as a method used to extract a systematic signal from the noise prescribed by data. There are two primary problems involved in extracting such a signal. First, it is typically the case that the factor whose influence one wishes to test or measure is not the only major factor affecting the dependent variable. * * * Second, even if one can somehow account for the effects of the other important systematic factors, there typically remain chance components.

* * *

> In multiple regression one first specifies the major variables that are believed to influence the dependent variable. * * * There inevitably remain minor influences, each one perhaps small, but creating in combination a non-negligible effect. These minor influences are treated by placing them in what is called a random disturbance term and assuming that their joint effect is not systematically related to the effects of the major variables being investigated—in other words by treating their effects as due to chance. Obviously, it is very desirable to have the random part of the relationships small, particularly relative to the systematic part. Indeed, the size of the random part provides an indication of how correctly one has judged what the systematic part is. Multiple regression thus provides a means not only for extracting the systematic effects from the data but also for assessing how well one has succeeded in doing so in the presence of the remaining random effects.
>
> The relationship between the dependent variable and the independent variable of interest is then estimated by extracting the effects of the other major variables (the systematic part). When this has been done, one has the best available substitute for controlled experimentation. The results of multiple regressions can be read as showing the effects of each variable on the dependent variable, holding the others constant. Moreover, those results allow one to make statements about the probability that the effect described has merely been observed as a result of chance fluctuation.

Fisher, Multiple Regression in Legal Proceedings, 80 Colum.L.Rev. 702, 705–06 (1980). See also, Finkelstein, The Judicial Reception of Multiple Regression Studies in Race and Sex Discrimination Cases, 80 Colum.L.Rev. 737 (1980). What did the plaintiffs in *Ottaviani* believe were the "major variables" affecting faculty salaries? Why did the plaintiffs seek to convince the court that faculty rank should not be considered in determining whether gender had influenced salary decisions?

In BAZEMORE v. FRIDAY, 478 U.S. 385, 106 S.Ct. 3000, 92 L.Ed.2d 315 (1986), the decision relied on by the plaintiffs in *Ottaviani* for their pre-Title VII discrimination claim, resulted from a suit challenging class wide racial discrimination against black state agricultural agents, the plaintiffs relied in large part on regression analyses to demonstrate that black agents were paid less than similarly situated whites. During discovery defendants asserted that the salaries of agricultural agents were determined by four factors: education, tenure, job title and performance. Plaintiffs' regression analyses used four independent variables—race, education, tenure and job title. Both the district court and the Court of Appeals rejected the regression analyses as evidence of discrimination because they did not include "all measurable variables thought to have an effect on salary level." The Supreme Court reversed.

> The [Court of Appeals's] view of the evidentiary value of the regression analyses was plainly incorrect. While the omission of variables from a regression analysis may render the analysis less probative than it otherwise might be, it can hardly be said, absent some other infirmity, that an analysis which accounts for the major factors "must be considered unacceptable as evidence of discrimination." Normally, failure to include variables will affect the analysis' a, not its admissibility.
>
> Importantly, it is clear that a regression analysis that includes less than "all measurable variables" may serve to prove a plaintiff's case. A plaintiff in a Title VII suit need not prove discrimination with scientific

certainty; rather, his or her burden is to prove discrimination by a preponderance of the evidence.

478 U.S. at 400, 106 S.Ct. at 3009. In light of their discovery, what reason would the plaintiffs in *Bazemore* have for *not* including "job performance" as an independent variable in their statistical analysis? See also, EEOC v. General Telephone Co. of Northwest, Inc., 885 F.2d 575, 582 (9th Cir.1989), cert. denied, ___ U.S. ___, 111 S.Ct. 370, 112 L.Ed.2d 332 (1990) (failure of regression analysis to account for gender-based differences in career interests between men and women did not alone defeat showing of discrimination, but did render analysis less precise).

2. Most pattern and practice cases are proved by a combination of statistical evidence and "anecdotal" testimony of the named plaintiffs or class members about specific instances of discrimination. Such testimony may "[bring] the cold numbers convincingly to life." *Teamsters*, supra, 431 U.S. at 339, 97 S.Ct. at 1856. Courts have demonstrated a marked reluctance to find intentional discrimination solely on the basis of statistical evidence. See, EEOC v. Sears, Roebuck & Co., 839 F.2d 302 (7th Cir.1988) (noting that one of the basic problems with the plaintiff's case was the failure to bring forward any supporting testimony by individual victims of discrimination.) See also Griffin v. Board of Regents, 795 F.2d 1281 (7th Cir.1986) (while examples of individual discrimination are not always required in class action, the lack of such proof reinforces the doubt arising from questions about the validity of the statistical significance). Compare Catlett v. Missouri Highway & Transportation Com'n, 828 F.2d 1260 (8th Cir.1987), cert. denied, 485 U.S. 1021, 108 S.Ct. 1574, 99 L.Ed.2d 889 (1988) (anecdotal evidence revealed numerous instances suggesting that the department was not receptive to idea of female maintenance workers; this evidence confirmed plaintiff's statistical case).

3. The fact that statistical proof by itself would not support a finding of pattern-and-practice discrimination does not, of course, mean that it has no probative value in an individual disparate treatment case. In MacDissi v. Valmont Industries, Inc., 856 F.2d 1054 (8th Cir.1988) the district court found that the plaintiff had been discharged because of his age in part on the basis of evidence that the two oldest employees in a small department had been terminated at the same time. On appeal the company attacked the finding of age discrimination on the ground that the plaintiff's department was too small a universe for the terminations to create a reliable inference of discrimination. The court of appeals rejected the argument and explained:

> Valmont argues vigorously that inferences of discrimination cannot be reliably drawn from two discharges in a nine-member department, citing several cases in which statistics based on workplaces of up to 50 employees have been rejected as insignificant. Taken to its logical conclusion, Valmont's position is that plaintiffs employed in smaller workplaces can never use statistics to establish a circumstantial case of discrimination, since the size of the workplace precludes any pattern observed in the data from proving intentional discrimination to a statistical certainty. This approach would unjustifiably deny employees in smaller workplaces the protection of federal discrimination law * * *. There is no minimum sample size prescribed either in federal law or in statistical theory: the adequacy of numerical comparisons within small sets of data depends on the degree of certainty the factfinder requires, as well as the type of inference the statistics are meant to demonstrate. * * * MacDissi provides independent,

direct grounds for disbelieving Valmont's explanations for his layoff, and so his quantitative evidence does not need to reach the degree of certainty required of plaintiffs who present no proof of discrimination besides a statistical pattern.

856 F.2d at 1058.

4.   The increasing complexity of statistical cases has led to expressions of judicial concern over the burden placed on the statistically unsophisticated court and of fear that such evidence may actually be infringing on the judicial function.

Excursions into the new and sometimes arcane corners of different disciplines is a familiar task of American trial lawyers and its generalist judges. But more is afoot here, and this court is uncomfortable with its implications. This concern has grown with the realization that the a of econometrics and statistics which both parties have required this court to judge have a centripetal dynamic of their own. They push from the outside roles of tools for "judicial" decisions toward the core of decision making itself. Stated more concretely: the precision-like mesh of numbers tends to make fits of social problems when I intuitively doubt such fits. I remain wary of the siren call of the numerical display and hope that here the resistance was adequate; that the ultimate findings are the product of judgment, not calculation.

* * *

I write this unusual conclusion to this unusual opinion to make plain that this court did not select a numbers field for this contest but instead has been forced to judge a fight, there fought.

To place the court's findings in perspective, an additional observation is required. Despite their recent recognition, the econometric techniques employed in this case are not discrimination CAT scanners—ready to detect alien discrimination in corporate bodies. It may reveal shadows but its resolution is seldom more precise.

Ultimately the findings of fact here are not numerical products and sums but a human judgment that the facts found are more likely true than not true. With that standard, stripped to essentials, and within the decisional limits placed upon me by higher courts, this is what I think happened, approximately.

Vuyanich v. Republic National Bank of Dallas, 505 F.Supp. 224, 394 (N.D.Tex. 1980), vacated on other grounds, 723 F.2d 1195 (5th Cir.) (*en banc*), cert. denied, 469 U.S. 1073, 105 S.Ct. 567, 83 L.Ed.2d 507 (1984).

SECTION E.   RETALIATION

The preceding sections in this chapter have examined the way in which the courts have interpreted the broad language comprising Title VII's general proscription against discrimination in employment. The statute, however, also prohibits another, more specifically described form of job bias. Section 704(a) states:

"It shall be an unlawful employment practice for an employer to discriminate against any of his employees or applicants for employment, for an employment agency, or joint labor-management committee controlling apprenticeship or other training * * * to discriminate against any individual, or for a labor organization to discriminate against any member thereof or applicant for membership, because he has opposed any practice made an unlawful employment practice by this title, or because he has made a charge, testified, assisted, or participated in any manner in an investigation, proceeding or hearing under this title."

PAYNE v. McLEMORE'S WHOLESALE & RETAIL STORES

United States Court of Appeals, Fifth Circuit, 1981.
654 F.2d 1130, cert. denied, 455 U.S. 1000, 102 S.Ct. 1630, 71 L.Ed.2d 866 (1982).

SAM D. JOHNSON, CIRCUIT JUDGE:

This is a Title VII action alleging that in early 1971, defendant McLemore's Wholesale & Retail Stores, Inc. failed to rehire plaintiff Charles Payne because of his participation in activities protected by section 704(a) of the Civil Rights Act of 1964. The district court concluded that plaintiff successfully carried his ultimate burden of proving discrimination. The district court found that plaintiff established a prima facie case of discrimination under section 704(a) by showing that the employer's failure to rehire plaintiff was caused by plaintiff's participation in boycott and picketing activities in opposition to an unlawful employment practice of the defendant. In addition, the district court found that plaintiff proved that the employer's proffered explanation for its failure to rehire the plaintiff—that plaintiff failed to reapply for a job with the employer—was merely pretextual. Because the finding of retaliatory discrimination is supported by requisite subsidiary facts, we affirm the district court judgment for the plaintiff.

During the period of time in which the actions challenged by plaintiff took place, McLemore's Wholesale & Retail Stores was a commercial partnership whose * * * operations included McLemore Wholesale Grocery, McLemore Jitney Jungle (a retail grocery operation), McLemore Farm Store (a light hardware, sporting goods, western wear, feed, seed, fertilizer, and chemical sales store), and Big M. Mobile Homes (a retail mobile home outlet). McLemore's Wholesale & Retail Stores, Inc., a Louisiana corporation, was incorporated August 26, 1975. In 1976, when this lawsuit was filed, the operation of McLemore's Wholesale & Retail Stores, Inc. had not changed significantly from the time it was a partnership; it continued to maintain the same operations that it had for the past several years. * * *

* * * Plaintiff originally worked in McLemore's fertilizer plant. The operation of the plant was seasonal in nature since the demand for fertilizer was dependent upon the farmers' planting seasons. During the first two years of plaintiff's employment with defendant, he was laid off for three months each year during the seasonal decline in work. In later years, during the off-season plaintiff was not laid off, but was

instead shifted to positions in other parts of the defendant's operations.
* * *

In November 1970, plaintiff was once again laid off due to the seasonal business decline. Two other black employees and two white employees were laid off at the same time. About a month later, plaintiff became involved in the formation and organization of the Franklin Parish Improvement Organization, a non-profit civil rights organization. * * * The organization was interested in improving social conditions of blacks in Franklin Parish, and it focused especially on the need to get blacks hired in retail stores in money-handling and supervisory positions in order to improve the treatment that blacks received while shopping in stores. Shortly after its formation, the members of the organization decided to boycott several retail business-es, including those of defendant * * *. Plaintiff organized and imple-mented the boycott and was actively involved in picketing McLemore's Jitney Jungle Food Stores. Defendant knew of plaintiff's involvement in the boycott and picketing. Moreover, the boycott and picketing were effective and defendant's business suffered as a result.

In previous years when he had been laid off, plaintiff had always gone back to work for defendant when the work picked back up. In the year of the boycott, however, he was not recalled or rehired.[3] * * *

On June 17, 1976, plaintiff filed this action in federal district court alleging that defendant's failure to rehire plaintiff was a result of plaintiff's race and his civil rights activity. In its answer, McLemore's denied that it had committed any discriminatory actions, and asserted that the reason the plaintiff was not rehired was because he failed to reapply for a position with McLemore's after he was laid off. The district court held that plaintiff did reapply for his job, but that he was not rehired because of his participation in boycotting and picketing activities. The court further found that participation in the boycott and picketing was protected activity under section 704(a) of Title VII; in other words, the district court concluded that the boycott and picketing were in opposition to an unlawful employment practice of the defendant. The court awarded plaintiff back pay, costs, and attorney's fees totalling $16,260.90.

The opposition clause of section 704(a) of Title VII provides protec-tion against retaliation for employees who oppose unlawful employ-ment practices committed by an employer. (Section 704(a) also con-tains a participation clause that protects employees against retaliation for their participation in the procedures established by Title VII to

---

3. Of the four other employees who were laid off at the same time as plaintiff, only one was rehired—a black employee who was not involved in the boycott or picketing by the Franklin Parish Improve-ment Organization. Both plaintiff and Russell Brass (the other black employee who was laid off and not rehired) were involved in the boycott and picketing. Ac-cording to defendant, the employee who was rehired was the only one of the five employees who were laid off that reapplied for a job.

enforce its provisions. The participation clause is not involved in this lawsuit.) * * *

In this case, plaintiff contends that he was not rehired in retaliation for his boycott and picketing activities which were, according to plaintiff, in opposition to unlawful employment practices committed by McLemore's. Plaintiff asserted that the unlawful employment practices his boycott and picketing activities were intended to protest were McLemore's discrimination against blacks in hiring and promotion—specifically, McLemore's failure to employ blacks in money-handling, clerking, or supervisory positions. In demonstrating his contentions at trial, plaintiff had the initial burden of establishing a prima facie case of discrimination. McDonnell Douglas Corp. v. Green. The burden then shifted to the defendant to articulate a legitimate, nondiscriminatory reason for the failure to rehire the plaintiff. Finally, if the defendant carried his burden, the plaintiff was entitled to an opportunity to show that the defendant's stated reason for its failure to rehire plaintiff was in fact pretextual.

"To establish a prima facie case under [section 704(a)] the plaintiff must establish (1) statutorily protected expression, (2) an adverse employment action, and (3) a causal link between the protected expression and the adverse action." Smalley v. City of Eatonville, 640 F.2d 765, 769 (5th Cir.1981). The first element of the prima facie case—statutorily protected expression—requires conduct by the plaintiff that is in opposition to an unlawful employment practice of the defendant. Thus, for the plaintiff to prove that he engaged in statutorily protected expression, he must show that the boycott and picketing activity in which he participated was in opposition to conduct by McLemore's that was made unlawful by Title VII. According to the plaintiff, the purpose of the boycott and picketing was to oppose McLemore's discrimination against blacks in hiring and promotion. * * * [T]here is substantial evidence to support the district court finding that the purpose of the boycott and picketing was to oppose defendant's discrimination against blacks in certain employment opportunities [7]—an unlawful employment practice under section 703(a)(1).

Defendant argues, however, that plaintiff failed to establish his prima facie case because he failed to *prove* that defendant had committed any unlawful employment practices. Plaintiff responds that he was not required to *prove* the actual existence of those unlawful employ-

---

7. Defendant claims that plaintiff did not engage in the boycott and picketing to oppose unlawful employment practices of McLemore's. Instead, it is McLemore's contention that the boycott and picketing were conducted to publicize the issues of integration of public facilities and common courtesy to blacks. To support this allegation, defendant points to the incident that initiated the formation of the Franklin Parish Improvement Organization—two black children being turned away from the town's segregated public swimming pool. * * * Although the Improvement Organization was, in part, occasioned by the position of blacks in Winnsboro in general, and although the boycott and picketing may have been to some extent a protest of this position, the district court's conclusion that the boycott and picketing activity was in opposition to unlawful employment practices of McLemore's is supported by substantial evidence.

ment practices; instead, he asserts that it was sufficient to establish a prima facie case if he had a *reasonable belief* that defendant had engaged in the unlawful employment practices. We agree with plaintiff and conclude that it was not fatal to plaintiff's section 704(a) case that he failed to prove, under the *McDonnell Douglas* criteria for proving an unlawful employment practice under section 703(a)(1), that McLemore's discriminated against blacks in retail store employment opportunities.

The Ninth Circuit was apparently the first appellate court to decide whether the opposition clause of section 704(a) required proof of actual discrimination. Sias v. City Demonstration Agency, 588 F.2d 692 (9th Cir.1978). In *Sias*, the plaintiff alleged that he was discharged by the City Demonstration Agency (an agency of the City of Los Angeles) in retaliation for his opposition to acts of racial discrimination by the City of Los Angeles. The City did not deny that plaintiff "was discharged for writing a letter of grievance to the Regional Administrator of the Department of Housing and Urban Development (HUD). Rather, it contend[ed] that, inasmuch as the trial court made no finding of actual discrimination, it [could not] be held to have violated" section 704(a). The Ninth Circuit concluded that "[s]uch a narrow interpretation * * * would not only chill the legitimate assertion of employee rights under Title VII but would tend to force employees to file formal charges rather than seek conciliation or informal adjustment of grievances." The *Sias* court quoted extensively from Hearth v. Metropolitan Transit Commission, 436 F.Supp. 685 (D.Minn.1977), which held that "as long as the employee had a reasonable belief that what was being opposed constituted discrimination under Title VII, the claim of retaliation does not hinge upon a showing that the employer was in fact in violation of Title VII." The *Hearth* court went on to state:

> But this Court believes that appropriate informal opposition to perceived discrimination must not be chilled by the fear of retaliatory action in the event the alleged wrongdoing does not exist. It should not be necessary for an employee to resort immediately to the EEOC or similar State agencies in order to bring complaints of discrimination to the attention of the employer with some measure of protection. The resolution of such charges without governmental prodding should be encouraged.

> The statutory language does not compel a contrary result. The elimination of discrimination in employment is the purpose behind Title VII and the statute is entitled to a liberal interpretation. When an employee reasonably believes that discrimination exists, opposition thereto is opposition to an employment practice made unlawful by Title VII even if the employee turns out to be mistaken as to the facts.

The Seventh Circuit has also adopted this position. Berg v. La Crosse Cooler Co., 612 F.2d 1041 (7th Cir.1980). In *Berg*, the plaintiff was discharged when she challenged her employer's failure to provide pregnancy benefits as sex-based discrimination. After she was fired, the United States Supreme Court ruled that a disability benefits plan does not violate Title VII because of its failure to cover pregnancy related disabilities. The Seventh Circuit held that where the employee opposed a practice that she reasonably believed was an unlawful employment practice under Title VII, her opposition was protected from retaliatory discharge even where the practice was later determined not be an unlawful employment practice. The court concluded that to interpret the opposition clause to require proof of an actual unlawful employment practice undermines Title VII's central purpose, the elimination of employment discrimination by informal means; destroys one of the chief means of achieving that purpose, the frank and nondisruptive exchange of ideas between employers and employees; and serves no redeeming statutory or policy purposes of its own. Section 2000e–3(a) plays a central role in effectuating these objectives. By protecting employees from retaliation, it is designed to encourage employees to call to their employers' attention discriminatory practices of which the employer may be unaware or which might result in protracted litigation to determine their legality if they are not voluntarily changed.

The Fifth Circuit has not heretofore directly addressed the issue whether proof of an actual unlawful employment practice is necessary under the opposition clause, or whether an employee is protected from retaliation under the opposition clause if the employee reasonably believes that the employer is engaged in unlawful employment practices. To the extent that earlier Fifth Circuit cases provide guidance to this Court, however, they indicate that the reasonable belief test of the Seventh and Ninth Circuits comports with the decisions of this Circuit and the policies underlying Title VII. In Pettway v. American Cast Iron Pipe Co., 411 F.2d 998 (5th Cir.1969), this Court held that an employee was protected by the participation clause of section 704(a) from discharge in retaliation for filing a charge with the EEOC, regardless of the truth or falsity of the contents of the charge. The Court stated that:

> There can be no doubt about the purpose of § 704(a). In unmistakable language it is to protect the employee who utilizes the tools provided by Congress to protect his rights. The Act will be frustrated if the employer may unilaterally determine the truth or falsity of charges and take independent action.

Thus, the Court held that where the communication with the EEOC satisfied the requirements of a "charge," the charging party could not be discharged for the writing and the court could not "either sustain any employer disciplinary action or deny relief because of the presence of * * * malicious material." Id. at 1007.[9]

---

9. Although this Court considers the reasoning of the *Pettway* decision to support the reasonable belief test in opposition clause cases, at least one district court has viewed the *Pettway* case quite differently. The district court in EEOC v. C & D

The Ninth Circuit recognized that the "considerations controlling the interpretation of the opposition clause are not entirely the same as those applying to the participation clause," and that the opposition clause "serves a more limited purpose" than does the participation clause. However, interpreting the opposition clause to require proof of an actual unlawful employment practice would "chill the legitimate assertion of employee rights under Title VII," just as surely as would interpreting the participation clause to require a truthful charge. On the other hand, interpreting the opposition clause to protect an employee who reasonably believes that discrimination exists "is consistent with a liberal construction of Title VII to implement the Congressional purpose of eliminating discrimination in employment."

* * *

To effectuate the policies of Title VII and to avoid the chilling effect that would otherwise arise, we are compelled to conclude that a plaintiff can establish a prima facie case of retaliatory discharge under the opposition clause of section 704(a) if he shows that he had a reasonable belief that the employer was engaged in unlawful employment practices.[11] While the district court made no explicit finding that

Sportswear Corp., 398 F.Supp. 300 (M.D.Ga.1975), held that "baseless accusations" were protected "only as a means of protecting access to the Commission." Thus, that court concluded that the result in *Pettway* was limited to actions under the participation clause, and did not apply to actions under the opposition clause. The *C & D Sportswear* court held:

> Accordingly, the only reasonable interpretation to be placed on Section 704(a) is that where accusations are made in the context of charges before the EEOC, the truth or falsity of that accusation is a matter to be determined by the EEOC, and thereafter by the courts. However, where accusations are made outside the procedures set forth by Congress that accusation is made at the accuser's peril. In order to be protected, it must be established that the accusation is well-founded. If it is, there is, in fact, an unlawful employment practice and he has the right, protected by Section 704(a), to oppose it. However, where there is no underlying unlawful employment practice the employee has no right to make that accusation in derogation of the procedures provided by statute.

Id. at 306. We find the reasoning of the *C & D Sportswear* district court unpersuasive and the result unjustifiably restrictive. In *C & D Sportswear*, an employee called the president of the company a racist and was discharged for making that accusation. The district court reasoned that

access to the EEOC must be protected. On the other hand, accusations of racism ought not to be made lightly. Unfounded accusations might well incite racism where none had previously existed. Were employees free to make unfounded accusations of racism against their employers and fellow employees, racial discord, disruption, and disharmony would likely ensue. This would be wholly contrary to Congress' intention that race be removed, as far as possible, as an issue in employment.

While unfounded, inflammatory accusations of racism might, on balance, be found to provide the employer with a legitimate, nondiscriminatory reason for discharging an employee, this would neither require nor suggest that all unfounded accusations should be totally unprotected by the opposition clause of section 704(a). It is as important to protect an employee's right to oppose perceived discrimination by appropriate, informal means as it is to protect his right of access to the EEOC. An employee who engages in opposition activity should not be required to act at his own peril if it turns out that no unlawful employment practice actually exists, as long as the employee holds a reasonable belief that the unlawful employment practices do exist.

11. The First Circuit has adopted a somewhat different test than have the Seventh and Ninth Circuits. The First Circuit has not explicitly decided whether a sec-

plaintiff's opposition was based upon a reasonable belief that McLemore's hiring and promotional policies violated Title VII, such a finding is implicit and is sufficiently supported by evidence in the record. Thus, plaintiff established that he reasonably believed that defendant McLemore's discriminated against blacks in employment opportunities. Moreover, plaintiff showed that his boycott and picketing activities were in opposition to this unlawful employment practice. Defendant's failure to rehire the plaintiff was undoubtedly an adverse employment action. Finally, there was evidence to support an inference that defendant's failure to rehire plaintiff was causally related to plaintiff's boycott and picketing activities.[13] Thus, plaintiff successfully established a prima facie case, thereby raising an inference of unlawful discrimination under section 704(a). The burden then shifted to the defendant to "rebut the presumption of discrimination by producing evidence" of a legitimate, nondiscriminatory reason for its failure to rehire plaintiff.

Defendant McLemore's steadfastly maintained at trial that the *only* reason plaintiff was not rehired was because he failed to reapply for a position with defendant. This comprised the full and complete extent of the rebuttal evidence presented by the agents of the defendant in an effort to articulate a legitimate, nondiscriminatory reason for the failure to rehire the plaintiff. * * *

* * * This reason—the failure to reapply—would, if believed, be legally sufficient to justify a judgment for the defendant. Thus, the defendant carried its rebuttal burden at trial.

After the defendant has an opportunity to rebut plaintiff's prima facie case, the plaintiff has a corresponding opportunity to show that the defendant's proffered explanation was in fact pretextual. Here, plaintiff presented substantial evidence that he did reapply for a job with McLemore's. The trial court found "as a fact that Mr. Payne did reapply for his position with the defendant corporation." There is,

---

tion 704(a) plaintiff must "demonstrate that he harbored a 'reasonable belief' of discriminatory employer behavior" or whether the plaintiff must show that he harbored a " 'conscientiously held belief' of such misconduct." Monteiro v. Poole Silver Co., 615 F.2d 4, 8 (1st Cir.1980) (footnote omitted). The *Monteiro* court found that "[u]nder either standard—the employer's conduct being non-discriminatory in fact—the plaintiff must show that his so-called opposition was in response to some *honestly held*, if mistaken, feeling that discriminatory practices existed." Id. (emphasis added) (footnote omitted). Thus, according to that court, if a reasonable person might have believed that the employer was engaged in unlawful employment practices, but the plaintiff actually did not in good faith hold such a belief, then the plaintiff's opposition conduct is unprotect-

ed. We need not decide here whether it is necessary to adopt a good faith requirement in addition to the reasonable belief requirement since, in the case before this Court, the plaintiff believed—reasonably and in good faith—that McLemore's was engaged in unlawful employment practices, and plaintiff's opposition conduct was in response to this belief.

13. An inference that defendant's failure to rehire the plaintiff was caused by plaintiff's participation in the boycott and picketing activity was proper in view of the existence of evidence that the employer was aware of the plaintiff's activities and that, within a relatively short time after those activities took place, the adverse employment consequence occurred. The defendant was then entitled to an opportunity to introduce evidence to rebut this inference.

therefore, substantial evidence in the record to support the district court's conclusion that the defendant's explanation for its failure to rehire the plaintiff was merely pretextual. The district court further found that members of McLemore's knew of plaintiff's participation in the boycott and picketing, and that there was a causal relationship between defendant's failure to rehire plaintiff and plaintiff's participation in the protest activity. There is also substantial evidence in the record to support the district court's conclusion in this regard. Thus, on the facts and arguments presented to the trial court, that court correctly held that the defendant's failure to rehire the plaintiff violated section 704(a); that is, that the defendant's stated reason for not rehiring the plaintiff (the plaintiff's failure to reapply for a job) was merely pretextual and that the defendant's actual reason for not rehiring the plaintiff was the plaintiff's participation in activities in opposition to unlawful employment practices of the defendant.

Now on appeal, for the first time, defendant contends that even if plaintiff's activity was in opposition to unlawful employment practices of defendant, plaintiff's actions were not protected by section 704(a) because the *form* of plaintiff's opposition was not covered by the statute. It is well-established that not all activity in opposition to unlawful employment practices is protected by section 704(a). Certain conduct—for example, illegal acts of opposition or unreasonably hostile or aggressive conduct—may provide a legitimate, independent, and nondiscriminatory basis for an employee's discharge. "There may arise instances where the employee's conduct in protest of an unlawful employment practice so interferes with the performance of his job that it renders him ineffective in the position for which he was employed. In such a case, his conduct, or form of opposition, is not covered by § 704(a)." Rosser v. Laborers' International Union, Local 438, 616 F.2d 221, 223 (5th Cir.1980), cert. denied, 449 U.S. 886, 101 S.Ct. 241, 66 L.Ed.2d 112. In order to determine when such a situation exists, the court must engage in a balancing test: "[T]he courts have required that the employee conduct be reasonable in light of the circumstances, and have held that 'the employer's right to run his business must be balanced against the rights of the employee to express his grievances and promote his own welfare.'" Jefferies v. Harris County Community Action Association, 615 F.2d 1025, 1036 (5th Cir.1980).

It appears that a number of cases have assumed that it is part of defendant's rebuttal burden to show that the form of plaintiff's opposition was unprotected by the statute. If the defendant took an adverse employment action against the plaintiff because of opposition conduct by the plaintiff that was outside the protection of the statute, then the defendant may have had a legitimate, nondiscriminatory reason to justify its actions. Thus, in the case before this Court, if the *form* of plaintiff's activities placed them outside the protection of section 704(a), then the defendant may have had a legitimate, nondiscriminatory reason for its failure to rehire the plaintiff. However, if the form of plaintiff's activities was the nondiscriminatory reason for the defendant's failure to rehire the plaintiff, it was the defendant's responsibility to introduce evidence to that effect at trial.   * * *

In Gonzalez v. Bolger, 486 F.Supp. 595 (D.D.C.1980), the plaintiff, a former post office employee, brought an employment discrimination suit pursuant to section 704(a) alleging that he was discharged unlawfully in retaliation for his exercise of rights protected by Title VII. The district court made the following findings:

> At trial, plaintiff presented a *prima facie* case of retaliatory discrimination, by showing that he engaged in protected activities, that his employer was aware of the protected activities, and that he was subsequently discharged, within a relatively short time interval after his performance of the activities. This series of events is sufficient to enable a court to infer retaliatory motivation, absent further explanation from the employer.   * * *

> * * *

> In rebuttal, however, defendant presented substantial proof, through testimony and documentary exhibits, that plaintiff's insubordination and disruptive outbursts were in fact the cause for his termination. These reasons, if accepted on the proof as a whole, would constitute a valid non-discriminatory explanation for defendant's action.

Since the court further found that plaintiff failed to establish that defendant's proffered justification was in fact pretextual, the court concluded that "[b]ecause plaintiff exceeded the limits of reasonable opposition activity on a continuing basis and his dismissal is attributable to these transgressions, the Court is forced to conclude that his termination was not pretextual, but rather was for valid non-discriminatory reasons." The *Gonzalez* court clearly placed the burden on defendant to show as part of its rebuttal burden, that the "plaintiff's excessive conduct was the cause for his termination."

* * *

It therefore becomes apparent that in the instant case, after plaintiff established his prima facie case, it was the responsibility of the defendant to show that the *form* of plaintiff's activities placed them outside the protection of section 704(a) and provided defendant with a legitimate reason for its failure to rehire the plaintiff. If the defendant intended to rely upon this contention, it was the defendant's responsibility to raise the issue at trial. Here, the defendant failed to offer *any* evidence at trial that its legitimate and nondiscriminatory reason for not rehiring the plaintiff was that plaintiff had engaged in hostile, unprotected activity that was detrimental to the employer's interests.[14]

14. * * * The only contention made by the defendant that the conduct of the plaintiff was not protected by section 704(a) was that the boycott and picketing were not in opposition to an unlawful employment practice of the defendant and so did not satisfy the requirements of section 704(a). * * * While defendant did allege that plaintiff's activity was not in opposition to an unlawful employment practice of

With respect to the defendant's burden of rebutting plaintiff's prima facie case, the *Burdine* Court stated that: "An articulation not admitted into evidence will not suffice. Thus, the defendant cannot meet its burden merely through an answer to the complaint or by argument of counsel." If the defendant cannot meet its rebuttal burden by answer to the complaint or by argument of counsel at trial, the defendant undoubtedly cannot meet its rebuttal burden solely by argument of counsel for the first time *on appeal*. It is not permissible for this Court to relate the defendant's arguments on appeal back to the time of trial in order to determine whether defendant met its rebuttal burden at trial. Since the defendant failed to present *any* evidence at trial that the egregious and disruptive form of plaintiff's opposition constituted the legitimate reason for defendant's failure to rehire plaintiff, the defendant surely did not carry its rebuttal burden on this issue at trial.

* * *

[The court then refused to make its own determination as to whether the form of the plaintiff's activities provided the defendant with a legitimate, nondiscriminatory reason for not rehiring the plaintiff.]

* * * Since plaintiff made out his prima facie case of discrimination under section 704(a), and since the only explanation offered by the defendant for its failure to rehire plaintiff was correctly determined to be pretextual, the judgment of the district court for plaintiff is

Affirmed.

COLEMAN, CIRCUIT JUDGE, dissenting.

* * *

The gravamen of my concern is found in the concession of the majority opinion that "The Fifth Circuit has not heretofore directly addressed the issue whether proof of an actual unlawful employment practice is necessary under the opposition clause, or whether an employee is protected from retaliation under the opposition clause if the employee reasonably believes that the employer is engaged in unlawful employment practices".

The majority then proceeds to hold that reasonable belief is enough.

* * *

The statute speaks in terms of practices—not what someone "reasonably believes" to have been a practice when, in fact, the practice did not exist. I cannot believe that Congress intended (since it did not say so) to penalize employers for what an employee or applicant "believes"

McLemore's, defendant did *not* assert that   the scope of section 704(a).
the form of plaintiff's activity was outside

when, in fact, the employer is innocent. To hold otherwise is to deprive employers of their property rights in violation of the due process clause.

Finally, I dissent because, as the majority concedes, the District Court made no finding [the majority adds the word "explicit"] that the plaintiff's opposition was based upon "reasonable belief". In proceeding to make its own, inferential, findings of fact the majority cites not a single specific fact that would support a finding of reasonable belief. * * *

I respectfully dissent.

NOTES AND PROBLEMS FOR DISCUSSION

1. As *Payne* indicates, § 704(a) offers protection from retaliation directed at two types of conduct: "participation" in the formal Title VII enforcement process and informal "opposition" to a proscribed employment practice. Most of the cases arising under this section raise one or more of the following four interpretative questions: (a) whether the plaintiff's activities constitute participation or opposition; (b) the extent to which an employee should be immunized from retaliation when that participation or opposition is premised on a factually or legally erroneous belief that the employer is engaged in unlawful conduct; (c) whether the nature or form of the plaintiff's conduct removes it from the protection of the statute; and (d) whether the defendant's response constitutes retaliation. In many cases, (including *Payne*) of course, there also is an important factual dispute as to the causal connection between the plaintiff's conduct and the defendant's response. Where causation is at issue, what is the impact, if any, of the treatment accorded "mixed motive" cases by recently added § 703(m) of Title VII? Is it significant that this provision does not explicitly refer to retaliation claims? Does this suggest that the statutory reversal of *Price Waterhouse* mixed motive analysis does not apply to § 704 claims? Wouldn't that depend on whether the employer offered an alternative nondiscriminatory explanation for its conduct? Suppose the defendant's position is that the form of the plaintiff's conduct takes her out of the protection of § 704. Is this a nondiscriminatory explanation for the action or a justification for the retaliation that is in the nature of an affirmative defense? Did the court in *Payne* mean to say that the defendant bears the risk of nonpersuasion on this issue when it stated that "it is part of defendant's rebuttal burden to show that the form of plaintiff's opposition was unprotected by the statute"? Yet, in the following sentence, the court stated that "if the defendant took an adverse employment action against the plaintiff because of opposition conduct by the plaintiff that was outside the protection of the statute, then the defendant may have had a legitimate, nondiscriminatory reason to justify its actions."

In light of all of the above-mentioned issues, consider the following:

(a) Jane Leston, an electrical engineer with Chicago Industries, Inc., was denied a promotion to department supervisor in favor of her colleague, Bill Thomas. Shortly thereafter, Ms. Leston filed a sex discrimination charge under Illinois law with the appropriate Illinois administrative agency. When the company learned of Leston's charge, it asked Mr. Thomas to sign an affidavit prepared by the company to aid in its defense. Thomas refused and was demoted one week later. Can Thomas state a claim under § 704(a)? See Smith v. Columbus Metropolitan Housing Authority, 443 F.Supp. 61 (S.D.Ohio

1977). Suppose that Leston's charge had alleged that she was denied the promotion because of her age. If the company terminated Leston after she filed that age discrimination claim, could she challenge the discharge under § 704(a)? See Learned v. City of Bellevue, 860 F.2d 928 (9th Cir.1988); Hicks v. ABT Associates, Inc., 572 F.2d 960 (3d Cir.1978).

(b) Karlen Construction, Inc. was awarded a contract by the federal government to help build a post office. The contract contained an affirmative action plan requiring Karlen to employ a specified percentage of minority workers. In the middle of construction, the company concluded that it could not afford to retain all four of the electricians it had hired for the post office project. To maintain compliance with the affirmative action plan, Karlen chose to lay off its three white electricians and retain its one black electrician. One of the laid off electricians, Fred Hill, circulated a letter around the site charging Karlen with racial discrimination in connection with the lay off of electricians. One month later, when its economic condition improved, Karlen rehired all of the laid off electricians, except for Hill. Hill subsequently filed a Title VII action alleging that Karlen's refusal to rehire him violated § 704(a). The trial court ruled in favor of the defendant, holding that the company's original decision to lay off the three white electricians and retain the black electrician did not violate Title VII and, therefore, that Hill's conduct after being laid off was not protected by § 704. How should the appellate court rule on Hill's appeal? See Sisco v. J. S. Alberici Construction Co., Inc., 655 F.2d 146 (8th Cir.1981), cert. denied, 455 U.S. 976, 102 S.Ct. 1485, 71 L.Ed.2d 688 (1982).

Was the issue raised by this problem addressed by the court in *Payne*? Should the courts distinguish between mistakes of fact and law? Compare Parker v. Baltimore & Ohio Railroad Co., 652 F.2d 1012 (D.C.Cir. 1981) and Berg v. La Crosse Cooler Co., 612 F.2d 1041 (7th Cir.1980) with Winsey v. Pace College, 394 F.Supp. 1324 (S.D.N.Y.1975).

In *Payne*, the court implied that persons engaged in participation enjoy a somewhat more expansive immunity than individuals engaged in opposition activities. Is such a distinction supported by any statutory language or policy consideration? See EEOC v. C & D Sportswear Corp., 398 F.Supp. 300 (M.D.Ga. 1975).

(c) Williams Steelworks, Inc. (W.S.I.), as a federal government contractor, was obliged to develop an affirmative action program and appoint one of its executives as director of the firm's equal opportunity programs. As equal opportunity director, Richard Kane was required to design the company's affirmative action programs and monitor their effectiveness. According to Kane, the company evidenced a lack of commitment to its equal opportunity obligation by continually ignoring his reports that detailed management's failure to accomplish the reforms outlined in the affirmative action programs. This ultimately led to Kane's filing a complaint against W.S.I. with the federal agency authorized to audit government contract compliance. When notified of the filing of this charge, the company asked Kane if he knew the identity of the charging party. He denied knowledge of this fact and continued to conceal his role as charging party while actively participating with the federal agency's investigation of his charge. During this period Kane also organized a clandestine meeting of minority employees to solicit complaints of discrimination. When W.S.I. learned of Kane's involvement with the federal investigation, Kane was fired. He subsequently brought suit against W.S.I. under § 704. What result? See Jennings v. Tinley Park Community Consol. School Dist. No.

146, 796 F.2d 962 (7th Cir.1986), cert. denied, 481 U.S. 1017, 107 S.Ct. 1895, 95 L.Ed.2d 502 (1987); Jones v. Flagship Intern., 793 F.2d 714 (5th Cir.1986), cert. denied, 479 U.S. 1065, 107 S.Ct. 952, 93 L.Ed.2d 1001 (1987); Holden v. Owens–Illinois, Inc., 793 F.2d 745 (6th Cir.1986); E.E.O.C. v. Crown Zellerbach Corp., 720 F.2d 1008 (9th Cir.1983). What if Kane also had filed a charge against W.S.I. with the EEOC before his discharge? See Gonzalez v. Bolger, 486 F.Supp. 595 (D.D.C.1980), affirmed, 656 F.2d 899 (D.C.Cir. 1981).

(d) Irish Pleshette filed a sex discrimination charge with the EEOC against her employer, Heavenly Foods, Inc., on March 16, 1976. She filed another charge on August 20, 1978. In both instances, the EEOC found no reasonable cause to believe discrimination had occurred and dismissed the charge. After EEOC dismissal of the second charge, Pleshette filed a Title VII action in federal court. The trial court granted the defendant's motion for summary judgment on March 16, 1980. Ms. Pleshette was discharged on April 30, 1980. Ms. Pleshette applied for a job with Consolidated Containers, Inc. on May 1, 1980. On May 5, 1980, John Newman, President of Heavenly Foods, refused Ms. Pleshette's request for a letter of recommendation. On May 8, 1980, Mr. Newman sent a letter to the Personnel Director of Consolidated, stating that Ms. Pleshette had filed charges of sex discrimination with the EEOC on two separate occasions, that both charges had been dismissed by the EEOC after lengthy investigations and that Ms. Pleshette had unsuccessfully pursued one of these claims in federal district court. Ms. Pleshette subsequently filed a second action against Heavenly Foods alleging that Newman's refusal to provide a letter of recommendation, and his sending of an unsolicited letter to Consolidated Containers violated § 704(a). What result? See § 701(f); Sherman v. Burke Contracting, Inc., 891 F.2d 1527 (11th Cir.1990); Pantchenko v. C. B. Dolge Co., 581 F.2d 1052 (2d Cir.1978); Rutherford v. American Bank of Commerce, 565 F.2d 1162 (10th Cir.1977). What if the letter had been solicited by Consolidated? See Czarnowski v. Desoto, Inc., 518 F.Supp. 1252 (N.D.Ill. 1981). Does Ms. Pleshette have a claim against Consolidated if she does not obtain a position with them? Would she have to prove that she would have been hired had Heavenly not sent the letter, or is it enough that she prove that she was eliminated from consideration because of the information in the letter? See Ruggles v. California Polytechnic State University, 797 F.2d 782 (9th Cir.1986).

(e) Suppose an employee successfully challenges the employer's promotion policies by filing a Title VII claim which results in a trial court judgment ordering the employer to promote the plaintiff. After complying with the court's order, the employer makes a public announcement that he is being forced to promote the plaintiff even though he believes that she is unqualified. Can she successfully bring a § 704 claim? See Jordan v. Wilson, 851 F.2d 1290 (11th Cir.1988).

For a further discussion of these issues, see Walterscheid, A Question Of Retaliation: Opposition Conduct As Protected Expression Under Title VII Of The Civil Rights Act of 1964, 29 B.C.L.Rev. 391 (1988); Kattan, Employee Opposition to Discriminatory Employment Practices: Protection From Reprisal Under Title VII, 19 Wm. & Mary L.Rev. 217 (1977).

2. Lou Bernstein and his daughter, Judy, worked for Martinez Paper Co. After the company denied Ms. Bernstein's application for a promotion, she filed a charge with the EEOC alleging that the denial of the promotion was based exclusively on her sex. Shortly after receiving notice of this charge, the

company discharged Mr. Bernstein. Can he state a cause of action under § 704? See Clark v. R. J. Reynolds Tobacco Co., 27 FEP Cases 1628 (E.D.La. 1982).

3. Is an employer prohibited by § 704(a) from bringing a defamation suit against an employee who prosecutes a nonmeritorious Title VII claim? Would the institution of such an action violate § 704(a)? What if the defamation suit was commenced in response to a letter sent by the employee to a local newspaper charging that the employer was a racist? While several courts have suggested, in dictum, that § 704 would not preclude a defamation action, see e.g., Noel v. McCain, 538 F.2d 633, 636 (4th Cir.1976) (opposition case); Pettway v. American Cast Iron Pipe Co., 411 F.2d 998, 1008 n. 22 (5th Cir.1969) (participation case); and Bartulica v. Paculdo, 411 F.Supp. 392, 397 n. 3 (W.D.Mo.1976) (opposition case), in the two cases in which this issue was directly addressed, the courts held that defamation suits instituted for retaliatory purposes would violate § 704. See EEOC v. Levi Strauss & Co., 515 F.Supp. 640 (N.D.Ill.1981); EEOC v. Virginia Carolina Veneer Corp., 495 F.Supp. 775 (W.D.Va.1980), appeal dismissed, 652 F.2d 380 (4th Cir.1981). The court in *Levi Strauss*, however, noted that a good faith suit brought to attempt to rehabilitate the employer's reputation would not be proscribed by § 704. Similarly, in Proulx v. Citibank, N.A., 659 F.Supp. 972 (S.D.N.Y.1987), the court held that while § 704(a) immunizes an employee from retaliation for filing a malicious charge that facially falls within the statute, the employer may sue the employee for defamation.

Is there an alternative to defamation actions for employers who believe they have been improperly subjected to Title VII litigation? Instead of filing a defamation action, the employer in HUDSON v. MOORE BUSINESS FORMS, INC., 836 F.2d 1156 (9th Cir.1987), filed a counterclaim in the employee's Title VII action in which it sought $200,000 in compensatory and $4 million in punitive damages, costs and attorneys' fees. In its counterclaim, the company alleged that it was entitled to tort damages because the plaintiff had breached the implied covenant of good faith and fair dealing between her and the company, as well as her duty of loyalty, by deliberately refusing the company's offer to transfer in order to initiate the instant case for wrongful termination. The trial court dismissed the counterclaim as wholly frivolous and brought for the purpose of intimidating the plaintiff into dropping her suit. It also awarded sanctions under Federal Rule of Civil Procedure 11 against the company's lawyers in the amount of almost $15,000, the plaintiff's costs in litigating the counterclaim. On appeal, the Ninth Circuit ruled that the company's counterclaim was not wholly without merit but, rather, was an "attempt to expand a developing area of the law". At the same time, however, the court of appeals found no justification for the amount of the compensatory and punitive damage claims. Accordingly, it remanded the case to the trial court for review of the sanction award.

A somewhat more novel remedy was sought and received by the defendants in Becker v. Sherwin Williams, 717 F.Supp. 288 (D.N.J.1989). There, the trial court found that the plaintiff had filed 321 groundless charges of discrimination against this defendant over the past eight or nine years in an effort to extort some settlement and that the vast majority of these charges had been dismissed by the EEOC upon its finding of no reasonable cause to believe that discrimination had occurred. (The court noted that processing these claims had cost the EEOC approximately $250,000.) To prevent "further abuse of the federal court system" by the plaintiff, the court granted the defendants' request for an order permanently enjoining the plaintiff from submitting further employment applications with the defendant employer, from filing age discrimination complaints against the employer in any governmental agency or tribunal without permission of court, from filing any new employment discrimination charge with any office of the defendant EEOC or state or local fair employment practice agency without a supporting affidavit containing specific information regarding the facts supporting a charge of discrimination and from filing any lawsuit against the EEOC in any federal or state court without a supporting affidavit and without notifying that court of this permanent injunction.

4. When Title VII was amended in 1972, a new provision, § 717, was enacted to extend the statutory guarantee of equal employment opportunity to federal employees. Does the absence in § 717 of any language pertaining to retaliation suggest that federal employees are not protected against retaliation? See Canino v. E.E.O.C., 707 F.2d 468 (11th Cir.1983); Smith v. Secretary of Navy, 659 F.2d 1113 (D.C. Cir. 1981); Porter v. Adams, 639 F.2d 273 (5th Cir.1981); Ayon v. Sampson, 547 F.2d 446 (9th Cir.1976).

Chapter 3

THE PROHIBITED CLASSIFICATIONS: SPECIAL PROBLEMS

As noted in Chapter 1, Title VII was intended to proscribe a wide range of discriminatory employment practices. Congress intentionally drafted the provisions that define the covered employment institutions and decisions in broad and general terms. Nevertheless, Title VII, in one important respect, is a statute of limited application. It prohibits discrimination on the basis of five specifically enumerated classifications—race, color, sex, religion and national origin. Consequently, the courts have ruled, allegations of bias based on any other classification do not state a claim under this statute. On the other hand, however, keep in mind that the availability of disproportionate impact-based claims serves to expand the universe of practices perceived as discriminating on the basis of the enumerated categories. The materials in this chapter will examine several interpretative questions concerning the five statutory classifications.

SECTION A. RELIGION AND THE DUTY TO ACCOMMODATE

Title VII is the only federal statute that explicitly prohibits employment discrimination on the basis of religion. Section 701(j) defines religion as including "all aspects of religious observance and practice, as well as belief * * *." While the statute does not set out the limits of these general terms, the federal courts have uniformly adopted the interpretation given to the religious exemption provision of the selective service statutes by the Supreme Court in two conscientious objector cases, Welsh v. United States, 398 U.S. 333, 90 S.Ct. 1792, 26 L.Ed.2d 308 (1970); and United States v. Seeger, 380 U.S. 163, 85 S.Ct. 850, 13 L.Ed.2d 733 (1965). Accordingly, a plaintiff need only prove (1) that his belief is "religious" in his own scheme of things [a]; and (2) that it is sincerely held.

The statutory definition of religion was added to the Act by the 1972 amendments to Title VII. This new enactment, § 701(j), contains

---

[a] In *Welsh*, this was held to include moral or ethical beliefs which occupy the role of religion in an individual's life. Political or social ideologies, on the other hand, have been held to fall outside the limits of Title VII protected religious belief. See Bellamy v. Mason's Stores, Inc., 368 F.Supp. 1025 (W.D.Va.1973), affirmed on other grounds, 508 F.2d 504 (4th Cir.1974) (racist and antisemitic philosophy espoused by Ku Klux Klan does not constitute religion). Atheism, however, does fit within the statutory definition of religion. Young v. Southwestern Savings & Loan Association, 509 F.2d 140 (5th Cir.1975).

another provision which has been the subject of most of the controversy and litigation in the area of religious discrimination in employment.

TRANS WORLD AIRLINES, INC. v. HARDISON

Supreme Court of the United States, 1977.
432 U.S. 63, 97 S.Ct. 2264, 53 L.Ed.2d 113.

MR. JUSTICE WHITE delivered the opinion of the Court.

Section 703(a)(1) of the Civil Rights Act of 1964, makes it an unlawful employment practice for an employer to discriminate against an employee or a prospective employee on the basis of his or her religion. At the time of the events involved here, a guideline of the Equal Employment Opportunity Commission (EEOC), required, as the Act itself now does, that an employer, short of "undue hardship," make "reasonable accommodations" to the religious needs of its employees. The issue in this case is the extent of the employer's obligation under Title VII to accommodate an employee whose religious beliefs prohibit him from working on Saturdays.

I

Petitioner Trans World Airlines (TWA) operates a large maintenance and overhaul base in Kansas City, Mo. On June 5, 1967, respondent Larry G. Hardison was hired by TWA to work as a clerk in the Stores Department at its Kansas City base. Because of its essential role in the Kansas City operation, the Stores Department must operate 24 hours per day, 365 days per year, and whenever an employee's job in that department is not filled, an employee must be shifted from another department, or a supervisor must cover the job, even if the work in other areas may suffer.

Hardison, like other employees at the Kansas City base, was subject to a seniority system contained in a collective-bargaining agreement that TWA maintains with petitioner International Association of Machinists and Aerospace Workers (IAM). The seniority system is implemented by the union steward through a system of bidding by employees for particular shift assignments as they become available. The most senior employees have first choice for job and shift assignments, and the most junior employees are required to work when the union steward is unable to find enough people willing to work at a particular time or in a particular job to fill TWA's needs.

In the spring of 1968 Hardison began to study the religion known as the Worldwide Church of God. One of the tenets of that religion is that one must observe the Sabbath by refraining from performing any work from sunset on Friday until sunset on Saturday. The religion also proscribes work on certain specified religious holidays.

When Hardison informed Everett Kussman, the manager of the Stores Department, of his religious conviction regarding observance of the Sabbath, Kussman agreed that the union steward should seek a job swap for Hardison or a change of days off; that Hardison would have his religious holidays off whenever possible if Hardison agreed to work the traditional holidays when asked; and that Kussman would try to find Hardison another job that would be more compatible with his religious beliefs. The problem was temporarily solved when Hardison transferred to the 11 p. m.–7 a. m. shift. Working this shift permitted Hardison to observe his Sabbath.

The problem soon reappeared when Hardison bid for and received a transfer from Building 1, where he had been employed, to Building 2, where he would work the day shift. The two buildings had entirely separate seniority lists; and while in Building 1 Hardison had sufficient seniority to observe the Sabbath regularly, he was second from the bottom on the Building 2 seniority list.

In Building 2 Hardison was asked to work Saturdays when a fellow employee went on vacation. TWA agreed to permit the union to seek a change of work assignments for Hardison, but the union was not willing to violate the seniority provisions set out in the collective-bargaining contract, and Hardison had insufficient seniority to bid for a shift having Saturdays off.

A proposal that Hardison work only four days a week was rejected by the company. Hardison's job was essential, and on weekends he was the only available person on his shift to perform it. To leave the position empty would have impaired supply shop functions, which were critical to airline operations; to fill Hardison's position with a supervisor or an employee from another area would simply have undermanned another operation; and to employ someone not regularly assigned to work Saturdays would have required TWA to pay premium wages.

When an accommodation was not reached, Hardison refused to report for work on Saturdays. A transfer to the twilight shift proved unavailing since that schedule still required Hardison to work past sundown on Fridays. After a hearing, Hardison was discharged on grounds of insubordination for refusing to work during his designated shift.

Hardison, having first invoked the administrative remedy provided by Title VII, brought this action for injunctive relief in the United States District Court * * *, claiming that his discharge by TWA constituted religious discrimination in violation of Title VII. * * * Hardison's claim of religious discrimination rested on 1967 EEOC guidelines requiring employers "to make reasonable accommodations to the religious needs of employees" whenever such accommodation would not work an "undue hardship," and on similar language adopted by Congress in the 1972 amendments to Title VII.

After a bench trial, the District Court ruled in favor of the defendants. * * * [T]he District Court rejected at the outset TWA's contention that requiring it in any way to accommodate the religious needs of its employees would constitute an unconstitutional establishment of religion. As the District Court construed the Act, however, TWA had satisfied its "reasonable accommodations" obligation, and any further accommodation would have worked an undue hardship on the company.

The Court of Appeals for the Eighth Circuit reversed the judgment for TWA. It agreed with the District Court's constitutional ruling, but held that TWA had not satisfied its duty to accommodate.   * * *

In * * * [its] petition for certiorari TWA * * * contended that adequate steps had been taken to accommodate Hardison's religious observances and that to construe the statute to require further efforts at accommodation would create an establishment of religion contrary to the First Amendment of the Constitution. TWA also contended that the Court of Appeals improperly ignored the District Court's findings of fact.

* * * Because we agree with petitioner that * * * [its] conduct was not a violation of Title VII, we need not reach the other questions presented.

II

The Court of Appeals found that TWA had committed an unlawful employment practice under § 703(a)(1) of the Act * * *. The emphasis of both the language and the legislative history of the statute is on eliminating discrimination in employment; similarly situated employees are not to be treated differently solely because they differ with respect to race, color, religion, sex, or national origin. This is true regardless of whether the discrimination is directed against majorities or minorities.

The prohibition against religious discrimination soon raised the question of whether it was impermissible under § 703(a)(1) to discharge or refuse to hire a person who for religious reasons refused to work during the employer's normal workweek. In 1966 an EEOC guideline dealing with this problem declared that an employer had an obligation under the statute "to accommodate to the reasonable religious needs of employees * * * where such accommodation can be made without serious inconvenience to the conduct of the business."

In 1967 the EEOC amended its guidelines to require employers "to make reasonable accommodations to the religious needs of employees and prospective employees where such accommodations can be made without undue hardship on the conduct of the employer's business." The EEOC did not suggest what sort of accommodations are "reasonable" or when hardship to an employer becomes "undue."

This question—the extent of the required accommodation—remained unsettled when this Court, in Dewey v. Reynolds Metals Co., 402 U.S. 689, 91 S.Ct. 2186, 29 L.Ed.2d 267 (1971), affirmed by an equally divided Court the Sixth Circuit's decision. This discharge of an employee who for religious reasons had refused to work on Sundays was there held by the Court of Appeals not to be an unlawful employment practice because the manner in which the employer allocated Sunday work assignments was discriminatory in neither its purpose nor effect; and consistent with the 1967 EEOC guidelines, the employer had made a reasonable accommodation of the employee's beliefs by giving him the opportunity to secure a replacement for his Sunday work.

In part "to resolve by legislation" some of the issues raised in *Dewey*, Congress included the following definition of religion in its 1972 amendments to Title VII:

> "The term 'religion' includes all aspects of religious observance and practice, as well as belief, unless an employer demonstrates that he is unable to reasonably accommodate to an employee's or prospective employee's religious observance or practice without undue hardship on the conduct of the employer's business." § 701(j).

The intent and effect of this definition was to make it an unlawful employment practice under § 703(a)(1) for an employer not to make reasonable accommodations, short of undue hardship, for the religious practices of his employees and prospective employees. But like the EEOC guidelines, the statute provides no guidance for determining the degree of accommodation that is required of an employer. The brief legislative history of § 701(j) is likewise of little assistance in this regard.[9] * * *

* * * With this in mind, we turn to a consideration of whether TWA has met its obligation under Title VII to accommodate the religious observances of its employees.

III

The Court of Appeals held that TWA had not made reasonable efforts to accommodate Hardison's religious needs under the 1967 EEOC guidelines in effect at the time the relevant events occurred.[11] In its view, TWA had rejected three reasonable alternatives, any one of which would have satisfied its obligation without undue hardship. First, within the framework of the seniority system, TWA could have permitted Hardison to work a four-day week, utilizing in his place a

---

9. * * * The legislative history of the measure consists chiefly of a brief floor debate in the Senate, contained in less than two pages of the Congressional Record and consisting principally of the views of the proponent of the measure, Senator Jennings Randolph.

11. Ordinarily, an EEOC guideline is not entitled to great weight where, as here, it varies from prior EEOC policy and no new legislative history has been introduced in support of the change. But where "Congress has not just kept its silence by refusing to overturn the administrative con-

struction, but has ratified it with positive legislation," Red Lion Broadcasting Co. v. FCC, 395 U.S. 367, 381–382, 89 S.Ct. 1794, 1802, 23 L.Ed.2d 371 (1969), the guideline is entitled to some deference, at least sufficient in this case to warrant our accepting the guideline as a defensible construction of the pre–1972 statute, *i.e.*, as imposing on TWA the duty of "reasonable accommodation" in the absence of "undue hardship." We thus need not consider whether § 701(j) must be applied retroactively to the facts of this litigation.

supervisor or another worker on duty elsewhere. That this would have caused other shop functions to suffer was insufficient to amount to undue hardship in the opinion of the Court of Appeals. Second— according to the Court of Appeals, also within the bounds of the collective-bargaining contract—the company could have filled Hardison's Saturday shift from other available personnel competent to do the job, of which the court said there were at least 200. That this would have involved premium overtime pay was not deemed an undue hardship. Third, TWA could have arranged a "swap between Hardison and another employee either for another shift or for the Sabbath days." In response to the assertion that this would have involved a breach of the seniority provisions of the contract, the court noted that it had not been settled in the courts whether the required statutory accommodation to religious needs stopped short of transgressing seniority rules, but found it unnecessary to decide the issue because, as the Court of Appeals saw the record, TWA had not sought, and the union had therefore not declined to entertain, a possible variance from the seniority provisions of the collective-bargaining agreement. The company had simply left the entire matter to the union steward who the Court of Appeals said "likewise did nothing."

We disagree with the Court of Appeals in all relevant respects. It is our view that TWA made reasonable efforts to accommodate and that each of the Court of Appeals' suggested alternatives would have been an undue hardship within the meaning of the statute as construed by the EEOC guidelines.

A

It might be inferred from the Court of Appeals' opinion and from the brief of the EEOC in this Court that TWA's efforts to accommodate were no more than negligible. The findings of the District Court, supported by the record, are to the contrary. In summarizing its more detailed findings, the District Court observed:

> "TWA established as a matter of fact that it did take appropriate action to accommodate as required by Title VII. It held several meetings with plaintiff at which it attempted to find a solution to plaintiff's problems. It did accommodate plaintiff's observance of his special religious holidays. It authorized the union steward to search for someone who would swap shifts, which apparently was normal procedure."

It is also true that TWA itself attempted without success to find Hardison another job. The District Court's view was that TWA had done all that could reasonably be expected within the bounds of the seniority system.

The Court of Appeals observed, however, that the possibility of a variance from the seniority system was never really posed to the union. This is contrary to the District Court's findings and to the record. The District Court found that when TWA first learned of Hardison's religious observances in April 1968, it agreed to permit the union's steward to seek a swap of shifts or days off but that "the steward reported that he was unable to work out scheduling changes and that he understood that no one was willing to swap days with plaintiff." Later, in March 1969, at a meeting held just two days before Hardison first failed to report for his Saturday shift, TWA again "offered to accommodate plaintiff's religious observance by agreeing to any trade of shifts or change of sections that plaintiff and the union could work out. * * * Any shift or change was impossible within the seniority framework and the union was not willing to violate the seniority provision set out in the contract to make a shift or change." * * *

* * *

B

We are also convinced, contrary to the Court of Appeals, that TWA itself cannot be faulted for having failed to work out a shift or job swap for Hardison. Both the union and TWA had agreed to the seniority system; the union was unwilling to entertain a variance over the objections of men senior to Hardison; and for TWA to have arranged unilaterally for a swap would have amounted to a breach of the collective-bargaining agreement.

(1)

Hardison and the EEOC insist that the statutory obligation to accommodate religious needs takes precedence over both the collective-bargaining contract and the seniority rights of TWA's other employees. We agree that neither a collective-bargaining contract nor a seniority system may be employed to violate the statute, but we do not believe that the duty to accommodate requires TWA to take steps inconsistent with the otherwise valid agreement. Collective bargaining, aimed at effecting workable and enforceable agreements between management and labor, lies at the core of our national labor policy, and seniority provisions are universally included in these contracts. Without a clear and express indication from Congress, we cannot agree with Hardison and the EEOC that an agreed-upon seniority system must give way when necessary to accommodate religious observances. * * *

* * *

Had TWA * * * circumvented the seniority system by relieving Hardison of Saturday work and ordering a senior employee to replace him, it would have denied the latter his shift preference so that Hardison could be given his. The senior employee would also have been deprived of his contractual rights under the collective-bargaining agreement.

It was essential to TWA's business to require Saturday and Sunday work from at least a few employees even though most employees preferred those days off. Allocating the burdens of weekend work was a matter for collective bargaining. In considering criteria to govern this allocation, TWA and the union had two alternatives: adopt a neutral system, such as seniority, a lottery, or rotating shifts; or allocate days off in accordance with the religious needs of its employees. TWA would have had to adopt the latter in order to assure Hardison and others like him of getting the days off necessary for strict observance of their religion, but it could have done so only at the expense of others who had strong, but perhaps nonreligious, reasons for not working on weekends. There were no volunteers to relieve Hardison on Saturdays, and to give Hardison Saturdays off, TWA would have had to deprive another employee of his shift preference at least in part because he did not adhere to a religion that observed the Saturday Sabbath.

Title VII does not contemplate such unequal treatment. The repeated, unequivocal emphasis of both the language and the legislative history of Title VII is on eliminating discrimination in employment, and such discrimination is proscribed when it is directed against majorities as well as minorities. * * * It would be anomalous to conclude that by "reasonable accommodation" Congress meant that an employer must deny the shift and job preference of some employees, as well as deprive them of their contractual rights, in order to accommodate or prefer the religious needs of others, and we conclude that Title VII does not require an employer to go that far.

(2)

Our conclusion is supported by the fact that seniority systems are afforded special treatment under Title VII itself. Section 703(h) provides in pertinent part:

"Notwithstanding any other provision of this subchapter, it shall not be an unlawful employment practice for an employer to apply different standards of compensation, or different terms, conditions, or privileges of employment pursuant to a bona fide seniority or merit system * * * provided that such differences are not the result of an intention to discriminate because of race, color, religion, sex, or national origin * * *."

"[T]he unmistakable purpose of § 703(h) was to make clear that the routine application of a bona fide seniority system would not be unlawful under Title VII." International Brotherhood of Teamsters v. United States, 431 U.S. 324, 352, 97 S.Ct. 1843, 1863, 52 L.Ed.2d 396 (1977). * * * [A]bsent a discriminatory purpose, the operation of a seniority system cannot be an unlawful employment practice even if the system has some discriminatory consequences.

There has been no suggestion of discriminatory intent in this case. * * * The Court of Appeals' conclusion that TWA was not limited by the terms of its seniority system was in substance nothing more than a ruling that operation of the seniority system was itself an unlawful employment practice even though no discriminatory purpose had been shown. That ruling is plainly inconsistent with the dictates of § 703(h), both on its face and as interpreted in the recent decisions of this Court.[13]

As we have said, TWA was not required by Title VII to carve out a special exception to its seniority system in order to help Hardison to meet his religious obligations.[14]

C

The Court of Appeals also suggested that TWA could have permitted Hardison to work a four-day week if necessary in order to avoid working on his Sabbath. Recognizing that this might have left TWA short-handed on the one shift each week that Hardison did not work, the court still concluded that TWA would suffer no undue hardship if it were required to replace Hardison either with supervisory personnel or with qualified personnel from other departments. Alternatively, the Court of Appeals suggested that TWA could have replaced Hardison on his Saturday shift with other available employees through the payment of premium wages. Both of these alternatives would involve costs to TWA, either in the form of lost efficiency in other jobs or higher wages.

13. Franks v. Bowman Transportation Co., is not to the contrary. In *Franks* we held that "once an illegal discriminatory practice occurring after the effective date of the Act is proved," § 703(h) does not bar an award of retroactive seniority status to victims of that discriminatory practice. Here the suggested exception to the TWA–IAM seniority system would not be remedial; the operation of the seniority system itself is said to violate Title VII. In such circumstances, § 703(h) unequivocally mandates that there is no statutory violation in the absence of a showing of discriminatory purpose. See United Air Lines, Inc. v. Evans, 431 U.S. 553, 558–560, 97 S.Ct. 1885, 1889–1890, 52 L.Ed.2d 571 (1977).

14. Despite its hyperbole and rhetoric, the dissent appears to agree with—at last it stops short of challenging—the fundamental proposition that Title VII does not require an employer and a union who have agreed on a seniority system to deprive senior employees of their seniority rights in order to accommodate a junior employee's religious practices. This is the principal issue on which TWA and the union came to this Court. The dissent is thus reduced to (1) asserting that the statute requires TWA to accommodate Hardison even though substantial expenditures are required to do so; and (2) advancing its own view of the record to show that TWA could have done more than it did to accommodate Hardison without violating the seniority system or incurring substantial additional costs. We reject the former assertion as an erroneous construction of the statute. As for the latter, we prefer the findings of the District Judge who heard the evidence. Thus, the dissent suggests that through further efforts TWA or the union might have arranged a temporary or permanent job swap within the seniority system, despite the District Court's express finding, supported by the record, that "[t]he seniority provisions * * * precluded the possibility of plaintiff's changing his shift." Similarly, the dissent offers two alternatives—sending Hardison back to Building 1 or allowing him to work extra days without overtime pay—that it says could have been pursued by TWA or the union, even though neither of the courts below even hinted that these suggested alternatives would have been feasible under the circumstances. Furthermore, Buildings 1 and 2 had separate seniority lists, and insofar as the record shows, a return to Building 1 would not have solved Hardison's problems. Hardison himself testified that he "gave up" his Building 1 seniority when he came to Building 2, App. 104, and that the union would not accept his early return to Building 1 in part "because the problem of seniority came up again." We accept the District Court's findings that TWA had done all that it could do to accommodate Hardison's religious beliefs without either incurring substantial costs or violating the seniority rights of other employees.

To require TWA to bear more than a *de minimis* cost in order to give Hardison Saturdays off is an undue hardship.[15] Like abandonment of the seniority system, to require TWA to bear additional costs when no such costs are incurred to give other employees the days off that they want would involve unequal treatment of employees on the basis of their religion. By suggesting that TWA should incur certain costs in order to give Hardison Saturdays off the Court of Appeals would in effect require TWA to finance an additional Saturday off and then to choose the employee who will enjoy it on the basis of his religious beliefs. While incurring extra costs to secure a replacement for Hardison might remove the necessity of compelling another employee to work involuntarily in Hardison's place, it would not change the fact that the privilege of having Saturdays off would be allocated according to religious beliefs.

As we have seen, the paramount concern of Congress in enacting Title VII was the elimination of discrimination in employment. In the absence of clear statutory language or legislative history to the contrary, we will not readily construe the statute to require an employer to discriminate against some employees in order to enable others to observe their Sabbath.

Reversed.

MR. JUSTICE MARSHALL, with whom MR. JUSTICE BRENNAN joins, dissenting.

* * *

Today's decision deals a fatal blow to all efforts under Title VII to accommodate work requirements to religious practices. The Court holds, in essence, that although the EEOC regulations and the Act state that an employer must make reasonable adjustments in his work demands to take account of religious observances, the regulation and Act do not really mean what they say. An employer, the Court concludes, need not grant even the most minor special privilege to religious observers to enable them to follow their faith. As a question of social policy, this result is deeply troubling, for a society that truly values religious pluralism cannot compel adherents of minority religions to make the cruel choice of surrendering their religion or their job. And as a matter of law today's result is intolerable, for the Court adopts the very position that Congress expressly rejected in 1972, as if we were free to disregard congressional choices that a majority of this Court thinks unwise. I therefore dissent.

---

15. The dissent argues that "the costs to TWA of either paying overtime or not replacing respondent would [not] have been more than *de minimis*." This ignores, however, the express finding of the District Court that "[b]oth of these solutions would have created an undue burden on the conduct of TWA's business," and it fails to take account of the likelihood that a company as large as TWA may have many employees whose religious observances, like Hardison's, prohibit them from working on Saturdays or Sundays.

I

With respect to each of the proposed accommodations to respondent Hardison's religious observances that the Court discusses, it ultimately notes that the accommodation would have required "unequal treatment," in favor of the religious observer. That is quite true. But if an accommodation can be rejected simply because it involves preferential treatment, then the regulation and the statute, while brimming with "sound and fury," ultimately "signif[y] nothing."

The accommodation issue by definition arises only when a neutral rule of general applicability conflicts with the religious practices of a particular employee. * * * What all * * * [the accommodation] cases have in common is an employee who could comply with the rule only by violating what the employee views as a religious commandment. In each instance, the question is whether the employee is to be exempt from the rule's demands. To do so will always result in a privilege being "allocated according to religious beliefs," unless the employer gratuitously decides to repeal the rule *in toto*. What the statute says, in plain words, is that such allocations are required unless "undue hardship" would result.

* * *

II

Once it is determined that the duty to accommodate sometimes requires that an employee be exempted from an otherwise valid work requirement, the only remaining question is whether this is such a case: Did TWA prove that it exhausted all reasonable accommodations, and that the only remaining alternatives would have caused undue hardship on TWA's business? To pose the question is to answer it, for all that the District Court found TWA had done to accommodate respondent's Sabbath observance was that it "held several meetings with [respondent] * * * [and] authorized the union steward to search for someone who would swap shifts." To conclude that TWA, one of the largest air carriers in the Nation, would have suffered undue hardship had it done anything more defies both reason and common sense.

The Court implicitly assumes that the only means of accommodation open to TWA were to compel an unwilling employee to replace Hardison; to pay premium wages to a voluntary substitute; or to employ one less person during respondent's Sabbath shift.[5] Based on this assumption, the Court seemingly finds that each alternative would have involved undue hardship not only because Hardison would have been given a special privilege, but also because either another employee would have been deprived of rights under the collective-bargaining

---

5. It is true that these are the only options the Court of Appeals discussed. But that court found that TWA could have adopted these options without undue hard- ship; once that conclusion is rejected it is incumbent on this Court to decide whether any other alternatives were available that would not have involved such hardship.

agreement, or because "more than a *de minimis* cost," would have been imposed on TWA. But the Court's myopic view of the available options is not supported by either the District Court's findings or the evidence adduced at trial. Thus, the Court's conclusion cannot withstand analysis, even assuming that its rejection of the alternatives it does discuss is justifiable.[6]

To begin with, the record simply does not support the Court's assertion, made without accompanying citations, that "[t]here were no volunteers to relieve Hardison on Saturdays." Everett Kussman, the manager of the department in which respondent worked, testified that he had made no effort to find volunteers, and the union stipulated that its steward had not done so either.[8] * * * Thus, respondent's religious observance might have been accommodated by a simple trade of days or shifts without necessarily depriving any employee of his or her contractual rights [10] and without imposing significant costs on TWA. Of

6. I entertain grave doubts on both factual and legal grounds about the validity of the Court's rejection of the options it considers. As a matter of fact, I do not believe the record supports the Court's suggestion that the costs to TWA of either paying overtime or not replacing respondent would have been more than *de minimis*. While the District Court did state, as the Court notes, that both alternatives "would have created an undue burden on the conduct of TWA's business," the court did not explain its understanding of the phrase "undue burden," and may have believed that such a burden exists whenever any cost is incurred by the employer, no matter how slight. Thus the District Court's assertion falls far short of a factual "finding" that the costs of these accommodations would be more than *de minimis*. Moreover, the record is devoid of any evidence documenting the extent of the "efficiency loss" TWA would have incurred had it used a supervisor or an already scheduled employee to do respondent's work, and while the stipulations make clear what overtime would have cost, the price is far from staggering: $150 for three months, at which time respondent would have been eligible to transfer back to his previous department. The Court's suggestion that the cost of accommodation must be evaluated in light of the "likelihood that * * * TWA may have many employees whose religious observances * * * prohibit them from working on Saturdays or Sundays," is not only contrary to the record, which indicates that only one other case involving a conflict between work schedules and Sabbath observance had arisen at TWA since 1945, but also irrelevant, since the real question is not whether such employees exist but whether they could be accommodated without significant expense. Indeed, to the extent that TWA employed Sunday as well as Saturday Sabbatarians, the likelihood of accommodation being costly would diminish, since trades would be more feasible.

As a matter of law, I seriously question whether simple English usage permits "undue hardship" to be interpreted to mean "more than *de minimis* cost," especially when the examples the guidelines give of possible undue hardship is the absence of a qualified substitute. I therefore believe that in the appropriate case we would be compelled to confront the constitutionality of requiring employers to bear more than *de minimis* costs. The issue need not be faced here, however, since an almost cost-free accommodation was possible.

8. The Court relies, on the District Court's conclusory assertion that "[a]ny shift or change was impossible within the seniority framework." But the District Court also found that "TWA did not take part in the search for employees willing to swap shifts * * * and it was admitted at trial that the Union made no real effort." Thus, the District Court's statement concerning the impact of "the seniority framework" lends no support to the Court's assertion that there were no volunteers. See also n. 10, infra.

10. If, as appears likely, no one senior to the substitute employee desired respondent's Sabbath assignment or his Thursday–Monday shift, then the substitute could have transferred to respondent's position without depriving anyone of his or her seniority expectations. Similarly, if, as also appears probable, no one senior to

course, it is also possible that no trade—or none consistent with the seniority system—could have been arranged. But the burden under the EEOC regulation is on TWA to establish that a reasonable accommodation was not possible. Because it failed either to explore the possibility of a voluntary trade or to assure that its delegate, the union steward, did so, TWA was unable to meet its burden.

Nor was a voluntary trade the only option open to TWA that the Court ignores; to the contrary, at least two other options are apparent from the record. First, TWA could have paid overtime to a voluntary replacement for respondent—assuming that someone would have been willing to work Saturdays for premium pay—and passed on the cost to respondent. In fact, one accommodation Hardison suggested would have done just that by requiring Hardison to work overtime when needed at regular pay. Under this plan, the total overtime cost to the employer—and the total number of overtime hours available for other employees—would not have reflected Hardison's Sabbath absences. Alternatively, TWA could have transferred respondent back to his previous department where he had accumulated substantial seniority, as respondent also suggested.[11] Admittedly, both options would have violated the collective-bargaining agreement; the former because the agreement required that employees working over 40 hours per week receive premium pay, and the latter because the agreement prohibited employees from transferring departments more than once every six months. But neither accommodation would have deprived any other employee of rights under the contract or violated the seniority system in any way.[12] Plainly an employer cannot avoid his duty to accommodate by signing a contract that precludes all reasonable accommodations; even the Court appears to concede as much. Thus I do not believe it can be even seriously argued that TWA would have suffered "undue hardship" to its business had it required respondent to pay the

respondent desired the substitute's spot, respondent could have assumed it. Such a trade would not have deprived any employee of seniority expectations. The trade apparently still would have violated the collective-bargaining agreement, however, since the agreement authorized transfers only to vacant jobs. This is undoubtedly what the District Court meant when it found that "the seniority framework" precluded shift changes. Indeed, the first time in the District Court's opinion that such a finding appears, it is preceded by the finding that "there were no jobs open for bid."

Even if a trade could not have been arranged without disrupting seniority expectations TWA could have requested the Union Relief Committee to approve an exemption. The record reveals that the Committee's function was to ameliorate the rigidity of the system, and that on at least

one occasion it had approved a permanent transfer apparently outside the seniority system.

11. The Court states, that because of TWA's departmental seniority system, such a transfer "would not have solved Hardison's problems." But respondent testified without contradiction that had he returned to his previous department he would have regained his seniority in that department, and thereby could have avoided work on his Sabbath. According to respondent, the only objection that was raised to this solution was that it violated the rule prohibiting transfers twice within six months.

12. The accommodations would have disadvantaged respondent to some extent, but since he suggested both options I do not consider whether an employer would satisfy his duty to accommodate by offering these choices to an unwilling employee.

extra costs of his replacement, or had it transferred respondent to his former department.

What makes today's decision most tragic, however, is not that respondent Hardison has been needlessly deprived of his livelihood simply because he chose to follow the dictates of his conscience. Nor is the tragedy exhausted by the impact it will have on thousands of Americans like Hardison who could be forced to live on welfare as the price they must pay for worshiping their God.[14] The ultimate tragedy is that despite Congress' best efforts, one of this Nation's pillars of strength—our hospitality to religious diversity—has been seriously eroded. All Americans will be a little poorer until today's decision is erased.

I respectfully dissent.

NOTES AND PROBLEMS FOR DISCUSSION

1. Shirley Booker was hired by the Postal Service as a full time window clerk in 1971. Pursuant to an agreement between the Selective Service System and the Postal Service, the latter agency agreed to participate in the registration of young men for the draft. As of January 1, 1981, in addition to their other duties, all window clerks were required to provide, aid in the completion of and accept registration forms. They also were prohibited from refusing a tendered form for any reason. After receiving the standard training in handling such forms, Ms. Booker notified her supervisor of her conscientious objection to any involvement in the registration process, based on her moral opposition to war and conscription. She asked to be relieved of this duty in exchange for which she agreed to perform additional tasks not performed by window clerks. Her supervisor rejected this request, however, stating that such a compromise would violate the work assignment provisions of the collective bargaining agreement covering all postal employees. In addition, he told Booker that accepting her request could severely disrupt the efficient operation of the post office by setting a precedent that would encourage other employees to try to bargain their way out of undesired duties. Accordingly, he informed Booker that any failure to process registration forms would result in her dismissal. Nevertheless, Booker consistently avoided processing the forms by referring all potential registrants to other windows. Upon learning of Booker's conduct, and personally observing such a referral, the supervisor served Booker with a notice of dismissal for insubordination. After exhausting all available administrative remedies, Booker filed suit under Title VII in a federal district court claiming that the discharge constituted discrimination on the basis of her religion. How should the court rule? See McGinnis v. United States Postal Service, 512 F.Supp. 517 (N.D.Cal.1980).

2. Do you agree with Justice Marshall's contention that the majority in *Hardison* effectively nullified the statutory duty to accommodate through its interpretation of "undue hardship"? Can you conceive of an accommodation that would not impose an undue hardship under a literal reading of the Court's

---

14. Ironically, the fiscal costs to society of today's decision may exceed the costs that would accrue if employers were required to make all accommodations without regard to hardship, since it is clear that persons on welfare cannot be denied benefits because they refuse to take jobs that would prevent them from observing religious holy days.

tripartite formulation of that term? If not, does this suggest that a lower court might choose to avoid a strict application of this ruling? One such example can be found in DRAZEWSKI v. WAUKEGAN DEVELOPMENT CENTER, 651 F.Supp. 754 (N.D.Ill.1986). There, the defendant rejected the plaintiff's request that it permit him to arrange for voluntary swaps so that he would not have to work on the Sabbath. It based this rejection on the ground that such an accommodation would amount to an allocation of swapping privileges solely on the basis of religion and that this was prohibited by the decision in *Hardison.* The court rejected this argument, stating that "[i]f *Hardison* means, as defendants argue, that an employer may never arrange a schedule to accommodate an employee's religious practices, then *Hardison* amounts to an emasculation of the statutory duty of accommodation. This court is reluctant to read *Hardison* in a way which contradicts the language of the statute." 651 F.Supp. at 759. In addition, the court declared that in the absence of a provision in the collective agreement precluding voluntary trade-offs of shift assignments, the employer's contention that the union would or might object to voluntary swaps was not, by itself, a sufficient reason for rejecting such an accommodation. "[T]he union's grumbling about a benefit allowed to plaintiffs would not absolve defendants of their statutory duty to accommodate." 651 F.Supp. at 758.

If, as the trial court in *Drazewski* suggested, the *Hardison* Court's interpretation of § 701(j) is at odds with any realistic appraisal of the statutory purpose, can the Court's restrictive interpretation of § 701(j) perhaps be explained as a method of avoiding the constitutional issue that would arise when a defendant is ordered to make some accommodation?

3. The courts have uniformly adopted the following allocation of the burden of proof in religious discrimination cases:

> "In order to establish a prima facie case of religious discrimination under [§§ 703(a) and 701(j)], a plaintiff must plead and prove that (1) he had a bona fide belief that compliance with an employment requirement is contrary to his religious faith; (2) he informed his employer about the conflict; and (3) he was discharged because of his refusal to comply with the employment requirement."

Brown v. General Motors Corp., 601 F.2d 956, 959 (8th Cir.1979). The requirement that the plaintiff prove that she informed her employer about the conflict can be waived where the record reveals that the employer had notice of the employee's religious practices. See Drazewski v. Waukegan Development Center, 651 F.Supp. 754, 757 (N.D.Ill.1986) (plaintiff satisfied burden by establishing that she told employer that she could not work on Saturday during first of two interviews). Once the plaintiff has established a prima facie case,

> "[t]he burden [is] thereafter upon [the defendants] to prove that they made good faith efforts to accommodate [the plaintiff's] religious beliefs and, if these efforts were unsuccessful, to demonstrate that they were unable reasonably to accommodate his beliefs without undue hardship."

Anderson v. General Dynamics Convair Aerospace Div., 589 F.2d 397, 401 (9th Cir.1978).

Does the employee's conduct have to be required by her religious beliefs? Is it enough to establish that the conduct is permitted or motivated by religious belief? In FRAZEE v. ILLINOIS DEPARTMENT OF EMPLOYMENT SECURITY, 489 U.S. 829, 109 S.Ct. 1514, 103 L.Ed.2d 914 (1989), the Supreme Court held that an individual's sincerely held religious belief was protected by the free exercise clause of the First Amendment even though the plaintiff did not claim to be a member of any particular religious sect or church. The Court also noted that the belief would have been protected even if it had not been a clear commandment of a religious sect, as long as the plaintiff had a sincere belief that his religion required him to take or not take particular action, such as, in this case, working on Sunday.

4. Section 702 exempts religious institutions from § 703's ban on religious discrimination. Does this mean that these institutions also are not subject to the § 701(j) duty to accommodate? See Larsen v. Kirkham, 499 F.Supp. 960 (D. Utah 1980), affirmed without opinion, 35 FEP 1799 (10th Cir. 1982), cert. denied, 464 U.S. 849, 104 S.Ct. 157, 78 L.Ed.2d 144 (1983).

5. If the employee and the company each propose a reasonable accommodation, does Title VII require the employer to accept the employee's proposal where it does not impose an undue hardship? In ANSONIA BOARD OF EDUCATION v. PHILBROOK, 479 U.S. 60, 107 S.Ct. 367, 93 L.Ed.2d 305 (1986), the collective bargaining agreement entered into by the defendant school board allowed all teachers to take three days of paid leave for religious holidays and permitted teachers to take up to three paid days of "personal business" leave. The contract also provided, however, that such personal business leave could not be used for religious activity or other uses specified in the contract. The plaintiff's religious observance required him to take six days off per year for religious holidays. Pursuant to the contractual provisions, he could only take paid leave for three of these six days. He proposed that the company allow him to use his three personal leave days for religious observance or that he be permitted to pay the cost of a substitute and receive full pay for the three additional days off for religious observance. The school board rejected his proposals. The trial court concluded that the plaintiff failed to establish a case of religious discrimination. The Second Circuit reversed this ruling. It assumed that the employer's leave policy was a reasonable accommodation to the plaintiff's religious beliefs but added that where both the employer and employee propose reasonable accommodations, the employer must agree to the employee's proposal unless the employer can show that this proposal would impose an undue hardship upon it. The court then remanded the case for determination of the hardship generated by the employee's proposed accommodation. The Supreme Court held that the statute only required the employer to make a reasonable accommodation and did not require it to adopt the *most* reasonable accommodation. Any reasonable accommodation, the Court concluded, would satisfy the statutory obligation. Once it is determined that the employer has offered a reasonable accommodation, the employer need not show that each of the employee's proposed accommodations would result in undue hardship. Thus, it concluded, the circuit court had erred in requiring the school board to prove on remand that the plaintiff's accommodations were unreasonable. It added, moreover, that the type of accommodation provided by the school board's contract (i.e., unpaid leave for religious observance) generally would be reasonable. Nevertheless, it continued, if the plaintiff could show, on remand, that the policy of not permitting the use of personal business paid leave was limited to requests for religious observance, i.e., that paid leave was allowed for non-religious purposes, such a discriminatory policy would not be reasonable. It therefore remanded for further findings as to past and existing practice in the administration of this provision of the collective bargaining agreement. Justice Marshall, concurring and dissenting in part, suggested that an employer should not be required to adopt the employee's proposed accommodation only where its

proposal fully resolved the conflict between the worker's employment and religious obligations. Since this employee was required to accept a loss of compensation in order to honor his religious obligations, Marshall concluded that the employer's accommodation did not fully resolve the conflict and, therefore, that the company was obliged to consider the employee's reasonable proposals. Justice Stevens, also concurring and dissenting in part, concluded that it was unnecessary to remand the case since the finding below that the employer's accommodation was reasonable was sufficient to resolve the issue. He agreed with the majority that the accommodation resolved the religious conflict and that the contract did not discriminate against religious observers since it prohibited the use of personal business leave days for other than religious reasons. He thus concluded that it was unnecessary to make a special analysis of the past and present administration of the personal business leave provision.

There has been some disagreement as to whether the statute always requires an employer to make some attempt to accommodate. The Tenth Circuit has held that an employer must first show some attempt at accommodation and then establish that additional accommodation would impose an undue hardship. See United States v. City of Albuquerque, 545 F.2d 110, 113 (10th Cir.1976), cert. denied, 433 U.S. 909, 97 S.Ct. 2974, 53 L.Ed.2d 1092 (1977). On the other hand, other circuits have held that an employer can claim undue hardship without showing any effort to accommodate where it can present evidence, rather than relying merely on speculation, that any reasonable accommodation would impose an undue hardship. See United States v. Board of Educ. for School Dist. of Philadelphia, 911 F.2d 882 (3d Cir.1990); EEOC v. Townley Engineering & Mfg. Co., 859 F.2d 610 (9th Cir.1988), cert. denied, 489 U.S. 1077, 109 S.Ct. 1527, 103 L.Ed.2d 832 (1989); Smith v. Pyro Mining Co., 827 F.2d 1081 (6th Cir.1987). In these circuits, should the employer prevail when the only possible accommodation would require the employer to violate state law? In UNITED STATES v. BOARD OF EDUC. FOR THE SCHOOL DIST. OF PHILADELPHIA, 911 F.2d 882 (3d Cir.1990), for example, a devout Muslim schoolteacher's religiously held conviction required that she cover her entire body except for her face and hands. As a result, she wore a head scarf while teaching in order to cover her head and neck. When she reported to duty as a substitute teacher at another school, the principal informed her that, pursuant to state law, she could not teach in her religious clothing because a state statute prohibited a teacher in any public school from wearing any dress or insignia indicating the fact that such teacher is a member or adherent of any religious order or denomination. The statute added that any public school director who failed to comply with its provisions was subject to criminal sanction. The teacher was given a chance to go home and change; she refused to do so and was not allowed to teach. She filed a claim with the EEOC which, pursuant to § 706(f), was transferred to the Department of Justice because the respondent was a public entity. The Justice Department subsequently filed this action in which it (1)sought a declaration that the state law was in conflict with Title VII and (2)alleged that the school had failed to reasonably accommodate the teacher's desire to wear garb that was an aspect of her religious observance and practice. The school conceded that it had not proffered any accommodation. Instead, it claimed, the accommodation sought by the teacher could not be accomplished without undue hardship. The appellate court acknowledged that the issue before it was whether accommodating her religious beliefs by taking an action contrary to state law imposed an undue hardship and thus made such an accommodation unreasonable. The court began its analysis by referring to a decision by the U.S. Supreme Court concerning a nearly identical Oregon statute in which the Court had upheld an Oregon Supreme Court ruling that such an enactment did not violate the plaintiff's first amendment free exercise rights because the statute permissibly advanced a compelling state interest in maintaining the appearance of religious neutrality in the public school classroom. On the basis of this ruling, the court in the instant case continued, whatever the precise meaning of "undue hardship" in terms of non-economic burdens, it was convinced that forcing the employer school district to sacrifice the compelling state interest codified in the state statute would clearly constitute an undue hardship. Do you agree with this analysis? Is it sufficient to say that, as a public entity, this school district shared in the state interest underlying the statute? On the other hand, would it be reasonable to require the school to violate a law whose constitutionality has been upheld? With reference to this last issue, the Third Circuit did state that exposing the Board and its administrators to a substantial risk of criminal prosecution, fines and other penalties would have imposed an undue hardship on the School Board. The court reasoned that if violating the seniority provision of a collective bargaining agreement is an undue hardship, so is requiring a school board to violate an apparently valid criminal statute. Furthermore, the court added, since the statute was designed to prevent the appearance of sectarianism in the administration of public schools, this state law was not inconsistent with the objectives of, and therefore not in violation of the terms of Title VII. But see EEOC v. READS, Inc., 759 F.Supp. 1150 (E.D.Pa.1991)(involving private school subject to Pennsylvania Department of Education regulation that incorporated state statutory proscription against wearing "religious garb". "Religious garb" consists only of either facially religious attire worn for religious reasons or attire worn for religious reasons that is apt to be perceived as religious by many children. It does not include attire worn for religious reasons which is not recognizable until its wearer explains the religious significance, since statute was designed to avoid risk that children will infer endorsement of religion from attire and such risk is absent where clothing is unlikely to convey a message of religious affiliation.).

Has the employer satisfied its accommodation obligation by consenting to shift swaps arranged by the employee whose religious beliefs preclude him from working on the Sabbath? Should that employer be required to make its own attempt to find a replacement for the employee? Would it matter if the employee notifies his employer that his religious convictions prevent him from trying to induce another to work in his stead on the Sabbath, but is willing to allow someone to arrange it for him? See Smith v. Pyro Mining Co., 827 F.2d 1081 (6th Cir.1987); EEOC v. J.P. Stevens & Co., 740 F.Supp. 1135 (E.D.N.C. 1990). If it is a reasonable accommodation for an employer to attempt to find a voluntary swap for the plaintiff, but the employer is unsuccessful at doing so, does the duty of accommodation also require the employer to force a reluctant employee to swap shifts with the plaintiff? See Eversley v. MBank Dallas, 843 F.2d 172 (5th Cir. 1988).

6. Is a trial court's findings of undue hardship and reasonable accommodation to be upset on appeal only if they are clearly erroneous? Does the Supreme Court's opinion in *Anderson, supra* at 164 help resolve this problem? See Wisner v. Truck Central, A Subsidiary of Saunders Leasing Systems, 784 F.2d 1571, 1573 (11th Cir.1986), cert. denied, 480 U.S. 934, 107 S.Ct. 1574, 94

L.Ed.2d 766 (1987)(holding finding on de minimis cost subject to Rule 52 standard).

7.   Rabban County employs several social workers to provide counseling and therapy for the inmates in its prison facilities. One of these counselors, Lisa Germain, sincerely views herself as an evangelist with a mission to spread the Gospel. Accordingly, she offered religious counseling, including Bible reading and prayer, to amenable inmates as one method of combatting their psychological problems. Rabban County follows a policy of precluding all county-paid social workers from using religious counseling because it believes that it is constitutionally compelled to maintain an atmosphere of religious neutrality within its jails. The County also instructs all of its counselors to refer requests for religious counseling to the chaplains who make themselves available to the inmates. Ms. Germain maintains that praying and sharing scripture with the inmates is a religious practice and continues to offer religious counseling to inmates who desire it. After repeated warnings, she is discharged. Germain then brings a Title VII action against the County alleging religious discrimination. The County claims that, in light of the constitutional constraints upon its conduct, it has made a reasonable accommodation to her religious beliefs by allowing inmates access to voluntary chaplains of all faiths. How should the court rule? See Spratt v. County of Kent, 621 F.Supp. 594 (W.D.Mich.1985).

8.   Wessjak Manufacturing Company, a corporation owned entirely by Mark Wessman and Julie Jackson, produces plastic doughnuts. Wessman and Jackson are deeply religious individuals who have devoted all aspects of their life to God. When they founded this company, Wessman and Jackson made a covenant with God that their business would be "spiritually and faithfully operated under God's law". As part of this covenant, Wessman and Jackson include a Gospel tract in every box of plastic doughnuts. In addition, they require all employees to attend weekly devotional services that are held during working hours. Michael Collins was hired in 1986 when the Company opened a new factory in Chicago, Illinois. Devotional services were not held at the Chicago plant until January, 1987. At that time, Collins, a declared atheist, announced that he would not attend the services. He was discharged. Has the Company violated § 703(a)? Can Collins state a prima facie case of religious discrimination? See Shapolia v. Los Alamos National Laboratory, 773 F.Supp. 304 (D.N.M.1991)(non–Mormon plaintiff, who alleges that he was terminated on basis of a bad evaluation given because plaintiff did not share his supervisor's Mormon religious beliefs, states prima facie Title VII claim of religious discrimination even though plaintiff did not allege a bona fide religious belief of his own). If so, can the company assert that to accommodate Collins' atheistic beliefs would impose a spiritual cost on it that would constitute an undue hardship? Can the Company take advantage of the exemption contained within § 702 for "religious corporations"? See EEOC v. Townley Engineering & Mfg. Co., 859 F.2d 610 (9th Cir.1988), cert. denied, 489 U.S. 1077, 109 S.Ct. 1527, 103 L.Ed.2d 832 (1989).

TOOLEY v. MARTIN–MARIETTA CORP.

United States Court of Appeals, Ninth Circuit, 1981.
648 F.2d 1239, cert. denied, 454 U.S. 1098, 102 S.Ct. 671, 70 L.Ed.2d 639.

Before HUG, TANG and FARRIS, CIRCUIT JUDGES.

FARRIS, CIRCUIT JUDGE.

* * *

In 1976, the Martin–Marietta Corporation and Steelworkers Local 8141 executed a collective bargaining agreement containing a "union shop" clause, under which the company was obligated to discharge all employees who failed to join the union. Plaintiffs Tooley, Bakke, and Helt are Seventh Day Adventists who, under the tenets of their faith, are prohibited from becoming members in or paying a service fee to a union. Plaintiffs informed the company and the union of this proscription, and offered to pay an amount equal to union dues to a mutually acceptable charity. The union refused.

After exhausting their administrative remedies, plaintiffs instituted this action, alleging that the union's and the company's refusal to honor the requested accommodation constituted religious discrimination under Title VII of the Civil Rights Act of 1964. In particular, the plaintiffs argued that both the union and the company were required under section 701(j) of the Act to make good faith efforts to institute their requested exemption unless it would result in undue hardship to either the Steelworkers or the company. The Steelworkers contended that the "substituted charity" accommodation was unreasonable, that its implementation would cause the union undue hardship, and that by authorizing such an accommodation, section 701(j) violated the Establishment Clause. The district court enjoined the union and the company from attempting to discharge the plaintiffs for failing to pay union dues so long as they make equivalent contributions to a mutually acceptable charity.

[The appellate court upheld as not clearly erroneous the trial judge's findings that the plaintiff's proposed accommodation was reasonable and did not impose an undue hardship upon the defendants. Consequently, the court was then obliged to consider the constitutional question left unanswered by the Supreme Court in *Hardison*.]

* * *

The Steelworkers argue that section 701(j) as applied here violates the Establishment Clause.[8] The district court held that section 701(j) withstood constitutional attack under the three-pronged test enunciated

---

8. The plaintiffs contend that the constitutional validity of § 701(j) as applied here has been determined conclusively by the Supreme Court's dismissal of the appeal in Rankins v. Comm'n on Professional Competence, 24 Cal.3d 167, 593 P.2d 852, 154 Cal.Rptr. 907, appeal dismissed, 444 U.S. 986, 100 S.Ct. 515, 62 L.Ed.2d 416 (1979). There, the California state constitutional employment discrimination provision, construed to require the same accommodations as those required by Title VII's § 701(j), was held not to offend the Estab- lishment Clause in requiring a school district to accommodate a teacher who refused to work on religious holidays. The dismissal of the appeal in *Rankins* binds this court only on "the precise issues presented and necessarily decided." Mandel v. Bradley, 432 U.S. 172, 176, 97 S.Ct. 2238, 2240, 53 L.Ed.2d 199 (1977). Because this case and *Rankins* involve entirely different kinds of religious accommodations, the constitutional dimension of each is necessarily different.

in Committee for Public Education & Religious Liberty v. Nyquist, 413 U.S. 756, 772–73, 93 S.Ct. 2955, 2965, 39 L.Ed.2d 948 (1973).

The Establishment Clause ensures government neutrality in matters of religion. But government neutrality "is not so narrow a channel that the slightest deviation from an absolutely straight course leads to condemnation." Sherbert v. Verner, 374 U.S. 398, 422, 83 S.Ct. 1790, 1803, 10 L.Ed.2d 965 (1963) (Harlan, J., dissenting). Courts have defined the government's obligation as one of "benevolent neutrality." Walz v. Tax Commission, 397 U.S. 664, 669, 90 S.Ct. 1409, 1411, 25 L.Ed.2d 697 (1970). While the government must avoid "partiality to any one group," Zorach v. Clauson, 343 U.S. 306, 313, 72 S.Ct. 679, 683, 96 L.Ed. 954 (1952), it may deviate from absolute rigidity to accommodate the religious practices of each group. *Walz*, 397 U.S. at 669, 90 S.Ct. at 1411.

Government can accommodate the beliefs and practices of members of minority religions without contravening the prohibitions of the Establishment Clause. Cf. Wisconsin v. Yoder, 406 U.S. 205, 234 n.22, 92 S.Ct. 1526, 1542 n.22, 32 L.Ed.2d 15 (1972) (exempting Amish children from state compulsory education laws); Sherbert v. Verner, 374 U.S. 398, 409, 83 S.Ct. 1790, 1796, 10 L.Ed.2d 965 (1963) (exempting Seventh–Day Adventists from state unemployment compensation requirements). Government may legitimately enforce accommodations of religious beliefs when the accommodation reflects the "obligation of neutrality in the face of religious differences," and does not constitute "sponsorship, financial support, [or] active involvement of the sovereign in religious activities" with which the Establishment Clause is mainly concerned.

Like the accommodations allowed in Sherbert v. Verner and Wisconsin v. Yoder, the substituted charity accommodation satisfies these requirements. By exempting the plaintiffs from union membership or the payment of mandatory union dues, the accommodation places the plaintiffs on an equal footing with other employees whose religious convictions find no impediment in the workplace. To this extent, the accommodation reflects governmental neutrality in the face of religious differences. Further, the substituted charity accommodation does not involve government "sponsorship" or "financial support" of the Seventh–Day Adventist religion: the accommodation requires that the plaintiffs suffer the same economic loss as their co-workers who are not similarly restricted in paying union dues or in obtaining union membership. The accommodation demands neither direct nor indirect financial support of the plaintiffs' religion by the government, and cannot be reasonably construed as actively advancing or assisting their religion.

This same conclusion is compelled under the test enunciated in Committee for Public Education & Religious Liberty v. Nyquist. The *Nyquist* test, typically applied to state legislation, requires that for section 701(j) to be consistent with the demands of the Establishment

Clause, it must (1) reflect a clearly secular purpose, (2) have a primary effect that neither inhibits nor advances religion, and (3) avoid excessive government entanglement with religion.

1. Legislative Purpose

The primary motivation for the enactment of section 701(j) was to resolve many of the issues left open by prior "Sabbatarian" cases, where employees refused to work on their Sabbath and requested that their employers accommodate them. *Hardison*, 432 U.S. at 73–74, 97 S.Ct. at 2271. The Steelworkers contend that because section 701(j) was intended to secure special treatment for Sabbatarians and other religious proponents, the legislation has an improper sectarian purpose.

Although section 701(j)'s enactment may have resolved certain problems confronting sectarians, this alone is insufficient to establish that the legislation lacks a clearly secular purpose. Section 701(j) was intended to promote Title VII's broader policy of prohibiting discrimination in employment. The bill's sponsor in the Senate, recognizing the problems confronting Sabbatarians in particular, stated that the legislation was intended to "assure that freedom from religious discrimination in the employment of workers is for all time guaranteed in law." Section 701(j) functions to "secure equal economic opportunity to members of minority religions." *Hardison*, 432 U.S. at 90 n.4, 97 S.Ct. at 2280 n. 4 (Marshall, J., dissenting). Cf. Rankins v. Commission on Professional Competence, 24 Cal.3d 167, 177–78, 593 P.2d 852, 859, 154 Cal.Rptr. 907, 913–14 (recognizing as secular the purpose of "promot[ing] equal employment opportunities for members of all religious faiths"), appeal dismissed, 444 U.S. 986, 100 S.Ct. 515, 62 L.Ed.2d 416 (1979). It therefore has a legitimate secular purpose.

2. Primary Effect

The Steelworkers contend that the substituted charity accommodation has the primary effect of advancing the plaintiffs' religion by conferring various alleged economic benefits. It is argued that as a consequence of the accommodation, the plaintiffs have a greater choice than their co-workers in determining how their money is spent, and are more easily able to make charitable contributions.

We reject this argument. It confuses ancillary or incidental benefits with primary benefits to those accommodated. It could be argued, for example, that the exemption allowed the Amish children in Wisconsin v. Yoder permitted the children to contribute additional economic benefit to their families, and that the exemption allowed in Sherbert v. Verner permitted the Seventh–Day Adventist to exercise a greater choice in determining which day of the week was to be free of employment responsibilities.

The substituted charity accommodation allows the plaintiffs to work without violating their religious beliefs, at a cost equivalent to that paid by their co-workers without similar beliefs. It neither in-

creases nor decreases the advantages of membership in the Seventh–
Day Adventist faith in a manner so substantial and direct that it
"advances" or "inhibits" the plaintiffs' religion.

The Steelworkers also contend that the accommodation violates the
Establishment Clause because it will ultimately result in either the
union curtailing necessary services, or forcing the accommodation cost
on other employees. In either case, the Steelworkers argue that the
plaintiffs receive the benefit of their religious beliefs at the expense of
their co-workers. As a result, it is urged that the accommodation
impermissibly places the burdens of accommodation on unaccommodated private parties.

A religious accommodation does not violate the Establishment
Clause merely because it can be construed in some abstract way as
placing an inappreciable but inevitable burden on those not accommodated. Exemption of conscientious objectors from military conscription
has been upheld despite the effect of requiring nonobjectors to serve in
their stead. Sectarian institutions are exempt from the payment of
property taxes, even though the effect may be to increase marginally
the property taxes paid by unaccommodated private citizens. Walz v.
Tax Commission, 397 U.S. 664, 90 S.Ct. 1409, 25 L.Ed.2d 697 (1970).
Sunday closing laws have been upheld even though their effect may be
to burden those who sincerely observe another Sabbath.

The substituted charity does not have a primary effect which either
advances or inhibits the plaintiffs' religion.

3. Government Entanglement

Nor do we find that the accommodation here requires that the
government become impermissibly entangled with the accommodation's
administration. The Establishment Clause prohibits only *excessive*
government entanglement. The implementation of the substituted
charity accommodation requires a minimal amount of supervision and
administrative cost. Once the sincerity of a religious objector's belief is
established, the only administrative burden involves the employee and
the union agreeing on a mutually acceptable charity. The Steelworkers have not demonstrated that the burden of administering this
accommodation involves sufficiently significant amounts of time or
money or that the government involvement is sufficiently "comprehensive, discriminating, and continuing" to draw into question the validity
of the accommodation.

Affirmed.

NOTES AND PROBLEMS FOR DISCUSSION

1. The edited version of *Tooley* does not include that portion of the court's
opinion dealing with the *statutory* objection to discharges undertaken pursuant
to union security clauses. Typically, as in the principal case, the employee is
willing to contribute an amount equal to the union dues to a non-sectarian,
non-union charity chosen by the union and the employer. Does the *union* have

a § 701(j) duty to accommodate the employee's religious beliefs? If so, does the loss of the plaintiff's dues impose any undue hardship upon the union? Could this accommodation distress other employees, impair their job performance and thus result in an undue hardship upon the employer?

At least four federal circuit courts have concluded that the presence of the word "employer" in § 701(j) notwithstanding, unions are under a statutory duty to accommodate. See Nottelson v. Smith Steel Workers, 643 F.2d 445 (7th Cir.), cert. denied, 454 U.S. 1046, 102 S.Ct. 587, 70 L.Ed.2d 488 (1981); Burns v. Southern Pacific Transportation Co., 589 F.2d 403 (9th Cir.1978), cert. denied, 439 U.S. 1072, 99 S.Ct. 843, 59 L.Ed.2d 38 (1979), on remand, 22 FEP Cases 1229 (D.Ariz.1979); McDaniel v. Essex International, Inc., 571 F.2d 338 (6th Cir. 1978), on remand, 509 F.Supp. 1055 (W.D.Mich.1981), affirmed, 696 F.2d 34 (6th Cir.1982); and Cooper v. General Dynamics, 533 F.2d 163 (5th Cir.1976). Moreover, in each of these cases except *Cooper*, the court held that neither the loss of an employee's union dues, nor the grumblings of other employees not offered such a choice, constituted undue hardship to the union or employer as a matter of law. While the courts recognized that the loss of dues generated by a large number of requests for substitute payments could result in undue hardship as a matter of fact, they stated that undue hardship could be established only by offering evidence of actual, as opposed to anticipated multiple requests for substitute payments. Accord, Haring v. Blumenthal, 471 F.Supp. 1172, 1182 (D.D.C.1979), affirmed, 24 EPD ¶ 31,412 (D.C.Cir. 1980). Accordingly, in *Nottelson, Burns* and *McDaniel*, the unions' and employers' blanket refusal to permit substitute payments and their failure to prove that this accommodation would result in undue hardship as a matter of fact, resulted in judgments for the plaintiffs.

Are these rulings consistent with the *Hardison* de minimis standard? Moreover, won't the accommodations required by the courts in these cases compel both the union and employer to violate the contractual union security clause? If so, is this permissible under *Hardison* ? In *Nottelson*, the court distinguished *Hardison* on the ground that the defendant in the latter case would have been forced to ignore a seniority system protected by Title VII as well as the collective bargaining agreement. 643 F.2d at 452. Do you agree? See also McCormick v. Board of Educ. of Belvidere School Dist., 32 FEP Cases 504 (N.D.Ill.1983); McDaniel v. Essex International, Inc., 509 F.Supp. 1055, 1061 (W.D.Mich.1981). Finally, isn't it also true that the plaintiffs in *Nottelson, Burns* and *McDaniel* were accorded differential treatment because of their religion?

The National Labor Relations Act, 29 U.S.C. § 151 et seq., the federal statute governing the organizational and collective bargaining rights of employees, sanctions the type of union security clause discussed in this Note. Defendants frequently had relied on § 8(a)(3) (the provision recognizing the legality of union security clauses) of the N.L.R.A. as the basis for their claim that a substituted charity accommodation is inconsistent with the national labor policy favoring, or at least acquiescing to, union security agreements. The statute was amended in 1980, however, to provide (in § 19) a religion-based exemption from a contractual requirement to join or financially support a union. But this exemption is restricted solely to (1)members of any bona fide religion, body or sect (2)that has historically held conscientious objections to joining or supporting labor unions. Do you see any constitutional objection to limiting the exemption either to members of religious groups or to those groups that have traditionally objected to union membership or support? At least one court has ruled that each of the limitations in § 19 rendered the amendment unconstitutional under the establishment clause of the First Amendment. In WILSON v. NLRB, 920 F.2d 1282 (6th Cir.1990), the court held that this statute created a denominational preference by conferring benefits on members of such sects and that the NLRB had not identified any compelling governmental interest furthered by such a provision. Moreover, the court added, even if the statute could be said to promote the governmental interest in protecting religious freedom in the workplace, this purpose would have been more appropriately promoted by language parallel to the protection afforded by § 701(j) of Title VII, which contains neither the membership nor tenet-based requirements. Finally, the court stated that it could not fairly construe the statutory language to eliminate either of these requirements and, therefore, that it could not interpret the statute in a way to avoid the constitutional infirmity.

Keep in mind, of course, that *membership* in a religious group is not explicitly mentioned in § 701(j) of Title VII as a prerequisite to the application of *its* religious accommodation provisions. Assuming, *arguendo,* that the membership and tenet-based provisions of § 19 are constitutional, since the NLRA amendment postdates the enactment of § 701(j), can it be argued that Congress intended *sub silentio* to impose this membership limitation on § 701(j) and thereby limit the scope of its accommodation provision? See International Ass'n of Machinists & Aerospace Workers, Lodge 751 v. Boeing Co., 833 F.2d 165 (9th Cir.1987); EEOC v. Davey Tree Surgery Co., 671 F.Supp. 1260 (N.D.Cal. 1987).

Section 19 of the NLRA also provides that a collective bargaining agreement can require those employees that are eligible for the exemption to make equivalent payments to a non-religious, non-labor organization charitable fund chosen by the employee from a list of at least three such funds designated in the contract, or, in the absence of such a contractual designation, to any such fund chosen by the employee. 29 U.S.C. § 169. Does this suggest that an employer should be held to have satisfied its *Title VII* duty to accommodate an employee whose religious beliefs preclude him from paying union dues by requiring him to pay an equal amount to one of several nonreligious charities designated in the collective bargaining agreement? See Stern v. Teamsters General Local Union No. 200, 626 F.Supp. 1043 (E.D.Wis.1986).

Congress' legitimization of union security clauses in § 8(a)(3) has also been circumscribed by the Supreme Court. The Court has interpreted this provision to authorize the exaction of only that portion of union fees and dues used to subsidize the cost of the union's performance of its duties as exclusive bargaining representative in dealing with the employer on labor-management issues. See COMMUNICATIONS WORKERS OF AMERICA v. BECK, 487 U.S. 735, 108 S.Ct. 2641, 101 L.Ed.2d 634 (1988)(§ 8(a)(3) was designed only to provide unions with a means of forcing employees to subsidize costs of performing the union's duties as exclusive bargaining representative, not to support union expenditures on political causes which employees oppose. Accordingly, a union cannot require a dues-paying nonmember to pay that portion of dues or fees that supports non-bargaining activity to which the employee objects.) Additionally, a union's ability to use dues paid by reluctant employees is subject to the limitations imposed by the First Amendment. In LEHNERT v. FERRIS FACULTY ASSOCIATION, ___ U.S. ___, 111 S.Ct. 2878, 115 L.Ed.2d 1044 (1991), the Supreme Court stated that its previous interpretations of the *statutory* limits on governmentally authorized union-shop agreements were "instructive" in delineating the *constitutional* bounds on compulsory dues requirements. In a case involving a public sector employee, a majority of the Court agreed that the statutory limits on chargeable activities should be applied to the analysis used in making the required case-by-case determination of which activities the union could, within constitutional limits, require a dissenting employee to subsidize. Thus, a majority concluded, chargeable activities would have to (1)be germane to collective bargaining activity; (2)be justified by the government's interest in promoting labor peace and avoiding free riders; and (3)not significantly add to the burdening of free speech that is inherent in allowing an agency shop.

To what extent, if any, should these developments in the jurisprudence surrounding the NLRA affect analogous issues arising under Title VII? For example, suppose an employee subject to a union security clause objects to the union's use of dues to support pro-choice legislation because of his deeply and sincerely held religious beliefs that abortion is wrong. The union rejects his request to make a substituted payment to a charity of an amount equal to his entire dues payment. It offers, instead, to rebate that portion of his dues that is even remotely connected with its support of pro-choice legislation. Has the union fulfilled its obligations under Title VII? Has it made a reasonable accommodation? Must the union prove that the employee's offer would result in an undue hardship to it? See E.E.O.C. v. University of Detroit, 904 F.2d 331 (6th Cir.1990).

2. The constitutionality of § 701(j) has been upheld by every circuit court that has considered the question. See EEOC v. Ithaca Industries, Inc., 849 F.2d 116 (4th Cir.1988)(en banc); International Ass'n of Machinists & Aerospace Workers, Lodge 751 v. Boeing Co., 833 F.2d 165 (9th Cir.1987); Protos v. Volkswagen of America, Inc., 797 F.2d 129 (3d Cir.), cert. denied, 479 U.S. 972, 107 S.Ct. 474, 93 L.Ed.2d 418 (1986); Cummins v. Parker Seal Co., 516 F.2d 544 (6th Cir.1975), vacated and remanded in light of *Hardison*, 433 U.S. 903, 97 S.Ct. 2965, 53 L.Ed.2d 1087 (1977); and Nottelson v. Smith Steel Workers, 643 F.2d 445 (7th Cir.), cert. denied, 454 U.S. 1046, 102 S.Ct. 587, 70 L.Ed.2d 488 (1981). In *Cummins*, however, Judge Celebrezze authored a dissenting opinion in which he strongly disagreed with the majority's application of the *Nyquist* standard:

* * *

There is no doubt that Congress acted with a valid secular purpose in banning employment discrimination based on religion through Title VII of the Civil Rights Act of 1964. The expressed purpose of that legislation was to end discrimination based on certain factors that had no relation to an individual's ability and initiative and, accordingly, to end the burden on interstate commerce imposed by various forms of invidious discrimination. The object was to make religion a meaningless factor in employment decisions.

This secular purpose does not justify the 1972 religious accommodation amendment * * *. Section 2000e(j) defines religion so as to require that persons receive preferential treatment because of their religion. This contradicts the secular purpose behind the original Title VII. Rather than "putting teeth" into the Act, it mandates religious discrimination, thus departing from the Act's basic purpose.

The second purportedly secular justification for the rule is that it recognizes that "certain persons will not compromise their religious convictions" and ensures "that they will not be punished for the supremacy of conscience."

The absence of a religious accommodation rule, however, would not amount to punishment. It would simply be a "hands-off" attitude on government's part, allowing employers and employees to settle their own differences. The rule grants benefits to religious practitioners because of their religion. The second rationale the majority advances, therefore, amounts to an assertion that it is a valid secular purpose to grant preferences to persons whose religious practices do not fit prevailing patterns. Indeed, the legislative history of the 1972 amendment reveals Congressional thinking that the Establishment Clause was not violated because "[i]n dealing with the free exercise [of religion], really, this promotes the constitutional demand in that respect."

It is, of course, fundamental that the First Amendment protects the free exercise of all religions, whatever the number of their practitioners. * * * Thus, Government may not penalize persons on the basis of their religion.

* * *

The fact that Government may not penalize particular religions does not mean that Congress may favor particular religions. On the contrary, it means that Congress may not. The argument that aid to religious institutions is justified under a broad reading of the Free Exercise Clause has been raised on behalf of aid to parochial schools and other benefits to religious groups. The argument has appeared in dissenting opinions, and Supreme Court majorities have consistently rejected it. * * * The Free Exercise Clause provides a shield against government interference with religion, but it does not offer a sword to cut through the strictures of the Establishment Clause. * * * There is no valid secular legislative purpose behind the rule. Its purpose is to protect and advance particular religions.

This purpose is clearly evident in the remarks of Senator Randolph, who authored the 1972 amendment. Although the majority cites his argument that the amendment would advance freedom from religious discrimination (despite its requiring discrimination on religious grounds), the majority fails to quote the real reason why Senator Randolph introduced the amendment:

> I say to the distinguished chairman of the Labor and Public Welfare Committee, who manages this bill, that there has been a partial refusal at times on the part of employees whose religious practices rigidly require them to abstain from work in the nature of hire on particular days. So there has been, because of understandable pressures, such as commitments of a family nature and otherwise, a dwindling of the membership of some of the religious organizations because of the situation to which I have just directed attention.

* * *

The purpose evident in these remarks is the promotion of certain religions whose followers' practices conflict with employers' schedules. The promotion of a particular religion is not a justifiable ground for legislation. Otherwise, the neutrality principle, which is the core of the First Amendment, would be violated.

Not only does the religious accommodation rule lack a secular purpose. It also fails the second test under *Nyquist*. It lacks "a primary effect that neither advances nor inhibits religion." It is, in other words, neither "even-handed in operation" nor "neutral in primary impact." The religious accommodation rule violates these principles in two respects.

First, the religious accommodation requirement discriminates between religion and non-religion. Only those with "religious practices" may benefit from the rule. Others are forced to submit to uniform work rules and to bear the burdens imposed by their employers' accommodation to religious practitioners. Thus, the rule discriminates against those with no religion, although the freedom not to believe is within the First Amendment's protection.

Second, it discriminates among religions. Only those which require their followers to manifest their belief in acts requiring modification of an employer's work rules benefit, while other employees are inconvenienced by the employer's accommodation. By singling out particular sects for government protection, the Federal Government has forfeited the pretense that the rule is merely part of the general ban on religious discrimination.
* * *

* * *

Because the religious accommodation rule violates the First Amendment under the first two tests of *Nyquist*, it is unnecessary to consider whether it also fosters "excessive entanglement" of Church and State. It is fair to note, however, that the 1972 amendment is worded far more broadly than Regulation 1605.1. The 1972 amendment extends to "all aspects of religious observance and practice, as well as belief." * * * Disposition of complaints under the amendment will require inquiry into the sincerity with which beliefs are held and force consideration of the validity of the religious nature of claims, procedures which are not favored and may themselves be improper because they put courts in review of religious matters.

* * *

This is not to say that a wise employer could not decide that as a matter of sound business practice and good employee relations to accommodate to his employees' religious practices. Forbidding the government from *requiring* accommodation would not be a holding that accommodation may not be made by private or public employers.

Is Judge Celebrezze's discussion of the Free Exercise Clause on point? Does § 701(j) create a conflict between the Free Exercise and Establishment Clauses of the First Amendment? See Anderson v. General Dynamics Convair Aerospace Div., 489 F.Supp. 782, 790 (S.D.Cal.1980), reversed on other grounds, 648 F.2d 1247 (9th Cir.1981). The Sixth Circuit's opinion in *Cummins*, decided before *Hardison*, originally was affirmed by an equally divided Supreme Court. On rehearing, however, the Supreme Court vacated the appellate court's opinion and remanded the case for reconsideration in light of *Hardison*. On remand, the Sixth Circuit concluded that a reasonable accommodation could not be achieved without undue hardship and, therefore, did not reach the constitutional issue.

In ESTATE OF THORNTON v. CALDOR, INC., 472 U.S. 703, 105 S.Ct. 2914, 86 L.Ed.2d 557 (1985), the Court ruled that a Connecticut statute that prohibited an employer from requiring an employee to work on the day of the week observed as his or her Sabbath and that provided that refusal to work on the Sabbath could not constitute grounds for dismissal, violated the Establishment Clause of the First Amendment. By providing Sabbath observers with the unqualified right not to work on whatever day they designated as their Sabbath, regardless of the burden or inconvenience imposed thereby on the employer or other workers, the statute was held to have the primary effect of impermissibly advancing a particular religious practice. Does this decision undermine the precedential value of the *Tooley* court's treatment of the constitutionality of § 701(j)? Justice O'Connor, in a concurring opinion (joined in by Justice Marshall) in *Caldor,* stated that the Connecticut statute unconstitutionally conveyed a message of endorsement of the Sabbath observance by granting, only to Sabbath observers, the benefit of selecting the day of the week in which to refrain from labor. She added that she did not read the majority's opinion as suggesting that § 701(j) was similarly invalid since that provision promoted the valid secular purpose of assuring equal employment opportunity and required reasonable rather than absolute accommodation. She also distinguished § 701(j) from the Connecticut statute on the ground that the former extended protection to all religious observance while the latter mandated accommodation only to Sabbath observance. Do you agree? At least two courts, relying, in part, on Justice O'Connor's reasoning, have concluded that *Tooley* survives *Caldor.* See International Ass'n of Machinists & Aerospace Workers, Lodge 751 v. Boeing Co., 833 F.2d 165 (9th Cir.1987); Protos v. Volkswagen of America, Inc., 797 F.2d 129 (3d Cir.1986), cert. denied, 479 U.S. 972, 107 S.Ct. 474, 93 L.Ed.2d 418 (1986). They noted that unlike the absolute preference granted by the Connecticut statute in *Caldor,* § 701(j) is flexible, requiring only a reasonable accommodation in light of the interests of the employer and nonobservant employees. The Ninth Circuit in *Boeing,* for example, recognized that substituted charity contributions would not be permitted where there was a widespread refusal to pay union dues. In addition, the court in *Protos* declared that even where the employee's religious views were challenged as either insincere or nonreligious, judicial investigation into the nature or sincerity of such claimed beliefs for the purpose of verifying the basis of a request for accommodation did not create excessive governmental entanglement in religion.

Does the refinement of the Court's standard for determining violations of the establishment clause articulated in *Allegheny County,* see *supra,* at 74, change either the analysis or result in *Tooley* or *Cummins?* Recall that in *Allegheny County* the Court focused on whether the governmental action sent a message of endorsement of religious beliefs or denominations.

3. In Rankins v. Commission on Professional Competence, cited at footnote eight of the principal case, the California Supreme Court, relying on § 701(j) cases, held that the California Constitution's prohibition of religious discrimination in employment implied a duty to accommodate equivalent to that found in § 701(j). The court also ruled that the imposition of this duty did not contravene the Establishment Clause of the federal Constitution. The U.S. Supreme Court dismissed the appeal taken in *Rankins* for want of a substantial federal question. The court in *Tooley* concluded that it was not bound on the constitutional issue by the U.S. Supreme Court's actions in *Rankins* since *Rankins* involved a plaintiff's religious objection to working on specified holy days, whereas plaintiff Tooley asserted a religious objection to paying union

dues. Are you persuaded by this distinction? See Nottelson v. Smith Steel Workers, 643 F.2d 445, 453 (7th Cir.1981).

4. U.S. Air Force regulations prohibit the wearing of headgear indoors except by armed security police in the performance of their duties. Dr. S. Simcha Goldman, an Orthodox Jew and ordained rabbi, while on active service as a clinical psychologist at an air force base mental health clinic, was permitted to wear his yarmulke in the health clinic and avoided controversy by wearing his service cap over the yarmulke when out of doors. He also wore the yarmulke while testifying as a witness at a court-martial. After a complaint was lodged with the Hospital Commander by the opposing counsel in that proceeding, the Commander declared that wearing the yarmulke was in violation of the regulations and ordered the psychologist not to wear it outside the hospital. Dr. Goldman refused and the Commander subsequently revised his order to prohibit Dr. Goldman from wearing the yarmulke even in the hospital. After receiving a formal letter of reprimand and a negative recommendation from the Hospital Commander in connection with his application to extend the term of his active service, Dr. Goldman brought suit alleging that the application of the regulation to prevent him from wearing his yarmulke infringed his First Amendment right to freely exercise his religious beliefs. In GOLDMAN v. WEINBERGER, 475 U.S. 503, 106 S.Ct. 1310, 89 L.Ed.2d 478 (1986), the Supreme Court rejected Dr. Goldman's claim. The Court noted that its review of military regulations challenged on First Amendment grounds was more deferential than that which would accompany analogous claims in the civilian sector. It added that deference was especially appropriate in connection with the professional judgment of military authorities concerning the importance of a particular military interest. Accordingly, the Court concluded, the regulation was supported by the military's perceived need for uniformity. While recognizing that this regulation might make military life more objectionable for individuals such as Dr. Goldman, the Court stated that the First Amendment did not require the military to accommodate such religious practices where such accommodation would detract from the uniformity sought by the regulations.

5. In HOBBIE v. UNEMPLOYMENT APPEALS COMMISSION OF FLORIDA, 480 U.S. 136, 107 S.Ct. 1046, 94 L.Ed.2d 190 (1987), the Supreme Court held that the State of Florida violated the free exercise clause of the First Amendment by denying unemployment compensation to an individual who, after converting to the Seventh–Day Adventist Church, refused, on religious grounds, to work on her Sabbath day. The Court also stated that awarding benefits to this individual did not violate the establishment clause. Relying on *Hobbie,* the Fourth Circuit ruled that a Virginia statute that made employees who voluntarily quit their job in order to follow their spouse to a new locality ineligible for unemployment benefits violated the free exercise clause of the First Amendment. The statute was declared unconstitutional as applied to a plaintiff who established that she had moved with the husband because of her sincere belief that her religion required her to abide by her husband's decision to move to care for his mother. The court ruled that the state's desire to maintain the fiscal integrity of the unemployment compensation fund and to ensure stability of employment did not constitute a compelling justification for penalizing the plaintiff for adhering to her religious beliefs. Austin v. Berryman, 862 F.2d 1050 (4th Cir.1988). On rehearing *en banc*, however, the Fourth Circuit reversed the panel's opinion. 878 F.2d 786 (4th Cir.1989), cert. denied, 493 U.S. 941, 110 S.Ct. 343, 107 L.Ed.2d 331 (1989). The full court reasoned

that the cause of the plaintiff's disqualification was geographical distance from the employer, not an incompatibility between her religious beliefs and her working environment or job duties. In contrast to the plaintiff in *Hobbie*, the court stated, the employer in this case did nothing to cause the termination of the plaintiff's employment status. Ms. Austin's unilateral decision to change residence simply placed her too far away from the employer's situs to make continued employment practicable. In fact, the court noted, had the plaintiff's husband chosen to move to a new residence within a commuting from the plaintiff's workplace, there would have been no interference with her employment. Consequently, the court concluded, the plaintiff here, unlike the plaintiff in *Hobbie*, was not forced to choose between religious conviction and the employer's job demands. Geography, and not religion, was, in the court's view, the exclusive cause of the plaintiff's disqualification from eligibility. Moreover, the court added, while the employer in *Hobbie* could have made some accommodation to the plaintiff's religious beliefs in order to avoid her discharge, the employer in this case was incapable of making any accommodation to the plaintiff's unilateral decision to move to a location 150 miles away from the workplace. Finally, the court noted that the Virginia statute precluded eligibility for all employees who voluntarily quit to join their spouse in a new location, irrespective of the reason for that decision. To craft an exception for family reunion decisions based solely on religious grounds (as the original panel decision did), especially in the absence of a direct conflict between religious beliefs and a particular employment practice, the full court held, would violate the establishment clause of the First Amendment.

In a subsequent proceeding in *Austin*, the appellate court also rejected the plaintiff's claim that the Virginia statute violated the equal protection clause of the Fourteenth Amendment. The plaintiff argued that women comprised 86.8% of the injured class and that the legislature had enacted the statute in the knowledge that the statute would disproportionately disadvantage women. The circuit court rejected these arguments, relying on the Supreme Court's ruling in *Feeney*, see *infra*, at 813, that purposeful discrimination is a *sine qua non* for a constitutional violation and concluding that the plaintiff had failed to show that a gender-based discriminatory purpose in any way shaped the Virginia statute. 955 F.2d 223 (4th Cir.), cert. denied, ___ U.S. ___, 112 S.Ct. 2997, 120 L.Ed.2d 874 (1992).

SECTION B.　NATIONAL ORIGIN

ESPINOZA v. FARAH MANUFACTURING CO.

Supreme Court of the United States, 1973.
414 U.S. 86, 94 S.Ct. 334, 38 L.Ed.2d 287.

Mr. Justice Marshall delivered the opinion of the Court.

This case involves interpretation of the phrase "national origin" in Tit. VII of the Civil Rights Act of 1964. Petitioner Cecilia Espinoza is a lawfully admitted resident alien who was born in and remains a citizen of Mexico. She resides in San Antonio, Texas, with her husband, Rudolfo Espinoza, a United States citizen. In July 1969, Mrs. Espinoza sought employment as a seamstress at the San Antonio division of respondent Farah Manufacturing Co. Her employment application was rejected on the basis of a longstanding company policy against the employment of aliens. After exhausting their administrative remedies with the Equal Employment Opportunity Commission, petitioners commenced this suit in the District Court alleging that respondent had discriminated against Mrs. Espinoza because of her "national origin" in violation of § 703 of Tit. VII. The District Court granted petitioners' motion for summary judgment, holding that a refusal to hire because of lack of citizenship constitutes discrimination on the basis of "national origin." The Court of Appeals reversed, concluding that the statutory phrase "national origin" did not embrace citizenship. We granted the writ to resolve this question of statutory construction and now affirm.

    * * * Certainly the plain language of the statute supports the result reached by the Court of Appeals. The term "national origin" on its face refers to the country where a person was born, or, more broadly, the country from which his or her ancestors came.

    The statute's legislative history, though quite meager in this respect, fully supports this construction. The only direct definition given the phrase "national origin" is the following remark made on the floor of the House of Representatives by Congressman Roosevelt, Chairman of the House Subcommittee which reported the bill: "It means the country from which you or your forebears came. * * * You may come from Poland, Czechoslovakia, England, France, or any other country." 110 Cong. Rec. 2549 (1964). We also note that an earlier version of § 703 had referred to discrimination because of "race, color, religion, national origin, or *ancestry*." The deletion of the word "ancestry" from the final version was not intended as a material change, see H.R.Rep. No. 914, 88th Cong., 1st Sess., 87 (1963), suggesting that the terms "national origin" and "ancestry" were considered synonymous.

    There are other compelling reasons to believe that Congress did not intend the term "national origin" to embrace citizenship requirements. Since 1914, the Federal Government itself, through Civil Service Commission regulations, has engaged in what amounts to discrimination against aliens by denying them the right to enter competitive examination for federal employment. But it has never been suggested that the citizenship requirement for federal employment constitutes discrimination because of national origin, even though since 1943, various Executive Orders have expressly prohibited discrimination on the basis of national origin in Federal Government employment.

    Moreover, § 701(b) of Tit. VII, in language closely paralleling § 703, makes it "the policy of the United States to insure equal employment opportunities for Federal employees without discrimination because of * * * national origin * * *." The legislative history of that section reveals no mention of any intent on Congress' part to reverse the longstanding practice of requiring federal employees to be United States citizens. To the contrary, there is every indication that no such reversal was intended. Congress itself has on several occasions since 1964 enacted statutes barring aliens from federal employment. The Treasury, Postal Service, and General Government Appropriation

Act, 1973, for example, provides that "no part of any appropriation contained in this or any other Act shall be used to pay the compensation of any officer or employee of the Government of the United States * * * unless such person (1) is a citizen of the United States * * *." [3]

To interpret the term "national origin" to embrace citizenship requirements would require us to conclude that Congress itself has repeatedly flouted its own declaration of policy. This Court cannot lightly find such a breach of faith. So far as federal employment is concerned, we think it plain that Congress has assumed that the ban on national-origin discrimination in § 701(b) did not affect the historical practice of requiring citizenship as a condition of employment. And there is no reason to believe Congress intended the term "national origin" in § 703 to have any broader scope.

Petitioners have suggested that the statutes and regulations discriminating against noncitizens in federal employment are unconstitutional under the Due Process Clause of the Fifth Amendment. We need not address that question here, for the issue presented in this case is not whether Congress has the power to discriminate against aliens in federal employment, but rather, whether Congress intended to prohibit such discrimination in private employment. Suffice it to say that we cannot conclude Congress would at once continue the practice of requiring citizenship as a condition of federal employment and, at the same time, prevent private employers from doing likewise. Interpreting § 703 as petitioners suggest would achieve the rather bizarre result of preventing Farah from insisting on United States citizenship as a condition of employment while the very agency charged with enforcement of Tit. VII would itself be required by Congress to place such a condition on its own personnel.

The District Court drew primary support for its holding from an interpretative guideline issued by the Equal Employment Opportunity Commission which provides:

> "Because discrimination on the basis of citizenship has the effect of discriminating on the basis of national origin, a lawfully immigrated alien who is domiciled or residing in this country may not be discriminated against on the basis of his citizenship * * *." 29 CFR § 1606.1(d) (1972).

Like the Court of Appeals, we have no occasion here to question the general validity of this guideline insofar as it can be read as an expression of the Commission's belief that there may be many situations where discrimination on the basis of citizenship would have the effect of discriminating on the basis of national origin. In some

---

3. Petitioners argue that it is unreasonable to attribute any great significance to these provisions in determining congressional intent because the barrier to employment of noncitizens has been tucked away in appropriations bills rather than expressed in a more affirmative fashion. We disagree. Indeed, the fact that Congress has occasionally enacted exceptions to the general barrier indicates to us that Congress was well aware of what it was doing.

instances, for example, a citizenship requirement might be but one part of a wider scheme of unlawful national-origin discrimination. In other cases, an employer might use a citizenship test as a pretext to disguise what is in fact national-origin discrimination. Certainly Tit. VII prohibits discrimination on the basis of citizenship whenever it has the purpose or effect of discriminating on the basis of national origin. "The Act proscribes not only overt discrimination but also practices that are fair in form, but discriminatory in operation." Griggs v. Duke Power Co., 401 U.S. 424, 431, 91 S.Ct. 849, 853, 28 L.Ed.2d 158 (1971).

It is equally clear, however, that these principles lend no support to petitioners in this case. There is no indication in the record that Farah's policy against employment of aliens had the purpose or effect of discriminating against persons of Mexican national origin.[5] It is conceded that Farah accepts employees of Mexican origin, provided the individual concerned has become an American citizen. Indeed, the District Court found that persons of Mexican ancestry make up more than 96% of the employees at the company's San Antonio division, and 97% of those doing the work for which Mrs. Espinoza applied. While statistics such as these do not automatically shield an employer from a charge of unlawful discrimination, the plain fact of the matter is that Farah does not discriminate against persons of Mexican national origin with respect to employment in the job Mrs. Espinoza sought. She was denied employment, not because of the country of her origin, but because she had not yet achieved United States citizenship. In fact, the record shows that the worker hired in place of Mrs. Espinoza was a citizen with a Spanish surname.

The Commission's guideline may have significance for a wide range of situations, but not for a case such as this where its very premise— that discrimination on the basis of citizenship has the effect of discrimination on the basis of national origin—is not borne out.[6] It is also significant to note that the Commission itself once held a different view as to the meaning of the phrase "national origin." When first confronted with the question, the Commission, through its General Counsel, said: " 'National origin' refers to the country from which the individual or his forebears came * * *, not to whether or not he is a United States citizen * * *." EEOC General Counsel's Opinion Letter, 1 CCH Employment Prac. Guide ¶ 1220.20 (1967). The Commission's more recent interpretation of the statute in the guideline relied on by the District

---

5. There is no suggestion, for example, that the company refused to hire aliens of Mexican or Spanish-speaking background while hiring those of other national origins. * * * While the company asks job applicants whether they are United States citizens, it makes no inquiry as to their national origin.

6. It is suggested that a refusal to hire an alien always disadvantages that person because of the country of his birth. A person born in the United States, the argument goes, automatically obtains citizenship at birth, while those born elsewhere can acquire citizenship only through a long and sometimes difficult process. The answer to this argument is that it is not the employer who places the burdens of naturalization on those born outside the country, but Congress itself, through laws enacted pursuant to its constitutional power "[t]o establish an uniform Rule of Naturalization." U.S.Const., Art. 1, § 8, cl. 4. * * *

Court is no doubt entitled to great deference, but that deference must have limits where, as here, application of the guideline would be inconsistent with an obvious congressional intent not to reach the employment practice in question. Courts need not defer to an administrative construction of a statute where there are "compelling indications that it is wrong."

Finally, petitioners seek to draw support from the fact that Tit. VII protects all individuals from unlawful discrimination, whether or not they are citizens of the United States. We agree that aliens are protected from discrimination under the Act. That result may be derived not only from the use of the term "any individual" in § 703, but also as a negative inference from the exemption in § 702, which provides that Tit. VII "shall not apply to an employer with respect to the employment of aliens outside any State * * *." Title VII was clearly intended to apply with respect to the employment of aliens inside any State.

The question posed in the present case, however, is not whether aliens are protected from illegal discrimination under the Act, but what kinds of discrimination the Act makes illegal. Certainly it would be unlawful for an employer to discriminate against aliens because of race, color, religion, sex, or national origin—for example, by hiring aliens of Anglo–Saxon background but refusing to hire those of Mexican or Spanish ancestry. Aliens are protected from illegal discrimination under the Act, but nothing in the Act makes it illegal to discriminate on the basis of citizenship or alienage.

We agree with the Court of Appeals that neither the language of the Act, nor its history, nor the specific facts of this case indicate that respondent has engaged in unlawful discrimination because of national origin.

Affirmed.

MR. JUSTICE DOUGLAS, dissenting.

It is odd that the Court which holds that a State may not bar an alien from the practice of law or deny employment to aliens can read a federal statute that prohibits discrimination in employment on account of "national origin" so as to permit discrimination against aliens.

Alienage results from one condition only: being born outside the United States. Those born within the country are citizens from birth. It could not be more clear that Farah's policy of excluding aliens is *de facto* a policy of preferring those who were born in this country. Therefore the construction placed upon the "national origin" provision is inconsistent with the construction this Court has placed upon the same Act's protections for persons denied employment on account of race or sex.

In connection with racial discrimination we have said that the Act prohibits "practices, procedures, or tests neutral on their face, and even neutral in terms of intent," if they create "artificial, arbitrary, and unnecessary barriers to employment when the barriers operate invidiously to discriminate on the basis of racial *or other impermissible classification.*"   Griggs v. Duke Power Co., 401 U.S. 424, 430–431, 91 S.Ct. 849, 28 L.Ed.2d 158 (1971) (emphasis added).   There we found that the employer could not use test or diploma requirements which on their face were racially neutral, when in fact those requirements had a *de facto* discriminatory result and the employer was unable to justify them as related to job performance.   The tests involved in *Griggs* did not eliminate all blacks seeking employment, just as the citizenship requirement here does not eliminate all applicants of foreign origin. Respondent here explicitly conceded that the citizenship requirement is imposed without regard to the alien's qualifications for the job.

These petitioners against whom discrimination is charged are Chicanos.   But whether brown, yellow, black, or white, the thrust of the Act is clear: alienage is no barrier to employment here.   *Griggs*, as I understood it until today, extends its protective principles to all, not to blacks alone.   Our cases on sex discrimination under the Act yield the same result as *Griggs*.

The construction placed upon the statute in the majority opinion is an extraordinary departure from prior cases, and it is opposed by the Equal Employment Opportunity Commission, the agency provided by law with the responsibility of enforcing the Act's protections.   The Commission takes the only permissible position: that discrimination on the basis of alienage *always* has the effect of discrimination on the basis of national origin.   Refusing to hire an individual because he is an alien "is discrimination based on birth outside the United States and is thus discrimination based on national origin in violation of Title VII." The Commission's interpretation of the statute is entitled to great weight.

There is no legislative history to cast doubt on this construction.[3] Indeed, any other construction flies in the face of the underlying congressional policy of removing "artificial, arbitrary, and unnecessary barriers to employment."   McDonnell Douglas Corp. v. Green, 411 U.S. 792, 806, 93 S.Ct. 1817, 1826, 36 L.Ed.2d 668 (1973).

Mrs. Espinoza is a permanent resident alien, married to an American citizen, and her children will be native-born American citizens. But that first generation has the greatest adjustments to make to their new country.   Their unfamiliarity with America makes them the most vulnerable to exploitation and discriminatory treatment.   They, of course, have the same obligation as American citizens to pay taxes, and

---

3. The only legislative history the majority points to is Congressman Roosevelt's definition of "national origin": "It means the country from which you or your forebears came. * * * You may come from Poland, Czechoslovakia, England, France, or any other country."   But that only makes clear what petitioners here argue— that Mrs. Espinoza cannot be discriminated against because she comes from a foreign country.   The majority's mention of the deletion of the word "ancestry," ibid., is certainly irrelevant.   Obviously "national origin" comprehends "ancestry," but as Congressman Roosevelt pointed out it means more—not only where one's forebears were born, but where one himself was born.

they are subject to the draft on the same basis. But they have never received equal treatment in the job market. * * *

The majority decides today that in passing sweeping legislation guaranteeing equal job opportunities, the Congress intended to help only the immigrant's children, excluding those "for whom there [is] no place at all." I cannot impute that niggardly an intent to Congress.

NOTES AND PROBLEMS FOR DISCUSSION

1. While foreign citizens are not protected by Title VII against private sector alienage bars, similarly restrictive employment practices used by a public employer can be challenged under the equal protection guarantees of the Fifth or Fourteenth Amendments to the U.S. Constitution. The Supreme Court has invalidated statutes that prevented aliens from entering a state's classified civil service, Sugarman v. Dougall, 413 U.S. 634, 93 S.Ct. 2842, 37 L.Ed.2d 853 (1973), practicing law, Application of Griffiths, 413 U.S. 717, 93 S.Ct. 2851, 37 L.Ed.2d 910 (1973) and working as an engineer, Examining Board of Engineers v. Flores de Otero, 426 U.S. 572, 96 S.Ct. 2264, 49 L.Ed.2d 65 (1976). More recently, however, the Court upheld one state statute that excluded aliens from serving as "peace officers", Cabell v. Chavez–Salido, 454 U.S. 432, 102 S.Ct. 735, 70 L.Ed.2d 677 (1982), another that prohibited aliens who did not manifest an intention to apply for U.S. citizenship from working as elementary and secondary school teachers, Ambach v. Norwick, 441 U.S. 68, 99 S.Ct. 1589, 60 L.Ed.2d 49 (1979), and a third that precluded aliens from working for a state police force, Foley v. Connelie, 435 U.S. 291, 98 S.Ct. 1067, 55 L.Ed.2d 287 (1978). These latter decisions indicate, at least with respect to "political function" positions, i.e., those "intimately related to the process of democratic self-government," Bernal v. Fainter, 467 U.S. 216, 104 S.Ct. 2312, 81 L.Ed.2d 175 (1984), that the Supreme Court will apply a less demanding standard than the strict scrutiny traditionally accorded alienage classifications. See generally Griffith, The Alien Meets Some Constitutional Hurdles in Employment, Education and Aid Programs, 17 S.D.L.Rev. 201 (1980).

Congress enacted the Immigration Reform and Control Act of 1986, 8 U.S.C. § 1324a (1986) (IRCA), as amended by the Immigration Act of 1990, P.L. 101–649, 104 Stat. 5053,5056 (1990), to deal with some of the problems posed by the employment of illegal aliens in the United States. This statute forbids the hiring, recruitment or referral for employment for a fee of any person known to be an alien without legal status. It imposes civil and criminal sanctions for the violation of these provisions and requires employers, unions and employment agencies to take steps (by requiring the presentation of prescribed documents such as a driver's license or alien documentation) to verify that individuals seeking employment or job referral or recruitment are lawfully eligible for employment. However, the 1990 amendments added that if an employer requests more or different employment-eligibility documents than are required under the IRCA, or refuses to honor documents that reasonably appear to be genuine, that employer will be subject to a claim of discrimination. Aliens who do not enjoy lawful employment status were also offered the opportunity (for a one year period) to apply for legal status if they could prove continuous residence in the United States since before January 1, 1982. Separate provisions apply to seasonal agricultural workers.

The IRCA adds a protection not available under Title VII by prohibiting employers with more than three employees from discriminating on the basis of citizenship status with respect to all but illegal aliens and except where citizenship is required by law. The Act does, however, permit an employer to discriminate against a lawful alien when that alien is competing for a job with an "equally qualified" American citizen or national. The 1990 amendments also included a provision like § 704(a) of Title VII that prohibits an employer from intimidating or retaliating against anyone who seeks relief under the IRCA or participates in any proceeding, hearing or investigation related to that statute. Finally, an alien who prevails on a claim under the IRCA is entitled to attorney's fees, but only upon a showing that the losing party's argument was "without reasonable foundation in law and fact."

In an attempt to conform enforcement of the IRCA to Title VII, the EEOC issued a policy statement in May, 1989, announcing that while undocumented aliens remain protected by the provisions of Title VII, where an employer, pursuant to the requirements of the IRCA, refuses to employ an undocumented alien after November 6, 1986 (the effective date of the IRCA), it cannot be ordered by the EEOC to hire or reinstate such an alien even if the employer's actions would constitute a violation of the terms of Title VII. The EEOC added, however, that undocumented aliens hired before November 6, 1986 can remain in their jobs without placing the employer in jeopardy of violating the IRCA. Thus, these "grandfathered" undocumented aliens would continue to be eligible for remedial relief if the employer discriminates against them in violation of Title VII.

The EEOC's position extending the protection of Title VII to undocumented alien workers was approved in EEOC v. Tortilleria "La Mejor", 758 F.Supp. 585 (E.D.Ca. 1991). In the first reported case dealing with the *post*-IRCA application of Title VII to undocumented aliens, the trial court ruled that in light of the specificity with which Congress drafted the exemptions from coverage under Title VII, it was prepared to presume that the absence of explicit reference in these provisions to undocumented aliens manifested a Congressional intention to include such aliens within the protections of the statute. The court also referred to rulings by the Supreme Court and the Eleventh Circuit which had held that the underlying policy of the IRCA to discourage the employment of undocumented aliens was supported by its decision to include such workers within the ambit of Title VII. In this regard, the court referred to rulings by the Supreme Court and the Eleventh Circuit in which these courts held that the IRCA did not preclude application of the NLRA and FLSA, respectively, to undocumented workers.

2. The EEOC Guidelines discussed in *Espinoza* were modified after that decision was rendered to provide that citizenship requirements violate Title VII only when they have the purpose or effect of discriminating on the basis of national origin. 29 C.F.R. § 1606.5 (1980). But this option appears to be available only in claims against American employers. Recall that some lower courts have ruled that U.S. treaties granting foreign employers the right to discriminate on the basis of alienage preclude a Title VII challenge to such citizenship preferences on the ground that they discriminate on the basis of either race or national origin. See Chapter 1, Section D, *supra*, at 78 n.4.

3. Does an employer's rule prohibiting employees from speaking Spanish on the job unless they are communicating with Spanish-speaking customers constitute national origin discrimination? Compare Gutierrez v. Municipal Court of Southeast Judicial District, Los Angeles County, 838 F.2d 1031 (9th Cir.1988), vacated as moot, 490 U.S. 1016, 109 S.Ct. 1736, 104 L.Ed.2d 174 (1989)

with Garcia v. Gloor, 618 F.2d 264 (5th Cir.1980), cert. denied, 449 U.S. 1113, 101 S.Ct. 923, 66 L.Ed.2d 842 (1981). What about an employer that denies a job or promotion to an individual because of his or her foreign accent? Can this employee state a prima facie case claim of national origin discrimination? If so, what response could the employer offer? In FRAGANTE v. CITY AND COUNTY OF HONOLULU, 888 F.2d 591 (9th Cir.1989), cert. denied, 494 U.S. 1081, 110 S.Ct. 1811, 108 L.Ed.2d 942 (1990), the plaintiff was denied a position that, among other things, required him to provide information to the public over the telephone. After receiving the highest score on the written examination among all applicants, the plaintiff was denied a position on the basis of evaluations by two interviewers who reported that they had difficulty understanding him and therefore determined that his "heavy Filipino accent" would interfere with the performance of certain important aspects of the job. Applicants who were found to be superior in their verbal communication ability were selected for the two available positions. The trial court dismissed the complaint on the ground that the plaintiff's rejection was based on his inability to communicate effectively with the public and not because of his national origin. The Ninth Circuit affirmed this ruling. It agreed that the defendant was motivated exclusively by its reasonable business interest in hiring someone who could communicate effectively with the public. Thus, it concluded, regardless of whether the plaintiff had established a prima facie case, the defendant had convinced the court that the decision was motivated by a legitimate, nondiscriminatory interest. The court emphasized that the plaintiff had not been denied employment simply because the employer did not like foreign accents or because the employer was afraid that its customers would not like foreign accents. Interestingly, however, the court felt uncomfortable in ruling that the plaintiff's lack of qualifications prevented him from satisfying the *Burdine* elements of a prima facie case. It expressly refused to rule on that question, holding, instead, that the defendant had established a nondiscriminatory, nonpretextual explanation for its conduct. But see Carino v. University of Oklahoma Board of Regents, 750 F.2d 815 (10th Cir.1984); Berke v. Ohio Dept. of Public Welfare, 628 F.2d 980 (6th Cir.1980). Should the disposition of these cases be influenced by the degree to which the disqualifying characteristic is immutable? The principal case and the mutability/immutability question are examined in Note, Garcia v. Gloor: Mutable Characteristics Rationale Extended to National Origin Discrimination, 32 Merc.L.Rev. 1275 (1981).

Can a plaintiff state a claim of national origin discrimination where he alleges that he was discriminated against because he is Serbian even though Serbia's existence as a nation ended decades before the plaintiff's birth? See Pejic v. Hughes Helicopters, Inc., 840 F.2d 667 (9th Cir.1988). What about a plaintiff who alleges that she was discriminated against because she is a Gypsy? Would it matter whether or not the plaintiff's complaint referred to any particular country or region as the place of her ancestors' origin? See Janko v. Illinois State Toll Highway Authority, 704 F.Supp. 1531 (N.D.Ill.1989) (denying motion to dismiss complaint on ground that dictionary refers to Gypsies as an ethnic group from Mediterranean area and, therefore, that Gypsy constitutes a national origin within meaning of statute).

4. Is an employer liable under Title VII if one of its supervisors makes derogatory references to a subordinate employee's heritage? See Cariddi v. Kansas City Chiefs Football Club, Inc., 568 F.2d 87 (8th Cir.1977); Morales v. Dain, Kalman & Quail, Inc., 467 F.Supp. 1031 (D.Minn.1979). What if the speaker was a co-employee rather than a supervisor? In either situation,

should it matter whether the company encouraged, acquiesced to, condemned, or was unaware of this conduct?

The EEOC Guidelines specifically address these issues:

"(a) The Commission has consistently held that harassment on the basis of national origin is a violation of Title VII. An employer has an affirmative duty to maintain a working environment free of harassment on the basis of national origin.

"(b) Ethnic slurs and other verbal or physical conduct relating to an individual's national origin constitute harassment when this conduct: (1) has the purpose or effect of creating an intimidating, hostile or offensive working environment; (2) has the purpose or effect of unreasonably interfering with an individual's work performance; or (3) otherwise adversely affects an individual's employment opportunities.

"(c) An employer is responsible for its acts and those of its agents and supervisory employees with respect to harassment on the basis of national origin regardless of whether the specific acts complained of were authorized or even forbidden by the employer and regardless of whether the employer knew or should have known of their occurrence. * * *

"(d) With respect to conduct between fellow employees, an employer is responsible for acts of harassment in the workplace on the basis of national origin, where the employer, its agents or supervisory employees, knows or should have known of the conduct, unless the employer can show that it took immediate and appropriate corrective action."

29 C.F.R. § 1606.8 (1980).

5. Can the owner of an Italian restaurant refuse to hire a non-Italian chef? Waiter?

6. Relying on *Griggs* disproportionate impact analysis, several courts have invalidated minimum height requirements on the ground that they disproportionately exclude members of certain national origin groups and are not related to job performance. See Craig v. County of Los Angeles, 626 F.2d 659 (9th Cir.1980), cert. denied, 450 U.S. 919, 101 S.Ct. 1364, 67 L.Ed.2d 345 (1981); United States v. City of Buffalo, 457 F.Supp 612 (W.D.N.Y.1978), affirmed as modified on remedies, 633 F.2d 643 (2d Cir. 1980).

7. How does a plaintiff in a national origin discrimination case establish that she is a member of a particular ethnic group? Is it sufficient, for example, for her to rely on evidence of her subjective feelings about her own ethnicity, or must she proffer evidence relating to her physical appearance, speech or mannerisms in order to demonstrate her objective appearance to others? See Bennun v. Rutgers State University, 941 F.2d 154 (3d Cir.1991), cert. denied, ___ U.S. ___, 112 S.Ct. 956, 117 L.Ed.2d 124 (1992).

SECTION C. RACE AND COLOR
McDONALD v. SANTA FE TRAIL TRANSPORTATION CO.

Supreme Court of the United States, 1976.
427 U.S. 273, 96 S.Ct. 2574, 49 L.Ed.2d 493.

MR. JUSTICE MARSHALL delivered the opinion of the Court.

Petitioners, L. N. McDonald and Raymond L. Laird, brought this action in the United States District Court for the Southern District of

Texas seeking relief against Santa Fe Trail Transportation Co. (Santa Fe) and International Brotherhood of Teamsters Local 988 (Local 988), which represented Santa Fe's Houston employees, for alleged violations of * * * Title VII of the Civil Rights Act of 1964, in connection with their discharge from Santa Fe's employment. The District Court dismissed the complaint on the pleadings. The Court of Appeals for the Fifth Circuit affirmed. In determining whether the decisions of these courts were correct, we must decide * * * whether a complaint alleging that white employees charged with misappropriating property from their employer were dismissed from employment, while a black employee similarly charged was not dismissed, states a claim under Title VII.
* * *

Because the District Court dismissed this case on the pleadings, we take as true the material facts alleged in petitioners' complaint. On September 26, 1970, petitioners, both white, and Charles Jackson, a Negro employee of Santa Fe, were jointly and severally charged with misappropriating 60 one-gallon cans of antifreeze which was part of a shipment Santa Fe was carrying for one of its customers. Six days later, petitioners were fired by Santa Fe, while Jackson was retained.
* * *

* * *

Title VII of the Civil Rights Act of 1964 prohibits the discharge of "any individual" because of "such individual's race," § 703(a)(1). Its terms are not limited to discrimination against members of any particular race. Thus, although we were not there confronted with racial discrimination against whites, we described the Act in Griggs v. Duke Power Co., as prohibiting "[d]iscriminatory preference for *any* [racial] group, *minority* or *majority* " (emphasis added). Similarly the EEOC, whose interpretations are entitled to great deference, has consistently interpreted Title VII to proscribe racial discrimination in private employment against whites on the same terms as racial discrimination against nonwhites, holding that to proceed otherwise would

> "constitute a derogation of the Commission's Congressional mandate to eliminate all practices which operate to disadvantage the employment opportunities of any group protected by Title VII, including Caucasians." EEOC Decision No. 74–31, 7 FEP 1326, 1328, CCH EEOC Decisions ¶ 6404, p. 4084 (1973).

This conclusion is in accord with uncontradicted legislative history to the effect that Title VII was intended to "cover white men and white women and all Americans," 110 Cong. Rec. 2578 (1964) (remarks of Rep. Celler), and create an "obligation not to discriminate against whites," id., at 7218 (memorandum of Sen. Clark). See also id., at 7213 (memorandum of Sens. Clark and Case); id., at 8912 (remarks of Sen. Williams). We therefore hold today that Title VII prohibits racial discrimination against the white petitioners in this case upon the same standards as would be applicable were they Negroes and Jackson white.

* * *

NOTES AND PROBLEMS FOR DISCUSSION

1. The absence of a statutory definition of "race" notwithstanding, few definitional problems have arisen in connection with this term. Since the statute also protects individuals from discrimination on the basis of color, national origin and religion, choosing the specific classification into which any particular claim fits usually is not a controversial issue. There are, however, two exceptions to this general rule. The bona fide occupational qualification defense provided in § 703(e) cannot be used to justify a classification based on race. Thus, characterizing a claim as alleging national origin, as opposed to race discrimination, can be critical where the defendant wants to take advantage of this defense. Secondly, affirmative action policies often define the class included within their provisions by racial membership.

2. The very few reported cases dealing with "color," as divorced from race discrimination, have involved claims by a dark-skinned person that he was denied a position given to a light-skinned member of his race (or vice versa) with similar qualifications. See Walker v. Internal Revenue Service, 713 F.Supp. 403 (N.D.Ga.1989) (light-skinned black employee can state claim under Title VII on ground that dark-skinned black supervisor discharged her on the basis of her skin color); Ali v. National Bank of Pakistan, 508 F.Supp. 611 (S.D.N.Y.1981); EEOC Decision No. 72–0454 (Nov. 15, 1971). In light of this and the inapplicability of the BFOQ defense to race or color claims, would a movie producer violate Title VII by insisting on a dark-complexioned black actor to play the lead role in "The Idi Amin Story"?

3. Plaintiff, a white woman, was discharged from her job because she was involved in a social relationship with a black man. Can she state a claim under Title VII? Compare Parr v. Woodmen of the World Life Ins. Co., 791 F.2d 888 (11th Cir.1986), on remand, 657 F.Supp. 1022 (M.D.Ga.1987) (dismissing case after trial on ground that the plaintiff was not a bona fide applicant for the job since, rather than being genuinely interested in the position, he was only interested in creating a basis for Title VII suit by letting it be known that he was married to a black woman); Chacon v. Ochs, 780 F.Supp. 680 (C.D.Ca.1991); Erwin v. Mister Omelet of America, Inc., 54 FEP Cases 1456 (M.D.N.C.1991); and Whitney v. Greater New York Corp. of Seventh Day Adventists, 401 F.Supp. 1363 (S.D.N.Y.1975) with Ripp v. Dobbs Houses, Inc., 366 F.Supp. 205 (N.D.Ala.1973).

4. In Morton v. Mancari, 417 U.S. 535, 94 S.Ct. 2474, 41 L.Ed.2d 290 (1974), the Supreme Court rejected a claim that a 1934 federal statute granting qualified American Indians an employment preference in the Bureau of Indian Affairs was inconsistent with, and thus superseded by the anti-racial discrimination provisions of Title VII. In reaching this result, the Court noted that Title VII itself specifically exempts Indian tribes from its provisions and permits private businesses located on or near Indian reservations to give preferential treatment to Indians living on or near reservations.

SECTION D. SEX

KANOWITZ, SEX–BASED DISCRIMINATION IN AMERICAN LAW III: TITLE VII OF THE 1964 CIVIL RIGHTS ACT AND THE EQUAL PAY ACT OF 1963

20 Hastings L.Rev. 305, 310–12 (1968).

* * *

Any consideration of the sex provisions of Title VII of the 1964 Civil Rights Act requires a preliminary glance at what can only be described as their peculiar legislative history. In the light of its tremendous potential for profoundly affecting the daily lives of so many Americans—both men and women—Title VII's prohibition against sex-discrimination in employment had a rather inauspicious birth.

This is not to say that some species of federal legislation outlawing sex-based discrimination in employment might not have emerged eventually from a Congress in which male representatives out-numbered female representatives overwhelmingly. Agitation for such a law, after all, had been going on for many years. * * * But the prospects for the passage of legislation prohibiting sex discrimination in hiring and promotional practices in employment were exceedingly dim in 1964. Had the sex provisions of Title VII been presented then as a separate bill, rather than being coupled as they were in an effusion of Congressional gimmickry with legislation aimed at curbing racial and ethnic discrimination, their defeat in 1964 would have been virtually assured. We have no less an authority for this conclusion than Oregon's Representative Edith Green, whose strong advocacy of equal legal treatment for American women lends great force to her appraisal. In her view, stated in Congress, the legislation against sex discrimination in employment, "considered by itself, and * * * brought to the floor with no hearings and no testimony * * * would not [have] receive[d] one hundred votes."

In fact, it was not until the last day of the bill's consideration in Chairman Howard Smith's House Rules committee, where it had gone after a favorable report from the Judiciary Committee, that there first appeared a motion to add "sex" discrimination to the other types of employment discrimination that the original bill sought to curb. That motion was defeated in Committee by a vote of 8–7. But after almost two weeks of passionate floor debate in the House and just one day before the act was passed, Representative Smith, a principal opponent of the original bill, offered an amendment to include sex as a prohibited basis for employment discrimination. Under that amendment, the previously proposed sanctions against employers, unions, hiring agencies, or their agents, for discrimination in hiring or promotional practices against actual or prospective employees on the basis of race, creed, or national origin, were, with some exceptions, also to apply to discrimination based upon the "sex" of the job applicant or employee. Offering his amendment, Representative Smith remarked: "Now I am very serious * * * I do not think it can do any harm to this legislation; maybe it will do some good."

Despite Congressman Smith's protestations of seriousness, there was substantial cause to doubt his motives. For four months Congress had been locked in debate over the passage of the Civil Rights Act of 1964. Most southern Representatives and a few of their northern allies had been making every effort to block its passage. In the context of that debate and of the prevailing Congressional sentiment when the amendment was offered, it is abundantly clear that a principal motive in introducing it was to prevent passage of the basic legislation being considered by Congress, rather than solicitude for women's employment rights.

It is not surprising, therefore, that Representative Green, expressing her hope that "the day will come when discrimination will be ended against women," also registered her opposition to the proposed amendment, stating that it "will clutter up the bill and it may later—very well—be used to help destroy this section of the bill by some of the very people who today support it."

Despite these misgivings, and despite the apparent objectives of its sponsors to block passage of the entire Act, the legislation that finally emerged contained Representative Smith's amendment intact. As a result of this stroke of misfired political tactics, our federal positive law now includes a provision that had been desired for many years by those who were concerned with the economic, social and political status of American women, but which had been delayed because of the feeling that the time had not ripened for such legislation, and had been specifically opposed in this instance partly because of a belief that "discrimination based on sex involves problems sufficiently different from discrimination based on * * * other factors * * * to make separate treatment preferable."

What significance should be drawn from this peculiar legislative history of Title VII's prohibition against sex discrimination? It would be a most serious error to attribute to Congress as a corporate unit the apparently cynical motives of the amendment's sponsor. Though most members of Congress were intent on prohibiting employment discrimination based on race, religion and national origin, they did vote to do the same with respect to sex discrimination once the matter, regardless of its sponsor's apparent intentions, was brought to them for a vote. And when Congress adopts any legislation, especially a law with such important ramifications, one must infer a Congressional intention that such legislation be effective to carry out its underlying social policy— which in this case is to eradicate every instance of sex-based employment discrimination that is not founded upon a bona fide occupational qualification.

* * *

1. "Sex–Plus" Discrimination and Pregnancy

After the enactment of Title VII, the federal courts treated sex discrimination claims just like claims relating to the other classifications. The disparate treatment and disproportionate impact theories, which originated in race cases, were easily adapted to allegations of sex bias. In Dothard v. Rawlinson, 433 U.S. 321, 97 S.Ct. 2720, 53 L.Ed.2d 786 (1977), for example, the Supreme Court invalidated a minimum height and weight requirement for jobs with the Alabama Board of Corrections because of its disproportionate exclusionary impact on women. There was, however, one development in the treatment of Title VII claims that was peculiar to sex-based charges. Employers with a significant proportion of women employees began to implement policies that restricted employment opportunities to specific classes of women. For example, some companies refused to employ married or pregnant women, women over a certain age, or women with pre-school-age children. The employers contended that the presence of women on their payrolls negated claims that they discriminated on the basis of sex. Opponents of these policies, on the other hand, argued that the restrictions did violate Title VII since they applied only to female employees. Thus, the courts were faced with determining whether an employment policy that does not discriminate *solely* on the basis of sex, but on the basis of sex plus some other, facially neutral qualification, is violative of Title VII.

PHILLIPS v. MARTIN MARIETTA CORP.

Supreme Court of the United States, 1971.
400 U.S. 542, 91 S.Ct. 496, 27 L.Ed.2d 613.

Per Curiam.

Petitioner Mrs. Ida Phillips commenced an action in the United States District Court for the Middle District of Florida under Title VII of the Civil Rights Act of 1964 alleging that she had been denied employment because of her sex. The District Court granted summary judgment for Martin Marietta Corp. (Martin) on the basis of the following showing: (1) in 1966 Martin informed Mrs. Phillips that it was not accepting job applications from women with pre-school-age children; (2) as of the time of the motion for summary judgment, Martin employed men with pre-school-age children; (3) at the time Mrs. Phillips applied, 70–75% of the applicants for the position she sought were women; 75–80% of those hired for the position, assembly trainee, were women, hence no question of bias against women as such was presented.

The Court of Appeals for the Fifth Circuit affirmed, and denied a rehearing *en banc*. We granted certiorari.

Section 703(a) of the Civil Rights Act of 1964 requires that persons of like qualifications be given employment opportunities irrespective of their sex. The Court of Appeals therefore erred in reading this section as permitting one hiring policy for women and another for men—each having pre-school-age children. The existence of such conflicting family obligations, if demonstrably more relevant to job performance for a woman than for a man, could arguably be a basis for distinction under § 703(e) of the Act. But that is a matter of evidence tending to show that the condition in question "is a bona fide occupational qualification reasonably necessary to the normal operation of that particular business or enterprise." The record before us, however, is not adequate for resolution of these important issues. Summary judgment was therefore improper and we remand for fuller development of the record and for further consideration.

Vacated and remanded.

MR. JUSTICE MARSHALL, concurring.

While I agree that this case must be remanded for a full development of the facts, I cannot agree with the Court's indication that a "bona fide occupational qualification reasonably necessary to the normal operation of" Martin Marietta's business could be established by a showing that some women, even the vast majority, with pre-school-age children have family responsibilities that interfere with job performance and that men do not usually have such responsibilities. Certainly, an employer can require that all of his employees, both men and women, meet minimum performance standards, and he can try to insure compliance by requiring parents, both mothers and fathers, to provide for the care of their children so that job performance is not interfered with.

But the Court suggests that it would not require such uniform standards. I fear that in this case, where the issue is not squarely before us, the Court has fallen into the trap of assuming that the Act permits ancient canards about the proper role of women to be a basis for discrimination. Congress, however, sought just the opposite result.

By adding the prohibition against job discrimination based on sex to the 1964 Civil Rights Act Congress intended to prevent employers from refusing "to hire an individual based on stereotyped characterizations of the sexes." Equal Employment Opportunity Commission, Guidelines on Discrimination Because of Sex, 29 CFR § 1604.1(a)(1)(ii). Even characterizations of the proper domestic roles of the sexes were not to serve as predicates for restricting employment opportunity. The exception for a "bona fide occupational qualification" was not intended to swallow the rule.

That exception has been construed by the Equal Employment Opportunity Commission, whose regulations are entitled to "great deference," Udall v. Tallman, 380 U.S. 1, 16, 85 S.Ct. 792, 801, 13 L.Ed.2d 616 (1965), to be applicable only to job situations that require specific physical characteristics necessarily possessed by only one sex. Thus the exception would apply where necessary "for the purpose of authenticity or genuineness" in the employment of actors or actresses, fashion models, and the like. If the exception is to be limited as Congress intended, the Commission has given it the only possible construction.

When performance characteristics of an individual are involved, even when parental roles are concerned, employment opportunity may be limited only by employment criteria that are neutral as to the sex of the applicant.

NOTES FOR DISCUSSION

1. While the Supreme Court did not employ "sex-plus" terminology in *Phillips*, this case, the first Title VII sex discrimination suit decided by the Court, clearly fits within that framework. Into which of the two previously discussed proof schemes—disparate treatment or disproportionate impact—does this type of claim fall?

2. What is your reaction to the majority's suggestion that sex might be a BFOQ? Justice Marshall contends that even if the premise upon which the application of that defense is predicated—that the responsibility for pre-school-age children more frequently falls on mothers than fathers—is statistically correct, Congress did not intend to sanction employment practices based on stereotyped characterizations of sex roles. Do you agree? The BFOQ defense is most frequently asserted in sex discrimination cases. For an extensive discussion of § 703(e) see Chapter 2, *supra*, at 167–262.

3. An employer decides to shut down one of its three plants because the employees of that plant were almost exclusively women. Can the few male employees who lost their jobs as a result of the sex-based shutdown state a claim of sex discrimination under Title VII? See Allen v. American Home Foods, Inc., 644 F.Supp. 1553 (N.D.Ind.1986) ("[The] 'person aggrieved' [language of Title VII] confers standing to all persons injured by an unlawful employment practice. These male plaintiffs allege such an injury, and thus have standing. * * * These males suffered the same injury as did the females that lost their jobs; the injuries of the males and females were occasioned by the same corporate decision; and if, as the plaintiffs allege, considerations of sex motivated the corporate decision to close the * * * plant, the corporate decision that injured the male plaintiffs constituted an unlawful employment practice under Title VII.").

WILLINGHAM v. MACON TELEGRAPH PUBLISHING CO.

United States Court of Appeals, Fifth Circuit, 1975.
507 F.2d 1084.

SIMPSON, CIRCUIT JUDGE.

Alan Willingham, plaintiff-appellant, applied for employment with defendant-appellee Macon Telegraph Publishing Co., Macon, Georgia (Macon Telegraph) as a display or copy layout artist on July 28, 1970. Macon Telegraph refused to hire Willingham. The suit below alleged that the sole basis for refusal to hire was objection to the length of his hair. On July 30, 1970, he filed a complaint with the Equal Employment Opportunity Commission (E.E.O.C.), asserting discrimination by Macon in its hiring policy based on sex * * *.

The E.E.O.C. investigated the alleged discrimination and eventually advised Willingham that there was reasonable cause to believe that Macon Telegraph had violated the * * * Civil Rights Act of 1964, and that he was entitled to file suit. On December 17, 1971, Willingham filed suit, alleging *inter alia* that Macon Telegraph's hiring policy unlawfully discriminated on the basis of sex. On April 17, 1972, the district court granted summary judgment in favor of defendant Macon Telegraph, finding no unlawful discrimination. Upon Willingham's appeal from the district court decision a panel of this circuit reversed, finding the presence of a prima facie case of sexual discrimination and directing remand for an evidentiary hearing. Upon en banc consideration we vacate the remand order of the original panel and affirm the district court.

THE FACTS

* * *

* * * Macon Telegraph's management believed that the entire business community it served—and depended upon for business success—associated long hair on men with the counter-culture types who gained extensive unfavorable national and local exposure at the time of [a local music] * * * festival. Therefore the newspaper's employee grooming code, which required employees (male and female) who came into contact with the public to be neatly dressed and groomed in accordance with the standards customarily accepted in the business community, was interpreted to exclude the employing of men (but not women) with long hair. Willingham's longer than acceptable shoulder length hair was thus the grooming code violation upon which Macon Telegraph based its denial of employment.

* * * Willingham's argument is that Macon Telegraph discriminates amongst employees based upon their sex, in that female employees can wear their hair any length they choose, while males must limit theirs to the length deemed acceptable by Macon Telegraph. He asserts therefore that he was denied employment because of his sex: were he a girl with identical length hair and comparable job qualifications, he (she) would have been employed. A majority of the original panel which heard the case agreed, and remanded the cause to the district court for a finding of whether or not the discrimination might not be lawful under the "bona fide occupational qualification" (B.F.O.Q.) statutory exception to Sec. 703. Since we agree with the district court that Macon Telegraph's dress and grooming policy does not unlawfully discriminate on the basis of sex, the applicability of the B.F.O.Q. exception will not be considered in this opinion.

THE NATURE OF SEXUAL DISCRIMINATION

The unlawfulness vel non of employer practices with respect to the hiring and treatment of employees in the private sector, as contemplated by Sec. 703 and applied to the facts of this case, can be determined by way of a three step analysis: (1) has there been some form of discrimination, i.e., different treatment of similarly situated individuals; (2) was the discrimination based on sex; and (3) if there has been sexual discrimination, is it within the purview of the bona fide occupational qualification (BFOQ) exception and thus lawful? We conclude that the undisputed discrimination practiced by Macon Telegraph is based not upon sex, but rather upon grooming standards, and thus outside the proscription of Sec. 703. This determination pretermits any discussion of whether, if sexual discrimination were involved, it would be within the BFOQ exception.

Although our judicial inquiry necessarily focuses upon the proper statutory construction to be accorded Sec. 703, it is helpful first to define narrowly the precise issue to be considered. * * * [W]e are not concerned with discrimination based upon sex alone. That situation obtains when an employer refuses to hire, promote, or raise the wages of an individual solely because of sex, as, for instance, if Macon Telegraph had refused to hire any women for the job of copy layout artist because of their sex.

Willingham relies on a more subtle form of discrimination, one which courts and commentators have often characterized as "sex plus". In general, this involves the classification of employees on the basis of sex *plus* one other ostensibly neutral characteristic. The practical effect of interpreting Sec. 703 to include this type of discrimination is to impose an equal protection gloss upon the statute, i.e. similarly situated individuals of either sex cannot be discriminated against vis a vis members of their own sex unless the same distinction is made with respect to those of the opposite sex. Such an interpretation may be necessary in order to counter some rather imaginative efforts by employers to circumvent Sec. 703.

Inclusion of "sex plus" discrimination within the proscription of Sec. 703 has legitimate legislative and judicial underpinning. An amendment which would have added the word "solely" to the bill, modifying "sex", was defeated on the floor in the House of Representatives. Presumably, Congress foresaw the debilitating effect such a limitation might have upon the sex discrimination amendment. Further, the Supreme Court, in Phillips v. Martin Marietta Corp., 1971, 400 U.S. 542, 91 S.Ct. 496, 27 L.Ed.2d 613, found expressly that "sex plus" discrimination violates the Civil Rights Act. The employer in *Phillips* refused to accept job applications from women with pre-school age children, but had no such policy with respect to male applicants. The defendant argued that it was not discriminating between men and women, but only amongst women, and then only with respect to a neutral fact—pre-school age children. In a short per curiam decision, the Supreme Court held that if the legislative purpose of giving persons of like qualifications equal employment opportunity irrespective of sex were to be effected, employers could not have one hiring policy for men and another for women. Thus "sex plus" discrimination against being a woman *plus* having pre-school age children, was under the facts of that case just as unlawful as would have been discrimination based solely upon sex.

In this analytical context, then, the single issue in this case is precisely drawn: Does a particular grooming regulation applicable to men only constitute "sex plus" discrimination within the meaning of Sec. 703, as construed by the Supreme Court? Willingham and numerous amici curiae have advanced several arguments supporting an affirmative answer to the question. We proceed to consider these arguments.

The primary premise of Willingham's position is that "sex plus" must be read to intend to include "sex plus any sexual stereotype" and thus, since short hair is stereotypically male, requiring it of all male applicants violates Sec. 703. While the Supreme Court did not explicate the breadth of its rationale in *Phillips*, it seems likely that Mr. Justice Marshall at least might agree with Willingham. In his special concurrence he noted that any hiring distinction based upon stereotyped characterizations of the sexes violates the Act, and went on to say that such discrimination could never be a BFOQ exception, an issue expressly left open in the majority's per curiam opinion.

Willingham finds further comfort in Sprogis v. United Air Lines, Inc., 7 Cir.1971, 444 F.2d 1194. Plaintiff there was a female stewardess who challenged an airline rule that stewardesses were not allowed to marry, but with no such provision for male stewards or other employees. The *Sprogis* court found the rule to be an unlawful form of "sex plus" discrimination, relying in part on *Phillips*. In reference to "sex plus" the court noted that "[i]n forbidding employers to discriminate against individuals because of their sex, Congress intended to strike at the entire spectrum of disparate treatment of men and women *resulting from sex stereotypes*." Treating the emphasized language in its broadest sense, it is possible that the court felt that all sexual stereotypes violate Sec. 703. Several district courts apparently agree with this construction, at least insofar as personal dress and appearance codes are concerned. See Aros v. McDonnell Douglas Corp., C.D.Cal.1972, 348 F.Supp. 661 (dress and grooming code constitutes sexual discrimination when applied differently to males and females); Donohue v. Shoe Corp. of America, C.D.Cal.1972, 337 F.Supp. 1357 (rule requiring short hair on men, but not on women, is prima facie violation of Sec. 703); Roberts v. General Mills, Inc., N.D.Ohio 1971, 337 F.Supp. 1055 (rule allowing female employees to wear hairnets, but requiring men to wear hats—and therefore keep their hair short—violates Sec. 703).

Finally, the E.E.O.C. by administrative decision, regulation, and on amicus brief here, fully supports Willingham's position. In its administrative decisions, the Commission has uniformly held that dress and grooming codes that distinguish between sexes are within Sec. 703, and can only be justified if proven to be a BFOQ. * * *

SEXUAL STEREOTYPES AND LEGISLATIVE INTENT

The beginning (and often the ending) point of statutory interpretation is an exploration of the legislative history of the Act in question. We must decide, if we can there find any basis for decision, whether Congress intended to include *all* sexual distinctions in its prohibition of discrimination (based solely on sex or on "sex plus"), or whether a line can legitimately be drawn beyond which employer conduct is no longer within reach of the statute.

We discover, as have other courts earlier considering the problem before us, that the meager legislative history regarding the addition of "sex" in Sec. 703(a) provides slim guidance for divining Congressional intent. * * * And while it is argued that a lack of change in this section in the 1972 amendments to the Act evidences Congressional agreement with the position of the E.E.O.C., it may be argued with equal force that the law was insufficiently developed at the time the amendments were considered to support any change. We find the legislative history inconclusive at best and draw but one conclusion, and that by way of negative inference. Without more extensive consideration, Congress in all probability did not intend for its proscription of sexual discrimination to have significant and sweeping implications. We should not therefore extend the coverage of the Act to situations of questionable application without some stronger Congressional mandate.

We perceive the intent of Congress to have been the guarantee of equal job opportunity for males and females. Providing such opportunity is where the emphasis rightly lies. This is to say that the Act should reach any device or policy of an employer which serves to deny acquisition and retention of a job or promotion in a job to an individual *because* the individual is either male or female. * * *

Juxtaposing our view of the Congressional purpose with the statutory interpretations advanced by the parties to this action elucidates our reasons for adopting the more narrow construction. Equal employment *opportunity* may be secured only when employers are barred from discriminating against employees on the basis of immutable characteristics, such as race and national origin. Similarly, an employer cannot have one hiring policy for men and another for women *if* the distinction is based on some fundamental right. But a hiring policy that distinguishes on some other ground, such as grooming codes or length of hair, is related more closely to the employer's choice of how to run his business than to equality of employment opportunity. In *Phillips*, supra, the Supreme Court condemned a hiring distinction based on having pre-school age children, an existing condition not subject to change. In Sprogis v. United Air Lines, supra, the Seventh Circuit reached a similar result with respect to marital status. We have no difficulty with the result reached in those cases; but nevertheless perceive that a line must be drawn between distinctions grounded on such fundamental rights as the right to have children or to marry and those interfering with the manner in which an employer exercises his judgment as to the way to operate a business. Hair length is not immutable and in the situation of employer vis a vis employee enjoys no constitutional protection. If the employee objects to the grooming code he has the right to reject it by looking elsewhere for employment, or alternatively he may choose to subordinate his preference by accepting the code along with the job.

* * *

We adopt the view, therefore, that distinctions in employment practices between men and women on the basis of something other than immutable or protected characteristics do not inhibit employment *opportunity* in violation of Sec. 703(a). Congress sought only to give all persons equal access to the job market, not to limit an employer's right to exercise his informed judgment as to how best to run his shop.

* * *

CONCLUSION

Nothing that we say should be construed as disparagement of what many feel to be a highly laudable goal—maximizing individual freedom by eliminating sexual stereotypes. We hold simply that such an objective may not be read into the Civil Rights Act of 1964 without further Congressional action. Private employers are prohibited from using different hiring policies for men and women only when the distinctions used relate to immutable characteristics or legally protected rights. While of course not impervious to judicial scrutiny, even those distinctions do not violate Sec. 703(a) if they are applied to both sexes.

Affirmed.

NOTES AND PROBLEMS FOR DISCUSSION

1. As the court in *Willingham* noted, sex-plus theory has been used to strike down no-marriage rules applied only to female employees. Other courts have similarly invalidated policies that discriminate against unwed mothers, Dolter v. Wahlert High School, 483 F.Supp. 266 (N.D.Iowa 1980); female homosexuals, Valdes v. Lumbermen's Mutual Casualty Co., 507 F.Supp. 10 (S.D.Fla.1980); black women, Jefferies v. Harris County Community Action Association, 615 F.2d 1025 (5th Cir.1980); and women who did not use their husband's surname on personnel forms, Allen v. Lovejoy, 553 F.2d 522 (6th Cir.1977). In each of the aforementioned cases, the "plus" factor was used only to disqualify women. Would the application of these factors to members of both sexes, however, necessarily insulate them from Title VII liability?

2. Several other courts have adopted the limitation imposed on sex-plus theory by the Fifth Circuit in *Willingham*—i.e., that Title VII only prohibits policies which discriminate on the basis of "plus" characteristics that are either immutable or involve fundamental rights—and thereby upheld dress codes prohibiting women from wearing pants, Data La Von Lanigan v. Bartlett and Co. Grain, 466 F.Supp. 1388 (W.D.Mo.1979); the discharge of an "uppity woman" because of her aggressive personality, Oaks v. City of Fairhope, Alabama, 515 F.Supp. 1004 (S.D.Ala.1981); and a maximum weight policy for

female flight attendants, EEOC v. Delta Air Lines, Inc., 24 EPD ¶ 31,455 (S.D.Tex.1980). One court somewhat self-consciously attempted to justify its acceptance of sex-differentiated dress codes (a state trial judge's requirement that male attorneys wear a necktie before his court) as in keeping with contemporary fashion. See Devine v. Lonschein, 621 F.Supp. 894, 897 (S.D.N.Y. 1985), affirmed without opinion, 800 F.2d 1127 (2d Cir.1986)(equal protection claim under § 1983 because of lack of employment relationship). But in O'Donnell v. Burlington Coat Factory Warehouse, Inc., 656 F.Supp. 263 (S.D.Ohio 1987), the court held that an employer violated Title VII by requiring its female sales clerks to wear a smock while male sales clerks were required only to wear business attire consisting of pants, shirt and a tie. The court reasoned that the effect of this rule was to perpetuate sexual stereotypes by making female employees wear a uniform (the smock) while male employees in the same position were allowed to wear professional business attire. The court added that it found no justification for this policy in accepted social norms and that the company had alternative ways of achieving its goal of salesclerk identification, such as requiring both sexes to wear the smock or some other distinguishing form of attire. The smock rule, it concluded, created a disadvantage to the conditions of employment of female sales clerks. See generally, Bayer, Mutable Characteristics and the Definition of Discrimination Under Title VII, 20 U.C.Davis L.Rev. 769 (1987). With the notable exception of the ruling in *O'Donnell,* don't decisions adopting and extending the *Willingham* analysis suggest that the courts continue to be willing to permit the use of employment policies that are based on, and thereby perpetuate, sexual stereotypes? Do these cases survive the Court's ruling in *Hopkins* ? See generally, Taub, Keeping Women In Their Place: Stereotyping Per Se As A Form Of Employment Discrimination, 21 B.C.L.Rev. 345 (1980).

Can an employer forbid its employees from wearing religious medallions on the job? What if the rule applies only to crucifixes? Is § 701(j) relevant here?

3. What happens if the "plus" factor can be possessed only by members of one gender? This issue arose in cases involving employment distinctions based on pregnancy. In GENERAL ELECTRIC CO. v. GILBERT, 429 U.S. 125, 97 S.Ct. 401, 50 L.Ed.2d 343 (1976), the plaintiffs claimed that the company's non-occupational disability plan was in violation of Title VII because it did not provide payment for any absence due to pregnancy. They contended that the employer's failure to include pregnancy disabilities on the same terms and conditions as other non-occupational disabilities discriminated against them on the basis of their sex. The Supreme Court rejected this claim, holding that the exclusion of pregnancy from an otherwise nearly comprehensive disability plan was not a gender-based discrimination nor a pretext for such discrimination, but simply an economically-motivated decision to remove one expensive risk from the list of compensable disabilities. In addition, the Court ruled, by failing to prove that the benefit package was worth more to men than to women, either financially or in terms of aggregate risk protection, the plaintiffs had not demonstrated that the pregnancy-related exclusion had a *Griggs*-like disproportionate discriminatory effect on women. This ruling, which contradicted both the unanimous position of the six federal appellate courts that had addressed the issue and the E.E.O.C. Guidelines, received a great deal of attention and criticism. See e.g., Comment, Differential Treatment of Pregnancy in Employment: The Impact of General Electric Co. v. Gilbert and Nashville Gas Co. v. Satty, 13 Harv.Civ.R.–Civ.Lib.L.Rev. 717 (1978); Comment, 27 Loy. L.Rev. 532 (1981); Comment, 1977 Utah L.Rev. 119 (1977). The Court soon

thereafter had another opportunity to examine a pregnancy-based employment policy and used it to limit the impact of *Gilbert*. In NASHVILLE GAS CO. v. SATTY, 434 U.S. 136, 98 S.Ct. 347, 54 L.Ed.2d 356 (1977), company policy required pregnant employees to take a formal leave of absence without pay and to forfeit their accumulated job seniority upon returning to work after childbirth. Employees disabled by non-occupational sickness or injury, however, were entitled to sick pay and retention of accumulated seniority. The Court concluded that the sick leave policy was indistinguishable from General Electric's denial of disability benefits to pregnant employees. Accordingly, the Court ruled, *Gilbert* controlled and this portion of the case was remanded to allow the trial court to determine whether the sick leave plan was a pretext for sex discrimination. It was the Court's treatment of the seniority provision, however, that generated the most controversy. The Court held that while the company's practice of denying accumulated seniority to employees returning from pregnancy leave was neutral on its face, it nevertheless had a discriminatory effect upon women and thus violated Title VII. In reaching this conclusion, the *Satty* Court distinguished *Gilbert* in the following manner:

> In *Gilbert*, there was no showing that General Electric's policy of compensating for all non-job-related disabilities except pregnancy favored men over women. No evidence was produced to suggest that men received more benefits from General Electric's disability insurance fund than did women; both men and women were subject generally to the disabilities covered and presumably drew similar amounts from the insurance fund. We therefore upheld the plan under Title VII. * * *

> Here, by comparison, petitioner has not merely refused to extend to women a benefit that men cannot and do not receive, but has imposed on women a substantial burden that men need not suffer. The distinction between benefits and burdens is more than one of semantics. We held in *Gilbert* that sec. 703(a)(1) did not require that greater economic benefits be paid to one sex or the other "because of their differing roles in 'the scheme of human existence,' " 429 U.S., at 139 n. 17. But that holding does not allow us to read sec. 703(a)(2) to permit an employer to burden female employees in such a way as to deprive them of employment opportunities because of their different role.

In order to determine whether subsequent cases were governed by *Gilbert* or *Satty*, the courts sought to ascertain whether the challenged pregnancy-based classifications either denied women some additional economic benefit or deprived them of employment opportunities, or adversely affected their employee status by subjecting them to a burden not borne by male employees. Pursuant to this somewhat elusive benefit/burden analysis, the courts held that absent a business justification, Title VII prohibited a school board from vesting discretion in the Superintendent to determine when a teacher could return from maternity leave when the Superintendent was not provided with similar discretion with respect to teachers returning from sick leave, Clanton v. Orleans Parish School Board, 649 F.2d 1084 (5th Cir.1981); or from requiring pregnant teachers to go on mandatory maternity leave at a fixed point in the pregnancy term, deLaurier v. San Diego Unified School District, 588 F.2d 674 (9th Cir.1978); and precluded an employer from requiring women who had been on pregnancy leave to have sustained a normal menstrual cycle before they could return to work, Harper v. Thiokol Chemical Corp., 619 F.2d 489 (5th Cir.1980). On the other hand, one court held that Title VII was not violated by a company rule granting employees on nonoccupational disability leave full seniority credit for the period of their absence but limiting female employees on maternity leave to a maximum of thirty days' service credit. In re Southwestern Bell Telephone Co. Maternity Benefits Litigation, 602 F.2d 845 (8th Cir. 1979).

Congress responded to the controversy and confusion surrounding *Gilbert* and *Satty* by passing the Pregnancy Discrimination Act of 1978. This amendment to Title VII added a new provision—§ 701(k)—designed specifically to reverse the rulings in *Gilbert* and *Satty* by declaring that all pregnancy-based distinctions constitute discrimination on the basis of sex and that pregnancy must be treated like other temporary disabilities for all employment-related purposes.

Read § 701(k) of Title VII.

NEWPORT NEWS SHIPBUILIDNG AND DRY DOCK CO. v. EEOC

Supreme Court of the United States, 1983.
462 U.S. 669, 103 S.Ct. 2622, 77 L.Ed.2d 89.

JUSTICE STEVENS delivered the opinion of the Court.

In 1978 Congress decided to overrule our decision in General Electric Co. v. Gilbert, 429 U.S. 125, 97 S.Ct. 401, 50 L.Ed.2d 343 (1976), by amending Title VII of the Civil Rights Act of 1964 "to prohibit sex discrimination on the basis of pregnancy." [1] On the effective date of the act, petitioner amended its health insurance plan to provide its female employees with hospitalization benefits for pregnancy-related conditions to the same extent as for other medical conditions. The plan continued, however, to provide less favorable pregnancy benefits for spouses of male employees. The question presented is whether the amended plan complies with the amended statute.

Petitioner's plan provides hospitalization and medical-surgical coverage for a defined category of employees [3] and a defined category of dependents. Dependents covered by the plan include employees' spouses, unmarried children between 14 days and 19 years of age, and some older dependent children. [4] Prior to April 29, 1979, the scope of the plan's coverage for eligible dependents was identical to its coverage for employees. All covered males, whether employees or dependents, were

1. The new statute (the Pregnancy Discrimination Act) amended the "Definitions" section of Title VII, 42 U.S.C. § 2000e (1976), to add a new subsection (k) reading in pertinent part as follows:

"The terms 'because of sex' or 'on the basis of sex' include, but are not limited to, because of or on the basis of pregnancy, childbirth, or related medical conditions; and women affected by pregnancy, childbirth, or related medical conditions shall be treated the same for all employment-related purposes, including receipt of benefits under fringe benefit programs, as other persons not so affected

but similar in their ability or inability to work, and nothing in section 2000e–2(h) of this title shall be interpreted to permit otherwise * * *."

3. On the first day following three months of continuous service, every active, full-time, production, maintenance, technical, and clerical area bargaining unit employee becomes a plan participant.

4. For example, unmarried children up to age 23 who are full-time college students solely dependent on an employee and certain mentally or physically handicapped children are also covered.

treated alike for purposes of hospitalization coverage. All covered females, whether employees or dependents, also were treated alike. Moreover, with one relevant exception, the coverage for males and females was identical. The exception was a limitation on hospital coverage for pregnancy that did not apply to any other hospital confinement.[6]

After the plan was amended in 1979, it provided the same hospitalization coverage for male and female employees themselves for all medical conditions, but it differentiated between female employees and spouses of male employees in its provision of pregnancy-related benefits.[7] In a booklet describing the plan, petitioner explained the amendment that gave rise to this litigation in this way:

"B. Effective April 29, 1979, maternity benefits for female employees will be paid the same as any other hospital confinement as described in question 16. This applies only to deliveries beginning on April 29, 1979 and thereafter.

"C. Maternity benefits for the wife of a male employee will continue to be paid as described in part 'A' of this question."

In turn, Part A stated, "The Basic Plan pays up to $500 of the hospital charges and 100% of reasonable and customary for delivery and anesthesiologist charges." As the Court of Appeals observed, "To the extent that the hospital charges in connection with an uncomplicated delivery may exceed $500, therefore, a male employee receives less complete coverage of spousal disabilities than does a female employee."

After the passage of the Pregnancy Discrimination Act, and before the amendment to petitioner's plan became effective, the Equal Opportunity Employment Commission issued "interpretive guidelines" in the form of questions and answers. Two of those questions, numbers 21 and 22, made it clear that the EEOC would consider petitioner's amended plan unlawful. Number 21 read as follows:

"21. Q. Must an employer provide health insurance coverage for the medical expenses of pregnancy-related conditions of the spouses of male employees? Of the dependents of all employees?

"A. Where an employer provides no coverage for dependents, the employer is not required to institute such coverage. However, if an employer's insurance program covers the medical expenses of spouses of female employees, then it must equally cover the medi-

---

6. For hospitalization caused by uncomplicated pregnancy, petitioner's plan paid 100% of the reasonable and customary physicians' charges for delivery and anesthesiology, and up to $500 of other hospital charges. For all other hospital confinement, the plan paid in full for a semiprivate room for up to 120 days and for surgical procedures; covered the first $750 of reasonable and customary charges for hospital services (including general nursing care, x-ray examinations, and drugs) and other necessary services during hospitalization; and paid 80 percent of the charges exceeding $750 for such services up to a maximum of 120 days.

7. Thus, as the EEOC found after its investigation, "the record reveals that the present disparate impact on male employees had its genesis in the gender-based distinction accorded to female employees in the past."

cal expenses of spouses of male employees, including those arising from pregnancy-related conditions.

But the insurance does not have to cover the pregnancy-related conditions of non-spouse dependents as long as it excludes the pregnancy-related conditions of such non-spouse dependents of male and female employees equally." [9]

On September 20, 1979, one of petitioner's male employees filed a charge with the EEOC alleging that petitioner had unlawfully refused to provide full insurance coverage for his wife's hospitalization caused by pregnancy; a month later the United Steelworkers filed a similar charge on behalf of other individuals. Petitioner then commenced an action in the United States District Court for the Eastern District of Virginia, challenging the Commission's guidelines and seeking both declaratory and injunctive relief. The complaint named the EEOC, the male employee, and the United Steelworkers of America as defendants. Later the EEOC filed a civil action against petitioner alleging discrimination on the basis of sex against male employees in the company's provision of hospitalization benefits. Concluding that the benefits of the new Act extended only to female employees, and not to spouses of male employees, the District Court held that petitioner's plan was lawful and enjoined enforcement of the EEOC guidelines relating to pregnancy benefits for employees' spouses. 510 F.Supp. 66 (1981). It also dismissed the EEOC's complaint. The two cases were consolidated on appeal.

A divided panel of the United States Court of Appeals for the Fourth Circuit reversed, reasoning that since "the company's health insurance plan contains a distinction based on pregnancy that results in less complete medical coverage for male employees with spouses than for female employees with spouses, it is impermissible under the statute." After rehearing the case en banc, the court reaffirmed the conclusion of the panel over the dissent of three judges who believed the statute was intended to protect female employees "in their ability or inability to work," and not to protect spouses of male employees. Because the important question presented by the case had been decided differently by the United States Court of Appeals for the Ninth Circuit,

---

9. Question 22 is equally clear. It reads:

"22. Q. Must an employer provide the same level of health insurance coverage for the pregnancy-related medical conditions of the spouses of male employees as it provides for its female employees?

"A. No. It is not necessary to provide the same level of coverage for the pregnancy-related medical conditions of spouses of male employees as for female employees. However, where the employer provides coverage for the medical conditions of the spouses of its employees, then the level of coverage for pregnancy-related medical conditions of the spouses of male employees must be the same as the level of coverage for all other medical conditions of the spouses of female employees. For example, if the employer covers employees for 100 percent of reasonable and customary expenses sustained for a medical condition, but only covers dependent spouses for 50 percent of reasonable and customary expenses for their medical conditions, the pregnancy-related expenses of the male employee's spouse must be covered at the 50 percent level."

EEOC v. Lockheed Missiles and Space Co., 680 F.2d 1243 (1982), we granted certiorari.[10]

Ultimately the question we must decide is whether petitioner has discriminated against its male employees with respect to their compensation, terms, conditions, or privileges of employment because of their sex within the meaning of § 703(a)(1) of Title VII. Although the Pregnancy Discrimination Act has clarified the meaning of certain terms in this section, neither that Act nor the underlying statute contains a definition of the word "discriminate." In order to decide whether petitioner's plan discriminates against male employees because of *their* sex, we must therefore go beyond the bare statutory language. Accordingly, we shall consider whether Congress, by enacting the Pregnancy Discrimination Act, not only overturned the specific holding in General Electric v. Gilbert, supra, but also rejected the test of discrimination employed by the Court in that case. We believe it did. Under the proper test petitioner's plan is unlawful, because the protection it affords to married male employees is less comprehensive than the protection it affords to married female employees.

I

At issue in General Electric v. Gilbert was the legality of a disability plan that provided the company's employees with weekly compensation during periods of disability resulting from nonoccupational causes. Because the plan excluded disabilities arising from pregnancy, the District Court and the Court of Appeals concluded that it discriminated against female employees because of their sex. This Court reversed.

After noting that Title VII does not define the term "discrimination," the Court applied an analysis derived from cases construing the Equal Protection Clause of the Fourteenth Amendment to the Constitution. The *Gilbert* opinion quoted at length from a footnote in Geduldig v. Aiello, 417 U.S. 484, 94 S.Ct. 2485, 41 L.Ed.2d 256 (1974), a case which had upheld the constitutionality of excluding pregnancy coverage under California's disability insurance plan. "Since it is a finding of sex-based discrimination that must trigger, in a case such as this, the finding of an unlawful employment practice under § 703(a)(1)," the Court added, "*Geduldig* is precisely in point in its holding that an exclusion of pregnancy from a disability-benefits plan providing general coverage is not a gender-based discrimination at all."

The dissenters in *Gilbert* took issue with the majority's assumption "that the Fourteenth Amendment standard of discrimination is coterminous with that applicable to Title VII."[13] As a matter of statutory

---

10. Subsequently the Court of Appeals for the Seventh Circuit agreed with the Ninth Circuit. EEOC v. Joslyn Mfg. & Supply Co., 706 F.2d 1469 (1983).

13. As the text of the *Geduldig* opinion makes clear, in evaluating the constitutionality of California's insurance program, the Court focused on the "non-invidious" character of the State's legitimate fiscal

interpretation, the dissenters rejected the Court's holding that the plan's exclusion of disabilities caused by pregnancy did not constitute discrimination based on sex. As Justice Brennan explained, it was facially discriminatory for the company to devise "a policy that, but for pregnancy, offers protection for all risks, even those that are 'unique to' men or heavily male dominated." It was inaccurate to describe the program as dividing potential recipients into two groups, pregnant women and nonpregnant persons, because insurance programs "deal with future *risks* rather than historic facts." Rather, the appropriate classification was "between persons who face a risk of pregnancy and those who do not." The company's plan, which was intended to provide employees with protection against the risk of uncompensated unemployment caused by physical disability, discriminated on the basis of sex by giving men protection for all categories of risk but giving women only partial protection. Thus, the dissenters asserted that the statute had been violated because conditions of employment for females were less favorable than for similarly situated males.

When Congress amended Title VII in 1978, it unambiguously expressed its disapproval of both the holding and the reasoning of the Court in the *Gilbert* decision. It incorporated a new subsection in the "definitions" applicable "[f]or the purposes of this subchapter." The first clause of the Act states, quite simply: "The terms 'because of sex' or 'on the basis of sex' include, but are not limited to, because of or on the basis of pregnancy, childbirth, or related medical conditions." [14] The House Report stated, "It is the Committee's view that the dissenting Justices correctly interpreted the Act." Similarly, the Senate Report quoted passages from the two dissenting opinions, stating that they "correctly express both the principle and the meaning of title VII." Proponents of the bill repeatedly emphasized that the Supreme Court had erroneously interpreted Congressional intent and that amending legislation was necessary to reestablish the principles of Title VII law as they had been understood prior to the *Gilbert* decision. Many of them expressly agreed with the views of the dissenting Justices.

As petitioner argues, congressional discussion focused on the needs of female members of the work force rather than spouses of male employees. This does not create a "negative inference" limiting the scope of the act to the specific problem that motivated its enactment. Congress apparently assumed that existing plans that included benefits for dependents typically provided no less pregnancy-related coverage for the wives of male employees than they did for female employees.

interest in excluding pregnancy coverage. This justification was not relevant to the statutory issue presented in *Gilbert*. See n. 25, *infra*.

14. The meaning of the first clause is not limited by the specific language in the second clause, which explains the application of the general principle to women employees.

When the question of differential coverage for dependents was addressed in the Senate Report, the Committee indicated that it should be resolved "on the basis of existing title VII principles." [20] The legislative context makes it clear that Congress was not thereby referring to the view of Title VII reflected in this Court's *Gilbert* opinion. Proponents of the legislation stressed throughout the debates that Congress had always intended to protect *all* individuals from sex discrimination in employment—including but not limited to pregnant women workers.[21] Against this background we review the terms of the amended statute to decide whether petitioner has unlawfully discriminated against its male employees.

20. "Questions were raised in the committee's deliberations regarding how this bill would affect medical coverage for dependents of employees, as opposed to employees themselves. In this context it must be remembered that the basic purpose of this bill is to protect women employees, it does not alter the basic principles of title VII law as regards sex discrimination. Rather, this legislation clarifies the definition of sex discrimination for title VII purposes. Therefore the question in regard to dependents' benefits would be determined on the basis of existing title VII principles." Leg.Hist. at 42–43.

This statement does not imply that the new statutory definition has no applicability; it merely acknowledges that the new definition does not itself resolve the question.

The dissent quotes extensive excerpts from an exchange on the Senate floor between Senators Hatch and Williams. Taken in context, this colloquy clearly deals only with the second clause of the bill, see n. 14, supra, and Senator Williams, the principal sponsor of the legislation, addressed only the bill's effect on income maintenance plans. Senator Williams first stated, in response to Senator Hatch, "With regard to more maintenance plans for pregnancy-related disabilities, I do not see how this language could be misunderstood." Upon further inquiry from Senator Hatch, he replied, "If there is any ambiguity, with regard to income maintenance plans, I cannot see it." At the end of the same response, he stated, "It is narrowly drawn and would not give any employee the right to obtain income maintenance as a result of the pregnancy of someone who is not an employee." These comments, which clearly limited the scope of Senator Williams' responses, are omitted from the dissent's lengthy quotation.

Other omitted portions of the colloquy make clear that it was logical to discuss the pregnancies of employees' spouses in connection with income maintenance plans. Senator Hatch asked, "what about the status of the woman coworker who is not pregnant but rides with a pregnant woman and cannot get to work once the pregnant female commences her maternity leave or the employed mother who stays home to nurse her pregnant daughter?" The reference to spouses of male employees must be understood in light of these hypothetical questions; it seems to address the situation in which a male employee wishes to take time off from work because his wife is pregnant.

21. See, e.g., 123 Cong.Rec. 7539 (1977) (remarks of Sen. Williams) ("the Court has ignored the congressional intent in enacting title VII of the Civil Rights Act—that intent was to protect all individuals from unjust employment discrimination, including pregnant workers"); id., at 29385, 29652. In light of statements such as these, it would be anomalous to hold that Congress provided that an employee's pregnancy is sex-based, while a spouse's pregnancy is gender-neutral.

During the course of the Senate debate on the Pregnancy Discrimination Act, Senator Bayh and Senator Cranston both expressed the belief that the new act would prohibit the exclusion of pregnancy coverage for spouses if spouses were otherwise fully covered by an insurance plan. Because our holding relies on the 1978 legislation only to the extent that it unequivocally rejected the *Gilbert* decision, and ultimately we rely on our understanding of general Title VII principles, we attach no more significance to these two statements than to the many other comments by both Senators and Congressmen disapproving the Court's reasoning and conclusion in *Gilbert*.

II

Section 703(a) makes it an unlawful employment practice for an employer to "discriminate against any individual with respect to his compensation, terms, conditions, or privileges of employment, because of such individual's race, color, religion, sex, or national origin * * *." Health insurance and other fringe benefits are "compensation, terms, conditions, or privileges of employment." Male as well as female employees are protected against discrimination. Thus, if a private employer were to provide complete health insurance coverage for the dependents of its female employees, and no coverage at all for the dependents of its male employees, it would violate Title VII.[22] Such a practice would not pass the simple test of Title VII discrimination that we enunciated in Los Angeles Department of Water & Power v. Manhart, 435 U.S. 702, 711, 98 S.Ct. 1370, 1377, 55 L.Ed.2d 657 (1978), for it would treat a male employee with dependents "in a manner which but for that person's sex would be different." [23] The same result would be reached even if the magnitude of the discrimination were smaller. For example, a plan that provided complete hospitalization coverage for the spouses of female employees but did not cover spouses of male employees when they had broken bones would violate Title VII by discriminating against male employees.

Petitioner's practice is just as unlawful. Its plan provides limited pregnancy-related benefits for employees' wives, and affords more extensive coverage for employees' spouses for all other medical conditions requiring hospitalization. Thus the husbands of female employees receive a specified level of hospitalization coverage for all conditions; the wives of male employees receive such coverage except for pregnancy-related conditions.[24] Although *Gilbert* concluded that an otherwise inclusive plan that singled out pregnancy-related benefits for exclusion was nondiscriminatory on its face, because only women can become pregnant, Congress has unequivocally rejected that reasoning. The

---

22. Consistently since 1970 the EEOC has considered it unlawful under Title VII for an employer to provide different insurance coverage for spouses of male and female employees.

Similarly, in our Equal Protection Clause cases we have repeatedly held that, if the spouses of female employees receive less favorable treatment in the provision of benefits, the practice discriminates not only against the spouses but also against the female employees on the basis of sex. Frontiero v. Richardson, 411 U.S. 677, 688, 93 S.Ct. 1764, 1771, 36 L.Ed.2d 583 (1973) (opinion of Brennan, J.) (increased quarters allowances and medical and dental benefits); Weinberger v. Wiesenfeld, 420 U.S. 636, 645, 95 S.Ct. 1225, 1231, 43 L.Ed.2d 514 (1975) (Social Security benefits for surviving spouses); Califano v. Goldfarb, 430 U.S. 199, 207–208, 97 S.Ct. 1021, 1027, 51 L.Ed.2d 270 (1977) (opinion of Brennan, J.) (Social Security benefits for surviving spouses); Wengler v. Druggists Mutual Ins. Co., 446 U.S. 142, 147, 100 S.Ct. 1540, 1543, 64 L.Ed.2d 107 (1980) (workers' compensation death benefits for surviving spouses).

23. The *Manhart* case was decided several months before the Pregnancy Discrimination Act was passed. Although it was not expressly discussed in the legislative history, it set forth some of the "existing title VII principles" on which Congress relied. * * *

24. This policy is analogous to the exclusion of broken bones for the wives of male employees, except that both employees' wives and employees' husbands may suffer broken bones, but only employees' wives can become pregnant.

1978 Act makes clear that it is discriminatory to treat pregnancy-related conditions less favorably than other medical conditions. Thus petitioner's plan unlawfully gives married male employees a benefit package for their dependents that is less inclusive than the dependency coverage provided to married female employees.

There is no merit to petitioner's argument that the prohibitions of Title VII do not extend to discrimination against pregnant spouses because the statute applies only to discrimination in employment. A two-step analysis demonstrates the fallacy in this contention. The Pregnancy Discrimination Act has now made clear that, for all Title VII purposes, discrimination based on a woman's pregnancy is, on its face, discrimination because of her sex. And since the sex of the spouse is always the opposite of the sex of the employee, it follows inexorably that discrimination against female spouses in the provision of fringe benefits is also discrimination against male employees.[25] By making clear that an employer could not discriminate on the basis of an employee's pregnancy, Congress did not erase the original prohibition against discrimination on the basis of an employee's sex.

In short, Congress' rejection of the premises of General Electric v. Gilbert forecloses any claim that an insurance program excluding pregnancy coverage for female beneficiaries and providing complete coverage to similarly situated male beneficiaries does not discriminate on the basis of sex. Petitioner's plan is the mirror image of the plan at issue in *Gilbert*. The pregnancy limitation in this case violates Title VII by discriminating against male employees.[26]

The judgment of the Court of Appeals is affirmed.

JUSTICE REHNQUIST, with whom JUSTICE POWELL joins, dissenting.

In General Electric Co. v. Gilbert, we held that an exclusion of pregnancy from a disability-benefits plan is not discrimination "because

---

25. See n. 22, supra. This reasoning does not require that a medical insurance plan treat the pregnancies of employees' wives the same as the pregnancies of female employees. For example, as the EEOC recognizes, see n. 9, supra (Question 22), an employer might provide full coverage for employees and no coverage at all for dependents. Similarly, a disability plan covering employees' children may exclude or limit maternity benefits. Although the distinction between pregnancy and other conditions is, according to the 1978 Act, discrimination "on the basis of sex," the exclusion affects male and female *employees* equally since both may have pregnant dependent daughters. The EEOC's guidelines permit differential treatment of the pregnancies of dependents who are not spouses.

26. Because the 1978 Act expressly states that exclusion of pregnancy coverage is gender-based discrimination on its face, it eliminates any need to consider the average monetary value of the plan's coverage to male and female employees.

The cost of providing complete health insurance coverage for the dependents of male employees, including pregnant wives, might exceed the cost of providing such coverage for the dependents of female employees. But although that type of cost differential may properly be analyzed in passing on the constitutionality of a State's health insurance plan, see Geduldig v. Aiello, supra, no such justification is recognized under Title II once discrimination has been shown. *Manhart*, supra ("It shall not be a defense under Title VII to a charge of sex discrimination in benefits that the cost of such benefits is greater with respect to one sex than the other.").

of [an] individual's * * * sex" within the meaning of Title VII. In our view, therefore, Title VII was not violated by an employer's disability plan that provided all employees with non-occupational sickness and accident benefits, but excluded from the plan's coverage disabilities arising from pregnancy. Under our decision in *Gilbert*, petitioner's otherwise inclusive benefits plan that excludes pregnancy benefits for a male employee's spouse clearly would not violate Title VII. For a different result to obtain, *Gilbert* would have to be judicially overruled by this Court or Congress would have to legislatively overrule our decision in its entirety by amending Title VII.

Today, the Court purports to find the latter by relying on the Pregnancy Discrimination Act of 1978, a statute that plainly speaks only of female employees affected by pregnancy and says nothing about spouses of male employees. Congress, of course, was free to legislatively overrule *Gilbert* in whole or in part, and there is no question but what the Pregnancy Discrimination Act manifests congressional dissatisfaction with the result we reached in *Gilbert*. But I think the Court reads far more into the Pregnancy Discrimination Act than Congress put there, and that therefore it is the Court, and not Congress, which is now overruling *Gilbert*.

In a case presenting a relatively simple question of statutory construction, the Court pays virtually no attention to the language of the Pregnancy Discrimination Act or the legislative history pertaining to that language. * * *

The Court recognizes that this provision is merely definitional and that "[u]ltimately the question we must decide is whether petitioner has discriminated against its male employees * * * because of their sex within the meaning of § 703(a)(1)" of Title VII. Section 703(a)(1) provides in part:

"It shall be an unlawful employment practice for an employer * * * to fail or refuse to hire or to discharge any individual, or otherwise to discriminate against any individual with respect to his compensation, terms, conditions, or privileges of employment, because of such individual's race, color, religion, sex, or national origin * * *."

It is undisputed that in § 703(a)(1) the word "individual" refers to an employee or applicant for employment. As modified by the first clause of the definitional provision of the Pregnancy Discrimination Act, the proscription in § 703(a)(1) is for discrimination "against any individual * * * *because of such individual's* * * * *pregnancy,* childbirth, or related medical conditions." This can only be read as referring to the pregnancy of an *employee*.

That this result was not inadvertent on the part of Congress is made very evident by the second clause of the Act, language that the Court essentially ignores in its opinion. When Congress in this clause further explained the proscription it was creating by saying that "women affected by pregnancy * * * shall be treated the same * * * as other persons not so affected but *similar in their ability or inability to work* " it could only have been referring to *female employees.* The Court of Appeals below stands alone in thinking otherwise.[3]

The Court concedes that this is a correct reading of the second clause. Ante, at n. 14. Then in an apparent effort to escape the impact of this provision, the Court asserts that "[t]he meaning of the first clause is not limited by the specific language in the second clause." Ante, at n. 14. I do not disagree. But this conclusion does not help the Court, for as explained above, when the definitional provision of the first clause is inserted in § 703(a)(1), it says the very same thing: the proscription added to Title VII applies only to female employees.

The plain language of the Pregnancy Discrimination Act leaves little room for the Court's conclusion that the Act was intended to extend beyond female employees. The Court concedes that "congressional discussion focused on the needs of female members of the work force rather than spouses of male employees." In fact, the singular focus of discussion on the problems of the *pregnant worker* is striking.

When introducing the Senate Report on the bill that later became the Pregnancy Discrimination Act, its principal sponsor, Senator Williams, explained:

> "Because of the Supreme Court's decision in the *Gilbert* case, this legislation is necessary to provide fundamental protection against sex discrimination for our Nation's 42 million *working women.* This protection will go a long way toward insuring that American women are permitted to assume their rightful place in our Nation's economy.

> "In addition to providing protection to *working women* with regard to fringe benefit programs, such as health and disability insurance programs, this legislation will prohibit other employment policies which adversely affect *pregnant workers.*"

* * * [T]he Congressional Record is overflowing with similar statements by individual members of Congress expressing their intention to insure with the Pregnancy Discrimination Act that working women are not treated differently because of pregnancy. Consistent with these views, all three committee reports on the bills that led to the Pregnan-

---

3. See EEOC v. Joslyn Manufacturing & Supply Co., 706 F.2d 1469, 1479 (CA7, 1983); EEOC v. Lockheed Missiles & Space Co., 680 F.2d 1243, 1245 (CA9 1982).

The Court of Appeals' majority, responding to the dissent's reliance on this language, excused the import of the language by saying: "The statutory reference to 'ability or inability to work' denotes disability and does not suggest that the spouse must be an employee of the employ-er providing the coverage. In fact, the statute says 'as other persons not so affected'; it does not say 'as other *employees* not so affected.' " This conclusion obviously does not comport with a common-sense understanding of the language. The logical explanation for Congress' reference to "persons" rather than "employees" is that Congress intended that the amendment should also apply to applicants for employment.

cy Discrimination Act expressly state that the Act would require employers to treat pregnant employees the same as "other employees."

The Court tries to avoid the impact of this legislative history by saying that it "does not create a 'negative inference' limiting the scope of the act to the specific problem that motivated its enactment." This reasoning might have some force if the legislative history was silent on an arguably related issue. But the legislative history is not silent. The Senate Report provides:

> "Questions were raised in the committee's deliberations regarding how this bill would affect medical coverage for dependents of employees, as opposed to employees themselves. In this context it must be remembered that the basic purpose of this bill is to protect women employees, it does not alter the basic principles of Title VII law as regards sex discrimination. * * * [T]he question in regard to dependents' benefits would be determined on the basis of existing Title VII principles. * * * *[T]he question of whether an employer who does cover dependents, either with or without additional cost to the employee, may exclude conditions related to pregnancy from that coverage is a different matter.* Presumably because plans which provide comprehensive medical coverage for spouses of women employees but not spouses of male employees are rare, we are not aware of any Title VII litigation concerning such plans. It is certainly not this committee's desire to encourage the institution of such plans. If such plans should be instituted in the future, the question would remain whether, under Title VII, the affected employees were discriminated against on the basis of their sex as regards the extent of coverage for their dependents."

This plainly disclaims any intention to deal with the issue presented in this case. Where Congress says that it would not want "to encourage" plans such as petitioner's, it cannot plausibly be argued that Congress has intended "to prohibit" such plans. Senator Williams was questioned on this point by Senator Hatch during discussions on the floor and his answers are to the same effect.

> "MR. HATCH: * * * The phrase 'women affected by pregnancy, childbirth or related medical conditions,' * * * appears to be overly broad, and is not limited in terms of employment. It does not even require that the person so affected be pregnant.

> *"Indeed under the present language of the bill, it is arguable that spouses of male employees are covered by this civil rights amendment. * * **

> "Could the sponsors clarify exactly whom that phrase intends to cover?

>   * * *

> "MR. WILLIAMS: * * * I do not see how one can read into this any pregnancy other than that pregnancy that relates to the employee, and if there is any ambiguity, *let it be clear here and now*

that this is very precise. It deals with a woman, a woman who is an employee, an employee in a work situation where all disabilities are covered under a company plan that provides income maintenance in the event of medical disability; that her particular period of disability, when she cannot work because of childbirth or anything related to childbirth is excluded. * * *

* * *

"MR. HATCH: So the Senator is satisfied that, though the committee language I brought up, 'woman affected by pregnancy' seems to be ambiguous, what it means is that *this act only applies to the particular woman who is actually pregnant, who is an employee and has become pregnant after her employment?*"

* * *

"MR. WILLIAMS: *"Exactly."* 123 Cong.Rec. S15,038–39 (daily ed. Sept. 16, 1977), Leg.Hist., at 80 (emphasis added).[7]

It seems to me that analysis of this case should end here. Under our decision in General Electric Co. v. Gilbert petitioner's exclusion of pregnancy benefits for male employee's spouses would not offend Title VII. Nothing in the Pregnancy Discrimination Act was intended to reach beyond female employees. Thus, *Gilbert* controls and requires that we reverse the Court of Appeals. But it is here, at what should be the stopping place, that the Court begins. * * *

The crux of the Court's reasoning is that even though the Pregnancy Discrimination Act redefines the phrases "because of sex" and "on the basis of sex" only to include discrimination against female employees affected by pregnancy, Congress also expressed its view that in *Gilbert* "the Supreme Court * * * erroneously interpreted Congressional intent." Somehow the Court then concludes that this renders all of *Gilbert* obsolete.

In support of its argument, the Court points to a few passages in congressional reports and several statements by various members of the

---

7. The Court suggests that in this exchange Senator Williams is explaining only that spouses of male employees will not be put on "income maintenance plans" while pregnant. This is utterly illogical. Spouses of employees have no income from the relevant employer to be maintained. Senator Williams clearly says that the Act is limited to female employees and as to such employees it will ensure income maintenance where male employees would receive similar disability benefits. Senator Hatch's final question and Senator Williams' response could not be clearer. The Act was intended to affect *only* pregnant workers. This is exactly what the Senate Report said and Senator Williams confirmed that this is exactly what Congress intended.

The only indications arguably contrary to the views reflected in the Senate Report and the exchange between Senators Hatch and Williams are found in two isolated remarks by Senators Bayh and Cranston. These statements, however, concern these two Senators' views concerning Title VII sex discrimination as it existed prior to the Pregnancy Discrimination Act. Their conclusions are completely at odds with our decision in General Electric Co. v. Gilbert, and are not entitled to deference here. We have consistently said that "[t]he views of members of a later Congress, concerning different [unamended] sections of Title VII * * * are entitled to little if any weight. It is the intent of the Congress that enacted [Title VII] in 1964 * * * that controls." Teamsters v. United States.

95th Congress to the effect that the Court in *Gilbert* had, when it construed Title VII, misperceived the intent of the 88th Congress. The Court also points out that "[m]any of [the members of 95th Congress] expressly agreed with the views of the dissenting Justices." Certainly *various members of Congress* said as much. But the fact remains that *Congress as a body* has not expressed these sweeping views in the Pregnancy Discrimination Act.

Under our decision in General Electric Co. v. Gilbert, petitioner's exclusion of pregnancy benefits for male employee's spouses would not violate Title VII. Since nothing in the Pregnancy Discrimination Act even arguably reaches beyond female employees affected by pregnancy, *Gilbert* requires that we reverse the Court of Appeals. Because the Court concludes otherwise, I dissent.

NOTES AND PROBLEMS FOR DISCUSSION

1. It seems clear that absent the 1978 amendment, this case would have been controlled by the ruling in *Gilbert* that a distinction based on pregnancy does not constitute sex-based discrimination under Title VII. It also is clear that *Gilbert* would now be decided differently as a result of the 1978 amendment. The issue in *Newport News,* then, is the extent, if any, to which the second clause of section 701(k) limits the instances in which a pregnancy-based distinction constitutes discrimination on the basis of sex. More specifically, the question is whether a company's failure to provide pregnancy benefits to an employee's spouse constitutes sex-based discrimination in the terms and conditions of employment offered to the employee. Without clearly saying so, the Court appears to be stating that since *spousal* health care benefits, like other fringe benefits, are terms and conditions of employment, they are provided for "employment related purposes" and thus must cover pregnancy to the same extent as other medical conditions. Unfortunately, the somewhat confusing language employed in footnote 14 of its opinion, as the dissenters recognize, does not help the majority. On the other hand, is the dissent's evaluation of the legislative history convincing? Does the fact that the amendment was aimed predominantly at protecting women employees from discrimination mean that it should not be interpreted to prevent discrimination against male employees with respect to their receipt of fringe benefits? Finally, does it strike you that the language in the majority opinion sounds a bit too much like a gloating judicial "I told you so" on the part of those who had dissented in *Gilbert?*

To what extent, if any, would the reasoning in *Newport News* apply to the case of a male employee who can establish that both he and his wife were fired by their common employer solely because of the wife's pregnancy? Can he state a claim of sex discrimination under Title VII? If so, would it be a pregnancy-based claim or a general claim of gender discrimination? See Nicol v. Imagematrix, Inc., 773 F.Supp. 802 (E.D.Va.1991).

2. Suppose an employer has no paid sick leave policy, but permits all employees to take up to two weeks unpaid sick leave before discharging them. Further assume that the employer uniformly discharged all persons who exceeded the two week limit. If the employer denies a female employee's request for additional unpaid time off for pregnancy and maternity leave, and discharges her upon the expiration of the two week period, can she successfully

maintain a claim of sex discrimination? Is *Griggs* applicable? The EEOC has ruled that an employer's adherence to a facially neutral sick leave policy and its consequent refusal to provide pregnant employees with a reasonable leave of absence, in the absence of a showing of business necessity, discriminates on the basis of sex because of its disproportionate impact on women. See EEOC Dec. No. 74–112, 19 FEP Cases 1817 (April 15, 1974); EEOC Guidelines, 29 C.F.R. § 1604.10(c). Similarly, in EEOC v. WARSHAWSKY & CO., 768 F.Supp. 647 (N.D.Ill. 1991), the trial court held that an employer policy precluding all employees from taking any paid sick leave during the first year of employment violated Title VII because it created a disproportionate impact on women and was not supported by any evidence of a legitimate business explanation. The court pointed to a statistical showing that the employer had discharged 53 first year employees pursuant to this sick leave policy, 50 of whom were women and three of whom were men. Moreover, of the 20 discharged female employees, 20 were pregnant. The trial judge also noted that the company had offered no evidence to support its allegation that the policy was intended to reward those employees who had shown their staying power with the company. Accordingly, the court granted the plaintiff's motion for partial summary judgment. But as this motion only addressed the issue of liability, the court reserved decision on the matter of appropriate relief. See also Abraham v. Graphic Arts Intern. Union, 660 F.2d 811 (D.C. Cir. 1981). If policies of this type do violate Title VII, what are the possible remedies? If the employer is ordered to provide extra sick leave to pregnant employees, as opposed to being required to expand the amount of sick leave offered to all employees, would such a result comport with the language in § 701(k) requiring pregnant employees to "be treated the same for all employee-related purposes" as non-pregnant employees? Would it amount to "reverse" sex discrimination? This issue has been addressed by the Supreme Court in the context of a state statute requiring employers to provide female employees with up to four months of unpaid pregnancy disability leave. See Note 4, *infra*, for a discussion of this case.

3. If an employer provides infant care leave, should it be made available to workers of either gender? See Comment, The Pregnancy Discrimination Act: Protecting A Man's Right to Infant–Care Leave, 25 Santa Clara L.Rev. 435 (1985). In the absence of federal legislation requiring employers to provide paid or unpaid parental leave, the legislative initiative in this area has come exclusively from the states. In 1987, Minnesota, Oregon and Connecticut enacted parental leave laws requiring employers to grant unpaid leave to either parent after the birth or adoption of a child. The Minnesota law requires public and private employers with 21 or more employees to give up to six weeks unpaid leave to one of the natural or adoptive parents beginning not later than six weeks after the birth or adoption. Employers in Oregon must give parents up to twelve weeks leave after the birth of the child, as long as both parents do not take the leave at the same time. In Connecticut, state employees are entitled to take up to twenty-four weeks of unpaid leave after the birth or adoption of a child. Private sector workers are eligible for up to sixteen weeks of unpaid leave within any two year period for the birth, adoption or serious illness of a child. This unpaid leave is also available for the employees' own serious illness or the serious illness of the employee's spouse or parent. In 1988, the legislatures in Maine and Wisconsin also passed family medical leave laws. The Maine statute requires public and private employers with 25 or more employees to provide ten weeks of leave in any two year period for the birth or adoption of a child or for the serious illness of an immediate family

member. In Wisconsin, the statute provides for up to six weeks yearly leave for a birth or adoption and a separate two weeks of yearly leave for care of a child with a serious health condition for any employee who has worked at least 1000 hours for the employer during the preceding 52 weeks. The Washington Family Leave Act of 1989 requires public and private employers with one hundred employees to provide employees with up to twelve weeks of unpaid leave for the birth or adoption of a child or to care for a child with a terminal health condition. A 1990 family and medical leave law enacted in the District of Columbia provides private sector and District employees with up to sixteen weeks in a twenty-four month period for the birth or placement of a child or for the care of a family member with a serious health condition. Hawaii enacted a statute in 1991 providing, initially, only private sector workers with the right to take up to four weeks of unpaid leave (with continuation of other benefits) in a 12 month period for the birth or adoption of a child, or for a serious health condition of a child, parent or spouse. The statute also provides, however, that its terms will extend to public sector employers with 100 or more employees in 1994. Legislation passed in Alaska and Virginia in 1991 provides unpaid parental leave in the public sector.

4. What if a state antidiscrimination law prohibited employers from refusing to grant reasonable leaves of absence for pregnancy? In CALIFORNIA FEDERAL SAVINGS AND LOAN ASS'N v. GUERRA, 479 U.S. 272, 107 S.Ct. 683, 93 L.Ed.2d 613 (1987), the Court was confronted by a California statute that required employers subject to the provisions of Title VII to provide female employees with up to four months unpaid pregnancy disability leave. It also required employers to reinstate any employee returning from such pregnancy leave to the job she previously held unless that position was unavailable due to business necessity, in which case, the employer was required to make a reasonable, good faith effort to provide employment in a substantially similar job. The petitioner, a California employer, had a policy of providing unpaid disability leave for a variety of conditions (including pregnancy and disability) and attempting to provide employees returning from such unpaid leave with a similar position. The company, however, expressly reserved the right to terminate any returning employee for whom a similar position was not available. After returning from unpaid leave and being informed that neither her specific nor a similar job was available, one of the petitioner's female employees charged the petitioner with violating the California statute. Pending administrative hearings on that charge, the petitioner filed the instant action seeking a declaration that the California statute was inconsistent with and pre-empted by Title VII and an injunction against enforcement of the state law. The district court granted the plaintiff's motion for summary judgment, ruling that the preferential-to-pregnancy provisions of the state law were pre-empted by Title VII and thus were inoperative under the Supremacy Clause of the U.S. Constitution. The Ninth Circuit reversed on the ground that a state law guaranteeing women employees a certain amount of pregnancy disability leave not only was not inconsistent with Title VII but was in furtherance of the federal policy of ensuring equal employment opportunity to women.

A majority of six members of the Supreme Court, in three separate opinions, agreed to affirm the judgment of the court of appeals. The opinion of the Court, written by Justice Marshall and joined in by Justices Brennan, Blackmun and O'Connor, began by noting that § 708 of Title VII provided that Title VII only pre-empted a state law "which purports to require or permit the doing of any act which would be an unlawful employment practice under this title" and that § 1104 of Title XI, applicable to all titles of the 1964 Civil Rights Act, stated that state laws were pre-empted by the 1964 Act when a state law "is inconsistent with any of the purposes of this Act or any provision thereof." Accordingly, the plurality reasoned, state laws could provide more extensive protections than Title VII offered as long as these extra protections did not conflict with either the terms or policies of the federal law. The opinion then stated that in its prior ruling in *Newport News*, the Court had held that the PDA was intended to overrule the Court's prior ruling and analysis in *Gilbert*. In so doing, these Justices agreed, Congress did not intend to prohibit employers from affording preferential treatment to pregnant workers. To support this inference, the plurality pointed to the absence of any reference in the statutory language or legislative history reflecting an intention to preclude such preferential treatment. Rather, the plurality concluded, the legislative history indicated that the PDA was intended to guarantee women the right to fully participate in the workforce without being forced to sacrifice their participation in family life. Thus, since Title VII did not preclude this form of preferential treatment of pregnancy, the state law could not be pre-empted under either §§ 708 or 1104. Title VII merely created a minimum level of protections for pregnant workers that could be augmented by state legislation. Moreover, they concluded, by limiting the right to disability leave and reinstatement to the period of physical disability occasioned by pregnancy, the state law did not erect or reflect a stereotypical view of pregnancy that would be inconsistent with, and thus pre-empted by Title VII. Finally, the plurality added, since the state law did not prevent employers from according identical disability leave and reinstatement rights to non-pregnant employees, the statute did not mandate that pregnant workers be treated more generously than non-pregnant workers. Thus, the plurality rejected the claim that pre-emption was required because compliance with both statutes was a physical impossibility. Justice Stevens agreed with the plurality's view that the California statute did not conflict with the purposes of the PDA. He wrote separately, however, to emphasize that he did not find it necessary to determine whether the pre-emption provisions of the more general § 1104 of Title XI applied to Title VII and to state that it was not clear whether the plurality had ruled on the applicability of both pre-emption provisions. He also noted that preferential treatment of pregnant workers was only permitted by the PDA where that preference was designed to achieve equality of employment opportunities. Justice Scalia was the sixth Justice to agree to affirm the lower court's judgment. He agreed with Justice Stevens that since the PDA is a part of Title VII, § 708 was the appropriate pre-emption provision to apply. He then reasoned that it was unnecessary to determine whether the federal statute prohibited preferential disability treatment for pregnant employees since the state law did not "purport to require or permit any act that would be an unlawful employment practice under any conceivable interpretation of the PDA." 479 U.S. at 296, 107 S.Ct. at 697, 93 L.Ed.2d at 633. Justice White, joined by the Chief Justice and Justice Powell, stated that the second clause of the PDA demanded that pregnant employees be treated the same as non-pregnant employees and, therefore, that the state law requiring employers to have a disability policy for pregnant workers that it need not have for non-pregnant employees was inconsistent with, and thus pre-empted by, the federal mandate of neutrality.

Did the Supreme Court adequately resolve the statutory dilemma? For thoughtful insights into the "special treatment/equal treatment" debate, see

Kay, Equality and Difference: The Case of Pregnancy, 1 Berkeley Women's L.J. 21 (1985); Finley, Transcending Equality Theory: A Way Out Of The Maternity And The Workplace Debate, 86 Col.L.Rev. 1118 (1986); Williams, Dissolving The Sameness/Difference Debate: A Postmodern Path Beyond Essentialism in Feminist and Critical Race Theory, 1991 Duke L.J. 296 (1991); Scales, Towards a New Feminist Jurisprudence, 56 Ind.L.J. 375 (1981); Williams, Equality's Riddle: Pregnancy and the Equal Treatment/Special Treatment Debate, 13 NYU Rev. of L. & Soc. Ch. 325 (1984–1985); Note, Pregnancy and Equality: A Precarious Alliance, 60 So.Cal.L.Rev. 1345 (1987); Minda, Title VII At The Crossroads of Employment Discrimination Law and Postmodern Feminist Theory, 11 St. Louis U.Pub.L.Rev. 89 (1992).

5.   The Federal Unemployment Tax Act forbids states from denying unemployment compensation to individuals who leave work "solely on the basis of pregnancy."   Suppose a state unemployment compensation law disqualified anyone who voluntarily terminated their employment for a non-employment related reason.   Further suppose that an employer in that state had an established policy of permitting employees with nonoccupational disabilities to take only unpaid leave and made reinstatement dependent upon the availability of a position at the time the worker sought to return.   Finally, suppose that one of this employer's employees was denied reinstatement after a pregnancy leave because of the unavailability of a vacant position.   Does the federal statute preclude the state from disqualifying her from receiving unemployment benefits?   This question confronted the Supreme Court in WIMBERLY v. LABOR & INDUSTRIAL COMMISSION, 479 U.S. 511, 107 S.Ct. 821, 93 L.Ed.2d 909 (1987).   There, a unanimous Supreme Court (Justice Blackmun recused himself) held that the federal statute was intended to prohibit States from singling out pregnancy for unfavorable treatment and, therefore, for using pregnancy as a specific basis for exclusion.   In this case, the Court reasoned, pregnancy was not the statutory basis for exclusion;   non-work related voluntary separation was the statutory exclusion standard.   Pregnancy was only the claimant's reason for satisfying the facially neutral exclusion criterion.   Accordingly, the Court concluded, "if a State adopts a neutral rule that incidentally disqualifies pregnant or formerly pregnant claimants as a part of a larger group, the neutral application of that rule cannot readily be characterized as a decision made 'solely on the basis of pregnancy.' "   Since persons who left their jobs for any non-work related reason were disqualified, the fact that the reason for separation in this particular case was pregnancy was irrelevant to the state and, therefore, it could not be said that pregnancy was the "sole basis" for the disqualification.   Moreover, the Court added, to preclude pregnancy-based disqualification would be tantamount to requiring preferential treatment on the basis of pregnancy when there is no evidence that Congress intended to mandate preferential treatment.   Rather, the Court reasoned, the statute was intended only to prohibit disadvantageous treatment on the basis of pregnancy.

Do you agree with this reasoning?   Is the reasoning behind *Griggs, Newport News* or *Guerra* (none of which were cited or discussed in the instant case) applicable?   Is *Guerra* distinguishable on the ground that the issue there was whether Title VII permitted a State to grant preferential treatment on the basis of pregnancy whereas *Wimberly* asked only whether the FUTA required a State to accord preferential status to pregnant workers?   See Radford, *Wimberly* And Beyond: Analyzing The Refusal To Award Unemployment Compensation To Women Who Terminate Prior Employment Due To Pregnancy, 63 NYU L.Rev. 532 (1988).

6. Does the Court's ruling in *Guerra* shed light on the legality of an employer's voluntarily adopted nonoccupational disability policy that provides a longer period of disability leave for maternity than it does for all other covered conditions? See Harness v. Hartz Mountain Corp., 877 F.2d 1307 (6th Cir.1989), cert. denied, 493 U.S. 1024, 110 S.Ct. 728, 107 L.Ed.2d 747 (1990). What about an employer who provides only female employees with the option of taking a one year unpaid leave of absence for childrearing? Is this a violation of Title VII or does it constitute permissible preferential treatment pursuant to the *Guerra* Court's interpretation of the PDA? In SCHAFER v. BOARD OF PUBLIC EDUCATION OF SCHOOL DISTRICT OF PITTSBURGH, 903 F.2d 243 (3d Cir.1990), the court struck down as violative of Title VII a collective bargaining provision that granted only to female teachers the right to a one year unpaid leave of absence for childrearing if taken immediately after childbirth. The court distinguished this plan from the statutory scheme in *Guerra* on the ground that the *Guerra* plurality limited its holding to a preference that was specifically limited to the period of actual physical disability. The contractual provision in *Schafer*, however, did not require that the female be disabled in order to obtain the unpaid leave. Therefore, the court reasoned, the leave was not related to conditions of pregnancy as required by the PDA. Accordingly, the court held that the provision of the collective bargaining agreement violated Title VII's prohibition against sex discrimination and was *per se* void for any leave granted beyond the period of actual physical disability on account of pregnancy, childbirth or related medical condition.

7. The federal Employee Retirement Income Security Act of 1974, 88 Stat. 829, 29 U.S.C. § 1001 et seq. (1976 ed. and Supp. V) (ERISA) subjects "employee benefit plans", such as pension and welfare plans, to federal regulation with respect to participation, funding and vesting. Section 514(a) of ERISA expressly preempts any and all state laws which relate to employee benefit plans covered by ERISA. The statute also, however, exempts from ERISA coverage (and thereby permits state regulation of) employee benefit plans maintained solely for the purpose of complying with applicable state workers' compensation, unemployment compensation or disability insurance laws. Finally, section 514(d) of ERISA provides that the statute cannot be construed to impair any other federal law. Prior to the enactment of the Pregnancy Discrimination Act, the New York State anti-discrimination statute had been interpreted to prohibit an employer from excluding pregnancy from its nonoccupational disability plan. This, of course, meant that the state law's provisions went beyond those of the federal statute as then interpreted by the Supreme Court in *Gilbert*. In SHAW v. DELTA AIR LINES, INC., 463 U.S. 85, 103 S.Ct. 2890, 77 L.Ed.2d 490 (1983), the Supreme Court held that the express preemption clause of ERISA prohibited state regulation of employee benefit plans insofar as the state statute prohibited practices that were lawful under Title VII. This ruling, the Court reasoned, gave effect to both the preemption of state law provision and the requirement that ERISA not be interpreted so as to impair or modify another federal statute. While the subsequent enactment of the Pregnancy Discrimination Act in 1978 limits the significance of this ruling with respect to the pregnancy provision of the New York State law, the Court noted that its decision might have further repercussions with respect to other provisions of state fair employment statutes that contain proscriptions broader than those in Title VII and that relate to employee benefit plans covered by ERISA.

8. Note also that the extent of protection afforded pregnancy classifications by § 701(k) may be limited by the availability of the business necessity and § 703(e) BFOQ defenses. Compare Harriss v. Pan American World Airways, Inc., 649 F.2d 670 (9th Cir.1980) (policy requiring flight attendants to take maternity leave immediately upon discovery of pregnancy justified under BFOQ defense) with Burwell v. Eastern Air Lines, Inc., 633 F.2d 361 (4th Cir.1980), cert. denied, 450 U.S. 965, 101 S.Ct. 1480, 67 L.Ed.2d 613 (1981) (business necessity defense justifies mandatory maternity leave only from the commencement of the 28th week of pregnancy.). Can a hospital justifiably discharge a pregnant radiation technologist on the ground that her exposure to X-rays created a risk of injury to the fetus and resultant liability to the hospital? What if an employer excludes all fertile women from jobs classified as requiring or possibly requiring contact with and exposure to known or suspected abortifacient or teratogenic agents? See International Union, United Auto Workers v. Johnson Controls, Inc., *supra*, at 167. Does the *Guerra* Court's recognition that the PDA does not preclude preferential treatment for pregnant employees that is designed to promote their ability to work, offer any guidance concerning the treatment of fetal vulnerability policies? For an interesting suggestion that *Guerra* can be extended to support the imposition on employers of a duty to responsibly accommodate pregnant workers in work environments that pose a hazard to the health and safety of the fetus during the time that hazard exists, see Furnish, Beyond Protection: Relevant Difference And Equality In The Toxic Work Environment, 21 U.C.D.L. Rev. 1 (1987).

9. Some states have created income maintenance programs that pay benefits to persons who are unemployed because of a nonoccupational disability and finance such programs by employee contributions withheld from wages. Suppose that under such a statutory program the employer is required to withhold employee contributions from its employees' wages, transmit these funds to the state agency and perform record keeping functions, but does not make contributions of its own to the fund. If the program treats pregnancy differently than all other disabilities, is the employer liable under Title VII? See Barone v. Hackett, 602 F.Supp. 481 (D.R.I.1984).

10. Should the result in *Newport News* be given retroactive effect? Two federal appeals courts have concluded that retroactivity is justified in light of the presumption in favor of liability in Title VII cases announced by the Supreme Court in Albemarle Paper Co. v. Moody, see *infra* at p. 601, and the factors set forth in Chevron Oil Co. v. Huson, 404 U.S. 97, 92 S.Ct. 349, 30 L.Ed.2d 296 (1971) for determining the appropriateness of retroactivity. Applying the *Chevron* standards, the court in EEOC v. Puget Sound Log Scaling & Grading Bureau, 752 F.2d 1389 (9th Cir. 1985) stated that in light of extant EEOC guidelines on the Pregnancy Discrimination Act, analogous equal protection holdings by the Supreme Court, and several federal court decisions concerning the application of the PDA to nonemployees, the result in *Newport News* should not have come as a surprise to this defendant. In addition, the court noted, to deny retroactivity would frustrate the statutory make-whole purpose and would encourage employers to wait as long as possible to comply with the PDA. The court also reasoned that retroactivity would not impose an overly burdensome expense on the employer since it would only have to reimburse a relatively small, discrete number of male employees who had privately financed the cost of their nonemployee spouses' pregnancies. Accord, see EEOC v. Atlanta Gas Light Co., 751 F.2d 1188 (11th Cir. 1985).

11.   Pregnancy and maternity policies used by public employers have been challenged under the Equal Protection and Due Process Clauses of the Constitution as well as under Title VII.   In GEDULDIG v. AIELLO, 417 U.S. 484, 94 S.Ct. 2485, 41 L.Ed.2d 256 (1974), the Supreme Court rejected an equal protection attack upon an employee-funded California disability insurance system that specifically excluded pregnancy from its list of compensable disabilities. The Court held that the State's determination not to provide a totally comprehensive insurance program did not amount to invidious discrimination under the Equal Protection Clause.   Since the plan provided equivalent aggregate risk protection to both sexes, the exclusion of pregnancy, though admittedly affecting only women, was not a sex-based classification for constitutional purposes. The decision to exclude pregnancy, the Court added, was not irrational but was supported by legitimate financial considerations.   This reasoning later served as the foundation for the Court's ruling in *Gilbert*.   The constitutionality of mandatory maternity leave for public school teachers was addressed in CLEVE-LAND BOARD OF EDUCATION v. LAFLEUR, 414 U.S. 632, 94 S.Ct. 791, 39 L.Ed.2d 52 (1974).   The Court struck down the Board's policy requiring every pregnant teacher to take unpaid maternity leave at the end of the fourth month of pregnancy as violative of the Due Process Clause of the Fourteenth Amendment.   This inflexible cutoff date, the Court reasoned, contained an irrebuttable presumption—that all pregnant teachers become physically incapable of teaching at the same designated moment—and applied it even in the face of undisputed contrary medical evidence as to an individual teacher. Relying on several of its prior decisions, the Court concluded that the Due Process Clause could not tolerate an irrebuttable presumption that was not necessarily or universally true when the School Board had a reasonable alternative method of making individualized determinations as to physical competence.   The Court applied this same analysis in also invalidating the Board's policy permitting teachers to return from maternity leave no sooner than the beginning of the regular semester following the date the teacher's child attained the age of three months.   However, the Court's subsequent ruling in Weinberger v. Salfi, 422 U.S. 749, 95 S.Ct. 2457, 45 L.Ed.2d 522 (1975), in which it rejected a due process challenge to a Social Security Act provision that awarded benefits to a deceased wage earner's surviving widow and step-children only if they had been related to the deceased for at least nine months prior to his death, indicates that the Court has abandoned the irrebuttable presumption doctrine.   See New York City Transit Authority v. Beazer, 440 U.S. 568, 592 n. 38, 99 S.Ct. 1355, 1369 n. 38, 59 L.Ed.2d 587, 606 n. 38 (1979) ("The District Court also concluded that TA's rule [refusing employment to methadone users] violates the Due Process Clause because it creates an 'irrebuttable presumption' of unemployability on the part of methadone users. Respondents do not rely on the due process argument in this Court, and we find no merit in it.").   See generally Chase, the Premature Demise of Irrebuttable Presumptions, 47 U.Colo.L.Rev. 653 (1976).   Consequently, most future challenges to public sector mandatory maternity leave programs are likely to rely principally upon Title VII rather than the Constitution.

12.   Pregnancy, of course, is not the only "plus" characteristic restricted to members of one sex.   Would an employer's refusal to hire all bearded applicants constitute a prima facie violation of Title VII?   What if a restaurant owner imposed large breast size as a requirement for employment?   Can either of these policies be justified under the BFOQ defense?

Can a female employee who was discharged for having an abortion state a claim under Title VII? Has she been discriminated against "on the basis of sex", i.e., "on the basis of pregnancy, childbirth or related medical conditions"? If so, would she assert a disparate treatment or disproportionate impact claim? In a case of first impression, the trial court in DOE v. FIRST NATIONAL BANK OF CHICAGO, 668 F.Supp. 1110 (N.D.Ill.1987) concluded that *if* Title VII proscribed discrimination on the basis of procuring an abortion, the plaintiff would have to prove both the employer's animus towards abortions and its knowledge of the plaintiff's abortion in order to establish a prima facie case. The court imposed this addition to the standard elements of a disparate treatment prima facie case because, it reasoned, it was improper to presume from the facts of the abortion and an otherwise unexplained employment decision, without more, that the decision was taken because of the abortion. The court suggested that it was "unreasonable and offensive to an awareness of the facts of life to assume, with nothing more, that more likely than not employers easily possess animus towards abortions and that the fact that an abortion was had or was being planned would easily become known." After a bench trial, the trial judge ruled in favor of the defendant, finding that the plaintiff had not established that the persons responsible for her termination either knew of her abortion or possessed animus towards abortion, i.e., she did not prove that she had been discharged because of the abortion. While the trial court undoubtedly was correct that the fact of an abortion is less extrinsically discernible than membership in a racial or gender group, is it so manifestly apparent that employers are less likely to possess abortion-based, than race-based animus? Interestingly, because the court concluded that the plaintiff had not established employer animus towards or knowledge of the abortion, it found it unnecessary to rule on whether Title VII actually did support such a cause of action. There was no discussion of whether the plaintiff could have asserted an impact-based claim. On appeal, the circuit court limited its review to the trial court's factual determinations and found that they were not clearly erroneous. Accordingly, it affirmed the judgment of the lower court. 865 F.2d 864 (7th Cir.1989).

13. Suppose that relevant state law requires employers to maintain health insurance coverage for discharged employees for at least three months after the date of discharge, with the cost of such insurance borne by the employee. After his discharge, Harley Karz–Wagman was offered a health insurance policy that did not include coverage for spousal pregnancy. It did, however, cover all other short-term disabilities. Has the company violated Title VII? Would it matter whether spousal pregnancy coverage had been provided during Karz–Wagman's tenure as an employee? See EEOC v. South Dakota Wheat Growers Association, 683 F.Supp. 1302 (D.S.D.1988).

14. Estelle Smith is hired by the Laromme Company as secretary to its President, Omri Astruc. She and the president begin a consensual affair which results in Estelle becoming pregnant. She informs him that he is the father and that she intends to have the baby even though she is married to someone else. The next day she is terminated. Can she state a claim of sex discrimination under Title VII? See Freeman v. Continental Technical Services, Inc., 710 F.Supp. 328 (N.D.Ga.1988).

2. Sexual Harassment

MERITOR SAVINGS BANK, FSB v. VINSON

Supreme Court of the United States, 1986.
477 U.S. 57, 106 S.Ct. 2399, 91 L.Ed.2d 49.

Justice Rehnquist delivered the opinion of the Court.

This case presents important questions concerning claims of workplace "sexual harassment" brought under Title VII of the Civil Rights Act of 1964.

I

In 1974, respondent Mechelle Vinson met Sidney Taylor, a vice president of what is now petitioner Meritor Savings Bank (the bank) and manager of one of its branch offices. When respondent asked whether she might obtain employment at the bank, Taylor gave her an application, which she completed and returned the next day; later that same day Taylor called her to say that she had been hired. With Taylor as her supervisor, respondent started as a teller-trainee, and thereafter was promoted to teller, head teller, and assistant branch manager. She worked at the same branch for four years, and it is undisputed that her advancement there was based on merit alone. In September 1978, respondent notified Taylor that she was taking sick leave for an indefinite period. On November 1, 1978, the bank discharged her for excessive use of that leave.

Respondent brought this action against Taylor and the bank, claiming that during her four years at the bank she had "constantly been subjected to sexual harassment" by Taylor in violation of Title VII. She sought injunctive relief, compensatory and punitive damages against Taylor and the bank, and attorney's fees.

At the 11–day bench trial, the parties presented conflicting testimony about Taylor's behavior during respondent's employment.* Respondent testified that during her probationary period as a teller-trainee, Taylor treated her in a fatherly way and made no sexual advances. Shortly thereafter, however, he invited her out to dinner and, during the course of the meal, suggested that they go to a motel to have sexual relations. At first she refused, but out of what she described as fear of losing her job she eventually agreed. According to respondent, Taylor thereafter made repeated demands upon her for sexual favors, usually at the branch, both during and after business hours; she estimated that over the next several years she had intercourse with him some 40 or 50 times. In addition, respondent testified that Taylor fondled her in front of other employees, followed her into the women's restroom when she went there alone, exposed himself to her, and even forcibly raped

---

* Like the Court of Appeals, this Court was not provided a complete transcript of the trial. We therefore rely largely on the District Court's opinion for the summary of the relevant testimony.

her on several occasions. These activities ceased after 1977, respondent stated, when she started going with a steady boyfriend.

Respondent also testified that Taylor touched and fondled other women employees of the bank, and she attempted to call witnesses to support this charge. But while some supporting testimony apparently was admitted without objection, the District Court did not allow her "to present wholesale evidence of a pattern and practice relating to sexual advances to other female employees in her case in chief, but advised her that she might well be able to present such evidence in rebuttal to the defendants' cases." Vinson v. Taylor, 22 EPD ¶ 30,708, p. 14, 693, n. 1, 23 FEP Cases 37, 38–39, n. 1 (D DC 1980). Respondent did not offer such evidence in rebuttal. Finally, respondent testified that because she was afraid of Taylor she never reported his harassment to any of his supervisors and never attempted to use the bank's complaint procedure.

Taylor denied respondent's allegations of sexual activity, testifying that he never fondled her, never made suggestive remarks to her, never engaged in sexual intercourse with her and never asked her to do so. He contended instead that respondent made her accusations in response to a business-related dispute. The bank also denied respondent's allegations and asserted that any sexual harassment by Taylor was unknown to the bank and engaged in without its consent or approval.

The District Court denied relief, but did not resolve the conflicting testimony about the existence of a sexual relationship between respondent and Taylor. It found instead that

> "If [respondent] and Taylor did engage in an intimate or sexual relationship during the time of [respondent's] employment with [the bank], that relationship was a voluntary one having nothing to do with her continued employment at [the bank] or her advancement or promotions at that institution."

The court ultimately found that respondent "was not the victim of sexual harassment and was not the victim of sexual discrimination" while employed at the bank.

Although it concluded that respondent had not proved a violation of Title VII, the District Court nevertheless went on to address the bank's liability. After noting the bank's express policy against discrimination, and finding that neither respondent nor any other employee had ever lodged a complaint about sexual harassment by Taylor, the court ultimately concluded that "the bank was without notice and cannot be held liable for the alleged actions of Taylor."

The Court of Appeals for the District of Columbia Circuit reversed. 753 F.2d 141 (1985). Relying on its earlier holding in Bundy v. Jackson, 641 F.2d 934 (1981), decided after the trial in this case, the court stated that a violation of Title VII may be predicated on either of two types of sexual harassment: harassment that involves the conditioning of concrete employment benefits on sexual favors, and harassment that, while not affecting economic benefits, creates a hostile or offensive working environment. The court drew additional support for this position from the Equal Employment Opportunity Commission's Guidelines on Discrimination Because of Sex, 29 CFR § 1604.11(a) (1985), which set out these two types of sexual harassment claims. Believing that "Vinson's grievance was clearly of the [hostile environment] type," and that the District Court had not considered whether a violation of this type had occurred, the court concluded that a remand was necessary.

The court further concluded that the District Court's finding that any sexual relationship between respondent and Taylor "was a voluntary one" did not obviate the need for a remand. "[U]ncertain as to precisely what the [district] court meant" by this finding, the Court of Appeals held that if the evidence otherwise showed that "Taylor made Vinson's toleration of sexual harassment a condition of her employment," her voluntariness "had no materiality whatsoever." The court then surmised that the District Court's finding of voluntariness might have been based on "the voluminous testimony regarding respondent's dress and personal fantasies," testimony that the Court of Appeals believed "had no place in this litigation."

As to the bank's liability, the Court of Appeals held that an employer is absolutely liable for sexual harassment practiced by supervisory personnel, whether or not the employer knew or should have known about the misconduct. The court relied chiefly on Title VII's definition of "employer" to include "any agent of such a person," 42 U.S.C. § 2000e(b), as well as on the EEOC guidelines. The court held that a supervisor is an "agent" of his employer for Title VII purposes, even if he lacks authority to hire, fire, or promote, since "the mere existence—or even the appearance—of a significant degree of influence in vital job decisions gives any supervisor the opportunity to impose on employees."

In accordance with the foregoing, the Court of Appeals reversed the judgment of the District Court and remanded the case for further proceedings. A subsequent suggestion for rehearing en banc was denied, with three judges dissenting. We granted certiorari, and now affirm but for different reasons.

II

Title VII of the Civil Rights Act of 1964 makes it "an unlawful employment practice for an employer * * * to discriminate against any individual with respect to his compensation, terms, conditions, or privileges of employment, because of such individual's race, color, religion, sex, or national origin." 42 U.S.C. § 2000e–2(a)(1). The prohibition against discrimination based on sex was added to Title VII at the last minute on the floor of the House of Representatives. 110 Cong.Rec. 2577–2584 (1964). The principal argument in opposition to the amendment was that "sex discrimination" was sufficiently different from other types of discrimination that it ought to receive separate legislative treatment. See id., at 2577 (Statement of Rep. Celler quoting letter from United States Department of Labor); id., at 2584 (statement of Rep. Green). This argument was defeated, the bill quickly passed as amended, and we are left with little legislative history to guide us in interpreting the Act's prohibition against discrimination based on "sex."

Respondent argues, and the Court of Appeals held, that unwelcome sexual advances that create an offensive or hostile working environment violate Title VII. Without question, when a supervisor sexually harasses a subordinate because of the subordinate's sex, that supervisor "discriminate[s]" on the basis of sex. Petitioner apparently does not challenge this proposition. It contends instead that in prohibiting discrimination with respect to "compensation, terms, conditions, or privileges" of employment, Congress was concerned with what petitioner describes as "tangible loss" of "an economic character," not "purely psychological aspects of the workplace environment." Brief for Petitioner 30–31, 34. In support of this claim petitioner observes that in both the legislative history of Title VII and this Court's Title VII decisions, the focus has been on tangible, economic barriers erected by discrimination.

We reject petitioner's view. First, the language of Title VII is not limited to "economic" or "tangible" discrimination. The phrase "terms, conditions, or privileges of employment" evinces a congressional intent " 'to strike at the entire spectrum of disparate treatment of men and women' " in employment. Los Angeles Department of Water and Power v. Manhart, 435 U.S. 702, 707, n. 13, 98 S.Ct. 1370, 1375, n. 13, 55 L.Ed.2d 657 (1978), quoting Sprogis v. United Air Lines, Inc., 444 F.2d 1194, 1198 (CA7 1971). Petitioner has pointed to nothing in the Act to suggest that Congress contemplated the limitation urged here.

Second, in 1980 the EEOC issued guidelines specifying that "sexual harassment," as there defined, is a form of sex discrimination prohibited by Title VII. As an "administrative interpretation of the Act by the enforcing agency," Griggs v. Duke Power Co., 401 U.S. 424, 433–434, 91 S.Ct. 849, 855, 28 L.Ed.2d 158 (1971), these guidelines, " 'while not controlling upon the courts by reason of their authority, do constitute a body of experience and informed judgment to which courts and litigants may properly resort for guidance,' " General Electric Co. v. Gilbert, 429 U.S. 125, 141–142, 97 S.Ct. 401, 410–11, 50 L.Ed.2d 343 (1976), quoting Skidmore v. Swift & Co., 323 U.S. 134, 140, 65 S.Ct. 161, 164, 89 L.Ed. 124 (1944). The EEOC guidelines fully support the view that harassment leading to noneconomic injury can violate Title VII.

In defining "sexual harassment," the guidelines first describe the kinds of workplace conduct that may be actionable under Title VII. These include "[u]nwelcome sexual advances, requests for sexual favors, and other verbal or physical conduct of a sexual nature." 29 CFR § 1604.11(a) (1985). Relevant to the charges at issue in this case, the guidelines provide that such sexual misconduct constitutes prohibited "sexual harassment," whether or not it is directly linked to the grant or denial of an economic *quid pro quo,* where "such conduct has the purpose or effect of unreasonably interfering with an individual's work performance or creating an intimidating, hostile, or offensive working environment." § 1604.11(a)(3).

In concluding that so-called "hostile environment" (i.e., non *quid pro quo*) harassment violates Title VII, the EEOC drew upon a substantial body of judicial decisions and EEOC precedent holding that Title VII affords employees the right to work in an environment free from discriminatory intimidation, ridicule, and insult.   See generally 45 Fed.Reg. 74676 (1980).   Rogers v. EEOC, 454 F.2d 234 (CA5 1971), cert. denied, 406 U.S. 957, 92 S.Ct. 2058, 32 L.Ed.2d 343 (1972), was apparently the first case to recognize a cause of action based upon a discriminatory work environment.   In *Rogers,* the Court of Appeals for the Fifth Circuit held that a Hispanic complainant could establish a Title VII violation by demonstrating that her employer created an offensive work environment for employees by giving discriminatory service to its Hispanic clientele.   The court explained that an employee's protections under Title VII extend beyond the economic aspects of employment:

> "[T]he phrase 'terms, conditions or privileges of employment' in [Title VII] is an expansive concept which sweeps within its protective ambit the practice of creating a working environment heavily charged with ethnic or racial discrimination * * *.   One can readily envision working environments so heavily polluted with discrimination as to destroy completely the emotional and psychological stability of minority group workers * * *."   454 F.2d, at 238.

Courts applied this principle to harassment based on race, e.g., Firefighters Institute for Racial Equality v. St. Louis, 549 F.2d 506, 514–515(CA8), cert. denied sub nom. Banta v. United States, 178 U.S.App. D.C. 91, 98, 434 U.S. 819, 98 S.Ct. 60, 54 L.Ed.2d 76 (1977); Gray v. Greyhound Lines, East, 178 U.S.App.D.C. 91, 98, 545 F.2d 169, 176 (1976), religion, e.g., Compston v. Borden, Inc., 424 F.Supp. 157 (SD Ohio 1976), and national origin, e.g., Cariddi v. Kansas City Chiefs Football Club, 568 F.2d 87, 88 (CA8 1977).   Nothing in Title VII suggests that a hostile environment based on discriminatory *sexual* harassment should not be likewise prohibited.   The guidelines thus appropriately drew from, and were fully consistent with, the existing caselaw.

Since the guidelines were issued, courts have uniformly held, and we agree, that a plaintiff may establish a violation of Title VII by proving that discrimination based on sex has created a hostile or abusive work environment.   As the Court of Appeals for the Eleventh Circuit wrote in Henson v. Dundee, 682 F.2d 897, 902 (1982):

> "Sexual harassment which creates a hostile or offensive environment for members of one sex is every bit the arbitrary barrier to sexual equality at the workplace that racial harassment is to racial equality.   Surely, a requirement that a man or woman run a

gauntlet of sexual abuse in return for the privilege of being allowed to work and make a living can be as demeaning and disconcerting as the harshest of racial epithets."

Accord, Katz v. Dole, 709 F.2d 251, 254–255 (CA4 1983); Bundy v. Jackson, 205 U.S.App.D.C. 444, 641 F.2d, at 934–944 (1981); Zabkowicz v. West Bend Co., 589 F.Supp. 780 (ED Wisc.1984).

Of course, as the courts in both *Rogers* and *Henson* recognized, not all workplace conduct that may be described as "harassment" affects a "term, condition, or privilege" of employment within the meaning of Title VII. See Rogers v. EEOC, supra, at 238 ("mere utterance of an ethnic or racial epithet which engenders offensive feelings in an employee" would not affect the conditions of employment to sufficiently significant degree to violate Title VII); *Henson,* supra, at 904 (quoting same). For sexual harassment to be actionable, it must be sufficiently severe or pervasive "to alter the conditions of [the victim's] employment and create an abusive working environment." Ibid. Respondent's allegations in this case—which include not only pervasive harassment but also criminal conduct of the most serious nature—are plainly sufficient to state a claim for "hostile environment" sexual harassment.

The question remains, however, whether the District Court's ultimate finding that respondent "was not the victim of sexual harassment," effectively disposed of respondent's claim. The Court of Appeals recognized, we think correctly, that this ultimate finding was likely based on one or both of two erroneous views of the law. First, the District Court apparently believed that a claim for sexual harassment will not lie absent an *economic* effect on the complainant's employment. See ibid. ("It is without question that sexual harassment of female employees in which they are asked or required to submit to sexual demands as a *condition to obtain employment or to maintain employment or to obtain promotions* falls within protection of Title VII.") (emphasis added). Since it appears that the District Court made its findings without ever considering the "hostile environment" theory of sexual harassment, the Court of Appeals' decision to remand was correct.

Second, the District Court's conclusion that no actionable harassment occurred might have rested on its earlier "finding" that "[i]f [respondent] and Taylor did engage in an intimate or sexual relationship * * *, that relationship was a voluntary one." But the fact that sex-related conduct was "voluntary," in the sense that the complainant was not forced to participate against her will, is not a defense to a sexual harassment suit brought under Title VII. The gravamen of any sexual harassment claim is that the alleged sexual advances were "unwelcome." 29 CFR § 1604.11(a) (1985). While the question whether particular conduct was indeed unwelcome presents difficult problems of proof and turns largely on credibility determinations committed to the trier of fact, the District Court in this case erroneously focused on the "voluntariness" of respondent's participation in the claimed sexual episodes. The correct inquiry is whether respondent by her conduct indicated that the alleged sexual advances were unwelcome, not whether her actual participation in sexual intercourse was voluntary.

Petitioner contends that even if this case must be remanded to the District Court, the Court of Appeals erred in one of the terms of its remand. Specifically, the Court of Appeals stated that testimony about respondent's "dress and personal fantasies," which the District Court apparently admitted into evidence, "had no place in this litigation." Ibid. The apparent ground for this conclusion was that respondent's voluntariness *vel non* in submitting to Taylor's advances was immaterial to her sexual harassment claim. While "voluntariness" in the sense of consent is not a defense to such a claim, it does not follow that a complainant's sexually provocative speech or dress is irrelevant as a matter of law in determining whether he or she found particular sexual advances unwelcome. To the contrary, such evidence is obviously relevant. The EEOC guidelines emphasize that the trier of fact must determine the existence of sexual harassment in light of "the record as a whole" and "the totality of circumstances, such as the nature of the sexual advances and the context in which the alleged incidents occurred." 29 CFR § 1604.11(b) (1985). Respondent's claim that any marginal relevance of the evidence in question was outweighed by the potential for unfair prejudice is the sort of argument properly addressed to the District Court. In this case the District Court concluded that the evidence should be admitted, and the Court of Appeals' contrary conclusion was based upon the erroneous, categorical view that testimony about provocative dress and publicly expressed sexual fantasies "had no place in this litigation." While the District Court must carefully weigh the applicable considerations in deciding whether to admit evidence of this kind, there is no *per se* rule against its admissibility.

III

Although the District Court concluded that respondent had not proved a violation of Title VII, it nevertheless went on to consider the question of the bank's liability. Finding that "the bank was without notice" of Taylor's alleged conduct, and that notice to Taylor was not the equivalent of notice to the bank, the court concluded that the bank therefore could not be held liable for Taylor's alleged actions. The Court of Appeals took the opposite view, holding that an employer is strictly liable for a hostile environment created by a supervisor's sexual advances, even though the employer neither knew nor reasonably could have known of the alleged misconduct. The court held that a supervisor, whether or not he possesses the authority to hire, fire, or promote, is necessarily an "agent" of his employer for all Title VII purposes, since "even the appearance" of such authority may enable him to impose himself on his subordinates.

The parties and *amici* suggest several different standards for employer liability. Respondent, not surprisingly, defends the position of the Court of Appeals. Noting that Title VII's definition of "employer" includes any "agent" of the employer, she also argues that "so long as the circumstance is work-related, the supervisor is the employer and the employer is the supervisor." Brief for Respondent 27. Notice to Taylor that the advances were unwelcome, therefore, was notice to the bank.

Petitioner argues that respondent's failure to use its established grievance procedure, or to otherwise put it on notice of the alleged misconduct, insulates petitioner from liability for Taylor's wrongdoing. A contrary rule would be unfair, petitioner argues, since in a hostile environment harassment case the employer often will have no reason to know about, or opportunity to cure, the alleged wrongdoing.

The EEOC, in its brief as *amicus curiae,* contends that courts formulating employer liability rules should draw from traditional agency principles. Examination of those principles has led the EEOC to the view that where a supervisor exercises the authority actually delegated to him by his employer, by making or threatening to make decisions affecting the employment status of his subordinates, such actions are properly imputed to the employer whose delegation of authority empowered the supervisor to undertake them. Thus, the courts have consistently held employers liable for the discriminatory discharges of employees by supervisory personnel, whether or not the employer knew, should have known, or approved of the supervisor's actions. E.g., Anderson v. Methodist Evangelical Hospital, Inc., 464 F.2d 723, 725 (CA6 1972).

The EEOC suggests that when a sexual harassment claim rests exclusively on a "hostile environment" theory, however, the usual basis for a finding of agency will often disappear. In that case, the EEOC believes, agency principles lead to

> "a rule that asks whether a victim of sexual harassment had reasonably available an avenue of complaint regarding such harassment, and, if available and utilized, whether that procedure was reasonably responsive to the employee's complaint. If the employer has an expressed policy against sexual harassment and has implemented a procedure specifically designed to resolve sexual harassment claims, and if the victim does not take advantage of that procedure, the employer should be shielded from liability absent actual knowledge of the sexually hostile environment (obtained, e.g., by the filing of a charge with the EEOC or a comparable state agency). In all other cases, the employer will be liable if it has actual knowledge of the harassment or if, considering all the facts of the case, the victim in question had no reasonably available avenue for making his or her complaint known to appropriate management officials." Brief for United States and Equal Opportunity Employment Commission as *Amici Curiae,* 26.

As respondent points out, this suggested rule is in some tension with the EEOC guidelines, which hold an employer liable for the acts of its agents without regard to notice. 29 CFR § 1604.11(c) (1985). The guidelines do require, however, an "examin[ation of] the circumstances of the particular employment relationship and the job [f]unctions performed by the individual in determining whether an individual acts in either a supervisory or agency capacity." Ibid.

This debate over the appropriate standard for employer liability has a rather abstract quality about it given the state of the record in this case. We do not know at this stage whether Taylor made any sexual advances toward respondent at all, let alone whether those advances were unwelcome, whether they were sufficiently pervasive to constitute a condition of employment, or whether they were "so pervasive and so long continuing * * * that the employer must have become conscious of [them]," Taylor v. Jones, 653 F.2d 1193, 1197–1199 (CA8 1981) (holding employer liable for racially hostile working environment based on constructive knowledge).

We therefore decline the parties' invitation to issue a definitive rule on employer liability, but we do agree with the EEOC that Congress wanted courts to look to agency principles for guidance in this area. While such common-law principles may not be transferable in all their particulars to Title VII, Congress' decision to define "employer" to include any "agent" of an employer, 42 U.S.C. § 2000e(b), surely evinces an intent to place some limits on the acts of employees for which employers under Title VII are to be held responsible. For this reason, we hold that the Court of Appeals erred in concluding that employers are always automatically liable for sexual harassment by their supervisors. See generally Restatement (Second) of Agency §§ 219–237 (1958). For the same reason, absence of notice to an employer does not necessarily insulate that employer from liability. Ibid.

Finally, we reject petitioner's view that the mere existence of a grievance procedure and a policy against discrimination, coupled with respondent's failure to invoke that procedure, must insulate petitioner from liability. While those facts are plainly relevant, the situation before us demonstrates why they are not necessarily dispositive. Petitioner's general nondiscrimination policy did not address sexual harassment in particular, and thus did not alert employees to their employer's interest in correcting that form of discrimination. App. 25. Moreover, the bank's grievance procedure apparently required an employee to complain first to her supervisor, in this case Taylor. Since Taylor was the alleged perpetrator, it is not altogether surprising that respondent failed to invoke the procedure and report her grievance to him. Petitioner's contention that respondent's failure should insulate it from liability might be substantially stronger if its procedures were better calculated to encourage victims of harassment to come forward.

IV

In sum, we hold that a claim of "hostile environment" sex discrimination is actionable under Title VII, that the District Court's findings were insufficient to dispose of respondent's hostile environment claim, and that the District Court did not err in admitting testimony about respondent's sexually provocative speech and dress. As to employer liability, we conclude that the Court of Appeals was wrong to entirely disregard agency principles and impose absolute liability on employers for the acts of their supervisors, regardless of the circumstances of a particular case.

Accordingly, the judgment of the Court of Appeals reversing the judgment of the District Court is affirmed, and the case is remanded for further proceedings consistent with this opinion.

It is so ordered.

JUSTICE MARSHALL, with whom JUSTICE BRENNAN, JUSTICE BLACKMUN, and JUSTICE STEVENS join, concurring in the judgment.

I fully agree with the Court's conclusion that workplace sexual harassment is illegal, and violates Title VII. Part III of the Court's opinion, however, leaves open the circumstances in which an employer is responsible under Title VII for such conduct. Because I believe that question to be properly before us, I write separately.

The issue the Court declines to resolve is addressed in the EEOC Guidelines on Discrimination Because of Sex, which are entitled to great deference. See Griggs v. Duke Power Co., 401 U.S. 424, 433–434, 91 S.Ct. 849, 854–55, 28 L.Ed.2d 158 (1971) (EEOC Guidelines on Employment Testing Procedures of 1966). The Guidelines explain:

> "Applying general Title VII principles, an employer * * * is responsible for its acts and those of its agents and supervisory employees with respect to sexual harassment regardless of whether the specific acts complained of were authorized or even forbidden by the employer and regardless of whether the employer knew or should have known of their occurrence. The Commission will examine the circumstances of the particular employment relationship and the job functions performed by the individual in determining whether an individual acts in either a supervisory or agency capacity.

> "With respect to conduct between fellow employees, an employer is responsible for acts of sexual harassment in the workplace where the employer (or its agents or supervisory employees) knows or should have known of the conduct, unless it can show that it took immediate and appropriate corrective action." 29 CFR §§ 1604.11(c), (d) (1985).

The Commission, in issuing the Guidelines, explained that its rule was "in keeping with the general standard of employer liability with respect to agents and supervisory employees * * * [T]he Commission and the courts have held for years that an employer is liable if a supervisor or an agent violates the Title VII, regardless of knowledge or any other mitigating factor." 45 Fed.Reg. 74676 (1980). I would adopt the standard set out by the Commission.

An employer can act only through individual supervisors and employees; discrimination is rarely carried out pursuant to a formal vote of a corporation's board of directors. Although an employer may sometimes adopt company-wide discriminatory policies violative of Title VII, acts that may constitute Title VII violations are generally effected through the actions of individuals, and often an individual may take such a step even in defiance of company policy. Nonetheless, Title VII remedies, such as reinstatement and backpay, generally run against the employer as an entity. The question thus arises as to the circumstances under which an employer will be held liable under Title VII for the acts of its employees.

The answer supplied by general Title VII law, like that supplied by federal labor law, is that the act of a supervisory employee or agent is imputed to the employer. Thus, for example, when a supervisor discriminatorily fires or refuses to promote a black employee, that act is, without more, considered the act of the employer. The courts do not stop to consider whether the employer otherwise had "notice" of the action, or even whether the supervisor had actual authority to act as he did. E.g., Flowers v. Crouch–Walker Corp., 552 F.2d 1277, 1282 (CA7 1977); Young v. Southwestern Savings and Loan Assn., 509 F.2d 140 (CA5 1975); Anderson v. Methodist Evangelical Hospital, Inc., 464 F.2d 723 (CA6 1972). Following that approach, every Court of Appeals that has considered the issue has held that sexual harassment by supervisory personnel is automatically imputed to the employer when the harassment results in tangible job detriment to the subordinate employee. See Horn v. Duke Homes, Inc., Div. of Windsor Mobile Homes, 755 F.2d 599, 604–606 (CA7 1985); Vinson v. Taylor, 243 U.S.App.D.C. 323, 329–334, 753 F.2d 141, 147–152 (1985); Craig v. Y & Y Snacks, Inc., 721 F.2d 77, 80–81 (CA3 1983); Katz v. Dole, 709 F.2d 251, 255, n. 6 (CA4 1983); Henson v. City of Dundee, 682 F.2d 897, 910 (CA11 1982); Miller v. Bank of America, 600 F.2d 211, 213 (CA9 1979).

The brief filed by the Solicitor General on behalf of the EEOC in this case suggests that a different rule should apply when a supervisor's harassment "merely" results in a discriminatory work environment. The Solicitor General concedes that sexual harassment that affects tangible job benefits is an exercise of authority delegated to the supervisor by the employer, and thus gives rise to employer liability. But, departing from the EEOC Guidelines, he argues that the case of a supervisor merely creating a discriminatory work environment is different because the supervisor "is not exercising, or threatening to exercise, actual or apparent authority to make personnel decisions affecting the victim." Brief for United States and EEOC as *Amicus Curiae* 24. In the latter situation, he concludes, some further notice requirement should therefore be necessary.

The Solicitor General's position is untenable. A supervisor's responsibilities do not begin and end with the power to hire, fire, and discipline employees, or with the power to recommend such actions. Rather, a supervisor is charged with the day-to-day supervision of the work environment and with ensuring a safe, productive, workplace. There is no reason why abuse of the latter authority should have different consequences than abuse of the former. In both cases it is the authority vested in the supervisor by the employer that enables him to commit the wrong: it is precisely because the supervisor is understood to be clothed with the employer's authority that he is able to impose unwelcome sexual conduct on subordinates. There is therefore no justification for a special rule, to be applied *only* in "hostile environment" cases, that sexual harassment does not create employer liability until the employee suffering the discrimination notifies other supervisors. No such requirement appears in the statute, and no such requirement can coherently be drawn from the law of agency.

Agency principles and the goals of Title VII law make appropriate some limitation on the liability of employers for the acts of supervisors. Where, for example, a supervisor has no authority over an employee, because the two work in wholly different parts of the employer's business, it may be improper to find strict employer liability. See 29 CFR § 1604.11(c) (1985). Those considerations, however, do not justify the creation of a special "notice" rule in hostile environment cases.

Further, nothing would be gained by crafting such a rule. In the "pure" hostile environment case, where an employee files an EEOC complaint alleging sexual harassment in the workplace, the employee seeks not money damages but injunctive relief. See Bundy v. Jackson, 205 U.S.App.D.C. 444, 446, 641 F.2d 934, 936, n. 12 (1981). Under Title VII, the EEOC must notify an employer of charges made against it within 10 days after receipt of the complaint. 42 U.S.C. § 2000e–5(b). If the charges appear to be based on "reasonable cause," the EEOC must attempt to eliminate the offending practice through "informal methods of conference, conciliation, and persuasion." Ibid. An employer whose internal procedures assertedly would have redressed the discrimination can avoid injunctive relief by employing these procedures after receiving notice of the complaint or during the conciliation period. Where a complainant, on the other hand, seeks backpay on the theory that a hostile work environment effected a constructive termination, the existence of an internal complaint procedure may be a factor in determining not the employer's liability but the remedies available against it. Where a complainant without good reason bypassed an internal complaint procedure she knew to be effective, a court may be reluctant to find constructive termination and thus to award reinstatement or backpay.

I therefore reject the Solicitor General's position. I would apply in this case the same rules we apply in all other Title VII cases, and hold that sexual harassment by a supervisor of an employee under his supervision, leading to a discriminatory work environment, should be imputed to the employer for Title VII purposes regardless of whether the employee gave "notice" of the offense.

NOTES AND PROBLEMS FOR DISCUSSION

1. As the Court noted in *Meritor,* the notion that Title VII affords employees protection against a threatening or coercive work environment originated in the context of racial and ethnic epithets. Does this mean, however, that the same standard should apply in determining the existence of racially and sexually hostile work environments? See Davis v. Monsanto Chemical Co., 858 F.2d 345 (6th Cir.1988). The significance of *Meritor,* then, lies not only in the Court's recognition that sexual harassment is prohibited by Title VII, but that the protection of the statute extends to harassment that is not accompanied by a tangible job detriment. This was the first case in which the Supreme Court declared that the creation of an abusive work environment (gender-based or otherwise) constituted, *per se,* unlawful discrimination. Consequently, most of the decisions now turn on the resolution of two subsidiary issues: (a) whether the alleged conduct was sufficiently "severe and pervasive" to create an "intimidating, hostile or offensive working environment", and (b) the circumstances and legal theories under which the employer is held liable for acts of harassment committed by its employees.

(a) The *Meritor* Court, in adopting the position enunciated in the EEOC Guidelines, indicated that in a hostile environment case, as opposed to a *quid pro quo* case, the harassment must be sufficiently severe and pervasive as to affect the average employee's work performance or create an "intimidating, hostile, or offensive working environment." This standard, however, may be easier to articulate than to apply. See e.g., Sand v. Johnson, 33 FEP Cases 716 (E.D.Mich.1982) (distinguishing between explicit sexual conduct and flirtatious conduct); Robinson v. E.I. Dupont De Nemours & Co., 33 FEP Cases 880 (D.Del.1979) (numerous sexual innuendos held to have been "irrationally misconstrued" by the plaintiff); Downes v. F.A.A., 775 F.2d 288 (Fed.Cir. 1985) (requiring a persistent pattern of offensive conduct but then ruling that evidence of five instances of such behavior during a three year period did not establish a pattern of harassment); Nieto v. United Auto Workers Local 598, 672 F.Supp. 987 (E.D.Mich.1987) (a "wolf pack" attack of eleven union members surrounding desk of supervisor and subjecting her to sex-based and race/national-origin-based verbal abuse for fifteen minutes for purpose of driving her from her job is a single incident and not a pattern of conduct sufficient to "rise to the level of poisoning the entire working environment"); Moffett v. Gene B. Glick Co., Inc., 621 F.Supp. 244, 269–270 (N.D.Ind.1985) ("Regular, almost daily exposure to terms such as 'stupid cunt', 'whore', 'bitch' and 'nigger lover' over the course of six to seven months, is, by any definition, a concerted pattern of continuous harassment which pollutes a working environment.").

While these and other cases indicate that individual assessments of what constitutes "severe or pervasive conduct" sufficient to generate an abusive working environment can vary, most of the results can be explained as an attempt by the courts to weigh and examine the totality of circumstances. Moreover, in gauging the totality of circumstances, the courts inevitably focus on some or all of the following four factors: (1)the level of offensiveness of the unwelcome acts or words; (2)the frequency or pervasiveness of the offensive encounters; (3)the total length of time over which the encounters occurred; and (4)the context in which the harassing conduct occurred. For example, in VANCE v. SOUTHERN BELL TEL. & TEL. Co., 863 F.2d 1503 (11th Cir.1989), the trial court had granted the defendant's motion for judgment notwithstanding the verdict on the ground that a noose hung over a black employee's desk on two different occasions was not enough, as a matter of law, to establish that the alleged racial harassment was a persistent, pervasive practice. 672 F.Supp. 1408 (M.D.Fla. 1987). The appellate court ruled that the trial court had incorrectly applied the pervasiveness standard outlined in *Meritor.* It held that the determination of whether the defendant's conduct was sufficiently "severe and pervasive" did not turn solely on the number of incidents alleged by the plaintiff. Rather, it continued, this determination was to be based on a consideration of all of the circumstances, including the number and severity of individual incidents of harassment. It was error, the Eleventh Circuit reasoned, for the trial court to apply an absolute numerical standard to the number of acts that must be committed before a jury could reasonably find the existence of a hostile environment. (A jury was involved here because the plaintiff had asserted her claim under § 1981 rather than under Title VII). This is the generally accepted approach. See Ellison v. Brady, 924 F.2d 872, 878 (9th Cir. 1991)("the required showing of severity or seriousness of the harassing conduct varies inversely with the pervasiveness or frequency of the conduct); King v. Board of Regents of University of Wisconsin System, 898 F.2d 533, 537 (7th Cir. 1990)("although a single act can be enough * * * generally, repeated incidents create a stronger claim of hostile environment, with the strength of the claim depending on the number of incidents and the intensity of each incident."); Carrero v. New York City Housing Authority, 890 F.2d 569 (2d Cir. 1989)(rejecting suggestion that existence of hostile environment is determined solely by duration of challenged conduct; offensiveness of individual actions is also a factor to use in determining whether harassing conduct was pervasive.). Yet, with respect to the fourth (context of the harassment) factor, the courts have taken some widely divergent positions. Compare, for example, Rabidue v. Osceola Refining Co., 805 F.2d 611 (6th Cir. 1986), cert. denied, 481 U.S. 1041, 107 S.Ct. 1983, 95 L.Ed.2d 823 (1987)(a display of sexually oriented posters in work areas "had a de minimis effect on the plaintiff's work environment when considered in the context of a society that condones and publicly features and commercially exploits open displays of written and pictorial erotica at the newsstands, on prime-time television, at the cinema and in other public places") with Robinson v. Jacksonville Shipyards, Inc., 760 F.Supp. 1486,1526 (M.D.Fla. 1991)(rejecting *Rabidue* "social context" argument and holding that "behavior that may be permissible in some settings can be abusive in the workplace. * * * A pre-existing atmosphere that deters women from entering or continuing in a profession or job is no less destructive to and offensive to workplace equality than a sign declaring 'Men Only'.")

Additionally, although the courts have adopted a generally consistent analytic approach to determining when the conduct is sufficiently "severe or pervasive", they do not agree on the appropriate standard for determining when that conduct has created an "abusive working environment". The earlier cases tended to impose a more stringent standard upon the plaintiffs, often requiring evidence of psychological damage. See e.g. Scott v. Sears, Roebuck & Co., 798 F.2d 210,212 (7th Cir.1986)(court examined evidence to determine whether the offending conduct caused "such anxiety and debilitation to the plaintiff that working conditions were poisoned"); Rabidue v. Osceola Refining Co., 805 F.2d 611 (6th Cir.1986), cert. denied, 481 U.S. 1041, 107 S.Ct. 1983, 95 L.Ed.2d 823 (1987)(the display of nude or scantily clad women in work areas "was not so startling as to have affected seriously the psyches of the plaintiff or other female employees.") and Caleshu v. Merill Lynch, Pierce, Fenner & Smith, Inc., 737 F.Supp. 1070,1081 (E.D.Mo. 1990)(harassment must "affect seriously the psychological well being of an employee"). But see Barbetta v. Chemlawn Services Corp., 669 F.Supp. 569 (W.D.N.Y.1987) (proliferation of pornographic material featuring pictures of nude women may "create an atmosphere in which women are viewed as men's sexual playthings rather than as their equal co-workers" and, therefore, can create a hostile work environment.). More recent cases, however, suggest a change in the approach to this issue. For example, in ELLISON v. BRADY, 924 F.2d 872,878 (9th Cir. 1991), the Ninth Circuit specifically rejected the standards imposed by the courts in *Scott* and *Rabidue* as not "following directly from language in *Meritor*." Instead, the court declared, "[i]t is the harasser's conduct which must be pervasive or severe, not the alteration in the conditions of employment. Surely, employees need not endure sexual harassment until their psychological well-being is seriously affected to the extent that they suffer anxiety and debilitation. Title VII's protection * * * comes into play long before the point where victims of sexual harassment require psychiatric assistance." The appropriate standard, the court concluded, is whether the objectionable conduct unreasonably interfered with work performance and not whether the emotional and psychological stability of the victim is seriously affected.

Moreover, regardless of which measure of "abusive working environment" is chosen, the court also must resolve whether the existence of this environment is to be measured according to a subjective, objective or combined standard. In other words, must the plaintiff establish (1)that his or her own performance or psychological well-being was affected, or (2)that the challenged conduct would have affected the performance or well-being of a reasonable individual, or (3)both? Most courts have adopted the combined standard. See Daniels v. Essex Group, Inc., 937 F.2d 1264 (7th Cir.1991); White v. Federal Express Corp., 939 F.2d 157 (4th Cir.1991); Ellison v. Brady, 924 F.2d 872 (9th Cir.1991), Andrews v. City of Philadelphia, 895 F.2d 1469 (3d Cir.1990); Rabidue v. Osceola Refining Co., 805 F.2d 611 (6th Cir.1986), cert. denied, 481 U.S. 1041, 107 S.Ct. 1983, 95 L.Ed.2d 823 (1987). Moreover, in applying the objective component, is it appropriate for the court to apply a reasonable *person* or reasonable *woman* standard? Is there likely to be any difference between these criteria? The Ninth Circuit thought so when, in ELLISON v. BRADY, 924 F.2d 872 (9th Cir.1991), it declared that in evaluating the severity of sexual harassment, a court should focus "on the perspective of the victim". Accordingly, the court ruled, it was sufficient for the female plaintiff to allege conduct that a "reasonable woman" would consider sufficiently severe or pervasive. The court reasoned that "a sex-blind reasonable person standard tends to be male-biased" and to systematically ignore the experiences of women. It added that as men are rarely the victims of sexual assault, they are inclined to view sexual conduct in a vacuum "without a full appreciation of the social setting or the underlying threat of violence that a woman may perceive." Relying on this perspective "would run the risk of reinforcing the prevailing level of discrimination" and allow harassers to "continue to harass merely because a particular discriminatory practice was common." And, the court concluded, a "gender-conscious examination of sexual harassment enables women to participate in the workplace on an equal footing with men." Id., at 878–79. Accord, Harris v. International Paper Co., 765 F.Supp. 1509, 1515 (D.Me.1991)(applying "reasonable black person" standard in hostile environment racial harassment case; "the standard for assessing the unwelcomeness and pervasiveness of conduct and speech must be founded on a fair concern for the different social experiences of men and women in the case of sexual harassment, and of white Americans and black Americans in the case of racial harassment."); Robinson v. Jacksonville Shipyards, Inc., 760 F.Supp. 1486 (M.D.Fla. 1991)(adopting "reasonable woman" standard and holding that requirement of establishing that the plaintiff was subjected to unwelcome harassment based upon sex is satisfied by demonstrating that the challenged behavior is disproportionately more offensive or demeaning to one sex. Such conduct "creates a barrier to the progress of women in the workplace because it conveys the message that they do not belong, that they are welcome in the workplace only if they will subvert their identities to the sexual stereotypes prevalent in that environment.").

What impact, if any, will the presence of a male-dominated federal judiciary have on the utility of a "reasonable victim" standard? And what is the likely effect of the availability of jury trials (at least in harassment cases alleging intentional discrimination; see Note 5, *infra*) on future implementation of this standard? Is the response of the Senate Judiciary Committee or public opinion to the Clarence Thomas/Anita Hill confrontation instructive in this regard?

Finally, while the preceding paragraphs indicate that sexually oriented conduct can take many forms, is it clear that sexual harassment claims are limited to charges that the allegedly harassing conduct contained sexual references or overtones? Several courts have concluded that as long as the conduct would not have occurred but for the sex of the victim, any gender-based harassment, including the actual or threatened use of physical force, regardless of whether it was taken with sexual overtones, can constitute prohibited sexual harassment. See Hicks v. Gates Rubber Co., 928 F.2d 966 (10th Cir.1991); Andrews v. City of Philadelphia, 895 F.2d 1469 (3d Cir.1990); Lipsett v. University of Puerto Rico, 864 F.2d 881 (1st Cir.1988); Hall v. Gus Construction Co., 842 F.2d 1010 (8th Cir.1988); McKinney v. Dole, 765 F.2d 1129 (D.C.Cir. 1985). But are such cases, then, any different analytically from garden variety gender discrimination claims? If not, does their denomination as sex harassment, rather than sex discrimination, claims have any special significance? Compare Cline v. General Elec. Credit Auto Lease, Inc., 748 F.Supp. 650 (N.D.Ill.1990)(sexual harassment must be "sexual" in nature; if harassment is unrelated to sexual activity, plaintiff can assert a traditional sex discrimination claim but must establish discriminatory intent under the *McDonnell Douglas* framework) with Ellison v. Brady, 924 F.2d 872, 880 (9th Cir. 1991)(sexual harassment is unlawful "even when harassers do not realize that their conduct creates a hostile working environment. Well intentioned compliments * * * can form the basis of a sexual harassment cause of action if a reasonable victim of the same sex as the plaintiff would consider the comments sufficiently severe or pervasive to alter a condition of employment and create an abusive working environment.")(citing *Griggs*).

(b) The other significant issue left partially unresolved by *Meritor* is the extent to which an "employer" will be held liable for acts of harassment committed by its employees. While the *Meritor* Court "decline[d] the parties' invitation to issue a definitive rule on employer liability," it did offer a set of general guidelines for future cases. On the one hand, the Supreme Court reversed the circuit court's ruling that employers are always liable for supervisory acts of harassment. It also stated, however, that a lack of employer notice would not "necessarily insulate that employer from liability". Since the statutory definition of "employer" includes any "agent" of the employer, the Court reasoned, the appropriate approach was to "look to agency principles for guidance in this area."

It then fell, of course, to the lower courts to implement this general instruction and develop a method for handling the wide variety of harassment cases that followed *Meritor.* An examination of these cases suggests that two factors have been most significant to the courts in determining whether or not to impose liability upon the employer: (a) whether the challenged conduct was undertaken by a supervisor or nonsupervisory co-employee; and (b) whether the plaintiff is alleging *quid pro quo* or hostile environment harassment.

In the supervisory employee context, most courts, explicitly or implicitly, have focused (as the *Meritor* Court did) on the fact that the statutory definition of "employer" includes any "agent" of that employer and have attempted to determine whether, under the circumstances, the supervisor was acting as the employer's "agent". Where the courts have found, through the use of agency doctrine, that the supervisor acted as the employer's "agent", they have imposed direct, rather than vicarious, liability. In fact, by incorporating agents within the definition of employer, Congress effectively merged these two concepts and eliminated the need to impose liability vicariously upon the employer through the common law concept of *respondeat superior.* As a consequence of § 701(b) of Title VII, the agent is the employer and the only remaining question is whether, under the circumstances, the supervisor fits within the meaning of agent as defined by common law agency doctrine.

While the appellate courts have not adopted a uniform position with respect to this question, one variable has emerged as the single most influential determinant of whether the harassing supervisor will be found to have acted as the employer's agent. It is the form or type of the alleged harassment, i.e., whether it fits into the *quid pro quo* or hostile environment category. Thus, for example, where the courts find that the supervisor relied on his or her delegated powers to engage in the harassing conduct (i.e., when engaged in *quid pro quo* harassment), the employer, from whom these powers are derived, has been held strictly liable for such misuse of the supervisor's delegated authority. The exercise of delegated authority, even if done improperly, is seen as a sufficient basis for labeling the supervisor as the employer's agent. See e.g., Sparks v. Pilot Freight Carriers, Inc., 830 F.2d 1554 (11th Cir.1987); Shrout v. Black Clawson Co., 689 F.Supp. 774 (S.D.Ohio 1988). This, moreover, is consistent with the Restatement view that an act may be within the scope of employment, and thus evidence the existence of an agency relationship, even though it is forbidden. Restatement (Second) of Agency § 320. On the other hand, where the supervisor is not relying on specifically delegated authority (such as the right to hire, fire, or discipline), i.e., where the harassment does not involve a tangible job detriment but is alleged solely to create a hostile environment, the supervisor is found not to have acted as the employer's agent and, therefore, the supervisor's conduct is not directly imputed to the employer unless the court concludes that the employer knew or should have known about the conduct and failed to rectify the situation. See EEOC v. Hacienda Hotel, 881 F.2d 1504 (9th Cir.1989); Steele v. Offshore Shipbuilding Inc., 867 F.2d 1311 (11th Cir.1989); North v. Madison Area Ass'n for Retarded Citizens Developmental Centers Corp., 844 F.2d 401 (7th Cir.1988); Yates v. Avco Corp., 819 F.2d 630 (6th Cir.1987). This view, however, suggests that the supervisor does not have generally delegated authority to control the subordinates' work environment. But the dissenters in *Meritor* and one panel of the Eleventh Circuit rejected this notion and reasoned that control over the workers' environment is part of the power delegated to a supervisor and that his misuse of that power similarly should be imputed to the employer. Accordingly, the court held, the employer could be held strictly liable for both forms (*quid pro quo* and hostile environment) of supervisorial harassment. See Vance v. Southern Bell Tel. & Tel. Co., 863 F.2d 1503, 1515 (11th Cir.1989) (employer held strictly liable for supervisorial act creating hostile environment on ground that court should examine not only the degree of authority harasser wields over the plaintiff but also any other "evidence bearing on the overall structure of the workplace, including the relative positions of the parties involved."). But see Steele v. Offshore Shipbuilding, Inc., 867 F.2d 1311, 1316 (11th Cir.1989) ("strict liability is illogical" in a hostile environment case since the supervisor is not relying on actual or apparent authority and thus does not act as the company's agent; no reference made to other panel's ruling in *Vance*). Several commentators also have argued in favor of strict liability in hostile environment cases. See Comment, When Should An Employer Be Held Liable For The Sexual Harassment By A Supervisor Who Creates A Hostile Work Environment? A Proposed Theory Of Liability, 19 Ariz.St.L.Rev. 285 (1987); Note, Employer Liability Under Title VII For Sexual Harassment After Meritor Savings Bank v. Vinson, 87 Colum.L.Rev. 1258, 1276 (1987). At least one circuit, however, requires proof that the employer knew about the conduct and failed to take corrective action, regardless of whether the supervisor engaged in *quid pro quo* or hostile environment harassment. See Tomkins v. Public Service Electric & Gas Co., 568 F.2d 1044 (3d Cir.1977).

Thus, the employer will be directly (as opposed to vicariously) liable for acts of supervisory harassment either where the supervisor is viewed as its agent (i.e., in cases of *quid pro quo* harassment) or where it failed to spot and/or redress the improper conduct (i.e., in hostile environment cases). Some of this same analysis applies to cases involving harassment by nonsupervisory co-employees. Presumably, a co-employee, by definition, is not in a position to effectuate *quid pro quo* harassment and, therefore, direct liability cannot be imposed on the employer by characterizing the harasser as its agent. Nevertheless, the employer, as in cases of supervisory harassment, can be directly liable for failing to discover and redress the improper conduct where the plaintiff can establish that the defendant had actual or constructive knowledge of the harassment and failed to take corrective action. Thus, albeit it for different reasons, the nature of the liability that is imposed in cases of both supervisory and nonsupervisory harassment is direct rather than vicarious. See Vance v. Southern Bell Tel. & Tel. Co., 863 F.2d 1503, 1512 (11th Cir.1989); Swentek v. USAIR, Inc., 830 F.2d 552 (4th Cir.1987); Rabidue v. Osceola Refining Co., 805 F.2d 611 (6th Cir.1986), cert. denied, 481 U.S. 1041, 107 S.Ct. 1983, 95 L.Ed.2d 823 (1987); Hunter v. Allis Chalmers Corp., 797 F.2d 1417 (7th Cir.1986); Scott v. Sears, Roebuck & Co., 605 F.Supp. 1047 (N.D.Ill.1985), affirmed, 798 F.2d 210 (7th Cir.1986). A helpful discussion of the issue of employer liability for cases of nonsupervisory harassment can be found in Allegretti, Sexual Harassment of Female Employees By Nonsupervisory Co-workers: A Theory of Liability, 15 Creighton L.Rev. 437 (1982); Significant Development, Employer Liability For Sexual Harassment Under Title VII, 61

B.U.L.Rev. 535 (1981); Note, Sexual Harassment Claims of Abusive Work Environment Under Title VII, 97 Harv.L.Rev. 1449 (1984).

In determining (when relevant to the imposition of liability) whether the employer took adequate remedial action, should the court be limited to investigating the employer's *post hoc* conduct? Or, can the plaintiff suggest that the employer did not take adequate steps to try to prevent her or his harassment? In PAROLINE v. UNISYS CORP., 879 F.2d 100 (4th Cir.1989), opinion vacated in part and affirmed in relevant part, 900 F.2d 27 (4th Cir.1990) (en banc), the plaintiff established that a co-employee had been involved in previous incidents of sexual harassment of other female workers, even after the company had warned him to refrain from such behavior. In addition, the plaintiff showed that at least one company official knew that the alleged harasser had asked the plaintiff in her job interview how she would respond if subjected to sexual harassment at work. The trial court granted the defendant's motion for summary judgement on the ground that the defendant took prompt remedial action *after* the plaintiff complained of the harassment. The appellate court reversed, ruling that it would impute liability to the employer for failure to take steps reasonably calculated to *prevent* sexual harassment where it found that the employer anticipated or reasonably should have anticipated that the plaintiff would become a victim of sexual harassment. It added that an employer's knowledge that a male worker has previously harassed female employees other than the plaintiff could be sufficient for the fact finder to determine that the employer should have anticipated the harassment. In this particular case, the court concluded that there was sufficient evidence from which the fact finder could reasonably infer that the company should have recognized the possibility of harassment to the plaintiff. Accordingly, it ruled that the trial court had erred in granting summary judgment on the plaintiff's sexual harassment claim in favor of the defendant. With respect to the general issue of the meaning of appropriate remedial action, the courts typically state the standard as requiring a response "reasonably calculated to end the harassment", with the level of response assessed proportionately to the seriousness of the offense. See Barrett v. Omaha National Bank, 726 F.2d 424 (8th Cir.1984); Katz v. Dole, 709 F.2d 251 (4th Cir.1983). In somewhat less abstract terms, the courts usually examine whether the employer's response is likely to stop the harassment by the person who engaged in it, which, depending on the circumstances, can often mean that a simple request to refrain from further harassing conduct will not be viewed as a sufficient response. Sometimes the court also may take into account whether the remedy will persuade other potential harassers to refrain from such conduct. See, e.g., Ellison v. Brady, 924 F.2d 872 (9th Cir.1991).

(c) The plaintiff is required to establish as part of the prima facie case that the challenged conduct was "unwelcome". Can the defendant challenge this portion of the plaintiff's case by offering evidence that the plaintiff frequently used foul language and thus welcomed obscene remarks generally? In Swentek v. USAIR, Inc., 830 F.2d 552 (4th Cir.1987), the circuit found that the trial judge had misconstrued the meaning of unwelcome sexual harassment by ruling that the plaintiff's use of foul language indicated that she was the kind of person who could not be offended by such comments and thus welcomed them generally. Rather, it concluded, the appropriate question was whether the plaintiff had welcomed the particular conduct in question from the alleged harasser. What about where the plaintiff has appeared in nude photographs published in a periodical of general circulation? See Burns v. McGregor Electronic Industries, Inc., 57 FEP Cases 1373 (8th Cir.1992)(fact that plaintiff posed nude for published photographs is relevant to, but not dispositive of, whether some of the challenged conduct was unwelcome). But see Perkins v. General Motors Corp., 709 F.Supp. 1487,1499 (W.D.Mo.1989)(indicating that courts do consider "whether the plaintiff substantially contributed to the allegedly distasteful atmosphere by her own 'profane and sexually suggestive conduct' " in determining whether the complained of conduct was "unwelcome").

2. Can an employee state a claim under Title VII when she alleges that the harassment was committed by a non-employee? Would it matter whether the act occurred inside or outside of the workplace? See Whitaker v. Carney, 778 F.2d 216 (5th Cir.1985). The EEOC Guidelines state that an employer "may also be responsible for the acts of non-employees, with respect to sexual harassment of employees in the workplace, where the employer (or its agents or supervisory employees) knows or should have known of the conduct and fails to take immediate and appropriate corrective action. 29 C.F.R. § 1604.11(e) (1985).

3. Can a supervisor state a claim of harassment by a subordinate? See Erebia v. Chrysler Plastic Products Corp., 772 F.2d 1250 (6th Cir.1985) (supervisor can state claim under § 1981 for ethnic slurs by subordinates condoned by employer); Moffett v. Gene B. Glick Co., Inc., 621 F.Supp. 244, 272 (N.D.Ind. 1985) (supervisor subjected to racially based harassment by subordinates can maintain action under Title VII).

4. Title VII has been held not to prohibit discrimination on the basis of sexual orientation. See *infra*, at 444. Does this mean that a gay male employee cannot state a claim under Title VII by alleging that a male supervisor conditioned his continued employment upon acceding to the supervisor's sexual demands? See Joyner v. AAA Cooper Transportation, 597 F.Supp. 537 (M.D.Ala.1983); Wright v. Methodist Youth Services, Inc., 511 F.Supp. 307 (N.D.Ill.1981). What about a bisexual supervisor? See Henson v. City of Dundee, 682 F.2d 897, 904 (11th Cir.1982); Comment, Sexual Harassment and Title VII, 51 N.Y.U.L.Rev. 148 (1976). In light of the Court's ruling in *Price Waterhouse*, could a male gay victim of sexual harassment successfully allege that he was subjected to gender discrimination by asserting that in the eyes of his harassers he did not live up to an appropriate male "macho" image? See Dillon v. Frank, 952 F.2d 403 (6th Cir.1992)(unpublished opinion)(distinguishing *Price Waterhouse* on ground that it was not a hostile environment case and, therefore, did not reflect Court's view that any treatment based on sexual stereotypes would violate Title VII).

5. Prior to the enactment of the 1991 Civil Rights Act, monetary awards were limited under Title VII to back pay. The courts uniformly have held that pain and suffering was not compensable under this statute. This had a particularly harsh impact on victims of hostile environment harassment where, by definition, the plaintiff has not suffered a tangible job detriment. One strategy plaintiffs employed in response to this problem was attaching either constitutional or state law tort claims to their Title VII actions since compensatory and punitive damages were available in such actions. See e.g., Bohen v. City of East Chicago, Indiana, 799 F.2d 1180 (7th Cir.1986), on remand, 666 F.Supp. 154 (N.D.Ind.1987)(sexual harassment was actionable sex discrimination under the equal protection clause, as long as the plaintiff could establish intentional discrimination; on remand, plaintiff awarded more than $29,000 in compensatory damages); Phillips v. Smalley Maintenance Services, Inc., 711

F.2d 1524 (11th Cir.1983) (court can exercise pendent jurisdiction over state law invasion of privacy count in complaint including Title VII sexual harassment claim); Rogers v. Loews L'Enfant Plaza Hotel, 526 F.Supp. 523 (D.D.C.1981) (where male supervisor accused of making verbal and written sexually oriented advances to female employee and of making telephone calls to her home that included sexually offensive comments, plaintiff can state a claim for compensatory and punitive damages under common law theories of invasion of privacy, assault, battery and intentional infliction of emotional distress); Coley v. Consolidated Rail Corp., 561 F.Supp. 645 (E.D.Mich.1982) (plaintiff in sexual harassment case entitled to recover mental anguish and humiliation damages under state anti-discrimination law); Marinelli, Title VII: Legal Protection Against Sexual Harassment, 20 Akron L.Rev. 375 (1987); Montgomery, Sexual Harassment in the Workplace: A Practitioner's Guide to Tort Actions, 10 Gold. Gate L.Rev. 879 (1980); Note, Sexual Harassment Claims of Abusive Work Environment Under Title VII, 97 Harv.L.Rev. 1449 (1984); Note, Legal Remedies for Employment–Related Sexual Harassment, 64 Minn.L.Rev. 151 (1979).

Nevertheless, while the availability of monetary relief under state law was widely recognized, risks associated with filing such claims sometimes discouraged plaintiffs from going this route. For example, where a female plaintiff brought an action in a California court for sexual harassment and intentional infliction of severe emotional distress, the California Supreme Court held that since the plaintiff had placed her mental state in issue by seeking damages for continuing emotional distress, loss of sleep, anxiety, mental anguish, humiliation, reduced self-esteem and other consequences flowing from the alleged harassment, she was required, pursuant to a provision of the California Civil Code, to submit to a psychological examination so that the defendant could investigate the continued existence and severity of her alleged damages. The Court rejected her claim that submission to such an examination violated her constitutional right of privacy, reasoning that filing the lawsuit constituted an implicit waiver of her rights insofar as the discovery was directly relevant to her claim concerning damages and essential to the fair resolution of the lawsuit. It did, however, preclude the defendants from examining the plaintiff as to her sexual history and practices since the defendants had failed to explain how probing into this area was directly relevant to the plaintiff's claim or essential to its fair resolution. The Court also concluded that the presence of the plaintiff's attorney was not required during the examination and that the trial court had not abused its discretion in excluding her counsel from the examination since no evidence had been offered to suggest that the defendants' expert would not respect her legitimate rights to privacy or might disobey any court-imposed restrictions. It noted that the plaintiff was entitled to record the examination on audio tape to allay her fears that the examiner would probe into impermissible areas. Vinson v. Superior Court, 43 Cal.3d 833, 239 Cal. Rptr. 292, 740 P.2d 404 (1987).

Now that the 1991 Civil Rights Act provides Title VII plaintiffs with an opportunity to collect compensatory and punitive damages, state law no longer will play the preeminent role in providing relief to sexual harassment victims seeking damages for other than lost wages. Nevertheless, many of the problems associated with state law claims, as well as others unique to the new federal law, will continue to confront plaintiffs seeking such relief. For example, Federal Rule of Civil Procedure 35(a) states that "When the mental or physical condition of a party * * * is in controversy, the court in which the action is pending may order the party to submit to a physical or mental examination by a suitably licensed or certified examiner * * *. The order may be made only on motion for good cause shown * * * and shall specify the * * * scope of the examination and the person or persons by whom it is to be made." Does this suggest that the ruling by the California court in *Vinson* is likely to apply to a federal action involving either a claim under the 1991 Act or a supplementary state law claim for emotional distress? In ROBINSON v. JACKSONVILLE SHIPYARDS, INC., 118 F.R.D. 525 (M.D.Fla.1988), the court noted that the California court in *Vinson* had expressly stated that such examinations should not be ordered in sexual harassment claims where mental or emotional damages are not claimed and where the plaintiff is seeking only compensation for having to endure an oppressive work environment. It agreed with this analysis, recognizing, as the *Vinson* court had, that to do otherwise would result in the routine ordering of mental examinations in all hostile environment actions and also would suggest that every plaintiff in such actions was asserting that he or she was mentally unstable. The court also rejected the defendant's claim that the requirement that a plaintiff alleging hostile environment harassment establish that the environment seriously affected the psychological well-being of a person of reasonable sensitivities did not require her to prove that she was not hypersensitive or that she was personally affected. Rather, the court concluded, the plaintiff was only required to prove her claim as to a reasonable person. Finally, the court added, a backpay award did not constitute compensation for emotional harm suffered, but served as a remedy for the constructive discharge created by the objectively-defined oppressive environment. Accordingly, it held, the plaintiff did not put her mental condition "in controversy" within the meaning of Rule 35(a).

A difficulty associated particularly with the 1991 Act is its limitation of the damages provision to claims of intentional discrimination. While many sexual harassment victims will be able to establish intentional discrimination, what happens where the defendant claims that the challenged conduct or statements, though not appreciated by the plaintiff, were "well intentioned" and the plaintiff asserts and proves that they were offensive to her and to the reasonable victim? Should this be viewed as intentional discrimination? Can't the same problem arise in connection with the purported use of sexual or other stereotypes?

6. Can a female employee who was not subjected personally to any harassing conduct file a claim charging that the defendant's conduct nevertheless created a hostile working environment for her and other female employees who find such conduct repugnant and offensive? See Hicks v. Gates Rubber Co., 833 F.2d 1406 (10th Cir.1987) (evidence of incidents involving employees other than the plaintiff are relevant in establishing a hostile work environment). In answering that question, consider whether or not it should matter whether the actual subject of that conduct welcomed the allegedly harassing conduct. This latter scenario is especially likely to occur in the situation where a supervisor grants a tangible benefit to an employee on the basis of a consensual sexual relationship. Suppose, for example, that two female employees applied for the same promotion and the supervisor chose the one with whom he was having a consensual sexual relationship. Assuming that the other employee could establish that the promotion was granted solely on the basis of the consensual relationship, can she successfully file a claim of sexual harassment? See King v. Palmer, 778 F.2d 878 (D.C.Cir.1985); Broderick v. Ruder, 685 F.Supp. 1269 (D.D.C. 1988); Priest v. Rotary, 634 F.Supp. 571 (N.D.Cal.1986). Would it make a difference if the unsuccessful applicant had

been a man? See DeCintio v. Westchester County Medical Center, 807 F.2d 304 (2d Cir.1986), cert. denied, 484 U.S. 965, 108 S.Ct. 455, 98 L.Ed.2d 395 (1987) (refusing to extend meaning of "sex" discrimination to include discrimination on the basis of "an ongoing, voluntary, romantic engagement" in absence of any element of coerced "submission" to sexual advances; no discussion of impact analysis). Accord, Miller v. Aluminum Co. of America, 679 F.Supp. 495 (W.D.Pa.1988) (no gender-based discrimination in case of favoritism by male supervisor towards his female paramour since both male and female employees share the disadvantage of not holding this special place in the affections of the supervisor). What if the female or male plaintiff was not passed over in favor of the supervisor's paramour, but felt that the existence of such a relationship, *per se*, created an unprofessional and distasteful working environment. Could the plaintiff state a claim of hostile environment discrimination? See Drinkwater v. Union Carbide Corp., 904 F.2d 853 (3d Cir.1990). Would the recognition of these types of claims act as a deterrent to proscribed forms of sexual harassment? What about a state law claim? See Kersul v. Skulls Angels Inc., 130 Misc.2d 345, 495 N.Y.S.2d 886 (1985) (woman denied a benefit in favor of other woman with whom supervisor had a "close personal friendship" states a claim of sex discrimination under state law). For a detailed discussion of these issues, see Comment, The Meaning of "Sex" in Title VII: Is Favoring an Employee Lover a Violation of the Act?, 83 Nw.U.L.Rev. 612 (1989).

7. When Title VII was amended in 1972 to include public sector employees within its protections, the substantive rights of federal employees were set forth in § 717. This provision states that "[a]ll personnel actions affecting [federal] employees * * * shall be made free from any discrimination based on race, color, religion, sex, or national origin." Section 703(a), on the other hand, makes it an unlawful employment practice to discriminate against any individual "with respect to his compensation, terms, condition, or privileges of employment." Does this difference in terminology suggest that federal employees do not enjoy the same level of protection from sexual harassment that is available to nonfederal employees? See Jordan v. Clark, 847 F.2d 1368, 1373 n. 3 (9th Cir.1988) ("Title VII protects government employees from sexual harassment to the same degree private employees are protected.").

8. Amy Randolph was employed as Executive Vice–President of Pastek Fruit Co. Shortly after her divorce, she began to have an affair with John Fesh, the President and sole owner of Pastek. The affair lasted two years. At the end of that period, Ms. Randolph decided to terminate her relationship with Mr. Fesh. Over the course of the next several weeks, Mr. Fesh made several unsuccessful attempts to talk Ms. Randolph into resuming their relationship. None of these discussions occurred either on company time or on company premises. Having failed to revive the relationship, Mr. Fesh turned bitter and discharged Ms. Randolph. Can she bring a claim of sexual harassment against Pastec? If so, should she assert a claim of *quid pro quo* or hostile environment?

In HUEBSCHEN v. DEPARTMENT OF HEALTH AND SOCIAL SERVICES, 716 F.2d 1167 (7th Cir.1983), a male employee was fired pursuant to the recommendation of the female supervisor with whom he had recently terminated a consensual sexual relationship. There was no evidence that the supervisor had ever told the plaintiff that his refusal to comply with her sexual requests would result in his receiving an unfavorable recommendation. The Seventh Circuit held that the plaintiff had not established sex-based discrimination under the equal protection clause and so dismissed his § 1983 claim. The court was not convinced that the supervisor had discriminated against the plaintiff on the basis of his gender. Rather, it concluded, the action had been taken on the basis of the plaintiff's individual characteristics and his gender was "merely coincidental" to the supervisor's conduct. While admitting that the supervisor had acted "spitefully" towards the plaintiff, the court reasoned that the supervisor's motivation was not that the plaintiff was a male, but that he was a former lover who had jilted her. Does this mean that once an employee engages in consensual sexual activity with a supervisor, that employee forfeits any subsequent claim of sexual harassment against the supervisor? This issue was addressed by the trial court in KEPPLER v. HINDSDALE TP. SCHOOL DISTRICT 86, 715 F.Supp. 862 (N.D.Ill.1989). There, a female employee was terminated after a male co-worker engaged in a campaign against her in retaliation for her termination of their consensual relationship. As in *Huebschen,* there was no evidence that the co-worker ever made any demand for sexual favors. The court reasoned that a partner to a consensual relationship *could* assert a claim of *hostile environment* discrimination if his or her former paramour engaged in conduct that created a hostile working environment. With respect to *quid pro quo* claims, the court interpreted *Huebschen* as creating a rebuttable presumption that employer retaliation after the termination of a consensual relationship is predicated not on the basis of gender but on the basis of the failed relationship. Thus, it concluded, where the retribution was taken solely because the plaintiff jilted the former partner, the plaintiff could not rebut this presumption and, therefore, could not state a claim of *quid pro quo* discrimination. ("[A] desire to continue a prior consensual relationship is not, on its own part, an impermissible basis for personnel action under Title VII." 715 F.Supp. at 870 n. 7.) But, it added, the presumption would be rebutted (and, therefore, a claim of *quid pro quo* discrimination could be stated) by evidence that the alleged harasser had demanded further relationships before taking the challenged action and had threatened retaliation for refusing that demand. In such a case, the court declared, it could conclude that the alleged harasser was using gender as a basis for allocating job benefits. Does this distinction make sense? It was relied upon by the court in BABCOCK v. FRANK, 729 F.Supp. 279 (S.D.N.Y.1990). In that case, the parties agreed that the female plaintiff and the male supervisor had had a consensual sexual relationship. The defendant company also did not deny the plaintiff's claim that the supervisor at times after the termination of the relationship made physical and verbal sexual advances that were unwelcome, not consented to nor condoned by the plaintiff, and that the supervisor told the plaintiff that he would fire her or prevent her career advancement if she did not accede to his advances. The defendant claimed that the complaint alleged harassment based not on gender but, rather, on the termination of a prior consensual sexual relationship. The court rejected this contention, reasoning that evidence of a past consensual sexual relationship did not automatically defeat a claim of *quid pro quo* harassment. It relied on the language in *Keppler* and distinguished the instant case from *Huebschen* on the ground that this case involved evidence of demands for sexual favors after the termination of the relationship. Accordingly, it denied the defendant's motion for dismissal. See also Prichard v. Ledford, 767 F.Supp. 1425 (E.D.Tenn. 1990)(female plaintiff resigned after being subjected to continuing unwelcomed advances by company's owner subsequent to her termination of consensual affair with him, which affair had led to her initial hiring. Court held that the advances after termination of their consensual affair were unwelcomed and generated a hostile working environment for the plaintiff. Court added that her resignation was a constructive discharge caused by the hostile environment. It further stated that since the owner also offered to reinstate her subject to a renewal of their relationship, the plaintiff was also a victim of *quid pro quo* sexual harassment which prevented her from returning to work.)

9. In many of the cases discussed in these Notes, the courts were called upon to determine the extent, if any, to which a wide variety of speech either contributed to or created *per se* the unlawfully hostile environment. Yet can it be argued that some of these offensive, vulgar, sexist or racist statements fall within the protective ambit of the First Amendment and, therefore, that any attempt to restrict such speech under Title VII is prohibited by the First Amendment? For an interesting discussion of the problems raised in this area, see Browne, Title VII as Censorship: Hostile–Environment Harassment and the First Amendment, 52 Ohio St.L.J. 481 (1991); Strauss, Sexist Speech in the Workplace, 25 Harv.C.R.-C.L.L.Rev. 1 (1990).

3. Pension Funds

CITY OF LOS ANGELES, DEPARTMENT OF WATER AND POWER v. MANHART

Supreme Court of the United States, 1978.
435 U.S. 702, 98 S.Ct. 1370, 55 L.Ed.2d 657.

Mr. Justice Stevens delivered the opinion of the Court.

As a class, women live longer than men. For this reason, the Los Angeles Department of Water and Power required its female employees to make larger contributions to its pension fund than its male employees. We granted certiorari to decide whether this practice discriminated against individual female employees because of their sex in violation of § 703(a)(1) of the Civil Rights Act of 1964, as amended.

For many years the Department has administered retirement, disability, and death-benefit programs for its employees. Upon retirement each employee is eligible for a monthly retirement benefit computed as a fraction of his or her salary multiplied by years of service.[3] The monthly benefits for men and women of the same age, seniority, and salary are equal. Benefits are funded entirely by contributions from the employees and the Department, augmented by the income earned on those contributions. No private insurance company is involved in the administration or payment of benefits.

Based on a study of mortality tables and its own experience, the Department determined that its 2,000 female employees, on the average, will live a few years longer than its 10,000 male employees. The cost of a pension for the average retired female is greater than for the average male retiree because more monthly payments must be made to the average woman. The Department therefore required female employees to make monthly contributions to the fund which were 14.84% higher than the contributions required of comparable male employees. Because employee contributions were withheld from paychecks, a fe-

---

3. * * * The benefit is guaranteed for life.

male employee took home less pay than a male employee earning the same salary.

* * * In 1973, respondents brought this suit in the United States District Court for the Central District of California on behalf of a class of women employed or formerly employed by the Department. They prayed for an injunction and restitution of excess contributions.

While this action was pending, the California Legislature enacted a law prohibiting certain municipal agencies from requiring female employees to make higher pension fund contributions than males. The Department therefore amended its plan, effective January 1, 1975. The current plan draws no distinction, either in contributions or in benefits, on the basis of sex. On a motion for summary judgment, the District Court held that the contribution differential violated § 703(a)(1) and ordered a refund of all excess contributions made before the amendment of the plan. The United States Court of Appeals for the Ninth Circuit affirmed.

The Department and various *amici curiae* contend that: (1) the differential in take-home pay between men and women was not discrimination within the meaning of § 703(a)(1) because it was offset by a difference in the value of the pension benefits provided to the two classes of employees; (2) the differential was based on a factor "other than sex" within the meaning of the Equal Pay Act of 1963 and was therefore protected by the so-called Bennett Amendment; (3) the rationale of General Electric Co. v. Gilbert, 429 U.S. 125, 97 S.Ct. 401, 50 L.Ed.2d 343, requires reversal; and (4) in any event, the retroactive monetary recovery is unjustified. We consider these contentions in turn.

There are both real and fictional differences between women and men. It is true that the average man is taller than the average woman; it is not true that the average woman driver is more accident prone than the average man. Before the Civil Rights Act of 1964 was enacted, an employer could fashion his personnel policies on the basis of assumptions about the differences between men and women, whether or not the assumptions were valid.

It is now well recognized that employment decisions cannot be predicated on mere "stereotyped" impressions about the characteristics of males or females. Myths and purely habitual assumptions about a woman's inability to perform certain kinds of work are no longer acceptable reasons for refusing to employ qualified individuals, or for paying them less. This case does not, however, involve a fictional difference between men and women. It involves a generalization that the parties accept as unquestionably true: Women, as a class, do live longer than men. The Department treated its women employees differently from its men employees because the two classes are in fact different. It is equally true, however, that all individuals in the respective classes do not share the characteristic that differentiates the average class representatives. Many women do not live as long as the average man and many men outlive the average woman. The question, therefore, is whether the existence or nonexistence of "discrimination" is to be determined by comparison of class characteristics or individual characteristics. A "stereotyped" answer to that question may not be the same as the answer that the language and purpose of the statute command.

The statute makes it unlawful "to discriminate against any *individual* with respect to his compensation, terms, conditions, or privileges of employment, because of such *individual's* race, color, religion, sex, or national origin." The statute's focus on the individual is unambiguous." It precludes treatment of individuals as simply components of a racial, religious, sexual, or national class. If height is required for a job, a tall woman may not be refused employment merely because, on the average, women are too short. Even a true generalization about the class is an insufficient reason for disqualifying an individual to whom the generalization does not apply.

That proposition is of critical importance in this case because there is no assurance that any individual woman working for the Department will actually fit the generalization on which the Department's policy is based. Many of those individuals will not live as long as the average man. While they were working, those individuals received smaller paychecks because of their sex, but they will receive no compensating advantage when they retire.

It is true, of course, that while contributions are being collected from the employees, the Department cannot know which individuals will predecease the average woman. Therefore, unless women as a class are assessed an extra charge, they will be subsidized, to some extent, by the class of male employees.[14] It follows, according to the Department, that fairness to its class of male employees justifies the extra assessment against all of its female employees.

But the question of fairness to various classes affected by the statute is essentially a matter of policy for the legislature to address. Congress has decided that classifications based on sex, like those based on national origin or race, are unlawful. Actuarial studies could unquestionably identify differences in life expectancy based on race or national origin, as well as sex.[15] But a statute that was designed to make race irrelevant in the employment market, see Griggs v. Duke Power Co., 401 U.S. 424, 436, 91 S.Ct. 849, 856, 28 L.Ed.2d 158, could

---

14. The size of the subsidy involved in this case is open to doubt, because the Department's plan provides for survivors' benefits. Since female spouses of male employees are likely to have greater life expectancies than the male spouses of female employees, whatever benefits men lose in "primary" coverage for themselves, they may regain in "secondary" coverage for their wives.

15. For example, the life expectancy of a white baby in 1973 was 72.2 years; a nonwhite baby could expect to live 65.9 years, a difference of 6.3 years. See Public Health Service, IIA Vital Statistics of the United States, 1973, Table 5–3.

not reasonably be construed to permit a take-home-pay differential based on a racial classification.[16]

Even if the statutory language were less clear, the basic policy of the statute requires that we focus on fairness to individuals rather than fairness to classes. Practices that classify employees in terms of religion, race, or sex tend to preserve traditional assumptions about groups rather than thoughtful scrutiny of individuals. The generalization involved in this case illustrates the point. Separate mortality tables are easily interpreted as reflecting innate differences between the sexes; but a significant part of the longevity differential may be explained by the social fact that men are heavier smokers than women.

Finally, there is no reason to believe that Congress intended a special definition of discrimination in the context of employee group insurance coverage. It is true that insurance is concerned with events that are individually unpredictable, but that is characteristic of many employment decisions. Individual risks, like individual performance, may not be predicted by resort to classifications proscribed by Title VII. Indeed, the fact that this case involves a group insurance program highlights a basic flaw in the Department's fairness argument. For when insurance risks are grouped, the better risks always subsidize the poorer risks. Healthy persons subsidize medical benefits for the less healthy; unmarried workers subsidize the pensions of married workers; persons who eat, drink, or smoke to excess may subsidize pension benefits for persons whose habits are more temperate. Treating different classes of risks as though they were the same for purposes of group insurance is a common practice that has never been considered inherently unfair. To insure the flabby and the fit as though they were equivalent risks may be more common than treating men and women alike; [19] but nothing more than habit makes one "subsidy" seem less fair than the other.

An employment practice that requires 2,000 individuals to contribute more money into a fund than 10,000 other employees simply because each of them is a woman, rather than a man, is in direct conflict with both the language and the policy of the Act. Such a practice does not pass the simple test of whether the evidence shows "treatment of a person in a manner which but for that person's sex would be different." It constitutes discrimination and is unlawful unless exempted by the Equal Pay Act of 1963 or some other affirmative justification.

Shortly before the enactment of Title VII in 1964, Senator Bennett proposed an amendment providing that a compensation differential

---

16. Fortifying this conclusion is the fact that some States have banned higher life insurance rates for blacks since the 19th century.

19. The record indicates, however, that the Department has funded its death-benefit plan by equal contributions from male and female employees. A death benefit—unlike a pension benefit—has less value for persons with longer life expectancies. Under the Department's concept of fairness, then, this neutral funding of death benefits is unfair to women as a class.

based on sex would not be unlawful if it was authorized by the Equal Pay Act, which had been passed a year earlier. The Equal Pay Act requires employers to pay members of both sexes the same wages for equivalent work, except when the differential is pursuant to one of four specified exceptions. The Department contends that the fourth exception applies here. That exception authorizes a "differential based on any other factor other than sex."

The Department argues that the different contributions exacted from men and women were based on the factor of longevity rather than sex. It is plain, however, that any individual's life expectancy is based on a number of factors, of which sex is only one. The record contains no evidence that any factor other than the employee's sex was taken into account in calculating the 14.84% differential between the respective contributions by men and women. * * *

* * *

The Department argues that reversal is required by General Electric Co. v. Gilbert, 429 U.S. 125, 97 S.Ct. 401, 50 L.Ed.2d 343. We are satisfied, however, that neither the holding nor the reasoning of *Gilbert* is controlling.

In *Gilbert* the Court held that the exclusion of pregnancy from an employer's disability benefit plan did not constitute sex discrimination within the meaning of Title VII. Relying on the reasoning in Geduldig v. Aiello, 417 U.S. 484, 94 S.Ct. 2485, 41 L.Ed.2d 256, the Court first held that the General Electric plan did not involve "discrimination based upon gender as such." The two groups of potential recipients which that case concerned were pregnant women and nonpregnant persons. " 'While the first group is exclusively female, the second includes members of both sexes." ' In contrast, each of the two groups of employees involved in this case is composed entirely and exclusively of members of the same sex. On its face, this plan discriminates on the basis of sex whereas the General Electric plan discriminated on the basis of a special physical disability.

In *Gilbert* the Court did note that the plan as actually administered had provided more favorable benefits to women as a class than to men as a class. This evidence supported the conclusion that not only had plaintiffs failed to establish a prima facie case by proving that the plan was discriminatory on its face, but they had also failed to prove any discriminatory effect.

In this case, however, the Department argues that the absence of a discriminatory effect on women as a class justifies an employment practice which, on its face, discriminated against individual employees because of their sex. But even if the Department's actuarial evidence is sufficient to prevent plaintiffs from establishing a prima facie case on the theory that the effect of the practice on women as a class was discriminatory, that evidence does not defeat the claim that the practice, on its face, discriminated against every individual woman employed by the Department.[30]

In essence, the Department is arguing that the prima facie showing of discrimination based on evidence of different contributions for the respective sexes is rebutted by its demonstration that there is a like difference in the cost of providing benefits for the respective classes. That argument might prevail if Title VII contained a cost-justification defense comparable to the affirmative defense available in a price discrimination suit. But neither Congress nor the courts have recognized such a defense under Title VII.

Although we conclude that the Department's practice violated Title VII, we do not suggest that the statute was intended to revolutionize the insurance and pension industries. All that is at issue today is a requirement that men and women make unequal contributions to an employer-operated pension fund. Nothing in our holding implies that it would be unlawful for an employer to set aside equal retirement contributions for each employee and let each retiree purchase the largest benefit which his or her accumulated contributions could command in the open market.[33] Nor does it call into question the insurance industry practice of considering the composition of an employer's work force in determining the probable cost of a retirement or death benefit plan. Finally, we recognize that in a case of this kind it may be necessary to take special care in fashioning appropriate relief.

* * *

There can be no doubt that the prohibition against sex-differentiated employee contributions represents a marked departure from past practice. Although Title VII was enacted in 1964, this is apparently the first litigation challenging contribution differences based on valid actuarial tables. Retroactive liability could be devastating for a pension fund. The harm would fall in large part on innocent third parties. If, as the courts below apparently contemplated, the plaintiffs' contributions are recovered from the pension fund, the administrators of the

---

30. Some *amici* suggest that the Department's discrimination is justified by business necessity. They argue that, if no gender distinction is drawn, many male employees will withdraw from the plan, or even the Department, because they can get a better pension plan in the private market. But the Department has long required equal contributions to its death-benefit plan, see n. 19, supra, and since 1975 it has required equal contributions to its pension plan. Yet the Department points to no "adverse selection" by the affected employees, presumably because an employee who wants to leave the plan must also leave his job, and few workers will quit because one of their fringe benefits could theoretically be obtained at a marginally

lower price on the open market. In short, there has been no showing that sex distinctions are reasonably necessary to the normal operation of the Department's retirement plan.

33. Title VII and the Equal Pay Act primarily govern relations between employees and their employer, not between employees and third parties. We do not suggest, of course, that an employer can avoid his responsibilities by delegating discriminatory programs to corporate shells. Title VII applies to "any agent" of a covered employer, and the Equal Pay Act applies to "any person acting directly or indirectly in the interest of an employer in relation to an employee." * * *

fund will be forced to meet unchanged obligations with diminished assets. If the reserve proves inadequate, either the expectations of all retired employees will be disappointed or current employees will be forced to pay not only for their own future security but also for the unanticipated reduction in the contributions of past employees.

Without qualifying the force of the * * * presumption in favor of retroactive relief, we conclude that it was error to grant such relief in this case. Accordingly, although we agree with the Court of Appeals' analysis of the statute, we vacate its judgment and remand the case for further proceedings consistent with this opinion.

It is so ordered.

MR. JUSTICE BRENNAN took no part in the consideration or decision of this case.

MR. JUSTICE BLACKMUN, concurring in part and concurring in the judgment.

* * *

The Court's rationale, * * * is that Congress, by Title VII of the Civil Rights Act of 1964, as amended, intended to eliminate, with certain exceptions, "race, color, religion, sex, or national origin," as factors upon which employers may act. A program such as the one challenged here does exacerbate gender consciousness. But the program under consideration in *General Electric* did exactly the same thing and yet was upheld against challenge.

The Court's distinction between the present case and *General Electric*—that the permitted classes there were "pregnant women and nonpregnant persons," both female and male—seems to me to be just too easy. It is probably the only distinction that can be drawn. For me, it does not serve to distinguish the case on any principled basis. I therefore must conclude that today's decision cuts back on *General Electric*, and inferentially on *Geduldig*, the reasoning of which was adopted there, and, indeed, makes the recognition of those cases as continuing precedent somewhat questionable. I do not say that this is necessarily bad. If that is what Congress has chosen to do by Title VII—as the Court today with such assurance asserts—so be it. I feel, however, that we should meet the posture of the earlier cases head on and not by thin rationalization that seeks to distinguish but fails in its quest.

* * *

MR. CHIEF JUSTICE BURGER, with whom MR. JUSTICE REHNQUIST joins, concurring in part and dissenting in part.

* * *

MR. JUSTICE MARSHALL, concurring in part and dissenting in part.

* * *

NOTES AND PROBLEMS FOR DISCUSSION

1. Do you agree with the majority or Justice Blackmun with respect to whether *Manhart* can be distinguished in any meaningful way from *Gilbert*? See generally, Rutherglen, Sexual Equality in Fringe–Benefit Plans, 65 Va. L.Rev. 199 (1979). To the extent that the two opinions are inconsistent, hasn't this problem been resolved by the enactment of the 1978 Pregnancy Discrimination Act and its subsequent interpretation by the Supreme Court in *Newport News*?

2. What impact should *Manhart* have on a pension plan under which women made contributions equal to those of men but receive smaller monthly benefits upon retirement? Would your response to this question change if the employee-funded retirement plan is administered by a private insurance company rather than by the employer? Each of these questions subsequently was addressed by the Court in ARIZONA GOVERNING COMMITTEE v. NORRIS, 463 U.S. 1073, 103 S.Ct. 3492, 77 L.Ed.2d 1236 (1983). The Court extended its ruling in *Manhart* to a deferred compensation plan that provided employees of the State of Arizona with the option of postponing the receipt of a portion of their wages until retirement by selecting among various plans offered by several companies chosen by the State to participate in its plan. The employees were not required to participate in the plan but participation was limited to a choice of one of the companies selected by the State; an employee could not invest its deferred compensation in any other way. The State was responsible for withholding the appropriate sum from a participating employee's wages but it did not contribute any money to supplement the employee's contribution. All of the companies selected by the State used sex-based mortality tables to calculate the monthly payments received by employees who chose to participate in a monthly annuity program. (The companies also offered a single lump-sum payment upon retirement option and an option making periodic payments of a fixed sum over a fixed time period.) Sex, however, was the only factor used to determine the longevity of individuals of the same age; other factors correlating with longevity such as smoking or alcohol consumption, weight, or medical history were not considered. The Court held that the use of sex-based actuarial tables was "no more permissible at the pay-out stage of a retirement plan than at the pay-in stage." In so holding, it rejected the State's contention that the plan did not violate Title VII because a man and woman who deferred the same amount of wages would receive, upon retirement, annuity policies having approximately the same present actuarial value, since the lower value of each monthly payment received by a woman was offset by the likelihood that she would receive more payments. The defect in this argument, the Court declared, was that the plan calculated longevity solely on the basis of gender, a practice prohibited in *Manhart*. In addition, the Court noted that, as in *Manhart*, if a female employee wished to receive the same monthly benefits paid to a similarly situated man, she would have to make greater monthly contributions than that male employee.

The fact that participation in the plan was voluntary was irrelevant, the Court reasoned, since Title VII prohibits discrimination concerning all terms and conditions of employment and the option of participating in a deferred compensation plan constitutes a condition of employment. Similarly irrelevant was the fact that the plan provided other nondiscriminatory options such as the lump-sum and fixed-sum-over-fixed period alternatives. Offering nondiscriminatory benefits, the Court declared, did not excuse the provision of another benefit on a discriminatory basis. Finally, to avoid a potentially devastating financial impact on pension funds, a majority of the Court concluded that this case should fall outside the presumption in favor of awarding retroactive relief announced by the Court in Albemarle Paper Co. v. Moody, see infra at 601. Accordingly, it required employers to calculate benefits without regard to the sex of the employee only as to benefits derived from contributions collected after the effective date of the trial court's judgment. Benefits derived from contributions made prior to that date, a majority ruled, could be calculated as provided by the existing terms of the Arizona plan.

Justice O'Connor played the pivotal role in the resolution of this case. Four Justices—Marshall, Brennan, White and Stevens—concluded that the plan violated Title VII but also stated that this decision should apply retroactively to a limited extent. These four members of the Court declared that the Court's ruling in *Manhart* should have put the State of Arizona on notice that male and female employees who make the same contributions to a retirement plan must receive equal monthly benefits. Accordingly, they concluded, it was not unfair to require the State to eliminate any sex-based disparity in monthly benefits attributable to contributions made post-*Manhart*. Moreover, they said, the decision should apply to payments attributable to pre-*Manhart* contributions, if the trial court on remand would find that the employer, after *Manhart*, could have applied sex-neutral tables to pre-*Manhart* contributions without violating the contractual rights of male employees. While Justice O'Connor joined to form a majority on the issue of liability, she did not agree with this proposed remedy. The other four Justices—Powell, Burger, Blackmun and Rehnquist—in an opinion authored by Powell, concluded that the Arizona plan did not violate Title VII and that the trial court also erred in imposing liability on more than a purely prospective basis. Justice O'Connor joined with the Powell quartet on the remedies issue, thereby creating a majority on this question. In her separate concurring opinion, Justice O'Connor explained that the benefits should be calculated without regard to sex with respect only to those payments derived from contributions collected after the effective date of the judgment in this case. Does this mean that female benefits must be "topped up" to reach the level of men's benefits or can the men's benefits be reduced to. achieve equality of benefit payments? Is it significant that the remedy is prospective only in its application? On remand, the Ninth Circuit ruled that the trial court had not abused its discretion in refusing to top up women's benefits since the *prospective* application of a gender-neutral benefit calculation would not, unlike a *retroactive* application, impair rights to expected benefits. Norris v. Arizona Governing Committee, 796 F.2d 1119 (9th Cir.1986).

Topping up was ordered, however, by the Eleventh Circuit in LONG v. STATE OF FLA., 805 F.2d 1542 (11th Cir.1986). *Long* involved a pension plan administered by the State of Florida for all state employees and employees of participating local governments. The primary pension option, since its inception, calculated contributions and benefits without regard to sex. The plan also, however, offered three optional joint annuitant plans, each of which based benefits, in part, on life expectancy which, in turn, was calculated according to sex-based actuarial tables. The appellate court affirmed the trial judge's order requiring the defendant to top up all benefits paid as of October 1, 1978 to male employees who retired after that date and were receiving smaller annuity payments than similarly situated female employees. It stated that since the Florida system knew or should have known since May 1, 1978, the date of the *Manhart* decision, that sex-based *benefits* were impermissible under Title VII, it was on notice that it had to base its benefits on sex-neutral tables as of a reasonable period after the date of the decision in *Manhart*. The court added that while the *Norris* Court precluded the award of retroactive relief, requiring topping up as of October 1, 1978 (the effective date of *Manhart*) constituted prospective, rather than retroactive relief. It interpreted *Norris* as saying that requiring a change in benefits based on contributions made before the date of judgment in the instant case constitutes retroactive relief because to the extent that a retirement plan represents a return on contributions made during the worker's period of employment that were intended to completely fund the benefits which that employee would receive in the future, the excess must come from alternative sources. In contrast, the Eleventh Circuit noted, almost all contributions to the Florida retirement system were made by the employer using public funds allocated by the legislature to cover current and future operating expenses and funding and, therefore, the benefits paid out of the fund were not directly based on the contributions paid into the fund. Accordingly, it concluded, the order to top up constituted permissible prospective relief. The Eleventh Circuit also noted that since the legislature had increased the system's contribution rates in 1984, thereby creating a surplus of over $200 million, the impact on the Florida taxpayers, while burdensome, would not be devastating. Finally, the circuit court also upheld the trial judge's decision not to require the defendant to top up the benefits paid to male employees who retired before October 1, 1978. Since the *Manhart* Court refused to apply its ruling retroactively to employees who retired prior to the date of judgment in that case, the Eleventh Circuit reasoned that the topping up order similarly could not apply to male employees in Florida who retired before the date of the *Manhart* judgment. But as to male employees who retired after 1978, benefits paid as of October 1, 1978 were to be raised to the level that males would have received had sex-neutral mortality tables been applied to their original benefits, i.e., under the unisex method of calculation. It rejected the request by the plaintiff class that it order topping up to the level of benefits that female employees received under the original sex-based mortality table system. In this regard, the court reasoned, the plaintiff class was not entitled to equalization, but, rather, to be made whole; i.e., to be placed in the situation they would have occupied had there been no discrimination.

This ruling was reversed, however, by a 5–4 vote of the Supreme Court. Florida v. Long, 487 U.S. 223, 108 S.Ct. 2354, 101 L.Ed.2d 206 (1988). The majority, in an opinion by Justice Kennedy, rejected the Eleventh Circuit's underlying premise that the ruling in *Manhart* requiring nondiscriminatory pension plan *contribution* schemes put employers on notice that *benefits* must also be calculated in a nondiscriminatory manner. Rather, the Court concluded, this issue was not resolved until its subsequent decision in *Norris*. Moreover, the Court added, since the State's primary pension plan option had provided sex-neutral benefits since its inception, the plan administrators, before *Norris*, could reasonably interpret *Manhart* as not precluding the provision of optional annuity plans that were sex-based. Accordingly, it concluded that the presumption against awarding retroactive relief was not overcome by equitable considerations and, therefore, that employees who retired before the effective date of *Norris* were not entitled to benefit readjustment. (The optional sex-based plans had been discontinued immediately after the ruling in *Norris*.).

The Supreme Court also rejected the circuit court's determination that post–*Manhart* topping up did not constitute retroactive relief. It stated that since the State determined the contribution levels by assessing its expected future benefit payments, a readjustment of benefits would affect the State's ability to meet its future benefit obligations. Furthermore, it continued, the fact that the State had a surplus fund sufficient to withstand a $43 million judgment was irrelevant to its determination that the proposed benefit readjustment constituted retroactive relief. In dissent, Justice Blackmun, joined by Justices Brennan and Marshall, maintained that the clear import of *Manhart* was to preclude sex-based benefit payments and that this decision placed Florida on notice of the illegality of its sex-based annuity options. Thus, they concluded, retroactive relief was not inequitable, but, rather, appropriate for post-*Manhart* retirees. They did concur, however, in those portions of the majority's judgment that characterized the relief offered as retroactive and that upheld the lower courts' denial of retroactive relief to pre–*Manhart* retirees. In a separate dissenting opinion, Justice Stevens agreed entirely with the Eleventh Circuit's reasoning that the relief awarded to post–*Manhart* retirees was prospective and added that failure to top up was akin to the perpetuation of past discrimination.

3.   Will forbidding the use of sex-based mortality tables increase the cost of employing female workers? If so, can't it be argued that the decision in *Manhart* will have an adverse effect on the employment of women? For an interesting and insightful debate over the meaning and impact of *Manhart*, see Kimball, Reverse Sex Discrimination: Manhart, 1979 Am.B.Found.Res.J. 83; Benston, The Economics of Gender Discrimination in Employee Fringe Benefits: Manhart Revisited, 49 U.Chi.L.Rev. 489 (1982); Brilmayer, Hekeler, Laycock & Sullivan, Sex Discrimination in Employer–Sponsored Insurance Plans: A Legal and Demographic Analysis, 47 U.Chi.L.Rev. 505 (1980).

4.   Sexual Preference Discrimination

DeSANTIS v. PACIFIC TELEPHONE & TELEGRAPH CO., INC.

United States Court of Appeals, Ninth Circuit, 1979.
608 F.2d 327.

CHOY, CIRCUIT JUDGE.

Male and female homosexuals brought three separate federal district court actions claiming that their employers or former employers discriminated against them in employment decisions because of their homosexuality.   They alleged that such discrimination violated Title VII of the Civil Rights Act of 1964 * * *.

I.   *Statement of the Case*

A.   *Strailey v. Happy Times Nursery School, Inc.*

Appellant Strailey, a male, was fired by the Happy Times Nursery School after two years' service as a teacher. He alleged that he was fired because he wore a small gold ear-loop to school prior to the commencement of the school year. He filed a charge with the Equal Employment Opportunity Commission (EEOC) which the EEOC rejected because of an alleged lack of jurisdiction over claims of discrimination based on sexual orientation. He then filed suit on behalf of himself and all others similarly situated, seeking declaratory, injunctive, and monetary relief. The district court dismissed the complaint as failing to state a claim * * *.

B.   *DeSantis v. Pacific Telephone & Telegraph Co.*

DeSantis, Boyle, and Simard, all males, claimed that Pacific Telephone & Telegraph Co. (PT&T) impermissibly discriminated against them because of their homosexuality. DeSantis alleged that he was not hired when a PT&T supervisor concluded that he was a homosexual. According to appellants' brief, "BOYLE was continually harassed by his co-workers and had to quit to preserve his health after only three months because his supervisors did nothing to alleviate this condition." Finally, "SIMARD was forced to quit under similar conditions after almost four years of employment with PT&T, but he was harassed by his supervisors [as well] * * *. In addition, his personnel file has been marked as not eligible for rehire, and his applications for employment were rejected by PT&T in 1974 and 1976." Appellants DeSantis, Boyle, and Simard also alleged that PT&T officials have publicly stated that they would not hire homosexuals.

These plaintiffs also filed charges with the EEOC, also rejected by the EEOC for lack of jurisdiction. They then filed suit on behalf of themselves and all others similarly situated seeking declaratory, injunctive, and monetary relief under Title VII * * *. They also prayed that the district court issue mandamus commanding the EEOC to process charges based on sexual orientation. The district court dismissed their complaint. It held that the court lacked jurisdiction to compel the EEOC to alter its interpretation of Title VII. It also held that appellants had not stated viable claims under * * * Title VII * * *.

C.   *Lundin v. Pacific Telephone & Telegraph*

Lundin and Buckley, both females, were operators with PT&T. They filed suit in federal court alleging that PT&T discriminated against them because of their known lesbian relationship and eventually fired them. They also alleged that they endured numerous insults by PT&T employees because of their relationship. * * * Appellants sought monetary and injunctive relief. The district court dismissed their suit as not stating a claim upon which relief could be granted.
* * *

II.   *Title VII Claim*

Appellants argue first that the district courts erred in holding that Title VII does not prohibit discrimination on the basis of sexual preference. They claim that in prohibiting certain employment discrimination on the basis of "sex," Congress meant to include discrimination on the basis of sexual orientation. They add that in a trial they could establish that discrimination against homosexuals disproportionately effects men and that this disproportionate impact and correlation between discrimination on the basis of sexual preference and discrimination on the basis of "sex" requires that sexual preference be considered a subcategory of the "sex" category of Title VII.

A. Congressional Intent in Prohibiting "Sex" Discrimination

In Holloway v. Arthur Andersen & Co., 566 F.2d 659 (9th Cir.1977), plaintiff argued that her employer had discriminated against her because she was undergoing a sex transformation and that this discrimination violated Title VII's prohibition on sex discrimination. This court rejected that claim, writing:

> The cases interpreting Title VII sex discrimination provisions agree that they were intended to place women on an equal footing with men. [Citations omitted.]
>
> Giving the statute its plain meaning, this court concludes that Congress had only the traditional notions of "sex" in mind. Later legislative activity makes this narrow definition even more evident. Several bills have been introduced to *amend* the Civil Rights Act to prohibit discrimination against "sexual preference." None have [*sic*] been enacted into law.
>
> Congress has not shown any intent other than to restrict the term "sex" to its traditional meaning. Therefore, this court will not expand Title VII's application in the absence of Congressional mandate. The manifest purpose of Title VII's prohibition against sex discrimination in employment is to ensure that men and women are treated equally, absent a bona fide relationship between the qualifications for the job and the person's sex.

Following *Holloway*, we conclude that Title VII's prohibition of "sex" discrimination applies only to discrimination on the basis of gender and should not be judicially extended to include sexual preference such as homosexuality. See Smith v. Liberty Mutual Insurance Co., 569 F.2d 325, 326–27 (5th Cir.1978).

B. Disproportionate Impact

Appellants argue that recent decisions dealing with disproportionate impact require that discrimination against homosexuals fall within the purview of Title VII. They contend that these recent decisions, like Griggs v. Duke Power Co., 401 U.S. 424, 91 S.Ct. 849, 28 L.Ed.2d 158 (1971), establish that any employment criterion that affects one sex more than the other violates Title VII. * * * They claim that in a trial they could prove that discrimination against homosexuals disproportionately affects men both because of the greater incidence of homosexuality in the male population and because of the greater likelihood of an employer's discovering male homosexuals compared to female homosexuals.

Assuming that appellants can otherwise satisfy the requirement of *Griggs*, we do not believe that *Griggs* can be applied to extend Title VII protection to homosexuals. In finding that the disproportionate impact of educational tests on blacks violated Title VII, the Supreme Court in *Griggs* sought to effectuate a major congressional purpose in enacting Title VII: protection of blacks from employment discrimination. * * *

The *Holloway* court noted that in passing Title VII Congress did not intend to protect sexual orientation and has repeatedly refused to extend such protection. Appellants now ask us to employ the disproportionate impact decisions as an artifice to "bootstrap" Title VII protection for homosexuals under the guise of protecting men generally.

This we are not free to do. Adoption of this bootstrap device would frustrate congressional objectives as explicated in *Holloway*, not effectuate congressional goals as in *Griggs*. It would achieve by judicial "construction" what Congress did not do and has consistently refused to do on many occasions. It would violate the rule that our duty in construing a statute is to "ascertain * * * and give effect to the legislative will." We conclude that the *Griggs* disproportionate impact theory may not be applied to extend Title VII protection to homosexuals.

C. *Differences in Employment Criteria*

Appellants next contend that recent decisions have held that an employer generally may not use different employment criteria for men and women. They claim that if a male employee prefers males as sexual partners, he will be treated differently from a female who prefers male partners. They conclude that the employer thus uses different employment criteria for men and women and violates the Supreme Court's warning in Phillips v. Martin–Marietta Corp., 400 U.S. 542, 91 S.Ct. 496, 27 L.Ed.2d 613 (1971):

> The Court of Appeals therefore erred in reading this section as permitting one hiring policy for women and another for men * * *.

We must again reject appellants' efforts to "bootstrap" Title VII protection for homosexuals. While we do not express approval of an employment policy that differentiates according to sexual preference, we note that whether dealing with men or women the employer is using the same criterion: it will not hire or promote a person who prefers sexual partners of the same sex. Thus this policy does not involve different decisional criteria for the sexes.

D. *Interference with Association*

Appellants argue that the EEOC has held that discrimination against an employee because of the race of the employee's friends may constitute discrimination based on race in violation of Title VII. They contend that analogously discrimination because of the sex of the employees' sexual partner should constitute discrimination based on sex.

Appellants, however, have not alleged that appellees have policies of discriminating against employees because of the gender of their friends. That is, they do not claim that the appellees will terminate anyone with a male (or female) friend. They claim instead that the appellees discriminate against employees who have a certain type of relationship—i.e., homosexual relationship—with certain friends. As noted earlier, that relationship is not protected by Title VII. Thus, assuming that it would violate Title VII for an employer to discriminate against employees because of the gender of their friends, appellants' claims do not fall within this purported rule.

E. *Effeminacy*

Appellant Strailey contends that he was terminated by the Happy Times Nursery School because that school felt that it was inappropriate for a male teacher to wear an earring to school. He claims that the school's reliance on a stereotype—that a male should have a virile rather than an effeminate appearance—violates Title VII.

In *Holloway* this court noted that Congress intended Title VII's ban on sex discrimination in employment to prevent discrimination because of gender, not because of sexual orientation or preference. Recently the Fifth Circuit similarly read the legislative history of Title VII and concluded that Title VII thus does not protect against discrimination because of effeminacy. Smith v. Liberty Mutual Insurance Co., 569 F.2d at 326–27. We agree and hold that discrimination because of effeminacy, like discrimination because of homosexuality or transsexualism (*Holloway*), does not fall within the purview of Title VII.

F. *Conclusion as to Title VII Claim*

Having determined that appellants' allegations do not implicate Title VII's prohibition on sex discrimination, we affirm the district court's dismissals of the Title VII claims.

SNEED, CIRCUIT JUDGE (concurring and dissenting).

* * *

I respectfully dissent from subpart B which holds that male homosexuals have not stated a Title VII claim under the disproportionate impact theories of Griggs v. Duke Power Co. My position is not foreclosed by our holding, with which I agree, that Title VII does not afford protection to homosexuals, male or female. The male appellants' complaint, as I understand it, is based on the contention that the use of homosexuality as a disqualification for employment, which for *Griggs'* purposes must be treated as a facially neutral criterion, impacts disproportionately on *males* because of the greater visibility of male homosexuals and a higher incidence of homosexuality among males than females.

To establish such a claim will be difficult because the male appellants must prove that as a result of the appellee's practices there exists discrimination against males *qua* males. That is, to establish a prima facie case under *Griggs* it will not be sufficient to show that appellees have employed a disproportionately large number of female *homosexuals* and a disproportionately small number of male *homosexuals*. Rather it will be necessary to establish that the use of homosexuality as a bar to employment disproportionately impacts on *males*, a class that enjoys Title VII protection. Such a showing perhaps could be made were male homosexuals a very large proportion of the total applicable male population.

My point of difference with the majority is merely that the male appellants in their *Griggs* claim are not using that case "as an artifice to 'bootstrap' Title VII protection for homosexuals under the guise of protecting men generally." Their claim, if established properly, would in fact protect males generally. I would permit them to try to make their case and not dismiss it on the pleadings.

NOTES AND PROBLEMS FOR DISCUSSION

1. Did the majority in *DeSantis* correctly analyze the plaintiff's disproportionate impact claim? Isn't Judge Sneed's dissenting opinion more on target?

2. Public sector employment policies that discriminate on the basis of sexual orientation are subject also to constitutional scrutiny. Such practices have been challenged under the First Amendment, the equal protection guarantees of the Fifth and Fourteenth Amendments and the penumbral right of privacy.

First Amendment challenges to anti-gay policies have focused on the infringement of the individual's rights of freedom of expression and association and have met with limited success. In NATIONAL GAY TASK FORCE v. BOARD OF EDUC. OF OKLAHOMA CITY, 729 F.2d 1270 (10th Cir.1984), for example, the court struck down as constitutionally invalid a state statute that permitted the dismissal or rejection for employment of teachers found to have engaged in public homosexual conduct or activity and to have been rendered unfit to hold a teaching position because of that conduct or activity. The statute defined "public homosexual conduct" as "advocating, soliciting, imposing, encouraging or promoting public or private homosexual activity in a manner that creates a substantial risk that such conduct will come to the attention of school children or school employees." "Public homosexual activity" was defined as the commission of a sex act with a person of the same sex in public. The court held that while the statute could permit a teacher to be fired for "public homosexual activity" without violating the constitutional right of privacy, the statutory definition of "public homosexual conduct" was facially overbroad. By prohibiting the "advocating", "encouraging", and "promoting" of homosexual activity, the statute prohibited protected First Amendment speech and therefore was unconstitutionally overbroad on its face. The court also held that the portion of the statute dealing with "public homosexual activity" was severable from the portion prohibiting "public homosexual conduct". Accordingly, it upheld the constitutionality of the former portion and struck down the statute only insofar as it punished "homosexual conduct" as that phrase was defined to include "advocating * * * encouraging or promoting" homosexual activity. This judgment was affirmed by an equally divided Supreme Court. 470 U.S. 903, 105 S.Ct. 1858, 84 L.Ed.2d 776 (1985).

BEN–SHALOM v. MARSH, 881 F.2d 454 (7th Cir.1989), cert. denied, 494 U.S. 1004, 110 S.Ct. 1296, 108 L.Ed.2d 473 (1990), involved a policy that penalized speech in the form of an admission of homosexual status rather than speech in the form of statements about homosexuality in general. The case involved an Army regulation that contained a nonwaivable disqualification to reenlistment applicable to any individual who admitted to having a "desire" for homosexual bodily contact but as to whom there was no evidence of having engaged in a homosexual act either before or during military service. The trial court struck the regulation down as violative of the First Amendment. It reasoned that by disqualifying a member of the service for making an admission of homosexual status, this regulation chilled protected First Amendment speech and was not sufficiently narrowly tailored to protect the Army's legitimate interests in maintaining discipline, morale, trust, confidence, integrity of rank deployability of service members who frequently must live and work under conditions affording minimal privacy, recruiting and retaining members of the service, maintaining public acceptability of military services and preventing breaches of security. The regulation had been designed to disqualify those who either engaged in homosexual activity or who displayed a propensity to engage in such conduct. The trial judge declared, however, that the Army had offered no basis upon which he could conclude that admission of homosexual status equalled evidence of propensity. Accordingly, the trial judge declared the regulation to be unconstitutional on its face.

The Seventh Circuit reversed, emphasizing that it did not want to second guess the Army's determination that the presence of homosexuals within the service would compromise its aforementioned legitimate interests. The court stated that while members of the military services did not forfeit all protection under the First Amendment, the "different character of the military community and of the military mission" demanded a different application of this constitutional principle than traditionally is applied to the civilian population. In this regard, the court reasoned, since an admission of homosexuality "implies, at the very least, a desire to commit homosexual acts," the Army could reasonably conclude that an admitted homosexual would have a desire and propensity to commit homosexual acts. And since none of the parties disputed the constitutionality of denying reenlistment for engaging in a homosexual act, the court concluded that the Army had a legitimate interest in excluding individuals who had acknowledged their propensity to commit proscribed conduct. Or, as the court put it, "the Army should not be required by this court to assume the risk, a risk it would be assuming for all our citizens, that accepting admitted homosexuals into the armed forces might imperil morale, discipline, and the effectiveness of our fighting forces." 881 F.2d at 461.

The appellate court also rejected the plaintiff's First Amendment argument on the ground that the regulation imposed, at most, an incidental limitation on her protected First Amendment freedom of speech. It noted that the regulation did not prevent the plaintiff from making declarations about homosexuality in general or about the Army's policy towards homosexuality. Nor did it prevent her from associating with homosexuals for the purpose of discussing these or other topics. What it prevented her from doing was declaring her homosexual orientation. This, the court reasoned, was an act of identification and it was this act of identification, not the speaking about it, that rendered her ineligible for reenlistment. Of course, it was her declaration of this identity that triggered the identity-based ineligibility. But this, the court reasoned, merely demonstrated that the regulation affected speech "only incidentally", in the course of pursuing legitimate goals. And, the court continued, this incidental limitation on First Amendment speech was justified by the government's interest in regulating the nonspeech element. Accord, see Pruitt v. Cheney, 943 F.2d 989 (9th Cir.1991)(female officer publicly revealed her homosexual status in newspaper interview and subsequently was honorably discharged per Army regulation requiring separation if member states that he/she is a homosexual; court rules that plaintiff cannot state claim under First Amendment; citing *Ben Shalom*, court finds that plaintiff was discharged for being a homosexual, not for the content of her speech).

Constitutional challenges to similarly restrictive public sector policies based on the right to privacy have been unsuccessful. In Dronenburg v. Zech, 741 F.2d 1388 (D.C.Cir.1984), the court rejected the plaintiff's claim that his constitutional right to privacy was violated by a Navy regulation that empowered the Secretary of the Navy to discharge anyone found to have engaged in homosexual acts, subject to the Secretary's exercise of discretion in rare situations for reasons unrelated to that individual's fitness to serve. The court based this decision on its determination that the right to privacy did not extend to homosexual conduct. The D.C. Circuit's analysis subsequently was adopted by the Supreme Court. In BOWERS v. HARDWICK, 478 U.S. 186, 106 S.Ct. 2841, 92 L.Ed.2d 140 (1986), the Supreme Court denied relief in a suit for declaratory judgment challenging the constitutionality of a Georgia statute criminalizing sodomy as applied to consensual homosexual sodomy between adults in the respondent's home. A five member majority, in an opinion written by Justice White, reviewed its prior decisions concerning the constitutional right to privacy and concluded that those cases did not recognize a right to be free from state proscription of all kinds of private sexual conduct between consenting adults. More specifically, it concluded that there was no substantive fundamental right under the Due Process Clause to engage in consensual homosexual sodomy. Since homosexual consensual sodomy had been historically proscribed by state law, the Court reasoned, it could not be said to be either a fundamental liberty that was deeply rooted in the Nation's history and tradition or a right whose sacrifice would threaten the continued existence of liberty or justice. In addition, the fact that the statute proscribed activity undertaken in the privacy of the respondent's home was not of constitutional significance. The Court indicated that its prior ruling in Stanley v. Georgia, in which it overturned a statute that restricted the viewing of pornographic materials in the home, rested not on the right to privacy but on First Amendment concerns. The dissenters, led by Justice Blackmun, maintained that as the statute applied to heterosexual and homosexual sodomy, the case did not turn on the question of the right to engage in homosexual conduct. Rather, they declared, the issue was whether the right to privacy precluded state restriction of any sexual conduct in the home between consenting adults. The dissenters concluded that the right of an individual to conduct intimate relationships in the intimacy of his home is part of the fundamental right of privacy. Moreover, the state's purported interest in protecting a tradition of condemning homosexual activity as immoral did not justify an abridgment of this right. See also Woodward v. United States, 871 F.2d 1068 (5th Cir.1989), cert. denied, 494 U.S. 1003, 110 S.Ct. 1295, 108 L.Ed.2d 473 (1990), (citing *Bowers* and *Dronenburg*, court holds that homosexual conduct is not protected under the constitutional right to privacy).

Discrimination on the basis of sexual orientation, when conducted by a public employer, also has been challenged as violative of the equal protection guarantees of the Fifth and Fourteenth Amendments. As in most equal protection cases, determining the appropriate level of scrutiny to be applied to the challenged classification is a critical issue. In PADULA v. WEBSTER, 822 F.2d 97 (D.C.Cir.1987), the plaintiff brought an equal protection challenge to the FBI's refusal to employ her as a special agent because of her homosexuality. The D.C. Circuit concluded that the Supreme Court's ruling in *Bowers* that the Constitution does not afford a privacy right to engage in homosexual conduct foreclosed the plaintiff's argument that homosexuals should be viewed as a suspect classification for equal protection purposes. The court reasoned that it "would be quite anomalous, on its face, to declare status defined by conduct that states may constitutionally criminalize as deserving of strict scrutiny under the equal protection clause." 822 F.2d at 103. Since, it added, denomination as a suspect class was implicitly limited to those instances in which it was "plainly unjustifiable to discriminate invidiously against the particular class * * * [i]f the Court was unwilling to object to state laws that criminalize the behavior that defines the class, it is hardly open to a lower court to conclude that state sponsored discrimination against the class is invidious." Id. Accordingly, the court concluded that homosexual classifications should be subjected to rational basis scrutiny and that it was rational for the FBI to conclude that employing agents who engage in conduct criminalized in roughly 50% of the states would undermine the law enforcement credibility of the Bureau. Furthermore, the court continued, it was not irrational for the Bureau to conclude that the criminalization of homosexual conduct and the general public disapproval of homosexuality exposed many homosexuals, even admitted homosexuals, to the risk of possible blackmail to protect their partners, if not themselves. The Fifth Circuit, citing *Padula* with approval, agreed that classifications based on homosexual conduct were not subject to heightened scrutiny. The court added that members of suspect classes exhibit immutable characteristics and then characterized homosexuality as "primarily behavioral in nature." Accordingly, it concluded, members of a class defined on the basis of homosexual conduct are not members of a suspect class to which heightened scrutiny must be afforded. Woodward v. United States, 871 F.2d 1068 (Fed.Cir. 1989).

Other courts have attempted to limit the holding in *Padula* by distinguishing classifications based on homosexual status from those based on homosexual conduct. WATKINS v. UNITED STATES ARMY, 875 F.2d 699 (9th Cir.1989) (en banc), involved a plaintiff who had been drafted in 1967 and who had admitted his homosexuality to the Army in his preinduction medical form by responding affirmatively to a question asking whether he had homosexual tendencies. This information notwithstanding, the Army found him to be qualified for admission and inducted him. In the face of a longstanding policy that homosexuality was a nonwaivable disqualification for *reenlistment*, Watkins nevertheless was allowed to reenlist for a second three year term in 1971. At the end of that period, in 1974, the Army accepted Watkins' application for a second reenlistment, this time for a six year term. Prior to 1981, Army regulations "authorized" *discharge* for homosexuality. Pursuant to this discretionary policy, the Army, in 1975, convened an investigation to determine whether Watkins should be discharged because of his homosexual tendencies. The board of inquiry unanimously concluded that there was no evidence that Watkins' homosexuality had any deleterious effect upon unit performance, moral, discipline or upon Watkins' own job performance. Accordingly, the board unanimously recommended that Watkins not be discharged and this decision was adopted by the Secretary of the Army. In 1979, towards the end of Watkins' second reenlistment period, the Army accepted his application for a third reenlistment. In 1981, the Army regulations concerning *discharge* were amended to *require* discharge from the Army on the basis of homosexuality. Pursuant to the revised discharge regulations, another board was convened in 1981 to consider discharging Watkins. While the board explicitly rejected the evidence that Watkins had engaged in homosexual conduct during the term of his Army service, the board recommended in 1982 that Watkins be discharged because he had admitted being a homosexual. Before the discharge issued, Watkins filed this action.

The trial court enjoined the Army from discharging Watkins. It based this decision on the ground that this discharge violated the Army's regulation against double jeopardy because the 1982 discharge essentially repeated the discharge proceedings that had been brought against Watkins in 1975. 541 F.Supp. 249, 259 (W.D.Wash.1982). During its oral argument before the trial judge, the Army had informed the court that if it were enjoined from discharging Watkins, it would deny reenlistment pursuant to its policy that always had made homosexuality a nonwaivable disqualification for reenlistment. After the trial court enjoined Watkins' discharge, the Army rejected Watkins' fourth reenlistment application because of his admitted homosexuality. Shortly thereafter, the trial court enjoined the Army from refusing to reenlist Watkins on the ground that the Army was equitably estopped from relying on the nonwaivable disqualification provisions that it had overlooked on the three previous occasions in which it had granted Watkins' application for reenlistment. 551 F.Supp. 212, 223 (W.D.Wash.1982).

On appeal, the Ninth Circuit panel reversed the trial court's injunction, holding that the equity powers of the federal courts could not be exercised to order military officials to violate their own regulations without a finding that the regulations were repugnant to either the Constitution or to statutory authority. 721 F.2d 687, 791 (9th Cir.1983) ("Watkins I"). The circuit court also remanded the case to the trial court, which subsequently held that the reenlistment regulations were repugnant to neither the Constitution nor any statutory authority and granted summary judgment to the Army. Watkins appealed again and alleged, *inter alia,* that the regulations violated his Fifth Amendment equal protection guarantees by disqualifying him solely on the basis of his homosexual orientation. He did not, however, challenge the constitutionality of that portion of the Army regulations that mandated disqualification from reenlistment for engaging in homosexual conduct. Rather, he claimed that the regulations constituted an invidious discrimination on the basis of his status as a homosexual.

In its second round with this case, the Ninth Circuit noted that under the regulations, the status of homosexual orientation, irrespective of the presence or absence of evidence of homosexual conduct, was the operative trait for disqualification from Army service. (In fact, the regulations did not mandate discharge or denial of reenlistment to an individual found to have committed an isolated homosexual act if the individual could establish that his or her sexual orientation was heterosexual by, for example, proving that the conduct occurred because of intoxication and was unlikely to recur.) As a preliminary matter, the court rejected the Army's claim that *Bowers* precluded an equal protection challenge to its regulations. The court read *Bowers* as limited solely to a due process challenge to a statute criminalizing homosexual sodomy. While recognizing that the *Bowers* Court had held that the right to privacy did not extend to private homosexual sodomy, the Ninth Circuit also indicated that the Court had not ruled in *Bowers* on whether the right to privacy would also prevent criminalization of heterosexual sodomy. Thus, the Ninth Circuit concluded, the Supreme Court in *Bowers* did not determine whether the equal protection, as opposed to the due process, clause prohibited a state from criminalizing homosexual, but not heterosexual sodomy. (It added that *Bowers* also failed to address the constitutionality of restrictions based on sexual orientation. This led the majority of the Ninth Circuit panel to go one step further and infer that the *Bowers* Court would not have upheld the Georgia statute had its proscription against consensual sodomy applied only to homosexual, and not to heterosexual, individuals.)

Turning then to the merits of the plaintiff's equal protection claim, the Ninth Circuit concluded that a homosexual classification should be subjected to strict scrutiny. The court admitted that since *Bowers* and other opinions refused to extend the right of privacy to homosexual conduct, this foreclosed a claim that a regulation banning homosexual conduct burdened the exercise of a fundamental or important substantive right to engage in such conduct. Nevertheless, it continued, persons of homosexual orientation constitute a suspect class and, therefore, a regulation punishing individuals on the sole basis of their sexual orientation was subject to strict equal protection scrutiny. It found that homosexuals satisfied the traditional indicia of suspectness, i.e., that they have been historically subjected to pernicious and sustained hostility and invidious discrimination based on inaccurate stereotypes or prejudice, that they are defined by an immutable attribute or characteristic that frequently is unrelated to ability to perform and that they represent a discrete and insular minority that lacks the political power necessary to obtain redress from the government. The court then concluded that while judicial review of military regulations is more deferential than comparable review of the actions of civilian agencies, the Army's mandatory exclusion based on sexual orientation did not survive strict scrutiny. It rejected the government's assertion of a compelling interest in enforcing society's moral consensus that homosexuality is evil. The court also suggested that the regulations were poorly tailored to advance the state's purported interest in avoiding the danger to military discipline that might result from emotional relationships between homosexuals of different military rank, since the regulations disqualified all homosexuals regardless of whether they have developed such emotional or sexual liaisons with other soldiers. Similarly, a ban on admitted homosexuals did not promote the Army's concern about security risks among gays who might be susceptible to blackmail. It therefore granted summary judgment in favor of the plaintiff Watkins, declared the regulations to be constitutionally void on their face and issued an injunction requiring the Army to consider Watkins' application for reenlistment without regard to his sexual orientation. 837 F.2d 1428 (9th Cir.1988) ("*Watkins II* ").

After the release of the panel opinion in *Watkins II,* the full court granted rehearing *en banc* and vacated the panel's opinion pending its *en banc* decision. The eleven member *en banc* court subsequently held that the Army was estopped from barring Watkins' reenlistment. 875 F.2d 699 (9th Cir.1989). Accordingly, it reversed the *Watkins I* panel opinion and found it unnecessary to address the constitutional issues raised in *Watkins II.* The court declared that *Watkins I* no longer stated the law of this circuit. The panel's holding that trial courts could not use equitable estoppel against the military to challenge the application of a statute or regulation to one individual, the en banc court reasoned, improperly required the trial court and the appellate panel in *Watkins II* to reach the broad constitutional issue when the case could have been decided on the narrow issue of equitable estoppel. In light of Watkins' outstanding record of service as well as the Army's acceptance of three reenlistment applications from Watkins in the full knowledge of his admitted homosexuality, the *en banc* court concluded that estopping the Army from denying reenlistment on the basis of Watkins' homosexuality would not disrupt any important military policies or adversely affect internal military affairs or the public interest and would protect Watkins from the loss of his career. Accordingly, the court reinstated the trial court's 1982 order estopping the Army from relying on its reenlistment regulation as a bar to Watkins' reenlistment. It also vacated the trial court's 1985 order and withdrew the appellate court panel opinions in *Watkins I* and *II*. Thus, of course, the panel's ruling in *Watkins II* that homosexual status is a suspect classification has been withdrawn. The Supreme Court denied the Army's petition for a writ of certiorari. ___ U.S. ___, 111 S.Ct. 384, 112 L.Ed.2d 395 (1990).

The constitutional issue subsequently was addressed by the Ninth Circuit in HIGH TECH GAYS v. DEFENSE INDUSTRIAL SECURITY CLEARANCE OFFICE, 895 F.2d 563 (9th Cir.1990). Adopting the rationales offered by the D.C. Circuit in *Padula* and the Federal Circuit in *Woodward*, the court declared that as there was no fundamental right to engage in homosexual conduct, and since homosexual conduct could therefore be criminalized, homosexuals could not constitute either a suspect or quasi-suspect class. The court also stated that the class of homosexuals did not meet all the criteria of suspectness since homosexuality was behavioral and not an immutable characteristic, and that homosexuals were not politically powerless. Accordingly, it held that a Department of Defense policy of subjecting all gay (but not all heterosexual) applicants for Secret and Top Secret security clearance to expanded investigations was to be subjected to rational basis scrutiny. It then ruled that the Defense Department had convinced it that counterintelligence agencies target homosexuals and, therefore, that subjecting them to expanded security investigations was rationally related to the government's legitimate interest in excluding individuals that are susceptible to coercion, blackmail or are otherwise vulnerable to counterintelligence efforts.

The Seventh Circuit also has rejected the status/conduct distinction. As you recall, in *Ben–Shalom, supra,* the court determined that the admission of homosexual orientation, even in the absence of an admission of participation in homosexual conduct, could "rationally and reasonably be viewed as reliable evidence of a desire and propensity to engage in homosexual conduct." 881 F.2d at 464. And while the court admitted that there could be exceptions to this general proposition, admission of status was "compelling evidence that [a] plaintiff has in the past and is likely to again engage in such conduct." Id. Thus, the court concluded:

"the regulation does not classify plaintiff based merely upon her status as a lesbian, but upon reasonable inferences about her probable conduct in the past and in the future. The Army need not shut its eyes to the practical realities of this situation, nor be compelled to engage in the sleuthing of soldiers' personal relationships for evidence of homosexual conduct in order to enforce its ban on homosexual acts * * *."

881 F.2d at 464. On the basis of this analysis, the court determined that the regulation did not contain a classification based solely on status and should be treated, for equal protection purposes, like any homosexual classification. Then, as to this issue, it agreed with the D.C. Circuit in *Padula* that the Supreme Court's ruling in *Bowers* that homosexual conduct could constitutionally be criminalized foreclosed denomination of homosexuals as a suspect class. Accordingly, the court applied rational basis scrutiny to the regulation and concluded that the classification therein was supported by legitimate military considerations. It therefore reversed the trial court and ordered the dismissal of the plaintiff's complaint.

One trial court has suggested that the armed forces' blanket exclusion of homosexuals was rationally related to the state's legitimate interest in maintaining the health of the armed forces and protecting the members thereof from a fatal and incurable disease—the HIV. While noting that its ruling was not predicated on this finding, the court in STEFFAN v. CHENEY, 780 F.Supp. 1 (D.D.C.1991) stated that its conclusions were supported by this consideration in light of studies, including one undertaken by the Presidential Commission on the Human Immunodeficiency Virus Epidemic, which reported that the HIV epidemic was predominantly confined to people engaging in either homosexual sex or intravenous drug use. For further discussion of the statutory and constitutional issues raised by anti-gay employment practices, see Developments In The Law, Sexual Orientation And The Law, 102 Harv.L.Rev. 1508 (1989); Sunstein, Sexual Orientation and The Constitution: A Note on the Relationship Between Due Process and Equal Protection, 55 U.Chi.L.Rev. 1161 (1988); Friedman, Constitutional and Statutory Challenges to Discrimination In Employment Based on Sexual Orientation, 64 Iowa L.Rev. 527 (1979).

3. Employing the same analysis relied upon in the principal case, courts have held that Title VII does not prohibit discrimination against transsexuals, as long as the defendant does not distinguish between male and female transsexuals. See Ulane v. Eastern Airlines, Inc., 742 F.2d 1081 (7th Cir.1984), cert. denied, 471 U.S. 1017, 105 S.Ct. 2023, 85 L.Ed.2d 304 (1985); Holloway v. Arthur Andersen & Co., 566 F.2d 659 (9th Cir.1977); Sommers v. Budget Marketing, Inc., 667 F.2d 748 (8th Cir.1982); Powell v. Read's, Inc., 436 F.Supp. 369 (D.Md.1977). For further discussion of these cases and a suggested alternative analysis, see Note, Ulane v. Eastern Airlines: Title VII and Transsexualism, 80 Nw.U.L.Rev. 1037 (1986).

4. While a large number of cities and counties have enacted statutes prohibiting discrimination on the basis of sexual orientation, only six states (New Jersey, Hawaii, Massachusetts, Wisconsin, Vermont and Connecticut) and the District of Columbia have enacted such a statute. There is also the possibility that a plaintiff can bring a claim under state common law. See e.g. Collins v. Shell Oil Co., Triton Biosciences, Inc., 56 FEP Cases 440 (Cal.Sup.1991)(trial court awarded over $5 million in punitive and compensatory damages to executive who was fired for private homosexual conduct occuring away from his place of employment; complaint included fraud, contract and intentional infliction of emotional distress claims).

5. "Protective" State Labor Legislation

ROSENFELD v. SOUTHERN PACIFIC CO.

United States Court of Appeals, Ninth Circuit, 1971.
444 F.2d 1219.

HAMLEY, CIRCUIT JUDGE.

Leah Rosenfeld brought this action against Southern Pacific Company pursuant to section 706(f) of Title VII of the Civil Rights Act of 1964(Act). Plaintiff, an employee of the company, alleged that in filling the position of agent-telegrapher at Thermal, California, in March, 1966, Southern Pacific discriminated against her solely because of her sex, by assigning the position to a junior male employee.

* * *

On the merits, Southern Pacific argues that it is the company's policy to exclude women, generically, from certain positions. The company restricts these job opportunities to men for two basic reasons: (1) the arduous nature of the work-related activity renders women physically unsuited for the jobs; (2) appointing a woman to the position would result in a violation of California labor laws and regulations which limit hours of work for women and restrict the weight they are permitted to lift. Positions such as that of agent-telegrapher at Thermal fall within the ambit of this policy. The company concludes that effectuation of this policy is not proscribed by Title VII of the Civil Rights Act due to the exception created by the Act for those situations where sex is a "bona fide occupational qualification."

While the agent-telegrapher position at Thermal is no longer in existence, the work requirements which that position entailed are illustrative of the kind of positions which are denied to female employees under the company's labor policy described above. During the harvesting season, the position may require work in excess of ten hours a day and eighty hours a week.[6] The position requires the heavy physical effort involved in climbing over and around boxcars to adjust their vents, collapse their bunkers and close and seal their doors. In addition, the employee must lift various objects weighing more than twenty-five pounds and, in some instances, more than fifty pounds.

The critical question presented by this argument is whether, consistent with Title VII of the Civil Rights Act of 1964, the company may apply such a labor policy.* * *

* * *

* * * [T]he company points out that, apart from its intrinsic merit, its policy is compelled by California labor laws. One of the reasons

---

6. It was, indeed, this opportunity to earn overtime pay that made this position attractive to plaintiff.

Mrs. Rosenfeld was refused assignment to the Thermal position, and would presumably be refused assignment to like positions, is that she could not perform the tasks of such a position without placing the company in violation of California laws. Not only would the repeated lifting of weights in excess of twenty-five pounds violate the state's Industrial Welfare Order No. 9–63, but for her to lift more than fifty pounds as required by the job would violate section 1251 of the California Labor Code. Likewise, the peak-season days of over ten hours would violate section 1350 of the California Labor Code.

It would appear that these state law limitations upon female labor run contrary to the general objectives of Title VII of the Civil Rights Act of 1964 * * * and are therefore, by virtue of the Supremacy Clause, supplanted by Title VII. However, appellants * * * rely on section 703(e) and argue that since positions such as the Thermal agent-telegrapher required weight-lifting and maximum hours in excess of those permitted under the California statutes, being a man was indeed a bona fide occupational qualification. This argument assumes that Congress, having established by Title VII the policy that individuals must be judged as individuals, and not on the basis of characteristics generally attributed to racial, religious, or sex groups, was willing for this policy to be thwarted by state legislation to the contrary.

We find no basis in the statute or its legislative history for such an assumption. Section 1104 of the Act, provides that nothing contained in the Act should be construed as indicating an intent to occupy the field in which the Act operates, to the exclusion of State laws or the same subject matter, nor be construed as invalidating any provision of state law " * * * unless such provision is inconsistent with any of the purposes of this Act, or any provision thereof." This section was added to the Act to save state laws aimed at preventing or punishing discrimination, and as the quoted words indicate, not to save inconsistent state laws.

Still more to the point is section 708 of the Act, which provides that nothing in Title VII shall be deemed to exempt or relieve any person from any liability, duty, penalty, or punishment provided by any present or future state law " * * * other than any such law which purports to require or permit the doing of any act which would be an unlawful employment practice under this title." This section was designed to preserve the effectiveness of state antidiscrimination laws.[7]

The Commission, created by the provisions of Title VII of the Act, through its published Guidelines and Policy Statements has, albeit after considerable hesitation, taken the position that state "protective" legislation, of the type in issue here, conflicts with the policy of non-discrimination manifested by Title VII of the Act. * * * It is implicit in this Commission pronouncement that state labor laws inconsistent with the general objectives of the Act must be disregarded. The

---

7. The legislative history is replete with statements making it clear that Congress was specifically aware that Title VII would undercut many state labor laws.

Supreme Court has recently observed that the administrative interpretation of the Act by the enforcing agency "is entitled to great deference." Griggs v. Duke Power Co., 401 U.S. 424, 91 S.Ct. 849, 28 L.Ed.2d 158 (1971).[10]

* * *

Under the principles set forth above, we conclude that Southern Pacific's employment policy is not excusable under * * * the state statutes. * * *

In the district court one of the company's defenses was that of good faith reliance upon the Commission's Guidelines then in effect. This defense was relevant to plaintiff's prayer for damages. While the district court did not award damages, it did find that the company did not rely on any written interpretation or opinion of the Commission, and concluded that the company "discriminated" against plaintiff solely because of her sex by refusing to assign her to the Thermal position.

In our opinion the finding on the question of reliance is unnecessary to the disposition of the cause and, in any event, should not have been entered without according Southern Pacific an evidentiary hearing. Moreover, in view of the California statutes referred to above, the conclusion that the company engaged in "discrimination" in refusing to assign plaintiff to the Thermal position carries with it no invidious connotation. Prior to a judicial determination such as evidenced by this opinion, an employer can hardly be faulted for following the explicit provisions of applicable state law.

* * *

Affirmed.

CHAMBERS, CIRCUIT JUDGE (dissenting).

* * *

NOTES AND PROBLEMS FOR DISCUSSION

1. State "protective" labor statutes have been uniformly invalidated under the supremacy clause on the ground that their enforcement violates Title VII's ban on sex discrimination. Accordingly, the courts have struck down state laws imposing special requirements on women with respect to required rest periods, Ridinger v. General Motors Corp., 325 F.Supp. 1089 (S.D.Ohio 1971), reversed on other grounds, 474 F.2d 949 (6th Cir.1972); seating arrangements, Manning v. General Motors Corp., 3 FEP Cases 968 (N.D.Ohio 1971), affirmed, 466 F.2d 812 (6th Cir.1972), cert. denied, 410 U.S. 946, 93 S.Ct. 1366, 35 L.Ed.2d 613 (1973); and exclusion from certain occupations, Sail'er Inn, Inc. v. Kirby, 5 Cal.3d 1, 95 Cal.Rptr. 329, 485 P.2d 529 (1971). See generally,

---

10. In the *Griggs* case, Chief Justice Burger, speaking for the Court, also pointed out that it is immaterial that the state laws in question, or the employer's labor policy, were not enacted or prescribed with an intent to discriminate. Said the Court: "Under the Act, practices, procedures, or tests neutral on their face, and even neutral in terms of intent, cannot be maintained if they operate to 'freeze' the status quo of prior discriminatory employment practices." * * *

Kennedy, Sex Discrimination: State Protective Laws Since Title VII, 47 Not. D.Law. 514 (1972).

2. Do you agree with the ruling in the principal case that an employer should be insulated from back pay liability by its good faith reliance on extent state labor legislation? Is it appropriate to impose the cost of discrimination on innocent employees rather than on the innocent employer? Does this ruling create any disincentive on employees to challenge other potentially discriminatory state laws? The courts, as in *Rosenfeld*, refusing to compel employers to subject themselves to possible state prosecution in order to comply with Title VII, deny back pay upon a showing of employer good faith reliance on state protective legislation. See Williams v. General Foods Corp., 492 F.2d 399 (7th Cir.1974); Manning v. General Motors Corp., 466 F.2d 812 (6th Cir.1972), cert. denied, 410 U.S. 946, 93 S.Ct. 1366, 35 L.Ed.2d 613 (1973). What if a similar or identical statute of another state had been judicially invalidated before the employer's conduct occurred? See Alaniz v. California Processors, Inc., 785 F.2d 1412 (9th Cir.1986) (employer liable for back pay from date it became aware of suspension of agency order restricting women from heavy lifting).

3. Once a court determines that a state protective labor statute conflicts with Title VII, what action should it take with respect to that enactment? Ordinarily, a court can achieve sexual parity in one of two alternative ways. It can invalidate the law entirely or it can take the benefit or restriction originally applicable only to women and extend it to all employees. The latter option, however, is not realistically available in the context of exclusionary statutes—i.e.—statutes that exclude women from certain occupations, from lifting objects over a specified weight, or from working more than a certain number of hours or days. In Hays v. Potlatch Forests, Inc., 465 F.2d 1081 (8th Cir.1972), the court held that any conflict between Title VII and an Arkansas statute requiring employers to pay only women employees premium pay for time worked in excess of eight hours per day could be avoided by requiring employers to pay premium compensation to all employees after eight hours of daily work. The EEOC Guidelines go beyond *Hays* by requiring that the "benefits" of all sex-oriented State protective statutes be extended to both sexes. However, for all but minimum wage and premium pay statutes, the Guidelines recognize a business necessity defense to the extension requirement. See 29 C.F.R. § 1604.2(b)(3), (4) (1972). Do you agree with this result? Can it be argued that extension results in governmental imposition of terms and conditions of employment that should be left to private negotiation absent a clear declaration of legislative intent to intervene in this area? See Burns v. Rohr Corp., 346 F.Supp. 994 (S.D.Cal.1972) (refusing to order extension of California regulation requiring employers to give ten minute rest breaks every four hours to female employees). Doesn't extension of state laws by a federal court also raise a difficult issue of federal-state relations? See Homemakers, Inc. v. Division of Industrial Welfare, 509 F.2d 20 (9th Cir.1974), cert. denied, 423 U.S. 1063, 96 S.Ct. 803, 46 L.Ed.2d 655 (1976) (refusing to extend California statute requiring payment of premium pay to covered women employees).

Chapter 4

PROCEDURAL REQUIREMENTS FOR PRIVATE SECTOR EMPLOYEES

Section 705 of Title VII creates the Equal Employment Opportunity Commission as the agency responsible for the enforcement of the Act. Congress did not, however, give the EEOC the kind of cease and desist powers enjoyed by some government agencies such as the National Labor Relations Board. Under Section 706 the EEOC must accept and investigate complaints of discrimination and, if the commission finds "reasonable cause to believe the charge is true," it must "endeavor to eliminate any such alleged unlawful employment practice by informal methods of conference, conciliation and persuasion." The EEOC also has the authority to file suit in cases where cause has been found and conciliation has been unsuccessful. Realizing that the EEOC would not be able to resolve all complaints filed with it under the act, Congress also provided in Sections 706(e) and (f) for a private right of action by persons claiming unlawful discrimination. Those sections require, however, that persons filing their own suits under the act, first file timely charges of discrimination with the EEOC and observe other technical requirements of the act as prerequisites to litigation.

The procedural requirements of Title VII for private litigants and the EEOC are discussed in this chapter.

SECTION A. SUITS BY INDIVIDUALS

1. The "Timeliness" Requirements of Title VII

ALLEN v. AVON PRODUCTS, INC.

United States District Court for the Southern District of New York, 1988.
55 FEP Cases 1662.

SHIRLEY WOHL KRAM, DISTRICT JUDGE:

The above-captioned action is presently before this Court upon the motion of defendant Avon Products, Inc. ("Avon") for summary judgment with respect to plaintiff Lorraine Allen's federal employment discrimination claim and pendent state law slander claim, pursuant to Rule 56 of the Federal Rules of Civil Procedure. Avon moves to dismiss the pendent claim, pursuant to Rules 12(b)(1) and (6) of the Federal Rules of Civil Procedure. In addition, Avon moves to dismiss the action in its entirety, pursuant to 28 U.S.C. Sec. 1915(d). For the reasons stated below, Avon's motion to dismiss and for summary judgment with respect to the federal claim is denied. With respect to the pendent claim, Avon's motion to dismiss is granted and the Court will thus not reach Avon's motion for summary judgment.

UNDISPUTED FACTS

Avon employed Allen as an art director in its sales promotion department from July, 1968, until her discharge on or about January 28, 1972. On August 29, 1972, Allen filed a sex discrimination charge ("first charge") against Avon with the Equal Employment Opportunity Commission ("EEOC"). The EEOC forwarded the first charge to the New York State Division of Human Rights ("NYSDHR"). The NYSDHR acknowledged receipt of Allen's papers from the EEOC on August 31, 1972. On February 14, 1973, Allen filed a second sex discrimination charge ("second charge") against Avon with the EEOC.

On or about June 1, 1974, the EEOC filed an action against Avon in this Court, alleging gender and racial discrimination. The EEOC forwarded Allen's charges to its litigation center in the interest of including them in negotiations between the EEOC and Avon. Although the EEOC litigation was settled on June 21, 1977, the parties were unable to enter into a consent decree covering the issues raised in Allen's charges. Allen rejected numerous offers from the EEOC for a statutory notice of a right to sue Avon in federal court, and requested that the EEOC continue conciliation efforts. On July 1, 1981, over Allen's objection, the EEOC issued Allen a right to sue notice and dismissed her charges, finding that there was no reasonable cause to believe that discrimination had occurred.

On September 29, 1981, Allen, proceeding pro se, submitted a complaint and an application for leave to proceed forma pauperis to the Pro Se Office of this Court. In a letter dated September 30, 1981, the pro se clerk requested that Allen submit a supplemental affidavit clarifying her pauperis application. On or about October 5, 1981, Allen complied with this request. On November 9, 1981, this Court granted leave to proceed in forma pauperis and her complaint was docketed. On December 1981, Allen, proceeding pro se, filed an amended complaint. On March 11, 1983, she filed an order to show cause seeking leave to amend the amended complaint. Her application was granted and on April 8, 1983, a second amended complaint was filed. Allen alleges that Avon engaged in unlawful employment practices in violation of 42 U.S.C. Sec. 2000e–5 and slander in violation of state tort law. Allen subsequently retained an attorney who filed a notice of appearance in this case on December 3, 1987.

DISCUSSION

Avon moves for summary judgment with respect to the federal employment discrimination claim on the grounds that: Allen failed to file a timely charge with the NYSDHR as required under 42 U.S.C. § 2000e–5(c); Allen failed to commence this action within the 90-day right to sue period as required under 42 U.S.C. § 2000e–5(f); and laches. Avon moves to dismiss the complaint on the ground that Allen submitted a false affidavit of poverty, in violation of 28 U.S.C. § 1915(d).

* * *

Filing of Charge with NYSDHR

Avon alleges that Allen failed to file a timely charge with the NYSDHR. Title 42 Section 2000(e)–5(e) of the United States Code, requires that all claims for employment discrimination be filed with the EEOC within 180 days from the date the alleged unlawful employment discrimination occurred. An exception to this requirement allows local agencies in states which have them, known as deferral states, the opportunity to review discrimination claims and act on them before the EEOC proceeds. In such cases the statute requires that the claimant file with the EEOC within a total of 300 days, or within 30 days after receiving notice that the state agency has terminated proceedings, whichever is earlier.

A separate section provides that a claimant may not file a complaint with the EEOC in deferral states until 60 days after the proceedings have been commenced by the appropriate state agency unless that state has terminated its proceedings in less than the allotted 60 days. 42 U.S.C. § 2000(e)–5(c). If a claim is filed first with the EEOC, the EEOC will defer it to the state agency for action for a period of 60 days. Id. § 2000(e)–5(d).

The Supreme Court has interpreted these rules to require that a claimant in deferral states has 240 days within which to file with the state agency in order to preserve federal jurisdiction. Mohasco Corporation v. Silver, 447 U.S. 807, 815, n. 16, 100 S.Ct. 2486, 2491, n. 16, 65 L.Ed.2d 532 (1980). A complaint cannot be filed with the EEOC until after the state agency has had the statutorily prescribed 60–day deferral period. Id. at 825–26, 100 S.Ct. at 2497. When a charge is filed with the EEOC prior to exhaustion of state remedies, state proceedings may be initiated by the EEOC acting on behalf of the complainant rather than by the complainant herself. Love v. Pullman Co., 404 U.S. 522, 525, 92 S.Ct. 616, 618, 30 L.Ed.2d 679 (1972). "Upon termination of the state proceedings or expiration of the 60–day deferral period, whichever comes first, the EEOC automatically assumes concurrent jurisdiction of the complaint." New York Gaslight Club, Inc. v. Carey, 447 U.S. 54, 64, 100 S.Ct. 2024, 2031, 64 L.Ed.2d 723 (1980), (citing Love v. Pullman Co., supra, 404 U.S. at 526, 92 S.Ct. at 618).

In the instant case, Allen was discharged from her employment on or about January 28, 1972. She filed her first charge with the EEOC on August 29, 1972, 215 days later. The EEOC, acting on behalf of Allen, forwarded this charge to the NYSDHR. Love v. Pullman Co., supra at 525, 92 S.Ct. at 618. In a letter dated August 31, 1972, the NYSDHR verified having received Allen's papers from the EEOC. Accordingly, the Court finds that proceedings were initiated with the

NYSDHR within the requisite 240 day period. Mohasco v. Silver, supra at 815, n. 16, 100 S.Ct. at 2491 n. 16.

Filing of the Case at Bar

Avon alleges that Allen failed to commence this action within the 90–day right to sue period as required under 42 U.S.C. § 2000e–5(f). Title 42, section 2000e–5(f)(1) of the United States Code provides in relevant part that:

> If a charge filed with the [EEOC] . . . is dismissed by the [EEOC] or if within one hundred and eighty days from the filing of such charge . . . [the EEOC], has not filed a civil action . . ., or the [EEOC] has not entered into a conciliation agreement to which the person aggrieved is a party, the [EEOC] . . . shall so notify the person aggrieved and within ninety days after . . . [receipt] of such notice a civil action may be brought against respondent named in the charge . . .

In the case at bar, the EEOC issued Allen her Notice of Right to Sue on July 1, 1981. On September 29, 1981, Allen proceeding pro se submitted her original complaint and an application for leave to proceed in forma pauperis to the Pro Se Office of this Court. In a letter dated September 30, 1981, the pro se clerk requested that Allen submit a supplemental affidavit clarifying her in forma pauperis application. On or about October 5, 1981, Allen complied with this request. On November 9, 1981, this Court granted leave to proceed in forma pauperis and docketed her complaint. Although Allen's original complaint and the Order granting leave to proceed in forma pauperis were not docketed with the Clerk of the Court until November 9, 1981, the delay between Allen's application and that date resulted from delays brought about by requests from the Court, and not from any lack of diligence by the plaintiff. Therefore, this Court holds that Allen's filing of the suit occurred when she submitted her complaint to the pro se Office on September 30, 1981 and that her action was commenced within the 90–day period pursuant to 42 U.S.C. § 2000e–5(f)(1). Nielsen v. Flower Hospital, 639 F.Supp. 738, 740 (S.D.N.Y.1986) (Presentation of a Title VII complaint to the Pro Se Clerk of this Court, if accompanied by either an application for leave to proceed in forma pauperis or the filing fee, represents the commencement of an action for the purposes of satisfying the 90–day filing requirement); George Dzaba v. Blyth Eastman Paine Webber, No. 84 Civ. 3711(GLG)(S.D.N.Y.1985) (available October 11, 1987, on Westlaw, DCTU library) (Submission of an in forma pauperis application and complaint to Pro Se Office tolls the 90–day filing period for the duration of the administrative and judicial review), citing Rosenberg v. Martin, 478 F.2d 520, 522 n.1a (2d Cir. 1973), cert. denied, 414 U.S. 872, 94 S.Ct. 102, 38 L.Ed.2d 90 (1973).

Laches

Citing the fact that more than nine years passed between the time Allen filed her initial charge of discrimination with the EEOC and the time she finally filed suit in this Court, Avon moves for summary judgment based on laches. In order for an action to be barred under the equitable theory of laches, defendant must establish (1) that the plaintiff's delay in bringing the lawsuit was unreasonable and inexcusable, and (2) that this delay resulted in material prejudice to the defendant's case.

The facts ... indicate that proceedings were initiated with the appropriate administrative agencies within the requisite time period. As this Court stated in Cosgrove v. Sears Roebuck and Co., No. 81 Civ. 3482(CSH) (S.D.N.Y. May 26, 1982) (available October 11, 1987, on LEXIS, Genfed library, Dist file), a disgruntled employee should be commended rather than criticized for attempting to stay out of court by allowing the administrative agency charged with enforcement of Title VII to attempt to settle amicably her suit...." Allen brought suit within the time allotted after receiving a Notice of Right to Sue from the EEOC. She was not required to litigate prior to the termination of the EEOC's investigation and attempts at conciliation. Staples v. Avis Rent–a–Car System, Inc., 537 F.Supp. 1215, 1219 (W.D.N.Y.1982) (citations omitted). The Court finds that Allen's delay in filing this action was neither unreasonable nor inexcusable, and thus will not reach the issue of prejudice to Avon. Accordingly, Avon's motion for summary judgment with respect to the federal claim is denied.

[Sections of Judge Kram's opinion discussing the validity of the plaintiff's affidavit of poverty and of her state law claim are omitted.]

NOTES AND PROBLEMS FOR DISCUSSION

1. Section 706(e) of Title VII requires that a charge be filed with the EEOC within 180 days "after the alleged unlawful practice occurred." As explained in *Allen v. Avon Products*, in a state with a deferral agency the charging party has 300 days to file with the EEOC. Section 706(c) of Title VII provides that where a qualifying state or local agency exists to remedy unlawful discrimination, "no charge may be filed * * * by the person aggrieved * * * [until] sixty days after state proceedings have been commenced * * * unless such proceedings have been earlier terminated." "Initial resort to state and local remedies is mandated, and recourse to the federal forums is appropriate only when the state law does not provide prompt or complete relief." New York Gaslight Club, Inc. v. Carey, 447 U.S. 54, 65, 100 S.Ct. 2024, 2031, 64 L.Ed.2d 723 (1980). The practical effect of these limitation periods in a deferral state is that the charging party has 240 days in which to file with the state agency.

State fair employment laws typically provide limitation periods similar to those in Title VII for filing charges with the state agencies. Should compliance with the state filing period be required of one who takes advantage of the 300 day period for filing with the EEOC? Since the 300–day period was intended to give the state agency time to investigate and resolve complaints before resort to the federal process, does it make any sense to give the charging party, who has failed to comply with state law and thus cannot obtain a state investigation, an additional 120 days to file with the EEOC? In EEOC v. COMMERCIAL OFFICE PRODUCTS CO., 486 U.S. 107, 108 S.Ct. 1666, 100 L.Ed.2d 96 (1988) the Supreme Court also held that the 300–day filing period in deferral states should apply irrespective of whether the charge is initially filed within the period allowed by state law. A majority of the Court reasoned that a contrary result would confuse lay persons attempting to file charges and would require the EEOC to make numerous ad hoc determinations of whether state limitation periods were jurisdictional and of whether the periods were equitably tolled under state law—determinations that "the EEOC has neither the time nor the expertise to make * * * under the varying laws of the many deferral States * * *." Id. at 122, 108 S.Ct. at 1675.

2. As was the case in *Allen*, charging parties in deferral states frequently file their charges with the EEOC without complaining first to the state agency. The EEOC cannot begin its investigation of such a complaint, but will not reject it as premature. In LOVE v. PULLMAN, 404 U.S. 522, 92 S.Ct. 616, 30 L.Ed.2d 679 (1972), the Supreme Court approved the EEOC's "deferral" procedure, now incorporated in 29 C.F.R. § 1601.13, under which the Commission refers a charge to the appropriate state or local agency on behalf of the grievant and defers its own action until the period of reference to the agency expires. The charge is received by the EEOC but not "filed" within the meaning of the statute. In endorsing this procedure, the Court noted:

Nothing in the Act suggests that the state proceedings may not be initiated by the EEOC acting on behalf of the complainant rather than by the complainant himself, nor is there any requirement that the complaint to the state agency be made in writing rather than by oral referral. Further, we cannot agree with the respondent's claim that the EEOC may not properly hold a complaint in "suspended animation," automatically filing it upon termination of the state proceedings.

404 U.S. at 525–526, 92 S.Ct. at 618.

The EEOC maintains "work sharing" agreements with most state deferral agencies under which the agency initially receiving the charge will process it. When the EEOC first receives the charge, it refers it to the state agency under the procedure approved in *Love v. Pullman*. The state agency in turn waives initial processing of the charge and sends it back to the EEOC for investigation while retaining jurisdiction to proceed in the future after the EEOC has completed its processing of the charge. The EEOC treats the referral of a charge to the state agency as the filing of the charge with that agency under *Love v. Pullman* and the waiver of the right initially to process the charge as a "termination" by the state agency of its proceedings within the meaning of Section 706(c), so as to allow the filing of the charge with the federal agency. The validity of such agreements was tested in EEOC v. COMMERCIAL OFFICE PRODUCTS CO., *supra*, where the claimant filed her charge of sex discrimination with the EEOC on the 289th day after discharge and the EEOC sent the charge to the state agency. That agency returned the charge to the EEOC indicating that it was waiving its right initially to process the charge and the EEOC began its investigation which resulted in the suit. The Tenth Circuit, citing the "clear requirement" of § 706(c) and Mohasco Corp. v. Silver, 447 U.S. 807, 100 S.Ct. 2486, 65 L.Ed.2d 532 (1980), held that *either* 60 days must lapse after initial institution of proceedings with the state agency *or* that agency must have both commenced and terminated its proceedings before the complaint may be deemed filed with the EEOC. The Court further held that the acknowledgement of receipt of the charge by the state agency and waiver of initial processing could not be construed as a commencement and termination of proceedings that toll the 60 day referral period. Accordingly, the Court held that the charge had not been timely filed with the EEOC because the 60–day period had not expired before the 300th day. EEOC v. Commercial Office Products Co., 803 F.2d 581 (10th Cir.1986). The Supreme Court reversed, holding that 706(c)'s requirement that the state agency "terminate" its proceedings included an agency's decision not to proceed for some interval of time even if the agency retained authority to activate its investigatory mechanisms in the future. 486 U.S. at 114–15, 108 S.Ct. at 1670–71. The Court stated that the two goals underlying the deferral provisions of the statute—deference to the states and efficient processing of claims—supported its conclusion that waiver by the state agency of the 60 day deferral period was sufficient to "terminate" the state agency's proceeding. Id. at 116–21, 108 S.Ct. at 1671–74.

Under a work sharing agreement, may a charge be both initiated and terminated by the state agency without the state ever being formally referred the charge within the 300 day period? Courts that have addressed the issue after *Commercial Office Products* have held that the state agency's waiver of the right to initially process the charge may be self-executing so that the filing of a charge with the EEOC simultaneously initiates and terminates state proceedings. EEOC v. Techalloy Maryland, Inc., 894 F.2d 676 (4th Cir.1990); Green v. Los Angeles County Superintendent of Schools, 883 F.2d 1472 (9th Cir.1989); Griffin v. Air Products and Chemicals, Inc., 883 F.2d 940 (11th Cir.1989). Cf., Sofferin v. American Airlines, Inc., 923 F.2d 552 (7th Cir.1991) (question of fact whether state agency through work sharing agreement had "prospectively waived" deferral period on charges initiated with EEOC). Is such a result consistent with the Court's holding in *Mohasco* that the "statutory plan was not designed to give the worker in a deferral state the option of choosing between his state and federal remedy"? See, Hong v. Children's Memorial Hospital, 936 F.2d 967 (7th Cir.1991) (characterizing work sharing agreement as "administrative shell game").

3. In ZIPES v. TRANS WORLD AIRLINES, INC., 455 U.S. 385, 102 S.Ct. 1127, 71 L.Ed.2d 234 (1982), the Supreme Court held that "filing a timely charge of discrimination with the EEOC is not a jurisdictional prerequisite to suit in federal court, but a requirement that, like a statute of limitations is subject to waiver, estoppel, and equitable tolling." 455 U.S. at 393, 102 S.Ct. at 1132. Courts have recognized a number of equitable considerations that will interrupt or delay the period for filing the charge with EEOC. They include:

Filing With The Wrong Agency: In Morgan v. Washington Manufacturing Co., 660 F.2d 710 (6th Cir.1981), a discharged employee wrote a letter to President Carter within two months of her termination complaining of discrimination by her employer. The White House forwarded the letter to the Wage and Hour Office of the Department of Labor. The Labor Department sought more information from the potential plaintiff and finally referred the complaint to the EEOC shortly after the 180 day period had expired. The Sixth Circuit held that "in the absence of prejudice to the defendant or a showing of bad faith or lack of diligence by a claimant, equitable considerations should toll the 180 day period for filing a complaint under Title VII when the claimant makes a timely filing with a federal agency, like the Labor Department, which has jurisdiction in some fields of employment discrimination and when that complaint is forwarded to the EEOC shortly after the time period has expired." 660 F.2d at 712. In Husch v. Szabo Food Service Co., 851 F.2d 999 (7th Cir.1988) the employer's corporate headquarters was in Illinois where the charging party was employed. The alleged discrimination took place in the employer's regional office in Connecticut. The charging party should have filed her charge with the Connecticut state agency but instead filed it with Illinois' agency and did not learn of the mistake until the time period to file in Connecticut had expired. Noting that the employer was a nationwide concern and that the employee had filed her charge in one of the states where a reasonable person would believe that the discrimination occurred, the Seventh Circuit held that dismissal of the employee's action "simply because she was unable to decipher the contradictory and confusing corporate structure of [the employer] in order to determine the exact state in which she allegedly was discriminated against" would be unfair. 851 F.2d at 1004. Cf. Smith v. General Scanning, Inc., 832 F.2d 96, 97 (7th Cir.1987) (filing charge in state with no connection to alleged discrimination will not toll running of filing period).

Mistaken or Misleading Information from Agency: See, Gray v. Phillips Petroleum Co., 858 F.2d 610, 613 (10th Cir.1988) (where EEOC misled charging parties into untimely action, equitable considerations support tolling of time limits); Gonzalez–Aller Balseyro v. GTE Lenkurt, Inc., 702 F.2d 857, 858–59 (10th Cir.1983) (180–day limitation period tolled because letter from court clerk misled plaintiff into filing late); White v. Dallas Independent School District, 581 F.2d 556, 562 (5th Cir.1978) (charging party "entitled to rely on ... seemingly authoritative statements by agency presumed to know the most about these matters) Gray v. Phillips Petroleum Co., 858 F.2d 610, 613 (10th Cir.1988) (where EEOC misled charging parties into untimely action, equitable considerations support tolling of time limits). Cf. Cornett v. AVCO Financial Services, Inc., 792 F.2d 447, 450 (4th Cir.1986) (court lacks power to proceed with suit where EEOC mistakenly referred plaintiff's complaint to wrong state agency under deferral statute). The Fifth Circuit has held that, even if misinformation from the EEOC would equitably toll the filing period, misleading assurances by a state agency that it had forwarded the charge to the EEOC would not stop the period. Chappell v. EMCO Machine Works Co., 601 F.2d 1295 (5th Cir.1979).

Misconduct of Defendant: Misrepresentation, concealment, intimidation or other actions by the employer which it knew or reasonably should have known would cause a delay in filing the EEOC charge will toll the 180–day period. See, Felty v. Graves–Humphreys Co., 785 F.2d 516 (4th Cir.1986) (offer of generous severance payment conditioned on not talking with other employees about termination); Clark v. Resistoflex Co., 854 F.2d 762 (5th Cir.1988) (employer's warning that severance benefits could end if terminated employee took any action prejudicial to employer may estop the employer from raising untimeliness of charge as defense—reasonable trier of fact could conclude that employer worded severance agreement so as to deter employee from asserting rights under ADEA); McClinton v. Alabama By–Products Corp., 743 F.2d 1483 (11th Cir.1984) (failure to post notices of law in workplace as required by Act); Bilka v. Pepe's Inc., 601 F.Supp. 1254 (N.D.Ill. 1985) (threats). Cf. Pruet Production Co. v. Ayles, 784 F.2d 1275 (5th Cir.1986) (no misrepresentation or concealment that would have lulled employee into missing deadline); Dillman v. Combustion Engineering, Inc., 784 F.2d 57 (2d Cir.1986) (offer of severance benefits not misleading when EEOC notices posted in workplace); Foutty v. Equifax Services, Inc., 55 FEP Cases 1344 (D.Kan.1991) (plaintiff not entitled to equitable tolling of period for filing charge because defendant's counsel had requested her "patience and understanding" while defendant was considering her settlement proposal, where defendant did not promise to settle case and did not attempt to prevent her from filing charge).

What other circumstances might reasonably operate to toll the filing period? See, Moody v. Bayliner Marine Corp., 664 F.Supp. 232 (E.D.N.C.1987); Llewellyn v. Celanese Corp., 693 F.Supp. 369 (W.D.N.C.1988) (employee's mentally disabled condition brought on by sexual harassment justifies tolling of charge-filing period). Would failure to tell an employee why he was being demoted constitute the kind of misrepresentation that ought to toll the filing period? The kind of employment action that will start the running of the filing period and the kind of notice the charging party must have of such action will be discussed in Section 2 of this chapter, *infra*.

4. The period for filing the EEOC charge will not, however, be tolled by the pursuit of a remedy, separate and apart from Title VII, such as a grievance procedure contained in a collective bargaining agreement. In ALEXANDER v. GARDNER–DENVER CO., 415 U.S. 36, 94 S.Ct. 1011, 39 L.Ed.2d 147 (1974), the Court stressed that contractual rights and remedies are distinct from statutory rights and held that an employee does not waive his right to assert a Title VII claim by filing and pursuing a union grievance with respect to the practice alleged to be discriminatory. Since contractual rights are totally separate from and independent of the employee's rights under Title VII, the Court held in INTERNATIONAL UNION OF ELECTRICAL, RADIO AND MACHINE WORKERS, LOCAL 790 v. ROBBINS & MYERS, INC., 429 U.S. 229, 97 S.Ct. 441, 50 L.Ed.2d 427 (1976), that pursuit of relief through a grievance procedure does not interrupt the period for filing an EEOC charge. The *Robbins & Myers* Court rejected arguments that equitable tolling principles should be applied because the employee was not seeking to assert his statutory (Title VII) claim in the grievance proceeding. Presumably, the Court felt the employee could not be misled under these circumstances as to the legal effect of filing the grievance. Note that the filing of an EEOC charge does not toll the running of any other statute of limitations applicable to an federal or state claim. Chapter 8 *infra*.

5. Section 706(b) (Sec. 2000e–5(b)) provides in relevant part that "charges shall be in writing under oath or affirmation and shall contain such information and be in such form as the Commission requires." EEOC regulations provide that "[a] charge may be amended to cure technical defects or omissions, including failure to verify the charge ... Such amendments ... will relate back to the date the charge was first received." 29 C.F.R. Sec. 1601.12(b) Most courts that have addressed the issue have held that the EEOC has the authority to decide that a subsequent verification (outside of the 180–day period) relates back to the date of the initial filing of a written statement describing the charge and satisfies the statutory requirement. See e.g., Philbin v. General Electric Capital Auto Lease, Inc., 929 F.2d 321, 324 (7th Cir.1991); Peterson v. City of Wichita, 888 F.2d 1307 (10th Cir.1989), cert. denied, 495 U.S. 932, 110 S.Ct. 2173, 109 L.Ed.2d 502 (1990). Cf., Sparkman v. Combined International, 690 F.Supp. 723 (N.D.Ill. 1988) (charge must be verified within filing period to be timely). An amendment to a pending charge that adds a new and distinct claim will not, however, relate back to the original filing date. See, Hornsby v. Conoco, Inc., 777 F.2d 243, (5th Cir.1985).

6. Under what circumstances may an employee waive the right to file an EEOC charge? May an employer condition payment of severance benefits on the employee's waiver of his right to file an EEOC charge? In EEOC v.

Cosmair, Inc., 821 F.2d 1085 (5th Cir.1987), a discharged employee was offered continuation of his salary and medical benefits for 39 weeks in exchange for a release from all claims, including those arising under state and federal discrimination in employment laws. The employee signed the release and thereafter filed an EEOC charge alleging age discrimination (the ADEA is discussed in Chapter 10). The employer discontinued the severance benefits and the employee filed a second charge alleging retaliation. The EEOC sought and obtained from the district court an injunction barring the employer from refusing to pay the severance benefits and from seeking releases from other employees. The Fifth Circuit affirmed on two grounds: (1) since the EEOC charge was not a claim for relief, it did not violate the release and (2) a waiver of the right to file a charge is void as against public policy. The court noted that since the EEOC relies on charges to notify it of discrimination against not only the charging party but other employees as well, allowing the filing of charges to be obstructed by enforcing waivers would impede the EEOC in enforcement of the act. 821 F.2d at 1090. The court carefully distinguished, however, between the waiver of the right to file a charge and the waiver of a cause of action or right to relief. "[A]lthough an employee cannot waive the right to file a charge with the EEOC, the employee can waive not only the right to recover in his or her own lawsuit but also the right to recover in a suit brought by the EEOC on the employee's behalf." 821 F.2d at 1091. See also, EEOC v. Goodyear Aerospace Corp., 813 F.2d 1539, 1543 (9th Cir.1987) (backpay claim by EEOC on behalf of employee who settled own Title VII claim is moot).

7. Relief is available to some persons who join as plaintiffs in a Title VII action even if they have not individually filed EEOC charges. Thus, an intervenor, who could have filed a timely charge and who alleges in the complaint the same kind of discrimination alleged in the EEOC charge will be able to "piggy back" on the timely EEOC charge of his fellow plaintiff. In Wu v. Thomas, 863 F.2d 1543 (11th Cir.1989), a university professor alleged in her EEOC charge that she was discriminated against with respect to salary and promotional opportunities and, in a second charge, that she was the victim of retaliation. When she filed suit, her husband, who had not filed an EEOC charge but who was also on the university's faculty, joined as a plaintiff and alleged that he had been removed from his position as a department chairperson in retaliation for his wife's charges of discrimination. Because "Wu's charge of retaliation is based on the university's actions toward her husband," the Eleventh Circuit held that the case "presents an archetypal example of the situation in which multiple filings are unnecessary." 863 F.2d at 1548. See also, Snell v. Suffolk County, 782 F.2d 1094 (2d Cir.1986). Members of a properly certified class are also entitled to proceed in litigation without satisfying the requirements of § 706. See, Chapter 6, *infra*. Before a non-filing class member or intervenor can benefit from a Title VII cause of action, at least one named plaintiff must have filed a timely EEOC charge and satisfied the other statutory prerequisites to a Title VII action. See Allen v. United States Steel Corp., 665 F.2d 689, 695–696 (5th Cir.1982).

IRWIN v. VETERANS ADMINISTRATION

Supreme Court of the United States, 1990.
___ U.S. ___, 111 S.Ct. 453, 112 L.Ed.2d 435.

CHIEF JUSTICE REHNQUIST delivered the opinion of the Court.

In April 1986, petitioner, Shirley Irwin, was fired from his job by respondent Veteran's Administration (VA). Irwin contacted an Equal

Employment Opportunities Commission (EEOC) counselor and filed a complaint with the EEOC, alleging that the VA had unlawfully discharged him on the basis of his race and physical disability. The EEOC dismissed Irwin's complaint by a letter dated March 19, 1987. The letter, which was sent to both Irwin and his attorney, expressly informed them that Irwin had the right to file a civil action under Title VII, ... within 30 days of receipt of the EEOC notice. According to Irwin, he did not receive the EEOC's letter until April 7, 1987, and the letter to his attorney arrived at the attorney's office on March 23, 1987, while the attorney was out of the country. The attorney did not learn of the EEOC's action until his return on April 10, 1987.

Irwin filed a complaint in the United States District Court for the Western District of Texas on May 6, 1987, 44 days after the EEOC notice was received at his attorney's office, but 29 days after the date on which he claimed he received the letter. The complaint alleged that the VA discriminated against him because of his race, age, and handicap, ... and the First and Fifth Amendments. Respondent VA moved to dismiss, asserting, inter alia, that the District Court lacked jurisdiction because the complaint was not filed within 30 days of the EEOC's decision as specified in 42 U.S.C. Sec. 2000e–16(c). The District Court granted the motion.

The Court of Appeals for the Fifth Circuit affirmed. 874 F. 2d 1092 (1989). The court held that the 30–day period begins to run on the date that the EEOC right-to-sue letter is delivered to the offices of formally designated counsel or to the claimant, even if counsel himself did not actually receive notice until later. The Court of Appeals further determined that the 30–day span allotted under Sec. 2000e16(c) operates as an absolute jurisdictional limit. Accordingly, it reasoned that the District Court could not excuse Irwin's late filing because federal courts lacked jurisdiction over his untimely claim. That holding is in direct conflict with the decisions of four other Courts of Appeals.[1]

We granted certiorari to determine when the 30–day period under Sec. 2000e–16(c) begins to run and to resolve the Circuit conflict over whether late-filed claims are jurisdictionally barred.

Section 2000e–16(c) provides that an employment discrimination complaint against the Federal Government under Title VII must be filed "within thirty days of receipt of notice of final action taken" by the EEOC. The Court of Appeals determined that a notice of final action is "received" when the EEOC delivers its notice to a claimant or the claimant's attorney, whichever comes first. Id., at 10994. Petitioner argues that the clock does not begin until the claimant himself has notice of his right to sue.

---

1. See Martinez v. Orr, 738 F.2d 1107 (CA10 1984); Milam v. U.S. Postal Service, 674 F.2d 860 (CA11 1982); Saltz v. Lehman, 217 U.S.App.D.C. 354, 672 F.2d 207 (1982); and Boddy v. Dean, 821 F.2d 346–350 (CA6 1987).

We conclude that Irwin's complaint filed in the District Court was untimely. As the Court of Appeals observed, Sec. 2000e–16(c) requires only that the EEOC notification letter be "received"; it does not specify receipt by the claimant rather than by the claimant's designated representative. There is no question but that petitioner appeared by his attorney in the EEOC proceeding. Under our system of representative litigation, "each party is deemed bound by the acts of his lawyer-agent and is considered to have notice of all facts, 'notice of which can be charged upon the attorney.'" Link v. Wabash R. Co., 370 U.S. 626, 634, 82 S.Ct. 1386, 1390, 8 L.Ed.2d 734 (1962) (quoting Smith v. Ayer, 101 U.S. 320, 326, 25 L.Ed. 955 (1880)). Congress has endorsed this sensible practice in the analogous provisions of the Federal Rules of Civil Procedure, which provide that "whenever under these rules service is required or permitted to be made upon a party represented by an attorney the service shall be made upon the attorney unless service upon the party is ordered by the court." Fed. Rule Civ. Proc. 5(b). To read the term "receipt" to mean only "actual receipt by the claimant" would render the practice of notification through counsel a meaningless exercise. If Congress intends to depart from the common and established practice of providing notification through counsel, it must do so expressly.

We also reject Irwin's contention that there is a material difference between receipt by an attorney and receipt by that attorney's office for purposes of Sec. 2000e–16(c). The lower federal courts have consistently held that notice to an attorney's office which is acknowledged by a representative of that office qualifies as notice to the client. Federal Rule of Civil Procedure 5(b) also permits notice to a litigant to be made by delivery of papers to the litigant's attorney's office. The practical effect of a contrary rule would be to encourage factual disputes about when actual notice was received, and thereby create uncertainty in an area of the law where certainty is much to be desired.

The fact that petitioner did not strictly comply with Sec. 2000e–16(c)'s filing deadline does not, however, end our inquiry. Petitioner contends that even if he failed to timely file, his error may be excused under equitable tolling principles. The Court of Appeals rejected this argument on the ground that the filing period contained in Sec. 2000e–16(c) is jurisdictional, and therefore the District Court lacked authority to consider his equitable claims. The court reasoned that Sec. 2000e–16(c) applies to suits against the Federal Government and thus is a condition of Congress' waiver of sovereign immunity. Since waivers of sovereign immunity are traditionally construed narrowly, the court determined that strict compliance with Sec. 2000e–16(c) is a necessary predicate to a Title VII suit.

* * *

Title 42 U.S.C. Sec. 2000e–16(c) provides in relevant part:

"Within thirty days of receipt of notice of final action taken by ... the Equal Employment Opportunity Commission ... an employee or applicant for employment, if aggrieved by the final disposition of his complaint, or by the failure to take final action on his complaint, may file a civil action as provided in section 2000e–5 of this title. . . ."

* * *

Time requirements in law suits between private litigants are customarily subject to "equitable tolling," Hallstrom v. Tillamook County, 493 U.S. 20, 26, 110 S.Ct. 304, 309, 107 L.Ed.2d 237 (1989). Indeed, we have held that the statutory time limits applicable to lawsuits against private employers under Title VII are subject to equitable tolling.[2]

A waiver of sovereign immunity " 'cannot be implied but must be unequivocally expressed.' " United States v. Mitchell, 445 U.S. 535, 538, 108 S.Ct. 1349, 1351, 63 L.Ed.2d 607 (1980) (quoting United States v. King, 395 U.S. 1, 4, 89 S.Ct. 1501, 1502, 23 L.Ed.2d 52 (1969)). Once Congress has made such a waiver, we think that making the rule of equitable tolling applicable to suits against the Government, in the same way that it is applicable to private suits, amounts to little, if any, broadening of the congressional waiver. Such a principle is likely to be a realistic assessment of legislative intent as well as a practically useful principle of interpretation. We therefore hold that the same rebuttable presumption of equitable tolling applicable to suits against private defendants should also apply to suits against the United States. Congress, of course, may provide otherwise if it wishes to do so.

But an examination of the cases in which we have applied the equitable tolling doctrine as between private litigants affords petitioner little help. Federal courts have typically extended equitable relief only sparingly. We have allowed equitable tolling in situations where the claimant has actively pursued his judicial remedies by filing a defective pleading during the statutory period,[3] or where the complainant has been induced or tricked by his adversary's misconduct into allowing the filing deadline to pass.[4] We have generally been much less forgiving in receiving late filings where the claimant failed to exercise due diligence in preserving his legal rights. Baldwin County Welcome Center v. Brown, 466 U.S. 147, 151, 104 S.Ct. 1723, 1725, 80 L.Ed.2d 196 (1984). Because the time limits imposed by Congress in a suit against the Government involve a waiver of sovereign immunity, it is evident that

2. See Zipes v. Trans World Airlines, Inc., 455 U.S. 385, 394, 102 S.Ct. 1127, 1133, 71 L.Ed.2d 234 (1982); Crown, Cork & Seal, Co. v. Parker, 462 U.S. 345, 349 n. 3, 103 S.Ct. 2392, 2395 n. 3, 76 L.Ed.2d 628 (1983).

3. See Burnett v. New York Central R. Co., 380 U.S. 424, 85 S.Ct. 1050, 13 L.Ed.2d 941 (1965) (plaintiff timely filed complaint in wrong court); Herb v. Pitcairn, 325 U.S. 77, 65 S.Ct. 954, 89 L.Ed. 1483 (1945) (same); American Pipe & Construction Co.

v. Utah, 414 U.S. 538, 94 S.Ct. 756, 38 L.Ed.2d 713 (1974) (plaintiff's timely filing of an individual action tolled the limitations period in a related class action claim).

4. See Glus v. Brooklyn Eastern District Terminal, 359 U.S. 231, 79 S.Ct. 760, 3 L.Ed.2d 770 (1959) (adversary's misrepresentation caused plaintiff to let filing period lapse); Holmberg v. Armbrecht, 327 U.S. 392, 66 S.Ct. 582, 90 L.Ed. 743 (1946) (same).

no more favorable tolling doctrine may be employed against the Government than is employed in suits between private litigants.

Petitioner urges that his failure to file in a timely manner should be excused because his lawyer was absent from his office at the time that the EEOC notice was received, and that he thereafter filed within 30 days of the day on which he personally received notice. But the principles of equitable tolling described above do not extend to what is at best a garden variety claim of excusable neglect.

The judgment of the Court of Appeals is accordingly

Affirmed.

[The concurring opinion of JUSTICES WHITE and MARSHALL is omitted.]

JUSTICE STEVENS, concurring in part and dissenting in part.

While I agree with the Court's conclusion that the filing deadline in 42 U.S.C. Sec. 2000e–16(c) is subject to equitable tolling and that the petitioner has failed to establish a basis for tolling in this case, I do not agree that the 30–day limitations period began to run when petitioner's lawyer, rather than petitioner himself, received notice from the EEOC of petitioner's right to file a civil action.

The Court is entirely correct that notice to a litigant's attorney is generally considered notice to the litigant after litigation has been commenced. But the Court overlooks the fact that litigation is usually commenced by service of process on the adverse party himself. Indeed, the Federal Rules of Civil Procedure expressly require service on the opposing litigant. See Fed. Rule Civ. Proc. 4(d). This case involves a notice that is a condition precedent to the commencement of formal litigation. I therefore believe that Congress intended that this notice, like a summons and complaint, be served on the adverse party, not his representative.

The Court contends that reading "the term 'receipt' [in Sec. 2000e–16(c)] to mean only 'actual receipt by the claimant' would render the practice of notification through counsel a meaningless exercise." By the same logic, however, reading "receipt," as the Court does, to mean only "receipt by the claimant's representative" renders "a meaningless exercise" the EEOC's practice of notifying the claimant personally, a practice codified in EEOC regulations, see 29 C.F.R. § 1613.234(a) (1990). Actually, notifying both the claimant and his representative makes sense regardless of which notice begins the ticking of the limitations clock. Dual notification ensures that all persons concerned with the progress of the action are apprised of important developments. Cf. ibid. (also requiring notification of employing agency). However, a claimant's representative before the EEOC will not necessarily also represent the claimant in the ensuing civil suit; indeed, the representative in the administrative proceedings need not even be an attorney. See 29 CFR Sec. 1613.214(b) (1990). Notice to the claimant is therefore the more logical trigger for the limitations countdown. This construction is not only sensible in light of the notice requirement's function in the statutory scheme but is also consistent with our previous admonitions that Title VII, a remedial statute, should be construed in favor of those whom the legislation was designed to protect. See Zipes v. Trans World Airlines, Inc., 455 U.S. 385, 397–398, 102 S.Ct. 1127, 1134–1135, 71 L.Ed.2d 234 (1982); Love v. Pullman Co., 404 U.S. 522, 527, 92 S.Ct. 616, 619, 30 L.Ed.2d 679 (1972).

Accordingly, I respectfully dissent from the Court's judgment. I would instead reverse the judgment of the Court of Appeals and remand the case for resolution of the disputed factual issue of when the petitioner himself actually received notice from the EEOC of his right to file a civil action.

NOTES AND PROBLEMS FOR DISCUSSION

1. As illustrated in *Allen v. Avon Products* and *Irwin v. Veterans Administration*, the provisions of Title VII distinguish between suits against the federal government and suits against non-federal employers. Title VII litigation against the federal government is discussed in Chapter 5 *infra*. In both kinds of cases, however, the plaintiff may not file a suit without first having received a notice of right to sue from the EEOC. Compare Sections 706(f)(1) (Sec. 2000e–5(f)(1)) and 717(c) (Sec. 2000e–16(c)) quoted respectively in *Allen* and *Irwin*. The language of Section 706(f)(1) of Title VII seems to require the EEOC to issue notice to the charging party within a 180–day period beginning when the charge is filed. Notice that in *Allen* the plaintiff filed her charge with the EEOC in 1972 and was not issued the right to sue notice until 1981. In Zambuto v. American Telephone & Telegraph Co., 544 F.2d 1333, 1334 (5th Cir.1977), the Court of Appeals recognized that, given the EEOC's workload, the 180 day period for completion of the administrative process could not be strictly enforced, and held that the Commission is not required to issue unsolicited 180 day "progress reports" which initiate the running of the 90 day period during which the charging party must decide whether to file suit. This construction of the statute was given apparent approval by the Supreme Court in OCCIDENTAL LIFE INSURANCE CO. v. EEOC, 432 U.S. 355, 97 S.Ct. 2447, 53 L.Ed.2d 402 (1977). "An aggrieved person unwilling to await the conclusion of extended EEOC proceedings may institute a private lawsuit 180 days after a charge has been filed." 432 U.S. at 366, 97 S.Ct. at 2454. See also, Turner v. Texas Instruments, Inc., 556 F.2d 1349 (5th Cir.1977). The current EEOC Regulations only require the issuance of a notice of right to sue when the agency terminates its proceedings (as in *Allen*) or is *requested* to do so by the charging party after the expiration of the 180–day period. 29 C.F.R. § 1601.28(a)(1).

The purpose of the 180-day mandatory delay between the filing of the charge and the charging party's entitlement to a right to sue notice is to allow time for the EEOC to investigate and attempt conciliation. Courts have uniformly held, however, that the "action or inaction of the EEOC cannot affect the grievant's substantive rights under the statute." Miller v. International Paper Co., 408 F.2d 283, 291 (5th Cir.1969). See also, Roberts v. Arizona Board of Regents, 661 F.2d 796, 800 (9th Cir.1981). Thus, the failure or inability of the EEOC to investigate or attempt conciliation of a charge cannot prevent the charging party from obtaining a right to sue notice or bar the suit. See Miller v. International Paper Co., *supra*, 408 F.2d at 288–291; Allen v. Schwab Rehabilitation Hospital, 509 F.Supp. 151, 155 (N.D.Ill. 1981). Such failure will, however, bar a suit by the EEOC. See Section B of this Chapter, *infra*. Should the charging party's refusal to cooperate with the EEOC's investigation of her charge bar her suit on the charge? See, Jordan v. United States, 522 F.2d 1128, 1133 (8th Cir.1975) (plaintiff's failure to cooperate with agency frustrated "operation of a carefully planned administrative procedure designed to expose truth or falsity of the very acts of which plaintiff complains"); Davis v. Mid–South Milling Co., 54 FEP Cases 1561 (W.D.Tenn.1990); Dates v. Phelps Dodge Magnet Wire Co., 604 F.Supp. 22 (N.D.Ind. 1984) (because primary objective of Title VII is to accomplish compliance with law through conciliation, the failure of charging party to cooperate with the EEOC deprives the court of jurisdiction). Are these decisions consistent with the rule that allows the charging party to obtain a right to sue notice before any EEOC investigation has occurred?

EEOC Regulations permit issuance of a right to sue notice, on request of the charging party, *before* the expiration of the 180–day period "provided, that the District Director * * * has determined that it is probable that the Commission will be unable to complete its administrative processing of the charge within 180 days * * *." 29 C.F.R. § 1601.28(a)(2). A number of courts have held that early issuance of the notice does not preclude the filing of a suit. See, Bryant v. California Brewers Association, 585 F.2d 421, 425 (9th Cir.1978), vacated on other grounds, 444 U.S. 598, 100 S.Ct. 814, 63 L.Ed.2d 55 (1980); Weise v. Syracuse University, 522 F.2d 397, 412 (2d Cir.1975). Contra, True v. New York State of Correctional Services, 613 F.Supp. 27 (W.D.N.Y.1984); Grimes v. Pitney Bowes, Inc., 480 F.Supp. 1381, 1383–86 (N.D.Ga.1979). EEOC Regulations also allow the agency to "revoke" a notice of right to sue if it elects to reconsider a charge within 90 days of issuance of the notice and before the charging party files suit. 29 C.F.R. § 1610.21(b)(1). The decision to reconsider a charge after the original 90–day period has expired and the issuance of a second right-to-sue notice does not, however, "revoke" the original notice and does not entitle the charging party who did not file suit under the first notice to file suit under the second notice. See, Dougherty v. Barry, 869 F.2d 605 (D.C.Cir. 1989). What would be the purpose of such a reconsideration?

2. The district court in *Allen v. Avon Products* concluded that the plaintiff's decision to wait out for nine years the EEOC administrative process was neither "unreasonable nor inexcusable." Compare, Cleveland Newspaper Guild, Local 1 v. Plain Dealer Publishing Co., 839 F.2d 1147 (6th Cir.1988) cert. denied, 488 U.S. 899, 109 S.Ct. 245, 102 L.Ed.2d 234 (1988). In that case, the union filed a charge in 1972 that the newspaper discriminated against women in merit pay, promotions, assignments and other terms and conditions of employment. The employer was informed of the charge but the EEOC did not begin its investigation until 1976. The employer refused to produce documents or otherwise to cooperate in the investigation on the ground that its ability to respond to the charges had been impaired by the delay. Nothing further happened until 1979 when the union wrote the EEOC concerning the status of the charge. In 1980, the EEOC unsuccessfully attempted conciliation. In 1982, the EEOC issued a right-to-sue notice and the union filed the action. The district court granted summary judgment to the employer based on laches. The Sixth Circuit initially reversed on the ground that it would defeat Title VII's purpose to penalize plaintiffs for relying on the EEOC's performance of its statutory duties. The court also noted that the defendant's own failure to cooperate with the EEOC added to the delay in bringing the suit. Cleveland Newspaper Guild–Local 1 v. Plain Dealer Publishing Co., 813 F.2d 101 (6th Cir.1987). Subsequently, the court granted rehearing *en banc,* vacated the

panel opinion, and affirmed the district court's dismissal of the suit.   839 F.2d 1147 (6th Cir.1988).   The court reasoned that since the union had "sophisticated knowledge and responsibility in equal employment matters" it could not reasonably account for its continued inaction during the extended period that the charge was pending.   There was little EEOC activity during the time that could explain the union's failure to act and it knew it could obtain a right-to-sue notice at any time.   The opinion provoked three concurrences and four dissents.   See also, Whitfield v. Anheuser–Busch, Inc., 820 F.2d 243 (8th Cir.1987) (10–year delay in filing Title VII action justified dismissal on laches grounds where plaintiff made no attempt to check on status of charge); Garrett v. General Motors Corp., 844 F.2d 559 (8th Cir.1988), cert. denied, 488 U.S. 908, 109 S.Ct. 259, 102 L.Ed.2d 248 (1988) (passage of 15 years between filing of EEOC charge and institution of suit constituted inexcusable delay for purpose of laches defense where plaintiff's contacts with EEOC were minimal until he learned of successful litigation against company by other employees).

3. *Irwin v. Veterans Administration* does not directly address the question of whether anything other than actual receipt of the notice of right to sue by the charging party will begin the running of the 90–day period where the charging party has not designated an attorney or other representative.   The Fourth Circuit has held that receipt by the claimant's wife of the notice, 91 days before he filed suit, did not justify extending the filing period, where plaintiff knew of notice within six days of receipt and failed to show that the remaining 84 days in the period were insufficient time within which to act. The court of appeals noted the split in the circuits over whether anything other than actual receipt by the charging party will trigger the filing period, but reasoned that a flexible rule demanding "a thorough examination of the facts to determine if reasonable grounds exist for an equitable tolling" was consistent with the congressional purpose embodied in Section 706(f)(1) that claimants act expeditiously.   Harvey v. City of New Bern Police Dept., 813 F.2d 652, 654 (4th Cir.1987).   See also, Espinoza v. Missouri Pacific R.R. Co., 754 F.2d 1247 (5th Cir.1985).

Relying on EEOC regulations requiring the charging party to notify the agency of changes of address, 29 C.F.R. § 1601.7(b) (1981), the Seventh Circuit has held that the 90–day period begins running on the date the notice is delivered to the most recent address the claimant has provided the EEOC.   St. Louis v. Alverno College, 744 F.2d 1314 (7th Cir.1984).   In Stallworth v. Wells Fargo Armored Services Corp., 936 F.2d 522 (11th Cir.1991) the court held that delivery of a notice of right to sue to plaintiff's nephew at her home did not trigger the 90–day period, because even though she was living elsewhere temporarily, she had requested the agency to send a copy to her attorney and it had not done so.   In addition the plaintiff had checked for mail at her home a number of times during the relevant period and had not been told of the notice. The Court of Appeals reasoned that the plaintiff fulfilled her "minimum responsibility to ensure receipt."   Compare, Franks v. Bowman Transportation Co., 495 F.2d 398 (5th Cir.1974), reversed and remanded on other grounds, 424 U.S. 747, 96 S.Ct. 1251, 47 L.Ed.2d 444 (1976) (notice received by charging party's nine-year old nephew and lost; plaintiff allowed to proceed with suit one year later when he learned of notice) and Archie v. Chicago Truck Drivers Union, 585 F.2d 210 (7th Cir.1978) (plaintiff's wife received notice 10 days before giving it to him; period did not begin to run until actual receipt by charging party); Minor v. Southeastern Pennsylvania Transp. Authority, 45 FEP Cases 145 (E.D.Pa. 1985) (90–day period for filing suit did not begin to run until actual receipt of notice by plaintiff where notice was sent by certified mail to post office and he did not pick up notice because of state of depression requiring professional counseling). Are these various decisions consistent?

What if the date of receipt of the notice cannot be determined? See, Pacheco v. International Business Machines Corp., 55 FEP Cases 1564 (N.D.N.Y.1991) (presumption that charging party received notice three days after it was mailed).

BALDWIN COUNTY WELCOME CENTER v. BROWN

Supreme Court of the United States, 1984.
466 U.S. 147, 104 S.Ct. 1723, 80 L.Ed.2d 196.

Per Curiam.

On November 6, 1979, respondent Celinda Brown filed a complaint with the Equal Employment Opportunity Commission (EEOC) alleging discriminatory treatment by her former employer, petitioner Baldwin County Welcome Center (Welcome Center). A notice of right to sue was issued to her on January 27, 1981. It stated that if Brown chose to commence a civil action "such suit must be filed in the appropriate United States District Court within ninety days of [her] receipt of this Notice." [1] Later, Brown mailed the notice to the United States District Court, where it was received on March 17, 1981. [2] In addition, she requested appointment of counsel.

On April 15, 1981, a United States Magistrate entered an order requiring that Brown make application for court-appointed counsel using the District Court's motion form and supporting questionnaire. The Magistrate's order to Brown reminded her of the necessity of filing a complaint within 90 days of the issuance of the right-to-sue letter. The questionnaire was not returned until May 6, 1981, the 96th day after receipt of the letter. The next day, the Magistrate denied Brown's motion for appointment of counsel because she had not timely complied with his orders, but he referred to the District Judge the question whether the filing of the right-to-sue letter with the court constituted commencement of an action within the meaning of Rule 3 of the Federal Rules of Civil Procedure. On June 9, 1981, the 130th day after receipt of the right-to-sue letter, Brown filed an "amended complaint," which was served on June 18.

On December 24, 1981, the District Court held that Brown had forfeited her right to pursue her claim under Title VII of the Civil Rights Act of 1964 because of her failure to file a complaint meeting the requirements of Rule 8 of the Federal Rules of Civil Procedure within 90 days of her receipt of the right-to-sue letter. It noted that the right-

---

1. The presumed date of receipt of the notice was January 30, 1981. Fed. Rule Civ. Proc. 6(e).

2. Brown mailed the letter to the United States District Court for the Middle District of Alabama. The case was transferred to the Southern District of Alabama, however, because the events giving rise to the charge had occurred there.

to-sue letter did not qualify as a complaint under Rule 8 because there was no statement in the letter of the factual basis for the claim of discrimination, which is required by the Rule.

The Court of Appeals for the Eleventh Circuit reversed, holding that the filing of a right-to-sue letter "tolls" the time period provided by Title VII. Judgment order reported at 698 F.2d 1236 (1983). Although conceding that its interpretation was "generous," the court stated that "[t]he remedial nature of the statute requires such an interpretation." The court then stated that the filing of the right-to-sue letter "satisfied the ninety day statutory limitation."

The Welcome Center petitioned for a writ of certiorari from this Court. We grant the petition and reverse the judgment of the Court of Appeals.

The section of Title VII at issue here states that within 90 days after the issuance of a right-to-sue letter "a civil action may be brought against the respondent named in the charge." 42 U.S.C. Sec. 2000e–5(f)(1). Rule 3 of the Federal Rules of Civil Procedure states that "[a] civil action is commenced by filing a complaint with the court." A complaint must contain, inter alia, "a short and plain statement of the claim showing that the pleader is entitled to relief." Fed. Rule Civ. Proc. 8(a)(2). The District Court held that the right-to-sue letter did not satisfy that standard. The Court of Appeals did not expressly disagree, but nevertheless stated that the 90–day statutory period for invoking the court's jurisdiction was satisfied, apparently concluding that the policies behind Title VII mandate a different definition of when an action is "commenced." [3] However, it identified no basis in the statute or its legislative history, cited no decision of this Court, and suggested no persuasive justification for its view that the Federal Rules of Civil Procedure were to have a different meaning in, or were not to apply to, Title VII litigation. Because we also can find no satisfactory basis for giving Title VII actions a special status under the Rules of Civil Procedure, we must disagree with the conclusion of the Court of Appeals.[4]

---

3. Neither the parties nor the courts below addressed the application of Rule 15(c) to the "amended complaint" filed on June 9. That Rule provides that amendment of a pleading "relates back" to the date of the original pleading. We do not believe that Rule 15(c) is applicable to this situation. The rationale of Rule 15(c) is that a party who has been notified of litigation concerning a particular occurrence has been given all the notice that statutes of limitations were intended to provide. 3 J. Moore, Moore's Federal Practice P15.-15[3], p. 15–194 (1984). Although the Federal Rules of Civil Procedure do not require a claimant to set forth an intricately detailed description of the asserted basis for relief, they do require that the plead-

ings "give the defendant fair notice of what the plaintiff's claim is and the grounds upon which it rests." Conley v. Gibson, 355 U.S. 41, 47, 78 S.Ct. 99, 102, 2 L.Ed.2d 80 (1957). Because the initial "pleading" did not contain such notice, it was not an original pleading that could be rehabilitated by invoking Rule 15(c).

4. JUSTICE STEVENS makes much of a letter dated March 21, 1981, sent by Brown to the District Court in which she describes the basis of her claim. Suffice it to say that no one but the dissent has relied upon this letter to sustain Brown's position. There is nothing in the record to suggest that the letter was considered by the District Court or the Court of Appeals,

With respect to its apparent alternative holding that the statutory period for invoking the court's jurisdiction is "tolled" by the filing of the right-to-sue letter, the Court of Appeals cited no principle of equity to support its conclusion.[5] Brown does little better, relying only on her asserted "diligent efforts." Nor do we find anything in the record to call for the application of the doctrine of equitable tolling.

The right-to-sue letter itself stated that Brown had the right to sue within 90 days. Also, the District Court informed Brown that "to be safe, you should file the petition on or before the ninetieth day after the day of the letter from the EEOC informing you of your right to sue." Finally, the order of April 15 from the Magistrate again reminded Brown of the 90-day limitation.

This is not a case in which at claimant has received inadequate notice, or where a motion for appointment of counsel is pending and equity would justify tolling the statutory period until the motion is acted upon, or where the court has led the plaintiff to believe that she had done everything required of her. Nor is this a case where affirmative misconduct on the part of a defendant lulled the plaintiff into inaction. The simple fact is that Brown was told three times what she must do to preserve her claim, and she did not do it. One who fails to act diligently cannot invoke equitable principles to excuse that lack of diligence.

Brown also contends that the doctrine of equitable tolling should apply because the Welcome Center has not demonstrated that it was prejudiced by her failure to comply with the Rules.[6] This argument is unavailing. Although absence of prejudice is a factor to be considered in determining whether the doctrine of equitable tolling should apply once a factor that might justify such tolling is identified, it is not an

---

and Brown does not rely upon it before this Court as a basis for affirming the judgment. The issue before the Court of Appeals and before this Court is whether the filing of a right-to-sue letter with the District Court constituted the commencement of an action. The Court of Appeals held that it did and based its judgment on that ground. We reverse that judgment. Even if respondent had relied on the letter in this Court, we would not be required to assess its significance without having the views of the lower courts in the first instance.

JUSTICE STEVENS also suggests that we should be more solicitous of the pleadings of the pro se litigant. It is noteworthy, however, that Brown was represented by counsel at the time of the dismissal by the District Court, before the Court of Appeals, and before this Court. Neither Brown nor her counsel ever requested that the letter in the record be construed as a complaint.

5. It is not clear from the opinion of the Court of Appeals for how long the statute is tolled. Presumably, under its view, the plaintiff has a "reasonable time" in which to file a complaint that satisfies the requirements of Rule 8. See Huston v. General Motors Corp., 477 F.2d 1003 (CA8 1973). In this case, it was another 84 days until such a complaint was filed.

6. Brown also contends that application of the doctrine of equitable tolling is mandated by our decision in Zipes v. Trans World Airlines, Inc. In Zipes, we held that the requirement of a timely filing of a charge of discrimination with the EEOC under 42 U.S.C. Sec. 2000e-5(e) is not a jurisdictional prerequisite to a suit in district court and that it is subject to waiver and equitable tolling. Brown's argument is without merit, for we did not in Zipes declare that the requirement need not ever be satisfied; we merely stated that it was subject to waiver and tolling. There was neither waiver nor tolling in this case.

independent basis for invoking the doctrine and sanctioning deviations from established procedures.

Procedural requirements established by Congress for gaining access to the federal courts are not to be disregarded by courts out of a vague sympathy for particular litigants. As we stated in Mohasco Corp. v. Silver, 447 U.S. 807, 826, 100 S.Ct. 2486, 2497, 65 L.Ed.2d 532 (1980), "in the long run, experience teaches that strict adherence to the procedural requirements specified by the legislature is the best guarantee of evenhanded administration of the law."

The petition for certiorari is granted, respondent's motion to proceed in forma pauperis is granted, and the judgment of the Court of Appeals is reversed.

It is so ordered.

[The dissenting opinion of JUSTICES STEVENS, BRENNAN and MARSHALL is omitted. The dissenters argued two grounds: first, that the plaintiff's letter which accompanied the right-to-sue notice constituted a "short and plain statement of the claim" in compliance with Rule 8 of the Federal Rules of Civil Procedure and, second, that, in light of the remedial scheme of Title VII, "filing the right to sue letter and exercising reasonable diligence in the District Court in attempting to obtain counsel and file a formal complaint should toll the statute of limitations." 466 U.S. at 168, 104 S.Ct. at 1734.]

NOTES AND PROBLEMS FOR DISCUSSION

1. In light of Title VII's remedial purposes and the fact that frequently, as in Ms. Brown's case, plaintiffs must initiate proceedings without assistance of counsel, do you agree that lack of prejudice to the defendant should not be an "independent basis" for equitable tolling? The factors that will justify equitable tolling remain somewhat in doubt. In Brown v. J.I. Case Co., 756 F.2d 48 (7th Cir.1985), the Court of Appeals held that a good faith request for appointment of counsel made within the 90–day period tolled the running of the time for filing suit until disposition of the motion. *Baldwin County* was distinguished on the ground that the plaintiff had "engaged in inequitable conduct" by not returning the magistrate's questionnaire until after the period had expired. Cf. Millard v. La Pointe's Fashion Store, Inc., 736 F.2d 501 (9th Cir.1984). Contra, Firle v. Mississippi State Dept. of Education, 762 F.2d 487 (5th Cir.1985). In Judkins v. Beech Aircraft Corp., 745 F.2d 1330 (11th Cir.1984), the claimant filed his right-to-sue notice and a copy of his EEOC charge. The Eleventh Circuit held that the charge, which explained the factual basis for the discrimination claim in considerable detail, complied with the requirements of Rule 8(a)(2) of the Federal Rules of Civil Procedure so as to constitute a complaint. Should plaintiff's mental illness during the 90–day period justify extending it. See, Lopez v. Citibank, N.A., 808 F.2d 905 (1st Cir.1987) (no, where claimant was represented by counsel who was capable of pursuing claim on claimant's behalf)

2. In *Baldwin County* the majority held that the plaintiff could not take advantage of the "relation back" doctrine of Rule 15(c) FRCP because her initial letter to the court was not a pleading that "could be rehabilitated by invoking Rule 15(c)." *supra* n.3. The Seventh Circuit has held, however, that a

complaint that is filed within the 90–day window may be amended to add a Title VII cause of action *after* the expiration of the period and that such amendment will preserve the Title VII claim. In Donnelly v. Yellow Freight System, Inc., 874 F.2d 402 (7th Cir.1989), affirmed on other grounds, 494 U.S. 820, 110 S.Ct. 1566, 108 L.Ed.2d 834 (1990), the plaintiff filed an action in state court based on the Illinois Human Rights Act in which she alleged that the defendant had refused to hire her because of her sex. The state suit was filed within 90 days of plaintiff's receipt of a right-to-sue notice from the EEOC. After defendant filed a motion to dismiss the action on grounds that plaintiff had failed to exhaust state administrative remedies, plaintiff sought to amend the suit to include a Title VII cause of action. The motion to amend was filed after the 90–day period had expired. Defendant removed the action to federal court and moved to dismiss on the ground that the Title VII claim was untimely. The district court denied the motion and ruled for plaintiff after a trial. The Seventh Circuit affirmed. Relying on Rule 15(c) of the Federal Rules of Civil Procedure, the court held that plaintiff's Title VII claim "related back" to the filing of the original state court action because both state and federal claims arose out of the same "conduct, transaction or occurrence." Since the state action was filed within the 90–day window, the amendment was timely. The court also noted that defendant could show no prejudice since it was fully aware from the date of the state suit and of the nature of plaintiff's charges. Is it consistent with the purposes of the Title VII limitation periods to allow a claimant to hold her federal claim in reserve after receiving the right-to-sue notice? How else might plaintiff have postponed filing her Title VII claim?

3. Section 706(f) provides that federal district courts "shall have jurisdiction of actions" under Title VII and most circuit courts that had addressed the issue had held that the statute gave exclusive jurisdiction to the federal courts. In YELLOW FREIGHT SYSTEM, INC. v. DONNELLY, *supra*, the Supreme Court granted certiorari limited to that issue. In a brief and unanimous opinion the Supreme Court held that, because Title VII contains no express language confining jurisdiction to federal courts and because there was no reason to question the presumption that state courts are as able as federal courts to adjudicate Title VII claims, federal and state courts have concurrent jurisdiction over Title VII claims. Does *Yellow Freight System* mean that, as a practical matter, plaintiffs can control the forum in which they litigate their Title VII causes of action? Consider the history of *Yellow Freight*.

4. If nothing else, *Baldwin County* highlights the importance to the claimant of obtaining legal assistance before the expiration of the filing period. Section 706(f)(1) of the Act authorizes the district court to appoint counsel "upon application by the complainant and in such circumstances as the court may deem just." Congress, however, has not created a fund (as it has for the Criminal Justice Act) from which appointed counsel can be compensated. Thus, appointed counsel will be paid for their services only if the plaintiff wins the case and counsel will probably have to bear the costs of the litigation pending its outcome. See Chapter 7C, *infra*. Under these circumstances, courts have been reluctant to force private attorneys to take on employment discrimination cases and, in practice, "appointments" under Title VII are more like referrals to counsel who may accept or reject the cases. But locating a lawyer venturesome enough to take on a hard-to-prove case on a wholly

contingent basis can prove difficult. In Bradshaw v. United States District Court for Southern District of California, 742 F.2d 515 (9th Cir.1984), the district court strove for over thirteen months to find an attorney who would agree to represent the plaintiff (twenty lawyers turned the case down) before directing the plaintiff to proceed *pro se.* On the plaintiff's petition for a writ of mandamus to compel the district court to appoint counsel, the Ninth Circuit held that district courts may resort to coercive appointments of counsel under Title VII but that the lower court had not abused its discretion in light of the litigious history of the plaintiff and the court's diligent search for counsel. In deciding whether to appoint counsel, the District of Columbia Circuit has held that the district court should take into account, in addition to the plaintiff's financial circumstances, the merits of the case, the efforts of plaintiff to secure counsel and the plaintiff's capacity to represent himself. Poindexter v. Federal Bureau of Investigation, 737 F.2d 1173 (D.C.Cir. 1984). The Sixth Circuit has held that the denial of a motion to appoint counsel in a Title VII case is not immediately appealable. Henry v. City of Detroit Manpower Dept., 763 F.2d 757 (6th Cir.1985) (*en banc.*), cert. denied, 474 U.S. 1036, 106 S.Ct. 604, 88 L.Ed.2d 582 (1985). A dissent in *Henry* argued that denial of appointment should be immediately appealable under the "death knell" doctrine and stressed the importance of representation by an attorney at the trial on the merits.

> Congress expressly recognized that a distinctive characteristic of civil rights plaintiffs is membership in a disadvantaged class. By contrast, civil rights defendants are typically institutions capable of wielding great resources and mustering extensive legal talent. * * * The civil rights action itself involves discovery and motions practice so complex that the plaintiff may drop the case before trial. * * * I am unwilling to assume "that civil rights plaintiffs are capable of prosecuting their own cases through trial * * * [and] that should they somehow succeed in doing so, they will have the determination and capability to perfect and conduct appeals properly and fully after they lose." [citing Bradshaw v. Zoological Society of San Diego, 662 F.2d 1301, 1310 (9th Cir.1981).]

763 F.2d at 772 (Jones, J. dissenting).

   In MALLARD v. UNITED STATES DISTRICT COURT FOR SOUTHERN DISTRICT OF IOWA, 490 U.S. 296, 109 S.Ct. 1814, 104 L.Ed.2d 318 (1989) the Court held that 28 U.S.C. Sec. 1915(d), which provides that a court "may request an attorney to represent" an indigent litigant in a civil case, *does not* give the district court power to make coercive appointments of unwilling counsel. How should *Mallard* impact on the appointment provision of Section 706? In Scott v. Tyson Foods, Inc., 943 F.2d 17 (8th Cir.1991) the Eighth Circuit distinguished *Mallard* on the ground that that decision was based on the language of Section 1915(d). By contrast with the language of Section 1915(d), Section 706(f)(1) provides that "[u]pon application by the complainant and in such circumstances as the court may deem just, the court may appoint an attorney for the applicant." The Court of Appeals read that language as conferring on the district courts the coercive power to require attorneys to represent plaintiffs in Title VII cases.

2. The Date of Discrimination: When Does the Period for Filing the Charge Begin to Run?

UNITED AIR LINES, INC. v. EVANS

Supreme Court of the United States, 1977.
431 U.S. 553, 97 S.Ct. 1885, 52 L.Ed.2d 571.

MR. JUSTICE STEVENS delivered the opinion of the Court.

Respondent was employed by United Air Lines as a flight attendant from November 1966 to February 1968. She was rehired in February 1972. Assuming, as she alleges, that her separation from employment in 1968 violated Title VII of the Civil Rights Act of 1964,[1] the question now presented is whether the employer is committing a second violation of Title VII by refusing to credit her with seniority for any period prior to February 1972.

Respondent filed charges with the Equal Employment Opportunity Commission in February 1973 alleging that United discriminated and continues to discriminate against her because she is a female. After receiving a letter granting her the right to sue, she commenced this action in the United States District Court for the Northern District of Illinois. Because the District Court dismissed her complaint, the facts which she has alleged are taken as true. They may be simply stated.

During respondent's initial period of employment, United maintained a policy of refusing to allow its female flight attendants to be married.[2] When she married in 1968, she was therefore forced to resign. Although it was subsequently decided that such a resignation violated Title VII, Sprogis v. United Air Lines, 444 F.2d 1194 (CA7 1971), cert. denied, 404 U.S. 991, 92 S.Ct. 536, 30 L.Ed.2d 543, respondent was not a party to that case and did not initiate any proceedings of her own in 1968 by filing a charge with the EEOC within 90 days of her separation.[3] A claim based on that discriminatory act is therefore barred.[4]

---

1. 78 Stat. 253. Title VII, as amended, is codified in 42 U.S.C. § 2000e et seq. (1970 ed. and Supp.V).

2. At that time United required that all flight attendants be female, except on flights between the mainland and Hawaii and on overseas military charter flights. See Sprogis v. United Air Lines, 444 F.2d 1194, 1203 (CA7 1971) (Stevens, J., dissenting); cert. denied, 404 U.S. 991, 92 S.Ct. 536, 30 L.Ed.2d 543.

3. Section 706(d), 78 Stat. 260, 42 U.S.C. § 2000e-5(e), then provided in part:

"A charge under subsection (a) shall be filed within ninety days after the alleged unlawful employment practice occurred * * *."

The 1972 amendments to Title VII added a new subsection (a) to § 706. Consequently, subsection (d) was redesignated as subsection (e). At the same time it was amended to enlarge the limitations period to 180 days. See 86 Stat. 105, 42 U.S.C. § 2000e-5(e) (1970 ed., Supp.V).

4. Timely filing is a prerequisite to the maintenance of a Title VII action. Alexander v. Gardner–Denver Co., 415 U.S. 36, 47, 94 S.Ct. 1011, 1019, 39 L.Ed.2d 147. See Electrical Workers v. Robbins & Myers, Inc., 429 U.S. 229, 239–240, 97 S.Ct. 441, 448–449, 50 L.Ed.2d 427.

In November 1968, United entered into a new collective-bargaining agreement which ended the pre-existing "no marriage" rule and provided for the reinstatement of certain flight attendants who had been terminated pursuant to that rule. Respondent was not covered by that agreement. On several occasions she unsuccessfully sought reinstatement; on February 16, 1972, she was hired as a new employee. Although her personnel file carried the same number as it did in 1968, for seniority purposes she has been treated as though she had no prior service with United.[5] She has not alleged that any other rehired employees were given credit for prior service with United, or that United's administration of the seniority system has violated the collective-bargaining agreement covering her employment.[6]

Informal requests to credit her with pre–1972 seniority having been denied, respondent commenced this action.[7] The District Court dismissed the complaint, holding that the failure to file a charge within 90 days of her separation in 1968 caused respondent's claim to be time barred and foreclosed any relief under Title VII.[8]

A divided panel of the Court of Appeals initially affirmed; then, after our decision in Franks v. Bowman Transportation Co., 424 U.S. 747, 96 S.Ct. 1251, 47 L.Ed.2d 444, the panel granted respondent's petition for rehearing and unanimously reversed. 534 F.2d 1247 (CA7

---

5. Respondent is carried on two seniority rolls. Her "company" or "system" seniority dates from the day she was rehired, February 16, 1972. Her "stewardess" or "pay" seniority dates from the day she completed her flight attendant training, March 16, 1972. One or both types of seniority determine a flight attendant's wages; the duration and timing of vacations; rights to retention in the event of layoffs and rights to re-employment thereafter; and rights to preferential selection of flight assignments.

6. Under the provisions of the collective-bargaining agreement between United and the Air Line Stewardesses and Flight Stewards as represented by the Air Line Pilots Association International for the period 1972–1974, seniority is irrevocably lost or broken after the separation from employment of a flight attendant *"who resigns or whose services with the Company are permanently severed for just cause."* Brief for Respondent 6.

7. The relief requested in respondent's complaint included an award of seniority to the starting date of her initial employment with United and backpay "lost as a result of the discriminatory employment practices of [United]." In her brief in this Court, respondent states that she seeks backpay only since her date of rehiring, February 16, 1972, which would consist of the increment in pay and benefits attribut-

able to her lower seniority since that time. Brief for Respondent 4.

8. The District Court recited that the motion was filed pursuant to Fed. Rule Civ. Proc. 12(b)(1) and dismissed the complaint on the ground that it had no jurisdiction of a time-barred claim. The District Court also held, however, that the complaint did not allege any continuing violation. For that reason, the complaint was ripe for dismissal under Rule 12(b)(6). The District Court stated:

"Plaintiff asserts that by defendant's denial of her seniority back to the starting date of her original employment in 1966, United is currently perpetuating the effect of past discrimination.

"Plaintiff, however, has not been suffering from any 'continuing' violation. She is seeking to have this court merely reinstate her November, 1966 seniority date which was lost solely by reason of her February, 1968 resignation. The fact that that resignation was the result of an unlawful employment practice is irrelevant for purposes of these proceedings because plaintiff lost her opportunity to redress that grievance when she failed to file a charge within ninety days of February, 1968. United's subsequent employment of plaintiff in 1972 cannot operate to resuscitate such a time-barred claim."

1976).   We granted certiorari, 429 U.S. 917, 97 S.Ct. 308, 50 L.Ed.2d 282, and now hold that the complaint was properly dismissed.

Respondent recognizes that it is now too late to obtain relief based on an unlawful employment practice which occurred in 1968.   She contends, however, that United is guilty of a present, continuing violation of Title VII and therefore that her claim is timely.[9]   She advances two reasons for holding that United's seniority system illegally discriminates against her: First, she is treated less favorably than males who were hired after her termination in 1968 and prior to her re-employment in 1972; second, the seniority system gives present effect to the past illegal act and therefore perpetuates the consequences of forbidden discrimination.   Neither argument persuades us that United is presently violating the statute.

It is true that some male employees with less total service than respondent have more seniority than she.   But this disparity is not a consequence of their sex, or of her sex.   For females hired between 1968 and 1972 also acquired the same preference over respondent as males hired during that period.   Moreover, both male and female employees who had service prior to February 1968, who resigned or were terminated for a nondiscriminatory reason (or for an unchallenged discriminatory reason), and who were later re-employed, also were treated as new employees receiving no seniority credit for their prior service.   Nothing alleged in the complaint indicates that United's seniority system treats existing female employees differently from existing male employees, or that the failure to credit prior service differentiates in any way between prior service by males and prior service by females.   Respondent has failed to allege that United's seniority system differentiates between similarly situated males and females on the basis of sex.

Respondent is correct in pointing out that the seniority system gives present effect to a past act of discrimination.   But United was entitled to treat that past act as lawful after respondent failed to file a charge of discrimination within the 90 days then allowed by § 706(d).   A discriminatory act which is not made the basis for a timely charge is the legal equivalent of a discriminatory act which occurred before the statute was passed.   It may constitute relevant background evidence in a proceeding in which the status of a current practice is at issue, but separately considered, it is merely an unfortunate event in history which has no present legal consequences.

Respondent emphasizes the fact that she has alleged a *continuing* violation.   United's seniority system does indeed have a continuing impact on her pay and fringe benefits.   But the emphasis should not be placed on mere continuity; the critical question is whether any present

---

9. Respondent cannot rely for jurisdiction on the single act of failing to assign her seniority credit for her prior service at the time she was rehired, for she filed her discrimination charge with the Equal Employment Opportunity Commission on February 21, 1973, more than one year after she was rehired on February 16, 1972. The applicable time limit in February 1972, was 90 days; effective March 24, 1972, this time was extended to 180 days, see n. 3, supra.

violation exists. She has not alleged that the system discriminates against former female employees or that it treats former employees who were discharged for a discriminatory reason any differently from former employees who resigned or were discharged for a non-discriminatory reason. In short, the system is neutral in its operation.[10]

Our decision in Franks v. Bowman Transportation Co., supra, does not control this case. In *Franks* we held that retroactive seniority was an appropriate remedy to be awarded under § 706(g) of Title VII, 42 U.S.C. § 2000e–5(g) (1970 ed., Supp. V), after an illegal discriminatory act or practice had been proved, 424 U.S., at 762–768, 96 S.Ct., at 1263–1266. When that case reached this Court, the issues relating to the timeliness of the charge [11] and the violation of Title VII [12] had already been decided; we dealt only with a question of remedy. In contrast, in the case now before us we do not reach any remedy issue because respondent did not file a timely charge based on her 1968 separation and she has not alleged facts establishing a violation since she was rehired in 1972.[13]

The difference between a remedy issue and a violation issue is highlighted by the analysis of § 703(h) of Title VII in *Franks*.[14] As we held in that case, by its terms that section does not bar the award of retroactive seniority after a violation has been proved. Rather, § 703(h) "delineates which employment practices are illegal and thereby prohibited and which are not," 424 U.S., at 758, 96 S.Ct., at 1261.

That section expressly provides that it shall not be an unlawful employment practice to apply different terms of employment pursuant to a bona fide seniority system, provided that any disparity is not the result of intentional discrimination. Since respondent does not attack the bona fides of United's seniority system, and since she makes no

10. This case does not involve any claim by respondent that United's seniority system deterred her from asserting any right granted by Title VII. It does not present the question raised in the so-called departmental seniority cases. See, e.g., Quarles v. Philip Morris, Inc., 279 F.Supp. 505 (ED Va.1968).

11. The Court of Appeals had disposed of the timeliness issues in *Franks*, 495 F.2d 398, 405 (CA5 1974).

12. This finding of the District Court was unchallenged in the Court of Appeals, id., at 402, 403, and was assumed in this Court, 424 U.S., at 750, 96 S.Ct. at 1257.

In any event we noted in *Franks*: "The underlying legal wrong affecting [the class] is not the alleged operation of a racially discriminatory seniority system but of a racially discriminatory hiring system." Id., at 758, 96 S.Ct., at 1261.

13. At the time she was rehired in 1972, respondent had no greater right to a job than any other applicant for employment with United. Since she was in fact treated like any other applicant when she was rehired, the employer did not violate Title VII in 1972. And if the employer did not violate Title VII in 1972 by refusing to credit respondent with back seniority, its continued adherence to that policy cannot be illegal.

14. Section 703(h) 78 Stat. 257, 42 U.S.C. § 2000e–2(h), provides:

"Notwithstanding any other provision of this title, it shall not be an unlawful employment practice for an employer to apply different standards of compensation, or different terms, conditions, or privileges of employment pursuant to a bona fide seniority or merit system * * * provided that such differences are not the result of an intention to discriminate because of race, color, religion, sex, or national origin * * *."

charge that the system is intentionally designed to discriminate because of race, color, religion, sex, or national origin, § 703(h) provides an additional ground for rejecting her claim.

The Court of Appeals read § 703(h) as intended to bar an attack on a seniority system based on the consequences of discriminatory acts which occurred prior to the effective date of Title VII in 1965,[15] but having no application to such attacks based on acts occurring after 1965. This reading of § 703(h) is too narrow. The statute does not foreclose attacks on the current operation of seniority systems which are subject to challenge as discriminatory. But such a challenge to a neutral system may not be predicated on the mere fact that a past event which has no present legal significance has affected the calculation of seniority credit, even if the past event might at one time have justified a valid claim against the employer. A contrary view would substitute a claim for seniority credit for almost every claim which is barred by limitations. Such a result would contravene the mandate of § 703(h).

The judgment of the Court of Appeals is reversed.

It is so ordered.

MR. JUSTICE MARSHALL, with whom MR. JUSTICE BRENNAN joins, dissenting.

But for her sex, respondent Carolyn Evans presently would enjoy all of the seniority rights that she seeks through this litigation. Petitioner United Air Lines has denied her those rights pursuant to a policy that perpetuates past discrimination by awarding the choicest jobs to those possessing a credential married women were unlawfully prevented from acquiring: continuous tenure with United. While the complaint respondent filed in the District Court was perhaps inartfully drawn,[1] it adequately draws into question this policy of United's.

For the reasons stated in the Court's opinion and in my separate opinion in Teamsters v. United States, 431 U.S. 324, 378, 97 S.Ct. 1843, 1875, 52 L.Ed.2d 396, I think it indisputable that, absent § 703(h), the seniority system at issue here would constitute an "unlawful employment practice" under Title VII, 42 U.S.C. § 2000e–2(a)(2) (1970 ed., Supp. V). And for the reasons developed at length in my separate opinion in *Teamsters*, I believe § 703(h) does not immunize seniority systems that perpetuate post-Act discrimination.

The only remaining question is whether Ms. Evans' complaint is barred by the applicable statute of limitations, 42 U.S.C. § 2000e–5(e)

---

15.   534 F.2d, at 1251.

1.   Although the District Court dismissed respondent's complaint for lack of jurisdiction pursuant to Fed. Rule Civ. Proc. 12(b)(1), the basis for its ruling was that the complaint was time barred. Thus, the dismissal closely resembles a dismissal for failure to state a claim upon which relief can be granted, and the only issue before us is whether "it appears beyond doubt that the plaintiff can prove no set of facts in support of [her] claim which would entitle [her] to relief." Conley v. Gibson, 355 U.S. 41, 45–46, 78 S.Ct. 99, 101–102, 2 L.Ed.2d 80 (1957).

(1970 ed., Supp. V). Her cause of action accrued, if at all, at the time her seniority was recomputed after she was rehired. Although she apparently failed to file a charge with the EEOC within 180 days after her seniority was determined, Title VII recognizes that certain violations, once commenced, are continuing in nature. In these instances, discriminatees can file charges at any time up to 180 days after the violation ceases. (They can, however, receive backpay only for the two years preceding the filing of charges with the Equal Employment Opportunity Commission. 42 U.S.C. § 2000e–5(g) (1970 ed., Supp. V).) In the instant case, the violation—treating respondent as a new employee even though she was wrongfully forced to resign—is continuing to this day. Respondent's charge therefore was not time barred, and the Court of Appeals judgment reinstating her complaint should be affirmed.[2]

———————

In BAZEMORE v. FRIDAY, 478 U.S. 385, 106 S.Ct. 3000, 92 L.Ed.2d 315 (1986), a state agricultural extension service had been organized, prior to August 1965, in two racially segregated branches. Employees in the black division of the service had been paid significantly lower wages than their white counterparts. In response to the Civil Rights Act of 1964, the two branches were merged but the disparities in salaries continued largely as a result of the historic pattern of separate pay scales. The district court refused to certify a class and found for defendants on all issues. The Court of Appeals affirmed, holding that defendants were not obligated to eliminate salary disparities that originated prior to 1972, the date on which Title VII was made applicable to state agencies. The Supreme Court reversed on the ground that pre-Act salary discrimination did not excuse perpetuating the discrimination after the service became covered by Title VII. "To hold otherwise would have the effect of exempting from liability those employers who were historically the greatest offenders of the rights of blacks." 478 U.S. at 395, 106 S.Ct. at 3006. Exactly why the pre-Act discrimination in pay rates was not "merely an unfortunate event in history which has no present legal consequences" (Evans, *supra*, at) was not explained because the Court neither cited UNITED AIRLINES v. EVANS nor discussed the continuing violation theory. One feature distinguishing the cases is that the prior, uncomplained-of discrimination

2. It is, of course, true that to establish her entitlement to relief, respondent will have to prove that she was unlawfully forced to resign more than 180 days prior to filing her charge with the EEOC. But if that is sufficient to defeat her claim, then discriminatees will never be able to challenge "practices, procedures, or tests * * * [which] operate to 'freeze' the status quo of prior discriminatory employment practices," Griggs v. Duke Power Co., 401 U.S. 424, 430, 91 S.Ct. 849, 853, 28 L.Ed.2d 158 (1971), even though *Griggs* holds that such practices are impermissible, and the legislative history of the Equal Employment Opportunity Act of 1972, 86 Stat. 103, indicates that Congress agrees, see Teamsters v. United States, 431 U.S., at 391–393, 97 S.Ct., at 1883–1884 (Marshall, J., concurring in part and dissenting in part). The consequence of Ms. Evans' failure to file charges after she was discharged is that she has lost her right to backpay; not her right to challenge present wrongs.

against Evans was not viewed by the court as intentional discrimination, but violated Title VII under the *Griggs* rationale. The pre-Act discrimination in *Bazemore,* by contrast, was intentional and constituted a violation of the equal protection clause of the Fourteenth Amendment. Do these differences explain the seemingly different result? See discussion of Lorance v. AT & T Technologies, Inc., 490 U.S. 900, 109 S.Ct. 2261, 104 L.Ed.2d 961 (1989), *infra,* at 506.

DELAWARE STATE COLLEGE v. RICKS

Supreme Court of the United States, 1980.
449 U.S. 250, 101 S.Ct. 498, 66 L.Ed.2d 431.

JUSTICE POWELL delivered the opinion of the Court.

The question in this case is whether respondent, a college professor, timely complained under the civil rights laws that he had been denied academic tenure because of his national origin.

I

Columbus Ricks is a black Liberian. In 1970, Ricks joined the faculty at Delaware State College, a state institution attended predominantly by blacks. In February 1973, the Faculty Committee on Promotions and Tenure (the tenure committee) recommended that Ricks not receive a tenured position in the education department. The tenure committee, however, agreed to reconsider its decision the following year. Upon reconsideration, in February 1974, the committee adhered to its earlier recommendation. The following month, the Faculty Senate voted to support the tenure committee's negative recommendation. On March 13, 1974, the College Board of Trustees formally voted to deny tenure to Ricks.

Dissatisfied with the decision, Ricks immediately filed a grievance with the Board's Educational Policy Committee (the grievance committee), which in May 1974 held a hearing and took the matter under submission.[1] During the pendency of the grievance, the College administration continued to plan for Ricks' eventual termination. Like many colleges and universities, Delaware State has a policy of not discharging immediately a junior faculty member who does not receive tenure. Rather, such a person is offered a "terminal" contract to teach one additional year. When that contract expires, the employment relationship ends. Adhering to this policy, the Trustees on June 26, 1974 told Ricks that he would be offered a one-year "terminal" contract that would expire June 30, 1975.[2] Ricks signed the contract without objec-

---

1. According to the Court of Appeals, the grievance committee almost immediately recommended to the Board that Ricks' grievance be denied. Ricks v. Delaware State College, 605 F.2d 710, 711 (CA3 1979). Nothing in the record, however, reveals the date on which the grievance committee rendered its decision.

2. The June 26 letter stated:

"June 26, 1974

"Dr. Columbus Ricks

tion or reservation on September 4, 1974. Shortly thereafter, on September 12, 1974, the Board of Trustees notified Ricks that it had denied his grievance.

Ricks attempted to file an employment discrimination charge with the Equal Employment Opportunity Commission (EEOC) on April 4, 1975. Under Title VII, however, state fair employment practices agencies have primary jurisdiction over employment discrimination complaints. See 42 U.S.C. § 2000e–5(c). The EEOC therefore referred Ricks' charge to the appropriate Delaware agency. On April 28, 1975, the state agency waived its jurisdiction, and the EEOC accepted Ricks' complaint for filing. More than two years later, the EEOC issued a "right to sue" letter.

Ricks filed this lawsuit in the District Court on September 9, 1977.[3] The complaint alleged, *inter alia*, that the College had discriminated against him on the basis of his national origin in violation of Title VII and 42 U.S.C. § 1981.[4] The District Court sustained the College's motion to dismiss both claims as untimely. It concluded that the only

"Delaware State College

"Dover, Delaware

"Dear Dr. Ricks:

"On March 13, 1974, the Board of Trustees of Delaware State College officially endorsed the recommendations of the Faculty Senate at its March 11, 1974 meeting, at which time the Faculty Senate recommended that the Board not grant you tenure.

"As we are both aware, the Educational Policy Committee of the Board of Trustees has heard your grievance and it is now in the process of coming to a decision. The Chairman of the Educational Policy Committee has indicated to me that a decision may not be forthcoming until sometime in July. In order to comply with the 1971 Trustee Policy Manual and AAUP requirements with regard to the amount of time needed in proper notification of non-reappointment for non-tenured faculty members, the Board has no choice but to follow actions according to its official position prior to the grievance process, and thus, notify you of its intent not to renew your contract at the end of the 1974–75 school year.

"Please understand that we have no way of knowing what the outcome of the grievance process may be, and that this action is being taken at this time in order to be consistent with the present formal position of the Board and AAUP time requirements in matters of this kind. Should the Educational Policy Committee decide to recommend that you be granted tenure, and should the

Board of Trustees concur with their recommendation, then of course, it will supersede any previous action taken by the Board.

"Sincerely yours,

"/s/Walton H. Simpson, President

Board of Trustees of Delaware State College"

3. In addition to the College itself, other defendants (petitioners in this Court) are Trustees Walton H. Simpson, William H. Davis, William G. Dix, Edward W. Hagemeyer, James C. Hardcastle, Delma Lafferty, James H. Williams, William S. Young, Burt C. Pratt, Luna I. Mishoe, and Pierre S. duPont IV (ex officio); the academic dean, M. Milford Caldwell (now deceased); the education department chairman, George W. McLaughlin; and tenure committee members Romeo C. Henderson, Harriet R. Williams, Arthur E. Bragg, Ora Bunch, Ehsan Helmy, Vera Powell, John R. Price, Herbert Thompson, W. Richard Wynder, Ulysses Washington, and Jane Laskaris.

4. Section 1981 provides:

"All persons within the jurisdiction of the United States shall have the same right in every State and Territory to make and enforce contracts, to sue, be parties, give evidence, and to the full and equal benefit of all laws and proceedings for the security of persons and property as is enjoyed by white citizens, and shall be subject to like punishment, pains, penalties, taxes, licenses, and exactions of every kind, and to no other."

unlawful employment practice alleged was the College's decision to deny Ricks' tenure, and that the limitations periods for both claims had commenced to run by June 26, 1974, when the President of the Board of Trustees officially notified Ricks that he would be offered a one-year "terminal" contract. See n.2, supra. The Title VII claim was not timely because Ricks had not filed his charge with the EEOC within 180 days after that date. Similarly, the § 1981 claim was not timely because the lawsuit had not been filed in the District Court within the applicable three-year statute of limitations.[5]

The Court of Appeals for the Third Circuit reversed. 605 F.2d 710 (1979). It agreed with the District Court that Ricks' essential allegation was that he had been denied tenure illegally. Id., at 711. According to the Court of Appeals, however, the Title VII filing requirement, and the statute of limitations for the § 1981 claim, did not commence to run until Ricks' "terminal" contract expired on June 30, 1975. The Court reasoned:

> " '[A] terminated employee who is still working should not be required to consult a lawyer or file charges of discrimination against his employer as long as he is still working, even though he has been told of the employer's present intention to terminate him in the future.' " Id., at 712, quoting Bonham v. Dresser Industries, Inc., 569 F.2d 187, 192 (CA3 1977), cert. denied, 439 U.S. 821, 99 S.Ct. 87, 58 L.Ed.2d 113 (1978).

The Court of Appeals believed that the initial decision to terminate an employee sometimes might be reversed. The aggrieved employee therefore should not be expected to resort to litigation until termination actually has occurred. Prior resort to judicial or administrative remedies would be

> "likely to have the negative side effect of reducing that employee's effectiveness during the balance of his or her term. Working relationships will be injured, if not sundered, and the litigation process will divert attention from the proper fulfillment of job responsibilities." 605 F.2d., at 712.

Finally, the Court of Appeals thought that a rule focusing on the last day of employment would provide a "bright line guide both for the courts and for the victims of discrimination." Id., at 712–713. It therefore reversed and remanded the case to the District Court for trial on the merits of Ricks' discrimination claims. We granted certiorari. 444 U.S. 1070, 100 S.Ct. 1012, 62 L.Ed.2d 751 (1980).

For the reasons that follow, we think that the Court of Appeals erred in holding that the filing limitations periods did not commence to run until June 30, 1975. We agree instead with the District Court that

---

5. The statute of limitations in § 1981 cases is that applicable to similar claims under state law. Johnson v. Railway Express Agency, Inc., 421 U.S. 454, 462, 95 S.Ct. 1716, 1721, 44 L.Ed.2d 295 (1975). The parties in this case agree that the applicable limitations period under Delaware law is three years.

both the Title VII and § 1981 claims were untimely.[6]　Accordingly, we reverse.

II

Title VII requires aggrieved persons to file a complaint with the EEOC "within one hundred and eighty days after the alleged unlawful employment practice occurred." 42 U.S.C. § 2000e–5(e).[7]　Similarly, § 1981 plaintiffs in Delaware must file suit within three years of the unfavorable employment decision. See n.5, supra. The limitations periods, while guaranteeing the protection of the civil rights laws to those who promptly assert their rights, also protect employers from the burden of defending claims arising from employment decisions that are long past.

Determining the timeliness of Ricks' EEOC complaint, and this ensuing lawsuit, requires us to identify precisely the "unlawful employment practice" of which he complains. Ricks now insists that discrimination not only motivated the College in denying him tenure, but also in terminating his employment on June 30, 1975. Tr. of Oral Arg., at 25, 26, 31–32. In effect, he is claiming a "continuing violation" of the civil rights laws with the result that the limitations periods did not commence to run until his one-year "terminal" contract expired. This argument cannot be squared with the allegations of the complaint. Mere continuity of employment, without more, is insufficient to prolong the life of a cause of action for employment discrimination. United Air Lines v. Evans, supra, at 558, 97 S.Ct. at 1889. If Ricks intended to complain of a discriminatory discharge, he should have identified the alleged discriminatory acts that continued until, or occurred at the time of, the actual termination of his employment. But the complaint alleges no such facts.[8]

Indeed, the contrary is true. It appears that termination of employment at Delaware State is a delayed, but inevitable, consequence of the denial of tenure. In order for the limitations periods to commence with the date of discharge, Ricks would have had to allege and prove that the manner in which his employment was terminated differed discriminatorily from the manner in which the College terminated

---

6. Because the claims were not timely filed, we do not decide whether a claim of national origin discrimination is cognizable under § 1981.

7. Under certain circumstances, the filing period is extended to 300 days. 42 U.S.C. § 2000e–5(e); see Mohasco Corp. v. Silver, 447 U.S. 807, 100 S.Ct. 2486, 65 L.Ed.2d 532 (1980).

8. Sixteen paragraphs in the complaint describe in detail the sequence of events surrounding the tenure denial. Only one paragraph even mentions Ricks' eventual departure from Delaware State, and nothing in that paragraph alleges any fact suggesting discrimination in the termination of Ricks' employment.

The complaint does allege that a variety of unusual incidents occurred during the 1974–1975 school year, including one in which the education department chairman, George W. McLaughlin, physically attacked Ricks. This incident allegedly resulted in McLaughlin's conviction for assault. Counsel for Ricks conceded at oral argument that incidents such as this were not independent acts of discrimination, Tr. of Oral Arg., at 29–30, but at most evidence that could be used at a trial.

other professors who also had been denied tenure. But no suggestion has been made that Ricks was treated differently from other unsuccessful tenure aspirants. Rather, in accord with the College's practice, Ricks was offered a one-year "terminal" contract, with explicit notice that his employment would end upon its expiration.

In sum, the only alleged discrimination occurred—and the filing limitations periods therefore commenced—at the time the tenure decision was made and communicated to Ricks.[9] That is so even though one of the *effects* of the denial of tenure—the eventual loss of a teaching position—did not occur until later. The Court of Appeals for the Ninth Circuit correctly held, in a similar tenure case, that "[t]he proper focus is upon the time of the *discriminatory acts*, not upon the time at which the *consequences* of the acts became most painful." Abramson v. University of Hawaii, 594 F.2d 202, 209 (1979) (emphasis added); see United Air Lines v. Evans, supra, at 558, 97 S.Ct. at 1889. It is simply insufficient for Ricks to allege that his termination "gives present effect to the past illegal act and therefore perpetuates the consequences of forbidden discrimination." Id. at 557, 97 S.Ct. at 1888. The emphasis is not upon the effects of earlier employment decisions; rather, it "is [upon] whether any present *violation* exists." Id. at 558, 97 S.Ct. at 1889 (emphasis in original).

III

We conclude for the foregoing reasons that the limitations periods commenced to run when the tenure decision was made and Ricks was notified. The remaining inquiry is the identification of this date.

A

Three dates have been advanced and argued by the parties. As indicated above, Ricks contended for June 30, 1975, the final date of his "terminal" contract, relying on a continuing violation theory. This contention fails, as we have shown, because of the absence of any allegations of facts to support it. The Court of Appeals agreed with Ricks that the relevant date was June 30, 1975, but it did so on a different theory. It found that the only alleged discriminatory act was the denial of tenure, 605 F.2d, at 711, but nevertheless adopted the "final date of employment" rule primarily for policy reasons. Ante, at 503. Although this view has the virtue of simplicity,[10] the discussion in Part II of this opinion demonstrates its fallacy as a rule of general application. Congress has decided that time limitations periods commence with the date of the "alleged unlawful employment practice."

---

9. Complaints that employment termination resulted from discrimination can present widely varying circumstances. In this case the only alleged discriminatory act is the denial of tenure sought by a college professor, with the termination of employment not occurring until a later date. The application of the general principles discussed herein necessarily must be made on a case-by-case basis.

10. Brief for *amicus curiae* EEOC, at 19–22; Ricks v. Delaware State College, supra, at 712–713.

See 42 U.S.C. § 2000e–5(e). Where, as here, the only challenged employment practice occurs before the termination date, the limitations periods necessarily commence to run before that date.[11] It should not be forgotten that time-limitations provisions themselves promoted important interests; "the period allowed for instituting suit inevitably reflects a value judgment concerning the point at which the interests in favor of protecting valid claims are outweighed by the interests in prohibiting the prosecution of stale ones." Johnson v. Railway Express Agency, Inc., supra, at 463–464, 95 S.Ct. at 1721–1722.[12] See Mohasco Corp. v. Silver, 447 U.S. 807, at 820, 100 S.Ct. 2486, at 2494, 65 L.Ed.2d 532 (1980).

B

The EEOC, in its *amicus* brief, contends in the alternative for a different date. It was not until September 12, 1974, that the Board notified Ricks that his grievance had been denied. The EEOC therefore asserts that, for purposes of computing limitations periods, this was the date of the unfavorable tenure decision.[13] Two possible lines of reasoning underlie this argument. First, it could be contended that the Trustees' initial decision was only an expression of intent that did not become final until the grievance was denied. In support of this argument, the EEOC notes that the June 26 letter explicitly held out to Ricks the possibility that he would receive tenure if the Board sustained his grievance. See n.2, supra. Second, even if the Board's first decision expressed its official position, it could be argued that the pendency of the grievance should toll the running of the limitations periods.

We do not find either argument to be persuasive. As to the former, we think that the Board of Trustees had made clear well before September 12 that it had formally rejected Ricks' tenure bid. The June

---

11. The Court of Appeals also thought it was significant that a final date of employment rule would permit the teacher to conclude his affairs at a school without the acrimony engendered by the filing of an administrative complaint or lawsuit. 605 F.2d at 712. It is true that "the filing of a lawsuit might tend to deter efforts at conciliation." Johnson v. Railway Express Agency, Inc., supra, at 461, 95 S.Ct. at 1720. But this is the "natural effect [ ] of the choice Congress has made," ibid., in explicitly requiring that the limitations period commence with the date of the "alleged unlawful employment practice," 42 U.S.C. § 2000e–5(c).

12. It is conceivable that the Court of Appeals' "final day of employment" rule might discourage colleges even from offering a "grace period," such as Delaware State's practice of one-year "terminal" contracts, during which the junior faculty member not offered tenure may seek a teaching position elsewhere.

13. If September 12 were the critical date, the § 1981 claim would be timely. Counting from September 12, the Title VII claim also would be timely if Ricks is entitled to 300 days, rather than 180 days, in which to file with the EEOC. In its brief before this Court, the EEOC as *amicus curiae* noted that Delaware is a state with its own fair employment practices agency. According to the EEOC, therefore, Ricks was entitled to 300 days to file his complaint. See n.7, supra. Because we hold that the time limitations periods commenced to run no later than June 26, 1974, we need not decide whether Ricks was entitled to 300 days to file under Title VII. Counting from the June 26 date, Ricks' filing with the EEOC was not timely even with the benefit of the 300–day period.

26 letter itself characterized that as the Board's "official position." Ibid. It is apparent, of course, that the Board in the June 26 letter indicated a willingness to change its prior decision if Ricks' grievance were found to be meritorious. But entertaining a grievance complaining of the tenure decision does not suggest that the earlier decision was in any respect tentative. The grievance procedure, by its nature, is a *remedy* for a prior decision, not an opportunity to *influence* that decision before it is made.

As to the latter argument, we already have held that the pendency of a grievance, or some other method of collateral review of an employment decision, does not toll the running of the limitations periods. International Union of Electrical Workers v. Robbins & Myers, Inc., 429 U.S. 229, 97 S.Ct. 441, 50 L.Ed.2d 427 (1976).[14] The existence of careful procedures to assure fairness in the tenure decision should not obscure the principle that limitations periods normally commence when the employer's decision is made. Cf. id., at 234–235, 97 S.Ct. at 446.[15]

C

The District Court rejected both the June 30, 1975 date and the September 12, 1974 date, and concluded that the limitations periods had commenced to run by June 26, 1974, when the President of the Board notified Ricks that he would be offered a "terminal" contract for the 1974–1975 school year. We cannot say that this decision was erroneous. By June 26, the tenure committee had twice recommended that Ricks not receive tenure; the Faculty Senate had voted to support the tenure committee's recommendation; and the Board of Trustees formally had voted to deny Ricks tenure.[16] In light of this unbroken array of negative decisions, the District Court was justified in concluding that the College had established its official position—and made that position apparent to Ricks—no later than June 26, 1974.[17]

14. See also B. Schlei & P. Grossman, Employment Discrimination Law, 235 (1979 Supp.), and cases cited therein.

15. We do not suggest that aspirants for academic tenure should ignore available opportunities to request reconsideration. Mere requests to reconsider, however, cannot extend the limitations periods applicable to the civil rights laws.

16. We recognize, of course, that the limitations periods should not commence to run so soon that it becomes difficult for a layman to invoke the protection of the civil rights statutes. See Oscar Mayer & Co. v. Evans, 441 U.S. 750, 761, 99 S.Ct. 2066, 2073 (1979); Love v. Pullman Co., 404 U.S. 522, 526–527, 92 S.Ct. 616, 618, 30 L.Ed.2d 679 (1972). But, for the reasons we have stated, there can be no claim here that Ricks was not abundantly forewarned. In NLRB v. Yeshiva University, 444 U.S. 672, 674, 100 S.Ct. 856, at 859, 63 L.Ed.2d

115 (1980), we noted that university boards of trustees customarily rely on the professional expertise of the tenured faculty, particularly with respect to decisions about hiring, tenure, termination, and promotion. Thus, the action of the Board of Trustees on March 13, 1974, affirming the faculty recommendation, was entirely predictable. The Board's letter of June 26, 1974 simply repeated to Ricks the Board's official position and acknowledged the pendency of the grievance through which Ricks hopes to persuade the Board to change that position.

17. We need not decide whether the District Court correctly focused on the June 26 date, rather than the date the Board communicated to Ricks its unfavorable tenure decision made at the March 13, 1974 meeting. As we have stated, see n.13, supra, both the Title VII and § 1981 com-

We therefore reverse the decision of the Court of Appeals and remand to that Court so that it may reinstate the District Court's order dismissing the complaint.

Reversed.

JUSTICE STEWART, with whom JUSTICE BRENNAN and JUSTICE MARSHALL join, dissenting.

I agree with the Court that the unlawful employment practice alleged in the respondent's complaint was a discriminatory denial of tenure, not a discriminatory termination of employment. Nevertheless, I believe that a fair reading of the complaint reveals a plausible allegation that the College actually denied Ricks' tenure on September 12, 1974, the date on which the Board finally confirmed its decision to accept the faculty's recommendation that he not be given tenure.

Therefore, unlike the Court, I think Ricks should be allowed to prove to the District Court that the allegedly unlawful denial of tenure occurred on that date.[1] As noted by the Court, if Ricks succeeds in this proof, his § 1981 claim would certainly be timely, and the timeliness of his Title VII claim would then depend on whether his filing of a complaint with the Delaware Department of Labor entitled him to file his EEOC charge within 300 days of the discriminatory act, rather than within the 180 days limitation that the Court of Appeals and the District Court assumed to be applicable.[2]

A brief examination of the June 26, 1974 letter to Ricks from the Board of Trustees, quoted by the Court, provides a reasonable basis for the allegation that the College did not effectively deny Ricks' tenure until September 12. The letter informed Ricks of the Board's "intent not to renew" his contract at the end of the 1974–1975 academic year. And the letter suggested that the Board was so informing Ricks at that time only to ensure technical compliance with College and AAUP requirements in case it should *later* decide to abide by its earlier acceptance of the faculty's recommendation that Ricks be denied tenure. The Board expressly stated in the letter that it had "no way of knowing" what the outcome of the grievance process might be, but that

plaints were not timely filed even counting from the June 26 date.

1. The Court treats the District Court's determination of June 26, 1974, as the date of tenure denial as a factual finding which is not clearly erroneous. But it must be stressed that the District Court dismissed Ricks' claims on the pleadings, and so never made factual determinations on this or any other issue.

2. Title VII would allow Ricks 300 days if he had "initially instituted" proceedings with a local or state agency with authority to grant him relief. 42 U.S.C. § 2000e–5(b); see Mohasco Corp. v. Silver, 447 U.S. 807, 808, 100 S.Ct. 2486, at 2488, 65 L.Ed.2d 532. To benefit from this provision, however, Ricks would arguably have had to make a timely filing with the state agency. Delaware law requires that a charge of discrimination be filed with the Department of Labor within 90 days after the allegedly discriminatory practice occurred or within 120 days after the practice is discovered, whichever date is later. Del. Code Ann. tit. 19, § 712(d). Neither the District Court nor the Court of Appeals considered the timeliness Ricks' filing with the state agency, nor the significance of the state agency's action in waiving jurisdiction over Ricks' charge, and so these questions would be appropriately addressed on remand.

a decision of the Board's Educational Policy Committee favorable to Ricks would "of course * * * supersede any previous action taken by the Board."

Thus, the Board itself may have regarded its earlier actions as tentative or preliminary, pending a thorough review triggered by the respondent's request to the Committee. The Court acknowledges that this letter expresses the Board's willingness to change its earlier view on Ricks' tenure, but considers the grievance procedure under which the decision might have been changed to be a remedy for an earlier tenure decision and not a part of the overall process of making the initial tenure decision. Ricks, however, may be able to prove to the District Court that at his College, the original Board response to the faculty's recommendation was not a virtually final action subject to reopening only in the most extreme cases, but a preliminary decision to shift the burden from the College to the tenure candidate, and to advance the tenure question to the Board's grievance committee as the next conventional stage in the process.[3]

Whether this is an accurate view of the tenure process at Delaware State College is, of course, a factual question we cannot resolve here. But Ricks lost his case in the trial court on a motion to dismiss. I think that motion was wrongly granted, and that Ricks was entitled to a hearing and a determination of this factual issue. See Abramson v. University of Hawaii, 594 F.2d 202 (CA9).

I would, therefore, vacate the judgment of the Court of Appeals and remand the case to the District Court so that it can make this determination and then, if necessary, resolve whether Title VII allowed Ricks 300 days from the denial of tenure to file his charge with the Commission.

JUSTICE STEVENS, dissenting.

The custom widely followed by colleges and universities of offering a one-year terminal contract immediately after making an adverse tenure decision is, in my judgment, analogous to the custom in many other personnel relationships of giving an employee two weeks advance notice of discharge. My evaluation of this case can perhaps best be explained by that analogy.

Three different reference points could arguably determine when a cause of action for a discriminatory discharge accrues: (1) when the employer decides to terminate the relationship; (2) when notice of termination is given to the employee; and (3) when the discharge becomes effective. The most sensible rule would provide that the date of discharge establishes the time when a cause of action accrues and the

---

3. This view is consistent with the policies and model procedures of the American Association of University Professors, AAUP Policy Documents and Reports 15, 29 (1977); see Board of Regents v. Roth, 408 U.S. 564, 578–579, and n.17, 92 S.Ct. 2701, 2710, and n. 17, 33 L.Ed.2d 548; AAUP *Amicus* Brief, at 9–10, on whose requirements the Board of Trustees in this case expressly relied in explaining its action in the June 26 letter.

statute of limitations begins to run. Prior to that date, the allegedly wrongful act is subject to change; more importantly, the effective discharge date is the date which can normally be identified with the least difficulty or dispute.[1]

I would apply the same reasoning here in identifying the date on which respondent's allegedly discriminatory discharge became actionable. See Egelston v. State University College at Geneseo, 535 F.2d 752, 755 (CA2 1976). Thus under my analysis the statute of limitations began to run on June 30, 1975, the termination date of respondent's one year contract. In reaching that conclusion, I do not characterize the college's discharge decision as a "continuing violation"; nor do I suggest that a teacher who is denied tenure and who remains in a school's employ for an indefinite period could file a timely complaint based on the tenure decision when he or she is ultimately discharged. Rather, I regard a case such as this one, in which a college denies tenure and offers a terminal one year contract as part of the adverse tenure decision, as a discharge case. The decision to deny tenure in this situation is in all respects comparable to another employer's decision to discharge an employee and, in due course, to give the employee notice of the effective date of that discharge. Both the interest in harmonious working relations during the terminal period of the employment relationship,[2] and the interest in certainty that is so important in litigation of this kind,[3] support this result.

For these reasons, I would affirm the judgment of the Court of Appeals.

NOTES AND PROBLEMS FOR DISCUSSION

1. Is a denial of tenure fundamentally different from a notice of discharge? Should the period for filing in the latter case run from the date the

1. Although few courts have had the occasion to consider the issue in the context of notice of discharge preceding actual termination, some courts have recognized that the date on which the employee actually ceases to perform services for the employer, and not a later date when the payment of benefits or accrued vacation time ceases, should determine the running of the statute of limitations. See Bonham v. Dresser Industries, Inc., 569 F.2d 187, 192 (CA3 1977), cert. denied, 439 U.S. 821, 99 S.Ct. 87, 58 L.Ed.2d 113 (1978); Krzyzewski v. Metropolitan Government of Nashville and Davidson County, 584 F.2d 802, 804–805 (CA6 1978).

2. This interest has special force in the college setting. Because the employee must file a charge with the EEOC within 180 days after the occurrence, the Court's analysis will necessitate the filing of a charge while the teacher is still employed. The filing of such a charge may prejudice any pending reconsideration of the tenure decision and also may impair the teacher's performance of his or her regular duties. Neither of these adverse consequences would be present in a discharge following a relatively short notice such as two weeks.

3. The interest in certainty lies not only in choosing the most easily identifiable date, but also in avoiding the involvement of the EEOC until the school's decision to deny tenure is final. The American Association of University Professors, as *amicus curiae* here, has indicated that under the "prevailing academic employment practices" of American higher education, which allow for maximum flexibility in tenure decisions, initial tenure determinations are often reconsidered, and the reconsideration process may take the better part of the terminal contract year. American Association of University Professors *Amicus* Brief, at 6–11.

employee learns of his discharge or from his last day of work? In CHARDON
v. FERNANDEZ, 454 U.S. 6, 102 S.Ct. 28, 70 L.Ed.2d 6 (1981), a case filed under
42 U.S.C. § 1983, the Supreme Court, relying on *Ricks*, concluded that in a
discharge case, the "unlawful employment practice" (from which date the
limitation period runs) occurs when the decision to terminate is made and
communicated to the employee, not the date that actual termination occurs.
Justice Brennan dissented:

> It is one thing to hold, as was held in Delaware State College v. Ricks,
> * * * that for the purpose of computing the limitations period, a cause of
> action for denial of a benefit such as tenure, and consequent damage,
> accrues when the plaintiff learns that he *has been* denied that benefit; it is
> quite another to hold, as the Court does here, that a cause of action for
> damages resulting from an unconstitutional termination of employment
> accrues when the plaintiff learns that he *will* be terminated. To my
> knowledge, such a rule has no analogue in customary principles of limita-
> tions law. See 4 A. Corbin, Contracts sec. 989 ("The plaintiff should not be
> penalized for leaving to the defendant an opportunity to retract his wrong-
> ful repudiation; and he will be so penalized if the statutory period of
> limitation is held to begin to run against him immediately.")
>
> The thrust of the Court's decision is to require a potential civil rights
> plaintiff to measure the time for filing his claim from the moment some
> form of injunctive relief first becomes available. The effect of this ruling
> will be to increase the number of unripe and anticipatory lawsuits in the
> federal courts—lawsuits that should not be filed until some concrete harm
> has been suffered, and until the parties, and the forces of time, have had
> maximum opportunity to resolve the controversy.

454 U.S. at 6, 102 S.Ct. at 29.

2. In *Delaware State College* the statute of limitations began to run "at
the time the tenure decision was made *and communicated* to Ricks." (emphasis
added). Most courts have found implicit in *Delaware State College* the common
"discovery rule" under which the limitation period begins to run when the
employee discovers or by exercise of reasonable diligence could have discovered
the discriminatory act. In Cada v. Baxter Healthcare Corp., 920 F.2d 446 (7th
Cir.1990), cert. denied, ___ U.S. ___, 111 S.Ct. 2916, 115 L.Ed.2d 1079 (1991), for
example, the court reasoned that if the plaintiff "did not discover that he had
been injured, i.e. that a decision to terminate him had been made, until May 22
the statute of limitations did not begin to run till that day ...". The limitation
period begins to run when the plaintiff knows, or should know, of the discriminatory *act* whether or not she realizes the discriminatory animus underlying
the act. See, Merrill v. Southern Methodist University, 806 F.2d 600 (5th
Cir.1986); Chapman v. Homco, Inc., 886 F.2d 756 (5th Cir.1989), cert. denied,
494 U.S. 1067, 110 S.Ct. 1784, 108 L.Ed.2d 785 (1990).

If the employee's discharge results from a prior discriminatory act, a biased
performance evaluation for example, should the filing period run from the date
of the evaluation or the date of the discharge? In Colgan v. Fisher Scientific
Co., 935 F.2d 1407 (3d Cir.), cert. denied, ___ U.S. ___, 112 S.Ct. 379, 116 L.Ed.2d
330 (1991) the plaintiff, after a lengthy and successful work history with the
employer, was given an unfavorable evaluation. Three months later the
company instituted a reduction in force plan which called for the termination
of employees with negative evaluations and the plaintiff was one of the
employees terminated under the plan. The plaintiff filed his EEOC charge

alleging age discrimination within 300 days of notice of his termination but more than 300 days after he had received the evaluation. The district court held that the EEOC charge was untimely under *Ricks* and *Evans* because the alleged discriminatory act was the evaluation, which, like the denial of tenure in *Ricks*, had resulted in his termination. Accordingly, the district court dismissed the case. The Third Circuit reversed. The Court of Appeals distinguished *Ricks* and *Evans* on the ground that in those cases the harm from the alleged unlawful employment decision was known at the time of the decision.

> [W]hen Colgon received his poor evaluation, it did not put him on formal notice that it would make him one of the first to be discharged when the company later decided on the reduction in force. We therefore conclude in this case, considering the totality of the circumstances, in particular the tentative nature of the evaluation and the lack of evidence showing Colgon, when evaluated, knew or had reason to anticipate his vulnerability to discharge, that Fisher's allegedly discriminatory employment practice did not trigger the start of the limitations period.

935 F.2d at 1420.

3. How should the discovery rule apply to wage discrimination claims? In a case where the plaintiff claimed to have first learned of pay discrimination during discovery on a discharge claim, the Fourth Circuit held that the period for filing a charge should not begin to run until "a reasonable plaintiff should have known facts which would support a charge of discrimination." Hamilton v. 1st Source Bank, 895 F.2d 159 (4th Cir.1990). The court distinguished pay claims from discharged claims as follows:

> At the moment an employee is discharged, she or he is on notice to inquire whether there was discriminatory motive for the discharge, and is alerted to file a claim with the EEOC within 180 days if he or she so suspects. In marked contrast, there is no reason to suspect discrimination each time one is handed a pay check. The Bank does not argue that Hamilton should have known about the difference between his salary and that of other vice-presidents at any time prior to the pretrial discovery; indeed, it points out that the normal and prudent American business practice is to discourage sharing information about salaries.

895 F.2d at 164. But the Fourth Circuit granted rehearing *en banc* in *Hamilton* and reversed the panel decision. 928 F.2d 86 (4th Cir.1990)(*en banc*). The court reasoned that if Congress had wanted to build a discovery rule into the filing requirement, it would have done so. According to the court, plain and unequivocal nature of the statutory language establishes a period of 180 days for plaintiffs to file charges with the EEOC, starting from the time the alleged unlawful practice occurs, not from the time that the employee discovers its discriminatory nature. The Court rejected the argument that, because an employee has no reason to suspect a discriminatory pay practice on receiving a paycheck, that a special rule be created for pay claims.

> An occurrence rule is based upon the supposition that the adverse act serves to put the employee on notice. That supposition applies equally to claims of discriminatory discharge and unequal pay.

928 F.2d at 89. If "occurrence" means when the discriminatory act takes place and nothing more, why is not the "occurrence" in a pay case the setting of a discriminatory salary? See Hall v. Ledex, Inc., 669 F.2d 397, 398–399 (6th Cir.1982); Roberts v. North American Rockwell Corp., 650 F.2d 823, 827–828

(6th Cir.1981) (in wage discrimination case plaintiff suffers denial of equal pay with each check she receives).   Cf. Battle v. Clark Equipment, 524 F.Supp. 683 (N.D.Ind. 1981) (application of *Delaware State College* to alleged discriminatory distribution of supplemented unemployment pay).   The parameters of the "continuing violation" doctrine are explored in the following material.

ABRAMS v. BAYLOR COLLEGE OF MEDICINE

United States Court of Appeals, Fifth Circuit, 1986.
805 F.2d 528.

JOHN R. BROWN, CIRCUIT JUDGE:

In 1977, Baylor College of Medicine (Baylor or the college) agreed to provide special cardiovascular services to the King Faisal Hospital in Riyadh, Saudi Arabia.   These services were to be provided by a team of surgeons, anesthesiologists, and other support personnel who were sent to Saudi Arabia for three month "rotation" periods.   Since the first team departed for Riyadh in 1978, Baylor has not selected a single Jew to participate in the Faisal Hospital rotation program.   In 1982, two anesthesiologists filed suit against Baylor claiming that they had unlawfully been denied the opportunity to participate in the program because they were Jews.

In this appeal, we review the District Court's judgment based on its findings that their claims were timely filed, and that the actions of the college constituted intentional discrimination, on the basis of religion, in violation of Title VII.   On reviewing the record and concluding that the Court's findings are legally acceptable in light of the record viewed in its entirety, we affirm that judgment based on Title VII.

* * *

International medicine—across National, Political and Religious Lines

The King Faisal Hospital (Faisal Hospital) is a large medical complex owned by the Kingdom of Saudi Arabia.   Its facilities are devoted primarily to the care and treatment of members of the Saudi royal family, but are also made available to those members of the Saudi populace who are afflicted with particularly difficult illnesses.   As a result of its unique situation in Saudi Arabia, Faisal Hospital offers fertile ground for the training of American physicians.   Saudi Arabia has a high incidence of rheumatic fever, so the incidence of pediatric patients afflicted with congenital or heart-valve defects is markedly higher in that country than in the United States.   That, in turn, presents physicians with a greater opportunity for clinical experience in the treatment of childhood heart disease than is generally available in America.

The stature of Faisal Hospital, the training opportunities it presented, and certain eleemosynary considerations, led Baylor to agree to provide cardiovascular surgical services to the Saudi hospital in 1977.   The agreement, which continues in effect, provided that Baylor would send surgeons, anesthesiologists, and other operating room personnel to Riyadh for three month rotations. Baylor is reimbursed by the Saudis for the lion's share of the cost associated with the program, including the cost of providing salary, travel, and fringe benefits to the physicians and nurses participating in the rotations.

In order to ensure that the rotations are adequately staffed, the salaries for program participants are set at a very attractive level. Indeed, while stationed at the Faisal Hospital, Baylor physicians receive a salary almost twice that paid to their colleagues who remain behind to care for patients in Houston. The combination of clinical experience and an attractive salary has engendered substantial interest in the rotations among the Baylor faculty. Many Baylor physicians have taken several rotations in Riyadh.

Most of the participants in the Saudi rotations are drawn from Baylor's prestigious Fondren–Brown cardiovascular unit at the Methodist Hospital. The physicians at Fondren–Brown all have excellent professional and academic credentials, but the only criteria for participation in the program are membership on the Baylor faculty and certification—for the anesthesiologists—by the American Board of Anesthesiology or its foreign equivalent. Physicians who possess these qualifications are not required formally to apply for a Saudi rotation. Instead, those who desire to participate merely communicate their interest by word of mouth to the Baylor administrators in charge of the program. Shortly thereafter, the interested physician is placed on a constantly changing scheduling sheet. At the time the physician is placed on the schedule, his name is also submitted for inclusion in the block entry visa issued by the Saudi government for the benefit of the Faisal Hospital rotation program.

The plaintiffs in this litigation are each cardiovascular anesthesiologists who met the objective criteria for participation in a Saudi rotation. Dr. Lawrence Abrams is a Board certified anesthesiologist who became a member of the Baylor faculty in July of 1978. Dr. Stewart Linde, a South African citizen, holds the equivalent of Board certification in anesthesiology and was employed as a Baylor faculty member in September of 1979.

Race/Religion Raises its Head

Early in their employment, each of the plaintiffs indicated an interest in participating in a rotation, but each was informed that he could not participate because—as a Jew—he would be unable to secure an entry visa which would permit him to enter Saudi Arabia. There is no evidence in the record that that statement represented the actual position of the Saudi government with regard to the participation of Jews in the program. In addition, there is no evidence that Baylor even attempted to ascertain the official position of the Saudi government on this issue. Despite this "visa problem," Abrams and Linde persisted in their desire to undertake a Saudi rotation. Nevertheless, each time a team departed for Riyadh, Jewish personnel were excluded from participation.

Dr. Abrams became a vocal critic of this practice. His chief complaint concerned the marked inequity in compensation and workload between the physicians who participated in the program and those who were excluded, because of their inability to take rotations. Dr. Abrams was eventually transferred by Baylor, over his objections, from Fondren–Brown to the Ben Taub Hospital. While Dr. Linde did not undertake vocal opposition to the policy, he was likewise excluded from participating in the Saudi rotations.

Dr. Abrams and Dr. Linde eventually filed charges of discrimination with the EEOC. Abrams filed his charge on November 7, 1982; Linde filed his on February 18, 1982. Both of these filings occurred substantially more than 180 days after the plaintiffs first became aware of their "visa problems." Baylor had, however, sent teams to Riyadh within 180 days preceding the filing of the plaintiffs' charges. When the timeliness of the claims was asserted by Baylor as a defense at trial, the District Court concluded that Baylor's policy of excluding Jews from the rotations constituted a continuing violation of Title VII. It therefore held that the claims had been timely filed.

The case proceeded to trial on the merits, and the District Court found that Baylor had intentionally discriminated against Abrams and Linde on the basis of their Jewish religion. It therefore awarded them backpay relief based upon the number of rotations in which each could have participated during his tenure at Baylor. In addition, the Court awarded Abrams and Linde attorneys' fees in excess of $280,000. Baylor has appealed, contesting the findings of timeliness and intentional discrimination, and the award of attorneys' fees. The plaintiffs have undertaken a cross-appeal that is largely precautionary.

The Title VII Claims

A district court's finding of intentional discrimination under Title VII is to be reviewed under the clearly erroneous standard. Anderson v. City of Bessemer, 470 U.S. 564, 105 S.Ct. 1504, 84 L.Ed.2d 518 (1985). Indeed, the Supreme Court has stated

> If the district court's account of the evidence is plausible in light of the record viewed in its entirety, the court of appeals may not reverse it even though convinced that had it been sitting as the trier of fact, it would have weighed the evidence differently. Where there are two permissible views of the evidence, the factfinder's choice between them cannot be clearly erroneous.

470 U.S. at 574, 105 S.Ct. at 1512, 84 L.Ed.2d at 528.

In this Circuit, the clearly erroneous standard also governs review of a district court's finding of a continuing violation when relevant to the issue of the timeliness of a claim filed under Title VII. Glass v. Petro–Tex Chem. Corp., 757 F.2d 1554, 1560 (5th Cir.1985). With those standards of review in mind, we now examine Baylor's contentions that the District Court erred in its findings on the issues of timeliness and intentional discrimination.

Federal Complaint—In Time?

Title VII of the Civil Rights Act of 1964 prohibits employment discrimination against any individual "because of such individual's race, color, religion, sex, or national origin." 42 U.S.C. § 2000e–2. Title VII affords a private right of action to individuals aggrieved by unlawful discrimination but, in order to preserve their statutory rights, employees must file their charges of discrimination "within one hundred and eighty days after the alleged unlawful employment practice occurred." 42 U.S.C. § 2000e–5(e). Timely filing is a prerequisite to the maintenance of a Title VII action and the failure to file within the statutory period will ordinarily operate as a bar to suit.

In the Fifth Circuit, however, we have recognized that "equitable considerations may very well require that the filing periods not begin to run until facts supportive of a Title VII charge or civil rights action are or should be apparent to a reasonably prudent person similarly situated." *Glass,* 757 F.2d at 1560; Dumas v. Town of Mount Vernon, 612 F.2d 974, 978 (5th Cir.1980). One such equitable consideration arises in the context of a continuing violation of Title VII. Where the unlawful employment practice manifests itself over time, rather than as a series of discrete acts, the violation may be found to be a continuing one that "relieves a plaintiff who makes such a claim from the burden of proving that the entire violation occurred within the actionable period." Berry v. Board of Supervisors, 715 F.2d 971, 979 (5th Cir.1983).

* * *

This theory of continuing violation has to be guardedly employed because within it are the seeds of the destruction of statutes of limitation in Title VII cases. As we pointed out in *Berry,*

> courts have differed over whether the existence of the policy itself constitutes a continuing violation, making a suit timely if the policy remains in effect during the actionable period, or whether there must be some actual application of it to the plaintiff within the period.

715 F.2d at 979. If the mere existence of a policy is sufficient to constitute a continuing violation, it is difficult to conceive of a circumstance in which a plaintiff's claim of an unlawful employment policy could be untimely. Such a result would render § 2000e–5(e) a nullity, and we decline to adopt it.

We hold, instead, that to establish a continuing violation, a plaintiff must show some application of the illegal policy to him (or to his class) within the 180 days preceding the filing of his complaint. Gonzalez v. Firestone Tire & Rubber Co., 610 F.2d 241, 249 (5th Cir.1980). Just as there can be no negligence in the air,[8] so the existence of a

8. Cf. Palsgraf v. Long Island R.R. Co., 248 N.Y.339, 162 N.E.2d 99 (1928).

quiescent discriminatory policy is simply insufficient to toll the statute of limitations. To hold to the contrary would expose employers to a virtually open-ended period of liability and would, as we said, read the statute of limitations right out of existence. Thus, we now review the District Court's finding that Baylor engaged in a continuing violation by virtue of its exclusionary policy.

We must bear in mind that a reasonably prudent employee will not necessarily conclude that his employer is an illegal discriminator on the basis of one conversation and one at least arguably nondiscriminatory act. *Glass,* 757 F.2d at 1562. In this case, both Abrams and Linde were informed that their ineligibility for rotations arose from their visa problems although all now recognize that this came about from their Jewish religion. There was testimony at trial that various mechanisms were available by which Baylor could have attempted to resolve the visa difficulties, so Abrams and Linde had a reasonable basis for assuming that the decision to exclude them was not a final one. In short, at the time that Baylor asserts that Abrams and Linde should have filed their claim, the doctors did not yet have enough information by which a "reasonably prudent person similarly situated" could have realized that he was the victim of illegal discrimination. See *Glass,* 757 F.2d at 1560.

The trial court could conclude that the continuing nature of Baylor's violation is evident from the fact that the college persisted in its exclusionary practices without any attempt to ascertain an official position from the Saudis. In the case of Dr. Abrams, the college persisted in its refusal to designate him for the Faisal Hospital rotation program until the date on which he resigned his position as a member of the faculty. Dr. Linde, in turn, was not offered a rotation until after he had already filed suit against the college.

Finally, we have no difficulty in upholding the District Court's finding that the unlawful policy was applied to Abrams and Linde within the 180 days preceding the filing of their complaints. The District Court found that the departures of the teams for Riyadh were the relevant employment decisions for purposes of the filing requirement.[9] Baylor's own witnesses, among them Drs. Beall and Storey, testified that the list of those scheduled to go to Riyadh changed almost constantly to account for cancellations and rescheduling of personnel. Given that the list was not final until the moment the team actually departed, the District Court's finding that the departure of a team was the relevant decision, for purposes of the time bar, is plausible in light of the record viewed as a whole. We hold, therefore, that the plaintiffs' claims were timely filed.

* * *

9. We recognize that an argument can be made that the relevant decision was the confection of the list of personnel scheduled for the rotation, but we find such an argument unpersuasive in light of the evidence at trial.

[that part of the opinion discussing the district court's finding of intentional discrimination and the award of attorney's fees is omitted]

NOTES AND PROBLEMS FOR DISCUSSION

1. In Berry v. Board of Supervisors of Louisiana State University, 715 F.2d 971 (5th Cir.1983), the case cited in *Abrams*, the Fifth Circuit suggested a general approach to be taken in distinguishing related acts of discrimination constituting a continuing violation and discrete acts "which must be regarded as individual violations."

> This inquiry, of necessity, turns on the facts and context of each particular case. Relevant to the determination are the following three factors, which we discuss, but by no means consider to be exhaustive. The first is subject matter. Do the alleged acts involve the same type of discrimination, tending to connect them in a continuing violation? The second is frequency. Are the alleged acts recurring (e.g., a biweekly paycheck) or more in the nature of an isolated work assignment or employment decision? The third factor, perhaps of most importance, is degree of permanence. Does the act have the degree of permanence which should trigger an employee's awareness of and duty to assert his or her rights, or which should indicate to the employee that the continued existence of the adverse consequences of the act is to be expected without being dependent on a continuing intent to discriminate?

715 F.2d at 981. Were these factors applied in *Abrams*? Should the apparent permanence of policy make it more or less likely that the existence of the policy will constitute a continuing violation? In Waltman v. International Paper Co., 875 F.2d 468 (5th Cir.1989), the plaintiff filed an EEOC charge alleging sexual harassment three years after the first incident of harassment but within 180 days of the last incident. The district court granted partial summary judgment on the ground that the acts of harassment occurring more than 180 days before the EEOC charge were time-barred. Relying on *Berry* and *Abrams,* the Court of Appeals rejected the employer's argument that, for a continuing violation to occur in the context of a hostile work environment, the incidents of harassment must be the result of a conspiracy, a company policy or the work of the same persons. With respect to the "permanence" factor emphasized in *Berry,* the Court noted:

> Acts of harassment that create an offensive or hostile environment generally do not have the same degree of permanence as, for example, the loss of a promotion. If the person harassing a plaintiff leaves his job, the harassment ends; the harassment is dependent on a continuing intent to harass. In contrast, when a person who denies a plaintiff a promotion leaves, the plaintiff is still without a promotion even though there is no longer any intent to discriminate. In this latter example, there is an element of permanence to the discriminatory action, which should, in most cases, alert a plaintiff that her rights have been violated. We find that in the instant case there is a material issue whether the acts of sexual harassment, had the *Berry* quality of "permanence" that would alert Waltman that her rights had been violated.

875 F.2d at 476.

Is plaintiff's awareness of the discriminatory nature of prior decisions to be determined on a subjective or objective basis? In Roberts v. Gadsden Memorial

Hospital, 835 F.2d 793 (11th Cir.1988), modified on rehearing, 850 F.2d 1549 (11th Cir.1988), the plaintiff had been denied promotions in 1977, 1978 and 1981. An EEOC charge was not filed until after the 1981 incident. On appeal the court addressed the question of whether the 1978 incident constituted a continuing violation and was thus encompassed within the 1981 charge.

> [E]ven if we assume that the 1978 discriminatory act continued into the statutory filing period, we must still conclude that Roberts' claim based on that incident is time-barred. Roberts admitted that he was aware of his rights in 1978. He could have asserted them at that time. To the extent that GMH injured him on a continuing basis as a result of the 1978 incident, it was only because he knowingly failed to exercise his rights. A claim arising out of an injury which is "continuing" only because a putative plaintiff knowingly fails to seek relief is exactly the sort of claim that Congress intended to bar by the 180–day limitation period.

850 F.2d at 1550. See also, Sabree v. United Brotherhood of Carpenters and Joiners, Local 33, 921 F.2d 396 (1st Cir.1990) (since plaintiff admitted that he believed he was being discriminated against at every turn, he had an obligation to file promptly or loose his claim—case distinguished where plaintiff is unable to appreciate that he is being discriminated against until he has lived through a series of incidents and is able to perceive the overall discriminatory pattern). How exactly are the plaintiffs in *Roberts* and *Sabree* to be distinguished from the plaintiff in *Waltman*? Generally, will not the victim of sexual harassment have *more* reason to realize her rights have been violated after the first incident of such harassment than the person who has been denied a promotion for discriminatory reasons? Compare, Sosa v. Hiraoka, 920 F.2d 1451 (9th Cir.1990) (suggesting that continuing violation doctrine is applicable so long as discrimination within filing period is part of "systematic policy of discrimination"). Does the holding in the case described in Note 2 mean that cases like *Abrams, Berry* and *Waltman* would be decided differently now?

2. As discussed in Chapter 2 *supra*, seniority systems that disproportionately affect a protected class and that do not fall within the protection of Section 703(h) ("bona fide" seniority systems) may violate Title VII. In LORANCE v. AT & T TECHNOLOGIES, INC., 490 U.S. 900, 109 S.Ct. 2261, 104 L.Ed.2d 961 (1989), the Supreme Court addressed the problem of deciding what event triggers the limitation period for challenges to seniority systems. Prior to 1979 the employer's facility had operated under a collective bargaining agreement that provided for accumulation of competitive seniority by all employees, regardless of job classification, on the basis of years worked in the plant. In 1979, the collective bargaining agreement was modified with respect to higher paid "tester" positions so that seniority in that position was based on time spent as a tester. The bargaining agreement was altered shortly after women, for the first time, began transferring into the tester positions. The plaintiffs had become testers in 1978 and 1980. In 1982, as a result of a reduction in force, the plaintiffs were selected for demotion; they would not have been demoted had the former plant-wide seniority system remained in place.

The plaintiffs filed EEOC charges and then sued under Title VII alleging that the 1979 collective bargaining agreement was intended to protect incumbent male employees and to discourage women from transferring into the tester position and was thus not bona fide within the meaning of Section 703(h). The district court granted summary judgment for the employer on the ground that plaintiffs had not filed their EEOC charges within the applicable limitations period. The Seventh Circuit affirmed, concluding that "the relevant discriminatory act that triggers the period of limitations occurs at the time an employee becomes subject to a facially-neutral but discriminatory seniority system that the employee knows, or reasonably should know, is discriminatory." 827 F.2d 163, 167 (7th Cir.1987).

The Supreme Court granted certiorari and affirmed. Relying on Delaware State College v. Ricks and United Air Lines, Inc. v. Evans, the court reasoned that since there was no allegation that the seniority system had been *administered* in a discriminatory fashion (all employees with equal job seniority were treated equally), the claim depended on proof of intentionally discriminatory adoption of the system. Since the only violation of law occurred outside of the limitation period, the plaintiffs' claim on behalf of themselves and a class of female employees was time barred. The majority also concluded that its holding was consistent with the special protection accorded seniority systems and the interests of incumbent employees by Section 703(h).

> This "special treatment" [Section 703(h)] strikes a balance between the interests of those protected against discrimination by Title VII and those who work—perhaps for many years—in reliance upon the validity of a facially lawful seniority system. There is no doubt, of course, that a facially discriminatory seniority system (one that treats similarly situated employees differently) can be challenged at any time, and that even a facially neutral system, if it is adopted with discriminatory motive, can be challenged within the prescribed period after adoption. But allowing a facially neutral system to be challenged, and entitlements under it to be altered, many years after its adoption would disrupt those valid reliance interests that § 703(h) was meant to protect.

490 U.S. at 912, 109 S.Ct. at 2269.

Characterizing the decision as "the latest example of how [the] Court, flouting the intent of Congress, has gradually diminished the application of Title VII to seniority systems," Justice Marshall, on behalf of Justices Blackmun and Brennan, dissented. Noting that some of the plaintiffs were not even testers in 1979 and that none of the plaintiffs could reasonably have anticipated being demoted or concretely harmed by the modifications to the bargaining agreement in 1979, the dissent argued that the "bizarre and impractical" result of the majority's holding was that "employees must now anticipate, and initiate suit to prevent, future adverse applications of a seniority system, no matter how speculative or unlikely these applications may be." The cases relied on by the majority were distinguished.

> Like *Evans*, *Ricks* stands for the proposition that neutral employment practices that passively perpetuate the consequences of time-barred discrimination but are not themselves bred of discriminatory intent do not constitute actionable wrongs under Title VII. Neither case suggests that the operation of a seniority system set up *in order* to discriminate should be treated the same way as a legitimate seniority (or tenure) system, born of non-discriminatory motives, which in a particular case may have the effect of passively reinforcing prior time-barred acts of discrimination.

490 U.S. at 918, 109 S.Ct. at 2272.

Lorance was reversed by the Civil Rights Act of 1991. Section 112 of the Act amends Section 706(e) of Title VII by adding the following paragraph:

(2) For purposes of this section, an unlawful employment practice occurs, with respect to a seniority system that has been adopted for an intentionally discriminatory purpose in violation of this title (whether or not that discriminatory purpose is apparent on the face of the seniority provision), when the seniority system is adopted, when an individual becomes subject to the seniority system, or when a person aggrieved is injured by the application of the seniority system or provision of the system.

Does the 1991 Act merely reinstate the law as it was prior to *Lorance* or does it do more? Does the above provision purport to give standing to file a Title VII action to an employee in a completely different bargaining unit from the one that has adopted the offending seniority system?

After *Lorance* several courts applied the rationale of that decision to bar challenges to employment policies that were not incorporated in seniority systems. See, EEOC v. City Colleges of Chicago, 740 F.Supp. 508 (N.D.Ill. 1990) (ADEA action filed in 1988 which challenged early retirement program adopted in 1982 held to be untimely: *Lorance* rationale applies to any employment plan or system); Davis v. Boeing Helicopter Co., 56 FEP Cases 284 (E.D.Pa. 1989) (application of *Lorance* to promotion policy). Should such decisions survive the legislative reversal of *Lorance*?

3. The Relation Between the Substance of the EEOC Charge and Suit

JENKINS v. BLUE CROSS MUTUAL HOSPITAL INSURANCE, INC.

United States Court of Appeals, Seventh Circuit, 1976.
538 F.2d 164, cert. denied, 429 U.S. 986, 97 S.Ct. 506, 50 L.Ed.2d 598.

SPRECHER, CIRCUIT JUDGE.

This appeal reheard in banc concentrates on whether the alleged victim of racial and sex discrimination made sufficiently like or reasonably related allegations in her charges to the Equal Employment Opportunity Commission to support, and out of which could grow or reasonably be expected to grow, the racial and sex allegations in her judicial complaint.

I.

The plaintiff brought this action on her own behalf and on behalf of other persons similarly situated as a class action, charging the defendants, her former employers, with denying her promotions and better assignments, and with ultimately terminating her employment because of her "race, sex, black styles of hair and dress," in violation of Title VII of the Civil Rights Act of 1964, 42 U.S.C. § 2000e et seq. and 42 U.S.C. § 1981. The plaintiff sought declaratory and injunctive relief, reinstatement with backpay and other money damages.

On July 17, 1974, the district court denied the plaintiff's motion seeking an order pursuant to F.R.Civ.P. 23(c)(1) determining that the action be maintainable as a class action.[1]   The court stated that "a Title VII complaint must be viewed in relationship to the charges filed by the plaintiff against the defendant before the Equal Employment Opportunity Commission."   The court's reasoning in denying certification of a class action was that: (1) "[i]t is clear that she did not raise sex before the EEOC * * * "; (2) "[w]hile there is an arguable connection to race by the allegation of hair style discrimination, such is not sufficient to raise the panorama of alleged [racial] evils plaintiff seeks to adjudicate in her complaint"; (3) "[h]er class could, therefore, only be composed of those persons denied promotion or not hired for wearing an Afro hair style"; and (4) "[n]o proof has been presented to the Court to show that this group of people would be so large that joinder of them in this action would be impracticable."

On January 21, 1975, the district court denied the plaintiff's motion for a preliminary injunction.   The plaintiff's notice of appeal was from both the July 17, 1974 and January 21, 1975 orders.

Upon this appeal a panel of this court reversed the district court's judgment "[i]n light of the fact that the trial court dismissed the complaint because of the failure of the named plaintiff to qualify as representative of her class under Title VII, without giving consideration to the claim based on § 1981, and since we conclude that the relief claimed under § 1981 need not be based on any form of claim filed with the EEOC * * *."   Jenkins v. Blue Cross Mutual Hospital Insurance, Inc., 522 F.2d 1235, 1241 (7th Cir.1975).   The case was remanded for the district court to give consideration to whether the plaintiff could qualify as a representative of the class upon her § 1981 claim, which alleged only racial discrimination, and thereafter to consider "what equitable relief the plaintiff may be entitled to."   Id. at 1242.

* * *

* * * The district court had concluded that the plaintiff's EEOC charges limited her Title VII court complaint to charges of discrimination because of her wearing an Afro hair style.   The original appeal panel consisting of Judges Tuttle,[3] Tone and Bauer was "unanimously of the view that the [EEOC] charge does not form the proper basis under Title VII for any complaint of discrimination on the basis of sex." 522 F.2d at 1241.   Judges Tone and Bauer also agreed with the district court that the EEOC charge did not support allegations of racial discrimination beyond those due to wearing an Afro hair style.   "Judge Tuttle would hold that the charge was sufficient under the announced standard to support the [racial] allegations of the complaint."   Id.

---

1. Chronologically the defendants first filed a motion for a determination that the action *not* be maintainable as a class action and subsequently the plaintiff filed a cross motion for a determination that it be so maintainable.   The district court order recites the existence of both motions and generally orders that "this action not be maintained as a class action" but in the accompanying "memorandum entry" only the plaintiff's motion is recited as denied.

3. Honorable Elbert P. Tuttle, United States Circuit Judge, Fifth Circuit, had been sitting by designation, and wrote the panel's opinion.

Upon the rehearing in banc a majority of the entire court [4] conclud-ed that the judgment should be reversed and remanded not only because of the § 1981 claim but also because the plaintiff's EEOC charges adequately support her judicial complaints of racial and sex discrimination.

The plaintiff's charge form, filed on June 8, 1971, with the EEOC, showed a check mark in the box on the form to indicate that the discrimination was because of "Race or Color" but no check mark appeared in the box preceded by the word "Sex." The explanation the plaintiff gave on the form for the discrimination was:

> I feel that I am being discriminated in the terms and conditions of my employment because of my race, Negro. I have worked for Blue Cross and Blue Shield approx. 3 years during which time I[had] no problem until May 1970 when I got my natural hair style. Later when I came up for promotion it was denied because my supervisor, Al Frymier, said I could never represent Blue Cross with my Afro. He also accused me of being the leader of the girls on the floor. The pressures I was working under kept me upset, therefore, I asked for a leave of absence. I was told I had to take a vacation before I could be granted leave of absence. I was granted a week vacation and on my return I was asked to take a 90 day leave, quit, or be fired, time they said to get myself together; and at the end of this time they would be able to place me on another job. A White employee who associated with me might have been denied her promotion because of her association with me.

The plaintiff received her statutory notice of her right to sue from the EEOC on August 4, 1972 and filed her complaint in the district court on August 28, 1972.

The entire court accepts the standard referred to in the panel decision as the guiding principle in its determination, namely that set forth in Danner v. Phillips Petroleum Co., 447 F.2d 159, 162 (5th Cir.1971):

> The correct rule to follow in construing EEOC charges for purposes of delineating the proper scope of a subsequent judicial inquiry is that "the complaint in the civil action * * * may proper-ly encompass any * * * discrimination like or reasonably related to the allegations of the charge and growing out of such allegations."

The majority parts with the panel in its application of the stan-dard.

In Haines v. Kerner, 404 U.S. 519, 520, 92 S.Ct. 594, 596, 30 L.Ed.2d 652 (1972), the Supreme Court unanimously expressed its opinion that "we hold to less stringent standards [the allegations of a *pro se* com-plaint] than formal pleadings drafted by lawyers * * *." In a case also

---

4. The argument on rehearing and con-sideration of the case took place before the induction of Judge Harlington Wood, Jr., to fill the vacancy created by the elevation of Judge John Paul Stevens to the Su-preme Court on December 19, 1975.

unanimously decided a few days later, Love v. Pullman Co., 404 U.S. 522, 527, 92 S.Ct. 616, 619, 30 L.Ed.2d 679 (1972), involving EEOC procedure, the Court said that "technicalities are particularly inappropriate in a statutory scheme in which laymen, unassisted by trained lawyers, initiated the process."

We have held that Title VII is to "be construed and applied broadly," Motorola, Inc. v. McLain, 484 F.2d 1339, 1344 (7th Cir.1973), and in doing so, we have recognized that EEOC charges are in layman's language, Cox v. United States Gypsum Co., 409 F.2d 289, 290–291 (7th Cir.1969). The context in which we must operate was well stated by Judge Bauer in Willis v. Chicago Extruded Metals Co., 375 F.Supp. 362, 365–366 (N.D. Ill.1974) (footnotes omitted):

> [T]he Civil Rights Act is designed to protect those who are least able to protect themselves. Complainants to the EEOC are seldom lawyers. To compel the charging party to specifically articulate in a charge filed with the Commission the full panoply of discrimination which he may have suffered may cause the very persons Title VII was designed to protect to lose that protection because they are ignorant of or unable to thoroughly describe the discriminatory practices to which they are subjected. * * *

> [T]he EEOC charges simply stated in laymen's language the "unfair thing that happened" to the plaintiff, that is, the discriminatory discharge * * *.

This policy of being "solicitous of the Title VII plaintiff" has been expressed by many courts. Gamble v. Birmingham Southern R.R., 514 F.2d 678, 687–689 (5th Cir.1975); Danner v. Phillips Petroleum Co., supra, at 161–162; Sanchez v. Standard Brands, Inc., 431 F.2d 455, 463 (5th Cir.1970).

In the present case the plaintiff checked the EEOC form box stating that the "discrimination [was] because of * * * Race or Color." She began describing the "unfair thing done" to her by saying that "I feel that I am being discriminated in the terms and conditions of my employment because of my race, Negro." She said that her supervisor denied her a promotion because she "could never represent Blue Cross with my Afro." A lay person's description of racial discrimination could hardly be more explicit. The reference to the Afro hairstyle was merely the method by which the plaintiff's supervisor allegedly expressed the employer's racial discrimination. The plaintiff stated that for three years prior to wearing her Afro hairstyle, she had no problem. As we have said, "[a] single charge may 'launch a full scale inquiry" ' into racial discrimination. Motorola, Inc. v. McLain, supra, at 1346.

The majority agrees with Judge Tuttle's minority position in the panel decision that the EEOC charge was sufficient to support the racial discrimination allegations of the complaint. 522 F.2d at 1241. Judge Tuttle reached the same conclusion speaking for the Fifth Circuit in Smith v. Delta Air Lines, Inc., 486 F.2d 512 (5th Cir.1973), where the court held that a charge alleging discrimination stemming from grooming requirements which applied particularly to black persons constituted a sufficient charge of racial discrimination when accompanied by substantially the same general allegation of racial discrimination as here.

In regard to sex discrimination, it is true that the plaintiff did not check the sex discrimination box on the EEOC form. In Sanchez v. Standard Brands, Inc., supra, at 462–464, the reverse situation had occurred. The plaintiff had checked only the box labeled "sex" and in her judicial complaint alleged discrimination because of her "national origin." The Fifth Circuit said:

> * * * [W]e decline to hold that the failure to place a check mark in the correct box is a fatal error. In the context of Title VII, no one—not even the unschooled—should be boxed out.

In Wetzel v. Liberty Mutual Insurance Co., 511 F.2d 199, 202–203 (3d Cir.1975), vacated on other grounds, 424 U.S. 737, 96 S.Ct. 1202, 47 L.Ed.2d 435, 44 U.S.L.W. 4350 (1976), an alleged victim of sex discrimination checked the wrong box. The court held that lay persons were not to be denied access to the federal courts because of a technical error. Finally, in Vuyanich v. Republic National Bank, 409 F.Supp. 1083 (N.D.Tex.1976), the plaintiff's EEOC charge expressly stated only racial prejudice whereas her judicial complaint alleged both racial and sexual discrimination. The court held that she could proceed on both grounds inasmuch as her EEOC form stated that her superior told her that she [a black female] "probably did not need a job anyway, because her husband was a Caucasian." Id., at 1985. The court concluded that such a statement discriminated against both black persons and females since it could not be made to either a white person or a male. Id., at 1089.

In the present case, the plaintiff charged to the EEOC that her superior, in addition to referring to her Afro hairstyle, "also accused me of being a leader of the girls on the floor." The plaintiff then stated that "[a] White employee who associated with me might have been denied her promotion because of her association with me." These statements taken in conjunction with the charges of racial discrimination also charge sex discrimination.

In Danner v. Phillips Petroleum Co., supra, at 161–163, the case relied upon by the panel here in its original decision, the court held that the alleged victim of sex discrimination adequately charged it to the EEOC where all she charged was that "[t]herefore due to the fact that my position was not eliminated, just taken from me and given to a man, I feel that I have been mistreated and damaged."

The majority of this court conclude that the plaintiff sufficiently charged both racial and sex discrimination in her EEOC form in order to be eligible to represent a class composed of "all black and female persons who are employed, or might be employed, by Blue Cross–Blue Shield, Inc." * * *

The judgment is reversed and the case is remanded for further proceedings not inconsistent with this opinion.

TONE, CIRCUIT JUDGE, with whom PELL and BAUER, CIRCUIT JUDGES, (dissenting).

I agree with the majority's statement of the governing legal principles. My only disagreement is in the reading of plaintiff's charge filed with the EEOC, which is quoted in full in the majority opinion. The reader of these opinions can judge for himself whether the present challenges to defendant's recruitment and promotion practices, including testing, pay scale, and job-qualification standards (see 522 F.2d at 1240 n.9), are "like or reasonably related to the allegations of the [EEOC] charge and growing out of such allegations." * See Danner v. Phillips Petroleum Co., 447 F.2d 159, 162 (5th Cir.1971). It appears to me that plaintiff made it clear she was not complaining about such practices when she said in her EEOC charge:

> "I have worked for Blue Cross and Blue Shield approximately 3 years during which time I[had] no problem until May 1970 when I got my natural hair style."

I can find nothing elsewhere in the charge that contradicts or qualifies this statement and nothing that suggests a pattern and practice charge based on race or sex. (I attach no significance to the failure to check the box marked "Sex.") She seems to me to be saying that after three years of employment about which she has no complaints she had her hair styled in an Afro fashion, and was unfairly treated because of that. If the relatedness or growing-out-of requirement is to be abolished, I would have no objection. I cannot agree, however, that if there is to be such a requirement it has been satisfied with respect to the pattern and practice charges described above.

NOTES AND PROBLEMS FOR DISCUSSION

1. In Sanchez v. Standard Brands, Inc., 431 F.2d 455 (5th Cir. 1970) the Fifth Circuit decision cited by the majority in *Jenkins*, the court explained the "like or related" test as follows:

> [T]he civil action is much more intimately related to the EEOC investigation than to the words of the charge which originally triggered the investigation. Within this statutory scheme, it is only logical to limit the permissible scope of the civil action to the scope of the EEOC investigation which can reasonably be expected to grow out of the charge of discrimination.

431 F.2d at 466. See also Gamble v. Birmingham Southern Railroad Co., 514 F.2d 678, 688 (5th Cir.1975) (*Sanchez* test hinges on whether broader EEOC

---

* I do not include among the allegations which are not supported by the charge the one to the effect that black employees were required to observe white hair styles and dress styles (item b in footnote 9, 522 F.2d at 1240–1241), which I think does satisfy the *Danner* test.

investigation might be expected to grow from original charge). The Fifth Circuit's liberal standard for determining the proper scope of a Title VII complaint has been adopted by most circuits. See, e.g., Smith v. American President Lines, Ltd., 571 F.2d 102, 107 n.10 (2d Cir.1978); EEOC v. Bailey Co., Inc., 563 F.2d 439, 446 (6th Cir.1977), cert. denied, 435 U.S. 915, 98 S.Ct. 1468, 55 L.Ed.2d 506 (1978); Ostapowicz v. Johnson Bronze Co., 541 F.2d 394, 399 (3d Cir.1976), cert. denied, 429 U.S. 1041, 97 S.Ct. 741, 50 L.Ed.2d 753 (1977).

Is the purpose of the "like or related" rule to give notice to the employer of the "ballpark" of the charge, or is it to insure that the EEOC has an opportunity to investigate all charges that may be litigated, or both? In Babrocky v. Jewel Food Co., 773 F.2d 857, 863–64 (7th Cir.1985) the Court of Appeals stated that "allowing a complaint to encompass allegations outside the ambit of the predicate EEOC charge would circumvent the EEOC's investigatory and conciliatory role, as well as deprive the charged party of notice of the charge, as surely as would an initial failure to file a timely EEOC charge." See also, Reiter v. Center Consolidated School District No. 26–JT, 618 F.Supp. 1458 (D.Colo. 1985) (fact that plaintiff did not charge national origin discrimination in EEOC charge irrelevant since state FEP agency determined that plaintiff was discriminated against because of her perceived association with Hispanic community and employer was notified of finding before EEOC issued right to sue notice). Would it be consistent with the purposes of the Act to limit the court's jurisdiction to those matters *actually investigated* by either the EEOC or a state deferral agency? The courts have uniformly held that a limited EEOC investigation will not defeat a complaint where it contains allegations reasonably related to those in the EEOC charge. While "the investigation may help define the scope of the charge, it is primarily the charge to which [the court must look to determine] whether the scope requirement is satisfied." Schnellbaecher v. Baskin Clothing Co., 887 F.2d 124, 127 (7th Cir.1989). *Accord*, Sosa v. Hiraoka, 920 F.2d 1451 (9th Cir.1990); Ostapowicz v. Johnson Bronze Co., *supra*, 541 F.2d at 398–99.

The variations in application of the "like or related" standard are vast. With *Jenkins* compare Ang v. Procter & Gamble Co., 932 F.2d 540 (6th Cir.1991) where the court held that a charge of national origin discrimination could not encompass a claim of race discrimination. "The scope of Ang's complaint does not automatically expand due to his membership in more than one minority." 55 FEP Cases at 1671. The Sixth Circuit noted that courts generally give the EEOC charge a "broad reading" to protect claimants who are "unschooled in the technicalities of the law and [who] proceed without counsel," but that "liberal construction is not necessary where the claimant is aided by counsel in preparing his charge." Id. In Sandom v. Travelers Mortgage Services, Inc., 752 F.Supp. 1240 (D.N.J.1990) the court held that sexual harassment is sufficiently distinct from other forms of gender discrimination that it must be specifically included in the EEOC charge in order to be claimed in suit. "Because a claim of sexual harassment may constitute sexual discrimination does not imply that a charge consisting of facts which purportedly constitute sexual discrimination necessarily includes all forms of sexual discrimination." 752 F.Supp. at 1247. Why would it not be reasonable for the EEOC to investigate all the kinds of discrimination which the charging party *might* have alleged? See, McBride v. Delta Air Lines, Inc., 551 F.2d 113, 115 (6th Cir.), vacated on other grounds, 434 U.S. 916, 98 S.Ct. 387, 54 L.Ed.2d 273 (1977) (discharge claim justified review of all allegedly racially discriminatory practices); Kahn v. Pepsi Cola Bottling Group, 526 F.Supp. 1268, (E.D.N.Y.1981) (investigation of claim of national origin discrimination is "likely to have touched upon race"); Latino v. Rainbo Bakers, Inc., 358 F.Supp. 870 (D. Colo. 1973) (where EEOC investigation disclosed sex discrimination, plaintiff not barred from suing on that ground because her charge alleged only national origin discrimination). Whether an EEOC investigation of the claims made in a complaint could reasonably be expected to grow out of the claims in an EEOC charge may be an issue of fact and not appropriate for summary judgment. See, Gomez v. Amoco Oil Co., 767 F.Supp. 191 (N.D.Ind. 1991).

2. Must a plaintiff whose employer has retaliated against him for filing an EEOC charge file a second charge to preserve his right to litigate the retaliation claim? In Gupta v. East Texas State University, 654 F.2d 411 (5th Cir.1981), the plaintiff's EEOC charge alleged discrimination against him in terms of job assignments and salary. After the lawsuit was filed, the plaintiff was discharged. Although no EEOC charge was filed by the plaintiff regarding his termination, the retaliation issue was litigated at trial, and the Court of Appeals held that the district court had jurisdiction to hear the claim.

> [I]t is unnecessary for a plaintiff to exhaust administrative remedies prior to urging a retaliation claim growing out of an earlier charge; the district court has ancillary jurisdiction to hear such a claim when it grows out of an administrative charge that is properly before the court.

654 F.2d at 414. The court reasoned that requiring a plaintiff to file a second charge under the circumstances "would serve no purpose except to create additional procedural technicalities when a single filing would comply with the intent of Title VII." In addition, elimination of the procedural barrier would aid private enforcement of Title VII and would deter "employers from attempting to discourage employees from exercising their rights under Title VII." See also, EEOC v. St. Anne's Hospital of Chicago, Inc., 664 F.2d 128, 131 (7th Cir.1981) (separate retaliation charge unnecessary where employer informed during investigation that retaliation was an issue). But if no EEOC charge on retaliation is filed, will the employer have an opportunity to resolve that claim before suit is filed? In Ang v. Proctor & Gamble, *supra*, the Sixth Circuit interpreted the *Gupta* rule as applying only to retaliation claims arising *after* the filing of the original EEOC charge. "Retaliatory conduct occurring prior to the filing of the EEOC complaint is distinguishable from conduct occurring afterwards as no unnecessary double filing is required by demanding that plaintiffs allege retaliation in the original complaint." 55 FEP Cases at 1672.

3. Section 706(f)(1) of Title VII, 42 U.S.C. § 2000e–5(f)(1), provides in part that, "a civil action may be brought against the respondent named in the [EEOC] charge * * * by the person claiming to be aggrieved * * * " The degree of precision with which the employer must be identified in the charge is a matter of some uncertainty. In Dickey v. Greene, 710 F.2d 1003 (4th Cir.1983) the plaintiff named only the institutional employer in the space on the EEOC charge form for listing the respondent, but in the narrative portion of the charge made allegations of discrimination against her supervisor whom she subsequently sued. The district court denied a motion for summary judgment by the individual defendant and held that by naming the individual in the narrative section of the charge, the EEOC was fairly appraised of his identity. The Court of Appeals reversed. "The facts set forth by Dickey in her charge, including the reference to Greene in the narrative portion of the charge, can in no way be viewed as sufficient under the statute to charge Greene and thus to require the EEOC to enter into the obligatory conciliation proceedings with

Greene * * * there is nothing in the record to suggest that Greene was ever involved in the conciliation efforts." 710 F.2d at 1006. By contrast, the Seventh Circuit held in Eggleston v. Chicago Journeymen Plumbers' Local Union No. 130, 657 F.2d 890, 905 (7th Cir.1981), cert. denied, 455 U.S. 1017, 102 S.Ct. 1710, 72 L.Ed.2d 134 (1982) that, "where an unnamed party has been provided with adequate notice of the charge, under circumstances where the party has been given the opportunity to participate in conciliation proceedings aimed at voluntary compliance, the charge is sufficient to confer jurisdiction over that party." See also, Greenwood v. Ross, 778 F.2d 448 (8th Cir.1985) (assistant coach who named university in EEOC charge should have been allowed to sue chancellor and athletic director who were not named in charge where those officials had acted on the university's behalf in controversy with the coach, had notice of the proceedings and had been represented by counsel throughout) and Dague v. Riverdale Athletic Ass'n., 99 F.R.D. 325 (N.D.Ga. 1983) (denying motion to dismiss filed by principle officers of the institutional defendant named in the charge). In *Dague* the court explained: "To dismiss the claims against these defendants solely on the fact that they were not named in the EEOC charge, without some showing of whether or not they had actual notice of the charge and an opportunity to participate in conciliation, would be to elevate form over substance and ignore the remedial purpose of the Act." 99 F.R.D. at 327. Do you agree? What purpose is served by correctly identifying the respondent in the original charge? See, Alvarado v. Board of Trustees of Montgomery Community College, 848 F.2d 457 (4th Cir.1988) (discharged employee who named the college in his EEOC charge was allowed to sue the college's board of trustees where the board and the college were identical under state law and it was unreasonable to have expected the employee to have known that the board rather than the college was the appropriate body to sue). Compare, Mufich v. Commonwealth Edison Co., 735 F.Supp. 897 (N.D.Ill. 1990) (plaintiff's Title VII complaint against individual supervisors not named in EEOC charge dismissed because as "low-level supervisors" they did not share a common interest with the employer, because they did not know plaintiff was asserting a claim against them personally and because the EEOC never informed them that they were the subjects of an investigation).

Courts are in general agreement that a charge which does not correctly identify an institutional respondent, is not fatal to a subsequent suit so long as the correct respondent was put on notice of the charge. See, Sedlacek v. Hach, 752 F.2d 333 (8th Cir.1985) (charge named a "substantially identical related partnership"); Shannon v. Village of Broadview, 682 F.Supp. 391 (N.D.Ill. 1988) (village not named in charge may be sued where charge named village governing body where village knew or should have known of pendency of charge).

4. In *Jenkins*, the plaintiff sought to represent a class apparently composed of all black and all female employees of the defendant company. The extent to which such a plaintiff may represent, through a class action, persons with factually dissimilar claims is discussed in Chapter 6 *infra*.

4. Res Judicata, Collateral Estoppel and the Impact of State Proceedings on Title VII Litigation

Section 706 of Title VII makes resort to state administrative remedies, in a state with a deferral agency, a prerequisite to litigation under the Act. It is important to understand, however, that, under certain circumstances, the *exhaustion* of state remedies may affect the claimant's right to a decision on the merits of his Title VII claim in federal court. In KREMER v. CHEMICAL CONSTRUCTION CORP., 456 U.S. 461, 102 S.Ct. 1883, 72 L.Ed.2d 262 (1982), the claimant, who alleged a discriminatory failure to rehire after a layoff, filed a charge with the EEOC which it, in turn, referred to the New York State Division of Human Rights (NYHRD), a § 706 deferral agency. See, Allen v. Avon Products, Inc., *supra.* After an investigation, the NYHRD concluded there was no probable cause for the charge. Kremer sought a review of the agency's action in state court, as allowed by New York's fair employment law. The state court affirmed the agency decision on the ground that it was not "arbitrary, capricious or an abuse of discretion." Subsequently, the EEOC issued a no-cause determination and a right-to-sue notice and Kremer filed a timely Title VII action in federal district court. The district court's dismissal of the complaint on grounds of res judicata was upheld by the Second Circuit. The Supreme Court, in a five-four decision, affirmed. While conceding that *initial resort* to state administrative remedies cannot deprive a charging party of a federal trial *de novo* on his Title VII claim, the majority found nothing in the legislative history of Title VII to suggest that Congress "considered it necessary or desirable to provide an absolute right to relitigate in federal court an issue resolved by a state court." 456 U.S. at 473, 102 S.Ct. at 1893. Since there was not a "clear and manifest" legislative purpose behind Title VII to deny res judicata or collateral estoppel to state court judgments on discrimination claims, the Court held that it would apply "the usual rule ... that [the] merits of a claim once decided in a court of competent jurisdiction are not subject to redetermination in another forum." 456 U.S. at 485, 102 S.Ct. at 1899.

According to the majority in *Kremer*, its decision was mandated by 28 U.S.C. § 1738 which requires federal courts to give the same preclusive effect to state court judgments that those judgments would be given in the courts of the state from which the judgments come. Thus, the determination of whether to apply res judicata in this context requires a two-prong inquiry: (1) whether state law would give the prior judgement preclusive effect against the claims asserted in the federal action if they were raised in a subsequent state suit; and (2) whether the party against whom preclusion is asserted had a full and fair opportunity in the state court proceeding to litigate the claims raised in the federal complaint. 456 U.S. at 481–82, 102 S.Ct. at 1898.

Justice Blackmun, joined by Justices Brennan and Marshall in dissent, argued that state judicial review of an agency determination is merely part of the state "proceedings" under § 706(b) and (c) and that the Congressional intent was that a claimant could pursue his Title VII claim in federal court despite the conclusion of state "proceedings." Justice Blackmun warned:

> The lesson of the Court's ruling is: *An unsuccessful state discrimination complainant should not seek state judicial review.* If a

discrimination complainant pursues state judicial review and loses—a likely result given the deferential standard of review in state
court—he forfeits his right to seek redress in a federal court. If,
however, he simply bypasses the state courts, he can proceed to the
EEOC and ultimately to federal court. Instead of a deferential
review of an agency record, he will receive in federal court a *de
novo* hearing accompanied by procedural aids such as broad discovery rules and the ability to subpoena witnesses. Thus, paradox-
ically, the Court effectively has eliminated state reviewing courts
from the fight against discrimination in an entire class of cases.
Consequently, the state courts will not have chance to correct state
agency errors when the agencies rule against discrimination victims, and the quality of decisionmaking can only deteriorate. It is
a perverse sort of comity that eliminates the reviewing function of
state courts in the name of giving their decisions due respect.

456 U.S. at 504–505, 102 S.Ct. at 1909. Justice Blackmun's assumption
that charging parties can "simply bypass" state court review at the end
of the state administrative process has not proved wholly correct.
Courts have uniformly construed *Kremer* as applicable regardless of
which party initiates the appeal to the state court. Thus, if the
plaintiff prevails before the state agency and is *forced* into state court
by the employer's appeal, the court's reversal of the agency's ruling will
bar the federal Title VII action. See, Gonsalves v. Alpine Country
Club, 727 F.2d 27 (1st Cir.1984); Hickman v. Electronic Keyboarding,
Inc., 741 F.2d 230 (8th Cir. 1984). The "lesson" of *Kremer* may be that,
in a deferral state where judicial review of the agency process is
possible, the claimant must abandon the agency proceedings *before* an
appealable decision in order to guarantee his right to a federal forum.

In MCDONALD V. CITY OF WEST BRANCH, MICHIGAN, 466
U.S. 284, 104 S.Ct. 1799, 80 L.Ed.2d 302 (1984), the Court held that an
arbitration was not a "judicial proceeding" within the meaning of
§ 1738 and thus should have no preclusive effect on subsequent federal
litigation involving the same issue which was arbitrated. There remained however the question of whether the doctrine of "administrative res judicata" should be applied in employment discrimination cases
so that state agency decisions would be given preclusive effect where
the agency had acted in a *judicial capacity*. Under the law of some
states, decisions of administrative tribunals that have accorded litigants
the procedural safeguards of courts are given the same preclusive effect
as decisions of the courts of those states. See, Buckhalter v. Pepsi–Cola
General Bottlers, Inc., 768 F.2d 842 (7th Cir.1985), vacated, 41 FEP
Cases 272, 478 U.S. 1017, 106 S.Ct. 3328, 92 L.Ed.2d 735 (1986).

The Supreme Court dealt with the "administrative res judicata"
issue in UNIVERSITY OF TENNESSEE v. ELLIOTT, 478 U.S. 788, 106
S.Ct. 3220, 92 L.Ed.2d 635 (1986). In *Elliott*, the plaintiff contested his
proposed termination by the University of Tennessee before an administrative law judge under the state administrative procedures act.

After hearing extensive evidence, the ALJ ruled that the university's charges against the plaintiff were not racially motivated as he had contended. The plaintiff did not seek review in the Tennessee courts, but instead proceeded with a suit filed in federal court under Title VII and Section 1983. The district court dismissed the suit on res judicata grounds, but the Sixth Circuit reversed, holding that the policies underlying Title VII and Section 1983 prevented the giving of preclusive effect to non judicial decisions. With respect to the Title VII claim, the Supreme Court affirmed the Court of Appeals and held that Congress did not intend unreviewed state administrative decisions to have preclusive effect on Title VII claims regardless of the nature of the state procedures. 478 U.S. at 795–96, 106 S.Ct. at 3324–25. The preclusive effects of administrative decisions on Section 1983 claims and other federal causes of action is discussed in Chapter 8, *infra.*

Although referred to loosely as "res judicata" in both KREMER v. CHEMICAL CONSTRUCTION CORP. and UNIVERSITY OF TENNESSEE v. ELLIOTT, the doctrine applied in both of those cases was that of collateral estoppel or "issue preclusion." The doctrine generally means that a factual issue decided in a proceeding between parties will bar those parties (or either of them) from relitigating that issue in a subsequent proceeding. Thus, in both *Kremer* and *Elliott*, a finding in the earlier state proceeding that the plaintiff had not been discriminated against barred the plaintiff's relitigation of that issue in a subsequent federal proceeding. In most jurisdictions the doctrine of "true" res judicata or "claim preclusion" will bar litigation of a claim which was litigated *or which could have been litigated* in an earlier proceeding so long as the parties to the second proceeding are the same as in the first proceeding.

The claim preclusion doctrine has led some courts to rule that a plaintiff with two kinds of discrimination claims arising from the same incident may not split them between two proceedings where he could have combined them in the first case. For example, in Pirela v. Village of North Aurora, 935 F.2d 909 (7th Cir.), cert. denied, __ U.S. __, 112 S.Ct. 587, 116 L.Ed.2d 612 (1991) a police officer filed an EEOC charge alleging discrimination on the basis of race and national origin by his employer. While his EEOC charge was pending, the plaintiff was charged by his supervisors with various infractions of police department rules. After a hearing on the charges before a civil service board the plaintiff was discharged. He sought review of the board's decision in state court. The state court affirmed the board's decision as not "against the manifest weight of the evidence." After receiving a right-to-sue notice from the EEOC, the plaintiff filed suit under Title VII alleging racial discrimination in denials of promotions, wages, and the discharge. The district court dismissed the complaint on *res judicata* grounds and the Court of Appeals affirmed in part. The Court of Appeals reasoned that the bar of *res judicata* extends not only to questions actually decided in the state proceeding but to all grounds of recovery *and defenses* which might have been presented in the prior litigation.

> Pirela's claims arose out of the same operative facts: Pirela's misconduct and the [department's] procedures relating to suspension and termination. Because his Title VII ... claims in this litigation, as well as the possible defense he had in the state proceedings, concern this single procedural scenario, Pirela's action is barred ...

935 F.2d at 912. The Court held that the plaintiff's claims that the department had denied him promotions and discriminated against him in the setting of wages because of his race and national origin were separate claims that could not have been raised in the discharge proceeding and were thus not barred by *res judicata*. Id. See also, Miller v. United States Postal Service, 825 F.2d 62 (5th Cir.1987) (plaintiff who unsuccessfully challenged his discharge in a Title VII sex discrimination action is barred from litigating in a separate proceeding claim that discharge violated his rights under Rehabilitation Act (handicap discrimination) where both claims could have combined in first action); Langston v. Insurance Company of North America, 827 F.2d 1044 (5th Cir.1987) (former employee's age discrimination case brought after state wrongful-discharge claim was removed to federal court barred where actions arose out of same transaction and age claims could have been advanced in prior proceeding); Bolling v. City & County of Denver, 790 F.2d 67 (10th Cir.1986) (federal race discrimination claims, the substance of which could have been raised in a prior state wrongful-discharge, are precluded by res judicata). Cf. McNasby v. Crown Cork & Seal Co., Inc., 888 F.2d 270, 278 (3d Cir.1989), cert. denied, 494 U.S. 1066, 110 S.Ct. 1783, 108 L.Ed.2d 784 (1990) (plaintiff who prevailed in sex discrimination case under state law in state court was not precluded from filing subsequent Title VII action where neither the state agency which originally heard plaintiff's claim nor the state court that reviewed the agency's findings had jurisdiction to entertain the federal claim); Headley v. Bacon, 828 F.2d 1272 (8th Cir.1987) (female police officer who won Title VII action against employer not precluded from subsequent action arising from same incident, based on violation of constitutional rights, against police officials as individuals).

It is clear that the state decision can have no preclusive effect in subsequent litigation unless the state proceeding has afforded the plaintiff a "full and fair opportunity" to litigate the merits of the discrimination claim. At a minimum, the state proceedings must satisfy due process requirements. *Kremer*, 456 U.S. at 481–82, 102 S.Ct. at 1897–98. See, Jones v. City of Alton, 757 F.2d 878 (7th Cir.1985) (state court decision upholding plaintiff's discharge not entitled to res judicata effect where state court prevented plaintiff from presenting evidence of discrimination on mistaken theory that such evidence was irrelevant to grounds of discharge). Compare, Pirela v. Village of North Aurora, *supra*, (since plaintiff's discrimination claims would have been relevant and admissible in proceedings to determine whether there was "cause" for his discharge, plaintiff had opportunity to litigate claim).

5. The Effect of Compulsory Arbitration Agreements

In ALEXANDER v. GARDNER–DENVER CO., 415 U.S. 36, 94 S.Ct. 1011, 39 L.Ed.2d 147 (1974) the Supreme Court held that a discharged employee whose grievance had been arbitrated pursuant to an arbitration clause in a collective bargaining agreement was not foreclosed from bringing a Title VII action based on the conduct that was the subject of the grievance. The court noted that the employee's contractual rights under the collective-bargaining agreement were distinct from his statutory Title VII rights and that the arbitrator's role was to "effectuate the intent of the parties [as expressed in the collective-bargaining agreement]," not enforce public laws. The Court also stressed that "federal courts have been assigned plenary powers to secure compliance with Title VII" and that "[t]here is no suggestion in the statutory scheme that a prior arbitral decision either forecloses an individual's right to sue or divests federal courts of jurisdiction." 415 U.S. at 45, 47, 94 S.Ct. 1018, 1019. Most courts have construed *Gardner–Denver* as meaning that an employee who signed an employment contract containing a compulsory arbitration clause could not by that contract be compelled to submit a claim, which would otherwise be covered by a discrimination statute, to binding arbitration. See, Alford v. Dean Witter Reynolds, Inc., 905 F.2d 104 (5th Cir.1990), vacated and remanded, ___ U.S. ___, 111 S.Ct. 2050, 114 L.Ed.2d 456, reversed on remand, 939 F.2d 229 (5th Cir.1991) (Title VII); Nicholson v. CPC International, Inc., 877 F.2d 221 (3d Cir.1989) (ADEA).

In GILMER v. INTERSTATE/JOHNSON LANE CORP., 500 U.S. ___, 111 S.Ct. 1647, 114 L.Ed.2d 26 (1991) the Supreme Court held that a claim under the Age Discrimination in Employment Act (ADEA) could be subjected to compulsory arbitration pursuant to an arbitration agreement entered into at the time of employment. The plaintiff in *Gilmer* was required as part of his employment to register as a securities representative with several stock exchanges. A rule of one of those exchanges required the arbitration of any controversy between the employee and his employer arising out of termination of employment. After his termination the plaintiff filed an age discrimination charge with the EEOC and subsequently brought suit against his former employer under the ADEA. The employer, relying on the arbitration agreement and upon the Federal Arbitration Act (FAA), moved to compel arbitration of the ADEA claim. The district court denied the motion on the ground that Congress had intended in the ADEA to protect claimants from the waiver of a judicial forum. The Fourth Circuit reversed (895 F.2d 195) and the Supreme Court affirmed.

The Supreme Court held that the plaintiff had not demonstrated that Congress intended to preclude arbitration of claims made under the ADEA: nothing in the text or legislative history of the Act precluded arbitration and arbitration was not inherently inconsistent with the statutory framework and purposes of the ADEA. The Court distinguished Alexander v. Gardner–Denver on several grounds. First, the arbitration agreement in that case was intended to cover only claims arising under the collective bargaining agreement and not statutory claims. Second, in *Gardner–Denver* the plaintiffs were represented in the arbitration by their unions. "An important concern therefore was the tension between collective representation and individual statutory rights, a concern not applicable [in *Gilmer*]." 500 U.S. at ___, 111 S.Ct. at 1650. Finally, *Gardner–Denver* was not decided under the FAA, a statute designed to encourage federal enforcement of arbitration agreements. The FAA exempts from its coverage any "contract of employment," but the Court ruled that this provision did not apply because the arbitration clause was in the registration agreement with the stock exchange, not the plaintiff's contract with the employer. A more extensive discussion of *Gilmer* and its implications for ADEA cases is contained in Chapter 10, *infra*.

Following the decision in *Gilmer* the Supreme Court vacated a decision of the Fifth Circuit which held that compulsory arbitration was not applicable to Title VII claims and remanded for reconsideration in light of *Gilmer*. On remand the Court of Appeals reversed its earlier decision.

> Because both the ADEA and Title VII are similar civil rights statutes, and both are enforced by the EEOC, ... we have little trouble concluding that Title VII claims can be subjected to compulsory arbitration. Any broad policy arguments against such a conclusion were necessarily rejected by *Gilmer*.

Alford v. Dean Witter Reynolds, 939 F.2d 229 (5th Cir.1991). The arbitration clause in *Alford*, like that in *Gilmer*, was contained in a stock exchange registration, not an employment contract and could thus be enforced under the FAA. The question of whether a compulsory arbitration clause that *could not* be enforced under the FAA would, nevertheless, be enforceable under the rational of *Gilmer* remains to be decided.

SECTION B.   SUITS BY THE EEOC
EQUAL EMPLOYMENT OPPORTUNITY COMMISSION v. SHERWOOD MEDICAL INDUSTRIES, INC.

United States District Court, Middle District of Florida, 1978.
452 F.Supp. 678.

MEMORANDUM OPINION

GEORGE C. YOUNG, CHIEF JUDGE.

This is a Title VII enforcement action brought by the Equal Employment Opportunity Commission against Sherwood Medical Industries, Inc. (Sherwood), alleging that Sherwood engaged in discriminatory employment practices with respect to race and male gender. Now before the Court is Sherwood's "Motion to Strike and/or for Dismissal for Failure to State a Claim and/or for Summary Judgment," which puts in issue the permissible scope of the Commission's judicial complaint in this cause. The decisive question raised is whether the EEOC is now foreclosed from prosecuting its claim of male sex discrimination because it neither included this claim in its reasonable cause determination nor afforded Sherwood an opportunity to conciliate the matter prior to filing suit.

I. BACKGROUND

This Title VII case was set in motion on July 16, 1973 when Larry C. Dilligard, a black male, filed a charge with the EEOC, complaining that he had been denied employment by defendant Sherwood solely because of his race. The details of his charge of discrimination, assumed to be true for the purpose of this motion, are as follows: Dilligard entered the personnel office of Sherwood's Deland facility on the morning of July 9, 1973 and requested an application for employment. He informed a Caucasian female employee that he was seeking a clerical position and that he had a college degree in business. Dilligard was told that there were no vacancies in the clerical area and that there was no need to fill out an application because "we only accumulate a lot of applications and eventually throw them in the garbage can". Dilligard responded that he wished to complete an application in any event so that he could have one on file if a vacancy did occur. The employee refused to give him an application. Dilligard observed at the time a number of white job applicants waiting in a nearby reception center for interviews.

The EEOC responded to Dilligard's charge by sending Sherwood the statutory notice of charge and initiating a broad scale investigation into Sherwood's employment practices. In the course of its investigation the Commission compiled statistical data on the race and sex composition of Sherwood's clerical work force.

On February 18, 1975 the Commission issued a formal "reasonable cause determination" finding "reasonable cause to believe that respondent [Sherwood] failed to hire charging party because of his race." Despite the fact that the investigation clearly encompassed male gender discrimination, the determination made no finding on that issue and it invited conciliation only on Dilligard's narrow charge of race discrimination. Indeed, there were merely two references to male gender employment practices in the entire three page document:

> "The Commission also notes that all of respondent's clericals are female except one.

The foregoing statistics coupled with the fact that there were clerical vacancies after July 9, 1973, is sufficient to establish that exclusion of blacks, and particularly black males, has occurred."

Apparently at no point during the conciliation negotiations that followed the Commission's determination did male gender employment discrimination emerge as a subject of concern. The conciliation agreement ultimately proposed by the Commission (and rejected by Sherwood) was completely silent on that issue; the agreement focused exclusively on Dilligard's charge of race discrimination. And from all that appears in the record it was not until the judicial complaint in this cause was filed that Sherwood first learned of the Commission's claim that it had discriminated against males.

Sherwood now argues that the Commission's failure to put it on notice of the sex discrimination claim and to afford it an opportunity to conciliate the matter bars the Commission from pressing that claim in this action. In substance, Sherwood's contention is that the Commission has filed to satisfy all of the statutory pre-requisites to its power to sue under Title VII, hence this Court lacks subject matter jurisdiction over the sex discrimination claim. The Commission's response is that it has satisfied the minimum conditions on its power to bring a Title VII enforcement action. It takes issue with the contention that the reasonable cause determination did not sufficiently apprise Sherwood of its claim of male gender discrimination. And it maintains that it can assert its sex discrimination claim even if that issue were never made an explicit subject of conciliation. Moreover, the Commission argues, the scope of matters sought to be conciliated is not a proper subject of judicial scrutiny and hence the Court should not even inquire into whether the sex claim was a subject of attempted conciliation.

II. THE SCOPE OF THE CHARGE AND THE INVESTIGATION

It is now well settled that the allowable scope of a civil enforcement action by the Commission is not fixed strictly by the allegations of the charging party's charge of discrimination. Rather, as the Fifth Circuit held in the often-cited decision of Sanchez v. Standard Brands, Inc., 431 F.2d 455 (1970), the scope of the civil action is to be determined by the "scope of the EEOC investigation which can reasonably be expected to grow out of the charge of discrimination." 431 F.2d at 466.[1] The charge should be viewed merely as the starting point for a reasonable

---

1. The post-*Sanchez* decisions have applied slightly different tests to determine whether the Commission's judicial complaint was unreasonably broad in light of the charge of discrimination. Compare e.g., Gamble v. Birmingham Southern R.R. Company, 514 F.2d 678, 687–89 (5th Cir. 1975); Oubichon v. North American Rockwell Corp., 482 F.2d 569, 571 (9th Cir.1973); with MacBride v. Delta Airlines, Inc., 551 F.2d 113, 115 (6th Cir.1977); EEOC v. General Electric Co., 532 F.2d 359, 365–66 (4th Cir.1976). It is doubtful that there is any meaningful distinction between the tests employed. The inquiry in every case is essentially whether the additional charge of employment discrimination could reasonably have grown out of an investigation into the original charge.

investigation, not as a common-law pleading which narrowly circum-scribes the Commission's freedom of action in carrying out its statutory duties. If the Commission uncovers during a reasonable investigation facts which support a charge of some form of discrimination other than that alleged in the original charge, it is free to develop these facts and, if necessary, to require the respondent to account for them. Judge Russell of the Fourth Circuit has astutely summarized this principle this way:

> *"So long as the new discrimination arises out of the reasonable investigation of the charge filed,* it can be the subject of a 'reason-able cause determination,' to be followed by an offer by the Com-mission of conciliation, and, if conciliation fails, by a civil suit, without the filing of a new charge on such claim of discrimination. In other words, the original charge is sufficient to support action by the EEOC as well as a civil suit under the Act for *any discrimina-tion stated in the charge itself or developed in the course of the reasonable investigation of that charge,* provided such discrimina-tion was included in the reasonable cause determination of the EEOC and was followed by compliance with the conciliation proce-dures fixed in the Act." (emphasis in original)

EEOC v. General Elec. Co., 532 F.2d 359, 366 (4th Cir.1976).

In the present case the Commission's investigation clearly exceeded the scope of the charging party's charge of discrimination. For Dilli-gard's charge dealt solely with race and the Commission, in the course of its investigation of that charge, compiled statistical data on sex as well. But Sherwood does not say that the broader focus of the investi-gation was in any way improper or abusive in relation to the charge filed; indeed it appears to concede the reasonableness of the investiga-tion. So there is no real question here about the scope of the judicial complaint per se. If the Commission complied with the statutory pre-requisites to bringing suit, it was free to assert its sex claim against Sherwood because that claim arose out of a reasonable investigation of the original charge of discrimination. The scope of the complaint is in issue here only because it is contended that with respect to the sex discrimination claim the Commission has failed to comply with two statutory conditions on its power to sue: a reasonable cause determina-tion and an effort to conciliate.

III. THE REASONABLE CAUSE DETERMINATION

Under 42 U.S.C. § 2000e–5(b), after the Commission investigates a charge of discrimination, it should "so far as practical not later than 120 days from the filing of the charge" make a determination on whether it believes the charge is true. This reasonable cause determi-nation is a very crucial step in the administrative process. For it marks the conclusion of the Commission's investigation into a respondent's employment practices and it represents the Commission's formal opinion about what its investigation revealed. The determination may even bring the administrative process to an end with respect to many charges; if a "no cause" determination is made the charge of discrimination will be dismissed and the complaining party left to his private remedies in court. And where a "cause" determination is reached, the Commission, by law, must undertake an attempt to conciliate the dispute. See generally Occidental Life Ins. Co. v. EEOC, 432 U.S. 355 at 359, 97 S.Ct. 2447, 2451, 53 L.Ed.2d 402 at 407 (1977). In that event, the reasonable cause determination is intended to serve both as a formal means of placing the respondent on notice of the particular employment practice which the Commission views as violative of Title VII and as a framework for the conciliation efforts to follow.

Because of the importance of the reasonable cause determination, as a means of finally drawing the investigation to a close, as an embodiment of the Commission's legal conclusions from the evidence, as a means of notice to the respondent and as a device to frame the issues for conciliation, it seems evident that any and all of a respondents' employment practices viewed by the Commission as probably discriminatory, must be explicitly included in the determination. That is, the Commission must make an express finding in the determination concerning each employment practice which it concludes to be violative of Title VII. The Courts which have addressed themselves to this question have so concluded.

The reasonable cause determination at issue here falls far short of making any such finding on the sex discrimination claim now asserted against Sherwood. Indeed, the closest scrutiny of the determination could not have effectively placed Sherwood on notice that sex discrimination was a matter in issue. The only material reference to sex in the entire determination was the comment that statistical analysis indicated that there were clerical vacancies after July 9, 1973 sufficient to establish that "the exclusion of blacks, and particularly black males, has occurred." This comment was manifestly insufficient to afford Sherwood notice of the sex discrimination claim. If anything, the inference that should be drawn from the statement is that there was no discrimination against white males. Race discrimination was all that Sherwood could reasonably have viewed as being in dispute.

IV. THE FAILURE TO CONCILIATE

Conciliation is the final step in an EEOC administrative proceeding and a condition precedent to the Commission's power to sue. The language of the statute admits of no exception. If the Commission finds reasonable cause it "shall endeavor to eliminate any such unlawful employment practice by informal methods of conference, conciliation and persuasion", and only when conciliation "acceptable to the

Commission" fails may it bring a civil action against the respondent. 42 U.S.C. § 2000e–5(b). The Courts have interpreted the statute to mean precisely what it says and it is thus now well established that failure to conciliate is fatal to a Title VII action brought by the Commission;[2] the suit or claim must be dismissed as premature.

The record in this case, as counsel for the Commission concedes, establishes that conciliation on the sex discrimination claim was never offered and never attempted. The only subject of conciliation efforts was Dilligard's race discrimination charge; when the negotiations on that charge failed, the Commission filed suit without ever attempting to settle the sex discrimination claim. It would thus seem to follow that the sex discrimination aspects of the Commission's claim against Sherwood would have to be stricken from this case. But the Commission argues that it would be error to do so because the Commission need conciliate only the original charge of discrimination, not the additional discrimination claims which come to life during an investigation of the original charge. That is, as the Commission views it, its duty is to conciliate the charging party's charge only and if it is unable to reach a conciliation agreement on that charge it is under no obligation to seek settlement with respect to additional discriminatory employment practices developed during the investigation of the original charge. Under this theory only Dilligard's charge was required to be conciliated.

This contention, if accepted, would run contrary to Congressional intent and could well have the affect of rendering the conciliation requirement an empty formality. The mandate that conciliation be attempted is unique to Title VII and it clearly reflects a strong Congressional desire for out-of-court settlement of Title VII violations. See Culpepper v. Reynolds Metal Co., 421 F.2d 888 (5th Cir.1970); Oatis v. Crown Zellerbach, 398 F.2d 496 (5th Cir.1968). The legislative history of the 1972 amendments confirms that Congress viewed judicial relief as a recourse of last resort, sought only after a settlement has been attempted and failed.[3] Conciliation is clearly the heart of the

---

2. By contrast, conciliation by the Commission is not a condition precedent to the institution of a private action for relief under Title VII by an individual plaintiff. See, Gamble v. Birmingham Southern R.R. Co., supra at 688–89; Danner v. Phillips Petroleum Co., 447 F.2d 159 (5th Cir.1971).

3. A reference to the legislative history of the Act appearing in EEOC v. Westvaco Corp., supra is particularly instructive:

"* * * Senator Dominick, the principle architect of the 1972 amendment that empowered the Commission to bring suit in its own name, stated that '[M]y amendment would take over at the level where conciliations fail' 118 Cong.Rec.S. 170 (Jan. 20, 1972). 'What the amend-

ment does * * * is * * * provide for trial in the U.S. District Courts whenever the EEOC has investigated a charge, found reasonable cause to believe that an unlawful employment practice has occurred, and is *unable* to obtain voluntary compliance' 118 Cong.Rec.S. 221 (Jan. 21, 1972). Similarly, the Senior House Conferee on the 1972 amendment ventured the opinion that *'[O]nly if conciliation proves to be impossible* do we expect the Commission to bring action in federal district court to seek enforcement.' Cong. Rec.H. 1861 (Mar. 18, 1972). (remarks of Congressman Perkins, introduced in the Conference Report on House Resolution 1746)." (emphasis supplied) 372 F.Supp. at 988.

Title VII administrative process. In light of the clear Congressional preference for conciliation it would be anomalous to conclude that the Commission is under no obligation to conciliate a claim of discrimination simply because it originated during the course of its investigation rather than from an aggrieved person's charge.

Certainly one can find no support for the Commission's position in the decisions dealing with the scope of the judicial complaint. To the contrary, every decision recognizing a right in the Commission to expand its investigation—and ultimately its judicial complaint—beyond the scope of the charging party's charge, has presupposed that the additional employment practices complained of were included in the conciliation attempt along with the original charge. In EEOC v. Raymond Metal Prod. Co., 385 F.Supp. 907, 915 (D.Md.1974) for instance, the Court concluded:

> " * * * the judicial complaint in an EEOC civil action may properly embrace, in addition to those allegations contained in the initial charge, any allegations of other discriminatory employment practices for which there has been *an investigation, a determination of reasonable cause and a genuine attempt at conciliation.*" (emphasis supplied)

The Fourth Circuit in EEOC v. General Electric Co., supra at 366, similarly stressed that the new discrimination developed from the Commission's investigation could be included in a civil suit provided that it was included in the reasonable cause determination and in the efforts to conciliate. Like language can be found in a long line of decisions concerning the scope of the Commission's judicial complaint. These decisions recognize a right in the Commission to pursue its investigation beyond the bounds of the original charge of discrimination. But in so doing they do not vest the Commission with the authority to pick and choose the matters to be conciliated.

The only construction of the statute which is at all in harmony with the Congressional desire for conciliation is that the Commission's authority to sue is conditioned upon full compliance with the administrative process—investigation, determination, and conciliation—with respect to each discriminatory practice alleged. "Congress, committed as it was to voluntary compliance, could not have intended that the Commission could attempt conciliation on one set of issues and, having failed, litigate a different set." EEOC v. E. I. duPont deNemours and Company, supra at 1336. Once having determined that a respondent has violated Title VII the Commission must make a genuine effort to conciliate with respect to each and every employment practice complained of. In this way, the respondent is afforded a fair opportunity to weigh all the factors which must be taken into account in deciding whether to settle a dispute out of court, even if the charge of discrimination in dispute arose from the Commission's own investigation rather than the charging party's charge. And if litigation then results, all parties are assured that they have had a fair opportunity to settle every matter in dispute. The Congressional mandate that litigation be a matter of last resort will have been observed.

It is contended, however, that this Court lacks jurisdiction to inquire into the degree of the Commission's compliance with the conciliation requirements of Title VII, hence Sherwood's complaint that it was afforded no opportunity to conciliate the sex discrimination claim may not be heard. Essentially, the Commission takes the position that the scope of the matters sought to be conciliated is not a proper subject of judicial scrutiny; the Courts inquiry into its jurisdiction must cease upon proof that conciliation was attempted on at least some matters in dispute. This contention is without merit. The Court recognizes that the conciliation requirement of the statute is phrased in terms of conciliation "acceptable to the Commission"; and thus district courts are not empowered to second guess the Commission with respect to particular settlement negotiations. But the question in this case is not whether the Commission properly exercised its discretion during settlement negotiations, but whether it afforded the respondent Sherwood the opportunity to conciliate at all with respect to one of the claims asserted in its judicial complaint. It is frivolous to contend that the court lacks jurisdiction to decide this question. If the Commission is to seek relief in federal court it must be prepared to show that it has satisfied the jurisdictional prerequisites—including submitting the matters in issue to conciliation. It has not done so here and it therefore follows that suit on the sex discrimination claim was premature. This is a matter of subject matter jurisdiction, not of Commission discretion.

V.   CONCLUSION

As Judge Stapleton observed in EEOC v. E.I. duPont deNemours and Company, supra, the "Commission's power of suit and administrative process [are not] unrelated activities, [but] sequential steps in a unified scheme for securing compliance with Title VII". 373 F.Supp. at 1333. The Commission must substantially satisfy the requirements of each step in this process—investigation, determination and conciliation—before it can progress to the next. In the present case the Commission has bypassed two of the most essential—determination and conciliation. These defects may not be overlooked, and the sex discrimination claim must therefore be stricken. A separate order dismissing the Commission's sex discrimination claim will be entered. The race discrimination claim, of course, will remain pending and the issue for trial will be whether during the relevant period Sherwood discriminated against employees or prospective employees on the basis of race.

JOHNSON v. NEKOOSA–EDWARDS PAPER CO.

United States Court of Appeals, Eighth Circuit, 1977.

558 F.2d 841, cert. denied, 434 U.S. 920, 98 S.Ct. 394, 54 L.Ed.2d 276.

Before CLARK, ASSOCIATE JUSTICE, RETIRED,[*] GIBSON, CHIEF JUDGE, and HEANEY, CIRCUIT JUDGE.

HEANEY, CIRCUIT JUDGE.

This action was filed by Linda Johnson and the United Paperworkers International Union against Nekoosa Papers, Inc., alleging the existence of sex discrimination in its employment practices at Nekoosa's Ashdown, Arkansas, facilities. The named plaintiffs sought to represent a class including all past and present female employees and all female job applicants who were denied employment opportunities because of their sex. The Equal Employment Opportunity Commission (EEOC) was allowed to intervene. The District Court initially certified the class to include only present employees but later decertified the class entirely and ruled that "the EEOC may not expand the scope of this action beyond that which the Plaintiffs are permitted to pursue."[1] The District Court's decision to decertify the class and to limit the scope of the EEOC's intervention is challenged in this consolidated appeal.[2]

Prior to bringing this action, Johnson and the Union had filed a charge with the EEOC alleging that "[f]emale employees have been denied job opportunities, wages and fringe benefits because of their sex, including but not limited to the treatment of maternity conditions by the employer."[3] After an investigation, the EEOC found reasonable cause to believe that Nekoosa discriminated against women in violation of Title VII with respect to maternity benefits, job opportunities and wages. The EEOC issued its determination of probable cause on June 19, 1974, and indicated that an EEOC representative would be in contact with each party in the near future to begin conciliation. In early August, 1974, the attorney for Nekoosa contacted the EEOC by letter and telephone seeking to expedite the conciliation process. The EEOC did not respond to Nekoosa's overtures. The EEOC issued a right-to-sue letter to Johnson and the Union at their request on August 19, 1974. This action was filed on September 9, 1974.

* * *

[*] Tom C. Clark, Associate Justice, Retired, Supreme Court of the United States, sitting by designation.

1. Linda Johnson and United Paperworkers International Union, AFL–CIO, and Equal Employment Opportunity Commission v. Nekoosa Papers Inc. (Ashdown, Arkansas), CA No. T–74–57–C (W.D. Ark., order filed June 8, 1976). Thus, the Equal Employment Opportunity Commission (EEOC) would not be able to raise the claims of those who were denied job opportunities because of their sex and to challenge the virtual exclusion of females from production jobs.

2. The above entitled cases were consolidated by this Court for the purpose of this opinion.

3. The charge was filed with the EEOC on November 29, 1973, by Johnson and the Union acting through their attorney.

[The Court held that the class decertification was not an appealable order. See infra at 463].

II.

We next consider whether the District Court properly held that the EEOC may not expand the scope of the action beyond that of the charge filed by the plaintiffs with the EEOC. The District Court certified the following questions to this Court pursuant to 28 U.S.C. § 1292(b).[6]

1. Whether the commission's suit in intervention properly enlarges the scope of the private plaintiffs' suit so as to include all forms of discrimination described in the Commission's Determination of Plaintiffs' underlying charges.

2. Whether the Court properly held that "the EEOC may not expand the scope of this action beyond that which the Plaintiffs are permitted to pursue" in view of the fact that the EEOC had not prior to the filing of its Motion to Intervene endeavored "to eliminate any such alleged, unlawful employment practice by informal methods of conference, conciliation, and persuasion" as required by § 706(b) of Title VII of the Civil Rights Act of 1964, 42 U.S.C. § 2000e–5(b) and that the EEOC had not as required by its rules, 29 CFR § 1601–23 (1974), notified the Defendant in writing "that such efforts have been unsuccessful and will not be resumed except on the Respondent's written request within the time specified in such notice."

3. Whether the Court abused its discretion in permitting the EEOC to intervene in this action in view of the fact that the EEOC had not, prior to the filing of its Motion for Intervention, endeavored to eliminate any alleged unlawful employment practice by informal methods of conference, conciliation and persuasion as required by § 706(b) of Title VII of the Civil Rights Act of 1964, 42 U.S.C. § 2000e–5(b) and that the EEOC had not, as required by its own rules, 29 CFR § 1601–23 (1974), notified the Defendant, in writing "that such efforts have been unsuccessful and will not be resumed except on the Respondent's written request with the time specified in such notice."

In order to resolve these questions relating to the permissible scope of the EEOC's suit in intervention, we are faced with the task of reconciling our holding in Equal Employment Op. Comm'n v. Missouri Pacific R. Co., 493 F.2d 71 (8th Cir.1974), with the EEOC's general obligation to conciliate.

In *Missouri Pacific*, this Circuit held "that, once the charging party has filed suit pursuant to a 'right to sue' notice the Commission is relegated to its right of permissive intervention." Id. at 75. The Court relied

6. The EEOC was granted permission to   September 23, 1976.
appeal by this Court in an order dated

upon the express statutory scheme,[7] 42 U.S.C. § 2000e 5(f)(1), and the legislative history of the 1972 amendments to Title VII [8] in reaching its conclusion that duplicitous suits were barred by the statute. Accord, E.E.O.C. v. Continental Oil Co., 548 F.2d 884, 889–890 (10th Cir.1977); Equal Employment Opportunity v. Occidental Life, 535 F.2d 533, 536 (9th Cir.) (dicta), cert. granted, 429 U.S. 1022, 97 S.Ct. 638, 50 L.Ed.2d 623 (1976).[9]

A problem arises, however, because different issues may be raised by the private suit and the suit filed by the EEOC even though the same charge originally filed with the EEOC serves as the basis for both suits. In this case, in its suit in intervention, the EEOC seeks to raise the claims of unsuccessful job applicants and to challenge the apparent exclusion of females from production jobs.[10] Thus, the scope of the EEOC suit is broader than that of the private suit which the District Court has limited to those issues raised by the charge filed with the EEOC which only alleged discrimination against present female employees.[11] The Court in *Missouri Pacific* recognized that the scope of

---

7. The scheme of the statute itself * * * negates the Commission's double-barreled approach. Once either the Commission or the charging party has filed suit, § 2000e–5(f)(1) speaks only in terms of intervention—the absolute right of the charging party to intervene if the Commission elects to file suit within 180 days; the permissive right of intervention on the part of the Commission in the private action. The statute cannot be read to warrant duplicitous lawsuits when both actions find their genesis in one unlawful employment practice charge. Equal Employment Op. Comm'n v. Missouri Pacific R. Co., 493 F.2d 71, 74 (8th Cir.1974).

8. H.R.Rep.No.92–238, 92d Cong., 2d Sess., 1972 U.S. Code Cong. & Admin. News p. 2148.

9. Other Circuits, have however, developed different approaches to the problem of duplicitous suits. The Fifth and Sixth Circuits, allow the EEOC to file suit if the EEOC suit would be broader in scope than the private action, even if a private suit based upon the same EEOC charge has already been filed. E.E.O.C. v. McLean Trucking Co. 525 F.2d 1007 (6th Cir.1975); Equal Employment Op. Comm'n v. Kimberly–Clark Corp., 511 F.2d 1352 (6th Cir. 1975), cert. denied, 423 U.S. 994, 96 S.Ct. 420, 46 L.Ed.2d 368 (1976); Equal Employment Op. Comm'n v. Huttig Sash & Door Co., 511 F.2d 453 (5th Cir.1975). This approach was rejected by the Tenth Circuit because it was unable to find any statutory basis for defining the EEOC's right to sue in terms of the scope of its suit. E.E.O.C.

v. Continental Oil Co., 548 F.2d 884, 889 (10th Cir.1977).

The Third Circuit reads the statute and the legislative history differently and places no limitation on the right of the EEOC to bring suit after a private action has been filed. Equal Emp. Opp. Comm'n v. North Hills Passavant Hosp., 544 F.2d 664, 672 (3rd Cir.1976). Any problem with duplicitous suits is to be resolved under Fed.R.Civ.P. 42(a) which provides for the consolidation of actions involving common questions of law and fact. Id. See generally Reiter, The Equal Employment Opportunity Commission and "Duplicitous Suits": An Examination of EEOC v. Missouri Pacific Railroad Co., 49 N.Y.U.L.Rev. 1130 (1974).

We adhere to our decision in Equal Employment Op. Comm'n v. Missouri Pacific R. Co., 493 F.2d 71 (8th Cir.1974), for the reasons stated in that opinion.

10. The EEOC investigation revealed that only 4.5% of Nekoosa's employees were female even though the community work force was 22.4% female. Moreover, 78.5% of the female Nekoosa employees occupied clerical positions.

11. We emphasize that we are without jurisdiction to review this aspect of the District Court's order. We note, however, that it has been held that a private suit is not necessarily restricted to the scope of the charge filed with the EEOC and may extend to those issues revealed by a reasonable investigation by the EEOC. See Jenkins v. Blue Cross Mutual Hospital Ins.,

the EEOC suit might be broader than that of the private suit when it stated that it was "fully confident that [the District Court] * * * will permit intervention and enlargement of the scope of the action by the Commission if necessary to the rendering of full and complete justice." Equal Employment Op. Comm'n v. Missouri Pacific R. Co., supra at 75. My concurring opinion went one step further and would have required the District Court to broaden the scope of the suit to include those issues raised by the EEOC because the EEOC is charged with the responsibility of eliminating discriminatory employment practices and, thus, must be allowed to bring the broader issues before the court. Id. at 75 (J. Heaney concurring). Indeed, it would be anomalous if we did not allow the EEOC's suit in intervention to broaden the issues beyond those raised by the charge filed with the EEOC since the EEOC is not so restricted if it brings a direct suit. See E.E.O.C. v. General Elec. Co., 532 F.2d 359 (4th Cir.1976); Equal Employment Op. Comm'n v. Huttig Sash & Door Co., 511 F.2d 453 (5th Cir.1975); cf. Equal Employment Op. Comm'n v. Western Pub. Co., Inc., 502 F.2d 599 (8th Cir.1974). We cannot, however, simply order that the EEOC be permitted to broaden the scope of its suit in intervention because we must also consider the obligation of the EEOC to attempt conciliation.

Because of the enormous backlog of cases pending before the EEOC, a private party will usually be able to bring an action before the EEOC has attempted conciliation and completed the administrative process.[12] When this occurs, as it did here, the EEOC is precluded from bringing a direct action and is relegated to its right of permissive

Inc., 522 F.2d 1235, 1241 (7th Cir.1975) (en banc); Danner v. Phillips Petroleum Co., 447 F.2d 159, 161–162 (5th Cir.1971); Sanchez v. Standard Brands, Inc., 431 F.2d 455, 466 (5th Cir.1970); cf. Parham v. Southwestern Bell Telephone Co., 433 F.2d 421, 425 (8th Cir.1970).

12. A charging party cannot bring a private action unless permission is received from the EEOC. However, the EEOC is required to issue a right-to-sue letter if it either dismisses a charge or does not bring suit within 180 days of the date the charge was filed. The charging party then has 90 days in which to initiate his own court action. 42 U.S.C. § 2000e–5(f)(1). It is, thus, possible for a charging party to bring suit within a short period of time after the charge has been filed.

While the EEOC can bring an action within 30 days after the charge has been filed, it can only do so if it finds reasonable cause to believe the charge to be true and if conciliation has failed. Since it has often taken the EEOC two to three years to attempt conciliation, Equal Employment Op. Comm'n v. Kimberly–Clark Corp. supra at 1358; U.S. Comm'n on Civil Rights,

The Federal Civil Rights Enforcement Effort—1974, 529 (1975), the EEOC will usually be unable to bring its own action before a private action has been filed. The EEOC's delay in processing cases is reflected by its backlog of cases. As of June 30, 1975, over 126,000 cases were pending before the EEOC. As the following table indicates, some of the pending charges date back to 1968.

Fiscal Year in Which Charge was Filed	Number of Open Charges
1968	2,213
1969	3,260
1970	4,245
1971	5,917
1972	8,114
1973	18,550
1974	30,812
1975	46,919
Unspecified	6,310
TOTAL	126,340

Report to the Congress by the Comptroller General of the United States, The Equal Employment Opportunity Commission Has

intervention. If conciliation was required prior to intervention, the EEOC's motion to intervene might not be considered timely under Fed.R.Civ.P. 24 because the process of conciliation is often time-consuming. While conciliation is mandatory prior to direct suit by the EEOC, 42 U.S.C. § 2000e–5(f)(1); 29 C.F.R. § 1601.23; Patterson v. American Tobacco Company, 535 F.2d 257 (4th Cir.), cert. denied, 429 U.S. 920, 97 S.Ct. 314, 50 L.Ed.2d 286 (1976); Equal Employment Op. Comm'n v. Hickey–Mitchell Co., 507 F.2d 944 (8th Cir.1974); it is not mandatory under the statutory scheme prior to intervention by the EEOC.[13] 42 U.S.C. § 2000e–5(f)(1). Thus, the EEOC cannot be precluded from intervention because it failed to conciliate.

Conciliation is nonetheless an integral part of Title VII, Equal Employment Op. Comm'n v. Hickey–Mitchell Co., supra, and is desirable for a variety of policy reasons including giving the defendant notice and an opportunity to respond to any additional claims revealed by the EEOC investigation and in order to avoid expensive and time-consuming court actions.[14] Because we believe strongly in the value of conciliation, we hold that while the EEOC is not barred from intervention by its failure to attempt to conciliate, it is under a continuing obligation to attempt to conciliate even after it has intervened in the action. To this end, we order the District Court to stay the action for sixty days and to require the EEOC to make a prompt offer to conciliate. If the offer is accepted by Nekoosa and if thereafter EEOC fulfills its obligation to conciliate in good faith and if no settlement is forthcoming by the end of the sixty-day period, the District Court is directed to then enter an order permitting the EEOC to expand its intervention in accordance with its petition. If Nekoosa refuses to conciliate, then the District Court's order permitting the EEOC to expand the scope of its intervention shall be issued forthwith.

We believe such a stay is not so long as to unduly prejudice the individual claimants. We realize that requiring the EEOC to expedite its conciliation process after intervention might be difficult for them because of their backlog of cases. We feel, however, it is the best balance between the right of the EEOC to intervene, the obligation of the EEOC to attempt conciliation and the right of the individual claimants to proceed with their action.

Made Limited Progress in Eliminating Employment Discrimination 9 (September 28, 1976).

13. The EEOC has been permitted to intervene in three District Court cases even though it had not attempted to conciliate. Willis v. Allied Maintenance Corp., 13 FEP Cases 767 (S.D.N.Y. 1976); NOW v. Minnesota Mining & Mfg., 11 FEP Cases 720 (D.Minn.1975); Jones v. Holy Cross Hospital Silver Springs, Inc., 64 F.R.D. 586 (D.MD.1974). In each case, the EEOC was not permitted to expand the scope of the action because it had not attempted to conciliate. Because we are ordering a stay to permit conciliation, the EEOC will be permitted to expand the scope of its action here.

14. We are aware that the conciliation process has to date been relatively unsuccessful. See Peck, The Equal Employment Opportunity Commission: Developments in the Administrative Process 1965, 1975, 51 Wash. L. Rev. 831, 852–853 (1976); Report to Congress by the Comptroller General of the United States, supra at 7–37. Action by the legislative and executive branches of the federal government is apparently necessary to make the process a more effective one.

Accordingly, we reverse and remand this action to the District Court for action consistent with this opinion.

NOTES AND PROBLEMS FOR DISCUSSION

1. With *Johnson*, compare EEOC v. Kimberly–Clark Corp., 511 F.2d 1352, 1363 (6th Cir.), cert. denied, 423 U.S. 994, 96 S.Ct. 420, 46 L.Ed.2d 368 (1975) ("The Congressional intent that duplicitous proceedings be avoided does not mean, however, that the EEOC should be limited to permissive intervention in a private suit when its investigation on the one charge has disclosed a number of violations which require judicial attention."); EEOC v. Walker–Fischer General Agency, Inc., 43 FEP Cases 1761 (N.D.Tex.1987) (EEOC allowed to challenge pregnancy provisions of employer's group health policy based on charge that employer had discharged employee because she was pregnant; EEOC's claim reasonably related to individual charge and employer could reasonably have expected that its terms would be discovered). Although the EEOC's investigation of a charge, and thus the claims it may raise in a subsequent suit, may be considerably broader that the substance of the charge, claims which the EEOC has not attempted to conciliate with the defendant will be stricken from the suit. See, EEOC v. Allegheny Airlines, 436 F.Supp. 1300, 1305–1307 (W.D.Pa.1977). But what kind of effort by the Commission to arrange conciliation is necessary? To what extent should the court delve into the conciliation process to determine whether an appropriate effort was made? See EEOC v. Klingler Electric Corp., 636 F.2d 104, 107 (5th Cir.1981); EEOC v. Zia Co., 582 F.2d 527, 533 (10th Cir.1978); EEOC v. Celotex Corp., 27 FEP Cases 324, 327 (W.D.Tenn.1980). Would a court's review of the actual offers and counter offers of the parties during the conciliation process, to determine the EEOC's good faith, be fair to the parties?

2. Private litigation in which the EEOC is not a party cannot preclude the EEOC from maintaining its own action based on the private litigants' EEOC charges. See, EEOC v. North Hills Passavant Hospital, 544 F.2d 664 (3d Cir.1976); EEOC v. United Parcel Service, 860 F.2d 372 (10th Cir.1988)(since EEOC has standing to challenge ongoing discrimination, charging party's settlement does not moot agency's claim). What if the charging party's suit has been dismissed with prejudice? See EEOC v. Huttig Sash & Door Co., 511 F.2d 453 (5th Cir.1975). Under § 706(i) of the Act, 42 U.S.C. § 2000e–5(i), the EEOC may seek enforcement of a decree entered in a case in which it was not a party. The courts are divided on the question of whether the Commission can seek modification of such decrees. Compare EEOC v. United Association of Journeymen, Local 189, 438 F.2d 408 (6th Cir.), cert. denied, 404 U.S. 832, 92 S.Ct. 77, 30 L.Ed.2d 62 (1971), with EEOC v. First Alabama Bank, 595 F.2d 1050 (5th Cir.1979).

3. Title VII imposes strict limits on the time within which private parties may file charges with the EEOC, but it does not contain an express limitation on the time within which the Commission may bring suit. But the Commission suit may be barred by the doctrine of laches when it has been inexcusably delayed and the defendant has been materially prejudiced by the delay. Occidental Life Insurance Co. v. EEOC, 432 U.S. 355, 373, 97 S.Ct. 2447, 2457, 53 L.Ed.2d 402, 415 (1977). Laches is only available as a defense where *both* unreasonable delay and substantial or material prejudice to the defendant have occurred. The EEOC's workload has been rejected as an excuse for unreasonable delay. See, EEOC v. Liberty Loan Corp., 584 F.2d 853, 857–858 (8th

Cir.1978). The burden of proving prejudice is on the defendant, EEOC v. Massey–Ferguson, Inc., 622 F.2d 271, 276 (7th Cir.1980), and is normally established by demonstrating the unavailability of witnesses, changed personnel, or loss of pertinent records. See, EEOC v. Alioto Fish Co., Limited, 623 F.2d 86, 88 (9th Cir.1980) (virtually all witnesses dead or suffering from "dimmed memories;" charging party did not remember applying with defendant). EEOC v. Firestone Tire & Rubber Co., 626 F.Supp. 90 (N.D.Ga.1985) (individuals who could have been anticipated as favorable witnesses have become hostile because of intervening discharges and advancing age and poor health have made other witnesses' recall of past events impossible). Cf. EEOC v. Jacksonville Shipyards, Inc., 690 F.Supp. 995 (M.D.Fla.1988) (employer may not take advantage of laches defense if it unreasonably failed to avoid prejudice by destroying records and not preserving statements of key witnesses).

4. Section 707 of Title VII, as it was originally enacted, granted to the Attorney General the authority to file suit under the Act when he had "reasonable cause to believe that any person * * * is engaged in a pattern or practice of resistance to the full enjoyment of any rights secured in this title * * *." Such a suit need not be based on a charge filed by an aggrieved employee or to have been preceded by an investigation or attempted conciliation. The 1972 amendments to the Act made it applicable to local governments and transferred to the EEOC the authority to bring "pattern and practice" actions under Section 707. A dispute then developed as to whether the 1972 amendments left the Justice Department with any authority to bring suits under Section 707. In 1978, as part of the Executive Reorganization Plan, *all* enforcement authority under Section 707 with respect to state or local governments or other political subdivisions was transferred back to the Justice Department. Where a claimant files an EEOC charge against a public employer, however, the EEOC may investigate and attempt conciliation of the charge. But if the Commission is unable to secure conciliation, under Section 706(f)(1), only the Attorney General is authorized to file suit for the government. The EEOC does retain its investigative powers, including the right to issue subpoenas, with respect to public employers. See, EEOC v. Illinois State Tollway Authority, 800 F.2d 656 (7th Cir.1986); EEOC v. Board of Public Education for City of Savannah, 643 F.Supp. 134 (S.D.Ga.1986). When a claimant wishes to file his own suit under Title VII against a public employer, what agency, if any, should issue the right-to-sue notice? See, Flint v. California, 594 F.Supp. 443 (E.D.Cal.1984).

5. To enable the EEOC to investigate charges Section 709(a) of Title VII provides the agency a broad right of access to "any evidence of any person being investigated . . . that relates to unlawful employment practices covered by [the Act] and is relevant to the charge under investigation. If an employer refuses to voluntarily provide information the Commission is authorized to issue subpoenas and to seek judicial enforcement of subpoenas. Section 710 (incorporating 29 U.S.C. Sec. 161). In a subpoena enforcement proceeding the court's duty is to "satisfy itself that the charge is valid and that the material requested is 'relevant' to the charge . . . and more generally to assess any contentions by the employer that the demand for information is too indefinite or has been made for an illegitimate purpose." EEOC v. Shell Oil Co., 466 U.S. 54, 72 n.26, 104 S.Ct. 1621, 1633 n.26, 80 L.Ed.2d 41, 59 n.26 (1984). In UNIVERSITY OF PENNSYLVANIA v. EQUAL EMPLOYMENT OPPORTUNITY COMMISSION, 493 U.S. 182, 110 S.Ct. 577, 107 L.Ed.2d 571 (1990) the Commission subpoenaed confidential peer review materials during the investigation of

charge against the university arising from the denial of tenure for a faculty member. The University resisted the subpoena on privacy and first amendment grounds. The district court ordered it to comply with the subpoena and the Third Circuit affirmed. The Supreme Court granted review on the question of whether a university enjoys a privilege, grounded in either the common law or the First Amendment, not to disclose peer evaluation materials that are relevant to charges of discrimination in tenure decisions.

In a unanimous decision, the Court held that the standard of disclosure under EEOC subpoenas applicable to business enterprises also applies to universities. Reasoning that the extension of Title VII's coverage to educational institutions in the 1972 amendments exposed tenure decisions to the same enforcement procedures applicable to other employment decisions, the Court rejected the university's claim that it was entitled to a common law privilege against compelled disclosure of peer review materials and its argument that discovery of such data would violate academic freedom protected by the First Amendment.

> Acceptance of [the University's] claim would also lead to a wave of similar privilege claims by other employers who play significant roles in furthering speech and learning in society. What of writers, publishers, musicians, lawyers? It surely is not unreasonable to believe, for example, that confidential peer reviews play an important part in partnership determinations at some law firms. We perceive no limiting principle in petitioner's argument. Accordingly, we stand behind the breakwater Congress has established: unless specifically provided otherwise in the statute, the EEOC may obtain "relevant" evidence. Congress has made the choice. If it dislikes the result, it may of course revise the statute.

493 U.S. at 194, 110 S.Ct. at 585.

6. Section 706(b) of Title VII provides for the initiation of proceedings by an aggrieved person or by "a member of the Commission." The statutory requirements for and procedures applicable to private charges and "Commissioner charges" are the same. Courts have tended, however, to require a good deal more specificity of Commissioner charges than of charges filed by private individuals. Disputes over the validity of Commissioner charges frequently arise during efforts by the Commission to enforce subpoenas issued in the course of investigations. In EEOC V. SHELL OIL CO., 466 U.S. 54, 104 S.Ct. 1621, 80 L.Ed.2d 41 (1984), the Commissioner's charge alleged that the company had engaged in a generic variety of unlawful practices from the effective date of Title VII to the present. The Court of Appeals held that the agency had failed to comply with § 706(b) because the notice had not included sufficient factual and statistical information about the charges nor informed the company of the approximate dates of the unlawful practices. Accordingly, it ordered that the agency subpoena not be enforced. The Supreme Court agreed that a charge and notice meeting the requirements of § 706 are jurisdictional prerequisites to judicial enforcement of an agency subpoena, but determined that in this case the requirements had been met. The Court concluded that the Eighth Circuit's holding would, in effect, have obliged the Commissioner to substantiate his allegations before the EEOC could investigate, thus impairing the agency's enforcement powers. The purpose of the notice requirement in § 706(b) is to give an employer fair notice of the existence and nature of the allegations against it, and not to impose a substantive constraint on the EEOC's investiga-

tive authority. The statute requires that a Commissioner charging a pattern or practice of discrimination should:

> Insofar as he is able * * * identify the groups of persons that he has reason to believe have been discriminated against, the categories of employment positions from which they have been excluded, the methods by which the discrimination may have been effected, and the periods of time in which he suspects the discrimination to have been practiced.

466 U.S. at 73, 104 S.Ct. at 1633. Should EEOC "harassment" of an employer constitute an affirmative defense to the Commission's suit? A basis for a counterclaim under the Federal Tort Claims Act? See EEOC v. First National Bank, 614 F.2d 1004 (5th Cir.1980), cert. denied, 450 U.S. 917, 101 S.Ct. 1361, 67 L.Ed.2d 342 (1981).

EEOC ACTIONS AND THE RIGHTS OF INDIVIDUAL CLAIMANTS

ADAMS v. PROCTOR & GAMBLE MANUFACTURING CO.

United States Court of Appeals, Fourth Circuit, 1983.
697 F.2d 582, cert. denied, 465 U.S. 1041, 104 S.Ct. 1318, 79 L.Ed.2d 714 (1984).

PER CURIAM:

This case, concerning the preclusive effect upon charging parties of a consent decree in an action brought against an employer by the EEOC, was first heard by a panel of this court. A majority of the panel held there was no preclusive effect, while Senior Judge Haynsworth dissented. Adams v. The Proctor & Gamble Mfg. Co., 678 F.2d 1190 (4th Cir.1982). Thereafter, an order was entered granting rehearing *en banc*.

The question turns upon a proper interpretation of § 706(f)(1) of Title VII, 42 U.S.C.A. § 2000e–5(f)(1), which, insofar as pertinent, provides:

> (f)(1) If within thirty days after a charge is filed with the Commission * * *, the Commission has been unable to secure from the respondent a conciliation agreement acceptable to the Commission, the Commission may bring a civil action against any respondent not a government, governmental agency, or political subdivision named in the charge * * *. The person or persons aggrieved shall have the right to intervene in a civil action brought by the Commission * * *. If a charge filed with the Commission pursuant to subsection (b) of this section is dismissed by the Commission, or if within one hundred and eighty days from the filing of such charge * * *, the Commission has not filed a civil action under this section * * *, or the Commission has not entered into a conciliation agreement to which the person aggrieved is a party, the Commission * * * shall so notify the person aggrieved and within ninety days after the giving of such notice a civil action may be brought

against the respondent named in the charge (A) by the person claiming to be aggrieved * * *.

In 1976 the EEOC brought an action against Proctor & Gamble alleging employment discrimination. Some two dozen Proctor & Gamble employees had filed charges with the EEOC, but none of them chose to intervene in the EEOC action, though each had an unqualified right to do so under § 706(f)(1). Negotiations between the employer and the EEOC resulted in a settlement of the action by consent decree. There-after, the EEOC issued right-to-sue letters to those charging parties who rejected awards under the decree. When sixteen of those Proctor & Gamble workers with right-to-sue letters sued individually, the district court granted the company's motion to dismiss on the ground that the letters were invalid.

Substantially for the reasons set forth in Judge Haynsworth's dissenting opinion when the case was before the panel, we hold the district court's dismissal was appropriate. We read § 706(f)(1) in these circumstances to preclude suits by individuals who are charging parties, but who have not intervened in the pending EEOC action in their behalf, once the EEOC action has been concluded by a consent decree.

Under § 706(f)(1) right-to-sue letters may be issued by the Commission to charging parties under several different circumstances, but there is no provision for the issuance of such a letter under any circumstance after the EEOC has filed an action on behalf of the charging parties. As noted by the panel dissenter, there must be an exception if the EEOC's action is concluded on technical grounds without a judgment on the merits. In every sense, however, this consent decree was a judgment on the merits, and it awarded benefits which were then available to the charging parties.

The statutory scheme is fair and reasonable. A charging party has an unqualified right to intervene in the EEOC's action. If he wishes to participate in settlement negotiations or to have the right to reject any settlement agreement negotiated by the EEOC, he may fully protect himself by intervening. If he does not intervene, it is not unfair to him to conclude that he placed the conduct of the litigation entirely upon the EEOC and expressed a conclusive willingness to be bound by the outcome, whether or not the outcome was negotiated.

General Telephone Co. of the Northwest, Inc., v. EEOC, 446 U.S. 318, 100 S.Ct. 1698, 64 L.Ed.2d 319 (1980), is not to the contrary. In that case the employer had sought a ruling that the EEOC could not obtain broad class relief without compliance with Federal Rule of Civil Procedure 23. There were only four charging parties in that case, but there were allegations of pervasive discrimination affecting a great many persons. In those circumstances, if the EEOC were required to comply with rule 23, the efficacy of the EEOC's § 706(f)(1) remedy would be substantially impaired. Thus, the Supreme Court observed that it was "unconvinced that it would be consistent with the remedial purpose of the statutes to bind all 'class' members * * * by the relief obtained under an EEOC judgment or settlement against the employer." Id. at 333, 100 S.Ct. at 1707–08.

The question before the Supreme Court in *General Telephone* was exclusively related to the effect of a possible judgment upon persons who were not charging parties and who had no right of intervention. The Court's dicta must be read as referable to them and entirely inapplicable to the question of the preclusive effect of a judgment upon charging parties who had not exercised their right of intervention.

Our interpretation of § 706(f)(1) is not unprecedented. See e.g., Jones v. Bell Helicopter Co., 614 F.2d 1389 (5th Cir.1980); McClain v. Wagner Electric Corp., 550 F.2d 1115 (8th Cir.1977); Crump v. Wagner Electric Corp., 369 F.Supp. 637 (E.D.Mo.1973). Cf. Truvillion v. King's Daughters Hospital, 614 F.2d 520 (5th Cir.1980).

There has been some expression of concern among our dissenting brothers that a charging party may not recognize any reason to intervene in an EEOC action before an undesirable consent decree has been entered, by which time the right to intervene will have been lost. We appreciate their concern, but it cannot change the plain meaning of § 706(f)(1). Moreover, one who wishes to participate in tactical decisions which may substantially affect the outcome of the litigation or in settlement negotiations has reason for early intervention. In this, as in many other situations, one who invokes administrative and judicial machinery in his behalf should have a continuing interest or participation in it. If he does not intervene and leaves it to the EEOC to do whatever seems best to the EEOC for him, he should not be heard to complain of the consequences of his own indifference.

The judgment of the district court is affirmed.

Affirmed.

*   *   *

[The concurring opinion of JUDGE WIDENER is omitted]

PHILLIPS, CIRCUIT JUDGE, dissenting:

I respectfully dissent for the reasons expressed in the superseded panel opinion, 678 F.2d 1190, which held that plaintiffs' individual rights of action were not terminated by the institution of an EEOC action nor precluded by the entry in that action of a consent judgment to which they were not parties and whose terms they had affirmatively rejected. I continue to believe (as presumably does the EEOC, the federal agency charged with enforcing the statutory scheme in issue) that under the circumstances the EEOC was entitled under § 706(f)(1) to issue to these plaintiffs the right-to-sue letters upon which this action was brought and that the underlying rights of action are subsisting ones.

With all deference, nothing said in the per curiam opinion of the en banc court dissuades me from the interpretation given the controlling statutory provision by the original panel decision. As the majority opinion notes, those of us in dissent are particularly concerned that the contrary interpretation now reached imposes an utterly unrealistic burden upon Title VII charging parties. Under that interpretation, charging parties are required at their peril, and unaided by the principals, to follow the course of agency-employer conciliation or "settlement" efforts closely enough to protect their individual interests by formal intervention if, following institution of an agency action, those negotiations seem headed toward an unfavorable settlement.

There is nothing in the relevant statutory framework that lays upon the EEOC or the employer any obligation to keep charging parties advised of the details of those negotiations; of whether any "settlement" is imminent; of whether any settlement under consideration is to be expressed in a conciliation agreement or in a consent judgment; of the details or even the substance of a "settlement" that has been informally reached and remains only to be formalized by either means; of whether and when an agency action is to be commenced; of the fact that one has been commenced; or of anything else about the course of agency-employer dealings. The formal agency documents on file and a part of the record in this case contain no information along these lines of which charging parties might be held to have constructive notice. On oral argument we were given to understand by counsel for the EEOC, appearing as *amicus,* that the agency does not consider itself under any obligation and does not routinely keep all charging parties even generally apprised of the course of its conciliation-"settlement" negotiations. Certainly there is no suggestion that in this case—where presumably the normal course of proceedings was followed—these charging party-plaintiffs were ever sufficiently advised along these lines to make an informed decision that they must formally intervene— with the attendant expense—in order to protect their interests against an imminent consent judgment that did not satisfactorily protect them.

To the plain difficulty created for charging parties by its interpretation the en banc majority—which commendably concedes the difficulty—has only the meager response that the law after all affords these and comparably situated claimants the same means to protect their interests vis-a-vis agency action in their behalf that it does all persons in whose behalf federal agency action is undertaken. When the practicalities of the real-life situation involving these and comparably situated Title VII charging parties in their relation to EEOC-employer negotiations are frankly recognized, this assessment calls to mind— though with none of its implications of callousness—Anatole France's wry comment about actual as opposed to apparent impartiality of the law's general reach.[1]

If to all this it be rejoined that it is not our function to re-write statutes to cure perceived difficulties but simply to apply them accord-

---

1. "The law, in its majestic equality, forbids the rich as well as the poor to sleep under bridges, to beg in the streets, and to steal bread." A. France, *Le Lys Rouge* ch. 7 (1894), *quoted in* J. Cournos, *A Modern Plutarch* 27 (1928).

ing to their plain import, my response remains as it was in the panel majority opinion: that the dispositive statutory provision here is sufficiently ambiguous to require judicial interpretation drawing on the traditional aids. Among those traditional aids—in addition to the legislative history specifically alluded to in the panel opinion, see 678 F.2d at 1193–94—is that ancient and honorable canon of construction that when a literal interpretation ("conciliation" means only "conciliation") would lead to mischievous consequences, legislative intent is properly sought at deeper levels of purpose. See J. Sutherland, *Statutes and Statutory Construction* § 363 (2d ed. 1904). I continue to believe that in General Telephone Co. of the Northwest, Inc. v. EEOC, 446 U.S. 318, 100 S.Ct. 1698, 64 L.Ed.2d 319 (1980), the Supreme Court, by the clearest possible implication, and perhaps drawing *sub silentio* upon that canon, has already rejected the narrowly literal interpretation of § 706(f)(1) for which Proctor & Gamble has contended and which the en banc majority now adopts. See 678 F.2d at 1194–95 & n. 7. The *General Telephone* Court's careful discussion of the practical means by which employers entering into Title VII consent judgments with the EEOC may protect themselves against the private claims of employees—*including* charging parties—who may later reject the agency-employer settlement, see *General Telephone*, 446 U.S. at 333 & n. 15, 100 S.Ct. at 1708 & n. 15, is sensible only if it assumes that such judgments are not legally binding on those employees and that the employees' private rights of action are not terminated by mere institution of agency actions under § 706.

I am authorized to say that CHIEF JUDGE WINTER and JUDGE SPROUSE join in this opinion.

NOTES AND PROBLEMS FOR DISCUSSION

1. The Fourth Circuit's construction of Section 706(f)(1) in *Adams* has been rejected by one circuit. In Riddle v. Cerro Wire & Cable Group, Inc., 902 F.2d 918 (11th Cir.1990), the EEOC instituted an action based on Riddle's charge and sought specific relief for her. Riddle did not intervene. The EEOC and the employer settled the case but Riddle was not happy with the terms of the agreement, refused to sign it and requested a right-to-sue notice which was issued to her. Riddle's suit was dismissed by the district court on the ground that under Sec. 706(f)(1) her right to commence a private action was cut off by the EEOC's filing suit on her behalf. Her only option according to the district court was to have intervened in the agency's action. The Eleventh Circuit reversed. That court held that Riddle's suit was not barred by either the terms of the statute or the doctrine of *res judicata*. The Court of Appeals interpreted Section 706(f)(1) as precluding the issuance of a right to sue notice only if (1) the EEOC filed suit *within 180 days of the charge or* (2) if the EEOC had entered into a conciliation agreement with the employer and the charging party. In *Riddle* the EEOC had not filed suit within 180 days of the charge and no conciliation agreement had been entered into. Nor was Riddle bound by the consent decree negotiated by the EEOC because she had not been a party to the proceeding, she had refused to accept the benefits of the settlement and her interests and those of the EEOC were so different that the agency could not be treated as her representative for preclusion purposes.

2. What steps might a district court take to protect the rights of employees affected by resolution of an EEOC suit? May the Court direct that notice be given to the affected employees? See, Hoffman–La Roche, Inc. v. Sperling, 493 U.S. 165, 110 S.Ct. 482, 107 L.Ed.2d 480 (1989) and discussion in Chapter 6, *infra*. May the district court reject a settlement between the employer and the EEOC on the grounds that it is not fair to employees who would be bound by a consent decree? See, EEOC v. Pan American World Airways, Inc., 622 F.Supp. 633 (N.D.Cal.1985), appeal dismissed, 796 F.2d 314 (9th Cir.1986), cert. denied, 479 U.S. 1030, 107 S.Ct. 874, 93 L.Ed.2d 829 (1987).

3. *Adams* and *Riddle* involve the effect of an EEOC case on a subsequent individual action. As noted earlier an individual action, regardless how it is resolved, will not preclude EEOC litigation based on the same charge. Does that mean that an individual's action will have *no effect* on a subsequent EEOC suit? In EEOC v. United States Steel Corp., 921 F.2d 489 (3d Cir.1990) the agency sought to obtain individual relief under the ADEA for a group of former employees that included individuals who had been unsuccessful in their private actions against the employer. The Court of Appeals held that individuals who fully litigate their own claims under the ADEA are precluded by *res judicata* from obtaining individual relief in a subsequent EEOC action based on the same claims.

> The absence of any formal designation of the individual claimants as parties ... does not change the nature of the EEOC's role as the individuals' representative and should not change the effect of the doctrine of claim preclusion. By claiming or accepting individual relief won by the EEOC, the individuals would necessarily concede that the EEOC was their representative and that they were embraced by the EEOC's judgment. For those individuals who had previously brought their own suits against USX and lost on the merits, this concession would be fatal. Having had their day in court, these individuals could not relitigate the same claim through a representative any more than they could relitigate the same claim on their own behalf.

921 F.2d at 496.

Chapter 5

PROCEDURAL REQUIREMENTS FOR PUBLIC SECTOR EMPLOYEES

SECTION A. FEDERAL GOVERNMENT EMPLOYEES

Read Section 717 of Title VII.

Title VII, as originally enacted, did not prohibit discrimination by public employers. As part of the Equal Employment Opportunity Act of 1972, however, Congress expanded the coverage of Title VII to include many federal, and most state and local government employees. State and local governments were brought under the statute's jurisdiction through a broadened definition of "person" in § 701(a). A new provision—§ 717—was added to bring federal employees within the coverage of the Act. This latter section, in addition to its substantive provisions, designated the Civil Service Commission as the agency with jurisdiction over federal employee complaints of job discrimination. This function subsequently was transferred to the EEOC by § 3 of President Carter's Reorganization Plan No. 1 of 1978. And this Reorganization Plan was expressly ratified by the Congress in 1984. See Chapter 9, *infra*, at 877 n.k.

After this transfer of authority from the Civil Service Commission to the EEOC was effected, the EEOC adopted, with some minor changes, the procedural regulations previously used by the Civil Service Commission. These regulations, now codified at 29 C.F.R. § 1613 (1979), set forth the unique procedural rules that apply only to federal employees. Briefly, they require the aggrieved first to seek review of the challenged action within his or her own agency by consulting with that agency's Equal Employment Opportunity Counselor. If the employee is not satisfied with the Counselor's informal resolution of the matter, he or she can file a formal complaint with the official designated by the agency to receive such complaints. After an investigation and opportunity for a hearing, the agency EEO official renders a decision which is appealable to the agency head. An aggrieved who is not satisfied with the agency's final decision can either seek immediate judicial review of that decision or appeal to the EEOC.[a] EEOC regula-

[a] The 1978 reorganization plan also authorized the EEOC to delegate back to the Civil Service Commission (renamed the Merit Systems Protection Board by President Carter's Reorganization Plan # 2 of 1978, § 201) the task of making prelimi-nary rulings on any discrimination issue in so called "mixed cases"—i.e., those involving charges of discrimination prohibited by Title VII and employer conduct not covered by § 717. Additionally, the aggrieved individual retained the right to appeal the

tions also set forth time limits governing the various stages of this process. For example, the agency must complete its investigation within 180 days, unless the parties agree to an extension of up to 90 additional days. The agency also is required to issue a notice after 180 days providing the grievant with the right to request a hearing before an EEOC administrative judge. Additionally, if the aggrieved chooses to bypass the EEOC, both § 717 and the EEOC regulations authorize him or her to file a civil action in federal district court:

(a) Within thirty days of receipt [b] of notice of final action taken by the employer agency on a complaint; [c] or

Merit Board's disposition of the § 717 issue to the EEOC. In cases involving only charges of discrimination cognizable under § 717, on the other hand, jurisdiction lies exclusively with the EEOC, which applies the same substantive standards used in connection with charges filed by private sector employees. This procedure was altered somewhat by the passage of the Civil Service Reform Act of 1978, 5 U.S.C. § 1101 et seq. This statute provides that where an employee or applicant seeks further administrative review of the employer agency's disposition of a Title VII challenge to certain specified kinds of employment decisions (removal, suspension for more than fourteen days, and reduction in grade or pay), the charge must be appealed from the agency to the MSPB, rather than the EEOC, regardless of whether it is a "mixed" or "pure" discrimination case. The charging party then can appeal the Board's decision to the EEOC which, if it disagrees with the Board's decision, must refer the case back to the Board for reconsideration. If the Board refuses to adopt the Commission's decision, and reaffirms its original ruling, it must certify the matter to a special three member panel consisting of a member of the Board, a member of the Commission and a Presidentially-appointed neutral. This panel then renders the final administrative decision in the case. See 5 U.S.C. §§ 7512, 7513, 7702 (1978). The Civil Service Reform Act also sets forth a separate series of limitations periods governing the filing of suit with respect to these limited types of personnel actions. Specifically, an aggrieved can file a civil action in federal district court after:

(a) the 120th day following the filing of a complaint with the employer agency where that complaint is appealable to the MSPB and there is no final decision by the agency and the aggrieved has not filed an appeal with the MSPB; or

(b) the 120th day after the filing of an appeal with the MSPB and there is no judicially reviewable action by the MSPB; or

(c) the 180th day after the filing of a petition with the EEOC and there is no final action by the EEOC.

The federal district court has jurisdiction over the entire case, including both the § 717 and non-§ 717 issues. See Christo v. MSPB, 667 F.2d 882 (10th Cir.1981). Where, however, the Merit Systems Protection Board determines that the discrimination allegation in a "mixed" case is frivolous, review of the merits of the action lies exclusively with the Federal Circuit. The district court has appellate jurisdiction only where the discrimination claim in a "mixed" case is not frivolous. Hill v. Department of Air Force, 796 F.2d 1469 (Fed. Cir. 1986).

[b] As you should recall from the discussion of this case in Chapter 4, *supra*, at 468, in Irwin v. Veterans Administration, ___ U.S. ___, 111 S.Ct. 453, 112 L.Ed.2d 435 (1990), the Supreme Court ruled that the statutory requirement of "receipt" did not require personal receipt by the claimant but, rather, was satisfied when notice of final action was received by the office of the aggrieved's attorney. The Court added, however, that the thirty day limitations rule contained within § 717 was subject to equitable estoppel even though it operated as a waiver of the government's sovereign immunity. The Court characterized its prior cases dealing with the effect of limitations periods in suits against the government as inconsistent and decided against continuing to resolve each case on an *ad hoc* basis. Instead, the Court concluded, to promote predictability, it was more appropriate to adopt a general policy that the same rebuttable presumption of equitable tolling presently applicable to suits against private defendants should also extend to suits against the United States.

[c] The courts have split on the issue of whether a federal employee who petitions

(b) After one-hundred eighty days from the filing of a complaint with the employer agency if there has been no decision.

However, if the employee chooses to appeal the agency's action to the EEOC before bringing suit, the court action must be filed

(a) Within thirty days after receipt of notice of final action taken by the EEOC on the complaint; or

(b) After one-hundred eighty days from the date of filing an appeal with the EEOC if there has been no EEOC decision.

29 C.F.R. § 1613.281.

In either case, § 717(c) of Title VII requires that the defendant in a suit by a federal employee be the head of the agency or department employing that worker and not the employing agency or department. A conflict has arisen as to the appropriate consequence to a plaintiff who erroneously names the agency as the defendant and who fails to correct this error within the applicable filing period. Some courts have held that the filing period is a statute of limitations, rather than a jurisdictional prerequisite and, therefore, that it can be equitably tolled in cases, for example, where the plaintiff was not represented by counsel. These courts have permitted the plaintiff to amend his or her complaint to name the correct defendant after the expiration of the filing period. See Warren v. Department of Army, 867 F.2d 1156 (8th Cir.1989); Mondy v. Secretary of the Army, 845 F.2d 1051 (D.C.Cir. 1988). Other courts, however, have ruled that failure to name the proper defendant within the filing period results in a dismissal of the complaint, even where the plaintiff had no attorney at the time the defective complaint was filed. While these courts recognize that the Supreme Court in *Zipes* held that the filing period governing the filing of EEOC complaints is not jurisdictional for private sector workers, and that the circuit courts have extended this ruling to cover the period for filing suit by private sector employees, they appear to distinguish the claims of federal employees on the ground that the federal filing period is premised on a waiver of sovereign immunity and that such waivers should be narrowly construed. See Lubniewski v. Lehman, 891 F.2d 216 (9th Cir.1989) (naming of proper defendant is nonwaivable jurisdictional prerequisite except that *pro se* plaintiff will be found to have named proper defendant by attaching the federal agency, but not EEOC, disposition of the discrimination claim since the administrative

---

the EEOC to reconsider his claim must file suit within thirty days after the original decision or within thirty days from the disposition of the reconsideration petition. Compare Birch v. Lehman, 677 F.2d 1006 (4th Cir.1982), cert. denied, 459 U.S. 1103, 103 S.Ct. 725, 74 L.Ed.2d 951 (1983) (reconsideration petition cannot extend filing period) with Donaldson v. T.V.A., 759 F.2d 535 (6th Cir.1985) (reconsideration petition filed within 30 day period for bringing suit extends filing period to thirty days from receipt of notice of disposition of reconsideration petition) and Nordell v. Heckler, 749 F.2d 47 (D.C.Cir. 1984) (if reconsideration petition filed within time for bringing suit, such petition renders the initial decision no longer a "final action" and extends the deadline until thirty days from disposition of the reconsideration request) and with Martinez v. Orr, 738 F.2d 1107 (10th Cir.1984) (reconsideration petition might be a basis in some circumstances for tolling the thirty day limit).

disposition comes from the agency head and thus it "provides a clue that he is the proper defendant." But where agency head is not served within the limitations period, amendment of complaint cannot relate back to original filing per F.R.Civ.P. 15(c)). See also Brown v. Department of Army, 854 F.2d 77 (5th Cir.1988); Hancock v. Egger, 848 F.2d 87 (6th Cir.1988). But see Miles v. Department of Army, 881 F.2d 777 (9th Cir.1989) (plaintiff could amend his complaint as matter of right under F.R.Civ.P. 15(a) since case dismissed before defendant filed responsive pleading; amendment was entitled to relate back to date of filing of original complaint since, per requirements of Rule 15(c), proposed amended complaint arose out of same occurrence as original complaint and timely receipt of the original complaint by the U.S. Attorney satisfied government notice requirement).

As mentioned in Section A of Chapter 1, *supra*, at 35 n.6, § 717 did not bring all federal employees within the compass of Title VII. It expressly limited coverage to employees in executive agencies and in competitive service positions in the legislative and judicial branches of the federal government. The Civil Rights Act of 1991 extended the substantive provisions of the amended Title VII to employees of the U.S. House of Representatives and of legislative agencies. Pursuant to § 117(a)(2)(B) of the 1991 Act, however, a different enforcement scheme was established to handle claims by this group of federal employees. It establishes the remedies and procedures contained in the House Fair Employment Practices Resolution adopted in 1988 (or any other subsequently adopted provision that continues the effect of this resolution and which is enacted by the House in the exercise of its rulemaking authority) as the exclusive mechanism for enforcing the Title VII rights of House employees. In addition, § 117(b)(2) provides that the remedies and procedures established by the chief official of each legislative agency shall apply exclusively to claims by employees of these agencies. The 1991 Act contains no provision for either judicial trial of these claims, or for judicial review of administrative disposition of Title VII claims by employees of either the House or legislative agencies.

Senate employees and presidential appointees are now protected against job discrimination by the Government Employee Rights Act of 1991 (GERA), which was enacted as part of the 1991 Civil Rights Act package. The GERA incorporates the substantive provisions of Title VII and applies them to present and former employees of, and applicants for employment with the U.S. Senate. It also covers presidential appointees, a term which is defined to include all executive branch employees, including the Executive Office, except for appointees whose appointment requires the advise and consent of the Senate and members of the uniformed services. Once again, while these employees enjoy the same substantive protections afforded other federal and private sector employees, they are governed by a unique remedial and procedural scheme. Like House employees, Senate employees and presidential appointees do not enjoy a right to judicial trial of their claims. There is, however, a special provision of judicial review for claims brought by this category of employees.

The GERA established an Office of Senate Fair Employment Practices and gave it exclusive jurisdiction over complaints by Senate employees. A Senate employee alleging a violation of Title VII must, under § 305 of the GERA, initiate the process by requesting counseling by the Office within 180 days after the alleged violation. The Office is then given thirty days within which to complete the counseling. If this does not resolve the matter to the aggrieved's satisfaction, § 306(a) provides that he or she must file a request for mediation with the Office within 15 days after the end of the counseling period. Mediation must be completed within thirty days after receipt of the request, with the opportunity for a thirty day extension at the discretion of the Office. The Office is required under § 306(b) to notify the employee and the head of the employing office when the mediation period has terminated. If the aggrieved wishes to continue the process, he or she must file a formal complaint with the Office within 30 days after receipt from the Office of notice of termination of the mediation period. Such a filing, according to § 307(a), must be preceded by a timely invocation and completion of the counseling and mediation procedures. Section 307(d) requires that a hearing must be held within 30 days after filing of the complaint, except that the Office can extend this period up to an additional 60 days for good cause. The hearing board, per § 307(g), must issue a written opinion no later than 45 days after the conclusion of the hearing. The hearing board is authorized by § 307(h), where it determines that a violation has occurred, to order compensatory damages and such remedies as would be appropriate under §§ 706(g) and (k) of Title VII. It is explicitly prohibited from awarding punitive damages. Decisions of the Office can be appealed by either the employee or the head of the employing office to the Senate Select Committee on Ethics. Section 308(a) mandates that such an appeal be filed within 10 days after receipt of the hearing board's decision, except that the Office itself can file a request for review not later than 5 days after the time for the employee or employing office to appeal has expired. If no appeal is filed, the hearing board's decision becomes the final decision of the Office. If the Committee does issue a ruling, that becomes the final decision of the Office. In either case, the aggrieved then has the right, under § 309(a), to seek judicial review of the final Office decision by the Federal Circuit Court of Appeals. This petition for review must be filed within 90 days after entry of the final decision by the Office. Finally, § 309(c) provides, in terms of the standard of review, that the court shall set aside the Office's final decision if it determines that the decision was either (1)arbitrary, capricious, an abuse of discretion or not consistent with law; (2)not made according to the required procedures; or (3)unsupported by substantial evidence based on the record as a whole. The court is also authorized by § 1309(d) to award attorney fees to a prevailing employee in accordance with the standards set forth in § 706(k) of Title VII.

The procedures governing claims by presidential appointees are contained in § 320 of the GERA. Pursuant to § 320(a), presidential appointees must file their claims with the EEOC, or any other entity designated by a presidential Executive Order, and are required to do so within 180 days after the occurrence of the alleged violation. If the EEOC determines that a violation has occurred, it is authorized by § 320(a)(2) to issue a remedy consistent with the terms of §§ 706(g) and (k), including compensatory damages, but not including punitive damages. Any party aggrieved by the decision of the EEOC or designated entity can petition for review by the Federal Circuit Court of Appeals. Section 320(a)(3)(C) sets forth the same standard of review applicable to suits by Senate employees. Attorney fees are also made available to the prevailing appointee in accordance with the standards prescribed in § 706(k) of Title VII.

NOTES AND PROBLEMS FOR DISCUSSION

1. Federal employment discrimination, of course, can also violate the equal protection and due process guarantees of the Fifth Amendment as well as Executive Order 11478. A federal employee also might wish to challenge job discrimination under the 1866 or 1871 Civil Rights Acts and the Equal Pay Act. In BROWN v. G.S.A., 425 U.S. 820, 96 S.Ct. 1961, 48 L.Ed.2d 402 (1976), however, the Supreme Court held that Congress intended Title VII to be the exclusive and pre-emptive administrative and judicial remedy for federal employment discrimination claims. What about an employee of the government of the District of Columbia? See Cox v. University of District of Columbia, 24 FEP Cases 690 (D.D.C.1980). If, as noted supra, Title VII does not provide relief for the physical and emotional damages suffered by victims of sexual harassment, is a federal employee precluded by *Brown* from seeking relief under some other cause of action? See Langster v. Schweiker, 565 F.Supp. 407 (N.D.Ill. 1983) (Title VII does not preempt other relief for conduct beyond the scope of Title VII); Epps v. Ripley, 30 FEP Cases 1632 (D.D.C.1982) (*Brown* interpreted as making Title VII the exclusive federal remedy and does not preempt state tort remedies); Stewart v. Thomas, 538 F.Supp. 891 (D.D.C.1982).

2. In light of the extensive administrative procedures available to a federal employee, to what extent should a federal judge be obliged to defer to the agency determinations in adjudicating a federal employee's Title VII claim? In CHANDLER v. ROUDEBUSH, 425 U.S. 840, 96 S.Ct. 1949, 48 L.Ed.2d 416 (1976), the Court concluded that federal employees enjoyed the same right to a judicial trial *de novo* of Title VII claims as private sector or state government employees. Central to this holding was the Court's determination that in enacting the 1972 amendment to extend Title VII to public employees, Congress intended to give federal employees the same measure of rights enjoyed by private employees. How, then, does this square with the ruling in *Brown*, decided the same day as *Chandler*, in light of the fact that private sector employees are not restricted to seeking relief for job discrimination under Title VII? It has been suggested that *Brown*'s divergence from the *Chandler* parity principle can be explained as a desire to compel federal employees to utilize the more elaborate administrative procedure provided to them in Title VII actions than is available to nonfederal workers. See C.A. Sullivan, M.J. Zimmer and R.F. Richards, Federal Statutory Law of Employment Discrimination, § 2.13 at 252–253 (1980). But doesn't the ruling in *Chandler* according federal courts the

right to completely disregard agency findings of fact and law in suits brought by federal employees cut against that argument? Should the availability of *de novo* review depend upon whether the federal employee loses or wins before the EEOC? In Moore v. Devine, 780 F.2d 1559 (11th Cir.1986), the court held that a final EEOC order favorable to a federal employee is binding on that employee's agency and is subject to an enforcement order by the district court without *de novo* review if the agency fails to comply with the EEOC order. The court distinguished *Chandler*, stating that it was limited to cases where the federal employee had lost before the EEOC. Where the plaintiff wins, however, the court reasoned, the statute indicated that federal employees are to be treated differently than private or state employees, since it provides the EEOC with the authority to issue remedial orders upon a finding of discrimination by the federal government.

    3. Who should bear the burden of establishing exhaustion of administrative remedies? Is it significant that since a federal employee must first seek redress within her or his own agency, the defendant would have custody of the relevant records? See Brown v. Marsh, 777 F.2d 8 (D.C.Cir. 1985).

SECTION B. STATE AND LOCAL GOVERNMENT EMPLOYEES

    The Equal Employment Opportunity Act of 1972 extended the coverage of Title VII to state and local government employees. In Fitzpatrick v. Bitzer,[a] moreover, the Supreme Court ruled that the Eleventh Amendment did not preclude the granting of monetary damages against a state or local government defendant for back pay and attorney's fees in an action brought under that statute. While the Supreme Court has indicated that the proof standards applied to private Title VII claims also should govern claims against state and local governments,[b] there is one procedural difference between the enforcement of private and nonfederal public discrimination claims. Section 706(f)(1) authorizes the Attorney General, rather than the EEOC, to file a civil action against a nonfederal public employer.

    As mentioned in Chapter 1, § A, Note 7, *supra*, at 36, § 701(f) excludes elected officials and three groups of officials appointed to assist elected officials—members of their personal staff, immediate legal advisors and policy-making level assistants who are not subject to state or local civil service laws—from protection under Title VII. This exemption was limited to elected officials by § 321 of the GERA portion of the 1991 Civil Rights Act package. It extends the application of § 717 to these appointed officials and directs them to file complaints with the EEOC within 180 days of the date of the alleged discriminatory conduct. If the EEOC determines that a violation has occurred, it is authorized to provide for relief appropriate under the terms of §§ 706(g)

---

[a] Fitzpatrick v. Bitzer, 427 U.S. 445, 96 S.Ct. 2666, 49 L.Ed.2d 614 (1976).

[b] See New York City Transit Authority v. Beazer, 440 U.S. 568, 99 S.Ct. 1355, 59 L.Ed.2d 587 (1979); Dothard v. Rawlinson, 433 U.S. 321, 331 n.14, 97 S.Ct. 2720, 2728 n.14, 53 L.Ed.2d 786, 799 n.14 (1977) (" * * * Congress expressly indicated that the same Title VII principles be applied to governmental and private employers alike.").

and (k), including compensatory damages but not including punitive damages. Additionally, however, § 321(b)(2) requires that where State or local law prohibits the practice alleged and where an enforcing authority exists with the power to grant relief, the EEOC must not act on the complaint before it has notified the appropriate State or local officials and, upon request, given them at least 60 days to remedy the alleged practice. Any party aggrieved by the EEOC's final decision can petition for review to a federal court of appeals. The standard of review is the same prescribed for appeals by Senate employees and presidential appointees. Finally, § 321(e) authorizes the court to award attorney fees, under the standards prescribed by § 706(k), to a prevailing appointed official.

NOTE FOR DISCUSSION

1. Should the exclusivity doctrine announced in *Brown* apply to state and local government employee claims under § 1983? While the Supreme Court has not addressed this question, the circuit courts overwhelmingly have adopted the position that Title VII does not preempt an action brought under § 1983 based on a violation of rights that are independent of Title VII, as, for example, those guaranteed by the Fourteenth Amendment. See e.g., Roberts v. College of the Desert, 870 F.2d 1411 (9th Cir.1988); Keller v. Prince George's County, 827 F.2d 952 (4th Cir.1987); Ratliff v. City of Milwaukee, 795 F.2d 612 (7th Cir.1986); Nilsen v. City of Moss Point, Miss., 701 F.2d 556 (5th Cir.1983); Poolaw v. City of Anadarko, 660 F.2d 459 (10th Cir.1981), cert. denied, 469 U.S. 1108, 105 S.Ct. 784, 83 L.Ed.2d 779 (1985). See also Shapiro, Section 1983 Claims To Redress Discrimination In Public Employment: Are They Preempted by Title VII? 35 Amer.U.L.Rev. 93 (1985); Comment, Trigg v. Fort Wayne Community Schools: State Employee Discrimination Claims—Is The Conflict Between Title VII and § 1983 Resolved?, 61 Not.D.L.Rev. 88 (1986). For the treatment of § 1981 claims filed by state employees see Note 3 *infra*, at 789–790.

Chapter 6

CLASS ACTIONS

INTRODUCTION

Rule 23 of the Federal Rules of Civil Procedure provides in part:

(a) Prerequisites to a Class Action. One or more members of a class may sue or be sued as representative parties on behalf of all only if (1) the class is so numerous that joinder of all members is impracticable, (2) there are questions of law or fact common to the class, (3) the claims or defenses of the representative parties are typical of the claims or defenses of the class, and (4) the representative parties will fairly and adequately protect the interests of the class.

(b) Class Actions Maintainable. An action may be maintained as a class action if the prerequisites of subdivision (a) are satisfied, and in addition:

(1) The prosecution of separate actions by or against individual members of the class would create a risk of

(A) inconsistent or varying adjudications with respect to individual members of the class which would establish incompatible standards of conduct for the party opposing the class, or

(B) adjudications with respect to individual members of the class which would as a practical matter be dispositive of the interests of the other members not parties to the adjudications or substantially impair or impede their ability to protect their interests; or

(2) the party opposing the class has acted or refused to act on grounds generally applicable to the class, thereby making appropriate final injunctive relief or corresponding declaratory relief with respect to the class as a whole; or

(3) the court finds that the questions of law or fact common to the members of the class predominate over any questions affecting only individual members, and that a class action is superior to other available methods for the fair and efficient adjudication of the controversy. The matters pertinent to the findings include: (A) the interest of members of the class in individually controlling the prosecution or defense of separate actions; (B) the extent and nature of any litigation concerning the controversy already commenced by or against members of the class; (C) the desirability or undesirability of concentrating the

litigation of the claims in the particular forum; (D) the difficulties likely to be encountered in the management of a class action.

(c) Determination by Order Whether Class Action to Be Maintained; Notice; Judgment; Actions Conducted Partially as Class Actions.

(1) As soon as practicable after the commencement of an action brought as a class action, the court shall determine by order whether it is to be so maintained. An order under this subdivision may be conditional, and may be altered or amended before the decision on the merits.

* * *

The class action did not originate with the adoption of the Federal Rules, but was "an invention of equity to enable it to proceed to a decree in suits where the number of those interested in the subject of the litigation is so great that their joinder as parties in conformity to the usual rules of procedure is impracticable." Hansberry v. Lee, 311 U.S. 32, 41, 61 S.Ct. 115, 118, 85 L.Ed. 22 (1940). Following Brown v. Board of Education, 347 U.S. 483, 74 S.Ct. 686, 98 L.Ed. 873 (1954), the civil rights class action became a frequently used device for attacking racial discrimination in education, voting rights and housing. Typical of these cases were school desegregation suits where relief could not be granted to an individual plaintiff without, in effect, affording the same relief (i.e., desegregated schools) to a class composed of those sharing the same racial characteristic, whether the suit was denominated a "class" action or not. As the Fifth Circuit noted:

> There is at least considerable doubt that relief confined to individual specified Negro children either could be granted or, if granted, could be so limited in its operative effect. By the very nature of the controversy, the attack is on the unconstitutional practice of racial discrimination. Once that is found to exist, the court must order that it be discontinued. Such a decree, of course, might name the successful plaintiff as the party not to be discriminated against. But that decree may not—either expressly or impliedly— affirmatively authorize continued discrimination by reason of race against others. * * * Moreover, to require a school system to admit the specific successful plaintiff Negro child while others, having no such protection, were required to attend schools in a racially segregated system, would be for the court to contribute actively to the *class* discrimination * * *.

Potts v. Flax, 313 F.2d 284, 289 (5th Cir.1963).

Rule 23 was revised in 1966 in part by the addition of section (b)(2) which was created specifically to facilitate civil rights actions "where a party is charged with discriminating unlawfully against a class, usually one whose members are incapable of specific enumeration." 1966 Advisory Committee's Note, 39 F.R.D. 98, 102. Not surprisingly, suits in which class-wide relief was automatic if the plaintiff prevailed did not encourage close attention to the requirements of Rule 23.

The 1966 revision of Rule 23 followed closely the enactment of Title VII. That statute brought with it a complex type of class action in which different kinds of discriminatory conduct were attacked in one proceeding. Early employment discrimination class actions frequently attacked a whole range of employment practices (hiring, promotion, job assignment, pay scales, working conditions, etc.) and were referred to as "across the board" cases. The justification for allowing such cases to proceed as class actions was that a common discriminatory policy formed the basis for all the employer's actions. See, Hall v. Werthan Bag Corp., 251 F.Supp. 184, 186 (M.D.Tenn.1966) ("[W]hether the Damoclean threat of racially discriminatory policy hangs over the racial class is a question of fact common to all the members of the class."); Jenkins v. United Gas Corp., 400 F.2d 28, 33 (5th Cir.1968) ("Whether in name or not, the suit is perforce a sort of class action for fellow employees similarly situated.").

Typical of the "across the board" line of cases was Johnson v. Georgia Highway Express, Inc., 417 F.2d 1122 (5th Cir.1969). In *Johnson* a discharged black employee sought to represent a class composed of "all other similarly situated Negroes seeking equal employment opportunities." Johnson alleged that his former employer had discriminated on the basis of race in virtually all aspects of its operation, including hiring, discharge, promotion and maintenance of segregated facilities. The district court restricted the class to black employees who had been discharged. The Fifth Circuit reversed on the ground that the alleged underlying policy of racial discrimination was sufficiently common to, and typical of, the claims of all class members to permit joinder of all the claims. The court noted that its decision did not mean that the plaintiff was necessarily an adequate representative of the class, but the decision made plain that the factual and legal differences between the named plaintiff's claim arising from his discharge and the claims made on behalf of the non-discharged class members would not render him an inadequate representative. Judge Godbold, in a concurring opinion, voiced the concern that interests of absent class members might be difficult to protect in such a broadly based class of employees located in separate facilities.

In a series of cases following *Johnson*, the Fifth Circuit and other courts of appeal continued to apply the across-the-board approach to class certification and to allow plaintiffs to litigate class claims for relief to which they would not be entitled individually. The high water mark was reached in Long v. Sapp, 502 F.2d 34 (5th Cir.1974), a case in which the plaintiff alleged that her discharge resulted from both racial and sexual discrimination. The plaintiff sought to represent a class composed of "all black persons who have applied for employment with the defendants or who would have applied for employment had the defendants not practiced racial discrimination in employment and recruiting, and all black persons terminated by the defendants." The district court dismissed the class claim on the ground that the plaintiff had not suffered the same kind of discrimination that she alleged had been inflicted on the class. The Fifth Circuit reversed on the class issue. This decision was particularly dramatic because while reversing on the class issue, the Court of Appeals affirmed the dismissal of the plaintiff's individual claim. According to the Fifth Circuit, the plaintiff had demonstrated the necessary "nexus" with the proposed class members because she was black and she had alleged that she had suffered from discrimination. The "common nexus" approach to determining typicality was widely adopted. See, Donaldson v. Pillsbury Co., *supra*, 554 F.2d 825, 831 (8th Cir.), cert. denied, 434 U.S. 856, 98 S.Ct. 177, 54 L.Ed.2d 128 (1977); Gibson v. Local 40, Longshoremen's Union, 543 F.2d 1259, 1264 (9th Cir.), cert. denied, 429 U.S. 870, 97 S.Ct. 182, 50 L.Ed.2d 150 (1976); Senter v. General Motors Corp., 532 F.2d 511, 523–524 (6th Cir.1976). See also, Strickler, Protecting the Class: The Search For The Adequate Representative in Class Action Litigation, 34 De Paul L. Rev. 73, 110–124 (1984).

The free-wheeling approach to class certification in Title VII cases ended with the Supreme Court's decision in EAST TEXAS MOTOR FREIGHT SYSTEM INC. v. RODRIGUEZ, 431 U.S. 395, 97 S.Ct. 1891, 52 L.Ed.2d 453 (1977), a case filed against the employer by three hispanic truck drivers. The plaintiffs had been denied transfer to over-the-road or "line" driver positions and alleged that the employer's no transfer policy and collective bargaining agreements with the Teamsters Union effectively locked them and other minorities into lower paying "local" driver positions thus perpetuating the effects of discrimination in initial job assignment. The plaintiffs proposed in their complaint to represent a class composed of all hispanic and black local drivers as well as all minority applicants for line driver jobs, but failed to move for class certification and confined their evidence at trial to their individual claims. The district court found against the plaintiffs on the merits and dismissed the class claims. The Court of Appeals reversed, holding that the district court should have certified the class *sua sponte* and should have found class-wide liability on the basis of statistical proof introduced in support of the plaintiffs' individual claims. The Supreme Court unanimously reversed on the ground that the named plaintiffs were not proper class representatives because they were not members of the class.

> [T]he trial proceedings made clear that [the plaintiffs] were not members of the class of discriminatees they purported to represent. As this Court has repeatedly held, a class representative must be part of the class and "possess the same interest and suffer the same injury" as the class members ... The District Court found upon abundant evidence that these plaintiffs lacked the qualifications to be hired as line drivers. Thus, they could have suffered no injury as a result of the alleged discriminatory practices, and they were, therefore, simply not eligible to represent a class of persons who

did allegedly suffer injury.　Furthermore, each named plaintiff stipulated that he had not been discriminated against with respect to his initial hire.　In the light of that stipulation they were hardly in a position to mount a class-wide attack on the no-transfer rule and seniority system on the ground that these practices perpetuated past discrimination and locked minorities into less desirable jobs to which they had been discriminatorily assigned.

431 U.S. at 403–04, 97 S.Ct. at 1896–97.　A number of lower courts confined *East Texas Motor Freight* to its peculiar facts (the combination of a loss on the merits with the failure of the plaintiffs to move for class certification or put on class-wide proof) and held that across-the-board class actions survived.　See e.g., Payne v. Travenol Laboratories, Inc., 565 F.2d 895, 900 (5th Cir.), cert. denied, 439 U.S. 835, 99 S.Ct. 118, 58 L.Ed.2d 131 (1978) (claim challenging defendant's college degree requirement for employment sustained though plaintiff was not a candidate for a degree); Arnett v. American National Red Cross, 78 F.R.D. 73, 77 n.6 (D.D.C. 1978) (*East Texas Motor Freight* only precludes maintenance of class actions by parties who are not victims of discrimination).　That narrow interpretation of *East Texas Motor Freight* proved wrong.

SECTION A. THE SCOPE OF THE CLASS AND THE PROPER CLASS REPRESENTATIVE

GENERAL TELEPHONE CO. OF SOUTHWEST v. FALCON

Supreme Court of the United States, 1982.
457 U.S. 147, 102 S.Ct. 2364, 72 L.Ed.2d 740.

JUSTICE STEVENS delivered the opinion of the Court.

The question presented is whether respondent Falcon, who complained that petitioner did not promote him because he is a Mexican–American, was properly permitted to maintain a class action on behalf of Mexican–American applicants for employment whom petitioner did not hire.

I

In 1969 petitioner initiated a special recruitment and training program for minorities.　Through that program, respondent Falcon was hired in July 1969 as a groundman, and within a year he was twice promoted, first to lineman and then to lineman-in-charge.　He subsequently refused a promotion to installer-repairman.　In October 1972 he applied for the job of field inspector; his application was denied even though the promotion was granted several white employees with less seniority.

Falcon thereupon filed a charge with the Equal Employment Opportunity Commission stating his belief that he had been passed over for promotion because of his national origin and that petitioner's promotion policy operated against Mexican–Americans as a class. 626 F.2d 369, 372, n. 2 (CA5 1980). In due course he received a right to sue letter from the Commission and, in April 1975, he commenced this action under Title VII of the Civil Rights Act of 1964, 74 Stat. 253, as amended, 42 U.S.C. § 2000e et seq., in the United States District Court for the Northern District of Texas. His complaint alleged that petitioner maintained "a policy, practice, custom, or usage of: (a) discriminating against [Mexican–Americans] because of national origin and with respect to compensation, terms, conditions, and privileges of employment, and (b) * * * subjecting [Mexican–Americans] to continuous employment discrimination." [1] Respondent claimed that as a result of this policy whites with less qualification and experience and lower evaluation scores than respondent had been promoted more rapidly. The complaint contained no factual allegations concerning petitioner's hiring practices.

Respondent brought the action "on his own behalf and on behalf of other persons similarly situated, pursuant to Rule 23(b)(2) of the Federal Rules of Civil Procedure." The class identified in the complaint was "composed of Mexican–American persons who are employed, or who might be employed, by GENERAL TELEPHONE COMPANY at its place of business located in Irving, Texas, who have been and who continue to be or might be adversely affected by the practices complained of herein." [3]

After responding to petitioner's written interrogatories,[4] respondent filed a memorandum in favor of certification of "the class of all

1. App. 14. In paragraph VI of the complaint, respondent alleged:

"The Defendant has established an employment, transfer, promotional, and seniority system, the design, intent, and purpose of which is to continue and preserve, and which has the effect of continuing and preserving, the Defendant's policy, practice, custom and usage of limiting the employment, transfer, and promotional opportunities of Mexican–American employees of the company because of national origin."

Id., at 15.

3. App. 13–14. The paragraph of the complaint in which respondent alleged conformance with the requirements of Rule 23 continued:

"There are common questions of law and fact affecting the rights of the members of this class who are, and who continue to be, limited, classified, and discriminated against in ways which deprive and/or tend to deprive them of equal employment opportunities and which otherwise adversely affect their status as employees because of national origin. These persons are so numerous that join-

der of all members is impracticable. A common relief is sought. The interests of said class are adequately represented by Plaintiff. Defendant has acted or refused to act on grounds generally applicable to the Plaintiff."

Id., at 14.

4. Petitioner's Interrogatory No. 8 stated:

"Identify the common questions of law and fact which affect the rights of the members of the purported class."

Id., at 26.

Respondent answered that interrogatory as follows:

"The facts which affect the rights of the members of the class are the facts of their employment, the ways in which evaluations are made, the subjective rather than objective manner in which recommendations for raises and transfers and promotions are handled, and all of the facts surrounding the employment of Mexican–American persons by General Telephone Company. The questions

hourly Mexican American employees who have been employed, are employed, or may in the future be employed and all those Mexican Americans who have applied or would have applied for employment had the Defendant not practiced racial discrimination in its employment practices." His position was supported by the ruling of the United States Court of Appeals for the Fifth Circuit in Johnson v. Georgia Highway Express, Inc., 417 F.2d 1122 (1969), that any victim of racial discrimination in employment may maintain an "across the board" attack on all unequal employment practices alleged to have been committed by the employer pursuant to a policy of racial discrimination. Without conducting an evidentiary hearing, the District Court certified a class including Mexican–American employees and Mexican–American applicants for employment who had not been hired.[5]

Following trial of the liability issues, the District Court entered separate findings of fact and conclusions of law with respect first to respondent and then to the class. The District Court found that petitioner had not discriminated against respondent in hiring, but that it did discriminate against him in its promotion practices. The court reached converse conclusions about the class, finding no discrimination in promotion practices, but concluding that petitioner had discriminated against Mexican–Americans at its Irving facility in its hiring practices.[6]

After various post-trial proceedings, the District Court ordered petitioner to furnish respondent with a list of all Mexican–Americans who had applied for employment at the Irving facility during the period between January 1, 1973, and October 18, 1976. Respondent was then ordered to give notice to those persons advising them that they might be entitled to some form of recovery. Evidence was taken concerning the applicants who responded to the notice and backpay was ultimately awarded to 13 persons, in addition to respondent Falcon. The total recovery by respondent and the entire class amounted to $67,925.49, plus costs and interest.[7]

---

of law specified in Interrogatory No. 8 call for a conclusion on the part of the Plaintiff."

Id., at 34.

5. The District Court's pretrial order of February 2, 1976, provided, in part:

"The case is to proceed as a class action and the Plaintiff is to represent the class. The class is to be made up of those employees who are employed and employees who have applied for employment in the Irving Division of the Defendant company, and no other division.

* * *

"Plaintiff and Defendant are to hold further negotiations to see if there is a possibility of granting individual relief to

the Plaintiff, MARIANO S. FALCON." App. to Pet. for Cert. 48a–49a.

The District Court denied subsequent motions to decertify the class both before and after the trial.

6. The District Court ordered petitioner to accelerate its affirmative action plan by taking specified steps to more actively recruit and promote Mexican–Americans at its Irving facility. See id., at 41a–45a.

7. Respondent's individual recovery amounted to $1,040.33. A large share of the class award, $28,827.50, represented attorneys' fees. Most of the remainder resulted from petitioner's practice of keeping all applications active for only 90 days; the District Court found that most of the applications had been properly rejected at the

Both parties appealed. The Court of Appeals rejected respondent's contention that the class should have encompassed all of petitioner's operations in Texas, New Mexico, Oklahoma, and Arkansas.[8] On the other hand, the court also rejected petitioner's argument that the class had been defined too broadly. For, under the Fifth Circuit's across-the-board rule, it is permissible for "an employee complaining of one employment practice to represent another complaining of another practice, if the plaintiff and the members of the class suffer from essentially the same injury. In this case, all of the claims are based on discrimination because of national origin." Id., at 375.[9] The court relied on Payne v. Travenol Laboratories, Inc., 565 F.2d 895 (1978), cert. denied, 439 U.S. 835, 99 S.Ct. 118, 58 L.Ed.2d 131, in which the Fifth Circuit stated:

"Plaintiffs' action is an 'across the board' attack on unequal employment practices alleged to have been committed by Travenol pursuant to a policy of racial discrimination. As parties who have allegedly been aggrieved by some of these discriminatory practices, plaintiffs have demonstrated a sufficient nexus to enable them to represent other class members suffering from different practices motivated by the same policies." Id., at 900, quoted in 626 F.2d, at 375.

On the merits, the Court of Appeals upheld respondent's claim of disparate treatment in promotion,[10] but held that the District Court's findings relating to disparate impact in hiring were insufficient to

time they were considered, but that petitioner could not justify the refusal to extend employment to disappointed applicants after an interval of 90 days. See 463 F.Supp. 315 (1978).

8. The Court of Appeals held that the District Court had not abused its discretion since each of petitioner's divisions conducted its own hiring and since management of the broader class would be much more difficult. 626 F.2d, at 376.

9. The court continued:

"While similarities of sex, race or national origin claims are not dispositive in favor of finding that the prerequisites of Rule 23 have been met, they are an extremely important factor in the determination, that can outweigh the fact that the members of the plaintiff class may be complaining about somewhat different specific discriminatory practices. In addition here, the plaintiff showed more than an alliance based simply on the same type of discriminatory claim. He also showed a similarity of interests based on job location, job function and other considerations."

626 F.2d, at 375–376 (citations omitted).

The court did not explain how job location, job function, and the unidentified other considerations were relevant to the Rule 23(a) determination.

10. The District Court found that petitioner's proffered reasons for promoting the whites, rather than respondent, were insufficient and subjective. The Court of Appeals held that respondent had made out a prima facie case under the test set forth in McDonnell Douglas Corp. v. Green, 411 U.S. 792, 802, 93 S.Ct. 1817, 1824, 36 L.Ed.2d 668, and that the District Court's conclusion that petitioner had not rebutted that prima facie case was not clearly erroneous. In so holding, the Court of Appeals relied on its earlier opinion in Burdine v. Texas Department of Community Affairs, 608 F.2d 563 (1979). Our opinion in *Burdine* had not yet been announced.

The Court of Appeals disposed of a number of other contentions raised by both parties, and reserved others pending the further proceedings before the District Court on remand. Among the latter issues was petitioner's objection to the District Court's theory for computing the class backpay awards. See n. 7, supra.

support recovery on behalf of the class.[11]   After this Court decided Texas Department of Community Affairs v. Burdine, 450 U.S. 248, 101 S.Ct. 1089, 67 L.Ed.2d 207, we vacated the judgment of the Court of Appeals and directed further consideration in the light of that opinion. 450 U.S. 1036, 101 S.Ct. 1752, 68 L.Ed.2d 234.   The Fifth Circuit thereupon vacated the portion of its opinion addressing respondent's promotion claim but reinstated the portions of its opinion approving the District Court's class certification.   With the merits of both respondent's promotion claim and the class hiring claims remaining open for reconsideration in the District Court on remand, we granted certiorari to decide whether the class action was properly maintained on behalf of both employees who were denied promotion and applicants who were denied employment.

II

The class action device was designed as "an exception to the usual rule that litigation is conducted by and on behalf of the individual named parties only."   Califano v. Yamasaki, 442 U.S. 682, 700–701, 99 S.Ct. 2545, 2557–2558, 61 L.Ed.2d 176.   Class relief is "peculiarly appropriate" when the "issues involved are common to the class as a whole" and when they "turn on questions of law applicable in the same manner to each member of the class."   Id., at 701, 99 S.Ct., at 2557. For in such cases, "the class-action device saves the resources of both the courts and the parties by permitting an issue potentially affecting every [class member] to be litigated in an economical fashion under Rule 23."   Ibid.

Title VII of the Civil Rights Act of 1964, as amended, authorizes the Equal Employment Opportunity Commission to sue in its own name to secure relief for individuals aggrieved by discriminatory practices forbidden by the Act.   See 42 U.S.C. § 2000e–5(f)(1).   In exercising this enforcement power, the Commission may seek relief for groups of employees or applicants for employment without complying with the strictures of Rule 23.   General Telephone Co. v. EEOC, 446 U.S. 318, 100 S.Ct. 1698, 64 L.Ed.2d 319.   Title VII, however, contains no special authorization for class suits maintained by private parties.   An individual litigant seeking to maintain a class action under Title VII must meet "the prerequisites of numerosity, commonality, typicality, and adequacy of representation" specified in Rule 23(a).   Id., at 330, 100 S.Ct., at 1706.   These requirements effectively "limit the class claims to those fairly encompassed by the named plaintiff's claims."   Ibid.

---

11. The District Court's finding was based on statistical evidence comparing the number of Mexican–Americans in the company's employ, and the number hired in 1972 and 1973, with the percentage of Mexican–Americans in the Dallas–Fort Worth labor force. See App. to Pet. for Cert. 39a. Since recovery had been al- lowed for the years 1973 through 1976 based on statistical evidence pertaining to only a portion of that period, and since petitioner's evidence concerning the entire period suggested that there was no dispar- ate impact, the Court of Appeals ordered further proceedings on the class hiring claims. 626 F.2d, at 380–382.

We have repeatedly held that "a class representative must be part of the class and 'possess the same interest and suffer the same injury' as the class members." East Texas Motor Freight System, Inc. v. Rodriguez, 431 U.S. 395, 403, 97 S.Ct. 1891, 1896, 52 L.Ed.2d 453 (quoting Schlesinger v. Reservists Committee to Stop the War, 418 U.S. 208, 216, 94 S.Ct. 2925, 2929–2930, 41 L.Ed.2d 706). In *East Texas Motor Freight*, a Title VII action brought by three Mexican–American city drivers, the Fifth Circuit certified a class consisting of the trucking company's black and Mexican–American city drivers allegedly denied on racial or ethnic grounds transfers to more desirable line-driver jobs. We held that the Court of Appeals had "plainly erred in declaring a class action." 431 U.S., at 403, 97 S.Ct., at 1896. Because at the time the class was certified it was clear that the named plaintiffs were not qualified for line-driver positions, "they could have suffered no injury as a result of the allegedly discriminatory practices, and they were, therefore, simply not eligible to represent a class of persons who did allegedly suffer injury." Id., at 403–404, 97 S.Ct., at 1897.

Our holding in *East Texas Motor Freight* was limited; we noted that "a different case would be presented if the District Court had certified a class and only later had it appeared that the named plaintiffs were not class members or were otherwise inappropriate class representatives." Id., at 406, n. 12, 97 S.Ct., at 1898, n. 12. We also recognized the theory behind the Fifth Circuit's across-the-board rule, noting our awareness "that suits alleging racial or ethnic discrimination are often by their very nature class suits, involving classwide wrongs," and that "[c]ommon questions of law or fact are typically present." Id., at 405, 97 S.Ct., at 1898. In the same breath, however, we reiterated that "careful attention to the requirements of Fed. Rule Civ. Proc. 23 remains nonetheless indispensable" and that the "mere fact that a complaint alleges racial or ethnic discrimination does not in itself ensure that the party who has brought the lawsuit will be an adequate representative of those who may have been the real victims of that discrimination." Id., at 405–406, 97 S.Ct., at 1898.

We cannot disagree with the proposition underlying the across-the-board rule—that racial discrimination is by definition class discrimination.[12] But the allegation that such discrimination has occurred neither determines whether a class action may be maintained in accordance with Rule 23 nor defines the class that may be certified. Conceptually, there is a wide gap between (a) an individual's claim that he has been denied a promotion on discriminatory grounds, and his otherwise unsupported allegation that the company has a policy of discrimination, and (b) the existence of a class of persons who have suffered the same injury as that individual, such that the individual's claim and the class claims will share common questions of law or fact and that the individual's claim will be typical of the class claims.[13] For respondent

---

12. See Hall v. Werthan Bag Corp., 251 F.Supp. 184, 186 (MD Tenn.1966).

13. The commonality and typicality requirements of Rule 23(a) tend to merge.

to bridge that gap, he must prove much more than the validity of his own claim. Even though evidence that he was passed over for promotion when several less deserving whites were advanced may support the conclusion that respondent was denied the promotion because of his national origin, such evidence would not necessarily justify the additional inferences (1) that this discriminatory treatment is typical of petitioner's promotion practices, (2) that petitioner's promotion practices are motivated by a policy of ethnic discrimination that pervades petitioner's Irving division, or (3) that this policy of ethnic discrimination is reflected in petitioner's other employment practices, such as hiring, in the same way it is manifested in the promotion practices. These additional inferences demonstrate the tenuous character of any presumption that the class claims are "fairly encompassed" within respondent's claim.

Respondent's complaint provided an insufficient basis for concluding that the adjudication of his claim of discrimination in promotion would require the decision of any common question concerning the failure of petitioner to hire more Mexican–Americans. Without any specific presentation identifying the questions of law or fact that were common to the claims of respondent and of the members of the class he sought to represent,[14] it was error for the District Court to presume that respondent's claim was typical of other claims against petitioner by Mexican–American employees and applicants. If one allegation of specific discriminatory treatment were sufficient to support an across-the-board attack, every Title VII case would be a potential company-wide class action. We find nothing in the statute to indicate that Congress intended to authorize such a wholesale expansion of class-action litigation.[15]

Both serve as guideposts for determining whether under the particular circumstances maintenance of a class action is economical and whether the named plaintiff's claim and the class claims are so interrelated that the interests of the class members will be fairly and adequately protected in their absence. Those requirements therefore also tend to merge with the adequacy-of-representation requirement, although the latter requirement also raises concerns about the competency of class counsel and conflicts of interest. In this case, we need not address petitioner's argument that there is a conflict of interest between respondent and the class of rejected applicants because an enlargement of the pool of Mexican–American employees will decrease respondent's chances for promotion. See General Telephone Co. v. EEOC, 446 U.S. 318, 331, 100 S.Ct. 1698, 1706–1707, 64 L.Ed.2d 319 ("In employment discrimination litigation, conflicts might arise, for example, between employees and applicants who were denied employment and who will, if granted relief, compete with employees for fringe benefits or seniority. Under Rule 23, the same plaintiff could not represent these classes."); see also East Texas Motor Freight System, Inc. v. Rodriguez, 431 U.S. 395, 404–405, 97 S.Ct. 1891, 1897–1898, 52 L.Ed.2d 453.

14. See n. 4, supra.

15. If petitioner used a biased testing procedure to evaluate both applicants for employment and incumbent employees, a class action on behalf of every applicant or employee who might have been prejudiced by the test clearly would satisfy the commonality and typicality requirements of Rule 23(a). Significant proof that an employer operated under a general policy of discrimination conceivably could justify a class of both applicants and employees if the discrimination manifested itself in hiring and promotion practices in the same general fashion, such as through entirely subjective decisionmaking processes. In this regard it is noteworthy that Title VII

The trial of this class action followed a predictable course. Instead of raising common questions of law or fact, respondent's evidentiary approaches to the individual and class claims were entirely different. He attempted to sustain his individual claim by proving intentional discrimination. He tried to prove the class claims through statistical evidence of disparate impact. Ironically, the District Court rejected the class claim of promotion discrimination, which conceptually might have borne a closer typicality and commonality relationship with respondent's individual claim, but sustained the class claim of hiring discrimination. As the District Court's bifurcated findings on liability demonstrate, the individual and class claims might as well have been tried separately. It is clear that the maintenance of respondent's action as a class action did not advance "the efficiency and economy of litigation which is a principal purpose of the procedure." American Pipe & Construction Co. v. Utah, 414 U.S. 538, 553, 94 S.Ct. 756, 766, 38 L.Ed.2d 713.

We do not, of course, judge the propriety of a class certification by hindsight. The District Court's error in this case, and the error inherent in the across-the-board rule, is the failure to evaluate carefully the legitimacy of the named plaintiff's plea that he is a proper class representative under Rule 23(a). As we noted in Coopers & Lybrand v. Livesay, 437 U.S. 463, 98 S.Ct. 2454, 57 L.Ed.2d 351, "the class determination generally involves considerations that are 'enmeshed in the factual and legal issues comprising the plaintiff's cause of action.'" Id., at 469, 98 S.Ct., at 2458 (quoting Mercantile Nat. Bank v. Langdeau, 371 U.S. 555, 558, 83 S.Ct. 520, 522, 9 L.Ed.2d 523). Sometimes the issues are plain enough from the pleadings to determine whether the interests of the absent parties are fairly encompassed within the named plaintiff's claim, and sometimes it may be necessary for the court to probe behind the pleadings before coming to rest on the certification question. Even after a certification order is entered, the judge remains free to modify it in the light of subsequent developments in the litigation.[16] For such an order, particularly during the period before any notice is sent to members of the class, "is inherently tentative." 437 U.S., at 469, n. 11, 98 S.Ct., at 2458 n. 11. This flexibility enhances the usefulness of the class-action device; actual, not presumed, conformance with Rule 23(a) remains, however, indispensable.

III

The need to carefully apply the requirements of Rule 23(a) to Title VII class actions was noticed by a member of the Fifth Circuit panel

---

prohibits discriminatory employment *practices*, not an abstract policy of discrimination. The mere fact that an aggrieved private plaintiff is a member of an identifiable class of persons of the same race or national origin is insufficient to establish his standing to litigate on their behalf all possible claims of discrimination against a common employer.

16. "As soon as practicable after the commencement of an action brought as a class action, the court shall determine by order whether it is to be so maintained. An order under this subdivision may be conditional, and may be altered or amended before the decision on the merits." Fed. Rule Civ. Proc. 23(c)(1).

that announced the across-the-board rule. In a specially concurring opinion in Johnson v. Georgia Highway Express, Inc., supra, at 1125–1127, Judge Godbold emphasized the need for "more precise pleadings," id., at 1125, for "without reasonable specificity the court cannot define the class, cannot determine whether the representation is adequate, and the employer does not know how to defend," id., at 1126. He termed as "most significant" the potential unfairness to the class members bound by the judgment if the framing of the class is over-broad. Ibid. And he pointed out the error of the "tacit assumption" underlying the across-the-board rule that "all will be well for surely the plaintiff will win and manna will fall on all members of the class." Id., at 1127. With the same concerns in mind, we reiterate today that a Title VII class action, like any other class action, may only be certified if the trial court is satisfied, after a rigorous analysis, that the prerequisites of Rule 23(a) have been satisfied.

The judgment of the Court of Appeals affirming the certification order is reversed and the case is remanded for further proceedings consistent with this opinion.

It is so ordered.

CHIEF JUSTICE BURGER, concurring in part and dissenting in part.

I agree with the Court's decision insofar as it states the general principles which apply in determining whether a class should be certified in this case under Rule 23. However, in my view it is not necessary to remand for further proceedings since it is entirely clear on this record that no class should have been certified in this case. I would simply reverse the Court of Appeals with instructions to dismiss the class claim.

As the Court notes, the purpose of Rule 23 is to promote judicial economy by allowing for litigation of common questions of law and fact at one time. Califano v. Yamasaki, 442 U.S. 682, 701, 99 S.Ct. 2545, 2557–2558, 61 L.Ed.2d 176 (1979). We have stressed that strict attention to the requirements of Rule 23 is indispensable in employment discrimination cases. East Texas Motor Freight System, Inc. v. Rodriguez, 431 U.S. 395, 405–406, 97 S.Ct. 1891, 1897–1898, 52 L.Ed.2d 453 (1977). This means that class claims are limited to those "fairly encompassed by the named plaintiff's claims." Ante at 2370; General Telephone Co. v. EEOC, 446 U.S. 318, 330, 100 S.Ct. 1698, 1706, 64 L.Ed.2d 319 (1980).

Respondent claims that he was not promoted to a job as field inspector because he is a Mexican–American. To be successful in his claim, which he advances under the "disparate treatment" theory, he must convince a court that those who were promoted were promoted not because they were better qualified than he was, but, instead, that he was not promoted for discriminatory reasons. The success of this claim depends on evaluation of the comparative qualifications of the applicants for promotion to field inspector and on analysis of the credibility of the reasons for the promotion decisions provided by those who made the decisions. Respondent's class claim on behalf of unsuccessful applicants for jobs with petitioner, in contrast, is advanced under the "adverse impact" theory. Its success depends on an analysis of statistics concerning petitioner's hiring patterns.[*]

The record in this case clearly shows that there are no common questions of law or fact between respondent's claim and the class claim; the only commonality is that respondent is a Mexican–American and he seeks to represent a class of Mexican–Americans. See ante, 2368–2369 & n. 9. We have repeatedly held that the bare fact that a plaintiff alleges racial or ethnic discrimination is not enough to justify class certification. Ante at 2370; *East Texas Motor Freight*, supra, 431 U.S., at 405–406, 97 S.Ct., at 1897–1898. Accordingly, the class should not have been certified.

Moreover, while a judge's decision to certify a class is not normally to be evaluated by hindsight, ante, at 2372, since the judge cannot know what the evidence will show, there is no reason for us at this stage of these lengthy judicial proceedings not to proceed in light of the evidence actually presented. The Court properly concludes that the Court of Appeals and the District Court failed to consider the requirements of Rule 23. In determining whether to reverse and remand or to simply reverse, we can and should look at the evidence. The record shows that there is no support for the class claim. Respondent's own statistics show that 7.7% of those hired by petitioner between 1972 and 1976 were Mexican–American while the relevant labor force was 5.2% Mexican–American. Falcon v. General Telephone Company of the Southwest, 626 F.2d 369, 372, 381 n. 16. Petitioner's unchallenged evidence shows that it hired Mexican–Americans in numbers greater than their percentage of the labor force even though Mexican–Americans applied for jobs with petitioner in numbers smaller than their percentage of the labor force. Id., at 373 n. 4. This negates any claim of Falcon as a class representative.

Like so many Title VII cases, this case has already gone on for years, draining judicial resources as well as resources of the litigants. Rather than promoting judicial economy, the "across-the-board" class action has promoted multiplication of claims and endless litigation. Since it is clear that the class claim brought on behalf of unsuccessful applicants for jobs with petitioner cannot succeed, I would simply reverse and remand with instructions to dismiss the class claim.

NOTES AND PROBLEMS FOR DISCUSSION

1. What precisely is the holding of General Telephone Co. v. Falcon? Is it that a named plaintiff may represent a class composed only of those persons

---

[*] There is no allegation that those who made the hiring decisions are the same persons who determined who was promoted to field inspector. Thus there is no claim that the same person or persons who made the challenged decisions were motivated by prejudice against Mexican–Americans, and that this prejudice manifested itself in both the hiring decisions and the decisions not to promote respondent.

who have been affected by a discriminatory policy in exactly the same manner as the plaintiff? Or does the decision merely stand for the proposition that the district court may not assume a sufficient nexus between the individual and class claims absent a factual showing of a link between the two?

The Court in *General Telephone* states that proof sufficient to establish Falcon's individual claim would not necessarily support a finding of class discrimination. Presumably, in a case where proof of the individual claim would support an inference of class discrimination, the commonality and typicality requirements of Rule 23(a) would be satisfied. Thus, if a company's policy was to refuse employment to pregnant women, presumably a female employee discharged because of pregnancy would be allowed under *General Telephone* to represent a class composed of discharged employees and persons refused employment because of that policy. But is the converse true? If proof of class-wide discrimination is sufficiently relevant to plaintiff's individual claim to be admissible in support of that claim, would the commonality and typicality requirements be satisfied? In MCDONNELL DOUGLAS CORP. v. GREEN, the Court noted that "statistics as to petitioner's employment policy and practice may be helpful to a determination of whether petitioner's refusal to rehire respondent * * * conformed to a general pattern of discrimination against blacks." After *General Telephone*, could the plaintiff in a case like *McDonnell Douglas* represent a class composed of disappointed black applicants as well as discharged employees, assuming that he alleged such a general pattern of discrimination?

2. It is often difficult at the certification stage to determine the adequacy of the individual plaintiff's attorney to represent the interests of the class. The district court should decertify the class if the attorney proves unable to properly protect class interests. See, Jordan v. County of Los Angeles, 669 F.2d 1311, 1323 n. 13 (9th Cir.) (adequacy of class counsel may be reviewed continually throughout pendency of action), vacated for further consideration in light of *Falcon*, 459 U.S. 810, 103 S.Ct. 35, 74 L.Ed.2d 48 (1982); Colby v. J.C. Penney Co., 128 F.R.D. 247, 250 (N.D.Ill. 1989), affirmed, 926 F.2d 645 (7th Cir.1991) (ineffectiveness of counsel in conducting discovery and responding to motion for summary judgment warrants decertification of class). In IMPACT v. Firestone, 893 F.2d 1189 (11th Cir.), cert. denied, ___ U.S. ___, 111 S.Ct. 133, 112 L.Ed.2d 100 (1990), the district court found that class counsel lacked the financing necessary to adequately carry the case to conclusion and decertified the class. On appeal, following a trial on the merits, the Eleventh Circuit remanded with instructions that the district court consider recertification of the class in light of fact that case was tried in many respects as if it were a class action and claims by plaintiffs that costs could be reduced requiring defendants to respond to additional discovery. Even after a trial on the merits, the court may decertify the class, thus relieving it of the preclusive effects of an adverse judgment, if class counsel has proved incompetent. See, Johnson v. Shreveport Garment Co., 422 F.Supp. 526, 533 (W.D.La.1976), affirmed, 577 F.2d 1132 (5th Cir.1978).

3. Does the Court's decision in *General Telephone* suggest that the remedial purposes of Title VII are irrelevant to class certification under Rule 23? Does the language or legislative history of Rule 23 require such a result? See, Advisory Committee's Note to 1966 Amendments to Rule 23, 39 F.R.D. 98, 102. In *General Telephone*, the plaintiff actively sought to represent a class even larger than that certified by the district court and at trial put on substantial proof to support the class claims. Assuming that Falcon was an "adequate"

representative of the class in the sense that he had both the desire and the means to vigorously pursue the class claims, does the decision in *General Telephone* further the goals of Title VII? For a discussion of the different meanings of "adequacy" see Strickler, Protecting the Class: The Search For The Adequate Representative in Class Action Litigation, 34 De Paul L.Rev. 73 (1984).

4. *Falcon* has not resulted in the complete demise of the broad-based class action. Focusing on footnote 15 of the Supreme Court's opinion, a number of courts have certified or refused to decertify classes composed of persons whose relation to defendant differ distinctly from that of the named plaintiff on the ground that the various discriminatory practices were infected by the same "subjective decision making processes." See e.g., Carpenter v. Stephen F. Austin State University, 706 F.2d 608 (5th Cir.1983) (former custodial workers were proper representatives of class composed of past, present and future black and female employees in all job classifications); Meiresonne v. Marriott Corp., 124 F.R.D. 619 (N.D.Ill. 1989) (evidence that employer maintains subjective evaluation system applied by central board to all class members satisfies commonality requirement); Wynn v. Dixieland Food Stores, Inc., 125 F.R.D. 696 (M.D.Ala.1989) (evidence that employer uses one subjective selection system for all selection decisions, that incumbent employees and outsiders compete for same jobs, and that selection process is same regardless of type or level of job warrants definition of class consisting of both incumbents and applicants).

Other courts have mechanically applied *Falcon* to deny certification of classes composed of applicants and employees; Walker v. Jim Dandy Co., 747 F.2d 1360 (11th Cir.1984), Hawkins v. Fulton County, 95 F.R.D. 88 (N.D.Ga. 1982); employees in different positions, Roby v. St. Louis Southwestern Railway Co., 775 F.2d 959 (8th Cir.1985); and employees and those terminated, Briggs v. Anderson, 796 F.2d 1009 (8th Cir.1986). In Watson v. Fort Worth Bank & Trust, 798 F.2d 791 (5th Cir.1986), vacated on other grounds, 487 U.S. 977, 108 S.Ct. 2777, 101 L.Ed.2d 827 (1988), a class action filed on behalf of black employees and applicants for employment by an employee who alleged that she was discriminated against in the promotion process. The district court originally certified the class because of evidence that a single individual was responsible for both hiring and promotion decisions. But after the trial, the court decertified the class and the Court of Appeals affirmed.

Watson asserts the district court erred because the commonality requirement may be satisfied by a showing that the same *persons* make both types of decisions. Assuming, *arguendo*, that Watson is correct, this Court's inquiry does not end with that conclusion. We cannot conclude that certification of a class of both employees and applicants is mandated merely because common questions exist. Rather, the other factors enunciated in Rule 23(a) also must be considered.

Thus, assuming a common question was presented in the instant case, *e.g.*, whether the same limited group of white supervisors discriminated in both hiring and promotions, that common question was not in fact a central feature in the actual proof presented at trial. The applicant class claims relied primarily on applicant flow statistics. In contrast, the proof asserted in support of the promotions claims focused on statistical evidence of the Bank's treatment of black individuals in the employee evaluation process, promotions process, compensation process and other employment practices. Consequently, the actual proof presented demonstrates that

Watson's promotion claim was not typical of the applicant claims, and she was not an adequate class representative.

798 F.2d at 796. Does *Watson* suggest that unless plaintiff employs the *same kind* of evidence on behalf of applicants and employees, that she cannot adequately represent the class? Does *Falcon* compel this conclusion? See also, Johnson, Rebuilding the Barriers: The Trend in Employment Discrimination Class Actions, 19 Colum. Hum.Rts.L.Rev. 1, 29–43 (1987).

Can representational adequacy problems under *Falcon* be cured by allowing intervention of additional named plaintiffs as subclass representatives? See, Hill v. Western Electric Co., 672 F.2d 381 (4th Cir.), cert. denied, 459 U.S. 981, 103 S.Ct. 318, 74 L.Ed.2d 294 (1982) and Note, Reinstating Vacated Findings in Employment Discrimination Class Actions: Reconciling General Telephone Co. v. Falcon with Hill v. Western Electric Co., 1983 Duke L.J. 821 (1983).

SECTION B. THE SIZE OF THE CLASS

A prerequisite for a class action under Rule 23(a)(1) is that the class be "so numerous that joinder of all members is impracticable." No arbitrary rules have been established regarding the number of persons necessary to satisfy the numerosity requirement: the determination will be made on the facts of each case. "Practicability of joinder depends on the size of the class, ease of identifying its members and determining their addresses, facility of making service on them if joined and their geographic dispersion." Garcia v. Gloor, 618 F.2d 264 (5th Cir.1980), cert. denied, 449 U.S. 1113, 101 S.Ct. 923, 66 L.Ed.2d 842 (1981) (proposed class of 31 persons whose identity and addresses were readily ascertainable and who lived in same area rejected on ground that joinder was practicable). The courts have divided on the issue of whether the remedial purposes of Title VII should influence the numerosity determination. Compare, Garcia v. Gloor, *supra*, ("Whether a class should be certified depends entirely on whether the proposal satisfies the requirements" of Rule 23) with Gay v. Waiters' and Dairy Lunchmen's Union, Local 30, 549 F.2d 1330, 1334 (9th Cir.1977) (district court's denial of class certification on numerosity grounds reversed: court "must consider the broad remedial purposes of Title VII and must liberally interpret and apply Rule 23 so as not to undermine the purpose and effectiveness of Title VII in eradicating class-based discrimination.") A number of courts have recognized that the fear by putative class members of filing individual actions is a relevant consideration in determining practicability of joinder and justifies the certification of relatively small classes. See, Arkansas Education Ass'n v. Board of Education, 446 F.2d 763, 765 (8th Cir.1971) (approximately 17 in class); Slanina v. William Penn Parking Corp., 106 F.R.D. 419 (W.D.Pa.1984) (class of 25 employees sufficiently large because of fear of reprisals if forced to sue individually); Rosario v. Cook County, 101 F.R.D. 659 (N.D.Ill. 1983) (class of 20 Hispanic correctional officers sufficiently numerous because of reluctance of individuals to bring employer into court); Simmons v. City of Kansas City, 129 F.R.D. 178

(D.Kan.1989) (class of 49 police officers sufficiently numerous in light of evidence of likelihood of retaliation against individual members).

Relatively small classes may also be justified by the fact that plaintiffs seek relief for persons whose identity and number are unknown at the time of class certification. In INTERNATIONAL BROTHERHOOD OF TEAMSTERS v. UNITED STATES, 431 U.S. 324, 364, 97 S.Ct. 1843, 1869, 52 L.Ed.2d 396 (1977), the Supreme Court stated that persons deterred from seeking employment because of the known discriminatory policies of an employer are entitled to relief in a Title VII action on the same basis as actual applicants, where they can demonstrate that they had an interest in the job in question and that application would have been futile. Such persons are, as a practical matter, unidentifiable at the class certification stage. See, Jones v. Diamond, 519 F.2d 1090, 1100 (5th Cir.1975) (smaller classes are less objectionable when plaintiff seeks relief for future class members). See also, Barnett v. W. T. Grant Co., 518 F.2d 543, 547 (4th Cir.1975) (class could include "all those blacks who had been kept ignorant of driver positions or discouraged from applying from them due to these practices.").

Although Rule 23(a) does not explicitly limit the *maximum* size of a class, the representational adequacy requirement may as a practical matter place limits on certification. The larger and more wide-spread the class, the more costly and time-consuming will be its representation. Certification may be denied if the court determines the plaintiff lacks the resources to adequately represent the class. Eisen v. Carlisle & Jacquelin, 417 U.S. 156, 94 S.Ct. 2140, 40 L.Ed.2d 732 (1974). Cf., IMPACT v. Firestone, 893 F.2d 1189 (11th Cir.), cert. denied, ___ U.S. ___, 111 S.Ct. 133, 112 L.Ed.2d 100 (1990) (decertification on ground that class lacked adequate financing vacated for reconsideration of whether costs could be reduced by further discovery from employer). In assessing manageability, the financial resources of the plaintiff, his attorney's ability to pursue extensive and costly discovery, the geographic dispersion of class members, problems of communication and the reconciling of adverse interests will be considered. When an extremely large class is proposed, courts may permit discovery, prior to certification, of plaintiff and his counsel as to their ability to manage the class. See, Guse v. J.C. Penney Co., 409 F.Supp. 28 (E.D.Wis.1976), reversed on other grounds, 562 F.2d 6 (7th Cir.1977).

One way to avoid the numerosity problem as well as the typicality and commonality barrier created by General Telephone Company Of The Southwest v. Falcon is to encourage intervention of putative class members. In HOFFMAN–LA ROCHE, INC. v. SPERLING, 493 U.S. 165, 110 S.Ct. 482, 107 L.Ed.2d 480 (1989), the Supreme Court held that a district court has inherent authority to direct and supervise the sending of notice to potential plaintiffs in order to facilitate their joinder in the action. *Hoffman–La Roche* was a suit under the Age

Discrimination in Employment Act (ADEA) in which the plaintiffs alleged that the Act was violated when company discharged or demoted some 1,200 workers in a reduction in force.   Under the ADEA, which incorporates provisions of the Fair Labor Standards Act (FLSA), a Rule 23 class action is impossible because a provision of the FLSA allows joinder only of those persons who have consented in writing to become plaintiffs.   At the request of the plaintiffs, the district court directed the employer to produce the names and addresses of all employees who had been discharged in the reduction in force and authorized the plaintiffs to send a court-approved notice to all employees who had not previously filed consent forms.   The Court of Appeals affirmed.

The Supreme Court noted that the benefits of collective action (both to age discrimination claimants and the courts) "depend on employees receiving accurate and timely notice concerning the pendency of the collective action, so that they may make informed decisions about whether or not to participate."   493 U.S. at 170, 110 S.Ct. at 486. Once such an action has been filed, "the court has a managerial responsibility to oversee the joinder of additional parties to assure that the task is accomplished in an efficient and proper way."   493 U.S. at 170–71, 110 S.Ct. at 484.   General authority for such notice was found in Rule 83 of the Federal Rules of Civil Procedure which provides that courts "may regulate their practice in any manner not inconsistent with" other federal or local rules, and in Rule 16 which allows the adoption of special procedures for the management of complex, multi-party actions.

Referring to the majority decision as an "extraordinary application of federal judicial power," Justice Scalia, joined by Chief Justice Rehnquist, dissented.   Justice Scalia argued that nothing in either the ADEA or the federal rules conferred on courts the authority "either directly or by lending its judicial power to the efforts of a party's counsel—to *search out* potential claimants, ensure that they are accurately informed of the litigation, and inquire whether they would like to bring their claims before the court."   493 U.S. at 177, 110 S.Ct. at 490 (Scalia, J., dissenting).

Although *Hoffman–La Roche* arose in the confines of an ADEA action, nothing in the majority's reasoning or the sources of authority for court-approved notice, limits the holding to such cases.   Justice Scalia indeed worried that:

> If the benefits of judicial efficiency and economy constitute sufficient warrant for the District Court's action, then one can imagine numerous areas in which district courts should similarly take on the function of litigation touts—*whenever,* in fact, they have before them a claim that is similar to claims which other identifiable individuals might possess.

493 U.S. at 180–81, 110 S.Ct. at 491–92 (Scalia, J., dissenting).   See also, Diaz v. Trust Territory of Pacific Islands, 876 F.2d 1401 (9th Cir.1989) (notice to putative class of pre-certification class dismissal necessary

where such persons may have relied on class action and refrained from filing individual actions or intervening). The administrative filing requirements of Title VII, discussed in Chapter 4, *supra*, also impact on the permissible scope of class actions filed under that statute. Those issues are discussed in Section C of this Chapter.

The problems associated with joinder of large numbers of individuals in a single proceeding are discussed in Chapter 7B, *infra*.

SECTION C. THE CLASS ACTION AND THE PREREQUISITES TO TITLE VII LITIGATION

OATIS v. CROWN ZELLERBACH CORP.

United States Court of Appeals, Fifth Circuit, 1968.
398 F.2d 496.

Before BELL, AINSWORTH, and GODBOLD, CIRCUIT JUDGES.

GRIFFIN B. BELL, CIRCUIT JUDGE.

This appeal presents the issue whether membership in a class action brought under § 706(e) of the Civil Rights Act of 1964, 42 U.S.C.A. § 2000e–5(e), is restricted to individuals who have filed charges with the Equal Employment Opportunity Commission. The District Court answered in the affirmative. Mondy v. Crown Zellerbach Corporation, E.D.La., 1967, 271 F.Supp. 258, 264–266. Being of the view that the class was unduly restricted, we reverse.

The suit giving rise to this issue was instituted on March 1, 1967 by four Negro employees (Hill, Oatis, Johnson and Young) of Crown Zellerbach Corporation. The suit was filed against the company and the two local unions representing employees at the Bogalusa, Louisiana plant of the company. Each plaintiff sued on behalf of himself and all present and prospective Negro employees of the plant, as a class, seeking injunctive relief against unfair employment practices as defined by Title VII of the Civil Rights Act of 1964, 42 U.S.C.A. §§ 2000e–2 and 3.

Prior to this action Hill filed a formal charge against the defendants with the Equal Employment Opportunity Commission (EEOC) in the manner provided for under § 706(a) of the Act, 42 U.S.C.A. § 2000e–5(a). The Commission informed Hill by letter that it had been unable to obtain voluntary compliance from appellees within the 60 days required by the Act. The suit was commenced two weeks later.

Crown and the unions filed motions to dismiss. They contended that an action under Title VII of the Act, 42 U.S.C.A. § 2000e et seq., cannot be brought on behalf of a class, and that in any event plaintiffs Oatis, Johnson and Young could not join in the action as co-plaintiffs inasmuch as they had not filed a charge with the EEOC. The Attorney General, representing the EEOC, was permitted to intervene. See § 706(e) of the Act, supra.

The District Court ruled that the action could be maintained as a class action, but that the class was limited to those Negro employees who had filed charges with EEOC pursuant to § 706(a) of the Act, 271 F.Supp., supra, at pp. 264–266. Oatis, Johnson and Young had not filed such a charge and the motions to dismiss were granted as to them. It is from this dismissal that they appeal.[1]

Under the enforcement provisions of Title VII an aggrieved person is required to file a written charge with the EEOC. § 706(a), supra. Assuming the EEOC finds reasonable cause to believe the charge is true, informal efforts to settle with the employer or union are to be made through conference, conciliation, and persuasion.[2] The filing of such a charge is a condition precedent to seeking judicial relief. See § 706(e).[3] It is thus clear that there is great emphasis in Title VII on private settlement and the elimination of unfair practices without litigation.

The plaintiffs-appellants maintain that a class action will lie if at least one aggrieved person has filed a charge with the EEOC. Defendants, on the other hand, assert that the administrative, private remedy intent and purposes of the statute will be circumvented and avoided if only one person may follow the administrative route dictate of the Act and then sue on behalf of the other employees. This, they urge, would result in the courts displacing the EEOC role in fostering the purposes of the Act. Defendants also argue that the Act provides for protection of the rights of a class in that § 707(a), 42 U.S.C.A. § 2000e–6, envisions a suit by the Attorney General when he finds that a pattern or practice of discrimination exists. This provision, they say, militates against the position of plaintiffs.

---

1. The express determination and direction required by Rule 54(b) F.R.Civ.P., in connection with the entry of judgment has been made and appeal is proper although the case is still pending as to Hill's complaint. See Dore v. Link Belt Company, 5 Cir., 1968, 391 F.2d 671.

2. § 706(a):

Whenever it is charged in writing under oath by a person claiming to be aggrieved, or a written charge has been filed by a member of the Commission where he has reasonable cause to believe a violation of this subchapter has occurred * * * that an employer, employment agency, or labor organization has engaged in an unlawful employment practice, the Commission shall furnish such employer, employment agency, or labor organization * * * with a copy of such charge and shall make an investigation of such charge, provided that such charge shall not be made public by the Commission. If the Commission shall determine, after such investigation, that there is reasonable cause to believe that the charge is true, the Commission shall endeavor to eliminate any such alleged unlawful employment practice by informal methods of conference, conciliation, and persuasion. * * *

3. § 706(e):

If within thirty days after a charge is filed with the Commission * * * the Commission has been unable to obtain voluntary compliance with this subchapter, the Commission shall so notify the person aggrieved and a civil action may, within thirty days thereafter, be brought against the respondent named in the charge (1) by the person claiming to be aggrieved, or (2) if such charge was filed by a member of the Commission, by any person whom the charge alleges was aggrieved by the alleged unlawful employment practice * * *.

The arguments of defendants are not persuasive for several reasons. A similar argument regarding a suit by the Attorney General was rejected by this court in a case brought under Title II of the Civil Rights Act of 1964. Lance v. Plummer, 5 Cir., 1965, 353 F.2d 585. We again reject it. The Act permits private suits and in nowise precludes the class action device.

Moreover, it does not appear that to allow a class action, within proper confines, would in any way frustrate the purpose of the Act that the settlement of grievances be first attempted through the office of the EEOC. It would be wasteful, if not vain, for numerous employees, all with the same grievance, to have to process many identical complaints with the EEOC. If it is impossible to reach a settlement with one discriminatee, what reason would there be to assume the next one would be successful. The better approach would appear to be that once an aggrieved person raises a particular issue with the EEOC which he has standing to raise, he may bring an action for himself and the class of persons similarly situated and we proceed to an examination of this view.

Plaintiff Hill raised several claims in the charge which he filed with the EEOC. One of these was that he was being discriminated against by the use of segregated locker rooms. Under the District Court's ruling Hill might bring suit and be placed in the white locker room. Other Negroes would have to wait until they could process their charges through EEOC before they could obtain the same relief from the same employer. We do not believe that Congress intended such a result from the application of Title VII. The class should not be so narrowly restricted. This conclusion is in line with several District Court decisions.

The Supreme Court recently made an apt comment on the nature of suits brought under the Civil Rights Act of 1964. See Newman v. Piggie Park Enterprises, 1968, 390 U.S. 400, 88 S.Ct. 964, 19 L.Ed.2d 1263, where the court stated:

> "A Title II suit is thus private in form only. When a plaintiff brings an action under that Title, he cannot recover damages. If he obtains an injunction, he does so not for himself alone, but also as a 'private attorney general', vindicating a policy that Congress considered of the highest priority."

Clearly the same logic applies to Title VII of the Act. Racial discrimination is by definition class discrimination, and to require a multiplicity of separate, identical charges before the EEOC, filed against the same employer, as a prerequisite to relief through resort to the court would tend to frustrate our system of justice and order.

We thus hold that a class action is permissible under Title VII of the Civil Rights Act of 1964 within the following limits. First, the class action must, as it does here, meet the requirements of Rule 23(a) and (b)(2). Next, the issues that may be raised by plaintiff in such a class action are those issues that he has standing to raise (i.e., the issues as to which he is aggrieved, see § 706(a), supra), and that he has raised in the charge filed with the EEOC pursuant to § 706(a). Here then the issues that may be considered in the suit are those properly asserted by Hill in the EEOC charge and as are reasserted in the complaint.

Additionally, it is not necessary that members of the class bring a charge with the EEOC as a prerequisite to joining as co-plaintiffs in the litigation. It is sufficient that they are in a class and assert the same or some of the issues. This emphasizes the reason for Oatis, Johnson and Young to appear as co-plaintiffs. They were each employed in a separate department of the plant. They were representative of their respective departments, as Hill was of his, in the class action. They, as co-plaintiffs, must proceed however, within the periphery of the issues which Hill could assert. Under Rule 23(a) they would be representatives of the class consisting of the Negro employees in their departments so as to fairly and adequately protect their interests. This follows from the fact that due to the inapplicability of some of the issues to all members of the class, the proceeding might be facilitated by the use of subclasses. In such event one or more of the co-plaintiffs might represent a subclass. It was error, therefore, to dismiss appellants. They should have been permitted to remain in the case as plaintiffs but with their participation limited to the issues asserted by Hill.

Reversed and remanded for further proceedings not inconsistent herewith.

GRIFFIN v. DUGGER

United States Court of Appeals, Eleventh Circuit, 1987.
823 F.2d 1476, cert. denied, 486 U.S. 1005, 108 S.Ct. 1729, 100 L.Ed.2d 193 (1988).

TJOFLAT, CIRCUIT JUDGE:

I.

In April 1971, Peners L. Griffin became the first black Road Prison Officer at the Tallahassee Road Prison, operated by the Florida Department of Corrections (FDOC or Department). Beginning in 1973, Griffin frequently sought promotion to higher-grade correctional officer positions, as well as various other positions. On each occasion, the FDOC turned him down.

In December 1974, Griffin's supervisor fired him for disciplinary reasons. The next day, the Regional Superintendent reinstated Griffin because the supervisor had not followed proper termination procedures. In early 1975, the FDOC again terminated Griffin's employment, without notice, for disciplinary reasons. He appealed the termination to the State of Florida Career Service Commission. The Commission found no just cause for Griffin's discharge and ordered the FDOC to reinstate him with back pay. The Florida District Court of Appeal affirmed the Commission's decision, and the FDOC reinstated Griffin to his position.

Soon after his reinstatement, Griffin filed a complaint with the FDOC's Equal Employment Opportunity Program Office, charging that his two dismissals were racially discriminatory. An investigator in that office wrote Griffin a month later and informed him of his conclusion that racial discrimination had not been a factor in the dismissals. Within a day or two of having received that letter, Griffin filed a complaint with the Equal Employment Opportunity Commission (EEOC), detailing the events leading up to his allegedly discriminatory discharges. A notation at the beginning of Griffin's complaint, probably made by an EEOC counselor, describes Griffin's allegations of racial discrimination as also encompassing "[s]incerity of recruiting, hiring, and promoting of minority groups within the Florida's Division of Adult Corrections. Specific attention within the Community Service Program."

Griffin asked the EEOC for a right-to-sue letter and received one in July 1979. On October 15, 1979, Griffin brought this action in the district court against Louis L. Wainwright, as Secretary of the FDOC, the FDOC, and the State of Florida. Griffin alleged that the FDOC had denied him several promotions because of his race. He also alleged that the FDOC impermissibly considered race in all of its promotion decisions, as well as in its hiring and job assignment decisions. In hiring correctional officers, according to Griffin, the Department used written entry-level examinations having a detrimental impact upon blacks.[1]

Griffin sued "individually and on behalf of all others similarly situated," pursuant to Rule 23(b)(2) of the Federal Rules of Civil Procedure, seeking declaratory and injunctive relief and money damages under Title VII of the Civil Rights Act of 1964, 42 U.S.C. § 1981 (1976), and 42 U.S.C. § 1983 (1976). The class identified in his complaint was composed "of all past, present and potential black American citizens and residents who have been, are or may be employees of the Defendants or applicants for employment."

On June 17, 1980, Griffin obtained leave of court to amend his complaint to add Henry L. Dejerinett as a party-plaintiff and class representative. Dejerinett, who is black, had applied for an FDOC clerical position but was not hired.[5] On March 10, 1981, based on a stipulation between the parties and without a hearing, the district

---

1. The district court found the following facts concerning the FDOC's written entry-level examination: "Every person seeking a position as a correctional officer is required to take a written examination. The Department of Administration developed the Correctional Officer I entry level test which consists of seventy-five questions. An applicant must receive a score of at least thirty-eight for employment consideration."

5. Dejerinett subsequently filed a timely charge of racial discrimination against the FDOC with the Florida Commission on Human Relations, a deferral agency for the EEOC. He requested and received a right-to-sue letter from the EEOC in April 1980.

court preliminarily certified the case as a class action with Griffin and Dejerinett representing the class of "all past, present, and potential black employees of the State of Florida Department of Corrections."

On June 25, 1982, the defendants filed a "Notice Regarding the Adequacy of the Preliminary Class Certified," which called to the court's attention a Supreme Court decision rendered eleven days previously. That decision, General Tel. Co. v. Falcon, 457 U.S. 147, 102 S.Ct. 2364, 72 L.Ed.2d 740 (1982), announced the appropriate standards courts should apply when determining class action certifications in the context of a Title VII suit, reversing a former Fifth Circuit decision permitting "across-the-board" class actions that had been binding precedent in the new Eleventh Circuit. On July 8, 1982, the defendants moved the court, in light of *Falcon,* to vacate its order certifying the class.

To avoid the risk that the district court might vacate its order certifying the class, Griffin and Dejerinett took steps to obtain an additional named plaintiff to represent those in the class who had applied for the position of correctional officer, failed the written entry-level examination, and not been hired. Accordingly, on July 8, 1982, Alvin Smith, joined by Griffin and Dejerinett, moved the court to intervene as an additional named plaintiff and class representative. In 1980 and 1981, Smith, who is black, applied for the same entry-level position that Griffin held. The FDOC did not hire Smith, because he did not have a high school diploma or a general equivalency diploma (GED), a prerequisite for employment as a correctional officer. Smith later obtained a GED, but when he reapplied with the FDOC in July 1981, he failed the written entry-level correctional officer examination and was again denied the job.[8]

On July 28, 1982, the district court denied the defendants' motion to decertify the class and permitted Smith to intervene because

> Smith, [as] an unsuccessful applicant, certainly has an interest in this suit which seeks to challenge defendants' employment practices, including hiring. Unless he is permitted to intervene, his interest may not be adequately represented by the named parties. Mr. Smith eases this court's concern that the class claim against the [FDOC]'s objective criteria was not fairly and adequately protected by the named plaintiffs. Alvin Smith is a proper representative for potential black employees.

As to the defendants' contention that Smith could not be a class representative because he had not timely filed an EEOC complaint, the district court found that the charges of discrimination Griffin had filed with the EEOC included "the hiring claim in addition to promotion, job classification, discipline, and termination claims." The court thus reasoned that the Fifth Circuit's single-filing rule excused Smith from having failed to exhaust his administrative remedies. See Oatis v.

---

8. Smith never filed a timely charge of racial discrimination with the EEOC.

Crown Zellerbach Corp., 398 F.2d 496, 498 (5th Cir.1968) ("[O]nce an aggrieved person raises a particular issue with the EEOC which he has standing to raise, he may bring an action for himself and the class of persons similarly situated * * *.").

On July 30, 1982, the district court entered partial summary judgment for the plaintiffs, including Griffin and Dejerinett, on the liability issue as to the written entry-level examination. The court found that the FDOC examination "has a disparate impact upon class members which has not been justified by business necessity." The plaintiffs had sought summary judgment on two other issues—the class hiring and promotion claims—but the court denied summary judgment on those issues because they presented material issues of fact.

A trial was held over the five-week period beginning August 17 and ending September 17, 1982. The court entered judgment on August 25, 1983, disposing of the following issues in favor of the defendants: whether the FDOC's policies and practices discriminated against past, present, and potential black employees; whether the FDOC's employment practices as to Peners L. Griffin were racially discriminatory; and whether the FDOC's hiring practices as to Henry L. Dejerinett were racially discriminatory. The court entered judgment for the plaintiffs on the liability issue concerning the correctional officer examination, on which it had previously granted summary judgment for the plaintiffs. The issue of relief for the class of black persons who took and failed the correctional officer written examination is still pending. The parties agreed that notice should be given to the affected members of the class and to seek interlocutory appeal of the district court's decision permitting Griffin, Dejerinett, and Smith to serve as named plaintiffs for a class that included applicants with testing claims. We granted this appeal pursuant to 28 U.S.C. § 1292(b) (1982 & Supp. III 1985). Because we conclude that the district court incorrectly applied the dictates of *Falcon,* we vacate the district court's order certifying the class.

II.

As with any private class action, the legitimacy of a private Title VII suit brought on behalf of a class depends upon the satisfaction of two distinct prerequisites. First, there must be an individual plaintiff with a cognizable claim, that is, an individual who has constitutional standing to raise the claim (or claims) and who has satisfied the procedural requirements of Title VII.[12] Second, the requirements of Rule 23 of the Federal Rules of Civil Procedure must be fulfilled; in

---

12. This circuit has held that the conditions precedent to filing a Title VII suit are not jurisdictional, but rather are akin to a statute of limitations. A plaintiff's failure to satisfy the conditions precedent does not, standing alone, deprive federal district courts of subject matter jurisdiction. Jack- son v. Seaboard Coast Line R.R., 678 F.2d 992 (11th Cir.1982). Nevertheless, "a plaintiff must generally allege in his complaint that 'all conditions precedent to the institution of the lawsuit have been fulfilled.' " Id. at 1010 (quoting Fed.R.Civ.P. 9(c)).

other words, the individual plaintiff must be qualified to represent the members of the class in accordance with the four prerequisites of Rule 23(a), and the action must be one of the three types Rule 23(b) identifies. We emphasize that any analysis of class certification must begin with the issue of standing and the procedural requirements of Title VII. Thus, the threshold question is whether the named plaintiffs have individual standing, in the constitutional sense, to raise certain issues. See Brown v. Sibley, 650 F.2d 760, 771 (5th Cir. Unit A July 1981) ("This constitutional threshold must be met before any consideration of the typicality of claims or commonality of issues required for procedural reasons by Fed.R.Civ.P. 23."). Only after the court determines the issues for which the named plaintiffs have standing should it address the question whether the named plaintiffs have representative capacity, as defined by Rule 23(a), to assert the rights of others. See generally 2 A. Larson & L. Larson, *Employment Discrimination* §§ 49.-50–.51 (1986 & Supp. Nov. 1986).

* * *

[The Court held that, since he had suffered no injury as a result of the FDOC's use of the written entry-level examination, plaintiff Griffin had no constitutional standing under Article III to assert the testing claim on behalf of himself or others. The Court further held that, because the FDOC's decision-making process for promotions was subjective while its hiring process was objective, the case did not come within the "same general fashion" classification of related forms of discrimination mentioned in footnote 15 of *Falcon.* Thus Griffin, who could assert discipline and promotion claims under Title VII, did not have representative capacity, within the meaning of Rule 23(a), to assert testing claims on behalf of others. The Court then proceeded to examine whether the joinder of Dejerinett and Smith as plaintiff-intervenors affected the class certification question.]

III.

A.

Eight months after filing his complaint in district court, Griffin sought leave to amend his complaint to add Henry L. Dejerinett as a party-plaintiff and as a class representative. In November 1978, Dejerinett applied for an FDOC clerical position, entitled "Property Manager III." Dejerinett was not required, as part of the application process, to produce an educational degree or to take the written entry-level examination required of correctional officer applicants. He was required, however, to have an interview. Dejerinett was not hired; instead, the FDOC hired a white male. A month later, Dejerinett filed a charge of racial discrimination against the FDOC with the Florida Commission on Human Relations, a deferral agency for the EEOC. He requested and received a right-to-sue letter from the EEOC in April 1980. The district court, with no written analysis of standing or Rule 23, granted

Griffin leave to amend his complaint and add Dejerinett as a named plaintiff.

Dejerinett had standing to assert a subjective hiring claim. He applied for a clerical position, requiring no correctional officer examination or educational degrees, and was not hired. Because Dejerinett never took the correctional officer examination, and never applied for that position, he suffered no injury as a result of that test. He thus lacked constitutional standing to assert a testing or a hiring claim arising out of the FDOC's correctional officer application process.

Accordingly, we hold that the district court erred when it permitted Dejerinett to raise the testing claim on behalf of himself and on behalf of others. We hold in the alternative that even if Dejerinett somehow had constitutional standing to assert the testing claim, he did not, in light of General Tel. Co. v. Falcon, have representative capacity to assert the testing claim on behalf of those who took the FDOC's written entry-level examination, failed it, and were not hired. In other words, Dejerinett did not meet the prerequisites of Rule 23(a).

The district court, in effect, presumed the similarity of hiring claims of those denied clerical positions to hiring claims of those denied correctional officer positions. In our view, applicants who were subjectively denied clerical positions cannot sufficiently identify with other applicants who failed an objective written examination and, on that basis, were not hired for the higher-ranking position of correctional officer. See Walker v. Jim Dandy Co., 747 F.2d 1360, 1364 (11th Cir.1984) ("The [district] court [correctly] reasoned that because [the plaintiffs] were applicants for supervisory positions, they did not sufficiently identify with other applicants for lower level labor jobs or employees complaining of disparate job assignments or pay.") The district court abused its discretion when, in light of *Falcon*, it continued to permit Dejerinett to represent those members of the class who took and failed the written entry-level correctional officer examination.

B.

Intervenor Alvin Smith twice applied for the entry-level correctional officer position held by Griffin. Smith was first denied the job because he did not have a high school diploma or a general equivalency diploma (GED), both requirements for the job. Later he obtained a GED, but he then failed the written correctional officer examination. Consequently, he was denied the position a second time.

Smith had constitutional standing to assert a testing claim under Title VII. He could, and did, allege injury as a result of the FDOC's testing requirement: he took and failed the written examination required of entry-level correctional officers. Although Smith may very well have had representative capacity, under Rule 23(a), to assert testing claims on behalf of other black applicants who failed the same test and were consequently not hired, we need not address that point. Smith did not file a timely charge of racial discrimination with the

EEOC, a precondition to a Title VII suit. Furthermore, as we discuss below, Smith could not avail himself of the single-filing rule. For these reasons, we hold that the district court erred when it allowed Smith to intervene as a class representative.

In Oatis v. Crown Zellerbach Corp., our predecessor circuit held that it is not necessary for each person with the same grievance to file an EEOC charge as a prerequisite to class membership. Nor is it necessary that an intervenor bring a charge with the EEOC as a prerequisite to serving as a class representative. Id. As long as at least one named plaintiff timely filed an EEOC charge, the precondition to a Title VII action is met for all other named plaintiffs and class members. Id.[36]

This rule, which has become known as the "single-filing rule," contains two essential requirements: "First, at least one plaintiff must have timely filed an EEOC complaint that is not otherwise defective * * *. Second, the individual claims of the filing and non-filing plaintiffs must have arisen out of similar discriminatory treatment in the same time frame." In the case before us, the first requirement was met: Griffin, one of the named plaintiffs, timely filed an adequate EEOC complaint, as far as it detailed his promotion and discipline claims. The second requirement, however, was not satisfied. Smith, a non-filing plaintiff, had an objective testing claim while Griffin, on the other hand, had subjective promotion and discipline claims.

We hold that Griffin and Smith were not sufficiently similarly situated. That is, employee Griffin's claims and applicant Smith's claims did not arise out of similar discriminatory treatment. Griffin alleged that the FDOC's subjective promotion and discipline practices were illegally discriminatory. Smith alleged that the FDOC's objective correctional officer examination illegally discriminated against black applicants. The FDOC's promotion and discipline practices were not manifested in similar fashion to its hiring and testing practices. See Ezell v. Mobile Housing Bd., 709 F.2d 1376, 1381 (11th Cir.1983) (non-filing incumbent plaintiff's discriminatory examination claim was not sufficiently similar to filing plaintiffs' discriminatory discharge and broad-based, ongoing campaign of discrimination claims to invoke single-filing rule to excuse filing requirement); Dalton v. Employment Sec. Comm'n, 671 F.2d 835, 838 (4th Cir.), cert. denied, 459 U.S. 862, 103 S.Ct. 138, 74 L.Ed.2d 117 (1982) (because non-charging plaintiff's hiring claim was not "substantially identical" to incumbent employee's claims of discriminatory treatment, single-filing rule did not apply). Although both employment practices could have been racially discriminatory,

36. The Oatis reasoning was extended to intervention in non-class suits in Wheeler v. American Home Prods. Corp., 582 F.2d 891, 897–98 (5th Cir.1977) (similarly situated a who had not filed EEOC charges nevertheless could assert back pay claims if one or more of original plaintiffs had filed timely charges). The Oatis rationale was further extended in Crawford v. United States Steel Corp., 660 F.2d 663, 665–66 (5th Cir. Unit B Nov. 1981), which held that every original plaintiff in a multi-plaintiff, non-class action suit need not file charges with the EEOC.

that alone is not enough to implicate the second requirement of the single-filing rule. Otherwise, "intervention [could] bootstrap the court's jurisdiction to encompass claims regarding practices broader than the ... claims properly assertable by the named plaintiffs." Vuyanich v. Republic Nat'l Bank, 723 F.2d 1195, 1201 (5th Cir.) (former employees who sought to intervene in class action but who did not file timely charges with EEOC could only proceed within periphery of issues that named plaintiffs could assert), cert. denied, 469 U.S. 1073, 105 S.Ct. 567, 83 L.Ed.2d 507 (1984); see also Wakeen v. Hoffman House, Inc., 724 F.2d 1238, 1246 (7th Cir.1983) ("[A] class member who does not meet the procedural prerequisites for waging a Title VII suit may not use the guise of a motion to intervene to take over as the sole class representative for someone who initiates but is not legitimately able to continue a class action.").

We also note that merely because a notation at the beginning of Griffin's EEOC complaint stated that Griffin's charge also encompassed "[s]incerity of recruiting, hiring, and promoting of minority groups within the Florida's Division of Adult Corrections," Smith's status as a class representative was not saved. As the pleadings make clear, Griffin never had constitutional standing to raise a testing or a hiring claim, a fundamental requirement underlying the single-filing rule: "once an aggrieved person raises a particular issue with the EEOC which he has standing to raise, he may bring an action for himself and the class of persons similarly situated." *Oatis,* 398 F.2d at 498.[37] Smith cannot point to Griffin's EEOC charge, which arguably contained a testing claim brought on behalf of others, to excuse his failure to have filed his own testing charge with the EEOC when Griffin did not have standing to raise the testing issue. We cannot permit the single-filing rule to be used to circumvent the constitutional requirement of standing.

IV.

In sum, based on standing principles and on the dictates of *Falcon,* we hold that the district court erred when it certified the class with the named plaintiffs as representatives. None of the named plaintiffs—Griffin, Dejerinett, or Smith—should have been allowed to represent the class of black correctional officer applicants with testing claims. The district court's order certifying the class is therefore

VACATED.

---

37. By "standing," the *Oatis* court meant "the issues as to which [the employee] is aggrieved," *Oatis,* 398 F.2d at 499, citing Title VII's enforcement provision that requires the EEOC to investigate the charges of a person claiming to be aggrieved, 42 U.S.C. § 2000e–5(a). By "standing," the *Oatis* court also meant, even if implicit-ly, personal injury, that is, constitutional standing. See id. at 498–99; see also Vuyanich v. Republic Nat'l Bank, 723 F.2d 1195, 1200–01 (5th Cir.) (interpreting *Oatis'* single-filing rule as implicating constitutional standing), cert. denied, 469 U.S. 1073, 105 S.Ct. 567, 83 L.Ed.2d 507 (1984).

HATCHETT, CIRCUIT JUDGE, dissenting:

I dissent. The majority holds that Smith did not meet the second element of the single-filing rule. That rule states, "the individual *claims* of the filing and non-filing plaintiffs must have arisen out of similar discriminatory treatment in the same time frame." *Jackson,* 678 F.2d at 1011–12 (emphasis added). One of Griffin's claims in his EEOC complaint was that the FDOC discriminated against black job applicants. Non-filing intervenor Smith's claim arose "out of similar discriminatory treatment," because he alleges that the FDOC discriminated against him and other applicants through administration of a test with a discriminatory impact on blacks. The majority ignores the fact that Griffin raised the claim of discrimination against black applicants in his EEOC complaint.

The majority erroneously assumes that if Griffin lacks standing to raise the hiring claim in federal court, then his raising of that claim before the EEOC is somehow ineffective for purposes of the single filing rule. The majority's reasoning is based upon its failure to differentiate between the policy underlying the standing requirement in federal court and the policy underlying the single filing rule in an EEOC action. The policy underlying the standing requirement is to ensure that a party litigating an issue has a concrete stake in the outcome of the case, and is therefore motivated to vigorously litigate the issues. The policy underlying the EEOC filing requirement is to ensure "that the settlement of grievances be first attempted through the office of the EEOC * * *." Ezell v. Mobile Housing Board, 709 F.2d 1376, 1381 (11th Cir.1983); Oatis v. Crown Zellerbach Corp., 398 F.2d 496, 498 (5th Cir.1968). The purpose underlying the EEOC filing requirement is therefore to promote the resolution of Title VII claims out of court. The EEOC proceeding is not designed as a way-station on the road to the federal courthouse.

By asserting a hiring grievance in his EEOC complaint, Griffin ensured "that the settlement of [hiring] grievances [would] be first attempted through the office of the EEOC." *Ezell,* 709 F.2d at 1381. The fact that Griffin may not have had standing in federal district court to raise the hiring issue is irrelevant to the fact that his EEOC complaint gave the EEOC an opportunity to settle the hiring grievance before that grievance was sued upon in federal district court. Since Smith's claim in federal district court of discriminatory hiring practices is identical to the claim of discriminatory hiring practices asserted in Griffin's complaint before the EEOC, invoking the single filing rule will not frustrate the purpose of the EEOC filing requirement: to give the EEOC a chance to resolve Title VII claims before they go to court. The fact that Griffin may not have had standing to raise the hiring claim in court is irrelevant to the issue of whether the EEOC has had a chance to resolve that claim before it is taken to court, whether by Griffin, Smith, or anyone else.

In short, the majority has grafted the constitutional standing requirement for parties litigating in federal district court onto the filing requirements for persons alleging Title VII claims before the EEOC. Such a requirement does not, and never has, existed. The majority, however, misinterprets Fifth Circuit dicta to reach just that conclusion. That dicta says, "Once an aggrieved person raises a particular issue with the EEOC which he has standing to raise, he may bring an action for himself and the class of persons similarly situated." *Oatis,* 398 F.2d at 498. The majority fails to mention that the sole issue in the *Oatis* case was whether a Title VII class action could include in the class persons who had not previously filed charges with the EEOC. The court held that the class could include such persons. The *Oatis* court gave its reasoning for this holding in the sentence immediately preceding the language relied upon by the majority in this case. That sentence states, "If it is impossible to reach a settlement with one discriminatee, what reason would there be to assume the next one would be successful." *Oatis,* 398 F.2d at 498. In short, the court in *Oatis* was not faced with the question of whether an EEOC complainant could effectively file claims with the EEOC even though the complainant would not have standing to assert the claim in federal district court. The majority's application of constitutional standing requirements to the EEOC complainant puts the EEOC in the nonsensical position of having to anticipate how the federal district court will rule on the complainant's standing to litigate various claims if the EEOC does not resolve them. Such a rule will result in the EEOC narrowing its resolution of claims to those which it anticipates the complainant will have standing to sue upon in federal district court, regardless of the apparent existence of the alleged discrimination with respect to other employees or job applicants. Such a situation would hardly further the purpose of the EEOC filing requirement: to resolve Title VII claims out of court.

Title 42 U.S.C. § 2000e–5(b) says:

> Whenever a charge is filed by or on behalf of a person *claiming* to be aggrieved, or by a member of the Commission, alleging that an employer * * * has engaged in an unlawful employment practice, the Commission *shall* serve a notice of the charge * * * and *shall* make an investigation thereof.

This provision requires the Commission to investigate all charges which a person "claims" to be aggrieved of. In no way does the provision suggest that the Commission is limited to the investigation of claims which the complainant will have standing to bring in a federal court. Any suggestion in *Oatis* of such a requirement is dicta that is in conflict with the intent of the statute that the EEOC resolve "claimed" discrimination out of court. Smith should therefore be allowed to proceed in federal district court as a class representative for the class of applicants who failed the objective test.

NOTES AND PROBLEMS FOR DISCUSSION

1. In *Oatis* the court held that the a, "must proceed * * * within the periphery of the issues which Hill could assert." As discussed in Chapter 4A(3),

supra, the claims in a Title VII action are limited to some degree by the allegations in the EEOC charge filed pursuant to § 706(a). The complaint may raise issues which can "reasonably be expected to grow out of the [EEOC] charge of discrimination." Sanchez v. Standard Brands, Inc., 431 F.2d 455, 466 (5th Cir.1970).

Although all the circuits adhere to the "like or related" test of *Sanchez* for determining the proper scope of class allegations in a Title VII action, there is substantial divergence among the courts as to the application of that standard. In Fellows v. Universal Restaurants, Inc., 701 F.2d 447 (5th Cir.1983), cert. denied, 464 U.S. 828, 104 S.Ct. 102, 78 L.Ed.2d 106 (1983), the court held that neither a class allegation in the EEOC charge nor a class investigation by the EEOC was a prerequisite to a class suit. All that was required was that the substance of the charge afford "a reasonable expectation that the EEOC's investigation could encompass not only Universal's alleged discrimination against Ms. Fellows but also that against all female applicants and employees." 701 F.2d at 451. But in Evans v. United States Pipe & Foundry Co., 696 F.2d 925 (11th Cir.1983), the district court dismissed class allegations of discrimination in initial job assignments, promotions, layoffs, discipline and termination on behalf of all black employees of the defendant, because the plaintiff's EEOC charge had only alleged racial discrimination in the areas of promotion and job assignment and because the EEOC investigation had been limited to those matters. The Eleventh Circuit, while recognizing contrary authority, affirmed.

> The record reveals that the substantive inquiry by the Commission was limited to defendant's claims of discrimination in promotion and harassment. Appellant's concept of widespread discrimination rooted in the subjective decisionmaking of the white supervisory staff was not a part of the investigation by the Commission. Among the principles underlying the "like or related" rule is the belief that the Commission should have the first opportunity to investigate the alleged discriminatory practices to permit it to perform its role in obtaining voluntary compliance and promoting conciliation efforts. In light of these principles, we cannot say that the district court erred in finding that plaintiff's broad class included members whose claims were beyond the scope of Evans' EEOC charge.

696 F.2d at 929. Does the majority's opinion in *Dugger* rest merely on the fact that Dugger's EEOC charge was not broad enough to encompass the claims made by Smith? Does the *Dugger* rule render less effective joinder or intervention as mechanisms for "firming up" a class action? See, Hoffman–La Roche, Inc. v. Sperling, *supra* (discussed in Section B of this chapter).

2. Under the single-filing rule, persons who have not filed EEOC charges may be represented in a Title VII class action by one who has and may even intervene as named plaintiffs under the "umbrella" of the first plaintiff's EEOC charge. But it is also clear that the class may include only those persons who had viable claims at the time the class representative on whom they depend filed a charge with the EEOC. See e.g., Laffey v. Northwest Airlines, Inc., 567 F.2d 429, 472–73 (D.C.Cir. 1976), cert. denied, 434 U.S. 1086, 98 S.Ct. 1281, 55 L.Ed.2d 792 (1978); Moses v. Avco Corp., 97 F.R.D. 20 (D.Conn.1982); Gill v. Monroe County Dept. of Social Services, 79 F.R.D. 316, 331 (W.D.N.Y.1978). For example, in a Title VII class action on behalf of persons unlawfully denied employment, the named plaintiff would have necessarily filed an EEOC charge within 180 days (in a non-deferral state) of the defendant's rejection of his

application. Thus, only those persons who were denied employment within 180 days prior to the date on which the named plaintiff filed his EEOC charge (i.e., those persons who *could* have filed an EEOC charge at the same time the plaintiff did) may be included in the class. McDonald v. United Air Lines, Inc., 587 F.2d 357, 361 n. 10 (7th Cir.1978), cert. denied, 442 U.S. 934, 99 S.Ct. 2869, 61 L.Ed.2d 303 (1979); Wetzel v. Liberty Mutual Insurance Co., 508 F.2d 239, 246 (3d Cir.), cert. denied, 421 U.S. 1011, 95 S.Ct. 2415, 44 L.Ed.2d 679 (1975); Zahorik v. Cornell University, 579 F.Supp. 349 (N.D.N.Y.1983), affirmed, 729 F.2d 85 (2d Cir.1984). For those persons rejected by the employer more than 180 days prior to the date on which the named plaintiff filed his charge, their rights to either file their own suit or participate in a class action under Title VII ended 180 days after they were turned down for employment. As the Supreme Court noted in UNITED AIR LINES, INC. v. EVANS, *supra*, Chapter 4, the discrimination against such persons "is merely an unfortunate event in history which has no present legal consequences." It follows that a person without a valid claim at the time the class representative's charge was filed may not intervene as a named plaintiff. Hill v. AT & T Technologies, Inc., 731 F.2d 175 (4th Cir.1984).

In UNITED AIRLINES, INC. v. MCDONALD, 432 U.S. 385, 97 S.Ct. 2464, 53 L.Ed.2d 423 (1977), the Supreme Court held that where the class representative refuses to appeal the denial of certification, a putative class member, even one who has not filed an EEOC charge, should be allowed to intervene for purposes of carrying forward the appeal. But should the same rule apply where the named plaintiff's individual claim is dismissed before any class determination is made? In other words, should a person who could not file a Title VII action on his own, for failure to file an EEOC charge, be allowed to intervene to represent a class where the named plaintiff, who did file a charge, is otherwise precluded, as a matter of law, from litigating his claim? See, Wakeen v. Hoffman House, Inc., 724 F.2d 1238 (7th Cir.1983).

CROWN, CORK & SEAL CO., INC. v. PARKER

Supreme Court of the United States, 1983.

462 U.S. 345, 103 S.Ct. 2392, 76 L.Ed.2d 628.

JUSTICE BLACKMUN delivered the opinion of the Court.

The question that confronts us in this case is whether the filing of a class action tolls the applicable statute of limitations, and thus permits all members of the putative class to file individual actions in the event that class certification is denied, provided, of course, that those actions are instituted within the time that remains on the limitations period.

I

Respondent Theodore Parker, a Negro male, was discharged from his employment with petitioner Crown, Cork & Seal Company, Inc., in July 1977. In October of that year, he filed a charge with the Equal Employment Opportunity Commission (EEOC) alleging that he had been harassed and then discharged on account of his race. On November 9, 1978, the EEOC issued a Determination Letter finding no reasonable cause to believe respondent's discrimination charge was true, and, pursuant to § 706(f) of the Civil Rights Act of 1964(Act), sent respondent a Notice of Right to Sue.

Two months earlier, while respondent's charge was pending before the EEOC, two other Negro males formerly employed by petitioner filed a class action in the United States District Court for the District of Maryland. Pendleton v. Crown, Cork & Seal Co., Civ. No. M–78–1734. The complaint in that action alleged that petitioner had discriminated against its Negro employees with respect to hiring, discharges, job assignments, promotions, disciplinary actions, and other terms and conditions of employment, in violation of Title VII of the Act. The named plaintiffs purported to represent a class of "black persons who have been, continue to be and who in the future will be denied equal employment opportunities by defendant on the grounds of race or color." App. to Brief for Petitioner 2a. It is undisputed that respondent was a member of the asserted class.

In May 1979, the named plaintiffs in Pendleton moved for class certification. Nearly a year and a half later, on September 4, 1980, the District Court denied the motion. App. to Brief for Petitioner 7a. The court ruled that the named plaintiffs' claims were not typical of those of the class, that the named plaintiffs would not be adequate representatives, and that the class was not so numerous as to make joinder impracticable. Thereafter, Pendleton proceeded as an individual action on behalf of its named plaintiffs.[1]

On October 27, 1980, within 90 days after the denial of class certification but almost two years after receiving his Notice of Right to Sue, respondent filed the present Title VII action in the United States District Court for the District of Maryland, alleging that his discharge was racially motivated. Respondent moved to consolidate his action with the pending Pendleton case, but petitioner opposed the motion on the ground that the two cases were at substantially different stages of preparation. The motion to consolidate was denied. The District Court then granted summary judgment for petitioner, ruling that respondent had failed to file his action within 90 days of receiving his Notice of Right to Sue, as required by the Act's § 706(f)(1).

The United States Court of Appeals for the Fourth Circuit reversed. 677 F.2d 391 (1982). Relying on American Pipe & Constr. Co. v. Utah, 414 U.S. 538, 94 S.Ct. 756, 38 L.Ed.2d 713 (1974), the Court of Appeals held that the filing of the Pendleton class action had tolled Title VII's statute of limitations for all members of the putative class. Because the Pendleton suit was instituted before respondent received his Notice, and because respondent had filed his action within 90 days after the denial of class certification, the Court of Appeals concluded that it was timely.

---

1. The named plaintiffs in Pendleton later settled their claims, and their action was dismissed with prejudice. Respondent Parker, as permitted by United Airlines, Inc. v. McDonald, 432 U.S. 385, 392–395, 97 S.Ct. 2464, 2468–2470, 53 L.Ed.2d 423 (1977), then intervened in that lawsuit for the limited purpose of appealing the denial of class certification. He failed, however, to take a timely appeal.

Two other Courts of Appeals have held that the tolling rule of American Pipe applies only to putative class members who seek to intervene after denial of class certification, and not to those who, like respondent, file individual actions.[2] We granted certiorari to resolve the conflict.

II

A

American Pipe was a federal antitrust suit brought by the State of Utah on behalf of itself and a class of other public bodies and agencies. The suit was filed with only 11 days left to run on the applicable statute of limitations. The District Court eventually ruled that the suit could not proceed as a class action, and eight days after this ruling a number of putative class members moved to intervene. This Court ruled that the motions to intervene were not time-barred. The Court reasoned that unless the filing of a class action tolled the statute of limitations, potential class members would be induced to file motions to intervene or to join in order to protect themselves against the possibility that certification would be denied. The principal purposes of the class action procedure—promotion of efficiency and economy of litigation—would thereby be frustrated. Ibid. To protect the policies behind the class action procedure, the Court held that "the commencement of a class action suspends the applicable statute of limitations as to all asserted members of the class who would have been parties had the suit been permitted to continue as a class action."

Petitioner asserts that the rule of American Pipe was limited to a, and does not toll the statute of limitations for class members who file actions of their own.[3] Petitioner relies on the Court's statement in American Pipe that "the commencement of the original class suit tolls the running of the statute for all purported members of the class *who make timely motions to intervene* after the court has found the suit inappropriate for class action status." While American Pipe concerned only a, we conclude that the holding of that case is not to be read so narrowly. The filing of a class action tolls the statute of limitations "as to all asserted members of the class," not just as to intervenors.

The American Pipe Court recognized that unless the statute of limitations was tolled by the filing of the class action, class members would not be able to rely on the existence of the suit to protect their rights. Only by intervening or taking other action prior to the running

---

2. See Pavlak v. Church, 681 F.2d 617 (CA9 1982), cert. pending, No. 82–650; Stull v. Bayard, 561 F.2d 429, 433 (CA2 1977), cert. denied, 434 U.S. 1035, 98 S.Ct. 769, 54 L.Ed.2d 783 (1978); Arneil v. Ramsey, 550 F.2d 774, 783 (CA2 1977).

3. Petitioner also argues that American Pipe does not apply in Title VII actions, because the time limit contained in § 706(f)(1), 42 U.S.C. § 2000e–5(f)(1) [42 U.S.C.A. § 2000e–5(f)(1)], is jurisdictional and may not be tolled. This argument is foreclosed by the Court's decisions in Zipes v. Trans World Airlines, Inc., 455 U.S. 385, 398, 102 S.Ct. 1127, 1135, 71 L.Ed.2d 234 (1982), and Mohasco Corp. v. Silver, 447 U.S. 807, 811, 100 S.Ct. 2486, 2489 and n. 9, 65 L.Ed.2d 532 (1980).

of the statute of limitations would they be able to ensure that their rights would not be lost in the event that class certification was denied. Much the same inefficiencies would ensue if American Pipe's tolling rule were limited to permitting putative class members to intervene after the denial of class certification. There are may reasons why a class member, after the denial of class certification, might prefer to bring an individual suit rather than intervene. The forum in which the class action is pending might be an inconvenient one, for example, or the class member might not wish to share control over the litigation with other plaintiffs once the economies of a class action were no longer available. Moreover, permission to intervene might be refused for reasons wholly unrelated to the merits of the claims.[4] A putative class member who fears that class certification may be denied would have every incentive to file a separate action prior to the expiration of his own period of limitations. The result would be a needless multiplicity of actions—precisely the situation that Federal Rule of Civil Procedure 23 and the tolling rule of American Pipe were designed to avoid.

B

Failure to apply American Pipe to class members filing separate actions also would be inconsistent with the Court's reliance on American Pipe in Eisen v. Carlisle & Jacquelin, 417 U.S. 156, 94 S.Ct. 2140, 40 L.Ed.2d 732 (1974). In Eisen, the Court held that Rule 23(c)(2) required individual notice to absent class members, so that each class member could decide whether to "opt out" of the class and thereby preserve his right to pursue his own lawsuit. The named plaintiff in Eisen argued that such notice would be fruitless because the statute of limitations had long since run on the claims of absent class members. This argument, said the Court, was "disposed of by our recent decision in American Pipe * * * which established that commencement of a class action tolls the applicable statute of limitations as to all members of the class."

If American Pipe's tolling rule applies only to a, this reference to American Pipe is misplaced and makes no sense. Eisen's notice requirement was intended to inform the class member that he could "preserve his opportunity to press his claim *separately*" by opting out of the class. But a class member would be unable to "press his claim separately" if the limitations period had expired while the class action was pending. The Eisen Court recognized this difficulty, but concluded

---

4. Putative class members frequently are not entitled to intervene as of right under Fed. Rule Civ. Proc. 24(a), and permissive intervention under Fed. Rule Civ. Proc. 24(b) may be denied in the discretion of the District Court. American Pipe, 414 U.S. at 559–560, 94 S.Ct. at 769; id., at 562, 94 S.Ct. at 770 (concurring opinion); see Railroad Trainmen v. Baltimore & Ohio R. Co., 331 U.S. 519, 524–525, 67 S.Ct. 1387, 1389–1390, 91 L.Ed. 1646 (1947). In exer- cising its discretion the District Court considers "whether the intervention will unduly delay or prejudice the adjudication of the rights of the original parties," Fed. Rule Civ. Proc. 24(b), and a court could conclude that undue delay or prejudice would result if many class members were brought in as plaintiffs upon the denial of class certification. Thus, permissive intervention well may be an uncertain prospect for members of a proposed class.

that the right to opt out and press a separate claim remained meaningful because the filing of the class action tolled the statute of limitations under the rule of American Pipe. If American Pipe were limited to a, it would not serve the purpose assigned to it by Eisen; no class member would opt out simply to intervene. Thus, the Eisen Court necessarily read American Pipe as we read it today, to apply to class members who choose to file separate suits.[5]

C

The Court noted in American Pipe that a tolling rule for class actions is not inconsistent with the purposes served by statutes of limitations. Limitations periods are intended to put defendants on notice of adverse claims and to prevent plaintiffs from sleeping on their rights, but these ends are met when a class action is commenced. Class members who do not file suit while the class action is pending cannot be accused of sleeping on their rights; Rule 23 both permits and encourages class members to rely on the named plaintiffs to press their claims. And a class complaint "notifies the defendants not only of the substantive claims being brought against them, but also of the number and generic identities of the potential plaintiffs who may participate in the judgment." The defendant will be aware of the need to preserve evidence and witnesses respecting the claims of all the members of the class. Tolling the statute of limitations thus creates no potential for unfair surprise, regardless of the method class members choose to enforce their rights upon denial of class certification.

Restricting the rule of American Pipe to a might reduce the number of individual lawsuits filed against a particular defendant but, as discussed above, this decrease in litigation would be counterbalanced by an increase in protective filings in all class actions. Moreover, although a defendant may prefer not to defend against multiple actions in multiple forums once a class has been decertified, this is not an interest that statutes of limitations are designed to protect. Other avenues exist by which the burdens of multiple lawsuits may be avoided; the defendant may seek consolidation in appropriate cases, see Fed. Rule Civ. Proc. 42(a); 28 U.S.C. § 1404[28 U.S.C.A. § 1404] (change

5. Several members of the Court have indicated that American Pipe's tolling rule can apply to class members who file individual suits, as well as to those who seek to intervene. See Johnson v. Railway Express Agency, Inc., 421 U.S. 454, 474–475, 95 S.Ct. 1716, 1727, 44 L.Ed.2d 295 (1975) (Marshall, J., joined by Douglas and Brennan, JJ., concurring in part and dissenting in part) ("In American Pipe we held that initiation of a timely class action tolled the running of the limitation period as to individual members of the class, enabling them to institute separate actions after the District Court found class action an inappropriate mechanism for the litigation"); United Airlines, Inc. v. McDonald, 432 U.S. 385, 402, 97 S.Ct. 2464, 2474, 53 L.Ed.2d 423 (1977) (Powell, J., joined by The Chief Justice and White, J., dissenting) ("Under American Pipe, the filing of a class action complaint tolls the statute of limitations until the District Court makes a decision regarding class status. If class status is denied, * * * the statute of limitations begins to run again as to class members excluded from the class. In order to protect their rights, such individuals must seek to intervene in the individual action (or possibly file an action of their own) before the time remaining in the limitations period expires").

of venue), and multidistrict proceedings may be available if suits have
been brought in different jurisdictions, see 28 U.S.C. § 1407[28 U.S.C.A.
§ 1407].[6]

III

We conclude, as did the Court in American Pipe, that "the commencement of a class action suspends the applicable statute of limitations as to all asserted members of the class who would have been
parties had the suit been permitted to continue as a class action."
Once the statute of limitations has been tolled, it remains tolled for all
members of the putative class until class certification is denied. At
that point, class members may choose to file their own suits or to
intervene as plaintiffs in the pending action.

In this case, respondent clearly would have been a party in Pendleton if that suit had been permitted to continue as a class action. The
filing of the Pendleton action thus tolled the statute of limitations for
respondent and other members of the Pendleton class. Since respondent did not receive his Notice of Right to Sue until after the Pendleton
action was filed, he retained a full 90 days in which to bring suit after
class certification was denied. Respondent's suit was thus timely filed.

The judgment of the Court of Appeals is affirmed.

SEPARATE OPINION

JUSTICE POWELL, with whom JUSTICE REHNQUIST and JUSTICE O'CONNOR
join, concurring.

I join the Court's opinion. It seems important to reiterate the view
expressed by Justice Blackmun in American Pipe & Constr. Co. v. Utah,
414 U.S. 538, 94 S.Ct. 756, 38 L.Ed.2d 713 (1974). He wrote that our
decision "must not be regarded as encouragement to lawyers in a case
of this kind to frame their pleadings as a class action, intentionally, to
attract and save members of the purported class who have slept on
their rights." The tolling rule of American Pipe is a generous one,
inviting abuse. It preserves for class members a range of options
pending a decision on class certification. The rule should not be read,
however, as leaving a plaintiff free to raise different or peripheral
claims following denial of class status.

In American Pipe we noted that a class suit "notifies the defendants not only of the substantive claims being brought against them,
but also of the number and generic identities of the potential plaintiffs
who participate in the judgment. Within the period set by the statute
of limitations, the defendants have the essential information necessary
to determine both the subject matter and size of the prospective
litigation." When thus notified, the defendant normally is not preju-

---

6. Petitioner's complaints about the
burden of defending multiple suits ring
particularly hollow in this case, since petitioner opposed respondent's efforts to consolidate his action with Pendleton.

diced by tolling of the statute of limitations. It is important to make certain, however, that American Pipe is not abused by the assertion of claims that differ from those raised in the original class suit. As Justice Blackmun noted, a district court should deny intervention under Rule 24(b) to "preserve a defendant whole against prejudice arising from claims for which he has received no prior notice." Similarly, when a plaintiff invokes American Pipe in support of a separate lawsuit, the district court should take care to ensure that the suit raises claims that "concern the same evidence, memories, and witnesses as the subject matter of the original class suit," so that "the defendant will not be prejudiced." Ibid. Claims as to which the defendant was not fairly placed on notice by the class suit are not protected under American Pipe and are barred by the statute of limitations.

In this case, it is undisputed that the Pendleton class suit notified petitioner of respondent's claims. The statute of limitations therefore was tolled under American Pipe as to those claims.

NOTES AND PROBLEMS FOR DISCUSSION

1. What if Parker had received his right-to-sue letter *before* the class action was filed? Would the 90–day period have been merely suspended during the pendency of the action or would the period have begun to run anew when class certification was denied? In AMERICAN PIPE & CONSTRUCTION CO. v. UTAH, the anti-trust action discussed in *Crown, Cork & Seal,* the Court held that the filing of class action suspended the running of the limitation period. In that case the controlling statute of limitations was established by the Clayton Act which also provided for suspension when the period was tolled. *American Pipe* did not establish a general rule on tolling applicable to all federal actions. In CHARDON v. FUMERO SOTO, 462 U.S. 650, 103 S.Ct. 2611, 77 L.Ed.2d 74 (1983), a suit filed under 42 U.S.C. § 1983, the Court held that where federal law is silent, state law must be looked to for both the applicable statute of limitations and to determine the tolling effect of a class action unless they are "inconsistent with the Constitution and laws of the United States." Under Puerto Rican law applicable in *Chardon,* the statute of limitations began to run anew when tolling ceases. Unlike § 1983, Title VII provides the applicable limitations period, but does not provide for the "tolling effect" of a class action. What rule should apply?

2. How similar must the claims raised in the original class action be to those in the subsequent suit for the tolling doctrine to apply? In Davis v. Bethlehem Steel Corp., et al., 769 F.2d 210 (4th Cir.), cert. denied, 474 U.S. 1021, 106 S.Ct. 573, 88 L.Ed.2d 557 (1985), the Court of Appeals held that a class action filed in 1971 containing a "laundry list" of pattern and practice allegations was not specific enough to put the defendants on notice of the discriminatory acts alleged in a 1982 complaint, thus precluding the application of *Crown, Cork & Seal.* Should the rule that the statute of limitations is tolled for all class members until class certification is denied or until they opt out of the class be limited to those members who can prove reliance on the pendency of the class action? See, Tosti v. City of Los Angeles, 754 F.2d 1485 (9th Cir.1985).

3. Under *Crown, Cork & Seal,* the filing of a class action tolls the statutes of limitation for individual actions by putative class members. But does the

pendency of a class action also toll the limitation period *for the filing of other class actions* by putative class members?   See, Korwek v. Hunt, 827 F.2d 874, 879 (2d Cir.1987) (Court in *Crown, Cork & Seal* certainly did not intend to afford plaintiffs the opportunity to argue and reargue the question of class certification by filing of repetitive complaints);   Andrews v. Orr, 851 F.2d 146 (6th Cir.1988) (pendency of previously filed class action does not toll limitation period for additional class actions by putative members of originally asserted class).

SECTION D. CERTIFICATION UNDER RULE 23(B)(2) AND 23(B)(3): NOTICE TO THE CLASS AND THE RIGHT TO OPT OUT

Once class certification is requested and the court finds that the mandatory requirements of Rule 23(a) are satisfied, it must determine whether the proposed class can be maintained under subsection (b)(1), (b)(2) or (b)(3) of the rule.[1]   Because of its language, subsection (b)(1) is seldom utilized and, as a practical matter, the choice in almost all class litigation is between certification under (b)(2) or (b)(3).

A(b)(2) class is permitted when the defendant has "acted or refused to act on grounds generally applicable to the class, thereby making appropriate final injunctive relief or corresponding declaratory relief with respect to the class as a whole."   The drafters of the rule intended (b)(2) to be applicable to actions involving very cohesive classes when injunctive relief applicable to all class members was sought.   The civil rights class action challenging racial discrimination which affected all class members in the same way typified the kind of case to which (b)(2) was to be applicable.   See, Advisory Committee's Note to Proposed Amendments to Rule 23, 39 F.R.D. 69, 102 (1966).   Rule 23(b)(3) was intended to apply to a more heterogeneous class when questions of law or fact common to the class predominate over questions affecting only individual members.   It was contemplated that (b)(3) certification would be appropriate when monetary relief was requested on behalf of class members who had suffered similar injuries.   Advisory Committee Note, supra, at 103.

Under Rule 23, a final judgment in a class action, regardless of subsection utilized for certification, is binding on all members of the

---

1. Rule 23(b)(1) emphasizes the effect individual adjudications of the claims of putative class members might have on defendants and other class members and was apparently designed to encompass cases where separate actions by individual members of the class would be dismissed for failure to join indispensable parties.   See, Homburger, State Class Actions and the Federal Rules, 71 Colum.L.Rev. 609, 633 (1971).   Thus, if the court determines that individual lawsuits by or against class members do not pose a threat of inconsistent adjudications that might cause hardship on the opposing party or that separate proceedings would not prejudice the other class members, the action cannot be maintained as a class action unless it qualifies under another subsection of 23(b).   Because few actions fall within the requirements of (b)(1) or, if they do, overlap with one of the other subsections, there is little litigation concerning the (b)(1) classes.   See, 7A Wright & Miller, Federal Practice and Procedure, § 1772, p. 5.

class. The major difference between certification under (b)(2) and (b)(3) lies in the notice and opt out provisions of section (c) of the rule. Because a(b)(2) action does not require notice to the class, a final judgment can be entered binding class members without any notice or opportunity to participate in or to be excluded from the proceeding. In a(b)(3) action, however, Rule 23(c)(2) requires that "the best notice practicable under the circumstances" be directed to class members at the time of certification, and that such members be allowed to exclude themselves from the action (and thus not be bound by any decision) with a timely notice to the court. The rule's authors believed that, because of differences that might exist between class members in the (b)(3) class, particularly where personal monetary relief was sought for class members, individual members might wish to pursue their personal claims in their own suits. Such class members were thus entitled to notice and the opportunity to opt out of the class action at the certification stage. Advisory Committee Note, *supra*, at 104–05. By contrast, the (b)(2) class was viewed as so unified in interest as to make notice and the opt out provision unnecessary because any injunctive relief granted would necessarily affect all class members identically whether they remained members of the class or not. See, Katz v. Carte Blanche Corp., 496 F.2d 747, 759 (3d Cir.), cert. denied, 419 U.S. 885, 95 S.Ct. 152, 42 L.Ed.2d 125 (1974); Advisory Committee Note, *supra*, at 104–05.

The Title VII class action has posed problems under Rule 23(b) because typically both broad injunctive relief and individual monetary awards in the form of back pay are requested for the class. Back pay, which will normally be in different amounts for individual class members depending on their length of employment, job classification and personal employment history, resembles the kind of relief thought by the drafters to be peculiarly appropriate for (b)(3) treatment. On the other hand, injunctive relief, either to prohibit class-wide discrimination in the future or as a remedy for past wrongs, is the kind of relief the (b)(2) class was designed to facilitate. The question of which subsection to utilize for certification is far from academic because of the Supreme Court's ruling in EISEN v. CARLISLE & JACQUELIN, 417 U.S. 156, 94 S.Ct. 2140, 40 L.Ed.2d 732 (1974), that in (b)(3) actions the plaintiff must bear all the costs of notice. The defendant in a class action thus has a strong incentive to see the action certified under (b)(3): where the class is large and geographically spread out, the cost of the notice required by (c)(2) may as a practical matter kill the action because of the plaintiff's inability to bear the expense. The employer-defendant will also benefit from class members opting out. Experience has shown that few if any employees will opt out because they want to bring individual cases and, if a sufficient number opt out, the class itself can fail for lack of numerosity.

The problem of designating which subsection is applicable in an employment case is illustrated by Wetzel v. Liberty Mutual Insurance Co., 508 F.2d 239 (3d Cir.), cert. denied, 421 U.S. 1011, 95 S.Ct. 2415, 44

L.Ed.2d 679 (1975) where plaintiffs sought certification of a nation-wide class of female employees in several job classifications. During the course of the litigation, the employer made changes in its hiring and promotional practices obviating the need for injunctive relief. On appeal, the employer argued that the case should have been certified as a(b)(3) action and notice required because, by the time the case reached judgment, the class no longer satisfied the requirements of 23(b)(2). The Third Circuit affirmed the district court's (b)(2) certification.

> [A] Title VII suit against discriminatory hiring and promotion is necessarily a suit to end discrimination because of a common class characteristic, in this case sex. * * * The conduct of the employer is actionable 'on grounds generally applicable to the class,' and the relief sought is 'relief with respect to the class as a whole.' Thus a Title VII action is particularly fit for (b)(2) treatment, and the drafters of Rule 23 specifically contemplated that suits against discriminatory hiring and promotion policies would be appropriately maintained under (b)(2). * * * Since a Title VII suit is essentially equitable in nature, it cannot be characterized as one seeking exclusively or predominantly money damages.

508 F.2d at 250–51. The Court also noted that the language of (b)(2) did not limit use of the subsection only to those cases where final injunctive relief was necessary, but merely required that the type of conduct by the party opposing the class be the kind that is subject to equitable relief.

> Liberty Mutual's policies at the time these charges were made were such that final injunctive relief was appropriate. This satisfies the language of the rule.

Ibid. It is far from clear that the drafters of Rule 23 contemplated anything like the modern Title VII class action when they devised (b)(2), but most courts have agreed with the Third Circuit that Title VII class actions should be certified under (b)(2) where both monetary and injunctive relief is sought. See generally, Rutherglen, Notice, Scope and Preclusion in Title VII Class Actions, 69 Va.L.Rev 11, 23 (1983). The Fifth Circuit has held that such "hybrid" class actions fall within the ambit of (b)(2) because the "demand for back pay is not in the nature of a claim for damages, but rather is an integral part of the statutory equitable remedy, to be determined through the exercise of the courts discretion." Johnson v. Georgia Highway Express, Inc., 417 F.2d 1122, 1125 (5th Cir.1969). See also, Pettway v. American Cast Iron Pipe Co., 494 F.2d 211, 256–57 (5th Cir.1974), cert. denied, 439 U.S. 1115, 99 S.Ct. 1020, 59 L.Ed.2d 74 (1979). (*Pettway III*).[2]

---

2. The civil rights cases cited in the Advisory Committee Note to the proposed revisions of Rule 23 involved challenges to overt, state-imposed policies of racial segregation in which all members of the class were necessarily affected by the discriminatory practices in the same way. Advisory Committee Note, *supra*, at 102. See, Strickler, Protecting the Class: The Search For the Adequate Representative in Class Action Litigation, 34 De Paul L. Rev. 73, 114 (1984);

Though not mandatory in a(b)(2) action, notice to the class at the time of certification may be ordered at the district court's discretion under Rule 23(d)(2).[3] See, Clark v. American Marine Corp., 297 F.Supp. 1305 (E.D.La.1969); Walthall v. Blue Shield of California, 16 FEP Cases 625 (N.D.Cal.1977). The notice may be issued for purely informational purposes, Avagliano v. Sumitomo Shoji America, Inc., 614 F.Supp. 1397 (S.D.N.Y. 1985), or to encourage intervention, Woods v. New York Life Insurance Co., 686 F.2d 578 (7th Cir.1982). The courts are divided over whether it is within the district court's discretion, at least at the certification stage, to allow class members to opt out of a(b)(2) action. Compare, Dosier v. Miami Valley Broadcasting Corp., 656 F.2d 1295, 1299 (9th Cir.1981); Laskey v. International Union, United Automotive, Aerospace & Agricultural Implement Workers of America, 638 F.2d 954, 956 (6th Cir.1981); Fowler v. Birmingham News Co., 608 F.2d 1055, 1058 (5th Cir.1979); Kincade v. General Tire & Rubber Co., 635 F.2d 501, 507 (5th Cir.1981).

Title VII class actions are usually tried in two stages. Liability is litigated first. If the court finds class-wide liability, the relief to which class members are entitled, including back pay, is determined in the second stage. See *infra*, Chapter 7D. Because stage two, with its individualized relief determinations, is functionally similar to the type of litigation for which (b)(3) classes (common issues of fact and law) were designed, some courts have held that (b)(2) class members are entitled to notice and the right to opt out (or to pursue their individual monetary claims in stage two with their own attorneys) after liability is established in stage one. Holmes v. Continental Can Co., 706 F.2d 1144, 1155 (11th Cir.1983); Officers for Justice v. Civil Service Commission, 688 F.2d 615, 634–35 (9th Cir.1982), cert. denied, 459 U.S. 1217, 103 S.Ct. 1219, 75 L.Ed.2d 456 (1983). The Eleventh Circuit has held that, until the monetary relief stage in a(b)(2) class action brought under Title VII is reached, opting out is always inappropriate. Cox v. American Cast Iron Pipe Co., 784 F.2d 1546, 1554 (11th Cir.), cert. denied, 479 U.S. 883, 107 S.Ct. 274, 93 L.Ed.2d 250 (1986). In *Cox* the district court allowed the employer to send notices and opt out questionnaires to the previously certified class of employees. On the basis of the returns (roughly half of the potential class opted out), the court decertified the class for lack of numerosity. The Court of Appeals reversed.

Such a procedure would only tend to promote what was actually accomplished here—the improper use of a court-approved opt-out

---

3. Rule 23(d) provides in part:

ORDERS IN CONDUCT OF CLASS ACTIONS. In the conduct of actions to which this rule applies, the court may make appropriate orders: ... (2) requiring, for the protection of the members of the class or otherwise for the fair conduct of the action, that notice be given in such manner as the court may direct to some or all of the members of any step in the action, or of the proposed extent of the judgment, or of the opportunity of members to signify whether they consider the representation fair and adequate, to intervene and present claims or defenses, or otherwise to come into the action; * * *

procedure designed to force class members to take a stand against their employers in order to stay in a controversial lawsuit. To authorize such a procedure was abuse of discretion.

784 F.2d at 1554–55. The problem of determining class-wide relief at stage two is discussed *infra,* in Chapter 7D.

When a class action is settled, regardless of what type of class it is, Rule 23(e) requires notice to the class members of the terms of the settlement and judicial approval of the agreement before it is implemented. Rule 23(e) notice does not serve the same function as notice of an opt out right at the time of certification. Most courts have held that in a(b)(2) action, class members have no automatic right to opt out of the settlement because they disagree with its terms. Kincade v. General Tire and Rubber Co., *supra,* 635 F.2d at 507; Pettway v. American Cast Iron Pipe Co., 576 F.2d 1157 (5th Cir.1978) (*Pettway IV*), cert. denied, 439 U.S. 1115, 99 S.Ct. 1020, 59 L.Ed.2d 74 (1979). The notice of the proposed settlement is intended to alert class members whose rights will be determined by the agreement to its terms and allow them to oppose judicial approval. See, Parker v. Anderson, 667 F.2d 1204 (5th Cir.1982), cert. denied, 459 U.S. 828, 103 S.Ct. 63, 74 L.Ed.2d 65 (1982). In Holmes v. Continental Can Co., supra, however, the court held that it was an abuse of discretion for the trial judge not to allow class members to opt out of a settlement they opposed where their individual monetary claims were not typical of those made by other class members and the settlement provided the objectors with relatively little relief.[4] Where a class action is settled, can there be any reason for *not* allowing class members who are not satisfied with the settlement terms from opting out and pursuing their claims in individual suits?

SECTION E. THE PRECLUSIVE EFFECT OF THE CLASS ACTION JUDGMENT ON THE CLAIMS OF INDIVIDUAL CLASS MEMBERS

In Johnson v. Georgia Highway Express, Inc., 417 F.2d 1122 (5th Cir. 1969), a case discussed in the introduction to this chapter, Judge Godbold cautioned that:

> The broad brush approach of some of the Title VII cases is in sharp contrast to the diligence with which in other areas we carefully protect those whose rights may be affected by litigation.... But when the problem is multiplied many-fold [by a class action], counsel, and at times the courts, are moving blithely ahead tacitly assuming all will be well for surely the plaintiff will win and manna will fall on all members of the class. It is not quite that easy.

---

4. The Court of Appeals was influenced by the fact that approximately one half of a relatively small lump-sum back pay award was to be divided among the eight named plaintiffs with the remainder to be distributed to 118 members of the class.

417 F.2d at 1127 (Godbold, J., concurring). As a general rule, a judgment entered in a properly certified class action binds, by way of res judicata or collateral estoppel, all class members on the issues decided in the case. Thus a class member who will benefit by a finding of class-wide discrimination will also be bound by a decision adverse to the class in the same way as if he had been a named plaintiff.

But a finding that class-wide discrimination did not occur, does not mean that the employer has not discriminated against one or more individuals who are class members. In COOPER v. FEDERAL RE-SERVE BANK OF RICHMOND, 467 U.S. 867, 104 S.Ct. 2794, 81 L.Ed.2d 718 (1984), a properly certified (b)(2) action on behalf of former and current employees of the bank, the plaintiffs tried but failed to prove a pattern and practice of racial discrimination in promotions. Thereafter, several class members filed separate actions, each alleging that he had been denied promotions because of race. The Bank moved to dismiss the complaints on the ground that each of the plaintiffs was a member of the class certified in the prior action and that they were bound by the determination that no class-wide discrimination had occurred. The district court denied the motions to dismiss but certified its order for an interlocutory appeal under 28 U.S.C. § 1292(b). The Fourth Circuit reversed, holding that under the doctrine of res judicata the judgment in the class action precluded the individual class members from maintaining their claims. The Supreme Court in turn reversed the Court of Appeals holding that it had erred in the preclusive effect accorded the class action judgment.

> That judgment (1) bars the class members from bringing another class action against the Bank alleging a pattern or practice of discrimination for the relevant time period and (2) precludes the class members in any other litigation with the Bank from relitigat-ing the question whether the Bank engaged in a pattern and practice of discrimination against black employees during the relevant time period. The judgment is not, however, dispositive of the individual claims the * * * petitioners have alleged in their separate action. Assuming they establish a prima facie case of discrimination under *McDonnell Douglas,* the Bank will be required to articulate a legitimate reason for each of the challenged decisions, and if it meets that burden, the ultimate questions regarding motivation in their individual cases will be resolved by the District Court.

467 U.S. at 880, 104 S.Ct. at 2802. To rule otherwise the Court stated "would be tantamount to requiring that every member of the class be permitted to intervene [in the class action] to litigate the merits of his individual claim" and would defeat the purpose of the class device as a procedure for the efficient adjudication of common questions of law or fact. *Ibid.*

Left somewhat unsettled by *Cooper* is the effect of the class ruling on the evidence in individual cases. The Court rather cryptically stated that the determination in the class action that the Bank had not engaged in a general pattern of discrimination "would be relevant on the issue of pretext."   467 U.S. at 880, 104 S.Ct. at 2802.   Will *Cooper* preclude the plaintiff from introducing evidence of discrimination against other employees, who were also members of the class, as circumstantial evidence of discrimination against him?   At what point would the use of such evidence constitute relitigation of the pattern and practice issue?

If a class member is allowed to opt out of the class and the court subsequently finds class-wide discrimination, of what use is that determination to the claimant in his individual case?   Consider, Parklane Hosiery Co. v. Shore, 439 U.S. 322, 99 S.Ct. 645, 58 L.Ed.2d 552 (1979).

An agreement settling a class action which has been judicially approved under Rule 23(e) will ordinarily bar a class member who is dissatisfied with the settlement from pursuing an individual claim encompassed within the class action.   What individual claims will be encompassed within the class action will not always be easy to determine.   In King v. South Central Bell Telephone and Telegraph Co., 790 F.2d 524 (6th Cir.1986), the plaintiff was forced to take maternity leave.   Under the company's policy a person taking maternity leave, unlike leave resulting from other temporary disabilities, did not continue to acquire seniority while on leave and was not assured of being returned to her prior position.   When King returned, she was assigned to a lower paying job.   While her EEOC charge was pending, King received notice of the settlement of a class action filed on behalf of female employees who had taken maternity leave and had been denied reinstatement or had been delayed in returning to work.   King responded to the notice by filing a claim for backpay for an 8–day delay between her request to return to work from leave and her actual return.   She included with the claim a statement that the settlement did not satisfy her claim for lost wages resulting from her being placed in a lower job and her assertion that she did not wish to waive her claim by participating in the settlement.   King subsequently filed her own case.   The district court granted summary judgment to the employer on *res judicata* grounds.   Despite the fact that the settlement notice was ambiguous as to the scope of claims to which the settlement applied, the Sixth Circuit affirmed.   "Even if it can be argued that the notice was somewhat ambiguous, King could not opt out because the action (23(b)(2)) did not include that privilege.   The most she could do was object to the decree and she did."   790 F.2d at 530.   One member of the panel dissented on the ground that, because of the nature of the monetary claims, the action should have been certified as a(b)(3) action and class members like King should have been given an opportunity to opt out.   What, if anything, could King have done to protect her ability to litigate her individual claim?

Should a class member who has opposed the terms of a class settlement be allowed to appeal *on behalf of the class* from the district court's approval of the settlement? See, Cotton v. United States Pipe & Foundry Co., 856 F.2d 158 (11th Cir.1988) (appeal from approval of consent decree is an appeal only for individuals who have no standing to appeal on behalf of the class in the absence of new certification).

SECTION F. APPEALABILITY OF CLASS CERTIFICATION DETERMINATIONS

In GARDNER v. WESTINGHOUSE BROADCASTING CO., 437 U.S. 478, 98 S.Ct. 2451, 57 L.Ed.2d 364 (1978), the Supreme Court held that the denial of class certification does not constitute a refusal to grant injunctive relief within the meaning of 28 U.S.C. § 1292(a) and thus cannot be reviewed by an interlocutory appeal. The Court expressly limited its opinion to cases in which the request for class certification was not accompanied by a motion for preliminary injunction. 437 U.S. at 479, n.3, 98 S.Ct. at 2453, n.3. *Gardner* means that, in most employment discrimination class actions, review of a denial of class certification may be obtained only after a determination on the merits of the plaintiffs' individual case—i.e., a "final" decision. But if, as suggested in EAST TEXAS MOTOR FREIGHT v. RODRIQUEZ, *supra,* the scope of review of a class denial after trial is in part determined by the decision on the merits of the plaintiff's claim, may full review of the class issue always be obtained? The Court in *Gardner* implied that full review of a class denial could be obtained through post-judgment intervention by putative class members. United Airlines, Inc. v. McDonald, 432 U.S. 385, 97 S.Ct. 2464, 53 L.Ed.2d 423 (1977). But in light of the practical difficulty of such would-be class members learning of the action, retaining counsel and taking the necessary steps to intervene and appeal within the time allowed by the Federal Rules, is that mechanism for review likely to be used?

SECTION G. CLASS ACTIONS AND THE E.E.O.C.

Section 706(c) of Title VII authorizes the EEOC, after unlawful employment practice charges against a private employer are filed with it and it is unable to secure conciliation, to bring a civil action against the employer seeking all relief authorized by the Act. Chapter 4, *supra.* In GENERAL TELEPHONE CO. OF THE NORTHWEST, INC. v. EEOC, 446 U.S. 318, 100 S.Ct. 1698, 64 L.Ed.2d 319 (1980), the Supreme Court resolved a conflict among the circuits by holding that the EEOC may seek class-wide relief without being certified as a class representative and without complying with the requirements of Rule 23(a) and (b). The Court concluded that to force compliance by the EEOC with Rule 23 requirements would be contrary to the purpose of Section 706, under which the Commission was to act not merely as a representative of private interests, but to vindicate public policy. Moreover, some actions authorized by Section 706 would be foreclosed by requiring EEOC compliance with Rule 23 requirements, such as numerosity or typicality. The Court also noted that it would not be consistent with the remedial purpose of Title VII to bind all "class" members with discrimination grievances against an employer by the relief obtained by an EEOC judgment or settlement against the employer, especially in view of the possible differences between the public and private interests involved.

Chapter 7

REMEDIES

SECTION A. MONETARY RELIEF

ALBEMARLE PAPER CO. v. MOODY

Supreme Court of the United States, 1975.
422 U.S. 405, 95 S.Ct. 2362, 45 L.Ed.2d 280.

MR. JUSTICE STEWART delivered the opinion of the Court.

These consolidated cases raise two important questions under Title VII of the Civil Rights Act of 1964: First: When employees or applicants for employment have lost the opportunity to earn wages because an employer has engaged in an unlawful discriminatory employment practice, what standards should a federal district court follow in deciding whether to award or deny backpay?

* * *

I

The respondents—plaintiffs in the District Court—are a certified class of present and former Negro employees at a paper mill in Roanoke Rapids, N.C.; the petitioners—defendants in the District Court—are the plant's owner, the Albemarle Paper Co., and the plant employees' labor union, Halifax Local No. 425. In August 1966, after filing a complaint with the Equal Employment Opportunity Commission (EEOC), and receiving notice of their right to sue, the respondents brought a class action in the United States District Court for the Eastern District of North Carolina, asking permanent injunctive relief against "any policy, practice, custom or usage" at the plant that violated Title VII. The respondents assured the court that the suit involved no claim for any monetary awards on a class basis, but in June 1970, after several years of discovery, the respondents moved to add a class demand for backpay. The court ruled that this issue would be considered at trial.

At the trial, in July and August 1971, the major issues were the plant's seniority system, its program of employment testing, and the question of backpay. In its opinion of November 9, 1971, the court found that the petitioners had "strictly segregated" the plant's departmental "lines of progression" prior to January 1, 1964, reserving the higher paying and more skilled lines for whites. The "racial identifiability" of whole lines of progression persisted until 1968, when the lines were reorganized under a new collective-bargaining agreement. The court found, however, that this reorganization left Negro employees " 'locked' in the lower paying job classifications." The formerly "Negro" lines of progression had been merely tacked on to the bottom of the formerly "white" lines, and promotions, demotions, and layoffs continued to be governed—where skills were "relatively equal"—by a system of "job seniority." Because of the plant's previous history of overt segregation, only whites had seniority in the higher job categories. Accordingly, the court ordered the petitioners to implement a system of "plantwide" seniority.

The court refused, however, to award backpay to the plaintiff class for losses suffered under the "job seniority" program.[3] The court explained:

> "In the instant case there was no evidence of bad faith non-compliance with the Act. It appears that the company as early as 1964 began active recruitment of blacks for its Maintenance Apprentice Program. Certain lines of progression were merged on its own initiative, and as judicial decisions expanded the then existing interpretations of the Act, the defendants took steps to correct the abuses without delay. . . .

> "In addition, an award of back pay is an equitable remedy. . . . The plaintiffs' claim for back pay was filed nearly five years after the institution of this action. It was not prayed for in the pleadings. Although neither party can be charged with deliberate dilatory tactics in bringing this cause to trial, it is apparent that the defendants would be substantially prejudiced by the granting of such affirmative relief. The defendants might have chosen to exercise unusual zeal in having this court determine their rights at an earlier date had they known that back pay would be at issue."

* * *

II

Whether a particular member of the plaintiff class should have been awarded any backpay and, if so, how much, are questions not involved in this review. The equities of individual cases were never reached. Though at least some of the members of the plaintiff class obviously suffered a loss of wage opportunities on account of Albemarle's unlawfully discriminatory system of job seniority, the District Court decided that *no* backpay should be awarded to *anyone* in the class. The court declined to make such an award on two stated grounds: the lack of "evidence of bad faith non-compliance with the Act," and the fact that "the defendants would be substantially prejudiced" by an award of backpay that was demanded contrary to an earlier representation and late in the progress of the litigation. Rely-

3. Under Title VII backpay liability exists only for practices occurring after the effective date of the Act, July 2, 1965, and accrues only from a date two years prior to the filing of a charge with the EEOC. See 42 U.S.C. § 2000e–5 (g) (1970 ed., Supp. III). Thus no award was possible with regard to the plant's pre–1964 policy of "strict segregation."

ing directly on Newman v. Piggie Park Enterprises, 390 U.S. 400, 88 S.Ct. 964, 19 L.Ed.2d 1263 (1968), the Court of Appeals reversed, holding that backpay could be denied only in "special circumstances." The petitioners argue that the Court of Appeals was in error—that a district court has virtually unfettered discretion to award or deny backpay, and that there was no abuse of that discretion here.[8]

Piggie Park Enterprises, supra, is not directly in point. The Court held there that attorneys' fees should "ordinarily" be awarded—i.e., in all but "special circumstances"—to plaintiffs successful in obtaining injunctions against discrimination in public accommodations, under Title II of the Civil Rights Act of 1964. While the Act appears to leave Title II fee awards to the district court's discretion, 42 U.S.C. § 2000a–3(b), the court determined that the great public interest in having injunctive actions brought could be vindicated only if successful plaintiffs, acting as "private attorneys general," were awarded attorneys' fees in all but very unusual circumstances. There is, of course, an equally strong public interest in having injunctive actions brought under Title VII, to eradicate discriminatory employment practices. But this interest can be vindicated by applying the *Piggie Park* standard to the *attorneys' fees* provision of Title VII, 42 U.S.C. § 2000e–5(k), see Northcross v. Memphis Board of Education, 412 U.S. 427, 428, 93 S.Ct. 2201, 2202, 37 L.Ed.2d 48 (1973). For guidance as to the granting and denial of *backpay*, one must, therefore, look elsewhere.

The petitioners contend that the statutory scheme provides no guidance, beyond indicating that backpay awards are within the district court's discretion. We disagree. It is true that backpay is not an

---

8. The petitioners also contend that no backpay can be awarded to those unnamed parties in the plaintiff class who have not themselves filed charges with the EEOC. We reject this contention. The Courts of Appeals that have confronted the issue are unanimous in recognizing that backpay may be awarded on a class basis under Title VII without exhaustion of administrative procedures by the unnamed class members. See, e.g., Rosen v. Public Service Electric & Gas Co., 409 F.2d 775, 780 (CA3 1969), and 477 F.2d 90, 95–96 (CA3 1973); Robinson v. Lorillard Corp., 444 F.2d 791, 802 (CA4 1971); United States v. Georgia Power Co., 474 F.2d 906, 919–921 (CA5 1973); Head v. Timken Roller Bearing Co., supra, at 876; Bowe v. Colgate–Palmolive Co., 416 F.2d 711, 719–721 (CA7 1969); United States v. N. L. Industries, Inc., 479 F.2d 354, 378–379 (CA8 1973). The Congress plainly ratified this construction of the Act in the course of enacting the Equal Employment Opportunity Act of 1972, Pub.L. 92–261, 86 Stat. 103. The House of Representatives passed a bill, H.R. 1746, 92d Cong., 1st Sess., that would have barred, in § 3(e), an award of backpay to any individual who "neither filed a charge [with the EEOC] nor was named in a charge or amendment thereto." But the Senate Committee on Labor and Public Welfare recommended, instead, the re-enactment of the backpay provision without such a limitation, and cited with approval several cases holding that backpay was awardable to class members who had not personally filed, nor been named in, charges to the EEOC, S.Rep. No. 92–415, p. 27 (1971). See also 118 Cong.Rec. 4942 (1972). The Senate passed a bill without the House's limitation, id., at 4944, and the Conference Committee adopted the Senate position. A Section–by–Section Analysis of the Conference Committee's resolution notes that "[a] provision limiting class actions was contained in the House bill and specifically rejected by the Conference Committee," id., at 7168, 7565. The Conference Committee bill was accepted by both Chambers. Id., at 7170, 7573.

automatic or mandatory remedy; like all other remedies under the Act, it is one which the courts "may" invoke.[9] The scheme implicitly recognizes that there may be cases calling for one remedy but not another, and—owing to the structure of the federal judiciary—these choices are, of course, left in the first instance to the district courts. However, such discretionary choices are not left to a court's "inclination, but to its judgment; and its judgment is to be guided by sound legal principles." United States v. Burr, 25 F.Cas. No. 14,692d, pp. 30, 35 (CC Va.1807) (Marshall, C. J.). The power to award backpay was bestowed by Congress, as part of a complex legislative design directed at a historic evil of national proportions. A court must exercise this power "in light of the large objectives of the Act," Hecht Co. v. Bowles, 321 U.S. 321, 331, 64 S.Ct. 587, 592, 88 L.Ed. 754 (1944). That the court's discretion is equitable in nature, see Curtis v. Loether, 415 U.S. 189, 197, 94 S.Ct. 1005, 1010, 39 L.Ed.2d 260 (1974), hardly means that it is unfettered by meaningful standards or shielded from thorough appellate review. In Mitchell v. Robert DeMario Jewelry, 361 U.S. 288, 292, 80 S.Ct. 332, 335, 4 L.Ed.2d 323 (1960), this Court held, in the face of a silent statute, that district courts enjoyed the "historic power of equity" to award lost wages to workmen unlawfully discriminated against under § 17 of the Fair Labor Standards Act of 1938, 52 Stat. 1069, as amended, 29 U.S.C. § 217 (1958 ed). The Court simultaneously noted that "the statutory purposes [leave] little room for the exercise of discretion not to order reimbursement." 361 U.S., at 296, 80 S.Ct. at 337.

It is true that "[e]quity eschews mechanical rules * * * [and] depends on flexibility." Holmberg v. Armbrecht, 327 U.S. 392, 396, 66 S.Ct. 582, 584, 90 L.Ed. 743 (1946). But when Congress invokes the Chancellor's conscience to further transcendent legislative purposes, what is required is the principled application of standards consistent with those purposes and not "equity [which] varies like the Chancellor's

---

9. Title 42 U.S.C. § 2000e–5(g) (1970 ed., Supp. III) provides:

"If the court finds that the respondent has intentionally engaged in or is intentionally engaging in an unlawful employment practice charged in the complaint, the court may enjoin the respondent from engaging in such unlawful employment practice, and order such affirmative action as may be appropriate, which may include, but is not limited to, reinstatement or hiring of employees, with or without back pay (payable by the employer, employment agency, or labor organization, as the case may be, responsible for the unlawful employment practice), or any other equitable relief as the court deems appropriate. Back pay liability shall not accrue from a date more than two years prior to the filing of a charge with the Commission. Interim earnings or amounts earnable with reasonable diligence by the person or persons discriminated against shall operate to reduce the back pay otherwise allowable. No order of the court shall require the admission or reinstatement of an individual as a member of a union, or the hiring, reinstatement, or promotion of an individual as an employee, or the payment to him of any back pay, if such individual was refused admission, suspended, or expelled, or was refused employment or advancement or was suspended or discharged for any reason other than discrimination on account of race, color, religion, sex, or national origin or in violation of section 2000e–3(a) of this title."

foot." [10]   Important national goals would be frustrated by a regime of discretion that "produce[d] different results for breaches of duty in situations that cannot be differentiated in policy." Moragne v. States Marine Lines, 398 U.S. 375, 405, 90 S.Ct. 1772, 1790, 26 L.Ed.2d 339 (1970).

The District Court's decision must therefore be measured against the purposes which inform Title VII. As the Court observed in Griggs v. Duke Power Co., 401 U.S., at 429–430, 91 S.Ct., at 853, the primary objective was a prophylactic one:

> "It was to achieve equality of employment opportunities and remove barriers that have operated in the past to favor an identifiable group of white employees over other employees."

Backpay has an obvious connection with this purpose. If employers faced only the prospect of an injunctive order, they would have little incentive to shun practices of dubious legality. It is the reasonably certain prospect of a backpay award that "provide[s] the spur or catalyst which causes employers and unions to self-examine and to self-evaluate their employment practices and to endeavor to eliminate, so far as possible, the last vestiges of an unfortunate and ignominious page in this country's history." United States v. N. L. Industries, Inc., 8 Cir., 479 F.2d at 354, 379 (CA8 1973).

It is also the purpose of Title VII to make persons whole for injuries suffered on account of unlawful employment discrimination. This is shown by the very fact that Congress took care to arm the courts with full equitable powers. For it is the historic purpose of equity to "secur[e] complete justice," Brown v. Swann, 10 Pet. 497, 503, 9 L.Ed. 508 (1836); see also Porter v. Warner Holding Co., 328 U.S. 395, 397–398, 66 S.Ct. 1086, 1088–1089, 90 L.Ed. 1332 (1946). "[W]here federally protected rights have been invaded, it has been the rule from the beginning that courts will be alert to adjust their remedies so as to grant the necessary relief." Bell v. Hood, 327 U.S. 678, 684, 66 S.Ct. 773, 777, 90 L.Ed. 939 (1946). Title VII deals with legal injuries of an economic character occasioned by racial or other antiminority discrimination. The terms "complete justice" and "necessary relief" have acquired a clear meaning in such circumstances. Where racial discrimination is concerned, "the [district] court has not merely the power but the duty to render a decree which will so far as possible eliminate the discriminatory effects of the past as well as bar like discrimination in the future." Louisiana v. United States, 380 U.S. 145, 154, 85 S.Ct. 817, 822, 13 L.Ed.2d 709 (1965). And where a legal injury is of an economic character,

> "[t]he general rule is, that when a wrong has been done, and the law gives a remedy, the compensation shall be equal to the injury. The latter is the standard by which the former is to be measured.

10.   Eldon, L. C., in Gee v. Pritchard, 2 Swans.   * 403, * 414, 36 Eng.Rep. 670, 674 (1818).

The injured party is to be placed, as near as may be, in the situation he would have occupied if the wrong had not been committed." Wicker v. Hoppock, 6 Wall. 94, 99, 18 L.Ed. 752 (1867).

The "make whole" purpose of Title VII is made evident by the legislative history. The backpay provision was expressly modeled on the backpay provision of the National Labor Relations Act.[11] Under that Act, "[m]aking the workers whole for losses suffered on account of an unfair labor practice is part of the vindication of the public policy which the Board enforces." Phelps Dodge Corp. v. NLRB, 313 U.S. 177, 197, 61 S.Ct. 845, 854, 85 L.Ed. 1271 (1941). See also Nathanson v. NLRB, 344 U.S. 25, 27, 73 S.Ct. 80, 82, 97 L.Ed. 23; NLRB v. J. H. Rutter–Rex Mfg. Co., 396 U.S. 258, 263, 90 S.Ct. 417, 420, 24 L.Ed.2d 405 (1969). We may assume that Congress was aware that the Board, since its inception, has awarded backpay as a matter of course—not randomly or in the exercise of a standardless discretion, and not merely where employer violations are peculiarly deliberate, egregious, or inexcusable.[12] Furthermore, in passing the Equal Employment Opportunity Act of 1972, Congress considered several bills to limit the judicial power to award backpay. These limiting efforts were rejected, and the backpay provision was re-enacted substantially in its original form.[13] A

---

11. Section 10(c) of the NLRA, 49 Stat. 454, as amended, 29 U.S.C. § 160(c), provides that when the Labor Board has found that a person has committed an "unfair labor practice," the Board "shall issue" an order "requiring such person to cease and desist from such unfair labor practice, and to take such affirmative action including reinstatement of employees with or without back pay, as will effectuate the policies of this subchapter." The backpay provision of Title VII provides that when the court has found "an unlawful employment practice," it "may enjoin" the practice "and order such affirmative action as may be appropriate, which may include, but is not limited to, reinstatement or hiring of employees, with or without back pay * * *." 42 U.S.C. § 2000e–5(g) (1970 ed., Supp. III). The framers of Title VII stated that they were using the NLRA provision as a model. 110 Cong.Rec. 6549 (1964) (remarks of Sen. Humphrey); id., at 7214 (interpretative memorandum by Sens. Clark and Case). In early versions of the Title VII provision on remedies, it was stated that a court "may" issue injunctions, but "shall" order appropriate affirmative action. This anomaly was removed by Substitute Amendment No. 656, 110 Cong.Rec. 12814, 12819 (1964). The framers regarded this as merely a "minor language change," id., at 12723–12724 (remarks of Sen. Humphrey). We can find here no intent to back away from the NLRA model or to denigrate in any way the status of backpay relief.

12. "The finding of an unfair labor practice and discriminatory discharge is presumptive proof that some back pay is owed by the employer," NLRB v. Mastro Plastics Corp., 354 F.2d 170, 178 (CA2 1965). While the backpay decision rests in the NLRB's discretion, and not with the courts, NLRB v. J. H. Rutter–Rex Mfg. Co., 396 U.S. 258, 263, 90 S.Ct. 417, 420, 24 L.Ed.2d 405 (1969), the Board has from its inception pursued "a practically uniform policy with respect to these orders requiring affirmative action." NLRB, First Annual Report 124 (1936).

"[I] all but a few cases involving discriminatory discharges, discriminatory refusals to employ or reinstate, or discriminatory demotions in violation of section 8(3), the Board has ordered the employer to offer reinstatement to the employee discriminated against and to make whole such employee for any loss of pay that he has suffered by reason of the discrimination." NLRB Annual Report, Second p. 148 (1937).

13. As to the unsuccessful effort to restrict class actions for backpay, see n. 8, *supra*. In addition, the Senate rejected an amendment which would have required a jury trial in Title VII cases involving backpay, 118 Cong.Rec. 4917, 4919–4920 (1972)

Section–by–Section Analysis introduced by Senator Williams to accompany the Conference Committee Report on the 1972 Act strongly reaffirmed the "make whole" purpose of Title VII:

> "The provisions of this subsection are intended to give the courts wide discretion exercising their equitable powers to fashion the most complete relief possible. In dealing with the present section 706(g) the courts have stressed that the scope of relief under that section of the Act is intended to make the victims of unlawful discrimination whole, and that the attainment of this objective rests not only upon the elimination of the particular unlawful employment practice complained of, but also requires that persons aggrieved by the consequences and effects of the unlawful employment practice be, so far as possible, restored to a position where they would have been were it not for the unlawful discrimination." 118 Cong.Rec. 7168 (1972).

As this makes clear, Congress' purpose in vesting a variety of "discretionary" powers in the courts was not to limit appellate review of trial courts, or to invite inconsistency and caprice, but rather to make possible the "fashion[ing][of] the most complete relief possible."

It follows that, given a finding of unlawful discrimination, backpay should be denied only for reasons which, if applied generally, would not frustrate the central statutory purposes of eradicating discrimination throughout the economy and making persons whole for injuries suffered through past discrimination.[14] The courts of appeals must maintain a consistent and principled application of the backpay provision, consonant with the twin statutory objectives, while at the same time recognizing that the trial court will often have the keener appreciation of those facts and circumstances peculiar to particular cases.

The District Court's stated grounds for denying backpay in this case must be tested against these standards. The first ground was that Albemarle's breach of Title VII had not been in "bad faith."[15] This is not a sufficient reason for denying backpay. Where an employer *has* shown bad faith—by maintaining a practice which he knew to be illegal or of highly questionable legality—he can make no claims whatsoever

---

(remarks of Sens. Ervin and Javits), and rejected a provision that would have limited backpay liability to a date two years prior to filing a complaint in court. Compare H.R. 1746, which passed the House, with the successful Conference Committee bill, analyzed at 118 Cong.Rec. 7168 (1972), which adopted a substantially more liberal limitation, i.e., a date two years prior to filing a charge with the EEOC. See 42 U.S.C. § 2000e–5(g) (1970 ed., Supp. III).

14. It is necessary, therefore, that if a district court does decline to award backpay, it carefully articulate its reasons.

15. The District Court thought that the breach of Title VII had not been in "bad faith" because judicial decisions had only recently focused directly on the discriminatory impact of seniority systems. The court also noted that Albemarle had taken some steps to recruit black workers into one of its departments and to eliminate strict segregation through the 1968 departmental merger.

on the Chancellor's conscience. But, under Title VII, the mere absence of bad faith simply opens the door to equity; it does not depress the scales in the employer's favor. If backpay were awardable only upon a showing of bad faith, the remedy would become a punishment for moral turpitude, rather than a compensation for workers' injuries. This would read the "make whole" purpose right out of Title VII, for a worker's injury is no less real simply because his employer did not inflict it in "bad faith." [16] Title VII is not concerned with the employer's "good intent or absence of discriminatory intent" for "Congress directed the thrust of the Act to the *consequences* of employment practices, not simply the motivation." Griggs v. Duke Power Co., 401 U.S., at 432, 91 S.Ct., at 854. See also Watson v. City of Memphis, 373 U.S. 526, 535, 83 S.Ct. 1314, 1319–1320, 10 L.Ed.2d 529 (1963); Wright v. Council of City of Emporia, 407 U.S. 451, 461–462, 92 S.Ct. 2196, 2202–2203, 33 L.Ed.2d 51 (1972).[17] To condition the awarding of backpay on a showing of "bad faith" would be to open an enormous chasm between injunctive and backpay relief under Title VII. There is nothing on the face of the statute or in its legislative history that justifies the creation of drastic and categorical distinctions between those two remedies.[18]

The District Court also grounded its denial of backpay on the fact that the respondents initially disclaimed any interest in backpay, first asserting their claim five years after the complaint was filed. The court concluded that the petitioners had been "prejudiced" by this conduct. The Court of Appeals reversed on the ground "that the broad aims of Title VII require that the issue of back pay be fully developed and determined even though it was not raised until the post-trial stage of litigation," 474 F.2d, at 141.

It is true that Title VII contains no legal bar to raising backpay claims after the complaint for injunctive relief has been filed, or indeed

---

16. The backpay remedy of the NLRA on which the Title VII remedy was modeled, see n. 11, supra, is fully available even where the "unfair labor practice" was committed in good faith. See, e.g., NLRB v. J. H. Rutter–Rex Mfg. Co., 396 U.S., at 265, 90 S.Ct. 417, 421, 24 L.Ed.2d 405; American Machinery Corp. v. NLRB, 5 Cir., 424 F.2d 1321, 1328–1330 (CA5 1970); Laidlaw Corp. v. NLRB, 7 Cir., 414 F.2d 99, 107 (CA7 1969).

17. Title VII itself recognizes a complete, but very narrow, immunity for employer conduct shown to have been undertaken "in good faith, in conformity with, and in reliance on any written interpretation or opinion of the [Equal Employment Opportunity] Commission." 42 U.S.C. § 2000e–12(b). It is not for the courts to upset this legislative choice to recognize

only a narrowly defined "good faith" defense.

18. We note that some courts have denied backpay, and limited their judgments to declaratory relief, in cases where the employer discriminated on sexual grounds in reliance on state "female protective" statutes that were inconsistent with Title VII. See, e.g., Kober v. Westinghouse Electric Corp., 3 Cir., 480 F.2d 240 (CA3 1973); LeBlanc v. Southern Bell Telephone & Telegraph Co., 5 Cir., 460 F.2d 1228 (CA5 1972); Manning v. General Motors Corp., 466 F.2d 812 (CA6 1972); Rosenfeld v. Southern Pacific Co., 9 Cir., 444 F.2d 1219 (CA9 1971). There is no occasion in this case to decide whether these decisions were correct. As to the effect of Title VII on state statutes inconsistent with it, see 42 U.S.C. § 2000e–7.

after a trial on that complaint has been had.[19] Furthermore, Fed. Rule Civ. Proc. 54(c) directs that

"every final judgment shall grant the relief to which the party in whose favor it is rendered is entitled, even if the party has not demanded such relief in his pleadings."

But a party may not be "entitled" to relief if its conduct of the cause has improperly and substantially prejudiced the other party. The respondents here were not merely tardy, but also inconsistent, in demanding backpay. To deny backpay because a *particular* cause has been prosecuted in an eccentric fashion, prejudicial to the other party, does not offend the broad purposes of Title VII. This is not to say, however, that the District Court's ruling was necessarily correct. Whether the petitioners were in fact prejudiced, and whether the respondents' trial conduct was excusable, are questions that will be open to review by the Court of Appeals, if the District Court, on remand, decides again to decline to make any award of backpay.[20] But the standard of review will be the familiar one of whether the District Court was "clearly erroneous" in its factual findings and whether it "abused" its traditional discretion to locate "a just result" in light of the circumstances peculiar to the case, Langnes v. Green, 282 U.S. 531, 541, 51 S.Ct. 243, 247, 75 L.Ed. 520 (1931). On these issues of procedural regularity and prejudice, the "broad aims of Title VII" provide no ready solution.

Judgment vacated and case remanded.

[The concurring opinion of JUSTICES MARSHALL and REHNQUIST and the concurring and dissenting opinion of CHIEF JUSTICE BURGER are omitted.]

NOTES AND PROBLEMS FOR DISCUSSION

1. Under the *Albemarle* standard, does the district court in fact have any equitable discretion over whether or not to award back pay in a case where the plaintiff has proved a violation of Title VII? In ARIZONA GOVERNING COMMITTEE v. NORRIS, 463 U.S. 1073, 103 S.Ct. 3492, 77 L.Ed.2d 1236 (1983), the Court held that a state retirement plan that paid lower benefits to women than to men solely because of their longer life expectancy, violated Title VII. The Court limited retroactive application of the decision on the grounds that, prior to the decision that such plans were unlawful, the employer could have reasonably assumed that the plan was lawful, and full retroactive application would have a devastating effect on the employer and the pension plan. See also, Goff v. USA Truck, Inc., 929 F.2d 429 (8th Cir.1991) (no abuse of discretion in denying back pay to successful Title VII plaintiff who presented no evidence of lost wages).

19. See Rosen v. Public Service Electric & Gas Co., 409 F.2d, at 780 n. 20; Robinson v. Lorillard Corp., 444 F.2d, at 802–803; United States v. Hayes International Corp., 5 Cir., 456 F.2d 112, 116, 121 (CA5 1972).

20. The District Court's stated grounds for denying backpay were, apparently, cumulative rather than independent. The District Court may, of course, reconsider its backpay determination in light of our ruling on the "good faith" question.

2. The only special circumstance that courts have generally recognized as relieving an employer, which has violated Title VII, of back pay liability is where good faith compliance with a state law has caused the violation. In Alaniz v. California Processors, Inc., 785 F.2d 1412 (9th Cir.1986), for example, back pay was denied where the employer had refused to assign female employees to certain jobs because of the state's prohibition of employment of women in any position requiring lifting of more than 25 pounds. The defendant's good faith was demonstrated by the fact that it abandoned its practice as soon as it was advised that the state had ended enforcement of the regulation. See also, Le Beau v. Libbey–Owens–Ford Co., 727 F.2d 141 (7th Cir.1984) (within district court's discretion to deny back pay where employer complied with state law restricting overtime work of women); Schaeffer v. San Diego Yellow Cabs, Inc., 462 F.2d 1002 (9th Cir.1972) (continued reliance on state law after notice of contrary EEOC regulations concerning state protective laws demonstrated lack of good faith). Are these decisions consistent with *Albemarle's* holding that the employer's "good faith" or lack of intent to violate the Act is not a special circumstance justifying a denial of back pay?

To what extent should an employee's malfeasance which the employer did not discover until after his discharge affect the employer's backpay liability? In Summers v. State Farm Mutual Automobile Ins. Co., 864 F.2d 700 (10th Cir.1988), the plaintiff claimed that he was discharged because of his age and religion. Four years after the discharge, as it was preparing for trial, the employer discovered numerous instances of fraud committed by the plaintiff, which, if known by the company, would have justified discharge. The district court granted summary judgment for the company and the court of appeals affirmed, reasoning that, "while such after acquired evidence cannot be said to have been a 'cause' for Summers' discharge in 1982, it is relevant to Summers' claim of 'injury,' and does itself preclude the grant of any present relief or remedy to Summers." 864 F.2d at 708. Is this ruling consistent with the holding of the Supreme Court in PRICE WATERHOUSE v. HOPKINS, *supra,* that an employer in a mixed-motive case may not prevail by offering a legitimate reason for its decision "if that reason did not motivate it at the time of the decision."?

3. Theoretically, in order to "make whole" an employee for lost wages, the back pay period would have to begin with the first act of discrimination that resulted in lost pay, regardless of how far in the past that incident occurred. A continuing pay violation, for example, may have begun decades before the employee initiated a Title VII claim by filing an EEOC charge. Section 706(g) of Title VII, however, provides in part that "[b]ack pay liability shall not accrue from a date more than two years prior to the filing of a charge with the [EEOC]." The back pay period thus cannot begin earlier than two years prior to the EEOC charge on which the suit is based. Generally, the back pay period will extend to the date of final judgment. See e.g., EEOC v. Monarch Machine Tool Co., 737 F.2d 1444, 1453 (6th Cir.1980) (where an employer has discriminated in refusal to hire, award of back pay will be computed from the date of first refusal until final judgment); Nord v. United States Steel Corp., 758 F.2d 1462, 1473 (11th Cir.1985) (district court erred in ending back pay four months before judgment entered); Thorne v. City of El Segundo, 802 F.2d 1131, 1136 (9th Cir.1986) (absent compelling circumstances, court should compute back pay from date of discriminatory act until date of final judgment).

———

LEGAL DAMAGES, JURY TRIALS AND
THE CIVIL RIGHTS ACT OF 1991

The Seventh Amendment "preserves" the right to trial by jury in "suits at common law, where the value in controversy ... exceeds twenty dollars." The amendment has long been interpreted as guaranteeing the right to jury trial, not just in actions recognized at common law in 1791 when the Bill of Rights was adopted, but in all "suits in which *legal* rights [are] to be ascertained and determined, in contradistinction to those where equitable rights alone [are] recognized, and equitable remedies [are] administered." Parsons v. Bedford, Breedlove & Robeson, 28 U.S. (3 Pet.) 433, 447, 7 L.Ed. 732 (1830). As a practical matter, where legal damages (compensatory or punitive) are claimed, either party is entitled to a jury trial.

As stated in *Albemarle*, the remedies outlined in Section 706(g) of Title VII, including back pay, have generally been characterized by the courts as equitable relief. In CHAUFFEURS, TEAMSTERS AND HELPERS LOCAL NO. 391 v. TERRY, 494 U.S. 558, 110 S.Ct. 1339, 108 L.Ed.2d 519 (1990), the Court stated that "backpay sought from an employer under Title VII would generally be restitutionary in nature." 494 U.S. at 573, 110 S.Ct. at 1349. The Court also commented that by including back pay within the list of available equitable remedies in Section 706(g), Congress "specifically characterized back pay under Title VII as a form of 'equitable relief'." *Id.* While the Supreme Court never directly addressed the question whether a jury trial was available in a Title VII action, the lower courts almost universally held that, where Title VII provided the only cause of action, neither party was entitled to a trial by jury. See, e.g, Keller v. Prince George's County, 827 F.2d 952, 955 (4th Cir.1987); Slack v. Havens, 522 F.2d 1091, 1094 (9th Cir.1975); Johnson v. Georgia Highway Express, Inc., 417 F.2d 1122, 1125 (5th Cir.1969). *Contra*, Beesley v. Hartford Fire Insurance Co., 723 F.Supp. 635 (N.D.Ala.1989); Walton v. Cowin Equipment Co., 733 F.Supp. 327 (N.D.Ala.1990), reversed, 930 F.2d 924 (11th Cir.1991); Note, Judge Acker's Last Stand: the Northern District of Alabama's Lonesome Battle for the Right to Trial by Jury Under Title VII, 39 Wash. U.J. Contemp. L. 135 (1991).

Title VII overlapped, however, other causes of action in which legal damages were available. In equal protection claims against public employers under 42 U.S.C. § 1983, race-based claims against private employers under 42 U.S.C. § 1981 and in suits under some state civil rights statutes plaintiffs could obtain both compensatory and punitive damages. Where claims under these statutes were joined with Title VII claims, the parties were entitled to jury trial on all issues of fact common to both claims. While bound by the jury's findings of fact in such cases, the trial judge determined whether equitable relief, including back pay should be awarded. See Chapter 8D, *infra*. The anomaly of allowing full legal relief in some types of employment cases (suits against public employers and race-based claims against private employers) but not others (sex, national origin, or religious-based claims against private employers) as well as the inadequacy of an award of back pay in some employment contexts such as sexual harassment, led Congress to include in the Civil Rights Act of 1991 a damage remedy for Title VII actions.   Section 102 of the new Act provides in part that:

(a) RIGHT OF RECOVERY

(1) CIVIL RIGHTS.—In an action brought by a complaining party under section 706 or 717 of the Civil Rights Act of 1964 (42 U.S.C. Sec. 2000e–5) against a respondent who engaged in unlawful intentional discrimination (not an employment practice that is unlawful because of its disparate impact) prohibited under section 703, 704, or 717 of the Act (42 U.S.C. Sec. 2000e–2 or 2000e–3), and provided that the complaining party cannot recover under section 1977 of the Revised Statutes (42 U.S.C. Sec. 1981), the complaining party may recover compensatory and punitive damages as allowed in subsection (b), in addition to any relief authorized by section 706(g) of the Civil Rights Act of 1964, from respondent.

* * *

(b) COMPENSATORY AND PUNITIVE DAMAGES.

(1) DETERMINATION OF PUNITIVE DAMAGES.—A complaining party may recover punitive damages under this section against a respondent (other than a government, government agency or political subdivision) if the complaining party demonstrates that the respondent engaged in a discriminatory practice or discriminatory practices with malice or with reckless indifference to the federally protected rights of an aggrieved individual.

(2) EXCLUSIONS FROM COMPENSATORY DAMAGES.—Compensatory damages awarded under this section shall not include backpay, interest on backpay, or any other type of relief authorized under section 706(g) of the Civil Rights Act of 1964.

(3) LIMITATIONS.—The sum of the amount of compensatory damages awarded under this section for future pecuniary losses, emotional pain, suffering, inconvenience, mental anguish, loss of enjoyment of life, and other nonpecuniary losses, and the amount of punitive damages awarded under this section, shall not exceed, for each complaining party—

[the Act places the following maximum limitations on damage awards depending on the size of the employer: more than 14 and fewer than 101 employees: $50,000; more than 100 and fewer than 201 employees: $100,000; more than 200 and fewer than 501 employees: $200,000; more than 500 employees: $300,000]

* * *

(c) JURY TRIAL.—If a complaining party seeks compensatory or punitive damages under this section—

(1) any party may demand a trial by jury; and

(2) the court shall not inform the jury of the limitations described in subsection (b)(3).

The 1991 Act provides for legal damages and jury trials in all disparate treatment cases except those in which the plaintiff can obtain damages under Section 1981. Section 1981, the other Reconstruction Era civil rights statutes and the calculation of legal and punitive damages are discussed in Chapter 8, *infra*. Does the explicit exclusion of back pay from the definition of compensatory damages in the 1991 Act mean that, in a jury trial under Title VII, the trial judge will continue to determine the amount of back pay? Since the jury plainly cannot include lost wages in its award of compensatory damages, what, if anything, should it be told about lost wages? Should the jury be told that it should ignore altogether past financial loss in determining damages? Is such an instruction logical? The problem of calculating the amount of back pay is discussed in the following case.

EQUAL EMPLOYMENT OPPORTUNITY COMMISSION v. FORD MOTOR CO.

UNITED STATES COURT OF APPEALS, FOURTH CIRCUIT, 1981.
645 F.2d 183.

Before WINTER and BUTZNER, CIRCUIT JUDGES, and HOFFMAN, SENIOR DISTRICT JUDGE.

WINTER, CIRCUIT JUDGE.

The Equal Employment Opportunity Commission (EEOC) brought suit against Ford Motor Company for violating Title VII. EEOC alleged that Ford had discriminated against several women in its hiring practices at a parts warehouse in Charlotte, North Carolina. The district court found that Ford had discriminated against ten individual women and awarded them back pay. We affirm, but remand the case to the district court for consideration of additional relief.

I.

Ford operates a parts warehouse in Charlotte. A number of the workers at the warehouse are "picker-packers." These employees fill order for automotive parts by "picking" out ordered parts from storage and "packing" them for delivery. Until 1972 when two women were hired as temporary workers, no woman had ever worked as a picker-packer at the warehouse. Ford did not hire a woman to work as a picker-packer on a permanent basis until 1975.

In 1971, Judy Gaddis applied for employment as a picker-packer at the warehouse. When she did not receive a job, she filed a sex discrimination charge with the EEOC. The EEOC, after unsuccessfully trying to secure an acceptable conciliation agreement, sued Ford under Title VII on behalf of two groups of women. The first group consisted of Gaddis and two others who applied for picker-packer jobs which Ford filled with men in the summer of 1971. The second group consisted of eleven women who applied for a single picker-packer opening in 1973. Again in 1973 Ford had chosen a man, not a woman, to work at the warehouse.

The 1971 woman applicants were Gaddis, Rebecca Starr and Zettie Smith. In response to proof that as of 1971 it had never hired women as picker-packers and proof of a discriminatory hiring policy, Ford attempted to demonstrate that it had not in fact discriminated against women in its hiring practices at the Charlotte warehouse. Further, Ford tried to show that these particular women had not applied before the 1971 openings were filled. The district court rejected Ford's arguments, finding that Ford had followed a discriminatory hiring policy and that the three women had applied prior to the time in 1971 when Ford hired three men.

With the aid of a special master, the district court calculated the back pay due Gaddis, Starr, and Smith. Based upon the employment history of the three men who were hired in 1971,[1] the district court decided that, if the women had been hired in 1971, they would have worked at Ford until the time of trial. The special master thus began the back pay period with the date of the 1971 hirings and ended it at the date of trial in 1977.

With respect to Gaddis and Starr only, Ford attempted to terminate its back pay liability at three different junctures: in 1973 when they were recalled for one year by their former employer General Motors, later in 1973 when they rejected job offers from Ford, and in 1975 when they entered a CETA nurses training program. The district court refused to truncate the back pay periods at any of these points. Further, the district court rejected Ford's request to subtract unemployment compensation from the back pay awards.

In 1973, Ford filled a vacancy by hiring a man, Robert Simpson, even though eleven women had applied for the position. The district court ruled that EEOC proved a prima facie case of sex discrimination, in this instance based upon Ford's hiring procedures. After referral, the special master found that Simpson was hired in part because a warehouse employee took an interest in his application and that Ford did not seriously consider the applications of the eleven women. The special master determined that Ford did not intentionally discriminate against the women when it hired Simpson. But the special master concluded that Ford's practice of hiring new employees on the recom-

---

1. Ford filled four positions with men in August, 1971. One of those positions was created especially for a man, Parks, who transferred from a Ford warehouse in another city. The district court instructed the special master to base the back pay periods of the three women on the employment histories of Blanchard, Coe, and Rogers, the three men hired to fill the other three positions in which vacancies had occurred in the regular course of operations.

mendation of present workers, who were all male, without giving other applications full consideration, had a discriminatory effect upon the women applicants. The district court accepted the conclusion of the special master.

Pursuant to the district court's instructions, the special master determined the back pay due each of the women who had applied for the 1973 opening. Smith was among the eleven who had applied, but she was not included in the 1973 group because her injury was remedied by the award she received as a member of the 1971 group. Of the remaining ten applicants, seven appeared before the special master and demonstrated their financial injury.[2] Under the district court's directions, the special master divided each woman's award by seven, since the seven women had applied for a single vacancy.

Ford attempted to reduce its back pay liability by arguing that the back pay periods of the seven women should terminate with the end of Simpson's employment at Ford. Simpson was laid off by Ford in 1974. He was not recalled; instead, Ford hired a woman, its first permanent female picker-packer, to fill his job. The special master found, however, that it was Ford's usual practice to recall employees who had been laid off. Therefore, the special master refused to end the back pay period with Simpson's termination, and the district court approved that decision.

The district court granted the two groups of women no additional relief beyond back pay. No mention of additional relief was made in the report of the special master, nor did the district court discuss other remedies in its findings of fact and conclusions of law, its referral order, or its final order.

Finally, the district court ordered Ford to report in the future about the company's efforts to hire women. The court declined however, to grant general prospective relief against sex discrimination at the warehouse, due to the vigorous affirmative action program Ford had pursued since 1975.

* * *

[The court affirmed the district court's findings that Gaddis, Starr and Smith had applied for warehouse positions in 1971 and had been denied employment because they were women as not "clearly erroneous."]

(2) *Back Pay*

In order to remedy the effects of discrimination against Gaddis, Starr, and Smith, the district court awarded them back pay. With the help of a special master, following the direction of this court in UTU v.

---

2. The seven women were Gloria Gaither, Betty Erwin, Mary Luckey, Frances McGinnis Gantz, Mary Cox, Arlene Brown, and Frankie Benson Grier. Because Mary Luckey had died in the interim, a representative of her estate appeared before the special master.

Norfolk & Western Railway, 532 F.2d 336, 341 (4 Cir.1975), cert. denied, 425 U.S. 934, 96 S.Ct. 1664, 48 L.Ed.2d 175 (1976), the court constructed the hypothetical work histories which the three women would have had at Ford if they had not been victims of discrimination. The court then used these hypothetical work histories to calculate back pay. The district court determined that if the women had been hired in 1971, they would have been working at Ford at the time of trial in 1977, as were two of the men who were hired in 1971. Accordingly, the court granted the women back pay from the time the men were hired in 1971 through 1977.

Ford urges that the back pay periods of Gaddis and Starr should have been terminated at three different points short of the date of trial. In addition, Ford insists that the awards of all three women should be reduced by the amount of unemployment compensation they received during the period.

(a) *Subsequent Recall*

Before Gaddis and Starr applied for the Ford warehouse jobs, they had worked in similar positions for General Motors. In 1971 Gaddis and Starr applied for work at the Ford warehouse because they had been laid off from their General Motors jobs. In January, 1973, Gaddis and Starr were recalled to General Motors. They worked at General Motors for approximately one year and were then laid off for a final time.

The district court subtracted their earnings at General Motors from their back pay awards. Ford insists that the district court should have gone further. Ford contends that the back pay period of Gaddis and Starr should have been terminated when they rejoined General Motors.

Ford's argument misses the point of a Title VII back pay award. Under Title VII, a district court awards back pay in order to put the discrimination victim in the position she would have occupied if the defendant had not discriminated against her. Albemarle Paper Co. v. Moody. Pursuant to this purpose, the district court constructed the claimants' hypothetical employment histories, calculated what they would have earned if they had not been victims of discrimination, subtracted what they actually earned during the period, and awarded the difference in back pay. We prescribed this formula in *UTU*, 532 F.2d at 341, because it makes the discrimination victim whole while denying her a double recovery. If the back pay period ended when a discrimination victim obtained substantially equivalent temporary employment, as Ford suggests, the discrimination victim would not be made whole, because her back pay period would be shorter than her hypothetical work history. Ford's proposed rule is thus contrary to the intent of Title VII, since it does not fully compensate the discrimination victim.

Moreover, the procedure followed by the district court is completely in accord with the statute. In 42 U.S.C. § 2000e–5(g), Congress provided: "Interim earnings or amounts earnable with reasonable diligence by the person or persons discriminated against shall operate to reduce the back pay otherwise allowable." Thus, the statute requires only that interim earnings be deducted from the back pay award, the very procedure implemented by the district court; but it does not require, as Ford urges, that the back pay period end when a discrimination victim accepts other temporary employment. The back pay period may continue past the acceptance of another job by a discrimination victim, as long as the victim's earnings are subtracted from the back pay award.

In this case, the district court properly found that the hypothetical employment histories of the women would extend beyond their employment at General Motors. The two men who were hired instead of Gaddis and Starr worked until the time of trial. Unlike the women, who were unable to continue at General Motors, the two male Ford workers were steadily employed from 1971 until 1977. Thus, if Ford had hired Gaddis and Starr in 1971, in all probability they would have worked until 1977.[6]

Ford also argues that the result reached by the district court is contrary to the method followed by the National Labor Relations Board under the National Labor Relations Act, 29 U.S.C. § 160. Ford contends that the NLRB has implemented a rule of ending back pay periods when a discrimination victim obtains substantially equivalent employment, even if the discrimination victim is subsequently laid off.

In fact, the approach under the NLRA is identical to the approach adopted by the district court. In NLRB v. Mastro Plastics Corp., 354 F.2d 170 (2 Cir.1965), cert. denied, 384 U.S. 972, 86 S.Ct. 1862, 16 L.Ed.2d 682 (1966),[7] the guilty employer made the same argument

6. Ford submits that this focus on the work histories of the men who were actually hired is punitive. But the best evidence of the female applicants' probable work histories at Ford was the work histories of the men who held the 1971 positions. By constructing the hypothetical work histories of the women through reliance on the work histories of the men, the district court acted only to compensate the discrimination victims, not to punish Ford.

7. See note 11, *infra*.

Furthermore, the back pay formula employed by the district court in this case is the back pay formula used under the NLRA. The Board estimates the back pay the discrimination victim would have earned but for the discrimination and subtracts actual earnings to determine the back pay award. NLRB v. Gullett Gin Co., 340 U.S. 361, 71 S.Ct. 337, 95 L.Ed. 337 (1951); Phelps Dodge Corp. v. NLRB, 313 U.S. 177, 61 S.Ct.

845, 85 L.Ed. 1271 (1941); F. W. Woolworth Co., 90 NLRB 289 (1950).

We also note that the NLRB decisions cited by Ford are inapposite to this case. In Circle Bindery, Inc., 232 NLRB 1185, 1187–88 (1977), the Board terminated the back pay period when the discrimination victim accepted permanent employment, but because the discrimination victim would have left the temporary job from which he had been discriminatorily discharged when he accepted the permanent job. Thus, the acceptance of the permanent job marked the end of his hypothetical work history for the temporary employer. In Star Baby Co., 140 NLRB 678, 683–84 (1963), the Board ended the back pay periods when the discrimination victims found permanent employment, but did not address the problem faced in the instant case. *Star Baby* was complicated by the fact that the employer had gone out of business.

advanced by Ford. Both the Board and the court rejected the employer's position. The court explained:

> Several discriminatees secured substantially equivalent employment or became self-employed during the back pay period and yet suffered additional losses thereafter. Mastro argues that the taking of such employment terminates completely its back pay obligation. We do not agree. The only issue here is whether the discriminatee willfully incurred a loss of earnings. It would be unjust to require him to mitigate his damages to the greatest extent possible but then to penalize him for substantial but short-lived success. Unless in taking substantially equivalent or self-employment the discriminatee willfully forwent greater earnings, his back pay should not be reduced beyond the interim earnings he in fact received.

Id. at 179.

This passage highlights the central weakness of Ford's argument. If the back pay period ended completely when a discrimination victim accepted substantially equivalent employment, then a discrimination victim would be discouraged from mitigating damages. She could accept equivalent employment only by forfeiting continued back pay rights, with the risk that her new job might end and leave her without income from any source. Many discrimination victims might choose unemployment and continuing back pay over employment which might be short-lived. Title VII, like the NLRA, should be interpreted so as to encourage mitigation of damages by discrimination victims in order to reduce the back pay liability of Title VII defendants. [That policy] would be ill-served by a rule which encouraged discrimination victims to remain idle.[8]

Therefore, by refusing to terminate the back pay period when Gaddis and Starr returned to General Motors, the district court furthered two policies underlying Title VII. It made Gaddis and Starr whole, by awarding them back pay during their entire hypothetical work histories at Ford. At the same time, the district court followed a rule which induces Title VII discrimination victims to mitigate damages. Without reservation, we affirm the district court's decision.

(b) *Job Offers*

Later in 1973, while Gaddis and Starr were working at General Motors, Ford offered a permanent warehouse job to Gaddis. She

---

8. Of course, if a discrimination victim accepts permanent employment with substantially equivalent wages and remains at that job, the back pay period would end when she accepted the permanent job, because thereafter she would suffer no damages. Her actual earnings from that point on would be equal to or more than what she would have earned if she had not been a victim of discrimination. See Butta v. Anne Arundel County, 473 F.Supp. 83, 89 (D.Md.1979); Milton v. Bell Laboratories, Inc., 428 F.Supp. 502, 515 & n. 19 (D.N.J. 1977). In this case, however, Gaddis and Starr were unable to remain at General Motors, because they were once again laid off after working for about a year. They thus suffered additional damages during the period following their layoff from General Motors, a period when they would probably have been employed if Ford had not discriminated against them in 1971.

declined the offer. Then Ford offered the job to Starr, who likewise declined. Ford asserts that its back pay liability cannot extend past the time when Gaddis and Starr turned down the offers.

The district court found that one principal reason why Gaddis and Starr rejected Ford's offer was because they would have been forced to abandon their seniority at General Motors. By accepting a job with Ford and leaving General Motors, Gaddis and Starr would have forfeited all their rights at General Motors. Ford's offer did not include retroactive seniority to the time of the 1971 hirings. Ford presented Gaddis and Starr with an offer of mere beginning employment.

We have twice held under Title VII that victims of discrimination need not accept job offers which include a loss of seniority in order to preserve their back pay rights. In *UTU*, 532 F.2d at 340, we explained:

> A refusal to commit seniority suicide is not an acceptable reason to deny back pay. Victims of discrimination should not be required to forfeit wage and security benefits accruing because of their seniority in order to remain eligible for purely speculative future back pay relief. A general rule requiring such action would frustrate the central purposes of Title VII.

Accord, Hairston v. McLean Trucking Co., 520 F.2d 226, 232 (4 Cir.1975) (plaintiff's refusal of promotion or transfer because of a discriminatory loss of seniority is not a defense to plaintiff's back pay claim).

Ford would present Gaddis and Starr with a similarly intolerable choice. Under Ford's legal theory, if Gaddis and Starr rejected Ford's offer and stayed at General Motors, they would forego their rights to further back pay benefits. On the other hand, if they accepted the job offered by Ford, which they had not held for the previous two years because of Ford's discriminatory hiring policy, they would lose their seniority rights at General Motors. Thus, Ford's job offer was tainted by the effects of the discrimination it had practiced in 1971. Gaddis and Starr could accept the offer only by forfeiting the seniority they had accumulated at General Motors and without a compensating offer of seniority at Ford to alleviate the effects of the discrimination against them in 1971. As in *Hairston* and *UTU*, the result advocated by Ford would "frustrate the central purposes of Title VII."

Our decision is in accord with the decisions of three other circuits. In Comacho v. Colorado Electronic Technical College, Inc., 590 F.2d 887 (10 Cir.1979) (per curiam), a woman sued a college under Title VII for discriminatorily firing her. She prevailed and was awarded back pay. The college argued that her right to back pay was terminated when the college made her an offer of reinstatement. The Tenth Circuit replied:

> 42 U.S.C. § 2000e–5(g) * * * gives the trial court discretion as to the remedies. The obvious purpose of the Act is to compensate persons for injuries suffered on account of unlawful discrimination. Congress clearly intended that the remedies employed would "make whole" as nearly as possible any person injured under the

Act. * * * An offer of reinstatement without back pay does not "make whole" the person injured by an illegal firing. Such a holding would circumvent the objectives of Title VII. The college thus did not offer to fully compensate plaintiff, but merely offered to reemploy her. * * * Thus we must hold that a reinstatement offer without back pay does not relieve a guilty employer from further liability.

Id. at 889.

In Jurinko v. Edwin L. Wiegand Co., 477 F.2d 1038 (3 Cir.), vacated on other grounds, 414 U.S. 970, 94 S.Ct. 293, 38 L.Ed.2d 214 (1973), the district court held that discrimination against the plaintiffs ceased when they were offered jobs by the defendant. The Third Circuit rejected this portion of the district court's opinion, stating:

The terms of the 1969 job offers were within Wiegand's control, and it did not offer the plaintiffs back seniority or back pay. The offer that was made did not rectify the effects of its past discrimination, and the plaintiffs were under no duty to accept such an offer.

Id. at 1047.

Similarly, in Claiborne v. Illinois Central Railroad, 583 F.2d 143, 153 (5 Cir.1978), cert. denied, 442 U.S. 934, 99 S.Ct. 2869, 61 L.Ed.2d 303 (1979), the Fifth Circuit held that: "Failure to accept an offer of reinstatement in a Title VII case does not necessarily terminate the right to relief, so long as those amounts earned elsewhere or earnable with reasonable diligence are deducted from each plaintiff's award." Furthermore, the Fifth Circuit explained that "the disadvantages to an employee returning to the railroad without retroactive seniority" would "more than justify" an employee's decision to refuse an offer of reinstatement. Thus, the Fifth Circuit, like the Third and the Tenth, would find, as we do, that Ford's job offers to Gaddis and Starr did not end their back pay periods.[9]

---

9. Ford points to several NLRA decisions in which the NLRB has held that an offer of reinstatement terminates an employer's back pay liability to a discriminatorily discharged employee. E.g., D'Armigene, Inc., 148 NLRB 2 (1964), enf'd as modified, 353 F.2d 406 (2 Cir.1965). For several reasons we do not find these decisions persuasive.

The decisions cited by Ford discuss offers of reinstatement. In the instant case, Ford did not make the women offers of reinstatement, but only offers of beginning employment. An offer of reinstatement carries with it seniority rights, whereas an offer of beginning employment includes no seniority rights. This failure of Ford to offer retroactive seniority prevents Ford from relying on its offers to Gaddis and Starr.

In fact, our decision in this case is consistent with at least one decision of the NLRB. See note 11 infra. In NLRB v. Hilton Mobile Homes, 387 F.2d 7 (8 Cir. 1967), the employer offered a discharged employee reinstatement, but *without* seniority rights. The Board held that this offer did not terminate the company's back pay liability because the offer did not include seniority. The court agreed and enforced the Board's order. The offer in the instant case is almost identical to the offer in *Hilton Mobile Homes*, but significantly different from the offer of reinstatement addressed in *D'Armigene*.

Also, Gaddis and Starr mitigated damages. In some situations, refusal of an offer of employment or reinstatement might amount to a failure to mitigate damages, and, under 42 U.S.C. § 2000e–5(g), the discrimination victim's recovery might

Further, it should be noted that Ford was benefited by the employment of Gaddis and Starr at General Motors. Their earnings at General Motors were deducted in the calculation of their back pay awards. Gaddis and Starr reduced Ford's back pay liability by working at General Motors.

In sum, the district court reached an eminently reasonable result. It did not permit Ford to cut off the back pay period by making Gaddis and Starr an incomplete and unacceptable offer, and it denied Gaddis and Starr a double recovery by deducting their General Motors wages from their back pay awards. We affirm this aspect of the district court's decision.[10]

(c) *Nurses Training*

In September, 1975, Gaddis and Starr entered a nurses training program, a CETA program for the unemployed. Ford asked the district court to terminate the back pay period of Gaddis and Starr upon their entry into the program. The district court refused. Instead, the court accepted the special master's report which treated the training program as employment and reduced the back pay awards by forty hours of minimum wage earnings for each week the women spent in the program.

On appeal, Ford again presses the argument that its back pay liability should not extend beyond the date when Gaddis and Starr entered the nurses training program. We think that there are four reasons why Ford should not prevail.

First of all, Gaddis and Starr did not remove themselves from the labor market when they entered the CETA program. Both testified that they would have accepted work had it been offered to them. The special master's report credited their testimony. He found that the two women had not removed themselves from the labor market, and his finding was adopted by the district court. Because this determination

be reduced by the amount of wages she could have earned in the offered job, as "amounts earnable with reasonable diligence." In the case of Gaddis and Starr, they reduced Ford's liability by continuing to work at General Motors.

10. In addition to its finding that the women did not want to lose their General Motors seniority, the district court found that neither Gaddis nor Starr wanted to be the only woman employed at the warehouse. In fact, Ford's warehouse manager testified that he warned Gaddis and Starr that they might be subject to sexual harassment if they worked at the warehouse. He told them that "they may very well [be] subjected to passes, offensive remarks, off-color language" and that "there are not now nor, * * * have there ever been women working in the warehouse."

Incredibly, Ford tries to rely upon the discriminatory atmosphere of the warehouse to argue that Gaddis and Starr unreasonably rejected Ford's job offers. It would be ironic indeed if Ford could defeat the remedial purposes of Title VII by resting upon sexual harassment of women in its warehouse. Ford cannot escape the fact that its offer included no seniority rights to make Gaddis and Starr whole.

We note further that the warehouse manager told Gaddis and Starr that if Ford hired one of them it would hire the other to avoid subjecting a lone woman to sexual harassment. In 1973, Ford offered a single position to each of the women. It did not offer positions to both.

was a reasonable credibility determination, we cannot treat it as clearly erroneous.

Two courts have decided similar cases in which Title VII claimants entered school after suffering discrimination at the hands of an employer. Those courts have decided that the critical determination is whether the claimant remained "ready, willing, and available" for employment. Taylor v. Safeway Stores, Inc., 524 F.2d 263, 267 (10 Cir.1975); United States v. Wood, Wire & Metal Lathers Local 46, 328 F.Supp. 429, 439, 443–44 (S.D.N.Y.1971). If the claimant is ready, willing, and available for work, these courts have suggested, the back pay period does not come to a close when the claimant enters school.

The district court in this case followed the rationale of these cases by instructing the special master to ascertain whether Gaddis and Starr had removed themselves from the labor market. We conclude that the district court acted correctly in ordering the special master to examine the availability of these two particular women for work, rather than mechanically ending the back pay period upon their entry into the CETA training program. The "ready, willing, and able" test followed by the district court permits the relief in each case to be fitted to fit the circumstances of particular claimants.

Second, the CETA training program closely resembled employment. Both women received the minimum wage for the time they spent in the training program. Both testified that they regarded the program as employment. Indeed, the apparent intent of the CETA program is to provide the unemployed with work while at the same time preparing them for future employment.

The special master treated the training program as employment like the claimants' temporary employment at General Motors. As with the wages the women earned at General Motors, the special master subtracted the wages the women earned in the training program from Ford's back pay liability. 42 U.S.C. § 2000e–5(g). In addition, the district court took every precaution to insure that Ford was not unfairly burdened by back pay liability. Even though Gaddis and Starr sometimes attended the program for less than forty hours per week, the district court subtracted forty-hours of earnings for each week they spent in the program. In this fashion, the district court properly treated the nurses training program as the equivalent of employment and also guaranteed that Gaddis and Starr did not receive more than one full recovery.

Third, Gaddis and Starr were enrolled in the program as a result of their presence on the unemployment compensation rolls. Gaddis and Starr were receiving unemployment compensation when they began the training program. Both testified that they did not sign up for the CETA program on their own and that they enrolled at the urging of the state unemployment compensation office. In fact, a representative of the state agency testified that their unemployment benefits would have been cancelled if they had not enrolled in the CETA program. As the special master found, "[T]his course of action was recommended very strongly by the North Carolina Employment Security Commission."

Gaddis and Starr were unemployed as a direct result of the discrimination against them by Ford. As the employment histories of the men hired in 1971 demonstrate, if Ford had not discriminated against Gaddis and Starr in 1971, they probably would not have been receiving unemployment compensation. But for Ford's discriminatory hiring practices, they would have had no need of a CETA program. However, because they were unable to find work and because they were a burden on the state unemployment compensation fund, Gaddis and Starr were convinced by the state to enroll in the CETA training program. Ford cannot equitably be relieved of Title VII back pay liability because of an event which flowed directly from its discriminatory actions. The district court reached the proper result when it refused to terminate Ford's back pay liability upon the entry of Gaddis and Starr into the CETA training program.

Fourth, as has been detailed above, the district court did not abuse its discretion, see Franks v. Bowman Transportation Co., when it chose not to end these claimants' back pay period with their enrollment in the nurses training program. As the Tenth Circuit indicated in *Taylor*, 524 F.2d at 268, district courts have discretion to examine the particulars of a claimant's entry into school and to decide whether the employer's back pay liability should end or continue. In this case, the enrollment of Gaddis and Starr into nurses training is colored by several facts, including their availability for work, the similarity between the CETA program and employment, and the close connection between the state unemployment compensation agency and the CETA training program. When all these factors are considered, it is apparent that the district court did not abuse its discretion when it permitted Ford's back pay liability to continue during the training program, while giving Ford credit for the claimants' possible minimum wage earnings during the period.

(d) *Unemployment Compensation*

Ford argues that the awards of all three women should be reduced by the amount of unemployment compensation they received during the back pay period. The district court did not deduct unemployment compensation from the back pay awards. We conclude that the district court ruled correctly.

There is a division of authority over the deduction of unemployment compensation from Title VII back pay awards. Some district courts have subtracted unemployment compensation in computing back pay. See, e.g., Heelan v. Johns–Manville Corp., 451 F.Supp. 1382 (D.Colo.1978).

On the other hand, one district court in this circuit has decided that monies received as "state unemployment compensation 'are made to carry out an independent social policy' and are not deductible from a back pay award under Title VII." Abron v. Black & Decker Manufacturing Co., 439 F.Supp. 1095, 1115 (D.Md.1977), quoting Inda v. United Air Line, Inc., 405 F.Supp. 426 (N.D.Cal.1975) aff'd in part and vacated in part, 565 F.2d 554 (9 Cir.1977), cert. denied, 435 U.S. 1007, 98 S.Ct. 1877, 56 L.Ed.2d 388 (1978). See also Tidwell v. American Oil Co., 332 F.Supp. 424 (D.Utah 1971).

In an analogous context, the Supreme Court has decided that unemployment compensation need not be deducted from back pay awarded under the NLRA. NLRB v. Gullett Gin Co., 340 U.S. 361, 71 S.Ct. 337, 95 L.Ed. 337 (1951). The Supreme Court's analysis is particularly convincing:

> * * * To decline to deduct state unemployment compensation benefits in computing back pay is not to make the employees more than whole, as contended by respondent. Since no consideration has been given to collateral *losses* in framing an order to reimburse employees for their lost earnings, manifestly no consideration need be given to collateral benefits which employees may have received.

> * * * Payments of unemployment compensation were not made to the employees by respondent but by the state out of state funds derived from taxation. True, these taxes were paid by employers, and thus to some extent respondent helped to create the fund. However, the payments to the employees were not made to discharge any liability or obligation of respondent, but to carry out a policy of social betterment for the benefit of the entire state. [citations omitted]. We think these facts plainly show the benefits to be collateral. It is thus apparent from what we have already said that failure to take them into account in ordering back pay does not make the employees more than "whole" as that phrase has been understood and applied.

Id. at 364, 71 S.Ct. at 339 (emphasis in original).[11]

Based on the *Abron* decision, the analysis of the Supreme Court, and the remedial policies of Title VII, we agree with the district court that "awards of back pay under Title VII should not be affected by a system of compensation which is designed to serve a wholly independent social policy." To decide otherwise would undercut to some degree the corrective force of a Title VII back pay award.

(3) *Conclusion*

Many of Ford's objections contest the factual findings and credibility determinations of the district court and the special master. Because we find none of them clearly erroneous, we do not overturn any of these resolutions of conflicting facts and testimony. Most of the rest of Ford's contentions challenge the district court's exercise of discretion in

---

11. This decision is particularly persuasive, because Congress turned to the "make whole" provisions of the NLRA when it framed the relief provisions of Title VII. *Albemarle Paper Co.*, 422 U.S. at 419–22, 95 S.Ct. at 2372–73.

framing a remedy. As indicated above, we find that the district court did not abuse its discretion but, on the contrary, closely examined each issue to determine an equitable adjustment of Ford's back pay liability. Consequently, we affirm the district court's decision with respect to Gaddis, Starr, and Smith.

* * *

[The court affirmed the district court's finding that Ford had passed over eleven female job applicants in 1973 because of employment practices that had a disparate impact on women.]

(2) *Back Pay*

The district court awarded the 1973 women applicants back pay. Seven appeared before the special master to prove their damages. Under the instructions of the district court, the special master calculated each woman's back pay and awarded one-seventh of each sum, because Ford only filled one vacancy in 1973. Ford does not contest this aspect of the district court's decision.

Ford does object to the length of the back pay period. After working several months, Simpson was laid off on February 6, 1974. Simpson's recall rights expired by the time Ford was ready to fill his vacant position. At that time, in September, 1975, Ford did not recall Simpson, but in his place hired Doris Baumgardner, who was Ford's first female permanent picker-packer.

The special master found that in the usual situation Ford recalled laid-off employees, even when their recall rights had expired. Because the hiring of Baumgardner was an unusual case, the special master did not terminate the back pay period with Simpson's layoff. Instead, the special master included Baumgardner's employment within the back pay period for the eleven women.

Ford argues that this extension of the back pay period was improper. According to Ford, "the court was required to track the actual work experience of the employee allegedly favored by Ford's alleged discrimination." Ford's proposed rule is unacceptable because it bears no relation to the purpose of a Title VII back pay award.

The purpose of a back pay award is to make the discrimination victim whole, to erase the effects of illegal discrimination. To accomplish that purpose, courts construct the hypothetical employment history of the discrimination victim to determine the appropriate back pay period. *UTU*, 532 F.2d at 341.

Frequently, the employment history of the applicant who was actually hired will provide the best guide to the hypothetical employment history of the discrimination victim. In fact, the district court in this case used the employment history of the men hired in 1971 to determine the back pay periods for Gaddis, Starr, and Smith. But the employment history of the employee is not controlling in and of itself. Actual employment histories are used only when they are the best available guide to the hypothetical employment history of the discrimination victim. The focus is on the probable job career of the victim, who is to be made whole, not on the career of the actual employee, who is of course not a party to the Title VII case.

In this instance, the special master tracked Simpson's work history, but only to a point. Simpson's employment history was used as the best indicator of the probable work history of the female applicants until Doris Baumgardner was hired to fill his job. At that point, the special master found that Simpson's employment history was abnormal. The testimony of Ford's warehouse manager revealed, as the special master found, that normally employees are recalled even after their recall rights had expired. In this case, Simpson was not recalled, and a woman was hired in his place. Ford's departure from its usual practice took place after EEOC filed this sex discrimination suit.

It was apparent, then, that Ford's decision not to recall Simpson was out of the ordinary, a product of unusual circumstances. As a result, Simpson's work history failed as an indicator of the probable work history that one of the seven women would have had. Since laid-off employees were usually recalled, the special master made the only reasonable decision when he abandoned Simpson's actual work history and concluded that one of the seven women would have probably been recalled if she had been hired. If the special master had instead followed Simpson's work history, the special master would have based the back pay period not on the hypothetical work history of the discrimination victim, but on the peculiarities of Simpson's situation. That approach would have been contrary to *UTU* and to the "make whole" doctrine of *Albemarle Paper Co.*

The special master adhered to the dictates of *UTU* and *Albemarle Paper Co.*, by constructing the hypothetical work histories of the women. In our view, the special master reasonably decided that if one of the women had been hired in 1973 she would have been recalled in 1975 even though Simpson was not.

III.

In its complaint, EEOC asked the district court to "make whole those persons adversely affected by [sex discrimination], by providing appropriate back pay, with interest, * * * and other affirmative relief necessary to eradicate the effects of unlawful employment practices." As described above, the district court meticulously formulated a back pay award to correct the effects of sex discrimination against the women applicants.

But the district court offered the women no further remedies. Under Title VII, district courts have discretion in the formulation of remedial orders. E.g., Franks v. Bowman Transportation Co. At the same time, district courts have a duty to grant the "fullest relief possible to the victims of discrimination," to insure that the effects of discrimination are totally removed from the lives of discrimination victims. *Albemarle Paper Co.*

In this case, the district court did not discuss possible remedies other than back pay. In its findings of fact and conclusions of law, in its referral order to the special master, and in its order adopting the special master's report, the district court did not address other remedial steps. Under *Albemarle Paper Co.*, then, the district court was obliged to consider other remedies and if it rejected them to articulate its reasons.

The district court may not have discussed other possible remedies because it concluded that Ford had made diligent efforts since 1975 to hire women. Although Ford's affirmative action program might justify the district court's decision not to order general affirmative relief against sex discrimination, Ford's anti-discrimination efforts do not alter the district court's responsibility to redress the discrimination suffered by these individual women. Ford's good faith since 1975 does not remove the burden placed upon the ten women by discrimination practices in 1971 and 1973. See *UTU*, 532 F.2d at 340.

In fact, these women are not aided in any fashion by Ford's program. They still do not possess the seniority they would have accumulated had they been hired in earlier years, and they do not yet have the jobs they might well have had if Ford had not discriminated against them. Ford's affirmative action program, then, does not excuse the district court's failure to consider additional relief for the individual women.

One seemingly desirable remedy in this instance would be to grant the women hiring preferences at the parts warehouse, with retroactive seniority.

This remedy may be particularly appropriate for the three women who were not hired in 1971. Gaddis and Starr have had difficulty finding jobs since 1971. After their final layoffs from General Motors, they were forced to enter a CETA training program, apparently unable to find work in the auto parts field. If Ford had not discriminated against them in 1971, they might well have avoided this checkered employment career. Smith had been employed during much of the time since 1971, but at relatively low wages. She also might be entitled to a hiring preference with retroactive seniority.

The seven women who were not hired in 1973 present a more difficult case. Ford filled only one opening in 1973, and thus all seven cannot reasonably claim that they would have been employed by Ford since 1973 if Ford had not discriminated against them. However, the district court may be able to fashion a remedy, such as hiring preferences without seniority, which would grant them more complete relief than a back pay award.

If the district court decides to order Ford to hire any or all of these discrimination victims as positions come open, it should also consider whether the women should receive an additional monetary award to compensate them for the estimated earnings lost between the date of the district court's decision and the date of employment at the warehouse. See White v. Carolina Paperboard Corp., 564 F.2d 1073, 1091 (4 Cir.1977). Such an award, along with back pay, preferential hiring, and retroactive seniority, would constitute the "fullest relief possible."

We emphasize that the terms and conditions of relief for discrimination victims is determined by district courts, not by this court. We only instruct the district court to consider these possible remedies; not necessarily to provide them. On remand, the district court should articulate its reasons for rejecting or accepting the additional relief proposed by EEOC.

IV.

We affirm the district court's decision as a proper exercise of discretion founded on not clearly erroneous factual determinations. We remand for consideration of further remedies, so that the district court can fully exercise its discretion to formulate the most complete relief possible for these discrimination victims.

Affirmed and remanded.

[The dissenting opinion of Judge Hoffman is omitted.]

FORD MOTOR CO. v. EQUAL EMPLOYMENT OPPORTUNITY COMMISSION

Supreme Court of the United States, 1982.
458 U.S. 219, 102 S.Ct. 3057, 73 L.Ed.2d 721.

Justice O'Connor delivered the opinion of the Court.

This case presents the question whether an employer charged with discrimination in hiring can toll the continuing accrual of backpay liability under § 706(g) of Title VII, 42 U.S.C. § 2000e–5(g), simply by unconditionally offering the claimant the job previously denied, or whether the employer also must offer seniority retroactive to the date of the alleged discrimination.[1]

---

1. The dissent asserts that by so "fram[ing] the question presented" we have "simply and completely misstate[d] the issue." Apparently, neither party agrees with the dissent. The petitioner summarizes the question presented as "whether back pay due an employment discrimination claimant continues to accrue after the claimant has rejected an unconditional job offer that does not include retroactive seniority or back pay." Brief for Petitioner i. The respondent sums up the question presented as "[w]hether an employer who unlawfully refused to hire job applicants because they were women can terminate its liability for back pay by subsequently offering the applicants positions without seniority at a time when they had obtained, and accumulated seniority in, other jobs." Brief for Respondent i.

To buttress the assertion that the Court has addressed a question not presented, the dissent claims that we have "misrea[d]" the Court of Appeals' decision, "transform[ing] a narrow Court of Appeals ruling into a broad one, just so [we could] reverse and install a broad new rule of [our] own choosing," rather than attempt, as best we are able, to decide the particular case actu-

The question has considerable practical significance because of the lengthy delays that too often attend Title VII litigation.[2] The extended time it frequently takes to obtain satisfaction in the courts may force a discrimination claimant to suffer through years of underemployment or unemployment before being awarded the job the claimant deserves. Court delays, of course, affect all litigants. But for the victim of job discrimination, delay is especially unfortunate. The claimant cannot afford to stand aside while the wheels of justice grind slowly toward the ultimate resolution of the lawsuit. The claimant needs work that will feed a family and restore self-respect. A job is needed—now. In this case, therefore, we must determine how best to fashion the remedies available under Title VII to fulfill this basic need.

* * *

[The Court's statement of the Facts and of the procedural history of the case is omitted.]

* * *

In this case, Ford and the EEOC offer competing standards to govern backpay liability. Ford argues that if an employer unconditionally offers a claimant the job for which he previously applied, the claimant's rejection of that offer should toll the continuing accrual of backpay liability.[9] The EEOC, on the other hand, defends the lower court's rule,[10] contending that backpay liability should be tolled only by the rejection of an offer that includes seniority retroactive to the date on which the alleged discrimination occurred. Our task is to determine which of these standards better coincides with the "large objectives" of Title VII.

III

The "primary objective" of Title VII is to bring employment discrimination to an end, *Albemarle Paper,* supra, by "achiev[ing] equality of employment opportunities and remov[ing] barriers that have operated in the past to favor an identifiable group * * * over other employ-

ally before us. Because we believe we have correctly and fairly framed the question, we decline the opportunity to address further this *ad hominem* argument.

2. The discriminatory refusals to hire involved in this case occurred 11 years ago.

9. It should be clear that the contested backpay in this suit stems from the period following Ford's offer, and during which Gaddis and Starr were unemployed, i.e., after the GM warehouse closed. Our decision today does not affect their right to claim backpay for the period before they rejected Ford's offers.

10. For reasons of its own, the dissenting opinion reads the decision below nar-

rowly and takes us to task for discerning the outlines of a "general rule" in the opinion of the Court of Appeals. In this regard, we note that already at least one district court evidently not only has read the opinion below as prescribing a general rule, but in addition has interpreted that rule more broadly than we do. See Saunders v. Hercules, Inc., 510 F.Supp. 1137, 1142 (W.D. Virginia 1981) ("in view of the recent Fourth Circuit Court of Appeals decision in Equal Employment Opportunity Commission v. Ford Motor Company, 645 F.2d 183 (4th Cir.1981) * * * [i]t is clear * * * that a person who has been discriminated against does not have to accept an offer of reemployment where back pay has not been offered").

ees." Ibid. "[T]he preferred means for achieving" this goal is through "[c]ooperation and voluntary compliance." Alexander v. Gardner–Denver Co.

To accomplish this objective, the legal rules fashioned to implement Title VII should be designed, consistent with other Title VII policies, to encourage Title VII defendants promptly to make curative, unconditional job offers to Title VII claimants, thereby bringing defendants into "voluntary compliance" and ending discrimination far more quickly than could litigation proceeding at its often ponderous pace. Delays in litigation unfortunately are now commonplace, forcing the victims of discrimination to suffer years of underemployment or unemployment before they can obtain a court order awarding them the jobs unlawfully denied them. In a better world, perhaps, law suits brought under Title VII would speed to judgment so quickly that the effects of legal rules on the behavior of the parties during the a of litigation would not be as important a consideration. We do not now live in such a world, however, as this case illustrates.

The rule tolling the further accrual of backpay liability if the defendant offers the claimant the job originally sought well serves the objective of ending discrimination through voluntary compliance, for it gives an employer a strong incentive to hire the Title VII claimant. While the claimant may be no more attractive than the other job applicants, a job offer to the claimant will free the employer of the threat of liability for further backpay damages. Since paying backpay damages is like paying an extra worker who never came to work, Ford's proposed rule gives the Title VII claimant a decided edge over other competitors for the job he seeks.

The rule adopted by the court below, on the other hand, fails to provide the same incentive, because it makes hiring the Title VII claimant more costly than hiring one of the other applicants for the same job. To give the claimant retroactive seniority before an adjudication of liability, the employer must be willing to pay the additional costs of the fringe benefits that come with the seniority that newly hired workers usually do not receive. More important, the employer must also be prepared to cope with the deterioration in morale, labor unrest, and reduced productivity that may be engendered by inserting the claimant into the seniority ladder over the heads of the incumbents who have earned their places through their work on the job. In many cases, moreover, disruption of the existing seniority system will violate a collective bargaining agreement, with all that such a violation entails for the employer's labor relations.[11] Under the rule adopted by the

11. See American Tobacco Co. v. Patterson, 456 U.S. 63, 76, 102 S.Ct. 1534, 1541, 71 L.Ed.2d 748 (1982) ("Seniority provisions are of 'overriding importance' in collective bargaining, * * * and they 'are universally included in these contracts'") (quoting Humphrey v. Moore, 375 U.S. 335, 346, 84 S.Ct. 363, 370, 11 L.Ed.2d 370 (1964), and Trans World Airlines, Inc. v. Hardison, 432 U.S. 63, 79, 97 S.Ct. 2264, 2274, 53 L.Ed.2d 113 (1977)).

court below, the employer must be willing to accept all these additional costs if he hopes to toll his backpay liability by offering the job to the claimant. As a result, the employer will be less, rather than more, likely to hire the claimant.

In sum, the Court of Appeals' rule provides no incentive to employers to hire Title VII claimants. The rule advocated by Ford, by contrast, powerfully motivates employers to put Title VII claimants to work, thus ending ongoing discrimination as promptly as possible.[12]

IV

Title VII's primary goal, of course, *is* to end discrimination; the victims of job discrimination want jobs, not lawsuits.[13] But when unlawful discrimination does occur, Title VII's secondary, fallback purpose is to compensate the victims for their injuries. To this end, § 706(g) aims "to make the victims of unlawful discrimination whole" by restoring them, "so far as possible * * * to a position where they would have been were it not for the unlawful discrimination." *Albemarle Paper*, supra, at 421. We now turn to consider whether the rule urged by Ford not only better serves the goal of ending discrimination, but also properly compensates injured Title VII claimants.

A

If Gaddis and Starr had rejected an unconditional offer from Ford before they were recalled to their jobs at GM, tolling Ford's backpay liability from the time of Ford's offer plainly would be consistent with providing Gaddis and Starr full compensation for their injuries. An unemployed or underemployed claimant, like all other Title VII claimants, is subject to the statutory duty to minimize damages set out in

---

12. In his dissent, Justice Blackmun suggests that it is we who speak from the "comfor[t]" of the "sidelines," somewhere outside "the real world" of sex discrimination. For all the dissent's rhetoric, however, nowhere does the dissent seriously challenge our conclusion that the rule we adopt will powerfully motivate employers to offer Title VII claimants the jobs they have been denied. But Rebecca Starr's trial testimony eloquently explains what claimants need: "I was just wanting that job so bad because you can't, a woman, when you've got three children, I needed the money, and I was wanting the job so bad." IV Tr. 356. Thus, it is the rule applied by the court below which manifests a "studied indifference to the real-life concerns" of the victims of sex discrimination.

13. See 118 Cong.Rec. 7569 (remarks of Rep. Dent during debate on 1972 amendments to Title VII) ("Most people just want to work. That is all. They want an opportunity to work. We are trying to see that all of us, no matter of what race, sex, or religious or ethnic background, will have an equal opportunity in employment").

§ 706(g).[14] This duty, rooted in an ancient principle of law,[15] requires the claimant to use reasonable diligence in finding other suitable employment. Although the un- or underemployed claimant need not go into another line of work, accept a demotion, or take a demeaning position,[16] he forfeits his right to backpay if he refuses a job substantially equivalent to the one he was denied.[17] Consequently, an employer charged with unlawful discrimination often can toll the accrual of backpay liability by unconditionally offering the claimant the job he sought, and thereby providing him with an opportunity to minimize damages.[18]

14. The provision expressly states that "[i]nterim earnings or amounts earnable with reasonable diligence by the person or persons discriminated against shall operate to reduce the back pay otherwise allowable." 42 U.S.C. § 2000e–5(g).

Claimants often take other lesser or dissimilar work during the a of their claims, even though doing so is not mandated by the statutory requirement that a claimant minimize damages or forfeit his right to compensation. See, e.g., Merriweather v. Hercules, Inc., 631 F.2d 1161 (CA5 1980) (voluntary minimization of damages in dissimilar work); Thornton v. East Texas Motor Freight, 497 F.2d 416, 422 (CA6 1974) (voluntary minimization of damages by moonlighting).

15. See generally, e.g., C. McCormick, Handbook on the Law of Damages 127–158 (1935). McCormick summarizes "the general rule" as follows:

"Where one person has committed a tort, breach of contract, or other legal wrong against another, it is incumbent upon the latter to use such means as are reasonable under the circumstances to avoid or minimize the damages. The person wronged cannot recover for any item of damage which could thus have been avoided." Id., at 127.

In connection with the remedial provisions of the NLRA, we said: "Making the workers whole for losses suffered on account of an unfair labor practice is part of the vindication of the public policy which the Board enforces. Since only actual losses should be made good, it seems fair that deductions should be made not only for actual earnings by the worker but also for losses which he willfully incurred." Phelps Dodge Corp. v. NLRB, 313 U.S. 177, 197–198, 61 S.Ct. 845, 853–854, 85 L.Ed. 1271 (1941).

16. See, e.g., NLRB v. The Madison Courier, Inc., 153 U.S.App.D.C. 232, 245–246, 472 F.2d 1307, 1320–1321 (1972) (employee need not "seek employment which is not consonant with his particular skills, background, and experience" or "which involves conditions that are substantially more onerous than his previous position"); Wonder Markets, Inc., 236 N.L.R.B. 787, 787 (1978) (offer of reinstatement ineffective when discharged employee offered a different job, though former position still existed), enforced sub nom. NLRB v. Eastern Smelting & Refining Corp., 598 F.2d 666, 676 (CA1 1979), supplemental decision, 249 N.L.R.B. 294 (1980); Good Foods Manufacturing & Processing Corp., 195 N.L.R.B. 418, 419 (1972) (offer of reinstatement ineffective because job offered had different conditions of employment and benefits), supplemental decision, 200 N.L.R.B. 623 (1972), enforced, 492 F.2d 1302 (CA7 1974); Harvey Carlton, 143 N.L.R.B. 295, 304 (1963) (offer of reinstatement ineffective because employees would return on probation).

Some lower courts have indicated, however, that after an extended period of time searching for work without success, a claimant must consider taking a lower-paying position. See, e.g., NLRB v. The Madison Courier, Inc., supra, at 245–246, 472 F.2d, at 1320–1321; NLRB v. Southern Silk Mills, Inc., 242 F.2d 697, 700(CA6), cert. denied, 355 U.S. 821, 78 S.Ct. 28, 2 L.Ed.2d 37 (1957). If the claimant decides to go into a dissimilar line of work, or to accept a demotion, his earnings must be deducted from any eventual backpay award. See § 706(g); Merriweather v. Hercules, Inc., 631 F.2d 1161, 1168 (CA5 1980); Taylor v. Philips Industries, Inc., 593 F.2d 783, 787 (CA7 1979) (per curiam).

17. NLRB v. Arduini Mfg. Corp., 394 F.2d 420 (CA1 1968).

18. The claimant's obligation to minimize damages in order to retain his right to compensation does not require him to settle his claim against the employer, in whole or in part. Thus, an applicant or discharged employee is not required to accept a job offered by the employer on the

An employer's unconditional offer of the job originally sought to an un- or underemployed claimant, moreover, need not be supplemented by an offer of retroactive seniority to be effective, lest a defendant's offer be irrationally disfavored relative to other employers' offers of substantially similar jobs. The claimant, after all, plainly would be required to minimize his damages by accepting another employer's offer even though it failed to grant the benefits of seniority not yet earned.[19] Of course, if the claimant fulfills the requirement that he minimize damages by accepting the defendant's unconditional offer, he remains entitled to full compensation if he wins his case.[20] A court may grant him backpay accrued prior to the effective date of the offer,[21] retroactive seniority,[22] and compensation for any losses suffered as a result of his lesser seniority before the court's judgment.[23]

In short, the un- or underemployed claimant's statutory obligation to minimize damages requires him to accept an unconditional offer of the job originally sought, even without retroactive seniority. Acceptance of the offer preserves, rather than jeopardizes, the claimant's right to be made whole; in the case of an un- or underemployed claimant, Ford's suggested rule merely embodies the existing requirement of § 706(g) that the claimant minimize damages, without affecting his right to compensation.

condition that his claims against the employer be compromised. See, e.g., NLRB v. St. Marys Sewer Pipe Co., 146 F.2d 995, 996 (CA3 1945).

19. For the same reasons, a defendant's job offer is effective to force minimization of damages by an un- or underemployed claimant even without a supplemental offer of backpay, since the claimant would be required to accept another employer's offer of a substantially similar job without a large front-end, lump-sum bonus. See, e.g., NLRB v. Midwest Hanger Co., 550 F.2d 1101, 1103(CA8) ("It is clear that had the Company's offer of reinstatement been conditioned solely on its refusal to give back pay, as the Company strenuously argues, then the offer of reinstatement would not have been invalidated"), cert. denied, 434 U.S. 830, 98 S.Ct. 112, 54 L.Ed.2d 90 (1977); Reliance Clay Products Co., 105 N.L.R.B. 135, 137 (1953) ("The Board has consistently held that a discriminatorily discharged employee may not refuse" an unconditioned offer of reinstatement even though unaccompanied by backpay; refusal of such an offer tolls the employer's liability for back pay).

20. In tailoring a Title VII remedy a court " 'has not merely the power but the duty to render a decree which will so far as possible eliminate the discriminatory effects of the past as well as bar like discrimination in the future.' " Albemarle Paper Co. v. Moody, 422 U.S., at 418, 95 S.Ct., at 2372 (1975) (quoting Louisiana v. United States, 380 U.S. 145, 154, 85 S.Ct. 817, 822, 13 L.Ed.2d 709 (1965)).

21. See, e.g., NLRB v. Huntington Hospital, Inc., 550 F.2d 921, 924 (CA4 1977).

22. See, e.g., Zipes v. Trans World Airlines, Inc., 455 U.S. 385, 102 S.Ct. 1127, 71 L.Ed.2d 234 (1982); Teamsters v. United States, 431 U.S. 324, 97 S.Ct. 1843, 52 L.Ed.2d 396 (1977); Franks v. Bowman Transportation Co., 424 U.S. 747, 96 S.Ct. 1251, 47 L.Ed.2d 444 (1976).

Decisions construing the remedial provision of the NLRA, § 10(c), 29 U.S.C. § 160(c), are in accord. See, e.g., In re Nevada Consolidated Copper Corp., 26 N.L.R.B. 1182, 1235 (1940) (persons unlawfully refused jobs must be offered jobs with "any seniority or other rights and privileges they would have acquired, had the respondent not unlawfully discriminated against them") (quoted in Franks v. Bowman Transportation Co., supra, at 770, 96 S.Ct., at 1267), enf. denied, 122 F.2d 587 (CA10 1941), rev'd, 316 U.S. 105, 62 S.Ct. 960, 86 L.Ed. 1305 (1942).

23. Both Ford and the EEOC agree on this point. See Brief for Respondent 19; Reply Brief for Petitioner 9.

B

Ford's proposed rule also is consistent with the policy of full compensation when the claimant has had the good fortune to find a more attractive job than the defendant's, because the availability of the better job terminates the ongoing ill effects of the defendant's refusal to hire the claimant. For example, if Gaddis and Starr considered their jobs at GM to be so far superior to the jobs originally offered by Ford that, even if Ford had hired them at the outset, they would have left Ford's employ to take the new work, continuing to hold Ford responsible for backpay after Gaddis and Starr lost their GM jobs would be to require, in effect, that Ford insure them against the risks of unemployment in a new and independent undertaking. Such a rule would not merely restore Gaddis and Starr to the " 'position where they would have been were it not for the unlawful discrimination.' " Albemarle Paper Co. v. Moody; it would catapult them into a better position than they would have enjoyed in the absence of discrimination.

Likewise, even if Gaddis and Starr considered their GM jobs only somewhat better or even substantially equivalent to the positions they would have held at Ford had Ford hired them initially,[24] their rejection of Ford's unconditional offer could be taken to mean that they believed that the lingering ill effects of Ford's prior refusal to hire them had been extinguished by later developments. If, for example, they thought that the Ford and GM jobs were identical in every respect, offering identical pay, identical conditions of employment, and identical risks of layoff, Gaddis and Starr would have been utterly indifferent as to which job they had—Ford's or GM's. Assuming that they could work at only one job at a time, the ongoing economic ill effects caused by Ford's prior refusal to hire them would have ceased when they found the identical jobs at GM, and they would have had no reason to accept Ford's offers. As in the case of a claimant who lands a better job, therefore, requiring a defendant to provide what amounts to a form of unemployment insurance to claimants, after they have found identical jobs and refused the defendant's unconditional job offer, would be, absent special circumstances, to grant them something more than compensation for their injuries.

In both of these situations, the claimant has the power to accept the defendant's offer and abandon the superior or substantially equivalent replacement job. As in the case of an un- or underemployed claimant, under the rule advocated by Ford acceptance of the defendant's unconditional offer would preserve fully the ultimately victorious claimant's right to full redress for the effects of discrimination.

---

24. It is possible that they did so value the GM jobs, since they applied at Ford only after being laid off at GM, and since after being recalled to the GM jobs they rejected Ford's offer. Therefore, contrary to the dissent's erroneous suggestion, the possibility that Gaddis and Starr considered their GM jobs superior to the positions they would have had at Ford had Ford hired them at the outset is not merely a "hypothetical case." We cannot infer that they so valued their GM jobs, however, solely from their rejection of Ford's offer.

The claimant who chooses not to follow this path does so, then, not because it provides inadequate compensation, but because the value of the replacement job outweighs the value of the defendant's job supplemented by the prospect of full court-ordered compensation. In other words, the victim of discrimination who finds a better or substantially equivalent job no longer suffers ongoing injury stemming from the unlawful discrimination.

C

Thus, the rule advocated by Ford rests comfortably both on the statutory requirement that a Title VII claimant must minimize damages and on the fact that a claimant is no longer incurring additional injury if he has been able to find other suitable work that, all things considered, is at least as attractive as the defendant's. For this reason, in almost all circumstances the rule is fully consistent with Title VII's object of making injured claimants whole.

The sole question that can be raised regarding whether the rule adequately compensates claimants arises in that narrow category of cases in which the claimant believes his replacement job to be superior to the defendant's job without seniority, but inferior to the defendant's job with the benefits of seniority. In the present case, for example, it is possible that Gaddis and Starr considered their GM jobs more attractive than the jobs offered by Ford, but less satisfactory than the positions they would have held at Ford if Ford had hired them initially. If so, they were confronted with two options. They could have accepted Ford's unconditional offer, preserving their right to full compensation if they prevailed on their Title VII claims, but forfeiting their favorable positions at GM. Alternatively, they could have kept their jobs at GM, retaining the possibility of continued employment there, but, under the operation of the rule advocated here by Ford, losing the right to claim further backpay from Ford after the date of Ford's offer. The court below concluded that under these circumstances Ford's rule would present Gaddis and Starr with an "intolerable choice," 645 F.2d 183, 192 (CA4 1981), depriving them of the opportunity to receive full compensation.

We agree that Gaddis and Starr had to choose between two alternatives. We do not agree, however, that their opportunity to choose deprived them of compensation. After all, they had the option of accepting Ford's unconditional offer and retaining the right to seek full compensation at trial, which would comport fully with Title VII's goal of making discrimination victims whole. Under the rule advocated by Ford, if Gaddis and Starr chose the option of remaining at their GM jobs rather than accept Ford's offer, it was because they thought that the GM jobs, plus their claims to backpay accrued prior to Ford's offer, were *more* valuable to them than the jobs they originally sought from Ford, plus the right to seek full compensation from the court.[26] It is

---

26. Employees value a job for many reasons besides the rate of pay, including, for example, the presence of other workers of the employee's own sex, the availability

hard to see how Gaddis and Starr could have been deprived of adequate compensation because they chose to venture upon a path that seemed to them more attractive than the Ford job plus the right to seek full compensation in court.

If the choice presented to Gaddis and Starr was difficult, it was only because it required them to assess their likelihood of prevailing at trial. But surely it cannot be contended for this reason alone that they were deprived of their right to adequate compensation. It is a fact of life that litigation is risky and that a plaintiff with a claim to compensation for his losses must consider the possibility that the claim might be lost at trial, either wrongly, because of litigation error, or rightly, because the defendant was innocent. Ford's rule merely requires the Title VII claimant to decide whether to take the job offered by the defendant, retaining his rights to an award by the court of backpay accrued prior to the effective date of the offer, and any court-ordered retroactive seniority plus compensation for any losses suffered as a result of his lesser seniority before the court's judgment, or, instead, whether to accept a more attractive job from another employer and the limitation of the claim for backpay to the damages that have already accrued. The rule urged by the EEOC and adopted by the court below, by contrast, would have the perverse result of requiring the employer in effect to insure the claimant against the risk that the employer might win at trial.

Therefore, we conclude that, when a claimant rejects the offer of the job he originally sought, as supplemented by a right to full court-ordered compensation, his choice can be taken as establishing that he considers the ongoing injury he has suffered at the hands of the defendant to have been ended by the availability of better opportunities elsewhere. For this reason, we find that, absent special circumstances,[27] the simple rule that the ongoing accrual of backpay liability

---

of recreational facilities at the worksite, staggered work hours, better health benefits, longer vacations, and so forth. What makes one job better than another varies from one employee to another.

Gaddis and Starr presumably rejected Ford's offer because they thought their jobs at GM were worth more to them than full compensation (Ford's offer plus a court award) discounted by the risks of litigation. In essence, the position adopted by the court below and advocated here by the EEOC turns on the fact that we cannot be sure that, had Gaddis and Starr known they were going to win their lawsuit, they still would have rejected Ford's offer. Had they known they were going to win, of course, they would have rejected the Ford job only if they valued the GM jobs more than they valued the combination of Ford's job plus the value of court-ordered compen-

sation *un* discounted by the risks of litigation. To agree with the EEOC is, in effect, to contend that a claimant is not made whole for purposes of Title VII unless he decided to stay at a replacement job that was worth to him more than the sum of (1) the defendant's job, (2) the right to seek full court-ordered compensation, and, in addition, (3) a sum analogous to insurance against the risk of loss at trial. We discern, however, no reason for concluding that Title VII requires the defendant to insure the claimant against the possibility that the defendant might prevail in the lawsuit.

27. If, for example, the claimant has been forced to move a great distance to find a replacement job, a rejection of the employer's offer might reflect the costs of relocation more than a judgment that the replacement job was superior, all things

is tolled when a Title VII claimant rejects the job he originally sought comports with Title VII's policy of making discrimination victims whole.

V

Although Title VII remedies depend primarily upon the objectives discussed above, the statute also permits us to consider the rights of "innocent third parties." City of Los Angeles Department of Water & Power v. Manhart, 435 U.S. 702, 723, 98 S.Ct. 1370, 1383, 55 L.Ed.2d 657 (1978). See also Teamsters v. United States, 431 U.S. 324, 371–376, 97 S.Ct. 1843, 1872–1875, 52 L.Ed.2d 396 (1977). The lower court's rule places a particularly onerous burden on the innocent employees of an employer charged with discrimination. Under the court's rule, an employer may cap backpay liability only by forcing his incumbent employees to yield seniority to a person who has not proven, and may never prove, unlawful discrimination. As we have acknowledged on numerous occasions, seniority plays a central role in allocating benefits and burdens among employees.[28] In light of the "overriding importance" of these rights, American Tobacco Co. v. Patterson, 456 U.S. 63, 76, 102 S.Ct. 1534, 1541, 71 L.Ed.2d 748 (1982) (quoting Humphrey v. Moore, 375 U.S. 335, 346, 84 S.Ct. 363, 370, 11 L.Ed.2d 370 (1964)), we should be wary of any rule that encourages job offers that compel innocent workers to sacrifice their seniority to a person who has only claimed, but not yet proven, unlawful discrimination.

The sacrifice demanded by the lower court's rule, moreover, leaves the displaced workers without any remedy against claimants who fail to establish their claims. If, for example, layoffs occur while the Title VII suit is pending, an employer may have to furlough an innocent worker indefinitely while retaining a claimant who was given retroactive seniority. If the claimant subsequently fails to prove unlawful discrimination, the worker unfairly relegated to the unemployment lines has no redress for the wrong done him. We do not believe that " 'the large objectives' " of Title VII, Albemarle Paper Co. v. Moody, 422

considered, to the defendant's job. In exceptional circumstances, the trial court, in the exercise of its sound discretion, could give weight to such factors when deciding whether backpay damages accrued after the rejection of an employer's offer should be awarded to the claimant.

The dissent attempts to characterize "the loss of accumulated seniority at [a] replacement jo[b]" as such a cost of relocation. By so doing, the dissent simply confuses the costs of changing from one job to another—whatever the respective advantages and disadvantages of the two jobs might be—with the differences between the two jobs.

28. Seniority may govern, "not only promotion and layoff, but also transfer, demotion, rest days, shift assignments, prerogative in scheduling vacation, order of layoff, possibilities of lateral transfer to avoid layoff, 'bumping' possibilities in the face of layoff, order of recall, training opportunities, working conditions, length of layoff endured without reducing seniority, length of layoff recall rights will withstand, overtime opportunities, parking privileges, and [even] a preferred place in the punch-out line." Franks v. Bowman Transportation Co., 424 U.S., at 766–767, 96 S.Ct., at 1265 (1976) (quoting Stacy, Title VII Seniority Remedies in a Time of Economic Downturn, 28 Vand.L.Rev. 487, 490 (1975)).

U.S., at 416, 95 S.Ct., at 2371 (citation omitted), require innocent employees to carry such a heavy burden.[29]

VI

In conclusion, we find that the rule adopted by the court below disserves Title VII's primary goal of getting the victims of employment discrimination into the jobs they deserve as quickly as possible. The rule, moreover, threatens the interests of other, innocent employees by disrupting the established seniority hierarchy, with the attendant risk that an innocent employee will be unfairly laid off or disadvantaged because a Title VII claimant unfairly has been granted seniority.

On the other hand, the rule that a Title VII claimant's rejection of a defendant's job offer normally ends the defendant's ongoing responsibility for backpay suffers neither of these disadvantages, while nevertheless adequately satisfying Title VII's compensation goals. Most important, it also serves as a potent force on behalf of Title VII's objective of bringing discrimination to an end more quickly than is often possible through litigation. For these reasons we hold that, absent special circumstances, the rejection of an employer's unconditional job offer ends the accrual of potential backpay liability. We reverse the judgment of the Court of Appeals and remand for proceedings consistent with this opinion.

So ordered.

JUSTICE BLACKMUN, with whom JUSTICE BRENNAN and JUSTICE MARSHALL join, dissenting.

After finding that petitioner Ford Motor Company had discriminated unlawfully against Judy Gaddis and Rebecca Starr because of their sex, the Court of Appeals affirmed the District Court's backpay award to the two women "as a proper exercise of discretion founded on not clearly erroneous factual determinations." The Court today reverses this unremarkable holding with a wide-ranging advisory ruling stretching far beyond the confines of this case. The Court's rule provides employers who have engaged in unlawful hiring practices with

---

29. In addition to the rights of innocent employees, the rule urged by the EEOC and adopted by the court below burdens innocent employers. An innocent employer—or one who believes himself innocent—has the right to challenge in court claims he considers weak or baseless. The approach endorsed by the lower court undermines this right by requiring the employer, if he wishes to offer some relief to the claimant and toll the mounting backpay bill, to surrender his defense to the charge that the claimant is entitled to retroactive seniority. If the employer offers the claimant retroactive seniority as well as a job, and then prevails at trial, he will have no recourse against the claimant for the costs of the retroactive seniority that the claimant erroneously received. The rule urged by Ford permits the parties to stem the ongoing effects of the alleged discrimination without compelling either claimant or employer to compromise his claims or surrender his defenses. Cf. Moro Motors Ltd., 216 N.L.R.B. 192, 193 (1975) ("were [an employer] required to offer to an employee, allegedly discharged for discriminatory reasons, reinstatement *with accrued back pay*, the [employer's] right to litigate the issue of whether the discharge was unlawful would for all practical purposes be nullified") (emphasis in original); National Screen Products Co., 147 N.L.R.B. 746, 747–748 (1964).

a unilateral device to cut off their backpay liability to the victims of their past discrimination.

To justify its new rule, the Court mischaracterizes the holding of the Court of Appeals, undertakes an intricate economic analysis of hypothetical situations not presented here, and invokes the rights of " 'innocent third parties,' " who are not before the Court. By so doing, the Court not only supplants traditional district court discretion to mold equitable relief, but also ensures that Judy Gaddis and Rebecca Starr—the only Title VII claimants whose rights are at issue in this lawsuit—will not be made whole for injury they indisputably have suffered. I find the Court's ruling both unnecessary and unfair. I dissent.

I

A

The Court frames the question presented as "whether an employer charged with discrimination in hiring can toll the continuing accrual of backpay liability * * * simply by unconditionally offering the [Title VII] claimant the job previously denied, or whether the employer also must offer seniority retroactive to the date of the alleged discrimination."

In my view, the Court simply and completely misstates the issue. The question before us is not which of two inflexible standards should govern accrual of backpay liability in *all* Title VII cases, but whether the District Court's award of backpay relief to Gaddis and Starr *in this case* constituted an abuse of discretion.

The Court makes frequent and puzzling reference to the "onerous burden[s]" and "sacrifice demanded by the lower court's rule." * * * In fact, the Court of Appeals adopted no inflexible "rule" at all. Rather, it simply applied the well-settled and flexible principles of appellate review of Title VII remedies prescribed in Albemarle Paper Co. v. Moody and Franks v. Bowman Transportation Co.

In *Albemarle*, this Court directed that, in most Title VII matters, "the standard of [appellate] review will be the familiar one of whether the District Court was 'clearly erroneous' in its factual findings and whether it 'abused' its traditional discretion to locate 'a just result' in light of the circumstances peculiar to the case." With regard to Title VII backpay relief, however, the Court specified that " 'the [district] court has not merely the power but the duty to render a decree which will so far as possible eliminate the discriminatory effects of the past as well as bar like discrimination in the future.' " To achieve this purpose, "Congress took care to arm the courts with full equitable powers. For it is the historic purpose of equity to 'secur[e] complete justice.' " [1]

1. In passing the Equal Employment Opportunity Act of 1972, 86 Stat. 103, Congress specifically rejected several legisla- tive efforts to limit the judicial power to award backpay. See Albemarle Paper Co. v. Moody, 422 U.S. 405, 420, 95 S.Ct. 2362,

The Court in *Albemarle* and *Franks* made clear that, in Title VII cases, the equitable discretion of district courts should be guided by a heavy presumption in favor of full backpay awards. "Rather than limiting the power of district courts to do equity, the presumption insures that complete equity normally will be accomplished." Franks v. Bowman Transportation Co., 424 U.S., at 786, 96 S.Ct., at 1275 (POWELL, J., concurring in part and dissenting in part). By exercising their discretion to award full backpay relief, district courts further two broad purposes underlying Title VII. First, "the reasonably certain prospect of a backpay award * * * 'provide[s] the spur or catalyst which causes employers * * * to self-examine and to self-evaluate their employment practices and to endeavor to eliminate, so far as possible, the last vestiges' " of discrimination. Albemarle Paper Co. v. Moody, 422 U.S., at 417–418, 95 S.Ct., at 2371–2372 (citation omitted). Second, backpay awards "make persons whole for injuries suffered on account of unlawful employment discrimination."

Thus, the goal of appellate review is to ensure that the district courts have exercised their remedial discretion in the way that "allow[s] the most complete achievement of the objectives of Title VII that is attainable under the facts and circumstances of the specific case." Franks v. Bowman Transportation Co., 424 U.S., at 770–771, 96 S.Ct., at 1266–1267. "The courts of appeals must maintain a consistent and principled application of the backpay provision, consistent with [Title VII's] twin statutory objectives, while at the same time recognizing that the trial court will often have the keener appreciation of those facts and circumstances peculiar to particular cases." Albemarle Paper Co. v. Moody, 422 U.S., at 421–422, 95 S.Ct., at 2373.

B

In this case, the trial court's findings of fact were uncontroverted. In July 1971, Judy Gaddis and Rebecca Starr sought jobs at petitioner Ford's automotive parts warehouse in Charlotte, N.C. "Because of their experience, each was qualified to work at Ford as a 'picker-packer.'" Ford's stated hiring practice was to fill job vacancies at the warehouse by "taking the earliest filed applications first," and selecting employees by interviewing qualified candidates. At the time Gaddis and Starr applied, however, Ford had never hired any woman to work at the

---

2373, 45 L.Ed.2d 280 (1975). The Section-by-Section Analysis accompanying the Conference Committee Report reaffirmed the "make whole" purpose of § 706(g), Title VII's backpay provision:

"The provisions of this subsection are intended to give the courts wide discretion exercising their equitable powers to fashion the most complete relief possible. In dealing with the present section 706(g) the courts have stressed that the scope of relief under that section of the

Act is intended to make the victims of unlawful discrimination whole, and that the attainment of this objective * * * requires that persons aggrieved by the consequences and effects of the unlawful employment practice be, so far as possible, restored to a position where they would have been were it not for the unlawful discrimination." 118 Cong. Rec. 7168 (1972), quoted in Albemarle Paper Co. v. Moody, 422 U.S., at 421, 95 S.Ct., at 2373.

warehouse.[2] When Gaddis and Starr received their application forms, "a receptionist at Ford * * * told them in substance that Ford did not hire women to work in the warehouse."

Despite Gaddis' persistent requests for job interviews, petitioner interviewed neither woman immediately, supposedly because no job vacancy existed. The unit supervisor testified: "Ms. Gaddis called me on several occasions and asked if I was hiring, and I said no, * * * I just have too much work to do to sit down and interview people if I'm not hiring." Shortly thereafter, however, in August 1971, Ford hired male applicants to fill four job openings. "At least two of the men * * * were offered their jobs *after* Gaddis and Starr applied."

Gaddis filed a sex discrimination charge with respondent EEOC in September 1971. In January 1973, Gaddis and Starr were recalled to jobs at a nearby General Motors warehouse. In July 1973, petitioner made a vague job offer first to Gaddis, then to Starr.[3] The District Court found as a fact that "[t]he offer to the two women was made after Ford learned that a charge of sex discrimination had been filed with the Commission (and was prompted by a desire to bring some women into the warehouse in response to the charge)." [4]

2. The District Court found, for example, that the job application of Zettie Smith, who sought employment at Ford about a month before Gaddis and Starr, and who was the first woman to apply for a warehouse job there, "was never seriously considered because she is a woman." App. to Pet. for Cert. A–157–A–158.

3. At trial, Gaddis was asked:

"Q. Did [the clerk to the warehouse manager] say that the job was being offered to you, or did he discuss simply with you, in the form of an interview, the possibility of hiring you into some job?

A. It was so vague that I couldn't pinpoint anything down. They never did say what type of work it would be, whether it would be [parts] picking or whether it would be in sheet metal or whether it would be putting up stock or whether it would be on a day shift or night shift, whether it was a permanent or temporary job. At the time, I had a good seniority with General Motors and I had a secure job, and so on those grounds, I refused it." App. 43.

Similarly, Starr testified on cross-examination:

"I remember [the clerk to the warehouse manager] wasn't specific on the job about what it would be. I did have, at General Motors I had fifteen, I don't know if it was fourteen or fifteen people

under me. I had seniority, and I also, this is the truth about [it,] I was scared. Whenever I had worked at Ford before, I had been badgered and I don't know, I was just, I wanted to look into the job. Yet, I had a fear to go back. I didn't know what I would be facing." Id., at 54.

4. The trial testimony of Ford's warehouse operations manager illuminates petitioner's motives:

"Q. Whose decision was it to call Ms. Gaddis and Ms. Starr?

A. It was my decision.

Q. Why?

A. Well, mainly because we had a suit, EEOC suit filed against us, and we wanted to give one of them an opportunity to go to work for us, and we only had one, maybe two openings at that time.

* * *

Q. Mr. Ely, you indicated in your testimony that you offered a job to one of the women, either Ms. Gaddis or Ms. Starr, in July, 1973. Is that correct?

A. Yes, that's correct.

Q. You also stated that you offered such job because of the EEOC charge which had been filed against Ford Motor Company. Is that correct?

A. That's correct." App. 17–18.

Gaddis, and then Starr, turned down petitioner's job offer. The District Court found that the offer was "refused by both women since they were at that time back at work in the General Motors warehouse, having been recalled to work in January, 1973. Neither woman wished to lose accrued seniority at General Motors and neither wanted to be the only woman employed in the Ford warehouse."

Based on its factual findings, the District Court concluded as a matter of law that "Ford discriminated against * * * Gaddis and Starr on the basis of their sex by failing to employ them in its warehouse in the positions filled in August, 1971." In rulings not contested here, the District Court also found that 10 other women had established prima facie cases of unlawful sex discrimination by Ford.

To determine the backpay remedy to which Gaddis and Starr were entitled, the District Court attached no legal significance to the women's decision to decline beginning employment at Ford nearly two years after they unlawfully had been denied those same jobs and six months after they had begun accumulating seniority elsewhere.[5] In the ruling which the Court today implicitly deems an abuse of discretion, the District Court held that "[b]ack pay due to Gaddis and Starr shall not be affected by their refusal to accept the single position offered them in July, 1973, inasmuch as neither would have been confronted by that decision and its implications had both been hired in August, 1971."

Applying the standard of review specified in *Franks*, supra, and *Albemarle*, supra, the Court of Appeals affirmed "the district court's decision as a proper exercise of discretion founded on not clearly erroneous factual determinations." In particular, the Court of Appeals found no abuse of discretion in the District Court's failure to terminate the backpay awards in July 1973.[6]

The Court of Appeals rested its narrow ruling on two key facts: that "Gaddis and Starr could accept [Ford's] offer only by *forfeiting the seniority* they had accumulated at General Motors and *without a compensating offer of seniority at Ford* to alleviate the effects of the discrimination against them in 1971." The court expressed no view as to whether Ford's backpay liability would have been tolled if Gaddis and Starr could have accepted Ford's job offer without forfeiting seniority accumulated elsewhere. Nor did the Court of Appeals decide whether the women would have been obliged to accept Ford's offer had

---

5. The District Court applied two equitable principles to shape relief in this case. It first concluded that an award of all backpay accruing after August 1971 would make Gaddis and Starr whole. The District Court therefore reconstructed a probable employment history at Ford for each woman, calculating what each would have received but for petitioner's unlawful discrimination. Second, the court obliged Gaddis and Starr to take all reasonable steps to mitigate damages. Accordingly, it subtracted from the backpay awards any amounts Gaddis and Starr actually earned or reasonably could have earned after August 1971. App. to Pet. for Cert. A–170.

6. "[T]he district court reached an eminently reasonable result. It did not permit Ford to cut off the back pay period by making Gaddis and Starr an incomplete and unacceptable offer, and it denied Gaddis and Starr a double recovery by deducting their General Motors wages from their back pay awards." 645 F.2d 183, at 193.

it encompassed *some* compensating offer of seniority, short of full retroactive seniority.

Contrary to this Court's suggestion today, the Court of Appeals announced no general *rule* that an employer's "backpay liability should be tolled *only* by the rejection of an offer that includes seniority retroactive to the date on which the alleged discrimination occurred." The Court of Appeals merely refused to announce a broad new rule, urged by Ford, requiring victims of Title VII discrimination to "accept job offers which include a loss of seniority in order to preserve their back pay rights." Such an inflexible approach, the court decided, would frustrate Title VII's central purposes by permitting employers to present discriminatees with an "intolerable choice." [7]

II

The Court today accepts Ford's invitation, wisely declined by the Court of Appeals, and adopts its broad new rule governing awards of backpay relief in Title VII cases: henceforth, "absent special circumstances, the rejection of an employer's unconditional job offer ends the accrual of potential backpay liability." [8] This ruling is disturbing in four respects.

First: The Court's new rule is flatly inconsistent with *Albemarle*'s unambiguous directive "that, given a finding of unlawful discrimination, backpay should be denied only for reasons which, if applied generally, would not frustrate the central statutory purposes of eradicating discrimination throughout the economy and making persons whole for injuries suffered through past discrimination." Applied generally, the Court's rule interferes with both objectives.

The Court's approach authorizes employers to make "cheap offers" to the victims of their past discrimination. Employers may now terminate their backpay liability unilaterally by extending to their discrimination victims offers they cannot reasonably accept. Once an employer has refused to hire a job applicant, and that applicant has mitigated damages by obtaining and accumulating seniority in another job, the employer may offer the applicant the same job that she was denied unlawfully several years earlier. In this very case, for example, Ford offered Gaddis and Starr jobs only after they had obtained employment

7. "[I]f Gaddis and Starr rejected Ford's offer and stayed at General Motors, they would forego their rights to further back pay benefits. On the other hand, if they accepted the job offered by Ford, which they had not held for the previous two years because of Ford's discriminatory hiring policy, they would lose their seniority rights at General Motors." 645 F.2d, at 192.

8. The Court's explanation for its misreading of the Court of Appeals' decision is that the United States District Court for the Western District of Virginia has interpreted that decision as stating a somewhat different proposition. But if one District Court in the Fourth Circuit has misconstrued the Fourth Circuit's opinion, surely that is a matter properly to be corrected by the United States Court of Appeals for the Fourth Circuit. This Court is not entitled to transform a narrow Court of Appeals ruling into a broad one, just so that it may reverse and install a broad new rule of its own choosing.

elsewhere and only because they had filed charges with the EEOC. If, as here, the applicant declines the offer to preserve existing job security, the employer has successfully cut off all future backpay liability to that applicant. By insulating a discriminating employer from proper liability for his discriminatory acts, the Court's rule reduces his "incentive to shun practices of dubious legality," and hinders the eradication of discrimination.

The Court's rule also violates Title VII's second objective—making victims of discrimination whole. Again, the rule's anomalies are well-illustrated by the facts of this case. Had petitioner not discriminated against Gaddis and Starr, both would have begun to work at Ford in August 1971. By July 1973, both would have accumulated nearly two years of seniority. Because of Ford's discrimination, however, each experienced long periods of unemployment and temporary employment before obtaining jobs elsewhere.[9] The District Court therefore determined that only full backpay awards, mitigated by wages earned or reasonably earnable elsewhere, would make Gaddis and Starr whole.

This Court now truncates those awards simply because Gaddis and Starr refused to accept Ford's offers of beginning employment in 1973. Yet even if Gaddis and Starr had accepted those offers, they would not have been made whole. Deprived of two years of seniority, Gaddis and Starr would have enjoyed lesser health, life, and unemployment insurance benefits, lower wages, less eligibility for promotion and transfer, and greater vulnerability to layoffs than persons hired after they were unlawfully refused employment. Even if Gaddis and Starr had continued to litigate the question of their retroactive seniority after accepting Ford's offer, they still would have spent many years at Ford "subordinate to persons who, but for the illegal discrimination, would have been[,] in respect to entitlement to [competitive seniority] benefits[,][their] inferiors." Franks v. Bowman Transportation Co.

The Court claims that its new rule "powerfully motivates employers to put Title VII claimants to work, thus ending ongoing discrimination as promptly as possible." In fact, the discrimination is not ended, because a discrimination victim who accepts a "cheap offer" will be obliged to work at a seniority disadvantage, and therefore will suffer ongoing effects from the employer's discriminatory act. The Court also alleges that its rule promotes "cooperation and voluntary compliance" with Title VII by giving both employers and claimants incentives to make and accept "unconditional" job offers. If the Court's rule furthers this end, however, it does so only by weakening the bargaining position of a claimant vis-a-vis the employer. Discrimination victims will be forced to accept otherwise unacceptable offers, because they will know that rejection of those offers truncates their backpay recovery. A

---

9. Gaddis, for example, sought employment in South Carolina, "at various parts places, independent part places, car dealers, such as Chrysler–Plymouth, the Ford place which was Lewis Ford at that time, all the car dealers, * * * some of the hosiery mills, * * * [and] Radiator Specialty Company," III Tr. 362, before obtaining her job at General Motors.

rule that shields discriminating employers from liability for their past discrimination and coerces bona fide Title VII claimants to accept incomplete job offers is fundamentally incompatible with the purposes of Title VII.

Second: The Court's rule unjustifiably limits a district court's discretion to make individual discrimination victims whole through awards of backpay. The Court suggests that, "absent special circumstances," a district court abuses its discretion *per se* if it fails to terminate an employer's backpay liability at the point where that employer has extended an unconditional job offer to a discrimination claimant. Yet "[i]n *Albemarle Paper* the Court read Title VII as creating a *presumption in favor* of backpay." Franks v. Bowman Transportation Co., 424 U.S., at 786, 96 S.Ct., at 1275 (Powell, J., concurring in part and dissenting in part) (emphasis added).[10] *Franks* supplied "emphatic confirmation that federal courts are empowered to fashion such relief as the *particular circumstances of a case may require* to effect restitution, making whole insofar as possible the victims of * * * discrimination in hiring." Id. at, 764, 96 S.Ct., at 1264 (opinion of the Court) (emphasis added).

The Court recognizes that its new rule interferes with district court discretion to make complete backpay awards in individual cases. Thus, the Court expressly preserves the principle of appellate deference to the "sound discretion" of the trial court in "exceptional circumstances." Yet, curiously, the Court offers no explanation why the facts of this very case fail to satisfy its own "exceptional circumstances" test.[11] Given the Court's concession that district courts must retain their discretion to make bona fide Title VII claimants whole in some cases, I see no advantage in prescribing a blanket rule that displaces that discretion in other cases where complete relief is equally justified.

Third: I am disturbed by the Court's efforts to justify its rule by relying on situations not presented by this case. For example, the Court partially rests its rule on an "un- or underemployed claimant's

10. The Court cites language from *Albemarle* suggesting that a district court's discretion is not limitless. But the Court conspicuously omits *Albemarle*'s clear statement that if Congress intended to limit the equitable discretion of district courts in any way, it did so only by leaving " 'little room for the exercise of discretion *not* to order reimbursement.' " See Albemarle Paper Co. v. Moody, 422 U.S., at 417, 95 S.Ct., at 2371, quoting Mitchell v. DeMario Jewelry, 361 U.S. 288, 296, 80 S.Ct. 332, 337, 4 L.Ed.2d 323 (1960) (emphasis added).

11. The Court suggests, for example, that if a hypothetical Title VII "claimant has been forced to move a great distance to find a replacement job, a rejection of the employer's offer might reflect the costs of

relocation more than a judgment that the replacement job was superior, all things considered, to the defendant's job." For Gaddis and Starr, however, the loss of their accumulated seniority at their replacement jobs certainly reflected "costs of relocation" at least as substantial as high moving expenses.

I expect that federal courts will find no meaningful distinction between a worker's refusal to accept a job offer because he believes that acceptance would force him to incur costs, and a similar refusal based on the worker's judgment that changing jobs would prove costly. In either case, for purposes of awarding Title VII relief, the reasonableness of the worker's refusal should be left to the trial court's discretion.

statutory obligation to minimize damages" by accepting an unconditional job offer without seniority. Because Gaddis and Starr were fully employed when Ford finally offered them jobs, however, neither the District Court nor the Court of Appeals exempted unemployed or underemployed victims of discrimination from accepting offers like Ford's.[12] Similarly, the Court analyzes the hypothetical case of a Title VII claimant who "has had the good fortune to find a more attractive job than the defendant's." But, as the Court later recognizes, there is no assurance that the present case fits this category either. After speculating at length about how Gaddis and Starr may have valued the relative worth of their Ford and General Motors jobs, the Court finally acknowledges that on this paper record, "[w]e cannot infer" how much Gaddis and Starr "valued their GM jobs * * * solely from their rejection of Ford's offer."

Equally unconvincing is the Court's repeated invocation of, and preoccupation with, "the rights of 'innocent third parties,'" and the "disruption of the existing seniority system[s]," that would result from adoption of the Court of Appeals' "rule." The Court nowhere demonstrates how *petitioner's* labor relations would have suffered had Ford extended offers of retroactive seniority to Gaddis and Starr. The details of Ford's collective-bargaining agreement were not litigated in either the District Court or the Court of Appeals. Thus, those courts never passed on petitioner's obligation to offer retroactive seniority to Gaddis and Starr if such an offer would have disrupted its labor relations or existing seniority systems.[13] Nor did the Court of Appeals decide, as a general matter, whether or not offers of retroactive seniority to discrimination claimants adversely affect the rights of incumbent employees.[14] The Court cannot justify reversal in the case at hand by

---

12. The purpose of § 706(g)'s "mitigation of damages" requirement is to encourage claimants to work while their Title VII claims are being adjudicated. The Court cannot deny that Gaddis and Starr fully mitigated damages by seeking and obtaining other employment while litigating their claims against Ford.

13. The Court of Appeals did not foreclose the possibility that Ford could have terminated its backpay liability to Gaddis and Starr by offering them employment plus an award of *provisional* seniority, defeasible in the event that they lost their continuing lawsuit for backpay. Nor did the Court of Appeals deny that offering a job without seniority might terminate Ford's backpay liability, should any provision of Ford's collective-bargaining agreement preclude it from making offers of retroactive seniority. Had petitioner pointed to such a collective-bargaining agreement provision, or proved that its incumbent employees actually had objected to offers of retroactive seniority to Title

VII claimants, the Court of Appeals would have considered those factors in determining whether the District Court abused its discretion in shaping Gaddis' and Starr's relief.

14. In any event, the Court's claim that offers of retroactive seniority would injure the rights of incumbent employees is vastly overstated. If any employer sued by a Title VII claimant could toll the accrual of backpay liability by making a unilateral offer that included some form of retroactive seniority, he still would have every incentive to make such an offer as soon as possible after the discriminatory act. The amount of retroactive seniority offered would necessarily be small, and the seniority rights of relatively few incumbent employees would be affected.

Under the Court's approach, in contrast, employers will no longer have any incentive to offer retroactive seniority. Any awards of retroactive seniority to bona fide Title VII claimants will thus be court-or-

vague reference to classes of claimants and third parties who are not before the Court. To the extent that it seeks to do so. Its intricate argument is both irrelevant and advisory.

Fourth and finally: I am struck by the contrast between the Court's concern for parties who are not here and its studied indifference to the real-life concerns of the parties whose interests are directly affected. When the Court finally confronts the choice that actually faced Gaddis and Starr, it blithely suggests that "[a]fter all, they had the option of accepting Ford's unconditional offer and retaining the right to seek full compensation at trial" in the form of retroactive seniority. Yet the Court earlier acknowledges that "[d]elays in litigation unfortunately are now commonplace, forcing the victims of discrimination to suffer years of underemployment or unemployment before they can obtain a court order awarding them the jobs unlawfully denied them."

"If the choice presented to Gaddis and Starr was difficult," the Court continues, "it was only because it required them to assess their likelihood of prevailing at trial." Without consulting the record, the Court then states:

"Gaddis and Starr presumably rejected Ford's offer because they thought their jobs at GM were worth more to them than full compensation (Ford's offer plus a court award) discounted by the risks of litigation. * * * Had they known they were going to win [their lawsuit], of course, they would have rejected the Ford job only if they valued the GM jobs more than they valued the combination of Ford's job plus the value of court-ordered compensation *un* discounted by the risks of litigation."

This is a comfortable rationale stated from the sidelines. Unfortunately, the abstract and technical concerns that govern the Court's calculations bear little resemblance to those that actually motivated Judy Gaddis and Rebecca Starr. When asked on cross-examination why she had turned down Ford's 1973 offer, Gaddis testified: "I had seniority [at General Motors] and I knew that I wasn't in danger of any layoff, where if I had accepted the job at Ford *I might have worked a week or two weeks and been laid off because I would have been low seniority.*" Similarly, Starr testified on cross-examination: "I had seniority at General Motors. I had about fifteen people working under me. *I could go to work at Ford and work a week and I knew that they could lay me off.*"

To a person living in the real world, the value of job security today far outstrips the value of full court-ordered compensation many years in the future. The Court's elaborate speculation about the concerns

dered, and will be entered only after "the lengthy delays that too often attend Title VII litigation." By delaying awards of retroactive seniority until final judgment in a significant number of cases, the Court's approach ensures that the seniority rights of comparatively greater numbers of incumbent employees will be affected adversely.

that "presumably" motivated Gaddis and Starr nowhere recognizes what a Ford job without seniority actually meant to Gaddis and Starr— a job from which they could be laid off at any moment. Unlike the Court, Gaddis and Starr recognized that if they traded their jobs with seniority for jobs without seniority, they could quickly become unemployed again, long before they had the chance to vindicate their rights at trial.

To people like Gaddis and Starr, the knowledge that they might someday establish their Title VII claims on the merits provides little solace for their immediate and pressing personal needs. Starr's trial testimony reveals just how much job security meant to her:

> "It was just a couple of days after I had [started working] there [at a temporary job] and this is, I was just wanting that job so bad because you can't, a woman, when you've got three children, I needed the money, and I was wanting the job so bad. I worked so hard. I'll never forget one day when [the unit supervisor] came to me. I'll never forget that, and he said, I had just been there a few days, I'll have to let you go. * * * It broke my heart because I knew I had worked so hard." [15]

I agree with the Court that "the victims of job discrimination want jobs, not lawsuits." * * * When Ford made its 1973 offers to Gaddis and Starr, however, they *had* jobs, in which they had accumulated seniority despite Ford's discrimination. I therefore cannot accept the Court's conclusion that these women should have traded those jobs for uncertain employment in which back seniority could be won only by lawsuit. Nor can I justify penalizing Gaddis and Starr because they "discounted" the ultimate likelihood of obtaining court-ordered retroactive seniority at a different rate than the Court does today.

After hearing all the witnesses and appraising all the evidence, the District Court exercised its equitable discretion to shape complete backpay relief for Gaddis and Starr. In light of all the circumstances, the District Court refused to penalize Gaddis and Starr for declining Ford's 1973 job offer. Applying the correct standard of review over Title VII remedies, the Court of Appeals concluded that the District Court had exercised its remedial discretion properly. Sitting at this remove, I cannot say that Gaddis and Starr acted unreasonably. I would affirm the judgment of the Court of Appeals and thereby, for these two victims of discrimination, fulfill, and not defeat, the promise of Title VII.

---

15. Without embarrassment, the Court cites Rebecca Starr's testimony to support its argument that the Court of Appeals' "rule," and not its own new rule, is indifferent to the real-life concerns of victims of sex discrimination. Under the Court of Appeals' "rule," however, Rebecca Starr was awarded full backpay as compensation for Ford's sex discrimination. Under this Court's rule, a large portion of Starr's compensation will simply be cut off. By claiming that the Court of Appeals was somehow *more* indifferent to Starr's real-life concerns, the Court only confirms how far removed from the real world it is.

NOTES AND PROBLEMS FOR DISCUSSION

1. Both the majority and the dissenting opinions of the Supreme Court in *Ford Motor Co.* rely on the Court's decision in Albemarle Paper Co. v. Moody. Which opinion is most consistent with the "make whole" philosophy of *Albemarle*? The majority opinion holds that an employer faced with a discrimination claim by an unsuccessful job applicant may choose not to gamble on the outcome of future litigation and may limit his potential liability for back pay by offering the claimant a position equivalent to that for which she originally applied. The claimant, who has obtained other employment, on the other hand, must give up his current job (and any seniority rights which have accrued) in order to preserve her right to 'full" back pay and retroactive seniority if she prevails at trial. But the question of what constitutes full relief will only arise after the employer has been found guilty of discrimination. Why then should it be the innocent employee who is forced to gamble? Is the majority's opinion based on the assumption that the relief afforded to Gaddis and Starr by the courts below made them *more* than whole? Was there a middle ground which the Court could have adopted?

Under the Supreme Court's rule in *Ford Motor Co.*, can the employer terminate its backpay liability by offering the claimant a position different from the job originally sought? Compare, EEOC v. Exxon Shipping Co., 745 F.2d 967 (5th Cir.1984) (offer of job not substantially equivalent to one sought by claimant does not terminate liability) with Cowen v. Standard Brands, Inc., 572 F.Supp. 1576 (N.D.Ala.1983) (offer of job in another city, while not as attractive to the plaintiff as one sought in local of his residence, was "comparable" in legal sense). Should the issue of "substantial equivalence" be one of fact or law? An employer will not toll the accrual of back pay without establishing that it offered the plaintiff a substantially equivalent position. Dickerson v. Deluxe Check Printers, Inc., 703 F.2d 276 (8th Cir.1983); EEOC v. Service News Co., 898 F.2d 958, 963 (4th Cir.1990) (vague offer to reinstate made to state investigator did not toll back pay period because not made to claimant). Are there circumstances that would allow a claimant to refuse an offer of an equivalent position without tolling back pay? See, Giandonato v. Sybron Corp., 804 F.2d 120 (10th Cir.1986) (discharged employee who refused offer of reinstatement because he did not want to work under particular supervisor and was concerned for terminally ill wife not entitled to either back pay or reinstatement); Fiedler v. Indianhead Truck Line, Inc., 670 F.2d 806 (8th Cir.1982) (an employee cannot refuse an offer of reinstatement for the personal reasons that he desired to have the EEOC investigation continue, that he was depressed by the death of his wife, and that he did not wish to give up his current job); Maturo v. National Graphics, Inc., 722 F.Supp. 916 (D.Conn.1989) (in sexual harassment case employer's unconditional offer to reinstate plaintiff after a constructive discharge did not toll back pay where employer did not ensure that plaintiff would be protected from future harassment).

In United Transportation Union Local No. 974 v. Norfolk & Western Railway Co., 532 F.2d 336, 340 (4th Cir.1975), cert. denied, 425 U.S. 934, 96 S.Ct. 1664, 48 L.Ed.2d 175 (1976), the court held that the refusal by black employees to accept promotions to predominantly white jobs, with a concomitant loss of seniority, did not cut off their back pay liability because "[a] refusal to commit seniority suicide is not an acceptable reason to deny back pay. Victims of discrimination should not be required to forfeit wage and seniority benefits *accruing* because of their seniority in order to remain eligible for purely speculative back pay relief." Is this case distinguishable from *Ford Motor Co.*?

Should the majority's reasoning in *Ford Motor Co.* also apply to a discriminatorily *discharged* employee offered reinstatement without accumulated back pay and seniority?

2. Section 706(g) provides in relevant part that "[i]nterim earnings *or amounts earnable with reasonable diligence* by the person or persons discriminated against shall operate to *reduce* the back pay otherwise allowable." In *Ford Motor Co.* the Court holds that "absent special circumstances, the rejection of an employer's unconditional offer ends the accrual of potential back pay liability." Despite the language of Section 706(g) and the limited nature of the Supreme Court's holding in *Ford Motor Co.* some courts hold that a failure to mitigate will terminate rather than reduce back pay. See e.g., Sellers v. Delgado College, 902 F.2d 1189 (5th Cir.), cert. denied, ___ U.S. ___, 111 S.Ct. 525, 112 L.Ed.2d 536 (1990) (plaintiff's failure to mitigate in year following her discharge cut off all back pay even though in later years she made diligent, though unsuccessful, efforts to find work). In Hopkins v. Price Waterhouse, 920 F.2d 967 (D.C.Cir.1990), however, the district court, on remand from the Supreme Court, found that the plaintiff's maximum earning potential following her constructive discharge was $100,000 per year. The plaintiff had in fact set up her own business and earned less than what she would have had she sought work with an established firm. Rather than cutting off all back pay, the district court reduced her back pay award by the amount she could have earned. In affirming, the Court of Appeals distinguished the forfeiture cases as all involving situations where plaintiffs failed to seek jobs that would have compensated them completely for their losses. The district judge in *Hopkins* had found that the plaintiff could not have found a job with pay equal to what she would have earned as a Price Waterhouse partner. 920 F.2d at 981–82. See also, Ezold v. Wolf, Block, Schorr and Solis–Cohen, 56 FEP Cases 580 (E.D.Pa.1991) (if plaintiff did not exercise reasonable diligence in securing interim employment, a determination of what amounts were earnable with reasonable diligence is to be made and the back pay award is to be reduced by that amount). Which approach to the mitigation requirement best furthers the purposes of Title VII?

What kind of effort to obtain comparable employment constitutes "reasonable diligence"? In Brooks v. Woodline Motor Freight, Inc., 852 F.2d 1061 (8th Cir.1988) the plaintiff actively sought employment for only one month after his discharge. His efforts consisted of a number of phone calls to potential employers. Receiving no offers, plaintiff started his own business. Thereafter he turned down offers of employment comparable to his former job. The Court of Appeals held that plaintiff's effort to mitigate were reasonable. 852 F.2d at 1065. See also, Nord v. United States Steel Co., 758 F.2d 1462 (11th Cir.1985) (2 1/2 years spent helping husband establish business not unreasonable in light of plaintiff's inability to find comparable work); Orzel v. Wauwatosa Fire Department, 697 F.2d 743 (7th Cir.), cert. denied, 464 U.S. 992, 104 S.Ct. 484, 78 L.Ed.2d 680 (1983) (one temporary job, one application for work and registration with state job service while "less than vigorous" did not constitute violation of duty to mitigate). But see, Hansard v. Pepsi–Cola Metropolitan Bottling Co., 865 F.2d 1461 (5th Cir.), cert. denied, 493 U.S. 842, 110 S.Ct. 129, 107 L.Ed.2d 89 (1989) (establishment of part-time business and stopping job search does not constitute reasonable diligence). As noted by the Supreme Court in *Ford Motor Co.*, there is no obligation to seek out work in another community, Hegler v. Board of Education, 447 F.2d 1078, 1081 (8th Cir.1971), or to accept a position inferior in terms of pay, status or conditions to the position sought. See, EEOC

v. Exxon Shipping Co., supra, 745 F.2d 967, 978 (5th Cir.1984). What if the plaintiff's job-hunting efforts have proved fruitless? May she attend school or go into a different line of work? See, Carden v. Westinghouse Electric Corp., 850 F.2d 996 (3d Cir.1988) (decision to become self-employed does not indicate lack of diligence); Smith v. American Services Co., 796 F.2d 1430 (11th Cir.1986) (claimant's decision to attend school full-time was not a failure to mitigate since she made reasonable efforts to get work before beginning school).

Failure to mitigate is in the nature of an affirmative defense and the employer has the burden of production and persuasion on the issue. What kind of evidence will satisfy the burden? Once the plaintiff establishes that she is the victim of unlawful discrimination, can the employer prove failure to mitigate by an attack on the plaintiff's credibility? In Floca v. Homcare Health Services, Inc., 845 F.2d 108 (5th Cir.1988) the Court of Appeals reversed a district court's finding that the plaintiff had failed to mitigate:

> [T]he district judge's opinion appears to incorrectly place the burden of proof on plaintiff on this issue. The major reason given for finding of failure to mitigate was that the judge did not believe Floca's testimony that she could not find comparable work. The lack of credibility of Floca's testimony, however, is insufficient to meet the defendant's burden of proof on this issue.

845 F.2d at 112. Does *Floca* mean that, in order to prove a failure to mitigate, the defendant must introduce evidence of the availability of comparable jobs for which the plaintiff did not apply? See, Ford v. Nicks, 866 F.2d 865 (6th Cir.1989) (plaintiff failed to mitigate where she refused offer of virtually identical job with another employer); Joshi v. FSU Health Center, 48 FEP Cases 656 (D.Fla.1986), cert. denied, 488 U.S. 1029, 109 S.Ct. 836, 102 L.Ed.2d 969 (1989) (defendant offered uncontradicted proof that equivalent positions were available for which plaintiff did not apply).

3. If a back pay award must be reduced by "interim earnings," why should such an award not be reduced by a substitute for interim earnings, i.e., unemployment compensation? By awarding the claimants what they presumably would have earned had they been employed by Ford, in addition to unemployment compensation already received, did not the district court in *Ford Motor Co.* make them more than whole? There is a substantial division of authority over the application of the "collateral source" rule to unemployment compensation payments and pension benefits received by the claimant. Compare, Brown v. A. J. Gerrard Mfg. Co., 715 F.2d 1549 (11th Cir.1983) (*en banc*); McDowell v. Avtex Fibers, Inc., 740 F.2d 214 (3d Cir.1984), vacated and remanded on other grounds, 469 U.S. 1202, 105 S.Ct. 1159, 84 L.Ed.2d 312 (1985); Maxfield v. Sinclair International, 766 F.2d 788 (3d Cir.1985), cert. denied, 474 U.S. 1507, 106 S.Ct. 796, 88 L.Ed.2d 773 (1986) (unemployment compensation, social security and pension benefits accruing between act of discrimination and award of relief not deducted from back pay) with Satty v. Nashville Gas Co., 522 F.2d 850 (6th Cir.1975), vacated in part on other grounds, 434 U.S. 136, 98 S.Ct. 347, 54 L.Ed.2d 356 (1977) and EEOC v. Enterprise Association Steamfitters, Local 638, 542 F.2d 579 (2d Cir.1976), cert. denied, 430 U.S. 911, 97 S.Ct. 1186, 51 L.Ed.2d 588 (1977) (back pay award should be reduced by unemployment benefits). The Fifth Circuit has held that social security payments to which an employee became entitled after his termination should not be deducted from back pay but that payments to the employee from the employer's retirement fund should reduce back pay because

such payments were not "collateral" in nature. Guthrie v. J.C. Penney Co., 803 F.2d 202, 210 (5th Cir.1986). Other circuits have held that the "collateral source" rule does not apply to pension benefits and that payments made to a plaintiff from a pension fund should not be offset against back pay. See, EEOC v. O'Grady, 857 F.2d 383, 391 (7th Cir.1988) ("collateral source rule should not afford a 'discrimination bonus' by allowing an adjudicated violator of the ADEA to pay less than it would have paid had it acted lawfully"); Doyne v. Union Electric Co., 953 F.2d 447, 451–52 (8th Cir.1992) (pension benefits have been earned by employee and should not be deducted from back pay award).

Assume that employee X is unlawfully discharged from her job in which she earned $15000 per annum. X is out of work for more than a year and has very small earnings from part-time jobs. X is then fortunate in obtaining a position that pays $23000 per year. When her case comes to trial, X has earned more in the period between discharge and trial than she would have earned had she never been discharged. Is X entitled to any back pay? See, Sims v. Mme. Paulette Dry Cleaners, 638 F.Supp. 224 (S.D.N.Y.1986). If an unlawfully discharged employee is able to obtain "moonlighting" work of a kind that he could not have performed had he not been discharged, should his earnings from such work be counted as interim earnings and thus deducted from back pay? See, Chesser v. State of Illinois, 895 F.2d 330, 338 (7th Cir.1990).

4. In order to "make whole" the economic loss suffered by the victim of discrimination, all fringe benefits which would have been enjoyed, but for the discrimination, should be included in the back pay award. See, Crabtree v. Baptist Hospital of Gadsden, Inc., 749 F.2d 1501 (11th Cir.1985) (executive retirement benefits); Patterson v. American Tobacco Co., 535 F.2d 257, 269 (4th Cir.), cert. denied, 429 U.S. 920, 97 S.Ct. 314, 50 L.Ed.2d 286 (1976) (employer pension and profit sharing contributions); Pettway v. American Cast Iron Pipe Co., 494 F.2d 211, 263 (5th Cir.1974), cert. denied, 439 U.S. 1115, 99 S.Ct. 1020, 59 L.Ed.2d 74 (1979) (overtime, shift differentials, sick pay and vacation pay); Love v. Pullman Co., 13 FEP Cases 423 (D.Colo.1976), affirmed, 569 F.2d 1074 (10th Cir.1978) (insurance premiums, estimated tips, sick and vacation pay). Where one of the fringe benefits of employment is the employer's contribution to group life insurance, what is the appropriate measure of monetary compensation for loss of the coverage—the premiums paid by the employer, the proceeds of the policy, or the cost of equivalent non-group coverage? Compare, Fariss v. Lynchburg Foundry, Inc., 769 F.2d 958, 961 (4th Cir.1985) (value of paid life insurance lost as result of unlawful termination is the value of insurance premiums that would have been paid by employer, not proceeds of policy) with EEOC v. Service News Co., 898 F.2d 958, 964 (4th Cir.1990) (where plaintiff tried, but was unable to obtain comparable health insurance because of pregnancy, measure of damages calculated as benefits which would have been paid under policy rather than cost of premiums). If overtime work is at the option of the employee, how should the lost opportunity for such work be compensated in the back pay award? See, Bruno v. Western Electric Co., 829 F.2d 957 (10th Cir.1987).

5. A victim of discrimination is hardly "made whole" by the award of the amount she should have earned years after she should have earned it. Courts have addressed this problem by awarding pre-judgment interest on the back pay award. See, Pettway v. American Cast Iron Pipe Co., 494 F.2d 211, 263 (5th Cir.1974), cert. denied, 439 U.S. 1115, 99 S.Ct. 1020, 59 L.Ed.2d 74 (1979) (interest on back pay award should be awarded to further compensatory

purpose of Title VII). The award of interest is in the discretion of the trial court. See, e.g., Conway v. Electro Switch Corp., 825 F.2d 593, 602 (1st Cir.1987) (cannot be said that prejudgment interest must, as a matter of law, be part of relief in Title VII case—question whether interest is necessary to make the plaintiff whole lies within discretion of trial court). Awards of prejudgment interest to compensate the claimant for the lost use of wages are, however, increasingly common and some courts have begun to suggest that the discretion to deny interest is, like the discretion to deny back pay, a limited one. The Eleventh Circuit has noted that Congress intended to model Title VII remedies on those afforded by the National Labor Relations Act and that the consistent practice under the NLRA is to require prejudgment interest. Smith v. American Service Company of Atlanta, 796 F.2d 1430, 1432–33 (11th Cir.1986) (remanding denial of prejudgment interest for determination of whether denial was justified under NLRA standards). In a subsequent decision, the Court stated that in *Smith,* it had "reserved ruling on whether the decision to award prejudgment interest in a Title VII back pay case lies within the discretion of the district court." EEOC v. Guardian Pools, Inc., 828 F.2d 1507, 1512 (11th Cir.1987). In Sellers v. Delgado Community College, 839 F.2d 1132, 1142 (5th Cir.1988), cert. denied, ___ U.S. ___, 111 S.Ct. 525, 112 L.Ed.2d 536 (1990) a constructive discharge case, the Fifth Circuit held that a magistrate's denial of prejudgment interest on the ground that the employer had not "intended" to force the plaintiff's resignation was an abuse of discretion.

There is no consensus on the manner or rate of interest to be used in the calculation. See, EEOC v. Guardian Pools, Inc., *supra,* 828 F.2d at 1512 (IRS prime rates for back pay period); Marshall v. Meyer Memorial Hospital, 32 FEP Cases 1335 (W.D.N.Y.1983) (adjusted prime interest rate, calculated from midpoint of back pay period); Pegues v. Mississippi State Employment Service, 35 EPD ¶ 34,645 (N.D.Miss.1984) (10% compounded annually); Association Against Discrimination in Employment, Inc. v. Bridgeport, 572 F.Supp. 494 (D.Conn.1983) (sliding scale interest rate tied to rates applicable to private money markets). In Gelof v. Papineau, 829 F.2d 452 (3d Cir.1987), the district court awarded prejudgment interest at the rate of 17% based on the rate of interest allowed on judgment under state law (5% over the Federal Reserve discount rate). On appeal, the Third Circuit rejected the defendant's argument that the trial court's discretion on the rate of interest should be limited to selection of that rate that represents the claimant's lost investment opportunities.

> Gelof was deprived of a periodic salary needed for daily existence, not merely deprived of investment opportunities. She was deprived of use of that salary from time to time, and presumably had to resort to other sources of funds in order to live. The district court did not, therefore, abuse its discretion in selecting the rate of interest allowed on judgments under Delaware law as an appropriate measure of the loss of use of funds.

829 F.2d at 456. The Court remanded the interest award for recalculation because the district court had applied the interest rate from the date of the plaintiff's termination rather than from when the salary should have been paid.

Prior to the passage of the Civil Rights Act of 1991, awards of back pay against the federal government could not include interest. See, Library of Congress v. Shaw, 478 U.S. 310, 106 S.Ct. 2957, 92 L.Ed.2d 250 (1986) ("In making the Government liable as a defendant under Title VII, * * * Congress did not waive the Government's traditional immunity from interest."). Section 114 of the 1991 Act, however, amends Section 717 of Title VII (remedies against the federal agencies) to specify that "the same interest to compensate for delay in payment shall be available [against federal employers] as in cases involving nonpublic bodies."

6. The tax consequences of back pay awards have proved troublesome to the courts. The payment of a lump-sum award representing years of lost wages may throw the plaintiff into a higher tax bracket than he otherwise would have been in resulting in a larger share of the award going to the government than would have been the case absent the discrimination. The Tenth Circuit has upheld a "tax component" of the back pay award to compensate plaintiffs for their additional tax liability as a result of receiving over seventeen years of back pay in one lump sum. Sears v. Atchison, Topeka & Santa Fe Railway, Co., 749 F.2d 1451 (10th Cir.1984), cert. denied, 471 U.S. 1099, 105 S.Ct. 2322, 85 L.Ed.2d 840 (1985). See also, Gelof v. Papineau, *supra*, (district court award of $85,000 to supplement back pay because of "tax effect" of receiving the back pay in one year vacated because of doubt concerning basis for calculation).

To what extent should monetary awards in employment discrimination cases be taxable? The Internal Revenue Code defines gross income as "all income from whatever source derived ..." 26 U.S.C. § 61(a). Section 104(a) of the Revenue Code provides that "gross income does not include ... (2) the amount of any damages received (whether by suit or agreement and whether in lump sums or as periodic payments) on account of personal injuries or sickness ..." 26 U.S.C. § 104(a). The Code does not define a "personal injury," but the Internal Revenue Service has long taken the position that back pay awards (whether by way of judgment or settlement), are taxable income because they are in lieu of wages. Rev.Rul. 72–341.

The "personal injury" exclusion in Section 104(a) of the Code led, however, to a split in the circuits concerning the taxability of back pay awards. The Tax Court and several circuits held the back pay portion of monetary awards under civil rights statutes such as Title VII was includable in gross income but not compensatory damages awarded under the ADEA or the Equal Pay Act. In Thompson v. Commissioner of Internal Revenue, 866 F.2d 709 (4th Cir.1989), for example, the plaintiff had received back pay under Title VII and the Equal Pay Act and an amount equal to the back pay as liquidated damages under the EPA. The Tax Court held that the back pay half of the award was taxable and the Fourth Circuit affirmed. See also, Wirtz v. Commissioner of Internal Revenue, 49 FEP Cases 729, 731 (T.C.1989) (in ADEA case where jury did not award liquidated damages, entire back pay award including compensation for lost insurance benefits was taxable income); Sparrow v. Commissioner of Internal Revenue, 50 FEP Cases 197, 202 (T.C.1989) (entire monetary settlement of Title VII claim against Navy taxable); Metzger v. Commissioner of Internal Revenue, 88 T.C. 834 (1987), affirmed, 845 F.2d 1013 (3d Cir.1988) (where parties settled Title VII back pay claim and pendent state tort claim for one lump sum without calculating amount of back pay, court will assume that half of settlement amount was back pay and thus taxable income). Other courts held, however, that employment discrimination was discrimination was a "personal injury" within the meaning of Section 104(a) and that all the monetary relief, whether denominated as back pay or not was thus excludable from taxable income. See, Byrne v. Commissioner of Internal Revenue, 883 F.2d 211 (3d Cir.1989) (entire amount received in settlement of suit filed under EPA and state wrongful discharge claim not taxable); Rickel v. Commissioner of Internal Revenue, 900 F.2d 655 (3d Cir.1990) (same with respect to settlement of ADEA claim).

The Supreme Court resolved the conflict in UNITED STATES v. BURKE, ___ U.S. ___, 112 S.Ct. 1867, 119 L.Ed.2d 34 (1992). In *Burke* the Sixth Circuit had held that an amount received in settlement of a Title VII suit was not taxable. The Court of Appeals reasoned that unlawful sex discrimination constituted a personal, tort-like injury and that, accordingly, all relief obtained on the basis of such a claim was "on account" of a personal injury within the meaning of Section 104(a). Burke v. United States, 929 F.2d 1119, 1121–23 (6th Cir.1991) The Supreme Court reversed. The majority focused on the fact that Title VII (as it existed when the suit was settled) allowed only recovery of lost wages and not recompense "for any of the other traditional harms associated with personal injury, such as pain and suffering, emotional distress, harm to reputation, or other consequential damages (*e.g.* ruined credit rating)." ___ U.S. at ___, 112 S.Ct. at 1873. The majority concluded that:

> Notwithstanding a common-law tradition of broad tort damages and the existence of other federal antidiscrimination statutes offering similarly broad remedies, Congress declined to recompense Title VII plaintiffs for anything beyond the wages due them—wages that, if paid in the ordinary course, would have been fully taxable.... Thus, we cannot say that a statute such as Title VII, whose sole remedial focus is the award of backwages, redresses a tort-like personal injury within the meaning of § 104(a)(2) and the applicable regulations.

Id. at ___, 112 S.Ct. at 1874. Justices O'Connor and Thomas in dissent argued that the remedies available to a Title VII plaintiff could not logically fix the character of the right sought to be enforced and that employment discrimination laws operated "functionally" as "in the traditional manner of torts." The dissenters also noted that in determining the appropriate periods of limitation for other civil rights statutes, the Court had found civil rights suits, including claims for employment discrimination, analogous to personal injury tort actions. See, Chapter 8E, *infra*.

The damages awarded to a person injured in an automobile accident will typically include an element of lost income as a result of the accident, but under IRS regulations the *entire* award is excluded from taxable income. Threlkeld v. Commissioner, 848 F.2d 81 (6th Cir.1988) Is the sharp distinction in tax treatment between victims of unlawful discrimination and claimants in common law tort cases a fair one? Should the 1991 revisions to Title VII which allow the recovery of compensatory and punitive damages be treated as a sufficient change in the "remedial focus" of the Act to exclude all monetary recovery, including back pay, from taxable income?

7. In *Ford Motor Co.* back pay was calculated by creating a "hypothetical work history" for the plaintiffs based on the employment histories of the men who were actually hired instead of the plaintiffs. The plaintiffs' interim earnings were subtracted from their hypothetical earnings to arrive at the amount of back pay. There is, of course, no way, particularly in a hiring case, to say with certainty that the plaintiffs' work histories, absent discrimination, would have resembled those of the male workers with whom they were compared. At the stage where back pay is calculated, however, the burden of proof on the issue of quantum is significantly different than at the trial of the merits. The plaintiff's burden is to produce evidence sufficient to allow the court to reasonably estimate the wages lost as a result of the discrimination. The burden of proof then shifts to the defendant to rebut the evidence establishing the "hypothetical work history" or to show the plaintiff's failure to mitigate. Horn v. Duke Homes, Div. of Windsor Mobile Homes, Inc., 755 F.2d 599, 606–08 (7th Cir.1985). Because of the speculative nature of the enterprise, the calculation cannot be precise, but unrealistic exactitude is not required in this context and "ambiguities in what an employee * * * would have earned but for the discrimination should be resolved against the discriminating employer." Stewart v. General Motors Corp., 542 F.2d 445, 452 (7th Cir.1976), cert. denied, 433 U.S. 919, 97 S.Ct. 2995, 53 L.Ed.2d 1105 (1977); Grimes v. Athens Newspaper, Inc., 604 F.Supp. 1166 (M.D.Ga.1985) (because of the impossibility of creating hypothetical work histories for female editors, back pay calculated by comparing actual earnings to "highest male salary being paid for the job"); Danna v. New York Telephone Company, 755 F.Supp. 615 (S.D.N.Y. 1991) (since plaintiff would have had, absent discrimination, the opportunity to fill numerous positions in two departments, back pay computed on basis of average salary of all employees in the two departments).

Some courts have been unwilling to assume that, absent discrimination, claimants would have enjoyed maximum success in their work. For example in EEOC v. Mike Smith Pontiac GMC, Inc., 896 F.2d 524 (11th Cir.1990), the employer refused to hire a female as a car salesperson. The EEOC requested back pay for the full 47 months between the refusal to hire and the date the dealership was sold when it was conceded that the charging party would have been terminated. Based on evidence that no salesperson was employed for as long as 47 months and that the tenure of most salespersons was less than 18 months, the district court limited the back pay period to the average length of employment of all salespersons. With respect to the back pay period, the Court of Appeals affirmed.

> [T]he EEOC simply provided no factual basis, besides mere speculation, for concluding that [the charging party] would have remained employed for the entire forty-seven month period. We find that the district court properly exercised its discretion when it opted to use averages in computing the back pay period.

896 F.2d at 530. In Jepsen v. Florida Board of Regents, 754 F.2d 924 (11th Cir.1985), the district court found that the plaintiff, a female university profes-

sor, had been denied promotions for a long period because of her sex. The plaintiff, who had retired prior to trial as an Associate Professor, urged that her back pay be determined by comparing her earnings to those of male professors who were hired near the time she was hired and who had advanced to full professor. The court found that the plaintiff, absent discrimination, would have been promoted at an earlier date to associate professor but could not conclude that she would have been promoted to full professor. Based on that conclusion, the plaintiff's back pay was determined by averaging the salaries of male faculty hired close to the time of plaintiff and who were promoted to associate professor close to the time she should have been promoted to arrive at an "adjusted salary." The Court of Appeals affirmed on the ground that the trial judge's finding that "Dr. Jepsen might well have remained an associate professor until her retirement" was not clearly erroneous. But if the employer has a history of discriminating against its employees, as did the university in *Jepsen*, why should it be entitled to the benefit of the doubt on the issue of whether the plaintiff would have been promoted? Are these cases consistent with the general rule that, at the relief stage, uncertainties are to be resolved in favor of the victim of discrimination?

A recurring question in back pay calculations is whether the employer is entitled to the *benefit* of expenses saved by the plaintiff as a result of being out of work. In EEOC v. Service News Co., 898 F.2d 958 (4th Cir.1990) the plaintiff was discharged because she was pregnant. The employer argued that back pay should be offset by the plaintiff's child care expenses which she was not required to pay because she was out of work and cared for her child herself. Does Section 706(g) allow for such an offset? What is the fair response to such a claim?

8. One circumstance which will create uncertainty about backpay but which will not necessarily work in favor of the aggrieved employee is the situation where there are multiple claimants for a limited number of positions. In Dougherty v. Barry, 869 F.2d 605 (D.C.Cir.1989) the district court found that the District of Columbia had discriminated on the basis of race in promoting two black firefighters to deputy fire chief. As relief, the court ordered full back pay and retirement benefits for eight white firefighters as though each had received one of the two promotions. On appeal the D.C. Circuit reversed the backpay award as "overly generous." The court of appeals reasoned that if the district court had been able to determine with certainty which of the two plaintiffs would have received the promotions, the proper course would have been to award those two firefighters full relief and the others none, but since such a determination could not be made, the monetary value of the promotions should be divided among the plaintiffs pro rata.

> By awarding each plaintiff full back pay, however, the district court treated each as though he possessed a hundred percent chance of receiving one of the promotions, counter to that court's own conclusion that one could not determine for certain which appellees, if any, would have been promoted. Thus, in order to restore appellees to the position they would have occupied absent discrimination * * * the district court should have awarded each plaintiff a fraction of the promotions' value commensurate with the likelihood of his receiving one of the promotions.

869 F.2d at 615. Under the court's ruling which party should bear the burden of establishing which of the plaintiffs would have received the promotions absent discrimination? Why should not the employer that has been found to

have acted unlawfully be required to pay full back pay to the employees unless it can convince the court which of the claimants would have received the positions in the absence of discrimination?

The problems associated with back pay determinations are magnified in class actions. See discussion, *infra*, Section E.

SECTION B. INJUNCTIVE RELIEF
FRANKS v. BOWMAN TRANSPORTATION CO., INC.

Supreme Court of the United States, 1976.
424 U.S. 747, 96 S.Ct. 1251, 47 L.Ed.2d 444.

MR. JUSTICE BRENNAN delivered the opinion of the Court.

This case presents the question whether identifiable applicants who were denied employment because of race after the effective date and in violation of Title VII of the Civil Rights Act of 1964, may be awarded seniority status retroactive to the dates of their employment applications.[1]

Petitioner Franks brought this class action in the United States District Court for the Northern District of Georgia against his former employer, respondent Bowman Transportation Co., and his unions, the International Union of District 50, Allied and Technical Workers of the United States and Canada, and its local, No. 13600,[2] alleging various racially discriminatory employment practices in violation of Title VII. Petitioner Lee intervened on behalf of himself and others similarly situated alleging racially discriminatory hiring and discharge policies limited to Bowman's employment of over-the-road (OTR) truck drivers. Following trial, the District Court found that Bowman had engaged in a pattern of racial discrimination in various company policies, including the hiring, transfer, and discharge of employees, and found further that the discriminatory practices were perpetrated in Bowman's collective-bargaining agreement with the unions. The District Court certified the action as a proper class action under Fed.R.Civ.P. 23(b)(2), and of import to the issues before this Court, found that petitioner Lee represented all black applicants who sought to be hired or to transfer to OTR driving positions prior to January 1, 1972. In its final order and decree, the District Court subdivided the class represented by petitioner Lee into a class of black nonemployee applicants for OTR positions prior to January 1, 1972 (class 3), and a class of black employees who applied for transfer to OTR positions prior to the same date (class 4).

---

1. Petitioners also alleged an alternative claim for relief for violations of 42 U.S.C. § 1981. In view of our decision we have no occasion to address that claim.

2. In 1972, the International Union of District 50 merged with the United Steelworkers of America, AFL–CIO, and hence the latter as the successor bargaining representative is the union respondent before this Court. Brief for Respondent United Steelworkers of America, AFL–CIO, and for American Federation of Labor and Congress of Industrial Organizations as *Amicus Curiae* 5.

In its final judgment entered July 14, 1972, the District Court permanently enjoined the respondents from perpetuating the discriminatory practices found to exist, and, in regard to the black applicants for OTR positions, ordered Bowman to notify the members of both subclasses within 30 days of their right to priority consideration for such jobs. The District Court declined, however, to grant to the unnamed members of classes 3 and 4 any other specific relief sought, which included an award of backpay and seniority status retroactive to the date of individual application for an OTR position.

On petitioners' appeal to the Court of Appeals for the Fifth Circuit, raising for the most part claimed inadequacy of the relief ordered respecting unnamed members of the various subclasses involved, the Court of Appeals affirmed in part, reversed in part, and vacated in part. 495 F.2d 398 (1974). The Court of Appeals held that the District Court had exercised its discretion under an erroneous view of law insofar as it failed to award backpay to the unnamed class members of both classes 3 and 4, and vacated the judgment in that respect. The judgment was reversed insofar as it failed to award any seniority remedy to the members of class 4 who after the judgment of the District Court sought and obtained priority consideration for transfer to OTR positions.[3] As respects unnamed members of class 3—nonemployee black applicants who applied for and were denied OTR positions prior to January 1, 1972—the Court of Appeals affirmed the District Court's denial of any form of seniority relief. Only this last aspect of the Court of Appeals' judgment is before us for review under our grant of the petition for certiorari. 420 U.S. 989, 95 S.Ct. 1421, 43 L.Ed.2d 699 (1975).

[The named plaintiffs included only one representative of class 3(Lee). After being discriminatorily refused employment, Lee was hired by Bowman, but then was discharged before trial for cause. The district court awarded him back pay for the intervening period of discrimination. The defendant's argument that the class claim for seniority relief was moot, because the sole class representative's claim had become moot, was rejected by the Supreme Court. "The unnamed members of the class are entitled to the relief already afforded Lee, hiring and back pay, and thus to that extent have 'such a personal stake in the outcome of the controversy [whether they are also entitled to seniority relief] as to assure that concrete adverseness which sharpens the presentation of issues upon which the court so largely depends for illumination of difficult * * * questions.' [citation omitted] Given a properly certified class action, * * * mootness turns on whether, in the specific circumstances of the given case at the time it is before this Court, an adversary relationship sufficient to fulfill this function ex-

---

3. In conjunction with its directions to the District Court regarding seniority relief for the members of other subclasses not involved in the issues presently confronting this Court, the Court of Appeals directed that class 4 members who transferred to OTR positions under the District Court's decree should be allowed to carry over all accumulated company seniority for all purposes in the OTR department. 495 F.2d, at 417.

ists."   424 U.S. at 755–756, 96 S.Ct. 1259–1260. The Court also held that § 703(h) of Title VII, which recognizes the legality of bona fide seniority and merit systems, does not bar seniority relief to persons who were not seeking "modification or elimination of the existing seniority system, but only * * * an award of the seniority status they would have individually enjoyed under the present system but for the illegal discriminatory refusal to hire."   424 U.S. at 758, 96 S.Ct. at 1261.]

* * *

II

In affirming the District Court's denial of seniority relief to the class 3 group of discriminatees, the Court of Appeals held that the relief was barred by § 703(h) of Title VII, 42 U.S.C. § 2000e–2(h). We disagree. Section 703(h) provides in pertinent part:

> "Notwithstanding any other provision of this title, it shall not be an unlawful employment practice for an employer to apply different standards of compensation, or different terms, conditions, or privileges of employment pursuant to a bona fide seniority or merit system * * * provided that such differences are not the result of an intention to discriminate because of race, color, religion, sex, or national origin * * *."

The Court of Appeals reasoned that a discriminatory refusal to hire "does not affect the bona fides of the seniority system. Thus, the differences in the benefits and conditions of employment which a seniority system accords to older and newer employees is protected [by § 703(h)] as 'not an unlawful employment practice.'" 495 F.2d, at 417. Significantly, neither Bowman nor the unions undertake to defend the Court of Appeals' judgment on that ground. It is clearly erroneous.

The black applicants for OTR positions composing class 3 are limited to those whose applications were put in evidence at the trial.[10] The underlying legal wrong affecting them is not the alleged operation of a racially discriminatory seniority system but of a racially discriminatory hiring system. Petitioners do not ask for modification or elimination of the existing seniority system, but only an award of the seniority status they would have individually enjoyed under the present system but for the illegal discriminatory refusal to hire. It is this context that must shape our determination as to the meaning and effect of § 703(h).

---

10. By its terms, the judgment of the District Court runs to all black applicants for OTR positions prior to January 1, 1972, and is not qualified by a limitation that the discriminatory refusal to hire must have taken place after the effective date of the Act. However, only post-Act victims of racial discrimination are members of class 3. Title VII's prohibition on racial discrimination in hiring became effective on July 2, 1965, one year after the date of its enactment. Pub.L. 88–352, §§ 716(a)–(b), 78 Stat. 266. Petitioners sought relief in this case for identifiable applicants for OTR positions "whose applications were put in evidence at the trial." App. 20a. There were 206 unhired black applicants prior to January 1, 1972, whose written applications are summarized in the record and none of the applications relates to years prior to 1970. Id. at 52a, Table VA.

On its face, § 703(h) appears to be only a definitional provision; as with the other provisions of § 703, subsection (h) delineates which employment practices are illegal and thereby prohibited and which are not.[11] Section 703(h) certainly does not expressly purport to qualify or proscribe relief otherwise appropriate under the remedial provisions of Title VII, § 706(g), 42 U.S.C. § 2000e–5(g), in circumstances where an illegal discriminatory act or practice is found. Further, the legislative history of § 703(h) plainly negates its reading as limiting or qualifying the relief authorized under § 706(g). The initial bill reported by the House Judiciary Committee as H.R. 7152[12] and passed by the full House on February 10, 1964,[13] did not contain § 703(h). Neither the House bill nor the majority Judiciary Committee Report[14] even mentioned the problem of seniority. That subject thereafter surfaced during the debate of the bill in the Senate. This debate prompted Senators Clark and Case to respond to criticism that Title VII would destroy existing seniority systems by placing an interpretive memorandum in the Congressional Record. The memorandum stated: "Title VII would have no effect on established seniority rights. Its effect is prospective and not retrospective." 110 Cong. Rec. 7213 (1964).[15] Senator Clark also placed in the Congressional Record a Justice Department statement concerning Title VII which stated: "[I]t has been asserted that Title VII would undermine vested rights of seniority. This is not correct. Title VII would have no effect on seniority rights existing at the time it takes effect." Id., at 7207.[16] Several weeks thereafter,

---

11. See Last Hired, First Fired Seniority, Layoffs, and Title VII: Questions of Liability and Remedy, 11 Colum.J.L.&Soc.Probs. 343, 376, 378 (1975).

12. See H.R.Rep.No. 914, 88th Cong., 1st Sess., U.S. Code Cong. & Admin. News 1964, p. 2355 (1963).

13. 110 Cong.Rec. 2804 (1964).

14. H.R.Rep.No.914, supra.

15. The full text of the memorandum pertaining to seniority states:

"Title VII would have no effect on established seniority rights. Its effect is prospective and not retrospective. Thus, for example, if a business has been discriminating in the past and as a result has an all-white working force, when the title comes into effect the employer's obligation would be simply to fill future vacancies on a nondiscriminatory basis. He would not be obliged—or indeed, permitted—to fire whites in order to hire Negroes, or to prefer Negroes for future vacancies, or, once Negroes are hired, to give them special seniority rights at the expense of the white workers hired earlier. (However, where waiting lists for employment or training are, prior to the effective date of the title, maintained on a discriminatory basis, the use of such

lists after the title takes effect may be held an unlawful subterfuge to accomplish discrimination.)"

16. The full text of the statement pertinent to seniority reads:

"First, it has been asserted that title VII would undermine vested rights of seniority. This is not correct. Title VII would have no effect on seniority rights existing at the time it takes effect. If, for example, a collective bargaining contract provides that in the event of layoffs, those who were hired last must be laid off first, such a provision would not be affected in the least by title VII. This would be true even in the case where owing to discrimination prior to the effective date of the title, white workers had more seniority than Negroes. Title VII is directed at discrimination based on race, color, religion, sex, or national origin. It is perfectly clear that when a worker is laid off or denied a chance for promotion because under established seniority rules he is 'low man on the totem pole' he is not being discriminated against because of his race. Of course, if the seniority rule itself is discriminatory, it would be unlawful under title VII. If a rule were to state that all Negroes

following several informal conferences among the Senate leadership, the House leadership, the Attorney General and others, see Vaas, Title VII: Legislative History, 7 B.C.Ind. & Com.L.Rev. 431, 445 (1966), a compromise substitute bill prepared by Senators Mansfield and Dirksen, Senate majority and minority leaders respectively, containing § 703(h) was introduced on the Senate floor.[17] Although the Mansfield–Dirksen substitute bill, and hence § 703(h), was not the subject of a committee report, see generally Vaas, supra, Senator Humphrey, one of the informal conferees, later stated during debate on the substitute that § 703(h) was not designed to alter the meaning of Title VII generally but rather "merely clarifies its present intent and effect." 110 Cong. Rec. 12723 (1964). Accordingly, whatever the exact meaning and scope of § 703(h) in light of its unusual legislative history and the absence of the usual legislative materials, see Vaas, supra, at 457–458, it is apparent that the thrust of the section is directed toward defining what is and what is not an illegal discriminatory practice in instances in which the post-Act operation of a seniority system is challenged as perpetuating the effects of discrimination occurring prior to the effective date of the Act. There is no indication in the legislative materials that § 703(h) was intended to modify or restrict relief otherwise appropriate once an illegal discriminatory practice occurring after the effective date of the Act is proved—as in the instant case, a discriminatory refusal to hire. This accords with the apparently unanimous view of commentators, see Cooper & Sobol, Seniority and Testing Under Fair Employment Laws: A General Approach to Objective Criteria of Hiring and Promotion, 82 Harv.L.Rev. 1598, 1632 (1969); Stacy, Title VII Seniority Remedies in a Time of Economic Downturn, 28 Vand.L.Rev.

---

must be laid off before any white man, such a rule could not serve as the basis for a discharge subsequent to the effective date of the title. I do not know how anyone could quarrel with such a result. But, in the ordinary case, assuming that seniority rights were built up over a period of time during which Negroes were not hired, these rights would not be set aside by the taking effect of title VII. Employers and labor organizations would simply be under a duty not to discriminate against Negroes because of their race. Any differences in treatment based on established seniority rights would not be based on race and would not be forbidden by the title." 110 Cong. Rec. 7207 (1964).

Senator Clark also introduced into the Congressional Record a set of answers to a series of questions propounded by Senator Dirksen. Two of these questions and answers are pertinent to the issue of seniority:

"Question. Would the same situation prevail in respect to promotions, when that management function is governed by a labor contract calling for promotions on the basis of seniority? What of dismissals? Normally, labor contracts call for 'last hired, first fired.' If the last hired are Negroes, is the employer discriminating if his contract requires they be first fired and the remaining employees are white?

"Answer. Seniority rights are in no way affected by the bill. If under a 'last hired, first fired' agreement a Negro happens to be the 'last hired,' he can still be 'first fired' as long as it is done because of his status as 'last hired' and not because of his race.

"Question. If an employer is directed to abolish his employment list because of discrimination what happens to seniority?

"Answer. The bill is not retroactive, and it will not require an employer to change existing seniority lists." Id., at 7217.

17. Id., at 11926, 11931.

487, 506 (1975).[18] We therefore hold that the Court of Appeals erred in concluding that, as a matter of law, § 703(h) barred the award of seniority relief to the unnamed class 3 members.

III

There remains the question whether an award of seniority relief is appropriate under the remedial provisions of Title VII, specifically, § 706(g).[19]

We begin by repeating the observation of earlier decisions that in enacting Title VII of the Civil Rights Act of 1964, Congress intended to prohibit all practices in whatever form which create inequality in employment opportunity due to discrimination on the basis of race, religion, sex, or national origin, Alexander v. Gardner–Denver Co., 415 U.S. 36, 44, 94 S.Ct. 1011, 1017, 39 L.Ed.2d 147, 155 (1974); McDonnell Douglas Corp. v. Green, 411 U.S. 792, 800, 93 S.Ct. 1817, 1823, 36 L.Ed.2d 668, 676 (1973); Griggs v. Duke Power Co., 401 U.S. 424, 429–430, 91 S.Ct. 849, 852–853, 28 L.Ed.2d 158, 163–164 (1971), and ordained that its policy of outlawing such discrimination should have the "highest priority," Alexander, supra, 415 U.S., at 47, 94 S.Ct. at 1019, 39 L.Ed.2d at 158; Newman v. Piggie Park Enterprises, Inc., 390 U.S. 400, 402, 88 S.Ct. 964, 966, 19 L.Ed.2d 1263, 1265 (1968). Last Term's Albemarle Paper Co. v. Moody, 422 U.S. 405, 95 S.Ct. 2362, 45 L.Ed.2d 280 (1975), consistently with the congressional plan, held that one of the central purposes of Title VII is "to make persons whole for injuries suffered on account of unlawful employment discrimination." Id., at 418, 95 S.Ct., at 2372, 45 L.Ed.2d, at 297. To effectuate this "make whole" objective, Congress in § 706(g) vested broad equitable discretion

18. Cf. Gould, Employment Security, Seniority and Race: The Role of Title VII of the Civil Rights Act of 1964, 13 How.L.J. 1, 8–9, and n. 32 (1967); see also Jurinko v. Edwin L. Wiegand Co., 477 F.2d 1038 (C.A.3), vacated and remanded on other grounds, 414 U.S. 970, 94 S.Ct. 293, 38 L.Ed.2d 214 (1973), wherein the court awarded back seniority in a case of discriminatory hiring after the effective date of Title VII without any discussion of the impact of § 703(h) on the propriety of such a remedy.

19. Section 706(g) of Title VII, 42 U.S.C. § 2000e–5(g) (1970 ed., Supp. IV), provides:

"If the court finds that the respondent has intentionally engaged in or is intentionally engaging in an unlawful employment practice charged in the complaint, the court may enjoin the respondent from engaging in such unlawful employment practice, and order such affirmative action as may be appropriate, which may include, but is not limited to, reinstatement or hiring of employees, with or without back pay (payable by the employer, employment agency, or labor organization, as the case may be, responsible for the unlawful employment practice), or any other equitable relief as the court deems appropriate. Back pay liability shall not accrue from a date more than two years prior to the filing of a charge with the Commission. Interim earnings or amounts earnable with reasonable diligence by the person or persons discriminated against shall operate to reduce the back pay otherwise allowable. No order of the court shall require the admission or reinstatement of an individual as a member of a union, or the hiring, reinstatement, or promotion of an individual as an employee, or the payment to him of any back pay, if such individual was refused admission, suspended, or expelled, or was refused employment or advancement or was suspended or discharged for any reason other than discrimination on account of race, color, religion, sex, or national origin or in violation of section 2000e–3(a) of this title."

in the federal courts to "order such affirmative action as may be appropriate, which may include, but is not limited to, reinstatement or hiring of employees, with or without back pay * * *, or any other equitable relief as the court deems appropriate." The legislative history supporting the 1972 amendments of § 706(g) of Title VII [20] affirms the breadth of this discretion. "The provisions of [§ 706(g)] are intended to give the courts wide discretion exercising their equitable powers to fashion the most complete relief possible. * * * [T]he Act is intended to make the victims of unlawful employment discrimination whole, and * * * the attainment of this objective * * * requires that persons aggrieved by the consequences and effects of the unlawful employment practice be, so far as possible, restored to a position where they would have been were it not for the unlawful discrimination." Section–by–Section Analysis of H.R. 1746, accompanying the Equal Employment Opportunity Act of 1972—Conference Report, 118 Cong. Rec. 7166, 7168 (1972). This is emphatic confirmation that federal courts are empowered to fashion such relief as the particular circumstances of a case may require to effect restitution, making whole insofar as possible the victims of racial discrimination in hiring.[21] Adequate relief may well

20. Equal Employment Opportunity Act of 1972, 86 Stat. 103, amending 42 U.S.C. § 2000e *et seq.*

21. It is true that backpay is the only remedy specifically mentioned in § 706(g). But to draw from this fact and other sections of the statute any implicit statement by Congress that seniority relief is a prohibited, or at least less available, form of remedy is not warranted. Indeed, any such contention necessarily disregards the extensive legislative history underlying the 1972 amendments to Title VII. The 1972 amendments added the phrase speaking to "other equitable relief" in § 706(g). The Senate Report manifested an explicit concern with the "earnings gap" presently existing between black and white employees in American society. S.Rep.No.92–415, p. 6 (1971). The Reports of both Houses of Congress indicated that "rightful place" was the intended objective of Title VII and the relief accorded thereunder. Ibid.; H.R.Rep.No.92–238, p. 4 (1971), U.S. Code Cong. & Admin. News 1972, p. 2137. * * * [R]ightful-place seniority, implicating an employee's *future* earnings, job security, and advancement prospects, is absolutely essential to obtaining this congressionally mandated goal.

The legislative history underlying the 1972 amendments completely answers the argument that Congress somehow intended seniority relief to be less available in pursuit of this goal. In explaining the need for the 1972 amendments, the Senate Report stated:

"Employment discrimination as viewed today is a * * * complex and pervasive phenomenon. Experts familiar with the subject now generally describe the problem in terms of 'systems' and 'effects' rather than simply intentional wrongs, and the literature on the subject is replete with discussions of, for example, the mechanics of seniority and lines of progression, perpetuation of the present effect of pre-act discriminatory practices through various institutional devices, and testing and validation requirements." S.Rep.No.92–415, supra, at 5. See also H.R.Rep.No.92–238, supra, at 8. In the context of this express reference to seniority, the Reports of both Houses cite with approval decisions of the lower federal courts which granted forms of retroactive "rightful place" seniority relief. S.Rep.No.92–415, supra, at 5 n. 1; H.R.Rep.No.92–238, supra, at 8 n.2. (The dissent would distinguish these lower federal court decisions as not involving instances of discriminatory *hiring.* Obviously, however, the concern of the entire thrust of the dissent—the impact of rightful-place seniority upon the expectations of other employees—is in no way a function of the specific type of illegal discriminatory practice upon which the judgment of liability is predicated.) Thereafter, in language that could hardly be more explicit, the analysis accompanying the Conference Report stated:

"In any area where the new law does not address itself, or in any areas where a

be denied in the absence of a seniority remedy slotting the victim in that position in the seniority system that would have been his had he been hired at the time of his application. It can hardly be questioned that ordinarily such relief will be necessary to achieve the "make-whole" purposes of the Act.

Seniority systems and the entitlements conferred by credits earned thereunder are of vast and increasing importance in the economic employment system of this Nation. S. Slichter, J. Healy, & E. Livernash, The Impact of Collective Bargaining on Management 104–115 (1960). Seniority principles are increasingly used to allocate entitlements to scarce benefits among competing employees ("competitive status" seniority) and to compute noncompetitive benefits earned under the contract of employment ("benefit" seniority). Ibid. We have already said about "competitive status" seniority that it "has become of overriding importance, and one of its major functions is to determine who gets or who keeps an available job." Humphrey v. Moore, 375 U.S. 335, 346–347, 84 S.Ct. 363, 370, 11 L.Ed.2d 370, 380 (1964). "More than any other provision of the collective[-bargaining] agreement * * * seniority affects the economic security of the individual employee covered by its terms." Aaron, Reflections on the Legal Nature and Enforceability of Seniority Rights, 75 Harv.L.Rev. 1532, 1535 (1962). "Competitive status" seniority also often plays a broader role in modern employment systems, particularly systems operated under collective-bargaining agreements:

> "Included among the benefits, options, and safeguards affected by competitive status seniority, are not only promotion and layoff, but also transfer, demotion, rest days, shift assignments, prerogative in scheduling vacation, order of layoff, possibilities of lateral transfer to avoid layoff, 'bumping' possibilities in the face of layoff, order of recall, training opportunities, working conditions, length of layoff endured without reducing seniority, length of layoff recall rights will withstand, overtime opportunities, parking privileges, and, in one plant, a preferred place in the punch-out line." Stacy, 28 Vand.L.Rev., supra, at 490 (footnotes omitted).

Seniority standing in employment with respondent Bowman, computed from the departmental date of hire, determines the order of layoff and recall of employees.[22] Further, job assignments for OTR drivers are posted for competitive bidding and seniority is used to determine the highest bidder.[23] As OTR drivers are paid on a per-mile basis,[24] earnings are therefore to some extent a function of seniority. Additionally, seniority computed from the company date of hire deter-

---

specific contrary intention is not indicated, it was assumed *that the present case law as developed by the courts would continue to govern the applicability and construction of Title VII."* Section–By–Section Analysis of H.R.1746, accompanying The Equal Employment Opportunity Act of 1972—Conference Report,

118 Cong.Rec. 7166 (1972) (emphasis added).

22. App. 46a–50a.

23. Ibid.

24. 2 Record 161.

mines the length of an employee's vacation [25] and pension benefits.[26] Obviously merely to require Bowman to hire the class 3 victim of discrimination falls far short of a "make whole" remedy.[27] A concomitant award of the seniority credit he presumptively would have earned but for the wrongful treatment would also seem necessary in the absence of justification for denying that relief. Without an award of seniority dating from the time when he was discriminatorily refused employment, an individual who applies for and obtains employment as an OTR driver pursuant to the District Court's order will never obtain his rightful place in the hierarchy of seniority according to which these various employment benefits are distributed. He will perpetually remain subordinate to persons who, but for the illegal discrimination, would have been in respect to entitlement to these benefits his inferiors.[28]

The Court of Appeals apparently followed this reasoning in holding that the District Court erred in not granting seniority relief to class 4 Bowman employees who were discriminatorily refused transfer to OTR positions. Yet the class 3 discriminatees in the absence of a comparable seniority award would also remain subordinated in the seniority system to the class 4 discriminatees. The distinction plainly finds no support anywhere in Title VII or its legislative history. Settled law dealing with the related "twin" areas of discriminatory hiring and discharges violative of the National Labor Relations Act, 49 Stat. 449, as amended, 29 U.S.C. § 151 et seq., provides a persuasive analogy. "[I]t would indeed be surprising if Congress gave a remedy for the one which it denied for the other." Phelps Dodge Corp. v. NLRB, 313 U.S. 177, 187, 61 S.Ct. 845, 849, 85 L.Ed. 1271, 1279 (1941). For courts to differentiate without justification between the classes of discriminatees "would be a differentiation not only without substance but in defiance of that against which the prohibition of discrimination is directed." Id., at 188, 61 S.Ct., at 850, 85 L.Ed., at 1280.

---

25. App. 47a, 51a.

26. 2 Record 169.

27. Further, at least in regard to "benefit"-type seniority such as length of vacation leave and pension benefits in the instant case, any general bar to the award of retroactive seniority for victims of illegal hiring discrimination serves to undermine the mutually reinforcing effect of the dual purposes of Title VII; it reduces the restitution required of an employer at such time as he is called upon to account for his discriminatory actions perpetrated in violation of the law. See Albemarle Paper Co. v. Moody, 422 U.S. 405, 417–418, 95 S.Ct. 2362, 2371–2372, 45 L.Ed.2d 280, 296–297 (1975).

28. Accordingly, it is clear that the seniority remedy which petitioners seek does not concern only the "make-whole" purposes of Title VII. The dissent errs in treating the issue of seniority relief as implicating only the "make whole" objective of Title VII and in stating that "Title VII's 'primary objective' of eradicating discrimination is not served at all * * *." Nothing could be further from reality—the issue of seniority relief cuts to the very heart of Title VII's primary objective of eradicating present and future discrimination in a way that backpay, for example, can never do. "[S]eniority, after all, is a right which a worker exercises in each job movement in the future, rather than a simple one-time payment for the past." Poplin, Fair Employment in a Depressed Economy: The Layoff Problem, 23 U.C.L.A.L.Rev. 177, 225 (1975).

Similarly, decisions construing the remedial section of the National Labor Relations Act, § 10(c), 29 U.S.C. § 160(c)—the model for § 706(g), *Albemarle Paper*, 422 U.S., at 419, 95 S.Ct., at 2372, 45 L.Ed.2d, at 297 [29]—make clear that remedies constituting authorized "affirmative action" include an award of seniority status, for the thrust of "affirmative action" redressing the wrong incurred by an unfair labor practice is to make "the employees whole, and thus restor[e] the economic status quo that would have obtained but for the company's wrongful [act]." NLRB v. Rutter–Rex Mfg. Co., 396 U.S. 258, 263, 90 S.Ct. 417, 420, 24 L.Ed.2d 405, 411 (1969). The task of the NLRB in applying § 10(c) is "to take measures designed to recreate the conditions and relationships that would have been had there been no unfair labor practice." Carpenters v. NLRB, 365 U.S. 651, 657, 81 S.Ct. 875, 879, 6 L.Ed.2d 1, 5 (1961) (Harlan, J., concurring). And the NLRB has often required that the hiring of employees who have been discriminatorily refused employment be accompanied by an award of seniority equivalent to that which they would have enjoyed but for the illegal conduct. See, e.g., In re Phelps Dodge Corp., 19 N.L.R.B. 547, 600, and n. 39, 603–604 (1940), modified on other grounds, 313 U.S. 177, 61 S.Ct. 845, 85 L.Ed. 1271 (1941) (ordering persons discriminatorily refused employment hired "without prejudice to their seniority or other rights and privileges"); In re Nevada Consolidated Copper Corp., 26 N.L.R.B. 1182, 1235 (1940), enforced, 316 U.S. 105, 62 S.Ct. 960, 86 L.Ed. 1305 (1942) (ordering persons discriminatorily refused employment hired with "any seniority or other rights and privileges they would have acquired, had the respondent not unlawfully discriminated against them"). Plainly the "affirmative action" injunction of § 706(g) has no lesser reach in the district courts. "Where racial discrimination is concerned, 'the [district] court has not merely the power but the duty to render a decree which will so far as possible eliminate the discriminatory effects of the past as well as bar like discrimination in the future.'" *Albemarle Paper*, supra, 422 U.S., at 418, 95 S.Ct., at 2372, 45 L.Ed.2d at 297.

IV

We are not to be understood as holding that an award of seniority status is requisite in all circumstances. The fashioning of appropriate remedies invokes the sound equitable discretion of the district courts. Respondent Bowman attempts to justify the District Court's denial of seniority relief for petitioners as an exercise of equitable discretion, but the record is its own refutation of the argument.

---

29. To the extent that there is a difference in the wording of the respective provisions, § 706(g) grants, if anything, broader discretionary powers than those granted the National Labor Relations Board. Section 10(c) of the NLRA authorizes "such affirmative action including reinstatement of employees with or without back pay, as will effectuate the policies of this subchapter," 29 U.S.C. § 160(c), whereas § 706(g) as amended in 1972 authorizes "such affirmative action as may be appropriate, which may include, *but is not limited to,* reinstatement *or hiring* of employees, with or without back pay * * *, *or any other equitable relief as the court deems appropriate.*" 42 U.S.C. § 2000e–5(g) (1970 ed., Supp. IV) (emphasis added).

Albemarle Paper, supra, at 416, 95 S.Ct., at 2371, 45 L.Ed.2d, at 296, made clear that discretion imports not the court's " 'inclination, but * * * its judgment; and its judgment is to be guided by sound legal principles.' " Discretion is vested not for purposes of "limit[ing] appellate review of trial courts, or * * * invit[ing] inconsistency and caprice," but rather to allow the most complete achievement of the objectives of Title VII that is attainable under the facts and circumstances of the specific case. 422 U.S., at 421, 95 S.Ct., at 2373, 45 L.Ed.2d, at 298. Accordingly, the District Court's denial of any form of seniority remedy must be reviewed in terms of its effect on the attainment of the Act's objectives under the circumstances presented by this record. No less than with the denial of the remedy of backpay, the denial of seniority relief to victims of illegal racial discrimination in hiring is permissible "only for reasons which, if applied generally, would not frustrate the central statutory purposes of eradicating discrimination throughout the economy and making persons whole for injuries suffered through past discrimination." Ibid.

The District Court stated two reasons for its denial of seniority relief for the unnamed class members.[30] The first was that those individuals had not filed administrative charges under the provisions of Title VII with the Equal Employment Opportunity Commission and therefore class relief of this sort was not appropriate. We rejected this justification for denial of class-based relief in the context of backpay awards in *Albemarle Paper*, and for the same reasons reject it here. This justification for denying class-based relief in Title VII suits has been unanimously rejected by the courts of appeals, and Congress ratified that construction by the 1972 amendments. *Albemarle Paper*, supra, at 414 n. 8, 95 S.Ct., at 2370, 45 L.Ed.2d, at 294.

The second reason stated by the District Court was that such claims "presuppose a vacancy, qualification, and performance by every member. There is no evidence on which to base these multiple conclusions." Pet. for Cert. A54. The Court of Appeals rejected this reason insofar as it was the basis of the District Court's denial of backpay, and of its denial of retroactive seniority relief to the unnamed members of class 4. We hold that it is also an improper reason for denying seniority relief to the unnamed members of class 3.

We read the District Court's reference to the lack of evidence regarding a "vacancy, qualification, and performance" for every individual member of the class as an expression of concern that some of the unnamed class members (unhired black applicants whose employment applications were summarized in the record) may not in fact have been actual victims of racial discrimination. That factor will become materi-

---

30. Since the Court of Appeals concluded that an award of retroactive seniority to the unnamed members of class 3 was barred by § 703(h), a conclusion which we today reject, the court did not address specifically the District Court's stated reasons for refusing the relief. The Court of Appeals also stated, however, that the District Court did not "abuse its discretion" in refusing such relief, 495 F.2d 398, 418 (1974), and we may therefore appropriately review the validity of the District Court's reasons.

al however only when those persons reapply for OTR positions pursuant to the hiring relief ordered by the District Court. Generalizations concerning such individually applicable evidence cannot serve as a justification for the denial of relief to the entire class. Rather, at such time as individual class members seek positions as OTR drivers, positions for which they are presumptively entitled to priority hiring consideration under the District Court's order,[31] evidence that particular individuals were not in fact victims of racial discrimination will be material. But petitioners here have carried their burden of demonstrating the existence of a discriminatory hiring pattern and practice by the respondents and, therefore, the burden will be upon respondents to prove that individuals who reapply were not in fact victims of previous hiring discrimination. Cf. McDonnell Douglas Corp. v. Green, 411 U.S. 792, 802, 93 S.Ct. 1817, 1824, 36 L.Ed.2d 668, 677 (1973); Baxter v. Savannah Sugar Rfg. Corp., 495 F.2d 437, 443–444 (C.A.5), cert. denied, 419 U.S. 1033, 95 S.Ct. 515, 42 L.Ed.2d 308 (1974).[32] Only if this burden is met may retroactive seniority—if otherwise determined to be an appropriate form of relief under the circumstances of the particular case—be denied individual class members.

Respondent Bowman raises an alternative theory of justification. Bowman argues that an award of retroactive seniority to the class of discriminatees will conflict with the economic interests of other Bowman employees. Accordingly, it is argued, the District Court acted within its discretion in denying this form of relief as an attempt to accommodate the competing interests of the various groups of employees.[33]

We reject this argument for two reasons. First, the District Court made no mention of such considerations in its order denying the seniority relief. As we noted in *Albemarle Paper*, 422 U.S., at 421 n. 14,

---

31. The District Court order is silent as to whether applicants for OTR positions who were previously discriminatorily refused employment must be presently qualified for those positions in order to be eligible for priority hiring under that order. The Court of Appeals, however, made it plain that they must be. Id., at 417. We agree.

32. Thus Bowman may attempt to prove that a given individual member of class 3 was not in fact discriminatorily refused employment as an OTR driver in order to defeat the individual's claim to seniority relief as well as any other remedy ordered for the class generally. Evidence of a lack of vacancies in OTR positions at the time the individual application was filed, or evidence indicating the individual's lack of qualification for the OTR positions—under nondiscriminatory standards *actually applied* by Bowman to individuals who were in fact hired—would of course be

relevant. It is true, of course, that obtaining the third category of evidence with which the District Court was concerned— what the individual discriminatee's job performance would have been but for the discrimination—presents great difficulty. No reason appears, however, why the victim rather than the perpetrator of the illegal act should bear the burden of proof on this issue.

33. Even by its terms, this argument could apply only to the award of retroactive seniority for purposes of "competitive status" benefits. It has no application to a retroactive award for purposes of "benefit" seniority—extent of vacation leave and pension benefits. Indeed, the decision concerning the propriety of this latter type of seniority relief is analogous, if not identical, to the decision concerning an award of backpay to an individual discriminatee hired pursuant to an order redressing previous employment discrimination.

95 S.Ct., at 2373, 45 L.Ed.2d, at 299, if the district court declines, due to the peculiar circumstances of the particular case, to award relief generally appropriate under Title VII, "[i]t is necessary * * * that * * * it carefully articulate its reasons" for so doing. Second, and more fundamentally, it is apparent that denial of seniority relief to identifiable victims of racial discrimination on the sole ground that such relief diminishes the expectations of other, arguably innocent, employees would if applied generally frustrate the central "make whole" objective of Title VII. These conflicting interests of other employees will, of course, always be present in instances where some scarce employment benefit is distributed among employees on the basis of their status in the seniority hierarchy. But, as we have said, there is nothing in the language of Title VII, or in its legislative history, to show that Congress intended generally to bar this form of relief to victims of illegal discrimination, and the experience under its remedial model in the National Labor Relations Act points to the contrary.[34] Accordingly, we find untenable the conclusion that this form of relief may be denied merely because the interests of other employees may thereby be affected. "If relief under Title VII can be denied merely because the majority group of employees, who have not suffered discrimination, will

34. With all respect, the dissent does not adequately treat with and fails to distinguish the standard practice of the National Labor Relations Board granting retroactive seniority relief under the National Labor Relations Act to persons discriminatorily discharged or refused employment in violation of the Act. The Court in Phelps Dodge Corp. v. NLRB, 313 U.S. 177, 196, 61 S.Ct. 845, 853, 85 L.Ed. 1271, 1284 (1941), of course, made reference to "restricted judicial review" as that case arose in the context of review of the policy determinations of an independent administrative agency, which are traditionally accorded a wide-ranging discretion under accepted principles of judicial review. "Because the relation of remedy to policy is peculiarly a matter for administrative competence, courts must not enter the allowable area of the Board's discretion." Id., at 194, 61 S.Ct., at 852, 85 L.Ed., at 1283. As we made clear in *Albemarle Paper*, however, the pertinent point is that in utilizing the NLRA as the remedial model for Title VII, reference must be made to actual operation and experience as it has evolved in administrating the Act. E.g., "We may assume that Congress was aware that the Board, since its inception, has awarded backpay as a matter of course." 422 U.S., at 419–420, 95 S.Ct., at 2372, 45 L.Ed.2d, at 298. "[T]he Board has from its inception pursued 'a practically uniform policy with respect to these orders requiring affirmative action.'" Id., at 2373 n. 12.

The dissent has cited no case, and our research discloses none, wherein the Board has ordered hiring relief and yet withheld the remedy of retroactive seniority status. Indeed, the Court of Appeals for the First Circuit has noted that a Board order requiring hiring relief "without prejudice to * * * seniority and other rights and privileges" is "language * * * in the standard form which has long been in use by the Board." NLRB v. Draper Corp., 159 F.2d 294, 296–297, and n. 1 (1947). The Board "routinely awards both back pay and retroactive seniority in hiring discrimination cases." Poplin, supra, n. 28, at 223. See also Edwards & Zaretsky, Preferential Remedies for Employment Discrimination, 74 Mich.L.Rev. 1, 45 n. 224 (1975) (a "common remedy"); Last Hired, First Fired Seniority, Layoffs and Title VII, supra, n. 11, at 377 ("traditionally and uniformly required"). This also is a "presumption" in favor of this form of seniority relief. If victims of racial discrimination are under Title VII to be treated differently and awarded less protection than victims of unfair labor practice discrimination under the NLRA, some persuasive justification for such disparate treatment should appear. That no justification exists doubtless explains the position of every union participant in the proceedings before the Court in the instant case arguing for the conclusion we have reached.

be unhappy about it, there will be little hope of correcting the wrongs to which the Act is directed." United States v. Bethlehem Steel Corp., 446 F.2d 652, 663 (C.A. 2 1971).[35]

With reference to the problems of fairness or equity respecting the conflicting interests of the various groups of employees, the relief which petitioners seek is only seniority status retroactive to the date of individual application, rather than some form of arguably more complete relief.[36] No claim is asserted that nondiscriminatee employees holding OTR positions they would not have obtained but for the illegal discrimination should be deprived of the seniority status they have earned. It is therefore clear that even if the seniority relief petitioners seek is awarded, most if not all discriminatees who actually obtain OTR jobs under the court order will not truly be restored to the actual seniority that would have existed in the absence of the illegal discrimination. Rather, most discriminatees even under an award of retroactive seniority status will still remain subordinated in the hierarchy to a position inferior to that of a greater total number of employees than would have been the case in the absence of discrimination. Therefore, the relief which petitioners seek, while a more complete form of relief than that which the District Court accorded, in no sense constitutes "complete relief." [37] Rather, the burden of the past discrimination in hiring is with respect to competitive status benefits divided among discriminatee and nondiscriminatee employees under the form of relief sought. The dissent criticizes the Court's result as not sufficiently cognizant that it will "directly implicate the rights and expectations of perfectly innocent employees." We are of the view, however, that the result which we reach today—which, standing alone,[38] establishes that

---

35. See also Vogler v. McCarty, Inc., 451 F.2d 1236, 1238–1239 (C.A. 5 1971): "Adequate protection of Negro rights under Title VII may necessitate, as in the instant case, some adjustment of the rights of white employees. The Court must be free to deal equitably with conflicting interests of white employees in order to shape remedies that will most effectively protect and redress the rights of the Negro victims of discrimination."

36. Another countervailing factor in assessing the expected impact on the interests of other employees actually occasioned by an award of the seniority relief sought is that it is not probable in instances of class-based relief that all of the victims of the past racial discrimination in hiring will actually apply for and obtain the prerequisite hiring relief. Indeed, in the instant case, there appear in the record the rejected applications of 166 black applicants who claimed at the time of application to have had the necessary job qualifications. However, the Court was informed at oral argument that only a small number of those individuals have to this date actu-

ally been hired pursuant to the District Court's order ("five, six, seven, something in that order"), Tr. of Oral Arg. 23, although ongoing litigation may ultimately determine more who desire the hiring relief and are eligible for it. Id., at 15.

37. In no way can the remedy established as presumptively necessary be characterized as "total restitution," or as deriving from an "absolutist conception of 'make whole'" relief.

38. In arguing that an award of the seniority relief established as presumptively necessary does nothing to place the burden of the past discrimination on the wrongdoer in most cases—the employer— the dissent of necessity addresses issues not presently before the Court. Further remedial action by the district courts, having the effect of shifting to the employer the burden of the past discrimination in respect of competitive-status benefits, raises such issues as the possibility of an injunctive "hold harmless" remedy respecting all affected employees in a layoff situaa sharing of the burden of the past discrimination is presumptively necessary—is entirely consistent with any fair characterization of equity jurisdiction,[39] particularly when considered in light of our traditional view that "[a]ttainment of a great national policy * * * must not be confined within narrow canons for equitable relief deemed suitable by chancellors in ordinary private controversies." Phelps Dodge Corp. v. NLRB, 313 U.S., at 188, 61 S.Ct., at 850, 85 L.Ed., at 1280.

Certainly there is no argument that the award of retroactive seniority to the victims of hiring discrimination in any way deprives other employees of indefeasibly vested rights conferred by the employment contract. This Court has long held that employee expectations arising from a seniority system agreement may be modified by statutes furthering a strong public policy interest.[40] Tilton v. Missouri Pacific R. Co., 376 U.S. 169, 84 S.Ct. 595, 11 L.Ed.2d 590 (1964) (construing §§ 9(c)(1) and (c)(2) of the Universal Military Training and Service Act, 1948, 50 U.S.C. App. §§ 459(c)(1) and (2), which provided that a re-employed returning veteran should enjoy the seniority status he would have acquired but for his absence in military service); Fishgold v. Sullivan Drydock & Repair Corp., 328 U.S. 275, 66 S.Ct. 1105, 90 L.Ed. 1230 (1946) (construing the comparable provision of the Selective Training and Service Act of 1940). The Court has also held that a collective-bargaining agreement may go further, enhancing the seniority status of certain employees for purposes of furthering public policy interests beyond what is required by statute, even though this will to some extent be detrimental to the expectations acquired by other employees under the previous seniority agreement. Ford Motor Co. v. Huffman, 345 U.S. 330, 73 S.Ct. 681, 97 L.Ed. 1048 (1953). And the ability of the union and employer voluntarily to modify the seniority system to the end of ameliorating the effects of past racial discrimination, a national policy objective of the "highest priority," is certainly no less than in other areas of public policy interests. Pellicer v. Brotherhood of Ry. & S.S. Clerks, 217 F.2d 205 (C.A.5 1954), cert. denied, 349 U.S. 912, 75

---

tion, Brief for Local 862, United Automobile Workers, as *Amicus Curiae*; the possibility of an award of monetary damages (sometimes designated "front pay") in favor of each employee and discriminatee otherwise bearing some of the burden of the past discrimination, *ibid.*; and the propriety of such further remedial action in instances wherein the union has been adjudged a participant in the illegal conduct. Brief for United States et al. as *Amici Curiae*. Such issues are not presented by the record before us, and we intimate no view regarding them.

39. " 'The qualities of mercy and practicality have made equity the instrument for nice adjustment and reconciliation between the public interest and private needs

as well as between competing private claims.' " " 'Moreover, * * * equitable remedies are a special blend of what is necessary, what is fair, and what is workable * * *.

" 'In equity, as nowhere else, courts eschew rigid absolutes and look to the practical realities and necessities inescapably involved in reconciling competing interests. * * * ' "

40. "[C]laims under Title VII involve the vindication of a major public interest * * *." Section–by–Section Analysis of H.R. 1746, accompanying the Equal Employment Opportunity Act of 1972—Conference Report, 118 Cong.Rec. 7166, 7168 (1972).

S.Ct. 601, 99 L.Ed. 1246 (1955).　See also Cooper & Sobol, 82 Harv. L.Rev. at 1605.

V

In holding that class-based seniority relief for identifiable victims of illegal hiring discrimination is a form of relief generally appropriate under § 706(g), we do not in any way modify our previously expressed view that the statutory scheme of Title VII "implicitly recognizes that there may be cases calling for one remedy but not another, and—owing to the structure of the federal judiciary—these choices are, of course, left in the first instance to the district courts." *Albemarle Paper*, 422 U.S., at 416, 95 S.Ct., at 2370, 45 L.Ed.2d at 295.　Circumstances peculiar to the individual case may, of course, justify the modification or withholding of seniority relief for reasons that would not if applied generally undermine the purposes of Title VII.[41]　In the instant case it appears that all new hirees establish seniority only upon completion of a 45–day probationary period, although upon completion seniority is retroactive to the date of hire.　Certainly any seniority relief ultimately awarded by the District Court could properly be cognizant of this fact. *Amici* and the respondent union point out that there may be circumstances where an award of full seniority should be deferred until completion of a training or apprenticeship program, or other preliminaries required of all new hirees.[42]　We do not undertake to delineate all such possible circumstances here.　Any enumeration must await particular cases and be determined in light of the trial courts' "keener appreciation" of peculiar facts and circumstances.　*Albemarle Paper*, supra, at 421–422, 95 S.Ct., at 2373, 45 L.Ed.2d, at 299.

Accordingly, the judgment of the Court of Appeals affirming the District Court's denial of seniority relief to class 3 is reversed, and the case is remanded to the District Court for further proceedings consistent with this opinion.

It is so ordered.

Reversed and remanded.

MR. JUSTICE STEVENS took no part in the consideration or decision of this case.

MR. CHIEF JUSTICE BURGER, concurring in part and dissenting in part.

---

41. Accordingly, to no "significant extent" do we "[strip] the district courts of [their] equity powers."　Rather our holding is that in exercising their equitable powers, district courts should take as their starting point the presumption in favor of rightful-place seniority relief, and proceed with further legal analysis from that point; and that such relief may not be denied on the abstract basis of adverse impact upon interests of other employees but rather only on the basis of unusual adverse impact arising from facts and circumstances that would not be generally found in Title VII cases.　To hold otherwise would be to shield "inconsisten[t] and capri[cious]" denial of such relief from "thorough appellate review." *Albemarle Paper*, 422 U.S., at 421, 416, 95 S.Ct., at 2373, 2371, 45 L.Ed.2d, at 299, 296.

42. Brief for United States et al. as *Amici Curiae* 26; Brief for Respondent United Steelworkers of America, AFL–CIO, and for American Federation of Labor and Congress of Industrial Organizations as *Amicus Curiae* 28 n. 32.

I agree generally with MR. JUSTICE POWELL, but I would stress that although retroactive benefit-type seniority relief may sometimes be appropriate and equitable, competitive-type seniority relief at the expense of wholly innocent employees can rarely, if ever, be equitable if that term retains traditional meaning. More equitable would be a monetary award to the person suffering the discrimination. An award such as "front pay" could replace the need for competitive-type seniority relief. Such monetary relief would serve the dual purpose of deterring wrongdoing by the employer or union—or both—as well as protecting the rights of innocent employees. In every respect an innocent employee is comparable to a "holder-in-due-course" of negotiable paper or a bona fide purchaser of property without notice of any defect in the seller's title. In this setting I cannot join in judicial approval of "robbing Peter to pay Paul."

I would stress that the Court today does not foreclose claims of employees who might be injured by this holding from securing equitable relief on their own behalf.

* * *

MR. JUSTICE POWELL, with whom MR. JUSTICE REHNQUIST joins, concurring and dissenting in part.

Although I am in accord with much of the Court's discussion in Parts III and IV, I cannot accept as correct its basic interpretation of § 706(g) as virtually requiring a district court, in determining appropriate equitable relief in a case of this kind, to ignore entirely the equities that may exist in favor of innocent employees. Its holding recognizes no meaningful distinction, in terms of the equitable relief to be granted, between "benefit"-type seniority and "competitive"-type seniority.[1] The Court reaches this result by taking an absolutist view of the "make whole" objective of Title VII, while rendering largely meaningless the discretionary authority vested in district courts by § 706(g) to weigh the equities of the situation. Accordingly, I dissent from Parts III and IV.

* * *

III

A

In *Albemarle Paper* the Court read Title VII as creating a presumption in favor of backpay. Rather than limiting the power of district courts to do equity, the presumption insures that complete equity

---

1. My terminology conforms to that of the Court. "Benefit"-type seniority refers to the use of a worker's earned seniority credits in computing his level of economic "fringe benefits." Examples of such benefits are pensions, paid vacation time, and unemployment insurance. "Competitive"-type seniority refers to the use of those same earned credits in determining his right, relative to other workers, to job-related "rights" that cannot be supplied equally to any two employees. Examples can range from the worker's right to keep his job while someone else is laid off, to his right to a place in the punch-out line ahead of another employee at the end of a workday.

normally will be accomplished. Backpay forces the employer[4] to account for economic benefits that he wrongfully has denied the victim of discrimination. The statutory purposes and equitable principles converge, for requiring payment of wrongfully withheld wages deters further wrongdoing at the same time that their restitution to the victim helps make him whole.

Similarly, to the extent that the Court today finds a like presumption in favor of granting *benefit*-type seniority, it is recognizing that normally this relief also will be equitable. As the Court notes, this type of seniority, which determines pension rights, length of vacations, size of insurance coverage and unemployment benefits, and the like, is analogous to backpay in that its retroactive grant serves "the mutually reinforcing effect of the dual purposes of Title VII." Benefit-type seniority, like backpay, serves to work complete equity by penalizing the wrongdoer economically at the same time that it tends to make whole the one who was wronged.

But the Court fails to recognize that a retroactive grant of *competitive*-type seniority invokes wholly different considerations. This is the type of seniority that determines an employee's preferential rights to various economic advantages at the expense of other employees. These normally include the order of layoff and recall of employees, job and trip assignments, and consideration for promotion.

It is true, of course, that the retroactive grant of competitive-type seniority does go a step further in "making whole" the discrimination victim, and therefore arguably furthers one of the objectives of Title VII. But apart from extending the make-whole concept to its outer limits, there is no similarity between this drastic relief and the granting of backpay and benefit-type seniority. First, a retroactive grant of competitive-type seniority usually does not directly affect the employer at all. It causes only a rearrangement of employees along the seniority ladder without any resulting increase in cost.[5] Thus, Title VII's "pri-

---

4. In an appropriate case, of course, Title VII remedies may be ordered against a wrongdoing union as well as the employer.

5. This certainly would be true in this case, as conceded by counsel for Bowman at oral argument. There the following exchange took place:

"QUESTION: How is Bowman injured by this action?

"MR. PATE [Counsel for Bowman]: By seniority? By the grant of this remedy?

"QUESTION: Either way.

"MR. PATE: It is not injured either way and the company, apart from the general interest of all of us in the importance of the question, has no specific tangible interest in it in this case as to whether seniority is granted to this group or not. That is correct." Tr. of Oral Arg. 42. In a supplemental memorandum filed after oral argument, petitioners referred to this statement by Bowman's counsel and suggested that he apparently was referring to the competitive aspects of seniority, such as which employees were to get the best job assignments, since Bowman certainly *would* be economically disadvantaged by the benefit-type seniority, such as seniority-related increases in backpay. I agree that in the context Bowman's counsel spoke, he was referring to the company's lack of a tangible interest, in whether or not competitive-type seniority was granted.

mary objective" of eradicating discrimination is not served at all,[6] for the employer is not deterred from the practice.

The second, and in my view controlling, distinction between these types of relief is the impact on other workers. As noted above, the granting of backpay and of benefit-type seniority furthers the prophylactic and make-whole objectives of the statute without penalizing other workers. But competitive seniority benefits, as the term implies, directly implicate the rights and expectations of perfectly innocent employees.[7] The economic benefits awarded discrimination victims would be derived not at the expense of the employer but at the expense of other workers. Putting it differently, those disadvantaged—sometimes to the extent of losing their jobs entirely—are not the wrongdoers who have no claim to the Chancellor's conscience, but rather are innocent third parties.

As noted above in Part II, Congress in § 706(g) expressly referred to "appropriate" affirmative action and "other equitable relief as the court deems appropriate." And the 1972 Section–by–Section Analysis still recognized that the touchstone of any relief is equity. Congress could not have been more explicit in leaving the relief to the equitable discretion of the court, to be determined in light of all relevant facts and circumstances. Congress did underscore "backpay" by specific reference in § 706(g), but no mention is made of the granting of other benefits upon ordering reinstatement or hiring. The entire question of retroactive seniority was thus deliberately left to the discretion of the district court, a discretion to be exercised in accordance with equitable principles.

> "The essence of equity jurisdiction has been the power of the Chancellor to do equity and to mould each decree to the necessities of the particular case. Flexibility rather than rigidity has distinguished it. The qualities of mercy and practicality have made equity the instrument for nice adjustment and reconciliation between the public interest and private needs as well as between competing private claims." Hecht Co. v. Bowles, 321 U.S. 321, 329–

---

6. The Court in *Albemarle* noted that this primary objective had been recognized in Griggs v. Duke Power Co., 401 U.S. 424, 91 S.Ct. 849, 28 L.Ed.2d 158 (1971). See 422 U.S., at 417, 95 S.Ct., at 2371, 45 L.Ed. 2d, at 296; see also supra, at 1273. In *Griggs*, the Court found this objective to be "plain from the language of the statute." 401 U.S., at 429, 91 S.Ct., at 853, 28 L.Ed. 2d, at 163. In creating a presumption in favor of a retroactive grant of competitive-type seniority the Court thus exalts the make-whole purpose, not only above fundamental principles of equity, but also above the primary objective of the statute recently found to be plain on its face.

7. Some commentators have suggested that the expectations of incumbents some-

how may be illegitimate because they result from past discrimination against others. Cooper & Sobol, Seniority and Testing under Fair Employment Laws: A General Approach to Objective Criteria of Hiring and Promotion, 82 Harv.L.Rev. 1598, 1605–1606 (1969). Such reasoning is badly flawed. Absent some showing of collusion, the incumbent employee was not a party to the discrimination by the employer. Acceptance of the job when offered hardly makes one an accessory to a discriminatory failure to hire someone else. Moreover, the incumbent's expectancy does not result from discrimination against others, but is based on his own efforts and satisfactory performance.

330, 64 S.Ct. 587, 592, 88 L.Ed. 754 (1944). "Moreover, * * * equitable remedies are a special blend of what is necessary, what is fair, and what is workable. * * * " Lemon v. Kurtzman, 411 U.S. 192, 200, 93 S.Ct. 1463, 1469, 36 L.Ed.2d 151, 161 (1973) (opinion of Burger, C. J.)

"In equity, as nowhere else, courts eschew rigid absolutes and look to the practical realities and necessities inescapably involved in reconciling competing interests * * *." Id., at 201, 93 S.Ct., at 1469, 36 L.Ed.2d 161.

The decision whether to grant competitive-type seniority relief therefore requires a district court to consider and weigh competing equities. In any proper exercise of the balancing process, a court must consider both the claims of the discrimination victims and the claims of incumbent employees who, if competitive seniority rights are awarded retroactively to others, will lose economic advantages earned through satisfactory and often long service.[8] If, as the Court today holds, the district court may not weigh these equities much of the language of § 706(g) is rendered meaningless. We cannot assume that Congress intended either that the statutory language be ignored or that the earned benefits of incumbent employees be wiped out by a presumption created by this Court.[9]

IV

In expressing the foregoing views, I suggest neither that Congress intended to bar a retroactive grant of competitive-type seniority in all cases,[13] nor that district courts should indulge a presumption against

---

8. The Court argues that a retroactive grant of competitive-type seniority always is equitable because it "divides the burden" of past discrimination between incumbents and victims. Aside from its opacity, this argument is flawed by what seems to be a misperception of the nature of Title VII relief. Specific relief necessarily focuses upon the individual victim, not upon some "class" of victims. A grant of full retroactive seniority to an individual victim of Bowman's discriminatory hiring practices will place that person exactly where he would have been had he been hired when he first applied. The question for a district court should be whether it is equitable to place that individual in that position despite the impact upon all incumbents hired after the date of his unsuccessful application. Any additional effect upon the entire work force—incumbents and the newly enfranchised victims alike—of similar relief to still *earlier* victims of the discrimination, raises distinctly different issues from the equity, vis-a-vis incumbents, of granting retroactive seniority to each victim.

9. Indeed, the 1972 amendment process which produced the Section–by–Section

Analysis containing the statement of the Act's "make whole" purpose, also resulted in an addition to § 706(g) itself clearly showing congressional recognition that total restitution to victims of discrimination is not a feasible goal. As originally enacted, § 706(g) contained simply an authorization to district courts to order reinstatement with or without backpay, with no limitation on how much backpay the courts could order. In 1972, however, the Congress added a limitation restricting the courts to an award to a date two years prior to the filing of a charge with EEOC. While it is true that Congress at the same time rejected an even more restrictive limitation, see Albemarle Paper Co. v. Moody, supra, 422 U.S., at 420 n. 13, 95 S.Ct., at 2373, 45 L.Ed.2d, at 298, its adoption of any limitation at all suggests an awareness that the desire to "make whole" must yield at some point to other considerations.

13. Nor is it suggested that incumbents have "indefeasibly vested rights" to their seniority status that invariably would foreclose retroactive seniority. But the cases cited by the Court for that proposition do

such relief.[14] My point instead is that we are dealing with a congressional mandate to district courts to determine and apply equitable remedies. Traditionally this is a balancing process left, within appropriate constitutional or statutory limits, to the sound discretion of the trial court. At this time it is necessary only to avoid imposing, from the level of this Court, arbitrary limitations on the exercise of this traditional discretion specifically explicated in § 706(g). There will be cases where, under all of the circumstances, the economic penalties that would be imposed on innocent incumbent employees will outweigh the claims of discrimination victims to be made entirely whole even at the expense of others. Similarly, there will be cases where the balance properly is struck the other way.

The Court virtually ignores the only previous judicial discussion directly in point. The Court of Appeals for the Sixth Circuit, recently faced with the issue of retroactive seniority for victims of hiring discrimination, showed a fine appreciation of the distinction discussed above. Meadows v. Ford Motor Co., 510 F.2d 939 (1975), cert. pending, No. 74–1349.[15] That court began with the recognition that retroactive competitive-type seniority presents "greater problems" than a grant of backpay because the burden falls upon innocent incumbents rather than the wrongdoing employer. Id., at 949.[16] The court further recognized that Title VII contains no prohibition against such relief. Then, noting that "the remedy for the wrong of discriminatory refusal to hire

not hold, or by analogy imply, that district courts operating under § 706(g) lack equitable discretion to take into account the rights of incumbents. In Tilton v. Missouri Pacific R. Co., 376 U.S. 169, 84 S.Ct. 595, 11 L.Ed.2d 590 (1964), and Fishgold v. Sullivan Corp., 328 U.S. 275, 66 S.Ct. 1105, 90 L.Ed. 1230 (1946), the Court only confirmed an express congressional determination, presumably made after weighing all relevant considerations, that for reasons of public policy veterans should receive seniority credit for their time in military service. See 376 U.S., at 174–175, 84 S.Ct., at 599–600, 11 L.Ed.2d, at 593–594. In Ford Motor Co. v. Huffman, 345 U.S. 330, 73 S.Ct. 681, 97 L.Ed. 1048 (1953), the Court affirmed the authority of a collective-bargaining agent, presumably after weighing the relative equities, see id., at 337–339, 73 S.Ct., at 685–687, 97 L.Ed., at 1057–1058, to advantage certain employees more than others. All I contend is that under § 706(g) a district court, like Congress in Tilton and Fishgold, and the bargaining agent in Huffman, also must be free to weigh the equities.

14. The Court suggests I am arguing that retroactive competitive-type seniority should be "less available" as relief than backpay. This is not my position. All

relief not specifically prohibited by the Act is equally "available" to the district courts. My point is that equitable considerations can make competitive-type seniority relief less "appropriate" in a particular situation than backpay or other relief. Again, the plain language of § 706(g) compels careful determination of the "appropriateness" of each "available" remedy in a specific case, and does not permit the inflexible approach taken by the Court.

15. From the briefs of the parties it appears that Meadows is one of only three reported appellate decisions dealing with the question of retroactive seniority relief to victims of discriminatory hiring practices. In the instant case, of course, the Court of Appeals for the Fifth Circuit held such relief barred by § 703(h). In Jurinko v. Edwin L. Wiegand Co., 477 F.2d 1038, vacated and remanded on other grounds, 414 U.S. 970, 94 S.Ct. 293, 38 L.Ed.2d 214 (1973), the Court of Appeals for the Third Circuit ordered the relief without any discussion of equitable considerations.

16. The Sixth Circuit noted that no equitable considerations stand in the way of a district court's granting retroactive benefit-type seniority. 510 F.2d at 949.

lies in the first instance *with the District Judge*," ibid. (emphasis added), the Court of Appeals for the Sixth Circuit stated:

> "For his guidance on this issue we observe * * * that a grant of retroactive seniority would not depend solely upon the existence of a record sufficient to justify back pay * * *. The court would, in dealing with job [i.e., competitive-type] seniority, need also to consider the interests of the workers who might be displaced * * *. We do not assume * * * that such reconciliation is impossible, but as is obvious, we certainly do foresee genuine difficulties. * * * "
> Ibid.

The Sixth Circuit suggested that the District Court seek enlightenment on the questions involved in the particular fact situation, and that it should allow intervention by representatives of the incumbents who stood to be disadvantaged.[17]

In attempted justification of its disregard of the explicit equitable mandate of § 706(g) the Court today relies almost exclusively on the practice of the National Labor Relations Board under § 10(c) of the National Labor Relations Act, 29 U.S.C. § 160(c).[18] It is true that in the two instances cited by the Court, and in the few others cited in the

---

17. One of the commentators quoted by the Court today has endorsed the even-handed approach adopted by the Sixth Circuit: "In fashioning a remedy, * * * the courts should consciously assess the costs of relief to *all* the parties in the case, and then tailor the decree to minimize these costs while affording plaintiffs adequate relief. The best way to do this will no doubt vary from case to case depending on the facts: the number of plaintiffs, the number of [incumbents] affected and the alternatives available to them, the economic circumstances of the industry." Poplin, Fair Employment in a Depressed Economy: The Layoff Problem, 23 U.C.L.A.L.Rev. 177, 202 (1975) (emphasis in original); see id. at 224.

Another commentator has said that judges who fail to take account of equitable claims of incumbents are engaging in an "Alice in Wonderland" approach to the problem of Title VII remedies. See Rains, Title VII v. Seniority Based Layoffs: A Question of Who Goes First, 4 Hofstra L.Rev. 49, 53 (1975).

18. By gathering bits and pieces of the legislative history of the 1972 amendments, the Court attempts to patch together an argument that full retroactive seniority is a remedy equally "available" as backpay. There are two short responses. First, as emphasized elsewhere, supra, at 1278 n. 14, no one contends that such relief is less *available*, but only that it may be less *equitable* in some situations. Second, insofar as the Court intends the legislative

history to suggest some presumption in favor of this relief, it is irrefutably blocked by the plain language of § 706(g) calling for the exercise of *equitable* discretion in the fashioning of *appropriate* relief. There are other responses. As to the committee citations of lower court decisions and the Conference Report Analysis reference to "present case law," it need only be noted that as of the 1972 amendments no appellate court had considered a case involving retroactive seniority relief to victims of discriminatory hiring practices. Moreover, the cases were cited only in the context of a general discussion of the complexities of employment discrimination, never for their adoption of a "rightful place" theory of relief. And by the terms of the Conference Report Analysis itself, the existing case law could not take precedence over the explicit language of § 706(g), added by the amendments, that told courts to exercise *equitable* discretion in granting *appropriate* relief.

Moreover, I find no basis for the Court's statement that the Committee Reports indicated "rightful place" to be the objective of Title VII relief. In fact, in both instances cited by the Court the term was used in the context of a general comment that minorities were still "far from reaching their rightful place in society." S.Rep.No. 92–416, p. 6 (1971). There was no reference to the scope of relief under § 706(g), or indeed even to Title VII remedies at all.

briefs of the parties,[19] the Board has ordered reinstatement of victims of discrimination "without prejudice to their seniority or other rights and privileges." But the alleged precedents are doubly unconvincing. First, in none of the cases is there a discussion of equities either by the Board or the enforcing court. That the Board has granted seniority relief in several cases may indicate nothing more than the fact that in the usual case no one speaks for the individual incumbents. This is the point recognized by the court in *Meadows*, and the impetus for its suggestion that a representative of their interests be entertained by the district court before it determines "appropriate" § 706(g) relief.

I also suggest, with all respect, that the Court's appeal to Board practice wholly misconceives the lesson to be drawn from it. In the seminal case recognizing the Board's power to order reinstatement for discriminatory refusals to hire, this Court in a reasoned opinion by Mr. Justice Frankfurter was careful to emphasize that the decision on the type and extent of relief rested in the Board's discretion, subject to limited review only by the courts.

> "But in the nature of things Congress could not catalogue all the devices and stratagems for circumventing the policies of the Act. Nor could it define the whole gamut of remedies to effectuate these policies in an infinite variety of specific situations. Congress met these difficulties by leaving the adaptation of means to end to the empiric process of administration. The exercise of the process was committed to the Board, subject to limited judicial review. * * *

> * * *

> " * * * All these and other factors outside our domain of experience may come into play. Their relevance is for the Board, not for us. *In the exercise of its informed discretion the Board may find that effectuation of the Act's policies may or may not require reinstatement.* We have no warrant for speculating on matters of fact the determination of which Congress has entrusted to the Board. All we are entitled to ask is that the statute speak through the Board where the statute does not speak for itself." Phelps Dodge Corp. v. NLRB, 313 U.S. 177, 194–196, 61 S.Ct. 845, 852–853, 85 L.Ed. 1271, 1283–1284 (1941) (emphasis added).

The fallacy of the Court's reliance upon Board practice is apparent: the district courts under Title VII stand in the place of the Board under the NLRA. Congress entrusted to their discretion the appropriate remedies for violations of the Act, just as it previously had entrusted discretion to the Board. The Court today denies that discretion to the district courts, when 35 years ago it was quite careful to leave discretion where Congress had entrusted it. It may be that the district courts, after weighing the competing equities, would order full retroac-

---

19. The respondent Steelworkers cited seven Board decisions in addition to those mentioned in the Court's opinion. Brief for Respondent United Steelworkers of America AFL–CIO, and for American Federation of Labor and Congress of Industrial Organizations as *Amicus Curiae*, 27 n. 31.

tive seniority in most cases. But they should do so only after determining in each instance that it *is* appropriate, and not because this Court has taken from them the power—granted by Congress—to weigh the equities.

In summary, the decision today denying district courts the power to balance equities cannot be reconciled with the explicit mandate of § 706(g) to determine "appropriate" relief through the exercise of "equitable powers." Accordingly, I would remand this case to the District Court with instructions to investigate and weigh competing equities before deciding upon the appropriateness of retroactive competitive-type seniority with respect to individual claimants.[20]

NOTES AND PROBLEMS FOR DISCUSSION

1. Following *Franks,* courts have treated retroactive seniority, like back pay, as a remedy to be denied the victim of discrimination only for the most compelling reasons. In EEOC v. M.D. Pneumatics, Inc., 779 F.2d 21 (8th Cir.1985), the district court denied retroactive seniority to women who had been refused employment with the defendant because the employer "had gone the extra mile in remedying its past discrimination" and because there was "no evidence * * * from which a reasonable determination could be made as to a date on which a class member might have been hired absent the sex discrimination which was then practiced by the defendant." The Court of Appeals reversed. "Pneumatic's effort to remedy the effects of past discrimination, although commendable, are not the kind of compelling reasons which justify the denial of retroactive seniority." 779 F.2d at 23. With respect to computation of seniority dates, the court noted that all the district court needed was the womens' dates of application and the dates on which men were subsequently hired. That data was either in the record of the case or could be obtained from the parties. With retroactive seniority, as with back pay, "unrealistic exactitude" is not required. See also, Easley v. Anheuser–Busch, Inc., 758 F.2d 251, 263–64 (8th Cir.1985).

In *Franks* the Court held that retroactive seniority may not be denied merely because of an adverse impact on the interests of other employees, but in a footnote qualified that rule by saying that, in exercising its equitable discretion, a court could deny such relief "on the basis of unusual adverse impact that would not be generally found in Title VII cases." In Romasanta v. United Air Lines, Inc., 717 F.2d 1140 (7th Cir.1983), cert. denied, 466 U.S. 944, 104 S.Ct. 1928, 80 L.Ed.2d 474 (1984), the Seventh Circuit relied on that footnote in denying immediate reinstatement, with full competitive seniority, to

---

20. This is not to suggest that district courts should be left to exercise a standardless, unreviewable discretion. But in the area of competitive-type seniority, unlike backpay and benefit-type seniority, the twin purposes of Title VII do not provide the standards. District courts must be guided in each instance by the mandate of § 706(g). They should, of course, record the considerations upon which they rely in granting or refusing relief, so that appellate review could be informed and precedents established in the area.

In this case, for example, factors that could be considered on remand and that could weigh in favor of full retroactive seniority, include Bowman's high employee turnover rate and the asserted fact that few victims of Bowman's discrimination have indicated a desire to be hired. Other factors, not fully developed in the record, also could require consideration in determining the balance of the equities. I would imply no opinion on the merits and would remand for full consideration in light of the views herein expressed.

a class of 1400 former airline stewardesses who had been terminated pursuant to an unlawful no-marriage rule. The plaintiffs argued that, on reinstatement, each class member should receive the full seniority she would have enjoyed had she never been fired. The Court concluded that, though such an award of retroactive seniority would appear to be necessary to make the discriminatees whole, to award more competitive seniority than the time actually worked before termination would have an unusual adverse impact on incumbents, resulting in furloughs, possible discharges, involuntary transfers and curtailment of job opportunities for recently hired minorities. In balancing the interests of all affected parties, the Court approved competitive seniority for time actually worked, but awarded noncompetitive seniority (used for pay and fringe benefit purposes) to cover the time from date of hire for each class member who was reinstated.

2. In INTERNATIONAL BROTHERHOOD OF TEAMSTERS v. UNITED STATES, 431 U.S. 324, 97 S.Ct. 1843, 52 L.Ed.2d 396 (1977) and AMERICAN TOBACCO CO. v. PATTERSON, 456 U.S. 63, 102 S.Ct. 1534, 71 L.Ed.2d 748 (1982), discussed in Chapter 2C, *supra*, the Court held that under § 703(h) of Title VII a "bona fide" seniority system (one not designed or maintained for a discriminatory purpose) was not illegal because it perpetuated the effects of past discrimination. In both *Teamsters* and *American Tobacco* the discrimination which was perpetuated by the seniority systems either had occurred before the enactment of Title VII or had not been the subject of a timely EEOC charge. The Court's determination that such seniority systems did not themselves violate the Act in no way affected the holding in *Franks* that, where discrimination in hiring or job assignment *over which the court has jurisdiction* is established, retroactive seniority is a proper remedy to make the victim of the discrimination whole. The Court in *Teamsters* was careful to distinguish between pre-Act discrimination, which was not illegal and for which the courts could not provide a remedy, and post-Act discrimination. "Post–Act discriminatees * * * may obtain full 'make whole' relief, including retroactive seniority * * * without attacking the seniority system as applied to them." 431 U.S. at 347, 97 S.Ct. at 1860.

Assume that employee A, who is black, was hired in 1962 and assigned to an all-black maintenance job. Employees B and C, who are white, were hired the next day and were given machine operator positions to which only whites were assigned. A, B and C all started with identical qualifications. Under the employer's seniority system, competitive seniority is only acquired in the job and an employee who transfers from one job to another loses all seniority acquired in the old position. In 1968 and again in 1975 A attempted to transfer into a machine operator position but was denied the transfer because of his race. After his 1975 rejection, A filed an EEOC charge and subsequently a law suit under Title VII. If the court finds that he was discriminated against in 1962, 1968 and 1975, what seniority relief is A entitled to?

3. In his separate opinion in *Franks* Justice Powell argued that "Title VII's 'primary objective' of eradicating discrimination is not served at all [by an award of retroactive seniority] for the employer is not deterred from the practice." 424 U.S. at 788, 96 S.Ct. at 1275. Is the premise of that argument true? See, Chambers v. Parco Foods, Inc., 935 F.2d 902 (7th Cir.1991) (maintenance of system of departmental seniority guarantees experienced work force in each department even during periods of employee lay-offs). Many structural seniority systems are, moreover, the products of collective bargaining between employers and unions. Unions have a great stake in protecting the seniority

rights of their incumbent members. The unpleasant alternative of court-ordered changes in seniority should have the same "prophylactic" effect on a union's policies as the threat of back pay theoretically will have on an employer.

Tenure in educational institutions and partnership in large law and accounting firms are, at least in part, the product of seniority. Because factors other than seniority influence decisions to award tenure and partnership, requests for court-awarded tenure and partnership have proved particularly troublesome to courts. As the First Circuit explained:

> Neither the district court nor this court is empowered to sit as a super tenure board. I believe that courts must be extremely wary of intruding into the world of university tenure decisions. These decisions necessarily hinge on subjective judgments regarding the applicant's academic excellence, teaching ability, creativity, contributions to the university community, rapport with students and colleagues, and other factors that are not susceptible of quantitative measurement. Absent discrimination, a university must be given a free hand in making such tenure decisions. Where, as here, the university's judgment is supportable and the evidence of discrimination negligible, a federal court should not substitute its judgment for that of the university.

Kumar v. Board of Trustees, University of Massachusetts, 774 F.2d 1, 12 (1st Cir.1985) (Campbell, J., concurring), cert. denied, 475 U.S. 1097, 106 S.Ct. 1496, 89 L.Ed.2d 896 (1986). In Fields v. Clark University, 817 F.2d 931 (1st Cir.1987) the district court found that the plaintiff had been denied tenure because of a "pervasively sexist attitude" on the part of the male members of her department and that male faculty members with similar qualifications to those of the plaintiff had been awarded tenure. But despite the finding that the decision to deny the plaintiff tenure was "impermissibly infected with sex discrimination," the court noted that there were questions as to her capacity as a teacher, and ordered the university to rehire her on a probationary basis for two years and then to renew the tenure process under circumstances free of discrimination. The First Circuit reversed. While it agreed with the district court that a finding that the decision to deny tenure was infected by sex discrimination did not, by itself, entitle her to reinstatement with tenure, the Court of Appeals held the district court erred in placing on the plaintiff the burden of proving her entitlement to tenure during the court-created probationary period. The case was remanded to the trial court for a hearing at which the employer would have an opportunity to prove by a preponderance of evidence that the plaintiff would have been denied tenure absent discrimination. Compare, Price Waterhouse v. Hopkins, Chapter 2B, *supra*. In another case, Brown v. Trustees of Boston University, 891 F.2d 337 (1st Cir.1989), cert. denied, 446 U.S. 937, 110 S.Ct. 3217, 110 L.Ed.2d 664 (1990) the Court of Appeals rejected a university's argument that the award of tenure was an infringement on its First Amendment right to determine for itself who may teach, the First Circuit affirmed. "[T]o deny tenure because of the intrusiveness of the remedy and because of the University's interest in making its own tenure decisions would frustrate Title VII's purpose of 'making persons whole for injuries suffered through past discrimination.' *Albermarle Paper Co.*, 422 U.S. at 421." 891 F.2d at 360.

On remand from the Supreme Court's decision in PRICE WATERHOUSE v. HOPKINS (Chapter 2B, *supra*) the district court directed that Ms. Hopkins be made a partner retroactive to 1982. Hopkins v. Price Waterhouse, 737

F.Supp. 1202 (D.D.C.1990). The defendant appealed. Relying on HISHON v. KING AND SPAULDING, *Price Waterhouse* argued that an injunction requiring that a plaintiff be made a partner was beyond the equitable powers of the court under Title VII because, once made a partner, the plaintiff would be outside the protection of the Act. The Court of Appeals rejected this argument on the ground that it "would directly subvert what Congress intended in the 1972 amendments if we were to hold that partnership could not be awarded to a person who was denied it because of unlawful discrimination" and affirmed the district court's injunction as well as the award of $371,000 in back pay. Hopkins v. Price Waterhouse, 920 F.2d 967, 977 (D.C.Cir.1990). The Court took pains, however, to delineate the reach of its decision.

> It is, of course, true, as Justice Powell noted in his concurrence to *Hishon*, that a partnership *relationship* is "markedly" different from the relationship of an employer and employee. See 467 U.S. at 79, 104 S.Ct. at 2235 (Powell, J., concurring). But this consideration is not controlling in this case. The instant case involves only an employee's elevation to partnership; it does not involve Ms. Hopkins retention of partnership or the regulation of the relationship among partners at Price Waterhouse. Thus, we are not confronted by the concerns expressed in Justice Powell's concurring opinion. Justice Powell emphasized that the Court in *Hishon* did not reach the question whether Title VII protects employees *after they become partners*; nor do we reach that question in this case.

920 F.2d at 979. See also, Ezold v. Wolf, Block, Schorr & Solis–Cohen, 56 FEP Cases 580 (E.D.Pa.1991) (attorney denied promotion to partner in law firm because of her sex ordered instated as partner as of date when she would have become partner in absence of discrimination).

4. The seniority systems of many industrial employers are organized in "lines of progression." In such systems, employees can use their competitive seniority to bid on jobs in a line of progression only in the order in which the jobs are ranked in the line: the employee must start at the bottom or "entry level" position and then can only use his seniority to bid on the next job up in the progression. The common rationale for such systems is that the employee needs to know the lower jobs in the progression before he can competently perform the "higher" positions. Sometimes progression line seniority is linked with the provision that an employee acquires competitive seniority only in a line of progression and relinquishes his seniority when he transfers to a new line of progression.

Line of progression seniority complicates the job of "making whole" the victim of discrimination. For example, an employee may have been excluded because of race or sex from a progression line. The court can, of course, order that the employee be placed in the seniority line from which he has been discriminatorily excluded, but if the progression line seniority system is not itself illegal (i.e. it is "bona fide" under *Teamsters*), how is he to be made whole for his earlier exclusion from the line? But for the discrimination the employee would be at a position in the line well above the entry level job which will typically be the lowest paying and most arduous job in the line. This kind of problem is addressed in Locke v. Kansas City Power & Light Co.

LOCKE v. KANSAS CITY POWER AND LIGHT CO.

United States Court of Appeals, Eighth Circuit, 1981.
660 F.2d 359.

McMILLIAN, CIRCUIT JUDGE.

Kansas City Power & Light Co. (KCP&L) appeals from a judgment entered in the District Court for the Western District of Missouri finding that KCP&L unlawfully discriminated against appellee Julius B. Locke on the basis of his race. The district court found that KCP&L had denied appellee employment in violation of Title VII of the Civil Rights Act of 1964, and awarded appellee backpay, reinstatement and attorney's fees.

For reversal appellant argues that the district court erred in (1) requiring appellant to show by a "preponderance of evidence" a legitimate, nondiscriminatory reason for refusing Locke's bid for employment; (2) finding the reason given by KCP&L for refusing Locke's bid to be a pretext; (3) ordering appellee reinstated to a higher position than that for which he had applied, with backpay computed, in part, at a rate commensurate with that higher position; and (4) eliminating the probationary period applied to all other employees.

For the reasons discussed below, we affirm in part and reverse in part and remand the case to the district court for further consideration of the remedy issue.

I. Background

On November 3, 1976, KCP&L hired Locke, a black male, as a "Temporary Plant Helper" at KCP&L's Hawthorn generating facility to work for a period of sixty days. Locke worked the full sixty-day term which ended on December 30, 1976. Shortly thereafter, on January 26, 1977, KCP&L rehired Locke, again as a "Temporary Plant Helper," this time for a period of ninety days. Locke completed this term of employment on April 27, 1977.

Temporary employees are hired by KCP&L for a specified period of time at the end of which the company automatically lays off the temporary employee unless he or she is transferred to a permanent position. (By contrast, in a permanent position at KCP&L after a probationary period the employee attains full permanent status, under which the employee automatically stays on unless appropriate steps are taken to end employment.)[2] While employed as a temporary plant

2. As KCP&L describes its policy, its plant supervisors may hire temporary employees only in an emergency or nonrecurring situation and must obtain authorization from the company which permits hiring of only a limited number of temporaries. The district court was not convinced, however, that this policy was actually followed, because the record suggested that at least in some instances KCP&L hired temporary plant helpers to do essentially the same job as permanent plant helpers on a regular basis. In addition to the groups of temporary plant helpers (in-

helper at KCP&L Locke applied to fill openings in three permanent job positions—one in November, 1976, for a janitor, and two in March, 1977, for plant helpers. Each time KCP&L returned the application to Locke, indicating that it would not be considered because a company policy prohibited accepting applications from temporary employees until the end of their temporary stints. Concerning the November, 1976, application, the company explained it had been filed after the closing date on the job announcement for accepting applications and that Locke was not eligible to apply until his temporary job ended. Concerning the March, 1977, applications, KCP&L explained only that Locke was not eligible to apply until his temporary job ended.[3] The company personnel department returned each application to Locke with an explanatory note dated the same day the application was submitted.

KCP&L continued to seek applicants for the available positions and ultimately filled them. Acting contrary to company policy as it was represented to Locke, KCP&L hired three white male temporary employees for the permanent positions which Locke also had sought. The applications of these temporary employees were considered even before their projects had been substantially completed.

Locke's second period of temporary employment ended April 27, 1977, and he was not rehired by the company. On May 9, 1977, Locke filed a charge of discrimination with the Equal Employment Opportunity Commission, alleging generally that the company had discriminated against him on the basis of race and specifically that a "probationary period" was used as a pretext to discharge him. The EEOC processed this charge and found no reasonable cause to believe that Locke's allegations were true and on June 7, 1978, notified Locke of his right to sue. Locke commenced this proceeding on August 29, 1978, complaining that KCP&L had discriminatorily failed to hire him into a permanent position and discharged him from temporary employment on the basis of race, all in violation of Title VII of the Civil Rights Act of 1964 and of 42 U.S.C. § 1981.[4]

At trial it was stipulated that KCP&L had hired into the permanent plant helper positions in question three white males who had, like

cluding Locke) hired in late 1976 and 1977, a third group was hired later in 1977 in what appeared to be an ongoing process despite absence of any evidence in the record of a year-long emergency under the company's stated policy.

3. There is some indication that Locke made these latter two applications after the closing date listed on the job announcement. The district court, however, found specifically that KCP&L continued to accept applications after Locke was turned down. Locke v. Kansas City Power & Light Co., No. 78–0636–CV–W–1 (W.D.Mo. Apr. 19, 1980), slip op. at 3, and KCP&L

does not challenge that finding on appeal. Indeed, KCP&L does not assign any error to the district court's finding that Locke established a *prima facie* case of racial discrimination under the analysis of McDonnell Douglas Corp. v. Green, 411 U.S. 792, 93 S.Ct. 1817, 36 L.Ed.2d 668 (1973) (McDonnell Douglas).

4. KCP&L does not assert that the allegations in the complaint were not "like or related" to the substance of the EEOC charge. See Satz v. ITT Financial Corp., 619 F.2d 738, 741 (8th Cir.1980). The EEOC determination of the charge is not in the record before us.

Locke, been temporary employees at the time of their applications and, like Locke, had not yet completed their temporary stints. KCP&L did not, however, attempt to justify its failure to hire Locke on the basis of the supposed policy against accepting applications from temporary workers before their jobs ended.[5] Instead, the company offered a new justification that it had actually given consideration to appellant's application and decided to reject him because of poor work performance. In particular KCP&L relied upon testimony by Glendon Paul Curry, the maintenance supervisor at the plant where Locke worked, that Curry had decided not to accept Locke's bid on the permanent plant helper jobs because of Locke's poor performance as a temporary employee. Curry testified that he had reports from foremen that Locke had been away from his work station, had argued with them, and had refused work assignments from more senior employees authorized by the foremen to direct him. The company also presented testimony of foremen and workers as direct evidence of Locke's poor performance.

The district court, however, determined this explanation was a pretext for a number of reasons which the court specified in an oral decision delivered from the bench.[6] The company had obtained written reports from foremen on Locke's supposedly poor performance after Locke's employment ended; the timing, of course, casts some doubt on whether those reports were actually considered in deciding not to give a permanent position to Locke. Moreover, KCP&L witnesses could not name any other employee who had been the subject of such post-termination reports. Locke's supposedly poor performance had not been grounds for failing to rehire him for a second period of temporary employment or for dismissing him. In the district court's view Locke's supposed absence from his work station and failure to follow orders from senior nonsupervisory workers would not be unusual in a job like plant helper where new workers were shuffled between various tasks, some requiring movement around various areas of the plant. It was

---

5. It was stipulated that

During the periods of [Locke's] employment, [KCP&L] maintained the following bidding procedure on permanent positions:

(a) Initially, regular bids will be considered.

(b) After regular employee bids are accepted or rejected, consideration may then be given to probationary employee bidders.

(c) Probationary employees are hired without time limitation and after six months of satisfactory service become employees.

(d) For the purposes of bidding, temporary employees are also probationary except that they are hired for a specific period of time only.

(e) The Company may elect to defer consideration of any bid submitted by a temporary employee until the project upon [which] they are working has been completed or nearly completed.

(f) The plant superintendent or his representative makes the decision regarding acceptance or rejection of bids.

6. Although the district court issued a document identified as written findings of fact and conclusions of law which had been approved as to form by counsel for both sides, the document does not fully reflect the substance of the factual findings and legal reasoning relied on by the court in announcing from the bench its decision on liability. In evaluating the district court's decision we consider both the document and the transcript of Judge Oliver's remarks which do not contradict the document but supplement it.

not clear from the record which KCP&L official was responsible for the decisions about Locke's future employment or what standards or considerations were normally applied in making the decision.[7] Finally, KCP&L's proffered justification for the failure to hire Locke was entirely different from what Locke was told when his application was returned to him.

The district court concluded that Locke had established a *prima facie* case of racial discrimination under the test of McDonnell Douglas v. Green, 411 U.S. 792, 93 S.Ct. 1817, 36 L.Ed.2d 668 (1973) (McDonnell Douglas), and that the reasons proffered by KCP&L for denying him a permanent position were pretextual. In its memorandum the court specified also that the "claim that [Locke] was less than a perfect employee fails to rebut [Locke's] prima facie case as it isn't necessary for [Locke] to 'show perfect performance or even average performance,' " Locke v. Kansas City Power & Light Co., No. 78–0636–CV–W–1 (W.D.Mo. Apr. 19, 1980), slip op. at 3, citing Flowers v. Crouch–Walker Corp., 552 F.2d 1277 (7th Cir.1977), and that KCP&L's "claim that [Locke] was not entitled to further employment because of an alleged failure to get along with his co-workers fails to rebut [Locke's] prima facie case as [Locke] is not required to have a 'pleasing personality' in order to be entitled to further employment." Locke v. Kansas City Power & Light Co., supra, slip op. at 3, citing Kyriazi v. Western Electric Co., 461 F.Supp. 894 (D.N.J.1978). The district court also concluded that KCP&L had "failed to show by a 'preponderance of the evidence' that [the] failure to accept plaintiff's bid for regular employment was for a legitimate nondiscriminatory reason." Locke v. Kansas City Power & Light Co., supra, slip op. at 4, citing Vanguard Justice Society v. Hughes, 471 F.Supp. 670 (D.Md.1979).

Accordingly, the district court found that KCP&L had violated Title VII by denying Locke a permanent plant helper position as of April, 1977, because of his race. In fashioning a remedy the court sought to put Locke in the position he would have occupied but for the discrimination against him. As the white temporary employees hired in place of Locke had all been promoted from plant helper to relief man positions at KCP&L, the district court ruled that Locke also was entitled to a relief man position. The court also held that Locke would not be required to undergo the normal six-month probationary period for new permanent employees. Finally, the court awarded backpay from April 27, 1977, the date KCP&L filled the permanent plant helper

---

7. For example, although KCP&L stipulated the decision would be made by the plant supervisor or his representative, KCP&L at trial took the position that the decision was delegated by the plant supervisor to the supervisor of maintenance in the plant. The district court remarked on the absence of any evidence that the plant manager made even a cursory review of a decision that was apparently his responsibility or that there were any standards at all to guide the decision. Although the court considered this as background evidence, it clearly did not hold the subjectiveness or vagueness of the decision making process *per se* improper, but rather went on to consider the ultimate question of whether race was a factor in this particular case.

position sought by Locke. Backpay was computed at the rate for a plant helper until January 18, 1978 (the date found by the court to be the "average date" for promotion to relief man of the three white plant helpers hired in April, 1977, ahead of Locke), and after January 18, 1978, at the rate for a relief man.[8]

* * *

[The court upheld the district court's finding that plaintiff was denied permanent employment because of his race and that the reasons put forward by the employer for its decisions were pretextual.]

III. *Remedy*

A. *Instatement as Permanent Plant Helper and Backpay at Plant Helper Rates*

As explained above, the district court found that absent discrimination Locke would have been hired as a plant helper on April 27, 1977 and continued in that position until January 20, 1978. The court awarded backpay at the plant helper rate until January 20, 1978; afterward it awarded backpay at the higher relief man rate. Including interest, a deduction for Locke's interim earnings, and probable overtime, the backpay award was $6,131.63 for 1977. During 1978 the award was zero because Locke's interim earnings fully offset his lost backpay even at the higher relief man rate. For 1979, the award was $7,359.14 and for 1980 up to the date of the district court's judgment the award was $2,060.80, all calculated at the relief man rate. In addition, the court ordered Locke instated as a relief man on a theory that Locke would have been promoted by that time in the absence of discrimination. The court further ordered that Locke should not have to undergo a six-month probationary period provided in KCP&L's contract with the union representing plant employees, because Locke would have served his probationary period long ago in the absence of discrimination.

On appeal KCP&L challenges certain aspects of this remedy, including the backpay award at the relief man rate, the instatement of Locke as a relief man, and the cancellation of the probationary period. KCP&L does not argue that backpay at the plant helper rate or instatement as a plant helper was improper as a remedy for the discrimination found by the district court and KCP&L did not appeal these matters. KCP&L's brief nevertheless seeks reversal of the entire judgment on grounds that, even if the district court was correct in finding discrimination, the remedy was an abuse of discretion. We take this to apply only to those parts of the remedy KCP&L objects to, and note that neither instatement of Locke as a plant helper nor backpay at the plant helper rate have been appealed. In view of our

8. The award was increased by adding prejudgment interest and decreased by subtracting interim earnings of Locke.

affirmance of the district court's finding of discrimination, no challenge remains to the portions of the judgment ordering Locke instated as a plant helper and $6,131.63 in backpay at the plant helper rate for 1977, and those parts of the judgment stand. However, as discussed below, the record before us is not adequate to support the other portions of the judgment. Therefore, we vacate and remand these questions for further consideration in light of this opinion.

B. *Standard of Review*

Preliminarily we note that we review the district court's remedial order only to correct abuse of discretion. Harper v. General Grocers Co., 590 F.2d 713, 717 (8th Cir.1979). That discretion is not unbounded but must be exercised consistently with the strong remedial aims of Title VII.

> One of the central purposes of Title VII is "to make persons whole for injuries suffered on account of unlawful employment discrimination." Albemarle Paper Company v. Moody, supra, [422 U.S. 405] at 418, 95 S.Ct. [2362] at 2372, 45 L.Ed.2d 280. Accord, Franks v. Bowman Transportation Co., [424 U.S. 747,] 763, 96 S.Ct. 1251, [1264, 47 L.Ed.2d 444] [(1976)]. "To effectuate this 'make whole' objective, Congress [has] vested broad equitable discretion in the federal courts to 'order such affirmative action as may be appropriate, which may include, but is not limited to, reinstatement * * * with or without back pay * * *, or any other equitable relief as the court deems appropriate." ' Id. at 763, 96 S.Ct. at 1264.

Harper v. General Grocers Co., supra, 590 F.2d at 716. Under this standard none of the remedial measures ordered by the district court *per se* went beyond the broad equitable powers specifically granted in § 706(g) of Title VII, 42 U.S.C. § 2000e–5(g). The problem is that there are insufficient findings in the record for us to evaluate the soundness of the district court's exercise of discretion and we therefore vacate parts of the judgment and remand for further findings and reconsideration. See Rule v. International Ass'n of Bridge, Structural & Ornamental Ironworkers, Local Union No. 396, 568 F.2d 558, 568 (8th Cir.1977).

C. *The Probationary Period*

The district court obviously had some basis for concern on this record that requiring Locke to go through a six-month probationary period, presumably giving him something less than the protection of a "just cause" clause in a typical collective bargaining agreement, would provide a ready pretext for further discrimination. There of course may well be valid nondiscriminatory reasons for requiring a probationary period. The probationary period has not been used to discriminate against Locke, however, and eliminating it may therefore be at odds with the equitable principle that the scope of the remedy should be tailored to the scope of the violation.

If the probationary period is a uniform requirement imposed by KCP&L on new employees for valid business purposes, we think Locke would be in the same position as other employees if he too was subject to it. If the probationary period in fact was not imposed uniformly, the district court may have been justified in exempting Locke from it in order to put him in the position he would have held but for the discrimination against him. Cf. Kansas City Power & Light Co. v. NLRB, 641 F.2d 553 (8th Cir.1981) (another case involving same employer suggesting a possibility of erratic enforcement). We cannot tell what the outcome should be on this record, and the district court has not made adequate subsidiary findings to support this remedial measure.

Rather than make the substantial inquiry that may be required to resolve a matter of only peripheral importance in this case, we suggest that it may be more appropriate for the district court simply to require Locke to serve the six-month probationary period and retain jurisdiction over the case during that time. Such a resolution would provide opportunity for close scrutiny of any employment decision which Locke may claim to have a discriminatory taint, while allowing KCP&L to use the probationary period for valid business objectives. Of course any action disfavoring Locke would have to be viewed in the context of the finding of discrimination already made in this case.[11]

D. *Promotion to Relief Man*

The district court apparently considered Locke qualified for a relief man job and thought Locke would have been promoted to relief man but for the discrimination against him. We cannot tell whether the court was of the view that the relief man job required essentially the same qualifications as the plant helper job or that Locke had any additional qualifications required for the relief man job or for some other reason. In any event the findings concerning Locke's qualifications and KCP&L's promotion practices are inadequate for us to evaluate the promotion of Locke to relief man as a remedial measure.

A court can in appropriate circumstances order a promotion as make whole relief for a victim of discrimination, but cannot under Title VII properly order the promotion of an employee to a position for which he or she is not qualified. Our research has not, however, discovered any cases precisely similar to this one, where a court has ordered a Title VII plaintiff who has suffered discrimination in the hiring process instated to a higher position than entry level.

11. In this light, if the district court allows the probationary period and retains jurisdiction, further proceedings will not be on a clean slate and KCP&L should be required to carry the burden of persuasion that any dismissal of Locke is based entirely on legitimate, nondiscriminatory factors. Compare International Bhd. of Teamsters v. United States, 431 U.S. 324, 362, 97 S.Ct. 1843, 52 L.Ed.2d 396 (1977) (after finding of discrimination against class the burden may be on the employer to demonstrate legitimate reasons for denying employment opportunity to a member of the class) with Burdine, supra, 101 S.Ct. at 1095 (plaintiff's burden of persuasion as to existence of discriminatory disparate treatment).

There is some support for the district court's action in a series of cases providing for "job-skipping" where an employer has discriminatorily excluded some employees from whole lines of progression within the employer's work force.   E.g., Watkins v. Scott Paper Co., 530 F.2d 1159 (5th Cir.), cert. denied, 429 U.S. 861, 97 S.Ct. 163, 50 L.Ed.2d 139 (1976); Rogers v. International Paper Co., 510 F.2d 1340, 1354 (8th Cir.), vacated on other grounds, 423 U.S. 809, 96 S.Ct. 19, 46 L.Ed.2d 29 (1975); Long v. Georgia Kraft Co., 450 F.2d 557 (5th Cir.1971); see also United States v. City of Philadelphia, 573 F.2d 802 (3d Cir.), cert. denied, 439 U.S. 830, 99 S.Ct. 105, 58 L.Ed.2d 123 (1978).   Such "job-skipping" cases have involved lines of progression between lower and higher level jobs in a plant, where a certain amount of time in a lower level job is generally required before moving up to the next higher job. Victims of discriminatory exclusion from the whole line of progression, especially those who have worked in other jobs within a facility, may be left without any real remedy if, for example, they must take a reduction in pay to transfer into the line of progression at entry level. Courts have in this context carefully scrutinized the lower level jobs prerequisite for advancement within lines of progression and have allowed job-skipping to make whole victims of discrimination where it has specifically been found that the lower level jobs prerequisite is not justified by business necessity.   But job-skipping is only appropriate where the beneficiary has demonstrated the skills or other qualifications legitimately required or the higher level job and the promotion is in a line of progression where a promotion is normally forthcoming after some interval of time in the lower level job.   Young v. Edgcomb Steel Co., 499 F.2d 97 (4th Cir.1974).

Under the job-skipping cases the district court has discretion to order Locke instated as a relief man only if it makes the following findings: (1) that Locke had the particular skills or other job-related qualifications required by KCP&L for a relief man, (2) that the relief man position was in a line of progression upward from the plant helper position, that is, a plant helper would normally be promoted to relief man after some interval of acceptable performance as a plant helper, and (3) that the prerequisite service as a plant helper is not itself justified by business necessity aside from the skills or other qualifications to perform the relief man job.   Moreover, in exercising its discretion we think the court should consider the possibility for making Locke whole economically by other means such as retroactive seniority, see Franks v. Bowman Transportation Co., supra, 424 U.S. 747, 96 S.Ct. 1251, 47 L.Ed.2d 444, or front pay discussed below.

In any event, KCP&L does not appear to contend that Locke is not entitled to instatement as a plant helper on the basis of the district court's discrimination finding that we have affirmed above and to nondiscriminatory consideration for promotion in the future.   Therefore, regardless of the decision on the relief man issue, Locke is in this posture of the case entitled to no less than instatement in a plant helper position.

E. *Backpay*

In view of our treatment of the promotion issue, the backpay award must be amended. If the district court finds that Locke is entitled under the above standards to a relief man position, Locke would be entitled to backpay at the relief man rate from the date his entitlement began, as under the present order. Otherwise, the backpay award must be recomputed at the lower plant helper rate for the year 1979 and any subsequent period of backpay award.

For the reasons stated above, the judgment of the district court is affirmed in part, vacated in part and remanded to the district court.

NOTES AND PROBLEMS FOR DISCUSSION

1. On remand, the district court, in order to sustain that portion of its judgment placing plaintiff in the relief man position, was instructed by the Eighth Circuit to make certain findings with respect to Locke's qualifications for the relief man position and the functional relation of that job to the position of plant helper. Who should have the burden of proof on these issues? Does Franks v. Bowman Transportation supply an answer? See, Ingram v. Missouri Pacific R. Co., 897 F.2d 1450, 1457 (8th Cir.1990) (retroactive promotion available to successful plaintiff unless employer shows by preponderance of the evidence that the employee would not have been promoted even in the absence of discrimination); McClure v. Mexia Independent School District, 750 F.2d 396 (5th Cir.1985) (district court did not abuse discretion in instating discharged employee in position she had never held where she had de facto exercised functions of the job and had been denied title because of her sex).

2. If the claimant lacks the qualifications to move directly into a non-entry level job he may be delayed in attaining his "rightful place" in the employment hierarchy. To financially compensate for this delay, monetary remedies have been developed.

Red Circling. In plants with functionally related lines of progression the minority employee, formerly excluded from bidding into a desirable department because of race or sex, may not be able to go directly into the job in that department to which he would have progressed absent discrimination (see the discussion of job-skipping in Locke v. Kansas City Power & Light Co.), but may be required to start at the entry level job for that line despite the award of retroactive seniority. But the employee may be dissuaded from seeking his rightful place, because the entry level job may pay less than the dead end position the employee now holds at the top of his formerly segregated line of progression. In such situations, the employer generally is required to "red circle" the employee's current wage rate, i.e., to allow the employee to carry it with him until he attains a job in the progression with a higher wage rate. See e.g., Grann v. City of Madison, 738 F.2d 786, 790 (7th Cir.), cert. denied, 469 U.S. 918, 105 S.Ct. 296, 83 L.Ed.2d 231 (1984); Rogers v. International Paper Co., 510 F.2d 1340, 1355–1356 (8th Cir.), on remand, 526 F.2d 722 (8th Cir.1975). Red circling can be combined with the job-skipping remedy described in *Locke*.

Front Pay. The Eighth Circuit's opinion in *Locke* suggests that front pay (paying the employee the wage rate of the higher job even though he holds the lower position) might be an alternative to placing the plaintiff directly into the relief man job. (Compare Chief Justice Burger's separate opinion in *Franks*, suggesting front pay as an alternative to retroactive seniority). Front pay has become virtually mandatory in cases when the "rightful place" position pays a higher wage rate than the claimant's current salary and, for whatever reason, the employee cannot immediately attain his "rightful place."

> Some employees who have been victims of discrimination will be unable to move immediately into jobs to which their seniority and ability entitle them. The back pay award should be fashioned to compensate them until they can obtain a job commensurate with their status. * * * [B]ack pay * * * until the date of judgment * * * should be supplemented by an award equal to the estimated present value of lost earnings that are reasonably likely to occur between the date of judgment and the time when the employee can assume his new position. * * * Alternatively, the court may exercise continuing jurisdiction over the case and make periodic back pay awards until the workers are promoted to the jobs their seniority and qualifications merit.

Patterson v. American Tobacco Co., 535 F.2d 257, 269 (4th Cir.), cert. denied, 429 U.S. 920, 97 S.Ct. 314, 50 L.Ed.2d 286 (1976). Front pay is normally calculated, at specific post-judgment intervals, as the difference between the employee's actual earnings and those of a hypothetical employee in the claimant's "rightful place." See generally, Note, Front Pay—Prophylactic Relief Under Title VII of the Civil Rights Act of 1964, 29 Vand.L.Rev. 211 (1976). Do front pay and red circling completely compensate an employee for the delay in reaching his "rightful place?" What if the "rightful place" position not only pays more, but is intellectually more challenging and physically less demanding than the claimant's current job?

3. Assuming *Locke* is qualified for the relief man position and that service as plant helper is not a legitimate prerequisite to the relief man job, could the court displace a white employee from that position in order to put Locke in his "rightful place?" Reconciling the rights of the victim of discrimination to be "made whole" with the interests of the incumbent employee has proved difficult for the courts. The legislative history of Title VII indicates that the Act's sponsors did not intend that employees hired *before* the effective date of the Act be bumped by those claiming under the Act. 110 Cong.Rec. 6992 (1964) (interpretive memorandum of Senators Clark and Case). Title VII's operation was to be "prospective and not retrospective." But employees hired after the Act's passage are, however, the beneficiaries of *illegal* discrimination, as was, presumably, the white temporary employed instead of Locke as plant helper. In FRANKS v. BOWMAN TRANSPORTATION CO. the Court stressed that "make whole" relief cannot "be denied merely because the majority group of employees, who have not suffered discrimination, will be unhappy about it" and that "adjustment of the rights of white employees" may be necessary "to shape remedies that will most effectively protect and redress the rights of the Negro victims of discrimination." 424 U.S. at 775 n.35, 96 S.Ct. at 1269, n.35. Are the equitable considerations surrounding the "bumping" of an employee from his job different from those surrounding deprivation of the employee's earned place on a seniority roster?

In Spagnuolo v. Whirlpool Corp., 717 F.2d 114 (4th Cir.1983) the district court in an ADEA case entered an order requiring that plaintiff be offered a "comparable position" to the one from which he had been terminated when one became available and paid front pay in the interim. After sixteen months, the district judge concluded that the defendant was dragging its feet in complying with the order and entered a new order requiring that the plaintiff be immediately reinstated to his old job. This order necessitated the bumping of the plaintiff's successor from his position. The Court of Appeals reversed, holding that regardless of the lapse in time and the trial judge's well-founded suspicion regarding defendant's conduct, the district court's equitable discretion did not extend to ordering displacement of an "innocent" incumbent employee. The Court went on to explain, however, that on remand, the district judge could explore whether the defendant had in fact filled positions after the original order which should have been offered to the plaintiff and whether it could have offered jobs in other locations to the incumbent holding the plaintiff's old position.

> We think that should the response to the first inquiry reveal that Whirlpool has filled a vacancy in a job that the district court concludes is comparable to the original position, the district court is empowered to bump the "new" incumbent from that position and order that Spagnuolo be employed in that job. It is important to note that this is not bumping the original employee who was the unknowing beneficiary of discrimination, as that bumping is prohibited by Title VII. Rather, this is bumping an employee whose promotion or hiring was in violation of the court's rightful place order. This "authorized" bumping presumes that the employee who is promoted or hired after the judicial pronouncement of discrimination is no longer an innocent beneficiary. We conclude that such equitable action is authorized under both Title VII and under the district court's inherent powers to enforce its orders.

717 F.2d at 122. Why would the beneficiary of the company's effort to avoid compliance with the court order be any less "innocent" than the beneficiary of the original illegal employment decision? With *Spagnuolo* compare the approach of the District of Columbia Court of Appeals in Lander v. Lujan, 888 F.2d 153 (D.C.Cir.1989). In *Lujan* the plaintiff was demoted from the top administrative position in the Bureau of Mines because of his criticism of an affirmative action plan developed for the agency by the Department of Interior. The district court found the demotion was unlawful retaliation under Section 704(a) of Title VII and ordered that plaintiff be reinstatement to his former job. Since there was only one such position, the court order necessarily displaced the incumbent who had replaced the plaintiff when he was demoted. The government appealed. Relying largely on Spagnuolo v. Whirlpool, it argued that the district court had erroneously balanced the equities because it did not properly weigh the disruption of the work place and the impact on the "innocent incumbent." The Court of Appeals affirmed.

> It may well be appropriate, perhaps even required, that a district court consider the impact of a bumping remedy on incumbents who are innocent beneficiaries of the employment discrimination.... But we see no indication in the statute nor in logic to lead us to conclude that ordinarily the innocent beneficiary has a superior equitable claim to the job vis-a-vis the victim of discrimination. Therefore, if the district court must choose between the two, we do not see how the court can be reversed for choosing complete relief for the victim. In any event, the Fourth Circuit's approach [in *Spagnuolo*] seems more suited to a situation where vacancies in the relevant jobs appear rather frequently, but not to a case such as ours where there is really only one top administrative job in the Bureau.

> Nor do we understand how an employer's claim that his workplace would be disrupted could possibly defeat the victim's entitlement to com-

plete relief when, after all, the employer's intentional discrimination created the disturbance by harming the plaintiff. A district court's discrimination remedy cannot turn on the employer's preferences.

888 F.2d at 157–58. In his concurring opinion in CITY OF RICHMOND v. J.A. CROSON COMPANY, discussed in Part IV, *infra,* Justice Scalia commented:

> [O]f course, a State may "undo the effects of past discrimination" in the sense of giving the identified victim of state discrimination that which it wrongfully denied him—for example, giving to a previously rejected black applicant the job that, by reason of discrimination, had been awarded to a white applicant, even if this means terminating the latter's employment. In such a context, the white job-holder is not being selected for disadvantageous treatment because of his race, but because he was wrongfully awarded a job to which another is entitled.

488 U.S. at 526, 109 S.Ct. at 738 (Scalia, J., concurring). Do you agree?

One theme common to a number of decisions upholding bumping is a finding of "recalcitrance" on the part of the employer. See, e.g., Walters v. City of Atlanta, 803 F.2d 1135, 1150 (11th Cir.1986) (repeated discrimination and retaliation against plaintiff are factors favoring bumping relief); Brewer v. Muscle Shoals Board of Education, 790 F.2d 1515 (11th Cir.1986) (court may order bumping in order to redress breach of Title VII settlement agreement); Lee v. Macon County Board of Education, 453 F.2d 1104 (5th Cir.1971) (authorizing bumping since school board hired incumbent after it had knowledge of plaintiff's claims).

Is an incumbent employee who might be "bumped" as the result of a Title VII action a necessary party to the proceeding? See Rule 19, Federal Rules of Civil Procedure and Martin v. Wilks, Section D, *infra.*

4. Reinstatement will not be ordered unless, absent discrimination, the plaintiff would have been employed by the defendant at the time of trial. See e.g., Easley v. Anheuser–Busch, Inc., 758 F.2d 251 (8th Cir.1985) (plaintiffs not entitled to reinstatement because positions for which they had applied had been eliminated in reduction of force before trial). Compare, EEOC v. Mike Smith Pontiac GMC, Inc., 896 F.2d 524 (11th Cir.1990) (back pay only available for the period of time that plaintiff would have been employed absent discrimination). See discussion of back pay calculation in Section A of this chapter.

If the "rightful place" position with the employer is available, however, reinstatement is the preferred remedy and successful plaintiffs do not have the option to choose front pay in lieu of reinstatement. See, e.g., EEOC v. Prudential Federal Savings & Loan Ass'n, 763 F.2d 1166, 1172 (10th Cir.), cert. denied, 474 U.S. 946, 106 S.Ct. 312, 88 L.Ed.2d 289 (1985); O'Donnell v. Georgia Osteopathic Hospital, Inc., 748 F.2d 1543, 1551–52 (11th Cir.1984). What other circumstances might justify the denial of injunctive relief to a victim of discrimination?

Reinstatement will frequently require former adversaries to work together. A number of courts have held that animosity between the parties may constitute a ground for denial of reinstatement. See e.g., EEOC v. Kallir, Philips, Ross, Inc., 420 F.Supp. 919 (S.D.N.Y.1976), affirmed, 559 F.2d 1203 (2d Cir.1977) (*per curiam*), cert. denied, 434 U.S. 920, 98 S.Ct. 395, 54 L.Ed.2d 277 (1977) (unlawfully discharged advertising account executive not entitled to reinstatement in view of close working relationship required between plaintiff and employer); Cooper v. Asplundh Tree Expert Co., 836 F.2d 1544, 1553 (10th

Cir.1988) (tension and animosity between parties in workplace with relatively few employees and where close contact with supervisors required justified denial of reinstatement); Brooks v. Woodline Motor Freight, Inc., 852 F.2d 1061, 1065 (8th Cir.1988) (award of front pay in lieu of reinstatement supported by evidence that nature of business requires high degree of mutual trust and where employer's president testified that he wanted to choke the plaintiff); Deloach v. Delchamps, Inc., 897 F.2d 815, 822 (5th Cir.1990) (reinstatement not appropriate where plaintiff's reinstatement would disrupt the employment of others and where, after trial, there was less likelihood than ever that plaintiff would be satisfactory employee).

Other courts have held that hostility, particularly that generated by the litigation itself, will not bar reinstatement. In Anderson v. Group Hospitalization, Inc., 820 F.2d 465 (D.C.Cir.1987), for example, the employer urged the court of appeals to vacate the district court's order requiring reinstatement of the plaintiff because it would result in an "intolerable environment" in the workplace. The court of appeals affirmed.

> While it is perhaps true that feelings between Anderson and her former supervisors ... are such that no meaningful work relationship could be reestablished, Judge Parker's order requires only that GHI reinstate Anderson to her former post or "an equivalent position." The fact that this litigation may have engendered ill will toward Sylvia Anderson on the part of GHI management generally is simply an insufficient reason to deny her the equitable remedial relief she sought and which the trial court, in its sound discretion, was entitled to award her. Such ill will is a frequent by-product of employment discrimination litigation and, standing alone, should not deprive a successful plaintiff of her right to hold a position she would otherwise have held but for her employer's unlawful action.

836 F.2d at 473. See also, Farber v. Massillon Board of Education, 917 F.2d 1391 (6th Cir.1990), cert. denied, ___ U.S. ___, 111 S.Ct. 2851, 115 L.Ed.2d 1019 (1991) (if reinstatement is to be denied on the basis of workplace tensions, "those tensions must be so serious as to manifest themselves in the public function of the employer"). On remand from the Supreme Court's decision in Price Waterhouse v. Hopkins, Chapter 2B, *supra*, the district court was faced with the question of whether it should force Price Waterhouse to make Ann Hopkins a partner. The district judge noted that, while "extreme workplace hostility and disruption may influence a court to deny reinstatement," this was not such a case. Price Waterhouse had over 900 partners spread among 90 offices and only a few partners had ever met Ms. Hopkins. The judge concluded that "Price Waterhouse lacks the intimacy and interdependence of smaller partnerships, so concerns about freedom of association have little force." Hopkins v. Price Waterhouse, 737 F.Supp. 1202, 1210 (D.D.C.1990). The judge also concluded that front pay was not a viable alternative for the following reasons:

> Since Ms. Hopkins' claim that partnership was always her objective cannot be tested, the alternative of front pay for the rest of Ms. Hopkins' business life does not appear to make her whole and, in any event, might well provide a wholly unwarranted windfall. The Court cannot determine whether she will be a successful, inadequate or superior partner. Nor can it determine how factors affecting her health, availability or the firm's own fortunes will impinge on her earnings. In addition, the Court is skeptical as to whether monetary relief alone provides a sufficient deterrent against

future discrimination for a group of highly-paid partners. Given these considerations, equity favors the course that will most vindicate the purpose of the sex discrimination statute, consistent with established national policy.

Id. The Court ordered that Ms. Hopkins be made a partner. That decision was affirmed. Hopkins v. Price Waterhouse, 920 F.2d 967 (D.C.Cir.1990).

5. Where reinstatement is denied, as opposed to being merely postponed until a position is available, how should front pay be calculated? Because of factors such as the economy, the age and skills of the claimant and the job market in her area of work, a victim of employment discrimination may never be able to find work comparable to the position she was denied. In such circumstances is the claimant entitled to front pay indefinitely? Until her retirement age? Is there any way for a court to predict what her earnings will be in non-comparable work? In Shore v. Federal Express Corp., 777 F.2d 1155, 1160 (6th Cir.1985), the court of appeals noted that:

> Some of the factors which the district courts have employed to alleviate the speculative nature of future damage awards include an employee's duty to mitigate, "the availability of employment opportunities, the period within which one by reasonable efforts may be re-employed, the employee's work and life expectancy, the discount tables to determine the present value of future damages and other factors that are pertinent on prospective damage awards." (quoting from Koyen v. Consolidated Edison Co. of New York, Inc., 560 F.Supp. 1161, 1168–69 (S.D.N.Y.1983)).

In Dominic v. Consolidated Edison Co. of New York, Inc., 822 F.2d 1249 (2d Cir.1987) the plaintiff appealed from the trial judge's award of front pay award in an amount equal to the difference between the salary of his old job and what he was earning at the time of trial for a two year period. The Second Circuit affirmed.

> Consolidated Edison's failure to show that Dominic had not mitigated damages does not entitle him to a lifetime front-pay award. In calculating the size of a front pay award the court must estimate the plaintiff's ability to mitigate damages in the future. Such a determination is committed to that court's discretion. * * * [W]e can conclude that Judge Walker [did not] abuse his discretion in finding that two years was a reasonable amount of time for Dominic to find comparable employment.

822 F.2d at 1258. See also, Graefenhain v. Pabst Brewing Co., 870 F.2d 1198 (7th Cir.1989) (front pay properly limited to five months in light of reduction in force which would most likely have cost plaintiff his job). Compare, Buckley v. Reynolds Metals Co., 690 F.Supp. 211 (S.D.N.Y.1988) (nine-year award of front pay to discharged salesman does not involve undue speculation); Folz v. Marriott Corp., 594 F.Supp. 1007 (W.D.Mo.1984) (court award of front pay to 53 year-old plaintiff from date of judgment to date of prospective retirement at age 65). In SCHOOL BOARD OF NASSAU COUNTY v. ARLINE, 480 U.S. 273, 107 S.Ct. 1123, 94 L.Ed.2d 307 (1987) (discussed *infra*, Chapter 11), the Supreme Court held that an elementary school teacher discharged in 1978 when she had a relapse of tuberculosis was an "otherwise qualified" employee within the meaning of the Rehabilitation Act. On remand, the district court awarded back pay and afforded the school district the choice of either reinstating the plaintiff or paying her front pay in the amount of $768,724.00 calculated as the present value of what plaintiff would earn from the 1988–89 school year until her retirement at age 65. Arline v. School Board of Nassau County, 692

F.Supp. 1286 (M.D.Fla.1988). Is such a "choice" consistent with the purposes of statutes prohibiting employment discrimination?

6. The language of the Civil Rights Act of 1991 creates some uncertainty concerning *who* should decide entitlement to front pay and the amount: judge of jury? Section 102 of the 1991 Act specifies that compensatory damages shall not include back pay "or any other type of relief authorized under section 706(g) of [Title VII]." While not explicitly mentioned in 706(g), courts have held that front pay is "authorized" by 706(g) and that the remedies contained in that section are equitable in nature. Another subpart of Section 102, however, refers to compensatory damages as including "future pecuniary losses" which certainly is a fair description of front pay. Under the Seventh Amendment and the explicit language of the 1991 Act, compensatory damages constitute legal relief and, at the option of either party, must be determined by a jury. Should front pay be left, like back pay, to the limited discretion of the trial judge or should it be characterized as a component of damages and decided by the jury? If front pay is part of the damage remedy, it will be subject to the limitations on amount specified in the 1991 Act. See, Chapter 7A, *supra* at 612.

7. In a hiring or promotion case the plaintiff who establishes that he was unlawfully denied the position will ordinarily be entitled to an injunction placing him in the position or, where an "innocent" incumbent would be affected, at least to a preference for the next vacancy. But what if discrimination is established and there was more than one minority applicant for the position? Could *both* be entitled to injunctive relief? In Milton v. Weinberger, 696 F.2d 94 (D.C.Cir.1982), the Court noted:

> [I]f two employees are denied the same promotion for concededly discriminatory reasons, the employer may nonetheless establish that one of the claimants is not entitled to a promotion * * * by offering clear and convincing evidence that there was only one job opening and that the other applicant was more qualified. Since only one of the two victims of discrimination would have been promoted 'but for' the discrimination, the other would not be entitled to an award of the job notwithstanding the unlawful reason for the denial.

696 F.2d at 99. The Court offered no explanation of what the outcome should be if the employer failed to meet its burden. Could the employer ever be ordered to hire both applicants if only one vacancy was originally available? If, as *Milton* assumes, both applicants are "victims of discrimination," would it be fair to at least award the less qualified of two applicants a hiring or promotion preference for a future vacancy? Compare, Dougherty v. Barry, 869 F.2d 605 (D.C.Cir.1989) (multiple claimants to single position must split back pay award). Is the winner-take-all approach to injunctive relief suggested in *Milton* required by the Supreme Court's decision in PRICE WATERHOUSE V. HOPKINS, Chapter 2B *supra*?

CONSTRUCTIVE DISCHARGE

The above material discusses various equitable defenses to reinstatement or other "rightful place" relief. A prerequisite for any kind of injunctive relief, however, is a finding that the employer's unlawful conduct *caused* the denial of employment. As discussed in the following case, the causal relationship between the employer's conduct and the employee's termination may be in dispute.

DERR v. GULF OIL CORPORATION

United States Court of Appeals, Tenth Circuit, 1986.
796 F.2d 340.

McKAY, CIRCUIT JUDGE.

Gail Derr filed an action against her employer, Gulf Oil Corporation, alleging, among other claims, that Gulf discriminated against her because of her sex in violation of Title VII of the Civil Rights Act of 1964. The trial court found that Gulf discriminated against Ms. Derr when it demoted her from an associate lease analyst position to an accounting clerk position. The court entered a judgment against Gulf from which the company appeals.

Gulf hired Ms. Derr as a clerk floater in the accounting department of Gulf Mineral Resources Company (GMRC), a division of Gulf Oil Corporation. Ms. Derr was later promoted to associate lease analyst in GMRC's lease records unit where she worked with three male lease analysts. Subsequently, as GMRC's business declined, Mr. Dale Lyon, GMRC's assistant comptroller, removed Ms. Derr from the lease records unit and assigned her to the accounting clerk position. Dissatisfied with her demotion, Ms. Derr resigned.

Gulf first contends that the trial court's finding that Gulf discriminated against Ms. Derr when it transferred her to the accounting clerk position is clearly erroneous. We conclude there is ample evidence from which the trial court could conclude that Ms. Derr's sex was a determinative factor in Gulf's decision to demote her. As an associate lease analyst, Ms. Derr was in a career ladder position, a few months away from becoming a lease analyst. She was doing better than satisfactory work and was being groomed by her supervisor to become a lease analyst. Gulf knew that an opening for Ms. Derr's promotion to lease analyst would occur very soon because two lease analysts were nearing retirement age, and one of them had indicated that he wanted to take advantage of Gulf's early retirement program. In deciding to demote Ms. Derr, Mr. Lyon did not consult Ms. Derr's immediate supervisor even though Mr. Lyon knew little about the duties and workload of the lease records unit. Instead he consulted only Mr. A.C. Weiler, the manager of accounting. The evidence shows that Mr. Weiler was biased against Ms. Derr because of her sex. For example, Mr. Weiler scolded Ms. Derr for attempting to achieve her career goals while having two small children at home. He also commented repeatedly that problems arise if a woman gets too much education. Additionally he was antagonistic toward Ms. Derr after she was demoted and refused to acknowledge her presence.

The evidence also shows that Mr. Lyon chose Ms. Derr for demotion without considering any other Gulf employee for the accounting clerk position. At least one other Gulf employee was not only interested in the accounting clerk job but, unlike Ms. Derr, was also trained for the job. Also, unlike Ms. Derr, the other employee was not very busy with her work at Gulf.

Finally, the following juggling of employees occurred all within a few months: Ms. Derr replaced a Mr. Whittaker, at a lower salary; Mr. Whittaker was transferred into a Mr. Villamor's department; and Mr. Villamor was transferred into the lease records unit, the unit from which Ms. Derr had been removed. Although varying inferences may be drawn from this evidence, the record clearly supports the judgment.

Gulf next contends the trial court erred when it ordered Gulf to reinstate Ms. Derr and awarded her back pay of $7,980 plus interest. These remedies, Gulf argues, are not available to Ms. Derr because she was not constructively discharged. Gulf's contentions require us to examine the basis for the trial court's award to Ms. Derr and the law of constructive discharge.

Ms. Derr resigned from Gulf on November 30, 1982. Apparently, the demotion to accounting clerk would not have made a difference in her salary until March 1, 1983, at which time, absent the discriminatory demotion, she would have been promoted to lease analyst. Thus, the trial court calculated damages for the period from March 1, 1983, to February 1, 1985, the date reinstatement was to take effect. The court determined that Ms. Derr's damages were the difference between what she would have earned as a lease analyst and what she would have earned had she remained in the accounting clerk position. Thus, all of the damages awarded relate to the period of time after Ms. Derr resigned but before she was to be reinstated.

We agree with Gulf that the remedies of back pay and reinstatement are not available to Ms. Derr unless she was constructively discharged. In Muller v. United States Steel Corp., 509 F.2d 923 (10th Cir.), cert. denied, 423 U.S. 825, 96 S.Ct. 39, 46 L.Ed.2d 41 (1975), we reversed the trial court's holding that an employee had been constructively discharged and then examined the effect of our conclusion on the trial court's damage award. We stated:

> Unless [the employee] was constructively discharged, he would not be entitled to back pay, interest and retirement from the date of [his resignation]. His damage would be measured by the difference between actual pay and the amount he would have made [had he not been discriminated against] until he quit * * *.

Id. at 930. Our conclusion in *Muller* is in harmony with the law in other jurisdictions. See, e.g., Satterwhite v. Smith, 744 F.2d 1380, 1381 n. 1 (9th Cir.1984) ("an employee who quits cannot secure back pay unless his employer constructively discharged him."); Bourque v. Powell Electrical Manufacturing Co., 617 F.2d 61, 66 & n. 8 (5th Cir.1980); Harrington v. Vandalia–Butler Board of Education, 585 F.2d 192, 197 (6th Cir.1978), cert. denied, 441 U.S. 932, 99 S.Ct. 2053, 60 L.Ed.2d 660 (1979). We agree with the Fifth Circuit's statement in *Bourque,* supra, that "society and the policies underlying Title VII will be best served if, wherever possible, unlawful discrimination is attacked within the context of existing employment relationships." 617 F.2d at 66.

Applying this rationale to the present case, we conclude that unless Ms. Derr was constructively discharged, she is entitled to only the difference in pay between what she earned as an accounting clerk and what she would have earned as an associate lease analyst until she resigned. That difference is, according to the record, zero.[2]

In addition, Ms. Derr is not entitled to reinstatement if she was not constructively discharged. Irving v. Dubuque Packing Co., 689 F.2d 170, 175 (10th Cir.1982); Dean v. Civiletti, 670 F.2d 99, 101 (8th Cir.1982) (per curiam); Fancher v. Nimmo, 549 F.Supp. 1324, 1333 (E.D.Ark.1982).

In response to Gulf's contention that Ms. Derr was not entitled to back pay and reinstatement because she was not constructively discharged, the trial court stated:

> [W]here the court has found discrimination in demoting her, changing her to another job, and the court has allowed a setoff or a deduction on what she would have made had she stayed with the company, *even though she was not constructively fired,* even though she was not forced out, she had other alternatives. She could have stayed. Nevertheless, *it was certainly not unreasonable* that being denied this job that she had held for a long period of time in anticipation of promotion and reduced back to an accounting clerk—*it was not unreasonable that she quit her job.*

Record, vol. 11, at 1247–48 (emphasis added). The trial court's findings that Ms. Derr was not constructively discharged and that she acted reasonably in resigning are inconsistent when viewed in light of the proper test for determining when an employee is constructively discharged, which we enunciate below.

The constructive discharge doctrine has been applied to Title VII cases by every circuit court of appeals but one. There is, however, a divergence of opinion among the circuits as to the findings necessary to apply the doctrine. While some courts require the employee to prove the employer's specific intent to force him to leave, Bristow v. Daily Press, Inc., 770 F.2d 1251, 1255 (4th Cir.1985), others have adopted a less stringent objective standard requiring the employee to prove that the employer has made working conditions so difficult that a reasonable person in the employee's shoes would feel forced to resign. Goss v. Exxon Office Systems Co., 747 F.2d 885, 887–88 (3d Cir.1984). In Satterwhite v. Smith, 744 F.2d 1380, 1383 n. 4 (9th Cir.1984), the court noted that "[t]he state of the law in the Tenth Circuit on this subject is confusing. * * * [L]anguage in the cases purports to embrace the

---

2. Ms. Derr's counsel apparently agrees that Ms. Derr is not entitled to "back pay" absent constructive discharge. He argued to the trial court that, even if Ms. Derr prevailed on her discrimination claim, a finding that she was not constructively discharged "foreclosed her from any monetary recovery at all." Record, vol. 10, at 1044.

reasonable employee standard *as well as* the employer's subjective-intent standard."

It is true that the Tenth Circuit's position on this issue has been less than clear. But in Irving v. Dubuque Packing Co., 689 F.2d 170 (10th Cir.1982), our most recent pronouncement in this area, we intended to clarify our position by adopting the standard set out in Bourque v. Powell Electrical Manufacturing Co., 617 F.2d 61 (5th Cir.1980). *Irving* cites *Bourque* with approval and concludes:

> A finding of constructive discharge depends upon whether a reasonable [person] would view the working conditions as intolerable, not upon the subjective view of the employee-claimant.[3]

689 F.2d at 172. While some language in Muller v. United States Steel Corp., 509 F.2d 923, 929 (10th Cir.), cert. denied, 423 U.S. 825, 96 S.Ct. 39, 46 L.Ed.2d 41 (1975), and *Irving*, supra at 172, suggests that our focus may once have been on the explicit subjective intent of the employer to force the employee to leave, our conclusion and discussions in *Irving* indicate that we have been struggling with the problem of what the employee must prove.

The examples of the quality and quantity of proof given in *Irving* demonstrate that typically proof of any element in these cases is circumstantial. What *Bourque* has done for the problem of proof is to cut through the details and difficulty of analyzing the employer's state of mind and focus on an objective standard. Thus, proof of constructive discharge "depends upon whether a reasonable [person] would view the working conditions as intolerable." Irving v. Dubuque Packing Co., 689 F.2d 170, 172 (10th Cir.1982). This shift in emphasis is consistent with the District of Columbia Circuit's observation that "[t]o the extent that [the employer] denies a conscious design to force [the employee] to resign, we note that an employer's subjective intent is irrelevant; [*the employer*] *must be held to have intended those consequences it could reasonably have foreseen.* See, e.g., *Bourque*, 617 F.2d at 65." Clark v. Marsh, 665 F.2d 1168, 1175 n. 8 (D.C. Cir. 1981) (emphasis added).

We trust that our unqualified adoption of this objective standard will clarify any ambiguity which may have remained in our cases to this point. We also believe the standard will simplify the task of the finder of fact in determining not only whether the employer discriminated against the employee but also whether the manner of discrimination rendered work conditions intolerable. In brief, this standard addresses the concerns expressed in both our *Muller* and *Irving* cases. Our position, then, is that the question on which constructive discharge cases turn is simply whether the employer by its illegal discriminatory

---

3. *Bourque* has become the leading case on the subject of constructive discharge under Title VII. In *Bourque*, the court ruled that, in order to find constructive discharge, "the trier of fact must be satisfied that the * * * working conditions would have been so difficult or unpleasant that a reasonable person in the employee's shoes would have felt compelled to resign." 617 F.2d at 65 (quoting Alicea Rosado v. Garcia Santiago, 562 F.2d 114, 119 (1st Cir.1977)).

acts has made working conditions so difficult that a reasonable person in the employee's position would feel compelled to resign. In light of our clarification of the standard for finding a constructive discharge, we remand to the trial court to determine whether Ms. Derr was constructively discharged.

[The Court held that, regardless of the trial court's constructive discharge finding, the plaintiff was the "prevailing party" because she had succeeded on a significant issue in the litigation and was therefore entitled to an award of attorney's fees. The fee shifting provisions of Title VII and other statutes are discussed in Chapter 15, infra.]

NOTES AND PROBLEMS FOR DISCUSSION

1. Is the Court's "objective" test for constructive discharge fair to the victim of discrimination who in fact is more emotionally vulnerable or sensitive than the hypothetical "reasonable" person? The Sixth Circuit has developed a different test for constructive discharge which focuses on the intent of the employer and the reasonably foreseeable impact of the employer's conduct upon the employee. "[A]n employee can establish a constructive discharge claim by showing that a reasonable employer would have foreseen that a reasonable employee (or this employee, if facts peculiar to her are known) would feel constructively discharged." Wheeler v. Southland Corp., 875 F.2d 1246, 1249 (6th Cir.1989). Which test for constructive discharge is more consistent with the remedial purposes of Title VII? A standard principle of tort law is that the wrongdoer "takes his victim as he finds him" and cannot complain if his actions cause more harm to his victim than the tortfeasor would have expected. Why should not this same principle apply to the constructive discharge analysis?

2. What in fact makes continuation of employment "intolerable" to the "reasonable" employee? A significant increase in workload? See, Wardwell v. School Board of Palm Beach County, 786 F.2d 1554 (11th Cir.1986). The disappearance of reasonable expectations for promotion? See, Hopkins v. Price Waterhouse, 920 F.2d 967 (D.C.Cir.1990). A change in the job from full-time to part-time? See, Schneider v. Jax Shack, Inc., 794 F.2d 383 (8th Cir.1986). Being required to train subordinates who would become the employee's superiors? See, Bruhwiler v. University of Tennessee, 859 F.2d 419 (6th Cir.1988). Exclusion from management meetings and false accusations of stealing and drinking on the job? Levendos v. Stern Entertainment, Inc., 860 F.2d 1227 (3d Cir.1988).

Who should have the burden of proof on the constructive discharge issue? Since the question of whether a constructive discharge has occurred will not arise until there has been a determination that the employer unlawfully discriminated against the plaintiff, does it make sense to place the burden of persuasion on the victim of discrimination? See, Garner v. Wal–Mart Stores, Inc., 807 F.2d 1536, 1539 (11th Cir.1987).

3. As noted by the Tenth Circuit in *Derr*, most courts have held that employees are entitled to reinstatement only if they were actually or constructively discharged from employment. See e.g., Jurgens v. EEOC, 903 F.2d 386 (5th Cir.1990); Morrison v. Genuine Parts Co., 828 F.2d 708 (11th Cir.1987), cert. denied, 484 U.S. 1065, 108 S.Ct. 1025, 98 L.Ed.2d 990 (1988). One rationale behind the general rule is that "society and the policies underlying Title VII will be best served if, wherever possible, unlawful discrimination is

attacked within the context of existing employment relationships." Bourque v. Powell Electrical Manufacturing Co., 617 F.2d 61, (5th Cir.1980). But does this rationale make sense where the victim of discrimination has no opportunity, within the employment relationship, to overcome discrimination? Is *any* interest served by making plaintiff stay on the job while she sues her employer?

In Ezold v. Wolf, Block, Schorr & Solis–Cohen, 751 F.Supp. 1175 (E.D.Pa. 1990), the plaintiff, a six-year associate with a large law firm, was informed that she would not be made a partner, though she could stay on at the firm in a subordinate status. She remained at the firm for approximately eight months before resigning to accept another job. After a trial on the merits, the district court found that the plaintiff had been denied partnership because she was a woman. The court concluded, however, that she had not been constructively discharged because "a reasonable person in her position would not have felt compelled to leave." 751 F.Supp. at 1190. The relief and liability phases of the trial were bifurcated. At the relief stage of the trial, the law firm argued that, since she was not constructively discharged, the only relief available to the plaintiff was back pay for the four-month period between the date her partnership would have become effective and the date of her resignation. The district court rejected this argument.

> Strict application of the constructive discharge rule in denial of promotion cases would mean that no matter how severe an employer's discrimination is with respect to the denial of a promotion, an employee would be forced to remain in the inferior employment position so long as the employer does not permit the working conditions of the inferior employment position to become intolerable. If the employee instead resigns the inferior employment position, her entitlement to a remedy for the discriminatory denial of the superior position would cease at the date of resignation. Such a rule flouts the Supreme Court's instruction that a complete Title VII remedy "should only be denied for reasons which, if applied generally, would not frustrate the central statutory purposes of eradicating discrimination throughout the economy and making persons whole for the injuries suffered through past discrimination." (*quoting*, Albemarle Paper Co. v. Moody)

Ezold v. Wolf, Block, Schorr & Solis–Cohen, 758 F.Supp. 303, 308 (E.D.Pa. 1991). The district court also reasoned that rigid application of the rule would conflict with plaintiff's obligation to mitigate.

> The application of the constructive discharge rule here, where the plaintiff was discriminatorily denied the one significant promotion available to an attorney practicing in a private firm setting, would be contrary to the most basic principles of equity underlying Title VII. Not only would a complete remedy be withheld from the plaintiff, but she would also be robbed of the freedom, once her promotion was denied, to seek out, both as a mitigative measure as well as for personal/professional advancement, employment opportunities that approach the position which the plaintiff was discriminatorily denied and that are superior to the position in which the employer discriminatorily forced the plaintiff to remain.

758 F.Supp. at 310. The law firm argued that the court's application of the constructive discharge rule would render the doctrine meaningless. The district judge rejected this argument also.

> The constructive discharge inquiry as to the tolerability of Ms. Ezold's working conditions at Wolf, Block is not rendered meaningless by an

inquiry as to whether her decision to resign was reasonable under the circumstances for purposes of determining the appropriate Title VII relief for the period after her resignation. The constructive discharge inquiry may be informative for purposes of determining whether Ms. Ezold properly mitigated her damages, but it is not appropriately applied as a strict limitation on the scope of Title VII relief available to her here.

758 F.Supp. at 312.

At the final stage of the proceeding the district court ordered that plaintiff be instated as a partner in the defendant's Litigation Department with the full rights of all partners admitted in 1989, the year when the court found, absent discrimination, the plaintiff would have been made partner. In addition, the plaintiff was awarded $131,784 in back pay. Ezold v. Wolf, Block, Schorr and Solis–Cohen, 56 FEP Cases 580 (E.D.Pa. 1991).

4. Courts are sometimes asked not only to make the victims of discrimination whole through reinstatement and monetary relief, but also to issue prospective relief to insure that the employer will not revert to discriminatory practices. Such relief is certainly appropriate in a class action where the class is composed of persons who will be subject in the future to the same procedures and practices that have been exercised in a discriminatory fashion in the past by the employer. For example, in Jordon v. Wilson, 667 F.Supp. 772 (M.D.Ala. 1987), reversed on other grounds, 851 F.2d 1290 (11th Cir.1988), a class action on behalf of female police officers in Montgomery, Alabama, the court severely restricted the role of the city's mayor in future police promotions because of his deep-seated bias against female officers and his past efforts to discourage females from pursuing discrimination claims against the department. Because of the EEOC's special role in enforcing Title VII, it has standing to seek permanent injunctions against future discrimination even in cases where injunctions might not be appropriate under traditional equitable principles. See, EEOC v. Goodyear Aerospace Corp., 813 F.2d 1539, 1543 (9th Cir.1987) (fact that employer took curative action after being sued fails to provide sufficient assurances that it will not repeat the violation); EEOC v. FLC & Brothers Rebel, Inc., 663 F.Supp. 864 (W.D.Va.1987), affirmed without opinion, 846 F.2d 70 (4th Cir.1988) (in sexual harassment case fact that EEOC did not allege a pattern of discrimination does not prevent issuance of injunction where evidence showed there were other employees who were subject to unwelcome sexual advances by nightclub manager but who did not report harassment out of fear of retaliation).

In non-class, individual actions, courts have been generally reluctant to grant prospective relief beyond that necessary to protect the named plaintiffs. In Brown v. Trustees of Boston University, 891 F.2d 337 (1st Cir.1989), cert. denied, 496 U.S. 937, 110 S.Ct. 3217, 110 L.Ed.2d 664 (1990), for example, the district court, in addition to reinstating the plaintiff to a faculty position with tenure, enjoined the university from discriminating in the future against Brown and from discriminating on the basis of sex in the appointment, promotion and tenure of other faculty. While affirming all of the individual relief awarded the plaintiff, the Court of Appeals reversed the injunction to the extent it prohibited discrimination against persons other than the plaintiff as "overbroad." The decree barring further discrimination against the plaintiff was "the outer limit of the relief to which she is entitled." 891 F.2d at 361. And in Hopkins v. Price Waterhouse, *supra*, the district court, while enjoining the firm from retaliation against Hopkins, denied her request that it be required to develop a written policy against sex discrimination against women candidates for partner and use of sexual stereotyping in the admission process. 737 F.Supp. 1202, 1216 (D.D.C.1990). See also, Spencer v. General Electric Co., 894 F.2d 651 (4th Cir.1990) (in sexual harassment case, refusal to issue prospective injunction was not error where employer had responded promptly to employee's complaint and there was no proof of systemic discrimination but only "an isolated incident of one supervisor run amok").

Are there any circumstances justifying the award of prospective relief to a plaintiff who has *not* been the victim of discrimination? In Thomas v. Washington County School Board, 915 F.2d 922 (4th Cir.1990) the court found that the employer's failure to consider the plaintiff for hiring was a mistake rather than an act of intentional discrimination and denied her relief of any kind. The court also concluded that the school board's hiring policies constituted arbitrary and unnecessary barriers to minority applicants under *Griggs*. Even though the plaintiff had not filed a class action and had not shown the discriminatory practices had affected her application, the Fourth Circuit held that she was entitled to an injunction prohibiting continuation of the challenged policies. The court based its decision partly on the fact that the plaintiff remained a "prospective applicant" and was entitled to lawful hiring practices if she renewed her application and, partly on prior Fourth Circuit authority, that a Title VII action is of "a public character in which remedies are devised to vindicate the policies of the Act, not merely to afford private relief to the employee." 915 F.2d at 925.

THE IMPACT OF INJUNCTIVE RELIEF ON THIRD PARTIES

The grant of most kinds of injunctive relief to an employee or applicant will affect the future progress of other employees or applicants in some way. For example, an order directing that a single employee be reinstated in his "rightful place" or placed in the next such position that becomes vacant as in Locke v. Kansas City Power & Light, *infra*, will, as a practical matter, deny that position to all other eligible persons. Where injunctive relief is granted to a whole class of persons as was sought in Franks v. Bowman Transportation Co. the relief may disadvantage virtually all employees who are not in the plaintiff's class. Such affected employees will not normally be joined as parties in the action in which the injunctive relief is sought and may not even be aware of the litigation until the court's order is implemented. This will particularly be the case where the litigation between plaintiffs and the employer is settled and the injunctive relief is incorporated in a consent decree. One of the most troubling issues in modern, institutional reform litigation concerns the accommodation of the interests of those whose legal rights have been violated by government or private institutions and the interests of other persons whose lives and livelihoods are controlled by those same institutions and who will necessarily be affected by injunctive relief intended to correct past wrongs done to others. See generally, Chayes, The Role of the Judge in Public Law Litigation, 89 Harv.L.Rev. 1281, 1289–94 (1976).

May employees who are not in the plaintiffs' class and whose job opportunities will be impaired by relief granted the plaintiffs' class block implementation of such decrees on the ground that, as non-parties to the litigation they cannot be "bound" by the results of the suit? May such employees file independent actions claiming that they are the victims of discrimination? In the past the answers to these questions has generally been "no." Prior to 1989 most circuits followed the "impermissible collateral attack" doctrine under which the failure to intervene seasonably in an action that could affect one's interests barred not only subsequent collateral attacks on the decree entered in the original litigation but also all challenges to actions taken pursuant to such a decree. See e.g., Thaggard v. City of Jackson, 687 F.2d 66, 68–69 (5th Cir.1982), cert. denied, 464 U.S. 900, 104 S.Ct. 255, 78 L.Ed.2d 241 (1983); Dennison v. City of Los Angeles Dept. of Water & Power, 658 F.2d 694, 696 (9th Cir.1981); Laycock, Consent Decrees Without Consent: The Rights of Nonconsenting Third Parties, 1987 U. Chi. Legal F. 103, 108–14.

The "impermissible collateral attack" doctrine was rejected by the Supreme Court in MARTIN v. WILKS, 490 U.S. 755, 109 S.Ct. 2180, 104 L.Ed.2d 835 (1989). In the background of the Supreme Court's decision in *Martin* were several Title VII class actions filed by blacks and women who were either employees or rejected applicants for employment with the City of Birmingham, Alabama. The plaintiffs in those suits alleged discrimination in the hiring and promotion practices of various city agencies including the police and fire departments. After seven years of litigation and two trials the parties negotiated a comprehensive settlement which included long-term and interim goals for the hiring and promotion of blacks in the police and fire departments. The settlement was incorporated in a consent decree the immediate effect of which was to reduce substantially the promotional opportunities of incumbent white employees. Before the consent decree was approved by the district court, white firefighters represented by their union filed objections to the proposed decree and moved to intervene in the litigation. The district court overruled all objections to the proposed decree and denied the motions to intervene as untimely. The Eleventh Circuit affirmed.

While appeals from the ruling on intervention were pending, white firefighters filed suit alleging that the implementation of the consent decree and its operation violated their rights under Title VII and the equal protection clause of the Fourteenth Amendment. Specifically, the plaintiffs alleged that they were being denied promotional opportunities solely because of their race in favor of less qualified black firefighters. In their answer the city defendants admitted they had made race-conscious promotions pursuant to the consent decree, but denied they had violated either Title VII or the constitution in doing so. After a trial of the white firefighters' suit the district court found that, because the consent decree authorized the promotion of minimally qualified black candidates over better qualified white candidates to meet the goals contained in the decree, the challenged promotions did not violate the decree and that the decree "immunize[d] the City from liability for actions taken pursuant to it." The decree itself could not be collaterally attacked because the plaintiffs had failed to timely intervene in the original class actions.

On appeal the Eleventh Circuit reversed. In re Birmingham Reverse Discrimination Employment Litigation, 833 F.2d 1492 (11th Cir. 1987). The Court of Appeals reasoned that since the plaintiffs were neither parties nor in privity with parties to the consent decrees, their independent claims of unlawful discrimination could not be precluded without violating their due process rights. The plaintiffs' claims of unlawful discrimination were remanded and the district court instructed to treat the consent decree as a voluntary affirmative action plan and to determine the legality of the actions take pursuant to it under standards established by the Supreme Court for challenges to race-conscious affirmative action plans. See, Part IV, *infra*.

In *Martin v. Wilks* the Supreme Court affirmed the Eleventh Circuit but did so without adopting the due process rationale of the circuit court. According to the Court, the impermissible collateral attack doctrine had to be rejected, not because of constitutional considerations, but because of the plain language of Rules 19 and 24 of the Federal Rules of Civil Procedure. The Court reasoned that the impermissible collateral attack doctrine operated as a rule of compulsory joinder because its effect was to compel intervention in a case by non-parties. Rule 24, however, casts intervention in permissive terms: while some non-parties may intervene "of right," the rule does not require intervention or forfeiture of rights by any person. Rule 19, on the other hand, requires existing parties to a litigation to join non-parties when a judgment rendered in their absence may as a practical matter impair the non-parties' interests or leave the parties subject to substantial risk of incurring inconsistent obligations. From these rules, Chief Justice Rehnquist, writing for the majority, concluded that "a party seeking a judgment binding on another cannot obligate that person to intervene; he must be joined" and that "[j]oinder as a party, rather than knowledge of a lawsuit and an opportunity to intervene is the method by which potential parties are subjected to the jurisdiction of the court and bound by a judgment or decree." 490 U.S. at 762 & 764, 109 S.Ct. at 2185 & 2186.

The number of white incumbent employees potentially affected by the consent decree at issue in *Martin v. Wilks* was well over 1100. According to the Court all these persons should have been joined as necessary party defendants under Rule 19. The petitioners in *Martin* argued that a rule requiring joinder of such large numbers of outsiders would prove too burdensome to plaintiffs and would discourage civil rights class actions. Justice Rehnquist's response to this argument was two-fold. In the first place, the policy argument was misplaced: even were the Court "wholly persuaded by these arguments as a matter of policy, acceptance of them would require a rewriting rather than an interpretation of the relevant rules." 109 S.Ct. at 2187. In the second place, the practical problem of joinder resulted not from the rules, but "from the nature of the relief sought" by plaintiffs in such cases. "The breadth of a lawsuit and concomitant relief may be at least partially shaped in advance through Rule 19 to avoid needless clashes with future litigation." Id.

The import of the Court's opinion was clear. A person such as an incumbent employee whose interests might as a practical matter be impaired by litigation and who had not voluntarily intervened or been joined as a party, may attack a decree (whether by consent or judgment after trial) in the case at any time without regard to his knowledge concerning the original litigation or his actual opportunity to intervene. The Court's message to civil rights plaintiffs was that they could avoid the hardship caused by Rule 19 by limiting the "breadth" of their cases and the nature of relief sought. See, Strickler, Martin v. Wilks, 64 Tul.L.Rev. 1557 (1990).

Martin v. Wilks was followed by a spate of "reverse discrimination" suits in which plaintiffs sought to overturn established consent decrees or court orders. See, e.g., Mann v. City of Albany, 883 F.2d 999 (11th Cir.1989) (plaintiffs entitled under Title VII to collaterally attack court decree entered in litigation in which they were not parties); Van Pool v. City and County of San Francisco, 752 F.Supp. 915 (N.D.Cal.1990) (white firefighters barred from attacking consent decree because their interests were adequately represented in prior litigation by their union which was allowed to intervene in that case).

In the Civil Rights Act of 1991, Congress attempted to reverse *Martin v. Wilks* by severely restricting the circumstances under which a court decree can be collaterally attacked. Section 108 of the Act amends Section 703 of Title VII to provide that "an employment practice that implements and is within the scope of a litigated or consent judgment or order that resolves a claim of employment discrimination under the Constitution or Federal civil rights laws may not be challenged" by a person who had "actual notice of the proposed judgment or order sufficient to apprise such person that such judgment or order might adversely affect the interests and legal rights of such person and that an opportunity was available to present objections to such judgment or order." Even without such notice, an outsider is barred from collaterally attacking a decree if his "interests were adequately represented by another person who had previously challenged the judgment or order on the same legal grounds and with a similar factual situation, unless there has been an intervening change in law or fact." The Act explicitly provides that nothing in it affects the rights of existing parties or of those persons who do intervene and that no provision should be construed as "authoriz[ing] or permit[ting] the denial to any person of the due process of law required by the Constitution."

The 1991 Act leaves open at least three questions which must be resolved by the courts. First, does notice of the proposed decree to an incumbent employee and the opportunity to object to the decree satisfy such an employee's right to procedural due process? Generally, due process has been construed as requiring notice and an opportunity to appear and contest a proceeding on the merits before one may be bound by the decree. It is far from clear that an opportunity to object to a proposed judgment without being allowed to litigate the merits of the underlying claim will satisfy due process. See, Issacharoff, When Substance Mandates Procedure: *Martin v. Wilks* and the Rights of Vested Incumbents in Civil Rights Consent Decrees, 77 Corn.L.Rev. 189, 229–230 (1991) (arguing that permitting incumbent employees to register objections to a consent decree at a fairness hearing would not constitute due process for incumbents absent full evidentiary hearing on any substantive claim). Second, the Act provides that a non-party whose interests have been "adequately represented" may be bound by a judgment or consent decree, but what constitutes "adequate representation"? Without a formal designation of representative status, as in a class action, can a party be said to "represent" a non-party simply because their interests in the litigation coincide? See, Van Pool v. City of San Francisco, *supra*, (discussing doctrine on "virtual representation"). Finally, to what extent will the rationale of *Martin v. Wilks* survive the 1991 Act? The majority in *Martin* strongly implies that the underlying Title VII actions should not have been litigated without joinder of the incumbent employees pursuant to Rule 19. The proper procedure under Rule 19 is for the defendant to move to dismiss for failure of the plaintiff to join indispensable parties. The court must then determine under Rule 19(a) whether the non-parties should be joined. If the answer is in the affirmative and the absent parties can be joined (they are within the territorial jurisdiction of the court), the court must order the plaintiffs to join them or dismiss the suit. Nothing in the 1991 Act purports to affect Rule 19. The fact that *after* a judgment or consent decree, absent persons may be barred from challenging the decree does not prevent defendants, at the outset of litigation, from moving pursuant to Rule 19 for joinder of all potentially affected individuals. Such a tactic would, if successful, vastly increase the cost and complexity of class actions seeking institutional relief. See, Strickler, Martin v. Wilks, *supra*.

SECTION C. ATTORNEY FEES
HENSLEY v. ECKERHART

United States Supreme Court, 1983
461 U.S. 424, 103 S.Ct. 1933, 76 L.Ed.2d 40.

JUSTICE POWELL delivered the opinion of the Court.

Title 42 U.S.C. Sec. 1988 provides that in federal civil rights actions "the court, in its discretion, may allow the prevailing party, other than

the United States, a reasonable attorney's fee as part of the costs."
The issue in this case is whether a partially prevailing plaintiff may
recover an attorney's fee for legal services on unsuccessful claims.

[The facts and procedural history of the case are omitted. The suit was
a class action challenging various conditions in the forensic unit of a
state hospital. Some claims in the case were settled before trial, others
became moot during the course of the litigation and some were tried.
At trial the plaintiff obtained some but not all of the relief requested in
the remaining claims.]

B

In February 1980 respondents filed a request for attorney's fees for
the period from January 1975 through the end of the litigation. Their
four attorneys claimed 2,985 hours worked and sought payment at rates
varying from $40 to $65 per hour. This amounted to approximately
$150,000. Respondents also requested that the fee be enhanced by 30
to 50 percent, for a total award of somewhere between $195,000 and
$225,000. Petitioners opposed the request on numerous grounds, in-
cluding inclusion of hours spent in pursuit of unsuccessful claims.

The District Court first determined that respondents were prevailing parties under 42 U.S.C. Sec. 1988 even though they had not
succeeded on every claim. It then refused to eliminate from the award
hours spent on unsuccessful claims:

> "[Petitioners'] suggested method of calculating fees is based
> strictly on a mathematical approach comparing the total number of
> issues in the case with those actually prevailed upon. Under this
> method no consideration is given for the relative importance of
> various issues, the interrelation of the issues, the difficulty in
> identifying issues, or the extent to which a party may prevail on
> various issues."

Finding that respondents "have obtained relief of significant import,"
the District Court awarded a fee of $133,332.25. This award differed
from the fee request in two respects. First, the court reduced the
number of hours claimed by one attorney by 30 percent to account for
his inexperience and failure to keep contemporaneous records. Second,
the court declined to adopt an enhancement factor to increase the
award.

The Court of Appeals for the Eighth Circuit affirmed on the basis
of the District Court's memorandum opinion and order. We granted
certiorari and now vacate and remand for further proceedings.

II

In Alyeska Pipeline Service Co. v. Wilderness Society, 421 U.S. 240,
95 S.Ct. 1612, 44 L.Ed.2d 141 (1975), this Court reaffirmed the "American Rule" that each party in a lawsuit ordinarily shall bear its own
attorney's fees unless there is express statutory authorization to the

contrary. In response Congress enacted the Civil Rights Attorney's Fees Awards Act of 1976, 42 U.S.C. Sec. 1988, authorizing the district courts to award a reasonable attorney's fee to prevailing parties in civil rights litigation. The purpose of Sec. 1988 is to ensure "effective access to the judicial process" for persons with civil rights grievances. H.R. Rep. No. 94–1558, p. 1 (1976). Accordingly, a prevailing plaintiff " 'should ordinarily recover an attorney's fee unless special circumstances would render such an award unjust.' " S.Rep. No. 94–1011, p. 4 (1976) (quoting Newman v. Piggie Park Enterprises, Inc., 390 U.S. 400, 402, 88 S.Ct. 964, 966, 19 L.Ed.2d 1263 (1968)).[2]

The amount of the fee, of course, must be determined on the facts of each case. On this issue the House Report simply refers to 12 factors set forth in Johnson v. Georgia Highway Express, Inc., 488 F.2d 714 (CA5 1974).[3] The Senate Report cites to Johnson as well and also refers to three District Court decisions that "correctly applied" the 12 factors.[4] One of the factors in Johnson, "the amount involved and the results obtained," indicates that the level of a plaintiff's success is relevant to the amount of fees to be awarded. The importance of this relationship is confirmed in varying degrees by the other cases cited approvingly in the Senate Report.

* * *

In this case petitioners contend that "an award of attorney's fees must be proportioned to be consistent with the extent to which a plaintiff has prevailed, and only time reasonably expended in support of

2. A prevailing defendant may recover an attorney's fee only where the suit was vexatious, frivolous, or brought to harass or embarrass the defendant. See H.R.Rep. No. 94–1558, p. 7 (1976); Christiansburg Garment Co. v. EEOC, 434 U.S. 412, 421, 98 S.Ct. 694, 700, 54 L.Ed.2d 648 (1978) ("[A] district court may in its discretion award attorney's fees to a prevailing defendant in a Title VII case upon a finding that the plaintiff's action was frivolous, unreasonable, or without foundation, even though not brought in subjective bad faith").

3. The 12 factors are: (1) the time and labor required; (2) the novelty and difficulty of the questions; (3) the skill requisite to perform the legal service properly; (4) the preclusion of employment by the attorney due to acceptance of the case; (5) the customary fee; (6) whether the fee is fixed or contingent; (7) time limitations imposed by the client or the circumstances; (8) the amount involved and the results obtained; (9) the experience, reputation, and ability of the attorneys; (10) the "undesirability" of the case; (11) the nature and length of the professional relationship with the client; and (12) awards in similar cases.

488 F.2d, at 717–719. These factors derive directly from the American Bar Association Code of Professional Responsibility, Disciplinary Rule 2–106 (1980).

4. "It is intended that the amount of fees awarded ... be governed by the same standards which prevail in other types of equally complex Federal litigation, such as antitrust cases[,] and not be reduced because the rights involved may be nonpecuniary in nature. The appropriate standards, see Johnson v. Georgia Highway Express, 488 F.2d 714 (5th Cir.1974), are correctly applied in such cases as Stanford Daily v. Zurcher, 64 F.R.D. 680 (ND Cal. 1974); Davis v. County of Los Angeles, 8 E.P.D. P9444 (CD Cal.1974); and Swann v. Charlotte–Mecklenburg Board of Education, 66 F.R.D. 483 (W.D.N.C.1975). These cases have resulted in fees which are adequate to attract competent counsel, but which do not produce windfalls to attorneys. In computing the fee, counsel for prevailing parties should be paid, as is traditional with attorneys compensated by a fee-paying client, 'for all time reasonably expended on a matter.' Davis, supra; Stanford Daily, supra at 684." S.Rep. No. 94–1011, p. 6 (1976).

successful claims should be compensated." Respondents agree that plaintiff's success is relevant, but propose a less stringent standard focusing on "whether the time spent prosecuting [an unsuccessful] claim in any way contributed to the ultimate results achieved." Both parties acknowledge the discretion of the district court in this area. We take this opportunity to clarify the proper relationship of the results obtained to an award of attorney's fees.[6]

III

A

A plaintiff must be a "prevailing party" to recover an attorney's fee under Sec. 1988.[7] The standard for making this threshold determination has been framed in various ways. A typical formulation is that "plaintiffs may be considered 'prevailing parties' for attorney's fees purposes if they succeed on any significant issue in litigation which achieves some of the benefit the parties sought in bringing suit." Nadeau v. Helgemoe, 581 F.2d 275, 278–279 (CA1 1978). This is a generous formulation that brings the plaintiff only across the statutory threshold. It remains for the district court to determine what fee is "reasonable."

The most useful starting point for determining the amount of a reasonable fee is the number of hours reasonably expended on the litigation multiplied by a reasonable hourly rate. This calculation provides an objective basis on which to make an initial estimate of the value of a lawyer's services. The party seeking an award of fees should submit evidence supporting the hours worked and rates claimed. Where the documentation of hours is inadequate, the district court may reduce the award accordingly.

The district court also should exclude from this initial fee calculation hours that were not "reasonably expended." Cases may be overstaffed, and the skill and experience of lawyers vary widely. Counsel for the prevailing party should make a good-faith effort to exclude from a fee request hours that are excessive, redundant, or otherwise unnecessary, just as a lawyer in private practice ethically is obligated to exclude such hours from his fee submission. "In the private sector, 'billing judgment' is an important component in fee setting. It is no

---

6. The parties disagree as to the results obtained in this case. Petitioners believe that respondents "prevailed only to an extremely limited degree." Respondents contend that they "prevailed on practically every claim advanced." As discussed in Part IV, infra, we leave this dispute for the District Court on remand.

7. As we noted in Hanrahan v. Hampton, 446 U.S. 754, 758, n. 4, 100 S.Ct. 1987, 1989, n. 4, 64 L.Ed.2d 670 (1980) (per curiam), "[t]he provision for counsel fees in Sec. 1988 was patterned upon the attor-

ney's fees provisions contained in Titles II and VII of the Civil Rights Act of 1964 and Sec. 402 of the Voting Rights Act Amendments of 1975." The legislative history of Sec. 1988 indicates that Congress intended that "the standards for awarding fees be generally the same as under the fee provisions of the 1964 Civil Rights Act." S.Rep. No. 94–1011, p. 4 (1976). The standards set forth in this opinion are generally applicable in all cases in which Congress has authorized an award of fees to a "prevailing party."

less important here. Hours that are not properly billed to one's client also are not properly billed to one's adversary pursuant to statutory authority." Copeland v. Marshall, 205 U.S.App.D.C. 390, 401, 641 F.2d 880, 891 (1980) (en banc) (emphasis in original).

B

The product of reasonable hours times a reasonable rate does not end the inquiry. There remain other considerations that may lead the district court to adjust the fee upward or downward, including the important factor of the "results obtained." [9] This factor is particularly crucial where a plaintiff is deemed "prevailing" even though he succeeded on only some of his claims for relief. In this situation two questions must be addressed. First, did the plaintiff fail to prevail on claims that were unrelated to the claims on which he succeeded? Second, did the plaintiff achieve a level of success that makes the hours reasonably expended a satisfactory basis for making a fee award?

In some cases a plaintiff may present in one lawsuit distinctly different claims for relief that are based on different facts and legal theories. In such a suit, even where the claims are brought against the same defendants—often an institution and its officers, as in this case—counsel's work on one claim will be unrelated to his work on another claim. Accordingly, work on an unsuccessful claim cannot be deemed to have been "expended in pursuit of the ultimate result achieved." Davis v. County of Los Angeles, 8 E.P.D., at 5049. The congressional intent to limit awards to prevailing parties requires that these unrelated claims be treated as if they had been raised in separate lawsuits, and therefore no fee may be awarded for services on the unsuccessful claim.

It may well be that cases involving such unrelated claims are unlikely to arise with great frequency. Many civil rights cases will present only a single claim. In other cases the plaintiff's claims for relief will involve a common core of facts or will be based on related legal theories. Much of counsel's time will be devoted generally to the litigation as a whole, making it difficult to divide the hours expended on a claim-by-claim basis. Such a lawsuit cannot be viewed as a series of discrete claims. Instead the district court should focus on the significance of the overall relief obtained by the plaintiff in relation to the hours reasonably expended on the litigation.

Where a plaintiff has obtained excellent results, his attorney should recover a fully compensatory fee. Normally this will encompass all hours reasonably expended on the litigation, and indeed in some cases of exceptional success an enhanced award may be justified. In these circumstances the fee award should not be reduced simply be-

---

9. The district court also may consider other factors identified in Johnson v. Georgia Highway Express, Inc., 488 F.2d 714, 717–719 (CA5 1974), though it should note that many of these factors usually are sub- sumed within the initial calculation of hours reasonably expended at a reasonable hourly rate. See Copeland v. Marshall, 205 U.S.App.D.C. 390, 400, 641 F.2d 880, 890 (1980) (en banc).

cause the plaintiff failed to prevail on every contention raised in the lawsuit. See Davis v. County of Los Angeles, supra, at 5049. Litigants in good faith may raise alternative legal grounds for a desired outcome, and the court's rejection of or failure to reach certain grounds is not a sufficient reason for reducing a fee. The result is what matters.[11]

If, on the other hand, a plaintiff has achieved only partial or limited success, the product of hours reasonably expended on the litigation as a whole times a reasonable hourly rate may be an excessive amount. This will be true even where the plaintiff's claims were interrelated, nonfrivolous, and raised in good faith. Congress has not authorized an award of fees whenever it was reasonable for a plaintiff to bring a lawsuit or whenever conscientious counsel tried the case with devotion and skill. Again, the most critical factor is the degree of success obtained.

Application of this principle is particularly important in complex civil rights litigation involving numerous challenges to institutional practices or conditions. This type of litigation is lengthy and demands many hours of lawyers' services. Although the plaintiff often may succeed in identifying some unlawful practices or conditions, the range of possible success is vast. That the plaintiff is a "prevailing party" therefore may say little about whether the expenditure of counsel's time was reasonable in relation to the success achieved. In this case, for example, the District Court's award of fees based on 2,557 hours worked may have been reasonable in light of the substantial relief obtained. But had respondents prevailed on only one of their six general claims, for example the claim that petitioners' visitation, mail, and telephone policies were overly restrictive, a fee award based on the claimed hours clearly would have been excessive.

There is no precise rule or formula for making these determinations. The district court may attempt to identify specific hours that should be eliminated, or it may simply reduce the award to account for the limited success. The court necessarily has discretion in making this equitable judgment. This discretion, however, must be exercised in light of the considerations we have identified.

C

A request for attorney's fees should not result in a second major litigation. Ideally, of course, litigants will settle the amount of a fee. Where settlement is not possible, the fee applicant bears the burden of establishing entitlement to an award and documenting the appropriate

---

11. We agree with the District Court's rejection of "a mathematical approach comparing the total number of issues in the case with those actually prevailed upon." Record 220. Such a ratio provides little aid in determining what is a reasonable fee in light of all the relevant factors. Nor is it necessarily significant that a pre-vailing plaintiff did not receive all the relief requested. For example, a plaintiff who failed to recover damages but obtained injunctive relief, or vice versa, may recover a fee award based on all hours reasonably expended if the relief obtained justified that expenditure of attorney time.

hours expended and hourly rates. The applicant should exercise "billing judgment" with respect to hours worked, see supra, at 434, and should maintain billing time records in a manner that will enable a reviewing court to identify distinct claims.[12]

We reemphasize that the district court has discretion in determining the amount of a fee award. This is appropriate in view of the district court's superior understanding of the litigation and the desirability of avoiding frequent appellate review of what essentially are factual matters. It remains important, however, for the district court to provide a concise but clear explanation of its reasons for the fee award. When an adjustment is requested on the basis of either the exceptional or limited nature of the relief obtained by the plaintiff, the district court should make clear that it has considered the relationship between the amount of the fee awarded and the results obtained.

IV

In this case the District Court began by finding that "[t]he relief [respondents] obtained at trial was substantial and certainly entitles them to be considered prevailing ..., without the need of examining those issues disposed of prior to trial in order to determine which went in [respondents'] favor." It then declined to divide the hours worked between winning and losing claims, stating that this fails to consider "the relative importance of various issues, the interrelation of the issues, the difficulty in identifying issues, or the extent to which a party may prevail on various issues." Finally, the court assessed the "amount involved/results obtained" and declared: "Not only should [respondents] be considered prevailing parties, they are parties who have obtained relief of significant import. [Respondents'] relief affects not only them, but also numerous other institutionalized patients similarly situated. The extent of this relief clearly justifies the award of a reasonable attorney's fee."

These findings represent a commendable effort to explain the fee award. Given the interrelated nature of the facts and legal theories in this case, the District Court did not err in refusing to apportion the fee award mechanically on the basis of respondents' success or failure on particular issues.[13] And given the findings with respect to the level of

---

12. We recognize that there is no certain method of determining when claims are "related" or "unrelated." Plaintiff's counsel, of course, is not required to record in great detail how each minute of his time was expended. But at least counsel should identify the general subject matter of his time expenditures. See Nadeau v. Helgemoe, 581 F.2d 275, 279 (CA1 1978) ("As for the future, we would not view with sympathy any claim that a district court abused its discretion in awarding unreasonably low attorney's fees in a suit in which plaintiffs were only partially successful if counsel's records do not provide a proper basis for determining how much time was spent on particular claims").

13. In addition, the District Court properly considered the reasonableness of the hours expended, and reduced the hours of one attorney by 30 percent to account for his inexperience and failure to keep contemporaneous time records.

respondents' success, the District Court's award may be consistent with our holding today.

We are unable to affirm the decisions below, however, because the District Court's opinion did not properly consider the relationship between the extent of success and the amount of the fee award. The court's finding that "the [significant] extent of the relief clearly justifies the award of a reasonable attorney's fee" does not answer the question of what is "reasonable" in light of that level of success. We emphasize that the inquiry does not end with a finding that the plaintiff obtained significant relief. A reduced fee award is appropriate if the relief, however significant, is limited in comparison to the scope of the litigation as a whole.

V

We hold that the extent of a plaintiff's success is a crucial factor in determining the proper amount of an award of attorney's fees under 42 U.S.C. Sec. 1988. Where the plaintiff has failed to prevail on a claim that is distinct in all respects from his successful claims, the hours spent on the unsuccessful claim should be excluded in considering the amount of a reasonable fee. Where a lawsuit consists of related claims, a plaintiff who has won substantial relief should not have his attorney's fee reduced simply because the district court did not adopt each contention raised. But where the plaintiff achieved only limited success, the district court should award only that amount of fees that is reasonable in relation to the results obtained. On remand the District Court should determine the proper amount of the attorney's fee award in light of these standards.

The judgment of the Court of Appeals is vacated, and the case is remanded for further proceedings consistent with this opinion.

It is so ordered.

CHIEF JUSTICE BURGER, concurring.

I read the Court's opinion as requiring that when a lawyer seeks to have his adversary pay the fees of the prevailing party, the lawyer must provide detailed records of the time and services for which fees are sought. It would be inconceivable that the prevailing party should not be required to establish at least as much to support a claim under 42 U.S.C. Sec. 1988 as a lawyer would be required to show if his own client challenged the fees. A district judge may not, in my view, authorize the payment of attorney's fees unless the attorney involved has established by clear and convincing evidence the time and effort claimed and shown that the time expended was necessary to achieve the results obtained.

A claim for legal services presented by the prevailing party to the losing party pursuant to Sec. 1988 presents quite a different situation from a bill that a lawyer presents to his own client. In the latter case, the attorney and client have presumably built up a relationship of mutual trust and respect; the client has confidence that his lawyer has exercised the appropriate "billing judgment," and unless challenged by the client, the billing does not need the kind of extensive documentation necessary for a payment under Sec. 1988. That statute requires the losing party in a civil rights action to bear the cost of his adversary's attorney and there is, of course, no relationship of trust and confidence between the adverse parties. As a result, the party who seeks payment must keep records in sufficient detail that a neutral judge can make a fair evaluation of the time expended, the nature and need for the service, and the reasonable fees to be allowed.

[The separate opinion (concurring in part and dissenting in part) of JUSTICES BRENNAN, MARSHALL, BLACKMUN and STEVENS is omitted.]

NOTES AND PROBLEMS FOR DISCUSSION

1. As noted in footnote 7 in *Hensley*, the fee shifting provision in Section 1988 is identical to that contained in Section 706(k) of Title VII and in most other federal civil rights statutes. By contrast, the remedies section of the Fair Labor Standards Act, 29 U.S.C. § 216, which is incorporated in the Equal Pay Act and the Age Discrimination in Employment Act, provides in part that "[t]he court in such action shall, in addition to any judgment awarded to the plaintiff or plaintiffs, allow a reasonable attorney's fee to be paid by the defendant, and costs of the action."

2. The Court in *Hensley* did not provide a specific standard for determining when a party has "prevailed" for purposes of the fee shifting statute. Most circuits have only required that a party succeed on a significant issue and receive some of the relief sought in the lawsuit to qualify for a fee award. See, e.g., Gingras v. Lloyd, 740 F.2d 210, 212 (2d Cir.1984); Nadeau v. Helgemoe, 581 F.2d 275, 278 (1st Cir.1978). The Fifth and Eleventh Circuits, however, required that a party succeed on the "central issue" in the litigation and achieve the "primary relief sought" to be eligible for a fee award. See, Simien v. San Antonio, 809 F.2d 255, 258 (5th Cir.1987); Martin v. Heckler, 773 F.2d 1145, 1149 (11th Cir.1985) (en banc). The Supreme Court clarified the issue in TEXAS STATE TEACHERS ASSOCIATION v. GARLAND INDEPENDENT SCHOOL DISTRICT, 489 U.S. 782, 109 S.Ct. 1486, 103 L.Ed.2d 866 (1989), a suit by teachers and their union challenging as unconstitutional policies of the school board that barred union access to school facilities and forbade teachers to discuss or promote the union during school hours. The Fifth Circuit upheld the ban on union access to the schools but determined that teachers could not constitutionally be prohibited from discussing or promoting unions during school hours. When the teachers sought attorney's fees, the court held that the teachers did not prevail on the "central issue" of union access and therefore were not "prevailing parties" entitled to fees. Declaring the circuit court's "central issue" test "directly contrary to the thrust" of *Hensley*, the Supreme Court reversed.

> The touchstone of the prevailing party inquiry must be the material alteration of the legal relationship of the parties in a manner which Congress sought to promote in the fee statute. Where such a change has occurred, the degree of the plaintiff's overall success goes to the reasonableness of the award under *Hensley*, not to the availability of a fee award *vel non*.

489 U.S. at 792–93, 109 S.Ct. at 1493. The Court cautioned, however, that "a technical victory may be so insignificant . . . as to be insufficient to support prevailing party status." *Ibid.* Can a party "succeed" on a significant issue in the litigation without obtaining any relief for himself?

In HEWITT v. HELMS, 482 U.S. 755, 107 S.Ct. 2672, 96 L.Ed.2d 654 (1987), a prison inmate filed a Section 1983 action against prison officials alleging that his disciplinary detention in isolation without a prompt hearing and his subsequent conviction for misconduct on the basis of uncorroborated hearsay testimony violated his constitutional right to due process. Summary judgment was rendered against him on the merits. On appeal, the court of appeals held that, as a matter of law, plaintiff had been denied due process and remanded for a determination of whether the defendants had qualified immunity from damages. The district court ruled that the defendants were immune and dismissed the damage claim. The district court also dismissed the claim for injunctive relief because plaintiff had by this time been released from prison and the court considered his claim for injunctive relief to be moot. The district court also denied a request for attorney's fees under Section 1988. Plaintiff appealed again. While the appeal was pending, the Board of Prisons revised its regulations concerning the use of hearsay in inmate disciplinary proceedings. The court of appeals affirmed on the merits, but reversed the attorney fee denial on the ground that its prior holding that plaintiff's constitutional rights were violated was "a form of judicial relief which serves to affirm the plaintiff's assertion that the defendant's actions were unconstitutional and which will serve as a standard of conduct to guide prison officials in the future." 780 F.2d 367, 370 (3d Cir.1986) The court also directed the district court on remand to reconsider whether the suit had been a "catalyst" for the change in the regulations on disciplinary hearings. The Supreme Court reversed. Writing for the majority, Justice Scalia reasoned that "prevailing party" status results from obtaining relief from the opposing party and that a favorable judicial pronouncement was not the equivalent of declaratory relief.

> To suggest such an equivalency is to lose sight of the nature of the judicial process. In all civil litigation, the judicial decree is not the end but the means. At the end of the rainbow lies not a judgment, but some action (or cessation of action) by the defendant that the judgment produces—the payment of damages, or some specific performance, or the termination of some conduct. Redress is sought *through* the court, but *from* the defendant. This is no less true of a declaratory judgment suit than of any other action. The real value of the judicial pronouncement—what makes it a proper judicial resolution of a "case or controversy" rather than an advisory opinion—is in the settling of some dispute *which affects the behavior of the defendant towards the plaintiff.* The "equivalency" doctrine is simply an acknowledgment of the primacy of the redress over the means by which it is obtained. * * * [A] judicial statement that does not affect the relationship between the plaintiff and the defendant is *not* an equivalent. As a consequence of the present lawsuit, Helms obtained nothing from the defendants. The only "relief" he received was the moral satisfaction of knowing that a federal court concluded that his rights had been violated.

482 U.S. at 761, 107 S.Ct. at 2676 (emphasis in original). The Court concluded that "a favorable judicial statement of law in the course of litigation that results in judgment against the plaintiff does not suffice to render him a 'prevailing party.'" *Id.* at 762, 107 S.Ct. at 2677. With respect to the argument that the suit might have served as a "catalyst" for the change in regulations,

the Court ruled that no further proceedings were necessary because, even if the plaintiff could establish a causal link between the litigation and the modification of the regulations, he could not thereby become the "prevailing party." The plaintiff did not (and could not have) obtained redress from the change because he had long been released before it was made. If a plaintiff obtains success on a legal issue on appeal that may or may not benefit her on subsequent proceedings in the case, has she "prevailed" within the meaning of *Hewitt?* See, Richardson v. Penfold, 900 F.2d 116 (7th Cir.1990) (circuit court's reversal of district court's dismissal of civil rights action does not entitle plaintiff to an interim fee award because reversal was a procedural victory that leaves the merits, and thus the question of whether plaintiff will "prevail" under *Hewitt v. Helms*, to be decided).

Does it follow from *Texas State Teachers* and *Hewitt* that any time a party obtains some of the relief requested in his suit, he will have "prevailed"? Assume the employer settles a Title VII action for only a fraction of the back pay claimed by the plaintiff because it would cost twice that amount to defend the case. Should the plaintiff be entitled to an award of attorney fees? See, Ashley v. Atlantic Richfield Co., 794 F.2d 128 (3d Cir.1986). In the wake of *Texas State Teachers* and *Hewitt* the circuits have divided on the question of whether a plaintiff who has received only nominal relief is a prevailing party under fee shifting statutes. Compare, Estate of Farrar v. Cain, 941 F.2d 1311 (5th Cir.1991), cert. granted, Farrar v. Hobby, ___ U.S. ___, 112 S.Ct. 1159, 117 L.Ed.2d 407 (1992) (when sole relief sought is money damages, plaintiff does not "prevail" when she obtains nominal damages of $1) and Ruggiero v. Krzeminski, 928 F.2d 558 (2d Cir.1991) (plaintiff "prevails" for purposes of attorney fees by establishing that violation of law has occurred even if relief is nominal). If an employee obtains reinstatement through a preliminary injunction but loses at the trial on the merits, will she have "prevailed"? See, Fiarman v. Western Publishing Co., 810 F.2d 85 (6th Cir.1987). If the plaintiff's Title VII case becomes moot because he obtains all the relief he could achieve in the suit through a labor arbitration, has he "prevailed" under the fee shifting statutes? See, Hampton v. U.S. Steel Corp., 40 FEP Cases 1272 (N.D.Ind. 1986).

Section 107 of the Civil Rights Act of 1991 delineates one circumstance in which a plaintiff may be entitled to an award of attorneys' fees even though no other relief is granted. In a "mixed motive" case if the plaintiff demonstrates that race or another prohibited classification was a "motivating factor" behind the challenged employment practice but the employer establishes that it would have taken the same action in the absence of the unlawful motivation, the court may grant declaratory relief and attorneys fees and costs.

3. The basic "lodestar" method of calculating fees has been universally adopted in cases where fees are sought under the fee shifting statutes. Determining how much time in a given case was "reasonable" and whether the hourly rates claimed by the prevailing party are "reasonable" is not, however, without difficulty.

Reasonable Hours

The practical difficulty in applying *Hensley* results from the fact that lawyers' work in litigation can seldom be so compartmentalized that all hours can be attributed to either "winning" or "losing" claims. For example, in depositions of the employer's officials all the contentions of the plaintiff are likely to be explored. Is such time to be fully compensated so long as some of the discovery was relevant to the winning claim? Who should have the burden of proving that given hours are related to the winning claim? The Court apparently recognized in *Hensley* that its rule allowing compensation only for time spent on successful claims would require rough approximations where proof on winning and losing claims overlapped. Such a ball-park calculation is illustrated in Bohen v. City of East Chicago, 666 F.Supp. 154 (N.D.Ind. 1987). In that case plaintiff prevailed on her sexual harassment claim but not on her discharge claim. The fee award should thus, in theory, compensate counsel only for the amount of time they would have spent had they pursued only the harassment claim. Judge Easterbrook's stream-of-consciousness approach to the problem was as follows:

> We know that pursuing the discharge claim took extra time—some parts of some witnesses' testimony were devoted exclusively to this claim—but it is very hard to say just how much. * * * My recollection is that no more than 10% of the time was spent exclusively on this subject, though more than that was spent on lines of questioning pertinent to both claims. From the City's perspective, however, the marginal time is all that matters. It wants to know what its legal bill would have been had there been no discharge claim. My best estimate is that it would have been 10% less.

666 F.Supp. at 156. Cf. Brown v. Bolger, 102 F.R.D. 849 (D.D.C.1984) (hours for which court is unable to discern compensable time from noncompensable time excluded from fee award); Turgeon v. Howard University, 571 F.Supp. 679 (D.D.C.1983) (inability of court to divide hours on claim-by-claim basis precludes separation out of fee request).

Even in a case where the plaintiff has prevailed on all the issues, the district court exercises considerable discretion in deciding whether the claimed hours are "reasonable." In Copeland v. Marshall, 641 F.2d 880 (D.C.Cir. 1980)(*en banc*) the district judge, while finding that the plaintiffs' counsel had been highly successful, reduced the lodestar by 22% because of his determination that the inexperienced lawyers handling the case had "lacked experienced trial direction." The Court of Appeals affirmed the reduction as within the judge's discretion. 641 F.2d at 902.

Reasonable Hourly Rates

In BLUM v. STENSON, 465 U.S. 886, 104 S.Ct. 1541, 79 L.Ed.2d 891 (1984), the successful plaintiffs were represented by a non-profit legal services organization. The district court calculated the lodestar on the basis of prevailing commercial rates in the community (New York City) and the Court of Appeals affirmed. In the Supreme Court defendants argued that the rate portion of the lodestar should be based on the cost of providing the legal services and that use of market rates would result in a windfall for counsel employed by a non-profit organization who were not engaged in the commercial practice of law. The Court held, however, that the legislative history of the fee-shifting statutes showed that Congress intended that fees be calculated according to market rates in the relevant community, not according to a cost-plus formula, regardless of whether the prevailing party is represented by private counsel or by non-profit organizations. The fee claimant has the burden of establishing the prevailing rate for attorneys of comparable experience and expertise in the community. 465 U.S. at 895–96 n.11, 104 S.Ct. at 1547 n.11.

To what extent should the successful attorney's own billing rates determine what is reasonable? Many lawyers whose client base is composed of individuals, non-profit organizations or unions charge hourly rates substantially below those charged by large law firms that specialize in corporate work. At one time the rule in the District of Columbia Circuit was that a firm's normal billing rates for its regular clients, even though significantly below the "community rates" for lawyers of similar experience, set the market rate for that firm because the regular billing rates demonstrated the economic incentive necessary to cause that firm to take on civil rights litigation. Laffey v. Northwest Airlines, Inc., 746 F.2d 4 (D.C. Cir.1984), cert. denied, 472 U.S. 1021, 105 S.Ct. 3488, 87 L.Ed.2d 622 (1985). The District of Columbia Circuit has now overruled *Laffey* as inconsistent with the intent of Congress as described in BLUM v. STENSON. Save Our Cumberland Mountains, Inc. v. Hodel, 857 F.2d 1516 (D.C. Cir.1988) (en banc) (market rate method used in awarding fees to traditional for-profit firms and public interest legal service organizations under *Blum* should also apply to attorneys who practice privately and for-profit but at reduced rates reflecting non-economic goals). In Student Public Interest Research Group of New Jersey, Inc. v. AT & T Bell Laboratories, 842 F.2d 1436 (3d Cir.1988) the Third Circuit criticized the "billing rate" rule and explicitly refused to apply a private public interest firm's regular billing rates ($60–$80/hour) in calculating a lodestar fee. The Court read *Blum* as requiring it to assess the experience and skill of the successful attorneys and compare their rates to those of comparable lawyers in the private business sphere. While recognizing that this approach might result in compensation of public interest attorneys beyond what was necessary to attract them to a case, the Court nonetheless felt its method of fee calculation was proper for three reasons. First, *Blum* requires the use of market rates and, to that extent, discounts concerns about potential windfalls. Second, the rule represented the best compromise among the conflicting policies behind fee-shifting statutes. Finally, the "community market" rule is the simplest and most workable approach to the problem. Cf. Coulter v. State of Tennessee, 805 F.2d 146 (6th Cir.1986), cert. denied, 482 U.S. 914 107 S.Ct. 3186, 96 L.Ed.2d 674 (1987) (billing rate of lead counsel in case applied to more experienced lawyer who claimed a higher hourly rate on ground that rate for lead counsel demonstrated rate necessary in that community to encourage competent counsel to undertake the work in question).

Should a prevailing attorney from outside the community be awarded fees based on the customary rates where he normally practices or on the prevailing rate in the community where the litigation takes place? Compare, Chrapliwy v. Uniroyal, Inc., 670 F.2d 760 (7th Cir.1982), cert. denied, 461 U.S. 956, 103 S.Ct. 2428, 77 L.Ed.2d 1315 (1983) (error to award fees to out-of-town counsel at lower local rates without a finding that a local attorney with requisite skill to handle highly complex case was available) and Maceira v. Pagan, 698 F.2d 38 (1st Cir.1983) (affirming award of out-of-town rates to counsel where there was no evidence that lawyers of similar expertise in the community where case was tried were willing to take on such litigation) with Ramos v. Lamm, 713 F.2d 546 (10th Cir.1983) (attorneys in civil rights litigation entitled to fees based on rates received by local attorneys with similar qualifications). Where a prevailing plaintiff's requested fees are challenged, should he be entitled to discover from defense counsel the hours charged their client for defense of the case and rates charged by defense counsel? See, Ruiz v. Estelle, 553 F.Supp. 567, 584 (S.D.Tex. 1982) ("though an assumption of precise congruity between the amounts of time spent by the two parties would obviously not be warranted, the value of the comparison cannot be assailed."); Stastny v. Southern Bell Tel. & Tel. Co., 77

F.R.D. 662, 663 (W.D.N.C.1978) ("obvious that the time that the opposition found necessary to prepare its case would be probative" on plaintiff's fee request).

A major difference between the collection of fees under the fee-shifting statutes and in normal commercial work is that counsel in civil rights cases are not paid as they go and must wait a substantial time to realize their fees for successful cases. In recognition of this delay in payment factor, most courts have awarded fees based on current rates rather than on rates prevailing at the time the legal work for which compensation is sought was performed. See, Murray v. Weinberger, 741 F.2d 1423 (D.C.Cir.1984) (rather than adjust lodestar upward to account for delay in payment, courts should award current rates); Johnson v. University College, 706 F.2d 1205 (11th Cir.), cert. denied, 464 U.S. 994, 104 S.Ct. 489, 78 L.Ed.2d 684 (1983) (delay in payment should be reflected through use of current rates or contingency adjustment of lodestar). In MISSOURI v. JENKINS, 491 U.S. 274, 109 S.Ct. 2463, 105 L.Ed.2d 229 (1989), the Supreme Court stated.

> Clearly, compensation received several years after the services were rendered—as it frequently is in complex civil rights litigation—is not equivalent to the same dollar amount received reasonably promptly as the legal services are performed, as would normally be the case with private billings. We agree, therefore, that an appropriate adjustment for delay in payment—whether by the application of current rather than historic hourly rates or otherwise—is within the contemplation of the statute.

491 U.S. at 283–84, 109 S.Ct. at 2469. Cf. Thompson v. Kennickell, 836 F.2d 616 (D.C.Cir.1988) (since Congress has not waived government's immunity from award of interest, historical hourly rates must be used in suits against United States, because the use of current rates is justified only by the delay in payment).

4. An issue not directly addressed in *Hensley* is what circumstances, if any, will justify the "enhancement" of a lodestar fee. Some courts have allowed an enhancement based on the contingent nature of the fee and the delay in payment. In Copeland v. Marshall, 641 F.2d 880 (D.C.Cir.1980)(*en banc*), for example, the Court of Appeals explained:

> An attorney contemplating representation of a Title VII plaintiff must recognize that no fee will be forthcoming unless the litigation is successful. An adjustment in the lodestar, therefore, may be appropriate to compensate for the risk that the lawsuit would be unsuccessful and that no fee at all would be obtained.

* * *

> The delay in receipt of payment for services rendered is an additional factor that may be incorporated into a contingency adjustment. The hourly rates used in the "lodestar" represent the prevailing rate for clients who typically pay their bills promptly. Court-awarded fees normally are received long after the legal services are rendered. That delay can represent cash-flow problems for attorneys. In any event, payment today for services rendered long in the past deprives the eventual recipient of the value of the use of the money in the meantime, which use, particularly in an inflationary era, is valuable. A percentage adjustment to reflect the delay in receipt of payment therefore may be appropriate.

641 F.2d at 893.

See also, Crumbaker v. Merit Systems Protection Board, 781 F.2d 191 (Fed.Cir. 1986) (lodestar multiplied to compensate for contingency risk and delay in payment); Clayton v. Thurman, 775 F.2d 1096 (10th Cir.1985) (33% enhancement for contingency and excellent results); Berger, Court Awarded Attorneys' Fees: What is "Reasonable?", 126 U.Pa.L.Rev. 281, 326 (1977) (proposing that multiplier should be determined by risk of non-success: 100% multiplier where plaintiff had 50% chance of non-success).

The Supreme Court proved to be much more reluctant to approve fee enhancements than the lower courts. In BLUM v. STENSON, *supra,* without flatly prohibiting upward adjustments, the Court established a presumption against them. The Court noted that the lodestar is presumed to represent the "reasonable" fee and that the fee applicant had the burden of showing that "such an adjustment is necessary to the determination of a reasonable fee." 465 U.S. at 898, 104 S.Ct. at 1548. In PENNSYLVANIA v. DELAWARE VALLEY CITIZENS' COUNCIL FOR CLEAN AIR (Delaware Valley I), 478 U.S. 546, 106 S.Ct. 3088, 92 L.Ed.2d 439 (1986) the district court had doubled the lodestar fee based on the high quality of representation plaintiffs' counsel had provided and the "low likelihood of success" plaintiffs faced when they filed the suit. Concluding that the quality of representation should be reflected in the hourly rate and thus in the lodestar, the Court reversed the enhancement based on that factor. The case was reargued on the question of whether enhancement could be based on contingency risk. In PENNSYLVANIA v. DELAWARE VALLEY CITIZENS' COUNCIL FOR CLEAN AIR (Delaware Valley II), 483 U.S. 711, 107 S.Ct. 3078, 97 L.Ed.2d 585 (1987), the Court in a plurality decision reversed the enhancement. The plurality reasoned that enhancements penalize defendants with the strongest cases and thus encourage the filing of weak cases. 483 U.S. at 718–22, 107 S.Ct. at 3083–85. But five justices (four dissenting and one concurring) agreed that under some circumstances a "reasonable" attorney's fee must include compensation above the lodestar. Justice O'Connor in her concurring opinion stated that "Congress did not intend to foreclose consideration of contingency in setting a reasonable fee" and that "compensation for contingency must be based on the difference in market treatment of contingent fee cases as a class rather than on an assessment of the 'riskiness' of any particular case." 483 U.S. at 731–32, 107 S.Ct. at 3089–90. Justice O'Connor's opinion was followed by most circuits. See *e.g.,* Lattimore v. Oman Construction Co., 868 F.2d 437, 439 (11th Cir.1989) (since relevant market for legal services compensated attorneys for contingent fee cases "by 100% at the very least" and "without enhancement, plaintiff would have faced substantial, and probably insurmountable difficulties in finding counsel in the relevant market" lodestar fee was doubled); Fadhl v. City & County of San Francisco, 859 F.2d 649 (9th Cir.1988) (fact that plaintiff had approached 35 lawyers before finding one that would take her case was strong support for proposition that without enhancement she would have faced substantial difficulty in obtaining counsel).

The Supreme Court returned to the enhancement issue in CITY OF BURLINGTON v. DAGUE, ___ U.S. ___, 112 S.Ct. 2638, 120 L.Ed.2d 449 (1992). The Court's composition had changed since its decision in *Delaware Valley II.* In an opinion by Justice Scalia, a six-member majority held that enhancement for contingency risk is not permitted under fee-shifting statutes. The majority reasoned that contingency enhancements are inconsistent with the requirement that only a prevailing party may recover a fee.

An attorney operating on a contingency fee basis pools the risks presented by his various cases: cases that turn out to be successful pay for the time he gambled on those that did not. To award a contingency enhancement under a fee-shifting statute would in effect pay for the attorney's time (or anticipated time) in cases where his client does not prevail.

___ U.S. at ___, 112 S.Ct. at 2639. In dissent Justice Blackmun argued that the very market factors relied upon to determine a "reasonable" fee may require that a lodestar fee be enhanced in order to qualify as a "reasonable fee."

Two principles, in my view, require the conclusion that the "enhanced" fee awarded to respondents was reasonable. First, this Court consistently has recognized that a "reasonable" fee is to be a "fully compensatory fee," Hensley v. Eckerhart, . . . , and is to be "calculated on the basis of rates and practices prevailing in the relevant market." Missouri v. Jenkins, 491 U.S. 274, 286, 109 S.Ct. 2463, 2470, 105 L.Ed.2d 229 (1989). Second, it is a fact of the market that an attorney who is paid only when his client prevails will tend to charge a higher fee than one who is paid regardless of outcome, and relevant professional standards long have recognized that this practice is reasonable.

___ U.S. at ___, 112 S.Ct. at 2644 (footnotes omitted).

Are there any circumstances, other than a failure to prevail on discrete issues, which would justify the *reduction* of a lodestar fee? One circumstance that has troubled courts is a great disparity between the fee award and monetary relief awarded to the plaintiff. See, Copper Liquor, Inc. v. Adolph Coors Co., 684 F.2d 1087 (5th Cir.1982) (25% downward adjustment of lodestar in light of low damage recovery). In CITY OF RIVERSIDE v. RIVERA, 477 U.S. 561, 106 S.Ct. 2686, 91 L.Ed.2d 466 (1986), the Supreme Court considered whether an award of $245,456.25 in attorney fees pursuant to 42 U.S.C. § 1988 could be "reasonable" in light of the fact that a jury had awarded plaintiffs a total of $33,350 in compensatory and punitive damages. The award was made in a police misconduct case filed under 42 U.S.C. § 1983 where the only relief requested was damages. The question sharply divided the Court and resulted in a 4–1–4 plurality decision. Five justices did vote to uphold the award and four of those Justices (the plurality) reasoned that limiting attorneys fees in civil rights cases to a proportion of the damages awarded would undermine the Congressional purpose behind Section 1988. *City of Riverside* is discussed in more detail in Chap. 8F, *infra.* Several courts have attempted to apply *City of Riverside* in Title VII cases. In Cowan v. Prudential Insurance Co., 935 F.2d 522 (2d Cir.1991), a suit filed under Title VII and 42 U.S.C. § 1981, the district court found that plaintiff's rights had been violated when he was not considered for three promotions. The plaintiff was awarded $15,000 in damages under Section 1981 but no back pay. The district judge calculated a lodestar fee of approximately $54,000 but reduced that award to $20,000 in light of limited monetary relief awarded the plaintiff. Relying on the plurality in *City of Riverside*, the Second Circuit reversed. "A presumptively correct 'lodestar' figure should not be reduced simply because a plaintiff recovered a low damage award." 56 FEP Cases at 232. See also, Davis v. Septa, 924 F.2d 51 (3d Cir.1991) (district court may not reduce lodestar fee solely on basis of requiring fee awards to be proportional to monetary relief); Starks v. George Court Company, Inc., 937 F.2d 311 (7th Cir.1991) (award of fee four times amount of back pay received by plaintiff was reasonable).

Once a lodestar has been calculated, may it be reduced because of the simplicity of the case or the fact that defendant attempted to settle early in the case? See, Cooper v. Utah, 894 F.2d 1169 (10th Cir.1990) (reduction of lodestar fees calculated by trial court on basis of simplicity of issue was error).

5. Should fees be awarded for attorneys' time spent in administrative proceedings related to the litigation? In NEW YORK GASLIGHT CLUB, INC. v. CAREY, 447 U.S. 54, 100 S.Ct. 2024, 64 L.Ed.2d 723 (1980), the claimant filed an EEOC charge alleging that she had been denied a job because of her race and the Commission referred the matter to the appropriate state agency under Title VII's deferral procedure. See, Chap. 4, *infra*. During the course of the state administrative proceedings, the EEOC issued a right to sue notice and the plaintiff filed suit in federal court. Before the case could progress to trial, the state agency determined that the employer had discriminated against plaintiff and directed that she be offered a job and awarded back pay. The state agency's order was affirmed by a state court. The federal action was then dismissed as moot and the district judge denied a request for attorney fees on the ground that the mere filing of a suit in federal court did not entitle the plaintiff to fees for the legal representation in the state proceeding. The Supreme Court read the "any action or proceeding" provision of Section 706(k) to encompass state deferral proceedings and held that a federal court may allow a claimant who prevails in state proceedings to which she was referred under Title VII to recover an award of attorneys' fees for work done in such state proceedings. In Chrapliwy v. Uniroyal, Inc., 670 F.2d 760 (7th Cir.1982), cert. denied, 461 U.S. 956, 103 S.Ct. 2428, 77 L.Ed.2d 1315 (1983), a Title VII class action, plaintiffs supplemented their litigation efforts by persuading the Office of Federal Contract Compliance to take action against the employer for violation of executive orders barring discrimination by federal contractors. The Title VII action was subsequently settled and the defendant admitted that it would not have settled had it not been for the threat of disbarment by the OFCCP. The district court awarded substantial fees to plaintiffs but denied compensation for time spent prodding the agency to take action as "not contemplated under Title VII's attorney fee provisions." Reasoning that "pursuit of disbarment was a service that contributed to the ultimate termination of the Title VII action, and in that sense was within the Title VII action," the Seventh Circuit reversed. 670 F.2d at 767. In non-Title VII cases where the plaintiff is not required by statute to pursue state remedies as a prerequisite to federal litigation, the Supreme Court has held that fees will not be awarded for work in the state proceedings. See, Webb v. Board of Education of Dyer County, 471 U.S. 234, 105 S.Ct. 1923, 85 L.Ed.2d 233 (1985) ("Because Section 1983 stands as 'an independent avenue of relief and petitioner could go straight to court to assert it,' the school board proceedings in this case simply do not have the integral function under Section 1983 that state administrative proceedings have under Title VII."); North Carolina Dept. of Transportation v. Crest Street Community Council, Inc., 479 U.S. 6, 107 S.Ct. 336, 93 L.Ed.2d 188 (1986) (under Section 1988 fees may only be awarded by court in case in which relief is sought under civil rights laws: action for attorney's fee standing alone not contemplated by statute).

There remains some question as to whether, in a suit in which a Title VII claim is combined with claims arising under the common law or statutes not covered by fee-shifting provisions, fees can be awarded for work on the non-civil rights claims. In Zabkowicz v. West Bend Co., 789 F.2d 540 (7th Cir.1986), plaintiff sued her employer, supervisors and some fellow workers for sexual harassment. Claims were stated under state tort law for intentional infliction of emotional distress against all the defendants and under Title VII against the employer only. After trial, the district court dismissed the state tort claims, and thus the suit against the supervisors and employees, but entered judgment against the employer under Title VII. The court also denied attorney fees because it considered the request to be exaggerated. The Seventh Circuit reversed and remanded for a determination of appropriate fees including compensation for time spent on the state causes of action.

> Although these claims are based on distinct legal theories, they undeniably involve a common core of facts. The tort claims sought to remedy the same course of conduct that gave rise to the Title VII action. Accordingly, Mrs. Zabkowicz may be entitled to recover all or a portion of the attorneys' fees incurred in prosecuting her tort claims. The precise amount of her fee award will, of course, depend upon the district court's analysis of the "significance of the overall relief obtained by the plaintiff in relation to the hours reasonably expended on the litigation." *Hensley,* 461 U.S. at 435, 103 S.Ct. at 1940.

789 F.2d at 551. See also, Seaway Drive–In, Inc. v. Township of Clay, 791 F.2d 447 (6th Cir.), cert. denied, 479 U.S. 884, 107 S.Ct. 274, 93 L.Ed.2d 251 (1986) (award of attorney's fees appropriate where fee and nonfee claim arose out of a common nucleus of operative facts).

  6.   Attorney fees may be awarded under § 706(k) of Title VII and Section 1988 against state and local governments. Unlike monetary damages, awards of attorney fees which ultimately run against the state are not barred by the Eleventh Amendment. Hutto v. Finney, 437 U.S. 678, 98 S.Ct. 2565, 57 L.Ed.2d 522 (1978); Fitzpatrick v. Bitzer, 427 U.S. 445, 96 S.Ct. 2666, 49 L.Ed.2d 614 (1976). Where plaintiffs obtain injunctive relief against government officials in their official capacities, the fee award will run against the government agency even though it is not a formal party to the litigation. Hutto v. Finney, *supra,* 437 U.S. at 693–94, 98 S.Ct. at 2574–2575. But where officials are sued for damages in their individual capacities and where the government entity could not be liable for damages on the merits, it can not be assessed fees under Section 1988. Kentucky v. Graham, 473 U.S. 159, 105 S.Ct. 3099, 87 L.Ed.2d 114 (1985). The qualified "good faith" immunity of the public official from damage liability is irrelevant to the award of attorney fees if injunctive or declaratory relief has been awarded. See, Aware Woman Clinic, Inc. v. Cocoa Beach, 629 F.2d 1146 (5th Cir.1980), Bond v. Stanton, 630 F.2d 1231 (7th Cir.1980), cert. denied, 454 U.S. 1063, 102 S.Ct. 614, 70 L.Ed.2d 601 (1981). Nor will the absolute immunity from damages which certain public officials (judges, prosecutors, legislators) enjoy for discretionary actions in the scope of their official duties bar an award of attorney fees against them in their official capacities where injunctive relief has been granted. See Morrison v. Ayoob, 627 F.2d 669 (3d Cir.1980), cert. denied, 449 U.S. 1102, 101 S.Ct. 898, 66 L.Ed.2d 828 (1981).

  In MISSOURI v. JENKINS, 491 U.S. 274, 109 S.Ct. 2463, 105 L.Ed.2d 229 (1989), an attorney fee award against a state agency under Section 1988 was enhanced to compensate counsel for long delay in payment. The state argued that such an enhancement was barred by the Eleventh Amendment even if Section 1988 constituted generally a "waiver" of Eleventh Amendment rights. The Supreme Court disagreed. Relying on HUTTO v. FINNEY, the Court held that the Eleventh Amendment has no application to an award of attorney fees ancillary to a grant of prospective relief against a state and the same is true for the calculation of the amount of such a fee. A more complete discussion of the Eleventh Amendment and its bearing on relief against state agencies is contained in Chap. 8D, *infra*.

7. Once a plaintiff has "prevailed" under a fee-shifting statute, there is usually no difficulty in determining *against whom* the fee should be assessed. In the ordinary case where the plaintiff prevails, fees will be awarded against the defendant employer and, where the defendant prevails, attorneys fees may, under some circumstances be awarded against the plaintiff. See, Christiansburg Garment Co. v. EEOC, *infra*. But class action pattern and practice cases may be filed against multiple defendants and intervention by unions or incumbent employees who stand to be affected by relief requested by plaintiffs is increasingly common. May a party who has not violated the plaintiff's rights, but who, by opposing plaintiffs' claims, has caused additional expense and legal fees for the prevailing party, be assessed fees under Section 706(k)? That question was answered in INDEPENDENT FEDERATION OF FLIGHT ATTENDANTS v. ZIPES, 491 U.S. 754, 109 S.Ct. 2732, 105 L.Ed.2d 639 (1989). *Zipes* was a protracted Title VII class action in which the plaintiffs and employer after almost ten years of litigation reached a settlement calling for backpay and retroactive seniority to class members. The union representing non-class employees who were potentially affected by the settlement intervened to oppose its adoption by the district court. The intervention was allowed, but the settlement was eventually approved. The court of appeals affirmed; the Supreme Court granted review but rejected the union's claims and upheld the settlement in all respects. Zipes v. Trans World Airlines, Inc., 455 U.S. 385, 102 S.Ct. 1127, 71 L.Ed.2d 234 (1982). Plaintiffs then petitioned the district court for an award of attorneys fees against the union. Rejecting the union's argument that fees could not be assessed against it because it had not violated plaintiffs' rights under Title VII, the court awarded plaintiffs approximately $180,000 in fees against the union and a divided court of appeals affirmed.

The Supreme Court reversed holding that a fee award against a losing intervenor is appropriate only where an award against a losing plaintiff is appropriate—that is where the intervenors' action was frivolous, unreasonable, or without foundation. Justice Scalia, writing for the majority and relying on *Christiansburg Garment Co.*, reasoned that, while only a prevailing party may recover a fee, the prevailing party's interests are not always paramount in determining entitlement to recovery.

> In this case, for example, [the union] became a party to the lawsuit not because it bore any responsibility for the practice alleged to have violated Title VII, but because it sought to protect the bargained-for seniority rights of its employees. Awarding attorney's fees against such an intervenor would further neither the general policy that wrongdoers make whole those whom they have injured nor Title VII's aim of deterring employers from engaging in discriminatory practices.

491 U.S. at 762, 109 S.Ct. at 2737. While recognizing that "a labor union's good-faith advocacy of its members' vital interests was not the specific type of conduct § 706(k) was intended to encourage," Justice Scalia's opinion ultimately rests on the conclusion that Section 706(k)'s purpose of compensating prevailing plaintiffs is overridden by the public interest in encouraging intervention in Title VII actions. "An intervenor of the sort before us here is particularly welcome, since we have stressed the necessity of protecting, in

Title VII litigation, 'the legitimate expectations of ... employees innocent of any wrongdoing,' (quoting from *Teamsters v. United States*)." 491 U.S. at 764, 109 S.Ct. at 2737.

Justice Blackmun concurred in the judgment but argued that the additional costs of litigating third-party claims should be placed on the defendant whose actions had resulted in the litigation.

> It seems to me that the first step towards solving the problem of intervenor fee liability is to recognize that it is the Title VII wrongdoer, and not the Title VII plaintiff, whose conduct has made it necessary to unsettle the expectations of a third party who itself is not responsible for the Title VII plaintiff's injuries. ... I see nothing in the language of the statute or in our precedents to foreclose a prevailing plaintiff from turning to the Title VII defendant for reimbursement of all the costs of obtaining a remedy, including the costs of assuring that third-party interests are dealt with fairly.

491 U.S. at 767, 109 S.Ct. at 2739–40. (Blackmun, J. concurring)

In dissent, Justices Marshall and Brennan argued that the majority's decision was wrong under the plain language of the Act and as a matter of policy.

> In its rush to protect an intervenor who contributed almost $200,000 in costs and nearly three years to the plaintiffs' struggle to achieve a settlement, the Court leaves behind the plaintiffs themselves, thereby reversing congressional priorities. The critical question in determining whether fees are awarded pursuant to § 706(k) should be whether the plaintiff prevailed, either against a named defendant or an intervenor. If the plaintiff has done so, fees should—and certainly may—be awarded.

491 U.S. at 779, 109 S.Ct. at 2746 (Marshall, J. dissenting). The dissenters also predicted that the decision will discourage remedial litigation because employers will rely on intervenors to bear the brunt of the defense thus "forcing prevailing plaintiffs to litigate ... their claims against parties from whom they have no chance of recovering fees."

In dictum, Justice Scalia suggested that *Zipes* may have an impact on plaintiffs beyond cases where a third party intervenes:

> Our decision in Martin v. Wilks ... establishes that a party affected by the decree in a Title VII case need not intervene but may attack the decree collaterally—in which suit the original Title VII plaintiff defending the decree would have no basis for claiming attorney's fees.

491 U.S. at 762, 109 S.Ct. at 2737. The holding of *Martin v. Wilks* was legislatively reversed by Section 108 of the Civil Rights Act of 1991. See Chap. 7B, The Impact of Injunctive Relief on Third Parties. Since that legislation is likely to encourage intervention in Title VII cases by unions and incumbent employees, the economic problems for plaintiffs caused by *Zipes* will continue. The House version of the 1991 Act (H.R. 1) contained a provision allowing an attorney fee award to the prevailing party in an action in which a judgment granting relief under Title VII was challenged against "an unsuccessful party challenging such relief or a party against whom relief was granted in the original action or from more than one such party under an equitable allocation determined by the court." This provision was not incorporated in the final compromise legislation that became law.

COSTS OF LITIGATION OTHER THAN ATTORNEYS' FEES

Section 706(k) provides for the award of reasonable attorneys' fees "as part of the costs of the litigation." What costs other than attorneys fees may be shifted to a losing party? Rule 54(d) of the Federal Rules of Civil Procedure and 28 U.S.C. § 1920 provide that certain costs, including fees for witnesses, can be taxed against the losing party. 28 U.S.C. § 1821 sets the amount of compensation to be paid witnesses at $30 per day. As in other kinds of complex litigation, litigants in employment discrimination cases frequently must resort to expert witnesses for assistance at trial. In class actions where intentional pattern and practice or disparate impact are alleged, plaintiffs are unlikely to make out even a prima facie case without the testimony of statisticians. See, Chap. 2C, *supra*. Experts, like lawyers, do not charge for their services at $30 per day. The anomaly of allowing the prevailing party in a civil rights case to recover attorneys fees but not allowing the recovery of the costs of expert assistance essential to success in the case led some courts to hold that all costs of litigation, including expert witness fees, could be shifted to the losing party under Section 706(k) or 42 U.S.C. § 1988. See e.g., Friedrich v. Chicago, 888 F.2d 511 (7th Cir.1989), vacated, ___ U.S. ___, 111 S.Ct. 1383, 113 L.Ed.2d 440 (1991) (time spent by experts is a substitute for lawyer time); SapaNajin v. Gunter, 857 F.2d 463 (8th Cir.1988) (witness fee cap of $30 per day does not apply when fees and costs awarded under Sec. 1988). But in WEST VIRGINIA UNIVERSITY HOSPITALS, INC. v. CASEY, 499 U.S. ___, 111 S.Ct. 1138, 113 L.Ed.2d 68 (1991), the Supreme Court rejected these circuit court decisions and held that the prevailing party in a civil rights case is *not* entitled to recover expert witness fees as part of a "reasonable attorney's fee" under the fee-shifting statutes. Justice Scalia, writing for the Court, compared the language of the fee-shifting provisions in the modern civil rights laws with the language of a number of federal statutes that explicitly shift to the losing party's attorney's fees and expert witness fees. He concluded that attorney's fees and expert's fees are regarded in statutory usage as separate elements of litigation costs and that, if Congress had intended to shift the fees for experts beyond which it had done in 28 U.S.C. § 1920 ($30 per day for witnesses), it would have done so. In Section 113 of the Civil Rights Act of 1991 Congress did exactly that by providing the court authority under both Section 706(k) of Title VII and 42 U.S.C. § 1988 to award expert fees in addition to attorney fees. Since the Act makes no reference to expert *witnesses* is it fair to assume that it ensures recovery of fees for both testimonial and non-testimonial assistance by experts?

CHRISTIANSBURG GARMENT CO. v. EQUAL EMPLOYMENT OPPORTUNITY COMMISSION

Supreme Court of the United States, 1978.
434 U.S. 412, 98 S.Ct. 694, 54 L.Ed.2d 648.

Mr. Justice Stewart delivered the opinion of the Court.

The question in this case is under what circumstances an attorney's fee should be allowed when the defendant is the prevailing party in a Title VII action—a question about which the federal courts have expressed divergent views.

I

Two years after Rosa Helm had filed a Title VII charge of racial discrimination against the petitioner Christiansburg Garment Co. (company), the Equal Employment Opportunity Commission notified her that its conciliation efforts had failed and that she had the right to sue the company in federal court. She did not do so. Almost two years later, in 1972, Congress enacted amendments to Title VII. Section 14 of these amendments authorized the Commission to sue in its own name to prosecute "charges pending with the Commission" on the effective date of the amendments. Proceeding under this section, the Commission sued the company, alleging that it had engaged in unlawful employment practices in violation of the amended Act. The company moved for summary judgment on the ground, inter alia, that the Rosa Helm charge had not been "pending" before the Commission when the 1972 amendments took effect. The District Court agreed, and granted summary judgment in favor of the company. 376 F.Supp. 1067 (W.D.Va.).

The company then petitioned for the allowance of attorney's fees against the Commission pursuant to § 706(k) of Title VII. Finding that "the Commission's action in bringing the suit cannot be characterized as unreasonable or meritless," the District Court concluded that "an award of attorney's fees to petitioner is not justified in this case." A divided Court of Appeals affirmed, 550 F.2d 949(CA), and we granted certiorari to consider an important question of federal law.

II

It is the general rule in the United States that in the absence of legislation providing otherwise, litigants must pay their own attorney's fees. Alyeska Pipeline Co. v. Wilderness Society, 421 U.S. 240, 95 S.Ct. 1612, 44 L.Ed.2d 141. Congress has provided only limited exceptions to this rule "under selected statutes granting or protecting various federal rights." Some of these statutes make fee awards mandatory for prevailing plaintiffs; others make awards permissive but limit them to certain parties, usually prevailing plaintiffs. But many of the statutes are more flexible, authorizing the award of attorney's fees to either plaintiffs or defendants, and entrusting the effectuation of the statutory policy to the discretion of the district courts. Section 706(k) of Title VII of the Civil Rights Act of 1964 falls into this last category, providing as it does that a district court may in its discretion allow an attorney's fee to the prevailing party.

In Newman v. Piggie Park Enterprises, 390 U.S. 400, 88 S.Ct. 964, 19 L.Ed.2d 1263, the Court considered a substantially identical statute authorizing the award of attorney's fees under Title II of the Civil Rights Act of 1964.[8] In that case the plaintiffs had prevailed, and the Court of Appeals had held that they should be awarded their attorney's fees "only to the extent that the respondents' defenses had been advanced 'for purposes of delay and not in good faith.' " We ruled that this "subjective standard" did not properly effectuate the purposes of the counsel-fee provision of Title II. Relying primarily on the intent of Congress to cast a Title II plaintiff in the role of "a 'private attorney general,' vindicating a policy that Congress considered of the highest priority," we held that a prevailing plaintiff under Title II "should ordinarily recover an attorney's fee unless special circumstances would render such an award unjust." We noted in passing that if the objective of Congress had been to permit the award of attorney's fees only against defendants who had acted in bad faith, "no new statutory provision would have been necessary," since even the American common-law rule allows the award of attorney's fees in those exceptional circumstances.

In Albemarle Paper Co. v. Moody, the Court made clear that the Piggie Park standard of awarding attorney's fees to a successful plaintiff is equally applicable in an action under Title VII of the Civil Rights Act. It can thus be taken as established, as the parties in this case both acknowledge, that under § 706(k) of Title VII a prevailing *plaintiff* ordinarily is to be awarded attorney's fees in all but special circumstances.

III

The question in the case before us is what standard should inform a district court's discretion in deciding whether to award attorney's fees to a successful *defendant* in a Title VII action. Not surprisingly, the parties in addressing the question in their briefs and oral arguments have taken almost diametrically opposite positions.

The company contends that the *Piggie Park* criterion for a successful plaintiff should apply equally as a guide to the award of attorney's fees to a successful defendant. Its submission, in short, is that every prevailing defendant in a Title VII action should receive an allowance of attorney's fees "unless special circumstances would render such an

---

8. "In any action commenced pursuant to this subchapter, the court, in its discretion, may allow the prevailing party, other than the United States, a reasonable attor-ney's fee as part of the costs, and the United States shall be liable for costs the same as a private person." 42 U.S.C. § 2000a–3(b).

award unjust." The respondent Commission, by contrast, argues that the prevailing defendant should receive an award of attorney's fees only when it is found that the plaintiff's action was brought in bad faith. We have concluded that neither of these positions is correct.

A

Relying on what it terms "the plain meaning of the statute," the company argues that the language of § 706(k) admits of only one interpretation: "A prevailing defendant is entitled to an award of attorney's fees on the same basis as a prevailing plaintiff." But the permissive and discretionary language of the statute does not even invite, let alone require, such a mechanical construction. The terms of § 706(k) provide no indication whatever of the circumstances under which either a plaintiff *or* a defendant should be entitled to attorney's fees. And a moment's reflection reveals that there are at least two strong equitable considerations counseling an attorney's fee award to a prevailing Title VII plaintiff that are wholly absent in the case of a prevailing Title VII defendant.

First, as emphasized so forcefully in *Piggie Park*, the plaintiff is the chosen instrument of Congress to vindicate "a policy that Congress considered of the highest priority." Second, when a district court awards counsel fees to a prevailing plaintiff, it is awarding them against a violator of federal law. As the Court of Appeals clearly perceived, "these policy considerations which support the award of fees to a prevailing plaintiff are not present in the case of a prevailing defendant." A successful defendant seeking counsel fees under § 706(k) must rely on quite different equitable considerations.

But if the company's position is untenable, the Commission's argument also misses the mark. It seems clear, in short, that in enacting § 706(k) Congress did not intend to permit the award of attorney's fees to a prevailing defendant only in a situation where the plaintiff was motivated by bad faith in bringing the action. As pointed out in *Piggie Park*, if that had been the intent of Congress, no statutory provision would have been necessary, for it has long been established that even under the American common-law rule attorney's fees may be awarded against a party who has proceeded in bad faith.

Furthermore, while it was certainly the policy of Congress that Title VII plaintiffs should vindicate "a policy that Congress considered of the highest priority," *Piggie Park*, 390 U.S., at 402, 88 S.Ct., at 966, it is equally certain that Congress entrusted the ultimate effectuation of that policy to the adversary judicial process, Occidental Life Ins. Co. v. EEOC, 432 U.S. 355, 97 S.Ct. 2447, 53 L.Ed.2d 402. A fair adversary process presupposes both a vigorous prosecution and a vigorous defense. It cannot be lightly assumed that in enacting § 706(k), Congress intended to distort that process by giving the private plaintiff substantial incentives to sue, while foreclosing to the defendant the possibility of recovering his expenses in resisting even a groundless action unless he can show that it was brought in bad faith.

B

The sparse legislative history of § 706(k) reveals little more than the barest outlines of a proper accommodation of the competing considerations we have discussed. The only specific reference to § 706(k) in the legislative debates indicates that the fee provision was included to "make it easier for a plaintiff of limited means to bring a meritorious suit." During the Senate floor discussions of the almost identical attorney's fee provision of Title II, however, several Senators explained that its allowance of awards to defendants would serve "to deter the bringing of lawsuits without foundation," "to discourage frivolous suits," and "to diminish the likelihood of unjustified suits being brought." If anything can be gleaned from these fragments of legislative history, it is that while Congress wanted to clear the way for suits to be brought under the Act, it also wanted to protect defendants from burdensome litigation having no legal or factual basis. The Court of Appeals for the District of Columbia Circuit seems to have drawn the maximum significance from the Senate debates when it concluded:

> "[From these debates] two purposes for § 706(k) emerge. First, Congress desired to 'make it easier for a plaintiff of limited means to bring a meritorious suit' * * *. But second, and equally important, Congress intended to 'deter the bringing of lawsuits without foundation' by providing that the 'prevailing party'—be it plaintiff or defendant—could obtain legal fees." Grubbs v. Bout, 79 U.S.App.D.C. 18, 20, 548 F.2d 973, 975.

The first federal appellate court to consider what criteria should govern the award of attorney's fees to a prevailing Title VII defendant was the Court of Appeals for the Third Circuit in United States Steel Corp. v. United States, 519 F.2d 359. There a District Court had denied a fee award to a defendant that had successfully resisted a Commission demand for documents, the court finding that the Commission's action had not been "'unfounded, meritless, frivolous or vexatiously brought.'" Id., at 363. The Court of Appeals concluded that the District Court had not abused its discretion in denying the award. Id., at 365. A similar standard was adopted by the Court of Appeals for the Second Circuit in Carrion v. Yeshiva University, 535 F.2d 722. In upholding an attorney's fee award to a successful defendant, that court stated that such awards should be permitted "not routinely, not simply because he succeeds, but only where the action brought is found to be unreasonable, frivolous, meritless or vexatious." Id., at 727.

To the extent that abstract words can deal with concrete cases, we think that the concept embodied in the language adopted by these two Courts of Appeals is correct. We would qualify their words only by pointing out that the term "meritless" is to be understood as meaning groundless or without foundation, rather than simply that the plaintiff has ultimately lost his case, and that the term "vexatious" in no way implies that the plaintiff's subjective bad faith is a necessary prerequisite to a fee award against him. In sum, a district court may in its discretion award attorney's fees to a prevailing defendant in a Title VII case upon a finding that the plaintiff's action was frivolous, unreasonable, or without foundation, even though not brought in subjective bad faith.

In applying these criteria, it is important that a district court resist the understandable temptation to engage in post hoc reasoning by concluding that because a plaintiff did not ultimately prevail, his action must have been unreasonable or without foundation. This kind of hindsight logic could discourage all but the most airtight claims, for seldom can a prospective plaintiff be sure of ultimate success. No matter how honest one's belief that he has been the victim of discrimination, no matter how meritorious one's claim may appear at the outset, the course of litigation is rarely predictable. Decisive facts may not emerge until discovery or trial. The law may change or clarify in the midst of litigation. Even when the law or the facts appear questionable or unfavorable at the outset, a party may have an entirely reasonable ground for bringing suit.

That § 706(k) allows fee awards only to *prevailing* private plaintiffs should assure that this statutory provision will not in itself operate as an incentive to the bringing of claims that have little chance of success. To take the further step of assessing attorney's fees against plaintiffs simply because they do not finally prevail would substantially add to the risks inhering in most litigation and would undercut the efforts of Congress to promote the vigorous enforcement of the provisions of Title VII. Hence, a plaintiff should not be assessed his opponent's attorney's fees unless a court finds that his claim was frivolous, unreasonable, or groundless, or that the plaintiff continued to litigate after it clearly became so. And, needless to say, if a plaintiff is found to have brought or continued such a claim in *bad faith*, there will be an even stronger basis for charging him with the attorney's fees incurred by the defense.[20]

---

20. Initially, the Commission argued that the "costs" assessable against the Government under § 706(k) did not include attorney's fees. See, e.g., United States Steel Corp. v. United States, 519 F.2d 359, 362(CA3); Van Hoomissen v. Xerox Corp., 503 F.2d 1131, 1132–1133(CA9). But the Courts of Appeals rejected this position and, during the course of appealing this case, the Commission abandoned its contention that it was legally immune to adverse fee awards under § 706(k). 550 F.2d, at 951.

It has been urged that fee awards against the Commission should rest on a standard different from that governing fee awards against private plaintiffs. One amicus stresses that the Commission, unlike private litigants, needs no inducement to enforce Title VII since it is required by statute to do so. But this distinction between the Commission and private plaintiffs merely explains why Congress drafted § 706(k) to preclude the recovery of attorney's fees by the Commission; it does not support a difference in treatment among private and Government plaintiffs when a prevailing defendant seeks to recover his attorney's fees. Several courts and commentators have also deemed significant the Government's greater ability to pay adverse fee awards compared to a private litigant. See, e.g., United States Steel

IV

In denying attorney's fees to the company in this case, the District Court focused on the standards we have discussed. The court found that "the Commission's action in bringing the suit cannot be characterized as unreasonable or meritless" because "the basis upon which petitioner prevailed was an issue of first impression requiring judicial resolution" and because the "Commission's statutory interpretation of § 14 of the 1972 amendments was not frivolous." The court thus exercised its discretion squarely within the permissible bounds of § 706(k). Accordingly, the judgment of the Court of Appeals upholding the decision of the District Court is affirmed.

It is so ordered.

MR. JUSTICE BLACKMUN took no part in the consideration or decision of this case.

NOTES AND PROBLEMS FOR DISCUSSION

1. Under *Christianburg Garment,* should an employer ever be entitled to fees if the plaintiff has been able to establish a prima facie case? In Blue v. United States Department of the Army, 914 F.2d 525 (4th Cir.1990), cert. denied, ___ U.S. ___, 111 S.Ct. 1580, 113 L.Ed.2d 645 (1991), the court held that mere establishment of a *prima facie* case of discrimination in employment will not, by itself, insulate litigants from sanctions for an otherwise frivolous case. In EEOC v. Caribe Hilton International, 821 F.2d 74 (1st Cir.1987), the Court affirmed an award of fees to the prevailing defendant against the EEOC even though the agency had made out a prima facie case. The district court based its decision on findings that the employee was not a credible witness and that he had been "intransigent" with the employer despite the employer's efforts at accommodation.

Under *Christiansburg* the employer need not establish that the plaintiff acted in bad faith in order to qualify for a fee award. The Court did not, however, quantify the proof that the losing plaintiff must produce to escape exposure. To what extent should the plaintiff's good faith in initiation of the litigation preclude an award of fees to the prevailing employer? Compare, Mitchell v. Office of Los Angeles County Superintendent of Schools, 805 F.2d 844 (9th Cir.1986), cert. denied, 484 U.S. 858, 108 S.Ct. 168, 98 L.Ed.2d 122

Corp. v. United States, supra, 519 F.2d, at 364 n. 24; Heinsz, Attorney's Fees for Prevailing Title VII Defendants: Toward a Workable Standard, 8 U.Toledo L.Rev. 259, 290 (1977); Comment, Title VII, Civil Rights Act of 1964; Standards for Award of Attorney's Fees to Prevailing Defendants, 1976 Wis.L.Rev. 207, 228. We are informed, however, that such awards must be paid from the Commission's litigation budget, so that every attorney's fee assessment against the Commission will inevitably divert resources from the agency's enforcement of Title VII. See 46 Comp.Gen. 98, 100 (1966); 38 Comp.Gen. 343, 344–345 (1958). The other side of this coin is the fact that many defendants in Title VII

claims are small- and moderate-size employers for whom the expense of defending even a frivolous claim may become a strong disincentive to the exercise of their legal rights. In short, there are equitable considerations on both sides of this question. Yet § 706(k) explicitly provides that "the Commission and the United States shall be liable for costs the same as a private person." Hence, although a district court may consider distinctions between the Commission and private plaintiffs in determining the reasonableness of the Commission's litigation efforts, we find no grounds for applying a different general standard whenever the Commission is the losing plaintiff.

(1987) (award of fees to employer reversed on ground that plaintiff had received a determination of reasonable cause from the EEOC and was qualified for position for which he applied); Eichman v. Linden & Sons, Inc., 752 F.2d 1246 (7th Cir.1985) (fact that employee filed suit in face of EEOC's determination of no probable cause does not necessarily compel conclusion that action was frivolous); Charves v. Western Union Telegraph Co., 711 F.2d 462 (1st Cir.1983) (a favorable EEOC evaluation of charge does not insure that court will not later conclude that case was frivolous and without foundation); Lane v. Sotheby Parke Bernet, Inc., 758 F.2d 71 (2d Cir.1985) (district court which denied fees to employer on ground that plaintiff had pled nonfrivolous cause of action erred in failing to determine whether plaintiff should have continued action once discovery was complete).

2.   Where a defendant has established entitlement to fees, should its award be calculated in the same manner as that of a prevailing plaintiff? Most courts that have addressed the issue have ruled that the financial condition of the plaintiff should be taken into account in fixing the fee. See e.g., Johnson v. New York City Transit Authority, 823 F.2d 31 (2d Cir.1987) (award of $3450 in attorney fees to defendant union was not necessarily excessive, but award vacated and remanded for a determination of whether the amount was more of a sanction than appropriate in light of a discharged transit worker's ability to pay); Durrett v. Jenkins Brickyard, Inc., 678 F.2d 911 (11th Cir.1982) (in light of plaintiff's ability to pay, reduced fee will fulfill the deterrent purpose of the Act without subjecting plaintiff to financial ruin); Faraci v. Hickey–Freeman Co., 607 F.2d 1025 (2d Cir.1979) (abuse of discretion for district court not to take into account financial resources of plaintiff: fee of $200 dollars assessed instead of $11,500 awarded in lower court); Quiroga v. Hasbro, Inc., 934 F.2d 497 (3d Cir.), cert. denied, ___ U.S. ___, 112 S.Ct. 376, 116 L.Ed.2d 327 (1991) (award of $10,000 in case where employer's fees and costs were approximately $125,000). Compare, Arnold v. Burger King Corp., 719 F.2d 63 (4th Cir.1983), cert. denied, 469 U.S. 826, 105 S.Ct. 108, 83 L.Ed.2d 51 (1984) (not an abuse of discretion for court to award full lodestar fee to employer given plaintiff's financial ability to pay); Charves v. Western Union Telegraph Co., *supra*, ($25,000 award upheld on ground that it would not completely ruin plaintiff financially). By contrast, the weak financial condition of a defendant has not been considered a factor in assessing fees. See, Jones v. Local 4B, Graphic Arts International Union, 595 F.Supp. 792 (D.D.C.1984); McPherson v. School District No. 186, 465 F.Supp. 749 (S.D.Ill.1978).

3.   The uncertain financial condition of many employment discrimination plaintiffs may frustrate the collection of any kind of an award made to a defendant and awards against plaintiffs do not have the kind of *in terrorem* effect often sought by prevailing defendants. These factors have resulted in efforts to assess fees and costs against unsuccessful plaintiffs' counsel. In ROADWAY EXPRESS, INC. v. PIPER, 447 U.S. 752, 100 S.Ct. 2455, 65 L.Ed.2d 488 (1980), the defendant argued that an award of fees should be shifted to plaintiffs' lawyers under Title VII and 28 U.S.C. § 1927, which allows the assessment of excess "costs" against attorneys who vexatiously multiply court proceedings. The Supreme Court construed "costs" under § 1927 not to include attorney fees and held that only a party may be assessed attorney fees under § 706(k) or § 1988. The Court noted, however, that in "narrowly defined circumstances federal courts have inherent power to assess attorney's fees against counsel" for abusive litigation practices. 447 U.S. at 765, 100 S.Ct. at 2463. After *Piper*, Congress amended § 1927 to expressly provide that an

attorney who multiplies court proceedings "unreasonably or vexatiously may be required to satisfy personally the excess costs, expenses, and attorney's fees reasonably incurred because of such conduct." Acting under § 1927 or Rule 11 of the Federal Rules of Civil Procedure (which provides for sanctions including the assessment of attorney fees against attorneys who file pleadings not "well grounded in fact" or "warranted by existing law"), courts have increasingly made awards against counsel deemed responsible for frivolous or bad faith law suits. See e.g., Blue v. U.S. Department of Army, 914 F.2d 525 (4th Cir.1990), cert. denied, ___ U.S. ___, 111 S.Ct. 1580, 113 L.Ed.2d 645 (1991) (award of fees against plaintiff and plaintiffs' counsel affirmed: district court properly concluded that counsel could not rely on client's patently incredible testimony when a reasonable investigation of claims or examination of material obtained in discovery would reveal implausibility of case); Quiroga v. Hasbro, Inc., *supra*, (because of plaintiff counsel's major role in causing client's discharge as well as bringing action, case remanded for determination of whether fee award against plaintiff should also run against his lawyer); Lewis v. Brown & Root, Inc., 711 F.2d 1287 (5th Cir.1983), cert. denied, 467 U.S. 1231, 104 S.Ct. 2690, 81 L.Ed.2d 884, and cert. denied, 464 U.S. 1069, 104 S.Ct. 975, 79 L.Ed.2d 213 (1984) (irresponsible manner in which litigation conducted further multiplied needless proceedings and justified award against counsel); Morris v. Adams–Millis Corp., 758 F.2d 1352 (10th Cir.1985) (fees awarded against counsel who commenced action without sufficient legal basis, continued to prosecute action when it was clear no grounds for prosecution would develop and abandoned client's cause when it became clear that defendant would not respond with nuisance value settlement of sufficient magnitude to justify his further involvement); Eastway Construction Corp. v. City of New York, 821 F.2d 121 (2d Cir.), cert. denied, 484 U.S. 918, 108 S.Ct. 269, 98 L.Ed.2d 226 (1987) (equitable allocation of fee award between counsel and client). Cf. Textor v. Board of Regents, 711 F.2d 1387 (7th Cir.1983) (lawyer should not be assessed fees without prior hearing to show that he acted in bad faith or otherwise abused judicial process so as to justify sanction).

Litigation under Rule 11 of the Federal Rules has increased since the amendment to the rule. A disproportionate percentage of sanctions under the revised rule have been levied against plaintiffs' lawyers in employment discrimination and other civil rights cases. See generally, Cochran, Rule 11: The Road To Amendment, 61 Miss. L.J. 1 (1991) (noting that most Rule 11 motions are filed against single practitioners and small firms, which are the only available source of representation of those without means); Vario, Rule 11: A Critical Analysis, 118 F.R.D. 189 (1988) (reporting that 28% of all Rule 11 motions were filed in civil rights and employment discrimination cases and 86% of such motions were directed against plaintiffs' counsel); LaFrance, Federal Rule 11 and Public Interest Litigation, 22 Val. U.L. Rev. 331 (1988). Rule 11 has been widely criticized as not providing sufficient standards to guide the courts. See, Cochran, Rule 11: The Road To Amendment, *supra*, (no clear distinction drawn between case that is "merely losing" and that which is both "losing and sanctionable"); Note, Plausible Pleadings: Developing Standards for Rule 11 Sanctions, 100 Harv.L.Rev. 630, 651 (1987) ("[e]rratic application of Rule 11 threatens to turn it from a constructive principle for caseload management into a random instrument of judicial intimidation"); Kassim, An Empirical Study of Rule 11 Sanctions, 26 Federal Judicial Center 1985 (reporting survey of federal judges showing that on same set of facts, half judges surveyed would have sanctioned complaint as frivolous while other half would not have granted sanctions: "good deal of interjudge disagreement over what . . . constitute[s] a violation of rule"). In an effort to relieve some of the confusion regarding application of the rule, the Fifth Circuit has established the following guidelines. First, the rule requires evaluation of the attorney's conduct at the time of the filing of a "pleading, motion or other paper." The rule therefore does not impose a continuing obligation on an attorney to abandon a case that was not in violation of the rule when filed. Second, the employer has a duty to mitigate its damages by keeping its legal response in line with the merits of the action. Third, the party seeking a sanction must give timely notice to the court and opposing counsel of the alleged violation rather than wait to the end of expensive litigation before making the claim. Finally, the court cautioned that Rule 11 is not a fee-shifting statute and that in granting a sanction, the district court should not render an award more severe than is necessary to dissuade such conduct in the future. Thomas v. Capital Security Services, Inc., 836 F.2d 866 (5th Cir.1988) (en banc). See also, Eastway Construction Corp. v. City of New York, 821 F.2d 121 (2d Cir.), cert. denied, 484 U.S. 918, 108 S.Ct. 269, 98 L.Ed.2d 226 (1987) (only that portion of defendant's attorney fees thought reasonable to serve sanctioning purpose of Rule 11 should be awarded even if award is substantially below defendant's lodestar amount).

PROBLEMS INVOLVING THE SETTLEMENT OF ATTORNEY FEE CLAIMS

Plaintiff's counsel in an employment discrimination, or other action where a fee-shifting statute is applicable, is in a markedly different position during settlement negotiations than a plaintiff's lawyer who is either paid by his client or who has a standard contingent fee contract which guarantees him a percentage of the recovery. Where the attorney looks to the defendant for his fee and must negotiate for his client and himself at the same time, there is the potential for a conflict of interest.

> [I]t is axiomatic that the overwhelming concern of counsel for the defendant in considering a proposed compromise is the total dollar cost of settlement. The defendant is uninterested in what portion of the total payment will go to the class and what percentage will go [to] the attorney. * * * [T]he spectre persists, absent appropriate judicial inquiry, that plaintiff's attorney may accept an insufficient judgment for the class in trade for immediate and certain compensation for himself in the form of legal fees deducted from the total available funds proffered by defendant. The actual presence and the potential consequences of such conflict of interest cannot be ignored.

Foster v. Boise–Cascade, Inc., 420 F.Supp. 674, 686 (S.D.Tex.1976), affirmed, 577 F.2d 335 (5th Cir.1978). In recognition of the potential conflict, a number of courts have expressed disapproval of the simultaneous negotiation of the merits of the case and fees. See, Obin v. District No. 9 of International Association of Machinists and Aerospace

Workers, 651 F.2d 574, 582 (8th Cir.1981) (counsel should not be "placed in the position of negotiating a fee ultimately destined for his pocket at the same time that all thoughts ought to be singlemindedly focused on the client's interests"); Prandini v. National Tea Co., 557 F.2d 1015, 1021 (3d Cir.1977) ("Only after court approval of the damage settlement should discussion and negotiation of appropriate compensation for the attorneys begin.").

The Supreme Court has, however, rejected the idea that courts can prevent simultaneous negotiations and set aside fee waivers which are coerced by defendants. In EVANS v. JEFF D., 475 U.S. 717, 106 S.Ct. 1531, 89 L.Ed.2d 747 (1986) defendants proposed a settlement of a class action attacking institutional conditions and health care of emotionally handicapped children by the State of Idaho, conditioned on a complete waiver of attorney fees by class counsel. Counsel agreed to the settlement because he felt no better relief could be obtained through litigation, but then moved the district court to award fees despite the settlement because the waiver had been coerced. The district court denied the motion but the Ninth Circuit reversed, holding that courts in class actions could not approve coerced waiver of fees. The Court of Appeals also stated that ordinarily simultaneous negotiations were improper. The Supreme Court reversed.

The Court reasoned that, in the first place, the simultaneous negotiation of the merits and fees is not legally improper. "We agree that when the parties find such negotiations conducive to settlement, the public interest, as well as that of the parties, is served by simultaneous negotiations." 475 U.S. at 738 n.30, 106 S.Ct. at 1543 n.30. With regard to the waiver issue, the Court could find nothing in the language or history of Section 1988 that mandated payment to successful counsel. On the other hand a general prohibition against attorney fee waivers in exchange for settlement would, according to the Court, actually "impede vindication of civil rights, at least in some cases, by reducing the attractiveness of settlement." 475 U.S. at 732, 106 S.Ct. at 1540. The Court recognized the difficulty faced by plaintiff's counsel but could see no "ethical dilemma" because the lawyer "had no *ethical* obligation to seek a statutory fee award." 475 U.S. at 728, 106 S.Ct. at 1537. The Court indeed suggested that the attorney would have acted unethically had he turned down the favorable offer because of the demand that fees be waived. *Ibid.*

In a dissent Justice Brennan, joined by Justices Marshall and Blackmun, criticized the majority's opinion as undermining the effectiveness of the fee-shifting statutes in encouraging of attorneys to take on civil rights cases.

> The cumulative effect this practice (coerced waivers) will have on the civil rights bar is evident. It does not denigrate the high ideals that motivate many civil rights practitioners to recognize that lawyers are in the business of practicing law, and that, like other business people, they are and must be concerned with earning a

living. The conclusion that permitting fee waivers will seriously impair the ability of civil rights plaintiffs to obtain legal assistance is embarrassingly obvious.

475 U.S. at 758, 106 S.Ct. at 1553. Can plaintiff's counsel solve the problem, or at least shift the burden of the problem, by entering into retainer agreements which make the client ultimately responsible for fees in the event of a successful resolution of the case where fees are for any reason not awarded? See, VENEGAS v. MITCHELL, 495 U.S. 82, 110 S.Ct. 1679, 109 L.Ed.2d 74 (1990) (counsel and client can contract for fee that is greater than what court would award as "reasonable fee" under fee-shifting statute); Note, Fee Waivers and Civil Rights Settlement Offers: State Ethics Prohibitions After Evans v. Jeff D., 87 Colum.L.Rev. 1214 (1987) Could such a strategy be used in a class action? See, Silver, A Restitutions Theory of Attorney's Fees in Class Actions, 76 Cornell L.Rev. 656 (1991).

The original House version of the Civil Rights Act of 1991 (H.R. 1) would have added the following provision to Section 706(k) of Title VII:

> No consent order or judgment settling a claim under this title shall be entered, and no stipulation of dismissal of a claim under this title shall be effective, unless the parties and their counsel attest to the court that a waiver of all or substantially all attorney's fees was not compelled as a condition of the settlement.

The above section was *not* included in the compromise legislation that was enacted. Would the addition of such a provision have facilitated or hindered the incidence of settlement?

Plaintiff's counsel in civil rights cases may also face offers of judgment under Rule 68 of the Federal Rules of Civil Procedure which allows the defendant to serve on the plaintiff an offer to "allow judgment to be taken against [him] for the money or property or to the effect specified in his offer, with costs then accrued." If the offer is rejected and "the judgment finally obtained by the offeree is not more favorable than the offer, the offeree must pay the costs incurred after the making of the offer." In MAREK v. CHESNY, 473 U.S. 1, 105 S.Ct. 3012, 87 L.Ed.2d 1 (1985), the Court held that the word "costs" in Rule 68 encompasses fees awarded under the fee-shifting statutes. Thus, where the defendant makes an offer to plaintiff before trial *inclusive of fees*, and the plaintiff subsequently recovers less than the amount offered, the court may deny all counsel fees incurred after the date of the offer. Should relief obtained by the plaintiff as result of the voluntary action of the employer be considered in determining whether the terms of the employer's offer of judgment were more favorable to the plaintiff than "judgment finally obtained"? See, Spencer v. General Electric Co., 894 F.2d 651 (4th Cir.1990) (judgment and relief are different: in making comparison required by Rule 68 court must compare only the offer of judgment to the "judgment finally obtained").

MAREK v. CHESNY did not involve the question of whether the plaintiff may be made to pay the defendant's post-offer costs and whether those costs may include the defendant's post-offer attorney fees. In Crossman v. Marcoccio, 806 F.2d 329 (1st Cir.1986), cert. denied, 481 U.S. 1029, 107 S.Ct. 1955, 95 L.Ed.2d 527 (1987), the Court noted that Rule 68 applies to costs which are properly awardable under the substantive law. Where the plaintiff has prevailed under a civil rights statute, there is no statutory basis for an award of attorney's fees as part of the costs to the defendant who is not the prevailing party. The court of appeals thus held that when the plaintiff recovers in judgment less than the defendant offered under Rule 68, the defendant's post-offer costs may be shifted to the plaintiff, but not the defendant's attorney's fees.

SECTION D. CLASS RELIEF

Employment discrimination class actions are normally litigated in bifurcated proceedings. Liability to the class, whether through a disparate impact or pattern and practice theory, as well as the claims of the individual class representatives, are tried in the first stage. Neither the class representatives nor individual class members are called upon to prove damages at this stage and remedy-oriented proof is usually not admitted. If classwide discrimination is found, a second proceeding, called "Stage II," is conducted for the purpose of determining the relief due the plaintiffs and individual class members. See generally, Craik v. Minnesota State University Board, 731 F.2d 465 (8th Cir.1984); Sagers v. Yellow Freight System, Inc., 529 F.2d 721, 733–34 (5th Cir.1976); Comment, Special Project: Back Pay in Employment Discrimination Cases, 35 Vand.L.Rev. 893, 978–92 (1982).

A finding that the employer has engaged in a pattern and practice of discrimination does not mean that every class member will be entitled to relief. For example, in a hiring case the employer may have discriminated against applicants generally on the basis of race, but some of the class members would not have been hired, absent discrimination, because they could not satisfy legitimate requirements of the position or because at the time of their applications there were no vacancies. Thus, in the Stage II proceeding, the court must determine both which class members are entitled to relief and the kind and amount of relief to be awarded. Because discrimination against the class has been determined, however, the burden of proof on the issues before the court no longer rests solely with the plaintiffs as it does in the liability phase of the case. In INTERNATIONAL BROTH. OF TEAMSTERS v. UNITED STATES, 431 U.S. 324, 97 S.Ct. 1843, 52 L.Ed.2d 396 (1977), the defendants contended that at the remedial stage of class litigation individual class members should have to establish their entitlement to relief through the *McDonnell Douglas–Burdine* formula. The Supreme Court rejected the argument and held that when class-wide discrimination has been established, the burden "rests on the employer to demonstrate that the individual applicant was denied an employment opportunity for lawful reasons such as his lack of qualifications or the fact that a more qualified applicant would have been chosen for a vacancy." 431 U.S. at 362, 369 n.53, 97 S.Ct. at 1868, 1872 n.53. As the three cases in this chapter demonstrate, however, disagreement remains over the exact nature of the employers' burden in Stage II.

The accepted method for determining the amount of back pay and/or retroactive seniority, once entitlement is established, is by the construction of hypothetical work histories as was done in EEOC v. Ford Motor Co., *supra,* for each class member. The larger the employer and the more complex its organization, the more difficult Stage II will be. Under the best of conditions, this process can be a monumental task, but because of such factors as highly subjective decision-making, lack of records and fading memories, anything approaching an accurate reconstruction of what an individual employee's work history would have been absent discrimination is often impossible. In Pettway v. American Cast Iron Pipe Co., 494 F.2d 211, 260 (5th Cir.1974) (*Pettway III*), the Court of Appeals described some of the problems facing courts in typical Stage II litigation.

> There is no way of determining which jobs the class members would have bid on and have obtained if discriminatory testing, seniority, posting and bidding system, and apprentice and on-the-job training programs not been in existence. Class members out-number promotion vacancies; jobs have become available only over a period of time; the vacancies enjoy different pay rates; and a determination of who was entitled to the vacancy would have to be determined on a judgment of seniority and ability at that time. This process creates a quagmire of hypothetical judgments.

The efforts of courts to solve problems associated with class relief are illustrated by the following cases.

KYRIAZI v. WESTERN ELECTRIC CO.

United States District Court for New Jersey, 1979.
465 F.Supp. 1141.

OPINION

STERN, DISTRICT JUDGE.

At the conclusion of "Stage I" of this Title VII litigation—the liability phase—this Court found that Western Electric discriminated against its female employees, applicants and former employees in the areas of hiring, promotion, participation in job training programs, layoffs, wages and opportunities for testing.[1] We now enter "Stage II",

---

1. That opinion is reported at 461 F.Supp. 894 (D.N.J.1978). An earlier opinion of this Court on the discovery aspects of Stage I is reported at 74 F.R.D. 468 (D.C. 1977).

the damage phase. Stage II requires adjudication of the claims of thousands of class members.[2]

To assist it in this formidable task, the Court has appointed three Special Masters pursuant to Rule 53(a) of the Federal Rules of Civil Procedure. The Court now addresses some of the procedural hurdles which confront it at this stage.

1. *Burden of Proof*

The Supreme Court has made clear that once there has been a finding of classwide discrimination, the burden then shifts to the employer to prove that a class member was not discriminated against; that is, a finding of discrimination creates a rebuttable presumption in favor of recovery. The Court first addressed this in Franks v. Bowman, in which it held that:

> [P]etitioners here have carried their burden of demonstrating the existence of a discriminatory hiring pattern and practice by the respondents and, therefore, the burden will be upon respondents to prove that individuals who reapply were not in fact victims of previous hiring discrimination.

More recently, in International Brotherhood of Teamsters v. United States, the Court specifically rejected the contention that in the remedial stage of a pattern-or-practice case, the government must prove that the individual was actually the victim of discrimination:

> That basic contention was rejected in the *Franks* case. As was true of the particular facts in *Franks,* and as is typical of Title VII pattern-or-practice suits, the question of individual relief does not arise until it has been proved that the employer has followed an employment policy of unlawful discrimination. The force of that proof does not dissipate at the remedial stage of the trial. The employer cannot, therefore, claim that there is no reason to believe that its individual employment decisions were discriminatorily based; it has already been shown to have maintained a policy of discriminatory decisionmaking.
>
> The proof of the pattern or practice supports an inference that any particular employment decision, during the period in which the discriminatory policy was in force, was made in pursuit of that policy. The Government need only show that an alleged individual discriminatee unsuccessfully applied for a job and therefore was a potential victim of the proved discrimination. As in *Franks,* the burden then rests on the employer to demonstrate that the individual applicant was denied an employment opportunity for lawful reasons.

---

2. Western reports that there are approximately 10,000 class members (Tr. 1/31/79 at 5), of which:
—1,131 are retired
—1,887 are active employees

—3,200 were laid off by Western

—3,500 were rejected by Western.

(Tr. 1/31/79 at 9–10).

(Footnote omitted; citation omitted).

Accordingly, the sole burden upon class members will be to demonstrate that they are members of the class, that is, that now or at any time since June 9, 1971, they were either employed by Western, applied for employment at Western or were terminated by Western. In practical terms, this will be reflected in the Proof of Claim forms which class members will be required to fill out. Those forms require only that the putative class member state the dates of her employment and/or application, the positions she held and/or sought.[3] The Court will not require individual class members to specify the manner in which they were discriminated against. As was held in Stage I, employees remained for the most part ignorant of the fact that they were being passed over for promotion and training programs, and unsuccessful applicants may well be unaware that they were rejected on the basis of their sex. The fact is that employment decisions are rarely put in discriminatory terms, no matter how discriminatorily bottomed. Individual employees should not be put to the almost impossible task of delving into the corporate consciousness to demonstrate how an already proven policy of discrimination exactly impacted each one of them.[4] Thus, once an individual demonstrates that she is a class member, the burden will then shift to Western to demonstrate that the individual class member was not the victim of discrimination.

2. Notice

Pursuant to Rule 23(d)(2), Federal Rules of Civil Procedure, Western is required to give notice to class members in the following manner. All class members whose addresses are known to Western will be sent a notice and Proof of Claim form together with a prepaid envelope. The remaining class members will be notified by publication in six local newspapers for two consecutive weeks in the Sunday editions and three weekday editions.[5] All costs of notification are, of course, to be borne by Western.

The Court has scanned the early returns from the newspaper notices and the mailings and has determined that it would be advisable to supplement the notice to the nearly 1,900 class members who are presently employed by Western by providing an opportunity for class

---

3. Copies of the notice to the class and the Proof of Claim forms to be distributed to class members are reproduced in the Appendix to this opinion.

4. Compare Pettway v. American Cast Iron Pipe Co., 494 F.2d 211, 259 (5th Cir. 1974), which held that each class member has the "initial burden * * * to bring himself within the class and to describe the harmful effect of the discrimination on his individual employment position." It is noteworthy, however, that *Pettway* was decided before the Supreme Court's decisions in *Franks* and *Teamsters*.

5. Those newspapers are *The* New York *Times, The* Daily *News, The* Newark *Star Ledger, The* Bergen *Record, The* New York *Post,* and *The* Jersey *Journal.*

A substantial number of class members, approximately 3,500 are women who applied for positions at Western and were rejected. Western reports that it does not have the addresses of these women, only their social security numbers. Counsel for the plaintiff has been directed to prepare a form of notice acceptable to the Social Security Administration to be forwarded to the last known business addresses of these women.

counsel to communicate with them directly at the plant.[6] Accordingly, Western will permit counsel for the class to enter the plant for the purpose of meeting with class members who are presently employed by Western. Western may accomplish this in any manner that will minimize loss of productivity and disruption of its normal activities, provided that the manner selected gives employees advance notice and a reasonable opportunity to meet with counsel. Undoubtedly, mass meetings will be required in order to minimize the number of visits which counsel will have to make. These meetings may take place before or after working hours, if Western prefers, but sufficient time must be allocated and a suitable facility must be provided. With these guidelines in mind, counsel are directed to meet and work out a schedule which will commence not later than March 12, 1979 and terminate not later than March 31, 1979, nine days before the April 9, 1979 cutoff date for the filing of claims by class members.

3. Computation of Back Pay Awards

The courts have adopted a number of approaches in connection with the computation of back pay awards.[7] One approach, the "pro rata" formula referred to in Pettway v. American Cast Iron Pipe Co., 494 F.2d 211 (5th Cir.1974), and United States v. United States Steel, 520 F.2d 1043 (5th Cir.1975), looks to the difference between the salary of the class members computed collectively and that received by employees of comparable skills and seniority, not the victims of discrimination. The class member then receives his pro rata share of that collective difference, based upon his salary differential and the number of competitors for the position. Another approach is the "test period" approach, used in Bowe v. Colgate, Palmolive Co., 489 F.2d 896 (7th Cir.1973), in which the court awards class members the difference between the pay they receive after implementation of the Title VII decree and the pay they received while the discriminatory policies were in force. A variation of the "test period" approach was used in Stewart v. General Motors, 542 F.2d 445 (7th Cir.1976), cert. denied, 433 U.S. 919, 97 S.Ct. 2995, 53 L.Ed.2d 1105 (1977), in which the court awarded the class members the difference between the wages of salaried white workers during a test period and that actually received by the class. Yet another approach was used in Stamps v. Detroit Edison Co., 365

---

6. In this Circuit, counsel is permitted to confer with members of the class—indeed, a restriction upon counsel's ability to communicate with class members has been held violative of the First Amendment. Coles v. Marsh, 560 F.2d 186 (3rd Cir.), cert. denied, 434 U.S. 985, 98 S.Ct. 611, 54 L.Ed.2d 479 (1977); Rodgers v. United States Steel Corp., 508 F.2d 152 (3rd Cir.), cert. denied, 423 U.S. 832, 96 S.Ct. 54, 46 L.Ed.2d 50 (1975). See also, Developments in the Law—Class Actions, 89 Harv.L.Rev. 1317, 1592–1604 (1976).

7. The back pay period commences two years before the filing of the EEOC charge.

42 U.S.C. § 2000e–5(g). At Stage I, the Court concluded that the nature of the discrimination alleged and proved brought this case within the "continuing violation" theory of Title VII, therefore, allowing class members to secure relief for acts of discrimination occurring since the effective date of Title VII. While it is clear that the back pay award is statutorily limited, the Court is considering what other forms of relief may be awarded for discrimination which occurred before the two year back pay period.

F.Supp. 87, 121 (E.D.Mich.1973), rev'd on other grounds sub nom. EEOC v. Detroit Edison Co., 515 F.2d 301 (6th Cir.1975), in which the court awarded class members the difference between their own actual earnings and the earnings of the skilled trade opportunity jobs from the effective date of Title VII.

The Court finds none of these approaches appropriate here. As we found in connection with Stage I, we deal with discrimination which manifests itself in a number of ways. For example, a woman might initially be hired at the lowest grade—32—while a comparable male would have been hired at grade 33. During the course of a ten-year period, the woman—perhaps unbeknownst to her—would be passed over for promotion, denied entry into job training programs and, finally, notwithstanding her seniority, would be the first to be laid off because she was in the lowest job category. She may in fact have been laid off and rehired a number of times.[8] By contrast, the male, during the same period and having started at a higher grade, would be promoted several grades—perhaps even trained for a supervisory position—and would thus remain unscathed in times of layoffs. It is, therefore, apparent that a back pay award must take into account the fact that a male and a female entering Western with comparable skills would, over a period of time, take dramatically divergent paths.

While this approach will not yield an exact measure of damages, neither could any other approach. However, the law is clear that where one has been damaged by the wrong of another, the victim is not to be denied any recompense merely because the exact measure of damages is uncertain. The approach we adopt at least gives individual consideration to each claimant and, if not precise, it is no more imprecise than lumping claimants into groups and extracting averages, or otherwise depersonalizing victims of discrimination by running them through a mathematical blender.

Moreover, Western itself objects to any formula type or averaging approach in awarding back pay—that is, to any but an individual approach under which the merits of each woman's claim is separately considered. In the face of Western's objections, it may be that due process considerations require that any award to an individual be on the merits of that individual's case. In any event, it does seem that an individual approach is more fair both to class members and to Western.

In its proposed Order of Reference, Western proposes that:

45. If there is more than one eligible claimant for a given designated vacancy, net back pay awards shall be computed for each claimant. One award shall be made in an amount equal to the highest individual net award. Each claimant shall share that award in the proportion that her individual net back pay award bears to her total of all claimants' net back pay awards pursuant to

---

8. The preliminary responses already received from class members indicate that this is no rare experience for women at Western.

the formula set forth in United States v. United States Steel, 520 F.2d 1043 (5th Cir.1975).

The Court rejects this approach. According to Western, if there were three women who should have been considered for one promotion and none were, and if we cannot now determine which of the three women should have received the promotion, then each one receives one-third of the benefits. As Western notes, this approach does shield Western from having to pay three increases when only one was actually possible, but it also unjustly penalizes the one woman who was entitled to *all*— not just one-third—of the benefits of that promotion. Under Western's approach, two of the claimants get a windfall while the actual victim receives only one-third of the back pay to which she is statutorily entitled. If we know that all three claimants were discriminated against in that they were not considered for promotion but that only one—which, we do not know—would have actually received the promotion, then all three should get the full benefit of the promotional opportunity. Where it is proved that an employer unlawfully disregarded women for promotion, it is better that it pay a little more than to permit an innocent party to shoulder the burdens of the guilty. Western *will* be permitted to demonstrate that the promotion would have gone to one class member, rather than the others. However, if Western cannot demonstrate which claimant would have received the promotion, Western cannot divide the benefits of the one job. It is no more unreal to construe three promotions out of one, than to divide the salary increase of one promotion among three prospects. Either smacks of some artificiality but the latter protects the wrongdoer at the expense of the innocent.

The Order of Reference to the Special Masters is reproduced in the Appendix. Among other requirements, in an effort to assure back pay awards on as individualized basis as possible, where appropriate class members will be compared to the male employee with comparable skills upon initial hire and comparable seniority. The class member will then be awarded the difference between her salary and that received by the male counterpart, including bonuses and any other fringe benefits. See Pettway v. American Cast Iron Pipe Co., supra.

4. Compensation of Special Masters

The final problem which confronts us at the outset of Stage II is the compensation of the Special Masters.

All parties have recognized that the number of potential claimants virtually mandates the appointment of Special Masters. The parties agree that if any significant portion of the 10,000 potential claimants respond, the existing court mechanism of a district judge and a magistrate is totally inadequate to deal with the issues which will confront the Court. Even 3,000 claimants out of the 10,000 eligible, for example, would exceed the yearly civil filings for this entire district of nine active judges and five magistrates. Moreover, unlike a rough sampling of the typical civil case cross section, many of which will be voluntarily dismissed, others of which will be settled without any judicial supervision, and the overwhelming majority of which will be settled without any judicial factfinding,[9] it appears that each one of the claims of Western's present or former employees will have to be individually considered and adjudicated. Western has objected to any formula approach, and has requested that each claim be considered upon its own merits. The Court agrees that not only is Western entitled to this approach, but that each claimant is also entitled to individual consideration. In many instances this approach requires that efforts be made to project the actual benefits lost by each Western employee who has been found to have been a victim of Western's discrimination. Whole work histories will have to be recast, based on evaluations of the background, education, potential and abilities of each claimant, as compared with the opportunities available to and realized by similarly situated males at Western. In a very real sense, Stage II proceedings under this approach resemble a host of individual cases, sharing many common questions of law and fact, as much as it does the pure class action of more common experience.

Faced with this task, the parties agree not merely to the appointment of a Special Master, but to the appointment of three Special Masters. The parties also agree that these Special Masters should not only be lawyers, but experienced trial lawyers. Western has demanded, and the Court has granted, an opportunity for it to conduct "discovery regarding the * * * claims pursuant to the Federal Rules of Civil Procedure." If the past is any gauge of the future, the Special Masters will be occupied with discovery matters concerning many hundreds of claimants even before they get down to dealing with the merits of each.

[The Court found that the Special Masters should be compensated "in a manner roughly comparable to that which they receive in the practices from which they are being diverted"—i.e. at hourly rates of $125 and $115. The defendant was ordered to pay all the Masters' fees.]

Appendix "A"

TO: Female Applicants, Employees or Former Employees of Western Electric's Kearny Plant (including the Clark Shops)

RE: Sex Discrimination Action Against Western

If you are a woman and now or any time since June 9, 1971 you either: (a) applied for employment at Western's Kearny plant and were rejected; *or* (b) were employed in any position at Western's Kearny plant; *or* (c) were laid off or discharged from any position at Western's Kearny plant, please read this notice carefully.

---

9. In 1978, approximately 90% of the civil actions filed in this District were terminated sometime prior to trial. *Management Statistics for United States Courts* (1978).

On October 30, 1978, in a lawsuit brought by Kyriaki Cleo Kyriazi, a former employee of Western, the United States District Court for the District of New Jersey found that Western has been discriminating against its women employees at its Kearny plant in violation of federal law. It was found that women, *as a group*, were discriminated against in the following ways:

1) *Hiring*—Women are hired into the lowest grades, while men with equal skills and experience were hired into the higher grades.

2) *Promotion*—Women employees were not given promotional opportunities equal to male employees.

3) *Layoffs*—Women were not treated fairly when employees had to be laid off.

4) *Transfer into Kearny*—Women who transferred into the Kearny plant were placed in lower grades than they were in before they transferred.

5) *Discharge*—More women were fired than men.

6) *Participation in Job Training Programs*—Women were not given the opportunities given to men to participate in job training programs.

7) *Opportunities for Testing*—Women were not given the opportunity to take tests for promotion to better positions.

The Court has completed the first stage of this lawsuit by finding that Western had discriminated against women in its Kearny plant. Copies of the Court's opinion are on file in the United States District Court of the District of New Jersey.

There will be soon be a second stage, "Stage II", at which time the Court will determine the damages and other relief which it will award to individual women. If you are or were at any time since June 9, 1971 an employee of Western, or if you ever applied for a position at Western, you may be entitled to certain benefits, including monetary payments. The "Stage II" proceedings will determine this question. At these "Stage II" proceedings, any eligible woman will be presumed to have been discriminated against. It will be Western's duty to show that it did not deny a woman employment opportunities because of her sex. If Western fails to demonstrate this, that women will be entitled to recovery, which may include back pay and reinstatement.

If you wish to be considered, you must fill out the enclosed form. Your claim will not be considered if you do not do so and return the form by April 2nd, 1979. If you do fill out the form, you may be required, with no cost to yourself, to participate in court proceedings. You will be furnished an attorney without cost to you. That attorney will be Judith Vladeck, Attorney for plaintiff Kyriazi. If you prefer, you may retain an attorney of your own choosing. If you wish further information, you may contact the attorney for the plaintiff, Judith Vladeck, at (212) 354–8330

AS PART OF THE COURT'S ORDER, YOUR EMPLOYER MAY NOT PENALIZE YOU IN ANY WAY IF YOU CHOOSE TO FILE A CLAIM AGAINST IT.

APPENDIX "B"

Kyriazi v. Western Electric 475–73

_____

NAME

_____

ADDRESS

_____

TELEPHONE NUMBER
Answer each question to the
best of your ability.

1) Did you use any other name while employed at Western's Kearny Plant? (Indicate yes or no) _____. If so, please set forth the names you used and the dates you used each name.

NAME	DATES
_____	_____ - _____
_____	_____ - _____

2) What is your social security number?_____

3) Were you rejected for a position at Western's Kearny Plant? (Indicate yes or no) _____. If so, please set forth the date of your application and the position for which you applied._____

_____

4) Are you presently employed at Western's Kearny Plant? _____. If so, when did your employment begin? _____. Please list all positions you have held at Western, (the grade, if the position was graded), and the dates you held each position.

POSITION	GRADE	DATES
_____	_____	_____ - _____
_____	_____	_____ - _____
_____	_____	_____ - _____

5) Were you laid off or otherwise terminated by Western?_____. If so, when did your employment end? _____. What was the reason given for your termination? _____
Set forth each of the positions you held at Western's Kearny plant and the dates you held each position.

_____	_____ - _____
_____	_____ - _____
_____	_____ - _____

6) Have you been employed since you left Western? _____. If so, please set forth the positions you have held since you left Western and the dates you held each position.

_____   _____ - _____

_____   _____ - _____

_____   _____ - _____

Please send the completed form to:

Angelo Locascio, Clerk

United States District Court

U.S. Post Office and Courthouse

Newark, New Jersey 07101

[Appendix "C" to the opinion, containing detailed guidelines for the Special Masters to follow in resolving the various types of claims to be raised by class members, is omitted.]

INGRAM v. MADISON SQUARE GARDEN CENTER, INC.

United States Court of Appeals for the Second Circuit, 1983.
709 F.2d 807, cert. denied, 464 U.S. 937, 104 S.Ct. 346, 78 L.Ed.2d 313.

Before VAN GRAAFEILAND, MESKILL and PRATT, CIRCUIT JUDGES.

VAN GRAAFEILAND, CIRCUIT JUDGE:

Local 3 of the International Brotherhood of Electric Workers appeals from a judgment of the United States District Court for the Southern District of New York (Sand, J.) which awarded plaintiffs in a class employment discrimination suit retroactive seniority rights with back pay, front pay, and attorneys' fees, the total monetary award, with interest, being substantially in excess of $1 million. Four opinions written by the district court are reported at 482 F.Supp. 414, 482 F.Supp. 426, 482 F.Supp. 918, and 535 F.Supp. 1082. Although we find the evidence of discrimination somewhat less persuasive than did the district court, we are not prepared to hold that the district court's findings on this issue were clearly erroneous. See Pullman–Standard v. Swint, 456 U.S. 273, 102 S.Ct. 1781, 72 L.Ed.2d 66 (1982). Accordingly, we affirm the district court's adjudication of liability. However, for reasons hereafter discussed, we find it necessary to modify the relief which the court below granted.

Since 1965, Local 3 of the International Brotherhood, which has more than 4,300 black and Hispanic members, has represented the "maintenance group of utility men" (hereafter "laborers") at Madison Square Garden. These laborers prepare the Garden for its various featured events. The several contracts between the Union and the Garden placed no restrictions on the employer's method of hiring, merely requiring that all laborers become members of the Union within 31 days of their employment. However, in practice, the hirelings, of which there was an average of about 5 per year, were referred to the Garden by the Union representative for the Garden laborers. About 1 in 6 of the hirelings was either black or Hispanic.

Until 1969, the Garden also employed other groups of people as cleaners or porters, bowling alley and lavatory attendants, and elevator operators. In 1969, the Garden subcontracted its cleaning work to Allied Maintenance Corporation, retaining only the elevator operators as its own employees. All of the cleaners are represented by Local 54 of Service Employees International Union, and most of them are either black or Hispanic.

On August 13, 1973, appellees Ingram, Britt, Moody, and Floyd, all of whom were porters working at the Garden, filed charges against the Garden and Allied with the Equal Employment Opportunity Commission, pursuant to Title VII of the Civil Rights Act of 1964, 42 U.S.C. § 2000e et seq., alleging that these employers had discriminated against them and other black porters by paying them less than the white laborers for doing similar work and by maintaining segregated job classifications. The EEOC concluded that the Garden and Allied were violating Title VII, and, on October 4, 1976, following unsuccessful conciliation efforts, issued right-to-sue letters to the four complainants. On December 30, 1976, the porters filed a proposed class action suit against the Garden and Allied, alleging violations of 42 U.S.C. §§ 1981 and 1985 as well as Title VII. On June 22, 1977, Local 3 was added to the litigation by means of an amended complaint, which charged that the Union was discouraging competent minority cleaners from seeking and obtaining jobs as laborers and was conspiring with the Garden and Allied towards this end by advising cleaners that the Garden was solely responsible for hiring, that no jobs were available, and that cleaners must do apprenticeships before becoming members of Local 3.

On November 24, 1975, appellees Anderson and Perry, black porters who worked at the Garden, also filed discrimination charges with the EEOC, their charges being directed against the Garden, Allied, and Local 3. On January 16, 1978, a right-to-sue letter issued, and on March 31, 1978, a proposed class action complaint on behalf of the Anderson group was filed.

The district court certified a Title VII class and a §§ 1981 and 1985 class in both actions. In the *Ingram* action, the Title VII class, whose claims, of necessity, were limited to the Garden and Allied, consisted of all blacks who, after February 14, 1973, had been or would be employed as cleaners at the Garden. The §§ 1981 and 1985 class consisted of all blacks and Hispanics who, after December 30, 1973, had been or would be employed as cleaners at the Garden. The §§ 1981 and 1985 class consisted of all blacks and Hispanics who, after December 30, 1973, had been or would be employed as cleaners at the Garden. Certification of both classes in *Ingram* was conditioned on the intervention of lavatory and bowling alley attendants and elevator operators as named plaintiffs. Thereafter, Williams, a black lavatory attendant, Milon, a black bowling alley attendant, Mitchell, a black elevator operator, Bruton, a retired black cleaner, and Garcia, an Hispanic cleaner, intervened. The *Anderson* classes were defined in the same manner as those of *Ingram,* except that the Title VII *Anderson* class limitation was May 28, 1975, and the §§ 1981 and 1985 *Anderson* class limitation was March 31, 1975, and both classes claimed against the Garden, Allied, and Local 3.

On July 13, 1978, the *Ingram* and *Anderson* actions were consolidated. On July 16, 1979, the district court denied the Union's motion to decertify the classes. Subsequently, the plaintiffs entered into a proposed consent decree with the Garden and Allied, in which the defendants agreed, among other things, to pay $117,500 in settlement of plaintiffs' monetary claims plus $47,500 in attorneys' fees. On October 23, 1979, the settlement was approved by the district court, subject only to the submission of an affidavit in support of counsel fees. See 482 F.Supp. at 426. In the meantime, the case had proceeded to trial against Local 3, the issue being limited to that of liability.

On October 3, 1979, in an opinion reported at 482 F.Supp. 414, the district court dismissed plaintiffs' § 1985 claims, relying on Great American Federal Savings & Loan Assoc. v. Novotny, but held the Union liable under both Title VII and § 1981.

[The Court's discussion of the statistical evidence (which showed that blacks and Hispanics had been referred by the Union in numbers significantly below their percentage in the relevant labor market) and of anecdotal testimony by class members is omitted.]

The Back Pay Award

In fashioning a remedy for employment discrimination, "the court must, as nearly as possible, 'recreate the conditions and relationships that would have been had there been no' unlawful discrimination." Int'l Bhd. of Teamsters v. United States. We believe that the remedy in the instant case went beyond that.

The district court referred the factual remedial issues to a Magistrate and instructed the Magistrate to award seniority to every class member who desired a laborer's job as of the date of the next laborer hire that followed his application or "qualifying desire", subject to a maximum date of July 2, 1965. The court instructed the Magistrate to make back pay awards on the same basis, subject to the 2–year limitation period of Title VII and the 3–year limitation period applicable in New York to § 1981. The computations, made as directed, produced some interesting results. Two class members were awarded retroactive competitive seniority dates to 1970, a year in which 5 laborers were hired, one of whom was Hispanic. If the district court was recreating the conditions that would have existed had there been no discrimination, presumably he intended that three of the five 1970 hirelings should have been either black or Hispanic. In 1974, 6 laborers were hired, one of whom was black. Nevertheless, 4 class members were awarded retroactive competitive seniority to 1974. In recreating the conditions for that year, the district court must have intended that 5 out of the 6 hirelings should have been either black or Hispanic. Although only one laborer, a white man, was hired in 1976, seniority retroactive to 1976 was awarded 4 class members.

According to appellees' own computations, in 1969, the laborer work force at the Garden consisted of 48 whites, 2 blacks and 2 Hispanics. Between 1970 and 1978, the Garden hired 33 laborers referred to it by the Union, of whom 6 were either black or Hispanic. The minority hiring rate during these years was thus 18.2%. The district court held that, for purposes of retroactive competitive seniority, 17 class members should have been hired during this period, for purposes of non-competitive seniority, 10 class members should have been hired, and for purposes of back pay awards, 13 class members should have been hired. Had 17 class members been hired, the racial composition of labor hirings during this period would have been 69% black or Hispanic. Had 13 class members been hired, the composition would have 57% black or Hispanic. Had 10 been hired, 48% of the hirelings would have been black or Hispanic. This is hardly a recreation of the conditions that would have existed had there been no discrimination.

A court that finds unlawful discrimination is not required to grant retroactive relief. City of Los Angeles v. Manhart, 435 U.S. 702, 718, 98 S.Ct. 1370, 1380, 55 L.Ed.2d 657 (1978). "To the point of redundancy, the statute stresses that retroactive relief 'may' be awarded if it is 'appropriate.' " Id. at 719, 98 S.Ct. at 1380. Moreover, such remedy as is given should not constitute a windfall at the expense of the employer, its union, or its white employees. Title VII imposes no duty to maximize the hiring of minority employees. Furnco Construction Corp. v. Waters. Remedial relief should be granted only to those class members who would have filled vacancies had there been no discrimination. The district court's judgment, based on the concept that all class members with unexpressed employment desires should have been hired regardless of the number of vacancies and competing applicants, is based upon a hypothetical hiring practice which the law did not require and which, in actuality, never would have been followed absent any trace of discrimination.

James O'Hara, the Union representative for the Garden laborers and the person who made job referrals, received over 300 requests for jobs during the period at issue, not a single one of which came from a class member. There is nothing in the record to indicate that, discrimination aside, class members would have been given preference over other applicants. Indeed, since the Union counted 4,300 blacks and Hispanics among its own members, it is unlikely that preferred treatment would have been given to members of another union. In view of the limited number of vacancies that occurred, we conclude that, to the extent that back pay was awarded to more than 7 class members, it constituted an unwarranted windfall and did not recreate the conditions that would have existed in the absence of discrimination.

Because of the statistical limitations inherent in the small samples available to plaintiffs' expert witness, her testimony concerning disproportionate hiring did not focus on any particular year. Faced with the same limitations, neither this Court nor the district court can state accurately when the 7 class members should have been hired. Under such circumstances, we think it would be inequitable to award back pay to only the first 7 class members who indicated a "desire" to become laborers. The fairer procedure, we believe, would be to compute a gross award for all the injured class members and divide it among them on a pro rata basis. See Stewart v. General Motors Corp., 542 F.2d 445, 452–53 (7th Cir.1976), cert. denied, 433 U.S. 919, 97 S.Ct. 2995, 53 L.Ed.2d 1105 (1977); Pettway v. American Cast Iron Pipe Co., 494 F.2d 211, 263 n. 154 (5th Cir.1974). In determining the amount of the gross award, however, we think it fair to both the Union and the class members to assume that the Union would have referred the 7 class members who first desired employment, had they applied, and to base the class award on the loss attributable to these 7 men.

The first 7 "applicants", determined by their seniority dates, and the back pay awards made them by the district court, are:

1.	Clarence Lamar	$ 55,120
2.	Wilfred Boudreaux	51,010
3.	William Moody	53,298
4.	Herbert Holmes	57,604
5.	Henry Ingram	27,202
6.	Kenneth Williams	61,494
7.	James Britt	39,988
		$345,716

The total award to these men, $345,716, is equal to approximately 52.14% of the total award of $663,085 which the district court made to all 18 back pay recipients. Proration by 52.14% of the 18 individual awards produces the following figures:

1.	Shelly Anderson	$ 16,578.43
2.	Wilfred Boudreaux	26,596.61
3.	James Britt	20,849.74
4.	John Carroll	9,630.78
5.	Russell Footman	11,123.03
6.	Waverly Green	10,675.67
7.	Graydon Griffith	18,963.84

8.	Lawrence Hawkins	24,746.17
9.	Francisco Hernandez	23,836.84
10.	Herbert Holmes	30,034.73
11.	Henry Ingram	14,183.12
12.	Clarence Lamar	28,739.57
13.	William Moody	27,789.58
14.	James Parrott	19,611.94
15.	James Perry	8,775.16
16.	James Pettigrew	11,628.78
17.	George Sharpe, Sr.	9,905.56
18.	Kenneth Williams	32,062.97

$345,732.52

The district court's award of back pay is modified in accordance with the foregoing figures.

Front Pay

Since this action was begun, at least 6 class members to whom the district court made back pay awards have been hired by the Garden, 5 of them on November 5, 1979, and one on December 20, 1980. The district court has indicated that it intends to make front pay awards for future losses to the twelve remaining back pay recipients. For the reasons already expressed, we believe it is completely unrealistic to assume that all 18 back pay beneficiaries would have been hired had there been no discrimination practiced against them. Accordingly, we deem it unfair to the members of the defendant Union, black, Hispanic, and white, to impose a continuing liability upon their association for the loss of future benefits. This unfairness is exacerbated by the fact that the Union has no control over future hirings, which are the sole prerogative of the Garden, and is therefore in no position to bring its liability for front pay to an end. Under these circumstances, we believe that it would be an abuse of discretion for the district court to make front pay awards against the Union to class members not already hired.

Retroactive Seniority

The same factors which dictate the limitation of back pay and front pay awards also militate against the grant of retroactive seniority to future hirelings. In addition, we view pendent grants of retroactive seniority as self-defeating, in that they militate against the likelihood that the beneficiaries of the grants will be employed. Under the consent decree which terminated plaintiffs' action against the Garden, the Garden agreed that every second job opening would be offered to minorities until their representation among the Garden's laborers reached 27%. Because at least 9 minority laborers have been hired since the execution of the consent decree, 6 of whom were class members, it is not at all unlikely that the 27% quota has been reached and the compulsory hiring of class members has come to an end. Relations between the Garden and its presently employed laborers will not be improved by the voluntary hiring of additional class members who will be granted automatic seniority under the terms of the district court's judgment. For all the foregoing reasons, we think that the proper exercise of discretion would limit the grant of retroactive seniority to the 6 or more class members already hired.

[The Court's discussion of the attorney fee issue is omitted.]

NOTES AND PROBLEMS FOR DISCUSSION

1. How does the district court's treatment of the "limited vacancy" problem in *Kyriazi* differ from that of the Second Circuit in *Ingram?* Has the Second Circuit in fact put the burden of proof on the employer? Compare the Ninth Circuit's approach in Domingo v. New England Fish Co., 727 F.2d 1429 (9th Cir.), modified, 742 F.2d 520 (9th Cir.1984).

> In order to be eligible for backpay, claimants need only prove they applied for a position or would have applied if not for Nefco's discriminatory practices. They may be required to show what their qualifications were, but do not have the burden of proving they were qualified for the position sought. Because class-wide discrimination has already been shown, the employer has the burden of proving that the applicant was unqualified or showing some other valid reason why the claimant was not, or would not have been, acceptable.... All uncertainties should be resolved against the employer.

727 F.2d at 1445. See also, Easley v. Anheuser–Busch, Inc., 758 F.2d 251 (8th Cir.1985) (at remedial stage employer has burden of showing that applicant would not have been hired absent discrimination). Which process is fairest for the class member?

2. The employer defendants in *Ingram* settled before trial for an amount that was roughly a third of the back pay award subsequently made against the union. The district court credited the settlement amount against the union's liability, but the union still claimed it was entitled to indemnity and/or contribution from the employers. In NORTHWEST AIRLINES, INC. v. TRANSPORT WORKERS UNION OF AMERICA, 451 U.S. 77, 101 S.Ct. 1571, 67 L.Ed.2d 750 (1981), the Supreme Court held that an employer guilty of violating Title VII does not possess an explicit or implied right of contribution from a union which was responsible in part for the violation. Noting that the legislative history of the Act was silent on the issue of contribution, the Court reasoned that it would be improper to imply a right of action for contribution because Congress had created a comprehensive remedial scheme which evidenced an intent not to allow additional remedies and because employers as a group were not the intended beneficiaries of the Act. But *Northwest Airlines* was distinguishable from *Ingram* because no charge of discrimination was ever

filed against the union in that case and the Supreme Court stated in its opinion that: "A court's broad power * * * to fashion relief against all respondents named in a properly filed charge is not, of course, at issue in this litigation since no charge was filed against either of the respondent unions." 451 U.S. at 93 n. 28, 101 S.Ct. at 1581 n. 28. The district court in the *Ingram* litigation, nevertheless relied on *Northwest Airlines* in rejecting the union's claims and the Second Circuit affirmed. Anderson v. Local Union No. 3, IBEW, 751 F.2d 546 (2d Cir.1984). The Court of Appeals based its affirmance in part on the fear that recognition of a right of indemnity would encourage suits between defendants which would in turn discourage voluntary settlements. Is the Second Circuit's concern realistic? Is an employer's knowledge that it will not be able to obtain contribution from a union more likely to encourage settlement or to encourage it to take its chances on the court's apportionment of liability at trial?

3. In a subsequent decision in *Kyriazi,* the district court created a hypothetical work history for the named plaintiff, in a manner similar to that employed in EEOC v. FORD MOTOR CO., *supra,* by modifying the actual work history of a male employee who held the same job as the plaintiff and had similar qualifications. Kyriazi v. Western Electric Co., 476 F.Supp. 335 (D.N.J. 1979), affirmed, 647 F.2d 388 (3d Cir.1981). Pursuant to that formula, Ms. Kyriazi was awarded $103,506.75 in back pay and interest and reinstated to the position she would have occupied with all seniority and benefits she would have enjoyed had she been continuously employed by Western Electric. The Stage II proceedings for class members who had filed claim forms proceeded. By June 1980, 108 final judgments had been entered on behalf of class members who were rejected applicants for employment and back pay awards totalling $234,-271.25 had been entered. The claims of 60 rejected applicants had not been adjudicated and only a few of the claims of the thousands of women actually employed by Western Electric had been heard. At that point the parties settled. Western Electric agreed to pay $7 million to be distributed among class members who had filed claim forms, to give priority consideration for hiring to class members who had been rejected for employment or laid off and to engage in a 4–year affirmative action program. The history of the *Kyriazi* litigation is recounted in the district court's approval of the settlement. Kyriazi v. Western Electric Co., 527 F.Supp. 18 (D.N.J.1981).

Is such a marathon proceeding in fact as Judge Stern states in *Kyriazi* "fair both to class members and [the employer]?" In Kraszewski v. State Farm General Insurance Co., 41 FEP Cases 1088 (N.D.Cal.1986), the district court directed that the parties begin individual stage II hearings in a case where there were potentially 50,000 claimants who might make claims based on 1250 vacancies during the relevant back pay period. The defendant estimated that the process would take 19 years: the district judge was more optimistic and estimated that the claim procedure would take between 2 and 3 years. The judge based his decision on his finding that "the only way to determine the actual victims is to give each class member the opportunity to demonstrate she was discriminated against with respect to any of the 1250 vacancies filled by men," but cautioned that "if on receipt of the claim forms, it is obvious that many more than one thousand claims establish a *prima facie* case, this court will be open to a motion from the defendants to reconsider [the procedure for determining class relief] on the basis that individual hearings will be unwieldy." 41 FEP Cases at 1091, 1092. After the court's order requiring individual hearings, the parties settled. Kraszewski v. State Farm General Insurance Co.,

912 F.2d 1182 (9th Cir.1990), cert. denied, ___ U.S. ___, 111 S.Ct. 1414, 113 L.Ed.2d 467 (1991). What alternatives are there to individual hearings? See Segar v. Smith, *infra*.

4. The economic burdens of protracted class actions like *Kyriazi* and *Kraszewski* on plaintiffs' counsel is enormous. Recognizing the severe financial problems of counsel in such cases, courts have awarded interim fees after the liability phase of the case. In James v. Stockham Valves & Fittings Co., 559 F.2d 310 (5th Cir.1977), cert. denied, 434 U.S. 1034, 98 S.Ct. 767, 54 L.Ed.2d 781 (1978), the Fifth Circuit explained the award of fees pendente lite.

> There is a danger that litigants will be discouraged from bringing such suits because of the risks of protracted litigation and the extended financial drain represented by such a risk. An award of interim attorneys' fees will prevent extreme cash-flow problems for plaintiffs and their attorneys. * * * Here, where the litigation has consumed more than eleven years, such an award is appropriate. Otherwise, the danger exists that defendants in Title VII suits may be tempted to seek victory through an economic war of attrition against plaintiffs.

559 F.2d at 358–59. See also, Carpenter v. Stephen F. Austin State University, 706 F.2d 608 (5th Cir.1983) (district court directed on remand to award interim fees for pre-trial, trial and appellate work should relief be afforded plaintiffs). The denial or granting of interim fees is not immediately appealable as a final order. See, Morgan v. Kopecky Charter Bus Co., 760 F.2d 919 (9th Cir.1985). Are such interim awards inconsistent with the Supreme Court's decision in HEWITT v. HELMS, 482 U.S. 755, 107 S.Ct. 2672, 96 L.Ed.2d 654 (1987), where the Court held that a decision that plaintiff's rights were violated, unaccompanied by an award of relief will not entitle the plaintiff to attorney fees? See, Section C of this chapter, *supra*.

One area which remains very unsettled is how fees of plaintiffs' counsel should be calculated *for* the remedial stage of a successful class action. If individualized hearings are conducted on class member claims at Stage II, should counsel be compensated for time spent on unsuccessful claims? In Wooldridge v. Marlene Industries Corp., 898 F.2d 1169 (6th Cir.1990), the district court made back pay awards to 38 claimants out of a class of approximately 130. Plaintiffs' counsel received fees for litigating all the back pay claims, regardless of their success, in the relief stage of the proceeding. Relying on Hewitt v. Helms, *supra*, the Sixth Circuit reversed:

> [W]e do not believe it appropriate to look to the class as a group to determine whether the plaintiffs have prevailed. A contrary result could force the defendants to compensate the class attorneys for work that did not benefit and was not intended to benefit the class as a group but was for the individual benefit of persons who were not harmed by the policy and who obtained no benefit from the litigation.... On remand the District Court should reduce the fees by the time spent litigating those [unsuccessful] claims. This portion of our ruling does not affect the fee award for the liability portion of the litigation since the time spent litigating issues common to the class benefitted those who received back pay awards as well as those who did not receive backpay.

898 F.2d at 1174–75. See also, Foster v. Board of School Commissioners of Mobile County, 810 F.2d 1021, 1024 (11th Cir.), cert. denied, 484 U.S. 829, 108 S.Ct. 99, 98 L.Ed.2d 60 (1987) (where less than one third of class members obtained back pay in Stage II proceedings, not an abuse of discretion to reduced

lodestar for remedial phase by 12%). But in McKenzie v. Kennickell, 645 F.Supp. 427, 432 (D.D.C.1986), the court reasoned that Stage II hearings are not "unrelated claims that should be separated from the class claims for purposes of a fee award" and held that the defendant should pay all fees and costs of individual claimants at the remedial stage "except where the claims are found to be frivolous or vexatious."

SEGAR v. SMITH

United States Court of Appeals for the District of Columbia Circuit, 1984.
738 F.2d 1249, cert. denied, 471 U.S. 1115, 105 S.Ct. 2357, 86 L.Ed.2d 258 (1985).

Before WRIGHT, WALD, and EDWARDS, CIRCUIT JUDGES.

J. SKELLY WRIGHT, CIRCUIT JUDGE:

Title VII of the Civil Rights Act of 1964 proclaims one of this nation's most fundamental, if yet unrealized, principles: a person shall not be denied full equality of employment opportunity on account of race, color, religion, sex, or national origin. Title VII bars both intentional discrimination and artificial, arbitrary, or unnecessary barriers to equal opportunity. In this case we review a decision of the United States District Court for the District of Columbia, Segar v. Civiletti, 508 F.Supp. 690 (D.D.C.1981), holding that the federal Drug Enforcement Agency (DEA) had engaged in a pattern or practice of discrimination against its black agents in violation of Title VII. A class comprising black agents initiated this suit in 1977 and the case came to trial in 1979. Finding that DEA had discriminated against black agents in salary, promotions, initial (GS) grade assignments, work assignments, supervisory evaluations, and imposition of discipline, the District Court ordered a comprehensive remedial scheme consisting of a class-wide backpay award, promotion goals and timetables to ensure that qualified black agents received promotions to the upper levels of DEA, and a class-wide frontpay award to compensate such qualified agents while they awaited the promotions they deserved. In the course of the proceedings the court also denied plaintiffs' request for prejudgment interest and issued a preliminary injunction barring transfer or demotion of Carl Jackson (the Jackson injunction), a black agent who was the subject of adverse employment decisions immediately after his testimony for plaintiffs in this lawsuit.

On appeal DEA challenges the liability determination, the remedial scheme, and the Jackson injunction. Plaintiffs cross-appeal the denial of prejudgment interest. As to the liability determination, DEA urges that the trial court erred in finding that plaintiffs had presented sufficient probative evidence to support any inference of discrimination at DEA, and urges that DEA had in any event effectively rebutted plaintiffs' showing. As to the remedial scheme, DEA argues that class-wide relief was inappropriate and that imposition of promotion goals and timetables both exceeded the court's remedial authority under Title VII and violated the equal protection component of the Fifth Amendment Due Process Clause. DEA also argues that Carl Jackson did not make a showing of retaliation sufficient to justify the preliminary injunction.

To resolve this appeal we have had to plumb some of the deepest complexities of Title VII adjudication. After careful review, we affirm the District Court's liability determination in its entirety. We also affirm the trial court's decision to use a class-wide backpay remedy, but we vacate the backpay formula imposed and remand for reformulation of the particular backpay award. We also vacate the part of the District Court's remedy that mandates promotion goals and timetables. We do not hold that such remedies exceed a court's remedial authority under Title VII. Nor do we hold that such remedies violate the Constitution. Nonetheless, we find that the District Court's particular order of goals and timetables was not appropriate on the current factual record. Because the frontpay remedy was specifically linked to the promotion goals and timetables, we vacate that part of the remedial order as well, and remand to the District Court for further consideration of appropriate remedies.[3] We affirm the preliminary injunction against demotion or transfer of Carl Jackson and we expect the District Court to undertake resolution of the status of the Jackson injunction on remand. We affirm the trial court's denial of prejudgment interest.

* * *

This Lawsuit

In January 1977 two black special agents of DEA, and an association representing all black special agents, brought suit alleging that DEA had engaged in a pattern or practice of racial discrimination against black special agents in violation of Title VII of the Civil Rights Act of 1964. These agents alleged discrimination in recruitment, hiring, initial grade assignments, salary, work assignments, evaluations, discipline, and promotions.

On September 9, 1977 the trial court, pursuant to Federal Rule of Civil Procedure 23(b)(2), certified the class of all blacks who then served or had been discharged as special agents at DEA, and who had applied for positions or would in the future apply. Before trial the parties settled the claims involving discriminatory recruitment and hiring, but could not come to terms on the other issues. As is common in Title VII class actions, the District Court bifurcated the trial into separate liability and remedial phases. After lengthy discovery, the liability issues came to trial in April 1979. The trial was in large measure a duel of experts armed with sophisticated statistical means of proof.

1. *The plaintiffs' case.* The plaintiffs presented a range of statistical and anecdotal evidence of discrimination. The statistical evidence included several multiple linear regression analyses as well as a num-

3. We vacate the frontpay remedy only because the trial court specifically linked it to the promotion timetables, and without prejudice to reinstatement of a new frontpay remedy if the trial court finds such a course appropriate on remand.

ber of studies considering the effects of particular employment practices.

Multiple regression is a form of statistical analysis used increasingly in Title VII actions that measures the discrete influence independent variables have on a dependent variable such as salary levels. See Valentino v. U.S. Postal Service, 674 F.2d 56, 70 (D.C.Cir.1982). Typically the independent variables in Title VII cases will be race, age, education level, and experience levels. The first step in a multiple regression analysis is specification of the independent (or explanatory) variables thought likely to affect significantly the dependent variable. The choice of proper explanatory variables determines the validity of the regression analysis. A coherent theory, devised prior to observation of the particular data, must be employed to select the relevant explanatory variables. See Vuyanich v. Republic Nat'l Bank of Dallas (Vuyanich I), 505 F.Supp. 224, 269 (N.D.Tex.1980), vacated on other grounds, 723 F.2d 1195 (5th Cir.1984). When the proper variables have been selected, the multiple regression analysis is conducted, generally by a computer. In essence, the regression measures the impact of each potential explanatory variable upon the dependent variable by holding all other explanatory variables constant. The analysis yields figures demonstrating how much of an observed disparity in salaries can be traced to race, as opposed to any of the other potential explanatory variables.

The computer analysis will generally also yield two other measurements that assist in evaluation of the explanatory power of the regression. The first is "T–Ratio." The T–Ratio measures the probability that the result obtained could have occurred by chance.[7] The second is R^2. The R^2 figure measures, to a certain extent, the degree to which a multiple regression analysis taken as a whole explains observed disparities in a dependent variable.

Having observed an average disparity in salary of about $3,000 between white and black special agents at DEA, plaintiffs' experts, Professors Bergmann and Straszheim,[8] formulated a regression analysis to discover whether and to what extent race explained the observed salary disparity. The experts based their analysis on a "human capital model." A widely accepted approach, the model builds on labor economists' findings that the human capital an employee brings to a job—such as education and experience—in large measure determines the employee's success. See Note, Beyond the Prima Facie Case in Employment Discrimination Law: Statistical Proof and Rebuttal, 89 Harv. L.Rev. 387, 408 n. 90 (1975); *Vuyanich I,* supra, 505 F.Supp. at 265–267.

---

7. The T–Ratio figure for a particular measure of race-related disparity corresponds to the number of standard deviations for that figure. D. Baldus & J. Cole, Statistical Proof of Discrimination 297 n. 14 (1980).

8. Professors Bergmann and Straszheim both hold Ph.D.'s and teach labor economics at the University of Maryland. Findings ¶ 6, 508 F.Supp. at 695.

Plaintiffs' experts selected education, prior federal experience, prior nonfederal experience, and race as the four independent variables that might explain the salary differential. Information regarding these independent variables came from the computerized JUNIPER personnel information tapes of the Department of Justice. Professors Bergmann and Straszheim then ran the regressions. They first evaluated the causes of salary disparities among all agents as of five dates: the first of January in 1975, 1976, 1977, and 1978 and the first of October in 1978. This study generated the following results:

DATE	RACE COEFFICIENT	T–RATIO
1/1/75	−$1,628	4.65
1/1/76	−$1,744	5.37
1/1/77	−$1,119	5.15
1/1/78	−$1,934	5.15
10/1/78	−$1,877	4.50

The race coefficient measures the salary disparities between white and black agents when education and prior experience are held constant. The T–Ratio figures here correspond to standard deviations of four or five. See D. Baldus & J. Cole, Statistical Proof of Discrimination 297 n. 14 (1980) (hereinafter "D. Baldus & J. Cole"). Since a standard deviation level higher than three indicates that the odds are less than one in a thousand that an observed result could have occurred by chance, these figures indicate that the odds are far less than one in a thousand that the observed disparities for any year could have occurred by chance. A study is generally considered to be statistically significant when the odds that the result occurred by chance are at best one in 20. See D. Baldus & J. Cole, supra, at 297.

Professors Bergmann and Straszheim then ran a second regression to measure salary disparities over the same time frame for agents hired after 1972. They intended this study to generate some measure of the effects of race discrimination at DEA after 1972. Title VII applies to DEA in this action only as of that date.[9] Because the first regression measured disparities in the salaries of all black agents, including those hired before 1972, the race coefficient in that study may have reflected disparities resulting from the continuing effects of discrimination that occurred prior to 1972, rather than actionable post–1972 discrimination. This second regression generated the following results:

9. Plaintiffs are subject to the statutory limit on the period of actionable discrimination; under Title VII liability may not accrue for a period of more than two years before the date of filing of an administrative complaint with the Equal Employment Opportunity Commission. In this case the actionable period began on July 15, 1972. Although not formally created until 1973, DEA was at its creation a consolidation of other federal agencies engaged in drug enforcement efforts, and agents serving these agencies became DEA agents.

DATE	RACE COEFFICIENT	T-RATIO
1/1/75	−$ 378	.84
1/1/76	−$1,864	2.54
1/1/77	−$1,119	3.18
1/1/78	−$ 866	2.07
10/1/78	−$1,026	2.30

Again a significant salary disparity between agents with comparable education and experience was revealed. The T-Ratios indicate that for every year, save 1975, the possibility that the result could have occurred by chance was at most one in 20. Though these figures are not at as high a level of significance as were those of the first regression, they still meet the generally accepted test for statistical significance. The second regression, moreover, tends to understate the amount of post-1972 discrimination at DEA. Because the post-1972 study measures discrimination among newer agents, the study focuses on the speed with which the new recruits make their way through the lower levels of DEA. Promotions at these levels are relatively automatic, and discrimination thus has less opportunity to work its effects. Discrimination will most adversely affect older agents contending for upper level positions; promotion decisions at these levels incorporate far more discretionary elements and leave more room for bias. The study does not measure any post-1972 discrimination against those hired before 1972. Since these agents would have been the ones contending for the upper level positions during the time frame studied, they would have been the ones on whom discrimination would have been most likely to operate. The problem is particularly severe with respect to the 1975 race coefficient. Almost half of those studied to obtain this figure were hired in 1974. Since they were in their first year at the time of the study, they would not yet have been eligible for a grade promotion.

Having uncovered evidence of significant discrimination in salary levels, plaintiffs' experts undertook a more exacting inquiry into DEA's employment practices to pinpoint where discrimination was taking place. They first examined DEA's initial grade assignment practices. Through regression analyses they determined at a sufficient level of statistical significance that blacks were 16 percent less likely than comparably qualified whites to have been hired at GS-9 rather than GS-7. For those hired after 1972, blacks were 12 percent less likely to be hired at GS-9. The experts then evaluated work assignments, supervisory evaluations, and discipline. In all three categories statistical analysis revealed significant levels of discrimination against black agents. Finally, plaintiffs' experts studied promotions at DEA. Promotions up to the GS-11 level were found to be relatively automatic. The promotion rate from GS-11 to GS-12 was 70 percent for blacks and 82 percent for whites. This differential met generally accepted levels of statistical significance. Differentials in promotion rates for positions above GS-12 were also found, but—largely because of the small sample size—these differentials did not achieve statistical significance at generally accepted levels.

To buttress the statistical proof plaintiffs introduced anecdotal testimony of discrimination. This evidence consisted of accounts by several black agents of perceived discrimination against them in initial grade assignments, work assignments, supervisory evaluations, and discipline. These agents also testified about their general perceptions of racial hostility at DEA.

2. *Defendant DEA's case.* DEA responded to plaintiffs' case in several ways. The rebuttal consisted of expert testimony attacking the methodological integrity and explanatory value of plaintiffs' statistics, alternative statistical analyses tending to show an absence of discrimination, testimonial evidence concerning DEA's equal employment opportunity programs, and cross-examination of plaintiffs' anecdotal accounts of individual discrimination

* * *

Testimonial evidence buttressed DEA's statistical rebuttal. DEA presented extensive general testimony on its efforts to establish equal opportunity programs and implement equal opportunity goals at the agency. Through cross-examination of plaintiffs' witnesses, DEA also sought to rebut every particular anecdotal account of discrimination.

The District Court Decision

1. *The liability determination.* Judge Robinson held that DEA had discriminated against black special agents in violation of Title VII across a range of employment practices. The court found that the salary differentials between white and black agents were a result of race discrimination, and that DEA had discriminated against black agents in grade-at-entry, work assignments, supervisory evaluations, and promotions. The finding of discrimination in promotions extended to promotions above the GS–12 level, even though the court did not credit plaintiffs' statistical evidence of discrimination at that level because the statistics had not achieved acceptable levels of statistical significance. The court based its finding of discrimination at the upper levels on inferences from proven discrimination at the immediately preceding levels and discrimination in the factors that bear most directly on promotions (work assignments, evaluations, and discipline).

To make these determinations the District Court credited the bulk of plaintiffs' statistical evidence [10] and rejected both DEA's critique of this evidence and DEA's alternative statistics. * * *

2. *The remedies determination.* Having found pervasive discrimination at DEA, the District Court—in a separate remedial proceeding—set out to formulate an appropriate remedial plan.[11] The essential

---

10. The court did, however, refuse to credit most of plaintiffs' anecdotal accounts of specific instances of discrimination. Findings ¶ 51d, 508 F.Supp. at 710.

11. DEA sought at the remedial hearing to introduce its own regression analy-

ses. These regressions purportedly showed an absence of race-related disparity at DEA. The District Court rejected this proffered evidence of DEA's nonliability as untimely.

elements of the plan were class-wide backpay, promotion goals and timetables, and class-wide frontpay.

Class-wide Backpay. Rather than order individualized relief hearings, see Int'l Brhd. of Teamsters v. United States, the District Court ordered a class-wide award of backpay for members of the plaintiff class. For successive one-year periods beginning in July 1972, a class-wide backpay pool figure would be calculated. The calculations would derive from plaintiffs' first salary regression study (which measured disparities among all agents including those hired before 1972). For every year for which figures were available—1975 to 1979—the class-wide pool figure would be the race coefficient multiplied by the number of black special agents. For the years before 1975 and after 1979 the race coefficient would be derived by extrapolating backward and forward from the available figures, and this extrapolated coefficient would be multiplied by the number of black agents.

The annual backpay pool would be distributed evenly among eligible black agents. Only agents above the GS–9 level during the year in question were made eligible. The court excluded agents at GS–7 and GS–9 because most discrimination was found to occur at the higher levels of DEA. The court did, however, permit individual plaintiffs to come forward and seek backpay for discrimination suffered in initial grade assignment (viz. assignment to GS–7 instead of GS–9). Any such individual awards would be subtracted from the class-wide pool in order to prevent double liability.

Promotion Goals and Timetables. Finding discrimination at the upper levels of DEA, the District Court ordered remedial promotion goals and timetables. Since black agents made up at least 10 percent of agents at every level through GS–12 the court held that a 10 percent goal was appropriate for all levels above GS–12. To meet this goal the court ordered DEA to promote one black agent for every two white agents until 10 percent black representation had been met at GS–13 and above (or until five years had passed).

Class-wide Frontpay. To compensate black agents awaiting promotion under the goals and timetables plan the court established a class-wide frontpay formula. Frontpay pool calculations were also based on extrapolations from the salary regression, but the pool was to be adjusted to reflect progress DEA had made under the promotions goals and timetables. The pool was to be distributed to all black agents at GS–12 for at least two years and all black agents above GS–12.

3. *Other issues.* In the course of the proceeding two other issues arose. Plaintiffs sought and were refused an award of prejudgment interest on the backpay awards. Also, during the time between the liability and remedial determinations the court issued a preliminary injunction barring demotion or transfer of black special agent Carl Jackson. Shortly after Jackson had testified at trial in this case he became the target of harassment and eventually of adverse employment actions including demotion and transfer. The District Court

concluded that there was a high likelihood that these actions were in retaliation for Jackson's testimony, and therefore preliminarily enjoined Jackson's demotion or transfer.

[The Court's analysis of the district court's liability determination is omitted.]

II.　The Remedies Determination

Section 706(g) of Title VII empowers a court that has found illegal discrimination to "order such affirmative action as may be appropriate, which may include, but is not limited to, reinstatement or hiring of employees, with or without back pay * * * or any other equitable relief as the court deems appropriate." * * *

Having found pervasive discrimination at DEA, the District Court fashioned a tripartite remedial scheme: class-wide backpay for those at GS–11 and above,[35] promotion goals and timetables at DEA's upper levels, and class-wide frontpay for those at GS–11 and above. DEA raises three challenges to these remedies. First, the class-wide backpay award impermissibly circumvents the individualized remedial hearings required by *Teamsters,* supra. Second, the backpay award compensates for nonactionable pre–1972 discrimination. Third, the promotion goals and timetables exceed the court's remedial authority under Section 706(g) and violate the equal protection component of the Fifth Amendment to the Constitution.

A.　*Individualized Hearings*

DEA objects to the District Court's decision to forego in this case the individualized relief hearings prescribed in *Teamsters,* supra. The gravamen of DEA's objection is that class-wide relief may benefit some black agents who were not victims of illegal discrimination. The Court in *Teamsters* stated that when plaintiffs seek relief as "victims of the discriminatory practice, a district court must usually conduct additional proceedings after the liability phase of the trial to determine the scope of individual relief." In the wake of *Teamsters* individualized hearings have been common features of Title VII class actions. See, e.g., McKenzie v. Sawyer, 684 F.2d 62, 75 (D.C.Cir.1982).

Though *Teamsters* certainly raises a presumption in favor of individualized hearings, the case should not be read as an unyielding limit on a court's equitable power to fashion effective relief for proven discrimination.[36] The language of *Teamsters* is not so inflexible; after

---

35. Finding most discrimination took place at GS–11 and above, the court did not order classwide relief for discrimination against black agents at GS–7 or GS–9 during any given backpay year. The court did, however, permit these agents to bring individual claims for relief. Any individual awards at these levels are to be deducted from the class-wide backpay pool distributed to agents at GS–11 and above.

36. McKenzie v. Sawyer, 684 F.2d 62 (D.C.Cir.1982), does not mandate individual hearings in every case. The panel in *Sawyer* affirmed a District Court's decision to require individual relief hearings. When, in an exercise of its remedial discretion, a trial court orders hearings, an appellate court is properly reluctant to interfere with that judgment. But the appellate

stating that individual hearings are "usually" required, *Teamsters,* supra, the Court went on to note that "[i]n determining the specific remedies to be afforded, a district court is 'to fashion such relief as the particular circumstances of a case may require to effect restitution.' " Later courts have often faced situations in which the *Teamsters* hearing preference had to bend to accommodate Title VII's remedial purposes. Primarily, courts have not required hearings when discrimination has so percolated through an employment system that any attempt to reconstruct individual employment histories would drag the court into "a quagmire of hypothetical judgments."

Applying these principles to the present controversy, we note at the outset that the District Court did not rush willy-nilly to impose class-wide relief. The court specifically ordered individual relief hearings where feasible. All claims of backpay for discrimination at levels below GS–11 will be resolved in individualized hearings. At these levels individualized hearings are appropriate because a small number of discernible decisions as to initial grade assignment and promotions will be in issue for each agent. These determinations are akin to those in *Teamsters,* where the required hearings were to involve a single determination as to whether individual plaintiffs had applied and were qualified for particular line driver positions in the trucking industry.

After careful consideration, the District Court here ordered class-wide relief only for discrimination above GS–11. The court had found that discrimination impeded black agents at every turn; blacks faced extra hurdles in DEA's initial grade assignments, work assignments, supervisory evaluations, imposition of discipline, and promotions. At the higher levels the cumulative effect of these pervasive discriminatory practices became severe, and the increased subjectivity in evaluations gave discrimination more room to work its effects. In such a situation "exact reconstruction of each individual claimant's work history, as if discrimination had not occurred, is not only imprecise but impractical." *Pettway,* supra, 494 F.2d at 262. The District Court here specifically found that "[e]ach major criterion in the promotion process at DEA was tainted by discrimination, making discrimination in the promotion process cumulative. Any attempt to recreate the employment histories of individual employees absent discrimination would result in mere guesswork." Our role in reviewing this determination is limited. "The framing of a remedial decree is left largely in the hands of the district judge, whose assessment of the needs of the situation is a factual judgment reviewable only for clear error * * *." McKenzie v. Sawyer, supra, 684 F.2d at 75.

We perceive no error in the District Court's finding that it would be impossible to reconstruct the employment histories of DEA's senior black agents. Examination of discrete promotion decisions, as difficult

panel in *Sawyer* was not faced with a trial court's decision that individual hearings would effectively preclude relief for most members of the plaintiff class. Thus, *Saw-*yer's reiteration of the *Teamsters* hearing preference should not be taken as implying that class-wide relief in the present context would be improper.

as even that might be, will not suffice. The decisive criteria for promotions decisions—supervisory evaluations, breadth of experience, and disciplinary history—were themselves found to be tainted with illegal discrimination. The court found that discrimination had skewed evaluations of black agents, but the court could have had no way of knowing how much more favorable a particular agent's evaluation should have been, or how a fair evaluation might have affected the agent's chances for obtaining a particular promotion. Similarly, the court found that discrimination in work assignments—leaving black agents with a disproportionately large share of undercover assignments—had impeded black agents in promotions, but the court could have had no way to divine what other broadening experiences a particular agent might have had, and no way to gauge how this hypothetical additional experience would have affected particular promotion decisions. And though the court found that black agents have been disciplined more frequently and more severely than white agents committing similar infractions, the court could have had no way of knowing exactly what effect the disproportionate disciplinary sanctions had on a particular agent's chances for particular promotions. Finally, because promotions at DEA are cumulative, the effects of discrimination in promotions are also cumulative. Denial of promotion to one grade affects the agent's eligibility for later promotions to higher grades.

To require individualized hearings in these circumstances would be to deny relief to the bulk of DEA's black agents despite a finding of pervasive discrimination against them. In effect, DEA would have us preclude relief unless the remedial order is perfectly tailored to award relief only to those injured and only in the exact amount of their injury. Though Section 706(g) generally does not allow for backpay to those whom discrimination has not injured, this section should not be read as requiring effective denial of backpay to the large numbers of agents whom DEA's discrimination has injured in order to account for the risk that a small number of undeserving individuals might receive backpay. Such a result cannot be squared with what the Supreme Court has told us about the nature of a court's remedial authority under Title VII. "[T]he scope of a district court's remedial powers under Title VII is determined by the purposes of the Act." A core purpose of Title VII is "to make persons whole for injuries suffered on account of unlawful employment discrimination." *Albemarle Paper Co.,* supra. "[F]ederal courts are empowered to fashion such relief as the particular circumstances require to effect restitution, making whole insofar as possible the victims of racial discrimination * * *." *Franks,* supra; accord *Albemarle Paper Co.,* supra, (the District Courts have "not merely the power but the duty to render a decree which will so far as possible eliminate the discriminatory effects of the past as well as bar like discrimination in the future"); *Teamsters,* supra. The trial court found that the particular circumstances of this case required classwide relief for black agents at GS–11 and above to ensure that they were made whole for the pervasive discrimination they have suffered. If effective relief for the victims of discrimination necessarily entails the risk that a few nonvictims might also benefit from the relief, then the employer, as a proven discriminator, must bear that risk. See Stewart v. General Motors Corp., supra, 542 F.2d at 452–453.

B. *The Allegation of Class-wide Overcompensation*

In calculating the backpay pool the District Court used the race coefficient of the first of plaintiffs' two salary regressions as the measure of average discrimination per agent. The first regression measured discrimination against all black agents, including those hired before 1972. This study may therefore have reflected the continuing effects of some discrimination occurring prior to 1972. Since the actionable period in this case commenced on July 15, 1972, use of the first regression might, according to DEA's argument, amount to compensation for some nonactionable discrimination.[37] Though the remedial order specifically states that backpay begins to accrue only as of July 15, 1972, DEA argues that a portion of the disparities between black and white agents as of that time (and thereafter) was caused by discrimination before 1972, and that DEA is therefore not liable for that portion.

The District Court found in the Liability Determination that "while pre–1972 discrimination may have affected the statistics * * *, post 1972 discrimination largely contributed to those statistics." The court also noted in the Remedial Order that plaintiffs' regressions "provide an accurate measure of the extent to which blacks at DEA were paid less than comparably qualified whites [and] * * * provide an appropriate basis for classwide relief." We are reluctant to disturb the trial court's finding on this factual issue. See McKenzie v. Sawyer, supra, 684 F.2d at 75. Nonetheless on the record as it now stands, we cannot affirm the District Court's decision to use the first regression as a basis for calculating the backpay pool.

Although the court properly found that the plaintiff's evidence sufficed to support an inference of actionable discrimination, the court's reliance on the first regression to determine backpay is problematic. The court never found that *all* of that regression's race coefficient reflected actionable post–1972 discrimination.[38] To do so the court

---

37. DEA also makes an argument that use of the first salary regression overcompensates plaintiffs based on the R^2 values for this study. DEA argues that, because the R^2 value was roughly .50, only about half of the race coefficient for the years in question actually represents race-related disparity. This argument reveals a basic misunderstanding of the meaning of R^2 figures. An R^2 of .50 does not mean that only half of the race coefficient is attributable to race. Rather, it means that half of the total salary disparity between black and white agents is attributable to the totality of the factors examined in the regression. See generally Fisher, Multiple Regression in Legal Proceedings, 80 Colum.L.Rev. 702,720 (1980). In any event, R^2 is far from a wholly reliable measure of a study's accuracy. For these reasons, we hold that DEA's objection based on R^2 values is without force.

38. Of course, the court need not have found that all of the discrimination reflected in the regression occurred after 1972 in order to find the regression suffi-

would have had to find either that all discrimination reflected in the salary disparities occurred after 1972 or that the small portion of "continuing effects" of pre–1972 discrimination reflected in the disparities was the result of a "continuing violation." The court made neither finding, and having found in the Liability Determination that pre–1972 discrimination had been "neither admitted nor proven," the court cannot plausibly rely on a continuing violation theory in the Remedial Order as grounds for using the first salary regression as a benchmark for the backpay pool.

It may be that plaintiffs' first regression does reflect only post–1972 discrimination. DEA's complete failure to present evidence showing pre–1972 discrimination in the regression certainly supports this view. It may also be that the portion of the disparity that reflects continuing effects of pre–1972 discrimination might be actionable on a continuing violation theory. Or it may be that the small amount of continuing effects cannot plausibly be factored out of the study; if so, and if no more precise methods of ascertaining the amount of actionable discrimination are reasonably available to the court, the court would be faced with using either a mildly overcompensatory formula based on the first regression or a significantly undercompensatory formula based on the second regression. Use of the first regression under these circumstances might be permissible.

We cannot, however, resolve these matters on the present appeal. As the Supreme Court stressed in Lehman v. Trout, supra, 465 U.S. at 1060, 104 S.Ct. at 1407, this court must scrupulously respect the factfinding prerogative of the District Court. In this case the District Court has not yet determined whether the first regression reflects only post–1972 discrimination, whether a continuing violation occurred that might permit compensation for whatever continuing effects the regression reflects, or whether the small portion of nonactionable continuing effects that might be reflected in the regression cannot be factored out. On remand, if the District Court is unable to find that any of these three factual circumstances exists, the court must devise a new backpay formula.

C. *Promotion Goals and Timetables*

The District Court ordered that one black be promoted for every two whites to positions above GS–12 at DEA until blacks made up 10 percent of all agents at each grade above GS–12 or until five years after the order was entered. DEA objects to this aspect of the remedy for the same reason that it objects to class-wide backpay: some individual agents might receive promotions they do not deserve. DEA argues that promotion goals and timetables exceed a court's remedial power under Title VII unless every person who potentially benefits from the relief has been individually shown to have been discriminatorily denied a specific promotion. According to DEA, Section 706(g) mandates this

cient to make out a prima facie case of actionable discrimination. See Part II–B– 1–b; Valentino v. U.S. Postal Service, 674 F.2d 56, 71 n. 26 (D.C.Cir.1982).

result. ("No order of the court shall require the * * * promotion of an individual as an employee, * * * if such individual was refused * * * advancement * * * for any reason other than discrimination * * *."). DEA also argues that such goals and timetables violate the equal protection component of the Fifth Amendment to the Constitution.

Though DEA's claims are not without some superficial appeal, Section 706(g) must not be read as requiring an exact fit between those whom an employer's discrimination has victimized and those eligible under promotion goals and timetables. The language on which DEA relies was aimed at ensuring that Title VII was not read as giving courts authority to remedy racial imbalance as an evil in itself, i.e., absent any finding that illegal discrimination caused the imbalance. See EEOC v. AT & T, 556 F.2d 167, 175 (3d Cir.1977), cert. denied, 438 U.S. 915, 98 S.Ct. 3145, 57 L.Ed.2d 1161 (1978). The language should not be stretched to support a requirement of absolute precision in fashioning promotion goals and timetables when such a requirement would frustrate effective relief for those who were victimized by discrimination.[39] Every federal Court of Appeals in this nation has approved remedial use of goals and timetables without requiring that each and every potentially eligible person be shown to have been a victim of discrimination. Nor can the imposition of quotas to remedy proven discrimination be said to violate the Constitution's guarantees of equal protection. Whatever the current status of affirmative action absent a finding of discrimination, the Supreme Court has made clear that such relief is not unconstitutional when used to remedy proven discrimination. See Swann v. Charlotte–Mecklenburg School District, 402 U.S. 1, 91 S.Ct. 1267, 28 L.Ed.2d 554 (1971); Bakke v. Board of Regents of the University of California, 438 U.S. 265, 302, 98 S.Ct. 2733, 2754, 57 L.Ed.2d 750 (1978) (Powell, J., concurring); id. at 363–386, 98 S.Ct. at 2785–2797 (Brennan, White, Marshall and Blackmun, JJ, concurring).

Nonetheless promotion goals and timetables—even if as admirably crafted as those at issue here—must be used cautiously. Such relief intrudes into the structure of employment relations and may at times upset the legitimate promotion expectations of individuals in the majority group. We must take a careful look at the District Court's decision to use goals and timetables in this case.

---

39. DEA has amassed an array of quotes from Title VII's legislative history in support of its contention that promotion goals and timetables are invalid if they benefit any individuals who are not proven victims of discrimination. See reply brief for appellants at 20–22. Many in Congress spoke in 1964, and again in 1972 when Title VII was amended, to assure wavering supporters that Title VII could not be applied to grant preferences for those who were not victims of discrimination. These statements are, however, inapposite to the question before us in this case. Those in Congress who made such statements were not considering the issue whether in affording relief for proven discrimination against a broad class some individual non-victims might benefit in order to ensure that all actual victims benefitted. Rather, these statements were made with reference to the question whether Title VII could be used as a mandate to correct overall racial imbalance in an employer's workforce when such an imbalance had not been shown to be the result of discrimination.

We are persuaded that the District Court's order that one black be promoted for every two whites to positions above GS–12 was not appropriate. Strict goals and timetables should not be imposed when "alternative, equally effective methods could * * * supplant resort to a quota." Thompson v. Sawyer, supra, 678 F.2d at 294. The District Court did not consider whether less severe remedies might prove equally efficacious in this case. We therefore vacate the District Court's imposition of goals and timetables, and remand for additional consideration of the propriety of such remedies in this case.

In determining whether less severe remedies might prove equally effective the court must evaluate the likelihood that the employer will implement the remedy in good faith. One important indicia is the employer's past behavior in implementing equal opportunity programs, either voluntarily or in response to court order. This court has some doubt that DEA's past record on equal employment opportunity warrants application of strict goals and timetables. DEA has not been before this court in the past on identical or related claims of discrimination, and thus has not shown any recalcitrance in remedying discrimination pursuant to court order. Nor does DEA's overall approach to equal employment matters lead us to conclude that DEA will be unlikely to remedy the proven discrimination in promotions once this court orders it to do so. The record contains significant uncontradicted evidence of DEA's institutional good faith in implementing equal employment opportunity programs. Of course, the determination of appropriate relief is for the District Court in the first instance. We also vacate the District Court's order of class-wide frontpay because the frontpay order was premised on the existence of promotion goals and timetables. The District Court is free to impose a new frontpay order on remand if it deems one appropriate.

On remand we encourage the District Court to consider other remedial options to ensure that black agents attain their rightful places at the upper levels of DEA. We note in particular that a promotion bottleneck appears to exist at the GS–12 level. While black agents manage to arrive at this level eventually, few progress beyond this point. In remedying promotion discrimination at this point and at all levels, the court is of course free to establish promotion guidelines and to monitor DEA's progress in meeting those guidelines, or to fashion any other appropriate relief.

* * *

[The Court affirmed the district court's grant of a preliminary injunction barring the demotion and transfer of Special Agent Jackson. The Court reasoned that irreparable harm would follow from a refusal to grant such relief because other class members would be deterred from coming forward with claims at the relief stage. The district court's denial of prejudgment interest was also affirmed on the ground that sovereign immunity barred such an award against the federal government. See, supra, n. 4. The concurring opinion of Judge Edwards is omitted.]

NOTES AND PROBLEMS FOR DISCUSSION

1. Courts have consistently held that difficulty in calculating back pay is not a ground for denying such relief altogether. See, e.g., Pettway v. American Cast Iron Pipe Co., 494 F.2d 211 (5th Cir.1974), cert. denied, 439 U.S. 1115, 99 S.Ct. 1020, 59 L.Ed.2d 74 (1979) (*Pettway III*); Salinas v. Roadway Express, Inc., 735 F.2d 1574, 1578 (5th Cir.1984), cert. denied, 479 U.S. 1103, 107 S.Ct. 1335, 94 L.Ed.2d 185 (1987). In a much-quoted section of *Pettway III,* the Fifth Circuit stated, "in computing a back pay award two principles are lucid: (1) unrealistic exactitude is not required, (2) uncertainties in determining what an employee would have earned but for the discrimination, should be resolved against the discriminating employer." 494 F.2d at 260–61. But does this reasoning justify the decision in *Segar* not to individualize the relief determinations? Was not the DEA entitled to show that particular class members would not have been promoted by introduction of objective evidence of their poor job performance? Despite the preference expressed in TEAMSTERS v. UNITED STATES, *supra,* for individualized Stage II proceedings, courts have often adopted class-wide formulas for providing relief. See, e.g., Domingo v. New England Fish Co., 742 F.2d 520 (9th Cir.1984); *Pettway* III, *supra* ; EEOC v. Chicago Minature Lamp Works, 668 F.Supp. 1150 (N.D.Ill.1987).

2. The "goals and timetables" type of affirmative relief will often impact on the employment opportunities of incumbent employees and of non-class applicants for employment. Is that why the injunctive part of the district court's order in *Segar* was vacated? In McKenzie v. Sawyer, 684 F.2d 62 (D.C.Cir.1982), a class action against the United States Government Printing Office, the court found that the defendant had engaged in a prolonged history of racial discrimination in hiring and promotional decisions. To address the continuing effects of that discrimination the court imposed on the defendant goals and timetables for promotion of members of the plaintiff class similar to those adopted in *Segar.* In order to insure that the defendant would meet its goals, the court ordered mandatory selection rates for certain positions: 80% of the vacancies were to be filled with members of the plaintiff class. Implementation of the order eventually resulted in a class member who was not on the list of those "best qualified" for a position being promoted over non-minority employees who were among those "best qualified" for the position. The defendant appealed and the Court of Appeals reversed.

> Title VII remedies are to be designed and enforced with appropriate attention to the interests of nonvictim employees—in the words of this court, 'with care to see that they wound as little as possible.' (quoting Thompson v. Sawyer, 678 F.2d 257, 293 (D.C.Cir.1982) The need for flexible enforcement of employment goals is at its maximum when the legitimate interests of third-party employees are at stake. Here when the district court saw that the promotional goals of its final order might not be realized in a timely fashion—for reasons involving no bad faith on the part of the governmental defendant—it was obliged to countenance some delay in their attainment before it could adopt additional remedial measures that would increase the burden borne by other employees whose opportunities for promotion had already been curtailed during the long journey toward nondiscriminatory employment.

McKenzie v. Kennickell, 825 F.2d 429 (D.C.Cir.1987), affirmed, 875 F.2d 330 (D. D.C.1989). Should it matter whether the class member who benefitted from implementation of the order was himself the victim of discrimination? The subject of "bumping" and other effects of injunctive relief on non-party employees is discussed in Section B of this Chapter, *supra*. In connection with *Segar* and *McKenzie* consider the Supreme Court's opinions in FRANKS v. BOWMAN TRANSPORTATION CO., *supra*, and MARTIN v. WILKS, *supra*.

3. The hiring "goals and timetables" ordered by the district court in *Segar* were designed to cure one of the effects of the DEA's discrimination, the absence of black agents above the rank of GS–12. As the Court of Appeals recognizes, some of the beneficiaries of such affirmative relief would be agents who had not actually been hurt by discrimination just as some of the recipients of back pay would not be victims of discrimination. The government's objections to non-victim relief were disposed of with the statement that "such relief is not unconstitutional when used to remedy proven discrimination." The justification for and problems surrounding "affirmative action" plans are explored in Chapter Part IV, *infra*.

Part III

OTHER FEDERAL ANTI–DISCRIMINATION LEGISLATION

Chapter 8

THE RECONSTRUCTION CIVIL RIGHTS ACTS— 42 U.S.C. §§ 1981, 1983, 1985(C)

SECTION A. THE CIVIL RIGHTS ACT OF 1866— 42 U.S.C. § 1981

REISS, REQUIEM FOR AN "INDEPENDENT REMEDY": THE CIVIL RIGHTS ACTS OF 1866 AND 1871 AS REMEDIES FOR EMPLOYMENT DISCRIMINATION

50 So.Cal.L.Rev. 961, 971–974 (1977).

* * *

In 1865, with the ratification of the thirteenth amendment, Congress obtained authority to pass laws designed to eradicate slavery and its incidents. The Civil Rights Act of 1866 [46] was enacted pursuant to that authority. Section 1 furthered two goals: first, it granted citizenship to all persons born in the United States; and second, it granted those persons the same rights as white citizens. There was some question at the time whether the thirteenth amendment authorized legislation this broad. These doubts, coupled with fears that the Act could easily be repealed in the future, constituted part of the impetus

---

[46.] Act of Apr. 9, 1866, ch. 31, § 1, 14 Stat. 27. Section 1 of the Civil Rights Act of 1866 provided:

That all persons born in the United States and not subject to any foreign power, excluding Indians not taxed, *are* hereby declared to be *citizens* of the United States; *and such citizens,* of every race and color, without regard to any previous condition of slavery or involuntary servitude, except as a punishment for crime whereof the party shall have been duly convicted, *shall have the same right,* in every State and Territory in the United States, *to make and enforce contracts, to sue, be parties, and give evi-*

dence, to inherit, purchase, lease, sell, hold, and convey real and personal property, *and to full and equal benefit of all laws and proceedings for the security of person and property, as is enjoyed by white citizens, and shall be subject to like punishment, pains, and penalties, and to none other,* any law, statute, ordinance, regulation, or custom, to the contrary notwithstanding.

14 Stat. 27 (1866) (emphasis added). The italicized portion is similar to, though not identical with, § 1981. The portion dealing with property rights is similar to what is now 42 U.S.C. § 1982.

for the subsequent adoption of the fourteenth amendment in 1868. Two years later, Congress reenacted the 1866 Act with only a minor change in wording, removing any doubts concerning its constitutionality. Years later, as part of a general recodification of federal law, the original section 1 was split into two separate statutes—sections 1981 and 1982. Section 1982 grants all persons the same *property* rights as white citizens, while section 1981 involves *other* rights, including the right to make and enforce contracts. Courts have held that the right "to make and enforce contracts" on an equal basis, referred to in section 1981, includes the right to enter into and enforce *employment* contracts. Thus, section 1981 prohibits discriminatory employment practices in recruitment, hiring, compensation, assignment, promotion, layoff, and discharge of employees.

* * *

* * * Although section 1981, by its terms, would seem to prohibit a broad range of *private* as well as public acts of discrimination, courts have narrowly construed the statute throughout most of its history. In 1883, in the *Civil Rights Cases,* the Supreme Court struck down other civil rights legislation which prohibited discrimination in public accommodations. The Court reasoned that Congress lacked the constitutional authority to reach wholly *private* conduct. Although the Civil Rights Act of 1866 was not directly involved in that case, the Court indicated that the statute should also be limited to situations involving state action. In 1948 the Court expressly declared that "governmental action" was required in a suit based on the Civil Rights Act of 1866.[54]

More than one hundred years after passage of the statute, the Supreme Court, in Jones v. Alfred H. Mayer Co.,[55] finally dispensed with the state action requirement and held that the Civil Rights Act of 1866 reached purely private acts of discrimination. While Jones v. Mayer involved the application of section 1982, it was immediately apparent that the rationale of the decision applied equally to section 1981. Following Jones v. Mayer, section 1981 was increasingly used by plaintiffs, in addition to Title VII, to attack discriminatory employment practices in the private sector. In each instance where a court of appeals had the opportunity to rule on the question, the court held that section 1981 did provide the basis for an independent federal cause of action against racial discrimination in employment. Finally, in Johnson v. Railway Express Agency, Inc.,[57] the Supreme Court affirmed that view. Courts have held section 1981 applicable not only to discrimination by private employers, but also to discrimination by labor unions. In other contexts, not directly involving employment, courts have held section 1981 applicable to contracts involving the purchase of tickets to an amusement park, the admission of patients to a private hospital,

54. Hurd v. Hodge, 334 U.S. 24, 31, 68 S.Ct. 847, 851, 92 L.Ed. 1187 (1948).

55. 392 U.S. 409, 88 S.Ct. 2186, 20 L.Ed.2d 1189 (1968).

57. 421 U.S. 454, 95 S.Ct. 1716, 44 L.Ed.2d 295 (1975).

membership in private clubs, and, most recently, attendance in private schools. Thus, in the private sector, the coverage of section 1981 is at least as broad as the coverage of Title VII. In fact, it is certainly broader.

Title VII has always applied to employers and unions whose "operations affect commerce," if of a minimum size. The original minimum of one hundred members or employees has been reduced to fifteen. Section 1981 contains no statutory minimum, simply providing that "all persons * * * shall have the same right * * * to make and enforce contracts * * * as * * * white citizens." While it is not likely that all enterprises employing fewer than fifteen employees will be covered by section 1981,[66] the statute clearly does extend its protection to millions of workers in millions of small business establishments not covered by Title VII.

* * *

Read 42 U.S.C. § 1981 at p. 1261–1262.

As noted in the preceding excerpt, since 1968 (the date of the Supreme Court's decision in Jones v. Alfred Mayer), the broad "right to make and enforce contracts" language of § 1981 had been interpreted to encompass employment contracts, thereby subjecting a wide range of employment decisions to the requirements of the 1866 Act. In 1989, however, the Supreme Court revisited the fundamental question of the scope of the antidiscrimination principle contained within § 1981. In PATTERSON v. MCLEAN CREDIT UNION, 491 U.S. 164, 109 S.Ct. 2363, 105 L.Ed.2d 132 (1989), the Court, while reaffirming its previously stated position that § 1981 prohibited discrimination in the making and enforcement of *private* contracts, dramatically reversed decades of jurisprudence through its interpretation of the "right to make and enforce contracts" language of § 1981. The five member majority, over a stinging dissent, declared that the right to "make" contracts referred only to discriminatory conduct associated with the formation of a contractual relationship. It did not extend, the Court continued, to conduct occurring after the formation of the contractual relation, such

---

66. At the far end of the size spectrum, small employment relationships can include not only family businesses, small partnerships, and sole proprietorships, but also the hiring of babysitters, live-in caretakers, and the like. It is simply not likely that all such employment relationships will be covered by § 1981. Two techniques are available for judicially establishing such limits: statutory construction and constitutional analysis. Courts may conclude either that § 1981 was not intended to reach certain of these very small, associational relationships or that the Constitution prohibits such regulation, regardless of Congress' intent. The Supreme Court has, to date, avoided reaching a decision on this question. In Sullivan v. Little Hunting Park, Inc., 396 U.S. 229, 90 S.Ct. 400, 24 L.Ed.2d 386 (1969), and Tillman v. Wheaton–Haven Recreation Ass'n, Inc., 410 U.S. 431, 93 S.Ct. 1090, 35 L.Ed.2d 403 (1973), the district courts had refused to apply § 1981 to "bona fide private clubs." The Supreme Court avoided deciding whether such an exemption existed, and if it did, whence it derived, by holding instead that the two organizations did not qualify as private clubs under Title II of the Civil Rights Act of 1964. More recently, in Runyon v. McCrary, 427 U.S. 160, 96 S.Ct. 2586, 49 L.Ed.2d 415 (1976), the Court again skirted the issue of whether § 1981 covered small, "truly private" schools.

as a breach of the terms of the contract or the imposition of discriminatory working conditions. Such postformation conduct involving the performance of contractual obligations did not invoke the right to "make" a contract and, therefore, was not governed by § 1981. Rather, the Court continued, these claims were more naturally subject to challenge under state contract law and Title VII. The majority also rejected dissenting Justice Brennan's suggestion that postformation conduct could be so severe or pervasive as to establish that the contract was not entered into in a nondiscriminatory manner. This type of discriminatory postformation conduct, according to the majority, could only be used by the plaintiff as evidence that a divergence in some discrete term of the contract was motivated by racial animus at the time of contract formation. As for the right to "enforce" contracts, the Court ruled that this guarantee embraced only the right of access to the legal process to enforce contractual obligations. Accordingly, this portion of § 1981 was construed to proscribe only conduct that impairs an individual's ability to enforce contractual rights through the legal process.

The plaintiff in *Patterson* asserted two claims under § 1981. She alleged that she had been the victim of racial harassment and that she had been denied a promotion on the basis of race. Since the alleged harassment involved postformation conduct relating to the terms and conditions of her continued employment, the Court concluded that this claim was not cognizable under § 1981. The promotion claim, however, was, in the Court's view "a different matter". A denial of a promotion, the Court reasoned, could constitute a denial of the right to "make" a contract where the promotion would have created a new and distinct relationship between the parties, i.e., where it would have presented the opportunity to enter into a new contractual relationship. Accordingly, while the harassment claim was dismissed, the promotion claim was remanded for further proceedings.

The ruling in *Patterson* generated an avalanche of lower court rulings in which the courts struggled to apply this new construction of the statute to a wide variety of situations. While *Patterson* clearly indicated that certain claims—such as harassment and discharge—did not invoke the right to "make" a contract, many other scenarios arose that presented trial and appellate courts with opportunities to engage their ingenuity and imagination in efforts to avoid what often was perceived as an unduly restrictive interpretation of the statute. For example, could a discharged employee successfully claim that the employer's refusal to rehire him after his discharge constituted a refusal to "make" a contract? What about an employee who claims that he was not recalled from a layoff because of his race? How do you treat employees at will who do not have a contract with the employer? Does § 1981 support a claim that the plaintiff was retaliated against because of his protests against the employer's discriminatory refusal to enter into a contractual relationship with a third party? Could retaliation implicate the right to "enforce" the contract? If so, must the retaliation have been undertaken in response to the plaintiff's efforts at enforcing contractual, as opposed to statutory rights? When does the denial of a promotion impair the ability to enter into a new contractual relationship? In making this determination, should it matter whether the position also was open to nonemployee applicants (who surely could allege that they were denied the right to "make" a contract) or whether it was restricted to incumbent employees? Does § 1981 apply to racially-based demotions? And where a company is sold and the successor owner chooses not to retain an employee on the basis of race, has the employee been denied the right to "make" a contract?

The confusion and uncertainty generated by the ruling in *Patterson* was matched by the widespread condemnation it received in the academic and legislative communities. Along with several other decisions rendered during its 1989 term, *Patterson* served as a launching pad for the ultimate enactment of the Civil Rights Act of 1991. In the first substantive provision of the statute, § 101, Congress emphatically reversed the decision in *Patterson* by amending § 1981 to include new subsection "(b)". This provision defines the phrase "make and enforce contracts" to include the making, performance, modification and termination of contracts as well as the enjoyment of all benefits, privileges, terms and conditions of the contractual relationship. The 1991 Act also added subsection 1981(c) which, *inter alia*, codified the *Patterson* Court's ruling that § 1981 applies to private acts of discrimination. Of course, the courts still must resolve whether this portion of the 1991 statute should apply to pre-Act conduct. This issue is discussed in detail, with respect to its impact on Title VII claims, in Chapter 2, Section A(2), *supra*, at 83. But in the § 1981 context, is it significant that the conduct now prohibited by § 1981 as a result of this new legislation was unlawful (albeit under Title VII) prior to the passage of the 1991 Act? Compare e.g., Graham v. Bodine Electric Company, 782 F.Supp. 74 (N.D.Ill.1992)(granting retroactivity) and Goldsmith v. City of Atmore, 782 F.Supp. 106 (S.D.Ala.1992)(Id.) with Luddington v. Indiana Bell Telephone Co., 966 F.2d 225 (7th Cir.1992) (denying retroactivity) and Fray v. Omaha World Herald Co., 960 F.2d 1370 (8th Cir.1992) (Id.).

BOBO v. ITT, CONTINENTAL BAKING CO.

United States Court of Appeals, Fifth Circuit, 1981.
662 F.2d 340.

AINSWORTH, CIRCUIT JUDGE.

The principal issue raised by this appeal is whether 42 U.S.C. § 1981, derived primarily from the Civil Rights Act of 1866, 14 Stat. 27, encompasses claims of sex discrimination. The clear answer is that it does not.

Alice Bobo, a black woman, brought this action against her former employer, ITT, Continental Baking Company (ITT). She alleged that

ITT discharged her because she had refused to wear a hat that co-employees allegedly were not required to wear. She also averred that prior to her firing, she had been the victim of other discriminatory employment conditions because of her race and sex. Bobo sought relief under Title VII of the Civil Rights Act of 1964 and 42 U.S.C. § 1981. Upon motion by ITT, partial summary judgment was entered against Bobo by the district court. The court ruled that Bobo's Title VII claim was barred because of her failure to sue within 90 days of receipt of her right to sue letter from the Equal Employment Opportunity Commission. The court also held that since § 1981 did not reach claims of sex discrimination, Bobo was entitled to a trial only on the issue of whether she had been subjected to racial discrimination.

* * *

On appeal, Bobo attacks the district court's * * * determination that sex discrimination is not cognizable under § 1981.

Sex Discrimination Under § 1981

Section 1981 generally forbids racial discrimination in the making and enforcement of private contracts, including private employment contracts, whether the aggrieved party is black or white. Runyon v. McCrary, 427 U.S. 160, 168, 96 S.Ct. 2586, 2593, 49 L.Ed.2d 415 (1976); McDonald v. Santa Fe Trial Transportation Co., 427 U.S. 273, 295, 96 S.Ct. 2574, 2586, 49 L.Ed.2d 493 (1976); Johnson v. Railway Express Agency, 421 U.S. 454, 459–60, 95 S.Ct. 1716, 1719–20, 44 L.Ed.2d 295 (1975). * * *

Although § 1981 strikes at many forms of racial discrimination, no court has held that allegations of gender based discrimination fall within its purview. Courts at every level of the federal judiciary have considered the question and reached the opposite result. The Supreme Court, in framing the question for decision in *Runyon*, explained that the case did not involve "the right of a private school to limit its student body to boys, to girls, or to adherents of a particular religious faith, since 42 U.S.C. § 1981 is in no way addressed to such categories of selectivity." Even if we were to heed Bobo's invitation to regard this statement as dictum and therefore not dispositive of the issue, we could not ignore the Supreme Court's consistent emphasis on the racial character of § 1981, as indicated by the law's language and legislative history. The Court has interpreted the phrase "as is enjoyed by white citizens * * *" in § 1981 as reflecting its drafters' intention that the statute ban racial discrimination.

The Court's view of the 1866 Act's purpose was expressed in Georgia v. Rachel, 384 U.S. 780, 86 S.Ct. 1783, 16 L.Ed.2d 925 (1966), which construed its removal provisions. In examining the legislative history, the Court noted that the "white citizens" language was not a part of the original Senate bill, but was added later "apparently to emphasize the racial character of the rights being protected." The Court considered the legislative history of the 1866 Act and concluded that it "clearly indicates that Congress intended to protect a limited category of rights, specifically defined in terms of racial equality." Two terms later, while determining the breadth of 42 U.S.C. § 1982[4] in Jones v. Alfred H. Mayer Co., the Court repeatedly referred to the 1866 Act's aim of eliminating racial discrimination. The Court observed that unlike the Fair Housing Title (Title VIII) of the Civil Rights Act of 1968, § 1982 was addressed only to racial discrimination. Finally, in perhaps its most extensive discussion of the legislative history of the 1866 Act, the Court reaffirmed the limits on § 1981 in *McDonald*. Though extending the statute's protection to claims of racial discrimination by whites, the Court ruled that the 1866 Act's goal was to promote equality among the races by precluding discrimination in the making and enforcement of contracts either for or against any particular race.

Bobo nevertheless argues that the term "white citizens" should be deemed synonymous with "most favored group," thereby permitting those who find themselves somehow less favored to advance discrimination charges under § 1981. A sweeping interpretation of this sort, however, would thwart the statute's evident meaning and purpose. As the Supreme Court has explained, Congress enacted § 1 of the 1866 Act with the ambitious goal of ensuring equal citizenship for the newly freed slaves. Statements in the legislative history, carefully reviewed in *McDonald*, reflect this objective and confirm that the "white citizens" language was added specifically to preclude a construction that might expand the statute's coverage to other groups. Representative Wilson, who proposed amending the original bill to add the "white citizens" language, stated that "the reason for offering [the amendment] was this: it was thought by some persons that unless these qualifying words were incorporated in the bill, those rights might be extended to all citizens, whether male or female, majors or minors."
* * *

Bobo further contends that since women obviously lacked equal legal rights during the Reconstruction era, "white citizens" should be read as "white men." But as the legislative history quoted above indicates, Congress meant precisely what it said. The drafters of § 1981 had no intention to disturb public or private authority to discriminate against women. Outlawing such discrimination in the United States in 1866 would have signaled an extraordinary social transformation, a result clearly not desired by Congress. Public sensitivity to the ills of gender discrimination is of more recent origin. We cannot ascribe contemporary attitudes to a Congress acting over a century ago when its views to the contrary are so plainly stated.

* * * [T]here is no direct holding by this court that gender based discrimination is not within the acts forbidden by § 1981. At least two

---

4. Section 1982 proscribes discrimination with respect to real or personal property interests. Like § 1981, § 1982 is principally derived from § 1 of the Civil Rights Act of 1866.

other circuits, however, have so held. Movement for Opportunity and Equality v. General Motors Corp., 622 F.2d 1235, 1278 (7th Cir.1980) (adopting district court opinion); DeGraffenreid v. General Motors Assembly Div., St. Louis, 558 F.2d 480, 486 n. 2 (8th Cir.1977). A procession of district court opinions is in agreement with this view. * * *

Bobo cites Guerra v. Manchester Terminal Corp., 498 F.2d 641 (5th Cir.1974) in support of a broader reading of § 1981. In *Guerra* a Mexican citizen lawfully residing in the United States complained that he was the victim of discrimination as a result of a collective bargaining agreement which targeted American citizens for more desirable jobs. The court held that § 1981 reached charges of discrimination based on alienage by private employers. In light of *Runyon* and *McDonald*, discussed above, we have previously characterized *Guerra* as a broad construction of § 1981 in a case with "strong racial overtones." Whatever vitality it may retain, *Guerra* did not propose extending § 1981 to sex discrimination, and thus lends no support to Bobo's contentions.

In the face of seemingly unambiguous statutory language, emphatic contemporaneous statements by legislators and an unbroken tide of case law rejecting Bobo's arguments, we conclude that the district court properly held that sex discrimination is not cognizable under § 1981.

* * *

For the foregoing reasons, the judgment of the district court is affirmed.

Affirmed.

NOTES AND PROBLEMS FOR DISCUSSION

1. To what extent should the reasoning in *Bobo* apply to other non-racial classifications? Note that the court in *Bobo* cited the Fifth Circuit's ruling in *Guerra* that § 1981 was applicable to alienage-based discrimination. But thirteen years after rendering its decision in *Guerra*, the Fifth Circuit reconsidered this issue in BHANDARI v. FIRST NATIONAL BANK OF COMMERCE, 829 F.2d 1343 (5th Cir.1987). In an en banc opinion, the court reversed *Guerra* and held that while it was required to follow the Supreme Court's rulings in *Runyon* and *Jones* that § 1981 applied to *private* acts of *racial* discrimination, it was not prepared to extend those rulings to include *private* acts of *alienage* discrimination within the compass of § 1981. The circuit court indicated that, in its view, the Supreme Court had incorrectly interpreted § 1981 since the legislative history of that statute revealed that it was intended to grant all individuals the same rights in the courts and under the laws as was enjoyed by white citizens, but was not intended to apply to private acts of discrimination. Nevertheless, the court declared, it was bound to follow the dictates of the High Court on the issue decided in those previous cases—i.e., that § 1981 applies to private acts of racial discrimination. The court noted, however, that the Supreme Court had not ruled on whether the statute similarly applied to private acts of *alienage* discrimination. On this question, the court continued, there was justification in the legislative history to differentiate between racial and non-racial discrimination. It pointed out that § 1981 derived both from

§ 1 of the 1866 Act and § 16 of the 1870 Act and that it was from the latter enactment that the protection for aliens was derived. Moreover, while the 1866 Act was concerned primarily with enforcing the 13th Amendment rights of newly freed black slaves, the 1870 enactment was passed as a statutory implementation of the 14th Amendment and Congress intended for this statute to curtail only *state* action that discriminated against aliens. The court also suggested that if Congress believed that § 1981 already covered private alienage discrimination, there would have been no need for it to enact the anti-discrimination provisions of the 1986 Immigration Reform and Control Act. Finally, while recognizing that construing the same "all persons" language of § 1981 to mean something for one class of persons (blacks) and something else for another class (non-citizens) was "awkward and undesirable," the Fifth Circuit declared that "racial and citizenship distinctions are things of a different kind; * * * the former our polity and increasingly our society as well are resolved * * * to have done [away] with, root and branch as representing an evil, always and everywhere. The latter is not so readily and roundly condemned; when all is said and done, patriotism remains a civic virtue * * *." 829 F.2d at 1352. The plaintiff in this case had alleged that he was denied credit by the defendant on the basis of his lack of American citizenship. At the end of its 1989 term, the Supreme Court vacated the Fifth Circuit's *en banc* opinion and remanded it for further consideration in light of *Patterson*. 492 U.S. 901, 109 S.Ct. 3207, 106 L.Ed.2d 558 (1989). On remand, the Fifth Circuit issued a per curiam opinion in which the entire circuit court unanimously agreed that the decision in *Patterson* did not affect its earlier ruling. 887 F.2d 609 (5th Cir.1989). The court stated that since the *Patterson* Court reaffirmed its decision in *Runyon,* the precedential landscape had not changed from what existed at the time of the circuit court's original decision in *Bhandari.*

Suppose the plaintiff in *Bhandari* had been a U.S. citizen of Indian ancestry and claimed that he had been discriminated against on the basis of his national origin. Could he state a claim under § 1981? For several years, while the lower federal courts agreed that § 1981 was intended to prohibit discrimination on the basis of race but not national origin, they nevertheless permitted national origin claims to proceed under § 1981 where those claims could be characterized as racial in nature. See e.g. Bullard v. OMI Georgia, Inc., 640 F.2d 632 (5th Cir.1981)(Black and white employees discharged and replaced by persons of Korean ancestry can state claim under § 1981 because complaint included allegation of race as well as national origin discrimination); Gonzalez v. Stanford Applied Engineering, Inc., 597 F.2d 1298 (9th Cir.1979)(Mexican–American alleging discrimination because of his having brown skin can state a claim under § 1981); Manzanares v. Safeway Stores, Inc., 593 F.2d 968, 970 (10th Cir.1979)(Mexican–American stated a claim of racial discrimination under § 1981 since the group to which he belonged is "of such an identifiable nature that the treatment afforded its members may be measured against that afforded Anglos."). One judge offered the following assessment of the treatment of national origin claims under § 1981:

"The terms 'race' and 'racial discrimination' may be of such doubtful sociological validity as to be scientifically meaningless, but these terms nonetheless are subject to a commonly-accepted, albeit sometimes vague, understanding. Those courts which have extended the coverage of § 1981 have done so on a realistic basis, within the framework of this common meaning and understanding. On this admittedly unscientific basis, whites are plainly a 'race' susceptible to 'racial discrimination'; Hispanic persons and Indians, like blacks, have been traditional victims of group discrimination, and, however inaccurately or stupidly, are frequently and even commonly subject to a 'racial' identification as 'non-whites.' There is accordingly both a practical need and a logical reason to extend § 1981's proscription against exclusively 'racial' employment discrimination to these groups of potential discriminatees."

Budinsky v. Corning Glass Works, 425 F.Supp. 786, 787–788 (W.D.Pa.1977). See also Ortiz v. Bank of America, 547 F.Supp. 550 (E.D.Cal.1982)(§ 1981 protects members of any distinctive group that has been treated differently than and is perceived as distinguishable from white citizens.). But see Anooya v. Hilton Hotels Corp., 733 F.2d 48 (7th Cir.1984)(§ 1981 complaint dismissal upheld where the plaintiff did not explicitly or implicitly allege facts from which court could equate the evil of race discrimination to the alleged national origin animus experienced on account of his Iraqi descent).

The Supreme Court tried to clear up some of the confusion concerning the treatment of ethnicity-based claims under § 1981 in two companion cases dealing, respectively, with claims of discrimination against Arabs and Jews. In SAINT FRANCIS COLLEGE v. AL–KHAZRAJI, 481 U.S. 604, 107 S.Ct. 2022, 95 L.Ed.2d 582 (1987), an Iranian-born U.S. citizen who had been denied tenure by the defendant college brought, *inter alia,* a claim of racial discrimination under § 1981. The trial court had dismissed the claim on the ground that § 1981 did not reach claims of discrimination based on Arabian ancestry. The Third Circuit reversed, holding that the plaintiff had alleged racial discrimination on the ground that the 1866 Congress had intended to forbid discrimination against "an individual because he or she is genetically part of an ethnically and physiognomically distinctive sub-grouping of *homo sapiens.*" The Supreme Court affirmed the Court of Appeals, declaring that while § 1981 did not use the word "race", it had been interpreted to forbid "racial" discrimination and that it was necessary, therefore, to determine the meaning of "race" in the nineteenth century to resolve whether the plaintiff had alleged racial discrimination within the meaning of the statute. In this regard, the Court reported, nineteenth century dictionaries defined "race" as "a family, tribe, people or nation, believed or presumed to belong to the same stock". It was not until the twentieth century that dictionaries began referring to the Caucasian, Mongolian and Negro races. The Court also noted that the legislative history of § 1981 similarly referred to ethnic groups as races. Accordingly, the Court concluded that Congress intended to protect individuals who were subjected to intentional discrimination "solely because of their ancestry or ethnic characteristics. Such discrimination is racial discrimination that Congress intended § 1981 to forbid, whether or not it would be classified as racial in terms of modern scientific theory." 481 U.S. at 613, 107 S.Ct. at 2028, 95 L.Ed.2d at 592. The Court added that a distinctive physiognomy was not essential to qualify for protection under § 1981, and that the plaintiff would prevail if, on remand, he could prove that he was subjected to intentional discrimination because he was born an Arab, rather than solely because of the place or nation of his origin, or because of his religion.

In the companion case, SHAARE TEFILA CONGREGATION v. COBB, 481 U.S. 615, 107 S.Ct. 2019, 95 L.Ed.2d 594 (1987), members of a Jewish congregation brought suit under § 1982 (the companion provision to § 1981 that guarantees to all U.S. citizens the same right to sell, lease, inherit and convey real and personal property that is enjoyed by white citizens) alleging that individuals who, acting out of racial prejudice, had desecrated the outside walls of their synagogue by spraying it with anti-Semitic slogans and symbols thereby had deprived the plaintiffs of their right to hold property because of their race. The trial court and Fourth Circuit had dismissed the complaint on the ground that Jews are not a distinct racial group and thus could not state a claim under § 1982. The Supreme Court reversed, applied the interpretation of "race" that it had announced in *St. Francis* and concluded that Jews, as well as Arabs, "were among the peoples [that Congress] then considered to be distinct races and hence within the protection of the statute."

In Nieto v. United Auto Workers Local 598, 672 F.Supp. 987 (E.D.Mich. 1987), the court concluded that Mexicans were also among the groups identified as distinct races in the legislative history of § 1981. Accordingly, pursuant to *St. Francis* and *Shaare Tefila*, the trial judge held that the Mexican plaintiff could state a claim under § 1981 if she could prove that she had been subjected to slurs because of her Mexican ancestry rather than because she had been born in Mexico. Similarly, the trial court in Quintana v. Byrd, 669 F.Supp. 849 (N.D.Ill.1987), denied the defendant's motion to dismiss a § 1981 complaint of racial discrimination brought by a white Hispanic, on the ground that ethnic characteristics, as opposed to country of birth, constitute "race" within the meaning of § 1981. See also Cardona v. American Express Travel Related Services Co., 720 F.Supp. 960 (S.D.Fla.1989)(plaintiff with Colombian ancestry or ethnic background can state § 1981 claim alleging that he was discriminated against in favor of employees of Cuban ancestry; both groups have distinct ethnic and cultural characteristics despite fact that both are Spanish-speaking peoples); MacDissi v. Valmont Industries, Inc., 856 F.2d 1054 (8th Cir.1988)(plaintiff who alleges discrimination on basis of his Lebanese descent states a claim under § 1981); DeSalle v. Key Bank, 685 F.Supp. 282 (D.Me.1988)(Italian who claims discrimination on basis of ethnicity rather than country of origin states claim under § 1981); Franceschi v. Hyatt Corp., 782 F.Supp. 712 (D.Puerto Rico 1992)(Puerto Rican heritage constitutes race within meaning of § 1981). Are these fair readings of the two Supreme Court decisions? For a discussion of alternative methods of determining which classes are protected by § 1981, see Note, When Is A Race Not A Race?: Contemporary Issues Under The Civil Rights Act of 1866, 61 N.Y.U.L.Rev. 976 (1986).

Suppose an employer discriminated against a job applicant on the basis of the mistaken belief that the applicant was a member of a particular racial or ethnic group. Would the fact that the plaintiff is not, in fact, a member of the protected group be fatal to her claim? See Franceschi v. Hyatt Corp., 782 F.Supp. 712 (D.Puerto Rico 1992) (court "will focus its attention at trial not on physiognomic characteristics but on defendant's perceptions of plaintiff as belonging to a given racial or ethnic group.") (dictum).

Recall that the Fifth Circuit in *Bhandari, supra,* a post-*St. Francis* case, held that § 1981 does not cover private acts of citizenship discrimination. How does this opinion square with the Supreme Court's rulings in *St. Francis* and *Shaare Tefila?* Don't these latter cases suggest that Bhandari's mistake was in claiming alienage, as opposed to ancestry/racial discrimination?

While most courts now recognize that § 1981 applies to national origin claims that involve ethnic or racial characteristics, the courts also have ruled that § 1981 does not cover claims of discrimination on the basis of age, Barkley v. Carraux, 533 F.Supp. 242 (S.D.Tex.1982); religion, Khawaja v. Wyatt, 494 F.Supp. 302 (W.D.N.Y.1980); or sexual preference, Grossman v. Bernards Township Board of Education, 11 FEP Cases 1196 (D.N.J.1975), affirmed, 538 F.2d 319 (3d Cir.1976), cert. denied, 429 U.S. 897, 97 S.Ct. 261, 50 L.Ed.2d 181 (1976).

2.   Can § 1981 be used to fill in some of the gaps in Title VII's coverage? For example, § 701(b) exempts Indian tribes from the antidiscrimination provisions of Title VII.   Can a non-Indian denied employment by an Indian tribe bring a race discrimination action under § 1981?   See Wardle v. Ute Indian Tribe, 623 F.2d 670 (10th Cir.1980).   Is a race discrimination claim brought by a uniformed member of the armed services cognizable under § 1981?   See Taylor v. Jones, 653 F.2d 1193 (8th Cir.1981).   What about an employee of a private, tax-exempt membership club?   Compare Guesby v. Kennedy, 580 F.Supp. 1280 (D.Kan.1984) with Kemerer v. Davis, 520 F.Supp. 256 (E.D.Mich.1981).

3.   In BROWN v. GENERAL SERVICES ADMINISTRATION, 425 U.S. 820, 96 S.Ct. 1961, 48 L.Ed.2d 402 (1976), the Supreme Court ruled that Title VII is the exclusive judicial remedy available to *federal* employees complaining of job discrimination.   Should this ruling extend to state and local government employees?   Prior to the enactment of the 1991 Civil Rights Acts, the courts uniformly ruled that state and local government employees were not limited to the remedies available under Title VII and thus could bring claims of racial or alienage discrimination under § 1981.   See e.g., Bridgeport Guardians, Inc. v. Bridgeport Civil Service Commission, 482 F.2d 1333 (2d Cir.1973), cert. denied, 421 U.S. 991, 95 S.Ct. 1997, 44 L.Ed.2d 481 (1975)(municipal police force); Carter v. Gallagher, 452 F.2d 315 (8th Cir.1971), cert. denied, 406 U.S. 950, 92 S.Ct. 2045, 32 L.Ed.2d 338 (1972)(municipal civil service commission).   It was unclear, however, whether these state government employees were limited by the Eleventh Amendment to claims for equitable relief.   The Eleventh Amendment has been interpreted to bar suits for damages in federal courts against states, or state officials where the damage award would be paid out of the state treasury, absent a waiver of sovereign immunity.   This left the courts, before the enactment of the 1991 Act, with the question of whether Congress implicitly had overridden the states' constitutional immunity to damage suits by enacting § 1981.   Unfortunately, the Supreme Court had not directly addressed this issue and its most analogous cases pointed in opposite directions.   In FITZPATRICK v. BITZER, 427 U.S. 445, 96 S.Ct. 2666, 49 L.Ed.2d 614 (1976), the Supreme Court ruled that Congress could and did abrogate the states' Eleventh Amendment immunity to damage actions through the 1972 amendment to Title VII authorizing private damage actions against states since that statute was enacted for the purpose of enforcing the provisions of the Fourteenth Amendment.   On the other hand, in QUERN v. JORDAN, 440 U.S. 332, 99 S.Ct. 1139, 59 L.Ed.2d 358 (1979), the Court reaffirmed its prior ruling in Edelman v. Jordan, 415 U.S. 651, 94 S.Ct. 1347, 39 L.Ed.2d 662 (1974) that the Eleventh Amendment precluded the assertion of a federal court action for damages against a state under 42 U.S.C. § 1983 even where the complaint alleged a violation of the Fourteenth Amendment.   Some courts found it significant that Title VII, unlike §§ 1981 and 1983, specifically authorized the awarding of money damages against a state.   But others noted that § 1981 did not specifically provide a damage remedy for private sector employees, even though such a remedy was uniformly recognized.   See Rucker v. Higher Educational Aids Board, 669 F.2d 1179 (7th Cir.1982); Gibson v. State of Wisconsin Department of Health, 489 F.Supp. 1048 (E.D.Wis.1980).

The question of whether § 1981 protects state government employees was resolved by the passage of the 1991 Civil Rights Act.   In addition to overruling the *Patterson* Court's interpretation of the "make or enforce" language of

§ 1981, Congress added new subsection 1981(c), which states that this statute applies to private discrimination and discrimination "under color of State law". While the 1991 Act does not expressly provide for the recovery of monetary damages in § 1981 cases, it recognizes the availability of such recovery (under 42 U.S.C. § 1988) since its authorization of monetary and punitive damage awards in § 102 is limited to cases where the complaining party cannot recover under § 1981. But this reference to § 1981 does not answer the question of whether state and local government workers, as opposed to private sector employees, are entitled to recover monetary damages under § 1981. Thus, the courts will again have to determine whether this enactment constitutes a waiver of the states' sovereign immunity under the Eleventh Amendment. In this connection, however, is it significant the amended § 1981 adopts the "under color of state law" terminology of § 1983?

Local and municipal governments, on the other hand, cannot claim any Eleventh Amendment immunity from damage actions. Nevertheless, a common law immunity from such suits is generally recognized. In enacting either the original or amended § 1981, did Congress intend to override municipal immunity? The Supreme Court has ruled that municipalities do not enjoy a common law immunity from compensatory damage claims in actions brought under § 1983 where the challenged conduct is attributable directly to the municipality. Monell v. Department of Social Services of City of New York, 436 U.S. 658, 98 S.Ct. 2018, 56 L.Ed.2d 611 (1978). The Court, however, has also held that municipalities retain their immunity from punitive damages in § 1983 suits. City of Newport v. Fact Concerts, Inc., 453 U.S. 247, 101 S.Ct. 2748, 69 L.Ed.2d 616 (1981). With respect to § 1981, the courts are split. Compare Sethy v. Alameda County Water District, 545 F.2d 1157 (9th Cir. 1976)(§ 1981 abolishes immunity) and Boyd v. Shawnee Mission Public Schools, 522 F.Supp. 1115 (D.Kan.1981)(§ 1981 abolishes immunity from punitive damages) with Poolaw v. City of Anadarko, 738 F.2d 364 (10th Cir.1984), cert. denied, 469 U.S. 1108, 105 S.Ct. 784, 83 L.Ed.2d 779 (1985)(municipality immune from punitive damages under § 1981) and Heritage Homes of Attleboro, Inc. v. Seekonk Water District, 670 F.2d 1 (1st Cir.1982)(municipality immune from punitive damages in § 1981 action).

4. Can a municipality be vicariously liable for the acts of its employees in violation of § 1981? In JETT v. DALLAS INDEPENDENT SCHOOL DIST., 798 F.2d 748 (5th Cir.1986), the Fifth Circuit reasoned that imposing municipal liability on a *respondeat superior* theory was inconsistent with the Supreme Court's ruling in *Monell.* In a subsequent opinion in which it denied a request for rehearing *en banc,* the Fifth Circuit added that since the Supreme Court in *Monell* had concluded that Congress did not intend to impose vicarious liability upon municipalities in connection with a statutory provision (§ 1983) that expressly and intentionally subjected municipalities to liability, there was "no reason to assume that Congress intended to impose vicarious municipal liability" under § 1981, a provision that "contains no language which can be construed as covering municipalities." 837 F.2d 1244, 1248 (5th Cir.1988).

This decision was affirmed by the Supreme Court, 491 U.S. 701, 109 S.Ct. 2702, 105 L.Ed.2d 598 (1989). In an opinion by Justice O'Connor (joined by the Chief Justice and Justices White and Kennedy), a four member plurality of the Court emphasized that the legislative history of § 1983 demonstrated that at the time it enacted § 1983, Congress thought it was providing a damages remedy for violations of federal constitutional and statutory rights by state actors for the first time and, therefore, that the remedial provision of § 1983 would control actions for damages brought against state officials under § 1981. Accordingly, the plurality concluded, § 1981 did not provide an independent cause of action for damages against public units and, therefore, the damages action created by § 1983 was the exclusive federal damages remedy for violations of the terms of § 1981 by state governmental units. Justice Scalia, in a separate concurring opinion, agreed with this interpretation of the law, but stated that his decision was made exclusively as a matter of statutory construction, expressly disassociating himself from the plurality's reliance on legislative history. Nevertheless, this resulted in a majority of the Court voting to link § 1981–based claims against governmental units to the remedial provisions of § 1983. And this, in turn, subjected such § 1981 claims to the Court's prior rulings under § 1983 that rejected the imposition of financial liability on a theory of *respondeat superior* and limited recovery against the government to situations where the plaintiff can establish that the violation was caused by a custom or policy of that unit within the meaning of *Monell* and subsequent § 1983 cases. Finally, with respect to whether the actions by the principal represented the official policy of the school board (which would support liability for money damages), the same majority relied on the Court's holding in St. Louis v. Praprotnik, 485 U.S. 112, 123, 108 S.Ct. 915, 924, 99 L.Ed.2d 107 (1988). In that case, the Court stated that "whether a particular official has final policymaking authority is a question of state law * * * to be resolved by the trial judge before the case is submitted to the jury." In undertaking this task, the trial judge must review "state and local positive law, as well as custom or usage having the force of law" and identify those officials who speak with final policymaking authority for the local governmental unit concerning the action that is alleged to have violated § 1981. Since the trial in *Jett* and the decision by the Court of Appeals had occurred years before the Court's decision in *Praprotnik,* the Supreme Court declined to make its own evaluation of Texas law to determine whether the principal possessed this final policymaking authority in the area of employee transfers and remanded the case to the circuit court for this determination in light of the *Praprotnik* principles.

Justice Brennan issued a dissenting opinion that was joined by Justices Marshall, Blackmun and Stevens. Noting that the defendant had never suggested in any of the proceedings below that the plaintiff did not have a private cause of action for damages under § 1981, the dissenters objected to, and characterized as "rash", the majority's decision to adjudicate an issue "on the basis of largely one-sided briefing, without the benefit of the views of the court's below." On the merits, they found that the language and legislative history of § 1981 supported the conclusion that this statute impliedly provided an independent claim for money damages against state units, stating that "before today, no one had questioned that a person could sue a government official for damages due to a violation of section 1981." They added that the creation of an independent claim five years after the enactment of § 1981 through the passage of § 1983 should not be viewed as an implicit repeal of the provisions of the 1866 Act (§ 1981), particularly in light of the language in the 1871 Act to the effect that nothing contained therein "shall be construed to supersede or repeal any former act or law except so far as the same may be repugnant thereto." Finally, the dissenters rejected the notion that the restrictions on § 1983 liability (in terms of vicarious responsibility) contained in the Court's decision in *Monell* governed actions brought under § 1981 since § 1981 covers a more limited range of official conduct than § 1983 and because § 1981, unlike § 1983, does not contain any language evidencing a Congressional intent to preclude liability on the basis of respondeat superior. Consequently, they concluded that the plaintiff could bring his action directly under § 1981 and that this statute permitted recovery against a local governmental unit on a theory of respondeat superior.

Applying the teachings of *Jett* and *Praprotnik,* the trial court in Luna v. City and County of Denver, 718 F.Supp. 854 (D.Colo.1989), dismissed the plaintiff's claim against the city and county on the ground that the city officials who were sued in their individual capacities did not have final policymaking authority and thus their decision not to promote the plaintiff did not represent the city's official policy. Rather, the court reasoned, since the city charter provided employees with the right to appeal denials of promotion to the Career Service Board, it was the Board, rather than the individual named defendants, that possessed the final policymaking authority. But the plaintiff had failed to exercise this right of appeal. Accordingly, the court found that the absence of a decision by the final policymaking authority meant that no action had been taken pursuant to official municipal custom, policy or standard operating procedure and, therefore, that the complaint had to be dismissed.

How does the addition of § 1981(c) by the 1991 Civil Rights Act affect the Court's analysis? What is the significance of the incorporation of § 1983 "under color of state law" terminology in this provision?

5. Can an employee bring a § 1981 action against its union? If so, is a federal employee limited by Brown v. G.S.A. to a Title VII action against its union? See Jennings v. American Postal Workers Union, 672 F.2d 712 (8th Cir.1982).

6. As noted in the introductory material in this Chapter, the Court's ruling in *Patterson* does not clearly resolve whether claims of retaliation fall within its interpretation of the "make or enforce" language of § 1981. Similarly, the amendment to § 1981 effected by the 1991 Civil Rights Act does not explicitly address this matter; "retaliation" is not included within the nonexclusive list of proscribed practices.

In the post-*Patterson*, pre–1991 Act period, most lower courts held that the Supreme Court's interpretation of § 1981 precluded all but a limited range of retaliation claims from challenge under that statute. This inherently postformation conduct, they reasoned, clearly did not affect the right to "make" a contract. See e.g., Carter v. South Central Bell, 912 F.2d 832 (5th Cir.1990), cert. denied, __ U.S. __, 111 S.Ct. 2916, 115 L.Ed.2d 1079 (1991)(§ 1981 does not extend to retaliatory termination because § 1981 should not be interpreted to duplicate protection offered by Title VII unless such overlap is necessary); and Miller v. SwissRe Holding, Inc., 731 F.Supp. 129 (S.D.N.Y.1990)(claim of retaliatory discharge does not implicate the right to make contracts).

With respect to the right to "enforce" contracts, the lower courts focused on the *Patterson* Court's statement that the right to enforce contracts is limited to employer conduct that "impairs an employee's ability to enforce through legal process his or her established contract rights." This language, they stated, supported the conclusion that an act of retaliation is covered by the § 1981 right to enforce a contract only when it was undertaken to prevent or discourage an employee from using legal process to enforce a specific contractual right. See Carter v. South Central Bell, 912 F.2d 832 (5th Cir.1990), cert. denied, __ U.S. __, 111 S.Ct. 2916, 115 L.Ed.2d 1079 (1991)(retaliation against plaintiff for filing a Title VII charge may discourage the aggrieved and others from using the legal process but does not impede the ability to enforce contractual rights); McKnight v. General Motors Corp., 908 F.2d 104 (7th Cir.1990)(Id.); Sherman v. Burke Contracting, Inc., 891 F.2d 1527 (11th Cir.1990)(dismissing a § 1981 claim where the plaintiff had alleged retaliation in response to his filing a claim with the EEOC; the EEOC complaint did not relate to any right created by the plaintiff's employment contract with the defendant); Overby v. Chevron U.S.A., Inc., 884 F.2d 470 (9th Cir.1989)(§ 1981 right to enforce contracts violated only by efforts to impede access to dispute resolution process for vindication of contractual rights; retaliation for filing EEOC charge is protected by Title VII, not § 1981); Miller v. SwissRe Holding, Inc., 731 F.Supp. 129 (S.D.N.Y.1990)(retaliation for filing an EEOC charge is not a sufficient obstacle to the enforcement of contractual rights to disregard the *Patterson* Court's admonition that § 1981 not be stretched to reach conduct proscribed by Title VII); Williams v. National R.R. Passenger Corp., 716 F.Supp. 49 (D.D.C.1989), affirmed without opinion, 901 F.2d 1131 (D.C.Cir. 1990)(§ 1981 right to enforce contracts does not apply where alleged retaliation impeded plaintiff's attempt to process a discrimination claim not based on a contractual right). But see Jordan v. U.S. West Direct Co., 716 F.Supp. 1366 (D.Colo.1989) (statutory right to enforce contract protects against efforts that impede nonjudicial methods of adjudicating disputes concerning discrimination; plaintiff demoted after complaining to employer about discriminatory conditions and instigating an investigation of his charges; court does not discuss whether complaint was founded on assertion of contractual or noncontractual rights). And at least one trial court held that retaliation claims cannot lie under § 1981, irrespective of whether the challenged conduct was taken in response to an effort to enforce contractual or statutory rights. See Danger-field v. Mission Press, 50 FEP Cases 1171 (N.D.Ill.1989)(retaliation for filing EEOC charge did not impair plaintiff's access to legal enforcement of contractual rights either in state court or through Title VII).

The distinction between efforts to enforce contractual versus noncontractual rights, even if it is relevant, may nevertheless be clouded in the many cases where a collective bargaining agreement contains a nondiscrimination clause that prohibits conduct violative of federal and state antidiscrimination law. Additionally, it has been suggested that the rights guaranteed by Title VII are implied terms of all employment contracts and, therefore, that any attempt to enforce these statutory rights is *ipso facto* an attempt to enforce contractual rights. See Shanor & Marcosson, Battleground for a Divided Court: Employment Discrimination in the Supreme Court, 1988–89, 6 The Labor Lawyer 145, 174 n. 118 (1990).

Assuming that an act of retaliation is found to have infringed on either the right to make or enforce a contract within the meaning of the amended § 1981, does the § 1981 plaintiff also have to prove that she was retaliated against because of her race? In other words, since § 1981 only prohibits discrimination on the basis of race and national origin involving racial or ethnic characteristics, could the employer defeat her claim if it could establish that it followed a race or ethnic-neutral policy of discharging any individual who filed any private or public claim of discrimination against it? While § 704 of Title VII creates an independent right to be free from retaliation regardless of the motivation behind the retaliation, § 1981 does not contain such an express, independent prohibition against retaliation. Accordingly, any protection against retaliation under § 1981 must be derivative of the right to make or enforce contracts on a race or ethnic-neutral basis. The pre-*Patterson* courts were split on this question. Some concluded that the right to be free from racial discrimination included the right to enforce and protect that *statutory* right. Accordingly, they ruled that § 1981 prohibited retaliatory conduct taken in response to efforts to enforce that right, irrespective of whether the retaliation itself was racially motivated. See Choudhury v. Polytechnic Institute, 735 F.2d 38 (2d Cir.1984); Goff v. Continental Oil Co, 678 F.2d 593 (5th Cir.1982). Others, however, reasoned that since the statute did not contain an anti-retaliation provision, it only prohibited retaliation that was racially motivated. See Tafoya v. Adams, 816 F.2d 555 (10th Cir.), cert. denied, 484 U.S. 851, 108 S.Ct. 152, 98 L.Ed.2d 108 (1987); Sisco v. J.S. Alberici Construction Co., Inc., 655 F.2d 146 (8th Cir.1981), cert. denied, 455 U.S. 976, 102 S.Ct. 1485, 71 L.Ed.2d 688 (1982); London v. Coopers & Lybrand, 644 F.2d 811 (9th Cir.1981).

Finally, if retaliation for seeking to "enforce" contractual rights is prohibited by § 1981, what happens where the employer retaliates against an employee who complains to the employer about, but does not bring any specific legal challenge to, an employment practice that he believes is in contravention of some contractual right? In other words, would § 1981 protect an employee who engages in, to use Title VII terminology, informal "opposition" that does not rise to the level of any formal effort to "enforce" a contractual right? For a suggestion that this should fall within the "to make" clause of § 1981, see Player, What Hath *Patterson* Wrought? A Study in the Failure to Understand the Employment Contract, 6 The Labor Lawyer 183, 210 (1990).

Prior to the Supreme Court's ruling in Washington v. Davis, 426 U.S. 229, 96 S.Ct. 2040, 48 L.Ed.2d 597 (1976)(requiring plaintiffs alleging violations of the Fourteenth Amendment to prove discriminatory intent in their prima facie case), most federal circuit courts applied Title VII proof standards to cases brought under § 1981 and therefore did not require proof of discriminatory purpose for such claims. The decision in *Washington* caused many circuit courts to reexamine the proof standard for § 1981 claims and led almost all of them to require a showing of intent in the prima facie case. The issue was finally addressed by the Supreme Court in the following case:

GENERAL BUILDING CONTRACTORS ASSOCIATION, INC. v. PENNSYLVANIA

Supreme Court of the United States, 1982.
458 U.S. 375, 102 S.Ct. 3141, 73 L.Ed.2d 835.

JUSTICE REHNQUIST delivered the opinion of the Court.

Respondents, the Commonwealth of Pennsylvania and a class of racial minorities who are skilled or seek work as operating engineers in the construction industry in Eastern Pennsylvania and Delaware, commenced this action under a variety of federal statutes protecting civil rights, including 42 U.S.C. § 1981. The complaint sought to redress racial discrimination in the operation of an exclusive hiring hall established in contracts between Local 542 of the International Union of Operating Engineers and construction industry employers doing business within the Union's jurisdiction. Respondents also alleged discrimination in the operation of an apprenticeship program established by Local 542 and several construction trade associations. Named as defendants were Local 542, the trade associations, the organization charged with administering the trade's apprenticeship program, and a class of approximately 1,400 construction industry employers. Petitioners, the defendant contractors and trade associations, seek review of a judgment granting an injunction against them. The questions we resolve are whether liability under 42 U.S.C. § 1981 requires proof of discriminatory intent and whether, absent such proof, liability can nevertheless be imposed vicariously on the employers and trade associations for the discriminatory conduct of the Union.

I

The hiring hall system that is the focus of this litigation originated in a collective bargaining agreement negotiated in 1961 by Local 542 and four construction trade associations in the Philadelphia area, three of whom are petitioners in this Court. The agreement was concluded only after a ten-week strike prompted by the resistance of the trade associations to the Union's demand for an exclusive hiring hall. Under the terms of the agreement, the Union was to maintain lists of operating engineers, or would-be engineers, classified according to the extent of their recent construction experience. Signatory employers were contractually obligated to hire operating engineers only from among those referred by the Union from its current lists. Workers affiliated with the Union were barred from seeking work with those employers except through Union referrals. Thus, the collective bargaining agreement effectively channeled all employment opportunities through the hiring hall. Since 1961 this requirement has been a constant feature of contracts negotiated with Local 542 by the trade associations, as well as of contracts signed with the Union by employers who were not represented by one of those associations in collective bargaining.

Among the means of gaining access to the Union's referral lists is an apprenticeship program established in 1965 by Local 542 and the trade associations. The program, which involves classroom and field training, is administered by the Joint Apprenticeship and Training Committee (JATC), a body of trustees half of whom are appointed by the Union and half by the trade associations. While enrolled in the program, apprentices are referred by the Union for unskilled construction work. Graduates of the program become journeymen operating engineers and are referred for heavy equipment jobs.

This action was filed in 1971 by the Commonwealth of Pennsylvania and 12 black plaintiffs representing a proposed class of minority group members residing within the jurisdiction of Local 542. The complaint charged that the Union and the JATC had violated numerous state and federal laws prohibiting employment discrimination, including Title VII of the Civil Rights Act of 1964 and 42 U.S.C. § 1981.

The complaint alleged that these defendants had engaged in a pattern and practice of racial discrimination, by systematically denying access to the Union's referral lists, and by arbitrarily skewing referrals in favor of white workers, limiting most minority workers who did gain access to the hiring hall to jobs of short hours and low pay. The contractor employers and trade associations were also named as defendants, although the complaint did not allege a Title VII cause of action against them.[4]

The District Court divided the trial into two stages. The first stage, from which petitioners appeal, addressed issues of liability; assessment of damages was deferred to a second stage. For purposes of the first phase of the proceedings, the court certified a plaintiff class of minority operating engineers and would-be engineers, as well as a defendant class consisting of all trade associations and employers who had been parties to labor contracts with Local 542. A single employer, petitioner Glasgow, Inc., was certified to represent the defendant subclass of approximately 1,400 contractor employers.

The District Court's opinion in the liability phase of the trial is lengthy. For our purposes, however, the relevant findings and conclusions can be summarized briefly. First, the court found that the hiring hall system established by collective bargaining was neutral on its face. Indeed, after May 1, 1971, the contracts contained a provision expressly prohibiting employment discrimination on the basis of race, religion, color, or national origin. But the court found that Local 542, in administering the system, "practiced a pattern of intentional discrimination and that union practices in the overall operation of a hiring hall for operating engineers created substantial racial disparities." The court made similar findings regarding the JATC's administration of the job training program. On the basis of these findings, the District Court held that Local 542 and the JATC had violated Title VII, both because they intentionally discriminated and because they enforced practices that resulted in a disparate racial impact. The court also interpreted 42 U.S.C. § 1981 to permit imposition of liability "on roughly the same basis as a Title VII claim," and therefore concluded that the Union and the JATC had also violated § 1981.

Turning to petitioners' liability under § 1981, the court found that the plaintiffs had failed to prove "that the associations or contractors viewed simply as a class were actually aware of the union discrimination," and had failed to show "intent to discriminate by the employers as a class." Nevertheless, the court held the employers and the associations liable under § 1981 for the purpose of imposing an injunctive remedy "as a result of their contractual relationship to and use of a hiring hall system which in practice effectuated intentional discrimination, whether or not the employers and associations knew or should

---

4. The complaint did not assert a Title VII cause of action against petitioners because they were not named in the com-   plaint filed by the plaintiffs with the EEOC, a precondition to suit in federal court.

have known [of the Union's conduct]." The court reasoned that liability under § 1981 "requires no proof of purposeful conduct on the part of any of the defendants." Instead, it was sufficient that "(1) the employers delegated an important aspect of their hiring procedure to the union; [and that] (2) the union, in effectuating the delegation, intentionally discriminated or, alternatively, produced a discriminatory impact." "[P]laintiffs have shown that the requisite relationship exists among employers, associations, and union to render applicable the theory of *respondeat superior*, thus making employers and associations liable injunctively for the discriminatory acts of the union."

Following an appeal authorized by 28 U.S.C. § 1292(b), the Court of Appeals for the Third Circuit, sitting en banc, affirmed the judgment of liability against petitioners by an equally divided vote. We granted certiorari and we now reverse.

II

The District Court held that petitioners had violated 42 U.S.C. § 1981 notwithstanding its finding that, as a class, petitioners did not intentionally discriminate against minority workers and neither knew nor had reason to know of the Union's discriminatory practices. The first question we address, therefore, is whether liability may be imposed under § 1981 without proof of intentional discrimination.[8]

Title 42 U.S.C. § 1981 provides:

"All persons within the jurisdiction of the United States shall have the same right in every State and Territory to make and enforce contracts, to sue, be parties, give evidence, and to the full and equal benefit of all laws and proceedings for the security of persons and property as is enjoyed by white citizens, and shall be subject to like punishment, pains, penalties, taxes, licenses, and exactions of every kind, and to no other."

8. The District Court concluded, by analogy to Title VII, that a violation of § 1981 could be made out by "proof of disparate impact alone." The court referred to Griggs v. Duke Power Co., 401 U.S. 424, 91 S.Ct. 849, 28 L.Ed.2d 158 (1971), in which we held that Title VII forbids the use of employment tests that produce a disproportionate racial impact unless the employer shows "a manifest relationship to the employment in question."

The District Court's holding on this issue is contrary to the holding of every Court of Appeals that has addressed the matter, including that of the Third Circuit in a subsequent case. See Guardians Assn. v. Civil Service Comm'n, 633 F.2d 232, 263–268 (CA2 1980), cert. granted, No. 81–431 (Jan. 11, 1982); Croker v. Boeing Co., 662 F.2d 975, 984–989 (CA3 1981) (en banc); Williams v. DeKalb Cty., 582 F.2d 2 (CA5

1978); Mescall v. Burrus, 603 F.2d 1266, 1269–1271 (CA7 1979); Craig v. County of Los Angeles, 626 F.2d 659, 668 (CA9 1980), cert. denied, 450 U.S. 919, 101 S.Ct. 1364, 67 L.Ed.2d 345 (1981); Chicano Police Officer's Assn. v. Stover, 552 F.2d 918, 920–921 (CA10 1977). Two other circuits have approved a requirement of discriminatory intent in dicta. See Des Vergnes v. Seekonk Water Dist., 601 F.2d 9, 14 (CA1 1979); Detroit Police Officers' Assn. v. Young, 608 F.2d 671, 692 (CA6 1979), cert. denied, 452 U.S. 938, 101 S.Ct. 3079, 69 L.Ed.2d 951 (1981). See also Johnson v. Alexander, 572 F.2d 1219, 1223–1224(CA8), cert. denied, 439 U.S. 986, 99 S.Ct. 576, 58 L.Ed.2d 658 (1978); Donnell v. General Motors Corp., 576 F.2d 1292, 1300 (CA8 1978). But see Kinsey v. First Regional Securities, Inc., 557 F.2d 830, 838, n. 22 (CADC 1977).

We have traced the evolution of this statute and its companion, 42 U.S.C. § 1982, on more than one occasion, and we will not repeat the narrative again except in broad outline.

The operative language of both laws apparently originated in § 1 of the Civil Rights Act of 1866, 14 Stat. 27, enacted by Congress shortly after ratification of the Thirteenth Amendment.[10] "The legislative history of the 1866 Act clearly indicates that Congress intended to protect a limited category of rights, specifically defined in terms of racial equality." Georgia v. Rachel, 384 U.S. 780, 791, 86 S.Ct. 1783, 1789, 16 L.Ed.2d 925 (1966). The same Congress also passed the joint resolution that was later adopted as the Fourteenth Amendment. As we explained in Hurd v. Hodge, 334 U.S. 24, 32–33, 68 S.Ct. 847, 851–852, 92 L.Ed. 1187 (1948) (footnotes omitted):

> "Frequent references to the Civil Rights Act are to be found in the record of the legislative debates on the adoption of the Amendment. It is clear that in many significant respects the statute and the Amendment were expressions of the same general congressional policy. Indeed, as the legislative debates reveal, one of the primary purposes of many members of Congress in supporting the adoption of the Fourteenth Amendment was to incorporate the guaranties of the Civil Rights Act of 1866 in the organic law of the land. Others supported the adoption of the Amendment in order to eliminate doubt as to the constitutional validity of the Civil Rights Act as applied to the States."

Following ratification of the Fourteenth Amendment, Congress passed what has come to be known as the Enforcement Act of 1870, 16 Stat. 140, pursuant to the power conferred by § 5 of the Amendment. Section 16 of that Act contains essentially the language that now appears in § 1981.[11] Indeed, the present codification is derived from

---

10. Section 1 of the Act of Apr. 9, 1866, read in part:

"That all persons born in the United States and not subject to any foreign power, * * * are hereby declared to be citizens of the United States; and such citizens, of every race and color, without regard to any previous condition of slavery or involuntary servitude, * * * shall have the same right, in every State and Territory in the United States, to make and enforce contracts, to sue, be parties, and give evidence, to inherit, purchase, lease, sell, hold, and convey real and personal property, and to full and equal benefit of all laws and proceedings for the security of person and property, as is enjoyed by white citizens, and shall be subject to like punishment, pains, and penalties, and to none other, any law, statute, ordinance, regulation, or custom, to the contrary notwithstanding."

11. "That all persons within the jurisdiction of the United States shall have the same right in every State and Territory in the United States to make and enforce contracts, to sue, be parties, give evidence, and to the full and equal benefit of all laws and proceedings for the security of person and property as is enjoyed by white citizens, and shall be subject to like punishment, pains, penalties, taxes, licenses, and exactions of every kind, and none other, any law, statute, ordinance, regulation, or custom to the contrary notwithstanding. No tax or charge shall be imposed or enforced by any State upon any person immigrating thereto from a foreign country which is not imposed and enforced upon every person immigrating to such State from any other foreign country; and any law of any State in conflict with this provision is hereby declared null and void." 16 Stat. 144.

§ 1977 of the Revised Statutes of 1874, which in turn codified verbatim § 16 of the 1870 Act. Section 16 differed from § 1 of the 1866 Act in at least two respects. First, where § 1 of the 1866 Act extended its guarantees to "citizens, of every race and color," § 16 of the 1870 Act— and § 1981—protects "all persons." Second, the 1870 Act omitted language contained in the 1866 Act, and eventually codified as § 1982, guaranteeing property rights equivalent to those enjoyed by white citizens. Thus, "[a]lthough the 1866 Act rested only on the Thirteenth Amendment * * * and, indeed, was enacted before the Fourteenth Amendment was formally proposed, * * * the 1870 Act was passed pursuant to the Fourteenth, and changes in wording may have reflected the language of the Fourteenth Amendment." Tillman v. Wheaton– Haven Recreation Assn., 410 U.S. 431, 439–440, n. 11, 93 S.Ct. 1090, 1095, n. 11, 35 L.Ed.2d 403 (1973).

In determining whether § 1981 reaches practices that merely result in a disproportionate impact on a particular class, or instead is limited to conduct motivated by a discriminatory purpose, we must be mindful of the "events and passions of the time" in which the law was forged. The Civil War had ended in April 1865. The First Session of the Thirty-ninth Congress met on December 4, 1865, some six months after the preceding Congress had sent to the States the Thirteenth Amendment and just two weeks before the Secretary of State certified the Amendment's ratification. On January 5, 1866, Senator Trumbull introduced the bill that would become the 1866 Act.

The principal object of the legislation was to eradicate the Black Codes, laws enacted by Southern legislatures imposing a range of civil disabilities on freedmen. Most of these laws embodied express racial classifications and although others, such as those penalizing vagrancy, were facially neutral, Congress plainly perceived all of them as consciously conceived methods of resurrecting the incidents of slavery. Senator Trumbull summarized the paramount aims of his bill:

> "Since the abolition of slavery, the Legislatures which have assembled in the insurrectionary States have passed laws relating to the freedmen, and in nearly all the States they have discriminated against them. They deny them certain rights, subject them to severe penalties, and still impose upon them the very restrictions which were imposed upon them in consequence of the existence of slavery, and before it was abolished. The purpose of the bill under consideration is to destroy all these discriminations, and to carry into effect the [Thirteenth] amendment." Cong. Globe, 39th Cong., 1st Sess. 474 (1866).

Senator Trumbull emphasized: "This bill has nothing to do with the political rights or *status* of parties. It is confined exclusively to their civil rights, such rights as should appertain to every free man."

Section 18 of the 1870 Act also re-enacted the 1866 Act and declared that § 16 "shall be enforced according to the provisions of said act." 16 Stat. 144.

Of course, this Court has found in the legislative history of the 1866 Act evidence that Congress sought to accomplish more than the destruction of state-imposed civil disabilities and discriminatory punishments. We have held that both § 1981 and § 1982 "prohibit all racial discrimination, whether or not under color of law, with respect to the rights enumerated therein." Jones v. Alfred H. Mayer Co., 392 U.S., at 436, 88 S.Ct., at 2201. See Johnson v. Railway Express Agency, 421 U.S. 454, 459–460, 95 S.Ct. 1716, 1719–1720, 44 L.Ed.2d 295 (1975); Runyon v. McCrary, 427 U.S., at 168, 96 S.Ct., at 2593. Nevertheless, the fact that the prohibitions of § 1981 encompass private as well as governmental action does not suggest that the statute reaches more than purposeful discrimination, whether public or private. Indeed, the relevant opinions are hostile to such an implication. Thus, although we held in *Jones,* supra, that § 1982 reaches private action, we explained that § 1 of the 1866 Act "was meant to prohibit all *racially motivated* deprivations of the rights enumerated in the statute." Similarly, in Runyon v. McCrary, supra, we stated that § 1981 would be violated "if a private offeror refuses to extend to a Negro, *solely because he is a Negro,* the same opportunity to enter into contracts as he extends to white offerees."

The immediate evils with which the Thirty-ninth Congress was concerned simply did not include practices that were "neutral on their face, and even neutral in terms of intent," Griggs v. Duke Power Co., 401 U.S. 424, 430, 91 S.Ct. 849, 853, 28 L.Ed.2d 158 (1971), but that had the incidental effect of disadvantaging blacks to a greater degree than whites. Congress instead acted to protect the freedmen from intentional discrimination by those whose object was "to make their former slaves dependent serfs, victims of unjust laws, and debarred from all progress and elevation by organized social prejudices." Cong. Globe, 39th Cong., 1st Sess. 1839 (1866) (Rep. Clarke). The supporters of the bill repeatedly emphasized that the legislation was designed to eradicate blatant deprivations of civil rights, clearly fashioned with the purpose of oppressing the former slaves. To infer that Congress sought to accomplish more than this would require stronger evidence in the legislative record than we have been able to discern.[15]

---

15. We attach significance to the fact that throughout much of the congressional debates, S.B. 61, which became the 1866 Act, contained an opening declaration that "there shall be no discrimination in civil rights or immunities among citizens of the United States in any State or Territory of the United States *on account of race, color, or previous condition of slavery.*" This passage had occasioned controversy in both the Senate and the House because of the breadth of the phrase "civil rights and immunities." After the Senate had passed the bill and as debates in the House were drawing to a close, the bill's floor manager, Rep. Wilson, introduced an amendment proposed by the House Judiciary Committee, of which he was also the chairman. That amendment deleted the language quoted above and left the bill as it would read when ultimately enacted. Rep. Wilson explained that the broad language of the original bill could have been interpreted to encompass the right of suffrage and other political rights. "To obviate that difficulty and the difficulty growing out of any other construction beyond the specific rights named in the section, our amendment strikes out all of those general terms and leaves the bill with the rights specified in the section." Cong. Globe 39th Cong. 1st Sess., 1367. The deleted language, em-

Our conclusion that § 1981 reaches only purposeful discrimination is supported by one final observation about its legislative history. As noted earlier, the origins of the law can be traced to both the Civil Rights Act of 1866 and the Enforcement Act of 1870. Both of these laws, in turn, were legislative cousins of the Fourteenth Amendment. The 1866 Act represented Congress' first attempt to ensure equal rights for the freedmen following the formal abolition of slavery effected by the Thirteenth Amendment. As such, it constituted an initial blueprint of the Fourteenth Amendment, which Congress proposed in part as a means of "incorporat[ing] the guaranties of the Civil Rights Act of 1866 in the organic law of the land." The 1870 Act, which contained the language that now appears in § 1981, was enacted as a means of enforcing the recently ratified Fourteenth Amendment. In light of the close connection between these Acts and the Amendment, it would be incongruous to construe the principal object of their successor, § 1981, in a manner markedly different from that of the Amendment itself.[17]

With respect to the latter, "official action will not be held unconstitutional solely because it results in a racially disproportionate impact," Arlington Heights v. Metropolitan Housing Dev. Corp., 429 U.S. 252, 264–265, 97 S.Ct. 555, 562–563, 50 L.Ed.2d 450 (1977). "[E]ven if a neutral law has a disproportionately adverse impact upon a racial minority, it is unconstitutional under the Equal Protection Clause only if that impact can be traced to a discriminatory purpose." Personnel Administrator of Mass. v. Feeney, 442 U.S. 256, 272, 99 S.Ct. 2282, 2292, 60 L.Ed.2d 870 (1979). See Washington v. Davis, 426 U.S. 229, 96 S.Ct. 2040, 48 L.Ed.2d 597 (1976). The same Congress that proposed the Fourteenth Amendment also passed the Civil Rights Act of 1866, and the ratification of that amendment paved the way for the Enforcement

phasized above, strongly suggests that Congress was primarily concerned with intentional discrimination. That the passage was removed in an effort to *narrow* the scope of the legislation sharply undercuts the view that the 1866 Act reflects broader concerns.

17. It is true that § 1981, because it is derived in part from the 1866 Act, has roots in the Thirteenth as well as the Fourteenth Amendment. Indeed, we relied on that heritage in holding that Congress could constitutionally enact § 1982, which is also traceable to the 1866 Act, without limiting its reach to "state action." See Jones v. Alfred H. Mayer Co., 392 U.S. 409, 438, 88 S.Ct. 2186, 2202, 20 L.Ed.2d 1189 (1968). As we have already intimated, however, the fact that Congress acted in the shadow of the Thirteenth Amendment does not demonstrate that Congress sought to eradicate more than purposeful discrimination when it passed the 1866 Act. For example, Congress also enacted 42 U.S.C. § 1985(3) in part to implement the commands of the Thirteenth Amendment. See Griffin v. Breckenridge, 403 U.S. 88, 104–105, 91 S.Ct. 1790, 1799, 29 L.Ed.2d 338 (1971). While holding that § 1985(3) does not require state action but also reaches private conspiracies, we have emphasized that a violation of the statute requires "some racial, or perhaps otherwise class-based, invidiously discriminatory animus behind the conspirators' action."

We need not decide whether the Thirteenth Amendment itself reaches practices with a disproportionate effect as well as those motivated by discriminatory purpose, or indeed whether it accomplished anything more than the abolition of slavery. We conclude only that the existence of that Amendment, and the fact that it authorized Congress to enact legislation abolishing the "badges and incidents of slavery," *Civil Rights Cases*, 109 U.S. 3, 20, 3 S.Ct. 18, 27, 27 L.Ed. 835 (1883), do not evidence congressional intent to reach disparate effects in enacting § 1981.

Act of 1870. These measures were all products of the same milieu and were directed against the same evils. Although Congress might have charted a different course in enacting the predecessors to § 1981 than it did in proposing the Fourteenth Amendment, we have found no convincing evidence that it did so.

We conclude, therefore, that § 1981, like the Equal Protection Clause, can be violated only by purposeful discrimination.

III

The District Court held petitioners liable under § 1981 notwithstanding its finding that the plaintiffs had failed to prove intent to discriminate on the part of the employers and associations as a class. In light of our holding that § 1981 can be violated only by intentional discrimination, the District Court's judgment can stand only if liability under § 1981 can properly rest on some ground other than the discriminatory motivation of the petitioners themselves. Both the District Court and respondents have relied on such grounds, but we find them unconvincing.

A

The District Court reasoned that liability could be vicariously imposed upon the employers and associations, based upon the intentional discrimination practiced by Local 542 in its operation of the hiring hall. The court's theory was that petitioners had delegated to the "union hiring hall" the authority to select workers as "the agent for two principals—the union and the contractors, with their respective associations." Since the hiring hall came into existence only through the agreement of petitioners, and since the exclusive hiring hall was the means by which "the intentional discrimination of the union was able to work its way broadly into the common workforce of operating engineers," the court concluded that "[t]he acts of the union therefore justify imposition of responsibility upon those employers participating in the original delegation." The effect of this holding, as the court recognized, was to impose a "duty to see that discrimination does not take place in the selection of one's workforce," regardless of where the discrimination originates.

As applied to the petitioner associations, the District Court's theory is flawed on its own terms. The doctrine of *respondeat superior*, as traditionally conceived and as understood by the District Court, enables the imposition of liability on a principal for the tortious acts of his agent and, in the more common case, on the master for the wrongful acts of his servant. "Agency is the fiduciary relation which results from the manifestation of consent by one person to another that the other shall act on his behalf and subject to his control, and consent by the other so to act." Restatement (Second) of Agency § 1 (1958). A master-servant relationship is a form of agency in which the master employs the servant as "an agent to perform service in his affairs" and "controls or has the right to control the physical conduct of the other in the performance of the service." Id., § 2. See 2 F. Harper & F. James, The Law of Torts § 26.6 (1956). Local 542, in its operation of the hiring hall, simply performed no function as the agent or servant of the associations. The record demonstrates that the associations themselves do not hire operating engineers, and never have. Their primary purpose is to represent certain employers in contract negotiations with the Union. Even if the doctrine of *respondeat superior* were broadly applicable to suits based on § 1981, therefore, it would not support the imposition of liability on a defendant based on the acts of a party with whom it had no agency or employment relationship.[18]

We have similar difficulty in accepting the application of traditional *respondeat superior* doctrine to the class of contract or employers. In the run of cases, the relationship between an employer and the union that represents its employees simply cannot be accurately characterized as one between principal and agent or master and servant. Indeed, such a conception is alien to the fundamental assumptions upon which the federal labor laws are structured.

At the core of agency is a "fiduciary relation" arising from the "consent by one person to another that the other shall act on his behalf and subject to his control." Restatement (Second) of Agency § 1. Equally central to the master-servant relation is the master's control over or right to control the physical activities of the servant. The District Court found that the requirement of control was satisfied because "the employers retained power to oppose the union discrimination." However, the "power to oppose" the Union, even when the opposition is grounded in the terms of the collective bargaining agreement, is not tantamount to a "right to control" the Union.[19] Indeed, a rule equating the two would convert every contractual relationship into an agency relationship, a result clearly unsupported by the common-law doctrines on which the District Court relied.

The District Court's assumptions about the relation between the Union and the class of employers with whom it has contracted also runs counter to the premises on which the federal labor laws have been constructed. While authorizing collective bargaining and providing

---

18. In this case, the associations were held liable because they negotiated an agreement, fair on its face, which was later implemented by another party in a manner that was not only discriminatory but in violation of the agreement itself *and* in a manner of which the associations were neither aware nor had reason to be aware. Since the associations' only role was as agent for employers whose hiring would actually be governed by the agreement, the District Court's theory presumably would also permit the imposition of liability on the attorneys who actually conducted the contract negotiations. We are unaware of any authority supporting such an extended application of *respondeat superior*.

19. According to respondents, the District Court's conclusion that petitioners retained the power to control the hiring hall was a finding of fact that cannot be set aside unless clearly erroneous. We disagree. The District Court found that petitioners had the "power to oppose" the Union, a conclusion we do not question. Whether the power to oppose the Union is equivalent to a right of control sufficient to invoke the doctrine of *respondeat superior* is, however, a legal question to which we must devote our independent judgment.

means of enforcing the resultant contracts, the National Labor Relations Act expressly prohibits employers from compromising the independence of labor unions. The entire process of collective bargaining is structured and regulated on the assumption that "[t]he parties—even granting the modification of views that may come from a realization of economic interdependence—still proceed from contrary and to an extent antagonistic viewpoints and concepts of self-interest." NLRB v. Insurance Agents, 361 U.S. 477, 488, 80 S.Ct. 419, 426, 4 L.Ed.2d 454 (1960). We have no reason to doubt the validity of that assumption in the instant case.

Respondents also suggest that petitioners can be held vicariously liable for the discriminatory conduct of the JATC. They argue that the JATC is properly viewed as an agent of both Local 542 and the associations, emphasizing that half of the trustees charged with administering the JATC are appointed by the associations and that the JATC is wholly funded by mandatory contributions from the employers. We note initially that the District Court premised petitioners' liability not on the actions of the JATC, but on the discriminatory conduct of the Union. The record, therefore, contains no findings regarding the relationship between the JATC and petitioners, beyond those noted above, that might support application of *respondeat superior*.

The facts emphasized by respondents, standing alone, are inadequate. That the employers fund the activities of the JATC does not render the JATC the employers' servant or agent any more than an independent contractor is rendered an agent simply because he is compensated by the principal for his services. The employers must also enjoy a right to control the activities of the JATC, and there is no record basis for believing that to be the case. Neither is a right of control inferable merely from the power of the associations to appoint half of the JATC's trustees. It is entirely possible that the trustees, once appointed, owe a fiduciary duty to the JATC and the apprentices enrolled in its programs, rather than to the entities that appointed them. On the assumption that *respondeat superior* applies to suits based on § 1981, there is no basis for holding either the employers or the associations liable under that doctrine without evidence that an agency relationship existed at the time the JATC committed the acts on which its own liability was premised.

B

The District Court also justified its result by concluding that § 1981 imposes a "nondelegable duty" on petitioners "to see that discrimination does not take place in the selection of [their] workforce." The concept of a nondelegable duty imposes upon the principal not merely an obligation to exercise care in his own activities, but to answer for the well being of those persons to whom the duty runs. See Restatement (Second) of Agency § 214. The duty is not discharged by using care in delegating it to an independent contractor. Consequently, the doctrine creates an exception to the common-law rule that a principal normally will not be liable for the tortious conduct of an independent contractor. So understood, a nondelegable duty is an affirmative obligation to ensure the protection of the person to whom the duty runs.

In a sense, to characterize such a duty as "nondelegable" is merely to restate the duty. Thus, in this litigation the question is not whether the employers and associations are free to delegate their duty to abide by § 1981, for whatever duty the statute imposes, they are bound to adhere to it. The question is *what* duty does § 1981 impose. More precisely, does § 1981 impose a duty to refrain from intentionally denying blacks the right to contract on the same basis as whites or does it impose an affirmative obligation to ensure that blacks enjoy such a right? The language of the statute does not speak in terms of duties. It merely declares specific rights held by "[a]ll persons within the jurisdiction of the United States." We are confident that the Thirty-ninth Congress meant to do no more than prohibit the employers and associations in these cases from intentionally depriving black workers of the rights enumerated in the statute, including the equal right to contract. It did not intend to make them the guarantors of the workers' rights as against third parties who would infringe them.

Our earlier holding that § 1981 reaches only intentional discrimination virtually compels this conclusion. It would be anomalous to hold that § 1981 could be violated only by intentional discrimination and then to find this requirement satisfied by proof that the individual plaintiffs did not enjoy "the same right * * * to make and enforce contracts * * * as is enjoyed by white citizens" and that the defendants merely failed to ensure that the plaintiffs enjoyed employment opportunities equivalent to that of whites. Such a result would be particularly inappropriate in the case of the associations, who are not engaged in the construction business, do not employ operating engineers, and consequently did not delegate to the Union any hiring functions which they otherwise would have performed themselves. Neither the District Court nor respondents identify anything in the language or legislative history of the statute to support a contrary conclusion.[21]

* * *

21. Respondents also contend that petitioners can be held liable on the theory that the hiring hall was a "joint enterprise" involving petitioners as well as the Union. They point to language in the District Court's opinion holding that "the union hiring hall was the agent for two principals—the union and the contractors with their respective associations." Even this theory, however, requires, among other things, the existence of a mutual right of control as between the members of the enterprise. See Restatement (Second) of Torts § 491. For reasons we have already stated, there is no record basis for finding that petitioners had a right to control Local 542 in its administration of the hiring hall. We also doubt the validity of the assumption that the hiring hall is a separate entity, except perhaps as a physical structure. The District Court did not find, and respondents do not assert, that the hiring hall has a separate juridical existence.

The judgment of the Court of Appeals is reversed and the case is remanded for proceedings consistent with this opinion.

It is so ordered.

JUSTICE O'CONNOR, with whom JUSTICE BLACKMUN joins, concurring.

* * *

I would briefly note the limits of the Court's holding. Once this case has been remanded to the District Court, nothing in the Court's opinion prevents the respondents from litigating the question of the employers' liability under § 1981 by attempting to prove the traditional elements of *respondeat superior*.

* * *

JUSTICE STEVENS, concurring in part and concurring in the judgment.

As I noted in my separate opinion in Runyon v. McCrary, 427 U.S. 160, 189, 96 S.Ct. 2586, 2603, 49 L.Ed.2d 415, the Congress that enacted § 1 of the Civil Rights Act of 1866 "intended only to guarantee all citizens the same legal capacity to make and enforce contracts, to obtain, own, and convey property, and to litigate and give evidence." Any violation of that guarantee—whether deliberate, negligent, or purely accidental—would, in my opinion, violate 42 U.S.C. § 1981. The statute itself contains no requirement that an intent to discriminate must be proved.

The Court has broadened the coverage of § 1981 far beyond the scope actually intended by its authors; in essence, the Court has converted a statutory guarantee of equal rights into a grant of equal opportunities. Whether or not those decisions faithfully reflect the intent of Congress, the enlarged coverage of the statute "is now an important part of the fabric of our law." *Runyon*, supra, at 190 (Stevens, J., concurring).

Since I do not believe Congress intended § 1981 to have any application at all in the area of employment discrimination generally covered by Title VII of the Civil Rights Act of 1964, an analysis of the motives and intent of the Reconstruction Congress cannot be expected to tell us whether proof of intentional discrimination should be required in the judicially-created portion of the statute's coverage. Since Congress required no such proof in the statute it actually enacted, a logician would be comfortable in concluding that no such proof should ever be required. Nevertheless, since that requirement tends to define the entire coverage of § 1981 in a way that better reflects the basic intent of Congress than would a contrary holding, I concur in the conclusion reached by the Court in Part II of its opinion insofar as it relates to the statutory protection of equal opportunity but, perhaps illogically, would reach a different conclusion in a case challenging a denial of a citizen's civil rights.

Accordingly, I join the Court's judgment and Parts III and IV of its opinion.

———

Justice Marshall, with whom Justice Brennan joins, dissenting.

Today the Court reaches out and decides that 42 U.S.C. § 1981 requires proof of an intent to discriminate—an issue that is not at all necessary to the disposition of this case. Because I find no support for the majority's resolution of this issue, and because I disagree with its disposition of this case even if proof of intent should ordinarily be required, I respectfully dissent.

I

The question whether intent generally should be required in § 1981 actions is at most tangentially related to this case. There was unquestionably intentional discrimination on the part of both the union (Local 542) and the Joint Apprenticeship and Training Committee (JATC), a body, composed of officials from the union and the petitioner contracting associations, which jointly administered the apprenticeship and training program. As a result, the only question that the Court need address today is whether limited injunctive liability may be vicariously imposed upon an employer when the person or entity to whom it delegates a large portion of its hiring decisions intentionally discriminates on the basis of race. However, because the majority has chosen to reach first the more general question whether proof of intent is a prerequisite to recovery in a § 1981 action, I likewise will address this issue first.

* * * The plain language does not contain or suggest an intent requirement. A violation of § 1981 is not expressly conditioned on the motivation or intent of any person. The language focuses on the effects of discrimination on the protected class, and not on the intent of the person engaging in discriminatory conduct. Nothing in the statutory language implies that a right denied because of sheer insensitivity, or a pattern of conduct that disproportionately burdens the protected class of persons, is entitled to any less protection than one denied because of racial animus.

The Court attaches no significance to the broad and unqualified language of § 1981. Furthermore, the majority finds no support for its conclusion that intent should be required in the legislative history to § 1 of the 1866 Act, the precursor to § 1981. Instead, in the face of this unqualified language and the broad remedial purpose § 1981 was intended to serve, the majority assumes that Congress intended to restrict the scope of the statute to those situations in which racial animus can be proved on the ground that the legislative history contains no "convincing evidence" to the contrary. In my view, this approach to statutory construction is not only unsound, it is also contrary to our prior decisions, which have consistently given § 1981 as broad an interpretation as its language permits.

The fallacy in the Court's approach is that, in construing § 1981 and its legislative history, the Court virtually ignores Congress' broad remedial purposes and our paramount national policy of eradicating racial discrimination and its pernicious effects. When viewed in this light, it is clear that proof of intentional discrimination should not be required in order to find a violation of § 1981.

Although the Thirty-ninth Congress that passed the Civil Rights Act of 1866 did not specifically address the question whether intent should be required, the conclusion is inescapable that the congressional leadership intended to effectuate "the *result* of a change from a centuries old social system based on involuntary labor, with all the notions of racial unsuitability for the performance of anything but menial labor under close supervision, to the free labor system." Croker v. Boeing Co., 662 F.2d 975, 1006 (CA3 1981) (Gibbons, J., with whom Higginbotham and Sloviter, JJ., joined, dissenting in part) (emphasis in original). When this Congress convened, the Thirteenth Amendment had been ratified, abolishing slavery as a legal status. However, it was clear that in reality, Negroes were hardly accorded the employment and other opportunities accorded white persons generally. Thus, this Congress undertook to provide *in fact* the rights and privileges that were available to Negroes in theory. Four separate but related measures were proposed in an effort to accomplish this purpose.[1]

In this general climate, the 1866 Civil Rights Act was not an isolated technical statute dealing with only a narrow subject. Instead, it was an integral part of a broad congressional scheme intended to work a major revolution in the prevailing social order.[2] It is inconceivable that the Congress which enacted this statute would permit this purpose to be thwarted by excluding from the statute private action that concededly creates serious obstacles to the pursuit of job opportunities by Negroes solely because the aggrieved persons could not prove that the actors deliberately intended such a result. Even less conceiva-

1. These measures included the Civil Rights Act of 1866 passed over President Johnson's veto; the Freedman's Bureau bill, which would have created a federal agency to ensure that a free labor system in which Negroes had equal participation would *in fact* be accomplished, and which commanded a clear majority in Congress, but failed to pass over a presidential veto; a constitutional amendment sponsored by Representative Bingham but not recommended; and the Fourteenth Amendment.

2. As the majority recognizes, one of the principal changes Congress hoped to achieve was the elimination of the infamous Black Codes. These included state laws regulating the terms and conditions of employment. In many States, these oppressive laws were facially neutral, literally applying to all laborers without regard to race. The laws prohibited such conduct as refusing to perform work and disobeying an employer, or inducing an employee away from his employer, and many provided for forfeiture of wages if the employee did not fulfill the terms of his employment contract. Other Codes included vagrancy laws, which were vague and broad enough to encompass virtually all Negro adults, and many were facially neutral, applying to white persons as well as to Negroes. The Black Codes were constantly discussed during the debates over the Civil Rights Act of 1866, and Congress clearly intended that the Act would eliminate even those Codes which were facially neutral.

ble is the notion, embraced by the Court's opinion today, that this Congress intended to absolve employers from even injunctive liability imposed as a result of intentional discrimination practiced by the persons to whom they had delegated their authority to hire employees.

The legislative history demonstrates that the Thirty-ninth Congress intended not merely to provide a remedy for preexisting rights, but to eradicate the "badges of slavery" that remained after the Civil War and the enactment of the Thirteenth Amendment. Congress was acutely aware of the difficulties that federal officials had encountered in effectuating the change from the system of slavery to a system of free labor even though the legal and constitutional groundwork for this change had already been laid. * * *

* * * [T]he leaders of Congress set about to enact legislation that would ensure to Negroes the opportunity to participate equally in the free labor system by providing an instrument by which they could strike down barriers to their participation, whether those barriers were erected with the conscious intent to exclude or with callous indifference to exclusionary effects. Congress knew that this attitude could manifest itself in a number of different ways and intended to protect Negro workers against not only flagrant, intentional discrimination, but also against more subtle forms of discrimination which might successfully camouflage the intent to oppress through facially neutral policies. * * *

Unfortunately, this awareness seems utterly lacking in the Court's opinion today. In order to hold that § 1981 requires a showing of intent, the majority must assume that the rights guaranteed under § 1981—to make and enforce contracts on the same basis as white persons—can be adequately protected by limiting the statute to cases where the aggrieved person can prove intentional discrimination. In taking this extraordinarily naive view, the Court shuts its eyes to reality, ignoring the manner in which racial discrimination most often infects our society. Today, although flagrant examples of intentional discrimination still exist, discrimination more often occurs "on a more sophisticated and subtle level," the effects of which are often as cruel and "devastating as the most crude form of discrimination." Pennsylvania v. Local 542, Int'l Union of Operating Engineers, 469 F.Supp. 329, 337 (ED Pa.1978) (Higginbotham, Circuit J., sitting by designation). I think that Judge Higginbotham most accurately recognized this problem when he noted that "[t]he facts of the instant case * * * demonstrate the complexity and subtlety of the interrelationship of race, collective bargaining, craft unions, the employment process and that ultimate goal—real jobs." He further noted that "[a]t the critical level of viable jobs and equal opportunities, there were intentional and persistent efforts to exclude and discourage most of the minorities who, but for their race, would have been considered for entry into the union and for the more lucrative jobs."

* * * The purposes behind § 1981, and the profound national policy of blotting out all vestiges of racial discrimination, are no less frustrated when equal opportunities are denied through cleverly masked or merely insensitive practices, where proof of actual intent is nearly impossible to obtain, than when instances of intentional discrimination escape unremedied. For this reason, I cannot accept the Court's glib and unrealistic view that requiring proof of intent in § 1981 actions does not frustrate that statute's purpose of protecting against the devastating effects of racial discrimination in employment.

II

Even if I agreed with the Court that intent must be proved in a § 1981 action, I could not agree with its conclusion that the petitioner contracting associations should be immunized, even from injunctive liability, for the intentional discrimination practiced by the union hall to which they delegated a major portion of their hiring decisions. Under § 1981, minorities have an unqualified right to enter into employment contracts on the same basis as white persons. It is undisputed that in this case, the respondent class was denied this right through intentional discrimination. The fact that the associations chose to delegate a large part of the hiring process to the local union hiring hall, which then engaged in intentional discrimination, does not alter the fact that respondents were denied the right to enter into employment contracts with the associations on the same basis as white persons.

At the very least, § 1981 imposes on employers the obligation to make employment decisions free from racial considerations. The hiring decisions made by the contracting associations in this case were fraught with racial discrimination. Solely because of their race, hundreds of minority operating engineers were totally excluded from the industry and could not enter into employment contracts with any employer. Those minorities allowed into the industry suffered discrimination in referrals, and thus they too were denied the same right as white persons to contract with the contracting associations. Not one of the petitioner contracting associations has ever claimed, nor could they, that minorities had the same right as white operating engineers to contract for employment.

Instead, the contracting associations attempt to hide behind the veil of ignorance, shifting their responsibility under § 1981 to the very entity which they chose to assist them in making hiring decisions. The suggestion that an employer's responsibility under § 1981 depends upon its own choice of a hiring agent finds no support in the statute, nor does any other source of law authorize the circumvention of § 1981 that the contracting associations seek here. Their obligation to make employment contracts free from racial discrimination is a nondelegable one—it does not disappear when, as is often the case, the actual employer designates a particular agent to assist in the hiring process.

In my view, the fact that the discriminating entity here is a union hiring hall, and not a person or corporation which has a traditional agent-principal relationship with the employer, does not alter this analysis.

The majority does not really analyze the question whether petitioners should be held injunctively liable because § 1981 imposes upon them a nondelegable duty. Instead the majority argues that, because it has held that § 1981 is intended only to reach intentional discrimination, the statute cannot make employers "guarantors of the workers' rights as against third parties who would infringe them." This argument does not withstand analysis. The majority does not assert that employers may escape liability under § 1981 by delegating their hiring decisions to a third party agent. Indeed, in light of the importance attached to the rights § 1981 is intended to safeguard, the duty to abide by this statute must be nondelegable, as the majority apparently recognizes. Instead, the majority argues that because § 1981 imposes only the duty to refrain from intentional discrimination in hiring, it somehow automatically follows that this duty could not have been violated in this case. However, it was precisely this duty that was violated here. The District Court found, and this Court does not disagree, that the entity to whom the petitioner associations effectively delegated their hiring decisions *intentionally discriminated* against the respondent class on the basis of race in making these decisions. Even under the Court's own narrow view of the scope of the duty imposed by § 1981, then, the duty was unquestionably violated in this case.

The majority obfuscates the issue by suggesting that the District Court imposed upon the contracting associations an obligation to seek out and eliminate discrimination by unrelated third parties wherever it may occur. In reality, the District Court did nothing more than impose limited injunctive liability upon the associations for violating their nondelegable duty under § 1981 when the union hiring hall, which effectively made hiring decisions for the associations, engaged in intentional discrimination on the basis of race in making these decisions.

By immunizing the employer from the injunctive relief necessary to remedy the intentional discrimination practiced by those through whom the employer makes its hiring decisions, the Court removes the person most necessary to accord full relief—the entity with whom the aggrieved persons will ultimately make a contract. I believe that the District Court appropriately rejected the petitioners' argument when it explained: "With intensity some employers urge that they agreed to the exclusive hiring hall system solely as a matter of economic survival at the end of a destructive ten week strike when the union would not compromise for any other hiring alternative. Yet economic pressures, however strong and harmful they might be, do not create immunity for employers, at least not in [the injunctive] liability phase."

Section 1981 provides Negroes "the same right" to make contracts as white persons enjoy. In the present case, this unqualified right was violated, and the violation is made no more palatable because the persons who actually made the hiring decisions and referrals, and not the employer itself, engaged in intentional discrimination.[5] The devastating violation of their rights under § 1981 remains the same and will go at least partially unremedied when the person with whom the ultimate employment contract must be made is immunized from even injunctive relief. I cannot impute to the Congress which enacted § 1981 the intention to reach such an inequitable and nonsensical result. Accordingly, I must dissent.

NOTES AND PROBLEMS FOR DISCUSSION

1. What impact is the decisions in *General Building Contractors Association* likely to have on the viability of § 1981 as a remedy for employment discrimination? For a suggestion that § 1981 should not be limited to claims of intentional discrimination, see Friedman, The Burger Court and the Prima Facie Case in Employment Discrimination Litigation: A Critique, 65 Corn. L.Rev. 1, 31–43 (1979).

2. In JOHNSON v. RYDER TRUCK LINES, INC., 575 F.2d 471 (4th Cir.1978), cert. denied, 440 U.S. 979, 99 S.Ct. 1785, 60 L.Ed.2d 239 (1979), the Fourth Circuit ruled that the bona fide seniority system exemption provided by § 703(h) of Title VII should be read into § 1981 to promote uniformity of result under the two statutes. This interpretation of § 1981 subsequently was adopted by several other circuit courts. See NAACP v. DPOA, 900 F.2d 903 (6th Cir.1990); Freeman v. Motor Convoy, Inc., 700 F.2d 1339 (11th Cir.1983); Boilermakers, Wattleton v. International Broth. of Boiler Makers, 686 F.2d 586 (7th Cir.1982), cert. denied, 459 U.S. 1208, 103 S.Ct. 1199, 75 L.Ed.2d 442 (1983); Terrell v. United States Pipe and Foundry Co., 644 F.2d 1112 (5th Cir.1981). But see Bolden v. Pennsylvania State Police, 578 F.2d 912 (3d Cir.1978) (§ 703(h) does not apply to § 1981 claims). What effect should the decision in *General Building Contractors Association* have on this issue?

3. Plaintiffs who can assert claims under either Title VII or § 1981 often look to the latter statute because of certain procedural and remedial advantages it offers. For example, they have immediate access to the courts, as § 1981, unlike Title VII, does not require invocation of administrative remedies as a prerequisite to judicial relief. But since the 1866 law is silent on the matter of procedure, the courts have played a significant role in delineating the procedural relationship between these two related statutes. In JOHNSON v. RAILWAY EXPRESS AGENCY, INC., 421 U.S. 454, 95 S.Ct. 1716, 44 L.Ed.2d 295 (1975), the Supreme Court emphasized that Congress intended for Title VII and § 1981 to be separate and independent, rather than mutually exclusive, remedies for employment discrimination. Accordingly, it held that the prosecution of a Title VII suit did not toll the limitations period applicable to an action based on the same facts brought under § 1981. The Court recognized that its ruling on the tolling issue would likely encourage a plaintiff interested in retaining its § 1981 claim to file a separate action under that statute

---

5. I agree with the Justice O'Connor's observation that nothing in the Court's opinion prevents the District Court on remand from holding the petitioner associations liable for discrimination practiced by the JATC. Specifically, they may be held liable because the trustees administering the JATC are appointed by the petitioner associations, the JATC is funded by employer contributions, and the associations exercise control over the JATC's actions. * * *

pending EEOC action on the related Title VII claim, a result inconsistent with Congress' expressed desire (when it enacted Title VII) to encourage administrative resolution of discrimination claims. It suggested, however, with some misgivings, that this undesirable consequence could be moderated if the plaintiff requested the court in the § 1981 action to stay that proceeding until the Title VII administrative efforts had been completed. Moreover, the Court concluded, the potential for discouraging reliance on the Title VII administrative machinery was overwhelmed by Congress' clear intent to retain § 1981 as an independent remedy for civil rights claimants.

The independent nature of these two remedies has been underscored by rulings that state administrative proceedings undertaken in connection with a Title VII claim do not operate as a bar to the related § 1981 action. See Kern v. Research Libraries, 27 FEP Cases 1007 (S.D.N.Y.1979). Where, however, a state administrative agency's decision has been reviewed by a state court, the principles of res judicata and collateral estoppel have been applied to preclude relitigation of the same issues in a § 1981 action. See Mitchell v. National Broadcasting Co., 553 F.2d 265 (2d Cir.1977) (§ 1981 case dismissed as result of state court's action upholding state agency dismissal of complaint brought under state antidiscrimination law since issue of race discrimination identical in both actions.) Is this analysis consistent with the Supreme Court's resolution of the same question with respect to Title VII in *Kremer* or in connection with § 1983 in *Elliot, supra* at 856? A ruling on the merits of a § 1981 claim has been held to preclude the assertion of an identical Title VII cause of action under the doctrine of collateral estoppel. See Lartius v. Iowa Dept. of Transp., 705 F.2d 1018 (8th Cir.1983).

Other advantages associated with filing under § 1981 have been eliminated as a result of the enactment of the 1991 Civil Rights Act. Jury trials and the opportunity for recovery of compensatory and punitive damages are now available under Title VII as well as § 1981. And while they are available only in Title VII claims alleging intentional discrimination, the Court's ruling in *General Building Contractors Ass'n* imposes the same limitation in § 1981 suits. Keep in mind, however, that the damage cap contained in the 1991 Act does not apply to actions brought under § 1981. In addition, the availability of a longer limitations period and the absence of a minimum employer size continue to make § 1981 an attractive alternative cause of action for those plaintiffs who fall within its protection.

SECTION B. THE CIVIL RIGHTS ACT OF 1871, SECTION ONE—42 U.S.C. § 1983

Read 42 U.S.C. § 1983 at p. 1264.

PERSONNEL ADMINISTRATOR OF MASSACHUSETTS v. FEENEY

Supreme Court of the United States, 1979.
442 U.S. 256, 99 S.Ct. 2282, 60 L.Ed.2d 870.

MR. JUSTICE STEWART delivered the opinion of the Court.

This case presents a challenge to the constitutionality of the Massachusetts Veterans Preference Statute, Mass.Gen.Laws, ch. 31,

§ 23, on the ground that it discriminates against women in violation of the Equal Protection Clause of the Fourteenth Amendment. Under ch. 31, § 23,[1] all veterans who qualify for state civil service positions must be considered for appointment ahead of any qualifying nonveterans. The preference operates overwhelmingly to the advantage of males.

The appellee Helen B. Feeney is not a veteran. She brought this action pursuant to 42 U.S.C. § 1983 alleging that the absolute preference formula established in ch. 31, § 23 inevitably operates to exclude women from consideration for the best Massachusetts civil service jobs and thus unconstitutionally denies them the equal protection of the laws.[2] The three-judge District Court agreed, one judge dissenting. Anthony v. Commonwealth of Massachusetts, 415 F.Supp. 485 (1976).[3]

The District Court found that the absolute preference afforded by Massachusetts to veterans has a devastating impact upon the employment opportunities of women. Although it found that the goals of the preference were worthy and legitimate and that the legislation had not been enacted for the purpose of discriminating against women, the court reasoned that its exclusionary impact upon women was nonetheless so severe as to require the State to further its goals through a more limited form of preference. Finding that a more modest preference formula would readily accommodate the State's interest in aiding veterans, the court declared ch. 31, § 23 unconstitutional and enjoined its operation.[4]

Upon an appeal taken by the Attorney General of Massachusetts,[5] this Court vacated the judgment and remanded the case for further consideration in light of our intervening decision in Washington v.

1. For the text of ch. 31, § 23, see n. 10, infra. The general Massachusetts Civil Service law, Mass.Gen.Laws, ch. 31, was recodified on Jan. 1, 1979, 1978 Mass. Acts, ch. 383, and the veterans' preference is now found at Mass.Gen.Laws Ann., ch. 31, § 26 (West 1979). Citations in this opinion, unless otherwise indicated, are to the ch. 31 codification in effect when this litigation was commenced.

2. No statutory claim was brought under Title VII of the Civil Rights Act of 1964, 42 U.S.C. § 2000e et seq. Section 712 of the Act, 42 U.S.C. § 2000e–11, provides that "nothing contained in this subchapter shall be construed to repeal or modify any Federal, State, territorial or local law creating special rights or preference for veterans." The parties have evidently assumed that this provision precludes a Title VII challenge.

3. The appellee's case had been consolidated with a similar action brought by Carol B. Anthony, a lawyer whose efforts to obtain a civil service Counsel I position had been frustrated by ch. 31, § 23. In

1975, Massachusetts exempted all attorney positions from the preference, 1975 Mass. Acts, ch. 134, and Anthony's claims were accordingly found moot by the District Court. Anthony v. Commonwealth of Massachusetts, 415 F.Supp. 485, 495.

4. The District Court entered a stay pending appeal, but the stay was rendered moot by the passage of an interim statute suspending ch. 31, § 23 pending final judgment and replacing it with an interim provision granting a modified point preference to veterans. 1976 Mass.Acts, ch. 200, now codified at Mass.Gen.Law Ann., ch. 31, § 26 (West 1979).

5. The Attorney General appealed the judgment over the objection of other state officers named as defendants. In response to our certification of the question whether Massachusetts law permits this, see Commonwealth of Massachusetts v. Feeney, 429 U.S. 66, 97 S.Ct. 345, 50 L.Ed.2d 224, the Supreme Judicial Court answered in the affirmative. Feeney v. Commonwealth, 373 Mass. 359, 366 N.E.2d 1262 (Mass.1977).

Davis, 426 U.S. 229, 96 S.Ct. 2040, 48 L.Ed.2d 597. Commonwealth of Massachusetts v. Feeney, 434 U.S. 884, 98 S.Ct. 252, 54 L.Ed.2d 169 (1977). The *Davis* case held that a neutral law does not violate the Equal Protection Clause solely because it results in a racially disproportionate impact; instead the disproportionate impact must be traced to a purpose to discriminate on the basis of race. 426 U.S., at 238–244, 96 S.Ct., at 2046–2050.

Upon remand, the District Court, one judge concurring and one judge again dissenting, concluded that a veterans' hiring preference is inherently nonneutral because it favors a class from which women have traditionally been excluded, and that the consequences of the Massachusetts absolute preference formula for the employment opportunities of women were too inevitable to have been "unintended." Accordingly, the court reaffirmed its original judgment. Feeney v. Commonwealth of Massachusetts, 451 F.Supp. 143. The Attorney General again appealed to this Court pursuant to 28 U.S.C. § 1253, and probable jurisdiction of the appeal was noted. 434 U.S. 884, 98 S.Ct. 252, 54 L.Ed.2d 169.

I

A

The Federal Government and virtually all of the States grant some sort of hiring preference to veterans.[6] The Massachusetts preference, which is loosely termed an "absolute lifetime" preference, is among the most generous.[7] It applies to all positions in the State's classified civil service, which constitute approximately 60% of the public jobs in the State. It is available to "any person, male or female, including a nurse," who was honorably discharged from the United States Armed Forces after at least 90 days of active service, at least one day of which

---

6. The first comprehensive federal veterans' statute was enacted in 1944. Veterans' Preference Act of 1944, ch. 287, 58 Stat. 387. The Federal Government has, however, engaged in preferential hiring of veterans, through official policies and various special laws, since the Civil War. See, e.g., Res. of March 3, 1865. No. 27, 13 Stat. 571 (hiring preference for disabled veterans). See generally The Provision of Federal Benefits for Veterans, An Historical Analysis of Major Veterans' Legislation, 1862–1954, Committee Print No. 171, 84th Cong., 1st Sess. (House Comm. on Vets. Affairs, Dec. 28, 1955) 258–265. For surveys of state veterans' preference laws, many of which also date back to the late 19th century, see State Veterans' Laws, Digest of State Laws Regarding Rights, Benefits and Privileges of Veterans and Their Dependents, House Committee on Veterans' Affairs, 91st Cong., 1st Sess.

(1969); Fleming & Shanor, Veterans Preferences in Public Employment: Unconstitutional Gender Discrimination? 26 Emory L.J. 13 (1977).

7. The forms of veterans' hiring preferences vary widely. The Federal Government and approximately 41 States grant veterans a point advantage on civil service examinations, usually 10 points for a disabled veteran and 5 for one who is not disabled. See Fleming & Shanor, supra n. 6, 26 Emory L.J., at 17, and n. 12 (citing statutes). A few offer only tie-breaking preferences. Id. n. 14 (citing statutes). A very few States, like Massachusetts, extend absolute hiring or positional preferences to qualified veterans. Id. n. 13. See, e.g., N.J.Stat.Ann. 11:27–4 (West 1977); S.D.Comp.Laws Ann. § 33-3-1 (1968); Utah Code Ann. § 34-30-11; Wash.Rev. Code §§ 41.04.010, 73.16.010 (1976).

was during "wartime." [8]   Persons who are deemed veterans and who are otherwise qualified for a particular civil service job may exercise the preference at any time and as many times as they wish.[9]

Civil service positions in Massachusetts fall into two general categories, labor and official. For jobs in the official service, with which the proofs in this action were concerned, the preference mechanics are uncomplicated. All applicants for employment must take competitive examinations. Grades are based on a formula that gives weight both to objective test results and to training and experience. Candidates who pass are then ranked in the order of their respective scores on an "eligible list." Ch. 31, § 23 requires, however, that disabled veterans, veterans, and surviving spouses and surviving parents of veterans be ranked—in the order of their respective scores—above all other candidates.[10]

Rank on the eligible list and availability for employment are the sole factors that * * * determine which candidates are considered for

8. Mass.Gen.Laws Ann., ch. 4, § 7, cl. 43 (West 1976), which supplies the general definition of the term "veteran," reads in pertinent part: "Veteran" shall mean any person, male or female, including a nurse, (a) whose last discharge or release from his wartime service, as defined herein, was under honorable conditions and who (b) served in the army, navy, marine corps, coast guard, or air force of the United States for not less than ninety days active service, at least one day of which was for wartime service * * *. Persons awarded the Purple Heart, ch. 4, § 7, cl. 43, or one of a number of specified campaign badges or the Congressional Medal of Honor are also deemed veterans. Mass.Gen.Laws Ann., ch. 31, § 21.

"Wartime service" is defined as service performed by a "Spanish War veteran," a "World War I veteran," a "World War II veteran," a "Korean veteran," a "Vietnam veteran," or a member of the "WAAC." Mass.Gen.Laws Ann., ch. 4, § 7, cl. 43 (West 1976). Each of these terms is further defined to specify a period of service. The statutory definitions, taken together, cover the entire period from September 16, 1940 to May 7, 1975. See ibid.

"WAAC" is defined as follows: "any woman who was discharged and so served in any corps or unit of the United States established for the purpose of enabling women to serve with, or as auxiliary to, the armed forces of the United States and such woman shall be deemed to be a veteran. Ibid.

9. The Massachusetts preference law formerly imposed a residency requirement, see 1954 Mass.Acts, ch. 627, § 3 (eligibility conditioned upon Massachusetts domicile prior to induction or five years residency in State). The distinction was invalidated as violative of the Equal Protection Clause in Stevens v. Campbell, 332 F.Supp. 102, 105 (D.C. Mass.1971). Cf. August v. Bronstein, 369 F.Supp. 190 (S.D.N.Y.1974) (upholding, inter alia, nondurational residency requirement in N.Y. veterans' preference statute), summarily aff'd, 417 U.S. 901, 94 S.Ct. 2596, 41 L.Ed.2d 208.

10. Chapter 31, § 23, provides in full:

"The names of persons who pass examinations for appointment to any position classified under the civil service shall be placed upon the eligible lists in the following order:—

"(1) Disabled veterans * * * in the order of their respective standing; (2) veterans in the order of their respective standing; (3) person described in section twenty-three B[the widow or widowed mother of a veteran killed in action or who died from a service-connected disability incurred in wartime service and who has not remarried] in the order of their respective standing; (4) other applicants in the order of their respective standing. Upon receipt of a requisition, names shall be certified from such lists according to the method of certification prescribed by the civil service rules. A disabled veteran shall be retained in employment in preference to all other persons, including veterans."

A 1977 amendment extended the dependents' preference to "surviving spouses," and "surviving parents." 1977 Mass. Acts, ch. 815.

appointment to an official civil service position. When a public agency has a vacancy, it requisitions a list of "certified eligibles" from the state personnel division. Under formulas prescribed by civil service rules, a small number of candidates from the top of an appropriate list, three if there is only one vacancy, are certified. The appointing agency is then required to choose from among these candidates.[11] Although the veterans' preference thus does not guarantee that a veteran will be appointed, it is obvious that the preference gives to veterans who achieve passing scores a well-nigh absolute advantage.

B

The appellee has lived in Dracut, Mass., most of her life. She entered the work force in 1948, and for the next 14 years worked at a variety of jobs in the private sector. She first entered the state civil service system in 1963, having competed successfully for a position as Senior Clerk Stenographer in the Massachusetts Civil Defense Agency. There she worked for four years. In 1967, she was promoted to the position of Federal Funds and Personnel Coordinator in the same agency. The agency, and with it her job, was eliminated in 1975.

During her 12–year tenure as a public employee, Ms. Feeney took and passed a number of open competitive civil service examinations. On several she did quite well, receiving in 1971 the second highest score on an examination for a job with the Board of Dental Examiners, and in 1973 the third highest on a test for an Administrative Assistant position with a mental health center. Her high scores, however, did not win her a place on the certified eligible list. Because of the veterans' preference, she was ranked sixth behind five male veterans on the Dental Examiner list. She was not certified, and a lower scoring veteran was eventually appointed. On the 1973 examination, she was placed in a position on the list behind 12 male veterans, 11 of whom had lower scores. Following the other examinations that she took, her name was similarly ranked below those of veterans who had achieved passing grades.

Ms. Feeney's interest in securing a better job in state government did not wane. Having been consistently eclipsed by veterans, however, she eventually concluded that further competition for civil service positions of interest to veterans would be futile. In 1975, shortly after her civil defense job was abolished, she commenced this litigation.

C

The veterans' hiring preference in Massachusetts, as in other jurisdictions, has traditionally been justified as a measure designed to reward veterans for the sacrifice of military service, to ease the transi-

---

11. A 1978 amendment requires the appointing authority to file a written statement of reasons if the person whose name was not highest is selected. 1978 Mass. Acts, ch. 393, § 11, currently codified at Mass.Gen.Laws Ann., ch. 31, § 27 (West 1979).

tion from military to civilian life, to encourage patriotic service, and to attract loyal and well-disciplined people to civil service occupations.[12]
* * *

* * *

* * * The Massachusetts law dates back to 1884, when the State, as part of its first civil service legislation, gave a statutory preference to civil service applicants who were Civil War veterans if their qualifications were equal to those of nonveterans. 1884 Mass. Acts, ch. 320, § 16. This tie-breaking provision blossomed into a truly absolute preference in 1895, when the State enacted its first general veterans preference law and exempted veterans from all merit selection requirements. 1895 Mass. Acts, ch. 501, § 2. In response to a challenge brought by a male non-veteran, this statute was declared violative of state constitutional provisions guaranteeing that government should be for the "common good" and prohibiting hereditary titles. Brown v. Russell, 166 Mass. 14, 43 N.E. 1005 (1896).

The current veterans' preference law has its origins in an 1896 statute, enacted to meet the state constitutional standards enunciated in Brown v. Russell. That statute limited the absolute preference to veterans who were otherwise qualified.[13] 1896 Mass. Acts, ch. 517, § 2. A closely divided Supreme Judicial Court, in an advisory opinion issued the same year, concluded that the preference embodied in such a statute would be valid. Opinion of the Justices, 166 Mass.589, 44 N.E. 625 (1896). In 1919, when the preference was extended to cover the veterans of World War I, the formula was further limited to provide for a priority in eligibility, in contrast to an absolute preference in hiring. 1919 Mass. Acts, ch. 150, § 2.[14] See Corliss v. Civil Service Comm'rs, 242 Mass.61, 136 N.E. 356 (1922). In Mayor of Lynn v. Comm'r of Civil Service, 269 Mass. 410, 414, 169 N.E. 502, 503–504 (1929), the Supreme

12. Veterans' preference laws have been challenged so often that the rationale in their support has become essentially standardized. See, e.g., Koelfgen v. Jackson, 355 F.Supp. 243 (D.C. Minn.1972), summarily aff'd, 410 U.S. 976, 93 S.Ct. 1502, 36 L.Ed.2d 173; August v. Bronstein, 369 F.Supp. 190 (S.D.N.Y.1974), summarily aff'd, 417 U.S. 901, 94 S.Ct. 2596, 41 L.Ed.2d 208; Rios v. Dillman, 499 F.2d 329 (CA5 1974); cf. Mitchell v. Cohen, 333 U.S. 411, 419 n. 12, 68 S.Ct. 518, 522 n. 12, 92 L.Ed. 774. See generally Blumberg, De Facto and De Jure Sex Discrimination Under the Equal Protection Clause: A Reconsideration of the Veterans' Preference in Public Employment, 26 Buffalo L.Rev. 3 (1977). For a collection of early cases, see Annot., Veterans' Preference Laws, 161 A.L.R. 494 (1946).

13. 1896 Mass. Acts, ch. 517, § 2. The statute provided that veterans who passed examinations should "be preferred in ap-

pointment to all persons not veterans * * *." Ibid. A proviso stated: "But nothing herein contained shall be construed to prevent the certification and employment of women."

14. 1919 Mass. Act, ch. 150, § 2. The amended statute provided that "The names of veterans who pass examinations * * * shall be placed upon the * * * eligible lists in the order of their respective standing, above the names of all other applicants," and further provided that "upon receipt of a requisition not especially calling for women, names shall be certified from such lists * * *." The exemption for "women's requisitions" was retained in substantially this form in subsequent revisions, see, e.g., 1954 Mass. Act, ch. 627, § 4. It was eliminated in 1971, 1971 Mass. Acts, ch. 219, when the State made all-single sex examinations subject to the prior approval of the Massachusetts Commission Against Discrimination, 1971 Mass. Acts, ch. 221.

Judicial Court, adhering to the views expressed in its 1896 advisory opinion, sustained this statute against a state constitutional challenge.

Since 1919, the preference has been repeatedly amended to cover persons who served in subsequent wars, declared or undeclared. See 1943 Mass. Acts, ch. 194; 1949 Mass. Acts, ch. 642, § 2 (World War II); 1954 Mass. Acts, ch. 627 (Korea); 1968 Mass. Acts, ch. 531, § 1 (Vietnam).[15] The current preference formula in ch. 31, § 23 is substantially the same as that settled upon in 1919. This absolute preference—even as modified in 1919—has never been universally popular. Over the years it has been subjected to repeated legal challenges, see Hutcheson v. Director of Civil Service, supra (collecting cases), criticism by civil service reform groups, see, e.g., Report of the Massachusetts Committee on Public Service on Initiative Bill Relative to Veterans' Preference, S. No. 279 (Feb. 1926); Report of Massachusetts Special Commission on Civil Service and Public Personnel Administration 37–43 (June 15, 1967) (hereinafter 1967 Report), and in 1926 to a referendum in which it was reaffirmed by a majority of 51.9%. See 1967 Report, supra, at 38. The present case is apparently the first to challenge the Massachusetts veterans' preference on the simple ground that it discriminates on the basis of sex.[16]

D

The first Massachusetts veterans' preference statute defined the term "veterans" in gender-neutral language. See 1896 Mass. Acts, ch. 517, § 2 ("any person" who served in the United States army or navy), and subsequent amendments have followed this pattern, see, e.g., 1919 Mass. Acts, ch. 150, § 1 ("any person" who served * * *); 1954 Mass. Acts, ch. 531, § 1 ("any person, male or female, including a nurse"). Women who have served in official United States military units during wartime, then, have always been entitled to the benefit of the preference. In addition, Massachusetts, through a 1943 amendment to the definition of "wartime service," extended the preference to women who served in unofficial auxiliary women's units. 1943 Mass. Acts, ch. 194.[17]

---

15. A provision requiring public agencies to hire disabled veterans certified as eligible was added in 1922. 1922 Mass. Acts, ch. 463. It was invalidated as applied in Hutcheson v. Civil Service Comm'n, 361 Mass.480, 281 N.E.2d 53 (1973) (suit by veteran arguing that absolute preference for disabled veterans arbitrary on facts). It has since been eliminated and replaced with a provision giving disabled veterans an absolute preference in retention. See Mass.Gen.Laws Ann., ch. 31, § 26 (West 1979). See n. 10, supra.

16. For cases presenting similar challenges to the veterans' preference laws of other States, see Ballou v. State Department of Civil Service, 75 N.J.365, 382 A.2d

1118 (1978) (sustaining New Jersey absolute preference); Feinerman v. Jones, 356 F.Supp. 252 (M.D.Pa.1973) (sustaining Pennsylvania point preference); Branch v. DuBois, 418 F.Supp. 1128 (N.D.Ill. 1976) (sustaining Illinois modified point preference); Wisconsin Nat'l Organization for Women v. Wisconsin, 417 F.Supp. 978 (W.D.Wis.1976) (sustaining Wisconsin point preference).

17. The provision, passed shortly after the creation of the Women's Auxiliary Army Corps (WAAC), see n. 21, infra, is currently found at Mass.Gen.Laws Ann., ch. 4, § 7, cl. 43 (West 1976), see n. 8, supra. "Wartime service" is defined as

When the first general veterans' preference statute was adopted in 1896, there were no women veterans.[18] The statute, however, covered only Civil War veterans. Most of them were beyond middle age, and relatively few were actively competing for public employment.[19] Thus, the impact of the preference upon the employment opportunities of nonveterans as a group and women in particular was slight.[20]

Notwithstanding the apparent attempts by Massachusetts to include as many military women as possible within the scope of the preference, the statute today benefits an overwhelmingly male class. This is attributable in some measure to the variety of federal statutes, regulations, and policies that have restricted the numbers of women who could enlist in the United States Armed Forces,[21] and largely to

service performed by a * * * member of the "WAAC." A "WAAC" is "any woman who was discharged and so served in any corps or unit of the United States established for the purpose of enabling women to serve with, or as auxiliary to, the armed forces of the United States and such woman shall be deemed to be a veteran." Ibid.

18. Small numbers of women served in combat roles in every war before the 20th century in which the United States was involved, but usually unofficially or disguised as men. See Binkin and Bach, Women and the Military 5 (1977). Among the better-known are Molly Pitcher (Revolutionary War); Deborah Sampson (Revolutionary War), and Lucy Brewer (War of 1812). Passing as one "George Baker," Brewer served for three years as a gunner on the U.S.S. Constitution ("Old Ironsides") and distinguished herself in several major naval battles in the War of 1812. See Laffin, Women in Battle 116–122 (1967).

19. By 1887, the average age of Civil War veterans in Massachusetts was already over 50. Third Annual Report, Mass. Civil Service Comm'n 22 (Jan. 10, 1887). The tie-breaking preference which had been established under the 1884 statute had apparently been difficult to enforce, since many appointing officers "prefer younger men." Ibid. The 1896 statute which established the first valid absolute preference, see text, at p. 2289, supra, again covered only Civil War veterans. 1896 Mass. Acts, ch. 517, § 1.

20. In 1896, for example, 2,804 persons applied for civil service positions: 2,031 were men, of whom only 32 were veterans; 773 were women. Of the 647 persons appointed, 525 were men, of whom only 9 were veterans; 122 were women. Thirteenth Annual Report, Mass. Civil Service Comm'n 5, 6 (Dec. 4, 1896). The average age of the applicants was 38. Ibid.

21. The Army Nurse Corps, created by Congress in 1901, was the first official military unit for women, but its members were not granted full military rank until 1944. See M. Binkin and S. Bach, Women and the Military 4–21 (1977) (hereinafter Binkin and Bach); M. E. Treadwell, The Women's Army Corps 6 (Dept. of Army, Office of Chief of Military History, 1954) (hereinafter Treadwell). During World War I, a variety of proposals were made to enlist women for work as doctors, telephone operators and clerks, but all were rejected by the War Department. See ibid. The Navy, however, interpreted its own authority broadly to include a power to enlist women as Yeoman F's and Marine F's. About 13,000 women served in this rank, working primarily at clerical jobs. These women were the first in the United States to be admitted to full military rank and status. See Treadwell 10.

Official military corps for women were established in response to the massive personnel needs of the Second World War. See generally Binkin and Bach; Treadwell. The Women's Army Auxiliary Corps (WAAC)—the unofficial predecessor of the Women's Army Corps (WAC)—was created on May 14, 1942, followed two months later by the WAVES (Women Accepted for Voluntary Emergency Service). See Binkin and Bach 7. Not long after, the U.S. Marine Corps Women's Reserve and the Coast Guard Women's Reserve (SPAR) were established. See ibid. Some 350,000 women served in the four services; some 800 women also served as Women's Airforce Service Pilots (WASPS). Ibid. Most worked in health care, administration, and communications; they were also employed as airplane mechanics, parachute riggers, gunnery instructors, air traffic controllers, and the like.

The authorizations for the women's units during World War II were temporary. The

the simple fact that women have never been subjected to a military draft. See generally M. Binkin and S. Bach, Women and the Military 4–21 (1977).

When this litigation was commenced, then, over 98% of the veterans in Massachusetts were male; only 1.8% were female. And over one-quarter of the Massachusetts population were veterans. During the decade between 1963 and 1973 when the appellee was actively participating in the State's merit selection system, 47,005 new permanent appointments were made in the classified official service. Forty-three percent of those hired were women, and 57% were men. Of the women appointed, 1.8% were veterans, while 54% of the men had veteran status. A large unspecified percentage of the female appointees were serving in lower paying positions for which males traditionally had not applied.[22] On each of 50 sample eligible lists that are part of the record in this case, one or more women who would have been certified as eligible for appointment on the basis of test results were displaced by veterans whose test scores were lower.

At the outset of this litigation the State conceded that for "many of the permanent positions for which males and females have competed" the veterans' preference has "resulted in a substantially greater proportion of female eligibles than male eligibles" not being certified for consideration. The impact of the veterans' preference law upon the public employment opportunities of women has thus been severe. This impact lies at the heart of the appellee's federal constitutional claim.

Women's Armed Services Integration Act of 1948, 62 Stat. 356–375, established the women's services on a permanent basis. Under the Act, women were given regular military status. However, quotas were placed on the numbers who could enlist; 62 Stat. 357, 360–361 (no more than 2% of total enlisted strength); eligibility requirements were more stringent than those for men, and career opportunities were limited. Binkin and Bach 11–12. During the 1950's and 1960's, enlisted women constituted little more than 1% of the total force. In 1967, the 2% quota was lifted, Act of Nov. 8, 1967, Pub.L. 90–130, § 1(b), 81 Stat. 376, and in the 1970's many restrictive policies concerning women's participation in the military have been eliminated or modified. See generally Binkin and Bach, supra. In 1972, women still constituted less than 2% of the enlisted strength. Id., at 14. By 1975, when this litigation was commenced, the percentage had risen to 4.0%. Ibid.

22. The former exemption for "women's requisitions," see nn. 13, 14, supra, may have operated in the 20th century to protect these types of jobs from the impact of the preference. However, the statutory history indicates that this was not its purpose. The provision dates back to the 1896 veterans' preference law and was retained in the law substantially unchanged until it was eliminated in 1971. See n. 14, supra. Since veterans in 1896 were a small but an exclusively male class, such a provision was apparently included to ensure that the statute would not be construed to outlaw a pre-existing practice of single-sex hiring explicitly authorized under the 1884 Civil Service Statute. See Rule XIX.3, Mass. Civil Service Law, Rules and Regs. of Comm'rs (1884) ("In case the request for any * * * certification, or any law or regulation shall call for persons of one sex, those of that sex shall be certified; otherwise sex shall be disregarded in certification.") The veterans' preference statute at no point endorsed this practice. Historical materials indicate, however, that the early preference law may have operated to encourage the employment of women in positions from which they previously had been excluded. See Thirteenth Annual Report, Mass. Civil Service Comm'n 5, 6 (Dec. 4, 1896); Third Annual Report, Mass. Civil Service Comm'n 23 (Jan. 10, 1887).

II

The sole question for decision on this appeal is whether Massachusetts, in granting an absolute lifetime preference to veterans, has discriminated against women in violation of the Equal Protection Clause of the Fourteenth Amendment.

A

The Equal Protection guarantee of the Fourteenth Amendment does not take from the States all power of classification. Massachusetts Bd. of Retirement v. Murgia, 427 U.S. 307, 314, 96 S.Ct. 2562, 2567, 49 L.Ed.2d 520. Most laws classify, and many affect certain groups unevenly, even though the law itself treats them no differently from all other members of the class described by the law. When the basic classification is rationally based, uneven effects upon particular groups within a class are ordinarily of no constitutional concern. New York City Transit Authority v. Beazer, 440 U.S. 568, 99 S.Ct. 1355, 59 L.Ed.2d 587; Jefferson v. Hackney, 406 U.S. 535, 548, 92 S.Ct. 1724, 1732, 32 L.Ed.2d 285. Cf. James v. Valtierra, 402 U.S. 137, 91 S.Ct. 1331, 28 L.Ed.2d 678. The calculus of effects, the manner in which a particular law reverberates in a society, is a legislative and not a judicial responsibility. Dandridge v. Williams, 397 U.S. 471, 90 S.Ct. 1153, 25 L.Ed.2d 491; San Antonio Bd. of Education v. Rodriguez, 411 U.S. 1, 93 S.Ct. 1278, 36 L.Ed.2d 16. In assessing an equal protection challenge, a court is called upon only to measure the basic validity of the legislative classification. Barrett v. Indiana, 229 U.S. 26, 29–30, 33 S.Ct. 692, 693, 57 L.Ed. 1050; Railway Express Co. v. New York, 336 U.S. 106, 69 S.Ct. 463, 93 L.Ed. 533. When some other independent right is not at stake, see, e.g., Shapiro v. Thompson, 394 U.S. 618, 89 S.Ct. 1322, 22 L.Ed.2d 600 and when there is no "reason to infer antipathy," Vance v. Bradley, 440 U.S. 93, 99 S.Ct. 939, 59 L.Ed.2d 171, it is presumed that "even improvident decisions will eventually be rectified by the democratic process * * *." Ibid.

Certain classifications, however, in themselves supply a reason to infer antipathy. Race is the paradigm. A racial classification, regardless of purported motivation, is presumptively invalid and can be upheld only upon an extraordinary justification. Brown v. Board of Education, 347 U.S. 483, 74 S.Ct. 686, 98 L.Ed. 873; MacLaughlin v. Florida, 379 U.S. 184, 85 S.Ct. 283, 13 L.Ed.2d 222. This rule applies as well to a classification that is ostensibly neutral but is an obvious pretext for racial discrimination. Yick Wo v. Hopkins, 118 U.S. 356, 6 S.Ct. 1064, 30 L.Ed. 220; Guinn v. United States, 238 U.S. 347, 35 S.Ct. 926, 59 L.Ed. 1340; cf. Lane v. Wilson, 307 U.S. 268, 59 S.Ct. 872, 83 L.Ed. 1281; Gomillion v. Lightfoot, 364 U.S. 339, 81 S.Ct. 125, 5 L.Ed.2d 110. But, as was made clear in Washington v. Davis, 426 U.S. 229, 96 S.Ct. 2040, 48 L.Ed.2d 597 and Village of Arlington Heights v. Metropolitan Housing Development Corp., 429 U.S. 252, 97 S.Ct. 555, 50 L.Ed.2d 450, even if a neutral law has a disproportionately adverse effect upon a racial minority, it is unconstitutional under the Equal Protection Clause only if that impact can be traced to a discriminatory purpose.

Classifications based upon gender, not unlike those based upon race, have traditionally been the touchstone for pervasive and often subtle discrimination. Caban v. Mohammed, 441 U.S. 380, 398, 99 S.Ct. 1760, 1771, 60 L.Ed.2d 297 (Stewart, J., dissenting). This Court's recent cases teach that such classifications must bear a "close and substantial relationship to important governmental objectives," Craig v. Boren, supra; and are in many settings unconstitutional. Although public employment is not a constitutional right, Massachusetts Bd. of Retirement v. Murgia, supra, and the States have wide discretion in framing employee qualifications, see, e.g., New York City Transit Authority v. Beazer, supra, these precedents dictate that any state law overtly or covertly designed to prefer males over females in public employment would require an exceedingly persuasive justification to withstand a constitutional challenge under the Equal Protection Clause of the Fourteenth Amendment.

B

The cases of Washington v. Davis, supra, and Village of Arlington Heights v. Metropolitan Housing Development Corp., supra, recognize that when a neutral law has a disparate impact upon a group that has historically been the victim of discrimination, an unconstitutional purpose may still be at work. But those cases signalled no departure from the settled rule that the Fourteenth Amendment guarantees equal laws, not equal results. *Davis* upheld a job-related employment test that white people passed in proportionately greater numbers than Negroes, for there had been no showing that racial discrimination entered into the establishment or formulation of the test. *Arlington Heights* upheld a zoning board decision that tended to perpetuate racially segregated housing patterns, since apart from its effect, the board's decision was shown to be nothing more than an application of constitutionally neutral zoning policy. Those principles apply with equal force to a case involving alleged gender discrimination.

When a statute gender-neutral on its face is challenged on the ground that its effects upon women are disproportionately adverse, a two-fold inquiry is thus appropriate. The first question is whether the statutory classification is indeed neutral in the sense that it is not gender-based. If the classification itself, covert or overt, is not based upon gender, the second question is whether the adverse effect reflects invidious gender-based discrimination. See Village of Arlington Heights v. Metropolitan Housing Development Corp., supra, 429 U.S., at 266, 97 S.Ct., at 564. In this second inquiry, impact provides an "important starting point," 429 U.S., at 266, 97 S.Ct. 564 but purposeful discrimination is "the condition that offends the Constitution." Swann v. Board of Education, 402 U.S. 1, 16, 91 S.Ct. 1267, 1276, 28 L.Ed.2d 554.

It is against this background of precedent that we consider the merits of the case before us.

III

A

The question whether ch. 31, § 23 establishes a classification that is overtly or covertly based upon gender must first be considered. The appellee has conceded that ch. 31, § 23 is neutral on its face. She has also acknowledged that state hiring preferences for veterans are not *per se* invalid, for she has limited her challenge to the absolute lifetime preference that Massachusetts provides to veterans. The District Court made two central findings that are relevant here: first, that ch. 31, § 23 serves legitimate and worthy purposes; second, that the absolute preference was not established for the purpose of discriminating against women. The appellee has thus acknowledged and the District Court has thus found that the distinction between veterans and nonveterans drawn by ch. 31, § 23 is not a pretext for gender discrimination. The appellee's concession and the District Court's finding are clearly correct.

If the impact of this statute could not be plausibly explained on a neutral ground, impact itself would signal that the real classification made by the law was in fact not neutral. See Washington v. Davis, supra, 426 U.S., at 242, 96 S.Ct., at 2049; Village of Arlington Heights v. Metropolitan Housing Development Corp., supra, 429 U.S., at 266, 97 S.Ct., at 564. But there can be but one answer to the question whether this veteran preference excludes significant numbers of women from preferred state jobs because they are women or because they are nonveterans. Apart from the fact that the definition of "veterans" in the statute has always been neutral as to gender and that Massachusetts has consistently defined veteran status in a way that has been inclusive of women who have served in the military, this is not a law that can plausibly be explained only as a gender-based classification. Indeed, it is not a law that can rationally be explained on that ground. Veteran status is not uniquely male. Although few women benefit from the preference the nonveteran class is not substantially all-female. To the contrary, significant numbers of nonveterans are men, and all nonveterans—male as well as female—are placed at a disadvantage. Too many men are affected by ch. 31, § 23 to permit the inference that the statute is but a pretext for preferring men over women.

Moreover, as the District Court implicitly found, the purposes of the statute provide the surest explanation for its impact. Just as there are cases in which impact alone can unmask an invidious classification, cf. Yick Wo v. Hopkins, supra, there are others, in which—notwithstanding impact—the legitimate noninvidious purposes of a law cannot be missed. This is one. The distinction made by ch. 31, § 23, is, as it seems to be, quite simply between veterans and nonveterans, not between men and women.

B

The dispositive question, then, is whether the appellee has shown that a gender-based discriminatory purpose has, at least in some measure, shaped the Massachusetts veterans' preference legislation. As did the District Court, she points to two basic factors which in her view distinguish ch. 31, § 23 from the neutral rules at issue in the Washington v. Davis and *Arlington Heights* cases. The first is the nature of the preference, which is said to be demonstrably gender-biased in the sense that it favors a status reserved under federal military policy primarily to men. The second concerns the impact of the absolute lifetime preference upon the employment opportunities of women, an impact claimed to be too inevitable to have been unintended. The appellee contends that these factors, coupled with the fact that the preference itself has little if any relevance to actual job performance, more than suffice to prove the discriminatory intent required to establish a constitutional violation.

1

The contention that this veterans' preference is "inherently non-neutral" or "gender-biased" presumes that the State, by favoring veterans, intentionally incorporated into its public employment policies the panoply of sex-based and assertedly discriminatory federal laws that have prevented all but a handful of women from becoming veterans. There are two serious difficulties with this argument. First, it is wholly at odds with the District Court's central finding that Massachusetts has not offered a preference to veterans for the purpose of discriminating against women. Second, it cannot be reconciled with the assumption made by both the appellee and the District Court that a more limiting hiring preference for veterans could be sustained. Taken together, these difficulties are fatal.

To the extent that the status of veteran is one that few women have been enabled to achieve, every hiring preference for veterans, however modest or extreme, is inherently gender-biased. If Massachusetts by offering such a preference can be said intentionally to have incorporated into its state employment policies the historical gender-based federal military personnel practices, the degree of the preference would or should make no constitutional difference. Invidious discrimination does not become less so because the discrimination accomplished is of a lesser magnitude.[23] Discriminatory intent is simply not amenable to calibration. It either is a factor that has influenced the legislative choice or it is not. The District Court's conclusion that the absolute veterans' preference was not originally enacted or subsequently reaffirmed for the purpose of giving an advantage to males as such necessarily compels the conclusion that the State intended nothing

---

23. This is not to say that the degree of impact is irrelevant to the question of intent. But it is to say that a more modest preference, while it might well lessen impact and, as the State argues, might lessen the effectiveness of the statute in helping veterans, would not be any more or less "neutral" in the constitutional sense.

more than to prefer "veterans." Given this finding, simple logic suggests that an intent to exclude women from significant public jobs was not at work in this law. To reason that it was, by describing the preference as "inherently non-neutral" or "gender-biased," is merely to restate the fact of impact, not to answer the question of intent.

To be sure, this case is unusual in that it involves a law that by design is not neutral. The law overtly prefers veterans as such. As opposed to the written test at issue in *Davis*, it does not purport to define a job related characteristic. To the contrary, it confers upon a specifically described group—perceived to be particularly deserving—a competitive head start. But the District Court found, and the appellee has not disputed, that this legislative choice was legitimate. The basic distinction between veterans and nonveterans, having been found not gender-based, and the goals of the preference having been found worthy, ch. 31 must be analyzed as is any other neutral law that casts a greater burden upon women as a group than upon men as a group. The enlistment policies of the armed services may well have discriminated on the basis of sex. See Frontiero v. Richardson, 411 U.S. 677, 93 S.Ct. 1764, 36 L.Ed.2d 583; cf. Schlesinger v. Ballard, 419 U.S. 498, 95 S.Ct. 572, 42 L.Ed.2d 610. But the history of discrimination against women in the military is not on trial in this case.

2

The appellee's ultimate argument rests upon the presumption, common to the criminal and civil law, that a person intends the natural and foreseeable consequences of his voluntary actions. Her position was well stated in the concurring opinion in the District Court:

"Conceding * * * that the goal here was to benefit the veteran, there is no reason to absolve the legislature from awareness that the means chosen to achieve this goal would freeze women out of all those state jobs actively sought by men. To be sure, the legislature did not wish to harm women. But the cutting-off of women's opportunities was an inevitable concomitant of the chosen scheme—as inevitable as the proposition that if tails is up, heads must be down. Where a law's consequences are *that* inevitable, can they meaningfully be described as unintended?" 451 F.Supp. 143, 151.

This rhetorical question implies that a negative answer is obvious, but it is not. The decision to grant a preference to veterans was of course "intentional." So, necessarily, did an adverse impact upon nonveterans follow from that decision. And it cannot seriously be argued that the legislature of Massachusetts could have been unaware that most veterans are men. It would thus be disingenuous to say that the adverse consequences of this legislation for women were unintended, in the sense that they were not volitional or in the sense that they were not foreseeable.

"Discriminatory purpose," however, implies more than intent as volition or intent as awareness of consequences. See United Jewish Organizations v. Carey, 430 U.S. 144, 179, 97 S.Ct. 996, 1016, 51 L.Ed.2d 229 (concurring opinion).[24] It implies that the decisionmaker, in this case a state legislature, selected or reaffirmed a particular course of action at least in part "because of," not merely "in spite of," its adverse effects upon an identifiable group.[25] Yet, nothing in the record demonstrates that this preference for veterans was originally devised or subsequently re-enacted because it would accomplish the collateral goal of keeping women in a stereotypic and predefined place in the Massachusetts Civil Service.

To the contrary, the statutory history shows that the benefit of the preference was consistently offered to "any person" who was a veteran. That benefit has been extended to women under a very broad statutory definition of the term veteran.[26] The preference formula itself, which is the focal point of this challenge, was first adopted—so it appears from this record—out of a perceived need to help a small group of older Civil War veterans. It has since been reaffirmed and extended only to cover new veterans.[27] When the totality of legislative actions establishing and extending the Massachusetts veterans' preference are considered, see Washington v. Davis, supra, 426 U.S., at 242, 96 S.Ct., at 2049, the law remains what it purports to be: a preference for veterans of either sex over nonveterans of either sex, not for men over women.

24. Proof of discriminatory intent must necessarily usually rely on objective factors, several of which were outlined in Village of Arlington Heights v. Metropolitan Housing Development Corp., 429 U.S. 252, 266, 97 S.Ct. 555, 564, 50 L.Ed.2d 397. The inquiry is practical. What a legislature or any official entity is "up to" may be plain from the results its actions achieve, or the results they avoid. Often it is made clear from what has been called, in a different context, "the give and take of the situation." Cramer v. United States, 325 U.S. 1, 32–33, 65 S.Ct. 918, 934, 89 L.Ed. 1441. (Jackson, J.)

25. This is not to say that the inevitability or foreseeability of consequences of a neutral rule has no bearing upon the existence of discriminatory intent. Certainly, when the adverse consequences of a law upon an identifiable group are as inevitable as the gender-based consequences of ch. 31, § 23, a strong inference that the adverse effects were desired can reasonably be drawn. But in this inquiry—made as it is under the Constitution—an inference is a working tool, not a synonym for proof. When as here, the impact is essentially an unavoidable consequence of a legislative policy that has in itself always

been deemed to be legitimate, and when, as here, the statutory history and all of the available evidence affirmatively demonstrate the opposite, the inference simply fails to ripen into proof.

26. See nn. 8, 17, supra.

27. The appellee has suggested that the former statutory exception for "women's requisitions," see nn. 13, 14, supra, supplies evidence that Massachusetts, when it established and subsequently reaffirmed the absolute preference legislation, assumed that women would not or should not compete with men. She has further suggested that the former provision extending the preference to certain female dependents of veterans, see n. 10, supra, demonstrates that ch. 31, § 23 is laced with "old notions" about the proper roles and needs of the sexes. See Califano v. Goldfarb, 430 U.S. 199, 97 S.Ct. 1021, 51 L.Ed.2d 270; Weinberger v. Wiesenfeld, 420 U.S. 636, 95 S.Ct. 1225, 43 L.Ed.2d 514. But the first suggestion is totally belied by the statutory history, see supra, at 2290–2292, and nn. 19, 20, and the second fails to account for the consistent statutory recognition of the contribution of women to this Nation's military efforts.

IV

Veterans' hiring preferences represent an awkward—and, many argue, unfair—exception to the widely shared view that merit and merit alone should prevail in the employment policies of government. After a war, such laws have been enacted virtually without opposition. During peacetime they inevitably have come to be viewed in many quarters as undemocratic and unwise.[28] Absolute and permanent preferences, as the troubled history of this law demonstrates, have always been subject to the objection that they give the veteran more than a square deal. But the Fourteenth Amendment "cannot be made a refuge from ill-advised * * * laws." District of Columbia v. Brooke, 214 U.S. 138, 150, 29 S.Ct. 560, 563, 53 L.Ed. 941. The substantial edge granted to veterans by ch. 31, § 23 may reflect unwise policy. The appellee, however, has simply failed to demonstrate that the law in any way reflects a purpose to discriminate on the basis of sex.

The judgment is reversed, and the case is remanded for further proceedings consistent with this opinion.

MR. JUSTICE STEVENS, with whom MR. JUSTICE WHITE joins, concurring.

While I concur in the Court's opinion, I confess that I am not at all sure that there is any difference between the two questions posed at p. 2293, ante. If a classification is not overtly based on gender, I am inclined to believe the question whether it is covertly gender-based is the same as the question whether its adverse effects reflect invidious gender-based discrimination. However the question is phrased, for me the answer is largely provided by the fact that the number of males disadvantaged by Massachusetts' Veterans Preference (1,867,000) is sufficiently large—and sufficiently close to the number of disadvantaged females (2,954,000)—to refute the claim that the rule was intended to benefit males as a class over females as a class.

MR. JUSTICE MARSHALL, with whom MR. JUSTICE BRENNAN joins, dissenting.

Although acknowledging that in some circumstances, discriminatory intent may be inferred from the inevitable or foreseeable impact of a statute, ante, at 2296 n. 25, the Court concludes that no such intent has been established here. I cannot agree. In my judgment, Massachusetts' choice of an absolute veterans' preference system evinces purposeful gender-based discrimination. And because the statutory scheme bears no substantial relationship to a legitimate governmental objective, it cannot withstand scrutiny under the Equal Protection Clause.

I

The District Court found that the "prime objective" of the Massachusetts Veterans Preference Statute, Mass.Gen.Laws, ch. 31, § 23, was

---

28. See generally Veterans' Preference Oversight Hearings before Subcomm. on Civil Service, 95th Cong., 1st Sess. (1977); Report of Comptroller General, Conflicting Congressional Policies: Veterans' Preference and Apportionment vs. Equal Employment Opportunity (Sept. 29, 1977).

to benefit individuals with prior military service.   415 F.Supp. 485, 497 (Mass.1976).   See 451 F.Supp. 143, 145 (Mass.1978).   Under the Court's analysis, this factual determination "necessarily compels the conclusion that the State intended nothing more than to prefer 'veterans.' Given this finding, simple logic suggests than an intent to exclude women from significant public jobs was not at work in this law."   Ante, at 2295.   I find the Court's logic neither simple nor compelling.

That a legislature seeks to advantage one group does not, as a matter of logic or of common sense, exclude the possibility that it also intends to disadvantage another.   Individuals in general and lawmakers in particular frequently act for a variety of reasons.   As this Court recognized in Arlington Heights v. Metropolitan Housing Development Corp., 429 U.S. 252, 265, 97 S.Ct. 555, 563, 50 L.Ed.2d 450 (1977), "[r]arely can it be said that a legislature or administrative body operating under a broad mandate made a decision motivated by a single concern."   Absent an omniscience not commonly attributed to the judiciary, it will often be impossible to ascertain the sole or even dominant purpose of a given statute.   See McGinnis v. Royster, 410 U.S. 263, 276–277, 93 S.Ct. 1055, 1062–1063, 35 L.Ed.2d 282 (1973); Ely, Legislative and Administrative Motivation in Constitutional Law, 79 Yale L.J. 1205, 1214 (1970).   Thus, the critical constitutional inquiry is not whether an illicit consideration was the primary or but-for cause of a decision, but rather whether it had an appreciable role in shaping a given legislative enactment.   Where there is "proof that a discriminatory purpose has been *a* motivating factor in the decision, * * * judicial deference is no longer justified."   Arlington Heights v. Metropolitan Housing Corp., supra, 429 U.S., at 265–266, 97 S.Ct., at 563 (emphasis added).

Moreover, since reliable evidence of subjective intentions is seldom obtainable, resort to inference based on objective factors is generally unavoidable.   See Beer v. United States, 425 U.S. 130, 148–149, n. 4, 96 S.Ct. 1357, 1367, n. 4, 47 L.Ed.2d 629 (1976) (Marshall, J., dissenting); cf. Palmer v. Thompson, 403 U.S. 217, 224–225, 91 S.Ct. 1940, 1944–1945, 29 L.Ed.2d 438 (1971); United States v. O'Brien, 391 U.S. 367, 383–384, 88 S.Ct. 1673, 1682–1683, 20 L.Ed.2d 672 (1968).   To discern the purposes underlying facially neutral policies, this Court has therefore considered the degree, inevitability, and foreseeability of any disproportionate impact as well as the alternatives reasonably available.   See Monroe v. Board of Commissioners, 391 U.S. 450, 459, 88 S.Ct. 1700, 1705, 20 L.Ed.2d 733 (1968); Goss v. Board of Education, 373 U.S. 683, 688–689, 83 S.Ct. 1405, 1408–1409, 10 L.Ed.2d 632 (1963); Gomillion v. Lightfoot, 364 U.S. 339, 81 S.Ct. 125, 5 L.Ed.2d 110 (1960); Griffin v. Illinois, 351 U.S. 12, 17 n. 11, 76 S.Ct. 585, 590 n. 11, 100 L.Ed. 891 (1956).   Cf. Albemarle Paper Co. v. Moody, 422 U.S. 405, 425, 95 S.Ct. 2362, 2375, 45 L.Ed.2d 280 (1975).

In the instant case, the impact of the Massachusetts statute on women is undisputed.   Any veteran with a passing grade on the civil service exam must be placed ahead of a nonveteran, regardless of their respective scores. The District Court found that, as a practical matter, this preference supplants test results as the determinant of upper-level civil service appointments. 415 F.Supp., at 488–489. Because less than 2% of the women in Massachusetts are veterans, the absolute preference formula has rendered desirable state civil service employment an almost exclusively male prerogative. 451 F.Supp., at 151 (Campbell, J., concurring).

As the District Court recognized, this consequence followed foreseeably, indeed inexorably, from the long history of policies severely limiting women's participation in the military.[1] Although neutral in form, the statute is anything but neutral in application. It inescapably reserves a major sector of public employment to "an already established class which, as a matter of historical fact, is 98% male." Ibid. Where the foreseeable impact of a facially neutral policy is so disproportionate, the burden should rest on the State to establish that sex-based considerations played no part in the choice of the particular legislative scheme. Cf. Castaneda v. Partida, 430 U.S. 482, 97 S.Ct. 1272, 51 L.Ed.2d 498 (1977); Washington v. Davis, 426 U.S. 229, 241, 96 S.Ct. 2040, 2048, 48 L.Ed.2d 597 (1976); Alexander v. Louisiana, 405 U.S. 625, 632, 92 S.Ct. 1221, 1226, 31 L.Ed.2d 536 (1972); see generally Brest, Palmer v. Thompson: An Approach to the Problem of Unconstitutional Legislative Motive, 1971 Sup.Ct.L.Rev. 95, 123.

Clearly, that burden was not sustained here. The legislative history of the statute reflects the Commonwealth's patent appreciation of the impact the preference system would have on women, and an equally evident desire to mitigate that impact only with respect to certain traditionally female occupations. Until 1971, the statute and implementing civil service regulations exempted from operation of the preference any job requisitions "especially calling for women." 1954 Mass. Acts, ch. 627, § 5. See also 1896 Mass. Acts, ch. 517, § 6; 1919 Mass. Acts, ch. 150, § 2; 1945 Mass. Acts, ch. 725, § 2(e); 1965 Mass. Acts, ch. 53, § 2; ante, at 2289, nn. 13, 14. In practice, this exemption,

1. See Anthony v. Massachusetts, 415 F.Supp. 485, 490, 495–499 (Mass.1976); Feeney v. Massachusetts, 451 F.Supp. 143, 145, 148 (Mass.1978). In addition to the 2% quota on women's participation in the armed forces, see ante, at 2291 n. 21, enlistment and appointment requirements have been more stringent for females than males with respect to age, mental and physical aptitude, parental consent, and educational attainment. M. Binkin and S. Bach, Women and the Military (1977) (hereinafter Binkin and Bach); Note, The Equal Rights Amendment and the Military, 82 Yale L.J. 1533, 1539 (1973). Until the 1970's, the armed forces precluded enlistment and appointment of women, but not men, who were married or had dependent children. See 415 F.Supp. at 490; App.

85; Exs. 98, 99, 103, 104. Sex-based restrictions on advancement and training opportunities also diminished the incentives for qualified women to enlist. See Binkin and Bach 10–17; Beans, Sex Discrimination in the Military, 67 Milit.L.Rev. 19, 59–83 (1979). Cf. Schlesinger v. Ballard, 419 U.S. 498, 508, 95 S.Ct. 572, 577, 42 L.Ed.2d 610 (1975).

Thus, unlike the employment examination in Washington v. Davis, 426 U.S. 229, 96 S.Ct. 2040, 48 L.Ed.2d 597 (1976), which the Court found to be demonstrably job-related, the Massachusetts preference statute incorporates the results of sex-based military policies irrelevant to women's current fitness for civilian public employment. See 415 F.Supp., at 498–499.

coupled with the absolute preference for veterans, has created a gender-based civil service hierarchy, with women occupying low grade clerical and secretarial jobs and men holding more responsible and remunerative positions. See 415 F.Supp., at 488; 451 F.Supp., at 148 n. 9.

Thus, for over 70 years, the Commonwealth has maintained, as an integral part of its veteran's preference system, an exemption relegating female civil service applicants to occupations traditionally filled by women. Such a statutory scheme both reflects and perpetuates precisely the kind of archaic assumptions about women's roles which we have previously held invalid. See Orr v. Orr, 440 U.S. 268, 99 S.Ct. 1102, 59 L.Ed.2d 306 (1979); Califano v. Goldfarb, 430 U.S. 199, 210–211, 97 S.Ct. 1021, 1028–1029, 51 L.Ed.2d 270 (1977); Stanton v. Stanton, 421 U.S. 7, 14, 95 S.Ct. 1373, 1377, 43 L.Ed.2d 688 (1975); Weinberger v. Wiesenfeld, 420 U.S. 636, 645, 95 S.Ct. 1225, 1231, 43 L.Ed.2d 514 (1975). Particularly when viewed against the range of less discriminatory alternatives available to assist veterans,[2] Massachusetts' choice of a formula that so severely restricts public employment opportunities for women cannot reasonably be thought gender-neutral. Cf. Albemarle Paper Co. v. Moody, supra, 422 U.S., at 425, 95 S.Ct., at 2375. The Court's conclusion to the contrary—that "nothing in the record" evinces a "collateral goal of keeping women in a stereotypic and predefined place in the Massachusetts Civil Service," ante, at 2296—displays a singularly myopic view of the facts established below.[3]

II

To survive challenge under the Equal Protection Clause, statutes reflecting gender-based discrimination must be substantially related to the achievement of important governmental objectives. See Califano v. Webster, 430 U.S. 313, 316–317, 97 S.Ct. 1192, 1194–1195, 51 L.Ed.2d 360 (1977); Craig v. Boren, 429 U.S. 190, 197, 97 S.Ct. 451, 456, 50 L.Ed.2d 397 (1976); Reed v. Reed, 404 U.S. 71, 76, 92 S.Ct. 251, 254, 30 L.Ed.2d 225 (1971). Appellants here advance three interests in support of the absolute preference system: (1) assisting veterans in their readjustment to civilian life; (2) encouraging military enlistment; and (3) rewarding those who have served their country. Brief for Appellants

2. Only four States afford a preference comparable in scope to that of Massachusetts. See Fleming and Shanor, Veterans' Preferences and Public Employment: Unconstitutional Gender Discrimination?, 26 Emory L.J. 13, 17 n. 13 (1977) (citing statutes). Other States and the Federal Government grant point or tie-breaking preferences that do not foreclose opportunities for women. See id., at 13, and nn. 13, 14; ante, at 2287 n. 7; Hearings before the Subcommittee on Civil Service of the House Committee on Post Office and Civil Service, 95th Cong., 1st Sess., 4 (1977) (statement of Alan Campbell, Chairman, U.S. Civil Service Commission).

3. Although it is relevant that the preference statute also disadvantages a substantial group of men, see ante, at 2285 (Stevens, J., concurring), it is equally pertinent that 47% of Massachusetts men over 18 are veterans, as compared to 0.8% of Massachusetts women. App. 83. Given this disparity, and the indicia of intent noted at p. 2287, supra, the absolute number of men denied preference cannot be dispositive, especially since they have not faced the barriers to achieving veteran status confronted by women. See n. 1, supra.

24. Although each of those goals is unquestionably legitimate, the "mere recitation of a benign compensatory purpose" cannot of itself insulate legislative classifications from constitutional scrutiny. Weinberger v. Wiesenfeld, supra, 420 U.S., at 648, 95 S.Ct., at 1233. And in this case, the Commonwealth has failed to establish a sufficient relationship between its objectives and the means chosen to effectuate them.

With respect to the first interest, facilitating veterans' transition to civilian status, the statute is plainly overinclusive. Cf. Trimble v. Gordon, 430 U.S. 762, 770–772, 97 S.Ct. 1459, 1465–1466, 52 L.Ed.2d 31 (1971); Jimenez v. Weinberger, 417 U.S. 628, 637, 94 S.Ct. 2496, 2502, 41 L.Ed.2d 363 (1974). By conferring a permanent preference, the legislation allows veterans to invoke their advantage repeatedly, without regard to their date of discharge. As the record demonstrates, a substantial majority of those currently enjoying the benefits of the system are not recently discharged veterans in need of readjustment assistance.[4]

Nor is the Commonwealth's second asserted interest, encouraging military service, a plausible justification for this legislative scheme. In its original and subsequent re-enactments, the statute extended benefits retroactively to veterans who had served during a prior specified period. See ante, at 2289. If the Commonwealth's "actual purpose" is to induce enlistment, this legislative design is hardly well-suited to that end. See Califano v. Webster, supra, 430 U.S., at 317, 97 S.Ct., at 1195; Weinberger v. Wiesenfeld, supra, 420 U.S., at 648, 95 S.Ct., at 1233. For I am unwilling to assume what appellants made no effort to prove, that the possibility of obtaining an *ex post facto* civil service preference significantly influenced the enlistment decisions of Massachusetts residents. Moreover, even if such influence could be presumed, the statute is still grossly overinclusive in that it bestows benefits on men drafted as well as those who volunteered.

Finally, the Commonwealth's third interest, rewarding veterans, does not "adequately justify the salient features" of this preference system. Craig v. Boren, 429 U.S., at 202, 97 S.Ct., at 459. See Orr v. Orr, 440 U.S., at 281, 99 S.Ct., at 1113. Where a particular statutory scheme visits substantial hardship on a class long subject to discrimination, the legislation cannot be sustained unless "carefully tuned to alternative considerations." Trimble v. Gordon, supra, 430 U.S., at 772, 97 S.Ct., at 1466. See Caban v. Mohammed, 441 U.S. 380, 392 n. 13, 99 S.Ct. 1760, 1768, n. 13, 60 L.Ed.2d 297 (1979); Mathews v. Lucas, 427 U.S. 495, 96 S.Ct. 2755, 49 L.Ed.2d 651 (1976). Here, there are a wide variety of less discriminatory means by which Massachusetts could effect its compensatory purposes. For example, a point preference system, such as that maintained by many States and the Federal

---

4. The eligibility lists for the positions Ms. Feeney sought included 95 veterans for whom discharge information was available. Of those 95 males, 64(67%) were discharged prior to 1960. App. 106, 150–151, 169–170.

Government, see n. 2, supra, or an absolute preference for a limited duration, would reward veterans without excluding all qualified women from upper level civil service positions. Apart from public employment, the Commonwealth, can, and does, afford assistance to veterans in various ways, including tax abatements, educational subsidies, and special programs for needy veterans. See Mass.Gen.Laws Ann., ch. 59, § 5 (West Supp. 1979); Mass.Gen.Laws Ann., ch. 69, §§ 7, 7B (West Supp. 1979); and Mass.Gen.Laws Ann., chs. 115, 115A (West Supp. 1978). Unlike these and similar benefits, the costs of which are distributed across the taxpaying public generally, the Massachusetts statute exacts a substantial price from a discrete group of individuals who have long been subject to employment discrimination,[5] and who, "because of circumstances totally beyond their control, have [had] little if any chance of becoming members of the preferred class." 415 F.Supp., at 499. See n. 1, supra.

In its present unqualified form, the Veterans Preference Statute precludes all but a small fraction of Massachusetts women from obtaining any civil service position also of interest to men. See 451 F.Supp., at 151 (Campbell, J., concurring). Given the range of alternatives available, this degree of preference is not constitutionally permissible.

I would affirm the judgment of the court below.

NOTES AND PROBLEMS FOR DISCUSSION

1. If a private business enacted its own veterans' preference rule, would a suit similar to *Feeney*, but with a cause of action based on Title VII, be likely to produce a different result? Could the plaintiff establish a *prima facie* case by the introduction of evidence similar to that introduced in *Feeney*? Would the employer's desire to reward veterans for their military service constitute a defense under Title VII? See, *infra*, Chapter 2, Section C.

2. Had the majority of the Court in *Feeney* found that a bias against women, at least in part, underlay the veteran's preference law, would the plaintiff necessarily have prevailed? As indicated in the majority opinion, in equal protection cases under the Fifth and Fourteenth Amendments, "strict scrutiny" is applied to classifications drawn along lines of race, referred to as "suspect" classifications. Such classifications are allowed to stand only if the state can demonstrate that they serve a "compelling" governmental interest that cannot be achieved by other means. See McLaughlin v. Florida, 379 U.S. 184, 85 S.Ct. 283, 13 L.Ed.2d 222 (1964). Despite the similarities between classifications based on sex and those based on race, the Supreme Court has declined to treat sex as a "suspect" classification so as to call for "strict-scrutiny", although, at one time, four members of the Court expressed this view. See, Frontiero v. Richardson, 411 U.S. 677, 93 S.Ct. 1764, 36 L.Ed.2d 583 (1973). The Court instead has applied an intermediate standard of review under which sex based classifications which serve "important" governmental

5. See Frontiero v. Richardson, 411 U.S. 677, 689 n. 23, 93 S.Ct. 1764, 1772 n. 23, 36 L.Ed.2d 583 (1973); Kahn v. Shevin, 416 U.S. 351, 353–354, 94 S.Ct. 1734, 1736–1737, 40 L.Ed.2d 189 (1974); United States Bureau of the Census, Current Population Reports, No. 107, Money Income and Poverty Status of Families and Persons in the United States: 1976 (Advance Report) (Table 7) (Sept. 1977).

interests and are "substantially related" to the achievement of those objectives, are upheld as not violative of equal protection. See, Craig v. Boren, 429 U.S. 190, 97 S.Ct. 451, 50 L.Ed.2d 397 (1976); Orr v. Orr, 440 U.S. 268, 99 S.Ct. 1102, 59 L.Ed.2d 306 (1979); Mississippi University for Women v. Hogan, 458 U.S. 718, 102 S.Ct. 3331, 73 L.Ed.2d 1090 (1982). See also, Tribe, American Constitutional Law, p. 1063–1066 (1978). What level of scrutiny do Justices Marshall and Brennan feel the veterans' preference should be subjected to?

3. In WASHINGTON v. DAVIS, 426 U.S. 229, 96 S.Ct. 2040, 48 L.Ed.2d 597 (1976), unsuccessful black applicants for the Washington, D.C. police force alleged that employment policies of the department violated the due process clause of the Fifth Amendment, 42 U.S.C. § 1981, and certain provisions of the D.C. Code. Although it was uncontradicted that black applicants failed a pre-employment screening test at a rate four times greater than white applicants, the district court granted summary judgment to defendants in part on the ground that there was no evidence of intentional discrimination. Relying on Griggs v. Duke Power Co., the Court of Appeals reversed, holding that the disproportionate impact of the test on black applicants was sufficient to establish a constitutional violation, absent evidence that the test was job related, and that the plaintiffs were not required to show that racial considerations prompted defendants to use the test. The Supreme Court reversed. To make out a *prima facie* case of discrimination under the Due Process Clause of the Fifth Amendment or the Equal Protection Clause of the Fourteenth Amendment, plaintiffs must produce evidence that the defendants' actions resulted from discriminatory purposes. If the plaintiff makes such a showing, the burden shifts to the defendant "to rebut the presumption of unconstitutional action." 426 U.S. at 241, 96 S.Ct. at 2048. But, standing alone, disproportionate impact, though relevant, "does not trigger the rule * * * that racial classifications are to be subjected to the strictest scrutiny and are justifiable only by the weightiest of considerations." 426 U.S. at 242, 96 S.Ct. at 2049. In VILLAGE OF ARLINGTON HEIGHTS v. METROPOLITAN HOUSING DEVELOPMENT CORP., 429 U.S. 252, 97 S.Ct. 555, 50 L.Ed.2d 450 (1977), a suit alleging that the refusal of a municipality to allow the construction of low income multi-family dwellings was racially discriminatory, the Court reaffirmed that evidence of disproportionate impact alone was insufficient to establish a *prima facie* case of discrimination under the Fourteenth Amendment. The Court noted, however, that the plaintiff is not required to show that a discriminatory purpose was the *sole* basis for the challenged action. "When there is proof that a discriminatory purpose has been a motivating factor in the decision" the rules regarding strict scrutiny are applicable. 429 U.S. at 265–266, 97 S.Ct., at 563–564.

As noted in both the majority and dissenting opinion in *Feeney*, courts have frequently inferred intent and motivation from an individual's ability to foresee the natural consequences of his acts. What more does the majority in *Feeney* require that the plaintiff show to establish intent? Does the decision mean that intent may not be proved by circumstantial evidence alone? As a practical matter, direct proof of illegal intent, the proverbial "smoking gun," is rare.

> [I]t is difficult and often futile—to obtain direct evidence of the official's intentions. Rather than announce his intention of violating antidiscrimination laws, it is far more likely that the state official "will pursue his discriminatory practices in ways that are devious, by methods subtle and illusive—for we deal with an area in which subtleties of conduct * * * play no small part."

United States v. Texas Education Agency, 532 F.2d 380, 388 (5th Cir.1976), vacated for reconsideration in light of Washington v. Davis, 429 U.S. 990, 97 S.Ct. 517, 50 L.Ed.2d 603 (1976). The Fifth Circuit has also stated that:

> Neither the Supreme Court nor this Court, however, has denied relief when the weight of the evidence proved a plan to intentionally discriminate, even when its true purpose was cleverly cloaked in the guise of propriety. The existence of a right to redress does not turn on the degree of subtlety with which a discriminatory plan is effectuated. Circumstantial evidence, of necessity, must suffice, so long as the inference of discriminatory intent is clear.

Lodge v. Buxton, 639 F.2d 1358, 1363 (5th Cir.1981), affirmed, 458 U.S. 613, 102 S.Ct. 3272, 73 L.Ed.2d 1012 (1982). If the district court in *Feeney* had found a discriminatory purpose underlying the veterans' preference act, would that finding have been "clearly erroneous" under Rule 52(a) of the Federal Rules of Civil Procedure? See, Arlington Heights v. Metropolitan Housing Development Corp., *supra*, 429 U.S. at 266, 97 S.Ct. at 563.

Should impact-type evidence be more probative of improper intent in a non-legislative context? For example, assume a public employer has hired an unbroken string of white applicants to fill job openings for each of which there were equally qualified black applicants. The employer denies any racial motivation and explains that in each case his decision was based on his subjective determination of who would do the best job. Would such evidence establish a *prima facie* case of an equal protection violation under the *Feeney* rationale? Is there any reason to impose on plaintiffs with constitutional causes of action a higher burden than is placed on plaintiffs alleging disparate treatment under Title VII? See Chapter 2, Section D, *supra*.

4. As noted in *Feeney,* Section 1983 is a remedial statute that does not create substantive rights but provides a remedy for the violation of rights created elsewhere. Most 1983 actions, like *Feeney,* are based on constitutional violations. In MAINE v. THIBOUTOT, 448 U.S. 1, 100 S.Ct. 2502, 65 L.Ed.2d 555 (1980), the Court held that Section 1983 also provides a remedy for actions taken under color of state law which contravene federal substantive statutes. The right to base a Section 1983 action on a Title VII violation would significantly expand the relief available to plaintiffs with employment discrimination claims against public agencies. In Day v. Wayne County Board of Auditors, 749 F.2d 1199 (6th Cir.1984), the plaintiff filed an action against his employer under Title VII and Section 1983. The district court found that the employer had retaliated against the plaintiff for filing EEOC charges in violation of § 704 and granted back pay and injunctive relief. The court also found that the plaintiff had failed to establish discrimination on the basis of race or age and denied damage relief under § 1983. The plaintiff appealed, arguing that under Maine v. Thiboutot the Title VII violation constituted, as a matter of law, a violation of § 1983. The Court of Appeals affirmed.

> Though the issue is not without doubt, we believe Title VII provides the exclusive remedy when the only § 1983 cause of action is based on a violation of Title VII. * * * It would be anomalous to hold that when the only unlawful employment practice consists of the violation of a right created by Title VII, the plaintiff can by-pass all of the administrative processes of Title VII and go directly into court under § 1983.

749 F.2d at 1204. See also, Polson v. Davis, 895 F.2d 705, 710 (10th Cir.1990) (since the exclusive remedies for violation of Title VII are the enforcement

provisions of that statute, rights created by Title VII cannot serve as the basis of an action under Section 1983); Morgan v. Humboldt County School District, 623 F.Supp 440 (D.Nev.1985) (statutory scheme of age discrimination act would be thwarted if employee could pursue § 1983 suit based on ADEA violation).

The Sixth Circuit in *Day* was careful to distinguish that case from one in which the § 1983 claim was based on a constitutional violation.

> Where an employee establishes employer conduct which violates both Title VII and rights derived from another source—the Constitution or a federal statute—which existed at the time of the enactment of Title VII, the claim based on the other source is independent of the Title VII claim, and the plaintiff may seek the remedies provided by § 1983 in addition to those created by Title VII.

749 F.2d at 1205. It is generally accepted, that Title VII is not the exclusive remedy for employment discrimination by state and local governments and that Section 1983 provides an alternative cause of action in such suits where the 1983 claim is based on a violation of rights independent of Title VII—for example, the Fourteenth Amendment. See e.g., Johnston v. Harris County Flood Control District, 869 F.2d 1565 (5th Cir.1989), cert. denied, 493 U.S. 1019, 110 S.Ct. 718, 107 L.Ed.2d 738 (1990); Carrero v. New York City Housing Authority, 890 F.2d 569 (2d Cir.1989); Starrett v. Wadley, 876 F.2d 808 (10th Cir.1989).

If a Title VII suit is dismissed for failure to comply with the administrative prerequisites, should a subsequent Section 1983 suit, based on the same facts alleged in the Title VII action, be barred by the doctrine of *res judicata?* See, Nilsen v. Moss Point, 701 F.2d 556 (5th Cir.1983) (*en banc*).

5. A continuing problem for plaintiffs in Section 1983 litigation is determining the appropriate party defendant. In MONROE v. PAPE, 365 U.S. 167, 81 S.Ct. 473, 5 L.Ed.2d 492 (1961), the Supreme Court held that because of the explicit language of the Act ("Every person who ... subjects or causes to be subjected any citizen ..."), only human beings and not institutions or corporate political bodies were proper party defendants in a § 1983 case. See also City of Kenosha v. Bruno, 412 U.S. 507, 93 S.Ct. 2222, 37 L.Ed.2d 109 (1973). Thus, for a number of years § 1983 actions were normally filed against the public officials whose actions were challenged rather than the agency or political body which they represented. See Aldinger v. Howard, 427 U.S. 1, 96 S.Ct. 2413, 49 L.Ed.2d 276 (1976). Note that *Feeney,* filed in 1975, was a suit against the administrator, not his agency. But in 1977, the Supreme Court, following the lead of a number of circuits, recognized that a direct action under the Fourteenth Amendment could be instituted against a public body if jurisdiction was proper under 28 U.S.C. § 1331 (general federal question jurisdiction), Mt. Healthy City School District Board of Education v. Doyle, 429 U.S. 274, 277–278, 97 S.Ct. 568, 571, 50 L.Ed.2d 471 (1977), and in MONELL v. DEPARTMENT OF SOCIAL SERVICES, 436 U.S. 658, 98 S.Ct. 2018, 56 L.Ed.2d 611 (1978), the Court finally overruled Monroe v. Pape and held that local governing bodies could be sued as "persons" under 42 U.S.C. § 1983 for monetary, declaratory, and injunctive relief where the unlawful action implemented or executed "a policy or custom" of the governing unit. The Court made clear, however, that public agencies would not be liable for all illegal acts of their employees on the theory of *respondeat superior.* "Instead, it is when execution of a government's policy or custom, whether made by its lawmakers or by those whose edicts or acts may fairly be said to represent official policy, inflicts the

injury that the government as an entity is responsible under § 1983." 436 U.S. at 691–95, 98 S.Ct. 2036–2038. Since individual officials will often be unable to pay damage awards, a critical question in post-*Monell* litigation is whether the actions of the officials in question reflect or establish the "policy" of the public body. See e.g., Oklahoma City v. Tuttle, 471 U.S. 808, 105 S.Ct. 2427, 85 L.Ed.2d 791 (1985) (fact that official has discretion in exercise of particular functions does not without more give rise to municipal liability based on exercise of that discretion); Pembaur v. Cincinnati, et al., 475 U.S. 469, 106 S.Ct. 1292, 89 L.Ed.2d 452 (1986) (if decision to adopt particular course of action is directed by those who establish government policy, the municipality is responsible whether that action is taken only once or repeatedly); Schnapper, Civil Rights Litigation After Monell, 79 Colum.L.Rev. 213, 217–19 (1979).

In CITY OF ST. LOUIS v. PRAPROTNIK, 485 U.S. 112, 108 S.Ct. 915, 99 L.Ed.2d 107 (1988), the Supreme Court returned again to the problem of articulating the proper standard for determining when decisions by municipal officials will constitute the "official policy" of the municipality, thus subjecting it to liability under *Monell*. In *Praprotnik* the plaintiff, a city architect, alleged that he had been transferred to a lesser job and then laid-off in retaliation for his having successfully appealed earlier disciplinary actions to the city's Civil Service Commission. A jury found the city liable for violations of plaintiff's First Amendment and due process rights. On appeal, the city argued that it could not be held liable for the unlawful and unauthorized acts of Praprotnik's supervisors. The Court of Appeals affirmed on the ground that under *Monell* the city was responsible for the actions of those officials whose employment decisions are "final" in the sense that they are not subject to *de novo* review by higher officials. The Supreme Court reversed. The Court began by holding that the identification of policy-making officials in a government is a matter of state law. "[W]e can be confident that state law (which may include valid local ordinances and regulations) will always direct a court to some official or body that has the responsibility for making law or setting policy in any given area of a local government's business." 485 U.S. at 125, 108 S.Ct. at 925, 99 L.Ed.2d at 119. A federal court thus has very limited range of movement in assigning "policy-maker" status to particular officials.

> [A] federal court would not be justified in assuming that municipal policy-making authority lies somewhere other than where the applicable law purports to put it. And certainly there can be no justification for giving a jury the discretion to determine which officials are high enough in the government that their actions can be said to represent a decision of the government itself.

Ibid. The city could not be responsible for damages in this case because the plaintiff did not even contend that the officials with policymaking power (the Mayor, Board of Aldermen and the Civil Service Commission) had promulgated or directed a policy of retaliating against employees who appealed adverse employment decisions, nor did the plaintiff attempt to prove that such retaliation was ever directed at anyone other than himself. The Court acknowledged that if a city's policymakers could insulate the government from liability by delegating their policymaking authority to others, Section 1983 could not serve its intended purpose. The opinion leaves unclear, however, under what circumstances the actions of an official, who has received his authority from a policymaker, will constitute official policy. On the one hand, the existence of a widespread practice that is so long-standing as to constitute a custom or usage of the municipality must be treated as an official policy. On the other hand, "simply going along with discretionary decisions made by one's subordinates * * * is not a delegation to them of the authority to make policy."

It would be a different matter if a particular decision by a subordinate was cast in the form of a policy statement and expressly approved by the supervising policymaker. It would be a different matter if a series of decisions by a subordinate official manifested a "custom or usage" of which the supervisor must have been aware. ... In both those cases, the supervisor could realistically be deemed to have adopted a policy that happened to have been formulated or initiated by a lower-ranking official. But the mere failure to investigate the basis of a subordinate's discretionary decisions does not amount to a delegation of policymaking authority, especially where (as here) the wrongfulness of the subordinate's decision arises from a retaliatory motive or other unstated rationale. In such circumstances, the purposes of 1983 would not be served by treating a subordinate employee's decision as if it were a reflection of municipal policy.

485 U.S. at 130, 108 S.Ct. at 928, 99 L.Ed.2d at 122. Does *Praprotnik* mean that in a non-pattern-and-practice case in which the plaintiff alleges race or sex discrimination in employment, no relief, as a practical matter, will be available against the municipal employer? In Williams v. Butler, 863 F.2d 1398 (8th Cir.1988) (*en banc*) cert. denied, 492 U.S. 906, 109 S.Ct. 3215, 106 L.Ed.2d 565 (1989), the Eighth Circuit held that a municipality's complete delegation of authority to an official renders the actions of that official the "policy" of the city.

A very fine line exists between delegating final policymaking authority to an official, for which a municipality may be held liable, and entrusting discretionary authority to that official, for which no liability attaches. The distinction, we believe, lies in the amount of authority retained by the authorized policymakers. The clear message from *Praprotnik* is that an incomplete delegation of authority will not result in municipal liability whereas an absolute delegation will.

863 F.2d at 1402. In *Williams* the city had allowed a municipal judge "carte blanche" authority over the employment of court clerks. The Eighth Circuit concluded that by delegating final, un-reviewable policy-making authority to the judge, the city exposed itself to liability for any unconstitutional action taken by him pursuant to that authority. Compare, Gray v. County of Dane, 854 F.2d 179 (7th Cir.1988) (§ 1983 action against county properly dismissed where plaintiff failed to plead that discrimination against her was attributable to policy or established practice of county rather than unauthorized conduct of officials). The *Monell–Praprotnik* line of cases apply only to Section 1983 actions against municipalities and other local governing bodies. Neither the state itself nor a state official acting in his official capacity is a "person" for purposes of Section 1983. WILL v. MICHIGAN DEPARTMENT OF STATE POLICE, 491 U.S. 58, 109 S.Ct. 2304, 105 L.Ed.2d 45 (1989). Suits for injunctive relief and monetary damages against state officials under Section 1983 must be brought against them as individuals "acting under color of state law."

6. Unlike Title VII, exhaustion of available administrative remedies is not a prerequisite to suit under Section 1983. In PATSY v. BOARD OF REGENTS OF STATE OF FLORIDA, 457 U.S. 496, 102 S.Ct. 2557, 73 L.Ed.2d 172 (1982), the Court held that neither the language of the statute nor its legislative history indicated a desire by Congress that a claimant aggrieved by the action

of a state official be required to resort to grievance mechanisms supplied by the state even if the relief available in such proceedings would fully compensate the claimant. The claimant may, of course, decide to use the internal grievance procedure of the state before filing her federal suit, but it is important to note that resort to such procedure will not necessarily toll the running of the statute of limitations applicable to the Section 1983 action. Whether the limitation period will be tolled will depend on state law. See discussion, *infra*, at Section D of this chapter. It is also important to remember that resort to state administrative remedies may preclude subsequent federal action under res judicata and collateral estoppel principles. That possibility will certainly exist if the final stage of the state's procedure is *judicial* review of the claim and may be the case if under state law the findings of the administrative board will be given preclusive effect by the courts of the state. See, University of Tennessee v. Elliott, discussed *infra* in Section E.

SECTION C. THE CIVIL RIGHTS ACT OF 1871, SECTION TWO—42 U.S.C. § 1985(C)

Section 2 of the Civil Rights Act of 1871,[a] now codified at 42 U.S.C. § 1985(c), was enacted primarily to provide protection to southern blacks and Union sympathizers from the violent activities of the Ku Klux Klan, by outlawing conspiracies to deprive persons of "the equal protection of the laws, or of equal privileges and immunities under the law." Since § 1985(c)—like its statutory counterpart, § 1983 (originally § 1 of the 1871 Act)—was enacted pursuant to the Fourteenth Amendment, it was interpreted initially to prohibit only those conspiracies involving state action. In Griffin v. Breckenridge,[b] however, the Supreme Court ruled that black plaintiffs claiming that they were beaten by a group of private white citizens could state a cause of action under § 1985(c) without alleging either state action or that the defendants acted under color of state law, since their complaint alleged a "class-based invidiously discriminatory" conspiracy to deprive them of their thirteenth amendment right to be free from slavery and constitutional right of interstate travel. Since the decision in *Griffin*, several questions have arisen in connection with the application of § 1985(c) to employment discrimination claims.[c] For example, did the Court intend to preclude the extension of § 1985(c) to private conspiracies aimed at depriving persons of other constitutionally or statutorily guaranteed rights? In addition, is the requirement of a "class-based" discriminatory intent restricted to conspiracies motivated by racial animus? Finally, can a plaintiff satisfy the statutory "two or more persons" requirement where the complaint alleges a conspiracy between a corporation and its agents?

Read 42 U.S.C. § 1985(c) at p. 1264.

[a] Act of April 20, 1871, ch. 22, § 2, 17 Stat. 13 (1871).

[b] 403 U.S. 88, 91 S.Ct. 1790, 29 L.Ed.2d 338 (1971).

[c] For a provocative critique of the application of § 1985(c) to employment discrimination claims, see Comment, A Construction of § 1985(c) In light of Its Original Purpose, 46 U.Chi.L.Rev. 402 (1979).

GREAT AMERICAN FEDERAL SAVINGS & LOAN ASSOCIATION v. NOVOTNY

Supreme Court of the United States, 1979.
442 U.S. 366, 99 S.Ct. 2345, 60 L.Ed.2d 957.

MR. JUSTICE STEWART delivered the opinion of the Court.

More than a century after their passage, the Civil Rights Acts of the Reconstruction era continue to present difficult problems of statutory construction. Cf. Chapman v. Houston Welfare Rights Org., 441 U.S. 600, 99 S.Ct. 1905, 60 L.Ed.2d 508. In the case now before us, we consider the scope of 42 U.S.C. § 1985(c), the surviving version of § 2 of the Civil Rights Act of 1871.

I

The respondent, John R. Novotny, began his career with the Great American Federal Savings and Loan Association (hereinafter the Association) in Allegheny County, Pa., in 1950. By 1975, he was secretary of the Association, a member of its board of directors, and a loan officer. According to the allegations of the complaint in this case the Association "intentionally and deliberately embarked upon and pursued a course of conduct the effect of which was to deny to female employees equal employment opportunity * * *." When Novotny expressed support for the female employees at a meeting of the board of directors, his connection with the Association abruptly ended. He was not re-elected as secretary; he was not re-elected to the board; and he was fired. His support for the Association's female employees, he alleges, was the cause of the termination of his employment.

Novotny filed a complaint with the Equal Employment Opportunity Commission under Title VII of the Civil Rights Act of 1964. After receiving a right-to-sue letter, he brought this lawsuit against the Association and its directors in the District Court for the Western District of Pennsylvania. He claimed damages under 42 U.S.C. § 1985(c), contending that he had been injured as the result of a conspiracy to deprive him of equal protection of and equal privileges and immunities under the laws.[4] The District Court granted the defendants' motion to dismiss. It held that § 1985(c) could not be invoked because the directors of a single corporation could not, as a matter of law and fact, engage in a conspiracy.[5]

Novotny appealed. After oral argument before a three-judge panel, the case was reargued before the en banc Court of Appeals for the Third Circuit, which unanimously reversed the District Court's judg-

---

4. His complaint also alleged, as a second cause of action, that his discharge was in retaliation for his efforts on behalf of equal employment opportunity, and thus violated § 704(a) of Title VII. * * *

5. As to the Title VII claim, the District Court held that Novotny was not a proper plaintiff under § 704(a).

ment. The Court of Appeals ruled that Novotny had stated a cause of action under § 1985(c). It held that conspiracies motivated by an invidious animus against women fall within § 1985(c), and that Novotny, a male allegedly injured as a result of such a conspiracy, had standing to bring suit under that statutory provision. It ruled that Title VII could be the source of a right asserted in an action under § 1985(c), and that intracorporate conspiracies come within the intendment of the section. Finally, the court concluded that its construction of § 1985(c) did not present any serious constitutional problem.[6]

We granted certiorari, 439 U.S. 1066, 99 S.Ct. 830, 59 L.Ed.2d 30, to consider the applicability of § 1985(c) to the facts alleged in Novotny's complaint.

II

The legislative history of § 2 of the Civil Rights Act of 1871, of which § 1985(c) was originally a part, has been reviewed many times in this Court. The section as first enacted authorized both criminal and civil actions against those who have conspired to deprive others of federally guaranteed rights. Before the 19th century ended, however, the Court found the criminal provisions of the statute unconstitutional because they exceeded the scope of congressional power, and the provisions thus invalidated were later formally repealed by Congress. The civil action provided by the Act remained, but for many years was rarely, if ever, invoked.

The provisions of what is now § 1985(c) were not fully considered by this Court until 1951, in the case of Collins v. Hardyman, 341 U.S. 651, 71 S.Ct. 937, 95 L.Ed.2d 1253. There the Court concluded that the section protected citizens only from injuries caused by conspiracies "under color of state law." Twenty years later, in Griffin v. Breckenridge, 403 U.S. 88, 91 S.Ct. 1790, 29 L.Ed.2d 338, the Court unanimously concluded that the *Collins* Court had accorded to the provisions of § 1985(c) too narrow a scope. The fears concerning congressional power that had motivated the Court in the *Collins* case had been dissolved by intervening cases. Therefore, the Court found that § 1985(c) did provide a cause of action for damages caused by purely private conspiracies.

The Court's opinion in *Griffin* discerned the following criteria for measuring whether a complaint states a cause of action under § 1985(c):

6. The Court of Appeals ruled that Novotny had also stated a valid cause of action under Title VII. It held that § 704(a) applies to retaliation for both formal and informal actions taken to advance the purposes of the Act. That holding is not now before this Court.

We note the relative narrowness of the specific issue before the Court. It is unnec-

essary for us to consider whether a plaintiff would have a cause of action under § 1985(c) where the defendant was not subject to suit under Title VII or a comparable statute. Nor do we think it necessary to consider whether § 1985(c) creates a remedy for statutory rights other than those fundamental rights derived from the Constitution.

"To come within the legislation a complaint must allege that the defendants did (1) 'conspire or go in disguise on the highway or on the premises of another' (2) 'for the purpose of depriving, either directly or indirectly, any person or class of persons of the equal protection of the laws, or of equal privileges and immunities under the laws.' It must then assert that one or more of the conspirators (3) did, or caused to be done, 'any act in furtherance of the object of [the] conspiracy,' whereby another was (4a) 'injured in his person of property' or (4b) 'deprived of having and exercising any right or privilege of a citizen of the United States.'"

Section 1985(c) provides no substantive rights itself; it merely provides a remedy for violation of the rights it designates. The primary question in the present case, therefore, is whether a person injured by a conspiracy to violate § 704(a) of Title VII of the Civil Rights Act of 1964 is deprived of "the equal protection of the laws, or of equal privileges and immunities under the laws" within the meaning of § 1985(c).[11]

Under Title VII, cases of alleged employment discrimination are subject to a detailed administrative and judicial process designed to provide an opportunity for nonjudicial and nonadversary resolution of claims. * * *

* * * The majority of the federal courts have held that the Act does not allow a court to award general or punitive damages. The Act expressly allows the prevailing party to recover his attorney's fees, and, in some cases, provides that a district court may appoint counsel for a plaintiff. Because the Act expressly authorizes only equitable remedies, the courts have consistently held that neither party has a right to a jury trial.

If a violation of Title VII could be asserted through § 1985(c), a complainant could avoid most if not all of these detailed and specific provisions of the law. Section 1985(c) expressly authorizes compensatory damages; punitive damages might well follow. The plaintiff or defendant might demand a jury trial. The short and precise time limitations of Title VII would be grossly altered. Perhaps most importantly, the complainant could completely bypass the administrative process, which plays such a crucial role in the scheme established by Congress in Title VII.

The problem in this case is closely akin to that in Brown v. GSA, 425 U.S. 820, 96 S.Ct. 1961, 48 L.Ed.2d 402. There, we held that § 717 of Title VII provides the exclusive remedy for employment discrimination claims of those federal employees that it covers. Our conclusion was based on the proposition that

11. For the purposes of this question, we assume but certainly do not decide that the directors of a single corporation can form a conspiracy within the meaning of § 1985(c).

"[t]he balance, completeness, and structural integrity of § 717 are inconsistent with the petitioner's contention that the judicial remedy afforded by § 717(c) was designed merely to supplement other putative judicial relief."

Here the case is even more compelling. In *Brown*, the Court concluded that § 717 displaced other causes of action arguably available to assert substantive rights similar to those granted by § 717. Section 1985(c), by contrast, *creates* no rights. It is a purely remedial statute, providing a civil cause of action when some otherwise defined federal right—to equal protection of the laws or equal privileges and immunities under the laws—is breached by a conspiracy in the manner defined by the section. Thus, we are not faced in this case with a question of implied repeal. The right Novotny claims under § 704(a) did not even arguably exist before the passage of Title VII. The only question here, therefore, is whether the rights created by Title VII may be asserted within the *remedial* framework of § 1985(3).

This case thus differs markedly from the cases recently decided by this Court that have related the substantive provisions of last century's Civil Rights Acts to contemporary legislation conferring similar substantive rights. In those cases we have held that substantive rights conferred in the 19th century were not withdrawn, *sub silentio*, by the subsequent passage of the modern statutes.   * * *

* * *

This case, by contrast, does not involve two "independent" rights, and for the same basic reasons that underlay the Court's decision in Brown v. GSA, supra, reinforced by the other considerations discussed in this opinion, we conclude that § 1985(c) may not be invoked to redress violations of Title VII. It is true that a § 1985(c) remedy would not be coextensive with Title VII, since a plaintiff in an action under § 1985(c) must prove both a conspiracy and a group animus that Title VII does not require. While this incomplete congruity would limit the damage that would be done to Title VII, it would not eliminate it. Unimpaired effectiveness can be given to the plan put together by Congress in Title VII only by holding that deprivation of a right created by Title VII cannot be the basis for a cause of action under § 1985(c).

Accordingly, the judgment of the Court of Appeals is vacated, and the case is remanded to that Court for further proceedings consistent with this opinion.

It is so ordered.

MR. JUSTICE POWELL, concurring.

* * *

The Court's specific holding is that 42 U.S.C. § 1985(c) may not be invoked to redress violations of Title VII. The broader issue argued to us in this case was whether this Civil War era remedial statute, providing no substantive rights itself, was intended to provide a remedy generally for the violation of subsequently created statutory rights. For essentially the reasons suggested by Mr. Justice Stevens, I would hold that § 1985(c) should not be so construed, and that its reach is limited to conspiracies to violate those fundamental rights derived from the Constitution.

The Court's unanimous decision in Griffin v. Breckenridge, 403 U.S. 88, 91 S.Ct. 1790, 29 L.Ed.2d 338 (1971), is to this effect. The alleged conspiracy there was an attempt by white citizens, resorting to force and violence, to deprive Negro citizens of the right to use interstate highways. In sustaining a cause of action under § 1985(c), the Court found that the alleged conspiracy—if implemented—would violate the constitutional "right of interstate travel" as well as the right of Negro citizens to be free from "invidiously discriminatory" action. The Court declared:

> "That the statute was meant to reach private action does not, however, mean that it was intended to apply to all tortious, conspiratorial interferences with the rights of others. For, though the supporters of the legislation insisted on coverage of private conspiracies, they were equally emphatic that they did not believe, in the words of Representative Cook, 'that Congress has a right to punish an assault and battery when committed by two or more persons within a State.' The constitutional shoals that would lie in the path of interpreting § 1985[(c)] as a general federal tort law can be avoided by giving full effect to the congressional purpose— by requiring, as an element of the cause of action, the kind of invidiously discriminatory motivation stressed by the sponsors of the limiting amendment. The language requiring intent to deprive of *equal* protection, or *equal* privileges and immunities, means that there must be some racial, or perhaps otherwise class-based, invidiously discriminatory animus behind the conspirators' action. The conspiracy, in other words, must aim at a deprivation of the equal enjoyment of rights secured by the law to all."

* * *

By contrast, this Court has never held that the right to any particular private employment is a "right of national citizenship," or derives from any other right created by the Constitution. Indeed, even Congress, in the exercise of its powers under the Commerce Clause of the Constitution, has accorded less than full protection to private employees. It excluded several classes of employers from the coverage of Title VII, for example, employers of fewer than 15 employees. Nor does the Constitution create any right to be free of gender-based discrimination perpetuated solely through private action.

The rationale of *Griffin* accords with the purpose, history, and common understanding of this Civil War era statute. Rather than leave federal courts in any doubt as to the scope of actions under

§ 1985(c), I would explicitly reaffirm the constitutional basis of *Griffin*.*

MR. JUSTICE STEVENS, concurring.

* * *

Sections 1983 and 1985(c) of Title 42 of the United States Code are the surviving direct descendants of §§ 1 and 2 of the Civil Rights Act of 1871. Neither of these sections created any substantive rights. Earlier this Term we squarely held that § 1983 merely provides a remedy for certain violations of certain federal rights, and today the Court unequivocally holds that § 1985(c) "provides no substantive rights itself; it merely provides a remedy for violation of the rights it designates."

* * * The import of the language [of §§ 1983 and 1985(c)] as well as the relevant legislative history, suggests that the Congress which enacted both provisions was concerned with providing federal remedies for deprivations of rights protected by the Constitution and, in particular, the newly ratified Fourteenth Amendment. If a violation was effected "under color of any law, statute, ordinance, regulation, custom, or usage of any State," § 1983 afforded redress; if a violation was caused by private persons who "conspire or go in disguise on the highway," § 1985(c) afforded redress. Thus, the former authorized a remedy for state action depriving an individual of his constitutional rights, the latter for private action.

Some privileges and immunities of citizenship, such as the right to engage in interstate travel and the right to be free of the badges of slavery, are protected by the Constitution against interference by private action, as well as impairment by state action. Private conspiracies to deprive individuals of these rights are, as this Court held in Griffin v. Breckenridge, 403 U.S. 88, 91 S.Ct. 1790, 29 L.Ed.2d 338, actionable under § 1985(c) without regard to any state involvement.

Other privileges and immunities of citizenship such as the right to due process of law and the right to the equal protection of the laws are protected by the Constitution only against state action. Shelley v. Kraemer, 334 U.S. 1, 13, 68 S.Ct. 836, 842, 92 L.Ed. 1161. If a state agency arbitrarily refuses to serve a class of persons—Chinese Americans, for example, see Yick Wo v. Hopkins, 118 U.S. 356, 6 S.Ct. 1064, 30 L.Ed. 220—it violates the Fourteenth Amendment. Or if private persons take conspiratorial action that prevents or hinders the constituted authorities of any State from giving or securing equal treatment, the private persons would cause those authorities to violate the Fourteenth Amendment; the private persons would then have violated § 1985(c).

---

* The doubts which will remain after the Court's decision are far from insubstantial. At least one federal court, for example, has held that although Title VII rights may not be asserted through § 1985(c), claims based on § 3 of the Equal Pay Act of 1963, may be raised in a § 1985(c) suit. I would take advantage of the present opportunity to make clear that this Civil War era statute was intended to provide a remedy *only* for conspiracies to violate fundamental rights derived from the Constitution.

If, however, private persons engage in purely private acts of discrimination—for example, if they discriminate against women or
against lawyers with a criminal practice, they do not violate the Equal
Protection Clause of the Fourteenth Amendment. The rights secured
by the Equal Protection and Due Process Clauses of the Fourteenth
Amendment are rights to protection against unequal or unfair treatment by the State, not by private parties. Thus, while § 1985(c) does
not require that a defendant act under color of state law, there still can
be no claim for relief based on a violation of the Fourteenth Amendment if there has been no involvement by the State. The requirement
of state action, in this context, is no more than a requirement that
there be a constitutional violation.

Here, there is no claim of such a violation. Private discrimination
on the basis of sex is not prohibited by the Constitution. The right to
be free of sex discrimination by other private parties is a statutory
right that was created almost a century after § 1985(c) was enacted.
Because I do not believe that statute was intended to provide a remedy
for the violation of statutory rights—let alone rights created by statutes
that had not yet been enacted—I agree with the Court's conclusion that
it does not provide respondent with redress for injuries caused by
private conspiracies to discriminate on the basis of sex.

With this additional explanation of my views, I join the Court's
opinion.

MR. JUSTICE WHITE, with whom MR. JUSTICE BRENNAN and MR. JUSTICE
MARSHALL join, dissenting.

The Court today releases employers acting with invidious discriminatory animus in concert with others from liability under 42 U.S.C.
§ 1985(c) for the injuries they inflict. Because for both respondent in
this case and as a general matter § 1985(c) is an entirely consistent
supplement to Title VII, I dissent.

* * * [T]he majority holds that the claim under § 1985(c) must be
dismissed because "deprivation of a right created by Title VII cannot be
the basis for a cause of action under § 1985(c)."

Unfortunately, the majority does not explain whether the "right
created by Title VII" to which it refers is the right guaranteed to
women employees under § 703(a) or the right guaranteed to respondent
under § 704(a). Although in stating its view of the issue before the
Court, the majority intimates that it is relying on the fact that respondent has a claim directly under § 704(a), the reasoning of the majority
opinion in no way indicates why the existence of a § 704(a) claim
should prevent respondent from seeking to vindicate under § 1985(c)
the entirely separate right provided by § 703(a).

Clearly, respondent's right under § 704(a)—to be free from retaliation for efforts to aid others asserting Title VII rights—is distinct from
the Title VII right implicated in his claim under § 1985(c), which is the
right of women employees not to be discriminated against on the basis

of their sex. Moreover, that respondent in this case is in a position to assert claims under both § 1985(c) and § 704(a) is due solely to the peculiar facts of this case, rather than to any necessary relationship between the two provisions. First, it is of course possible that a person could be injured in the course of a conspiracy to deny § 703(a) rights— as respondent claims under his § 1985(c) cause of action—by some means other than retaliatory discrimination prohibited under § 704(a). Second, § 704(a) itself protects only employees and applicants for employment; others, such as customers or suppliers, retaliated against in the course of a conspiracy to violate § 703(a) are not expressly protected under any provision of Title VII. Indeed, if respondent in this case had been only a director, rather than both a director and an employee, of the Great American Federal Savings and Loan Association, he apparently would not be able to assert a claim under § 704(a).

Because the existence of a § 704(a) claim is due entirely to the peculiar facts of this case, I interpret the majority's broad holding that "deprivation of a right created by Title VII cannot be the basis for a cause of action under § 1985(c)" to preclude respondent from suing under § 1985(c) not because he coincidentally has a § 704(a) claim, but because the purpose of conspiracy alleging resulting in injury to him was to deny § 703(a) rights.

The pervasive and essential flaw in the majority's approach to reconciliation of § 1985(c) and Title VII proceeds from its characterization of the former statute as solely a "remedial" provision. It is true that the words "equal privileges and immunities under the laws" in § 1985(c) refer to substantive rights created or guaranteed by other federal law, be it the Constitution or federal statutes other than § 1985(c);[5] and in this case it is a conspiracy to deny a substantive right created in § 703(a) of Title VII[6] that is part of the basis for respon-

5. The majority opinion does not reach the issue whether § 1985(c) encompasses federal statutory rights other than those proceeding in "fundamental" fashion from the Constitution itself. I am not certain in what manner the Court conceives of sex discrimination by private parties to proceed from explicit constitutional guarantees. In any event, I need not pursue this issue because I think it clear that § 1985(c) encompasses all rights guaranteed in federal statutes as well as rights guaranteed directly by the Constitution. As originally introduced, § 2 of the Civil Rights Act of 1871, encompassed "rights, privileges, or immunities * * * under the Constitution and laws of the United States." The substitution of the terms "the equal protection of the laws" and "equal privileges and immunities under the laws," did not limit the scope of the rights protected but added a requirement of certain "class-based, invidiously discriminatory animus behind the conspirators' action." We have repeatedly

held that 18 U.S.C. § 241 (derived from § 6 of the Civil Rights Act of 1870, 16 Stat. 141), which is the "closest remaining criminal analogue to § 1985[c]," Griffin v. Breckenridge, supra, at 98, 91 S.Ct., at 1796, encompasses all federal statutory rights. Similarly, we have stated that 42 U.S.C. § 1983, derived from § 1 of the 1871 Civil Rights Act, encompasses federal statutory as well as constitutional rights.

6. Although Griffin v. Breckenridge, supra, at 102 n. 9, 91 S.Ct., at 1798, did not reach the issue whether discrimination on a basis other than race may be vindicated under § 1985(c), the Court correctly assumes that the answer to this question is yes. The statute broadly refers to all privileges and immunities, without any limitation as to the class of persons to whom these rights may be granted. It is clear that sex discrimination may be sufficiently invidious to come within the prohibition of § 1985(c).

dent's suit under § 1985(c).[7] However, § 1985(c), unlike a remedial statute such as 42 U.S.C. § 1983, does not merely provide a cause of action for persons deprived of rights elsewhere guaranteed. Because § 1985(c) provides a remedy for *any person* injured as a result of deprivation of a substantive federal right, it must be seen as itself creating rights in persons other than those to whom the underlying federal right extends.

In this case, for instance, respondent is seeking to redress an injury inflicted upon *him*, which injury is distinct and separate from the injury inflicted upon the female employees whose § 703(a) rights were allegedly denied. The damages available to a person such as respondent suing under § 1985(c) are not dependent upon the amount of injury caused persons deprived of "equal privileges and immunities under the laws," but upon the gravity of the separate injury inflicted upon the person suing.

In this circumstance—where the § 1985(c) plaintiff is seeking redress for injury caused as a result of the denial of other persons' Title VII rights—it makes no sense to hold that the remedies provided in Title VII are exclusive, for such a § 1985(c) plaintiff has no Title VII remedy. It thus can hardly be asserted that allowing this § 1985(c) plaintiff to seek redress of his injury would allow such individual to "completely bypass" the administrative and other "detailed and specific" enforcement mechanisms provided in Title VII.

In enacting § 1985(c), Congress specifically contemplated that persons injured by private conspiracies to deny the federal rights of others could redress their injuries, quite apart from any redress by those who are the object of the conspiracy. Nothing in the Court's opinion suggests any warrant for refusal to recognize this cause of action simply because Title VII rights are involved.

I am also convinced that persons whose own Title VII rights have allegedly been violated retain the separate right to seek redress under § 1985(c). In seeking to accommodate the civil rights statutes enacted in the decade after the Civil War and the civil rights statutes of the recent era, the Court has recognized that the later statutes cannot be said to have impliedly repealed the earlier unless there is an irreconcilable conflict between them. Of course, the mere fact of overlap in modes of redressing discrimination does not constitute such irreconcilable conflict. * * *

It is clear that such overlap as may exist between Title VII and § 1985(c) occurs only because the latter is directed at a discrete and particularly disfavored form of discrimination, and examination of § 1985(c) shows that it constitutes a compatible and important supplement to the more general prohibition and remedy provided in Title VII.

---

7. This is analogous to United States v. Johnson, supra, where the basis for a prosecution under 18 U.S.C. § 241 was a conspiracy to deny the substantive right to equality in public accommodations guaranteed under Title II of the Civil Rights Act of 1964.

Thus, while it may be that in many cases persons seeking redress under § 1985(c) also have a claim directly under Title VII,[10] this is not sufficient reason to deprive those persons of the right to sue for the compensatory and punitive damages to which they are entitled under the post-Civil War statute.

As previously indicated, the majority's willingness to infer a silent repeal of § 1985(c) is based on its view that the provision only gives a remedy to redress deprivations prohibited by other federal law. But this narrow view of § 1985(c) is incorrect even as to § 1985(c) plaintiffs themselves denied Title VII rights. Because only conspiracies to deprive persons of federal rights are subject to redress under § 1985(c), that statute, like 18 U.S.C. § 241, is itself a prohibition, separate and apart from the prohibitions stated in the underlying provisions of federal law. Moreover, only those deprivations imbued with "invidiously discriminatory motivation" amounting to "class-based * * * animus," are encompassed by § 1985(c). Viewed in this manner, the right guaranteed by § 1985(c) is the right not to be subjected to an invidious conspiracy to deny other federal rights. This discrete category of deprivations to which § 1985(c) is directed stands in sharp contrast to the broad prohibition on discrimination provided in § 703(a) of Title VII, see Griggs v. Duke Power Co., 401 U.S. 424, 91 S.Ct. 849, 28 L.Ed.2d 158 (1971). If, as the majority suggests, it would not recognize an implied repeal of an earlier statute granting a separate but overlapping right, then it should not do so in this case; for respondent has alleged a violation of § 703(a) in a manner independently prohibited by § 1985(c), and under the majority's approach should be allowed to redress *both* deprivations.

* * *

Because respondent exhausted his administrative remedies under Title VII, there is no need in this case to reach the question whether persons whose Title VII rights have been violated may bring suit directly in federal court alleging an invidious conspiracy to deny those Title VII rights. I note, however, that the majority's desire not to undercut the administrative enforcement scheme, including the encouragement of voluntary conciliation, provided by Title VII would be completely fulfilled by insisting that § 1985(c) plaintiffs exhaust whatever Title VII remedies they may have. The concerns expressed in the majority opinion do not provide a basis for precluding redress altogether under § 1985(c).

NOTES AND PROBLEMS FOR DISCUSSION

1. Should the holding in *Novotny* be extended to cases where the plaintiff alleges a conspiracy to deprive him or someone else of a right guaranteed by some federal statute other than Title VII? While Justices Powell and Stevens

---

10. It is, of course, theoretically possible that an individual could be injured by a conspiracy to violate his Title VII rights even though that conspiracy was never brought to fruition and thus there was no violation of Title VII itself.

would restrict § 1985(c) to claimed deprivations of constitutional rights, and Justices White, Brennan and Marshall would not, the four other members of the majority did not address this issue. One year after its decision in *Novotny*, however, in MAINE v. THIBOUTOT, 448 U.S. 1, 100 S.Ct. 2502, 65 L.Ed.2d 555 (1980) the Court interpreted the language in § 1983 requiring plaintiffs to allege a deprivation of rights secured by the Constitution "and laws" to embrace claims of statutory as well as constitutional violations. Nevertheless, relying on the Court's ruling in *Novotny*, several lower federal courts have held that a § 1985(c) action cannot be based on a conspiracy to deprive persons of their rights under the Age Discrimination in Employment Act, Wippel v. Prudential Ins. Co., 33 FEP Cases 412 (D.Md.1982) and the Equal Pay Act, Whitten v. Petroleum Club of Lafayette, 508 F.Supp. 765 (W.D.La.1981). In both of these situations, however, the court was dealing with a statute that was enacted substantially after § 1985(c) and which provided for administrative review of discrimination claims prior to the institution of suit. What if a § 1985(c) complaint alleged a private conspiracy to deprive persons of their rights under a statute—such as § 1981—that was enacted before § 1985(c) and that did not require pre-suit exhaustion of administrative remedies? See Nieto v. United Auto Workers Local 598, 672 F.Supp. 987 (E.D.Mich.1987)(*Novotny* does not preclude the use of § 1981 as the substantive predicate for a § 1985 cause of action as § 1981 and Title VII were intended by Congress to be supplementary rather than mutually exclusive); Witten v. A.H. Smith & Co., 567 F.Supp. 1063 (D.Md.1983)(§ 1981 is proper substantive basis for § 1985(c) claim since Congress' purpose in enacting the 1871 Act was to enforce the provisions of the 1866 Act); Hudson v. Teamsters Local Union No. 957, 536 F.Supp. 1138 (S.D.Ohio 1982)(plaintiff can bring § 1985(c) action for conspiracy to violate § 1981). Cf. Brett v. Sohio Construction Co., 518 F.Supp. 698 (D. Alaska 1981)(§ 1985(c) covers claim based on Labor Management Reporting & Disclosure Act). What about an alleged deprivation of a state statutory right? See Life Insurance Co. of North America v. Reichardt, 591 F.2d 499 (9th Cir.1979). The principal case is noted at 61 B.U.L.Rev. 1007 (1981); 65 Corn.L.Rev. 114 (1979).

2. Paul Jones, a black man, received a notice from his foreman that because of excessive lateness he was recommending to the plant manager that Jones be discharged. After unsuccessfully requesting his union representative to intervene on his behalf, Jones spoke personally with the plant manager and convinced the manager to reject the foreman's recommendation in light of the company's lenient policy with respect to lateness. Jones subsequently brought a § 1985(c) action in federal court against the foreman and union representative charging that they conspired to deprive him of his rights under Title VII by strictly applying the tardiness rule to him because of his race. Jones' complaint alleged that no white employee had ever been fired because of excessive lateness. How should the court rule on the defendant's motion to dismiss for failure to state a cause of action? Note that in footnote six of *Novotny*, the Court explained that it was not ruling on whether a claim would lie under § 1985(c) where the defendant was not subject to suit under Title VII. Should the result be different under those circumstances?

The other manner in which this issue arises was addressed in Justice White's dissenting opinion—i.e., the availability of a § 1985(c) cause of action to a third party injured by a conspiracy directed at others. Do you agree with Justice White's conclusion that Congress intended to protect advocates of the victimized class? Does this interpretation promote the policy behind the Act?

What about Justice White's claim that without such a cause of action, the plaintiff is left remediless?

3. In his concurring opinion in *Novotny*, Justice Powell cited the passage in *Griffin v. Breckenridge* where a unanimous Court declared that a claim brought under § 1985(c) must allege "some racial, or perhaps otherwise class-based, invidiously discriminatory animus behind the conspirators' action." The majority in *Novotny* did not have to decide whether that language could be interpreted to permit a § 1985(c) claim challenging discrimination on the basis of a non-racial classification.

In UNITED BROTHERHOOD OF CARPENTERS AND JOINERS OF AMERICA, LOCAL 610 v. SCOTT, 463 U.S. 825, 103 S.Ct. 3352, 77 L.Ed.2d 1049 (1983), two non-union employees were beaten by local residents during a citizen protest against an employer's policy of hiring workers without regard to union membership. The company and these two employees brought suit under § 1985(c) against several local unions, a local trades council and various individuals, alleging that these defendants conspired to deprive the plaintiffs of their First Amendment right to associate with their fellow non-union employees and that this curtailment was a deprivation of the equal protection of the laws within the meaning of § 1985(c). This caused the Court to examine whether § 1985(c) reaches conspiracies other than those motivated by racial animus. In a 5–4 decision, the majority opined that "it is a close question whether Section 1985(c) was intended to reach any class-based animus other than animus against Negroes and those who championed their cause, most notably Republicans." The Court examined the legislative history and concluded that as the predominant purpose of the statute was to combat the then prevalent animus against Blacks and their supporters, it could not be construed to protect every political group from any injury perpetrated by a rival organization. While the majority did not hold that all political groups were excluded from the coverage of § 1985(c), it ruled that this provision did not reach conspiracies motivated by economic or commercial, as opposed to racial animus. Group actions resting on economic motivations were deemed outside the reach of the statute. Of course, this decision continued to leave unresolved the issue of whether § 1985(c) prohibits conspiracies aimed at non-racial groups that are motivated by other than economic animus. The four dissenters, on the other hand, would interpret § 1985(c) to include conspiracies to hinder any group or class of persons in the exercise of their legal rights because of an invidious animus towards members of that class.

Relying on *Scott*, the Tenth Circuit subsequently held that the class of handicapped persons was not a protected class under § 1985(c). Wilhelm v. Continental Title Co., 720 F.2d 1173 (10th Cir.1983). Other pre-*Scott* lower federal courts, however, have extended § 1985(c) to discrimination on the basis of sex, Padway v. Palches, 665 F.2d 965 (9th Cir.1982); religion and national origin, Marlowe v. Fisher Body, 489 F.2d 1057 (6th Cir.1973), Schneider v. Bahler, 564 F.Supp. 1449 (N.D.Ind.1983); and age, Pavlo v. Stiefel Laboratories, Inc., 22 FEP Cases 489 (S.D.N.Y.1979). And while some courts have refused to apply the protection of § 1985(c) to homosexuals, DeSantis v. Pacific Tel. & Tel. Co., Inc., 608 F.2d 327 (9th Cir.1979), or to public drunks, Wagar v. Hasenkrug, 486 F.Supp. 47 (D.Mont.1980), one trial court has held that women seeking abortions are a class protected by § 1985(c). See Planned Parenthood Ass'n v. Holy Angels Catholic Church, 765 F.Supp. 617 (N.D.Cal.1991)(only women get pregnant and gender classifications have been accorded heightened scrutiny by the courts). Can a rational distinction be drawn between the protected and unprotected classes? See Note, Protected Rights and Classes under 42 U.S.C. § 1985(3); United Brotherhood of Carpenters v. Scott, 17 Conn.L.Rev. 165 (1984); Gormley, Private Conspiracies and the Constitution: A Modern Vision of 42 U.S.C. § 1985(c), 64 Tex.L.Rev. 527 (1985).

4. While the circuit court in *Novotny* ruled that agents of a single corporation could form a conspiracy within the meaning of § 1985(c), the Supreme Court reserved decision on this question as well as on whether a conspiracy could occur between the corporation and its agents. Where the employees are found to have acted in the scope of their employment, rather than in pursuit of their personal interests, most courts have refused to recognize intracorporate conspiracies. The majority of courts reason that because a corporation acts through its officers, directors and employees, action taken by a corporation and its agents within the scope of their employ constitutes conduct by only a single entity. Thus, these courts conclude, the statutory requirement of a conspiracy between "two or more persons" is not satisfied—i.e., an entity cannot conspire with itself. See e.g., Herrmann v. Moore, 576 F.2d 453 (2d Cir.), cert. denied, 439 U.S. 1003, 99 S.Ct. 613, 58 L.Ed.2d 679 (1978); Dombrowski v. Dowling, 459 F.2d 190 (7th Cir.1972). On the other hand, where the employees are named as individual defendants, some courts have recognized the existence of an intracorporate conspiracy where the individual employees are found to have acted in concert either (1) outside the scope of their employment and discriminated for personal reasons, see Garza v. City of Omaha, 814 F.2d 553 (8th Cir.1987), (2) within the scope of their supervisory authority but in ways which did not further the company's legitimate business concerns, see Volk v. Coler, 845 F.2d 1422 (7th Cir.1988), or (3) in connection with multiple acts of discrimination, see An–Ti Chai v. Michigan Technological University, 493 F.Supp. 1137 (W.D.Mich.1980).

A union is treated as a single entity for these purposes. Ironically, therefore, where eleven union members joined to subject a supervisor to verbal abuse, the court's determination that this racially-motivated conduct had been discussed and planned at a union meeting and had been executed on behalf of the union immunized the individuals as well as the union from liability under § 1985(c). Nieto v. United Auto Workers Local 598, 672 F.Supp. 987 (E.D.Mich. 1987). For further discussion of intracorporate conspiracies see Note, Intracorporate Conspiracies Under 42 U.S.C. § 1985(c), 13 Ga.L.Rev. 591 (1979); Note, Intracorporate Conspiracies Under 42 U.S.C. § 1985(c), 92 Harv.L.Rev. 470 (1978).

5. Must a § 1985(c) plaintiff prove discriminatory intent as part of its prima facie case? See Taylor v. St. Louis, 702 F.2d 695 (8th Cir.1983).

SECTION D. THE APPLICABLE STATUTES OF LIMITATION

Unlike Title VII the Reconstruction Era civil rights acts discussed above do not contain their own statutes of limitation and there is no "catch all" federal limitation period. 42 U.S.C. § 1988 provides, however, that if in a civil rights case federal law is "deficient," the court should apply the law "of the State wherein the court having jurisdiction of such [claim] is held, so far as the same is not inconsistent with the Constitution and laws of the United States * * *." It is settled that federal courts will look to state law to determine the statutes of limitations for suits filed pursuant to Sections 1981, 1983 and 1985. See, Board of Regents v. Tomanio, 446 U.S. 478, 100 S.Ct. 1790, 64 L.Ed.2d 440 (1980) (courts should borrow "the state law of limitations governing an analogous cause of action"); Johnson v. Railway Express Agency, Inc., 421 U.S. 454, 95 S.Ct. 1716, 44 L.Ed.2d 295 (1975) (federal court should use "that [limitation period] which the State would apply if the action had been brought in a state court"). States typically have different limitations periods for different causes of action (contract, tort, land matters, etc.) and a residual or "catch-all" period for claims not fitting into one of the established causes of action. Because more than one such limitation period could arguably apply to civil rights actions, the decision of which period to adopt has not been without difficulty.

In WILSON v. GARCIA, 471 U.S. 261, 105 S.Ct. 1938, 85 L.Ed.2d 254 (1985), the Court resolved matters, at least for Section 1983 cases, by adopting a bright-line approach to the problem. The Court held that all Section 1983 actions should be treated as claims for violation of personal rights and that the state statute governing tort actions for the recovery of damages for personal injuries provides the appropriate limitation period. "[T]his choice is supported by the nature of the [Section] 1983 remedy, and by the federal interest in insuring that the borrowed period of limitations not discriminate against the federal civil rights remedy." 471 U.S. at 276, 105 S.Ct. at 1947. *Wilson* was a police brutality damage action, but the court made clear that its ruling applied to all Section 1983 actions, including employment discrimination claims, since allowing courts to choose the applicable limitation period based on the facts of each case would lead to "uncertainty and time-consuming litigation that is foreign to the central purpose of [Section] 1983." 471 U.S. at 272, 105 S.Ct. at 1945. The Court expressly rejected the possibility that states' residuary statutes of limitations be applied in Section 1983 actions. "The relative scarcity of statutory claims when § 1983 was enacted makes it unlikely that Congress would have intended to apply the catchall periods of limitations for statutory claims that were later enacted by many States." 471 U.S. at 278, 105 S.Ct. at 1948. *Wilson* did not end all confusion about the matter because a number of states provide more than one limitation period for personal injury claims, distinguishing, for example, between intentional and non-intentional torts. After *Wilson,* the circuits divided on which type of tort limitation period was applicable to Section 1983 claims. See, Gates v. Spinks, 771 F.2d 916 (5th Cir.1985), cert. denied, 475 U.S. 1065, 106 S.Ct. 1378, 89 L.Ed.2d 603 (1986) (statute governing intentional torts should apply); Hamilton v. City of Overland Park, 730 F.2d 613 (10th Cir.1984), cert. denied, 471 U.S. 1052, 105 S.Ct. 2111, 85 L.Ed.2d 476 (1985) (residual limitation period governing non-intentional torts applicable).

In OWENS v. OKURE, 488 U.S. 235, 109 S.Ct. 573, 102 L.Ed.2d 594 (1989), a police misconduct action filed pursuant to Section 1983, the Supreme Court addressed the problem of whether a limitation period for intentional torts or a general residuary period applicable to all personal injury claims not covered by specific statutes of limitation should be used in such a case. The Court characterized the choice between specific and residuary tort limitations statutes as "essentially a practical inquiry." In his opinion for the Court, Justice Marshall stated that *Wilson* had announced a single broad characterization of all § 1983 actions in order to eliminate the uncertainty and chaos that had resulted from the application of different statutes of limitations under the theretofore prevailing analysis. Thus, he reasoned, it was incumbent on the Court to devise a rule for determining the appropriate personal injury limitations statute that could be applied "with ease and predictability in all 50 states." Choosing the intentional tort limitations statute would be inappropriate, he reasoned, since the existence in every state of more than one such statute would not eliminate the potential for confusion and contradiction in choosing among these provisions. By way of contrast, Marshall noted, every State has only one, easily identifiable, general or residual limitations statute governing personal injury actions. Adopting the general or residual period would permit litigants to readily ascertain the applicable limitations period. Rejecting the defendants' claim that the intentional tort limitations period should be applied because § 1983 claims are more analogous to intentional torts, the Court emphasized the wide spectrum of claims that fall within the embrace of § 1983, including those that do not contain an element of intent in their prima facie case or defense. Thus, the Court concluded, where a State has more than one statute of limitations for personal injury actions, courts considering § 1983 claims should borrow the general or residual statute for personal injury actions.

In GOODMAN v. LUKENS STEEL CO., 482 U.S. 656, 107 S.Ct. 2617, 96 L.Ed.2d 572 (1987), the Court extended *Wilson* to § 1981 cases. The Court noted that while § 1981 did refer to contractual rights, it also referred to such personal rights as the rights to sue, to testify and to equal rights under the laws. Moreover, the Court added, the statute was part of a federal law barring racial discrimination which, it reasoned, constituted a fundamental injury to a person's individual rights. Thus, a majority of the Court concluded, *Wilson's* characterization of § 1983 claims was equally applicable to actions brought under § 1981.

As held in Delaware State College v. Ricks, Chapter 4, *supra*, the question of when the applicable statute of limitations accrues or begins to run in a suit under the federal civil rights statutes is a matter of federal law. The question of what "tolls" or stops the running of the limitation period is, however, controlled by state law. In Board of Regents v. Tomanio, *supra*, the Court held that when a federal court borrows a state statute of limitations it must also use the state's tolling rules as well, unless to do so would conflict with the federal policies of compensation and deterrence underlying the civil rights acts. 446 U.S. at 484, 100 S.Ct. at 1795. State law also controls the effect of tolling, i.e. the amount of time remaining in the period to file suit after the event that tolls the limitation period is over. In Chardon v. Fumero Soto, 462 U.S. 650, 103 S.Ct. 2611, 77 L.Ed.2d 74 (1983), the Court held that Puerto Rican law under which the limitation period starts running anew once tolling has occurred was not inconsistent with the policies behind Section 1983.

The application of a state tolling doctrine was demonstrated by the Ninth Circuit in Donoghue v. County of Orange, 848 F.2d 926 (9th Cir.1987). In that case, the district court dismissed the plaintiff's Section 1983, 1985, 1986 and state pendent claims as time barred under the applicable California statute of limitations. Because a timely EEOC charge had been filed, the Title VII cause of action was allowed to proceed to trial. The Court of Appeal reversed and remanded for a determination by the trial court of whether the filing of the EEOC charge tolled the prescriptive period for the other claims under the state's equitable tolling doctrine. The court reasoned that under California law if the defendant received timely notice of the original claim, was not prejudiced by the delay and the plaintiff acted in good faith, the " [tolling] doctrine suspends the statute of limitations pending exhaustion of administrative remedies, even though no statute makes exhaustion a condition of the right to sue." 848 F.2d at 931. See also, Brown v. Hartshorne Public School District No.1, 926 F.2d 959 (10th Cir.1991) (Sec. 1983 action filed after expiration of state's two-year limitations period but within one month of dismissal of previous action stating same cause of action not time barred where state's savings statute allows a refiling of dismissed action within one year).

While statutes of limitation and tolling principles applicable to Sections 1983 and 1981 claims will vary from state to state, restrictions on the enforcement of the federal claims in state courts that might produce different outcomes based solely on whether the federal claims are pursued in state or federal courts *within a state* are constitutionally prohibited. In FELDER v. CASEY, 487 U.S. 131, 108 S.Ct. 2302, 101 L.Ed.2d 123 (1988), a police misconduct case filed in state court under Section 1983 and various state causes of action, the plaintiff's claims, including the Section 1983 cause of action, were dismissed because of his failure to comply with a notice-of-claim statute which required, as a prerequisite to suit against a public agency or officer, notice of intent to sue within 120 days of date of injury. The Supreme Court held that the notice-of-claim statute conflicted both in its purpose and effect with Section 1983's remedial objectives and, because it would produce different outcomes in Section 1983 litigation based solely on whether the claim is asserted in state or federal court, the statute was pre-empted by the Supremacy Clause. The Court reasoned that: (1) unlike statutes of limitation, notice-of-claim rules are far from universal and there is no reason to believe that Congress intended federal courts to apply such rules since they significantly inhibit the ability to bring federal actions; (2) enforcement of such restrictions in state-court 1983 actions would "frequently and predictably produce different outcomes in federal civil rights litigation" depending on whether the claim was initiated in state or federal court; (3) a state law that predictably alters the outcome of Section 1983 actions depending on whether they are filed in state or federal court within the state is inconsistent with the federal interest in intrastate uniformity; and (4) such lack of uniformity so frustrates the substantive right that Congress created that, under the Supremacy Clause, it must yield to the federal interest. The Court also noted that the notice-of-claim statute operated like an exhaustion requirement by forcing claimants to seek satisfaction in the first instance from the governmental defendant and that in Patsy v. Board of Regents, *supra*, the Court had held that such exhaustion requirements were incompatible with Section 1983's remedial purposes.

SECTION E. THE ROLE OF RES JUDICATA AND COLLATERAL ESTOPPEL

28 U.S.C. § 1738 which requires federal courts to give the same preclusive effect to state court judgments that such judgments would be given in the courts of the state applies in cases under the Reconstruction civil rights statutes as well as in Title VII suits. See discussion in Chapter 4, *supra*. Thus, under the doctrine of collateral estoppel or "issue preclusion," a factual issue actually litigated in a prior proceeding will normally bar relitigation in a federal case of the same issue. Under the doctrine of "claim preclusion" prior litigation *may* bar litigation of a claim which could have been, but was not, raised in the first proceeding. Whether the second action will be precluded depends on whether it would have been barred had it been filed in state court. See, Migra v. Warren City School District, 465 U.S. 75, 104 S.Ct. 892, 79 L.Ed.2d 56 (1984).

In UNIVERSITY OF TENNESSEE v. ELLIOTT, 478 U.S. 788, 106 S.Ct. 3220, 92 L.Ed.2d 635 (1986), an employment discrimination case filed under Title VII and Section 1983, the plaintiff contested his discharge before a state administrative law judge before filing his federal action. The courts of Tennessee would have given preclusive effect to the administrative ruling even though it was not reviewed by a state court. Distinguishing between the two kinds of federal claims, the Supreme Court held that Congress did not intend *unreviewed* state administrative decisions to have preclusive effect on Title VII claims regardless of the nature of the state procedures or state law. But as to the Section 1983 claim, the Court could "see no reason to suppose that Congress, in enacting the Reconstruction civil rights statutes, wished to foreclose the adaptation of traditional principles of preclusion to such subsequent developments as the burgeoning use of administrative adjudication in the 20th century." Accordingly, the Court held that when a state agency acting in a judicial capacity resolves disputed issues of fact which the parties had an adequate opportunity to litigate, federal courts in suits filed under the Reconstruction Era civil rights statutes must give the agency's factfinding the same preclusive effect to which it would be entitled in the courts of the state.

The Supreme Court's extension of the collateral estoppel doctrine to administrative findings in *Elliott* has resulted in speculation as to whether state claim preclusion doctrines should be extended to administrative proceedings so as to bar litigation of a federal claim, the substance of which could have been raised, but was not, in an earlier unreviewed administrative proceeding. In Gjellum v. City of Birmingham, 829 F.2d 1056 (11th Cir.1987), a police officer had challenged his discharge before an administrative review board and won. Under state law, the officer was precluded from bringing a damage action arising out of the discharge under the claim preclusion doctrine. The question before the Eleventh Circuit was whether the officer's Section 1983 action was barred by extension of the *Elliott* holding to claim preclusion rules. The Court upheld the officer's right to proceed in the federal forum.

> With respect to the claim preclusive effect of unreviewed state agency rulings, we conclude that the importance of the federal rights at issue, the desirability of avoiding the forcing of litigants to file suit initially in federal court rather than seek relief in an unreviewed administrative proceeding, and the limitations of state agencies as adjudicators of federal rights over-ride the lessened federalism concerns implicated outside the contours of the full faith and credit statute. In addition, claim preclusion, unlike issue preclusion, does not create a risk of inconsistent results in this context after *Elliott* because claim preclusion seeks to prevent litigation of issues that were not adjudicated before the state agency. We hold therefore that, at least in the context of section 1983 suits, the federal common law of preclusion does not require application of state claim preclusion rules to unreviewed state administrative decisions.

829 F.2d at 1064–65. The circuits are split on the question of whether an unreviewed administrative decision should preclude resort to court under the Age Discrimination in Employment Act. Compare, Stillians v. State of Iowa, 843 F.2d 276 (8th Cir.1988) with Duggan v. Board of Education of East Chicago Heights, 818 F.2d 1291 (7th Cir.1987) and Solimino v. Astoria Federal Savings and Loan Ass'n, 901 F.2d 1148 (2d Cir.1990).

SECTION F. REMEDIES

1. Monetary Relief

WILLIAMSON v. HANDY BUTTON MACHINE COMPANY

United States Court of Appeals, Seventh Circuit, 1987.

817 F.2d 1290.

Before EASTERBROOK and MANION, CIRCUIT JUDGES, and ESCHBACH, SENIOR CIRCUIT JUDGE.

EASTERBROOK, Circuit Judge. Beatrice Williamson worked for 21 years at the Handy Button Machine Co., principally as an assembly operator. She was fired in 1977 after she failed to reply to a telegram from Handy Button. The jury in this case under 42 U.S.C. Sec. 1981 and Title VII of the Civil Rights Act of 1964, 42 U.S.C. Sec. 2000e et seq., was entitled to find that Williamson did not answer the telegram because she had been driven to distraction by racial discrimination and the abusive behavior of her supervisor. She has been unable to work since. She recovered $150,000 in compensatory and $100,000 in punitive damages. While the jury was deliberating on the case under Sec. 1981, the district judge found that Williamson had not established sex discrimination in violation of Title VII and had demonstrated only two episodes of racial discrimination, which had not caused the discharge. The judge nonetheless declined to set aside the jury's verdict, holding that its view of the evidence was as permissible as his own.

I

The evidence, which we narrate in the light most favorable to the verdict, shows that during her entire career at Handy Button, Williamson was assigned unskilled entry-level work, although she was able to do higher-paying work such as inspection (and did so on occasion). Between 1968 and 1976 Williamson repeatedly applied for work as an inspector and saw white employees with less seniority promoted over her. In 1975 she and about ten other assembly workers were demoted to the sorting department because of a slowdown in work at the plant. Sorting is a dirty, boring job. Although sorting and assembly pay the same base wage, assemblers may earn a maximum bonus of $12 per week. Most weeks Williamson had earned the maximum bonus; she was not eligible for a bonus in sorting. Williamson was the only black employee demoted—and the most senior. Under the collective bargaining agreement, she should have been the first returned to assembly. But as work picked up, only white employees junior to Williamson were returned to assembly. She protested to the supervisor of assembly, to no avail.

In July 1975, as white employees were being returned to the assembly department, Williamson began to have uncontrollable crying spells. By February 1976 she was under medical care for depression and was taking drugs for the condition. She began to stay home ill. In late 1976 another inspector's job was filled by a white employee junior to her, without any opportunity to apply for the vacancy, despite the collective bargaining agreement's requirement that openings be posted for applications. Williamson filed a charge of discrimination with the EEOC; Handy Button learned of this charge no later than January 1977. In early March 1977 Williamson took a week of vacation time she had accrued, informing the company at the last minute. When she returned, supervisor Mervyn Mendel handed her a stiff note denying permission to take the vacation because she had not given "advance notice". The firm had no requirements that employees seek permission before taking vacations. (The memo was a blot on her record but had no immediate effect on her income, because the vacation had been unpaid.) On March 15, 1977, Williamson went to the upstairs washroom (where she had been assigned a locker by the company) to remove her work clothes and wash up at the end of the day. Mendel confronted her after she left and in loud, scatological language berated her for using the upstairs washroom rather than a different one.

This event, according to a psychiatrist's testimony, was the "straw that broke the camel's back." Williamson went home, never to return to work. The psychiatrist stated that she had a "major depressive disorder" that was "a 10 on a 10–point scale" of seriousness. On March 28 the firm sent her a telegram instructing her to call the company by March 30 to let it know when she would return to work. She did not respond and was fired. The jury could conclude that, as a result of Mendel's handiwork, Williamson was unable to understand the telegram, let alone to respond. Williamson testified that although she had been able to read, for many years after the incident she could neither read nor understand anything except the Bible. The firm did not call to find out why she had not answered the telegram, and it did not reinstate her after a psychiatrist explained the lack of response— although it had done both for other employees. Williamson, who was 52 when fired, has not been able to work since. Handy Button does not contend that she is a malingerer. (She worked as a teachers' aide for a year but was emotionally unable to continue.) The Social Security administration concluded in 1978 that she is completely disabled and awarded disability benefits.

The jury answered seven interrogatories. It found that Williamson (1) was denied a transfer back to assembly because of her race; (2) was denied promotion to inspector because of her race; (3) was denied a week's vacation because of her race; (4) was refused permission to use the upstairs bathroom because of her race; (5) was "berated and verbally abused" because of her race; (6) was fired because of her race; and (7) was treated adversely because of her complaint alleging discrimination. The jury fixed damages at $10,000 for psychological disability and emotional pain, $130,000 for "earnings lost and the present cash value of the earnings reasonably certain to be lost in the future", and $10,000 for the expenses of medical and psychological treatment. It awarded $100,000 more as punitive damages. Handy Button conceded at oral argument that the compensatory damages are supported by the record, if the evidence demonstrates that Handy Button's discriminatory conduct caused Williamson's breakdown and discharge. It does. Whether it is more than minimally sufficient we need not say.

Handy Button insists that the judge's more confined view of the evidence controls because rendered first, while the jury was deliberating. Not so. Title VII proceedings are "equitable" and Sec. 1981 proceedings are "legal", so that the plaintiff has a right to a jury trial only on the Sec. 1981 claim. But when the two are tried together, the jury's verdict governs factual issues common to them. Hunter v. Allis–Chalmers Corp., 797 F.2d 1417, 1421 (7th Cir.1986). The constitutional right to a jury trial may not be abridged by a court's deciding the equitable portion of a case first. Dairy Queen, Inc. v. Wood, 369 U.S. 469, 82 S.Ct. 894, 8 L.Ed.2d 44 (1962). Timing might be important if the Title VII claim had been filed as a separate suit, so that principles of preclusion applied to the Sec. 1981 claim. Parklane Hosiery Co. v. Shore, 439 U.S. 322, 333–37, 99 S.Ct. 645, 58 L.Ed.2d 552 (1979). Ours is not a problem of preclusion, however, for there was but one trial. The jury's verdict governs.

The jury could infer discrimination. Handy Button never offered an explanation for keeping Williamson in the plant's lowest-paying job, despite her entitlement by seniority to the assembly job. It never offered an explanation for failing to promote her to inspector between 1968 and late 1976, when it first stated that it wanted inspectors to have high school degrees, itself a potential ground of liability. See Griggs v. Duke Power Co., 401 U.S. 424, 91 S.Ct. 849, 28 L.Ed.2d 158 (1971). The jury was entitled to infer discrimination from the fact that a qualified black employee repeatedly, and without explanation, was passed over in favor of whites for better jobs, including one to which the black employee was contractually entitled and in which she served competently. McDonnell Douglas Corp. v. Green, 411 U.S. 792, 93 S.Ct. 1817, 36 L.Ed.2d 668 (1973). This discrimination contributed to Williamson's mental deterioration. Perhaps she was unusually sensitive, but a tortfeasor takes its victims as it finds them. E.g., Vosburg v. Putney, 80 Wis. 523, 50 N.W. 403 (1891); Stoleson v. United States, 708 F.2d 1217, 1221 (7th Cir.1983); Lancaster v. Norfolk & Western Ry., 773 F.2d 807, 820 (7th Cir.1985). In some cases unusual sensitivity will enhance the loss; in others unusual hardiness will reduce it; payment of the actual damage in each case will both compensate the victim and lead the injurer to take account of the full consequences of its acts. (The injurer expects to pay the average injury caused by conduct of the sort.)

Williamson's breakdown led to her discharge. Handy Button played on this. The district court observed: "It was [Handy Button's] litigation strategy to agree that [Williamson] was emotionally disturbed and, indeed, the more disturbed the better. [Handy Button] seemed anxious to bring out and capitalize upon the suggestion of the psychiatrist that [Williamson] may even have been psychotic ..." This led Handy Button to embrace "expect" testimony that has questionable value—see Bohen v. City of East Chicago, 622 F.Supp. 1234, 1243 n.4 (N.D.Ind. 1985), reversed in part on other grounds, 799 F.2d 1180 (7th Cir.1986) (" 'Experts' on this subject know no more than judges about what causes mental changes—which is to say that they know almost nothing.")—and to emphasize other evidence of instability. Perhaps Handy Button believed that if the jury thought Williamson crazy, it would see why Handy Button dismissed her. The risk was that the jury would conclude that Handy Button had driven Williamson to distraction; the jury so found.

Handy Button is liable under the civil rights laws for Williamson's principal injury—her continued inability to work—only if the emotional instability came from racial discrimination. Handy Button might have tried to argue that Williamson's breakdown was attributable to boorish conduct by Mendel, her supervisor in 1977. Personal animosity, even monstrous conduct, is not actionable under Sec. 1981 and Title VII unless based on race. Dale v. Chicago Tribune Co., 797 F.2d 458, 465 & n.9 (7th Cir.1986). A breakdown caused by non-racial offensiveness might explain why Williamson could not respond to the telegram and therefore support an award of damages until Williamson could have found another job (had she been emotionally stable), but it would not justify an award of a lifetime's lost income. Handy Button did not try to pry apart the racial and non-racial causes of Williamson's distress, however. It stood by as evidence of personal animosity came in, and it did not request limiting instructions or suggest that the jury be told to separate racial and other causes of Williamson's inability to work after she had been fired.

The evidence was not so thin that we must step in to protect defendants who did not protect themselves. Even if there had been no intervening acts of discrimination, the jury would have been entitled to find that the discriminatory failure to return Williamson to the assembly department was a cause of her breakdown. The jury also was entitled to infer that the vacation and washroom incidents, and the firm's refusal to call her or reinstate her after learning of the cause of her failure to respond, had race at their core. True, none of these events involved racial epithets, and the employer offered neutral explanations for each. But once a jury decides that an employer makes use of race in its everyday decisions—in this case, that it held Williamson's race against her over a decade—it is permissible to infer that race also explains other disparate treatment. Handy Button did not try to show, for example, that Mendel cursed white employees who used the upstairs washroom. The firm also was more tolerant of white employees who became ill. The jury's finding of liability must stand.

This makes it unnecessary to explore liability under Title VII for racial discrimination, because an award for racial discrimination under a different statute would be redundant. Williamson also charged that Handy Button engaged in sex discrimination, in violation of Title VII, by not promoting her to inspector. This question was not submitted to the jury under Sec. 1981, which does not deal with sex discrimination. The judgment on the sex discrimination claim could have a small influence on the award of damages. We affirm the district court's conclusions as not clearly erroneous. This is one of many cases that could go either way.

II

The court gave this instruction on punitive damages:

If you find that the defendant was guilty of discrimination against the plaintiff because of her race or that defendant terminated plaintiff in retaliation for her having filed discrimination charges ..., and if you believe that justice and the public good require it, you may, in addition to any compensatory damages to which you find plaintiff entitled, award plaintiff an amount which will serve to punish the defendant and to deter others from the commission of like offenses.

The instruction left the jury at sea. Although the court gave some guidance on how to set the amount of punitive damages (by reference to punishment and deterrence), it offered none on when punitive damages are appropriate. Telling jurors to award punitive damages "if you believe that justice and the public good require it" is the equivalent of telling them to award punitive damages "if you want to." "Justice" and the "public good" are not terms with widely understood meanings. Handy Button did not object to this instruction. It objected to giving any instruction at all, which is not the same as objecting to the language of the instruction given. The objection must be sufficiently detailed to draw the court's attention to the defect. A blunderbuss objection does not do this.

No doctrine of "plain error" protects parties from the consequences of their decisions in civil litigation.

* * *

This instruction therefore states the law of the case. "[I]n a civil case, each party must live with the legal theory reflected in instructions to which it does not object." Will v. Comprehensive Accounting Corp., 776 F.2d 665, 675 (7th Cir.1985).

The evidence was sufficient to support an award of punitive damages under this instruction. (It is hard to see what evidence would be insufficient, provided the jury found liability and awarded compensatory damages.) Handy Button does not contend that an award of $100,-000 is excessive. When an offense is concealable or difficult to prosecute successfully, it is necessary to multiply the damages to deter wrongdoers. The multiplier of 1.67 produced by this award is hardly the work of a runaway jury. The law has many double and treble damages provisions. Handy Button argues only that there should have been no punitive award. That argument cannot succeed, given the instruction to the jury.

Handy Button has preserved only an objection to a punitive damages instruction of any flavor. A party may challenge the sufficiency of the evidence even without objecting to the content of the instructions. Dual Manufacturing & Engineering, Inc. v. Burris Industries, Inc., 619 F.2d 660, 662–63 (7th Cir.1980) (en banc). The evidence was sufficient to permit the submission of the question on an appropriate instruction, informing the jury that the award of punitive damages should be reserved for willful wrongdoing or reckless indifference to the plaintiff's known rights. See Smith v. Wade, 461 U.S. 30, 51–55, 103 S.Ct. 1625, 75 L.Ed.2d 632 (1983) (a case decided under Sec. 1983, but equally applicable to Sec. 1981, see Yarbrough v. Tower Oldsmobile, Inc., 789 F.2d 508, 514 (7th Cir.1986)). The jury was entitled to find that Handy Button had been discriminating against Williamson for a decade. It had passed her over for promotion many times, and later it kept her in the sorting department despite both her protests and the seniority rule in the collective bargaining agreement. This extended course of conduct suggests an official policy of discrimination as opposed to the work of a renegade supervisor. The rule against racial discrimination in employment is well understood; no employer has a good faith belief that discrimination is lawful. Cf. Walton v. United Consumers Club, Inc., 786 F.2d 303, 308–12 (7th Cir.1986) (discussing other definitions of "willful"). We sustained an award of punitive damages in Yarbrough on a thinner record.

Smith v. Wade suggests that any conduct violating Sec. 1983 may support an award of punitive damages. This is deceiving, however, because the Court also observed that the plaintiff under Sec. 1983 must surmount the defense of official immunity (461 U.S. at 55, 103 S.Ct. at 1639). The complete rule applicable to a defendant without the formal benefit of immunity therefore may be that intentional, illegal conduct may support an award of punitive damages when the application of the law to the facts at hand was so clear at the time of the act that reasonably competent people would have agreed on its application. See Soderbeck v. Burnett County, 752 F.2d 285, 289–91 (7th Cir.1985) (punitive damages usually depend on specific intent to violate a knowable right). Cf. Colaizzi v. Walker, 812 F.2d 304, 308 (7th Cir.1987). An approach of this character still supports the submission of the question to the jury, given the clarity of the rule against racial discrimination in employment.

III

Williamson asked the district court to add prejudgment interest to the award of back pay. The court declined, explaining: "The verdict, both compensatory and punitive, is in the upper range of what can reasonably be sustained. Adding interest would, in the court's view, result in an excessive award." The compensatory award in question is $130,000, which covers both past and future earnings and the reduction in the value of Williamson's pension. It is hard to see how $130,000 could be thought in the "upper range". Williamson was five days from her 53rd birthday when fired in 1977. She was making about $13,000 per year. Had she worked as a sorter from April 1977 through the time of trial in March 1986, she would have earned a little more than $127,000 (this includes the increases negotiated by the union in subsequent collective bargaining agreements and excludes her earnings as a teachers' aide). Employment for another three years, until retirement in 1989 at age 65, had a present value of about $54,274 at the time of trial (using the 1986 wage of $18,820 and discounting at 2 % per year). The loss of 13 years' work reduced Williamson's pension by about $2,700 per year, starting in 1989. Considering Williamson's life expectancy, that reduction had a present value of about $24,000 at the time of trial. These computations would have supported an award of some $205,000 for lost income.

We also disagree with the premise of the district court's decision—that a court has discretion in Sec. 1981 litigation to deny an award of prejudgment interest on an award of back wages because the court does not approve of the jury's award. Under 42 U.S.C. Sec. 1988 a federal court is supposed to follow principles of state law when federal law does not supply a rule of decision. We observed in Hunter, 797 F.2d at 1426, that the common law requires judges to add prejudgment interest to awards of back pay. Neither the district court nor Handy Button cited any contrary statement of the law in Illinois, the forum state. We strongly hinted in Hunter that federal law would require the addition of prejudgment interest even if state law did not, because prejudgment interest is necessary to make the award fully compensatory. Id. at 1425–27. The award should make the victim whole. Williamson lost $9,436.93 for the nine months she was out of work in 1977. An award of $9,436.93 in 1987 does not make her whole. If she had received the money as wages in 1977 and invested it at 10 %, readily available during those years on safe investments, she would have had $24,547.00 ten years later. (We disregard taxes.) A return of 15 %, which was available on many investments, would have produced $38,286.87 in the same period. The increase substantially exceeds the 1.67 multiplier produced by the punitive damages. Handy Button had Williamson's money during these ten years and has been able to earn the market return. If Handy Button can turn over only $9,436.93, it has made a tidy profit on the arrangement. The effect of prejudgment interest on the wages for later years is less, but still significant.

We have held that prejudgment interest is part of full compensation under other statutes, necessary to carry out the federal policies of compensation and deterrence. Twice in the last four years, the Supreme Court has held that "prejudgment interest is an element of complete compensation". West Virginia v. United States, 479 U.S. 305, 107 S.Ct. 702, 706, 93 L.Ed.2d 639 (1987) (contractual debt); General Motors Corp. v. Devex Corp., 461 U.S. 648, 655–56, 76 L.Ed.2d 211, 103 S.Ct. 2058 (1983) (damages for infringement of patent). Money today is simply not a full substitute for the same sum that should have been paid some time ago. Prejudgment interest therefore must be an ordinary part of any award of back pay (or other incurred expense) under Sec. 1981.

"Ordinary" does not imply inevitable. Devex allowed that an award might be inappropriate at some times. See also Heritage Homes v. Seekonk Water District, 648 F.2d 761, 764 (1st Cir.1981) (the only other appellate case dealing with prejudgment interest under Sec. 1981), vacated on other grounds, 454 U.S. 807, 102 S.Ct. 81, 70 L.Ed.2d 76, reaffirmed, 670 F.2d 1 (1982). Substantial, unexplained delay in filing suit might be such a reason, because delay shifts the investment risk to the defendant, allowing the plaintiff to recover interest without bearing the corresponding risk. Williamson, though, filed this suit in 1978. The size of the jury's verdict may be another, if only the supposition that the jury has compensated plaintiff for the time value of money can explain the result. This verdict is not so large; it does not seem to cover even actual loss.

There is one other reason why prejudgment interest may be denied—because "the amount of backpay is not readily determinable." Domingo v. New England Fish Co., 727 F.2d 1429, 1446 (9th Cir.1984). Interest is not available on lost future wages and pensions; the time value of money is taken into account when these are discounted to present value. Only back pay and expenses incurred in the past may be augmented by prejudgment interest. Yet Williamson proposed a verdict form that lumped past and future wages together. The judge used the form Williamson proposed, and the jury returned a verdict that does not distinguish past and future sources of loss. The district judge did not rely on this when denying Williamson's motion, but we must consider the implications of the general award of damages.

* * *

One could say that unless the amount of back pay is exactly determinable no interest should be awarded. That rule appears in contract cases, where common law courts disallowed prejudgment interest on disputed contract damages unless the sum in question had been liquidated or been made certain in another way. Afram Export Corp. v. Metallurgiki Halyps, S.A., 772 F.2d 1358, 1370–71 (7th Cir.1985), collects both cases and secondary sources. The award of back pay under Title VII is an "equitable" rather than a "legal" remedy, however, and the common law requirement of certainty has never been applied to it. If it were, it would be impossible to award interest even if the jury had returned separate verdicts in this case on back pay, front pay, and the value of the pension. Williamson was out of work for a decade; how much of the back pay should be apportioned to each year? Without an answer to that question, it is impossible to compute prejudgment interest, which is higher on the salary lost in 1977 than the salary lost in 1982. Absolute certainty is unavailable no matter what kind of instruction is given to the jury; it is also unnecessary. No purpose would be served by allowing the wrongdoer to keep the entire time value of the money, just because the exact amount is subject to fair dispute. Once we know that back pay is at least some minimum, it is safe to award interest on that amount.

It is also significant that the district judge did not deny interest on the ground that it was too hard to figure out what the jury had awarded as back pay. The judge gave a different reason: that the jury had awarded too much money. That reason is reviewable and wrong. Had the district judge given the reason Handy Button advances, we might be inclined to defer to it; but he did not, and we hesitate to affirm a judgment on a ground that was neither offered to the district judge nor adopted by him. Handy Button's briefs in this court do not maintain that it is too hard to determine what the jury awarded as back pay; Handy Button instead supported the district court's rationale and added the thought that interest should be discretionary. A court should not decide a civil case on the basis of an argument made in neither the district court nor the court of appeals.

If the district judge determines that it is possible to ascertain a minimum amount of back pay awarded, it will be necessary to apportion that sum. Each year's pay requires a different amount of prejudgment interest. The computational process, however, is the same in principle as the one used to discount future income (which occurs at different times in the future) to present value. The parties should be able to agree on this mechanical computation if the district court can determine how much back pay the jury awarded, allocate it among years, and fix the rate of prejudgment interest.

The jury's verdict of $250,000 is affirmed to the extent it is challenged by Handy Button's appeal. The judge's disposition of the claim of sex discrimination under Title VII, one subject of appeal is affirmed. The denial of prejudgment interest, the other subject of appeal, is reversed, and the case is remanded for further proceedings consistent with this opinion. Williamson shall recover her costs in both appeals.

NOTES AND PROBLEMS FOR DISCUSSION

1. In *Handy Button* the damage claim submitted to the jury under Section 1981 included back pay. As noted previously in Chapter 7A, the Civil Rights Act of 1991 provides for the award of both compensatory and punitive damages in disparate treatment cases under Title VII. The new act, however, explicitly excludes from compensatory damages back pay and interest on back pay and places limits on the total amount of compensatory and punitive damages that may be awarded depending on the size of the employer. The 1991 Act also makes the Title VII damage remedy available only where the complaining party "cannot recover" under 42 U.S.C. § 1981. What effect would the new act have had on Ms. Williamson's claim in *Handy Button*? Should the back pay determination be submitted to the jury? Should Ms. Williamson's claim for damages be subject to the size-of-employer limitations for Title VII? Do the answers to these questions depend on what is meant by the new act's limitation of damages under Title VII to those cases where the plaintiff "cannot recover" under Section 1981? Should that provision be interpreted as barring damages under Title VII where the plaintiff *could have filed a claim under Section 1981* or only where the plaintiff has in fact recovered damages under Section 1981?

2. As noted in *Handy Button*, common law tort principles apply to damage actions under Sections 1981, 1983 and 1985. Carey v. Piphus, 435 U.S. 247, 98 S.Ct. 1042, 55 L.Ed.2d 252 (1978); Smith v. Wade, 461 U.S. 30, 48–49, 103 S.Ct. 1625, 1636–7, 75 L.Ed.2d 632 (1983). Presumably those same principles will

also govern the determination of damages under the 1991 Act. Accordingly, in all intentional employment discrimination cases, recovery can be had for emotional distress, humiliation and other psychic injury, as well as for physical injury and other economic loss. With the principal case compare, Stallworth v. Shuler, 777 F.2d 1431 (11th Cir.1985) ($100,000 in compensatory damages to black employee denied promotions because of racial discrimination is within "acceptable universe" for injuries in light of plaintiff's testimony that he suffered stress, loss of sleep, marital strain and humiliation); Muldrew v. Anheuser–Busch, Inc., 728 F.2d 989 (8th Cir.1984) ($125,000 award to employee discharged for racially discriminatory reasons where there was evidence that, as result of discharge, he lost his car and house, began experiencing marital problems and felt he had lost respect of his children). The Supreme Court has held, however, that compensatory damages must always be designed to compensate for actual injuries caused by unlawful actions, and not for the violation of a legal right in the abstract. In MEMPHIS COMMUNITY SCHOOL DISTRICT v. STACHURA, 477 U.S. 299, 106 S.Ct. 2537, 91 L.Ed.2d 249 (1986), the Court held that damages based on the abstract "value" or "importance" of constitutional rights are not a permissible element of compensatory damages in Section 1983 cases.

In *Handy Button* Judge Easterbrook states the general common law rule that a tortfeasor takes its victims as it finds them. This means that the same kind of unlawful conduct may produce widely different damage awards depending on the "sensitivity" of the individual victims. With *Handy Button* compare Brown v. Trustees of Boston University, 674 F.Supp. 393 (D.Mass.1987), affirmed in part, vacated in part, 891 F.2d 337 (1st Cir.1989), cert. denied, 496 U.S. 937, 110 S.Ct. 3217, 110 L.Ed.2d 664 (1990) (award of $15,000 under state FEP law for emotional injury resulting from gender-biased denial of tenure despite court's conclusion that part of emotional distress was caused by plaintiff's "highly strung personality and her highly developed expectations for herself").

3. Why does Judge Easterbrook find fault with the punitive damage instruction given by the district judge in *Handy Button*? See, PACIFIC MUTUAL LIFE INSURANCE CO. v. HASLIP, ___ U.S. ___, 111 S.Ct. 1032, 113 L.Ed.2d 1 (1991) (suggesting that unlimited jury discretion in fixing punitive damages might constitute due process violation). In SMITH v. WADE, 461 U.S. 30, 103 S.Ct. 1625, 75 L.Ed.2d 632 (1983) the Court held that reckless or callous disregard for the plaintiff's rights, as well as intentional violations of federal law "should be sufficient to trigger ... consideration of the appropriateness of punitive damages." 461 U.S. at 51, 103 S.Ct. at 1637. Liability is not established under Section 1981 or 1983, however, without a showing of intentional discrimination. Does this mean that any conduct violating one of the Reconstruction Era statutes merits punitive damages? How does the court in *Handy Button* answer this question? In *Smith v. Wade* the Court noted that "in situations where the standard for compensatory liability is as high as or higher than the usual threshold for punitive damages, most courts will permit awards of punitive damages without requiring any extra showing." 461 U.S. at 53, 103 S.Ct. at 1639. The First Circuit, recognizing that "the state of mind necessary to trigger liability for the wrong (Sec. 1981) is at least as culpable as that required to make punitive damages applicable," has held that in each case where intentional discrimination has been found, the trier of fact has the discretion to determine whether punitive damages are necessary to punish for outrageous conduct and to deter similar conduct in the future. Rowlett v.

Anheuser–Busch, Inc., 832 F.2d 194, 205 (1st Cir.1987). There, the court of appeals reversed a punitive damage award of three million dollars in a Title VII–Section 1981 case as grossly excessive and remanded for a redetermination under the following guidelines.

> In future cases, once the district court determines that awarding punitive damages is within the jury's discretion, the court should instruct jurors that, if they conclude that such damages are to be granted, in determining the amount to be granted, they should engage in a balancing test taking into consideration such factors as the grievousness of the conduct, the solvency of the guilty party, and the potential for deterrence of the verdict. In addition, the court should instruct the jury as to the maximum verdict allowable as reasonable using such balancing factors.

832 F.2d at 207. The court concluded that $300,000 was sufficient for deterrence and punishment under the circumstances of the case. Because the purpose of punitive damages is to punish and deter, the size and wealth of the defendant are proper factors to be considered by the court in determining the amount of such damages. See, McKnight v. General Motors Corp., 705 F.Supp. 464, 468 (E.D.Wis.1989), affirmed in part and reversed in part (post-*Patterson*), 908 F.2d 104 (7th Cir.1990), cert. denied, ___ U.S. ___, 111 S.Ct. 1306, 113 L.Ed.2d 241 (1991) ($500,000 award of punitive damages appropriate in light of defendant's resources).

A public employer has a common law immunity from an award of punitive damages under Section 1983. City of Newport v. Fact Concerts, Inc., 453 U.S. 247, 101 S.Ct. 2748, 69 L.Ed.2d 616 (1981). A plaintiff may recover punitive damages from individual wrongdoers who are joined as defendants in such cases. See, Cornwell v. City of Riverside, 896 F.2d 398 (9th Cir.), cert. denied, ___ U.S. ___, 110 S.Ct. 3274, 111 L.Ed.2d 784 (1990).

4. As in other types of personal injury litigation, the difficulty of fixing dollar amounts for emotional injury and, in the case of punitive damages, for deterrence, has resulted in enormous variations in the amounts awarded. The punitive damage award in *Handy Button* was 67% of the amount of actual damages awarded. According to Judge Easterbrook, such an award was not "the work of a runaway jury." But what kind of award would have been excessive? Compare, Rawson v. Sears, Roebuck & Co., 822 F.2d 908 (10th Cir.1987), cert. denied, 484 U.S. 1006, 108 S.Ct. 699, 98 L.Ed.2d 651 (1988) (reversing jury award of $5,000,000 for pain, suffering and humiliation, $10,-000,000 in punitive damages and $849,910 in lost wages to victim of age discrimination); Rogders v. Fisher Body Div., General Motors Corp., 739 F.2d 1102 (6th Cir.1984), cert. denied, 470 U.S. 1054, 105 S.Ct. 1759, 84 L.Ed.2d 821 (1985) (awards of $300,000 compensatory and $500,000 punitive damages to black employee discharged for racially discriminatory reasons overturned as excessive); Phillips v. Smalley Maintenance Services, Inc., 711 F.2d 1524 (11th Cir.1983) (award of $25,000 to victim of sexual harassment for mental suffering under state pendent cause of action upheld).

5. Where legal damages are claimed, as opposed to equitable relief, either party is entitled as a matter of right to a jury trial under the Seventh Amendment. Until the passage of the Civil Rights Act of 1991, Title VII expressly authorized only equitable remedies and courts agreed that neither party, in a pure Title VII case, was entitled to a jury trial. See e.g., Slack v. Havens, 522 F.2d 1091, 1094 (9th Cir.1975); Johnson v. Georgia Highway Express, Inc., 417 F.2d 1122, 1125 (5th Cir.1969). See discussion Chapter 7A,

supra. The circuits remain divided, however, on the question of whether a claim for back pay in a § 1981 or 1983 case is a claim for equitable or legal relief. Compare, Moore v. Sun Oil Co., 636 F.2d 154 (6th Cir.1980) (claim for back pay constitutes equitable rather than legal relief and plaintiff is entitled to jury trial in § 1981 case only if he asserts claim for compensatory or punitive damages) and Setser v. Novack Investment Co., 638 F.2d 1137 (8th Cir.), cert. denied, 454 U.S. 1064, 102 S.Ct. 615, 70 L.Ed.2d 601 (1981) (back pay constitutes legal damages in § 1981 action).

Where a damage claim is joined with an equitable claim (reinstatement for example) and either party requests a jury trial, the jury will determine all the common factual issues of the claims as well as the amount of damages. As illustrated by *Handy Button*, the trial judge in such a case must decide the equitable claim but will be bound by the jury's findings of fact on common issues. Since entitlement to equitable relief in an employment case will usually turn on the same facts as will the claim for damages (whether the employer's conduct was unlawful), a jury verdict on the legal claim will, as a practical matter, determine whether equitable relief will be available.

In LYTLE v. HOUSEHOLD MANUFACTURING, INC., 494 U.S. 545, 110 S.Ct. 1331, 108 L.Ed.2d 504 (1990) the district court dismissed the plaintiff's Section 1981 claim on the ground that Title VII provided the exclusive remedy, conducted a bench trial on the Title VII claim, and ruled against the plaintiff on the merits. The Court of Appeals, noting that the dismissal of the Sec. 1981 claims was "apparently erroneous" because Title VII and Sec. 1981 remedies were separate, independent, and distinct, nevertheless affirmed because the district court's findings on the Title VII claims collaterally estopped the plaintiff from relitigation of the Sec. 1981 claims. A unanimous Supreme Court reversed. The Court reasoned that, but for the dismissal of the plaintiff's Sec. 1981 claims, he would have been entitled to a jury trial on all factual issues common to the 1981 and Title VII causes of action. As in *Handy Button*, the plaintiff would also have been entitled to have the jury verdict control the judge's decision on the equitable (Title VII) issues. Accordingly, the Court held that the Seventh Amendment prevented giving collateral-estoppel effect to a district court's determination of issues common to equitable and legal claims where the court resolved the equitable claims first solely because it erroneously dismissed the legal claims. Note Judge Easterbrook's comment in *Handy Button* that the case would be different if the plaintiff had filed two suits and the Title VII action had been tried first.

It has long been settled that the Seventh Amendment's right to trial by jury does not apply to actions against the federal government. See, Galloway v. United States, 319 U.S. 372, 388–89, 63 S.Ct. 1077, 1086, 87 L.Ed. 1458 (1943); Cuddy v. Carmen, 694 F.2d 853 (D.C.Cir.1982).

6. The Eleventh Amendment to the Constitution provides in part that "[t]he judicial power of the United States shall not be construed to extend to any suit in law or equity, commenced or prosecuted against one of the United States by Citizens of another State." That language has been construed to bar an award of monetary relief against a state or state agency. Edelman v. Jordan, 415 U.S. 651, 94 S.Ct. 1347, 39 L.Ed.2d 662 (1974). Thus, an award of back pay or damages against a state under Sec. 1983 is precluded by the Eleventh Amendment. Quern v. Jordan, 440 U.S. 332, 99 S.Ct. 1139, 59 L.Ed.2d 358 (1979); Sessions v. Rusk State Hospital, 648 F.2d 1066, 1069 (5th Cir.1981). By contrast backpay awards against a state under Title VII are not

barred by the Eleventh Amendment because Congress exercised its power under the Fourteenth Amendment to abrogate Eleventh Amendment immunity. See discussion *supra*, Chapter 7. Should the same waiver rationale apply to the award of compensatory damages against a state agency under the Civil Rights Act of 1991?

The Eleventh Amendment does not apply to suits against political subdivisions of a state such as cities, counties, school districts, and like entities. Moor v. County of Alameda, 411 U.S. 693, 93 S.Ct. 1785, 36 L.Ed.2d 596 (1973); Goss v. San Jacinto Junior College, 588 F.2d 96 (5th Cir.1979), modified on rehearing, 595 F.2d 1119 (1979). Thus, in employment discrimination actions filed under Sec. 1983 against such public employers other than the state, back pay and damages are available to the same extent as in Section 1981 actions against private employers. Presumably, the size-of-employer limitations on damages under Title VII incorporated in the Civil Rights Act of 1991 will also apply to public employers. Whether a particular public entity is an agency of the state or of local government for Eleventh Amendment purposes is a fact question the answer to which will depend on various factors. See, Keller v. Prince George's County, 923 F.2d 30 (4th Cir.1991) (Eleventh Amendment bars suit under Sec. 1983 against county department of social services in view of fact that county department was operated by state department of human resources, that employees were paid by state, that department operated pursuant to state personnel policies and that only 2% of department's funding came from county).

While the Eleventh Amendment does not bar prospective injunctive relief against a state official, it does preclude an award of back pay or damages against him under Section 1983 in his *official capacity*, because such a judgment would necessarily have to be paid with state funds. Edelman v. Jordan, *supra*. The Amendment does not immunize such officials from *personal* liability for their illegal acts, though they may benefit from other types of official immunity. See, Scheuer v. Rhodes, 416 U.S. 232, 94 S.Ct. 1683, 40 L.Ed.2d 90 (1974) (executive immunity); Tenney v. Brandhove, 341 U.S. 367, 71 S.Ct. 783, 95 L.Ed. 1019 (1951). Public officials generally enjoy qualified immunity for "good faith" actions. See, Wood v. Strickland, 420 U.S. 308, 95 S.Ct. 992, 43 L.Ed.2d 214 (1975); Nicholson v. Georgia Department of Human Resources, 918 F.2d 145 (11th Cir.1990) (officials not entitled to qualified immunity for intentional discrimination in connection with transfer and demotion of female employee, since law was quite clear that such conduct violated constitution and such officials either knew or should have known that their actions were unlawful). Does the provision for compensatory damages under Title VII make the Eleventh Amendment protection of state officials and agencies and the common law "good faith" immunity of public officials less important?

The Supreme Court has held that municipalities enjoy a "common law" immunity from an award of punitive damages. City of Newport v. Fact Concerts, Inc., 453 U.S. 247, 101 S.Ct. 2748, 69 L.Ed.2d 616 (1981). Under the 1991 Act punitive damages may not be recovered on a Title VII claim from a government, government agency or political subdivision.

The Eleventh Amendment bars only an award of damages against the state by a federal court and has no application to actions in state courts. The Supreme Court has now held, however, that an award of damages cannot be recovered in state court against a state or its agencies under Section 1983 because the state, unlike municipalities and other political subdivisions, is not a "person" under Section 1983. WILL v. MICHIGAN DEPARTMENT OF

STATE POLICE, 491 U.S. 58, 109 S.Ct. 2304, 105 L.Ed.2d 45 (1989). Thus, states have the same immunity in state courts from damage actions under Section 1983 that they enjoy in federal court. The Court in *Will* also conformed its construction of Section 1983 to its Eleventh Amendment decisions with respect to state officials sued in their official capacities. Reasoning that a suit against an official in her official capacity was not a suit against a person but against the official's office and thus against the state itself, the Court held that a state official in her official capacity is not a "person" for purposes of Section 1983. Compare, Edelman v. Jordan, *supra.*

2. Injunctive Relief

Section 1983 provides that persons who, acting under color of state law, violate the constitutional or federal statutory rights of others "shall be liable to the party injured in an action at law, suit in equity, or other proper proceeding for redress." Section 1981 contains no remedy language but where the provisions of the civil rights statutes "are not adapted to the object, or are deficient in the provisions necessary to furnish suitable remedies and punish offenses against the law, the common law, as modified and changed by the constitution and statutes of the State ... so far as not inconsistent with the Constitution and laws of the United States, shall be extended to and govern ... in the trial and disposition of the cause ..." 42 U.S.C. § 1988. Equitable relief is thus available in Section 1981 and 1983 actions to the same extent that it is available under Title VII. See *supra*, Chapter 7B.

Suits against state entities under Section 1983 are, however, complicated by the Eleventh Amendment to the United States Constitution. That amendment bars federal actions at law or in equity against states. The effect of the amendment is avoided by naming as the defendant an appropriate state official rather than her agency. Ex Parte Young, 209 U.S. 123, 28 S.Ct. 441, 52 L.Ed. 714 (1908) held that the illegal action of a state official is not action of the state for Eleventh Amendment purposes (even though it is simultaneously treated as "state action" for Fourteenth Amendment purposes). Cf., Pennhurst State School and Hospital v. Halderman, 465 U.S. 89, 104 S.Ct. 900, 79 L.Ed.2d 67 (1984) (Eleventh Amendment bars even injunctive relief against state officials if based on state pendent cause of action). Thus, equitable relief is available under Section 1983 against states and their agencies by way of suits against the responsible state officials. By contrast, equitable relief is directly available against private employers under Title VII, Section 1981 and other civil rights statutes and against non-state public employers under Title VII and Section 1983.

3. Attorney Fees and Costs

Section 1988 provides in part that "[i]n any action or proceeding to enforce a provision of sections 1981, 1982, 1983, 1985 ..., the court, in its discretion, may allow the prevailing party, other than the United States, a reasonable attorney's fee as part of the costs." That language is identical to the fee shifting provision in § 706(k) of Title VII. The legislative history of Section 1988 makes it clear that Congress intended

that "the standards for awarding fees under [the Act] should be generally the same as under the fee provisions of the 1964 Civil Rights Act."
S.Rep. No. 1011, 94th Cong., 2d Sess. 4 (1976). In HENSLEY V.
ECKERHART, 461 U.S. 424, 433 n.7, 103 S.Ct. 1933, 1939 n.7, 76
L.Ed.2d 40 (1983) the Supreme Court noted that the standards for
award of fees are the same in all cases where Congress has authorized
such fees to the "prevailing party." Thus the law regarding entitlement to and calculation of attorney fees under Section 1988 is the same
as that under Title VII. See *supra*, Chapter 7C.

One factor which formerly distinguished litigation under the Reconstruction civil rights statutes from that under Title VII was that
monetary relief, including compensatory and punitive damages, was
awarded under common law tort principles. See Section F(1), *supra*.
In the United States fees for plaintiffs in personal injury tort cases are
generally "contingent" fees and, by agreement of the plaintiff and her
attorney, are usually calculated as a percentage of the monetary
recovery. After Section 1988 was amended to include the fee shifting
provision, a question that caused some division in the federal courts
was whether a fee award under that section should be influenced by the
amount of the monetary recovery for the plaintiff. In CITY OF
RIVERSIDE v. RIVERA, 477 U.S. 561, 106 S.Ct. 2686, 91 L.Ed.2d 466
(1986), the Supreme Court considered whether an award of $245,456.25
in attorney fees pursuant to 42 U.S.C. § 1988 could be "reasonable" in
light of the fact that a jury had awarded plaintiffs a total of $33,350 in
compensatory and punitive damages. The award was made in a police
misconduct case filed under Section 1983. The district court made
findings required by *HENSLEY* and determined that plaintiffs' counsel
were entitled to the full lodestar fee requested. The Court of Appeals
affirmed on the basis of the district court's findings. Arguing that in
civil rights cases in which only monetary relief is requested a "reasonable" fee should necessarily be proportionate to the damage award
recovered, petitioners asked the Court to abandon the use of the
lodestar method of calculation in such cases and suggested that fee
awards in civil rights damage cases should be modeled upon the
contingent fee arrangements commonly used in personal injury litigation.

In a plurality opinion, the Court rejected the analogy between civil
rights cases seeking monetary relief and garden-variety tort litigation
because, "damage awards do not reflect fully the public benefit advanced by civil rights litigation." 477 U.S. at 575, 106 S.Ct. at 2695.
The Court also held that limiting attorney fees in civil rights cases to a
proportion of the damages awarded would undermine the Congressional
purpose behind Section 1988.

> A rule of proportionality would make it difficult, if not impossible,
> for individuals with meritorious civil rights claims but relatively
> small potential damages to obtain redress from the courts. This is
> totally inconsistent with the Congress' purpose in enacting § 1988.

Congress recognized that private-sector fee arrangements were inadequate to ensure sufficiently vigorous enforcement of civil rights. In order to ensure that lawyers would be willing to represent persons with legitimate civil rights grievances, Congress determined that it would be necessary to compensate lawyers for all time reasonably expended on a case.

Ibid.

In a dissenting opinion, Justice Rehnquist argued that the fees awarded were necessarily unreasonable because "[t]he very 'reasonableness' of the hours expended on a case by a plaintiff's attorney necessarily will depend, to a large extent, on the amount that may reasonably be expected to be recovered if the plaintiff prevails." According to the dissent, a "reasonable" fee under Section 1988 "means a fee that would have been deemed reasonable if billed to affluent plaintiffs by their own attorneys." Should the overall "reasonableness" of a fee award under the civil rights laws be determined by the same standard applied to fees charged to "affluent" clients motivated solely by the economics of the situation? Which view of "reasonableness," that of Justice Rehnquist or that of the plurality opinion, most closely accords with the purpose of the fee-shifting statutes?

What should be the effect on a fee award under Section 1988 of a normal contingent fee agreement between the plaintiff and counsel that specified that the fee would be a percentage of the recovery? Should such an agreement put a ceiling on the fee that the defendant can be required to pay under the fee shifting statute? That question had also divided the circuits. The Supreme Court resolved the matter in BLANCHARD v. BERGERON, 489 U.S. 87, 109 S.Ct. 939, 103 L.Ed.2d 67 (1989). There the plaintiff in a Section 1983 police misconduct case obtained a $10,000 damage award. The Fifth Circuit ruled that the successful plaintiff's attorney, who had claimed more than $40,000 in fees, was limited to a maximum award of $4,000 because of his 40% contingent fee contract with the plaintiff which put a "cap" on the fee that could be shifted to the defendant. The Supreme Court reversed on the ground that the imposition of an automatic ceiling on attorney's fees because of a contingent fee contract would be inconsistent with the policy and the purpose of the fee shifting statutes. In the first place, the Court reasoned that the statute contemplated reasonable compensation in light of all the circumstances for the time and effort expended by the prevailing attorney and that, should a fee agreement provide less than a reasonable fee calculated in that manner, the defendant should nevertheless be required to pay the higher amount. In the second place:

If a contingent fee agreement were to govern as a strict limitation on the award of attorney's fees, an undesirable emphasis might be placed on the importance of the recovery of damages in civil rights litigation. The intention of Congress was to encourage successful civil rights litigation, not to create a special incentive to prove damages and shortchange efforts to seek effective injunctive or declaratory relief.

489 U.S. at 95, 109 S.Ct. at 945.

If a contingent fee agreement between a plaintiff and her attorney must be ignored for purposes of setting a fee award under the fee-shifting statutes, can such an agreement that would require a plaintiff to pay *more* than the statutory "reasonable attorney's fee" be enforced? In VENEGAS v. MITCHELL, 495 U.S. 82, 110 S.Ct. 1679, 109 L.Ed.2d 74 (1990), the plaintiff in a Section 1983 damage action signed a contingent fee agreement providing that the attorney would receive 40 percent of any recovery, offset by any fee awarded under Section 1988. The district court awarded the plaintiff over $2 million in damages and, on the fee application, awarded $75,000 for work done by plaintiff's counsel. The plaintiff attempted to get out of the fee contract by asserting that its enforcement would be inconsistent with the purpose of the fee-shifting statute which is to relieve successful civil rights plaintiffs of having to pay their attorneys. Both the district court and court of appeal rejected that argument and held that Section 1988 does not prevent collection of a contingent fee even if it exceeds the statutory award. The Supreme Court affirmed unanimously.

> [S]ection 1988 controls what the losing defendant must pay, not what the prevailing plaintiff must pay his lawyer. What a plaintiff may be bound to pay and what an attorney is free to collect under a fee agreement are not necessarily measured by the "reasonable attorney's fee" that a defendant must pay pursuant to a court order. Section 1988 itself does not interfere with the enforceability of a contingent-fee contract.

495 U.S. at 90, 110 S.Ct. at 1684. The Court also reasoned that "depriving plaintiffs of the option of promising to pay more than the statutory fee would not further Section 1988's general purpose of enabling such plaintiffs in civil rights cases to secure competent counsel." *Id.* Does *Venegas* turn on the fact that the fee agreement offset the statutory fee award against the contingent fee? Does the decision mean that counsel in a Title VII case can contract for a percentage of a back pay recovery as a fee and collect such a contingent fee in addition to the court awarded fee?

Chapter 9

THE EQUAL PAY ACT

In 1963, Congress passed the first modern statute directed at eliminating discrimination in the job market—the Equal Pay Act (EPA).[a] Enacted as an amendment to the Fair Labor Standards Act,[b] the EPA proscribes a limited range of discriminatory employment practices—sex-based wage differentials between employees performing "equal work." Subject to four statutorily created exceptions, an employer is prohibited from paying an employee of one sex less than an employee of the opposite sex for "equal work on jobs the performance of which requires equal skill, effort, and responsibility, and which are performed under similar working conditions * * *." The Act also provides that compliance with its equal pay mandate cannot be achieved by reducing the wages of the higher paid employee.

As it is part of the Fair Labor Standards Act (FLSA), coverage under and enforcement of the Equal Pay Act is tied to the provisions of the FLSA.

Employers can fall within the general jurisdiction of the FLSA under either of two theories. The first ("employee") test focuses on the individual employee and asks whether he or she is "engaged in commerce" or engaged "in the production of goods for commerce." All employees who satisfy this requirement are protected by the FLSA. The use of this criterion, however, can result in one employer having both protected and unprotected employees, depending upon the nature of their particular job duties. To eliminate this problem, the FLSA was amended in 1966 to add a new basis for coverage that focuses on the general nature of the employer's business. Under this "enterprise" standard, all the employees of a particular enterprise are covered, regardless of their individual job responsibilities, if the enterprise is (a) engaged in interstate commerce or in the production of goods for interstate commerce, (b) has 2 or more employees so engaged, and (c) except for a few specified industries, makes at least $325,000 in annual gross.

Coverage under the EPA, however, may not be limited to the "employee" and "enterprise" standards that govern inclusion within the minimum wage provisions of the FLSA. The EPA states that an employer cannot discriminate against "employees subject to any provision of this section" within any "establishment" in which such employees are employed. The absence of any reference in this section to

---

[a] Pub.L. 88–38, 77 Stat. 56, 29 U.S.C. § 206(d).

[b] Pub.L. 75–718, 52 Stat. 1060, 29 U.S.C. §§ 201–209.

875

"engaged in commerce", as well as the use of "establishment" instead of "enterprise", has led Professor Larson, among others, to conclude that an employer is covered so long as it has at least one male and one female worker engaged in commerce or in the production of goods for commerce.[c]

In 1974, the FLSA was amended to apply to federal, state and local government employees. The Supreme Court, in National League of Cities v. Usery,[d] struck down the extension of the statute's wage and hour provisions to state and local government workers on the ground that the Tenth Amendment precluded Congress' exercise of its Commerce Clause authority to regulate the relationship between a state and its employees. This ruling was overruled, however, in GARCIA v. SAN ANTONIO METROPOLITAN TRANSIT AUTHORITY,[e] where the Court held that the extension of the FLSA wage and hour provisions to state and local governments did not constitute an unconstitutional exercise of Congress' authority under the Commerce Clause. Prior to the ruling in *Garcia*, the majority of lower federal courts distinguished the Equal Pay Act portions of the FLSA from the wage and hour provisions addressed in *National League of Cities*. Consistent with their treatment of similar amendments to Title VII and the Age Discrimination In Employment Act, these courts upheld the constitutionality of the application of the EPA to state and local agencies on either of two grounds. Some distinguished *Usery* by reasoning that Congress extended the coverage of the EPA pursuant to its authority under § 5 of the Fourteenth Amendment, rather than the Commerce Clause.[f] Others maintained that the EPA does not constitute an impermissible federal intrusion into state sovereignty because paying sex-differentiated wages is not a function essential to the separate and independent existence of the states.[g]

The Equal Pay Act, unlike the other portions of the FLSA, specifically mentions labor organizations, forbidding them from causing or attempting to cause an employer to violate the Act.[h]

In Northwest Airlines, Inc. v. Transport Workers Union of America,[i] the Supreme Court stated that the EPA does not expressly create a private right of action for monetary relief against unions but reserved decision on whether the EPA provided employees with an implied right of action for monetary relief. It noted, however, that the lower federal

---

[c] See 1 A. Larson, Employment Discrimination, § 6.41 (1981).

[d] 426 U.S. 833, 96 S.Ct. 2465, 49 L.Ed.2d 245 (1976).

[e] 469 U.S. 528, 105 S.Ct. 1005, 83 L.Ed.2d 1016 (1985).

[f] See e.g. Marshall v. Owensboro–Daviess County Hospital, 581 F.2d 116 (6th Cir. 1978); Marshall v. City of Sheboygan, 577 F.2d 1 (7th Cir.1978).

[g] See Marshall v. A & M Consolidated Independent School District, 605 F.2d 186 (5th Cir.1979).

[h] The EPA does not contain a minimum member requirement for labor organizations.

[i] 451 U.S. 77, 101 S.Ct. 1571, 67 L.Ed.2d 750 (1981).

courts generally had refused to find that the Act created such an implied right of action.[j]

The Department of Labor was designated by the FLSA as the agency responsible for interpreting and enforcing its provisions. This task was transferred, however, to the EEOC by President Carter's Reorganization Plan No. 1 of 1978. (This reorganization plan was expressly ratified by the Congress in 1984. See note k, *infra*.) While an aggrieved employee is entitled to file a complaint of an EPA violation with the EEOC, these proceedings need not be invoked prior to filing suit. An employee can bring a private action under the EPA in either federal or state court for amounts withheld in violation of the Act. The EEOC can bring such an action on that employee's behalf, but its exercise of this authority terminates the employee's right to file suit and the EPA, unlike Title VII, does not grant the individual a right to intervene in the EEOC action.[k] In addition, the EEOC can seek injunctive relief and liquidated damages as well as backpay. Finally, a two year statute of limitations applies to EPA suits for backpay, except that a case arising out of a willful violation is subject to a three year limitations period.[l]

The remaining materials in this Chapter will address the three most frequently litigated issues in cases brought under the EPA: (1) the meaning of the statutory equal work standard, (2) the scope of the

[j] The Court also ruled that where an employer was held liable under the EPA for sex-based wage differentials that were collectively bargained with a union, the employer did not possess either a federal statutory or federal common law right to contribution from that union.

[k] Intervention may be sought, however, under Fed.Rule Civ.Proc. 24. In the absence of any express conciliation requirement, one court has held that the EPA does not require the EEOC to attempt conciliation before instituting suit. EEOC v. Home of Economy, Inc., 712 F.2d 356 (8th Cir.1983).

In Immigration and Naturalization Service v. Chadha, 462 U.S. 919, 103 S.Ct. 2764, 77 L.Ed.2d 317 (1983), the Supreme Court held that a legislative provision that gave one house of the Congress the power to veto the act of the Attorney General suspending deportation proceedings violated the constitutional separation of powers doctrine and the constitutional requirement that legislation be accomplished by action of both houses of Congress and by presentment to the President. Reorganization Plan No. 1 was promulgated by President Carter pursuant to the Reorganization Act of 1977, which statute authorized the President to reorganize federal agen-

cies subject to veto by only one house of Congress. For some time, the lower courts split as to whether the EEOC's authority to file lawsuits under the EPA survived the ruling in *Chadha*. Compare EEOC v. Allstate Ins. Co., 570 F.Supp. 1224 (S.D.Miss. 1983) (entire Act is unconstitutional as one-house veto provision was not severable from remainder of statute), appeal dismissed for want of jurisdiction, 467 U.S. 1232, 104 S.Ct. 3499, 82 L.Ed.2d 810 (1984) with EEOC v. Hernando Bank, Inc., 724 F.2d 1188 (5th Cir.1984) (one-house veto provision is severable from rest of Reorganization Act). This conflict was resolved, however, when Congress enacted a statute that specifically ratified and affirmed the transfer of authority to the EEOC by the Reorganization Plan. See Ratification of Reorganization Plans As A Matter of Law, 5 U.S.C. § 906 note, Pub.L. No. 98–532, 98 Stat. 2705 (1984).

[l] To establish a willful violation, the plaintiff must prove that the defendant knew or should have known that its conduct was governed by the Act. McLaughlin v. Richland Shoe Co., 486 U.S. 128, 108 S.Ct. 1677, 100 L.Ed.2d 115 (1988)(action brought under FLSA but Court states that FLSA provision governs suits under EPA).

statutory exceptions, and (3) the relationship between the EPA and Title VII.

Read 29 U.S.C. §§ 206(d) and 216 at pp. 1265–1266.

BRENNAN v. PRINCE WILLIAM HOSPITAL CORP.

United States Court of Appeals, Fourth Circuit, 1974.
503 F.2d 282, cert. denied, 420 U.S. 972, 95 S.Ct. 1392, 43 L.Ed.2d 652 (1975).

BUTZNER, CIRCUIT JUDGE.

The Secretary of Labor appeals from the dismissal of an action against Prince William Hospital to equalize pay of male hospital orderlies and female nurses' aides in conformity with the Equal Pay Act of 1963. The district court noted that the facts were not in dispute and that the controversy centered on the inferences to be drawn from them. It found that although aides and orderlies do the same type of patient care work, the following differences exist between the jobs: the proportions of routine care tasks are not the same; aides do work which orderlies are neither required nor permitted to do; and, most important, orderlies do work, including extra tasks, which aides are neither required nor permitted to do. It concluded, therefore, that the Secretary had failed to establish that the aides and orderlies perform substantially equal work.

We believe that the district court gave undue significance to these differences because it misapprehended the statutory definition of equal work, which embraces the concepts of "skill, effort, and responsibility." Since it applied an improper legal standard to the relevant facts, we reverse and remand for the entry of judgment for the Secretary.

In applying the Congressional mandate of equal pay for equal work on jobs which require equal skill, effort, and responsibility, there are two extremes of interpretation that must be avoided. Congress realized that the majority of job differentiations are made for genuine economic reasons unrelated to sex. It did not authorize the Secretary or the courts to engage in wholesale reevaluation of any employer's pay structure in order to enforce their own conceptions of economic worth. But if courts defer to overly nice distinctions in job content, employers may evade the Act at will. The response to this dilemma has been to require the Secretary to prove substantial equality of skill, effort, and responsibility as the jobs are actually performed.

One of the most common grounds for justifying different wages is the assertion that male employees perform extra tasks. These may support a wage differential if they create significant variations in skill, effort, and responsibility between otherwise equal jobs. But the semblance of the valid job classification system may not be allowed to mask the existence of wage discrimination based on sex. The Secretary may therefore show that the greater pay received by the male employees is not related to any extra tasks and thus is not justified by them. Higher pay is not related to extra duties when one or more of the following circumstances exists:

> Some male employees receive higher pay without doing the extra work.

> Female employees also perform extra duties of equal skill, effort, and responsibility.

> Qualified female employees are not given the opportunity to do the extra work.

> The supposed extra duties do not in fact exist.

> The extra task consumes a minimal amount of time and is of peripheral importance.

> Third persons who do the extra task as their primary job are paid less than the male employees in question.

In all of these * * * [circumstances] the basic jobs were substantially equal. Despite claims to the contrary, the extra tasks were * * * makeweights. This left sex—which in this context refers to the availability of women at lower wages than men—as the one discernible reason for the wage differential. That, however, is precisely the criterion for setting wages that the Act prohibits.

Although a number of courts have applied the Equal Pay Act to hospital and nursing home aides and orderlies, varied employment practices among institutions have prevented the development of an industry-wide standard. The Act must be applied on a case by case basis to factual situations that are, for practical purposes, unique. It is therefore necessary to examine in some detail the employment practices of Prince William Hospital, even though the material facts are not in dispute.

Prince William is a 154 bed general hospital in Manassas, Virginia. It contains four medical and surgical units, intensive care and cardiac facilities, an obstetric floor with a nursery, four operating rooms, and an emergency room. Average occupancy is 120 patients, 60% female.

Floor orderlies and nurses' aides provide routine patient care under the supervision of nurses. The hospital hires only men as orderlies and only women as aides. Their numbers varied during the time covered by this case, ranging between 30–40 aides and 5–10 orderlies. When the case was tried, there were four full-time floor orderlies and thirty-four full-time aides, plus three part-time orderlies and three part-time aides. Full-time employees work five eight-hour shifts per week.

The hospital has maintained a pay differential between the two jobs since 1969. It uses a pay system with thirteen pay grades and five steps within each grade. Grades are assigned to positions and steps within grade show merit or longevity. All nurses' aides are in grade I, in which the hourly pay ranges from $1.98 to $2.31, and all orderlies are in grade II, in which the hourly pay ranges from $2.08 to $2.43, depending on the step in which the employee has been placed.

Before 1969 aides and orderlies had been paid the same wages, but the hospital had difficulty in hiring orderlies. The hospital's administrator believed that a higher wage was needed to attract orderlies because of the limited number of men willing to do housekeeping and personal care work. When the orderlies' wage was raised, they were given the additional duty of catheterizing male patients.

Hiring criteria for aides and orderlies are identical: a tenth grade education, personal cleanliness, and a desire to work with people. Experience, though desirable, is unnecessary. Although the educational level of the aides was somewhat lower, both groups included individuals who had not finished high school. The pay differential follows neither experience nor education. An aide with prior hospital experience starts in grade I step 2 ($2.06), while a completely inexperienced orderly starts in grade II step 1 ($2.08).

Aides and orderlies are the least skilled persons who care for patients. They participate in a common orientation program, but much of their training is acquired on the job. Each is assigned six to eight patients who require routine care. Whenever possible orderlies are assigned to male patients and aides to female, but the shortage of orderlies requires aides to care for males. Most of the time, aides and orderlies are occupied with tasks related to routine patient care that do not require the skills of a trained nurse.

The principal duties of both, which the hospital's director of nursing stated were identical, can be divided into four groups: patient care, which includes oral hygiene, back rubs, baths, bed-making, answering calls, giving bed pans, feeding, transporting the patient, and assistance with ambulation; minor treatment, which includes weighing, taking pulse, temperature, or blood pressure, draping and positioning the patient, administering heat pads and ice packs, assistance with dressing changes, and giving enemas; housekeeping, which includes room cleaning, equipment care and cleaning, work area cleaning, and obtaining supplies; and miscellaneous tasks, including answering the phone, running errands, and transportation to the morgue.

The hospital emphasized statistical evidence which shows that aides and orderlies do not perform all of their routine tasks with equal frequency. One of its exhibits, for example, shows that aides write charts, make beds, give baths, rub backs, and fetch bed pans more often than orderlies. Orderlies, on the other hand, bring supplies, run errands, and assist the nurses with their duties more often than aides. These distinctions, however, do not show any difference in skill, effort, or responsibility. All of the routine tasks are relatively simple. None performed more frequently by the orderlies requires the exertion of significantly more skill, effort, or responsibility than those performed more frequently by the aides. As hired, trained, and employed, the orderlies and aides are practical substitutes for one another in the performance of their basic duties. Disproportionate frequency in the performance of the same routine tasks does not make the job unequal.

The district court also found that aides perform certain duties which orderlies do not. Specifically, it found that some of the aides work in the obstetric department and care for infants in the nursery. Orderlies were not assigned to obstetrics, according to the director of nursing, for two reasons: there were no male patients and their lifting ability was unneeded there. Aides assigned to obstetrics performed the same duties as those on the medical and surgical wards.

These facts do not show any differences in skill, effort, or responsibility. Unless there is a difference of working conditions involved, which is not contended here, there is no reason why the performance of the same duties in a different location should be a significant difference in the jobs.

The final—and in some respects the most difficult—aspect of this case pertains to extra duties throughout the hospital that are assigned to the orderlies but not to the aides. These duties are specified in the job description of the orderlies. The district court found that the following extra duties were the most significant: heavy lifting, assisting in the emergency room, performing surgical preps on male patients, providing physical security by dealing with combative or hysterical persons, and catheterization of male patients.

Job descriptions and titles, however, are not decisive. Actual job requirements and performance are controlling. This aspect of the case, therefore, turns primarily on the extent to which the aides and orderlies actually perform the extra duties nominally assigned to the orderlies and on the skill, effort, and responsibility involved in those tasks which the orderlies alone perform.

In addition to caring for assigned patients, orderlies are required to answer calls to different parts of the hospital. On these excursions, called floating, they perform either their basic duties or the extra tasks. Floating itself adds nothing to the level of skill or responsibility, for that depends on the work done in the other locations. It might add to the degree of effort involved if the orderlies, in addition, had to perform their full basic workload. This, however, is not the case. According to the director of nursing, an orderly's routine duties at his assigned station are reassigned to other staff personnel, including the aides, when he is in another part of the hospital.

The job description states that orderlies are expected to perform total lifting of heavy or helpless patients and to set up traction equipment. The district court, however, found that the same tasks are performed by aides when no orderly is available and that aides assist orderlies in these tasks. Due to the small number of orderlies, there are rarely more than two on duty each shift, and from time to time no orderly is available on some of the shifts. It sometimes takes more than one aide, or mechanical assistance, to replace an orderly, but there is no evidence that any heavy lifting cannot be done without male assistance. The performance of tasks involving physical strength, therefore, though necessary to the operation of the hospital, is not a peculiar aspect of the orderlies' job. Strength is not a factor in the hiring of orderlies, except in the very general sense that the hospital assumes that a man is usually stronger than a woman. A large, burly woman would not be hired as an orderly, nor would a small, delicate man be hired as an aide. But the converse is not true. One of the orderlies is 5'2" tall and weighs 125 lbs., while one aide is 6'1" and weighs 225 lbs. The wage differential therefore can not be justified on the grounds that the hospital is maintaining a reserve of strong men for essential tasks.

Heavy lifting does not add significantly to the effort involved in the orderlies' job. In the ten working days covered by the hospital's survey of activities, the orderlies set up traction only once and lifted or assisted patients of unknown weight 54 times. Aides set up traction and lifted or ambulated patients a proportionate number of times. The extra effort, if any, is not substantial.

The emergency room is staffed by an orderly whose status is not questioned in this action. The hospital's claim that floor orderlies "assisted" there is supported only by the job description, but a mere job description without evidence of actual performance does not establish the existence of extra duties. Aides were also called to work in the emergency room. The record proves no more than that both aides and orderlies performed their normal duties with minor variations in a different location.

All surgical preps during the day shifts are done by the operating room staff. On the evening and night shifts, surgical preps on men are done by orderlies, and on women by aides or nurses. Aides also do surgical preps in the obstetric ward. A person performing a prep explains to the patient what is about to be done, shaves the area where the incision will be made, and washes it with antiseptic soap. The skill, effort, and responsibility involved are identical regardless of the patient's sex.

Physical security, as an extra duty, has two components. Because of his size and sex, the presence of a male orderly is claimed to reassure the other staff and exert a calming and deterrent effect on potentially violent patients or intruders. Because of his superior strength, he is given the primary responsibility for restraining actually violent persons. According to the hospital, he therefore possesses a special skill and is required to exert extra effort.

The hospital's contention, however, is contradicted by the record. Although in theory the orderly deals with disturbances, in practice the nearest staff member is expected to do so until assistance comes. Aides are expected to restrain violent or disoriented patients themselves when possible. They also deal with intruders. The hospital's tabulation of orderly and aide activity shows aides spending a larger proportion of their time than orderlies in applying restraining devices to patients. There is no evidence that orderlies do more actual physical restraint than aides.

No doubt the physical presence of a man in the house does have a comforting effect on the staff. It is doubtful, though, that this is a significant component of the orderly job. Unlike hospitals in which providing physical security has been found significant, Prince William Hospital does not handle psychiatric, alcoholic, criminal, or other potentially dangerous patients. There is no evidence that episodes caused by violent or confused patients are so frequent or dangerous that orderlies are necessary for the safety of the staff. Security guards are called to deal with violent episodes even when orderlies are available. Moreover, the ability to deal with confused or violent patients, according to the director of nursing, is as much a function of attitude and experience as of size and strength. If the orderly's superior strength is an extra skill, it is a peripheral part of his employment.

The hospital places great emphasis on the fact that orderlies insert Foley catheters in male patients. It contends that the task is a highly skilled and responsible procedure, requiring 30 to 45 minutes of an orderly's time.

A Foley catheter is a sterile tube which is inserted in the patient's urethra to drain the bladder. Orderlies catheterize male patients with unobstructed urinary tracts. If any difficulty is foreseen or experienced a physician catheterizes the patient. Nurses catheterize female patients. They are competent to catheterize males, but prefer not to do so for reasons of modesty. Since the hospital has enough nurses to catheterize women, aides are not assigned this duty. The orderly's job therefore does call for the exercise of skill and responsibility which is not required of the aides.

However, no more than one or two routine catheterizations are usually performed each week. When no floor orderly is present, other qualified male personnel are available to do them. The hospital looks for no special skill in this regard from its prospective orderlies but concedes that "any reasonably dextrous person can learn male catheterization on the job." Orderlies were assigned this duty only when the hospital decided that a higher wage rate was needed to attract men for routine care work, and new orderlies who have not yet learned to catheterize are nevertheless paid at the higher rate.

Like any other extra duty, catheterization must be evaluated as part of the entire job. In Hodgson v. Fairmont Supply Co., 454 F.2d 490, 496 (4th Cir.1972), we pointed out that when jobs were substantially equal, a minimal amount of extra skill, effort, or responsibility cannot justify wage differentials. Infrequent performance of catheterizations, unaccompanied by other extra skills and responsibilities, has never been held to support a pay differential between aides and orderlies. The orderlies in Hodgson v. William and Mary Nursing Hotel, 20 W.H. Cases 10 (M.D.Fla.1971), for example, a case in which the district court found catheterization to be a significant extra duty, also moved heavy equipment, administered suction therapy, and did other demanding work not done by aides. Catheterizations, moreover, were frequent and difficult in that geriatric nursing home. Similarly, catheterization was only one element of the orderlies' duties, which differed fundamentally from the aides', in Hodgson v. Good Shepherd Hospital, 327 F.Supp. 143 (E.D.Tex.1971). In contrast, catheterization which only consumed a minimal amount of time was considered to be an insubstantial difference in Shultz v. Brookhaven General Hospital, 305 F.Supp. 424 (E.D.Tex.1969), aff'd in part and remanded in part sub nom. Hodgson v. Brookhaven General Hospital, 436 F.2d 719 (5th Cir.1970), on remand 20 W.H. Cases 54 (E.D.Tex.1971), aff'd, 470 F.2d 729 (5th Cir.1972). We conclude, therefore, that the orderlies' pay differential cannot be justified on the basis of the occasional extra work involved in catheterizing male patients.

In sum, the work performed by aides and orderlies is not identical. But, as we have previously held, application of the Equal Pay Act is not restricted to identical work. The basic routine tasks of the aides and orderlies are equal. The variations that the district court found, when tested by the Act's standard of "equal skill, effort, and responsibility," do not affect the substantial equality of their overall work.

The judgment of the district court is reversed, and this case is remanded for entry of judgment for the Secretary.

NOTES AND PROBLEMS FOR DISCUSSION

1. State University operates campuses in three different cities in the State—North, South and West. Undergraduate instruction is offered at the North and South campuses, while the graduate and professional schools are located on the West campus. Robert Force, a Professor of English at North with 10 years seniority, receives an annual salary of $25,000. Ruth Morris, a Professor of English at South with comparable credentials and identical seniority is paid $20,000 per year. Prof. Morris brings an action under the EPA. What result? See Brennan v. Goose Creek Consolidated Independent School District, 519 F.2d 53 (5th Cir.1975). Could Morris successfully bring an action under Title VII? See Bartelt v. Berlitz School of Languages of America, Inc., 698 F.2d 1003 (9th Cir.), cert. denied, 464 U.S. 915, 104 S.Ct. 277, 78 L.Ed.2d 257 (1983). What if Force was a Professor of Chemistry at South? See Soble v. University of Maryland, 778 F.2d 164 (4th Cir.1985); Melanson v. Rantoul, 536 F.Supp. 271 (D.R.I.1982). Does the statute suggest that a lesser degree of similarity is required with respect to working conditions than skill, effort and responsibility? See Lanegan—Grimm v. Library Ass'n of Portland, 560 F.Supp. 486, 493 (D.Or.1983).

2. Federal Airlines pays identical salaries to its male and female flight attendants. During layovers, female flight attendants are required to share double rooms while male attendants are provided with single rooms. In addition, male attendants are given a monthly uniform cleaning allowance. No such allowance is provided to female attendants. Can a female attendant state a claim under the EPA? See Laffey v. Northwest Airlines, Inc., 642 F.2d 578 (D.C.Cir.1980); Donovan v. KFC Services, Inc., 547 F.Supp. 503 (E.D.N.Y.1982).

3. Does the application of the EPA to a religious organization violate the establishment or free exercise clauses of the First Amendment? See Dole v.

Shenandoah Baptist Church, 899 F.2d 1389 (4th Cir.1990); Russell v. Belmont College, 554 F.Supp. 667 (M.D.Tenn.1982).

KOUBA v. ALLSTATE INSURANCE CO.
United States Court of Appeals, Ninth Circuit, 1982.
691 F.2d 873.

CHOY, CIRCUIT JUDGE:

This appeal calls into question the scope of the "factor other than sex" exception to the Equal Pay Act of 1963 as incorporated into Title VII of the Civil Rights Act of 1964 by the Bennett Amendment.[2] Because the district court misconstrued the exception, we reverse and remand.

I

Allstate Insurance Co. computes the minimum salary guaranteed to a new sales agent on the basis of ability, education, experience, and prior salary. During an 8–to–13 week training period, the agent receives only the minimum. Afterwards, Allstate pays the greater of the minimum and the commissions earned from sales. A result of this practice is that, on the average, female agents make less than their male counterparts.

Lola Kouba, representing a class of all female agents, argued below that the use of prior salary caused the wage differential and thus constitutes unlawful sex discrimination. Allstate responded that prior salary is a "factor other than sex" within the meaning of the statutory exception. The district court entered summary judgment against Allstate, reasoning that (1) because so many employers paid discriminatory salaries in the past, the court would presume that a female agent's prior salary was based on her gender unless Allstate presented evidence to rebut that presumption, and (2) absent such a showing (which Allstate did not attempt to make), prior salary is not a factor other than sex.

II

The Equal Pay Act prohibits differential payments between male and female employees doing equal work except when made pursuant to any of three specific compensation systems or "any other factor other than sex." These exceptions are affirmative defenses which the employer must plead and prove. Corning Glass Works v. Brennan, 417

---

2. The Bennett Amendment, which incorporates into Title VII the affirmative defenses fixed in the Equal Pay Act, states:

It shall not be an unlawful employment practice under this subchapter [Title VII] for any employer to differentiate upon the basis of sex in determining the amount of the wages or compensation paid or to be paid to employees of such employer if such differentiation is authorized by the provisions of section 206(d) of title 29[Equal Pay Act].

U.S. 188, 196–97, 94 S.Ct. 2223, 2229, 41 L.Ed.2d 1 (1974) (claim brought under the Equal Pay Act).

Because Kouba brought her claim under Title VII rather than directly under the Equal Pay Act,[3] Allstate contends that the standard Title VII rules govern the allocation of evidentiary burdens. It cites Texas Department of Community Affairs v. Burdine, 450 U.S. 248, 253, 101 S.Ct. 1089, 1091, 67 L.Ed.2d 207 (1981), for the proposition that under Title VII an employee alleging sex discrimination bears the burden of persuasion at all times as to all issues and concludes that Kouba failed to carry the burden of showing that the wage differential did not result from a factor other than sex.[4]

Allstate misallocates the burden. In County of Washington v. Gunther, 452 U.S. 161, 170–71, 101 S.Ct. 2242, 2248–49, 68 L.Ed.2d 751 (1981), the Supreme Court recognized that very different principles govern the standard structure of Title VII litigation, including burdens of proof, and the structure of Title VII litigation implicating the "factor other than sex" exception to an equal-pay claim (though the Court reserved judgment on specifically how to structure an equal-pay claim under Title VII). Accordingly, we have held that even under Title VII, the employer bears the burden of showing that the wage differential resulted from a factor other than sex. Piva v. Xerox Corp., 654 F.2d 591, 598–601 (9th Cir.1981); Gunther v. County of Washington, 623 F.2d 1303, 1319 (9th Cir.1979) (supplemental opinion denying rehearing), aff'd, 452 U.S. 161, 101 S.Ct. 2242, 68 L.Ed.2d 751 (1981). Nothing in *Burdine* converts this affirmative defense, which the employer must plead and prove under *Corning Glass,* into an element of the cause of action, which the employee must show does not exist.

III

In an effort to carry its burden, Allstate asserts that if its use of prior salary caused the wage differential,[5] prior salary constitutes a factor other than sex. An obstacle to evaluating Allstate's contention is the ambiguous statutory language. The parties proffer a variety of possible interpretations of the term "factor other than sex."

A

We can discard at the outset three interpretations manifestly incompatible with the Equal Pay Act. At one extreme are two that would tolerate all but the most blatant discrimination. Kouba asserts that Allstate wrongly reads "factor other than sex" to mean any factor

---

3. Her apparent reasons for bringing a Title VII action were the uncertainty at that time how the Equal Pay Act affected Title VII and the apparently less-demanding class-consent requirements under Title VII. Kuhn v. Philadelphia Electric Co., 475 F.Supp. 324, 326 (E.D.Pa.1979).

4. Allstate does not dispute that otherwise Kouba established a prima facie case. Thus, for purposes of this appeal, we assume that she has.

5. Allstate questions whether its use of prior salary caused the wage differential. We leave that issue for the district court on remand.

that either does not refer on its face to an employee's gender or does not result in all women having lower salaries than all men. Since an employer could easily manipulate factors having a close correlation to gender as a guise to pay female employees discriminatorily low salaries, it would contravene the Act to allow their use simply because they also are facially neutral or do not produce complete segregation. Not surprisingly, Allstate denies relying on either reading of the exception.

At the other extreme is an interpretation that would deny employers the opportunity to use clearly acceptable factors. Kouba insists that in order to give the Act its full remedial force, employers cannot use any factor that perpetuates historic sex discrimination. The court below adopted a variation of this interpretation: the employer must demonstrate that it made a reasonable attempt to satisfy itself that the factor causing the wage differential was not the product of sex discrimination. Kouba v. Allstate Insurance Co., 523 F.Supp. 148, 162 (E.D.Cal. 1981). But while Congress fashioned the Equal Pay Act to help cure longstanding societal ills, it also intended to exempt factors such as training and experience that may reflect opportunities denied to women in the past. H.R.Rep. No. 309, 88th Cong., 1st Sess. 3, reprinted in 1963 U.S. Code Cong. & Ad. News 687, 689. Neither Kouba's interpretation nor the district court's variation can accommodate practices that Congress and the courts have approved.

B

All three interpretations miss the mark in large part because they do not focus on the reason for the employer's use of the factor. The Equal Pay Act concerns business practices. It would be nonsensical to sanction the use of a factor that rests on some consideration unrelated to business. An employer thus cannot use a factor which causes a wage differential between male and female employees absent an acceptable business reason.[6] Conversely, a factor used to effectuate some business policy is not prohibited simply because a wage differential results.

Even with a business-related requirement, an employer might assert some business reason as a pretext for a discriminatory objective. This possibility is especially great with a factor like prior salary which can easily be used to capitalize on the unfairly low salaries historically paid to women. See Futran v. RING Radio Co., 501 F.Supp. 734, 739 n. 2 (N.D.Ga.1980) (expressing concern that the use of prior salary would perpetuate the traditionally lower salaries paid women). The ability of courts to protect against such abuse is somewhat limited, however. The Equal Pay Act entrusts employers, not judges, with making the often uncertain decision of how to accomplish business objectives. We have found no authority giving guidance on the proper judicial inquiry

---

6. Not every reason making economic sense is acceptable. See Corning Glass Works v. Brennan, 417 U.S. at 205, 94 S.Ct. at 2233. This appeal does not, however, require us to compile a complete list of unacceptable factors or even formulate a standard to distinguish them from acceptable ones. We leave those tasks for another day.

absent direct evidence of discriminatory intent. A pragmatic standard, which protects against abuse yet accommodates employer discretion, is that the employer must use the factor reasonably in light of the employer's stated purpose as well as its other practices. The specific relevant considerations will of course vary with the situation. In Part IV of this opinion, we outline how the court below should apply this test to the business reasons given by Allstate for its use of prior salary.

C

Relying on recent Supreme Court precedent, Kouba would limit the category of business reasons acceptable under the exception to those that measure the value of an employee's job performance to his or her employer. In County of Washington v. Gunther, 452 U.S. at 170–71 n. 11, 101 S.Ct. at 2248–49 n. 11, the Court reported that Congress added the exception "because of a concern that bona fide job evaluation systems used by American businesses would otherwise be disrupted." In Corning Glass Works v. Brennan, 417 U.S. at 199, 94 S.Ct. at 2230, the Court explained that these systems "took into consideration four separate factors in determining job value—skill, effort, responsibility and working conditions—and each of these four components was further systematically divided into various subcomponents." Our study of the legislative history of the Equal Pay Act confirms that Congress discussed only factors that reflect job value.

In drafting the Act, however, Congress did not limit the exception to job-evaluation systems. Instead, it excepted "any other factor other than sex" and thus created a "broad general exception." H.R.Rep. No. 309, 88th Cong., 1st Sess. 3, reprinted in 1963 U.S. Code Cong. & Ad. News 687, 689. While a concern about job-evaluation systems served as the impetus for creating the exception, Congress did not limit the exception to that concern.

Other language in the Act supports this conclusion. The statutory definition of equal work incorporates the four factors listed in *Corning Glass* as the standard components in job-evaluation systems. (The Act refers to "equal work on jobs the performance of which requires equal skill, effort, and responsibility, and which are performed under similar working conditions.") It would render the "factor other than sex" exception surplusage to limit the exception to the same four factors. And while we might be able to distinguish other factors that also reflect job value, the scope of the exception would be exceedingly narrow if limited to other apparently uncommon factors. The broad language of the exception belies such limitation.

Accordingly, no court or other authority has inferred a job-evaluation requirement. We, too, reject that limitation on the "factor other than sex" exception.

IV

Allstate provides two business reasons for its use of prior salary that the district court must evaluate on remand.[7] We will discuss each explanation in turn without attempting to establish a comprehensive framework for its evaluation. The district court should mold its inquiry to the particular facts that unfold at trial.

A

Allstate asserts that it ties the guaranteed monthly minimum to prior salary as part of a sales-incentive program. If the monthly minimum far exceeds the amount that the agent earned previously, the agent might become complacent and not fulfill his or her selling potential. By limiting the monthly minimum according to prior salary, Allstate hopes to motivate the agent to make sales, earn commissions, and thus improve his or her financial position. Presumably, Allstate cannot set a uniform monthly minimum so low that it motivates all sales agents, because then prospective agents with substantially higher prior salaries might not risk taking a job with Allstate.

This reasoning does not explain Allstate's use of prior salary during the initial training period. Because the agents cannot earn commissions at that time, there is no potential reward to motivate them to make sales.

When commissions become available, we wonder whether Allstate adjusts the guaranteed minimum regularly and whether most agents earn commission-based salaries. On remand, the district court should inquire into these and other issues that relate to the reasonableness of the use of prior salary in the incentive program.

B

Reasoning that salary corresponds roughly to an employee's ability, Allstate also claims that it uses prior salary to predict a new employee's performance as a sales agent. Relevant considerations in evaluating the reasonableness of this practice include (1) whether the employer also uses other available predictors of the new employee's performance, (2) whether the employer attributes less significance to prior salary once the employee has proven himself or herself on the job, and (3) whether the employer relies more heavily on salary when the prior job resembles the job of sales agent.

V

In conclusion, the Equal Pay Act does not impose a strict prohibition against the use of prior salary. Thus while we share the district

---

7. A third reason given by Allstate is that an individual with a higher prior salary can demand more in the marketplace. Courts disagree whether market demand can ever justify a wage differential. Compare, e.g., Horner v. Mary Institute, 613 F.2d 706, 714 (8th Cir.1980) (allowing it in limited situations), with Futran v. RING Radio Co., 501 F.Supp. 734, 739 (N.D.Ga. 1980) (disallowing it always). We need not rule whether Congress intended to prohibit the use of market demand. Because Allstate did not present any evidence to support its use of prior salary in response to market demand, the district court properly disposed of that reason on summary judgment.

court's fear that an employer might manipulate its use of prior salary to underpay female employees the court must find that the business reasons given by Allstate do not reasonably explain its use of that factor before finding a violation of the Act.

Reversed and Remanded.

* * *

NOTES AND PROBLEMS FOR DISCUSSION

1. What if the employer in *Kouba* had a policy of basing salary on the prior salary *it* paid to its employees so that when an employee transferred to another position, the new salary was based, at least in part, on that individual's prior salary? Compare Glenn v. General Motors Corp., 841 F.2d 1567 (11th Cir.), cert. denied, 488 U.S. 948, 109 S.Ct. 378, 102 L.Ed.2d 367 (1988) with Covington v. S.I.U., 816 F.2d 317 (7th Cir.), cert. denied, 484 U.S. 848, 108 S.Ct. 146, 98 L.Ed.2d 101 (1987).

2. Mel's Clothing Store has separate departments for men's and women's clothing. The merchandise in the men's department is of better quality and higher price than the women's merchandise, and yields a higher profit margin than the women's clothing. Only women were hired for the women's department and only men were permitted to work in the men's department. It is conceded that the sales personnel in both departments perform equal work. Mel's, however, pays all its salesmen a higher base salary than is paid to its saleswomen. The store maintains that this differential is justified by the greater profitability and dollar volume of gross sales produced by the salespersons in the men's department. Is Mel's violating the EPA? Is the plaintiff in this problem really asserting a claim of unequal pay? Or is she alleging that she was a victim of a discriminatory job assignment? If the latter, shouldn't the action be brought under Title VII rather than the EPA? See Hodgson v. Robert Hall Clothes, Inc., 473 F.2d 589 (3d Cir.), cert. denied, 414 U.S. 866, 94 S.Ct. 50, 38 L.Ed.2d 85 (1973). Does the principal case address any of these issues? See Sullivan, The Equal Pay Act of 1963: Making and Breaking A Prima Facie Case, 31 Ark.L.Rev. 545 (1978).

3. Buff Spas Inc. operates a chain of health spas, each of which is divided into a men's and women's division. Men operate the men's division and women operate the women's division. The manager of each division is paid by commissions based on gross sales of memberships. Male managers are paid 6% of their spa's gross sales of memberships to men; female managers are paid 4% of gross sales of memberships to women. Over the course of the company's existence, the gross volume of membership sales to women was 50% higher than the gross volume of membership sales to men. There is no difference in the job duties of male and female managers and they perform their jobs under similar working conditions. The total remuneration received by males and females was substantially equal, however, because while females received a commission based on a lower percentage of gross sales, they sold more memberships than the males. The company says that it pays different commission rates so that men and women will be paid substantially equal compensation for equal work performed. Is the company in violation of the Equal Pay Act? See Bence v. Detroit Health Corp., 712 F.2d 1024 (6th Cir.1983), cert. denied, 465 U.S. 1025, 104 S.Ct. 1282, 79 L.Ed.2d 685 (1984).

4. In connection with the opening of a family planning center, Good Samaritan Hospital sought to hire two additional gynecologists. From a pool of twenty male and two female applicants for the posts, the hospital made offers to Dr. Arlene DeRoy and Dr. Paul Barron. After both joined the Hospital's staff, Dr. Barron discovered that Dr. DeRoy's salary was $10,000 higher than his. Both Drs. Barron and DeRoy were 1975 graduates of the same medical school with comparable prior experience and medical school records. The Hospital contends that because of the great demand and extremely limited supply of female gynecologists, it was compelled to offer Dr. DeRoy a higher salary to lure her away from other offers of employment. Has the Hospital violated the Equal Pay Act? Compare Horner v. Mary Institute, 613 F.2d 706 (8th Cir.1980) with Hodgson v. Brookhaven General Hospital, 436 F.2d 719 (5th Cir.1970).

5. In CORNING GLASS WORKS v. BRENNAN, 417 U.S. 188, 94 S.Ct. 2223, 41 L.Ed.2d 1 (1974), discussed in the principal case, the employer paid a higher base wage to male night shift inspectors than it paid to female inspectors who performed the same job duties during the day shift. It also paid a separate premium to all workers on the night shift. The defendant argued that since day shift work was not "performed under similar working conditions" as night shift work, the plaintiff Secretary of Labor had failed to prove that Corning was paying unequal pay for equal work. The Secretary contended that day and night shift work were performed under similar working conditions and that while night shift work could constitute a "factor other than sex" defense, Corning had failed to prove that the higher base wage paid to male night shift inspectors was based on a non-sex factor. The Court agreed with the Secretary:

> While a layman might well assume that time of day worked reflects one aspect of a job's "working conditions," the term has a different and much more specific meaning in the language of industrial relations. As Corning's own representative testified at the hearings, the element of working conditions encompasses two subfactors: "surroundings" and "hazards." "Surroundings" measures the elements, such as toxic chemicals or fumes, regularly encountered by a worker, their intensity, and their frequency. "Hazards" takes into account the physical hazards regularly encountered, their frequency, and the severity of injury they can cause. This definition of "working conditions" is not only manifested in Corning's own job evaluation plans but is also well accepted across a wide range of American industry.

> Nowhere in any of these definitions is time of day worked mentioned as a relevant criterion. The fact of the matter is that the concept of "working conditions," as used in the specialized language of job evaluation systems, simply does not encompass shift differentials. Indeed, while Corning now argues that night inspection work is not equal to day inspection work, all of its own job evaluation plans, including the one now in effect, have consistently treated them as equal in all respects, including working conditions. * * * We agree with the Second Circuit that the inspection work at issue in this case, whether performed during the day or night, is "equal work" as that term is defined in the Act.

> This does not mean, of course, that there is no room in the Equal Pay Act for nondiscriminatory shift differentials. Work on a steady night shift no doubt has psychological and physiological impacts making it less attractive than work on a day shift. The Act contemplates that a male night

worker may receive a higher wage than a female day worker, just as it contemplates that a male employee with 20 years' seniority can receive a higher wage than a woman with two years' seniority. Factors such as these play a role under the Act's four exceptions—the seniority differential under the specific seniority exception, the shift differential under the catch-all exception for differentials "based on any other factor other than sex."

417 U.S. at 202–204, 94 S.Ct. at 2231–2233, 41 L.Ed.2d at 14–15.

What is the significance of this ruling?

The Court concluded that Corning had not sustained its burden of proving that the higher base rate paid for night work was based on a factor other than sex, since prior to 1966, Corning allowed only men to work the night shift and the men would not work at the low wage paid to women inspectors. Would the Court have reached a different conclusion if state law had precluded women from working at night? Can an employer justify a sex-based wage differential on the ground that the state minimum wage law establishes a higher minimum wage for women? See Wirtz v. Rainbo Baking Co. of Lexington, 303 F.Supp. 1049 (E.D.Ky.1967). Should the response to these questions differ from the treatment of the conflict between state "protective" labor legislation and Title VII? Does the language of the EPA offer any guidance as to how such state laws are to be interpreted in order to comply with the federal Act's equal pay standard? See Peters v. City of Shreveport, 818 F.2d 1148 (5th Cir.1987) (reliance upon gender-neutral state minimum wage statute that was not shown to have a state-wide sex discriminatory impact qualifies as a "factor other than sex"). See generally, EEOC v. J.C. Penney Co., Inc., 843 F.2d 249, 253 (6th Cir.1988)("the 'factor other than sex' defense does not include literally any other factor, but a factor that, at a minimum, was adopted for a legitimate business reason.").

6. The Robin Morris Institute determined that the salaries of its female researchers were significantly lower than those of its similarly qualified male researchers. Accordingly, it designed a formula for increasing the salaries of its female researchers to remedy that discrimination. Raises resulting from the application of that formula were given to the female researchers. A group of male researchers claims that the Morris Institute violated the EPA by giving raises solely to its female researchers. What result? See Ende v. Board of Regents, 757 F.2d 176 (7th Cir.1985).

7. As mentioned in the introduction to this Chapter, the Equal Pay Act was enacted as an amendment to the Fair Labor Standards Act (FLSA) and incorporates the remedial provisions of the FLSA. The EPA expressly provides that any amount owing to an employee under the EPA is to be treated just like unpaid minimum wages or unpaid overtime compensation owing under the FLSA. This is important because § 16 of the FLSA provides that any employer who violates the provisions of this statute shall be liable to the employee "for the amount of their unpaid minimum wages, or their unpaid overtime compensation, as the case may be, and in an additional equal amount as liquidated damages." Since this provision does not condition the award of punitive damages on a finding of a willful violation, as is the case under the ADEA (see p. 956, *infra*), it suggests that a successful EPA plaintiff will collect back pay and punitive damages as as matter of course. But the FLSA was amended by the Portal to Portal Act, 29 U.S.C. § 260 (1975), to make an award of liquidated damages discretionary where the court finds that the defendant both acted in

"good faith" and had "reasonable grounds for believing that [its] act or omission was not a violation" of the FLSA. This language has been interpreted to warrant the awarding of liquidated damages unless the employer comes forward and persuades the court that it has met both the subjective good faith standard and the objective standard of having reasonable grounds to believe its conduct did not violate the Act. See Soto v. Adams Elevator Equipment Co., 941 F.2d 543 (7th Cir.1991). Prejudgment interest on a backpay award will not be granted where liquidated damages are awarded. Moreover, as noted in the introductory paragraph in this Chapter, back pay is limited by the two or three year limitations provision of the FLSA and injunctive relief is unavailable in a private action. Injunctive relief is available, however, if the EEOC files suit under § 17 of the FLSA.

8. The issue of attorney fees is treated differently under the FLSA than it is under either Title VII, the Reconstruction Acts, the ADA or the Rehabilitation Act. First of all, § 16 of the FLSA makes the awarding of attorney fees by the court nondiscretionary in those instances where it is available. And second, the FLSA explicitly restricts the availability of attorney fees to prevailing *plaintiffs*, rather than to prevailing parties.

9. A jury trial is available under the EPA on the issues of liability and back pay. The court decides whether or not to award liquidated damages. See Lorillard v. Pons, 434 U.S. 575, 98 S.Ct. 866, 55 L.Ed.2d 40 (1978); Altman v. Stevens Fashion Fabrics, 441 F.Supp. 1318,1323 (N.D.Cal.1977).

COUNTY OF WASHINGTON v. GUNTHER

Supreme Court of the United States, 1981.
452 U.S. 161, 101 S.Ct. 2242, 68 L.Ed.2d 751.

JUSTICE BRENNAN delivered the opinion of the Court.

The question presented is whether § 703(h) of Title VII of the Civil Rights Act of 1964 restricts Title VII's prohibition of sex-based wage discrimination to claims of equal pay for equal work.

I

This case arises over the payment by petitioner, the County of Washington, Or., of substantially lower wages to female guards in the female section of the county jail than it paid to male guards in the male section of the jail. Respondents are four women who were employed to guard female prisoners and to carry out certain other functions in the jail.[2] In January 1974, the county eliminated the female section of the jail, transferred the female prisoners to the jail of a nearby county, and discharged respondents.

Respondents filed suit against petitioner in Federal District Court

2. Oregon requires that female inmates be guarded solely by women, Or.Rev.Stat. §§ 137.350, 137.360, and the District Court opinion indicates that women had not been employed to guard male prisoners. For purposes of this litigation, respondents concede that gender is a bona fide occupation-

under Title VII, seeking backpay and other relief.[3] They alleged that they were paid unequal wages for work substantially equal to that performed by male guards, and in the alternative, that part of the pay differential was attributable to intentional sex discrimination. The latter allegation was based on a claim that, because of intentional discrimination, the county set the pay scale for female guards, but not for male guards, at a level lower than that warranted by its own survey of outside markets and the worth of the jobs.

After trial, the District Court found that the male guards supervised more than 10 times as many prisoners per guard as did the female guards, and that the females devoted much of their time to less-valuable clerical duties. It therefore held that respondents' jobs were not substantially equal to those of the male guards, and that respondents were thus not entitled to equal pay. The Court of Appeals affirmed on that issue, and respondents do not seek review of the ruling.

The District Court also dismissed respondents' claim that the discrepancy in pay between the male and female guards was attributable in part to intentional sex discrimination. It held as a matter of law that a sex-based wage discrimination claim cannot be brought under Title VII unless it would satisfy the equal work standard of the Equal Pay Act. The Court therefore permitted no additional evidence on this claim, and made no findings on whether petitioner's pay scales for female guards resulted from intentional sex discrimination.

The Court of Appeals reversed, holding that persons alleging sex discrimination "are not precluded from suing under Title VII to protest * * * discriminatory compensation practices" merely because their jobs were not equal to higher-paying jobs held by members of the opposite sex. The Court remanded to the District Court with instructions to take evidence on respondents' claim that part of the difference between their rate of pay and that of the male guards is attributable to sex discrimination. We granted certiorari, and now affirm.

We emphasize at the outset the narrowness of the question before us in this case. Respondents' claim is not based on the controversial concept of "comparable worth," under which plaintiffs might claim increased compensation on the basis of a comparison of the intrinsic worth or difficulty of their job with that of other jobs in the same organization or community. Rather, respondents seek to prove, by direct evidence, that their wages were depressed because of intentional sex discrimination, consisting of setting the wage scale for female guards, but not for male guards, at a level lower than its own survey of outside markets and the worth of the jobs warranted. The narrow

al qualification for some of the female guard positions.

3. Respondents could not sue under the Equal Pay Act because the Equal Pay Act did not apply to municipal employees until passage of the Fair Labor Standards Amendments of 1974. Title VII has applied to such employees since passage of the Equal Employment Opportunity Act of 1972.

question in this case is whether such a claim is precluded by the last sentence of § 703(h) of Title VII, called the "Bennett Amendment." [8]

Title VII makes it an unlawful employment practice for an employer "to discriminate against any individual with respect to his compensation, terms, conditions, or privileges of employment, because of such individual's * * * sex * * *." The Bennett Amendment to Title VII, however provides:

> "It shall not be an unlawful employment practice under this subchapter for any employer to differentiate upon the basis of sex in determining the amount of the wages or compensation paid or to be paid to employees of such employer if such differentiation is authorized by the provisions of section 206(d) of title 29."

To discover what practices are exempted from Title VII's prohibitions by the Bennett Amendment, we must turn to * * * the Equal Pay Act * * *. On its face, the Equal Pay Act contains three restrictions pertinent to this case. First, its coverage is limited to those employers subject to the Fair Labor Standards Act. Thus, the Act does not apply, for example, to certain businesses engaged in retail sales, fishing, agriculture, and newspaper publishing. Second, the Act is restricted to cases involving "equal work on jobs the performance of which requires equal skill, effort, and responsibility, and which are performed under similar working conditions." Third, the Act's four affirmative defenses exempt any wage differentials attributable to seniority, merit, quantity or quality of production, or "any other factor other than sex."

Petitioner argues that the purpose of the Bennett Amendment was to restrict Title VII sex-based wage discrimination claims to those that could also be brought under the Equal Pay Act, and thus that claims not arising from "equal work" are precluded. Respondents, in contrast, argue that the Bennett Amendment was designed merely to incorporate the four affirmative defenses of the Equal Pay Act into Title VII for sex-based wage discrimination claims. Respondents thus contend that claims for sex-based wage discrimination can be brought under Title VII even though no member of the opposite sex holds an equal but higher-paying job, provided that the challenged wage rate is not based on seniority, merit, quantity or quality of production, or "any other factor other than sex." The Court of Appeals found respondents' interpretation the "more persuasive." While recognizing that the language and legislative history of the provision are not unambiguous, we conclude that the Court of Appeals was correct.

The language of the Bennett Amendment suggests an intention to incorporate only the affirmative defenses of the Equal Pay Act into Title VII. The Amendment bars sex-based wage discrimination claims

---

8. We are not called upon in this case to decide whether respondents have stated a prima facie case of sex discrimination under Title VII, or to lay down standards for the further conduct of this litigation. The sole issue we decide is whether respondents' failure to satisfy the equal work standard of the Equal Pay Act in itself precludes their proceeding under Title VII.

under Title VII where the pay differential is "authorized" by the Equal Pay Act. Although the word "authorize" sometimes means simply "to permit," it ordinarily denotes affirmative enabling action. * * * The question, then, is what wage practices have been affirmatively authorized by the Equal Pay Act.

The Equal Pay Act is divided into two parts: a definition of the violation, followed by four affirmative defenses. The first part can hardly be said to "authorize" anything at all: it is purely prohibitory. The second part, however, in essence "authorizes" employers to differentiate in pay on the basis of seniority, merit, quantity or quality of production, or any other factor other than sex, even though such differentiation might otherwise violate the Act. It is to these provisions, therefore, that the Bennett Amendment must refer.

Petitioner argues that this construction of the Bennett Amendment would render it superfluous. Petitioner claims that the first three affirmative defenses are simply redundant of the provisions elsewhere in § 703(h) of Title VII that already exempt bona fide seniority and merit systems and systems measuring earnings by quantity or quality of production, and that the fourth defense—"any other factor other than sex"—is implicit in Title VII's general prohibition of sex-based discrimination.

We cannot agree. The Bennett Amendment was offered as a "technical amendment" designed to resolve any potential conflicts between Title VII and the Equal Pay Act. Thus, with respect to the first three defenses, the Bennett Amendment has the effect of guaranteeing that courts and administrative agencies adopt a consistent interpretation of like provisions in both statutes. Otherwise, they might develop inconsistent bodies of case law interpreting two sets of nearly identical language.

More importantly, incorporation of the fourth affirmative defense could have significant consequences for Title VII litigation. Title VII's prohibition of discriminatory employment practices was intended to be broadly inclusive, proscribing "not only overt discrimination but also practices that are fair in form, but discriminatory in operation." Griggs v. Duke Power Co. The structure of Title VII litigation, including presumptions, burdens of proof, and defenses, has been designed to reflect this approach. The fourth affirmative defense of the Equal Pay Act, however, was designed differently, to confine the application of the Act to wage differentials attributable to sex discrimination. Equal Pay Act litigation, therefore, has been structured to permit employers to defend against charges of discrimination where their pay differentials are based on a bona fide use of "other factors other than sex." Under the Equal Pay Act, the courts and administrative agencies are not permitted "to substitute their judgment for the judgment of the employer * * * who [has] established and employed a bona fide job rating system," so long as it does not discriminate on the basis of sex. 109 Cong.Rec. 9209 (statement of Rep. Goodell, principal exponent of the

Act). Although we do not decide in this case how sex-based wage discrimination litigation under Title VII should be structured to accommodate the fourth affirmative defense of the Equal Pay Act, we consider it clear that the Bennett Amendment, under this interpretation, is not rendered superfluous.

We therefore conclude that only differentials attributable to the four affirmative defenses of the Equal Pay Act are "authorized" by that Act within the meaning of § 703(h) of Title VII.[14]

* * *

Our interpretation of the Bennett Amendment draws additional support from the remedial purposes of Title VII and the Equal Pay Act. Section 703(a) of Title VII makes it unlawful for an employer "to fail or refuse to hire or to discharge any individual, or *otherwise to discriminate* against any individual with respect to his compensation, terms, conditions, or privileges of employment" because of such individual's sex. (emphasis added). As Congress itself has indicated, a "broad approach" to the definition of equal employment opportunity is essential to overcoming and undoing the effect of discrimination. S.Rep.No. 867, 88th Cong., 2d Sess., 12 (1964). We must therefore avoid interpretations of Title VII that deprive victims of discrimination of a remedy, without clear congressional mandate.

Under petitioner's reading of the Bennett Amendment, only those sex-based wage discrimination claims that satisfy the "equal work" standard of the Equal Pay Act could be brought under Title VII. In practical terms, this means that a woman who is discriminatorily underpaid could obtain no relief—no matter how egregious the discrimination might be—unless her employer also employed a man in an equal job in the same establishment, at a higher rate of pay. Thus, if an employer hired a woman for a unique position in the company and then admitted that her salary would have been higher had she been male, the woman would be unable to obtain legal redress under petitioner's interpretation. Similarly, if an employer used a transparently sex-biased system for wage determination, women holding jobs not equal to those held by men would be denied the right to prove that the system is a pretext for discrimination. Moreover, to cite an example arising from a recent case, Los Angeles Department of Water & Power v. Manhart, 435 U.S. 702, 98 S.Ct. 1370, 55 L.Ed.2d 657 (1978), if the employer required its female workers to pay more into its pension program than male workers were required to pay, the only women who

---

14. The argument in the dissent that under our interpretation, the Equal Pay Act would be impliedly repealed and rendered a nullity is mistaken. Not only might the substantive provisions of the Equal Pay Act's affirmative defenses affect the outcome of some Title VII sex-based wage discrimination cases, but the procedural characteristics of the Equal Pay Act also remain significant. For example, the statute of limitations for backpay relief is more generous under the Equal Pay Act than under Title VII, and the Equal Pay Act, unlike Title VII, has no requirement of filing administrative complaints and awaiting administrative conciliation efforts. Given these advantages, many plaintiffs will prefer to sue under the Equal Pay Act rather than Title VII.

could bring a Title VII action under petitioner's interpretation would be those who could establish that a man performed equal work: a female auditor thus might have a cause of action while a female secretary might not. Congress surely did not intend the Bennett Amendment to insulate such blatantly discriminatory practices from judicial redress under Title VII.[19]

Moreover, petitioner's interpretation would have other far-reaching consequences. Since it rests on the proposition that any wage differentials not prohibited by the Equal Pay Act are "authorized" by it, petitioner's interpretation would lead to the conclusion that discriminatory compensation by employers not covered by the Fair Labor Standards Act is "authorized"—since not prohibited—by the Equal Pay Act. Thus it would deny Title VII protection against sex-based wage discrimination by those employers not subject to the Fair Labor Standards Act but covered by Title VII. There is no persuasive evidence that Congress intended such a result, and the EEOC has rejected it since at least 1965. Indeed, petitioner itself apparently acknowledges that Congress intended Title VII's broader coverage to apply to equal pay claims under Title VII, thus impliedly admitting the fallacy in its own argument.

* * *

Petitioner argues strenuously that the approach of the Court of Appeals places "the pay structure of virtually every employer and the entire economy * * * at risk and subject to scrutiny by the federal courts." It raises the spectre that "Title VII plaintiffs could draw any type of comparison imaginable concerning job duties and pay between any job predominantly performed by women and any job predominantly performed by men." But whatever the merit of petitioner's arguments in other contexts, they are inapplicable here, for claims based on the type of job comparisons petitioner describes are manifestly different from respondents' claim. Respondents contend that the County of Washington evaluated the worth of their jobs; that the county determined that they should be paid approximately 95% as much as the male correctional officers; that it paid them only about 70% as much, while paying the male officers the full evaluated worth of their jobs; and that the failure of the county to pay respondents the full evaluated worth of their jobs can be proven to be attributable to intentional sex discrimination. Thus, respondents' suit does not require a court to make its own subjective assessment of the value of the male and female guard jobs, or to attempt by statistical technique or other method to quantify the effect of sex discrimination on the wage rates.

---

19. The dissent attempts to minimize the significance of the Title VII remedy in these cases on the ground that the Equal Pay Act already provides an action for sex-biased wage discrimination by women who hold jobs not *currently* held by men. But the dissent's position would still leave remediless all victims of discrimination who hold jobs *never* held by men.

We do not decide in this case the precise contours of lawsuits challenging sex discrimination in compensation under Title VII. It is sufficient to note that respondents' claims of discriminatory undercompensation are not barred by § 703(h) of Title VII merely because respondents do not perform work equal to that of male jail guards. The judgment of the Court of Appeals is therefore

Affirmed.

JUSTICE REHNQUIST, with whom THE CHIEF JUSTICE, JUSTICE STEWART, and JUSTICE POWELL join, dissenting.

The Court today holds a plaintiff may state a claim of sex-based wage discrimination under Title VII without even establishing that she has performed "equal or substantially equal work" to that of males as defined in the Equal Pay Act. Because I believe that the legislative history of both the Equal Pay Act and Title VII clearly establishes that there can be no Title VII claim of sex-based wage discrimination without proof of "equal work," I dissent.

Because the Court never comes to grips with petitioners' argument, it is necessary to restate it here. Petitioners argue that Congress in adopting the Equal Pay Act of 1963 specifically addressed the problem of sex-based wage discrimination and determined that there should be a remedy for claims of unequal pay for equal work, but not for "comparable" work. Petitioners further observe that nothing in the legislative history of Title VII, enacted just one year later in 1964, reveals an intent to overrule that determination. Quite the contrary, petitioner notes that the legislative history of Title VII, including the adoption of the so-called Bennett Amendment, demonstrates Congress' intent to require all sex-based wage discrimination claims, whether brought under the Equal Pay Act or under Title VII, to satisfy the "equal work" standard. Because respondents have not satisfied the "equal work" standard, petitioners conclude that they have not stated a claim under Title VII.

In rejecting that argument, the Court ignores traditional canons of statutory construction and relevant legislative history. * * * It insists that there simply *must* be a remedy for wage discrimination *beyond* that provided in the Equal Pay Act. The Court does not explain *why* that must be so, nor does it explain *what* that remedy might be. And, of course, the Court cannot explain why it and not Congress is charged with determining what is and what is not sound public policy.

The closest the Court can come in giving a reason for its decision is its belief that interpretations of Title VII which "deprive victims of discrimination of a remedy, without clear congressional mandate" must be avoided. But that analysis turns traditional canons of statutory construction on their head. It has long been the rule that when a legislature enacts a statute to protect a class of persons, the burden is on the plaintiff to show statutory coverage, not on the defendant to show that there is a "clear congressional mandate" for *excluding* the plaintiff from coverage. Such a departure from traditional rules is particularly unwarranted in this case, where the doctrine of *in pari materia* suggests that all claims of sex-based wage discrimination are governed by the substantive standards of the previously enacted and more specific legislation, the Equal Pay Act.

Because the decision does not rest on any reasoned statement of logic or principle, it provides little guidance to employers or lower courts as to what types of compensation practices might now violate Title VII. The Court correctly emphasizes that its decision is narrow, and indeed one searches the Court's opinion in vain for a hint as to what pleadings or proof other than that adduced in this particular case, would be sufficient to state a claim of sex-based wage discrimination under Title VII. * * * All we know is that Title VII provides a remedy when, as here, plaintiffs seek to show by *direct* evidence that their employer *intentionally* depressed their wages. And, for reasons that go largely unexplained, we also know that a Title VII remedy may not be available to plaintiffs who allege theories different than that alleged here, such as the so-called "comparable worth" theory. One has the sense that the decision today will be treated like a restricted railroad ticket, "good for this day and train only."

In the end, however, the flaw with today's decision is not so much that it is so narrowly written as to be virtually meaningless, but rather that its legal analysis is wrong. The Court is obviously more interested in the consequences of its decision than in discerning the intention of Congress. In reaching its desired result, the Court conveniently and persistently ignores relevant legislative history and instead relies wholly on what it believes Congress *should* have enacted.

The starting point for any discussion of sex-based wage discrimination claims must be the Equal Pay Act of 1963, enacted as an amendment to the Fair Labor Standards Act of 1938. It was there that Congress, after 18 months of careful and exhaustive study, specifically addressed the problem of sex-based wage discrimination. The Equal Pay Act states that employers shall not discriminate on the basis of sex by paying different wages for jobs that require equal skill, effort, and responsibility. In adopting the "equal pay for equal work" formula, Congress carefully considered and ultimately rejected the "equal pay for comparable worth" standard advanced by respondents and several *amici*. As the legislative history of the Equal Pay Act amply demonstrates, Congress realized that the adoption of the comparable worth doctrine would ignore the economic realities of supply and demand and would involve both governmental agencies and courts in the impossible task of ascertaining the worth of comparable work, an area in which they have little expertise.

* * *

* * * Instead, Congress concluded that governmental intervention to equalize wage differentials was to be undertaken only within one circumstance: when men's and women's jobs were identical or nearly

so, hence unarguably of equal worth. It defies common sense to believe that the same Congress—which, after 18 months of hearings and debates, had decided in 1963 upon the extent of federal involvement it desired in the area of wage rate claims—intended *sub silentio* to reject all of this work and to abandon the limitations of the equal work approach just one year later, when it enacted Title VII.

* * * The question is whether Congress intended to completely turn its back on the "equal work" standard enacted in the Equal Pay Act of 1963 when it adopted Title VII only one year later.

The Court answers that question in the affirmative, concluding that Title VII must be read more broadly than the Equal Pay Act. In so holding, the majority wholly ignores this Court's repeated adherence to the doctrine of *in pari materia*, namely, that "where there is no clear intention otherwise, a specific statute will not be controlled or nullified by a general one, regardless of the priority of enactment." * * *

Applying those principles to this case, there can be no doubt that the Equal Pay Act and Title VII should be construed *in pari materia*. The Equal Pay Act is the more specific piece of legislation, dealing solely with sex-based wage discrimination, and was the product of exhaustive congressional study. Title VII, by contrast, is a general antidiscrimination provision, passed with virtually no consideration of the specific problem of sex-based wage discrimination. See *General Electric Co. v. Gilbert*, 429 U.S. 125, 143, 97 S.Ct. 401, 411, 50 L.Ed.2d 343 (1976) (the legislative history of the sex discrimination amendment is "notable primarily for its brevity").[4] Most significantly, there is absolutely nothing in the legislative history of Title VII which reveals an intent by Congress to repeal by implication the provisions of the Equal Pay Act. Quite the contrary, what little legislative history there is on the subject * * * indicates that Congress intended to incorporate the substantive standards of the Equal Pay Act into Title VII so that sex-based wage discrimination claims would be governed by the equal work standard of the Equal Pay Act and by that standard alone. * * *

* * *

In response to questions by Senator Dirksen, Senator Clark, the floor manager for the bill, prepared a memorandum in which he attempted to put to rest certain objections which he believed to be unfounded. Senator Clark's answer to Senator Dirksen reveals that Senator Clark believed that all cases of wage discrimination under Title VII would be treated under the standards of the Equal Pay Act:

---

4. Indeed, Title VII was originally intended to protect the rights of Negroes. On the final day of consideration by the entire House, Representative Smith added an amendment to prohibit sex discrimination. It has been speculated that the amendment was added as an attempt to thwart passage of Title VII. The amendment was passed by the House that same day, and the entire bill was approved two days later and sent to the Senate without any consideration of the effect of the amendment on the Equal Pay Act. The attenuated history of the sex amendment to Title VII makes it difficult to believe that Congress thereby intended to wholly abandon the carefully crafted equal work standard of the Equal Pay Act.

"*Objection.* The sex anti-discrimination provisions of the bill duplicate the coverage of the Equal Pay Act of 1963. But more than this, they extend far beyond the scope and coverage of the Equal Pay Act. *They do not include the limitation in that Act with respect to equal work on jobs requiring equal skills in the same establishments, and thus, cut across different jobs.*

"*Answer.* The Equal Pay Act is a part of the Wage Hour Law, with different coverage and with numerous exemptions unlike Title VII. Furthermore, under Title VII, jobs can no longer be classified as to sex, except where there is a rational basis for discrimination on the ground of bona fide occupational qualification. *The standards in the Equal Pay Act for determining discrimination as to wages, of course, are applicable to the comparable situation under Title VII.*" 110 Cong. Rec. 7217 (1964) (emphasis added).

In this passage, Senator Clark asserted that the sex discrimination provisions of Title VII were necessary, notwithstanding the Equal Pay Act, because (a) the Equal Pay Act had numerous exemptions for various types of businesses, and (b) Title VII covered discrimination in access (e.g., assignment and promotion) to jobs, not just compensation. In addition, Senator Clark made clear that in the compensation area the equal work standard would continue to be the applicable standard. He explained, in answer to Senator Dirksen's concern, that when *different jobs* were at issue, the Equal Pay Act's legal standards—the "equal work" standard—would apply to limit the reach of Title VII. Thus Senator Clark rejected as unfounded the objections that the sex provisions of Title VII were unnecessary on the one hand, or extended beyond the equal work standard on the other.

Notwithstanding Senator Clark's explanation, Senator Bennett remained concerned that, absent an explicit cross reference to the Equal Pay Act, the "wholesale assertion" of the word "sex" in Title VII could nullify the carefully conceived Equal Pay Act standard. 110 Cong.Rec. 13647 (1964). Accordingly, he offered, and the Senate accepted, the * * * amendment to Title VII * * *.

Although the language of the Bennett Amendment is ambiguous, the most plausible interpretation of the Amendment is that it incorporates the substantive standard of the Equal Pay Act—the equal pay for equal work standard—into Title VII. A number of considerations support that view. In the first place, that interpretation is wholly consistent with, and in fact confirms, Senator Clark's earlier explanation of Title VII. Second, in the limited time available to Senator Bennett when he offered his amendment—the time for debate having been limited by cloture—he explained the Amendment's purpose.

"Mr. President, after many years of yearning by members of the fair sex in this country, and after careful study by the appropriate committees of Congress, last year Congress passed the so-called Equal Pay Act, which became effective only yesterday.

"By this time, programs have been established for the effective administration of this Act. Now when the Civil Rights Bill is under consideration in which the word sex has been inserted in many places, I do not believe sufficient attention may have been paid to possible conflicts between the wholesale insertion of the word sex in the bill and the Equal Pay Act. *The purpose of my amendment is to provide that in the event of conflicts, the provisions of the Equal Pay Act shall not be nullified.*" 110 Cong.Rec. 13647 (1964) (emphasis supplied).

It is obvious that the principal way in which the Equal Pay Act could be "nullified" would be to allow plaintiffs unable to meet the "equal pay for equal work" standard to proceed under Title VII asserting some other theory of wage discrimination, such as "comparable worth." If plaintiffs can proceed under Title VII without showing that they satisfy the "equal work" criterion of the Equal Pay Act, one would expect all plaintiffs to file suit under the "broader" Title VII standard. Such a result would, for all practical purposes, constitute an implied repeal of the equal work standard of the Equal Pay Act and render that Act a nullity. This was precisely the result Congress sought to avert when it adopted the Bennett Amendment, and the result the Court today embraces.

Senator Bennett confirmed this interpretation just one year later. The Senator expressed concern as to the proper interpretation of his Amendment and offered his written understanding of the Amendment.

"The Amendment therefore means that it is not an unlawful employment practice: * * * (b) to have different standards of compensation for nonexempt employees, where such differentiation is not prohibited by the Equal Pay Amendment to the Fair Labor Standards Act.

"Simply stated, *the [Bennett] Amendment means that discrimination and compensation on account of sex does not violate Title VII unless it also violates that Equal Pay Act.*" 111 Cong.Rec. 13359 (1965) (emphasis supplied).

Senator Dirksen agreed that this interpretation was "precisely" the one that he, Senator Humphrey, and their staffs had in mind when the Senate adopted the Bennett Amendment. He added, "I trust that that will suffice to clear up in the minds of anyone, whether in the Department of Justice or elsewhere, what the Senate intended when that Amendment was accepted." [6]

* * *

6. There is undoubtedly some danger in relying on subsequent legislative history. But that does not mean that such subsequent legislative history is wholly irrelevant, particularly where, as here, the *sponsor* of the legislation makes a clarifying statement which is not inconsistent with the prior ambiguous legislative history.

The Court suggests Senator Bennett's 1965 comments should be discounted because Senator Clark criticized them. Senator Clark did indeed criticize Senator Ben-

The Court blithely ignores all of his legislative history and chooses to interpret the Bennett Amendment as incorporating only the Equal Pay Act's four affirmative defenses, and not the equal work requirement.[10] That argument does not survive scrutiny. In the first place, the language of the amendment draws no distinction between the Equal Pay Act's standard for liability—equal pay for equal work—and the Act's defenses. Nor does any Senator or Congressman even come close to suggesting that the Amendment incorporates the Equal Pay Act's affirmative defenses into Title VII, but not the equal work standard itself. Quite the contrary, the concern was that Title VII would render the Equal Pay Act a nullity. It is only too obvious that reading just the four affirmative defenses of the Equal Pay Act into Title VII does not protect the careful draftsmanship of the Equal Pay Act. * * * In this case, it stands Congress' concern on its head to suppose that Congress sought to incorporate the affirmative defenses, but not the equal work standard. It would be surprising if Congress in 1964 sought to reverse its decision in 1963 to require a showing of "equal work" as a predicate to an equal pay claim and at the same time carefully preserve the four affirmative defenses.

Moreover, even on its own terms the Court's argument is unpersuasive. The Equal Pay Act contains four statutory defenses: different compensation is permissible if the differential is made by way of (1) a seniority system, (2) a merit system, (3) a system which measures earnings by quantity or quality of production, or (4) is based on any other factor other than sex. The flaw in interpreting the Bennett Amendment as incorporating only the four defenses of the Equal Pay Act into Title VII is that Title VII, even without the Bennett Amendment, contains those very same defenses. The opening sentence of § 703(h) protects differentials and compensation based on seniority, merit, or quantity or quality of production. These are three of the four

nett, but only because Senator Clark read Senator Bennett's explanation as suggesting that Title VII protection would not be available to those employees not within the Equal Pay Act's coverage. Senator Clark's view was that employees not covered by the Equal Pay Act could still bring Title VII claims. He did not dispute, however, the proposition that the "equal work" standard of the Equal Pay Act was incorporated into Title VII claims. Quite the contrary, Senator Clark placed into the record a letter from the Chairman of the National Committee for Equal Pay which stated that:

"Our best understanding of the implications of the [Bennett Amendment] at the time it was adopted was that its intent and effect was to make sure that equal pay would be applied and interpreted under the Civil Rights Act in the same way as under the earlier statute, the Equal Pay Act. *That is, the Equal*

*Pay Act standards, requiring equal work * * * would also be applied under the Civil Rights Act."*

10. In reaching this conclusion, the Court relies far too heavily on a definition of the word "authorize." Rather than "make a fortress out of the dictionary," the Court should instead attempt to implement the legislative intent of Congress. Even if dictionary definitions were to be our guide, the word "authorized" has been defined to mean exactly what petitioners contend. Black's Law Dictionary defines "authorized" to mean "to permit a thing to be done in the future." (4th ed. 1968). Accordingly, the language of the Bennett Amendment suggests that those differentiations which are authorized under the Equal Pay Act—and thus Title VII—are those based on "skill, effort, responsibility and working conditions" and those related to the four affirmative defenses. * * *

EPA defenses. The fourth EPA defense, "a factor other than sex," is already implicit in Title VII because the statute's prohibition of sex discrimination applies only if there is discrimination on the basis of sex. Under the Court's interpretation, the Bennett Amendment, the second sentence of § 703(h), is mere surplusage. The Court's answer to this argument is curious. It suggests that repetition ensures that the provisions would be consistently interpreted by the courts. But that answer only speaks to the purpose for incorporating the defenses in each statute, not for stating the defenses twice in the same statute. Courts are not quite as dense as the majority assumes.

In sum, Title VII and the Equal Pay Act, read together, provide a balanced approach to resolving sex-based wage discrimination claims. Title VII guarantees that qualified female employees will have access to all jobs, and the Equal Pay Act assures that men and women performing the same work will be paid equally. Congress intended to remedy wage discrimination through the Equal Pay Act standards, whether suit is brought under that statute or under Title VII. What emerges is that Title VII would have been construed *in pari materia* even without the Bennett Amendment, and that the Amendment serves simply to insure that the equal work standard would be the standard by which all wage compensation claims would be judged.

Perhaps recognizing that there is virtually no support for its position in the legislative history, the Court rests its holding on its belief that any other holding would be unacceptable public policy. It argues that there must be remedy for wage discrimination beyond that provided for in the Equal Pay Act. Quite apart from the fact that that is an issue properly left to Congress and not the Court, the Court is wrong even as a policy matter. The Court's parade of horribles that would occur absent a distinct Title VII remedy simply do not support the result it reaches.

First, the Court contends that a separate Title VII remedy is necessary to remedy the situation where an employer admits to a female worker, hired for a unique position, that her compensation would have been higher had she been male. Stated differently, the Court insists that an employer could isolate a predominantly female job category and arbitrarily cut its wages because no men currently perform equal or substantially equal work. But a Title VII remedy is unnecessary in these cases because an Equal Pay Act remedy is available. Under the Equal Pay Act, it is not necessary that every Equal Pay Act violation be established through proof that members of the opposite sex are *currently* performing equal work for greater pay. However, unlikely such an admission might be in the bullpen of litigation, an employer's statement that "if my female employees performing a particular job were males, I would pay them more simply because they are males" would be admissible in a suit under that Act. Overt discrimination does not go unremedied by the Equal Pay Act. In addition, insofar as hiring or placement discrimination caused the isolated job category, Title VII already provides numerous remedies (such as backpay, transfer and constructive seniority) without resort to job comparisons. In short, if women are limited to low paying jobs against their will, they have adequate remedies under Title VII for denial of job opportunities even under what I believe is the correct construction of the Bennett Amendment.

The Court next contends that absent a Title VII remedy, women who work for employers exempted from coverage of the Equal Pay Act would be wholly without a remedy for wage discrimination. The Court misapprehends petitioners' argument. As Senator Clark explained in his memorandum, Congress sought to incorporate into Title VII the substantive standard of the Equal Pay Act—the "equal work" standard—not the employee coverage provisions. Thus, to say that the "equal pay for equal work" standard is incorporated into Title VII does not mean that employees are precluded from bringing compensation discrimination claims under Title VII. It means only that if employees choose to proceed under Title VII, they must show that they have been deprived of "equal pay for equal work."

There is of course a situation in which petitioners' position *would* deny women a remedy for claims of sex-based wage discrimination. A remedy would not be available where a lower paying job held primarily by women is "comparable," but not substantially equal to, a higher paying job performed by men. That is, plaintiffs would be foreclosed from showing that they received unequal pay for work of "comparable worth" or that dissimilar jobs are of "equal worth." The short, and best, answer to that contention is that Congress in 1963 explicitly chose not to provide a remedy in such cases. And contrary to the suggestion of the Court, it is by no means clear that Title VII was enacted to remedy *all* forms of alleged discrimination. * * * Congress balanced the need for a remedy for wage discrimination against its desire to avoid the burdens associated with governmental intervention into wage structures. The Equal Pay Act's "equal pay for equal work" formula reflects the outcome of this legislative balancing. In construing Title VII, therefore, the courts cannot be indifferent to this sort of political compromise.

Even though today's opinion reaches what I believe to be the wrong result, its narrow holding is perhaps its saving feature. The opinion does not endorse the so-called "comparable worth" theory: though the Court does not indicate how a plaintiff might establish a prima facie case under Title VII, the Court does suggest that allegations of unequal pay for unequal, but comparable, work will not state a claim on which relief may be granted. The Court, for example, repeatedly emphasizes that this is not a case where plaintiffs ask the court to compare the value of dissimilar jobs or to quantify the effect of sex discrimination on wage rates. * * *

Given that implied repeals of legislation are disfavored, we should not be surprised that the Court disassociates itself from the entire notion of "comparable worth." In enacting the Equal Pay Act in 1963, Congress specifically prohibited the courts from comparing the wage rates of dissimilar jobs: there can only be a comparison of wage rates where jobs are "equal or substantially equal." Because the legislative history of Title VII does not reveal an intent to overrule that determination, the courts should strive to harmonize the intent of Congress in enacting the Equal Pay Act with its intent in enacting Title VII. Where, as here, the policy of prior legislation is clearly expressed, the Court should not "transfuse the successor statute with a gloss of its own choosing."

Because there are no logical underpinnings to the Court's opinion, all we may conclude is that even absent a showing of equal work there is a cause of action under Title VII where there is direct evidence that an employer has *intentionally* depressed a woman's salary because she is a woman. The decision today does not approve a cause of action based on a *comparison* of the wage rates of dissimilar jobs.

For the foregoing reasons, however, I believe that even that narrow holding cannot be supported by the legislative history of the Equal Pay Act and Title VII. This is simply a case where the Court has superimposed upon Title VII a "gloss of its own choosing."

NOTES AND PROBLEMS FOR DISCUSSION

1. The Court in *Gunther* only went so far as to permit a litigant to bring an action for intentional sex-based wage discrimination under Title VII without satisfying the EPA's equal work standard. It left to the lower courts, however, the difficult task of formulating the proof standards to be applied to plaintiffs in such cases. In WILKINS v. UNIVERSITY OF HOUSTON, 654 F.2d 388 (5th Cir.1981), vacated and remanded, 459 U.S. 809, 103 S.Ct. 34, 74 L.Ed.2d 47 (1982), affirmed on remand, 695 F.2d 134 (5th Cir.1983), a post-*Gunther* case, the plaintiffs' Title VII claim was similar in theory to the one that had been asserted in *Gunther*. Their complaint alleged that the University evaluated all of the jobs held by its professional and administrative staff employees and classified each of them into one of nine levels. Although they did not offer evidence that women were paid less than men for equal work, the plaintiffs did show that in the University's academic division, a disproportionate number of those employees paid less than the minimum salary established for the level of their jobs were women and that all of the employees who received a salary in excess of the maximum assigned to their job levels were men. This statistical evidence of disparate wage treatment effected through the discriminatory application of a job classification system, the court held, established a prima facie Title VII violation.

Another issue that was not raised directly in *Gunther* is whether the EPA "single establishment" requirement applies to Title VII gender-based wage discrimination claims. Nevertheless, relying on the general analytic approach taken by the Court in *Gunther,* several circuit courts have held that plaintiffs asserting sex-based wage discrimination claims under Title VII are not subject to the "single establishment" requirement of the Equal Pay Act. See e.g., Marcoux v. State of Maine, 797 F.2d 1100 (1st Cir.1986); Bartelt v. Berlitz

School of Languages of America, Inc., 698 F.2d 1003 (9th Cir.1983), cert. denied, 464 U.S. 915, 104 S.Ct. 277, 78 L.Ed.2d 257 (1983).

A more difficult question is posed by plaintiffs seeking recovery under a "comparable worth" theory. The *Gunther* court emphasized that the complaint before it did not rely on that concept and thus it specifically reserved decision on whether such a claim was cognizable under Title VII. The availability of a comparable worth cause of action has generated a measure of support among the commentators. See e.g., Gasaway, Comparable Worth: A Post–Gunther Overview, 69 Geo.L.J. 1123 (1981); Note, Equal Pay, Comparable Work, and Job Evaluation, 90 Yale L.J. 657 (1981). Under this theory, employees would be entitled to equal pay for jobs that are not substantially equal but are comparable in their value to the employer. This, its proponents contend, would respond to the general undervaluation of jobs traditionally dominated by women, which goes unremedied under traditional Equal Pay doctrine because of the absence of male workers in those positions. See Blumrosen, Wage Discrimination, Job Segregation and Title VII of the Civil Rights Act of 1964, 12 U.Mich.J.L.Ref. 397 (1979). Its opponents argue that such a theory would result in an unacceptable intrusion into the labor market and require courts to engage in a comparative appraisal of the value of unrelated jobs, an area in which they have little institutional expertise. In BRIGGS v. CITY OF MADISON, 536 F.Supp. 435 (W.D.Wis.1982), the first reported post-*Gunther* case addressing the comparable worth issue, the court rejected the contention that plaintiffs could establish a prima facie case of wage discrimination under Title VII simply by showing that women occupied a sex-segregated job classification in which they were paid less than men occupying a sex-segregated job classification. It added, however, that a prima facie violation could be established if the plaintiffs also proved that the female and male sex-segregated jobs were "similar" in their requirements of skill, effort, responsibility and working conditions and were of comparable value to the employer. In POWER v. BARRY COUNTY, 539 F.Supp. 721 (W.D.Mich.1982), on the other hand, the court refused to recognize the plaintiff's Title VII comparable worth-based claim. Referring to *Gunther*, the court stated:

> A review of the legislative history leads me to conclude that the Supreme Court's recognition of intentional discrimination may well signal the outer limit of the legal theories cognizable under Title VII. There is no indication in Title VII's legislative history that the boundaries of the Act can be expanded to encompass the theory of comparable worth. Nor is there convincing evidence that Congress intended to make such a theory available to those seeking redress for real or imaginary wage inequalities. Nothing in the legislative history indicates support for an independent claim of recovery where the outcome of the case is dependent upon a court's evaluation of the relative worth of two distinct jobs. * * * [I]f Plaintiffs are able to demonstrate their wages are lower solely because they are women, then a claim under Title VII will exist. That is a quantum leap from the theory of comparable worth advanced by plaintiffs, wherein the Court is required to evaluate the worth of different jobs and rank them according to their relative values. Similarly, the legislative history provided by Plaintiffs fails to buttress their intention that comparable worth is a cognizable and independent cause of action.

539 F.Supp. at 726. This same analysis was employed in Connecticut State Employees Ass'n v. State of Connecticut, 530 F.Supp. 618 (D.Ct.1982)(plaintiffs stated a Title VII claim of intentional discrimination where complaint alleged

that lower rates of compensation were paid for work which the employer had determined to be of comparable or equal value to dissimilar, higher-paying jobs.). See also Cox v. American Cast Iron Pipe Co., 784 F.2d 1546 (11th Cir.1986)(plaintiff can state Title VII claim when alleging that traditionally male jobs are compensated "objectively" based on system of detailed job descriptions, standardized evaluations, job classifications, pay scales and review provisions. While compensation for women's jobs is subjectively determined); Spaulding v. University of Washington, 740 F.2d 686 (9th Cir.), cert. denied, 469 U.S. 1036, 105 S.Ct. 511, 83 L.Ed.2d 401 (1984).

Suppose the plaintiff convinces the trial court that the employer has violated Title VII by intentionally depressing the wages in those job classifications in which women predominate. Would it make a difference if the plaintiff was a male employed in that female-dominated classification? Would a male plaintiff be a "person aggrieved" from discrimination "on the basis of sex"? The prevailing view in such cases is that the male plaintiffs do not have standing because they cannot allege that they are being discriminated because of *their* gender. See Patee v. Pacific Northwest Bell Tel. Co., 803 F.2d 476 (9th Cir.1986); AFSCME v. County of Nassau, 664 F.Supp. 64 (E.D.N.Y.1987). But see Allen v. American Home Foods, Inc., 644 F.Supp. 1553 (N.D.Ind.1986) (discharged male plaintiffs can state claim that company's decision to close one of its plants was based on predominance of women employees in that plant). For a suggestion that the prevailing view is inconsistent with the judiciary's treatment of standing in third party retaliation and hostile work environment cases, see Torrey, Indirect Discrimination Under Title VII: Expanding Male Standing To Sue For Injuries Received As A Result Of Employer Discrimination Against Females, 64 Wash.L.Rev. 365 (1989).

In Plemer v. Parsons–Gilbane, 713 F.2d 1127 (5th Cir.1983), a female plaintiff based her Title VII action on the claim that the dissimilarities between her and a male employee's jobs did not justify the differential in salary paid to these two employees. The court rejected this claim, stating that unless the plaintiff could show that the employer had assessed the value of the two jobs, it was not prepared to make a subjective assessment of the value of differing duties and responsibilities. Does this ruling imply that an employer is under no duty to make such assessments? Moreover, doesn't it discourage employers from undertaking job valuation studies for fear of facing statutory liability for their failure to adjust salary structures in light of the report?

The latter scenario befell the State of Washington in AFSCME v. STATE OF WASHINGTON, 578 F.Supp. 846 (W.D.Wa.1983). The State commissioned an independent study of civil service positions which concluded that clear indications of pay differences existed between job groups predominantly held by men and those predominantly held by women and that the jobs were of comparable worth. The report also computed the cost of eliminating discrimination. The outgoing Governor then included a budget appropriation to implement the report's recommendations in his proposed budget, but the incoming Governor took the appropriation out of her budget despite a state budget surplus large enough to finance the remedial measures. In addition, the state legislature took no action to implement the report until after the filing of the instant lawsuit. The court held that the State's failure to eliminate an admittedly discriminatory compensation system constituted an intentional violation of Title VII since it did not present convincing evidence of a good faith reason for its failure to pay women their evaluated worth. This judgment was reversed on appeal. 770 F.2d 1401 (9th Cir.1985). The Ninth

Circuit reasoned that employers should be commended rather than penalized for undertaking job evaluation studies and held, therefore, that the State's failure to adopt the recommendations of a study that it had commissioned did not establish the discriminatory motive required in a disparate treatment claim. It also rejected the plaintiff's attempt to challenge the State's compensation scheme under disproportionate impact analysis. The plaintiff had claimed that the State's policy of requiring that state employee salaries reflect prevailing market rates generated an adverse impact on women by perpetuating the historical pattern of paying lower wages to women. The court reasoned that disproportionate impact analysis was only applicable to cases challenging a "specific, clearly delineated" employment standard and not to situations, as here, where the employer's policy was based on a multitude of such complex factors as market surveys, administrative hearings and recommendations, budget proposals, executive actions and legislative enactments. Moreover, the court added, in terms of disparate treatment analysis, reliance on market rates did not raise an inference of discriminatory motive since the employer did not create the extant market disparity and had not been shown to have been motivated by sex-based considerations in its decision to rely on the market. To the contrary, the court declared, nothing in the legislative history of Title VII indicated that Congress intended to prevent employers from competing in the labor market and relying on market forces in establishing their compensation schemes. Shortly after the ruling by the Ninth Circuit, the parties reached an out-of-court settlement in which the State agreed to spend over $46 million to correct the sex-based inequities in its wage scales. The settlement provided for review and approval of its terms by the state legislature and the trial court. For more on this case, see Gender Discrimination: "Comparable Worth"—AFSCME v. Washington, 9 Harv.J.L. & Pub. Pol. 253 (1986).

Similarly, in BEARD v. WHITLEY COUNTY REMC, 656 F.Supp. 1461 (N.D.Ind.1987), the court held that an employer's decision not to grant a wage increase to office and clerical workers that was made in reliance on wage surveys did not constitute the type of policy that was subject to impact analysis. Employers, the court reasoned, are confronted by the market and respond to it simply as "price-takers." As a result, they cannot be said to be following their own "policy" in any meaningful sense. The court added that while the office and clerical staff consisted primarily of female employees, the single decision not to grant a wage increase did not constitute the type of "policy" or "practice" that is required to assert a claim of disproportionate impact. See generally, Weiler, The Wages Of Sex: The Uses and Limits of Comparable Worth, 99 Harv.L.Rev. 1728 (1986); Note, Market Value As A Factor "Other Than Sex" In Sex–Based Wage Discrimination Claims, 1985 U.Ill.L.Rev. 1027 (1985).

The Ninth Circuit's reasoning in *AFSCME* had been adumbrated by an Illinois federal trial court's decision in AMERICAN NURSES ASS'N v. STATE OF ILLINOIS, 606 F.Supp. 1313 (N.D.Ill.1985). There, the defendant had not implemented the findings of an evaluative study that it had funded and conducted. The court reasoned that the mere funding and performance of a study did not compel the employer to adopt its results and implement a wage scale that the study found to be more equitable than the existing schedule. To do otherwise, the court declared, would create a disincentive to employers to conduct job evaluation studies. Title VII, the court ruled, only required that any action taken as the result of such a study be undertaken on a nondiscriminatory basis. Thus, since the defendant here did not implement any of the findings of its report, it was found not to have violated the Act. This decision, however, was reversed by the Seventh Circuit. 783 F.2d 716 (7th Cir.1986). The appellate court agreed that "if all that the plaintiffs in this case are complaining about is the State of Illinois' failure to implement a comparable worth study, they have no case and it was properly dismissed." Similarly, it stated, no claim for intentional discrimination would lie if the refusal to implement the study had been intended as a reaffirmation of the State's commitment to pay market wages. But, the court concluded, the imprecise wording of the complaint permitted the interpretation that the plaintiffs were alleging intentionally discriminatory conduct actionable under Title VII, i.e., either that the State had refused to implement the study's recommendations because it believed that women should be paid less than men for equal work or that the State had refused to hire women for jobs traditionally reserved for men. Accordingly, it reversed the trial court's dismissal of the complaint and provided the plaintiffs with the opportunity to make additional efforts to prove a case of intentional discrimination. See also UAW v. State of Michigan, 886 F.2d 766 (6th Cir.1989)(plaintiff in so-called comparable worth action must prove intentional discrimination and comparable worth statistics alone are insufficient to establish intentional discrimination; intent also may not be inferred from either defendant's reliance on market factors or its failure to rectify disparities resulting from such reliance).

Is the Equal Pay Act ever relevant to a comparable worth claim? See Comparable Worth in the Equal Pay Act, 51 U.Chi.L.Rev. 1078 (1984). For more on the potential viability of comparable worth claims, see Loudon & Loudon, Applying Disparate Impact to Title VII Comparable Worth Claims: An Incomparable Task, 61 Ind.L.J. 165 (1986); Newman & Vonhof, Separate But Equal—Job Segregation and Pay Equity in the Wake of *Gunther*, 1981 U.Ill. L.Rev. 269 (1981); Note, Women, Wages and Title VII: The Significance of County of Washington v. Gunther, 43 U.Pitt.L.Rev. 467 (1982); Rhode, Occupational Inequality, 1988 Duke L.J. 1207 (1988); Fischel & Lazear, Comparable Worth and Discrimination in Labor Markets, 53 U.Chi.L.Rev. 891 (1986); Holzhauer, The Economic Possibilities of Comparable Worth, 53 U.Chi.L.Rev. 919 (1986); Becker, Barriers Facing Women in the Wage Labor Market and the Need for Additional Remedies: A Reply To Fischel and Lazear, 53 U.Chi.L.Rev. 934 (1986); Comparable Worth: A Rejoinder, 53 U.Chi.L.Rev. 950 (1986). For an interesting discussion of the applicability of the EPA, Title VII and comparable worth theory to part-time employees, see Chamallas, Women and Part–Time Work: The Case for Pay Equity and Equal Access, 64 N.Car.L.Rev. 709 (1986). And for a criticism of the view expressed by, *inter alia,* the Ninth Circuit in *AFSCME,* that disproportionate impact analysis is inapplicable to market-based compensation decisions, see Brown, Baumann & Melnick, Equal Pay For Jobs Of Comparable Worth: An Analysis Of The Rhetoric, 21 Harv.Civ.R.–Civ. L.L.Rev. 127 (1986); Comment, Comparable Worth, Disparate Impact and the Market Rate Salary Problem: A Legal Analysis & Statistical Application, 71 Cal.L.Rev. 730 (1983).

2. Assuming a plaintiff established a prima facie case of wage discrimination under Title VII, does the Court's treatment of the Bennett Amendment issue in *Gunther* suggest that the defendant in such a case must shoulder a heavier burden of proof than it would confront in a non-wage Title VII claim? Does *Gunther* suggest that *Burdine* will not apply to wage claims under Title VII? Moreover, did the Court imply that defendants in Title VII wage discrimi-

nation cases are limited to the four EPA defenses? Compare Fallon v. Illinois, 882 F.2d 1206 (7th Cir.1989); Crockwell v. Blackmon–Mooring Steamatic, Inc., 627 F.Supp. 800, 806 (W.D.Tenn.1985); Briggs v. City of Madison, 536 F.Supp. 435, 447–48, (W.D.Wis.1982) and Boyd v. Madison County Mutual Insurance Co., 653 F.2d 1173, 1177–78 (7th Cir.1981), cert. denied, 454 U.S. 1146, 102 S.Ct. 1008, 71 L.Ed.2d 299 (1982), with Kouba v. Allstate Insurance Co., 691 F.2d 873, 875 (9th Cir.1982); and Schulte v. Wilson Industries, Inc., 547 F.Supp. 324 (S.D.Tex.1982). If so, does this mean that the BFOQ defense is inapplicable to Title VII-based claims of compensation discrimination? Does the language of § 703(e) support such a conclusion? See Hodgson v. Robert Hall Clothes, Inc., 326 F.Supp. 1264 (D.Del.1971), modified on other grounds, 473 F.2d 589 (3d Cir.), cert. denied, 414 U.S. 866, 94 S.Ct. 50, 38 L.Ed.2d 85 (1973). Would it make a difference if the plaintiff's Title VII claim was or was not based on a claim of unequal pay for equal work? See McKee v. Bi–State Development Agency, 801 F.2d 1014, 1019 (8th Cir.1986)("Where a claim is for unequal pay for equal work based upon sex, the standards of the Equal Pay Act apply whether the suit alleges a violation of the Equal Pay Act or of Title VII".). See also Barnett, Comparable Worth and the Equal Pay Act—Proving Sex–Based Wage Discrimination Claims After Gunther, 28 Wayne L.Rev. 1669, 1692–1700 (1982).

3. Several states, including California (public employment only), North Dakota, Oklahoma, Oregon and South Dakota have passed statutes requiring employers to provide equal pay for comparable work.

4. To the extent that a federal employee's wage discrimination claim falls within the jurisdiction of Title VII as well as the Equal Pay Act, does the exclusivity rule announced by the Supreme Court in Brown v. G.S.A., supra at 549, preclude that individual from bringing an action under the EPA? See Epstein v. Secretary, U.S. Dept. of Treasury, 552 F.Supp. 436 (N.D.Ill.1982).

Chapter 10

THE AGE DISCRIMINATION
IN EMPLOYMENT ACT

SECTION A. OVERVIEW OF STATUTORY PROVISIONS

The Age Discrimination in Employment Act of 1967 (ADEA),[a] as amended in 1974 [b], 1978 [c], 1986,[d] and 1990[e], is the exclusive federal statutory remedy for age discrimination in employment. Before the enactment of the ADEA, federal protection against age discrimination was limited to government workers (through the equal protection and due process clauses of the Constitution) and employees of federal contractors and subcontractors (through Executive Order 11141[f]).[g] The ADEA, like Title VII, applies to employers, labor organizations and employment agencies. It defines employers as private business organizations that are engaged in commerce and have at least twenty employees,[h] their agents, and state and local government entities.[i] A separate

---

[a] Pub.L. 90–202, 81 Stat. 602, 29 U.S.C. §§ 621–634 (1976).

[b] Pub.L. 93–259, 88 Stat. 74, 29 U.S.C. §§ 630(b), (c), (f), 633a, 634 (1976).

[c] Pub.L. 95–256, 92 Stat. 189, 29 U.S.C. §§ 623, (f)(2), 624, 626(c), (d), (e), 631, 633a(a), (f), (g), 634 (1981).

[d] Pub.L. 99–592, 100 Stat. 3342, 29 U.S.C. § 623 (1986).

[e] Pub.L. 101–433, 104 Stat. 978, 29 U.S.C. § 621 et seq. (1990).

[f] 3 C.F.R. § 179 (1964), 29 Fed.Reg. 2477 (1964).

This Order, promulgated by President Johnson, provides that federal contractors and subcontractors shall not discriminate on the basis of age except upon the basis of a bona fide occupational qualification, retirement plan or statutory requirement. For further discussion of this and other Executive Orders, see infra at 1219–1233.

[g] A few states, such as Arizona, Hawaii, Idaho, Kentucky, Texas and Utah, had enacted state laws prohibiting age discrimination in employment before the passage of the ADEA.

[h] For a helpful discussion of the standard used to determine employee status see EEOC v. Zippo Mfg. Co., 713 F.2d 32 (3d Cir.1983) (adopting hybrid common law

"right to control"/"economic realities" standard). See also Gazder v. Air India, 574 F.Supp. 134 (S.D.N.Y.1983) (airline owned by foreign government is an "employer" under ADEA).

From 1967 until 1984, the federal courts ruled that an American working outside of the U.S. for an American company was not covered by the ADEA because the ADEA incorporates the FLSA provisions that prohibit application of that statute outside the boundaries of the U.S. See Zahourek v. Arthur Young & Co., 750 F.2d 827 (10th Cir.1984); Thomas v. Brown & Root, Inc., 745 F.2d 279 (4th Cir.1984); Cleary v. U.S. Lines, Inc., 728 F.2d 607 (3d Cir.1984). Congress reversed this interpretation of the ADEA when it amended that statute by enacting the Older American Act Amendments of 1984, Pub.L. 98–459, 98 Stat. 1767. Section 802 of this statute explicitly extends the coverage of the ADEA to U.S. citizens employed abroad by American corporations or their subsidiaries except in cases where application of the ADEA would violate the law of the nation in which the U.S. citizen is employed. In Pfeiffer v. Wm. Wrigley Co., 755 F.2d 554 (7th Cir.1985), the court held that the amendment should not be applied retroac-

[i] See note i on page 914.

913

tively, on the ground that the legislative history was silent as to whether the amendment was intended either to change the scope of the original ADEA, to state the intended meaning of the original statute more clearly, or to limit the ADEA's intended extraterritorial effect to countries that did not possess inconsistent domestic law.

i The constitutionality of the extension of the ADEA to state and local government employees was upheld by the Supreme Court in EEOC v. Wyoming, 460 U.S. 226, 103 S.Ct. 1054, 75 L.Ed.2d 18 (1983). The Court rejected the contention that the statutory amendment violated the Tenth Amendment on the ground that the Tenth Amendment prohibits federal interference in certain core state functions and that requiring state and local governments to comply with the ADEA did not directly impair a state's ability to structure integral operations in areas of traditional governmental functions. In this case, a Wyoming statute required employer approval of the employment of game wardens who reach age 55. The Court ruled that the degree of federal intrusion occasioned by the application of the ADEA to this state law was not significant enough to override Congress' choice to extend its anti-age bias policy to the states. The ADEA would only require the state to make individualized tests of fitness and did not prohibit the state from pursuing its goal of maintaining worker fitness. Moreover, the court noted, the state could retain its policy if it could prove that age was a BFOQ for that position.

In Fitzpatrick v. Bitzer, 427 U.S. 445, 96 S.Ct. 2666, 49 L.Ed.2d 614 (1976), the Court upheld the constitutionality of the extension of Title VII to state government employment practices by ruling that the extension was effected through Congress' exercise of its authority under Section 5 of the Fourteenth Amendment rather than its power under the Commerce Clause. The *Wyoming* Court did not rule on whether the Fourteenth Amendment or the Commerce Clause was the constitutional basis for Congress' ADEA action. Accordingly, it did not use the *Fitzpatrick* rationale to reject the defendant's Tenth Amendment defense. This refusal to rule on whether the statute was an exercise of Congress' Fourteenth Amendment authority left unresolved whether a state can be held liable for money damages under the ADEA, since the Court in *Fitzpatrick* held only that the states enjoyed no Eleventh Amendment sovereign immunity from an award of money damages issued pursuant to a federal statute enacted under Con-

gress' Fourteenth Amendment authority. In Ramirez v. Puerto Rico Fire Service, 715 F.2d 694 (1st Cir.1983), the First Circuit addressed this question, ruling that the amendment extending the ADEA to public employees was enacted pursuant to Congress' authority under § 5 of the Fourteenth Amendment. Moreover, the court held, the legislative history evidenced sufficient Congressional intent to abrogate the states' Eleventh Amendment immunity to enforce the Fourteenth Amendment and, thus, that a state could be held liable for money damages under the ADEA.

Section 11(f) originally exempted from the statutory definition of "employee" any "person elected to public office in any State or political subdivision * * * or any person chosen by such officer to be on such officer's personal staff, **or an appointee on the policymaking level** or an immediate adviser with respect to the exercise of the constitutional or legal powers of the office." (emphasis added) Section 321 of the GERA, as part of the 1991 Civil Rights Act, eliminated this exclusion as to all but elected officials. Thus, this provision overrode the interpretation of the "appointee on the policymaking level" language by the Supreme Court in GREGORY v. ASHCROFT, ___ U.S. ___, 111 S.Ct. 2395, 115 L.Ed.2d 410 (1991). In *Gregory*, the Court had concluded that this exclusionary provision extended to appointed state court judges and, therefore, that these judges were not protected from age discrimination by the ADEA.

The plaintiffs in *Gregory* also asserted an equal protection challenge to the mandatory retirement provision of the Missouri Constitution. The Constitution required most state judges to retire at age 70. The plaintiff judges, pursuant to another provision in the Missouri Constitution, had been initially appointed by the Governor and subsequently retained in office by means of a retention election in which they ran unopposed, subject only to a "yes/no" vote. The plaintiffs' constitutional claim alleged that the mandatory retirement provision contained two irrational classifications— i.e., between judges over and under age 70 and between judges and those other state employees who were not subject to mandatory retirement. The Court agreed with the plaintiffs' admission that the classification was subject only to rational basis scrutiny, but rejected their claim that it was irrational. Emphasizing that the plaintiffs were challenging the constitutionality of a state constitutional, rather than statutory provision, the Court announced that it would not overturn such a provision unless the distinction contained therein was "so unrelated to the achievement of any combi-

provision, patterned exactly after § 717 of Title VII, extends the coverage of the Act to federal employees.[j] Similarly, the ADEA's definition of labor organizations and employment agencies, with one minor exception, duplicates the language of the corresponding Title VII provisions.[k]

The substantive portions of the ADEA, including the prohibitions against retaliation [l] and discriminatory advertising, are also virtually

nation of legitimate purposes that we can only conclude that the actions were irrational." The majority then concluded that the people of Missouri rationally could conclude that retention elections, voluntary retirement and impeachment were not adequate checks on the continuing ability of judges to fulfill their judicial functions and that mandatory retirement was a reasonable response to the compelling interest in maintaining a competent judiciary. It also found a rational explanation for distinguishing judges from those state officials who were not subject to mandatory retirement. These other officials, according to the majority, were subject to greater public scrutiny and to more standard elections. Accordingly, it was reasonable for Missouri to conclude that mandatory retirement was not a necessary check on their continuing ability to fulfill their professional obligations. The classification, therefore, did not violate the equal protection clause. Justices Blackmun and Marshall, having found the Missouri constitutional provision subject to and violative of the ADEA, did not address the plaintiffs' constitutional claim.

As amended, § 630(b) of the ADEA defines "employer" to include (1) agents of "persons" and (2) states and their political subdivisions. Section 630(a) defines "person" to include all forms of business associations, but does not explicitly include state and local governments. Does this failure to include state and local governments within the "person" or "agent" definitions suggest that agents of a state's instrumentalities are not "employers" within the meaning of the Act and therefore cannot be sued individually? The court in Price v. Erie County, 654 F.Supp. 1206 (W.D.N.Y. 1987) thought so, noting that the plaintiff's failure to cite any legislative history reinforced its decision not to negate the clear language of the statute as amended. Moreover, it added, while several courts had held that Congress' intent in amending the statute in 1974 was to extend to government employees the same protection previously enjoyed by private sector workers, the denial of a remedy against agents of states only "marginally" distinguished the protections afforded public and private sector employees. By contrast, the court

noted, when Congress amended Title VII to include public sector workers, it explicitly added state and local governments to the definition of both "person" and "employer". See also Court v. Administrative Office, 764 F.Supp. 168 (D.Utah 1991)(agents of public sector employers are not covered by ADEA; as this provision is not *in haec verba* with corresponding definitional provision in Title VII, it is appropriate to accord it a different interpretation than is given to Title VII); Wanner v. State of Kansas, 766 F.Supp. 1005 (D.Kan.1991)(Id.).

[j] This provision, in language identical to that found in § 717 of Title VII, extends the application of the Act to employees or applicants for employment in the "military departments." Nevertheless, relying on a series of lower court cases arising under Title VII, the courts have held that Congress did not intend for this provision to extend the protections of the Act to uniformed personnel. See Kawitt v. United States, 842 F.2d 951 (7th Cir.1988); Helm v. California, 722 F.2d 507 (9th Cir.1983). But whereas the definition of "employer" in the original version of § 630(b) (i.e., concerning private sector employers) expressly includes a twenty employee requirement, the amendment to this provision that extends the statute to public employers does not contain any such requirement. Nevertheless, at least one circuit court has reasoned that since the statutory history indicates that Congress intended the law to extend the save coverage to private and public employees, "common sense" dictated that the minimum employee size be equally applicable to public employers. See EEOC v. Monclova Township, 920 F.2d 360,362 (6th Cir.1990).

[k] The ADEA requires statutory labor organizations that do not operate a hiring hall to have twenty-five members, whereas only fifteen members are required by Title VII. The ADEA, like the Equal Pay Act, incorporates the remedial scheme of the FLSA. The FLSA authorizes an employee to bring an action for damages against an "employer" and expressly excludes labor organizations from the definition of "employer." Accordingly, it has been held that an employee cannot recover damages against a union under the ADEA. See

[l] See note l on page 916.

identical to the antidiscrimination provisions of Title VII. The major difference, of course, is that the ADEA only prohibits discrimination on the basis of age and only as to persons 40 years of age or older. Finally, an aggrieved can bring a private cause of action under the ADEA, but only, as with Title VII claims, after he or she has pursued certain administrative remedies. The materials in this chapter are designed to offer a more detailed examination of the substantive and procedural components of the ADEA.

SECTION B. SUBSTANTIVE PROVISIONS

Read § 4 of the ADEA at pp. 1267–1274.

TRANS WORLD AIRLINES, INC. v. THURSTON

Supreme Court of the United States, 1985.
469 U.S. 111, 105 S.Ct. 613, 83 L.Ed.2d 523.

JUSTICE POWELL delivered the opinion of the Court.

Trans World Airlines, Inc. (TWA), a commercial airline, permits captains disqualified from serving in that capacity for reasons other than age to transfer automatically to the position of flight engineer. In this case, we must decide whether the Age Discrimination in Employment Act of 1967 (ADEA) requires the airline to afford this same "privilege of employment" to those captains disqualified by their age. We also must decide what constitutes a "willful" violation of the ADEA, entitling a plaintiff to "liquidated" or double damages.

I

A

TWA has approximately 3,000 employees who fill the three cockpit positions on most of its flights.[1] The "captain" is the pilot and controls the aircraft. He is responsible for all phases of its operation. The "first officer" is the copilot and assists the captain. The "flight engineer" usually monitors a side-facing instrument panel. He does not operate the flight controls unless the captain and the first officer become incapacitated.

In 1977, TWA and the Air Line Pilots Association (ALPA) entered into a collective-bargaining agreement, under which every employee in a cockpit position was required to retire when he reached the age of 60.

Neuman v. Northwest Airlines, Inc., 28 FEP Cases 1488 (N.D.Ill.1982).

[1] See EEOC v. Board of Governors, 957 F.2d 424 (7th Cir.1992) (provision in collective bargaining agreement that authorizes employer to cease processing any grievance when employee challenges same employer conduct in an administrative or judicial forum constitutes unlawful retaliation).

1. On certain long-distance flights, a fourth crew member, the "international relief officer," is in the cockpit. On some types of aircraft, there are only two cockpit positions.

This provision for mandatory retirement was lawful under the ADEA, as part of a "bona fide seniority system." See United Air Lines, Inc. v. McMann, 434 U.S. 192, 98 S.Ct. 444, 54 L.Ed.2d 402 (1977). On April 6, 1978, however, the Act was amended to prohibit the mandatory retirement of a protected individual because of his age. TWA officials became concerned that the company's retirement policy, at least as it applied to flight engineers, violated the amended ADEA.[3]

On July 19, 1978, TWA announced that the amended ADEA prohibited the forced retirement of flight engineers at age 60. The company thus proposed a new policy, under which employees in all three cockpit positions, upon reaching age 60, would be allowed to continue working as flight engineers. TWA stated that it would not implement its new policy until it "had the benefit of [ALPA's] views." ALPA's views were not long in coming. The Union contended that the collective-bargaining agreement prohibited the employment of a flight engineer after his 60th birthday and that the proposed change was not required by the recently amended ADEA.

Despite opposition from the Union, TWA adopted a modified version of its proposal. Under this plan, any employee in "flight engineer status" at age 60 is entitled to continue working in that capacity. The new plan, unlike the initial proposal, does not give 60–year–old captains[6] the right automatically to begin training as flight engineers. Instead, a captain may remain with the airline only if he has been able to obtain "flight engineer status" through the bidding procedures outlined in the collective-bargaining agreement. These procedures require a captain, prior to his 60th birthday, to submit a "standing bid" for the position of flight engineer. When a vacancy occurs, it is assigned to the most senior captain with a standing bid. If no vacancy occurs prior to his 60th birthday, or if he lacks sufficient seniority to bid successfully for those vacancies that do occur, the captain is retired.[7]

Under the collective-bargaining agreement, a captain displaced for any reason besides age need not resort to the bidding procedures. For example, a captain unable to maintain the requisite first-class medical certificate, see 14 CFR § 67.13 (1984), may displace automatically, or

---

3. A regulation promulgated by the Federal Aviation Administration prohibits anyone from serving after age 60 as a pilot on a commercial carrier. 14 CFR § 121.-383(c) (1984). Captains and first officers are considered "pilots" subject to this regulation; flight engineers are not. Therefore, TWA officials were concerned primarily with the effect that the 1978 amendments had on the company's policy of mandatory retirement of flight engineers.

6. The term "captain" will hereinafter be used to refer to both the positions of captain and first officer.

7. In 1980, TWA imposed an additional restriction on captains bidding for flight engineer positions. Successful bidders were required to "fulfill their bids in a timely manner." Under this amended practice, captains who bid successfully for positions as flight engineers were required to "activate" their bids immediately. As a result, many captains under age 60 were trained for and assumed flight engineer positions, with resulting lower pay and responsibility.

"bump," a less senior flight engineer.[8]   The medically disabled captain's ability to bump does not depend upon the availability of a vacancy.[9]   Similarly, a captain whose position is eliminated due to reduced manpower needs can "bump" a less senior flight engineer.[10] Even if a captain is found to be incompetent to serve in that capacity, he is not discharged,[11] but is allowed to transfer to a position as flight engineer without resort to the bidding procedures.[12]

Respondents Harold Thurston, Christopher J. Clark, and Clifton A. Parkhill, former captains for TWA, were retired upon reaching the age of 60.   Each was denied an opportunity to "bump" a less senior flight engineer.   Thurston was forced to retire on May 26, 1978, before the company adopted its new policy.   Clark did not attempt to bid because TWA had advised him that bidding would not affect his chances of obtaining a transfer.   These two captains thus effectively were denied an opportunity to become flight engineers through the bidding procedures.   The third captain, Parkhill, did file a standing bid for the position of flight engineer.   No vacancies occurred prior to Parkhill's 60th birthday, however, and he too was forced to retire.

B

Thurston, Clark, and Parkhill filed this action against TWA and ALPA in the United States District Court for the Southern District of New York.   They argued that the company's transfer policy violated ADEA § 4(a)(1).   The airline allowed captains displaced for reasons other than age to "bump" less senior flight engineers.   Captains compelled to vacate their positions upon reaching age 60, they claimed, should be afforded this same "privilege of employment." * * *

The District Court entered a summary judgment in favor of defendants TWA and ALPA.   Air Line Pilots Assn. v. Trans World Air Lines, 547 F.Supp. 1221 (SDNY 1982).   The court held that the plaintiffs had failed to establish a prima facie case of age discrimination under the test set forth in McDonnell Douglas Corp. v. Green.   None could show that at the time of his transfer request a vacancy existed for the position of flight engineer.   Furthermore, the court found that two

---

8. The pilot must be able to obtain the second-class medical certificate that is required for the position of flight engineer. See 14 CFR § 67.15 (1984).

9. If the disabled captain lacks sufficient seniority to displace, he is not discharged.   Rather, he is entitled to go on unpaid medical leave for up to five years, during which time he retains and continues to accrue seniority.

10. Only those flight engineers in the current and last former domiciles of the displaced captain may be "bumped." If a captain has insufficient seniority to displace a flight engineer at either of these domiciles, he is not discharged.   Instead, he is placed in furlough status for a period of up to 10 years, during which time he continues to accrue seniority for purposes of a recall.

11. Although the collective-bargaining agreement does not address disciplinary downgrades, TWA's Vice President of Flight Operations, J.E. Frankum, stated that such downgrades had occurred "many times over many years."

12. Captains disqualified for other reasons also are allowed to "bump" less senior flight engineers.   For example, the collective-bargaining agreement provides that a captain who fails to "requalify" in that position will not be discharged.

affirmative defenses justified the company's transfer policy. 29 U.S.C. § 623(f)(1) and (f)(2). The United States Court of Appeals for the Second Circuit reversed the District Court's judgment. 713 F.2d 940 (1983). It found the *McDonnell Douglas* formula inapposite because the plaintiffs had adduced *direct* proof of age discrimination. Captains disqualified for reasons other than age were allowed to "bump" less senior flight engineers. Therefore, the company was required by ADEA § 4(a)(1) to afford 60–year–old captains this same "privilege of employment." The Court of Appeals also held that the affirmative defenses of the ADEA did not justify the company's discriminatory transfer policy.[14] TWA was held liable for "liquidated" or double damages because its violation of the ADEA was found to be "willful." According to the court, an employer's conduct is "willful" if it "knows or shows reckless disregard for the matter of whether its conduct is prohibited by the ADEA." Because "TWA was clearly aware of the 1978 ADEA amendments," the Court of Appeals found the respondents entitled to double damages.

TWA filed a petition for a writ of certiorari in which it challenged the Court of Appeals' holding that the transfer policy violated the ADEA and that TWA's violation was "willful." The Union filed a cross-petition raising only the liability issue. We granted certiorari in both cases, and consolidated them for argument. We now affirm as to the violation of the ADEA, and reverse as to the claim for double damages.

II

A

The ADEA "broadly prohibits arbitrary discrimination in the workplace based on age." Lorillard v. Pons, 434 U.S. 575, 577, 98 S.Ct. 866,

---

14. The Court of Appeals also found that ALPA had violated ADEA § 4(c), 29 U.S.C. § 623(c), which prohibits unions from causing or attempting to cause an employer to engage in unlawful discrimination. The court found, however, that ALPA was not liable for damages. It held that the ADEA does not permit the recovery of monetary damages, including back pay, against a labor organization. It noted that the ADEA incorporates the remedial scheme of the FLSA, which does not allow actions against unions to recover damages.

In its petition for a writ of certiorari, TWA raised the issue of a union's liability for damages under the ADEA. Although we granted the petition in full, we now conclude that the Court is without jurisdiction to consider this question. TWA was not the proper party to present this question. The airline cannot assert the right of others to recover damages against the Union.

Both the individual respondents and the EEOC argue that the issue of union liability is properly before the Court. But the respondents failed to file a cross-petition raising this question. A prevailing party may advance any ground in support of a judgment in his favor. Dandridge v. Williams, 397 U.S. 471, 475 n. 6, 90 S.Ct. 1153, 1156 n. 6, 25 L.Ed.2d 491 (1970). An argument that would modify the judgment, however, cannot be presented unless a cross-petition has been filed. Federal Energy Admin. v. Algonquin SNG, Inc., 426 U.S. 548, 560 n. 11, 96 S.Ct. 2295, 2302 n. 11, 49 L.Ed.2d 49 (1976). In this case, the judgment of the Court of Appeals would be modified by the arguments advanced by the EEOC and the individual plaintiffs, as they are contending that the Union should be liable to them for monetary damages.

868, 55 L.Ed.2d 40 (1978).   Section 4(a)(1) of the Act proscribes differential treatment of older workers "with respect to * * * [a] privileg[e] of employment."   Under TWA's transfer policy, 60–year–old captains are denied a "privilege of employment" on the basis of age.   Captains who become disqualified from serving in that position for reasons other than age automatically are able to displace less senior flight engineers. Captains disqualified because of age are not afforded this same "bumping" privilege.   Instead, they are forced to resort to the bidding procedures set forth in the collective-bargaining agreement.   If there is no vacancy prior to a bidding captain's 60th birthday, he must retire.[15]

The Act does not require TWA to grant transfer privileges to disqualified captains.   Nevertheless, if TWA does grant some disqualified captains the "privilege" of "bumping" less senior flight engineers, it may not deny this opportunity to others because of their age.   In Hishon v. King & Spalding, 467 U.S. 69, 104 S.Ct. 2229, 81 L.Ed.2d 59 (1984), we held that "[a] benefit that is part and parcel of the employment relationship may not be doled out in a discriminatory fashion, even if the employer would be free * * * not to provide the benefit at all."   This interpretation of Title VII of the Civil Rights Act of 1964 applies with equal force in the context of age discrimination, for the substantive provisions of the ADEA "were derived *in haec verba* from Title VII."   Lorillard v. Pons, supra.

TWA contends that the respondents failed to make out a prima facie case of age discrimination under McDonnell Douglas v. Green, because at the time they were retired, no flight engineer vacancies existed.   This argument fails, for the *McDonnell Douglas* test is inapplicable where the plaintiff presents direct evidence of discrimination. See Teamsters v. United States, 431 U.S. 324, 358 n. 44, 97 S.Ct. 1843, 1866 n. 44, 52 L.Ed.2d 396 (1977).   The shifting burdens of proof set forth in *McDonnell Douglas* are designed to assure that the "plaintiff [has] his day in court despite the unavailability of direct evidence." Loeb v. Textron, Inc., 600 F.2d 1003, 1014 (CA1 1979).   In this case there is direct evidence that the method of transfer available to a disqualified captain depends upon his age.   Since it allows captains who become disqualified for any reason other than age to "bump" less senior flight engineers, TWA's transfer policy is discriminatory on its face.

B

Although we find that TWA's transfer policy discriminates against disqualified captains on the basis of age, our inquiry cannot end here. Petitioners contend that the age-based transfer policy is justified by two

---

15. The discriminatory transfer policy may violate the Act even though 83% of the 60–year–old captains were able to obtain positions as flight engineers through the bidding procedures.   See Phillips v. Martin Marietta Corp., 400 U.S. 542, 91 S.Ct. 496, 27 L.Ed.2d 613 (1971) (*per curiam*).

It also should be noted that many of the captains who obtained positions as flight engineers were forced to assume that position prior to reaching age 60.   See n. 7, supra.   They were adversely affected by the discriminatory transfer policy despite the fact that they obtained positions as flight engineers.

of the ADEA's five affirmative defenses. Petitioners first argue that the discharge of respondents was lawful because age is a "bona fide occupational qualification" (BFOQ) for the position of captain. Furthermore, TWA claims that its retirement policy is part of a "bona fide seniority system," and thus exempt from the Act's coverage.

Section 4(f)(1) of the ADEA provides that an employer may take "any action otherwise prohibited" where age is a "bona fide occupational qualification." In order to be permissible under § 4(f)(1), however, the age-based discrimination must relate to a "particular business." Every court to consider the issue has assumed that the "particular business" to which the statute refers is the job from which the protected individual is excluded. In Weeks v. Southern Bell Tel. & Tel. Co., 408 F.2d 228 (CA5 1969), for example, the court considered the Title VII claim of a female employee who, because of her sex, had not been allowed to transfer to the position of switchman. In deciding that the BFOQ defense was not available to the defendant, the court considered only the job of switchman.

TWA's discriminatory transfer policy is not permissible under § 4(f)(1) because age is not a BFOQ for the "particular" position of flight engineer. It is necessary to recognize that the airline has two age-based policies: (i) captains are not allowed to serve in that capacity after reaching the age of 60; and (ii) age-disqualified captains are not given the transfer privileges afforded captains disqualified for other reasons. The first policy, which precludes individuals from serving as captains, is not challenged by respondents.[17] The second practice does not operate to exclude protected individuals from the position of captain; rather it prevents qualified 60–year–olds from working as flight engineers. Thus, it is the "particular" job of flight engineer from which the respondents were excluded by the discriminatory transfer policy. Because age under 60 is not a BFOQ for the position of flight engineer,[18] the age-based discrimination at issue in this case cannot be justified by § 4(f)(1).

TWA nevertheless contends that its BFOQ argument is supported by the legislative history of the amendments to the ADEA. In 1978, Congress amended ADEA § 4(f)(2) to prohibit the involuntary retirement of protected individuals on the basis of age. Some Members of Congress were concerned that this amendment might be construed as limiting the employer's ability to terminate workers subject to a valid BFOQ. The Senate proposed an amendment to § 4(f)(1) providing that an employer could establish a mandatory retirement age where age is a BFOQ. S.Rep. No. 95–493, pp. 11, 24 (1977), U.S.Code Cong. & Ad-

17. In this litigation, the respondents have not challenged TWA's claim that the FAA regulation establishes a BFOQ for the position of captain. The EEOC guidelines, however, do not list the FAA's age–60 rule as an example of a BFOQ because the EEOC wishes to avoid any appearance that

it endorses the rule. 46 Fed.Reg. 47724, 47725 (1981).

18. The petitioners do not contend that age is a BFOQ for the position of flight engineer. Indeed, the airline has employed at least 148 flight engineers who are over 60 years old.

min.News 1978, p. 504. In the Conference Committee, however, the proposed amendment was withdrawn because "the [Senate] conferees agreed that * * * [it] neither added to nor worked any change upon present law." H.R.Conf.Rep. No. 95–950, p. 7 (1978), U.S.Code Cong. & Admin.News 1978, p. 529. The House Committee Report also indicated that an individual could be compelled to retire from a position for which age was a BFOQ. H.R.Rep. No. 95–527 pt. 1, p. 12 (1977).

The legislative history of the 1978 Amendments does not support petitioners' position. The history shows only that the ADEA does not prohibit TWA from retiring all disqualified captains, including those who are incapacitated because of age. This does not mean, however, that TWA can make dependent upon the age of the individual the availability of a transfer to a position for which age is not a BFOQ. Nothing in the legislative history cited by petitioners indicates a congressional intention to allow an employer to discriminate against an older worker seeking to transfer to another position, on the ground that age was a BFOQ for his *former* job.

TWA also contends that its discriminatory transfer policy is lawful under the Act because it is part of a "bona fide seniority system." The Court of Appeals held that the airline's retirement policy is not mandated by the negotiated seniority plan. We need not address this finding; any seniority system that includes the challenged practice is not "bona fide" under the statute. The Act provides that a seniority system may not "require or permit" the involuntary retirement of a protected individual because of his age. Although the FAA "age 60 rule" may have caused respondents' retirement, TWA's seniority plan certainly "permitted" it within the meaning of the ADEA. Moreover, because captains disqualified for reasons other than age are allowed to "bump" less senior flight engineers, the mandatory retirement was age-based. Therefore, the "bona fide seniority system" defense is unavailable to the petitioners.

In summary, TWA's transfer policy discriminates against protected individuals on the basis of age, and thereby violates the Act. The two statutory defenses raised by petitioners do not support the argument that this discrimination is justified. The BFOQ defense is meritless because age is not a bona fide occupational qualification for the position of flight engineer, the job from which the respondents were excluded. Nor can TWA's policy be viewed as part of a bona fide seniority system. A system that includes this discriminatory transfer policy permits the forced retirement of captains on the basis of age.

III
A

Section 7(b) of the ADEA provides that the rights created by the Act are to be "enforced in accordance with the powers, remedies, and procedures" of the Fair Labor Standards Act. See Lorillard v. Pons, 434 U.S., at 579, 98 S.Ct., at 869 (1978). But the remedial provisions of the two statutes are not identical.   Congress declined to incorporate into the ADEA several FLSA sections.   Moreover, § 16(b) of the FLSA, which makes the award of liquidated damages mandatory, is significantly qualified in ADEA § 7(b) by a proviso that a prevailing plaintiff is entitled to double damages "only in cases of willful violations."   In this case, the Court of Appeals held that TWA's violation of the ADEA was "willful," and that the respondents therefore were entitled to double damages.   We granted certiorari to review this holding.

The legislative history of the ADEA indicates that Congress intended for liquidated damages to be punitive in nature.   The original bill proposed by the administration incorporated § 16(a) of the FLSA, which imposes criminal liability for a willful violation.   See 113 Cong.Rec. 2199 (1967).   Senator Javits found "certain serious defects" in the administration bill.   He stated that "difficult problems of proof * * * would arise under a criminal provision," and that the employer's invocation of the Fifth Amendment might impede investigation, conciliation, and enforcement.   113 Cong.Rec. 7076 (1967).   Therefore, he proposed that "the [FLSA's] criminal penalty in cases of willful violation * * * [be] eliminated and a double damage liability substituted." Ibid.   Senator Javits argued that his proposed amendment would "furnish an effective deterrent to willful violations [of the ADEA]," ibid., and it was incorporated into the ADEA with only minor modification, S. 788, 90th Cong., 1st Sess. (1967).

This Court has recognized that in enacting the ADEA, "Congress exhibited * * * a detailed knowledge of the FLSA provisions and their judicial interpretation * * *."   Lorillard v. Pons, 434 U.S. 575, 581, 98 S.Ct. 866, 870, 55 L.Ed.2d 40 (1978).   The manner in which FLSA § 16(a) has been interpreted therefore is relevant.   In general, courts have found that an employer is subject to criminal penalties under the FLSA when he "wholly disregards the law * * * without making any reasonable effort to determine whether the plan he is following would constitute a violation of the law."   Nabob Oil Co. v. United States, 190 F.2d 478, 479 (CA10), cert. denied, 342 U.S. 876, 72 S.Ct. 167, 96 L.Ed. 659 (1951); see also Darby v. United States, 132 F.2d 928 (CA5 1943).[19] This standard is substantially in accord with the interpretation of "willful" adopted by the Court of Appeals in interpreting the liquidated damages provision of the ADEA.   The court below stated that a violation of the Act was "willful" if "the employer * * * knew or showed reckless disregard for the matter of whether its conduct was prohibited by the ADEA."   Given the legislative history of the liquidated damages provision, we think the "reckless disregard" standard is reasonable.

19.   Courts below have held that an employer's action may be "willful," within the meaning of § 16(a) of the FLSA, even though he did not have an evil motive or bad purpose.   See Nabob Oil Co. v. United States, 190 F.2d 478 (CA10), cert. denied, 342 U.S. 876, 72 S.Ct. 167, 96 L.Ed. 659 (1951).   We do not agree with TWA's argument that unless it intended to violate the Act, double damages are inappropriate under § 7(b) of the ADEA.   Only one court of appeals has expressed approval of this position.   See Loeb v. Textron, Inc., 600 F.2d 1003, 1020 n. 27 (CA1 1979).

The definition of "willful" adopted by the above cited courts is consistent with the manner in which this Court has interpreted the term in other criminal and civil statutes. In United States v. Murdock, 290 U.S. 389, 54 S.Ct. 223, 78 L.Ed. 381 (1933), the defendant was prosecuted under the Revenue Acts of 1926 and 1928, which made it a misdemeanor for a person "willfully" to fail to pay the required tax. The *Murdock* Court stated that conduct was "willful" within the meaning of this criminal statute if it was "marked by careless disregard [for] whether or not one has the right so to act." In United States v. Illinois Central R., 303 U.S. 239, 58 S.Ct. 533, 82 L.Ed. 773 (1938), the Court applied the *Murdock* definition of "willful" in a civil case. There, the defendant's failure to unload a cattle car was "willful," because it showed a disregard for the governing statute and an indifference to its requirements.

The respondents argue that an employer's conduct is willful if he is "cognizant of an appreciable possibility that the employees involved were covered by the [ADEA]." In support of their position, the respondents cite § 6 of the Portal–to–Portal Act of 1947(PPA), 29 U.S.C. § 255(a), which is incorporated in both the ADEA and the FLSA. Section 6 of the PPA provides for a 2–year statute of limitations period unless the violation is willful, in which case the limitations period is extended to three years. Several courts have held that a violation is willful within the meaning of § 6 if the employer knew that the ADEA was "in the picture." See, e.g., Coleman v. Jiffy June Farms, Inc., 458 F.2d 1139, 1142 (CA5 1971), cert. denied, 409 U.S. 948, 93 S.Ct. 292, 34 L.Ed.2d 219 (1972); EEOC v. Central Kansas Medical Center, 705 F.2d 1270, 1274 (CA10 1983). Respondents contend that the term "willful" should be interpreted in a similar manner in applying the liquidated damages provision of the ADEA.

We are unpersuaded by respondents' argument that a violation of the Act is "willful" if the employer simply knew of the potential applicability of the ADEA. Even if the "in the picture" standard were appropriate for the statute of limitations, the same standard should not govern a provision dealing with liquidated damages.[21] More importantly, the broad standard proposed by the respondents would result in an award of double damages in almost every case. As employers are required to post ADEA notices, it would be virtually impossible for an employer to show that he was unaware of the Act and its potential applicability. Both the legislative history and the structure of the statute show that Congress intended a two-tiered liability scheme. We decline to interpret the liquidated damages provision of ADEA § 7(b) in

---

21. The Courts of Appeals are divided over whether Congress intended the "willfulness" standard to be identical for determining liquidated damages and for purposes of the limitations period. Compare Spagnuolo v. Whirlpool Corp., 641 F.2d 1109, 1113(CA4), cert. denied, 454 U.S. 860, 102 S.Ct. 316, 70 L.Ed.2d 158 (1981) (standards are identical), with Kelly v. Ameri-

a manner that frustrates this intent.[22]

B

As noted above, the Court of Appeals stated that a violation is "willful" if "the employer either knew or showed reckless disregard for the matter of whether its conduct was prohibited by the ADEA." Although we hold that this is an acceptable way to articulate a definition of "willful," the court below misapplied this standard. TWA certainly did not "know" that its conduct violated the Act. Nor can it fairly be said that TWA adopted its transfer policy in "reckless disregard" of the Act's requirements. The record makes clear that TWA officials acted reasonably and in good faith in attempting to determine whether their plan would violate the ADEA.

Shortly after the ADEA was amended, TWA officials met with their lawyers to determine whether the mandatory retirement policy violated the Act. Concluding that the company's existing plan was inconsistent with the ADEA, David Crombie, the airline's Vice President for Administration, proposed a new policy. Despite opposition from the Union, the company adopted a modified version of this initial proposal. Under the plan adopted on August 10, 1978, any pilot in "flight engineer status" on his 60th birthday could continue to work for the airline. On the day the plan was adopted, the Union filed suit against the airline claiming that the new retirement policy constituted a "major" change in the collective-bargaining agreement, and thus was barred by the § 6 of the Railway Labor Act, 45 U.S.C. § 156. Nevertheless, TWA adhered to its new policy.

As evidence of "willfulness," respondents point to comments made by J.E. Frankum, the Vice President of Flight Operations. After Crombie was hospitalized in August 1978, Frankum assumed responsibility for bringing TWA's retirement policy into conformance with the ADEA. Despite legal advice to the contrary, Frankum initially believed that the company was not required to allow any pilot over 60to work. Frankum later abandoned this position in favor of the plan approved on August 10, 1978. Frankum apparently had been con-

can Standard, Inc., 640 F.2d 974, 979 (CA9 1981) (standards are different).

22. The "in the picture" standard proposed by the respondents would allow the recovery of liquidated damages even if the employer acted reasonably and in complete "good faith." Congress hardly intended such a result.

The Court interpreted the FLSA, as originally enacted, as allowing the recovery of liquidated damages any time that there was a violation of the Act. See *Overnight Motor Transportation Co. v. Missel*, 316 U.S. 572, 62 S.Ct. 1216, 86 L.Ed. 1682 (1942). In response to its dissatisfaction with that harsh interpretation of the provision, Congress enacted the Portal–to–Portal Act of 1947. See *Lorillard v. Pons*, 434 U.S. 575, 581–582 n. 8, 98 S.Ct. 866, 870 n. 8, 55 L.Ed.2d 40 (1978). Section 11 of the PPA, 29 U.S.C. § 260, provides the employer with a defense to a mandatory award of liquidated damages when it can show good faith and reasonable grounds for believing it was not in violation of the FLSA. Section 7(b) of the ADEA does not incorporate § 11 of the PPA, contra *Hays v. Republic Steel Corp.*, 531 F.2d 1307 (CA5 1976). Nevertheless, we think that the same concerns are reflected in the proviso to § 7(b) of the ADEA.

cerned only about whether flight engineers could work after reaching the age of 60. There is no indication that TWA was ever advised by counsel that its new transfer policy discriminated against captains on the basis of age.

There simply is no evidence that TWA acted in "reckless disregard" of the requirements of the ADEA. The airline had obligations under the collective-bargaining agreement with the Air Line Pilots Association. In an attempt to bring its retirement policy into compliance with the ADEA, while at the same time observing the terms of the collective-bargaining agreement, TWA sought legal advice and consulted with the Union. Despite opposition from the Union, a plan was adopted that permitted cockpit employees to work as "flight engineers" after reaching age 60. Apparently TWA officials and the airline's attorneys failed to focus specifically on the effect of each aspect of the new retirement policy for cockpit personnel. It is reasonable to believe that the parties involved, in focusing on the larger overall problem, simply overlooked the challenged aspect of the new plan.[23] We conclude that TWA's violation of the Act was not willful within the meaning of § 7(b), and that respondents therefore are not entitled to liquidated damages.

IV

The ADEA requires TWA to afford 60–year–old captains the same transfer privileges that it gives to captains disqualified for reasons other than age. Therefore, we affirm the Court of Appeals on this issue. We do not agree with its holding that TWA's violation of the Act was willful. We accordingly reverse its judgment that respondents are entitled to liquidated or double damages.

It is so ordered.

NOTES AND PROBLEMS FOR DISCUSSION

1. The Court in the principal case noted that since the substantive provisions of the ADEA were derived "in haec verba" from Title VII, it was appropriate to apply Title VII jurisprudence to analogous issues arising under the ADEA. Does this mean, for example, that the *Price Waterhouse* language governing the allocation of burdens of proof in "mixed motive" cases, as modified by the 1991 Civil Rights Act, should extend to age cases? Must the plaintiff establish that age played a substantial or motivating role through the introduction of direct evidence, or can the plaintiff trigger the burden-shifting by relying on circumstantial evidence to establish that age was considered? In *Thurston* the Court did state that "the *McDonnell Douglas* test is inapplicable where the plaintiff presents direct evidence of discrimination." This statement, however, was made in the context of a ruling on whether the plaintiffs'

---

23. In his dissent, Judge Van Graafeiland also focused on the larger problem, rather than on the discriminatory transfer policy. Judge Van Graafeiland stated: "TWA is the only trunk airline that voluntarily has permitted [persons] * * * over 60 to continue working as flight engineers. Instead of receiving commendation for what it has done, TWA is held liable as a matter of law for age discrimination," 713 F.2d 940, 957 (1983).

failure to satisfy all four of the elements of the *McDonnell Douglas* prima facie case standard was fatal to the establishment of a prima facie case. The nature of the defendant's evidentiary burden was neither discussed nor at issue in this portion of the opinion. But compare Ostrowski v. Atlantic Mutual Insurance Companies, 968 F.2d 171 (2d Cir.1992) (extending the Price Waterhouse burden-shifting formulation to cases arising under the ADEA regardless of whether the ADEA plaintiff establishes that age was a "motivating factor" through either direct or circumstantial evidence); Summers v. Communication Channels, Inc., 729 F.Supp. 1234 (N.D.Ill.1990)(*Price Waterhouse* should apply to age discrimination cases, but the ruling in that case was limited to instances where the plaintiff produced some *direct* evidence that the defendant considered an improper factor in making its decision; cases relying on *indirect* evidence of discrimination fall under the *McDonnell Douglas* framework) and Hill v. Bethlehem Steel Corp., 729 F.Supp. 1071 (E.D.Pa.1989), affirmed without opinion, 902 F.2d 1560 (3d Cir.1990)(Id.) with Spanier v. Morrison's Management Services, Inc., 822 F.2d 975 (11th Cir.1987)(pre-*Price Waterhouse* case holding that defendant bears burden of persuasion on "same decision" defense once plaintiff establishes that age was a "determining" factor either through direct or circumstantial evidence).

2. In addition to the circumstances presented in the principal case, there are other areas in which strict application of Title VII analysis would be inappropriate in an age discrimination case. For example, where a plaintiff alleges that she was chosen to be the victim of a reduction-in-force or other form of structural reorganization, it often would be impossible to satisfy the fourth element of the *McDonnell Douglas* prima facie case standard, i.e., that after her rejection, the position remained open and that the employer continued to seek applicants from persons of the plaintiff's qualifications. By definition, most victims are not replaced in reduction-in-force cases. Noting that the *McDonnell Douglas* Court stated that its standard was not "necessarily applicable in every respect to differing factual situations," most federal circuits that have considered the issue have not required plaintiffs in age-based reduction-in-force or structural reorganization cases to establish that they were replaced by younger individuals. Rather, noting the intended flexibility of the *McDonnell Douglas* standard, the courts have required the plaintiff to offer either direct or circumstantial evidence that the discharge occurred in circumstances that give rise to an inference of age discrimination. See e.g., Duke v. Uniroyal Inc., 928 F.2d 1413 (4th Cir.1991)(evidence that (1)the effect of the reduction was to increase the ratio of unprotected [by the ADEA] to protected workers in the group affected by the reduction, and (2)that some unprotected persons who were performing at substantially the same or a lower level than the plaintiff were retained is sufficient to generate an inference of age discrimination); Barnes v. GenCorp Inc., 896 F.2d 1457 (6th Cir.1990); Benjamin v. Traffic Executive Ass'n Eastern Railroads, 869 F.2d 107 (2d Cir.1989); Oxman v. WLS–TV, 846 F.2d 448 (7th Cir.1988). In *Benjamin*, for example, the Second Circuit upheld the lower court's determination that the plaintiff had established a prima facie case. It reasoned that the facts that the plaintiff's job duties were transferred to an overworked younger employee and then retransferred to a newly hired younger employee and that the plaintiff had not been offered the new position, even though she was qualified for it, were sufficient to give rise to an inference that she had been a victim of age discrimination.

Similarly, a plaintiff may be replaced by a younger employee who, nevertheless, is over the age of forty and, therefore, is also a member of the statutorily protected group. The third of the four prongs of the *McDonnell Douglas* standard requires evidence that the plaintiff was replaced by a person outside the protected group. The courts have recognized that age, unlike sex, race, religion or national origin, is not a discrete characteristic that separates members of the protected group from nonmembers. Rather, it is a continuum along which relative distinctions can be made. Not all sixty year old employees are replaced by twenty-five year olds. Accordingly, noting again the intended flexibility of the *McDonnell Douglas* formula, the circuit courts have held that the plaintiff's failure to show that he or she was replaced by someone under the age of forty is not an absolute bar to the establishment of a prima facie case. Instead, as in the reduction-in-force cases, they require that the plaintiff proffer evidence that the decision occurred in circumstances that give rise to an inference of age discrimination. See Carter v. City of Miami, 870 F.2d 578 (11th Cir.1989); Carden v. Westinghouse Electric Corp., 850 F.2d 996 (3d Cir.1988); Furr v. AT & T Technologies, Inc., 824 F.2d 1537 (10th Cir.1987); Diaz v. AT & T, 752 F.2d 1356 (9th Cir.1985). In most cases, of course, this takes the form of evidence that the plaintiff was replaced by a younger person. And, in such cases, the strength of the inference of discrimination is directly related to the extent of the age difference between the plaintiff and the successful candidate.

Should a different result obtain when the plaintiff seeks to bring a disproportionate impact claim? Suppose, for example, that an employer's use of a physical endurance examination excluded almost all candidates over the age of fifty but that two thirds of its employees were over age forty. Can the plaintiff, a fifty five year old individual who was rejected for failure to pass the physical examination, state a prima facie case of disproportionate impact under the ADEA? See Lowe v. Commack Union Free School Dist., 886 F.2d 1364 (2d Cir.1989), cert. denied, 494 U.S. 1026, 110 S.Ct. 1470, 108 L.Ed.2d 608 (1990) (rejecting the plaintiff's suggestion that it extend impact analysis to the effect of the challenged policy on a "sub-protected group" on the ground that the conceptual link between impact and discrimination is appropriate only when those preferred by the challenged policy are not members of the statutorily protected group).

Reduction-in-force cases also raise an interesting question concerning the second part of the *McDonnell Douglas* formula—i.e., that the plaintiff was qualified and performing satisfactorily. Now that the plaintiff has been discharged and her position no longer exists, how does she prove she is qualified? Qualified for what? Her nonexistent position? A position held by a younger employee? Any position the employer offers or any position to which she would agree to be transferred? Or is it enough to establish that she was adequately performing a job that has been eliminated? See Ayala v. Mayfair Molded Products Corp., 831 F.2d 1314 (7th Cir.1987)(plaintiff must prove he was qualified to assume another post at the time of the reduction to establish a prima facie case).

3. The company asserted two arguments in *Thurston*. First, it contended that the plaintiff had failed to establish a prima facie case. Second, it alternatively argued that even if a prima facie case had been established, its policy was justified by two of the ADEA's five affirmative defenses. Suppose that instead of relying on the statutory defenses, the company had sought to rebut the plaintiffs' disparate treatment-based prima facie case with evidence of "some legitimate nondiscriminatory reason" for its decision. Would it have been subjected to the same burden of proof?

In Douglas v. Anderson, 656 F.2d 528 (9th Cir.1981), the manager of a law school bookstore alleged that he had been discharged because of his age. The defendants claimed that Douglas had been terminated after an audit of the financial records of the bookstore revealed several substantial management problems which led the auditors to conclude that the plaintiff had performed unsatisfactorily as business manager of the store. The court, applying the *McDonnell Douglas* formula, found that the plaintiff had established a prima facie case and that this shifted the burden to the employer "to produce evidence of a legitimate nondiscriminatory reason for terminating Douglas's employment." (Note, however, that this same circuit court, in Kouba v. Allstate Ins., *supra* at 885, stated that the employer bears the burden of "showing" that its challenged policy falls within the analogous "factor other than sex" defense of the Equal Pay Act.)

Section 4(f) of the ADEA sets forth four defenses to claims of age bias. Under this provision, a defendant will be found not to have violated the statute:

(1) where age is a bona fide occupational qualification reasonably necessary to the normal operations of the particular business;

(2) where the differentiation is based on reasonable factors other than age;

(3) where the defendant has observed the terms of a bona fide seniority system or bona fide employee benefit plan that is not a subterfuge to evade the purposes of the Act and is not used to involuntarily retire an employee because of his or her age; or

(4) where the discharge or discipline was based on good cause.

Wasn't the defendant in *Douglas* asserting the second of these four defenses? If so, then why did it bear only the burden of production when the *Thurston* Court implied that the defendant would bear the burden of persuasion as to its assertion of the first and third listed defenses? Is there a justifiable distinction between these three types of defenses? Consider this analysis offered by the Fifth Circuit:

"The reason for that distinction is clear. A defendant who seeks to establish a BFOQ is essentially asserting an 'affirmative defense'—one in the nature of confession and avoidance. An age-related BFOQ permits an employer to admit that he had discriminated on the basis of age, but to avoid any penalty. Establishment of a BFOQ relating to age justifies an employer's violation of the heart of the ADEA, allowing him to apply a general exclusionary rule to otherwise statutorily protected individuals solely on the basis of class membership. The good cause and differentiating factor exceptions, on the other hand, are denials of the plaintiff's prima facie case. Plaintiff says that the employer fired him because of his age; employer replies, in effect, not so, plaintiff was fired for excessive absences, general inability, or some other non-discriminatory reason. The natural tendency of the court to place the burden of proof upon the party desiring change and the special policy considerations disfavoring the statutory exceptions both justify the distinction between these defenses."

Marshall v. Westinghouse Electric Corp., 576 F.2d 588, 591 (5th Cir.1978). Is the court's reference, in the above quoted paragraph, to "special policy considerations disfavoring the statutory exceptions" consistent with its conclusion that the defendant should be subjected only to the burden of production on its claim? For a thorough discussion of this affirmative defense/denial controversy and an argument in support of treating the reasonable factor other than age provision as an affirmative defense in all but individual, disparate treatment/circumstantial evidence cases, see Eglit, The Age Discrimination in Employment Act's Forgotten Affirmative Defense: The Reasonable Factors Other Than Age Exception, 66 B.U.L.Rev. 155 (1986).

4. Were you satisfied with the Court's treatment of the BFOQ issue in *Thurston?* Did the Court rest its decision on the company's failure to contend that age was a BFOQ for the flight engineer position? Or did it take into account that the company had employed over 148 flight engineers over the age of sixty? Should it have made such a factual determination or should it have remanded for further consideration?

The question of the nature and quantity of evidence necessary to establish a BFOQ was not addressed in *Thurston.* In most post-*Thurston* cases, the courts have tended to agree that in certain situations, such as those where the employer asserts safety as a consideration for its challenged decision, a lesser showing is required. In Spurlock v. United Airlines, Inc., 475 F.2d 216, 219 (10th Cir.1972), a disproportionate impact Title VII case in which the defendant raised the defense of business necessity, the court stated that where the job in question "requires a small amount of skill and training and the consequences of hiring an unqualified applicant are insignificant, the * * * employer should have a heavy burden to demonstrate * * * that his employment criteria are job-related. On the other hand, when the job clearly requires a high degree of skill and the economic and human risks involved in hiring an unqualified applicant are great, the employer bears a correspondingly lighter burden * * *." See also Tuohy v. Ford Motor Co., 675 F.2d 842, 845 (6th Cir.1982) ("The presence of an overriding safety factor might well lead a court to conclude as a matter of policy that the level of proof required to establish the reasonable necessity of a BFOQ is relatively low."). But see Usery v. Tamiami Trail Tours, Inc., 531 F.2d 224 (5th Cir.1976) (distinguishing Spurlock as a non-BFOQ case).

Most of the courts agree that, as in Title VII cases, two elements must be proven by the defendant to establish a BFOQ: (1) that the job qualifications used to justify discrimination are reasonably necessary to the essence of the business; and (2) that there is a substantial factual basis for believing that all or substantially all members of the excluded class are unable to safely and efficiently perform the job, or that there is no practical basis other than the challenged classification for determining an individual applicant's ability to safely and efficiently perform the job. Nevertheless, at least in ADEA cases, they disagree with respect to the nature and amount of evidence needed to satisfy the second element of the defense. Compare Hodgson v. Greyhound Lines, Inc., 499 F.2d 859, 865 (7th Cir.1974), cert. denied, 419 U.S. 1122, 95 S.Ct. 805, 42 L.Ed.2d 822 (1975) (bus company that refuses to hire new drivers over age 35 need only show that its policy was based on a good faith judgment that passenger safety could be assured by its age limitation and was not merely the result of "an arbitrary belief lacking in objective reason or rationale.") with Smallwood v. United Air Lines, Inc., 661 F.2d 303 (4th Cir.1981) (airline policy denying employment to pilot applicants over age 35 violates ADEA as employer did not offer significant evidence tending to prove that substantially all applicants over age 35 would be unable to satisfy job requirements and company's extant physical examination program could be used to screen out unsafe applicants on an individual basis) and Usery v. Tamiami Trail Tours, Inc., 531 F.2d 224 (5th Cir.1976) (bus company's refusal to hire new drivers over age 40 upheld because employer demonstrated that age was the only practical basis for determining which applicants would be unsafe drivers even though court found employer did not demonstrate a factual basis for assuming that all applicants over 40 would be unsafe drivers).   For further discussion of these cases see Note, The Scope of the Bona Fide Occupational Qualification Exemption Under the ADEA, 57 Chi.Kent L.Rev. 1145 (1981); Note, The Age Discrimination in Employment Act of 1967, 90 Harv.L.Rev. 380, 400–410 (1976).

The Supreme Court addressed this controversy in WESTERN AIR LINES, INC. v. CRISWELL, 472 U.S. 400, 105 S.Ct. 2743, 86 L.Ed.2d 321 (1985).   It upheld the two pronged BFOQ inquiry developed in *Tamiami* and described herein.   More significantly, perhaps, it rejected the employer's contention that the ADEA required only that an employer establish a "rational basis in fact" for believing that identification of those individuals lacking suitable qualifications could not occur on an individualized basis.   Thus, the Court held, to establish a BFOQ defense, an employer must first demonstrate that the qualification used to justify the age requirement is reasonably necessary to the essence of its business and then prove that it was compelled to rely on age as a proxy for this qualification by establishing either that all or substantially all individuals over a particular age lack the qualification or that it is impracticable or impossible to treat persons over this age on an individualized basis. Applying this test, the Third Circuit ruled that a State Police Department could not assert good health and physical conditioning as reasonably necessary job characteristics for its older police officers when it did not require police officers of all ages to demonstrate some minimum level of health and physical conditioning.   Since the Department had not developed, implemented or enforced minimum health and fitness standards for all its officers, it was imposing selective age-based enforcement of health and fitness requirements and not relying on a BFOQ.   EEOC v. Commonwealth of Pennsylvania, 829 F.2d 392 (3d Cir.1987).

Moreover, in JOHNSON v. MAYOR AND CITY COUNCIL OF BALTIMORE, 472 U.S. 353, 105 S.Ct. 2717, 86 L.Ed.2d 286 (1985), decided the same day as *Western Air Lines,* the Court stated that a federal mandatory retirement rule applicable to a class of federal employees did not establish an absolute BFOQ defense to a state or local government rule imposing an identical pre-age 70 mandatory retirement age on analogous state and local government workers. It concluded that the federal statute relied on by the defendants in this case was not intended by Congress to apply to nonfederal employees.   The Court also concluded that the decision to impose an age 55 mandatory retirement provision was not based on a Congressional determination that age was a bona fide occupational qualification for the subject class (federal firefighters), but, rather, on the idiosyncratic problems of federal civil servants and Congress' desire to create an image of a "young man's service."   Accordingly, the Court stated that the presence of a federal statute authorizing pre-age 70 mandatory retirement for federal firefighters was not relevant to the question of whether age is a BFOQ for firefighters.   The Court did add, however, that if, in another case, there was evidence that Congress had based its early retirement statute on the same considerations that would support the finding of a BFOQ, then such evidence "might" be admissible as evidence to determine the existence of a BFOQ for nonfederal employees and that the extent of the probativity of such a Congressional determination would depend upon the level of congruity between the federal and nonfederal occupations under question.   Finally, it declared that if Congress had expressly extended the BFOQ to nonfederal occupations, that determination would be dispositive.

5. Luther Clark, a 45 year old former Air Force pilot, applied for a pilot position with Ace Airlines, Inc. The company rejected his application in a letter stating that while Clark was otherwise qualified for the job, airline policy precluded hiring pilots over the age of 35. Ace maintains a pilot training and progression system under which all pilot applicants are hired as Second Officers, are promoted to First Officers after 8 to 10 years of service with Ace and are advanced to Captain after an additional 6 to 8 years. The company contends that substantial costs are involved in operating its pilot training and progression system and, when coupled with an F.A.A. requirement that all pilots retire at 60, a maximum age of 35 at initial hire is necessary to achieve peak pilot productivity. Has Ace violated the ADEA? Compare Smallwood v. United Air Lines, Inc., 661 F.2d 303 (4th Cir.1981), cert. denied, 456 U.S. 1007, 102 S.Ct. 2299, 73 L.Ed.2d 1302 (1982), with Murnane v. American Airlines, Inc., 667 F.2d 98 (D.C.Cir.1981), cert. denied, 456 U.S. 915, 102 S.Ct. 1770, 72 L.Ed.2d 174 (1982).

6. Kevin Conroy was discharged as Manager of the men's clothing department of Watson's Department Store one month after his 55th birthday. At the time of his discharge, Conroy had worked at Watson's for 25 years and was earning $47,000. Conroy's position eventually was filled by Mark Dix, a 25 year old who had worked as an assistant buyer at Watson's for 3 years. The store contends that a sharp decrease in revenues forced it to adopt several cost-cutting techniques, including the discharge of its five highest paid employees, and that Conroy was discharged pursuant to that policy. Has Watson's violated the ADEA? See Leftwich v. Harris–Stowe State College, 702 F.2d 686 (8th Cir.1983); Geller v. Markham, 635 F.2d 1027 (2d Cir.1980).

Would it matter if the employer's desire to cut costs was the basis for discharging an individual employee rather than the basis of a general policy governing a large scale reduction in force? In METZ v. TRANSIT MIX, INC., 828 F.2d 1202 (7th Cir.1987), the trial court recognized that the ADEA prohibited an employer from replacing higher paid employees with lower paid employees in order to reduce its costs, but accepted the defendant's contention that the desire to save costs was a permissible motive when made in the context of an individual employment decision as opposed to a policy of general applicability. The appellate court rejected this distinction. In this case, the plaintiff's salary was the product of annual raises given regardless of the company's financial condition. Consequently, the plaintiff's high salary was, to a significant degree, a direct function of his accrued seniority. The Seventh Circuit reasoned that where, as in the instant case, salary is tied directly to the plaintiff's seniority (and thus his age), the use of salary operates as a "proxy" for age and the plaintiff can establish a prima facie case of disparate treatment discrimination. Moreover, the court added, where salary is used as the functional equivalent of age, reliance on high salary as the basis for discharge cannot, as a matter of law, constitute either a nondiscriminatory explanation or a reasonable factor other than age. Presumably, this reasoning should have been sufficient to lead the court to rule in favor of the plaintiff on one of two grounds—i.e., either that the defendant had not supplied a nondiscriminatory explanation to rebut the plaintiff's prima facie case, or that its attempt to use cost-justification as a "factor other than age" affirmative defense had been rejected as a matter of law. Nevertheless, the majority also pointed out that the company had not offered to plaintiff the opportunity to retain his job at the lower salary offered to his younger replacement. While this fact might suggest that cost-saving was not the defendant's true motive, such a determination should have been unnecessary since the court already had rejected the cost-saving "defense" as a matter of law.

In his dissent, Judge Easterbrook also took note of the majority's interest in this matter. He emphasized that the majority's discussion of this issue suggests that the majority would not have found a violation if the company had reduced the plaintiff's salary instead of discharging him. This led him to criticize the majority for stating, on the one hand, that employers cannot act on the basis of salary, while implying, on the other hand, that although salary could not be used as the basis for discharge, it could be used as the basis for salary reduction. ("If one is off limits, so is the other; neither the language nor the structure of the Act creates the sort of distinction my colleagues suggest." 828 F.2d at 1213–14.) On a more fundamental level, Judge Easterbrook rejected the majority's treatment of salary as the functional equivalent of age and its analysis of the plaintiff's complaint as a disparate treatment case. In his view, wage discrimination constitutes age discrimination "only when wage depends directly on age, so that the use of one is a pretext for the other; high covariance is not sufficient * * *." Id., at 1212. Here, Easterbrook continued, the company used the plaintiff's wage with indifference to his age, rather than because of it. Accordingly, since this was a situation where wage was only related to, rather than "directly dependent" upon age, the only conceivable concern with treating high wage earners adversely was the disproportionate impact of such a policy on older workers. Consequently, he declared, this decision should have been analyzed under impact, rather than disparate treatment theory. Yet when that evidentiary model is used, Easterbrook maintained, the facts do not support a prima facie showing of impact. He pointed to statistics indicating that wages rise through age forty and then decline. He also reported that there was no evidence in the record of the instant case indicating that the wage-age profile at Transmit Mix had an upward slope. (This may be explained by the fact that the plaintiff plead and tried the case as a disparate treatment claim.) Thus, he concluded, other than taking judicial notice of a wage-age profile that did not exist, there was no showing of disproportionate impact. Additionally, he reasoned, even if a prima facie case of impact had been established, the defendant's decision to replace a high salaried employee because the productivity obtained from that position did not justify such a salary when someone was available to perform the job at a lower salary, constituted a sound business reason justifying the creation of this impact. For more on this question, see Kaminshine, The Cost of Older Workers, Disparate Impact, And the Age Discrimination In Employment Act, 42 Fla.L.Rev. 229 (1990).

What if Watson's had offered to retain Conroy at the $21,000 salary it subsequently offered to Dix? Would that violate § 4(a)(3) of the ADEA, which makes it unlawful for an employer "to reduce the wage rate of any employee in order to comply with the Act"? See generally, Note, The Cost Defense Under the ADEA, 1982 Duke L.J. 580 (1982).

7. Johanson Insurance Co. decides to reduce the number of its insurance salesmen in response to a decline in sales. It offers an early retirement option to any of its sales personnel whose age plus total years of service is equal to or greater than 75. The plan pays $750 per month to all qualifying employees. David Filvaroff, a 60 year old employee, brings an ADEA claim against the company, alleging that by providing equal monthly early retirement benefits, younger qualifying employees will receive greater total benefits since they will

be receiving monthly payments over a longer period of time. What result? See Dorsch v. L.B. Foster Co., 782 F.2d 1421 (7th Cir.1986).

8. Congress made some significant changes to the ADEA when it amended the statute in 1986. Prior to this legislative change, the Act only protected private and non-federal public employees between the ages of forty and seventy from involuntary retirement. In 1986, Congress removed the upper age limit previously applicable to private and non-federal public employees so that all persons over 40 years of age are protected from involuntary retirement and all other forms of unlawful age discrimination. It also required employers to continue to provide group health care insurance coverage to all employees over age 40, regardless of age. The amendment additionally permits involuntary retirement of tenured professors and allows state and local governments to refuse to hire or to discharge firefighters and law enforcement officers where either the individual has attained the age of hiring or retirement set by state or local law as of March 3, 1983, or where the decision is taken pursuant to a bona fide hiring or retirement plan. Both of these exemptions, however, will expire on December 31, 1993.

The statute, of course, only prohibits mandatory retirement. (But keep in mind that this prohibition remains subject to the statutory BFOQ exception.) Does this mean, therefore, that an employer can offer voluntary retirement plans? In HENN v. NATIONAL GEOGRAPHIC SOCIETY, 819 F.2d 824 (7th Cir.), cert. denied, 484 U.S. 964, 108 S.Ct. 454, 98 L.Ed.2d 394 (1987), the employer offered ad salesmen over the age of 55 the option of retaining their jobs or taking early retirement. The court held that since the employees had the option of retaining their jobs with no loss of employee benefits or any other change from the status quo, this additional option was only a benefit and did not constitute a prima facie case of age discrimination against those to whom the offer was made. The limited issue in this case left two interesting questions unanswered. First, would the result have changed if the employer had not permitted the plaintiff to retain his position, i.e., had presented him with the option of "voluntary" retirement with benefits or discharge? Would it matter if the employee had accepted this offer only after the employer had agreed to additional terms contained in the employee's counter-proposal? Second, does the offer of early retirement discriminate on the basis of age against those employees who are not old enough to be eligible for the offer?

In HEBERT v. MOHAWK RUBBER CO., 872 F.2d 1104 (1st Cir.1989), the First Circuit, citing the Seventh Circuit's ruling in *Henn*, held that absent the option to choose to remain working under lawful conditions, an employer's offer of a choice between early retirement with benefits and not working without benefits amounted to compulsory retirement. The court added that the fact that the plaintiff had bargained for all he could obtain in the face of his "retire-or-be-fired" choice, did not transform the decision from a forced to a voluntary retirement. (As the court noted, the plaintiff still had to establish that this decision was made on the basis of his age.) In so ruling, the First Circuit expressly rejected a contrary ruling by the Sixth Circuit in Ackerman v. Diamond Shamrock Corp., 670 F.2d 66 (6th Cir.1982). There, the court held that even though the plaintiff employee was presented only with the choice of accepting early retirement or being fired without benefits, the fact that he accepted the company's offer and signed the document setting forth the retirement arrangement "of his own free will" rendered his retirement voluntary.

The question of whether the provision of an early retirement plan discriminates against those employees who are over age forty but are not old enough to participate in the plan was addressed by the court in WEHRLY v. AMERICAN MOTORS SALES CORP., 678 F.Supp. 1366 (N.D.Ind.1988). There, a 54 year old employee challenged his ineligibility for early retirement under a plan that limited early retirement to employees 55 years of age or older. The court held that a plaintiff who is denied early retirement because he is too young, and therefore ineligible, to participate in an early retirement program, does not state a prima facie case under the ADEA. A contrary result, the court reasoned, would not serve the purpose of the Act of promoting the employment of older persons. Moreover, the trial judge continued, it would impose the unreasonable burden of requiring every employer who wished to implement an early retirement plan to establish a sound business purpose for setting some minimum age limit for participation in the plan. In addition, the court read the Seventh Circuit's ruling in *Henn* to mean that an optional early retirement plan would violate the Act only where the alternative to accepting early retirement was constructive discharge. Here, since the plaintiff could continue to work at his present job until he was old enough to take advantage of the early retirement plan, no constructive discharge was or could be alleged.

The prevailing judicial approach towards early retirement was codified by Congress in the Older Workers Benefit Protection Act, Pub.L. 101–433, 104 Stat. 978 (October 16, 1990), as amended by Pub.L. 101–521, 104 Stat. 2287 (November 5, 1990)(OWBPA). This enactment, *inter alia*, amends the ADEA by adding a new provision, § 4(l) [29 U.S.C. § 623(l)], which permits voluntary early retirement incentive plans as long as the employer can demonstrate that the plan is consistent with the relevant purpose or purposes of the OWBPA. The statute also explicitly lists the following as its goals: (1)to promote the employment of older workers based on ability rather than age; (2)to prohibit arbitrary age-based discrimination in employment; and (3)to assist employers and employees in addressing problems associated with the impact of age on employment. Thus, as long as the employer's plan is consistent with the relevant purpose or purposes, eligibility for an early retirement program can be limited to employees of a certain minimum age without violating the terms of the Act. But voluntary early retirement plans remain otherwise subject to the anti-discrimination provisions of the ADEA as well as to the equal benefit or equal cost defense of § 4(f)(2). (See Note 10(a), *infra*.)

9. A question frequently associated with early retirement plans arises when the employer offers enhanced benefits in exchange for the employees' waiver of statutory rights. The prevailing judicial attitude is that a knowing and willful waiver of a worker's rights under the ADEA, even when contained in a release that was executed without EEOC supervision, is permissible and not void as contrary to public policy. These courts point to the fact that private settlement of age claims is not inconsistent with the terms and policy of the ADEA. They admit that the ADEA incorporates by reference the enforcement provisions of the FLSA and that the Supreme Court has consistently held that private waiver of claims under the FLSA is contrary to public policy and, therefore, unenforceable. Nevertheless, they reason, because the FLSA protects the lowest paid class of workers and the ADEA protects a class of employees that includes many highly paid individuals that are capable of obtaining legal assistance without hardship, the statutes can be treated differently for waiver purposes. They also note that Title VII claims can be waived. See O'Hare v. Global Natural Resources, Inc., 898 F.2d 1015 (5th Cir.1990);

Bormann v. AT & T Communications, Inc., 875 F.2d 399 (2d Cir.), cert. denied, 493 U.S. 924, 110 S.Ct. 292, 107 L.Ed.2d 272 (1989); Coventry v. U.S. Steel Corp., 856 F.2d 514 (3d Cir.1988); Lancaster v. Buerkle Buick Honda Co., 809 F.2d 539 (8th Cir.), cert. denied, 482 U.S. 928, 107 S.Ct. 3212, 96 L.Ed.2d 699 (1987).

The OWBPA also codified this general acceptance of statutory waivers. Title II of this enactment provides that a waiver of rights under the ADEA, including those sought as a condition for receipt of early retirement or severance pay, is permissible where the waiver is "knowing and voluntary". The statute then sets forth a list of threshold requirements for courts to consider in determining whether the waiver was "knowing and voluntary". Among these are that the waiver must (a)be written in a manner calculated to be understood by the average worker; (b)specifically refer to rights or claims arising under the ADEA; (c)not include a waiver of rights or claims that may arise after the date of execution of the waiver; (d)be made in exchange for consideration beyond anything to which the individual already was entitled; (e)contain a written statement advising the individual to consult with an attorney prior to executing the agreement; and (f)provide the individual with at least 21 days within which to consider the agreement (or 45 days where the waiver is part of an exit incentive or other employment termination program offered to a group of employees) and with another seven days after the execution of the agreement to revoke the agreement. In addition, the waiver agreement will not become enforceable until the expiration of the revocation period and the burden of proving that the waiver was knowing and voluntary is on the party asserting the validity of the waiver. Note, in this regard, that the statute requires the employer to prove that the waiver was written in a manner calculated to be understood by the average worker. This suggests that an individual employee may not be bound to a waiver when the employer only demonstrates that she personally understood the meaning of the waiver. Rather, it suggests that the employer must prove that the average worker subject to the waiver would understand it. An individual waiver also does not bar the EEOC from taking action to enforce the Act. Finally, if a waiver is sought in settlement of a pending EEOC charge or judicial proceeding, the waiver must comply with all of the aforesaid requirements, except for the mandatory consideration and revocation periods. Rather, the statute provides only that the individual must be given "a reasonable period of time within which to consider the settlement agreement" when it relates to a pending administrative or judicial proceeding. These provisions apply to all ADEA waivers entered into after October 16, 1990.

What is the significance, if any, of this new statutory language with respect to an employee's acceptance of a proposal that she submit all employment-related disputes and claims to binding arbitration? Would it matter whether the parties to such an agreement were the employee and her employer rather than the employee and some third party such as a professional licensing organization? Consider, in this regard, that in 1925, Congress enacted the Federal Arbitration Act (FAA), a statute whose purpose is to reverse the common law rule denying specific performance to arbitration agreements and which requires that such agreements be recognized and enforced on the same terms as all other contracts.

The question of whether an agreement for binding arbitration of all employment-related claims can operate as a valid waiver of *judicial* enforcement of statutory (as opposed to contractual, see discussion of Alexander v. Gardner–Denver at p. 521, *supra*) rights confronted the Supreme Court in

GILMER v. INTERSTATE/JOHNSON LANE CORPORATION, 500 U.S. ___, 111 S.Ct. 1647, 114 L.Ed.2d 26 (1991). There, the plaintiff was required by his employer (the defendant) to register with the New York Stock Exchange (NYSE) as a securities representative. The Exchange's registration application, in turn, provided, *inter alia*, that the applicant thereby agreed to arbitrate any claim arising between him and his employer that was subject to binding arbitration under any other NYSE regulation. One of these other regulations, NYSE Rule 347, provided for arbitration of any employment-related controversy between a registered representative and a NYSE member organization. Thus, by complying with his employer's demand that he register with the NYSE, the plaintiff was subjected to the NYSE rule requiring binding arbitration of any employment-related claim between a registered representative and his employer. After being discharged (at age 62), Gilmer filed an age discrimination charge with the EEOC and, subsequently, an ADEA claim in federal district court. The trial judge denied the defendant's motion to dismiss the claim and to compel arbitration, ruling that Congress indicated its intention in the ADEA to protect employees from the waiver of a judicial forum to enforce statutory rights. The Fourth Circuit disagreed, finding no evidence in the text, legislative history or underlying purposes of the ADEA of any congressional intent to preclude the enforcement of arbitration agreements. The Supreme Court affirmed the appellate court's ruling by focusing on three issues: (a)whether statutory claims could be the subject of an arbitration agreement enforceable under the FAA; (b)if so, whether the FAA's explicit exclusion of "employment contracts" applied to the instant arbitration provision; and (c)if not, whether there was, nevertheless, any evidence that Congress, in enacting the ADEA, intended to preclude the waiver of judicial enforcement of these statutory rights by a binding arbitration agreement.

The Court began by noting that it previously had held enforceable arbitration agreements relating to claims arising under such statutes as the Securities Acts of 1933 and 1934 and RICO. Thus, it was clear to the seven member majority that an arbitration clause requiring the arbitration of statutory claims could be enforced under the FAA. The resolution of the second question turned on the interpretation of a provision in the FAA that exempted any "contract of employment" from the operation of that law. The majority ruled that this exclusionary clause did not apply to the arbitration agreement at issue. The Court noted that the defendant had never contended that its employment contract with Gilmer included a written arbitration clause. Rather, the majority reasoned, the arbitration obligation arose only as a result of the relationship created between Gilmer and the NYSE when he registered with the Exchange and so the arbitration promise was a part of Gilmer's contract with the NYSE, not with the defendant employer. Thus, they concluded, this agreement to arbitrate was not part of an "employment contract" within the meaning of the exclusionary clause and was, therefore, enforceable under the terms of the FAA. In dissent, Justice Stevens (joined by Justice Marshall) maintained that the statutory exclusionary clause should be interpreted to cover *any* agreement by an employee to arbitrate employment-related disputes, irrespective of whether that arbitration obligation was contained in the employee's contract with the employer or in an application for registration with a third party, at least when such a third party registration was a condition of employment.

Having concluded that the instant arbitration agreement was otherwise enforceable under the FAA, the Court then had to examine whether, in enacting the ADEA, Congress intended to preclude a waiver of judicial remedies for the enforcement of the rights contained therein. Since the plaintiff had conceded that nothing in the text nor legislative history of the ADEA explicitly precluded arbitration, the Court declared that Gilmer was bound by his promise to arbitrate all employment-related claims unless he otherwise could establish that Congress intended to preclude the waiver of a judicial forum for ADEA claims. This could be done, the Court added, by demonstrating an "inherent conflict between arbitration and the ADEA's underlying purposes," albeit in light of the federal policy favoring arbitration. The Court, however, then rejected Gilmer's contention that compulsory arbitration of ADEA claims would be inconsistent with the statutory framework and purposes of the ADEA. The majority reasoned that arbitration, like litigation, could further social policies as well as resolve specific individual disputes. The majority pointed to the fact that claims under other statutes serving broad social purposes, such as RICO and the Securities Acts of 1933 and 1934, had been held to be appropriate for arbitration. It also rejected the notion that arbitrating ADEA claims would undermine the EEOC's role in enforcing that statute, stating that while an individual subject to an arbitration agreement could not bring suit, she was not precluded from filing a charge with the EEOC, and that the arbitration agreement would not preclude the EEOC from filing an action seeking classwide relief. The majority also emphatically dismissed the claim that reliance on the arbitration forum would weaken the level of protection afforded by the ADEA as "far out of step with our current strong endorsement of the federal statutes favoring this method of resolving disputes." It noted that the NYSE regulations provided protections against biased arbitration panels (as well as adequate methods of discovery such as document production, information requests, depositions and subpoenas) and that the rules required that all arbitration awards be in writing and be made available to the public. While admitting that judicial review of arbitration decisions is limited, the majority reiterated its previously stated view that such review was sufficient to ensure that arbitrators comply with the requirements of the statute at issue. Responding to the claim that the arbitration process could not adequately promote the objectives of the ADEA because it could not provide for broad equitable relief or class actions, the Court declared that the NYSE regulations did not restrict the form of relief awardable by arbitrators and that the existence of an arbitration agreement would not preclude the EEOC from filing a class action seeking class-wide and equitable relief. The Court also refused to ignore all arbitration agreements on the basis of a general claim that all such provisions are the product of unequal bargaining power. Rather, the Court provided, arbitration agreements should be treated like all other contracts, and be subject to ad hoc examination to determine if the individual contract resulted from the type of fraud or unequal bargaining power that would provide grounds for the revocation of any contract. No such evidence of coercion or fraud, the Court determined, was found in the case at bar.

Finally, the Court distinguished the decision in the case at bar from its prior ruling in Alexander v. Gardner–Denver in which it had held that arbitration under a collective bargaining agreement did not preclude the initiation of a Title VII action. *Gardner–Denver,* the Court reasoned, involved an arbitration provision applicable only to contractual disputes, whereas the instant agreement encompassed statutory as well as contractual claims. Since the employees in *Gardner–Denver* had not agreed to submit statutory claims to arbitration, the issue there was whether arbitration of contractual claims precluded subsequent judicial resolution of statutory claims over which the arbitrator had no jurisdiction. The Court also noted that *Gardner–Denver* had not been decided under the FAA and that the arbitration therein was conducted on the employee's behalf by his union, which raised a concern about the tension between collective representation and individual statutory rights, a concern that did not arise in the present case.

In his dissent, Justice Stevens maintained that since the issuance of broad injunctive relief was fundamental to eliminating age discrimination and class-wide injunctive relief is generally not available in arbitral forums, compulsory arbitration of ADEA claims would frustrate an essential purpose of that law. He also expressed his doubts that Congress intended the FAA to apply to statutory claims, especially in the context of employment disputes and when contained in form contracts between parties of unequal bargaining power.

As noted above, the majority in *Gilmer* sought to distinguish its ruling therein from its prior decision in *Gardner–Denver*. Consequently, the *Gilmer* Court did not decide whether a *collectively bargained* arbitration agreement was enforceable under the FAA, regardless of whether or not that agreement provided for the arbitration of purely contractual, or statutory as well as contractual, disputes. *Gilmer* also, of course, only dealt with the arbitrability of ADEA claims. Not suprisingly, it did not take long for a case to arise in which the defendants sought to have *Gilmer* extended to the Title VII context. Shortly after issuing its opinion in *Gilmer*, the Supreme Court, in DEAN WITTER REYNOLDS INC. v. ALFORD, __ U.S. __, 111 S.Ct. 2050, 114 L.Ed.2d 456 (1991), vacated and remanded for further consideration in light of *Gilmer* a Fifth Circuit decision in which that court (pre-*Gilmer*) had relied on *Gardner–Denver* and refused to dismiss the plaintiff's Title VII claim. The circuit court ruled that a stockbroker employed by a securities firm was not required under the FAA to submit her Title VII claim to arbitration pursuant to an arbitration clause contained in her contract with the securities exchange (that was identical to the one discussed in *Gilmer*). It also noted that post-*Gardner-Denver* decisions by the Supreme Court reflected the Court's broad interpretation of the FAA and its policy favoring the enforcement of arbitration agreements. Nevertheless, the Fifth Circuit panel concluded, it remained bound by the as-yet unmodified *Gardner–Denver* ruling insofar as Title VII claims were concerned. The Fifth Circuit did not examine the issue of whether the exclusionary clause of the FAA was applicable to this arbitration agreement. 905 F.2d 104 (5th Cir.1990). On remand from the Supreme Court, however, the Fifth Circuit panel unanimously reversed its position and concluded that the Court's decision in *Gilmer* required it to order the trial court to dismiss the plaintiff's Title VII complaint and to compel arbitration of the plaintiff's claim. 939 F.2d 229 (5th Cir.1991). The appellate court reasoned that in light of the many similarities between Title VII and the ADEA, the *Gilmer* rule should extend to Title VII claims. Accordingly, the court concluded that it had "little trouble concluding that Title VII claims can be subjected to compulsory arbitration." Significantly, however, the court noted that it was only enforcing an arbitration provision contained in the plaintiff's contract with the securities exchange and not in her contract with her employer. Thus, the appellate court again avoided ruling on the applicability of the "contracts of employment" exclusionary clause in the FAA. It also reaffirmed the *Gilmer* Court's distinction of *Gilmer* from *Gardner–Denver* on the ground that the latter case involved the arbitration of solely contract-based claims in a collective bargaining context where the claimant would be represented by a union. The impact of *Gilmer* in the Title VII context and its relationship to *Gardner–*

Denver is also discussed in Chapter 4, *supra*, at 521. See also Mago v. Shearson Lehman Hutton Inc., 956 F.2d 932 (9th Cir.1992)(extending *Gilmer* to Title VII action and distinguishing *Gardner–Denver* from *Gilmer* on ground that former case involved collectively bargained agreement; but court fails to address significance of fact that instant arbitration agreement extended to both statutory and contractual disputes).

In WILLIS v. DEAN WITTER REYNOLDS, INC., 948 F.2d 305 (6th Cir.1991), however, a case involving the same arbitration clause contained in the same securities registration form that was examined in *Gilmer* and *Alford*, the Sixth Circuit addressed the controversy surrounding the meaning of the "contracts of employment" exclusionary clause in the FAA. The plaintiff maintained that the arbitration clause contained in the securities registration application was a part of her employment contract since registering with the various stock exchanges was a condition of her employment as an account executive with the defendant securities firm. Thus, she argued, the FAA did not apply to this contractual arbitration clause. The Sixth Circuit initially agreed with the plaintiff in ruling that the language, legislative history and purpose of the FAA all clearly pointed to the conclusion that the FAA was not intended to apply to either collective bargaining or individual employment contracts. Thus, the court declared, any employment contract that was subject to the provisions of Title VII or the ADEA could not be subject to the requirements of the FAA. Nevertheless, the court continued, while contracts for employment are excluded from the coverage of the FAA, the ruling in *Gilmer* precluded a finding that the arbitration clause embodied in the securities regulation form was part of an employment contract. On the other hand, the trial court in DANCU v. COOPERS & LYBRAND, 778 F.Supp. 832 (E.D.Pa. 1991) reasoned that since the exclusionary clause refers to contracts of employment of "seamen, railroad employees, or any other class of workers engaged in foreign or interstate commerce," the drafters intended only to exclude contracts of workers involved in interstate transportation. Otherwise, the court declared, there would have been no reason for Congress to make specific reference only to two transportation-related classes of employees. Accordingly, the court ruled that a partnership agreement executed between the defendant consulting firm and a partner who provided consulting services to state and local governments did not involve workers engaged in interstate transportation and, therefore, was not covered by the FAA's exclusionary clause.

The flip side of this problem arises when the collective bargaining agreement authorizes the employer to cease processing a grievance when an employee also seeks to resolve the dispute in an administrative or judicial forum. In EEOC v. BOARD OF GOVERNORS, 957 F.2d 424 (7th Cir.1992), the court held that since the contract applied, *inter alia*, to age-based complaints, it authorized the employer to penalize an employee for participating in statutorily protected activity. The fact that the contract applied to all attempts to seek recourse in outside forums and was justified by the company as an attempt to avoid duplicative litigation did not save the provision. The court refused to recognize a good faith defense to the prohibition against retaliation. Moreover, with respect to the question of waiver of statutory rights, the court declared that the union could not waive the employees' rights under the ADEA, distinguishing *Gilmer* on the ground that it was not decided in the context of a collective bargaining agreement.

Section 118 of the 1991 Civil Rights Act states that "where appropriate and to the extent authorized by law", the use of alternative dispute resolution mechanisms, such as arbitration, is "encouraged" to resolve disputes under the ADEA and all other statutes amended by the Act. What significance, if any, should this declaration have on the enforceability of arbitration clauses?

Suppose the plaintiff in *Gilmer* had not been required to become a registered securities representative of the NYSE, but had voluntarily chosen to become one. Would he still be subject to the arbitration clause of the NYSE rules and, therefore, be compelled to arbitrate his age discrimination claim? Should it matter at what stage in the plaintiff's ADEA action the employer sought to dismiss the complaint and to compel arbitration? See Moore v. Merrill Lynch, Pierce, Fenner & Smith, Inc., 56 FEP Cases 1466 (D.N.J.1991) (plaintiff, as a registered representative, is subject to compulsory arbitration clause of NYSE rules even though she had registered voluntarily, but arbitration is not compelled because of prejudice to plaintiff occasioned by filing of motion to compel arbitration after plaintiff had filed amended complaint and undertaken extensive discovery efforts, including deposing witnesses and parties in preparation for trial).

10. While the bona fide employee benefit and seniority plan defense of § 4(f)(2) is not available with respect to involuntary retirement, the BFOQ defense does apply to involuntary retirement decisions. Additionally, of course, while not applicable to involuntary retirement, the bona fide seniority and benefit plan defense is applicable to all other age-based decisions. This has generated several interesting problems. For example:

(a) Suppose the employees of Dimitri Enterprises are covered by an employer-funded disability, life and health insurance benefits plan. Since the cost of premiums for employees over the age of 60 is substantially higher than the cost of such premiums for those under age 60, DiMitri's employee benefits plan terminates disability, life and health insurance benefits to all employees at age 60. Recall that the 1986 amendments require employers to continue to provide group health care insurance coverage to all employees over age 40, irrespective of age. Does the ADEA, as amended, prohibit the policy employed by Dimitri Enterprises? Must Dimitri absorb the extra cost of these higher premiums or, at least, make equal premium contributions for over–60 employees and simply provide reduced coverage or require the employees to fund the difference? Prior to the enactment of the 1986 amendment, the EEOC issued a set of interpretative guidelines for the ADEA which included, *inter alia*, the statement that "the legislative history [of § 4(f)(2)] indicates that its purpose is to permit age-based reductions in employee benefit plans where such reductions are justified by significant cost considerations." 29 C.F.R. § 1625.10(a)(1),(d)(4); 46 Fed. Reg. 47724 (Sept. 29, 1981). This interpretation of § 4(f)(2) was adopted by several courts which ruled that the 1986 amendment, while requiring employers to provide some level of health coverage regardless of age, did not preclude age-based disparities in benefit levels if such differences were required to achieve approximate cost equivalency of benefits for older and younger workers. Of course, these courts required that the employer demonstrate a nexus between data concerning the cost of insuring older workers and the specific level of reductions in its particular programs to prove that it reduced benefits no more than necessary to compensate for the higher cost of insuring older workers. See e.g., EEOC v. City of Mt. Lebanon, Pa., 842 F.2d 1480 (3d Cir.1988).

But, in PUBLIC EMPLOYEES RETIREMENT SYSTEM OF OHIO v. BETTS, 492 U.S. 158, 109 S.Ct. 2854, 106 L.Ed.2d 134 (1989), the Supreme Court rejected this interpretation of § 4(f)(2) and held that the EEOC interpretative regulation was invalid as contrary to the plain language of § 4(f)(2). The key issue, obviously, was whether an age-driven, cost-based benefit differential constituted a "subterfuge to evade the purposes of the Act." After noting that a benefit plan adopted before the enactment of the ADEA could not constitute a subterfuge, the Court stated that the mere existence of § 4(f)(2) indicated that Congress believed that not all age discrimination was arbitrary and that relieving employers of the obligation to provide equal insurance benefits to older and younger employees would encourage the employment of older workers. Consequently, the Court concluded, age-based distinctions in post-Act fringe benefit plans would not constitute a subterfuge to evade the purposes of the Act unless they were shown to have been implemented for the purpose of discriminating with respect to some *other* aspect of the employment relationship. Thus, under the *Betts* Court's interpretation of § 4(f)(2), an employer does not have to offer any justification for an age-based provision in its otherwise bona fide employee benefit plan unless the plaintiff can establish that the discriminatory benefit provision is really a subterfuge for discrimination in another area of the employment relation.

The Congressional reaction to this decision, as to several others issued during the 1989 term, was swift. In October, 1990, President Bush signed the aforementioned Older Workers Benefit Protection Act. Title I of this enactment was designed, in primary part, to overturn the Supreme Court's ruling in *Betts* and to codify the EEOC's administrative interpretation of § 4(f)(2). Congress' intention is reflected in § 101 (the preamble) of the new law, which announces Congress' determination that

"as a result of the decision of the Supreme Court in * * * *Betts*, legislative action is necessary to restore the original congressional intent in passing and amending the ADEA, which was to prohibit discrimination against older workers in all employee benefits except when age-based reductions in employee benefit plans are justified by significant cost considerations."

Congress achieved this aim in two steps. First, it added a new subsection to the list of definitions in the ADEA wherein it defined "compensation, terms, conditions, or privileges of employment" to encompass all benefits provided pursuant to a bona fide employee benefit plan. The effect of this is to put age-based discrimination in such employee benefits expressly within the proscription against age discrimination found in § 4(a)(1) of the ADEA.

Second, Congress revised § 4(f)(2), the exception to the general prohibition against age discrimination. It divided the original version of § 4(f)(2) into two new sub-parts; the first dealing with seniority systems and the second with employee benefit plans. The only change in the subsection dealing with bona fide *seniority* systems is the elimination of the word "subterfuge," so that an employer can now discriminate on the basis of age in order to observe the terms of a bona fide seniority system unless that system is "intended to evade the purposes of" the Act. (It also retains the prohibition against involuntary retirement because of age.) With respect to bona fide *employee benefit* plans, the new provision eliminates entirely the "subterfuge to evade the purposes of the Act" terminology and replaces it with language permitting age-based discrimination in such plans as long as the cost incurred or payment made on account of an older worker is no less than that made or incurred on behalf of a younger worker "as permissible under section 1625.10, title 29, Code of Federal Regulations." This latter citation, of course, is to the EEOC interpretative regulation.   Thus, the statute reverses *Betts* and codifies the EEOC's "equal benefit or equal cost" principle, i.e., that an employer can provide either (1)equal benefits to all employees regardless of age, or (2)unequal benefits to older workers as long as the cost of benefits provided to older employees is at least equal to the cost of benefits for younger workers.   Moreover, the elimination of the "subterfuge for the purposes of evading the Act" language means that a plaintiff no longer has to establish that the benefit differential was implemented for the purpose of discriminating in some other area of the employment relationship.   The statute goes on to provide that any employer relying on the § 4(f)(2) exemption has the burden of proving that it has fulfilled the statutory requirements.

The new Act also added § 4(k) to the ADEA.   This provision extends the application of the Act to all seniority and employee benefit plans, regardless of the date of their adoption.   In *Betts*, the Court had stated (reaffirming a prior ruling), that the "subterfuge to evade the purposes of the Act" language of the ADEA could not apply to a benefit plan or seniority system adopted *before* the enactment of the ADEA.   The new statutory language, then, overrules this portion of the holding in *Betts*.   Employee benefits contained within collective bargaining agreements became subject to the statutory requirements as of June 1, 1992.

11.   In EEOC v. County of Allegheny, 705 F.2d 679 (3d Cir.1983), the court rejected the defendant's claim that its reliance upon a state statute that conflicted with the provisions of the ADEA constituted a "differentiation based on factors other than age."

12.   Public sector age classifications also are subject to constitutional scrutiny under the equal protection and due process guarantees of the Fifth and Fourteenth Amendments of the U.S. Constitution. In MASSACHUSETTS BOARD OF RETIREMENT v. MURGIA, 427 U.S. 307, 96 S.Ct. 2562, 49 L.Ed.2d 520 (1976), noted in the principal case, a Massachusetts statute requiring uniformed state police officers to retire at age fifty was held not to violate the equal protection clause. (No claim was made under the ADEA.) The Supreme Court stated that an age classification need only pass the rationality, rather than strict scrutiny standard; and that mandatory retirement at age 50 rationally furthered Massachusetts' interest in protecting the public by assuring the physical preparedness of the uniformed police. Similarly, in VANCE v. BRADLEY, 440 U.S. 93, 99 S.Ct. 939, 59 L.Ed.2d 171 (1979), a federal statute mandating retirement at age 60 of Foreign Service personnel was upheld in the face of an equal protection challenge. The Supreme Court held that the retirement provision rationally furthered Congress' legitimate objective of maintaining a competent Foreign Service. However, in light of the virtual identity in language between § 15 of the ADEA and § 717 of Title VII, should the ruling in Brown v. General Services Administration, 425 U.S. 820, 96 S.Ct. 1961, 48 L.Ed.2d 402 (1976), be extended to make the ADEA the exclusive remedy for federal employee claims of age discrimination, or should age claimants enjoy a parallel constitutional remedy? See Purtill v. Harris, 658 F.2d 134 (3d Cir.1981); Paterson v. Weinberger, 644 F.2d 521 (5th Cir.1981). Similarly, should the ADEA apply to an age discrimination claim of a uniformed member of the armed forces? See Lear v. Schlesinger, 17 FEP Cases 337 (W.D.Mo.1978).

13.   The ADEA, unlike Title VII, does not contain an express exemption for religious institutions or Indian tribes. Does the application of the ADEA to

religious institutions create a conflict with either of the religion clauses of the First Amendment? Compare Soriano v. Xavier University Corp., 687 F.Supp. 1188 (S.D.Ohio 1988)(denying defendant Jesuit–affiliated university's motion for summary judgment on ground that enforcement of the "limited provisions" of the ADEA does not entangle nor endanger the religion clauses of the First Amendment; court does not identify employment status of plaintiff); and Lukaszewski v. Nazareth Hospital, 764 F.Supp. 57 (E.D.Pa.1991)(application of ADEA to claim of secular employee of religiously affiliated hospital does not violate establishment clause as adjudication of this claim will not lead to excessive governmental entanglement into hospital's affairs. Hospital claimed that plaintiff was discharged for using racial epithets in violation of its religious tenets. Court rejected hospital's claim that adjudication of case would require court to evaluate hospital's religious philosophy; use of racial epithets is *per se* justifiable, nondiscriminatory reason for discharge and so inquiry into wisdom of hospital's policy against racial slurs would not be at issue. Court also held that application of ADEA would not violate free exercise clause since statute is generally applicable and not directed specifically at religious practices.) with Cochran v. St. Louis Preparatory Seminary, 717 F.Supp. 1413 (E.D.Mo. 1989)(ADEA not applicable to church-operated schools because (a) application of ADEA to employment practices of religious seminary would raise serious problems under the First Amendment religion clauses as it could cause seminary to steer wide of the zone of prohibited conduct, thereby chilling its performance of its religious mission, and (b) Congressional silence on inclusion of religious institutions within class of covered employers indicates that Congress did not contemplate that the Act would apply to such institutions). The two appellate courts that have ruled on the narrower issue of the applicability of the ADEA to matters affecting clergy agree that the First Amendment prohibits such an extension of the statute. See Scharon v. St. Luke's Episcopal Presbyterian Hospitals, 929 F.2d 360 (8th Cir.1991)(application of ADEA to employment relationship between religious institution and ordained priest who performed religious and secular duties would violate free exercise and establishment clauses of First Amendment) and Minker v. Baltimore Annual Conference of United Methodist Church, 894 F.2d 1354 (D.C.Cir.1990) (affirming trial court ruling that dismissed ADEA claim by pastor allegedly denied an appointment to another congregation because of his age on ground that application of ADEA to employment relationship between pastor and church is barred by free exercise clause of First Amendment). Does tribal sovereign immunity preclude application of the ADEA to an Indian tribe? In EEOC v. CHEROKEE NATION, 871 F.2d 937 (10th Cir.1989), the appellate court reversed the trial court and held that the lower court should not have enforced a subpoena duces tecum issued by the EEOC in connection with its investigation of an age bias complaint. The Tenth Circuit pointed to a treaty between the Cherokee Nation and the U.S. that recognized the tribe's right of self-government and noted a long recognized principle of statutory construction concerning Indian rights that ambiguous provisions in federal legislation should be interpreted to the benefit of the Indians. Accordingly, the Tenth Circuit reasoned, since the ADEA, unlike Title VII, was silent on its applicability to Indian tribes and since Congress had not made any clear indication of its desire to abrogate Indian sovereignty rights, the court was obliged to apply the special canons of construction to the benefit of Indian interests and to rule that the ADEA was inapplicable to the defendant tribe.

14. Recall the discussion concerning the availability of a "market defense" in the context of the Equal Pay Act. Suppose an employer states that it will pay the market rate for all new employees but will not adjust the salaries of incumbent workers to meet the market rate. Does such a practice violate the Act? Does it have a disproportionate impact on older workers? If so, is it justified by the "factor other than age" or alternative defense? Compare MacPherson v. University of Montevallo, 922 F.2d 766 (11th Cir.1991)(practice of paying market rates to newly-hired faculty members but not to others has a disparate impact on older professors, but is supported by the defendant's "legitimate business interest" in attracting and hiring good new faculty members) with Davidson v. Board of Governors of State Colleges & Universities, 920 F.2d 441,446 (7th Cir.1990)(the "limited" disparate impact created by the defendant's policy of paying market rate "does not come close to demonstrating a taint of age discrimination.").

SECTION C. PROCEDURAL REQUIREMENTS

Read §§ 7, 14 and 15 of the ADEA.

As a consequence of the combination of the amendments made to the ADEA in 1978 and those effected by the 1991 Civil Rights Act, litigants proceeding under the ADEA are subject to most of the same procedural requirements placed before Title VII claimants. For example, pursuant to § 7(d), a grievant (other than a federal employee) intent on filing a civil action under the ADEA must first file a charge with the EEOC within 180 days after the alleged unlawful practice,[a] or within 300 days of the alleged unlawful practice where a recognized state agency exists, or within 30 days after receipt of notice of termination of proceedings under State law, whichever comes first. The earliest date for filing a judicial action is 60 days after filing the EEOC charge. The maximum period for filing suit was changed by the 1991 Civil Rights Act. Prior to the enactment of the 1991 statute, § 7(e) of the ADEA incorporated the limitations periods set forth in §§ 55 and 56 of the FLSA, which meant that a plaintiff was required to file an age discrimination claim within two years (or, in the case of willful violations, within three years) of the date of the alleged discriminatory act. Among Congress' objectives in passing the 1991 Civil Rights Act was the desire to standardize the limitations periods applicable to ADEA and Title VII claims. Section 115 of the 1991 Act amended § 7(e) of the ADEA to provide that ADEA plaintiffs, like those proceeding under Title VII, must file suit within 90 days after receiving notice from the EEOC that it has concluded or terminated its proceedings. This provi-

---

[a] The Fourth Circuit rejected the suggestion that it adopt a "discovery rule" and held that the language of § 7(d) clearly indicates that the limitations period begins to run from the date of the alleged event and not from the time the claimant discovered its discriminatory nature. Hamilton v. 1st Source Bank, 928 F.2d 86 (4th Cir. 1990)(en banc). The court reasoned that where Congress has intended a discovery rule, it has explicitly provided for it. The court added, however, that since this plaintiff did not assert a claim of equitable tolling, it was not ruling on the availability of that doctrine.

sion also requires the EEOC to provide such notification to the aggrieved.

OSCAR MAYER & CO. v. EVANS

Supreme Court of the United States, 1979.
441 U.S. 750, 99 S.Ct. 2066, 60 L.Ed.2d 609.

Mr. Justice Brennan delivered the opinion of the Court.

* * *

This case presents three questions * * *. First, whether § 14(b) requires an aggrieved person to resort to appropriate state remedies before bringing suit under § 7(c) of the ADEA. Second, if so, whether the state proceedings must be commenced within time limits specified by state law in order to preserve the federal right of action. Third, if so, whether any circumstances may excuse the failure to commence timely state proceedings.

We hold that § 14(b) mandates that a grievant not bring suit in federal court under § 7(c) of the ADEA until he has first resorted to appropriate state administrative proceedings. We also hold, however, that the grievant is not required by § 14(b) to commence the state proceedings within time limits specified by state law. In light of these holdings, it is not necessary to address the question of the circumstances, if any, in which failure to comply with § 14(b) may be excused.

Respondent Joseph Evans was employed by petitioner Oscar Mayer & Co. for 23 years until his involuntary retirement in January 1976. On March 10, 1976, respondent filed with the United States Department of Labor a notice of intent to sue the company under the ADEA. Respondent charged that he had been forced to retire because of his age in violation of the Act. At approximately this time respondent inquired of the Department whether he was obliged to file a state complaint in order to preserve his federal rights. The Department informed respondent that the ADEA contained no such requirement. Relying on this official advice, respondent refrained from resorting to state proceedings. On March 7, 1977, after federal conciliation efforts had failed, respondent brought suit against petitioner company and company officials in the United States District Court for the Southern District of Iowa.

Petitioners moved to dismiss the complaint on the grounds that the Iowa State Civil Rights Commission was empowered to remedy age discrimination in employment and that § 14(b) required resort to this state remedy prior to the commencement of the federal suit. The District Court denied the motion, and the Court of Appeals for the Eighth Circuit affirmed. * * * We reverse.

Petitioners argue that § 14(b) mandates that in States with agencies empowered to remedy age discrimination in employment (deferral States) a grievant may not bring suit under the ADEA unless he has first commenced a proceeding with the appropriate state agency. Respondent, on the other hand, argues that the grievant has the option of whether to resort to state proceedings, and that § 14(b) requires only that grievants choosing to resort to state remedies wait 60 days before bringing suit in federal court. The question of construction is close, but we conclude that petitioners are correct.

Section 14(b) of the ADEA was patterned after and is virtually *in haec verba* with § 706(c) of Title VII of the Civil Rights Act of 1964 * * *.

* * *

* * * Because state agencies cannot even attempt to resolve discrimination complaints not brought to their attention, the section has been interpreted to require individuals in deferral States to resort to appropriate state proceedings before bringing suit under Title VII.

Since the ADEA and Title VII share a common purpose, the elimination of discrimination in the workplace, since the language of § 14(b) is almost *in haec verba* with § 706(c), and since the legislative history of § 14(b) indicates that its source was § 706(c), we may properly conclude that Congress intended that the construction of § 14(b) should follow that of § 706(c). We therefore conclude that § 14(b), like § 706(c), is intended to screen from the federal courts those discrimination complaints that might be settled to the satisfaction of the grievant in state proceedings. We further conclude that prior resort to appropriate state proceedings is required under § 14(b), just as under § 706(c).

The contrary arguments advanced by respondent in support of construing § 14(b) as merely optional are not persuasive. Respondent notes first that under Title VII persons aggrieved must file with a state antidiscrimination agency before filing with the Equal Employment Opportunity Commission (EEOC). Under the ADEA, by contrast, grievants may file with state and federal agencies simultaneously.[4] From this respondent concludes that the ADEA pays less deference to state agencies and that, as a consequence, ADEA claimants have the option to ignore state remedies.

We disagree. The ADEA permits concurrent rather than sequential state and federal administrative jurisdiction in order to expedite the processing of age-discrimination claims. The premise for this difference is that the delay inherent in sequential jurisdiction is particularly prejudicial to the rights of "older citizens to whom, by definition, relatively few productive years are left."

The purpose of expeditious disposition would not be frustrated were ADEA claimants required to pursue state and federal administrative remedies simultaneously. Indeed, simultaneous state and federal conciliation efforts may well facilitate rapid settlements. There is no

4. ADEA grievants may file with the State before or after they file with the Secretary of Labor.

reason to conclude, therefore, that the possibility of concurrent state and federal cognizance supports the construction of § 14(b) that ADEA grievants may ignore state remedies altogether.

Respondent notes a second difference between the ADEA and Title VII. Section 14(a) of the ADEA, for which Title VII has no counterpart, provides that upon commencement of an action under ADEA, all state proceedings are superseded. From this, respondent concludes that it would be an exercise in futility to require aggrieved persons to file state complaints since those persons may, after only 60 days, abort their involuntary state proceeding by filing a federal suit.

We find no merit in the argument. Unless § 14(b) is to be stripped of all meaning, state agencies must be given at least some opportunity to solve problems of discrimination. While 60 days provides a limited time for the state agency to act, that was a decision for Congress to make and Congress apparently thought it sufficient. * * *

* * *

We consider now the consequences of respondent's failure to file a complaint with the Iowa State Civil Rights Commission. Petitioners argue that since Iowa's 120–day age-discrimination statute of limitations has run, it is now too late for respondent to remedy his procedural omission and that respondent's federal action is therefore jurisdictionally barred. Respondent pleads that since his failure to file was due to incorrect advice by the Department of Labor, his tardiness should be excused.

Both arguments miss the mark. Neither questions of jurisdiction nor questions of excuse arise unless Congress mandated that resort to state proceedings must be within time limits specified by the State. We do not construe § 14(b) to make that requirement. Section 14(b) requires only that the grievant *commence* state proceedings. Nothing whatever in the section requires the respondent here to commence those proceedings within the 120 days allotted by Iowa law in order to preserve a right of action under § 7(c).

* * * By its terms, * * * the section requires only that state proceedings be commenced 60 days before federal litigation is instituted; besides commencement no other obligation is placed upon the ADEA grievant. In particular, there is no requirement that, in order to commence state proceedings and thereby preserve federal rights, the grievant must file with the State within whatever time limits are specified by state law. * * *

This implication is made express by the last sentence of § 14(b), which specifically provides:

"If any requirement for the commencement of such proceedings is imposed by a State authority other than a requirement of the filing of a written and signed statement of the facts upon which the proceeding is based, the proceeding shall be deemed to have been commenced for the purposes of this subsection at the time such statement is sent by registered mail to the appropriate State authority."

State limitations periods are, of course, requirements "other than a requirement of the filing of a written and signed statement of the facts upon which the proceeding is based." Therefore, even if a State were to make timeliness a precondition for commencement, rather than follow the more typical pattern of making untimeliness an affirmative defense, a state proceeding will be deemed commenced for purposes of § 14(b) as soon as the complaint is filed.

* * *

This construction of the statute is fully consistent with the ADEA's remedial purposes and is particularly appropriate "in a statutory scheme in which laymen, unassisted by trained lawyers, initiate the process."

It is also consistent with the purposes of § 14(b). Section 14(b) does not stipulate an exhaustion requirement. The section is intended only to give state agencies a limited opportunity to settle the grievances of ADEA claimants in a voluntary and localized manner so that the grievants thereafter have no need or desire for independent federal relief. Individuals should not be penalized if States decline, for whatever reason, to take advantage of these opportunities. Congress did not intend to foreclose federal relief simply because state relief was also foreclosed.

The structure of the ADEA reinforces the conclusion that state procedural defaults cannot foreclose federal relief and that state limitations periods cannot govern the efficacy of the federal remedy. * * * Congress could not have intended to consign federal lawsuits to the "vagaries of diverse state limitations statutes," ibid, particularly since, in many States, including Iowa, the limitations periods are considerably shorter than the 180–day period allowed grievants in nondeferral States by 29 U.S.C. § 626(d)(1).

That Congress regarded incorporation as inconsistent with the federal scheme is made clear by the legislative history of § 706(c)'s definition of commencement—the same definition later used in § 14(b). Proponents of Title VII were concerned that localities hostile to civil rights might enact sham discrimination ordinances for the purpose of frustrating the vindication of federal rights. The statutory definition of commencement as requiring the filing of a state complaint and nothing more was intended to meet this concern while at the same time avoiding burdensome case-by-case inquiry into the reasonableness of various state procedural requirements.[11]

* * *

11. Moreover, even the danger that state remedies will be *inadvertently* by passed by otherwise proper ADEA plain- tiffs will soon become nonexistent. After July 1, 1979, the EEOC will administer the ADEA. Discrimination charges will have

We therefore hold that respondent may yet comply with the requirements of § 14(b) by simply filing a signed complaint with the Iowa State Civil Rights Commission. That Commission must be given an opportunity to entertain respondent's grievance before his federal litigation can continue. Meanwhile, the federal suit should be held in abeyance. If, as respondent fears, his state complaint is subsequently dismissed as untimely, respondent may then return to federal court. But until that happens, or until 60 days have passed without a settlement, respondent must pursue his state remedy.

Accordingly, the judgment of the Court of Appeals is reversed, and the case is remanded to that court with instructions to enter an order directing the District Court to hold respondent's suit in abeyance until respondent has complied with the mandate of § 14(b).

It is so ordered.

MR. JUSTICE BLACKMUN, concurring.

* * *

MR. JUSTICE STEVENS, with whom THE CHIEF JUSTICE, MR. JUSTICE POWELL, and MR. JUSTICE REHNQUIST join, concurring in part and dissenting in part.

Section 14(b) of the Age Discrimination in Employment Act of 1967, 81 Stat. 607, 29 U.S.C. § 633(b), explicitly states that "no suit may be brought" under the Act until the individual has first resorted to appropriate state remedies. Respondent has concededly never resorted to state remedies. In my judgment, this means that his suit should not have been brought and should now be dismissed.

* * *

* * * If respondent should decide at this point to resort to state remedies, and if his complaint there is found to be time barred, and if he should then seek relief in federal court, the question addressed in * * * the Court's opinion—whether § 14(b) requires resort to state remedies "within time limits specified by the State"—would then be presented. But that question is not presented now, and I decline to join or to render any advisory opinion on its merits. I would simply order that this suit be dismissed in accordance with "the mandate of § 14(b)."

NOTES AND PROBLEMS FOR DISCUSSION

1. Does the Court's ruling that the plaintiff need not file a state administrative charge within the state limitations period mean that there is no time limit for filing that state administrative charge? What about the combined effect of the requirement in § 14(b) that the plaintiff must wait for sixty days

to be filed with the EEOC within time limits specified by federal law, and the EEOC already has a regular procedure whereby discrimination complaints are automatically referred to appropriate agencies as soon as they are received. See Love v. Pullman Co., 404 U.S. 522, 92 S.Ct. 616, 30 L.Ed.2d 679 (1972); 29 CFR 1601.13 (1978). Thus, the deference to state agencies required by § 14(b) will soon become automatic. * * *

after the state filing before filing its federal action and the requirement in § 7(e) that suit be commenced within ninety days after receipt of notice from the EEOC that it has concluded or terminated its proceedings? Moreover, do the answers to these questions affect the availability of the 300 day period for filing with the EEOC? Must a plaintiff file a timely state law charge with the state agency to qualify for the 300 day limit for filing with the EEOC? In fact, must a plaintiff file with the state agency before filing its EEOC charge in order to take advantage of the 300 day filing limit? Is it significant, in this regard, that the state and federal administrative filings can otherwise be made simultaneously? See Aronsen v. Crown Zellerbach, 662 F.2d 584 (9th Cir.1981), cert. denied, 459 U.S. 1200, 103 S.Ct. 1183, 75 L.Ed.2d 431 (1983)(plaintiff can utilize 300 day period regardless of when state charge is filed); Fugate v. Allied Corp., 582 F.Supp. 780 (N.D.Ill.1984)(ADEA contains no time requirement for commencement of state proceedings as long as state charge filed at least sixty days before filing federal suit).

2. Should the invocation of state remedies requirement announced in *Oscar Mayer* be extended to ADEA actions brought by the EEOC? See Marshall v. Chamberlain Manufacturing Corp., 601 F.2d 100 (3d Cir.1979). What is the extent of the EEOC's statutory duty to attempt to achieve conciliation prior to instituting suit? Should the trial court dismiss or stay an EEOC age suit where it finds the EEOC has not fulfilled this statutory obligation? See Marshall v. Sun Oil Co., 592 F.2d 563 (10th Cir.), cert. denied, 444 U.S. 826, 100 S.Ct. 49, 62 L.Ed.2d 33 (1979); Brennan v. Ace Hardware Corp., 495 F.2d 368 (8th Cir.1974).

3. Is a grievant's failure to file a timely charge with the EEOC fatal to a court's exercise of ADEA jurisdiction or is the filing requirement subject to equitable tolling? In ZIPES v. TRANS WORLD AIRLINES, INC., 455 U.S. 385, 102 S.Ct. 1127, 71 L.Ed.2d 234 (1982), the Supreme Court held that the timely filing of an EEOC charge is not a jurisdictional prerequisite to a Title VII suit in federal court but, rather, a precondition subject to waiver, estoppel and equitable tolling. In light of the comments made by the Supreme Court in the principle case concerning the relationship between Title VII and the ADEA, should the *Zipes* ruling be extended to ADEA actions? See Vance v. Whirlpool Corp., 716 F.2d 1010 (4th Cir.1983). If so, under what circumstances would tolling be appropriate? See Dillman v. Combustion Engineering, Inc., 784 F.2d 57 (2d Cir.1986); Price v. Litton Business Systems, Inc., 694 F.2d 963 (4th Cir.1982)(filing period can be tolled if untimeliness is result of employer's deliberate design or conduct employer unmistakably should have understood would cause delay); Franci v. Avco Corp., Avco Lycoming Division, 538 F.Supp. 250 (D.Conn.1982); Barber v. Commercial Union Insurance Co., 27 FEP Cases 703 (D.C.Pa.1981).

4. Section 7(d) requires an individual to wait at least sixty days after filing an EEOC charge before commencing suit in order to give the EEOC a chance to resolve the dispute at the administrative level. Is this sixty day waiting period a jurisdictional requirement? In this regard, should private litigants be subject to the same rule that is applied to EEOC suits (an issue raised in Note 2)? See Vance v. Whirlpool Corp., 707 F.2d 483 (4th Cir.1983), cert. denied, 465 U.S. 1102, 104 S.Ct. 1600, 80 L.Ed.2d 130 (1984). Antecedent to the enactment of the 1991 Civil Rights Act, plaintiffs confronted a two or three year limitations period that dated from the time of the alleged discriminatory act, without reference to the completion of the EEOC's administrative process. This occasionally created a problem when the plaintiff preferred to pursue the EEOC's

conciliation efforts, rather than filing suit at the earliest possible moment, and the agency's backlog did not permit it to resolve or otherwise dispose of charges before the expiration of the two/three year limitations period set forth in § 7(e). In response to this dilemma, Congress enacted a series of provisions that initially tolled the limitations period for up to one year during the period of the agency's conciliation efforts and then extended this tolling period for additional periods. But when Congress decided, in § 115 of the 1991 Civil Rights Act, to tie the limitations period to the termination of the administrative proceedings, it also removed these tolling provisions.

5. The amendments to the ADEA effected by § 115 of the 1991 Civil Rights Act also significantly reduced the importance of determining whether the definition of "willfulness" articulated by the Supreme Court in *Thurston* in connection with the availability of punitive damages should also apply for purposes of the extended statutory limitations period applicable to willful violations. But as the retroactivity of the 1991 Act remains in doubt, this question is not yet moot. In McLAUGHLIN v. RICHLAND SHOE CO., 486 U.S. 128, 108 S.Ct. 1677, 100 L.Ed.2d 115 (1988), the Court extended *Thurston* and rejected the use of the "in the picture" standard of willfulness in connection with the three year statute of limitations applicable to civil actions to enforce the FLSA. While this case arose directly out of an action under the FLSA rather than under the ADEA, the Court noted that the subject provision applied to actions to enforce both statutes (and, for that matter, to the Equal Pay Act as well). Moreover, it noted that the petition for certiorari asked the Court to resolve the post-*Thurston* conflict among the circuits and cited several ADEA cases as representative of that conflict. The Court unanimously rejected the "in the picture" standard, noting that the two-tiered statute of limitations manifested Congress' intention to distinguish between ordinary and willful violations. And the "in the picture standard," they agreed, "virtually obliterated" any distinction between willful and non-willful violations since it would be nearly impossible for any employer to establish that it was unaware either of the Act or its potential applicability. Moreover, they concluded, to adopt such a standard would serve to immunize only ignorant employers from the extended limitations period, a result clearly not intended by Congress. This reasoning led a majority of six Members to conclude that extension of the *Thurston* "knowing or reckless disregard" standard was a "fair reading" of the "plain language" of the statute since common dictionary definitions of "willfulness" referred to conduct that was intentional or deliberate and not merely negligent. In dissent, Justice Marshall, joined by Justices Brennan and Blackmun, preferred the intermediate standard urged by the petitioner, i.e., that a violation was "willful" where the employer knew that there was an "appreciable possibility" that it was covered by the Act and failed to take steps "reasonably calculated" to resolve the doubt. The majority had rejected this alternative on the ground that since it seemed to require an inquiry solely into whether the employer acted "reasonably" in determining the legality of its wage policies, it would still permit a finding of willfulness on the basis of negligent, rather than intentional wrongdoing. In the majority's view, the statute required that the defendant must act recklessly, and not merely unreasonably, to be subject to the extended limitations period. The dissenters criticized the majority for engaging in an unprecedented "plain language" definition of "willful" rather than the traditional "contextual" approach to statutory interpretation. They maintained that the intermediate alternative was appropriate in light of the contextual difference between the instant case and *Thurston*. In *Thurston*, the

dissenters suggested, the meaning of willful was influenced by the fact that it arose in the context of a punitive remedy, whereas the instant case involved merely the length of the filing period in which an unlawfully underpaid employee could obtain compensatory damages. Finally, the dissenters opined, there was likely to be no practical difference between the definitions of "willful" adopted by the majority or by them since, they suggested, it would be unlikely to find an employer who acted "unreasonably" but not "recklessly."

Applying the *McLaughlin* standard for willfulness, the Third Circuit, in EEOC v. Westinghouse Elec. Corp., 869 F.2d 696, 712 (3d Cir.), judgment vacated and remanded for reconsideration on other grounds, 493 U.S. 801, 110 S.Ct. 37, 107 L.Ed.2d 7 (1989), stated that an employer's unwillingness to change its own plans in the face of court rulings that similar plans violate the ADEA is "strong evidence" of willful behavior.

6. Section 7(c)(1) provides that suit by the EEOC terminates the individual's right to bring a separate action under the ADEA. Does an EEOC suit similarly preclude the aggrieved from pursuing his or her state law remedies? See Dunlop v. Pan American World Airways, Inc., 672 F.2d 1044 (2d Cir.1982). Must a trial court dismiss a pending private ADEA action when the EEOC subsequently decides to file suit? See EEOC v. Eastern Airlines, Inc., 736 F.2d 635 (11th Cir.1984); Burns v. Equitable Life Assurance Society, 696 F.2d 21 (2d Cir.1982), cert. denied, 464 U.S. 933, 104 S.Ct. 336, 78 L.Ed.2d 306 (1983). Does the EEOC's intervention into an ADEA action filed in state court by the aggrieved preclude the aggrieved from subsequently filing an ADEA action in federal court? See Chapman v. City of Detroit, 808 F.2d 459 (6th Cir.1986)(by intervening in the state court action, the EEOC has "commenced" an action for the enforcement of the plaintiffs' ADEA rights within the meaning of § 7(c) and, therefore, terminated the individuals' subsequently filed private right of action in federal court). Suppose, on the other hand, the private individual files the first action. Does this preclude the EEOC from bringing its own action on behalf of this aggrieved individual? See EEOC v. Wackenhut Corp., 939 F.2d 241 (5th Cir.1991).

7. Section 15 of the ADEA provides federal employees with a different remedial scheme than is prescribed for non-federal employees. Specifically, federal employees are not required to invoke any state or federal administrative remedy prior to instituting suit. Rather, a federal employee can either seek administrative resolution of a claim by the employing agency (with an appeal to the EEOC from a final agency decision) before filing suit, or bypass the administrative mechanism and file suit in federal district court directly. However, if the second option is chosen, the federal employee, like all other claimants, must file a notice of intent to sue with the EEOC at least thirty days prior to instituting suit. Moreover, as the Supreme Court held in STEVENS v. DEPARTMENT OF TREASURY, ___ U.S. ___, 111 S.Ct. 1562, 114 L.Ed.2d 1 (1991), Section 15(d) requires the claimant to file this notice with the EEOC within 180 days of the alleged discriminatory occurrence and then to wait at least 30 days from said filing before bringing a federal civil action.

An issue has come up, however, as to whether a federal employee who chooses to invoke the EEOC machinery (rather than simply filing a notice of intention to sue and waiting for thirty days) is required to exhaust that administrative mechanism before bringing suit. While nearly all of the circuit courts have concluded that a federal ADEA complainant must completely exhaust the administrative process prior to filing suit, see e.g., Wrenn v.

Secretary, Dept. of Veterans Affairs, 918 F.2d 1073 (2d Cir.1990), cert. denied, ___ U.S. ___, 111 S.Ct. 1625, 113 L.Ed.2d 721 (1991)(requiring exhaustion because permitting the plaintiff to abandon the administrative remedies he has initiated would tend to frustrate the ability of that agency to deal with complaints); Tolbert v. United States, 916 F.2d 245 (5th Cir.1990); McGinty v. U.S. Dept. of Army, 900 F.2d 1114 (7th Cir.1990) and Purtill v. Harris, 658 F.2d 134 (3d Cir.1981), cert. denied, 462 U.S. 1131, 103 S.Ct. 3110, 77 L.Ed.2d 1365 (1983) (Id.), one circuit does not require exhaustion. See Langford v. U.S. Army Corps of Engineers, 839 F.2d 1192 (6th Cir.1988). In *Stevens,* the Court noted this disagreement and admitted that the issue was an important one. Nevertheless, the Solicitor General, representing the defendant agency, informed the Supreme Court that the government was abandoning the position it had taken on this issue before the trial and appellate courts below and was now adopting the plaintiff's view that exhaustion was not required. Under the circumstances, since there now was no one before it defending the contrary position, the Court decided not to rule on the merits and to remand the case for further proceedings. It suggested, however, that the government's changed position would likely result in a ruling in favor of the plaintiff on this issue.

The lower courts also disagree as to the appropriate limitations period to apply to such federal employee actions. Compare Lavery v. Marsh, 918 F.2d 1022 (1st Cir.1990)(federal employee ADEA suits are subject to 30 day limitations period applicable to federal employee claims under Title VII because it is "most reasonable to impute to Congress an intent that ADEA federal employee actions be subject to the same limitations period as other federal employee discrimination claims" and Title VII is the proper comparison statute because the ADEA and Title VII both share the common purpose of combatting employment discrimination and § 15 of ADEA was patterned after § 717 of Title VII) with Lubniewski v. Lehman, 891 F.2d 216 (9th Cir.1989)(rejecting claim that federal employee ADEA claims should be subjected to thirty day limitations period applicable to federal employee Title VII actions; also ruling that § 15(f) precludes reference to any other provision in ADEA, including limitations period governing private actions and holding, therefore, that federal employee ADEA claims are subject to six year catch-all statute of limitations for nontort civil claims against the U.S.); Bornholdt v. Brady, 869 F.2d 57,60 (2d Cir.1989)(rejecting application of 30 day filing period without adopting any alternative, stating that it was "unable to determine precisely what Congress had in mind"); Wiersema v. TVA, 648 F.Supp. 66 (E.D.Tenn.1986)(federal employees held subject to the pre–1991 Act two/three year statute of limitations on ground that by extending coverage of ADEA to federal employees, Congress intended that the scope of protection afforded to federal employees against discrimination be as broad as enjoyed by private sector workers). This issue was raised before the Supreme Court in *Stevens.* The Court noted that while the ADEA does not contain an express limitations period applicable to civil actions filed by federal employees, it would "assume that Congress intended to impose an appropriate period borrowed either from a state statute or from an analogous federal one." But since the plaintiff in *Stevens* had filed suit within one year and six days after the allegedly discriminatory event, the Court concluded that the action had been filed "well within whatever statute of limitations might apply" and, therefore, that it was not required to decide which limitations period was applicable to this action.

Is a federal employee with an age discrimination claim limited to seeking relief under the ADEA? Is it, like Title VII, the exclusive remedy for federal employees? See Chennareddy v. Bowsher, 935 F.2d 315, 318 (D.C.Cir. 1991)("It is undisputed that the ADEA provides the exclusive remedy for a federal employee who claims age discrimination.").

8. In light of the many procedural prerequisites to filing an action under the ADEA, should a state employee be permitted to file an age discrimination charge under § 1983? See Zombro v. Baltimore City Police Department, 868 F.2d 1364 (4th Cir.), cert. denied, 493 U.S. 850, 110 S.Ct. 147, 107 L.Ed.2d 106 (1989)(police officer cannot assert age claim under § 1983 based on alleged constitutional violation by defendant); Price v. Erie County, 654 F.Supp. 1206 (W.D.N.Y.1987)(cause of action based solely upon violation of ADEA cannot be brought under § 1983); Frye v. Grandy, 625 F.Supp. 1573, 1576 (D.Md.1986).

9. Should an unreviewed state agency finding of fact have preclusive effect in a subsequent ADEA action in federal court? Is the Supreme Court's ruling in *Elliott, supra* at 518, applicable? In ASTORIA FEDERAL SAVINGS & LOAN ASS'N v. SOLIMINO, ___ U.S. ___, 111 S.Ct. 2166, 115 L.Ed.2d 96 (1991), a unanimous Supreme Court ruled that judicially unreviewed state administrative agency findings have no preclusive effect on ADEA claims filed in federal court. The Court, in an opinion authored by Justice Souter, noted its longstanding support of the common law doctrines of preclusion as applied to final administrative determinations where the federal or state agency acted in a judicial capacity and the parties had an adequate opportunity to litigate before the administrative body. Moreover, it added, since Congress is understood to legislate in full knowledge of the operation of this well established common law principle, it was appropriate to presume that Congress meant for preclusion to be a part of any statutory framework in the absence of a statutory purpose to the contrary. This, of course, then raised the critical question of which standard the Court would apply to determine whether such a contrary intention had been manifested by Congress. You may recall that this same issue was addressed by the Court, also during its 1991 term, in the context of the presumption against extraterritoriality as applied to Title VII. See EEOC v. Arabian American Oil Co., Chapter 1, § D, *supra* at 80. In contrast to its analysis in *Arabian American Oil,* however, the Court in *Solimino* reasoned that the presumption in favor of administrative preclusion did not require a "clear statement" by Congress to demonstrate its intention to overcome the presumption. Unlike the presumption against extraterritoriality (which, the Court stated, was designed to protect the heightened value of avoiding unintended conflicts between U.S. and foreign law), the presumption in favor of administrative preclusion did not invoke values of sufficient magnitude to require a precise statement by Congress of its intention to overcome the presumption's application to this statutory scheme. The Court declared that while favored as a matter of general policy, administrative preclusion was a flexible concept whose suitability depended upon, inter alia, the nature of the agency involved and the relative adequacy of its procedures. Accordingly, the Court concluded, this "lenient" presumption was so weak that, absent complete legislative default on the issue, it would have, in effect, no presumptive effect at all.

The Court then looked at the text of the ADEA and found that while there was no express provision addressing the deference to be accorded administrative determinations, several provisions carried an implication that Congress did not intend for federal courts to be precluded by state administrative findings. For example, it pointed to the language in § 14(b) that refers to the termination of proceedings under State law as one of the alternative prerequisites to filing an action under the federal statute in federal court. Similarly, the statute lists the termination of state proceedings as one of the reference points for the commencement of the period within which a charge must be filed with the EEOC. This language, in the Court's judgment, reflected Congress' assumption that federal consideration could occur after the termination of state agency proceedings. And invoking preclusion would render the invocation of federal proceedings under these circumstances "strictly *pro forma*." Moreover, the Court urged, granting administrative preclusion would simply encourage claimants committed to preserving their federal claim to perfunctorily file their state claim, wait the minimum sixty day period and then initiate their federal suit, thereby defeating the main purpose of state law deferral—to resolve complaints outside the federal system.

In *Elliott*, the Court had emphasized that the Title VII language requiring federal courts to give "substantial weight" to state administrative findings demonstrated Congress' disinclination to attach preclusive weight to such determinations. Several lower courts had seized on the absence of such language in the ADEA as support for their determination that the ruling in *Elliott* should not be extended to ADEA cases. But the *Solimino* Court rejected that distinction as immaterial, stating that there was "nothing talismanic" about that language and that the result in *Elliott* would have been the same even in the absence of this provision, since § 706(c), like § 14(b) of the ADEA, provides for federal court action after the termination of state proceedings.

The Court also indicated that denying preclusive effect to state agency findings was consistent with the general remedial scheme of the ADEA. It observed that the lower courts uniformly denied preclusive effect to federal agency determinations in subsequent age discrimination suits brought by federal employees and suggested that there was no reason to accord greater deference to state agency findings.

In addition to these statutory arguments, the Court gratuitously offered some policy justifications for its decision. Denying administrative preclusion, it maintained, would avoid future litigation over whether the instant agency had acted in a judicial capacity and whether the parties had been afforded an adequate opportunity to litigate. Additionally, since this ruling was limited to judicially unreviewed agency findings, the Court emphasized that it was only providing claimants with "no more than a second chance to prove the claim" and that the state administrative findings could always be considered by the federal court in an attempt to minimize any duplication of effort.

Finally, the Court emphasized that it previously had ruled, in the "closely parallel" Title VII context, that state court judgments enjoyed preclusive effect in federal courts because the federal statute requiring federal courts to accord full faith and credit to state court judgments had not been impliedly repealed by Title VII. The instant case, the Court stressed, did not involve the judgment of a state court and, therefore, since the federal "full faith and credit" statute was inapplicable, it was not confronted with a question of implied repeal of that law by the ADEA.

10. We already have seen that the ADEA, like the Equal Pay Act, incorporates the remedial provisions of the FLSA. Yet, while (as in the case of the EPA) this includes the reference in the FLSA to awards of back pay and liquidated damages, § 7 of the ADEA (the provision that incorporates the remedies and procedures of the FLSA) adds the condition that "liquidated damages shall be payable only in cases of willful violations" of this statute.

Thus, an ADEA plaintiff, unlike an EPA plaintiff, shoulders the burden of persuading the court that the defendant has committed a willful violation of the Act. Of course, as we mentioned in Note 5, the meaning of "willful" violation was addressed by the Supreme Court in *Thurston*. Notice, however, the way in which the *Thurston* Court phrased its holding on this issue. Recall that it only said that the lower court's interpretation of willful—to mean that the plaintiff must establish that the defendant acted either in the knowledge that its conduct violated the Act or in reckless disregard of the requirements of the Act—was "an acceptable way to articulate a definition of 'willful'." Does this suggest that the Court offered this as an acceptable, though not exclusive definition of the term? It did, of course, reject as unacceptable the plaintiff's suggestion of an "in the picture" standard.

The ruling in *Thurston* left open several other aspects of the meaning of willfulness. For example, we have seen that § 11 of the Portal–to–Portal Act provides employers with a good faith defense to an otherwise mandatory award of liquidated damages in an Equal Pay Act case. But, since § 7(b) of the ADEA does not incorporate § 11 of the Portal–to–Portal Act, the employer's good faith is not an absolute defense to a claim for liquidated damages in an ADEA action. It was suggested, nevertheless, by the Court in *Thurston,* that good faith is a factor to consider in determining whether the defendant acted willfully, a condition that does apply to requests for liquidated damages under the ADEA.

Another problem related to proving willfulness arises in connection with ADEA claims of intentional discrimination. As noted in *Thurston*, an ADEA plaintiff can establish liability either by proving intentional discrimination on the basis of age or by proving that the defendant's facially neutral policy had a disproportionately exclusionary impact on older workers. *Thurston*, however, was an impact case and thus did not raise the issue of the overlap between intentional and willful violations in disparate treatment cases. Since both willfulness and intentional discrimination have a subjective, state-of-mind component to them, will a plaintiff who has proven intentional discrimination *ipso facto* satisfy the requirement of establishing willfulness for liquidated damages purposes? What about the *Thurston* Court's articulated reluctance to make liquidated damages readily available and its statement that the legislative history and structure of the ADEA reflect a Congressional intent to provide a "two-tiered liability scheme"? While the lower courts uniformly recognize that *Thurston* rejected the notion that a plaintiff alleging willfulness must prove specific intent to violate the statute, they have not agreed on whether willfulness is established by proving merely that the employer intentionally discriminated on the basis of age. The Third Circuit, for example, requires plaintiffs to prove that the defendant intentionally discriminated on the basis of age and that this conduct was "outrageous" in order to recover liquidated damages. See e.g., Lockhart v. Westinghouse Credit Corp., 879 F.2d 43 (3d Cir.1989). Similarly, the Fifth Circuit appears to have added an "egregious" requirement to the *Thurston* formulation. See Hansard v. Pepsi–Cola Metropolitan Bottling Co., 865 F.2d 1461, 1470 (5th Cir.), cert. denied, 493 U.S. 842, 110 S.Ct. 129, 107 L.Ed.2d 89 (1989)("liquidated damages are a punitive sanction and should be reserved for the most egregious violations of the ADEA."). On other hand, however, a couple of circuits have expressly rejected the Third Circuit's "outrageousness" standard and require instead that the plaintiff prove that age was the *predominant* factor to establish willfulness, while only requiring proof that age was a *determinative* factor to establish liability. See e.g., Schrand v. Federal Pacific Electric Co., 851 F.2d 152 (6th Cir.1988); Cooper v. Asplundh

Tree Expert Co., 836 F.2d 1544 (10th Cir.1988). Still others have held that willfulness is shown where the employer is found to have made no effort to learn whether it was acting in violation of the Act's requirements. See e.g., Benjamin v. United Merchants & Manufacturers, Inc., 873 F.2d 41, 44 (2d Cir.1989)("double damages may properly be awarded when the proof shows that an employer was indifferent to the requirements of the governing statute and acted in a purposeful, deliberate, or calculated manner). The Eighth Circuit, alternatively, has held that while a jury can make inferences from circumstantial evidence sufficient to justify an award of compensatory damages, a finding of willfulness must be predicated on direct evidence. Hudson v. Normandy School District, 57 FEP Cases 1132 (8th Cir.1992). Finally, several other circuits have chosen merely to adopt, without refinement, the *Thurston* "knowing or reckless disregard" standard. See Biggins v. Hazen Paper Co., 57 FEP Cases 1160 (1st Cir.1992); Taylor v. Home Insurance Company, 777 F.2d 849 (4th Cir.1985), cert. denied, 476 U.S. 1142, 106 S.Ct. 2249, 90 L.Ed.2d 695 (1986); Brown v. M & M/Mars, 883 F.2d 505 (7th Cir.1989); and Gilchrist v. Jim Slemons Imports, Inc., 803 F.2d 1488 (9th Cir.1986).

11. The federal appellate courts uniformly agree that an ADEA plaintiff cannot recover compensatory damages (aside from unpaid wages) such as pain and suffering or mental distress, primarily because the FLSA does not allow for recovery of general compensatory damages. For the same reason, the courts also agree that punitive (as opposed to liquidated) damages are unavailable in ADEA actions. This position is buttressed by the *Thurston* Court's statement that the ADEA's provision of liquidated damages for willful violations is intended to serve a punitive purpose.

The provisions of the 1991 Civil Rights Act giving Title VII, ADA and Rehabilitation Act plaintiffs the right to seek compensatory and punitive damages do not contain any reference to actions brought under the ADEA. Nevertheless, in light of the considerable degree to which Title VII jurisprudence has been transplanted into age discrimination litigation, should these provisions of the 1991 Act be extended to ADEA suits? On the other hand, Congress did expressly mention the ADEA in other provisions of the 1991 Act and when it wanted to extend these remedies to other statutory contexts (such as the ADA and Rehabilitation Act), it knew how to do so in clear and unambiguous language. See Morgan v. The Servicemaster Co. Ltd. Partnership, 58 EPD ¶ 41,262 (N.D.Ill.1992) (nothing in text or legislative history of 1991 Act suggests that Congress intended to extend compensatory and punitive damage remedies to ADEA cases; statute was designed to overrule Supreme Court cases that did not involve age discrimination claims); Guillory–Wuerz v. Brady, 785 F.Supp. 889 (D.Colo.1992) (Id., relying on *Morgan*); Thompson v. Prudential Ins. Co. of America, 59 FEP Cases 263 (D.N.J.1992) (1991 Act provision amending statute of limitations applicable to seniority claims is inapplicable to ADEA claims since this section of 1991 Act does not refer to the ADEA while other portions of the 1991 Act expressly amend the ADEA).

12. With respect to unpaid wages, an ADEA plaintiff has the duty to mitigate. The courts have held, however, that the employer has the burden of proving failure to mitigate by establishing that comparable positions were available and discoverable by the claimant and that she failed to use reasonable care to find them. Jackson v. Shell Oil Co., 702 F.2d 197 (9th Cir.1983); Coleman v. Omaha, 714 F.2d 804 (8th Cir.1983).

13.   As mentioned in connection with the Equal Pay Act, in contrast to the treatment of back pay claims under Title VII as "equitable relief," private actions by employees for back pay under the FLSA (and, therefore, under the EPA and ADEA) have consistently been held to include a right to trial by jury. See Lorillard v. Pons, 434 U.S. 575, 98 S.Ct. 866, 55 L.Ed.2d 40 (1978); Note, The Right to Jury Trial Under the Age Discrimination in Employment and Fair Labor Standards Acts, 44 U.Chi. L.Rev. 365, 376 (1977).   In 1978, the ADEA was amended to specifically authorize trial by jury "of any issue of fact in any * * * action for recovery of amounts owing as a result of a violation of this chapter."   29 U.S.C. § 626(c)(2).   Thus, under the ADEA, all claims for monetary relief, whether back wages or liquidated damages, may be tried to a jury. See Criswell v. Western Air Lines, Inc., 514 F.Supp. 384, 393 (C.D.Cal.1981), affirmed, 709 F.2d 544 (9th Cir.1983).   A jury trial, however, is not available in an age claim against the federal government.   Lehman v. Nakshian, 453 U.S. 156, 101 S.Ct. 2698, 69 L.Ed.2d 548 (1981)(jury trial is proper against federal government only where Congress expressly authorizes it and § 15 of ADEA only mentions right to jury trial in action against private employers).   Additionally, since § 7(b) of the ADEA authorizes the issuance of such "equitable relief as may be appropriate to effectuate the purposes of this [statute], including * * * judgments compelling employment, reinstatement or promotion", where the plaintiff seeks only equitable relief, the right to jury trial does not attach.   And where the plaintiff seeks both equitable and legal relief, the jury will rule on the legal claims while the equitable claims go to the court. In such a case, factual issues common to both claims are submitted initially to the jury for determination of the legal claims.   These findings are then binding on the court in order to prevent inconsistent findings by the court with respect to the request for equitable relief and thereby preserve the right to jury trial. See Cancellier v. Federated Department Stores, 672 F.2d 1312 (9th Cir.), cert. denied, 459 U.S. 859, 103 S.Ct. 131, 74 L.Ed.2d 113 (1982).   Occasionally a dispute arises as to whether a given claim is legal or equitable in nature.   For example, while attorney fees and costs are consistently viewed as equitable in nature, the courts are divided on the question of whether a request for front pay or pension benefits is legal or equitable.

14.   Again, as in the case of the EPA, the ADEA incorporates the FLSA provisions concerning attorney fees, i.e., that a grant of attorney fees is mandatory when the plaintiff prevails and that it is available only when the prevailing party is the plaintiff.

Chapter 11

THE STATUTORY RESPONSE TO DISABILITY–
BASED DISCRIMINATION

SECTION A. THE AMERICANS WITH DISABILITIES ACT

1. Overview

In 1990, Congress passed the Americans with Disabilities Act (ADA),[a] in an effort to expand the protections against job discrimination offered to persons with disabilities. This statute, like the Civil Rights Act of 1964, is a comprehensive package of protections intended to address (as stated in § 2(b)'s declaration of legislative purpose) the "major areas" of discrimination against individuals with disabilities. Its various Titles prohibit discrimination in public services, public accommodations and telecommunications services, as well as employment. Title I, however, is the portion of the ADA that contains most of the rules concerning discrimination in employment. (A few other relevant provisions are found in Title V, the statute's final chapter consisting of a collection of miscellaneous provisions.)

Until the emergence of the ADA, the major piece of federal legislation prohibiting employment discrimination on the basis of mental and physical disability was the Federal Rehabilitation Act of 1973. (Individuals with disabilities employed by state and local governments, of course, also had the possibility of stating a claim under the equal protection clause of the fourteenth amendment. Additionally, most states had local legislation providing varying levels of protection against public and, sometimes, private sector disability-based discrimination.) This statute, however, is of limited usefulness because it applies only to the federal government, the U.S. Postal Service, federal contractors and entities receiving federal funds. Consequently, it left employees of a large portion of the private sector without any federal statutory protection against disability-based employment bias. The ADA was enacted to close this gap and to provide disabled individuals with more expansive protection against discrimination in the workplace. (Section 501(a) expressly states that except as otherwise provided in the Act, nothing in the ADA shall be construed to apply a lesser standard than is applied under the Rehabilitation Act.) Congress sought to accomplish this by merging the substantive proscriptions developed in the Rehabilitation Act caselaw with the evidentiary for-

[a] Pub.L. 101–336; 104 Stat. 327; 42 U.S.C. § 12101 (1990).

mulae associated with Title VII jurisprudence and extending these rules to the broad class of employment entities covered by Title VII.

In recognition, however, of the dramatic changes this legislation would demand, and to give private employers an adequate opportunity to adjust their employment policies to the requirements of the new legislation, the statute provided that its terms would not become effective until two years after the date of passage, i.e., July 26, 1992. Thus, prior to that date, the Rehabilitation Act remained the most significant federal statutory basis for challenging disability-based employment discrimination. In addition, not only did Congress contemplate that the ADA would not preempt the applicability of the Rehabilitation Act, the fact that much of the proscriptive language of the ADA derives from the Rehabilitation Act suggests that Congress did not intend for the body of Rehabilitation Act caselaw to be ignored by courts in deciding cases under the new statute. Thus, since much of the ADA is patterned after the language found in sections 503 and 504 of the Rehabilitation Act, the jurisprudence interpreting that statute is likely to have a significant impact on judges when they begin to interpret the more detailed provisions of the ADA. And, of course, it remains vitally important to litigants who chose to proceed under the Rehabilitation Act.

At this early stage of the new statute's history, in the absence of any published judicial commentary on the ADA, the remainder of this section will, of necessity, be limited to a summary of the Act's substantive and procedural provisions. The entirety of Title I, and the relevant provisions of other portions of the ADA are reprinted in the Appendix, *infra*, at 1288–1303.

2. The Substantive Provisions

The substantive content of the ADA is, in predominant part, the product of an amalgam of concepts found in both the text and jurisprudence of The Rehabilitation Act and Title VII, with the further inclusion of some language found in neither of these two enactments. Congress adopted and codified nearly all of the judicially created embellishments of the bare bones language of sections 503 and 504 of the Rehabilitation Act, including the duty to make a reasonable accommodation, added the disproportionate impact theory of discrimination, anti-retaliation rule and business necessity defense found in Title VII and extended all of these terms to nearly the identical population of employers, unions and employment agencies covered by the 1964 Civil Rights Act.

(a) The Covered Entities and Extraterritoriality

The applicability of the ADA is almost co-extensive with that of Title VII, i.e., it applies to private, state and local government employers engaged in an industry affecting commerce, labor organizations and employment agencies, and is inapplicable to Indian tribes and bona fide private membership clubs. (The statute incorporates by reference the definition found in Title VII for each of these terms). With respect to employers, however, for the first two years after its effective date, i.e., until July 26, 1994, the statute applies to employers with 25 or more employees. Thereafter, it will apply to employers with 15 or more employees. The major difference in coverage between the two statutes is that the ADA, unlike Title VII, does not apply to federal employees, other than those employed by the U.S. Senate, the House of Representatives and Congressional instrumentalities (such as the General Accounting Office, Library of Congress, Congressional Budget Office and Government Printing Office). Additionally, § 109 of the 1991 Civil Rights Act amends the definition of "employee" in § 101(4) of the ADA to provide for the same degree of extraterritorial protection that is accorded to employees under Title VII. Thus, American employees of U.S. companies, or foreign companies controlled by U.S. companies, are covered when working outside the territorial limits of the U.S., except where compliance with the requirements of the ADA would compel the defendant to violate foreign domestic law. But § 109(c) of the 1991 Act also explicitly states that the provision for extraterritorial application shall not apply to pre-Act conduct.

The statute provides protection to any "qualified individual with a disability," a term defined in the statute to include any individual with a "disability" who, with or without reasonable accommodation, can perform the essential functions of the job held or sought by that individual. The statute goes on to say that in determining what constitutes an "essential function," the employer's judgment on this matter, including any written job description prepared before advertising or interviewing applicants for the particular job, must be considered. And as to the meaning of "disability," Congress incorporated the formulation set forth in Section 7(B) of the Rehabilitation Act—i.e., a physical or mental impairment that substantially limits one or more of an individual's major life activities, a record of such an impairment, or being regarded as having such an impairment. Additionally, however, the ADA explicitly excludes the following from the meaning of "disability": homosexuality, bisexuality, transvestism, current illegal drug use (if discriminated against on the basis of that condition), transsexualism, pedophilia, exhibitionism, voyeurism, gender identity disorders not resulting from physical impairments or other sexual behavior disorders, compulsive gambling, kleptomania, or pyromania, and psychoactive substance use disorders resulting from current illegal use of drugs. Nevertheless, while current use of illegal drugs is not a protected "disability," the statute also provides that an individual who has either successfully completed, or is presently participating in, a supervised drug rehabilitation program and is not currently using illegal drugs, as well as someone who is erroneously regarded as engaging in such use, does fall within the meaning of individual with a "disability" and, therefore, enjoys the protections of the ADA.

(b) Proving and Defending Claims of Discrimination

Section 102 sets forth the substantive requirements of the ADA. It contains a broad, Title VII-like nondiscrimination duty, prohibiting a covered entity from discriminating against a "qualified individual with a disability" (see *infra*) on the basis of that individual's disability with respect to any term, condition, or privilege of employment. While the provision does specifically enumerate a few covered employment-related decisions, including hiring, discharge, promotion, job application procedures, and medical examinations and inquiries, the residual "term and condition of employment" category was clearly intended to extend the coverage of the Act to all aspects of the employment relationship.

Further evidence of Congress' intention to provide comprehensive coverage to the protected class can be found in § 102(b). This provision, which has no precise analogue in Title VII, contains a detailed definition of discrimination. It includes, *inter alia*, a subsection identical to that found in § 703(a)(2) of Title VII, as well as language expressly codifying the disproportionate impact theory of discrimination that was developed in the Title VII cases, codified in the 1991 Civil Rights Act and was assumed to extend in some form to § 504 of the Rehabilitation Act by the Supreme Court in Alexander v. Choate. For example, § 102(b)(3) prohibits the use of employment criteria "that have the effect of discriminating on the basis of disability" and § 102(b)(6) proscribes the use of standards, tests or other selection criteria "that screen out or tend to screen out" individuals or groups of individuals with disabilities. In addition, § 103(b) states that an impact-based claim also can be asserted against an employer requirement that individuals not pose a direct threat to the health or safety of others in the workplace. And in § 102(b)(7), Congress provided that an employer's failure to select and administer employment tests in the manner most likely to ensure that their results accurately reflect the factors they purport to measure, rather than any impaired sensory, manual or speaking skills of disabled individuals, constitutes unlawful discrimination unless the object of the test is to measure such skills. Thus, it is clear that Congress chose to explicate in some detail the manner by which an ADA plaintiff can establish a prima facie claim.

The defenses to such claims are set forth with comparable specificity. Section 103 provides that the defendant can defend a charge that its employment standard tends to select out an individual or group with a disability by showing that the standard is job-related, consistent with business necessity and that performance on the standard cannot be accomplished by the kind of reasonable accommodation required by the ADA. Thus, for example, an employer could deny employment to an otherwise qualified individual on the ground that his contagious disease creates a direct threat to the health of other workers if the employer can establish that no reasonable accommodation would remove that risk. (This "direct threat" language of § 103 was chosen by Congress to codify the standard set forth by the Supreme Court in School Board of Nassau County v. Arline, 480 U.S. 273, 107 S.Ct. 1123, 94 L.Ed.2d 307 (1987), see *infra*, at 988. Furthermore, the legislative history makes clear that the determination that the individual will pose a safety threat to others must be made on an ad hoc basis and must not be based on generalizations, misperceptions, patronizing attitudes, myths or fears.) As you can see, not only did Congress clearly chose to codify the pre-*Atonio* proof formulation by placing the burden of proof upon the defendant, but by requiring proof of job-relatedness, business necessity and inability to make a reasonable accommodation, Congress has prescribed an even heavier burden under the ADA than was imposed by the pre-*Atonio* Title VII jurisprudence.

The statutory definition of discrimination also encompasses the duty to make a reasonable accommodation as developed in *Prewitt* and other Rehabilitation Act cases. Section 102(b)(5)(A) defines discrimination to include the failure to make reasonable accommodations to the known physical or mental limitations of a member of the protected class unless the employer (or other covered entity) proves that the accommodation would impose an undue hardship on the operation of its business. Pursuant to § 102(b)(5)(B), an employer cannot refuse to hire an otherwise qualified person with a disability on the ground that hiring that individual would require the employer to make a reasonable accommodation to her physical or mental impairment. Another unique provision of the ADA is the language of § 102(b)(4) which prohibits associational discrimination, i.e., discrimination taken against a qualified, nondisabled individual because of the known disability of a person with whom the qualified individual is known to have a relationship or association.

But while Congress adopted the "reasonable accommodation" and "undue hardship" language of Section 701(j) of Title VII, it exceeded the textual limits of Title VII by defining both of these terms in the ADA. Section 101(9) defines "reasonable accommodation" by setting forth a non-exclusive list of responses including (a)redesigning physical facilities to make them accessible to and usable by individuals with disabilities, (b)restructuring such aspects of the work environment as job requirements and assignments, work schedules, working equipment and devices, examinations and training materials, and (c)providing qualified readers or interpreters. And in language clearly more expansive than the standard imposed under Title VII by the Supreme Court in *Hardison*, § 101(10)(A) defines "undue hardship" to mean a response that requires "significant difficulty or expense" when considered in light of the, apparently non-exclusive, list of factors set forth in § 101(10)(B). Notice, by the way, that these factors refer not only to the nature and cost of the requisite accommodation, but to the financial resources of the particular facility at which the accommodation is sought as well as the resources, size and structure of the defendant's overall business. The entirety of this language reveals Congress' intention to mandate a fact-specific, case-by-case approach to determining the reasonableness of accommodations.

(c) Rules Governing Medical Examinations and Inquiries

Section 102(c) extends the general statutory prohibition against discrimination to medical examinations and inquiries concerning the existence, nature or severity of a disability and provides a very specific set of rules governing the use of such procedures. This provision prohibits covered entities from requiring applicants to undergo preemployment medical exams or inquiries (with the exception of tests for the presence of illegal drugs) to determine the presence, nature or severity of a disability. But the employer can inquire about the individual's ability to perform relevant job functions and also can require a medical examination after the offer has been made and before the commencement of employment. Moreover, the employer can condition the offer of employment on the results of such an examination. But a medical examination is permitted under these circumstances only if all of the following three requirements are satisfied: (a)the inquiry or examination is shown by the employer to be job-related and consistent with business necessity, (b)all employees in a particular job category are subjected to it, and (c)if the information obtained from the examination or inquiry is treated confidentially and kept apart from the employees' other employment records. The confidentiality requirement, however, is subject to the employer's right to provide relevant information to (a)an individual's supervisor concerning necessary restrictions on, and/or accommodations to, the individual's work or duties, (b)first aid or safety personnel if the disability requires emergency treatment, or (c)government officials investigating compliance with the ADA.

The statute also creates an exception for voluntary medical examinations, permitting covered entities to conduct such examinations (including medical histories) as long as they are part of an employee health program. But the information obtained from voluntary examinations is subject to the same requirements of separate maintenance and confidentiality applicable to mandatory tests.

(d) Rules Governing Food Handlers

Pursuant to § 103(d), the Secretary of Health & Human Services must publish and widely disseminate an annually updated report including a list of infectious and communicable diseases that may be transmitted through handling the food supply and the methods by which they are transmitted. Section 103(d)(2) permits an employer to refuse to assign an individual with a listed disease to a job involving food handling where the risk of transmission cannot be "eliminated" by a reasonable accommodation. Additionally, § 103(d)(3) provides that the ADA does not preempt or modify any State or local law or regulation governing food handling which is designed to protect the public health from individuals who pose a significant risk to the health or safety of others with respect to those diseases included on the Secretary's list and as to which the risk of transmission cannot be "eliminated" by a reasonable accommodation.

In the summer of 1991, the first annual list of communicable diseases was released by the Public Health Service. It included fifteen diseases that are "often" or "occasionally" transmitted through food, including Hepatitis A, Norwalk viruses, Salmonella, Staphylococcus and Streptococcus. AIDS was not among the diseases on the list.

(e) Alcohol and Illegal Drug Use and Drug Testing

As noted in Section A, *supra*, although current users of illegal drugs do not fall within the protected class of otherwise qualified individuals with a disability, the statute does protect individuals who have either successfully completed or are presently participating in a supervised drug rehabilitation program and are not currently using illegal drugs. The statute also protects individuals who do not use illegal drugs but are incorrectly regarded as using them. Pursuant to § 104(b), it is not unlawful for a covered entity to use "reasonable policies or procedures", including drug testing, to ensure that a rehabilitated or rehabilitating individual is not currently using illegal drugs. Covered entities also are permitted to prohibit illegal drug use and alcohol use at the workplace and to enforce policies requiring that employees not be under the influence of alcohol or be engaged in using illegal drugs at the workplace. Further, an employer can impose the same job qualifications and job performance standards on alcoholics and illegal drug users that are required of all other employees. Finally, employees employed in an industry subject to regulations of the Department of Defense, Nuclear Regulatory Commission or Department of Transportation, can be held to the policies adopted by these agencies concerning alcohol and illegal drug use, including those regulations, if any, that apply to employment in sensitive positions in such an industry.

Tests used to determine the use of illegal drugs, as mentioned in Section C, *supra*, are not subject to the statutory restrictions on the use of medical examinations or inquiries. But § 104(d)(2) declares that the ADA neither prohibits, encourages nor permits the testing of employees or applicants for illegal drug use. It similarly provides that the Act does not prohibit, encourage or permit the making of any employment decision on the basis of the results of such tests. Neither does it affect in any way the opportunity for entities subject to the jurisdiction of the Department of Transportation to test employees in, or applicants for, positions involving safety-sensitive jobs for illegal drug use or on-duty impairment by alcohol.

(f) Religious Institution Exemptions

Section 103(c) provides the same exemption for religious entities that is found in § 702 of Title VII, namely a blanket authorization for such entities to prefer individuals of a particular religion for employment in connection with any activity, religious or secular, undertaken by that entity. It goes beyond the express terms of § 702, however, by also permitting such an entity to require that all applicants and employees conform to its religious tenets.

3. The Enforcement Mechanism

(a) Administrative Enforcement

Section 107(a) incorporates by reference the enforcement mechanism of Title VII. This scheme governs all claims of violations of both the ADA and those implementing regulations promulgated by the EEOC pursuant to the terms of § 106. Section 107(b) directs the agencies responsible for enforcing the ADA and the Rehabilitation Act to coordinate their procedures to avoid duplication of effort in the handling of administrative complaints filed under these statutes. It also specifies that these agencies shall develop procedures to prevent the imposition of inconsistent or conflicting standards with respect to those requirements that are common to both statutes. Pursuant to this statutory directive, the EEOC and the Office of Federal Contract Compliance Programs (OFCCP) adopted joint procedures for coordinating the processing of complaints that fall within the common jurisdiction of the ADA and Rehabilitation Act. 57 Fed.Reg. 2960, 41 C.F.R. § 1641 (1/24/92). For example, discrimination claims against federal contractors and subcontractors with more than twenty-five employees are cognizable under both statutes. Under the joint procedural regulations, the OFCCP will play the lead role in investigating and adjudicating claims of disability discrimination. The regulations provide that the OFCCP will serve as the EEOC's agent for handling claims filed under the ADA, except for those claims "deemed of particular importance to EEOC's enforcement of the ADA." Additionally, claims filed directly with the OFCCP under § 503 will be treated as having been filed simultaneously under the ADA. If the OFCCP determines that a violation exists and its conciliation efforts are unsuccessful, it can either pursue administrative enforcement through litigation or refer the case to the EEOC for possible litigation by the Commission. If an individual seeks to file a charge with the EEOC under the ADA after filing a complaint with the OFCCP under § 503, the EEOC is directed to dismiss the charge.

(b) Availability of Compensatory and Punitive Damages

Section 107(a) also incorporates the remedial provisions of Title VII. Prior to the enactment of the 1991 Civil Rights Act, this meant that ADA plaintiffs, like those proceeding under Title VII, could not collect compensatory or punitive damages. But since the 1991 Act provides for the recovery of compensatory and punitive damages in Title VII cases alleging intentional discrimination, such awards can now be recovered in claims of intentional discrimination under the ADA. Moreover, § 102(a)(2) of the 1991 Civil Rights Act expressly amends the ADA to provide for the recovery of compensatory and punitive damages in connection with claims of intentional discrimination or failure to make a reasonable accommodation under the same rules governing their availability in Title VII cases, except that such relief is unavailable under the ADA where the defendant establishes that it made a good faith effort, after consulting with the plaintiff, to make a reasonable accommodation.

4. Miscellaneous Provisions

(a) Relationship to the Rehabilitation Act and Other Laws

In addition to the general statement that the ADA shall not be construed to apply a lesser standard than is applied under the Rehabilitation Act or regulations issued pursuant thereto, § 501 states that the ADA shall not preempt equally or more expansive remedies, rights or procedures provided by state and local laws. It also provides that the ADA shall not be construed to prevent the prohibition of, or imposition of restrictions on, smoking in places of employment covered by this law.

(b) Waiver of State Sovereign Immunity

Section 502 expressly removes a State's Eleventh Amendment immunity from suit under the ADA and provides for the availability of equitable and legal damages against a State to the same extent that these remedies are available against private and non-State public entities.

(c) Prohibition Against Retaliation

Retaliation taken in response to acts of opposition and participation, as defined in § 704(a) of Title VII, is similarly prohibited by § 503. Individuals asserting claims of retaliation shall be subject to the same remedies and procedures available to all other claims of employment discrimination brought under the ADA.

(d) Attorney Fees

Section 505 is patterned after § 706(k) of Title VII, except that this section expressly provides for the issuance of attorney fees to the prevailing party with respect to administrative proceedings. And unlike § 706(k), this provision does not expressly exclude the EEOC from obtaining an award of attorney fees.

(e) Definition of Illegal Drugs

Illegal drugs are defined in §§ 101(6) and 510(d) as drugs, the possession or distribution of which is unlawful under the Controlled Substances Act. Drugs taken under supervision by a licensed health care professional or used in other ways authorized by the Controlled Substances Act, are expressly excluded from this definition.

(f) Amendments to the Rehabilitation Act

To conform the definition of "individual with handicaps" under the Rehabilitation Act to the definition of "individual with a disability" under the ADA, the definition of the Rehabilitation Act provision is amended to exclude individuals who are currently using illegal drugs and alcoholics whose current use prevents them from performing the duties of the job in question or would constitute a direct threat to the property or safety of others. It also expands the definition of this term to include individuals who have either rehabilitated or are in the process of rehabilitating and are not presently using illegal drugs.

5. The Administrative Regulations

Section 106 of the ADA directed the EEOC to issue substantive regulations implementing Title I within one year from July 26, 1990, the date of enactment. The EEOC fulfilled this mandate by issuing the final regulations and guidelines implementing and explaining the provisions of Title I on July 26, 1991. 29 C.F.R. Part 1630. In so doing, it was guided by Congress' admonition that these regulations be modeled after the regulations implementing § 504 of the Rehabilitation Act. Thus, for example, the definition of such key phrases as "disability," "physical or mental impairment," and "major life activity" in the ADA regulations are identical to the definitions contained within the Rehabilitation Act regulations. But there are differences. For example, in determining when a proposed accommodation would impose an undue hardship, the ADA regulations state that cost is a factor and that where the expense of a proposed accommodation would impose an undue hardship on the defendant, the individual should be offered the opportunity to pay for the undue hardship portion of that expense. Additionally, of course, as there are issues covered by the ADA that are not addressed by the Rehabilitation Act, the regulations associated with these provisions are not derived from the Rehabilitation Act guidelines. The ADA regulations provide that where an individual claims to be a rehabilitated drug user who is not a current user (a classification that is included within the statutorily protected group of otherwise qualified individuals with a disability), the employer can request evidence of negative drug tests to corroborate such a claim. And where an individual claims that she has been erroneously regarded as disabled, the regulations state that the individual bears the burden of proving that she is so regarded.

SECTION B. THE REHABILITATION ACT OF 1973

Read §§ 7(7), 501 and 503–505 of the Rehabilitation Act.

PREWITT v. UNITED STATES POSTAL SERVICE

United States Court of Appeals, Fifth Circuit, 1981.
662 F.2d 292.

TATE, CIRCUIT JUDGE.

Claiming that the United States Postal Service unlawfully denied him employment due to his physical handicap, the plaintiff, George Dunbar Prewitt, Jr., brought this action against the postal service. Prewitt contended that he was physically able to perform the job for which he applied despite his handicap, even though the postal service's physical requirements indicate that only persons in "good physical condition" can perform the job because it involves "arduous" work. Prewitt alleged, inter alia, that the postal service thus violated his rights under the Rehabilitation Act of 1973, Prewitt filed this suit as a class action, after he was denied employment as a clerk/carrier at the Greenville, Mississippi post office. The district court granted the postal service's motion for summary judgment. On Prewitt's appeal, we find that the plaintiff has raised genuine issues of material fact as to 1) whether the postal service's physical requirements for postal employment are sufficiently "job related" to provide lawful grounds for the refusal to hire Prewitt, and 2) whether the postal service has breached its duty to make "reasonable accommodation" for handicapped persons such as Prewitt. Accordingly, we reverse the summary judgment of the district court, and remand the case for further proceedings in accordance with this opinion.

The Factual Background

The plaintiff Prewitt is a disabled Vietnam war veteran. Due to gunshot wounds, he must endure limited mobility of his left arm and shoulder. Nevertheless, in May *1970* (prior to his rejection for re-employment in 1978 that gave rise to this lawsuit), Prewitt applied for a position as a distribution clerk in the Jackson, Mississippi post office, a position which, according to the job description, "require[s] arduous physical exertion involving prolonged standing, throwing, reaching, and may involve lifting sacks of mail up to 80 pounds." [1] Prewitt was hired after passing the requisite written and medical examinations, and it is undisputed that, despite his handicap, he performed his duties in a competent, entirely satisfactory manner.

Prewitt resigned his position at the Jackson post office in September 1970 to return to school. He testified in his affidavit, which we must regard as true for summary judgment purposes, that his physical condition did not diminish in any significant way between May 1970 and September 1978, when he applied for the position at the Greenville post office that gave rise to this lawsuit. Prewitt questions the failure of the postal service to re-employ him in 1978, due to a physical handicap, for a position as clerk/carrier, a position with similar physical requirements to those of the job that he had satisfactorily performed in 1970.

* * *

According to the postal services qualification standards, the duties of a carrier "are arduous and require that the incumbent be in good physical condition." Thus, a medical form which was given to Prewitt indicates that applicants for this position must meet a wide range of physical criteria, including, inter alia, the ability to see, hear, lift heavy weights, carry moderate weights, reach above shoulder, and use fingers and both hands. According to the affidavit of Postmaster Charles Hughes, the duties of a clerk/carrier require stooping, bending, squatting, lifting up to seventy pounds, standing for long periods, stretching arms in all directions, reaching above and below the shoulder, and some twisting of the back.

To determine whether Prewitt could meet these physical standards, the Greenville postal authorities asked Prewitt to authorize the Veteran's Administration (VA) to release his medical records to the postal service for examination, and Prewitt complied with this request. The VA records, which apparently were made in 1970 before Prewitt was awarded disability benefits, indicated that Prewitt had a 30% service-related disability that caused "limitation of motion of left shoulder and atrophy of trapezius," as well as that he had a kidney disease, hypertension, and an eye condition not related to his armed forces service. The VA report was analyzed by Dr. Cenon Baltazar, a postal medical officer, who reported: "Limited records pertaining to [Prewitt] showed limitation of left shoulder and atrophy of trapezius muscle. This is not suitable for full performance as required of postal service positions unless it is a desk job." Prewitt subsequently received from Hughes a terse, two sentence letter informing him that Dr. Baltazar had determined that he was "medically unsuitable for postal employment." The letter did not state any reasons for this finding of unsuitability.

---

1. These physical requirements of Prewitt's 1970 position as distribution clerk are similar to those for the position of clerk/carrier for which he applied in 1978.

After receiving word of this adverse determination, Prewitt contacted Hughes to dispute the conclusion of the medical officer. Hughes told Prewitt that there was no appeal from the decision, but that the decision would be reconsidered at the local level if Prewitt would undergo an examination, at his own expense, by a private physician. In fact, Prewitt did have the right to appeal to the postal service's regional medical director. After belatedly learning of this right, Prewitt exercised his right to appeal, but he chose not to undergo a new physical examination. The regional medical officer, Dr. Gedney, examined the VA report and concluded that Prewitt was medically unsuitable. Unlike Dr. Baltazar, who relied solely on Prewitt's shoulder injury as the basis for his adverse determination, Dr. Gedney also mentioned the kidney disease (which Dr. Gedney stated is an unpredictably progressive disease that could possibly be aggravated by arduous duty) and hypertension. Based on Dr. Gedney's report, the regional office sustained the adverse determination and told Prewitt that there were no further medical appeal rights. Again, the letter did not inform Prewitt of the medical reasons upon which this conclusion was based.

Although the regional office correctly stated that there were no further *medical* appeal rights, in fact Prewitt had available to him an entirely independent chain of administrative review of the adverse determination through the postal service's equal employment opportunity (EEO) office. Prewitt filed an EEO complaint, alleging that the postal service had discriminated against him on the basis of his handicap by finding him unsuitable for postal employment. The EEO office conducted an investigation and found that the same medical officer who had disqualified Prewitt had ruled three other disabled or physically handicapped applicants suitable for postal employment. The investigation also revealed that the Greenville post office had hired fourteen persons classified as disabled and/or physically handicapped. Relying on these findings, the EEO office found no discrimination and advised Prewitt that he could appeal its decision to the Office of Appeals and Review of the Equal Employment Opportunity Commission (EEOC).

As permitted by statute, 42 U.S.C. § 2000e–16(c), made applicable to the handicapped by 29 U.S.C. § 794a(a)(1), instead of appealing to the EEOC, Prewitt filed this suit in the district court. No contention is made by the postal service that Prewitt did not exhaust administrative remedies. The postal service responded to Prewitt's complaint with a motion for summary judgment, contending that it had rejected Prewitt for valid medical reasons, and that Prewitt's refusal to take a physical examination had precluded it from making a re-evaluation. The plaintiff responded that postal service regulations required that applicants be given a current physical examination before a medical determination is made, and therefore, even though Prewitt was afforded an opportunity to take a physical after his determination was made, the determination of medical unfitness was invalid. Prewitt further argued that the regulations entitled him to a free physical examination, so that he was not required to bear the expense of an examination by a private physician. Finally, Prewitt noted that in view of the undisputed fact that he had been able to perform competently a similar job in 1970, the postal service had failed to articulate any legitimate reason for its finding of medical unsuitability.

* * *

Only since 1978 have handicapped individuals been entitled to bring private actions against federal agencies for violations of the Rehabilitation Act. This is apparently the first case in which a federal appellate court has been called upon to determine the nature and extent of this newly-created private right. We shall therefore examine the history of this legislation in some detail.

Congress passed the Rehabilitation Act of 1973 for the express purpose, inter alia, of "promot[ing] and expand[ing] employment opportunities in the public and private sectors for handicapped individuals." In addition to creating a number of wide-ranging federally-funded programs designed to aid handicapped persons in assuming a full role in society, the Act, in its Title V, established the principle that (a) the federal government, (b) federal contractors, and (c) recipients of federal funds cannot discriminate against the handicapped.

The duties of each of these three classes of entities were set forth in separate sections. Section 503 of the Act, required federal contractors to include in their contracts with the United States a provision mandating that, in employing persons to carry out the contract, "the party contracting with the United States shall take affirmative action to employ and advance in employment qualified handicapped individuals. * * * " Section 504, which imposed duties on recipients of federal funds, provided: "No otherwise qualified handicapped individual * * * shall, solely by reason of his handicap, be excluded from participation in, be denied the benefits of, or be subjected to discrimination under any program or activity receiving federal financial assistance."

The duties of the federal government itself were set forth in section 501(b), which stated:

> Each department, agency, and instrumentality (including the United States Postal Service and the Postal Rate Commission) in the executive branch shall * * * submit to the Civil Service Commission and to the [Interagency Committee on Handicapped Employees] an affirmative action program plan for the hiring, placement, and advancement of handicapped individuals in such department, agency, or instrumentality. Such plan shall include a description of the extent to which and methods whereby the special needs of handicapped employees are being met. * * *

* * *

Under the original 1973 Rehabilitation Act, a private cause of action founded on handicap discrimination was not recognized upon section 501 as against a federal government employer; the literal statutory wording merely required federal agencies to *submit* affirmative actions plans. However, due to differences in statutory wording, all courts that considered the issue found that section 504 established a private cause of action for handicapped persons subjected to discrimination by recipients of federal funds, while the federal courts split on the question whether the same was true under section 503 for individuals subjected to handicap discrimination by federal contractors.

In 1978, the Rehabilitation Act was amended to provide a private cause of action in favor of persons subjected to handicap discrimination by the federal government employing agencies. In the House, an amendment was adopted and ultimately enacted by the Congress that extended section 504's proscription against handicap discrimination to "any program or activity conducted by an Executive agency or by the United States Postal Service;" the legislative history, as well as the judicial interpretations, fully recognized that a private right of action had been created by section 504.

The Senate, at the same time, added a new section 505(a)(1) to the Rehabilitation Act, which created a private right of action under section 501. The provision states:

> The remedies, procedures, and rights set forth in section 717 of the Civil Rights Act of 1964, including the application of sections 706(f) through 706(k), shall be available, with respect to any complaint under section 501 of this Act, to any employee or applicant for employment aggrieved by the final disposition of such complaint, or by the failure to take final action on such complaint.

Section 717 of Title VII of the Civil Rights Act, to which section 501 is explicitly tied by the new section 505, mandates that all federal personnel actions be made "free from any discrimination based on race, color, religion, sex, or national origin." The provision further provides for a private right of action in favor of those whose claims of discrimination have not been satisfactorily resolved by administrative procedures. However, before an individual can bring a section 717 action in court, strict procedural requirements with respect to exhaustion of administrative remedies must be fulfilled. Once administrative remedies have been exhausted, however, an individual is entitled to de novo consideration of his discrimination claims in the district court; however, prior administrative findings made with respect to an employment discrimination claim may be admitted into evidence at the trial de novo.

* * *

The scope of the federal government's obligations under section 501 received Senate attention during debate on a proposed amendment to the proposed new section 505(a)(1). An amendment offered by Senator McClure would have added the following clause at the end of section 505(a)(1): "provided, however, that no equitable relief or affirmative action remedy disproportionately exceeding actual damages in the case shall be available under this section." Senator McClure explained that his amendment "would provide that the federally financed affirmative action remedy * * * could not be used to initiate massive construction projects for relatively minor temporal damages."

Senators Cranston and Stafford spoke in opposition to the McClure amendment. Senator Cranston remarked:

> I believe that the requirement with respect to Federal Contractors and grantees should be no less stringent than the requirements attached to the Federal Government. The amendment offered by the Senator from Idaho would create an unwise and unrealistic distinction with respect of [sic] employment between the obligations of the Federal Government and the obligations of Federal contractors and grantees. Ironically, the Senator's amendment would limit— with a financial test—the Federal Government's obligation of being an equal opportunity employer. Federal contractors and grantees would—appropriately—continue to be required to be equal opportunity employers. Rather than a leader in this field, the Federal Government would become a distant also-ran requiring more of its grantees and contractors than it would be willing to require of itself.

The dispute was resolved when Senator McClure and the managers of the bill agreed upon the following compromise language: "In fashioning an equitable or affirmative action remedy under such section [section 501], a court may take into account the reasonableness of the cost of any necessary workplace accommodation, and the availability of alternative therefor or other appropriate relief." Id. at S15667. As thus amended, the new section 505(a)(1) was enacted into law * * *.

In summary, the 1978 amendments to the Rehabilitation Act 1) established a private right of action, subject to the same procedural constraints (administrative exhaustion, etc.) set forth in Title VII of the Civil Rights Act, in favor of section 501 claimants, and 2) extended section 504's proscription against handicap employment discrimination to cover the activities of the federal government itself.

Thus, by its 1978 amendments to the Rehabilitation Act, Congress clearly recognized both in section 501 and in section 504 that individuals now have a private cause of action to obtain relief for handicap discrimination on the part of the federal government and its agencies. The amendments to section 504 were simply the House's answer to the same problem that the Senate saw fit to resolve by strengthening section 501. The joint House–Senate conference committee could have chosen to eliminate the partial overlap between the two provisions, but instead the conference committee, and subsequently Congress as a whole, chose to pass both provisions, despite the overlap. "When there are two acts upon the same subject, the rule is to give effect to both if possible." United States v. Borden Co., 308 U.S. 188, 198, 60 S.Ct. 182, 188, 84 L.Ed. 181 (1939). By this same principle, in order to give effect to *both* the House and the Senate 1978 amendments finally enacted, we must read the exhaustion of administrative remedies requirement of section 501 into the private remedy recognized by both section 501 and section 504 for federal government handicap discrimination.

In the present suit, Prewitt claims that, despite his handicap, he is physically able to perform the job for which he applied, but that the postal service's physical requirements, neutral on their face, had *disparate impact* upon a person with his particular handicap and that they excluded him from employment that in fact he was physically able to perform. The present case was dismissed on summary judgment, through a failure to take into account the principles applicable to the federal government by the Rehabilitation Act of 1973, as amended in 1978; due to disputed issues of material fact, as will be stated, summary judgment was improvidently granted.

* * *

One of the chief physical factors upon which the postal service bases its refusal to hire Prewitt is that, due to Prewitt's inability to lift his left arm above shoulder level, the employing authority feels that he cannot "case" (sort) the mail that he would be required to deliver on his route. Because a carrier is required to lift above shoulder level with both hands to remove stacks of mail from a six-foot-high top ledge, the postal service contends that Prewitt would not be able to do this part of the job without some workplace modification—however, the postal service witness admitted, for instance, that Prewitt could be accommodated simply by lowering the legs to which the shelves are attached.[18] Only if Prewitt, despite his handicap, can perform the essential duties of the position in question, without the need for any workplace accommodation, can it be said that he was a victim of "disparate impact" discrimination. However, even if Prewitt cannot so perform, he might still be entitled to relief if he was a victim of "surmountable barrier" discrimination, i.e., if he was rejected even though he could have performed the essentials of the job if afforded reasonable accommodation.[19]

---

18. The second principal factor upon which the postal service relies is the severe pain that a VA report indicates that Prewitt suffers after lifting. Prewitt denies the pain or at least its severity. This type of handicap may be either a surmountable or insurmountable employment barrier.

19. Commentators have identified four distinct types of discriminatory barriers that handicapped persons must confront when seeking employment: 1. Intentional discrimination for reasons of social bias (racial, sexual, religion, handicap, etc.); 2. neutral standards with disparate impact; 3. surmountable impairment barriers; and 4. insurmountable impairment barriers.

The present complaints by Prewitt involve alleged "disparate impact" and a "surmountable barrier" handicap-discrimination.

The Title VII jurisprudence is, we believe, for the most part applicable to intentional social-bias discrimination against handicapped persons. *See* Texas Department of Corrections v. Burdine, 450 U.S. 248, 101 S.Ct. 1089, 67 L.Ed.2d 207 (1981) and McDonnell Douglas Corp. v. Green, 411 U.S. 792, 93 S.Ct. 1817, 36 L.Ed.2d 668 (1973). Likewise, as will be noted in the text, the Title VII disparate impact decisions are relevant in the determination of disparate impact handicap discrimination. Surmountable and insurmountable barriers raise issues that for the most part are peculiar to handicap discrimination.

Since both issues will arise on the remand, we will therefore note the principles applicable to judicial determination of both cases involving claims of "disparate impact" and also of "surmountable barrier" ("the duty to make reasonable accommodation") discrimination against a handicapped person.

Preliminarily, however, we should observe that section 501 requires affirmative action on the part of federal agencies; unlike section 504 of the Rehabilitation Act and Title VII of the Civil Rights Act which usually require only nondiscrimination. In Ryan v. Federal Deposit Insurance Corp., 565 F.2d 762, 763 (D.C.Cir.1977), the court held, and we agree, especially in light of the 1978 amendments, that section 501 requires that federal agencies do more than just *submit* affirmative plans—section 501 "impose[s] a duty upon federal agencies to structure their procedures and programs so as to ensure that handicapped individuals are afforded equal opportunity in both job assignment and promotion." Although *Ryan*, which was decided prior to the 1978 amendments, did not recognize a private right of action under section 501, the court held that the defendant federal agency should amend its procedures to provide an administrative forum through which handicapped individuals could enforce their section 501 rights. Subsequent to *Ryan*, the Civil Service Commission, and its successor enforcement agency, the EEOC, promulgated administrative regulations that define the section 501 duties of federal agencies, which for instance (see below) include the duty to make reasonable accommodation to employ a handicapped person. These regulations are the administrative interpretation of the Act by the enforcing agency and are therefore entitled to some deference in our attempt to determine the applications of this statute.

* * *

The EEOC regulations adopt a *Griggs*-type approach in the disparate impact handicap discrimination context. They require federal agencies not to use any selection criterion that "screens out or tends to screen out qualified handicapped persons or any class of handicapped persons" unless the criterion, as used by the agency, is shown to be "job-related for the position in question." The test is whether a handicapped individual who meets all employment criteria except for the challenged discriminatory criterion "can perform the essential functions of the position in question without endangering the health and safety of the individuals or others." If the individual can so perform, he must not be subjected to discrimination.

In our opinion, in the disparate impact context, there should be only minor differences in the application of the *Griggs* principles to handicap discrimination claims. One difference, however, is that, when assessing the disparate impact of a facially-neutral criterion, courts must be careful not to group all handicapped persons into one class, or even into broad subclasses. This is because "the fact that an employer employs fifteen epileptics is not necessarily probative of whether he or she has discriminated against a blind person."

In a section 504 handicap discrimination case, the Supreme Court held that the Rehabilitation Act does not require redress of "insurmountable barrier" handicap discrimination—that the statutory language prohibiting discrimination against an "otherwise qualified handicapped individual" means qualified *"in spite" of* his handicap, not qualified in all respects except for being handicapped. Southeastern Community College v. Davis, 442 U.S. 397, 406, 99 S.Ct. 2361, 2367, 60 L.Ed.2d 980 (1979) (emphasis added).

The *Davis* rationale is equally controlling in the employment discrimination context. Accordingly, employers subject to the Rehabilitation Act need not hire handicapped individuals who cannot fully perform the required work, even with accommodation. However, while *Davis* demonstrates that only individuals who are qualified "in spite of" their handicaps need be hired, *Griggs* and its progeny dictate that the employer must bear the burden of proving that the physical criteria are job related. If the employer does this, then the burden of persuasion to show that he can satisfy these criteria rests on the handicapped applicant.

Federal employers, including the postal service, are obliged by section 501(b) to provide reasonable accommodation for the handicapped.[21] As the *Davis* Court pointed out, section 501(b), unlike section 504, explicitly requires federal government employers to undertake "affirmative action" on behalf of the handicapped. And the new section 505, added by Congress in 1978, explicitly permits courts to fashion "an equitable or affirmative action remedy" for violations of section 501, with the caveat that "the reasonableness of the cost of any necessary workplace accommodation" should be taken into account. The legislative intent reflected in the creation of a handicap discrimination private action clearly shows that federal government employers must make reasonable accommodation for handicapped job applicants.

There is a dearth of decisional law on this issue.[22] However, the EEOC administrative regulations, which, as noted above, are entitled to

21. This court has consistently held that section 504 also mandates reasonable accommodation, thus prohibiting surmountable barrier discrimination by federal grantees against the handicapped.

22. Outside the handicap discrimination context, the "reasonable accommodation" issue has arisen in cases involving persons who claim a right to accommodation of their religious duty to refrain from working on certain days. In Trans World Airlines v. Hardison, 432 U.S. 63, 84, 97 S.Ct. 2264, 2277, 53 L.Ed.2d 113 (1977), the Supreme Court interpreted § 701(j) of the Civil Rights Act of 1964, 42 U.S.C. § 2000e(j), which requires employers to ac-

commodate such religious practices, unless to do so would impose "undue hardship." The Court held that an employer need not accommodate such persons if the accommodation would require "more than a *de minimis* cost."

The *Hardison* principles are not applicable in the federal-employer handicap discrimination context. Congress clearly intended the federal government to take measures that would involve more than a *de minimis* cost. As the debate over the McClure amendment shows, Congress was even unwilling to approve language that would have limited the government's duty

deference, provide some basis for outlining the contours of the surmountable barrier accommodation duty.

The relevant EEOC regulation, 29 C.F.R. § 1613.704, provides:

(a) An agency shall make reasonable accommodation to the known physical or mental limitations of a qualified handicapped applicant or employee unless the agency can demonstrate that the accommodation would impose an undue hardship on the operation of its program.

(b) Reasonable accommodation may include, but shall not be limited to: (1) Making facilities readily accessible to and usable by handicapped persons, and (2) job restructuring, part-time or modified work schedules, acquisition or modification of equipment or devices, appropriate adjustment or modification of examinations, the provision of readers and interpreters, and other similar actions.

(c) In determining pursuant to paragraph (a) of this section whether an accommodation would impose an undue hardship on the operation of the agency in question, factors to be considered include: (1) The overall size of the agency's program will respect to the number of employees, number and type of facilities and size of budget; (2) the type of agency operation, including the composition and structure of the agency's work force; and (3) the nature and the cost of the accommodation.

Thus, under subsection (a) of this provision, the burden of proving inability to accommodate is upon the employer. The administrative reasons for so placing the burden likewise justify a similar burden of proof in a private action based upon the Rehabilitation Act. The employer has greater knowledge of the essentials of the job than does the handicapped applicant. The employer can look to its own experience, or, if that is not helpful, to that of other employers who have provided jobs to individuals with handicaps similar to those of the applicant in question. Furthermore, the employer may be able to obtain advice concerning possible accommodations from private and government sources.

Although the burden of persuasion in proving inability to accommodate always remains on the employer, we must add one caveat. Once the employer presents credible evidence that indicates accommodation of the plaintiff would not reasonably be possible, the plaintiff may not remain silent. Once the employer presents such evidence, the plaintiff has the burden of coming forward with evidence concerning his individual capabilities and suggestions for possible accommodations to rebut the employer's evidence.

In addition, subsections (a) and (c) of 29 C.F.R. § 1613.704, which limit the employer's duty to accommodate to instances where accommodation would not impose "undue hardship" and define the factors to be

to make reasonable accommodation to instances in which the cost of accommodation does not "disproportionately exceed[ ] actual damages."

used in determining whether a particular accommodation would impose "undue hardship," accurately express congressional intent. The second sentence of section 505, which admonishes the courts to "take into account the reasonableness of the cost of any necessary workplace accommodation," was added as compromise language in response to Senator McClure's concern that federal employers might be obliged "to initiate massive construction projects." The EEOC regulations adequately respond to this concern.

The factual showing before the district court was that the postal service rejected Prewitt's application for employment because it felt, on the basis of the medical records supplied to it, that Prewitt could not perform the "arduous" duties of the position. In view of the undisputed fact that Prewitt had satisfactorily performed a similar postal job in 1970 despite his physical handicap, as well as of his *uncontradicted* affidavit that his physical condition was substantially unchanged since then, Prewitt raised a genuine dispute issue of material fact as to whether the postal service's physical standards for employment are sufficiently "job related" to justify the employer's refusal to hire him. Under the applicable legal principles earlier set forth, therefore, the postal service is not shown under the facts thus far educed to have been justified as a matter of law in denying Prewitt's application. The summary judgment must therefore be reversed.

We should note that the postal service contends that the postal service rejected him because he refused its request that he take a current physical examination to establish his medical suitability for employment. This contention is based upon the showing that, *after* Prewitt was found medically unsuitable for employment, he was informally advised by the local postmaster that he would be reconsidered if he secured a new medical examination.

However, the record reveals that Prewitt's application was rejected because he was found to be medically unsuitable (without notifying Prewitt of the specific medical reasons), not because he refused to furnish any further or more current medical information. Indeed, Prewitt's essential position was that his physical condition and the effect of his disability was unchanged since 1970 and that, even accepting the disability reflected by the VA medical reports upon which the postal service relied, he was physically qualified to perform the duties of the position for which he applied, as instanced by his earlier satisfactory performance of the duties of a similar postal position.

On the basis of the factual showing thus far made, we reverse the summary judgment dismissing Prewitt's handicap-discrimination claim. We remand for further proceedings in accordance with the views set forth in this opinion. To summarize:

(1) Prewitt, the disabled claimant, may establish a prima facie of unlawful discrimination by proving that: (a) except for his physical handicap, he is qualified to fill the position; (b) he has a handicap that prevents him from meeting the physical criteria for employment; and

(c) the challenged physical standards have a disproportionate impact on persons having the same handicap from which he suffers. To sustain this prima facie case, there should also be a facial showing or at least plausible reasons to believe that the handicap can be accommodated or that the physical criteria are not "job related."

(2) Once the prima facie case of handicap discrimination is established, the burden of persuasion shifts to the federal employer to show that the physical criteria offered as justification for refusal to hire the plaintiff are "job related," *i.e.*, that persons who suffer from the handicap plaintiff suffers and who are, therefore, unable to meet the challenged standards, cannot safely and efficiently perform the essentials of the position in question. If the issue of reasonable accommodation is raised, the agency must then be prepared to make a further showing that accommodation cannot reasonably be made that would enable the handicapped applicant to perform the essentials of the job adequately and safely; in this regard, the postal service must "demonstrate that the accommodation would impose an undue hardship on the operation of its program," 29 C.F.R. § 1613.704(a), taking into consideration the factors set forth by 704(c) of the cited regulation.

(3) If the employer proves that the challenged requirements are job related, the plaintiff may then show that other selection criteria without a similar discriminatory effect would also serve the employer's legitimate interest in efficient and trustworthy workmanship. When the issue of reasonable accommodation is raised, the burden of persuasion in proving inability to accommodate always remains on the employer; however, once the employer presents credible evidence that reasonable accommodation is not possible or practicable, the plaintiff must bear the burden of coming forward with evidence that suggests that accommodation may in fact be reasonably made.

We of course express no opinion as to the merits of Prewitt's claim. If he is unable to perform the essentials of the position for which he has applied, with or without reasonable accommodation, the postal service need not hire him. The ultimate test is whether, with or without reasonable accommodation, a handicapped individual who meets all employment criteria except for the challenged discriminatory criterion "can perform the essential functions of the position in question without endangering the health and safety of the individuals or others." 28 C.F.R. § 1613.702(f). Since a disputed issue of material fact is shown as to this issue, the summary judgment granted by the district court must be reversed.

* * *

NOTES AND PROBLEMS FOR DISCUSSION

1. While most of the issues that confronted the Fifth Circuit in *Prewitt* were subsequently addressed by Congress through its enactment of the ADA, as noted in the introductory portion of this Chapter, Congress anticipated that the Rehabilitation Act jurisprudence would shape the interpretation of comparable

provisions in the new statute. *Prewitt,* therefore, still serves as a useful guide to the resolution of two related interpretive problems under the ADA: (1)the extent of a defendant's duty of accommodation; and (2)the method of proving disability discrimination. These two issues are discussed in the following two Notes.

2. The duty of accommodation that the *Prewitt* court read into § 504 is now explicitly codified in § 102 of the ADA. And while the statute includes a definition of "reasonable accommodation" and "undue hardship", the language of these definitions is merely illustrative and is, therefore, still susceptible to judicial gloss. Consequently, it is appropriate to consider the manner in which the courts interpreted these phrases in cases arising under the Rehabilitation Act. As the court in *Prewitt* noted, few cases have addressed the scope of a § 501 or § 504 defendant's duty to make a reasonable accommodation for disabled employees or job applicants. In SOUTHEASTERN COMMUNITY COLLEGE v. DAVIS, 442 U.S. 397, 99 S.Ct. 2361, 60 L.Ed.2d 980 (1979), the Supreme Court discussed the accommodation issue in the context of a § 504 action brought by a hearing-impaired applicant who had been denied admission by the defendant college to its associate degree nursing program. The college maintained that the plaintiff was not "otherwise qualified" for its program because her inability to understand speech directed to her without the aid of lipreading prevented her from participating safely in both the clinical training program and her proposed profession. The Court agreed, thereby finding that the decision to exclude her was not discrimination within the meaning of § 504. Moreover, the Court rejected the plaintiff's claim that § 504 compelled the college to make whatever adjustments would be necessary to permit her safe participation in its nursing program. While personal supervision by a nursing instructor or a waiver of the clinical requirement might have enabled the plaintiff to participate in the training program, this accommodation would have resulted in a substantial modification of an essential feature of the training program. In other words, the Court implicitly concluded that the plaintiff was a victim of "insurmountable barrier" discrimination since the proposed accommodation would not have rendered her capable of successfully performing all the normal and necessary duties of a registered nurse. Accordingly, the failure to redress this discrimination did not violate § 504. Nevertheless, while the Court ruled that the defendant was not obliged to make an accommodation under those circumstances, it noted that "situations may arise where a refusal to modify an existing program might become unreasonable and discriminatory." It did not elaborate, however, on the duty to accommodate in the face of surmountable barrier discrimination, i.e., on where to draw the line between reasonable accommodation and undue hardship.

This issue, however, as the *Prewitt* court noted, has been addressed by the EEOC in its Equal Federal Employment Opportunity Guidelines. 29 C.F.R. § 1613.704(c) (1981). Notice the similarities between the tripartite formula for undue hardship proposed by these Guidelines (which is reproduced in the principal case at 979, *supra*) and the factors expressly designated by Congress' in the definition of "undue hardship" contained in § 101(10)(A) of the ADA. Is there any important difference between these standards?

The *Prewitt* court implied that the guidelines articulated in *Hardison* with respect to accommodation to religious beliefs would not apply in the disability context. Is this a proper implication? Is it likely that Congress intended to demand less of employers in an area (religion) where it clearly and explicitly created a duty to accommodate? On the other hand, now that Congress has codified the duty to accommodate in the 1991 Act, does this suggest that the *Hardison* guidelines should apply in both contexts? How does the definition of "reasonable accommodation" in § 101(9) of the ADA affect your answer to this question? What about the language in § 101(10)(A) that defines "undue hardship" to mean action that requires "significant difficulty or expense" in light of the list of factors contained in § 101(10)(B)? And what about the statement in § 501 that the ADA shall not be construed to apply a "lesser standard" than is applied under the Rehabilitation Act? Finally, does the absence of a First Amendment limitation support a more extensive accommodation duty in the disability, as opposed to religion, context? See Note, Protecting the Handicapped From Employment Discrimination in Private Sector Employment: A Critical Analyses of § 503 of the Rehabilitation Act of 1973, 54 Tul.L.Rev. 717, 734–37 (1980); Note, Accommodating the Handicapped: The Meaning of Discrimination under § 504 of the Rehabilitation Act, 55 N.Y.U.L.Rev. 881 (1980).

If, nevertheless, the *Prewitt* court is correct in stating, in footnote 22, that "[t]he *Hardison* principles are not applicable in the federal-employer handicap discrimination context [and that] Congress clearly intended the federal government to take measures that would involve more than a *de minimis* cost," does this mean, for example, that the defendant would not be required to undertake an accommodation that would violate the terms of a seniority clause in a collective bargaining agreement? See Shea v. Tisch, 870 F.2d 786 (1st Cir.1989)(employer not required to make an accommodation that would violate seniority provision of collective agreement); Carter v. Tisch, 822 F.2d 465, 467 (4th Cir.1987)("employer cannot be required to accommodate a handicapped employee by restructuring a job in a manner which would usurp legitimate rights of other employees under a collective bargaining agreement."); Hurst v. U.S. Postal Service, 653 F.Supp. 259 (N.D.Ga.1986)(in action brought by Vietnam veteran against Postal Service under §§ 501 and 505, the plaintiff's proposed accommodation would violate the seniority provision of the collective bargaining agreement and was, therefore, not "reasonable").

Must an employer consider the disabled plaintiff for positions other than those for which she applied? See Carter v. Tisch, 822 F.2d 465 (4th Cir.1987) (§ 504 does not require employer to provide alternative employment to disabled employee where it does not provide such alternative employment to other disabled employees under its existing policies); Dexler v. Carlin, 40 FEP Cases 633 (D.Conn.1986).

Does the accommodation obligation require an employer to adjust the ethical or "moral" standards it sets for its employees? In COPELAND v. PHILADELPHIA POLICE DEPT., 840 F.2d 1139 (3d Cir.1988), the defendant police department discharged the plaintiff police officer for using illegal drugs (his blood had tested positive for the presence of marijuana). The officer brought suit under, *inter alia*, § 504, contending that he was discriminated against on the basis of a perceived disability and that the Department did not make a reasonable accommodation to this disability. He argued that since the Department assigned police officers who were alcoholics or who were found to have violated state laws regarding alcohol abuse to a Department-operated rehabilitation program, a similar, reasonable accommodation to his disability was possible. The defendants asserted that a police officer who violates the criminal laws he has sworn to uphold does not possess the moral or ethical requirements of the job and that these criteria could not be accommodated without a substantial modification of the essential functions of the Department. The plaintiff, in response, contended that an examination of his ethical or moral qualifications for the job was beyond the scope of the Rehabilitation Act. The trial court rejected his claim and granted summary judgment in favor of the defendants. The Third Circuit agreed, reasoning that allowing this officer to remain and enter a drug rehabilitation program would cast doubt on the integrity of the police force and that since an essential function of the Department is to enforce the criminal laws, retaining an illegal drug user would constitute a substantial modification of the Department's essential functions. Accordingly, it concluded that the Department could not reasonably accommodate the plaintiff's disability and that, therefore, he was not otherwise qualified for the position of police officer.

Finally, must the employee accept the employer's offer of a reasonable accommodation? Is the Court's ruling in *Ansonia* (in the Title VII context) relevant here? See Severino v. North Fort Myers Fire Control Dist., 935 F.2d 1179 (11th Cir.1991)(defendant did not violate § 504 when it discharged AIDS-infected employee who refused to accept modified job duties; reassigning plaintiff firefighter from rescue work to light duty was a reasonable accommodation to the risk of transmission of the AIDS virus because the defendant relied upon reasonable medical opinion in making this decision; as plaintiff was terminated for refusing to accept reasonable transfer, the discharge was not made solely on the basis of his AIDS condition).

3.   The allocation of evidentiary burdens in disability discrimination litigation, like the duty of accommodation, is an area where the role traditionally played by the courts (as exemplified by Rehabilitation Act cases such as *Prewitt*) has been supplanted, at least in part, by Congress. Just as it codified the evidentiary rules governing Title VII actions in the 1991 Civil Rights Act, Congress attempted to codify the evidentiary rules governing claims of disability discrimination in the ADA. Accordingly, while one must look solely to caselaw to determine the rules controlling proof of Rehabilitation Act claims, there is legislative guidance with respect to the handling of claims under the ADA.

As we know, § 505(a)(2) links the enforcement of § 504 rights to the rules governing claims under Title VI of the 1964 Civil Rights Act. In GUARDIANS ASS'N v. CIVIL SERVICE COM'N, 463 U.S. 582, 103 S.Ct. 3221, 77 L.Ed.2d 866 (1983) (discussed in some detail in *Consolidated Rail, infra*, at 997), the Court addressed the question of the standard of proof governing Title VI claims. The Justices wrote six separate opinions, none of which was adopted in full by a majority of the Court. Nevertheless, seven Justices agreed that proof of discriminatory intent was necessary to establish a statutory violation. A majority of five, however, also concluded that a *Griggs*-type showing of disproportionate impact would suffice in a suit brought to enforce administrative regulations issued pursuant to this statute. Should this ruling apply also to claims brought under § 504? This question was not addressed by the Court in *Consolidated Rail* since the plaintiff therein had alleged intentional discrimination.

The issue was raised, however, by the parties in ALEXANDER v. CHOATE, 469 U.S. 287, 105 S.Ct. 712, 83 L.Ed.2d 661 (1985). There, the director of the Tennessee Medicaid program decided to institute a variety of cost-cutting measures to respond to projected Medicaid costs in excess of the State's Medicaid budget. One of the proposed changes was to reduce from twenty to fourteen the number of inpatient hospital days per fiscal year that Tennessee Medicaid would pay to hospitals on behalf of Medicaid patients. A class of Tennessee Medicaid recipients brought an action under § 504 to enjoin this proposed change on the ground that the reduced limitation on inpatient coverage would have a disproportionately disadvantageous impact on the disabled. It was undisputed that 27.4% of all handicapped users of hospital services who received Medicaid in the 1979–1980 fiscal year required more than 14 days of care, whereas only 7.8% of the nonhandicapped users of hospital services required more than 14 days of inpatient care. The defendant State of Tennessee, relying on the Court's ruling in *Guardians Ass'n,* claimed that § 504 prohibited only purposeful discrimination against the disabled. The trial court dismissed the complaint for failure to state a claim under § 504. The Sixth Circuit reversed, holding that the plaintiffs had established a prima facie case by claiming that the State's proposed action would have a disproportionately discriminatory effect on the disabled. It remanded the case to give the State an opportunity to rebut the prima facie case either by demonstrating the unavailability of an alternative cost-saving proposal with a less disproportionate impact on the disabled or offering a substantial justification for its adoption of the proposed plan. The Supreme Court overturned the appellate court's judgment, but refused to rule explicitly on whether an impact-based claim was cognizable under either § 504 or its implementing regulations. The Court stated that its opinion in *Guardians Ass'n.* was not dispositive of this issue since the decision in *Guardians Ass'n.*—that a Title VI violation required proof of discriminatory purpose—was controlled by the *stare decisis* effect of the Court's prior decision in *Bakke,* a restriction which did not apply to the interpretation of § 504. It also mentioned that the legislative history of § 504 reflected both Congress' recognition that most discrimination against the disabled was the product of indifference rather than animus and its intention to proscribe this manifestation of bias. Moreover, it noted that all the federal circuit courts that had addressed the issue had agreed that § 504 reaches some form of impact discrimination. Nevertheless, the Court expressed its concern that a broad ruling that § 504 reached all action with a disproportionate impact on the handicapped would create a potentially unwieldy administrative and adjudicative burden. Consequently, the Court was unwilling to adopt such a broad interpretation of the statute. In addition, it chose not to decide whether § 504 would ever extend to an impact-based discrimination claim. Instead, it assumed *arguendo* that § 504 or its implementing regulations reached some conduct that creates a disproportionate impact and ruled that the disproportionate effect of Tennessee's challenged action did not fall within the class of impact that the federal statute or regulations might reach. The reduction in inpatient coverage, the Court reasoned, did not adversely affect the handicapped since all users of hospital services were subject to the same limitation. To do otherwise, the Court declared, would require singling out the handicapped for more than fourteen days of coverage and improperly read into § 504 an obligation to guarantee equal results from the provision of state Medicaid payments to the handicapped. Because the handicapped, like all other hospital service users, retained meaningful and equal access to fourteen days of Medicaid coverage for inpatient care, the Court concluded, Tennessee's proposed action did not create the type of disproportionate impact on the handicapped which might be prohibited by Section 504 or its implementing regulations. Is this analysis reminiscent of the Court's approach in General Electric v. Gilbert, *supra* at 385? Since the Supreme Court has not issued any post-*Alexander* ruling on this issue, most appellate courts follow the *Prewitt* proof guidelines and permit impact-based claims. For a detailed discussion of the methods of proving discrimination in § 504 cases, see Wegner, the Antidiscrimination Model Reconsidered: Ensuring Equal Opportunity Without Respect to Handicap Under § 504 of the Rehabilitation Act of 1973, 69 Corn.L.Rev. 401 (1984).

In § 102(b) of the ADA, however, the definition of discrimination expressly codifies the disproportionate impact analysis employed by the court in *Prewitt*. The statute, in § 103, also sets forth with some precision the nature of the showing a defendant must make in response to an impact-based ADA claim. Little, if any, guidance is offered in the ADA, however, with respect to claims of intentional discrimination. Similarly, in *Prewitt*, the court only discussed the defenses available to an employer in a disproportionate impact-based claim of disability discrimination. What defenses are available when the plaintiff asserts a claim of disparate treatment, i.e., intentional discrimination? For example, can an employer justify its refusal to employ disabled persons by pointing to an anticipated increase in workmen's compensation insurance premiums? See Panettieri v. C. V. Hill Refrigeration, 159 N.J.Super. 472, 388 A.2d 630 (1978). What if the employer refuses to hire a disabled person on this ground, but also can point to that individual's history of unsafe job performance?

4. One of the most central and complex interpretive problems associated with the Rehabilitation Act is the meaning of "individual with handicap." Its significance lies in the fact that it defines the class of protected individuals. The complexity has centered mainly around the meaning of two pivotal phrases in the statutory definition—"impairment" and "substantially limits."

(a) The Rehabilitation Act protects individuals who have, have had or are regarded as having a mental or physical "impairment." Much of the controversy concerning the meaning of "impairment" initially arose in connection with so-called "voluntary" disabilities such as alcoholism and drug addiction. There was substantial debate over whether the Rehabilitation Act, as originally enacted, was intended to protect alcoholics and drug addicts. Congress addressed this concern in 1978, when it amended the statutory definition to exclude from protection under §§ 503 and 504 any *current* alcohol or drug abuser whose current use prevents the user from performing his or her job duties or whose use constitutes a threat to property or the safety of others. The clear implication of this language, which is consistent with the pre-amendment jurisprudence, is that current users whose use does not either impair their job performance or constitute a threat to property or persons fall within the definition and, therefore, are protected from discrimination based solely on this disability. The pre-amendment cases similarly held that former or perceived alcoholics and drug addicts could not be discriminated against unless they were "otherwise qualified". See Whitaker v. Board of Higher Education, 461 F.Supp. 99 (E.D.N.Y.1978)(alcoholism is a covered "impairment"); Davis v. Bucher, 451 F.Supp. 791 (E.D.Pa.1978)(drug addiction is an "impairment"); Anderson v. University of Wisconsin, 841 F.2d 737 (7th Cir.1988)(recovered alcoholic who was denied readmission after being expelled from law school for failing to maintain required grade average is "handicapped" but is not "otherwise qualified" to continue in law school); Heron v. McGuire, 803 F.2d 67 (2d Cir.1986)(heroin addict not "otherwise qualified" for position as police officer). Additionally, while one trial court has suggested that compulsive gambling may constitute a "mental impairment" within the meaning of the Rehabilitation Act, see Rezza v. United States Department of Justice, 46 FEP Cases 1366 (E.D.Pa.1988), § 511 of the ADA expressly excludes compulsive gambling from the class of covered disabilities.

The ADA further amended the Rehabilitation Act by expressly excluding individuals currently engaged in the illegal use of drugs from the protected class, although only when the defendant's action is based on such illegal use. Moreover, the amended provision states that this exclusion of illegal drug users does not apply to individuals who have successfully completed or are presently participating in a supervised rehabilitation program, as long as they are not presently engaging in illegal drug use. Additionally, individuals who are erroneously regarded as engaging in illegal drug use are protected under this amendment. Finally, the ADA provides that employers do not violate the Act by requiring employees to undergo medical examinations or inquiries related to the presence of illegal drugs. Similarly, employers are permitted to prohibit illegal drug use and alcohol use at the workplace and may enforce policies that employees not be under the influence of alcohol or be engaged in using illegal drugs at the workplace.

Note that the 1978 amendment only excluded current users from protection under §§ 503 and 504. At least one circuit court has ruled that this exclusion should not be extended to § 501 in recognition of the federal government's heightened responsibility towards hiring the handicapped. Crewe v. U.S. Office of Personnel Management, 834 F.2d 140 (8th Cir.1987). Does this mean that a federal employee who is a current drug or alcohol abuser can state a claim under § 501 and require the government to make a reasonable accommodation to his or her condition? See Whitlock v. Donovan, 598 F.Supp. 126 (D.D.C.1984)(federal government required to make reasonable accommodation to alcoholic employee under § 501).

The Rehabilitation Act and the ADA, however, are not the only federal enactments dealing with alcoholism in federal employment. The Comprehensive Alcohol Abuse and Alcoholism Prevention, Treatment and Rehabilitation Act of 1970, 42 U.S.C. § 290dd–1(a), requires federal agencies, including the armed forces, to maintain alcoholism treatment programs for their employees and has been interpreted to permit an agency to dismiss an alcoholic employee only where either (a)the employee refuses to accept treatment and subsequently fails to perform adequately on the job, or (b)the employee accepts treatment but repeatedly fails in the treatment after having been granted sick leave and also continues to fail to demonstrate adequate job performance. See generally, Rodgers v. Lehman, 869 F.2d 253 (4th Cir.1989).

Another question that has arisen in connection with the meaning of "impairment" is whether the disability must result in a present impairment. Consider the following:

A city police department refused to hire an applicant when a pre-employment physical examination revealed that he suffered from a degenerative knee condition. According to the examining physician's report, while the applicant's knees were fully functional at present, there was a significant likelihood of degenerative changes in his knees in the future. These changes, the report concluded, would prevent the applicant from performing several job duties that put pressure on a patrol officer's knees. Assuming the police department receives federal funding, has it violated § 504? Compare Chicago, Milwaukee, St. Paul & Pacific Railroad Co. v. Washington State Human Rights Commission, 11 EPD ¶ 10, 727 (Wash.Super.1975), reversed in part and vacated in part on other grounds, 87 Wn.2d 802, 557 P.2d 307 (1976); with Chrysler Outboard Corp. v. Department of Industry, Labor & Human Relations, 13 EPD ¶ 11, 526 (Wis.Cir.1976). See also Miller, Hiring the Handicapped: An Analysis of Laws

Prohibiting Discrimination Against the Handicapped in Employment, 16 Gonz. L.Rev. 23 (1980).

While the courts have tended to define "impairment" on an ad hoc basis, the federal agencies have chosen to include in their regulations a list of specific disabilities they view as falling within the ambit of the statute. For example, the Department of Health and Human Services' regulations include cosmetic disfigurement, sight, speech, hearing, reproductive and learning impairment, and mental retardation as covered disabilities. They also specifically exclude economic, cultural and environmental disadvantages, prison records, homosexuality and age. See 45 C.F.R. § 84.3(i) (1979). Yet while agency regulations typically exclude sexual orientation from the list of covered "impairments," the courts have disagreed on this question. Compare, for example, Blackwell v. United States Dept. of Treasury, 830 F.2d 1183 (D.C.Cir.1987)(sexual preference or orientation does not constitute a "handicap" within the meaning of the statute) with Doe v. United States Postal Service, 37 FEP Cases 1867 (D.D.C.1985)(denying the defendant's motion to dismiss a § 501 claim brought by a transsexual who alleged that she was handicapped by reason of her medically and psychologically established need for gender reassignment surgery and that this impairment substantially limited her major life activity of working). The ADA, on the other hand, offers a somewhat different approach to this problem. While Congress transplanted the Rehabilitation Act definition of "disability," it also set forth a nonexclusive list of conditions (such as, *inter alia,* homosexuality, bisexuality, sexual behavior and identity disorders, compulsive gambling, kleptomania and pyromania) that are explicitly excluded from the meaning of "disability."

Perhaps the most controversial question surrounding the meaning of "impairment" under the Rehabilitation Act is whether the Act protects individuals with contagious conditions such as AIDS. The Supreme Court addressed this issue in the context of an individual who suffered from tuberculosis.

In SCHOOL BOARD OF NASSAU COUNTY v. ARLINE, 480 U.S. 273, 107 S.Ct. 1123, 94 L.Ed.2d 307 (1987), the Supreme Court, by a vote of 7 to 2, held that a woman who had been hospitalized for and was suffering from the effects of a relapse of tuberculosis had established a "record of physical impairment" that substantially limited a major life activity and, therefore, was a "handicapped individual" within the meaning of § 504. The Court rejected the petitioners' claim that the statute did not apply to a person who had been discharged because of the threat of contagion from her disease, as distinguished from the disease's physical effects on her. It reasoned, rather, that since the disease was the source of both the physical impairment and the contagiousness, the employee had been discharged on the basis of her "handicap." The Court noted that the statute had been amended to protect individuals who are "regarded" as having a physical impairment from being limited in a major life activity, such as employment. This amendment, the Court stated, evinced Congress' recognition that social myths and fears about diseases can be as handicapping as the physical limitations that flow from the condition. Therefore, it concluded, permitting discrimination on the basis of the contagious effects of a physical impairment would be inconsistent with the statutory goal of protecting otherwise qualified disabled individuals from being denied jobs because of the prejudiced attitudes or ignorance of others. The majority declared that "the effects of one's impairment on others is as relevant to a determination of whether one is handicapped as is the physical effect of one's handicap on oneself." 480 U.S. at 283, n. 10, 107 S.Ct. at 1129 n. 10, 94 L.Ed.2d at 318 n. 10. The Court specifically reserved decision, however, on the question of whether an individual who is only a carrier of a disease, i.e., is capable of transmitting it to others, but who does not suffer any physical impairment, can be deemed a "handicapped person" solely on the basis of contagiousness. Thus, the Court sidestepped the obvious link between this case and the potential application of § 504 to AIDS carriers.

Having found that a person with a record of physical impairment who is also contagious is a "handicapped individual", the Court then examined whether the risk of contagion precluded that individual from being declared "otherwise qualified" within the meaning of § 504. In this regard, the Court stated that the language and legislative history of the Act precluded a blanket exclusion from statutory coverage of all actual or perceived contagious individuals, without a determination of whether the specific individual posed a serious health threat to others. Accordingly, it held that § 504 required an individualized inquiry, based on reasonable medical judgments given the state of medical knowledge, with respect to the following factors: "(a) the nature of the risk (how the disease is transmitted), (b) the duration of the risk (how long is the carrier infectious), (c) the severity of the risk (the degree of the potential harm to third parties) and (d) the probabilities the disease will be transmitted and will cause varying degrees of harm." It added that courts could reasonably be expected to defer to the judgments of public health officials in making this determination unless those judgments were medically unsupportable. (It expressly chose not to rule on whether courts also should defer to the reasonable medical judgments of private physicians upon whom the employer relied.) A person who was found to pose a significant risk of communicating an infectious disease to others in the workplace would be found not to be "otherwise qualified" if a reasonable accommodation would not eliminate that risk. The Court then remanded the case to the trial court to determine whether the respondent/plaintiff was "otherwise qualified" under these standards. Chief Justice Rehnquist, joined by Justice Scalia, dissented on a narrow ground. He maintained that recipients of federal funding could be subjected to only those conditions that are unambiguously expressed in federal legislation. And since the language, regulations and legislative history of the Rehabilitation Act were silent on the central issue of whether the statute was meant to prohibit discrimination on the basis of contagiousness as opposed to discrimination on the basis of any diminished physical capability resulting from the contagious disease, it was inappropriate to conclude that recipients of federal funding should be found to have knowingly agreed to condition their receipt of such funding on such a broad interpretation of the Act.

On remand, the trial court concluded that on the basis of the medical information available at the time of the plaintiff's discharge, the plaintiff had been cured of tuberculosis, posed no threat of communicating tuberculosis to the schoolchildren she was teaching and posed no risk of harm to others. Accordingly, it held that she was "otherwise qualified" to teach and that the discharge on the basis of her medical history of tuberculosis was not based on reasonable medical judgments but upon society's myths and fears about tuberculosis. The trial court entered judgment in favor of plaintiff on her § 504 claim and awarded her four years back pay and ordered the defendant school district to reinstate her to her position as a third grade teacher or to provide front pay in lieu of reinstatement. 692 F.Supp. 1286 (M.D.Fla.1988).

Applying the *Arline* standards to an AIDS victim who was transferred by the defendant school board from a teaching to administrative position and barred from classroom teaching, a trial court denied the plaintiff teacher's request for a preliminary injunction because the trial judge was not completely convinced by the evidence that there was no risk of transmission of AIDS to the plaintiff's deaf students. Doe v. Orange County Dept. of Educ., 44 FEP Cases 1579 (C.D.Cal.1987). On appeal, the Ninth Circuit reversed and ordered the trial judge to enter a preliminary injunction directing the defendant to restore the plaintiff to his teaching position. Chalk v. United States District Court, 832 F.2d 1158 (9th Cir.1987). The Ninth Circuit was convinced that the evidence "overwhelmingly indicated that the casual contact incident to the performance of his teaching duties in the classroom presents no significant risk of harm to others, and * * * [therefore,] appellant is otherwise qualified to perform his job within the meaning of § 504." Id. In a subsequent opinion in which it more fully explained its reasoning for reversing the trial court and ordering him to issue the preliminary injunction, the Ninth Circuit stated that by basing his refusal to grant the injunction on his lingering doubts about the transmittability of the AIDS virus, the trial court had not followed the legal standards set forth in *Arline* and had placed an impossible burden of proof on the plaintiff since, the court concluded, "little in science can be proved with complete certainty, and § 504 does not require a test." 840 F.2d 701, 707 (9th Cir.1988). It emphasized that *Arline* interpreted § 504 to permit the exclusion of a protected individual only where there is a "*significant* risk of communicating an infectious disease to others" and required deferral to reasonable medical judgments of public health officials on this question. By ignoring the overwhelming consensus of medical opinion and relying on his own speculation, the trial court, according to the Ninth Circuit, failed to adhere to the requirements set forth in *Arline*. The court thus concluded that the trial judge had relied on erroneous legal principles to conclude that the plaintiff had not demonstrated a likelihood of success on the merits. It also found the trial court's determination that the plaintiff had not demonstrated that he was threatened with the possibility of irreparable injury was clearly erroneous. It reasoned that the trial judge had erred in focusing on the fact that the transfer did not involve a diminution in salary and not on the nature of the alternative work that was given to the plaintiff. It found the non-monetary deprivation of personal satisfaction caused by his loss of student contact to be a substantial and cognizable injury. Finally, the court determined that in balancing the hardships, the plaintiff's injury outweighed any harm to the defendant school district since this latter injury was based solely on the theoretical and unproven risk of injury to others. Accordingly, it ordered the trial judge to enter a preliminary injunction ordering the defendants to restore the plaintiff to his former teaching duties.

The Supreme Court in *Arline* was quite careful to avoid deciding whether a disease carrier is "handicapped" within the meaning of the statute. Should § 504 apply to persons who carry a contagious disease, such as AIDS, but do not also have a physical impairment that substantially limits a major life activity? Could a recipient of federal funding refuse an applicant based on the employer's belief that the applicant was capable of transmitting a disease? Is it significant that the statute, as amended, defines "handicapped individual" to include persons "regarded as" having a physical or mental impairment that substantially limits a major life activity? For example, in HARRIS v. THIGPEN, 941 F.2d 1495 (11th Cir.1991), the Alabama Department of Corrections implemented a policy of uniformly segregating from the general prison population those prisoners who tested positive for exposure to Human Immunodeficiency Virus

(HIV). As a consequence of this segregation, the prisoners who tested HIV-positive were not able to participate in most of the programs available to general population prisoners. A group of HIV-positive prisoners claimed that their categorical exclusion from prison programs violated § 504. The trial court denied relief on the ground that assuming the seropositive plaintiffs were "handicapped", they were not "otherwise qualified" within the meaning of the Act because a significant risk of transmission remained after reasonable accommodations were made. The circuit court concluded, in narrowly drafted language, that since the plaintiffs were excluded from programs solely because of their HIV-positive status, the prison authorities were treating them as though they were unable to engage in these "major life activities" relative to the rest of the prison population. Accordingly, the court reasoned, it was appropriate to conclude that the seropositive prisoners were "regarded as having" a physical or mental impairment and, therefore, in this case, seropositivity was a "handicap" within the meaning of the Act. The court then examined, pursuant to the standards set forth in *Arline*, whether the plaintiffs were otherwise qualified, i.e., whether a significant risk of transmission of the infectious disease remained after the implementation of reasonable accommodations. It criticized the trial court's conclusory treatment of this issue, stating that while the court's conclusions might ultimately prove to be correct, it had not offered any support for its conclusion and its analysis was devoid of the kind of individualized inquiry required by *Arline* to determine whether the plaintiffs were otherwise qualified or could become so through reasonable accommodation. Consequently, it remanded the case for a determination of the risk of transmission with respect to each program from which the plaintiffs had been automatically excluded and whether reasonable accommodations could minimize this risk as to each such program. See AIDS Discrimination Under Federal, State, And Local Law After Arline, 15 Fla.St.U.L.Rev. 221 (1987); Note, AIDS and Employment Discrimination: Should AIDS Be Considered A Handicap? 33 Wayne L.Rev. 1095 (1987).

In LOCAL 1812, AFGE v. U.S. DEPT. OF STATE, 662 F.Supp. 50 (D.D.C. 1987), the plaintiff brought an action under, *inter alia*, § 504 to enjoin the State Department from expanding its employee medical fitness program for all Foreign Service employees to include mandatory bloodtesting for the presence of the virus (HIV) believed to cause AIDS. In response to the defense claim that the plaintiff was not "handicapped" within the meaning of the statute, Judge Gesell stated that "there is no doubt that a known carrier of the virus which causes [AIDS] * * * is perceived to be handicapped." Id., at 54. Interestingly, because the State Department wished to assert that all HIV carriers were not "otherwise qualified", it conceded the applicability of the Rehabilitation Act to symptomless HIV carriers on the ground that the great majority of HIV carriers are physically impaired due to measurable deficiencies in their immune systems even where disease symptoms have not yet developed. The plaintiff disputed the proposition that symptomless HIV carriers are physically impaired, but the court chose not to resolve this issue. Rather, it concluded that the carriers were not "otherwise qualified" for foreign service. The State Department, Judge Gesell concluded, had demonstrated serious ground for its concern about the risk to HIV carriers from foreign service where medical care would be inadequate to diagnose and treat subsequent medical problems that the carriers could develop and that any further accommodation, such as only allowing foreign service at posts with adequate medical facilities or upgrading the medical facilities at all overseas posts exceeded the statutory reasonable accommodation standard. Accordingly, he denied the request for a preliminary injunction.

Does the employer's exclusion *ipso facto* prove or suggest that the individual is "regarded as" having such an impairment? In BLACKWELL v. UNITED STATES DEPT. OF TREASURY, 639 F.Supp. 289 (D.D.C.1986), for example, another opinion written by Judge Gesell, the court denied the defendant's motion to dismiss and held that a transvestite stated a claim under § 504 by alleging that the defendant employer refused to rehire him. The court reasoned that the fact of the plaintiff's exclusion for being a transvestite demonstrated that the employer regarded his being a transvestite as a handicap. Moreover, the court added, the plaintiff would not have to allege or prove that his disability actually impaired his ability to function. Interestingly, however, after a bench trial, the court entered judgment for the defendant on the ground that the plaintiff had a statutory duty to inform his prospective employer of a disability that is not automatically apparent. Since the plaintiff had not indicated during the job interview that he was a transvestite, he was held not to be entitled to relief. 656 F.Supp. 713 (D.D.C.1986). On appeal, however, the D.C. Circuit vacated the trial court's judgment on the ground that such a requirement of explicit notice was inconsistent with the language and intent of the statute. Ironically, the court ultimately affirmed the trial judge's dismissal of the complaint, but only because it concluded that sexual orientation does not fall within the compass of the Rehabilitation Act. 830 F.2d 1183 (D.C.Cir.1987). For a general discussion of the meaning of "handicap" see Larson, What Disabilities Are Protected Under The Rehabilitation Act of 1987?, 16 Memph. St.U.L.Rev. 229 (1986). Can being left-handed constitute an "impairment"? See de la Torres v. Bolger, 781 F.2d 1134 (5th Cir.1986).

In the Civil Rights Restoration Act of 1987, 20 U.S.C. §§ 1687, 1688 (an enactment designed principally to reverse the Supreme Court's ruling in *Grove City College* concerning the "program or activity" language in Title IX, see p. 1008, *supra*), Congress included a provision that amended the definitions provision of the Rehabilitation Act. This amendment states that the term "handicapped individual", as it relates to employment, shall *not* include an individual who "has" a currently contagious disease or infection who, by reason of that disease or infection, either (1) would constitute a direct threat to the health or safety of others, or (2) is unable to perform the duties of the job. The statute does not specify either who is to make the determination of whether an individual has a currently contagious disease or infection or upon what evidentiary basis such a determination may or shall be made. Neither does it clearly resolve whether a "carrier" is to be viewed as a person who "has" a currently contagious disease or infection. But the inclusion of the term "infection" within this amendment suggests that Congress intended to include asymptomatic individuals who are infected with the HIV virus (i.e., "carriers") within the coverage of the statute unless they constitute a direct threat to the health or safety of others or are unable to perform the duties of the job.

Some state legislatures have chosen to amend their own fair employment laws to make them expressly applicable to asymptomatic AIDS victims. Effective June 1, 1988, the Missouri Fair Employment Practices Act's proscription against employment discrimination was extended to all individuals with HIV infection, AIDS and AIDS–related complex except those who are "currently contagious" or who, by reason of their currently contagious disease or infection either would constitute a direct threat to the health or safety of other individuals or are unable to perform their job duties. The Washington State legislature amended its Law Against Discrimination to include discrimination based on "actual or perceived" HIV infection among its proscribed practices. It also prohibits the imposition of testing for HIV infection as a condition of hiring, promotion or continued employment, unless performance of the job in question is shown to present a significant risk, as defined by the board of health, of transmitting HIV infection to others and there exists no means of eliminating the risk by restructuring the job. A 1989 enactment by the North Carolina legislature prohibits discrimination against "any person having AIDS virus or HIV infection on account of that infection for continued employment." And a 1990 Nebraska statute prohibits discrimination in employment against any individual who is suffering or is suspected of suffering from human immunode- ficiency virus infection or AIDS unless such individual poses a direct threat to the health or safety of himself, herself, or others, or is unable to perform the duties of the job.

In addition, pursuant to a request from President Reagan that the Justice Department review all existing federal anti-discrimination laws applicable to the HIV infection context, the Justice Department's Office of Legal Counsel issued a memorandum on September 27, 1988, stating its view as to the applicability of § 504 to asymptomatic AIDS carriers. The memorandum states that § 504, in light of the enactment of the Civil Rights Restoration Act, should be interpreted to include symptomatic and asymptomatic HIV–infected individ- uals within the meaning of "handicapped" and, therefore, that all such individ- uals are protected from discrimination on the basis of that handicap as long as they are "otherwise qualified," i.e., so long as they can perform the job duties and do not constitute a direct threat to the health or safety of others. For further discussion of the applicability of § 504 to AIDS victims and carriers see Carey & Arthur, The Developing Law On Aids In The Workplace, 46 Md.L.Rev. 284 (1987); Leonard, Employment Discrimination Against Persons With AIDS, 10 U. Of Dayton L.Rev. 681 (1985); Note, AIDS: Does It Qualify As A "Handicap" Under The Rehabilitation Act Of 1973?, 61 Not.D.L.Rev. 572 (1986).

(b) In order for an individual to fall within the protections of the Rehabili- tation Act, she must have an impairment that "substantially limits" one or more of her major life activities. The Department of Labor's Office of Federal Contract Compliance Programs regulations state that a disabled person is "substantially limited" if she or he is "likely to experience difficulty in securing, retaining or advancing in employment" because of the disability. Does this mean that a worker who is denied a particular position because of her disability, but who can successfully perform several other similar or related jobs, is covered by the Act? In E.E. Black, Limited v. Marshall, 497 F.Supp. 1088 (D.Hawaii 1980), the trial court reversed the Assistant Secretary of Labor's determination that an individual was substantially limited if the impairment operated to bar him from the particular job of his choice. At the same time, the court refused to limit statutory protection to persons whose disability precluded almost any type of employment. The court concluded that Congress' use of "substantially" to modify "limits" reflected its intent to cover individuals whose disability impaired employment in their chosen field. See also Jasany v. United States Postal Service, 755 F.2d 1244, 1249 (6th Cir.1985)(whether a particular impairment is a handicap under the Act depends on "the number and type of jobs from which the impaired individual is disqualified"). In Forrisi v. Bowen, 794 F.2d 931 (4th Cir.1986), for example, the court concluded that an individual with acrophobia—fear of heights—was not "substantially limited" simply because he could not perform his chosen occupation in a setting that also required him to climb stairways and ladders. And in Wright v. Tisch, 45 FEP Cases 151 (D.Va.1987), the court held that a plaintiff whose allergies were triggered by the particular environmental conditions of a specific location did not suffer substantial limitation of a major life activity.

5. Section 504 prohibits discrimination against an "otherwise qualified" individual with a disability. Is an individual who can perform the assigned job duties "otherwise qualified" if her performance creates a risk of injuries to other employees? The U.S. Postal Service refused to hire an epileptic applicant who had a history of one grand mal seizure per year for a position that would involve driving a vehicle or using dangerous machinery with moving parts. It contended that this person was not an "otherwise qualified" handicapped person on the ground that she would create an "elevated risk" of injury to herself or others. The court stated that in some cases it is necessary to screen out job applicants on the basis of possible future injury. To do so, however, the court added, the defendant must show a "reasonable probability of substantial harm" based on an ad hoc analysis of the plaintiff's work and medical history and the requirements of the job in question. Mantolete v. Bolger, 767 F.2d 1416 (9th Cir.1985).

6. In addition to proving that she is an "individual with handicaps" who is "otherwise qualified", a § 504 plaintiff also must establish that she was discriminated against "solely by reason of" this handicap. Suppose that an employee is discharged for excessive, unexcused absences. If the plaintiff can show, however, that these absences were the direct result of her disabling condition, can she prove that she was fired "solely by reason of her handicap"? If so, is this evidence relevant to any other issue? Can, for example, the employer offer it to rebut the plaintiff's showing that she is "otherwise qualified"? See Teahan v. Metro–North Commuter Railroad Co., 951 F.2d 511, 516 (2d Cir.1991)("an employer relies on a handicap when it justifies termination based on conduct caused by the handicap"; whether such conduct was causally related to the handicap is a question of fact; any conduct demonstrated to be a manifestation of the disability that is likely to occur in the future is relevant to the "otherwise qualified" determination). Note that under the ADA, the plaintiff must show that she can perform "the essential functions of the job" with or without a reasonable accommodation.

7. The Fifth Circuit in *Prewitt* construed the 1978 amendments to the Rehabilitation Act to provide a private cause of action for federal and Postal Service employees under both §§ 501 and 504. The Sixth and Eighth Circuits agree with this interpretation. See Morgan v. United States Postal Service, 798 F.2d 1162 (8th Cir.1986), cert. denied, 480 U.S. 948, 107 S.Ct. 1608, 94 L.Ed.2d 794 (1987); Smith v. United States Postal Service, 742 F.2d 257 (6th Cir.1984). The Seventh, Ninth and Tenth Circuits, however, have held that only § 501 provides a private cause of action for federal employees alleging disability discrimination. See Johnston v. Horne, 875 F.2d 1415 (9th Cir.1989); Johnson v. United States Postal Service, 861 F.2d 1475 (10th Cir.1988), cert. denied, 493 U.S. 811, 110 S.Ct. 54, 107 L.Ed.2d 23 (1989); McGuinness v. United States Postal Service, 744 F.2d 1318 (7th Cir.1984). (Keep in mind that the ADA does not apply to federal employees other than those employed by the two houses of Congress and legislative agencies.).

Section 505, however, does more than expressly provide a private right of action for claims under §§ 501 and 504. It also subjects such claims to the remedial and procedural regimes of Titles VII and VI, respectively. That is, claims under § 501 are governed by the Title VII enforcement mechanism, whereas § 504 plaintiffs are subject to the remedial and procedural provisions of Title VI. This creates a potential problem in those circuits (mentioned in the preceding paragraph) which permit federal employees to file disability claims under either §§ 501 or 504. Should such claims be governed by the procedural requirements of Title VI or VII? To promote uniform treatment of federal employee disability claims, these circuits agree that disability claims by federal employees, whether brought under §§ 501 or 504, are subject to the procedural constraints imposed upon federal employees by § 717 of Title VII. This means that all such claims are subject to the limitations period applied to federal employee Title VII claims and that these plaintiffs are required to invoke administrative remedies prior to filing suit.

Employees of federal grantees, on the other hand, can only state a Rehabilitation Act claim under § 504 and, therefore, per § 505, they are subject to the procedural requirements set forth in Title VI. Most, if not all funding agencies have formulated their own administrative mechanism for investigating and adjudicating claims of disability discrimination brought against their recipient institutions. Does this mean that, pursuant to Title VI, a § 504 plaintiff must invoke these administrative remedies prior to instituting suit? In CANNON v. UNIVERSITY OF CHICAGO, 441 U.S. 677, 99 S.Ct. 1946, 60 L.Ed.2d 560 (1979), the Supreme Court held that a Title IX plaintiff was not required to pursue administrative remedies prior to filing suit. Because of the similarity between the enforcement schemes provided in Titles VI and IX, and in light of the fact that the available administrative remedy—termination of funding—does not compensate the individual discriminatee, the lower federal courts have held that Title VI does not impose an exhaustion of administrative remedies requirement. Thus, they conclude, an individual seeking to bring a claim under § 504 is not required to invoke these administrative remedies prior to filing suit. See Camenisch v. University of Texas, 616 F.2d 127 (5th Cir.1980), vacated and remanded for mootness, 451 U.S. 390, 101 S.Ct. 1830, 68 L.Ed.2d 175 (1981); Cain v. Archdiocese of Kansas City, Kansas, 508 F.Supp. 1021 (D.Kan.1981); Whitaker v. Board of Education of City of New York, 461 F.Supp. 99 (E.D.N.Y. 1978). But see Peterson v. Gentry, 28 FEP Cases 273 (S.D.Iowa 1981)(§ 504 action dismissed for failure to exhaust state law administrative remedies that can provide remedy plaintiff seeks). In addition, such suits are subject to the terms of the most closely analogous state statute of limitations. Section 107(a) of the ADA, on the other hand, incorporates the remedial and enforcement mechanism of Title VII and declares that it shall govern all claims under this statute. Accordingly, plaintiffs proceeding under the ADA will be required to invoke the EEOC administrative machinery prior to filing suit.

Finally, does the incorporation of the Title VII enforcement scheme by § 505(a)(1) of the Rehabilitation Act have any substantive impact on the scope of protection offered to federal employees by this statute? For example, should the judicially crafted exemptions from Title VII coverage applicable to federal employees, such as the exclusion of uniformed personnel of the armed forces, extend to the Rehabilitation Act? See Doe v. Ball, 725 F.Supp. 1210 (M.D.Fla. 1989)(scope of Rehabilitation Act's application to federal employees is restricted by federal employees and, therefore, uniformed member of armed forces has no remedy under this statute.).

8. After his unsuccessful application for employment as a clerk/carrier with the Greenville, Mississippi post office, the plaintiff in the principal case applied for a substitute rural carrier job. Once again, he was found medically

unsuitable for employment. He filed a second action alleging discrimination because of his handicap, which was dismissed with prejudice by the federal trial judge. The appellate court reversed this dismissal and noted that if the plaintiff prevailed on the merits, he would receive an award of back pay. Prewitt v. United States Postal Service, 662 F.2d 311 (5th Cir.1981) (Prewitt II). Was the court correct in assuming (without discussion) that back pay, as opposed to other forms of equitable relief such as injunctions or declaratory judgments, is recoverable under § 504? If so, does this mean that a § 504 plaintiff can also recover compensatory and/or punitive damages? See how the first of these two issues is resolved and the second is discussed in *Consolidated Rail*, the following principal case. See generally, Safeguarding Equality For The Handicapped: Compensatory Relief Under Section 504 Of The Rehabilitation Act, 1986 Duke L.J. 197 (1986).

9. In light of the Supreme Court's ruling in *Elliott,* should a state administrative agency's decision have preclusive effect on a plaintiff's subsequent action under § 504? In Daniels v. Barry, 659 F.Supp. 999 (D.D.C.1987), the court correctly perceived the issue as whether § 504 claims should be viewed and treated like Title VII or § 1983 claims. The court concluded that since § 501 expressly incorporated Title VII remedies and § 504, like § 501, provided for a private right of action, that §§ 501 and 504 should be seen as more like Title VII than § 1983. Accordingly, it concluded, *Elliott* demanded that the state administrative decision not have preclusive effect. The court added that as plaintiffs in § 504 actions were not required to exhaust administrative remedies, this suggested that Congress intended for the federal courts in § 504 actions to have the type of de novo review authority that was assigned to them in Title VII actions. This further supported the court's view that § 504 actions should not be precluded by state administrative adjudications. On the other hand, the Fifth Circuit applied the doctrine of res *judicata* to preclude the filing of a § 501 claim by a discharged Postal Service employee who could have, but did not, include that claim in a previously filed Title VII action that challenged the same discharge on the ground of sex discrimination and was dismissed on a motion for summary judgment in favor of the Postal Service. See Miller v. U.S. Postal Service, 825 F.2d 62 (5th Cir.1987).

10. Dr. Keith Werhan, a cancer researcher, is employed by Omega Laboratories. Omega has received a grant from the U.S. Department of Public Health to develop innovative cancer detection procedures. Upon discovering that Dr. Werhan, the leader of the research team, has contracted Kaposi's Sarcoma, an AIDS-related illness, the Department cancels the grant because of its concern over Werhan's illness. Can Werhan bring a § 504 claim against the Public Health Department? See Doe v. Attorney General, 941 F.2d 780 (9th Cir.1991)(plaintiff does have a private right of action under § 504 against the agency that provides the funding to his employer even though plaintiff is not an employee of the funding agency; plaintiff is not limited to administrative remedies against funding agency). But see Cousins v. Secretary of Transportation, 880 F.2d 603 (1st Cir.1989)(individual prevented from working as truck driver pursuant to U.S. Department of Transportation regulation excluding deaf persons does not have private right of action under § 504 against agency for harm caused by agency's regulatory action. Remedy lies in appeal of agency action under Administrative Procedures Act.).

11. Does a disabled beneficiary of a program receiving federal funding have a private right of action under § 504 against the Secretary of the funding federal department for allegedly failing to investigate the beneficiary's com-

plaint? See Salvador v. Bell, 622 F.Supp. 438 (N.D.Ill.1985)(availability of § 504 action against recipient of funding renders such a suit incompatible with the integrity of the § 504 enforcement scheme and is therefore not permitted).

CONSOLIDATED RAIL CORP. v. DARRONE

Supreme Court of the United States, 1984.
465 U.S. 624, 104 S.Ct. 1248, 79 L.Ed.2d 568.

JUSTICE POWELL delivered the opinion of the Court.

This case requires us to clarify the scope of the private right of action to enforce § 504 of the Rehabilitation Act of 1973, that prohibits discrimination against the handicapped by federal grant recipients. There is a conflict among the circuits.

I

The Rehabilitation Act of 1973 establishes a comprehensive federal program aimed at improving the lot of the handicapped. Among its purposes are to "promote and expand employment opportunities in the public and private sectors for handicapped individuals and place such individuals in employment." To further these purposes, Congress enacted § 504 of the Act. That section provides that:

No otherwise qualified handicapped individual * * * shall, solely by reason of his handicap, be excluded from the participation in, be denied the benefits of, or be subjected to discrimination under any program or activity receiving Federal financial assistance.

The language of the section is virtually identical to that of § 601 of Title VI of the Civil Rights Act of 1964, that similarly bars discrimination (on the ground of race, color, or national origin) in federally-assisted programs.

In 1978, Congress amended the Rehabilitation Act to specify the means of enforcing its ban on discrimination. In particular, § 505(a)(2), made available the "remedies, procedure, and rights set forth in Title VI of the Civil Rights Acts of 1964" to victims of discrimination in violation of § 504 of the Act.[1]

Petitioner, Consolidated Rail Corporation ("Conrail"), was formed pursuant to subchapter III of the Regional Rail Reorganization Act, 45 U.S.C. §§ 701 et seq. The Act, passed in response to the insolvency of a number of railroads in the Northeast and Midwest, established Conrail to acquire and operate the rail properties of the insolvent railroads and

---

1. Section 505(a)(2) provides in full: "The remedies, procedures, and rights set forth in title VI of the Civil Rights Act of 1964 shall be available to any person aggrieved by any act or failure to act by any recipient of Federal assistance or Federal provider of such assistance under § 794 of this title."

Section 505(a)(1) generally makes available the remedies of Title VII of the Civil Rights Act to persons aggrieved by violation of § 791 of the Rehabilitation Act, which governs the federal government's employment of the handicapped.

to integrate these properties into an efficient national rail transportation system.   Under § 216 of the Act, 45 U.S.C. § 726, the United States, acting through the United States Railway Association, purchases debentures and series A preferred stock of the corporation "at such times and in such amounts as may be required and requested by the corporation," but "in accordance with the terms and conditions * * * prescribed by the Association * * *."   Id. § 726(b)(1).   The statute permits the proceeds from these sales to be devoted to maintenance of rail properties, capital needs, refinancing of indebtedness, or working capital.   Ibid.   Under this statutory authorization, Conrail has sold the United States $3.28 billion in securities.

Conrail also received federal funds under subchapter V of the Act, now repealed, to provide for reassignment and retraining of railroad workers whose jobs were affected by the reorganization.   And Conrail now receives federal funds under § 1143(a) of the Northeast Rail Service Act, 45 U.S.C. § 797a, that provides termination allowances of up to $25,000 to workers who lose their jobs as a result of reorganization.

II

In 1979, Thomas LeStrange filed suit against petitioner for violation of rights conferred by § 504 of the Rehabilitation Act.[2]   The complaint alleged that the Erie Lackawanna Railroad, to which Conrail is the successor in interest, had employed the plaintiff as a locomotive engineer; that an accident had required amputation of plaintiff's left hand and forearm in 1971; and that, after LeStrange was disabled, the Erie Lackawanna Railroad, and then Conrail, had refused to employ him although it had no justification for finding him unfit to work.

The District Court, following the decision of Trageser v. Libbie Rehabilitation Center, Inc., 590 F.2d 87 (CA4 1978), cert. denied, 442 U.S. 947, 99 S.Ct. 2895, 61 L.Ed.2d 318 (1979), granted petitioner's motion for summary judgment on the ground that the plaintiff did not have "standing" to bring a private action under § 504.[3]   In Trageser, the Fourth Circuit had held that § 505(a)(2) of the Rehabilitation Act incorporated into that act the limitation found in § 604 of Title VI, which provides that employment discrimination is actionable only when the employer receives federal financial assistance the "primary objective" of which is "to provide employment."   The District Court concluded that the aid provided to petitioner did not satisfy the "primary objective" test.[4]

2. Respondent, the administratrix of LeStrange's estate, was substituted as a party before this Court upon the death of LeStrange.

3. The District Court previously had dismissed constitutional claims raised by LeStrange, 501 F.Supp. 964 (MD Pa.1980).

4. Under the analysis of Trageser, a private plaintiff also may have "standing" to sue for employment discrimination if he can show "that discrimination in employment necessarily causes discrimination against" the intended beneficiaries of the federal aid, even where that aid itself was not intended to further employment.   App.

The Court of Appeals reversed and remanded to the District Court. 687 F.2d 767 (CA3 1982). There was no opinion for the court, but all three judges of the panel agreed that the cause of action for employment discrimination under § 504 was not properly limited to situations "where a primary objective of the federal financial assistance is to provide employment." Judge Bloch, noting that North Haven Board of Education v. Bell, 456 U.S. 512, 102 S.Ct. 1912, 72 L.Ed.2d 299 (1982), had construed Title IX to create a private cause of action for employment discrimination in all federally funded education programs, concluded that the language and legislative history of § 504 required the same broad construction of that section. Judge Adams, concurring in the judgment, found the result compelled by *North Haven Board of Education* and by the Third Circuit's decision in Grove City College v. Bell, aff'd, ante, p. 555.[5] Judge Weis, concurring, argued that Congress had not intended the Rehabilitation Act to incorporate Title VI's "primary objective" limitation: that limitation was designed to temper the government's decision to terminate federal funds, a decision that has more drastic consequences for the funded programs than do private suits for individual relief.

We granted certiorari to resolve the conflict among the circuits and to consider other questions under the Rehabilitation Act.[6] We affirm.

III

We are met initially by petitioner's contention that the death of the plaintiff LeStrange has mooted the case and deprives the Court of jurisdiction for that reason.[7] Petitioner concedes, however, that there remains a case or controversy if LeStrange's estate may recover money that would have been owed to LeStrange.[8] Without determining the extent to which money damages are available under § 504, we think it clear that § 504 authorizes a plaintiff who alleges intentional discrimination to bring an equitable action for backpay. The case therefore is not moot.

to Pet. for Cert. 33. The District Court found as well that this prong of the *Trageser* test was not satisfied here.

5. The Third Circuit Court of Appeals had held in *Grove City College* that an entire educational institution is subject to the anti-discrimination provisions of Title IX if any department of the institution receives federal aid.

6. Three other Courts of Appeals have agreed substantially with the Fourth Circuit decision in *Trageser*. See Scanlon v. Atascadero State Hospital, 677 F.2d 1271 (CA9 1982); United States v. Cabrini Medical Center, 639 F.2d 908 (CA2 1981); Carmi v. Metropolitan St. Louis Sewer District, 620 F.2d 672 (CA8), cert. denied, 449 U.S. 892, 101 S.Ct. 249, 66 L.Ed.2d 117 (1980).

7. In addition, Conrail argued below, and again in its opening brief, that § 504 does not create a private right of action for employment discrimination. This argument was abandoned at page 3 of Conrail's reply brief. See also Tr. of Oral Arg. 13. In view of this concession it is unnecessary to address the question here beyond noting that the courts below relied on Cannon v. University of Chicago, 441 U.S. 677, 99 S.Ct. 1946, 60 L.Ed.2d 560 (1979), in holding that such a private right exists under § 504.

8. Petitioner also concedes that respondent, as representative of LeStrange's estate, may assert any right to monetary relief under § 504 that was possessed by LeStrange.

In Guardians Ass'n v. Civil Service Comm'n, 463 U.S. 582, 103 S.Ct. 3221, 77 L.Ed.2d 866 (1983), a majority of the Court expressed the view that a private plaintiff under Title VI could recover backpay; and no member of the Court contended that backpay was unavailable, at least as a remedy for intentional discrimination.[9] It is unnecessary to review here the grounds for this interpretation of Title VI. It suffices to state that we now apply this interpretation to § 505(a)(2), that, as we have noted, provides to plaintiffs under § 504 the remedies set forth in Title VI. Therefore, respondent, having alleged intentional discrimination, may recover backpay in the present § 504 suit.[10]

IV

A

The Court of Appeals rejected the argument that petitioner may be sued under § 504 only if the primary objective of the federal aid that it receives is to promote employment. Conrail relies particularly on § 604 of Title VI. This section limits the applicability of Title VI to "employment practice[s] * * * where a *primary objective* of the federal financial assistance is to provide employment" (emphasis added).[11] As noted above, § 505(a)(2) of the Rehabilitation Act, as amended in 1978, adopted the remedies and rights provided in Title VI. Accordingly, Conrail's basic position in this case is that § 604's limitation was incorporated expressly into the Rehabilitation Act. The decision of the Court of Appeals therefore should be reversed, Conrail contends, as the

---

9. A majority of the Court agreed that retroactive relief is available to private plaintiffs for all discrimination, whether intentional or unintentional, that is actionable under Title VI. Justice Marshall, and Justice Stevens, joined by Justices Brennan and Blackmun, argued that both prospective and retroactive relief were fully available to Title VI plaintiffs. 463 U.S., at 624–634, 635–639, 103 S.Ct., at 3245–3249. Justice O'Connor agreed that both prospective and retroactive equitable relief were available, while reserving judgment on the question whether there is a private cause of action for damages relief under Title VI. Id., at 621, n. 1, 103 S.Ct., at 3237, n. 1. Justice White, joined by Justice Rehnquist, while contending that only relief ordering future compliance with legal obligations was available in other private actions under Title VI, put aside the situation of the private plaintiff who alleged intentional discrimination. Id., at 597, 103 S.Ct., at 3237. The Chief Justice and Justice Powell did not reach the question, as they would have held that petitioners in that case had no private right of action and had not made the showing of intentional discrimination required to establish a vio-

lation of Title VI. Id., at 596, 103 S.Ct., at 3236.

10. Although the legislative history of the 1978 amendments does not explicitly indicate that Congress intended to preserve the full measure of courts' equitable power to award backpay, the few references to the question are consistent with our holding. Congress clearly intended to make backpay available to victims of discrimination by the federal government, see S.Rep. No. 95–890, p. 19 (1978); and statements made in relation to subsequent legislation by the Senate Committee on Labor and Human Resources, the committee responsible for the 1978 amendments, endorse the availability of backpay. S.Rep. No. 96–316, pp. 12–13 (1979).

11. Section 604 provides in full: "Nothing contained in this subchapter shall be construed to authorize action under this subchapter by any department or agency with respect to any employment practice of any employer, employment agency, or labor organization except where a primary objective of the Federal financial assistance is to provide employment." 42 U.S.C. § 2000d–3.

primary objective of the federal assistance received by Conrail was not to promote employment.

It is clear that § 504 itself contains no such limitation. Section 504 neither refers explicitly to § 604 nor contains analogous limiting language; rather, that section prohibits discrimination against the handicapped under "*any* program or activity receiving Federal financial assistance." And it is unquestionable that the section was intended to reach employment discrimination.[12] Indeed, enhancing employment of the handicapped was so much the focus of the 1973 legislation that Congress the next year felt it necessary to amend the statute to clarify whether § 504 was intended to prohibit other types of discrimination as well. See § 111(a), Pub.L. 93–516, 88 Stat. 1617, 1619 (1974), *amending* 29 U.S.C. § 706(6).[13] Thus, the language of § 504 suggests that its bar

12. Congress recognized that vocational rehabilitation of the handicapped would be futile if those who were rehabilitated could not obtain jobs because of discrimination. Employment discrimination thus would have "a profound effect on the provision of relevant and effective [rehabilitation] services." 119 Cong.Rec. 5862 (1973) (remarks of Sen. Williams). See, e.g., S.Rep. No. 93–318, p. 4 (1973); 119 Cong.Rec. 24587 (1973) (remarks of Sen. Taft), 24588 (remarks of Sen. Williams). Several other sections of Title V of the Rehabilitation Act also were aimed at discrimination in employment: § 501 and § 503 require all federal employers and federal contractors to adopt affirmative action programs for the handicapped.

13. We note further that the Court in an analogous statutory context rejected the contention that the terms used in § 504 implicitly contain a "primary objective" limitation. § 901 of Title IX, like § 504, borrowed the language of § 601 of Title VI. North Haven Board of Education v. Bell, 456 U.S. 512, 102 S.Ct. 1912, 72 L.Ed.2d 299 (1982), found, however, that Title IX's prohibition of employment discrimination did not incorporate § 604's "primary objective" requirement. The Court stated that, had Congress wished so to limit Title IX, it would have enacted in that Title counterparts to both § 601 and § 604. Id., at 530, 102 S.Ct., at 1922–1923.

Petitioner suggests that *North Haven* is inapplicable to the construction of § 504 because the Congress considered but rejected a provision explicitly incorporating the language of § 604 of Title VI into Title IX. And other aspects of the legislative history also supported the Court's interpretation of § 901, see id., at 523–529, 102 S.Ct., at 1919–1922. In contrast, Congress did not advert to a "primary objective" limitation when drafting § 504.

Clearly, petitioner's observations do not touch on that aspect of *North Haven*—its analysis of the language of § 601—that is relevant to the present case. But even without the analysis of *North Haven*, petitioner's interpretation of § 504's language is unfounded. For language is broad as that of § 504 cannot be read in isolation from its history and purposes. In these respects, § 504 differs from Title VI in ways that suggest that § 504 cannot sensibly be interpreted to ban employment discrimination only in programs that receive federal aid the "primary objective" of which is to promote employment. The "primary objective" limitation of Title VI gave the antidiscrimination provision of that Title a scope that well fits its underlying purposes—to ensure "that funds of the United States are not used to support racial discrimination" but "are spent in accordance with the Constitution and the moral sense of the Nation." 110 Cong.Rec. 6544 (1964) (remarks of Sen. Humphrey). As the Court of Appeals observed, it was unnecessary to extend Title VI more generally to ban employment discrimination, as Title VII comprehensively regulates such discrimination.

In contrast, the primary goal of the Act is to increase employment of the handicapped, see supra, at 1253 and n. 13. However, Congress chose to ban employment discrimination against the handicapped, not by all employers, but only by the federal government and recipients of federal contracts and grants. As to the latter, Congress apparently determined that it would require contractors and grantees to bear the costs of providing employment for the handicapped as a *quid pro quo* for the receipt of federal funds. Cf. 118 Cong.Rec. 32305 (1972) (remarks of Sen. Javits). But

on employment discrimination should not be limited to programs that receive federal aid the primary purpose of which is to promote employment.

The legislative history, executive interpretation, and purpose of the 1973 enactment all are consistent with this construction. The legislative history contains no mention of a "primary objective" limitation, although the legislators on numerous occasions adverted to § 504's prohibition against discrimination in employment by programs assisted with federal funds. See, e.g., S.Rep. No. 93–318, at 4, 18, 50, 70 (1973), U.S.Code Cong. & Admin.News 1973, 2076; 119 Cong.Rec. 5862 (remarks of Sen. Cranston), 24587–24588 (1973) (remarks of Sen. Williams, chairman of the Committee on Labor and Public Welfare). Moreover, the Department of Health, Education and Welfare, the agency designated by the President to be responsible for coordinating enforcement of § 504, see Exec. Order No. 11914, from the outset has interpreted that section to prohibit employment discrimination by all recipients of federal financial aid, regardless of the primary objective of that aid.[14] This Court generally has deferred to contemporaneous regulations issued by the agency responsible for implementing a congressional enactment. See, e.g., NLRB v. Bell Aerospace Co., 416 U.S. 267, 274–275, 94 S.Ct. 1757, 1761–1762, 40 L.Ed.2d 134 (1974). The regulations particularly merit deference in the present case: the responsible congressional committees participated in their formulation, and both these committees and Congress itself endorsed the regulations in their final form.[15] Finally, application of § 504 to all programs receiving federal financial assistance fits the remedial purpose of the Rehabilitation Act "to promote and expand employment opportunities" for the handicapped. 29 U.S.C. § 701(8).

B

Nor did Congress intend to enact the "primary objective" requirement of § 604 into the Rehabilitation Act when it amended that Act in 1978. The amendments, as we have noted, make "available" the remedies, procedures and rights of Title VI for suits under § 504 against "*any* recipient of federal assistance." § 505(a)(2). These terms do not incorporate § 604's "primary objective" limitation. Rather, the

this decision to limit § 504 to the recipients of federal aid does not require us to limit that section still further, as petitioner urges.

14. See 39 Fed.Reg. 18562, 18582 (1974) (revising pre-existing provisions to implement § 504); 41 Fed.Reg. 29548, 29552, 29563 (1976) (proposed department regulations), *promulgated, 42 Fed.Reg. 22678 (§ 84.2), 22680 (§ 84.11), 22688 ("Employment Practices") (1977); 43 Fed.Reg. 2132, 2138 (1978) (final coordinating regulations).*

The Department of Justice, now responsible for coordinating agency implementation of § 504, see Executive Order No. 12250, 45 Fed.Reg. 72995 (1980), adopted the HEW guidelines, 46 Fed.Reg. 440686 (1981). The Department of Transportation, from which Conrail receives federal aid, also has construed § 504 to prohibit employment discrimination in all programs receiving federal financial assistance. 44 Fed.Reg. 31442, 31468 (1979), codified at 49 C.F.R. Pt. 27. See id. § 27.31.

15. See S.Rep. No. 93–1297, p. 25 (1974). In adopting § 505(a)(2) in the amendments of 1978, Congress incorporated the substance of the Department's regulations into the statute. See infra, at n. 17.

legislative history reveals that this section was intended to codify the regulations of the Department of Health, Education and Welfare governing enforcement of § 504, see S.Rep. No. 95–890, at 19, that prohibited employment discrimination regardless of the purpose of federal financial assistance.[16] And it would be anomalous to conclude that the section, "designed to enhance the ability of handicapped individuals to assure compliance with [§ 504]," id., at 18, silently adopted a drastic limitation on the handicapped individual's right to sue federal grant recipients for employment discrimination.

V

Section 504, by its terms, prohibits discrimination only by a "program or activity receiving Federal financial assistance." This Court on two occasions has considered the meaning of the terms "program or activity" as used in Title IX. Grove City College v. Bell, 465 U.S. 553, 104 S.Ct. 1211, 78 L.Ed.2d 516 (1984); North Haven Board of Education v. Bell, 456 U.S., at 535–540, 102 S.Ct., at 1925–1928. Clearly, this language limits the ban on discrimination to the specific program that receives federal funds. Neither opinion, however, provides particular guidance as to the appropriate treatment of the programs before us. *Grove City College* considered grants of financial aid to students. The Court specifically declined to analogize these grants to nonearmarked direct grants and, indeed, characterized them as *"sui generis."* 465 U.S., at 573, 104 S.Ct., at 1221. North Haven Board of Education did not undertake to define the term "program" at all, finding that, in the procedural posture of that case, that task should be left to the District Court in the first instance.[17]

The procedural posture of the case before us is the same as that of *North Haven Board of Education.* The District Court granted a motion for summary judgment on grounds unrelated to the issue of "program specificity." That judgment was reversed by the Court of Appeals and the case remanded for further proceedings. Thus, neither the District Court nor the Court of Appeals below considered the question whether respondent's decedent had sought and been denied employment in a "program * * * receiving federal financial assistance." [18] Nor did the

---

16. The Committee noted that "the regulations promulgated by the Department of Health, Education and Welfare with respect to procedures, remedies, and rights under § 504 conform with those promulgated under Title VI. Thus, this amendment codifies existing practice as a specific statutory requirement." S.Rep. No. 95–890, at 19. Although these Department regulations incorporated Title VI regulations governing "complaint and enforcement procedures," see 42 Fed.Reg., at 22685, 22694–22701, the regulations implementing § 504 did not incorporate § 80.3 of the Title VI regulations, which limit Title VI's application to employment dis-

crimination in federal programs to increase employment. The § 504 regulations banned employment discrimination in programs receiving any form of federal financial assistance. See n. 15, supra.

17. The Court held that the Court of Appeals in that case had erroneously suggested that HEW regulations issued under Title XI to govern employment discrimination need not be program specific.

18. Although Judge Adams cited the Third Circuit opinion in *Grove City College,* he did so merely to support his rejection of the *Trageser* "standing" analysis. See supra, at 1252.

District Court develop the record or make the factual findings that would be required to define the relevant "program." We therefore do not consider whether federal financial assistance was received by the "program or activity" that discriminated against LeStrange.[19]

VI

We conclude that respondent may recover backpay due to her decedent under § 504 and that this suit for employment discrimination may be maintained even if petitioner receives no federal aid the primary purpose of which is to promote employment. The judgment of the Court of Appeals is therefore affirmed.

It is so ordered.

NOTES AND PROBLEMS FOR DISCUSSION

1. As alluded to in Note 8 after *Prewitt*, while the *Consolidated Rail* Court did rule on the availability of back pay in § 504 actions with respect to claims of intentional discrimination, it did not resolve whether compensatory or punitive damages are recoverable in § 504 cases. Concerning back pay, the Court stated that since § 505(a)(2) of the Rehabilitation Act incorporated the remedies provided under Title VI, its prior ruling in *Guardians Association* (that a Title VI plaintiff alleging intentional discrimination could recover back pay) should apply to § 504 actions. *Guardians* involved an action brought under Title VI of the 1964 Civil Rights Act. This statute, in language almost identical to that later used in § 504, prohibits discrimination on the basis of race, color and national origin in federally funded programs. The Court held that grantees should be permitted to terminate their receipt of federal assistance rather than be compelled to assume the obligations necessary for compliance as well as any liability for noncompliance. The Court recognized that in cases of intentional discrimination the grantee could not deny its awareness of the antidiscrimination obligation or its failure to meet that obligation and thus the victim of such intentional discrimination might be entitled to compensation. Nevertheless, it also concluded that in a case of unintentional discrimination, it was not obvious that a grantee was aware that it was administering its program in violation of the statute or accompanying regulations and, therefore, the grantee should not be subject to financial sanction.

Post-*Consolidated Rail* lower federal courts did not agree, however, on how the ruling in *Guardians* should apply to § 504 claims for compensatory and punitive damages. Compare Greater Los Angeles Council on Deafness, Inc. v. Zolin, 812 F.2d 1103 (9th Cir.1987)("plaintiffs suing under § 504 may pursue the full panoply of remedies, including equitable relief and monetary damages") and Miener v. State of Missouri, 673 F.2d 969 (8th Cir.), cert. denied, 459 U.S. 909, 103 S.Ct. 215, 74 L.Ed.2d 171 (1982)(compensatory damages awardable under § 504 because vindication of an individual's rights may often only be accomplished by a monetary award) with Eastman v. Virginia Polytechnic Institute, 939 F.2d 204 (4th Cir.1991)(specifically rejecting *Miener* ruling on ground that it ignored legislative history; reads *Guardians* as addressing only the question of equitable relief and as holding, therefore, that only back pay,

---

19. Conrail does not contest that it receives Federal financial assistance within the meaning of § 504. Apparently, the government's payments to Conrail exceed the fair market value of the securities issued by Conrail to the government.

and not monetary damages in the form of compensatory or punitive relief, is available for a claim of intentional discrimination under § 504. Court also notes that *Guardians* Court stated that Title VII is a useful guidepost in analyzing Title VI and that Title VII is not amenable to a claim of compensatory or punitive damages. Additionally states that while Title VI goes beyond employment discrimination, the fact that both statutes address claims of racial discrimination against federally funded employers was sufficient overlap to support a basic congruity of remedies and, moreover, that most Title VI cases disallow claims for compensatory relief.); Doe v. Southeastern University, 732 F.Supp. 7, 9–10 (D.D.C.1990)("To hold that compensatory and punitive damages are available [under § 504] would be to engage in judicial activism."); Shuttleworth v. Broward County, 649 F.Supp. 35 (S.D.Fla.1986)(lacking guidance from Rehabilitation Act cases, look to Title VII jurisprudence since instant claim alleges employment discrimination and since compensatories other than back pay denied in Title VII cases, deny them under § 504); Martin v. Cardinal Glennon Memorial Hospital, 599 F.Supp. 284 (E.D.Mo.1984)(neither punitive nor compensatory damages for pain and suffering available under § 504) and Ruth Anne M. v. Alvin Independent School District, 532 F.Supp. 460 (S.D.Tex.1982)(private § 504 action limited to equitable relief). See generally, Richards, Handicap Discrimination in Employment: The Rehabilitation Act of 1973, 39 U. of Ark.L.Rev. 1, 45–52 (1985); Solomon, Constraints on Damage Claims Under Title VI of the Civil Rights Act, 3 Law and Inequality 183 (1985); Comment, Compensating the Handicapped: An Approach to Determining the Appropriateness of Damages for Violations of Section 504, 1981 B.Y.U.L.Rev. 133 (1981); and Safeguarding Equality For The Handicapped: Compensatory Relief Under Section 504 Of The Rehabilitation Act, 1986 Duke L.J. 197 (1986).

The Supreme Court finally offered guidance on this issue in FRANKLIN v. GWINNETT COUNTY PUBLIC SCHOOLS, __ U.S. __, 112 S.Ct. 1028, 117 L.Ed.2d 208 (1992). This case involved a female high school student who brought an action for damages under Title IX against the defendant school district alleging that she had been sexually harassed and abused by a teacher in her school. The Eleventh Circuit had affirmed the decision of the trial court to dismiss her complaint on the ground that Title IX did not authorize an award of damages. The Supreme Court unanimously reversed, stating that where, as here, a cause of action to enforce the underlying federal statutory right has been recognized, a federal court is presumed to have the authority to order any appropriate relief, regardless of the constitutional source of Congress' power to enact that statute. And, the Court continued, this presumption can be rebutted only by showing that Congress "has expressly indicated otherwise." Since the Court had previously recognized the existence of an implied right of action to enforce Title IX in *Cannon* (see Note 7 after *Prewitt, supra,* at 992), the only remaining issue for the Court was whether Congress had demonstrated its intention to limit the courts' remedial authority under Title IX. The Court then looked at the pre and post-*Cannon* actions by Congress and concluded that Congress had not manifested any intention to abandon the traditional presumption in favor of all available remedies. Specifically, it pointed to the passage of two post-*Cannon* statutes containing amendments to Title IX, neither of which altered the existing rights of action or corresponding remedies available under this statute. The Court also rejected the proposition that permitting damage awards would violate separation of powers principles by unduly expanding judicial power into a sphere traditionally reserved to the other two branches. In its judgment, the power to award damages, unlike the decision to recognize a cause of action, did not expand judicial authority. To the contrary, the Court added, ad hoc abdication of its traditional authority to award damages could create separation of powers problems because this would permit the judiciary to render individual statutes a nullity by declining to authorize the recovery of damages. The Court did, however, reemphasize a limitation on the scope of this ruling—the same one set forth in *Guardians Association* and *Consolidated Rail* in connection with backpay awards. It declared that the presumption in favor of all appropriate remedies, including damages, was only available in actions, such as the case at bar, involving allegations of intentional discrimination.

In his dissenting opinion, Justice Scalia (joined by the Chief Justice and Justice Thomas) was prepared to indulge this presumption, but only with respect to rights of action expressly created in the subject statute. But, he maintained, where the right of action is judicially implied, limitations on the range of available remedies also could be judicially implied. In his view, the majority's requirement that limitations on available remedies be expressly provided in a statute that did not even expressly provide a right of action would inevitably result in "the most questionable of private rights * * * [being] * * * the most expansively remediable." Nevertheless, he concluded, since post-*Cannon* amendments to Title IX made it clear that damages were available under this statute, it was "too late in the day" to impose any limitation on the permissible remedies.

In light of the manner in which the Court has interpreted the two statutes, is there any reason to suggest that the ruling in *Franklin* will not apply to Title VI and, therefore, § 504 of the Rehabilitation Act? See Tanberg v. Weld County Sheriff, 787 F.Supp. 970 (D.Colo.1992)(extending *Franklin* analysis to § 504 claim and ruling that since Congress did not expressly prohibit the recovery of compensatory damages in Title VI and because compensatory damages are an appropriate remedy to redress intentional discrimination, the plaintiff can recover compensatory damages for pain and suffering if he can prove that the defendant intentionally discriminated against him when he was discharged for testing HIV-positive). If so, should it also apply to § 504 claims brought by federal employees? Would the federal government enjoy a sovereign immunity defense? See Doe v. Attorney General of United States, 941 F.2d 780 (9th Cir.1991)(§ 504 contains an unequivocal expression of congressional intent to provide private right of action against federal government and thereby waive sovereign immunity; absence of cases addressing whether monetary damages are awardable against federal government under Title VI is understandable since Title VI focuses on discrimination by recipients of federal funding and not by federal government which rarely runs or controls such programs; 1978 amendment extending application of § 504 to federal agencies reflects congressional intent to put federal government on equal footing with other defendants, including susceptibility to private right of action for damages.)

Does the Eleventh Amendment provide States with sovereign immunity against damage claims under § 504? In a 5–4 decision in ATASCADERO STATE HOSPITAL v. SCANLON, 473 U.S. 234, 105 S.Ct. 3142, 87 L.Ed.2d 171 (1985), the Court stated that while Congress can abrogate a State's Eleventh Amendment immunity from suit in federal court by acting pursuant to § 5 of the Fourteenth Amendment, it can do so only "by making its intention unmistakably clear in the language of the statute." Such an explicit intention was required, the Court declared, because the Eleventh Amendment "implicates the fundamental constitutional balance between the Federal Government and the States". Undertaking this inquiry, the Court rejected the plaintiff's claim that the language in § 505 providing remedies for § 504 violations by "*any* recipient of Federal assistance" constituted such a clear expression of Congressional intent to subject States to federal suit. The Court reasoned that States cannot be treated like any other class of recipients and that such a general authorization for federal suit did not constitute "the kind of unequivocal statutory language sufficient to abrogate the Eleventh Amendment. When Congress chooses to subject the States to federal jurisdiction, it must do so specifically." The Court went further and stated that if the Rehabilitation Act were viewed as an enactment pursuant to the Spending Clause of Article I, rather than to § 5 of the Fourteenth Amendment, the fact that various provisions of the Act were addressed to the States did not render participation by a State in programs funded under the Act an express or implied consent to be sued under that statute. Again, the Court reasoned that the Act did not contain any express language clearly manifesting an intent to condition participation in funded programs on a State's consent to waive its constitutional immunity. Thus, the State could not be said to have consented to federal jurisdiction by participating in funded programs. Finally, the majority declared that a California State Constitution provision authorizing suits against the State in such manner as "directed by law" did not constitute a waiver of the State's constitutional immunity from federal court jurisdiction. They ruled that to constitute such a waiver, the state statute or constitutional provision must specify the State's intention to subject itself to suit in federal court. This state constitutional provision was interpreted as merely authorizing the state legislature to waive the State's sovereign immunity and did not constitute an unequivocal waiver specifically applicable to federal court jurisdiction.

In response to this decision, Congress enacted the Civil Rights Remedies Equalization Act, Pub.L. 99–506, 100 Stat. 1845, 42 U.S.C. § 2000d–7 (1986) as part of the Rehabilitation Act Amendments of 1986. This statute, one of those mentioned by the Court in *Franklin*, explicitly removes a State's Eleventh Amendment immunity from suit for violation of § 504, Title IX, Title VI, the ADEA, or any other federal statute prohibiting discrimination by recipients of federal financial assistance. It specifically provides that legal and equitable remedies in suits against a State will be available to the same extent that they are available in actions against non-State defendants. See generally, Brower, Now You See It, Now You Don't: Title IX As An Alternate Remedy For Sex Discrimination In Educational Employment, 31 New York L.Rev. 657 (1986). Similarly, § 502 of the ADA explicitly removes a State's Eleventh Amendment immunity from suit under the ADA and provides that equitable and legal damages shall be available against a State to the same extent that they are available against private and non-State public entities.

While the ruling in *Franklin* strongly suggests that monetary damages will be available in § 504 claims under the Rehabilitation Act, the 1991 Civil Rights Act contains an amendment to the ADA that expressly provides for the recovery of compensatory and punitive damages in claims under that statute. As originally enacted, the ADA did not provide for the recovery of compensatory or punitive damages. But, since § 107(a) of the ADA incorporates the remedial provisions of Title VII, and the 1991 Civil Rights Act provides for such relief in Title VII cases alleging intentional discrimination, such awards can now be recovered in claims of intentional discrimination under the ADA. Moreover, § 102(a)(2) of the 1991 Civil Rights Act expressly amends the ADA to provide for the recovery of compensatory and punitive damages in connection with claims of intentional discrimination or failure to make a reasonable accommodation under the same rules governing their availability in Title VII cases, except that such relief is unavailable under the ADA where the defendant establishes that it made a good faith effort, after consulting with the plaintiff, to make a reasonable accommodation. This provision also amends the Rehabilitation Act to allow for the recovery of compensatory and punitive damages, but only with respect to claims under § 501, i.e., claims against the federal government. Such recovery is precluded, however, where the government establishes that it made a good faith effort, after consulting with the plaintiff, to make a reasonable accommodation.

2. Louise Ross, an associate professor of physics, was dismissed shortly after she was involved in an automobile accident that left her blind and paralyzed from the waist down. The University contended that her disability made it impossible for Professor Ross to engage in the type of research activity expected of a teacher in her chosen field. In addition, the University indicated that while it received a substantial amount of federal funding, all of those monies were used to finance scholarships for minority students in the foreign language, mathematics and history departments. Is there any basis upon which the University could move to dismiss Ross' § 504 claim for failure to state a cause of action? What is the significance of the language in § 504 prohibiting discrimination in "any program or activity receiving Federal financial assistance"? The Supreme Court did not address the issue of program-specificity in *Consolidated Rail*, since that question had not been considered by the courts below. Instead, it remanded the case and directed the trial court to define the relevant "program". During that same term, however, the Court did examine this issue in a related statutory context.

Title IX of the Education Amendments of 1972, 20 U.S.C. §§ 1001–1686 (1976), in language nearly identical to that found in § 504, prohibits sex discrimination "under any education program or activity receiving Federal financial assistance * * *." In GROVE CITY COLLEGE v. BELL, 465 U.S. 555, 104 S.Ct. 1211, 79 L.Ed.2d 516 (1984), the Supreme Court held that a private college which enrolled students who received federal loans and grants to pay for their educational expenses was "receiving Federal financial assistance" within the meaning of the statute. It also ruled, however, that the receipt of loans and grants by some of the college's students did not trigger institution-wide coverage under Title IX. Rather, the Court reasoned, the program-specific language of Title IX required it to determine which of the institution's programs or activities were intended to be benefitted by this indirect grant of federal financial assistance. The case was complicated by the fact that the funds went from the students into the College's general operating budget. The Court concluded, nevertheless, that the intent behind the student loan program was to enhance the ability of educational institutions to provide financial aid. Accordingly, it held that the College's financial aid office was the only "program or activity" receiving federal financial assistance and, therefore, that only this program could be regulated under Title IX.

Substantial Congressional dissatisfaction with the *Grove City College* Court's narrow interpretation of Title IX led directly to the passage of the Civil Rights Restoration Act of 1987, Pub.L. 100–259, 20 U.S.C. §§ 1687, 1688. (Portions of the Act are reprinted in the Appendix, *infra*, at 1303.) This enactment was designed to reverse the Court's interpretation of the "program or activity" language in Title IX. It explicitly amended the "program or activity" language in Titles VI and IX, § 504 of the Rehabilitation Act and § 309 of the ADEA. The amendment provides that "program or activity" as defined in all of these statutes means all the operations of any governmental entity or educational institution where any part of that entity or institution receives federal financial assistance. It does, however, specifically exempt, for Title IX purposes only, an entity controlled by a religious organization if the application of Title IX to that entity's operation would be inconsistent with the religious tenets of the religious organization.

3. Is a charitable organization that receives an exemption from federal income taxation covered by § 504? Is it "receiving federal financial assistance"? See Martin v. Delaware Law School, 625 F.Supp. 1288, 1302 (D.Del. 1985), affirmed without opinion, 884 F.2d 1384 (3d Cir.1989), cert. denied, 493 U.S. 966, 110 S.Ct. 411, 107 L.Ed.2d 376 (1989). What about a private social service agency that receives funding from a state agency? What if the state agency is reimbursed by the federal government? See Graves v. Methodist Youth Services, Inc., 624 F.Supp. 429 (N.D.Ill.1985). Must the defendant have received federal funding at the time of the challenged employment decision in order for the plaintiff to state a claim under § 504? See Niehaus v. Kansas Bar Ass'n, 793 F.2d 1159 (10th Cir.1986).

DAVIS v. UNITED AIR LINES, INC.

United States Court of Appeals, Second Circuit, 1981.
662 F.2d 120, cert. denied, 456 U.S. 965, 102 S.Ct. 2045, 72 L.Ed.2d 490 (1982).

OAKES, CIRCUIT JUDGE.

This case involves the issue whether section 503 of the Vocational Rehabilitation Act of 1973, as amended, gives an employee a private right of action against an employer contracting with the federal government for alleged discrimination in employment on the basis of physical disability. The question has been answered contrarily by a number of district courts, with differing views among the district judges in the Second Circuit, but the only courts of appeal passing on the question, the Fifth, Sixth, and Seventh, Circuits, have held that there is no such private judicial remedy. We agree with the extended analysis of this question by Judge Alvin Rubin for the panel majority in the Fifth Circuit in Rogers v. Frito–Lay, Inc., 611 F.2d 1074 (5th Cir.1980), and our examination of the cases decided in the Supreme Court and in our own court since *Rogers* was handed down reenforces the conclusion in *Rogers* that no private right of action may be inferred from section 503. Accordingly, we reverse the judgment of the United States District Court for the Eastern District of New York, Jack B. Weinstein, Chief Judge, which found the reasoning of courts upholding a private right of action "persuasive" in light of the factors identified by the Supreme Court in Cort v. Ash, 422 U.S. 66, 95 S.Ct. 2080, 45 L.Ed.2d 26 (1975).
* * *

* * * Thomas Davis had worked for United Air Lines, Inc. ("United") since 1966 as a ramp serviceman, servicing aircraft and loading and unloading cargo. In 1969 he was diagnosed as having epilepsy and from time to time until mid-September 1974, he experienced seizures

that did not interfere with his satisfactory performance of duties as a ramp serviceman. After he experienced a seizure in mid-September 1974, he was placed on restricted duties, and he was ultimately confined to working in the bag room. In June 1977, he was placed on "extended illness status" because of his epilepsy; he was officially discharged on February 15, 1980.

In December 1978 Davis filed a complaint with the Department of Labor as provided by section 503(b), charging that United had discriminated against him on the basis of his physical handicap. The Department of Labor has not acted on his complaint. In October 1979, he filed a private suit against United in the Eastern District of New York claiming that United had violated his rights under section 503. Judge Weinstein denied United's motion for judgment on the pleadings, and certified his order for appeal in accordance with 28 U.S.C. § 1292(b). It is assumed for purposes of this appeal that Davis is physically "handicapped" within the meaning of the Act, that United holds government contract subject to the requirements of section 503, and that Davis was discharged because of his handicap.

The law may be briefly stated as follows. Under section 503(a), any contract in excess of $2,500 entered into by the federal government must "contain a provision requiring that * * * [the contractor] shall take affirmative action to employ and advance in employment qualified handicapped individuals. * * * " Section 503(b) provides that if any handicapped individual "believes any contractor has failed or refuse[d] to comply with the provisions of his [federal] contract," that "such individual may file a complaint with the Department of Labor" which shall "promptly investigate" and "take such action * * * as the facts and circumstances warrant * * *."

Because section 503 creates no explicit private judicial remedy against federal contractors charged with employment discrimination against the handicapped, the federal courts have had to determine whether a private right of action may be inferred. The starting points for our analysis must be the four factors set out in Cort v. Ash * * *.

Under *Cort* the initial consideration is whether the plaintiff is a member of a class for "whose *especial* benefit the statute was enacted." Although section 503 was generally intended to benefit handicapped persons, that alone does not establish that Congress intended to "create a federal right in favor of the plaintiff."

The Supreme Court has suggested that a private right of action may be more readily implied when the language of a statute is "right-creating" rather than merely "duty-creating." See Cannon v. University of Chicago. Statutory language has been found right-creating when it focuses explicitly on the benefited class. See, e.g., id. at 682 n. 3, 99 S.Ct. at 2487 ("no person * * * shall, on the basis of sex, be excluded * * *," 20 U.S.C. § 1681).

Section 504 of the Vocational Rehabilitation Act of 1973, which is not at issue in this case, invokes just such right-creating language: "No otherwise qualified handicapped individual * * * shall, solely by reason of his handicap, be excluded from the participation in, be denied the benefits of, or be subjected to discrimination under any program or activity receiving Federal financial assistance." Accordingly, a number of courts have held that section 504 creates a private cause of action for handicapped persons.

By contrast, section 503 contains only duty-creating language, directing federal departments and agencies to provide in all federal contracts that contractors are obligated to take affirmative steps to employ and advance handicapped persons. Nowhere does section 503 confer an express right upon the handicapped, nor impose a direct duty on federal contractors. As Judge Rubin noted in *Rogers*, the use of duty-creating rather than right-creating phrases, though "not conclusive," makes "inference of a private cause of action more difficult." Indeed, the Supreme Court has stated that language such as that contained in section 503 militates against inferring a private right of action:

> There would be far less reason to infer a private remedy in favor of individual persons if Congress, instead of drafting Title IX with an unmistakable focus on the benefited class, had written it simply as a ban on discriminatory conduct by recipients of federal funds or as a prohibition against the disbursement of public funds to educational institutions engaged in discriminatory practices.

Cannon v. University of Chicago.

The second inquiry under *Cort* is whether there is any legislative history evidencing congressional intent to create or deny a private remedy. We read *Cort* * * * as requiring a very close, even microscopic, examination of the legislative history of the particular statute involved. This reading of the legislative history must be done with an enlightened judicial eye, giving full attention to the underlying congressional purpose, the very heart of statutory analysis, but also with a healthy skepticism of "casual statements from floor debates," as Justice Jackson warned us so pointedly in Schwegmann Bros. v. Calvert Distillers Co., 341 U.S. 384, 396, 71 S.Ct. 745, 751, 95 L.Ed. 1035 (1951).

Taking such a view of section 503, we find nothing in the history of the original Rehabilitation Act of 1973 that casts any light on whether Congress intended to create a private right of action. Given Congress's initial silence, we may seek some guidance from the 1974 and 1978 amendments to the Act. In giving weight to these amendments, we would choose a middle road between the panel majority in Rogers v. Frito–Lay, Inc. ("[W]hat happened after a statute was enacted may be history and it may come from members of the Congress, but it is not part of the legislative history of the original enactment"), and Judge Goldberg's dissent in *Rogers* ("it is a well-established principle that the post-enactment treatment of a statute by Congress is cogent evidence of the intent of Congress at the time of its passage"). We believe our view is called for by Cannon v. University of Chicago, in which the Court, while partially relying on subsequent legislative history, noted that "we cannot accord these remarks the weight of contemporary legislative history * * *."

The subsequent legislative history of the Rehabilitation Act is internally conflicting. The 1974 amendments deal expressly with section 504, equating it with Title VI (race discrimination) and Title IX (sex discrimination). Senate Report No. 93–1297, which urged overriding the President's veto of the 1974 amendments, expressly noted that section 504 permits a private right of action.

In contrast, the Senate Conference Committee never explicitly stated that section 503 confers a private right of action. Although the report did state that "[i]t is intended that sections 503 and 504 be administered in such a manner that a consistent uniform and effective Federal approach to discrimination against handicapped persons would result," this appears to refer simply to the desirability of cooperation between the Department of Health, Education, and Welfare, which was assigned to enforce section 504, and the Department of Labor, which was assigned to enforce section 503. This separate assignment may even indicate that section 503, unlike 504, was not intended to be privately enforced; the Department of Labor, unlike the Department of Health, Education, and Welfare, lacked experience in dealing with private lawsuits.

The only indication that a "uniform" approach to combatting employment discrimination against the handicapped might entail a private right of action under section 503 as well as section 504 is the remarks of a senator who was not a member of the conference committee, although he was one of the principal sponsors of the original Act and its subsequent amendments. Senator Robert Stafford of Vermont stated on the floor in 1974 that enforcement under both sections 503 and 504 should be similar to enforcement under Title VI and Title IX. These remarks were not, however, included in the conference committee report. Furthermore, although an exchange of correspondence between the Senate Committee on Labor and Public Welfare and the Secretary of Labor regarding the enforcement of section 503 is appended to the report, nowhere in that correspondence is there any hint that the statute was to be enforced through private lawsuits. * * *

With the exception of Senator Stafford's statement on the floor, then, the legislative intent demonstrated by the history of the 1974 amendments simply does not support implication of a private right of action under section 503. In 1978, however, when Congress again amended the Act by adding section 505 to provide for attorney's fees "[i]n any action or proceeding to enforce or charge a violation of [the Act]," the accompanying Senate Report clearly assumed that a private judicial remedy was available under section 503: "[T]he availability of attorney's fees should assist in vindicating private rights of action in the case of section 502 and 503 cases, as well as those arising under section 501 and 504." H.R. Rep.No. 95–1149 (Education and Labor Committee), spoke in exactly the same terms.[8]

Neither the Senate nor the House Reports, however, contained any reference to the existing case law from the district courts. Although two district court cases had found that there was a private right of action under section 503, three cases had held that no implied right of action existed.

This failure to note the conflicting case law of the time indicates that the reference to private rights of action being available in section 502 and 503 cases as well as those arising under sections 501 and 504 was inadvertent. This seems especially true in light of the Senate Report's extensive reference to the testimony of Deborah Kaplan of the Disability Rights Center before the Subcommittee on the Handicapped. Her testimony quoted in the Senate Report related only to sections 501 and 504:

> Unfortunately, the disabled citizens who are protected by section 501 as well as section 504 stand alone among minority groups in this country, since they remain largely unaffected by the recently enacted Civil Rights Attorney's Fees Awards Act of 1976, Public Law 94–559, and because the legislation which protects their civil rights contains no attorney's fees provision. Thus many disabled people, who desperately need to vindicate their rights through the courts, have been utterly frustrated and disillusioned because they could neither afford an attorney, locate one able to represent them without a fee, nor seek an attorney's fee award from the courts.

We note also the Seventh Circuit's point in Simpson v. Reynolds Metals Co., 629 F.2d 1226, 1242 (7th Cir.1980), that allowing attorney's fees in actions or proceedings brought under section 503 may have been intended to provide for attorney's fees either in a section 503(b) proceeding before the Department of Labor or in a judicial proceeding brought pursuant to the Department of Labor's regulations permitting the director of the Office of Federal Contract Compliance Programs (OFCCP) to seek appropriate judicial action to enforce the affirmative action contractual provisions required under the Act. In short, even giving appropriate weight to the subsequent legislative history reflected in the 1978 amendment, we find nothing that compels us to the conclusion that a private right of action exists under section 503. The assumption in the 1978 congressional reports simply "cannot be relied upon as a faithful indicator of prior congressional intent." Simpson v. Reynolds Metals Co.

Given the somewhat ambiguous legislative history, however, we must proceed to the third question under Cort v. Ash: whether it is

---

8. The House Report stated: "The new section permits courts, at their discretion, to award to the prevailing party, other than the United States, in any action to enforce sections 501, 503 or 504 of the act, a reasonable allowance to cover the costs of attorneys' fees."

consistent with the underlying purposes of the legislative scheme to infer a private right of action for the handicapped person discriminated against by his employor. Here we note, as did the *Rogers* majority, that Congress provided a rather complete administrative scheme to remedy section 503 violations and that the implementing regulations, emphasize resolving complaints to the Department of Labor "by informal means, including conciliation, and persuasion, whenever possible." The regulations provide as remedies withholding of progess payments, termination of existing contracts, or debarment from receiving future contracts, rather than remedies running to the discriminated-against employee. In this regard, the administrative procedures established by the Act and implementing regulations are remarkably consistent with those under the Comprehensive Employment and Training Act (CETA) discussed in CETA Workers' Organizing Committee v. New York, 617 F.2d 926 (2d Cir.1980). * * * [A]s in *CETA Workers*, we believe that the underlying congressional purpose was to provide an administrative procedure for the determination of complaints under which the administering agency was to use its powers to enforce the section in question. And though the Rehabilitation Act failed directly to provide for judicial review of such an administrative procedure, the Department of Labor evidently thought that such review might be possible * * *. The implementing regulations do incorporate the elaborate and sophisticated hearing practice and procedure used to enforce equal opportunity under Executive Order No. 11,246; these elaborate hearing provisions culminate, or may culminate, in a final administrative order, which is in our view reviewable like other administrative orders under the Administrative Procedure Act and particularly 5 U.S.C. §§ 701–706.

To be sure, the regulations' failure to specify time limits has presented a problem that is particularly evident in the case at bar. The Department of Labor has, contrary to the will of Congress, been unable to comply speedily with the provisions of the Rehabilitation Act. This has resulted in the Department's taking the position in the past, although it takes no position here, that a private cause of action should be permitted in order to remedy section 503 violations more effectively and indeed an acknowledgment that "[t]he net effect of [OFCCP] discretion is that there is no assurance that compliance decisions are not tempered by political, procurement, personal or other potentially competing or conflicting requirements," OFCCP Task Force, Preliminary Report on the Revitalization of the Federal Contract Compliance Program (1977). The agency backlog and its position in favor of recognition of a private remedy are set forth in an affidavit by the director of the OFCCP * * *. While lack of executive resources to enforce an act of Congress is regrettable, it is hardly the judiciary's role to redress that lack by inferring a judicial remedy.

Moreover, although a department's position on whether an implied private cause of action exists is entitled to judicial consideration, an agency's expertise, "[e]ven if the agency spoke with a consistent voice, * * * is of limited value when the narrow legal issue is one peculiarly reserved for judicial resolution, namely whether a cause of action should be implied by judicial interpretation in favor of a particular class of litigants." Piper v. Chris–Craft Industries, 430 U.S. at 41 n. 27, 97 S.Ct. at 949. * * *

In any case, an after-the-fact acknowledgment of inadequacy because of limited departmental resources is not the equivalent of a long-held, firmly established, well-reasoned position that the agency has made known to Congress and to the courts over the years, such as in *Cannon* * * *.

We need not deal with the fourth Cort v. Ash factor; it is plain enough that discrimination against the disabled has not been a matter traditionally relegated to state law. But we conclude, as have the other three courts of appeals that have passed upon the question, that no implied private right of action exists under section 503, recognizing that the glass through which we see is by no means crystal clear but is so cloudy as to be barely translucent.

Judgment reversed.

IRVING R. KAUFMAN, CIRCUIT JUDGE (dissenting).

* * *

The threshold question under *Cort* is whether the plaintiff was one of the class for whose "especial benefit" § 503 was enacted. This inquiry focuses on whether Congress intended to benefit a clearly defined class rather than to protect the general public. Looking to the language of the statute may provide evidence of this intent. Here, the language of § 503(a) and (b) specifically identifies the class, "handicapped individuals," and provides equal employment opportunities for all who fall within it. Indeed, relying on this approach to the first *Cort* factor, virtually all of the district courts analyzing § 503, including those that ultimately found no private right of action, have concluded that the statute was enacted for the "especial benefit" of the handicapped.

The majority, however, contends that when § 503 is examined for "right- or duty-creating language," Cannon v. University of Chicago, no indication of an intention to establish a federal right in favor of the plaintiff can be found. While the absence of such a "talismanic incantation," is less relevant than the substance of the obligations created, the affirmative action language of § 503 may appear to create, when scrutinized closely, a duty for federal agencies, it is argued, not for employers.

Although the duty-creating phrases are not conclusive in either direction, an analysis of the second and more important *Cort* factor, contrary to the majority's position, offers exceedingly strong evidence for giving a right of action to the handicapped individual. In considering whether the legislative history of § 503 sheds light on the private right of action question, three statutes carry weight and are directly relevant to our determination: the 1973 Rehabilitation Act, the Rehabilitation Act Amendments of 1974, and the attorney's fees provisions of the Rehabilitation, Comprehensive Services, and Developmental Disabilities Amendments of 1978.

I do not quarrel with the assertion that the legislative history of the 1973 Act provides little assistance. Debate primarily focused on the establishment of federally-funded programs for the handicapped, not on the relatively non-controversial antidiscrimination provisions of §§ 503 and 504. Nor is an examination of the history surrounding the 1974 Amendments to the Act particularly enlightening, because discussion centered on redefining "handicapped individual," not on explicating the full meaning of §§ 503 and 504. The conference report, however, lends guidance. It states that § 504 permits a "judicial remedy through private action," and notes, as the majority recognizes, that both sections will be administered to effect a uniform approach to discrimination against handicapped persons. Such language, I believe, should fairly be read to suggest that, since Congress recognized a private right of action under § 504, such a remedy would not be inconsistent with Congress's purpose in § 503. In addition, during the Senate debate, Senator Robert Stafford, one of the principal sponsors of the original Act and its later amendments, stated that enforcement of both sections would be similar to that of § 601 of the Civil Rights Act and § 901 of the Education Amendments of 1972. Although a private right of action was found to exist for the Education Amendments in *Cannon,* supra, the majority denigrates the value of Senator Stafford's remarks.

More conclusive evidence of a congressional intent to authorize a private action is found in the 1978 attorney's fees amendments. This provision explicitly presumes private judicial actions because attorney's fees are made available to parties "other than the United States" and because the language looks to actions before "courts," not administrative agencies. The Senate Report and Senate debates also indicate that private actions were envisioned. The majority concedes that the accompanying Senate Report explicitly stated that the availability of attorney's fees was intended to aid handicapped individuals in "vindicating private rights of action in the case of section * * * 503 cases." The majority further acknowledges that H.R.Rep.No.1149, took precisely the same position.

My brothers have decided that this legislative material is "unpersuasive" and virtually dismiss it. They adopt the rationale that failure to discuss the then-existing case law indicates that references to the availability of a § 503 private right of action were "inadvertent." I realize that "even Homer nods," but such a bald refusal to acknowledge a clear, express statement of congressional intent is inexcusable. Granted, the evidence surrounding the passage of the 1978 attorney's fees amendments carries less weight than contemporary legislative history, but this evidence is strongly relevant in determining what members of Congress assumed they had done several years previously.

It is clear from the legislative history that Congress premised the attorney's fees provision on the existence of an implied remedy. Furthermore, interpreting an attorney's fees amendment to reveal Congress's intent is surely not a novel method of construction, as the majority's position would appear to suggest. In *Cannon*, interpretation of the legislative background of the attorney's fees amendment to § 901 of Title IX served as the basis for the Court's recognition of a private right of action. Indeed, Congress is generally considered to be a creditable interpreter of its actions, and judicial deference to these interpretations is appropriate.

Here, the notion that the view of a subsequent Congress forms a weak foundation for inferring the intent of an earlier one, is not a persuasive argument. Many members of the relevant committees in 1978 were also members of those committees in 1973. I doubt that these distinguished members of Congress who labored over trail-blazing legislation would have forgotten what they had intended a mere five years before the 1978 amendments. Contrary to the majority's poorly-supported and tenuous conclusion that the legislative history is ambiguous, the legislative history clearly indicates that Congress, in passing the attorney's fees amendments of 1978, assumed that a private right of action was created with the passage of § 503 in 1973. This assumption does not reflect a subsequent desire to amend the original enactment; rather, it illuminates the initial intent of the draftsmen.

The third factor of the *Cort* analysis considers whether a private right of action would support Congress's purpose in enacting the statutory scheme. Implication of a private right of action is not inconsistent with the underlying purpose of § 503—effective administrative enforcement. The Department of Labor and its office of Federal Contract Compliance Programs, it is interesting to note, have stated that the existence of an implied remedy would enhance informal conciliation and administrative enforcement in general. Although the majority lightly dismisses these agency opinions, courts generally believe they are deserving of substantial weight.

My brothers, in concluding that the mandates of the third *Cort* factor are not fulfilled, rely on an analysis contained in CETA Workers' Org. Comm. v. City of New York. Such reliance is misplaced because *CETA* is readily distinguishable. The statutory presumption in favor of administrative enforcement is much more potent under the Comprehensive Employment and Training Act ("CETA") than it is under the Rehabilitation Act. Section 106 provides, in great detail, a sophisticated scheme for enforcement of CETA. In particular, the Secretary of Labor is required to reach a final determination on a complaint within 120 days. This complex enforcement mechanism suggests the "primacy" and "exclusivity" of the administrative grievance procedures.

No such detailed machinery exists under the Rehabilitation Act, and even the accompanying Regulations contain no deadlines for the processing of complaints. Surely, it does not require straining the legislative interpretation to envision a private right of action complementing the statutory enforcement mechanism for § 503. Indeed, the Department of Labor endorses this view. I submit that analysis of the third *Cort* factor differs for the two statutes. More importantly, it indicates that Congress would be more inclined to create a private right of action for a statute where provisions for administrative enforcement are not detailed and precise. But the majority, admitting that the CETA scheme is more fully developed, still finds the distinctions between the two of little significance even in light of the Department of Labor's statement that an implied right of action for § 503 violations should be permitted. The majority, it appears, attaches greater weight to tangential *exempla* than to direct, explicit evidence.

* * *

* * * I believe the only reasonable conclusion to be reached from applying the *Cort* analysis is that Congress intended handicapped individuals to have a private remedy under § 503. * * *

NOTES AND PROBLEMS FOR DISCUSSION

1. Does the opinion in the principal case evidence the operation of a presumption against the recognition of an implied private right of action? In his dissenting opinion in CANNON v. UNIVERSITY OF CHICAGO, 441 U.S. 677, 749, 99 S.Ct. 1946, 1985, 60 L.Ed.2d 560, 608 (1979), Justice Powell recommended that the Court "not condone the implication of any private action from a federal statute absent the most compelling evidence that Congress in fact intended such an action to exist." Should such a presumption operate in the context of a civil rights statute whose administrative remedy not only does not redress, but may compound, the injury suffered by the individual discriminatee? For a proposal urging the adoption of a presumption in favor of recognizing private rights of action under these circumstances, see Note, Implied Rights of Action Under the Rehabilitation Act of 1973, 68 Geo.L.J. 1229, 1254–1260 (1980). See also, Note, Implied Rights of Action to Enforce Civil Rights: The Case For a Sympathetic View, 87 Yale L.J. 1378 (1978).

2. Could a plaintiff avoid the ruling in *Davis* by asserting a claim as a third party beneficiary of the affirmative action provision in the employer's contract with the government? See D'Amato v. Wisconsin Gas Co., 760 F.2d 1474 (7th Cir.1985)(rejecting third party beneficiary claim on the grounds that the parties to the contract did not intend to make the handicapped direct beneficiaries of their contracts and that Congress intended that the administrative scheme be the sole avenue of redress for the handicapped); Hodges v. Atchison, T. & S.F. Ry. Co., 728 F.2d 414 (10th Cir.1984), cert. denied, 469 U.S. 822, 105 S.Ct. 97, 83 L.Ed.2d 43 (1985)(rejecting third party beneficiary claim as "but another aspect of the implied right of action argument").

3. Assume a state university entered into a contract to provide scientific research for the federal government and discriminated against a disabled applicant for a job in that federally financed program. Can the applicant bring a private action against the university under 42 U.S.C. § 1983 alleging that the university deprived him of rights secured by § 503 of the Rehabilitation Act? Is the holding in *Davis* relevant to this issue? See Meyerson v. State of

Arizona, 709 F.2d 1235 (9th Cir.1983), vacated and remanded on other grounds in light of Consolidated Rail v. Darrone, 465 U.S. 1095, 104 S.Ct. 1584, 80 L.Ed.2d 118 (1984).

4.   While the Rehabilitation Act and the ADA are the primary federal statutory sources of protection for disabled individuals, state and local government employees can look to the Fourteenth Amendment for redress. Absolute rules precluding all employment on the basis of specified disabilities, it has been held, use irrebutable presumptions in violation of the Due Process Clause. See e.g., Gurmankin v. Costanzo, 556 F.2d 184 (3d Cir.1977) (local school board's refusal to allow blind applicants to take qualifying exam violates Due Process Clause of Fourteenth Amendment). The irrebutable presumption doctrine, however, is no longer favored by the Supreme Court. Accordingly, constitutional challenges to disability discrimination by state and local government workers are likely to focus on the Equal Protection Clause. Such was the case, for example, in NEW YORK CITY TRANSIT AUTHORITY v. BEAZER, 440 U.S. 568, 99 S.Ct. 1355, 59 L.Ed.2d 587 (1979). The trial court had ruled that the defendant's blanket exclusion of methadone users from all positions violated the Due Process Clause because it created an irrebutable presumption of unemployability as to all methadone users. The Supreme Court noted that the respondent employees no longer asserted that argument and, moreover, that it was without merit. The Court then turned to the respondent's equal protection claim and found that it survived scrutiny under the rationality standard. See also Judd v. Packard, 669 F.Supp. 741 (D.Md.1987) (*assuming* inmate who tests positive for the HTLV–III antibody is "handicapped", placing of him in isolation for diagnostic and treatment purposes by state prison authorities is supported by legitimate governmental purpose to avoid health danger to other inmates and it was rational for the authorities to believe that such isolation would promote that purpose).

Can a federal employee state a constitutional cause of action for disability discrimination? Does § 505 of the Rehabilitation Act suggest that the Court's ruling in Brown v. G.S.A. should be extended to make the Rehabilitation Act the exclusive remedy for such federal employee claims? See McGuinness v. U.S. Postal Service, 744 F.2d 1318 (7th Cir.1984).

5.   While the enactment of the ADA greatly expanded the availability of federal statutory protection against disability-based job discrimination, state law continues to play an important role in this area. Over forty states have enacted legislation that prohibits discrimination against disabled persons.

6.   In addition to its obligations under § 503, any federal contractor or subcontractor involved with a federal contract in the amount of $10,000 or more for the procurement of personal property and non-personal services (including construction), is required by the Vietnam Veterans' Readjustment Assistance Act (VRA), 38 U.S.C. § 2011 et seq., to take affirmative action to employ and advance in employment disabled veterans of the Vietnam era. If a covered veteran believes that a contractor has not complied with this requirement, the statute authorizes him to file an administrative complaint with the Secretary of Labor. In the absence, however, of any express private right of action, one court has refused to find an implied private cause of action for violation of the VRA, especially since the statute does provide an administrative enforcement mechanism. Harris v. Adams, 873 F.2d 929 (6th Cir.1989). The Act also requires all federal executive departments and agencies to include in the affirmative action hiring and advancement plans required by § 501 of

the Rehabilitation Act, a separate specification of their plans to employ and advance disabled Vietnam era veterans. 38 U.S.C. § 2014.

7. Can an aggrieved employee file suit to compel the Secretary of Labor to institute § 503(b) enforcement proceedings against a government contractor? Compare Andrews v. Consolidated Rail Corp., 831 F.2d 678 (7th Cir.1987)(Department of Labor decision not to prosecute § 503 claim is subject to agency's total discretion and is not subject to judicial review under Administrative Procedure Act) with Moon v. Donovan, 29 FEP Cases 1780 (N.D.Ga.1982) (plaintiff can bring such a cause of action under Administrative Procedure Act). See also Salvador v. Bennett, 800 F.2d 97 (7th Cir.1986)(handicapped individual participating in program that received funding from U.S. Department of Education does not have private right of action under § 504 against Secretary of Education for allegedly failing to investigate his handicap discrimination complaint). But see Giacobbi v. Biermann, 57 FEP Cases 1201 (D.D.C. 1992)(while agency's decision not to take enforcement action is left to agency discretion and is not subject to judicial review, language in § 503 requiring Department of Labor to "promptly investigate" complaints requires agency to undertake and complete investigation in a reasonable time and these issues are subject to judicial review; upon finding that agency did not complete investigation within reasonable time, court concludes that it cannot provide any relief to plaintiff since investigation ultimately was completed and plaintiff did not demonstrate any injury resulting from delay; since court cannot require agency to take enforcement action, only permissible remedy would be injunction ordering agency to expedite investigation, but this is available only where plaintiff brings suit while investigation is pending).

PART IV

AFFIRMATIVE ACTION

Read §§ 703(j) and 706(g) of Title VII.

Section 706(g) of Title VII provides that if a defendant is found to have intentionally engaged in or be intentionally engaging in an unlawful employment practice, the court may "order such affirmative action as may be appropriate, which may include, but is not limited to, reinstatement or hiring of employees * * * or any other equitable relief as the court deems appropriate." This remedial provision has generated several of the most complex and controversial issues in the entire field of employment discrimination law. The questions raised by the use of affirmative action fall into two broad categories. First, to what extent, if any, will a court's exercise of this statutory remedial authority conflict with the antidiscrimination provisions of § 703, the anti-preferential treatment mandate of § 703(j), the protection afforded seniority systems by § 703(h), or the equal protection guarantees of the Fifth or Fourteenth Amendments? Second, will any of these statutory or constitutional provisions be violated if an employer or union undertakes an affirmative action program on a voluntary basis?

LOCAL 28 OF SHEET METAL WORKERS
INTERN. ASS'N v. EEOC

Supreme Court of the United States, 1986.
478 U.S. 421, 106 S.Ct. 3019, 92 L.Ed.2d 344.

JUSTICE BRENNAN announced the judgment of the Court and delivered the opinion of the Court with respect to Parts I, II, III, and VI, and an opinion with respect to Parts IV, V, and VII in which JUSTICE MARSHALL, JUSTICE BLACKMUN, and JUSTICE STEVENS join.

In 1975, petitioners were found guilty of engaging in a pattern and practice of discrimination against black and Hispanic individuals (nonwhites) in violation of Title VII of the Civil Rights Act of 1964, and ordered to end their discriminatory practices, and to admit a certain percentage of nonwhites to union membership by July 1982. In 1982 and again in 1983, petitioners were found guilty of civil contempt for disobeying the District Court's earlier orders. They now challenge the District Court's contempt finding, and also the remedies the court ordered both for the Title VII violation and for contempt. Principally, the issue presented is whether the remedial provision of Title VII, see 42 U.S.C. 2000e–5(g), empowers a district court to order race-conscious relief that may benefit individuals who are not identified victims of unlawful discrimination.

I

Petitioner Local 28 of the Sheet Metal Workers' International Association (Local 28) represents sheet metal workers employed by contractors in the New York City metropolitan area. Petitioner Local 28 Joint Apprenticeship Committee (JAC) is a management-labor committee which operates a 4–year apprenticeship training program designed to teach sheet metal skills. Apprentices enrolled in the program receive training both from classes and from on the job work experience. Upon completing the program, apprentices become journeyman members of Local 28. Successful completion of the program is the principal means of attaining union membership.[1]

In 1964, the New York State Commission for Human Rights determined that petitioners had excluded blacks from the union and the apprenticeship program in violation of state law. The State Commission found, among other things, that Local 28 had never had any black members or apprentices, and that "admission to apprenticeship is conducted largely on a nepot[is]tic basis involving sponsorship by incumbent union members," creating an impenetrable barrier for nonwhite applicants.[2] Petitioners were ordered to "cease and desist" their racially discriminatory practices. The New York State Supreme Court affirmed the State Commission's findings, and directed petitioners to implement objective standards for selecting apprentices. State Comm'n for Human Rights v. Farrell, 43 Misc.2d 958, 252 N.Y.S.2d 649 (1964).

When the court's orders proved ineffective, the State commission commenced other state-court proceedings in an effort to end petitioners' discriminatory practices. Petitioners had originally agreed to indenture two successive classes of apprentices using nondiscriminatory selection procedures, but stopped processing applications for the second apprentice class, thus requiring that the State Commission seek a court order requiring petitioners to indenture the apprentices. The court subsequently denied the union's request to reduce the size of the second apprentice class, and chastized the union for refusing "except for token gestures, to further the integration process." Petitioners proceeded to disregard the results of the selection test for a third apprentice class on the ground that nonwhites had received "unfair tutoring" and had

---

1. In addition to completing the apprenticeship program, an individual can gain membership in Local 28 by (1) transferring directly from a "sister" union; (2) passing a battery of journeyman level tests administered by the union; and (3) gaining admission at the time a nonunion sheet metal shop is organized by Local 28. In addition, during periods of full employment, Local 28 issues temporary work permits which allow nonmembers to work within its jurisdiction.

2. The Sheet Metal Workers' International Union was formed in 1888, under a Constitution which provided for the establishment of "white local unions" and relegated blacks to membership in subordinate locals. Local 28 was established in 1913 as a "white local union." Although racial restrictions were formally deleted from the International Constitution in 1946, Local 28 refused to admit blacks until 1969.

passed in unreasonably high numbers. The state court ordered petitioners to indenture the apprentices based on the examination results.

In 1971, the United States initiated this action under Title VII and Executive Order 11246, 3 C.F.R. § 339 (1964–1965 Comp.) to enjoin petitioners from engaging in a pattern and practice of discrimination against black and Hispanic individuals (nonwhites).[3] The New York City Commission on Human Rights (City) intervened as plaintiff to press claims that petitioners had violated municipal fair employment laws, and had frustrated the City's efforts to increase job opportunities for minorities in the construction industry. In 1970, the City had adopted a plan requiring contractors on its projects to employ one minority trainee for every four journeyman union members. Local 28 was the only construction local which refused to comply voluntarily with the plan. In early 1974, the City attempted to assign six minority trainees to sheet metal contractors working on municipal construction projects. After Local 28 members stopped work on the projects, the District Court directed the JAC to admit the six trainees into the apprenticeship program, and enjoined Local 28 from causing any work stoppage at the affected job sites. The parties subsequently agreed to a consent order that required the JAC to admit up to 40 minorities into the apprenticeship program by September 1974. The JAC stalled compliance with the consent order, and only completed the indenture process under threat of contempt.

Following a trial in 1975, the District Court concluded that petitioners had violated both Title VII and New York law by discriminating against nonwhite workers in recruitment, selection, training, and admission to the union. 401 F.Supp. 467 (1975). Noting that as of July 1, 1974, only 3.19% of the union's total membership, including apprentices and journeymen, was nonwhite, the court found that petitioners had denied qualified nonwhites access to union membership through a variety of discriminatory practices. First, the court found that petitioners had adopted discriminatory procedures and standards for admission into the apprenticeship program. The court examined some of the factors used to select apprentices, including the entrance examination and high-school diploma requirement, and determined that these criteria had an adverse discriminatory impact on nonwhites, and were not related to job performance. The court also observed that petitioners had used union funds to subsidize special training sessions for friends and relatives of union members taking the apprenticeship examination.[4]

3. The Equal Employment Opportunity Commission was substituted as named plaintiff in this case. The Sheet Metal and Air Conditioning Contractors' Association of New York City (Contractor's Association) was also named as a defendant. The New York State Division of Human Rights (State), although joined as a third and fourth-party defendant in this action, realigned itself as a plaintiff.

4. The court also noted that petitioners' failure to comply with EEOC regulations requiring them to keep records of each applicant's race had made it difficult for the court to evaluate the discriminatory impact of petitioners' selection procedures.

Second, the court determined that Local 28 had restricted the size of its membership in order to deny access to nonwhites. The court found that Local 28 had refused to administer yearly journeymen's examinations despite a growing demand for members' services.[5] Rather, to meet this increase in demand, Local 28 recalled pensioners who obtained doctors' certificates that they were able to work, and issued hundreds of temporary work permits to nonmembers; only one of these permits was issued to a nonwhite. Moreover, the court found that "despite the fact that Local 28 saw fit to request [temporary workers] from sister locals all across the country, as well as from allied New York construction unions such as plumbers, carpenters, and iron workers, it never once sought them from Sheet Metal Local 400," a New York City union comprised almost entirely of nonwhites. The court concluded that by using the temporary permit system rather than continuing to administer journeymen's tests, Local 28 successfully restricted the size of its membership with the "illegal effect, if not the intention, of denying non-whites access to employment opportunities in the industry." Ibid.

Third, the District Court determined that Local 28 had selectively organized nonunion sheet metal shops with few, if any, minority employees, and admitted to membership only white employees from those shops. The court found that "[p]rior to 1973 no non-white ever became a member of Local 28 through the organization of a non-union shop." The court also found that, despite insistent pressure from both the International Union and local contractors, Local 28 had stubbornly refused to organize sheet metal workers in the local blowpipe industry because a large percentage of such workers were nonwhite.

Finally, the court found that Local 28 had discriminated in favor of white applicants seeking to transfer from sister locals. The court noted that from 1967 through 1972, Local 28 had accepted 57 transfers from sister locals, all of them white, and that it was only after this litigation had commenced that Local 28 accepted its first nonwhite transfers, two journeymen from Local 400. The court also found that on one occasion, the union's president had incorrectly told nonwhite Local 400 members that they were not eligible for transfer.

The District Court entered an order and judgment (O & J) enjoining petitioners from discriminating against nonwhites, and enjoining the specific practices the court had found to be discriminatory. Recognizing that "the record in both state and federal court against these

5. The Court noted that Local 28 had offered journeymen's examinations in 1968 and 1969 as a result of arbitration proceedings initiated by the Contractors' Association to force Local 28 to increase its manpower. Only 24 of 330 individuals, all of them white, passed the first examination and were admitted to the union. The court found that this examination had an adverse impact on nonwhites and had not been validated in accordance with EEOC guidelines, and was therefore violative of Title VII. Some nonwhites did pass the second examination, and the court concluded that Local 28's failure to keep records of the number of white and nonwhites tested made it impossible to determine whether that test had also had an adverse impact on nonwhites.

defendants is replete with instances of * * * bad faith attempts to prevent or delay affirmative action," [6] the court concluded that "the imposition of a remedial racial goal in conjunction with an admission preference in favor of non-whites is essential to place the defendants in a position of compliance with [Title VII]." The court established a 29% nonwhite membership goal, based on the percentage of nonwhites in the relevant labor pool in New York City, for the union to achieve by July 1, 1981. The parties were ordered to devise and to implement recruitment and admission procedures designed to achieve this goal under the supervision of a court-appointed administrator.[7]

The administrator proposed, and the court adopted, an Affirmative Action Program which, among other things, required petitioners to offer annual, nondiscriminatory journeyman and apprentice examinations, select members according to a white-nonwhite ratio to be negotiated by the parties, conduct extensive recruitment and publicity campaigns aimed at minorities,[8] secure the administrator's consent before issuing temporary work permits, and maintain detailed membership records, including separate records for whites and nonwhites. Local 28 was permitted to extend any of the benefits of the program to whites and other minorities, provided that this did not interfere with the program's operation.

The Court of Appeals for the Second Circuit affirmed the District Court's determination of liability, finding that petitioners had "consistently and egregiously violated Title VII." 532 F.2d 821, 825 (1976). The court upheld the 29% nonwhite membership goal as a temporary remedy, justified by a "long and persistent pattern of discrimination," and concluded that the appointment of an administrator with broad powers was clearly appropriate, given petitioners' refusal to change their membership practices in the face of prior state and federal court orders. However, the court modified the District Court's order to

---

6. The court remarked:

"After [state] Justice Markowitz [in the 1964 state-court proceeding] ordered implementation of [a plan intended to] create a 'truly nondiscriminatory union[,]' Local 28 flouted the court's mandate by expending union funds to subsidize special training sessions designed to give union members' friends and relatives a competitive edge in taking the [apprenticeship examination]. JAC obtained an exemption from state affirmative action regulations directed towards the administration of apprentice programs on the ground that its program was operating pursuant to court order; yet Justice Markowitz had specifically provided that all such subsequent regulations, to the extent not inconsistent with his order, were to be incorporated therein and applied to JAC's program. More recently, the defendants unilaterally suspended court-ordered time tables for admission

of forty non-whites to the apprentice program pending trial of this action, only completing the admission process under threat of contempt citations." 401 F.Supp., at 488.

7. The O & J also awarded backpay to those nonwhites who could demonstrate that they were discriminatorily excluded from union membership.

8. The District Court had concluded that petitioners had earned a well-deserved reputation for discriminating against non-whites, and that this reputation "operated and still operates to discourage non-whites seeking membership in the local union or its apprenticeship program." The publicity campaign was consequently designed to dispel this reputation, and to encourage nonwhites to take advantage of opportunities for union membership.

permit the use of a white-nonwhite ratio for the apprenticeship program only pending implementation of valid, job-related entrance tests. Local 28 did not seek certiorari in this Court to review the Court of Appeals' judgment.

On remand, the District Court adopted a Revised Affirmative Action Program and Order (RAAPO) to incorporate the Court of Appeals' mandate. RAAPO also modified the original Affirmative Action Program to accommodate petitioners' claim that economic problems facing the construction industry had made it difficult for them to comply with the court's orders. Petitioners were given an additional year to meet the 29% membership goal. RAAPO also established interim membership goals designed to "afford the parties and the Administrator with some device to measure progress so that, if warranted, other provisions of the program could be modified to reflect change (sic) circumstances." The JAC was directed to indenture at least 36 apprentices by February 1977, and to determine the size of future apprenticeship classes subject to review by the administrator.[9] A divided panel of the Court of Appeals affirmed RAAPO in its entirety, including the 29% nonwhite membership goal. 565 F.2d 31 (1977). Petitioners again chose not to seek certiorari from this Court to review the Court of Appeals' judgment.

In April 1982, the City and State moved in the District Court for an order holding petitioners in contempt.[10] They alleged that petitioners had not achieved RAAPO's 29% nonwhite membership goal, and that this failure was due to petitioners' numerous violations of the O & J, RAAPO, and orders of the administrator. The District Court, after receiving detailed evidence of how the O & J and RAAPO had operated over the previous six years, held petitioners in civil contempt. The court did not rest its contempt finding on petitioners' failure to meet the 29% membership goal, although nonwhite membership in Local 28 was only 10.8% at the time of the hearing. Instead, the court found that petitioners had "failed to comply with RAAPO * * * almost from its date of entry," identifying six "separate actions or omissions on the part of the defendants [that] have impeded the entry of non-whites into Local 28 in contravention of the prior orders of this court." Specifically, the court determined that petitioners had (1) adopted a policy of underutilizing the apprenticeship program in order to limit nonwhite membership and employment opportunities;[11] (2) refused to conduct the

---

9. The Affirmative Action Program originally had required the JAC to indenture at least 300 apprentices by July 1, 1976, and at least 200 apprentices in each year thereafter, up to and including 1981. These figures were adjusted downward after petitioners complained that economic conditions made it impossible for them to indenture this number of apprentices. The District Court also permitted petitioners to defer administration of the journeyman's examination for the same reason.

10. The Contractor's Association and individual Local 28 contractors were also named as respondents to the contempt proceeding.

11. The court explained that the "journeymen benefiting from this policy of underutilizing the apprenticeship program comprise Local 28's white incumbent membership." The court rejected Local 28's contention that any underutilization of the apprenticeship program could be blamed

general publicity campaign required by the O & J and RAAPO to inform nonwhites of membership opportunities; (3) added a job protection provision to the union's collective-bargaining agreement that favored older workers and discriminated against nonwhites (older workers provision); (4) issued unauthorized work permits to white workers from sister locals; and (5) failed to maintain and submit records and reports required by RAAPO, the O & J, and the administrator, thus making it difficult to monitor petitioners' compliance with the court's orders.

To remedy petitioners' contempt, the court imposed a $150,000 fine to be placed in a fund designed to increase nonwhite membership in the apprenticeship program and the union. The administrator was directed to propose a plan for utilizing the fund. The court deferred imposition of further coercive fines pending receipt of the administrator's recommendations for modifications to RAAPO.[12]

In 1983, the City brought a second contempt proceeding before the administrator, charging petitioners with additional violations of the O & J, RAAPO, and various administrative orders. The administrator found that the JAC had violated RAAPO by failing to submit accurate reports of hours worked by apprentices, thus preventing the court from evaluating whether non-white apprentices had shared in available employment opportunities, and that Local 28 had: (1) failed, in a timely manner, to provide the racial and ethnic data required by the O & J and RAAPO with respect to new members entering the union as a result of its merger with five predominately white sheet metal locals, (2) failed to serve copies of the O & J and RAAPO on contractors employing Local 28 members, as ordered by the administrator, and (3) submitted inaccurate racial membership records.[13]

The District Court adopted the administrator's findings and once again adjudicated petitioners guilty of civil contempt. The court ordered petitioners to pay for a computerized recordkeeping system to be

on difficult economic circumstances, emphasizing that the court had "not overlooked the obstacles or problems with which [petitioners] have had to contend," and that it had "given much consideration to the economic condition of the sheet metal trade in particular and the construction industry in general over the past six years."

12. The District Court found it necessary to modify RAAPO in light of the fact that the 29% nonwhite membership goal was no longer viable on the present timetable, and also because five other locals with predominantly white memberships had recently merged with Local 28. The court denied petitioners cross-motion for an order terminating both the O & J and RAAPO, finding that these orders had not caused petitioners unexpected or undue hardship.

13. The administrator's comments revealed that he was more concerned with Local 28's "inability to provide accurate data" than with the specific errors he had discovered. He emphasized that Local 28 had "no formal system to verify the racial and ethnic composition of [its] membership," and that "[s]uch verification that was done, was done on a totally haphazard basis." He concluded that "[t]he lack of any proper verification controls confirms * * * that Local 28 has not acted in the affirmative manner contemplated by the court." More generally, he observed that "[t]he violations found herein cannot be viewed in isolation, rather they must be seen as part of a pattern of disregard for state and federal court orders and as a continuation of conduct which led the court to find defendants in contempt."

maintained by outside consultants, but deferred ruling on additional contempt fines pending submission of the administrator's fund proposal. The court subsequently adopted the administrator's proposed Employment, Training, Education, and Recruitment Fund (Fund) to "be used for the purpose of remedying discrimination." The Fund was used for a variety of purposes. In order to increase the pool of qualified nonwhite applicants for the apprenticeship program, the Fund paid for nonwhite union members to serve as liaisons to vocational and technical schools with sheet metal programs, created part-time and summer sheet metal jobs for qualified nonwhite youths, and extended financial assistance to needy apprentices. The Fund also extended counseling and tutorial services to nonwhite apprentices, giving them the benefits that had traditionally been available to white apprentices from family and friends. Finally, in an effort to maximize employment opportunities for all apprentices, the Fund provided financial support to employers otherwise unable to hire a sufficient number of apprentices, as well as matching funds to attract additional funding for job training programs.[14]

The District Court also entered an Amended Affirmative Action Plan and Order (AAAPO) which modified RAAPO in several respects. AAAPO established a 29.23% minority membership goal to be met by August 31, 1987. The new goal was based on the labor pool in the area covered by the newly expanded union. The court abolished the apprenticeship examination, concluding that "the violations that have occurred in the past have been so egregious that a new approach must be taken to solve the apprentice selection problem." Apprentices were to be selected by a three-member Board, which would select one minority apprentice for each white apprentice indentured. Finally, to prevent petitioners from underutilizing the apprenticeship program, the JAC was required to assign to Local 28 contractors one apprentice for every four journeymen, unless the contractor obtained a written waiver from respondents.

Petitioners appealed the District Court's contempt orders, the Fund order, and the order adopting AAAPO.[15] A divided panel of the Court of Appeals affirmed the District Court's contempt findings,[16] except the

---

14. The Fund was to be financed by the $150,000 fine from the first contempt proceeding, plus an additional payment of $.02 per hour for each hour worked by a journeyman or apprentice. The Fund would remain in existence until the union achieved its nonwhite membership goal, and the District Court determined that the Fund was no longer necessary.

15. Petitioners did not appeal the denial of their cross-motion to terminate the O & J and RAAPO. The city cross-appealed from that part of AAAPO establishing a temporary 29.23% nonwhite membership goal, claiming that the percentage should

be higher. The Court of Appeals denied the cross-motion.

16. With respect to the finding of underutilization of the apprenticeship program, the court noted that the District Court had mistakenly compared the total number of apprentices enrolled during the period before the O & J was entered against the number of new enrollees admitted during the period after entry of the O & J. However, the court found this error inconsequential, since the statistical comparison was "only a small part of the overall evidence showing underutilization of the apprenticeship program." 753 F.2d 1172,

finding based on adoption of the older workers' provision.[17] The court concluded that "[p]articularly in light of the determined resistance by Local 28 to all efforts to integrate its membership, * * * the combination of violations found by [the District Court] amply demonstrates the union's foot-dragging egregious noncompliance * * * and adequately supports [its] findings of civil contempt against both Local 28 and the JAC." The court also affirmed the District Court's contempt remedies, including the Fund order, and affirmed AAAPO with two modifications: it set aside the requirement that one minority apprentice be indentured for every white apprentice,[18] and clarified the Disrict Court's orders to allow petitioners to implement objective, nondiscriminatory apprentice selection procedures.[19] The court found the 29.23% nonwhite membership goal to be proper in light of Local 28's "long continued and egregious racial discrimination," and because it "will not unnecessarily trammel the rights of any readily ascertainable group of nonminority individuals." The court rejected petitioners' argument that the goal violated Title VII or the Constitution. The court also distinguished AAAPO from the race-conscious order invalidated by this Court in Firefighters v. Stotts, 467 U.S. 561, 104 S.Ct. 2576, 81 L.Ed.2d 483 (1984), on three grounds: (1) unlike the order in *Stotts*, AAAPO did not conflict with a bona fide seniority plan; (2) the *Stotts* discussion of § 706(g) of Title VII, applied only to "make whole" relief and did not address the prospective relief contained in AAAPO and the Fund order; and (3) this case, unlike *Stotts*, involved intentional discrimination.

Local 28 and the JAC filed a petition for a writ of certiorari. They present several claims for review: (1) that the District Court relied on incorrect statistical data; (2) that the contempt remedies ordered by the District Court were criminal in nature and were imposed without due process; (3) that the appointment of an administrator to supervise membership practices interferes with their right to self-governance;

1180 (1985). The court determined that the District Court's finding of underutilization was supported by strong evidence that despite a need for more apprentices, petitioners refused to advertise the apprenticeship program and thereby help fill the need. See n. 22, infra. The court also noted that "[m]any of the uncertainties about underutilization that are urged by defendants are due in large part to the union's noncompliance with the reporting provisions of RAAPO."

17. The court held that plaintiffs had failed to prove that the older workers' provision had either a discriminatory purpose or effect, because although negotiated, it was never actually implemented. The court instructed the District Court on remand to determine the status and effect of the provision. Because adoption of this provision was the only contemptuous conduct that the Contractors' Association had been charged with, the Court of Appeals vacated all contempt relief against the Association.

18. The court recognized that "temporary hiring rations may be necessary in order to achieve integration of a work force from which minorities have been unlawfully barred," but cautioned that "such race-conscious ratios are extreme remedies that must be used sparingly and 'carefully tailored to fit the violations found.'" Noting that petitioners had voluntarily indentured 45% nonwhites since January of 1981, the court concluded that a strict one-to-one hiring requirement was not needed to insure that a sufficient number of nonwhites were selected for the apprenticeship program.

19. The EEOC had argued that AAAPO prohibited the use of any new selection procedures until the 29.23% membership goal was reached.

and (4) that the membership goal and Fund are unconstitutional. Principally, however, petitioners, supported by the Solicitor General, maintain that the membership goal and Fund exceed the scope of remedies available under Title VII because they extend race-conscious preferences to individuals who are not the identified victims of petitioners' unlawful discrimination. We granted the petition, and now affirm the Court of Appeals.

II

Petitioners argue that the District Court relied on incorrect statistical evidence in violation of Title VII and of petitioners' right to due process.

A

Under the O & J and RAAPO, petitioners were directed to attain a 29% nonwhite membership goal by July of 1981. This goal was based on the percentage of minorities in the relevant labor pool within New York City. Petitioners argue that because members and applicants for Local 28 membership have always been drawn from areas outside of New York City, the nonwhite membership goal should have accounted for the percentage of minorities in the relevant labor pool in these areas. Although they concede that there is no evidence in the record from which the correct percentage could be derived, they insist that the District Court's figure is erroneous, and that this error was "significant." [20]

The 29% nonwhite membership goal was established more than a decade ago and was twice affirmed by the Court of Appeals. Petitioners did not seek certiorari from this Court to review either of the Court of Appeals' judgments. Consequently, we do not have before us any issue as to the correctness of the 29% figure. See Pasadena City Board of Education v. Spangler, 427 U.S. 424, 432, 96 S.Ct. 2697, 2703, 49 L.Ed.2d 599 (1976). Under AAAPO, petitioners are now obligated to attain a 29.23% nonwhite-membership goal by August 1987. AAAPO adjusted the original 29% membership goal to account for the fact that Local 28's members were now drawn from areas outside of New York City. Thus, even assuming that the original 29% membership goal was

---

20. In their brief, petitioners also suggest that the District Court's 29% membership goal was used to confirm its original finding of discrimination, and was therefore invalid under Hazelwood School District v. United States, 433 U.S. 299, 97 S.Ct. 2736, 53 L.Ed.2d 768 (1977) (proof of a pattern of discrimination by statistical evidence must be drawn from relevant geographical locations). However, the Court of Appeals recognized that the District Court's finding of liability "did not rely on inferences from racial ratios of population and employment in the area," but rather "was based on direct and overwhelming evidence of purposeful racial discrimination over a period of many years." In any event, petitioners conceded at oral argument that they do not "challeng[e] any finding that there was deliberate discrimination."

erroneous, it would not affect petitioners' existing obligations under AAAPO, or any other issue now before us.[21]

B

Petitioners argue that the District Court also relied on incorrect data in finding that they had underutilized the apprenticeship program. The Court of Appeals recognized this error, see n. 20, supra, but affirmed the finding based on other evidence presented to the District Court.[22] Petitioners do not explain whether, and if so, why, the Court of Appeals' evaluation of the evidence was incorrect. Based on our own review of the record, we cannot say that the District Court's resolution of the evidence presented on this issue was clearly erroneous. Moreover, because petitioners do not challenge three of the findings on which the first contempt order was based, any alleged use of incorrect statistical evidence by the District Court provides no basis for disturbing the contempt citation. As the Court of Appeals observed, petitioners' "failure to have the apprentices employed is both an independent ground for contempt and a symptom of the effects of defendants' other kinds of contemptuous conduct."

III

The District Court imposed a variety of contempt sanctions in this case, including fines to finance the Fund, a computerized recordkeeping requirement, and attorney's fees and expenses. Petitioners claim that these sanctions, while ostensibly imposed for civil contempt, are in fact punitive, and were issued without the procedures required for criminal contempt proceedings, see Fed.Rule Crim.Proc. 42(b); 42 U.S.C. § 2000h. We reject this contention.

21. Petitioners contend that "[i]nasmuch as [they] have now been held in contempt for not achieving the [29% membership] quota, the propriety of the evidence upon which it was derived is relevant." In the first place, the District Court expressly stated that petitioners were not held in contempt for failing to attain the 29% membership goal. In any event, a "contempt proceeding does not open to reconsideration the legal or factual basis of the order alleged to have been disobeyed and thus become a retrial of the original controversy." Maggio v. Zeitz, 333 U.S. 56, 69, 68 S.Ct. 401, 408, 92 L.Ed. 476 (1948); see also Walker v. City of Birmingham, 388 U.S. 307, 313–314, 87 S.Ct. 1824, 1828, 18 L.Ed.2d 1210 (1967); United States v. Rylander, 460 U.S. 752, 756–757, 103 S.Ct. 1548, 1552–1553, 75 L.Ed.2d 521 (1983); C. Wright & A. Miller, Federal Practice and Procedure § 2960, pp. 597–598.

22. The court pointed to evidence before the District Court showing that after the O & J was entered: (1) there was a "sharp increase" in the ratio of journeymen to apprentices employed by contractors; (2) the average number of hours worked annually by journeymen "increased dramatically"; (3) the percentage of unemployed apprentices decreased; and (4) the union issued hundreds of temporary work permits, mostly to white journeymen. Based on this evidence, the Court of Appeals concluded that despite the need for more apprentices, Local 28 had deliberately shifted employment opportunities from apprentices to predominately white journeymen, and had refused to conduct the general publicity campaign required by RAAPO to attract nonwhites to the apprenticeship program.

Criminal contempt sanctions are punitive in nature and are imposed to vindicate the authority of the court. United States v. Mine Workers, 330 U.S. 258, 302, 67 S.Ct. 677, 700, 91 L.Ed. 884 (1947). On the other hand, sanctions in civil-contempt proceedings may be employed "for either or both of two purposes: to coerce the defendant into compliance with the court's order, and to compensate the complainant for losses sustained." Id., at 303–304, 67 S.Ct., at 701; see also McComb v. Jacksonville Paper Co., 336 U.S. 187, 191, 69 S.Ct. 497, 499, 93 L.Ed. 599 (1949); Penfield Co. of California v. S.E.C., 330 U.S. 585, 590, 67 S.Ct. 918, 921, 91 L.Ed. 1117 (1947); Nye v. United States, 313 U.S. 33, 42, 61 S.Ct. 810, 813, 85 L.Ed. 1172 (1941); McCrone v. United States, 307 U.S. 61, 64, 59 S.Ct. 685, 686–687, 83 L.Ed. 1108 (1939); 42 U.S.C. § 2000h. Under this standard, the sanctions issued by the District Court were clearly civil in nature.

The District Court determined that petitioners' had underutilized the apprenticeship program to the detriment of nonwhites, and that this was one of the factors that had prevented petitioners even from approaching the court-ordered 29% nonwhite membership goal. The Fund—and the fines used to finance it—sought to remedy petitioners' contemptuous conduct by increasing nonwhite membership in the apprenticeship program in a variety of ways. In an attempt to encourage nonwhite interest in the apprenticeship program, petitioners were required to finance recruiting efforts at vocational schools, and to create summer and part-time sheet metal jobs for qualified vocational students. Nonwhite apprentices were provided with tutorial, counseling, and financial support services. In an effort to stimulate employment opportunities for *all* apprentices, the Fund helped subsidize contractors who could not afford to hire one apprentice for every four journeymen, and helped the union secure matching training funds. The court carefully considered "the character and magnitude of the harm threatened by continued contumacy, and the probable effectiveness of any suggested sanction in bringing about the result desired," *Mine Workers,* supra, 330 U.S., at 304, 67 S.Ct., at 701, and concluded that the Fund was necessary to secure petitioners' compliance with its earlier orders. Under the terms of the Fund order, petitioners could purge themselves of the contempt by ending their discriminatory practices and by achieving the court-ordered membership goal; they would then be entitled, with the court's approval, to recover any moneys remaining in the Fund. Thus, the sanctions levied by the District Court were clearly designed to coerce compliance with the court's orders, rather than to punish petitioners for their contemptuous conduct.[23]

23. The District Court had also determined that petitioners had failed to comply with the detailed recordkeeping requirements of the O & J and RAAPO. The computerized recordkeeping system was clearly designed to foster petitioners' compliance with these provisions. Finally, the assessment of attorney fees and expenses compensated respondents for costs occasioned by petitioners' contemptuous conduct.

IV

Petitioners, joined by the Solicitor General, argue that the membership goal, the Fund order, and other orders which require petitioners to grant membership preferences to nonwhites are expressly prohibited by § 706(g), which defines the remedies available under Title VII. Petitioners and the Solicitor General maintain that § 706(g) authorizes a district court to award preferential relief only to the actual victims of unlawful discrimination.[24] They maintain that the membership goal and the Fund violate this provision, since they require petitioners to admit to membership, and otherwise to extend benefits to black and Hispanic individuals who are not the identified victims of unlawful discrimination.[25] We reject this argument, and hold that § 706(g) does not prohibit a court from ordering, in appropriate circumstances, affirmative race-conscious relief as a remedy for past discrimination. Specifically, we hold that such relief may be appropriate where an employer or a labor union has engaged in persistent or egregious discrimination, or where necessary to dissipate the lingering effects of pervasive discrimination.

A

Section 706(g) states:

"If the court finds that the respondent has intentionally engaged in or is intentionally engaging in an unlawful employment practice

---

24. Both petitioners and the Solicitor General present this challenge from a rather curious position. Petitioners did not seek review in this Court of the 29% membership goal twice approved by the Court of Appeals, even though that goal was similar to the 29.23% goal they now challenge. However, we reject the State's contention that either res judicata or the law of the case prohibits us from now addressing the legality of the membership goal.

The Solicitor General challenges the membership goal and Fund order even though the EEOC has, throughout this litigation, joined the other plaintiffs in asking the courts to order numerical goals, implementing ratios, and timetables. In the complaint, the Government sought the "selection of sufficient apprentices from among qualified non-white applicants to overcome the effects of past discrimination." In its post-trial memorandum, the Government urged the court to "establish a goal of no less than 30 per cent non white membership in Local 28." To achieve this, the Government asked the court to order petitioners to select apprentices based on a one-to-one white to nonwhite ratio, and argued that "a reasonable preference in favor of minority persons to remedy past discriminatory injustices is permissable [*sic*]." Ibid.

25. The last sentence of § 706(g) addresses only court orders requiring the "admission or reinstatement of an individual as a member of a union." 42 U.S.C. § 2000e–5(g). Thus, even under petitioners' reading of § 706(g), that provision would not apply to several of the benefits conferred by the Fund, to wit the tutorial, liaison, counseling, stipend, and loan programs extended to nonwhites. Moreover, the District Court established the Fund in the exercise of its contempt powers. Thus, even assuming that petitioners correctly read § 706(g) to limit the remedies a court may impose *for a violation of Title VII*, that provision would not necessarily limit the District Court's authority to order petitioners to implement the Fund. The Solicitor General, without citing any authority, maintains that "contempt sanctions imposed to enforce Title VII must not themselves violate the statute's policy of providing relief only to the actual victims of discrimination." We need not decide whether § 706(g) restricts a court's contempt powers, since we reject the proposition that § 706(g) always prohibits a court from ordering affirmative race-conscious relief which might incidentally benefit in-

* * *, the court may enjoin the respondent from engaging in such unlawful employment practice, and order such affirmative action as may be appropriate, which may include, but is not limited to, reinstatement or hiring of employees, with or without back pay * * *, or any other equitable relief as the court deems appropriate. * * * No order of the court shall require the admission or reinstatement of an individual as a member of a union, or the hiring, reinstatement, or promotion of an individual as an employee, or the payment to him of any back pay, if such individual was refused admission, suspended, or expelled, or was refused employment or advancement or was suspended or discharged for any reason other than discrimination on account of race, color, religion, sex, or national origin in violation of * * * this title." 42 U.S.C. § 2000e–5(g).

The language of § 706(g) plainly expresses Congress's intent to vest district courts with broad discretion to award "appropriate" equitable relief to remedy unlawful discrimination. Teamsters v. United States, 431 U.S. 324, 364, 97 S.Ct. 1843, 1869, 52 L.Ed.2d 396 (1977); Franks v. Bowman Transportation Co., 424 U.S. 747, 771, 96 S.Ct. 1251, 1267, 47 L.Ed.2d 444 (1976); Albermarle Paper Co. v. Moody, 422 U.S. 405, 421, 95 S.Ct. 2362, 2373, 45 L.Ed.2d 280 (1975).[26] Nevertheless, petitioners and the Solicitor General argue that the last sentence of § 706(g) prohibits a court from ordering an employer or labor union to take affirmative steps to eliminate discrimination which might incidentally benefit individuals who are not the actual victims of discrimination. This reading twists the plain language of the statute.

The last sentence of § 706(g) prohibits a court from ordering a union to admit an individual who was "refused admission * * * for any reason other than discrimination." It does not, as petitioners and the Solicitor General suggest, say that a court may order relief only for the actual victims of past discrimination. The sentence on its face addresses only the situation where a plaintiff demonstrates that a union (or an employer) has engaged in unlawful discrimination, but the union can

---

dividuals who were not the actual victims of discrimination.

26. Section 706(g) was modeled after § 10(c) of the National Labor Relations Act, 29 U.S.C. § 160(c). See Franks v. Bowman Transportation Co., 424 U.S., at 769, 96 S.Ct., at 1266; Albermarle Paper Co. v. Moody, 422 U.S., at 419, 95 S.Ct., at 2372. Principles developed under the National Labor Relations Act "guide, but do not bind, courts tailoring remedies under Title VII." Ford Motor Co. v. EEOC, 458 U.S. 219, 226, n. 8, 102 S.Ct. 3057, 3062–3063, n. 8, 73 L.Ed.2d 721 (1982). Section 10(c) as we have noted, was intended to give the National Labor Relations Board broad authority to formulate appropriate remedies:

"[I]n the nature of things Congress could not catalogue all the devices and stratagems for circumventing the policies of the Act. Nor could it define the whole gamut of remedies to effectuate these policies in an infinite variety of specific situations. Congress met these difficulties by leaving the adaption of means to end to the empiric process of administration." Phelps Dodge Corp. v. NLRB, 313 U.S. 177, 194, 61 S.Ct. 845, 852, 85 L.Ed. 1271 (1941).

See also *Franks,* supra, 424 U.S., at 769, n. 29, 96 S.Ct., at 1266 ("§ 706(g) grants * * * broader discretionary powers than those granted the [NLRB under section 10(c)].")

show that a particular individual would have been refused admission even in the absence of discrimination, for example because that individual was unqualified. In these circumstances § 706(g) confirms that a court could not order the union to admit the unqualified individual. In this case, neither the membership goal nor the Fund order required petitioners to admit to membership individuals who had been refused admission for reasons unrelated to discrimination. Thus, we do not read § 706(g) to prohibit a court from ordering the kind of affirmative relief the District Court awarded in this case.

B

The availability of race-conscious affirmative relief under § 706(g) as a remedy for a violation of Title VII also furthers the broad purposes underlying the statute. Congress enacted Title VII based on its determination that racial minorities were subject to pervasive and systematic discrimination in employment. "[I]t was clear to Congress that '[t]he crux of the problem [was] to open employment opportunities for Negroes in occupations which have been traditionally closed to them,' * * * and it was to this problem that Title VII's prohibition against racial discrimination in employment was primarily addressed." Steelworkers v. Weber, 443 U.S. 193, 203, 99 S.Ct. 2721, 2727, 61 L.Ed.2d 480 (1979) (quoting 110 Cong.Rec. 6548 (1964) (remarks of Sen. Humphrey)). Title VII was designed "to achieve equality of employment opportunities and remove barriers that have operated in the past to favor an identifiable group of white employees over other employees." Griggs v. Duke Power Co., 401 U.S. 424, 429–430, 91 S.Ct. 849, 853, 28 L.Ed.2d 158 (1971); see *Teamsters,* supra, 431 U.S., at 364–365, 97 S.Ct., at 1869–1870; *Franks,* supra, 424 U.S., at 763, 771, 96 S.Ct., at 1263–1264, 1267; *Albemarle Paper,* 422 U.S., at 417–18, 95 S.Ct., at 2371–2372. In order to foster equal employment opportunities, Congress gave the lower courts broad power under § 706(g) to fashion "the most complete relief possible" to remedy past discrimination. *Franks,* supra, 424 U.S., at 770, 96 S.Ct., at 1267; *Albemarle Paper,* supra, 422 U.S., at 418, 95 S.Ct., at 2372.

In most cases, the court need only order the employer or union to cease engaging in discriminatory practices, and award make-whole relief to the individuals victimized by those practices. In some instances, however, it may be necessary to require the employer or union to take affirmative steps to end discrimination effectively to enforce Title VII. Where an employer or union has engaged in particularly long-standing or egregious discrimination, an injunction simply reiterating Title VII's prohibition against discrimination will often prove useless and will only result in endless enforcement litigation. In such cases, requiring recalcitrant employers or unions to hire and to admit qualified minorities roughly in proportion to the number of qualified minorities in the work force may be the only effective way to ensure the full enjoyment of the rights protected by Title VII.

Further, even where the employer or union formally ceases to engage in discrimination, informal mechanisms may obstruct equal employment opportunities. An employer's reputation for discrimination may discourage minorities from seeking available employment. In these circumstances, affirmative race-conscious relief may be the only means available "to assure equality of employment opportunities and to eliminate those discriminatory practices and devices which have fostered racially stratified job environments to the disadvantage of minority citizens." McDonnell Douglas Corp. v. Green, 411 U.S. 792, 800, 93 S.Ct. 1817, 1823, 36 L.Ed.2d 668 (1973); see *Teamsters,* 431 U.S., at 348, 97 S.Ct., at 1861.[27] Affirmative action "promptly operates to change the outward and visible signs of yesterday's racial distinctions and thus, to provide an impetus to the process of dismantling the barriers, psychological or otherwise, erected by past practices." NAACP v. Allen, 493 F.2d 614, 621 (CA5 1974).

Finally, a district court may find it necessary to order interim hiring or promotional goals pending the development of nondiscriminatory hiring or promotion procedures. In these cases, the use of numerical goals provides a compromise between two unacceptable alternatives: an outright ban on hiring or promotions, or continued use of a discriminatory selection procedure.

We have previously suggested that courts may utilize certain kinds of racial preferences to remedy past discrimination under Title VII. See Fullilove v. Klutznick, 448 U.S. 448, 483, 100 S.Ct. 2758, 2777, 65 L.Ed.2d 902 (1980) (opinion of Burger, C.J.) ("Where federal antidiscrimination laws have been violated, an equitable remedy may in the appropriate case include a racial or ethnic factor"); id., at 513, 100 S.Ct., at 2792–2793 (Powell, J., concurring) ("The Courts of Appeals have approved temporary hiring remedies insuring that the percentage of minority group workers in a business or governmental agency will be reasonably related to the percentage of minority group members in the relevant population"); University of California Regents v. Bakke, 438 U.S. 265, 353, 98 S.Ct. 2733, 2780, 57 L.Ed.2d 750 (1978) (opinion of Brennan, White, Marshall, and Blackmun, JJ.) ("the Court has required that preferences be given by employers to members of racial minorities as a remedy for past violations of Title VII"). The Courts of Appeals have unanimously agreed that racial preferences may be used, in appropriate cases, to remedy past discrimination under Title VII.

---

27. We have steadfastly recognized that affirmative race-conscious relief may provide an effective means of remedying the effects of past discrimination. See Wygant v. Jackson Board of Education, 476 U.S. 267, 106 S.Ct. 1842, 90 L.Ed.2d 260 (1986) (opinion of Powell, J.) ("to eliminate every vestige of racial segregation and discrimination * * * race-conscious remedial action may be necessary"); *id.,* at 301, 106 S.Ct., at 1861 (Marshall, J., dissenting) ("racial distinctions * * * are highly relevant to the one legitimate state objective of eliminating the pernicious vestiges of past discrimination"); Fullilove v. Klutznick, 448 U.S. 448, 100 S.Ct. 2758, 65 L.Ed.2d 902 (1980) (upholding 10% set aside of federal contract funds for minority businesses).

C

Despite the fact that the plain language of § 706(g) and the purposes of Title VII suggest the opposite, petitioners and the Solicitor General maintain that the legislative history indicates that Congress intended that affirmative relief under § 706(g) benefit only the identified victims of past discrimination. To support this contention, petitioners and the Solicitor General rely principally on statements made throughout the House and Senate debates to the effect that Title VII would not require employers or labor unions to adopt quotas or preferences that would benefit racial minorities.

Our examination of the legislative history of Title VII convinces us that, when examined in context, the statements relied upon by petitioners and the Solicitor General do not indicate that Congress intended to limit relief under § 706(g) to that which benefits only the actual victims of unlawful discrimination. Rather, these statements were intended largely to reassure opponents of the bill that it would not require employers or labor unions to use racial quotas or to grant preferential treatment to racial minorities in order to avoid being charged with unlawful discrimination. See United Steelworkers of America, AFL CIO CLC v. Weber, (1979), 443 U.S. 193, at 205, 99 S.Ct. 2721, 2728, 61 L.Ed.2d 480. The bill's supporters insisted that this would not be the intent and effect of the legislation, and eventually agreed to state this expressly in § 703(j). Contrary to the arguments made by petitioners and the Solicitor General, these statements do not suggest that a court may not order preferential relief under § 706(g) when appropriate to remedy past discrimination. Rather, it is clear that the bill's supporters only wished to emphasize that an employer would not violate the statute merely by having a racially imbalanced work force, and, consequently, that a court could not order an employer to adopt racial preferences merely to correct such an imbalance.

1

H.R. 7152, the bill that ultimately became the Civil Rights Act of 1964, was introduced in the House by Representatives on June 20, 1963, and referred to the Committee on the Judiciary. The bill contained no provisions addressed to discrimination in employment, but the Judiciary Committee amended it by adding Title VII. Title VII as reported by the Judiciary Committee included a version of § 706(g), which read, in relevant part: "No order of the court shall require the admission or reinstatement of an individual as a member of a union * * * if such individual was refused admission, suspended, or expelled * * * for *cause.*" The word "cause" was deleted from the bill on the House floor and replaced by the language "any reason other than discrimination on account of race, color, religion, or national origin." Representative Celler, the Chairman of the House Judiciary Committee and the sponsor of this amendment, explained:

"[T]he purpose of the amendment is to specify cause. Here the court, for example, cannot find any violation of the act which is based on facts other—and I emphasize 'other'—than discrimination on the grounds of race, color, religion, or national origin. The discharge might be based, for example, on incompetence or a morals charge or theft, but the court can only consider charges based on race, color, religion, or national origin. That is the purpose of this amendment."

2

Even before the Judiciary Committee's bill reached the House floor, opponents charged that Title VII would require that an employer maintain a racially balanced work force. The Minority Report of the Judiciary Committee observed that "the word discrimination is nowhere defined in the bill," and charged that "the administration intends to rely upon its own construction of 'discrimination' as including the lack of racial balance." To demonstrate how the bill would operate in practice, the Report posited a number of hypothetical employment situations, concluding each time that Title VII would compel employers "to 'racially balance' those who work for him *in every job classification* or be in violation of Federal law." [30] In response, Republican proponents of the bill issued a statement emphasizing that the EEOC could not enforce the statute merely to achieve racial balance:

"[T]he Commission must confine its activities to correcting abuse, not promoting equality with mathematical certainty. In this regard, nothing in the title permits a person to demand employment. Of greater importance, the Commission will only jeopardize its continued existence if it seeks to impose forced racial balance upon employers or labor unions."

When H.R. 7152 actually reached the House floor, Representative Celler attempted to respond to charges that the existence of racial imbalance would constitute "discrimination" under Title VII, or that

---

30. For illustrative purposes, we include two of these "examples":

"Under the power granted in this bill, if a carpenters' hiring hall, say, had 20 men awaiting call, the first 10 in seniority being white carpenters, the union could be forced to pass them over in favor of carpenters beneath them in seniority, but of the stipulated race. And if the union roster did not contain the names of the carpenters of the race needed to 'racially balance' the job, the union agent must, then, go into the street and recruit members of the stipulated race in sufficient number * * * else his local could be held in violation of Federal law."

"Assume two women of separate races apply to [a] firm for the position of stenographer; further assume that the employer for some indefinable reason, prefers one above the other, whether because of personality, superior alertness, intelligence, work history, or general neatness. Assume the employer has learned good things about the character of one and derogatory things about the character of the other which are not subject to proof. If his firm is not 'racially balanced,' [the employer] has no choice, he must employ the person of that race which, by ratio, is next up, even though he is certain in his own mind that the woman he is not allowed to employ would be a superior employee."

the EEOC would be authorized to "order the hiring and promotion only of employees of certain races or religious groups." [31] Nevertheless, accusations similar to those made in the Judiciary Committee's Minority Report were repeatedly raised on the House floor. For example, Representative Alger charged that Title VII would "demand by law, special privileges for Negroes":

> "The Negro represents about 10 percent of the population of the United States and it cannot be said he is being kept from opportunity if he is represented in 10 percent of the working force. Now we are asked to ignore population ratios and force the hiring of Negroes even when it will mean, as in Government, that they are given preferential hiring far beyond the 10 percent of the population they represent."

Representative Abernathy raised the scenario of a "union [having] to send out a 'racially' balanced staff of organizers to sign up a crew of 'racially balanced' carpenters, a crew of 'racially balanced' laborers, 'racially balanced' plumbers, electricians, plasterers, roofers, and so forth, before a construction job could begin. Supporters of the bill stridently denied any intent to require "racial balancing." [32] Thus, in response to charges that an employer or labor union would be guilty of "discrimination" under Title VII simply because of a racial imbalance in its work force or membership roster, supporters of the bill insisted repeatedly that Title VII would not require employers or unions to implement hiring or promotional quotas in order to achieve racial balance. The question whether there should be any comparable restrictions with respect to a court's use of racial preferences as an appropriate *remedy for past discrimination* under § 706(g) simply did not arise during the House debates.

3

After passing the House by a vote of 290–130, the bill ran into equally strong opposition in the Senate. Opponents initially sought to

---

31. Representative Celler explained that the Commission would have no power "to rectify existing 'racial or religious imbalance' in employment by requiring the hiring of certain people * * * simply because they are of a given race or religion." He emphasized that "[n]o order could be entered against an employer except by a court," and that "[e]ven then, the court could not order that any preference be given to any particular race, religion or other group, but would be limited to ordering an end to discrimination."

32. See 110 Cong.Rec. 1540 (1964) (remarks of Rep. Lindsay) (The bill "does not impose quotas or any special privileges of seniority or acceptance. There is nothing whatever in this bill about racial balance as appears so frequently in the minority

report of the committee"); id., at 1600 (remarks of Rep. Minish) ("[U]nder title VII. * * * no quota system will be set up, no one will be forced to hire incompetent help because of race or religion, and no one will be given a vested right to demand employment for a certain job"); id., at 1994 (remarks of Rep. Healy) ("Opponents of the bill say that it sets up racial quotas for job[s] * * *. The bill does not do that"); id., at 2558 (remarks of Rep. Goodell) ("There is nothing here as a matter of legislative history that would require racial balancing * * *. We are not talking about a union having to balance its membership or an employer having to balance the number of employees. There is no quota involved").

have it sent to the Senate Judiciary Committee, which was hostile to civil rights legislation. The debate on this motion focused on the merits of the bill; many Senators again raised the specter of "racial balancing." Senator Ervin charged that under the substantive provisions of Title VII, "the Commission could * * * tell an employer that he had too few employees * * * and enter an order * * * requiring him to hire more persons, not because the employer thought he needed more persons, but because the Commission wanted to compel him to employ persons of a particular race." Similarly, Senator Robertson stated:

> "This title suggests that hiring should be done on some percentage basis in order that racial imbalance will be overcome. It is contemplated by this title that the percentage of colored and white population in a community shall be in similar percentages in every business establishment that employs over 25 persons. Thus, if there were 10,000 colored persons in a city and 15,000 whites, an employer with 25 employees would, in order to overcome racial imbalance, be required to have 10 colored personnel and 15 white. And, if by chance that employer had 20 colored employees he would have to fire 10 of them in order to rectify the situation."

Senator Humphrey, one of the most vocal proponents of H.R. 7152, rose to the bill's defense. He introduced a newspaper article quoting the answers of a Justice Department expert to common objections to Title VII. In response to the "objection" that "[w]hite people would be fired, to make room for Negroes," the article stated that "[t]he bill would not authorize anyone to order hiring or firing to achieve racial or religious balance." Later, responding to a political advertisement suggesting that federal agencies would interpret "discrimination" under Title VII as synonymous with racial imbalance, Senator Humphrey stressed that Title VII "does [not] in any way authorize the Federal Government to prescribe, as the advertisement charges, a 'racial balance' of job classifications or office staffs or 'preferential treatment of minorities'" to achieve such a balance. After 17 days of debate, the Senate voted to take up the bill directly without referring it to a committee.

Senators Humphrey and Kuchel, who served as bipartisan floor managers for H.R. 7152, opened formal debate on the merits of the bill and addressed opponent's charges that Title VII would require employers to implement quotas to achieve a certain racial balance. Senator Humphrey stressed that "[c]ontrary to the allegations of some opponents of this title, there is nothing in it that will give any power to the Commission or to any court to require hiring, firing, or promotion of employees in order to meet a racial 'quota' or to achieve a certain racial balance." Senator Kuchel elaborated:

> "[Title VII] is pictured by its opponents and detractors as an intrusion of numerous Federal inspectors into our economic life. These inspectors would presumably dictate to labor unions and their members with regard to * * * racial balance in job classifica-

tions, racial balance in membership, and preferential advancement for members of so called minority groups. Nothing could be further from the truth * * *. [T]he important point * * * is that the court cannot order preferential hiring or promotion consideration for any particular race, religion, or other group."

These sentiments were echoed by Senators Case and Clark, who spoke as bipartisan team "captains" in support of Title VII. The Senators submitted an interpretative memorandum which explained that "[t]here is no requirement in title VII that an employer maintain a racial balance in his work force." Senator Clark also introduced a Justice Department memorandum which repeated what supporters of the bill had tried to make clear:

"There is no provision, either in title VII or in any other part of this bill, that requires or authorizes any Federal agency or Federal court to require preferential treatment for any individual or any group for the purpose of achieving racial balance. No employer is required to hire an individual because that individual is a Negro. No employer is required to maintain any ratio of Negroes to whites, Jews to gentiles, Italians to English, or women to men."

Opponents of the bill invoked a 2–month filibuster, again raising the charge that "discrimination" would be defined to include racial imbalance. Senator Robertson remarked: "What does discrimination mean? If it means what I think it does, and which it could mean, it means that a man could be required to have a quota *or he would be discriminating.*" Senators Smathers and Sparkman conceded that Title VII did not in so many words require the use of quotas, but feared that employers would adopt racial quotas or preferences to avoid being charged with discrimination. Even outsiders joined in the debate, Senator Javits referred to charges raised by Governor Wallace of Alabama that the bill "vested power in a federal inspector who, under an allegation of racial imbalance * * * can establish a quota system whereby a certain percentage of a certain ethnic group must be employed." The bill's supporters insisted that employers would not be required to implement racial quotas to avoid being charged with liability.[33] Nonetheless, opponents remained skeptical.

Recognizing that their own verbal assurances would not end the dispute over "racial balancing," supporters of the bill eventually agreed to insert an explicit disclaimer into the language of the bill to assuage opponents' fears. Senator Dirksen introduced the comprehensive

33. See id., at 7420 (remarks of Sen. Humphrey) ("if [Senator Robertson] can find in title VII * * * any language which provides that an employer will have to hire on the basis of percentage or quota related to color, race * * * I will start eating the pages"); id., at 8500–8501 (remarks of Sen. Allott) ("if anyone sees in the bill quotas or percentages, he must read that language into it. It is not in the bill"); id., at 8921 (remarks of Sen. Williams) ("there is nothing whatever in the bill which provides for racial balance or quotas in employment"); id., at 11471 (remarks of Sen. Javits) (the bill "in no respect imposes a quota system or racial imbalance standard"); id., at 11848 (remarks of Sen. Humphrey) (the title "does not provide that any quota systems may be established to maintain racial balance in employment").

"Dirksen–Mansfield" amendment as a substitute for the entire bill, which added several provisions defining and clarifying the scope of Title VII's substantive provisions. One of those provisions, § 703(j), specifically addressed the charges of "racial balancing":

> "Nothing contained in this subchapter shall be interpreted to require any * * * labor organization, or joint labor-management committee * * * to grant preferential treatment to any individual or to any group because of the race * * * of such individual or group on account of an imbalance which may exist with respect to the total number or percentage of persons of any race [admitted to the labor organization, or to any apprenticeship program] in comparison with the total number or percentage of persons of such race * * * in any community, State, section, or other area, or in the available work force in any community, State, section, or other area."

As Senator Humphrey explained:

> "A new subsection 703(j) is added to deal with the problem of racial balance among employees. The proponents of this bill have carefully stated on numerous occasions that title VII does not require an employer to achieve any sort of racial balance in his work force by giving preferential treatment to any individual or group. Since doubts have persisted, subsection (j) is added to state this point expressly. This subsection does not represent any change in the substance of the title. It does state clearly and accurately what we have maintained all along about the bill's intent and meaning."

* * * Section 703(j) apparently calmed the fears of most opponents, for complaints of "racial balance" and "quotas" died down considerably after its adoption.

In contrast to the heated debate over the substantive provisions of § 703, the Senate paid scant attention to the remedial provisions of § 706(g). Several Senators did emphasize, in reference to the last sentence of section 706(g), that "[t]he title does not provide for the reinstatement or employment of a person * * * if he was fired or refused employment or promotion for any reason other than discrimination prohibited by the Title." 110 Cong.Rec., at 11848 (remarks of Sen. Humphrey).[35] While both petitioners and the Solicitor General liberally quote from these excerpts, we do not read these statements as supporting their argument that a district court may not order affirmative race-conscious relief which may incidentally benefit individuals

---

35. See id., at 6549 (remarks of Sen. Humphrey) ("No court order can require hiring, reinstatement, admission to membership, or payment of back pay for anyone who was not fired, refused employment or advancement or admission to a union by an act of discrimination forbidden by this title. This is stated expressly in the last sentence of [§ 706(g)], which makes clear what is implicit throughout the whole title; namely, that employers may hire and fire, promote and refuse to promote for any reason, good or bad, provided only that individuals may not be discriminated against because of race, religion, sex, or national origin").

who are not identified victims of unlawful discrimination. To the contrary, these statements confirm our reading of the last sentence of § 706(g): that a court has no power to award relief to an individual who was denied an employment opportunity for reasons other than discrimination.

After 83 days of debate, the Senate adopted Title VII by a vote of 73 to 27. Rather than setting up a Conference Committee, the House voted directly upon, and passed, the Senate version of the bill. The bill's sponsors repeated, for the last time, that Title VII "[did] not require quotas, racial balance, or any of the other things that the opponents have been saying about it."

To summarize, many opponents of Title VII argued that an employer could be found guilty of discrimination under the statute simply because of a racial imbalance in his work force, and would be compelled to implement racial "quotas" to avoid being charged with liability. At the same time, supporters of the bill insisted that employers would not violate Title VII simply because of racial imbalance, and emphasized that neither the Commission nor the courts could compel employers to adopt quotas solely to facilitate racial balancing. The debate concerning what Title VII did and did not require culminated in the adoption of § 703(j), which stated expressly that the statute did not require an employer or labor union to adopt quotas or preferences simply because of a racial imbalance. However, while Congress strongly opposed the use of quotas or preferences merely to maintain racial balance, it gave no intimation as to whether such measures would be acceptable as *remedies* for Title VII violations.[36]

Congress' failure to consider this issue is not surprising, since there was relatively little civil rights litigation prior to the adoption of the 1964 Civil Rights Act. More importantly, the cases that had been litigated had not resulted in the sort of affirmative-action remedies that, as later became apparent, would sometimes be necessary to eliminate effectively the effects of past discrimination. Thus, the use of racial preferences as a *remedy* for past discrimination simply was not an issue at the time Title VII was being considered. Our task then, is to determine whether Congress intended to preclude a district court from ordering affirmative action in appropriate circumstances as a remedy for past discrimination. Our examination of the legislative policy behind Title VII leads us to conclude that Congress did not intend to prohibit a court from exercising its remedial authority in that way.[37] Congress deliberately gave the district courts broad authority

---

36. Cf. *Bakke,* 438 U.S., at 342, n. 17, 98 S.Ct., at 2774–2775, n. 17 (opinion of Brennan, White, Marshall, and Blackmun, JJ.) ("Even assuming that Title VII prohibits employers from deliberately maintaining a particular racial composition in their work force as an end in itself, this does not imply, in the absence of any consideration of the question, that Congress intended to ban the use of racial preferences as a tool for achieving the objective of remedying past discrimination or other compelling ends").

37. We also reject petitioners' argument that the District Court's remedies contravened § 703(j), since they require pe-

under Title VII to fashion the most complete relief possible to eliminate "the last vestiges of an unfortunate and ignominious page in this country's history," *Albemarle Paper,* 422 U.S., at 418, 95 S.Ct., at 2372. As we noted above, affirmative race-conscious relief may in some instances be necessary to accomplish this task. In the absence of any indication that Congress intended to limit a district court's remedial authority in a way which would frustrate the court's ability to enforce Title VII's mandate, we decline to fashion such a limitation ourselves.

4

Our reading of the scope of the district court's remedial powers under § 706(g) is confirmed by the contemporaneous interpretations of the EEOC and the Justice Department.[38] Following the enactment of the Civil Rights Act of 1964, both the Justice Department and the EEOC, the two federal agencies charged with enforcing Title VII, steadfastly maintained that race-conscious remedies for unlawful discrimination are available under the statute. Both agencies have, in appropriate cases, sought court orders and consent decrees containing such provisions. See, e.g., United States v. City of Alexandria, 614 F.2d 1358 (CA5 1980); see also Affirmative Action Appropriate Under Title VII of the Civil Rights Act of 1964, 29 CFR § 1608 (1985); Uniform Guidelines on Employee Selection Procedures, id., § 1607.17; 42 Op.

titioners to grant preferential treatment to blacks and Hispanics based on race. Our examination of the legislative history convinces us that § 703(j) was added to Title VII to make clear that an employer or labor union does not engage in "discrimination" simply because of a racial imbalance in its workforce or membership, and would not be required to institute preferential quotas to avoid Title VII liability. See *Weber,* 443 U.S., at 205, n. 5, 99 S.Ct., at 2728, n. 5 ("§ 703(j) speaks to substantive liability under Title VII"); *Teamsters,* 431 U.S., at 339–340, n. 20, 97 S.Ct., at 1856–1857, n. 20 ("§ 703(j) makes clear that Title VII imposes no requirement that a work force mirror the general population"); *Franks,* 424 U.S., at 758, 96 S.Ct., at 1261 ("the * * * provisions of § 703 * * * delineat[e] which employment practices are illegal and thereby prohibited and which are not"). We reject the notion that § 703(j) somehow qualifies or proscribes a court's authority to order relief otherwise appropriate under § 706(g) in circumstances where an illegal discriminatory act or practice is established.

38. Although the Solicitor General now makes a contrary argument, we note that the brief for the EEOC submitted by the Solicitor General in *Weber,* supra, described the 1964 legislative history as follows:

"To be sure, there was considerable concern that the Act would be construed to require the use of quota systems to establish and maintain racial balance in employers' work forces. [citations omitted]. The sponsors of the bill repeatedly assured its opponents that this was not the intent and would not be the effect of the statute. [citations omitted]. But these assurances did not suggest restrictions on remedies that could be ordered after a finding of discrimination. Instead, they made it clear that the statute would not impose a duty on employers to establish racially balanced work forces and that it would not require or even permit employers to establish racial quotas for employment in the absence of discrimination of the kind prohibited by the Act. [citations omitted]." Brief for the United States and the Equal Employment Opportunity Commission in United Steelworkers of America v. Weber, O.T. 1978. Nos. 432, 435 and 436, pp. 29–30.

The brief concludes that "the last sentence of Section 706(g) simply state[s] that a court could not order relief under the authority of the Act if employers took action against employees or applicants on grounds other than those prohibited by the Act."

Atty.Gen. 405 (1969). The agencies' contemporaneous reading of the statute lends strong support for our interpretation.

5

Finally, our interpretation of § 706(g) is confirmed by the legislative history of the Equal Employment Opportunity Act of 1972, which amended Title VII in several respects. One such change modified the language of § 706(g) to empower a court to order "such affirmative action as may be appropriate, which may include, *but is not limited to* reinstatement or hiring of employees * * * *or any other equitable relief as the court deems appropriate.*" (emphasized language added in 1972). This language was intended "to give the courts wide discretion exercising their equitable powers to fashion the most complete relief possible." While the section-by-section analysis undertaken in the Conference Committee Report stressed the need for "make-whole" relief for the "victims of unlawful discrimination," nowhere did Congress suggest that a court lacked the power to award preferential remedies that might benefit nonvictims. Indeed, the Senate's rejection of two other amendments supports a contrary conclusion.

During the 1972 debates, Senator Ervin introduced an amendment to counteract the effects of the Department of Labor's so-called Philadelphia Plan. The Philadelphia Plan was established pursuant to Executive Order No. 11246, 3 CFR 339 (1964–1965 comp.), and required prospective federal contractors to submit affirmative-action programs including "specific goals of minority manpower utilization." Attacking the Plan as "[t]he most notorious example of discrimination in reverse," Senator Ervin proposed an amendment to Title VII that read, in relevant part: "No department, agency, or officer of the United States shall require an employer to practice discrimination in reverse by employing persons of a particular race * * * in either fixed or variable numbers, proportions, percentages, quotas, goals, or ranges." Senator Ervin complained that the amendment was needed because both the Department of Labor and the EEOC were ignoring § 703(j)'s prohibition against requiring employers to engage in preferential hiring for racial minorities.

Senator Javits vigorously opposed Senator Ervin's proposal. First, he recognized that the amendment, while targeted at the Philadelphia Plan, would also jettison "the whole concept of 'affirmative action' as it has been developed under Executive Order 11246 *and as a remedial concept under Title VII.*" (emphasis added). He explained that the amendment would "deprive the courts of the opportunity to order affirmative action under title VII of the type which they have sustained in order to correct a history of unjust and illegal discrimination in employment." * * * The Ervin amendment was defeated by a margin of 2 to 1.

Senator Ervin proposed a second amendment that would have extended § 703(j)'s prohibition against racial preferences to "Executive

Order Numbered 11246, or any other law or Executive Order," this amendment was also defeated resoundingly. Thus, the legislative history of the 1972 amendments to Title VII confirms the availability of race-conscious affirmative action as a remedy under the statute. Congress was aware that both the Executive and Judicial Branches had used such measures to remedy past discrimination,[41] and rejected amendments that would have barred such remedies. Instead, Congress reaffirmed the breadth of the court's remedial powers under § 706(g) by adding language authorizing courts to order "any other equitable relief as the court deems appropriate." 42 U.S.C. § 2000e–5(g). The section-by-section analysis undertaken by the Conference Committee Report confirms Congress' resolve to accept prevailing judicial interpretations regarding the scope of Title VII: "[I]n any area where the new law does not address itself, or in any area where a specific contrary intention is not indicated, it was assumed that the present case law as developed by the courts would continue to govern the applicability and construction of Title VII." 118 Cong.Rec., at 7166, 7564. Thus, "[e]xecutive, judicial, and congressional action subsequent to the passage of Title VII conclusively established that the Title did not bar the remedial use of race." *Bakke,* 438 U.S., at 353, n. 28, 98 S.Ct., at 2780 (opinion of Brennan, White, Marshall, and Blackmun, JJ.)[42]

D

Finally, petitioners and the Solicitor General find support for their reading of § 706(g) in several of our decisions applying that provision. Petitioners refer to several cases for the proposition that court-ordered remedies under § 706(g) are limited to make-whole relief benefiting actual victims of past discrimination. See Ford Motor Co. v. EEOC, 458 U.S. 219, 102 S.Ct. 3057, 73 L.Ed.2d 721 (1982); Connecticut v. Teal, 457 U.S. 440, 102 S.Ct. 2525, 73 L.Ed.2d 130 (1982); Teamsters v. United States, 431 U.S. 324, 97 S.Ct. 1843, 52 L.Ed.2d 396 (1977); Franks v. Bowman Transportation Co., 424 U.S. 747, 96 S.Ct. 1251, 47 L.Ed.2d 444 (1976); Albemarle Paper Co. v. Moody, 422 U.S. 405, 95 S.Ct. 2362, 45

41. In addition, * * * other federal courts had, prior to the passage of the 1972 amendments, approved of the use of racial preferences to remedy the effects of illegal employment discrimination. See e.g., Carter v. Gallagher, 452 F.2d 315, 330 (CA8 1971) (en banc), cert. denied, 406 U.S. 950, 92 S.Ct. 2045, 32 L.Ed.2d 338 (1972); Local 53, Heat & Frost Insulators v. Volger, 407 F.2d 1047, 1055 (CA5 1969); United States v. Central Motor Lines, Inc., 338 F.Supp. 532, 560–562 (WDNC 1971); United States v. Sheet Metal Workers International Association, Local 10, 3 Empl.Prac.Dec. ¶ 8068 (D NJ 1970).

42. Again, we note that the brief submitted by the Solicitor General in *Weber* urged this reading of the 1972 legislative history. The Solicitor General argued that

"[a]ny doubts that Title VII authorized the use of race-conscious remedies were put to rest with the enactment of the Equal Employment Opportunity Act of 1972." Referring specifically to the amendment to the language of § 706(g), the Government argued:

"In light of Congress's keen awareness of the kinds of remedies courts had been granting in Title VII cases, and in light of the protests from Senator Ervin and others over the use of race-conscious remedies, this amendment to Section 706(g) provides substantial support for the proposition that Congress intended that numerical, race-conscious relief is available under Title VII to remedy employment discrimination."

L.Ed.2d 280 (1975). This reliance is misguided. The cases cited hold only that a court may order relief designed to make individual victims of racial discrimination whole. See *Teamsters,* supra (competitive seniority); *Franks,* supra, 424 U.S., at 779, 96 S.Ct., at 1271 (competitive seniority); *Albemarle Paper,* supra, 422 U.S., at 422, 95 S.Ct., at 2373–2374 (backpay). None of these decisions suggested that individual "make-whole" relief was the *only* kind of remedy available under the statute, on the contrary, several cases emphasized that the district court's remedial powers should be exercised both to eradicate the effects of unlawful discrimination as well as to make the victims of past discrimination whole. Neither do these cases suggest that § 706(g) prohibits a court from ordering relief which might benefit nonvictims; indeed several cases acknowledged that the district court has broad authority to "devise prospective relief designed to assure that employers found to be in violation of [Title VII] eliminate their discriminatory practices and the effects therefrom." *Teamsters,* supra, 431 U.S., at 361, n. 47, 97 S.Ct., at 1868, n. 47; see also *Franks,* supra, 424 U.S., at 770, 96 S.Ct. at 1267; *Albemarle Paper,* supra, 422 U.S., at 418, 95 S.Ct., at 2372.

Petitioners claim to find their strongest support in Firefighters v. Stotts, 467 U.S. 561, 104 S.Ct. 2576, 81 L.Ed.2d 483 (1984). * * *

First, we rejected the claim that the District Court was merely enforcing the terms of the consent decree since the parties had expressed no intention to depart from the existing seniority system in the event of layoffs. Second, we concluded that the District Court's order conflicted with § 703(h) of Title VII, which "permits the routine application of a seniority system absent proof of an intention to discriminate." Since the District Court had found that the proposed layoffs were not motivated by a discriminatory purpose, we held that the court erred in enjoining the city from applying its seniority system in making the layoffs.

We also rejected the Court of Appeals' suggestion that the District Court's order was justified by the fact that, had plaintiffs prevailed at trial, the court could have entered an order overriding the city's seniority system. Relying on *Teamsters,* supra, we observed that a court may abridge a bona fide seniority system in fashioning a Title VII remedy only to make victims of intentional discrimination whole, that is, a court may award competitive seniority to individuals who show that they had been discriminated against. However, because none of the firefighters protected by the court's order was a proven victim of illegal discrimination, we reasoned that at trial the District Court would have been without authority to override the city's seniority system, and therefore the court could not enter such an order merely to effectuate the purposes of the consent decree.

While not strictly necessary to the result, we went on to comment that "[o]ur ruling in *Teamsters* that a court can award competitive seniority only when the beneficiary of the award has actually been a victim of illegal discrimination is consistent with the policy behind § 706(g)" which, we noted, "is to provide 'make-whole' relief only to those who have been actual victims of illegal discrimination." Relying on this language, petitioners, joined by the Solicitor General, argue that both the membership goal and the Fund order contravene the policy behind § 706(g) since they extend preferential relief to individuals who were not the actual victims of illegal discrimination. We think this argument both reads *Stotts* too broadly and ignores the important differences between *Stotts* and this case.

Stotts discussed the "policy" behind § 706(g) in order to supplement the holding that the District Court could not have interfered with the city's seniority system in fashioning a Title VII remedy. This "policy" was read to prohibit a court from awarding make-whole relief, such as competitive seniority, backpay, or promotion, to individuals who were denied employment opportunities for reasons unrelated to discrimination. The District Court's injunction was considered to be inconsistent with this "policy" because it was tantamount to an award of make-whole relief (in the form of competitive seniority) to individual black firefighters who had not shown that the proposed layoffs were motivated by racial discrimination.[44] However, this limitation on *individual* make-whole relief does not affect a court's authority to order race-conscious affirmative action. The purpose of affirmative action is not to make identified victims whole, but rather to dismantle prior patterns of employment discrimination and to prevent discrimination in the future. Such relief is provided to the class as a whole rather than to individual members; no individual is entitled to relief, and beneficiaries need not show that they were themselves victims of, discrimination.[45] In this case, neither the membership goal nor the Fund order required the petitioners to indenture or train particular individuals, and neither required them to admit to membership individuals who were refused admission for reasons unrelated to discrimination. We decline petitioners' invitation to read *Stotts* to prohibit a court from ordering any kind of race-conscious affirmative relief that might benefit nonvictims.[46] This reading would distort the language of § 706(g), and

44. We note that, consistent with *Stotts*, the District Court in this case properly limited make-whole relief to the actual victims of discrimination. The court awarded back pay, for example, only to those class members who could establish that they were discriminated against.

45. Even where the district court orders such relief, we note that § 706(g) protects the right of the employer or the union to exclude a particular individual from its workforce or membership for reasons unrelated to discrimination.

46. The Government urged a different interpretation of *Stotts* earlier in this lawsuit. In July 1984, petitioners' counsel, in a letter to the Court of Appeals, argued that *Stotts* "affects the propriety [of the remedies ordered] by the district court." In response, counsel for the EEOC submitted that "the decision in *Stotts* does not affect the disposition of the issues in this appeal." Counsel explained that "the court's discussion [in *Stotts*] of § 706(g) is not relevant to the relief challenged by the appellants since it relates only to the award of retroactive or 'make whole' relief and not to the use of prospective remedies," like those ordered by the District Court. With respect to the last sentence of § 706(g), counsel stated:

"The last sentence of § 706(g) * * * deals with 'make whole' relief and does

would deprive the courts of an important means of enforcing Title VII's guarantee of equal employment opportunity.[47]

E

Although we conclude that § 706(g) does not foreclose a district court from instituting some sorts of racial preferences where necessary to remedy past discrimination, we do not mean to suggest that such relief is always proper. While the fashioning of "appropriate" remedies for a particular Title VII violation invokes the "equitable discretion of the district courts," *Franks,* 424 U.S., at 770, 96 S.Ct., at 1267, we emphasize that a court's judgment should be guided by sound legal principles. In particular, the court should exercise its discretion with an eye towards Congress' concern that race-conscious affirmative measures not be invoked simply to create a racially balanced work force. In the majority of Title VII cases, the court will not have to impose affirmative action as a remedy for past discrimination, but need only order the employer or union to cease engaging in discriminatory practices and award make-whole relief to the individuals victimized by those practices. However, in some cases, affirmative action may be necessary in order effectively to enforce Title VII. As we noted before, a court may have to resort to race-conscious affirmative action when confronted with an employer or labor union that has engaged in persistent or egregious discrimination. Or, such relief may be necessary to dissipate the lingering effects of pervasive discrimination. Whether there might be other circumstances that justify the use of court-ordered affirmative action is a matter that we need not decide here. We note only that a court should consider whether affirmative action is necessary to remedy past discrimination in a particular case before imposing such measures, and that the court should also take care to tailor its orders to fit the nature of the violation it seeks to

not even address prospective relief, let alone state that all prospective remedial orders must be limited so that they only benefit the specific victims of the employer's or union's past discriminatory acts. Moreover, the language and the legislative history of § 706(g) support the Commission's position that carefully tailored prospective race-conscious measures are permissible Title VII remedies. * * * [T]he fact that this interpretation was consistently followed by the Commission and the Department of Justice, during the years immediately following enactment of Title VII entitles the interpretation to great deference."

47. The federal courts have declined to read *Stotts* broadly, and have instead limited the decision to its facts. See Pennsylvania v. International Union of Operating Engineers, 770 F.2d 1068 (CA3 1985), cert. denied 474 U.S. 1060, 106 S.Ct. 803, 88

L.Ed.2d 779 (1986); Paradise v. Prescott, 767 F.2d, at 1527–1530; Turner v. Orr, 759 F.2d 817, 823–826 (CA11 1985); Vanguards of Cleveland v. City of Cleveland, 753 F.2d, at 485–489; Diaz v. American Telephone & Telegraph, 752 F.2d 1356, 1360 n. 5 (CA9 1985); Van Aken v. Young, 750 F.2d 43, 44–45 (CA6 1984); Wygant v. Jackson Bd. of Educ., 746 F.2d 1152, 1157–1159 (CA6 1984), rev'd on other grounds, 476 U.S. 267, 106 S.Ct. 1842, 90 L.Ed.2d 260 (1986); Kromnick v. School Dist. of Philadelphia, 739 F.2d 894, 911 (CA3 1984), cert. denied, 469 U.S. 1107, 105 S.Ct. 782, 83 L.Ed.2d 777 (1985); Grann v. City of Madison, 738 F.2d 786, 795, n. 5(CA7), cert. denied, 469 U.S. 918, 105 S.Ct. 296, 83 L.Ed.2d 231 (1984); Deveraux v. Geary, 596 F.Supp. 1481, 1485–1487 (Mass.1984) aff'd, 765 F.2d 268 (CA1 1985); NAACP v. Detroit Police Officers Assn., 591 F.Supp. 1194, 1202–1203 (ED Mich.1984).

correct.[48] In this case, several factors lead us to conclude that the relief ordered by the District Court was proper.

First, both the District Court and the Court of Appeals agreed that the membership goal and Fund order were necessary to remedy petitioners' pervasive and egregious discrimination. The District Court set the original 29% membership goal upon observing that "[t]he record in both state and federal courts against [petitioners] is replete with instances of their bad faith attempts to prevent or delay affirmative action." The court extended the goal after finding petitioners in contempt for refusing to end their discriminatory practices and failing to comply with various provisions of RAAPO. In affirming the revised membership goal, the Court of Appeals observed that "[t]his court has twice recognized Local 28's long continued and egregious racial discrimination * * * and Local 28 has presented no facts to indicate that our earlier observations are no longer apposite." In light of petitioners' long history of "foot-dragging resistance" to court orders, simply enjoining them from once again engaging in discriminatory practices would clearly have been futile. Rather, the District Court properly determined that affirmative race-conscious measures were necessary to put an end to petitioners' discriminatory ways.

Both the membership goal and Fund order were similarly necessary to combat the lingering effects of past discrimination. In light of the District Court's determination that the union's reputation for discrimination operated to discourage nonwhites from even applying for membership, it is unlikely that an injunction would have been sufficient to extend to nonwhites equal opportunities for employment. Rather, because access to admission, membership, training, and employment in the industry had traditionally been obtained through informal contacts with union members, it was necessary for a substantial number of nonwhite workers to become members of the union in order for the effects of discrimination to cease. The Fund, in particular, was designed to insure that nonwhites would receive the kind of assistance that white apprentices and applicants had traditionally received through informal sources. On the facts of this case, the District Court properly determined that affirmative, race-conscious measures were necessary to assure the equal employment opportunities guaranteed by Title VII.

Second, the District Court's flexible application of the membership goal gives strong indication that it is not being used simply to achieve and maintain racial balance, but rather as a benchmark against which

---

48. This cautious approach to the use of racial preferences has been followed by the Courts of Appeals. As one commentator has noted:

"While the circuit courts of appeals have indicated that they possess [the] power [to award race-conscious affirmative relief], they have been reluctant to exercise it. The federal appellate courts have preferred to issue less harsh orders such as recruiting and posting of notices of vacancies. They have tended to impose hiring orders only after employer recalcitrance has been demonstrated." Blumrosen, 34 Rutgers L.Rev., at 41.

the court could gauge petitioners' efforts to remedy past discrimination. The court has twice adjusted the deadline for achieving the goal, and has continually approved of changes in the size of the apprenticeship classes to account for the fact that economic conditions prevented petitioners from meeting their membership targets; there is every reason to believe that both the court and the administrator will continue to accommodate *legitimate* explanations for the petitioners' failure to comply with the court's orders. Moreover, the District Court expressly disavowed any reliance on petitioners' failure to meet the goal as a basis for the contempt finding, but instead viewed this failure as symptomatic of petitioners' refusal to comply with various subsidiary provisions of RAAPO. In sum, the District Court has implemented the membership goal as a means by which it can measure petitioners' compliance with its orders, rather than as a strict racial quota.[49]

Third, both the membership goal and the Fund order are temporary measures. Under AAAPO "[p]referential selection of union members [w]ill end as soon as the percentage of [minority union members] approximates the percentage of [minorities] in the local labor force." *Weber,* 443 U.S., at 208–209, 99 S.Ct., at 2730. Similarly, the Fund is scheduled to terminate when petitioners achieve the membership goal, and the court determines that it is no longer needed to remedy past discrimination. The District Court's orders thus operate "as a temporary tool for remedying past discrimination without attempting to 'maintain' a previously achieved balance." *Weber,* supra, at 216, 99 S.Ct., at 2734 (Blackmun, J., concurring).

Finally, we think it significant that neither the membership goal nor the Fund order "unnecessarily trammel the interests of white employees." Id., 443 U.S., at 208, 99 S.Ct., at 2730; *Teamsters,* 431 U.S., at 352–353, 97 S.Ct., at 1863–1864. Petitioners concede that the District Court's orders did not require any member of the union to be laid off, and did not discriminate against *existing* union members. See *Weber,* supra, 443 U.S., at 208, 99 S.Ct., at 2729–2730. While whites

---

49. Other factors support the finding that the membership goal has not been applied as a strict racial quota. For example, the Court of Appeals has twice struck down provisions requiring petitioners to indenture one nonwhite apprentice for each white apprentice indentured. Petitioners, however, characterize the following comments by the District Court as evidence that the 29.23% membership goal is in reality an inflexible quota:

"Although defendants were given seven years to attain [the 29% membership] goal * * * they have not. Indeed, they have a long way to go. In addition, they consistently have violated numerous court orders that were designed to assist in the achievement of that goal. The court therefore sees no reason to be lenient with defendants, for whatever rea-

son, and orders that the * * * merged locals must reach a nonwhite membership of 29.23% by August 31, 1987. If the goal is not attained by that date, defendants will face fines that will threaten their very existence."

The District Court's comments express the understandable frustration of a court faced with 15 years of petitioners' deliberate resistance to ending discrimination. We do not view these statements as evidence that the court intends to apply the nonwhite membership goal as an inflexible quota. The record shows that the District Court has been willing to accommodate *legitimate* reasons for petitioners' failure to comply with court orders, and we have no reason to expect that this will change in the future.

seeking admission into the union may be denied benefits extended to their nonwhite counterparts, the court's orders do not stand as an absolute bar to such individuals; indeed, a majority of new union members have been white. Many provisions of the court's orders are race-neutral (for example, the requirement that the JAC assign one apprentice for every four journeymen workers), and petitioners remain free to adopt the provisions of AAAPO and the Fund Order for the benefit of white members and applicants.

V

Petitioners also allege that the membership goal and Fund order contravene the equal protection component of the Due Process Clause of the Fifth Amendment because they deny benefits to white individuals based on race. We have consistently recognized that government bodies constitutionally may adopt racial classifications as a remedy for past discrimination. See Wygant v. Jackson Board of Education, 476 U.S. 267, 106 S.Ct. 1842, 90 L.Ed.2d 260 (1986); Fullilove v. Klutznick, 448 U.S. 448, 100 S.Ct. 2758, 65 L.Ed.2d 902 (1980); University of California Regents v. Bakke, 438 U.S. 265, 98 S.Ct. 2733, 57 L.Ed.2d 750 (1978); Swann v. Charlotte–Mecklenburg Board of Education, 402 U.S. 1, 91 S.Ct. 1267, 28 L.Ed.2d 554 (1971). We have not agreed however, on the proper test to be applied in analyzing the constitutionality of race-conscious remedial measures. See *Wygant,* 476 U.S., at 274, 106 S.Ct., at 1847 (opinion of Powell, J.) (means chosen must be "narrowly tailored" to achieve "compelling government interest"); id., at 284–287, 106 S.Ct., at 1852 (O'Connor, J., concurring); id., at 301–302, 106 S.Ct., at 1861–1862 (Marshall, J., dissenting); id., at 313, 106 S.Ct., at 1867 (Stevens, J., dissenting) (public interest served by racial classification and means pursued must justify adverse effects on the disadvantaged group); *Fullilove,* supra, 448 U.S., at 491, 100 S.Ct., at 2781 (opinion of Burger, C.J.) (racial preferences subject to "a most searching examination"); id., at 519, 100 S.Ct., at 2795–2796 (Marshall, J., concurring in the judgment) (remedial use of race must be substantially related to achievement of important governmental objectives); *Bakke,* supra, 438 U.S., at 305, 98 S.Ct., at 2756 (opinion of Powell, J.) (racial classification must be necessary to accomplishment of substantial state interest); id., at 359, 98 S.Ct., at 2783 (opinion of Brennan, White, Marshall and Blackmun, JJ.) (remedial use of race must be substantially related to achievement of important governmental objectives). We need not resolve this dispute here, since we conclude that the relief ordered in this case passes even the most rigorous test—it is narrowly tailored to further the Government's compelling interest in remedying past discrimination.

In this case, there is no problem, as there was in *Wygant,* with a proper showing of prior discrimination that would justify the use of remedial racial classifications. Both the District Court and Court of Appeals have repeatedly found petitioners guilty of egregious violations of Title VII, and have determined that affirmative measures were necessary to remedy their racially discriminatory practices. More importantly, the District Court's orders were properly tailored to accomplish this objective. First, the District Court considered the efficacy of alternative remedies, and concluded that, in light of petitioners' long record of resistance to official efforts to end their discriminatory practices, stronger measures were necessary. The court devised the temporary membership goal and the Fund as tools for remedying past discrimination. More importantly, the District Court's orders will have only a marginal impact on the interests of white workers. Again, petitioners concede that the District Court's orders did not disadvantage *existing* union members. While white applicants for union membership may be denied certain benefits available to their nonwhite counterparts, the court's orders do not stand as an absolute bar to the admission of such individuals; again, a majority of those entering the union after entry of the court's orders have been white. We therefore conclude that the District Court's orders do not violate the equal protection safeguards of the Constitution.[50]

VI

Finally, Local 28 challenges the District Court's appointment of an administrator with broad powers to supervise its compliance with the court's orders as an unjustifiable interference with its statutory right to self-governance. See 29 U.S.C. § 401(a). Preliminarily, we note that while AAAPO gives the administrator broad powers to oversee petitioners' membership practices, Local 28 retains complete control over its other affairs. Even with respect to membership, the administrator's job is to insure that petitioners comply with the court's orders and admit sufficient numbers of nonwhites; the administrator does not select the particular individuals that will be admitted, that task is left to union officials. In any event, in light of the difficulties inherent in monitoring compliance with the court's orders, and especially petitioners' established record of resistance to prior state and federal court orders designed to end their discriminatory membership practices, appointment of an administrator was well within the District Court's discretion. See Fed.Rule Civ. Proc. 53. While the administrator may substantially interfere with petitioners' membership operations, such "interference" is necessary to put an end to petitioners' discriminatory ways.

VII

To summarize our holding today, six members of the Court agree that a district court may, in appropriate circumstances, order preferential relief benefitting individuals who are not the actual victims of discrimination as a remedy for violations of Title VII, see supra, Parts

---

50. Petitioners also argue that "the construction of Title VII adopted by the Court of Appeals has the effect of making the Civil Rights Act an unconstitutional bill of attainder, visiting upon white persons the sins of past discrimination by others." We reject this contention as without merit.

IV–A—IV–D (opinion of BRENNAN, J., joined by Marshall, J., Blackmun, J., and Stevens, J.); post, at 1054 (Powell, J., concurring in part and concurring in the judgment); post, at 1063 (White, J., dissenting), that the District Court did not use incorrect statistical evidence in establishing petitioners' nonwhite membership goal, see supra, Part II–A, that the contempt fines and Fund order were proper remedies for civil contempt, see supra, Part III, and that the District Court properly appointed an administrator to supervise petitioners' compliance with the court's orders, see supra Part VI. Five members of the Court agree that in this case, the District Court did not err in evaluating petitioners' utilization of the apprenticeship program, see supra, Part II–B, and that the membership goal and the Fund order are not violative of either Title VII or the Constitution, see supra, Parts IV–E, V (opinion of Brennan, J., joined by Marshall, J., Blackmun, J., and Stevens, J.); post, at 1054 (Powell, J., concurring in part and concurring in the judgment). The judgment of the Court of Appeals is hereby

Affirmed.

JUSTICE POWELL, concurring in part and concurring in the judgment.

I join Parts I, II, III, and VI of Justice Brennan's opinion. I further agree that § 706(g) does not limit a court in all cases to granting relief only to actual victims of discrimination. I write separately * * * to explain why I think the remedy ordered under the circumstances of this case [did not violate] the Constitution.

I

* * * I have recently reiterated what I believe to be the standard for assessing a constitutional challenge to a racial classification:

> " 'Any preference based on racial or ethnic criteria must necessarily receive a most searching examination to make sure that it does not conflict with constitutional guarantees.' Fullilove v. Klutznick, 448 U.S. 448, 491 (100 S.Ct. 2758, 2781, 65 L.Ed.2d 902) (1980) (opinion of Burger, C.J.). There are two prongs to this examination. First, any racial classification 'must be justified by a compelling governmental interest' Palmore v. Sidoti, 466 U.S. 429, 432 (104 S.Ct. 1879, 1882, 80 L.Ed.2d 421) (1984); see Loving v. Virginia, 388 U.S. 1, 11 (87 S.Ct. 1817, 1823, 18 L.Ed.2d 1010) (1967); cf. Graham v. Richardson, 403 U.S. 365, 375 (91 S.Ct. 1848, 1853–1854, 29 L.Ed.2d 534) (1971) (alienage). Second, the means chosen by the State to effectuate its purpose must be 'narrowly tailored to the achievement of that goal.' *Fullilove,* supra, 448 U.S., at 480 (100 S.Ct., at 2776)." Wygant v. Jackson Board of Education, 476 U.S. 267, 273–274, 106 S.Ct. 1842, 1846, 90 L.Ed.2d 260 (1986).

The finding by the District Court and the Court of Appeals that petitioners have engaged in egregious violations of Title VII establishes, without doubt, a compelling governmental interest sufficient to justify the imposition of a racially classified remedy. It would be difficult to find defendants more determined to discriminate against minorities. My inquiry, therefore, focuses on whether the District Court's remedy is "narrowly tailored," to the goal of eradicating the discrimination engaged in by petitioners. I believe it is.

The Fund order is supported not only by the governmental interest in eradicating petitioners' discriminatory practices, it also is supported by the societal interest in compliance with the judgments of federal courts. The Fund order was not imposed until *after* petitioners were held in contempt. In requiring the Union to create the Fund, the District Court expressly considered " 'the consequent seriousness of the burden' to the defendants." Moreover, the focus of the Fund order was to give minorities opportunities that for years had been available informally only to nonminorities. The burden this imposes on nonminorities is slight. Under these circumstances, I have little difficulty concluding that the Fund order was carefully structured to vindicate the compelling governmental interests present in this case.

The percentage goal raises a different question. In Fullilove v. Klutznick, 448 U.S. 448, 100 S.Ct. 2758, 65 L.Ed.2d 902 (1980), this Court upheld the constitutionality of the "minority business enterprise" provision of the Public Works Employment Act of 1977, which required, absent administrative waiver, that at least 10% of federal funds granted for local public works projects be used by grantees to procure services or supplies from businesses owned by minority group members. In my concurring opinion, I relied on four factors that had been applied by courts of appeals when considering the proper scope of race-conscious hiring remedies. Those factors were: (i) the efficacy of alternative remedies; (ii) the planned duration of the remedy; (iii) the relationship between the percentage of minority workers to be employed and the percentage of minority group members in the relevant population or work force; and (iv) the availability of waiver provisions if the hiring plan could not be met. A final factor of primary importance that I considered in *Fullilove,* as well as in *Wygant,* was "the effect of the [remedy] upon innocent third-parties." Application of those factors demonstrates that the goal in this case comports with constitutional requirements.

First, it is doubtful, given petitioners' history in this litigation, that the District Court had available to it any other effective remedy. That court, having had the parties before it over a period of time, was in the best position to judge whether an alternative remedy, such as a simple injunction, would have been effective in ending petitioners' discriminatory practices. Here, the court imposed the 29% goal in 1975 only after declaring that "[i]n light of Local 28's and JAC's failure to 'clean house' this court concludes that the imposition of a remedial racial goal * * * is essential to place the defendants in a position of compliance with the 1964 Civil Rights Act." On these facts, it is fair to conclude that absent authority to set a goal as a benchmark against which it could measure progress in eliminating discriminatory practices, the District Court may have been powerless to provide an effective remedy. Second, the goal was not imposed as a permanent requirement, but is of limited duration. Third, the goal is directly related to the percentage of nonwhites in the relevant workforce.

As a fourth factor, my concurring opinion in *Fullilove* considered whether waiver provisions were available in the event that the hiring goal could not be met. The requirement of a waiver provision or, more generally, of flexibility with respect to the imposition of a numerical goal reflects a recognition that neither the Constitution or Title VII requires a particular racial balance in the workplace. Indeed, the Constitution forbids such a requirement if imposed for its own sake. *Fullilove,* supra, 448 U.S., at 507, 100 S.Ct., at 2789–2790. "We have recognized, however, that in order to remedy the effects of prior discrimination, it may be necessary to take race into account." *Wygant,* supra, at 106 S.Ct., at 1850. Thus, a court may not choose a remedy for the purpose of attaining a particular racial balance; rather, remedies properly are confined to the elimination of proven discrimination. A goal is a means, useful in limited circumstances, to assist a court in determining whether discrimination has been eradicated.

The flexible application of the goal requirement in this case demonstrates that it is not a means to achieve racial balance. The contempt order was not imposed for the Union's failure to achieve the goal, but for its failure to take the prescribed steps that would facilitate achieving the goal. Additional flexibility is evidenced by the fact that this goal, originally set to be achieved by 1981, has been twice delayed and is now set for 1987.

It is also important to emphasize that on the record before us, it does not appear that nonminorities will be burdened directly, if at all. Petitioners' counsel conceded at oral argument that imposition of the goal would not require the layoff of nonminority union workers, and that therefore the District Court's order did not disadvantage existing union members. This case is thus distinguishable from *Wygant* where the plurality opinion noted that "layoffs impose the entire burden of achieving racial equality on particular individuals, often resulting in serious disruption of their lives." In contrast to the layoff provision in *Wygant,* the goal at issue here is akin to a hiring goal. In *Wygant* the plurality observed:

> "In cases involving valid *hiring* goals, the burden to be borne by individuals is diffused to a considerable extent among society generally. Though hiring goals may burden some innocent individuals, they simply do not impose the same kind of injury that layoffs impose." Id., at 14.[3]

---

3. Of course, it is too simplistic to conclude from the combined holdings in *Wygant* and this case that hiring goals withstand constitutional muster whereas layoff goals and fixed quotas do not. There may be cases, for example, where a hiring goal in a particularly specialized area of employment would have the same pernicious effect as the layoff goal in *Wygant.* The proper constitutional inquiry focuses on

My view that the imposition of flexible goals as a remedy for past discrimination may be permissible under the Constitution is not an endorsement of their indiscriminate use. Nor do I imply that the adoption of such a goal will always pass constitutional muster.[4]

Justice O'Connor, concurring in part and dissenting in part.

I join Parts II–A, III, and VI of the Court's opinion. I would reverse the judgment of the Court of Appeals on statutory grounds insofar as the membership "goal" and the Fund order are concerned, and I would not reach petitioners' constitutional claims. I agree with Justice White, however, that the membership "goal" in this case operates as a rigid racial quota that cannot feasibly be met through good-faith efforts by Local 28. In my view, § 703(j), and § 706(g), read together, preclude courts from ordering racial quotas such as this. I therefore dissent from the Court's judgment insofar as it affirms the use of these mandatory quotas.

In Firefighters v. Stotts, 467 U.S. 561, 104 S.Ct. 2576, 81 L.Ed.2d 483 (1984), the Court interpreted § 706(g) as embodying a policy against court-ordered remedies under Title VII that award racial preferences in employment to individuals who have not been subjected to unlawful discrimination. The dissenting opinion in *Stotts* urged precisely the position advanced by Justice Brennan's plurality opinion today—that any such policy extends only to awarding make-whole relief to particular non-victims of discrimination, and does not bar class-wide racial preferences in certain cases. Id., at 612–614, 104 S.Ct., at 2605–2607 (Blackmun, J., dissenting). The Court unquestionably rejected that view in *Stotts*. Although technically dicta, the discussion of § 706(g) in *Stotts* was an important part of the Court's rationale for the result it reached, and accordingly is entitled to greater weight than the Court gives it today.

It is now clear, however, that a majority of the Court believes that the last sentence of § 706(g) does not in all circumstances prohibit a court in a Title VII employment discrimination case from ordering relief that may confer some racial preferences with regard to employment in favor of non-victims of discrimination. Even assuming that some forms of race-conscious affirmative relief, such as racial hiring goals, are permissible as remedies for egregious and pervasive violations of Title VII, in my view the membership "goal" and fund order in

the effect, if any, and the diffuseness of the burden imposed on innocent nonminorities, not on the label applied to the particular employment plan at issue.

4. If the record now before us supported the position taken by Justice O'Connor, I might well view this case differently. Justice O'Connor apparently assumes that the goal can be achieved by August 31, 1987, only if the District Court requires "the replacement of journeymen by apprentices on a strictly racial basis." If and when

that happens, petitioners will be free to argue that an impermissible quota has been imposed on the union and the JAC. An examination of what *has occurred* in this litigation over the years makes plain that the District Court has not enforced the goal in the rigid manner that concerns Justice O'Connor. Based on the record actually before us, I am satisfied that the goal imposed by the District Court is a flexible one.

this case were impermissible because they operate not as goals but as racial quotas. Such quotas run counter to § 703(j) of Title VII, and are thus impermissible under § 706(g) when that section is read in light of § 703(j), as I believe it should be.

The plurality asserts that § 703(j) in no way "qualifies or proscribes a court's authority to order relief otherwise appropriate under § 706(g) in circumstances where an illegal discriminatory act or practice is established." According to the plurality, § 703(j) merely provides that an employer or union does not engage in unlawful discrimination simply on account of a racial imbalance in its workforce or membership, and thus is not required to institute preferential quotas to avoid Title VII liability. Thus, the plurality concedes that § 703(j) is aimed at racial quotas, but interprets it as limiting only the substantive liability of employers and unions, not the remedial powers of courts.

This interpretation of § 703(j) is unduly narrow. * * *

In Steelworkers v. Weber, 443 U.S. 193, 205 n. 5, 99 S.Ct. 2721, 2728, n. 5, 61 L.Ed.2d 480 (1979) the Court stated that "Section 703(j) speaks to substantive liability under Title VII." While this is *one* purpose of § 703(j), the Court in *Weber* had no occasion to consider whether it was the *exclusive* purpose. In my view, the words "Nothing contained in this title shall be interpreted to require" plainly make § 703(j) applicable to the interpretation of *any* provision of Title VII, including § 706(g). Therefore, when a court interprets § 706(g) as authorizing it to require an employer to adopt a racial quota, that court contravenes § 703(j) to the extent that the relief imposed as a purported remedy for a violation of Title VII's substantive provisions in fact operates to require racial preferences "on account of [a racial] imbalance." In addition, since § 703(j) by its terms limits the circumstances in which an employer or union may be required to extend "preferential treatment to any individual *or to any group* because of * * * race," the plurality's distinction between make-whole and class-wide relief is plainly ruled out insofar as § 703(j) is concerned.

The plurality's restrictive reading of § 703(j) rests largely on its view of the legislative history, which the plurality claims establishes that Congress simply did not consider the use of racial preferences to remedy past discrimination when it enacted Title VII. According to the plurality, the sole focus of concern over racial quotas involved the scope of substantive liability under Title VII: the fear was that employers or unions would be found liable for violating Title VII merely on account of a racial imbalance. This reading of the legislative history ignores authoritative statements—relied on by the Court in *Stotts*, supra, 467 U.S., at 580–582, 104 S.Ct., at 2589–2590—addressing the relief courts could order, and making plain that racial *quotas*, at least, were not among the permissible remedies for past discrimination. See, e.g., 110 Cong.Rec. 6549 (1964) ("Contrary to the allegations of some opponents of this title, there is nothing in it that will give any power to the Commission or to any court to require hiring, firing, or promotion of employees in order to meet a racial 'quota' or to achieve a certain racial balance") (Sen. Humphrey); id., at 6566 ("[T]itle VII does not permit the ordering of racial quotas in businesses or unions * * *.") (memorandum of Republican House sponsors); id., at 14665 ("under title VII, not even a court, much less the Commission, could order racial quotas or the hiring, reinstatement, admission to membership or payment of back pay for anyone who is not discriminated against in violation of this title") (statement of Senate sponsors in a bipartisan newsletter delivered to Senators supporting the bill during an attempted filibuster).

The plurality's reading of the legislative history also defies common sense. Legislators who objected to racial quotas obviously did so because of the harm that such quotas would impose on innocent nonminority workers as well as because of the restriction on employer freedom that would follow from an across-the-board requirement of racial balance in every workplace. Racial quotas would inflict such harms on nonminority workers whether such quotas were imposed directly by federal law in the form of a requirement that every workforce be racially balanced, or imposed as part of a court-ordered remedy for an employer's violations of Title VII. The legislative history, fairly read, indicates that such racial quotas are impermissible as a means of enforcing Title VII, and that even racial preferences short of quotas should be used only where clearly necessary if these preferences would benefit nonvictims at the expense of innocent nonminority workers.

At bottom, the plurality recognizes that this is so, although it prefers to cut the congressional rejection of racial quotas loose from any statutory moorings and make this policy simply another factor that should inform the remedial discretion of district courts. Indeed, notwithstanding its claim that § 703(j) is irrelevant to interpretation of § 706(g), the plurality tacitly concedes that racial quotas are improper, and that they are improper by virtue of § 703(j). The plurality says that in considering whether to grant race-conscious affirmative relief "the court should exercise its discretion with an eye towards Congress' concern that race-conscious affirmative measures not be invoked simply to create a racially balanced work force." Since this is precisely the congressional concern that the plurality locates in § 703(j), the plurality appears to recognize that § 703(j) *is* relevant, after all, to the choice of remedies under § 706(g). Moreover, the plurality indicates that a hiring or membership goal must be applied flexibly in order that the goal not be "used simply to achieve and maintain racial balance, but rather as a benchmark against which the court [can] gauge [an employer's or union's] efforts to remedy past discrimination." It is fair to infer that the plurality approves the use of the membership goal in this case only because, in its view, that goal can be characterized as "a means by which [the court] can measure petitioners' compliance with its orders, rather than as a strict racial quota."

The plurality correctly indicates that, as to any racial goal ordered by a court as a remedy for past discrimination, the employer *always* has a potential defense by virtue of § 706(g) against a claim that it was required to hire a particular employee, to wit, that the employee was not hired for "reasons unrelated to discrimination." Although the plurality gives no clues as to the scope of this defense, it is clear that an employer would remain free to refuse to hire unqualified minority applicants, even if as a result the employer failed to meet a racial hiring goal. Thus, an employer's undoubted freedom to refuse to hire unqualified minority applicants, even in the face of a court-ordered racial hiring goal, operates as one important limitation on the extent of any racially preferential treatment that can result from such a goal.

The plurality offers little guidance as to what separates an impermissible quota from a permissible goal. Reference to benchmarks such as the percentage of minority workers in the relevant labor pool will often be entirely proper in order to *estimate* how an employer's workforce would be composed absent past discrimination. But it is completely unrealistic to assume that individuals of each race will gravitate with mathematical exactitude to each employer or union absent unlawful discrimination. That, of course, is why there must be a substantial statistical disparity between the composition of an employer's workforce and the relevant labor pool, or the general population, before an intent to discriminate may be inferred from such a disparity. Teamsters v. United States, 431 U.S. 324, 339–340, and n. 20, 97 S.Ct. 1843, 1856–1857, and n. 20, 52 L.Ed.2d 396 (1977). Thus, the use of a rigid quota turns a sensible rule of thumb into an unjustified conclusion about the precise extent to which past discrimination has lingering effects, or into an unjustified prediction about what would happen in the future in the absence of continuing discrimination. The imposition of a quota is therefore not truly remedial, but rather amounts to a requirement of racial balance, in contravention of § 703(j)'s clear policy against such requirements.

To be consistent with § 703(j), a racial hiring or membership goal must be intended to serve merely as a benchmark for measuring compliance with Title VII and eliminating the lingering effects of past discrimination, rather than as a rigid numerical requirement that must unconditionally be met on pain of sanctions. To hold an employer or union to achievement of a particular percentage of minority employment or membership, and to do so regardless of circumstances such as economic conditions or the number of available qualified minority applicants, is to impose an impermissible quota. By contrast, a permissible goal should require only a good faith effort on the employer's or union's part to come within a range demarcated by the goal itself.

This understanding of the difference between goals and quotas essentially comports with the definitions jointly adopted by the EEOC and the Departments of Justice and Labor in a 1973 memorandum, and reaffirmed on several occasions since then by the EEOC and the

Department of Labor. Memorandum—Permissible Goals and Timetables in State and Local Government Employment Practices (Mar. 23, 1973), reprinted in 2 CCH Employment Practices ¶ 3776 (1985) (hereinafter Memorandum); see 41 Fed.Reg. 38815 (1976) (EEOC Policy Statement on Affirmative Action Programs for State and Local Government Agencies); Office of Federal Contract Compliance Programs v. Priester Construction Co., No. 78–OFCCP–11 (Feb. 22, 1983), summarized in OFCCP Order No. 970a3, reprinted in 2 BNA AACM D:9121 (1983). In the view of these federal agencies, which are charged with responsibility for enforcing equal employment opportunity laws, a quota "would impose a fixed number or percentage which must be attained, or which cannot be exceeded," and would do so "regardless of the number of potential applicants who meet necessary qualifications." Memorandum, 2 CCH Employment Practices, at 3856. By contrast, a goal is "a numerical objective, fixed realistically in terms of the number of vacancies expected, and the number of qualified applicants available in the relevant job market." Ibid. An employer's failure to meet a goal despite good faith efforts "is not subject to sanction, because [the employer] is not expected to displace existing employees or to hire unneeded employees to meet [the] goal." Ibid. This understanding of the difference between goals and quotas seems to me workable and far more consistent with the policy underlying § 703(j) and § 706(g) than the plurality's forced distinction between make-whole relief and class-wide relief. If, then, some racial preferences may be ordered by a court as a remedy for past discrimination even though the beneficiaries may be nonvictims, I would employ a distinction such as this between quotas and goals in setting standards to inform use by district courts of their remedial powers under § 706(g) to fashion such relief.

If, as the Court holds, Title VII sometimes allows district courts to employ race-conscious remedies that may result in racially preferential treatment for non-victims, it does so only where such remedies are truly necessary. In fashioning any such remedy, including racial hiring goals, the court should exercise caution and "take care to tailor its orders to fit the nature of the violation it seeks to correct." As the plurality suggests, goals should generally be temporary measures rather than efforts to maintain a previously achieved racial balance, and should not unnecessarily trammel the interests of nonminority employees. Furthermore, the use of goals is least likely to be consistent with § 703(j) where the adverse effects of any racially preferential treatment attributable to the goals will be "concentrated upon a relatively small, ascertainable group of non-minority persons." In sum, the creation of racial preferences by courts, even in the more limited form of goals rather than quotas, must be done sparingly and only where manifestly necessary to remedy violations of Title VII if the policy underlying § 703(j) and § 706(g) is to be honored.

In this case, I agree with Justice White that the membership "goal" established by the District Court's successive orders in this case has been administered and will continue to operate "not just [as] a minority membership goal but also [as] a strict racial quota that the union was required to attain." It is important to realize that the membership "goal" ordered by the District Court goes well beyond a requirement, such as the ones the plurality discusses approvingly, that a union "admit qualified minorities roughly in proportion to the number of qualified minorities in the work force." The "goal" here requires that the racial composition of Local 28's entire membership mirror that of the relevant labor pool by August 31, 1987, without regard to variables such as the number of qualified minority applicants available or the number of new apprentices needed. The District Court plainly stated that "[i]f the goal is not attained by that date, defendants will face fines that will threaten their very existence."

I see no reason not to take the District Court's mandatory language at face value, and certainly none is supplied by the plurality's conclusory assertion that "the District Court has been willing to accommodate *legitimate* reasons for petitioners' failure to comply with court orders." As Judge Winter persuasively argued in dissent below, the District Court was clearly *not* willing to take due account of the economic conditions that led to a sharp decline in the demand for the union skills involved in this case. Indeed, notwithstanding that petitioners have "voluntarily indentured 45% nonwhites in the apprenticeship classes since January 1981," the District Court ordered the JAC to indenture one nonwhite apprentice for every white apprentice. 753 F.2d, at 1189. The Court of Appeals set this portion of the District Court's order aside as an abuse of discretion, ibid., but the District Court's willingness to impose such a rigid hiring quota certainly suggests that the District Court intended the membership "goal" to be equally absolute.

It is no answer to these observations that the District Court on two previous occasions postponed the final date for full compliance with the membership goal. At the time of the Court of Appeals' decision, Local 28's membership was approximately 10.8% nonwhite, and at oral argument counsel for petitioners represented that Local 28's membership of about 3,100 workers is now approximately 15.5% nonwhite. Absent an enormous expansion in the size of the apprentice program—which would be feasible only if the demand for the services of Local 28's members were dramatically to increase—it is beyond cavil that neither the "voluntary" 45% minority ratio now employed for apprenticeship classes nor the District Court's one-to-one order could achieve the 29.23% membership goal by Aug. 31, 1987. Indeed, at oral argument counsel for respondent conceded as much.

I do not question that petitioners' past violations of Title VII were egregious, or that in some respects they exhibited inexcusable recalcitrance in the face of the District Court's earlier remedial orders. But the timetable with which petitioners were ordered to comply was quite unrealistic and clearly could not be met by good-faith efforts on petitioners' part. In sum, the membership goal operates as a rigid membership quota, which will in turn spawn a sharp curtailment in the opportunities of nonminorities to be admitted to the apprenticeship program. Indeed, in order for the District Court's timetable to be met, this fixed quota would appear to require "the replacement of journeymen by apprentices on a strictly racial basis." 753 F.2d, at 1195 (Winter, J., dissenting).

Whether the unequivocal rejection of racial quotas by the Congress that enacted Title VII is said to be expressed in § 706(g), in § 703(j), or in both, a "remedy" such as this membership quota cannot stand. For similar reasons, I believe that the Fund order, which created benefits for minority apprentices that nonminority apprentices were precluded from enjoying, operated as a form of racial quota. Accordingly, I would reverse the judgment of the Court of Appeals on statutory grounds insofar as the membership "goal" and Fund order are concerned, without reaching petitioners' constitutional claims.

JUSTICE WHITE, dissenting.

As the Court observes, the general policy under Title VII is to limit relief for racial discrimination in employment practices to actual victims of the discrimination. But I agree that § 706(g) does not bar relief for nonvictims in all circumstances. Hence, I generally agree with Parts I through IV–D of the Court's opinion. It may also be that this is one of those unusual cases where nonvictims of discrimination were entitled to a measure of the relief ordered by the District Court and affirmed by the Court of Appeals. But Judge Winter, in dissent below, was correct in concluding that critical parts of the remedy ordered in this case were excessive under § 706(g), absent findings that those benefiting from the relief had been victims of discriminatory practices by the union. As Judge Winter explained and contrary to the Court's views, the cumulative effect of the revised affirmative action plan and the contempt judgments against the union established not just a minority membership goal but also a strict racial quota that the union was required to attain. We have not heretofore approved this kind of racially discriminatory hiring practice, and I would not do so now. Beyond this, I am convinced, as Judge Winter was, that holding the union in contempt for failing to attain the membership quota during a time of economic doldrums in the construction industry and a declining demand for the union skills involved in this case was for all practical purposes equivalent to a judicial insistence that the union comply even if it required the displacement of nonminority workers by members of the plaintiff class. The remedy is inequitable in my view, and for this reason I dissent from the judgment affirming the Court of Appeals.

JUSTICE REHNQUIST, with whom THE CHIEF JUSTICE joins, dissenting.

Today, in Local Number 93 v. City of Cleveland, (REHNQUIST, J., dissenting), I express my belief that § 706(g) forbids a court from ordering racial preferences that effectively displace non-minorities except to minority individuals who have been the actual victims of a particular employer's racial discrimination. Although the pervasiveness of the racial discrimination practiced by a particular union or employer is likely to increase the number of victims who are entitled to a remedy under the Act, § 706(g) does not allow us to go further than that and sanction the granting of relief to those who were not victims at the expense of innocent non-minority workers injured by racial preferences. I explain that both the language and the legislative history of § 706(g) clearly support this reading of § 706(g), and that this Court stated as much just two Terms ago in Firefighters v. Stotts, 467 U.S. 561, 104 S.Ct. 2576, 81 L.Ed.2d 483 (1984). Because of this, I would not reach the equal protection question, but would rely solely on § 706(g) to reverse the Court of Appeals' judgment approving the order of class-based relief for petitioners' past discrimination.

NOTES AND PROBLEMS FOR DISCUSSION

1. The opinions written by Justices Brennan and Powell state that an employer cannot be found in violation of Title VII "simply" because of a racial imbalance in its workforce and, therefore, that racial preferences cannot be imposed solely for the purpose of attaining or maintaining racial balance. Nevertheless, the opinions continue, racial preferences can be ordered by the courts as remedies for Title VII violations. But if racial imbalance is not *per se* violative of Title VII, i.e., if discrimination means something more than the mere fact of imbalance, should racial balance constitute the objective of a remedy for discrimination? Is that the effect of including a specific numerical hiring or promotion goal in a court ordered affirmative action plan? Or is the Court using a numerical goal merely as a gauge by which it can measure the nondiscriminatory effect of the defendant's future personnel policy? Yet, if discrimination is not to be measured solely by the level of racial representation, should the effectiveness of efforts to remedy discrimination be gauged by racial proportionality?

2. The Court interpreted the last sentence of § 706(g) as permitting the awarding of race-conscious affirmative relief that might benefit non-victims as long as that relief was designed to remedy prior discrimination. In footnote 45, however, the Court added that specific individuals could be precluded from such relief where they are proven non-victims, i.e., where action taken against them was proven to be unrelated to discrimination. Yet if, as the Court also indicated, affirmative action is designed "to dismantle prior patterns of employment discrimination and to prevent discrimination in the future" and "is provided to the class as a whole rather than to individual members", is there a justification for distinguishing between proven and unproven non-victims? Does Justice O'Connor's opinion shed light on this question?

Note that on this critical question of whether a court can order race-conscious relief that might benefit non-victims, six members (Brennan, Marshall, Blackmun, Stevens, Powell and White) agreed that "in appropriate circumstances", Title VII would not preclude such relief. Only Justice Rehnquist and Chief Justice Burger agreed with the Solicitor General's contention that Title VII relief must be limited to proven victims of discrimination. Note that while Justice O'Connor concluded that the goal and Fund in this case exceeded the statutory limits on the court's remedial authority, she carefully avoided ruling on whether a Title VII remedy could ever provide relief to non-victims.

3. Justice Powell upheld the trial court's order, at least in part, because he concluded that incumbent nonminority workers would not be burdened directly, if at all, by the race-based hiring goal. Justices O'Connor and White, on the other hand, maintained that the plan would result in a "sharp curtailment in the opportunities of nonminorities to be admitted to the apprenticeship program." Justice Brennan, writing for the Court, concluded that while incumbents would not suffer any disadvantage under the challenged plan, whites seeking admission into the union might be temporarily disadvantaged in favor of minority candidates. What is the significance of this difference of opinion?

4. Do the opinions in *Local 28* reflect a consensus on the issue of whether court ordered affirmative action can respond to societal discrimination? The plurality opinion states that race-conscious relief "may be appropriate where an employer or a labor union has engaged in persistent or egregious discrimination, *or where necessary to dissipate the lingering effects of pervasive discrimination.*" (emphasis added). Justice Powell, whose critical swing vote produced a majority in favor of upholding the judgments below, while concentrating on the constitutional question, said only that such relief was permitted under Title VII "in cases involving particularly egregious conduct." Justice O'Connor declared that "assuming that some forms of race-conscious affirmative relief, such as racial hiring goals, are permissible as remedies for egregious and pervasive violations", such relief must be intended to serve as a benchmark for "eliminating the lingering effects of past discrimination." Justice White "agreed generally" with the plurality's statement on the issue. Justice Rehnquist and the Chief Justice dissented on the ground that affirmative relief that effectively displaced nonminority individuals could be awarded only to "actual victims of a particular employer's racial discrimination." The Court did address the issue of the propriety of voluntarily adopted affirmative responses to societal discrimination in *Weber* and *Wygant, infra.*

5. The legislative debates surrounding the passage by Congress of the 1990 and 1991 Civil Rights Acts, as well as the statements issued by the White House in connection with President Bush's veto of the 1990 Act and endorsement of the 1991 statute, are replete with references to the authors' perceptions of the intended and/or desired impact of the new legislation on affirmative action jurisprudence. The result of the intensive and extensive negotiations that surrounded the ultimate passage and signing of the 1991 Act is codified in the one sentence designated as § 116. It states that the new statute shall not be construed to affect court-ordered remedies, conciliation agreements, or voluntary affirmative action that are "in accordance with the law." At first blush, this appears to mean that Congress decided to leave the extant jurisprudence intact. But when Congress states that the Act does not affect affirmative action that is in accord with "the law", does "the law" include relevant provisions of the 1991 statute or does it refer only to pre-Act jurisprudence? The ramifications of these alternative interpretations are particularly meaningful in the context of voluntary affirmative action, a matter that is addressed in more detail in Note 7 following *Johnson, infra,* at 1218. Nevertheless, this language could also affect court ordered remedies. For example, if § 116 encompasses the other provisions of the 1991 Act, this would suggest that a court could not order an employer to engage in "race-norming" (i.e., the use of adjusted scores, different cutoff scores, or other alterations of the results of employment related tests on the basis of race or any other proscribed classifica-

tion in connection with the selection or referral of applicants) since this practice is expressly prohibited by § 106 of the 1991 Act.

6. Frequently, the parties to litigation choose to settle their case in order to save the time, expense and risks associated with litigation. Where the parties in a class action choose to do so through the execution of a consent decree, their settlement must be approved by the trial judge. As part of the approval process, the court will hold a hearing in which interested third parties can assert objections to the terms of the proposed consent decree. In LOCAL NUMBER 93, INTERNATIONAL ASSOCIATION OF FIREFIGHTERS v. CLEVELAND, 478 U.S. 501, 106 S.Ct. 3063, 92 L.Ed.2d 405 (1986), a union representing a majority of the firefighters of the City of Cleveland objected to the terms of a proposed consent decree between the City of Cleveland and an organization of African–American and Hispanic firefighters in Cleveland. This union claimed that the consent decree violated the terms of Title VII and the Fourteenth Amendment Equal Protection Clause by giving a race-based preference in promotion to minority firefighters who had not been found to be victims of discrimination. These objections were overruled by the trial judge, who adopted the consent decree. The union then appealed the trial court's ruling to the Seventh Circuit, which affirmed the trial court. The Supreme Court was then asked to rule on the limited question of whether the limits on judicially ordered relief contained in § 706(g) applied to consent decrees. (Recall that in *Local 28*, decided the same day as *Local 93*, a majority agreed that § 706(g) did not preclude a trial court from granting relief after trial, in exceptional cases, to a group that included non-victims of discrimination.) The Court concluded that § 706(g) was inapplicable to consent decrees and, therefore, that the terms of this decree were subject only to the limitations imposed by § 703(a) of Title VII and the Fourteenth Amendment. (These issues are the focus of the Supreme Court's opinions in the remaining principal cases in this Chapter.) The Court reasoned that while a consent decree bears some of the earmarks of judgments after litigation, it also enjoys many of the characteristics of a private contract. Moreover, the Court added, since the language of § 706(g) did not clearly include consent decrees, it was appropriate to consider the legislative history of Title VII which reflected Congress' desire not to preclude all voluntary race-conscious affirmative action. Accordingly, it held that a consent decree should not be viewed as an "order" within the meaning of § 706(g).

The Court in *Local 93* also noted that judicial approval of a consent decree did not and could not dispose of the claims of nonconsenting intervenors; which, if properly raised, remained subject to separate litigation efforts by the intervenor. This left open the question of the extent to which third parties are free to bring their own legal challenge to the terms of a consent decree. Suppose Local 93 had neither participated in the hearings concerning the proposed consent decree, nor objected to the terms of the proposed consent decree, nor appealed the trial court's approval of the consent decree. Assume, rather, that after the consent decree was approved between the employer and the Vanguards, a group of nonminority individuals filed a separate action under Title VII alleging that hiring and promotion decisions were made on the basis of race pursuant to the terms of the consent decree and that those decisions constituted prohibited racial discrimination. Further assume that in response to this complaint, the defendant employer filed a motion to dismiss on the ground that the plaintiffs' failure to intervene in the original action prohibited them from making this collateral challenge to the terms of the consent decree. How should the court rule on this motion?

As discussed in Chapter 7B, *supra*, at 708, this issue was addressed by the Supreme Court in MARTIN v. WILKS, 490 U.S. 755, 109 S.Ct. 2180, 104 L.Ed.2d 835 (1989). There, the City of Birmingham and the County Personnel Board had been sued by the NAACP and seven black individuals in separate actions alleging that these governmental entities engaged in racially discriminatory hiring and promotion practices in violation of Title VII. After a bench trial, but before judgment, the black individuals entered into one consent decree with the City and another with the County, each of which contained, *inter alia*, long-term and interim annual goals for the hiring and promotion of black firefighters. Notice of the final fairness hearings, along with a general description of the proposed decrees, was published in two local newspapers. A group representing some white firefighters, as well as two of its members, appeared and filed objections at the hearing. Additionally, after the hearing, but before final approval of the decrees, this association and these two members moved to intervene. The trial court denied the motions to intervene as untimely. Seven other members of the group then filed a separate complaint against the City and the Personnel Board seeking injunctive relief against enforcement of the decrees. The trial court also denied their request for relief. The appeal of the denial of intervention was consolidated with the appeal from the denial of injunctive relief and the Eleventh Circuit ruled that the trial court had not abused its discretion in connection with either decision. With respect to the denial of intervention, the appellate court rested its decision, in part, on the ground that these firefighters could safeguard their interests by instituting an independent Title VII action. Similarly, as to the request for injunctive relief, the availability of a separate forum led the appellate court to conclude that the plaintiffs had not demonstrated that operation of the challenged decrees would cause them irreparable injury.

Subsequently, a different group of white firefighters in Birmingham filed the instant suit against the City and the Personnel Board, alleging that they were denied promotions on the basis of their race in violation of the Constitution and Title VII. They, of course, had not participated in any of the prior proceedings concerning the consent decrees. The defendants admitted that the challenged promotion decisions were made on the basis of race, but maintained that these decisions were immunized from statutory challenge because they were undertaken pursuant to the terms of the consent decrees. Moreover, they filed a motion to dismiss the complaint as an impermissible collateral attack on the consent decree. The trial court denied the motion to dismiss. However, it also ruled that the decrees provided a defense to the merits of the claim of discrimination with respect to those promotion decisions mandated by the decrees. Consequently, after trial, the trial court dismissed the complaint upon finding that the promotion decisions were required by the consent decree. The Eleventh Circuit reversed, rejecting the doctrine of impermissible collateral attack and holding that nonparties to the consent decrees could not be precluded from bringing an independent challenge to the terms of the decree. It also remanded the case for trial on the discrimination claims and suggested that the legality of the terms of the consent decree should be determined by reference to the substantive law applicable to voluntary affirmative action plans.

The Supreme Court, by a vote of five to four, affirmed the Eleventh Circuit. In an opinion authored by Chief Justice Rehnquist and joined in by Justices White, O'Connor, Scalia and Kennedy, the majority noted that a "great majority" of the federal circuit courts had adopted the "impermissible collateral attack" doctrine to preclude those individuals who chose not to intervene from later litigating the issues in an independent action. Nevertheless, the Court agreed with the Eleventh Circuit's view that "[t]he linchpin of the 'impermissible collateral attack' doctrine—the attribution of preclusive effect to a failure to intervene—is * * * quite inconsistent with [Federal] Rule [of Civil Procedure] 19 and Rule 24." The majority emphasized that the language of Rule 24 (intervention) and Rule 19 (mandatory joinder) incorporated the "principle of general application in Anglo–American jurisprudence that one is not bound by a judgment in personam in a litigation in which he is not designated as a party or to which he has not been made a party by service of process." Moreover, the majority continued, this same principle mandated that "a party seeking a judgment binding on another cannot obligate that person to intervene; he must be joined." Thus, the majority concluded, joinder as a party, and not mere knowledge of the lawsuit and an opportunity to intervene, was a prerequisite to binding someone to the terms of a judgment or consent decree. Preclusive effect could not be predicated upon a failure to intervene. Putting the burden of fulfilling the requirements for preclusive effect on the named parties, rather than on the potential intervenor, the Court reasoned, was appropriate since the parties are in the best position to know the nature and scope of the relief sought and, therefore, at whose expense such relief might be awarded. The majority discounted the contention that such a ruling would be unduly burdensome and discouraging to civil rights litigants since potential adverse claimants might be numerous and/or difficult to identify and that failure to join all such claimants raised the spectre of repetitive litigation and potentially inconsistent judgments. It suggested, in response, that these difficulties were not a function of the choice between mandatory intervention and joinder, but, rather, of the nature and scope of the relief sought by the plaintiff. The Court indicated that the rules for joinder were adequate to the task and that, in its opinion, a mandatory intervention rule would not be "less awkward" since it would not prevent relitigation by individuals without knowledge of the initial action and would generate additional litigation over such issues as the timeliness and adequacy of the intervenors' notice of the lawsuit. In the end, the question, in the majority's view, was simply who should bear the burden of overcoming these difficulties and it concluded that the parties, rather than any potential intervenors, were best able to do so. Accordingly, in affirming the decision of the Eleventh Circuit, the Court remanded the case for trial of the respondents' "reverse discrimination" claims, thereby rejecting the trial court's ruling that the existence of the consent decree acted as a defense to promotion decisions made pursuant to that decree. Instead, the clear and intended result of the Court's decision was to permit the non-intervenors to bring their own substantive challenge to the terms of the consent decree.

The Court's ruling in *Wilks* was another one of the direct targets of Congress' efforts in 1990 and 1991 to enact a new civil rights bill. Section 108 of the 1991 Act substantially limits this ruling by severely restricting the opportunities for collateral challenges to litigated or consent judgments. It adds a new subsection to § 703 of Title VII that precludes challenges (under the Constitution or federal civil rights laws) to any employment practice that "implements or is within the scope of" a litigated or consent judgment by nonparties, nonintervenors or non-class members who received actual notice of their opportunity to present objections to the judgment. Moreover, the provision precludes such a collateral challenge by anyone whose interests were adequately represented by someone else who had challenged the judgment on the same legal grounds and with a similar fact situation, unless there is an intervening change in the law or facts. The statute also contains the traditional exceptions permitting collateral challenges on the ground that the judgment (1)was obtained through collusion or fraud, (2)is transparently invalid, or (3)was entered by a court lacking subject matter jurisdiction. Finally, § 108 adds that where collateral challenges are available, they shall be filed in the same court and, if possible, in front of the same judge, that issued the original judgment. Keep in mind, however, that this provision only applies to collateral challenges and does not alter the extant rules governing when parties represented in the original action may reopen a decree.

The detailed language of § 108 raises interpretive problems that did not exist under the *Wilks* rule. For example, does this provision restrict collateral challenges only to express terms of the judgment, or does it also limit collateral attacks on subsequent implementation of the judgment by either the issuing court or the parties? The exception permitting collateral challenges in the face of intervening changes in the law or facts is contained only in amended § 703(n)(1)(B)(ii)—the subsection that otherwise bars collateral challenges by individuals whose interests were adequately represented by another party. Does this mean that individuals who received adequate notice of their opportunity to object would continue to be barred in the face of an intervening change in the law or facts? Could such an individual contend that the intervening change vitiated the adequacy of the notice that his interests might be adversely affected by the challenged judgment?

7. In the last section of its opinion in the principal case, the Court briefly addressed the petitioners' constitutional equal protection challenge to portions of the trial court's order. As the Court readily admitted, the Justices were (and for some time had been) unable to agree on the appropriate level of scrutiny to be applied to race-conscious remedies. But since a majority agreed that the order satisfied even the rigorous scrutiny associated with suspect classification analysis, they did not discuss this issue in depth.

During its next term, the Court had another opportunity to examine this issue; this time in the context of a constitutional challenge to a court ordered race-conscious promotion plan. In UNITED STATES v. PARADISE, 480 U.S. 149, 107 S.Ct. 1053, 94 L.Ed.2d 203 (1987), the trial court had found that the Alabama Public Safety Department had committed an egregious violation of the Fourteenth Amendment by systematically excluding blacks from trooper positions over a period of four decades. As a result of this finding, the trial court issued an order requiring the Department to hire one black trooper for each white trooper hired until blacks constituted approximately 25% of the state trooper force. Several years later, the parties entered into a consent decree wherein the Department agreed to develop a promotion procedure within one year that would not have an adverse impact on black applicants. The decree also provided for judicial enforcement of its terms. Two years later, the Department proposed a promotion procedure which the plaintiff class objected to on the ground that it had not been validated. This dispute was resolved when the Department agreed to execute a second consent decree in which it reaffirmed its commitment to developing a nondiscriminatory promotion policy and in which the parties agreed to implementation of the Department's proposed policy, subject to review of its impact. The decree also provided that if the parties could not agree on the validity of the promotion policy, the issue would be resolved by the trial court. In April, 1983, the Department announced that there was an immediate need to make eight to ten promotions to the rank of corporal and proposed to make these promotions pursuant to their disputed promotion procedure.

The plaintiffs asked the trial court to enforce the consent decrees by requiring the Department to promote one black trooper for each white trooper promoted to corporal until the Department implemented a nondiscriminatory promotion procedure. The trial court ruled that the Department's promotion policy had an adverse impact on blacks and ordered the Department to produce a nondiscriminatory procedure within about two weeks. In response, the Department offered a plan to promote fifteen troopers to corporal, including four black troopers, and asked for more time to develop a nondiscriminatory procedure. The plaintiff class opposed this proposal and the trial court granted the class' motion to enforce the consent decrees. Pursuant to the language in the second decree granting the trial court authority to resolve any dispute over the validity of proposed promotion policies, the trial court fashioned the relief at issue before the Supreme Court. It ordered that 50% of the promotions to corporal be awarded to qualified black troopers until either blacks occupied 25% of the corporal positions or until the Department implemented a promotion policy that did not have an adverse impact on black troopers. The Department, pursuant to this order, promoted eight black and eight white troopers to corporal. When the Department subsequently submitted a new set of promotion procedures, the trial court accepted them and suspended application of the one-for-one promotion requirement. The Eleventh Circuit affirmed the district court order.

The Supreme Court, by a vote of five to four, also affirmed the order. Four Justices (Brennan, Marshall, Blackmun and Powell) joined in the opinion of the Court. Once again, however, after noting that the Court had been unable to reach consensus on the appropriate level of scrutiny for such race-conscious remedies, they stated that the relief ordered in the instant case survived even a strict scrutiny standard. Thus, even though three of these Justices, Brennan, Marshall and Blackmun, had acknowledged the propriety of a less-than-strict standard in *Local 28,* they were not compelled to reiterate this position in *Paradise.* The plurality reasoned that the one-for-one promotion order withstood strict scrutiny since it was narrowly tailored to serve the compelling governmental purpose of remedying the defendant's unconstitutionally "pervasive, systematic and obstinate" discriminatory conduct. They rejected the claim that promotion-based relief could not be awarded in the context of a finding of discrimination in hiring, reasoning that this relief was necessary to remedy the discrimination that permeated the defendant's hiring and promotion policies. With respect to whether the remedy was sufficiently "narrowly tailored" to serve that compelling interest, the plurality declared that it would look to five factors: (1)the necessity of such relief; (2)the efficacy of alternative remedies; (3)the flexibility and duration of the remedy (including the availability of waiver provisions); (4)the relationship of the numerical goals to the labor market; and (5)the extent of the impact of the relief on the rights of third parties. They then concluded that in light of the Department's historically inadequate efforts at eliminating discrimination in hiring and promotions, the trial court's remedy was necessary to serve the compelling federal interest in remedying that discrimination. The plurality also noted that race-neutral alternatives, such as fines, awards of attorney fees and additional time to develop nondiscriminatory policies would not serve either the interest of preventing further foot-dragging or compensating the plaintiffs for the delays in implementing acceptable promotion policies.

The remedial plan also was determined to be sufficiently flexible since it was designed to terminate either when the defendant implemented a nondiscriminatory procedure or when blacks obtained 25% of the upper level positions. This 25% figure, moreover, was found to reflect the percentage of blacks in the relevant labor market. And although 50% of the promotions in the short run were reserved for black troopers, this figure was chosen simply to hasten the attainment of the ultimate 25% goal. The plurality also mentioned the fact that the racial preference was limited solely to qualified blacks.

Finally, the use of race as a factor in promotions did not impose burdens on innocent nonminority third parties of the sort involved in *Wygant* since it did not involve the layoff or discharge of white workers and was limited to qualified black troopers. Justice Powell also issued a separate opinion in which he explicitly reiterated his reliance on the five factors he had set forth in his separate opinion in *Local 28*. The fifth vote in support of the race-based remedy came from Justice Stevens, who declared that, as a proven discriminator, the defendant Department bore the burden of persuasion as to the unconstitutionality of the remedial order, i.e., that the relief exceeded "the bounds of reasonableness." He then concluded that this burden had not been met. In dissent, Justice O'Connor, Chief Justice Rehnquist, Justice Scalia and Justice White found the remedy not "sufficiently tailored" because (1)the 50% promotion quota was substantially in excess of the percentage of blacks in the relevant labor market, (2)the trial court had not expressly evaluated available alternative remedies, and (3)these alternatives would have fulfilled the stated purpose of compelling the Department to comply with the consent decree.

As you know, a review of the Court's constitutional jurisprudence makes manifest that the Court's choice of which level of scrutiny is to be applied to a particular classification is highly significant to, if not often determinative of the results in these cases. It is, therefore, critical to examine the form of equal protection analysis employed by the various Justices in these cases. The following case, which was decided during the same term as *Local 28* and which was cited therein, provides a clear exposition of the respective positions taken by the Members on this crucial question. But note that this case, unlike either *Local 28* or *Paradise*, arises not in the context of a race-conscious remedial order issued by a court upon a finding of discrimination, but, rather, in connection with a race-based action voluntary undertaken by a public sector employer.

WYGANT v. JACKSON BOARD OF EDUCATION

Supreme Court of the United States, 1986.

476 U.S. 267, 106 S.Ct. 1842, 90 L.Ed.2d 260.

JUSTICE POWELL announced the judgment of the Court and delivered an opinion in which THE CHIEF JUSTICE and JUSTICE REHNQUIST joined, and which JUSTICE O'CONNOR joined in parts I, II, III–A, III–B, and V.

This case presents the question whether a school board, consistent with the Equal Protection Clause, may extend preferential protection against layoffs to some of its employees because of their race or national origin.

I

In 1972 the Jackson Board of Education, because of racial tension in the community that extended to its schools, considered adding a layoff provision to the Collective Bargaining Agreement (CBA) between the Board and the Jackson Education Association (the Union) that would protect employees who were members of certain minority groups against layoffs.[1] The Board and the Union eventually approved a new provision, Article XII of the CBA, covering layoffs. It stated:

> "In the event that it becomes necessary to reduce the number of teachers through layoff from employment by the Board, teachers with the most seniority in the district shall be retained, except that at no time will there be a greater percentage of minority personnel laid off than the current percentage of minority personnel employed at the time of the layoff. In no event will the number given notice of possible layoff be greater than the number of positions to be eliminated. Each teacher so affected will be called back in reverse order for positions for which he is certificated maintaining the above minority balance." App. 13.[2]

When layoffs became necessary in 1974, it was evident that adherence to the CBA would result in the layoff of tenured non-minority teachers while minority teachers on probationary status were retained. Rather than complying with Article XII, the Board retained the tenured teachers and laid off probationary minority teachers, thus failing to maintain the percentage of minority personnel that existed at the time of the layoff. The Union, together with two minority teachers who had been laid off, brought suit in federal court, id., at 30, (Jackson Education Assn. v. Board of Education, (Jackson I) (mem. op.)), claiming that the Board's failure to adhere to the layoff provision violated the Equal Protection Clause of the Fourteenth Amendment and Title VII of the Civil Rights Act of 1964. They also urged the District Court to take pendent jurisdiction over state law contract claims. In its answer the Board denied any prior employment discrimination and argued that the layoff provision conflicted with the Michigan Teacher Tenure Act. App. 33. Following trial, the District Court *sua sponte* concluded that it lacked jurisdiction over the case, in part because there was insufficient evidence to support the plaintiffs' claim that the Board had engaged in discriminatory hiring practices prior to 1972, id., at 35–37, and in part because the plaintiffs had not fulfilled the jurisdictional prerequisite to a Title VII claim by filing discrimination charges with

1. Prior to bargaining on this subject, the Minority Affairs Office of the Jackson Public Schools sent a questionnaire to all teachers, soliciting their views as to a layoff policy. The questionnaire proposed two alternatives: continuation of the existing straight seniority system, or a freeze of minority layoffs to ensure retention of minority teachers in exact proportion to the minority student population. Ninety-six percent of the teachers who responded to the questionnaire expressed a preference for the straight seniority system.

2. Article VII of the CBA defined "minority group personnel" as "those employees who are Black, American Indian, Oriental, or of Spanish descendancy." App. 15.

the Equal Employment Opportunity Commission. After dismissing the federal claims, the District Court declined to exercise pendent jurisdiction over the state law contract claims.

Rather than taking an appeal, the plaintiffs instituted a suit in state court, Jackson Education Assn. v. Board of Education (Jackson County Circuit Court, 1979) (*Jackson II*), raising in essence the same claims that had been raised in *Jackson I.* In entering judgment for the plaintiffs, the state court found that the Board had breached its contract with the plaintiffs, and that Article XII did not violate the Michigan Teacher Tenure Act. In rejecting the Board's argument that the layoff provision violated the Civil Rights Act of 1964, the state court found that it "ha[d] not been established that the board had discriminated against minorities in its hiring practices. The minority representation on the faculty was the result of societal racial discrimination." The state court also found that "[t]here is no history of overt past discrimination by the parties to this contract." Nevertheless, the court held that Article XII was permissible, despite its discriminatory effect on nonminority teachers, as an attempt to remedy the effects of societal discrimination.

After *Jackson II,* the Board adhered to Article XII. As a result, during the 1976–1977 and 1981–1982 school years, nonminority teachers were laid off, while minority teachers with less seniority were retained. The displaced nonminority teachers, petitioners here, brought suit in Federal District Court, alleging violations of the Equal Protection Clause, Title VII, 42 U.S.C. § 1983, and other federal and state statutes. On cross motions for summary judgment, the District Court dismissed all of petitioners' claims. With respect to the equal protection claim,[3] the District Court held that the racial preferences granted by the Board need not be grounded on a finding of prior discrimination. Instead, the court decided that the racial preferences were permissible under the Equal Protection Clause as an attempt to remedy societal discrimination by providing "role models" for minority schoolchildren, and upheld the constitutionality of the layoff provision.

The Court of Appeals for the Sixth Circuit affirmed, largely adopting the reasoning and language of the District Court. 746 F.2d 1152 (1984). We granted certiorari to resolve the important issue of the constitutionality of race-based layoffs by public employers. We now reverse.

II

Petitioners' central claim is that they were laid off because of their race in violation of the Equal Protection Clause of the Fourteenth Amendment. Decisions by faculties and administrators of public schools based on race or ethnic origin are reviewable under the Four-

---

3. Petitioners have sought review in this Court only of their claim based on the   Equal Protection Clause.

teenth Amendment.[4] This Court has "consistently repudiated '[d]istinctions between citizens solely because of their ancestry' as being 'odious to a free people whose institutions are founded upon the doctrine of equality,'" Loving v. Virginia, 388 U.S. 1, 11, 87 S.Ct. 1817, 1823, 18 L.Ed.2d 1010 (1967) quoting Hirabayashi v. United States, 320 U.S. 81, 100, 63 S.Ct. 1375, 1385, 87 L.Ed. 1774 (1943). "Racial and ethnic distinctions of any sort are inherently suspect and thus call for the most exacting judicial examination." Regents of University of California v. Bakke, 438 U.S. 265, 291, 98 S.Ct. 2733, 2748, 57 L.Ed.2d 750 (1978) (opinion of Powell, J., joined by White, J.)

The Court has recognized that the level of scrutiny does not change merely because the challenged classification operates against a group that historically has not been subject to governmental discrimination. Mississippi University for Women v. Hogan, 458 U.S. 718, 724 n. 9, 102 S.Ct. 3331, 3336 n. 9, 73 L.Ed.2d 1090 (1982); *Bakke,* 438 U.S., at 291–299, 98 S.Ct., at 2748–2752; see Shelley v. Kraemer, 334 U.S. 1, 22, 68 S.Ct. 836, 846, 92 L.Ed. 1161 (1948); see also A. Bickel, The Morality of Consent 133 (1975). In this case, Article XII of the CBA operates against whites and in favor of certain minorities, and therefore constitutes a classification based on race. "Any preference based on racial or ethnic criteria must necessarily receive a most searching examination to make sure that it does not conflict with constitutional guarantees." Fullilove v. Klutznick, 448 U.S. 448, 491, 100 S.Ct. 2758, 2781, 65 L.Ed.2d 902 (1980) (opinion of Burger, C.J.). There are two prongs to this examination. First, any racial classification "must be justified by a compelling governmental interest." Palmore v. Sidoti, 466 U.S. 429, 432, 104 S.Ct. 1879, 1882, 80 L.Ed.2d 421 (1984); see Loving v. Virginia, 388 U.S. 1, 11, 87 S.Ct. 1817, 1823, 18 L.Ed.2d 1010 (1967); cf. Graham v. Richardson, 403 U.S. 365, 375, 91 S.Ct. 1848, 1853, 29 L.Ed.2d 534 (1971) (alienage). Second, the means chosen by the State to effectuate its purpose must be "narrowly tailored to the achievement of that goal." *Fullilove,* 448 U.S., at 480, 100 S.Ct., at 2776. We must decide whether the layoff provision is supported by a compelling state purpose and whether the means chosen to accomplish that purpose are narrowly tailored.

III

A

The Court of Appeals, relying on the reasoning and language of the District Court's opinion, held that the Board's interest in providing minority role models for its minority students, as an attempt to alleviate the effects of societal discrimination, was sufficiently important to justify the racial classification embodied in the layoff provision. The court discerned a need for more minority faculty role models by finding

---

4. School district collective bargaining agreements constitute state action for purposes of the Fourteenth Amendment. Abood v. Detroit Board of Ed., 431 U.S. 209, 218, and n. 12, 97 S.Ct. 1782, 1790, and n. 12, 52 L.Ed.2d 261 (1977).

that the percentage of minority teachers was less than the percentage of minority students.

This Court never has held that societal discrimination alone is sufficient to justify a racial classification. Rather, the Court has insisted upon some showing of prior discrimination by the governmental unit involved before allowing limited use of racial classifications in order to remedy such discrimination. This Court's reasoning in Hazelwood School District v. United States, 433 U.S. 299, 97 S.Ct. 2736, 53 L.Ed.2d 768 (1977), illustrates that the relevant analysis in cases involving proof of discrimination by statistical disparity focuses on those disparities that demonstrate such prior governmental discrimination. In *Hazelwood* the Court concluded that, absent employment discrimination by the school board, " 'nondiscriminatory hiring practices will in time result in a work force more or less representative of the racial and ethnic composition of the population in the community from which the employees are hired.' " Id., at 307, 97 S.Ct., at 2741, quoting Teamsters v. United States, 431 U.S. 324, 340, n. 20, 97 S.Ct. 1843, 1856, n. 20, 52 L.Ed.2d 396 (1977). See also *Wygant,* supra, 746 F.2d, at 1160 (Wellford, J., concurring) ("Had the plaintiffs in this case presented data as to the percentage of qualified minority teachers in the relevant labor market to show that defendant Board's hiring of black teachers over a number of years had equalled that figure, I believe this court may well have been required to reverse * * *."). Based on that reasoning, the Court in *Hazelwood* held that the proper comparison for determining the existence of actual discrimination by the school board was "between the racial composition of [the school's] teaching staff and the racial composition of the qualified public school teacher population in the relevant labor market." 433 U.S., at 308, 97 S.Ct., at 2742. *Hazelwood* demonstrates this Court's focus on prior discrimination as the justification for, and the limitation on, a State's adoption of race-based remedies. See also Swann v. Charlotte–Mecklenburg Board of Education, 402 U.S. 1, 91 S.Ct. 1267, 28 L.Ed.2d 554 (1971).

Unlike the analysis in *Hazelwood,* the role model theory employed by the District Court has no logical stopping point. The role model theory allows the Board to engage in discriminatory hiring and layoff practices long past the point required by any legitimate remedial purpose. Indeed, by tying the required percentage of minority teachers to the percentage of minority students, it requires just the sort of year-to-year calibration the Court stated was unnecessary in *Swann,* 402 U.S., at 31–32, 91 S.Ct., at 1283–1284:

> "At some point these school authorities and others like them should have achieved full compliance with this Court's decision in *Brown I.* * * * Neither school authorities nor district courts are constitutionally required to make year-by-year adjustments of the racial composition of student bodies once the affirmative duty to desegregate has been accomplished and racial discrimination through official action is eliminated from the system."

Moreover, because the role model theory does not necessarily bear a relationship to the harm caused by prior discriminatory hiring practices, it actually could be used to escape the obligation to remedy such practices by justifying the small percentage of black teachers by reference to the small percentage of black students. Carried to its logical extreme, the idea that black students are better off with black teachers could lead to the very system the Court rejected in Brown v. Board of Education, 347 U.S. 483, 74 S.Ct. 686, 98 L.Ed. 873 (1954) (*Brown I*).

Societal discrimination, without more, is too amorphous a basis for imposing a racially classified remedy. The role model theory announced by the District Court and the resultant holding typify this indefiniteness. There are numerous explanations for a disparity between the percentage of minority students and the percentage of minority faculty, many of them completely unrelated to discrimination of any kind. In fact, there is no apparent connection between the two groups. Nevertheless, the District Court combined irrelevant comparisons between these two groups with an indisputable statement that there has been societal discrimination, and upheld state action predicated upon racial classifications. No one doubts that there has been serious racial discrimination in this country. But as the basis for imposing discriminatory *legal* remedies that work against innocent people, societal discrimination is insufficient and over expansive. In the absence of particularized findings, a court could uphold remedies that are ageless in their reach into the past, and timeless in their ability to affect the future.

B

Respondents also now argue that their purpose in adopting the layoff provision was to remedy prior discrimination against minorities by the Jackson School District in hiring teachers. Public schools, like other public employers, operate under two interrelated constitutional duties. They are under a clear command from this Court, starting with Brown v. Board of Education, 349 U.S. 294, 75 S.Ct. 753, 99 L.Ed. 1083 (1955), to eliminate every vestige of racial segregation and discrimination in the schools. Pursuant to that goal, race-conscious remedial action may be necessary. North Carolina State Board of Education v. Swann, 402 U.S. 43, 46, 91 S.Ct. 1284, 1286, 28 L.Ed.2d 586 (1971). On the other hand, public employers, including public schools, also must act in accordance with a "core purpose of the Fourteenth Amendment" which is to "do away with all governmentally imposed distinctions based on race." Palmore v. Sidoti, 466 U.S., at 432, 104 S.Ct., at 1881–1882. These related constitutional duties are not always harmonious; reconciling them requires public employers to act with extraordinary care. In particular, a public employer like the Board must ensure that, before it embarks on an affirmative action program, it has convincing evidence that remedial action is warranted. That is, it must have sufficient evidence to justify the conclusion that there has been prior discrimination.

Evidentiary support for the conclusion that remedial action is warranted becomes crucial when the remedial program is challenged in court by nonminority employees. In this case, for example, petitioners contended at trial that the remedial program—Article XII—had the purpose and effect of instituting a racial classification that was not justified by a remedial purpose. In such a case, the trial court must make a factual determination that the employer had a strong basis in evidence for its conclusion that remedial action was necessary. The ultimate burden remains with the employees to demonstrate the unconstitutionality of an affirmative action program. But unless such a determination is made, an appellate court reviewing a challenge to remedial action by nonminority employees cannot determine whether the race-based action is justified as a remedy for prior discrimination.

Despite the fact that Article XII has spawned years of litigation and three separate lawsuits, no such determination ever has been made. Although its litigation position was different, the Board in *Jackson I* and *Jackson II* denied the existence of prior discriminatory hiring practices. This precise issue was litigated in both those suits. Both courts concluded that any statistical disparities were the result of general societal discrimination, not of prior discrimination by the Board. The Board now contends that, given another opportunity, it could establish the existence of prior discrimination. Although this argument seems belated at this point in the proceedings, we need not consider the question since we conclude below that the layoff provision was not a legally appropriate means of achieving even a compelling purpose.[5]

5. Justice Marshall contends that "the majority has too quickly assumed the absence of a legitimate factual predicate for affirmative action in the Jackson schools." In support of that assertion, he engages in an unprecedented reliance on non-record documents that respondent has "lodged" with this Court. This selective citation to factual materials not considered by the District Court or the Court of Appeals below is unusual enough by itself. My disagreement with Justice Marshall, however, is more fundamental than any disagreement over the heretofore unquestioned rule that this Court decides cases based on the record before it. Justice Marshall does not define what he means by "legitimate factual predicate," nor does he demonstrate the relationship of these non-record materials to his undefined predicate. If, for example, his dissent assumes that general societal discrimination is a sufficient factual predicate, then there is no need to refer to respondents' lodgings as to its own employment history. No one disputes that

there has been race discrimination in this country. If that fact alone can justify race-conscious action by the State, despite the Equal Protection Clause, then the dissent need not rely on non-record materials to show a "legitimate factual predicate." If, on the other hand, Justice Marshall is assuming that the necessary factual predicate is prior discrimination by the Board, there is no escaping the need for a factual determination below—a determination that does not exist.

The real dispute, then, is not over the state of the record. It is disagreement as to what constitutes a "legitimate factual predicate." If the necessary factual predicate is *prior discrimination*—that is, that race-based state action is taken to remedy prior discrimination by the governmental unit involved—then the very nature of appellate review requires that a factfinder determine whether the employer was justified in instituting a remedial plan. Nor can the respondent unilaterally insulate

IV

The Court of Appeals examined the means chosen to accomplish the Board's race-conscious purposes under a test of "reasonableness." That standard has no support in the decisions of this Court. As demonstrated in Part II above, our decisions always have employed a more stringent standard—however articulated—to test the validity of the means chosen by a state to accomplish its race-conscious purposes. See, e.g., *Palmore,* 466 U.S., at 432, 104 S.Ct., at 1882 ("to pass constitutional muster, [racial classifications] must be necessary * * * to the accomplishment of their legitimate purpose") (quoting McLaughlin v. Florida, 379 U.S. 184, 196, 85 S.Ct. 283, 290, 13 L.Ed.2d 222 (1964)); *Fullilove,* 448 U.S., at 480, 100 S.Ct., at 2775 (opinion of Burger, C.J.) ("We recognize the need for careful judicial evaluation to assure that any * * * program that employs racial or ethnic criteria to accomplish the objective of remedying the present effects of past discrimination is narrowly tailored to the achievement of that goal").[6] Under strict scrutiny the means chosen to accomplish the State's asserted purpose must be specifically and narrowly framed to accomplish that purpose. *Fullilove,* 448 U.S., at 480, 100 S.Ct., at 2775 (opinion of Burger, C.J.).[7] "Racial classifications are simply too pernicious to permit any but the

itself from this key constitutional question by conceding that it has discriminated in the past, now that it is in its interest to make such a concession. Contrary to the dissent's assertion, the requirement of such a determination by the trial court is not some arbitrary barrier set up by today's opinion. Rather, it is a necessary result of the requirement that race-based state action be remedial.

At any rate, much of the material relied on by Justice Marshall has been the subject of the previous lawsuit in *Jackson II,* where the court concluded that it "had not been established that the Board had discriminated against minorities in its hiring practices." Moreover, as noted supra, at 1852, in *Jackson I* the Board expressly denied that it had engaged in employment discrimination.

6. The term "narrowly tailored," so frequently used in our cases, has acquired a secondary meaning. More specifically, as commentators have indicated, the term may be used to require consideration whether lawful alternative and less restrictive means could have been used. Or, as Professor Ely has noted, the classification at issue must "fit" with greater precision than any alternative means. Ely, The Constitutionality of Reverse Racial Discrimination, 41 U.Chi.L.Rev. 723, 727, n. 26 (1974) (hereinafter Ely). "[Courts] should give particularly intense scrutiny to whether a nonracial approach or a more

narrowly tailored racial classification could promote the substantial interest about as well and at tolerable administrative expense." Greenawalt, Judicial Scrutiny of "Benign" Racial Preference in Law School Admissions, 75 Colum.L.Rev. 559, 578–579 (1975).

7. Several commentators have emphasized, no matter what the weight of the asserted governmental purpose, that the *means* chosen to accomplish the purpose should be narrowly tailored. In arguing for a form of intermediate scrutiny, Professor Greenawalt contends that, "while benign racial classifications call for some weighing of the importance of ends they call for even more intense scrutiny of means, especially of the administrability of less onerous alternative classifications." Greenawalt 565. Professor Ely has suggested that "special scrutiny in the suspect classification context has in fact consisted not in weighing ends but rather in insisting that the classification in issue fit a constitutional permissible state goal with greater precision than any available alternative." Ely 727, n. 26. Professor Gunther argues that judicial scrutiny of legislative means is more appropriate than judicial weighing of the importance of the legislative purpose. Gunther, Foreword: In Search of Evolving Doctrine on a Changing Court: A Model For a Newer Equal Protection, 86 Harv.L.Rev. 1, 20–21 (1972).

most exact connection between justification and classification." Id., at 537, 100 S.Ct., at 2805 (Stevens, J., dissenting).

We have recognized, however, that in order to remedy the effects of prior discrimination, it may be necessary to take race into account. As part of this Nation's dedication to eradicating racial discrimination, innocent persons may be called upon to bear some of the burden of the remedy. "When effectuating a limited and properly tailored remedy to cure the effects of prior discrimination, such a 'sharing of the burden' by innocent parties is not impermissible." Id., at 484, 100 S.Ct., at 2778, quoting Franks v. Bowman Transportation Co., 424 U.S. 747, 96 S.Ct. 1251, 47 L.Ed.2d 444 (1976).[8] In *Fullilove,* the challenged statute required at least 10 percent of federal public works funds to be used in contracts with minority-owned business enterprises. This requirement was found to be within the remedial powers of Congress in part because the "actual burden shouldered by nonminority firms is relatively light." 448 U.S., at 484, 100 S.Ct., at 2778.[9]

Significantly, none of the cases discussed above involved layoffs. Here, by contrast, the means chosen to achieve the Board's asserted purposes is that of laying off nonminority teachers with greater seniori-

---

8. Of course, when a state implements a race-based plan that requires such a sharing of the burden, it cannot justify the discriminatory effect on some individuals because other individuals had approved the plan. Any "waiver" of the right not to be dealt with by the government on the basis of one's race must be made by those affected. Yet Justice Marshall repeatedly contends that the fact that Article XII was approved by a majority vote of the Union somehow validates this plan. He sees this case not in terms of individual constitutional rights, but as an allocation of burdens "between two racial groups." Thus, Article XII becomes a political compromise that "avoided placing the entire burden of layoffs on either the white teachers as a group or the minority teachers as a group." But the petitioners before us today are not "the white teachers as a group." They are Wendy Wygant and other individuals who claim that they were fired from their jobs because of their race. That claim cannot be waived by petitioners' more senior colleagues. In view of the way union seniority works, it is not surprising that while a straight freeze on minority layoffs was overwhelmingly rejected, a "compromise" eventually was reached that placed the entire burden of the compromise on the most junior union members. The more senior union members simply had nothing to lose from such a compromise. The fact that such a painless accommodation was approved by the more senior union members six times since 1972 is irrelevant.

The Constitution does not allocate constitutional rights to be distributed like bloc grants within discrete racial groups; and until it does, petitioners' more senior union colleagues cannot vote away petitioners' rights.

Justice Marshall also attempts to portray the layoff plan as one that has no real invidious effect, stating that "within the confines of constant minority proportions, it preserves the hierarchy of seniority in the selection of individuals for layoff." That phrase merely expresses the tautology that layoffs are based on seniority except as to those nonminority teachers who are displaced by minority teachers with less seniority. This is really nothing more than group-based analysis: "each group would shoulder a portion of [the layoff] burden equal to its portion of the faculty." The constitutional problem remains: the decision that petitioners would be laid off was based on their race.

9. Similarly, the Court approved the hiring program in Steelworkers v. Weber, 443 U.S. 193, 208, 99 S.Ct. 2721, 2729, 61 L.Ed.2d 480 (1979), in part because the plan did not "unnecessarily trammel the interests of the white employees." Since *Weber* involved a private company, its reasoning concerning the validity of the hiring plan at issue there is not directly relevant to this case, which involves a state-imposed plan. No equal protection claim was presented in *Weber.*

ty in order to retain minority teachers with less seniority. We have previously expressed concern over the burden that a preferential layoffs scheme imposes on innocent parties. See Firefighters v. Stotts, 467 U.S. 561, 574–576, 578–579, 104 S.Ct. 2576, 2585–2586, 2587–2588, 81 L.Ed.2d 483 (1984); see also *Weber,* 443 U.S., at 208, 99 S.Ct., at 2730 ("The plan does not require the discharge of white workers and their replacement with new black hirees"). In cases involving valid *hiring* goals, the burden to be borne by innocent individuals is diffused to a considerable extent among society generally. Though hiring goals may burden some innocent individuals, they simply do not impose the same kind of injury that layoffs impose. Denial of a future employment opportunity is not as intrusive as loss of an existing job.

Many of our cases involve union seniority plans with employees who are typically heavily dependent on wages for their day-to-day living. Even a temporary layoff may have adverse financial as well as psychological effects. A worker may invest many productive years in one job and one city with the expectation of earning the stability and security of seniority. "At that point, the rights and expectations surrounding seniority make up what is probably the most valuable capital asset that the worker 'owns,' worth even more than the current equity in his home." Fallon & Weiler, Conflicting Models of Racial Justice, 1984 S.Ct.Rev. 1, 58. Layoffs disrupt these settled expectations in a way that general hiring goals do not.

While hiring goals impose a diffuse burden, often foreclosing only one of several opportunities,[11] layoffs impose the entire burden of achieving racial equality on particular individuals, often resulting in serious disruption of their lives. That burden is too intrusive. We therefore hold that, as a means of accomplishing purposes that otherwise may be legitimate, the Board's layoff plan is not sufficiently narrowly tailored.[12] Other, less intrusive means of accomplishing similar purposes—such as the adoption of hiring goals—are available. For these reasons, the Board's selection of layoffs as the means to accomplish even a valid purpose cannot satisfy the demands of the Equal Protection Clause.[13]

11. The "school admission" cases, which involve the same basic concepts as cases involving hiring goals, illustrate this principle. For example, in DeFunis v. Odegaard, 416 U.S. 312, 94 S.Ct. 1704, 40 L.Ed.2d 164 (1974), while petitioner's complaint alleged that he had been denied admission to the University of Washington Law School because of his race, he also had been accepted at the Oregon, Idaho, Gonzaga, and Willamette Law Schools. DeFunis v. Odegaard, 82 Wash.2d 11, 30, n. 11, 507 P.2d 1169, 1181, n. 11 (1973). The injury to DeFunis was not of the same kind or degree as the injury that he would have suffered had he been removed from law school in his third year. Even this analogy

may not rise to the level of harm suffered by a union member who is laid off.

12. We have recognized, however, that in order to provide make-whole relief to the actual, identified victims of individual discrimination, a court may in an appropriate case award competitive seniority. See Franks v. Bowman Transportation Co., 424 U.S. 747, 96 S.Ct. 1251, 47 L.Ed.2d 444 (1976).

13. The Board's definition of minority to include blacks, Orientals, American Indians, and persons of Spanish descent, n. 2, supra, further illustrates the undifferentiated nature of the plan. There is no explanation of why the Board chose to favor

V

We accordingly reverse the judgment of the Court of Appeals for the Sixth Circuit.

It is so ordered.

JUSTICE O'CONNOR, concurring in part and concurring in the judgment.

This case requires us to define and apply the standard required by the Equal Protection Clause when a governmental agency agrees to give preferences on the basis of race or national origin in making layoffs of employees. The specific question posed is, as Justice Marshall puts it, "whether the Constitution prohibits a union and a local school board from developing a collective-bargaining agreement that apportions layoffs between two racially determined groups as a means of preserving the effects of an affirmative hiring policy." Post, at 1860 (Marshall, J., dissenting). There is no issue here of the interpretation and application of Title VII of the Civil Rights Act; accordingly, we have only the constitutional issue to resolve.

The Equal Protection Clause standard applicable to racial classifications that work to the disadvantage of "nonminorities" has been articulated in various ways. Justice Powell now would require that: (1) the racial classification be justified by a " 'compelling governmental interest,' " and (2) the means chosen by the State to effectuate its purpose be "narrowly tailored." This standard reflects the belief, apparently held by all members of this Court, that racial classifications of any sort must be subjected to "strict scrutiny," however defined. See, e.g., Fullilove v. Klutznick, 448 U.S. 448, 491, 100 S.Ct. 2758, 2781, 65 L.Ed.2d 902 (1980) (opinion of Burger, C.J., joined by White, J.) ("Any preference based on racial or ethnic criteria must necessarily receive a most searching examination to make sure that it does not conflict with constitutional guarantees"); id., at 537, 100 S.Ct., at 2805 (Stevens, J., dissenting) ("Racial classifications are simply too pernicious to permit any but the most exact connection between justification and classification"); Regents of University of California v. Bakke, 438 U.S. 265, 291, 98 S.Ct. 2733, 2748, 57 L.Ed.2d 750 (1978) (opinion of Powell, J., joined by White, J.) ("Racial and ethnic distinctions of any sort are inherently suspect and thus call for the most exacting judicial examination"); id., at 361–362, 98 S.Ct., at 2784 ("[O]ur review under the Fourteenth Amendment should be strict—not ' "strict" in theory and fatal in fact,' because it is stigma that causes fatality—but strict and searching nonetheless") (opinion of Brennan, White, Marshall, and Blackmun, JJ). Justices Marshall, Brennan, and Blackmun, however, seem to adhere to the formulation of the "strict" standard that they authored, with Justice White, in *Bakke:* "remedial use of race is

these particular minorities or how in fact members of some of the categories can be identified. Moreover, respondents have never suggested—much less formally found—that they have engaged in prior, purposeful discrimination against members of each of these minority groups.

permissible if it serves 'important governmental objectives' and is 'substantially related to achievement of those objectives.'" Supra, at 359, 98 S.Ct., at 2783 (opinion of Brennan, White, Marshall, and Blackmun, JJ.).

I subscribe to Justice Powell's formulation because it mirrors the standard we have consistently applied in examining racial classifications in other contexts. In my view,

> "the analysis and level of scrutiny applied to determine the validity of [a racial] classification do not vary simply because the objective appears acceptable to individual Members of the Court. While the validity and importance of the objective may affect the outcome of the analysis, the analysis itself does not change." Mississippi University for Women v. Hogan, 458 U.S. 718, 724, n. 9, 102 S.Ct. 3331, 3336, n. 9, 73 L.Ed.2d 1090 (1982).

Although Justice Powell's formulation may be viewed as more stringent than that suggested by Justices Brennan, White, Marshall, and Blackmun, the disparities between the two tests do not preclude a fair measure of consensus. In particular, as regards certain state interests commonly relied upon in formulating affirmative action programs, the distinction between a "compelling" and an "important" governmental purpose may be a negligible one. The Court is in agreement that, whatever the formulation employed, remedying past or present racial discrimination by a state actor is a sufficiently weighty state interest to warrant the remedial use of a carefully constructed affirmative action program. This remedial purpose need not be accompanied by contemporaneous findings of actual discrimination to be accepted as legitimate as long as the public actor has a firm basis for believing that remedial action is required. Additionally, although its precise contours are uncertain, a state interest in the promotion of racial diversity has been found sufficiently "compelling," at least in the context of higher education, to support the use of racial considerations in furthering that interest. See, e.g., *Bakke,* 438 U.S., at 311–315, 98 S.Ct., at 2759–2761 (opinion of Powell, J.). And certainly nothing the Court has said today necessarily forecloses the possibility that the Court will find other governmental interests which have been relied upon in the lower courts but which have not been passed on here to be sufficiently "important" or "compelling" to sustain the use of affirmative action policies.

It appears, then, that the true source of disagreement on the Court lies not so much in defining the state interests which may support affirmative action efforts as in defining the degree to which the means employed must "fit" the ends pursued to meet constitutional standards. Yet even here the Court has forged a degree of unanimity; it is agreed that a plan need not be limited to the remedying of specific instances of identified discrimination for it to be deemed sufficiently "narrowly tailored," or "substantially related," to the correction of prior discrimination by the state actor.

In the final analysis, the diverse formulations and the number of separate writings put forth by various members of the Court in these difficult cases do not necessarily reflect an intractable fragmentation in opinion with respect to certain core principles. Ultimately, the Court is at least in accord in believing that a public employer, consistent with the Constitution, may undertake an affirmative action program which is designed to further a legitimate remedial purpose and which implements that purpose by means that do not impose disproportionate harm on the interests, or unnecessarily trammel the rights, of innocent individuals directly and adversely affected by a plan's racial preference.

Respondent School Board argues that the governmental purpose or goal advanced here was the School Board's desire to correct apparent prior employment discrimination against minorities while avoiding further litigation. The Michigan Civil Rights Commission determined that the evidence before it supported the allegations of discrimination on the part of the Jackson School Board, though that determination was never reduced to formal findings because the School Board, with the agreement of the Jackson Education Association (Union), voluntarily chose to remedy the perceived violation. Among the measures the School Board and the Union eventually agreed were necessary to remedy the apparent prior discrimination was the layoff provision challenged here; they reasoned that without the layoff provision, the remedial gains made under the ongoing hiring goals contained in the collective bargaining agreement could be eviscerated by layoffs.

The District Court and the Court of Appeals did not focus on the School Board's unquestionably compelling interest in remedying its apparent prior discrimination when evaluating the constitutionality of the challenged layoff provision. Instead, both courts reasoned that the goals of remedying "societal discrimination" and providing "role models" were sufficiently important to withstand equal protection scrutiny. I agree with the Court that a governmental agency's interest in remedying "societal" discrimination, that is, discrimination not traceable to its own actions, cannot be deemed sufficiently compelling to pass constitutional muster under strict scrutiny. I also concur in the Court's assessment that use by the courts below of a "role model" theory to justify the conclusion that this plan had a legitimate remedial purpose was in error. * Thus, in my view, the District Court and the Court of Appeals clearly erred in relying on these purposes and in failing to give greater attention to the School Board's asserted purpose of rectifying its own apparent discrimination.

---

* The goal of providing "role-models" discussed by the courts below should not be confused with the very different goal of promoting racial diversity among the faculty. Because this latter goal was not urged as such in support of the layoff provision before the District Court and the Court of Appeals, however, I do not believe it necessary to discuss the magnitude of that interest or its applicability in this case. The only governmental interests at issue here are those of remedying "societal" discrimination, providing "role models," and remedying apparent prior employment discrimination by the School District.

The error of the District Court and the Court of Appeals can be explained by reference to the fact that the primary issue argued by the parties on the cross motions for summary judgment was whether the School Board, a court, or another competent body had to have made a finding of past discrimination before or at the time of the institution of the plan in order for the plan to be upheld as remedial in purpose. The courts below ruled that a particularized, contemporaneous finding of discrimination was not necessary and upheld the plan as a remedy for "societal" discrimination, apparently on the assumption that in the absence of a specific, contemporaneous finding, any discrimination addressed by an affirmative action plan could only be termed "societal." I believe that this assumption is false and therefore agree with the Court that a contemporaneous or antecedent finding of past discrimination by a court or other competent body is not a constitutional prerequisite to a public employer's voluntary agreement to an affirmative action plan.

A violation of federal statutory or constitutional requirements does not arise with the making of a finding; it arises when the wrong is committed. Contemporaneous findings serve solely as a means by which it can be made absolutely certain that the governmental actor truly is attempting to remedy its own unlawful conduct when it adopts an affirmative action plan, rather than attempting to alleviate the wrongs suffered through general societal discrimination. Such findings, when voluntarily made by a public employer, obviously are desirable in that they provide evidentiary safeguards of value both to nonminority employees and to the public employer itself, should its affirmative action program be challenged in court. If contemporaneous findings were *required* of public employers in every case as a precondition to the constitutional validity of their affirmative action efforts, however, the relative value of these evidentiary advantages would diminish, for they could be secured only by the sacrifice of other vitally important values.

The imposition of a requirement that public employers make findings that they have engaged in illegal discrimination before they engage in affirmative action programs would severely undermine public employers' incentive to meet voluntarily their civil rights obligations. This result would clearly be at odds with this Court's and Congress' consistent emphasis on "the value of voluntary efforts to further the objectives of the law." *Bakke,* supra, 438 U.S., at 364, 98 S.Ct., at 2785 (opinion of Brennan, White, Marshall, and Blackmun, JJ.); see also Albemarle Paper Co. v. Moody, 422 U.S. 405, 417–418, 95 S.Ct. 2362, 2371–2372, 45 L.Ed.2d 280 (1975); Alexander v. Gardner–Denver Co., 415 U.S. 36, 44, 94 S.Ct. 1011, 1017, 39 L.Ed.2d 147 (1974). The value of voluntary compliance is doubly important when it is a public employer that acts, both because of the example its voluntary assumption of responsibility sets and because the remediation of governmental discrimination is of unique importance. See S.Rep. No. 92–415, p. 10 (1971) (accompanying the amendments extending coverage of Title VII to the States) ("Discrimination by government * * * serves a doubly destructive purpose. The exclusion of minorities from effective participation in the bureaucracy not only promotes ignorance of minority problems in that particular community, but also creates mistrust, alienation, and all too often hostility toward the entire process of government"). Imposing a contemporaneous findings requirement would produce the anomalous result that what private employers may voluntarily do to correct apparent violations of Title VII, Steelworkers v. Weber, supra, public employers are constitutionally forbidden to do to correct their statutory and constitutional transgressions.

Such results cannot, in my view, be justified by reference to the incremental value a contemporaneous findings requirement would have as an evidentiary safeguard. As is illustrated by this case, public employers are trapped between the competing hazards of liability to minorities if affirmative action *is not* taken to remedy apparent employment discrimination and liability to nonminorities if affirmative action *is* taken. Where these employers, who are presumably fully aware both of their duty under federal law to respect the rights of *all* their employees and of their potential liability for failing to do so, act on the basis of information which gives them a sufficient basis for concluding that remedial action is necessary, a contemporaneous findings requirement should not be necessary.

This conclusion is consistent with our previous decisions recognizing the States' ability to take voluntary race-conscious action to achieve compliance with the law even in the absence of a specific finding of past discrimination. See, e.g., United Jewish Organizations of Williamsburgh, Inc. v. Carey, 430 U.S. 144, 165–166, 97 S.Ct. 996, 1009–1010, 51 L.Ed.2d 229 (1977) (reapportionment); McDaniel v. Barresi, 402 U.S. 39, 91 S.Ct. 1287, 28 L.Ed.2d 582 (1971) (school desegregation). Indeed, our recognition of the responsible state actor's competency to take these steps is assumed in our recognition of the States' constitutional *duty* to take affirmative steps to eliminate the continuing effects of past unconstitutional discrimination. See, e.g., Swann v. Charlotte–Mecklenburg Board of Education, 402 U.S. 1, 15, 91 S.Ct. 1267, 1275, 28 L.Ed.2d 554 (1971); Green v. New Kent County School Board, 391 U.S. 430, 437–438, 88 S.Ct. 1689, 1693–1694, 20 L.Ed.2d 716 (1968).

Of course, as the Court notes, the public employer must discharge this sensitive duty with great care; in order to provide some measure of protection to the interests of its nonminority employees and the employer itself in the event that its affirmative action plan is challenged, the public employer must have a firm basis for determining that affirmative action is warranted. Public employers are not without reliable benchmarks in making this determination. For example, demonstrable evidence of a disparity between the percentage of qualified blacks on a school's teaching staff and the percentage of qualified minorities in the relevant labor pool sufficient to support a prima facie Title VII pattern or practice claim by minority teachers would lend a compelling basis for a competent authority such as the School Board to conclude that implementation of a voluntary affirmative action plan is appropriate to remedy apparent prior employment discrimination.

To be sure, such a conclusion is not unassailable. If a voluntary affirmative action plan is subsequently challenged in court by nonminority employees, those employees must be given the opportunity to prove that the plan does not meet the constitutional standard this Court has articulated. However, as the Court suggests, the institution of such a challenge does not automatically impose upon the public employer the burden of convincing the court of its liability for prior unlawful discrimination; nor does it mean that the court must make an actual finding of prior discrimination based on the employer's proof before the employer's affirmative action plan will be upheld. In "reverse discrimination" suits, as in any other suit, it is the plaintiffs who must bear the burden of demonstrating that their rights have been violated. The findings a court must make before upholding an affirmative action plan reflect this allocation of proof and the nature of the challenge asserted. For instance, in the example posed above, the nonminority teachers could easily demonstrate that the purpose and effect of the plan is to impose a race-based classification. But when the Board introduces its statistical proof as evidence of its remedial purpose, thereby supplying the court with the means for determining that the Board had a firm basis for concluding that remedial action was appropriate, it is incumbent upon the nonminority teachers to prove their case; they continue to bear the ultimate burden of persuading the court that the Board's evidence did not support an inference of prior discrimination and thus a remedial purpose, or that the plan instituted on the basis of this evidence was not sufficiently "narrowly tailored." Only by meeting this burden could the plaintiffs establish a violation of their constitutional rights, and thereby defeat the presumption that the Board's assertedly remedial action based on the statistical evidence was justified.

In sum, I do not think that the layoff provision was constitutionally infirm simply because the School Board, the Commission or a court had not made particularized findings of discrimination at the time the provision was agreed upon. But when the plan was challenged, the District Court and the Court of Appeals did not make the proper inquiry into the legitimacy of the Board's asserted remedial purpose; instead, they relied upon governmental purposes that we have deemed insufficient to withstand strict scrutiny, and therefore failed to isolate a sufficiently important governmental purpose that could support the challenged provision.

There is, however, no need to inquire whether the provision actually had a legitimate remedial purpose based on the record, such as it is, because the judgment is vulnerable on yet another ground: the courts below applied a "reasonableness" test in evaluating the relationship between the ends pursued and the means employed to achieve them that is plainly incorrect under any of the standards articulated by this Court. Nor is it necessary, in my view, to resolve the troubling questions of whether any layoff provision could survive strict scrutiny or whether this particular layoff provision could, when considered without reference to the hiring goal it was intended to further, pass the onerous "narrowly tailored" requirement. Petitioners have met their burden of establishing that this layoff provision is not "narrowly tailored" to achieve its asserted remedial purpose by demonstrating that the provision is keyed to a hiring goal that itself has no relation to the remedying of employment discrimination.

Although the constitutionality of the hiring goal as such is not before us, it is impossible to evaluate the necessity of the layoff provision as a remedy for the apparent prior employment discrimination absent reference to that goal. See, e.g., post, at 1858, (Marshall, J., dissenting). In this case, the hiring goal that the layoff provision was designed to safeguard was tied to the percentage of minority students in the school district, not to the percentage of qualified minority teachers within the relevant labor pool. The disparity between the percentage of minorities on the teaching staff and the percentage of minorities in the student body is not probative of employment discrimination; it is only when it is established that the availability of minorities in the relevant labor pool substantially exceeded those hired that one may draw an inference of deliberate discrimination in employment. See Hazelwood School District v. United States, 433 U.S. 299, 308, 97 S.Ct. 2736, 2741, 53 L.Ed.2d 768 (1977) (Title VII context). Because the layoff provision here acts to maintain levels of minority hiring that have no relation to remedying employment discrimination, it cannot be adjudged "narrowly tailored" to effectuate its asserted remedial purpose.

I therefore join in parts I, II, III–A, III–B, and V of the Court's opinion, and concur in the judgment.

JUSTICE WHITE, concurring in the judgment.

The school board's policy when layoffs are necessary is to maintain a certain proportion of minority teachers. This policy requires laying off non-minority teachers solely on the basis of their race, including teachers with seniority, and retaining other teachers solely because they are black, even though some of them are in probationary status. None of the interests asserted by the board, singly or together, justify this racially discriminatory layoff policy and save it from the strictures of the Equal Protection Clause. Whatever the legitimacy of hiring goals or quotas may be, the discharge of white teachers to make room for blacks, none of whom has been shown to be a victim of any racial discrimination, is quite a different matter. I cannot believe that in order to integrate a work force, it would be permissible to discharge whites and hire blacks until the latter comprised a suitable percentage of the work force. None of our cases suggest that this would be permissible under the Equal Protection Clause. Indeed, our cases look quite the other way. The layoff policy in this case—laying off whites

who would otherwise be retained in order to keep blacks on the job—
has the same effect and is equally violative of the Equal Protection
Clause. I agree with the plurality that this official policy is unconstitutional and hence concur in the judgment.

JUSTICE MARSHALL, with whom JUSTICE BRENNAN and JUSTICE BLACK-
MUN join, dissenting.

When this Court seeks to resolve far-ranging constitutional issues,
it must be especially careful to ground its analysis firmly in the facts of
the particular controversy before it. Yet in this significant case, we are
hindered by a record that is informal and incomplete. Both parties
now appear to realize that the record is inadequate to inform the
Court's decision. Both have lodged with the Court voluminous "submissions" containing factual material that was not considered by the
District Court or the Court of Appeals. Petitioners have submitted 21
separate items, predominantly statistical charts, which they assert are
relevant to their claim of discrimination. Respondents have submitted
public documents that tend to substantiate the facts alleged in the brief
accompanying their motion for summary judgment in the District
Court. These include transcripts and exhibits from two prior proceedings, in which certain questions of discrimination in the Jackson
schools were litigated, Jackson Education Association v. Board of Education, No. 4–72340 (ED Mich.1976) (*Jackson I*), and Jackson Education
Association v. Board of Education, (Jackson Cty.Cir.Ct.1979) (*Jackson
II*).

We should not acquiesce in the parties' attempt to try their case
before this Court. Yet it would be just as serious a mistake simply to
ignore altogether, as the plurality has done, the compelling factual
setting in which this case evidently has arisen. No race-conscious
provision that purports to serve a remedial purpose can be fairly
assessed in a vacuum.

The haste with which the District Court granted summary judgment to respondents, without seeking to develop the factual allegations
contained in respondents' brief, prevented the full exploration of the
facts that are now critical to resolution of the important issue before us.
Respondents' acquiescence in a premature victory in the District Court
should not now be used as an instrument of their defeat. Rather, the
District Court should have the opportunity to develop a factual record
adequate to resolve the serious issue raised by the case. I believe,
therefore, that it is improper for this Court to resolve the constitutional
issue in its current posture. But, because I feel that the plurality has
also erred seriously in its legal analysis of the merits of this case, I
write further to express my disagreement with the conclusions that it
has reached.

I, too, believe that layoffs are unfair. But unfairness ought not be
confused with constitutional injury. Paying no heed to the true circumstances of petitioners' plight, the plurality would nullify years of
negotiation and compromise designed to solve serious educational prob-

lems in the public schools of Jackson, Michigan. Because I believe that a public employer, with the full agreement of its employees, should be permitted to preserve the benefits of a legitimate and constitutional affirmative-action hiring plan even while reducing its work force, I dissent.

I

The record and extra-record materials that we have before us persuasively suggest that the plurality has too quickly assumed the absence of a legitimate factual predicate, even under the plurality's own view, for affirmative action in the Jackson schools. The first black teacher in the Jackson Public Schools was hired in 1954.[1] In 1969, when minority representation on the faculty had risen only to 3.9%, the Jackson branch of the NAACP filed a complaint with the Michigan Civil Rights Commission, alleging that the Board had engaged in various discriminatory practices, including racial discrimination in the hiring of teachers. The Commission conducted an investigation and concluded that each of the allegations had merit.[2]

In settlement of the complaint, the Commission issued an order of adjustment, under which the Jackson Board of Education (Board) agreed to numerous measures designed to improve educational opportunities for black public-school students. Among them was a promise to "[t]ake affirmative steps to recruit, hire and promote minority group teachers and counselors as positions bec[a]me available * * *." As a result of the Board's efforts to comply with the order over the next two years, the percentage of minority teachers increased to 8.8%.

In 1971, however, faculty layoffs became necessary. The contract in effect at that time, between the Board and the Jackson Education Association (Union), provided that layoffs would be made in reverse order of seniority. Because of the recent vintage of the school system's efforts to hire minorities, the seniority scheme led to the layoff of a substantial number of minority teachers, "literally wip[ing] out all the gain" made toward achieving racial balance. Respondent's Lodging No. 3, p. 24 (deposition of Superintendent of Schools). Once again, minority teachers on the faculty were a rarity.

---

1. Unless otherwise indicated, the historical facts herein recited have been taken from the Defendants' Brief in Support of its Motion for Summary Judgment before the District Court, Record, Doc. No. 4, pp. 1–6.

2. The Commission concluded that "[r]acial tension continues to be a part of the entire Jackson School System from the elementary level through high school. It would appear, therefore, that each of the allegations as stated in the complaint can be substantiated based upon organizational records, court files, school records, special committee reports and the appraisal conducted by the Superintendent of Schools." This conclusion is supported by extra-record materials suggesting that the shortage of minority teachers was the result of past discrimination in teacher hiring. For example, the then-Superintendent of Schools testified that "an administrator * * * told me she had tried to get a position in Jackson in the early 1950's and was told that they didn't hire colored people." This was the "type of thing," he stated, that led to adoption of Article XII.

By early 1972, when racial tensions in the schools had escalated to violent levels, school officials determined that the best course was full integration of the school system, including integration of the faculty. But they recognized that, without some modification of the seniority layoff system, genuine faculty integration could not take place. The Minority Affairs Office of the Jackson Public Schools submitted a questionnaire to all teachers, asking them to consider the possibility of abandoning the "last hired, first fired" approach to layoffs in favor of an absolute freeze on layoffs of minority teachers. The teachers overwhelmingly voted in favor of retaining the straight seniority system. Negotiations ensued between the two camps—on the one hand, the Board, which favored a freeze of minority layoffs and, on the other, the Union, urging straight seniority—and the negotiators ultimately reached accord. One union leader characterized the development of the layoff compromise as the most difficult balancing of equities that he had ever encountered.

The compromise avoided placing the entire burden of layoffs on either the white teachers as a group or the minority teachers as a group. Instead, each group would shoulder a portion of that burden equal to its portion of the faculty. Thus, the overall percentage of minorities on the faculty would remain constant. Within each group, seniority would govern which individuals would be laid off. This compromise was the provision at issue here, subsequently known as Article XII: * * *

The Board and the Union leadership agreed to the adoption of Article XII. The compromise was then presented to the teachers, who ratified it by majority vote. Each of the six times that the contract has been renegotiated, Article XII has been presented for reconsideration to the members of the Union, at least 80% of whom are white, and each time it has been ratified.

To petitioners, at the bottom of the seniority scale among white teachers, fell the lot of bearing the white group's proportionate share of layoffs that became necessary in 1982. Claiming a right not to lose their jobs ahead of minority teachers with less seniority, petitioners brought this challenge to Article XII under the Equal Protection Clause of the Fourteenth Amendment.

II

From the outset, it is useful to bear in mind what this case is not. There has been no court order to achieve racial balance, which might require us to reflect upon the existence of judicial power to impose obligations on parties not proven to have committed a wrong. There is also no occasion here to resolve whether a white worker may be required to give up his or her job in order to be replaced by a black worker. See Steelworkers v. Weber, 443 U.S. 193, 208, 99 S.Ct. 2721, 2729, 61 L.Ed.2d 480 (1979). Nor are we asked to order parties to suffer the consequences of an agreement that they had no role in adopting.

See Firefighters v. Stotts, 467 U.S. 561, 575, 104 S.Ct. 2576, 2586, 81 L.Ed.2d 483 (1984). Moreover, this is not a case in which a party to a collective-bargaining agreement has attempted unilaterally to achieve racial balance by refusing to comply with a contractual, seniority-based layoff provision. Cf. Teamsters v. United States, 431 U.S. 324, 350, 352, 97 S.Ct. 1843, 1862, 1863, 52 L.Ed.2d 396 (1977).

The sole question posed by this case is whether the Constitution prohibits a union and a local school board from developing a collective-bargaining agreement that apportions layoffs between two racially determined groups as a means of preserving the effects of an affirmative hiring policy, the constitutionality of which is unchallenged.[3]

III

Agreement upon a means for applying the Equal Protection Clause to an affirmative-action program has eluded this Court every time the issue has come before us. In University of California Regents v. Bakke, 438 U.S. 265, 98 S.Ct. 2733, 57 L.Ed.2d 750 (1978), four Members of the Court concluded that, while racial distinctions are irrelevant to nearly all legitimate state objectives and are properly subjected to the most rigorous judicial scrutiny in most instances, they are highly relevant to the one legitimate state objective of eliminating the pernicious vestiges of past discrimination; when that is the goal, a less exacting standard of review is appropriate. We explained at length our view that, because no fundamental right was involved and because whites have none of the immutable characteristics of a suspect class, the so-called "strict scrutiny" applied to cases involving either fundamental rights or suspect classifications was not applicable. Id., at 357, 98 S.Ct., at 2782 (opinion of Brennan, White, Marshall, and Blackmun, JJ.). Nevertheless, we eschewed the least rigorous, "rational basis" standard of

---

3. Justice O'Connor rests her disposition of this case on the propriety of the hiring plan, even though petitioners have not challenged it. She appears to rely on language in the preamble to the collective-bargaining agreement, which suggests that the "goal of such [affirmative-action] policy shall be to have at least the same percentage of minority racial representation on each individual staff as is represented by the student population of the Jackson Public Schools." Believing that the school system's hiring "goal" ought instead to be the percentage of qualified minorities in the labor pool, Justice O'Connor concludes that the challenged layoff provision itself is overly broad. Among the materials considered by the District Court and Court of Appeals, however, there is no evidence to show the actual proportion of minority teachers in the Jackson schools, either in relation to the qualified minority labor force or in relation to the number of minority students. If the distinction between the two goals is to be considered critical to the constitutionality of the affirmative-action plan, it is incumbent on petitioners—plaintiffs below—to demonstrate that, at the time they were laid off, the proportion of minority teachers had equaled or exceeded the appropriate percentage of the minority labor force, and that continued adherence to affirmative-action goals, therefore, unjustifiably caused their injuries. This petitioners have failed to do. Outside of the First Amendment context, I know of no justification for invalidating a provision because it might, in a hypothetical case, apply improperly to other potential plaintiffs. Petitioners have attempted to fill the gap in their case by supplying statistical charts to this Court. Clearly, however, we are not equipped for such factfinding, and if the hortatory ceiling of the affirmative-action plan is indeed to be considered a significant aspect of the case, then that would be an appropriate subject of inquiry on remand.

review, recognizing that any racial classification is subject to misuse. We determined that remedial use of race is permissible if it serves "important governmental objectives" and is "substantially related to achievement of those objectives." Id., at 359, 98 S.Ct., at 2783; see also id., at 387, 98 S.Ct., at 2797 (opinion of Marshall, J.); id., at 402, 98 S.Ct., at 2802 (opinion of Blackmun, J.). This standard is genuinely a "strict and searching" judicial inquiry, but is "not " 'strict" in theory and fatal in fact." ' Id., at 362, 98 S.Ct. at 2784 (opinion of Brennan, White, Marshall, and Blackmun, JJ.) (quoting Gunther, The Supreme Court, 1971 Term—Foreward: In Search of Evolving Doctrine on a Changing Court: A Model for a Newer Equal Protection, 86 Harv. L.Rev. 1, 8 (1972)). The only other Justice to reach the constitutional issue in *Bakke* suggested that, remedial purpose or no, any racial distinctions "call for the most exacting judicial examination." Id., at 291, 98 S.Ct., at 2748 (opinion of Powell, J.).

In Fullilove v. Klutznick, 448 U.S. 448, 100 S.Ct. 2758, 65 L.Ed.2d 902 (1980), the Court again disagreed as to the proper standard of review. Three Justices, of whom I was one, concluded that a statute reserving 10% of federal funds for minority contractors served important governmental objectives and was substantially related to achievement of those objectives, surviving attack under our *Bakke* test. 448 U.S., at 519, 100 S.Ct., at 2748 (Marshall, J., joined by Brennan and Blackmun, JJ., concurring in judgment). Three other Justices expressly declined to adopt any standard of review, deciding that the provision survived judicial scrutiny under either of the formulae articulated in *Bakke.* 448 U.S., at 492, 100 S.Ct., at 2781 (opinion of Burger, C.J., joined by White and Powell, JJ.).

Despite the Court's inability to agree on a route, we have reached a common destination in sustaining affirmative action against constitutional attack. In *Bakke,* we determined that a state institution may take race into account as a factor in its decisions, 438 U.S., at 326, 98 S.Ct., at 2766, and in *Fullilove,* the Court upheld a congressional preference for minority contractors because the measure was legitimately designed to ameliorate the present effects of past discrimination, 448 U.S., at 520, 100 S.Ct., at 2796.

In this case, it should not matter which test the Court applies. What is most important, under any approach to the constitutional analysis, is that a reviewing court genuinely consider the circumstances of the provision at issue. The history and application of Article XII, assuming verification upon a proper record, demonstrate that this provision would pass constitutional muster, no matter which standard the Court should adopt.

IV

The principal state purpose supporting Article XII is the need to preserve the levels of faculty integration achieved through the affirmative hiring policy adopted in the early 1970's. Justification for the hiring policy itself is found in the turbulent history of the effort to integrate the Jackson Public Schools—not even mentioned in the majority opinion—which attests to the bona fides of the Board's current employment practices.

The record and lodgings indicate that the Commission, endowed by the State Constitution with the power to investigate complaints of discrimination and the duty to secure the equal protection of the laws, Mich.Const., Art. V, § 29, prompted and oversaw the remedial steps now under attack.[4] When the Board agreed to take specified remedial action, including the hiring and promotion of minority teachers, the Commission did not pursue its investigation of the apparent violations to the point of rendering formal findings of discrimination.

Instead of subjecting an already volatile school system to the further disruption of formal accusations and trials, it appears that the Board set about achieving the goals articulated in the settlement. According to the then-Superintendent of Schools, the Board was aware, at every step of the way, that "[t]he NAACP had its court suit ready if either the Board postponed the [integration] operation or abandoned the attempts. They were willing to—they were ready to go into Federal court and get a court order, as happened in Kalamazoo." Rather than provoke the looming lawsuit, the Board and the Union worked with the committees to reach a solution to the racial problems plaguing the school system. In 1972, the Board explained to parents why it had adopted a voluntary integration plan:

> "Waiting for what appears the inevitable only flames passions and contributes to the difficulties of an orderly transition from a segregated to a desegregated school system. Firmly established legal precedents mandate a change. Many citizens know this to be true.

> "Waiting for a court order emphasizes to many that we are quite willing to disobey the law. * * * Further, court orders cost money for both the school system and the litigants." Respondents' Lodging No. 1, pp. 1–2 (Exhibit No. 8, *Jackson I*).

An explicit Board admission or judicial determination of culpability, which the petitioners and even the Solicitor General urge us to hold was required before the Board could undertake a race-conscious remedial plan, would only have exposed the Board in this case to further litigation and liability, including individual liability under 42 U.S.C. § 1983, for past acts. It would have contributed nothing to the ad-

---

4. The Commission currently describes its participation in the Jackson matter as follows: "[T]he Commission investigated the allegations and sought *to remedy the apparent violations* by negotiating an order of adjustment with the Jackson Board. * * * [T]he out-of-line seniority layoff provisions in the Jackson Board of Education's employment contracts with its teachers since 1972 are consistent with overall desegregation efforts undertaken *in compliance with* the Commission's order of adjustment." Brief for Michigan Civil Rights Commission, Michigan Dept. of Civil Rights as *Amicus Curiae* 14 (emphasis added).

vancement of the community's urgent objective of integrating its schools.

The real irony of the argument urging mandatory, formal findings of discrimination lies in its complete disregard for a longstanding goal of civil rights reform, that of integrating schools without taking every school system to court. Our school desegregation cases imposed an affirmative duty on local school boards to see that "racial discrimination would be eliminated root and branch." Green v. County School Board, 391 U.S. 430, 437–438, 88 S.Ct. 1689, 1693–1694, 20 L.Ed.2d 716 (1968); see Brown v. Board of Education, 349 U.S. 294, 299, 75 S.Ct. 753, 755, 99 L.Ed. 1083 (1955). Petitioners would now have us inform the Board, having belatedly taken this Court's admonitions to heart, that it should have delayed further, disputing its obligations and forcing the aggrieved parties to seek judicial relief. This result would be wholly inconsistent with the national policies against overloading judicial dockets, maintaining groundless defenses, and impeding good-faith settlement of legal disputes. Only last Term, writing for the Court, The Chief Justice reaffirmed that civil rights litigation is no exception to the general policy in favor of settlements: "Indeed, Congress made clear its concern that civil rights plaintiffs not be penalized for 'helping to lessen docket congestion' by settling their cases out of court. * * * In short, settlements rather than litigation will serve the interests of plaintiffs as well as defendants." Marek v. Chesny, 473 U.S. 1, 10, 105 S.Ct. 3012, 3018, 87 L.Ed.2d 1 (1985). It would defy equity to penalize those who achieve harmony from discord, as it would defy wisdom to impose on society the needless cost of superfluous litigation. The Court is correct to recognize, as it does today, that formal findings of past discrimination are not a necessary predicate to the adoption of affirmative-action policies, and that the scope of such policies need not be limited to remedying specific instances of identifiable discrimination.

Moreover, under the apparent circumstances of this case, we need not rely on any general awareness of "societal discrimination" to conclude that the Board's purpose is of sufficient importance to justify its limited remedial efforts. There are allegations that the imperative to integrate the public schools was urgent. Racially motivated violence had erupted at the schools, interfering with all educational objectives. We are told that, having found apparent violations of the law and a substantial underrepresentation of minority teachers, the state agency responsible for ensuring equality of treatment for all citizens of Michigan had instituted a settlement that required the Board to adopt affirmative hiring practices in lieu of further enforcement proceedings. That agency, participating as *amicus curiae* through the Attorney General of Michigan, still stands fully behind the solution that the Board and the Union adopted in Article XII, viewing it as a measure necessary to attainment of stability and educational quality in the public schools. See n. 4, supra. Surely, if properly presented to the District Court, this would supply the "[e]videntiary support for the conclusion that remedial action is warranted" that the plurality purports to seek. Since the District Court did not permit submission of this evidentiary support, I am at a loss as to why Justice Powell so glibly rejects the obvious solution of remanding for the factfinding he appears to recognize is necessary. See ante, at 1848–1849, n. 5.

Were I satisfied with the record before us, I would hold that the state purpose of preserving the integrity of a valid hiring policy—which in turn sought to achieve diversity and stability for the benefit of *all* students—was sufficient, in this case, to satisfy the demands of the Constitution.

V

The second part of any constitutional assessment of the disputed plan requires us to examine the means chosen to achieve the state purpose. Again, the history of Article XII, insofar as we can determine it, is the best source of assistance.

A

Testimony of both Union and school officials illustrates that the Board's obligation to integrate its faculty could not have been fulfilled meaningfully as long as layoffs continued to eliminate the last hired. In addition, qualified minority teachers from other States were reluctant to uproot their lives and move to Michigan without any promise of protection from imminent layoff. The testimony suggests that the lack of some layoff protection would have crippled the efforts to recruit minority applicants. Adjustment of the layoff hierarchy under these circumstances was a necessary corollary of an affirmative hiring policy.

B

Under Justice Powell's approach, the community of Jackson, having painfully watched the hard-won benefits of its integration efforts vanish as a result of massive layoffs, would be informed today, simply, that preferential layoff protection is never permissible because hiring policies serve the same purpose at a lesser cost. As a matter of logic as well as fact, a hiring policy achieves no purpose at all if it is eviscerated by layoffs. Justice Powell's position is untenable.

Justice Powell has concluded, by focusing exclusively on the undisputed hardship of losing a job, that the Equal Protection Clause always bars race-conscious layoff plans. This analysis overlooks, however, the important fact that Article XII does not cause the loss of jobs; someone will lose a job under any layoff plan and, whoever it is, that person will not deserve it. Any *per se* prohibition against layoff protection, therefore, must rest upon a premise that the tradition of basing layoff decisions on seniority is so fundamental that its modification can never be permitted. Our cases belie that premise.

The general practice of basing employment decisions on relative seniority may be upset for the sake of other public policies. For example, a court may displace innocent workers by granting retroactive seniority to victims of employment discrimination. Franks v. Bowman Transportation Co., 424 U.S. 747, 775, 96 S.Ct. 1251, 1269, 47 L.Ed.2d 444 (1976). Further, this Court has long held that "employee expectations arising from a seniority system agreement may be modified by statutes furthering a strong public policy interest." Id., at 778, 96 S.Ct., at 1271. And we have recognized that collective-bargaining agreements may go further than statutes in enhancing the seniority of certain employees for the purpose of fostering legitimate interests. See Ford Motor Co. v. Huffman, 345 U.S. 330, 339–340, 73 S.Ct. 681, 686–687, 97 L.Ed. 1048 (1953). Accordingly, we have upheld one collectively bargained provision that bestowed enhanced seniority on those who had served in the military before employment, id., at 340, 73 S.Ct., at 687, and another that gave preferred seniority status to union chairmen, to the detriment of veterans. Aeronautical Industrial District Lodge 727 v. Campbell, 337 U.S. 521, 529, 69 S.Ct. 1287, 1291, 93 L.Ed. 1513 (1949).

In Steelworkers v. Weber, 443 U.S. 193, 99 S.Ct. 2721, 61 L.Ed.2d 480 (1979), we specifically addressed a departure from the seniority principle designed to alleviate racial disparity. In *Weber,* a private employer and a union negotiated a collective agreement that reserved for black employees one half of all openings in a plant training program, replacing the prior system of awarding all seats on the basis of seniority. This plan tampered with the expectations attendant to seniority, and redistributed opportunities to achieve an important qualification toward advancement in the company. We upheld the challenged plan under the Civil Rights Act of 1964 because it was designed to "eliminate traditional patterns of racial segregation" in the industry and did not "unnecessarily trammel the interests of the white employees." Id., at 201, 208, 99 S.Ct., at 2726, 2730. We required no judicial finding or employer admission of past discrimination to justify that interference with the seniority hierarchy for the sake of the legitimate purposes at stake.

These cases establish that protection from layoff is not altogether unavailable as a tool for achieving legitimate societal goals. It remains to be determined whether the particular form of layoff protection embodied in Article XII falls among the permissible means for preserving minority proportions on the teaching staff.

C

Article XII is a narrow provision because it allocates the impact of an unavoidable burden proportionately between two racial groups. It places no absolute burden or benefit on one race, and, within the confines of constant minority proportions, it preserves the hierarchy of seniority in the selection of individuals for layoff. Race is a factor, along with seniority, in determining which individuals the school system will lose; it is not alone dispositive of any individual's fate. Cf. *Bakke,* 438 U.S., at 318, 98 S.Ct., at 2762 (opinion of Powell, J.).

Moreover, Article XII does not use layoff protection as a tool for *increasing* minority representation; achievement of that goal is entrusted to the less severe hiring policies.[5] And Article XII is narrow in the temporal sense as well. The very bilateral process that gave rise to Article XII when its adoption was necessary will also occasion its demise when remedial measures are no longer required. Finally, Article XII modifies contractual expectations that do not themselves carry any connotation of merit or achievement; it does not interfere with the "cherished American ethic" of "[f]airness in individual competition," *Bakke,* supra, at 319, n. 53, 98 S.Ct., at 2763, n. 53, depriving individuals of an opportunity that they could be said to deserve. In all of these important ways, Article XII metes out the hardship of layoffs in a manner that achieves its purpose with the smallest possible deviation from established norms.

The Board's goal of preserving minority proportions could have been achieved, perhaps, in a different way. For example, if layoffs had been determined by lottery, the ultimate effect would have been retention of current racial percentages. A random system, however, would place every teacher in equal jeopardy, working a much greater upheaval of the seniority hierarchy than that occasioned by Article XII; it is not at all a less restrictive means of achieving the Board's goal. Another possible approach would have been a freeze on layoffs of minority teachers. This measure, too, would have been substantially more burdensome than Article XII, not only by necessitating the layoff of a greater number of white teachers, but also by erecting an absolute distinction between the races, one to be benefited and one to be burdened, in a way that Article XII avoids. Indeed, neither petitioners nor any Justice of this Court has suggested an alternative to Article XII that would have attained the stated goal in any narrower or more equitable a fashion. Nor can I conceive of one.

VI

It is no accident that this least burdensome of all conceivable options is the very provision that the parties adopted. For Article XII was forged in the crucible of clashing interests. All of the economic powers of the predominantly white teachers' union were brought to bear against those of the elected Board, and the process yielded consensus.

The concerns that have prompted some Members of this Court to call for narrowly tailored, perhaps court-ordered, means of achieving racial balance spring from a legitimate fear that racial distinctions will

---

5. Justice White assumes that respondents' plan is equivalent to one that deliberately seeks to change the racial composition of a staff by firing and hiring members of predetermined rates. Ante, at 1857. That assumption utterly ignores the fact that the Jackson plan involves only the means for selecting the employees who will be chosen for layoffs already necessitated by external economic conditions. This plan does not seek to supplant whites with blacks, nor does it contribute in any way to the number of job losses.

again be used as a means to persecute individuals, while couched in benign phraseology. That fear has given rise to mistrust of those who profess to take remedial action, and concern that any such action "work the least harm possible to other innocent persons competing for the benefit." *Bakke*, supra, at 308, 98 S.Ct., at 2757 (opinion of Powell, J.). One Justice has warned that "if innocent employees are to be made to make any sacrifices * * * they must be represented and have had full participation rights in the negotiation process," Firefighters v. Stotts, 467 U.S., at 588, n. 3, 104 S.Ct., at 2593 (O'Connor, J., concurring), and another has called for a "principle for deciding whether preferential classifications reflect a benign remedial purpose or a malevolent stigmatic classification * * * " *Bakke*, supra, 438 U.S., at 294–295, n. 34, 98 S.Ct., at 2750, n. 34 (opinion of Powell, J.). This case answers that call.

The collective-bargaining process is a legitimate and powerful vehicle for the resolution of thorny problems, and we have favored "minimal supervision by courts and other governmental agencies over the substantive terms of collective-bargaining agreements." American Tobacco Co. v. Patterson, 456 U.S. 63, 76–77, 102 S.Ct. 1534, 1541, 71 L.Ed.2d 748 (1982). We have also noted that "[s]ignificant freedom must be afforded employers and unions to create differing seniority systems," California Brewers Assn. v. Bryant, 444 U.S. 598, 608, 100 S.Ct. 814, 820, 63 L.Ed.2d 55 (1980).[6] The perceived dangers of affirmative action misused, therefore, are naturally averted by the bilateral process of negotiation, agreement, and ratification. The best evidence that Article XII is a narrow means to serve important interests is that representatives of all affected persons, starting from diametrically opposed perspectives, have agreed to it—not once, but six times since 1972.

VII

The narrow question presented by this case, if indeed we proceed to the merits, offers no occasion for the Court to issue broad proclamations of public policy concerning the controversial issue of affirmative action. Rather, this case calls for calm, dispassionate reflection upon exactly what has been done, to whom, and why. If one honestly confronts each of those questions against the factual background suggested by the materials submitted to us, I believe the conclusion is inescapable that Article XII meets, and indeed surpasses, any standard for ensuring that race-conscious programs are necessary to achieve remedial purposes. When an elected school board and a teachers' union collectively bargain a layoff provision designed to preserve the effects of a valid minority recruitment plan by apportioning layoffs between two racial groups, as a result of a settlement achieved under the auspices of a supervisory

---

6. This deference is warranted only if the union represents the interests of the workers fairly; a union's breach of that duty in the form of racial discrimination gives rise to an action by the worker against the union. See Steele v. Louisville & Nashville R. Co., 323 U.S. 192, 207, 65 S.Ct. 226, 234, 89 L.Ed. 173 (1944).

state agency charged with protecting the civil rights of all citizens, that provision should not be upset by this Court on constitutional grounds.

The alleged facts that I have set forth above evince, at the very least, a wealth of plausible evidence supporting the Board's position that Article XII was a legitimate and necessary response both to racial discrimination and to educational imperatives. To attempt to resolve the constitutional issue either with no historical context whatever, as the plurality has done, or on the basis of a record devoid of established facts, is to do a grave injustice not only to the Board and teachers of Jackson and to the State of Michigan, but also to individuals and governments committed to the goal of eliminating all traces of segregation throughout the country. Most of all, it does an injustice to the aspirations embodied in the Fourteenth Amendment itself. I would vacate the judgment of the Court of Appeals and remand with instructions that the case be remanded to the District Court for further proceedings consistent with the views I have expressed.[7]

JUSTICE STEVENS, dissenting.

In my opinion, it is not necessary to find that the Board of Education has been guilty of racial discrimination in the past to support the conclusion that it has a legitimate interest in employing more black teachers in the future. Rather than analyzing a case of this kind by asking whether minority teachers have some sort of special entitlement to jobs as a remedy for sins that were committed in the past, I believe that we should first ask whether the Board's action advances the public interest in educating children for the future. If so, I believe we should consider whether that public interest, and the manner in which it is pursued, justifies any adverse effects on the disadvantaged group.[1]

I

The Equal Protection Clause absolutely prohibits the use of race in many governmental contexts. To cite only a few: the government may not use race to decide who may serve on juries,[2] who may use public

---

7. I do not envy the District Court its task of sorting out what this Court has and has not held today. It is clear, at any rate, that from among the many views expressed today, two noteworthy results emerge: a majority of the Court has explicitly rejected the argument that an affirmative-action plan must be preceded by a formal finding that the entity seeking to institute the plan has committed discriminatory acts in the past; and the Court has left open whether layoffs may be used as an instrument of remedial action.

1. In every equal protection case, we have to ask certain basic questions.

"What class is harmed by the legislation, and has it been subjected to a 'tradition of

disfavor' by our laws? What is the public purpose that is being served by the law? What is the characteristic of the disadvantaged class that justifies the disparate treatment?" Cleburne v. Cleburne Living Center, 473 U.S. 432, 453, 105 S.Ct. 3249, 3261–3262, 87 L.Ed.2d 313 (1985) (Stevens, J., concurring).

2. Batson v. Kentucky, 476 U.S. 79, 106 S.Ct. 1712, 90 L.Ed.2d 69 (1986); Vasquez v. Hillery, 474 U.S. 254, 106 S.Ct. 617, 88 L.Ed.2d 598 (1985); Rose v. Mitchell, 443 U.S. 545, 99 S.Ct. 2993, 61 L.Ed.2d 739 (1979); Strauder v. West Virginia, 10 Otto 303, 100 U.S. 303, 25 L.Ed. 664 (1880).

services,[3] who may marry,[4] and who may be fit parents.[5] The use of race in these situations is "utterly irrational" because it is completely unrelated to any valid public purpose;[6] moreover, it is particularly pernicious because it constitutes a badge of oppression that is unfaithful to the central promise of the Fourteenth Amendment.

Nevertheless, in our present society, race is not always irrelevant to sound governmental decisionmaking.[7] To take the most obvious example, in law enforcement, if an undercover agent is needed to infiltrate a group suspected of ongoing criminal behavior—and if the members of the group are all of the same race—it would seem perfectly rational to employ an agent of that race rather than a member of a different racial class. Similarly, in a city with a recent history of racial unrest, the superintendent of police might reasonably conclude that an integrated police force could develop a better relationship with the community and thereby do a more effective job of maintaining law and order than a force composed only of white officers.

In the context of public education,[8] it is quite obvious that a school board may reasonably conclude that an integrated faculty will be able

---

3. Turner v. City of Memphis, 369 U.S. 350, 82 S.Ct. 805, 7 L.Ed.2d 762 (1962) (per curiam); Burton v. Wilmington Parking Authority, 365 U.S. 715, 81 S.Ct. 856, 6 L.Ed.2d 45 (1961).

4. Loving v. Virginia, 388 U.S. 1, 87 S.Ct. 1817, 18 L.Ed.2d 1010 (1967).

5. Palmore v. Sidoti, 466 U.S. 429, 104 S.Ct. 1879, 80 L.Ed.2d 421 (1984).

6. *Cleburne,* supra, 473 U.S., at 452, 105 S.Ct., at 3261 (Stevens, J., concurring in judgment) ("It would be utterly irrational to limit the franchise on the basis of height or weight; it is equally invalid to limit it on the basis of skin color"). See also Palmore v. Sidoti, 466 U.S., at 432, 104 S.Ct., at 1882 (1984) ("Classifying persons according to their race is more likely to reflect racial prejudice than legitimate public concerns; the race, not the person, dictates the category").

7. As Justice Marshall explains, although the Court's path in University of California Regents v. Bakke, 438 U.S. 265, 98 S.Ct. 2733, 57 L.Ed.2d 750 (1978) and Fullilove v. Klutznick, 448 U.S. 448, 100 S.Ct. 2758, 65 L.Ed.2d 902 (1980) is tortuous, the path at least reveals that race consciousness does not automatically violate the Equal Protection Clause. In those opinions, only two Justices of the Court suggested that race conscious governmental efforts were inherently unconstitutional. See id., at 522, 100 S.Ct., at 2797 (Stewart, J., dissenting, joined by Rehnquist, J.). Cf. id., at 548, 100 S.Ct., at 2810 (Stevens, J., dissenting) ("Unlike Mr. Justice Stewart and Mr. Justice Rehnquist, * * * I am not

convinced that the Clause contains an absolute prohibition against any statutory classification based on race"). Notably, in this Court, petitioners have presented solely a constitutional theory, and have not pursued any statutory claims. Cf. *Bakke,* 438 U.S. at 408, 98 S.Ct., at 2808 (Stevens, J., concurring in judgment in part and dissenting in part) (suggesting that constitutional issue need not be reached because statutory issue was dispositive).

8. The Court has frequently emphasized the role of public schools in our national life. See Board of Education v. Pico, 457 U.S. 853, 864, 102 S.Ct. 2799, 2806, 73 L.Ed.2d 435 (1982) (plurality opinion) ("[P]ublic schools are vitally important * * * as vehicles for 'inculcating fundamental values necessary to the maintenance of a democratic political system' "); Ambach v. Norwick, 441 U.S. 68, 76, 99 S.Ct. 1589, 1594, 60 L.Ed.2d 49 (1979) ("The importance of public schools in the preparation of individuals for participation as citizens, and in the preservation of the values on which our society rests, long has been recognized by our decisions"); San Antonio Independent School District v. Rodriguez, 411 U.S. 1, 30, 93 S.Ct. 1278, 1295, 36 L.Ed.2d 16 (1973) (" 'the grave significance of education both to the individual and to our society' cannot be doubted"); Brown v. Board of Education, 347 U.S. 483, 493, 74 S.Ct. 686, 691, 98 L.Ed. 873 (1954) ("[E]ducation * * * is the very foundation of good citizenship. Today it is a principal instrument in awakening the

to provide benefits to the student body that could not be provided by an all white, or nearly all white, faculty. For one of the most important lessons that the American public schools teach is that the diverse ethnic, cultural, and national backgrounds that have been brought together in our famous "melting pot" do not identify essential differences among the human beings that inhabit our land. It is one thing for a white child to be taught by a white teacher that color, like beauty, is only "skin deep"; it is far more convincing to experience that truth on a day to day basis during the routine, ongoing learning process.

In this case, the collective-bargaining agreement between the Union and the Board of Education succinctly stated a valid public purpose—"recognition of the desirability of multi-ethnic representation on the teaching faculty," and thus "a policy of actively seeking minority group personnel." App. to Pet. for Cert. 22a. Nothing in the record—not a shred of evidence—contradicts the view that the Board's attempt to employ, and to retain, more minority teachers in the Jackson public school system served this completely sound educational purpose. Thus, there was a rational and unquestionably legitimate basis for the Board's decision to enter into the collective-bargaining agreement that petitioners have challenged, even though the agreement required special efforts to recruit and retain minority teachers.

II

It is argued, nonetheless, that the purpose should be deemed invalid because, even if the Board of Education's judgment in this case furthered a laudable goal, some other boards might claim that their experience demonstrates that segregated classes, or segregated faculties, lead to better academic achievement. There is, however, a critical difference between a decision to *exclude* a member of a minority race because of his or her skin color and a decision to *include* more members of the minority in a school faculty for that reason.

The exclusionary decision rests on the false premise that differences in race, or in the color of a person's skin, reflect real differences that are relevant to a person's right to share in the blessings of a free society. As noted, that premise is "utterly irrational," *Cleburne v. Cleburne Living Center,* 473 U.S. 432, 452, 105 S.Ct. 3249, 3261, 87 L.Ed.2d 313 (1987), and repugnant to the principles of a free and democratic society. Nevertheless, the fact that persons of different races do, indeed, have differently colored skin, may give rise to a belief that there is some significant difference between such persons. The inclusion of minority teachers in the educational process inevitably tends to dispel that illusion whereas their exclusion could only tend to foster it. The inclusionary decision is consistent with the principle that all men are created equal; the exclusionary decision is at war with that principle. One decision accords with the Equal Protection Clause of the

child to cultural values, in preparing him for later professional training, and in helping him to adjust normally to his environment").

Fourteenth Amendment; the other does not. Thus, consideration of whether the consciousness of race is exclusionary or inclusionary plainly distinguishes the Board's valid purpose in this case from a race-conscious decision that would reinforce assumptions of inequality.[9]

III

Even if there is a valid purpose to the race consciousness, however, the question that remains is whether that public purpose transcends the harm to the white teachers who are disadvantaged by the special preference the Board has given to its most recently hired minority teachers. In my view, there are two important inquiries in assessing the harm to the disadvantaged teacher. The first is an assessment of the procedures that were used to adopt, and implement, the race-conscious action.[10] The second is an evaluation of the nature of the harm itself.

In this case, there can be no question about either the fairness of the procedures used to adopt the race-conscious provision, or the propriety of its breadth. As Justice Marshall has demonstrated, the procedures for adopting this provision were scrupulously fair. The Union that represents the petitioners negotiated the provision and agreed to it; the agreement was put to a vote of the membership, and overwhelmingly approved. Again, not a shred of evidence in the record suggests *any* procedural unfairness in the adoption of the agreement. Similarly, the provision is specifically designed to achieve its objective—retaining the minority teachers that have been specially recruited to give the Jackson schools, after a period of racial unrest, an integrated faculty. Thus, in striking contrast to the procedural inadequacy and unjustified breadth of the race-based classification in Fullilove v. Klutznick, 448 U.S. 448, 100 S.Ct. 2758, 65 L.Ed.2d 902 (1980), the race-conscious layoff

---

9. Cf. Palmore v. Sidoti, 466 U.S., at 434, 104 S.Ct., at 1882 (1984) ("The effects of racial prejudice, however real, cannot justify a racial classification removing an infant child from the custody of its natural mother found to be an appropriate person to have such custody"); Buchanan v. Warley, 245 U.S. 60, 81, 38 S.Ct. 16, 20, 62 L.Ed. 149 (1917) (rejecting legitimacy of argument that the "proposed segregation will promote the public peace by preventing race conflicts").

10. Cf. *Fullilove,* 448 U.S., at 548–549, 100 S.Ct., at 2810–2811 (Stevens, J., dissenting) (a race-based classification "does impose a special obligation to scrutinize any governmental decision-making process that draws nationwide distinctions between citizens on the basis of their race and incidentally also discriminates against non-citizens in the preferred racial classes. For just as procedural safeguards are necessary to guarantee impartial decisionmak-

ing in the judicial process, so can they play a vital part in preserving the impartial character of the legislative process"). That observation is, of course, equally applicable to a context in which the governmental decision is reached through a nonlegislative process. Significantly, a reason given for what this Court frequently calls "strict scrutiny" of certain classifications is the notion that the disadvantaged class is one that has been unable to enjoy full procedural participation. See United States v. Carolene Products, Co., 304 U.S. 144, 152–153, n. 4, 58 S.Ct. 778, 783–784, n. 4, 82 L.Ed. 1234 (1938) ("[P]rejudice against discrete and insular minorities may be a special condition, which tends seriously to curtail the operation of those political processes ordinarily to be relied upon to protect minorities, and which may call for a correspondingly more searching judicial inquiry"); J. Ely, Democracy and Distrust 75–77 (1980).

policy here was adopted with full participation of the disadvantaged individuals and with a narrowly circumscribed berth for the policy's operation.

Finally, we must consider the harm to the petitioners. Every layoff, like every refusal to employ a qualified applicant, is a grave loss to the affected individual. However, the undisputed facts in this case demonstrate that this serious consequence to the petitioners is not based on any lack of respect for their race, or on blind habit and stereotype. Rather, petitioners have been laid off for a combination of two reasons: the economic conditions that have led Jackson to lay off some teachers, and the special contractual protections intended to preserve the newly integrated character of the faculty in the Jackson schools. Thus, the same harm might occur if a number of gifted young teachers had been given special contractual protection because their specialties were in short supply and if the Jackson Board of Education faced a fiscal need for layoffs. A Board decision to grant immediate tenure to a group of experts in computer technology, an athletic coach, and a language teacher, for example, might reduce the pool of teachers eligible for layoffs during a depression and therefore have precisely the same impact as the racial preference at issue here. In either case, the harm would be generated by the combination of economic conditions and the special contractual protection given a different group of teachers—a protection that, as discussed above, was justified by a valid and extremely strong public interest.[14]

IV

We should not lightly approve the government's use of a race-based distinction. History teaches the obvious dangers of such classifications. Our ultimate goal must, of course, be "to eliminate entirely from governmental decisionmaking such irrelevant factors as a human being's race." In this case, however, I am persuaded that the decision to include more minority teachers in the Jackson, Michigan, school system served a valid public purpose, that it was adopted with fair procedures and given a narrow breadth, that it transcends the harm to petitioners, and that it is a step toward that ultimate goal of eliminating entirely from governmental decisionmaking such irrelevant factors as a human

---

14. The fact that the issue arises in a layoff context, rather than a hiring context, has no bearing on the equal protection question. For if the Board's interest in employing more minority teachers is sufficient to justify providing them with an extra incentive to accept jobs in Jackson, Michigan, it is also sufficient to justify their retention when the number of available jobs is reduced. Justice Powell's suggestion, ante, at 1850–1852, that there is a distinction of constitutional significance under the Equal Protection Clause between a racial preference at the time of hiring and an identical preference at the time of discharge is thus wholly unpersuasive. He seems to assume that a teacher who has been working for a few years suffers a greater harm when he is laid off than the harm suffered by an unemployed teacher who is refused a job for which he is qualified. In either event, the adverse decision forecloses "only one of several opportunities" that may be available, ante, at 1851, to the disappointed teacher. Moreover, the distinction is artificial, for the layoff provision at issue in this case was included as part of the terms of the *hiring* of minority and other teachers under the collective-bargaining agreement.

being's race. I would therefore affirm the judgment of the Court of Appeals.

NOTES AND PROBLEMS FOR DISCUSSION

1. The decision in *Wygant*, the first Supreme Court opinion dealing with a constitutional challenge to race-based affirmative relief in the employment context, revealed the Justices' positions on two important issues and offered insight into their likely views on two other questions.

(a) The four member plurality clearly stated that racial classifications, whether predicated on so called "benign" or invidious considerations, are subject to traditional strict scrutiny analysis. Justices Marshall, Brennan and Blackmun, on the other hand, concluded that benign classifications; i.e., those designed to remedy the effects of prior discrimination, should be subjected to a less rigorous level of scrutiny. Justice White did not announce his view on this question. Justice Stevens' opinion, in this regard, may be the most intriguing. While citing the opinion in which he applied traditional strict scrutiny to the statutory minority-owned business set-aside program in *Fullilove*, his use in *Wygant* of such phrases as "legitimate interest," "sound purpose" and "valid purpose" and his reliance on an inclusionary/exclusionary consciousness dichotomy, at least suggested that he was moving closer to the dissenters' position. The Court's inability to reach a consensus on the appropriate level of constitutional scrutiny to be applied to race-based affirmative action is lamented in Friedman, Constitutional Equality and Affirmative Action in Employment: A Search for Standards, 1986 Det.C. of L.Rev. 1113 (1986); Choper, Continued Uncertainty as to the Constitutionality of Remedial Racial Classifications: Identifying the Pieces of the Puzzle, 72 Iowa L.Rev. 255 (1987). Three years later, with the addition of Justices Scalia and Kennedy to the Court, a majority finally was able to agree on the level of scrutiny to be applied to race-based affirmative action plans. See *Croson, infra*, at 1104.

(b) There seemed to be no disagreement with the notion that while eliminating the effects of prior employer-specific discrimination is a permissible justification for the use of race-based affirmative relief in the public sector, ameliorating the vestiges of societal discrimination is not a constitutionally sufficient state interest. Equally significantly, all of the seven Justices who discussed the issue (i.e., all but White and Stevens) agreed that the requisite employer-specific discrimination did not have to be documented in a contemporaneous judicial determination of discrimination. While the Justices may have quibbled over the exact characterization of the requisite standard of employer belief in the necessity for affirmative action, these seven concurred in rejecting the contention that affirmative relief must be predicated upon a judicial finding of liability. For an interesting discussion on the capacity of public institutions to make the determinations necessary to support an affirmative action plan, see Note, Principles of Competence: The Ability of Public Institutions To Adopt Remedial Affirmative Action Plans, 53 U.Chi.L.Rev. 581 (1986). The related, but perhaps more complex issue of the degree of legislative factfinding sufficient to support a legislatively enacted affirmative action plan was addressed by the Court in *Croson*, the next principal case.

(c) While the Justices differed on the level of scrutiny to be applied to this racial classification, they all adhered to the traditional two tiered formula. With respect to the second prong of this bifurcated approach—the degree to which the chosen means accomplished the legitimate state interest in remedying prior discrimination by the defendant employer—the opinions suggest that although a majority of five invalidated the layoff policy, all nine might uphold a race-based hiring plan. Three members of the plurality, Justices Powell, Burger and Rehnquist, reasoned that race-based layoffs are more injurious to the innocent, non-preferred employees and are thus less acceptable than race-based hiring decisions. This consideration was enough for them to conclude that the layoff policy was not sufficiently narrowly tailored to pass constitutional muster. Nevertheless, they contrasted the layoff policy to hiring goals, which they characterized as a "less intrusive means" of accomplishing the permissible purpose. Justice White's somewhat perplexing opinion suggests that he also might treat a race-based hiring policy differently than a layoff plan. Justice O'Connor broke with the plurality on this issue. While she agreed that the layoff policy was not narrowly tailored, she based this conclusion on the ground that by tying layoffs to a policy of maintaining a balance between the level of teacher and student integration, the policy was unrelated to the permissible goal of eradicating the effects of racial discrimination in hiring. Her opinion implies, therefore, that had the hiring, and thus the layoff, policy been keyed to the percentage of qualified black workers in the relevant labor pool, it would have survived constitutional challenge. The four dissenters, including Justice Stevens, not only upheld the validity of the layoff plan but rejected Justice Powell's view that there was a constitutional difference between race-based layoff and hiring policies.

When, therefore, Justice O'Connor's position is considered in conjunction with that of the four dissenters, it strongly suggests that a majority of five would have approved of the race-conscious layoff policy had it been more narrowly tailored, in Justice O'Connor's view, to the goal of remedying employment discrimination. Thus, had the layoff preference been designed to maintain a balance between the percentage of black teachers and the percentage of qualified blacks in the relevant labor pool, it probably would have been upheld by a majority of the Court. This certainly was the view of the Seventh Circuit. Prior to the Supreme Court's ruling in *Wygant*, the circuit court had granted an en banc rehearing in BRITTON v. SOUTH BEND COMMUNITY SCHOOL CORP., 775 F.2d 794 (7th Cir.1985), cert. denied, 484 U.S. 925, 108 S.Ct. 288, 98 L.Ed.2d 248 (1987), a case challenging the constitutionality of a school district collective bargaining agreement that provided that no black teacher would be laid off until every white teacher had been laid off. After the ruling was issued in *Wygant*, the Seventh Circuit rendered its en banc opinion in *Britton*, concluding that while *Wygant* implied that a racially based layoff policy could withstand constitutional scrutiny if it was tied to the percentage of qualified minority workers in the relevant labor pool, the instant contractual provision, as in *Wygant*, sought to accomplish the impermissible goal of raising the level of black representation on the faculty to the level of black representation in the student body. 819 F.2d 766 (7th Cir.1987). Moreover, a majority of the court added, the South Bend contract went further than the provision in *Wygant* since it provided an absolute preference in the event of layoffs to all black teachers and thus must have been intended to increase, rather than simply maintain, the level of black employment effected by prior race-conscious hiring decisions and, in doing so, imposed an unacceptable burden on the white employees. It therefore reversed the trial court's decision, which had upheld the constitutionality of the school board's action, and refused to remand the case to allow the plaintiff school district to prove that the no-minority layoff provision was actually designed to remedy past discrimination in hiring against black teachers. The four dissenting judges were not convinced that the subject provision was based on a "role model" theory designed simply to achieve identical levels of faculty and student integration. They preferred to remand the case to permit the trial court to decide whether or not the no-minority layoff provision was, in fact, intended to remedy past discrimination against black teachers and, if so, whether such a drastic remedy was necessary to accomplish that compelling state interest.

(d) Finally, while none of the opinions directly addressed the controversial issue of whether affirmative relief should be limited to identifiable victims of discrimination or made available on a group basis to members of the victimized class, footnote 12 of the plurality opinion implies that a race-based hiring remedy, as opposed to layoff protection, might not have to be limited to specific victims. The Court directly addressed this issue, in the statutory context, in *Local 28, supra.*

2. Suppose an employer discovers that its hiring examination generates a disproportionate impact on women and minority candidates. To attain a representative racial mix, it readjusts the weight it accords to the various components of the test in order to create a racially and gender-proportioned bottom line. Has the employer violated Title VII? See San Francisco Police Officers' Ass'n v. City and County of San Francisco, 812 F.2d 1125 (9th Cir.1987).

3. When nonminority individuals bring a *Wygant*-like claim of "reverse discrimination", should the validity of the affirmative action plan be viewed as part of plaintiff's *prima facie* case, as an element of the defendant's general denial, or as an affirmative defense? In other words, who should bear the burden of persuasion? An overwhelming majority of the Court in *Wygant* (all but Justices White and Stevens) placed this burden on the plaintiff. Prior to this decision, however, several lower courts had ruled that the defendant carried the burden of proving that the plan was appropriately tailored to a permissible state interest. The Court finally addressed this question, at least in the statutory context, in Johnson v. Transportation Agency, *infra*, at 1177.

4. The City of Apex announced that it had 19 vacancies for the position of Detective Grade I. It solicited applications from all persons holding the rank of Detective Grade II. The selection committee submitted 19 names to the Chief of Police. The Chief concluded that accepting these names would not promote the goals of the affirmative action plan that the City had voluntarily adopted. Accordingly, he agreed to promote the 19 individuals recommended by the selection committee but also requested that the selection committee propose four additional names to improve the representation of blacks and women at the Detective Grade I level. The committee proffered the names of three black officers and one woman officer and these four were also given promotions. Four white male officers whose names were on neither the original nor supplemental list filed suit against the City under § 1983, alleging that they had been discriminated against on the basis of their race and sex in violation of the equal protection clause. What result? See Ledoux v. District of Columbia, 40 FEP Cases 1258 (D.D.C.1986).

CITY OF RICHMOND v. J.A. CROSON COMPANY

Supreme Court of the United States, 1989.
488 U.S. 469, 109 S.Ct. 706, 102 L.Ed.2d 854.

JUSTICE O'CONNOR announced the judgment of the Court and delivered the opinion of the Court with respect to Parts I, III–B, and IV, an opinion with respect to Part II, in which The Chief Justice and Justice White join, and an opinion with respect to Parts III–A and V, in which The Chief Justice, Justice White and Justice Kennedy join.

In this case, we confront once again the tension between the Fourteenth Amendment's guarantee of equal treatment to all citizens, and the use of race-based measures to ameliorate the effects of past discrimination on the opportunities enjoyed by members of minority groups in our society. In Fullilove v. Klutznick, 448 U.S. 448, 100 S.Ct. 2758, 65 L.Ed.2d 902 (1980), we held that a congressional program requiring that 10% of certain federal construction grants be awarded to minority contractors did not violate the equal protection principles embodied in the Due Process Clause of the Fifth Amendment. Relying largely on our decision in *Fullilove*, some lower federal courts have applied a similar standard of review in assessing the constitutionality of state and local minority set-aside provisions under the Equal Protection Clause of the Fourteenth Amendment. See, e.g. South Florida Chapter, Associated General Contractors of America, Inc. v. Metropolitan Dade County, 723 F.2d 846 (CA11), cert. denied, 469 U.S. 871, 105 S.Ct. 220, 83 L.Ed.2d 150 (1984); Ohio Contractors Assn. v. Keip, 713 F.2d 167 (CA6 1983). Since our decision two Terms ago in Wygant v. Jackson Board of Education, 476 U.S. 267, 106 S.Ct. 1842, 90 L.Ed.2d 260 (1986), the lower federal courts have attempted to apply its standards in evaluating the constitutionality of state and local programs which allocate a portion of public contracting opportunities exclusively to minority-owned businesses. See, e.g., Michigan Road Builders Assn., Inc. v. Milliken, 834 F.2d 583 (CA6 1987), appeal docketed, No. 87–1860; Associated General Contractors of Cal. v. City and Cty. of San Francisco, 813 F.2d 922 (CA9 1987). We noted probable jurisdiction in this case to consider the applicability of our decision in *Wygant* to a minority set-aside program adopted by the city of Richmond, Virginia.

I

On April 11, 1983, the Richmond City Council adopted the Minority Business Utilization Plan (the Plan). The Plan required prime contractors to whom the city awarded construction contracts to subcontract at least 30% of the dollar amount of the contract to one or more Minority Business Enterprises (MBEs). The 30% set-aside did not apply to city contracts awarded to minority-owned prime contractors.

The Plan defined an MBE as "[a] business at least fifty-one (51) percent of which is owned and controlled * * * by minority group members." "Minority group members" were defined as "[c]itizens of the United States who are Blacks, Spanish-speaking, Orientals, Indians, Eskimos, or Aleuts." There was no geographic limit to the Plan; an otherwise qualified MBE from anywhere in the United States could avail itself of the 30% set-aside. The Plan declared that it was "remedial" in nature, and enacted "for the purpose of promoting wider participation by minority business enterprises in the construction of public projects." The Plan expired on June 30, 1988, and was in effect for approximately five years.[1]

The Plan authorized the Director of the Department of General Services to promulgate rules which "shall allow waivers in those individual situations where a contractor can prove to the satisfaction of the director that the requirements herein cannot be achieved." To this end, the Director promulgated Contract Clauses, Minority Business Utilization Plan (Contract Clauses). Section D of these rules provided:

> "No partial or complete waiver of the foregoing [30% set-aside] requirement shall be granted by the city other than in exceptional circumstances. To justify a waiver, it must be shown that every feasible attempt has been made to comply, and it must be demonstrated that sufficient, relevant, qualified Minority Business Enterprises * * * are unavailable or unwilling to participate in the contract to enable meeting the 30% MBE goal."

The Director also promulgated "purchasing procedures" to be followed in the letting of city contracts in accordance with the Plan. Bidders on city construction contracts were provided with a "Minority Business Utilization Plan Commitment Form." Within 10 days of the opening of the bids, the lowest otherwise responsive bidder was required to submit a commitment form naming the MBEs to be used on the contract and the percentage of the total contract price awarded to the minority firm or firms. The prime contractor's commitment form or request for a waiver of the 30% set-aside was then referred to the city Human Relations Commission (HRC). The HRC verified that the MBEs named in the commitment form were in fact minority owned, and then either approved the commitment form or made a recommendation regarding the prime contractor's request for a partial or complete waiver of the 30% set-aside. The Director of General Services made the final determination on compliance with the set-aside provisions or the propriety of granting a waiver. His discretion in this regard appears to have been plenary. There was no direct administrative appeal from the Director's denial of a waiver. Once a contract had been awarded to another firm a bidder denied an award for failure to comply with the MBE requirements had a general right of protest

---

1. The expiration of the ordinance has not rendered the controversy between the city and Croson moot. There remains a live controversy between the parties over whether Richmond's refusal to award Croson a contract pursuant to the ordinance was unlawful and thus entitles Croson to damages. See Memphis Light, Gas & Water Division v. Craft, 436 U.S. 1, 8–9, 98 S.Ct. 1554, 1559–1560, 56 L.Ed.2d 30 (1978).

under Richmond procurement policies. Richmond, Va., City Code, § 12–126(a) (1985).

The Plan was adopted by the Richmond City Council after a public hearing. Seven members of the public spoke to the merits of the ordinance: five were in opposition, two in favor. Proponents of the set-aside provision relied on a study which indicated that, while the general population of Richmond was 50% black, only .67% of the city's prime construction contracts had been awarded to minority businesses in the 5–year period from 1978 to 1983. It was also established that a variety of contractors' associations, whose representatives appeared in opposition to the ordinance, had virtually no minority businesses within their membership. The city's legal counsel indicated his view that the ordinance was constitutional under this Court's decision in Fullilove v. Klutznick. Councilperson Marsh, a proponent of the ordinance, made the following statement:

"There is some information, however, that I want to make sure that we put in the record. I have been practicing law in this community since 1961, and I am familiar with the practices in the construction industry in this area, in the State, and around the nation. And I can say without equivocation, that the general conduct of the construction industry in this area, and the State, and around the nation, is one in which race discrimination and exclusion on the basis of race is widespread."

There was no direct evidence of race discrimination on the part of the city in letting contracts or any evidence that the city's prime contractors had discriminated against minority-owned subcontractors.

Opponents of the ordinance questioned both its wisdom and its legality. They argued that a disparity between minorities in the population of Richmond and the number of prime contracts awarded to MBEs had little probative value in establishing discrimination in the construction industry. Representatives of various contractors' associations questioned whether there were enough MBEs in the Richmond area to satisfy the 30% set-aside requirement. Mr. Murphy noted that only 4.7% of all construction firms in the United States were minority owned and that 41% of these were located in California, New York, Illinois, Florida, and Hawaii. He predicted that the ordinance would thus lead to a windfall for the few minority firms in Richmond. Councilperson Gillespie indicated his concern that many local labor jobs, held by both blacks and whites, would be lost because the ordinance put no geographic limit on the MBEs eligible for the 30% set-aside. Some of the representatives of the local contractors organizations indicated that they did not discriminate on the basis of race and were in fact actively seeking out minority members. Councilperson Gillespie expressed his concern about the legality of the Plan, and asked that a vote be delayed pending consultation with outside counsel. His suggestion was rejected, and the ordinance was enacted by a vote of six to two, with councilmember Gillespie abstaining.

On September 6, 1983, the city of Richmond issued an invitation to bid on a project for the provision and installation of certain plumbing fixtures at the city jail. On September 30, 1983, Eugene Bonn, the regional manager of J.A. Croson Company (Croson), a mechanical plumbing and heating contractor, received the bid forms. The project involved the installation of stainless steel urinals and water closets in the city jail. Products of either of two manufacturers were specified, Acorn Engineering Company (Acorn) or Bradley Manufacturing Company (Bradley). Bonn determined that to meet the 30% set-aside requirement, a minority contractor would have to supply the fixtures. The provision of the fixtures amounted to 75% of the total contract price.

On September 30, Bonn contacted five or six MBEs that were potential suppliers of the fixtures, after contacting three local and state agencies that maintained lists of MBEs. No MBE expressed interest in the project or tendered a quote. On October 12, 1983, the day the bids were due, Bonn again telephoned a group of MBEs. This time, Melvin Brown, president of Continental Metal Hose (Continental), a local MBE, indicated that he wished to participate in the project. Brown subsequently contacted two sources of the specified fixtures in order to obtain a price quotation. One supplier, Ferguson Plumbing Supply, which is not an MBE, had already made a quotation directly to Croson, and refused to quote the same fixtures to Continental. Brown also contacted an agent of Bradley, one of the two manufacturers of the specified fixtures. The agent was not familiar with Brown or Continental, and indicated that a credit check was required which would take at least 30 days to complete.

On October 13, 1983, the sealed bids were opened. Croson turned out to be the only bidder, with a bid of $126,530. Brown and Bonn met personally at the bid opening, and Brown informed Bonn that his difficulty in obtaining credit approval had hindered his submission of a bid.

By October 19, 1983, Croson had still not received a bid from Continental. On that date it submitted a request for a waiver of the 30% set-aside. Croson's waiver request indicated that Continental was "unqualified" and that the other MBEs contacted had been unresponsive or unable to quote. Upon learning of Croson's waiver request, Brown contacted an agent of Acorn, the other fixture manufacturer specified by the city. Based upon his discussions with Acorn, Brown subsequently submitted a bid on the fixtures to Croson. Continental's bid was $6,183.29 higher than the price Croson had included for the fixtures in its bid to the city. This constituted a 7% increase over the market price for the fixtures. With added bonding and insurance, using Continental would have raised the cost of the project by $7,663.16. On the same day that Brown contacted Acorn, he also called city procurement officials and told them that Continental, an MBE, could supply the fixtures specified in the city jail contract. On November 2, 1983, the city denied Croson's waiver request, indicating that Croson had 10 days to submit an MBE Utilization Commitment Form, and warned that failure to do so could result in its bid being considered unresponsive.

Croson wrote the city on November 8, 1983. In the letter, Bonn indicated that Continental was not an authorized supplier for either Acorn or Bradley fixtures. He also noted that Acorn's quotation to Brown was subject to credit approval and in any case was substantially higher than any other quotation Croson had received. Finally, Bonn noted that Continental's bid had been submitted some 21 days after the prime bids were due. In a second letter, Croson laid out the additional costs that using Continental to supply the fixtures would entail, and asked that it be allowed to raise the overall contract price accordingly. The city denied both Croson's request for a waiver and its suggestion that the contract price be raised. The city informed Croson that it had decided to rebid the project. On December 9, 1983, counsel for Croson wrote the city asking for a review of the waiver denial. The city's attorney responded that the city had elected to rebid the project, and that there is no appeal of such a decision. Shortly thereafter Croson brought this action under 42 U.S.C. § 1983 in the Federal District Court for the Eastern District of Virginia, arguing that the Richmond ordinance was unconstitutional on its face and as applied in this case.

The District Court upheld the Plan in all respects. In its original opinion, a divided panel of the Fourth Circuit Court of Appeals affirmed. Croson I, 779 F.2d 181 (1985). Both courts applied a test derived from "the common concerns articulated by the various Supreme Court opinions" in Fullilove v. Klutznick, and University of California Regents v. Bakke, 438 U.S. 265, 98 S.Ct. 2733, 57 L.Ed.2d 750 (1978). Relying on the great deference which this Court accorded Congress' findings of past discrimination in *Fullilove*, the panel majority indicated its view that the same standard should be applied to the Richmond City Council, stating:

"Unlike the review we make of a lower court decision, our task is not to determine if there was sufficient evidence to sustain the council majority's position in any traditional sense of weighing the evidence. Rather, it is to determine whether 'the legislative history * * * demonstrates that [the council] reasonably concluded that * * * private and governmental discrimination had contributed to the negligible percentage of public contracts awarded minority contractors.' " Id. at 190 (quoting *Fullilove, supra*, 448 U.S. at 503, 100 S.Ct. at 2787 (Powell, J., concurring)).

The majority found that national findings of discrimination in the construction industry, when considered in conjunction with the statistical study concerning the awarding of prime contracts in Richmond, rendered the city council's conclusion that low minority participation in city contracts was due to past discrimination "reasonable." The panel opinion then turned to the second part of its "synthesized *Fullilove*" test, examining whether the racial quota was "narrowly tailored to the legislative goals of the Plan." First, the court upheld the 30% set-aside figure, by comparing it not to the number of MBEs in Richmond, but rather to the percentage of minority persons in the city's population. The panel held that to remedy the effects of past discrimination, "a set-aside program for a period of five years obviously must require more than a 0.67% set-aside to encourage minorities to enter the contracting industry and to allow existing minority contractors to grow." Thus, in the court's view the 30% figure was "reasonable in light of the undisputed fact that minorities constitute 50% of the population of Richmond." Ibid.

Croson sought certiorari from this Court. We granted the writ, vacated the opinion of the Court of Appeals, and remanded the case for further consideration in light of our intervening decision in Wygant v. Jackson Board of Education, 476 U.S. 267, 106 S.Ct. 1842, 90 L.Ed.2d 260 (1986). See 478 U.S. 1016, 106 S.Ct. 3327, 92 L.Ed.2d 733 (1986).

On remand, a divided panel of the Court of Appeals struck down the Richmond set-aside program as violating both prongs of strict scrutiny under the Equal Protection Clause of the Fourteenth Amendment. J.A. Croson Co. v. Richmond, 822 F.2d 1355 (CA4 1987) (*Croson II*). The majority found that the "core" of this Court's holding in *Wygant* was that, "[t]o show that a plan is justified by a compelling governmental interest, a municipality that wishes to employ a racial preference cannot rest on broad-brush assumptions of historical discrimination." As the court read this requirement, "[f]indings of *societal* discrimination will not suffice; the findings must concern 'prior discrimination *by the government unit involved.*' " Id., at 1358 (quoting *Wygant,* supra, 476 U.S., at 274, 106 S.Ct., at 1846) (emphasis in original)).

In this case, the debate at the city council meeting "revealed no record of prior discrimination by the city in awarding public contracts * * *." *Croson II,* supra, at 1358. Moreover, the statistics comparing the minority population of Richmond to the percentage of *prime* contracts awarded to minority firms had little or no probative value in establishing prior discrimination in the relevant market, and actually suggested "more of a political than a remedial basis for the racial preference." The court concluded that, "[i]f this plan is supported by a compelling governmental interest, so is every other plan that has been enacted in the past or that will be enacted in the future."

The Court of Appeals went on to hold that even if the city had demonstrated a compelling interest in the use of a race-based quota, the 30% set-aside was not narrowly tailored to accomplish a remedial purpose. The court found that the 30% figure was "chosen arbitrarily" and was not tied to the number of minority subcontractors in Richmond or to any other relevant number. Ibid. The dissenting judge argued that the majority had "misconstrue[d] and misapplie[d]" our decision in *Wygant.* 822 F.2d, at 1362. We * * * now affirm the judgment.

II

The parties and their supporting *amici* fight an initial battle over the scope of the city's power to adopt legislation designed to address the effects of past discrimination. Relying on our decision in *Wygant*, appellee argues that the city must limit any race-based remedial efforts to eradicating the effects of its own prior discrimination. This is essentially the position taken by the Court of Appeals below. Appellant argues that our decision in *Fullilove* is controlling, and that as a result the city of Richmond enjoys sweeping legislative power to define and attack the effects of prior discrimination in its local construction industry. We find that neither of these two rather stark alternatives can withstand analysis.

In *Fullilove*, we upheld the minority set-aside contained in § 103(f)(2) of the Public Works Employment Act of 1977, Pub.L. 95–28, 91 Stat. 116, 42 U.S.C. § 6701 et seq. (the Act) against a challenge based on the equal protection component of the Due Process Clause. The Act authorized a four billion dollar appropriation for federal grants to state and local governments for use in public works projects. The primary purpose of the Act was to give the national economy a quick boost in a recessionary period; funds had to be committed to state or local grantees by September 30, 1977. The Act also contained the following requirement: "Except to the extent the Secretary determines otherwise, no grant shall be made under this Act * * * unless the applicant gives satisfactory assurance to the Secretary that at least 10 per centum of the amount of each grant shall be expended for minority business enterprises." MBEs were defined as businesses effectively controlled by "citizens of the United States who are Negroes, Spanish-speaking, Orientals, Indians, Eskimos, and Aleuts."

The principal opinion in *Fullilove*, written by Chief Justice Burger, did not employ "strict scrutiny" or any other traditional standard of equal protection review. The Chief Justice noted at the outset that although racial classifications call for close examination, the Court was at the same time, "bound to approach [its] task with appropriate deference to the Congress, a co-equal branch charged by the Constitution with the power to 'provide for the * * * general Welfare of the United States' and 'to enforce by appropriate legislation,' the equal protection guarantees of the Fourteenth Amendment." The principal opinion asked two questions: first, were the objectives of the legislation within the power of Congress? Second, was the limited use of racial and ethnic criteria a permissible means for Congress to carry out its objectives within the constraints of the Due Process Clause?

On the issue of congressional power, the Chief Justice found that Congress' commerce power was sufficiently broad to allow it to reach the practices of prime contractors on federally funded local construction projects. Congress could mandate state and local government compliance with the set-aside program under its § 5 power to enforce the Fourteenth Amendment.

The Chief Justice next turned to the constraints on Congress' power to employ race-conscious remedial relief. His opinion stressed two factors in upholding the MBE set-aside. First was the unique remedial powers of Congress under § 5 of the Fourteenth Amendment:

"Here we deal * * * not with the limited remedial powers of a federal court, for example, but with the broad remedial powers of Congress. It is fundamental that *in no organ of government, state or federal, does there repose a more comprehensive remedial power than in the Congress,* expressly charged by the Constitution with competence and authority to enforce equal protection guarantees." 448 U.S., at 483, 100 S.Ct., at 2777 (plurality opinion) (emphasis added).

Because of these unique powers, the Chief Justice concluded that "Congress not only may induce voluntary action to assure compliance with existing federal statutory or constitutional antidiscrimination provisions, but also, where Congress has authority to *declare certain conduct unlawful,* it may, as here, authorize and induce state action to avoid such conduct." Id., at 483–484, 100 S.Ct., at 2777 (emphasis added).

In reviewing the legislative history behind the Act, the principal opinion focused on the evidence before Congress that a nationwide history of past discrimination had reduced minority participation in federal construction grants. The Chief Justice also noted that Congress drew on its experience under § 8(a) of the Small Business Act of 1953, which had extended aid to minority businesses. The Chief Justice concluded that "Congress had abundant historical basis from which it could conclude that traditional procurement practices, when applied to minority businesses, could perpetuate the effects of prior discrimination."

The second factor emphasized by the principal opinion in *Fullilove* was the flexible nature of the 10% set-aside. Two "congressional assumptions" underlay the MBE program: first, that the effects of past discrimination had impaired the competitive position of minority businesses, and second, that "adjustment for the effects of past discrimination" would assure that at least 10% of the funds from the federal grant program would flow to minority businesses. The Chief Justice noted that both of these "assumptions" could be "rebutted" by a grantee seeking a waiver of the 10% requirement. Thus a waiver could be sought where minority businesses were not available to fill the 10% requirement or, more importantly, where an MBE attempted "to exploit the remedial aspects of the program by charging an unreasonable price, *i.e.,* a price not attributable to the present effects of prior discrimination." The Chief Justice indicated that without this fine tuning to remedial purpose, the statute would not have "pass[ed] muster."

In his concurring opinion, Justice Powell relied on the legislative history adduced by the principal opinion in finding that "Congress reasonably concluded that private and governmental discrimination had contributed to the negligible percentage of public contracts awarded minority contractors." Justice Powell also found that the means chosen by Congress, particularly in light of the flexible waiver provisions, were "reasonably necessary" to address the problem identified. Justice Powell made it clear that other governmental entities might have to show more than Congress before undertaking race-conscious measures: "The degree of specificity required in the findings of discrimination and the breadth of discretion in the choice of remedies may vary with the nature and authority of the governmental body." Id., at 515–516, n. 14, 100 S.Ct., at 2794, n. 14.

Appellant and its supporting *amici* rely heavily on *Fullilove* for the proposition that a city council, like Congress, need not make specific findings of discrimination to engage in race-conscious relief. Thus, appellant argues "[i]t would be a perversion of federalism to hold that the federal government has a compelling interest in remedying the effects of racial discrimination in its own public works program, but a city government does not."

What appellant ignores is that Congress, unlike any State or political subdivision, has a specific constitutional mandate to enforce the dictates of the Fourteenth Amendment. The power to "enforce" may at times also include the power to define situations which *Congress* determines threaten principles of equality and to adopt prophylactic rules to deal with those situations. See Katzenbach v. Morgan, supra, 384 U.S., at 651, 86 S.Ct., at 1723 ("Correctly viewed, § 5 is a positive grant of legislative power authorizing Congress to exercise its discretion in determining whether and what legislation is needed to secure the guarantees of the Fourteenth Amendment"). See also South Carolina v. Katzenbach, 383 U.S. 301, 326, 86 S.Ct. 803, 817, 15 L.Ed.2d 769 (1966) (similar interpretation of congressional power under § 2 of the Fifteenth Amendment). The Civil War Amendments themselves worked a dramatic change in the balance between congressional and state power over matters of race. Speaking of the Thirteenth and Fourteenth Amendments in Ex parte Virginia, 100 U.S. 339, 345, 25 L.Ed. 676 (1880), the Court stated: "They were intended to be, what they really are, limitations of the powers of the States and enlargements of the power of Congress."

That Congress may identify and redress the effects of society-wide discrimination does not mean that, *a fortiori*, the States and their political subdivisions are free to decide that such remedies are appropriate. Section 1 of the Fourteenth Amendment is an explicit *constraint* on state power, and the States must undertake any remedial efforts in accordance with that provision. To hold otherwise would be to cede control over the content of the Equal Protection Clause to the 50 state legislatures and their myriad political subdivisions. The mere recitation of a benign or compensatory purpose for the use of a racial classification would essentially entitle the States to exercise the full power of Congress under § 5 of the Fourteenth Amendment and insulate any racial classification from judicial scrutiny under § 1. We believe that such a result would be contrary to the intentions of the Framers of the Fourteenth Amendment, who desired to place clear limits on the States' use of race as a criterion for legislative action, and to have the federal courts enforce those limitations.

We do not, as Justice Marshall's dissent suggests, find in § 5 of the Fourteenth Amendment some form of federal pre-emption in matters of race. We simply note what should be apparent to all—§ 1 of the Fourteenth Amendment stemmed from a distrust of state legislative enactments based on race; § 5 is, as the dissent notes, " 'a *positive* grant of legislative power' " to Congress. Thus, our treatment of an exercise of congressional power in *Fullilove* cannot be dispositive here. In the *Slaughter–House Cases,* 16 Wall. 36, 21 L.Ed. 394 (1873), cited by the dissent, the Court noted that the Civil War Amendments granted "additional powers to the Federal government," and laid "additional restraints upon those of the States."

It would seem equally clear, however, that a state or local subdivision (if delegated the authority from the State) has the authority to eradicate the effects of private discrimination within its own legislative jurisdiction.[2] This authority must, of course, be exercised within the constraints of § 1 of the Fourteenth Amendment. Our decision in *Wygant* is not to the contrary. *Wygant* addressed the constitutionality of the use of racial quotas by local school authorities pursuant to an agreement reached with the local teachers' union. It was in the context of addressing the school board's power to adopt a race-based layoff program affecting its own work force that the *Wygant* plurality indicated that the Equal Protection Clause required "some showing of prior discrimination by the governmental unit involved." As a matter of state law, the city of Richmond has legislative authority over its procurement policies, and can use its spending powers to remedy private discrimination, if it identifies that discrimination with the particularity required by the Fourteenth Amendment. To this extent, on the question of the city's competence, the Court of Appeals erred in following *Wygant* by rote in a case involving a state entity which has state-law authority to address discriminatory practices within local commerce under its jurisdiction.

Thus, if the city could show that it had essentially become a "passive participant" in a system of racial exclusion practiced by elements of the local construction industry, we think it clear that the city could take affirmative steps to dismantle such a system. It is beyond dispute that any public entity, state or federal, has a compelling interest in assuring that public dollars, drawn from the tax contributions of all citizens, do not serve to finance the evil of private prejudice.

2. In its original panel opinion, the Court of Appeals held that under Virginia law the city had the legal authority to enact the set-aside program. That determination was not disturbed by the court's subsequent holding that the Plan violated the Equal Protection Clause.

Cf. Norwood v. Harrison, 413 U.S. 455, 465, 93 S.Ct. 2804, 2810, 37 L.Ed.2d 723 (1973) ("Racial discrimination in state-operated schools is barred by the Constitution and [i]t is also axiomatic that a state may not induce, encourage or promote private persons to accomplish what it is constitutionally forbidden to accomplish") (citation and internal quotations omitted).

III

A

The Equal Protection Clause of the Fourteenth Amendment provides that "[N]o State shall * * * deny to *any person* within its jurisdiction the equal protection of the laws" (emphasis added). As this Court has noted in the past, the "rights created by the first section of the Fourteenth Amendment are, by its terms, guaranteed to the individual. The rights established are personal rights." Shelly v. Kraemer, 334 U.S. 1, 22, 68 S.Ct. 836, 846, 92 L.Ed. 1161 (1948). The Richmond Plan denies certain citizens the opportunity to compete for a fixed percentage of public contracts based solely upon their race. To whatever racial group these citizens belong, their "personal rights" to be treated with equal dignity and respect are implicated by a rigid rule erecting race as the sole criterion in an aspect of public decisionmaking.

Absent searching judicial inquiry into the justification for such race-based measures, there is simply no way of determining what classifications are "benign" or "remedial" and what classifications are in fact motivated by illegitimate notions of racial inferiority or simple racial politics. Indeed, the purpose of strict scrutiny is to "smoke out" illegitimate uses of race by assuring that the legislative body is pursuing a goal important enough to warrant use of a highly suspect tool. The test also ensures that the means chosen "fit" this compelling goal so closely that there is little or no possibility that the motive for the classification was illegitimate racial prejudice or stereotype.

Classifications based on race carry a danger of stigmatic harm. Unless they are strictly reserved for remedial settings, they may in fact promote notions of racial inferiority and lead to a politics of racial hostility. See University of California Regents v. Bakke, 438 U.S. at 298, 98 S.Ct., at 2752 (opinion of Powell, J.) ("[P]referential programs may only reinforce common sterotypes holding that certain groups are unable to achieve success without special protection based on a factor having no relation to individual worth"). We thus reaffirm the view expressed by the plurality in *Wygant* that the standard of review under the Equal Protection Clause is not dependent on the race of those burdened or benefited by a particular classification.

Our continued adherence to the standard of review employed in *Wygant*, does not, as Justice Marshall's dissent suggests, indicate that we view "racial discrimination as largely a phenomenon of the past" or that "government bodies need no longer preoccupy themselves with rectifying racial injustice." As we indicate below, States and their local subdivisions have many legislative weapons at their disposal both to punish and prevent present discrimination and to remove arbitrary barriers to minority advancement. Rather, our interpretation of § 1 stems from our agreement with the view expressed by Justice Powell in *Bakke,* that "[t]he guarantee of equal protection cannot mean one thing when applied to one individual and something else when applied to a person of another color."

Under the standard proposed by Justice Marshall's dissent, "[r]ace-conscious classifications designed to further remedial goals," are forthwith subject to a relaxed standard of review. How the dissent arrives at the legal conclusion that a racial classification is "designed to further remedial goals," without first engaging in an examination of the factual basis for its enactment and the nexus between its scope and that factual basis we are not told. However, once the "remedial" conclusion is reached, the dissent's standard is singularly deferential, and bears little resemblance to the close examination of legislative purpose we have engaged in when reviewing classifications based either on race or gender. See Weinberger v. Wiesenfeld, 420 U.S. 636, 648, 95 S.Ct. 1225, 1233, 43 L.Ed.2d 514 (1975) ("[T]he mere recitation of a benign, compensatory purpose is not an automatic shield which protects against any inquiry into the actual purposes underlying a statutory scheme"). The dissent's watered-down version of equal protection review effectively assures that race will always be relevant in American life, and that the "ultimate goal" of "eliminat[ing] entirely from governmental decisionmaking such irrelevant factors as a human being's race," *Wygant,* supra, 476 U.S. at 320, 106 S.Ct. at 1871 (Stevens, J., dissenting) (footnote omitted), will never be achieved.

Even were we to accept a reading of the guarantee of equal protection under which the level of scrutiny varies according to the ability of different groups to defend their interests in the representative process, heightened scrutiny would still be appropriate in the circumstances of this case. One of the central arguments for applying a less exacting standard to "benign" racial classifications is that such measures essentially involve a choice made by dominant racial groups to disadvantage themselves. If one aspect of the judiciary's role under the Equal Protection Clause is to protect "discrete and insular minorities" from majoritarian prejudice or indifference, see United States v. Carolene Products Co., 304 U.S. 144, 153, n. 4, 58 S.Ct. 778, 784, n. 4, 82 L.Ed. 1234 (1938), some maintain that these concerns are not implicated when the "white majority" places burdens upon itself.

In this case, blacks comprise approximately 50% of the population of the city of Richmond. Five of the nine seats on the City Council are held by blacks. The concern that a political majority will more easily act to the disadvantage of a minority based on unwarranted assumptions or incomplete facts would seem to militate for, not against, the application of heightened judicial scrutiny in this case.

In *Bakke,* supra, the Court confronted a racial quota employed by the University of California at Davis Medical School. Under the plan, 16 out of 100 seats in each entering class at the school were reserved exclusively for certain minority groups. Among the justifications offered in support of the plan were the desire to "reduc[e] the historic deficit of traditionally disfavored minorities in medical school and the medical profession" and the need to "counte[r] the effects of societal discrimination." Five Members of the Court determined that none of these interests could justify a plan that completely eliminated nonminorities from consideration for a specified percentage of opportunities. Id., at 271–272, 98 S.Ct., at 2738 (Powell, J.) (addressing constitutionality of Davis plan); id., at 408, 98 S.Ct. at 2808 (Stevens, J., Burger, C.J., Stewart and Rehnquist, JJ. concurring and dissenting) (addressing only legality of Davis admissions plan under Title VI of the Civil Rights Act of 1964).

Justice Powell's opinion applied heightened scrutiny under the Equal Protection Clause to the racial classification at issue. His opinion decisively rejected the first justification for the racially segregated admissions plan. The desire to have more black medical students or doctors, standing alone, was not merely insufficiently compelling to justify a racial classification, it was "discrimination for its own sake," forbidden by the Constitution. Nor could the second concern, the history of discrimination in society at large, justify a racial quota in medical school admissions. Justice Powell contrasted the "focused" goal of remedying "wrongs worked by specific instances of racial discrimination" with "the remedying of the effects of 'societal discrimination,' an amorphous concept of injury that may be ageless in its reach into the past." He indicated that for the governmental interest in remedying past discrimination to be triggered "judicial, legislative, or administrative findings of constitutional or statutory violations" must be made. Only then does the Government have a compelling interest in favoring one race over another.

In *Wygant,* four Members of the Court applied heightened scrutiny to a race-based system of employee layoffs. Justice Powell, writing for the plurality, again drew the distinction between "societal discrimination" which is an inadequate basis for race-conscious classifications, and the type of identified discrimination that can support and define the scope of race-based relief. The challenged classification in that case tied the layoff of minority teachers to the percentage of minority students enrolled in the school district. The lower courts had upheld the scheme, based on the theory that minority students were in need of "role models" to alleviate the effects of prior discrimination in society. This Court reversed, with a plurality of four Justices reiterating the view expressed by Justice Powell in *Bakke* that "[s]ocietal discrimination, without more, is too amorphous a basis for imposing a racially classified remedy."

The role model theory employed by the lower courts failed for two reasons. First, the statistical disparity between students and teachers had no probative value in demonstrating the kind of prior discrimination in hiring or promotion that would justify race-based relief. Second, because the role model theory had no relation to some basis for believing a constitutional or statutory violation had occurred, it could be used to "justify" race-based decisionmaking essentially limitless in scope and duration.

III
B

We think it clear that the factual predicate offered in support of the Richmond Plan suffers from the same two defects identified as fatal in *Wygant*. The District Court found the city council's "findings sufficient to ensure that, in adopting the Plan, it was remedying the present effects of past discrimination in the *construction industry.*" (emphasis added). Like the "role model" theory employed in *Wygant,* a generalized assertion that there has been past discrimination in an entire industry provides no guidance for a legislative body to determine the precise scope of the injury it seeks to remedy. It "has no logical stopping point." *Wygant,* supra, at 275, 106 S.Ct., at 1847 (plurality opinion). "Relief" for such an ill-defined wrong could extend until the percentage of public contracts awarded to MBEs in Richmond mirrored the percentage of minorities in the population as a whole.

Appellant argues that it is attempting to remedy various forms of past discrimination that are alleged to be responsible for the small number of minority businesses in the local contracting industry. Among these the city cites the exclusion of blacks from skilled construction trade unions and training programs. This past discrimination has prevented them "from following the traditional path from laborer to entrepreneur." Brief for Appellant 23–24. The city also lists a host of nonracial factors which would seem to face a member of any racial group attempting to establish a new business enterprise, such as deficiencies in working capital, inability to meet bonding requirements, unfamiliarity with bidding procedures, and disability caused by an inadequate track record.

While there is no doubt that the sorry history of both private and public discrimination in this country has contributed to a lack of opportunities for black entrepreneurs, this observation, standing alone, cannot justify a rigid racial quota in the awarding of public contracts in Richmond, Virginia. Like the claim that discrimination in primary and secondary schooling justifies a rigid racial preference in medical school admissions, an amorphous claim that there has been past discrimination in a particular industry cannot justify the use of an unyielding racial quota.

It is sheer speculation how many minority firms there would be in Richmond absent past societal discrimination, just as it was sheer speculation how many minority medical students would have been admitted to the medical school at Davis absent past discrimination in educational opportunities. Defining these sorts of injuries as "identified discrimination" would give local governments license to create a patchwork of racial preferences based on statistical generalizations about any particular field of endeavor.

These defects are readily apparent in this case. The 30% quota cannot in any realistic sense be tied to any injury suffered by anyone. The District Court relied upon five predicate "facts" in reaching its conclusion that there was an adequate basis for the 30% quota: (1) the ordinance declares itself to be remedial; (2) several proponents of the measure stated their views that there had been past discrimination in the construction industry; (3) minority businesses received .67% of prime contracts from the city while minorities constituted 50% of the city's population; (4) there were very few minority contractors in local and state contractors' associations; and (5) in 1977, Congress made a determination that the effects of past discrimination had stifled minority participation in the construction industry nationally.

None of these "findings," singly or together, provide the city of Richmond with a "strong basis in evidence for its conclusion that remedial action was necessary." *Wygant,* 476 U.S., at 277, 106 S.Ct., at 1848 (plurality opinion). There is nothing approaching a prima facie case of a constitutional or statutory violation by *anyone* in the Richmond construction industry.

The District Court accorded great weight to the fact that the city council designated the Plan as "remedial." But the mere recitation of a "benign" or legitimate purpose for a racial classification, is entitled to little or no weight. See Weinberger v. Wiesenfeld, 420 U.S., at 648, n. 16, 95 S.Ct., at 1233, n. 16 ("This Court need not in equal protection cases accept at face value assertions of legislative purposes, when an examination of the legislative scheme and its history demonstrates that the asserted purpose could not have been a goal of the legislation"). Racial classifications are suspect, and that means that simple legislative assurances of good intention cannot suffice.

The District Court also relied on the highly conclusionary statement of a proponent of the Plan that there was racial discrimination in the construction industry "in this area, and the State, and around the nation." It also noted that the city manager had related his view that racial discrimination still plagued the construction industry in his home city of Pittsburg. These statements are of little probative value in establishing identified discrimination in the Richmond construction industry. The fact finding process of legislative bodies is generally entitled to a presumption of regularity and deferential review by the judiciary. See Williamson v. Lee Optical of Oklahoma, Inc., 348 U.S. 483, 488–489, 75 S.Ct. 461, 464–465, 99 L.Ed. 563 (1955). But when a legislative body chooses to employ a suspect classification, it cannot rest upon a generalized assertion as to the classification's relevance to its goals. See McLaughlin v. Florida, 379 U.S. 184, 190–192, 85 S.Ct. 283, 287–289, 13 L.Ed.2d 222 (1964). A governmental actor cannot render race a legitimate proxy for a particular condition merely by declaring that the condition exists. See id., at 193, 85 S.Ct., at 289; *Wygant,* 476 U.S., at 277, 106 S.Ct., at 1848. The history of racial classifications in this country suggests that blind judicial deference to legislative or executive pronouncements of necessity has no place in equal protection analysis. See Korematsu v. United States, 323 U.S. 214, 235–240, 65 S.Ct. 193, 202–205, 89 L.Ed. 194 (1944) (Murphy, J., dissenting).

Reliance on the disparity between the number of prime contracts awarded to minority firms and the minority population of the city of Richmond is similarly misplaced. There is no doubt that "[w]here gross statistical disparities can be shown, they alone in a proper case may constitute prima facie proof of a pattern or practice of discrimination" under Title VII. Hazelwood School Dist. v. United States, 433 U.S. 299, 307–308, 97 S.Ct. 2736, 2741, 53 L.Ed.2d 768 (1977). But it is equally clear that "[w]hen special qualifications are required to fill particular jobs, comparisons to the general population (rather than to the smaller group of individuals who possess the necessary qualifications) may have little probative value." Id., at 308, n. 13, 97 S.Ct., at 2742, n. 13. See also Mayor v. Educational Equality League, 415 U.S. 605, 620, 94 S.Ct. 1323, 1333, 39 L.Ed.2d 630 (1974) ("[T]his is not a case in which it can be assumed that all citizens are fungible for purposes of determining whether members of a particular class have been unlawfully excluded").

In the employment context, we have recognized that for certain entry level positions or positions requiring minimal training, statistical comparisons of the racial composition of an employer's workforce to the racial composition of the relevant population may be probative of a pattern of discrimination. See Teamsters v. United States, 431 U.S. 324, 337–338, 97 S.Ct. 1843, 1855–1856, 52 L.Ed.2d 396 (1977) (statistical comparison between minority truck drivers and relevant population probative of discriminatory exclusion). But where special qualifications are necessary, the relevant statistical pool for purposes of demonstrating discriminatory exclusion must be the number of minorities qualified to undertake the particular task. See *Hazelwood,* supra, 433 U.S., at 308, 97 S.Ct., at 2741; Johnson v. Transportation Agency, 480 U.S. 616, 651–652, 107 S.Ct. 1442, 1462, 91 L.Ed.2d 615 (1987) (O'Connor, J., concurring).

In this case, the city does not even know how many MBEs in the relevant market are qualified to undertake prime or subcontracting work in public construction projects. Compare Ohio Contractors Assn. v. Keip, 713 F.2d, at 171 (relying on percentage of minority *businesses* in the State compared to percentage of state purchasing contracts awarded to minority firms in upholding set-aside). Nor does the city know what percentage of total city construction dollars minority firms now receive as subcontractors on prime contracts let by the city.

To a large extent, the set-aside of subcontracting dollars seems to rest on the unsupported assumption that white prime contractors simply will not hire minority firms.[3] Indeed, there is evidence in this record that overall minority participation in city contracts in Richmond is seven to eight percent, and that minority contractor participation in Community Block Development Grant *construction* projects is 17% to 22%. App. 16 (statement of Mr. Deese, City Manager). Without any information on minority participation in subcontracting, it is quite simply impossible to evaluate overall minority representation in the city's construction expenditures.

The city and the District Court also relied on evidence that MBE membership in local contractors' associations was extremely low. Again, standing alone this evidence is not probative of any discrimination in the local construction industry. There are numerous explanations for this dearth of minority participation, including past societal discrimination in education and economic opportunities as well as both black and white career and entrepreneurial choices. Blacks may be disproportionately attracted to industries other than construction. The mere fact that black membership in these trade organizations is low, standing alone, cannot establish a prima facie case of discrimination. Cf. Bazemore v. Friday, 478 U.S. 385, 407–408, 106 S.Ct. 3000, 3013, 92 L.Ed.2d 315 (1986) (mere existence of single race clubs in absence of evidence of exclusion by race cannot create a duty to integrate).

For low minority membership in these associations to be relevant, the city would have to link it to the number of local MBEs eligible for membership. If the statistical disparity between eligible MBEs and MBE membership were great enough, an inference of discriminatory exclusion could arise. In such a case, the city would have a compelling interest in preventing its tax dollars from assisting these organizations in maintaining a racially segregated construction market. See *Norwood*, 413 U.S., at 465, 93 S.Ct., at 2804; *Ohio Contractors*, 713 F.2d, at 171 (upholding minority set-aside based in part on earlier District Court finding that "the state had become 'a joint participant' with private industry and certain craft unions in a pattern of racially discriminatory conduct which excluded black laborers from work on public construction contracts").

Finally, the city and the District Court relied on Congress' finding in connection with the set-aside approved in *Fullilove* that there had been nationwide discrimination in the construction industry. The probative value of these findings for demonstrating the existence of discrimination in Richmond is extremely limited. By its inclusion of a

---

3. Since 1975 the city of Richmond has had an ordinance on the books prohibiting both discrimination in the award of public contracts and employment discrimination by public contractors. The city points to no evidence that its prime contractors have been violating the ordinance in either their employment or subcontracting practices. The complete silence of the record concerning enforcement of the city's own anti-discrimination ordinance flies in the face of the dissent's vision of a "tight-knit industry" which has prevented blacks from obtaining the experience necessary to participate in construction contracting.

waiver procedure in the national program addressed in *Fullilove,* Congress explicitly recognized that the scope of the problem would vary from market area to market area. See *Fullilove,* 448 U.S., at 487, 100 S.Ct., at 2779 (noting that the presumption that minority firms are disadvantaged by past discrimination may be rebutted by grantees in individual situations).

Moreover, as noted above, Congress was exercising its powers under § 5 of the Fourteenth Amendment in making a finding that past discrimination would cause federal funds to be distributed in a manner which reinforced prior patterns of discrimination. While the States and their subdivisions may take remedial action when they possess evidence that their own spending practices are exacerbating a pattern of prior discrimination, they must identify that discrimination, public or private, with some specificity before they may use race-conscious relief. Congress has made national findings that there has been societal discrimination in a host of fields. If all a state or local government need do is find a congressional report on the subject to enact a set-aside program, the constraints of the Equal Protection Clause will, in effect, have been rendered a nullity.

Justice Marshall apparently views the requirement that Richmond identify the discrimination it seeks to remedy in its own jurisdiction as a mere administrative headache, an "onerous documentary obligatio[n]." We cannot agree. In this regard, we are in accord with Justice Stevens' observation in *Fullilove,* that "[b]ecause racial characteristics so seldom provide a relevant basis for disparate treatment, and because classifications based on race are potentially so harmful to the entire body politic, it is especially important that the reasons for any such classification be clearly identified and unquestionably legitimate." *Fullilove,* supra, at 533–535, 100 S.Ct., at 2803–04 (Stevens, J., dissenting). The "evidence" relied upon by the dissent, the history of school desegregation in Richmond and numerous congressional reports, does little to define the scope of any injury to minority contractors in Richmond or the necessary remedy. The factors relied upon by the dissent could justify a preference of any size or duration.

Moreover, Justice Marshall's suggestion that findings of discrimination may be "shared" from jurisdiction to jurisdiction in the same manner as information concerning zoning and property values is unprecedented. We have never approved the extrapolation of discrimination in one jurisdiction from the experience of another. See Milliken v. Bradley, 418 U.S. 717, 746, 94 S.Ct. 3112, 3128, 41 L.Ed.2d 1069 (1974) ("Disparate treatment of white and Negro students occurred within the Detroit school system, and not elsewhere, and on this record the remedy must be limited to that system").

In sum, none of the evidence presented by the city points to any identified discrimination in the Richmond construction industry. We, therefore, hold that the city has failed to demonstrate a compelling interest in apportioning public contracting opportunities on the basis of race. To accept Richmond's claim that past societal discrimination alone can serve as the basis for rigid racial preferences would be to open the door to competing claims for "remedial relief" for every disadvantaged group. The dream of a Nation of equal citizens in a society where race is irrelevant to personal opportunity and achievement would be lost in a mosaic of shifting preferences based on inherently unmeasurable claims of past wrongs. "Courts would be asked to evaluate the extent of the prejudice and consequent harm suffered by various minority groups. Those whose societal injury is thought to exceed some arbitrary level of tolerability then would be entitled to preferential classifications * * *." *Bakke,* 438 U.S., at 296–297, 98 S.Ct., at 2751 (Powell, J.). We think such a result would be contrary to both the letter and spirit of a constitutional provision whose central command is equality.

The foregoing analysis applies only to the inclusion of blacks within the Richmond set-aside program. There is *absolutely no evidence* of past discrimination against Spanish-speaking, Oriental, Indian, Eskimo, or Aleut persons in any aspect of the Richmond construction industry. The District Court took judicial notice of the fact that the vast majority of "minority" persons in Richmond were black. Supp. App. 207. It may well be that Richmond has never had an Aleut or Eskimo citizen. The random inclusion of racial groups that, as a practical matter, may never have suffered from discrimination in the construction industry in Richmond, suggests that perhaps the city's purpose was not in fact to remedy past discrimination.

If a 30% set-aside was "narrowly tailored" to compensate black contractors for past discrimination, one may legitimately ask why they are forced to share this "remedial relief" with an Aleut citizen who moves to Richmond tomorrow? The gross overinclusiveness of Richmond's racial preference strongly impugns the city's claim of remedial motivation. See *Wygant,* 476 U.S., at 284, n. 13, 106 S.Ct., at 1852, n. 13 (haphazard inclusion of racial groups "further illustrates the undifferentiated nature of the plan").

IV

As noted by the court below, it is almost impossible to assess whether the Richmond Plan is narrowly tailored to remedy prior discrimination since it is not linked to identified discrimination in any way. We limit ourselves to two observations in this regard.

First, there does not appear to have been any consideration of the use of race-neutral means to increase minority business participation in city contracting. See United States v. Paradise, 480 U.S. 149, 171, 107 S.Ct. 1053, 1067, 94 L.Ed.2d 203 (1987) ("In determining whether race-conscious remedies are appropriate, we look to several factors, including the efficacy of alternative remedies"). Many of the barriers to minority participation in the construction industry relied upon by the city to justify a racial classification appear to be race neutral. If MBEs disproportionately lack capital or cannot meet bonding requirements, a race-neutral program of city financing for small firms would, *a fortiori,* lead to greater minority participation. The principal opinion in *Fullilove* found that Congress had carefully examined and rejected race-neutral alternatives before enacting the MBE set-aside. See *Fullilove,* 448 U.S., at 463–467, 100 S.Ct., at 2767–2769; see also id., at 511, 100 S.Ct., at 2792 (Powell, J., concurring) ("[B]y the time Congress enacted [the MBE set-aside] in 1977, it knew that other remedies had failed to ameliorate the effects of racial discrimination in the construction industry"). There is no evidence in this record that the Richmond City Council has considered any alternatives to a race-based quota.

Second, the 30% quota cannot be said to be narrowly tailored to any goal, except perhaps outright racial balancing. It rests upon the "completely unrealistic" assumption that minorities will choose a particular trade in lockstep proportion to their representation in the local population. See Sheet Metal Workers v. EEOC, 478 U.S. 421, 494, 106 S.Ct. 3019, 3060, 92 L.Ed.2d 344 (1986) (O'Connor, J., concurring in part and dissenting in part) ("[I]t is completely unrealistic to assume that individuals of one race will gravitate with mathematical exactitude to each employer or union absent unlawful discrimination").

Since the city must already consider bids and waivers on a case-by-case basis, it is difficult to see the need for a rigid numerical quota. As noted above, the congressional scheme upheld in *Fullilove* allowed for a waiver of the set-aside provision where an MBE's higher price was not attributable to the effects of past discrimination. Based upon proper findings, such programs are less problematic from an equal protection standpoint because they treat all candidates individually, rather than making the color of an applicant's skin the sole relevant consideration. Unlike the program upheld in *Fullilove,* the Richmond Plan's waiver system focuses solely on the availability of MBEs; there is no inquiry into whether or not the particular MBE seeking a racial preference has suffered from the effects of past discrimination by the city or prime contractors.

Given the existence of an individualized procedure, the city's only interest in maintaining a quota system rather than investigating the need for remedial action in particular cases would seem to be simple administrative convenience. But the interest in avoiding the bureaucratic effort necessary to tailor remedial relief to those who truly have suffered the effects of prior discrimination cannot justify a rigid line drawn on the basis of a suspect classification. See Frontiero v. Richardson, 411 U.S. 677, 690, 93 S.Ct. 1764, 1772, 36 L.Ed.2d 583 (1973) (plurality opinion) ("[W]hen we enter the realm of 'strict judicial scrutiny,' there can be no doubt that 'administrative convenience' is not a shibboleth, the mere recitation of which dictates constitutionality"). Under Richmond's scheme, a successful black, Hispanic, or Oriental entrepreneur from anywhere in the country enjoys an absolute preference over other citizens based solely on their race. We think it obvious that such a program is not narrowly tailored to remedy the effects of prior discrimination.

V

Nothing we say today precludes a state or local entity from taking action to rectify the effects of identified discrimination within its jurisdiction. If the city of Richmond had evidence before it that non-minority contractors were systematically excluding minority businesses from subcontracting opportunities it could take action to end the discriminatory exclusion. Where there is a significant statistical disparity between the number of qualified minority contractors willing and able to perform a particular service and the number of such contractors actually engaged by the locality or the locality's prime contractors, an inference of discriminatory exclusion could arise. See Bazemore v. Friday, 478 U.S., at 398, 106 S.Ct., at 3008; Teamsters v. United States, 431 U.S., at 337–339, 97 S.Ct., at 1856. Under such circumstances, the city could act to dismantle the closed business system by taking appropriate measures against those who discriminate on the basis of race or other illegitimate criteria. See, e.g., New York State Club Assn. v. New York City, 487 U.S. ___, ___, 108 S.Ct. 2225, ___, 101 L.Ed.2d 1 (1988). In the extreme case, some form of narrowly tailored racial preference might be necessary to break down patterns of deliberate exclusion.

Nor is local government powerless to deal with individual instances of racially motivated refusals to employ minority contractors. Where such discrimination occurs, a city would be justified in penalizing the discriminator and providing appropriate relief to the victim of such discrimination. See generally McDonnell Douglas Corp. v. Green, 411 U.S. 792, 802–803, 93 S.Ct. 1817, 1824–1825, 36 L.Ed.2d 668 (1973). Moreover, evidence of a pattern of individual discriminatory acts can, if supported by appropriate statistical proof, lend support to a local government's determination that broader remedial relief is justified. See *Teamsters.*

Even in the absence of evidence of discrimination, the city has at its disposal a whole array of race-neutral devices to increase the accessibility of city contracting opportunities to small entrepreneurs of all races. Simplification of bidding procedures, relaxation of bonding requirements, and training and financial aid for disadvantaged entrepreneurs of all races would open the public contracting market to all those who have suffered the effects of past societal discrimination or neglect. Many of the formal barriers to new entrants may be the product of bureaucratic inertia more than actual necessity, and may have a disproportionate effect on the opportunities open to new minority firms. Their elimination or modification would have little detrimental effect on the city's interests and would serve to increase the opportunities available to minority business without classifying individuals on the basis of race. The city may also act to prohibit discrimination in the provision of credit or bonding by local suppliers and banks. Business as usual should not mean business pursuant to the unthinking exclusion of certain members of our society from its rewards.

In the case at hand, the city has not ascertained how many minority enterprises are present in the local construction market nor the level of their participation in city construction projects. The city points to no evidence that qualified minority contractors have been passed over for city contracts or subcontracts, either as a group or in any individual case. Under such circumstances, it is simply impossible to say that the city has demonstrated "a strong basis in evidence for its conclusion that remedial action was necessary." *Wygant.*

Proper findings in this regard are necessary to define both the scope of the injury and the extent of the remedy necessary to cure its effects. Such findings also serve to assure all citizens that the deviation from the norm of equal treatment of all racial and ethnic groups is a temporary matter, a measure taken in the service of the goal of equality itself. Absent such findings, there is a danger that a racial classification is merely the product of unthinking stereotypes or a form of racial politics. "[I]f there is no duty to attempt either to measure the recovery by the wrong or to distribute that recovery within the injured class in an evenhanded way, our history will adequately support a legislative preference for almost any ethnic, religious, or racial group with the political strength to negotiate 'a piece of the action' for its members." *Fullilove*, 448 U.S., at 539, 100 S.Ct., at 2806 (Stevens, J., dissenting). Because the city of Richmond has failed to identify the need for remedial action in the awarding of its public construction contracts, its treatment of its citizens on a racial basis violates the dictates of the Equal Protection Clause. Accordingly, the judgment of the Court of Appeals for the Fourth Circuit is

AFFIRMED.

Justice Stevens, concurring in part and concurring in the judgment.

A central purpose of the Fourteenth Amendment is to further the national goal of equal opportunity for all our citizens. In order to achieve that goal we must learn from our past mistakes, but I believe the Constitution requires us to evaluate our policy decisions—including those that govern the relationships among different racial and ethnic groups—primarily by studying their probable impact on the future. I therefore do not agree with the premise that seems to underlie today's decision, as well as the decision in *Wygant*, that a governmental decision that rests on a racial classification is never permissible except as a remedy for a past wrong.[1] I do, however, agree with the Court's

1. In my view the Court's approach to this case gives unwarranted deference to race-based legislative action that purports to serve a purely remedial goal, and overlooks the potential value of race-based de- terminations that may serve other valid purposes. With regard to the former point—as I explained at some length in *Fullilove* —I am not prepared to assume that even a more narrowly tailored set-

explanation of why the Richmond ordinance cannot be justified as a remedy for past discrimination, and therefore join Parts I, III–B, and IV of its opinion. I write separately to emphasize three aspects of the case that are of special importance to me.

First, the city makes no claim that the public interest in the efficient performance of its construction contracts will be served by granting a preference to minority-business enterprises. This case is therefore completely unlike *Wygant,* in which I thought it quite obvious that the School Board had reasonably concluded that an integrated faculty could provide educational benefits to the entire student body that could not be provided by an all-white, or nearly all-white faculty. As I pointed out in my dissent in that case, even if we completely disregard our history of racial injustice, race is not always irrelevant to sound governmental decisionmaking.[2] In the case of public contracting, however, if we disregard the past, there is not even an arguable basis for suggesting that the race of a subcontractor or general contractor should have any relevance to his or her access to the market.

Second, this litigation involves an attempt by a legislative body, rather than a court, to fashion a remedy for a past wrong. Legislatures

aside program supported by stronger findings would be constitutionally justified. Unless the legislature can identify both the particular victims and the particular perpetrators of past discrimination, which is precisely what a court does when it makes findings of fact and conclusions of law, a *remedial* justification for race-based legislation will almost certainly sweep too broadly. With regard to the latter point: I think it unfortunate that the Court in neither *Wygant* nor this case seems prepared to acknowledge that some race-based policy decisions may serve a legitimate public purpose. I agree, of course, that race is so seldom relevant to legislative decisions on how best to foster the public good that legitimate justifications for race-based legislation will usually not be available. But unlike the Court, I would not totally discount the legitimacy of race-based decisions that may produce tangible and fully justified future benefits.

2. "Rather than analyzing a case of this kind by asking whether minority teachers have some sort of special entitlement to jobs as a remedy for sins that were committed in the past, I believe that we should first ask whether the Board's action advances the public interest in educating children for the future.

* * *

"[I]n our present society, race is not always irrelevant to sound governmental decisionmaking. To take the most obvious example, in law enforcement, if an undercover agent is needed to infiltrate a group suspected of ongoing criminal behavior—and if the members of the group are all of the same race—it would seem perfectly rational to employ an agent of that race rather than a member of a different racial class. Similarly, in a city with a recent history of racial unrest, the superintendent of police might reasonably conclude that an integrated police force could develop a better relationship with the community and thereby do a more effective job of maintaining law and order than a force composed only of white officers.

"In the context of public education, it is quite obvious that a school board may reasonably conclude that an integrated faculty will be able to provide benefits to the student body that could not be provided by an all-white, or nearly all-white, faculty. For one of the most important lessons that the American public schools teach is that the diverse ethnic, cultural, and national backgrounds that have been brought together in our famous 'melting pot' do not identify essential differences among the human beings that inhabit our land. It is one thing for a white child to be taught by a white teacher that color, like beauty, is only 'skin deep'; it is far more convincing to experience that truth on a day-to-day basis during the routine, ongoing learning process." Wygant v. Jackson Board of Education, 476 U.S. 267, 313–315, 106 S.Ct. 1842, 1867–1868, 90 L.Ed.2d 260 (1986) (Stevens, J., dissenting) (footnotes omitted).

are primarily policymaking bodies that promulgate rules to govern future conduct. The constitutional prohibitions against the enactment of *ex post facto* laws and bills of attainder reflect a valid concern about the use of the political process to punish or characterize past conduct of private citizens.[3] It is the judicial system, rather than the legislative process, that is best equipped to identify past wrongdoers and to fashion remedies that will create the conditions that presumably would have existed had no wrong been committed. Thus, in cases involving the review of judicial remedies imposed against persons who have been proved guilty of violations of law, I would allow the courts in racial discrimination cases the same broad discretion that chancellors enjoy in other areas of the law. See Swann v. Charlotte–Mecklenburg Board of Education, 402 U.S. 1, 15–16, 91 S.Ct. 1267, 1275–1276, 28 L.Ed.2d 554 (1971).[4]

Third, instead of engaging in a debate over the proper standard of review to apply in affirmative-action litigation, I believe it is more constructive to try to identify the characteristics of the advantaged and disadvantaged classes that may justify their disparate treatment. See Cleburne v. Cleburne Living Center, Inc., 473 U.S. 432, 452–453, 105 S.Ct. 3249, 3261, 87 L.Ed.2d 313 (1985) (Stevens, J., concurring). In this case that approach convinces me that, instead of carefully identifying the characteristics of the two classes of contractors that are respectively favored and disfavored by its ordinance, the Richmond City Council has merely engaged in the type of stereotypical analysis that is a hallmark of violations of the Equal Protection Clause. Whether we look at the class of persons benefited by the ordinance or at the disadvantaged class, the same conclusion emerges.

The justification for the ordinance is the fact that in the past white contractors—and presumably other white citizens in Richmond—have discriminated against black contractors. The class of persons benefited

---

3. Of course, legislatures frequently appropriate funds to compensate victims of past governmental misconduct for which there is no judicial remedy. See, e.g., Pub.L. 100–383, 102 Stat. 903 (provision of restitution to interned Japanese–Americans during World War II). Thus, it would have been consistent with normal practice for the city of Richmond to provide direct monetary compensation to any minority-business enterprise that the city might have injured in the past. Such a voluntary decision by a public body is, however, quite different from a decision to require one private party to compensate another for an unproven injury.

4. As I pointed out in my separate opinion concurring in the judgment in United States v. Paradise, 480 U.S. 149, 193–194, 107 S.Ct. 1053, 1078–1079, 94 L.Ed.2d 203 (1987):

"A party who has been found guilty of repeated and persistent violations of the law bears the burden of demonstrating that the chancellor's efforts to fashion effective relief exceed the bounds of 'reasonableness.' The burden of proof in a case like this is precisely the opposite of that in cases such as Wygant v. Jackson Board of Education, 476 U.S. 267, 106 S.Ct. 1842, 90 L.Ed.2d 260 (1986), and Fullilove v. Klutznick, 448 U.S. 448, 100 S.Ct. 2758, 65 L.Ed.2d 902 (1980), which did not involve any proven violations of law. In such cases the governmental decisionmaker who would make race-conscious decisions must overcome a strong presumption against them. No such burden rests on a federal district judge who has found that the governmental unit before him is guilty of racially discriminatory conduct that violates the Constitution."

by the ordinance is not, however, limited to victims of such discrimination—it encompasses persons who have never been in business in Richmond as well as minority contractors who may have been guilty of discriminating against members of other minority groups. Indeed, for all the record shows, all of the minority-business enterprises that have benefited from the ordinance may be firms that have prospered notwithstanding the discriminatory conduct that may have harmed other minority firms years ago. Ironically, minority firms that have survived in the competitive struggle, rather than those that have perished, are most likely to benefit from an ordinance of this kind.

The ordinance is equally vulnerable because of its failure to identify the characteristics of the disadvantaged class of white contractors that justify the disparate treatment. That class unquestionably includes some white contractors who are guilty of past discrimination against blacks, but it is only habit, rather than evidence or analysis, that makes it seem acceptable to assume that every white contractor covered by the ordinance shares in that guilt. Indeed, even among those who have discriminated in the past, it must be assumed that at least some of them have complied with the city ordinance that has made such discrimination unlawful since 1975. Thus, the composition of the disadvantaged class of white contractors presumably includes some who have been guilty of unlawful discrimination, some who practiced discrimination before it was forbidden by law,[8] and some who have never discriminated against anyone on the basis of race. Imposing a common burden on such a disparate class merely because each member of the class is of the same race stems from reliance on a stereotype rather than fact or reason.[9]

There is a special irony in the stereotypical thinking that prompts legislation of this kind. Although it stigmatizes the disadvantaged class with the unproven charge of past racial discrimination, it actually imposes a greater stigma on its supposed beneficiaries. For, as I explained in my *Fullilove* opinion:

> "[E]ven though it is not the actual predicate for this legislation, a statute of this kind inevitably is perceived by many as resting on an assumption that those who are granted this special preference are less qualified in some respect that is identified purely by their race." * * *

8. There is surely some question about the power of a legislature to impose a statutory burden on private citizens for engaging in discriminatory practices at a time when such practices were not unlawful. Cf. Teamsters v. United States, 431 U.S. 324, 356–357, 360, 97 S.Ct. 1843, 1865, 1867, 52 L.Ed.2d 396 (1977).

9. There is, of course, another possibility that should not be overlooked. The ordinance might be nothing more than a form of patronage. But racial patronage, like a racial gerrymander, is no more defensible than political patronage or a political gerrymander. A southern State with a long history of discrimination against Republicans in the awarding of public contracts could not rely on such past discrimination as a basis for granting a legislative preference to Republican contractors in the future.

Accordingly, I concur in parts I, III–B, and IV of the Court's opinion, and in the judgment.

JUSTICE KENNEDY, concurring in part and concurring in the judgment.

I join all but Part II of Justice O'Connor's opinion and give this further explanation.

Part II examines our caselaw upholding Congressional power to grant preferences based on overt and explicit classification by race. With the acknowledgement that the summary in Part II is both precise and fair, I must decline to join it. The process by which a law that is an equal protection violation when enacted by a State becomes transformed to an equal protection guarantee when enacted by Congress poses a difficult proposition for me; but as it is not before us, any reconsideration of that issue must await some further case. For purposes of the ordinance challenged here, it suffices to say that the State has the power to eradicate racial discrimination and its effects in both the public and private sectors, and the absolute duty to do so where those wrongs were caused intentionally by the State itself. The Fourteenth Amendment ought not to be interpreted to reduce a State's authority in this regard, unless, of course, there is a conflict with federal law or a state remedy is itself a violation of equal protection. The latter is the case presented here.

The moral imperative of racial neutrality is the driving force of the Equal Protection Clause. Justice Scalia's opinion underscores that proposition, quite properly in my view. The rule suggested in his opinion, which would strike down all preferences which are not necessary remedies to victims of unlawful discrimination, would serve important structural goals, as it would eliminate the necessity for courts to pass upon each racial preference that is enacted. Structural protections may be necessities if moral imperatives are to be obeyed. His opinion would make it crystal clear to the political branches, at least those of the States, that legislation must be based on criteria other than race.

Nevertheless, given that a rule of automatic invalidity for racial preferences in almost every case would be a significant break with our precedents that require a case-by-case test, I am not convinced we need adopt it at this point. On the assumption that it will vindicate the principle of race neutrality found in the Equal Protection Clause, I accept the less absolute rule contained in Justice O'Connor's opinion, a rule based on the proposition that any racial preference must face the most rigorous scrutiny by the courts. My reasons for doing so are as follows. First, I am confident that, in application, the strict scrutiny standard will operate in a manner generally consistent with the imperative of race neutrality, because it forbids the use even of narrowly drawn racial classifications except as a last resort. Second, the rule against race-conscious remedies is already less than an absolute one, for that relief may be the only adequate remedy after a judicial determination that a State or its instrumentality has violated the Equal Protection Clause. I note, in this connection, that evidence which would support a judicial finding of intentional discrimination may suffice also to justify remedial legislative action, for it diminishes the constitutional responsibilities of the political branches to say they must wait to act until ordered to do so by a court. Third, the strict scrutiny rule is consistent with our precedents, as Justice O'Connor's opinion demonstrates.

The ordinance before us falls far short of the standard we adopt. The nature and scope of the injury that existed; its historical or antecedent causes; the extent to which the City contributed to it, either by intentional acts or by passive complicity in acts of discrimination by the private sector; the necessity for the response adopted, its duration in relation to the wrong, and the precision with which it otherwise bore on whatever injury in fact was addressed, were all matters unmeasured, unexplored, or unexplained by the City Council. We are left with an ordinance and a legislative record open to the fair charge that it is not a remedy but is itself a preference which will cause the same corrosive animosities that the Constitution forbids in the whole sphere of government and that our national policy condemns in the rest of society as well. This ordinance is invalid under the Fourteenth Amendment.

JUSTICE SCALIA, concurring in the judgment.

I agree with much of the Court's opinion, and, in particular, with its conclusion that strict scrutiny must be applied to all governmental classification by race, whether or not its asserted purpose is "remedial" or "benign." I do not agree, however, with the Court's dicta suggesting that, despite the Fourteenth Amendment, state and local governments may in some circumstances discriminate on the basis of race in order (in a broad sense) "to ameliorate the effects of past discrimination." The benign purpose of compensating for social disadvantages, whether they have been acquired by reason of prior discrimination or otherwise, can no more be pursued by the illegitimate means of racial discrimination than can other assertedly benign purposes we have repeatedly rejected. The difficulty of overcoming the effects of past discrimination is as nothing compared with the difficulty of eradicating from our society the source of those effects, which is the tendency—fatal to a nation such as ours—to classify and judge men and women on the basis of their country of origin or the color of their skin. A solution to the first problem that aggravates the second is no solution at all. I share the view expressed by Alexander Bickel that "[t]he lesson of the great decisions of the Supreme Court and the lesson of contemporary history have been the same for at least a generation: discrimination on the basis of race is illegal, immoral, unconstitutional, inherently wrong, and destructive of democratic society." A. Bickel, The Morality of Consent 133 (1975). At least where state or local action is at issue, only a social emergency rising to the level of imminent danger to life and limb—for example, a prison race riot, requiring temporary segregation of inmates, cf. Lee v. Washington, supra—can justify an exception to the principle embodied in the Fourteenth Amendment that "[o]ur Constitution is color-blind, and neither knows nor tolerates classes among citizens," Plessy v. Ferguson, 163 U.S. 537, 559, 16 S.Ct. 1138, 1146, 41 L.Ed. 256 (1896) (Harlan, J., dissenting).

We have in some contexts approved the use of racial classifications by the Federal Government to remedy the effects of past discrimination. I do not believe that we must or should extend those holdings to the States. In *Fullilove,* we upheld legislative action by Congress similar in its asserted purpose to that at issue here. And we have permitted federal courts to prescribe quite severe race-conscious remedies when confronted with egregious and persistent unlawful discrimination, see, e.g., United States v. Paradise, 480 U.S. 149, 107 S.Ct. 1053, 94 L.Ed.2d 203 (1987); Sheet Metal Workers v. EEOC, 478 U.S. 421, 106 S.Ct. 3019, 92 L.Ed.2d 344 (1986). As the Court acknowledges, however, it is one thing to permit racially based conduct by the Federal Government—whose legislative powers concerning matters of race were explicitly enhanced by the Fourteenth Amendment, see U.S. Const., Amdt. 14, § 5—and quite another to permit it by the precise entities against whose conduct in matters of race that Amendment was specifically directed, see Amdt. 14, § 1. As we said in *Ex parte Virginia,* supra, 100 U.S., at 345, the Civil War Amendments were designed to "take away all possibility of oppression by law because of race or color" and "to be * * * limitations on the power of the States and enlargements of the power of Congress." Thus, without revisiting what we held in *Fullilove* or trying to derive a rationale from the three separate opinions supporting the judgment, none of which commanded more than three votes, I do not believe our decision in that case controls the one before us here.

A sound distinction between federal and state (or local) action based on race rests not only upon the substance of the Civil War Amendments, but upon social reality and governmental theory. It is a simple fact that what Justice Stewart described in *Fullilove* as "the dispassionate objectivity [and] the flexibility that are needed to mold a race-conscious remedy around the single objective of eliminating the effects of past or present discrimination"—political qualities already to be doubted in a national legislature, *Fullilove,* supra, at 527, 100 S.Ct., at 2800 (Stewart, J., with whom Rehnquist, J., joined, dissenting)—are substantially less likely to exist at the state or local level. The struggle for racial justice has historically been a struggle by the national society against oppression in the individual States. See, e.g., *Ex parte Virginia,* supra (denying writ of habeas corpus to a state judge in custody under federal indictment for excluding jurors on the basis of race). And the struggle retains that character in modern times. See, e.g., Brown v. Board of Education, 349 U.S. 294, 75 S.Ct. 753, 99 L.Ed. 1083 (1955) (*Brown II*). Not all of that struggle has involved discrimination against blacks, see, e.g., Yick Wo v. Hopkins, 118 U.S. 356, 6 S.Ct. 1064,

30 L.Ed. 220 (1886) (Chinese); Hernandez v. Texas, 347 U.S. 475, 74 S.Ct. 667, 98 L.Ed. 866 (1954) (Hispanics), and not all of it has been in the Old South, see, e.g., Columbus Board of Education v. Penick, 443 U.S. 449, 99 S.Ct. 2941, 61 L.Ed.2d 666 (1979); Keyes v. School District No. 1, Denver, Colorado, 413 U.S. 189, 93 S.Ct. 2686, 37 L.Ed.2d 548 (1973). What the record shows, in other words, is that racial discrimination against any group finds a more ready expression at the state and local than at the federal level. To the children of the Founding Fathers, this should come as no surprise. An acute awareness of the heightened danger of oppression from political factions in small, rather than large, political units dates to the very beginning of our national history. See G. Wood, The Creation of the American Republic, 1776–1787, pp. 499–506 (1969). As James Madison observed in support of the proposed Constitution's enhancement of national powers:

"The smaller the society, the fewer probably will be the distinct parties and interests composing it; the fewer the distinct parties and interests, the more frequently will a majority be found of the same party; and the smaller the number of individuals composing a majority, and the smaller the compass within which they are placed, the more easily will they concert and execute their plan of oppression. Extend the sphere and you take in a greater variety of parties and interests; you make it less probable that a majority of the whole will have a common motive to invade the rights of other citizens; or if such a common motive exists, it will be more difficult for all who feel it to discover their own strength and to act in unison with each other." The Federalist No. 10, pp. 82–84 (C. Rossiter ed. 1961).

The prophesy of these words came to fruition in Richmond in the enactment of a set-aside clearly and directly beneficial to the dominant political group, which happens also to be the dominant racial group. The same thing has no doubt happened before in other cities (though the racial basis of the preference has rarely been made textually explicit)—and blacks have often been on the receiving end of the injustice. Where injustice is the game, however, turn-about is not fair play.

In my view there is only one circumstance in which the States may act *by race* to "undo the effects of past discrimination": where that is necessary to eliminate their own maintenance of a system of unlawful racial classification. If, for example, a state agency has a discriminatory pay scale compensating black employees in all positions at 20% less than their nonblack counterparts, it may assuredly promulgate an order raising the salaries of "all black employees" by 20%. Cf. Bazemore v. Friday, 478 U.S. 385, 395–396, 106 S.Ct. 3000, 3006–3007, 92 L.Ed.2d 315 (1986). This distinction explains our school desegregation cases, in which we have made plain that States and localities sometimes have an obligation to adopt race-conscious remedies. While there is no doubt that those cases have taken into account the continuing "effects" of previously mandated racial school assignment, we have held those effects to justify a race-conscious remedy only because we have concluded, in that context, that they perpetuate a "dual school system." We have stressed each school district's constitutional "duty to *dismantle* its dual system," and have found that "[e]ach instance of a failure or refusal to fulfill this affirmative duty *continues the violation* of the Fourteenth Amendment." Columbus Board of Education v. Penick, supra, 443 U.S. at 458–459, 99 S.Ct. at 2946–2947 (emphasis added). Concluding in this context that race-neutral efforts at "dismantling the state-imposed dual system" were so ineffective that they might "indicate a lack of good faith," Green v. County School Board, 391 U.S. 430, 439, 88 S.Ct. 1689, 1695, 20 L.Ed.2d 716 (1968), we have permitted, as part of the local authorities' "affirmative duty to disestablish the dual school system[s]," such voluntary (that is, noncourt-ordered) measures as attendance zones drawn to achieve greater racial balance, and out-of-zone assignment by race for the same purpose. McDaniel v. Barresi, 402 U.S. 39, 40–41, 91 S.Ct. 1287, 1288, 28 L.Ed.2d 582 (1971). While thus permitting the use of race to *de* classify racially classified students, teachers, and educational resources, however, we have also made it clear that the remedial power extends no further than the scope of the continuing constitutional violation. See e.g., Columbus Board of Education v. Penick, supra, 443 U.S., at 465, 99 S.Ct. at 2950; Dayton Board of Education v. Brinkman, 433 U.S. 406, 420, 97 S.Ct. 2766, 2775, 53 L.Ed.2d 851 (1977); Milliken v. Bradley, 418 U.S. 717, 744, 94 S.Ct. 3112, 3127, 41 L.Ed.2d 1069 (1974); Keyes v. School District No. 1, Denver, Colorado, 413 U.S., at 213, 93 S.Ct., at 2699. And it is implicit in our cases that after the dual school system has been completely disestablished, the States may no longer assign students by race. Cf. Pasadena City Board of Education v. Spangler, 427 U.S. 424, 96 S.Ct. 2697, 49 L.Ed.2d 599 (1976) (federal court may not require racial assignment in such circumstances).

Our analysis in *Bazemore,* supra, reflected our unwillingness to conclude, outside the context of school assignment, that the continuing effects of prior discrimination can be equated with state maintenance of a discriminatory system. There we found both that the government's adoption of "wholly neutral admissions" policies for 4–H and Homemaker clubs sufficed to remedy its prior constitutional violation of maintaining segregated admissions, and that there was no further obligation to use racial reassignments to eliminate continuing effects— that is, any remaining all-black and all-white clubs. "[H]owever sound Green [v. County School Board, supra] may have been in the context of the public schools," we said, "it has no application to this wholly different milieu." The same is so here.

A State can, of course, act "to undo the effects of past discrimination" in many permissible ways that do not involve classification by race. In the particular field of state contracting, for example, it may adopt a preference for small businesses, or even for new businesses— which would make it easier for those previously excluded by discrimina-

tion to enter the field. Such programs may well have racially disproportionate impact, but they are not based on race. And, of course, a
State may "undo the effects of past discrimination" in the sense of
giving the identified victim of state discrimination that which it wrongfully denied him—for example, giving to a previously rejected black
applicant the job that, by reason of discrimination, had been awarded to
a white applicant, even if this means terminating the latter's employment. In such a context, the white job-holder is not being selected for
disadvantageous treatment because of his race, but because he was
wrongfully awarded a job to which another is entitled. That is worlds
apart from the system here, in which those to be disadvantaged are
identified solely by race.

I agree with the Court's dictum that a fundamental distinction
must be drawn between the effects of "societal" discrimination and the
effects of "identified" discrimination, and that the situation would be
different if Richmond's plan were "tailored" to identify those particular
bidders who "suffered from the effects of past discrimination by the city
or prime contractors." In my view, however, the reason that would
make a difference is not, as the Court states, that it would justify race-
conscious action—but rather that it would enable race-neutral remediation. Nothing prevents Richmond from according a contracting preference to identified victims of discrimination. While most of the beneficiaries might be black, neither the beneficiaries nor those disadvantaged by the preference would be identified *on the basis of their race*.
In other words, far from justifying racial classification, identification of
actual victims of discrimination makes it less supportable than ever,
because more obviously unneeded. * * * Apart from their societal
effects, however, * * * it is important not to lose sight of the fact that
even "benign" racial quotas have individual victims, whose very real
injustice we ignore whenever we deny them enforcement of their right
not to be disadvantaged on the basis of race. Johnson v. Transportation Agency, Santa Clara County, Cal., 480 U.S. 616, 677, 107 S.Ct.
1442, 1476, 94 L.Ed.2d 615 (1987) (SCALIA, J., dissenting). As Justice
Douglas observed: "A. DeFunis who is white is entitled to no advantage
by virtue of that fact; nor is he subject to any disability, no matter
what his race or color. Whatever his race, he had a constitutional
right to have his application considered on its individual merits in a
racially neutral manner." DeFunis v. Odegaard, 416 U.S. 312, 337, 94
S.Ct. 1704, 1716, 40 L.Ed.2d 164 (1974) (Douglas, J., dissenting). When
we depart from this American principle we play with fire, and much
more than an occasional DeFunis, Johnson, or Croson burns.

It is plainly true that in our society blacks have suffered discrimination immeasurably greater than any directed at other racial groups.
But those who believe that racial preferences can help to "even the
score" display, and reinforce, a manner of thinking by race that was the
source of the injustice and that will, if it endures within our society, be
the source of more injustice still. The relevant proposition is not that
it was blacks, or Jews, or Irish who were discriminated against, but that

it was individual men and women, "created equal," who were discriminated against. And the relevant resolve is that that should never happen again. Racial preferences appear to "even the score" (in some small degree) only if one embraces the proposition that our society is appropriately viewed as divided into races, making it right that an injustice rendered in the past to a black man should be compensated for by discriminating against a white. Nothing is worth that embrace. Since blacks have been disproportionately disadvantaged by racial discrimination, any race-neutral remedial program aimed at the disadvantaged *as such* will have a disproportionately beneficial impact on blacks. Only such a program, and not one that operates on the basis of race, is in accord with the letter and the spirit of our Constitution.

Since I believe that the appellee here had a constitutional right to have its bid succeed or fail under a decisionmaking process uninfected with racial bias, I concur in the judgment of the Court.

JUSTICE MARSHALL, with whom JUSTICE BRENNAN and JUSTICE BLACKMUN join, dissenting.

It is a welcome symbol of racial progress when the former capital of the Confederacy acts forthrightly to confront the effects of racial discrimination in its midst. In my view, nothing in the Constitution can be construed to prevent Richmond, Virginia, from allocating a portion of its contracting dollars for businesses owned or controlled by members of minority groups. Indeed, Richmond's set-aside program is indistinguishable in all meaningful respects from—and in fact was patterned upon—the federal set-aside plan which this Court upheld in *Fullilove.*

A majority of this Court holds today, however, that the Equal Protection Clause of the Fourteenth Amendment blocks Richmond's initiative. The essence of the majority's position [1] is that Richmond has failed to catalogue adequate findings to prove that past discrimination has impeded minorities from joining or participating fully in Richmond's construction contracting industry. I find deep irony in second-guessing Richmond's judgment on this point. As much as any municipality in the United States, Richmond knows what racial discrimination is; a century of decisions by this and other federal courts has richly documented the city's disgraceful history of public and private racial discrimination. In any event, the Richmond City Council *has* supported its determination that minorities have been wrongly excluded from local construction contracting. Its proof includes statistics showing that minority-owned businesses have received virtually no city contracting dollars and rarely if ever belonged to area trade associations; testimony by municipal officials that discrimination has been widespread in the local construction industry; and the same exhaustive and widely publicized federal studies relied on in *Fullilove,* studies

---

1. In the interest of convenience, I refer to the opinion in this case authored by Justice O'Connor as "the majority," recognizing that certain portions of that opinion have been joined by only a plurality of the Court.

which showed that pervasive discrimination in the Nation's tight-knit construction industry had operated to exclude minorities from public contracting. These are precisely the types of statistical and testimonial evidence which, until today, this Court had credited in cases approving of race-conscious measures designed to remedy past discrimination.

More fundamentally, today's decision marks a deliberate and giant step backward in this Court's affirmative action jurisprudence. Cynical of one municipality's attempt to redress the effects of past racial discrimination in a particular industry, the majority launches a grape-shot attack on race-conscious remedies in general. The majority's unnecessary pronouncements will inevitably discourage or prevent governmental entities, particularly States and localities, from acting to rectify the scourge of past discrimination. This is the harsh reality of the majority's decision, but it is not the Constitution's command.

I

As an initial matter, the majority takes an exceedingly myopic view of the factual predicate on which the Richmond City Council relied when it passed the Minority Business Utilization Plan. The majority analyzes Richmond's initiative as if it were based solely upon the facts about local construction and contracting practices adduced during the City Council session at which the measure was enacted. In so doing, the majority down-plays the fact that the City Council had before it a rich trove of evidence that discrimination in the Nation's construction industry had seriously impaired the competitive position of businesses owned or controlled by members of minority groups. It is only against this backdrop of documented national discrimination, however, that the local evidence adduced by Richmond can be properly understood. The majority's refusal to recognize that Richmond has proven itself no exception to the dismaying pattern of national exclusion which Congress so painstakingly identified infects its entire analysis of this case.

Six years before Richmond acted, Congress passed, and the President signed, the Public Works Employment Act of 1977, Pub.L. 95–28, 91 Stat. 116, 42 U.S.C. § 6701 et seq. (Act), a measure which appropriated $4 billion in federal grants to state and local governments for use in public works projects. Section 103(f)(2) of the Act was a minority business set-aside provision. It required state or local grantees to use 10% of their federal grants to procure services or supplies from businesses owned or controlled by members of statutorily identified minority groups, absent an administrative waiver. In 1980, in *Fullilove,* supra, this Court upheld the validity of this federal set-aside. Chief Justice Burger's opinion noted the importance of overcoming those "criteria, methods, or practices thought by Congress to have the effect of defeating, or substantially impairing, access by the minority business community to public funds made available by congressional appropriations." Finding the set-aside provision properly tailored to this goal, the plurality concluded that the program was valid under either strict or intermediate scrutiny.

The congressional program upheld in *Fullilove* was based upon an array of congressional and agency studies which documented the powerful influence of racially exclusionary practices in the business world. * * *

Congress further found that minorities seeking initial public contracting assignments often faced immense entry barriers which did not confront experienced nonminority contractors. A report submitted to Congress in 1975 by the United States Commission on Civil Rights, for example, described the way in which fledgling minority-owned businesses were hampered by "deficiencies in working capital, inability to meet bonding requirements, disabilities caused by an inadequate 'track record,' lack of awareness of bidding opportunities, unfamiliarity with bidding procedures, preselection before the formal advertising process, and the exercise of discretion by government procurement officers to disfavor minority businesses."

Thus, as of 1977, there was "abundant evidence" in the public domain "that minority businesses ha[d] been denied effective participation in public contracting opportunities by procurement practices that perpetuated the effects of prior discrimination." *Fullilove,* supra, at 477–478, 100 S.Ct., at 2774.[2] Significantly, this evidence demonstrated that discrimination had prevented existing or nascent minority-owned businesses from obtaining not only federal contracting assignments, but state and local ones as well. See *Fullilove,* supra, at 478, 100 S.Ct., at 2774.[3]

---

2. Other reports indicating the dearth of minority-owned businesses include H.R.Rep. No. 92–1615, p. 3 (1972) (Report of the Subcommittee on Minority Small Business Enterprise, finding that the "long history of racial bias" has created "major problems" for minority businessmen); H.R.Doc. No. 92–194, p. 1 (1972) (text of message from President Nixon to Congress, describing federal efforts "to press open new doors of opportunity for millions of Americans to whom those doors had previously been barred, or only half-open"); H.R.Doc. No. 92–169, p. 1 (1971) (text of message from President Nixon to Congress, describing paucity of minority business ownership and federal efforts to give "every man an equal chance at the starting line").

3. Numerous congressional studies undertaken after 1977 and issued before the Richmond City Council convened in April 1983 found that the exclusion of minorities had continued virtually unabated—and that, because of this legacy of discrimination, minority businesses across the nation had still failed, as of 1983, to gain a real toehold in the business world. See, e.g., H.R.Rep. No. 95–949, pp. 2, 8 (1978) (Report of House Committee on Small Business, finding that minority businesses "are severely undercapitalized" and that many minorities are disadvantaged "because they are identified as members of certain racial categories"); S.Rep. No. 95–1070, pp. 14–15 (1978), U.S.Code Cong. & Admin.News 1978, pp. 3835, 3848, 3849; (Report of Senate Select Committee on Small Business, finding that the federal effort "has fallen far short of its goal to develop strong and growing disadvantaged small businesses," and "recogniz[ing] the pattern of social and economic discrimination that continues to deprive racial and ethnic minorities, and others, of the opportunity to participate fully in the free enterprise system"); S.Rep. No. 96–31, pp. IX, 107 (1979) (report of Senate Select Committee on Small Business, finding that many minorities have "suffered the effects of discriminatory practices or similar invidious circumstances over which they have no control"); S.Rep. No. 96–974, p. 3 (1980), U.S.Code Cong. & Admin.News 1980, pp.

The members of the Richmond City Council were well aware of these exhaustive congressional findings, a point the majority, tellingly, elides. The transcript of the session at which the Council enacted the local set-aside initiative contains numerous references to the 6–year–old congressional set-aside program, to the evidence of nationwide discrimination barriers described above, and to the *Fullilove* decision itself.

The City Council's members also heard testimony that, although minority groups made up half of the city's population, only .67% of the $24.6 million which Richmond had dispensed in construction contracts during the five years ending in March 1983 had gone to minority-owned prime contractors. They heard testimony that the major Richmond area construction trade associations had virtually no minorities among their hundreds of members.[4] Finally, they heard testimony from city officials as to the exclusionary history of the local construction industry.[5] As the District Court noted, not a single person who testified before the City Council denied that discrimination in Richmond's construction industry had been widespread. Civ.Action No. 84–0021 (ED Va., Dec. 3, 1984) (reprinted in Supp.App. to Juris.Statement 164–165).[6] So long as one views Richmond's local evidence of discrimination against the back-drop of systematic nationwide racial discrimination which Congress had so painstakingly identified in this very industry, this case is readily resolved.

4953, 4954 (Report of Senate Select Committee on Small Business, finding that government aid must be "significantly increased" if minority-owned businesses are to "have the maximum practical opportunity to develop into viable small businesses"); H.R.Rep. No. 97–956, p. 35 (1982) (Report of House Committee on Small Business, finding that federal programs to aid minority businesses have had "limited success" to date, but concluding that success could be "greatly expanded" with "appropriate corrective actions"); H.R.Rep. No. 98–3, p. 1 (1983) (Report of House Committee on Small Business, finding that "the small business share of Federal contracts continues to be inadequate").

4. According to testimony by trade association representatives, the Associated General Contractors of Virginia had no blacks among its 130 Richmond-area members; the American Subcontractors Association had no blacks among its 80 Richmond members, id., at 36 (remarks of Patrick Murphy); the Professional Contractors Estimators Association had one black member among its 60 Richmond members; the Central Virginia Electrical Contractors Association had one black member among its 45 members; and the National Electrical Contractors Association had two black members among its 81 Virginia members.

5. Among those testifying to the discriminatory practices of Richmond's construction industry was councilmember Henry Marsh, who had served as Mayor of Richmond from 1977 to 1982. Marsh stated:

"I have been practicing law in this community since 1961, and I am familiar with the practices in the construction industry in this area, in the State, and around the nation. And I can say without equivocation, that the general conduct in the construction industry in this area, and the State and around the nation, is one in which race discrimination and exclusion on the basis of race is widespread.

"I think the situation involved in the City of Richmond is the same * * *. I think the question of whether or not remedial action is required is not open to question." App. 41.

Manuel Deese, who in his capacity as City Manager had oversight responsibility for city procurement matters, stated that he fully agreed with Marsh's analysis. Id., at 42.

6. The representatives of several trade associations did, however, deny that their particular organizations engaged in discrimination.

II

"Agreement upon a means for applying the Equal Protection Clause to an affirmative-action program has eluded this Court every time the issue has come before us." Wygant v. Jackson Bd. of Education, 476 U.S. 267, 301, 106 S.Ct. 1842, 1861, 90 L.Ed.2d 260 (1986) (Marshall, J., dissenting). My view has long been that race-conscious classifications designed to further remedial goals "must serve important governmental objectives and must be substantially related to achievement of those objectives" in order to withstand constitutional scrutiny. Analyzed in terms of this two-prong standard, Richmond's set-aside, like the federal program on which it was modeled, is "plainly constitutional." *Fullilove,* supra, at 519, 100 S.Ct., at 2795–2796 (Marshall, J., concurring in judgment).

A

1

Turning first to the governmental interest inquiry, Richmond has two powerful interests in setting aside a portion of public contracting funds for minority-owned enterprises. The first is the city's interest in eradicating the effects of past racial discrimination. It is far too late in the day to doubt that remedying such discrimination is a compelling, let alone an important, interest. In *Fullilove,* six members of this Court deemed this interest sufficient to support a race-conscious set-aside program governing federal contract procurement. The decision, in holding that the federal set-aside provision satisfied the Equal Protection Clause under any level of scrutiny, recognized that the measure sought to remove "barriers to competitive access which had their roots in racial and ethnic discrimination, and which continue today, even absent any intentional discrimination or unlawful conduct." 448 U.S., at 478, 100 S.Ct., at 2774. Indeed, we have repeatedly reaffirmed the government's interest in breaking down barriers erected by past racial discrimination, in cases involving access to public education, McDaniel v. Barresi, 402 U.S. 39, 41, 91 S.Ct. 1287, 1288, 28 L.Ed.2d 582 (1971); University of California Regents v. Bakke, 438 U.S., at 320, 98 S.Ct., at 2763 (Powell, J.); id., at 362–364, 98 S.Ct., at 2784–2785 (joint separate opinion of Brennan, White, Marshall, and Blackmun, JJ.), employment, United States v. Paradise, 480 U.S. 149, 167, 107 S.Ct. 1053, 1064, 94 L.Ed.2d 203 (1987) (plurality opinion); id., at 186–189, 107 S.Ct., at 1074–1076 (Powell, J., concurring), and valuable government contracts. *Fullilove,* supra, 448 U.S., at 481–484, 100 S.Ct., at 2776–2777 (opinion of Burger, C.J.); id., at 496–497, 100 S.Ct., at 2783–2784 (Powell, J., concurring); id., at 521, 100 S.Ct., at 2797 (Marshall, J., concurring in judgment).

Richmond has a second compelling interest in setting aside, where possible, a portion of its contracting dollars. That interest is the prospective one of preventing the city's own spending decisions from reinforcing and perpetuating the exclusionary effects of past discrimination. See *Fullilove*, 448 U.S., at 475, 100 S.Ct., at 2773 (noting Congress' conclusion that "the subcontracting practices of prime contractors could perpetuate the prevailing impaired access by minority businesses to public contracting opportunities").

The majority pays only lip service to this additional governmental interest. But our decisions have often emphasized the danger of the government tacitly adopting, encouraging, or furthering racial discrimination even by its own routine operations. In Shelley v. Kraemer, 334 U.S. 1, 68 S.Ct. 836, 92 L.Ed. 1161 (1948), this Court recognized this interest as a constitutional command, holding unanimously that the Equal Protection Clause forbids courts to enforce racially restrictive covenants even where such covenants satisfied all requirements of state law and where the State harbored no discriminatory intent. Similarly, in Norwood v. Harrison, 413 U.S. 455, 93 S.Ct. 2804, 37 L.Ed.2d 723 (1973), we invalidated a program in which a State purchased textbooks and loaned them to students in public and private schools, including private schools with racially discriminatory policies. We stated that the Constitution requires a State "to steer clear, not only of operating the old dual system of racially segregated schools, but also of giving significant aid to institutions that practice racial or other invidious discrimination." Id., at 467, 93 S.Ct., at 2811–2812; see also Gilmore v. City of Montgomery, 417 U.S. 556, 94 S.Ct. 2416, 41 L.Ed.2d 304 (1974) (upholding federal court order forbidding city from allowing private segregated schools which allegedly discriminated on the basis of race to use public parks).

The majority is wrong to trivialize the continuing impact of government acceptance or use of private institutions or structures once wrought by discrimination. When government channels all its contracting funds to a white-dominated community of established contractors whose racial homogeneity is the product of private discrimination, it does more than place its imprimatur on the practices which forged and which continue to define that community. It also provides a measurable boost to those economic entities that have thrived within it, while denying important economic benefits to those entities which, but for prior discrimination, might well be better qualified to receive valuable government contracts. In my view, the interest in ensuring that the government does not reflect and reinforce prior private discrimination in dispensing public contracts is every bit as strong as the interest in eliminating private discrimination—an interest which this Court has repeatedly deemed compelling. See, e.g., New York State Club Assn. v. New York City, 487 U.S. ___, n. 5, 108 S.Ct. 2225, 2235 n. 5, 101 L.Ed.2d 1 (1988); Board of Directors v. Rotary Club, 481 U.S. 537, 549, 107 S.Ct. 1940, ___, 95 L.Ed.2d 474 (1987); Roberts v. United States Jaycees, 468 U.S. 609, 623, 104 S.Ct. 3244, 3252, 82 L.Ed.2d 462 (1984); Bob Jones University v. United States, 461 U.S. 574, 604, 103 S.Ct. 2017, 2035, 76 L.Ed.2d 157 (1983); Runyon v. McCrary, 427 U.S. 160, 179, 96 S.Ct. 2586, 2598, 49 L.Ed.2d 415 (1976). The more government bestows its rewards on those persons or businesses that were positioned to thrive during a period of private racial discrimination, the tighter the dead-hand grip of prior discrimination becomes on the present and future. Cities like Richmond may not be constitutionally required to adopt set-aside plans. But there can be no doubt that when Richmond acted affirmatively to stem the perpetuation of patterns of discrimination through its own decision-making, it served an interest of the highest order.

2

The remaining question with respect to the "governmental interest" prong of equal protection analysis is whether Richmond has proffered satisfactory proof of past racial discrimination to support its twin interests in remediation and in governmental nonperpetuation. Although the Members of this Court have differed on the appropriate standard of review for race-conscious remedial measures, we have always regarded this factual inquiry as a practical one. Thus, the Court has eschewed rigid tests which require the provision of particular species of evidence, statistical or otherwise. At the same time we have required that government adduce evidence that, taken as a whole, is sufficient to support its claimed interest and to dispel the natural concern that it acted out of mere "paternalistic stereotyping, not on a careful consideration of modern social conditions." Fullilove v. Klutznick, 448 U.S., at 519, 100 S.Ct., at 2795 (Marshall, J., concurring in judgment).

The separate opinions issued in *Wygant* * * *, reflect this shared understanding. Justice Powell's opinion for a plurality of four Justices stated that "the trial court must make a factual determination that the employer had a strong basis in evidence for its conclusion that remedial action was necessary." Justice O'Connor's separate concurrence required "a firm basis for concluding that remedial action was appropriate." The dissenting opinion I authored, joined by Justices Brennan and Blackmun, required a government body to present a "legitimate factual predicate" and a reviewing court to "genuinely consider the circumstances of the provision at issue." Finally, Justice Stevens' separate dissent sought and found "a rational and unquestionably legitimate basis" for the school board's action. Our unwillingness to go beyond these generalized standards to require specific types of proof in all circumstances reflects, in my view, an understanding that discrimination takes a myriad of "ingenious and pervasive forms." University of California Regents v. Bakke, 438 U.S., at 387, 98 S.Ct., at 2797 (separate opinion of Marshall, J.).

The varied body of evidence on which Richmond relied provides a "strong," "firm," and "unquestionably legitimate" basis upon which the City Council could determine that the effects of past racial discrimination warranted a remedial and prophylactic governmental response. As I have noted, supra, Richmond acted against a backdrop of congressional and Executive Branch studies which demonstrated with such force the nationwide pervasiveness of prior discrimination that Congress presumed that " 'present economic inequities' " in construction contracting resulted from " 'past discriminatory systems.' " The city's local evidence confirmed that Richmond's construction industry did not deviate from this pernicious national pattern. The fact that just .67% of public construction expenditures over the previous five years had gone to minority-owned prime contractors, despite the city's racially mixed population, strongly suggests that construction contracting in the area was rife with "present economic inequities." To the extent this enormous disparity did not itself demonstrate that discrimination had occurred, the descriptive testimony of Richmond's elected and appointed leaders drew the necessary link between the pitifully small presence of minorities in construction contracting and past exclusionary practices. That *no one* who testified challenged this depiction of widespread racial discrimination in area construction contracting lent significant weight to these accounts. The fact that area trade associations had virtually no minority members dramatized the extent of present inequities and suggested the lasting power of past discriminatory systems. In sum, to suggest that the facts on which Richmond has relied do not provide a sound basis for its finding of past racial discrimination simply blinks credibility.

Richmond's reliance on localized, industry-specific findings is a far cry from the reliance on generalized "societal discrimination" which the majority describes as a basis for remedial action. But characterizing the plight of Richmond's minority contractors as mere "societal discrimination" is not the only respect in which the majority's critique shows an unwillingness to come to grips with why construction-contracting in Richmond is essentially a whites-only enterprise. The majority also takes the disingenuous approach of disaggregating Richmond's local evidence, attacking it piecemeal, and thereby concluding that no *single* piece of evidence adduced by the city, "standing alone," suffices to prove past discrimination. But items of evidence do not, of course, "stan[d] alone" or exist in alien juxtaposition; they necessarily work together, reinforcing or contradicting each other.

In any event, the majority's criticisms of individual items of Richmond's evidence rest on flimsy foundations. The majority states, for example, that reliance on the disparity between the share of city contracts awarded to minority firms (.67%) and the minority population of Richmond (approximately 50%) is "misplaced." It is true that, when the factual predicate needed to be proved is one of *present* discrimination, we have generally credited statistical contrasts between the racial composition of a work force and the general population as proving discrimination only where this contrast revealed "gross statistical disparities." Hazelwood School District v. United States, 433 U.S. 299, 307–308, 97 S.Ct. 2736, 2741–2742, 53 L.Ed.2d 768 (1977) (Title VII case). But this principle does not impugn Richmond's statistical contrast, for two reasons. First, considering how miniscule the share of Richmond public construction contracting dollars received by minority-owned businesses is, it is hardly unreasonable to conclude that this case involves a "gross statistical disparit[y]." There are roughly equal numbers of minorities and nonminorities in Richmond—yet minority-owned businesses receive *one-seventy-fifth* the public contracting funds that other businesses receive.

Second, and more fundamentally, where the issue is not present discrimination but rather whether *past* discrimination has resulted in the *continuing exclusion* of minorities from an historically tight-knit industry, a contrast between population and work force is entirely appropriate to help gauge the degree of the exclusion. In Johnson v. Transportation Agency, supra, Justice O'Connor specifically observed that, when it is alleged that discrimination has prevented blacks from "obtaining th[e] experience" needed to qualify for a position, the "relevant comparison" is not to the percentage of blacks in the pool of qualified candidates, but to "the total percentage of blacks in the labor force." This contrast is especially illuminating in cases like this, where a main avenue of introduction into the work force—here, membership in the trade associations whose members presumably train apprentices and help them procure subcontracting assignments—is itself grossly dominated by nonminorities. The majority's assertion that the city "does not even know how many MBE's in the relevant market are qualified," is thus entirely beside the point. If Richmond indeed has a monochromatic contracting community—a conclusion reached by the District Court,—this most likely reflects the lingering power of past exclusionary practices. Certainly this is the explanation Congress has found persuasive at the national level. See *Fullilove.* The city's requirement that prime public contractors set aside 30% of their subcontracting assignments for minority-owned enterprises, subject to the ordinance's provision for waivers where minority-owned enterprises are unavailable or unwilling to participate, is designed precisely to ease minority contractors into the industry.

The majority's perfunctory dismissal of the testimony of Richmond's appointed and elected leaders is also deeply disturbing. These officials—including councilmembers, a former mayor, and the present city manager—asserted that race discrimination in area contracting had been widespread, and that the set-aside ordinance was a sincere and necessary attempt to eradicate the effects of this discrimination. The majority, however, states that where racial classifications are concerned, "simple legislative assurances of good intention cannot suffice." It similarly discounts as minimally probative the City Council's designation of its set-aside plan as remedial. "[B]lind judicial deference to legislative or executive pronouncements," the majority explains, "has no place in equal protection analysis."

No one, of course, advocates "blind judicial deference" to the findings of the City Council or the testimony of city leaders. The majority's suggestion that wholesale deference is what Richmond seeks is a classic straw-man argument. But the majority's trivialization of the testimony of Richmond's leaders is dismaying in a far more serious respect. By disregarding the testimony of local leaders and the judgment of local government, the majority does violence to the very principles of comity within our federal system which this Court has long championed. Local officials, by virtue of their proximity to, and their expertise with, local affairs, are exceptionally well-qualified to make determinations of public good "within their respective spheres of authority." Hawaii Housing Authority v. Midkiff, 467 U.S. 229, 244, 104 S.Ct. 2321, 2331, 81 L.Ed.2d 186 (1984). The majority, however, leaves any traces of comity behind in its headlong rush to strike down Richmond's race-conscious measure.

Had the majority paused for a moment on the facts of the Richmond experience, it would have discovered that the city's leadership is deeply familiar with what racial discrimination is. The members of the Richmond City Council have spent long years witnessing multifarious acts of discrimination, including, but not limited to, the deliberate diminution of black residents' voting rights, resistance to school desegregation, and publicly sanctioned housing discrimination. Numerous decisions of federal courts chronicle this disgraceful recent history. In Richmond v. United States, 422 U.S. 358, 95 S.Ct. 2296, 45 L.Ed.2d 245 (1975), for example, this Court denounced Richmond's decision to annex part of an adjacent county at a time when the city's black population was nearing 50% because it was "infected by the impermissible purpose of denying the right to vote based on race through perpetuating white majority power to exclude Negroes from office." Id., at 373, 95 S.Ct., at 2305; see also id., at 382, 95 S.Ct., at 2309 (Brennan, J., dissenting) (describing Richmond's "flagrantly discriminatory purpose * * *. to avert a transfer of political control to what was fast becoming a black-population majority").

In Bradley v. School Board of City of Richmond, Virginia, 462 F.2d 1058, 1060, n. 1 (CA4 1972), aff'd by an equally divided Court, 412 U.S. 92, 93 S.Ct. 1952, 36 L.Ed.2d 771 (1973), the Court of Appeals for the Fourth Circuit, sitting en banc, reviewed in the context of a school desegregation case Richmond's long history of inadequate compliance with Brown v. Board of Education, 347 U.S. 483, 74 S.Ct. 686, 98 L.Ed. 873 (1954), and the cases implementing its holding. * * * The Court of Appeals majority in *Bradley* used * * * pungent words in describing public and private housing discrimination in Richmond. Though rejecting the black plaintiffs' request that it consolidate Richmond's school district with those of two neighboring counties, the majority nonetheless agreed with the plaintiffs' assertion that "within the City of Richmond there has been state (also federal) action tending to perpetuate apartheid of the races in ghetto patterns throughout the city."

When the legislatures and leaders of cities with histories of pervasive discrimination testify that past discrimination has infected one of their industries, armchair cynicism like that exercised by the majority has no place. It may well be that "the autonomy of a state is an essential component of federalism," Garcia v. San Antonio Metropolitan Transit Authority, 469 U.S. 528, 588, 105 S.Ct. 1005, 1037, 83 L.Ed.2d 1016 (1985) (O'Connor, J., dissenting), and that "each State is sovereign within its own domain, governing its citizens and providing for their general welfare," FERC v. Mississippi, 456 U.S., at 777, 102 S.Ct., at 2147 (O'Connor, J., dissenting), but apparently this is not the case when federal judges, with nothing but their impressions to go on, choose to disbelieve the explanations of these local governments and officials. Disbelief is particularly inappropriate here in light of the fact that appellee Croson, which had the burden of proving unconstitutionality at trial, *Wygant*, 476 U.S., at 277–278, 106 S.Ct., at 1848 (plurality opinion), has *at no point* come forward with *any* direct evidence that the City Council's motives were anything other than sincere.[9]

Finally, I vehemently disagree with the majority's dismissal of the congressional and Executive Branch findings noted in *Fullilove* as having "extremely limited" probative value in this case. The majority concedes that Congress established nothing less than a "presumption" that minority contracting firms have been disadvantaged by prior discrimination. The majority, inexplicably, would forbid Richmond to "share" in this information, and permit only Congress to take note of these ample findings. In thus requiring that Richmond's local evidence be severed from the context in which it was prepared, the majority would require cities seeking to eradicate the effects of past discrimination within their borders to reinvent the evidentiary wheel and engage in unnecessarily duplicative, costly, and time-consuming factfinding.

No principle of federalism or of federal power, however, forbids a state or local government from drawing upon a nationally relevant historical record prepared by the Federal Government.[10] Of course, Richmond could have built an even more compendious record of past discrimination, one including additional stark statistics and additional individual accounts of past discrimination. But nothing in the Fourteenth Amendment imposes such onerous documentary obligations upon States and localities once the reality of past discrimination is apparent.

B

In my judgment, Richmond's set-aside plan also comports with the second prong of the equal protection inquiry, for it is substantially related to the interests it seeks to serve in remedying past discrimina-

---

9. Compare *Fullilove*, 448 U.S., at 541, 100 S.Ct., at 2807 (Stevens, J., dissenting) (noting statements of sponsors of federal set-aside that measure was designed to give their constituents "a piece of the action").

10. Although the majority sharply criticizes Richmond for using data which it did not itself develop, it is noteworthy that the federal set-aside program upheld in *Fullilove* was adopted as a floor amendment "without any congressional hearings or investigation whatsoever." L. Tribe, American Constitutional Law 345 (2d ed. 1988). The principal opinion in *Fullilove* justified the set-aside by relying heavily on the aforementioned studies by agencies like the Small Business Administration and on legislative reports prepared in connection with prior, failed legislation.

tion and in ensuring that municipal contract procurement does not perpetuate that discrimination. The most striking aspect of the city's ordinance is the similarity it bears to the "appropriately limited" federal set-aside provision upheld in *Fullilove*. Like the federal provision, Richmond's is limited to five years in duration, and was not renewed when it came up for reconsideration in 1988. Like the federal provision, Richmond's contains a waiver provision freeing from its subcontracting requirements those nonminority firms that demonstrate that they cannot comply with its provisions. Like the federal provision, Richmond's has a minimal impact on innocent third parties. While the measure affects 30% of *public* contracting dollars, that translates to only 3% of overall Richmond area contracting.

Finally, like the federal provision, Richmond's does not interfere with any vested right of a contractor to a particular contract; instead it operates entirely prospectively. Ibid. Richmond's initiative affects only future economic arrangements and imposes only a diffuse burden on nonminority competitors—here, businesses owned or controlled by nonminorities which seek subcontracting work on public construction projects. The plurality in *Wygant* emphasized the importance of this not disrupting the settled and legitimate expectations of innocent parties. "While hiring goals impose a diffuse burden, often foreclosing only one of several opportunities, layoffs impose the entire burden of achieving racial equality on particular individuals, often resulting in serious disruption of their lives. That burden is too intrusive." *Wygant*, 476 U.S., at 283, 106 S.Ct., at 1851.

These factors, far from "justify[ing] a preference of any size or duration," are precisely the factors to which this Court looked in *Fullilove*. The majority takes issue, however, with two aspects of Richmond's tailoring: the city's refusal to explore the use of race-neutral measures to increase minority business participation in contracting, and the selection of a 30% set-aside figure. The majority's first criticism is flawed in two respects. First, the majority overlooks the fact that since 1975, Richmond has barred both discrimination by the city in awarding public contracts and discrimination by public contractors. See Richmond, Va., City Code, § 17.1 et seq. (1985). The virtual absence of minority businesses from the city's contracting rolls, indicated by the fact that such businesses have received less than 1% of public contracting dollars, strongly suggests that this ban has not succeeded in redressing the impact of past discrimination or in preventing city contract procurement from reinforcing racial homogeneity. Second, the majority's suggestion that Richmond should have first undertaken such race-neutral measures as a program of city financing for small firms, ignores the fact that such measures, while theoretically appealing, have been discredited by Congress as ineffectual in eradicating the effects of past discrimination in this very industry. For this reason, this Court in *Fullilove* refused to fault Congress for not undertaking race-neutral measures as precursors to its race-conscious set-aside. The Equal Protection Clause does not require Richmond to

retrace Congress' steps when Congress has found that those steps lead
nowhere. Given the well-exposed limitations of race-neutral measures,
it was thus appropriate for a municipality like Richmond to conclude
that, in the words of Justice Blackmun, "[i]n order to get beyond
racism, we must first take account of race. There is no other way."
University of California Regents v. Bakke, 438 U.S., at 407, 98 S.Ct., at
2807–2808 (1978) (separate opinion).[11]

As for Richmond's 30% target, the majority states that this figure
"cannot be said to be narrowly tailored to any goal, except perhaps
outright racial balancing." Ante, at 728. The majority ignores two
important facts. First, the set-aside measure affects only 3% of overall
city contracting; thus, any imprecision in tailoring has far less impact
than the majority suggests. But more important, the majority ignores
the fact that Richmond's 30% figure was patterned directly on the
Fullilove precedent. Congress' 10% figure fell "roughly halfway between the present percentage of minority contractors and the percentage of minority group members in the Nation." *Fullilove*, supra, 448
U.S., at 513–514, 100 S.Ct., at 2792–2793 (Powell, J., concurring). The
Richmond City Council's 30% figure similarly falls roughly halfway
between the present percentage of Richmond-based minority contractors (almost zero) and the percentage of minorities in Richmond (50%).
In faulting Richmond for not presenting a different explanation for its
choice of a set-aside figure, the majority honors *Fullilove* only in the
breach.

III

I would ordinarily end my analysis at this point and conclude that
Richmond's ordinance satisfies both the governmental interest and
substantial relationship prongs of our Equal Protection Clause analysis.
However, I am compelled to add more, for the majority has gone beyond
the facts of this case to announce a set of principles which unnecessarily restrict the power of governmental entities to take race-conscious
measures to redress the effects of prior discrimination.

A

Today, for the first time, a majority of this Court has adopted strict
scrutiny as its standard of Equal Protection Clause review of race-
conscious remedial measures. This is an unwelcome development. A
profound difference separates governmental actions that themselves
are racist, and governmental actions that seek to remedy the effects of

---

11. The majority also faults Richmond's
ordinance for including within its definition of "minority group members" not only
black citizens, but also citizens who are
"Spanish-speaking, Oriental, Indian, Eskimo, or Aleut persons." This is, of course,
precisely the same definition Congress
adopted in its set-aside legislation. *Fullilove*, 448 U.S., at 454, 100 S.Ct., at 2762.

Even accepting the majority's view that
Richmond's ordinance is overbroad because
it includes groups, such as Eskimos or
Aleuts, about whom no evidence of local
discrimination has been proffered, it does
not necessarily follow that the balance of
Richmond's ordinance should be invalidated.

prior racism or to prevent neutral governmental activity from perpetuating the effects of such racism.

Racial classifications "drawn on the presumption that one race is inferior to another or because they put the weight of government behind racial hatred and separatism" warrant the strictest judicial scrutiny because of the very irrelevance of these rationales. By contrast, racial classifications drawn for the purpose of remedying the effects of discrimination that itself was race-based have a highly pertinent basis: the tragic and indelible fact that discrimination against blacks and other racial minorities in this Nation has pervaded our Nation's history and continues to scar our society. As I stated in *Fullilove:* "Because the consideration of race is relevant to remedying the continuing effects of past racial discrimination, and because governmental programs employing racial classifications for remedial purposes can be crafted to avoid stigmatization, * * * such programs should not be subjected to conventional 'strict scrutiny'—scrutiny that is strict in theory, but fatal in fact." *Fullilove,* supra, 448 U.S., at 518–519, 100 S.Ct., at 2795.

In concluding that remedial classifications warrant no different standard of review under the Constitution than the most brute and repugnant forms of state-sponsored racism, a majority of this Court signals that it regards racial discrimination as largely a phenomenon of the past, and that government bodies need no longer preoccupy themselves with rectifying racial injustice. I, however, do not believe this Nation is anywhere close to eradicating racial discrimination or its vestiges. In constitutionalizing its wishful thinking, the majority today does a grave disservice not only to those victims of past and present racial discrimination in this Nation whom government has sought to assist, but also to this Court's long tradition of approaching issues of race with the utmost sensitivity.

B

I am also troubled by the majority's assertion that, even if it did not believe generally in strict scrutiny of race-based remedial measures, "the circumstances of this case" require this Court to look upon the Richmond City Council's measure with the strictest scrutiny. The sole such circumstance which the majority cites, however, is the fact that blacks in Richmond are a "dominant racial grou[p]" in the city. In support of this characterization of dominance, the majority observes that "blacks comprise approximately 50% of the population of the city of Richmond" and that "[f]ive of the nine seats on the City Council are held by blacks."

While I agree that the numerical and political supremacy of a given racial group is a factor bearing upon the level of scrutiny to be applied, this Court has never held that numerical inferiority, standing alone, makes a racial group "suspect" and thus entitled to strict scrutiny review. Rather, we have identified *other* "traditional indicia of suspectness": whether a group has been "saddled with such disabilities, or subjected to such a history of purposeful unequal treatment, or relegated to such a position of political powerlessness as to command extraordinary protection from the majoritarian political process." San Antonio Independent School District v. Rodriguez, 411 U.S. 1, 28, 93 S.Ct. 1278, 1294, 36 L.Ed.2d 16 (1973).

It cannot seriously be suggested that nonminorities in Richmond have any "history of purposeful unequal treatment." Nor is there any indication that they have any of the disabilities that have characteristically afflicted those groups this Court has deemed suspect. Indeed, the numerical and political dominance of nonminorities within the State of Virginia and the Nation as a whole provide an enormous political check against the "simple racial politics" at the municipal level which the majority fears. If the majority really believes that groups like Richmond's non-minorities, which comprise approximately half the population but which are outnumbered even marginally in political fora, are deserving of suspect class status for these reasons alone, this Court's decisions denying suspect status to women, see Craig v. Boren, 429 U.S. 190, 197, 97 S.Ct. 451, 456, 50 L.Ed.2d 397 (1976), and to persons with below-average incomes, see *San Antonio Independent School Dist.,* supra, 411 U.S., at 28, 93 S.Ct., at 1294, stand on extremely shaky ground.

In my view, the "circumstances of this case," underscore the importance of *not* subjecting to a strict scrutiny straitjacket the increasing number of cities which have recently come under minority leadership and are eager to rectify, or at least prevent the perpetuation of, past racial discrimination. In many cases, these cities will be the ones with the most in the way of prior discrimination to rectify. Richmond's leaders had just witnessed decades of publicly sanctioned racial discrimination in virtually all walks of life—discrimination amply documented in the decisions of the federal judiciary. This history of "purposefully unequal treatment" forced upon minorities, not imposed by them, should raise an inference that minorities in Richmond had much to remedy—and that the 1983 set-aside was undertaken with sincere remedial goals in mind, not "simple racial politics."

Richmond's own recent political history underscores the facile nature of the majority's assumption that elected officials' voting decisions are based on the color of their skins. In recent years, white and black councilmembers in Richmond have increasingly joined hands on controversial matters. When the Richmond City Council elected a black man Mayor in 1982, for example, his victory was won with the support of the City Council's four white members. Richmond Times–Dispatch, July 2, 1982, p. 1, col. 1. The vote on the set-aside plan a year later also was not purely along racial lines. Of the four white councilmembers, one voted for the measure and another abstained. The majority's view that remedial measures undertaken by municipalities with black leadership must face a stiffer test of Equal Protection

Clause scrutiny than remedial measures undertaken by municipalities with white leadership implies a lack of political maturity on the part of this Nation's elected minority officials that is totally unwarranted. Such insulting judgments have no place in constitutional jurisprudence.

C

Today's decision, finally, is particularly noteworthy for the daunting standard it imposes upon States and localities contemplating the use of race-conscious measures to eradicate the present effects of prior discrimination and prevent its perpetuation. The majority restricts the use of such measures to situations in which a State or locality can put forth "a prima facie case of a constitutional or statutory violation." In so doing, the majority calls into question the validity of the business set-asides which dozens of municipalities across this Nation have adopted on the authority of *Fullilove.*

Nothing in the Constitution or in the prior decisions of this Court supports limiting state authority to confront the effects of past discrimination to those situations in which a prima facie case of a constitutional or statutory violation can be made out. By its very terms, the majority's standard effectively cedes control of a large component of the content of that constitutional provision to Congress and to state legislatures. If an antecedent Virginia or Richmond law had defined as unlawful the award to nonminorities of an overwhelming share of a city's contracting dollars, for example, Richmond's subsequent set-aside initiative would then satisfy the majority's standard. But without such a law, the initiative might not withstand constitutional scrutiny. The meaning of "equal protection of the laws" thus turns on the happenstance of whether a State or local body has previously defined illegal discrimination. Indeed, given that racially discriminatory cities may be the ones least likely to have tough antidiscrimination laws on their books, the majority's constitutional incorporation of state and local statutes has the perverse effect of inhibiting those States or localities with the worst records of official racism from taking remedial action.

Similar flaws would inhere in the majority's standard even if it incorporated only federal anti-discrimination statutes. If Congress tomorrow dramatically expanded Title VII of the Civil Rights Act of 1964,—or alternatively, if it repealed that legislation altogether—the meaning of equal protection would change precipitously along with it. Whatever the Framers of the Fourteenth Amendment had in mind in 1868, it certainly was not that the content of their Amendment would turn on the amendments to or the evolving interpretations of a federal statute passed nearly a century later.[12]

12. Although the majority purports to "adher[e] to the standard of review employed in *Wygant*," the "prima facie case" standard it adopts marks an implicit rejection of the more generally framed "strong basis in evidence" test endorsed by the *Wygant* plurality, and the similar "firm basis" test endorsed by Justice O'CONNOR in her separate concurrence in that case. Under those tests, proving a prima facie violation of Title VII would appear to have been but one means of adducing sufficient

To the degree that this parsimonious standard is grounded on a view that either § 1 or § 5 of the Fourteenth Amendment substantially disempowered States and localities from remedying past racial discrimination, ante, at 719, 726–727, the majority is seriously mistaken. With respect, first, to § 5, our precedents have never suggested that this provision—or, for that matter, its companion federal-empowerment provisions in the Thirteenth and Fifteenth Amendments—was meant to pre-empt or limit state police power to undertake race-conscious remedial measures. To the contrary, in Katzenbach v. Morgan, 384 U.S. 641, 86 S.Ct. 1717, 16 L.Ed.2d 828 (1966), we held that § 5 "is a *positive* grant of legislative power authorizing Congress to exercise its discretion in determining whether and what legislation is needed to secure the guarantees of the Fourteenth Amendment." Indeed, we have held that Congress has this authority even where no constitutional violation has been found. See *Katzenbach,* supra (upholding Voting Rights Act provision nullifying state English literacy requirement we had previously upheld against Equal Protection Clause challenge). Certainly *Fullilove* did not view § 5 either as limiting the traditionally broad police powers of the States to fight discrimination, or as mandating a zero-sum game in which state power wanes as federal power waxes. On the contrary, the *Fullilove* plurality invoked § 5 only because it provided specific and certain authorization for the Federal Government's attempt to impose a race-conscious condition on the dispensation of federal funds by state and local grantees.

As for § 1, it is too late in the day to assert seriously that the Equal Protection Clause prohibits States—or for that matter, the Federal Government, to whom the equal protection guarantee has largely been applied, see Bolling v. Sharpe, 347 U.S. 497, 74 S.Ct. 693, 98 L.Ed. 884 (1954)—from enacting race-conscious remedies. Our cases in the areas of school desegregation, voting rights, and affirmative action have

proof to satisfy Equal Protection Clause analysis. See Johnson v. Transportation Agency, 480 U.S. 616, 632, 107 S.Ct. 1442, 1452, 94 L.Ed.2d 615 (1987) (plurality opinion) (criticizing suggestion that race-conscious relief be conditioned on showing of a prima facie Title VII violation).

The rhetoric of today's majority opinion departs from *Wygant* in another significant respect. In *Wygant,* a majority of this Court rejected as unduly inhibiting and constitutionally unsupported a requirement that a municipality demonstrate that its remedial plan is designed only to benefit specific victims of discrimination. Justice O'Connor noted that the Court's general agreement that a "remedial purpose need not be accompanied by contemporaneous findings of actual discrimination to be accepted as legitimate as long as the public actor has a firm basis for believing that remedial action is required * * *. [A] plan

need not be limited to the remedying of specific instances of identified discrimination for it to be deemed sufficiently 'narrowly tailored,' or 'substantially related,' to the correction of prior discrimination by the state actor." Id., at 286–287, 106 S.Ct., at 1853. The majority's opinion today, however, hints that a "specific victims" proof requirement might be appropriate in equal protection cases. Given that just three Terms ago this Court rejected the "specific victims" idea as untenable, I believe these references—and the majority's cryptic "identified discrimination" requirement—cannot be read to require States and localities to make such highly particularized showings. Rather, I take the majority's standard of "identified discrimination" merely to require some quantum of proof of discrimination within a given jurisdiction that exceeds the proof which Richmond has put forth here.

demonstrated time and again that race is constitutionally germane, precisely because race remains dismayingly relevant in American life.

In adopting its prima facie standard for States and localities, the majority closes its eyes to this constitutional history and social reality. So, too, does Justice Scalia. He would further limit consideration of race to those cases in which States find it "necessary to eliminate their own maintenance of a system of unlawful racial classification"—a "distinction" which, he states, "explains our school desegregation cases." But this Court's remedy-stage school desegregation decisions cannot so conveniently be cordoned off. These decisions (like those involving voting rights and affirmative action) stand for the same broad principles of equal protection which Richmond seeks to vindicate in this case: all persons have equal worth, and it is permissible, given a sufficient factual predicate and appropriate tailoring, for government to take account of race to eradicate the present effects of race-based subjugation denying that basic equality. Justice Scalia's artful distinction allows him to avoid having to repudiate "our school desegregation cases," but, like the arbitrary limitation on race-conscious relief adopted by the majority, his approach "would freeze the status quo that is the very target" of the remedial actions of States and localities. McDaniel v. Barresi, 402 U.S., at 41, 100 S.Ct., at 1288; see also Board of Education v. Swann, 402 U.S., at 46, 91 S.Ct., at 1286 (striking down State's flat prohibition on assignment of pupils on basis of race as impeding an "effective remedy"); United Jewish Organizations v. Carey, 430 U.S. 144, 159–162, 97 S.Ct. 996, 1006–1008, 51 L.Ed.2d 229 (1977) (upholding New York's use of racial criteria in drawing district lines so as to comply with § 5 of the Voting Rights Act).

The fact is that Congress' concern in passing the Reconstruction Amendments, and particularly their congressional authorization provisions, was that States would *not* adequately respond to racial violence or discrimination against newly freed slaves. To interpret any aspect of these Amendments as proscribing state remedial responses to these very problems turns the Amendments on their heads. As four Justices, of whom I was one, stated in University of California Regents v. Bakke:

> "[There is] no reason to conclude that the States cannot voluntarily accomplish under § 1 of the Fourteenth Amendment what Congress under § 5 of the Fourteenth Amendment validly may authorize or compel either the States or private persons to do. A contrary position would conflict with the traditional understanding recognizing the competence of the States to initiate measures consistent with federal policy in the absence of congressional preemption of the subject matter. *Nothing whatever in the legislative history of either the Fourteenth Amendment or the Civil Rights Acts even remotely suggests that the States are foreclosed from furthering the fundamental purpose of equal opportunity to which the Amendment and those Acts are addressed.* Indeed, voluntary initiatives by the States to achieve the national goal of equal opportunity have

been recognized to be essential to its attainment. 'To use the Fourteenth Amendment as a sword against such State power would stultify that Amendment.' Railway Mail Assn. v. Corsi, 326 U.S. 88, 98, 65 S.Ct. 1483, 1489, 89 L.Ed. 2072 (Frankfurter, J., concurring)." 438 U.S., at 368, 98 S.Ct., at 2788 (1978) (footnote omitted) (emphasis added).

In short, there is simply no credible evidence that the Framers of the Fourteenth Amendment sought "to transfer the security and protection of all the civil rights * * * from the States to the Federal government." The Slaughter–House Cases, 16 Wall. 36, 77–78, 21 L.Ed. 394 (1873).[13] The three Reconstruction Amendments undeniably "worked a dramatic change in the balance between congressional and state power," they forbade state-sanctioned slavery, forbade the state-sanctioned denial of the right to vote, and (until the content of the Equal Protection Clause was substantially applied to the Federal Government through the Due Process Clause of the Fifth Amendment) uniquely forbade States from denying equal protection. The Amendments also specifically empowered the Federal Government to combat discrimination at a time when the breadth of federal power under the Constitution was less apparent than it is today. But nothing in the Amendments themselves, or in our long history of interpreting or applying those momentous charters, suggests that States, exercising their police power, are in any way constitutionally inhibited from working alongside the Federal Government in the fight against discrimination and its effects.

IV

The majority today sounds a full-scale retreat from the Court's longstanding solicitude to race-conscious remedial efforts "directed toward deliverance of the century-old promise of equality of economic opportunity." *Fullilove*, 448 U.S., at 463, 100 S.Ct., at 2767. The new and restrictive tests it applies scuttle one city's effort to surmount its discriminatory past, and imperil those of dozens more localities. I, however, profoundly disagree with the cramped vision of the Equal Protection Clause which the majority offers today and with its application of that vision to Richmond, Virginia's, laudable set-aside plan. The battle against pernicious racial discrimination or its effects is nowhere near won. I must dissent.

JUSTICE BLACKMUN, with whom JUSTICE BRENNAN joins, dissenting.

I join Justice Marshall's perceptive and incisive opinion revealing great sensitivity toward those who have suffered the pains of economic discrimination in the construction trades for so long.

---

13. Tellingly, the sole support the majority offers for its view that the Framers of the Fourteenth Amendment intended such a result are two law review articles analyzing this Court's recent affirmative action decisions, and a court of appeals decision which relies upon statements by James Madison. Madison, of course, had been dead for 32 years when the Fourteenth Amendment was enacted.

I never thought that I would live to see the day when the city of Richmond, Virginia, the cradle of the Old Confederacy, sought on its own, within a narrow confine, to lessen the stark impact of persistent discrimination. But Richmond, to its great credit, acted. Yet this Court, the supposed bastion of equality, strikes down Richmond's efforts as though discrimination had never existed or was not demonstrated in this particular litigation. Justice Marshall convincingly discloses the fallacy and the shallowness of that approach. History is irrefutable, even though one might sympathize with those who—though possibly innocent in themselves—benefit from the wrongs of past decades.

So the Court today regresses. I am confident, however, that, given time, it one day again will do its best to fulfill the great promises of the Constitution's Preamble and of the guarantees embodied in the Bill of Rights—a fulfillment that would make this Nation very special.

NOTES AND PROBLEMS FOR DISCUSSION

1. The decision in *Croson* significantly changed the legal landscape and had a dramatic impact on the subsequent adoption and continuation of affirmative action plans. Most significantly, of course, a majority of the Court, for the first time, agreed on the level of scrutiny to be applied to race-based preferences. Perhaps equally important, however, was the analysis employed by the Court with respect to the evidentiary showing that now would be required to sustain this heightened level of scrutiny. Not surprisingly, this ruling led to the invalidation of several such plans. For example, In MICHIGAN ROAD BUILDERS ASS'N, INC. v. MILLIKEN, 834 F.2d 583 (6th Cir.1987), affirmed without opinion, 489 U.S. 1061, 109 S.Ct. 1333, 103 L.Ed.2d 804 (1989), the Michigan legislature had enacted a "set-aside" statute that required each state department to award not less than 7% of its expenditures for construction, goods and services to MBEs ("black, hispanic, oriental, eskimo or American Indian" fell within definition of "minority") and not less than 5% to WBEs (woman owned businesses). The circuit court applied strict scrutiny to the racial classification and upheld the trial court's grant of summary judgment in favor of the plaintiff, ruling that the statute was unconstitutional under the equal protection clause of the Fourteenth Amendment. In reviewing the record, the Sixth Circuit indicated that the Michigan legislature had relied on information collected with respect to prior, unrelated legislation dealing with the inability of small businesses, rather than MBEs, to break into the market and that the legislative history of the set-aside statute attributed the scarcity of MBE contracts with the state to the effects of societal discrimination. Accordingly, the court concluded that the State had not demonstrated a compelling interest in remedying past discrimination since the legislature did not have sufficient evidence to warrant a finding that the State itself had discriminated against MBEs in awarding state contracts for the purchase of goods and services. The Sixth Circuit interpreted the Supreme Court's ruling in *Wygant* as requiring the State to demonstrate that *it* had engaged in racial discrimination in order to justify a race-based set-aside program designed to remedy the effects of prior discrimination. With respect to the sex-based set aside, the court stated that intermediate scrutiny was appropriate, but that the statute even failed to meet that lesser burden since the legislature had offered absolutely no evidence of its past discrimination against women owned businesses. The Supreme Court affirmed these rulings, but did not issue a written opinion.

See also O'Donnell Construction Co. v. District of Columbia, 963 F.2d 420 (D.C.Cir.1992)(reversing trial court's denial of preliminary injunction against enforcement of D.C. statute requiring 35% of dollar volume of all construction contracts awarded by District to be reserved for local minority owned businesses; District failed to present sufficient evidence of past discrimination beyond unsupported statement in statutory "Findings" section and unexplained statistic relating to number and value of contracts awarded to MBE's).

On the other hand, some municipalities have been able to conform to the standards articulated in *Croson*. For example, in CONE CORP. v. HILLSBOROUGH COUNTY, 908 F.2d 908 (11th Cir.1990), cert. denied, __ U.S. __, 111 S.Ct. 516, 112 L.Ed.2d 528 (1990), an ordinance establishing an annual goal of twenty-five percent total MBE participation in County construction was upheld. This statute set an MBE participation goal for each project. In the fiscal year following the implementation of the ordinance, MBE participation in those projects in which goals were set totalled almost twenty per cent, that is, less than the 25% goal, but higher than the percentage of minority contractors in the County. The court concluded that this statute was materially different from the Richmond ordinance struck down in *Croson*. It noted that the statute was enacted after the County had undertaken a statistical survey of minority business participation in contracts awarded by the County which indicated that minorities were significantly underrepresented in such awards in comparison to the percentage of MBE contractors in the local community. Thus, the court concluded, the legislature had relied on statistics which indicated that there was discrimination specifically in the construction business commissioned by the County, not just in the construction industry in general. The legislature also had evidence before it of numerous complaints made by MBE contractors to the County regarding discrimination by prime contractors. On the basis of all of this information, the court stated, the legislature had more than enough evidence on the question of prior discrimination and the need for racial classification to remedy the situation. With respect to whether the use of a racial classification was narrowly tailored, the court added that the County had tried a race-neutral program for six years prior to adopting the set-aside program. In addition, the MBE law included all of the race-neutral measures suggested by the Court in *Croson*. Moreover, the goal was flexible and did not apply to every individual project. Rather, it applied only to projects based on the number of qualified MBE subcontractors available for each subcontractable area. Under the plan, no goal would be set if there were not at least three qualified MBE subcontractors available for the subcontractable area. Finally, this statute, unlike the Richmond plan, did not apply the 25% participation goal to all covered minority groups. Accordingly, the court held, the plan passed constitutional muster. See also Stuart v. Roache, 57 FEP Cases 902 (1st Cir.1991)(consent decree entered into by Boston Police Department containing goal for promotion of black police sergeants survives strict scrutiny; since decree compared percentage of black sergeants with percentage of black police officers possessing minimal qualifications needed for promotion to sergeant and in light of defendant's adjudicated past history of entry-level racial discrimination, there was sufficient evidence of prior discrimination by defendant to support determination that racially-based preference was designed to remedy prior discrimination. Court also finds plan to be narrowly tailored.).

In CORAL CONSTRUCTION CO. v. KING COUNTY, 941 F.2d 910 (9th Cir.1991), cert. denied, __ U.S. __, 112 S.Ct. 875, 116 L.Ed.2d 780 (1992), however, the Ninth Circuit appears to have relaxed, to some degree, the evidentiary requirements discussed in *Croson*. Specifically, it addressed the language in *Croson* that requires a municipality to demonstrate that it relied on evidence of discrimination within the industry affected by the affirmative action plan in order to establish the remedial nature of the plan. This case involved a program implemented by Kings County (which encompasses the city of Seattle) that established a preference for the use of minority-owned and women-owned businesses in letting county contracts or subcontracts. The appellate court ruled that *Croson* did not require the County to compile a factual record on its own. Rather, the court declared, it was permissible for the County to demonstrate that it had relied on data compiled by the City of Seattle, a city agency, and another municipality contained within the territorial limits of the County. Data sharing under these limited circumstances, the court reasoned, was not inconsistent with the underlying concern in *Croson* that an MBE program not be based on extraterritorial data. Extraterritorial data was precluded by *Croson*, the court continued, because it constituted evidence of "societal discrimination", a situation that was beyond the remedial authority of local jurisdictions. Here, the evidence related directly to discrimination within the County limits.

The court then addressed the question of the kind of evidence that could be relied upon to prove the existence of a systemic pattern of discrimination necessary for the adoption of an affirmative action plan. In this case, the factual record contained an extensive amount of anecdotal evidence from individual contractors with respect to specific incidents of discrimination, but was devoid of statistical evidence. The court ruled that while anecdotal evidence *suggested* the existence of a systemic pattern, it was not enough, in the absence of statistical evidence, to prove such a pattern and, therefore, did not meet the County's burden of proving that its program was justified by the compelling interest of remedying prior county-wide discrimination. Nevertheless, the court added, this defect was cured by the fact that the trial court had been presented by the County with such statistical evidence contained in studies undertaken *after* the adoption of the MBE program. The court reasoned that while the County was required to have *some* concrete evidence of discrimination within the construction industry *before* it adopted a remedial program, the ultimate determination of whether the plan complied with the stringent requirements of the constitutional strict scrutiny standard should be made by a court on the basis of all evidence presented to it, regardless of when it was adduced. Otherwise, in the Ninth Circuit's judgment, a municipality would face the dilemma of deciding whether (1)to wait for further development of the record before acting and thereby risk potential constitutional liability for failing to eradicate extant discrimination, or (2)to act and risk liability for acting prematurely. Thus, it concluded, it would not invalidate an MBE program solely because the record at the time of adoption did not measure up to constitutional standards, as long as an adequate factual record was subsequently provided. Accordingly, it remanded the case to the trial court for a determination of whether the statistical studies compiled after the adoption of the plan provided an adequate factual justification for the implementation of this MBE program.

2. A majority of the Supreme Court took great pains to distinguish *Croson* from *Fullilove* with respect to the method of proving that a racial classification was adopted for the purpose of remedying prior discrimination. What impact, if any, will this aspect of the Court's analysis have on future equal protection scrutiny of affirmative action preferences that are either judicially imposed or

are voluntarily undertaken by non-legislative public institutions? For example, suppose a city police department transferred white police officers out of a special investigatory unit because it desired to correct what it perceived to be a racial imbalance within that investigatory unit? Could the department overcome an equal protection challenge to this race-based decision on the ground that it was undertaking voluntary affirmative action to remedy this racial imbalance? In CYGNAR v. CITY OF CHICAGO, 865 F.2d 827 (7th Cir.1989), the Seventh Circuit held that the defendants could not justify such a race-based transfer of white police officers out of a special investigatory unit on the ground that it was attempting to correct what it perceived to be a previously existing racial imbalance within that investigatory unit. The court ruled that this "affirmative action defense" could not withstand equal protection scrutiny (even though the jury had found that the defendants' decision was motivated by a desire to correct the perceived racial imbalance) because the defendants had not offered any evidence as to which population groups, if any, they had compared with the percentage of minority employees in the investigatory unit in concluding that an imbalance existed. In fact, the court continued, the defendants even failed to convince it that they had attempted to make any comparison whatsoever. Is this result mandated by *Croson*? Should a police department be subjected to the same standard of factfinding that is demanded of a state or local legislature?

3. As the material in the two previous Notes indicates, the Court, in *Croson,* finally achieved a majority consensus on the level of scrutiny to be applied in an equal protection challenge to a remedial affirmative action plan. The Note materials also indicate, however, that the *Croson* Court clearly sought to distinguish its constitutional analysis from the approach it had taken in *Fullilove* on the ground that *Croson* involved an equal protection challenge to a racially-based set-aside enacted by a local legislature, rather than by Congress. The relatively broad language in *Croson,* however, suggested that the Court might subsequently extend strict scrutiny analysis to a federally promulgated affirmative action plan.

The Court explicitly rejected such an extension of strict scrutiny, however, by a vote of 5–4 in METRO BROADCASTING, INC. v. FEDERAL COMMUNICATIONS COMMISSION, 497 U.S. 547, 110 S.Ct. 2997, 111 L.Ed.2d 445 (1990). In *Metro Broadcasting,* the Court was asked to rule on an equal protection challenge to two minority preference policies that had been adopted by the Federal Communications Commission. The FCC was granted exclusive authority to grant broadcast licenses based on the public interest by the terms of the Communications Act of 1934. Pursuant to this authority, and after holding hearings and conferences on minority ownership policies, the FCC adopted a Statement of Policy on Minority Ownership of Broadcasting Facilities which included two provisions intended to improve the opportunity for minority businesses to obtain broadcast licenses. The first provision stated that in comparative proceedings for new licenses it would consider minority ownership and participation in management as a plus factor to be weighed with all other relevant factors. Second, the Commission announced a plan to increase minority opportunities to receive reassigned and transferred licenses by creating an exception to its general rule forbidding the transfer of a license by a licensee whose qualifications to maintain its license had come under question. Under this provision, a licensee who was willing to sell the license at a "distress sale" could assign the license, but only to an FCC-approved minority enterprise.

Each of these preferences was challenged as violative of the Fifth Amendment guarantee of equal protection.

The Court began its analysis by emphasizing that this FCC policy encouraging minority ownership was specifically approved and, in fact, mandated by Congress. (Congress had enacted and the President had signed FCC appropriations bills for fiscal years 1988 and 1989 that prohibited the Commission from spending any appropriated funds to examine or change its minority ownership policies.) Thus, the five member majority (Brennan, Marshall, Blackmun, White and Stevens) reasoned, this case was closer to *Fullilove* than it was to *Croson*. The majority then stated that strict scrutiny had not been applied by a majority in *Fullilove* because the racial classification in that case had been adopted by Congress and that *Croson* did not prescribe the level of scrutiny to be applied to a benign racial classification employed by Congress. In the critical sentence of the opinion, the majority then stated that "benign race-conscious measures mandated by Congress—even if those measures are not 'remedial' in the sense of being designed to compensate victims of past governmental or societal discrimination—are constitutionally permissible to the extent that they serve important governmental objectives within the power of Congress and are substantially related to achievement of those objectives." The majority went on to conclude that the preferences served the important governmental objective of promoting broadcast diversity and were substantially related to achieving that objective. Promoting programming diversity, the majority declared, was an important governmental objective because providing a diversity of views and information to both the minority and nonminority segments of the audience on the airwaves served important First Amendment values. It then deferred to the findings by the FCC and Congress that there was an empirical nexus between minority ownership and broadcasting diversity. The majority also stated that the Commission had established minority ownership preferences only after extended experience demonstrated that race-neutral means could not produce adequate broadcasting diversity. Finally, the majority added that the preferences at issue did not impose impermissible burdens on nonminority candidates. The comparative hearing preference was only a "plus" factor considered in concert with other neutral factors and the opportunity reserved for minority firms to receive assignments through distress sales was limited to situations where no competing application had been filed with the Commission at the time the qualifications of the incumbent licensee were designated for hearing. It noted that distress sales represented less than four tenths of one percent of all broadcast sales since 1979.

In her dissenting opinion, Justice O'Connor (joined by Justices Scalia, Kennedy and the Chief Justice) lamented that the majority's analysis "marks a renewed toleration of racial classifications" and that the application of a lessened equal protection standard to congressional actions "finds no support in our cases or in the Constitution." She maintained that the equal protection guarantee in the Fifth Amendment compelled application of the same level of scrutiny to racial classifications employed by Congressional enactments as the Fourteenth Amendment required with respect to racial preferences adopted by state and local governments. Moreover, she emphasized, a lessened standard of scrutiny was applied in *Fullilove* because the racial classification was adopted pursuant to Congress' exercise of its powers under § 5 of the Fourteenth Amendment and because the classification was used to remedy identified past discrimination, neither of which factor existed in the instant case. She also expressed her dissatisfaction with the majority's characterization of the racial preference as "benign," a term she found to be indeterminate, at best.

The FCC policy upheld in *Metro Broadcasting* also contained a gender preference in its comparative licensing program. This preference, which made female ownership and participation a "plus factor" in comparative hearings, was not before the Court in *Metro*. It was, however, addressed and struck down as violative of the Equal Protection Clause of the Fifth Amendment by the D.C. Circuit (in an opinion written by then-Judge Thomas). In LAMPRECHT v. FCC, 958 F.2d 382 (D.C.Cir. 1992), the appellate court applied the intermediate scrutiny standard employed in *Metro* and found that there was insufficient evidence to establish that granting preferences to women would increase programming diversity. Accordingly, the majority concluded, the gender preference was not "substantially related to achieving" the government's legitimate interest in achieving diversity of viewpoints. The court distinguished this case from *Metro* on the ground that while there was a "host of empirical evidence" supporting the judgment linking minority ownership of stations with the stations' programming practices, there was no "statistically meaningful" proof supporting the Commission's judgment that women owners would broadcast women's or minority or any other underrepresented type of programming at any different rate than male owners.

UNITED STEELWORKERS OF AMERICA v. WEBER

Supreme Court of the United States, 1979.
443 U.S. 193, 99 S.Ct. 2721, 61 L.Ed.2d 480.

MR. JUSTICE BRENNAN delivered the opinion of the Court.

Challenged here is the legality of an affirmative action plan—collectively bargained by an employer and a union—that reserves for black employees 50% of the openings in an in-plant craft-training program until the percentage of black craftworkers in the plant is commensurate with the percentage of blacks in the local labor force. The question for decision is whether Congress, in Title VII of the Civil Rights Act of 1964, left employers and unions in the private sector free to take such race-conscious steps to eliminate manifest racial imbalances in traditionally segregated job categories. We hold that Title VII does not prohibit such race-conscious affirmative action plans.

I

In 1974, petitioner United Steelworkers of America (USWA) and petitioner Kaiser Aluminum & Chemical Corp. (Kaiser) entered into a master collective-bargaining agreement covering terms and conditions of employment at 15 Kaiser plants. The agreement contained, *inter alia*, an affirmative action plan designed to eliminate conspicuous racial imbalances in Kaiser's then almost exclusively white craftwork forces. Black craft-hiring goals were set for each Kaiser plant equal to the percentage of blacks in the respective local labor forces. To enable plants to meet these goals, on-the-job training programs were established to teach unskilled production workers—black and white—the skills necessary to become craftworkers. The plan reserved for black employees 50% of the openings in these newly created in-plant training programs.

This case arose from the operation of the plan at Kaiser's plant in Gramercy, La. Until 1974, Kaiser hired as craftworkers for that plant only persons who had had prior craft experience. Because blacks had long been excluded from craft unions,[1] few were able to present such credentials. As a consequence, prior to 1974 only 1.83% (5 out of 273) of the skilled craftworkers at the Gramercy plant were black, even though the work force in the Gramercy area was approximately 39% black.

Pursuant to the national agreement Kaiser altered its craft-hiring practice in the Gramercy plant. Rather than hiring already trained outsiders, Kaiser established a training program to train its production workers to fill craft openings. Selection of craft trainees was made on the basis of seniority, with the proviso that at least 50% of the new trainees were to be black until the percentage of black skilled craftworkers in the Gramercy plant approximated the percentage of blacks in the local labor force.

During 1974, the first year of the operation of the Kaiser–USWA affirmative action plan, 13 craft trainees were selected from Gramercy's production work force. Of these, seven were black and six white. The most senior black selected into the program had less seniority than several white production workers whose bids for admission were rejected. Thereafter one of those white production workers, respondent Brian Weber (hereafter respondent), instituted this class action in the United States District Court for the Eastern District of Louisiana.

The complaint alleged that the filling of craft trainee positions at the Gramercy plant pursuant to the affirmative action program had resulted in junior black employees' receiving training in preference to senior white employees, thus discriminating against respondent and other similarly situated white employees in violation of §§ 703(a) and (d) of Title VII. The District Court held that the plan violated Title VII, entered a judgment in favor of the plaintiff class, and granted a permanent injunction prohibiting Kaiser and the USWA "from denying plaintiffs, Brian F. Weber and all other members of the class, access to on-the-job training programs on the basis of race." A divided panel of the Court of Appeals for the Fifth Circuit affirmed, holding that all employment preferences based upon race, including those preferences incidental to bona fide affirmative action plans, violated Title VII's prohibition against racial discrimination in employment.   * * * We reverse.

II

We emphasize at the outset the narrowness of our inquiry. Since the Kaiser–USWA plan does not involve state action, this case does not

---

1. Judicial findings of exclusion from crafts on racial grounds are so numerous as to make such exclusion a proper subject for judicial notice.

present an alleged violation of the Equal Protection Clause of the Fourteenth Amendment. Further, since the Kaiser–USWA plan was adopted voluntarily, we are not concerned with what Title VII requires or with what a court might order to remedy a past proved violation of the Act. The only question before us is the narrow statutory issue of whether Title VII *forbids* private employers and unions from voluntarily agreeing upon bona fide affirmative action plans that accord racial preferences in the manner and for the purpose provided in the Kaiser–USWA plan. That question was expressly left open in McDonald v. Santa Fe Trail Transp. Co., 427 U.S. 273, 281 n. 8, 96 S.Ct. 2574, 2579, 49 L.Ed.2d 493 (1976), which held, in a case not involving affirmative action, that Title VII protects whites as well as blacks from certain forms of racial discrimination.

Respondent argues that Congress intended in Title VII to prohibit all race-conscious affirmative action plans. Respondent's argument rests upon a literal interpretation of §§ 703(a) and (d) of the Act. Those sections make it unlawful to "discriminate * * * because of * * * race" in hiring and in the selection of apprentices for training programs. Since, the argument runs, McDonald v. Santa Fe Trail Transp. Co., supra, settled that Title VII forbids discrimination against whites as well as blacks, and since the Kaiser–USWA affirmative action plan operates to discriminate against white employees solely because they are white, it follows that the Kaiser–USWA plan violates Title VII.

Respondent's argument is not without force. But it overlooks the significance of the fact that the Kaiser–USWA plan is an affirmative action plan voluntarily adopted by private parties to eliminate traditional patterns of racial segregation. In this context respondent's reliance upon a literal construction of §§ 703(a) and (d) and upon *McDonald* is misplaced. See McDonald v. Santa Fe Trail Transp. Co., supra, at 281 n. 8, 96 S.Ct., at 2579. It is a "familiar rule, that a thing may be within the letter of the statute and yet not within the statute, because not within its spirit, nor within the intention of its makers." Holy Trinity Church v. United States, 143 U.S. 457, 459, 12 S.Ct. 511, 512, 36 L.Ed. 226 (1892). The prohibition against racial discrimination in §§ 703(a) and (d) of Title VII must therefore be read against the background of the legislative history of Title VII and the historical context from which the Act arose. Examination of those sources makes clear that an interpretation of the sections that forbade all race-conscious affirmative action would "bring about an end completely at variance with the purpose of the statute" and must be rejected.

Congress' primary concern in enacting the prohibition against racial discrimination in Title VII of the Civil Rights Act of 1964 was with "the plight of the Negro in our economy." Before 1964, blacks were largely relegated to "unskilled and semi-skilled jobs." Because of automation the number of such jobs was rapidly decreasing. As a consequence, "the relative position of the Negro worker [was] steadily worsening. * * * "

Congress feared that the goals of the Civil Rights Act—the integration of blacks into the mainstream of American society—could not be achieved unless this trend were reversed. And Congress recognized that that would not be possible unless blacks were able to secure jobs "which have a future." * * * Accordingly, it was clear to Congress that "[t]he crux of the problem [was] to open employment opportunities for Negroes in occupations which have been traditionally closed to them," and it was to this problem that Title VII's prohibition against racial discrimination in employment was primarily addressed.

It plainly appears from the House Report accompanying the Civil Rights Act that Congress did not intend wholly to prohibit private and voluntary affirmative action efforts as one method of solving this problem. The Report provides:

"No bill can or should lay claim to eliminating all of the causes and consequences of racial and other types of discrimination against minorities. There is reason to believe, however, that national leadership provided by the enactment of Federal legislation dealing with the most troublesome problems *will create an atmosphere conducive to voluntary or local resolution of other forms of discrimination.*"

Given this legislative history, we cannot agree with respondent that Congress intended to prohibit the private sector from taking effective steps to accomplish the goal that Congress designed Title VII to achieve. The very statutory words intended as a spur or catalyst to cause "employers and unions to self-examine and to self-evaluate their employment practices and to endeavor to eliminate, so far as possible, the last vestiges of an unfortunate and ignominious page in this country's history," Albemarle Paper Co. v. Moody, 422 U.S. 405, 418, 95 S.Ct. 2362, 2372, 45 L.Ed.2d 280 (1975), cannot be interpreted as an absolute prohibition against all private, voluntary, race-conscious affirmative action efforts to hasten the elimination of such vestiges. It would be ironic indeed if a law triggered by a Nation's concern over centuries of racial injustice and intended to improve the lot of those who had "been excluded from the American dream for so long," constituted the first legislative prohibition of all voluntary, private, race-conscious efforts to abolish traditional patterns of racial segregation and hierarchy.

Our conclusion is further reinforced by examination of the language and legislative history of § 703(j) of Title VII. Opponents of Title VII raised two related arguments against the bill. First, they argued that the Act would be interpreted to *require* employers with racially imbalanced work forces to grant preferential treatment to racial minorities in order to integrate. Second, they argued that employers with racially imbalanced work forces would grant preferential treatment to racial minorities, even if not required to do so by the Act. Had Congress meant to prohibit all race-conscious affirmative action, as respondent urges, it easily could have answered both objections by

providing that Title VII would not require or *permit* racially preferential integration efforts. But Congress did not choose such a course.
Rather Congress added § 703(j) which addresses only the first objection.
The section provides that nothing contained in Title VII "shall be
interpreted to *require* any employer * * * to grant preferential treatment * * * to any group because of the race * * * of such * * * group
on account of" a *de facto* racial imbalance in the employer's work force.
The section does *not* state that "nothing in Title VII shall be interpreted to *permit* " voluntary affirmative efforts to correct racial imbalances.
The natural inference is that Congress chose not to forbid all voluntary
race-conscious affirmative action.

The reasons for this choice are evident from the legislative record.
Title VII could not have been enacted into law without substantial
support from legislators in both Houses who traditionally resisted
federal regulation of private business. Those legislators demanded as a
price for their support that "management prerogatives, and union
freedoms * * * be left undisturbed to the greatest extent possible." H.
R. Rep. No. 914, 88th Cong., 1st Sess., pt. 2, p. 29 (1963). Section 703(j)
was proposed by Senator Dirksen to allay any fears that the Act might
be interpreted in such a way as to upset this compromise. The section
was designed to prevent § 703 of Title VII from being interpreted in
such a way as to lead to undue "Federal Government interference with
private businesses because of some Federal employee's ideas about
racial balance or racial imbalance." Clearly, a prohibition against all
voluntary, race-conscious, affirmative action efforts would disserve
these ends. Such a prohibition would augment the powers of the
Federal Government and diminish traditional management prerogatives while at the same time impeding attainment of the ultimate
statutory goals. In view of this legislative history and in view of
Congress' desire to avoid undue federal regulation of private businesses,
use of the word "require" rather than the phrase "require or permit" in
§ 703(j) fortifies the conclusion that Congress did not intend to limit
traditional business freedom to such a degree as to prohibit all voluntary, race-conscious affirmative action.

We therefore hold that Title VII's prohibition in §§ 703(a) and (d)
against racial discrimination does not condemn all private, voluntary,
race-conscious affirmative action plans.

III

We need not today define in detail the line of demarcation between
permissible and impermissible affirmative action plans. It suffices to
hold that the challenged Kaiser–USWA affirmative action plan falls on
the permissible side of the line. The purposes of the plan mirror those
of the statute. Both were designed to break down old patterns of racial
segregation and hierarchy. Both were structured to "open employment

opportunities for Negroes in occupations which have been traditionally closed to them." [8]

At the same time, the plan does not unnecessarily trammel the interests of the white employees. The plan does not require the discharge of white workers and their replacement with new black hirees. Nor does the plan create an absolute bar to the advancement of white employees; half of those trained in the program will be white. Moreover, the plan is a temporary measure; it is not intended to maintain racial balance, but simply to eliminate a manifest racial imbalance. Preferential selection of craft trainees at the Gramercy plant will end as soon as the percentage of black skilled craftworkers in the Gramercy plant approximates the percentage of blacks in the local labor force.

We conclude, therefore, that the adoption of the Kaiser–USWA plan for the Gramercy plant falls within the area of discretion left by Title VII to the private sector voluntarily to adopt affirmative action plans designed to eliminate conspicuous racial imbalance in traditionally segregated job categories.[9] Accordingly, the judgment of the Court of Appeals for the Fifth Circuit is

Reversed.

MR. JUSTICE POWELL and MR. JUSTICE STEVENS took no part in the consideration or decision of these cases.

MR. JUSTICE BLACKMUN, concurring.

* * *

In his dissent from the decision of the United States Court of Appeals for the Fifth Circuit, Judge Wisdom pointed out that this case arises from a practical problem in the administration of Title VII. The broad prohibition against discrimination places the employer and the union on what he accurately described as a "high tightrope without a net beneath them." If Title VII is read literally, on the one hand they face liability for past discrimination against blacks, and on the other they face liability to whites for any voluntary preferences adopted to mitigate the effects of prior discrimination against blacks.

In this litigation, Kaiser denies prior discrimination but concedes that its past hiring practices may be subject to question. Although the labor force in the Gramercy area was approximately 39% black, Kaiser's work force was less than 15% black, and its craftwork force was less than 2% black. Kaiser had made some effort to recruit black

---

8. See n. 1, supra. This is not to suggest that the freedom of an employer to undertake race-conscious affirmative action efforts depends on whether or not his effort is motivated by fear of liability under Title VII.

9. Our disposition makes unnecessary consideration of petitioners' argument that their plan was justified because they feared that black employees would bring suit under Title VII if they did not adopt an affirmative action plan. Nor need we consider petitioners' contention that their affirmative action plan represented an attempt to comply with Exec. Order No. 11246, 3 CFR 339 (1964–1965 Comp.).

painters, carpenters, insulators, and other craftsmen, but it continued to insist that those hired have five years prior industrial experience, a requirement that arguably was not sufficiently job related to justify under Title VII any discriminatory impact it may have had. The parties dispute the extent to which black craftsmen were available in the local labor market. They agree, however, that after critical reviews from the Office of Federal Contract Compliance, Kaiser and the Steelworkers established the training program in question here and modeled it along the lines of a Title VII consent decree later entered for the steel industry. Yet when they did this, respondent Weber sued, alleging that Title VII prohibited the program because it discriminated against him as a white person and it was not supported by a prior judicial finding of discrimination against blacks.

Respondent Weber's reading of Title VII, endorsed by the Court of Appeals, places voluntary compliance with Title VII in profound jeopardy. The only way for the employer and the union to keep their footing on the "tightrope" it creates would be to eschew all forms of voluntary affirmative action. Even a whisper of emphasis on minority recruiting would be forbidden. Because Congress intended to encourage private efforts to come into compliance with Title VII, Judge Wisdom concluded that employers and unions who had committed "arguable violations" of Title VII should be free to make reasonable responses without fear of liability to whites. Preferential hiring along the lines of the Kaiser program is a reasonable response for the employer, whether or not a court, on these facts, could order the same step as a remedy. The company is able to avoid identifying victims of past discrimination, and so avoids claims for backpay that would inevitably follow a response limited to such victims. If past victims should be benefited by the program, however, the company mitigates its liability to those persons. Also, to the extent that Title VII liability is predicated on the "disparate effect" of an employer's past hiring practices, the program makes it less likely that such an effect could be demonstrated. And the Court has recently held that work-force statistics resulting from private affirmative action were probative of benign intent in a "disparate treatment" case. Furnco Construction Corp. v. Waters, 438 U.S. 567, 579–580, 98 S.Ct. 2943, 2950–951, 57 L.Ed.2d 957 (1978).

The "arguable violation" theory has a number of advantages. It responds to a practical problem in the administration of Title VII not anticipated by Congress. It draws predictability from the outline of present law and closely effectuates the purpose of the Act. Both Kaiser and the United States urge its adoption here. Because I agree that it is the soundest way to approach this case, my preference would be to resolve this litigation by applying it and holding that Kaiser's craft training program meets the requirement that voluntary affirmative action be a reasonable response to an "arguable violation" of Title VII.

The Court, however, declines to consider the narrow "arguable violation" approach and adheres instead to an interpretation of Title

VII that permits affirmative action by an employer whenever the job category in question is "traditionally segregated." The sources cited suggest that the Court considers a job category to be "traditionally segregated" when there has been a societal history of purposeful exclusion of blacks from the job category, resulting in a persistent disparity between the proportion of blacks in the labor force and the proportion of blacks among those who hold jobs within the category.

"Traditionally segregated job categories," where they exist, sweep far more broadly than the class of "arguable violations" of Title VII. The Court's expansive approach is somewhat disturbing for me because, as Mr. Justice Rehnquist points out, the Congress that passed Title VII probably thought it was adopting a principle of nondiscrimination that would apply to blacks and whites alike. While setting aside that principle can be justified where necessary to advance statutory policy by encouraging reasonable responses as a form of voluntary compliance that mitigates "arguable violations," discarding the principle of nondiscrimination where no countervailing statutory policy exists appears to be at odds with the bargain struck when Title VII was enacted.

A closer look at the problem, however, reveals that in each of the principal ways in which the Court's "traditionally segregated job categories" approach expands on the "arguable violations" theory, still other considerations point in favor of the broad standard adopted by the Court, and make it possible for me to conclude that the Court's reading of the statute is an acceptable one.

A. The first point at which the Court departs from the "arguable violations" approach is that it measures an individual employer's capacity for affirmative action solely in terms of a statistical disparity. The individual employer need not have engaged in discriminatory practices in the past. While, under Title VII, a mere disparity may provide the basis for a prima facie case against an employer, Dothard v. Rawlinson, 433 U.S. 321, 329–331, 97 S.Ct. 2720, 2726–2727, 53 L.Ed.2d 786 (1977), it would not conclusively prove a violation of the Act. Teamsters v. United States, 431 U.S. 324, 339–340, n. 20, 97 S.Ct. 1843, 1856, 52 L.Ed.2d 396 (1977). As a practical matter, however, this difference may not be that great. While the "arguable violation" standard is conceptually satisfying, in practice the emphasis would be on "arguable" rather than on "violation." The great difficulty in the District Court was that no one had any incentive to prove that Kaiser had violated the Act. Neither Kaiser nor the Steelworkers wanted to establish a past violation, nor did Weber. The blacks harmed had never sued and so had no established representative. The Equal Employment Opportunity Commission declined to intervene, and cannot be expected to intervene in every case of this nature. To make the "arguable violation" standard work, it would have to be set low enough to permit the employer to prove it without obligating himself to pay a damages award. The inevitable tendency would be to avoid hairsplitting litigation by simply concluding that a mere disparity between the racial composition of the employer's work force and the composition of the qualified local labor force would be an "arguable violation," even though actual liability could not be established on that basis alone.

B. The Court also departs from the "arguable violation" approach by permitting an employer to redress discrimination that lies wholly outside the bounds of Title VII. For example, Title VII provides no remedy for pre-Act discrimination, yet the purposeful discrimination that creates a "traditionally segregated job category" may have entirely predated the Act. More subtly, in assessing a prima facie case of Title VII liability, the composition of the employer's work force is compared to the composition of the pool of workers who meet valid job qualifications. When a "job category" is traditionally segregated, however, that pool will reflect the effects of segregation, and the Court's approach goes further and permits a comparison with the composition of the labor force as a whole, in which minorities are more heavily represented.

Strong considerations of equity support an interpretation of Title VII that would permit private affirmative action to reach where Title VII itself does not. The bargain struck in 1964 with the passage of Title VII guaranteed equal opportunity for white and black alike, but where Title VII provides no remedy for blacks, it should not be construed to foreclose private affirmative action from supplying relief. It seems unfair for respondent Weber to argue, as he does, that the asserted scarcity of black craftsmen in Louisiana, the product of historic discrimination, makes Kaiser's training program illegal because it ostensibly absolves Kaiser of all Title VII liability. Absent compelling evidence of legislative intent, I would not interpret Title VII itself as a means of "locking in" the effects of segregation for which Title VII provides no remedy. Such a construction, as the Court points out, would be "ironic," given the broad remedial purposes of Title VII.

Mr. Justice Rehnquist's dissent, while it focuses more on what Title VII does not require than on what Title VII forbids, cites several passages that appear to express an intent to "lock in" minorities. In mining the legislative history anew, however, the dissent, in my view, fails to take proper account of our prior cases that have given that history a much more limited reading than that adopted by the dissent. For example, in Griggs v. Duke Power Co., 401 U.S. 424, 434–436, and n. 11, 91 S.Ct. 849, 855–856, 28 L.Ed.2d 158 (1971), the Court refused to give controlling weight to the memorandum of Senators Clark and Case which the dissent now finds so persuasive. And in quoting a statement from that memorandum that an employer would not be "permitted * * * to prefer Negroes for future vacancies," the dissent does not point out that the Court's opinion in Teamsters v. United States, 431 U.S., at 349–351, 97 S.Ct., at 1861–1862, implies that that language is limited to the protection of established seniority systems. Here, seniority is not in issue because the craft training program is new and does not involve an abrogation of pre-existing seniority rights. In short, the passages marshaled by the dissent are not so compelling as to merit the whip hand over the obvious equity of permitting employers to ameliorate the effects of past discrimination for which Title VII provides no direct relief.

* * *

MR. CHIEF JUSTICE BURGER, dissenting.

The Court reaches a result I would be inclined to vote for were I a Member of Congress considering a proposed amendment of Title VII. I cannot join the Court's judgment, however, because it is contrary to the explicit language of the statute and arrived at by means wholly incompatible with long-established principles of separation of powers. Under the guise of statutory "construction," the Court effectively rewrites Title VII to achieve what it regards as a desirable result. It "amends" the statute to do precisely what both its sponsors and its opponents agreed the statute was *not* intended to do.

When Congress enacted Title VII after long study and searching debate, it produced a statute of extraordinary clarity, which speaks directly to the issue we consider in this case. * * *

Often we have difficulty interpreting statutes either because of imprecise drafting or because legislative compromises have produced genuine ambiguities. But here there is no lack of clarity, no ambiguity. The quota embodied in the collective-bargaining agreement between Kaiser and the Steelworkers unquestionably discriminates on the basis of race against individual employees seeking admission to on-the-job training programs. And, under the plain language of § 703(d), that is "an *unlawful* employment practice."

Oddly, the Court seizes upon the very clarity of the statute almost as a justification for evading the unavoidable impact of its language. The Court blandly tells us that Congress could not really have meant what it said, for a "literal construction" would defeat the "purpose" of the statute—at least the congressional "purpose" as five Justices divine it today. But how are judges supposed to ascertain the *purpose* of a statute except through the words Congress used and the legislative history of the statute's evolution? One need not even resort to the legislative history to recognize what is apparent from the face of Title VII—that it is specious to suggest that § 703(j) contains a negative pregnant that permits employers to do what §§ 703(a) and (d) unambiguously and unequivocally *forbid* employers from doing. Moreover, as Mr. Justice Rehnquist's opinion—which I join—conclusively demonstrates, the legislative history makes equally clear that the supporters and opponents of Title VII reached an agreement about the statute's intended effect. That agreement, expressed so clearly in the language of the statute that no one should doubt its meaning, forecloses the reading which the Court gives the statute today.

* * *

MR. JUSTICE REHNQUIST, with whom THE CHIEF JUSTICE joins, dissenting.

* * *

* * * It may be that one or more of the principal sponsors of Title VII would have preferred to see a provision allowing preferential treatment of minorities written into the bill. Such a provision, however, would have to have been expressly or impliedly excepted from Title VII's explicit prohibition on all racial discrimination in employment. There is no such exception in the Act. And a reading of the legislative debates concerning Title VII, in which proponents and opponents alike uniformly denounced discrimination in favor of, as well as discrimination against, Negroes, demonstrates clearly that any legislator harboring an unspoken desire for such a provision could not possibly have succeeded in enacting it into law.

* * * In February 1974, under pressure from the Office of Federal Contract Compliance to increase minority representation in craft positions at its various plants,[2] and hoping to deter the filing of employment discrimination claims by minorities, Kaiser entered into a collective-bargaining agreement with the United Steelworkers of America (Steelworkers) which * * * required that no less than one minority applicant be admitted to the training program for every nonminority applicant until the percentage of blacks in craft positions equaled the percentage of blacks in the local work force.   * * *

* * *

* * * To be sure, the reality of employment discrimination against Negroes provided the primary impetus for passage of Title VII. But this fact by no means supports the proposition that Congress intended

2. The Office of Federal Contract Compliance (OFCC), subsequently renamed the Office of Federal Contract Compliance Programs (OFCCP), is an arm of the Department of Labor responsible for ensuring compliance by Government contractors with the equal employment opportunity requirements established by Exec. Order No. 11246, 3 CFR 339 (1964–1965 Comp.), as amended by Exec. Order No. 11375, 3 CFR 684 (1966–1970 Comp.), and by Exec. Order No. 12086, 3 CFR 230 (1979).

Executive Order 11246, as amended, requires all applicants for federal contracts to refrain from employment discrimination and to "take affirmative action to ensure that applicants are employed, and that employees are treated during employment, without regard to their race, color, religion, sex or national origin." The Executive Order empowers the Secretary of Labor to issue rules and regulations necessary and appropriate to achieve its purpose. He, in turn, has delegated most enforcement duties to the OFCC. See 41 CFR 60–20.1 et seq., 60–2.24 (1978).

The affirmative action program mandated * * * for nonconstruction contractors requires a "utilization" study to determine minority representation in the work force. Goals for hiring and promotion must be set to overcome any "underutilization" found to exist.

The OFCC employs the "power of the purse" to coerce acceptance of its affirmative action plans. Indeed, in this case, "the district court found that the 1974 collective bargaining agreement reflected less of a desire on Kaiser's part to train black craft workers than a self-interest in satisfying the OFCC in order to retain lucrative government contracts." 563 F.2d 216, 226 (CA5 1977).

to leave employers free to discriminate against white persons.[11] In most cases, "[l]egislative history * * * is more vague than the statute we are called upon to interpret." Here, however, the legislative history of Title VII is as clear as the language of §§ 703(a) and (d), and it irrefutably demonstrates that Congress meant precisely what it said in §§ 703(a) and (d)—that *no* racial discrimination in employment is permissible under Title VII, not even preferential treatment of minorities to correct racial imbalance.

* * *

In the opening speech of the formal Senate debate on the bill, Senator Humphrey addressed the main concern of Title VII's opponents, advising that not only does Title VII not require use of racial quotas, *it does not permit* their use. "The truth," stated the floor

---

11. The only shred of legislative history cited by the Court in support of the proposition that "Congress did not intend wholly to prohibit private and voluntary affirmative action efforts," ante, at 203, is the following excerpt from the Judiciary Committee Report accompanying the civil rights bill reported to the House:

"No bill can or should lay claim to eliminating all of the causes and consequences of racial and other types of discrimination against minorities. There is reason to believe, however, that national leadership provided by the enactment of Federal legislation dealing with the most troublesome problems *will create an atmosphere conducive to voluntary or local resolution of other forms of discrimination.*" H.R.Rep.No. 914, 88th Cong., 1st Sess., pt. 1, p. 18 (1963) (hereinafter H.R.Rep.), quoted ante, at 203–204.

The Court seizes on the italicized language to support its conclusion that Congress did not intend to prohibit voluntary imposition of racially discriminatory employment quotas. The Court, however, stops too short in its reading of the House Report. The words immediately following the material excerpted by the Court are as follows:

"It is, however, possible and necessary for the Congress to enact legislation which prohibits and provides the means of terminating *the most serious types of discrimination.* This H.R. 7152, as amended, would achieve in a number of related areas. It would reduce discriminatory obstacles to the exercise of the right to vote and provide means of expediting the vindication of that right. It would make it possible to remove the daily affront and humiliation involved in discriminatory denials of access to facilities ostensibly open to the general pub-

lic. It would guarantee that there will be no discrimination upon recipients of Federal financial assistance. It would prohibit discrimination in employment, and provide means to expedite termination of discrimination in public education. It would open additional avenues to deal with redress of denials of equal protection of the laws on account of race, color, religion, or national origin by State or local authorities." H.R.Rep., pt. 1, p. 18 (emphasis added).

When thus read in context, the meaning of the italicized language in the Court's excerpt of the House Report becomes clear. By dealing with "the most serious types of discrimination," such as discrimination in voting, public accommodations, employment, etc., H.R. 7152 would hopefully inspire "voluntary or local resolution of other forms of discrimination," that is, forms other than discrimination in voting, public accommodations, employment, etc.

One can also infer from the House Report that the Judiciary Committee hoped that federal legislation would inspire voluntary elimination of discrimination against minority groups other than those protected under the bill, perhaps the aged and handicapped to name just two. In any event, the House Report does not support the Court's proposition that Congress, by banning racial discrimination in employment, intended to permit racial discrimination in employment.

Thus, examination of the House Judiciary Committee's report reveals that the Court's interpretation of Title VII, far from being compelled by the Act's legislative history, is utterly without support in that legislative history. Indeed, as demonstrated in Part III, infra, the Court's interpretation of Title VII is totally refuted by the Act's legislative history.

leader of the bill, "is that this title forbids discriminating against anyone on account of race. This is the simple and complete truth about Title VII." * * *

At the close of his speech, Senator Humphrey returned briefly to the subject of employment quotas: "It is claimed that the bill would require racial quotas for all hiring, when in fact it provides that race shall not be a basis for making personnel decisions."

* * *

A few days later the Senate's attention focused exclusively on Title VII, as Senators Clark and Case rose to discuss the title of H.R. 7152 on which they shared floor "captain" responsibilities. In an interpretative memorandum submitted jointly to the Senate, Senators Clark and Case took pains to refute the opposition's charge that Title VII would result in preferential treatment of minorities. Their words were clear and unequivocal:

> "There is no requirement in Title VII that an employer maintain a racial balance in his work force. On the contrary, any deliberate attempt to maintain a racial balance, whatever such a balance may be, would involve a violation of Title VII because maintaining such a balance would require an employer to hire or to refuse to hire on the basis of race. It must be emphasized that discrimination is prohibited as to any individual." Id., at 7213.

Of particular relevance to the instant case were their observations regarding seniority rights. As if directing their comments at Brian Weber, the Senators said:

> "Title VII would have no effect on established seniority rights. Its effect is prospective and not retrospective. Thus, for example, if a business has been discriminating in the past and as a result has an all-white working force, when the title comes into effect the employer's obligation would be simply to fill future vacancies on a nondiscriminatory basis. He would not be obliged—*or indeed permitted*—to fire whites in order to hire Negroes, *or to prefer Negroes for future vacancies, or, once Negroes are hired, to give them special seniority rights at the expense of the white workers hired earlier.*" *Ibid.* (emphasis added).[19]

---

19. A Justice Department memorandum earlier introduced by Senator Clark, see n. 18, supra, expressed the same view regarding Title VII's impact on seniority rights of employees:

"Title VII would have no effect on seniority rights existing at the time it takes effect. * * * This would be true even in the case where owing to discrimination prior to the effective date of the title, white workers had more seniority than Negroes. * * * [A]ssuming that seniority rights were built up over a period

of time during which Negroes were not hired, these rights would not be set aside by the taking effect of Title VII. Employers and labor organizations would simply be under a duty not to discriminate against Negroes because of their race." 110 Cong.Rec. 7207 (1964).

The interpretation of Title VII contained in the memoranda introduced by Senator Clark totally refutes the Court's implied suggestion that Title VII would prohibit an employer from discriminating on the basis of race in order to *maintain* a racial bal-

Thus, with virtual clairvoyance the Senate's leading supporters of Title VII anticipated precisely the circumstances of this case and advised their colleagues that the type of minority preference employed by Kaiser would violate Title VII's ban on racial discrimination. To further accentuate the point, Senator Clark introduced another memorandum dealing with common criticisms of the bill, including the charge that racial quotas would be imposed under Title VII. The answer was simple and to the point: "Quotas are themselves discriminatory."

* * * Senators Smathers and Sparkman, while conceding that Title VII does not in so many words require the use of hiring quotas, repeated the opposition's view that employers would be coerced to grant preferential hiring treatment to minorities by agencies of the Federal Government. Senator Williams was quick to respond:

> "Those opposed to H.R. 7152 should realize that to hire a Negro solely because he is a Negro is racial discrimination, just as much as a 'white only' employment policy. Both forms of discrimination are prohibited by Title VII of this bill. The language of that title simply states that race is not a qualification for employment. * * * Some people charge that H.R. 7152 favors the Negro, at the expense of the white majority. But how can the language of equality favor one race or one religion over another? Equality can have only one meaning, and that meaning is self-evident to reasonable men. Those who say that equality means favoritism do violence to common sense." * * *

While the debate in the Senate raged, a bipartisan coalition under the leadership of Senators Dirksen, Mansfield, Humphrey, and Kuchel

---

ance in his work force, but would permit him to do so in order to *achieve* racial balance.

The maintain-achieve distinction is analytically indefensible in any event. Apparently, the Court is saying that an employer is free to *achieve* a racially balanced work force by discriminating against whites, but that once he has reached his goal, he is no longer free to discriminate in order to maintain that racial balance. In other words, once Kaiser reaches its goal of 39% minority representation in craft positions at the Gramercy plant, it can no longer consider race in admitting employees into its on-the-job training programs, even if the programs become as "all-white" as they were in April 1974.

Obviously, the Court is driven to this illogical position by the glaring statement, quoted in text, of Senators Clark and Case that "any deliberate attempt to *maintain* a racial balance * * * would involve a violation of Title VII because *maintaining* such a balance would require an employer to hire or to refuse to hire on the basis of

race." Achieving a certain racial balance, however, no less than maintaining such a balance, would require an employer to hire or to refuse to hire on the basis of race. Further, the Court's own conclusion that Title VII's legislative history, coupled with the wording of § 703(j), evinces a congressional intent to leave employers free to employ "private, voluntary, race-conscious affirmative action plans," is inconsistent with its maintain-achieve distinction. If Congress' primary purpose in enacting Title VII was to open employment opportunities previously closed to Negroes, it would seem to make little difference whether the employer opening those opportunities was achieving or maintaining a certain racial balance in his work force. Likewise, if § 703(j) evinces Congress' intent to permit imposition of race-conscious affirmative action plans, it would seem to make little difference whether the plan was adopted to achieve or maintain the desired racial balance.

was working with House leaders and representatives of the Johnson administration on a number of amendments to H.R. 7152 designed to enhance its prospects of passage. The so-called "Dirksen–Mansfield" amendment was introduced on May 26 by Senator Dirksen as a substitute for the entire House-passed bill. The substitute bill, which ultimately became law, left unchanged the basic prohibitory language of §§ 703(a) and (d), as well as the remedial provisions in § 706(g). It added, however, several provisions defining and clarifying the scope of Title VII's substantive prohibitions. One of those clarifying amendments, § 703(j), was specifically directed at the opposition's concerns regarding racial balancing and preferential treatment of minorities * * *.

*   *   *

Contrary to the Court's analysis, the language of § 703(j) is precisely tailored to the objection voiced time and again by Title VII's opponents. Not once during the 83 days of debate in the Senate did a speaker, proponent or opponent, suggest that the bill would allow employers *voluntarily* to prefer racial minorities over white persons. In light of Title VII's flat prohibition on discrimination "against any individual * * * because of such individual's race," § 703(a), such a contention would have been, in any event, too preposterous to warrant response. Indeed, speakers on both sides of the issue, as the legislative history makes clear, recognized that Title VII would tolerate no *voluntary* racial preference, whether in favor of blacks or whites. The complaint consistently voiced by the opponents was that Title VII, particularly the word "discrimination," would be *interpreted* by federal agencies such as the EEOC to *require* the correction of racial imbalance through the granting of preferential treatment to minorities. Verbal assurances that Title VII would not require—indeed, would not permit—preferential treatment of blacks having failed, supporters of H.R. 7152 responded by proposing an amendment carefully worded to meet, and put to rest, the opposition's charge. Indeed, unlike §§ 703(a) and (d), which are by their terms directed at entities—e.g., employers, labor unions—whose actions are restricted by Title VII's prohibitions, the language of § 703(j) is specifically directed at entities—federal agencies and courts—charged with the responsibility of interpreting Title VII's provisions.

In light of the background and purpose of § 703(j), the irony of invoking the section to justify the result in this case is obvious. The Court's frequent references to the "voluntary" nature of Kaiser's racially discriminatory admission quota bear no relationship to the facts of this case. Kaiser and the Steelworkers acted under pressure from an agency of the Federal Government, the Office of Federal Contract Compliance, which found that minorities were being "underutilized" at Kaiser's plants. See n. 2, supra. That is, Kaiser's work force was racially imbalanced. Bowing to that pressure, Kaiser instituted an admissions quota preferring blacks over whites, thus confirming that the fears of Title VII's opponents were well founded. Today, § 703(j), adopted to allay those fears, is invoked by the Court to uphold imposition of a racial quota under the very circumstances that the section was intended to prevent.

* * *

Reading the language of Title VII, as the Court purports to do, "against the background of [its] legislative history * * * and the historical context from which the Act arose," ante, at 201, one is led inescapably to the conclusion that Congress fully understood what it was saying and meant precisely what it said. Opponents of the civil rights bill did not argue that employers would be permitted under Title VII voluntarily to grant preferential treatment to minorities to correct racial imbalance. The plain language of the statute too clearly prohibited such racial discrimination to admit of any doubt. They argued, tirelessly, that Title VII would be interpreted by federal agencies and their agents to require unwilling employers to racially balance their work forces by granting preferential treatment to minorities. Supporters of H.R. 7152 responded, equally tirelessly, that the Act would not be so interpreted because not only does it not require preferential treatment of minorities, it does not *permit* preferential treatment of any race for any reason. * * *

To put an end to the dispute, supporters of the civil rights bill drafted and introduced § 703(j). Specifically addressed to the opposition's charge, § 703(j) simply enjoins federal agencies and courts from interpreting Title VII to require an employer to prefer certain racial groups to correct imbalances in his work force. The section says nothing about voluntary preferential treatment of minorities because such racial discrimination is plainly proscribed by §§ 703(a) and (d). Indeed, had Congress intended to except voluntary, race-conscious preferential treatment from the blanket prohibition of racial discrimination in §§ 703(a) and (d), it surely could have drafted language better suited to the task than § 703(j). It knew how. Section 703(i) provides:

> "Nothing contained in [Title VII] shall apply to any business or enterprise on or near an Indian reservation with respect to any publicly announced employment practice of such business or enterprise under which a preferential treatment is given to any individual because he is an Indian living on or near a reservation." 78 Stat. 257, 42 U.S.C. § 2000e–2(i).

* * *

WEBER v. KAISER ALUMINUM & CHEMICAL CORP.

United States Court of Appeals, Fifth Circuit, 1980.
611 F.2d 132, on remand from the Supreme Court of the United
States, 443 U.S. 193, 99 S.Ct. 2721, 61 L.Ed.2d 480 (1979).

Before WISDOM, GEE, and FAY, CIRCUIT JUDGES.

GEE, CIRCUIT JUDGE.

* * *

For myself only, and with all respect and deference, I here note my personal conviction that the decision of the Supreme Court in this case is profoundly wrong.

That it is wrong as a matter of statutory construction seems to me sufficiently demonstrated by the dissenting opinions of the Chief Justice and of Mr. Justice Rehnquist. To these I can add nothing. They make plain beyond peradventure that the Civil Rights Act of 1964 passed the Congress on the express representation of its sponsors that it would not and could not be construed as the Court has now construed it. What could be plainer than the words of the late Senator Humphrey—defending the bill against the charge that it adumbrated quotas and preferential treatment—that "the title would *prohibit* preferential treatment for any particular group * * * "? The Court now tells us that this is not so. That it feels it may properly do so seems to me a grievous thing.

But sadder still—tragic, in my own view—is the Court's departure from the long road that we have travelled from Plessy v. Ferguson, 163 U.S. 537, 16 S.Ct. 1138, 41 L.Ed. 256 (1896), toward making good Mr. Justice Harlan's anguished cry in dissent that "[o]ur Constitution is color-blind, and neither knows nor tolerates classes among citizens." Id. at 559, 16 S.Ct. at 1146. I voice my profound belief that this present action, like *Plessy*, is a wrong and dangerous turning, and my confident hope that we will soon return to the high, bright road on which we disdain to classify a citizen, *any* citizen, to any degree or for any purpose by the color of his skin.

Though for the above reasons I think it gravely mistaken, I do not say that the Court's decision is immoral or unjust—indeed, in some basic sense it may well represent true justice. But there are many actions roughly just that our laws do not authorize and our Constitution forbids, actions such as preventing a Nazi Party march through a town where reside former inmates of concentration camps or inflicting summary punishment on one caught redhanded in a crime.

Subordinate magistrates such as I must either obey the orders of higher authority or yield up their posts to those who will. I obey, since in my view the action required of me by the Court's mandate is only to follow a mistaken course and not an evil one.

Vacated and Remanded.

WISDOM, CIRCUIT JUDGE, specially concurring:

With deference to the views expressed by the majority of this Court, I express the view that the decision of the Supreme Court in this case is profoundly right for the reasons stated in my dissenting opinion. Weber v. Kaiser Aluminum & Chemical Corporation and United Steelworkers of America, AFL–CIO, 5 Cir.1977, 563 F.2d 216, 227.

NOTES AND PROBLEMS FOR DISCUSSION

1. Was the result in *Weber* a necessary consequence of the Court's prior rulings in *Griggs* and *Albemarle*? Can it be explained as a response to the dilemma (alluded to in Justice Blackmun's concurring opinion) that confronts employers who artificially increase their proportion of black employees in order to either avoid liability under a disproportionate impact discrimination claim predicated on a showing of racial imbalance in the employers' workforce, or to eschew the burden of validating the job relatedness of their employment criteria? If so, how does the Court's opinion in Connecticut v. Teal, supra, fit into this calculation? See Blumrosen, The "Bottom Line" After Connecticut v. Teal, 8 Emp.Rel.L.J. 572 (1983).

2. Is the "traditional pattern of segregation" standard more or less satisfactory than Judge Wisdom's "arguable violation" theory? Is an individual employer competent to make a determination as to the existence of either of these two criteria? What about Justice Blackmun's concern that the "traditional pattern" standard can, and likely will, include consideration of lawful pre-Act discrimination? On the other hand, is the majority saying that affirmative action is permissible where current employment practices perpetuate the discriminatory effects of a lawful pre-Act tradition of racial bias? Does the "traditional pattern" criterion permit the use of affirmative action in an historically segregated industry by a nondiscriminating employer that played no part in creating or maintaining that tradition? Would this issue arise under the "arguable violation" standard? See Cohen v. Community College of Philadelphia, 484 F.Supp. 411, 434 (E.D.Pa.1980) (" * * * I do not read *Weber* as requiring an employer to establish a history of actual discrimination on his own part before he is permitted to adopt an affirmative action plan designed to eliminate that discrimination. Rather, I hold that under *Weber*, an employer's affirmative action plan can be justified by the existence of a history of racial discrimination in the relevant occupation or profession at large.")

3. Are you convinced by either the majority's or Justice Rehnquist's opinion as to whether Congress seriously considered the issue of voluntary affirmative action during its deliberations over Title VII? If not, what impact should an inconclusive legislative history have on the construction of a statute?

4. The majority opinion notes that Kaiser's craft training program was established as part of an affirmative action plan designed specifically to increase the number of black craft workers. Prior to the creation of this training program, Kaiser hired only craftworkers with craft experience. The plaintiff sought admission to the training program because he couldn't satisfy the experience requirement for a craft job. Thus, he sought and was denied a benefit—training—that was created for the sole purpose of helping train black workers. Clearly, Weber would not have benefitted from the termination of the affirmative action plan since this would have eliminated any opportunity for him to obtain a craft job with Kaiser. Does this diminish the extent of the

injury Weber suffered from being denied admission to the program to the preference of a less senior black employee?

5. Was Kaiser's plan limited to providing training to identifiable victims of discrimination? If not, what was the purpose of the plan? Does this suggest anything about Kaiser's, and perhaps the Court's, view of equality?

6. The majority in *Weber* concluded that Kaiser's plan constituted a permissible form of affirmative action because, in part, it was a temporary measure—lasting until the percentage of black craftworkers in the plant approximated the percentage of blacks in the local labor force. The significance attached to the temporary nature of the preference indicates that the Court believed that racial preferences could be used to attain, but not maintain racial balance in traditionally segregated job classifications. Is this distinction justifiable or is it merely an attempt to effect a compromise of an extremely sensitive issue? Is Justice Rehnquist right in suggesting that this distinction is at variance with other portions of the majority's opinion?

7. In determining whether a "traditional pattern" of discrimination exists, must a court compare the minority composition of the defendant's or industry's workforce with that minority's representation in the local area population? Minnick v. California Department of Corrections, 95 Cal.App.3d 506, 157 Cal.Rptr. 260 (1979), cert. dismissed for want of finality, 452 U.S. 105, 101 S.Ct. 2211, 68 L.Ed.2d 706 (1981) (neither Title VII nor U.S. Constitution violated by voluntarily adopted affirmative action hiring plan designed to have the percentage of minority prison employees approximate the proportion of minority persons in the State prison inmate population).

8. In light of the extensive factual inquiry associated with judicial review of affirmative action plans, is the issue of the validity of such a plan a question of law or of fact? Where the defendant is a public entity, is the validity of the plan a question of law to be determined by a court or is the plaintiff entitled under the Seventh Amendment to a jury determination on this issue? See Bratton v. Detroit, 704 F.2d 878 (6th Cir.1983), modified, 712 F.2d 222 (6th Cir.1983), cert. denied, 464 U.S. 1040, 104 S.Ct. 703, 79 L.Ed.2d 168 (1984). Additionally, is the determination of the validity of a plan or hiring order subject to the "clearly erroneous" standard of review on appeal?

9. Among the most helpful and insightful of the many articles discussing *Weber* and its impact on affirmative action are Cox, The Question of "Voluntary" Racial Employment Quotas and Some Thoughts on Judicial Role, 23 Ariz. L.Rev. 87 (1981); Boyd, Affirmative Action in Employment—The *Weber* Decision, 66 Iowa L.Rev. 1 (1980); Belton, Discrimination and Affirmative Action: An Analysis of Competing Theories of Equality and *Weber*, 59 No.Car.L.Rev. 531 (1981); Blumrosen, Affirmative Action in Employment After *Weber*, 34 Rutg.L.Rev. 1 (1981); Meltzer, The *Weber* Case: The Judicial Abrogation of the Antidiscrimination Standard in Employment, 47 U.Chi.L.Rev. 423 (1980); Schatzki, United Steelworkers of America v. Weber: An Exercise in Understandable Indecision, 56 Wash.L.Rev. 51 (1980).

10. The Court had the opportunity to examine several of the issues addressed in the preceding Notes, as well as many of the premises underlying its decision in *Weber*, in the following case.

JOHNSON v. TRANSPORTATION AGENCY

Supreme Court of the United States, 1987.
480 U.S. 616, 107 S.Ct. 1442, 94 L.Ed.2d 615.

JUSTICE BRENNAN delivered the opinion of the Court.

Respondent, Transportation Agency of Santa Clara County, California, unilaterally promulgated an Affirmative Action Plan applicable, *inter alia,* to promotions of employees. In selecting applicants for the promotional position of road dispatcher, the Agency, pursuant to the Plan, passed over petitioner Paul Johnson, a male employee, and promoted a female employee applicant, Diane Joyce. The question for decision is whether in making the promotion the Agency impermissibly took into account the sex of the applicants in violation of Title VII of the Civil Rights Act of 1964.[1] The District Court for the Northern District of California, in an action filed by petitioner following receipt of a right-to-sue letter from the Equal Employment Opportunity Commission (EEOC), held that respondent had violated Title VII. The Court of Appeals for the Ninth Circuit reversed. We granted certiorari. We affirm.[2]

I

A

In December 1978, the Santa Clara County Transit District Board of Supervisors adopted an Affirmative Action Plan (Plan) for the County Transportation Agency. The Plan implemented a County Affirmative Action Plan, which had been adopted, declared the County, because "mere prohibition of discriminatory practices is not enough to remedy the effects of past practices and to permit attainment of an equitable representation of minorities, women and handicapped persons." Relevant to this case, the Agency Plan provides that, in making promotions to positions within a traditionally segregated job classification in which women have been significantly underrepresented, the Agency is authorized to consider as one factor the sex of a qualified applicant.

1. Section 703(a) of the Act, 78 Stat. 255, as amended, 86 Stat. 109, 42 U.S.C. § 2000e–2(a), provides that it "shall be an unlawful employment practice for an employer—

"(1) to fail or refuse to hire or to discharge any individual, or otherwise to discriminate against any individual with respect to his compensation, terms, conditions, or privileges of employment, because of such individual's race, color, religion, sex, or national origin; or

"(2) to limit, segregate, or classify his employees or applicants for employment in any way which would deprive or tend to deprive any individual of employment opportunities or otherwise adversely affect his status as an employee, because of such individual's race, color, religion, sex, or national origin."

2. No constitutional issue was either raised or addressed in the litigation below. We therefore decide in this case only the issue of the prohibitory scope of Title VII. Of course, where the issue is properly raised, public employers must justify the adoption and implementation of a voluntary affirmative action plan under the Equal Protection Clause. See Wygant v. Jackson Board of Education, 476 U.S. 267, 106 S.Ct. 1842, 90 L.Ed.2d 260 (1986).

In reviewing the composition of its work force, the Agency noted in its Plan that women were represented in numbers far less than their proportion of the county labor force in both the Agency as a whole and in five of seven job categories. Specifically, while women constituted 36.4% of the area labor market, they composed only 22.4% of Agency employees. Furthermore, women working at the Agency were concentrated largely in EEOC job categories traditionally held by women: women made up 76% of Office and Clerical Workers, but only 7.1% of Agency Officials and Administrators, 8.6% of Professionals, 9.7% of Technicians, and 22% of Service and Maintenance Workers. As for the job classification relevant to this case, none of the 238 Skilled Craft Worker positions was held by a woman. The Plan noted that this underrepresentation of women in part reflected the fact that women had not traditionally been employed in these positions, and that they had not been strongly motivated to seek training or employment in them "because of the limited opportunities that have existed in the past for them to work in such classifications." The Plan also observed that, while the proportion of ethnic minorities in the Agency as a whole exceeded the proportion of such minorities in the county work force, a smaller percentage of minority employees held management, professional, and technical positions.[4]

The Agency stated that its Plan was intended to achieve "a statistically measurable yearly improvement in hiring, training and promotion of minorities and women throughout the Agency in all major job classifications where they are underrepresented." As a benchmark by which to evaluate progress, the Agency stated that its long-term goal was to attain a work force whose composition reflected the proportion of minorities and women in the area labor force. Thus, for the Skilled Craft category in which the road dispatcher position at issue here was classified, the Agency's aspiration was that eventually about 36% of the jobs would be occupied by women.

The Plan acknowledged that a number of factors might make it unrealistic to rely on the Agency's long-term goals in evaluating the Agency's progress in expanding job opportunities for minorities and women. Among the factors identified were low turnover rates in some classifications, the fact that some jobs involved heavy labor, the small number of positions within some job categories, the limited number of entry positions leading to the Technical and Skilled Craft classifications, and the limited number of minorities and women qualified for positions requiring specialized training and experience. As a result, the Plan counselled that short-range goals be established and annually adjusted to serve as the most realistic guide for actual employment decisions. Among the tasks identified as important in establishing such short-term goals was the acquisition of data "reflecting the ratio of minorities, women and handicapped persons who are working in the

---

4. While minorities constituted 19.7% of the county labor force, they represented 7.1% of the Agency's Officials and Admin- istrators, 19% of its Professionals, and 16.9% of its Technicians. Id., at 48.

local area in major job classifications relating to those utilized by the County Administration," so as to determine the availability of members of such groups who "possess the desired qualifications or potential for placement." These data on qualified group members, along with predictions of position vacancies, were to serve as the basis for "realistic yearly employment goals for women, minorities and handicapped persons in each EEOC job category and major job classification."

The Agency's Plan thus set aside no specific number of positions for minorities or women, but authorized the consideration of ethnicity or sex as a factor when evaluating qualified candidates for jobs in which members of such groups were poorly represented. One such job was the road dispatcher position that is the subject of the dispute in this case.

B

On December 12, 1979, the Agency announced a vacancy for the promotional position of road dispatcher in the Agency's Roads Division. Dispatchers assign road crews, equipment, and materials, and maintain records pertaining to road maintenance jobs. The position requires at minimum four years of dispatch or road maintenance work experience for Santa Clara County. The EEOC job classification scheme designates a road dispatcher as a Skilled Craft worker.

Twelve County employees applied for the promotion, including Joyce and Johnson. Joyce had worked for the County since 1970, serving as an account clerk until 1975. She had applied for a road dispatcher position in 1974, but was deemed ineligible because she had not served as a road maintenance worker. In 1975, Joyce transferred from a senior account clerk position to a road maintenance worker position, becoming the first woman to fill such a job. During her four years in that position, she occasionally worked out of class as a road dispatcher.

Petitioner Johnson began with the County in 1967 as a road yard clerk, after private employment that included working as a supervisor and dispatcher. He had also unsuccessfully applied for the road dispatcher opening in 1974. In 1977, his clerical position was downgraded, and he sought and received a transfer to the position of road maintenance worker. He also occasionally worked out of class as a dispatcher while performing that job.

Nine of the applicants, including Joyce and Johnson, were deemed qualified for the job, and were interviewed by a two-person board. Seven of the applicants scored above 70 on this interview, which meant that they were certified as eligible for selection by the appointing authority. The scores awarded ranged from 70 to 80. Johnson was tied for second with score of 75, while Joyce ranked next with a score of 73. A second interview was conducted by three Agency supervisors, who ultimately recommended that Johnson be promoted. Prior to the second interview, Joyce had contacted the County's Affirmative Action

Office because she feared that her application might not receive disinterested review.[5] The Office in turn contacted the Agency's Affirmative Action Coordinator, whom the Agency's Plan makes responsible for, *inter alia,* keeping the Director informed of opportunities for the Agency to accomplish its objectives under the Plan. At the time, the Agency employed no women in any Skilled Craft position, and had never employed a woman as a road dispatcher. The Coordinator recommended to the Director of the Agency, James Graebner, that Joyce be promoted.

Graebner, authorized to choose any of the seven persons deemed eligible, thus had the benefit of suggestions by the second interview panel and by the Agency Coordinator in arriving at his decision. After deliberation, Graebner concluded that the promotion should be given to Joyce. As he testified: "I tried to look at the whole picture, the combination of her qualifications and Mr. Johnson's qualifications, their test scores, their expertise, their background, affirmative action matters, things like that * * * I believe it was a combination of all those."

The certification form naming Joyce as the person promoted to the dispatcher position stated that both she and Johnson were rated as well-qualified for the job. The evaluation of Joyce read: "Well qualified by virtue of 18 years of past clerical experience including 3½ years at West Yard plus almost 5 years as a[road maintenance worker]." The evaluation of Johnson was as follows: "Well qualified applicant; two years of [road maintenance worker] experience plus 11 years of Road Yard Clerk. Has had previous outside Dispatch experience but was 13 years ago." Graebner testified that he did not regard as significant the fact that Johnson scored 75 and Joyce 73 when interviewed by the two-person board.

Petitioner Johnson filed a complaint with the EEOC alleging that he had been denied promotion on the basis of sex in violation of Title VII. * * * The District Court found that Johnson was more qualified for the dispatcher position than Joyce, and that the sex of Joyce was the *"determining factor* in her selection." The court acknowledged

---

5. Joyce testified that she had had disagreements with two of the three members of the second interview panel. One had been her first supervisor when she began work as a road maintenance worker. In performing arduous work in this job, she had not been issued coveralls, although her male co-workers had received them. After ruining her pants, she complained to her supervisor, to no avail. After three other similar incidents, ruining clothes on each occasion, she filed a grievance, and was issued four pair of coveralls the next day. Joyce had dealt with a second member of the panel for a year and a half in her capacity as chair of the Roads Operations Safety Committee, where she and he "had several differences of opinion on how safety should be implemented." In addition, Joyce testified that she had informed the person responsible for arranging her second interview that she had a disaster preparedness class on a certain day the following week. By this time about ten days had passed since she had notified this person of her availability, and no date had yet been set for the interview. Within a day or two after this conversation, however, she received a notice setting her interview at a time directly in the middle of her disaster preparedness class. This same panel member had earlier described Joyce as a "rebel-rousing, skirt-wearing person".

that, since the Agency justified its decision on the basis of its Affirmative Action Plan, the criteria announced in Steelworkers v. Weber, 443 U.S. 193, 99 S.Ct. 2721, 61 L.Ed.2d 480 (1979), should be applied in evaluating the validity of the plan. It then found the Agency's Plan invalid on the ground that the evidence did not satisfy *Weber's* criterion that the Plan be temporary. The Court of Appeals for the Ninth Circuit reversed, holding that the absence of an express termination date in the Plan was not dispositive, since the Plan repeatedly expressed its objective as the attainment, rather than the maintenance, of a work force mirroring the labor force in the county. The Court of Appeals added that the fact that the Plan established no fixed percentage of positions for minorities or women made it less essential that the Plan contain a relatively explicit deadline. The Court held further that the Agency's consideration of Joyce's sex in filling the road dispatcher position was lawful. The Agency Plan had been adopted, the court said, to address a conspicuous imbalance in the Agency's work force, and neither unnecessarily trammeled the rights of other employees, nor created an absolute bar to their advancement.

II

As a preliminary matter, we note that petitioner bears the burden of establishing the invalidity of the Agency's Plan. Only last term in Wygant v. Jackson Board of Education, 476 U.S. 267, 277–278, 106 S.Ct. 1842, 1848, 90 L.Ed.2d 260 (1986), we held that "[t]he ultimate burden remains with the employees to demonstrate the unconstitutionality of an affirmative-action program," and we see no basis for a different rule regarding a plan's alleged violation of Title VII. This case also fits readily within the analytical framework set forth in McDonnell Douglas Corp. v. Green. Once a plaintiff establishes a prima facie case that race or sex has been taken into account in an employer's employment decision, the burden shifts to the employer to articulate a nondiscriminatory rationale for its decision. The existence of an affirmative action plan provides such a rationale. If such a plan is articulated as the basis for the employer's decision, the burden shifts to the plaintiff to prove that the employer's justification is pretextual and the plan is invalid. As a practical matter, of course, an employer will generally seek to avoid a charge of pretext by presenting evidence in support of its plan. That does not mean, however, as petitioner suggests, that reliance on an affirmative action plan is to be treated as an affirmative defense requiring the employer to carry the burden of proving the validity of the plan. The burden of proving its invalidity remains on the plaintiff.

The assessment of the legality of the Agency Plan must be guided by our decision in *Weber,* supra.[6] In that case, the Court addressed the question whether the employer violated Title VII by adopting a volun-

---

6. The dissent maintains that the obligations of a public employer under Title VII must be identical to its obligations under the Constitution, and that a public employer's adoption of an affirmative action plan therefore should be governed by

tary affirmative action plan designed to "eliminate manifest racial imbalances in traditionally segregated job categories." The respondent employee in that case challenged the employer's denial of his application for a position in a newly established craft training program, contending that the employer's selection process impermissibly took into account the race of the applicants. The selection process was guided by an affirmative action plan, which provided that 50% of the new trainees were to be black until the percentage of black skilled craftworkers in the employer's plant approximated the percentage of blacks in the local labor force. Adoption of the plan had been prompted by the fact that only 5 of 273, or 1.83%, of skilled craftworkers at the plant were black, even though the work force in the area was approximately 39% black. Because of the historical exclusion of blacks from craft positions, the employer regarded its former policy of hiring trained outsiders as inadequate to redress the imbalance in its work force.

We upheld the employer's decision to select less senior black applicants over the white respondent, for we found that taking race into account was consistent with Title VII's objective of "break[ing] down old patterns of racial segregation and hierarchy." Id., at 208, 99 S.Ct., at 2730. As we stated:

> "It would be ironic indeed if a law triggered by a Nation's concern over centuries of racial injustice and intended to improve

Wygant. This rests on the following logic: Title VI embodies the same constraints as the Constitution; Title VI and Title VII have the same prohibitory scope; therefore, Title VII and the Constitution are coterminous for purposes of this case. The flaw is with the second step of the analysis, for it advances a proposition that we explicitly considered and rejected in *Weber.* As we noted in that case, Title VI was an exercise of federal power "over a matter in which the Federal Government was already directly involved," since Congress "was legislating to assure federal funds would not be used in an improper manner." "Title VII, by contrast, was enacted pursuant to the commerce power to regulate purely private decisionmaking and was not intended to incorporate and particularize the commands of the Fifth and Fourteenth Amendments. Title VII and Title VI, therefore, cannot be read *in pari materia.*" This point is underscored by Congress' concern that the receipt of any form of financial assistance might render an employer subject to the commands of Title VI rather than Title VII. As a result, Congress added § 604 to Title VI, 42 U.S.C. § 2000d–3, which provides:

"Nothing contained in this subchapter shall be construed to authorize action under this subchapter by any department or agency with respect to any employment practice of any employer, employment agency, or labor organization except where a primary objective of the Federal financial assistance is to provide employment."

The sponsor of this section, Senator Cooper, stated that it was designed to clarify that "it was not intended that [T]itle VI would impinge on [T]itle VII." 110 Cong. Rec. 11615 (1964).

While public employers were not added to the definition of "employer" in Title VII until 1972, there is no evidence that this mere addition to the definitional section of the statute was intended to transform the substantive standard governing employer conduct. Indeed, "Congress expressly indicated the intent that the same Title VII principles be applied to governmental and private employers alike." Dothard v. Rawlinson, 433 U.S. 321, 332 n. 14, 97 S.Ct. 2720, 2728 n. 14, 53 L.Ed.2d 786 (1977). The fact that a public employer must also satisfy the Constitution does not negate the fact that the *statutory* prohibition with which that employer must contend was not intended to extend as far as that of the Constitution.

the lot of those who had 'been excluded from the American dream for so long' constituted the first legislative prohibition of all voluntary, private, race-conscious efforts to abolish traditional patterns of racial segregation and hierarchy." Id., at 204, 99 S.Ct., at 2728 (quoting remarks of Sen. Humphrey, 110 Cong.Rec. 6552 (1964)).[7]

We noted that the plan did not "unnecessarily trammel the interests of the white employees," since it did not require "the discharge of white workers and their replacement with new black hirees." Nor did the plan create "an absolute bar to the advancement of white employees," since half of those trained in the new program were to be white. Finally, we observed that the plan was a temporary measure, not designed to maintain racial balance, but to "eliminate a manifest racial imbalance." As Justice Blackmun's concurrence made clear, *Weber* held that an employer seeking to justify the adoption of a plan need not point to its own prior discriminatory practices, nor even to evidence of an "arguable violation" on its part. Rather, it need point only to a "conspicuous * * * imbalance in traditionally segregated job categories." Our decision was grounded in the recognition that voluntary

7. The dissent maintains that *Weber's* conclusion that Title VII does not prohibit voluntary affirmative action programs "rewrote the statute it purported to construe." *Weber's* decisive rejection of the argument that the "plain language" of the statute prohibits affirmative action rested on (1) legislative history indicating Congress' clear intention that employers play a major role in eliminating the vestiges of discrimination, and (2) the language and legislative history of § 703(j) of the statute, which reflect a strong desire to preserve managerial prerogatives so that they might be utilized for this purpose. As Justice Blackmun said in his concurrence in *Weber,* "[I]f the Court has misperceived the political will, it has the assurance that because the question is statutory Congress may set a different course if it so chooses." Congress has not amended the statute to reject our construction, nor have any such amendments even been proposed, and we therefore may assume that our interpretation was correct.

The dissent faults the fact that we take note of the absence of Congressional efforts to amend the statute to nullify *Weber.* It suggests that Congressional inaction cannot be regarded as acquiescence under all circumstances, but then draws from that unexceptional point the conclusion that *any* reliance on Congressional failure to act is necessarily a "canard." The fact that inaction may not always provide crystal-line revelation, however, should not obscure the fact that it may be probative to varying degrees. *Weber,* for instance, was

a widely-publicized decision that addressed a prominent issue of public debate. Legislative inattention thus is not a plausible explanation for Congressional inaction. Furthermore, Congress not only passed no contrary legislation in the wake of *Weber,* but not one legislator even proposed a bill to do so. The barriers of the legislative process therefore also seem a poor explanation for failure to act. By contrast, when Congress has been displeased with our interpretation of Title VII, it has not hesitated to amend the statute to tell us so. For instance, when Congress passed the Pregnancy Discrimination Act of 1978, 42 U.S.C. § 2000e(k), "it unambiguously expressed its disapproval of both the holding and the reasoning of the Court in General Electric v. Gilbert, 429 U.S. 125, 97 S.Ct. 401, 50 L.Ed.2d 343 (1976)." Newport News Shipbuilding & Dry Dock v. EEOC, 462 U.S. 669, 678, 103 S.Ct. 2622, 2628, 77 L.Ed.2d 89 (1983). Surely, it is appropriate to find some probative value in such radically different Congressional reactions to this Court's interpretations of the same statute.

As one scholar has put it, "When a court says to a legislature: 'You (or your predecessor) meant X,' it almost invites the legislature to answer: 'We did not.'" G. Calabresi, A Common Law for the Age of Statute 31–32 (1982). Any belief in the notion of a dialogue between the judiciary and the legislature must acknowledge that on occasion an invitation declined is as significant as one accepted.

employer action can play a crucial role in furthering Title VII's purpose of eliminating the effects of discrimination in the workplace, and that Title VII should not be read to thwart such efforts.[8]

In reviewing the employment decision at issue in this case, we must first examine whether that decision was made pursuant to a plan prompted by concerns similar to those of the employer in *Weber*. Next, we must determine whether the effect of the plan on males and non-minorities is comparable to the effect of the plan in that case.

The first issue is therefore whether consideration of the sex of applicants for skilled craft jobs was justified by the existence of a "manifest imbalance" that reflected underrepresentation of women in "traditionally segregated job categories." In determining whether an imbalance exists that would justify taking sex or race into account, a comparison of the percentage of minorities or women in the employer's work force with the percentage in the area labor market or general population is appropriate in analyzing jobs that require no special expertise, see Teamsters v. United States, 431 U.S. 324, 97 S.Ct. 1843, 52 L.Ed.2d 396 (1977) (comparison between percentage of blacks in employer's work force and in general population proper in determining extent of imbalance in truck driving positions), or training programs designed to provide expertise, see *Weber*, supra (comparison between proportion of blacks working at plant and proportion of blacks in area

---

8. See also Firefighters v. Cleveland, 478 U.S. 501, 515, 106 S.Ct. 3063, 3072, 92 L.Ed.2d 405 (1986) ("We have on numerous occasions recognized that Congress intended for voluntary compliance to be the preferred means of achieving the objectives of Title VII"); Alexander v. Gardner–Denver, 415 U.S. 36, 44, 94 S.Ct. 1011, 1017, 39 L.Ed.2d 147 (1974) ("Cooperation and voluntary compliance were selected as the preferred means for achieving [Title VII's] goal"). The dissent's suggestion that an affirmative action program may be adopted only to redress an employer's past discrimination was rejected in Steelworkers v. Weber, because the prospect of liability created by such an admission would create a significant disincentive for voluntary action. As Justice Blackmun's concurrence in that case pointed out, such a standard would "plac[e] voluntary compliance with Title VII in profound jeopardy. The only way for the employer and the union to keep their footing on the 'tightrope' it creates would be to eschew all forms of voluntary affirmative action." Similarly, Justice O'Connor has observed in the constitutional context that "[t]he imposition of a requirement that public employers make findings that they have engaged in illegal discrimination before they engage in affirmative action programs would severely undermine public employers' incentive to

meet voluntarily their civil rights obligations." *Wygant*, 476 U.S., at 290, 106 S.Ct., at 1855 (O'Connor, J., concurring in part and concurring in the judgment).

Contrary to the dissent's contention, our decisions last term in Firefighters, supra, and Sheet Metal Workers v. EEOC, 478 U.S. 421, 106 S.Ct. 3019, 92 L.Ed.2d 344 (1986), provide no support for a standard more restrictive than that enunciated in *Weber*. *Firefighters* raised the issue of the conditions under which parties could enter into a consent decree providing for explicit numerical quotas. By contrast, the affirmative action plan in this case sets aside no positions for minorities or women. In *Sheet Metal Workers*, the issue we addressed was the scope of judicial remedial authority under Title VII, authority that has not been exercised in this case. The dissent's suggestion that employers should be able to do no more voluntarily than courts can order as remedies, ignores the fundamental difference between volitional private behavior and the exercise of coercion by the state. Plainly, "Congress' concern that federal courts not impose unwanted obligations on employers and unions," *Firefighters*, supra, 478 U.S., at 524, 106 S.Ct., at 3077, reflects a desire to preserve a relatively large domain for voluntary employer action.

labor force appropriate in calculating imbalance for purpose of establishing preferential admission to craft training program). Where a job requires special training, however, the comparison should be with those in the labor force who possess the relevant qualifications. See Hazelwood School District v. United States, 433 U.S. 299, 97 S.Ct. 2736, 53 L.Ed.2d 768 (1977) (must compare percentage of blacks in employer's work ranks with percentage of qualified black teachers in area labor force in determining underrepresentation in teaching positions). The requirement that the "manifest imbalance" relate to a "traditionally segregated job category" provides assurance both that sex or race will be taken into account in a manner consistent with Title VII's purpose of eliminating the effects of employment discrimination, and that the interests of those employees not benefitting from the plan will not be unduly infringed.

A manifest imbalance need not be such that it would support a prima facie case against the employer, as suggested in Justice O'Connor's concurrence, since we do not regard as identical the constraints of Title VII and the federal constitution on voluntarily adopted affirmative action plans.[9] Application of the "prima facie" standard in Title VII cases would be inconsistent with *Weber*'s focus on statistical imbalance,[10] and could inappropriately create a significant disincentive for employers to adopt an affirmative action plan. See *Weber,* supra, 443 U.S., at 204, 99 S.Ct., at 2727–28 (Title VII intended as a "catalyst" for employer efforts to eliminate vestiges of discrimination). A corporation concerned with maximizing return on investment, for instance, is hardly likely to adopt a plan if in order to do so it must compile evidence that could be used to subject it to a colorable Title VII suit.[11]

9. See supra, n. 6.

10. The difference between the "manifest imbalance" and "prima facie" standards is illuminated by *Weber.* Had the Court in that case been concerned with past discrimination by the employer, it would have focused on discrimination in hiring skilled, not unskilled, workers, since only the scarcity of the former in Kaiser's work force would have made it vulnerable to a Title VII suit. In order to make out a prima facie case on such a claim, a plaintiff would be required to compare the percentage of black skilled workers in the Kaiser work force with the percentage of black skilled craft workers in the area labor market.

Weber obviously did not make such a comparison. Instead, it focused on the disparity between the percentage of black skilled craft workers in Kaiser's ranks and the percentage of blacks in the area labor force. Such an approach reflected a recognition that the proportion of black craft workers in the local labor force was likely as miniscule as the proportion in Kaiser's work force. The Court realized that the lack of imbalance between these figures would mean that employers in precisely those industries in which discrimination has been most effective would be precluded from adopting training programs to increase the percentage of qualified minorities. Thus, in cases such as *Weber,* where the employment decision at issue involves the selection of unskilled persons for a training program, the "manifest imbalance" standard permits comparison with the general labor force. By contrast, the "prima facie" standard would require comparison with the percentage of minorities or women qualified for the job for which the trainees are being trained, a standard that would have invalidated the plan in *Weber* itself.

11. In some cases, of course, the manifest imbalance may be sufficiently egregious to establish a prima facie case. However, as long as there is a manifest imbalance, an employer may adopt a plan even where the disparity is not so striking, without being required to introduce the non-

It is clear that the decision to hire Joyce was made pursuant to an Agency plan that directed that sex or race be taken into account for the purpose of remedying underrepresentation. The Agency Plan acknowledged the "limited opportunities that have existed in the past," for women to find employment in certain job classifications "where women have not been traditionally employed in significant numbers." [12] As a result, observed the Plan, women were concentrated in traditionally female jobs in the Agency, and represented a lower percentage in other job classifications than would be expected if such traditional segregation had not occurred. Specifically, 9 of the 10 Para–Professionals and 110 of the 145 Office and Clerical Workers were women. By contrast, women were only 2 of the 28 Officials and Administrators, 5 of the 58 Professionals, 12 of the 124 Technicians, none of the Skilled Craft Workers, and 1—who was Joyce—of the 110 Road Maintenance Workers. The Plan sought to remedy these imbalances through "hiring, training and promotion of ... women throughout the Agency in all major job classifications where they are underrepresented."

As an initial matter, the Agency adopted as a benchmark for measuring progress in eliminating underrepresentation the long-term goal of a work force that mirrored in its major job classifications the percentage of women in the area labor market.[13] Even as it did so, however, the Agency acknowledged that such a figure could not by itself necessarily justify taking into account the sex of applicants for positions in all job categories. For positions requiring specialized training and experience, the Plan observed that the number of minorities and women "who possess the qualifications required for entry into such job classifications is limited." The Plan therefore directed that annual short-term goals be formulated that would provide a more realistic indication of the degree to which sex should be taken into account in filling particular positions. The Plan stressed that such

statistical evidence of past discrimination that would be demanded by the "prima facie" standard. See, e.g., Teamsters v. United States, 431 U.S. 324, 339, 97 S.Ct. 1843, 1856, 52 L.Ed.2d 396 (1977) (statistics in pattern and practice case supplemented by testimony regarding employment practices). Of course, when there is sufficient evidence to meet the more stringent "prima facie" standard, be it statistical, nonstatistical, or a combination of the two, the employer is free to adopt an affirmative action plan.

12. For instance, the description of the Skilled Craft Worker category, in which the road dispatcher position is located, is as follows:

"Occupations in which workers perform jobs which require special manual skill and a thorough and comprehensive knowledge of the process involved in the work which is acquired through on-the-job training and experience or through apprenticeship or other formal training programs. Includes: mechanics and repairmen; electricians, heavy equipment operators, stationary engineers, skilled machining occupations, carpenters, compositors and typesetters and kindred workers."

As the Court of Appeals said in its decision below, "A plethora of proof is hardly necessary to show that women are generally underrepresented in such positions and that strong social pressures weigh against their participation."

13. Because of the employment decision at issue in this case, our discussion henceforth refers primarily to the Plan's provisions to remedy the underrepresentation of women. Our analysis could apply as well, however, to the provisions of the plan pertaining to minorities.

goals "should not be construed as 'quotas' that must be met," but as reasonable aspirations in correcting the imbalance in the Agency's work force. These goals were to take into account factors such as "turnover, layoffs, lateral transfers, new job openings, retirements and availability of minorities, women and handicapped persons in the area work force who possess the desired qualifications or potential for placement." The Plan specifically directed that, in establishing such goals, the Agency work with the County Planning Department and other sources in attempting to compile data on the percentage of minorities and women in the local labor force that were actually working in the job classifications comprising the Agency work force. From the outset, therefore, the Plan sought annually to develop even more refined measures of the underrepresentation in each job category that required attention.

As the Agency Plan recognized, women were most egregiously underrepresented in the Skilled Craft job category, since *none* of the 238 positions was occupied by a woman. In mid–1980, when Joyce was selected for the road dispatcher position, the Agency was still in the process of refining its short-term goals for Skilled Craft Workers in accordance with the directive of the Plan. This process did not reach fruition until 1982, when the Agency established a short-term goal for that year of three women for the 55 expected openings in that job category—a modest goal of about 6% for that category.

We reject petitioner's argument that, since only the long-term goal was in place for Skilled Craft positions at the time of Joyce's promotion, it was inappropriate for the Director to take into account affirmative action considerations in filling the road dispatcher position. The Agency's Plan emphasized that the long-term goals were not to be taken as guides for actual hiring decisions, but that supervisors were to consider a host of practical factors in seeking to meet affirmative action objectives, including the fact that in some job categories women were not qualified in numbers comparable to their representation in the labor force.

By contrast, had the Plan simply calculated imbalances in all categories according to the proportion of women in the area labor pool, and then directed that hiring be governed solely by those figures, its validity fairly could be called into question. This is because analysis of a more specialized labor pool normally is necessary in determining underrepresentation in some positions. If a plan failed to take distinctions in qualifications into account in providing guidance for actual employment decisions, it would dictate mere blind hiring by the numbers, for it would hold supervisors to "achievement of a particular percentage of minority employment or membership * * * regardless of circumstances such as economic conditions or the number of qualified minority applicants * * *" Sheet Metal Workers v. EEOC, 478 U.S. 421, 106 S.Ct. 3019, 92 L.Ed.2d 344 (1986) (O'Connor, J., concurring in part and dissenting in part).

The Agency's Plan emphatically did *not* authorize such blind hiring. It expressly directed that numerous factors be taken into account in making hiring decisions, including specifically the qualifications of female applicants for particular jobs. Thus, despite the fact that no precise short-term goal was yet in place for the Skilled Craft category in mid–1980, the Agency's management nevertheless had been clearly instructed that they were not to hire solely by reference to statistics. The fact that only the long-term goal had been established for this category posed no danger that personnel decisions would be made by reflexive adherence to a numerical standard.

Furthermore, in considering the candidates for the road dispatcher position in 1980, the Agency hardly needed to rely on a refined short-term goal to realize that it had a significant problem of underrepresentation that required attention. Given the obvious imbalance in the Skilled Craft category, and given the Agency's commitment to eliminating such imbalances, it was plainly not unreasonable for the Agency to determine that it was appropriate to consider as one factor the sex of Ms. Joyce in making its decision.[14] The promotion of Joyce thus satisfies the first requirement enunciated in *Weber,* since it was undertaken to further an affirmative action plan designed to eliminate Agency work force imbalances in traditionally segregated job categories.

We next consider whether the Agency Plan unnecessarily trammeled the rights of male employees or created an absolute bar to their advancement. In contrast to the plan in *Weber,* which provided that 50% of the positions in the craft training program were exclusively for blacks, and to the consent decree upheld last term in Firefighters v. Cleveland, 478 U.S. 501, 106 S.Ct. 3063, 92 L.Ed.2d 405 (1986), which required the promotion of specific numbers of minorities, the Plan sets aside no positions for women. The Plan expressly states that "[t]he 'goals' established for each Division should not be construed as 'quotas' that must be met." Rather, the Plan merely authorizes that consideration be given to affirmative action concerns when evaluating qualified applicants. As the Agency Director testified, the sex of Joyce was but one of numerous factors he took into account in arriving at his decision. The Plan thus resembles the "Harvard Plan" approvingly noted by Justice Powell in *University of California Regents v. Bakke,* 438 U.S. 265, 316–319, 98 S.Ct. 2733, 2761–63, 57 L.Ed.2d 750 (1978), which considers race along with other criteria in determining admission to the college. As Justice Powell observed, "In such an admissions program, race or ethnic background may be deemed a 'plus' in a particular applicant's file, yet it does not insulate the individual from comparison

14. In addition, the Agency was mindful of the importance of finally hiring a woman in a job category that had formerly been all-male. The Director testified that, while the promotion of Joyce "made a small dent, for sure, in the numbers," nonetheless "philosophically it made a larger impact in that it probably has encouraged other females and minorities to look at the possibility of so-called 'non-traditional' jobs as areas where they and the agency both have samples of a success story."

with all other candidates for the available seats." Similarly, the Agency Plan requires women to compete with all other qualified applicants. *No* persons are automatically excluded from consideration; *all* are able to have their qualifications weighed against those of other applicants.

In addition, petitioner had no absolute entitlement to the road dispatcher position. Seven of the applicants were classified as qualified and eligible, and the Agency Director was authorized to promote any of the seven. Thus, denial of the promotion unsettled no legitimate firmly rooted expectation on the part of the petitioner. Furthermore, while the petitioner in this case was denied a promotion, he retained his employment with the Agency, at the same salary and with the same seniority, and remained eligible for other promotions.[15]

Finally, the Agency's Plan was intended to *attain* a balanced work force, not to maintain one. The Plan contains ten references to the Agency's desire to "attain" such a balance, but no reference whatsoever to a goal of maintaining it. The Director testified that, while the "broader goal" of affirmative action, defined as "the desire to hire, to promote, to give opportunity and training on an equitable, non-discriminatory basis," is something that is "a permanent part" of "the Agency's operating philosophy," that broader goal "is divorced, if you will, from specific numbers or percentages."

The Agency acknowledged the difficulties that it would confront in remedying the imbalance in its work force, and it anticipated only gradual increases in the representation of minorities and women.[16] It is thus unsurprising that the Plan contains no explicit end date, for the Agency's flexible, case-by-case approach was not expected to yield success in a brief period of time. Express assurance that a program is only temporary may be necessary if the program actually sets aside

---

15. Furthermore, from 1978 to 1982 Skilled Craft jobs in the Agency increased from 238 to 349. The Agency's personnel figures indicate that the Agency fully expected most of these positions to be filled by men. Of the 111 new Skilled Craft jobs during this period, 105, or almost 95%, went to men. As previously noted, the Agency's 1982 Plan set a goal of hiring only three women out of the 55 new Skilled Craft positions projected for that year, a figure of about 6%. While this degree of employment expansion by an employer is by no means essential to a plan's validity, it underscores the fact that the Plan in this case in no way significantly restricts the employment prospects of such persons. Illustrative of this is the fact that an additional road dispatcher position was created in 1983, and petitioner was awarded the job.

16. As the Agency Plan stated, after noting the limited number of minorities and women qualified in certain categories, as well as other difficulties in remedying underrepresentation:

"As indicated by the above factors, it will be much easier to attain the Agency's employment goals in some job categories than in others. It is particularly evident that it will be extremely difficult to significantly increase the representation of women in technical and skilled craft job classifications where they have traditionally been greatly underrepresented. Similarly, only gradual increases in the representation of women, minorities or handicapped persons in management and professional positions can realistically be expected due to the low turnover that exists in these positions and the small numbers of persons who can be expected to compete for available openings."

positions according to specific numbers. See, e.g., *Firefighters,* supra, 478 U.S., at 510, 106 S.Ct., at 3069 (four-year duration for consent decree providing for promotion of particular number of minorities); *Weber,* 443 U.S., at 199, 99 S.Ct., at 2725 (plan requiring that blacks constitute 50% of new trainees in effect until percentage of employer work force equal to percentage in local labor force). This is necessary both to minimize the effect of the program on other employees, and to ensure that the plan's goals "[are] not being used simply to achieve and maintain ... balance, but rather as a benchmark against which" the employer may measure its progress in eliminating the underrepresentation of minorities and women. *Sheet Metal Workers,* supra, 478 U.S., at 477–478, 106 S.Ct., at 3051. In this case, however, substantial evidence shows that the Agency has sought to take a moderate, gradual approach to eliminating the imbalance in its work force, one which establishes realistic guidance for employment decisions, and which visits minimal intrusion on the legitimate expectations of other employees. Given this fact, as well as the Agency's express commitment to "attain" a balanced work force, there is ample assurance that the Agency does not seek to use its Plan to maintain a permanent racial and sexual balance.

III

In evaluating the compliance of an affirmative action plan with Title VII's prohibition on discrimination, we must be mindful of "this Court's and Congress' consistent emphasis on 'the value of voluntary efforts to further the objectives of the law.'" *Wygant,* 476 U.S., at 290, 106 S.Ct., at 1855 (O'Connor, J., concurring in part and concurring in judgment) (quoting *Bakke,* supra, 438 U.S., at 364, 98 S.Ct., at 2785–86). The Agency in the case before us has undertaken such a voluntary effort, and has done so in full recognition of both the difficulties and the potential for intrusion on males and non-minorities. The Agency has identified a conspicuous imbalance in job categories traditionally segregated by race and sex. It has made clear from the outset, however, that employment decisions may not be justified solely by reference to this imbalance, but must rest on a multitude of practical, realistic factors. It has therefore committed itself to annual adjustment of goals so as to provide a reasonable guide for actual hiring and promotion decisions. The Agency earmarks no positions for anyone; sex is but one of several factors that may be taken into account in evaluating qualified applicants for a position.[17] As both the Plan's language and its manner of

---

17. The dissent predicts that today's decision will loose a flood of "less qualified" minorities and women upon the workforce, as employers seek to forestall possible Title VII liability. The first problem with this projection is that it is by no means certain that employers could in every case necessarily avoid liability for discrimination merely by adopting an affirmative action plan. Indeed, our unwillingness to require an admission of discrimination as the price of adopting a plan has been premised on concern that the potential liability to which such an admission would expose an employer would serve as a disincentive for creating an affirmative action program. See supra, n. 6.

operation attest, the Agency has no intention of establishing a work force whose permanent composition is dictated by rigid numerical standards.

We therefore hold that the Agency appropriately took into account as one factor the sex of Diane Joyce in determining that she should be promoted to the road dispatcher position. The decision to do so was made pursuant to an affirmative action plan that represents a moderate, flexible, case-by-case approach to effecting a gradual improvement in the representation of minorities and women in the Agency's work force. Such a plan is fully consistent with Title VII, for it embodies the contribution that voluntary employer action can make in eliminating the vestiges of discrimination in the workplace. Accordingly, the judgment of the Court of Appeals is

Affirmed.

JUSTICE STEVENS, concurring.

While I join the Court's opinion, I write separately to explain my view of this case's position in our evolving antidiscrimination law and to emphasize that the opinion does not establish the permissible outer limits of voluntary programs undertaken by employers to benefit disadvantaged groups.

I

Antidiscrimination measures may benefit protected groups in two distinct ways. As a sword, such measures may confer benefits by specifying that a person's membership in a disadvantaged group must be a neutral, irrelevant factor in governmental or private decisionmaking or, alternatively, by compelling decisionmakers to give favorable consideration to disadvantaged group status. As a shield, an antidiscrimination statute can also help a member of a protected class by assuring decisionmakers in some instances that, when they elect for good reasons of their own to grant a preference of some sort to a minority citizen, they will not violate the law. The Court properly holds that the statutory shield allowed respondent to take Diane

---

A second, and more fundamental, problem with the dissent's speculation is that it ignores the fact that

"[i]t is a standard tenet of personnel administration that there is rarely a single, 'best qualified' person for a job. An effective personnel system will bring before the selecting official several fully-qualified candidates who each may possess different attributes which recommend them for selection. Especially where the job is an unexceptional, middle-level craft position, without the need for unique work experience or educational attainment and for which several

well-qualified candidates are available, final determinations as to which candidate is 'best qualified' are at best subjective." Brief for American Society for Personnel Administration as *Amicus Curiae* 9.

This case provides an example of precisely this point. Any differences in qualifications between Johnson and Joyce were minimal, to say the least. The selection of Joyce thus belies the dissent's contention that the beneficiaries of affirmative action programs will be those employees who are merely not "utterly unqualified."

Joyce's sex into account in promoting her to the road dispatcher position.

Prior to 1978 the Court construed the Civil Rights Act of 1964 as an absolute blanket prohibition against discrimination which neither required nor permitted discriminatory preferences for any group, minority or majority. The Court unambiguously endorsed the neutral approach, first in the context of gender discrimination [1] and then in the context of racial discrimination against a white person.[2] As I explained in my separate opinion in University of California Regents v. Bakke, 438 U.S. 265, 412–418, 98 S.Ct. 2733, 2810–2813, 57 L.Ed.2d 750 (1978), and as the Court forcefully stated in McDonald v. Santa Fe Trail Transportation Co., 427 U.S. 273, 280, 96 S.Ct. 2574, 2578, 49 L.Ed.2d 493 (1976), Congress intended " 'to eliminate all practices which operate to disadvantage the employment opportunities of any group protected by Title VII including Caucasians.' " (citations omitted). If the Court had adhered to that construction of the Act, petitioner would unquestionably prevail in this case. But it has not done so.

In the *Bakke* case in 1978 and again in Steelworkers v. Weber, a majority of the Court interpreted the antidiscriminatory strategy of the statute in a fundamentally different way. The Court held in the *Weber* case that an employer's program designed to increase the number of black craftworkers in an aluminum plant did not violate Title VII.[3] It remains clear that the Act does not *require* any employer to grant preferential treatment on the basis of race or gender, but since 1978 the Court has unambiguously interpreted the statute to *permit* the volun-

1. "Discriminatory preference for any group, minority or majority, is precisely and only what Congress has proscribed. What is required by Congress is the removal of artificial, arbitrary, and unnecessary barriers to employment when the barriers operate invidiously to discriminate on the basis of racial or other impermissible classification." Griggs v. Duke Power Co., 401 U.S. 424, 431, 91 S.Ct. 849, 853, 28 L.Ed.2d 158 (1971).

2. "Similarly the EEOC, whose interpretations are entitled to great deference, [401 U.S.,] at 433–434, 91 S.Ct., at 854–55, has consistently interpreted Title VII to proscribe racial discrimination in private employment against whites on the same terms as racial discrimination against non-whites, holding that to proceed otherwise would

'constitute a derogation of the Commission's Congressional mandate to eliminate all practices which operate to disadvantage the employment opportunities of any group protected by Title VII, including Caucasians.' EEOC Decision No. 74–31, 7 FEP Cases 1326, 1328, CCH EEOC Decisions ¶ 6404, p. 4084 (1973)."

"This conclusion is in accord with uncontradicted legislative history to the effect that Title VII was intended to 'cover white men and white women and all Americans,' 110 Cong.Rec. 2578 (1964) (remarks of Rep. Celler), and create an 'obligation not to discriminate against whites,' id., at 7218 (memorandum of Sen. Clark). See also id., at 7213 (memorandum of Sens. Clark and Case); id., at 8912 (remarks of Sen. Williams). We therefore hold today that Title VII prohibits racial discrimination against the white petitioners in this case upon the same standards as would be applicable were they Negroes and Jackson white." McDonald v. Santa Fe Trail Transportation Co., 427 U.S. 273, 279–280, 96 S.Ct. 2574, 2578–2579, 49 L.Ed.2d 493 (1976) (footnotes omitted).

3. Toward the end of its opinion, the Court mentioned certain reasons why the plan did not impose a special hardship on white employees or white applicants for employment. I have never understood those comments to constitute a set of conditions that every race-conscious plan must satisfy in order to comply with Title VII.

tary adoption of special programs to benefit members of the minority groups for whose protection the statute was enacted. Neither the "same standards" language used in *McDonald,* nor the "color blind" rhetoric used by the Senators and Congressmen who enacted the bill, is now controlling. Thus, as was true in Runyon v. McCrary, 427 U.S. 160, 189, 96 S.Ct. 2586, 2603, 49 L.Ed.2d 415 (1976) (Stevens, J., concurring), the only problem for me is whether to adhere to an authoritative construction of the Act that is at odds with my understanding of the actual intent of the authors of the legislation. I conclude without hesitation that I must answer that question in the affirmative, just as I did in *Runyon.*

Bakke and *Weber* have been decided and are now an important part of the fabric of our law. This consideration is sufficiently compelling for me to adhere to the basic construction of this legislation that the Court adopted in *Bakke* and in *Weber.* There is an undoubted public interest in "stability and orderly development of the law."

The logic of antidiscrimination legislation requires that judicial constructions of Title VII leave "breathing room" for employer initiatives to benefit members of minority groups. If Title VII had never been enacted, a private employer would be free to hire members of minority groups for any reason that might seem sensible from a business or a social point of view. The Court's opinion in *Weber* reflects the same approach; the opinion relied heavily on legislative history indicating that Congress intended that traditional management prerogatives be left undisturbed to the greatest extent possible. As we observed Last Term, " '[i]t would be ironic indeed if a law triggered by a Nation's concern over centuries of racial injustice and intended to improve the lot of those who had "been excluded from the American dream for so long" constituted the first legislative prohibition of all voluntary, private, race-conscious efforts to abolish traditional patterns of racial segregation and hierarchy.' " Firefighters v. Cleveland, 478 U.S. 501, 516, 106 S.Ct. 3063, 3072, 92 L.Ed.2d 405 (1986) (quoting *Weber,* 443 U.S., at 204, 99 S.Ct., at 2727). In *Firefighters,* we again acknowledged Congress' concern in Title VII to avoid "undue federal interference with managerial discretion."

As construed in *Weber* and in *Firefighters,* the statute does not absolutely prohibit preferential hiring in favor of minorities; it was merely intended to protect historically disadvantaged groups *against* discrimination and not to hamper managerial efforts to benefit members of disadvantaged groups that are consistent with that paramount purpose. The preference granted by respondent in this case does not violate the statute as so construed; the record amply supports the conclusion that the challenged employment decision served the legitimate purpose of creating diversity in a category of employment that had been almost an exclusive province of males in the past. Respondent's voluntary decision is surely not prohibited by Title VII as construed in *Weber.*

II

Whether a voluntary decision of the kind made by respondent would ever be prohibited by Title VII is a question we need not answer until it is squarely presented. Given the interpretation of the statute the Court adopted in *Weber,* I see no reason why the employer has any duty, prior to granting a preference to a qualified minority employee, to determine whether his past conduct might constitute an arguable violation of Title VII. Indeed, in some instances the employer may find it more helpful to focus on the future. Instead of retroactively scrutinizing his own or society's possible exclusions of minorities in the past to determine the outer limits of a valid affirmative-action program—or indeed, any particular affirmative-action decision—in many cases the employer will find it more appropriate to consider other legitimate reasons to give preferences to members of underrepresented groups. Statutes enacted for the benefit of minority groups should not block these forward-looking considerations. * * *

The Court today does not foreclose other voluntary decisions based in part on a qualified employee's membership in a disadvantaged group. Accordingly, I concur.

JUSTICE O'CONNOR, concurring in the judgment.

In Steelworkers v. Weber, this Court held that § 703(d) of Title VII does not prohibit voluntary affirmative action efforts if the employer sought to remedy a "manifest * * * imbalanc[e] in traditionally segregated job categories." As Justice Scalia illuminates with excruciating clarity, § 703 has been interpreted by *Weber* and succeeding cases to permit what its language read literally would prohibit. Section 703(d) prohibits employment discrimination "against *any individual* because of his race, color, religion, sex, or national origin." The *Weber* Court, however, concluded that voluntary affirmative action was permissible in some circumstances because a prohibition of every type of affirmative action would " 'bring about an end completely at variance with the purpose of the statute.' " This purpose, according to the Court, was to open employment opportunities for blacks in occupations that had been traditionally closed to them.

None of the parties in this case have suggested that we overrule *Weber* and that question was not raised, briefed, or argued in this Court or in the courts below. If the Court is faithful to its normal prudential restraints and to the principle of *stare decisis* we must address once again the propriety of an affirmative action plan under Title VII in light of our precedents, precedents that have upheld affirmative action in a variety of circumstances. This time the question posed is whether a public employer violates Title VII by promoting a qualified woman rather than a marginally better qualified man when there is a statistical imbalance sufficient to support a claim of a pattern or practice of discrimination against women under Title VII.

I concur in the judgment of the Court in light of our precedents. I write separately, however, because the Court has chosen to follow an expansive and ill-defined approach to voluntary affirmative action by public employers despite the limitations imposed by the Constitution and by the provisions of Title VII, and because the dissent rejects the Court's precedents and addresses the question of how Title VII should be interpreted as if the Court were writing on a clean slate. The former course of action gives insufficient guidance to courts and litigants; the latter course of action serves as a useful point of academic discussion, but fails to reckon with the reality of the course that the majority of the Court has determined to follow.

In my view, the proper initial inquiry in evaluating the legality of an affirmative action plan by a public employer under Title VII is no different from that required by the Equal Protection Clause. In either case, consistent with the congressional intent to provide some measure of protection to the interests of the employer's nonminority employees, the employer must have had a firm basis for believing that remedial action was required. An employer would have such a firm basis if it can point to a statistical disparity sufficient to support a prima facie claim under Title VII by the employee beneficiaries of the affirmative action plan of a pattern or practice claim of discrimination.

In *Weber,* this Court balanced two conflicting concerns in construing § 703(d): Congress' intent to root out invidious discrimination against *any* person on the basis of race or gender, McDonald v. Santa Fe Transp. Co., 427 U.S. 273, 96 S.Ct. 2574, 49 L.Ed.2d 493 (1976), and its goal of eliminating the lasting effects of discrimination against minorities. Given these conflicting concerns, the Court concluded that it would be inconsistent with the background and purpose of Title VII to prohibit affirmative action in all cases. As I read *Weber,* however, the Court also determined that Congress had balanced these two competing concerns by permitting affirmative action only as a remedial device to eliminate actual or apparent discrimination or the lingering effects of this discrimination.

Contrary to the intimations in Justice Stevens' concurrence, this Court did not approve preferences for minorities "for any reason that might seem sensible from a business or a social point of view." Indeed, such an approach would have been wholly at odds with this Court's holding in *McDonald* that Congress intended to prohibit practices that operate to discriminate against the employment opportunities of nonminorities as well as minorities. Moreover, in *Weber* the Court was careful to consider the effects of the affirmative action plan for black employees on the employment opportunities of white employees. Instead of a wholly standardless approach to affirmative action, the Court determined in *Weber* that Congress intended to permit affirmative action only if the employer could point to a "manifest ... imbalanc[e] in traditionally segregated job categories." This requirement both "provides assurance that sex or race will be taken into account in a manner consistent with Title VII's purpose of eliminating the effects of employment discrimination," and is consistent with this Court's and Congress' consistent emphasis on the value of voluntary efforts to further the antidiscrimination purposes of Title VII. Wygant v. Jackson Board of Education, 476 U.S. 267, 290, 106 S.Ct. 1842, 1855, 90 L.Ed.2d 260 (1986) (O'Connor, J., concurring in part and concurring in judgment).

The *Weber* view of Congress' resolution of the conflicting concerns of minority and nonminority workers in Title VII appears substantially similar to this Court's resolution of these same concerns in Wygant v. Jackson Board of Education, supra, which involved the claim that an affirmative action plan by a public employer violated the Equal Protection Clause. In *Wygant,* the Court was in agreement that remedying past or present racial discrimination by a state actor is a sufficiently weighty interest to warrant the remedial use of a carefully constructed affirmative action plan. The Court also concluded, however, that "[s]ocietal discrimination, without more, is too amorphous a basis for imposing a racially classified remedy." Instead, we determined that affirmative action was valid if it was crafted to remedy past or present discrimination by the employer. Although the employer need not point to any contemporaneous findings of actual discrimination, I concluded in *Wygant* that the employer must point to evidence sufficient to establish a firm basis for believing that remedial action is required, and that a statistical imbalance sufficient for a Title VII prima facie case against the employer would satisfy this firm basis requirement:

> "Public employers are not without reliable benchmarks in making this determination. For example, demonstrable evidence of a disparity between the percentage of qualified blacks on a school's teaching staff and the percentage of qualified minorities in the relevant labor pool sufficient to support a prima facie Title VII pattern or practice claim by minority teachers would lend a compelling basis for a competent authority such as the School Board to conclude that implementation of a voluntary affirmative action plan is appropriate to remedy apparent prior employment discrimination." Id., at 292, 106 S.Ct., at 1856.

The *Wygant* analysis is entirely consistent with *Weber.* In *Weber,* the affirmative action plan involved a training program for unskilled production workers. There was little doubt that the absence of black craft workers was the result of the exclusion of blacks from craft unions. Steelworkers v. Weber, 443 U.S., at 198, n. 1, 99 S.Ct., at 2725, n. 1 ("Judicial findings of exclusion from crafts on racial grounds are so numerous as to make such exclusion a proper subject for judicial notice"). The employer in *Weber* had previously hired as craft-workers only persons with prior craft experience, and craft unions provided the sole avenue for obtaining this experience. Because the discrimination occurred at entry into the craft union, the "manifest racial imbalance" was powerful evidence of prior race discrimination. Under our case law, the relevant comparison for a Title VII prima facie case in those circumstances—discrimination in admission to entry-level positions such as membership in craft unions—is to the total percentage of blacks in the labor force. See Teamsters v. United States, 431 U.S. 324, 97 S.Ct. 1843, 52 L.Ed.2d 396 (1977). Here, however, the evidence of past discrimination is more complex. The number of women with the qualifications for entry into the relevant job classification was quite small. A statistical imbalance between the percentage of women in the work force generally and the percentage of women in the particular specialized job classification, therefore, does not suggest past discrimination for purposes of proving a Title VII prima facie case. See Hazelwood School District v. United States.

Unfortunately, the Court today gives little guidance for what statistical imbalance is sufficient to support an affirmative action plan. Although the Court denies that the statistical imbalance need be sufficient to make out a prima facie case of discrimination against women, the Court fails to suggest an alternative standard. Because both *Wygant* and *Weber* attempt to reconcile the same competing concerns, I see little justification for the adoption of different standards for affirmative action under Title VII and the Equal Protection Clause.

While employers must have a firm basis for concluding that remedial action is necessary, neither *Wygant* nor *Weber* places a burden on employers to prove that they actually discriminated against women or minorities. Employers are "trapped between the competing hazards of liability to minorities if affirmative action is *not* taken to remedy apparent employment discrimination and liability to nonminorities if affirmative action *is* taken." Wygant v. Jackson Board of Education, 476 U.S., at 291, 106 S.Ct., at 1855 (O'Connor, J., concurring in part and concurring in judgment). Moreover, this Court has long emphasized the importance of voluntary efforts to eliminate discrimination. Thus, I concluded in *Wygant* that a contemporaneous finding of discrimination should not be required because it would discourage voluntary efforts to remedy apparent discrimination. A requirement that an employer actually prove that it had discriminated in the past would also unduly discourage voluntary efforts to remedy apparent discrimination. As I emphasized in *Wygant,* a challenge to an affirmative action plan "does not automatically impose upon the public employer the burden of convincing the court of its liability for prior unlawful discrimination; nor does it mean that the court must make an actual finding of prior discrimination based on the employer's proof before the employer's affirmative action plan will be upheld." Evidence sufficient for a prima facie Title VII pattern or practice claim against the employer itself suggests that the absence of women or minorities in a work force cannot be explained by general societal discrimination alone and that remedial action is appropriate.

In applying these principles to this case, it is important to pay close attention to both the affirmative action plan, and the manner in which that plan was applied to the specific promotion decision at issue in this case. In December 1978, the Santa Clara Transit District Board of Supervisors adopted an affirmative action plan for the Santa Clara County Transportation Agency (Agency). At the time the plan was adopted, not one woman was employed in respondents' 238 skilled craft positions, and the plan recognized that women "are not strongly motivated to seek employment in job classifications where they have not been traditionally employed because of the limited opportunities that have existed in the past for them to work in such classifications." Additionally, the plan stated that respondents "recognize[d] that mere prohibition of discriminatory practices is not enough to remedy the effects of past practices and to permit attainment of an equitable representation of minorities, women and handicapped persons," and that "the selection and appointment processes are areas where hidden discrimination frequently occurs." Thus, the respondents had the expectation that plan "should result in improved personnel practices that will benefit all Agency employees who may have been subjected to discriminatory personnel practices in the past."

The long-term goal of the plan was "to attain a work force whose composition in all job levels and major job classifications approximates the distribution of women * * * in the Santa Clara County work force." If this long-term goal had been applied to the hiring decisions made by the Agency, in my view, the affirmative action plan would violate Title VII. "[I]t is completely unrealistic to assume that individuals of each [sex] will gravitate with mathematical exactitude to each employer * * * absent unlawful discrimination." *Sheet Metal Workers,* supra, 478 U.S., at 494, 106 S.Ct., at 3060 (O'Connor, J., concurring in part and dissenting in part). Thus, a goal that makes such an assumption, and simplistically focuses on the proportion of women and minorities in the work force without more, is not remedial. Only a goal that takes into account the number of women and minorities qualified for the relevant position could satisfy the requirement that an affirmative action plan be remedial. This long-range goal, however, was never used as a guide for actual hiring decisions. Instead, the goal was merely a statement of aspiration wholly without operational significance. The affirmative action plan itself recognized the host of reasons why this goal was extremely unrealistic, and as I read the record, the long-term goal was not applied in the promotion decision challenged in this case. Instead, the plan provided for the development of short-term goals, which alone were to guide the respondents, and the plan cautioned that even these goals "should not be construed as 'quotas' that must be met." Instead, these short-term goals were to be focused on remedying past apparent discrimination, and would "[p]rovide an objective standard for use in determining if the representation of minorities, women and handicapped persons in particular job classifications is at a reasonable level in comparison with estimates of the numbers of persons from these groups in the area work force who can meet the educational and experience requirements for employment."

At the time of the promotion at issue in this case, the short-term goals had not been fully developed. Nevertheless, the Agency had already recognized that the long-range goal was unrealistic, and had determined that the progress of the Agency should be judged by a comparison to the *qualified* women in the area work force. As I view the record, the promotion decision in this case was entirely consistent with the philosophy underlying the development of the short-term goals.

* * *

The ultimate decision to promote Joyce rather than petitioner was made by James Graebner, the Director of the Agency. As Justice Scalia views the record in this case, the Agency Director made the decision to promote Joyce rather than petitioner solely on the basis of sex and with indifference to the relative merits of the two applicants. In my view, however, the record simply fails to substantiate the picture painted by Justice Scalia. The Agency Director testified that he "tried to look at the whole picture, the combination of [Joyce's] qualification's and Mr. Johnson's qualifications, their test scores, their experience, their background, affirmative action matters, things like that." Contrary to Justice Scalia's suggestion, the Agency Director knew far more than merely the sex of the candidates and that they appeared on a list of candidates eligible for the job. The Director had spoken to individuals familiar with the qualifications of both applicants for the promotion, and was aware that their scores were rather close. Moreover, he testified that over a period of weeks he had spent several hours making the promotion decision, suggesting that Joyce was not selected solely on the basis of her sex. Additionally, the Director stated that had Joyce's experience been less than that of petitioner by a larger margin, petitioner might have received the promotion. As the Director summarized his decision to promote Joyce, the underrepresentation of women in skilled craft positions was only one element of a number of considerations that led to the promotion of Ms. Joyce. While I agree with the dissent that an affirmative action program that automatically and blindly promotes those marginally qualified candidates falling within a preferred race or gender category, or that can be equated with a permanent plan of "proportionate representation by race and sex" would violate Title VII, I cannot agree that this is such a case. Rather, as the Court demonstrates, Joyce's sex was simply used as a "plus" factor.

In this case, I am also satisfied that the respondent had a firm basis for adopting an affirmative action program. Although the District Court found no discrimination against women in fact, at the time the affirmative action plan was adopted, there were *no* women in its skilled craft positions. The petitioner concedes that women constituted approximately 5% of the local labor pool of skilled craft workers in 1970. Thus, when compared to the percentage of women in the qualified work force, the statistical disparity would have been sufficient for a prima facie Title VII case brought by unsuccessful women job applicants. See *Teamsters,* 431 U.S., at 342, n. 23, 97 S.Ct., at 1858, n. 23 ("[F]ine tuning of the statistics could not have obscured the glaring absence of minority line drivers * * *. [T]he company's inability to rebut the inference of discrimination came not from a misuse of statistics but from 'the inexorable zero' ").

In sum, I agree that the respondents' affirmative action plan as implemented in this instance with respect to skilled craft positions satisfies the requirements of *Weber* and of *Wygant.* Accordingly, I concur in the judgment of the Court.

JUSTICE WHITE, dissenting.

I agree with Parts I and II of Justice Scalia's dissenting opinion. Although I do not join Part III, I also would overrule *Weber.* My understanding of *Weber* was, and is, that the employer's plan did not violate Title VII because it was designed to remedy intentional and systematic exclusion of blacks by the employer and the unions from certain job categories. That is how I understood the phrase "traditionally segregated jobs" we used in that case. The Court now interprets it to mean nothing more than a manifest imbalance between one identifiable group and another in an employer's labor force. As so interpreted, that case, as well as today's decision, as Justice Scalia so well demonstrates, is a perversion of Title VII. I would overrule *Weber* and reverse the judgment below.

JUSTICE SCALIA, with whom THE CHIEF JUSTICE joins, and with whom JUSTICE WHITE joins in Parts I and II, dissenting.

With a clarity which, had it not proven so unavailing, one might well recommend as a model of statutory draftsmanship, Title VII of the Civil Rights Act of 1964 declares:

"It shall be an unlawful employment practice for an employer—

"(1) to fail or refuse to hire or to discharge any individual, or otherwise to discriminate against any individual with respect to his compensation, terms, conditions, or privileges of employment, because of such individual's race, color, religion, sex, or national origin; or

"(2) to limit, segregate, or classify his employees or applicants for employment in any way which would deprive or tend to deprive any individual of employment opportunities or otherwise adversely affect his status as an employee, because of such individual's race, color, religion, sex, or national origin." 42 U.S.C. § 2000e–2(a).

The Court today completes the process of converting this from a guarantee that race or sex will *not* be the basis for employment determinations, to a guarantee that it often *will.* Ever so subtly, without even alluding to the last obstacles preserved by earlier opinions that we now push out of our path, we effectively replace the goal of a discrimination-free society with the quite incompatible goal of proportionate representation by race and by sex in the workplace. Part I of this dissent will describe the nature of the plan that the Court approves, and its effect upon this petitioner. Part II will discuss prior holdings that are tacitly overruled, and prior distinctions that are disregarded. Part III will describe the engine of discrimination we have finally completed.

I

On October 16, 1979, the County of Santa Clara adopted an Affirmative Action Program (County plan) which sought the "attainment of a County work force whose composition * * * includes women, disabled persons and ethnic minorities in a ratio in all job categories that reflects their distribution in the Santa Clara County area work force." In order to comply with the County plan and various requirements imposed by federal and state agencies, the Transportation Agency adopted, effective December 18, 1978, the Equal Employment Opportunity Affirmative Action Plan (Agency plan or plan) at issue here. Its stated long-range goal was the same as the County plan's: "to attain a work force whose composition in all job levels and major job classifications approximates the distribution of women, minority and handicapped persons in the Santa Clara County work force." The plan called for the establishment of a procedure by which Division Directors would review the ethnic and sexual composition of their work forces whenever they sought to fill a vacancy, which procedure was expected to include "a requirement that Division Directors indicate why they did *not* select minorities, women and handicapped persons if such persons were on the list of eligibles considered and if the Division had an underrepresentation of such persons in the job classification being filled."

Several salient features of the plan should be noted. Most importantly, the plan's purpose was assuredly not to remedy prior sex discrimination by the Agency. It could not have been, because there was no prior sex discrimination to remedy. The majority, in cataloguing the Agency's alleged misdeeds, neglects to mention the District Court's finding that the Agency "has not discriminated in the past, and does not discriminate in the present against women in regard to employment opportunities in general and promotions in particular." This finding was not disturbed by the Ninth Circuit.

Not only was the plan not directed at the results of past sex discrimination by the Agency, but its objective was not to achieve the state of affairs that this Court has dubiously assumed would result from an absence of discrimination—an overall work force "more or less representative of the racial and ethnic composition of the population in the community." Teamsters v. United States. Rather, the oft-stated goal was to mirror the racial and sexual composition of the entire county labor force, not merely in the Agency work force as a whole, but in each and every individual job category at the Agency. In a discrimination-free world, it would obviously be a statistical oddity for every job category to match the racial and sexual composition of even that portion of the county work force *qualified* for that job; it would be utterly miraculous for each of them to match, as the plan expected, the composition of the *entire* work force. Quite obviously, the plan did not seek to replicate what a lack of discrimination would produce, but rather imposed racial and sexual tailoring that would, in defiance of normal expectations and laws of probability, give each protected racial and sexual group a governmentally determined "proper" proportion of each job category.

That the plan was not directed at remedying or eliminating the effects of past discrimination is most clearly illustrated by its description of what it regarded as the *"Factors Hindering Goal Attainment"*— i.e., the existing impediments to the racially and sexually representative work force that it pursued. The plan noted that it would be "difficult," to attain its objective of across-the-board statistical parity in at least some job categories, because

* * *

* * * the qualifications and desires of women may fail to match the Agency's Platonic ideal of a work force. The plan concluded from this, of course, not that the ideal should be reconsidered, but that its attainment could not be immediate. It would, in any event, be rigorously pursued, by giving "special consideration to Affirmative Action requirements in every individual hiring action pertaining to positions where minorities, women and handicapped persons continue to be underrepresented." [1]

Finally, the one message that the plan unmistakably communicated was that concrete results were expected, and supervisory personnel would be evaluated on the basis of the affirmative-action numbers they produced. The plan's implementation was expected to "result in a statistically measurable yearly improvement in the hiring, training and promotion of minorities, women and handicapped persons in the major job classifications utilized by the Agency where these groups are underrepresented." Its Preface declared that "[t]he degree to which each Agency Division *attains the Plan's objectives* will provide a direct measure of that Division Director's personal commitment to the EEO Policy," and the plan itself repeated that "[t]he degree to which each Division *attains the Agency Affirmative Action employment goals* will provide a measure of that Director's commitment and effectiveness in carrying out the Division's EEO Affirmative Action requirements." As noted earlier, supervisors were reminded of the need to give attention to affirmative action in every employment decision, and to explain their reasons for *failing* to hire women and minorities whenever there was an opportunity to do so.

1. This renders utterly incomprehensible the majority's assertion that "the Agency acknowledged that [its long-term goal] could not by itself necessarily justify taking into account the sex of applicants for positions in all job categories."

The petitioner in the present case, Paul E. Johnson, had been an employee of the Agency since 1967, coming there from a private company where he had been a road dispatcher for seventeen years. He had first applied for the position of Road Dispatcher at the Agency in 1974, coming in second. Several years later, after a reorganization resulted in a downgrading of his Road Yard Clerk II position, in which Johnson "could see no future," he requested and received a voluntary demotion from Road Yard Clerk II to Road Maintenance Worker, to increase his experience and thus improve his chances for future promotion. When the Road Dispatcher job next became vacant, in 1979, he was the leading candidate—and indeed was assigned to work out of class full-time in the vacancy, from September of 1979 until June of 1980. There is no question why he did not get the job.

The fact of discrimination against Johnson is much clearer, and its degree more shocking, than the majority and Justice O'Connor's concurring opinion would suggest—largely because neither of them recites a single one of the District Court findings that govern this appeal, relying instead upon portions of the transcript which those findings implicitly rejected, and even upon a document (favorably comparing Joyce to Johnson), that was prepared *after* Joyce was selected. It is worth mentioning, for example, the trier of fact's determination that, if the Affirmative Action Coordinator had not intervened, "the decision as to whom to promote * * * would have been made by [the Road Operations Division Director]," who had recommended that Johnson be appointed to the position.[2] Likewise, the even more extraordinary findings that James Graebner, the Agency Director who made the appointment, "did not inspect the applications and related examination records of either [Paul Johnson] or Diane Joyce before making his decision," and indeed "did little or nothing to inquire into the results of the interview process and conclusions which [were] described as of critical importance to the selection process." In light of these determinations, it is impossible to believe (or to think that the District Court believed) Graebner's self-serving statements relied upon by the majority and concurrence * * *. It was evidently enough for Graebner to know that both candidates (in the words of Johnson's counsel, to which Graebner

---

2. The character of this intervention, and the reasoning behind it, was described by the Agency Director in his testimony at trial:

"Q. How did you happen to become involved in this particular promotional opportunity?

"A. I * * * became aware that there was a difference of opinion between specifically the Road Operations people [Mr. Shields] and the Affirmative Action Director [Mr. Morton] as to the desirability of certain of the individuals to be promoted.

* * *

"* * * Mr. Shields felt that Mr. Johnson should be appointed to that position.

"Q. Mr. Morton felt that Diane Joyce should be appointed?

"A. Mr. Morton was less interested in the particular individual; he felt that this was an opportunity for us to take a step toward meeting our affirmative action goals, and because there was only one person on the [eligibility] list who was one of the protected groups, he felt that this afforded us an opportunity to meet those goals through the appointment of that member of a protected group."

assented) "met the M.Q.'s, the minimum. Both were minimally qualified." When asked whether he had "any basis," ibid., for determining whether one of the candidates was more qualified than the other, Graebner candidly answered, "No * * *. As I've said, they both appeared, and my conversations with people tended to corroborate, that they were both capable of performing the work."

After a two-day trial, the District Court concluded that Diane Joyce's gender was *"the determining factor"* in her selection for the position. Specifically, it found that "[b]ased upon the examination results and the departmental interview, [Mr. Johnson] was more qualified for the position of Road Dispatcher than Diane Joyce," that "[b]ut for [Mr. Johnson's] sex, male, he would have been promoted to the position of Road Dispatcher," and that "[b]ut for Diane Joyce's sex, female, she would not have been appointed to the position * * *." The Ninth Circuit did not reject these factual findings as clearly erroneous, nor could it have done so on the record before us. We are bound by those findings under Federal Rule of Civil Procedure 52(a).

II

The most significant proposition of law established by today's decision is that racial or sexual discrimination is permitted under Title VII when it is intended to overcome the effect, not of the employer's own discrimination, but of societal attitudes that have limited the entry of certain races, or of a particular sex, into certain jobs. Even if the societal attitudes in question consisted exclusively of conscious discrimination by other employers, this holding would contradict a decision of this Court rendered only last Term. Wygant v. Jackson Board of Education, 476 U.S. 267, 106 S.Ct. 1842, 90 L.Ed.2d 260 (1986), held that the objective of remedying societal discrimination cannot prevent remedial affirmative action from violating the Equal Protection Clause. While Mr. Johnson does not advance a constitutional claim here, it is most unlikely that Title VII was intended to place a *lesser* restraint on discrimination by public actors than is established by the Constitution. The Court has already held that the prohibitions on discrimination in Title VI, are at least as stringent as those in the Constitution. See Regents of the University of California v. Bakke, 438 U.S. 265, 286–287, 98 S.Ct. 2733, 2746–2747, 57 L.Ed.2d 750 (1978) (opinion of Powell, J.) (Title VI embodies constitutional restraints on discrimination); id., at 329–340, 98 S.Ct. at 2768 (opinion of Brennan, White, Marshall, and Blackmun, JJ.) (same); id., at 416, 98 S.Ct., at 2812 (opinion of Stevens, J., joined by Burger, C.J., and Stewart and Rehnquist, JJ.) (Title VI "has independent force, with language and emphasis *in addition* to that found in the Constitution") (emphasis added). There is no good reason to think that Title VII, in this regard, is any different from Title VI.[3]

---

3. To support the proposition that Title VII is more narrow than Title VI, the majority repeats the reasons for the dictum to that effect set forth in Steelworkers v. Weber—a case which, as Justice O'Connor points out, could reasonably be read as

Because, therefore, those justifications (e.g., the remedying of past societal wrongs) that are inadequate to insulate discriminatory action from the racial discrimination prohibitions of the Constitution are also inadequate to insulate it from the racial discrimination prohibitions of Title VII; and because the portions of Title VII at issue here treat race and sex equivalently; *Wygant,* which dealt with race discrimination, is fully applicable precedent, and is squarely inconsistent with today's decision.[4]

Likewise on the assumption that the societal attitudes relied upon by the majority consist of conscious discrimination by employers, today's decision also disregards the limitations carefully expressed in last Term's opinions in Sheet Metal Workers v. EEOC, 478 U.S. 421, 106 S.Ct. 3019, 92 L.Ed.2d 344 (1986). While those limitations were dicta, it is remarkable to see them so readily (and so silently) swept away. The question in *Sheet Metal Workers* was whether the remedial provision of Title VII, 42 U.S.C. § 2000e–5(g), empowers courts to order race-conscious relief for persons who were not identifiable victims of discrimination. Six members of this Court concluded that it does, *under narrowly confined circumstances.* The plurality opinion for four justices found that race-conscious relief could be ordered at least when "an employer or labor union has engaged in persistent or egregious discrimination, or where necessary to dissipate the lingering effects of pervasive discrimination." Justice Powell concluded that race-conscious relief can be ordered "in cases involving particularly egregious conduct," and Justice

consistent with the constitutional standards of *Wygant.* Those reasons are unpersuasive, consisting only of the existence in Title VII of 42 U.S.C. § 2000e–2(j) (the implausibility of which, as a *restriction* upon the scope of Title VII, was demonstrated by Chief Justice Rehnquist's literally unanswered *Weber* dissent) and the fact that Title VI pertains to recipients of federal funds while Title VII pertains to employers generally. The latter fact, while true and perhaps interesting, is not conceivably a reason for giving to virtually identical categorical language the interpretation, in one case, that intentional discrimination is forbidden, and, in the other case, that it is not.

4. Justice O'Connor's concurrence at least makes an attempt to bring this term into accord with last. Under her reading of Title VII, an employer may discriminate affirmatively, so to speak, if he has a "firm basis" for believing that he might be guilty of (nonaffirmative) discrimination under the Act, and if his action is designed to remedy that suspected prior discrimination. This is something of a half-way house between leaving employers scot-free to discriminate against disfavored groups, as the majority opinion does, and prohibit-

ing discrimination, as do the words of Title VII. In the present case, although the District Court found that in fact no sex discrimination existed, Justice O'Connor would find a "firm basis" for the agency's *belief* that sex discrimination existed in the "inexorable zero": the complete absence, prior to Diane Joyce, of any women in the Agency's skilled positions. There are two problems with this: First, even positing a "firm basis" for the Agency's belief in prior discrimination, as I have discussed earlier the plan was patently not *designed to remedy* that prior discrimination, but rather to establish a sexually representative work force. Second, even an absolute zero is not "inexorable." While it may inexorably provide "firm basis" for belief in the mind of an outside observer, it cannot conclusively establish such a belief *on the employer's part,* since he may be aware of the particular reasons that account for the zero. That is quite likely to be the case here, given the nature of the jobs we are talking about, and the list of *"Factors Hindering Goal Attainment"* recited by the Agency plan. See supra, at 1467. The question is in any event one of fact, which, if it were indeed relevant to the outcome, would require a remand to the District Court rather than an affirmance.

White similarly limited his approval of race-conscious remedies to "unusual cases." There is no sensible basis for construing Title VII to permit employers to engage in race- or sex-conscious employment practices that courts would be forbidden from ordering them to engage in following a judicial finding of discrimination. * * *

The Agency here was not seeking to remedy discrimination—much less "unusual" or "egregious" discrimination. * * *.

In fact, however, today's decision goes well beyond merely allowing racial or sexual discrimination in order to eliminate the effects of prior societal *discrimination*. The majority opinion often uses the phrase "traditionally segregated job category" to describe the evil against which the plan is legitimately (according to the majority) directed. As originally used in Steelworkers v. Weber, that phrase described skilled jobs from which employers and unions had systematically and intentionally excluded black workers—traditionally segregated jobs, that is, in the sense of conscious, exclusionary discrimination. But that is assuredly not the sense in which the phrase is used here. It is absurd to think that the nationwide failure of road maintenance crews, for example, to achieve the Agency's ambition of 36.4% female representation is attributable primarily, if even substantially, to systematic exclusion of women eager to shoulder pick and shovel. It is a "traditionally segregated job category" *not* in the *Weber* sense, but in the sense that, because of longstanding social attitudes, it has not been regarded *by women themselves* as desirable work. Or as the majority opinion puts the point, quoting approvingly the Court of Appeals: " 'A plethora of proof is hardly necessary to show that women are generally underrepresented in such positions and that strong social pressures weigh against their participation.' " Given this meaning of the phrase, it is patently false to say that "[t]he requirement that the 'manifest imbalance' relate to a 'traditionally segregated job category' provides assurance that sex or race will be taken into account in a manner consistent with Title VII's purpose of eliminating the effects of employment discrimination." There are, of course, those who believe that the social attitudes which cause women themselves to avoid certain jobs and to favor others are as nefarious as conscious, exclusionary discrimination. Whether or not that is so (and there is assuredly no consensus on the point equivalent to our national consensus against intentional discrimination), the two phenomena are certainly distinct. And it is the alteration of social attitudes, rather than the elimination of discrimination, which today's decision approves as justification for state-enforced discrimination. This is an enormous expansion, undertaken without the slightest justification or analysis.

III

I have omitted from the foregoing discussion the most obvious respect in which today's decision o'erleaps, without analysis, a barrier that was thought still to be overcome. In *Weber*, this Court held that a private-sector affirmative-action training program that overtly discriminated against white applicants did not violate Title VII. However, although the majority does not advert to the fact, until today the applicability of *Weber* to public employers remained an open question. In *Weber* itself, and in later decisions, see Firefighters v. Cleveland; *Wygant;* this Court has repeatedly emphasized that *Weber* involved only a private employer. This distinction between public and private employers has several possible justifications. *Weber* rested in part on the assertion that the 88th Congress did not wish to intrude too deeply into private employment decisions. Whatever validity that assertion may have with respect to private employers (and I think it negligible), it has none with respect to public employers or to the 92d Congress that brought them within Title VII. See Equal Employment Opportunity Act of 1972, Pub.L. 92–261, § 2, 86 Stat. 103, 42 U.S.C. § 2000e(a). Another reason for limiting *Weber* to private employers is that state agencies, unlike private actors, are subject to the Fourteenth Amendment. As noted earlier, it would be strange to construe Title VII to permit discrimination by public actors that the Constitution forbids.

In truth, however, the language of 42 U.S.C. § 2000e–2 draws no distinction between private and public employers, and the only good reason for creating such a distinction would be to limit the damage of *Weber*. It would be better, in my view, to acknowledge that case as fully applicable precedent, and to use the Fourteenth Amendment ramifications—which *Weber* did not address and which are implicated for the first time here—as the occasion for reconsidering and overruling it. It is well to keep in mind just how thoroughly *Weber* rewrote the statute it purported to construe. The language of that statute, as quoted at the outset of this dissent, is unambiguous: it is an unlawful employment practice "to fail or refuse to hire or to discharge any individual, or otherwise to discriminate against any individual with respect to his compensation, terms, conditions, or privileges of employment, because of such individual's race, color, religion, sex, or national origin." *Weber* disregarded the text of the statute, invoking instead its " 'spirit,' " and "practical and equitable [considerations] only partially perceived, if perceived at all, by the 88th Congress". * * * In effect, *Weber* held that the legality of intentional discrimination by private employers against certain disfavored groups or individuals is to be judged not by Title VII but by a judicially crafted code of conduct, the contours of which are determined by no discernible standard, aside from (as the dissent convincingly demonstrated) the divination of congressional "purposes" belied by the face of the statute and by its legislative history. We have been recasting that self-promulgated code of conduct ever since—and what it has led us to today adds to the reasons for abandoning it.

The majority's response to this criticism of *Weber,* asserts that, since "Congress has not amended the statute to reject our construction, * * * we * * * may assume that our interpretation was correct." This assumption, which frequently haunts our opinions, should be put to rest. It is based, to begin with, on the patently false premise that the correctness of statutory construction is to be measured by what the current Congress desires, rather than by what the law as enacted meant. To make matters worse, it assays the current Congress' desires *with respect to the particular provision in isolation,* rather than (the way the provision was originally enacted) as part of a total legislative package containing many *quids pro quo.* Whereas the statute as originally proposed may have presented to the enacting Congress a question such as "Should hospitals be required to provide medical care for indigent patients, with federal subsidies to offset the cost?," the question theoretically asked of the later Congress, in order to establish the "correctness" of a judicial interpretation that the statute provides no subsidies, is simply "Should the medical care that hospitals are required to provide for indigent patients be federally subsidized?" Hardly the same question—and many of those legislators who accepted the subsidy provisions in order to gain the votes necessary for enactment of the care requirement would not vote for the subsidy in isolation, now that an unsubsidized care requirement is, thanks to the judicial opinion, safely on the books. But even accepting the flawed premise that the intent of the current Congress, with respect to the provision in isolation, is determinative, one must ignore rudimentary principles of political science to draw any conclusions regarding that intent from the *failure* to enact legislation. The "complicated check on legislation," The Federalist No. 62, p. 378 (C. Rossiter ed. 1961), erected by our Constitution creates an inertia that makes it impossible to assert with any degree of assurance that congressional failure to act represents (1) approval of the status quo, as opposed to (2) inability to agree upon how to alter the status quo, (3) unawareness of the status quo, (4) indifference to the status quo, or even (5) political cowardice. It is interesting to speculate on how the principle that congressional inaction proves judicial correctness would apply to another issue in the civil rights field, the liability of municipal corporations under § 1983. In 1961, we held that that statute did not reach municipalities. See Monroe v. Pape, 365 U.S. 167, 187, 81 S.Ct. 473, 484, 5 L.Ed.2d 492 (1961). Congress took no action to overturn our decision, but we ourselves did, in Monell v. New York City Dept. of Social Services, 436 U.S. 658, 663, 98 S.Ct. 2018, 2021–22, 56 L.Ed.2d 611 (1978). On the majority's logic, *Monell* was wrongly decided, since Congress' seventeen years of silence established that *Monroe* had not "misperceived the political will," and one could therefore "assume that [*Monroe's*] interpretation was correct." On the other hand, nine years have now gone by since *Monell,* and Congress *again* has not amended § 1983. Should we now "assume that [*Monell's*] interpretation was correct"? Rather, I think we should admit that vindication by congressional inaction is a canard.

Justice Stevens' concurring opinion emphasizes "the underlying public interest in 'stability and orderly development of the law,' " that often requires adherence to an erroneous decision. As I have described above, however, today's decision is a demonstration not of stability and order but of the instability and unpredictable expansion which the substitution of judicial improvisation for statutory text has produced. For a number of reasons, *stare decisis* ought not to save *Weber*. First, this Court has applied the doctrine of *stare decisis* to civil rights statutes less rigorously than to other laws. See Maine v. Thiboutot, 448 U.S. 1, 33, 100 S.Ct. 2502, 2519, 65 L.Ed.2d 555 (1980) (Powell, J., dissenting); Monroe v. Pape, supra, 365 U.S., at 221–222, 81 S.Ct., at 502–503 (Frankfurter, J., dissenting in part). Second, as Justice Stevens acknowledges in his concurrence, *Weber* was itself a dramatic departure from the Court's prior Title VII precedents, and can scarcely be said to be "so consistent with the warp and woof of civil rights law as to be beyond question." Monell v. New York City Dept. of Social Services. Third, *Weber* was decided a mere seven years ago, and has provided little guidance to persons seeking to conform their conduct to the law, beyond the proposition that Title VII does not mean what it says. Finally, "even under the most stringent test for the propriety of overruling a statutory decision * * * —'that it appear beyond doubt * * * that [the decision] misapprehended the meaning of the controlling provision,' " *Weber* should be overruled.

In addition to complying with the commands of the statute, abandoning *Weber* would have the desirable side-effect of eliminating the requirement of willing suspension of disbelief that is currently a credential for reading our opinions in the affirmative action field—from *Weber* itself, which demanded belief that the corporate employer adopted the affirmative action program "voluntarily," rather than under practical compulsion from government contracting agencies, to *Bakke,* a Title VI case cited as authority by the majority here, which demanded belief that the University of California took race into account as merely one of the many diversities to which it felt it was educationally important to expose its medical students, to today's opinion, which—in the face of a plan obviously designed to force promoting officials to prefer candidates from the favored racial and sexual classes, warning them that their "personal commitment" will be determined by how successfully they "attain" certain numerical goals, and in the face of a particular promotion awarded to the less qualified applicant by an official who "did little or nothing" to inquire into sources "critical" to determining the final candidates' relative qualifications other than their sex—in the face of all this, demands belief that we are dealing here with no more than a program that "merely authorizes that consideration be given to affirmative action concerns when evaluating qualified applicants." Any line of decisions rooted so firmly in naivete must be wrong.

The majority emphasizes, as though it is meaningful, that "*No* persons are automatically excluded from consideration; *all* are able to have their qualifications weighed against those of other applicants." One is reminded of the exchange from Shakespeare's King Henry the Fourth, Part I: "GLENDOWER: I can call Spirits from the vasty Deep.

HOTSPUR: Why, so can I, or so can any man. But will they come when you do call for them?" Act III, Scene I, lines 53–55. Johnson was indeed entitled to have his qualifications weighed against those of other applicants—but more to the point, he was virtually assured that, after the weighing, if there was any minimally qualified applicant from one of the favored groups, he would be rejected.

Similarly hollow is the Court's assurance that we would strike this plan down if it "failed to take distinctions in qualifications into account," because that "would dictate mere blind hiring by the numbers." For what the Court means by "taking distinctions in qualifications into account" consists of no more than eliminating from the applicant pool those who are not even *minimally qualified* for the job. Once that has been done, once the promoting officer assures himself that all the candidates before him are "M.Q.s" (minimally qualifieds), he can then ignore, as the Agency Director did here, how much better than minimally qualified some of the candidates may be, and can proceed to appoint from the pool solely on the basis of race or sex, until the affirmative action "goals" have been reached. The requirement that the employer "take distinctions in qualifications into account" thus turns out to be an assurance, not that candidates' comparative merits will always be considered, but only that none of the successful candidates selected over the others solely on the basis of their race or sex will be utterly unqualified. That may be of great comfort to those concerned with American productivity; and it is undoubtedly effective in reducing the effect of affirmative-action discrimination upon those in the upper strata of society, who (unlike road maintenance workers, for example) compete for employment in professional and semiprofessional fields where, for many reasons, including most notably the effects of past discrimination, the numbers of "M.Q." applicants from the favored groups are substantially less. But I fail to see how it has any relevance to whether selecting among final candidates solely on the basis of race or sex is permissible under Title VII, which prohibits discrimination on the basis of race or sex.[5]

Today's decision does more, however, than merely reaffirm *Weber,* and more than merely extend it to public actors. It is impossible not to be aware that the practical effect of our holding is to accomplish *de facto* what the law—in language even plainer than that ignored in *Weber,* see 42 U.S.C. § 2000e–2(j)—forbids anyone from accomplishing

---

5. In a footnote purporting to respond to this dissent's (nonexistent) "predict[ion] that today's decision will loose a flood of 'less qualified' minorities and women upon the workforce," ante, at n. 17, the majority accepts the contention of the American Society for Personnel Administration that there is no way to determine who is the best qualified candidate for a job such as Road Dispatcher. This effectively constitutes appellate reversal of a finding of fact by the District Court in the present case ("plaintiff was more qualified for the position of Road Dispatcher than Diane Joyce," App. to Pet. for Cert. 12a). More importantly, it has staggering implications for future Title VII litigation, since the most common reason advanced for failing to hire a member of a protected group is the superior qualification of the hired individual. I am confident, however, that the Court considers this argument no more enduring than I do.

de jure: in many contexts it effectively *requires* employers, public as well as private, to engage in intentional discrimination on the basis of race or sex. This Court's prior interpretations of Title VII, especially the decision in Griggs v. Duke Power Co., subject employers to a potential Title VII suit whenever there is a noticeable imbalance in the representation of minorities or women in the employer's work force. Even the employer who is confident of ultimately prevailing in such a suit must contemplate the expense and adverse publicity of a trial, because the extent of the imbalance, and the "job relatedness" of his selection criteria, are questions of fact to be explored through rebuttal and counter-rebuttal of a "prima facie case" consisting of no more than the showing that the employer's selection process "selects those from the protected class at a 'significantly' lesser rate than their counter-parts." B. Schlei & P. Grossman, Employment Discrimination Law 91 (2d ed. 1983). If, however, employers are free to discriminate through affirmative action, without fear of "reverse discrimination" suits by their nonminority or male victims, they are offered a threshold defense against Title VII liability premised on numerical disparities. Thus, after today's decision the *failure* to engage in reverse discrimination is economic folly, and arguably a breach of duty to shareholders or taxpayers, wherever the cost of anticipated Title VII litigation exceeds the cost of hiring less capable (though still minimally capable) workers. (This situation is more likely to obtain, of course, with respect to the least skilled jobs—perversely creating an incentive to discriminate against precisely those members of the nonfavored groups *least* likely to have profited from societal discrimination in the past.) It is predicta-ble, moreover, that this incentive will be greatly magnified by economic pressures brought to bear by government contracting agencies upon employers who refuse to discriminate in the fashion we have now approved. A statute designed to establish a color-blind and gender-blind workplace has thus been converted into a powerful engine of racism and sexism, not merely *permitting* intentional race- and sex-based discrimination, but often making it, through operation of the legal system, practically compelled.

It is unlikely that today's result will be displeasing to politically elected officials, to whom it provides the means of quickly accommodat-ing the demands of organized groups to achieve concrete, numerical improvement in the economic status of particular constituencies. Nor will it displease the world of corporate and governmental employers (many of whom have filed briefs as *amici* in the present case, all on the side of Santa Clara) for whom the cost of hiring less qualified workers is often substantially less—and infinitely more predictable—than the cost of litigating Title VII cases and of seeking to convince federal agencies by nonnumerical means that no discrimination exists. In fact, the only losers in the process are the Johnsons of the country, for whom Title VII has been not merely repealed but actually inverted. The irony is that these individuals—predominantly unknown, unaffluent, unorganized—suffer this injustice at the hands of a Court fond of thinking itself the champion of the politically impotent. I dissent.

NOTES AND PROBLEMS FOR DISCUSSION

1. Should the constitutional and statutory standards applicable to a public employer's voluntary affirmative action efforts be identical? Is it significant that the requirements of a prima facie case of discrimination under these separate causes of action are not the same? Compare the impact-based Title VII claim in *Hazlewood, supra* at 5 n. 299 with the requirement in *Feeney, supra,* at 813, that a prima facie showing in a constitutional case include proof of intent. What about the references by Justices O'Connor and Scalia to Title VII? For an argument rejecting distinctions between the statutory and constitutional standards for judging affirmative action, see Rutherglen and Ortiz, Affirmative Action Under The Constitution And Title VII: From Confusion To Convergence, 35 UCLA L.Rev. 467 (1988).

If you believe that the constitutional and statutory standards for public sector affirmative action should be identical, does this mean that the constitutional test applied to a public employer's voluntary plan should also be identical to the statutory standard applied to a private employer's voluntary plan? Did Congress intend to impose different requirements under Title VII upon public, as opposed to private employers? See generally, Schwartz, The 1986 and 1987 Affirmative Action Cases: It's All Over But The Shouting, 86 Mich.L.Rev. 524, 541–542 (1987).

2. Since the ruling in *Johnson* permits an employer to use its affirmative action plan as a defense or "shield" to a non-preferred individual's "reverse" discrimination claim, should a preferred employee be able to assert the affirmative action plan as a "sword" when the employer seeks to discharge or lay off that employee? In terms of the issue raised in Note 1, should the standards set forth in *Wygant* control this issue? In LIAO v. TENNESSEE VALLEY AUTHORITY, 867 F.2d 1366 (11th Cir.1989), a woman who had been hired pursuant to a voluntarily adopted affirmative action plan was laid off while her two male counterparts were retained. The employer asserted that the two males had more expertise than the plaintiff. She contended that the failure to give her a preference against layoff constituted a violation of the affirmative action plan and, therefore, a violation of Title VII. The trial court, relying on *Johnson,* agreed with the plaintiff's analysis and ruled in her favor. It concluded that the defendant was obliged to adhere to its affirmative action plan and that its failure to do so constituted a violation of Title VII. 658 F.Supp. 1554 (N.D.Ala.1987). The Eleventh Circuit reversed, ruling that while cases such as *Weber* and *Johnson* stated that an employer was *permitted* to implement a voluntary affirmative action plan, these cases did not also hold that failure to abide by the terms of such a plan constituted a *per se* violation of Title VII. Failure to grant a preference pursuant to a voluntarily adopted affirmative action plan, without independent evidence of either disparate treatment or disproportionate impact, the appellate court reasoned, did not constitute a Title VII violation. The court also noted that it was unclear as to whether the employer had even violated the terms of the affirmative action plan, since the plan appeared to require preferences only as to hiring and not as to layoff or termination. Nevertheless, the court concluded, it was unnecessary to resolve this question since even if the plan was read to create an implied obligation to protect recently hired minorities from termination, the violation

of the plan, by itself, did not trigger a Title VII violation. Thus, the court held, since the evidence could not support a finding that the defendant had otherwise engaged in unlawful discrimination, the defendant was entitled to judgment as a matter of law. Should the "sword" theory also be rejected where a female plaintiff contends that, in violation of the employer's voluntarily adopted sex-based affirmative action plan, she was not given preferential consideration in hiring? Several courts have held that while failure to live up to the terms of an affirmative action plan is not a *per se* violation of Title VII, evidence of such a failure to conform could be relevant to the question of the employer's discriminatory intent. See Gonzales v. Police Dept., 901 F.2d 758 (9th Cir. 1990); Yatvin v. Madison Metropolitan School District, 840 F.2d 412 (7th Cir.1988); Craik v. Minnesota State University Bd., 731 F.2d 465 (8th Cir.1984).

3. Suppose a university determines that the salaries of its female faculty members are significantly less than those of its male faculty members. It then decides to implement an affirmative action plan to eliminate this differential by creating a compensation scheme that provides each woman faculty member with a $6000 increase in salary. As a result of this scheme, Prof. Amy Michel receives a higher salary than Prof. Richard Winfield, even though both teach in the same department, hold the same academic rank, have essentially identical credentials and have worked at the university for the same length of time. Does this plan violate Title VII? See Grann v. Madison, 738 F.2d 786 (7th Cir.1984), cert. denied, 469 U.S. 918, 105 S.Ct. 296, 83 L.Ed.2d 231 (1984). What about the Equal Pay Act? See Ende v. Board of Regents, 565 F.Supp. 501 (N.D.Ill.1983).

4. Were the majorities in *Weber* and *Johnson* correct in ruling that the scope of permissible affirmative action can be greater when engaged in on a voluntary basis than when ordered by a trial court after a finding of discrimination? Even though the courts' power to issue affirmative relief is expressly authorized in § 706(g) and the literal language of the Act is, at best, ambiguous as to the permissibility of voluntary affirmative action?

5. Is it clear now what type of factual predicate is required, in the face of a Title VII as opposed to an equal protection challenge, to uphold voluntary affirmative action plans? In light of the findings of the trial court, as discussed by Justice Scalia, on what basis did the majority conclude that, to use the language of *Weber,* the Agency's plan was "designed to eliminate conspicuous * * * imbalance in traditionally segregated job categories"? At first blush, this appears to be the issue that separates Justice O'Connor from the majority. But are they really imposing different requirements? Don't O'Connor and the majority agree that in cases involving jobs that require special training, as in the instant case, the appropriate comparison populations for the purpose of determining that imbalance are the employer's work force and the pool of qualified minority or female workers? And isn't the significant statistical difference between these two figures the reason why O'Connor agreed with the majority that the Agency's plan did not violate Title VII? Nevertheless, O'Connor stated that she could not join in the majority's opinion because it fashioned an "expansive and ill-defined" standard for determining the validity of public employer affirmative action programs. She maintained that her analysis was different in that she would require a demonstration of evidence sufficient to establish a prima facie case while the majority explicitly declined to require evidence sufficient to establish a prima facie case. This wordsmanship notwithstanding, is there any difference between these two positions? Particularly when both would agree that affirmative relief applicable to entry

level positions could be justified by evidence of an imbalance between the defendant's work force and the general minority or female working population? Can Justice O'Connor's reliance on prima facie case terminology perhaps be explained as her desire to be consistent with her frequently quoted language in *Wygant* to the effect that affirmative relief can never be justified simply on the basis of societal discrimination? Yet, if voluntary affirmative action can be justified on the basis of traditional patterns of segregation, and these patterns can be established by evidence of a statistical imbalance that could be the function of societal, rather than defendant-specific discrimination, isn't it fair to say that voluntary affirmative action designed to remedy societal discrimination may satisfy the requirements of Title VII even though it would not pass constitutional muster? In JANOWIAK v. CORPORATE CITY OF SOUTH BEND, 836 F.2d 1034 (7th Cir.1984), cert. denied, 489 U.S. 1051, 109 S.Ct. 1310, 103 L.Ed.2d 579 (1989), the Seventh Circuit interpreted *Johnson* to require statistical evidence comparing the percentage of minorities in the employer's work force with the percentage of minorities in the qualified area labor pool, at least where the level of black representation in the defendant's workforce was greater than the "inexorable zero." Accordingly, it struck down (under Title VII) the city's affirmative action plan that had been justified on the basis of a statistical disparity between the percentage of blacks in the police and fire department and the percentage of blacks in the general population. The court added that the same type of statistical comparison was required by the Court's opinion in *Wygant* to survive constitutional scrutiny. It therefore also found that the affirmative action plan violated the Equal Protection Clause of the Fourteenth Amendment. For more on this issue, see Selig, Affirmative Action In Employment: The Legacy of A Supreme Court Majority, 63 Ind.L.J. 301 (1987).

6. Justice Scalia is particularly concerned that the long range goal of the Agency's plan was to create a condition that would not exist in a discrimination-free society—i.e., perfect gender and racial balance in all job classifications. Is this a relevant consideration? What does this say about his and the other Justices' views about the appropriate long and short term goals of Title VII? For a detailed discussion of an alternative vision of Title VII, see Friedman, Redefining Equality, Discrimination, and Affirmative Action Under Title VII: The Access Principle, 65 Texas L.Rev. 41 (1986).

7. As mentioned in Note 5 after *Local 28*, *supra*, at 1065, it is unclear whether Congress intended the 1991 Civil Rights Act to alter the manner in which the Supreme Court has construed Title VII to apply to voluntary affirmative action. You will recall that § 107 of the 1991 law substantially reversed the Court's ruling in *Price Waterhouse* concerning the treatment of mixed motive employment practices. Under this section of the statute, if sex, race, or any other proscribed classification is shown to have been a motivating factor in the decisionmaking process, the defendant will be found to have violated the Act. Voluntarily adopted affirmative action plans, by definition, take race or sex into account. Thus, since § 116 of the 1991 statute preserves affirmative action plans that are in accord with "the law", if "the law" includes § 107 of the 1991 Act, the new statute may have a devastating effect on the continued viability of voluntary affirmative action plans under Title VII.

Part V

THE PRESIDENTIAL RESPONSE TO DISCRIMINATION: EXECUTIVE ORDERS

Over the past four decades, U.S. Presidents, beginning with Franklin D. Roosevelt in 1941, have issued Executive Orders designed to eliminate employment discrimination by the federal government and private employers who have contracts with the federal government, or their subcontractors. The most comprehensive current Order is Executive Order No. 11246,[a] as amended by Order No. 11375 [b] and No. 12086,[c] which imposes nondiscrimination and affirmative action obligations on federal government contractors and their subcontractors with respect to race, color, religion, national origin and sex.[d] These dual obligations are contained within an equal opportunity clause that the Order requires all contracting federal agencies to include in their contracts with private employers. The Order also assigns to the Secretary of Labor the task of administering and enforcing its provisions and the authority to promulgate rules and regulations deemed necessary to achieve its purposes. The Secretary has delegated this responsibility to the Office of Federal Contract Compliance Programs (OFCCP),[e] which has issued an extensive body of regulations [f] to implement the requirements of the Order.

The OFCCP regulations provide that all contracts and subcontracts exceeding $10,000 must contain an equal opportunity clause that prohibits the contractors from discriminating and requires them to take affirmative action to ensure against discrimination on the basis of race, color, religion, sex and national origin. Contractors and subcontractors having 50 or more employees and a nonconstruction prime contract or

---

[a] 30 Fed.Reg. 12319, 3 C.F.R. § 339 (1965).

[b] 32 Fed.Reg. 14303, 3 C.F.R. § 684 (1967).

[c] 43 Fed.Reg. 46501 (1978).

[d] Executive Order No. 11478, 34 Fed.Reg. 12985, 3 C.F.R. § 841 (1969), declares that it is the policy of the federal government to prohibit employment discrimination in each executive department and agency based on race, color, religion, sex, national origin, handicap, or age. It requires all such departments and agencies to establish and maintain an "affirmative program of equal employment opportunity" and di-

rects the EEOC to issue rules and regulations deemed necessary to implement the Order. The extension of Title VII to federal employees by the Equal Employment Opportunity Act of 1972, however, has significantly reduced the importance of this Order. Similarly, the impact of Executive Order No. 11141, 29 Fed.Reg. 2477, 3 C.F.R. § 179 (1964), which states that federal contractors and their subcontractors shall not discriminate on the basis of age, was sharply curtailed by the subsequent enactment of the Age Discrimination in Employment Act.

[e] 41 C.F.R. § 60–1.2 (1981).

[f] 41 C.F.R. § 60–1 et seq. (1981).

1219

subcontract worth $50,000 or more also must develop a written affirmative action plan for each of their establishments within 120 days of the commencement of the contract. These plans must analyse the utilization of minority workers for each job category and include specific goals and timetables designed to increase minority participation in those categories in which minority workers are currently "underutilized". Underutilization is defined as "having fewer minorities or women in a particular job group than would reasonably be expected by their availability." These nonconstruction contractors also are required to submit annual reports of the results of such programs to the OFCCP.

Construction contractors and subcontractors holding federal or federally assisted contracts in excess of $10,000 also must engage in affirmative action. To obtain such a contract, the applicant's bid must include an affirmative action clause requiring the contractor to comply with goals and timetables for minority and female employment set periodically, according to the geographic location of the construction project, by the OFCCP.[g] Alternatively, if a construction contractor or subcontractor is participating in a "Hometown Plan"[h] approved by the Department of Labor, it must comply with the affirmative action requirements, including goals and timetables, set forth in that plan. And, if the Hometown Plan doesn't extend to women, the contractor must establish its own goals for female representation, at a level at least as high as the goals established by the OFCCP.[i]

Order No. 11246 provides that the Secretary of Labor can receive and investigate complaints by employees and job applicants of a contractor's failure to comply with its nondiscrimination or affirmative action obligations, or engage in such an investigation on its own initiative. The Secretary also is given the authority to impose a variety of penalties for noncompliance, including publishing the names of nonconforming contractors, recommending to the EEOC that proceedings be instituted under Title VII, requesting the Attorney General to bring suit to enforce the Order in cases of actual or threatened substantial violations of the contractual equal opportunity clause, directing the contracting agency to cancel, terminate or suspend the contract or any portion thereof, or debarring the noncomplying contractor from entering into further government contracts until the contractor has satisfied the Secretary that it will abide by the provisions of the Order. The Secretary must make reasonable efforts to secure compliance by conciliation, mediation and persuasion before requesting enforcement action by the Attorney General or cancelling or surrending a contract. A hearing is required before the Secretary can debar a contractor and may be granted before any other sanction is imposed. The OFCCP regulations, pursuant to a delegation of authority by the

---

[g] 41 C.F.R. § 60–4.2, 4.3 (1981).

[h] A program voluntarily developed by unions and contractors, in consultation with minority group representatives, whereby these groups agree to commit themselves to goals and timetables for minority participation in all construction projects in a designated geographical area.

[i] 41 C.F.R. § 60–4.4(b)(1981).

Secretary, set forth in detail the procedures used to administer and enforce the Order.

As a consequence of the emphasis placed on administrative enforcement of Executive Order No. 11246, the courts have played a limited role in defining the equal employment obligations of government contractors. Most of the cases involving the Order have addressed two questions: (1) the availability of a private right of action to enforce the provisions of the Order; and (2) the relationship between the Order and the requirements of Title VII and the Due Process Clause of the Fifth Amendment.

CONTRACTORS ASSOCIATION OF EASTERN PENNSYLVANIA v. SECRETARY OF LABOR

United States Court of Appeals, Third Circuit, 1971.
442 F.2d 159, cert. denied, 404 U.S. 854, 92 S.Ct. 98, 30 L.Ed.2d 95.

* * *

The complaint challenges the validity of the Philadelphia Plan, promulgated by the federal defendants under the authority of Executive Order No. 11246. That Plan is embodied in two orders issued by officials of the United States Department of Labor, dated June 27, 1969 and September 23, 1969, respectively. * * * In summary, they require that bidders on any federal or federally assisted construction contracts for projects in a five-county area around Philadelphia, the estimated total cost of which exceeds $500,000, shall submit an acceptable affirmative action program which includes specific goals for the utilization of minority manpower in six skilled crafts: ironworkers, plumbers and pipefitters, steamfitters, sheetmetal workers, electrical workers, and elevator construction workers.

* * * The Executive Order empowers the Secretary of Labor to issue rules and regulations necessary and appropriate to achieve its purpose. On June 27, 1969 Assistant Secretary of Labor Fletcher issued an order implementing the Executive Order in the five-county Philadelphia area. The order required bidders, prior to the award of contracts, to submit "acceptable affirmative action" programs "which shall include specific goals of minority manpower utilization." The order contained a finding that enforcement of the "affirmative action" requirement of Executive Order No. 11246 had posed special problems in the construction trades. Contractors and subcontractors must hire a new employee complement for each job, and they rely on craft unions as their prime or sole source for labor. The craft unions operate hiring halls. "Because of the exclusionary practices of labor organizations," the order finds "there traditionally has been only a small number of Negroes employed in these * * * trades." The June 27, 1969 order provided that the Area Coordinator of the Office of Federal Contract Compliance, in conjunction with the federal contracting and administering agencies in the Philadelphia area, would determine definite

standards for specific goals in a contractor's affirmative action program. After such standards were determined, each bidder would be required to commit itself to specific goals for minority manpower utilization. The order set forth factors to be considered in determining definite standards, including:

"1) The current extent of minority group participation in the trade.

2) The availability of minority group persons for employment in such trade.

3) The need for training programs in the area and/or the need to assure demand for those in or from existing training programs.

4) The impact of the program upon the existing labor force."

Acting pursuant to the June 29, 1969 order, representatives of the Department of Labor held public hearings in Philadelphia on August 26, 27 and 28, 1969. On September 23, 1969, Assistant Secretary Fletcher made findings with respect to each of the listed factors and ordered that the following ranges be established as the standards for minority manpower utilization for each of the designated trades in the Philadelphia area for the following four years:

| Identification of Trade | Range of Minority Group Employment | | | |
	Until 12/31/70	for 1971	for 1972	for 1973
Ironworkers	5%–9%	11%–15%	16%–20%	22%–26%
Plumbers & Pipefitters	5%–8%	10%–14%	15%–19%	20%–24%
Steamfitters	5%–8%	11%–15%	15%–19%	20%–24%
Sheetmetal workers	4%–8%	9%–13%	14%–18%	19%–23%
Electrical workers	4%–8%	9%–13%	14%–18%	19%–23%
Elevator construction workers	4%–8%	9%–13%	14%–18%	19%–23%

The order of September 23, 1969 specified that on each invitation to bid each bidder would be required to submit an affirmative action program. The order further provided:

"4. No bidder will be awarded a contract unless his affirmative action program contains goals falling within the range set forth * * * above. * * *

* * *

6. The purpose of the contractor's commitment to specific goals as to minority manpower utilization is to meet his affirmative action obligations under the equal opportunity clause of the contract. This commitment is not intended and shall not be used to discriminate against any qualified applicant or employee. Whenever it comes to the bidder's attention that the goals are being used in a discriminatory manner, he must report it to the Area Coordinator of the Office of Federal Contract Compliance of the U. S. Depart-

ment of Labor in order that appropriate sanction proceedings may be instituted.

* * *

8. The bidder agrees to keep such records and file such reports relating to the provisions of this order as shall be required by the contracting or administering agency."

In November, 1969, the General State Authority of the Commonwealth of Pennsylvania issued invitations to bid for the construction of an earth dam on Marsh Creek in Chester County, Pennsylvania. Although this dam is a Commonwealth project, part of the construction cost, estimated at over $3,000,000 is to be funded by federal monies under a program administered by the Department of Agriculture. The Secretary of Agriculture, one of the federal defendants, as a condition for payment of federal financial assistance for the project, required the inclusion in each bid of a Philadelphia Plan Commitment in compliance with the order of September 23, 1969. On November 14, 1969, the General State Authority issued an addendum to the original invitation for bids requiring all bidders to include such a commitment in their bids. It is alleged and not denied that except for the requirement by the Secretary of Agriculture that the Philadelphia Plan Commitment be included, the General State Authority would not have imposed such a requirement on bidders.

The Association consists of more than eighty contractors in the five-county Philadelphia area who regularly employ workers in the six specified crafts, and who collectively perform more than $150,000,000 of federal and federally assisted construction in that area annually. Each of the contractor plaintiffs is a regular bidder on federal and federally assisted construction projects. The complaint was filed prior to the opening of bids on the Marsh Creek dam. It sought injunctive relief against the inclusion of a Philadelphia Plan Commitment requirement in the invitation for bids. By virtue of a stipulation that the General State Authority would issue a new and superseding invitation for bids if the district court held the Plan to be unlawful, the parties agreed that bids could be received without affecting the justiciability of the controversy. Bids were received on January 7, 1970. One of the intervening contractor plaintiffs submitted a low bid and appeared at the time of the district court decision to be entitled to an award of the contract.

The complaints of the Association and the Contractors refer to the fact that the Comptroller General of the United States has opined that the Philadelphia Plan Commitment is illegal and that disbursement of federal funds for the performance of a contract containing such a promise will be treated as unlawful. The plaintiffs point out that the withholding of funds after a contractor has commenced performance would have catastrophic consequences, since contractors depend upon progress payments, and are in no position to complete their contracts without such payments. They allege that the Philadelphia Plan is illegal and void for the following reasons:

1. It is action by the Executive branch not authorized by the constitution or any statute and beyond Executive power.

2. It is inconsistent with Title VII of the Civil Rights Act of 1964.

3. It is inconsistent with Title VI of the Civil Rights Act of 1964.

* * *

5. It is substantively inconsistent with and was not adopted in procedural accordance with Executive Order No. 11246.

6. It violates due process because

    a) it requires contradictory conduct impossible of consistent attainment;

    b) it unreasonably requires contractors to undertake to remedy an evil for which the craft unions, not they, are responsible;

    c) it arbitrarily and without basis in fact singles out the five-county Philadelphia area for discriminatory treatment without adequate basis in fact or law; and

    d) it requires quota hiring in violation of the Fifth Amendment.

* * *

The plaintiffs contend that the Philadelphia Plan is social legislation of local application enacted by the Executive without the benefit of statutory or constitutional authority. They point out, probably correctly, that the Plan imposes on the successful bidder on a project of the Commonwealth of Pennsylvania record keeping and hiring practices which violate Pennsylvania law.[14] If the Plan was adopted pursuant to a valid exercise of presidential power its provisions would, of course, control over local law. But, say the plaintiffs, where there is neither statutory authorization nor constitutional authority for the Executive action, no substantive federal requirements may be imposed upon a contract between the Commonwealth and its contractor.

* * *

The limitations of Executive power have rarely been considered by the courts. One of those rare instances is Youngstown Sheet & Tube Co. v. Sawyer, 343 U.S. 579, 72 S.Ct. 863, 96 L.Ed. 1153 (1952). From the six concurring opinions and one dissenting opinion in that case, the most significant guidance for present purposes may be found in that of Justice Jackson:

---

14. The Pennsylvania Human Relations Act, specifically prohibits an employer from keeping any record of or using any form of application with respect to the race, color, religion, ancestry, sex or national origin of an applicant for employment. The Act also prohibits the use of a quota system for employment based on the same criteria. The record keeping prohibition may be of limited force due to certain requirements of Title VII of the Civil Rights Act of 1964. Moreover, we do not know how the Pennsylvania courts or the Pennsylvania Human Relations Commission would react to a scheme of "benign" quota hiring.

"We may well begin by a somewhat oversimplified grouping of practical situations in which a President may doubt, or others may challenge, his powers, and by distinguishing roughly the legal consequences of this factor of relativity.

1. When the President acts pursuant to an express or implied authorization of Congress, his authority is at its maximum, for it includes all that he possesses in his own right plus all that Congress can delegate. In these circumstances, and in these only, may he be said (for what it may be worth) to personify the federal sovereignty. If his act is held unconstitutional under these circumstances, it usually means that the Federal Government as an undivided whole lacks power. A seizure executed by the President pursuant to an Act of Congress would be supported by the strongest of presumptions and the widest latitude of judicial interpretation, and the burden of persuasion would rest heavily on any who might attack it.

2. When the President acts in absence of either a congressional grant or denial of authority, he can only rely upon his own independent powers, but there is a zone of twilight in which he and Congress may have concurrent authority, or in which its distribution is uncertain. Therefore, congressional inertia, indifference or quiescence may sometimes, at least as a practical matter, enable, if not invite, measures on independent presidential responsibility. In this area, any actual test of power is likely to depend on the imperatives of events and contemporary imponderables rather than on abstract theories of law.

3. When the President takes measures incompatible with the expressed or implied will of Congress, his power is at its lowest ebb, for then he can rely only upon his own constitutional powers minus any constitutional powers of Congress over the matter. Courts can sustain exclusive presidential control in such a case only by disabling the Congress from acting upon the subject. Presidential claim to a power at once so conclusive and preclusive must be scrutinized with caution, for what is at stake is the equilibrium established by our constitutional system."

Plaintiffs contend that the Philadelphia Plan is inconsistent with the will of Congress expressed in several statutes. We deal with these statutory contentions hereinafter. Thus for the moment we may set to one side consideration of Justice Jackson's third category, and turn to category (1), action expressly or impliedly authorized, and category (2), action in which the President has implied power to act in the absence of congressional preemption. To determine into which category the Philadelphia Plan falls a review of Executive Orders in the field of fair employment practices is helpful.

The first such order, Executive Order No. 8802, was signed by President Roosevelt on June 25, 1941. It established in the Office of Production Management a Committee on Fair Employment Practice, and it required that all Government contracting agencies include in all defense contracts a covenant not to discriminate against any worker because of race, creed, color, or national origin. The order contained no specific statutory reference, and describes the action "as a prerequisite to the successful conduct of our national defense production effort." In December 1941 Congress enacted "An Act to expedite the prosecution of the war effort," and on December 27, 1941, pursuant to that Act the President issued Executive Order No. 9001 which granted to the War and Navy Departments and the Maritime Commission broad contracting authority. This order among other provisions stated that a non-discrimination clause would be deemed incorporated by reference in all such contracts. On May 27, 1943, Executive Order No. 8802 was amended by Executive Order No. 9346 which established in the Office for Emergency Management of the Executive Office of the President a Committee on Fair Employment Practice. This order required the antidiscrimination clause in all government contracts rather than in defense contracts only. Still, the order was quite clearly bottomed on the President's war mobilization powers and was by its terms directed toward enhancing the pool of workers available for defense production.

On December 18, 1945, President Truman signed Executive Order No. 9664, which continued the Committee established by Executive Orders Nos. 8802 and 9346 "for the periods and subject to the conditions stated in the National War Agencies Appropriation Act, 1946. On February 2, 1951, the President signed Executive Order No. 10210, which transferred to the Department of Defense the contracting powers referred to in Executive Order No. 9001. The order continued the provision that a non-discrimination clause would be deemed incorporated by reference in all defense contracts. It referenced the First War Powers Act, 1941, as amended. By a subsequent series of Executive Orders, Executive Order No. 10210 was extended to other Government agencies engaged in defense related procurement. On December 3, 1951 the President signed Executive Order No. 10308, creating the Committee on Government Contract Compliance, which was charged with the duty of obtaining compliance with the non-discrimination contract provisions. The statutory authorities referenced in Executive Order No. 10308 are the Defense Production Act of 1950 and 31 U.S.C. § 691.[34] Reference to the Defense Production Act of 1950 shows that the President was still acting, pursuant to his national defense powers, to assure maximum utilization of available manpower.

President Eisenhower on August 13, 1953, by Executive Order No. 10479 revoked Executive Order No. 10308 and transferred the compliance functions of the Committee on Government Contract Compliance to the Government Contract Committee. In this order for the first time there is no mention of defense production. For the first time the Committee is authorized to receive complaints of violations, and to

34. This latter reference is to the source of appropriations for salaries and expenses for committee members and staff. It appears in numerous subsequent Executive Orders, but has no significance other than fiscal.

conduct activities not directly related to federal procurement. On September 3, 1954, by Executive Order No. 10557 the required form of Government contract provision was revised. The new provision was much more specific, required the imposition of the contractor's obligation on his subcontractors, and required the posting of appropriate notices. The Eisenhower orders, while they did not refer to defense production and did authorize the Compliance Committee to encourage nondiscrimination outside the field of Government contracts, were still restricted in direct application to federal government procurement. While the orders do not contain any specific statutory reference other than the appropriations statute, they would seem to be authorized by the broad grant of procurement authority with respect to Titles 40 and 41. No less than in the case of defense procurement it is in the interest of the United States in all procurement to see that its suppliers are not over the long run increasing its costs and delaying its programs by excluding from the labor pool available minority workmen. In the area of Government procurement Executive authority to impose non-discrimination contract provisions falls in Justice Jackson's first category: action pursuant to the express or implied authorization of Congress.

Executive Order No. 10925 signed by President Kennedy on March 6, 1961, among other things enlarged the notice requirements and specified that the President's Committee on Equal Employment Opportunity could by rule, regulation or order impose sanctions for violation. Coverage still extended only to federal government contracts. Significantly for purposes of this case, however, the required contract language was amended to add the provision:

> "The Contractor will take affirmative action to ensure that applicants are employed, and that employees are treated during employment, without regard to their race, creed, color, or national origin."

The Philadelphia Plan is simply a refined approach to this "affirmative action" mandate. Applied to federal procurement the affirmative action clause is supported by the same Presidential procurement authority that supports the non-discrimination clause generally.

The most significant change in the Executive Order program for present purposes occurred on June 22, 1963 when the President signed Executive Order No. 11114, which amended Executive Order No. 10925 by providing that the same non-discrimination contract provisions heretofore required in all federal procurement contracts must also be included in all federally assisted construction contracts. By way of Executive Order No. 11246 issued in 1965, President Johnson transferred to the Secretary of Labor the functions formerly specified in Executive Order Nos. 10925 and 11114, and he continued both the affirmative action requirement and the coverage of federally assisted construction contracts.

While all federal procurement contracts must include an affirmative action covenant, the coverage on federally assisted contracts has been extended to construction contracts only. This choice is significant, for it demonstrates that the Presidents were not attempting by the Executive Order program merely to impose their notions of desirable social legislation on the states wholesale. Rather, they acted in the one area in which discrimination in employment was most likely to affect the cost and the progress of projects in which the federal government had both financial and completion interests. In direct procurement the federal government has a vital interest in assuring that the largest possible pool of qualified manpower be available for the accomplishment of its projects. It has the identical interest with respect to federally assisted construction projects. When the Congress authorizes an appropriation for a program of federal assistance, and authorizes the Executive branch to implement the program by arranging for assistance to specific projects, in the absence of specific statutory regulations it must be deemed to have granted to the President a general authority to act for the protection of federal interests. In the case of Executive Order Nos. 11246 and 11114 three Presidents have acted by analogizing federally assisted construction to direct federal procurement. If such action has not been authorized by Congress (Justice Jackson's first category), at the least it falls within the second category. If no congressional enactments prohibit what has been done, the Executive action is valid. Particularly is this so when Congress, aware of Presidential action with respect to federally assisted construction projects since June of 1963, has continued to make appropriations for such projects. We conclude, therefore, that unless the Philadelphia Plan is prohibited by some other congressional enactment, its inclusion as a pre-condition for federal assistance was within the implied authority of the President and his designees. We turn, then to a consideration of the statutes on which plaintiffs rely.

Plaintiffs suggest that by enacting Title VII of the Civil Rights Act of 1964, * * * Congress occupied the field. The express reference in that statute to Executive Order No. 10925 or any other Executive Order prescribing fair employment practices for Government contractors, 42 U.S.C. § 2000e–8(d), indicates, however, that Congress contemplated continuance of the Executive Order program. Moreover we have held that the remedies established by Title VII are not exclusive.

But while Congress has not prohibited Presidential action in the area of fair employment on federal or federally assisted contracts, the Executive is bound by the express prohibitions of Title VII. The argument most strenuously advanced against the Philadelphia Plan is that it requires action by employers which violates the Act. Plaintiffs point to § 703(j). * * * The Plan requires that the contractor establish specific goals for utilization of available minority manpower in six trades in the five-county area. Possibly an employer could not be compelled, under the authority of Title VII, to embrace such a program, although § 703(j) refers to percentages of minorities in an area work force rather than percentages of minority tradesmen in an available trade work force. We do not meet that issue here, however, for the source of the required contract provision is Executive Order No. 11246.

Section 703(j) is a limitation only upon Title VII not upon any other remedies, state or federal.

Plaintiffs, and more particularly the union amici, contend that the Plan violates Title VII because it interferes with a bona fide seniority system. * * * The unions, it is said, refer men from the hiring halls on the basis of seniority, and the Philadelphia Plan interferes with this arrangement since few minority tradesmen have high seniority. Just as with § 703(j), however, § 703(h) is a limitation only upon Title VII, not upon any other remedies.

Plaintiffs contend that the Plan, by imposing remedial quotas, requires them to violate the basic prohibitions of Section 703(a). * * * Because the Plan requires that the contractor agree to specific goals for minority employment in each of the six trades and requires a good faith effort to achieve those goals, they argue, it requires (1) that they refuse to hire some white tradesmen, and (2) that they classify their employees by race, in violation of § 703(a). This argument rests on an overly simple reading both of the Plan and of the findings which led to its adoption.

The order of September 23, 1969 contained findings that although overall minority group representation in the construction industry in the five-county Philadelphia area was thirty per cent, in the six trades representation was approximately one per cent. It found, moreover, that this obvious underrepresentation was due to the exclusionary practices of the unions representing the six trades. It is the practice of building contractors to rely on union hiring halls as the prime source for employees. The order made further findings as to the availability of qualified minority tradesmen for employment in each trade, and as to the impact of an affirmative action program with specific goals upon the existing labor force. The Department of Labor found that contractors could commit to the specific employment goals "without adverse impact on the existing labor force." Some minority tradesmen could be recruited, in other words, without eliminating job opportunities for white tradesmen.

To read § 703(a) in the manner suggested by the plaintiffs we would have to attribute to Congress the intention to freeze the status quo and to foreclose remedial action under other authority designed to overcome existing evils. We discern no such intention either from the language of the statute or from its legislative history. Clearly the Philadelphia Plan is color-conscious. Indeed the only meaning which can be attributed to the "affirmative action" language which since March of 1961 has been included in successive Executive Orders is that Government contractors must be color-conscious. Since 1941 the Executive Order program has recognized that discriminatory practices exclude available minority manpower from the labor pool. * * * It has been said respecting Title VII that "Congress did not intend to freeze an entire generation of Negro employees into discriminatory patters that existed before the Act." * * * We reject the contention that Title

VII prevents the President acting through the Executive Order program from attempting to remedy the absence from the Philadelphia construction labor of minority tradesmen in key trades.

What we have said about Title VII applies with equal force to Title VI of the Civil Rights Act of 1964. That Title prohibits racial and other discrimination in any program or activity receiving federal financial assistance. This general prohibition against discrimination cannot be construed as limiting Executive authority in defining appropriate affirmative action on the part of a contractor.

We hold that the Philadelphia Plan does not violate the Civil Rights Act of 1964.

* * *

The absence of a judicial finding of past discrimination is also legally irrelevant. The Assistant Secretary acted not pursuant to Title VII but pursuant to the Executive Order. Regardless of the cause, exclusion from the available labor pool of minority tradesmen is likely to have an adverse effect upon the cost and completion of construction projects in which the federal government is interested. Even absent a finding that the situation found to exist in the five-county area was the result of deliberate past discrimination, the federal interest in improving the availability of key tradesmen in the labor pool would be the same. While a court must find intentional past discrimination before it can require affirmative action under 42 U.S.C. § 2000e–5(g), that section imposes no restraint upon the measures which the President may require of the beneficiaries of federal assistance. The decision of his designees as to the specific affirmative action which would satisfy the local situation * * * was not prohibited by 42 U.S.C. § 2000e–5(g).

The plaintiffs argue that the affirmative action mandate of § 202 of Executive Order No. 11246 is limited by the more general requirement in the same section, "The contractor will not discriminate against any employee or applicant for employment because of race, creed, color, or national origin." They contend that properly construed the affirmative action referred to means only policing against actual present discrimination, not action looking toward the employment of specific numbers of minority tradesmen.

Section 201 of the Executive Order provides:

"The Secretary of Labor shall be responsible for the administration of Parts II[Government contracts] and III[federal assistance] of this Order and shall adopt such rules and regulations and issue such orders as he deems necessary and appropriate to achieve the purposes thereof."

Acting under this broad delegation of authority the Labor Department in a series of orders of local application made it clear that it interpreted "affirmative action" to require more than mere policing against actual present discrimination. Administrative action pursuant to an Executive Order is invalid and subject to judicial review if beyond the scope of the Executive Order. But the courts should give more than ordinary deference to an administrative agency's interpretation of an Executive Order or regulation which it is charged to administer. The Attorney General has issued an opinion that the Philadelphia Plan is valid, and the President has continued to acquiesce in the interpretation of the Executive Order made by his designee. The Labor Department interpretation of the affirmative action clause must, therefore, be deferred to by the courts.

* * *

Plaintiffs urge that the Plan violates the Due Process Clause of the Fifth Amendment in several ways.

First, they allege that it imposes on the contractors contradictory duties impossible of attainment. This impossibility arises, they say, because the Plan requires both an undertaking to seek achievement of specific goals of minority employment and an undertaking not to discriminate against any qualified applicant or employee, and because a decision to hire any black employee necessarily involves a decision not to hire a qualified white employee. This is pure sophistry. The findings in the September 23, 1969 order disclose that the specific goals may be met, considering normal employee attrition and anticipated growth in the industry, without adverse effects on the existing labor force. According to the order the construction industry has an essentially transitory labor force and is often in short supply in key trades. The complaint does not allege that these findings misstate the underlying facts.

Next the plaintiffs urge that the Plan is arbitrary and capricious administrative action, in that it singles out the contractors and makes them take action to remedy the situation created by acts of past discrimination by the craft unions. They point to the absence of any proceedings under Title VII against the offending unions, and urge that they are being discriminated against. This argument misconceives the source of the authority for the affirmative action program. Plaintiffs are not being discriminated against. They are merely being invited to bid on a contract with terms imposed by the source of the funds. The affirmative action covenant is no different in kind than other covenants specified in the invitation to bid. The Plan does not impose a punishment for past misconduct. It exacts a covenant for present performance.

Some amici urge that selection of the five-county Philadelphia area was arbitrary and capricious and without basis in fact. The complaint contains a conclusive allegation to this effect. No supporting facts are alleged. It is not alleged, for example, that the specific goals for minority manpower utilization would be different if more or fewer counties were to be included in the September 23, 1969 order. The union amici do question the findings made by the Assistant Secretary of Labor, but the complaint, fairly read, does not put these findings in issue. We read the allegation with respect to the five-county area as putting in issue the legal authority of the Secretary to impose a specific affirmative action requirement in any separate geographic area. The simple answer to this contention is that federally assisted construction contracts are performed at specific times and in specific places. What is appropriate affirmative action will vary according to the local manpower conditions prevailing at the time.

Finally, the plaintiffs urge that the specific goals specified by the Plan are racial quotas prohibited by the equal protection aspect of the Fifth Amendment. The Philadelphia Plan is valid Executive action designed to remedy the perceived evil that minority tradesmen have not been included in the labor pool available for the performance of construction projects in which the federal government has a cost and performance interest. The Fifth Amendment does not prohibit such action.

* * *

The judgment of the district court will be affirmed.

NOTES AND PROBLEMS FOR DISCUSSION

1. Does the court's discussion in *Contractors Association* of the equal protection challenge to the Philadelphia Plan survive the Supreme Court's ruling in Fullilove v. Klutznick, *supra*? Is a determination by a federal agency as to the existence of and appropriate response to discrimination in the construction industry entitled to the same deference accorded to a Congressional finding? See note 1 following Fullilove, *supra*.

2. What is the impact of the Supreme Court's opinion in United Steelworkers v. Weber, *supra*, on the relationship between the affirmative action component of Order No. 11246 and Title VII? Does the nonvolitional nature of this obligation, as exemplified by the Philadelphia Plan, distinguish it from the affirmative action plan that survived a Title VII attack in *Weber*? Is the Order's affirmative action requirement consistent with the *Weber* majority's desire to reduce governmental interference with private business? On the other hand, what about the connection, noted in Justice Rehnquist's dissenting opinion in *Weber*, between the implementation of the craft training program and the pressure directed at Kaiser, a federal contractor, by the OFCCP to increase minority representation in its craft positions? See Note, Doing Good the Wrong Way: The Case for Delimiting Presidential Power Under Executive Order No. 11,246, 33 Vand.L.Rev. 921 (1980).

3. Do you agree with the court in the principal case that § 703(j) only limits the remedies available under Title VII? If not, must you conclude that the affirmative action requirements of Order No. 11246 violate Title VII? Assuming *arguendo* that the *Weber* Court's interpretation of § 703(j) would not be controlling, do decisions such as Association Against Discrimination v. City of Bridgeport, *supra*, nevertheless suggest that involuntarily imposed affirmative action requirements may not be prohibited by § 703(j)?

4. Is the *Contractors Association* court's analysis of the applicability of § 703(h) consistent with International Brotherhood of Teamsters v. United States, *supra*? Suppose the Secretary of Labor claims that a contractor did not comply with the antidiscrimination clause in the federal contract. Could the contractor justify its action on the ground that it acted pursuant to a facially

neutral, bona fide seniority plan? While the Third Circuit Court of Appeals in *Contractors Association* rejected the extension of the terms of § 703(h) to Order No. 11246, in UNITED STATES v. EAST TEXAS MOTOR FREIGHT SYSTEM, INC., 564 F.2d 179 (5th Cir.1977), the court disagreed, reasoning that a President could not make unlawful—or penalize—that which Congress had declared to be lawful. How does this aspect of *Contractors Association* comport with cases such as Johnson v. Ryder Truck Lines, Inc., 575 F.2d 471 (4th Cir.1978), cert. denied, 440 U.S. 979, 99 S.Ct. 1785, 60 L.Ed.2d 239 (1979), that hold that the § 703(h) defense should be read into 42 U.S.C. § 1981? See United States v. Trucking Management, Inc., 662 F.2d 36 (D.C.Cir.1981). For a discussion of this and other issues relating to the relationship between Title VII and Executive Order No. 11246, see Brody, Congress, The President and Federal Equal Employment Policymaking: A Problem In Separation of Powers, 60 B.U.L.Rev. 239 (1980).

5. Executive Order No. 11246 does not explicitly provide for a private right of action against a government contractor for an alleged failure to satisfy its nondiscrimination or affirmative action obligations and most courts have refused to recognize such an implied right of action. See Weise v. Syracuse University, 522 F.2d 397 (2d Cir.1975), Farkas v. Texas Instrument, Inc., 375 F.2d 629 (5th Cir.1967), cert. denied, 389 U.S. 977, 88 S.Ct. 480, 19 L.Ed.2d 471 (1967). On the other hand, the courts do permit private actions against the federal officials charged with enforcing the Order where the plaintiff seeks relief in the nature of *mandamus*—i.e., to compel performance of the non-discretionary aspects of administrative action required by the Order. See Legal Aid Society v. Brennan, 608 F.2d 1319 (9th Cir.1979), cert. denied, 447 U.S. 921, 100 S.Ct. 3010, 65 L.Ed.2d 1112 (1980). Moreover, individual relief is available in an enforcement action brought by the Justice Department pursuant to § 209(a)(2) of Executive Order No. 11246. While the Order authorizes the Justice Department to bring an "appropriate proceeding * * * including the enjoining * * * of organizations, individuals, or groups who * * * prevent directly or indirectly, compliances with the provisions of this Order * * * ," it has been held to support a suit for back pay for employee victims of discrimination by government contractors. See United States v. Duquesne Light Co., 423 F.Supp. 507 (W.D.Pa.1976).

For a comprehensive description and analysis of the history of administrative and judicial enforcement efforts under Executive Order # 11246 see Jones, Twenty–One Years of Affirmative Action: The Motivation of the Administrative Enforcement Process Under The Executive Order 11246 As Amended, 59 Chi.K.L.Rev. 67 (1982).

APPENDIX

TITLE VII OF CIVIL RIGHTS ACT OF 1964,
as Amended by the Civil Rights Act of 1991.

42 U.S.C.A. § 2000e et seq.

§ 701. Definitions

For the purposes of this Title—

(a) The term "person" includes one or more individuals, governments, governmental agencies, political subdivisions, labor unions, partnerships, associations, corporations, legal representatives, mutual companies, joint-stock companies, trusts, unincorporated organizations, trustees, trustees in cases under Title 11, or receivers.

(b) The term "employer" means a person engaged in an industry affecting commerce who has fifteen or more employees for each working day in each of twenty or more calendar weeks in the current or preceding calendar year, and any agent of such a person, but such term does not include (1) the United States, a corporation wholly owned by the Government of the United States, an Indian tribe, or any department or agency of the District of Columbia subject by statute to procedures of the competitive service (as defined in section 2102 of Title 5), or (2) a bona fide private membership club (other than a labor organization) which is exempt from taxation under section 501(c) of Title 26, except that during the first year after March 24, 1972, persons having fewer than twenty-five employees (and their agents) shall not be considered employers.

(c) The term "employment agency" means any person regularly undertaking with or without compensation to procure employees for an employer or to procure for employees opportunities to work for an employer and includes an agent of such a person.

(d) The term "labor organization" means a labor organization engaged in an industry affecting commerce, and any agent of such an organization, and includes any organization of any kind, any agency, or employee representation committee, group, association, or plan so engaged in which employees participate and which exists for the purpose, in whole or in part, of dealing with employers concerning grievances, labor disputes, wages, rates of pay, hours, or other terms or conditions of employment, and any conference, general committee, joint or system board, or joint council so engaged which is subordinate to a national or international labor organization.

1234

(e) A labor organization shall be deemed to be engaged in an industry affecting commerce if (1) it maintains or operates a hiring hall or hiring office which procures employees for an employer or procures for employees opportunities to work for an employer, or (2) the number of its members (or, where it is a labor organization composed of other labor organizations or their representatives, if the aggregate number of the members of such other labor organization) is (A) twenty-five or more during the first year after March 24, 1972, or (B) fifteen or more thereafter, and such labor organization—

(1) is the certified representative of employees under the provisions of the National Labor Relations Act, as amended, or the Railway Labor Act, as amended;

(2) although not certified, is a national or international labor organization or a local labor organization recognized or acting as the representative of employees of an employer or employers engaged in an industry affecting commerce; or

(3) has chartered a local labor organization or subsidiary body which is representing or actively seeking to represent employees of employers within the meaning of paragraph (1) or (2); or

(4) has been chartered by a labor organization representing or actively seeking to represent employees within the meaning of paragraph (1) or (2) as the local or subordinate body through which such employees may enjoy membership or become affiliated with such labor organization; or

(5) is a conference, general committee, joint or system board, or joint council subordinate to a national or international labor organization, which includes a labor organization engaged in an industry affecting commerce within the meaning of any of the preceding paragraphs of this subsection.

(f) The term "employee" means an individual employed by an employer, except that the term "employee" shall not include any person elected to public office in any State or political subdivision of any State by the qualified voters thereof, or any person chosen by such officer to be on such officer's personal staff, or an appointee on the policy making level or an immediate adviser with respect to the exercise of the constitutional or legal powers of the office. The exemption set forth in the preceding sentence shall not include employees subject to the civil service laws of a State government, governmental agency or political subdivision. With respect to employment in a foreign country, such term includes an individual who is a citizen of the United States.

(g) The term "commerce" means trade, traffic, commerce, transportation, transmission, or communication among the several States; or between a State and any place outside thereof; or within the District of Columbia, or a possession of the United States; or between points in the same State but through a point outside thereof.

(h) The term "industry affecting commerce" means any activity, business, or industry in commerce or in which a labor dispute would hinder or obstruct commerce or the free flow of commerce and includes any activity or industry "affecting commerce" within the meaning of the Labor–Management Reporting and Disclosure Act of 1959, and further includes any governmental industry, business, or activity.

(i) The term "State" includes a State of the United States, the District of Columbia, Puerto Rico, the Virgin Islands, American Samoa, Guam, Wake Island, the Canal Zone, and Outer Continental Shelf lands defined in the Outer Continental Shelf Lands Act.

(j) The term "religion" includes all aspects of religious observance and practice, as well as belief, unless an employer demonstrates that he is unable to reasonably accommodate to an employee's or prospective employee's religious observance or practice without undue hardship on the conduct of the employer's business.

(k) The terms "because of sex" or "on the basis of sex" include, but are not limited to, because of or on the basis of pregnancy, childbirth, or related medical conditions; and women affected by pregnancy, childbirth, or related medical conditions shall be treated the same for all employment-related purposes, including receipt of benefits under fringe benefit programs, as other persons not so affected but similar in their ability or inability to work, and nothing in section 703(h) of this Act shall be interpreted to permit otherwise. This subsection shall not require an employer to pay for health insurance benefits for abortion, except where the life of the mother would be endangered if the fetus were carried to term, or except where medical complications have arisen from an abortion: *Provided*, That nothing herein shall preclude an employer from providing abortion benefits or otherwise affect bargaining agreements in regard to abortion.

(*l*) The term "complaining party" means the Commission, the Attorney General, or a person who may bring an action or proceeding under this title.

(m) The term "demonstrates" means meets the burdens of production and persuasion.

(n) The term "respondent" means an employer, employment agency, labor organization, joint labor-management committee controlling apprenticeship or other training or retraining program, including an on-the-job training program, or Federal entity subject to section 717.

§ 702. Exemptions

(a) This Title shall not apply to an employer with respect to the employment of aliens outside any State, or to a religious corporation, association, educational institution, or society with respect to the employment of individuals of a particular religion to perform work connected with the carrying on by such corporation, association, educational institution, or society of its activities.

(b) It shall not be unlawful under section 703 or 704 for an employer (or a corporation controlled by an employer), labor organization, employment agency, or joint labor-management committee controlling apprenticeship or other training or retraining (including on-the-job training programs) to take any action otherwise prohibited by such section, with respect to an employee in a workplace in a foreign country if compliance with such section would cause such employer (or such corporation), such organization, such agency, or such committee to violate the law of the foreign country in which such workplace is located.

(c)(1) If an employer controls a corporation whose place of incorporation is a foreign country, any practice prohibited by section 703 or 704 engaged in by such corporation shall be presumed to be engaged in by such employer.

(2) Sections 703 and 704 shall not apply with respect to the foreign operations of an employer that is a foreign person not controlled by an American employer.

(3) For purposes of this subsection, the determination of whether an employer controls a corporation shall be based on—

(A) the interrelation of operations;

(B) the common management;

(C) the centralized control of labor relations; and

(D) the common ownership or financial control, of the employer and the corporation.

§ 703. Unlawful employment practices

(a) It shall be an unlawful employment practice for an employer—

(1) to fail or refuse to hire or to discharge any individual, or otherwise to discriminate against any individual with respect to his compensation, terms, conditions, or privileges of employment, because of such individual's race, color, religion, sex, or national origin; or

(2) to limit, segregate, or classify his employees or applicants for employment in any way which would deprive or tend to deprive any individual of employment opportunities or otherwise adversely affect his status as an employee, because of such individual's race, color, religion, sex, or national origin.

(b) It shall be an unlawful employment practice for an employment agency to fail or refuse to refer for employment, or otherwise to discriminate against, any individual because of his race, color, religion, sex, or national origin, or to classify or refer for employment any individual on the basis of his race, color, religion, sex, or national origin.

(c) It shall be an unlawful employment practice for a labor organization—

(1) to exclude or to expel from its membership, or otherwise to discriminate against, any individual because of his race, color, religion, sex, or national origin;

(2) to limit, segregate, or classify its membership or applicants for membership, or to classify or fail or refuse to refer for employment any individual, in any way which would deprive or tend to deprive any individual of employment opportunities, or would limit such employment opportunities or otherwise adversely affect his status as an employee or as an applicant for employment, because of such individual's race, color, religion, sex, or national origin; or

(3) to cause or attempt to cause an employer to discriminate against an individual in violation of this section.

(d) It shall be an unlawful employment practice for any employer, labor organization, or joint labor-management committee controlling apprenticeship or other training or retraining, including on-the-job training programs to discriminate against any individual because of his race, color, religion, sex, or national origin in admission to, or employment in, any program established to provide apprenticeship or other training.

(e) Notwithstanding any other provision of this Title, (1) it shall not be an unlawful employment practice for an employer to hire and employ employees, for an employment agency to classify, or refer for employment any individual, for a labor organization to classify its membership or to classify or refer for employment any individual, or for an employer, labor organization, or joint labor-management committee controlling apprenticeship or other training or retraining programs to admit or employ any individual in any such program, on the basis of his religion, sex, or national origin in those certain instances where religion, sex, or national origin is a bona fide occupational qualification reasonably necessary to the normal operation of that particular business or enterprise, and (2) it shall not be an unlawful employment practice for a school, college, university, or other educational institution or institution of learning to hire and employ employees of a particular religion if such school, college, university, or other educational institution or institution of learning is, in whole or in substantial part, owned, supported, controlled, or managed by a particular religion or by a particular religious corporation, association, or society, or if the curriculum of such school, college, university, or other educational institution or institution of learning is directed toward the propagation of a particular religion.

(f) As used in this Title, the phrase "unlawful employment practice" shall not be deemed to include any action or measure taken by an employer, labor organization, joint labor-management committee, or employment agency with respect to an individual who is a member of the Communist Party of the United States or of any other organization required to register as a Communist-action or Communist-front organization by final order of the Subversive Activities Control Board pursuant to the Subversive Activities Control Act of 1950.

(g) Notwithstanding any other provision of this Title, it shall not be an unlawful employment practice for an employer to fail or refuse to hire and employ any individual for any position, for an employer to discharge any individual from any position, or for an employment agency to fail or refuse to refer any individual for employment in any position, or for a labor organization to fail or refuse to refer any individual for employment in any position, if—

(1) the occupancy of such position, or access to the premises in or upon which any part of the duties of such position is performed or is to be performed, is subject to any requirement imposed in the interest of the national security of the United States under any security program in effect pursuant to or administered under any statute of the United States or any Executive order of the President; and

(2) such individual has not fulfilled or has ceased to fulfill that requirement.

(h) Notwithstanding any other provision of this Title, it shall not be an unlawful employment practice for an employer to apply different standards of compensation, or different terms, conditions, or privileges of employment pursuant to a bona fide seniority or merit system, or a system which measures earnings by quantity or quality of production or to employees who work in different locations, provided that such differences are not the result of an intention to discriminate because of race, color, religion, sex, or national origin, nor shall it be an unlawful employment practice for an employer to give and to act upon the results of any professionally developed ability test provided that such test, its administration or action upon the results is not designed, intended or used to discriminate because of race, color, religion, sex or national origin. It shall not be an unlawful employment practice under this Title for any employer to differentiate upon the basis of sex in determining the amount of the wages or compensation paid or to be paid to employees of such employer if such differentiation is authorized by the provisions of the Equal Pay Act.

(i) Nothing contained in this Title shall apply to any business or enterprise on or near an Indian reservation with respect to any publicly announced employment practice of such business or enterprise under which a preferential treatment is given to any individual because he is an Indian living on or near a reservation.

(j) Nothing contained in this Title shall be interpreted to require any employer, employment agency, labor organization, or joint labor-management committee subject to this subchapter to grant preferential treatment to any individual or to any group because of the race, color, religion, sex, or national origin of such individual or group on account of an imbalance which may exist with respect to the total number or percentage of persons of any race, color, religion, sex, or national origin employed by any employer, referred or classified for employment by any employment agency or labor organization, admitted to membership or classified by any labor organization, or admitted to, or employed in, any apprenticeship or other training program, in comparison with the total number or percentage of persons of such race, color, religion, sex, or national origin in any community, State, section, or other area, or in the available work force in any community, State, section, or other area.

(k)(1)(A) An unlawful employment practice based on disparate impact is established under this Title only if—

(i) a complaining party demonstrates that a respondent uses a particular employment practice that causes a disparate impact on the basis of race, color, religion, sex, or national origin and the respondent fails to demonstrate that the challenged practice is job related for the position in question and consistent with business necessity; or

(ii) the complaining party makes the demonstration described in subparagraph (C) with respect to an alternative employment practice and the respondent refuses to adopt such alternative employment practice.

(B)(i) With respect to demonstrating that a particular employment practice causes a disparate impact as described in subparagraph (A)(i), the complaining party shall demonstrate that each particular challenged employment practice causes a disparate impact, except that if the complaining party can demonstrate to the court that the elements of a respondent's decisionmaking process are not capable of separation for analysis, the decisionmaking process may be analyzed as one employment practice.

(ii) If the respondent demonstrates that a specific employment practice does not cause the disparate impact, the respondent shall not be required to demonstrate that such practice is required by business necessity.

(C) The demonstration referred to by subparagraph (A)(ii) shall be in accordance with the law as it existed on June 4, 1989, with respect to the concept of "alternative employment practice".

(2) A demonstration that an employment practice is required by business necessity may not be used as a defense against a claim of intentional discrimination under this title.

(3) Notwithstanding any other provision of this Title, a rule barring the employment of an individual who currently and knowingly uses or possesses a controlled substance, as defined in schedules I and II of section 102(6) of the Controlled Substances Act, other than the use or possession of a drug taken under the supervision of a licensed health care professional, or any other use or possession authorized by the Controlled Substances Act or any other provision of Federal law, shall be considered an unlawful employment practice under this title only if such rule is adopted or applied with an intent to discriminate because of race, color, religion, sex, or national origin.

[§ 105(b) of the Civil Rights Act of 1991 provides as follows:

No statements other than the interpretive memorandum appearing at Vol. 137 Congressional Record S 15276 (daily ed. Oct. 25, 1991) shall be considered legislative history of, or relied upon in any way as legislative history in construing or applying, any provision of this Act that relates to Wards Cove—Business necessity/cumulation/alternative business practice. For reproduction of relevant portion of Congressional Record, see § 105(b) of 1991 Civil Rights Act, *infra*, at 1258–1259.]

(*l*) It shall be an unlawful employment practice for a respondent, in connection with the selection or referral of applicants or candidates for employment or promotion, to adjust the scores of, use different cutoff scores for, or otherwise alter the results of, employment related tests on the basis of race, color, religion, sex, or national origin.

(m) Except as otherwise provided in this Title, an unlawful employment practice is established when the complaining party demonstrates that race, color, religion, sex, or national origin was a motivating factor for any employment practice, even though other factors also motivated the practice.

(n)(1)(A) Notwithstanding any other provision of law, and except as provided in paragraph (2), an employment practice that implements and is within the scope of a litigated or consent judgment or order that resolves a claim of employment discrimination under the Constitution or Federal civil rights laws may not be challenged under the circumstances described in subparagraph (B).

(B) A practice described in subparagraph (A) may not be challenged in a claim under the Constitution or Federal civil rights laws—

(i) by a person who, prior to the entry of the judgment or order described in subparagraph (A), had—

(I) actual notice of the proposed judgment or order sufficient to apprise such person that such judgment or order might adversely affect the interests and legal rights of such person and that an opportunity was available to present objections to such judgment or order by a future date certain; and

(II) a reasonable opportunity to present objections to such judgment or order; or

(ii) by a person whose interests were adequately represented by another person who had previously challenged the judgment or order on the same legal grounds and with a similar factual situation, unless there has been an intervening change in law or fact.

(2) Nothing in this subsection shall be construed to—

(A) alter the standards for intervention under rule 24 of the Federal Rules of Civil Procedure or apply to the rights of parties who have successfully intervened pursuant to such rule in the proceeding in which the parties intervened;

(B) apply to the rights of parties to the action in which a litigated or consent judgment or order was entered, or of members of a class represented or sought to be represented in such action, or of members of a group on whose behalf relief was sought in such action by the Federal Government;

(C) prevent challenges to a litigated or consent judgment or order on the ground that such judgment or order was obtained through collusion or fraud, or is transparently invalid or was entered by a court lacking subject matter jurisdiction; or

(D) authorize or permit the denial to any person of the due process of law required by the Constitution.

(3) Any action not precluded under this subsection that challenges an employment consent judgment or order described in paragraph (1) shall be brought in the court, and if possible before the judge, that entered such judgment or order. Nothing in this subsection shall preclude a transfer of such action pursuant to 28 U.S.C. § 1404 [the change of venue statute].

§ 704. Other unlawful employment practices

(a) It shall be an unlawful employment practice for an employer to discriminate against any of his employees or applicants for employment, for an employment agency, or joint labor-management committee controlling apprenticeship or other training or retraining, including on-the-job training programs, to discriminate against any individual, or for a labor organization to discriminate against any member thereof or applicant for membership, because he has opposed any practice made an unlawful employment practice by this Title, or because he has made a charge, testified, assisted, or participated in any manner in an investigation, proceeding, or hearing under this Title.

(b) It shall be an unlawful employment practice for an employer, labor organization, employment agency, or joint labor-management committee controlling apprenticeship or other training or retraining, including on-the-job training programs, to print or publish or cause to be printed or published any notice or advertisement relating to employment by such an employer or membership in or any classification or referral for employment by such a labor organization, or relating to any classification or referral for employment by such an employment agency, or relating to admission to, or employment in, any program established to provide apprenticeship or other training by such a joint labor-management committee, indicating any preference, limitation, specification, or discrimination, based on race, color, religion, sex, or national origin, except that such a notice or advertisement may indicate a preference, limitation, specification, or discrimination based on religion, sex, or national origin when religion, sex, or national origin is a bona fide occupational qualification for employment.

§ 705. Equal Employment Opportunity Commission

(a) There is hereby created a Commission to be known as the Equal Employment Opportunity Commission, which shall be composed of five members, not more than three of whom shall be members of the same political party. Members of the Commission shall be appointed by the President by and with the advice and consent of the Senate for a term of five years. Any individual chosen to fill a vacancy shall be appointed only for the unexpired term of the member whom he shall succeed, and all members of the Commission shall continue to serve until their successors are appointed and qualified, except that no such member of the Commission shall continue to serve (1) for more than sixty days when the Congress is in session unless a nomination to fill such vacancy shall have been submitted to the Senate, or (2) after the adjournment sine die of the session of the Senate in which such nomination was submitted. The President shall designate one member to serve as Chairman of the Commission, and one member to serve as Vice Chairman. The Chairman shall be responsible on behalf of the Commission for the administrative operations of the Commission, and, except as provided in subsection (b) of this section, shall appoint, in accordance with the provisions of Title 5 governing appointments in the competitive service, such officers, agents, attorneys, administrative law judges, and employees as he deems necessary to assist it in the performance of its functions and to fix their compensation in accordance with the provisions of chapter 51 and subchapter III of chapter 53 of Title 5, relating to classification and General Schedule pay rates: *Provided*, That assignment, removal, and compensation of administrative law judges shall be in accordance with sections 3105, 3344, 5372, and 7521 of Title 5.

(b)(1) There shall be a General Counsel of the Commission appointed by the President, by and with the advice and consent of the Senate, for a term of four years. The General Counsel shall have responsibility for the conduct of litigation as provided in sections 706 and 707 of this Act. The General Counsel shall have such other duties as the Commission may prescribe or as may be provided by law and shall concur with the Chairman of the Commission on the appointment and supervision of regional attorneys. The General Counsel of the Commission on the effective date of this Act shall continue in such position and perform the functions specified in this subsection until a successor is appointed and qualified.

(2) Attorneys appointed under this section may, at the direction of the Commission, appear for and represent the Commission in any case in court, provided that the Attorney General shall conduct all litigation to which the Commission is a party in the Supreme Court pursuant to this Title.

(c) A vacancy in the Commission shall not impair the right of the remaining members to exercise all the powers of the Commission and three members thereof shall constitute a quorum.

(d) The Commission shall have an official seal which shall be judicially noticed.

(e) The Commission shall at the close of each fiscal year report to the Congress and to the President concerning the action it has taken and the moneys it has disbursed. It shall make such further reports on the cause of and means of eliminating discrimination and such recommendations for further legislation as may appear desirable.

(f) The principal office of the Commission shall be in or near the District of Columbia, but it may meet or exercise any or all its powers at any other place. The Commission may establish such regional or State offices as it deems necessary to accomplish the purpose of this Title.

(g) The Commission shall have power—

(1) to cooperate with and, with their consent, utilize regional, State, local, and other agencies, both public and private, and individuals;

(2) to pay to witnesses whose depositions are taken or who are summoned before the Commission or any of its agents the same witness and mileage fees as are paid to witnesses in the courts of the United States;

(3) to furnish to persons subject to this subchapter such technical assistance as they may request to further their compliance with this Title or an order issued thereunder;

(4) upon the request of (i) any employer, whose employees or some of them, or (ii) any labor organization, whose members or some of them, refuse or threaten to refuse to cooperate in effectuating the provisions of this Title, to assist in such effectuation by conciliation or such other remedial action as is provided by this Title;

(5) to make such technical studies as are appropriate to effectuate the purposes and policies of this Title and to make the results of such studies available to the public;

(6) to intervene in a civil action brought under section 706 of this Act by an aggrieved party against a respondent other than a government, governmental agency or political subdivision.

(h)(1) The Commission shall, in any of its educational or promotional activities, cooperate with other departments and agencies in the performance of such educational and promotional activities.

(2) In exercising its powers under this title, the Commission shall carry out educational and outreach activities (including dissemination of information in languages other than English) targeted to—

(A) individuals who historically have been victims of employment discrimination and have not been equitably served by the Commission; and

(B) individuals on whose behalf the Commission has authority to enforce any other law prohibiting employment discrimination, concerning rights and obligations under this title or such law, as the case may be.

(i) All officers, agents, attorneys, and employees of the Commission shall be subject to the provisions of section 7324 of Title 5, notwithstanding any exemption contained in such section.

(j)(1) The Commission shall establish a Technical Assistance Training Institute, through which the Commission shall provide technical assistance and training regarding the laws and regulations enforced by the Commission.

(2) An employer or other entity covered under this title shall not be excused from compliance with the requirements of this title because of any failure to receive technical assistance under this subsection.

(3) There are authorized to be appropriated to carry out this subsection such sums as may be necessary for fiscal year 1992.

§ 706. Enforcement provisions

(a) The Commission is empowered, as hereinafter provided, to prevent any person from engaging in any unlawful employment practice as set forth in section 703 or 704 of this Act.

(b) Whenever a charge is filed by or on behalf of a person claiming to be aggrieved, or by a member of the Commission, alleging that an employer, employment agency, labor organization, or joint labor-management committee controlling apprenticeship or other training or retraining, including on-the-job training programs, has engaged in an unlawful employment practice, the Commission shall serve a notice of the charge (including the date, place and circumstances of the alleged unlawful employment practice) on such employer, employment agency, labor organization, or joint labor-management committee (hereinafter referred to as the "respondent") within ten days, and shall make an investigation thereof. Charges shall be in writing under oath or affirmation and shall contain such information and be in such form as the Commission requires. Charges shall not be made public by the Commission. If the Commission determines after such investigation that there is not reasonable cause to believe that the charge is true, it shall dismiss the charge and promptly notify the person claiming to be aggrieved and the respondent of its action. In determining whether reasonable cause exists, the Commission shall accord substantial weight to final findings and orders made by State or local authorities in proceedings commenced under State or local law pursuant to the requirements of subsections (c) and (d) of this section. If the Commission determines after such investigation that there is reasonable cause to believe that the charge is true, the Commission shall endeavor to eliminate any such alleged unlawful employment practice by informal methods of conference, conciliation, and persuasion. Nothing said or done during and as a part of such informal endeavors may be made public by the Commission, its officers or employees, or used as evidence in a subsequent proceeding without the written consent of the persons concerned. Any person who makes public information in violation of this subsection shall be fined not more than $1,000 or imprisoned for not more than one year, or both. The Commission shall make its determination on reasonable cause as promptly as possible and, so far as practicable, not later than one hundred and twenty days from the filing of the charge or, where applicable under subsection (c) or (d) of this section, from the date upon which the Commission is authorized to take action with respect to the charge.

(c) In the case of an alleged unlawful employment practice occurring in a State, or political subdivision of a State, which has a State or local law prohibiting the unlawful employment practice alleged and establishing or authorizing a State or local authority to grant or seek relief from such practice or to institute criminal proceedings with respect thereto upon receiving notice thereof, no charge may be filed under subsection (b) of this section by the person aggrieved before the expiration of sixty days after proceedings have been commenced under the State or local law, unless such proceedings have been earlier terminated, provided that such sixty-day period shall be extended to one hundred and twenty days during the first year after the effective date of such State or local law. If any requirement for the commencement of such proceedings is imposed by a State or local authority other than a requirement of the filing of a written and signed statement of the facts upon which the proceeding is based, the proceeding shall be deemed to have been commenced for the purposes of this subsection at the time such statement is sent by registered mail to the appropriate State or local authority.

(d) In the case of any charge filed by a member of the Commission alleging an unlawful employment practice occurring in a State or political subdivision of a State which has a State or local law prohibiting the practice alleged and establishing or authorizing a State or local authority to grant or seek relief from such practice or to institute criminal proceedings with respect thereto upon receiving notice thereof, the Commission shall, before taking any action with respect to such charge, notify the appropriate State or local officials and, upon request, afford them a reasonable time, but not less than sixty days (provided that such sixty-day period shall be extended to one hundred and twenty days during the first year after the effective day of such State or local law), unless a shorter period is requested, to act under such State or local law to remedy the practice alleged.

(e)(1) A charge under this section shall be filed within one hundred and eighty days after the alleged unlawful employment practice occurred and notice of the charge (including the date, place and circumstances of the alleged unlawful employment practice) shall be served upon the person against whom such charge is made within ten days thereafter, except that in a case of an unlawful employment practice with respect to which the person aggrieved has initially instituted proceedings with a State or local agency with authority to grant or seek relief from such practice or to institute criminal proceedings with respect thereto upon receiving notice thereof, such charge shall be filed by or on behalf of the person aggrieved within three hundred days after the alleged unlawful employment practice occurred, or within thirty days after receiving notice that the State or local agency has terminated the proceedings under the State or local law, whichever is earlier, and a copy of such charge shall be filed by the Commission with the State or local agency.

(2) For purposes of this section, an unlawful employment practice occurs, with respect to a seniority system that has been adopted for an intentionally discriminatory purpose in violation of this title (whether or not that discriminatory purpose is apparent on the face of the seniority provision), when the seniority system is adopted, when an individual becomes subject to the seniority system, or when a person aggrieved is injured by the application of the seniority system or provision of the system.

(f)(1) If within thirty days after a charge is filed with the Commission or within thirty days after expiration of any period of reference under subsection (c) or (d) of this section, the Commission has been unable to secure from the respondent a conciliation agreement acceptable to the Commission, the Commission may bring a civil action against any respondent not a government, governmental agency, or political subdivision named in the charge. In the case of a respondent which is a government, governmental agency, or political subdivision, if the Commission has been unable to secure from the respondent a conciliation agreement acceptable to the Commission, the Commission shall take no further action and shall refer the case to the Attorney General who may bring a civil action against such respondent in the appropriate United States district court. The person or persons aggrieved shall have the right to intervene in a civil action brought by the Commission or the Attorney General in a case involving a government, governmental agency, or political subdivision. If a charge filed with the Commission pursuant to subsection (b) of this section is dismissed by the Commission, or if within one hundred and eighty days from the filing of such charge or the expiration of any period of reference under subsection (c) or (d) of this section, whichever is later, the Commission has not filed a civil action under this section or the Attorney General has not filed a civil action in a case involving a government, governmental agency, or political subdivision, or the Commission has not entered into a conciliation agreement to which the person aggrieved is a party, the Commission, or the Attorney General in a case involving a government, governmental agency, or political subdivision, shall so notify the person aggrieved and within ninety days after the giving of such notice a civil action may be brought against the respondent named in the charge (A) by the person claiming to be aggrieved or (B) if such charge was filed by a member of the Commission, by any person whom the charge alleges was aggrieved by the alleged unlawful employment practice. Upon application by the complainant and in such circumstances as the court may deem just, the court may appoint an attorney for such complainant and may authorize the commencement of the action without the payment of fees, costs, or security. Upon timely application, the court may, in its discretion, permit the Commission, or the Attorney General in a case involving a government, governmental agency, or political subdivision, to intervene in such civil action upon certification that the case is of general public importance. Upon request, the court may, in its discretion, stay further proceedings for not more than sixty days pending the termination of State or local proceedings described in subsection (c) or (d) of this section or further efforts of the Commission to obtain voluntary compliance.

(2) Whenever a charge is filed with the Commission and the Commission concludes on the basis of a preliminary investigation that prompt judicial action is necessary to carry out the purposes of this Act, the Commission, or the Attorney General in a case involving a government, governmental agency, or political subdivision, may bring an action for appropriate temporary or preliminary relief pending final disposition of such charge. Any temporary restraining order or other order granting preliminary or temporary relief shall be issued in accordance with rule 65 of the Federal Rules of Civil Procedure. It shall be the duty of a court having jurisdiction over proceedings under this section to assign cases for hearing at the earliest practicable date and to cause such cases to be in every way expedited.

(3) Each United States district court and each United States court of a place subject to the jurisdiction of the United States shall have jurisdiction of actions brought under this Title. Such an action may be brought in any judicial district in the State in which the unlawful employment practice is alleged to have been committed, in the judicial district in which the employment records relevant to such practice are maintained and administered, or in the judicial district in which the aggrieved person would have worked but for the alleged unlawful employment practice, but if the respondent is not found within any

such district, such an action may be brought within the judicial district in which the respondent has his principal office. For purposes of sections 1404 and 1406 of Title 28, the judicial district in which the respondent has his principal office shall in all cases be considered a district in which the action might have been brought.

(4) It shall be the duty of the chief judge of the district (or in his absence, the acting chief judge) in which the case is pending immediately to designate a judge in such district to hear and determine the case. In the event that no judge in the district is available to hear and determine the case, the chief judge of the district, or the acting chief judge, as the case may be, shall certify this fact to the chief judge of the circuit (or in his absence, the acting chief judge) who shall then designate a district or circuit judge of the circuit to hear and determine the case.

(5) It shall be the duty of the judge designated pursuant to this subsection to assign the case for hearing at the earliest practicable date and to cause the case to be in every way expedited. If such judge has not scheduled the case for trial within one hundred and twenty days after issue has been joined, that judge may appoint a master pursuant to rule 53 of the Federal Rules of Civil Procedure.

(g)(1) If the court finds that the respondent has intentionally engaged in or is intentionally engaging in an unlawful employment practice charged in the complaint, the court may enjoin the respondent from engaging in such unlawful employment practice, and order such affirmative action as may be appropriate, which may include, but is not limited to, reinstatement or hiring of employees, with or without back pay (payable by the employer, employment agency, or labor organization, as the case may be, responsible for the unlawful employment practice), or any other equitable relief as the court deems appropriate. Back pay liability shall not accrue from a date more than two years prior to the filing of a charge with the Commission. Interim earnings or amounts earnable with reasonable diligence by the person or persons discriminated against shall operate to reduce the back pay otherwise allowable.

(2)(A) No order of the court shall require the admission or reinstatement of an individual as a member of a union, or the hiring, reinstatement, or promotion of an individual as an employee, or the payment to him of any back pay, if such individual was refused admission, suspended, or expelled, or was refused employment or advancement or was suspended or discharged for any reason other than discrimination on account of race, color, religion, sex, or national origin or in violation of section 704 of this Act.

(B) On a claim in which an individual proves a violation under section 703(m) and a respondent demonstrates that the respondent would have taken the same action in the absence of the impermissible motivating factor, the court—

(i) may grant declaratory relief, injunctive relief (except as provided in clause (ii)), and attorney's fees and costs demonstrated to be directly attributable only to the pursuit of a claim under section 703(m); and

(ii) shall not award damages or issue an order requiring any admission, reinstatement, hiring, promotion, or payment, described in subparagraph (A).

(h) The provisions of sections 101 to 115 of Title 29 shall not apply with respect to civil actions brought under this section.

(i) In any case in which an employer, employment agency, or labor organization fails to comply with an order of a court issued in a civil action brought under this section, the Commission may commence proceedings to compel compliance with such order.

(j) Any civil action brought under this section and any proceedings brought under subsection (i) of this section shall be subject to appeal as provided in sections 1291 and 1292, Title 28.

(k) In any action or proceeding under this Title the court, in its discretion, may allow the prevailing party, other than the Commission or the United States, a reasonable attorney's fee (including expert fees) as part of the costs, and the Commission and the United States shall be liable for costs the same as a private person.

§ 707. Civil Actions by Attorney General

(a) Whenever the Attorney General has reasonable cause to believe that any person or group of persons is engaged in a pattern or practice of resistance to the full enjoyment of any of the rights secured by this Title, and that the pattern or practice is of such a nature and is intended to deny the full exercise of the rights herein described, the Attorney General may bring a civil action in the appropriate district court of the United States by filing with it a complaint (1) signed by him (or in his absence the Acting Attorney General), (2) setting forth facts pertaining to such pattern or practice, and (3) requesting such relief, including an application for a permanent or temporary injunction, restraining order or other order against the person or persons responsible for such pattern or practice, as he deems necessary to insure the full enjoyment of the rights herein described.

(b) The district courts of the United States shall have and shall exercise jurisdiction of proceedings instituted pursuant to this section, and in any such proceeding the Attorney General may file with the clerk of such court a request that a court of three judges be convened to hear and determine the case. Such request by the Attorney General shall be accompanied by a certificate that, in his opinion, the case is of general public importance. A copy of the certificate and request for a three-judge court shall be immediately furnished by such clerk to the chief judge of the circuit (or in his absence, the presiding circuit judge of the circuit) in which the case is pending. Upon receipt of such request it shall be the duty of the chief judge of the circuit or the presiding circuit judge, as the case may be, to designate immediately three judges in such circuit, of whom at least one shall be a circuit judge and another of whom shall be a district judge of the court in which the proceeding was instituted, to hear and determine such case, and it shall be the duty of the judges so designated to assign the case for hearing at the earliest practicable date, to participate in the hearing and determination thereof, and to cause the case to be in every way expedited. An appeal from the final judgment of such court will lie to the Supreme Court.

In the event the Attorney General fails to file such a request in any such proceeding, it shall be the duty of the chief judge of the district (or in his absence, the acting chief judge) in which the case is pending immediately to designate a judge in such district to hear and determine the case. In the event that no judge in the district is available to hear and determine the case, the chief judge of the district, or the acting chief judge, as the case may be, shall certify this fact to the chief judge of the circuit (or in his absence, the acting chief judge) who shall then designate a district or circuit judge of the circuit to hear and determine the case.

It shall be the duty of the judge designated pursuant to this section to assign the case for hearing at the earliest practicable date and to cause the case to be in every way expedited.

(c) Effective two years after March 24, 1972, the functions of the Attorney General under this section shall be transferred to the Commission, together with such personnel, property, records, and unexpended balances of appropriations, allocations, and other funds employed, used, held, available, or to be made available in connection with such functions unless the President submits, and neither House of Congress vetoes, a reorganization plan pursuant to chapter 9 of Title 5, inconsistent with the provisions of this subsection. The Commission shall carry out such functions in accordance with subsections (d) and (e) of this section.

(d) Upon the transfer of functions provided for in subsection (c) of this section, in all suits commenced pursuant to this section prior to the date of such transfer, proceedings shall continue without abatement, all court orders and decrees shall remain in effect, and the Commission shall be substituted as a party for the United States of America, the Attorney General, or the Acting Attorney General, as appropriate.

(e) Subsequent to March 24, 1972, the Commission shall have authority to investigate and act on a charge of a pattern or practice of discrimination, whether filed by or on behalf of a person claiming to be aggrieved or by a member of the Commission. All such actions shall be conducted in accordance with the procedures set forth in section 706 of this Act.

§ 708. Effect on State laws

Nothing in this Title shall be deemed to exempt or relieve any person from any liability, duty, penalty, or punishment provided by any present or future law of any State or political subdivision of a State, other than any such law which purports to require or permit the doing of any act which would be an unlawful employment practice under this Title.

§ 709. Investigations

(a) In connection with any investigation of a charge filed under section 706 of this Act, the Commission or its designated representative shall at all reasonable times have access to, for the purposes of examination, and the right to copy any evidence of any person being investigated or proceeded against that relates to unlawful employment practices covered by this Title and is relevant to the charge under investigation.

(b) The Commission may cooperate with State and local agencies charged with the administration of State fair employment practices laws and, with the consent of such agencies, may, for the purpose of carrying out its functions and duties under this Title and within the limitation of funds appropriated specifically for such purpose, engage in and contribute to the cost of research and other projects of mutual interest undertaken by such agencies, and utilize the services of such agencies and their employees, and, notwithstanding any other provision of law, pay by advance or reimbursement such agencies and their employees for services rendered to assist the Commission in carrying out this Title. In furtherance of such cooperative efforts, the Commission may enter into written agreements with such State or local agencies and such agreements may include provisions under which the Commission shall refrain from processing a charge in any cases or class of cases specified in such agreements or under which the Commission shall relieve any person or class of persons in such State or locality from requirements imposed under this section. The Commission shall rescind any such agreement whenever it determines that the agreement no longer serves the interest of effective enforcement of this Title.

(c) Every employer, employment agency, and labor organization subject to this Title shall (1) make and keep such records relevant to the determinations of whether unlawful employment practices have been or are being committed, (2) preserve such records for such periods, and (3) make such reports therefrom as the Commission shall prescribe by regulation or order, after public hearing, as reasonable, necessary, or appropriate for the enforcement of this Title or the regulations or orders thereunder. The Commission shall, by regulation, require each employer, labor organization, and joint labor-management committee subject to this Title which controls an apprenticeship or other training program to maintain such records as are reasonably necessary to carry out the purposes of this Title, including, but not limited to, a list of applicants who wish to participate in such program, including the chronological order in which applications were received, and to furnish to the Commission upon request, a detailed description of the manner in which persons are selected to participate in the apprenticeship or other training program. Any employer, employment agency, labor organization, or joint labor-management committee which believes that the application to it of any regulation or order issued under this section would result in undue hardship may apply to the Commission for an exemption from the application of such regulation or order, and, if such application for an exemption is denied, bring a civil action in the United States district court for the district where such records are kept. If the Commission or the court, as the case may be, finds that the application of the regulation or order to the employer, employment agency, or labor organization in question would impose an undue hardship, the Commission or the court, as the case may be, may grant appropriate relief. If any person required to comply with the provisions of this subsection fails or refuses to do so, the United States district court for the district in which such person is found, resides, or transacts business, shall, upon application of the Commission, or the Attorney General in a case involving a government, governmental agency or political subdivision, have jurisdiction to issue to such person an order requiring him to comply.

(d) In prescribing requirements pursuant to subsection (c) of this section, the Commission shall consult with other interested State and Federal agencies and shall endeavor to coordinate its requirements with those adopted by such agencies. The Commission shall furnish upon request and without cost to any State or local agency charged with the administration of a fair employment practice law information obtained pursuant to subsection (c) of this section from any employer, employment agency, labor organization, or joint labor-management committee subject to the jurisdiction of such agency. Such information shall be furnished on condition that it not be made public by the recipient agency prior to the institution of a proceeding under State or local law involving such information. If this condition is violated by a recipient agency, the Commission may decline to honor subsequent requests pursuant to this subsection.

(e) It shall be unlawful for any officer or employee of the Commission to make public in any manner whatever any information obtained by the Commission pursuant to its authority under this section prior to the institution of any proceeding under this Title involving such information. Any officer or employee of the Commission who shall make public in any manner whatever any information in violation of this subsection shall be guilty of a misdemeanor and upon conviction thereof, shall be fined not more than $1,000, or imprisoned not more than one year.

§ 710. Conduct of hearings and investigations

For the purpose of all hearings and investigations conducted by the Commission or its duly authorized agents or agencies, section 161 of Title 29 shall apply.

§ 711. Posting of notices; penalties

(a) Every employer, employment agency, and labor organization, as the case may be,shall post and keep posted in conspicuous places upon its premises where notices to employees, applicants for employment, and members are customarily posted a notice to be prepared or approved by the Commission setting forth excerpts from or, summaries of, the pertinent provisions of this Title and information pertinent to the filing of a complaint.

(b) A willful violation of this section shall be punishable by a fine of not more than $100 for each separate offense.

§ 712. Veterans' special rights or preference

Nothing contained in this Title shall be construed to repeal or modify any Federal, State, territorial, or local law creating special rights or preference for veterans.

§ 713. Regulations and reliance on interpretations and instructions of Commission

(a) The Commission shall have authority from time to time to issue, amend, or rescind suitable procedural regulations to carry out the provisions of this Title. Regulations issued under this section shall be in conformity with the standards and limitations of subchapter II of chapter 5 of Title 5.

(b) In any action or proceeding based on any alleged unlawful employment practice, no person shall be subject to any liability or punishment for or on account of (1) the commission by such person of an unlawful employment practice if he pleads and proves that the act or omission complained of was in good faith, in conformity with, and in reliance on any written interpretation or opinion of the Commission, or (2) the failure of such person to publish and file any information required by any provision of this Title if he pleads and proves that he failed to publish and file such information in good faith, in conformity with the instructions of the Commission issued under this Title regarding the filing of such information. Such a defense, if established, shall be a bar to the action or proceeding, notwithstanding that (A) after such act or omission, such interpretation or opinion is modified or rescinded or is determined by judicial authority to be invalid or of no legal effect, or (B) after publishing or filing the description and annual reports, such publication or filing is determined by judicial authority not to be in conformity with the requirements of this Title.

* * *

§ 715. Coordination of efforts and elimination of competition among Federal departments, agencies, etc. in implementation and enforcement of equal employment opportunity legislation, orders, and policies; report to President and Congress

The Equal Employment Opportunity Commission shall have the responsibility for developing and implementing agreements, policies and practices designed to maximize effort, promote efficiency, and eliminate conflict, competition, duplication and inconsistency among the operations, functions and jurisdictions of the various departments, agencies and branches of the Federal Government responsible for the implementation and enforcement of equal employment opportunity legislation, orders, and policies. On or before October 1 of each year, the Equal Employment Opportunity Commission shall transmit to the President and to the Congress a report of its activities, together with such recommendations for legislative or administrative changes as it concludes are desirable to further promote the purposes of this section.

* * *

§ 717. Employment by Federal Government

(a) All personnel actions affecting employees or applicants for employment (except with regard to aliens employed outside the limits of the United States) in military departments as defined in section 102 of Title 5, in executive agencies as defined in section 105 of Title 5 (including employees and applicants for employment who are paid from nonappropriated funds), in the United States Postal Service and the Postal Rate Commission, in those units of the Government of the District of Columbia having positions in the competitive service, and in those units of the legislative and judicial branches of the Federal Government having positions in the competitive service, and in the Library of Congress shall be made free from any discrimination based on race, color, religion, sex, or national origin.

(b) Except as otherwise provided in this subsection, the Equal Employment Opportunity Commission shall have authority to enforce the provisions of subsection (a) of this section through appropriate remedies, including reinstatement or hiring of employees with or without back pay, as will effectuate the policies of this section, and shall issue such rules, regulations, orders and instructions as it deems necessary and appropriate to carry out its responsibilities under this section. The Equal Employment Opportunity Commission shall—

> (1) be responsible for the annual review and approval of a national and regional equal employment opportunity plan which each department and agency and each appropriate unit referred to in subsection (a) of this section shall submit in order to maintain an affirmative program of equal employment opportunity for all such employees and applicants for employment;

> (2) be responsible for the review and evaluation of the operation of all agency equal employment opportunity programs, periodically obtaining and publishing (on at least a semiannual basis) progress reports from each such department, agency, or unit; and

> (3) consult with and solicit the recommendations of interested individuals, groups, and organizations relating to equal employment opportunity.

The head of each such department, agency, or unit shall comply with such rules, regulations, orders, and instructions which shall include a provision that an employee or applicant for employment shall be notified of any final action taken on any complaint of discrimination filed by him thereunder. The plan submitted by each department, agency, and unit shall include, but not be limited to—

(1) provision for the establishment of training and education programs designed to provide a maximum opportunity for employees to advance so as to perform at their highest potential; and

(2) a description of the qualifications in terms of training and experience relating to equal employment opportunity for the principal and operating officials of each such department, agency, or unit responsible for carrying out the equal employment opportunity program and of the allocation of personnel and resources proposed by such department, agency, or unit to carry out its equal employment opportunity program.

With respect to employment in the Library of Congress, authorities granted in this subsection to the Equal Employment Opportunity Commission shall be exercised by the Librarian of Congress.

(c) Within ninety (90) days of receipt of notice of final action taken by a department, agency, or unit referred to in subsection (a) of this section, or by the Equal Employment Opportunity Commission upon an appeal from a decision or order of such department, agency, or unit on a complaint of discrimination based on race, color, religion, sex or national origin, brought pursuant to subsection (a) of this section, Executive Order 11478 or any succeeding Executive orders, or after one hundred and eighty days from the filing of the initial charge with the department, agency, or unit or with the Equal Employment Opportunity Commission on appeal from a decision or order of such department, agency, or unit until such time as final action may be taken by a department, agency, or unit, an employee or applicant for employment, if aggrieved by the final disposition of his complaint, or by the failure to take final action on his complaint, may file a civil action as provided in section 706 of this Act, in which civil action the head of the department, agency, or unit, as appropriate, shall be the defendant.

(d) The provisions of section 706(f) through (k) of this Act, as applicable, shall govern civil actions brought hereunder, and the same interest to compensate for delay in payment shall be available as in cases involving nonpublic parties.

(e) Nothing contained in this Act shall relieve any Government agency or official of its or his primary responsibility to assure nondiscrimination in employment as required by the Constitution and statutes or of its or his responsibilities under Executive Order 11478 relating to equal employment opportunity in the Federal Government.

§ 718. Procedure for denial, withholding, termination, or suspension of Government contract

No Government contract, or portion thereof, with any employer, shall be denied, withheld, terminated, or suspended, by any agency or officer of the United States under any equal employment opportunity law or order, where such employer has an affirmative action plan which has previously been accepted by the Government for the same facility within the past twelve months without first according such employer full hearing and adjudication under the provisions of section 554 of Title 5, and the following pertinent sections: *Provided*, That if such employer has deviated substantially from such previously agreed to affirmative action plan, this section shall not apply: *Provided further*, That for the purposes of this section an affirmative action plan shall be deemed to have been accepted by the Government at the time the appropriate compliance agency has accepted such plan unless within forty-five days thereafter the Office of Federal Contract Compliance has disapproved such plan.

CIVIL RIGHTS ACT OF 1991
42 U.S.C. § ___, P.L. 102–166; 105 Stat. 1071.

An Act to amend the Civil Rights Act of 1964 to strengthen and improve Federal civil rights laws, to provide for damages in cases of intentional employment discrimination, to clarify provisions regarding disparate impact actions, and for other purposes.

Be it enacted by the Senate and House of Representatives of the United States of America in Congress assembled,

§ 1. SHORT TITLE

This Act may be cited as the "Civil Rights Act of 1991."

§ 2. FINDINGS

The Congress finds that—

(1) additional remedies under Federal law are needed to deter unlawful harassment and intentional discrimination in the workplace;

(2) the decision of the Supreme Court in Wards Cove Packing Co. v. Atonio, 490 U.S. 642 (1989) has weakened the scope and effectiveness of Federal civil rights protections; and

(3) legislation is necessary to provide additional protections against unlawful discrimination in employment.

§ 3. PURPOSES

The purposes of this Act are—

(1) to provide appropriate remedies for intentional discrimination and unlawful harassment in the workplace;

(2) to codify the concepts of "business necessity" and "job related" enunciated by the Supreme Court in Griggs v. Duke Power Co., 401 U.S. 424 (1971), and in the other Supreme Court decisions prior to Wards Cove Packing Co. v. Atonio, 490 U.S. 642 (1989);

(3) to confirm statutory authority and provide statutory guidelines for the adjudication of disparate impact suits under Title VII of the Civil Rights Act of 1964; and

(4) to respond to recent decisions of the Supreme Court by expanding the scope of relevant civil rights statutes in order to provide adequate protection to victims of discrimination.

TITLE I—FEDERAL CIVIL RIGHTS REMEDIES

* * *

§ 102. DAMAGES IN CASES OF INTENTIONAL DISCRIMINATION

The Revised Statutes are amended by inserting after 42 U.S.C. § 1981 the following new section, 42 U.S.C. § 1981A. [Text of this provision can be found *infra*, at 1262–1263.]

* * *

§ 105. BURDEN OF PROOF IN DISPARATE IMPACT CASES

* * *

(b) No statements other than the interpretive memorandum appearing at Vol. 137 Congressional Record S 15276 (daily ed. Oct. 25, 1991) shall be considered legislative history of, or relied upon in any way as legislative history in construing or applying, any provision of this Act that relates to Wards Cove—Business necessity/cumulation/alternative business practice.

[The portion of the Congressional Record cited in § 105(b) provides as follows:

Mr. DANFORTH.

Mr. President, I ask unanimous consent that the attached interpretive memorandum be printed in the RECORD.

There being no objection, the memorandum was ordered to be printed in the RECORD, as follows:

INTERPRETIVE MEMORANDUM

The final compromise on S. 1745 agreed to by several Senate sponsors, including Senators DANFORTH, KENNEDY, and DOLE, and the Administration states that with respect to Wards Cove–Business necessity/cumulation/alternative business practice-the exclusive legislative history is as follows:

The terms "business necessity" and "job related" are intended to reflect the concepts enunciated by the Supreme Court in Griggs v. Duke Power Co., 401 U.S. 424 (1971), and in the other Supreme Court decisions prior to Wards Cove Packing Co. v. Atonio, 490 U.S. 642 (1989).

When a decision-making process includes particular, functionally-integrated practices which are components of the same criterion, standard, method of administration, or test, such as the height and weight requirements designed to measure strength in Dothard v. Rawlinson, 433 U.S. 321 (1977), the particular, functionally-integrated practices may be analyzed as one employment practice.]

* * *

§ 116. LAWFUL COURT–ORDERED REMEDIES, AFFIRMATIVE ACTION, AND CONCILIATION AGREEMENTS NOT AFFECTED

Nothing in the amendments made by this title shall be construed to affect court-ordered remedies, affirmative action, or conciliation agreements, that are in accordance with the law.

§ 117. COVERAGE OF HOUSE OF REPRESENTATIVES AND THE AGENCIES OF THE LEGISLATIVE BRANCH

(a) COVERAGE OF THE HOUSE OF REPRESENTATIVES—

(1) **IN GENERAL**—Notwithstanding any provision of Title VII of the Civil Rights Act of 1964 or of other law, the purposes of such title shall, subject to paragraph (2), apply in their entirety to the House of Representatives.

(2) **EMPLOYMENT IN THE HOUSE**—

(A) **APPLICATION**—The rights and protections under Title VII of the Civil Rights Act of 1964 shall, subject to subparagraph (B), apply with respect to any employee in an employment position in the House of Representatives and any employing authority of the House of Representatives.

(B) **ADMINISTRATION**—

(i) **IN GENERAL**—In the administration of this paragraph, the remedies and procedures made applicable pursuant to the resolution described in clause (ii) shall apply exclusively.

(ii) **RESOLUTION**—The resolution referred to in clause (i) is the Fair Employment Practices Resolution (House Resolution 558 of the One Hundredth Congress, as agreed to October 4, 1988), as incorporated into the Rules of the House of Representatives of the One Hundred Second Congress as Rule LI, or any other provision that continues in effect the provisions of such resolution.

(C) **EXERCISE OF RULEMAKING POWER**—The provisions of subparagraph (B) are enacted by the House of Representatives as an exercise of the rulemaking power of the House of Representatives, with full recognition of the right of the House to change its rules, in the same manner, and to the same extent as in the case of any other rule of the House.

(b) INSTRUMENTALITIES OF CONGRESS—

(1) **IN GENERAL**—The rights and protections under this title and Title VII of the Civil Rights Act of 1964 shall, subject to paragraph (2), apply with respect to the conduct of each instrumentality of the Congress.

(2) **ESTABLISHMENT OF REMEDIES AND PROCEDURES BY INSTRUMENTALITIES**—The chief official of each instrumentality of the Congress shall establish remedies and procedures to be utilized with respect to the rights and protections provided pursuant to paragraph (1). Such remedies and procedures shall apply exclusively, except for the employees who are defined as Senate employees, in section 301(c)(1).

(3) **REPORT TO CONGRESS**—The chief official of each instrumentality of the Congress shall, after establishing remedies and procedures for purposes of paragraph (2), submit to the Congress a report describing the remedies and procedures.

(4) **DEFINITION OF INSTRUMENTALITIES**—For purposes of this section, instrumentalities of the Congress include the following: the Architect of the Capitol, the Congressional Budget Office, the General Accounting Office, the Government Printing Office, the Office of Technology Assessment, and the United States Botanic Garden.

(5) **CONSTRUCTION**—Nothing in this section shall alter the enforcement procedures for individuals protected under section 717 of Title VII for the Civil Rights Act of 1964.

§ 118. ALTERNATIVE MEANS OF DISPUTE RESOLUTION

Where appropriate and to the extent authorized by law, the use of alternative means of dispute resolution, including settlement negotiations, conciliation, facilitation, mediation, factfinding, minitrials, and arbitration, is encouraged to resolve disputes arising under the Acts or provisions of Federal law amended by this Act.

* * *

TITLE IV—GENERAL PROVISIONS

§ 402. EFFECTIVE DATE

(a) **IN GENERAL**—Except as otherwise specifically provided, this Act and the amendments made by this Act shall take effect upon enactment.

(b) CERTAIN DISPARATE IMPACT CASES—Notwithstanding any other provision of this Act, nothing in this Act shall apply to any disparate impact case for which a complaint was filed before March 1, 1975, and for which an initial decision was rendered after October 30, 1983.

SELECTED CONSTITUTIONAL AMENDMENTS

Amendment V

No person shall * * * be deprived of life, liberty, or property, without due process of law; nor shall private property be taken for public use, without just compensation.

Amendment XIII [1865]

Section 1. Neither slavery nor involuntary servitude, except as a punishment for crime whereof the party shall have been duly convicted, shall exist within the United States, or any place subject to their jurisdiction.

Section 2. Congress shall have power to enforce this article by appropriate legislation.

Amendment XIV [1868]

Section 1. All persons born or naturalized in the United States, and subject to the jurisdiction thereof, are citizens of the United States and of the State wherein they reside. No State shall make or enforce any law which shall abridge the privileges or immunities of citizens of the United States; nor shall any State deprive any person of life, liberty, or property, without due process of law; nor deny to any person within its jurisdiction the equal protection of the laws.

* * *

Section 5. The Congress shall have power to enforce, by appropriate legislation, the provisions of this article.

RECONSTRUCTION CIVIL RIGHTS ACTS, as Amended by the Civil Rights Act of 1991

42 U.S.C.A. § 1981. Equal rights under the law, as amended

(a) All persons within the jurisdiction of the United States shall have the same right in every State and Territory to make and enforce contracts, to sue, be parties, give evidence, and to the full and equal benefit of all laws and proceedings for the security of persons and property as is enjoyed by white citizens, and shall be subject to like punishment, pains, penalties, taxes, licenses, and exactions of every kind, and to no other.

(b) For purposes of this section, the term "make and enforce contracts" includes the making, performance, modification, and termination of contracts, and the enjoyment of all benefits, privileges, terms, and conditions of the contractual relationship.

(c) The rights protected by this section are protected against impairment by nongovernmental discrimination and impairment under color of State law.

42 U.S.C.A. § 1981A. Damages In Cases Of Intentional Discrimination In Employment

(a) RIGHT OF RECOVERY—

(1) **CIVIL RIGHTS**—In an action brought by a complaining party under section 706 or 717 of the Civil Rights Act of 1964 against a respondent who engaged in unlawful intentional discrimination (not an employment practice that is unlawful because of its disparate impact) prohibited under section 703, 704, or 717 of the Act, and provided that the complaining party cannot recover under 42 U.S.C. § 1981, the complaining party may recover compensatory and punitive damages as allowed in subsection (b), in addition to any relief authorized by section 706(g) of the Civil Rights Act of 1964, from the respondent.

(2) **DISABILITY**—In an action brought by a complaining party under the powers, remedies, and procedures set forth in section 706 or 717 of the Civil Rights Act of 1964 (as provided in section 107(a) of the Americans with Disabilities Act of 1990, and section 505(a)(1) of the Rehabilitation Act of 1973, respectively) against a respondent who engaged in unlawful intentional discrimination (not an employment practice that is unlawful because of its disparate impact) under section 501 of the Rehabilitation Act of 1973 and the regulations implementing section 501, or who violated the requirements of section 501 of the Act or the regulations implementing section 501 concerning the provision of a reasonable accommodation, or section 102 of the Americans with Disabilities Act of 1990, or committed a violation of section 102(b)(5) of the Act, against an individual, the complaining party may recover compensatory and punitive damages as allowed in subsection (b), in addition to any relief authorized by section 706(g) of the Civil Rights Act of 1964, from the respondent.

(3) **REASONABLE ACCOMMODATION AND GOOD FAITH EFFORT**—In cases where a discriminatory practice involves the provision of a reasonable accommodation pursuant to section 102(b)(5) of the Americans with Disabilities Act of 1990 or regulations implementing section 501 of the Rehabilitation Act of 1973, damages may not be awarded under this section where the covered entity demonstrates good faith efforts, in consultation with the person with the disability who has informed the covered entity that accommodation is needed, to identify and make a reasonable accommodation that would provide such individual with an equally

effective opportunity and would not cause an undue hardship on the operation of the business.

(b) COMPENSATORY AND PUNITIVE DAMAGES—

(1) DETERMINATION OF PUNITIVE DAMAGES—A complaining party may recover punitive damages under this section against a respondent (other than a government, government agency or political subdivision) if the complaining party demonstrates that the respondent engaged in a discriminatory practice or discriminatory practices with malice or with reckless indifference to the federally protected rights of an aggrieved individual.

(2) EXCLUSIONS FROM COMPENSATORY DAMAGES—Compensatory damages awarded under this section shall not include backpay, interest on backpay, or any other type of relief authorized under section 706(g) of the Civil Rights Act of 1964.

(3) LIMITATIONS—The sum of the amount of compensatory damages awarded under this section for future pecuniary losses, emotional pain, suffering, inconvenience, mental anguish, loss of enjoyment of life, and other nonpecuniary losses, and the amount of punitive damages awarded under this section, shall not exceed, for each complaining party—

> (A) in the case of a respondent who has more than 14 and fewer than 101 employees in each of 20 or more calendar weeks in the current or preceding calendar year, $50,000;

> (B) in the case of a respondent who has more than 100 and fewer than 201 employees in each of 20 or more calendar weeks in the current or preceding calendar year, $100,000; and

> (C) in the case of a respondent who has more than 200 and fewer than 501 employees in each of 20 or more calendar weeks in the current or preceding calendar year, $200,000; and

> (D) in the case of a respondent who has more than 500 employees in each of 20 or more calendar weeks in the current or preceding calendar year, $300,000.

(4) CONSTRUCTION—Nothing in this section shall be construed to limit the scope of, or the relief available under 42 U.S.C. § 1981.

(c) JURY TRIAL—If a complaining party seeks compensatory or punitive damages under this section—

(1) any party may demand a trial by jury; and

(2) the court shall not inform the jury of the limitations described in subsection (b)(3).

(d) DEFINITIONS—As used in this section:

(1) COMPLAINING PARTY—The term "complaining party" means—

(A) in the case of a person seeking to bring an action under subsection (a)(1), the Equal Employment Opportunity Commission, the Attorney General, or a person who may bring an action or proceeding under Title VII of the Civil Rights Act of 1964; or

(B) in the case of a person seeking to bring an action under subsection (a)(2), the Equal Employment Opportunity Commission, the Attorney General, a person who may bring an action or proceeding under section 505(a)(1) of the Rehabilitation Act of 1973, or a person who may bring an action or proceeding under Title I of the Americans with Disabilities Act of 1990.

(2) **DISCRIMINATORY PRACTICE**—The term "discriminatory practice" means the discrimination described in paragraph (1), or the discrimination or the violation described in paragraph (2), of subsection (a).

42 U.S.C.A. § 1983. Civil action for deprivation of rights

Every person who, under color of any statute, ordinance, regulation, custom, or usage, of any State or Territory or the District of Columbia, subjects, or causes to be subjected, any citizen of the United States or other person within the jurisdiction thereof to the deprivation of any rights, privileges, or immunities secured by the Constitution and laws, shall be liable to the party injured in an action at law, suit in equity, or other proper proceeding for redress. For the purposes of this section, any Act of Congress applicable exclusively to the District of Columbia shall be considered to be a statute of the District of Columbia.

42 U.S.C.A. § 1985(c). Conspiracy to interfere with civil rights

If two or more persons in any State or Territory conspire or go in disguise on the highway or on the premises of another, for the purpose of depriving, either directly or indirectly, any person or class of persons of the equal protection of the laws, or of equal privileges and immunities under the laws; or for the purpose of preventing or hindering the constituted authorities of any State or Territory from giving or securing to all persons within such State or Territory the equal protection of the laws; or if two or more persons conspire to prevent by force, intimidation, or threat, any citizen who is lawfully entitled to vote, from giving his support or advocacy in a legal manner, toward or in favor of the election of any lawfully qualified person as an elector for President or Vice President, or as a Member of Congress of the United States; or to injure any citizen in person or property on account of such support or advocacy; in any case of conspiracy set forth in this section, if one or more persons engaged therein do, or cause to be done, any act in furtherance of the object of such conspiracy, whereby another is injured in his person or property, or deprived of having and exercising any right or privilege of a citizen of the United States, the party so injured or deprived may have an action for the recovery of damages occasioned by such injury or deprivation, against anyone or more of the conspirators.

42 U.S.C.A. § 1988. Proceedings in vindication of civil rights, attorney's fees, as amended

* * *

(b) In any action or proceeding to enforce a provision of sections 1981, 1981A, 1982, 1983, 1985, and 1986 of this title, title IX of Public Law 92–318, or title VI of the Civil Rights Act of 1964, the court, in its discretion, may allow the prevailing party, other than the United States, a reasonable attorney's fee as part of the costs.

(c) In awarding an attorney's fee under subsection (b) in any action or proceeding to enforce a provision of 42 U.S.C. §§ 1981 or 1981A, the court, in its discretion, may include expert fees as part of the attorney's fee.

EQUAL PAY ACT
29 U.S.C.A. § 206(d).

§ 206(d). Prohibition of sex discrimination

(1) No employer having employees subject to any provisions of this section shall discriminate, within any establishment in which such employees are employed, between employees on the basis of sex by paying wages to employees in such establishment at a rate less than the rate at which he pays wages to employees of the opposite sex in such establishment for equal work on jobs the performance of which requires equal skill, effort, and responsibility, and which are performed under similar working conditions, except where such payment is made pursuant to (i) a seniority system; (ii) a merit system; (iii) a system which measures earnings by quantity or quality of production; or (iv) a differential based on any other factor other than sex: *Provided*, That an employer who is paying a wage rate differential in violation of this subsection shall not, in order to comply with the provisions of this subsection, reduce the wage rate of any employee.

(2) No labor organization, or its agents, representing employees of an employer having employees subject to any provisions of this section shall cause or attempt to cause such an employer to discriminate against an employee in violation of paragraph (1) of this subsection.

(3) For purposes of administration and enforcement, any amounts owing to any employee which have been withheld in violation of this subsection shall be deemed to be unpaid minimum wages or unpaid overtime compensation under this Act.

(4) As used in this subsection, the term "labor organization" means any organization of any kind, or any agency or employee representation committee or plan, in which employees participate and which exists for

the purpose, in whole or in part, of dealing with employers concerning grievances, labor disputes, wages, rates of pay, hours of employment, or conditions of work.

29 U.S.C. § 216. Remedies [§ 16(b) of Fair Labor Standards Act of 1938, as amended]

(b) Any employer who violates the provisions of section 206 or section 207 of this title shall be liable to the employee or employees affected in the amount of their unpaid minimum wages, or their unpaid overtime compensation, as the case may be, and in an additional equal amount as liquidated damages. Any employer who violates the provisions of section 215(a)(3) of this title shall be liable for such legal or equitable relief as may be appropriate to effectuate the purposes of section 215(a)(3) of this title, including without limitation employment, reinstatement, promotion, and the payment of wages lost and an additional equal amount as liquidated damages. An action to recover the liability prescribed in either of the preceding sentences may be maintained against any employer (including a public agency) in any Federal or State court of competent jurisdiction by any one or more employees for and in behalf of himself or themselves and other employees similarly situated. No employee shall be a party plaintiff to any such action unless he gives his consent in writing to become such a party and such consent is filed in the court in which such action is brought. The court in such action shall, in addition to any judgment awarded to the plaintiff or plaintiffs, allow a reasonable attorney's fee to be paid by the defendant, and costs of the action. The right provided by this subsection to bring an action by or on behalf of any employee, and the right of any employee to become a party plaintiff to any such action, shall terminate upon the filing of a complaint by the Secretary of Labor in an action under section 217 of this title in which (1) restraint is sought of any further delay in the payment of unpaid minimum wages, or the amount of unpaid overtime compensation, as the case may be, owing to such employee under section 206 or section 207 of this title by an employer liable therefor under the provisions of this subsection or (2) legal or equitable relief is sought as a result of alleged violations of section 215(a)(3) of this title.

AGE DISCRIMINATION IN EMPLOYMENT ACT

29 U.S.C.A. § 621 et seq.

§ 2. Congressional statement of findings and purpose

(a) The Congress hereby finds and declares that—

(1) in the face of rising productivity and affluence, older workers find themselves disadvantaged in their efforts to retain employment, and especially to regain employment when displaced from jobs;

(2) the setting of arbitrary age limits regardless of potential for job performance has become a common practice, and certain otherwise desirable practices may work to the disadvantage of older persons;

(3) the incidence of unemployment, especially long-term unemployment with resultant deterioration of skill, morale, and employer acceptability is, relative to the younger ages, high among older workers; their numbers are great and growing; and their employment problems grave;

(4) the existence in industries affecting commerce, of arbitrary discrimination in employment because of age, burdens commerce and the free flow of goods in commerce.

(b) It is therefore the purpose of this chapter to promote employment of older persons based on their ability rather than age; to prohibit arbitrary age discrimination in employment; to help employers and workers find ways of meeting problems arising from the impact of age on employment.

* * *

§ 4. Prohibition of age discrimination

(a) Employer practices

It shall be unlawful for an employer—

(1) to fail or refuse to hire or to discharge any individual or otherwise discriminate against any individual with respect to his compensation, terms, conditions, or privileges of employment, because of such individual's age;

(2) to limit, segregate, or classify his employees in any way which would deprive or tend to deprive any individual of employment opportunities or otherwise adversely affect his status as an employee, because of such individual's age; or

(3) to reduce the wage rate of any employee in order to comply with this Act.

(b) Employment agency practices

It shall be unlawful for an employment agency to fail or refuse to refer for employment, or otherwise to discriminate against, any individual because of such individual's age, or to classify or refer for employment any individual on the basis of such individual's age.

(c) Labor organization practices

It shall be unlawful for a labor organization—

(1) to exclude or to expel from its membership, or otherwise to discriminate against, any individual because of his age;

(2) to limit, segregate, or classify its membership, or to classify or fail or refuse to refer for employment any individual, in any way

which would deprive or tend to deprive any individual of employment opportunities, or would limit such employment opportunities or otherwise adversely affect his status as an employee or as an applicant for employment, because of such individual's age;

(3) to cause or attempt to cause an employer to discriminate against an individual in violation of this section.

(d) Opposition to unlawful practices; participation in investigations, proceedings, or litigation

It shall be unlawful for an employer to discriminate against any of his employees or applicants for employment, for an employment agency to discriminate against any individual, or for a labor organization to discriminate against any member thereof or applicant for membership, because such individual, member or applicant for membership has opposed any practice made unlawful by this section, or because such individual, member or applicant for membership has made a charge, testified, assisted, or participated in any manner in an investigation, proceeding, or litigation under this Act.

(e) Printing or publication of notice or advertisement indicating preference, limitation, etc.

It shall be unlawful for an employer, labor organization, or employment agency to print or publish, or cause to be printed or published, any notice or advertisement relating to employment by such an employer or membership in or any classification or referral for employment by such a labor organization, or relating to any classification or referral for employment by such an employment agency, indicating any preference, limitation, specification, or discrimination, based on age.

(f) Lawful practices; age an occupational qualification; other reasonable factors; laws of foreign workplace; seniority system; employee benefit plans; discharge or discipline for good cause

It shall not be unlawful for an employer, employment agency, or labor organization—

(1) to take any action otherwise prohibited under subsections (a), (b), (c), or (e) of this section where age is a bona fide occupational qualification reasonably necessary to the normal operation of the particular business, or where the differentiation is based on reasonable factors other than age, or where such practices involve an employee in a workplace in a foreign country, and compliance with such subsections would cause such employer, or a corporation controlled by such employer, to violate the laws of the country in which such workplace is located;

(2) to take any action otherwise prohibited under subsection (a), (b), (c), or (e) of this section—

(A) to observe the terms of a bona fide seniority system that is not intended to evade the purposes of this Act, except that no such seniority system shall require or permit the involuntary retirement of any individual specified by section 12(a) of this Act because of the age of such individual; or

(B) to observe the terms of a bona fide employee benefit plan—

(i) where, for each benefit or benefit package, the actual amount of payment made or cost incurred on behalf of an older worker is no less than that made or incurred on behalf of a younger worker, as permissible under section 1625.10, Title 29, Code of Federal Regulations (as in effect on June 22, 1989); or

(ii) that is a voluntary early retirement incentive plan consistent with the relevant purpose or purposes of this Act.

Notwithstanding clause (i) or (ii) of subparagraph (B), no such employee benefit plan or voluntary early retirement incentive plan shall excuse the failure to hire any individual, and no such employee benefit plan shall require or permit the involuntary retirement of any individual specified by section 12(a) of this Act, because of the age of such individual. An employer, employment agency, or labor organization acting under subparagraph (A), or under clause (i) or (ii) of subparagraph (B), shall have the burden of proving that such actions are lawful in any civil enforcement proceeding brought under this chapter; or

(3) to discharge or otherwise discipline an individual for good cause.

[(g) Repealed.]

(h) Practices of foreign corporations controlled by American employers; foreign persons not controlled by American employers; factors determining control

(1) If an employer controls a corporation whose place of incorporation is in a foreign country, any practice by such corporation prohibited under this section shall be presumed to be such practice by such employer.

(2) The prohibitions of this section shall not apply where the employer is a foreign person not controlled by an American employer.

(3) For the purpose of this subsection the determination of whether an employer controls a corporation shall be based upon the—

(A) interrelation of operations,

(B) common management,

(C) centralized control of labor relations, and

(D) common ownership or financial control, of the employer and the corporation.

(i) Firefighters and law enforcement officers attaining hiring or retiring age under State or local law on March 3, 1983

It shall not be unlawful for an employer which is a State, a political subdivision of a State, an agency or instrumentality of a State or a political subdivision of a State, or an interstate agency to fail or refuse to hire or to discharge any individual because of such individual's age if such action is taken—

(1) with respect to the employment of an individual as a firefighter or as a law enforcement officer and the individual has attained the age of hiring or retirement in effect under applicable State or local law on March 3, 1983, and

(2) pursuant to a bona fide hiring or retirement plan that is not a subterfuge to evade the purposes of this chapter.

(j) Employee pension benefit plans; cessation or reduction of benefit accrual or of allocation to employee account; distribution of benefits after attainment of normal retirement age; compliance; highly compensated employees

(1) Except as otherwise provided in this subsection, it shall be unlawful for an employer, an employment agency, a labor organization, or any combination thereof to establish or maintain an employee pension benefit plan which requires or permits—

(A) in the case of a defined benefit plan, the cessation of an employee's benefit accrual, or the reduction of the rate of an employee's benefit accrual, because of age, or

(B) in the case of a defined contribution plan, the cessation of allocations to an employee's account, or the reduction of the rate at which amounts are allocated to an employee's account, because of age.

(2) Nothing in this section shall be construed to prohibit an employer, employment agency, or labor organization from observing any provision of an employee pension benefit plan to the extent that such provision imposes (without regard to age) a limitation on the amount of benefits that the plan provides or a limitation on the number of years of service or years of participation which are taken into account for purposes of determining benefit accrual under the plan.

(3) In the case of any employee who, as of the end of any plan year under a defined benefit plan, has attained normal retirement age under such plan—

(A) if distribution of benefits under such plan with respect to such employee has commenced as of the end of such plan year, then any requirement of this subsection for continued accrual of benefits under such plan with respect to such employee during such plan year shall be treated as satisfied to the extent of the actuarial equivalent of in-service distribution of benefits, and

(B) if distribution of benefits under such plan with respect to such employee has not commenced as of the end of such year in accordance with section 206(a)(3) of the Employee Retirement Income Security Act of 1974 and section 401(a)(14)(C) of the Internal Revenue Code of 1986, and the payment of benefits under such plan with respect to such employee is not suspended during such plan year pursuant to section 203(a)(3)(B) of the Employee Retirement Income Security Act of 1974 or section 411(a)(3)(B) of the Internal Revenue Code of 1986 then any requirement of this subsection for continued accrual of benefits under such plan with respect to such employee during such plan year shall be treated as satisfied to the extent of any adjustment in the benefit payable under the plan during such plan year attributable to the delay in the distribution of benefits after the attainment of normal retirement age.

The provisions of this paragraph shall apply in accordance with regulations of the Secretary of the Treasury. Such regulations shall provide for the application of the preceding provisions of this paragraph to all employee pension benefit plans subject to this subsection and may provide for the application of such provisions, in the case of any such employee, with respect to any period of time within a plan year.

(4) Compliance with the requirements of this subsection with respect to an employee pension benefit plan shall constitute compliance with the requirements of this section relating to benefit accrual under such plan.

(5) Paragraph (1) shall not apply with respect to any employee who is a highly compensated employee (within the meaning of section 414(q) of the Internal Revenue Code of 1986) to the extent provided in regulations prescribed by the Secretary of the Treasury for purposes of precluding discrimination in favor of highly compensated employees within the meaning of sections 401–425 of the Internal Revenue Code of 1986.

(6) A plan shall not be treated as failing to meet the requirements of paragraph (1) solely because the subsidized portion of any early retirement benefit is disregarded in determining benefit accruals.

(7) Any regulations prescribed by the Secretary of the Treasury pursuant to clause (v) of section 411(b)(1)(H) of the Internal Revenue Code and subparagraphs (C) and (D) of section 411(b)(2) of the Internal Revenue Code shall apply with respect to the requirements of this subsection in the same manner and to the same extent as such regulations apply with respect to the requirements

of such sections 411(b)(1)(H) and 411(b)(2) of the Internal Revenue Code.

(8) A plan shall not be treated as failing to meet the requirements of this section solely because such plan provides a normal retirement age described in section 3(24)(B) of the Employee Retirement Income Security Act and section 411(a)(8)(B) of the Internal Revenue Code.

(9) For purposes of this subsection—

(A) The terms "employee pension benefit plan," "defined benefit plan," "defined contribution plan," and "normal retirement age" have the meanings provided such terms in section 3 of the Employment Retirement Income Security Act.

(B) The term "compensation" has the meaning provided by section 414(s) of the Internal Revenue Code.

(k) Date of adoption of system or plan

A seniority system or employee benefit plan shall comply with this chapter regardless of the date of adoption of such system or plan.

(*l*) Minimum age requirements; early retirement benefits

Notwithstanding clause (i) or (ii) of subsection (f)(2)(B) of this section—

(1) It shall not be a violation of subsection (a), (b), (c), or (e) of this section solely because—

(A) an employee pension benefit plan (as defined in section 1002(2) of this title) provides for the attainment of a minimum age as a condition of eligibility for normal or early retirement benefits; or

(B) a defined benefit plan (as defined in section 3(35) of the Employment Retirement Income Security Act) provides for—

(i) payments that constitute the subsidized portion of an early retirement benefit; or

(ii) social security supplements for plan participants that commence before the age and terminate at the age (specified by the plan) when participants are eligible to receive reduced or unreduced old-age insurance benefits under title II of the Social Security Act (42 U.S.C. 401 et seq.), and that do not exceed such old-age insurance benefits.

(2)(A) It shall not be a violation of subsection (a), (b), (c), or (e) of this section solely because following a contingent event unrelated to age—

(i) the value of any retiree health benefits received by an individual eligible for an immediate pension;

(ii) the value of any additional pension benefits that are made available solely as a result of the contingent event unrelated to age and following which the individual is eligible for not less than an immediate and unreduced pension; or

(iii) the values described in both clauses (i) and (ii); are deducted from severance pay made available as a result of the contingent event unrelated to age.

(B) For an individual who receives immediate pension benefits that are actuarially reduced under subparagraph (A)(i), the amount of the deduction available pursuant to subparagraph (A)(i) shall be reduced by the same percentage as the reduction in the pension benefits.

(C) For purposes of this paragraph, severance pay shall include that portion of supplemental unemployment compensation benefits (as described in section 501(c)(17) of the Internal Revenue Code) that—

(i) constitutes additional benefits of up to 52 weeks;

(ii) has the primary purpose and effect of continuing benefits until an individual becomes eligible for an immediate and unreduced pension; and

(iii) is discontinued once the individual becomes eligible for an immediate and unreduced pension.

(D) For purposes of this paragraph and solely in order to make the deduction authorized under this paragraph, the term "retiree health benefits" means benefits provided pursuant to a group health plan covering retirees, for which (determined as of the contingent event unrelated to age)—

(i) the package of benefits provided by the employer for the retirees who are below age 65 is at least comparable to benefits provided under Title XVIII of the Social Security Act (42 U.S.C. 1395 et seq.);

(ii) the package of benefits provided by the employer for the retirees who are age 65 and above is at least comparable to that offered under a plan that provides a benefit package with one-fourth the value of benefits provided under Title XVIII of such Act; or

(iii) the package of benefits provided by the employer is as described in clauses (i) and (ii).

(E)(i) If the obligation of the employer to provide retiree health benefits is of limited duration, the value for each individual shall be calculated at a rate of $3,000 per year for benefit years before age 65, and $750 per year for benefit years beginning at age 65 and above.

(ii) If the obligation of the employer to provide retiree health benefits is of unlimited duration, the value for each individual shall be calculated at a rate of $48,000 for individuals below age 65, and $24,000 for individuals age 65 and above.

(iii) The values described in clauses (i) and (ii) shall be calculated based on the age of the individual as of the date of the contingent event unrelated to age. The values are effective on October 16, 1990, and shall be adjusted on an annual basis, with respect to a contingent event that occurs subsequent to the first year after October 16, 1990, based on the medical component of the Consumer Price Index for all-urban consumers published by the Department of Labor.

(iv) If an individual is required to pay a premium for retiree health benefits, the value calculated pursuant to this subparagraph shall be reduced by whatever percentage of the overall premium the individual is required to pay.

(F) If an employer that has implemented a deduction pursuant to subparagraph (A) fails to fulfill the obligation described in subparagraph (E), any aggrieved individual may bring an action for specific performance of the obligation described in subparagraph (E). The relief shall be in addition to any other remedies provided under Federal or State law.

(3) It shall not be a violation of subsection (a), (b), (c), or (e) of this section solely because an employer provides a bona fide employee benefit plan or plans under which long-term disability benefits received by an individual are reduced by any pension benefits (other than those attributable to employee contributions)—

(A) paid to the individual that the individual voluntarily elects to receive; or

(B) for which an individual who has attained the later of age 62 or normal retirement age is eligible.

* * *

§ 7. Recordkeeping, investigation, and enforcement

(a) Attendance of witnesses; investigations, inspections, records, and homework regulations

The Equal Employment Opportunity Commission shall have the power to make investigations and require the keeping of records necessary or appropriate for the administration of this chapter in accordance with the powers and procedures provided in sections 9 and 11 of the Fair Labor Standards Act of 1938, as amended.

(b) Enforcement; prohibition of age discrimination under fair labor standards; unpaid minimum wages and unpaid overtime compensation; liquidated damages; judicial relief; conciliation, conference, and persuasion

The provisions of this chapter shall be enforced in accordance with the powers, remedies, and procedures provided in sections 11(b), 16 (except for subsection (a) thereof), and 17 of the Fair Labor Standards Act of 1938, as amended, and subsection (c) of this section. Any act prohibited under section 4 of this Act shall be deemed to be a prohibited act under section 15 of the Fair Labor Standards Act of 1938, as amended. Amounts owing to a person as a result of a violation of this Act shall be deemed to be unpaid minimum wages or unpaid overtime compensation for purposes of sections 16 and 17 of the Fair Labor Standards Act of 1938, as amended: Provided, That liquidated damages shall be payable only in cases of willful violations of this Act. In any action brought to enforce this chapter the court shall have jurisdiction to grant such legal or equitable relief as may be appropriate to effectuate the purposes of this Act, including without limitation judgments compelling employment, reinstatement or promotion, or enforcing the liability for amounts deemed to be unpaid minimum wages or unpaid overtime compensation under this section. Before instituting any action under this section, the Equal Employment Opportunity Commission shall attempt to eliminate the discriminatory practice or practices alleged, and to effect voluntary compliance with the requirements of this chapter through informal methods of conciliation, conference, and persuasion.

(c) Civil actions; persons aggrieved; jurisdiction; judicial relief; termination of individual action upon commencement of action by Commission; jury trial

(1) Any person aggrieved may bring a civil action in any court of competent jurisdiction for such legal or equitable relief as will effectuate the purposes of this chapter: Provided, That the right of any person to bring such action shall terminate upon the commencement of an action by the Equal Employment Opportunity Commission to enforce the right of such employee under this Act.

(2) In an action brought under paragraph (1), a person shall be entitled to a trial by jury of any issue of fact in any such action for recovery of amounts owing as a result of a violation of this Act, regardless of whether equitable relief is sought by any party in such action.

(d) Filing of charge with Commission; timeliness; conciliation, conference, and persuasion

No civil action may be commenced by an individual under this section until 60 days after a charge alleging unlawful discrimination has been filed with the Equal Employment Opportunity Commission. Such a charge shall be filed—

(1) within 180 days after the alleged unlawful practice occurred; or

(2) in a case to which section 14(b) of this Act applies, within 300 days after the alleged unlawful practice occurred, or within 30

days after receipt by the individual of notice of termination of proceedings under State law, whichever is earlier.

Upon receiving such a charge, the Commission shall promptly notify all persons named in such charge as prospective defendants in the action and shall promptly seek to eliminate any alleged unlawful practice by informal methods of conciliation, conference, and persuasion.

(e) Statute of limitations; reliance in future on administrative ruling, etc.; tolling

Section 59 of the Fair Labor Standards Act of 1938, as amended, shall apply to actions under this Act. If a charge filed with the Commission under this Act is dismissed or the proceedings of the Commission are otherwise terminated by the Commission, the Commission shall notify the person aggrieved. A civil action may be brought under this section by a person defined in section 11(a) against the respondent named in the charge within 90 days after the date of the receipt of such notice.

(f) Waiver

(1) An individual may not waive any right or claim under this Act unless the waiver is knowing and voluntary. Except as provided in paragraph (2), a waiver may not be considered knowing and voluntary unless at a minimum—

(A) the waiver is part of an agreement between the individual and the employer that is written in a manner calculated to be understood by such individual, or by the average individual eligible to participate;

(B) the waiver specifically refers to rights or claims arising under this chapter;

(C) the individual does not waive rights or claims that may arise after the date the waiver is executed;

(D) the individual waives rights or claims only in exchange for consideration in addition to anything of value to which the individual already is entitled;

(E) the individual is advised in writing to consult with an attorney prior to executing the agreement;

(F)(i) the individual is given a period of at least 21 days within which to consider the agreement; or

(ii) if a waiver is requested in connection with an exit incentive or other employment termination program offered to a group or class of employees, the individual is given a period of at least 45 days within which to consider the agreement;

(G) the agreement provides that for a period of at least 7 days following the execution of such agreement, the individual may revoke the agreement, and the agreement shall not become effective or enforceable until the revocation period has expired;

(H) if a waiver is requested in connection with an exit incentive or other employment termination program offered to a group or class of employees, the employer (at the commencement of the period specified in subparagraph (F)) informs the individual in writing in a manner calculated to be understood by the average individual eligible to participate, as to—

(i) any class, unit, or group of individuals covered by such program, any eligibility factors for such program, and any time limits applicable to such program; and

(ii) the job titles and ages of all individuals eligible or selected for the program, and the ages of all individuals in the same job classification or organizational unit who are not eligible or selected for the program.

(2) A waiver in settlement of a charge filed with the Equal Employment Opportunity Commission, or an action filed in court by the individual or the individual's representative, alleging age discrimination of a kind prohibited under section 4 or 15 of this Act may not be considered knowing and voluntary unless at a minimum—

(A) subparagraphs (A) through (E) of paragraph (1) have been met; and

(B) the individual is given a reasonable period of time within which to consider the settlement agreement.

(3) In any dispute that may arise over whether any of the requirements, conditions, and circumstances set forth in subparagraph (A), (B), (C), (D), (E), (F), (G), or (H) of paragraph (1), or subparagraph (A) or (B) of paragraph (2), have been met, the party asserting the validity of a waiver shall have the burden of proving in a court of competent jurisdiction that a waiver was knowing and voluntary pursuant to paragraph (1) or (2).

(4) No waiver agreement may affect the Commission's rights and responsibilities to enforce this Act. No waiver may be used to justify interfering with the protected right of an employee to file a charge or participate in an investigation or proceeding conducted by the Commission.

§ 8. Notices to be posted

Every employer, employment agency, and labor organization shall post and keep posted in conspicuous places upon its premises a notice to be prepared or approved by the Equal Employment Opportunity Commission setting forth information as the Commission deems appropriate to effectuate the purposes of this Act.

§ 9. Rules and regulations; exemptions

In accordance with the provisions of the Administrative Procedure Act, the Equal Employment Opportunity Commission may issue such rules and regulations as it may consider necessary or appropriate for carrying out this chapter, and may establish such reasonable exemptions to and from any or all provisions of this chapter as it may find necessary and proper in the public interest.

* * *

§ 11. Definitions

For the purposes of this Act—

(a) The term "person" means one or more individuals, partnerships, associations, labor organizations, corporations, business trusts, legal representatives, or any organized groups of persons.

(b) The term "employer" means a person engaged in an industry affecting commerce who has twenty or more employees for each working day in each of twenty or more calendar weeks in the current or preceding calendar year: Provided, That prior to June 30, 1968, employers having fewer than fifty employees shall not be considered employers. The term also means (1) any agent of such a person, and (2) a State or political subdivision of a State and any agency or instrumentality of a State or a political subdivision of a State, and any interstate agency, but such term does not include the United States, or a corporation wholly owned by the Government of the United States.

(c) The term "employment agency" means any person regularly undertaking with or without compensation to procure employees for an employer and includes an agent of such a person; but shall not include an agency of the United States.

(d) The term "labor organization" means a labor organization engaged in an industry affecting commerce, and any agent of such an organization, and includes any organization of any kind, any agency, or employee representation committee, group, association, or plan so engaged in which employees participate and which exists for the purpose, in whole or in part, of dealing with employers concerning grievances, labor disputes, wages, rates of pay, hours, or other terms or conditions of employment, and any conference, general committee, joint or system board, or joint council so engaged which is subordinate to a national or international labor organization.

(e) A labor organization shall be deemed to be engaged in an industry affecting commerce if (1) it maintains or operates a hiring hall or hiring office which procures employees for an employer or procures for employees opportunities to work for an employer, or (2) the number of its members (or, where it is a labor organization composed of other labor organizations or their representatives, if the aggregate number of the members of such other labor organization) is fifty or more prior to

July 1, 1968, or twenty-five or more on or after July 1, 1968, and such labor organization—

(1) is the certified representative of employees under the provisions of the National Labor Relations Act, as amended, or the Railway Labor Act, as amended; or

(2) although not certified, is a national or international labor organization or a local labor organization recognized or acting as the representative of employees of an employer or employers engaged in an industry affecting commerce; or

(3) has chartered a local labor organization or subsidiary body which is representing or actively seeking to represent employees of employers within the meaning of paragraph (1) or (2); or

(4) has been chartered by a labor organization representing or actively seeking to represent employees within the meaning of paragraph (1) or (2) as the local or subordinate body through which such employees may enjoy membership or become affiliated with such labor organization; or

(5) is a conference, general committee, joint or system board, or joint council subordinate to a national or international labor organization, which includes a labor organization engaged in an industry affecting commerce within the meaning of any of the preceding paragraphs of this subsection.

(f) The term "employee" means an individual employed by any employer except that the term "employee" shall not include any person elected to public office in any State or political subdivision of any State by the qualified voters thereof, or any person chosen by such officer to be on such officer's personal staff, or an appointee on the policymaking level or an immediate adviser with respect to the exercise of the constitutional or legal powers of the office.

The exemption set forth in the preceding sentence shall not include employees subject to the civil service laws of a State government, governmental agency, or political subdivision. The term "employee" includes any individual who is a citizen of the United States employed by an employer in a workplace in a foreign country.

(g) The term "commerce" means trade, traffic, commerce, transportation, transmission, or communication among the several States; or between a State and any place outside thereof; or within the District of Columbia, or a possession of the United States; or between points in the same State but through a point outside thereof.

(h) The term "industry affecting commerce" means any activity, business, or industry in commerce or in which a labor dispute would hinder or obstruct commerce or the free flow of commerce and includes any activity or industry "affecting commerce" within the meaning of the Labor–Management Reporting and Disclosure Act of 1959.

(i) The term "State" includes a State of the United States, the District of Columbia, Puerto Rico, the Virgin Islands, American Samoa, Guam, Wake Island, the Canal Zone, and Outer Continental Shelf lands defined in the Outer Continental Shelf Lands Act.

(j) The term "firefighter" means an employee, the duties of whose position are primarily to perform work directly connected with the control and extinguishment of fires or the maintenance and use of firefighting apparatus and equipment, including an employee engaged in this activity who is transferred to a supervisory or administrative position.

(k) The term "law enforcement officer" means an employee, the duties of whose position are primarily the investigation, apprehension, or detention of individuals suspected or convicted of offenses against the criminal laws of a State, including an employee engaged in this activity who is transferred to a supervisory or administrative position. For the purpose of this subsection, "detention" includes the duties of employees assigned to guard individuals incarcerated in any penal institution.

(*l*) The term "compensation, terms, conditions, or privileges of employment" encompasses all employee benefits, including such benefits provided pursuant to a bona fide employee benefit plan.

§ 12. Age limits

(a) Individuals at least 40 years of age

The prohibitions in this chapter shall be limited to individuals who are at least 40 years of age.

(b) Employees or applicants for employment in Federal Government

In the case of any personnel action affecting employees or applicants for employment which is subject to the provisions of section 15 of this Act, the prohibitions established in section 15 of this Act shall be limited to individuals who are at least 40 years of age.

(c) Bona fide executives or high policymakers

(1) Nothing in this chapter shall be construed to prohibit compulsory retirement of any employee who has attained 65 years of age and who, for the 2–year period immediately before retirement, is employed in a bona fide executive or a high policymaking position, if such employee is entitled to an immediate nonforfeitable annual retirement benefit from a pension, profit-sharing, savings, or deferred compensation plan, or any combination of such plans, of the employer of such employee, which equals, in the aggregate, at least $44,000.

(2) In applying the retirement benefit test of paragraph (1) of this subsection, if any such retirement benefit is in a form other than a straight life annuity (with no ancillary benefits), or if

employees contribute to any such plan or make rollover contributions, such benefit shall be adjusted in accordance with regulations prescribed by the Equal Employment Opportunity Commission, after consultation with the Secretary of the Treasury, so that the benefit is the equivalent of a straight life annuity (with no ancillary benefits) under a plan to which employees do not contribute and under which no rollover contributions are made.

(d) Tenured employee at institution of higher education

Nothing in this chapter shall be construed to prohibit compulsory retirement of any employee who has attained 70 years of age, and who is serving under a contract of unlimited tenure (or similar arrangement providing for unlimited tenure) at an institution of higher education (as defined by section 1201(a) of the Higher Education Act of 1965).

§ 13. Annual report to Congress

The Equal Employment Opportunity Commission shall submit annually in January a report to the Congress covering its activities for the preceding year and including such information, data, and recommendations for further legislation in connection with the matters covered by this chapter as it may find advisable. Such report shall contain an evaluation and appraisal by the Commission of the effect of the minimum and maximum ages established by this chapter, together with its recommendations to the Congress. In making such evaluation and appraisal, the Commission shall take into consideration any changes which may have occurred in the general age level of the population, the effect of the chapter upon workers not covered by its provisions, and such other factors as it may deem pertinent.

§ 14. Federal–State relationship

(a) Federal action superseding State action

Nothing in this Act shall affect the jurisdiction of any agency of any State performing like functions with regard to discriminatory employment practices on account of age except that upon commencement of action under this Act such action shall supersede any State action.

(b) Limitation of Federal action upon commencement of State proceedings

In the case of an alleged unlawful practice occurring in a State which has a law prohibiting discrimination in employment because of age and establishing or authorizing a State authority to grant or seek relief from such discriminatory practice, no suit may be brought under section 7 of this Act before the expiration of sixty days after proceedings have been commenced under the State law, unless such proceedings have been earlier terminated: Provided, That such sixty-day period shall be extended to one hundred and twenty days during the first year after the effective date of such State law. If any requirement for the commencement of such proceedings is imposed by a State authority other than a requirement of the filing of a written and signed statement of the facts upon which the proceeding is based, the proceeding shall be deemed to have been commenced for the purposes of this subsection at the time such statement is sent by registered mail to the appropriate State authority.

§ 15. Nondiscrimination on account of age in Federal Government employment

(a) Federal agencies affected

All personnel actions affecting employees or applicants for employment who are at least 40 years of age (except personnel actions with regard to aliens employed outside the limits of the United States) in military departments as defined in section 102 of Title 5, in executive agencies as defined in section 105 of Title 5 (including employees and applicants for employment who are paid from nonappropriated funds), in the United States Postal Service and the Postal Rate Commission, in those units in the government of the District of Columbia having positions in the competitive service, and in those units of the legislative and judicial branches of the Federal Government having positions in the competitive service, and in the Library of Congress shall be made free from any discrimination based on age.

(b) Enforcement by Equal Employment Opportunity Commission and by Librarian of Congress in Library of Congress; remedies; rules, regulations, orders, and instructions of Commission: compliance by Federal agencies; powers and duties of Commission; notification of final action on complaint of discrimination; exemptions: bona fide occupational qualification

Except as otherwise provided in this subsection, the Equal Employment Opportunity Commission is authorized to enforce the provisions of subsection (a) of this section through appropriate remedies, including reinstatement or hiring of employees with or without backpay, as will effectuate the policies of this section. The Equal Employment Opportunity Commission shall issue such rules, regulations, orders, and instructions as it deems necessary and appropriate to carry out its responsibilities under this section. The Equal Employment Opportunity Commission shall—

(1) be responsible for the review and evaluation of the operation of all agency programs designed to carry out the policy of this section, periodically obtaining and publishing (on at least a semiannual basis) progress reports from each department, agency, or unit referred to in subsection (a) of this section;

(2) consult with and solicit the recommendations of interested individuals, groups, and organizations relating to nondiscrimination in employment on account of age; and

(3) provide for the acceptance and processing of complaints of discrimination in Federal employment on account of age.

The head of each such department, agency, or unit shall comply with such rules, regulations, orders, and instructions of the Equal Employment Opportunity Commission which shall include a provision that an employee or applicant for employment shall be notified of any final action taken on any complaint of discrimination filed by him thereunder. Reasonable exemptions to the provisions of this section may be established by the Commission but only when the Commission has established a maximum age requirement on the basis of a determination that age is a bona fide occupational qualification necessary to the performance of the duties of the position. With respect to employment in the Library of Congress, authorities granted in this subsection to the Equal Employment Opportunity Commission shall be exercised by the Librarian of Congress.

(c) Civil actions; jurisdiction; relief

Any person aggrieved may bring a civil action in any Federal district court of competent jurisdiction for such legal or equitable relief as will effectuate the purposes of this Act.

(d) Notice to Commission; time of notice; Commission notification of prospective defendants; Commission elimination of unlawful practices

When the individual has not filed a complaint concerning age discrimination with the Commission, no civil action may be commenced by any individual under this section until the individual has given the Commission not less than thirty days' notice of an intent to file such action. Such notice shall be filed within one hundred and eighty days after the alleged unlawful practice occurred. Upon receiving a notice of intent to sue, the Commission shall promptly notify all persons named therein as prospective defendants in the action and take any appropriate action to assure the elimination of any unlawful practice.

(e) Duty of Government agency or official

Nothing contained in this section shall relieve any Government agency or official of the responsibility to assure nondiscrimination on account of age in employment as required under any provision of Federal law.

(f) Applicability of statutory provisions to personnel action of Federal departments, etc.

Any personnel action of any department, agency, or other entity referred to in subsection (a) of this section shall not be subject to, or affected by, any provision of this Act, other than the provisions of section 12(b) of this Act and the provisions of this section.

* * *

[See also § 16(b) of the Fair Labor Standards Act of 1938, as amended, reprinted in this Appendix as part of the Equal Pay Act]

THE REHABILITATION ACT, as Amended by the Americans With Disabilities Act and the 1991 Civil Rights Act

29 U.S.C.A. §§ 706(8), 791, 793, 794, 794a.

§ 7. Definitions

(8)(A) Except as otherwise provided in subparagraph (B), the term "an individual with handicaps" means any individual who (i) has a physical or mental disability which for such individual constitutes or results in a substantial handicap to employment and (ii) can reasonably be expected to benefit in terms of employability from vocational rehabilitation services provided pursuant to Titles I and III of this Act.

(B) Subject to subparagraphs (C) and (D), the term "an individual with handicaps" means, for purposes of this Act, any person who (i) has a physical or mental impairment which substantially limits one or more of such person's major life activities, (ii) has a record of such an impairment, or (iii) is regarded as having such an impairment. For purposes of sections 503 and 504 as such sections relate to employment, such term does not include any individual who is an alcoholic or drug abuser whose current use of alcohol or drugs prevents such individual from performing the duties of the job in question or whose employment, by reason of such current alcohol or drug abuse, would constitute a direct threat to property or the safety of others.

(C)(i) For purposes of this statute, the term "individual with handicaps" does not include an individual who is currently engaging in the illegal use of drugs, when a covered entity acts on the basis of such use.

(ii) Nothing in clause (i) shall be construed to exclude as an individual with handicaps an individual who—

(I) has successfully completed a supervised drug rehabilitation program and is no longer engaging in the illegal use of drugs, or has otherwise been rehabilitated successfully and is no longer engaging in such use;

(II) is participating in a supervised rehabilitation program and is no longer engaging in such use; or

(III) is erroneously regarded as engaging in such use, but is not engaging in such use;

except that it shall not be a violation of this statute for a covered entity to adopt or administer reasonable policies or procedures, including but not limited to drug testing, designed to ensure that an individual described in subclause (I) or (II) is no longer engaging in the illegal use of drugs.

* * *

(v) For purposes of sections 503 and 504 of this statute as such sections relate to employment, the term "individual with handicaps" does not include any individual who is an alcoholic whose current use of alcohol prevents such individual from performing the duties of the job in question or whose employment, by reason of such current alcohol abuse, would constitute a direct threat to property or the safety of others.

(D) For the purpose of sections 503 and 504 of this statute, as such sections relate to employment, such term does not include an individual who has a currently contagious disease or infection and who, by reason of such disease or infection, would constitute a direct threat to the health or safety of other individuals or who, by reason of the currently contagious disease or infection, is unable to perform the duties of the job.

§ 501. Employment of handicapped individuals

(a) There is established within the Federal Government an Interagency Committee on Handicapped Employees (hereinafter in this section referred to as the "Committee"), comprised of such members as the President may select, including the following (or their designees whose positions are Executive Level IV or higher): the Chairman of the Civil Service Commission, the Administrator of Veterans' Affairs, and the Secretaries of Labor and Health, Education, and Welfare. The Secretary of Health, Education, and Welfare and the Chairman of the Civil Service Commission shall serve as co-chairmen of the Committee. The resources of the President's Committees on Employment of the Handicapped and on Mental Retardation shall be made fully available to the Committee. It shall be the purpose and function of the Committee (1) to provide a focus for Federal and other employment of handicapped individuals, and to review, on a periodic basis, in cooperation with the Civil Service Commission, the adequacy of hiring, placement, and advancement practices with respect to handicapped individuals, by each department, agency, and instrumentality in the executive branch of Government, and to insure that the special needs of such individuals are being met; and (2) to consult with the Civil Service Commission to assist the Commission to carry out its responsibilities under subsections (b), (c), and (d) of this section. On the basis of such review and consultation, the Committee shall periodically make to the Civil Service Commission such recommendations for legislative and administrative changes as it deems necessary or desirable. The Civil Service Commission shall timely transmit to the appropriate committees of Congress any such recommendations.

(b) Each department, agency, and instrumentality (including the United States Postal Service and the Postal Rate Commission) in the executive branch shall, within one hundred and eighty days after September 26, 1973, submit to the Civil Service Commission and to the Committee an affirmative action program plan for the hiring, placement, and advancement of handicapped individuals in such department, agency, or instrumentality. Such plan shall include a description of the extent to which and methods whereby the special needs of handicapped employees are being met. Such plan shall be updated annually, and shall be reviewed annually and approved by the Commission, if the Commission determines, after consultation with the Committee, that such plan provides sufficient assurances, procedures and commitments to provide adequate hiring, placement, and advancement opportunities for handicapped individuals.

(c) The Civil Service Commission, after consultation with the Committee, shall develop and recommend to the Secretary for referral to the appropriate State agencies, policies and procedures which will facilitate the hiring, placement, and advancement in employment of individuals who have received rehabilitation services under State vocational rehabilitation programs, veterans' programs, or any other program for handicapped individuals, including the promotion of job opportunities for such individuals. The Secretary shall encourage such State agencies to adopt and implement such policies and procedures.

(d) The Civil Service Commission, after consultation with the Committee, shall, on June 30, 1974, and at the end of each subsequent fiscal year, make a complete report to the appropriate committees of the Congress with respect to the practices of and achievements in hiring, placement, and advancement of handicapped individuals by each department, agency, and instrumentality and the effectiveness of the affirmative action programs required by subsection (b) of this section, together with recommendations as to legislation which have been submitted to the Civil Service Commission under subsection (a) of this section, or other appropriate action to insure the adequacy of such practices. Such report shall also include an evaluation by the Committee of the effectiveness of the Civil Service Commission's activities under subsections (b) and (c) of this section.

* * *

§ 503. Employment under Federal contracts

(a) Any contract in excess of $2,500 entered into by any Federal department or agency for the procurement of personal property and nonpersonal services (including construction) for the United States shall contain a provision requiring that, in employing persons to carry out such contract, the party contracting with the United States shall take affirmative action to employ and advance in employment qualified handicapped individuals as defined in section 7(7). The provisions of this section shall apply to any subcontract in excess of $2,500 entered into by a prime contractor in carrying out any contract for the procurement of personal property and nonpersonal services (including construction) for the United States. The President shall implement the provisions of this section by promulgating regulations within ninety days after September 26, 1973.

(b) If any handicapped individual believes any contractor has failed or refused to comply with the provisions of a contract with the United

States, relating to employment of individuals with handicaps, such individual may file a complaint with the Department of Labor. The Department shall promptly investigate such complaint and shall take such action thereon as the facts and circumstances warrant, consistent with the terms of such contract and the laws and regulations applicable thereto.

(c) The requirements of this section may be waived, in whole or in part, by the President with respect to a particular contract or subcontract, in accordance with guidelines set forth in regulations which he shall prescribe, when he determines that special circumstances in the national interest so require and states in writing his reasons for such determination.

§ 504. Nondiscrimination under Federal grants and programs

(a) No otherwise qualified individual with handicaps in the United States, as defined in section 7(8) shall, solely by reason of her or his handicap, be excluded from the participation in, be denied the benefits of, or be subjected to discrimination under any program or activity receiving Federal financial assistance or under any program or activity conducted by any Executive agency or by the United States Postal Service. The head of each such agency shall promulgate such regulations as may be necessary to carry out the amendments to this section made by the Rehabilitation, Comprehensive Services, and Developmental Disabilities Act of 1978. Copies of any proposed regulation shall be submitted to appropriate authorizing committees of the Congress, and such regulation may take effect no earlier than the thirtieth day after the date on which such regulation is so submitted to such committees.

(b) For the purposes of this section, the term "program or activity" means all of the operations of—

(1)(A) a department, agency, special purpose district, or other instrumentality of a State or of a local government; or

(B) the entity of such State or local government that distributes such assistance and each such department or agency (and each other State or local government entity) to which the assistance is extended, in the case of assistance to a State or local government;

(2)(A) a college, university, or other postsecondary institution, or a public system of higher education; or

(B) a local educational agency (as defined in section 198(a)(10) of the Elementary and Secondary Education Act of 1965), system of vocational education, or other school system;

(3)(A) an entire corporation, partnership, or other private organization, or an entire sole proprietorship—

(i) if assistance is extended to such corporation, partnership, private organization, or sole proprietorship as a whole; or

(ii) which is principally engaged in the business of providing education, health care, housing, social services, or parks and recreation; or

(B) the entire plant or other comparable, geographically separate facility to which Federal financial assistance is extended, in the case of any other corporation, partnership, private organization, or sole proprietorship; or

(4) any other entity which is established by two or more of the entities described in paragraph (1), (2), or (3);

any part of which is extended Federal financial assistance.

(c) Small providers are not required by subsection (a) to make significant structural alterations to their existing facilities for the purpose of assuring program accessibility, if alternative means of providing the services are available. The terms used in this subsection shall be construed with reference to the regulations existing on March 22, 1988.

§ 505. Remedies and attorney fees

(a)(1) The remedies, procedures, and rights set forth in section 717 of the Civil Rights Act of 1964, including the application of sections 706(f) through 706(k), shall be available, with respect to any complaint under section 501 of this Act, to any employee or applicant for employment aggrieved by the final disposition of such complaint, or by the failure to take final action on such complaint. In fashioning an equitable or affirmative action remedy under such section, a court may take into account the reasonableness of the cost of any necessary work place accommodation, and the availability of alternatives therefor or other appropriate relief in order to achieve an equitable and appropriate remedy.

(2) The remedies, procedures, and rights set forth in Title VI of the Civil Rights Act of 1964 shall be available to any person aggrieved by any act or failure to act by any recipient of Federal assistance or Federal provider of such assistance under section 504 of this Act.

(b) In any action or proceeding to enforce or charge a violation of a provision of this Act, the court, in its discretion, may allow the prevailing party, other than the United States, a reasonable attorney's fee as part of the costs.

AMERICANS WITH DISABILITIES ACT OF 1990, as Amended by the Civil Rights Act of 1991

42 U.S.C. § 12101 et seq.

§ 2. Findings and purposes

(a) Findings

The Congress finds that—

(1) some 43,000,000 Americans have one or more physical or mental disabilities, and this number is increasing as the population as a whole is growing older;

(2) historically, society has tended to isolate and segregate individuals with disabilities, and, despite some improvements, such forms of discrimination against individuals with disabilities continue to be a serious and pervasive social problem;

(3) discrimination against individuals with disabilities persists in such critical areas as employment, housing, public accommodations, education, transportation, communication, recreation, institutionalization, health services, voting, and access to public services;

(4) unlike individuals who have experienced discrimination on the basis of race, color, sex, national origin, religion, or age, individuals who have experienced discrimination on the basis of disability have often had no legal recourse to redress such discrimination;

(5) individuals with disabilities continually encounter various forms of discrimination, including outright intentional exclusion, the discriminatory effects of architectural, transportation, and communication barriers, overprotective rules and policies, failure to make modifications to existing facilities and practices, exclusionary qualification standards and criteria, segregation, and relegation to lesser services, programs, activities, benefits, jobs, or other opportunities;

(6) census data, national polls, and other studies have documented that people with disabilities, as a group, occupy an inferior status in our society, and are severely disadvantaged socially, vocationally, economically, and educationally;

(7) individuals with disabilities are a discrete and insular minority who have been faced with restrictions and limitations, subjected to a history of purposeful unequal treatment, and relegated to a position of political powerlessness in our society, based on characteristics that are beyond the control of such individuals and resulting from stereotypic assumptions not truly indicative of the individual ability of such individuals to participate in, and contribute to, society;

(8) the Nation's proper goals regarding individuals with disabilities are to assure equality of opportunity, full participation, independent living, and economic self-sufficiency for such individuals; and

(9) the continuing existence of unfair and unnecessary discrimination and prejudice denies people with disabilities the opportunity to compete on an equal basis and to pursue those opportunities for which our free society is justifiably famous, and costs the United

States billions of dollars in unnecessary expenses resulting from dependency and nonproductivity.

(b) Purpose

It is the purpose of this Act—

(1) to provide a clear and comprehensive national mandate for the elimination of discrimination against individuals with disabilities;

(2) to provide clear, strong, consistent, enforceable standards addressing discrimination against individuals with disabilities;

(3) to ensure that the Federal Government plays a central role in enforcing the standards established in this Act on behalf of individuals with disabilities; and

(4) to invoke the sweep of congressional authority, including the power to enforce the fourteenth amendment and to regulate commerce, in order to address the major areas of discrimination faced day-to-day by people with disabilities.

§ 3. Definitions

As used in this Act:

(1) Auxiliary aids and services

The term "auxiliary aids and services" includes—

(A) qualified interpreters or other effective methods of making aurally delivered materials available to individuals with hearing impairments;

(B) qualified readers, taped texts, or other effective methods of making visually delivered materials available to individuals with visual impairments;

(C) acquisition or modification of equipment or devices; and

(D) other similar services and actions.

(2) Disability

The term "disability" means, with respect to an individual—

(A) a physical or mental impairment that substantially limits one or more of the major life activities of such individual;

(B) a record of such an impairment; or

(C) being regarded as having such an impairment.

(3) State

The term "State" means each of the several States, the District of Columbia, the Commonwealth of Puerto Rico, Guam, American Samoa, the Virgin Islands, the Trust Territory of the Pacific Islands, and the Commonwealth of the Northern Mariana Islands.

TITLE I—EMPLOYMENT

§ 101. Definitions

As used in this Title:

(1) Commission

The term "Commission" means the Equal Employment Opportunity Commission established by § 705 of [Title VII of] the Civil Rights Act of 1964.

(2) Covered entity

The term "covered entity" means an employer, employment agency, labor organization, or joint labor-management committee.

(3) Direct threat

The term "direct threat" means a significant risk to the health or safety of others that cannot be eliminated by reasonable accommodation.

(4) Employee

The term "employee" means an individual employed by an employer. With respect to employment in a foreign country, such term includes an individual who is a citizen of the United States.

(5) Employer

(A) In general

The term "employer" means a person engaged in an industry affecting commerce who has 15 or more employees for each working day in each of 20 or more calendar weeks in the current or preceding calendar year, and any agent of such person, except that, for two years following the effective date of this Title, an employer means a person engaged in an industry affecting commerce who has 25 or more employees for each working day in each of 20 or more calendar weeks in the current or preceding year, and any agent of such person.

(B) Exceptions

The term "employer" does not include—

(i) the United States, a corporation wholly owned by the government of the United States, or an Indian tribe; or

(ii) a bona fide private membership club (other than a labor organization) that is exempt from taxation under section 501(c) of the Internal Revenue Code of 1986.

(6) Illegal use of drugs

(A) In general

The term "illegal use of drugs" means the use of drugs, the possession or distribution of which is unlawful under the Controlled Substances Act (21 U.S.C. 812). Such term does not include the use of a drug taken under supervision by a licensed health care professional, or other uses authorized by the Controlled Substances Act or other provisions of Federal law.

(B) Drugs

The term "drug" means a controlled substance, as defined in schedules I through V of section 202 of the Controlled Substances Act.

(7) Person, etc.

The terms "person," "labor organization," "employment agency," "commerce," and "industry affecting commerce," shall have the same meaning given such terms in § 701 of [Title VII of] the Civil Rights Act of 1964.

(8) Qualified individual with a disability

The term "qualified individual with a disability" means an individual with a disability who, with or without reasonable accommodation, can perform the essential functions of the employment position that such individual holds or desires. For the purposes of this Title, consideration shall be given to the employer's judgment as to what functions of a job are essential, and if an employer has prepared a written description before advertising or interviewing applicants for the job, this description shall be considered evidence of the essential functions of the job.

(9) Reasonable accommodation

The term "reasonable accommodation" may include—

(A) making existing facilities used by employees readily accessible to and usable by individuals with disabilities; and

(B) job restructuring, part-time or modified work schedules, reassignment to a vacant position, acquisition or modification of equipment or devices, appropriate adjustment or modifications of examinations, training materials or policies, the provision of qualified readers or interpreters, and other similar accommodations for individuals with disabilities.

(10) Undue hardship

(A) In general

The term "undue hardship" means an action requiring significant difficulty or expense, when considered in light of the factors set forth in subparagraph (B).

(B) Factors to be considered

In determining whether an accommodation would impose an undue hardship on a covered entity, factors to be considered include—

(i) the nature and cost of the accommodation needed under this Act;

(ii) the overall financial resources of the facility or facilities involved in the provision of the reasonable accommodation; the number of persons employed at such facility; the effect on expenses and resources, or the impact otherwise of such accommodation upon the operation of the facility;

(iii) the overall financial resources of the covered entity; the overall size of the business of a covered entity with respect to the number of its employees; the number, type, and location of its facilities; and

(iv) the type of operation or operations of the covered entity, including the composition, structure, and functions of the workforce of such entity; the geographic separateness, administrative, or fiscal relationship of the facility or facilities in question to the covered entity.

§ 102. Discrimination

(a) General rule

No covered entity shall discriminate against a qualified individual with a disability because of the disability of such individual in regard to job application procedures, the hiring, advancement, or discharge of employees, employee compensation, job training, and other terms, conditions, and privileges of employment.

(b) Construction

As used in subsection (a) of this section, the term "discriminate" includes—

(1) limiting, segregating, or classifying a job applicant or employee in a way that adversely affects the opportunities or status of such applicant or employee because of the disability of such applicant or employee;

(2) participating in a contractual or other arrangement or relationship that has the effect of subjecting a covered entity's qualified applicant or employee with a disability to the discrimination prohibited by this Title (such relationship includes a relationship with an employment or referral agency, labor union, an organization providing fringe benefits to an employee of the covered entity, or an organization providing training and apprenticeship programs);

(3) utilizing standards, criteria, or methods of administration—

(A) that have the effect of discrimination on the basis of disability; or

(B) that perpetuate the discrimination of others who are subject to common administrative control;

(4) excluding or otherwise denying equal jobs or benefits to a qualified individual because of the known disability of an individual with whom the qualified individual is known to have a relationship or association;

(5)(A) not making reasonable accommodations to the known physical or mental limitations of an otherwise qualified individual with a disability who is an applicant or employee, unless such covered entity can demonstrate that the accommodation would impose an undue hardship on the operation of the business of such covered entity; or

(B) denying employment opportunities to a job applicant or employee who is an otherwise qualified individual with a disability, if such denial is based on the need of such covered entity to make reasonable accommodation to the physical or mental impairments of the employee or applicant;

(6) using qualification standards, employment tests or other selection criteria that screen out or tend to screen out an individual with a disability or a class of individuals with disabilities unless the standard, test or other selection criteria, as used by the covered entity, is shown to be job-related for the position in question and is consistent with business necessity; and

(7) failing to select and administer tests concerning employment in the most effective manner to ensure that, when such test is administered to a job applicant or employee who has a disability that impairs sensory, manual, or speaking skills, such test results accurately reflect the skills, aptitude, or whatever other factor of such applicant or employee that such test purports to measure, rather than reflecting the impaired sensory, manual, or speaking skills of such employee or applicant (except where such skills are the factors that the test purports to measure).

(c) Covered entities in foreign countries

(1) In general

It shall not be unlawful under this section for a covered entity to take any action that constitutes discrimination under this section with respect to an employee in a workplace in a foreign country if compliance with this section would cause such covered entity to violate the law of the foreign country in which such workplace is located.

(2) Control of corporation

(A) Presumption

If an employer controls a corporation whose place of incorporation is a foreign country, any practice that constitutes discrimination under this section and is engaged in by such corporation shall be presumed to be engaged in by such employer.

(B) Exception

This section shall not apply with respect to the foreign operations of an employer that is a foreign person not controlled by an American employer.

(C) Determination

For purposes of this paragraph, the determination of whether an employer controls a corporation shall be based on—

(i) the interrelation of operations;

(ii) the common management;

(iii) the centralized control of labor relations; and

(iv) the common ownership or financial control, of the employer and the corporation.

(d) Medical examinations and inquiries

(1) In general

The prohibition against discrimination as referred to in subsection (a) of this section shall include medical examinations and inquiries.

(2) Preemployment

(A) Prohibited examination or inquiry

Except as provided in paragraph (3), a covered entity shall not conduct a medical examination or make inquiries of a job applicant as to whether such applicant is an individual with a disability or as to the nature or severity of such disability.

(B) Acceptable inquiry

A covered entity may make preemployment inquiries into the ability of an applicant to perform job-related functions.

(3) Employment entrance examination

A covered entity may require a medical examination after an offer of employment has been made to a job applicant and prior to the commencement of the employment duties of such applicant, and may condition an offer of employment on the results of such examination, if—

(A) all entering employees are subjected to such an examination regardless of disability;

(B) information obtained regarding the medical condition or history of the applicant is collected and maintained on separate forms and in separate medical files and is treated as a confidential medical record, except that—

(i) supervisors and managers may be informed regarding necessary restrictions on the work or duties of the employee and necessary accommodations;

(ii) first aid and safety personnel may be informed, when appropriate, if the disability might require emergency treatment; and

(iii) government officials investigating compliance with this Act shall be provided relevant information on request; and

(C) the results of such examination are used only in accordance with this Title.

(4) Examination and inquiry

(A) Prohibited examinations and inquiries

A covered entity shall not require a medical examination and shall not make inquiries of an employee as to whether such employee is an individual with a disability or as to the nature or severity of the disability, unless such examination or inquiry is shown to be job-related and consistent with business necessity.

(B) Acceptable examinations and inquiries

A covered entity may conduct voluntary medical examinations, including voluntary medical histories, which are part of an employee health program available to employees at that work site. A covered entity may make inquiries into the ability of an employee to perform job-related functions.

(C) Requirement

Information obtained under subparagraph (B) regarding the medical condition or history of any employee are subject to the requirements of subparagraphs (B) and (C) of paragraph (3).

§ 103. Defenses

(a) In general

It may be a defense to a charge of discrimination under this Act that an alleged application of qualification standards, tests, or selection criteria that screen out or tend to screen out or otherwise deny a job or benefit to an individual with a disability has been shown to be job-related and consistent with business necessity, and such performance cannot be accomplished by reasonable accommodation, as required under this Title.

(b) Qualification standards

The term "qualification standards" may include a requirement that an individual shall not pose a direct threat to the health or safety of other individuals in the workplace.

(c) Religious entities

(1) In general

This Title shall not prohibit a religious corporation, association, educational institution, or society from giving preference in employment to individuals of a particular religion to perform work connected with the carrying on by such corporation, association, educational institution, or society of its activities.

(2) Religious tenets requirement

Under this Title, a religious organization may require that all applicants and employees conform to the religious tenets of such organization.

(d) List of infectious and communicable diseases

(1) In general

The Secretary of Health and Human Services, not later than 6 months after July 26, 1990, shall—

(A) review all infectious and communicable diseases which may be transmitted through handling the food supply;

(B) publish a list of infectious and communicable diseases which are transmitted through handling the food supply;

(C) publish the methods by which such diseases are transmitted; and

(D) widely disseminate such information regarding the list of diseases and their modes of transmissibility to the general public.

Such list shall be updated annually.

(2) Applications

In any case in which an individual has an infectious or communicable disease that is transmitted to others through the handling of food, that is included on the list developed by the Secretary of Health and Human Services under paragraph (1), and which cannot be eliminated by reasonable accommodation, a covered entity may refuse to assign or continue to assign such individual to a job involving food handling.

(3) Construction

Nothing in this Act shall be construed to preempt, modify, or amend any State, county, or local law, ordinance, or regulation applicable to food handling which is designed to protect the public health from individuals who pose a significant risk to the health or safety of others, which cannot be eliminated by reasonable accommodation, pursuant to the list of infectious or communicable diseases and the modes of transmissibility published by the Secretary of Health and Human Services.

§ 104. Illegal use of drugs and alcohol

(a) Qualified individual with a disability

For purposes of this Title, the term "qualified individual with a disability" shall not include any employee or applicant who is currently engaging in the illegal use of drugs, when the covered entity acts on the basis of such use.

(b) Rules of construction

Nothing in subsection (a) of this section shall be construed to exclude as a qualified individual with a disability an individual who—

(1) has successfully completed a supervised drug rehabilitation program and is no longer engaging in the illegal use of drugs, or has otherwise been rehabilitated successfully and is no longer engaging in such use;

(2) is participating in a supervised rehabilitation program and is no longer engaging in such use; or

(3) is erroneously regarded as engaging in such use, but is not engaging in such use; except that it shall not be a violation of this Act for a covered entity to adopt or administer reasonable policies or procedures, including but not limited to drug testing, designed to ensure that an individual described in paragraph (1) or (2) is no longer engaging in the illegal use of drugs.

(c) Authority of covered entity

A covered entity—

(1) may prohibit the illegal use of drugs and the use of alcohol at the workplace by all employees;

(2) may require that employees shall not be under the influence of alcohol or be engaging in the illegal use of drugs at the workplace;

(3) may require that employees behave in conformance with the requirements established under the Drug–Free Workplace Act of 1988 (41 U.S.C. 701 et seq.);

(4) may hold an employee who engages in the illegal use of drugs or who is an alcoholic to the same qualification standards for employment or job performance and behavior that such entity holds other employees, even if any unsatisfactory performance or behavior is related to the drug use or alcoholism of such employee; and

(5) may, with respect to Federal regulations regarding alcohol and the illegal use of drugs, require that—

(A) employees comply with the standards established in such regulations of the Department of Defense, if the employees of the covered entity are employed in an industry subject to such regulations, including complying with regulations (if any) that apply to employment in sensitive positions in such an industry, in the case of employees of the covered entity who are employed in such positions (as defined in the regulations of the Department of Defense);

(B) employees comply with the standards established in such regulations of the Nuclear Regulatory Commission, if the employees of the covered entity are employed in an industry subject to such regulations, including complying with regulations (if any) that apply to employment in sensitive positions in such an industry, in the case of employees of the covered entity who are employed in such positions (as defined in the regulations of the Nuclear Regulatory Commission); and

(C) employees comply with the standards established in such regulations of the Department of Transportation, if the employees of the covered entity are employed in a transportation industry subject to such regulations, including complying with such regulations (if any) that apply to employment in sensitive positions in such an industry, in the case of employees of the covered entity who are employed in such positions (as defined in the regulations of the Department of Transportation).

(d) Drug testing

(1) In general

For purposes of this Title, a test to determine the illegal use of drugs shall not be considered a medical examination.

(2) Construction

Nothing in this Title shall be construed to encourage, prohibit, or authorize the conducting of drug testing for the illegal use of drugs by job applicants or employees or making employment decisions based on such test results.

(e) Transportation employees

Nothing in this Title shall be construed to encourage, prohibit, restrict, or authorize the otherwise lawful exercise by entities subject to the jurisdiction of the Department of Transportation of authority to—

(1) test employees of such entities in, and applicants for, positions involving safety-sensitive duties for the illegal use of drugs and for on-duty impairment by alcohol; and

(2) remove such persons who test positive for illegal use of drugs and on-duty impairment by alcohol pursuant to paragraph (1) from safety-sensitive duties in implementing subsection (c) of this section.

§ 105. Posting notices

Every employer, employment agency, labor organization, or joint labor-management committee covered under this Title shall post notices in an accessible format to applicants, employees, and members describing the applicable provisions of this Act, in the manner prescribed by § 711 of [Title VII of] the Civil Rights Act of 1964.

§ 106. Regulations

Not later than 1 year after July 26, 1990, the Commission shall issue regulations in an accessible format to carry out this Title in accordance with the provisions of the Administrative Procedure Act.

§ 107. Enforcement

(a) Powers, remedies, and procedures

The powers, remedies, and procedures set forth in §§ 705, 706, 707, 708, 709 and 710 of [Title VII of] the Civil Rights Act of 1964 shall be the powers, remedies, and procedures this Title provides to the Commission, to the Attorney General, or to any person alleging discrimination on the basis of disability in violation of any provision of this Act, or regulations promulgated under § 106, concerning employment.

(b) Coordination

The agencies with enforcement authority for actions which allege employment discrimination under this Title and under the Rehabilitation Act of 1973 shall develop procedures to ensure that administrative complaints filed under this Title and under the Rehabilitation Act of 1973 are dealt with in a manner that avoids duplication of effort and prevents imposition of inconsistent or conflicting standards for the same requirements under this Title and the Rehabilitation Act of 1973. The Commission, the Attorney General, and the Office of Federal Contract Compliance Programs shall establish such coordinating mechanisms (similar to provisions contained in the joint regulations promulgated by the Commission and the Attorney General at part 42 of Title 28 and part 1691 of Title 29, Code of Federal Regulations, and the Memorandum of Understanding between the Commission and the Office of Federal Contract Compliance Programs dated January 16, 1981 (46 Fed.Reg. 7435, January 23, 1981)) in regulations implementing this Title and Rehabilitation Act of 1973 not later than 18 months after July 26, 1990.

TITLE V—MISCELLANEOUS PROVISIONS

§ 501. Construction

(a) In general

Except as otherwise provided in this Act, nothing in this Act shall be construed to apply a lesser standard than the standards applied under Title V of the Rehabilitation Act of 1973 (29 U.S.C. 790 et seq.) or the regulations issued by Federal agencies pursuant to such Title.

(b) Relationship to other laws

Nothing in this Act shall be construed to invalidate or limit the remedies, rights, and procedures of any Federal law or law of any State or political subdivision of any State or jurisdiction that provides greater or equal protection for the rights of individuals with disabilities than are afforded by this Act. Nothing in this Act shall be construed to preclude the prohibition of, or the imposition of restrictions on, smoking in places of employment covered by Title I of this Act * * *.

* * *

(d) Accommodations and services

Nothing in this Act shall be construed to require an individual with a disability to accept an accommodation, aid, service, opportunity, or benefit which such individual chooses not to accept.

§ 502. State immunity

A State shall not be immune under the eleventh amendment to the Constitution of the United States from an action in Federal or State court of competent jurisdiction for a violation of this Act. In any action against a State for a violation of the requirements of this Act, remedies (including remedies both at law and in equity) are available for such a violation to the same extent as such remedies are available for such a violation in an action against any public or private entity other than a State.

§ 503. Prohibition against retaliation and coercion

(a) Retaliation

No person shall discriminate against any individual because such individual has opposed any act or practice made unlawful by this Act or because such individual made a charge, testified, assisted, or participated in any manner in an investigation, proceeding, or hearing under this Act.

(b) Interference, coercion, or intimidation

It shall be unlawful to coerce, intimidate, threaten, or interfere with any individual in the exercise or enjoyment of, or on account of his or her having exercised or enjoyed, or on account of his or her having aided or encouraged any other individual in the exercise or enjoyment of, any right granted or protected by this Act.

(c) Remedies and procedures

The remedies and procedures available under § 107 * * * of this Act shall be available to aggrieved persons for violations of subsections (a) and (b) of this section, with respect to Title I * * * of this Act.

* * *

§ 505. Attorney's fees

In any action or administrative proceeding commenced pursuant to this Act, the court or agency, in its discretion, may allow the prevailing party, other than the United States, a reasonable attorney's fee, including litigation expenses, and costs, and the United States shall be liable for the foregoing the same as a private individual.

* * *

§ 508. Transvestites

For the purposes of this Act, the term "disabled" or "disability" shall not apply to an individual solely because that individual is a transvestite.

* * *

§ 510. Illegal use of drugs

(a) In general

For purposes of this Act, the term "individual with a disability" does not include an individual who is currently engaging in the illegal use of drugs, when the covered entity acts on the basis of such use.

(b) Rules of construction

Nothing in subsection (a) of this section shall be construed to exclude as an individual with a disability an individual who—

(1) has successfully completed a supervised drug rehabilitation program and is no longer engaging in the illegal use of drugs, or has otherwise been rehabilitated successfully and is no longer engaging in such use;

(2) is participating in a supervised rehabilitation program and is no longer engaging in such use; or

(3) is erroneously regarded as engaging in such use, but is not engaging in such use; except that it shall not be a violation of this Act for a covered entity to adopt or administer reasonable policies or procedures, including but not limited to drug testing, designed to ensure that an individual described in paragraph (1) or (2) is no longer engaging in the illegal use of drugs; however, nothing in this section shall be construed to encourage, prohibit, restrict, or authorize the conducting of testing for the illegal use of drugs.

(c) Health and other services

Notwithstanding subsection (a) of this section and § 511(b)(3), an individual shall not be denied health services, or services provided in connection with drug rehabilitation, on the basis of the current illegal use of drugs if the individual is otherwise entitled to such services.

(d) Definition of illegal use of drugs

(1) In general

The term "illegal use of drugs" means the use of drugs, the possession or distribution of which is unlawful under the Controlled Substances Act (21 U.S.C. 812). Such term does not include the use of a drug taken under supervision by a licensed health care professional, or other uses authorized by the Controlled Substances Act or other provisions of Federal law.

(2) Drugs

The term "drug" means a controlled substance, as defined in schedules I through V of section 202 of the Controlled Substances Act.

§ 511. Definitions

(a) Homosexuality and bisexuality

For purposes of the definition of "disability" in § 3(2), homosexuality and bisexuality are not impairments and as such are not disabilities under this Act.

(b) Certain conditions

Under this Act, the term "disability" shall not include—

(1) transvestism, transsexualism, pedophilia, exhibitionism, voyeurism, gender identity disorders not resulting from physical impairments, or other sexual behavior disorders;

(2) compulsive gambling, kleptomania, or pyromania; or

(3) psychoactive substance use disorders resulting from current illegal use of drugs.

* * *

CIVIL RIGHTS RESTORATION ACT OF 1987

20 U.S.C. § 1687 et seq.

AN ACT

To restore the broad scope of coverage and to clarify the application of Title IX of the Education Amendments of 1972 * * * and Title VI of the Civil Rights Act of 1964.

Be it enacted by the Senate and House of Representatives of the United States of America in Congress assembled,

SHORT TITLE

Sec. 1. This Act may be cited as the "Civil Rights Restoration Act of 1987."

FINDINGS OF CONGRESS

Sec. 2. The Congress finds that—

(1) certain aspects of recent decisions and opinions of the Supreme Court have unduly narrowed or cast doubt upon the broad application of Title IX of the Education Amendments of 1972, section 504 of the Rehabilitation Act of 1973, the Age Discrimination Act of 1975, and Title VI of the Civil Rights Act of 1964; and

(2) legislative action is necessary to restore the prior consistent and long-standing executive branch interpretation and broad, institution-wide application of those laws as previously administered.

EDUCATION AMENDMENTS AMENDMENT

Sec. 3. (a) Title IX of the Education Amendments of 1972 is amended by adding at the end the following new sections:

"INTERPRETATION OF 'PROGRAM OR ACTIVITY'

"Sec. 908. For the purposes of this Title, the term 'program or activity' and 'program' mean all of the operations of—

"(1)(A) a department, agency, special purpose district, or other instrumentality of a State or of a local government; or

"(B) the entity of such State or local government that distributes such assistance and each such department or agency (and each other State or local government entity) to which the assistance is extended, in the case of assistance to a State or local government;

"(2)(A) a college, university, or other postsecondary institution, or a public system of higher education; or

"(B) a local educational agency (as defined in section 198(a)(10) of the Elementary and Secondary Education Act of 1965), system of vocational education, or other school system;

"(3)(A) an entire corporation, partnership, or other private organization, or an entire sole proprietorship—

"(i) if assistance is extended to such corporation, partnership, private organization, or sole proprietorship as a whole; or

"(ii) which is principally engaged in the business of providing education, health care, housing, social services, or parks and recreation; or

"(B) the entire plant or other comparable, geographically separate facility to which Federal financial assistance is extended, in the case of any other corporation, partnership, private organization, or sole proprietorship; or

"(4) any other entity which is established by two or more of the entities described in paragraph (1), (2), or (3);

any part of which is extended Federal financial assistance, except that such term does not include any operation of an entity which is controlled by a religious organization if the application of section 901 to such operation would not be consistent with the religious tenets of such organization."

(b) Notwithstanding any provision of this Act or any amendment adopted thereto:

"NEUTRALITY WITH RESPECT TO ABORTION

"Sec. 909. Nothing in this Title shall be construed to require or prohibit any person, or public or private entity, to provide or pay for any benefit or service, including the use of facilities, related to an abortion. Nothing in this section shall be construed to permit a penalty to be imposed on any person or individual because such person or individual is seeking or has received any benefit or service related to a legal abortion."

* * *

CIVIL RIGHTS ACT AMENDMENT

Sec. 6. Title VI of the Civil Rights Act of 1964 is amended by adding at the end the following new section:

"Sec. 606. For the purposes of this Title, the term 'program or activity' and the term 'program' mean all of the operations of—

"(1)(A) a department, agency, special purpose district, or other instrumentality of a State or of a local government; or

"(B) the entity of such State or local government that distributes such assistance and each such department or agency (and each other State or local government entity) to which the assistance is extended, in the case of assistance to a State or local government;

"(2)(A) a college, university, or other postsecondary institution, or a public system of higher education; or

"(B) a local educational agency (as defined in section 198(a)(10) of the Elementary and Secondary Education Act of 1965), system of vocational education, or other school system;

"(3)(A) an entire corporation, partnership, or other private organization, or an entire sole proprietorship—

"(i) if assistance is extended to such corporation, partnership, private organization, or sole proprietorship as a whole; or

"(ii) which is principally engaged in the business of providing education, health care, housing, social services, or parks and recreation; or

"(B) the entire plant or other comparable, geographically separate facility to which Federal financial assistance is extended, in the case of any other corporation, partnership, private organization, or sole proprietorship; or

"(4) any other entity which is established by two or more of the entities described in paragraph (1), (2), or (3);

any part of which is extended Federal financial assistance."

RULE OF CONSTRUCTION

Sec. 7. Nothing in the amendments made by this Act shall be construed to extend the application of the Acts so amended to ultimate beneficiaries of Federal financial assistance excluded from coverage before the enactment of this Act.

ABORTION NEUTRALITY

Sec. 8. No provision of this Act or any amendment made by this Act shall be construed to force or require any individual or hospital or any other institution, program, or activity receiving Federal Funds to perform or pay for an abortion.

* * *

EXECUTIVE ORDER NO. 11246

Under and by virtue of the authority vested in me as President of the United States by the Constitution and statutes of the United States, it is ordered as follows:

PART I—NONDISCRIMINATION IN GOVERNMENT EMPLOYMENT

[Superseded by Ex.Ord.No. 11478, Aug. 8, 1969, 34 F.R. 12985]

PART II—NONDISCRIMINATION IN EMPLOYMENT BY GOVERNMENT CONTRACTORS AND SUBCONTRACTORS
SUBPART A—DUTIES OF THE SECRETARY OF LABOR

Sec. 201. The Secretary of Labor shall be responsible for the administration and enforcement of Parts II and III of this Order. The Secretary shall adopt such rules and regulations and issue such orders as are deemed necessary and appropriate to achieve the purposes of Parts II and III of this Order.

SUBPART B—CONTRACTORS' AGREEMENTS

Sec. 202. Except in contracts exempted in accordance with Section 204 of this Order, all Government contracting agencies shall include in every Government contract hereafter entered into the following provisions:

"During the performance of this contract, the contractor agrees as follows:

"(1) The contractor will not discriminate against any employee or applicant for employment because of race, color, religion, sex, or national origin. The contractor will take affirmative action to ensure that applicants are employed, and that employees are treated during employment, without regard to their race, color, religion, sex or national origin. Such action shall include, but not be limited to the following: employment, upgrading, demotion, or transfer; recruitment or recruitment advertising; layoff or termination; rates of pay or other forms of compensation; and selection for training, including apprenticeship. The contractor agrees to post in conspicuous places, available to employees and applicants for employment, notices to be provided by the contracting officer setting forth the provisions of this nondiscrimination clause.

"(2) The contractor will, in all solicitations or advertisements for employees placed by or on behalf of the contractor, state that all qualified applicants will receive consideration for employment without regard to race, color, religion, sex or national origin.

"(3) The contractor will send to each labor union or representative of workers with which he has a collective bargaining agreement or other contract or understanding, a notice, to be provided by the agency contracting officer, advising the labor union or workers' representative of the contractor's commitments under Section 202 of Executive Order No. 11246 of September 24, 1965, and shall post copies of the notice in conspicuous places available to employees and applicants for employment.

"(4) The contractor will comply with all provisions of Executive Order No. 11246 of Sept. 24, 1965, and of the rules, regulations, and relevant orders of the Secretary of Labor.

"(5) The contractor will furnish all information and reports required by Executive Order No. 11246 of September 24, 1965, and by the rules, regulations, and orders of the Secretary of Labor, or pursuant thereto, and will permit access to his books, records, and accounts by the contracting agency and the Secretary of Labor for purposes of investigation to ascertain compliance with such rules, regulations, and orders.

"(6) In the event of the contractor's noncompliance with the nondiscrimination clauses of this contract or with any of such rules, regulations, or orders, this contract may be cancelled, terminated or suspended in whole or in part and the contractor may be declared ineligible for further Government contracts in accordance with procedures authorized in Executive Order No. 11246 of Sept. 24, 1965, and such other sanctions may be imposed and remedies invoked as provided in Executive Order No. 11246 of September 24, 1965, or by rule, regulation, or order of the Secretary of Labor, or as otherwise provided by law.

"(7) The contractor will include the provisions of paragraphs (1) through (7) in every subcontract or purchase order unless exempted by rules, regulations, or orders of the Secretary of Labor issued pursuant to Section 204 of Executive Order No. 11246 of September 24, 1965[section 204 of this Order], so that such provisions will be binding upon each subcontractor or vendor. The contractor will take such action with respect to any subcontract or purchase order as may be directed by the Secretary of Labor as a means of enforcing such provisions including sanctions for noncompliance: *Provided, however,* That in the event the contractor becomes involved in, or is threatened with, litigation with a subcontractor or vendor as a result of such direction, the contractor may request the United States to enter into such litigation to protect the interests of the United States."

Sec. 203. (a) Each contractor having a contract containing the provisions prescribed in Section 202 shall file, and shall cause each of his subcontractors to file, Compliance Reports with the contracting agency or the Secretary of Labor as may be directed. Compliance Reports shall be filed within such times and shall contain such information as to the practices, policies, programs, and employment policies, programs, and employment statistics of the contractor and each subcontractor, and shall be in such form, as the Secretary of Labor may prescribe.

(b) Bidders or prospective contractors or subcontractors may be required to state whether they have participated in any previous contract subject to the provisions of this Order, or any preceding similar Executive order, and in that event to submit, on behalf of themselves and their proposed subcontractors, Compliance Reports prior to or as an initial part of their bid or negotiation of a contract.

(c) Whenever the contractor or subcontractor has a collective bargaining agreement or other contract or understanding with a labor union or an agency referring workers or providing or supervising apprenticeship or training for such workers, the Compliance Report shall include such information as to such labor union's or agency's practices and policies affecting compliance as the Secretary of Labor may prescribe: *Provided,* That to the extent such information is within the exclusive possession of a labor union or an agency referring workers or providing or supervising apprenticeship or training and such labor union or agency shall refuse to furnish such information to the contractor, the contractor shall so certify to the Secretary of Labor as part of its Compliance Report and shall set forth what efforts he has made to obtain such information.

(d) The Secretary of Labor may direct that any bidder or prospective contractor or subcontractor shall submit, as part of his Compliance Report, a statement in writing, signed by an authorized officer or agent on behalf of any labor union or any agency referring workers or providing or supervising apprenticeship or other training, with which the bidder or prospective contractor deals, with supporting information, to the effect that the signer's practices and policies do not discriminate on the grounds of race, color, religion, sex or national origin, and that the signer either will affirmatively cooperate in the implementation of the policy and provisions of this order or that it consents and agrees that recruitment, employment, and the terms and conditions of employment under the proposed contract shall be in accordance with the purposes and provisions of the order. In the event that the union, or the agency shall refuse to execute such a statement, the Compliance

Report shall so certify and set forth what efforts have been made to secure such a statement and such additional factual material as the Secretary of Labor may require.

Sec. 204. The Secretary of Labor may, when he deems that special circumstances in the national interest so require, exempt a contracting agency from the requirement of including any or all of the provisions of Section 202 of this Order in any specific contract, subcontract, or purchase order. The Secretary of Labor may, by rule or regulation, also exempt certain classes of contracts, subcontracts, or purchase orders (1) whenever work is to be or has been performed outside the United States and no recruitment of workers within the limits of the United States is involved; (2) for standard commercial supplies or raw materials; (3) involving less than specified amounts of money or specified numbers of workers; or (4) to the extent that they involve subcontracts below a specified tier. The Secretary of Labor may also provide, by rule, regulation, or order, for the exemption of facilities of a contractor which are in all respects separate and distinct from activities of the contractor related to the performance of the contract: *Provided*, That such an exemption will not interfere with or impede the effectuation of the purposes of this Order: *And provided further*, That in the absence of such an exemption all facilities shall be covered by the provisions of this Order.

SUBPART C—POWERS AND DUTIES OF THE SECRETARY OF LABOR AND THE CONTRACTING AGENCIES

Sec. 205. The Secretary of Labor shall be responsible for securing compliance by all Government contractors and subcontractors with this Order and any implementing rules or regulations. All contracting agencies shall comply with the terms of this Order and any implementing rules, regulations, or orders of the Secretary of Labor. Contracting agencies shall cooperate with the Secretary of Labor and shall furnish such information and assistance as the Secretary may require.

Sec. 206. (a) The Secretary of Labor may investigate the employment practices of any Government contractor or subcontractor to determine whether or not the contractual provisions specified in Section 202 of this Order have been violated. Such investigation shall be conducted in accordance with the procedures established by the Secretary of Labor.

(b) The Secretary of Labor may receive and investigate complaints by employees or prospective employees of a Government contractor or subcontractor which allege discrimination contrary to the contractual provisions specified in Section 202 of this Order.

Sec. 207. The Secretary of Labor shall use his best efforts, directly and through interested Federal, State, and local agencies, contractors, and all other available instrumentalities to cause any labor union engaged in work under Government contracts or any agency referring workers or providing or supervising apprenticeship or training for or in the course of such work to cooperate in the implementation of the purposes of this Order. The Secretary of Labor shall, in appropriate cases, notify the Equal Employment Opportunity Commission, the Department of Justice, or other appropriate Federal agencies whenever it has reason to believe that the practices of any such labor organization or agency violate Title VI or Title VII of the Civil Rights Act of 1964 or other provision of Federal law.

Sec. 208. (a) The Secretary of Labor, or any agency, officer, or employee in the executive branch of the Government designated by rule, regulation, or order of the Secretary, may hold such hearings, public or private, as the Secretary may deem advisable for compliance, enforcement, or educational purposes.

(b) The Secretary of Labor may hold, or cause to be held, hearings in accordance with Subsection (a) of this Section prior to imposing, ordering, or recommending the imposition of penalties and sanctions under this Order. No order for debarment of any contractor from further Government contracts under Section 209(a)(6) shall be made without affording the contractor an opportunity for a hearing.

SUBPART D—SANCTIONS AND PENALTIES

Sec. 209. (a) In accordance with such rules, regulations, or orders as the Secretary of Labor may issue or adopt, the Secretary may:

(1) Publish, or cause to be published, the names of contractors or unions which it has concluded have complied or have failed to comply with the provisions of this Order or of the rules, regulations, and orders of the Secretary of Labor.

(2) Recommend to the Department of Justice that, in cases in which there is substantial or material violation or the threat of substantial or material violation of the contractual provisions set forth in Section 202 of this Order, appropriate proceedings be brought to enforce those provisions, including the enjoining, within the limitations of applicable law, of organizations, individuals, or groups who prevent directly or indirectly, or seek to prevent directly or indirectly, compliance with the provisions of this Order.

(3) Recommend to the Equal Employment Opportunity Commission or the Department of Justice that appropriate proceedings be instituted under Title VII of the Civil Rights Act of 1964.

(4) Recommend to the Department of Justice that criminal proceedings be brought for the furnishing of false information to any contracting agency or to the Secretary of Labor as the case may be.

(5) After consulting with the contracting agency, direct the contracting agency to cancel, terminate, suspend, or cause to be cancelled, terminated, or suspended, any contract, or any portion or portions thereof, for failure of the contractor or subcontractor to comply with equal employment opportunity provisions of the con-

tract. Contracts may be cancelled, terminated, or suspended absolutely or continuance of contracts may be conditioned upon a program for future compliance approved by the Secretary of Labor.

(6) Provide that any contracting agency shall refrain from entering into further contracts, or extensions or other modifications of existing contracts, with any noncomplying contractor, until such contractor has satisfied the Secretary of Labor that such contractor has established and will carry out personnel and employment policies in compliance with the provisions of this Order.

(b) Pursuant to rules and regulations prescribed by the Secretary of Labor, the Secretary shall make reasonable efforts, within a reasonable time limitation, to secure compliance with the contract provisions of this Order by methods of conference, conciliation, mediation, and persuasion before proceedings shall be instituted under subsection (a)(2) of this Section, or before a contract shall be cancelled or terminated in whole or in part under subsection (a)(5) of this Section.

Sec. 210. Whenever the Secretary of Labor makes a determination under Section 209, the Secretary shall promptly notify the appropriate agency. The agency shall take the action directed by the Secretary and shall report the results of the action it has taken to the Secretary of Labor within such time as the Secretary shall specify. If the contracting agency fails to take the action directed within thirty days, the Secretary may take the action directly.

Sec. 211. If the Secretary of Labor shall so direct, contracting agencies shall not enter into contracts with any bidder or prospective contractor unless the bidder or prospective contractor has satisfactorily complied with the provisions of this Order or submits a program for compliance acceptable to the Secretary of Labor.

Sec. 212. When a contract has been cancelled or terminated under Section 209(a)(5) or a contractor has been debarred from further Government contracts under Section 209(a)(6) of this Order, because of noncompliance with the contract provisions specified in Section 202 of this Order, the Secretary of Labor shall promptly notify the Comptroller General of the United States.

* * *

PART III—NONDISCRIMINATION PROVISIONS IN FEDERALLY ASSISTED CONSTRUCTION CONTRACTS

Sec. 301. Each executive department and agency which administers a program involving Federal financial assistance shall require as a condition for the approval of any grant, contract, loan, insurance, or guarantee thereunder, which may involve a construction contract, that the applicant for Federal assistance undertake and agree to incorporate, or cause to be incorporated, into all construction contracts paid for in whole or in part with funds obtained from the Federal Government or borrowed on the credit of the Federal Government pursuant to such grant, contract, loan, insurance, or guarantee, or undertaken pursuant to any Federal program involving such grant, contract, loan, insurance, or guarantee, the provisions prescribed for Government contracts by Section 202 of this Order or such modification thereof, preserving in substance the contractor's obligations thereunder, as may be approved by the Secretary of Labor, together with such additional provisions as the Secretary deems appropriate to establish and protect the interest of the United States in the enforcement of those obligations. Each such applicant shall also undertake and agree (1) to assist and cooperate actively with the Secretary of Labor in obtaining the compliance of contractors and subcontractors with those contract provisions and with the rules, regulations and relevant orders of the Secretary, (2) to obtain and to furnish to the Secretary of Labor such information as the Secretary may require for the supervision of such compliance, (3) to carry out sanctions and penalties for violation of such obligations imposed upon contractors and subcontractors by the Secretary of Labor pursuant to Part II, Subpart D, of this Order, and (4) to refrain from entering into any contract subject to this Order, or extension or other modification of such a contract with a contractor debarred from Government contracts under Part II, Subpart D, of this Order.

Sec. 302. (a) "Construction contract" as used in this Order means any contract for the construction, rehabilitation, alteration, conversion, extension, or repair of buildings, highways, or other improvements to real property.

(b) The provisions of Part II of this Order shall apply to such construction contracts, and for purposes of such application the administering department or agency shall be considered the contracting agency referred to therein.

(c) The term "applicant" as used in this Order means an applicant for Federal assistance or, as determined by agency regulation, other program participant, with respect to whom an application for any grant, contract, loan, insurance, or guarantee is not finally acted upon prior to the effective date of this Part, and it includes such an applicant after he becomes a recipient of such Federal assistance.

Sec. 303(a). The Secretary of Labor shall be responsible for obtaining the compliance of such applicants with their undertakings under this Order. Each administering department and agency is directed to cooperate with the Secretary of Labor and to furnish the Secretary such information and assistance as the Secretary may require in the performance of the Secretary's functions under this Order.

(b) In the event an applicant fails and refuses to comply with the applicant's undertakings pursuant to this Order, the Secretary of Labor may, after consulting with the administering department or agency, take any or all of the following actions: (1) direct any administering department or agency to cancel, terminate, or suspend in whole or in part the agreement, contract or other arrangement with such applicant with respect to which the failure or refusal occurred; (2) direct any administering department or agency to refrain from extending any further assistance to the applicant under the program with respect to which the failure or refusal occurred until satisfactory assurance of future compliance has been received by the Secretary of Labor from such applicant; and (3) refer the case to the Department of Justice or the Equal Employment Opportunity Commission for appropriate law enforcement or other proceedings.

(c) In no case shall action be taken with respect to an applicant pursuant to clause (1) or (2) of subsection (b) without notice and opportunity for hearing.

Sec. 304. Any executive department or agency which imposes by rule, regulation, or order requirements of nondiscrimination in employment, other than requirements imposed pursuant to this Order, may delegate to the Secretary of Labor by agreement such responsibilities with respect to compliance standards, reports, and procedures as would tend to bring the administration of such requirements into conformity with the administration of requirements imposed under this Order: *Provided*, That actions to effect compliance by recipients of Federal financial assistance with requirements imposed pursuant to Title VI of the Civil Rights Act of 1964 shall be taken in conformity with the procedures and limitations prescribed in Section 602 thereof and the regulations of the administering department or agency issued thereunder.

PART IV—MISCELLANEOUS

Sec. 401. The Secretary of Labor may delegate to any officer, agency, or employee in the Executive branch of the Government, any function or duty of the Secretary under Parts II and III of this Order.

* * *

*

INDEX

References are to pages

†